On the Cover

The worker bee shown on the cover is collecting flower pollen (seen in the pollen baskets on her legs) and nectar that she —all worker bees are female—will take back to her hive to feed the colony. In the process, honey bees also cross-pollinate plants as they collect pollen. Many of these plants are of great agricultural importance to humans, and some crops require pollination by honey bees. Hives are transported all around the country to get the bees at the right place and the right time for crop pollination.

The pollination services of honey bees have been in jeopardy in recent years due to excessive losses of hives—a condition known as colony collapse disorder. The causes are still being studied, but suspects include pesticides, parasites, diseases, and stress. Continued loss of honey bees could spell serious agricultural losses.

Life

The Science of Biology

TWELFTH EDITION

Life

The Science of Biology
TWELFTH EDITION

David M. Hillis
University of Texas, Austin

H. Craig Heller
Stanford University

Sally D. Hacker
Oregon State University

David W. Hall
University of Georgia

Marta J. Laskowski
Oberlin College

David Sadava
Emeritus, The Claremont Colleges

SINAUER

MACMILLAN

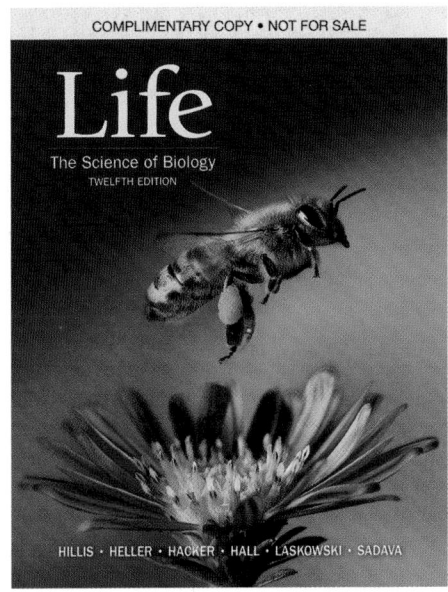

The Cover

See the inside front cover for an explanation of the honey bee.
Photo © Michael Durham/Minden Pictures.

The Frontispiece

Polar bear (*Ursus maritimus*) and arctic fox (*Alopex lagopus*) on an ice field, Hudson Bay, Churchill, Manitoba, Canada. Photo © Thomas Mangelsen/Minden Pictures.

Life: The Science of Biology, Twelfth Edition, Instructor's Edition

Copyright © 2020, 2017, 2014, 2011, 2008, 2004, 2001, 1998, 1995, 1992, 1987, 1983 Oxford University Press
Sinauer Associates is an imprint of Oxford University Press.
This book may not be reproduced in whole or in part without permission.

Address Editorial Correspondence To:

Oxford University Press, 23 Plumtree Road, Sunderland, MA 01375 U.S.A.

Address orders to:

MPS/W. H. Freeman & Co., Order Department, 16365 James Madison Highway, U.S. Route 15, Gordonsville, VA 22942 U.S.A.

Examination Copy Information: 1-800-446-8923

Cataloging-in-Publication Data

On file with the Library of Congess
ISBN 9781319307042

Printed in the United States of America
First Printing December 2019
Printed by LSC Communications

Contents in Brief

PHOTO CREDITS:
Table of Contents in Brief: Part One: © National Geographic Image Collection/Alamy Stock Photo, Part Two: © Dennis Kunkel Microscopy/Science Source, Part Three: E. Stone. 1763. Philos Trans R Soc Lond 53: 195–200, Part Four: © Steve Gschmeissner/Science Source, Part Five: © blickwinkel/Alamy Stock Photo, Part Six: "Milky seas" data prepared by Steven Miller of the Naval Research Laboratory, Monterey, CA. Background data (Earth at Night image) courtesy Marc Imhoff (NASA/GSFC) and Christopher Elvidge (NOAA/NGDC); image by Craig Mayhew (NASA/GSFC) and Robert Simmon (NASA/GSFC)., Part Seven: © MisoKnitl/Getty Images, Part Eight: © dpa picture alliance/Alamy Stock Photo, Part Nine: © Morley Read/Alamy Stock Photo.

Life The Science of Biology

Dear Instructor,

Biology inspires wonder. The image of a honey bee pollinating an aster [*Symphyotrichum* sp. (*Asteraceae*)] on our cover shows an example of mutualism between a plant and an animal. The plant needs the bee to successfully reproduce, and the bee gets nectar and pollen from the plant for food. This fascinating relationship is an example of what motivates biologists to study the complexities and interactions of life.

Biology is dynamic. It is constantly changing as new insights lead to new ideas and new tools to test those ideas. Think of the use of drones and satellites to photograph penguin populations in Antarctica. Think of the developments in biological imaging and computation. Think of genome sequencing and its effect on our understanding of everything from human diseases to the tree of life. Think of the use of ice cores to understand past global climate.

Biology is a system. Biological systems are made up of different levels of organization—from molecules to ecosystems—that are interconnected and complex. Biologists are beginning to use integrated approaches to understand the complex properties of biological systems.

Biology is life. We face many challenges as humans, including emerging diseases, feeding people in a sustainable way, population growth, degradation of natural systems, and climate change. We understand that humans are integrally connected to and dependent on all life on Earth.

Our goal—and challenge—in writing *Life* is to engage students in all these aspects of biology by motivating learning through active discovery. We focus on key concepts and contemporary examples that provide a foundation for further study. We have consulted and collaborated with faculty, students, and experts in the fields of biology and education. As you will see in the next several pages, in this, our Twelfth Edition, we engage students by explaining how biology affects their daily lives and how new knowledge is discovered. To help students master the concepts and principles of biology, we have continued to develop and expand our active learning activities.

Craig Heller

Dave Hall

David Sadava

David Hillis

Sally Hacker

Marta Laskowski

In the new edition of *Life: The Science of Biology*, you'll find the book's signature focus on skill-building, engagement, and active learning taken to a whole new level. With extensive updating, new pedagogical features, and powerful online advances in **Achieve**, it immerses students in the world of biological experimentation, providing impactful experiences with research and data they'll need to succeed in class and in their future STEM careers.

Life The Science of Biology is

FOCUSED ON SKILLS

To support teaching and learning in biology through asking questions:

- **New! Data in Depth** is a new online feature that offers students hands-on practice with key data skills. Companions to the in-text **Work with the Data** feature, these exercises help build students' data literacy and data manipulation skills through a range of interactive elements and assignable questions.

- Engaging and powerful **simulations** let students interact with important biological processes. They can be used as a tool in lectures or as homework assignments. The simulations now include quizzes that report to the **Achieve** gradebook.

- **New!** The online version of Appendix B, **Making Sense of Data: A Statistics Primer** gives students the opportunity to learn basic statistical concepts and skill through hands-on simulations and activities.

- The **Experiments** and **Work with the Data** exercises highlight important research and **instill the foundation of scientific investigation in students** by always following the hypothesis–method–results–conclusion framework.

- Questions in **Recap and Assess** range from questions that support retention of content to questions that foster higher-order thinking.

- Leading by example, *Life* exposes students to many thoughtful questions throughout the body of the text, **reinforcing the importance of asking questions** in biology.

- To make sure students get the most out of the multitude of questions available to them in the textbook, **answers to all in-book questions are included in Achieve.**

FOCUSED ON ENGAGEMENT

To help students take learning into their own hands:

- The **Investigating Life** narrative thread **weaves through the chapter** to keep students engaged from the first page to the last. In every chapter the opening story and question set the stage for the narrative, a related **Experiment** and **Work with the Data** exercise helps reinforce the concepts, and the **Future directions** feature at the end helps wrap up the investigation.

- **References** to media such as animations, simulations, and jaw-dropping videos appear throughout each chapter and **allow students to interact with content in a variety of ways**.

- Intriguing questions in figure captions **sharpen students' skills in critical thinking** about biology and subtly reinforce the process of doing science.

- **Connect the Concepts** foster **thinking about the big picture**—a task that can be overwhelming for introductory biology students—by demonstrating how certain important terms and concepts relate to discussions in another chapter.

FOCUSED ON ACTIVE LEARNING

To help instructors encourage students to "learn by doing":

- The **Active Learning Guide** (for instructors) provides invaluable resources and support for **implementing active learning techniques in the classroom**. Accompanying the Guide are a set of full **Active Learning Modules**, which are comprised of a pre-lecture video, a complete in-class exercise, a pre- and post-quiz, and extensive instructor support.

- **Learning objectives guide students to the essential content** as they read through each **Key Concept** section.

- **Recap and Assess** for each **Key Concept** includes **questions** (all Bloom's levels 2–4) that test students' mastery of the **Key Concept**.

EXPERIENCED THROUGH ACHIEVE

With this edition's **Achieve**, *Life* is more than ever a truly integrated text/media resource. **Achieve** gives students everything they need to prepare for class and exams while giving instructors everything they need to set up a course, customize the content, craft presentations, assign homework, assess students, and guide the progress of individuals and the class as a whole.

Life The Science of Biology
Achieve for *Life*

Introducing

achieve.macmillanlearning.com

ACHIEVE is a comprehensive set of interconnected teaching and assessment tools. It incorporates the most effective elements from Macmillan's market leading solutions—including LaunchPad, iClicker and others—in a single, easy-to-use platform. Our resources were co-designed with instructors and students, using a foundation of learning research and rigorous testing.

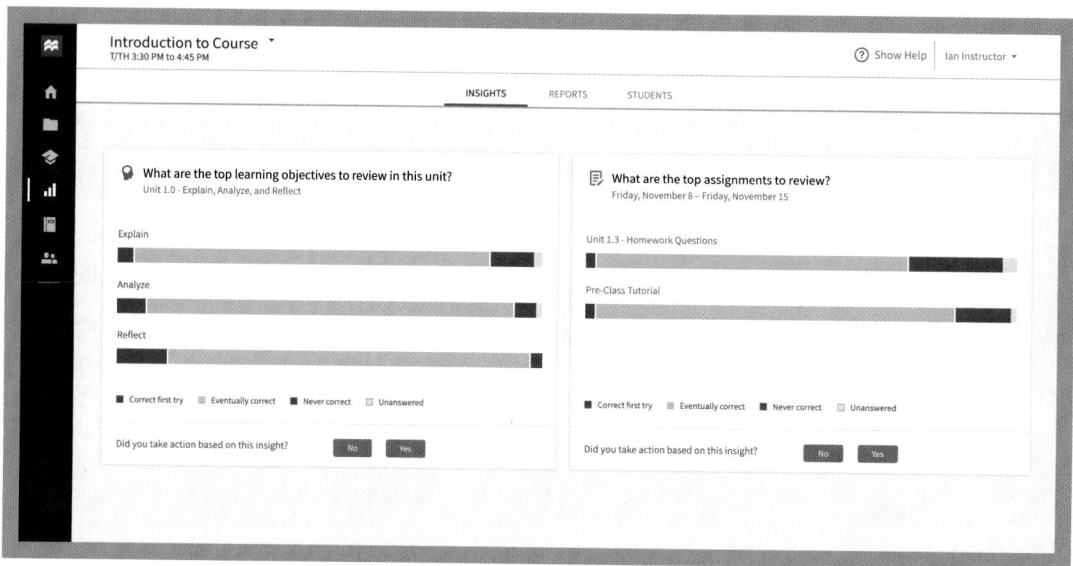

ENGAGING STUDENTS FOR BETTER OUTCOMES

Students interact more meaningfully with content when using Achieve.

For every 1% increase in the proportion of Achieve pre-class activities a student completes, she can expect a 1% increase in her final course grade.

SUPPORTING STUDENTS OF ALL LEVELS

Achieve was designed for all students whether they are high achievers or need extra support.

8%

Students who completed at least 81% of their pre-class activities scored 8% higher on their final exams.

This finding is true for all students—those less and more academically prepared to succeed.

PARTNERING WITH YOU

Macmillan remains dedicated to expert authorship and support of the customer experience.

88%

88% of students (1,241 students) reported that Achieve activities were engaging.

Life The Science of Biology
Achieve for *Life*

Achieve for *Life* features:

INSIGHTS & REPORTING

Powerful analytics, viewable in an elegant dashboard, offer instructors a window into student progress.

RESOURCES

Achieve includes access to carefully developed, book-specific content as well your own resources to use in the course as needed.

E-BOOK

The e-book offers highlighting, note-taking, offline access, and read aloud functionality.

DIVERSE, THOUGHTFUL QUESTIONS

Multiple question types enhance student engagement and critical thinking skills.

GRADEBOOK

An easy-to-use gradebook provides a clear window into performance for the whole class, for individual students, and for individual assignments.

INTEGRATION OPTIONS

You can work with us to integrate with your campus LMS—including Blackboard, Canvas, D2L/Brightspace, Moodle—as well as for Inclusive Access.

COURSE- & DISCIPLINE-SPECIFIC TOOLS

Depending on the discipline, Achieve also includes:

- Diagnostics
- Writing and revision tools
- A math assessment engine
- Molecular drawing software
- and more.

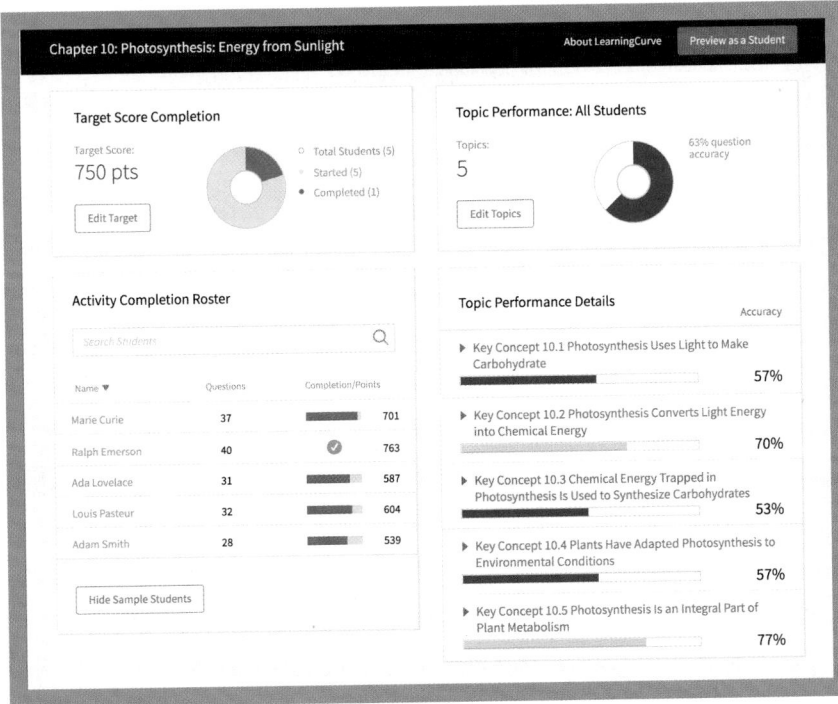

All students benefit from Achieve, but especially those who are less academically prepared.

↑ +12 There is a 12 percentage point boost in final exam scores for students who were less academically prepared.

↑ +9 There is a 9 percentage point boost in final exam scores for all students when they hit 81% completion of Achieve assignments.

↑ +6 There is a 6 percentage point boost in final exam scores for students who were more academically prepared.

Learn more about the research that went into the development of Achieve at **macmillanlearning.com/achieve**.

Life The Science of Biology
Focused on Skills

Developing Skills and Working with Data

Life has always been known for emphasizing the role of experimentation, data, and research in our understanding of biology.

The Experiments and Work with the Data exercises highlight important research and **instill the foundation of scientific investigation in students** by always following the hypothesis–method–results–conclusion framework.

> I especially like the Work with the Data exercises. Too often this sort of critical thinking is left to upper-level courses."
>
> —Susan Reigler, Indiana University Southeast

Experiment

Original Paper: P. N. Rao and R. T. Johnson. 1970. Mammalian cell fusion: Studies on the regulation of DNA synthesis and mitosis. *Nature* 225: 159–164.

Nuclei of cells in G1 do not undergo DNA replication, but nuclei in S phase do. Rao and Johnson wondered whether substances present in cells in S phase could be used to induce DNA replication in cells in G1.

HYPOTHESIS▶ A cell in S phase contains an activator of DNA replication.

METHOD▶

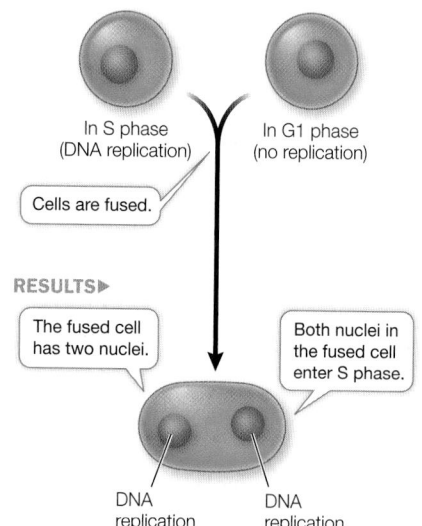

In S phase
(DNA replication)

In G1 phase
(no replication)

Cells are fused.

RESULTS▶

The fused cell has two nuclei.

Both nuclei in the fused cell enter S phase.

DNA replication

DNA replication

CONCLUSION▶ The S phase cell contains a substance that diffuses to the G1 nucleus and activates DNA replication.

Work with the Data

The fusion of cellular membranes is a natural process; it occurs during endocytosis and exocytosis, and in fertilization (the fusion of gametes). Membrane fusion also occurs when membrane-enclosed viruses infect their host cells. Occasionally these viruses also induce the fusion of adjacent host cells, creating a multinucleate cell. This observation led to the use of Sendai virus, a membrane-enclosed mouse respiratory virus, as a tool in the laboratory to fuse cells experimentally. Rao and Johnson used this strategy to study the regulation of the cell cycle.

In their experiment, Rao and Johnson used HeLa cells, which divide continuously (see the opening story of this chapter). First, they isolated cells in either G1 or S phase. Before fusion, the cells in S phase were exposed to a radioactively labeled component of DNA (thymidine). The radioactivity was incorporated into these cells' newly replicated DNA, labeling their nuclei. The S and G1 cells were then fused using Sendai virus (resulting in G1/S fusions) and again exposed to labeled thymidine. At various times after fusion, the scientists calculated the percent of previously unlabeled (G1) nuclei that had incorporated new label (i.e., had replicated their DNA) (**Figure A**). In a second series of experiments, S and G2 cells were fused in various combinations and then the numbers of cells in mitosis were counted and expressed as a percent of all cells in the population (**Figure B**).

Figure A

Figure B

Hours after cell fusion

Hours after cell fusion

QUESTIONS▶

1. According to Figure A, how long did it take for all the G1 nuclei in the G1/S cells to become labeled?

2. Examine the data for fused G1/G1 cells and unfused G1 cells in Figure A. Explain why these were appropriate controls for the experiment. When did these nuclei become labeled? Compare these times with each other and with that for the G1/S nuclei and discuss.

3. Examine the data in Figure B. Why did it take longer for the S phase cells to begin mitosis than the G2 cells?

4. According to Figure B, did fusion with G2 cells alter the timing of mitosis in the S cell nuclei? Explain what this means in terms of regulation of the cell cycle.

Go to Achieve for a companion Data in Depth exercise.

New Digital Feature
in **Achieve!** Data in Depth

Data in Depth is a new online feature that offers students hands-on practice with key data skills. Companions to the in-text **Work with the Data** feature, these exercises help build students' data literacy and data manipulation skills through a range of interactive elements and assignable questions.

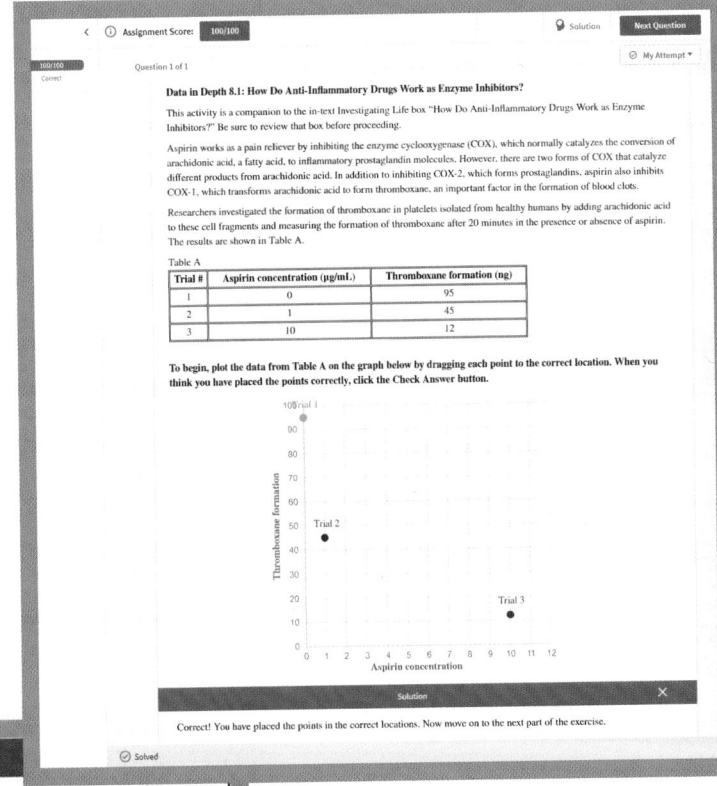

Simulations

The engaging and powerful simulations in **Achieve** allow students to interact with important biological processes. They can be used as a tool in lectures or as homework assignments. The simulations now include quizzes that report to the gradebook in **Achieve**.

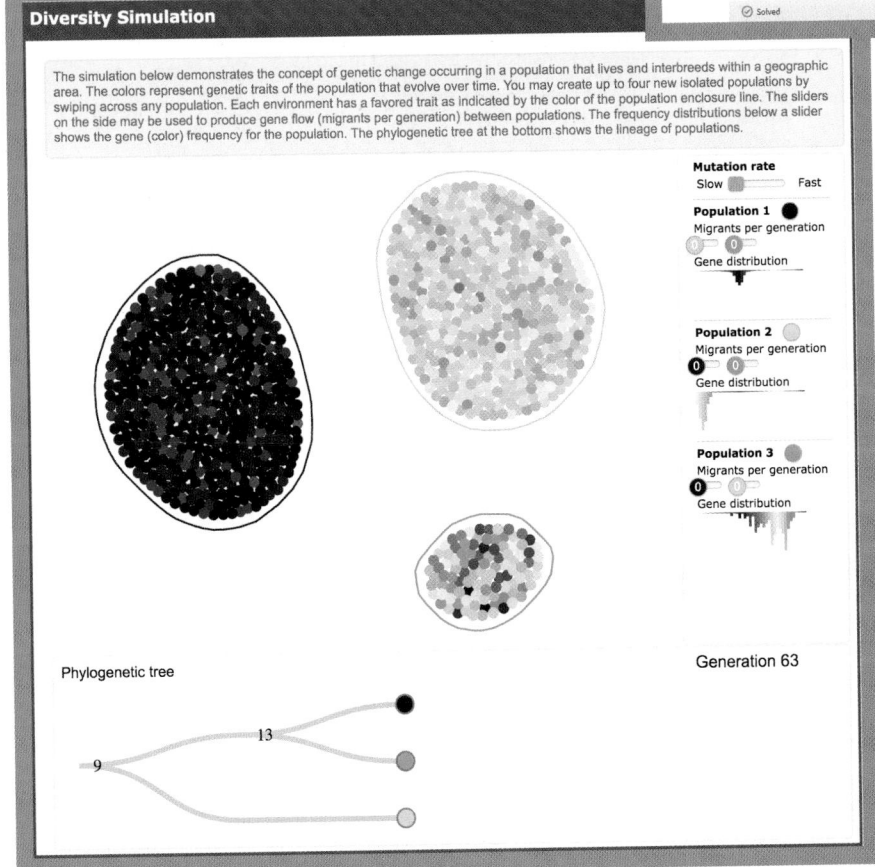

Life The Science of Biology
Focused on Engagement

New! Visual Summaries

Visual Summaries conclude every chapter, providing students with a visually compelling checklist, emphasizing major concepts through key figures, bullets, and mid-range Bloom's questions. To ensure mastery of the Key Concepts, the summary encourages students to refer to the original chapter text and figures, and to relevant animations and activities.

VISUAL SUMMARY 57

© Dr. Paul A. Zahl/Science Source

You should be able to relate each summary to the adjacent figures. If you go to this visual summary in **Achieve**, you can follow links to figures, animations, activities, and simulations that will help you consolidate the material.

KEY CONCEPT

57.1   Human Activities Are Changing the Biosphere, Resulting in Biodiversity Loss

- Biodiversity has great value to human society in the form of goods and services, but human activities have caused its rapid decline at genetic, population, species, ecosystem, and global scales.
- Human-caused events coupled with natural events can reduce a species' **effective population size** (number of individuals that can contribute offspring to the next generation), leading to population and species extinctions. Ever-smaller effective population sizes are affected by inbreeding depression, genetic drift, and **demographic stochasticity**.
- Humans are causing biodiversity loss at unprecedented rates, rivaling that of the five previous mass extinction events, which were the result of cataclysmic natural disasters.
- We can estimate the extinction probability of species by taking into account their population sizes, genetic variation, life history traits, and ecology.

Figure 57.2

Questions

1. How does the loss of biodiversity at one scale affect its loss at other scales?
2. How can reducing a species' effective population size result in population and species extinction?
3. Why is it difficult to determine how many species are extinct, and what factors indicate that a species could be at risk of extinction?

KEY CONCEPT

57.2   Most Biodiversity Loss to Date Is Caused by Habitat Loss and Degradation

Go to Animation 57.1

- **Habitat loss** (reduction in habitat quantity) and **habitat degradation** (reduction in habitat quality) have been the major causes of biodiversity loss. Estimates are that humans have transformed and fragmented 50%–60% of the land surface, primarily for agriculture, timber, and livestock grazing.
- Overharvesting of species for food, clothing, ornamentation, pets, and medicines was once the most important and rapid cause of species extinction and is still a concern for some species, and their food webs, if conservation measures are not enacted.
- Deliberate or inadvertent introductions of non-native species have increased exponentially over the last 200 years, with roughly 10% of those species becoming invasive.
- **Invasive** species can endanger native species through predation, competition, and disease. They can cause changes to ecosystem functions or genetic diversity through hybridization with wild populations.
- Human-generated emissions of greenhouse gases are contributing to global climate warming, sea level rise, increased storminess, and ocean acidification, all of which are becoming increasingly important causes of biodiversity loss.

Figure 57.5

© Ed Reschke/Getty Images

© Rolf Nussbaumer Photography/Alamy Stock Photo

VISUAL SUMMARY 57

- Scientific evidence shows that some species have been, or are currently being, affected by climate change through distributional changes, timing of life history events, and decreased growth and reproduction.

Figure 57.9

Questions

1. How do habitat loss, degradation, and fragmentation contribute to the extinction of species?
2. Give three reasons why invasive species can have negative effects on biodiversity and ecosystems.
3. Describe how overharvesting and climate change could affect a large carnivore species and its food web.

...cting Biodiversity Requires Conservation
...lanagement Strategies

Go to Activity 57.1 and Animation 57.2

...ientific theory, empirical data, and tools from a variety
...elp inform socioeconomic and institutional sectors in
...d management of biodiversity.

Figure 57.12

...ed areas and restoring degraded habitat can curtail
...Creating viable protected areas requires establishing
...s, buffer zones surrounding them, and habitat corridors

...logy involves renewing degraded ecosystems by re-
...original structure and function through active removal
...on-native species, revegetation to reestablish habitat
...s, reintroduction of native species, or reestablishment
...sses such as disturbance.

...programs and ending trade can help conserve and
...hly threatened or charismatic species.

...duce the damage caused by invasive species is to
...ir introduction through trade restrictions or eradicate
...y establishment phase.

...e conserved because of the economic value of the
...s it provides.

Figure 57.13

...rinciples, what are the best spatial configurations
...e designs?

...on ecology be used to reestablish the original
...ction of degraded ecosystems?

...t ways to reduce the damage caused by

Life The Science of Biology
Focused on Active Learning

Active Learning Modules

The **Active Learning Modules** provide everything an instructor needs to successfully implement an active approach to teaching key topics. Each module includes many resources, including:

- Pre-class video specifically created for the module
- Pre-quiz and post-quiz
- Handout for in-class work
- Detailed in-class exercise
- Detailed instructor's guide

These modules are easy to implement and are a great way to add more active learning to the classroom.

Active Learning Guide

The **Active Learning Guide** provides extensive resources and support for implementing active learning techniques in the classroom. It includes a thorough introduction to the concepts, techniques, and benefits of active learning, along with chapter-by-chapter guidance on teaching using the many active learning resources we provide for *Life*.

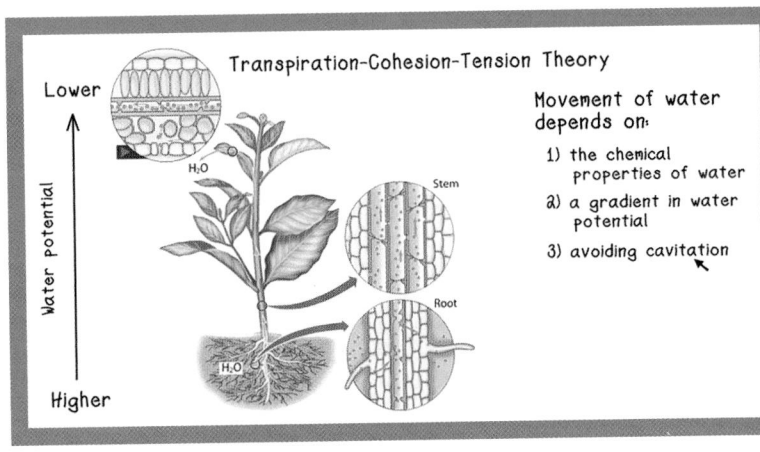

Integration with ▷ iClicker

Student confidence and end-of-course grades increase with the use of **iClicker**. iClicker includes a geolocation attendance feature to get students to class. During class, instructors can choose from flexible polling and quizzing options to engage students, check understanding, and get feedback in real time. Additionally, iClicker allows students to participate using laptops, mobile devices, or iClicker remotes—all in the same classroom. Instructors can easily sync grades between iClicker and **Achieve** as well as use student response questions specific to *Life*. To learn more or schedule a demo, visit **iClicker.com**.

❝

I absolutely love the active nature of the built-in Activity sections; they are quick to access from the digital version of the textbook.❞

—Jason Duncan, Willamette University

Life The Science of Biology
Content Updates

PART 1: The Science of Life and Its Chemical Basis

- Clarification and figure describing valence shell and the periodic table
- Clarification and new figure on representations of bonding
- Definition and more discussion of the importance of pH
- Clearer discussion of phosphodiester bond formation in nucleic acids
- Inclusion of lipoprotein structure and function
- Updates on the search for water on extraterrestrial bodies
- Recent evidence for the origin of cells

PART 2: Cells

- Background on the cell theory
- More extensive discussion of cell size
- Clear differentiation between chromosomes and chromatin in the nucleus
- Roles of the different regions of the Golgi apparatus in the secretory pathway
- Clarification of the roles of kinesin and dynein in movements
- Role of the extracellular matrix in organ formation
- Clarification of the role of integrins in cell attachment to the matrix
- Clearer description of the sodium–potassium ion pump
- Discussion of cross-talk between cell signaling pathways

PART 3: Cells and Energy

- Clearer linkage between free energy changes and biochemical transformations
- Specific examples of activation energy in enzyme-catalyzed reactions
- Additional detail on the structure and role of pyruvate dehydrogenase
- Clarification of the difference between chlorophyll *a* and chlorophyll *b*
- Clearer illustrations and discussion of the structure and function of a photosystem in the chloroplast
- Comparison of C_4 and CAM photosynthesis

PART 4: Genes, Genomes, and Heredity

- Reorganization to the unit so Chapter 17: *Genomes* and Chapter 18: *Recombinant DNA and Biotechnology* are included in Part 4

- Sections dealing with mutations substantially altered to clarify the relationships between DNA damage, DNA mismatches and DNA mutations, and the role of DNA repair
- Update of transcription initiation in eukaryotes to include mediator
- Substantial update of Chapter 17: *Genomes*, including addition of transcriptomics, SNP genotyping, and use of SNPs in ancestry and association studies
- Expansion of Chapter 18: *Recombinant DNA and Biotechnology* to include greater detail on transgenics, cloning, reporters, genetic screens, and other methods to identify genes of interest, and uses of CRISPR

PART 5: The Processes and Patterns of Evolution

- Major expansion and update of Chapter 21: *Evolution of Genes and Genomes*
- Expansion and integration of developmental mechanisms of evolution through changes in gene expression
- More integration of phylogeny and its uses throughout the questions and problem sets
- Addition of more data-based problems so that students can apply evolutionary concepts to practical problems in biology

PART 6: Diversity of Life

- Updated information on our current knowledge of the tree of life
- More discussion of the origins of the major lineages of life, with explanations of the contributions to eukaryotes from both archaea and bacteria
- New problem sets that allow students to explore the basis for our understanding of the tree of life

PART 7: Flowering Plants: Form and Function

- Enhanced emphasis on plants' ability to sense and respond to the environment, including a new figure that shows how roots grow in response to low levels of P and N
- Updated treatment of osmosis that corrects common misconceptions
- Updated description of plant meristems
- Introduced exciting new data showing that the rate of dark reversion of phytochrome may act as a temperature sensor
- Increased focus on plant response to climate change

PART 8: Animals: Form and Function

- New Chapter 38 Investigating Life box on Ebola and emergency workers who face heat stress due to wearing protective gear
- New figure and increased coverage of glia and the glymphatic system
- Updated coverage about birth control methods
- Improved coverage of thyroxin with revised figure showing the steps of biosynthesis of the hormone
- Revised coverage and figures on the evolution of the vertebrate heart
- New figure and more detail on the mechanism of penile erection
- Improved coverage of 3-D vision

PART 9: Ecology

- A consistent focus on the importance of scale and multiple levels of organization in ecology. Special emphasis has been placed on global change and the role of humans as part of Earth's systems
- Inclusion of quantitative and conceptual material in order to visualize (through figures) and analyze (through Work with the Data questions) concepts using active learning techniques
- Updated examples, including marine, invasive species, and endangered species studies
- Updated content on the effects of Earth's topography on physical processes such as temperature inversion, ocean upwelling, and rain shadow effects
- Updated content on population growth models and examples, including material on life table analysis
- Updated content on disturbance and succession including the concept of alternative stable states
- Updated content on nutrient cycling at ecosystem and global scales, including decomposition, nutrient transformations, and the causes of climate change
- Updated content on the causes and consequences of biodiversity loss, including pollution, overharvesting, invasive species, emerging diseases, and the effects of climate change

Life The Science of Biology
Media Updates

Updates to the Media and Assessment Resources

Activities

- A new format for most activities, designed to better engage the student

Simulations

- New simulations on topics such as macromolecules, active and passive transport, and natural selection
- Each simulation is now accompanied by an assignable quiz in **Achieve**.

Animations

- A new video format that incorporates captions directly into the video

Data in Depth

- Each in-book **Work with the Data** exercise has a new online companion exercise, **Data in Depth**, designed to deepen students' data manipulation skills.

Interactive Stats Primer

- The online version of Appendix B, **Making Sense of Data: A Statistics Primer** gives students the opportunity to learn basic statistical concepts and skill through hands-on simulations and activities.

Active Learning Guide and Instructor's Manual

- A thorough primer on active learning in biology
- Includes sections such as:
    - What is active learning?
    - Designing your course for active learning
    - Using active learning in the classroom
    - How to implement *Life* resources
- Chapter-by-chapter ideas, suggestions, and resources
- Now integrated with the Instructor's Manual

Active Learning Modules

- Robust modules designed to provide all the support an instructor needs to teach selected topics in an active learning setting
- Each module includes a detailed instructor's guide, a pre-quiz, a pre-class video, an in-class exercise, a post-quiz, and assessment questions.

Test Bank

- All questions aligned to new Learning Objectives
- Additional questions at higher Bloom's Levels

LearningCurve

- Expanded question banks for each chapter
- Hints added to all questions

LearningCurve, in particular, is very helpful to my students. Many of my students commented on my student evaluation that they found the online resources and LearningCurve assignments very helpful to them."

— Amanda Chau, Blinn College

About the Authors

David M. Hillis is the Alfred W. Roark Centennial Professor in Integrative Biology at the University of Texas at Austin, where he also has directed the Center for Computational Biology and Bioinformatics, the Biodiversity Center, and the School of Biological Sciences. Dr. Hillis has taught courses in introductory biology, genetics, evolution, systematics, and biodiversity. He is a member of the National Academy of Sciences and the American Academy of Arts and Sciences. He was awarded a John D. and Catherine T. MacArthur Fellowship, and has served as President of the Society for the Study of Evolution and of the Society of Systematic Biologists. He served on the National Research Council committee that wrote the report *BIO 2010: Transforming Undergraduate Biology Education for Research Biologists*, and currently serves on the Executive Committee of the National Academies Scientific Teaching Alliance.

H. Craig Heller is the Lorry I. Lokey/Business Wire Professor in Biological Sciences and Human Biology at Stanford University. He has taught in the core biology courses at Stanford since 1972 and served as Director of the Program in Human Biology, Chairman of the Biological Sciences Department, and Associate Dean of Research. Dr. Heller is a fellow of the American Association for the Advancement of Science and a recipient of the Walter J. Gores Award for excellence in teaching and the Kenneth Cuthberson Award for Exceptional Service to Stanford University. His research is on the neurobiology of sleep and circadian rhythms, mammalian hibernation, the regulation of body temperature, the physiology of human performance, and the neurobiology of learning. He has done research on a huge variety of animals and physiological problems, including sleeping kangaroo rats, diving seals, hibernating bears, photo-periodic hamsters, and exercising athletes. Dr. Heller has extended his enthusiasm for promoting active learning via the development of a two-year curriculum in human biology for the middle grades through the production of Virtual Labs—interactive computer-based modules to teach physiology.

Sally D. Hacker is a Professor at Oregon State University where she has been a faculty member since 2004. She has taught courses in introductory ecology, community ecology, invasion biology, field ecology, and marine biology. She was awarded the Murray F. Buell Award by the Ecological Society of America and the Young Investigator Prize by the American Society of Naturalists. Dr. Hacker's research explores the structure, function, and services of natural and managed ecosystems under varying contexts of species interactions and global change. She has conducted research with plants and animals in rocky intertidal, salt marsh, seagrass, and coastal dune ecosystems. Her work has most recently focused on the protective role of dune ecosystems in mitigating coastal vulnerability due to climate change. In addition to the textbooks *Life: The Science of Biology* and *Ecology* (Sinauer Associates), she is author or coauthor on numerous articles and book chapters exploring community ecology, species interactions, marine invasions, and ecosystem services important to coastal management. She is particularly interested in promoting active and experiential learning for students interested in ecology and field-immersion experiences.

David W. Hall is Associate Professor of Genetics at the University of Georgia, where he was the recipient of the Sandy Beaver Excellence in Teaching Award in 2013. Recent work includes using mathematical models to address the evolution of meiotic drive, the rate and pattern of molecular evolution in social insects, and early sex chromosome evolution. In the lab, he utilizes different yeast species to study spontaneous mutations using a combination of both mutation-accumulation and adaptation experiments. Since high school, he has been captivated by how the living world works. Like many students, he was initially overwhelmed by the diversity of life, but he came to realize that there are fundamental principles that unite organisms. His interest in determining how these principles shape the diversity of life led him into his research and teaching career.

Marta J. Laskowski is a Professor in the Biology Department at Oberlin College. Dr. Laskowski has mentored undergraduate students in research and has taught introductory biology, skills-based first year seminars (Feeding the World), plant physiology, and plant development. She heads an effort at Oberlin, funded by the HHMI Inclusive Excellence program, to enhance the climate for and success of a diverse student population in STEM. One of her numerous journal articles resulted in a Guinness World Record for the fastest opening flower (*Cornus canadensis*; bunchberry). A college class in developmental biology so captivated her that she decided to focus her research on discovering the intricate subcellular interactions that establish the plant root system.

David Sadava is the Pritzker Family Foundation Professor of Biology, Emeritus, at the Keck Science Center of Claremont McKenna, Pitzer, and Scripps, three of The Claremont Colleges. In addition, he is Adjunct Professor of Cancer Cell Biology at the City of Hope Medical Center. Twice winner of the Huntoon Award for superior teaching, Dr. Sadava has taught courses on introductory biology, biotechnology, biochemistry, cell biology, molecular biology, plant biology, and cancer biology. In addition to *Life: The Science of Biology*, he is the author or coauthor of books on cell biology and on plants, genes, and crop biotechnology. His research has resulted in many papers coauthored with his students, on topics ranging from plant biochemistry to pharmacology of narcotic analgesics to human genetic diseases. For the past 15 years, he has investigated multi-drug resistance in human small-cell lung carcinoma cells with a view to understanding and overcoming this clinical challenge. At the City of Hope, his current work focuses on new anti-cancer agents from plants.

Acknowledgments

Although our names are on the cover, and we take ultimate responsibility for the contents of this book, we relied on many people for help. We have received a multitude of valuable suggestions across the various editions of *Life* from our Advisory Board. These biologists, from institutions large and small, have helped us plan many of the pedagogical innovations for this edition. These colleagues provided exceptional critiques to our proposals, drawing on their vast teaching experiences in diverse learning environments. As our chapters became reality, the thoughtful insights of these advisors were invaluable. In addition, with their varied experiences incorporating online material into their teaching, the members of the Advisory Board were an important source of feedback as we developed the active learning and assessment materials associated with the book. We could not have done it without them.

Many thousands of people have reviewed the chapters of *Life* over its 12 editions, and another 180 reviewers guided us in this revision by providing between-edition reviews and suggestions for each of our chapters. They helped us decide what needed improving and gave us suggestions to make that happen. With our emphasis on active learning and pedagogy, we also asked experts in biology education to critique our pedagogical features and give us suggestions for improvement. We are grateful to each and every one of these reviewers.

The talented team at Sinauer Associates included Sydney Carroll, who provided the editorial oversight for the Twelfth Edition. Dean Scudder managed the Sinauer team and provided guidance and suggestions in the planning and development of *Life*. We also thank our Production Editors, Danna Niedzwiecki Lockwood, Johannah Walkowicz, and Tracy Marton, who edited our chapters, and helped us implement and maintain consistency in our features. We are grateful to Mark Siddall, who located new, fresh photographs to illustrate the chapters; Michele Beckta and Tracy Marton, who managed the permissions process and were ever vigilant in prompting us to track down data sources; Joan Gemme and Donna DiCarlo, who created the design and managed the production of the book's cover and pages; Liz Pierson, who skillfully copyedited all the chapters; and Suzanne Carter, who directed a team of talented media and supplements editors and writers.

We appreciate the ongoing support of John Challice and Petra Recter from Oxford University Press. Macmillan Learning has worked aggressively to bring *Life* to a broader audience. Executive Marketing Manager Will Moore, Executive Program Manager for Biology Lisa Lockwood, and Executive Program Director for Life Sciences Sandy Lindelof, along with the regional specialists, regional managers, and experienced sales force, are effective ambassadors and skillful transmitters of the strong features and unique strengths of this new edition. We depend upon their experience and energy to keep us in touch with how *Life* is perceived by its users.

Finally, we thank Andy Sinauer, who was our publisher for the first 11 editions of *Life*, and who recruited most of us to the author team. Although Andy has now retired, his love of biology, his commitment to education, and his standards of excellence in publishing continue to inspire us all.

DAVID HILLIS
CRAIG HELLER
SALLY HACKER
DAVID HALL
MARTA LASKOWSKI
DAVID SADAVA

Reviewers and Contributors

Between-Edition Reviewers

Danyelle N. Aganovic, University of North Georgia

Cristian Aguilar, Azusa Pacific University

Norma Allewell, University of Maryland, College Park

Christine Andrews, University of Chicago

Jason Arnold, Hopkinsville Community College

Miriam Ashley-Ross, Wake Forest University

Linda Auker, St. Lawrence University

Katherine Barker, Blinn College

Geoffrey Benn, University of California at Davis

Michael Berger, Washington State University

Alex Bezzerides, Lewis-Clark State College

Mary Bisson, University at Buffalo

Kristina Blanke, University at Buffalo

Andrew Blaustein, Oregon State University

Luis Bonachea, University of Pittsburgh at Johnstown

James Bottesch, Eastern Florida State College

Nicole Bournias-Vardiabasis, California State University, San Bernardino

Christopher Brandon, Florida Southern College

Mirjana M. Brockett, Georgia Institute of Technology

Chris Burcher, Virginia Highlands Community College

Stephen Burnett, Clayton State University

Shere Kuss Byrd, Fort Lewis College

Alisha Campbell, Northwest Missouri State University

Billy Carver, Lees-McRae College

Dale Casamatta, University of North Florida

Alyson Center, Normandale Community College

Rebekah Chapman, Georgia State University

Prescott Bryant, Chase Florida State University

Amanda Chau, Blinn College

Charles Chen, Azusa Pacific University

Byung Min Chung, The Catholic University of America

Cynthia Church, Metropolitan State University of Denver

Kari Clifton, University of West Florida

Heather Coan, Western Carolina University

Kelly Collins, Lees-McRae College

Pamela Connerly, Indiana University Southeast

Frank Corotto, University of North Georgia

Christopher M. Cottingham, University of North Alabama

Elizabeth Cowles, Eastern Connecticut State University

David P. Craig, Willamette University

Lorelei Crerar, George Mason University

Jennifer Cymbola, Grand Valley State University

Mary Ellen Czesak, Vassar College

Christine Dahlin, University of Pittsburgh at Johnstown

Candice Damiani, University of Pittsburgh

Douglas Darnowski, Indiana University Southeast

Alyce DeMarais, University of Puget Sound

William Dentler, University of Kansas

Tiffany Doan, New College of Florida

Cathleen Dobbs, Joliet Junior College

Jennifer Doherty, University of Washington

Jason Duncan, Willamette University

Kelli Duncan, Vassar College

Megan Dunn, Indiana University

Ana Esther Escandon, Los Angeles Harbor College

Melinda Faulkner, Bradley University

Kenneth Filchak, University of Notre Dame

Janet Fisher, University of West Georgia

Lee Ann Frederick, University of Texas at Arlington

Pamela Freeman, College of St. Scholastica

Marian M. Furimsky, Westminster College (PA)

Megan D. Gall, Vassar College

Kathryn Gardner, University of Pittsburgh

Renaud Geslain, College of Charleston

Raffaella Ghittoni, University of Southern California

William Gilliland, DePaul University, Chicago

Gwen Goodmanlowe, California State University, Long Beach

Suzanna Gribble, University of Pittsburgh

Eric Haag, University of Maryland, College Park

Gokhan Hacisalihoglu, Florida A&M University

Michael K. Hamed, Virginia Highlands Community College

Donna Hamilton, University of North Texas, Dallas

Phillip Harris, The University of Alabama

Wayne Hatch, Utah State University Eastern

Brian T. Hentschel, San Diego State University

Brad Hersh, Allegheny College

Ayana Hinton, Denison University

Mark A. Holbrook, University of Iowa

William Huddleston, University of Calgary

Victor Izzo, University of Vermont

Jamie Jensen, Brigham Young University

Heather Joesting, Georgia Southern University

Michael Johanson, Blinn College

Gregory Johnson, University of Puget Sound

Jerald B. Johnson, Brigham Young University

Gregory Jones, Santa Fe College

Carly Jordan, The George Washington University

Jennifer Jost, Bradley University

Joshua Kapfer, University of Wisconsin, Whitewater

Lori Kayes, Oregon State University

Moshe Khurgel, Bridgewater College

Henrik Kibak, California State University, Monterey Bay

Kelly C. Kissane, Blinn College–Brenham Campus

Amy Klocko, University of Colorado, Colorado Springs

Ross Koning, Eastern Connecticut State University

Jason Kuehner, Emmanuel College

Stacie Kutz, The Sage Colleges

Kim Lackey, University of Alabama

Adriana LaGier, Grand View University

Diane Lahaise, Georgia State University–Perimeter College

Kari Lavalli, Boston University

Chris Levesque, John Abbott College

Eric Liebl, Denison University

Faith Liebl, Southern Illinois University

Samantha Lin, Yale University

Craig Longtine, North Hennepin Community College

Laura Lorentzen, Kean University

Christopher Loretz, University at Buffalo

Peter Lyons, Andrews University

Elizabeth Machunis-Masuoka, Midwestern State University

Jay Mager, Ohio Northern University

Charles Mallery, University of Miami

Barry J. Margulies, Towson University

Carolyn Martineau, DePaul University

Lori McGrew, Belmont University

Gerard McNeil, York College/City University of New York

Jennifer Metzler, Ball State University

Roderick Morgan, Grand Valley State University

Brent Mortensen, Benedictine College

LaSharon Mosley, University of Cincinnati

Patricia Mote, Georgia State University

Orissa Moulton, Texas A&M University, Galveston

James Murphy, Bloomfield College

Barbara Musolf, Clayton State University

Benjamin Navia, Andrews University

Judy Nesmith, University of Michigan, Dearborn

Jennifer Ness, Bradley University

Robert H. Newman, North Carolina A&T State University

Wade Nichols, Illinois State University

Alexey Nikitin, Grand Valley State University

Eric Norstrom, DePaul University

Matthew Nusnbaum, Georgia State University

Alexander E. Olvido, University of North Georgia

Robert Osuna, University at Albany, State University of New York

Ellen Ott-Reeves, Blinn College

Irvin Pan, Stonehill College

Janet Paper, Benedictine College

Kristin Picardo, St. John Fisher College

Daniel Potter, University of California, Davis

Kimberly Quaranta, Arizona State University

Elizabeth Rielly, Holy Family University

Leslie Riley, Ohio Northern University

Laurel Roberts, University of Pittsburgh

Ben Rowley, University of Central Arkansas

Charlotte Russell, Simmons University

Susan Sadler, University of Denver

Cassandra Saitow, Simmons College

Donald Sakaguchi, Iowa State University

James Reid Schwebach, George Mason University

Erik P. Scully, Towson University

Anupama Shanmuganathan, Washington & Jefferson College

Sylvia Sharp, Saginaw Valley State University

Tonya Shepherd, Blinn College & Texas A&M University

James Shinkle, Trinity University

Erin Shortlidge, Portland State University

Cahleen Shrier, Azusa Pacific University

Bin Shuai, Wichita State University

William K. Smith, Wake Forest University

Robert Steven, University of Toledo

Michaela Gazdik Stofer, Utah Valley University

Fengjie Sun, Georgia Gwinnett College

Cynthia A. Surmacz, Bloomsburg University of Pennsylvania

Ken Gunter Sweat, Arizona State University

Zuzana Swigonova, University of Pittsburgh

Edward Tall, Seton Hall University

Rebekah Taylor, Frostburg State University

Ilya Temkin, Northern Virginia Community College

Jennifer T. Thomas, Belmont University

Beverly Thompson, Tri-County Technical College

Monica S. Torres, Rutgers University

Catherine Trivigno, Florida Atlantic University

Cynthia van Golen, Delaware State University

Doug Van Hoewyk, Coastal Carolina University

Matthew Venesky, Allegheny College

Brian G. Walker, Fairfield University

Lisa B. Whitenack, Allegheny College

Cathy Whiting, University of North Georgia

Larry Wimmers, Towson University

Steven Wood, Blinn College

Robert Zdor, Andrews University

Media and Supplements Contributors

Moira Conith, University of Massachusetts, Amherst

Jill DeVito, University of Texas, Arlington

Donna Francis, University of Massachusetts, Amherst

Richard Gill, Brigham Young University

Carol Hand, Science writer

Phillip Harris, University of Alabama

Margaret Hill, Science writer

Kendra Hutchins, Cornell University

Norman Johnson, University of Massachusetts, Amherst

Carly Jordan, The George Washington University

Laurie Leonelli, New York University

Betty Anne McGuire, Cornell University

Meredith Safford, Johns Hopkins University

John Townsend-Mehler, Montana State University

Mary Tyler, University of Maine, Orono

Robert Wise, University of Wisconsin, Oshkosh (emeritus)

Media and Supplements

to accompany *Life: The Science of Biology*, Twelfth Edition

 Achieve

Achieve is the easy-to-use online platform that integrates the e-book, all of the student and instructor media resources, and assessment functions into one clean, unified interface. For more about **Achieve**, see pages viii–xiii and visit macmillanlearning.com/Achieve.

Student Resources

ACTIVITIES. A range of interactive activities helps students learn and review key facts and concepts through labeling diagrams and identifying structures and stages of processes.

SIMULATIONS. Dynamic simulations allow students to explore how biological systems and processes work. Each is accompanied by a brief quiz.

ANIMATIONS. In-depth animations present complex topics in a clear, easy-to-follow format. Each is accompanied by a brief quiz.

MEDIA CLIPS. These engaging video clips depict fascinating examples of some of the many organisms, processes, and phenomena discussed in the textbook.

DATA IN DEPTH. These online companions to the in-text Work with the Data exercises help students improve data literacy and quantitative skills through interactive exercises and questions.

LEARNINGCURVE. A powerful adaptive quizzing system with a game-like format that engages students. See page xv for details.

SUMMATIVE QUIZZES. Pre-built quizzes that assess overall student understanding of each chapter.

APPLY WHAT YOU'VE LEARNED. Exercises that challenge students to put their knowledge into action by answering questions related to specific research findings.

VIDEOS. The wide-ranging collection of video segments helps demonstrate the complexity and beauty of life.

TREE OF LIFE. An interactive version of the tree of life from Appendix A, with links to a wealth of information on each group listed.

BIONEWS FROM *SCIENTIFIC AMERICAN*. BioNews makes it easy for instructors to bring the dynamic nature of the biological sciences and up-to-the-minute currency into their course via an automatically updated news feed in **Achieve**.

Instructor Resources

TEXTBOOK FIGURES AND TABLES. Every figure and table from the textbook (including all photos and all unnumbered figures) is provided in both JPEG and PowerPoint formats, in multiple versions, including whole, reformatted, and unlabeled.

POWERPOINT RESOURCES. For each chapter of the textbook, several different PowerPoint presentations are available, providing instructors the flexibility to build presentations in the manner that best suits their needs:

- Textbook Figures and Tables
- Lecture Presentations
- Layered Art Figures
- Active Learning Module In-Class Exercises

ACTIVE LEARNING GUIDE & INSTRUCTOR'S MANUAL. This guide provides an excellent overview of active learning techniques for introductory biology, along with chapter-specific support. Active learning resources and suggestions are all organized by Key Concept, with Learning Objectives included. Also included are the following sections for each chapter: *Chapter Overview*, *What's New in This Edition*, *Chapter Outline*, and *Key Terms*. See page xiii for details.

ACTIVE LEARNING MODULES. These comprehensive modules provide instructors everything they need to teach selected key topics using an active learning approach. See page xiii for details.

ANSWERS TO TEXTBOOK QUESTIONS. Answers to all of the in-text questions: Recap and Assess questions, Work with the Data questions, Figure questions, and Visual Summary questions.

ANSWERS TO APPLY WHAT YOU'VE LEARNED. Answers to all of the Apply What You've Learned exercises.

TEST BANK. The *Life* Test Bank includes over 7,000 questions, all referenced to specific Key Concepts, Learning Objectives, and Bloom's Levels. Each chapter includes a wide range of multiple-choice and short-answer questions.

COMPUTERIZED TEST BANK. The Test Bank is also available in Cognero format, with software included, for easy exam and quiz creation.

LEARNING MANAGEMENT SYSTEM SUPPORT. Easy LMS integration into any school's learning management system—such as Blackboard, Canvas, D2L/Brightspace, Moodle, and more—means your gradebook and roster are always in sync and your students also get the benefit of single sign-on.

Additional Resources

Instructors, get more out of your classroom.

iClicker's innovative solutions make it easy to track attendance, increase participation, facilitate quizzes, measure performance, and get more out of your classroom. For more information, visit **iclicker.com**.

Macmillan Learning Lab Solutions

Macmillan Learning Lab Solutions unites the same brands you know and trust—W. H. Freeman, Hayden-McNeil, Sapling Learning, and Late Nite Labs—and provides the resources to build a seamless, comprehensive lab experience for your students. For more information, visit **macmillanlearning.com/LabSolutions**.

CatchUp Math & Stats for the Life Sciences

Michael Harris, Gordon Taylor, and Jacquelyn Taylor
(ISBN 978-1-4292-0557-3)
Presented in brief, accessible units, this primer will help students quickly brush up on the quantitative skills they need to succeed in biology.

A Student Handbook for Writing in Biology, Fifth Edition

Karin Knisely (ISBN 978-1-3191-2181-5)
This book provides practical advice to students who are learning to write according to the conventions in biology, using the standards of journal publication as a model.

BioStats Basics: A Student Handbook

James L. Gould and Grant F. Gould (ISBN 978-0-7167-3416-1)
Engaging and informal, *BioStats Basics* provides introductory-level biology students with a practical, accessible introduction to statistical methodology.

Hayden-McNeil Life Sciences Lab Notebook

(ISBN 978-1-4292-3055-1)
This durable, high-quality carbonless laboratory notebook allows students to hand in originals or copies of their lab work, not entire composition books. The Lab Notebook contains Hayden-McNeil's unique white paper carbonless copies and biology-specific reference materials.

The *Scientific Teaching* Book Series

The Series is a collection of practical guides, intended for all science, technology, engineering and mathematics (STEM) faculty who teach undergraduate and graduate students in these disciplines. The purpose of these books is to help faculty become more successful in all aspects of teaching and learning science, including classroom instruction, mentoring students, and professional development. Authored by well-known science educators, the Series provides concise descriptions of best practices and how to implement them in the classroom, the laboratory, or the department. For readers interested in the research results on which these best practices are based, the books also provide a gateway to the key educational literature. The Series includes:

Scientific Teaching
Jo Handelsman, Sarah Miller, and Christine Pfund
(ISBN 978-1-4292-0188-9)

Transformations: Approaches to College Science Teaching
Deborah Allen and Kimberly Tanner
(ISBN 978-1-4292-5335-2)

Entering Research: A Curriculum to Support Undergraduate & Graduate Research Trainees, Second Edition
Janet L. Branchaw, Amanda R. Butz, and Amber Smith
(ISBN: 978-1-3192-6368-3)

Discipline-Based Science Education Research: A Scientist's Guide
Stephanie J. Slater, Timothy F. Slater, and Janelle M. Bailey
(ISBN 978-1-4292-6586-7)

Assessment in the College Classroom
Clarissa Dirks, Mary Pat Wenderoth, and Michelle Withers
(ISBN 978-1-4292-8197-3)

Contents

© Spencer Grant/Science Source

© Talley Lambert/Science Source

© Konrad Wothe/Minden Pictures

© Spencer Sutton/Science Source

© Michael Ventura/Alamy Stock Photo

© imageBROKER/Alamy Stock Photo

© StellaPhotography/Alamy Stock Photo

© Ingo Arndt/Minden Pictures

© Chris Newbert/Minden Pictures

© BOONCHUAY PROMJIAM/Shutterstock.com

39 Animal Hormones 863

▶Investigating**LIFE**

The Smart and Healthy Hormone 863

40 Immunology: Animal Defense Systems 886

▶Investigating**LIFE**

Vaccines and Immunity 886

© Chien Lee/Minden Pictures

© PCN Photography/Alamy Stock Photo

© Graeme Guy/Minden Pictures

51 Animal Behavior   1143

© Ingo Arndt/Minden Pictures

PART NINE   Ecology

© Brigitte Marcon/Minden Pictures

© Hiroya Minakuchi/Minden Pictures

Life

The Science of Biology
TWELFTH EDITION

Studying Life 1

Scientists are studying how corals are affected by global climate change.

KEY CONCEPTS

1.1 Living Organisms Have a Common Origin and Share Similarities

1.2 Genetics and Evolution Are Fundamental Principles of Biology

1.3 Biologists Investigate Life through Experiments That Test Hypotheses

1.4 Understanding Biology Is Important for Health, Well-Being, and Public-Policy Decisions

▶Investigating**LIFE**

Corals in Hot Water

Coral reefs support the largest diversity of life in the oceans. They provide fisheries and storm protection for about a billion people and are a magnificent source of natural beauty. But coral reefs are endangered. Over the past 25 years about half of the world's reef-building corals have been destroyed by rising water temperature and other factors. High temperatures disrupt a fascinating aspect of coral biology. Corals are animals, yet most corals have algae (dinoflagellates) growing within their cells. Dinoflagellates use the energy of sunlight to produce carbohydrates. Corals provide a home for the dinoflagellates, which in turn provide nutrients for the corals. When high temperature impairs the dinoflagellates, the corals eject them—a process called bleaching. Then, without nutrients from the dinoflagellates, the corals die, unless they can take in new dinoflagellates that are more resistant to the higher temperatures.

Understanding the effects of heat on corals was the motivation of graduate student Rachael Bay and her colleagues working with Professor Steve Palumbi at Stanford University's Hopkins Marine Station. While studying corals in small back-reef pools in American Samoa, they observed that during low tides some pools reached higher temperatures than others. The research-ers predicted that corals in the warmer pools had mechanisms enabling them to resist bleaching. To test their prediction, the researchers brought corals into the laboratory, subjected them to temperature fluctuations, and showed that the corals from the warm pools were more resistant to bleaching. They also transplanted corals between the different temperature environments in nature. As a result of these experiments, Bay and her colleagues proposed that two different processes contribute to the different abilities of the corals to survive heat stress. First, corals growing in the warmer pools could have genetic traits contributing to heat resistance, and second, individual corals may have the same genetic makeup but differ in their ability to adjust to their environment by changing the expression levels of certain genes. More knowledge of the mechanisms of heat stress and heat resistance in corals could lead to new strategies to decrease their losses as their environments change.

 How might experiments on heat stress in corals be used to predict the response of corals to global warming? (Find the answer on page 20.)

1.1 Living Organisms Have a Common Origin and Share Similarities

Learning Objectives

1.1.1 List the major characteristics shared among all living things.

1.1.2 Describe the general history of life on Earth and the origins of the three major groups of organisms.

1.1.3 Explain how photosynthesis influenced the history of life on Earth.

1.1.4 Discuss the relationship between multicellularity and homeostasis.

You likely have a sense of what we mean by "life," but try to define it; it isn't easy. You can easily designate the things around you as living or nonliving, but what are the essential differences? We call the living things organisms. In contrast to nonliving things, organisms sustain and renew themselves. The loss of the ability to sustain and renew means the loss of life, and organisms that die become part of the nonliving world. **Biology** is the scientific study of organisms, both living and after death (e.g., the study of fossils), with the goal of discovering and understanding the underlying unity as well as the amazing diversity of the complex processes that make up life.

Life on our planet is quite diverse (**Figure 1.1**), yet its many diverse forms share common features. What characteristics do organisms share that distinguish them from the nonliving world? Most organisms:

- are composed of a common set of chemical compounds: mainly carbohydrates, fatty acids, nucleic acids, and amino acids.

- are made up of cells.

- use molecules obtained from the environment to synthesize new biological molecules.

(A) *Sulfolobus*

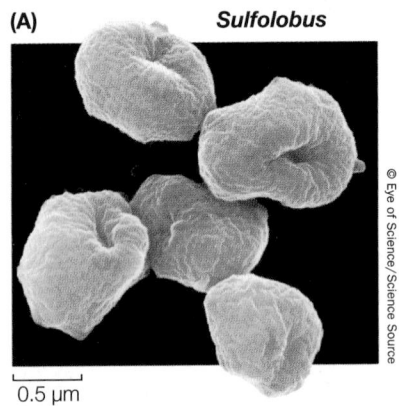

0.5 μm

(B) *Escherichia coli*

0.6 μm

(C) *Coronosphaera mediterranea*

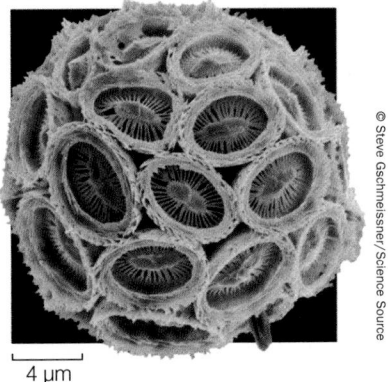

4 μm

(D) *Thelocactus conothelos argenteus*

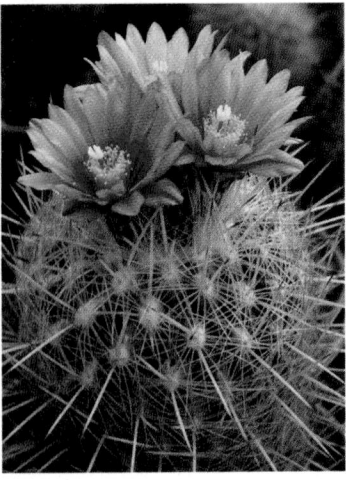

(E) *Pholiota squarrosa* (shaggy scalycap mushrooms)

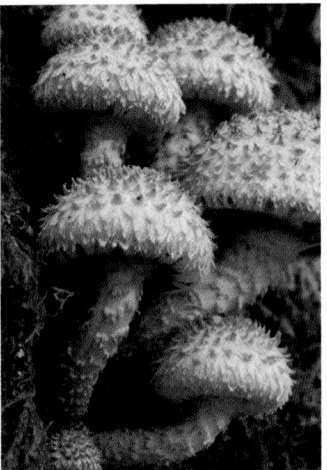

(F) *Heteractis magnifica* (magnificent sea anemone)
Eretmochlys imbricata (hawksbill sea turtle)
Chaetodon punctatofasciatus (spotband butterflyfish)

Figure 1.1 The Many Faces of Life   The processes of evolution have led to the millions of diverse organisms living on Earth today. Archaea **(A)** and bacteria **(B)** are all single-celled organisms, as described in Chapter 24. **(C)** Many eukaryotes are also unicellular, but as discussed in Chapter 25, their cell structures are more complex than those of archaea and bacteria. This unicellular eukaryote has manufactured "plates" of calcium carbonate that surround and protect its single cell. (D–F) Most of the visible life on Earth is multicellular. Chapters 26 and 27 cover the green plants **(D)**. The other broad groups of multicellular organisms are the fungi **(E)**, discussed in Chapter 28, and the animals **(F)**, covered in Chapters 29–31.

- extract energy from the environment and use it to do work.
- regulate their internal environments.
- contain genetic information—genomes—that enables them to develop, maintain themselves, function, and reproduce.
- use a universal molecular code to build proteins from their genomic information.
- exist in populations that evolve over time.

How do you think all organisms came to have these similarities? If life had multiple origins, we would not expect to see such striking similarities in chemical composition, cell structure, cell functions, and genetic codes across the living world. Instead, these common characteristics logically lead to the conclusion that all life has a common ancestry, and that the diverse organisms alive today all originated from one life form. Organisms from a separate origin of life—say, on another planet—might be similar in superficial ways to life on Earth, but they would not have the same genetic code, chemical composition, or cellular structures and functions that we see widely shared among living organisms on Earth. All evidence points to a common origin of life on our planet about 4 billion years ago.

Some forms of life may not display all the characteristics we have just listed all of the time. For example, the seed of a desert plant may go for many years without extracting energy from the environment, converting molecules, regulating its internal environment, or reproducing; yet the seed is alive. Viruses present a special case as well. Viruses are not composed of cells and cannot carry out physiological functions on their own. Viruses depend on the cells of host organisms to carry out these functions for them. Yet viruses contain genetic information, and their populations evolve over time, as we know from witnessing changes in the flu viruses each flu season. Even though viruses are not independent cellular organisms, their existence depends on cells, and it is highly probable that viruses evolved from cellular life forms. Thus most biologists consider viruses to be a part of life.

As you go through this book, you will explore details of the common characteristics of life, how these characteristics arose, and how they work together so that organisms survive and reproduce. You will also explore the amazing diversity of life on Earth and how that diversity has been produced through the processes of **evolution**—changes in the genetic makeup of populations through time. Because organisms do not all survive and reproduce with equal success, advantageous variations spread in a population from generation to generation and result in adaptations that better suit individuals to specific environments. The processes of evolution have generated the enormous diversity of life on Earth, and evolution is a central theme of biology.

Life arose from non-life via chemical evolution

Earth formed between 4.6 and 4.5 billion years ago, but at first it was not a place hospitable to life. The cooling of Earth, the formation of surface water, and the evolution of the first life forms took about 600 million years. If we picture the 4.6-billion-year history

Figure 1.2 Life's Timeline Depicting the 4.6 billion years of Earth's history on the scale of a 30-day month provides a sense of the immensity of evolutionary time.

of Earth as a 30-day month, life first appeared some time around the end of the first week (**Figure 1.2**).

The composition of Earth in terms of the chemical elements has not changed over its history, but random physical and chemical interactions of those atoms produced an enormous variety of molecules. The young Earth's atmosphere, oceans, and climate were very different than they are today, influencing how those molecules interacted. Experiments simulating those conditions have confirmed that the generation of complex molecules was inevitable. The critical step for the evolution of life was the appearance of **nucleic acids**—molecules that could reproduce themselves and serve as templates for the synthesis of **proteins**, large molecules with complex but stable shapes. The variation in the shapes of these proteins enabled them to participate in increasing numbers and kinds of chemical reactions with other molecules. These subjects are covered in Part One of this book.

Cellular structure evolved in the common ancestor of life

An important step in the evolution of life was the enclosure of complex proteins and other biological molecules by membranes that contained them in a compact internal environment separate from the surrounding (external) environment. Fatty acid molecules played a critical role in membrane evolution because these molecules do not dissolve in water. Think of shaking an oil and vinegar salad dressing. The oil breaks up into small droplets, but the droplets do not dissolve in the vinegar and they rapidly coalesce. Similarly, fatty acids can form membranous films on the surface of water. When these films are agitated, they can form spherical structures called **liposomes**. Such structures are now used for delivering drugs to cells (**Figure 1.3A**). In a primordial ocean, such membranous structures could have enveloped assemblages of complex biological molecules. The origin of an internal environment that concentrated reactants and products of chemical reactions led to the first cells with the ability to replicate themselves—the evolution of the first cellular organisms.

For billions of years all the organisms existing on Earth were unicellular and were enclosed by a single outer membrane. Such organisms, like the bacteria that are abundant on you, in you, and all around you, are called **prokaryotes** (Figure 1.3B). Two main groups diverged early in life's history: **Bacteria** and **Archaea**. The third major category of life on Earth, **Eukarya**, arose billions of years later, with contributions from both bacteria and archaea. (Note that we use initial capitals when referring to these three main groups, but lowercase when referring to members of the

groups.) In addition to its outer membrane, a eukaryotic cell (**Figure 1.3C**) has internal membranes that enclose specialized internal compartments called organelles. The organelle that gives eukaryotes their name is the **nucleus**—the organelle that contains the cell's genetic information. The word "eukaryote" comes from two Greek words meaning "a true kernel." Other organelles carry out specific functions such as synthesizing biological molecules or providing energy.

How might eukaryotes have arisen from prokaryotes? Infoldings of the prokaryotic cell membrane could have formed internal compartments—the organelles—that isolated cell functions from each other, resulting in greater integration or efficiency of cell functions. Another possibility, similar to that seen in the relationship between corals and dinoflagellates described at the beginning of this chapter, is that close, interdependent relationships may have developed between different prokaryotic cells, leading to a merger of sorts. Suppose a prokaryote good at converting energy was engulfed (but not digested) by a prokaryote good at synthesizing biological molecules. Each would supply a valuable service for the other, but now one would be an organelle inside the other. The structure of prokaryotic and eukaryotic cells, their membranes, and their evolution are the subjects of Part Two.

Photosynthesis allows some organisms to capture energy from the Sun

Living cells require energy to function. The earliest prokaryotes supplied their energy needs—their **metabolism**—by taking in small molecules from their environment, breaking the chemical

(A) Liposomes

200 nm

(B) Prokaryotic cells

Cell membrane

1 μm

(C) Eukaryotic cell

Cell membrane

Membrane of nucleus

Mitochondria (membrane-enclosed)

1 μm

Figure 1.3 Membranes Enclose the Building Blocks of Life These photographs were taken with electron microscopes (see Figure 5.4) and enhanced with added color to highlight details. **(A)** Liposomes are tiny round bubbles known as vesicles and are made out of the same material as a cell membrane. Liposomes can be filled with drugs and used to deliver drugs to cells. **(B)** Two prokaryotic cells of an *Enterococcus* bacterium that lives in the human digestive system. Prokaryotes are unicellular organisms with genetic and biochemical material enclosed inside a single membrane. **(C)** A human white blood cell (lymphocyte) represents one of the many specialized cell types that make up a multicellular eukaryote. Multiple membranes within the cell-enclosing outer membrane segregate the different biochemical processes of eukaryotic cells.

bonds of these molecules, and using the energy released from those chemical bonds to do cellular work. Many modern prokaryotes still function this way, and they function very successfully. But about 2.5 billion years ago, the emergence of **photosynthesis** changed the nature of life on Earth and also changed our planet.

Photosynthesis transforms the energy of sunlight into a form of chemical energy that can be used to do work such as the synthesis of large molecules. These large molecules can then be used to build cell structures or can be broken down to provide metabolic energy. Photosynthesis is the basis of most of life on Earth today because its energy-capturing processes provide food for other organisms. Early photosynthetic cells were probably similar to present-day prokaryotes called **cyanobacteria** (Figure 1.4). Over time, photosynthetic prokaryotes became so abundant that vast quantities of oxygen gas (O_2), a by-product of photosynthesis, began to accumulate in the atmosphere.

Connect the Concepts The pathways that harvest chemical energy to do all the kinds of biological work necessary to support metabolism are presented in Chapter 9.

During the early history of prokaryotic life, there was very little O_2 in Earth's atmosphere. In fact, O_2 was toxic to many of the prokaryotes living at that time, and its buildup in the atmosphere resulted in a huge mass extinction. But those organisms that could tolerate O_2 proliferated. Atmospheric O_2 opened up vast new avenues of evolution because **aerobic metabolism**—a biochemical process that uses O_2 to extract energy from nutrient molecules—is far more efficient than **anaerobic metabolism** (which does not use O_2). Most organisms today use aerobic metabolism.

Oxygen in the atmosphere also made it possible for life to move onto land. For most of life's history, ultraviolet (UV) radiation falling on Earth's surface was so intense that it destroyed any organism that was not shielded by water. The atmospheric accumulation of photosynthetically generated O_2 over a period of more than 2 billion years gradually led to the production of a layer of ozone (O_3) in the upper atmosphere. By about 500 million years ago, the ozone layer was sufficiently dense and absorbed enough of the Sun's UV radiation to make it possible for organisms to leave the protection of the water and live on land.

Cellular differentiation and specialization underlie multicellular life

Single-celled organisms were the only forms of life for more than half of the history of life on Earth (see Figure 1.2). However, at some point the cells of some eukaryotes didn't separate after cell division and instead remained attached to each other. Such colonial aggregations of cells made it possible for some of the associated cells to specialize in certain functions, such as reproduction, while other cells specialized in other functions, such as nutrient absorption or motility. This **cellular specialization** enabled multicellular eukaryotes to increase in size and become more efficient at gathering resources and adapting to specific environments.

Single-celled organisms must provide for all of their own needs, but the cells of multicellular organisms can evolve specializations to carry out certain functions exclusively and efficiently because they can depend on other cells to carry out other functions. Thus

(A) Cyanobacteria

© Dr. Robert Calentine/Visuals Unlimited, Inc.

5 μm

(B) Fossilized stromatolite

© Armands Pharyos/Alamy Stock Photo

(C) Living stromatolite

Stromatolites form as small grains of sediment are cemented together by communities of microorganisms, especially cyanobacteria.

© Krystyna Szulecka/Alamy Stock Photo

Figure 1.4 Photosynthetic Organisms Changed Earth's Atmosphere (**A**) Cyanobacteria are aquatic and photosynthetic: they live in the water and can manufacture their own food. Although they are quite small, they often grow in colonies large enough to see. (**B**) Colonies of photosynthetic cyanobacteria and other microorganisms produced structures called stromatolites that were preserved in the ancient fossil record. (**C**) Living stromatolites can still be found in appropriate environments.

the cells of a multicellular organism can have different developmental fates. Similar cell types can develop together into **tissues** that accomplish tasks that a single cell cannot. For example, muscle cells develop cellular mechanisms for generating force. A single muscle cell cannot generate much force, but many cells of a muscle

(A) Atoms to organisms

Atoms → Small molecules → Large molecules → Cells → Organism

Atoms: Oxygen, Carbon, Hydrogen

Small molecules: Water, Methane, Carbon dioxide

Large molecules: Proteins, Nucleic acids

Cells: Unicellular organisms, Colonial organisms, Cell specialization

Organism: Organ systems, Organs, Tissues, Multicellular organism (leopard frog, *Rana pipiens*)

Figure 1.5 Biology Is Studied at Many Levels of Organization
(A) Life's properties emerge when DNA and other molecules are organized in cells, which form building blocks for organisms. **(B)** Organisms exist in populations and interact with other populations to form communities, which interact with the physical environment to make up the many ecosystems of the biosphere.

▶ View in **Achieve**
Activity 1.1 **The Hierarchy of Biological Organization**

tissue can work together to generate considerable force, and working with structural tissues such as bones, they can produce large movements. Different tissue types develop together into **organs** that accomplish specific functions. The heart, brain, and stomach are each composed of several types of tissues, as are the roots, stems, and leaves of plants. Organs whose functions are interrelated can be grouped into **organ systems**; the esophagus, stomach, and intestines, for example, are all part of the digestive system. The hierarchy of biological organization from atoms to organisms is shown in **Figure 1.5A**. The biology of the two major groups of multicellular organisms, plants and animals, is discussed in detail in Parts Seven and Eight, respectively.

Organisms extract energy and raw materials from the environment

Living organisms acquire nutrients from the environment. Biochemical reactions break down complex nutrient molecules into smaller chemical units. Some of those smaller units are used as building blocks for structures the organism requires. The breakdown of nutrient molecules does more than supply raw materials. The breaking of the chemical bonds of nutrient molecules releases energy that the cell transfers to high-energy molecules that it uses to do work.

One kind of work cells do is mechanical—moving molecules from one cellular location to another, moving whole cells or tissues, or even moving the organism itself (**Figure 1.6A**). The cell also does biochemical work in the building, or synthesis, of new complex molecules and structures from smaller chemical units. For example, we are all familiar with the fact that carbohydrates eaten today may be deposited in the body as fat tomorrow (**Figure 1.6B**). Still another kind of work is the electrical work that is the essence of information processing in nervous systems.

(A) *Coracias garrulus*

© Bence Máté/Visuals Unlimited, Inc.

(B) *Urocitellus parryii*

© Rolf Nussbaumer Photography/Alamy Stock Photo

Figure 1.6 Energy Can Be Used Immediately or Stored
(A) Animal cells break down food molecules and use the energy contained in the chemical bonds of those molecules to do mechanical work, such as running, flying, and jumping. This image is a European Roller flying with mammal prey in its bill. **(B)** The cells of this Arctic ground squirrel have broken down the complex carbohydrates in the plants it consumed and converted those molecules into fats. The fats are stored in the animal's body to provide an energy supply for the cold months.

(B) Organisms to ecosystems

Population · Community · Ecosystem · **Biosphere**

NASA image by Reto Stöckli, based on data from NASA and NOAA

The many biochemical reactions that take place in cells are integrally linked in that the products of one reaction are the raw materials of the next. These complex networks of reactions must be integrated and precisely controlled; when they are not, the result is malfunction and disease.

 Media Clip 1.1 Leaping Lemurs
Life12e.com/mc1.1

Living organisms must regulate their internal environment

If different specialized cells, tissues, and organs provide for different needs of the multicellular organism, how are these specific services shared by the cells of the whole organism? All of the cells of the body share an **internal environment** that is made up of extracellular fluids. Cells derive their nutrients from these extracellular fluids, and they deposit their wastes into the extracellular fluid. This internal environment serves the needs of all cells of the body, and therefore its physical and chemical composition must be maintained within a narrow range of physiological conditions that support survival and function. The maintenance of this narrow range of conditions is known as **homeostasis**. A relatively stable internal environment means that cells can function efficiently even when external conditions could not support the lives of individual cells.

Homeostasis requires that the activities of the cells and systems of the body be regulated. Regulation requires information—information about internal conditions, external conditions, and what is optimal. Thus organisms must have **sensory mechanisms** to monitor conditions, **effector mechanisms** to alter those conditions, and **signaling mechanisms** to integrate information and enable communication between sensors and effectors. The major information systems of animals—nervous, hormonal, and immune—use chemical and electric signals to process information.

Connect the Concepts The regulation of body temperature is an important example of homeostasis that is discussed in Chapter 38.

The concept of homeostasis also applies to the intracellular environment. Both unicellular and multicellular organisms must regulate the composition of their intracellular environments within a range that allows those cells to survive and function. Individual cells regulate these properties through actions of their membranes and, in the case of eukaryotes, their organelles. Thus self-regulation to maintain a more or less constant internal environment is a general attribute of all life.

Living organisms interact

Organisms do not live in isolation. Besides the internal hierarchy of the individual organism, there is also an external hierarchy of the biological world (**Figure 1.5B**). The populations of all the species that live and interact in a defined area are called a **community**. Communities together with their abiotic, or physical, environment constitute an **ecosystem**.

Individuals in a population interact in many different ways. Animals eat plants and other animals and compete with other species for food and other resources. Some animals prevent other individuals of their own species from exploiting a resource, be it food, nesting sites, or mates. Animals may also cooperate with members of their own species, forming social units such as a termite colony or a flock of birds. Such interactions have resulted in the evolution of social behaviors such as communication and courtship displays.

Plants also interact with their external biotic and abiotic environment. Plants living on land depend on partnerships with fungi, bacteria, and animals. Some of these partnerships are necessary to obtain nutrients, some to produce fertile seeds, and still others to disperse seeds. Plants compete with each other for light and water and have ongoing evolutionary interactions with the animals that eat them. Through time, many adaptations such as thorns and toxins have evolved that protect plants from predation. Other adaptations such as flowers and fruits help attract the animals that assist in plant reproduction. The interactions of populations of plant and animal species in a community are major evolutionary forces that produce specialized adaptations.

The major ecosystems of Earth that cover broad geographic areas with distinguishing physical features and communities of organisms are known as **biomes**. Examples of biomes include Arctic tundra, coral reefs, and tropical rainforests. All of the biomes on our planet make up the **biosphere**. The ways in which species interact with one another and with their environment in populations, communities, and ecosystems is the subject of ecology, covered in Part Nine of this book.

KEY CONCEPT
1.1 Recap and Assess

All organisms are related by common descent from a single chemical origin of life. That origin involved the enclosure of complex biological molecules within an internal environment and led to the first cells with the ability to replicate themselves. Cells need energy and can extract that energy from the environment and use it to do biological work, including synthesizing complex molecules and structures. A major step in energy extraction was the evolution of photosynthesis, which changed our planet and made life on land possible. The rise of multicellularity enabled cellular specialization and the development of tissues, organs, and organ systems. Cellular specialization made it possible and necessary to have a regulated internal environment that serves the needs of all the cells of the body. Evolution has produced an enormous diversity of organisms that interact with each other, forming the many communities and ecosystems that constitute life on Earth.

1. Describe two ways in which the origin of photosynthesis influenced the history of life on Earth.

2. If we discovered life on another planet, how could we tell if it had a separate origin from life on Earth?

3. Why was maintenance of a regulated internal environment but not extracellular environment necessary for the evolution of large multicellular animals?

4. Explain the concept of homeostatic regulation.

This key concept outlined some of the major features of life—features that we will cover in depth in subsequent chapters. But first, to better understand how the enormous diversity of life evolved, we look at two of the central principles of biology: genetics and evolution.

KEY CONCEPT
1.2 Genetics and Evolution Are Fundamental Principles of Biology

---

Learning Objectives

1.2.1 Describe the relationships among genes, genomes, and genetics.

1.2.2 Explain how natural selection can produce evolutionary change.

1.2.3 Describe what information can be represented in a phylogenetic tree.

Before there was a science of biology, humans recognized that offspring resemble parents, and this fact was used by plant and animal breeders to produce variants with desirable qualities.

Figure 1.7 Genetics Developed as the Study of Discrete Heritable Traits Gregor Mendel discovered the basics of genetics through breeding experiments with pea plants. When he crossed tall plants with short plants, all of the offspring were tall. Then when he crossed these offspring plants, he got one short plant for every three tall plants. From these experiments Mendel concluded that there was a tall factor and a short factor. Each plant inherited one factor from each parent, and the tall factor was dominant.

However, not until the famous plant breeding experiments of the Austrian monk Gregor Mendel in the mid-1800s was it demonstrated that inherited traits existed in discrete units (**Figure 1.7**). These discrete units of inheritance were termed **genes** in the early 1900s, giving rise to the science of **genetics**.

The science of genetics preceded discovery of the chemical nature of genes

An enormous body of information about traits of organisms represented by single genes was created before the chemical structure of a gene was known, and hence before the nature of the information that is passed from parent to offspring was known. That mystery was solved in the mid-1900s with the discovery that the molecule **deoxyribonucleic acid (DNA)** is the genetic information that specifies what an organism will look like and how it will function. This "blueprint" for the existence of each individual organism is contained in the sum total of all the DNA molecules contained in each of the organism's cells—its **genome**. DNA molecules are long sequences of four different subunits called **nucleotides**. Genes are specific segments of DNA that encode information about structure and function, including the information the cell uses to build proteins. Therefore each gene is defined by a specific sequence of the four nucleotides. The genetic code spells out how sequences of nucleotides are translated into sequences of amino acids, which are the building blocks of proteins. This translation process involves first **transcribing** some of the DNA information of a gene into the structure of another smaller molecule called **ribonucleic acid** (**RNA**) (**Figure 1.8**). RNA serves as the template for synthesis of a protein. Protein molecules govern the chemical reactions within cells and form much of an organism's structure.

Connect the Concepts How the structure of DNA codes for and is translated into proteins is discussed in Key Concept 4.1 and in more detail in Chapters 13 and 14.

By analogy with a book, the nucleotides of DNA are like the letters of an alphabet, and protein molecules are the words. Combinations of proteins that form structures and control specific biochemical processes are the sentences and paragraphs. The structures and processes that are organized into different complex systems with specific tasks (such as digestion or movement) are the chapters of the book, and the complete book is the organism. If you were to write out your own genome using four letters to represent the four nucleotides, you would write more than 3 billion letters. Using the size type you are reading now, your genome would fill about 1,000 books the size of this one. The processes of evolution are the authors and editors of all the books in the library of life.

Even though all the cells of a multicellular organism contain essentially the same genome, different cells of the organism have different functions and form different structures—contractile proteins form in muscle cells, hemoglobin in red blood cells, digestive enzymes in gut cells, and so on. We thus surmise that different types of cells in an organism express different parts of the genome. How cells control gene expression to enable a complex organism to develop and function is a major focus of current biological research.

The genome of an organism consists of thousands of genes. This entire genome must be replicated as new cells are produced. However, the replication process is not perfect, and a few errors, known as **mutations**, are likely to occur when the genome is replicated. Mutations occur spontaneously and can be induced by environmental factors such as chemicals and radiation. Most mutations are either harmful or have no effect, but occasionally a mutation improves the functioning of the organism under the environmental conditions it encounters.

The discovery of the structure of DNA by James Watson, Francis Crick, and Rosalind Franklin in the middle of the twentieth century, and the subsequent elucidation of the mechanisms by which this material encodes and transmits information, transformed biology. These crucial discoveries are detailed in Part Four of this book.

Populations of all living organisms evolve

A **population** is a group of individuals of the same type of organism that interbreed. The processes of evolution result in changes in the genetic makeup of populations through time. Evolution is the major unifying principle of biology. Charles Darwin compiled

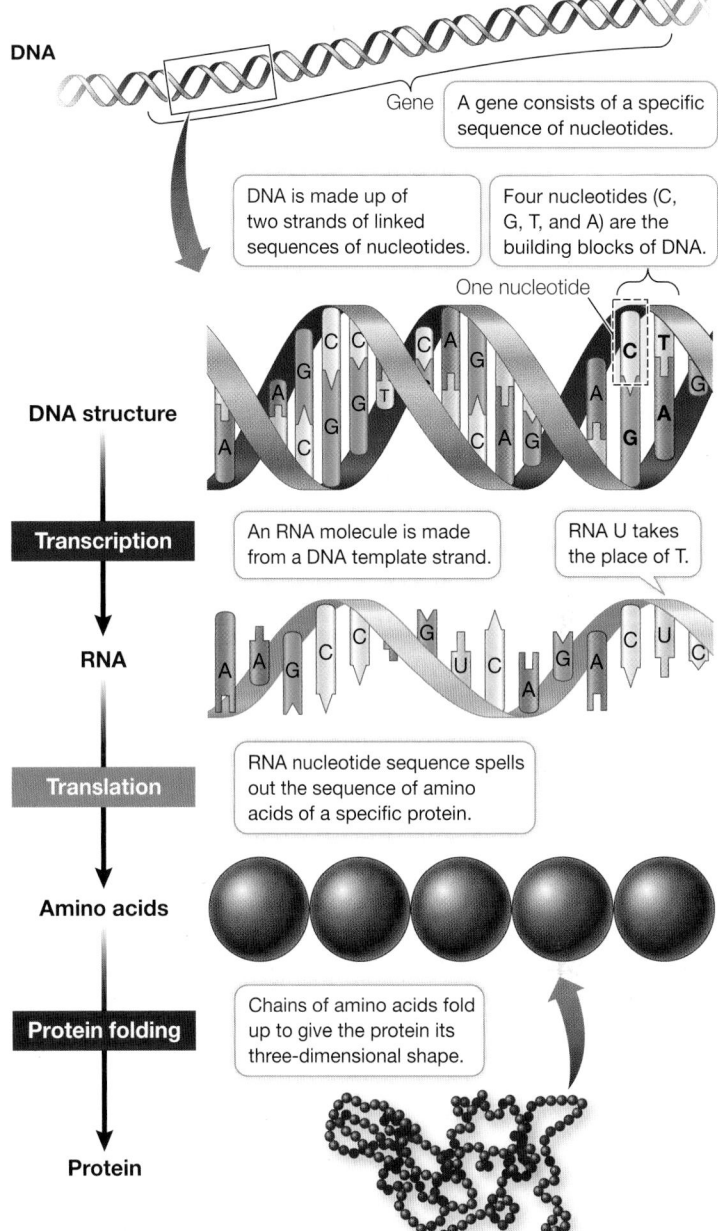

Figure 1.8 **DNA Is Life's Blueprint**   The instructions for life are contained in the sequences of nucleotides in DNA molecules. Specific DNA nucleotide sequences compose genes. The average length of a single human gene is 16,000 nucleotides. The information in each gene provides the cell with the information it needs to manufacture molecules of a specific protein.

factual evidence for evolution in his 1859 book *On the Origin of Species*. Darwin argued that differential survival and reproduction among individuals in a population, which he termed **natural selection**, could account for much of the evolution of biodiversity.

Connect the Concepts The story of Darwin's formulation of evolution by natural selection is covered in Key Concept 19.1.

Although Darwin proposed that all organisms are descended from a common ancestor and therefore are related to one another, he did not have knowledge of the mechanisms of genetic inheritance. Even so, he understood the process of selective breeding of plants and animals to obtain breeds with desired traits. Darwin himself was a pigeon breeder and knew that he could produce pigeons with different colorations, feather patterns, or tail shapes by selecting mates (see Figure 19.5). The steps in such selective breeding can be described as follows:

- Observe trait variation in a population.
- Selectively breed pairs based on a desired trait to produce that trait in their offspring.
- Repeat such crosses in subsequent generations to amplify the trait.

Darwin realized that if humans could select for specific traits in domesticated plants and animals, the same process could operate in nature; hence the term "natural selection" as opposed to artificial (human-imposed) selection. He reasoned that the reproductive capacity of plants and animals, if unchecked, would result in unlimited growth of populations, but we do not observe such growth in nature. In most species, only a small percentage of an individual's offspring survive to reproduce. Thus any trait that confers even a small increase in the probability that its possessor will survive and reproduce increases in the population across generations.

Because organisms with certain traits survive and reproduce best under specific sets of conditions, natural selection leads to **adaptations**: structural, physiological, or behavioral traits that enhance an organism's chances of survival and reproduction in its environment (**Figure 1.9**). The opening story of this chapter described experiments aimed at understanding adaptations that might enable corals to survive in a warmer environment. In addition to natural selection, evolutionary processes such as sexual selection (selection due to mate choice) and genetic drift (the random fluctuation of gene frequencies in a population due to chance events) contribute to biodiversity. These processes operating over

evolutionary history have contributed to the remarkable diversity of life on Earth. Part Five describes how natural selection and other evolutionary processes are supported and explained by the massive body of genetic and molecular genetic knowledge mostly produced over the past 100 years.

Over most of the history of biology, the diversity of life was described and catalogued based on structural characteristics of organisms. With the rapid development of molecular genetic tools in recent years, it is now possible to obtain the DNA sequences of parts or all of the genomes of organisms. Now it is possible to compare organisms on the basis of their DNA blueprints, which has given rise to the field of **genomics**. For example, a structural feature that differentiates humans with African or European origins versus East Asian origins is hair. Europeans have fine hair that can be curly, as is the hair of Africans. East Asians have thick hair that is straight. This difference is due to a gene called *EDAR* and to a single nucleotide substitution in that gene resulting in a single amino acid change in the protein product of that gene (**Figure 1.10**).

The ability to sequence the billions of letters in genetic codes generates enormous amounts of data, and to manage and analyze that data, the field of **bioinformatics** has grown in parallel with genomics. Genomics has enormous applications throughout biology, from evolutionary studies to investigations of human health. Advances in genomics and bioinformatics make current initiatives in precision medicine possible.

Biologists trace the evolutionary tree of life

Populations geographically isolated from one another evolve differences. As populations diverge from one another, individuals from one population become less likely to reproduce successfully with individuals of the other populations. Eventually these differences between the populations become so great that they are considered to be different species. Thus species that share a fairly

Figure 1.9 Adaptations to the Environment The limbs of frogs show adaptations to the different environments of each species. **(A)** This terrestrial frog walks across the ground using its short legs and peglike digits (toes). **(B)** Webbed rear feet are evident in this highly aquatic species of frog. **(C)** This arboreal species has toe pads, which are adaptations for climbing. **(D)** A different arboreal species has extended webbing between the toes, which increases surface area and allows the frog to glide from tree to tree.

(A) *Dyscophus guineti*

(B) *Pelophylax* sp.

(C) *Hyloscirtus lindae*

(D) *Rhacophorus nigropalmatus*

© Life on white/Alamy Stock Photo

© Stockbroker xtra/AGE Fotostock

© Nature Picture Library/Alamy Stock Photo

© Stephen Dalton/Minden Pictures

Figure 1.10 The Blueprint of Life
Using technologies that reveal the sequence of nucleotides that make up the genome of an organism, we can detect small alterations that are responsible for specific traits. The *EDAR* gene is involved in hair development, and a single nucleotide substitution results in a single amino acid difference between the EDAR proteins of humans with East Asian origins and those with African or European origins.

East Asian   African

East Asian   T C C A C G T A C A A C T C T G A G A A G G C T G T T G T G A A A A C G T G G C G C C A C C T C G C C

African   T C C A C G T A C A A C T C T G A G A A G G C T G C T G T G A A A A C G T G G C G C C A C C T C G C C

recent evolutionary history are generally more similar to each other than are species that share an ancestor in the more distant past. By identifying, analyzing, and quantifying similarities and differences among species, biologists can construct **phylogenetic trees** that portray the evolutionary histories of the different groups of organisms. As an example, we can show the evolutionary relationships among humans and our closest living relatives in a branching diagram that shows how they diverged from a common ancestor (**Figure 1.11**). In this tree, the living species are shown at the tips of the branches, and the branches show when these groups diverged from one another along a time scale. Our convention in this book will be to place phylogenetic trees on their sides, with the oldest lineages on the left and the most recent to the right.

Tens of millions of species exist on Earth today; many times that number lived in the past but are now extinct. Biologists give each of these species a distinctive scientific name formed from two Latinized names—a **binomial**. The first part of the name identifies the species' **genus** (plural *genera*)—a group of species that share a recent common ancestor. The second part of the scientific name identifies a particular species within the genus. For example, the scientific name for modern-day humans is *Homo sapiens*: *Homo* is our genus, *sapiens* refers to our species. *Homo* is Latin for "man," and *sapiens* is from the Latin word for "wise" or "rational." The binomial for our close but extinct relatives, the Neanderthals, is *Homo neanderthalensis*. Note that it is conventional to write the binomial in italics with the genus capitalized but the second part not capitalized.

Figure 1.11 Phylogenetic Trees Depict Evolutionary Relationships
Biologists use phylogenetic trees to show the evolutionary relationships of genes, populations, and species. As all of life is related through its evolutionary history, these diagrams are important for making comparisons at every level of biological investigation.

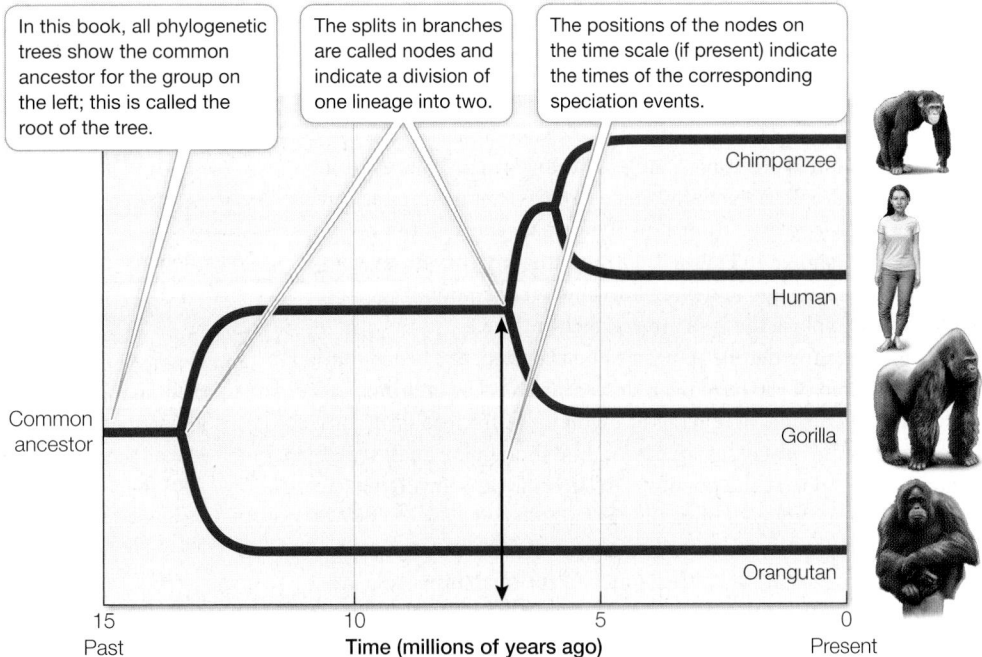

In this book, all phylogenetic trees show the common ancestor for the group on the left; this is called the root of the tree.

The splits in branches are called nodes and indicate a division of one lineage into two.

The positions of the nodes on the time scale (if present) indicate the times of the corresponding speciation events.

Chimpanzee

Human

Gorilla

Orangutan

Common ancestor

15   10   5   0
Past   Time (millions of years ago)   Present

Figure 1.12 The Tree of Life The earliest division of life was between Bacteria and Archaea. Later, one lineage of archaea incorporated specializations (including a cell nucleus) that allowed the repeated evolution of multicellularity; we call this specialized group Eukarya. The aqua branches within Eukarya represent various groups of microbial eukaryotes, sometimes called "protists." The organisms on any one branch share a common ancestor.

Q: According to this phylogenetic tree, are fungi more closely related to plants or to animals?

See the **Interactive Tree of Life**
Life12e.com/tree

Much of biology is based on comparisons among species. Meaningful interpretations of those comparisons require an understanding of evolutionary relationships of the respective species. Our ability to reconstruct evolutionary relationships has been greatly enhanced in recent decades by gene sequencing. Genomic sequence analysis and other molecular techniques have enabled biologists to augment evolutionary knowledge based on the fossil record with a vast array of molecular evidence. The result is the ongoing compilation of phylogenetic trees that document and diagram evolutionary relationships. The broadest categories of the tree of life are shown in **Figure 1.12**, and they will be surveyed in more detail in Part Six. (The tree is expanded in Appendix A, and you can also explore the tree interactively online.)

Although many details remain to be clarified, the broad outlines of the tree of life have been determined. Its branching patterns are based on a rich array of evidence from fossils, structures, metabolic processes, behavior, and molecular analyses of genomes. Recall that the primary division of life—into Archaea and Bacteria—occurred among the early single-celled prokaryotes. Members of these two groups differ so fundamentally that they are believed to have separated into distinct evolutionary lineages early in the history of life. One of the lineages of archaea incorporated a nucleus and internal, membrane-bound organelles and gave rise to the major group Eukarya. Plants, fungi, and animals are examples of familiar multicellular eukaryotes that evolved independently, from different groups of unicellular eukaryotes. We know that plants, fungi, and animals had independent origins of multicellularity because each of these three groups is most closely related to different groups of microbial eukaryotes, as can be seen from the branching pattern of Figure 1.12.

KEY CONCEPT
1.2 Recap and Assess

All organisms contain genetic information that encodes how they look and how they function. Genomics helps scientists establish the evolutionary relationships between organisms, which can be depicted in phylogenetic trees. Multicellularity evolved multiple times among the eukaryotes.

1. What are the relationships among DNA, RNA, amino acids, and proteins?

2. How does selective breeding of agricultural species by humans differ from natural selection?

3. Assume a population of fish becomes isolated in a dark cave environment, with no access to light from the surface. What major change might you expect in the population over time, and why?

4. What information do biologists use to construct phylogenetic trees?

This key concept described two central principles in biology, genetics and evolution—topics we will cover in detail in Parts Four and Five of this book. Throughout the book, you should be asking not just "What do we know about life?" but "How do we know it?" In all areas of biology, it is important to understand how scientists obtain information and how they use that information to broaden our understanding of life and put that understanding to practical use.

KEY CONCEPT
1.3
Biologists Investigate Life through Experiments That Test Hypotheses

Learning Objectives

1.3.1 Diagram the relationships among the steps in the scientific method and describe the roles played by inductive and deductive logic.

1.3.2 Differentiate between controlled and comparative experiments and describe their respective advantages and disadvantages.

1.3.3 Formulate a null hypothesis for a scientific question and explain its role in statistical analysis of data.

1.3.4 Explain why experiments on different kinds of animals may have relevance for understanding human biology.

Scientific investigations are based on observation, experimentation, data analysis, and logic. Scientists use many different tools and methods in making observations, collecting data, experimenting, analyzing data, and applying logic.

Observing and quantifying are important skills

Biologists observe the world around them. Our ability to observe has been greatly enhanced by technologies such as electron microscopes, rapid genome sequencing, magnetic resonance imaging, and global positioning satellites. These technologies allow us to observe everything from the distribution of molecules in the body to the movement of animals across continents and oceans.

Observation is a basic tool of biology, but as scientists we must be able to quantify the information, or **data**, we collect and observe. Whether we are testing a new drug or mapping the migrations of whales, it is essential to apply mathematical and statistical methods to the data we collect. In our opening discussion of the responses of corals to temperature, it was essential for Bay to measure temperatures accurately and to have a physical measure of bleaching so she could compare the responses of her corals to different conditions and conclude that the differences were more than just random variation.

Scientific methods combine observation, experimentation, and logic

Textbooks often describe "*the* scientific method," as if there were a single, simple flow chart that all scientists follow. This is an oversimplification. Although flow charts such as the one shown in **Figure 1.13** incorporate much of what scientists do, you should not conclude that scientists necessarily progress through the steps of the process in one prescribed, linear order.

Figure 1.13 Scientific Methodology The process of observation, speculation and questioning, hypothesis formation, prediction, and experimentation is a cornerstone of modern science, although scientists may initiate their research at several different points. Answers gleaned through experimentation lead to new questions, more hypotheses, further experiments, and expanding knowledge.

Observations lead to questions. To answer those questions, scientists make additional observations, formulate possible answers, and do experiments to test those possibilities. This investigative approach traditionally has five steps: (1) making observations; (2) asking questions; (3) forming hypotheses, which are tentative answers to the questions; (4) making predictions based on the hypotheses; and (5) testing the predictions by making additional observations or conducting experiments.

After posing a question, a scientist often uses **inductive logic** to propose a tentative answer. Inductive logic involves taking observations or facts and formulating a new proposition that is compatible with those observations or facts. Such a tentative proposition is a **hypothesis** (plural *hypotheses*). For example, in the opener to this chapter you learned that Rachael Bay observed corals growing in pools that reached temperatures known to kill corals. She formulated two hypotheses:

1. The populations of corals in the warm pools have evolved genetic differences that enable them to survive heat stress (adaptations), or

2. Individual corals have the ability to adjust physiologically to different thermal conditions (acclimation).

Bay and her colleagues conducted experiments and made observations to test these hypotheses. How do scientists design experiments to test hypotheses?

The next step in the scientific method is to apply a different form of logic—**deductive logic**—that starts with a statement believed to be true (the hypothesis) and then goes on to predict what facts would also have to be true to be compatible with that statement. Bay's team tested their hypotheses by measuring how corals from the warm and cool pools responded to laboratory experiments that simulated the heat-stress conditions that occurred sometimes in the warm pools. They predicted that the cool-pool corals would bleach at higher rates under the experimental conditions than the warm-pool corals would. That experiment revealed differences between the two populations, but did not reveal whether the differences were a result of long-term evolutionary changes in the populations (adaptations) or short-term acclimation of individuals to their current environments. The researchers therefore looked for genetic differences in the corals living in the warm and cool pools (adaptations). They also looked for differences in gene expression patterns when the corals were transplanted to different environments (acclimation). Did the two populations have fundamental genetic differences, or did the environments they lived in stimulate different patterns of gene expression and therefore physiological acclimation?

 View in Achieve
Animation 1.1 Using Scientific Methodology

Good experiments have the potential to falsify hypotheses

Once predictions are made from a hypothesis, experiments can be designed to test those predictions. The most informative experiments are those that have the ability to show that the prediction is wrong. If the prediction is wrong, the hypothesis must be questioned, modified, or rejected.

There are two general types of experiments, both of which compare data from different groups or samples:

1. **Controlled experiments** manipulate one factor of interest while holding other variables constant as a means of testing the influence of the manipulated variable.

2. **Comparative experiments** compare data gathered from different populations that differ in multiple, unknown ways.

Bay and her colleagues conducted both types of experiments, to reveal genetic differences between the coral populations as well as their abilities to acclimate to different temperature environments.

In a controlled experiment, we predict on the basis of our hypothesis that some critical factor, or variable, has an effect on the phenomenon we are investigating. We devise some method to manipulate *only that variable* in an "experimental" group and compare the resulting data with data from an unmanipulated "control" group. If the predicted difference occurs, we then apply statistical tests to ascertain the probability that the manipulation caused the difference (as opposed to the difference being the result of random chance). **Investigating Life: Corals in Hot Water**

►Investigating LIFE
Corals in Hot Water

Experiment

Original Paper: S. R. Palumbi et al. 2014. Mechanisms of reef coral resistance to future climate change. *Science* 344: 895–898.

Rachael Bay and her colleagues did a controlled experiment by bringing corals from the warm and the cool tidal pools into the laboratory and then subjecting them to cycles of heat stress that simulated the conditions that sometimes occurred in the warm tidal pools. The outcome measure was bleaching—the loss of photosynthetic symbionts (dinoflagellates) from the coral bodies.

HYPOTHESIS► Heat stress results in coral bleaching, but corals from warm pools are less subject to bleaching under heat stress than are corals from cool pools.

METHOD►

1. Transplant corals from warm and cool pools into laboratory aquariums maintained at a safe temperature.

2. Subject experimental corals to heat stress (the experimental condition) by simulating the daily temperature cycle in the warm pools.

3. Measure coral bleaching (the dependent variable) as the ratio of chlorophyll (the photosynthetic pigment of the symbionts) in the corals exposed to heat stress versus in the controls in non-stressed conditions. A ratio of less than 1.0 indicates higher bleaching in the heat-stressed corals than in the controls.

© Reinhard Dirscherl/Alamy Stock Photo

RESULTS► Corals from both cool pools and warm pools exhibited higher bleaching under heat stress than controls did, but the cool-pool corals showed higher average levels of bleaching than the warm-pool corals did. (You will calculate the statistical significance of this difference in the following Work with the Data exercise.)

CONCLUSION► The warm-pool corals showed lower effects of heat stress than the cool-pool corals did, although both populations showed increased bleaching under heat stress. The difference in the populations could be explained either by genetic adaptation to heat stress in the populations of warm-pool corals or by physiological acclimation of individuals exposed to warm-pool conditions, or by some combination of the two.

Work with the Data

The bar graph in the Results section of the experiment shows that both cool-pool corals and warm-pool corals showed increased levels of bleaching under heat stress, relative to controls. It also shows that the cool-pool corals showed greater relative bleaching under heat stress than did the warm-pool corals. But how do we know that these differences are greater than would be expected if the variation within and between samples represents nothing more than random variation? Here we will use some simple tests to see if the differences measured are significant (unlikely to be due to random variation).

Average chlorophyll ratio	Cool-pool corals	Warm-pool corals
0.0	0	0
0.1	0	0
0.2	1	0
0.3	1	0
0.4	4	0
0.5	7	0
0.6	1	0
0.7	1	1
0.8	2	3
0.9	0	3
1.0	0	1

QUESTIONS▶

1. Prepare a bar graph based on these data. Show the chlorophyll ratios on the x axis and the number of corals that exhibited each ratio on the y axis.

2. First, let's consider if there is a significant effect of heat stress in each of the two groups. At the outset we assume that there is no effect of heat stress in either group—this is called our null hypothesis (H_0). We use statistical tests to decide if we can reject the null hypothesis and conclude that there *is* an effect of heat stress. If the null hypothesis is true, then we would expect that any differences in chlorophyll levels between control and experimental populations are due to random variation, and so we would expect the chlorophyll ratios to be greater than 1.0 as often as they are less than 1.0. In other words, the expected distribution of values < 1 and > 1 is like the expected distribution of heads and tails in a coin toss. Let's first consider the cool-pool corals. There are 17 samples, and all 17 had chlorophyll ratios < 1.0. The probability of this happening at random is the same as getting 17 heads in 17 flips of a fair coin (by a "fair coin" we mean the probability of heads in one flip = 0.5). Using this criterion, calculate the probability of the null hypothesis (H_0: no effect of heat stress on bleaching) for each of the two populations.

3. Now let's consider if there is a significant difference in the level of bleaching in the cool-pool versus the warm-pool corals. Our null hypothesis in this case is that the levels of bleaching are the same in both groups. If the null hypothesis is true, then we would expect (on average) the same distribution of chlorophyll ratios in the samples of both groups. From the Results section in the experiment, we see that the average chlorophyll ratio observed in the cool-pool samples is 0.5, and the average chlorophyll ratio observed in the warm-pool samples is 0.85. Would we expect a difference this great if the distributions of the two samples were drawn from the same underlying distribution of values? To find out, write each of the 25 observed chlorophyll ratios (from both groups) on an index card. Thoroughly mix and shuffle the cards to randomize their order, and then deal them into two groups of the same size as the cool-pool samples (17) and warm-pool samples (8). Calculate the average ratios in these randomized samples. Repeat this procedure or combine the results of your randomization test with those of other students in your class. How often do you see a difference as great as the observed difference in the two samples (0.85–0.5, or a difference of 0.35)?

4. What do these results suggest about the possible response of coral populations in different environments to ocean warming?

Go to **Achieve** for a companion Data in Depth exercise.

describes a controlled experiment examining the effect of pool of origin on the response of corals to heat stress done by Rachael Bay and other members of the Palumbi laboratory. A good controlled experiment is not easy to design because biological variables are so interrelated that it is sometimes difficult to alter just one. In this experiment the controlled variable was whether the experimental corals came from the cool-pool or the warm-pool environment. They were then subjected to the same thermal stresses and their responses measured as extent of bleaching. The control groups were corals not exposed to the thermal stress protocol.

A comparative experiment starts with the prediction that there will be a difference between samples or groups based on the hypothesis. Unlike in a controlled experiment, we cannot control all the variables in a comparative experiment; often we cannot even identify all the variables involved. We are simply gathering and comparing data from different sample groups. Bay and her colleagues did a comparative experiment in addition to the controlled experiment shown in Investigating Life: Corals in Hot Water. They analyzed and compared the genetic makeup of corals taken from the warm and cool pools.

Statistical methods are essential scientific tools

Whether we do comparative or controlled experiments, we have to decide whether there is a real difference between the samples, individuals, groups, or populations in the study. How do we decide whether a measured difference is enough to support or falsify a hypothesis? In other words, how do we decide in an unbiased, objective way that the measured difference is significant?

Significance is measured with statistical methods. Random variation is almost always present in any set of measurements. Statistical tests calculate the probability that the differences observed in an experiment could be due to random variation. The results of statistical tests are therefore probabilities. A statistical test starts with a **null hypothesis**—the premise that observed differences are the result of random variation that arises from drawing two finite samples from the same population. When quantified observations, or data, are collected, statistical methods are applied to those data to see if there is sufficient evidence to reject the null hypothesis.

More specifically, statistical methods tell us the probability of obtaining the same results by chance even if the null hypothesis were true. *We need to eliminate, insofar as possible, the chance that any differences showing up in the data are merely the result of random variation in the samples tested.* Scientists generally conclude that the differences they measure are significant if statistical tests show that the probability of error (that is, the probability that a difference as large as the one observed could be obtained by mere chance) is 5% or lower. They often use more stringent criteria for rejecting the null hypothesis, however, depending on the consequences of accepting a wrong hypothesis. Appendix B of this book offers a short primer on statistical methods to which you can refer as you analyze data that will be presented throughout the text.

Discoveries in biology can be generalized

All life is related by descent from a common ancestor, shares a genetic code, and consists of similar biochemical building blocks. Therefore knowledge gained from investigations of one type of organism can, with thought and care, be generalized to other organisms. Biologists use **model systems** for research, knowing that they can extend their findings from such systems to other organisms. For example, our basic understanding of the chemical reactions in cells came from research on bacteria but is applicable to all cells, including those of humans. Similarly, the biochemistry of photosynthesis—the process by which all green plants use sunlight to produce biological molecules—was worked out largely from experiments on *Chlorella*, a unicellular green alga. Much of what we know about the genes that control plant development is the result of work on *Arabidopsis thaliana*, a relative of the mustard plant. Knowledge about how animals, including humans, develop has come from work on sea urchins, frogs, chickens, roundworms, mice, and fruit flies. Being able to generalize from model systems is a powerful tool in biology.

Not all forms of inquiry are scientific

Science is a unique human endeavor that has certain standards of practice. Other areas of scholarship share with science the practice of making observations and asking questions, but scientists are distinguished by what they do with their observations, how they frame their questions, and how they determine their answers. Quantifiable data, subjected to appropriate statistical analysis, are critical in evaluating hypotheses. The Investigating Life boxes and the Work with the Data exercises you will find throughout this book are intended to reinforce this way of thinking. *Scientific observation, hypothesis generation, and experimental testing constitute the most powerful approach humans have devised for learning about the world and how it works.*

Scientific explanations for natural processes are objective and reliable because *a hypothesis must be testable* and *a hypothesis must have the potential of being rejected* by direct observations and experiments. Scientists must clearly describe the methods they use to test hypotheses so that other scientists can repeat their results. Not all experiments are repeated, but surprising or controversial results are always subjected to independent verification. Scientists worldwide share this process of testing and rejecting hypotheses, contributing to a common body of scientific knowledge.

If you understand the methods of science, you can distinguish science from non-science. Art, music, and literature all contribute

to the quality of human life, but they are not science. They do not use scientific methods to establish what is fact. Religion is not science, although religions have historically attempted to explain natural events ranging from unusual weather patterns to crop failures to human diseases. Most such phenomena that at one time were mysterious can now be explained in terms of scientific principles. Fundamental tenets of religious faith, such as the existence of a supreme deity or deities, cannot be confirmed or refuted by experimentation and are thus outside the realm of science.

The power of science derives from strict objectivity and absolute dependence on evidence based on *reproducible and quantifiable observations*. A religious or spiritual explanation of a natural phenomenon may be coherent and satisfying for the person holding that view, but it is not testable and therefore it is not science. To invoke a supernatural explanation (such as a "creator" or "intelligent designer" with no known bounds) is to depart from the world of science. Science does not necessarily say that religious beliefs are wrong; they are simply not part of the world of science and are untestable using scientific methods.

Science describes how the world works. It is silent on the question of how the world "ought to be." Many scientific advances that contribute to human welfare also raise major ethical issues. Recent developments in genetics and developmental biology may enable us to select the sex of our children, to use stem cells to repair our bodies, and to modify the human genome. Although scientific knowledge may enable us to do these things, science cannot tell us whether or not we *should* do so, or if we choose to do them, how we should regulate them. Such issues are as crucial to human society as the science itself, and a responsible scientist does not lose sight of these questions or neglect the contributions of the humanities and social sciences in attempting to come to grips with them.

KEY CONCEPT
1.3 Recap and Assess

Scientific methods of inquiry start with the formulation of hypotheses based on observations and data. Comparative and controlled experiments are carried out to test hypotheses. Statistics are essential for drawing conclusions from the data obtained in experiments. Because organisms can be compared through their evolutionary relationships, the results of experiments can frequently be generalized to apply to other species. Science is built from provable facts, whereas religion is based on beliefs.

1. What is the relationship between a hypothesis and an experiment?
2. What is controlled in a controlled experiment?
3. What features characterize questions that can and must be answered using a comparative approach rather than a controlled experiment?
4. Why is it often possible to generalize the results of biological research on one species to very different species?

The vast body of scientific knowledge accumulated over centuries of human civilization allows us to understand and manipulate aspects of the natural world in ways that no other species can. These abilities present us with challenges, opportunities, and above all, responsibilities.

KEY CONCEPT 1.4 Understanding Biology Is Important for Health, Well-Being, and Public-Policy Decisions

Learning Objectives

1.4.1 Describe an example of how biology contributes to improvements in agriculture.

1.4.2 Explain how research in different areas of biology informs medical science.

1.4.3 Discuss an example of how knowledge of biology can be used to develop wise public policy.

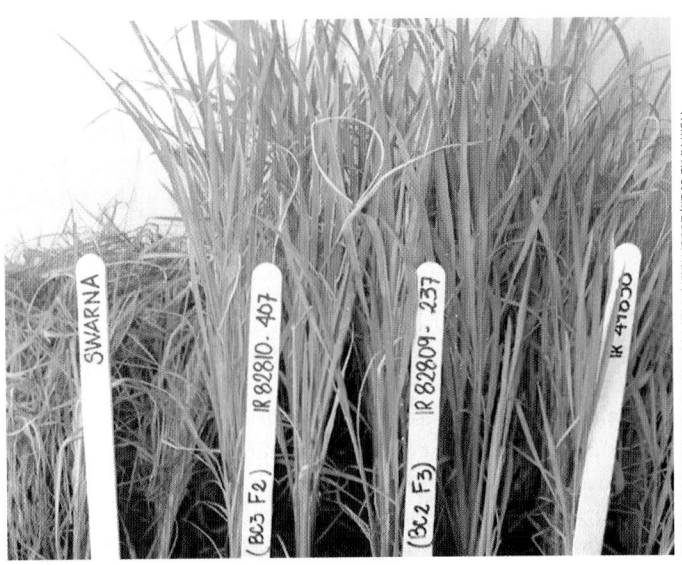

Figure 1.14 A Green Revolution Advances in agricultural plant genetics have vastly increased yields and nutritional value of crops such as the food grains that make up about 50% of calories in the human diet. New molecular genetic technologies make even greater advances possible. The strains of rice on the right have been modified to increase resistance to prolonged flooding; the rice plants on the left are unmodified, and have died from overexposure to flood conditions.

Human beings exist in and depend on a world of living organisms. The oxygen we breathe is produced by the photosynthetic activity of countless billions of individual organisms. The food that fuels our bodies comes from the tissues of other living organisms. The fuels that power our cars, trucks, and planes are carbon molecules produced by living organisms—mostly millions of years ago. Inside and out, our bodies are covered in complex communities of living unicellular organisms. Some help us be healthy, but others can invade our bodies and cause mild to serious diseases, or even death. These interactions with other species are not limited to humans. Ecosystems depend on thousands of complex interactions among the millions of species that inhabit Earth. Understanding biological principles is essential for us to lead healthy, productive lives and to be good stewards of our planet.

Modern agriculture depends on biology

Agriculture represents some of the earliest human applications of biological principles. Beginning about 10,000 years ago, humans began to cultivate and harvest grains. It is probable that even in those early times farmers selected the most productive or otherwise favorable plants and animals to use as seed stock for propagation, and over generations farmers continued and refined these practices. By 1960 the worldwide yield of food grains reached a billion tons, but human population growth outpaced agricultural productivity and starvation was common in developing countries. Catastrophic famine was predicted for the 1970s. In response to those predictions, developed countries initiated huge efforts to produce genetically improved, higher-yielding food grain varieties. These highly successful research programs resulted in what has been called the Green Revolution, and by the year 2000 the worldwide yield of food grains, which make up about 50% of the calories in the human diet, had reached 2 billion tons. In 2018 it reached 2.4 billion tons. Increasing knowledge of plant and animal biology has transformed agriculture in many ways and has resulted in huge boosts in food production.

A new threat to agriculture and the world food supply is global climate change. Some regions are becoming wetter and others drier, and those changes affect traditional agricultures. An example is rice, which normally grows in shallow water in rice paddies (**Figure 1.14**). But common rice varieties cannot survive complete submergence for more than a few days, and are therefore killed by flooding

caused by too much rain. In India and Bangladesh alone, annual flooding can destroy about 4 million tons of rice, enough to feed 30 million people. In recent years plant geneticists Pam Ronald, David Mackill, and their colleagues at the University of California at Davis have discovered a single gene from an ancient variety of rice that when genetically engineered into the current rice varieties makes them capable of surviving total submergence for many days. Advances such as this may help save the benefits of the Green Revolution from the new problems generated by global climate change.

Over the past few decades, detailed knowledge of the genomes of many domestic species and the development of technology for directly recombining genes have allowed biologists to develop new breeds and strains of animals, plants, and fungi of agricultural interest. New strains of crop plants are being developed that are resistant to pests or tolerant of drought or, in the case of rice, flooding. Moreover, understanding evolutionary theory allows biologists to devise strategies for the application of pesticides that minimize the evolution of pest resistance. And better understanding of plant–fungus relationships results in better plant health and higher productivity. These are just a few of the many ways that biology continues to inform and improve agricultural practice.

Biology is the basis of medical practice

People have speculated about the causes of diseases and searched for methods to combat them since ancient times. Long before the microbial causes of many diseases were known, people recognized that infections could be passed from one person to another, and the isolation of infected persons has been practiced as long as written records have been available.

Modern biological research informs us about how living organisms work, and about why they develop the problems and infections that we call disease. In addition to knowing about diseases caused by infectious organisms, we now know that many diseases are genetic—meaning that variants of genes in our genomes cause particular problems in the way we function. Developing appropriate treatments or cures for diseases depends on understanding the origin, basis, and effects of these diseases, as well as understanding the consequences of any changes we make. For example, the recent resurgence of tuberculosis is the result of the evolution of bacteria that are resistant to antibiotics. Dealing with future tuberculosis epidemics will require understanding aspects of molecular biology, physiology, microbial ecology, and evolution—in other words, many of the general principles of modern biology.

Many of the microbial organisms that are periodically epidemic in human populations have short generation times and high mutation rates. For example, we need yearly vaccines for flu because of the high rate of evolution of influenza viruses, the causative agent of flu. Evolutionary principles help us understand how influenza viruses are changing, and can even help us predict which strains of influenza virus are likely to lead to future flu epidemics. This medical understanding—which combines an application of molecular biology, evolutionary theory, and basic principles of ecology—allows medical researchers to develop effective vaccines and other strategies for the control of major epidemics (**Figure 1.15**).

© Associated Press

Figure 1.15 Medical Applications of Biology Improve Human Health Vaccination to prevent disease is a biologically based medical practice that began in the eighteenth century. Today evolutionary biology and genomics provide the basis for constant updates to vaccines that protect humans from virus-borne diseases such as flu and measles. In the developed world, vaccinations are so commonplace that some are offered on a "drive-through" basis.

(A)

Courtesy of Wayne Whippen

Figure 1.16 Bluefin Tunas Do Not Recognize Boundaries **(A)** Marine biologist Barbara Block attaches computerized data-recording tracking tags to a live bluefin tuna before returning it to the Atlantic Ocean, where its travels will be monitored. **(B)** Tracking data from eastern (Mediterranean) and western (Gulf of Mexico) breeding populations of bluefin tunas. At one time commercial fishing regulatory agencies assumed that bluefins from western- and eastern-breeding populations fed on their respective sides of the Atlantic. To speed recovery of the endangered western population, fishing quotas were created for each side of the mid-Atlantic Ocean (dashed line). (B after J. R. Rooker et al. 2007. *Rev Fish Sci* 15: 265–310; B. A. Block et al. 2005. *Nature* 434: 1121–1127.)

Q: Based on Dr. Block's data, does it seem likely that fishing quotas based on the mid-Atlantic boundary line would protect the western-breeding population of bluefin tunas?

(B)

Canada

U.S.A.

Europe

Africa

Atlantic Ocean

The two populations mix freely, especially in the heavily fished waters of the North Atlantic.

● Tracked fish from eastern spawning ground
● Tracked fish from western spawning ground

Biology can inform public policy

Thanks to the deciphering of genomes and our newfound ability to manipulate them, vast new possibilities now exist for controlling human diseases and increasing agricultural productivity—but these capabilities raise ethical and policy issues. How much and in what ways should we tinker with the genes of humans and other species? Does it matter whether the genomes of our crop plants and domesticated animals are changed by traditional methods of controlled breeding or by the biotechnology of gene transfer? What rules should govern the release of genetically modified organisms into the environment? Science alone cannot provide all the answers, but wise policy decisions must be based on accurate scientific information.

Biologists are increasingly called on to advise government agencies concerning the laws, rules, and regulations by which society deals with the increasing number of challenges that have a biological basis. As an example of the value of scientific knowledge for the assessment and formulation of public policy, consider a management problem. Scientists and fishermen have long known that Atlantic bluefin tunas (*Thunnus thynnus*) have a western breeding ground in the Gulf of Mexico and an eastern breeding ground in the Mediterranean Sea (**Figure 1.16**). Overfishing led to declining numbers of bluefin tunas, especially in the western-breeding populations, to the point of these populations being endangered.

Initially it was assumed by scientists, fishermen, and policy makers alike that the eastern and western populations had geographically separate feeding grounds as well as separate breeding grounds. Acting on this assumption, an international commission drew a line down the middle of the Atlantic Ocean and established strict fishing quotas on the western side of the line, with the intent of allowing the western population to recover. Modern tracking data, however, revealed that in fact the eastern and western bluefin populations mix freely on their feeding grounds across the entire North Atlantic—a swath of ocean that includes the most heavily fished waters in the world. Tunas caught on the eastern side of the line could just as likely be from the western-breeding population as from the eastern; thus the established policy could not achieve its intended goal.

Scientific knowledge can make significant contributions to the formulation of wise public policy, but economic and political factors frequently outweigh scientific recommendations. It is particularly lamentable when solid scientific evidence is discounted or ignored because it is inconvenient. An example is the rejection by many policy makers of strong evidence for and scientific consensus on global climate change.

Biology is crucial for understanding ecosystems

Earth has been changing since its formation and continues to change. Human activity, however, is resulting in an unprecedented *rate* of change in the world's ecosystems. For example, the mining and consumption of fossil fuels are releasing massive quantities of carbon dioxide into Earth's atmosphere. This anthropogenic (human-generated) increase in atmospheric carbon dioxide is largely responsible for the rapid rate of global climate warming recorded over the last six decades (**Figure 1.17**).

Our use of natural resources is putting stress on the ability of Earth's ecosystems to continue to produce the goods and services on which our society depends. Human activities are changing global climates at an unprecedented rate and are leading to the extinctions of large numbers of species (such as the reef-building corals featured in this chapter). The modern, warmer world is also experiencing the spread of new diseases and the resurgence of old ones. Biological knowledge is vital for determining the causes of these changes and for devising policies to deal with them.

Biodiversity helps us understand, enjoy, and appreciate our world

Beyond issues of policy and pragmatism lies the human "need to know." Most people are fascinated by the richness and diversity of life and want to know more about organisms, how they function,

(A) 1941

Riggs Glacier

Muir Glacier

(B) 2004

Riggs Glacier

Both photos courtesy of the U.S. Geological Survey

Figure 1.17 A Warmer World   Earth's climate has been steadily warming for the last 150 years. The rate of this warming trend has also steadily increased, resulting in the rapid melting of polar ice caps, glaciers, and alpine (mountaintop) snow and ice. **(A, B)** These photographs show the effects of 63 years of climate change on two ancient, longstanding glaciers in Alaska. Over that time, Muir Glacier retreated some 7 kilometers and can no longer be seen from the original vantage point. Understanding how biological populations respond to such change requires integration of biological principles from molecular biology to ecosystem ecology.

and how they interact (**Figure 1.18**). For the biologist, biodiversity offers an inexhaustible source of new questions and opportunities for new investigations and experiments. New discoveries and greater knowledge generate questions no one thought to ask before. Science is a never-ending quest.

Apart from scientific endeavors, biodiversity enriches our lives. You may be an avid birdwatcher, or enjoy gardening, or seek out particular species if you hunt or fish. Some people observe or collect butterflies, or mushrooms, or other groups of plants and animals. Displays of spring wildflowers bring out throngs of human viewers. Hiking and camping in natural areas full of diverse species are activities enjoyed by millions. Learning about biology greatly increases our enjoyment of the world around us.

KEY CONCEPT

1.4 Recap and Assess

Biology informs us about the structure, processes, and interactions of the living organisms that make up our world. Informed decisions about food and energy production, health, and our environment depend on biological knowledge. Biology also addresses the human need to understand the world around us, and helps us appreciate the diverse planet we call home.

1. Describe an example of how modern biology is applied to agriculture.
2. Discuss an example of a biological problem that is directly related to global climate change.
3. Explain why excessive use of antibiotics can be a problem.

This chapter has provided a brief roadmap of the rest of the book. Thinking about the principles outlined here may help you clarify and make sense of the pages of detailed description to come.

© Mark Moffett/Minden Pictures

Figure 1.18 Exploring Life on Earth These biologists are collecting insects in the top boughs of a spruce tree in the Carmanah Valley of Vancouver, Canada. Biologists estimate that the number of species discovered to date is only a small percentage of the species that inhabit Earth. To fill this gap in our knowledge, biologists around the world are applying thorough sampling techniques and new genetic tools to document and understand Earth's biodiversity.

▶ Investigating**LIFE**

 How might experiments on heat stress in corals be used to predict the response of corals to global warming?

How can we put studies like the one conducted by Rachael Bay and her colleagues to use? One way is to use the information to make predictions. As we've noted in this chapter, abundant evidence shows that Earth's climate is warming as a result of increased levels of CO_2 in our atmosphere. Can corals survive this global warming, or will they all lose their photosynthetic dinoflagellates and die? The experiments and observations done by Bay's team suggest that higher temperatures will lead to increased coral bleaching, but that some short-term acclimation of individuals can occur. If global warming is slowed sufficiently, longer-term processes of evolution will act on the surviving corals that have genetic adaptations that increase their tolerance to warmer waters. This selection process should result in genetic changes in populations, which will allow more corals to survive. How well acclimation and adaptation can work to ensure the survival of corals depends on many factors, including the average life span of individual coral colonies, the rate of global warming, and the availability of alternative heat-resistant dinoflagellates. The basic research conducted by Bay's team is a first, but critical, step in predicting the future response of corals to global warming.

Future directions

As we have described, the corals in Bay's study have certain species of dinoflagellates growing within their cells. The corals provide a suitable environment for the dinoflagellates, and the dinoflagellates provide nutrients for the corals. Such a mutually beneficial relationship is called **symbiosis**. The bleaching response to high temperature implies dysfunction in the dinoflagellates, leading to their expulsion from the corals. Understanding thermal tolerance of the corals therefore requires greater understanding of genetic changes and acclimation of the symbiotic dinoflagellates. Other studies have shown that some corals contain multiple strains of dinoflagellates, and these strains change in abundance when the corals are grown at different temperatures, perhaps contributing to thermal tolerance. There are many species and strains of dinoflagellates, but coral species usually are associated with specific species. Future research could focus on thermal tolerance of dinoflagellates to identify genes that confer thermal tolerance. Additional research could be to find ways of transferring those genes into other species of dinoflagellates or to find ways of infecting corals endangered by rising temperatures with strains of temperature-tolerant symbionts.

VISUAL SUMMARY 1

You should be able to relate each summary to the adjacent figures. If you go to this visual summary in **Achieve**, you can follow links to figures, animations, activities, and simulations that will help you consolidate the material.

KEY CONCEPT

1.1 Living Organisms Have a Common Origin and Share Similarities

Go to **Activity 1.1**

- All living organisms are related to one another through common descent.

- Cells evolved early in the history of life. **Cellular specialization** enabled the evolution of multicellular organisms.

- **Photosynthesis** provided a means of capturing energy directly from sunlight, and over time changed Earth's atmosphere.

- Life can be studied at different levels of organization.

- Living organisms, whether unicellular or multicellular, must regulate their internal environment to maintain **homeostasis**, the range of physical and chemical conditions necessary for survival and function.

- Individual organisms form populations and interact with other organisms of their own and other species.

Questions

1. What is the evidence that all life on Earth has a common origin?

2. How did photosynthesis make life on land possible?

3. What is the relationship between a population and an ecosystem?

Figure 1.2

KEY CONCEPT

1.2 Genetics and Evolution Are Fundamental Principles of Biology

- Genetic information consists of **genes**, which are sequences of **deoxyribonucleic acid** (**DNA**) that can code for proteins. All of the genetic information of an individual is its **genome**.

- Evolution is change in the genetic makeup of biological **populations** through time due to **natural selection** that produces **adaptations**.

- **Phylogenetic trees** show evolutionary relationships among biological lineages and help biologists make comparisons among genes, organisms, populations, and species.

Questions

1. What is a mutation, and what determines whether it contributes to evolutionary change?

2. What are two possible explanations for why very similar genes can be found in bacteria and plants?

3. Explain the molecular genetics meaning of transcription and translation.

Figure 1.8

Figure 1.11

KEY CONCEPT
1.3 Biologists Investigate Life through Experiments That Test Hypotheses

Go to Animation 1.1

- Scientific methodology combines observation, the gathering of information (**data**), experimentation, and the application of logic.

- **Hypotheses** are tentative explanations of observations or answers to questions. Predictions made on the basis of a hypothesis are tested with additional observations and experiments and the use of statistical methods.

- Statistical methods are applied to quantitative data to establish whether the differences observed could be the result of chance.

Questions

1. What is the role of inductive logic in forming a hypothesis?

2. Give an example of a controlled experiment and a comparative experiment.

3. Why do biologists use statistical tests to analyze their data?

Figure 1.13

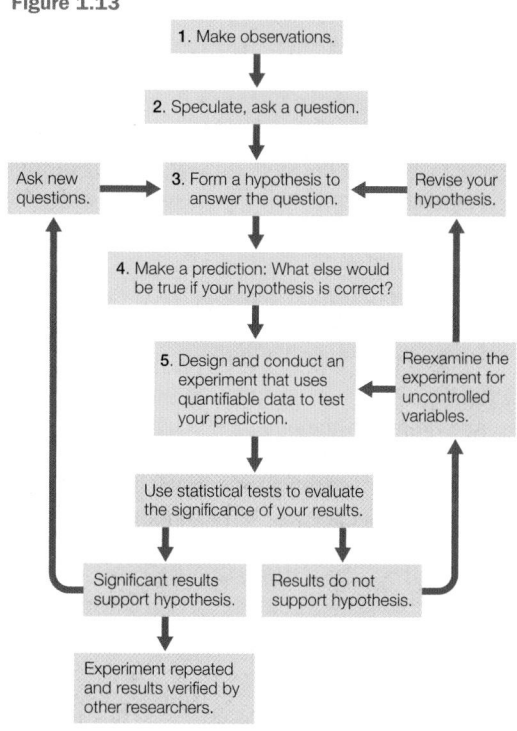

KEY CONCEPT
1.4 Understanding Biology Is Important for Health, Well-Being, and Public-Policy Decisions

- Biological knowledge is important for advancing agriculture and medicine.

- Biological knowledge is important for the formulation of effective public policy.

- Biology is increasingly important for understanding how organisms interact with each other and with the environment in a rapidly changing world.

Questions

1. Describe one way in which global climate change threatens agriculture.

2. Why is it wise to get a flu shot each year?

3. Describe an ecosystem service that can be threatened by human activities.

Figure 1.14

From K. Xu et al., 2006, *Nature* 442: 705–708. © Macmillan Publishers Ltd.

Go to **Achieve** for the eBook, **LearningCurve**, animations, activities, simulations, and additional resources and assignments.

Small Molecules and the Chemistry of Life 2

KEY CONCEPTS

2.1 An Element's Atomic Structure Determines Its Properties

2.2 Atoms Bond to Form Molecules

2.3 Chemical Reactions Transform Substances

2.4 The Properties of Water Are Critical to the Chemistry of Life

The atoms in water can become part of the bodies of animals that drink it.

▶ Investigating LIFE

Tracking a Dinosaur

"You are what you eat—and that applies to teeth" is a modification of a famous saying about body chemistry. One of the important atoms in organisms is oxygen (O), which is part of water (H₂O). Oxygen has two naturally occurring variants called isotopes; they have the same chemical properties but different weights because their nuclei have different numbers of neutrons. Both isotopes of O are incorporated into the bodies of animals that consume the isotopes in water and food.

The hard surface of teeth, called enamel, is made up largely of calcium phosphate, $Ca_3(PO_4)_2$. The isotope composition of the oxygen in calcium phosphate enamel varies depending on where an animal was living when the enamel was made. When water evaporates from the ocean, it forms clouds that move inland and release rain. Water with the heavier isotope of O tends to fall more readily than water containing the lighter isotope. As a result, regions of the world that are closer to the ocean receive rain containing more heavy water than do regions farther away, and these differences are reflected in the bodies of animals that dwell in these regions.

This property has been used to reveal an astounding fact about dinosaurs that lived in the great basins of southwestern North America about 150 million years ago. *Camarasaurus* was big—up to 25 meters long and weighing up to 45 metric

tons. Henry Ficke from Colorado College analyzed the oxygen isotopes in the enamel of *Camarasaurus* fossils and found two kinds of teeth: Some had the heavy oxygen content typical of rains and rocks in the basin region. But others, surprisingly, had a lower proportion of heavy oxygen, indicating that these animals had lived at higher elevations 300 kilometers to the west. This indicated for the first time that dinosaurs migrated a long way from west to east. The reason for this migration is not clear. *Camarasaurus* ate a plant-based diet, and perhaps the migration was directed at finding food.

Many biological phenomena are analyzed and understood in the context of chemistry. You will learn, for example, that adding even one atom to a large molecule can change its character and function. Analyzing the isotopes in dinosaur teeth is but one example of how chemical analysis has led to advances in biological science.

 What insights into biological systems have been discovered through isotope analysis? (Find the answer on page 40.)

2.1 An Element's Atomic Structure Determines Its Properties

Learning Objectives

2.1.1 Compare the elements found in living tissue with elements found in nonliving matter.

2.1.2 Relate the atomic structure of an atom to its identity as an element.

2.1.3 Explain the role that the outermost electron shell plays in determining how an atom may combine with other atoms.

2.1.4 Explain how elements can be grouped into columns on the periodic table according to their chemical properties.

All matter is composed of **atoms**. Atoms are tiny—more than a trillion (10^{12}) of them could make up the period at the end of this sentence. Atoms and their component particles have volume and mass, which are characteristics of all matter. **Mass** is a measure of the quantity of matter present; the greater the mass, the greater the quantity of matter. Atoms also have electric charges.

Atoms contain protons, neutrons, and electrons

Each atom consists of a dense, positively charged **nucleus**, around which are one or more negatively charged **electrons** (Figure 2.1). The nucleus contains one or more positively charged **protons** and may contain one or more **neutrons** with no electric charge.

The mass of a proton serves as a standard unit of measure called the **dalton** (named after the English chemist John Dalton). A single proton or neutron has a mass of about 1 dalton (Da), which is 1.7×10^{-24} grams (0.0000000000000000000000017 g), but an electron has even less mass at 9×10^{-28} g (0.0005 Da). Because the mass of an electron is negligible compared with the mass of a proton or a neutron, the contribution of electrons to the mass of an atom can usually be ignored when measurements and calculations are made. It is electrons, however, that determine how atoms will combine with other atoms to form stable associations.

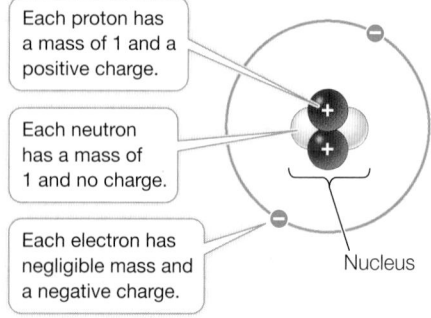

Each proton has a mass of 1 and a positive charge.

Each neutron has a mass of 1 and no charge.

Each electron has negligible mass and a negative charge.

Nucleus

Figure 2.1 The Structure of an Atom An atom has a nucleus composed of neutrons and protons surrounded by electrons. Although the nucleus accounts for virtually all of the atomic weight, it occupies only 1/10,000 of the atom's volume. This type of representation, which is called a Bohr model, depicts individual electrons moving in "orbits" at set distances from the nucleus.

Each proton has a positive electric charge, defined as +1 unit of charge. An electron has a negative charge equal and opposite to that of a proton (–1). The neutron, as its name suggests, is electrically neutral, so its charge is 0. Charges that are different (+/–) attract each other, whereas charges that are alike (+/+, –/–) repel each other. Generally, atoms are electrically neutral because the number of electrons in an atom equals the number of protons.

An element consists of only one kind of atom

An **element** is a fundamental substance that contains only one kind of atom. The element hydrogen consists only of hydrogen atoms; the element iron consists only of iron atoms. The atoms of each element have characteristics that distinguish them from the atoms of other elements. These physical and chemical properties (how they interact with other atoms) depend on the numbers of particles the atoms contain.

There are more than 100 different elements, although only 92 of them occur naturally. About 98% of the tissue of every living organism (except in skeletons) is composed of just six elements:

Carbon (symbol C)	Hydrogen (H)	Nitrogen (N)
Oxygen (O)	Phosphorus (P)	Sulfur (S)

Although living organisms are composed of the same elements as the nonliving universe, the proportions in living systems are very different. For example, oxygen makes up 65% of the human body (excluding bones). But it makes up 21% of Earth's atmosphere and 46% of Earth's crust. Carbon makes up 18% of the human body but less than 1% Earth's atmosphere and its crust. Silicon, by contrast, makes up less than 0.01% of the human body and is absent from our atmosphere, but it makes up 28% of Earth's crust. Clearly, living systems are selective in the amounts of elements they extract from the environment. This selectivity is a fundamental property of life.

Each element has a unique number of protons

A particular element differs from other elements by the number of protons in the nucleus of each of its atoms; the number of protons is designated the **atomic number**. This atomic number is unique to each element. The atomic number of helium is 2, and an atom of helium always has two protons; the atomic number of oxygen is 8, and an atom of oxygen always has eight protons. Since the number of protons (and electrons) determines how an element behaves in chemical reactions, it is possible to arrange the elements in a table such that those with similar chemical properties are grouped together. This is the familiar **periodic table** you see in Figure 2.2.

Media Clip 2.1 The Elements Song
Life12e.com/mc2.1

Along with a definitive number of protons, every element except hydrogen has one or more neutrons in its nucleus. The **mass number** of an atom is the total number of protons and neutrons in its nucleus. The nucleus of a carbon atom contains six protons and six neutrons and has a mass number of 12. Oxygen has eight protons and eight neutrons and has a mass number of 16. Since the mass of an electron is negligible, the mass number is essentially the mass of the atom in daltons.

Atomic number (number of protons)
Chemical symbol (for hydrogen)
Atomic weight

The six elements highlighted in yellow make up 98% of the tissue of most living organisms (except for skeletons).

Elements highlighted in orange are present in small amounts in many organisms.

1	2	3	4	5	6	7	8	9	10	11	12	13	14	15	16	17	18
1 H 1.0079																	2 He 4.003
3 Li 6.941	4 Be 9.012											5 B 10.81	6 C 12.011	7 N 14.007	8 O 15.999	9 F 18.998	10 Ne 20.179
11 Na 22.990	12 Mg 24.305											13 Al 26.982	14 Si 28.086	15 P 30.974	16 S 32.06	17 Cl 35.453	18 Ar 39.948
19 K 39.098	20 Ca 40.08	21 Sc 44.956	22 Ti 47.88	23 V 50.942	24 Cr 51.996	25 Mn 54.938	26 Fe 55.847	27 Co 58.933	28 Ni 58.69	29 Cu 63.546	30 Zn 65.38	31 Ga 69.72	32 Ge 72.59	33 As 74.922	34 Se 78.96	35 Br 79.909	36 Kr 83.80
37 Rb 85.4778	38 Sr 87.62	39 Y 88.906	40 Zr 91.22	41 Nb 92.906	42 Mo 95.94	43 Tc (99)	44 Ru 101.07	45 Rh 102.906	46 Pd 106.4	47 Ag 107.870	48 Cd 112.41	49 In 114.82	50 Sn 118.69	51 Sb 121.75	52 Te 127.60	53 I 126.904	54 Xe 131.30
55 Cs 132.905	56 Ba 137.34		72 Hf 178.49	73 Ta 180.948	74 W 183.85	75 Re 186.207	76 Os 190.2	77 Ir 192.2	78 Pt 195.08	79 Au 196.967	80 Hg 200.59	81 Tl 204.37	82 Pb 207.19	83 Bi 208.980	84 Po (209)	85 At (210)	86 Rn (222)
87 Fr (223)	88 Ra 226.025		104 Rf (261)	105 Db (262)	106 Sg (266)	107 Bh (264)	108 Hs (269)	109 Mt (268)	110 Ds (269)	111 Rg (272)	112 Cn (277)	113 Nh	114 Fl (285)	115 Mc (289)	116 Lv (293)	117 Ts	118 Og (293)

Masses in parentheses indicate unstable elements that decay rapidly to form other elements.

Lanthanide series

57 La 138.906	58 Ce 140.12	59 Pr 140.9077	60 Nd 144.24	61 Pm (145)	62 Sm 150.36	63 Eu 151.96	64 Gd 157.25	65 Tb 158.924	66 Dy 162.50	67 Ho 164.930	68 Er 167.26	69 Tm 168.934	70 Yb 173.04	71 Lu 174.97

Actinide series

89 Ac 227.028	90 Th 232.038	91 Pa 231.0359	92 U 238.02	93 Np 237.0482	94 Pu (244)	95 Am (243)	96 Cm (247)	97 Bk (247)	98 Cf (251)	99 Es (252)	100 Fm (257)	101 Md (258)	102 No (259)	103 Lr (260)

Figure 2.2 The Periodic Table The periodic table groups all the elements according to their physical and chemical properties. Elements 1–92 occur in nature; elements with atomic numbers greater than 94 were created in the laboratory.

Q: Why is this table called the periodic table?

By convention, we often print the symbol for an element with the atomic number at the lower left and the mass number at the upper left, both immediately preceding the symbol. Thus hydrogen, carbon, and oxygen can be written as ^1_1H, $^{12}_6\text{C}$, and $^{16}_8\text{O}$, respectively.

The number of neutrons differs among isotopes

In some elements, there are different forms in which the number of neutrons in the nucleus may vary. Different **isotopes** of the same element have the same number of protons but different numbers of neutrons, as you saw in the story opening this chapter. Many elements have several isotopes. Generally, isotopes are formed when atoms combine and/or release subatomic particles (decay). The isotopes of hydrogen (**Figure 2.3**) have special names, but for most elements their isotopes do not have special names.

For example, there are three isotopes of carbon: ^{12}C (six neutrons in the nucleus), ^{13}C (seven neutrons), and ^{14}C (eight neutrons). Note that all three (called carbon-12, carbon-13, and carbon-14) have six protons, so they are all carbon. Most carbon atoms are ^{12}C, about 1.1% are ^{13}C, and a tiny fraction are ^{14}C. The carbon atoms that make up complex biological molecules are mostly ^{12}C, but some are ^{13}C. The ratio of ^{13}C:^{12}C varies with location and can

be used to identify biological samples whose origin is not known (**Investigating Life: Determining Beef Source in Big Macs Using Isotope Analysis**). All carbon isotopes have virtually the same chemical reactivity, which is an important property for their use in experimental biology and medicine.

An element's **atomic weight** (or relative atomic mass) is equivalent to the average of the mass numbers of a representative

^1_1H **Hydrogen** 1 proton 0 neutrons

^2_1H **Deuterium** 1 proton 1 neutron

^3_1H **Tritium** 1 proton 2 neutrons

Figure 2.3 Isotopes of Hydrogen All three forms of H have the same number of protons (1), but their number of neutrons differs.

▶InvestigatingLIFE   Determining Beef Source in Big Macs Using Isotope Analysis

Experiment

Original Paper: L. Martinelli et al. 2011. Worldwide stable carbon and nitrogen isotopes of Big Mac patties: An example of a truly "glocal" food. *Food Chem* 127: 1712–1718.

The Big Mac hamburger can be purchased in 38,000 outlets in 120 countries. The recipe for the Big Mac is virtually the same everywhere; it is claimed that the burger has the same quality meat and nutritional quality everywhere it is served. To investigate this claim, Lesley Chesson and James Ehleringer at the University of Utah compared the ratio of $^{13}C:^{12}C$ in Big Mac patties around the world to determine whether the meat had a local or a common source. Beef cattle eat plant food, and carbon atoms from this food end up in meat. In some types of plants, the ratio of $^{13}C:^{12}C$ is higher than in others. Depending on which type of plants the cattle consume, the beef will also have a different $^{13}C:^{12}C$ ratio.

HYPOTHESIS▶   Beef in Big Macs served in different countries comes from the same source.

METHOD▶

RESULTS▶

CONCLUSION▶   The Big Mac burger patties in the two countries have a different isotopic ratio of 13C:12C atoms, which reflects local sources for the beef. The hypothesis is rejected.

---

sample of atoms of that element, with all the isotopes in their normally occurring proportions. More precisely, an element's atomic weight is defined as the ratio of the average mass per atom of the element to $\frac{1}{12}$ of the mass of an atom of ^{12}C. Because it is a ratio, atomic weight is a dimensionless physical quantity—it is not expressed in units. The atomic weight of hydrogen, taking into account all of its isotopes and their typical abundances, is 1.00794. This number is fractional because it is the average of the contributing masses of all of the isotopes. This definition implies that in any given sample of hydrogen atoms of a particular element found on Earth, the average composition of isotopes will be constant. But as you saw in the opening to this chapter, that is not necessarily so. Some water has more of the heavy O isotopes. So chemists are now listing atomic weights as ranges, for example, H: 1.00784–1.00811.

Most isotopes are stable. However, some, called **radioisotopes**, are unstable and spontaneously give off energy in the form of α (alpha), β (beta), or γ (gamma) radiation from the nucleus. Known as **radioactive decay**, this release of energy transforms the original atom. The type of transformation varies depending on the radioisotope, but some transformations result in a different number of protons, so that the original atom becomes a different element. This is especially true of elements with atomic numbers greater than 92, which exist only in the laboratory.

Scientists can detect released radiation from radioisotopes. For instance, if you feed an earthworm food containing a radioisotope, you can follow the worm's path through the soil by using a detector called a Geiger counter. Most atoms in living organisms are organized into stable associations called **molecules**. If a radioisotope is incorporated into a molecule, it acts as a tag or label, allowing

Work with the Data

The experiment compared the meat in Big Macs served in 26 different countries by measuring the ratio of stable carbon isotopes (^{13}C:^{12}C) in samples of ten beef patties from each country. The hypothesis was based on claims that the beef used in Big Macs comes from a single source, and that the ^{13}C:^{12}C ratio in patties found everywhere should thus be the same. **Table A** shows the average ^{13}C:^{12}C ratio for each of the 26 countries. A higher number means more of the rare, stable isotope ^{13}C than of the more common ^{12}C.

Table A

Country	^{13}C:^{12}C ratio[a]	Country	^{13}C:^{12}C ratio	Country	^{13}C:^{12}C ratio
All	15.8	Germany	21.7	Portugal	20.7
Argentina	17.2	Hungary	22.0	Scotland	25.2
Australia	19.4	Indonesia	19.5	Slovakia	21.0
Austria	22.0	Israel	20.4	South Africa	13.0
Brazil	11.1	Japan	11.8	Spain	21.1
Canada	21.6	Malaysia	21.5	Sweden	23.2
China	13.9	Mexico	13.9	Turkey	20.5
England	25.4	Netherlands	20.7	United States	14.5
France	21.8	Paraguay	12.1	Uruguay	16.7

[a]Measured in parts per million atoms (× 100).

Go to **Achieve** for a companion Data in Depth exercise.

QUESTIONS▶

1. Do the average local ratios differ from the 26-country average ratio? What statistical test would you perform to show that the differences between the individual country averages and the all-countries average are significant? (Refer to Appendix B.)

2. The countries from which the hamburgers were analyzed are in different locations on Earth. One way to compare locations is by geographic latitude. You may recall that in latitude, 0 degrees defines the equator and 90 degrees defines the poles. **Table B** shows average ^{13}C:^{12}C ratios of Big Mac beef patties from different latitudes. Plot the data on a graph of ratio versus latitude. What can you conclude from these data?

Table B

Latitude	^{13}C:^{12}C ratio[a]
20°S–20°N	11.4
20°–40°[ob]	15.3
40°–60°[ob]	21.8

[a]Average value measured in parts per million atoms (× 100).

[b]20°S–40°S and 20°N–40°N; 40°S–60°S and 40°N–60°N.

---

a researcher or physician to track the molecule in an experiment or in the body (**Figure 2.4**).

Connect the Concepts Radioisotopes are also used to analyze biochemical pathways (see Key Concept 10.3) and to date fossils (see Key Concept 24.1).

Although radioisotopes are useful in research and in medicine, even a low dose of the radiation they emit has the potential to damage molecules and cells. However, these damaging effects are sometimes used to our advantage; for example, the radiation from ^{60}Co (cobalt-60) and ^{131}I (iodine-131) is used in medicine to kill cancer cells.

The behavior of electrons determines chemical bonding and geometry

The number of electrons in an atom determines how it will combine with other atoms. Biologists are interested both in the structures of substances in living systems, and how chemical changes take place in living cells. Combinations of atoms, usually involving changes in the distribution of electrons in atoms, underlie both of these areas of interest.

The location of a given electron in an atom at any given time is impossible to determine. We can only describe a volume of space within the atom where the electron is likely to be. The region of space where the electron is found at least 90% of the time is the electron's **orbital**. Orbitals have characteristic shapes and orientations, and a given orbital can be occupied by a maximum of two

(A) Depressed   **(B) Not depressed**

Figure 2.4 Tagging the Brain   In these images from live persons, a radioactively labeled sugar has been used to detect differences between the brain activity of a depressed person (**A**) and a person who is not depressed (**B**). The more active a brain region is, the more sugar it takes up (shown as dark yellow areas). The brain of the depressed person (left) shows less activity than the brain of the person who is not depressed.

Q: How could this technique be used in the clinic?

Atoms in the same column have the same number of electrons in the outer (valence) shell and have similar chemical properties.

Electrons occupying the same orbital are shown as pairs.

First shell

Nucleus

Hydrogen (H)   1+

Helium (He)   2+

Second shell

Lithium (Li)   3+   Carbon (C)   6+   Nitrogen (N)   7+   Oxygen (O)   8+   Fluorine (F)   9+   Neon (Ne)   10+

Third shell

Sodium (Na)   11+   Phosphorus (P)   15+   Sulfur (S)   16+   Chlorine (Cl)   17+   Argon (Ar)   18+

Atoms whose outermost shells contain unfilled orbitals (unpaired electrons) are reactive.

When all the orbitals in the outermost shell are filled, the atom is stable.

Figure 2.5 Electron Shells Determine the Reactivity of Atoms
Each shell can hold a specific maximum number of electrons. Going out from the nucleus, each shell must be filled before electrons can occupy the next shell. The energy level of an electron is higher in a shell farther from the nucleus. An atom with unpaired electrons in its outermost shell can react (bond) with other atoms. Note that the atoms in this figure are arranged similarly to their arrangement in the periodic table.

Q: Which elements on this graph do not react with other elements? Why?

electrons. Thus any atom larger than helium (atomic number 2) must have electrons in two or more orbitals. As we move from lighter to heavier atoms in the periodic table, the orbitals are filled in a specific sequence, in a series of what are known as **electron shells**, or energy levels, around the nucleus.

- *First shell*: The innermost electron shell consists of just one orbital. A hydrogen atom ($_1$H) has one electron in its first shell; helium ($_2$He) has two. Atoms of all other elements have two or more shells to accommodate orbitals for additional electrons.

- *Second shell*: The second shell contains four orbitals and hence holds up to eight electrons.

- *Additional shells*: Elements with more than ten electrons have three or more electron shells. The farther a shell is from the nucleus, the higher the energy level is for an electron occupying that shell.

View in Achieve
Activity 2.1 Electron Orbitals

Every electron shell has a single, spherical *s* orbital. The second shell and subsequent shells also have three dumbbell-shaped *p* orbitals. The third shell and subsequent shells have additional orbitals. The *s* orbitals fill with electrons first, and their electrons have the lowest energy level. Subsequent shells have different numbers of orbitals, but the outermost shells usually hold only eight electrons. In any atom, the outermost electron shell (the **valence shell**) determines how the atom combines with other atoms—that is, how the atom behaves chemically. When a valence shell with four orbitals contains eight electrons, there are no unpaired electrons and the atom is stable—it is least likely to react with other atoms (**Figure 2.5**). Examples of chemically stable elements are helium, neon, and argon. By contrast, atoms that have one or more unpaired electrons in their outer shell are capable of reacting with other atoms.

Atoms with unpaired electrons (i.e., partially filled orbitals) in their outermost electron shell are unstable and will undergo reactions in order to fill their outermost shell. *Reactive atoms can attain stability either by sharing electrons with other atoms or by losing or gaining one or more electrons.* In either case, the atoms involved are bonded together into stable associations called molecules. The tendency of atoms to form stable molecules so that they have eight electrons in their outermost shell is known as the octet rule. Many atoms in biologically important molecules—for example, carbon (C) and nitrogen (N)—follow this rule. An important exception is hydrogen (H), which attains stability when two electrons occupy its single shell (consisting of just one *s* orbital).

KEY CONCEPT
2.1 Recap and Assess

Living organisms are composed of the same set of chemical elements as the rest of the universe. An atom consists of a nucleus of protons and neutrons and a characteristic configuration of electrons in orbitals around the nucleus. An atom's chemical properties are determined by its atomic structure. Elements are composed of atoms with the same number of protons. Elements are grouped in the periodic table according to the number of electrons in their outermost shell.

1. Describe how the configuration of the valence shell influences the placement of an element in the periodic table.

2. How does bonding help a reactive atom achieve stability?

3. Would you expect the elemental composition of Earth's crust to be the same as that of the human body? Explain your answer.

4. There is an isotope of oxygen with a mass number of 18. With respect to the number of protons, neutrons, and electrons, how does this isotope differ from oxygen atoms with a mass number of 16?

You have been introduced to the individual players on the biochemical stage—the atoms. We have shown how the number of unpaired electrons in an atom's valence shell drives its "quest for stability." Next we will describe the different types of chemical bonds that can lead to stability—joining atoms together into molecular structures with different properties.

KEY CONCEPT
2.2 Atoms Bond to Form Molecules

Learning Objectives

2.2.1 Compare chemical bonds and explain why covalent bonds are so strong.

2.2.2 Identify examples of polar covalent and nonpolar covalent bonds.

2.2.3 Distinguish between hydrophilic and hydrophobic interactions using examples.

2.2.4 Identify instances in which van der Waals forces are important.

A **chemical bond** is an attractive force that links two atoms together in a molecule. There are several kinds of chemical bonds (Table 2.1). We will begin with covalent bonds, the strong bonds that result from the sharing of electrons. Next we will examine ionic bonds, which form when an atom gains or loses one or more electrons to achieve stability. We will then consider other, weaker kinds of interactions, including hydrogen bonds.

▶ **View in Achieve**
Animation 2.1 **Chemical Bond Formation**

Covalent bonds consist of shared pairs of electrons

A **covalent bond** forms when two atoms attain stable electron numbers in their outermost shells by sharing one or more pairs of electrons. In a covalent bond, each atom contributes one member of each electron pair. Consider two hydrogen atoms coming close to one another, each with an unpaired electron in its single shell (Figure 2.6). When the electrons pair up, each hydrogen atom attains a stable number of electrons in its outermost shell—in this case, two electrons—and this links the two hydrogen atoms in a covalent bond, forming the molecule H_2.

A **compound** is a pure substance made up of two or more different elements bonded together in a fixed ratio. Chemical symbols identify the different elements in a compound, and subscript numbers indicate how many atoms of each element are present. For example, water (H_2O) has two atoms of hydrogen (H) bonded to a single oxygen atom (O). Every compound has a **molecular weight** that is the sum of the atomic weights of all atoms in the molecule. Looking at the periodic table in Figure 2.2, you can calculate the molecular weight of water to be 18.01. Molecules that make up living organisms can have molecular weights of up to half a billion.

TABLE **2.1** | Chemical Bonds and Interactions			
Name	**Basis of interaction**	**Structure**	**Bond energy**[a]
Covalent bond	Sharing of electron pairs	H O | || —N—C—	50–110
Ionic bond	Attraction of opposite charges	H | O | || —N—H ⊕ ⊖ O—C— | H	3–7
Hydrogen bond	Electrical attraction between a covalently bonded H atom and an electronegative atom	H | δ^+ δ^- | —N—H••••O=C—	3–7
Hydrophobic interaction	Interaction of nonpolar substances in the presence of polar substances (especially water)	H H H | | | —C—C—H C—C | | | | | H H H H H	1–2
van der Waals forces	Interaction of electrons of nonpolar substances	H—H C H H	1

[a]Bond energy is the amount of energy in kcal/mol needed to separate two bonded or interacting atoms under physiological conditions.

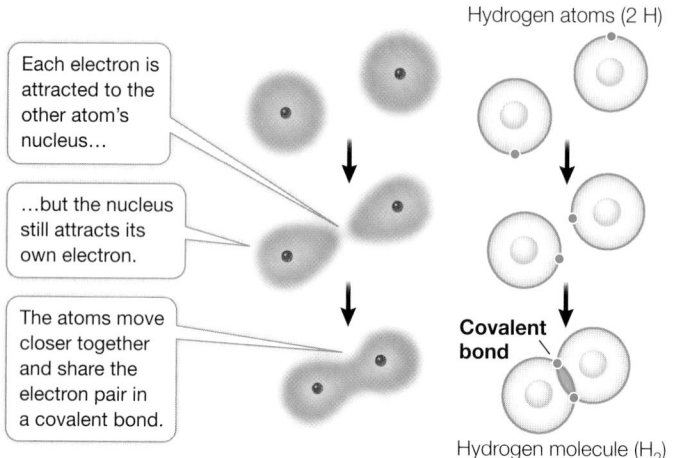

Hydrogen atoms (2 H)

Each electron is attracted to the other atom's nucleus...

...but the nucleus still attracts its own electron.

The atoms move closer together and share the electron pair in a covalent bond.

Covalent bond

Hydrogen molecule (H_2)

Figure 2.6 Electrons Are Shared in Covalent Bonds Two hydrogen atoms can combine to form a hydrogen molecule. A covalent bond forms when the electron orbitals of the two atoms overlap in an energetically stable manner.

How are the covalent bonds formed in a molecule of methane gas (CH_4)? The carbon atom has six electrons: two electrons fill its inner shell, and four unpaired electrons travel in its outer shell. Because its outer shell can hold up to eight electrons, carbon can share electrons with up to four other atoms—*it can form four covalent bonds*. When an atom of carbon reacts with four hydrogen atoms, methane forms. Thanks to electron sharing, the outer shell of methane's carbon atom is now filled with eight electrons, a stable configuration. The outer shell of each of the four hydrogen atoms is also filled. Four covalent bonds—four shared electron pairs—hold methane together. Figure 2.7 shows several different ways to represent molecular structures. Table 2.2 shows the covalent bonding capabilities of some biologically significant elements.

STRENGTH AND STABILITY Covalent bonds are very strong, meaning that it takes a lot of energy to break them. At temperatures where life exists, the covalent bonds of biological molecules are quite stable, as are their three-dimensional structures. However, this stability does not preclude change, as you will see.

Name (molecular formula)	Bohr model	Structural formula	Space-filling model	Ball-and-stick model
Hydrogen (H_2)	H H	H—H		H H
Oxygen (O_2)	O O	O=O		O O
Water (H_2O)	O H H	O—H | H		O H H
Methane (CH_4)	H H C H H	H—C—H with H above and below		H C H H H

Figure 2.7 Molecular Structures The four molecules shown here are all formed by covalent bonding.

Q: Draw the four representations for carbon dioxide (CO_2).

TABLE **2.2**	Covalent Bonding Capabilities of Some Biologically Important Elements	
Element	**Usual number of covalent bonds**
Hydrogen (H)	1
Oxygen (O)	2
Sulfur (S)	2
Nitrogen (N)	3
Carbon (C)	4
Phosphorus (P)	5

ORIENTATION For a given pair of elements—for example, carbon bonded to hydrogen—the length of the covalent bond is always the same. And for a given atom within a molecule, the angle of each of its covalent bonds, with respect to the other bonds, is generally the same. This is true regardless of the type of larger molecule that contains the atom. For example, the four filled orbitals around the carbon atom in methane are always distributed in space so that the bonded hydrogen atoms point to the corners of a regular tetrahedron, with carbon in the center (see Figure 2.7). Even when carbon is bonded to four atoms other than hydrogen, this three-dimensional orientation is more or less maintained. The orientation of covalent bonds in space gives the molecules their three-dimensional geometry, and the shapes of molecules contribute to their biological functions (see Key Concept 3.1).

Even though the orientations of bonds around each atom are fairly stable, the shapes of molecules can change. Think of a single covalent bond as an axle around which the two atoms, along with their other bonded atoms, can rotate (**Figure 2.8**). Bond rotation has enormous implications for the large molecules that make up living tissues. Since long chains of atoms (especially carbons) can rotate freely, there are many possibilities for the arrangement of atoms within the chain. This allows molecules to alter their structures, for example, to fit other molecules.

MULTIPLE COVALENT BONDS Two atoms can share more than one pair of electrons, forming multiple covalent bonds. These can be represented by lines between the chemical symbols for the linked atoms:

- A single bond involves the sharing of a single pair of electrons (for example, H—H or C—H).
- A double bond involves the sharing of four electrons (two pairs) (C=C).
- Triple bonds—six shared electrons—are rare, but there is one in nitrogen gas (N≡N), which is the major component of the air we breathe.

The bond energies are higher for multiple covalent bonds. For example, the bond energy of a C—C single bond is 80 kcal/mol while that of a C=C double bond is 145 kcal/mol.

UNEQUAL SHARING OF ELECTRONS When two atoms of the same element are covalently bonded, electrons in the bond are shared equally by both atoms. However, when the two atoms are of different elements, the sharing may not be equal. One nucleus may exert a greater attractive force on the electron pair than the other nucleus, so that the pair tends to be closer to that atom.

The attractive force that an atomic nucleus exerts on electrons is called its **electronegativity**. The electronegativity of an atom depends roughly on how many positive charges it has (atoms with more protons are more positive and thus more attractive to electrons) and on the distance between the nucleus and the electrons in the outer (valence) shell (the closer the electrons, the greater the electronegative pull). Table 2.3 shows the electronegativities (which are calculated to produce dimensionless quantities) of some elements important in biological systems. Note that oxygen (O) is very electronegative; in fact, oxygen is the second most electronegative element (after fluorine). Many organisms exploit the negativity of oxygen; moving electrons between C and O atoms powers living systems, as you will see in many subsequent examples in this text.

If two atoms are close to one another in electronegativity, they will share electrons equally in what is called a **nonpolar covalent bond**. Two oxygen atoms, for example, each with an electronegativity of 3.5, will share electrons equally. So will two hydrogen atoms (each with an electronegativity of 2.1). But when hydrogen bonds with oxygen to form water, the electrons involved are shared unequally; they tend to be nearer to the oxygen nucleus because it is more electronegative than hydrogen. When electrons are drawn to one nucleus more than to the other, the result is a **polar covalent bond** (**Figure 2.9**). Typically, a polar covalent

The Cl atoms are on opposite sides (*trans*).

The Cl atoms are in the same side orientation (*cis*).

Dichloroethane

Figure 2.8 Different Orientations of Atoms around a Covalent Bond
Rotation of atoms around a C—C bond allows different structures to form. These can have very different properties.

TABLE **2.3**	Some Electronegativities	
Element	**Electronegativity**
Oxygen (O)	3.5
Chlorine (Cl)	3.1
Nitrogen (N)	3.0
Carbon (C)	2.5
Phosphorus (P)	2.1
Hydrogen (H)	2.1
Sodium (Na)	0.9
Potassium (K)	0.8

(A) Unshared pairs of electrons

(B) Unshared pairs of electrons

Shared electron pairs

The electrons shared in bonds of water are shared unequally because they are more attracted to the nucleus of the oxygen atom than to those of the hydrogen atoms.

Figure 2.9 Water's Covalent Bonds Are Polar   When atoms with different electronegativities, such as oxygen and hydrogen, form a covalent bond, the electrons are drawn to one nucleus more than to the other. **(A)** A molecule held together by such a polar covalent bond has partial (δ^+ and δ^-) charges at different surfaces. **(B)** In water, the shared electrons are displaced toward the oxygen atom's nucleus.

bond occurs when the two atoms participating differ in electronegativity by more than 0.4.

Because of this unequal sharing of electrons, the oxygen end of the hydrogen–oxygen bond has a slightly negative charge (symbolized by δ^- and spoken of as "delta negative," meaning a partial unit of charge), and the hydrogen end has a slightly positive charge (δ^+). The bond is **polar** because these opposite charges are separated at the two ends, or poles, of the bond. The partial charges that result from polar covalent bonds produce polar molecules or polar regions of large molecules. Polar bonds within molecules greatly influence the interactions that such molecules have with other polar molecules. Water (H_2O) is a polar compound, and this polarity has significant effects on its physical properties and chemical reactivity, as you will see in later chapters. Molecules are termed *polar* if they contain polar covalent bonds and if one region is more polar than others.

Ionic bonds form by electrical attraction

When one interacting atom is much more electronegative than the other, a complete transfer of one or more electrons may take place. Consider sodium (electronegativity 0.9) and chlorine (electronegativity 3.1). A sodium atom has only one electron in its outermost shell; this condition is unstable. A chlorine atom has seven electrons in its outermost shell—another unstable condition. Since the electronegativity of chlorine is much greater than that of sodium, any electrons involved in bonding will tend to transfer completely from sodium's outermost shell to that of chlorine (**Figure 2.10**). This reaction between sodium and chlorine makes the resulting atoms more stable because they both have eight fully paired electrons in their outer shell. The result is two ions.

Ions are electrically charged particles that form when atoms gain or lose one or more electrons:

- The sodium ion (Na^+) in our example has a +1 unit of charge because it has one less electron than it has protons. The outermost electron shell of the sodium ion is full, with eight electrons, so the ion is stable. Positively charged ions are called **cations**. Other biologically important cations include Ca^{2+}, H^+, Mg^{2+}, and K^+.

- The chloride ion (Cl^-) has a −1 unit of charge because it has one more electron than it has protons. This additional electron gives Cl^- a stable outermost shell with eight electrons. Negatively charged ions are called **anions**.

Some elements can form ions with multiple charges by losing or gaining more than one electron. Examples are Ca^{2+} (the calcium ion, a calcium atom that has lost two electrons) and Mg^{2+} (the magnesium ion). Two biologically important elements can each yield more than one stable ion. Iron yields Fe^{2+} (the ferrous ion) and Fe^{3+} (the ferric ion), and copper yields Cu^+ (the cuprous ion) and Cu^{2+} (the cupric ion). Groups of covalently bonded atoms that carry an electric charge are called **complex ions**; examples include NH_4^+ (the ammonium ion), SO_4^{2-} (the sulfate ion), and PO_4^{3-} (the phosphate ion). Once formed, ions are usually stable and no more electrons are lost or gained.

Ionic bonds are bonds formed as a result of the electrical attraction between ions bearing opposite charges. Ions can form bonds that result in stable solid compounds, which we call salts. You're familiar with sodium chloride (NaCl)—table salt; its cations (Na^+) and anions (Cl^-) are held together by ionic bonds. In solids, the attractions are strong because the ions are close together. However, when ions are dispersed in water, the distances between them can be large, greatly reducing the strength of the attraction. Under

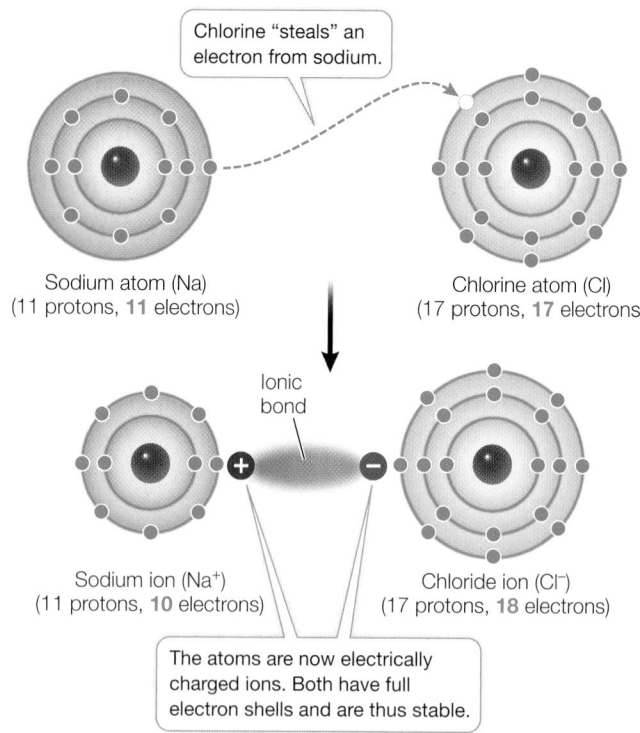

Chlorine "steals" an electron from sodium.

Sodium atom (Na)
(11 protons, **11** electrons)

Chlorine atom (Cl)
(17 protons, **17** electrons)

Ionic bond

Sodium ion (Na^+)
(11 protons, **10** electrons)

Chloride ion (Cl^-)
(17 protons, **18** electrons)

The atoms are now electrically charged ions. Both have full electron shells and are thus stable.

Figure 2.10 Formation of Sodium and Chloride Ions   When a sodium atom reacts with a chlorine atom, the more electronegative chlorine fills its outermost shell by "stealing" an electron from the sodium. In so doing, the chlorine atom becomes a negatively charged chloride ion (Cl^-). With one less electron, the sodium atom becomes a positively charged sodium ion (Na^+).

Q: What ions are formed when calcium reacts with chlorine? See the periodic table in Figure 2.2.

the conditions in living cells, an ionic bond is less strong than a covalent bond (see Table 2.1).

Not surprisingly, ions can interact with polar molecules, since both are charged. This interaction results when a solid salt such as NaCl dissolves in water. Water molecules surround the individual ions, separating them (**Figure 2.11**). The negatively charged chloride ions attract the positive poles of the water molecules, while the positively charged sodium ions attract the negative poles of the water molecules. This special property of water (its polarity) is one reason it is such a good biological solvent (see Key Concept 2.4).

Hydrogen bonds may form within or between molecules with polar covalent bonds

In liquid water, the negatively charged oxygen (δ^-) atom of one water molecule is attracted to the positively charged hydrogen (δ^+) atoms of another water molecule (**Figure 2.12A**). The bond resulting from this attraction is called a **hydrogen bond**. Later in this chapter you'll see how hydrogen bonding between water molecules contributes to many of the properties that make water so important for living systems. Hydrogen bonds are not restricted to water molecules. Such a bond can also form between a strongly

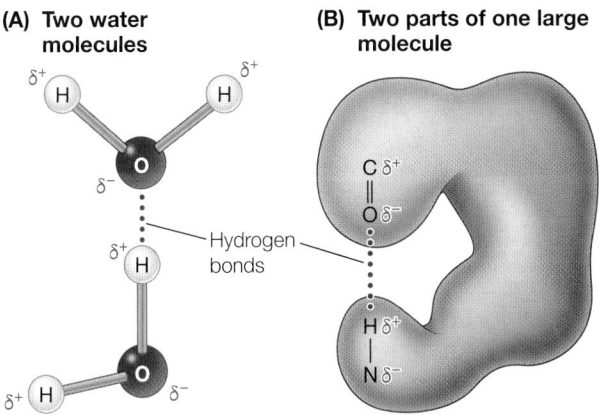

(A) Two water molecules

(B) Two parts of one large molecule

Figure 2.12 Hydrogen Bonds Can Form between or within Molecules   (A) A hydrogen bond between two molecules is an attraction between a negative charge on one molecule and the positive charge on a hydrogen atom of the second molecule. (B) Hydrogen bonds can form between different parts of the same large molecule.

Q: What happens to a large molecule if increasing heat is applied? Which bonds or interactions are affected?

electronegative atom in one molecule and a hydrogen atom that is involved in a polar covalent bond in another molecule, or another part of the same molecule (**Figure 2.12B**).

A hydrogen bond is weaker than most ionic bonds because its formation is due to partial charges (δ^+ and δ^-). It is much weaker than a covalent bond between a hydrogen atom and an oxygen atom (see Table 2.1). Although individual hydrogen bonds are weak, there can be many of them within a single molecule or between two molecules. In these cases, the hydrogen bonds together have considerable strength and can greatly influence the structure and properties of substances. For example, hydrogen bonds play important roles in determining and maintaining the three-dimensional shapes of giant molecules such as DNA and proteins (see Key Concept 3.2).

Hydrophobic interactions bring together nonpolar molecules

Just as water molecules can interact with one another through hydrogen bonds, any molecule that is polar can interact with other polar molecules through the weak (δ^+ to δ^-) attractions of hydrogen bonds. If a polar molecule interacts with water in this way, it is called **hydrophilic** ("water-loving") (**Figure 2.13A**).

Nonpolar molecules, in contrast, tend to interact with other nonpolar molecules. For example, carbon (electronegativity 2.5) forms nonpolar bonds with hydrogen (electronegativity 2.1), and molecules containing only hydrogen and carbon atoms—called **hydrocarbon molecules**—are nonpolar. In water these molecules tend to aggregate with one another rather than with the polar water molecules. Therefore nonpolar molecules are known as **hydrophobic** ("water-hating"), and the interactions between them are called **hydrophobic interactions** (**Figure 2.13B**). Of course, hydrophobic substances do not really "hate" water; they can form weak interactions with it, since the electronegativities of carbon

Chlorine (Cl)
Sodium (Na)
Oxygen (O)
Hydrogen (H)

Ionic bonds between Na⁺ and Cl⁺ hold ions together in a solid crystal.

Chloride ion (Cl⁻)

Sodium ion (Na⁺)

Undissolved sodium chloride (NaCl)

Water molecules

When NaCl is dissolved in water, the chloride anion (–) attracts the δ^+ pole of water…

… and the sodium cation (+) attracts the δ^- pole of water.

Figure 2.11 Water Molecules Surround Ions   When an ionic solid dissolves in water, polar water molecules cluster around the cations and anions, preventing them from reassociating.

Q: What happens at the chemical and physical levels when a salt solution evaporates?

(A) Hydrophilic

(B) Hydrophobic

Water is polar.

Polar molecules such as hydrogen fluoride are attracted to water.

Nonpolar molecules are more likely to associate with one another than with water.

Figure 2.13 Hydrophilic and Hydrophobic **(A)** Molecules with polar covalent bonds are attracted to polar water (they are hydrophilic). **(B)** Molecules with nonpolar covalent bonds show greater attraction to one another than to water (they are hydrophobic).

Q: Would a hydrocarbon with the formula $H_3C—(CH_2)_{10}—COOH$ be polar, nonpolar, or both?

and hydrogen are not exactly the same. But these interactions are far weaker than the hydrogen bonds between the water molecules (see Table 2.1), so the nonpolar substances tend to aggregate.

van der Waals forces involve contacts between atoms

The interactions between nonpolar substances are enhanced by **van der Waals forces**, which occur when the atoms of two molecules are in close proximity. These brief interactions result from random variations in the electron distribution in one molecule, which can create opposite charge distributions in the adjacent molecule. So there will be a weak, temporary δ^+ to δ^- attraction. van der Waals forces occur in polar and nonpolar molecules. In the latter case, they can induce cohesion between molecules that do not form ionic bonds or hydrogen bonds. Although a single van der Waals force is brief and weak, the sum of many such interactions over the entire span of a large nonpolar molecule can result in substantial attraction. This is important when hydrophobic regions of different molecules such as an enzyme and a substrate come together (see Chapter 8).

KEY CONCEPT
2.2 Recap and Assess

Some atoms form strong covalent bonds with other atoms by sharing one or more pairs of electrons. Unequal sharing of electrons resulting from differences in electronegativity produces polarity. Other atoms become ions by losing or gaining electrons. An ionic bond forms through the attractions of positively to negatively charged ions. Weak forces such as hydrogen bonds and van der Waals forces attract atoms to one another within the same molecules or between different molecules.

1. Why is a covalent bond stronger than an ionic bond when a molecule is in water?

2. Consider the following pairs of bonded atoms:

     C—H   C=O   O—P   C—C

   For each pair, use Tables 2.2 and 2.3 to determine:
   a. whether the bond is polar or nonpolar
   b. if the bond is polar, which end is δ^-

c. whether the atom pair contributes hydrophilic or hydrophobic properties to a molecule

3. Geckos are lizards that are amazing climbers. A gecko can climb up a glass surface and stick to it with a single toe. Professor Kellar Autumn at Lewis and Clark College and his students and collaborators have shown that each toe of a gecko has millions of micrometer-sized hairs, and that each hair splits into hundreds of 200-nanometer tips that provide intimate contact with a surface. Careful measurements show that a million of these tips could easily support the animal, but it has far more. The toes stick well on hydrophilic and hydrophobic surfaces. Bending the hairs allows the gecko to detach. What kind of noncovalent force is involved in gecko sticking?

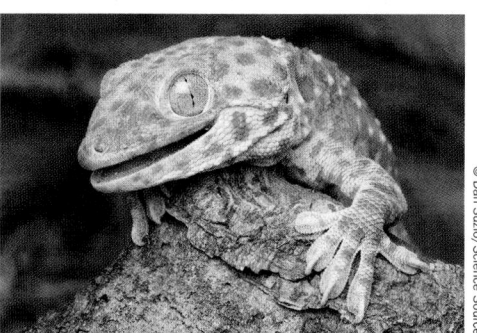

© Dan Suzio/Science Source

The bonding of atoms to form molecules is not necessarily permanent. The dynamic aspect of life involves constant change, even at the molecular level. In the next key concept we will examine how molecules interact with one another—how they break up, how they find new partners, and what the consequences of those changes can be.

KEY CONCEPT
2.3 Chemical Reactions Transform Substances

Learning Objectives

2.3.1 Provide an example of how chemical reactions obey the law of conservation of matter.

2.3.2 Explain how energy is involved in a chemical reaction.

A hallmark of life is that it is dynamic. Things don't sit still, especially at the chemical level. Atoms bonded to other atoms can leave a binding relationship and find a new partner. Bear in mind that this does not happen all the time: your skin is a biological tissue, and its atoms form a stable structure. But change is common, especially among the atoms and molecules dissolved in water. A **chemical reaction** occurs when moving atoms collide with sufficient energy to combine or to change their bonding partners.

Chemical reactions obey the laws of conservation of energy and conservation of matter

Consider the combustion reaction that takes place in the flame of a propane stove. When propane (C_3H_8) reacts with oxygen gas (O_2), the carbon atoms become bonded to oxygen atoms instead of hydrogen atoms, and the hydrogen atoms become bonded to oxygen instead of carbon (**Figure 2.14**). As the covalently bonded atoms change partners, the composition of the matter changes; propane and oxygen gas become carbon dioxide and water. This chemical reaction can be represented by the equation

$$C_3H_8 + 5\,O_2 \rightarrow 3\,CO_2 + 4\,H_2O + Energy$$
$$Reactants \rightarrow Products$$

In this equation, propane and oxygen are the **reactants**, and carbon dioxide and water are the **products**. This example is an **oxidation-reduction (redox) reaction**—a special type of chemical reaction that involves a transfer of electrons between two species:

- The electron acceptor, or oxidizing agent, gains electrons and is said to be *reduced* in a chemical reaction.
- The electron donor, or reducing agent, loses electrons and is said to be is *oxidized* in a chemical reaction.

Can you identify the oxidizing and reducing agents in our example? Because electrons and protons (i.e., hydrogen atoms) are transferred *from* propane, propane is the reducing agent and oxygen is the oxidizing agent, which in this example forms water upon accepting the hydrogens. You will see many examples of redox reactions involving electron/proton transfer in later chapters.

The products of a chemical reaction can have very different properties from the reactants. The reaction shown in Figure 2.14 is said to be *complete*: all the propane and oxygen are used up in forming the two products. The arrow symbolizes the direction of the chemical reaction. The numbers preceding the molecular formulas indicate how many molecules are used or produced.

Note that in this and all other chemical reactions, *matter is neither created nor destroyed.* The total number of carbon atoms on the left side of the equation (3) equals the total number of carbon atoms on the right (3). In other words, the equation is *balanced*.

Figure 2.14 Bonding Partners and Energy May Change in a Chemical Reaction One molecule of propane (a gas used for cooking) from this burner reacts with five molecules of oxygen gas to give three molecules of carbon dioxide and four molecules of water. This reaction releases energy in the form of heat and light.

However, there is another aspect of this reaction: the heat and light of the stove's flame reveal that the reaction between propane and oxygen releases a great deal of energy.

Energy is defined as the capacity to do work, but in the context of chemical reactions, it can be thought of as the capacity for change. Chemical reactions do not create or destroy energy, but *changes in the form of energy* usually accompany chemical reactions.

In the reaction between propane and oxygen, a large amount of heat energy is released. This energy was present in another form, called potential chemical energy, in the covalent bonds within the propane and oxygen gas molecules. Not all reactions release energy; indeed, many chemical reactions require that energy be supplied from the environment. Some of this energy is then stored as potential chemical energy in the bonds formed in the products. We will see in future chapters how reactions that release energy and reactions that require energy are often coupled.

Many chemical reactions take place in living cells, and some of these have a lot in common with the oxidation–reduction reaction we saw in the combustion of propane. In cells, the reactants are different (they may be sugars or fats), and the reactions proceed by many intermediate steps that permit the released energy to be harvested and put to use by the cells. But the products are the same: carbon dioxide and water.

KEY CONCEPT

2.3 Recap and Assess

In a chemical reaction, a set of reactants is converted to a set of products with different chemical compositions. A chemical reaction involves breaking old bonds and making new ones. A reaction may release energy or require its input.

1. Using the example of the chemical equation $C_6H_{12}O_6 + O_2 \rightarrow CO_2 + H_2O$, insert numbers so that the numbers of atoms on both sides of the equation are balanced.

2. Use an example to explain how the form of energy can change during a chemical reaction.

We will return to chemical reactions and how they occur in living systems in Chapter 8, 9, and 10, focusing particularly on energy transformations that fuel biological processes. First, however, we will examine the unique properties of the substance in which most biochemical reactions take place: water.

KEY CONCEPT | **The Properties of Water Are**
2.4 | **Critical to the Chemistry of Life**

Learning Objectives

2.4.1 Describe how hydrogen bonding in water affects its heat capacity, melting, evaporation, and cohesion.

2.4.2 Explain why water's solvent properties are important in understanding events taking place inside cells.

2.4.3 Perform quantitative analyses of biochemical compounds using the mole concept.

2.4.4 Predict and explain changes in pH caused by changes in concentration of weak acids or bases in living tissue.

Your body is more than 60% water by weight, excluding the minerals contained in bones. Water is the dominant component of virtually all living organisms, and most biochemical reactions take place in this watery, or aqueous, environment. Indeed, the search for life on other planets usually begins with the question of whether the planet has liquid water. Water is an unusual substance with unusual properties, many of them resulting from the polarity of the covalent bonds in the molecule and the ability to form hydrogen bonds with other molecules.

Water has a unique structure and special properties

The molecule H_2O has unusual physical and chemical properties.

ICE FLOATS   In water's solid state (ice), individual water molecules are held in place by hydrogen bonds. Each molecule is bonded to four other molecules in a rigid, crystalline structure (**Figure 2.15**). Although the molecules are held firmly in place, they are farther apart from one another than they are in liquid water, where the molecules are moving about. In ice, there are cavities between individual water molecules. In other words, solid water is less dense than liquid water, which is why ice floats.

In its gaseous state, water does not form hydrogen bonds.

In ice, water molecules are held in a rigid state by hydrogen bonds.

Hydrogen bonds continually break and form as water molecules move.

Gaseous water (vapor)

Solid water (ice)

Liquid water

© Pablo H Caridad/ Shutterstock.com

Figure 2.15 Hydrogen Bonding and the Properties of Water
Hydrogen bonding occurs between the molecules of water in both its liquid and solid states. Ice is more structured but less dense than liquid water, which is why ice floats. Water forms a gas when its hydrogen bonds are broken and the molecules move farther apart.

Think of the biological consequences if ice were to sink in water. A pond would freeze from the bottom up, becoming a solid block of ice in winter and killing most of the organisms living there. Once the whole pond was frozen, its temperature could drop well below the freezing point of water. But because ice floats, it forms an insulating layer on the top of the pond, and reduces heat flow to the cold air above. Thus fishes, plants, and other organisms in the pond are not subjected to temperatures lower than 0°C, which is the freezing point of pure water.

MELTING, FREEZING, AND HEAT CAPACITY   Compared with many other substances that have molecules of similar size, ice requires a great deal of heat energy to melt. The amount of heat energy required to raise the temperature of 1 gram of a substance by 1 degree Celsius is called its **specific heat**. Water has a relatively high specific heat because so many hydrogen bonds connecting the water molecules in ice must be broken to change water from solid to liquid. In the opposite process—freezing—a great deal of energy is released to the environment. We say water has a high heat capacity. For example, water has twice the specific heat of ethyl alcohol and five times that of sand. This is why when you are on the beach as the sun sets, the sand cools much more quickly than the water.

Water also has a high **heat of vaporization**, defined as the heat a liquid absorbs in order to form a gas. A lot of heat (actually 580 calories per gram) is required to change 1 gram of water from liquid to gas. Once again, much of the heat energy is used to break the many hydrogen bonds between the water molecules. This heat must be absorbed from the environment in contact with the water. **Evaporation** (forming a vapor, or gas) thus has a cooling effect on the environment—whether a leaf, a forest, or an entire land mass. This effect explains why sweating cools the human body: as sweat evaporates from the skin, it uses up some of the adjacent body heat (**Figure 2.16A**).

On an environmental scale, a lot of solar energy that arrives at Earth is absorbed by the oceans. This heat absorption keeps ocean temperatures moderate. This not only allows survival of many marine organisms that otherwise might die in high temperatures, but also keeps the temperatures on coastal lands more moderate. If you have been to the San Francisco Bay area you know this: on a summer day, the temperature in the city is often 10 degrees Celsius cooler than that of inland cities, such as Walnut Creek. As the global climate gets warmer, heat absorption by bodies of water is becoming increasingly important.

Connect the Concepts Living systems use the evaporation of water, which disrupts hydrogen bonds, to dissipate excess heat that would otherwise cause problems. See Key Concept 37.1 for examples in plants, and Key Concepts 38.3–38.5 for examples in animals.

COHESION AND SURFACE TENSION   In liquid water, individual molecules are able to move about. The hydrogen bonds between the molecules continually form and break (see Figure 2.15). Chemists estimate that this occurs about a trillion times a minute for a single water molecule!

At any given time, a water molecule forms on average 3.4 hydrogen bonds with other water molecules. These hydrogen bonds explain the cohesive strength of liquid water. This cohesive strength, or **cohesion**, is defined as the capacity of water molecules to resist coming apart from one another when placed under tension. Water's cohesive strength permits narrow columns of liquid water to move from the roots to the leaves of tall trees. When water evaporates from the leaves, the entire column moves upward in response to the pull of the molecules at the top (**Figure 2.16B**). A related property is **adhesion**, the attraction of water molecules to other molecules of a different type. For example, when you put a straw into a cup with water, it "climbs" up the straw so the column is higher than the level in the cup. This adhesive behavior of water—sticking to the sides of the straw—reflects the adhesion of water forming the column.

(A)

High heat of vaporization: Sweating uses evaporation of water to cool the body.

© iStock.com/shakzu

(B)

Cohesion: Water's cohesive strength helps it to flow from the roots to the leaves in a tree.

© kawhia/Shutterstock.com

(C)

Surface tension: Water molecules stick to one another and help prevent this wolf spider from sinking.

David McIntyre

Figure 2.16 Water in Biology These three properties of water make it beneficial to organisms.

Connect the Concepts As described in Key Concept 33.2, the transpiration–cohesion–tension mechanism accounts for the movement of water from roots to leaves. Because of the cohesion between water molecules, water is pulled upward in continuous columns.

The surface of liquid water exposed to the air is difficult to puncture because the water molecules at the surface are hydrogen-bonded to other water molecules below them. This surface tension of water permits a container to be filled slightly above its rim without overflowing, and it permits spiders to walk on the surface of a pond (**Figure 2.16C**).

The reactions of life take place in aqueous solutions

A **solution** is produced when a substance (the **solute**) is dissolved in a liquid (the **solvent**). If the solvent is water, then the solution is called an aqueous solution. Water is polar, and because many important molecules in biological systems are polar, they readily dissolve in water. Being soluble doesn't mean that the molecules lose their identity and properties. They can still react, and indeed many important biochemical reactions occur in aqueous solutions.

Biologists who are interested in the biochemical reactions within cells identify the reactants and products and determine their amounts using two different types of analyses:

1. *Qualitative analyses* focus on identifying the substances involved in chemical reactions. For example, a qualitative analysis would be used to investigate the steps involved and the products formed when carbon-containing compounds are broken down to release energy in living tissues.

2. *Quantitative analyses* measure concentrations or amounts of substances. For example, a biochemist would use a quantitative analysis to measure how much of a certain product is formed in a chemical reaction. What follows is a brief introduction to some of the quantitative chemical terms you will see in this book.

A **mole** is the amount of a substance (in grams) that is numerically equal to its molecular weight. So a mole of hydrogen gas (H_2) weighs 2 g, a mole of sodium ion (Na^+) weighs 23 g, and a mole of table sugar ($C_{12}H_{22}O_{11}$) weighs about 342 g.

Quantitative analyses do not yield counts of molecules. Because the amount of a substance in 1 mole is directly related to its molecular weight, it follows that the number of molecules in 1 mole is constant for all substances. So 1 mole of salt contains the same *number of molecules* as 1 mole of table sugar. This constant number of molecules in a mole is called **Avogadro's number**, and it is 6.02×10^{23} molecules per mole. Chemists work with moles of substances (which can be weighed in the laboratory) instead of actual molecules, which are too numerous to be counted. Consider 34.2 g (just over 1 ounce) of table sugar, $C_{12}H_{22}O_{11}$. This is one-tenth of a mole, or one-tenth of Avogadro's number: 6.02×10^{22} molecules.

A chemist can dissolve 1 mole of table sugar (342 g) in water to make 1 liter of solution, knowing that the mole contains 6.02×10^{23} individual sugar molecules. This solution—1 mole of a substance dissolved in water to make 1 liter—is called a 1 molar (1 M) solution. When a physician injects a certain volume and molar concentration of a drug into the bloodstream of a patient, a rough calculation can be made of the actual number of drug molecules that will interact with the patient's cells. As you know, the dose is important.

The many molecules dissolved in the water of living tissues are not present at concentrations anywhere near 1 molar. Most are in the micromolar (millionths of a mole per liter of solution; μM) to millimolar (thousandths of a mole per liter; mM) range. Some, such as hormone molecules, are even less concentrated than that. While these molarities seem to indicate very low concentrations, remember that even a 1 μM solution has 6.02×10^{17} molecules of the solute per liter.

Aqueous solutions may be acidic or basic

When some substances dissolve in water, they release hydrogen ions (H^+), which are actually single, positively charged protons. Hydrogen ions can interact with other molecules and change their properties. For example, the protons in "acid rain" can damage plants, and you probably have experienced the excess of hydrogen ions that we call "acid indigestion."

Here we will examine the properties of **acids** (defined as substances that release H^+) and **bases** (defined as substances that accept H^+). We will distinguish between strong and weak acids and bases, and provide a quantitative means for stating the concentration of H^+ in solutions: the pH scale.

ACIDS RELEASE H^+ When hydrochloric acid (HCl) is added to water, it dissolves, releasing the ions H^+ and Cl^-:

$$HCl \rightarrow H^+ + Cl^-$$

Because its H^+ concentration has increased, the solution is acidic.

Acids are substances that *release* H^+ ions in solution. HCl is an acid, as is H_2SO_4 (sulfuric acid). One molecule of sulfuric acid will ionize to yield two H^+ and one SO_4^{2-}. Biological compounds that contain —COOH (called a carboxyl group) are acids because the carboxyl group can ionize to —COO^-, releasing H^+:

$$-COOH \rightarrow -COO^- + H^+$$

Acids that fully ionize in solution, such as HCl and H_2SO_4, are called strong acids. However, not all acids ionize fully in water. For example, if acetic acid (CH_3COOH) is added to water, some of it will dissociate into two ions (CH_3COO^- and H^+), but some of the original acetic acid will remain as well. Because the reaction is not complete, acetic acid is a weak acid.

BASES ACCEPT H^+ Bases are substances that *accept* H^+ in solution. As with acids, there are strong and weak bases. If NaOH (sodium hydroxide) is added to water, it dissolves and ionizes, releasing OH^- and Na^+ ions:

$$NaOH \rightarrow Na^+ + OH^-$$

Because OH^- absorbs H^+ to form water, such a solution is basic. This reaction is complete, and so NaOH is a strong base.

Weak bases include the bicarbonate ion (HCO_3^-), which can accept an H^+ ion and become carbonic acid (H_2CO_3), and ammonia (NH_3), which can accept H^+ and become an ammonium ion (NH_4^+). Biological compounds that contain —NH_2 (the amino group) are also bases because —NH_2 accepts H^+:

$$-NH_2 + H^+ \rightarrow -NH_3^+$$

ACID–BASE REACTIONS MAY BE REVERSIBLE   When acetic acid is dissolved in water, two reactions happen. First, the acetic acid forms its ions:

$$CH_3COOH \rightarrow CH_3COO^- + H^+$$

Then, once the ions are formed, some of them re-form acetic acid:

$$CH_3COO^- + H^+ \rightarrow CH_3COOH$$

This pair of reactions is reversible. A **reversible reaction** can proceed in either direction—left to right or right to left—depending on the relative starting concentrations of the reactants and products. The formula for a reversible reaction can be written using a double arrow:

$$CH_3COOH \rightleftharpoons CH_3COO^- + H^+$$

In terms of acids and bases, there are two types of reactions, depending on the extent of the reversibility:

1. The ionization of strong acids and bases in water is virtually irreversible.

2. The ionization of weak acids and bases in water is somewhat reversible.

WATER IS A WEAK ACID AND A WEAK BASE   The water molecule has a slight but significant tendency to ionize into a hydroxide ion (OH^-) and a hydrogen ion (H^+). Actually, two water molecules participate in this reaction. One of the two molecules "captures" a hydrogen ion from the other molecule, forming a hydroxide ion and a hydronium ion (H_3O^+):

$$2\,H_2O \rightleftharpoons H_3O^+ + OH^-$$

The hydronium ion is, in effect, a hydrogen ion bound to a water molecule. For simplicity, biochemists tend to use a modified representation of the ionization of water:

$$H_2O \rightleftharpoons H^+ + OH^-$$

The ionization of water is important to all living creatures. This fact may seem surprising, since only about 1 water molecule in 500 million is ionized at any given time. But this is less surprising if we focus on the abundance of water in living systems, and the reactive nature of the H^+ ions produced by ionization.

pH: HYDROGEN ION CONCENTRATION   As we have seen, compounds can be either acids or bases, and thus solutions can be either acidic or basic. We can measure how acidic or basic a solution is by measuring its concentration of H^+ in moles per liter (its molarity; see p. 37). Here are some examples:

- Pure water has a H^+ concentration of 10^{-7} M.

- A 1 M HCl solution has a H^+ concentration of 1 M (recall that all the HCl dissociates into its ions).

- A 1 M NaOH solution has a H^+ concentration of 10^{-14} M.

This is a very wide range of numbers to work with—think about the decimals! It is easier to work with the logarithm of the H^+ concentration, because logarithms compress this range: the $\log_{10}$

of 100, for example, is 2; and the $\log_{10}$ of 0.01 is −2. Because most H^+ concentrations in living systems are less than 1 M, their $\log_{10}$ values are negative. For convenience, we convert these negative numbers into positive ones by using the *negative* of the logarithm of the H^+ molar concentration. This number is called the **pH** of the solution:

$$pH = -\log[H^+] \text{ where } [H^+] \text{ is the concentration of free } H^+ \text{ in solution}$$

Since the H^+ concentration of pure water is 10^{-7} M, its pH is −$\log(10^{-7}) = -(-7)$, or 7. A smaller negative logarithm means a larger number. In practical terms, a lower pH means a higher H^+ concentration, or greater acidity. In 1 M HCl, the H^+ concentration is 1 M, so the pH is the negative logarithm of 1 (−$\log 10^0$), or 0. The pH of 1 M NaOH is the negative logarithm of 10^{-14}, or 14.

A solution with a pH of less than 7 is acidic—it contains more H^+ ions than OH^- ions. A solution with a pH of 7 is referred to as neutral, and a solution with a pH value greater than 7 is basic. **Figure 2.17** shows the pH values of some common substances.

Why is this discussion of pH so relevant to biology? Many reactions involve the transfer of an ion or charged group from one molecule to another, and the presence of positive or negative ions in the environment can greatly influence the rates of such reactions. Furthermore, pH can influence the shapes of molecules. Many biologically important molecules contain charged groups (e.g., $—COO^-$) that can interact with the polar regions of water, and these interactions influence the way such molecules fold up into three-dimensional shapes. If these charged groups combine with H^+ or other ions in their environment to form uncharged groups (e.g., —COOH; see above), they will have a reduced tendency to interact with water. These uncharged (hydrophobic) groups might induce the molecule to fold up differently so that they are no longer in contact with the watery environment. Since the three-dimensional structures of biological molecules greatly affect the way they function, organisms do all they can to minimize changes in the pH of their cells and tissues. An important way to do this is with buffers.

BUFFERS   The maintenance of internal constancy—homeostasis—is a hallmark of all living things and extends to pH. If biological molecules lose or gain H^+ ions, their properties can change, thus upsetting homeostasis. For example, people who exercise strenuously produce lactic acid, which ionizes to produce H^+. Internal constancy within tissues can be achieved with buffers: solutions that maintain a relatively constant pH even when substantial amounts of acid or base are added. How does this work?

A **buffer** is a mixture of a weak acid and its corresponding base, or a weak base and its corresponding acid. For example, a weak acid is carbonic acid (H_2CO_3), and its corresponding base is the bicarbonate ion (HCO_3^-). If another acid is added to a solution containing this mixture (a buffered solution), not all the H^+ ions from the acid remain in solution. Instead, many of them combine with the bicarbonate ions to produce more carbonic acid:

$$HCO_3^- + H^+ \rightleftharpoons H_2CO_3$$

Figure 2.17 pH Values of Some Familiar Substances

This reaction uses up some of the H^+ ions in the solution and decreases the acidifying effect of the added acid. If a base is added, the reaction essentially reverses. Some of the carbonic acid ionizes to produce bicarbonate ions and more H^+, which counteracts some of the added base. The buffer minimizes the effect that an added acid or base has on pH. The carbonic acid/bicarbonate buffering system is present in the blood, where it is important for preventing significant changes in pH that could disrupt the ability of the blood to carry vital oxygen to tissues. A given amount of acid or base causes a smaller pH change in a buffered solution than in a non-buffered one (**Figure 2.18**).

Buffers illustrate an important chemical principle of reversible reactions, called the **law of mass action**. Addition of a reactant on one side of a reversible system drives the reaction in the direction that uses up that compound. In the case of buffers, addition of an acid drives the reaction in one direction; addition of a base drives the reaction in the other direction.

You may occasionally use a buffer to relieve indigestion. The lining of the stomach constantly secretes hydrochloric acid, making the stomach contents acidic. But excessive stomach acid can cause discomfort. We can relieve this discomfort by

In the presence of buffer, additions of even large quantities of base result in relatively small changes in pH.

Buffering range

When buffering capacity is exceeded, added base greatly increases pH.

In the absence of buffer, there is a rapid increase in pH as base is added.

Figure 2.18 Buffers Minimize Changes in pH   When base is added to a solution, the pH of the solution increases. Without a buffer, the change is large and the slope of the pH graph is steep. In the presence of a buffer, however, the slope within the buffering range is shallow.

Q: If acid is added instead of base, what will the two graphs look like?

ingesting a salt such as $NaHCO_3$ (sodium bicarbonate), which acts as a buffer.

KEY CONCEPT

2.4 Recap and Assess

Most of the chemistry of life occurs in water, which has unique properties that make it an ideal medium for supporting life. These properties include hydrogen bonding between molecules, high specific heat, and cohesion between molecules. Aqueous solutions can be acidic or basic, depending on the concentration of hydrogen ions. The cells and tissues of organisms are buffered, however, because changes in pH can change the properties of biological molecules.

1. The boiling point of water (H_2O) is 100°C, while the boiling point of methane (CH_4) is −161°C. Explain this difference in terms of hydrogen bonding between molecules.

2. What is a solution, and why do we call water "the medium of life"?

3. A substance in a cell has a concentration of 0.00000001 molar. What does this mean in terms of the number of molecules in a cell that has a volume of 0.000001 liters?

4. In human tissues, CO_2 is formed as a by-product of oxidation of more complex molecules. CO_2 enters the bloodstream and in red blood cells is removed from the blood by the reaction $CO_2 + H_2O \rightarrow HCO_3^- + H^+$. What is the consequence of this reaction on the pH of the blood? What chemical reaction would restore the pH of the blood?

▶InvestigatingLIFE

Q&A   **What insights into biological systems have been discovered through isotope analysis?**

The opening investigation of dinosaurs (oxygen atoms) and the Investigating Life experiment on hamburgers (carbon atoms) are examples of identifying the life history of organisms through isotope analysis. Recently, this has been applied to humans as well. Hair is a living tissue, with a lot of O and H atoms derived from water in the diet. Ecologist Jim Ehleringer and chemist Thure Cerling have shown that as in the dinosaurs, the isotope ratios of O and H in hair reflect the geographic region where a person drank the water. This can be useful evidence in a forensic investigation, placing a person at a location. Isotope ratios are also used to identify where plants are grown, because their tissues also have unique ratios. For example, ratios have revealed the geographic origin of poppies used to make heroin. The mass spectrometer, a chemical analysis instrument that detects isotopes, is fast becoming an important tool for biologists.

Future directions

Tracking the isotopes of oxygen and hydrogen in precipitation is useful in understanding patterns of climate change. Water evaporates in warmer regions at the tropical latitudes on Earth and moves toward the cooler poles. As an air mass moves from a warmer to a cooler region, water vapor condenses and is removed as precipitation. The heavy isotopes of H and O tend to fall as precipitation more readily than the lighter isotopes, so as the water vapor moves toward the poles, it becomes enriched in the lighter isotopes. The ratio of heavy to light isotopes that reach the poles depends on the climate—the cooler the climate, the lower the ratio, because more water precipitates as it moves toward the poles, depleting more of the heavier isotopes. Analyses of polar ice cores show that heavy-to-light isotope ratios vary over geological time scales. This has allowed scientists to reconstruct climate change in the past, and to relate it to fossil organisms that lived at those times. Isotope ratios may be useful in monitoring climate change that is happening today.

You should be able to relate each summary to the adjacent figures. If you go to this visual summary in **Achieve**, you can follow links to figures, animations, activities, and simulations that will help you consolidate the material.

KEY CONCEPT

2.1 An Element's Atomic Structure Determines Its Properties

Go to Activity 2.1

- Each **element** has a characteristic number of **protons** in its **nucleus**.

- The number of **electrons** in the outer shell of an element determines its chemical properties. Elements are grouped in the **periodic table**.

Questions

1. How many protons and neutrons are in the nucleus of the element aluminum (Al), with an atomic number of 13 and a mass number of 27?

2. How many electrons are in each of the three electron shells of Al?

3. Why do isotopes differ in mass number but not atomic number?

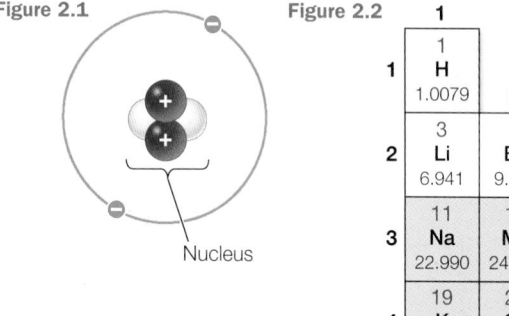

Figure 2.1

Nucleus

Figure 2.2

1			
1	1 **H** 1.0079	**2**	
2	3 **Li** 6.941	4 **Be** 9.012	
3	11 **Na** 22.990	12 **Mg** 24.305	**3**
4	19 **K** 39.098	20 **Ca** 40.08	21 **Sc** 44.956

KEY CONCEPT

2.2 Atoms Bond to Form Molecules

Go to Animation 2.1

- A **chemical bond** is an attractive force that links two atoms together in a molecule.

- **Covalent bonds** are strong bonds formed when two atoms share one or more pairs of electrons.

- **Ionic bonds** occur between oppositely charged **ions**. Ionic bonds are strong in solids (salts) but weaken when the ions are separated from one another in solution.

- A **hydrogen bond** is a weak electrical attraction that forms between a δ^+ hydrogen atom in one molecule and a δ^- atom in another molecule (or in another part of the same, large molecule). Hydrogen bonds are abundant in water.

Questions

1. Why aren't covalent bonds between atoms of the same element polar?

2. Why do elements such as sodium (Na) in the first group of the periodic table form ionic as opposed to covalent bonds?

3. How does the polarity of carbon dioxide (CO_2) compare with that of hexane (C_6H_{14})? Would you expect either of them to form hydrogen bonds with water?

Figure 2.7

H   H

Figure 2.10

Ionic
bond

Figure 2.12

KEY CONCEPT

2.3 Chemical Reactions Transform Substances

■ In **chemical reactions**, atoms combine or change their bonding partners.

■ Some chemical reactions release **energy** as one of their **products**; other reactions can occur only if energy is provided to the **reactants**.

■ Neither matter nor energy is created or destroyed in a chemical reaction, but both change form.

Questions

1. How can a freshwater fish, which does not regulate its body temperature, increase the rate of a chemical reaction in its muscles?

2. In the reaction $C_6H_{12}O_6 + O_2 \rightarrow CO_2 + H_2O$, the bond energy stored in the reactants is greater than the energy in the products. If there is an energy term in the equation, where would it go?

Figure 2.14

PROPANE

Reactants   Products

KEY CONCEPT

2.4 The Properties of Water Are Critical to the Chemistry of Life

■ Water's molecular structure and its capacity to form hydrogen bonds give it unique properties that are significant for life.

■ A **solution** is produced when a solid substance (the **solute**) dissolves in a liquid (the **solvent**). Water is the critically important solvent for life. The ability of molecules to lose or accept protons (H^+) is important in biological structure and function.

Questions

1. Why does water have a high heat capacity?

2. What is surface tension, and why does water have a high surface tension?

3. Why is water an excellent solvent for polar and ionic compounds?

Figure 2.15

Figure 2.18

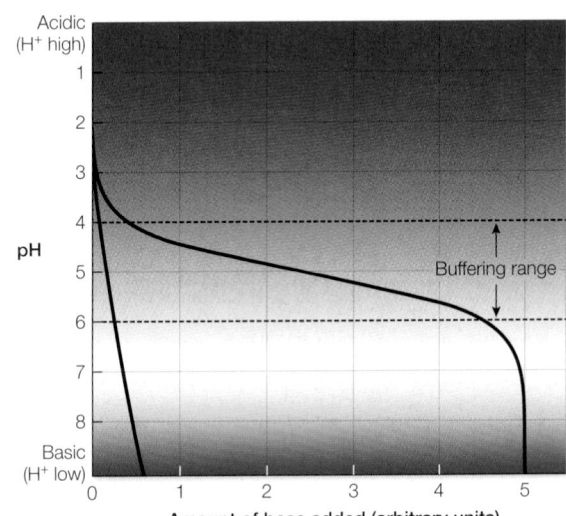

Acidic
(H^+ high)

pH

Buffering range

Basic
(H^+ low)

Amount of base added (arbitrary units)

Proteins, Carbohydrates, and Lipids 3

KEY CONCEPTS

3.1 Macromolecules Characterize Living Things

3.2 Proteins Are Polymers with Highly Variable Structures

3.3 Carbohydrates Are Made from Simple Sugars

3.4 Lipids Are Defined by Their Insolubility in Water

Molecular Superpower Spider silk protein has a structure that makes it one of the strongest fibers in nature.

© AF archive/Alamy Stock Photo

▶Investigating LIFE

Weaving a Web

A spider web is an amazing structure. It is not only beautiful to look at, but an architectural wonder serving as the spider's home, its mating place, and its way to capture food. Consider a fly that chances to interact with a spider web. The fibers of the web must slow down the fly, but they cannot break, so they need to stretch to dissipate the energy of the fly's movement. The fibers holding the fly cannot stretch too much; they must be strong enough to hold the web in place. Web fibers are far thinner than a human hair, yet they are very strong. The fibers can also be long; for example, the Darwin's bark spider makes strands up to 25 meters long.

Chemical investigations reveal that spider silk is made of variations on a single type of large molecule called a protein. Proteins are polymers: long chains of individual smaller units called amino acids. The proteins in spider silks have characteristic structures and amino acid compositions that determine particular functions. Proteins in the stretchy web fibers have amino acids that allow them to curl into spirals, and these spirals can slip along one another to change the fiber's length. Another kind of spider silk is the dragline silk, which is less stretchy and used

to construct the outline of the web, its spokes, and the lifeline of the spider. The proteins in these strong fibers are made up of amino acids that cause the proteins to fold into flat sheets with ratchets, so that parallel sheets can fit together like Lego blocks. This arrangement makes these fibers hard to pull apart.

Just how strong is spider silk? A popular series of films features the fictional character Spider-Man. He often uses his web to ensnare evildoers and protect the innocent. In one scene, he stops a train by using ten ropes made of spider silk, each about 1 centimeter thick. Scientists who study spider silk have estimated the number of silk fibers in each rope and calculated that this scene would indeed be possible. All of this from covalent bonds holding long chains of amino acids together and weaker forces between the chains! Given the amazing strength shown by these proteins, it is not surprising that there is a lot of interest in using spider silk for human activities.

 What are practical uses for spider silk?
(Find the answer on page 65.)

KEY CONCEPT 3.1 Macromolecules Characterize Living Things

Learning Objectives

3.1.1 Give an example of two molecules that have the same functional groups but different properties, and explain the reason for the differences.

3.1.2 Sketch the chemical structures of two biological monomers, and show how a condensation reaction produces a covalent bond between the two.

3.1.3 Distinguish between structural, *cis-trans*, and optical isomers.

Four kinds of molecules are characteristic of living things: proteins, carbohydrates, lipids, and nucleic acids. With the exception of the lipids, these biological molecules are **polymers** (*poly*, "many," + *mer*, "unit") constructed by the covalent bonding of smaller molecules called **monomers**. Each kind of biological molecule is made up of monomers with similar chemical structures:

- Proteins are formed from different combinations of 20 amino acids, all of which share chemical similarities.

- Carbohydrates can form giant molecules by linking together chemically similar sugar monomers (monosaccharides) to form polysaccharides.

- Nucleic acids are formed from four kinds of nucleotide monomers linked together in long chains.

- Lipids also form large structures from a limited set of smaller molecules, but in this case noncovalent forces maintain the interactions between the lipid monomers that are held together by covalent bonds.

Polymers containing thousands or more atoms are called **macromolecules**. The proteins, carbohydrates, and nucleic acids of living systems fall into this category. Although large lipid structures are not polymers in the strictest sense, it is convenient to treat them as macromolecules (see Key Concept 3.4). Green plants have the living world's most abundant protein (rubisco; see Chapter 10), most abundant carbohydrate (cellulose in plant cell walls), and most abundant lipid (monogalactosyl diglyceride in leaves).

Functional chemical groups determine the structures of macromolecules

Certain small groups of atoms, called **functional groups**, occur frequently in biological molecules (**Figure 3.1**). Each functional group has specific chemical properties, and when it is attached to a

Figure 3.1 Some Functional Groups Important to Living Systems Highlighted here are the eight functional groups most commonly found in biologically important molecules. "R" is a variable chemical grouping.

Q: Which functional group(s) are hydrophobic? Why?

 View in Achieve Activity 3.1 **Functional Groups**

 View in Achieve Animation 3.1 **Proteins, Carbohydrates, and Lipids**

Functional group	Class of compounds and an example	Properties
Hydroxyl R—OH	**Alcohols** Ethanol	Polar. Forms hydrogen bonds with water to help dissolve molecules. Enables linkage to other molecules by condensation.
Aldehyde	**Aldehydes** Acetaldehyde	Polar. C=O group is very reactive. Important in building molecules and in energy-releasing reactions.
Keto	**Ketones** Acetone	Polar. C=O group is important in carbohydrates and in energy reactions.
Carboxyl	**Carboxylic acids** Acetic acid	Charged; acidic. Ionizes in living tissues to form —COO⁻ and H⁺. Enters into condensation reactions by giving up —OH. Some carboxylic acids important in energy-releasing reactions.
Amino	**Amines** Methylamine	Charged; basic. Accepts H⁺ in living tissues to form —NH₃⁺. Enters into condensation reactions by giving up H⁺.
Phosphate	**Organic phosphates** 3-Phosphoglycerate	Charged; acidic. Enters into condensation reactions by giving up —OH. When bonded to another phosphate, hydrolysis releases much energy.
Sulfhydryl R—SH	**Thiols** Mercaptoethanol	By giving up H, two —SH groups can react to form a disulfide bridge, thus stabilizing protein structure.
Methyl	**Alkyl** Alanine	Nonpolar. Important in interacting with other nonpolar molecules and in energy transfer.

larger molecule, it confers those properties on the larger molecule. One of these properties is polarity. Looking at the structures in Figure 3.1, can you determine which functional groups are the most polar? (*Hint*: look for C—O, N—H, and P—O bonds.) The chemical properties of functional groups help us understand the properties of the molecules that contain them.

Macromolecules have many different functional groups. A single large protein may contain nonpolar, polar, and charged functional groups, each of which gives different specific properties to local sites on the macromolecule. As we will see, sometimes these different groups interact within the same macromolecule. They help determine the shape of the macromolecule as well as how it interacts with other macromolecules and with smaller molecules.

Using the same atoms, molecules can differ from one another because their functional groups can be arranged differently. **Isomers** are molecules that have the same ("iso") chemical formula—the same kinds and numbers of atoms—but with the atoms arranged differently. Of the different kinds of isomers, we will consider three: structural isomers, *cis-trans* isomers, and optical isomers.

1. **Structural isomers** differ in how their atoms are joined together. Consider two simple molecules, each composed of four carbon and ten hydrogen atoms bonded covalently, both with the formula C_4H_{10}. These atoms can be linked in two different ways, resulting in different molecules (**Figure 3.2A**).

2. ***cis-trans* isomers** typically involve a double bond between two carbon atoms, where the carbons share two pairs of electrons. When the remaining two bonds of each of these carbons are to two different atoms or groups of atoms (e.g., a hydrogen and a methyl group; **Figure 3.2B**), these can be oriented on the same side or different sides of the double-bonded molecule. If the different atoms or groups of atoms are on the same side, the double bond is called *cis*; if they are on opposite sides, the bond is *trans*. These molecules can have very different properties.

3. **Optical isomers** occur when a carbon atom has four different atoms or groups of atoms attached to it. This pattern allows for two different ways of making the attachments, each the mirror image of the other (**Figure 3.2C**). Such a carbon atom is called an asymmetric carbon, and the two resulting molecules are optical isomers of one another. You can envision your right and left hands as optical isomers. Just as a glove is specific for a particular hand, some biochemical molecules that can interact with one optical isomer of a carbon compound are unable to "fit" the other.

The structures of macromolecules reflect their functions

The four kinds of biological macromolecules are present in roughly the same proportions in all living organisms (**Figure 3.3**). Also, a particular protein that has a certain three-dimensional structure and function in an apple tree probably has a similar structure and function in a human being, because the protein's chemistry is the same wherever it is found. This impressive biochemical unity reflects the evolution of all life from a common ancestor, by descent with modification. An important advantage of biochemical

(A) Structural isomers

Butane

Isobutane

(B) *cis-trans* isomers

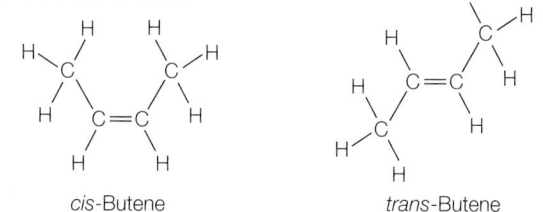

cis-Butene

trans-Butene

(C) Optical isomers

Hand   Mirror image   Molecule   Mirror image

Figure 3.2 Isomers Isomers have the same chemical formula, but the atoms are arranged differently. Pairs of isomers often have different chemical properties and functions.

Q: Draw the *cis* and *trans* isomers of dichloroethene: ClHC=CHCl.

unity is that some organisms can acquire needed raw materials by eating other organisms. When you eat bread, the molecules you take in include carbohydrates, lipids, and proteins that can be broken down into monomers which are then polymerized into the varieties of those molecules needed by humans. For example, the storage proteins in wheat grains have a particular composition and sequence of the 20 amino acids. When you eat them in bread, these wheat proteins are broken down into amino acids. In your muscle, these amino acids from wheat are used to make the human proteins actin and myosin, which compose muscle fibers.

The sequence and chemical properties of the chain of monomers in a macromolecule determine its three-dimensional shape and function. Some macromolecules fold into compact forms with surface features that make them water-soluble and capable of binding and interacting with other molecules. Some proteins and carbohydrates form long, fibrous structures (such as those found in spider silk or hair) that provide strength and rigidity. The specific structure of a macromolecule determines its function in a given environment, regardless of its origin. For example, composite spider silk fiber made by another organism (e.g., the silkworm, a moth larva) has the same properties as spider silk made by a spider (**Investigating Life: Making Spider Silk**).

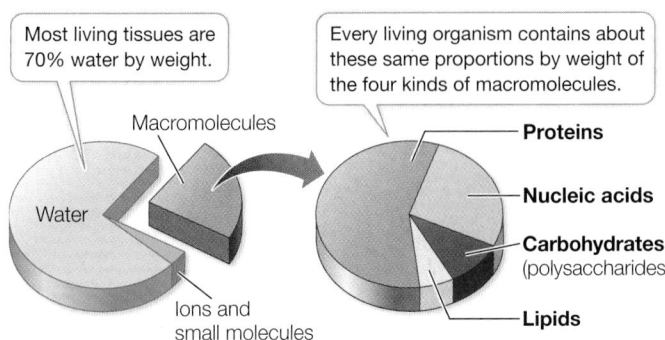

Figure 3.3 Substances Found in Living Tissues The substances shown here make up the non-mineral components of living tissues (bone is an example of a mineral component).

Most macromolecules are formed by condensation and broken down by hydrolysis

Polymers are formed from monomers by a series of **condensation reactions** (in this case called dehydration reactions; both terms refer to the loss of water). Condensation reactions result in the formation of covalent bonds between monomers. A molecule of water is released with each covalent bond formed (**Figure 3.4A**). The condensation reactions that produce the different kinds of polymers differ in detail, but in all cases polymers form only if water molecules are removed and energy is added to the system. In living systems, specific energy-rich molecules supply the necessary energy.

(A) Condensation reactions produce water.

(B) Hydrolysis reactions consume water.

Figure 3.4 Condensation and Hydrolysis of Polymers
(A) Condensation reactions link monomers into polymers and produce water. **(B)** Hydrolysis reactions break polymers into individual monomers and consume water.

The reverse of a condensation reaction is a **hydrolysis reaction** (*hydro*, "water," + *lysis*, "break"). Hydrolysis reactions result in the breakdown of polymers into their component monomers. Water reacts with the covalent bonds that link the polymer together. For each covalent bond that is broken, a water molecule splits into two ions (H^+ and OH^-), each of which becomes part of one of the products (**Figure 3.4B**).

KEY CONCEPT
3.1 Recap and Assess

The four kinds of large molecules that distinguish living tissues are proteins, lipids, carbohydrates, and nucleic acids. Most are polymers: chains of monomers linked by dehydration reactions. Very large polymers are called macromolecules. Biological molecules carry out a variety of functions.

1. What are the differences between structural, *cis-trans*, and optical isomers?

2. Examine the isomers mannose and galactose below. What makes them isomers of each other? Which functional groups do these carbohydrates contain, and what properties do these functional groups give to the molecules?

α-Mannose α-Galactose

3. Below are the general structures of three monomers in a biological polymer where A, B, and C are numerous atoms. Draw the two reactions that link them together to form a polymer ABC.
   H—A—OH   H—B—OH   H—C—OH

The four types of macromolecules can be seen as the building blocks of life. We will cover the unique properties of the nucleic acids in Chapter 4. The remainder of this chapter will describe the structures and functions of the proteins, carbohydrates, and lipids.

KEY CONCEPT
3.2 Proteins Are Polymers with Highly Variable Structures

Learning Objectives

3.2.1 Describe how amino acids differ in their side chains.

3.2.2 Describe how amino acids are joined to form a peptide.

3.2.3 Distinguish primary, secondary, tertiary, and quaternary structure and predict how a protein's structure will be affected by a change in an amino acid in its primary structure.

3.2.4 Predict the effects of various environmental factors on a protein's structure.

Proteins have many roles. You'll learn about the many functions of proteins (Table 3.1) in virtually every chapter of this book. **Proteins**

▶Investigating LIFE   Making Spider Silk

Experiment

Original Paper: F. Teule et al. 2012. Silkworms transformed with chimeric silkworm/spider silk genes spin composite silk fibers with improved mechanical properties. *Proc Natl Acad Sci USA* 109: 923–928.

Spider silk is one of the strongest materials known, but it is very hard to harvest in quantity. Industrial biologists are therefore using genetic engineering to produce the protein fibers. The scientists have coaxed silkworms, insect larvae that make silk fibers used in clothing, to make a much stronger composite of silkworm and spider silk.

HYPOTHESIS▶   Genetically engineered silkworms can produce silk with physical properties like those of silk made by spiders.

METHOD▶

RESULTS▶   Both silks had identical physical properties of stress (force needed to break) and strain (stretching).

CONCLUSION▶   Silkworms can make composite silk fiber with the same properties as those of the native spider silk protein.

© blickwinkel/Alamy Stock Photo

© iStock.com/Noppharat05081977

1 Extract silk fibers produced by both spiders and genetically engineered silkworms.

2 Measure tensile strength of fibers by stretching them on an analyzer.

Silk fiber

Force

Work with the Data

Spider silk is a protein-based material that is very strong because of its secondary structure. Because of its potential uses by humans, it is desirable to obtain large amounts of these fibers. Spiders spin out the silk fibers for their web, but the amounts are insufficient for human use. Silkworms make abundant silk fibers that are used in textiles but are much weaker than spider silk. An international team of scientists led by Randy Lewis at the University of Wyoming genetically engineered silkworms to make composite silkworm–spider silk fibers in large quantities. They then tested the properties of these fibers and compared them with those of native spider silk.

QUESTIONS▶

1. To evaluate the properties of the protein fibers, researchers stretched them and measured the forces involved as well as the resulting lengthening of the fibers. You can liken this to stretching a rubber band until it breaks. Stress is the force required to break the fiber; it is measured in millipascals (mPa; 1 Pa is the force in newtons per unit of area in m^2). Strain is a measure of how much the fiber lengthens (as a percentage of its original length). **Table A** compares the results from silk from spiders and from genetically engineered silkworms. Did the genetically engineered silkworms make fibers that were similar to native spider silk?

2. Why was fiber thickness (diameter) reported in the data?

3. What statistical test would you perform to determine if the measured properties were significantly different (see Appendix B)?

4. The scientists measured the properties of composite silkworm-spider silk compared with those of Kevlar (a synthetic fiber with many uses, including in bicycle tires, racing sails, and body armor) and steel. The results are shown in **Table B**. What can you conclude about the composite silkworm-spider silk?

Table A

Silk source	Diameter (μm)	Max. strain (%)
Silkworms	21.8 ± 1.6	22.0 ± 5.8
Silkworms, genetically engineered	21.1 ± 1.4	31.8 ± 5.2
Spiders	8.1 ± 0.4	19.7 ± 4.8

Table B

Material	Energy required to break filament (joules/kg)	Weight (g/mm³)
Composite silkworm-spider silk	120,000	1.3
Kevlar	40,000	1.4
Steel	3,500	7.84

Source: https://www.kraiglabs.com/spider-silk/

Go to Achieve for a companion Data in Depth exercise.

TABLE **3.1** | **Proteins and Their Functions**

Category	Function
Enzymes	Catalyze (speed up) biochemical reactions
Structural proteins	Provide physical stability and movement
Defensive proteins	Recognize and respond to nonself substances (e.g., antibodies)
Signaling proteins	Control physiological processes (e.g., hormones)
Receptor proteins	Receive and respond to chemical signals
Membrane transporters	Regulate passage of substances across cellular membranes
Storage proteins	Store amino acids for later use
Transport proteins	Bind and carry substances within the organism
Gene regulatory proteins	Determine the rate of expression of a gene
Motor proteins	Cause movement of structures in the cell

are polymers made up of 20 amino acids in different proportions and sequences. Proteins range in size, from small ones such as the human hormone insulin, which has 51 amino acids and a molecular weight of 5,733, to huge molecules such as the muscle protein titin, with 24,000–36,000 amino acids and a molecular weight of 2,993,451. Proteins consist of one or more **polypeptide chains**—unbranched (linear) polymers of covalently bonded amino acids. Variation in the sequences of amino acids in the polypeptide chains allows for the vast diversity in protein structure and function. Each chain folds into a particular three-dimensional shape that is specified by the sequence of amino acids present in the chain.

Monomers of proteins link together to make the macromolecule

Each **amino acid** has both a carboxyl functional group and an amino functional group (see Figure 3.1) attached to the same carbon atom, called the α (alpha) carbon. Also attached to the α carbon atom are a hydrogen atom and a **side chain**, or **R group**, designated by the letter R (**Figure 3.5**).

The α carbon in an amino acid has four available electrons for covalent bonding. It is asymmetrical because it is bonded to four atoms or groups of atoms. Therefore amino acids can exist as optical isomers (see Figure 3.2) called D-amino acids and L-amino

acids. D and L are abbreviations of the Latin terms for right (*dextro*) and left (*levo*). Only L-amino acids (with the configuration shown in Figure 3.5) are found in the proteins of most organisms, and their presence is an important chemical "signature" of life.

At the pH levels typically found in cells (usually pH 7.0–7.4), both the carboxyl and amino groups of amino acids are ionized: the carboxyl group has lost a hydrogen ion:

$$-COOH \rightarrow -COO^- + H^+$$

and the amino group has gained a hydrogen ion:

$$-NH_2 + H^+ \rightarrow -NH_3^+$$

Thus amino acids show both acid and basic properties.

 View in **Achieve**
Activity 3.2 **Features of Amino Acids**

Connect the Concepts You can review the chemistry and properties of acids and bases in Key Concept 2.4.

The side chains (or R groups) of amino acids contain functional groups that are important in determining the three-dimensional structure and thus the function of the protein. As **Table 3.2** shows, the 20 amino acids found in living organisms are grouped and distinguished by their side chains:

- Five amino acids have electrically charged (ionized, +1 or −1) side chains at pH levels typical of living cells. These side chains attract water (are hydrophilic) and attract oppositely charged ions of all sorts.

Figure 3.6 A Disulfide Bridge Two cysteine molecules in a polypeptide chain can form a disulfide bridge (—S—S—) by oxidation (removal of H atoms).

Q: Why is it that all cysteines in a protein are not involved in forming disulfide bridges?

Figure 3.5 An Amino Acid The structure of glycine, an amino acid that has an R group (side chain) of –H. Note that at the pH in living tissues, both the amino group and carboxyl group are ionized.

Q: At a low pH, what will be the ionization status of the amino and carboxyl groups?

TABLE **3.2** | The Twenty Amino Acids

(A) Amino acids with electrically charged hydrophilic side chains

(B) Amino acids with polar but uncharged side chains (hydrophilic)

(C) Special cases

(D) Amino acids with nonpolar hydrophobic side chains

- Five amino acids have polar side chains (δ^+ and δ^-). They tend to form hydrogen bonds with water and other polar substances. They are also hydrophilic.

- Seven amino acids have side chains that are nonpolar hydrocarbons and are thus hydrophobic. In the watery environment of the cell, these hydrophobic groups may cluster together in the interior of the protein.

Three amino acids—cysteine, glycine, and proline—are special cases, although the side chains of the latter two are generally hydrophobic.

- The cysteine side chain, which has a terminal —SH group, can react with another cysteine side chain in an oxidation reaction to form a covalent bond (**Figure 3.6**). Such a bond, called a

disulfide bridge or disulfide bond (—S—S—), helps determine how a polypeptide chain folds. Note that most cysteines in a protein are not involved in disulfide bridges.

- The glycine side chain consists of a single hydrogen atom. It is small enough to fit into tight corners in the interiors of protein molecules where larger side chains could not fit. The small side chain allows the protein to be more flexible at the locations where glycine occurs.

- Proline possesses a modified amino group that lacks a hydrogen atom and instead forms a covalent bond with the hydrocarbon side chain, resulting in a ring structure. This limits both its hydrogen-bonding ability and its ability to rotate around the α carbon. So proline is often found where a protein bends or loops.

Peptide bonds form the backbone of a protein

Amino acids can form short polymers of 20 or fewer amino acids called **oligopeptides** or simply **peptides**. These include some hormones and other molecules involves in signaling between parts of an organism. Even with their short chains, peptides have distinctive three-dimensional structures. More common are the longer polymers called **polypeptides**, each with a unique sequence of amino acids.

Linking amino acids involves a reaction between carboxyl and amino groups attached to the α carbon. The amino group of an adding amino acid interacts in a condensation reaction with the carboxyl group of the last amino acid in the growing chain, forming a **peptide bond**. **Figure 3.7** depicts this reaction.

Just as a sentence begins with a capital letter and ends with a period, polypeptide chains have a beginning and an end. The "capital letter" marking the beginning of a polypeptide is the amino group of the first amino acid added to the chain and is known as the N terminus. The "period" is the carboxyl group of the last amino acid added; this is the C terminus.

Two characteristics of the peptide bond are especially important in the three-dimensional structures of proteins:

1. In the C—N bond, the adjacent α carbons (α C—C—N— α C) are not free to rotate fully, which limits the folding of the polypeptide chain.

2. The oxygen bound to the carbon (C＝O) in the carboxyl group carries a slight negative charge (δ^-), whereas the hydrogen bound to the nitrogen (N—H) in the amino group is slightly positive (δ^+). This asymmetry of charge favors hydrogen bonding within the protein molecule itself and between molecules. These bonds contribute to the structures and functions of many proteins.

In addition to these characteristics of the peptide bond, the particular sequence of amino acids—with their various R groups—in the polypeptide chain also plays a vital role in determining a protein's structure (see Figure 3.8A) and function.

The primary structure of a protein is its amino acid sequence

The precise sequence of amino acids in a polypeptide chain held together by peptide bonds constitutes the **primary structure** of a protein (**Figure 3.8A**). The single-letter abbreviations for amino acids (see Table 3.2) are used to record the amino acid sequence of a protein. Here, for example, are the first 20 amino acids (out of a total of 124) in the protein ribonuclease from a cow:

KETAAAKFERQHMDSSTSAA

The theoretical number of different proteins is enormous. Since there are 20 different amino acids, there could be $20 \times 20 = 400$ distinct dipeptides (two linked amino acids) and $20 \times 20 \times 20 = 8,000$ different tripeptides (three linked amino acids). Imagine this process of multiplying by 20 extended to a protein made up of 100 amino acids (which would be considered a small protein). There could be 20^{100} (that's approximately 10^{130}) such small proteins, each with its own distinctive primary structure. How large is the number 20^{100}? Physicists tell us there aren't that many electrons in the entire universe!

The sequence of amino acids in the polypeptide chain determines its final shape. The properties associated with each functional group in the side chains of the amino acids (see Table 3.2) determine how the protein can twist and fold, thus adopting a specific stable structure that distinguishes it from every other protein. In contrast to primary structure, which is determined by covalent bonds, most of the forces involved with folding are noncovalent, such as hydrogen bonds and ionic bonds.

The secondary structure of a protein requires hydrogen bonding

A protein's **secondary structure** consists of regular, repeated spatial patterns in different regions of a polypeptide chain. There are two basic types of secondary structure, both determined by hydrogen bonding between the amino acids that make up the primary structure: the α helix and the β pleated sheet (**Figure 3.8B**).

THE ALPHA HELIX   The **α (alpha) helix** is a right-handed coil that turns in the same clockwise direction as a standard wood screw (see Figure 3.8B and **Figure 3.9**). The R groups extend outward from the peptide backbone of the helix. The coiling results from hydrogen bonds that form between the δ^+ hydrogen of the N—H of one amino acid and the δ^- oxygen of the C＝O of another. When this pattern of hydrogen bonding is established repeatedly over a segment of the protein, it stabilizes the coil.

THE BETA PLEATED SHEET   A **β (beta) pleated sheet** is formed from two or more polypeptide chains that are almost completely extended and aligned side by side. The sheet is stabilized by hydrogen bonds

Figure 3.7 Peptide Bond Formation   Peptide bonds are formed by condensation reactions in which the amino group of one amino acid reacts with the carboxyl group of another amino acid, releasing a molecule of water.

Level	Description	Stabilized by	Example
(A) Primary	Amino acid monomers are joined, forming polypeptide chains.	Peptide bonds	Amino acid monomers Peptide bond (H N C O H C N R C H N C O H C N R C H N C O R)
(B) Secondary	Polypeptide chains may form α helices or β pleated sheets.	Hydrogen bonds	**β Pleated sheet** **α Helix** Amino acid Hydrogen bonds
(C) Tertiary	Polypeptides fold, forming specific shapes.	Hydrogen bonds; disulfide bridges; hydrophobic interactions	β Pleated sheet Hydrogen bond α Helix Disulfide bridge
(D) Quaternary	Two or more polypeptides assemble to form larger protein molecules.	Hydrogen bonds; disulfide bridges; hydrophobic interactions; ionic bonds	Subunit 1 Subunit 2 Subunit 3 Subunit 4

Figure 3.8 The Four Levels of Protein Structure Secondary, tertiary, and quaternary structure all arise from the primary structure of the protein.

Q: If a protein is gently heated to break hydrogen bonds, what level(s) of structure will be unaffected, and why?

between the N—H groups on one chain and the C=O groups on the other (see Figure 3.8B). A β pleated sheet may form between separate polypeptide chains or between different regions of a single polypeptide chain that is bent back on itself. The ratcheted, stacked sheets in dragline spider silks (described at the beginning of the chapter and in Investigating Life: Making Spider Silk) are made up of β pleated sheets. Many proteins contain regions of both α helix and β pleated sheet in the same polypeptide chain.

The tertiary structure of a protein is formed by bending and folding

In many proteins, the polypeptide chain is bent at specific sites and then folded back and forth, resulting in the **tertiary structure** of the protein (**Figure 3.8C**). Although α helices and β pleated sheets contribute to the tertiary structure, usually only portions of the

DNA and proteins usually coil into right-handed helices.

A right-handed helix curves in the direction of the fingers in a right hand when the thumb points upward.

Figure 3.9 Left- and Right-Handed Helices A protein will often have one or more right-handed helices as part of its secondary structure.

macromolecule have these secondary structures, and large regions consist of tertiary structure unique to a particular protein. For example, the proteins found in stretchy spider silks (see the opening story) have repeated amino acid sequences that cause the proteins to fold into spirals. Tertiary structure is a macromolecule's definitive three-dimensional shape, often including a buried interior as well as a surface that is exposed to the environment.

The protein's exposed outer surfaces present functional groups capable of interacting with other molecules in the cell. These molecules might be other macromolecules, including proteins, nucleic acids, carbohydrates, and lipid structures, or smaller chemical substances.

You saw that hydrogen bonding between the N—H and C═O groups within and between chains is responsible for secondary structure. For tertiary structure, the interactions between R groups—the amino acid side chains—and between R groups and the environment are key. Recall the various strong and weak interactions between atoms described in Key Concept 2.2. Here is how these interactions are involved in determining and maintaining tertiary structure:

- Covalent disulfide bridges can form between specific cysteine side chains (see Figure 3.6), holding a folded polypeptide in place.

- Hydrogen bonds between side chains also stabilize folds in proteins.

- Hydrophobic side chains can aggregate together in the interior of the protein, away from water, folding the polypeptide in the process. Close interactions between the hydrophobic side chains are stabilized by van der Waals forces.

- Ionic bonds can form between positively and negatively charged side chains, forming salt bridges between amino acids. Salt bridges can be near the surfaces of polypeptides or buried deep within a protein, away from water. These interactions occur

between positively and negatively charged amino acids, for example glutamic acid (which has a negatively charged R group) and arginine (which is positively charged) (see Table 3.2):

A protein folds into its final shape in a way that maximizes all the interactions noted and minimizes inappropriate interactions, such as two positively charged residues (a term identifying monomers in a polymer) being near one another, or a hydrophobic residue being near water. A complete description of a protein's tertiary structure would specify the location of every atom in the molecule in three-dimensional space relative to all the other atoms. **Figure 3.10** shows three ways of modeling the structure of the protein lysozyme. Each way has its uses. The space-filling model might be used to study how other molecules interact with specific sites and R groups on the protein's surface. The stick model emphasizes the sites where bends occur, resulting in folds in the polypeptide chain. The ribbon model, perhaps the most widely used, shows the different types of secondary structure and how they fold into the tertiary structure.

If a protein is heated slowly and moderately, the heat energy will disrupt only the weak interactions, causing the secondary and tertiary structure to break down. A protein whose structure is disrupted is said to be **denatured**. A comparison of native (untreated) and denatured proteins shows major differences:

- Native proteins are compact; denatured proteins have a larger volume.

- Native proteins exist in one, preferred shape; denatured proteins can take many shapes.

Figure 3.10 Three Representations of Lysozyme Different molecular representations of a protein emphasize different aspects of its tertiary structure: surface features, sites of bends and folds, or sites where alpha or beta structures predominate. These three representations of lysozyme are similarly oriented. (Data from PDB 1IVM. T. Obita et al. 2003. *Cell Mol Life Sci* 60: 176–184.)

**Media Clip 3.1
Protein Structures in 3D**
Life12e.com/mc3.1

(A) Space-filling model

A realistic depiction of lysozyme shows dense packing of its atoms.

(B) Stick model

β Pleated sheet

α Helix

The "backbone" of lysozyme consists of repeating N—C—C units of amino acids.

(C) Ribbon model

β Pleated sheet

α Helix

- Native proteins have hydrogen bonds that stabilize the structure internally; denatured proteins have hydrogen bonds on the exterior, to water.

You can't "unboil" an egg after it has been hard-boiled; the egg proteins are irreversibly denatured. Amazingly, in some cases a protein can return to its normal tertiary structure when it cools, demonstrating that all the information needed to specify the unique shape of a protein is contained in its primary structure. This was first shown (using chemicals instead of heat to denature the protein) by biochemist Christian Anfinsen for the protein ribonuclease (**Figure 3.11**).

If a protein has changes in amino acid sequence such that regions that ordinarily are on the inside of the protein (hydrophobic) are now on the outside, the protein may adopt a flat, beta configuration instead of a three-dimensional tertiary structure. These flat sheets act like fibrous proteins and aggregate, forming **amyloids**. Amyloids are characteristic of a rare brain disease called spongiform encephalopathy (or "mad cow disease," since amyloids made from fragments of a protein called a prion can enter humans from cows). More commonly, amyloids of a different protein are a hallmark of the brains of people with Alzheimer's disease.

The quaternary structure of a protein consists of subunits

Many functional proteins contain two or more polypeptide chains, called subunits, each of them folded into its own unique tertiary structure. The protein's **quaternary structure** results from the ways in which these subunits bind together and interact (**Figure 3.8D**).

Hemoglobin has four polypeptide chains interacting to form quaternary structure (**Figure 3.12**). Hydrophobic interactions, van der Waals forces, hydrogen bonds, and ionic bonds all help hold the four subunits together to form a hemoglobin molecule. However, the weak nature of these forces permits small changes in the quaternary structure to aid the protein's function—which is to carry oxygen in red blood cells. As hemoglobin binds one O_2 molecule, the four subunits shift their relative positions slightly, changing the quaternary structure. Ionic bonds are broken, exposing buried side chains that enhance the binding of additional O_2 molecules. The quaternary structure changes back when hemoglobin releases its O_2 molecules to the cells of the body.

Shape and surface chemistry contribute to protein function

The shapes of proteins allow specific sites on their exposed surfaces to bind noncovalently to other molecules, which may be large or small. The binding is usually very specific because only certain compatible chemical groups will bind to one another. The specificity of protein binding depends on two general properties of the protein: its shape, and the chemistry of its exposed surface groups.

- *Shape.* When a small molecule collides with and binds to a much larger protein, it is like a baseball being caught by a catcher's mitt: the mitt has a shape that binds to the ball and fits around it. Just as a hockey puck or a ping-pong ball does not fit a baseball catcher's mitt, a given molecule will not bind to a protein unless there is a general "fit" between their three-dimensional shapes.

Experiment

Figure 3.11A Primary Structure Specifies Tertiary Structure

Original Papers: C. B. Anfinsen et al. 1961. The kinetics of formation of native ribonuclease during oxidation of the reduced polypeptide chain. *Proc Natl Acad Sci USA* 47: 1309–1314.

F. White, Jr. 1961. Regeneration of native secondary and tertiary structures by air oxidation of reduced ribonuclease. *J Biol Chem* 236: 1353–1360.

Using the protein ribonuclease, Christian Anfinsen showed that proteins spontaneously fold into functionally correct three-dimensional configurations. As long as the primary structure is not disrupted, the information for correct folding (under the right conditions) is retained.

HYPOTHESIS▶ Under controlled conditions that simulate the normal cellular environment, a denatured protein can refold into a functional three-dimensional structure.

METHOD▶ Chemically denature a functional ribonuclease so that only its primary structure (i.e., an unfolded polypeptide chain) remains. Once denaturation is complete, remove the disruptive chemicals.

1 Extract and purify a functional protein, ribonuclease, from tissue.

α Helix

β Pleated sheet

Disulfide bridge

2 Add chemicals that disrupt hydrogen bonds and ionic bonds (urea) and disulfide bridges (mercaptoethanol).

—SH group

3 Slowly remove the chemical agents.

Denatured protein

RESULTS▶ When the disruptive agents are removed, three-dimensional structure is restored and the protein once again is functional.

CONCLUSION▶ In normal cellular conditions, the primary structure of a protein specifies how it folds into a functional, three-dimensional structure.

Figure 3.11B Work with the Data follows on next page.

Work with the Data

Figure 3.11B   Primary Structure Specifies Tertiary Structure

Original Papers: C. B. Anfinsen et al. 1961. The kinetics of formation of native ribonuclease during oxidation of the reduced polypeptide chain. *Proc Natl Acad Sci USA* 47: 1309–1314.

F. White, Jr. 1961. Regeneration of native secondary and tertiary structures by air oxidation of reduced ribonuclease. *J Biol Chem* 236: 1353–1360.

After the tertiary structures of proteins were shown to be highly specific, the question arose as to how the order of amino acids determined the three-dimensional structure. The second protein whose structure was determined was ribonuclease A (RNase A). This enzyme was readily available from cow pancreases at slaughterhouses and, because it works in the highly acidic environment of the cow stomach, was stable compared with most proteins and easy to purify. RNase A has 124 amino acids. Among these are eight cysteine residues, which form four disulfide bridges. Were these covalent bonds between cysteines essential for the three-dimensional structure of RNase A? As outlined in Figure 3.11A, Christian Anfinsen and his colleagues set out to answer this question.

QUESTIONS▶

1. Initially, the disulfide bonds (S—S) in RNase A were eliminated because the sulfur atoms in cysteine residues were all reduced (—SH). At time zero, reoxidation began; and at various times, the amount of S—S bond re-formation and the activity of the enzyme were measured by chemical methods. The data are shown in **Figure A**.

Figure A

At what time did disulfide bonds begin to form? At what time did enzyme activity begin to appear? Explain the difference between these times.

2. The three-dimensional structure of RNase A was examined by ultraviolet spectroscopy. In this technique, the protein was exposed to different wavelengths of ultraviolet light (measured in nanometers) and the amount of light absorbed by the protein at each wavelength was measured (*E*). The results are plotted in **Figure B**.

Figure B

Look carefully at the plots. What are the differences between the peak absorbances of native (untreated) and reduced (denatured) RNase A? What happened when reduced RNase A was reoxidized (renatured)? What can you conclude about the structure of RNase A from these experiments?

Go to Achieve for a companion **Data in Depth** exercise.

Figure 3.12 Quaternary Structure of a Protein   Hemoglobin consists of four folded polypeptide subunits that assemble themselves into the quaternary structure represented by the ribbon model (**A**) and space-filling model (**B**). In both representations, each type of subunit is a different color (α subunits are blue and β subunits are green). The heme groups (red) contain iron and are the oxygen-carrying sites. (Data from PDB 2HHB. G. Fermi et al. 1984. *J Mol Biol* 175: 159–174.)

Q: What forces hold the subunits of hemoglobin together?

Figure 3.13 Noncovalent Interactions between Proteins and Other Molecules Noncovalent interactions allow a protein (red) to bind tightly to another molecule (green) with specific properties. Noncovalent interactions also allow regions within the same protein to interact with one another.

- *Chemistry.* The exposed R groups on the surface of a protein permit chemical interactions with other substances (**Figure 3.13**). Three types of interactions may be involved: ionic, hydrophobic, or hydrogen bonding. Many important functions of proteins involve interactions between surface R groups and other molecules. In later chapters you will learn about proteins called enzymes that bind small molecules and enhance their chemical reactivity, as well as proteins that bind to nucleic acids and participate in the expression and regulation of their activities. In these and many other cases, the interactions between the molecules are noncovalent.

Environmental conditions affect protein structure

Because they are largely determined by weak forces, the three-dimensional structures of proteins are influenced by environmental conditions. Conditions that would not break covalent bonds can disrupt the weaker, noncovalent interactions that determine secondary, tertiary, and quaternary structure. Such alterations may affect a protein's shape and thus its function. Various conditions can alter the weak, noncovalent interactions:

- Increases in temperature cause more rapid molecular movements and thus can break hydrogen bonds and hydrophobic interactions.

- Changes in pH can change the ionization pattern of exposed carboxyl and amino groups in the R groups of amino acids, thus disrupting the pattern of ionic bonds and repulsions. For example, as the pH rises, H^+ ions are removed from the charged H_3N^+ groups of lysine and arginine, making them less charged and less polar; and COOH groups on aspartic and glutamic acids ionize, making them negative and therefore more polar. These differences in polarity change the tertiary

structure of the protein, with more polar groups on the outside (interacting with water) and fewer polar groups on the inside (away from water).

- High concentrations of polar substances such as urea can disrupt the hydrogen bonding that is crucial to protein structure. Urea was used in the experiment on reversible protein denaturation shown in Figure 3.11.

- Nonpolar substances may also disrupt normal protein structure in cases where hydrophobic interactions are essential to maintain the structure.

Protein shapes can change

As we saw in the case of hemoglobin, which undergoes subtle shape changes when it binds oxygen, the shapes of proteins can change as a result of their interactions with other molecules. Proteins can also change shape if they undergo covalent modifications.

- *Proteins interact with other molecules.* Proteins do not exist in isolation. In fact, if a biochemist "goes fishing" with a particular protein, by attaching the protein to a chemical "hook" and inserting it into cells, the protein will often be attached to something else when it is "reeled in." These molecular interactions are reminiscent of the interactions that make up quaternary structure (see above). If a polypeptide comes into contact with another molecule, R groups on its surface may form weak interactions (e.g., hydrophobic, van der Waals) with groups on the surface of the other molecule. This may disrupt some of the interactions between R groups within the polypeptide, causing it to undergo a change in shape (**Figure 3.14A**). You will see many instances of this in the coming chapters.

Figure 3.14 Protein Structure Can Change Proteins can change their tertiary structure when they bind to other molecules (**A**) or are modified chemically (**B**).

• *Proteins undergo covalent modifications.* After it is made, the structure of a protein can be modified by the covalent bonding of a chemical group to the side chain of one or more of its amino acids. The chemical modification of just one amino acid can alter the shape and function of a protein. An example is the addition of a charged phosphate group to a relatively nonpolar R group. This can cause the amino acid to become more hydrophilic and to move to the outer surface of the protein, altering the shape of the protein in the region near the amino acid (**Figure 3.14B**).

Connect the Concepts Covalent modifications of proteins with subsequent changes in shape and function underlie many biological processes, ranging from signaling within the cell (see Key Concept 7.3) to the action of plant hormones on growth (see Key Concept 36.2).

Molecular chaperones help shape proteins

Within a living cell, a polypeptide chain is sometimes in danger of binding the wrong substance. There are two major situations when this can occur:

1. *Just after a protein is made.* When a protein has not yet folded completely, it can present a surface that binds the wrong molecule.

2. *Following denaturation.* Certain conditions, such as moderate heat, can cause some proteins in a living cell to denature without killing the organism. Before the protein can refold, it may present a surface that binds the wrong molecule. In these cases, the inappropriate binding may be irreversible.

Many cells have a special class of proteins, called **chaperones**, that protect the three-dimensional structures of other proteins. They bind to their partner proteins just as they are being made and also when they become denatured. Like the chaperones at a high school dance, chaperone proteins prevent inappropriate interactions and enhance appropriate ones. Typically, a chaperone protein has a cagelike structure that pulls in a polypeptide, causes it to fold into the correct shape, and then releases it (**Figure 3.15**).

Tumors make chaperone proteins, possibly to stabilize proteins important in the cancer process, and so chaperone-inhibiting drugs are being designed for use in chemotherapy. In some clinical situations, treatment with these inhibitors results in the inappropriate folding of proteins in tumor cells, causing the tumors to stop growing. As noted above, misfolding of proteins to form amyloid aggregates underlies certain brain diseases, and there is an effort to use the principles of chaperones to induce the proteins to fold correctly and prevent aggregation.

KEY CONCEPT
3.2 Recap and Assess

Proteins are polymers of amino acids. The sequence of amino acids in a protein is its primary structure. Secondary, tertiary, and quaternary structures arise through noncovalent and covalent interactions between the amino acids. A protein's three-dimensional shape and exposed chemical groups establish its binding specificity for other substances.

1. Suppose that, in a given protein, one lysine is replaced by aspartic acid (see Table 3.2). Does this change occur in the primary structure or in the secondary structure? How might it result in a change in tertiary structure? In quaternary structure?

2. A single amino acid change in a protein can change its shape. For example, the amino acid glycine may normally reside at a certain position in a protein. If glycine is replaced with either glutamic acid or arginine, the protein shape near that amino acid changes significantly. There are two possible explanations for this:

   a. A small amino acid at that position in the polypeptide is necessary for normal shape.

   b. An uncharged amino acid is necessary for normal shape.

   Further amino acid substitutions are done to distinguish between these possibilities. Replacing glycine with serine or alanine results in normal shape, but replacing glycine with valine changes the shape. Which of the two possible explanations is supported by the observations? Explain your answer.

3. Human hair is composed of the protein keratin. At the hair salon, two techniques are used to modify the three-dimensional shape of hair. Styling involves heat, and a perm involves cleaving and re-forming disulfide bonds. How would you investigate these phenomena in terms of protein structure?

The seemingly infinite number of protein configurations made possible by the biochemical properties of the 20 amino acids has

Figure 3.15 Molecular Chaperones Protect Proteins from Inappropriate Binding Chaperone proteins surround new or denatured proteins and prevent them from binding to the wrong substances. Heat shock proteins such as HSP60, shown here, make up one class of chaperone proteins.

Q: Why are heat shock proteins important for a cell?

Denatured protein

"Lid"

HSP60 "cage"

1 A denatured protein binds to HSP60 and enters it.

2 The inside of the structure has hydrophobic amino acids that bind to hydrophobic amino acids on the target protein.

3 A "lid" seals the "cage."

4 The protein folds into its appropriate shape and is released.

driven the evolution of life's diversity. The linkage configurations of sugar monomers (monosaccharides) determine the structures of the next group of macromolecules, the carbohydrates, which provide energy for life.

KEY CONCEPT 3.3 Carbohydrates Are Made from Simple Sugars

Learning Objectives

3.3.1 Identify the primary functions of carbohydrates in living organisms.

3.3.2 Explain why polysaccharides are useful structures for energy storage.

3.3.3 Use the chemical structures of polysaccharides to explain their properties.

Carbohydrates make up a large group of molecules that all have similar atomic compositions but differ greatly in size, chemical properties, and biological functions. Carbohydrates usually have the general formula $(C_1H_2O_1)_n$, (n stands for a number), which makes them appear as "hydrates of carbon" (a hydrate refers to water), hence their name. However, carbohydrates are not really "hydrates" because the water molecules are not intact. Rather, the linked carbon atoms are bonded with hydrogen atoms (—H) and hydroxyl groups (—OH), the components of water.

Carbohydrates have four major biochemical roles:

1. They are a source of stored energy that can be released in a form usable by organisms.

2. They are used to transport stored energy within complex organisms.

3. They serve as carbon skeletons that can be rearranged to form new molecules.

4. They form extracellular assemblies such as cell walls that provide structure to organisms.

Some carbohydrates are relatively small, with molecular weights of less than 100. Others are true macromolecules, with molecular weights in the hundreds of thousands.

There are four categories of biologically important carbohydrates, defined by the number of monomers:

1. **Monosaccharides** (mono, "one," + saccharide, "sugar"), such as glucose, are simple sugars. They are the monomers from which the larger carbohydrates are constructed.

2. **Disaccharides** (di, "two") consist of two monosaccharides linked together by covalent bonds. The most familiar is sucrose, which is made up of covalently bonded glucose and fructose molecules.

3. **Oligosaccharides** (oligo, "several") are made up of several (3–20) monosaccharides.

4. **Polysaccharides** (poly, "many"), such as starch, glycogen, and cellulose, are polymers made up of hundreds or thousands of monosaccharides.

Monosaccharides are simple sugars

All living cells contain the monosaccharide **glucose**; it is the "blood sugar" used to store and transport energy in humans. Cells use glucose as an energy source, breaking it down through a series of reactions that convert stored energy to more usable chemical-bond energy and produce carbon dioxide; this is a cellular form of the combustion reaction you saw in Key Concept 2.3.

Glucose exists in straight chains and in ring forms. The ring forms predominate in virtually all biological circumstances because they are more stable in water. There are two forms of the glucose ring, called α- and β-glucose, which differ only in the orientation of the —H and —OH groups attached to carbon 1 (**Figure 3.16**). The α and β forms interconvert and exist in equilibrium when dissolved in water.

Figure 3.16 From One Form of Glucose to the Other   All glucose molecules have the formula $C_6H_{12}O_6$, but their structures vary. When dissolved in water, the α and β "ring" forms of glucose interconvert. The convention used here for numbering the carbon atoms is standard in biochemistry.

View in Achieve
Activity 3.3 Forms of Glucose

Five-carbon sugars (pentoses)

Ribose and deoxyribose each have five carbons, but different chemical properties and biological roles.

Six-carbon sugars (hexoses)

α-Mannose   α-Glucose   Fructose

These hexoses are structural isomers. All have the formula $C_6H_{12}O_6$, but each has distinct biochemical properties.

Figure 3.17 Monosaccharides Are Simple Sugars
Monosaccharides are made up of varying numbers of carbons. Some hexoses are structural isomers that have the same kind and number of atoms, but the atoms are arranged differently. Fructose, for example, is a hexose but forms a five-membered ring like the pentoses.

Different monosaccharides contain different numbers of carbons. Some monosaccharides are structural isomers, with the same kinds and numbers of atoms but in different arrangements (**Figure 3.17**). Such seemingly small structural changes can significantly alter their properties. Most of the monosaccharides in living systems belong to the D (right-handed) series of optical isomers.

- **Pentoses** (*pente*, "five") are five-carbon sugars. Two pentoses are of particular biological importance: the backbones of the nucleic acids RNA and DNA contain ribose and deoxyribose, respectively (see Key Concept 4.1). These two pentoses are not isomers of each other; rather, one oxygen atom is missing from carbon 2 in deoxyribose (*de-*, "absent"). The absence of this oxygen atom is an important distinction between RNA and DNA.

- The **hexoses** (*hex*, "six") shown in Figures 3.16 and 3.17 are a group of structural isomers with the formula $C_6H_{12}O_6$. Common hexoses are glucose, fructose (so named because it was first found in fruits), mannose, and galactose.

Glycosidic bonds link monosaccharides

The disaccharides, oligosaccharides, and polysaccharides are all constructed from monosaccharides that are covalently bonded together by condensation reactions that form **glycosidic bonds** (**Figure 3.18**). A single glycosidic bond between two monosaccharides forms a disaccharide. For example, sucrose—common table sugar (the real

The presence of a carbon atom (C) at a junction such as this is implied.

In sucrose, glucose and fructose are linked by an α-1,2 glycosidic bond.

CH₂OH + CH₂OH → Formation of α bond → α-1,2 Glycosidic bond

α-D-Glucose   Fructose   α-D-Glucose   Fructose
Sucrose

Maltose is produced when an α-1,4 glycosidic bond forms between two glucose molecules. The hydroxyl group on carbon 1 of one D-glucose in the α (down) position reacts with the hydroxyl group on carbon 4 of the other glucose.

α-D-Glucose   β-D-Glucose → Formation of α bond → α-1,4 Glycosidic bond

α-D-Glucose   β-D-Glucose
Maltose

In cellobiose, two glucoses are linked by a β-1,4 glycosidic bond.

β-D-Glucose   β-D-Glucose → Formation of β bond → β-1,4 Glycosidic bond

β-D-Glucose   β-D-Glucose
Cellobiose

Figure 3.18 Disaccharides Form by Glycosidic Bonds
Glycosidic bonds between two monosaccharides can create many different disaccharides. The particular disaccharide formed depends on which monosaccharides are bonded, on the site of bonding (i.e., which carbon atoms are involved), and on the form (α or β) of the bond.

stuff, not artificial sweetener) in the human diet and the major disaccharide in plants—is formed from a glucose and a fructose molecule.

The disaccharides maltose and cellobiose are made from two glucose molecules (see Figure 3.18). Maltose and cellobiose are structural isomers, both having the formula $C_{12}H_{22}O_{11}$. However, they have different chemical properties and are recognized by different enzymes in biological tissues. For example, maltose can be hydrolyzed into its monosaccharides in the human body, whereas cellobiose cannot.

Connect the Concepts Enzymes are an important class of proteins that may change shape when they come into contact with a reactant in a biochemical reaction. Each enzyme is specific for the reactant it binds. See Key Concept 8.4.

Oligosaccharides contain several monosaccharides bound by glycosidic bonds at various sites. Many oligosaccharides have additional functional groups, which give them special properties.

Oligosaccharides are often covalently bonded to proteins and lipids on the outer cell surface, where they serve as recognition signals. The different human blood groups (e.g., the ABO blood types) get their specificities from oligosaccharide chains.

Polysaccharides store energy and provide structural materials

Polysaccharides are large (sometimes gigantic) polymers of monosaccharides connected by glycosidic bonds (**Figure 3.19**). In contrast to polypeptides, polysaccharides are not necessarily linear chains of monomers. Each monomer unit has several sites that are capable of forming glycosidic bonds, and thus branched molecules are possible.

STARCH   Starches make up a family of large molecules with similar structures. While all starches are polysaccharides of glucose

(A) Molecular structure

Cellulose

Cellulose is an unbranched polymer of glucose with β-1,4 glycosidic bonds that are chemically very stable.

Starch and glycogen

Glycogen and starch are polymers of glucose with α-1,4 glycosidic bonds. α-1,6 Glycosidic bonds produce branching at carbon 6.

(B) Macromolecular structure

Linear (cellulose)

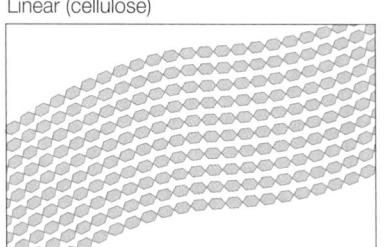

Parallel cellulose molecules form hydrogen bonds, resulting in thin fibrils.

Branched (starch)

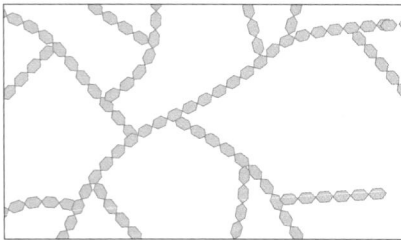

Branching limits the number of hydrogen bonds that can form in starch molecules, making starch less compact than cellulose.

Highly branched (glycogen)

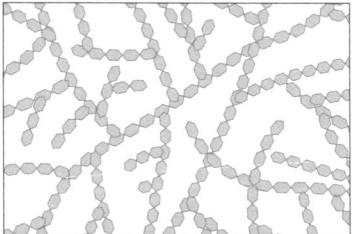

The high amount of branching in glycogen makes its solid deposits more compact than starch.

(C) Polysaccharides in cells

Layers of cellulose fibrils, as seen in this scanning electron micrograph, give plant cell walls great strength.

Within these potato cells, starch deposits (colored red in this scanning electron micrograph) have a granular shape.

© Biophoto Associates/ Science Source

© Dennis Kunkel Microscopy/ Science Source

The dark clumps in this electron micrograph are glycogen deposits in a liver cell.

© Don W. Fawcett/Science Source

Figure 3.19 Representative Polysaccharides Cellulose, starch, and glycogen have different levels of branching and compaction of the polysaccharides.

Q: When beer is made, initially mashed-up barley seeds are soaked in water and maltose is produced. What kind of reaction is involved in maltose production in this case?

with α-glycosidic bonds (α-1,4 and α-1,6 glycosidic bonds; see Figure 3.19A), the different starches can be distinguished by the amount of branching that occurs at carbons 1 and 6 (see Figure 3.19B). Starch is the principal energy storage compound of plants. Some plant starches, such as amylose, are unbranched; others are moderately branched (for example, amylopectin). Starch readily binds water; if you're a cook you know this. However, when water is removed, hydrogen bonds form between the unbranched polysaccharide chains, which then aggregate. Large starch aggregates called starch grains can be observed in the storage tissues of plant seeds (see Figure 3.19C). These aggregates are broken up when starch is heated, breaking the hydrogen bonds. The starch becomes less solid and crystalline and water is absorbed, making the starch even more amorphous. This is what happens in baking with wheat flour, and is what gives bread its texture. Next time you eat some bread, think of hydrogen bonds!

GLYCOGEN **Glycogen** is a water-insoluble, highly branched polymer of glucose. It is used to store glucose in the liver and muscles and is thus an energy storage compound for animals, as starch is for plants. Both glycogen and starch are readily hydrolyzed into glucose monomers, which in turn can be broken down to liberate their stored energy.

But if it is glucose that is needed for fuel, why store it in the form of glycogen? The reason is that 1,000 glucose molecules would exert 1,000 times the osmotic pressure of a single glycogen molecule, causing water to enter cells where glucose is stored (see Key Concept 6.3). If it were not for polysaccharides, many organisms would expend a lot of energy expelling excess water from their cells.

CELLULOSE As the predominant component of plant cell walls, **cellulose** is by far the most abundant organic compound on Earth. Like starch and glycogen, cellulose is a polysaccharide of glucose, but its individual monosaccharides are connected by β- rather than by α-glycosidic bonds. Starch is easily degraded by the actions of chemicals or enzymes. Cellulose, however, is chemically more stable because of its β-glycosidic bonds. Thus whereas starch is easily broken down to supply glucose for energy-producing reactions, cellulose is an excellent structural material that can withstand harsh environmental conditions without substantial change.

Chemically modified carbohydrates contain additional functional groups

Some carbohydrates are chemically modified by the addition of functional groups such as phosphate, amino, or *N*-acetyl groups (**Figure 3.20**). For example, a phosphate group may be added to

---

(A) Sugar phosphate

Fructose 1,6-bisphosphate is involved in the reactions that liberate energy from glucose. (The numbers in its name refer to the carbon sites of phosphate bonding; *bis-* indicates that two phosphates are present.)

Phosphate groups

Fructose 1,6-bisphosphate

Figure 3.20 Chemically Modified Carbohydrates Added functional groups can modify the form and properties of a carbohydrate.

(B) Amino sugars

The monosaccharides glucosamine and galactosamine are amino sugars with an amino group in place of a hydroxyl group.

Glucosamine   Amino group   **Galactosamine**

Galactosamine is an important component of cartilage, a connective tissue in vertebrates.

(C) Chitin

Chitin is a polymer of *N*-acetylglucosamine; *N*-acetyl groups provide additional sites for hydrogen bonding between the polymers.

The external skeletons of insects are made up of chitin.

Chitin

one or more of the —OH sites (see Figure 3.20A). Some of the resulting sugar phosphates, such as fructose 1,6-bisphosphate, are important intermediates in cellular energy reactions, which you'll see in Chapter 9.

When an amino group (NH_2) is substituted for an —OH group, amino sugars, such as glucosamine and galactosamine, are produced (see Figure 3.20B). These compounds are important in the extracellular matrix (see Key Concept 5.4), where they form parts of glycoproteins, which are molecules involved in keeping tissues together. Galactosamine is a major component of cartilage, the material that forms caps on the ends of bones and stiffens the ears and nose. A derivative of glucosamine is present in the polymer chitin (see Figure 3.20C), the principal structural polysaccharide in the external skeletons of insects and many crustaceans (such as crabs and lobsters), and a component of the cell walls of fungi.

KEY CONCEPT
3.3 Recap and Assess

Carbohydrates are composed of carbon, hydrogen, and oxygen and have the general formula $(C_1H_2O_1)_n$. They provide energy and structure to cells and are precursors of numerous important biological molecules. Monosaccharide monomers can be connected by glycosidic bonds to form disaccharides, oligosaccharides, and polysaccharides.

1. What qualities of the polysaccharides starch and glycogen make them useful for energy storage?

2. After looking at the cellulose molecule in Figure 3.19A, can you see why a large number of hydrogen bonds are present in the linear structure of cellulose shown in Figure 3.19B? Why is this structure so strong?

You have seen how amino acid monomers form protein polymers and how sugar monomers form the polymers of carbohydrates. Now we will look at the lipids, which are unique among the four classes of large biological molecules in that they are not, strictly speaking, polymers.

KEY CONCEPT
3.4 Lipids Are Defined by Their Insolubility in Water

Learning Objectives

3.4.1 Compare and contrast triglycerides in fats and oils.

3.4.2 Describe how the polar and nonpolar natures of phospholipids result in the formation of a membrane bilayer.

3.4.3 Explain why carotenoids, steroids, and waxes are classified as lipids.

Lipids—colloquially called fats—are hydrocarbons that are insoluble in water because of their many nonpolar covalent bonds. As you saw in Key Concept 2.2, nonpolar hydrocarbon molecules are hydrophobic and preferentially aggregate together, away from water, which is polar (see Figure 2.13). The huge macromolecular aggregations that can form are not polymers in a strict chemical sense, because the individual lipid molecules are not covalently bonded.

There are several different types of lipids, and they play numerous roles in living organisms:

- Fats and oils store energy.
- Phospholipids play important structural roles in cell membranes.
- Carotenoids and chlorophylls help plants capture light energy.
- Steroids and modified fatty acids play regulatory roles as hormones and vitamins.
- Fat in animal bodies serves as thermal insulation.
- A lipid coating around nerves provides electrical insulation.
- Oil or wax on the surfaces of skin, fur, feathers, and leaves repels water and prevents excessive evaporation of water from terrestrial animals and plants.

Fats and oils are triglycerides

Chemically, fats and oils are **triglycerides**, also known as simple lipids. Triglycerides that are solid at room temperature (around 20°C) are called **fats**; those that are liquid at room temperature are called **oils**. Triglycerides are composed of two types of building blocks: fatty acids and glycerol. **Glycerol** is a small molecule with three hydroxyl (—OH) groups (thus it is an alcohol). A **fatty acid** is made up of a long nonpolar hydrocarbon chain and an acidic polar carboxyl group (—COOH). These chains are very hydrophobic because of their abundant C—H and C—C bonds, which have similar electronegativity values and are therefore nonpolar.

Connect the Concepts As discussed in Key Concept 2.2, electronegativity is a measure of the attraction an atomic nucleus exerts on electrons in a covalent bond. When one interacting atom is much more electronegative than the other, a complete transfer of one or more electrons may take place.

A triglyceride contains three fatty acid molecules and one molecule of glycerol. Making a triglyceride involves three condensation (dehydration) reactions. In each reaction, the carboxyl group of a fatty acid bonds with a hydroxyl group of glycerol, resulting in a covalent bond called an **ester linkage** and the release of a water molecule (**Figure 3.21**). The three fatty acids in a triglyceride molecule need not all have the same hydrocarbon chain length or structure; some may be saturated fatty acids, whereas others may be unsaturated:

- In **saturated fatty acids**, all the bonds between the carbon atoms in the hydrocarbon chain are single bonds—there are no double bonds. That is, all the bonds are saturated with hydrogen atoms (**Figure 3.22A**). These fatty acid molecules are relatively straight, and they pack together tightly, like pencils in a box. They are called saturated because additional hydrogen atoms cannot be added to the carbon atoms in the chain.

- In **unsaturated fatty acids**, the hydrocarbon chain contains one or more double bonds. Linoleic acid is an example of a polyunsaturated fatty acid that has two double bonds near the middle of the hydrocarbon chain, causing kinks in the molecule (**Figure 3.22B**). Such kinks prevent the unsaturated fat molecules from

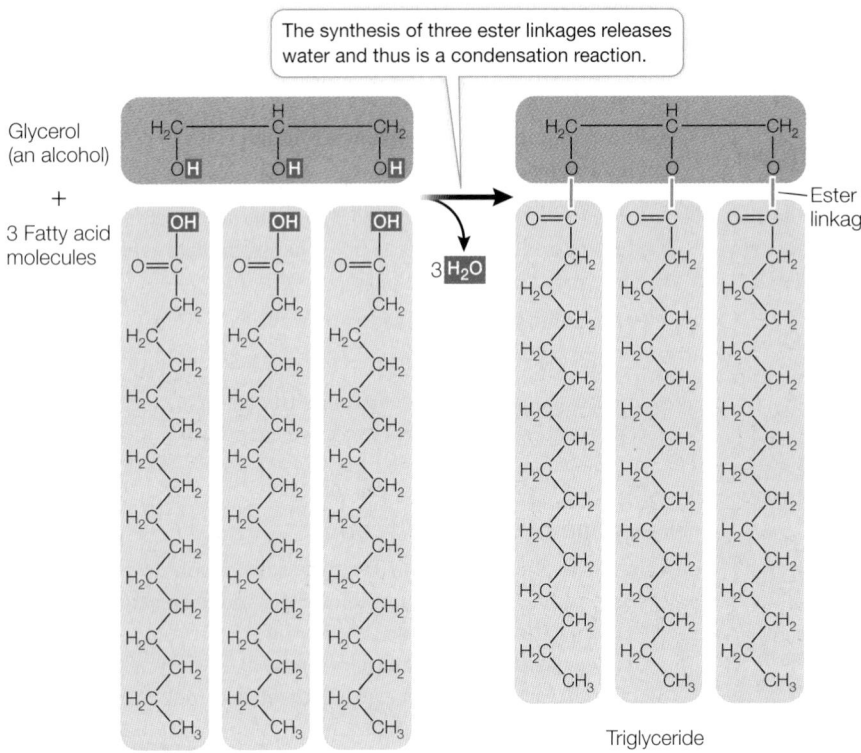

Figure 3.21 Synthesis of a Triglyceride   In living things, the reaction that forms a triglyceride is more complex, but the end result is the same as shown here.

packing together tightly. Plants store unsaturated fats, as in corn oil and soybean oil.

The kinks in fatty acid molecules are important in determining the fluidity and melting points of lipids. The triglycerides of animal fats (as in meat) tend to have many long-chain saturated fatty acids packed tightly together; these fats are usually solids at room temperature and have high melting points. The triglycerides of plants, such as corn oil, tend to have short or unsaturated fatty acids. Because of their kinks, these fatty acids pack together poorly and have low melting points, and these triglycerides are usually liquids at room temperature.

The kinks in fatty acids are possible because the H atoms around the C=C double bond are in the same plane of the molecule (*cis*; see Figures 3.22 and 2.8). However, in some fatty acids the H atoms are on opposite sides of the plane of the molecule (*trans*). In these fatty acids, there are no kinks and the fat containing them—called **trans fat**—packs tightly and is more fluid at room temperature. As plant oils became more available, consistent, and cheaper than animal fat, the food industry devised methods to make the oils semisolid by adding hydrogen to saturate the

Figure 3.22 Saturated and Unsaturated Fatty Acids   **(A)** The straight hydrocarbon chain of a saturated fatty acid allows the molecule to pack tightly with other, similar molecules. **(B)** In unsaturated fatty acids, kinks in the chain prevent close packing. The color convention in the models shown here (gray, H; red, O; black, C) is commonly used.

Q: If hydrogen gas (H_2) is bubbled over a suspension of unsaturated fatty acids, which will happen to their structure?

double bonds (by bubbling H_2 gas). Thus margarine and shortening were developed. A side effect of this industrial process was that some of the *cis* fatty acid double bonds were converted to the *trans* configuration. So the foods ended up with some trans fats. As more people consumed trans fats, they had higher levels of low-density lipoproteins (LDL; see Figure 3.23C), which may result in accumulation of lipids on the inner walls of arteries, leading to heart disease and stroke. Food labels now show the content of trans fats, and restaurants have banned them.

Unsaturated fatty acids are identified by the position of the carbon atom of the first double bond, with the first carbon atom—called the omega carbon—being at the opposite end of the chain from the carboxylic acid group. For example, in Figure 3.22B the first C=C bond in linoleic acid is at carbon 6, so it is called an omega-6 fatty acid. Certain other fatty acids have their first C=C bond at position 3 and so are called **omega-3 fatty acids**. There is good evidence that omega-3 fatty acids protect against heart attacks and stroke, so government agencies in many countries recommend consuming foods containing them.

Fatty acids are excellent storehouses for chemical-bond energy. As you will see in Chapter 9, when the C—H bond is broken, it releases significant energy that an organism can use for its own purposes, such as movement or building up other complex molecules.

Phospholipids form biological membranes

We have mentioned the hydrophobic nature of the many C—C and C—H bonds in fatty acids. But what about the carboxyl functional group at the end of the molecule? When it ionizes and forms COO^-, it is strongly hydrophilic. So a fatty acid is a molecule with a hydrophilic end and a long hydrophobic "tail." It has two opposing chemical properties—part hydrophobic and part hydrophilic; the technical term for this is **amphipathic**.

Like triglycerides, **phospholipids** contain fatty acids bound to glycerol by ester linkages. In phospholipids, however, any one of several phosphate-containing compounds replaces the first or third fatty acid, giving phospholipids amphipathic properties (**Figure 3.23A**). The phosphate functional group has a negative electric charge, so this portion of the molecule is hydrophilic, attracting

Figure 3.23 Phospholipids (A) Phosphatidylcholine (lecithin) demonstrates the structure of a phospholipid molecule. In other phospholipids, the amino acid serine, the sugar alcohol inositol, or other compounds replace choline. (B) In an aqueous environment, hydrophobic interactions bring the "tails" of phospholipids together in the interior of a bilayer. The hydrophilic "heads" face outward on both sides of the bilayer, where they interact with the surrounding water molecules. (C) Phospholipids, in conjunction with specialized proteins, can form lipoproteins, which transport lipids such as cholesterol primarily in the blood.

polar water molecules. But the two fatty acids are hydrophobic, so they tend to avoid water and aggregate together or with other hydrophobic substances.

In an aqueous environment, phospholipids line up in such a way that the nonpolar, hydrophobic "tails" pack tightly together and the phosphate-containing "heads" face outward, where they interact with water. The phospholipids can form a **bilayer**: a sheet two molecules thick, with water excluded from the core (**Figure 3.23B**). Biological membranes have this kind of **phospholipid bilayer** structure, and we will devote Chapter 6 to their biological functions. In animals, phospholipids form single-layered spherical structures called **lipoproteins** that have hydrophilic exteriors and hydrophobic interiors (**Figure 3.23C**). The latter can bind to hydrophobic molecules such as cholesterol (see the next section) and transport it in the blood to various tissues in the body.

Some lipids have roles in energy conversion, regulation, and protection

In the paragraphs above we focused on triglycerides and phospholipids—lipids that are involved in energy storage and cell structure. However, there are other nonpolar and amphipathic lipids that have different structures and roles (**Figure 3.24**).

(A) Two carotenoids

β-Carotene

Carotenoids are composed of a repeating, branched five-carbon unit.

Vitamin A

(B) Two steroids

The core of a steroid typically contains 17 carbon atoms bonded in four "fused" rings.

Cholesterol

Estradiol

(C) A wax

A wax is a long-chain alcohol bound to a fatty acid.

Figure 3.24 More Lipids Because of their insolubility in water, carotenoids (**A**), steroids (**B**), and waxes (**C**) are classified as lipids.

Q: Why might it be dangerous for a person to eat meat from animals treated with steroid hormones?

CAROTENOIDS The carotenoids are a family of light-absorbing pigments found in plants and animals. Beta-carotene (β-carotene) is one of the pigments that traps light energy in leaves during photosynthesis. In humans, a molecule of β-carotene can be broken down into two vitamin A molecules. Vitamin A is used to make the pigment *cis*-retinal, which is required for vision. Carotenoids are responsible for the colors of carrots, tomatoes, pumpkins, egg yolks, and butter. The brilliant yellows and oranges of autumn leaves are also from carotenoids.

STEROIDS The steroids are a family of organic compounds whose multiple rings are linked through shared carbons. The steroid cholesterol is an important constituent of membranes, helping maintain membrane integrity (see Key Concept 6.1). Other steroids function as hormones: chemical signals that carry messages from one part of the body to another (see Chapter 40). Cholesterol is synthesized in the liver and is the starting material for making steroid hormones such as testosterone and estrogen.

WAXES Birds and mammals have glands in their skins that secrete waxy coatings onto their feathers or hair. These coatings repel water and help keep the hair and feathers pliable. The shiny leaves of plants such as holly, familiar during winter holidays, also have waxy coatings. Waxy coatings on plants can help them retain water and exclude pathogens. Bees make their honeycombs out of wax. Waxes are substances that are hydrophobic and plastic, or malleable, at room temperature. Each wax molecule consists of a saturated, long-chain fatty acid and a saturated, long-chain alcohol joined by an ester linkage. The result is a very long molecule with 40–60 CH_2 groups.

KEY CONCEPT

3.4 Recap and Assess

Lipids include both hydrophobic and amphipathic molecules that are largely composed of carbon and hydrogen. They are important in energy storage, light absorption, intercellular communication, and biological structures. A phospholipid is composed of two hydrophobic fatty acids linked to glycerol and a hydrophilic phosphate group. Cell membranes contain phospholipid bilayers.

1. If phospholipids were placed in a nonpolar solvent, would a membrane-type bilayer structure form? Explain your answer, using a diagram.

2. What is the difference between fats and oils?

3. Why are steroids classified as lipids?

In this chapter we discussed three of the classes of macromolecules that are characteristic of living organisms. All organisms are made up of these three types of macromolecules, a fact that shows the wonderful biochemical unity of life. This unity in turns implies that all life has a common origin (see Key Concept 1.1). Essential to this origin was a fourth class of macromolecule, the nucleic acids. In the next chapter we will turn to the related topics of nucleic acids and the origin of life.

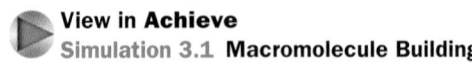 **View in Achieve**
Simulation 3.1 Macromolecule Building

▶Investigating**LIFE**

Q and A What are practical uses for spider silk?

Spider silk protein has many glycine and alanine residues, which are hydrophobic and cause the protein to fold into a fibrous shape. More than 1,000 individual polypeptide chains hydrogen-bond and hydrophobically interact with one another to form long silk fibers. The strength—the ability of silk to withstand forces tending to make it longer—and toughness—the ability of silk to resist breakage—are comparable to steel, and this has prompted engineers to propose human uses for spider silk. Using genetic engineering, biologists have been able to harvest composite silk fibers produced by silkworms in industrial quantities. Now that this composite silkworm–spider silk is available, numerous applications (functions related to structure) can be contemplated. For example, a recent study compared surgical sutures made from spider silk with widely used sutures made from synthetic fibers to hold together injured tendons.

The spider silk sutures were far superior, holding their strength over many cycles of tendon movement during healing. Another application on the horizon is bulletproof vests: the energy required to break a spider silk filament is at least 100 times greater than the energy of a typical bullet in impact.

Future directions

Perhaps the most widespread use for spider silk may be in textiles. By definition, textiles are flexible materials made of natural or artificial fibers (threads) that are woven together. The clothes you are wearing are textiles, perhaps made of cotton fibers (made up of cellulose) or polyester fibers (an artificial polymer) or a combination. Of course, silk fibers from silkworms have a long history in textiles, particularly in Asia. The addition of spider silk fibers, or combined spider–silkworm silk to existing textiles, holds great promise to increase the strength and in some cases the flexibility of textiles.

VISUAL SUMMARY 3

You should be able to relate each summary to the adjacent figures. If you go to this visual summary in **Achieve**, you can follow links to figures, animations, activities, and simulations that will help you consolidate the material.

KEY CONCEPT

3.1 Macromolecules Characterize Living Things

Go to **Activity 3.1** and **Animation 3.1**

- **Functional groups** have particular chemical properties that they confer on any larger molecule of which they are a part.

- **Macromolecules** are **polymers** constructed by the formation of covalent bonds between smaller molecules called **monomers**.

Questions

1. One of the most common chemical reactions in cells is phosphorylation, whereby a phosphate functional group is covalently added to an existing molecule. If the molecule is nonpolar, how will the addition of phosphate alter the molecule's properties?

2. Could hydrolysis reactions to break down a polymer occur in a nonpolar environment?

Figure 3.1

Functional group	Class of compounds and an example
Hydroxyl R — OH	**Alcohols** Ethanol
Aldehyde R — C(=O)H	**Aldehydes** Acetaldehyde

Figure 3.4

KEY CONCEPT

3.2 Proteins Are Polymers with Highly Variable Structures

Go to Activity 3.2

- **Peptide bonds** covalently link **amino acids** into **polypeptide chains**. These bonds form by condensation reactions between the carboxyl and amino groups.

- Proteins have four levels of structure that result in a three-dimensional macromolecule.

- The specific shape and structure of a protein allow it to bind noncovalently to other molecules.

Figure 3.7

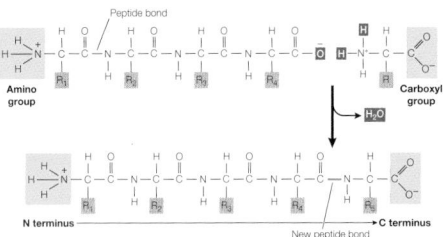

Questions

1. Is the tertiary structure of a protein determined by covalent bonding, noncovalent interactions, or both? Give examples, using specific amino acids.

2. Polypeptide chains are said to "grow in the N to C direction". Explain.

Figure 3.8

α Helix

KEY CONCEPT

3.3 Carbohydrates Are Made from Simple Sugars

Go to Activity 3.3

- **Carbohydrates** contain carbon bonded to hydrogen and oxygen atoms and have the general formula $(C_1H_2O_1)_n$.

- **Monosaccharides** are built into larger molecules by **glycosidic bonds**.

- **Starch**, **glycogen**, and **cellulose** are polymers used to store energy-rich molecules and to provide structure.

Figure 3.18

Questions

1. What is the difference between the isomers maltose and cellobiose?

2. Whole-grain wheat flour contains abundant starch and cellulose, while processed flour contains much less cellulose. Why is bread baked from whole-grain flour more fibrous?

Figure 3.19

Cellulose   Starch and glycogen

KEY CONCEPT

3.4 Lipids Are Defined by Their Insolubility in Water

Go to Simulation 3.1

- **Lipids** are hydrocarbons that are insoluble in water because of their many nonpolar covalent bonds. They play roles in energy storage, membrane structure, light harvesting, intercellular communication, and protection.

- A **triglyceride** is composed of three **fatty acids** covalently bonded to a molecule of **glycerol** by ester linkages.

- A **saturated fatty acid** has a hydrocarbon chain with no double bonds. These molecules can pack together tightly. The hydrocarbon chain of an **unsaturated fatty acid** has one or more double bonds that bend the chain, preventing close packing.

- A **phospholipid** has a hydrophobic hydrocarbon "tail" and a hydrophilic phosphate "head"; that is, it is **amphipathic**. In water, the interactions of the tails and heads of phospholipids generate a **phospholipid bilayer**. The heads are directed outward, where they interact with the surrounding water. The tails are packed together in the interior of the bilayer, away from water.

Questions

1. How are a triglyceride and a phospholipid similar and different?

2. Olive oil and vinegar (acetic acid) are both liquids. Why don't they mix in salad dressing?

Figure 3.21   Figure 3.22   Figure 3.23

Go to **Achieve** for the eBook, **LearningCurve**, animations, activities, simulations, and additional resources and assignments.

Nucleic Acids and the Origin of Life

4

KEY CONCEPTS

4.1 Nucleic Acids Are Informational Macromolecules

4.2 The Small Molecules of Life Originated on Primitive Earth

4.3 The Large Molecules of Life Originated from Small Molecules

4.4 Cells Originated from Their Molecular Building Blocks

NASA/JPL-Caltech/MSSS

Self-portrait of the Mars rover *Curiosity* on the Martian surface For reference, each wheel is 50 centimeters in diameter.

▶Investigating LIFE

Looking for Life

On Earth you can find organisms and the chemical signatures of life everywhere—even deep under the sea, inside volcanoes, buried in ice, and floating in the air. Determining life's origin is difficult because (with few exceptions) the simple organisms that first existed left no fossils. On Mars, however, things might be different.

Mars has fascinated scientists (and science-fiction writers) since its discovery by astronomers more than 3,000 years ago. A cold planet, Mars has a geology that has changed little over several billion years, and so any evidence of life may be preserved. As you know from Chapter 2, life as we know it has two distinctive chemical features. One is the presence of water, and the other is carbon-based chemistry.

Initial observations of Mars with telescopes showed polar caps that changed with the seasons and were proposed to be made of water ice, as well as markings on the Martian surface that looked like rivers to some imaginative observers on Earth. Better telescopes, chemical analyses based on light emission (spectroscopy), orbiting satellites, and landers controlled from Earth have confirmed water at the poles, although it is mixed

with CO_2. While the "rivers" seen in the nineteenth century are mostly geological features, twenty-first-century observations have provided evidence for stream and lake beds on the surface, indicating that water was once there. In addition, there is a large amount of water ice below the Martian surface. The high pressures there may be sufficient to support a small amount of liquid water.

What about carbon-based chemistry? The Martian atmosphere is more than 95% CO_2, much higher than the concentration in Earth's atmosphere. In addition, methane (CH_4) is in the Martian atmosphere, and fluctuates during the Martian solar year. While there are nonbiological explanations for methane and its fluctuation, there is a biological one as well—methane-producing bacteria are well established on Earth, and their activities vary with seasons. So far, no such bacteria have been found on or slightly below the Martian surface. But the search goes on.

 Can we find evidence of life on Mars?
(Find the answer on page 80.)

4.1 Nucleic Acids Are Informational Macromolecules

Learning Objectives

4.1.1 Compare the chemical structures of purines versus pyrimidines and DNA versus RNA.

4.1.2 Explain how biological information is encoded in DNA.

4.1.3 Identify cellular functions of nucleotides other than information processing.

DNA, a nucleic acid, is often used as a metaphor for the essence of something ("It's in her DNA"), and indeed, DNA contains life's genetic code. From medicine to evolution, from agriculture to forensics, the properties of nucleic acids affect our lives every day. It is with nucleic acids that the concept of "information" entered the biological vocabulary. Nucleic acids are uniquely capable of coding for and transmitting biological information.

The two groups of bases

Figure 4.1 Nucleotide Chemistry Nucleotide monomers, each consisting of a base, a sugar, and a phosphate group, are the building blocks of DNA and RNA polymers. The bases fall into two groups: the pyrimidines and the purines.

Q: What kinds of bonds link the base, sugar, and phosphate together?

 View in Achieve
Activity 4.1 **Nucleic Acid Building Blocks**

 View in Achieve
Animation 4.1 **Nucleic Acids**

Nucleic acids carry and express genetic information

Nucleic acids are polymers specialized for the storage, transmission, and use of genetic information. There are two types of nucleic acids—**DNA (deoxyribonucleic acid)** and **RNA (ribonucleic acid)**—and both are macromolecules, polymers of monomers called nucleotides. The roles of DNA and RNA in the preservation, replication, and expression of genetic material will be descried in later chapters. Here we focus on the chemistry of the nucleic acids, revealing how their structures reflect their functions.

A **nucleotide** has three components: a nitrogen-containing (**nitrogenous**) **base**, a pentose sugar, and one to three phosphate groups (**Figure 4.1**). Molecules consisting of a pentose sugar and a nitrogenous base—but no phosphate group—are called **nucleosides**. The nucleotides that make up nucleic acids contain just one phosphate group—they are nucleoside monophosphates. The bases of the nucleic acids take one of two chemical forms: a six-membered single-ring structure called a **pyrimidine**, or a fused double-ring structure called a **purine** (see Figure 4.1). In DNA, the pentose sugar is deoxyribose, which differs from the ribose found in RNA by the absence of one oxygen atom (see Figure 3.17).

A nucleic acid forms in a similar way that other macromolecule polymers (proteins and polysaccharides) form: by the addition of monomers, one at a time. The reaction, called a transesterification, is between the 3′ —OH on the sugar of the existing chain and the alpha (first) phosphate of the incoming nucleoside triphosphate. The resulting bond is called a **phosphodiester bond** (**Figure 4.2**). During the reaction, the terminal two phosphate groups, still covalently bonded, are released. Hydrolysis of this pyrophosphate to its two individual phosphates releases energy for the polymerization reaction. Because each nucleotide is added to the 3′ carbon of the last sugar, nucleic acids are said to *elongate in the 5′-to-3′ direction.*

Nucleic acids can range in polymer length. Oligonucleotides are relatively short, with about 20 nucleotide monomers, whereas polynucleotides can be much longer.

- Oligonucleotides include RNA molecules that function as "primers" to begin the duplication of DNA; RNA molecules that regulate the expression of genes; and synthetic DNA molecules used for amplifying and analyzing other, longer nucleotide sequences.

- Polynucleotides, more commonly referred to as nucleic acids, include DNA and some RNA. Polynucleotides can be very long, and indeed are the longest polymers in the living world. Some DNA molecules in plants and animals contain hundreds of millions of nucleotides.

Base pairing occurs in both DNA and RNA

DNA and RNA differ somewhat in their sugar groups, bases, and strand structure (**Table 4.1**). Four bases are found in DNA: adenine (**A**), cytosine (**C**), guanine (**G**), and thymine (**T**). RNA is also made up of four different monomers, but its nucleotides include uracil (**U**) instead of thymine.

A key to understanding the structure and function of nucleic acids is the principle of **complementary base pairing**. In DNA, thymine and adenine pair (T-A), and cytosine and guanine pair (C-G). In RNA, the base pairs are A-U and C-G (**Figure 4.3**). Base

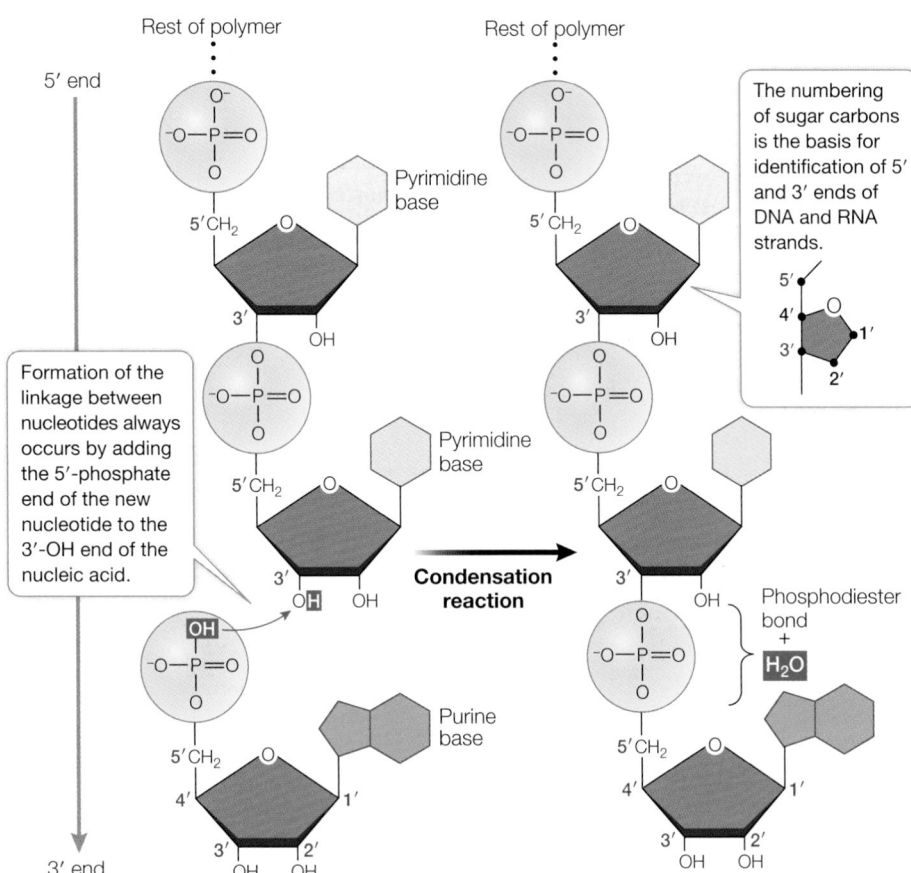

Rest of polymer

Rest of polymer

5′ end

3′ end

Formation of the linkage between nucleotides always occurs by adding the 5′-phosphate end of the new nucleotide to the 3′-OH end of the nucleic acid.

Pyrimidine base

Pyrimidine base

Purine base

Condensation reaction

Phosphodiester bond

$+$

H_2O

The numbering of sugar carbons is the basis for identification of 5′ and 3′ ends of DNA and RNA strands.

Figure 4.2 Linking Nucleotides Together
Growth of a nucleic acid (RNA in this figure) from its monomers occurs in the 5′ (phosphate) to 3′ (hydroxyl) direction. Note that the added nucleotide is not initially a monophosphate but actually a triphosphate. The details of this process will be described in Chapter 13.

pairs are held together primarily by hydrogen bonds. There are polar $C=O$ and $N-H$ covalent bonds in the bases; these can form hydrogen bonds between the δ^- on an oxygen or nitrogen of one base and the δ^+ on a hydrogen of another base when the atoms are in close proximity.

Individual hydrogen bonds are relatively weak, but there are so many of them in a DNA or RNA molecule that collectively they provide a considerable force of attraction, which can bind together two polynucleotide strands, or a single strand that folds back onto itself. This attraction is not as strong as a covalent bond, however. This means that individual base pairs can be broken with a modest input of energy. As you will see, the breaking and making of hydrogen bonds in nucleic acids is vital to their role in living systems.

RNA Even though RNA is generally single-stranded (**Figure 4.4A**), base pairing can occur between different regions of the molecule. Portions of the single-stranded RNA molecule can fold back and pair with one another (**Figure 4.4B**). Thus complementary hydrogen bonding between ribonucleotides plays an important role in determining the three-dimensional shapes of some RNA molecules. Complementary base pairing can also take place between ribonucleotides in RNA and deoxyribonucleotides in DNA. Adenine in an RNA strand can pair either with uracil (in another RNA strand) or with thymine (in a DNA strand). Similarly, an

There are two hydrogen bonds between the pyrimidine T and the purine A.

Thymine   T ⁞⁞⁞ A   **Adenine**

Hydrogen bond

There are three hydrogen bonds between the pyrimidine C and the purine G.

Cytosine   C ⁞⁞⁞⁞ G   **Guanine**

Figure 4.3 Base Pairing by Hydrogen Bonding between Nucleotides
T-A and C-G base pairs form because the bases fit together such that atoms forming hydrogen bonds are in close proximity.

TABLE **4.1**	Distinguishing RNA from DNA			
Nucleic acid	**Sugar**	**Bases**	**Name of nucleoside**	**Strands**
RNA	Ribose	Adenine	Adenosine	One
		Cytosine	Cytidine	
		Guanine	Guanosine	
		Uracil	Uridine	
DNA	Deoxyribose	Adenine	Deoxyadenosine	Two
		Cytosine	Deoxycytidine	
		Guanine	Deoxyguanosine	
		Thymine	Deoxythymidine	

(A) Single-stranded RNA

(B) Complementary base pairing in regions of a single RNA molecule

Folding of the linear molecule brings distant base sequences closer together.

Double-stranded segments form when sequences of RNA nucleotides pair with one another.

In RNA, the bases are attached to ribose. The bases in RNA are the purines adenine (A) and guanine (G) and the pyrimidines cytosine (C) and uracil (U).

Figure 4.4 RNA **(A)** RNA is usually a single strand. **(B)** When a single-stranded RNA folds back on itself, hydrogen bonds between complementary sequences can stabilize it into a three-dimensional shape with complex surface characteristics. The surfaces and exposed bases can be recognized by other molecules, such as proteins, that bind to the nucleic acid.

Q: What would happen if a folded RNA molecule were heated? Recall the effect of heat on hydrogen bonds.

adenine in DNA can pair either with thymine (in the complementary DNA strand) or with uracil (in RNA).

DNA Usually, DNA is double-stranded; that is, it consists of two separate polynucleotide strands of the same length that are held together by hydrogen bonds between base pairs (**Figure 4.5A**). In contrast to RNA's diversity in three-dimensional structure, DNA is remarkably uniform. The A-T and G-C base pairs are about the same size (each is a purine paired with a pyrimidine), and the two polynucleotide strands form a "ladder" that twists into a double helix (**Figure 4.5B**). The sugar–phosphate groups form the sides of the ladder, and the bases with their hydrogen bonds form the "rungs" on the inside. DNA carries genetic information in its sequence of base pairs rather than in its three-dimensional structure. The key differences among DNA molecules are their different nucleotide base sequences.

Connect the Concepts As explained in Key Concept 13.2, the two strands of a DNA molecule fit together because they run in opposite directions—that is, they are antiparallel to one another. Equal distance between strands is maintained because a purine on one strand is always found opposite a pyrimidine on the other strand.

 View in Achieve
Activity 4.2 DNA Structure

DNA carries information and is expressed through RNA

DNA is an informational macromolecule. The information is encoded in the sequence of bases carried in its strands. For example, the information encoded in a DNA strand with the base sequence TCAGCA is different from the information in the sequence CCAGCA. DNA transmits information in two ways:

1. DNA can be reproduced exactly. This process, called **DNA replication**, is done by polymerization using an existing strand as a base-pairing template.

2. Certain DNA sequences can be copied into RNA, in a process called **transcription**. The nucleotide sequence in the RNA can then be used to specify a sequence of amino acids in a polypeptide chain, in the process called **translation** (**Figure 4.6**). The overall process of transcription and translation is called **gene expression**.

The details of these important processes will be described in later chapters, but it is important to realize two things at this point:

1. *DNA replication and transcription depend on the base-pairing properties of nucleic acids.* Recall that the hydrogen-bonded base pairs are A-T and G-C in DNA and A-U and G-C in RNA. Consider, for example, this double-stranded DNA region:

$$5'\text{-TCAGCA-}3'$$
$$3'\text{-AGTCGT-}5'$$

Transcription of the lower strand will result in a single strand of RNA with the sequence 5'-UCAGCA-3'. Can you figure out the sequence that the top strand would produce?

2. *The entire DNA molecule is replicated.* Since DNA contains essential information, it must be replicated completely and accurately so that each new cell or new organism receives a complete set of DNA from its parent (**Figure 4.7A**). The complete set of DNA in a living organism is called its **genome**. However, not all of the information in the genome is needed at all times and in all tissues, and only small sections of the DNA are transcribed into RNA molecules (**Figure 4.7B**). The sequences of DNA that are transcribed into RNA are called **genes**.

In humans, the gene that encodes the major protein in hair (keratin) is expressed in skin cells that produce hair. The genetic information in the keratin-encoding gene is transcribed into RNA and then translated into a keratin polypeptide. In other tissues such as the muscles, the keratin gene is not transcribed, but other genes are—for example, the genes that encode proteins present in muscles but not in skin or hair. The expressions of these genes are turned on and off by elegant controls, described in Chapter 16.

(A) A linear view of double-stranded DNA　　　**(B) The DNA double helix**

In DNA, the bases are attached to deoxyribose, and the base thymine (T) is found instead of uracil. Hydrogen bonds between purines and pyrimidines hold the two strands of DNA together.

Figure 4.5 DNA (A) DNA usually consists of two strands running in opposite directions that are held together by hydrogen bonds between purines and pyrimidines on the two strands. (B) The two strands in DNA are coiled in a right-handed double helix.

Q: For replication or transcription, DNA must "unwind" to expose bases. What bonds must be broken for this to occur?

than they are to those of your great-grandparents. And on a more general level, your DNA sequences are more closely related to those of other primates than to those of fruit flies. (But yes, you do have sequences in common with fruit flies!) The details of how scientists use DNA sequence information to trace evolutionary relationships will be covered in Chapter 20.

DNA sequencing and analysis of sequences by computer programs have enabled scientists to determine the entire DNA base sequences—the genome—of many organisms, including humans, whose genome contains about 3 billion base pairs. These studies have confirmed many of the evolutionary relationships that had been inferred previously from more traditional comparisons of body structure, biochemistry, and physiology. Increasingly, scientists turn to DNA analyses to elucidate evolutionary relationships when other comparisons are not possible or are not conclusive. For example, DNA studies revealed a close relationship between starlings and mockingbirds that was not expected on the basis of their anatomy or behavior.

The DNA base sequence reveals evolutionary relationships

DNA carries hereditary information from one generation to the next, accumulating changes in its base sequence over long periods of time. A series of DNA molecules stretches back through the lineage of every organism to the beginning of biological evolution on Earth, more than 3.5 billion years ago. Therefore closely related living species have more similar base sequences than do species that are more distantly related. For example, your DNA base sequences are more similar to those of your biological parents

Figure 4.6 DNA, RNA, and Protein Replication, transcription, and translation describe the manner in which genetic information is used and together have been called the "central dogma of molecular biology": the premise that information flows from DNA to RNA to polypeptide (protein).

Figure 4.7 DNA Replication and Transcription DNA is usually completely replicated (**A**) but only partially transcribed (**B**). RNA transcripts are produced from genes that code for specific proteins. Transcription of different genes occurs at different times and, in multicellular organisms, in different cells of the body.

Q: What do you think determines whether a particular cell transcribes a sequence of DNA into RNA?

Nucleotides have other important roles

Nucleotides are more than just the building blocks of nucleic acids. As we will describe in later chapters, there are several nucleotides (or modified nucleotides) with other functions:

- ATP (adenosine triphosphate) acts as an agent of energy transfer in many biochemical reactions (see Key Concept 8.2).

- GTP (guanosine triphosphate) serves as an energy source, especially in protein synthesis. It also plays a role in the transfer of information from the environment to cells (see Key Concept 7.2).

- cAMP (cyclic adenosine monophosphate) is a special nucleotide with an additional bond between the sugar and the phosphate group. It is essential in many processes, including the actions of hormones and the transmission of information by the nervous system (see Key Concept 7.3).

- Nucleotides play roles as carriers in the synthesis and breakdown of carbohydrates and lipids (see Key Concept 9.1).

KEY CONCEPT
4.1 Recap and Assess

The nucleic acids DNA and RNA are polymers made up of nucleotide monomers. The sequence of nucleotides in DNA carries the information that is used by RNA to specify the sequence of amino acids in a protein. The genetic information in DNA is passed from generation to generation in cells and can be used to understand evolutionary relationships.

1. What are the key differences between purines and pyrimidines, and how does this relate to the structure of DNA?

2. How can DNA molecules be very diverse, even though they appear to be structurally similar?

3. Single-stranded nucleic acids about 25 bases long are called aptamers. Because many sequences are possible, particular aptamers can be used to bind to specific targets, either as drugs to a protein target or for quantitating a small molecule in tissues or fluids. How can aptamers have such diversity and specificity for binding?

We have seen that the nucleic acids RNA and DNA carry the blueprint of life, and that the inheritance of these macromolecules reaches back to the beginning of evolutionary time. But when, where, and how did nucleic acids arise on Earth? How did the building blocks of life, such as amino acids and sugars, originally arise?

KEY CONCEPT
4.2 The Small Molecules of Life Originated on Primitive Earth

Learning Objectives

4.2.1 Explain how Redi's and Pasteur's experiments disproved spontaneous generation.

4.2.2 Describe conditions on early Earth and theories about how these conditions affected the origin of life on Earth.

4.2.3 Justify the conditions used by Miller and Urey in their experiments.

You learned in Chapter 2 that living things are composed of the same elements as the inanimate universe (e.g., C, H, O, P, N, and S). But in proteins, carbohydrates, and nucleic acids, for instance, the arrangements of these atoms into molecules are unique in biological systems. You don't find DNA in rocks. Two possibilities for these new arrangements of atoms from inanimate nature are that they happen repeatedly, or that they happened only once and all life has come from life since then.

Living organisms do not repeatedly come from inanimate nature

We can't know for certain how life on Earth began. But one thing is sure: life (or at least life as we know it) is not constantly being restarted. That is, **spontaneous generation** of life from inanimate nature is not happening repeatedly before our eyes. Now and in the past, all life has come from life that existed before. But people, including scientists, did not always believe this. The ancient Greek philosopher Aristotle, who had great influence on scientific thinking for more than a millennium, proposed that insects came from "putrifying earth." In Shakespeare's play *Antony and Cleopatra*, a Roman states that "Your Serpent of Egypt, is bred now of your mud by the operation of your sun: so is your crocodile." Scientists in the seventeenth century wrote that mice arose from sweaty clothes placed in dim light and that rotting meat produced flies.

One scientist who doubted these assumptions was the Italian physician and poet Francesco Redi. Redi hypothesized that flies arose not by some mysterious transformation of decaying meat, but from other flies that laid their eggs on the meat. In 1668, Redi performed a scientific experiment—a relatively new concept at the time—to test his hypothesis (**Figure 4.8**). His finding that maggots could occur only where flies had been present laid to rest the idea that a complex organism such as a fly could appear spontaneously from a nonliving substance in the meat, or from "something in the air." Well, perhaps not quite laid to rest.

In the 1660s, the newly invented microscope revealed a vast biological world that had never been seen before. Virtually every environment on Earth was found to be teeming with tiny organisms. Some scientists believed these organisms arose spontaneously from their rich chemical environment, by the action of a "life force." But experiments in the nineteenth century by the great French scientist Louis Pasteur showed that microorganisms can arise only from other microorganisms, and that an environment without life remains lifeless (**Figure 4.9**).

Pasteur's and Redi's experiments showed that living organisms cannot arise from nonliving materials under the conditions that exist on Earth now. But their experiments did not prove that spontaneous generation never occurred. Eons ago, conditions on Earth and in the atmosphere above it were vastly different than they are today. Indeed, conditions similar to those found on primitive Earth may have existed, or may exist now, on other bodies in our solar system and elsewhere.

 View in Achieve
Animation 4.2 Pasteur's Experiment

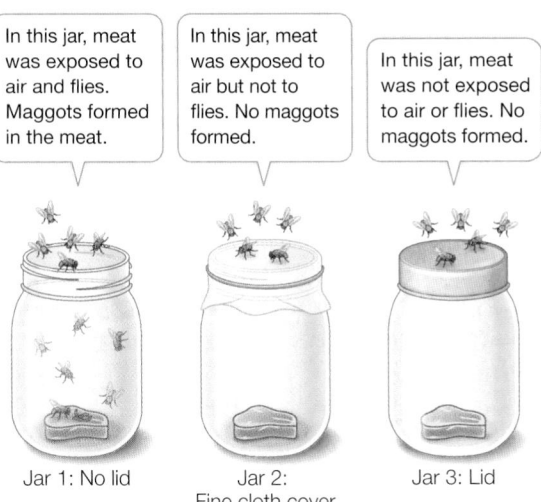

In this jar, meat was exposed to air and flies. Maggots formed in the meat.

In this jar, meat was exposed to air but not to flies. No maggots formed.

In this jar, meat was not exposed to air or flies. No maggots formed.

Jar 1: No lid

Jar 2: Fine cloth cover

Jar 3: Lid

Figure 4.8 Disproving Spontaneous Generation: Redi's Experiment   By showing that maggots came from flies and not air, Francesco Redi disproved spontaneous generation of life.

Life began in water

As we emphasized in Chapter 2, water is an essential component of life as we know it. This is why there was great excitement when remotely controlled spacecraft sent from Earth detected water ice on Mars. Astronomers believe our solar system began forming about 4.6 billion years ago, when a cloud of space gas and dust was disturbed, possibly by a shock wave from an exploding star. The gas and dust collapsed on themselves to form the Sun. But the gas was rotating, and some of it more distant from the Sun formed a disc. Material on the disc cooled and formed rocks called planetesimals. These planetesimals collided with one another to form the inner planets, including Earth and Mars. The first chemical signatures indicating the presence of life on Earth are about 4 billion years old. So it took 600 million years for the chemical conditions on Earth to become just right for life. Key among those conditions was the presence of water.

Ancient Earth probably had a lot of water vapor in its atmosphere. Where did the water come from? One view is that comets (loose agglomerations of dust and ice that have orbited the Sun since the planets formed) struck Earth, bringing not only water but also other chemical components of life, such as nitrogen and carbon-containing molecules. The hot planetary surface evaporated any water that arrived. But over time, this atmospheric water vapor condensed as rain on a cooler planet, and lakes and oceans were formed.

As Earth cooled, chemicals from the rocks dissolved in the water, and simple chemical reactions would have taken place. Some of these reactions might have led to life, but impacts by large comets and rocky meteorites released enough energy to heat the developing oceans almost to boiling, thus destroying any early life that might have existed. On Earth, these large impacts eventually subsided, and about 3.8 billion years ago life gained a foothold. There has been life on Earth ever since.

Several models have been proposed to explain the origin of life on Earth. The next sections will discuss two alternative theories:

Experiment

Figure 4.9 Disproving Spontaneous Generation: Pasteur's Experiment

Source: Pasteur gave a talk on his research at the Sorbonne Scientific Soirée on April 7, 1864. This talk has been translated into English: rc.usf.edu/~levineat/pasteur.pdf.

Previous experiments disproving the spontaneous generation of larger organisms were called into question when microorganisms were discovered. Louis Pasteur's classic experiment disproved the spontaneous generation of microorganisms.

HYPOTHESIS▶ Microorganisms come only from other microorganisms and cannot arise by spontaneous generation.

METHOD▶

1 Create flasks of nutrient medium with "swan" necks that are open to air but exclude microorganism-bearing dust particles.

Control

Experimental

2 Boil to kill all microorganisms in the nutrient medium.

3 Break the swan neck off one flask, exposing the contents to microorganisms in dust.

Dust

Dust

Dust settles in the bend.

RESULTS▶ Microbial life grows only in the flasks exposed to microorganisms. There is no "spontaneous generation" of life in the sterile flask.

Microbial life grows in the flask exposed to microbes.

No microbial growth occurs in the "sterile" (lifeless) flask.

CONCLUSION▶ Living organisms arise from preexisting living organisms.

that life arose on Earth through chemical evolution, or that life came from outside Earth.

Prebiotic synthesis experiments model early Earth

One theory for the origin of life on Earth, **chemical evolution**, holds that conditions on primitive Earth led to the formation of simple molecules such as the monomers of proteins, carbohydrates, and nucleic acids (see Key Concept 3.1), and that these molecules led to the formation of life forms. Scientists have sought to reconstruct those primitive conditions, both physically (by varying temperature) and chemically (by re-creating the mixes of elements that may have been present).

HOT CHEMISTRY   Earth's early atmosphere came mostly from erupting volcanoes. Even today, the gases released from volcanoes are consistent: mostly H_2O vapor, with much smaller amounts of other gases. Most notably, there is no O_2 released from volcanoes, and scientists believe that it wasn't until the emergence of photosynthetic life that O_2 began to accumulate in the atmosphere. In the 1950s Stanley Miller and Harold Urey at the University of Chicago set up an experimental "atmosphere" containing the gases they thought were present in Earth's early atmosphere: hydrogen gas, ammonia, methane gas, and water vapor. They passed an electrical spark through these gases to simulate lightning, a source of energy to drive chemical reactions. Then they cooled the system so the gases would condense and collect in a watery solution, or "ocean" (**Figure 4.10**). After a week of continuous operation, the system contained numerous organic molecules, including a variety of amino acids—the building blocks of proteins.

 View in Achieve
Animation 4.3 Synthesis of Prebiotic Molecules

COLD CHEMISTRY   Stanley Miller also performed a long-term experiment in which the electrical spark was not used. In 1972 he filled test tubes with ammonia gas, water vapor, and cyanide (HCN), another molecule that is thought to have formed on primitive Earth. After checking that there were no contaminating substances or organisms that might confound the results, he sealed the tubes and cooled them to –78°C, the temperature of the ice that covers Europa, one of Jupiter's moons. Opening the tubes 27 years later, Miller found amino acids and nucleotide bases. Apparently, pockets of liquid water within the ice had allowed high concentrations of the starting materials to accumulate, thereby speeding up chemical reactions. The important conclusion is that the cold water within ice on ancient Earth may have provided environments for the prebiotic synthesis of molecules required for the subsequent formation of simple living systems.

The results of these experiments were profoundly important in giving weight to speculations about the chemical origin of life on Earth and elsewhere in the universe. Decades of experimental work and critical evaluation followed Miller and Urey's original experiments. In science, an experiment and its results must be repeatable and be reinterpreted and refined as more knowledge

Experiment

Figure 4.10 Modeling the Formation of Biological Molecules from Chemicals Present in Earth's Early Atmosphere

Original Papers: S. L. Miller. 1953. A production of amino acids under possible primitive earth conditions. *Science* 117: 528–529.

S. L. Miller and H. C. Urey. 1959. Organic compound synthesis on the primitive earth. *Science* 130: 245–251.

With an increased understanding of the atmospheric conditions that existed on primitive Earth, the researchers devised an experiment to see if these conditions could lead to the formation of organic molecules.

HYPOTHESIS▶ Organic chemical compounds can be generated under conditions similar to those that existed in the atmosphere of primitive Earth.

METHOD▶

H_2O

2 Electrical sparks simulating lightning provide energy for synthesis of new compounds.

"Atmospheric" compartment

NH_3 CH_4 H_2

1 Heat a solution of simple chemicals to produce an "atmosphere" of methane, ammonia, hydrogen, and water vapor.

← Cold water

3 A condenser cools the "atmospheric" gases in a "rain" containing new compounds. The compounds collect in an "ocean."

"Oceanic" compartment

Condensation

Heat

4 Collect and analyze the condensed liquid.

RESULTS▶

Reactions in the condensed liquid eventually formed organic chemical compounds, including amino acids.

CONCLUSION▶ The chemical building blocks of life could have been generated in the probable atmosphere of early Earth.

accumulates. For example, ideas about Earth's original atmosphere have changed. Volcanic gases now are known to include carbon dioxide (CO_2), nitrogen (N_2), hydrogen sulfide (H_2S), and sulfur dioxide (SO_2). Experiments using these gases in addition to the ones in the original Miller–Urey experiment have produced a more diverse list of organic products:

- All five bases present in DNA and RNA (i.e., A, T, C, G, and U)
- All of the 20 amino acids used in protein synthesis
- Many three- to six-carbon sugars, including ribose
- Certain fatty acids and glycerol phosphate, a lipid precursor
- Vitamin B_6 (pantothenic acid, a component of coenzyme A)
- Nicotinamide (part of NAD, which is involved in energy metabolism)
- Carboxylic acids such as succinic and lactic acids (also involved in energy metabolism)

Life may have come from outside Earth

In 1969 a remarkable event led to the discovery that a meteorite from space carried molecules that are characteristic of life on Earth. On September 28 of that year, fragments of a meteorite fell around the town of Murchison, Australia. Using gloves to avoid Earth-derived contamination, scientists immediately shaved off tiny pieces of the rock, put them in test tubes, and extracted them in water (**Figure 4.11**). They found several of the molecules that are unique to life, including purines, pyrimidines, sugars, and ten amino acids.

 Media Clip 4.1 DNA Building Blocks from Space
Life12e.com/mc4.1

Were these molecules truly brought from space as part of the meteorite, or did they get there after the rock landed on Earth? There are several reasons to believe the molecules were not Earthly contaminants:

- The scientists took great care to avoid contamination. They used gloves and sterile instruments, took pieces from below the rock's surface, and did their work very soon after the meteorite landed (they hoped before organisms from Earth could contaminate the samples).
- Amino acids in most living organisms on Earth are L-amino acids; that is, the amino acids of living things are found in only one of the two possible optical isomeric forms (see Figure 3.2). The amino acids in the meteorite, however, were a mixture of L- and D-isomers, with a slight majority of the L form. Thus the amino acids in the meteorite were not likely to have come from a living organism on Earth.
- In the story that opened Chapter 2, we described how the ratio of isotopes in a living organism reflects the ratio of the same isotopes in the environment where the organism lives. The isotope ratios for carbon and hydrogen in the sugars from the meteorite were different from the ratios of those elements found on Earth.

More than 90 meteorites from Mars have been recovered on Earth. Many show signs of water—for example, in minerals such as carbonates that are precipitated from aqueous solution. Some also contain organic molecules that are the chemical signatures of life. While the presence of such molecules suggests that these rocks once harbored life, it does not prove that there were living organisms in the rocks when they landed on Earth. You may find it hard to believe

Courtesy of the Argonne National Laboratory

Figure 4.11 The Murchison Meteorite Pieces from a fragment of the meteorite that landed in Australia in 1969 were put into test tubes with water. Soluble molecules present in the rock—including amino acids, nucleotide bases, and sugars—dissolved in the water.

that a living organism could survive thousands of years of traveling through space encased in a meteorite, followed by intense heat as the meteorite passed through Earth's atmosphere. But there is evidence that the heat at the centers of some meteorites may not have been extreme. If this were the case, then a long interplanetary trip by living organisms might have been possible.

Life does not have to reach Earth from space to prove it exists elsewhere. There is an ongoing search for life in celestial bodies. For example, as mentioned in the opening story of this chapter, both orbiting satellites and vehicles probing the landscape of Mars search for conditions suitable for present or past life on Mars. Perhaps the most dramatic attempt to discover life on Mars came in 1976, when NASA landed two stationary probes, or landers, called *Viking 1* and *Viking 2* on the planet. **Investigating Life: Can We Find Evidence of Life on Mars?** describes how scientists on Earth directed onboard instruments to evaluate soil on Mars for signs of life. As noted in the opening story of this chapter, other landers have followed, with similar missions.

KEY CONCEPT
4.2 Recap and Assess

Life does not arise repeatedly through spontaneous generation but comes from preexisting life. Water is an essential ingredient for the emergence of life. Chemical synthesis experiments provide support for the idea that life's simple molecules formed in the prebiotic environment on Earth. Meteorites that have landed on Earth provide some evidence for an extraterrestrial origin of life, as do experiments with landers on Mars showing possible chemical interconversions that may reflect life.

1. What conditions existing on Earth today might preclude the origin of life from the prebiotic molecules Miller and Urey used?

2. The interpretation of Pasteur's experiment (see Figure 4.9) depended on the inactivation of microorganisms by heat. We now know of microorganisms that can survive extremely high temperatures (see Chapter 24). Does this change the interpretation of Pasteur's experiment? What experiments would you do to inactivate such microbes?

(Continued on page 77)

▶Investigating LIFE   Can We Find Evidence of Life on Mars?

Experiment

Original Papers: G. V. Levin and O. Straat. 1976. Viking labeled release biology experiment: Interim results. *Science* 194: 1322–1329.

C. Ponnamperuma et al. 1977. Possible surface reactions on Mars: Implications for Viking biology results. *Science* 197: 455–457.

The Viking landers on Mars scooped up some of the soil and tested it for chemical interconversions consistent with life. Gilbert Levin and colleagues designed experiments to show remotely, at a distance of millions of miles, that there could be life on Mars at the present time.

HYPOTHESIS▶ Martian soil can be tested by a probe on Mars to show chemical changes consistent with life.

METHOD▶

1 Send Viking landers to Mars.

2 Landers scoop up Martian soil.

Courtesy of NASA/JPL-Caltech/ University of Arizona

Courtesy of NASA/JPL- Caltech/University of Arizona

Broth of radioactive nutrients

Radioactivity detector

3 In sealed containers add radioactive nutrients to Martian soil.

Martian soil

4 After 4 days, record levels of radioactive gases.

RESULTS▶

Radioactive gas detected (counts per minute) after 4 Martian days

Control (no soil)	Martian sample 1	Martian sample 2
500	9,500	12,000

CONCLUSION▶ Martian soil shows chemical changes consistent with life.

Work with the Data

While it's challenging to design experiments in the lab here on Earth, imagine the challenge of designing experiments done remotely on Mars! A team of biologists and chemists led by Levin and Straat sent instruments to Mars to test for the presence of life by measuring the emission of gases after nutrients were supplied to soils possibly containing Martian organisms. A scoop was used to obtain a 0.2-mL sample of soil, which was then placed in a sealed container. The mixture was warmed to about 18°C (much higher than the surrounding Martian environment). Radioactive nutrients (formate, glycolate, glycine, alanine, and lactate) with their carbon atoms labeled in ^{14}C were added. At intervals after nutrient injection, a radioactive detector was employed to test for the release of ^{14}C radioactive gases.

QUESTIONS▶

1. **Table A** shows data from two of the experiments. Plot the data as ^{14}C radioactive gas versus Martian days after nutrient addition. What can you conclude? Laboratory experiments prior to the two Viking departures showed that the total radioactivity that could be released if all of the nutrients were completely converted to gases was 257,000 counts per minute (cpm). Calculate the fraction of this that appeared in the Martian sample and comment on the result.

2. Table A shows data from Martian soil that had been heated for 3 h at 160°C before nutrient addition. Plot these data on the same graph you made for Question 1. What types of molecules are destroyed by heat, and how does this occur? How do these data affect your conclusions from Question 1?

3. Back on Earth, Ponnamperuma and colleagues simulated Martian soil by using a major component of Martian soil called hematite (Fe_2O_3) and added the nutrients in the same way as had been done in the Mars experiment. Their results, including a preheated experiment, are shown in **Table B**. How do these results affect the conclusions you drew after considering Questions 1 and 2?

Table A

Time (days)	^{14}C Gases Detected (counts per minute)		
	Experiment 1	**Experiment 2**	**Preheated soil**
INITIAL	185	1,100	655
0.2	3,000	5,500	540
0.5	4,800	7,200	500
1.0	6,200	9,500	525
2.0	7,000	11,300	590
3.0	7,600	11,800	610
4.0	8,000	12,000	620

Table B

	^{14}C Gases Detected (counts per minute)	
	Hematite + ^{14}C nutrients	**Hematite without nutrients**
Experiment	10,140	207
Preheated 160°C	308	107

Go to Achieve for a companion Data in Depth exercise.

(4.2 Recap and Assess continued)

3. The Miller–Urey experiment (see Figure 4.10) showed that it was possible for amino acids to be formed from gases that were hypothesized to have been in Earth's early atmosphere. These amino acids were dissolved in water. Knowing what you do about the polymerization of amino acids into proteins (see Figure 3.7), how would you set up an experiment to show that proteins can form under the conditions of early Earth?

Chemistry experiments modeling the conditions of ancient Earth provide clues about the origins of the monomers (such as amino acids) that make up the polymers (such as proteins) that characterize life. How did these polymers develop?

KEY CONCEPT 4.3 The Large Molecules of Life Originated from Small Molecules

Learning Objectives

4.3.1 Justify the need for catalysts in the origin of life.

4.3.2 Describe the proposed role for RNA in the formation of long-chain polymers.

4.3.3 Provide evidence supporting RNA as a catalyst in prebiotic chemical reactions that gave rise to other biological polymers.

The Miller–Urey experiment and others that followed provide a plausible scenario for the formation of the building blocks of life under conditions that prevailed on primitive Earth. The next step in forming and supporting a general theory on the origin of life would be an explanation for how polymers formed from these monomers.

Complex molecules could be formed from simpler ones on primitive Earth

Scientists have used numerous model systems to try to simulate conditions under which the first biological polymers might have been made. Each of these systems is based on several observations and speculations:

- Solid mineral surfaces, such as powderlike clays, have large surface areas. Scientists speculate that the silicates in clay may have catalyzed (sped up) the condensation reactions that resulted in organic polymers.

- Hydrothermal vents deep in the ocean, where hot water emerges from beneath Earth's crust, lack oxygen gas and contain metals such as iron and nickel. In laboratory experiments, these metals have been shown to catalyze the polymerization of amino acids in the absence of oxygen.

- In hot pools at the edges of oceans, evaporation may have concentrated monomers to the point where polymerization was favored (the "primordial soup" hypothesis).

In whatever ways the earliest stages of chemical evolution occurred, they resulted in the emergence of monomers and polymers that have probably remained unchanged in their general structures and functions for several billion years.

RNA may have been the first biological catalyst

A hallmark of life is change, particularly change induced by chemical reactions. You have already read about chemical changes in this and other chapters: for example, condensation and hydrolysis involving biological macromolecules, and DNA replication and transcription. As you will see in Chapter 8, some of these chemical changes can occur spontaneously in aqueous solutions like those that exist in biological systems, but most would occur extremely slowly. Catalysts—molecules that speed up biochemical conversions—solve this problem. So a key to the origin of life is the appearance of catalysts.

Today the main catalysts in organisms are proteins called enzymes. The many shapes of proteins allow them to bind to diverse substances in solution and speed up chemical reactions. But we know that proteins are made based on information in nucleic acids. So we have a chicken-or-egg problem: If proteins are needed for life, nucleic acids must have appeared first, so that the proteins could be made. But if nucleic acids appeared before proteins, proteins could not have been the first catalysts. Could nucleic acids be catalysts, in addition to their role as blueprints for protein synthesis? The answer is yes.

As in a protein, the three-dimensional structure of a folded RNA molecule presents a unique surface to the external environment (see Figure 4.4). The surfaces of RNA molecules can be every bit as specific as those of proteins. The three-dimensional shapes and other chemical properties of certain RNA molecules allow them to function as catalysts. Catalytic RNAs, called **ribozymes**, can speed up reactions involving their own nucleotides as well as other cellular substances. Given that RNA can be both informational (in its nucleotide sequence) and catalytic (because of its ability to form unique three-dimensional shapes), it has been hypothesized that early life consisted of an "RNA world"—a world before DNA. It is thought that when RNA was first made, it could have acted as a catalyst for its own replication as well as for the synthesis of proteins. DNA could eventually have evolved from RNA (**Figure 4.12**). Several lines of evidence support this scenario:

- Ribose, the sugar that is part of RNA nucleotides (see Figure 4.1), can be formed in prebiotic chemical synthesis experiments (see Key Concept 4.2). Ribose is the precursor to deoxyribose, the sugar in DNA.

- In living organisms today, the formation of peptide bonds between amino acids (see Figure 3.7) is catalyzed by ribozymes.

- In certain viruses called retroviruses, there is an enzyme called reverse transcriptase that catalyzes the synthesis of DNA from RNA.

- When a short, naturally occurring RNA molecule is added to a mixture of nucleotides, RNA polymers are formed at a rate 7 million times greater than in the formation of polymers without the added RNA. This indicates that the added RNA is a catalyst, not just a template.

- An artificial ribozyme has been developed that can catalyze the assembly of short RNAs into a longer molecule that is an exact copy of itself. This may be how nucleic acid replication evolved.

1 Ribose, nucleotide bases, and phosphate come together to form RNA.

2 Some RNA molecules gain the ability to replicate.

3 RNA molecules begin to make catalytic proteins.

Protein

4 Catalytic proteins increase the efficiency of RNA replication and protein synthesis. They also aid the formation of double-stranded RNA, which then evolves into double-stranded DNA.

DNA   RNA   RNA   Protein

5 DNA becomes the primary molecule for information storage. DNA uses RNA to make proteins, which in turn help with DNA replication and transcription.

DNA   RNA   Protein

Figure 4.12 The "RNA World" Hypothesis This view postulates that in a world before DNA, RNA alone was both the blueprint for protein synthesis and a catalyst for its own replication. Eventually, the information storage molecules of DNA could have evolved from RNA.

Q: Ribose sugar was made in the Miller–Urey hot chemistry experiment. Why is this important for the "RNA world" hypothesis?

KEY CONCEPT
4.3 Recap and Assess

The formation of the large polymers that are characteristic of life may have occurred on the surfaces of clay particles, near hydrothermal vents, or in hot pools at the edges of oceans. RNA may have been the first genetic material and catalyst.

1. Why was the ability to both encode information and catalyze reactions important for the origin of life?

2. Why was the discovery of ribozymes important for the development of the "RNA world" hypothesis?

3. In living organisms, the catalyst for the formation of the peptide bond is an RNA that does not have an informational role. How does this relate to the "RNA world" hypothesis?

The discovery of mechanisms for the formation of small and large molecules is essential to answering questions about the origin of life on Earth. But we also need to understand how organized living systems formed. Such systems display the characteristic properties of life, including reproduction, energy processing, and responsiveness to the environment. These are properties of cells, whose origin we will explore in the next key concept.

KEY CONCEPT
4.4 Cells Originated from Their Molecular Building Blocks

Learning Objectives

4.4.1 Justify the reasoning behind the hypothesis that a membrane was critical in the evolution of life on Earth.

4.4.2 Describe the evidence suggesting that microfossils may be the remains of early cells.

Biochemical reactions are organized and do not occur in dilute solutions with the molecular participants far apart. In order for living systems to form, there had to be a compartment of some sort that brought together and concentrated the substances involved. Initially, this compartment may have simply been a tiny droplet of water on the surface of a rock, but this would have been unstable. The evolution of the cell membrane provided a stable system.

Life as we know it is separated from the environment within structurally defined units called **cells**. The internal contents of a cell are separated from the nonbiological environment by a special barrier—a **membrane**. The membrane is not just a barrier; it regulates what goes into and out of the cell, as we will describe in Chapter 6. This role of the surface membrane is very important because it permits the interior of the cell to maintain a chemical composition that is different from that of its external environment.

How did the first cells with membranes come into existence?

Jack Szostak and his colleagues at Harvard University built a laboratory model that gives insights into the origin of cells. To do this, they first put fatty acids (which can be made in prebiotic experiments) into water. Recall from Chapter 3 that fatty acids are amphipathic: they have a hydrophilic polar head and a long, nonpolar tail that is hydrophobic (see Figure 3.23). When placed in water, fatty acids will arrange themselves in a round "huddle" much like a football team: the hydrophilic heads point outward to interact with the aqueous environment, and the fatty acid tails point inward, away from the water molecules.

What if some water becomes trapped in the interior of this "huddle"? Now the layer of hydrophobic fatty acid tails is in water, which is an unstable situation. To stabilize this structure, a second layer of fatty acids forms. This **lipid bilayer** has the polar heads of the fatty acids facing both outward and inward, because they are attracted to the polar water molecules present on each side of the double layer. The nonpolar tails form the interior of the bilayer

(A) Hypothetical formation of a protocell

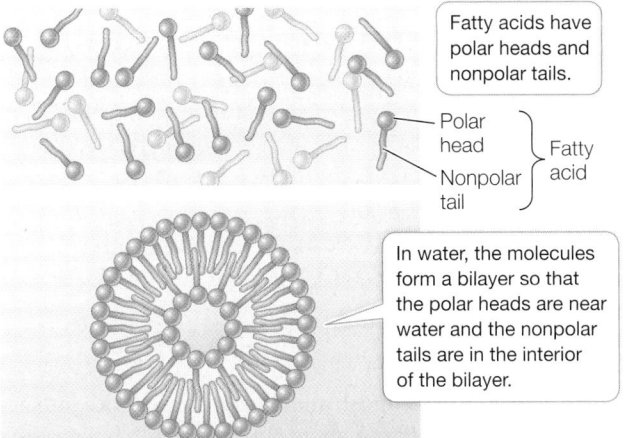

Fatty acids have polar heads and nonpolar tails.

Polar head
Nonpolar tail
} Fatty acid

In water, the molecules form a bilayer so that the polar heads are near water and the nonpolar tails are in the interior of the bilayer.

(B) Model of a protocell

Outside surface of protocell

Bilayer

RNA

Interior of protocell

Courtesy of Janet Iwasa, Szostak group, MGH/Harvard

Figure 4.13 Protocells **(A)** In a series of experiments, Jack Szostak and his colleagues mixed fatty acid molecules in water. The molecules formed spherical structures called protocells, with water surrounded by bilayers of fatty acids. **(B)** A model of a protocell. A portion of the "membrane" has been cut away to reveal the inside of the protocell and the membrane's bilayer structure. Nutrients and nucleotides pass through the "membrane" and enter the protocell, where they copy an already present RNA template. The new copies of RNA remain in the protocell.

(**Figure 4.13**). These prebiotic, water-filled structures, defined by a lipid bilayer membrane, very much resemble living cells. Scientists refer to these compartments as **protocells**. Examining their properties revealed that:

• Large molecules such as DNA and RNA could not pass through the bilayer to enter the protocells, but small molecules such as sugars and individual nucleotides could.

• Nucleic acids inside the protocells could replicate using the nucleotides from outside. When the investigators placed a short nucleic acid strand capable of self-replication inside protocells and added nucleotides to the watery environment outside, the nucleotides crossed the barrier, entered the protocells, and became incorporated into new

polynucleotide chains. This replication, which can occur without protein catalysis, may have been the first step toward cell reproduction.

Were these protocells truly cells, and was the lipid bilayer produced in these experiments a true cell membrane? Certainly not. The protocells could not fully reproduce, nor could they carry out all the metabolic reactions that take place in modern cells. The simple lipid bilayer had few of the sophisticated functions of modern cell membranes. Nevertheless, the protocell may be a reasonable facsimile of a cell as it evolved billions of years ago:

• It can act as an organized system of parts, with substances interacting and reacting, in some cases catalytically.

• It includes an interior that is distinct from the exterior environment.

• It is capable of limited replication.

These are all fundamental characteristics of living cells.

Connect the Concepts Protocells more closely resemble bacteria than they do plant or animal cells. The evolution of the latter two cell types is believed to have occurred in a series of steps, as explained in Key Concept 25.1.

Some ancient cells left a fossil imprint

In the 1990s scientists made a rare find: a formation of ancient rocks in Australia that had remained relatively unchanged since the rocks first formed 3.5 billion years ago. In one of these rock samples, geologist J. William Schopf of the University of California, Los Angeles, saw chains and clumps of what looked tantalizingly like contemporary cyanobacteria, or "blue-green" bacteria (**Figure 4.14**). Cyanobacteria are believed to have been among the first organisms because they can perform photosynthesis, converting CO_2 and water into carbohydrates. Schopf needed to prove that the chains were once alive, not just the results of simple chemical reactions. He and his colleagues looked for chemical evidence of biochemical processes in the rock samples.

Figure 4.14 The Earliest Cells? This fossil from Western Australia is 3.5 billion years old. Its form is similar to that of modern filamentous cyanobacteria (inset).

Figure 4.15 The Origin of Life
This highly simplified time line gives a sense of the major events that culminated in the origin of life more than 3.5 billion years ago.

The ratio of carbon isotopes (^{13}C:^{12}C) in molecular structures produced by living systems differs from that of the inanimate environment. Using a sophisticated technique called secondary ion mass spectrometry (SIMS), Schopf and colleagues analyzed various samples of possible microfossils, carefully isolated from the ancient rocks, and found not only that the carbon isotope ratios differed from the rocks, but that there were several distinct ratios. Comparing these ratios with those in currently living organisms, they showed that the samples represented not just one species, but a diversity of simple organisms. For example, some samples had a carbon isotope ratio similar to that of current bacteria that use methane gas as a source of carbon, while other ancient samples had an isotope ratio more typical of bacteria that carry out photosynthesis, using CO_2. Still others appeared to use sulfur. These findings indicate that biological diversity was already present 3.5 billion years ago and suggest that the first cells arose even earlier.

Taking geological, chemical, and biological evidence into account, it is plausible that it took about 500 million to a billion years from the formation of Earth until the appearance of the first cells (**Figure 4.15**). Life has been cellular ever since. In the next chapter we will begin our study of cell structure and function.

KEY CONCEPT
4.4 Recap and Assess

The chemical reactions that preceded living organisms probably occurred in specialized compartments, such as water droplets on the surfaces of minerals. Life as we know it did not begin until the emergence of cells. Protocells made in the laboratory have some of the properties of modern cells. Cell-like structures fossilized in ancient rocks date early cells to about 3.5 billion years ago.

1. Why is the cell membrane important to the evolution of living organisms?

2. If you wanted to find evidence for the existence of cells more than 3 billion years ago, what would you look for?

▶Investigating**LIFE**

 Can we find evidence of life on Mars?

In 2014 NASA declared that finding evidence for current or past life on Mars is a primary goal. At this writing, the *Curiosity* rover is still there, doing experiments and analyses. In 2018 it dug up and analyzed some Martian soil and detected significant amounts of complex organic (carbon-containing) molecules, including propane (C_3H_8) and benzene (C_6H_6). While these molecules are not present in most living organisms on Earth, they indicate the presence of a complex chemistry needed for the formation of life's molecules as we know them. Later Martian rovers with more sophisticated instruments for sampling and analysis are scheduled for launch in the near future. The European Space Agency, collaborating with Russia, is planning to launch the *Rosalind Franklin* rover, which will drill 2 meters into the surface of Mars to get cores to analyze. Most exciting, scheduled as early as 2026, is a Mars Sample Return mission, in which soil samples will be brought back to Earth for careful experimentation and analysis in laboratories, just as samples from the moon were brought back about 50 years ago. If you had a Martian soil sample here on Earth, what analyses and experiments would you perform?

Future directions

Mars is not the only celestial body subject to the search for life. Three moons of large outer planets—Jupiter's Europa and Saturn's Enceladus and Titan—have some conditions suitable for life. Powerful Earth-based observations and satellites have indicated the presence of abundant subsurface water (in some cases, liquid) and carbon-based chemistry. Future missions are planned to sample these moons directly.

A daring space mission is underway to obtain and return to Earth a soil sample from the asteroid Bennu. There are more than 600,000 known asteroids, most of them rocks from the early solar system orbiting the Sun between Mars and Jupiter. But a few thousand have been kicked out of the typical location and are relatively near Earth, some getting closer than our moon. Bennu is just the right size and composition to contain organic molecules. At this writing, the *OSIRIS-REx* probe has arrived and is orbiting around Bennu, getting images and data to find a suitable landing spot. After landing, it will return to Earth with its cargo in 2023. This sample of the early solar system will provide scientists with a window onto not just what the asteroid is made of, but perhaps the earliest molecules that could have led to life.

You should be able to relate each summary to the adjacent figures. If you go to this visual summary in **Achieve**, you can follow links to figures, animations, activities, and simulations that will help you consolidate the material.

KEY CONCEPT

4.1 Nucleic Acids Are Informational Macromolecules

Go to Activities 4.1 and 4.2 and Animation 4.1

- **Nucleic acids** (**DNA** and **RNA**) are polymers of **nucleotides**. The polymers can fold or interact with other chains by **complementary base pairing**.

- DNA is the genetic material, and as such is purely an informational macromolecule. The information in DNA resides in its base sequence.

- The information in DNA is expressed as RNA during **transcription**. During **translation**, RNA can then specify the amino acid sequence of a protein.

Questions

1. One strand of DNA has the base sequence 5′-AAGGTC-3′. What is the sequence of the other strand? What would the sequence be of an RNA molecule transcribed from this strand?

2. If, through an error in DNA replication, an A-G base pair is formed, what will be the consequence for the secondary structure of DNA?

Figure 4.3

Figure 4.5

Figure 4.6

KEY CONCEPT

4.2 The Small Molecules of Life Originated on Primitive Earth

Go to Animations 4.2 and 4.3

- The historical belief that life can originate repeatedly by **spontaneous generation** was disproven experimentally.

- One hypothesis for the origin of life on Earth is **chemical evolution**: the idea that organic molecules were formed on Earth before life began. Chemical experiments modeling the prebiotic conditions on Earth support the idea of chemical evolution.

Questions

1. Does the Miller–Urey experiment show that the organic molecules of life could have originated only on Earth? Explain your answer.

2. When you purchase pasteurized milk, why is the container sealed? Relate this to the Pasteur experiments. Why must you store an opened milk container in the refrigerator?

Figure 4.9

Figure 4.10

KEY CONCEPT

4.3   The Large Molecules of Life Originated from Small Molecules

- Chemical evolution may have led to the polymerization of small molecules into polymers on clay particles, in hydro-thermal vents, or in hot pools at the edges of oceans.

- On early Earth, RNA may have acted as a catalyst for its own replication as well as for the synthesis of proteins. DNA could eventually have evolved from RNA.

Question

1. What key line of evidence rules out proteins and instead favors RNA as the first biological molecule?

Figure 4.12

KEY CONCEPT

4.4   Cells Originated from Their Molecular Building Blocks

- A key to the emergence of living **cells** was the prebiotic generation of compartments enclosed by **membranes**.

- In the laboratory, fatty acids assemble into **protocells** that have some of the characteristics of cells.

- Ancient rocks (3.5 billion years old) have been found with imprints that are probably fossils of early cells.

Questions

1. Why was the evolution of a cell membrane important for the emergence of life?

2. What is the evidence that the putative cellular fossils found in rocks in Australia were not the first cells, but the results of evolution from the first cells that existed previously?

Figure 4.13

Figure 4.14

© Stanley M. Awramik/Biological Photo Service; inset © Dennis Kunkel Microscopy/Science Source

Go to **Achieve** for the eBook, **LearningCurve**, animations, activities, simulations, and additional resources and assignments.

Cells: The Working Units of Life 5

KEY CONCEPTS

5.1 Cells Are the Fundamental Units of Life

5.2 Prokaryotic Cells Are the Simplest Cells

5.3 Eukaryotic Cells Contain Organelles

5.4 Extracellular Materials Provide Structure

5.5 Eukaryotic Cells Evolved in Several Steps

© Dennis Kunkel Microscopy/Science Source

Compartmentalization is a prominent feature of this liver cell, which shows the prominent nucleus at the center and energy-producing mitochondria (red). Also visible are ribosomes (purple dots) which synthesize proteins. The cytosol (pink) is where much of the chemistry of the cell occurs.

▶InvestigatingLIFE

Natural Sunscreen

Sunlight plays a key role in life, providing the energy that is transformed into stored chemical-bond energy in green plants through the process of photosynthesis. When we eat food, the energy stored in its chemical bonds ultimately came from the Sun. But sunlight has a nasty side effect: part of it, the highly energetic ultraviolet light, damages the genetic material, DNA. Even without knowing this chemistry, some people take measures to minimize exposure to excess sunlight, either by staying in the shade or using chemical sunscreens. But there is also a biological mechanism that has evolved to reduce the Sun's damage to organisms. In most animals, dark brown or black chemical pigments called melanins are made inside cells, the basic units of life. Melanins absorb ultraviolet light, thereby protecting DNA.

In humans, melanin is made in certain skin cells called melanocytes. Humans first evolved in Africa, and the intense sunlight near the equator acted as an evolutionary selective agent for the development of large numbers of melanocytes. As some of these dark-skinned people migrated to more northern regions where the Sun is not as intense, the selection pressure for melanocytes was reduced, and over millennia, genetic changes leading

to fewer melanocytes persisted in offspring, resulting in lighter skin. Exposure to intense sunlight in these people results in the production of more melanin, the familiar tanning response.

Melanocytes are specialized cells. You find them in the skin and the eye but not typically in internal organs. We will return to the process of how different cells have different functions in later chapters. But even inside the melanocyte, there is specialization. Melanin is made inside a special cell compartment called the melanosome. These compartments can be expelled from melanocytes and transferred to other skin cells, so they too become loaded with pigment. This occurs spontaneously in dark-skinned people, while in paler people it is stimulated by exposure to intense sunlight.

The observation that the chemistry of life takes place within cells, and in some cases within specialized compartments in them, is a key concept of biological science.

 Are pigments compartmentalized in all types of cells? (Find the answer on page 109.)

KEY CONCEPT 5.1 Cells Are the Fundamental Units of Life

Learning Objectives

5.1.1 List the three tenets of the original cell theory.

5.1.2 Explain how surface area-to-volume ratio constrains cell size.

5.1.3 Explain the importance of membranes in cell function.

Chapter 1 introduced some of the characteristics of life: chemical complexity, growth and reproduction, the ability to refashion substances from the environment, and the ability to move specific substances into and out of the organism. Cells have all of these characteristics. Just as atoms are the building blocks of chemistry, cells are the building blocks of life.

What is the cell theory?

The **cell theory** is an important unifying principle of biology. There are three components of the cell theory:

1. Cells are the fundamental units of life.

2. All living organisms are composed of cells.

3. All cells come from preexisting cells.

To the original cell theory, first stated in 1838, should be added:

4. Modern cells evolved from a common ancestor.

Cells contain water and other small and large molecules, which we examined in Chapters 2–4. Each cell contains at least 10,000 different types of molecules, most of them present in many copies. Cells use these molecules to transform matter and energy, to respond to their environments, and to reproduce. The cell theory has three important implications:

1. *Studying cell biology is in some sense the same as studying life.* The principles that underlie the functions of the single cell of a bacterium are similar to those governing the approximately 37 trillion human cells of your body.

2. *Life is continuous.* All the cells in your body came from a single cell, a fertilized egg (zygote). That zygote came from the fusion of two cells, a sperm and an egg, from your biological parents. The cells of your parents' bodies were all derived from their parents, and so on back through generations and evolution to the initial cell.

3. *The origin of life on Earth was marked by the origin of the first cells* (see Chapter 4).

Even the largest creatures on Earth are composed of cells, but the cells themselves are usually too small for the naked eye to see. Why are cells so small?

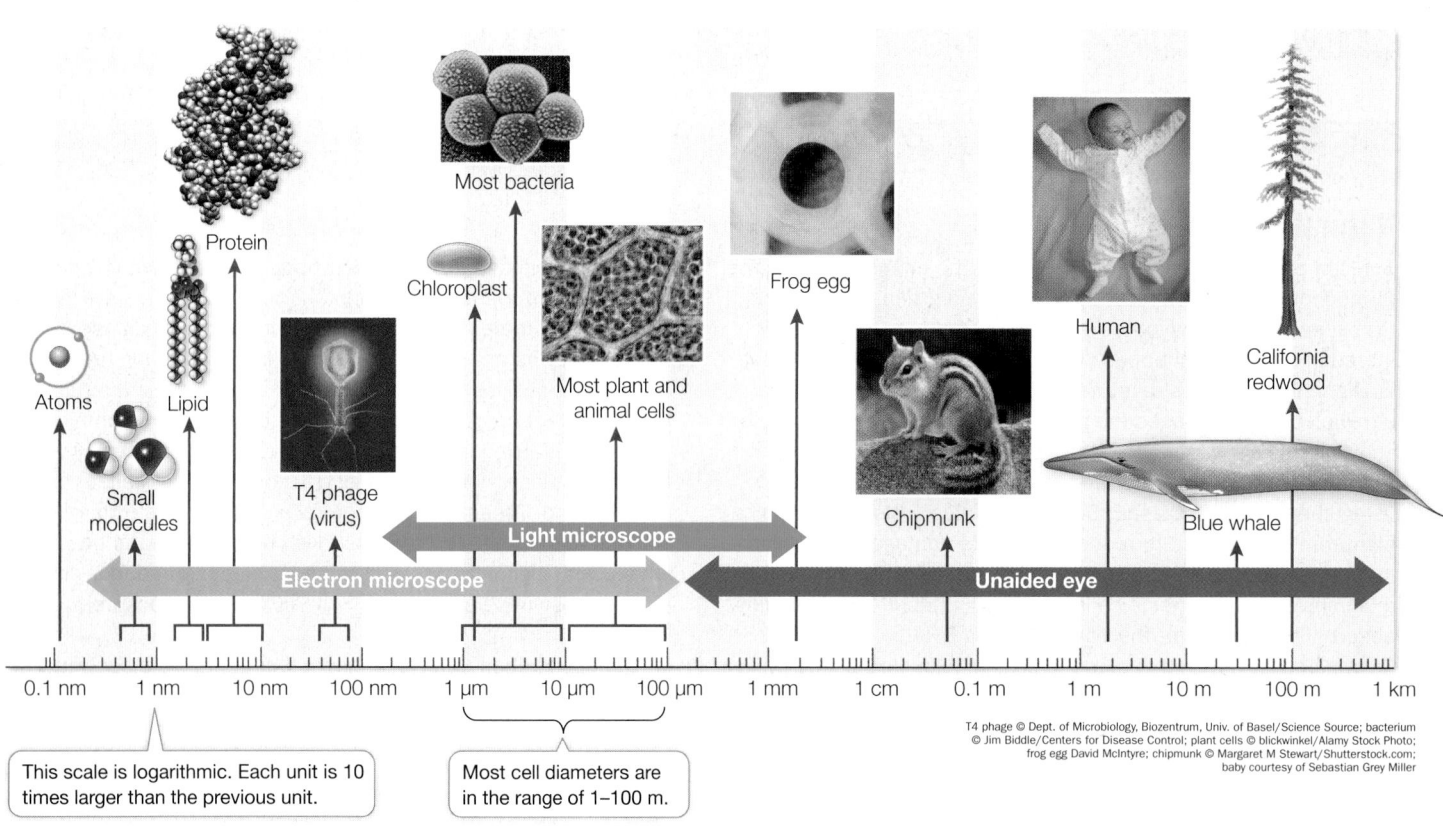

Most bacteria

Protein

Chloroplast

Frog egg

Human

California redwood

Atoms

Lipid

Small molecules

T4 phage (virus)

Most plant and animal cells

Chipmunk

Blue whale

Light microscope

Electron microscope

Unaided eye

0.1 nm   1 nm   10 nm   100 nm   1 μm   10 μm   100 μm   1 mm   1 cm   0.1 m   1 m   10 m   100 m   1 km

T4 phage © Dept. of Microbiology, Biozentrum, Univ. of Basel/Science Source; bacterium © Jim Biddle/Centers for Disease Control; plant cells © blickwinkel/Alamy Stock Photo; frog egg David McIntyre; chipmunk © Margaret M Stewart/Shutterstock.com; baby courtesy of Sebastian Grey Miller

This scale is logarithmic. Each unit is 10 times larger than the previous unit.

Most cell diameters are in the range of 1–100 m.

Figure 5.1 The Scale of Life This logarithmic scale shows the relative sizes of molecules, cells, and multicellular organisms. Protein data from PDB 1IVM. T. Obita et al. 2003. *Cell Mol Life Sci* 60: 176–184)

View in Achieve
Activity 5.1 The Scale of Life

Diameter	2 μm	20 μm	200 μm
Surface area $4 \pi r^2$	12.6 μm^2	1,260 μm^2	126,000 μm^2
Volume $^4/_3 \pi r^3$	4.2 μm^3	4,200 μm^3	4,200,000 μm^3
Surface area-to-volume ratio	3.0:1	0.3:1	0.003:1

Figure 5.2 Why Cells Are Small   As an object grows larger, its volume increases more rapidly than its surface area. Cells must maintain a large surface area-to-volume ratio in order to function. This explains why large organisms are composed of many small cells rather than a few huge ones.

Q: If a cell with a diameter of 200 μm has many folds in its cell membrane and increases its surface area tenfold, what will its surface area-to-volume be?

Cell size is limited by the surface area-to-volume ratio

In 1665 Robert Hooke estimated that in 1 square inch of cork, which he examined under his magnifying lens, there were 1,259,712,000 cells! The diameters of typical cells range from about 1 to 100 micrometers (μm). There are some exceptions: the eggs of fishes and amphibians (several millimeters in diameter) and of birds and other reptiles (several centimeters in diameter) are large single cells that store nutrients for development. Some individual cells of several types of algae and bacteria are large enough to be seen with the unaided eye (**Figure 5.1**).

Small cell size is a practical necessity arising from the change in the **surface area-to-volume ratio** of any object as it increases in size. As an object increases in volume, its surface area also increases, but not at the same rate (**Figure 5.2**). This phenomenon has great biological significance. To appreciate this point, let's assume that the amount of chemical activity carried out by a cell is proportional to its volume. The surface area of the cell determines the amount of substances that can enter it from the outside environment, and the amount of waste products that can exit to the environment.

As a living cell grows larger, its chemical activities, and thus its need for resources and its rate of waste production, usually increase faster than its surface area, assuming the shape remains the same. The surface area, being two-dimensional, increases in proportion to the square of the radius, whereas the volume, being three-dimensional, increases much more—in proportion to the cube of the radius. This explains why large organisms must consist of many small cells: cells must be small in volume in order to maintain a large enough surface area-to-volume ratio and an ideal internal volume. The large surface area represented by the many small cells of a multicellular organism allows the organism to carry out the many different functions required for survival.

While surface area-to-volume ratio limits cell size, some cells change their shape as they become larger, allowing them to maintain a sufficiently high ratio. Shape change can involve increased infoldings of the cell membrane, or size increases that occur in only one dimension. For example, nerve cells in humans, which can be a meter long, have very narrow projections, keeping the surface area-to-volume ratio high. Some cells get around the surface area-to-volume challenge by simply increasing the rate at which substances move across their boundary into and out of the cells.

Microscopes reveal the features of cells

Most cells are too small to be seen with the unaided eye. Microscopes allow cells and details within them to be seen. The property that allows detail to be seen is called resolution. Formally defined, resolution is the minimum distance two objects can be apart and still be seen as two objects. Resolution for the human eye is about 0.2 mm (200 μm).

There are two basic types of microscopes—light microscopes and electron microscopes—that use different forms of radiation (see Figure 5.4). While the resolution is better in electron microscopy, only dead cells are visualized because they must be prepared in a vacuum. Light microscopes, by contrast, can be used to visualize living cells (for example, by phase-contrast microscopy; see Figure 5.4).

Before we look at cell structure, it is useful to consider the many uses of microscopy. Here is an example: an entire branch of medicine, pathology, makes use of many different methods of microscopy to aid in the analysis of cells and the diagnosis of diseases. For instance, a surgeon might remove from a body some tissue suspected of being cancerous. The pathologist might:

- examine the tissue quickly by phase-contrast microscopy to determine the size, shape, and spread of the cells;
- stain the tissue with a general dye and examine it by bright-field microscopy to bring out features such as the shapes of the nuclei, or cell division characteristics (**Figure 5.3**);
- examine the tissue under the transmission electron microscope to observe internal structures such as the mitochondria or the chromatin (these are described in Key Concept 5.3);
- stain the tissue with a specific dye and examine it by microscopy for the presence of proteins that are diagnostic of particular cancers. The results can influence the choice of therapy.

A general stain shows the outlines of clumps of breast cancer cells with nuclei (dark purple).

A selective stain (brown) that targets the estrogen receptor shows it heavily concentrated in the nuclei of breast cancer cells.

Both photos from R. Sandhu and J. S. Parker. 2010. *Lab Med* 41: 364–372

Figure 5.3 Staining Cells for Microscopy   Stains can reveal cell and tissue structure, as well as composition.

Research Tools

Figure 5.4 Looking at Cells The six images on this page show some techniques used in light microscopy. The three images on the following page were created using electron microscopes. All of these images are of a particular type of cultured cell known as HeLa cells. Note that the images in most cases are flat, two-dimensional views.

As you look at images of cells, keep in mind that they are three-dimensional structures.

View in Achieve
Activity 5.2 Know Your Techniques

Light microscope

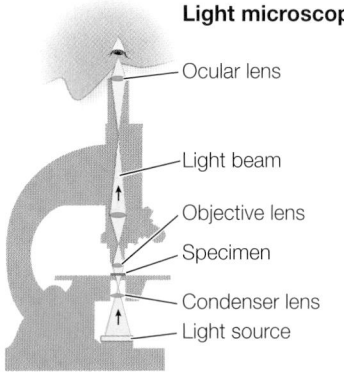

- Ocular lens
- Light beam
- Objective lens
- Specimen
- Condenser lens
- Light source

© Radu Razvan/Shutterstock.com

In a *light microscope*, glass lenses and visible light are used to form an image. The resolution is about 0.2 μm, which is 1,000 times greater than that of the human eye. Light microscopy allows visualization of cel sizes and shapes and some internal cell structures. Internal structures are hard to see under visible light, so cells are often chemically treated and stained with various dyes to make certain structures stand out by increasing contrast.

Courtesy of the IST Cell Bank, Genoa

30 μm

Bright-field microscopy: Light passes directly through these human cells. Unless natural pigments are present, there is little contrast and details are not distinguished.

© Eye of Science/Science Source

30 μm

Phase-contrast microscopy: Contrast in the image is increased by emphasizing differences in refractive index (the capacity to bend light), thereby enhancing light and dark regions in the cell.

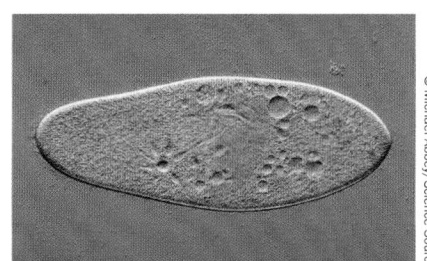

© Michael Abbey/Science Source

30 μm

Differential interference-contrast microscopy: Uses two beams of polarized light. The combined images look as if the cell is casting a shadow on one side.

© Richard J. Green/Science Source

30 μm

Stained bright-field microscopy: A stain enhances contrast and reveals details not otherwise visible. Stains differ greatly in their chemistry and their capacity to bind to cell materials, so many choices are available.

© Robert S. McNeil/Baylor College of Medicine Science Source

20 μm

Fluorescence microscopy: A natural substance in the cell or a fluorescent dye that binds to a specific cell material is stimulated by a beam of light, and the longer-wavelength fluorescent light is observed coming directly from the dye.

© Dr. Gopal Murti/Science Source

20 μm

Confocal microscopy: Uses fluorescent materials but adds a system of focusing both the stimulating and emitted light so that a single plane through the cell is seen. The result is a sharper two-dimensional image than with standard fluorescence microscopy.

Most cells are much smaller than 200 μm and thus are invisible to the human eye. Microscopes magnify and increase resolution so that cells and their internal structures can be seen clearly (**Figure 5.4**).

The cell membrane forms an outer boundary of every cell

While light microscopy shows many types of cells and even some structure inside them, the **cell membrane** is best observed with

Research Tools *(continued)*

Transmission electron microscope

- Electron gun
- First condenser lens (electromagnet)
- Electron beam
- Specimen
- Objective lens
- Projector lens (electromagnet)
- Screen or digital camera

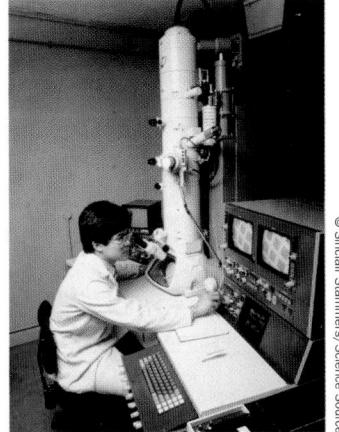

In an *electron microscope*, electromagnets are used to focus an electron beam, much as a light microscope uses glass lenses to focus a beam of light. Since we cannot see electrons, the electron microscope directs them through a vacuum at a fluorescent screen or digital camera to create a visible image. The resolution of electron microscopes is about 2 nm, which is about 100,000 times greater than that of the human eye. This resolution permits the details of many subcellular structures to be distinguished.

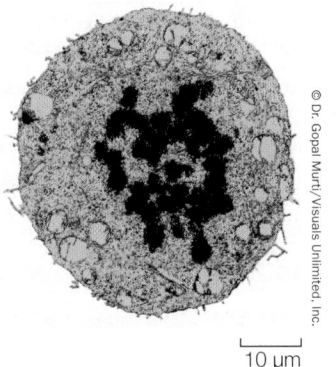

|← 10 μm →|

Transmission electron microscopy (TEM): A beam of electrons is focused on the object by magnets. Objects appear darker if they absorb the electrons. If the electrons pass through they are detected on a fluorescent screen.

|← 20 μm →|

Scanning electron microscopy (SEM): Directs electrons to the surface of the sample, where they cause other electrons to be emitted. These electrons are viewed on a screen. The three-dimensional surface of the sample can be visualized.

|← 0.1 μm →|

Freeze-fracture microscopy: Cells are frozen and then a knife is used to crack them open. The crack often passes through the interior of cell and internal membranes. The "bumps" that appear are usually large proteins or aggregates embedded in the interior of the membrane.

---

an electron microscope. This very thin structure forms the outer boundary of the cytoplasm of every cell, and it has similar thickness and molecular structure in all cells. You will learn about membranes in more detail in Chapter 6. For now, keep in mind that (with the exception of some species of archaea discussed in Chapter 24) the cell membrane consists of a phospholipid bilayer (see Key Concept 3.4), and that a variety of proteins are embedded within the bilayer.

The membrane has several important roles:

- The cell membrane acts as a selectively permeable barrier, preventing some substances from crossing it while permitting other substances to enter and leave the cell.

- By regulating transport across it, the cell membrane allows the cell to maintain a more or less constant internal environment. The maintenance of a constant internal environment (known as homeostasis) is a key characteristic of life and will be discussed in detail in Chapter 38.

- As the cell's boundary with the outside environment, the cell membrane is important in communicating with adjacent cells and receiving signals from the environment. You will learn about this in Chapter 7.

- The cell membrane often has proteins protruding from it that are responsible for binding and adhering to adjacent cells. Thus the cell membrane plays an important structural role and contributes to cell shape.

Everything inside the cell, except for the nucleus if the cell has one, is termed the **cytoplasm**. The **cytosol** is the fluid cytoplasm not contained inside another compartment.

Cells may be classified as either prokaryotic or eukaryotic

As you saw in Key Concept 1.1, biologists classify all living things into three domains: Archaea, Bacteria, and Eukarya. The organisms in Archaea and Bacteria are collectively called **prokaryotes**, and they have in common a prokaryotic cell organization. A prokaryotic cell typically does not have membrane-enclosed internal compartments; in particular, it does not have a nucleus. The first cells were probably similar in organization to those of modern prokaryotes.

Eukaryotic cell organization is found in members of the domain Eukarya (**eukaryotes**), which includes the protists, plants, fungi, and animals. In contrast to prokaryotic cells, eukaryotic cells contain membrane-enclosed compartments called **organelles**. The most

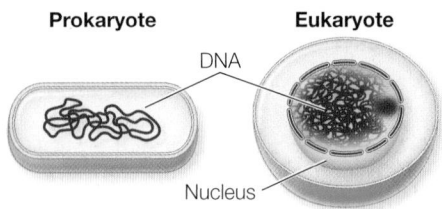

Prokaryote   Eukaryote

DNA

Nucleus

Figure 5.5 Prokaryotic versus Eukaryotic The presence of a cell nucleus and other membrane-bound internal compartments, or organelles, distinguishes eukaryotic cells from prokaryotic cells.

Q: Which two components are present in both eukaryotic and prokaryotic cells?

noticeable organelle is the cell **nucleus**, where most of the cell's DNA is located and where gene expression begins (**Figure 5.5**).

Just as a cell is an enclosed compartment, separating its contents from the surrounding environment, so each organelle provides a compartment that separates molecules and biochemical reactions from the rest of the cell. This "division of labor" provides possibilities for regulation and efficiency that were important in the evolution of complex organisms and helps explain the complexity of eukaryotic cells relative to prokaryotic cells.

KEY CONCEPT
5.1 Recap and Assess

The cell theory is a unifying principle of biology. Cell size is limited in order to maintain a high surface area-to-volume ratio. Both prokaryotic and eukaryotic cells are enclosed within a cell membrane, but prokaryotic cells lack the membrane-enclosed organelles that are found in eukaryotic cells.

1. How does cell biology embody all the principles of life?
2. What is the importance of the cell membrane and the membranes that surround organelles?

As we mentioned in this key concept, there are two structural themes in cell architecture: prokaryotic and eukaryotic. We will now turn to the organization of prokaryotic cells.

KEY CONCEPT
5.2 Prokaryotic Cells Are the Simplest Cells

Learning Objectives

5.2.1 Describe the major features of a prokaryotic cell.

5.2.2 Identify specialized features found in some prokaryotic cells.

With diameters or lengths in the range of 1–10 μm, prokaryotic cells are generally smaller than eukaryotic cells, whose diameters are usually in the range of 10–100 μm. Each individual prokaryote is a single cell, but many types of prokaryotes form chains or small clusters of cells, and some occur in large clusters containing hundreds of cells. In this key concept we will first consider the features shared by cells in the domains Bacteria and Archaea. Then we will examine structural features that are found in some, but not all, prokaryotes.

Prokaryotic cells share certain features

All prokaryotic cells have the same basic structure (**Figure 5.6**):

• The cell membrane encloses the cell, regulating the traffic of materials into and out of the cell, and separating its interior from the external environment.

• The **nucleoid** is a region in the cell where the DNA is located. As we described in Key Concept 4.1, DNA is the hereditary material that controls cell growth, maintenance, and reproduction.

• The rest of the material enclosed in the cell membrane is the cytoplasm.

Figure 5.6 A Prokaryotic Cell
This electron micrograph and drawing of the bacterium *Pseudomonas aeruginosa* illustrate the typical structures shared by all prokaryotic cells. In addition, this bacterium has a protective outer membrane that is not present in all prokaryotes. The flagellum and capsule are also structures found in some, but not all, prokaryotic cells.

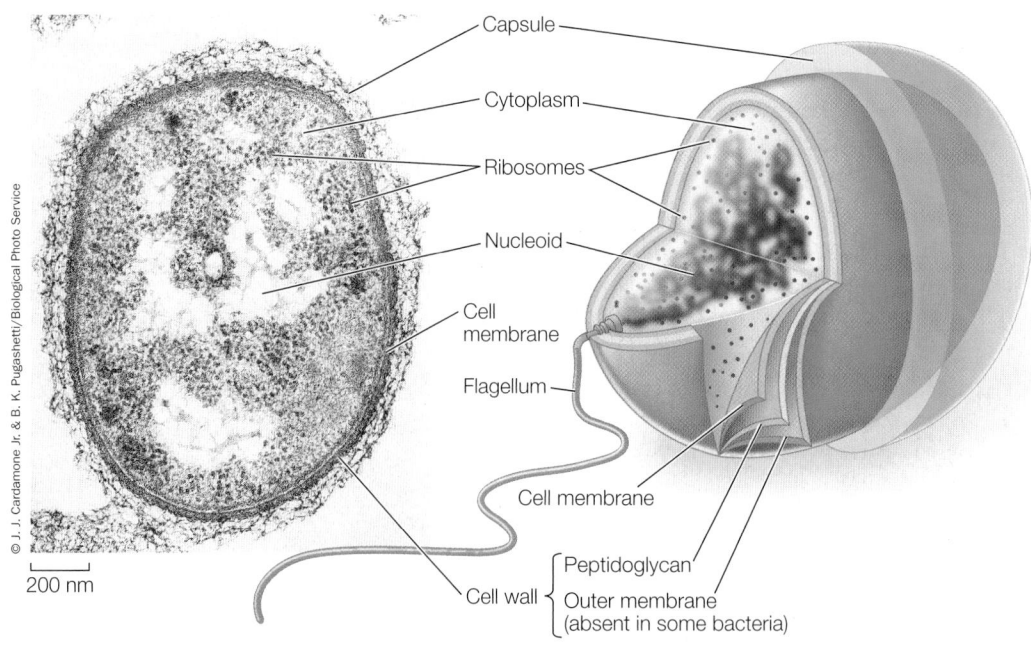

© J. J. Cardamone Jr. & B. K. Pugashetti/Biological Photo Service

200 nm

Capsule
Cytoplasm
Ribosomes
Nucleoid
Cell membrane
Flagellum
Cell membrane
Peptidoglycan
Cell wall {
Outer membrane (absent in some bacteria)

- **Ribosomes** are complexes of RNA and proteins in the cytoplasm that are about 25 nanometers (nm) in diameter. They can be visualized only with the electron microscope. They are the sites of protein synthesis, where information coded for in nucleic acids directs the sequential linking of amino acids to form proteins.

Connect the Concepts   In terms of sheer numbers, prokaryotes are the most successful organisms on Earth. As we examine prokaryotic cells in this key concept, bear in mind that there are vast numbers of prokaryotic species, and that bacteria and archaea are distinguished in numerous ways. These differences, and the vast diversity of organisms in these two domains, are the subject of Chapter 24.

The cytoplasm is not static. Rather, the substances in this environment are in constant motion. For example, a typical protein moves around the entire cell within a minute, and it collides with many other molecules along the way. This motion helps ensure that biochemical reactions proceed at rates sufficient to meet the needs of the cell. Although they are structurally less complex than eukaryotic cells, prokaryotic cells are functionally complex, carrying out thousands of biochemical reactions.

Specialized features are found in some prokaryotes

As they evolved, some prokaryotes developed specialized structures that gave them a selective advantage: cells with these structures were better able to survive and reproduce in particular environments than cells lacking them.

CELL WALL   Most prokaryotic cells have a **cell wall** located outside the cell membrane. The rigid wall supports the cell and determines its shape. The cell walls of most bacteria, but not archaea, contain peptidoglycan, a polymer of amino sugars that is linked at regular intervals to short peptides. Cross-linking among these peptides results in a single giant molecule around the entire cell. In some bacteria, another layer, the **outer membrane** (a polysaccharide-rich phospholipid membrane), encloses the peptidoglycan layer (see Figure 5.6). Unlike the cell membrane, this outer membrane is not a major barrier to the movement of molecules across it. Enclosing the cell wall in some bacteria is a slimy layer composed mostly of polysaccharides and referred to as a **capsule**. In some cases these capsules protect the bacteria from attack by white blood cells in the animals they infect. Capsules also help keep the cells from drying out, and sometimes they help bacteria attach to other cells.

INTERNAL MEMBRANES   Some groups of bacteria—including the cyanobacteria—carry out photosynthesis: they use energy from the Sun to convert carbon dioxide and water into carbohydrates. These bacteria have an **internal membrane** system that contains molecules needed for photosynthesis. The development of photosynthesis, which requires membranes, was an important event in the early evolution of life on Earth. Other prokaryotes have internal membrane folds that are attached to the cell membrane. These folds may function in cell division or in various energy-releasing reactions.

FLAGELLA AND PILI   Some prokaryotes swim by using appendages called **flagella**, which sometimes look like tiny corkscrews (**Figure 5.7A**). In bacteria, the filament of the flagellum is made of a protein called flagellin. (As you will see in Key Concept 5.3, the flagella of eukaryotes are quite different in structure, but similar in function.) A complex motor protein spins the bacterial flagellum

(A) Flagella of a prokaryotic cell

Flagella

© Dennis Kunkel Microscopy/ Science Source

(B) Rotary "motor" of a flagellum

Outside of cell

Outer membrane

Peptidoglycan

Cell membrane

Inside of cell

The flagellum is rotated by a complex motor protein secured in the cell membrane.

45 nm

Filament of flagellum
L ring
Drive shaft
P ring
Rotor
Transport apparatus
C ring

Courtesy of David DeRosier, Brandeis U.

Figure 5.7 Prokaryotic Flagella
(A) Flagella contribute to the movement and adhesion of prokaryotic cells. **(B)** Complex protein ring structures anchored in the cell membrane form a motor unit that rotates the flagellum and propels the cell.

on its axis like a propeller, driving the cell along. The motor protein is anchored to the cell membrane and, in some bacteria, to the outer membrane of the cell wall (**Figure 5.7B**). We know that the flagella cause the motion of cells because if they are removed, the cells do not move.

Pili are structures made of protein that project from the surfaces of some types of bacterial cells. These hairlike structures are shorter than flagella and are used for adherence. Conjugative pili (sex pili) help bacteria join to one another to exchange genetic material. Fimbriae are composed of the same proteins as pili but are shorter, and help cells adhere to surfaces such as animal cells, for food and protection.

CYTOSKELETON   The **cytoskeleton** is the collective name for protein filaments that play roles in cell division, cell movement, and in maintaining the shapes of cells. Prokaryotes have filamentous proteins that are homologous (similar in amino acid sequence) to the proteins that make up the cytoskeleton in eukaryotic cells. These proteins include FtsZ, which forms a contractile ring in the center of the cell when it divides, and MreB, which forms filaments just inside the cell membrane and maintains the shape of the cell.

KEY CONCEPT
5.2 Recap and Assess

Prokaryotic cells share basic features, including the cell membrane and a region called the nucleoid. The rest of the material enclosed by the cell membrane, including the ribosomes, is called the cytoplasm. Other features, such as cell walls, internal membranes, and flagella, are present in some but not all prokaryotes.

1. What are the structure and function of the following specialized prokaryotic cell features: cell wall, capsule, and flagellum?

2. What are the chemical compositions of the nucleoid and cytoplasm in a prokaryotic cell?

As we have already noted, the prokaryotic cell is one of two types of cells recognized in cell biology. The other is the eukaryotic cell. Eukaryotic cells are more structurally and functionally complex than prokaryotic cells.

KEY CONCEPT
5.3 Eukaryotic Cells Contain Organelles

Learning Objectives

5.3.1 Discuss the importance of compartmentalization in eukaryotic cells.

5.3.2 Compare the sizes, structures, typical numbers, and roles of subcellular structures.

5.3.3 Trace the path of a molecule as it moves between organelles in a eukaryotic cell.

Eukaryotic cells generally are larger than prokaryotes, and as noted in Figure 5.5, the distinguishing feature of eukaryotic cells is the presence of membrane-bound subcellular compartments called organelles. As you will see throughout this book, there are

many types of eukaryotic cells in terms of structure and function. Here we will emphasize the features they have in common.

 View in Achieve
Activity 5.3 **Eukaryotic Cell Tour**

Compartmentalization is important to eukaryotic cell function

The most obvious organelle in almost all eukaryotic cells is the nucleus, which houses the genetic material, DNA, and thereby controls overall cell functions. Other organelles carry out particular functions, and you will see that separating these biochemical reactions from the rest of the cell is important. For example, one type of organelle hydrolyzes polymers such as proteins and lipids. If its reactions were not compartmentalized, the proteins and lipids of the rest of the cell would also be broken down. Another type of organelle, in plant cells, carries out the reactions of photosynthesis, converting light energy into chemical-bond energy which is then used to synthesize monosaccharides. In still another organelle, its membrane is used to separate electric charges between the interior of the organelle and the surrounding cytoplasm, allowing the production of molecules rich in chemical-bond energy. As we noted in Key Concept 4.4 when discussing the role of a membrane in separating and concentrating molecules to favor their interaction in chemical reactions, compartmentalization within a cell favors the reactions inside that compartment.

Organelles can be studied by microscopy or isolated for chemical analysis

Cell organelles and structures were first detected by light and then by electron microscopy (see Figure 5.4). The functions of the organelles could sometimes be inferred by observations and experiments, leading, for example, to the hypothesis (later confirmed) that the nucleus contains the genetic material. Later, the use of stains targeted to specific macromolecules allowed cell biologists to determine the chemical compositions of organelles (see Figure 5.4).

Another way to analyze cells is to take them apart in a process called cell fractionation. This process permits cell organelles and other cytoplasmic structures to be separated from each other and examined using chemical methods. Cell fractionation begins with the destruction of the cell membrane, which allows the cytoplasmic components to flow out into a test tube. The various organelles can then be separated from one another on the basis of size or density (**Figure 5.8**). Biochemical analyses can then be done on the isolated organelles. Microscopy and cell fractionation have complemented each other, giving us a more complete picture of the composition and function of each organelle and structure.

Microscopy of eukaryotic cells has revealed that many of the organelles are similar in appearance in each cell type (**Figure 5.9**). By comparing Figures 5.9 and 5.6 you can see some of the prominent differences between eukaryotic cells and prokaryotic cells.

Ribosomes are factories for protein synthesis

The ribosomes of prokaryotes and eukaryotes are similar in that both types

Figure 5.8 Cell Fractionation   Organelles can be separated from one another after cells are broken open and their contents suspended in an aqueous medium. The medium is placed in a tube and spun in a centrifuge, which rotates about an axis at high speed. Centrifugal forces (measured in multiples of gravity, × g) cause particles to sediment (form a pellet) at the bottom of the tube, which may be collected for biochemical study. Heavier particles sediment at lower speeds (lower centrifugal forces) than lighter particles. By adjusting the speed of centrifugation, researchers can separate and partially purify cellular organelles.

Q: How would you use this method to isolate ribosomes?

consist of two different-sized subunits, are about 25 nm in diameter, and can number up to thousands per cell. Because they lack membranes and are not a compartment, ribosomes are not classified as organelles. Rather, like the cytoskeleton (discussed later in this key concept), they are called cell structures.

Chemically, ribosomes consist of a special type of RNA called ribosomal RNA (rRNA). Ribosomes also contain more than 50 different protein molecules, which fit together noncovalently, employing forces for protein interaction such as hydrophobic interactions (see Figure 3.13). Additionally, some of the proteins bind noncovalently to the rRNA.

Connect the Concepts As discussed in Key Concept 14.5, the ribosome is the molecular workbench where mRNA is translated into protein.

In prokaryotic cells, ribosomes generally exist unattached in the cytoplasm. In eukaryotic cells, they are found in several places: in the cytoplasm; attached to the surface of the endoplasmic reticulum (a membrane-bound organelle, discussed later in this key concept); and inside other organelles, including the mitochondria and chloroplasts in plant cells. In each of these locations, the ribosomes are molecular factories where proteins are synthesized.

The nucleus contains most of the genetic information

As we discussed in Chapter 4, hereditary information is stored in the sequence of nucleotides in DNA molecules. Most of the DNA in a eukaryotic cell resides in the single nucleus, about 5 μm in diameter (**Figure 5.10A**). The nucleus has several functions in the cell:

- It is the location of most of the cell's DNA and the site of DNA replication.
- It is the site where gene transcription is turned on or off.
- A region within the nucleus, the **nucleolus**, is where ribosomes (see the previous section) begin to be assembled from RNA and proteins.

The contents of the nucleus, aside from the nucleolus, are referred to as the nucleoplasm. Similar to the cytosol, the nucleoplasm consists of the liquid content of the nucleus and the insoluble molecules suspended within it. The nucleus is enclosed by an integrated structure composed of two membranes, called the **nuclear envelope**. The two membranes of the nuclear envelope are perforated by thousands of nuclear pores (**Figure 5.10B**), each measuring approximately 9 nm in diameter, which connect the nucleoplasm with the cytoplasm.

The pores are not really porous. Instead, they act as "traffic cops," allowing some molecules to pass into and out of the nucleus and blocking others. This allows the nucleus to regulate its information-processing functions. Small substances, including ions and other molecules with molecular weights of less than 10,000 daltons, move through the pores. But larger molecules, such as most proteins that are made in the cytoplasm, can't get through. In some cases, however, there is a special transport mechanism to get such proteins into the nucleus; you'll learn about this in Chapter 14.

AN ANIMAL CELL

Mitochondria are the cell's power plants.

© K. Porter, D. Fawcett/Visuals Unlimited, Inc.

Mitochondrion

0.8 μm

The nucleus is the site of most cellular DNA, which, with associated proteins, comprises chromatin.

© Richard Rodewald/Biological Photo Service

Nucleolus

Nucleus

1.5 μm

A cytoskeleton composed of microtubules, intermediate filaments, and microfilaments supports the cell and is involved in cell and organelle shape and movement.

© Don Fawcett/Science Source

Cytoskeleton

25 nm

Free ribosomes

Peroxisome

Centrioles

Ribosomes (bound to RER)

Golgi apparatus

Cell membrane

Smooth endoplasmic reticulum

Rough endoplasmic reticulum

© Don Fawcett/Science Source

Ribosomes

30 nm

The rough endoplasmic reticulum is the site of much protein synthesis.

© Barry F. King/Biological Photo Service

Centrioles are associated with nuclear division.

0.1 μm

Inside of cell

Outside of cell

© 2006 Warren Rosenberg/Fundamental Photographs

30 nm

The cell membrane separates the cell from its environment and regulates traffic of materials into and out of the cell.

Figure 5.9 Eukaryotic Cells   In electron micrographs, many plant cell organelles are nearly identical in form to those observed in animal cells. Cellular structures found in plant but not animal cells include the cell wall and the chloroplasts. Note that the images are two-dimensional "slices," whereas cells are three-dimensional structures.

Media Clip 5.1 The Inner Life of a Cell
Life12e.com/mc5.1

A PLANT CELL

Carbohydrates and other molecules are metabolized in the smooth endoplasmic reticulum.

© Don Fawcett, D. Friend/Science Source

Smooth endoplasmic reticulum

0.5 μm

Ribosomes manufacture proteins.

© 1990 American Society for Microbiology. Used with permission. No further reproduction or distribution is permitted without prior written permission of American Society of Microbiology

Free ribosomes

25 nm

A cell wall supports the plant cell.

© Biophoto Associates/Science Source

Cell wall

0.75 μm

Nucleolus

Nucleus

Vacuole

Cell membrane

Rough endoplasmic reticulum

Peroxisome

© E. H. Newcomb & S. E. Frederick/Biological Photo Service

Peroxisomes break down toxic peroxides.

Mitochondrion

Plasmodesmata

Chloroplast

© W. P Wergin, E. H. Newcomb/Biological Photo Service

Chloroplasts harvest the energy of sunlight to produce sugar.

1 μm

Golgi apparatus

Courtesy of L. Andrew Staehelin, U. Colorado

The Golgi apparatus processes and packages proteins.

0.5 μm

(A) Chromatin distributed within the nucleoplasm

Dense chromatin (dark) near the nuclear envelope is attached to the nuclear lamina.

Diffuse chromatin (light) is in the nucleoplasm.

Nuclear envelope   Nucleolus   1 μm

© Barry King, U. California, Davis/ Biological Photo Service

(B) Nuclear pores of the nuclear envelope

Nuclear pores   0.5 μm

© Don Fawcett/Science Source

(C) Chromatin fibers highly condensed into chromosomes during cell division

1.4 μm

© Biophoto Associates/Science Source

Figure 5.10 The Nucleus, Chromatin, and Chromosomes
(A) Chromatin consists of nuclear DNA and the proteins associated with it. When the cell is not dividing, the chromatin is dispersed throughout the nucleus. This two-dimensional image was made using a transmission electron microscope. (B) The nuclear envelope has many pores that regulate traffic of large molecules such as RNA and proteins in and out of the nucleus. (C) The chromatin in dividing cells becomes highly condensed, so that the individual chromosomes can be seen. This three-dimensional image of isolated metaphase chromosomes was produced using a scanning electron microscope.

Inside the nucleus, each DNA molecule (in humans there are 46 of them) combines with proteins to form a fibrous complex called **chromatin**, which makes up long, thin threads called **chromosomes**. Despite the seeming disorganization of the nucleus as seen in Figure 5.10A, there is an underlying architecture, with chromosomes arranged specifically. We know this because if a laser beam is directed at a small region of the nucleus, only one or two chromosomes—the ones in that region—are damaged. The effects of this subnuclear organization are only beginning to be understood. One of them seems to be that chromosomes near one another may swap DNA regions; in some cases this leads to abnormal cell reproduction and cancer.

If and when a cell reproduces—a process called cell division—the chromatin becomes tightly compacted and condensed so that the individual chromosomes are visible under a light microscope (**Figure 5.10C**). At the inside edge of the nucleus, the chromatin is attached to a protein meshwork, called the nuclear lamina, which is formed by the polymerization of proteins called lamins into long, thin structures called intermediate filaments (discussed later in this key concept). The nuclear lamina maintains the shape of the nucleus by its attachment to both the chromatin and the nuclear envelope. On the outside of the nucleus, the outer membrane of the nuclear envelope folds outward into the cytoplasm and is continuous with the membrane of another organelle, the endoplasmic reticulum, which we will discuss next.

The endomembrane system is a group of interrelated organelles

Much of the volume of some eukaryotic cells is taken up by an extensive **endomembrane system**. This is an interconnected system of membrane-enclosed compartments that are sometimes flattened into sheets and sometimes have other characteristic shapes (see Figure 5.9). The endomembrane system includes:

- the cell membrane
- the nuclear envelope
- the endoplasmic reticulum
- the Golgi apparatus
- the lysosomes

Tiny, membrane-surrounded droplets called **vesicles** shuttle substances between the various components of the endomembrane system (**Figure 5.11**). In drawings and electron microscope pictures, this system appears static, fixed in space and time. But these depictions are just snapshots; in the living cell, the membranes and the materials they contain are in constant motion. Membrane components have been observed to shift from one organelle to another within the endomembrane system. Thus these membranes and compartments are functionally related.

ENDOPLASMIC RETICULUM   Electron micrographs of eukaryotic cells reveal networks of interconnected membranes branching throughout the cytoplasm, forming tubes and flattened sacs. These membranes are collectively called the **endoplasmic reticulum**, or **ER**. The interior compartment of the ER, called the lumen, can compose up to 10% of the interior volume of the cell, and its folds result in a surface area many times greater than that of the cell membrane. There are two types of endoplasmic reticulum, the so-called rough and smooth.

Rough endoplasmic reticulum (RER) is called "rough" because of the many ribosomes attached to the outer surface of the membrane, giving it a "rough" appearance in electron microscopy (see Figure 5.9). The bound ribosomes are actively involved in protein synthesis, but that is not the entire story:

The Golgi apparatus processes and packages proteins.

0.5 μm

Nucleus

Cytosol

Rough endoplasmic reticulum is studded with ribosomes that are sites for protein synthesis. They produce its rough appearance.

1 Protein-containing vesicles from the endoplasmic reticulum transfer substances to the *cis* face of the Golgi apparatus.

Lumen

Cisterna

cis face

2 The Golgi apparatus chemically modifies proteins in its lumen…

medial face

3 …and "targets" them to the correct destinations.

trans face

Proteins for use within the cell

Smooth endoplasmic reticulum is a site for lipid synthesis and chemical modification of proteins.

Cell membrane

Lysosome

Proteins for use outside the cell

Outside of cell

Figure 5.11 The Endomembrane System Membranes of the nucleus, endoplasmic reticulum, lysosomes, and Golgi apparatus form a network connected by vesicles.

Q: What processes in the endomembrane system are mediated by vesicles?

- The RER receives into its lumen certain newly synthesized proteins (including proteins destined for lysosomes, the cell membrane, and export from the cell), segregating them away from the cytoplasm. The RER also participates in transporting these proteins to other locations in the cell.

- While inside the RER, proteins can be chemically modified to alter their functions and "tag" them for delivery to specific cellular destinations.

- Proteins are sent to destinations elsewhere in the cell enclosed within vesicles that pinch off from the RER.

- Most membrane-bound proteins are made in the RER.

A protein enters the lumen of the RER through a pore as it is synthesized. As with a protein passing through a nuclear pore, there is a special transport mechanism to get proteins into the

ER, which you'll learn about in Chapter 14. Once in the lumen of the RER, proteins undergo several changes, including the formation of disulfide bridges and folding into their tertiary structures (see Figure 3.6).

Some proteins become covalently linked to carbohydrate groups in the RER, thereby becoming glycoproteins. In the case of proteins directed to the lysosomes, the carbohydrate groups are part of an "addressing" system that ensures that the right proteins are directed to those organelles. This addressing system is very important because the enzymes within the lysosomes are some of the most destructive the cell makes. Were they not properly addressed and contained, they could destroy the cell. Cells that make a lot of proteins, such as the cells that make digestive enzymes for the human intestine and antibodies for the immune system, are full of RER.

Smooth endoplasmic reticulum (SER) lacks ribosomes and is more tubular (and less like flattened sacs) than the RER, but it shows continuity with portions of the RER (see Figure 5.11). The SER has several important roles:

- It is responsible for the chemical modification of small molecules taken in by the cell that may be toxic to the cell. These modifications make the targeted molecules more polar, so they are more water-soluble and easily removed.

- It is the site for glycogen degradation in animal cells. We will discuss this important process in Chapter 9.

- It is the site where lipids and steroids are synthesized, as well as some polysaccharides in plant cells.

- It stores calcium ions, which when released trigger numerous cell responses.

Connect the Concepts Regulating muscle contraction is one of the important roles played by the calcium ions stored by the SER. See Key Concept 46.1.

GOLGI APPARATUS   The **Golgi apparatus** is another part of the diverse, dynamic, and extensive endomembrane system (see Figure 5.11 insert). This structure was named after its discoverer, Camillo Golgi. Its appearance varies, but it almost always consists of two components: flattened membranous sacs called cisternae (singular *cisterna*) that are piled up like saucers, and small membrane-enclosed vesicles. The entire apparatus is about 1 μm long.

 View in Achieve
Animation 5.1 The Golgi Apparatus

The Golgi apparatus has several roles:

- It receives protein-containing vesicles from the RER.

- It modifies, concentrates, packages, and sorts proteins before they are sent to their cellular or extracellular destinations.

- It adds carbohydrates to proteins and modifies other carbohydrates that were attached to proteins in the RER.

- It is where some polysaccharides for the plant cell wall are synthesized.

- It cuts certain large precursor proteins transferred from the RER into smaller, functional fragments. For example, in humans the pituitary gland makes a 241-amino acid polypeptide called proopiomelanocortin. In the Golgi apparatus, this is cut into several molecules, including corticotropin (39 amino acids), melanocyte-stimulating hormone (22 amino acids), and β-endorphin (31 amino acids). You will learn more about these molecules in Chapter 39.

The cisternae of the Golgi apparatus have three functionally distinct regions, called *faces*:

1. The *cis* face lies nearest to the nucleus or a patch of RER.

2. The *trans* face lies closest to the cell membrane.

3. The *medial* face lies in between (see Figure 5.11).

The terms *cis*, *trans*, and *medial* derive from Latin words meaning, respectively, "on the same side," "on the opposite side," and "in the middle." These three parts of the Golgi apparatus contain different enzymes and perform different functions.

Protein-containing vesicles from the RER fuse with the *cis* membrane of the Golgi apparatus, releasing their cargo into the lumen of the Golgi apparatus cisterna. Other vesicles may move between the cisternae, transporting proteins, and it appears that some proteins move from one cisterna to the next through tiny channels. Vesicles budding off from the *trans* face carry their contents away from the Golgi apparatus. These vesicles go to the cell membrane or to the lysosome, another organelle in the endomembrane system.

$$\text{ER} \rightarrow \textit{cis-}\text{Golgi} \rightarrow \textit{medial-}\text{Golgi} \rightarrow \textit{trans-}\text{Golgi} \Big\langle \begin{array}{l} \text{cell membrane} \\ \text{lysosome} \end{array}$$

How do the vesicles in this system recognize their targets for fusion? In other words, when a vesicle buds off from the ER, how does it "know" to fuse with the *cis-*Golgi membrane? The answer lies in proteins on both membranes appropriately called SNAREs Pairs of SNAREs are complementary—that is, they bind to one another like a lock and key. So the SNARE on the ER surface that forms a vesicle can bind to a SNARE on the *cis-*Golgi.

LYSOSOMES   The **primary lysosomes** originate from the Golgi apparatus. They contain digestive enzymes and are the sites where macromolecules—proteins, polysaccharides, nucleic acids, and lipids—are hydrolyzed into their monomers (see Figure 3.4).

$$R_1 \text{—} R_2 \text{ (linked monomers)} + H_2O \rightarrow R_1 \text{—OH} + R_2 \text{—H}$$

Lysosomes are about 1 μm in diameter, are surrounded by a single membrane, and have a densely staining, featureless interior (**Figure 5.12**). There may be dozens of lysosomes in a cell, depending on its needs. The interior of the lysosome is more acidic (pH 5) than the external cytoplasm (pH 7.2).

Lysosomes are cellular "disposals," compartments for the breakdown of food, other cells, or foreign objects that are taken up by the cell. These materials enter the cell by a process called **phagocytosis** (*phago*, "eat," + *cytosis*, "cellular"). In this process, a pocket forms in the cell membrane and then deepens and encloses material from outside the cell. The pocket becomes a small vesicle called a phagosome, containing food or other material, which breaks free of the cell membrane to move into the cytoplasm. The phagosome fuses with a primary lysosome to form a **secondary lysosome**, where digestion occurs. These reactions are enhanced by the acidity of the lysosome's interior. The products of digestion pass through the membrane of the lysosome, providing energy and raw materials for other cellular processes. For example, a protease might hydrolyze proteins to amino acids, which are released to the cytoplasm for reassembly into other proteins. The "used" secondary lysosome, now containing undigested particles, then moves to the cell membrane, fuses with it, and releases the undigested contents to the environment, a process called **exocytosis**.

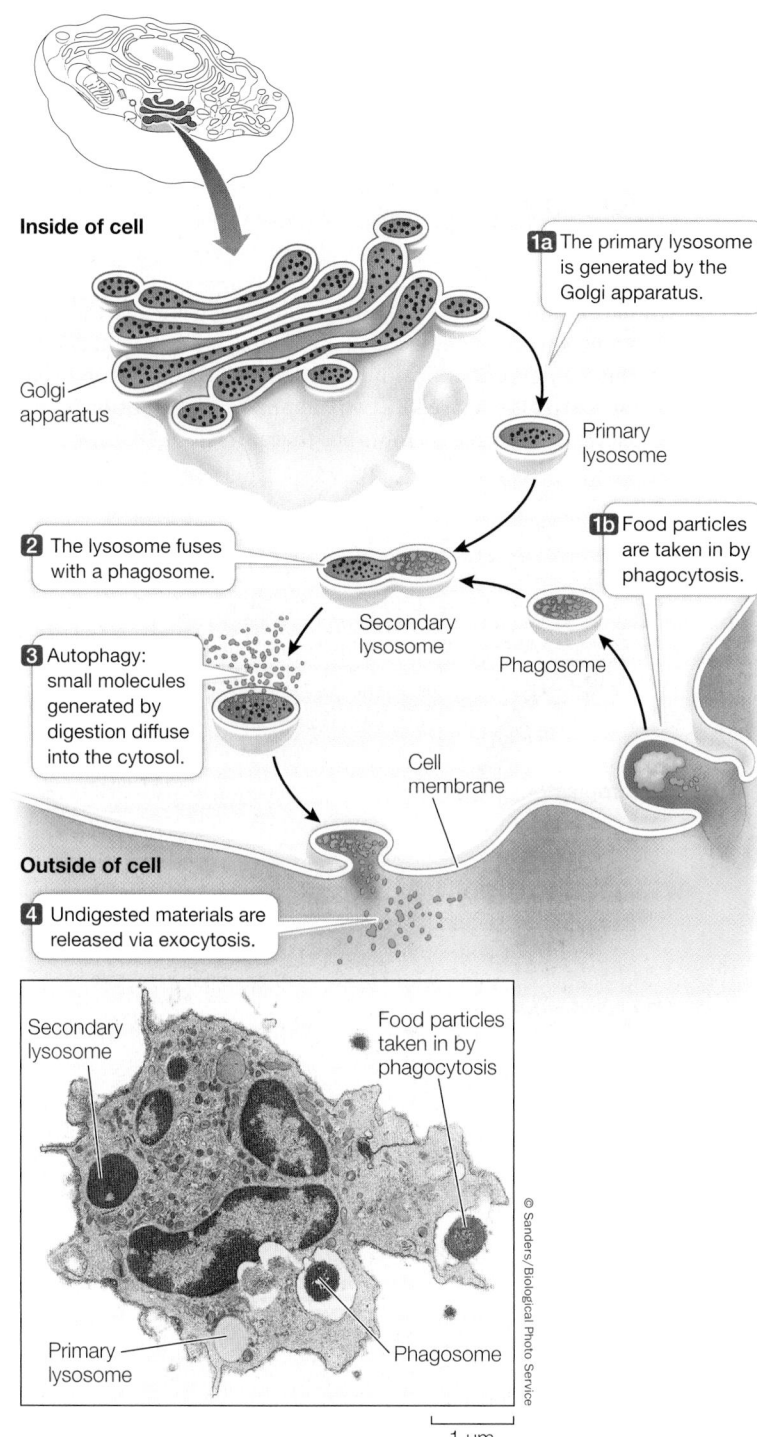

Inside of cell

Golgi apparatus

1a The primary lysosome is generated by the Golgi apparatus.

Primary lysosome

2 The lysosome fuses with a phagosome.

1b Food particles are taken in by phagocytosis.

Secondary lysosome

Phagosome

3 Autophagy: small molecules generated by digestion diffuse into the cytosol.

Cell membrane

Outside of cell

4 Undigested materials are released via exocytosis.

Secondary lysosome

Food particles taken in by phagocytosis

Primary lysosome

Phagosome

© Sanders/Biological Photo Service

1 μm

Figure 5.12 Lysosomes Isolate Digestive Enzymes from the Cytoplasm
Lysosomes are sites for the hydrolysis of material taken into the cell by phagocytosis. Discarded components exit the cell by exocytosis.

▶ View in **Achieve**
  Activity 5.4 Lysosomal Digestion

Phagocytes (see Key Concept 40.1) are specialized cells that have an essential role in taking up and breaking down materials; they are found in nearly all animals and many protists. You will encounter them and their activities again at many places in this book, but at this point one example suffices: in the human liver and spleen,

phagocytes digest approximately 10 billion aged or damaged blood cells each day! The digestion products are then used to make new cells to replace those that are digested.

Lysosomes are active even in cells that do not perform phagocytosis. Cells are dynamic systems; some cell components are continually being broken down and replaced by new ones. The programmed destruction of cell components is called **autophagy**, and lysosomes are where the cell breaks down its own materials. With the proper signal, lysosomes can engulf entire organelles, hydrolyzing their constituents.

How important is autophagy? An entire class of human diseases called **lysosomal storage diseases** are caused by the failure of lysosomes to digest specific cellular components; these diseases are invariably harmful or fatal. An example is Tay-Sachs disease, in which a particular lipid called a ganglioside is not broken down in the lysosomes and instead accumulates in brain cells. In the most common form of this disease, a baby starts exhibiting neurological symptoms and becomes blind, deaf, and unable to swallow after 6 months of age. Death occurs before age 4.

Plant cells do not appear to contain lysosomes, but the vacuole of a plant cell (which we describe later in this key concept) may function in an equivalent capacity because it, like lysosomes, hydrolyzes macromolecules.

Some organelles transform energy

A cell requires energy for activities such as growth, reproduction, responsiveness, and movement. Energy is harvested from fuel molecules in the mitochondria (found in all eukaryotic cells) and from sunlight in the chloroplasts of plant cells. Energy in biological systems is stored and transferred in the form of covalent bonds in organic molecules.

 MITOCHONDRIA   In eukaryotic cells, the breakdown of energy-rich molecules such as glucose begins in the cytoplasm. The molecules that result from this partial degradation enter the **mitochondria** (singular *mitochondrion*), whose primary function is to harvest the chemical-bond energy of those molecules in a form that the cell can use, namely the energy-rich molecule ATP (adenosine triphosphate) (see Key Concept 8.2). The production of ATP in the mitochondria, using fuel molecules and molecular oxygen (O_2), is called **cellular respiration** (see Chapter 9).

Typical mitochondria are somewhat less than 1.5 μm in diameter and are 2–8 μm in length—about the size of many bacteria (**Figure 5.13**). They can reproduce and divide independently of the central nucleus. The number of mitochondria per cell ranges from one large organelle in some unicellular protists to a few hundred thousand in large egg cells. A typical human liver cell contains more than 1,000 mitochondria. Cells that are active in movement and growth

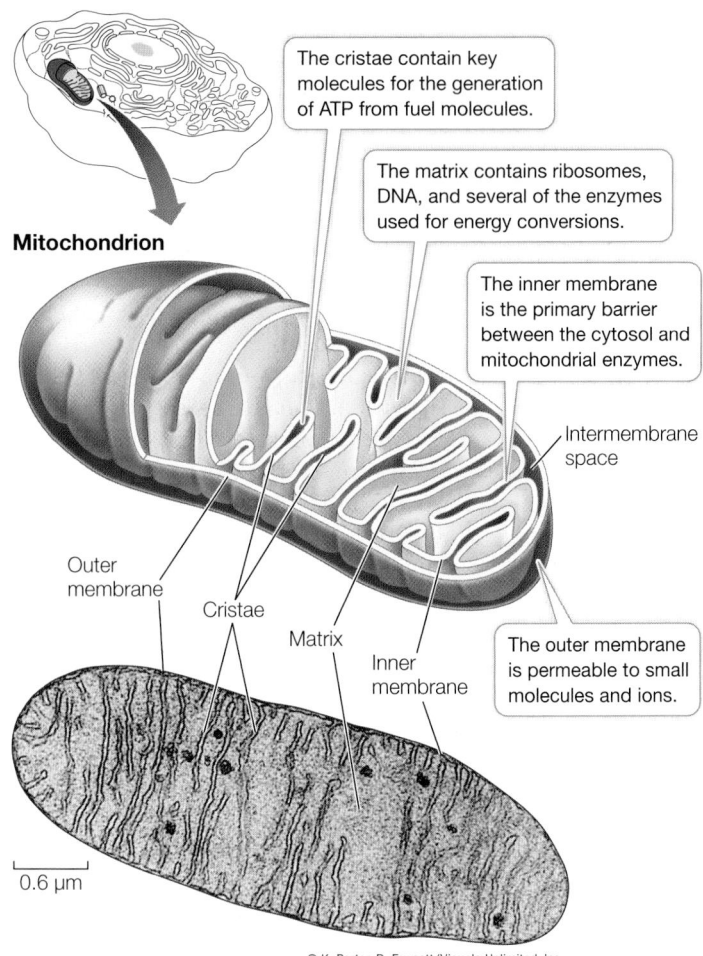

Mitochondrion

The cristae contain key molecules for the generation of ATP from fuel molecules.

The matrix contains ribosomes, DNA, and several of the enzymes used for energy conversions.

The inner membrane is the primary barrier between the cytosol and mitochondrial enzymes.

Intermembrane space

The outer membrane is permeable to small molecules and ions.

Outer membrane

Cristae

Matrix

Inner membrane

0.6 μm

© K. Porter, D. Fawcett/Visuals Unlimited, Inc.

Figure 5.13 A Mitochondrion Converts Energy from Fuel Molecules into ATP The electron micrograph is a two-dimensional slice through a three-dimensional organelle. As the drawing emphasizes, the cristae are extensions of the inner mitochondrial membrane.

Q: What kinds of human cells would you expect to have a lot of mitochondria?

require the most chemical-bond energy and tend to have the most mitochondria.

Mitochondria have two membranes. The outer membrane is smooth in appearance and permits the movement of substances into and out of the organelle. Immediately inside the outer membrane is an inner membrane, which folds inward in many places and thus has a surface area much greater than that of the outer membrane. The folds tend to be quite regular, giving rise to shelflike structures called cristae (from the Latin word for "crest" or "plume"). The inner membrane exerts much more control over what enters and leaves the space it encloses than does the outer membrane. Embedded in the inner mitochondrial membrane are many large protein complexes that participate in cellular respiration.

The space enclosed by the inner membrane is called the mitochondrial matrix. In addition to many molecules involved in cellular respiration, the matrix contains ribosomes and DNA that are used to make some of the mitochondrial proteins needed for cellular respiration.

PLASTIDS Plastids occur only in the cells of plants and certain protists. Like mitochondria, plastids can divide independently of the cell nucleus. There are several types of plastids, with different functions.

Just as melanosomes are a compartment for melanin pigment in animal cells (see the chapter opening), so are **chloroplasts**, which contain the green pigment chlorophyll and are the sites of photosynthesis (**Figure 5.14**). In photosynthesis, light energy is converted into chemical-bond energy. Like a mitochondrion, a chloroplast is enclosed by two membranes. In addition, there is a series of internal membranes that often look like stacks of

Chloroplast

Chemical energy is used in converting CO_2 and H_2O to carbohydrate in the stroma, the area outside the thylakoid membranes.

Thylakoid membranes are sites where light energy is harvested by the green pigment chlorophyll and converted into chemical energy.

Thylakoid

Outer membrane

Inner membrane

Stroma

Granum (stack of thylakoids)

© W. P. Wergin, E. H. Newcomb/Biological Photo Service

1 μm

Figure 5.14 Chloroplasts Feed the World The electron micrograph shows a chloroplast from a leaf of corn. Chloroplasts are large compared with mitochondria and contain extensive networks of thylakoid membranes. These membranes contain the green pigment chlorophyll, and are the sites where light energy is converted into chemical energy for the synthesis of carbohydrates from CO_2 and H_2O.

Q: Chloroplasts are present only in plant cells. Why do these cells also contain mitochondria?

(A) Production and storage of pigments

Chromoplasts

Left © iStock.com/SilentWolf; right From Gunning, B. E. S. Plant Cell Biology on DVD: Information for students and a resource for teachers. Springer, 2009 (www.springer.com/life+sciences/plant+sciences/book/978-3-642-03690-3)

20 μm

(B) Storage of starch

Leucoplast

Starch grains

Left © iStock.com/John Shepherd; right Courtesy of R. R. Dute

1 μm

Figure 5.15 Other Types of Plastids (A) Chromoplasts in flower petals contain pigments. (B) Leucoplasts in potatoes store starch.

flat, hollow pita bread. Each stack is called a granum (plural *grana*) and the pita bread–like compartments are called **thylakoids** (see Figure 5.14). Thylakoid lipids are distinctive: only 10% are phospholipids, whereas the rest are galactose-substituted diglycerides and sulfolipids. Because of the abundance of chloroplasts, these are the most abundant lipids in the biosphere.

In addition to lipids and proteins, the membranes of the thylakoids contain chlorophyll and other pigments that harvest light energy for photosynthesis (we will see how they do this in Key Concept 10.2). The thylakoids of one granum may be connected to those of other grana, making the interior of the chloroplast a highly developed network, much like the ER. The fluid in which the grana are suspended is called the stroma. Like the mitochondrial matrix, the chloroplast stroma contains ribosomes and DNA, which are used to synthesize some chloroplast polypeptides.

Other types of plastids, such as chromoplasts and leucoplasts, have functions different from those of chloroplasts (**Figure 5.15**). Chromoplasts make and store red, yellow, and orange pigments, especially in flowers and fruits—again, just as the melanocytes in the opening story store pigment. Leucoplasts are storage organelles that store starch.

There are several other membrane-enclosed organelles

There are three other organelles whose boundary membranes separate their specialized chemical reactions and contents from the rest of the cytoplasm: peroxisomes, glyoxysomes, and vacuoles.

Peroxisomes are organelles that accumulate toxic peroxides, such as hydrogen peroxide (H_2O_2), that occur as by-products of some biochemical reactions. These peroxides are safely broken down inside the peroxisomes without mixing with other parts of the cell.

$$RH_2 + O_2 \rightarrow R + H_2O_2 \text{ (cellular reactions)}$$
$$2\,H_2O_2 \rightarrow 2\,H_2O + O_2 \text{ (inside peroxisome)}$$

Peroxisomes are small organelles, about 1 μm in diameter.

Glyoxysomes are similar to peroxisomes and are found only in plants. They are most abundant in young plants and are the locations where stored lipids are converted into carbohydrates for transport to growing cells. The direct conversion of fat to carbohydrate is unique to these plants.

Vacuoles occur in many eukaryotic cells but particularly those of plants, fungi, and protists. They arise from the ER or Golgi apparatus. Plant vacuoles (**Figure 5.16**) have several functions:

- *Structure*: In many plant cells, vacuoles take up more than 90% of the cell volume and grow as the cell grows. The presence of dissolved substances in the vacuole causes water to enter it from the cytosol, making the vacuole swell like a balloon. A mature plant cell does not swell when the vacuole fills with water, since it has a rigid cell wall. Instead, it stiffens from the increase in water pressure (called turgor), and this supports the plant body (see Figure 6.10).

- *Reproduction*: Vacuoles contain some of the pigments (especially blue and pink ones) in the petals and fruits of flowering plants. These pigments—the anthocyanins—are visual cues that help attract animals that assist in pollination or seed dispersal.

- *Digestion*: In some plants, vacuoles in seeds contain molecules that hydrolyze stored proteins into monomers. During seed

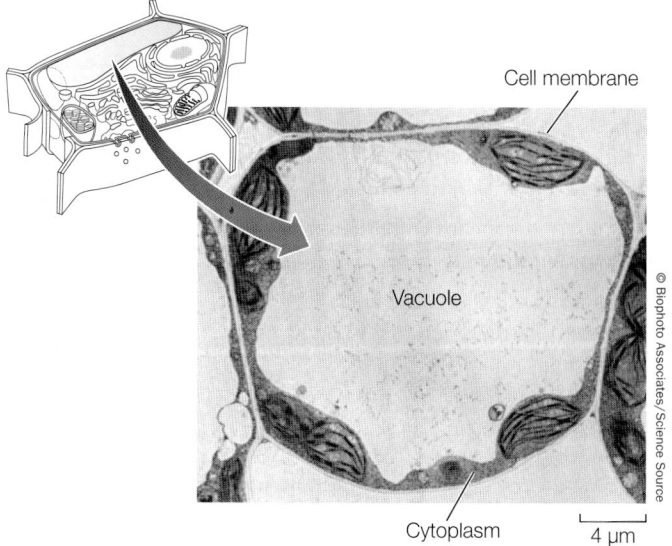

Cell membrane

Vacuole

Cytoplasm

4 μm

© Biophoto Associates/Science Source

Figure 5.16 Vacuoles in Plant Cells Are Usually Large The large central vacuole in this cell is typical of some types of plant cells.

germination, the monomers are used as food by the developing plant seedlings.

- *Storage*: In addition to storing water, vacuoles store toxic molecules and waste products. Because they are poisonous or distasteful, these stored materials deter some animals from eating the plants and may thus contribute to plant defense and survival. An example is tannins, a class of polyphenols that are made in many plants and may be familiar to you as the aftertaste in tea and red wine. Their bitter taste deters predators, and their dark color acts like animal melanin to protect the plant from ultraviolet light damage. Tannins are made in the chloroplast and end up in the vacuole. A newly discovered organelle, appropriately named the tannosome, contains tannins (Investigating Life: Discovering a New Organelle, the Tannosome).

So far we have discussed numerous membrane-enclosed organelles. Now we will turn to a group of cytoplasmic structures without membranes.

The cytoskeleton is important in cell structure and movement

Cell shapes can sometimes change, and there appear to be rapid movements of structures inside cells. These phenomena involve a meshwork of rods within cells that can be seen in electron microscopy. Experimentation showed that this meshwork—called the cytoskeleton—fills several important roles:

- It supports the cell and maintains its shape.

- It holds cell organelles and other particles in position within the cell.

- It moves organelles and other particles around in the cell.

- It is involved with movements of the cytoplasm, called cytoplasmic streaming.

- It interacts with extracellular structures, helping anchor the cell in place.

There are three components of the eukaryotic cytoskeleton: microfilaments (smallest diameter), intermediate filaments, and microtubules (largest diameter). These filaments have very different functions (**Figure 5.17**).

▶Investigating**LIFE**   Discovering a New Organelle, the Tannosome

Experiment

Original Paper: J.-M. Brillouet et al. 2013. The tannosome is an organelle forming condensed tannins in the chlorophyllous organs of *Tracheophyta*. *Ann Bot* 112: 1003–1014.

Through a series of investigations involving microscopy, cell fractionation, and chemical analysis, biologists discovered that plant tannins are compartmentalized in a heretofore undiscovered structure, the tannosome.

QUESTION▶   Are pigments compartmentalized in all types of cells?

METHOD▶

1 Examine plants that make tannins (e.g., grapevines).

2 Examine cells in electron microscope.

3 Stain with dye specific for tannins and examine in light microscope.

4 Separate organelles using cell fractionation.

5 Analyze the chemistry of the organelles for tannins.

Separate molecules   Detector

RESULTS▶

Tannin grains observed in chloroplast

Tannins inside organelles

Tannin organelles separate from chloroplasts

Tannins identified

CONCLUSION▶   Tannins are present in an organelle that begins in the chloroplast.

Work with the Data

The team of biologists and chemists (Brillouet et al. 2013) at the French National Institute for Agricultural Research, led by Geneviève Conejero, sought to investigate the cellular basis of tannin formation. It was well known from electron micrographs that these pigments accumulate in vacuoles, but how they got there was not established. The team used a combination of microscopy (light and electron; see Figure 5.4), cell fractionation (see Figure 5.8), and chemical analysis to show that tannins are formed in discrete vesicles, which the researchers named tannosomes.

QUESTIONS▶

1. Plant organs rich in tannins were examined by electron microscopy. Representative photographs are shown in **Figure A**. What do these images indicate about the origin and final resting spot of tannins in the cell? Based on what you know of vesicle trafficking in the cell, how do you think the tannins get from the chloroplast to the vacuole?

2. The scientists used specific dyes targeted to chlorophyll and tannins and examined slices of plant tissues by light microscopy. **Figure B** shows the results. What can you conclude about the subcellullar origin of tannins, and how does your answer relate to your answer to Question 1?

3. Cell fractionation was used to try to isolate tannin-containing structures separate from chloroplasts. In a very dense (72%), syrupy sucrose medium, fractionated cell contents showed two membrane-bound fractions (see the experiment). Both were examined by microscopy for tannin staining, and the contents were analyzed for chlorophyll and tannins. The results are shown in the table. What can you conclude about the tannin compartment?

Go to Achieve for a companion Data in Depth exercise.

Figure A

Vacuole with tannin vesicles

Chloroplast with tannin granules

Figure B

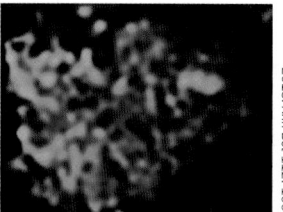

Staining of plant cell for chlorophyll   Staining of plant cell for tannins

	Upper fraction	Lower fraction
Staining for tannins	No	Yes
Staining for chlorophyll	Yes	Yes
Chemical analysis for tannins	No	Yes

(A) Microfilaments

−End   +End

7 nm

Actin monomer

Cell membrane

Nucleus

10 μm

Made up of strands of the protein actin; often interact with strands of other proteins.

(B) Intermediate filaments

8–12 nm

Fibrous subunit

10 μm

Made up of fibrous proteins organized into tough, ropelike assemblages that stabilize a cell's structure and help maintain its shape.

(C) Microtubules

−End   +End

25 nm

β-tubulin monomer   α-tubulin monomer

Tubulin dimer

10 μm

Long, hollow cylinders made up of many molecules of the protein tubulin. Tubulin consists of two subunits, α-tubulin and β-tubulin.

A, B, and C courtesy of John Victor Small

Figure 5.17 The Cytoskeleton Three highly visible and important structural components of the cytoskeleton are shown here in detail. The photographs are all of the same cell, treated with different fluorescent antibodies that detect microfilaments (**A**), intermediate filaments (**B**), or microtubules (**C**). These structures maintain and reinforce cell shape and contribute to cell movement. The position of the cell's nucleus is near the center of the photos.

MICROFILAMENTS **Microfilaments** can exist as single filaments, in bundles, or in networks. They are about 7 nm in diameter and up to several micrometers long. Microfilaments have two major roles:

1. They help the entire cell or parts of the cell move.
2. They determine and stabilize cell shape.

Microfilaments are assembled from monomers of **actin**, a protein that exists in several forms and has many functions, especially in animals. The actin found in microfilaments (which are also known as actin filaments) has distinct ends, designated "plus" and "minus." These ends permit actin monomers to interact with one another to form long, double-helical chains (see Figure 5.17A). Within cells, the polymerization of actin into microfilaments is reversible, and the microfilaments can disappear from cells by breaking down into monomers of free actin. Special actin-binding proteins mediate these processes.

> **Connect the Concepts** In animal muscle cells, actin filaments are associated with another protein, the "motor protein" myosin, and the interactions of these two proteins account for the contraction of muscles, as described in Key Concept 46.1.

In non-muscle cells, actin filaments are associated with localized changes in cell shape. For example, microfilaments are involved in the flowing movement of the cytoplasm called cytoplasmic streaming, in amoeboid movement, and in the "pinching" contractions that divide an animal cell into two daughter cells. Microfilaments are also involved in the formation of cellular extensions called pseudopodia (*pseudo*, "false," + *podia*, "feet") that enable some cells to move. As you will see in Key Concept 40.3, cells of the immune system must move toward other cells during the immune response.

In some cell types, microfilaments form a meshwork just inside the cell membrane. Actin-binding proteins then cross-link the microfilaments to form a rigid netlike structure that supports the cell. For example, microfilaments support the tiny microvilli that line the human intestine, giving it a larger surface area through which to absorb nutrients (**Figure 5.18**).

INTERMEDIATE FILAMENTS There are at least 50 different kinds of **intermediate filaments**, many of them specific to a few cell types. They generally fall into six molecular classes (based on amino acid sequence) that share the same general structure. One of these classes consists of fibrous proteins of the keratin family, which also includes the proteins that make up hair and fingernails. Intermediate filaments are tough, ropelike protein structures 8–12 nm in diameter (see Figure 5.17B). They are more permanent than the other two types in that they do not continually form and re-form, as the microtubules and microfilaments do.

Intermediate filaments have two major structural functions:

1. They anchor cell structures in place. In some cells, intermediate filaments radiate from the nuclear envelope and help maintain the positions of the nucleus and other organelles in the cell. The lamins of the nuclear lamina

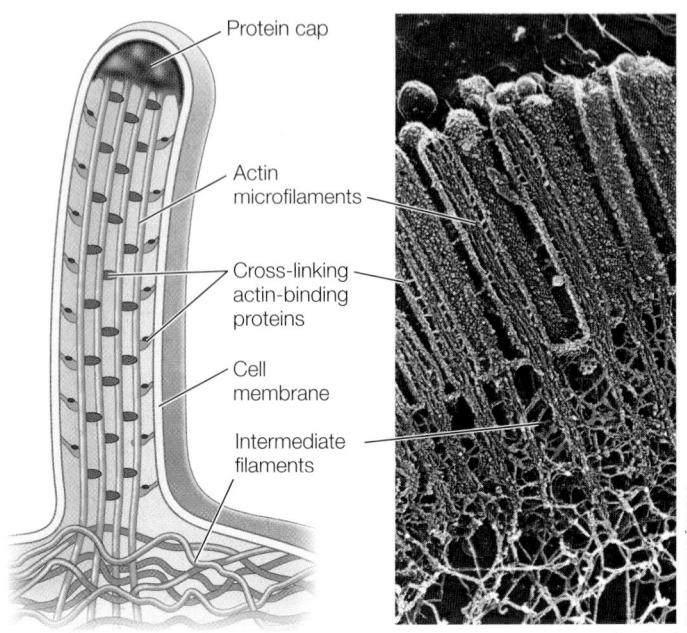

Protein cap

Actin microfilaments

Cross-linking actin-binding proteins

Cell membrane

Intermediate filaments

Courtesy of N. Hirokawa

0.25 μm

Figure 5.18 Microfilaments for Support Cells that line the intestine are folded into tiny projections called microvilli, which are supported by microfilaments. The microfilaments interact with intermediate filaments at the base of each microvillus.

are intermediate filaments. Other kinds of intermediate filaments help hold in place the complex apparatus of microfilaments in the microvilli of intestinal cells (see Figure 5.18).

2. They resist tension. For example, they maintain rigidity in body surface tissues by stretching through the cytoplasm and connecting specialized membrane structures called desmosomes (see Figure 6.6).

MICROTUBULES The largest-diameter components of the cytoskeletal system, **microtubules**, are long, hollow, unbranched cylinders about 25 nm in diameter and up to several micrometers long. Microtubules have two roles in the cell:

1. They form a rigid internal skeleton for some cells.
2. They act as a framework along which motor proteins can move structures within the cell.

Microtubules are assembled from dimers—two similar molecules in a complex—of the protein **tubulin**, called α-tubulin and β-tubulin. Thirteen chains of tubulin doublets surround the central cavity of the microtubule (see Figures 5.17C and 5.19B).

$$\alpha\text{-tubulin} + \beta\text{-tubulin} \rightarrow \alpha\beta \text{ doublet} \rightarrow \text{polymer of doublets}$$
$$\text{(microtubule)}$$

As in microfilaments, the two ends of a microtubule are different: one is designated the "plus" end and the other the "minus" end. Tubulin dimers can be rapidly added or subtracted, mainly at the plus end, lengthening or shortening the microtubule.

Many microtubules appear to radiate from a region of the cell called the microtubule organizing center. Tubulin polymerization results in a rigid structure, and tubulin depolymerization leads to its collapse.

Microtubule ↔ tubulin doublets

The capacity to change length rapidly makes microtubules dynamic structures: they are readily adapted for new purposes in the cell. For example, by disassembly and reassembly, microtubules can move to new parts of the cell; or by disassembly, they can drag along substances attached to them.

In plants, microtubules act as a framework for the assembly of cellulose and help orient the cellulose fibers of the cell wall (see Figure 3.19). Electron micrographs of plants frequently show microtubules lying just inside the cell membranes of cells that are forming or extending their cell walls. If the orientation of these microtubules is altered experimentally, it leads to a similar change in the cell wall and a new shape for the cell.

Microtubules serve as tracks for **motor proteins**, specialized molecules that use cellular energy to change their shapes and move. Motor proteins bind to and move along the microtubules, carrying materials from one part of the cell to another. There are two main types of motor proteins:

1. **Kinesins** move materials toward the "plus" end.
2. **Dyneins** move materials toward the minus end.

The movement of organelles such as vesicles inside neurons occurs via kinesins; both kinesins and dyneins are involved in the movement of chromosomes during cell division; and as you will see next, dynein allows microtubule doublets to slide past one another in cilia and flagella.

CILIA AND FLAGELLA Microtubules and their associated proteins line the interior of certain movable appendages on eukaryotic cells: the **cilia** (Figure 5.19A) and flagella. Many cells have one or the other of these appendages, which form from projections of the cell membrane:

- Cilia are 0.25 μm in length. They occur by the hundreds on individual cells and move stiffly to either propel the cell (for example, in protists) or to move fluid over a stationary cell (as in the human respiratory system).
- Flagella are longer—100 to 200 μm—and occur singly or in pairs. They can push or pull a cell through its aqueous environment.

In cross section, a typical cilium or eukaryotic flagellum is surrounded by the cell membrane and contains a "9 + 2" array of microtubules. As Figure 5.19B shows, nine fused pairs of microtubules form an outer cylinder, and one pair of unfused microtubules runs up the center. Each doublet is connected to the center of the structure by a radial spoke. This structure is essential to the bending motion of both cilia and flagella. How does this bending occur?

The motion of cilia and flagella results from the sliding of the microtubule doublets past one another. This sliding is driven by the motor protein dynein, which, like other motor proteins, works by undergoing reversible shape changes that require chemical-bond energy. Dynein molecules bind between two neighboring microtubule pairs, and as the dynein molecules change shape, the pairs

(A) The beating of the cilia covering the surface of this unicellular protist propels it through the water of its environment.

Three cilia

25 μm

© SPL/Science Source

© W. L. Dentler/Biological Photo Service

250 nm

(B) Cross section reveals the "9 + 2" pattern of microtubules, including nine pairs of fused microtubles...

...and two unfused inner microtubules.

© W. L. Dentler/Biological Photo Service

Microtubule doublet

Motor protein (dynein; see Figure 5.20)

Radial "spokes"

Linker protein (nexin)

~50 nm

Figure 5.19 Cilia **(A)** This unicellular eukaryotic organism (a ciliated protist) can coordinate the beating of its cilia, allowing rapid movement. **(B)** A cross section of a single cilium shows the arrangement of micro-tubules and other proteins.

Dynein Microtubule doublet Nexin

In isolated cilia without nexin cross-links, movement of dynein motor proteins causes microtubule doublets to slide past one another.

When nexin is present to cross-link the doublets, they cannot slide and the force generated by dynein movement causes the cilium to bend.

Figure 5.20 **Motor Protein Moves Microtubules in Cilia and Flagella** A motor protein, dynein, causes microtubule doublets to slide past one another. In a flagellum or cilium, anchorage of the microtubule doublets to one another results in bending. (After B. Alberts et al. 2008. *The Molecular Biology of the Cell, 5th Edition.* Garland Science: New York.)

Q: In some people, the nexin links are absent and micro-tubule doublets are not attached to one another. What do you think the consequences of this are?

(A)

Microtubule
Kinesin
Vesicle

Kinesin cross-links the vesicle to the microtubule.

Detachment and reattachment of kinesin causes it to "walk" along the microtubule.

(B)

Microtubule

Initial time: the vesicle attaches to the microtubule via kinesin.

2.5 seconds later: the vesicle has moved 2 μm along the microtubule.

From N. Pollack et al. 1999. *J Cell Biol* 147: 493–506; courtesy of R. D. Vale

Figure 5.21 **A Motor Protein Pulls Vesicles along Microtubules** **(A)** Kinesin delivers vesicles to various parts of the cell by moving along microtubule "railroad tracks." **(B)** A vesicle is pulled by kinesin along a microtubule in the protist *Dictyostelium*. The time sequence, in half-second intervals, is shown by the color changes from purple to blue.

move past one another (**Figure 5.20**). Another protein, nexin, cross-links the pairs and appears to limit how far the doublets can slide. This causes the cilium or flagellum to bend.

Other motor proteins, including kinesin, carry protein-laden vesicles or other organelles from one part of the cell to another (**Figure 5.21**). These proteins bind to the organelle and "walk" it along a microtubule by a repeated series of shape changes. Recall that microtubules are directional, with a plus end where there is a net addition of tubulin and a minus end where there is removal. Cytoplasmic dynein (which has a different role than the one found in cilia and flagella) moves organelles attached to it toward the minus end, whereas kinesin moves them toward the plus end (see Figure 5.17). The ability of microtubules to carry vesicles is used by some fishes and amphibians to avoid predators. Motor proteins carrying pigment vesicles aggregate them in the center of the cell in response to environmental or nervous system stimuli. This makes the animal appear lighter. When the stimuli are removed, other motor proteins move the vesicles along microtubules to a more even distribution, restoring a darker hue.

> **Connect the Concepts** Perhaps the most dramatic role of microtubules is in the process of chromosome movement during cell division. See Key Concept 11.3.

Biologists can manipulate living systems to establish cause and effect

How do we know that the elements of the cytoskeleton, such as microtubules and microfilaments, can perform all these functions? We can observe an individual structure under the microscope, and we can observe the functions of living cells that contain that structure. These observations may suggest that the structure carries out a particular function, but mere correlation does not show cause and effect. For example, light microscopy of living cells reveals that the cytoplasm is actively streaming around the cell, and that cytoplasm flows into an extended portion of an amoeboid cell during movement. The observed presence of cytoskeletal components *suggests, but does not prove,* their role in this process. Science seeks to show the specific links that relate one process, A, to a function, B. In cell biology, two approaches are often used to show that a structure or process A causes function B:

1. *Inhibition*: Use a drug that inhibits A and see if B still occurs. If it does not, then A is probably a causative factor for B. **Figure 5.22** shows an experiment with such a drug (an inhibitor) that demonstrates cause and effect in the case of the cytoskeleton and cell movement.

2. *Mutation*: Examine a cell that lacks the gene (or genes) for A and see if B still occurs. If it does not, then A is probably a causative factor for B. Part Four of this book will describe many experiments using this genetic approach.

Experiment

Figure 5.22A The Role of Microfilaments in Cell Movement— Showing Cause and Effect in Biology

Original Paper: T. D. Pollard and R. R. Weihing. 1974. Actin and myosin in cell movement. *CRC Crit Rev Biochem* 2: 1–65.

After a test tube demonstration that the drug cytochalasin B prevented microfilament formation from monomeric precursors, the question was asked: Will the drug work like this in living cells and inhibit cell movement in *Amoeba*? Complementary experiments showed that the drug did not poison other cellular processes.

HYPOTHESIS▶ Amoeboid cell movements are caused by the cytoskeleton.

METHOD▶

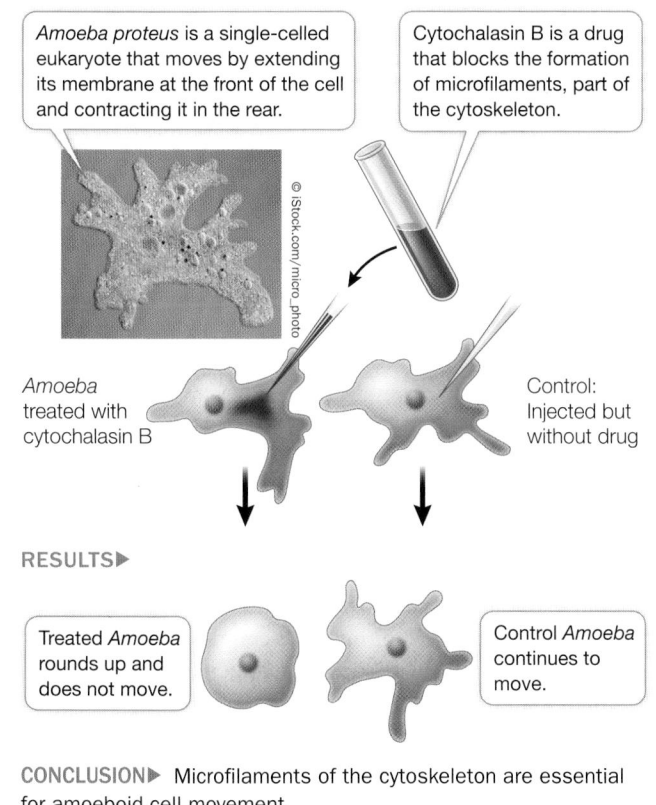

Amoeba proteus is a single-celled eukaryote that moves by extending its membrane at the front of the cell and contracting it in the rear.

Cytochalasin B is a drug that blocks the formation of microfilaments, part of the cytoskeleton.

Amoeba treated with cytochalasin B

Control: Injected but without drug

RESULTS▶

Treated *Amoeba* rounds up and does not move.

Control *Amoeba* continues to move.

CONCLUSION▶ Microfilaments of the cytoskeleton are essential for amoeboid cell movement.

Working with the Data

Figure 5.22B The Role of Microfilaments in Cell Movement— Showing Cause and Effect in Biology

Original Paper: T. D Pollard and R. R. Weihing. 1974. Actin and myosin in cell movement. CRC Crit Rev Biochem 2: 1–65.

In a search for natural molecules that have effects on cells— particularly cancer cells—a team of chemists and biologists at Imperial Chemical Industries examined extracts of the fungus Helminthosporium dematioideum. When the extracts appeared to inhibit cell division, the scientists purified the active ingredient and called it cytochalasin B (from the Greek cyto, "cell," and *chalasis*, "dislocation"). Remarkably, application of cytochalasin B to dividing cells blocked the division of the cytoplasm but not division of the nucleus, so the result was a binucleate cell. In addition, the drug inhibited cell movement and phagocytosis. These dynamic processes were both hypothesized to involve cytoplasmic microfilaments (actin filaments); the experiment that tested this hypothesis is outlined in Figure 5.22A.

Several important controls were done to validate the conclusions of the experiment. The experiment was repeated in the presence of the following drugs: cycloheximide, which inhibits new protein synthesis; dinitrophenol, which inhibits new ATP formation (energy); and colchicine, which inhibits the polymerization of microtubules. The results are shown in the table.

Condition	Rounded cells (%)
No drug	3
Cytochalasin B	95
Colchicine	4
Cycloheximide	3
Cycloheximide + cytochalasin B	94
Dinitrophenol	5
Dinitrophenol + cytochalasin B	85

QUESTIONS▶

1. Explain the reasoning behind each experiment. Why were these controls important?

2. Interpret the results of each experiment. What can you conclude about movements in *Amoeba* and the cytoskeleton?

Go to **Achieve** for a companion **Data in Depth** exercise.

KEY CONCEPT

5.3 Recap and Assess

The hallmark of eukaryotic cells is compartmentalization. Membrane-enclosed organelles process information, transform energy, form internal compartments for transporting proteins, and carry out intracellular digestion. An internal cytoskeleton plays several structural roles.

1. Using examples, explain why compartmentalization is important in eukaryotic cells.

2. Through how many membranes would a molecule have to pass in moving (a) from the interior (stroma) of a chloroplast to the interior (matrix) of a mitochondrion? (b) From the interior of a lysosome to the outside of a cell? (c) From one ribosome to another?

3. The drug vincristine is used to treat many cancers. It appears to work by causing microtubules to depolymerize. Vincristine use has many side effects, including loss of dividing cells and nerve problems. Explain why this might be so.

4. The movements of newly synthesized proteins can be followed through cells using a "pulse–chase" experiment. During synthesis, proteins are tagged with a radioactive isotope (the "pulse"), then the cells are allowed to process the proteins for varying periods of time. The locations of the radioactive proteins are then determined by isolating cell organelles and quantifying their levels of radioactivity. What would be the expected pathway for (a) a lysosomal enzyme and (b) a protein that is released from the cell?

All cells interact with their environments. Many eukaryotic cells are parts of multicellular organisms and must closely coordinate their activities with other cells. The cell membrane plays a crucial role in these interactions, but other structures outside that membrane are involved as well.

Figure 5.23 The Plant Cell Wall The semirigid cell wall provides support for plant cells. It is composed of cellulose fibrils embedded in a matrix of polysaccharides and proteins.

<table>
<tr><td>**KEY CONCEPT**
5.4</td><td>**Extracellular Materials Provide Structure**</td></tr>
</table>

Learning Objectives

5.4.1 Explain structure–function relationships in cell walls.

5.4.2 Compare and contrast plant and animal cell extracellular matrices.

5.4.3 Analyze changes to cells involving extracellular components.

Although the cell membrane is the functional barrier between the inside and the outside of a cell, many structures are produced by cells and secreted to the outside of the cell membrane, where they play essential roles in protecting, supporting, or attaching cells to each other. Because they are outside the cell membrane, these structures are said to be extracellular. The peptidoglycan cell wall of bacteria is an example of an extracellular structure (see Figure 5.6), as is the chitinous matrix outside the cells of arthropods. In many eukaryotes, other extracellular structures, such as the cell walls of plants and the extracellular matrices found between the cells of animals, play similar roles. Each of these structures is made up of two main components: a prominent fibrous macromolecule and a gel-like medium in which the fibers are embedded.

The plant cell wall provides structure and protection

The plant cell wall is a semirigid structure outside the cell membrane (**Figure 5.23**). We will consider the structure and role of the cell wall in more detail in Chapter 32. For now, we note that it consists of cellulose fibers (see Figure 3.19) embedded in other complex polysaccharides and proteins. The plant cell wall has three major roles:

1. It provides support for the cell and plant by remaining rigid. Yet it is flexible enough that it can allow the plant to bend in the wind, for example.

2. It acts as a barrier to infection by fungi and other organisms that can cause plant diseases.

3. It contributes to plant form by growing as the plant cells expand.

In some cells, such as those in a leaf, the cell wall is porous to allow the passage of molecules into and out of the cell. In other cells, such as those of the plant's vascular system (which transports water and small molecules between organs), the wall is not porous.

Because of their thick cell walls, plant cells viewed under a light microscope appear to be entirely isolated from one another. But electron microscopy reveals that this is not the case. The cytoplasms of adjacent plant cells are connected by numerous cell membrane–lined channels called **plasmodesmata**, which are about 20–40 nm in diameter and extend through the cell walls (see Figure 5.9). Plasmodesmata permit the diffusion of water, ions, small molecules, RNA, and proteins between connected

cells, allowing for the use of these substances far from their sites of synthesis.

The extracellular matrix supports tissue functions in animals

Animal cells lack the semirigid wall that is characteristic of plant cells, but many animal cells are surrounded by, or in contact with, an **extracellular matrix**. This matrix is composed of three types of molecules: fibrous proteins such as **collagen** (the most abundant protein in mammals, constituting over 25% of the protein in the human body); a matrix of glycoproteins termed **proteoglycans**, consisting primarily of sugars; and a third group of proteins that link the fibrous proteins and the gel-like proteoglycan matrix together (**Figure 5.24**). These proteins and proteoglycans are secreted, along with other substances that are specific to certain body tissues, by cells that are present in or near the matrix.

The extracellular matrix has several functions:

- It holds cells together in tissues. In Chapter 6 we will describe how there is an intercellular "glue" that is involved in both cell recognition and adhesion.

- It contributes to the physical properties of cellular aggregates called tissues. Cartilage and bone are part of connective tissue. For example, the mineral component of bone is laid down on an organized extracellular matrix. This property can be used in reverse, to create organs in the laboratory. In tissue engineering, cells are removed from the extracellular matrix and the latter serves as a scaffold for the development of new organs with the correct architecture. This is a frontier in organ transplantation in humans whose organs fail.

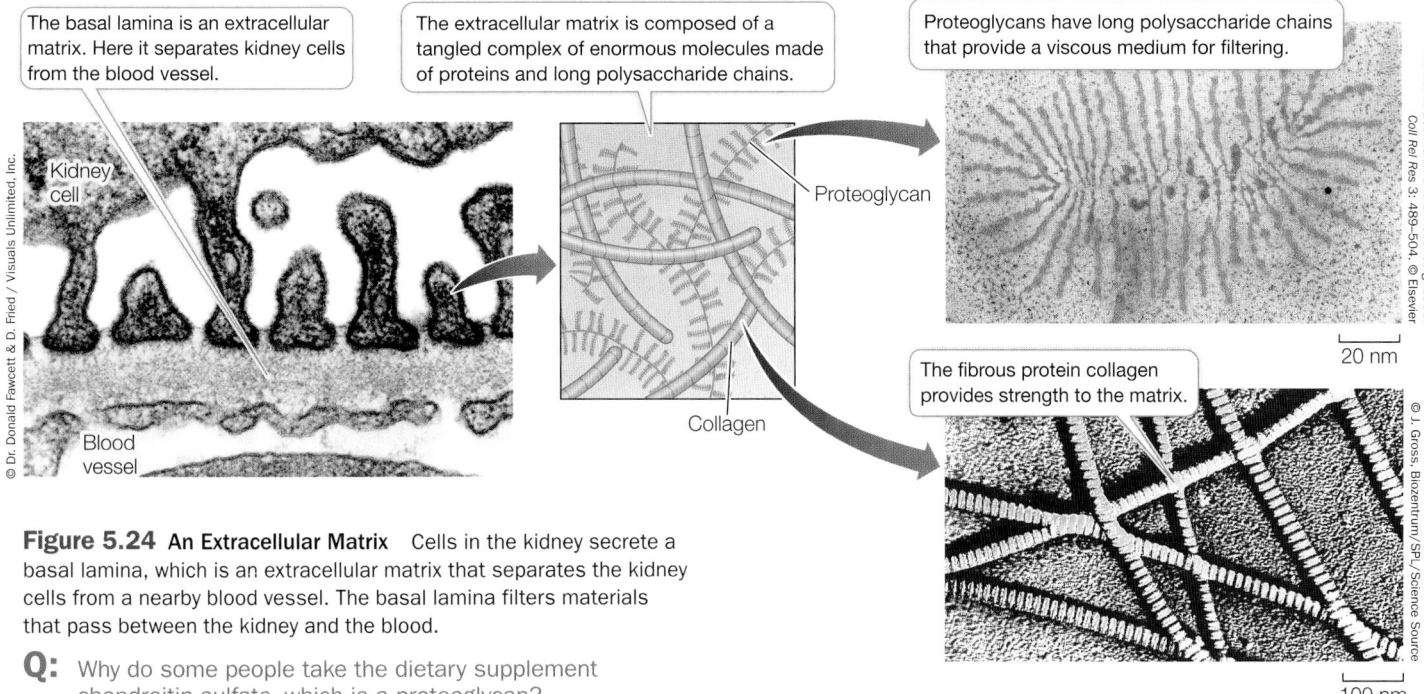

The basal lamina is an extracellular matrix. Here it separates kidney cells from the blood vessel.

The extracellular matrix is composed of a tangled complex of enormous molecules made of proteins and long polysaccharide chains.

Proteoglycans have long polysaccharide chains that provide a viscous medium for filtering.

Kidney cell

Blood vessel

Proteoglycan

Collagen

The fibrous protein collagen provides strength to the matrix.

20 nm

100 nm

© Dr. Donald Fawcett & D. Fried / Visuals Unlimited, Inc.

From J. A. Buckwalter and L. Rosenberg, 1983. *Coll Rel Res* 3: 489–504, © Elsevier

© J. Gross, Biozentrum/SPL/Science Source

Figure 5.24 An Extracellular Matrix Cells in the kidney secrete a basal lamina, which is an extracellular matrix that separates the kidney cells from a nearby blood vessel. The basal lamina filters materials that pass between the kidney and the blood.

Q: Why do some people take the dietary supplement chondroitin sulfate, which is a proteoglycan?

- It helps filter materials passing between different tissues. This is especially important in the kidney.
- It helps orient cell movements during embryonic development and during tissue repair.
- It plays a role in chemical signaling from one cell to another. Proteins connect the cell's cell membrane to the extracellular matrix. These proteins (for example, integrin) span the cell membrane and are involved with transmitting signals to the interior of the cell. This allows communication between the extracellular matrix and the cytoplasm of the cell.

KEY CONCEPT
5.4 Recap and Assess

Extracellular structures are produced by cells and secreted outside the cell membrane. Most consist of a fibrous component in a gel-like medium.

1. When a cancer spreads from the initial site to another location in the body, initial events are the detachment of the cancer cells from its surrounding extracellular matrix and digestion of the matrix as the cell migrates. How might these events occur?

2. How does the structure of a cell wall contribute to its function?

3. How could a biologist use chemical analysis to differentiate between a plant cell and an animal cell?

We have now discussed the structures and some functions of prokaryotic and eukaryotic cells. Both exemplify the cell theory, showing that cells are the basic units of life and of biological continuity. Much of the rest of this part of the book will deal with these two aspects of cells. There is abundant evidence that the simpler prokaryotic cells are more ancient than eukaryotic cells, and that the first cells were probably prokaryotic. We will now turn to the next step in cellular evolution, the origin of eukaryotic cells.

KEY CONCEPT
5.5 Eukaryotic Cells Evolved in Several Steps

Learning Objectives

5.5.1 Explain how the cell membrane could have been involved in the evolution of the endomembrane system in eukaryotes.

5.5.2 Relate endosymbiotic theory to observations of modern cells.

Life on Earth was entirely prokaryotic for about 1 billion years—from the time when prokaryotic cells first appeared until about 2.7 billion years ago, when evidence of eukaryotic cells appears in ancient rocks. The advent of compartmentalization—the hallmark of eukaryotes—was a major event in the history of life. It permitted many more biochemical functions to exist in the same cell than had previously been possible. Compared with a typical eukaryote, a single prokaryotic cell is often biochemically specialized, limited in the resources it can use and the functions it can perform.

What is the origin of compartmentalization? We will describe the evolution of eukaryotic organelles in more detail in Key Concept 24.2. Here we outline two major themes in this process.

Internal membranes and the nuclear envelope probably came from the cell membrane

We noted earlier in this chapter that some bacteria contain internal membranes. How could these arise? In electron micrographs, the internal membranes of prokaryotes often appear to be inward folds of the cell membrane. This observation has led to a theory

Figure 5.25 The Origins of Organelles (A) The endomembrane system and nuclear envelope may have been formed by infolding and then fusion of the cell membrane. (B) The endosymbiosis theory proposes that some organelles may be descended from prokaryotes that were engulfed by other, larger cells.

that the endomembrane system and the cell nucleus originated by related processes (**Figure 5.25A**). The close relationship between the endoplasmic reticulum (ER) and the nuclear envelope in today's eukaryotes is consistent with this theory.

A bacterium with enclosed compartments would have several evolutionary advantages. Chemicals could be concentrated in particular regions of the cell, allowing chemical reactions to proceed more efficiently. A biochemical process could be segregated within an organelle with, for example, a different pH from the rest of the cell, creating more favorable conditions for that process. Finally, DNA transcription could be separated from translation, providing more opportunities for separate control of these steps in gene expression.

Some organelles arose by endosymbiosis

Symbiosis means "living together," and often refers to two organisms that coexist, each one supplying something that the other needs. With the **theory of endosymbiosis** biologists have proposed that some organelles—the mitochondria and the plastids—arose not by an infolding of the cell membrane but by one cell *in*gesting (but not *di*gesting) another cell, giving rise to a symbiotic relationship. Eventually, the ingested cell lost its autonomy and some of its functions. In addition, many of the ingested cell's genes were transferred to the host's DNA. Mitochondria and plastids in today's eukaryotic cells are the remnants of these symbionts, retaining some specialized functions that benefit their host cells.

Consider the case of the plastid. About 2.5 billion years ago some prokaryotes (the cyanobacteria) developed photosynthesis. The emergence of these prokaryotes was a key event in the evolution of complex organisms because they increased the O_2 concentration in Earth's atmosphere (see Key Concept 24.2).

According to the endosymbiosis theory, photosynthetic prokaryotes also provided the precursor of the modern-day plastid. Cells without cell walls can engulf relatively large particles by phagocytosis (see Figure 5.12). In some cases, such as that of phagocytes in the human immune system, the engulfed particle can be an entire cell, such as a bacterium. Plastids may have arisen by a similar event involving an ancestral eukaryote and a cyanobacterium (**Figure 5.25B**).

KEY CONCEPT
5.5 Recap and Assess

Eukaryotic cells arose long after prokaryotic cells. Some organelles may have evolved by infolding of the cell membrane, whereas others probably evolved by endosymbiosis.

1. How could membrane infolding in a prokaryotic cell lead to the formation of the endomembrane system?

2. When they are removed from a cell, organelles such as mitochondria no longer function as they did inside the cell. What aspect of endosymbiotic theory explains this observation?

(A) Hypothetical evolution of the ER

1 An ancient prokaryotic cell has no internal membranes.

Cell membrane

DNA in nucleoid

2 The cell membrane folds inward. Many modern-day prokaryotes have membrane infoldings.

3 Further membrane infoldings begin the formation of the ER, creating a segregated compartment. The ER surrounds the nucleiod and forms the nuclear envelope.

(B) Evolution of the chloroplast according to the theory of endosymbiosis

Nucleus

Mitochondrion

Cyanobacterium

1 An ancestral eukaryotic cell endocytoses a photosynthetic cyanobacterium.

Chloroplast

2 The endocytosed cyanobacterium loses most of its genetic material to the host nucleus but retains the ability to photosynthesize. It is now a chloroplast.

In this chapter we presented an overview of the components of cells, with some ideas about their structures, functions, and origins. As you now embark on the study of major cellular processes, keep in mind that cellular components do not exist in isolation: they are part of a dynamic, interacting system. In Chapter 6 you will see that the cell membrane is far from a passive barrier, but instead is a multifunctional system that connects the inside of the cell with its extracellular environment.

▶Investigating LIFE

 Are pigments compartmentalized in all types of cells?

In this chapter you learned of several situations in which pigments are concentrated in discrete organelles: in humans, melanin is packaged in melanosomes in human skin cells; in plants, tannins are packaged in tannosomes, chlorophyll is packaged in thylakoids, other pigments are contained in chromoplasts, and anthocyanins that may attract pollinators and seed dispersers are packaged in the vacuoles in petals and fruits. You learned, too, of the remarkable ability of motor proteins to move pigment granules into the center of cells in fishes and amphibians, to lighten their skin color as a defensive mechanism.

Many biological traits and adaptations are linked to pigments in organelles. For example, the distribution of melanosomes is related to eye color, and genetically determined errors in the formation of melanosomes can lead to albinism and a lack of protection against ultraviolet light. In plants, the formation of tannosomes is associated with plant defenses (see Chapter 37). Understanding the pathway by which tannosomes are formed could have beneficial applications in agriculture. For example, tannins are important to the taste of red wine, and manipulating tannin concentrations can result in new flavors.

Future directions

The most common form of human cancer is skin cancer. Most skin cancers are easily treated, but a rare type, melanoma, can be lethal. As its name implies, melanoma occurs when melanocytes in the skin multiply excessively. This can happen if melanocytes are exposed to ultraviolet light from the Sun in excess of the ability of their melanin pigment to absorb it. When localized in the skin, melanoma is not harmful; it's just a growth. But when the tumor cells spread to other organs in a process called metastasis, melanoma often is lethal. Carmit Levy at the Sackler School of Medicine in Israel has found that the tumor sends a signal, contained in melanosomes, to neighboring skin cells that changes them and allows the tumor to spread. An experimental drug that blocks melanosome release also inhibits metastasis in animal studies. The drug is under development for human use.

 VISUAL SUMMARY 5

© Dennis Kunkel Microscopy/Science Source

You should be able to relate each summary to the adjacent figures. If you go to this visual summary in **Achieve**, you can follow links to figures, animations, activities, and simulations that will help you consolidate the material.

KEY CONCEPT

5.1 Cells Are the Fundamental Units of Life

Go to Activities 5.1 and 5.2

- The **cell theory** is the unifying theory of cell biology. All living things are composed of cells, and all cells come from preexisting cells.

- A cell is small and maintains a large **surface area-to-volume ratio**. This allows it to exchange adequate quantities of materials with its environment.

- Whereas certain biochemical processes, molecules, and structures are shared by all kinds of cells, there are two categories of organisms—**prokaryotes and eukaryotes**—that can be distinguished by characteristic cell structures.

Figure 5.2

	2 µm	20 µm	200 µm
Diameter	2 µm	20 µm	200 µm
Surface area $4\pi r^2$	12.6 µm^2	1,260 µm^2	126,000 µm^2
Volume $\frac{4}{3}\pi r^3$	4.2 µm^3	4,200 µm^3	4,200,000 µm^3
Surface area-to-volume ratio	3.0:1	0.3:1	0.003:1

Questions

1. One cell type has twice the diameter of another. Yet the first cell type has a larger surface area-to-volume ratio. How can this occur?

2. A cell has a diameter of 2 µm. Is the cell prokaryotic or eukaryotic? Explain.

Figure 5.5

KEY CONCEPT

5.2 Prokaryotic Cells Are the Simplest Cells

■ Prokaryotic cells have no internal compartments but have a **nucleoid** region containing DNA. The rest of the material inside the cell membrane, including the **ribosomes**, is called the cytoplasm. Some prokaryotes have additional protective structures, including a **cell wall**, an **outer membrane**, and a **capsule**.

■ Some prokaryotes have folded **internal membranes**, and some have **flagella** or **pili** for motility or attachment.

Questions

1. Penicillin and related antibiotics inhibit the synthesis of the bacterial cell wall. How do you think this kills bacteria?

2. There are more prokaryotic cells than eukaryotic cells in the human body. Explain.

Figure 5.6

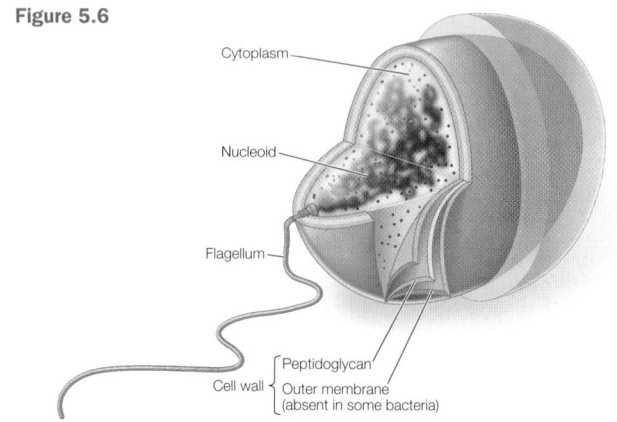

KEY CONCEPT

5.3 Eukaryotic Cells Contain Organelles

Go to Activities 5.3 and 5.4 and Animation 5.1

■ Eukaryotic cells are larger than prokaryotic cells and contain many membrane-enclosed organelles that compartmentalize functions.

■ The nucleus contains most of the cell's DNA and participates in the control of protein synthesis, which occurs in the cytoplasm at ribosomes.

■ The **endomembrane system**—consisting of the cell membrane, the **nuclear envelope**, the **endoplasmic reticulum**, the **Golgi apparatus**, and **lysosomes**—is a series of interrelated compartments enclosed by membranes. It segregates proteins and modifies them. Lysosomes contain many digestive enzymes.

■ **Mitochondria** and **chloroplasts** are organelles that process energy.

■ The **microfilaments**, **intermediate filaments**, and **microtubules** of the cytoskeleton provide the cell with shape, strength, and movement.

Questions

1. What organelles or structures are unique to eukaryotic plant cells?

2. A human genetic disease, Zellweger syndrome, arises when there is an absence of peroxisomes. What do you suppose are the biochemical consequences of this situation?

3. Another human genetic disease, I-cell disease, arises from an inability of the Golgi apparatus to correctly modify certain proteins to target them to lysosomes. What would be the consequences?

Figure 5.9

Figure 5.11

Figure 5.17

10 μm

KEY CONCEPT

5.4 Extracellular Materials Provide Structure

■ The plant cell wall consists principally of cellulose.

■ In animal cells, the **extracellular matrix** consists of different kinds of proteins, including **collagen** and **proteoglycans**.

Questions

1. Compare the plant cell wall with the animal extracellular matrix with respect to the fibrous and non-fibrous components.

2. There are proteins and polysaccharides in both the plant cell wall and animal extracellular matrix. Where are these molecules made, and how do they get into the extracellular structures?

Figure 5.23

Figure 5.24

KEY CONCEPT

5.5 Eukaryotic Cells Evolved in Several Steps

■ Infoldings of the cell membrane could have led to the formation of some membrane-enclosed organelles, such as the endomembrane system and the nucleus.

■ The **theory of endosymbiosis** states that mitochondria and chloroplasts originated when larger cells engulfed, but did not digest, smaller cells.

Questions

1. Could the lysosome have evolved by endosymbiosis? Explain.

2. Could mitochondria have evolved nonsymbiotically? Explain.

Figure 5.25

6 Cell Membranes

KEY CONCEPTS

6.1 Biological Membranes Are Lipid–Protein Bilayers

6.2 The Cell Membrane Is Important in Cell Adhesion and Recognition

6.3 Substances Can Cross Membranes by Passive Processes

6.4 Active Transport across Membranes Requires Energy

6.5 Large Molecules Enter and Leave a Cell through Vesicles

Blood, Sweat, and Membranes Water lost through sweating, leaves body tissues by passing through their cell membranes.

© Scott Barbour/Getty Images

▶ Investigating LIFE

Sweating and Membranes

As you saw in Chapter 2, sweating is a way to reduce body heat by using excess heat to evaporate water. At peak activity, in the gym or doing other physical work, you may lose as much as 2 liters of water an hour. Total water content of a typical person (it varies with body weight, fat content, etc.) is about 30 liters.

The sweat glands lie just below the surface of the skin. They are essentially cell-lined tubes surrounded by extracellular fluid. When sweating is triggered, these tubes fill with water and dissolved substances. To get from the extracellular fluid into the tube, water must go through the cells that line the tube.

A hallmark of living cells is the ability to regulate what enters and leaves the cytoplasm. This is a function of the cell membrane, a hydrophobic lipid bilayer with associated proteins. Because it is insoluble in the aqueous environment both inside and outside cells, the membrane is a physical barrier. But it is also a functional barrier—that is, the cell membrane is selectively permeable. Whereas water is polar, the interior of the membrane is nonpolar, so water has a natural tendency to avoid the membrane. The rate of movement of water across a lipid bilayer is modest. When you engage in normal activities such as reading this book, the cell membranes enclosing the cells lining

the sweat glands do not allow much water to enter or leave. But when you exercise vigorously, tiny membrane-enclosed vesicles inside the cells fill with water and some dissolved salts. In a process called exocytosis, these vesicles fuse with the cell membrane and release their watery contents (sweat) into the tubes. From there the sweat flows to the surface of the skin and evaporates.

Vesicles are not the only way to get polar water across a nonpolar membrane. For most types of animal cells, the modest rate of movement of water across the cell membrane is sufficient to meet the changing needs of the cell. But in some organs, like the mammalian kidney, and in plant roots, stems, and leaves, water needs can be so great and urgent that movement through the lipid bilayer is not enough. Instead, these organs have special pores called aquaporins present in the cell membrane. Water can flow through these pores readily because the proteins lining the channel have a hydrophilic inner surface.

 What is the importance of aquaporin membrane channels? (Find the answer on page 129.)

Biological Membranes Are Lipid–Protein Bilayers

Learning Objectives

6.1.1 Explain how the hydrophobic and hydrophilic regions of phospholipids are involved in membrane formation.

6.1.2 Differentiate among integral, peripheral, and anchored proteins.

6.1.3 Design an experiment to compare the properties of membranes in different types of cells.

6.1.4 Give an example of information provided by cell fusion experiments.

The physical organization and functioning of all biological membranes depend on their constituents: lipids, proteins, and carbohydrates. You are already familiar with these molecules from Chapter 3 and with membranes that enclose cells and organelles from Chapter 5. Lipids establish the physical integrity of the membrane and create a barrier to the rapid passage of hydrophilic materials such as polar molecules and ions. In addition, the phospholipid bilayer serves as a lipid "lake" in which a variety of proteins "float" (**Figure 6.1**). This general design is known as the **fluid mosaic model**. It is *mosaic* because it is made up of many discrete components, and *fluid* because the components can move freely.

Although the fluid mosaic model is largely valid for membrane structure, it does not say much about membrane composition.

As you read about the various molecules in membranes in the next sections, keep in mind that some membranes have more protein than lipids, others are lipid-rich, others have significant amounts of cholesterol or other sterols, and still others are rich in carbohydrates.

Lipids form the hydrophobic core of the membrane

Phospholipids are the major lipid components of biological membranes. Phospholipids form thin bilayers, with their charged, hydrophilic "heads" on the external surface interacting with the aqueous environment, and their nonpolar, fatty acid "tails" interacting with each other on the inside of the membrane (**Figure 6.2**).

> **Connect the Concepts** Recall from Key Concept 2.2 that some compounds are hydrophilic ("water-loving") and others are hydro-phobic ("water-hating"), and from Key Concept 3.4 that a phospholipid molecule has both hydrophilic and hydrophobic regions.

The thickness of a biological membrane is about 8 nanometers (0.008 μm), which is twice the length of a typical phospholipid—another indication that the membrane consists of a lipid bilayer. To give you an idea of the scale, a typical sheet of paper is about 8,000 times thicker than a membrane.

Although all biological membranes have a similar structure, membranes from different cells and different organelles within a cell may vary greatly in their lipid composition. For example, phospholipids can differ in fatty acid chain length (number of carbon atoms), degree of unsaturation (number of double bonds) in the fatty acids, and the polar groups present (see Key Concept

Outside of cell

Carbohydrates are attached to the outer surface of proteins (forming glycoproteins) or lipids (forming glycolipids).

Cholesterol alters membrane fluidity.

Phospholipid bilayer

Inside of cell

Peripheral membrane proteins are noncovalently attached to either membrane surface.

Membrane proteins may consist of multiple polypeptide subunits.

Some integral membrane proteins span the entire membrane.

Some integral membrane proteins are partially embedded in the bilayer.

Anchored membrane proteins are covalently bonded to lipids that are inserted into the membrane.

Figure 6.1 The Fluid Mosaic Model The general molecular structure of a biological membrane is a continuous phospholipid bilayer that has proteins embedded in or associated with it.

Q: What kinds of chemical interactions hold some membrane proteins embedded in the membrane and others on the membrane surface?

View in Achieve
Activity 6.1 The Fluid Mosaic Model

Aqueous environment

The nonpolar, hydrophobic fatty acid "tails" interact with one another in the interior of the bilayer.

The charged, or polar, hydrophilic "head" portions interact with polar water.

Aqueous environment

Figure 6.2 Phospholipid Bilayer The phospholipid bilayer separates two aqueous regions. The eight phospholipid molecules shown on the right represent a small cross section of a membrane bilayer. (Right after L. Stryer. 1981. *Biochemistry*, 2nd Ed., W. H. Freeman: New York.)

3.4). The saturated chains allow close packing of fatty acids in the bilayer, whereas the "kinks" in unsaturated fatty acids (see Figure 3.22) make for a less dense, more fluid packing.

The steroid cholesterol (see Figure 3.24) is an abundant component (20%–50%) of animal cell membranes. The hydroxyl group of cholesterol interacts with the polar ends of phospholipids, and the nonpolar rings and hydrocarbon chain insert into the fatty acids chains in the interior of the membrane. Cholesterol is important for membrane integrity and modulates membrane fluidity; the cholesterol in your membranes is not hazardous to your health.

The fatty acids of the phospholipids make the hydrophobic interior of the membrane somewhat fluid—about as fluid as lightweight olive oil. This fluidity permits some molecules to move laterally within the plane of the membrane. A given phospholipid molecule in the cell membrane can travel from one end of the cell to the other in a little more than a second! However, a phospholipid molecule in one half of the bilayer is unlikely to spontaneously flip over to the other side. For that to happen, the polar part of the molecule would have to move through the hydrophobic interior of the membrane. Since spontaneous phospholipid flip-flops are rare, the inner and outer halves of the bilayer may be quite different in the kinds of phospholipids they contain.

Membrane fluidity is affected by several factors, two of which are particularly important:

1. *Lipid composition*: Cholesterol and long-chain, saturated fatty acids pack tightly beside one another, with little room for movement. This close packing results in less fluid

membranes. A membrane with shorter-chain fatty acids, unsaturated fatty acids, or less cholesterol is more fluid.

2. *Temperature*: Because molecules move more slowly and fluidity decreases at reduced temperatures, cellular processes that take place within the membrane may slow down or stop under cold conditions in organisms that cannot keep their bodies warm. To address this problem, in some organisms the lipid composition of their membranes changes when they get cold, replacing saturated with unsaturated fatty acids and using fatty acids with shorter tails. These changes play a role in the survival of plants, bacteria, and hibernating animals during the winter.

▶ **View in Achieve**
Simulation 6.1 Lipid Bilayer Composition

Membrane proteins are asymmetrically distributed

Typically, cell membranes have 1 protein molecule for every 25 lipid molecules. This ratio varies depending on membrane function. In the inner membrane of the mitochondrion, which is specialized for energy processing, there is 1 protein for every 15 lipids. However, myelin—a modified cell membrane that encloses portions of some neurons (nerve cells) and acts as an electrical insulator—has only 1 protein for every 70 lipids.

Membrane proteins are very diverse. In fact, about one-fourth of the protein-coding genes in the eukaryotic genome encode membrane proteins. There are three general types of membrane proteins: integral proteins, peripheral proteins, and anchored proteins.

Integral membrane proteins are at least partly embedded in the phospholipid bilayer (see Figure 6.1). Like phospholipids, these proteins have both hydrophilic and hydrophobic regions (domains) (**Figure 6.3**).

• *Hydrophilic domains*: Stretches of amino acids with hydrophilic side chains (R groups; see Table 3.2) give certain regions of the protein a polar character. These hydrophilic domains

Hydrophilic R groups (side chains) in exposed parts of the protein interact with aqueous environments.

Outside of cell (aqueous)

Hydrophobic interior of bilayer

Hydrophobic R groups interact with the hydrophobic core of the membrane, away from water.

Inside of cell (aqueous)

Figure 6.3 Interactions of Integral Membrane Proteins An integral membrane protein is held in the membrane by the distribution of the hydrophilic and hydrophobic side chains on its amino acids.

interact with water and stick out into the aqueous environment inside or outside the cell or organelle.

- *Hydrophobic domains*: Stretches of amino acids with hydrophobic side chains give other regions of the protein a nonpolar character. These domains interact with the fatty acids in the interior of the phospholipid bilayer, away from water.

Peripheral membrane proteins lack exposed hydrophobic groups and are not embedded in the bilayer. Instead, they have polar or charged regions that interact with exposed parts of integral membrane proteins, or with the polar heads of phospholipid molecules (see Figure 6.1).

Anchored membrane proteins are covalently attached to fatty acids or other lipid groups. The hydrophobic lipid groups insert into the phospholipid bilayer and hold these proteins in association with the membrane.

Proteins are asymmetrically distributed on the inner and outer surfaces of membranes, giving the two surfaces different properties. An integral protein that extends all the way through the phospholipid bilayer and protrudes on both sides is known as a **transmembrane protein**. In addition to having one or more **transmembrane domains** that extend through the bilayer, such a protein may have domains with other specific functions on the inner and outer sides of the membrane. Peripheral membrane proteins, by contrast, are located on one side of the membrane or the other. This asymmetrical arrangement of membrane proteins gives the two surfaces of the membrane different properties. As you will see, these differences have great functional significance.

Like lipids, some membrane proteins move around relatively freely within the phospholipid bilayer. Experiments that involve the technique of cell fusion illustrate this migration dramatically. When two cells are fused, a single continuous membrane forms and surrounds both cells, and some proteins from each cell distribute themselves uniformly around this membrane (**Figure 6.4**).

Although some proteins are free to migrate in the membrane, others are not, but rather are confined to a specific region of the membrane. These membrane regions are like an enclosure of animals at the zoo: the animals are free to move around within the fenced area but not outside it. An example is the protein in the cell membrane of a muscle cell that recognizes a chemical signal from a neuron. This protein is normally found only at the specific region where the neuron meets the muscle cell. Proteins inside the cell can restrict the movement of proteins within a membrane. The cytoskeleton has components just below the inner face of the membrane that are attached to membrane proteins protruding into the cytoplasm. The stability of the cytoskeletal components may thus restrict movement of attached membrane proteins.

Membranes are constantly changing

Membranes in eukaryotic cells are constantly forming, transforming from one type to another, fusing with one another, and breaking down. As we discussed in Chapter 5, fragments of membrane move, in the form of vesicles, from the endoplasmic reticulum (ER) to the Golgi apparatus, and from the Golgi apparatus to the cell membrane (see Figure 5.11). Secondary lysosomes form when

Experiment

Figure 6.4 Rapid Diffusion of Membrane Proteins

Original Paper: L. D. Frye and M. Edidin. 1970. The rapid intermixing of cell surface antigens after formation of mouse-human heterokaryons. *J Cell Sci* 7: 319–335.

Two animal cells can be fused together in the laboratory, forming a single large cell (heterokaryon). This phenomenon was used to test whether membrane proteins can diffuse independently in the plane of the cell membrane.

HYPOTHESIS▶ Proteins embedded in a membrane can diffuse freely within the membrane.

METHOD▶

The mouse cell has a membrane protein that can be labeled with a green dye.

The human cell has a membrane protein that can be labeled with a red dye.

Membrane proteins

Mouse cell   **Human cell**

1 The cells are fused together to create a heterokaryon.

RESULTS▶

2 Initially, the mouse and human membrane proteins are on different sides of the heterokaryon.

3 After 40 minutes, the mouse and human membrane proteins are intermixed.

CONCLUSION▶ Membrane proteins can diffuse rapidly in the plane of the membrane.

primary lysosomes from the Golgi apparatus fuse with phagosomes from the cell membrane.

Because all membranes appear similar under the electron microscope, and because they interconvert readily, we might expect all subcellular membranes to be chemically identical. However, that is not the case: there are major chemical differences among the membranes of even a single eukaryotic cell. Membranes are changed chemically when they form parts of certain organelles. In the Golgi apparatus, for example, the membranes of the *cis* face closely resemble those of the ER in chemical composition, but those of the *trans* face are more similar to the cell membrane.

Cell membrane carbohydrates are recognition sites

In addition to lipids and proteins, the cell membrane contains carbohydrates (see Figure 6.1). The carbohydrates are located on the outer surface of the cell membrane and serve as recognition sites for other cells and molecules, as you will see in Key Concept 6.2.

Membrane-associated carbohydrates may be covalently bonded to lipids or to proteins:

- A **glycolipid** consists of a carbohydrate covalently bonded to a lipid. Extending out from the cell surface, the carbohydrate may serve as a recognition signal for interactions between cells. For example, the carbohydrates on some glycolipids change when cells become cancerous. This change may allow white blood cells to target cancer cells for destruction.

- A **glycoprotein** consists of one or more short carbohydrate chains covalently bonded to a protein. The bound carbohydrates are oligosaccharides, usually not exceeding 20 monosaccharide units in length (see Key Concept 3.3). A proteoglycan (see Key Concept 5.4) is a more heavily glycosylated protein: it has more carbohydrate molecules attached to it, and the carbohydrate chains are often longer than they are in glycoproteins. The carbohydrates of glycoproteins and proteoglycans often function in cell recognition and adhesion.

The "alphabet" of monosaccharides on the outer surfaces of membranes can generate a large diversity of messages. Recall from Key Concept 3.3 that monosaccharides are simple carbohydrates, often containing five or six carbons in a ring structure and which can bond with one another in various configurations. They may form linear or branched oligosaccharides with many different three-dimensional shapes. An oligosaccharide of a specific shape on one cell can bind to a complementary shape on an adjacent cell. This binding is the basis of cell–cell adhesion.

KEY CONCEPT
6.1 Recap and Assess

The fluid mosaic model applies to the cell membrane and the membranes of organelles. In the aqueous environment of the cell, phospholipids spontaneously assemble into a bilayer. The cell membrane is considered fluid because the phospholipids and some of the proteins that compose it can move within their monolayer. An integral membrane protein has both hydrophilic and hydrophobic domains, which affect its position and function in the membrane. Peripheral membrane proteins are bound to one side or the other of the membrane. Anchored membrane proteins are covalently attached to membrane lipids. Carbohydrates that attach to lipids and proteins on the outside of the membrane serve as recognition and adhesion sites for adjacent cells.

1. How do the hydrophobic and hydrophilic regions of phospholipids form a membrane bilayer?

2. What differentiates an integral protein from a peripheral protein?

3. If a cell membrane is frozen and then fractured so that the two leaflets of the cell membrane are peeled away from each other, bumps appear in electron microscopy. What are the bumps?

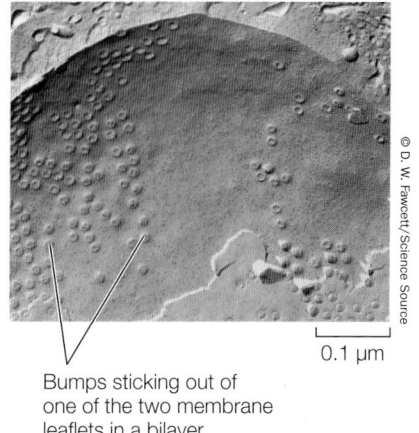

Bumps sticking out of one of the two membrane leaflets in a bilayer

0.1 µm

4. When a normal lung cell becomes a lung cancer cell, there are several important changes in cell membrane properties. How would you investigate the observation that the cancer cell membrane is more fluid, with more rapid diffusion in the plane of the membrane of both lipids and proteins?

Now that you understand the structure of biological membranes, let's see how their components function. In the next key concept we'll focus on the membrane that surrounds individual cells—the cell membrane—and look at how the cell membrane allows individual cells to be grouped together into multicellular systems of tissues.

KEY CONCEPT
6.2 The Cell Membrane Is Important in Cell Adhesion and Recognition

Learning Objectives

6.2.1 Design investigations to analyze the function of proteins and carbohydrates in cell adhesion and cell recognition.

6.2.2 Compare and contrast the three types of cell junctions found in animals.

Often the cells of multicellular organisms exist in specialized groups with similar functions, called tissues. Your body has about 37 trillion cells organized into various kinds of tissues—such as muscle, nerve, and epithelium. Two processes allow cells to arrange themselves in groups:

1. **Cell recognition**, in which one cell specifically recognizes and binds to another cell of a certain type

2. **Cell adhesion**, in which the connection between the two cells is strengthened

Simple organisms are useful in understanding cell recognition and adhesion

Both cell adhesion and cell recognition involve the cell membrane. One way to study these processes is to break down a tissue into its individual cells and then allow them to adhere to one another again. This type of experiment is most easily done in relatively simple organisms, such as sponges, which provide good models for studying processes that also occur in the complex tissues of larger species.

Sponges are multicellular marine animals that have only a few distinct cell layers (see Key Concept 29.1). The cells of a sponge adhere to one another but can be separated mechanically by passing the animal several times through a fine wire screen (**Figure 6.5**). Through this process, what was a single animal becomes hundreds of individual cells suspended in seawater. If such cells are stirred gently for a few hours, cell recognition occurs: the cells bump into and recognize one another, sticking together in the same shape and tissue organization as in the original sponge. This recognition is species-specific; if disaggregated sponge cells from two different species are placed in the same container and shaken, individual cells will stick only to other cells of the same species. Two different sponges form, just like the ones at the start of the experiment.

Tissue-specific and species-specific cell recognition and cell adhesion are essential to the formation and maintenance of tissues in multicellular organisms. Think of your own body. What keeps muscle cells bound to muscle cells and skin to skin? Specific cell adhesion is so obvious a characteristic of complex organisms that it is easy to overlook. You will see many examples of specific cell adhesion throughout this book; here we describe its general principles. As you will see, cell recognition and cell adhesion depend on cell membrane proteins.

Cell recognition and adhesion involve proteins and carbohydrates at the cell surface

The molecules responsible for cell recognition and adhesion in sponges are proteoglycans (often 80% carbohydrate by molecular weight) that carry two kinds of carbohydrates. One kind is relatively small and binds to membrane components, keeping the proteoglycan attached to the cell. The other kind of carbohydrate is a larger, sulfated polysaccharide. If the sulfated polysaccharide from a particular species of sponge is purified and attached to cellulose beads, the beads will aggregate together or with sponge cells—but only with cells of the same species from which the polysaccharide was purified. This demonstrates that the sulfated polysaccharide is responsible for both the specific recognition and adhesion of the sponge cells.

Cell adhesion can result from interactions between the carbohydrates that are parts of glycolipids, glycoproteins, or proteoglycans—as is the case in sponge cells. In other cases, a carbohydrate on one cell interacts with a membrane protein on another cell. Or two proteins can interact directly. As we described in Key Concept 3.2, a protein not only has a specific shape,

it also has specific chemical groups exposed on its surface where they can interact with other substances, including other proteins. Both of these features allow binding to other specific molecules. Cell adhesion occurs in all kinds of multicellular organisms. In plants, cell adhesion may be mediated by both integral membrane proteins and specific carbohydrates in the cell walls.

Usually, the binding of cells in a tissue is **homotypic**; that is, the same molecule sticks out of both cells, and the exposed surfaces fit together and bind to each other. This is a factor that keeps skin cells together in a sheet of cells. But **heterotypic** binding (between different molecules on different cells) also occurs. In this case, chemical groups on different surface molecules have an affinity for one another. For example, when the mammalian sperm meets the egg, different proteins on the two types of cells have complementary binding surfaces. Similarly, some algae form male and female reproductive cells (analogous to sperm and eggs) that have flagella to propel them toward each other. Male and female cells can recognize each other by heterotypic glycoproteins on their flagella.

Three types of cell junctions connect adjacent cells

In a complex multicellular organism, cell recognition molecules allow specific types of cells to bind to one another. Often, after the initial binding, both cells contribute material to form additional membrane structures that connect them to one another. These specialized structures, called **cell junctions**, are most evident in electron micrographs of animal epithelial tissues, which are layers of cells that line body cavities or cover body surfaces. These

1. Tissue from a red sponge contains similar cells bound to each other.

2. The sponge tissue can be separated into single cells by passing it through a fine mesh screen.

3. Exposed regions of membrane proteoglycans bind to each other, causing cells to adhere.

4. A new sponge forms.

© WaterFrame/Alamy Stock Photo

Figure 6.5 Cell Recognition and Adhesion
In most cases (including the aggregation of animal cells into tissues), the binding between molecules is homotypic (same to same).

surfaces often receive stresses or must retain their contents under pressure, so it is particularly important that their cells adhere tightly. We will examine three types of cell junctions that enable animal cells to seal intercellular spaces, reinforce attachments to one another, and communicate with each other. Tight junctions, desmosomes, and gap junctions, respectively, perform these three functions (Figure 6.6).

1. **Tight junctions** prevent substances from moving through the spaces between cells. For example, cells lining the bladder have tight junctions so urine cannot leak out into the body cavity. Another important function of tight junctions is to maintain distinct faces of a cell within a tissue by restricting the migration of membrane proteins over the cell surface from one face to the other. This may result in a certain function (e.g., endocytosis) being confined to one region of the cell surface.

2. **Desmosomes** hold neighboring cells firmly together, acting like spot welds or rivets. Materials can still move around in the extracellular matrix. This provides mechanical stability for tissues such as skin that receive physical stress.

3. **Gap junctions** are channels that run between membrane pores in adjacent cells, allowing substances to pass between cells. In the heart, for example, gap junctions allow the rapid spread of electric current (mediated by ions) so the heart muscle cells beat in unison.

Cell membranes adhere to the extracellular matrix

In Key Concept 5.4 you learned about the extracellular matrix of animal cells, which is composed of collagen protein arranged in fibers in a gelatinous matrix of proteoglycans. The attachment of a cell to the extracellular matrix is important in maintaining the integrity of a tissue. In addition, some cells can detach from their neighbors, move, and attach to other cells; this is often mediated by interactions with the extracellular matrix.

A transmembrane protein called **integrin** often mediates the attachment of epithelial cells to the extracellular matrix (**Figure 6.7**). More than 24 different integrins have been described in human cells. All of them bind to a protein in the extracellular matrix outside the cell, and to actin filaments, which are part of the cytoskeleton, inside the cell. So in addition to playing a role in

(A) Tight junctions

The proteins of tight junctions form a "quilted" seal, barring the movement of dissolved materials through the space between epithelial cells.

(B) Desmosomal adhesion

Desmosomes link adjacent cells tightly but permit materials to move around them in the intercellular space.

(C) Gap junctions

Gap junctions let adjacent cells communicate.

Figure 6.6 Junctions Link Animal Cells Together Tight junctions (A) and desmosomes (B) are abundant in epithelial tissues. Gap junctions (C) are also found in some muscle and nerve tissues, in which rapid communication between cells is important. Although all three junction types are shown in the cell at the top left, all three are not necessarily seen at the same time in actual cells.

 View in **Achieve**
Activity 6.2 Animal Cell Junctions

(A)

(B)

Outside of cell

Outside of cell
Extracellular matrix

Integrin

Integrin has binding sites for the extracellular matrix and for the cell cytoskeleton; the cell is bound to the matrix.

When integrin's three-dimensional structure changes, it cannot bind to the extracellular matrix and the cell detaches.

Actin

Inside of cell

Inside of cell

Figure 6.7 Integrins and the Extracellular Matrix (A) Integrins mediate the attachment of cells to the extracellular matrix. (B) When integrins no longer mediate attachment, the cell can separate itself from its extracellular matrix.

Q: When a tumor spreads in the body, cells detach from the extracellular matrix and then reattach at another organ in the body. For each tumor type, there are preferred organs to which it spreads. What does this indicate about integrins and the extracellular matrix?

adhesion, integrin has a role in maintaining cell structure via its interaction with the cytoskeleton. The binding of integrin to the extracellular matrix is noncovalent and reversible. When a cell moves its location within a tissue or organism, the integrin-matrix interaction is released and the cell is free from the constraints of the matrix. When the cell arrives at the new location, a new integrin may be made to allow the cells to interact with the particular extracellular matrix in that tissue.

KEY CONCEPT
6.2 Recap and Assess

In multicellular organisms, cells arrange themselves into tissues via the processes of cell recognition and cell adhesion. These processes are mediated by membrane-associated proteins and carbohydrates. Cell membrane proteins also interact with the extracellular matrix. Cell junctions assist in strengthening tissues and allow cells to communicate with one another.

1. Describe an experiment showing a role for carbohydrates in cell recognition and adhesion.
2. To which of the three types of animal cell junctions are plasmodesmata most similar (see Figure 5.9)?

You have seen how the cell membrane and molecules associated with it facilitate binding between cells and the maintenance of cell adhesion. We'll turn now to another major function of membranes: regulating the substances that enter or leave a cell or organelle.

KEY CONCEPT
6.3 Substances Can Cross Membranes by Passive Processes

Learning Objectives

6.3.1 Predict rates of diffusion of substances under different conditions.

6.3.2 Discuss the effect of different environmental conditions on the movement of water into and out of living cells.

6.3.3 Explain the role of channel proteins in facilitating diffusion across membranes.

Membranes separate an internal environment from the external environment, giving cells or organelles the ability to regulate their internal composition. Biological membranes allow some substances, but not others, to pass through them. This characteristic of membranes is called **selective permeability**. Selective permeability allows the membrane to determine what substances enter or leave a cell or organelle.

There are two fundamentally different processes by which substances cross biological membranes:

1. The processes of **passive transport** do not require the input of chemical-bond energy to drive them.

2. The processes of **active transport** are driven by chemical-bond energy (metabolic energy).

This key concept focuses on the passive processes by which substances cross membranes. The energy for the passive transport of a substance comes from the difference between its concentration on one side of the membrane and its concentration on the other—its **concentration gradient**. Passive transport can involve either of two types of diffusion: simple diffusion through the phospholipid bilayer, or facilitated diffusion via channel proteins or carrier proteins.

 View in Achieve
Animation 6.1 **Passive Transport**

Diffusion is the process of random movement toward a state of equilibrium

In a solution, there is a tendency for all of the components to be evenly distributed. You can see this when a drop of food coloring falls into a glass of water. Initially the pigment molecules are very concentrated, but they will move about at random, slowly spreading until the intensity of the color is eventually the same throughout the glass (**Figure 6.8**). A solution in which the solute particles are uniformly distributed is said to be at equilibrium because there will be no future net change in their concentration. Being at equilibrium does not mean that the particles have stopped moving; it just means that they are moving in such a way that their overall distribution does not change.

Diffusion is the process of random movement toward a state of equilibrium. Although the motion of each individual particle is

1 **Initial:** The dye molecules are concentrated in one region.

2 **Diffusion:** The dye molecules move to become evenly distributed.

3 **Final:** The dye molecules are evenly distributed.

Figure 6.8 Diffusion Molecules tend to move from a region of higher concentration to one of lower concentration, until the molecules are evenly distributed in the environment, as shown here by dye molecules in a beaker of water.

Q: The food dye in this experiment has a molecular weight of 600. If a dye with a molecular weight of 10,000 was used instead, what would the result be?

absolutely random, the net movement of particles is directional until equilibrium is reached. Diffusion is thus a net movement from regions of higher concentration to regions of lower concentration. In a solution with many different substances dissolved in it (solutes), the diffusion of each solute is independent of those of the others. How fast a substance diffuses depends on five factors:

1. The *size and mass* of the molecules or ions: smaller molecules diffuse faster.

2. The *temperature* of the solution: higher temperatures lead to faster diffusion because ions or molecules have more energy, and thus move more rapidly, at higher temperatures.

3. The *density of the solution*: as the density of the solution through which a substance is diffusing increases, the diffusion rate decreases.

4. The *concentration gradient* in the system—that is, the change in solute concentration with distance in a given direction: the greater the concentration gradient, the more rapidly a substance diffuses.

5. The *area* across which a substance diffuses and the *distance* it diffuses: a larger surface area permits more rapid diffusion. As you will see in Chapter 30, keeping the distance a substance must diffuse as short as possible maximizes the diffusion rate.

In our example in Figure 6.8, the gradient is the concentration of food coloring in the droplet when first dropped into the water as compared with the concentration of food coloring in the water on the edge of the glass. When the food coloring is first dropped into the water, there is a high (or steep) concentration gradient. All the coloring molecules are in one region. As time passes and the coloring molecules diffuse through the solution, the concentration gradient decreases.

DIFFUSION WITHIN CELLS AND TISSUES   In a small volume such as that inside a cell, solutes distribute themselves rapidly by diffusion. Small molecules and ions may move from one end of a cell to another in a millisecond (10^{-3} s, or one-thousandth of a second). However, the usefulness of diffusion as a transport

mechanism declines drastically as distances become greater. In the absence of mechanical stirring, diffusion across more than a centimeter may take an hour or more, and diffusion across meters may take years! Diffusion would not be adequate to distribute materials over the length of a human body, much less that of a larger organism. But within our cells or across layers of one or two cells, diffusion is rapid enough to distribute small molecules and ions almost instantaneously.

DIFFUSION ACROSS MEMBRANES   In a solution without barriers, all the solutes diffuse at rates determined by temperature, their physical properties, their concentration gradients, the density of the solution, and the area and distance of diffusion. If a biological membrane divides the solution into separate compartments (e.g., the cytoplasm of a cell vs. the extracellular environment), then the movement of the different solutes can also be affected by the properties of the membrane. The membrane is said to be permeable to solutes that can cross it more or less easily, but impermeable to substances that cannot move across it. Molecules to which the membrane is impermeable remain in separate compartments, and their concentrations may be different on the two sides of the membrane. Molecules to which the membrane is permeable diffuse from one compartment to the other until their concentrations are equal on both sides of the membrane, and equilibrium is reached. After that point, individual molecules will continue to pass through the membrane, but *there will be no net change in concentration.*

Simple diffusion takes place through the phospholipid bilayer

In **simple diffusion**, small molecules pass through the phospholipid bilayer of the membrane. A molecule that is itself hydrophobic, and is therefore soluble in lipids, enters the membrane readily and is able to pass through it. The more lipid-soluble the molecule is, the more rapidly it diffuses through the membrane bilayer. This statement holds true over a wide range of molecular weights.

By contrast, electrically charged or polar molecules, such as amino acids, sugars, and ions, do not pass readily through a membrane, for two reasons. First, such charged or polar molecules are not very soluble in the hydrophobic interior of the bilayer. Second, such substances form many hydrogen bonds with water and ions in the aqueous environment, be it the cytoplasm or the cell exterior. The multiplicity of these hydrogen bonds prevents the substances from moving into the hydrophobic interior of the membrane. **Figure 6.9** summarizes these phenomena.

Osmosis is the diffusion of water across membranes

Movement of water molecules through a membrane toward a region of higher solute concentration is called **osmosis**. This is a passive process that uses no metabolic energy. Because large or polar solute molecules can't cross the membrane, their otherwise random movement becomes biased away from the membrane (see Figure 6.9). If the solute concentration on one side of the membrane is higher, and all other factors are equal, then more solute molecules move away from the membrane on the side with the

Figure 6.9 Permeability of Phospholipid Bilayers Small uncharged molecules can diffuse through the membrane, but ions and large polar molecules cannot.

In general, when we discuss tonicity in cells, we refer to the outside solution in comparison with the inside of the cell. Therefore a solution that has a higher concentration of solutes than the concentration inside the cell is hypertonic. To reach equilibrium, water would move out of the cell into the surrounding solution. Water moves from a hypotonic solution across a membrane to a hypertonic solution.

When we say that "water moves," bear in mind that we are referring to the net movement of water. Since it is so abundant, water is constantly moving across the cell membrane into and out of cells. What concerns us here is whether the overall movement is greater in one direction or the other.

The total concentration of solutes in the environment determines the direction of osmosis. Consider red blood cells (see Figure 6.10). The environment outside the cell, the blood plasma, must be isotonic to the blood cells if the cells are not to burst (if the environment is hypotonic) or shrink (hypertonic). Regulation of the solute concentration of the blood plasma is therefore an important process for maintaining the integrity of the red blood cells. As you will see in Chapter 50, the body expends a great deal of energy maintaining

greater solute concentration, and there is a net movement of water toward the side with the higher solute concentration.

Connect the Concepts Osmosis plays key roles in plant physiology (e.g., in the root; see Key Concept 33.1) and in animal physiology (e.g., in the kidney; see Key Concept 50.1).

Three terms are used to compare the total solute concentrations of two solutions separated by a membrane:

1. **Isotonic** solutions have equal solute concentrations (Figure 6.10A).

2. A **hypotonic** solution has a lower solute concentration than the other solution with which it is being compared (Figure 6.10B).

3. A **hypertonic** solution has a higher solute concentration than the other solution with which it is being compared (Figure 6.10C).

Figure 6.10 Osmosis Can Modify the Shapes of Cells In a solution that is isotonic with the cytoplasm (**A**), a plant or animal cell maintains a consistent, characteristic shape because there is no net movement of water into or out of the cell. In these models, it is assumed that the solutes do not move across the membrane. In a solution that is hypotonic to the cytoplasm (**B**), water enters the cell. An environment that is hypertonic to the cytoplasm (**C**) results in water leaving the cell.

Q: If you overfertilize the soil of a potted plant, the plant often wilts. Why?

(A) Isotonic (equivalent solute concentration)

Inside of cell | Outside of cell

Animal cell in living animal (red blood cell in bloodstream)

The rates of water movement in and out are equal.

Plant cell in unstressed leaf (leaf epithelial cells)

The rates of water movement in and out are equal.

(B) Hypotonic on the outside (dilute solutes outside)

Inside of cell | Outside of cell

Animal cell in hypotonic solution

Cells take up water, swell, and burst.

Plant cell of plant watered with distilled water

The cell stiffens but generally retains its shape because a cell wall is present.

(C) Hypertonic on the outside (concentrated solutes outside)

Inside of cell | Outside of cell

Animal cell in hypertonic solution

Cells lose water and shrivel.

Plant cell of plant watered with salt water

The cell shrinks, pulling the cell membrane away from the cell wall (plasmolysis).

this environment. To put it more generally, cells and organisms strive to maintain an isotonic external environment.

Unlike animal cells, the cells of plants, archaea, bacteria, fungi, and some protists have cell walls outside their cell membrane that limit their volumes. Cells with sturdy walls take up a limited amount of water, and in so doing they build up internal pressure against the cell wall, which prevents further water from entering. This pressure within the cell is called **turgor pressure**. Turgor pressure keeps plants upright (and lettuce crisp) and is the driving force for the enlargement of plant cells. It is a normal and essential component of plant growth. If enough water leaves the cells, turgor pressure drops and the plant wilts. Turgor pressure reaches about 100 pounds per square inch (0.7 kg/cm^2)—several times greater than the pressure in automobile tires. This pressure is so great that the cells would change shape and detach from one another were it not for adhesive molecules in the plant cell walls and the plasmodesmata linking the cell cytoplasms (see Key Concept 5.4).

Diffusion may be aided by channel proteins

As we saw earlier, polar or charged substances such as water, amino acids, sugars, and ions do not readily diffuse across membranes. But they can cross the hydrophobic phospholipid bilayer passively (that is, without the input of energy) in one of two ways, depending on the substance:

1. **Channel proteins** are integral membrane proteins that form channels across the membrane through which certain substances can pass. Note that these are not channels in the widely used sense of the word (meaning open to the environment like a canal) but tunnels (surrounded by the membrane protein).

2. **Carrier proteins** bind substances and speed up their diffusion through the phospholipid bilayer.

Diffusion that is aided by channel proteins or carrier proteins is called **facilitated diffusion**. The substances diffuse according to their concentration gradients, but their diffusion is facilitated by protein channels or carriers. Although these proteins enhance the rate of diffusion, facilitated diffusion, like simple diffusion, does not require any input of energy.

ION CHANNELS   The best-studied channel proteins are the **ion channels**. As you will see in later chapters, the movement of ions across membranes is important in many biological processes such as respiration within the mitochondria, the electrical activity of the nervous system, and the opening of pores in leaves to allow gas exchange with the environment. Several types of ion channels have been identified—each specific for a particular ion. All show the same basic structure of a hydrophilic pore that allows a particular ion to move through its center.

> **Connect the Concepts** Ion channels play an important role in the excitability of nervous tissues. See Key Concept 44.2.

Just as a fence may have a gate that can be opened or closed, most ion channels are gated: they can be opened or closed to ion passage (**Figure 6.11**). A **gated channel** opens when a stimulus

causes a change in the three-dimensional shape of the channel. In some cases, this stimulus is the binding of a chemical signal, or **ligand**. Channels controlled in this way are called ligand-gated channels. Other channels are mechanically gated and open in response to physical stimuli such as sound waves in the ear, or are light-gated, as in the eye. A voltage-gated channel is stimulated to open or close by a change in the voltage (electric charge difference) across the membrane.

AQUAPORINS FOR WATER   As you saw in the opening story of this chapter, water can cross membranes through protein channels called **aquaporins**. These channels function as a cellular plumbing system for moving water. The aquaporin channel is highly specific. Water molecules move in single file through the channel, which excludes ions so that the electrical properties of the cell are maintained. Aquaporins were first identified when a protein from red blood cell membranes was inserted into frog oocytes (immature egg cells). The membranes of these cells are normally impermeable to water, but the membranes of the cells treated with aquaporins became much more permeable (**Investigating Life: Aquaporins Increase Membrane Permeability to Water**).

Carrier proteins aid diffusion by binding substances

As we mentioned earlier, another type of facilitated diffusion involves the binding of the transported substance to a membrane protein called a carrier protein. Like channel proteins, carrier

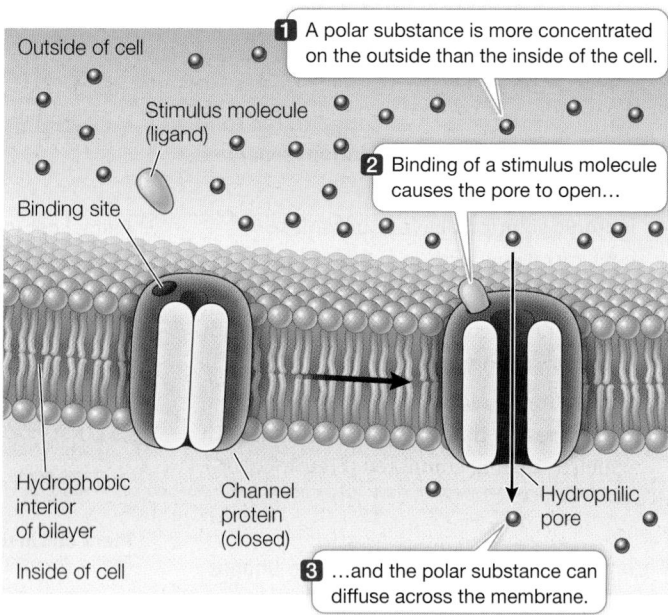

Figure 6.11 A Gated Channel Protein Opens in Response to a Stimulus The channel protein has a pore of polar amino acids and water. It is anchored in the hydrophobic bilayer by its outer coating of nonpolar R groups. The protein changes its three-dimensional shape when a stimulus molecule (ligand) binds to it, opening the pore so that specific hydrophilic substances can pass through. Other channels open in response to an electric potential (voltage) or mechanical stimuli.

Q: Are gated ion channels directional, allowing ion transport either in or out of the cell?

▶Investigating LIFE Aquaporins Increase Membrane Permeability to Water

Experiment

Original Paper: G. M. Preston et al. 1992. Appearance of water channels in *Xenopus* oocytes expressing red cell CHIP28 protein. *Science* 256: 385–387.

A protein was isolated from the membranes of cells in which water diffuses rapidly across the membranes. When the protein was inserted into oocytes, which do not normally have it, the water permeability of the oocytes was greatly increased.

HYPOTHESIS▶ Aquaporin increases membrane permeability to water.

METHOD▶   **RESULTS▶**

Aquaporin channel

Aquaporin mRNA injected into the oocyte is translated to make aquaporin protein.

Aquaporin mRNA

This oocyte does not have aquaporins in the cell membrane.

This oocyte has aquaporins inserted experimentally into the cell membrane.

Water diffuses into the cell through the aquaporin channels and it swells.

Water does not diffuse into the cell so it does not swell.

3.5 minutes in hypotonic solution

Photos courtesy of P. Agre.

CONCLUSION▶ Aquaporin increases the rate of water diffusion across the cell membrane.

Work with the Data

Although diffusion can account for limited water movement across cell membranes, simple diffusion seemed unlikely to explain the considerable water movement in kidney and red blood cells. By chance, Peter Agre and his colleagues found a major membrane protein, CHIP28, shared by these two cell types, and hypothesized that it was responsible for cell membrane water transport. So they did a "what if" experiment, taking the mRNA for CHIP28 and injecting it into frog oocytes that do not normally make the protein.

QUESTIONS▶

1. Frog oocytes in isotonic liquid were injected with either a small amount of water (control) or with CHIP28 mRNA in a small amount of water. The oocytes were then transferred to a hypotonic medium, and changes in relative cell volume were measured by microscopy. **Table A** shows the results.

Table A

Time (min)	Cell volume	
	CHIP28 mRNA	Water only (control)
0	1.0	1.0
0.5	1.05	1.0
1	1.15	1.02
1.5	1.23	—
2	1.32	1.02
2.5	1.36	—
3	1.41	1.02
4	(burst)	1.03

Plot the data on a graph of relative cell volume versus time after injection. How do the mRNA and control eggs compare? What explains the increase in the volume of the mRNA-injected oocytes? What explains the situation with both cells at 4 minutes after injection?

2. Water permeability (P_f) was calculated by the rate of osmotic swelling. **Table B** shows the results when increasing amounts of CHIP28 mRNA were injected.

Table B

Amount of mRNA (ng)	P_f (cm/sec × 10^{-4})[a]
0	13.7 (3.3)
0.1	50.0 (10.1)
0.5	112 (29.2)
2.0	175 (38.4)
10.0	221 (14.8)

[a]Numbers in parentheses indicate +/− standard deviation.

What can you conclude from these data? What statistical test (see Appendix B) would you do to show the significance of your conclusion?

3. To further investigate the role of CHIP28 in water transport, oocytes were given a known inhibitor of protein-mediated water transport, mercuric chloride, and then tested for water permeability with CHIP28 mRNA. Some of the eggs were also treated with mercaptoethanol, a molecule that overcomes the inhibition of water transport by mercuric chloride. The question was, would the inhibitor actually block water transport mediated by CHIP28, and would mercaptoethanol restore transport? The results are shown in **Table C**.

Table C

mRNA injected	Mercuric chloride	Mercapto-ethanol	P_f (cm/sec × 10^{-4})
None	None	None	27.9
None	Yes	None	20.3
None	Yes	Yes	25.4
CHIP28	None	None	210
CHIP28	Yes	None	80.7
CHIP28	Yes	Yes	188

What can you conclude about the molecular nature of water transport mediated by CHIP28 mRNA? What data support your conclusion? Explain all the controls that were done.

Go to **Achieve** for a companion Data in Depth exercise.

(A) Glucose uptake by the glucose transporter

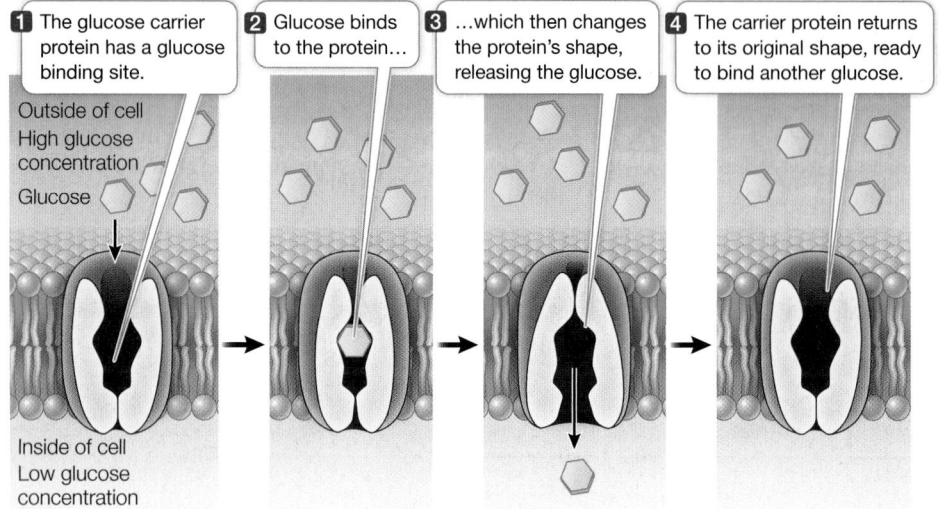

1 The glucose carrier protein has a glucose binding site.

2 Glucose binds to the protein...

3 ...which then changes the protein's shape, releasing the glucose.

4 The carrier protein returns to its original shape, ready to bind another glucose.

Outside of cell
High glucose concentration
Glucose

Inside of cell
Low glucose concentration

(B) Gradual saturation of glucose transporters

Rate of diffusion into the cell

All carriers are occupied.

Some carriers are occupied.

Glucose concentration outside the cell

Figure 6.12 A Carrier Protein Facilitates Diffusion The glucose transporter is a carrier protein that allows glucose to enter the cell at a faster rate than would be possible by simple diffusion. **(A)** The transporter binds to glucose, brings it into the membrane interior, then changes shape, releasing glucose into the cell cytoplasm. **(B)** The graph shows the rate of glucose entry via a carrier versus the concentration of glucose outside the cell. As the glucose concentration increases, the rate of diffusion increases until the point at which all the available transporters are being used (the system is saturated).

View in Achieve
Simulation 6.2 Membrane Transport

proteins facilitate the passive diffusion of substances into or out of cells or organelles. Carrier proteins transport polar molecules such as sugars and amino acids.

Glucose is the major energy source for most cells, and living systems require a great deal of it. Glucose is polar and cannot readily diffuse across membranes. Eukaryotic cell membranes contain a carrier protein—the glucose transporter—that facilitates glucose uptake into the cell. Binding of glucose to a specific three-dimensional site on one side of the transporter protein causes the protein to change its shape and release glucose on the other side of the membrane (Figure 6.12A). Since glucose is either broken down or otherwise removed almost as soon as it enters a cell, there is almost always a strong concentration gradient favoring glucose entry (that is, a higher concentration outside the cell than inside).

Transport by carrier proteins is different from simple diffusion. In simple diffusion, the rate of movement depends on the concentration gradient across the membrane. This is also true for carrier-mediated transport, up to a point. In carrier-mediated transport, as the concentration gradient increases, the diffusion rate also increases, but its *rate* of increase slows, and a point is reached at which the diffusion rate becomes constant. At this point, the facilitated diffusion system is said to be *saturated* (Figure 6.12B). This is explained by the fact that a particular cell has a specific number of carrier protein molecules in its cell membrane.

The rate of diffusion reaches a maximum when all the carrier molecules are fully loaded with solute molecules. Think of waiting for the elevator on the ground floor of a hotel with 50 other people. You can't all get in the elevator (carrier) at once, so the rate of transport (say, ten people at a time) is at its maximum, and

the transport system is "saturated." As a consequence, cells that require large amounts of energy, such as muscle cells, have high concentrations of glucose transporters in their membranes so that the maximum rate of facilitated diffusion is greater. Likewise, the human brain has high glucose needs, and the blood vessels that nourish it have high concentrations of glucose transporters.

KEY CONCEPT
6.3 Recap and Assess

Diffusion is the movement of ions or molecules from a region of higher concentration to a region of lower concentration. Osmosis is the diffusion of water through a selectively permeable cell membrane. Channel proteins and carrier proteins can facilitate the diffusion of charged and polar substances, including water, across cell membranes.

1. What properties determine whether, and how fast, a substance will diffuse across a membrane?

2. What is the effect on red blood cells if the kidney removes too many ions from the blood and makes it hypotonic to the cells?

3. Cells in the nervous system may have a higher concentration of K$^+$ ions inside the cell than outside. What is the role of the cell membrane in maintaining this imbalance? How can K$^+$ membrane channels eliminate this imbalance?

The process of diffusion tends to equalize the concentrations of substances outside and inside cells. However, one hallmark of a living cell is that it can have an internal composition quite different from that of its environment. To achieve this, a cell must sometimes move substances against their concentration gradients. This process requires an input of energy and is known as active transport.

KEY CONCEPT 6.4 Active Transport across Membranes Requires Energy

Learning Objectives

6.4.1 Compare and contrast diffusion and active transport.

6.4.2 Explain why active transport requires energy.

6.4.3 Describe and give examples of the different types of proteins that carry out active transport.

6.4.4 Differentiate between primary and secondary active transport.

In many biological situations, the concentration of a particular ion or small molecule inside the cell differs from that outside the cell. Such imbalances are maintained by a protein in the cell membrane that moves the substance against its concentration and/or electrical gradient. Movement of molecules or ions against a gradient is called **active transport** because it requires an input of energy. Often the energy source is adenosine triphosphate (ATP), which has chemical-bond energy stored in its terminal phosphate bond. In eukaryotes, ATP is produced in the mitochondria. Energy is released in a hydrolysis reaction that breaks the terminal phosphate bond of ATP, converting it to adenosine diphosphate (ADP). We will detail how ATP provides energy to cells in Key Concept 8.2.

The differences between diffusion and active transport are summarized in Table 6.1.

 View in Achieve
Animation 6.2 Active Transport

Active transport is directional

In diffusion, ions or molecules can move down their concentration gradients in either direction across the cell membrane. In contrast, active transport is directional, and moves a substance either into or out of the cell or organelle, depending on need. There are three kinds of membrane proteins that carry out active transport (**Figure 6.13**):

1. A **uniporter** moves a single substance in one direction. For example, a calcium-binding protein found in the cell membrane and the ER membranes of many cells actively transports Ca^{2+} to locations where it is more highly concentrated, either outside the cell or inside the lumen of the ER.

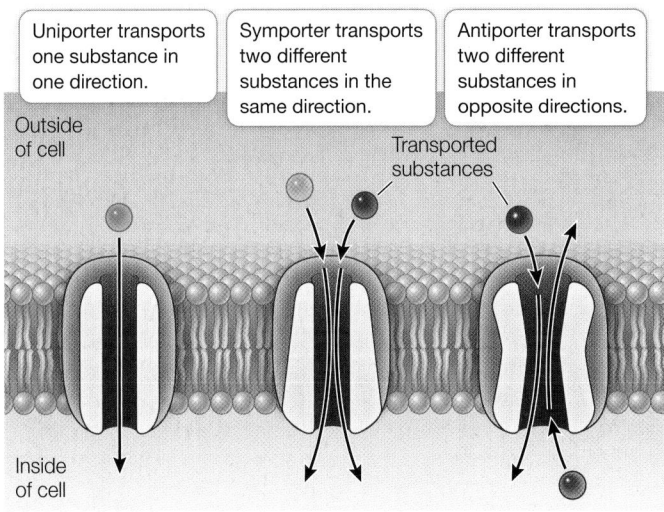

Figure 6.13 Three Types of Proteins for Active Transport
Note that in each of the three cases, transport is directional. Symporters and antiporters are examples of coupled transporters. All three types of transporters are coupled to energy sources in order to move substances against their concentration gradients.

2. A **symporter** moves two substances in the same direction. For example, a symporter in the cells that line the intestine must bind Na^+ in addition to an amino acid in order to absorb amino acids from the intestine.

3. An **antiporter** moves two substances in opposite directions, one into the cell (or organelle) and the other out of the cell (or organelle). For example, many cells have a sodium–potassium pump that moves Na^+ out of the cell and K^+ into it.

Symporters and antiporters are also known as **coupled transporters** because they move two substances at once.

Different energy sources distinguish different active transport systems

There are two basic types of active transport:

1. **Primary active transport** involves the direct hydrolysis of ATP, which provides the energy required for transport.

2. **Secondary active transport (co-transport)** does not use ATP directly. Instead, its energy is supplied by an ion concentration gradient established by primary (ATP-driven) active transport.

In primary active transport, energy released by the hydrolysis of ATP drives the movement of specific ions against their concentration gradients. For example, we mentioned earlier that concentrations of potassium ions (K^+) inside a cell are often much higher than in the fluid bathing the cell. However, the concentration of sodium ions (Na^+) is often much higher outside the cell. A protein in the cell membrane pumps Na^+ out of the cell and K^+ into the cell against these concentration gradients, ensuring that the gradients are maintained (**Figure 6.14**). This **sodium–potassium (Na^+–K^+) pump** is found in all animal cells. The pump is an integral membrane glycoprotein. It breaks down a molecule of ATP to ADP and a free phosphate ion (P_i) and uses the energy released to bring two K^+ ions into the cell and export three Na^+ ions. The Na^+–K^+ pump is thus an antiporter because it moves two substances in different directions.

TABLE 6.1	Membrane Transport Mechanisms		
	Simple diffusion	Facilitated diffusion (through channel or carrier)	Active transport
Cellular energy required?	No	No	Yes
Driving force	Conc. gradient	Conc. gradient	ATP hydrolysis
Membrane protein required?	No	Yes	Yes
Specificity	No	Yes	Yes

1. 3 Na$^+$ and 1 ATP bind to the protein "pump."

2. Hydrolysis of ATP releases ADP and phosphorylates an amino acid in the pump protein.

3. The shape change causes Na$^+$ ions to be released outside the cell and two K$^+$ ions to enter the pump.

4. Two K$^+$ ions bind to the pump.

5. Dephosphorylation of the pump releases P$_i$, causing two K$^+$ ions to be released to the interior of the cell and returning the pump to its original form. The cycle can then repeat.

Figure 6.14 **Primary Active Transport: The Sodium–Potassium Pump** In active transport, energy is used to move a solute against its concentration gradient. Here, energy from ATP is used to move Na$^+$ and K$^+$ against their concentration gradients.

Q: Ouabain is a natural product from a tree that has been used by traditional cultures in eastern Africa as a poison on arrows. Ouabain binds to a cell membrane protein. Tissues treated with ouabain have greatly increased intracellular Na$^+$. How does ouabain work?

An important drug used to treat a weak heart inhibits the Na$^+$–K$^+$ pump. Digitalis, purified from the foxglove plant, blocks the release of phosphate ions (P$_i$) from the protein (see Figure 6.14, step 5). This "freezes" the shape of the pump, and it can no longer bind Na$^+$. So Na$^+$ accumulates inside heart cells. This ultimately leads to a greater force of contraction of heart muscle, which aids a patient whose heart is not pumping well.

In secondary active transport (co-transport), the movement of a substance against its concentration gradient is accomplished using energy "regained" by letting ions move across the membrane with their concentration gradients. Think of it this way: A large dam may prevent a river from flowing. The accumulated water represents energy, and when the water is allowed to flow past the dam, the energy it releases can be used to drive turbines that

make electricity. It's similar for secondary active transport. Consider, for example, the absorption of glucose into the bloodstream from the digestive tract. Once the Na$^+$–K$^+$ pump establishes a concentration gradient of sodium ions, the passive diffusion of some Na$^+$ back into the cell can provide energy for the secondary active transport of glucose into the cell (**Figure 6.15**). Secondary active

Figure 6.15 **Secondary Active Transport (Co-Transport)** The Na$^+$ concentration gradient established by primary active transport by the sodium–potassium pump (left) powers the secondary active transport of glucose (right). A symporter protein couples the movement of glucose across the membrane against its concentration gradient to the passive movement of Na$^+$ into the cell.

Q: If the Na$^+$–K$^+$ pump is blocked by a drug, how will intracellular concentrations of Na$^+$ and glucose be affected in cells with this co-transport mechanism?

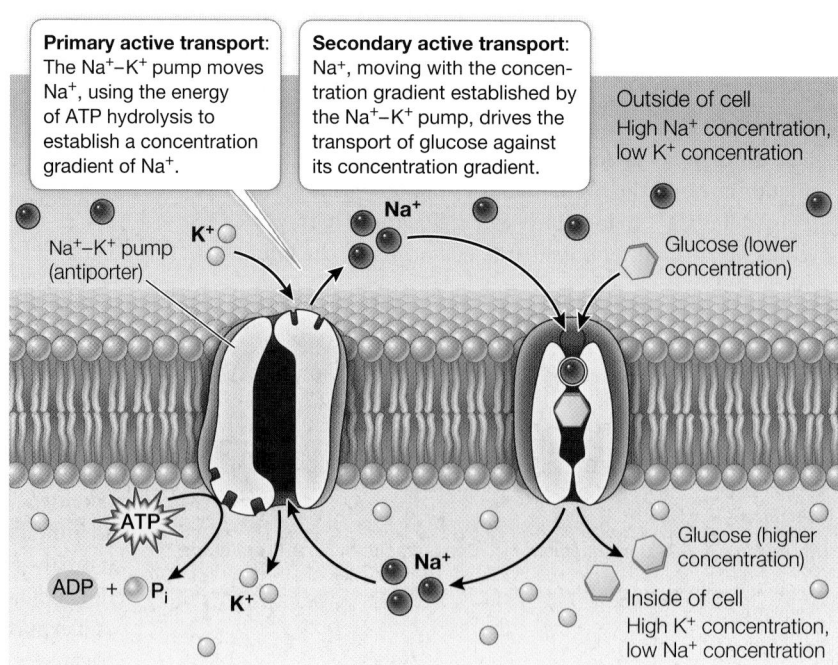

Primary active transport: The Na$^+$–K$^+$ pump moves Na$^+$, using the energy of ATP hydrolysis to establish a concentration gradient of Na$^+$.

Secondary active transport: Na$^+$, moving with the concentration gradient established by the Na$^+$–K$^+$ pump, drives the transport of glucose against its concentration gradient.

Outside of cell
High Na$^+$ concentration, low K$^+$ concentration

Na$^+$–K$^+$ pump (antiporter)

Glucose (lower concentration)

Glucose (higher concentration)

Inside of cell
High K$^+$ concentration, low Na$^+$ concentration

transport aids in the uptake of amino acids and sugars, which are essential raw materials for cell maintenance and growth. Both types of coupled transport proteins—symporters and antiporters—are used for secondary active transport.

Knowledge of co-transport was applied in developing oral rehydration therapy (ORT). Childhood diarrhea, often a result of infections, is a major problem throughout the world, especially in poor regions. As you know, diarrhea results in a lot of fluid loss from the intestine. The loss of water with dissolved ions can have severe consequences. When the mechanism of Na$^+$/glucose transport was described, physicians invented ORT, whereby water is consumed with dissolved Na$^+$ and glucose. When this fluid reaches the intestine, cells in the intestinal lining use the Na$^+$–K$^+$ pump, which, along with the added Na$^+$ in the oral fluid, keeps the level of Na$^+$ high. The diffusion of Na$^+$ into the intestinal cells is accompanied by the rapid diffusion of glucose. These solutes are accompanied by water, accomplishing rehydration. ORT costs less than 10 cents U.S. per liter and has saved millions of lives.

KEY CONCEPT
6.4 Recap and Assess

Active transport across a membrane is directional and requires an input of energy to move substances against their concentration gradients. Active transport allows a cell to maintain small molecules and ions at concentrations very different from those in the surrounding environment.

1. Why is energy required for active transport?
2. Why is the sodium–potassium (Na$^+$–K$^+$) pump classified as an antiporter?
3. What are the differences between primary active transport and secondary active transport?
4. What are the similarities and differences between active transport and facilitated diffusion?

We have examined several passive and active ways in which ions and small molecules can enter and leave cells. But what about large molecules such as proteins? Many proteins are so large that they diffuse very slowly, and their bulk makes it difficult for them to pass through the phospholipid bilayer. A completely different mechanism is needed to move intact large molecules across membranes.

KEY CONCEPT
6.5 Large Molecules Enter and Leave a Cell through Vesicles

Learning Objectives

6.5.1 Compare and contrast the three types of endocytosis.
6.5.2 Describe the process of receptor-mediated endocytosis.
6.5.3 Provide examples of processes that involve endocytosis and/or exocytosis.

Macromolecules such as proteins, polysaccharides, and nucleic acids are too large and too charged or polar to pass through biological membranes. This is actually fortunate—think of the consequences if such molecules diffused out of cells: a red blood cell would not retain its hemoglobin! As you saw in Chapter 5, the development of a selectively permeable membrane was essential for the functioning of the first cells when life on Earth began. The interior of a cell can be maintained as a separate compartment with a different composition from that of the exterior environment, which is subject to abrupt changes. However, cells must sometimes take up or secrete (release to the external environment) intact large molecules. In Key Concept 5.3 we described phagocytosis, the mechanism by which solid particles can be brought into the cell by means of vesicles that pinch off from the cell membrane. The general terms for the mechanisms by which substances enter and leave the cell via membrane vesicles are endocytosis and exocytosis.

 View in Achieve
Animation 6.3 **Endocytosis and Exocytosis**

Macromolecules and particles enter the cell by endocytosis

Endocytosis is a general term for a group of processes that bring small molecules, macromolecules, large particles, and even small cells into the eukaryotic cell (**Figure 6.16A**). Generally, there are three types of endocytosis: phagocytosis, pinocytosis, and receptor-mediated endocytosis. In all three, the cell membrane invaginates (folds inward), forming a small pocket around materials from the environment. The pocket deepens, forming a vesicle. This vesicle separates from the cell membrane and migrates with its contents to the cell's interior.

1. In **phagocytosis** ("cellular eating"), part of the cell membrane engulfs large particles or even entire cells. Unicellular protists use phagocytosis for feeding, and some white blood cells use phagocytosis to defend the body by engulfing foreign cells and substances. The food vacuole or phagosome that forms usually fuses with a lysosome, where its contents are digested (see Figure 5.12).

2. In **pinocytosis** ("cellular drinking"), vesicles also form. However, these vesicles are smaller, and the process operates to bring fluids and dissolved substances into the cell. Like phagocytosis, pinocytosis can be relatively nonspecific regarding what it brings into the cell. For example, pinocytosis occurs constantly in the endothelium, the single layer of cells that separates a tiny blood capillary from the surrounding tissue. Pinocytosis allows cells of the endothelium to rapidly acquire fluids and dissolved solutes from the blood.

3. In **receptor-mediated endocytosis**, molecules at the cell surface recognize and trigger the uptake of specific materials.

Receptor-mediated endocytosis is highly specific

Receptor-mediated endocytosis is used by animal cells to capture specific macromolecules from the cell's environment. This process depends on **receptor proteins**, which are proteins that can bind to specific molecules within the cell or in the cell's external environment. In receptor-mediated endocytosis, the receptors are integral membrane proteins located at particular regions on the extracellular surface of the cell membrane. These membrane regions are called coated pits because they form slight depressions in

(A) Endocytosis

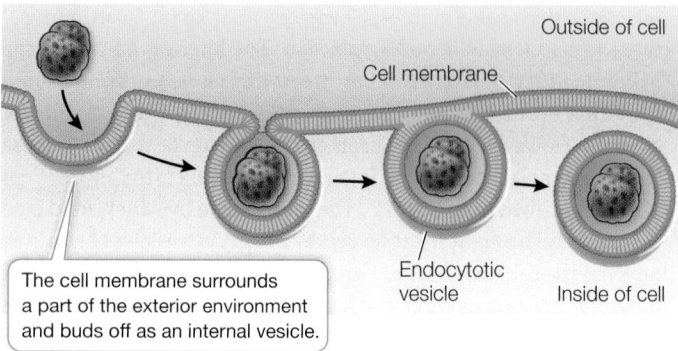

Outside of cell

Cell membrane

The cell membrane surrounds a part of the exterior environment and buds off as an internal vesicle.

Endocytotic vesicle

Inside of cell

(B) Exocytosis

Secretory vesicle

A vesicle fuses with the cell membrane. The contents of the vesicle are released, and its membrane becomes part of the cell membrane.

Figure 6.16 Endocytosis and Exocytosis Endocytosis (**A**) and exocytosis (**B**) are used by eukaryotic cells to take up and release fluids, large molecules, and particles. Smaller cells, such as invading bacteria, can be taken up by endocytosis.

 Media Clip 6.1 An Amoeba Eats by Phagocytosis
Life12e.com/mc6.1

An example of receptor-mediated endocytosis is the way in which cholesterol is taken up by many mammalian cells. Cholesterol and triglycerides, which have a low solubility in water, are packaged by liver cells into lipoprotein particles (see Figure 3.23C), which are released into the bloodstream. When a particular cell requires cholesterol, it produces specific low-density lipoprotein (LDL) receptors, which are inserted into the cell membrane in clathrin-coated pits. Binding of LDLs to the receptor proteins triggers the uptake of the LDLs via receptor-mediated endocytosis. Within the resulting vesicle, the LDL particles are freed from the receptors. The receptors segregate to a region that buds off and forms a new vesicle, which is recycled to the cell membrane. The freed LDL particles remain in the original vesicle, which fuses with a lysosome. There, the LDLs are digested and the cholesterol made available for cell use.

In healthy individuals, the liver takes up unused LDLs for recycling. People with the inherited disease familial hypercholesterolemia have a deficient LDL receptor in their livers. This prevents receptor-mediated endocytosis of LDLs, resulting in dangerously high levels of cholesterol in the blood. The cholesterol builds up in the arteries that nourish the heart and causes heart attacks. In extreme cases where only the deficient receptor is present, children and teenagers can have severe cardiovascular disease.

Exocytosis moves materials out of the cell

Exocytosis is the process by which materials packaged in vesicles are secreted from a cell when the vesicle membrane fuses with the cell membrane (**Figure 6.16B**). This fusing allows the vesicle contents to be released into the environment, and the vesicle membrane is smoothly incorporated into the cell membrane.

the cell membrane and their cytoplasmic surfaces are coated by other proteins, such as clathrin. The uptake process is similar to that in phagocytosis.

When a receptor protein binds to its specific ligand (in this case, the macromolecule to be taken into the cell), its coated pit invaginates and forms a coated vesicle around the bound macromolecule. The clathrin molecules strengthen and stabilize the vesicle, which carries the macromolecule away from the cell membrane and into the cytoplasm (**Figure 6.17**). Once inside, the vesicle loses its clathrin coat and may fuse with a lysosome, where the engulfed material is digested (by the hydrolysis of polymers to monomers) and the products are released into the cytoplasm. Because of its specificity for particular macromolecules, receptor-mediated endocytosis is an efficient method of taking up substances that may exist at low concentrations in the cell's environment.

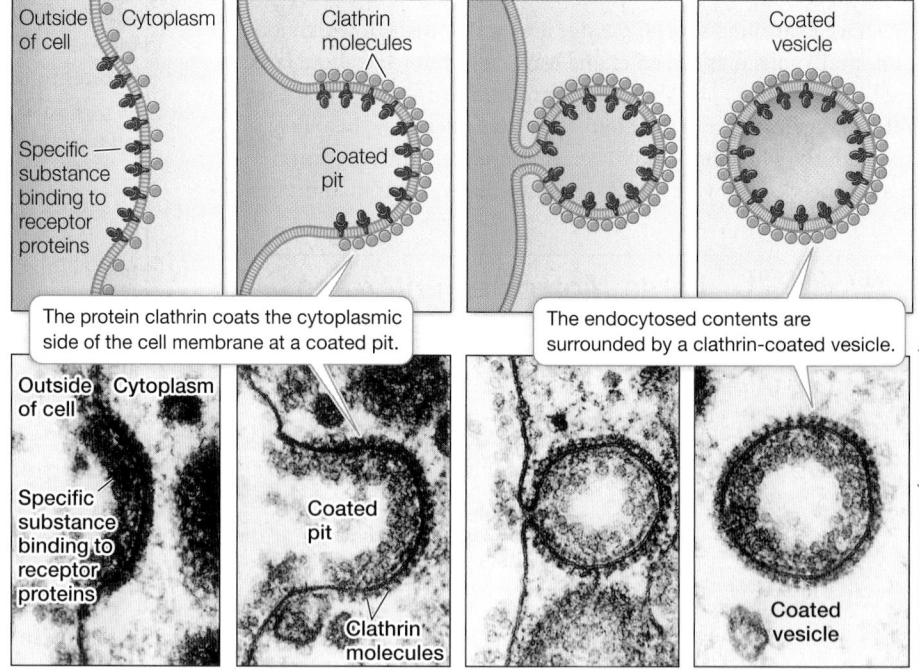

Outside of cell | Cytoplasm

Specific substance binding to receptor proteins

Clathrin molecules

Coated pit

Coated vesicle

The protein clathrin coats the cytoplasmic side of the cell membrane at a coated pit.

The endocytosed contents are surrounded by a clathrin-coated vesicle.

Outside of cell | Cytoplasm

Specific substance binding to receptor proteins

Coated pit

Clathrin molecules

Coated vesicle

All photos from M. M. Perry, 1979. *J Cell Sci* 39: 257–272

Figure 6.17 Receptor-Mediated Endocytosis The receptor proteins in a coated pit bind specific macromolecules, which are then carried into the cell by a coated vesicle.

TABLE 6.2 | Endocytosis and Exocytosis

Type of process	Example
ENDOCYTOSIS	
Receptor-mediated endocytosis	Specific uptake of large molecules (e.g., LDL)
Pinocytosis	Nonspecific uptake of extracellular fluid (e.g., fluids and dissolved substances from blood)
Phagocytosis	Nonspecific uptake of large undissolved particles (e.g., invading bacteria by cells of the immune system)
EXOCYTOSIS	
Release of large molecules	Vesicle fusion with cell membrane (e.g., digestive enzymes in the pancreas)
Release of small molecules	Vesicle fusion with cell membrane (e.g., neurotransmitters at the synapse)

In another form of exocytosis, the vesicle touches the cell membrane and a pore forms, releasing the vesicle's contents. There is no membrane fusion in this process, termed "kiss and run." We saw an example of exocytosis in describing sweat glands at the start of the chapter.

Table 6.2 summarizes examples of endocytosis and exocytosis.

KEY CONCEPT
6.5 Recap and Assess

Endocytosis and exocytosis are the processes by which large particles and molecules are transported into and out of the cell. Endocytosis may be mediated by a receptor protein in the cell membrane.

1. What are the differences between phagocytosis and pinocytosis?

2. Describe receptor-mediated endocytosis and give an example of a process involving this phenomenon.

3. Key Concept 25.2 describes the diatoms, which are protists that have complex glassy structures in their cell walls (see Figure 25.8 and the photo below of eight diatom cells inside their ornate cell walls). These structures form within the Golgi apparatus. How do they reach the cell wall without having to pass through a membrane?

© blickwinkel/Alamy Stock Photo

▶Investigating**LIFE**

What is the importance of aquaporin membrane channels?

There are ten genes encoding aquaporins in humans, each channel of the "plumbing system" having its particular location in the body. Genetic deficiency resulting in a lack of one of the aquaporins can have significant consequences. For example, one of the aquaporins occurs in the part of the kidney where water is removed from the developing urine and returned to the blood. When this aquaporin is absent, there is more water in the urine and the person urinates more and more often; bedwetting is a common result. The existence of aquaporins in plants was indicated when plant roots failed to take up water from the soil when they were exposed to solutions of mercuric chloride, a poison that binds to and inactivates membrane proteins. The proteins in the root cell membranes were identified as aquaporins; others have been found in the membrane that encloses the large central vacuole. Root aquaporins form channels for water on its way from the soil to the interior tissues, from which it is transported to the rest of the plant. In the vacuole, aquaporin channels are important in the organelle swelling, resulting in turgor pressure, which is important in plant organ structure and plant cell expansion. All of these aquaporins, and those of other organisms, share a common structure that spans the cell membrane and has a channel through which water molecules pass in single file.

Future directions

The water relations of plants, especially crop plants, are under intense study. Heavy use of chemical fertilizers that dissolve in water can lead to a hypertonic environment in the soil relative to the interior of plant root cells. Water tends to leave plant roots by osmosis through aquaporins. However, some plants can adapt to this by gating the aquaporin channel, shutting it off to preserve cellular water. Similarly, some plants can shut off their root aquaporins to preserve water during periods of drought, which are increasing in some regions due to climate change. Understanding these mechanisms and applying them to other plants can be important in future food production. Efforts are underway to insert aquaporins into synthetic membranes used for industrial applications. Because aquaporins allow only water and low concentrations of ions to pass through, such membranes could be used to purify contaminated fresh water, or to desalinate water, which as you know has very high ion concentrations. Aquaporins are expressed in skin, where they play a role in keeping the skin moist. This is also a goal of some cosmetics (moisturizers) and has led to a search for, and patenting of, small molecules that stimulate aquaporins. These molecules are components of some widely marketed skin creams.

You should be able to relate each summary to the adjacent figures. If you go to this visual summary in **Achieve**, you can follow links to figures, animations, activities, and simulations that will help you consolidate the material.

KEY CONCEPT

6.1 Biological Membranes Are Lipid–Protein Bilayers

Go to Activity 6.1 and Simulation 6.1

- Biological membranes consist of lipids, proteins, and carbohydrates. The **fluid mosaic model** of membrane structure describes a phospholipid bilayer in which proteins can move within the plane of the membrane.

- The properties of membranes depend on the nonpolar lipids as well as **integral membrane proteins**, **peripheral membrane proteins**, and **anchored membrane proteins** inserted in or associated with the bilayer.

Questions

1. For an integral membrane protein, which class of amino acids might you expect to find on the portion of the protein embedded in the membrane (see Table 3.2)? Give examples.

2. What will happen if a cell is incubated in a nonpolar detergent?

Figure 6.1

Outside of cell

Inside of cell

KEY CONCEPT

6.2 The Cell Membrane Is Important in Cell Adhesion and Recognition

Go to Activity 6.2

- In order for cells to assemble into tissues, they must recognize and adhere to one another. **Cell recognition** and **cell adhesion** depend on membrane-associated proteins and carbohydrates.

- **Cell junctions** connect adjacent cells. In some animal cells, **tight junctions** prevent the passage of molecules through the intercellular spaces between cells, and they restrict the movement of membrane proteins over the cell surface. **Desmosomes** cause cells to adhere firmly to one another. **Gap junctions** provide channels for communication between adjacent cells.

Questions

1. If a sponge is disaggregated and the cells are allowed to reaggregate in the presence of an enzyme that digests exposed cell membrane proteins, what will happen?

2. Matrix metalloproteases are molecules made by cancer cells that hydrolyze collagen and proteoglycans in the extracellular matrix. Why is it significant that these molecules are made by cancer cells that migrate to other locations in the body?

Figure 6.5

Figure 6.6

Tight junctions

© Dr. Donald Fawcett & J.P. Revel/ Visuals Unlimited, Inc.

Junctional

Desmosomal adhesion

© Dr. Donald Fawcett/Visuals Unlimited, Inc.

Intercellular space

Cytoplasmic plaque

Gap junctions

Courtesy of C. Peracchia

Cell membranes

Intercellular space

Connexins (channel proteins)

KEY CONCEPT

6.3 Substances Can Cross Membranes by Passive Processes

Go to Animation 6.1 and Simulation 6.2

- Membranes exhibit **selective permeability**, regulating which substances pass through them.

- **Diffusion** is the movement of a solute from a region of higher concentration to a region of lower concentration.

- In **osmosis**, water diffuses across a membrane from a region of higher water concentration to a region of lower water concentration. In an **isotonic** environment, total solute concentrations on both sides of the cell membrane are equal. If the solution surrounding a cell is **hypotonic** to the cell interior, more water enters the cell than leaves it, causing it to swell. In a **hypertonic** solution, more water leaves the cell than enters it, causing it to shrivel.

- A substance can diffuse passively across a membrane by either **simple diffusion** or **facilitated diffusion**, via a **channel protein** or a **carrier protein**.

Questions

1. Proteins and ions do not readily diffuse across the cell membrane. For each case, what is the major property of the chemical that limits its diffusion?

2. The total concentration of substances dissolved (solutes) in red blood cells is 0.3 M. What is the total concentration of solutes in the blood plasma surrounding the red blood cells? If this concentration is reduced by 33%, what will happen to the cells?

Figure 6.10

Figure 6.11

KEY CONCEPT

6.4 Active Transport across Membranes Requires Energy

Go to Animation 6.2

- **Active transport** requires the use of chemical-bond energy to move substances across membranes against their concentration or electrical gradients.

- In **primary active transport**, energy from the hydrolysis of ATP is used to move ions into or out of cells. The **sodium–potassium (Na^+–K^+) pump** is an example.

- **Secondary active transport** (**co-transport**) couples the passive movement of one substance down its concentration gradient to the movement of another substance against its concentration gradient through active transport.

Questions

1. The concentration of calcium ions (Ca^{2+}) in the endoplasmic reticulum of an unfertilized egg cell of the marine brown alga *Fucus* is much higher than that in the surrounding cytosol. When the egg is fertilized, Ca^{2+} is released rapidly into the cytosol. What two types of membrane transport are involved?

2. The imbalance of Na^+ and K^+ concentrations, with the former higher and the latter lower outside than inside cells, is important to the functioning of the nervous system. Why is the nervous system dependent on a supply of energy via ATP?

Figure 6.14

Figure 6.15

KEY CONCEPT

6.5 Large Molecules Enter and Leave a Cell through Vesicles

Go to Animation 6.3

- **Endocytosis** is the transport of small molecules, macro-molecules, large particles, and small cells into eukaryotic cells via invagination of the cell membrane and the formation of vesicles.

- In **exocytosis**, materials in vesicles are secreted from the cell when the vesicles fuse with the cell membrane.

- In **receptor-mediated endocytosis**, a specific **receptor protein** on the cell membrane binds to a particular macro-molecule.

Questions

1. Why do the fatty acid and protein compositions of lipids differ in endocytotic and exocytotic vesicles?

2. Developing red blood cells require iron to make hemoglobin. They take up iron carried by the protein transferrin via receptor-mediated endocytosis. If you mapped transferrin receptors on the cell membrane, would they be evenly distributed over the cell surface?

Figure 6.16

Outside of cell

Cell membrane

Endocytotic vesicle

Inside of cell

Figure 6.17

Outside of cell

Cytoplasm

Specific substance binding to receptor proteins

Coated pit

Clathrin molecules

Coated vesicle

All photos from M. M. Perry, 1979, *J Cell Sci* 39: 257–272

Go to **Achieve** for the eBook, **LearningCurve**, animations, activities, simulations, and additional resources and assignments.

Cell Communication and Multicellularity 7

KEY CONCEPTS

7.1 Cells Detect a Variety of Signals

7.2 Receptors Bind Signals to Initiate a Cellular Response

7.3 Signal Transduction Spreads the Response to a Signal through the Cell

7.4 Cells Change in Response to Signals in Several Ways

7.5 Adjacent Cells in a Multicellular Organism Can Communicate Directly

Courtesy of Todd Ahern

Voles Prairie voles display bonding behaviors after mating. These behaviors are mediated by peptides acting as intercellular signals.

▶Investigating LIFE

A Signal for Bonding

Prairie voles (*Microtus ochrogaster*) are small rodents that live in temperate climates, where they dig tunnels in fields. When a male prairie vole encounters a female, the female enters her reproductive cycle and mating often ensues. After mating the pair stays together, building a nest and raising their pups, born after 22 days gestation. The bond between the two voles is so strong that they stay together for life, producing a litter of pups about once a month for 2 to 3 years. Contrast this behavior with that of the montane vole (*M. montanus*), which is closely related to the prairie vole and lives in the hills not far away. In this species, mating is quick, and afterward the pair separates. The male looks for new mates and the female abandons her young soon after they are born.

The reason for these dramatic behavioral differences lies in the brains of these two species. When prairie voles mate, the brains of both males and females release specific peptides consisting of nine amino acids. In females, the peptide is oxytocin; in males, it is vasopressin. The peptides circulate in the bloodstream and reach all tissues in the body, but they bind to only a few cell types. These cells have surface proteins called receptors, to which the peptides specifically bind, like a key inserting into a lock.

The binding of peptide to receptor causes the receptor, which extends across the cell membrane, to change shape. Within the cytoplasm, this change sets off a series of events that ultimately result in changes in behavior. The receptors for oxytocin and vasopressin in prairie voles are most concentrated in the regions of the brain that are responsible for behaviors such as bonding and caring for young. In montane voles, there are far fewer receptors for these peptides, and as a result, fewer bonding and caring behaviors. Clearly, oxytocin and vasopressin are signals that induce these behaviors.

Intercellular signaling is a hallmark of multicellular organisms. A cell's response to a signal molecule takes place in three sequential steps. First, the signal binds to a receptor in the cell, often embedded in the outside surface of the cell membrane. Second, signal binding conveys a message to the cell. Third, the cell changes its activity in response to the signal. In a multicellular organism, these steps lead to changes in that organism's functioning, with signaling allowing different types of cells and tissues to work together.

 Is oxytocin the "trust" signal in humans? (Find the answer on page 149.)

KEY CONCEPT 7.1 Cells Detect a Variety of Signals

Learning Objectives

7.1.1 Use the source and distribution mechanism of a signal to identify its type.

7.1.2 Give an example of how a particular type of signal (autocrine, juxtacrine, paracrine, or hormone) functions in an organism.

7.1.3 Explain how specificity is achieved in a signal transduction pathway.

7.1.4 Compare cells found in the same organism that can and cannot respond to a specific chemical signal.

The environment around an organism and cell varies both in space and time. All organisms, prokaryotic and eukaryotic, can detect and respond to a multitude of environmental variables, including light, temperature, sound, touch, magnetic fields, gravity, pH, and chemicals. For example, plants grow toward light, bacteria alter gene transcription when the temperature rises, barnacle larvae sense and then attach to solid surfaces, pigeons navigate using Earth's magnetic field, and carrion beetles fly toward the odor of dead animals. While these responses involve the whole organism or particular organs, environmental variables are detected by individual cells, which undergo changes that lead to responses.

The presence of a signal does not always lead to a response; a cell does not respond to every signal, just as you are not paying close attention to every stimulus in your environment as you read this. To respond to a signal, a cell must have a specific receptor that can detect it and a way to use that information to influence cellular processes. A **signal transduction pathway** is a sequence of molecular events and chemical reactions that lead to a cell's response to a signal. Signal transduction pathways vary greatly in their details, but every such pathway involves a signal, a receptor, and a response. In this key concept we provide a brief overview of signal transduction. We'll consider receptors in Key Concept 7.2, and other aspects of signal transduction in Key Concepts 7.3 and 7.4.

Cells receive several types of signals

The environment is full of signals. For example, our sense organs allow us to respond to light (a physical signal), or odors and tastes (chemical signals). Bacteria and protists can respond to small chemical changes in their surroundings. Plants respond to light as a signal as well as an energy source, for example, by growing toward the source of light. A cell that is deep inside a large multicellular organism and far away from the exterior environment receives signals from neighboring cells and the surrounding extracellular fluids. In multicellular organisms, chemical signals are often made in one part of the body and arrive at target cells by local diffusion or by circulation in the blood or the plant vascular system. Chemical cell signals are usually present in tiny concentrations (as low as 10^{-10} M) (see Key Concept 2.4 for an explanation of molar concentrations) and differ in their sources and mode of delivery (**Figure 7.1**):

(A) Cell signaling on the local level

(B) Cell signaling from a distance

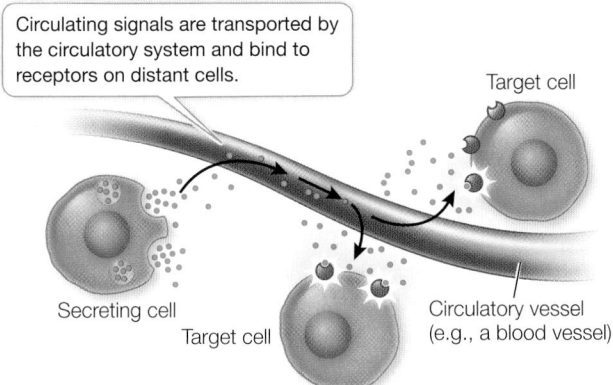

Figure 7.1 Chemical Signaling Systems **(A)** A signal molecule can diffuse to and act on the cell that produces it, an adjacent cell, or a nearby cell. **(B)** Chemical signals that act on distant cells must be transported by the organism's circulatory system.

Q: Based on the opening story, is oxytocin signaling autocrine, juxtacrine, or signaling at a distance?

 View in Achieve
Activity 7.1 Chemical Signaling Systems

- **Autocrine** signals diffuse to and affect the cells that make them. For example, many tumor cells reproduce uncontrollably because they both make, and respond to, signals that stimulate cell division.

- **Juxtacrine** signals affect only cells right next to and in contact with the cell producing the signal. This type of signaling is especially common during development, when cells are in groups and changing to become specialized.

- **Paracrine** signals diffuse to and affect nearby cells. An example occurs in inflammation when the skin is cut. Signals from skin cells are sent to nearby blood cells to aid in healing (see Key Concept 40.2).

- Signals that travel through the circulatory systems of animals or the vascular systems of plants are generally called **hormones**.

A signal transduction pathway involves a signal, a receptor, and responses: Overview

As you saw in the opening story, the elements of a signal transduction pathway are a signal, a receptor, and a response (**Figure 7.2**). For the information from a signal to be transmitted to a cell, the target cell must be able to receive the signal and respond to it. This is the job of receptors. All cells may be exposed to a signal, but most cells in the organism may not be able to respond to it. *Only cells with the appropriate receptors can respond.* Signal–receptor interaction, which often but not always occurs at the cell membrane, sets off a series of events inside the cell. Usually the events of signal transduction amplify the signal's effects. As Figure 7.2 shows, the ultimate responses of the cell (and organism) may be short-term or long-term. Think of the rapid "fight-or-flight" response that occurs when you see a bear in the woods a few feet away, compared with the bonding behaviors mediated by oxytocin in the prairie voles in the opening story.

In this chapter we consider signal transduction pathways in isolation from one another. In life, however, signal transduction pathways are often interconnected. A great deal of **crosstalk**—interactions between different signal transduction pathways—is common. For example, a single activated protein (receptor or enzyme) might activate enzymes or transcription factors in multiple pathways, leading to multiple responses to a single stimulus.

Multiple signal transduction pathways might converge on a single transcription factor, allowing the transcription of a single gene to be adjusted in response to several different signals. Crosstalk can also result in the activation of one pathway and the inhibition of another. The phenomenon of crosstalk inside the cell is analogous to the "crosstalk" that occurs at the level of the whole body. For example, in your limbs you have opposing muscles. When you bend your elbow, you contract one set of muscles and relax the opposing muscles, so that your arm will bend. Because of crosstalk, biologists often refer to "signaling networks" rather than signal transduction pathways, reflecting the high degree of complexity in cellular signaling.

KEY CONCEPT

7.1 Recap and Assess

Cells are constantly exposed to molecular signals that can come from the external environment or, in a multicellular organism, from within the body. To respond to a signal, the cell must have a specific receptor that detects the signal and activates some type of cellular response. Signal transduction pathways involve regulation of enzymes and transcription factors, and crosstalk often occurs between pathways.

1. Under what conditions would autocrine signaling be most advantageous for a cell?
2. How are hormones delivered to target cell receptors?
3. All cells have the potential to respond to all signals in an organism. What makes signaling specific?
4. Some cells can detect pH levels in their surroundings. How might a receptor detect changes in pH?

The general features of signal transduction pathways described in this key concept will recur in more detail throughout the chapter. First, let's consider more closely the nature of the receptors that bind signal molecules.

KEY CONCEPT 7.2   Receptors Bind Signals to Initiate a Cellular Response

Learning Objectives

7.2.1 Explain how and why different cells respond to different chemical signals.

7.2.2 Using equations, describe the chemical kinetics of receptor–ligand interactions.

7.2.3 Analyze dissociation constants as a measure of binding affinity.

7.2.4 Compare and contrast cell membrane receptors and intracellular receptors.

Any given cell in a multicellular organism is bombarded with many signals. However, it responds to only some of them, because no cell makes receptors for all signals. A **receptor** protein recognizes its signal very specifically, in much the same way that a membrane transport protein recognizes and binds to the substance it transports. This specificity ensures that only those cells that make a specific receptor will respond to a given signal.

Signal molecule

Receptor

1 A signal arrives at a target cell.

2 The signal molecule binds to a receptor protein on the cell surface (shown) or inside the cell.

3 Signal binding changes the three-dimensional shape (conformation) of the receptor and exposes its active site.

Inactive signal transduction molecule

4 The activated receptor activates a signal transduction pathway.

Activated signal transduction molecule

Short-term changes: enzyme activation, cell movement

Long-term changes: altered DNA transcription

5 The signal transduction pathway activates a cell response.

Figure 7.2 A Signal Transduction Pathway This general pathway is common to many cells and situations. The ultimate effects on the cell are either short-term or long-term molecular changes, or both.

Receptors that recognize chemical signals have specific binding sites

A **ligand** is a specific chemical signal molecule that fits into a three-dimensional site on its protein receptor (**Figure 7.3A**). Binding of the signaling ligand causes the receptor protein to change its three-dimensional shape, and that conformational change initiates a cellular response. The ligand does not contribute further to this response. In fact, the ligand is usually not changed; its role is purely to "knock on the door."

(A) The signal, adenosine, binding to its receptor

Outside of cell

The membrane-bound receptor has both extracellular and intracellular regions connected by a hydrophobic region.

The signal (ligand) fits into the receptor at its extracellular region.

Cell membrane

Inside of cell

(B) Chemical similarity between caffeine and adenosine

Caffeine   Adenosine

The similar structures of caffeine and adenosine allow them both to bind the receptor, but only adenosine triggers signal transduction.

© iStock.com/ Georgii Dolgykh

Figure 7.3 A Signal and Its Receptor **(A)** The adenosine 2A receptor occurs in the human brain, where it is involved in inhibiting active wakefulness. **(B)** Adenosine is the normal (endogenous) ligand for the receptor. Caffeine has a structure similar to that of adenosine and can act as an antagonist that binds the receptor and prevents its normal functioning. (A data from PDB 3EML. V. P. Jaakola et al. 2008. *Science* 322: 1211–1217.)

Q: Is the binding of adenosine and caffeine covalent or noncovalent? Explain your answer.

The sensitivity of a cell to a signal is determined in part by the affinity of the cell's receptors for the signal ligand—the likelihood that the receptor will bind to the ligand at any given ligand concentration. Receptors (R) bind to their ligands (L) according to chemistry's law of mass action. This means that the binding is reversible:

$$R + L \rightleftharpoons RL \qquad (7.1)$$

For most ligand–receptor complexes (RL), binding is favored. Reversibility is important, however, because if the ligand were never released, the receptor would be continuously stimulated and the cell would never stop responding.

As with any reversible chemical reaction, the binding and dissociation processes each have a rate constant, here designated k_1 and k_2:

$$\text{Binding: } R + L \xrightarrow{k_1} RL \qquad (7.2)$$

$$\text{Dissociation: } RL \xrightarrow{k_2} R + L \qquad (7.3)$$

A rate constant relates the rate of a reaction to the concentration(s) of the reactant(s):

$$\text{Rate of binding} = k_1[R][L] \qquad (7.4)$$

$$\text{Rate of dissociation} = k_2[RL] \qquad (7.5)$$

where "[ ]" indicates the concentration of the substance inside the brackets. Binding of a receptor to a ligand is reversible, and when equilibrium is reached the rate of binding equals the rate of dissociation:

$$k_1[R][L] = k_2[RL] \qquad (7.6)$$

If this is rearranged, we get:

$$\frac{[R][L]}{[RL]} = \frac{k_2}{k_1} = K_D \qquad (7.7)$$

K_D, the **dissociation constant**, is a measure of the affinity of the receptor for its ligand. The lower the K_D, the higher the affinity of the ligand for its receptor. Some receptors have very low K_D values, which allows them to bind their ligands at very low ligand concentrations; other receptors have higher K_D values and need more ligand to be present to set off their signal transduction pathways.

An entire field of biology and medicine—called pharmacology—is devoted to the study of drugs. These molecules are usually thought of as synthetic, but some are natural substances, such as caffeine that come from plants used by traditional societies (see Figure 7.3B). Drugs function as ligands that bind specific receptors. In the discovery and design of new drugs, it is helpful to know the specific receptor that the drug will bind, because then it is possible to determine the K_D value of its binding. This is one factor that can be taken into consideration when determining dosage levels. Of course, many drugs have side effects, and these are also dosage-dependent.

What happens when a ligand binds to a receptor? When we discussed small molecules binding to proteins in Key Concept 3.2, we described how proteins often change shape when bound. This is exactly what happens to receptors. The change in the receptor's shape may expose a previously hidden group of amino acids on the protein that participate in a biochemical activity. This activity may be the binding of another molecule, such as another protein (e.g., a G protein, discussed in the next section), or a substrate for an enzyme.

Instead of the ligand, other chemicals that resemble it can bind to the receptor. **Agonists** are chemicals that set a receptor into signal transduction mode just as the ligand does. **Antagonists** are inhibitors that bind to the receptor and "freeze" it in place, preventing the real ligand from binding, but do not set off signal transduction.

Many substances that alter human behavior bind to specific receptors in the brain and prevent the binding of the receptors' specific ligands. One example is caffeine, which is probably the world's most widely consumed stimulant. In the brain, the nucleoside adenosine acts as a ligand that binds to a receptor on nerve cells, initiating a signal transduction pathway that reduces brain activity, especially feelings of active wakefulness. Because caffeine has a molecular structure similar to that of adenosine, it also binds to the adenosine receptor (**Figure 7.3B**) and acts as an antagonist, preventing adenosine binding and thereby allowing continued nerve cell activity and an active feeling.

Receptors can be classified by location and function

There are many kinds of chemical signals. Some ligands are hydrophobic (nonpolar) and can diffuse through membranes, whereas others cannot. Physical signals such as light also vary in their ability to penetrate cells and tissues. Correspondingly, a receptor can be classified by its location in the cell, which largely depends on the nature of its signal (**Figure 7.4**):

- *Membrane receptors*: Large or polar ligands cannot cross the lipid bilayer. Insulin, for example, is a protein hormone that cannot diffuse through the cell membrane; instead, it binds to a transmembrane receptor with an extracellular binding domain.

- *Intracellular receptors*: Small or nonpolar ligands can diffuse across the nonpolar phospholipid bilayer of the cell membrane and enter the cell. The hormone estrogen, for example, is a lipid-soluble steroid (see Figure 3.24) that can diffuse across the cell membrane; it binds to a receptor inside the cell.

In complex eukaryotes such as mammals and higher plants, there are three well-studied categories of cell membrane receptors that are grouped according to their functions: ion channels, protein kinase receptors, and G protein-coupled receptors.

ION CHANNELS   As you saw in Key Concept 6.3, the cell membranes of many types of cells have gated **ion channels** that allow ions such as Na⁺, K⁺, Ca²⁺, or Cl⁻ to enter or leave the cell. The gate-opening mechanism is an alteration in the three-dimensional shape of the channel protein upon interaction with a signal; thus these proteins function as receptors. An example is the acetylcholine receptor, a ligand-gated Na⁺ channel located in the cell membrane of skeletal muscle cells. Acetylcholine is a neurotransmitter—a chemical signal released from nerve cells (**Figure 7.5**). Opening of the channel allows Na⁺, which is more concentrated outside the cell than inside it, to diffuse into the cell. This initiates a series of events that result in muscle contraction (see Figure 46.5).

Figure 7.4 Two Locations for Receptors   Receptors can be located inside the cell (in the cytoplasm or nucleus) or in the cell membrane.

Q: Steroid hormones are nonpolar. Could a receptor for a steroid be located at the cell membrane?

Connect the Concepts Ion channels are key to the functioning of the nervous system. An example is the connection between nerve and muscle described in Key Concepts 43.3 and 46.1.

PROTEIN KINASE RECEPTORS   Some eukaryotic receptor proteins, called **protein kinases**, catalyze the phosphorylation (addition of phosphate) of themselves or other proteins, thus changing their shapes and therefore their functions.

Figure 7.5 A Gated Ion Channel   The acetylcholine receptor (AChR) is a ligand-gated ion channel for sodium ions (Na⁺). It is made up of five polypeptide subunits. When acetylcholine molecules (ACh) bind to two of the subunits, the gate opens and Na⁺ flows into the cell. This channel helps regulate membrane polarity.

$$\text{Target protein} + \text{ATP} \xrightarrow{\text{Protein kinase}} \text{Protein} - \textcircled{P} + \text{ADP}$$
$$\text{(altered shape}$$
$$\text{and function)}$$

Phosphorylation is a reaction that is especially important in biology. Of the estimated 20,500 genes that code for proteins in humans, more than 500 of them encode protein kinases. When you think of all the functions that make up a person, this is indeed an impressive number. There are three amino acids in proteins that can be phosphorylated (**Figure 7.6A**). The receptor for insulin is an example of a protein kinase receptor. Insulin is a protein hormone made by the pancreas. Its receptor has two copies each of two different polypeptide subunits called α and β (**Figure 7.6B**). When insulin binds to the receptor, the receptor becomes activated and is able to phosphorylate itself and certain cytoplasmic proteins that are appropriately called insulin-response substrates. These proteins then initiate many cellular responses, including the insertion of glucose transporters (see Figure 6.12A) into the cell membrane.

(A)

(B)

Figure 7.6 A Protein Kinase Receptor **(A)** The three amino acids that can be phosphorylated by protein kinase activity. **(B)** The hormone insulin binds to a receptor on the outside surface of the cell and initiates a response.

G PROTEIN-COUPLED RECEPTORS Another category of eukaryotic cell membrane receptors is the **G protein-coupled receptors**. These receptors have many roles, including light detection in the mammalian retina (photoreceptors), detection of odors (olfactory receptors), and regulation of mood and behavior (such as mating in mammals and even single-celled yeasts). The receptors that bind the hormones oxytocin and vasopressin, which affect mating behavior in voles (see the opening story), are G protein-coupled receptors. Humans have hundreds of G protein-coupled receptors.

Ligand binding on the extracellular side of the receptor changes the shape of its cytoplasmic region, exposing a site that binds to a mobile membrane protein called a **G protein**. The G protein is partially inserted into the lipid bilayer and partially exposed on the cytoplasmic surface of the membrane.

Many G proteins have three polypeptide subunits and can bind three different types of molecules (**Figure 7.7A**):

1. The receptor

2. GDP and GTP (guanosine diphosphate and triphosphate, respectively; these are nucleoside phosphates like ADP and ATP)

3. An effector protein (see next paragraph)

When the G protein binds to an activated receptor protein, GDP is exchanged for GTP (**Figure 7.7B**). At the same time, the ligand is usually released from the extracellular side of the receptor. GTP binding causes a conformational change in the G protein. The GTP-bound α subunit then separates from the rest of the G protein, diffusing in the plane of the phospholipid bilayer until it encounters an **effector protein** to which it can bind. An effector protein is just what its name implies: it causes an effect in the cell. The binding of the GTP-bearing G protein subunit activates the effector, thereby causing changes in cell function (**Figure 7.7C**).

After activation of the effector protein, the GTP bound to the G protein is hydrolyzed to GDP. The now inactive G protein α subunit separates from the effector protein and diffuses in the membrane to bind to the other two G protein subunits. When the three components of the G protein are reassembled, the protein is capable of binding again to an activated receptor. After binding, the activated receptor exchanges the GDP on the G protein for a GTP, and the cycle begins again.

Intracellular receptors are located in the cytoplasm or the nucleus

Intracellular receptors are located inside the cell and respond to physical signals such as light (e.g., some photoreceptors in plants) or chemical signals that can diffuse across the cell membrane (e.g., steroid hormones in animals). Many intracellular receptors are transcription factors. Some are located in the cytoplasm until they are activated; after binding their ligands, these transcription factors move to the nucleus where they bind to DNA and alter the expression of specific genes. A typical example is the receptor for the steroid hormone cortisol. This receptor is normally bound to a chaperone protein that blocks it from entering the nucleus. Binding of the hormone causes the receptor to change its shape so that the chaperone is released

(A) The three units of a G protein-coupled receptor

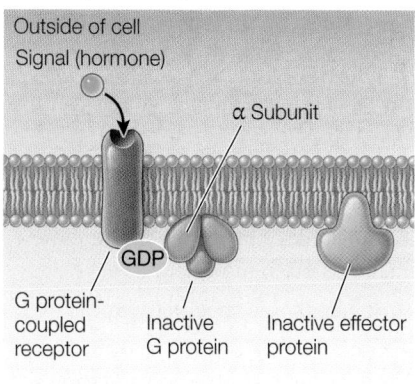

(B) Activation of the G protein

(C) Activation of the effector protein

Figure 7.7 A G Protein-Coupled Receptor   The G protein is an intermediary between the receptor and its effector.

Q: How does ligand binding alter the α subunit of the G protein, and what are two effects of this alteration?

▶ **View in Achieve**
Animation 7.1 A Signal Transduction Pathway

(Figure 7.8). This release allows the receptor to enter the nucleus, where it affects DNA transcription. Another group of intracellular receptors is always located in the nucleus, and their ligands must enter the nucleus before binding.

Figure 7.8 An Intracellular Receptor   The receptor for cortisol is in the cytoplasm, bound to a chaperone protein that is released when cortisol binds to the receptor.

KEY CONCEPT
7.2 Recap and Assess

Receptors are proteins that bind, or are changed by, specific ligands or physical signals. The changed receptor initiates a response in the cell. These receptors are located in the cell membrane or inside the cell.

1. What is the dissociation constant K_D, and what does it tell us about the likelihood that a signal will produce a cellular response?
2. What is the chemical nature and importance of specificity in the binding of a receptor to its particular ligand?
3. What are the differences between receptors located in the cytoplasm and those at the cell membrane?
4. An intact cell is treated to remove all proteins on the cell surface. Will the cell be able to detect any signals from other cells?

Now that we have discussed signals and receptors, let's examine the characteristics of the molecules (transducers) that mediate the cellular response.

KEY CONCEPT

7.3 Signal Transduction Spreads the Response to a Signal through the Cell

Learning Objectives

7.3.1 Describe how a protein cascade amplifies a signal.
7.3.2 Explain how the same second-messenger molecule can be used in many different signal transduction pathways.
7.3.3 Explain how signal transduction pathways are regulated in a cell.

As you have seen, there are different kinds of signals and receptors. Not surprisingly, the ways that signals are transduced, and the resulting cellular responses, also vary. Some signal transduction pathways are quite simple and direct, whereas others involve multiple steps. In addition, **second messengers** can diffuse throughout the cytoplasm and mediate further steps in pathways.

In many cases, a signal initiates a cascade (chain) of events, in which proteins interact with other proteins, which interact with still other proteins until the final responses are achieved. Through such a cascade, an initial signal can be both amplified and distributed to cause several different responses in the target cell. In this key concept we examine the kinds of molecules that transduce signals and look at several different signal transduction pathways.

The cell amplifies its response to ligand binding in a cascade

Scientists worked out the signal transduction pathway for one growth factor by studying a cell that went wrong. Many human bladder cancers contain an abnormal form of a protein called Ras (so named because a similar protein was previously isolated from a *rat* sarcoma tumor). Ras is a G protein, and as described in Key Concept 7.2, G proteins function as switches with "on" and "off" states. In the "off" state, G protein is bound to GDP, whereas in the "on" state the protein becomes bound to GTP. The abnormal form of the Ras protein under study was always active because it was permanently bound to GTP and thus caused continuous cell division (Figure 7.9).

 View in Achieve
Animation 7.2 Signal Transduction and Cancer

Other types of cancer cells have abnormalities in different parts of the same signal transduction pathway. By comparing the defects in abnormal cells with the normal signaling process in non-cancer cells, biologists worked out the entire signaling pathway (Figure 7.10). Recall from Key Concept 7.2 that a G protein mediates a response after activation by the protein kinase receptor. In Figure 7.10, the activated G protein Ras initiates a series of additional events composing a signal transduction pathway known as a **protein kinase cascade**, wherein one protein kinase activates the next, and so on. In this pathway, the ligands stimulate cell division or mitosis, and so the ligands are called **mitogens**. The

various kinases are called MAPKs—*m*itogen *a*ctivated *p*rotein *k*inases. Protein kinase cascades are useful signal transducers for four reasons:

1. At each step in the cascade of events, the signal is amplified, because each newly activated protein kinase is an enzyme that can catalyze the phosphorylation of many target proteins (see Figure 7.10, steps 5 and 6).

2. The information from a signal that originally arrived at the cell membrane is communicated to the nucleus, where the expression of multiple genes is often modified.

3. The multitude of steps provides some specificity to the process.

4. Different target proteins at each step in the cascade can provide variation in the response.

Second messengers can amplify signals between receptors and target molecules

Often there is a small molecule intermediary between the activated receptor and the cascade of events that ensues. Earl Sutherland and his colleagues at Case Western Reserve University discovered one such molecule when they were investigating the activation of the liver enzyme glycogen phosphorylase by the hormone epinephrine. The hormone is released when an animal faces life-threatening conditions and needs energy fast for the fight-or-flight response (see Figure 39.3). Glycogen phosphorylase catalyzes the breakdown of glycogen stored in the liver so that the resulting glucose molecules can be released to the blood. The enzyme is present in the liver cell cytoplasm but is inactive unless the liver cells are exposed to epinephrine:

The researchers found that epinephrine bound to a receptor at the cell membrane but that enzyme activation occurred in the

(A) Ras function in a normal cell

Figure 7.9 Signal Transduction and Cancer **(A)** Ras is a G protein that regulates cell division. **(B)** In some tumors, the Ras protein is permanently active, resulting in uncontrolled cell division.

(B) Abnormal Ras function in a cancer cell

Q: What would be the effect of a molecule that inhibits the interaction between GTP and Ras?

Outside of cell

Growth factor

1 A growth factor binds its receptor…

2 …which phosphorylates itself.

Ras
GDP
Inactive

P P
P P
P P
P P

3 The activated receptor initiates a series of events that allow Ras to bind GTP and become activated.

Ras
GTP
Active   (MAP3K)

Ras
(MAP3K)

4 Activated Ras binds and activates MAP3K.

(MAP2K)   (MAP2K) P

(MAPK)   (MAPK) P

5 Activated MAP3K is a protein kinase that phosphorylates many molecules of MAP2K.

6 Activated MAP2K is a protein kinase that phosphorylates many molecules of MAP kinase.

(MAPK) P

7 MAP kinase, when activated by phosphorylation, can enter the nucleus.

Cellular responses (including stimulation of cell division)

Nucleus

Inactive kinase

Activated kinase

Amplification

Inside of cell

Figure 7.10 A Protein Kinase Cascade   In a protein kinase cascade, a series of proteins are sequentially activated.

Q: Sorafenib is a drug that was designed to inhibit MAP3K, which is very active in kidney cancer. How does this drug work on the protein kinase cascade?

cytoplasm. How was the information of ligand binding communicated to the enzyme in the cytoplasm? Sutherland and others found that a key was a chemical intermediary, a "second messenger" that transmits the epinephrine binding signal (epinephrine being the "first messenger"). The second messenger was identified as **cyclic AMP (cAMP)**, which is produced from ATP by the enzyme adenylyl cyclase (**Figure 7.11**).

In contrast to the specificity of receptor binding, second messengers such as cAMP allow a cell to respond to a single event at the cell membrane with many events inside the cell. Thus second messengers amplify and distribute the signal—for example, binding of a single epinephrine molecule leads to the production of many molecules of cAMP, which then activate many enzyme targets by binding to them noncovalently. In the case of epinephrine and the liver cell, glycogen phosphorylase is just one of several enzymes that are activated.

Second messengers are often involved in crosstalk between different signaling pathways. Activation of the epinephrine receptor is not the only way for a cell to produce cAMP; and as noted, there

Figure 7.11 The Formation of Cyclic AMP   The formation of cAMP from ATP is catalyzed by adenylyl cyclase, an enzyme that is activated by G proteins.

are multiple targets of cAMP in the cell, and these targets are parts of other pathways.

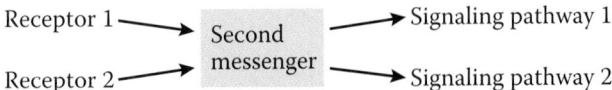

LIPID-DERIVED SECOND MESSENGERS

In addition to their role as structural components of the cell membrane, phospholipids are also involved in signal transduction. When certain phospholipids are hydrolyzed into their component parts by enzymes called phospholipases, second messengers are formed. The best-studied examples of these second messengers come from hydrolysis of the phospholipid **phosphatidyl inositol-bisphosphate** (**PIP₂**). Like all phospholipids, PIP_2 has a hydrophobic portion embedded in the cell membrane: two fatty acid tails attached to a molecule of glycerol, which together form **diacylglycerol**, or **DAG**. The hydrophilic portion of PIP_2 is **inositol trisphosphate**, or **IP₃**, which projects into the cytoplasm.

Receptor binding activates phospholipase C, an enzyme that is also located in the membrane. This enzyme cleaves off the IP_3 from PIP_2, leaving the diacylglycerol (DAG) in the phospholipid bilayer:

$$\underset{\text{In membrane}}{PIP_2} \xrightarrow{\text{Phospholipase C}} \underset{\substack{\text{Released to} \\ \text{cytoplasm}}}{IP_3} + \underset{\text{In membrane}}{DAG}$$

IP_3 and DAG are both second messengers; they have different modes of action that build on each other to activate protein kinase C (PKC). PKC refers to a family of protein kinases that can phosphorylate a wide variety of target proteins, leading to a multiplicity of cellular responses that vary depending on the tissue or cell type.

CALCIUM IONS

Calcium ions (Ca^{2+}) are scarce inside most cells, which have cytosolic Ca^{2+} concentrations of only about 0.1 micromolar (μM). Ca^{2+} concentrations outside cells and within the endoplasmic reticulum (ER) are usually much higher. Active transport proteins in the cell membrane and ER membrane maintain this concentration difference by pumping Ca^{2+} out of the cytosol. Opening and closing of gated ion channels allow Ca^{2+} to diffuse into the cell cytosol.

> **Connect the Concepts** Review the functions of gated ion channels and membrane pumps in Key Concepts 6.3 and 6.4.

Many signals can cause calcium channels to open, including IP_3. The entry of a sperm into an egg is a very important signal that causes a massive opening of calcium channels, resulting in numerous and dramatic changes that prepare the now-fertilized egg for cell division and development (**Figure 7.12**). Whatever the initial signal that causes calcium channels to open, their opening results in a dramatic increase in cytosolic Ca^{2+} concentration, which can increase up to 100-fold within a fraction of a second. This increase activates PKC. In addition, Ca^{2+} controls other ion channels and stimulates secretion by exocytosis in many cell types.

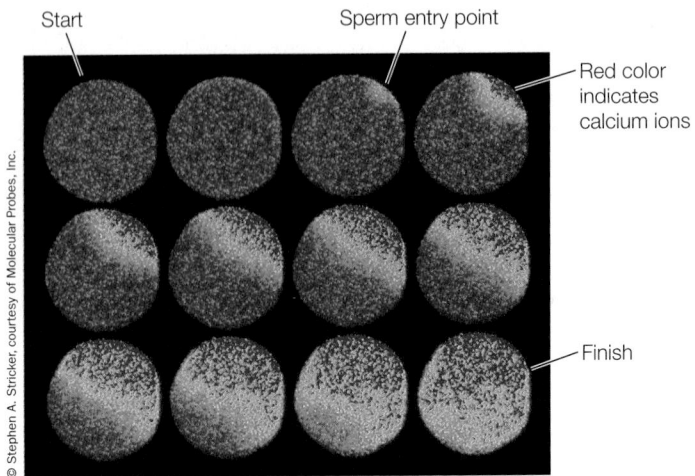

Figure 7.12 Calcium Ions as Second Messengers   The concentration of Ca^{2+} can be measured using a dye that fluoresces when it binds the ion. Here, fertilization in a sea star egg causes a rush of Ca^{2+} from the environment into the cytoplasm. Areas of high Ca^{2+} concentration are indicated by the red color, and the events are photographed at 5-second intervals. Calcium signaling occurs in virtually all animal groups and triggers cell division in fertilized eggs, initiating the development of new individuals.

© Stephen A. Stricker, courtesy of Molecular Probes, Inc.

NITRIC OXIDE

Most signaling molecules and second messengers are solutes that remain dissolved in either the aqueous or hydrophobic components of cells. It was a great surprise to find that a gas could also be active in signal transduction. Nitric oxide (NO) is a second messenger in the signal transduction pathway between the neurotransmitter acetylcholine (see Key Concept 7.2) and the relaxation of smooth muscles lining blood vessels, which allows more blood flow (**Figure 7.13**). In the body, NO is made from the amino acid arginine by the enzyme NO synthase. When the acetylcholine receptor on the surface of an endothelial cell is activated, IP_3 is released from the membrane (via the pathway shown in Figure 7.13), causing a calcium channel in the ER membrane to open and a subsequent increase in cytosolic Ca^{2+}. The Ca^{2+} then activates NO synthase to produce NO, which diffuses to the underlying smooth muscle cells, where it activates guanylyl cyclase (a close relative of adenylyl cyclase). This enzyme catalyzes the formation of the second messenger cyclic GMP (cGMP), which contributes to the relaxation of muscle cells.

The discovery of NO as a participant in signal transduction explained the action of nitroglycerin, a drug that has been used for more than a century to treat angina, the chest pain caused by insufficient blood flow to the heart. Nitroglycerin releases NO, which results in relaxation of the blood vessels and increased blood flow. The drug sildenafil (Viagra®) was developed to treat angina via the NO signal transduction pathway but was only modestly useful for that purpose. However, men taking it reported more pronounced penile erections. During sexual stimulation, NO acts as a signal, causing an increase in cGMP and a subsequent relaxation of the smooth muscles surrounding the arteries in the corpus cavernosum of the penis. As a result of this signal, the penis fills with blood, producing an erection.

Blood vessel   Smooth   Endothelial
muscle   cell

Outside of cell

Acetylcholine
(ACh)

1 Acetylcholine binds to receptors on endothelial cells of blood vessels; activation of the receptor causes production of IP₃.

Acetylcholine
receptor (AChR)

2 IP₃ opens Ca²⁺ channels on the ER membrane, releasing Ca²⁺ into the cytoplasm.

Inside of cell

IP₃

3 Ca²⁺ stimulates NO synthase, the enzyme that makes nitric oxide gas (NO) from arginine.

Ca²⁺

NO synthase

Ca²⁺

Arginine

NO

Smooth ER

4 NO diffuses to the smooth muscle cells, where it stimulates cGMP synthesis.

Guanylyl
cyclase

NO

**Smooth
muscle cell**

GTP   cGMP + PPᵢ

5 cGMP promotes muscle relaxation.

Figure 7.13 Nitric Oxide in Signal Transduction   Nitric oxide (NO) is an unstable gas, which nevertheless serves as a mediator between a signal, acetylcholine (ACh), and its effect: the relaxation of smooth muscles.

Q: Babies born prematurely (before 37 weeks gestation) can have pulmonary hypertension, whereby the blood vessels in the lungs are constricted and not enough blood reaches the lungs. These babies are given NO gas and this reduces hypertension. How does this work?

Signal transduction is highly regulated

Cells can regulate the activity of a molecule involved in signal transduction. The concentration of NO, which breaks down quickly, can be regulated only by how much of it is made. By contrast, membrane pumps and ion channels regulate the cytosolic concentration of Ca²⁺, as you have seen. To regulate protein kinase cascades, G proteins, and cAMP, there are enzymes that inactivate the activated transducer (**Figure 7.14**).

The balance between the activities of enzymes that activate and inactivate transducers determines the ultimate cellular response to a signal. Cells can alter this balance in several ways:

- *Synthesis or breakdown of the enzymes.* For example, synthesis of adenylyl cyclase (which synthesizes cAMP) and breakdown of phosphodiesterase (which breaks down cAMP) will tilt the balance in favor of more cAMP in the cell.

- *Activation or inhibition of the enzymes by other molecules.* An example is that NO signaling from sildenafil inhibits the phosphodiesterase that normally breaks down cGMP.

Because cell signaling is so important in diseases such as cancer, a search is under way for new drugs that can modulate the activities of enzymes that participate in signal transduction pathways.

(A) Phosphatase inactivates a protein kinase

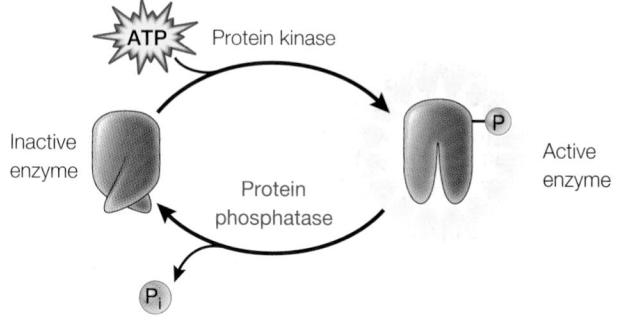

ATP   Protein kinase

Inactive
enzyme

Active
enzyme

Protein
phosphatase

Pᵢ

(B) GTPase inactivates a G protein

Receptor binding

Inactive
G protein

GDP

Active
G protein

GTP

GTPase

(C) Phosphodiesterase inactivates cAMP

Adenylyl
cyclase

Phosphodiesterase

ATP   cAMP   AMP

Figure 7.14 Regulation of Signal Transduction   Some signals lead to the production of active transducers such as **(A)** protein kinases, **(B)** G proteins, and **(C)** cAMP. Other enzymes inactivate or remove these transducers.

7.3 Recap and Assess

Signal transduction is the series of steps between the binding of a signal to a receptor and the ultimate cellular response. A protein kinase cascade amplifies a signal through a series of protein phosphorylation reactions. In many cases, a second messenger amplifies and distributes the downstream effects of the signal. The activity of transducer molecules is regulated.

1. How can an activated G protein such as Ras amplify a response to ligand binding?
2. Cyclic AMP is a second messenger in many different responses. How can the same messenger act in different ways in different cells?
3. How are signal transduction cascades regulated?

You have seen how the binding of a signal to its receptor initiates the response of a cell to the signal, and how signal transduction pathways amplify the signal and distribute its effects to numerous targets in the cell. In the next key concept we will look at the third step in the signal transduction process, the actual effects of the signal on cell function.

KEY CONCEPT
7.4 Cells Change in Response to Signals in Several Ways

Learning Objectives

7.4.1 Describe the signal transduction pathway stimulated by oxytocin.

7.4.2 Compare various mechanisms that cells use to respond to signals.

The effects of a signal on cell function take three primary forms: the opening of ion channels, changes in the activities of enzymes, or differential gene expression. These events set the cell on a path for further changes in form and function.

Ion channels respond to signals by opening or closing

You have seen that ion channels can function as receptors in cell signaling (see Figure 7.5). In Chapters 43 and 44 you will learn how signaling affects ion channels, particularly for Na^+ in the nervous system, where stimulation of a receptor by light, sound, or touch can lead to channel opening. Inside some cells, Ca^{2+} channels in the ER membrane open in response to signal transduction to modulate muscle contraction.

Oxytocin, which we described in the opening of this chapter, combines the two ion channel responses. Oxytocin binds to a G protein-coupled receptor (see Figure 7.7), which is expressed in brain tissue as well as muscles involved in birth and lactation. Activation of the receptor results in signal transduction through the IP_3–DAG pathway, releasing Ca^{2+} into the cytoplasm via ion channels. In the brain, the effect of Ca^{2+} is to indirectly stimulate nerve cell activity by the opening of ion channels for Na^+, as you will learn in Chapter 43. To summarize:

Oxytocin → Receptor → G protein activation → IP_3 signal transduction → Ca^{2+} channel opening → Na^+ channel opening

You saw in the opening of this chapter that the behavioral effect of oxytocin in voles involves bonding between them. Does this also happen in people? Neuroscientist Paul Zak at the Center for Neuroeconomics Studies thinks so. He has done experiments with human volunteers and shown that oxytocin signaling is important in trusting behavior (**Investigating Life: Is Oxytocin a "Trust" Signal in Humans?**). Recently, it was shown that people who have an inherited defect in the oxytocin receptor act in some ways like the montane voles that lack oxytocin receptors: they are less trusting.

Enzyme activities change in response to signals

Enzymes are often modified during signal transduction—either covalently or noncovalently. You have seen examples of both types of protein modifications earlier in this chapter. For example, addition of a phosphate group to an enzyme by a protein kinase is a covalent change; cAMP binding is noncovalent. Both types of modifications change the enzyme's shape, activating or inhibiting its function. In the case of activation, the shape change exposes a previously inaccessible active site, and the target enzyme goes on to perform a new cellular role.

The G protein-mediated protein kinase cascade that is stimulated by epinephrine in liver cells results in the activation by cAMP of a key signaling molecule, protein kinase A. In turn, protein kinase A phosphorylates two other enzymes, with opposite effects (**Figure 7.15**):

1. *Inhibition*: Glycogen synthase, which catalyzes the joining of glucose molecules to synthesize the energy-storing molecule glycogen, is inactivated when a phosphate group is added to it by protein kinase A. Thus the epinephrine signal prevents glucose from being stored in the form of glycogen (see Figure 7.15, step 1).

2. *Activation*: Phosphorylase kinase is activated when a phosphate group is added to it. It is part of a protein kinase cascade that ultimately leads to the activation of glycogen phosphorylase, another key enzyme in glucose metabolism. This enzyme results in the liberation of glucose molecules from glycogen (see Figure 7.15, steps 2 and 3).

Connect the Concepts Enzyme regulation determines the rate of chemical transformations in cells, and thus cell functions. See Key Concept 8.5.

The amplification of the signal in this pathway is impressive; as detailed in Figure 7.15, each molecule of epinephrine that arrives at the cell membrane ultimately results in the release of 10,000 molecules of glucose into the bloodstream:

1	molecule of epinephrine bound to the membrane leads to
20	molecules of cAMP, which activate
20	molecules of protein kinase A, which activate
100	molecules of phosphorylase kinase, which activate
1,000	molecules of glycogen phosphorylase, which produce
10,000	molecules of glucose 1-phosphate, which produce
10,000	molecules of blood glucose

►Investigating LIFE   Is Oxytocin a "Trust" Signal in Humans?

Experiment

Original Paper: P. Zak et al. 2005. Oxytocin is associated with human trustworthiness. *Horm Behav* 48: 522–527.

Cell signaling in the brain leads to changes in behavior. This experiment investigates whether the peptide oxytocin correlates with the development of trust between humans.

HYPOTHESIS►   The signal oxytocin is involved in trust between humans.

METHOD►

1 156 people are given $10 to participate.

2 Participants are randomly assigned to pairs who do not meet.

3 Donor and recipient are told that donor can give up to $10 to the recipient, which will be tripled in recipient's account, and that the recipient can reward the donor.

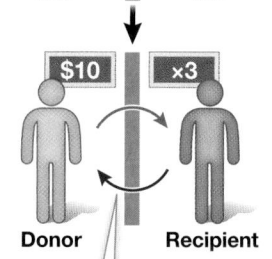

Donor   Recipient

4 **Establish Trust**: Donor hopes recipient will reward donor out of the tripled account more than donor gave. Trustworthiness is seen when recipient feels good about donor's generosity and gives back to donor.

5 **Establish a Control Group**: In the control group donors are told at random exactly what to give, and recipients are aware of this. So there is no donor intention to be generous.

6 Measure oxytocin levels in blood of donors in both experimental and control groups immediately after the donor decides what to give the recipient.

RESULTS►

	Experimental (donor intent)	Control (no intent)
Amount given by donor	$5.52	$5.63
Amount returned by recipient	$6.96	$3.53
Oxytocin level in recipient (pg/mL)	278	198

CONCLUSIONS►

1. People (recipients) who trust another person (donor, experimental) will be more trustworthy than people who do not have that feeling.

2. Oxytocin levels are higher in people who are trustworthy.

Work with the Data

Original Paper: M. Kosfeld et al. 2005. Oxytocin increases trust in humans. *Nature* 435: 673–676.

Paul Zak used an economics experiment to investigate trust and found that when people felt that a stranger had trusted them with money, the recipients not only reciprocated by giving the donor some money back, but also had elevated levels of the intercellular signaling molecule oxytocin. As in many experiments, although these data were suggestive of a relationship, correlation does not necessarily mean causation. So Zak and his colleagues tried a direct experiment in which subjects were given oxytocin before the experiment, to determine if oxytocin induces greater trust.

QUESTIONS►

1. In the experiment, donors were divided into control and experimental groups and paired with recipients. All donors were given 12 money units and asked to donate to a paired recipient, whom they did not know or see. Donors knew that whatever amount they donated would be tripled in the recipient's account (up to 36 units) and trusted that the recipient would generously give some money back to the donor. The experimental donor group was given nasal spray containing oxytocin just before the experiment; the control donor group received a nasal spray without oxytocin. The table shows the results.

	Average number of units (SD) sent to recipient
Experimental group (with oxytocin spray)	9.6 (2.8)
Control (no oxytocin spray)	8.1 (3.1)

What can you conclude from these data about oxytocin and trust in the donors? What statistical test would you use to show that the two averages are significantly different?

2. The experiment described in Question 1 was repeated, but this time both donor groups were told exactly how much to give the recipient. The results are shown in the table.

	Average number of units (SD) sent to recipient
Experimental group (with oxytocin spray)	7.5 (3.3)
Control (no oxytocin spray)	7.5 (3.4)

What can you conclude about the effect of oxytocin in this case, and what does it indicate about the trust relationship?

Go to Achieve for a companion Data in Depth exercise.

Figure 7.15 A Cascade of Reactions Leads to Altered Enzyme Activity   Liver cells respond to epinephrine by activating G proteins, which in turn activate the synthesis of the second messenger cAMP. Cyclic AMP initiates a protein kinase cascade, greatly amplifying the epinephrine signal, as indicated by the bold, black numbers. The cascade both inhibits the conversion of glucose to glycogen and stimulates the release of previously stored glucose.

Q: Theobromine, a molecule in cocoa beans that are used to make chocolate, is a phosphodiesterase inhibitor. Chocolate is poisonous to dogs, even at low doses, because dogs do not break down theobromine effectively. How does theobromine work as a poison?

View in Achieve
Simulation 7.1
Cell Signaling and Amplification

Signals can initiate DNA transcription

You learned in Key Concept 4.1 that the genetic material, DNA, is transcribed into RNA, which is then translated into a protein whose amino acid sequence is specified by the original DNA sequence. Proteins are important in all cellular functions, so a key way to regulate specific functions in a cell is to regulate which proteins are made, and therefore which DNA sequences are transcribed.

Signal transduction plays an important role in determining which DNA sequences are transcribed. Common targets of signal transduction are proteins called transcription factors, which bind to specific DNA sequences in the cell nucleus and activate or inactivate transcription of the adjacent DNA regions. For example, the Ras signaling pathway (see Figure 7.10) ends in the nucleus. The final protein kinase in the Ras signaling cascade, MAPK, enters the nucleus and phosphorylates a protein that stimulates the expression of several genes involved in cell proliferation.

Connect the Concepts   In this chapter you've learned about signaling pathways that occur in animal cells. Signal transduction pathways play equally important roles in other organisms, including plants, as we will explore extensively in Chapters 35 and 37.

KEY CONCEPT
7.4 Recap and Assess

Cells respond to signal transduction by opening membrane channels, activating or inactivating enzymes, or stimulating or inhibiting gene transcription.

1. How does oxytocin signaling involve several signaling pathways?

2. Which method(s) of cell response to signaling are rapid and which are slower? Explain.

We have described how signals from a cell's environment can influence the cell. But the environment of a cell in a multicellular organism is more than the extracellular medium—it includes neighboring cells as well. In the next key concept we'll see how specialized junctions between cells allow them to pass signals from one to another.

KEY CONCEPT 7.5   Adjacent Cells in a Multicellular Organism Can Communicate Directly

Learning Objectives

7.5.1   Explain the biological advantages of gap junctions in animals.

7.5.2   Design investigations to answer questions about intercellular communication.

7.5.3   Compare the structure and function of gap junctions and plasmodesmata.

The hallmark of multicellular organisms is their ability to have specialized functions in subsets of cells within their bodies. How do these cells communicate with one another so that they can work together for the good of the entire organism? As you learned in Key Concept 7.1, some intercellular signals travel through the circulatory system to reach their target cells. But cells also have more direct ways of communicating. Cells that are packed together within a tissue can communicate directly with their neighbors via specialized intercellular junctions: gap junctions in animals (see Figure 6.6) and plasmodesmata in plants (see Figure 5.9).

Animal cells communicate through gap junctions

Gap junctions are channels between adjacent cells that occur in many animals, occupying up to 25% of the area of the cell membrane (**Figure 7.16A**). Gap junctions traverse the narrow space between the cell membranes of two adjacent cells (the "gap") by

means of channel structures called **connexons**. The walls of a connexon are composed of six subunits of the integral membrane protein connexin. In adjacent cells, two connexons come together to form a gap junction that links the cytoplasms of the two cells. There may be hundreds of these channels between a cell and its neighbors. The channel pores are about 1.5 nanometers (nm) in diameter—too narrow for the passage of large molecules but adequate for passage of small molecules and ions.

Here is an example of gap junctions at work: In the lens of the mammalian eye, only the cells at the periphery are close enough to the blood supply for adequate diffusion of nutrients and wastes. But because lens cells are connected by large numbers of gap junctions, material can diffuse between them rapidly and efficiently. Hormones and second messengers can move through gap junctions. Sometimes just a few cells in a tissue have the receptor for a particular signal; in such cases, gap junctions allow a coordinated response to the signal by all the cells in the tissue.

Plant cells communicate through plasmodesmata

Instead of gap junctions, plants have **plasmodesmata** (singular *plasmodesma*), which are membrane-lined tunnels that traverse the thick cell walls separating plant cells from one another. A typical plant cell has several thousand plasmodesmata. Plasmodesmata differ from gap junctions in one fundamental way: unlike gap junctions, in which the wall of the channel is made of integral membrane proteins from the adjacent cell membranes, plasmodesmata are lined by the fused cell membranes themselves.

The diameter of a plasmodesma is about 6 nm, far larger than a gap junction channel. But the actual space available for diffusion is about the same—1.5 nm. Examination of the interior of the plasmodesma by transmission electron microscopy reveals that a tubule called the **desmotubule**, apparently derived from the endoplasmic reticulum, fills up most of the opening of the plasmodesma (**Figure 7.16B**). Typically, only small metabolites and ions can move between plant cells.

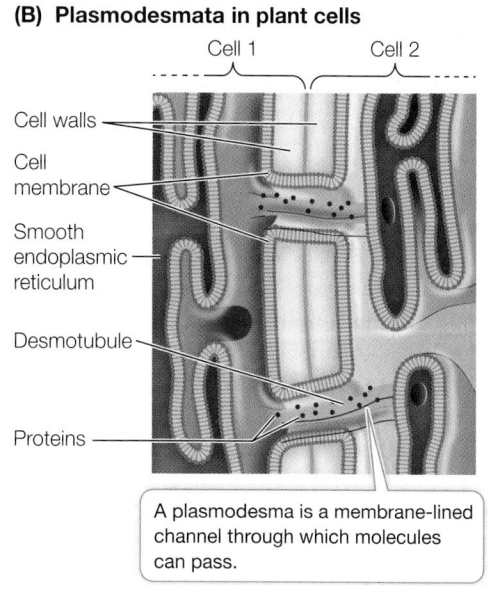

(A) Gap junctions in animal cells

Cell 1   Cell 2

Connexins

Cell membranes

Connexon

Space between cells ("gap"; ~2 nm)

The connexons of two cells come together to form a narrow (~1.5 nm) channel through which ions and small signal molecules can pass.

(B) Plasmodesmata in plant cells

Cell 1   Cell 2

Cell walls

Cell membrane

Smooth endoplasmic reticulum

Desmotubule

Proteins

A plasmodesma is a membrane-lined channel through which molecules can pass.

Figure 7.16 Communicating Junctions **(A)** An animal cell may contain hundreds of gap junctions connecting it to neighboring cells. The pores of gap junctions allow small molecules to pass from cell to cell, ensuring similar concentrations of important signaling molecules in adjacent cells so that the cells can coordinate their activities. **(B)** Plasmodesmata connect plant cells. The desmotubule, derived from the smooth endoplasmic reticulum, fills up most of the space inside a plasmodesma, leaving a tiny gap through which small metabolites and ions can pass.

Figure 7.17 Multicellularity
The evolution of intercellular interactions in a multicellular organism can be inferred from these green algae.

Q: Why was the evolution of direct communication important for tissue formation?

Plasmodesmata are vital in plants because their circulatory transport system, the vascular system, lacks the tiny vessels (capillaries) that many animals have for bringing gases and nutrients to every cell. For instance, simple diffusion from plant cell to cell across cell membranes is inadequate to account for the movement of a plant hormone from the site of production to the site of action. Instead, plants rely on more rapid diffusion through plasmodesmata to ensure that all cells of a tissue respond to a signal at the same time. There are cases in which larger molecules or particles can pass between cells via plasmodesmata. For example, some viruses can move through plasmodesmata by using "movement proteins" to assist their passage.

Chlamydomonas is single-celled.

Gonium is a cluster of cells.

Pandorina is a larger cluster of 16 cells.

Eudorina is a still larger cluster of cells.

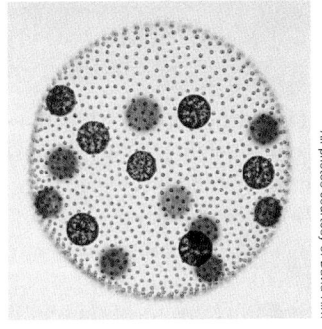
Pleodorina has some cells specialized for reproduction.

Volvox is larger, with internal specialized reproductive cells.

All photos courtesy of David Kirk

Modern organisms provide clues about the evolution of cell–cell interactions and multicellularity

Multicellular organisms can indeed be multicellular—a human has about 60 trillion eukaryotic cells and many more prokaryotic ones. But it's not just cells that make up a human or a rose plant—it is groups of cells specialized into tissues and then groups of tissues in organs (e.g., the nerve cells in the brain or the petals in a flower) that have specific roles. As you will learn in Chapter 42, the embryonic development of tissues and organs takes place in several steps:

- Migration of cells to form a group
- Organization of cells in the cluster
- Specialization of cells into tissues
- Connections between cells

Even though single-celled organisms continue to be highly successful on Earth, over time complex multicellular organisms evolved, along with their division of biological labor among specialized cells. The transition from single-celled to multicellular life took a long time. Indeed, while there is evidence that single-celled organisms arose about 500 million to a billion years after the formation of Earth (see Chapter 4), the first evidence of true multicellular organisms dates from more than a billion years later. Multicellularity probably arose several times.

Studying the evolutionary origin of multicellularity is a challenge because it happened so long ago. The closest unicellular relatives of most modern animals and plants probably existed hundreds of millions of years ago. The transition from single-celled to multicellular organisms may have occurred in several steps:

- Aggregation of cells into a cluster
- Intercellular communication within the cluster
- Specialization of some cells within the cluster
- Organization of specialized cells into groups (tissues)

Does this list look familiar? (See the first list in this section for the origin of organs in the embryo.)

A key event would have been the evolution of intercellular communication, which is necessary to coordinate the activities of different cells within a multicellular organism.

We can visualize how the evolution of multicellularity might have occurred by examining the Volvocine line of aquatic green algae (Chlorophyta). These plants range from single cells to complex multicellular organisms with differentiated cell clusters (**Figure 7.17**). Included in this range are a single-celled organism (*Chlamydomonas*); an organism that occurs in small cell clusters (*Gonium*); species with larger cell clusters (*Pandorina* and *Eudorina*); a colony of somatic and reproductive cells (*Pleodorina*);

and a larger, 1,000-celled alga with somatic and reproductive cells organized into separate tissues (*Volvox*).

Chlamydomonas is the single-celled member of this group. It has two cellular phases: a swimming phase, when the cells have flagella and move about, and a non-swimming phase, when the flagella are reabsorbed (disaggregated) and the cell undergoes cell division (reproduction). Compare this with *Volvox*: most of the cells of this multicellular, spherical organism are on the surface; the beating of their flagella gives the organism a rolling motion as it swims toward light, where it can perform photosynthesis. But some *Volvox* cells are larger and located inside the sphere. These cells are specialized for reproduction: they lose their flagella and then divide to form offspring.

 Media Clip 7.1 Social Amoebas Aggregate on Cue
Life12e.com/mc7.1

In addition to cell specialization, the ability of cells to be independent has changed on the way from the simplest colony (*Gonium*) to *Volvox*. If a single cell of *Gonium*, *Pandorina*, *Eudorina*, or *Pleodorina* detaches from the colony, it can divide and form a new colony just like the parent. Not so with *Volvox*. Most *Volvox* cells, particularly the reproductive ones, have lost the ability to live and divide independently. They are now inextricably part of an organism.

What has happened on that way from cell to organism? The separation of somatic and reproductive functions in *Volvox*, as well as the loss of independence of single cells, is possible because of a key intercellular signaling mechanism that coordinates the activities of the separate tissues within the organism. *Volvox* has a gene whose protein product is produced by the outer, motile cells and travels to the reproductive cells, causing them to lose their flagella and divide. This gene is not active in *Gonium* and *Pandorina*, which show cell aggregation but no cell specialization.

KEY CONCEPT
7.5 Recap and Assess

Cells can communicate with their neighbors through specialized cell junctions. In animals, these structures are gap junctions; in plants, they are plasmodesmata. The evolution of intercellular communication and tissue formation can be inferred from existing organisms, such as certain related green algae.

1. List the characteristics of direct communication by cell junctions and chemical signaling between cells. What is the advantage of direct communication over chemical signaling?

2. How does the Volvocine line of green algae show possible steps in the evolution of cell communication and tissue formation?

3. The tiny invertebrate *Hydra* have an apical region with tentacles and a long, slender body. *Hydra* can reproduce asexually when cells on the body wall differentiate and form a bud, which then breaks off as a new organism. Buds form only at certain distances from the apex, leading to the idea that the apex releases a signal molecule that diffuses down the body and, at high concentrations (i.e., near the apex), inhibits bud formation. *Hydra* lack a circulatory system, so this inhibitor must diffuse from cell to cell. If you have an antibody that binds to connexons and plugs up the gap junctions, how would you test the

hypothesis that the inhibitory factor of *Hydra* passes through these junctions?

Apex

Bud

© iStock.com/micro_photo

 View in Achieve
Activity 7.2 Concept Matching:
Cell Communication and Multicellularity

▶ Investigating**LIFE**

Q and **A**   **Is oxytocin the "trust" signal in humans?**

Paul Zak's experiments showing the involvement of oxytocin in the trust involved in money transfers between people opened up a new field of study called neuroeconomics. In 1759 the philosopher Adam Smith wrote that social and economic interactions between people are driven by what he called "fellow feeling." Now, 260 years later, the oxytocin studies validate this and have put it into the language of cell signaling. What other things besides economic generosity release oxytocin? Zak and others have shown that many pleasant activities, including sexual interactions and even massage and hugs, release oxytocin and induce positive behaviors as a result. Not surprisingly, oxytocin is available for purchase. A fragrance called "Liquid Trust" is marketed to sales people as well as those seeking love, and the book *Make Love Like a Prairie Vole* offers steps to a happier love life. In a somewhat more serious vein, oxytocin and other peptides that modulate behavior are being investigated as a treatment for autism, a disorder in which children can show alterations in trusting behaviors.

Future directions

In this chapter you have seen how a natural substance such as caffeine acts on receptors to alter cell function. As signal transduction pathways have been described for important processes such as the regulation of cell division, it has become possible to perturb intermediate steps in the pathway between signal and cell effects. In the signaling that stimulates cells to reproduce, two pathways are the focus of intense interest. One is at the cell membrane and involves protein kinase receptors and the ensuing signaling kinase pathway (see Figure 7.10). One or more steps along this pathway are often activated in cancer cells. For example, a kinase called Bcr-Abl is present and active in a type of leukemia and not in normal white blood cells. A drug has been developed that targets this kinase and results in a cure for the disease.

VISUAL SUMMARY 7

Courtesy of Todd Ahern

You should be able to relate each summary to the adjacent figures. If you go to this visual summary in **Achieve**, you can follow links to figures, animations, activities, and simulations that will help you consolidate the material.

KEY CONCEPT

7.1 Cells Detect a Variety of Signals

Go to **Activity 7.1**

- Cells receive many signals from the environment and from other cells.
- **Autocrine** signals affect the cells that make them; **juxtacrine** signals affect adjacent cells; **paracrine** signals diffuse to and affect nearby cells; and **hormones** are carried through the circulatory system of animals or the vascular system of plants.
- A **signal transduction pathway** involves the interaction of a signal molecule with a receptor; the transduction of the signal via a series of steps within the cell; and effects on the function of the cell.

Questions
1. Why don't all cells respond to all cell signals?
2. Are all signals chemical?

Figure 7.1

KEY CONCEPT

7.2 Receptors Bind Signals to Initiate a Cellular Response

Go to **Animation 7.1**

- Binding of a signal **ligand** to its **receptor** obeys the chemical law of mass action. A key measurement of the strength of binding is the **dissociation constant** (K_D).
- Depending on the nature of its signal or ligand, a receptor may be located in the cell membrane or inside the target cell.
- Receptors located in the cell membrane include **ion channels**, **protein kinases**, and **G protein-coupled receptors**.
- **Intracellular receptors** include steroid hormone receptors in animals. A lipid-soluble ligand such as a steroid hormone may enter the cytoplasm or the nucleus before binding.

Questions
1. What are the three protein domains of a typical membrane-bound receptor, and what are their respective functions?
2. What is the general effect of activation of a receptor?
3. Why do cytoplasmic receptors bind only nonpolar signals?

Figure 7.4

KEY CONCEPT

7.3 Signal Transduction Spreads the Response to a Signal through the Cell

Go to **Animation 7.2**

- A **protein kinase cascade** amplifies the response to receptor binding.
- **Second messengers** between signal binding at the cell membrane and signal transduction in the cytoplasm include **cyclic AMP (cAMP)**, **inositol trisphosphate (IP_3)**, **diacylglycerol (DAG)**, nitric oxide, and calcium ions.
- Signal transduction can be regulated in several ways.

Questions
1. In addition to binding to the adenosine receptor, caffeine is a phosphodiesterase inhibitor. What effect does this have on cell signaling?
2. In addition to activating the MAPK pathway, Ras activates the calcium signaling pathway. What phenomenon is this an example of?

Figure 7.10

Figure 7.14

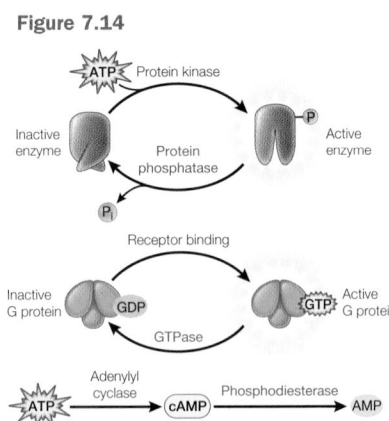

KEY CONCEPT

7.4 Cells Change in Response to Signals in Several Ways

Go to **Simulation 7.1**

- The cellular responses to signals may include the opening of ion channels, the alteration of enzyme activities, or changes in gene expression.

- Activated enzymes may activate other enzymes in a signal transduction pathway, leading to impressive amplification of a signal.

Questions

1. What is the major difference between the activation of a protein kinase in a signal transduction cascade and the activation of an enzyme by cAMP?

2. If there were not a multi-step signal transduction pathway, would there be an amplification of many molecules of glycogen phosphorylation?

Figure 7.15

KEY CONCEPT

7.5 Adjacent Cells in a Multicellular Organism Can Communicate Directly

Go to **Activity 7.2**

- Many adjacent animal cells can communicate with one another directly through small pores in their cell membranes called **gap junctions**. Protein structures called **connexons** form thin channels between two adjacent cells through which small signal molecules and ions can pass.

- Plant cells are connected by somewhat larger pores called **plasmodesmata**, which traverse both cell membranes and cell walls. The **desmotubule** narrows the opening of the plasmodesma.

- The evolution of cell communication and tissue formation can be inferred from existing organisms, such as certain green algae.

Questions

1. Most signaling molecules are polar and cannot readily diffuse through the cell membrane. When a signal binds to a cell, it is therefore difficult for a second messenger, other small molecule involved in signal transduction, or ions to pass on to an adjacent cell. What mechanism do animal and plant cells have for rapid movement of these substances from one cell to another?

2. If you compared *Chlamydomonas*, *Gonium*, and *Volvox* with regard to intercellular signaling and plasmodesmata, what would you expect to find?

Figure 7.16

Figure 7.17

All photos courtesy of David Kirk

Go to **Achieve** for the eBook, **LearningCurve**, animations, activities, simulations, and additional resources and assignments.

8 Energy, Enzymes, and Metabolism

KEY CONCEPTS

Edward Stone's letter to the Royal Society, 1763
This report ultimately led to the mass production of aspirin. More than 100 billion tablets are taken every year.

E. Stone. 1763. *Philos Trans R Soc Lond* 53: 195–200

▶Investigating**LIFE**

How Aspirin Works

Despite suffering from the "ague," the Reverend Edward Stone went walking in 1758 in the English countryside. Feverish, tired, with aching muscles and joints, he came across a willow tree. Although apparently unaware that many ancient healers such as the Greek physician Hippocrates in 400 BCE had used willow bark extracts to reduce fever, the clergyman knew of the tradition of natural remedies for various diseases. The willow reminded him of the bitter extracts from the bark of South American trees then being sold (at high prices) to treat fevers. Removing some willow bark, Stone sucked on it and found it did indeed taste bitter—and that it relieved his symptoms.

Later he gathered a pound of willow bark and ground it into a powder, which he gave to about 50 people who complained of fever and joint pain; all said they felt better. Stone reported the results of this "clinical test" in a letter to the Royal Society, England's most respected scientific body. Stone had discovered salicylic acid, the basis of the most widely used drug in the world. The date of his letter (which still exists) was April 25, 1763.

The chemical structure of salicylic acid (named for *Salix*, the willow genus) was worked out about 70 years later, and soon chemists could synthesize it in the laboratory. Although the compound alleviated pain, its acidity irritated the digestive system. In the late 1890s, the German chemical company Bayer synthesized a milder yet equally effective form, acetylsalicylic acid, which it marketed as aspirin. The new medicine's success launched Bayer to world prominence as a pharmaceutical company, a position it maintains today. Uses for this drug have expanded to include prevention of blood clotting in people after a heart attack. For several years it's been popular for people without symptoms of heart abnormalities to take aspirin in low doses to prevent clots in arteries, but this use was recently proven to be unsupported by clinical trials.

Fever, joint pain, headache, blood clots: what do these symptoms have in common? They all are mediated by fatty acid products called prostaglandins and molecules derived from them. Salicylic acid blocks the synthesis of the primary prostaglandin. The biochemical mechanism by which aspirin works was described in 1971. As we will see, an understanding of this mechanism requires an understanding of protein and enzyme function—two subjects of this chapter.

 How do anti-inflammatory drugs work as enzyme inhibitors? (Find the answer on page 171.)

© TH Foto/Alamy Stock Photo

8.1 Chemical Transformations Involve Energy and Energy Transfers

Learning Objectives

8.1.1 Apply the second law of thermodynamics to biological systems.

8.1.2 Differentiate between exergonic and endergonic reactions.

A **chemical reaction** occurs when atoms have sufficient energy to combine or change their bonding partners. Consider the hydrolysis of the disaccharide sucrose to its component monomers, glucose and fructose (see Figure 3.18):

$$\text{Sucrose} + \text{H}_2\text{O} \rightarrow \text{glucose} + \text{fructose}$$
$$(\text{C}_{12}\text{H}_{22}\text{O}_{11}) \qquad (\text{C}_6\text{H}_{12}\text{O}_6) \ (\text{C}_6\text{H}_{12}\text{O}_6)$$

In this equation, sucrose and water are the **reactants**, and glucose and fructose are the **products**. During the reaction, some of the bonds in sucrose and water are broken and new bonds are formed, resulting in products with chemical properties that are very different from those of the reactants. The sum total of all the chemical reactions occurring in a biological system at a given time is called **metabolism**. Metabolic reactions involve energy changes; for example, the energy contained in the chemical bonds of sucrose (reactants) is greater than the energy in the bonds of the two products, glucose and fructose.

Physicists define **energy** as the capacity to do work, which occurs when a force operates on an object over a distance. In biochemistry, it is more useful to think of energy as *the capacity for change*. In biochemical reactions, energy changes are usually associated with changes in the chemical compositions and properties of molecules.

There are two basic types of energy

Energy comes in many forms: chemical, electrical, heat, light, and mechanical (**Table 8.1**). But all forms of energy can be considered as one of two basic types (**Figure 8.1**):

TABLE 8.1 | Energy in Biology

Form of energy	Example in biology
Chemical-bond: Stored in bonds	Chemical energy stored in covalent bonds is released during the hydrolysis of polymers
Electrical: Separation of charges	Electrical gradients across cell membranes help drive the movement of ions through channels
Heat: Transfer due to temperature difference	Heat can be released by chemical reactions, and this can alter the internal temperature of an organism
Light: Electromagnetic radiation stored as photons	Light energy is captured by pigments in the eye and by plant pigments in photosynthesis
Mechanical: Energy of motion	Mechanical energy is used in muscle movements and movements within cells

1. **Potential energy** is the energy of state or position—that is, stored energy. It can be stored in many forms: in covalent bonds, as a concentration gradient, or even as an electric charge imbalance.

2. **Kinetic energy** is the energy of movement—that is, the type of energy that does work, that makes things change. For example, heat causes molecular motions and can even break chemical bonds.

To produce a change, energy must be transformed, either by conversion from one form to another or from one place to another. Potential energy can be converted into kinetic energy and vice versa, and the form that the energy takes can also be converted. Think of reading this book: light energy is converted to chemical energy in your eyes, and then is converted to electrical energy in the nerve cells that carry messages to your brain. When you decide to turn a page, the electrical and chemical energy of nerves and muscles are converted to kinetic energy for movement of your hand and arm.

Chemical-bond potential energy is converted into kinetic mechanical energy when the cat leaps.

Chemical-bond potential energy is stored in the muscles of the cat.

Courtesy of Violet Bedell-McIntyre

Figure 8.1 Energy Conversions and Work A leaping cat illustrates both the conversion between potential and kinetic energy and the conversion of energy from one form (chemical-bond) to another (mechanical).

Q: What are the energy conversions that occur when a woman dives from a board into a pool, splashes, and begins swimming?

There are two basic types of metabolism

Energy changes in living systems usually occur mostly as chemical changes, in which energy is stored in, or released from, chemical bonds.

Anabolic reactions (collectively anabolism) typically link smaller molecules to form larger, more complex molecules. Anabolic reactions require an input of energy. Energy is captured in the chemical bonds that are formed (for example, the glycosidic bond between the two monosaccharides forming sucrose). This captured energy is stored in the chemical bonds as potential energy:

$$\text{Glucose} + \text{fructose} + \text{energy} \rightarrow \text{Sucrose}$$

Catabolic reactions (collectively catabolism) break down larger, more complex molecules into smaller ones and often release the energy stored in the chemical bonds. For example, when sucrose is hydrolyzed, energy is released. In a biological system the released energy may be recaptured in new chemical bonds, or it may be used as kinetic energy—moving atoms, molecules, cells, or the whole organism:

$$\text{Sucrose} + H_2O \rightarrow \text{Glucose} + \text{fructose} + \text{energy}$$

Catabolic and anabolic reactions are often linked. The energy released in catabolic reactions is often used to drive anabolic reactions—that is, to do biological work. For example, the energy released by the breakdown of glucose (catabolism) is used to drive anabolic reactions such as the synthesis of triglycerides. This is why you can accumulate fat if you eat food in excess of your energy requirements.

The **laws of thermodynamics** (*thermo*, "energy," + *dynamics*, "change") were derived from studies of the fundamental physical properties of energy and the ways it interacts with matter. The laws apply to all matter and all energy transformations in the universe. Their application to living systems helps us understand how organisms and cells harvest and transform energy to sustain life.

The first law of thermodynamics: Energy is neither created nor destroyed

The first law of thermodynamics states that in any energy conversion, energy is neither created nor destroyed. In other words, during any conversion of energy—whether from one form to another or from one location to another—the total energy in the system under consideration before and after the conversion is the same (**Figure 8.2A**). As you will see in the next two chapters, the potential energy present in the chemical bonds of carbohydrates and lipids can be converted to potential energy in the form of adenosine triphosphate (ATP). This can then be converted into kinetic energy to do mechanical work (such as muscle contractions) or biochemical work (such as anabolism).

The second law of thermodynamics: Disorder tends to increase

Although energy cannot be created or destroyed, the second law of thermodynamics states that when energy is converted from one form to another, some of that energy becomes unavailable for doing work (**Figure 8.2B**). In other words, no physical process or

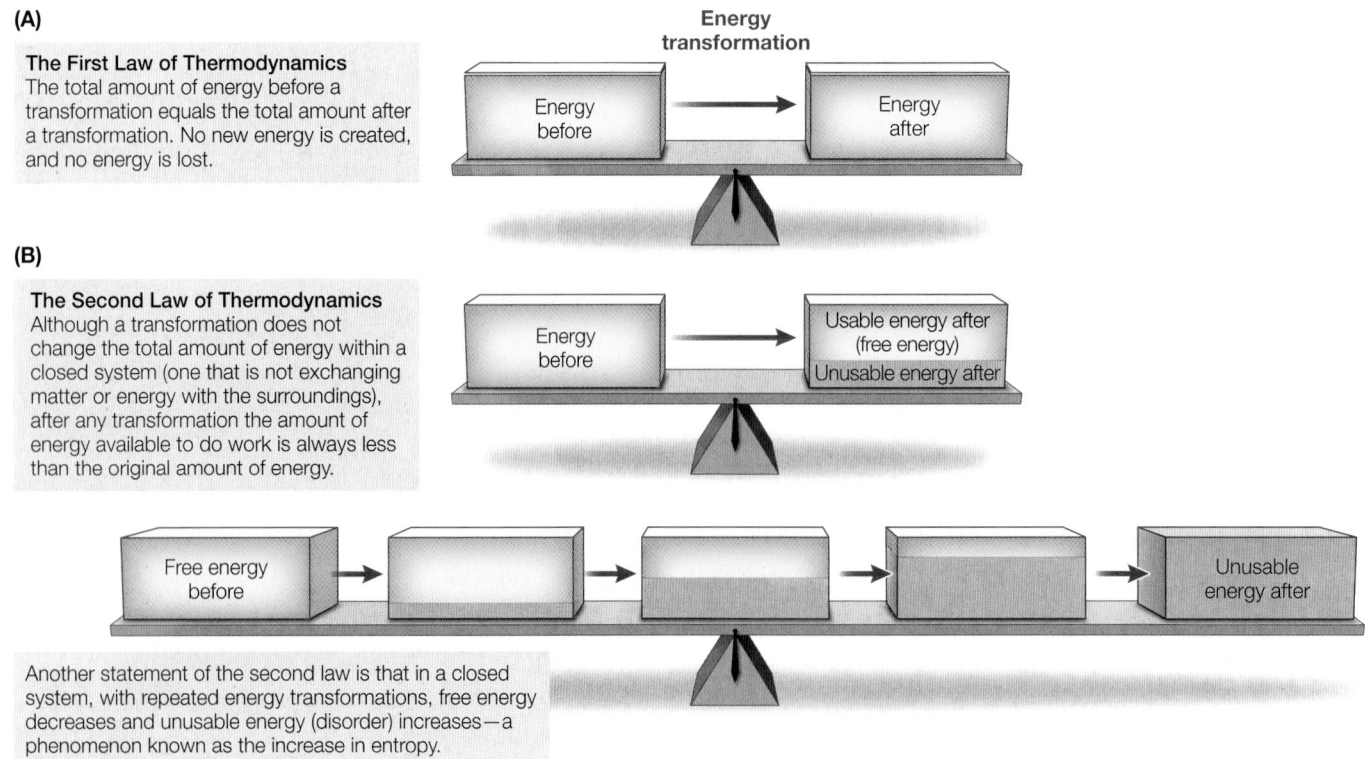

(A)

The First Law of Thermodynamics
The total amount of energy before a transformation equals the total amount after a transformation. No new energy is created, and no energy is lost.

Energy transformation

Energy before → Energy after

(B)

The Second Law of Thermodynamics
Although a transformation does not change the total amount of energy within a closed system (one that is not exchanging matter or energy with the surroundings), after any transformation the amount of energy available to do work is always less than the original amount of energy.

Energy before → Usable energy after (free energy) / Unusable energy after

Free energy before → Unusable energy after

Another statement of the second law is that in a closed system, with repeated energy transformations, free energy decreases and unusable energy (disorder) increases—a phenomenon known as the increase in entropy.

Figure 8.2 The Laws of Thermodynamics **(A)** The first law states that energy cannot be created or destroyed. **(B)** The second law states that after energy transformations, some energy becomes unavailable to do work.

chemical reaction is 100% efficient; some of the released energy is lost to a form associated with disorder. Think of disorder as a kind of randomness that is due to the thermal motion of particles; this energy is of such a low value and so spread out that it is unusable. **Entropy** is a measure of the disorder in a system.

It takes energy to impose order on a system. Unless energy is applied to a system, it will be randomly arranged or disordered. The second law applies to all energy transformations, but we will focus here on transformations in living systems. The second law applies on the micro scale, in chemical reactions and pathways in the cell. But it also applies on the macro scale, in communities of organisms interacting in the environment.

Connect the Concepts See Key Concept 56.3, which discusses the flow of energy in food chains, where there is a decline in usable energy in each step.

NOT ALL ENERGY CAN BE USED   In any system, the total energy includes the usable energy that can do work and the unusable energy that is lost to disorder:

Total energy = usable energy + unusable energy

In biological systems, the total energy is called **enthalpy (H)**. The usable energy that can do work is called **free energy (G)**. Free energy is what cells require for all the chemical reactions involved in growth, cell division, and maintenance. The unusable energy is represented by entropy (S) multiplied by the absolute temperature (T). Thus we can rewrite the word equation above more precisely as:

$$H = G + TS \qquad (8.1)$$

Because we are interested in usable energy, we rearrange Equation 8.1:

$$G = H - TS \qquad (8.2)$$

Although we cannot measure G, H, or S absolutely, we can determine the *change* in each at a constant temperature. Such energy changes are measured in calories (cal) or joules (J).[1] A change is represented by the Greek letter delta (Δ). The change in free energy (ΔG) of any chemical reaction is equal to the difference in free energy between the products and the reactants:

$$\Delta G_{reaction} = G_{products} - G_{reactants} \qquad (8.3)$$

A change in free energy can be either positive or negative; that is, the free energy of the products can be more or less than the free energy of the reactants. If the products have more free energy than the reactants (ΔG is positive), then there must have been some input of energy into the reaction. (Remember that energy cannot be created, so some energy must have been added from an external source.)

At a constant temperature ΔG is defined in terms of the change in total energy (ΔH) and the change in entropy (ΔS):

$$\Delta G = \Delta H - T\Delta S \qquad (8.4)$$

---

[1] A calorie is the amount of heat energy needed to raise the temperature of 1 gram of pure water from 14.5°C to 15.5°C. In the SI system, energy is measured in joules. 1 J = 0.239 cal; conversely, 1 cal = 4.184 J. Thus, for example, 486 cal = 2,033 J, or 2.033 kJ. Although they are defined here in terms of heat, the calorie and the joule are measures of mechanical, electrical, or chemical energy. When you compare data on energy, always compare joules with joules and calories with calories.

Equation 8.4 tells us whether free energy is released or required by a chemical reaction:

- If ΔG is negative (ΔG < 0), free energy is released.
- If ΔG is positive (ΔG > 0), free energy is required.

If the necessary free energy is not available, the reaction does not occur. The sign and magnitude of ΔG depend on the two factors on the right side of the equation:

- ΔH: In a chemical reaction, ΔH is the total amount of energy added to the system (ΔH > 0) or released (ΔH < 0).
- ΔS: Depending on the sign and magnitude of ΔS, the entire term, TΔS, may be negative or positive, large or small. In the chemistry lab, temperature can affect ΔG. But living systems don't vary their temperature that much, so the magnitude and sign of ΔG can depend on changes in entropy.

If a reaction increases entropy, its products are more disordered or random than its reactants. For example, when a protein is hydrolyzed to its amino acids, the products have considerable freedom to move around. The disorder in a solution of amino acids will be large compared with that in the protein, in which peptide bonds and other forces prevent free movement. So in hydrolysis, the change in entropy (ΔS) will be positive. Conversely, if there are fewer products and they are more restrained in their movements than the reactants (as for amino acids being joined in a protein), ΔS will be negative. This means that according to Equation 8.4, ΔG is positive and energy input is required.

DISORDER TENDS TO INCREASE   Consider the human body, with its highly organized tissues and organs composed of large, complex molecules. You might think that this order and complexity are in conflict with the second law—after all, entropy, or disorder, should be maximized—but they are not, for two reasons:

1. *Getting ordered is coupled to the generation of disorder.* Making 1 kg of a human body (soft tissues, not bones) requires the catabolism of about 10 kg of highly ordered biological materials (our food), which are converted into CO_2, H_2O, and other simple molecules. So this process creates far more disorder (more energy is lost to entropy in the small molecules) than the amount of order (total energy; enthalpy) stored in large molecules in 1 kg of a person.

2. *Life requires a constant input of energy to maintain order.* Without this energy, the complex structures of living systems would break down. Because energy is used to generate and maintain order, there is no conflict with the second law of thermodynamics.

Having seen that the laws of thermodynamics apply to organisms, let's see how these laws apply to biochemical reactions inside the cell.

Chemical reactions release or consume energy

As you saw earlier, anabolic reactions link simple molecules to form more complex molecules, so they tend to increase complexity (order) in the cell. By contrast, catabolic reactions break down complex molecules into simpler ones, so they tend to decrease complexity (generate disorder).

- Catabolic reactions may break down an ordered reactant into smaller, more randomly distributed products. Reactions that release free energy ($-\Delta G$) are called **exergonic** reactions (**Figure 8.3A**). For example:

  Complex molecules → free energy + small molecules

- Anabolic reactions may make a single product (a highly ordered substance) out of many smaller reactants (less ordered). Reactions that require or consume free energy ($+\Delta G$) are called **endergonic** reactions (**Figure 8.3B**). For example:

  Free energy + small molecules → complex molecules

In principle, chemical reactions are reversible and can run both forward and backward. For example, if compound A can be converted into compound B (A → B), then B, in principle, can be converted into A (B → A), although *the concentrations of A and B*

(A) Exergonic reaction

> In an exergonic reaction, *energy is released* as the reactants form lower-energy products. ΔG is negative.

Reactants

Amount of energy released

Products

Free energy

Time course of reaction   Time course of reaction

(B) Endergonic reaction

> *Energy must be added* for an endergonic reaction, in which reactants are converted to products with a higher energy level. ΔG is positive.

Products

Amount of energy required

Reactants

Free energy

Time course of reaction   Time course of reaction

Figure 8.3 Exergonic and Endergonic Reactions (**A**) In an exergonic reaction, the reactants behave like a ball rolling down a hill, and energy is released. (**B**) A ball will not roll uphill by itself. Driving an endergonic reaction, like moving a ball uphill, requires the addition of free energy.

determine which of these directions will be favored. You can think of the overall reaction as resulting from competition between the forward and reverse reactions (A ⇌ B). According to the law of mass action, increasing the concentration of A makes the forward reaction (A → B) happen more often than the reverse reaction, just as increasing the concentration of B favors the reverse reaction (B → A).

There are concentrations of A and B at which the forward and reverse reactions take place at the same rate. At these concentrations, no further *net change* in the system is observable, although individual molecules are still forming and breaking apart. This balance between forward and reverse reactions is known as **chemical equilibrium**. Chemical equilibrium is a state of no net change, and a state in which $\Delta G = 0$.

Chemical equilibrium and free energy are related

Chemical reactions do not necessarily proceed to completion, with all reactants converted into products. Each reaction has a specific equilibrium point, which is related to the relative free energy contents of the reactants and products. To understand the principle of equilibrium, consider the interconversion of glucose 1-phosphate and glucose 6-phosphate, a rearrangement of a phosphate group from one position on the ring of carbon atoms to another:

Glucose 1-phosphate ⇌ glucose 6-phosphate

Unraveling what goes on chemically in the cell is made possible by that fact that in many cases, after a cell's membrane has been ruptured to release its contents, the **cell-free system** with the cell contents (cytoplasm) in a test tube, usually in a buffered solution, has the same chemical properties as the intact cell. So the reaction can be studied in a test tube. Suppose we start out with an aqueous solution of glucose 1-phosphate that has a concentration of 0.02 M. (M stands for molar concentration; see Key Concept 2.4.) The solution is maintained under constant environmental conditions (25°C and pH 7). As the reaction proceeds to equilibrium, the concentration of the product, glucose 6-phosphate, rises from 0 M to 0.019 M, while the concentration of the reactant, glucose 1-phosphate, falls from 0.02 M to 0.001 M, at which point equilibrium is reached (**Figure 8.4**). *At equilibrium, the reverse reaction, from glucose 6-phosphate to glucose 1-phosphate, progresses at the same rate as the forward reaction.*

At equilibrium, then, this reaction has a product-to-reactant ratio of 19:1 (0.019/0.001), so the forward reaction has gone 95% of the way to completion ("to the right," as written above). This result is obtained every time the experiment is run under the same conditions.

The change in free energy (ΔG) for any reaction is related directly to its point of equilibrium. The further toward completion the point of equilibrium lies, the more free energy is released. In an exergonic reaction, ΔG is a negative number. The total value of ΔG also depends on the beginning concentrations of the reactants and products and other conditions such as temperature, pressure, and pH of the solution. Biochemists

Figure 8.4 Chemical Reactions Run to Equilibrium No matter what quantities of glucose 1-phosphate and glucose 6-phosphate are dissolved in water, when equilibrium is attained, there will always be 95% glucose 6-phosphate and 5% glucose 1-phosphate.

Q: What would happen in this system if, after formation, the glucose 6-phosphate was removed by a subsequent reaction?

Reaction to equilibrium

Initial condition:
100% Glucose 1-phosphate
(0.02 M concentration)

At equilibrium:
95% Glucose 6-phosphate
(0.019 M concentration)
5% Glucose 1-phosphate
(0.001 M concentration)

Equilibrium:
The reactions continue in both directions, but the concentrations remain the same.

often calculate ΔG using standard laboratory conditions: 25°C, 1 atmosphere pressure, 1 molar (1 M) concentrations of the solutes, and pH 7. The **standard free energy** change calculated using these conditions is designated ΔG^0. In our example of the conversion of glucose 1-phosphate to glucose 6-phosphate, $\Delta G^0 = -1.7$ kcal/mol, or -7.1 kJ/mol.

A large, positive ΔG for a reaction means that it does not proceed to the right (A → B). If the concentration of B is initially high relative to that of A, such a reaction runs "to the left" (A ← B), and at equilibrium nearly all of B is converted into A. A ΔG value near zero is characteristic of a readily reversible reaction: reactants and products have almost the same free energies.

In Chapters 9 and 10 you will learn the biochemical conversions that extract energy from food and light. In turn, this energy is used to synthesize carbohydrates, lipids, and proteins. All of the chemical reactions carried out by living organisms are governed by the principles of thermodynamics and equilibrium.

KEY CONCEPT
8.1 Recap and Assess

Two laws of thermodynamics govern energy transformations in biological systems. A biochemical reaction can release or consume energy, and it may not run to completion, but instead end up at a point of equilibrium.

1. What is the difference between endergonic and exergonic reactions, and what is the importance of positive and negative ΔG?
2. What makes it possible for endergonic reactions to proceed in organisms?

The principles of thermodynamics that we have been discussing apply to all energy transformations in the universe, so they are very powerful and useful. Now let's apply them to reactions in cells that involve the currency of biological energy, ATP.

KEY CONCEPT
8.2 ATP Plays a Key Role in Biochemical Energetics

Learning Objectives

8.2.1 Explain the characteristics of ATP that account for the high free energy released during its hydrolysis to form ADP and P_i.

8.2.2 Analyze evidence to identify reactions as exergonic or endergonic.

8.2.3 Predict biochemical transformations that require coupling to ATP hydrolysis.

Cells use adenosine triphosphate (ATP) for the capture and transfer of the free energy they require to do chemical work. ATP operates as a kind of "energy currency." Just as it is more efficient and convenient for you to trade money for a lunch in a café than to trade your actual labor, it's useful for cells to have a single currency for transferring energy between different reactions and cell processes. So some of the free energy that is released by exergonic reactions is captured in the formation of ATP from adenosine diphosphate (ADP) and inorganic phosphate (HPO_4^{2-}, which is commonly abbreviated to P_i). The ATP can then be hydrolyzed in the cell to release free energy to drive endergonic reactions.

ATP has another important role in the cell beyond its use as an energy currency: it can be converted into a building block for nucleic acids (see Chapter 4). The structure of ATP is similar to that of other nucleoside triphosphates, but two things about ATP make it especially useful to cells:

1. ATP releases a relatively large amount of energy when hydrolyzed to ADP and P_i.

The structure of ATP

Forming ADP and P$_i$ results in a lower free energy state, and energy is released.

Adenine

Phosphate groups

Ribose

Adenosine

AMP (Adenosine monophosphate)

ADP (Adenosine diphosphate)

ATP (Adenosine triphosphate)

Figure 8.5 ATP ATP is richer in energy than ADP and AMP. The conversion of ATP to ADP releases energy.

2. ATP can phosphorylate (donate a phosphate group to) many different molecules, which gain some of the energy that was stored in the ATP.

ATP hydrolysis releases energy

ATP (**Figure 8.5**) is a nucleoside triphosphate (see Figure 4.1). The hydrolysis of a molecule of ATP yields free energy, as well as ADP and an inorganic phosphate ion (P$_i$). Thus:

$$ATP + H_2O \rightarrow ADP + P_i + \text{free energy}$$

The important property of this reaction is that it is exergonic, releasing free energy. Under standard laboratory conditions, the change in free energy (ΔG) for this reaction is about –7.3 kcal/mol (–30 kJ/mol). This change in free energy is negative because the chemical bonds in ATP and H$_2$O are weaker than the chemical bonds in ADP and P$_i$. A molecule of ATP can be hydrolyzed either to ADP and P$_i$, or to adenosine monophosphate (AMP) and a pyrophosphate ion (P$_2$O$_7^{4-}$, commonly abbreviated as PP$_i$). Two characteristics of ATP account for the free energy released by the loss of one or two of its phosphate groups:

1. Because phosphate groups are negatively charged and so repel each other, it takes energy to get two phosphates near enough to each other to make the covalent bond that links them together. Some of this energy is stored as potential energy in the P~O bonds between the phosphates in ATP (the wavy line indicates a high-energy bond).

2. The free energy of this P~O bond (called a phosphoanhydride bond) is much higher than the energy of

the O—H bond that forms as a result of hydrolysis. So it is the lower free energy state of the system that releases energy.

Cells use the energy released by ATP hydrolysis to fuel endergonic reactions (such as the biosynthesis of complex molecules), for active transport, for movement, and even for the production of light (bioluminescence). Another interesting example of the use of ATP involves converting its chemical energy into light energy.

▶ **Media Clip 8.1 Bioluminescence in the Deep Sea**
Life12e.com/mc8.1

ATP couples exergonic and endergonic reactions

As you have just seen, the hydrolysis of ATP is exergonic and yields ADP, P$_i$, and more free energy (or AMP, PP$_i$, and more free energy). The reverse reaction, the formation of ATP from ADP and P$_i$, is endergonic and consumes as much free energy as is released by the hydrolysis of ATP:

$$ADP + P_i + \text{free energy} \rightarrow ATP + H_2O$$

Many exergonic reactions in the cell can provide the energy to convert ADP into ATP. For eukaryotes and many prokaryotes, the most important of these reactions is cellular respiration, in which some of the energy released from fuel molecules is captured in ATP. The formation and hydrolysis of ATP constitute what might be called an "energy-coupling cycle," in which ADP picks up energy from exergonic reactions to become ATP, which then donates energy to endergonic reactions. ATP is the common component of these reactions and is the agent of coupling, as illustrated in **Figure 8.6**.

Coupling of exergonic and endergonic reactions is very common in metabolism. Free energy is captured and retained in the P~O bonds of ATP, which is hydrolyzed in conjunction with

Exergonic reaction:
(releases energy)
• Cell respiration
• Catabolism

Energy

Endergonic reaction:
(requires energy)
• Active transport
• Cell movements
• Anabolism

Energy

ADP + P$_i$

Synthesis of ATP from ADP and P$_i$ requires energy.

Hydrolysis of ATP to ADP and P$_i$ releases energy.

ATP

Figure 8.6 Coupling of Reactions Exergonic reactions in the cell release the energy needed to convert ADP to ATP. The energy released from the conversion of ATP back to ADP can be used to fuel endergonic reactions.

▶ **View in Achieve**
Activity 8.1 ATP and Coupled Reactions

another reaction. The free energy released drives an endergonic reaction. For example, the formation of glucose 6-phosphate from glucose (**Figure 8.7**), which has a positive ΔG (is endergonic), will not proceed without the input of free energy from ATP hydrolysis, which has a negative ΔG (is exergonic). The overall ΔG for the coupled reactions (when the two ΔGs are added together) is negative. Hence the reactions proceed exergonically when they are coupled by occurring at the same time and place, and glucose 6-phosphate is synthesized. As you will see in Chapter 9, this is the initial reaction in the catabolism of glucose.

An active cell requires the production of millions of molecules of ATP per second to drive its biochemical machinery. From previous chapters, you may already be familiar with some of the activities in the cell that require energy from the hydrolysis of ATP:

- Active transport across a membrane (see Figure 6.14)

- Condensation reactions that use enzymes to form polymers (see Figure 3.4A)

- Modifications of cell signaling proteins by protein kinases (see Figure 7.15)

- Motor proteins that move vesicles along microtubules (see Figure 5.21)

An ATP molecule is typically consumed within a second of its formation. At rest, an average person produces and hydrolyzes about 40 kg of ATP per day—as much as some people weigh. This means that each ATP molecule undergoes about 10,000 cycles of synthesis and hydrolysis every day!

KEY CONCEPT
8.2 Recap and Assess

ATP is the "energy currency" of cells. Potential energy is stored in the P~O bonds of ATP. Some of the free energy released by exergonic reactions can be captured in the form of ATP. This energy can then be released by ATP hydrolysis and used to drive endergonic reactions.

1. What chemical properties allow ATP to store energy?

2. The following is a biochemical reaction that involves ATP:

    Phosphoenolpyruvate → pyruvate ($\Delta G = -14$ kcal/mol)

    a. Is the reaction exergonic or endergonic?

    b. Is ATP hydrolyzed or formed during the reaction?

ATP is synthesized and used up very rapidly. But these biochemical reactions—and nearly all the others that take place inside a cell—could not proceed so rapidly without the help of enzymes.

KEY CONCEPT
8.3 Enzymes Speed Up Biochemical Transformations

Learning Objectives

8.3.1 Describe a catalyst.

8.3.2 Describe how an enzyme–substrate complex forms.

8.3.3 Explain the relationship between an enzyme and the equilibrium point of the reaction it catalyzes.

When we know the change in free energy (ΔG) of a reaction, we know where the equilibrium point of the reaction lies: the more negative the ΔG value is, the further the reaction proceeds to products and toward completion. We call such a reaction spontaneous. However, ΔG tells us nothing about the *rate* of a reaction—how fast it moves toward equilibrium. Most reaction rates in chemical transformations in living systems are slow—indeed, too slow to result in the rapid changes needed for an organism to respond to environmental changes and perform its cellular functions. In chemistry, **catalysts** are substances that speed up reactions without themselves being permanently altered. Often, a catalyst provides a surface on which to line up reactants so they will be more likely to collide and react than they would in solution. A catalyst does not cause a reaction to occur that would not proceed without it, *but merely increases the rate of the reaction*, allowing equilibrium to be approached more rapidly. This is an important point: *No catalyst makes a reaction occur that cannot otherwise occur.*

Most biological catalysts are proteins called **enzymes**. A biological catalyst is a molecular framework or scaffold within which chemical catalysis takes place. The enzyme binds the reactants and sometimes participates in the reaction itself; however, such participation does not permanently change the enzyme. That's the hallmark of any catalyst: it ends up in exactly the same chemical condition after a reaction as before it.

Exergonic reaction
(releases energy)

The negative ΔG indicates an exergonic reaction.

$ATP + H_2O$ → ATP hydrolysis → $ADP + P_i$ $\Delta G = -7.3$ kcal/mol

Energy

Endergonic reaction
(requires energy)

The positive ΔG indicates an endergonic reaction.

$\Delta G = +4.0$ kcal/mol

$+ P_i$

Glucose **Glucose 6-phosphate (G6P)**

The coupled reaction has an overall negative ΔG, indicating an exergonic reaction that proceeds toward completion.

Net $\Delta G = -3.3$ kcal/mol

Figure 8.7 Coupling of ATP Hydrolysis to an Endergonic Reaction
The addition of phosphate derived from the hydrolysis of ATP to glucose forms the molecule glucose 6-phosphate (in a reaction catalyzed by hexokinase). ATP hydrolysis is exergonic, and the energy released drives the second reaction, which is endergonic.

Q: What would be the magnitude of the ΔG of a different conversion that could drive the synthesis of ATP?

In this key concept we will discuss the energy barrier that controls the rate of a chemical reaction. Then we will focus on the roles of enzymes: how they interact with specific reactants, how they lower the energy barrier, and how they permit reactions to proceed more quickly.

To speed up a reaction, an energy barrier must be overcome

An exergonic reaction may release free energy, but without a catalyst it will take place very slowly because there is an energy barrier between reactants and products. Think about the hydrolysis of sucrose, which we described in Key Concept 8.1:

$$\text{Sucrose} + H_2O \rightarrow \text{glucose} + \text{fructose}$$

In your body, this reaction is part of digestion. Even if water is abundant, the sucrose molecule will only rarely bind the H atom and the —OH group of water at the appropriate locations to break the covalent bond between glucose and fructose *unless there is an input of energy to initiate the reaction*. This input of energy will place the sucrose into a reactive mode called the **transition state**. The energy input required for sucrose to reach this state is called the **activation energy** (E_a):

$$E_a + \text{sucrose} + H_2O \rightarrow \text{sucrose–}H_2O \text{ transition state}$$

Once the transition state is formed, the reaction proceeds rapidly:

$$\text{Sucrose–}H_2O \text{ transition state} \rightarrow \text{glucose} + \text{fructose}$$

In this case, the overall reaction is exergonic, releasing energy (**Figure 8.8**). But note that activation energy is needed to start endergonic reactions as well.

Where does activation energy come from? If reactants are at the human body temperature (37°C), they are moving around. A few are moving fast enough that their kinetic energy can supply activation energy, and these reactant molecules enter the transition state and react. If the system is heated, all the reactant molecules move faster and have more kinetic energy, and the reaction speeds up. You have probably used this method in the chemistry laboratory or the kitchen.

However, adding heat to increase the average kinetic energy of the molecules so they can react would not work in living systems. Such a nonspecific approach would accelerate all chemical reactions, including destructive ones such as the denaturation of proteins (see Chapter 3). A more effective way to speed up a reaction in a living system is to lower the energy barrier by bringing the reactants close together. In living cells, enzymes accomplish this task.

Enzymes bind specific reactants at their active sites

As we have already noted, some chemical catalysts get reactants into the transition state by providing a surface where the reactants line up beside one another in the proper orientation. The molecular structure of proteins, with their myriad three-dimensional shapes (see Figure 3.8), makes them ideally suited to act as biological catalysts. Enzymes are highly specific. An enzyme usually recognizes and binds to only one or a few closely related reactants, yielding specific products.

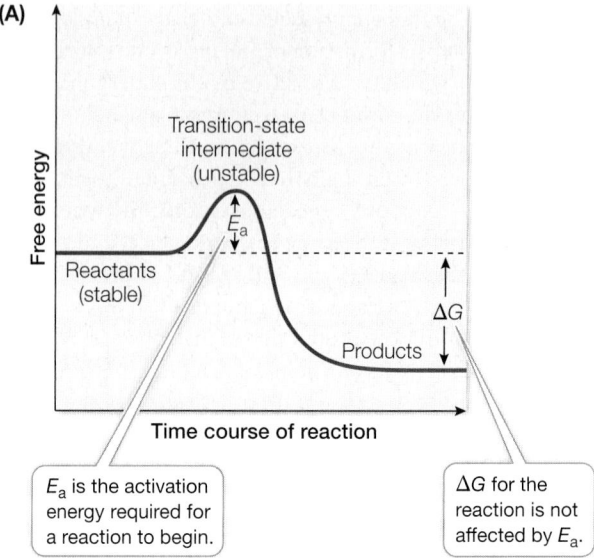

(A)

E_a is the activation energy required for a reaction to begin.

ΔG for the reaction is not affected by E_a.

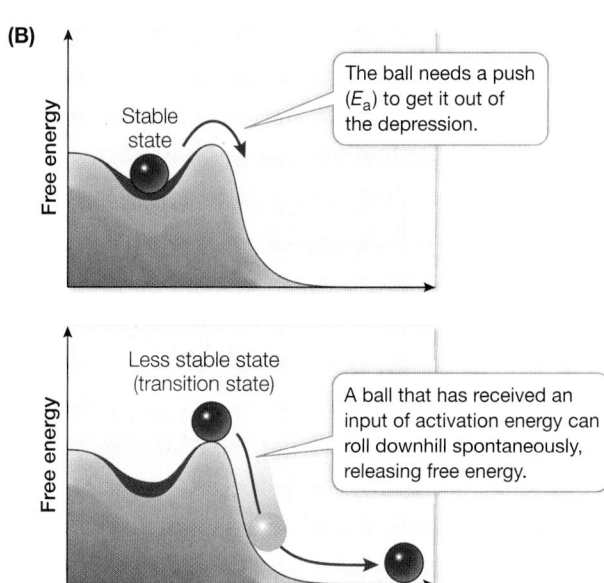

(B)

The ball needs a push (E_a) to get it out of the depression.

A ball that has received an input of activation energy can roll downhill spontaneously, releasing free energy.

Figure 8.8 Activation Energy Initiates Reactions (A) In any chemical reaction, an initial stable state must become less stable before change is possible. (B) A ball on a hillside provides a physical analogy for the biochemical principle graphed in (A).

Connect the Concepts To understand enzymes and their activity, you should review the structures and chemical properties of proteins. See Key Concept 3.2.

In an enzyme-catalyzed reaction, the reactants are called **substrates**. Substrate molecules bind to a specific three-dimensional location on the enzyme protein called the **active site**, where catalysis takes place (**Figure 8.9**). This specificity is comparable to the specific binding of a membrane transport protein or receptor protein to its specific ligand, as described in Chapters 6 and 7. The names of enzymes often reflect their functions and end with the suffix "ase." For example, the enzyme sucrase catalyzes the hydrolysis of sucrose, which we have referred to earlier:

1 The substrate and enzyme approach one another.

Active site

Substrate

Enzyme

2 The substrate binds to the enzyme's active site, forming an enzyme–substrate complex.

3 The products are released.

Products

Figure 8.9 Enzyme and Substrate   A reaction involving an enzyme is illustrated by lysozyme. Lysozyme catalyzes breakage of bonds in the peptidoglycans of bacterial cell walls. (See Key Concept 5.2 for a description of peptidoglycans.) (Data from PDB 148L. R. Kuroki et al. 1993. *Science* 262: 2030–2033.)

Q: Is "fitting in the lock" the only necessary function for enzyme–substrate interactions?

$$\text{Sucrose} + H_2O \xrightarrow{\text{Sucrase}} \text{glucose} + \text{fructose}$$

Thousands of enzymes have been identified, each catalyzing the transformation of its particular substrate(s). In general, enzymes fall into six categories:

1. *Oxidoreductases* transfer electrons between molecules, especially in energy metabolism. An example of an enzyme that catalyzes this reaction is oxidoreductase:

$$A^- + B \rightarrow A + B^-$$

   You will see other examples in Chapters 9 and 10.

2. *Transferases* transfer groups of atoms (functional groups) (see Figure 3.1) between molecules. The basic reaction can be shown as:

$$AX + B \rightarrow A + BX$$

   where A = the donor, B = the acceptor, and X = the functional group. For example, aminotransferases transfer $—NH_2$ groups between molecules, linking carbohydrates and amino acids.

3. *Hydrolases* add water to covalent bonds to break down molecules. An example (shown earlier) is sucrase, which hydrolyzes sucrose to its constituent monosaccharides.

4. *Lyases* are a diverse set of enzyme that catalyze non-hydrolytic bond breakage, often forming a new bond in the process. For example, a lyase catalyzes the cleavage of the phosphorus–oxygen bond of ATP (see Figure 7.11):

$$ATP \rightarrow cAMP + PP_i$$

5. *Isomerases* move functional groups from one place to another within a molecule, forming an isomer with the same atoms, differently bonded. For example, glucose and fructose are isomers of $C_6H_{12}O_6$ (see Figure 3.17).

6. *Ligases* join two molecules together. You will see examples of ligases when you learn about DNA replication in Chapter 13.

A special note on language: When biologists refer to an enzyme, they usually use a verb for its action. For example, as noted for ligases (#6), we used the words "ligases join…." It is important for you to realize that this wording is shorthand for what really happens: ligases catalyze the joining. *Enzymes don't "do" the reaction; they catalyze it.*

When a substrate binds to the active site of an enzyme, the result is called an **enzyme–substrate complex (ES)** (see Figure 8.9). The chemical forces that hold the complex together may include hydrogen bonding, electrical attraction, or temporary covalent bonding. The enzyme–substrate complex gives rise to product and free enzyme:

$$E + S \rightarrow ES \rightarrow E + P$$

where E is the enzyme, S is the substrate, P is the product, and ES is the enzyme–substrate complex. Using the example of sucrose hydrolysis, we can write out the steps of the reaction:

$$\text{Sucrose} + H_2O + \text{sucrase} \rightarrow \text{sucrase–sucrose–}H_2O \text{ complex} \rightarrow$$
$$\text{glucose} + \text{fructose} + \text{sucrase}$$

The free enzyme (E, sucrase) is in the same chemical form at the end of the reaction as at the beginning. While bound to the substrate, it may change chemically, but by the end of the reaction it has been restored to its initial form and is ready to bind more substrate.

Connect the Concepts   Binding of a substrate to an enzyme involves not just a "fit" but also noncovalent interactions between the enzyme and substrate. See Key Concept 3.2 for an outline of noncovalent interactions.

The relationship between enzyme and substrate may seem familiar; it is analogous to the binding of a receptor and ligand that we described in Chapter 7. In that instance, we described the affinity of a receptor for its ligand with the dissociation constant (K_D). The lower the K_D, the tighter the binding. For enzymes and their substrates, K_D values are often in the range 10^{-5} to 10^{-6} M, which favors the formation of the ES. In practical terms, the K_D values of the ES are such that the binding between enzyme and substrate is somewhat reversible; the substrate can be released before the reaction. However, many enzyme-catalyzed reactions will proceed because the ES is short-lived and the product(s) form quickly.

Enzymes lower the energy barrier but do not affect equilibrium

Reactants that are bound to the enzyme, forming an enzyme–substrate complex, require less activation energy than do the transition-state intermediates in the corresponding uncatalyzed reaction (**Figure 8.10**). Thus the enzyme lowers the activation energy needed for the reaction, speeding it up. Note that both the forward and the reverse reactions speed up, so the enzyme-catalyzed reaction proceeds toward equilibrium more rapidly than the uncatalyzed reaction. *The final equilibrium is the same with or without the enzyme.* Similarly, adding an enzyme to a reaction does not change the difference in free energy (ΔG) between the reactants and the products (see Figure 8.10).

What do we mean by "speeding it up"? Consider a protein that has arginine as its terminal amino acid. This is an organized situation, and a hydrolysis reaction—releasing the arginine—is spontaneous (entropy increases). But spontaneous does not mean fast. In solution, it takes about 7 years for half of the protein molecules to undergo the hydrolysis reaction. Enter the enzyme carboxypeptidase A. When it catalyzes the reaction, half the arginines are released in less than a second! Rate enhancement by enzymes varies from 1 million times to an amazing 10^{26} by sulfate monoesterases. The consequence of catalysis for living cells is not difficult to imagine. Such increased reaction rates make new realities possible.

Figure 8.10 Enzymes Lower the Energy Barrier   Although the activation energy is lower in an enzyme-catalyzed reaction than in an uncatalyzed reaction, the energy released is the same with or without catalysis. In other words, E_a is lower but ΔG is unchanged. Lower activation energy means the reaction will take place at a faster rate.

View in Achieve
Activity 8.2 Free Energy Changes

8.3 Recap and Assess

A chemical reaction requires a "push" over the energy barrier to get started. An enzyme reduces the activation energy needed to start a reaction by binding the reactants (substrates), which speeds up the reaction. Biological catalysts are highly specific; only a narrow range of substrates can fit into the enzyme's active site, so generally only one specific reaction can be catalyzed by a given enzyme. Enzymes affect only the *rates* at which reactions proceed—they do not affect the equilibrium or free energy associated with a given reaction.

1. Explain how the structure of an enzyme makes that enzyme specific.
2. What is the relationship between an enzyme and the equilibrium point of a reaction?
3. When potatoes are peeled, the enzyme polyphenol oxidase causes discoloration by catalyzing the oxidation of certain molecules, using O_2 as a substrate. Explain these observations:
   a. Browning is reduced in potatoes that are peeled under water and kept there.
   b. Potatoes that have been boiled at 100°C and then cooled do not brown when they are sliced.

Now that you have a general understanding of the structures, functions, and specificities of enzymes, let's look more closely at how they work.

KEY CONCEPT 8.4

Enzymes Bring Substrates Together so Reactions Readily Occur

Learning Objectives

8.4.1 Give examples of mechanisms for enzyme catalysis.
8.4.2 Describe coenzymes and cofactors and how they function.
8.4.3 Predict changes in the rate of an enzyme-catalyzed reaction as factors in the reaction are varied.

During and after the formation of the enzyme–substrate complex, chemical interactions occur. These interactions contribute directly to the breaking of old bonds and the formation of new ones.

Enzymes lower activation energy in several ways

In catalyzing a reaction, an enzyme may use one or more strategies.

SUBSTRATE ORIENTATION   When free in solution, substrates are moving from place to place randomly while at the same time vibrating, rotating, and tumbling. They only rarely have the proper orientation to interact when they collide. When bound to an enzyme, however, substrates are held in the correct orientation to bring the appropriate chemical groups of substrates together, facilitating bond breakage and formation (**Figure 8.11A**).

INDUCING STRAIN   Once a substrate has bound to its active site, an enzyme can cause bonds in the substrate to stretch, putting it in an unstable transition state (**Figure 8.11B**). This causes the strained bonds to have higher potential energy (they are weaker), making them prone to break.

ADDING CHEMICAL GROUPS   The side chains (R groups) of an enzyme's amino acids may be direct participants in making the enzyme's substrates more chemically reactive (**Figure 8.11C**).

- In *acid–base catalysis*, the acidic or basic side chains of the amino acids in the active site transfer H^+ to or from the substrate, destabilizing a covalent bond in the substrate, and permitting it to break.

- In *covalent catalysis*, a functional group in a side chain forms a temporary covalent bond with a portion of the substrate.

- In *metal ion catalysis*, metal ions such as copper, iron, and manganese, which are often firmly bound to side chains of enzymes, can lose or gain electrons without detaching from the enzymes. This ability makes them important participants in oxidation–reduction reactions, which involve the loss or gain of electrons.

Molecular structure determines enzyme function

Many enzymes are much larger than their substrates. An enzyme is typically a protein containing hundreds of amino acids. It may consist of a single folded polypeptide chain or of several subunits (see Key Concept 3.2). Its substrate is generally a small molecule or a small part of a large molecule. The active site of the enzyme is usually quite small, not more than 6 to 12 amino acids. You may be asking yourself:

- What features of the enzyme's active site allow it to recognize and bind the substrate?

- What is the role of the rest of the protein?

THE ACTIVE SITE IS SPECIFIC TO THE SUBSTRATE(S)   The remarkable ability of an enzyme to select exactly the right substrate(s) depends on a precise interlocking of molecular shapes and interactions of chemical groups at the active site. The binding of a substrate to the active site depends on the same kinds of forces that maintain the tertiary structure of the enzyme: hydrogen bonds, the attraction and repulsion of electrically charged groups, and hydrophobic interactions. The specific fit of the substrate in the active site of lysozyme is illustrated in Figures 8.9 and 8.11B.

AN ENZYME CHANGES SHAPE WHEN IT BINDS A SUBSTRATE
Just as a membrane receptor protein may undergo precise changes in conformation upon binding its ligand (see Chapter 7), some enzymes change their shapes when they bind their substrate(s). These shape changes, which are called **induced fit**, alter the shape of the active site(s) of the enzyme.

An example of induced fit can be seen in the enzyme hexokinase, which catalyzes the reaction

$$\text{Glucose} + \text{ATP} \rightarrow \text{glucose 6-phosphate} + \text{ADP}$$

Induced fit brings reactive side chains from the hexokinase active site into alignment with the substrates (**Figure 8.12**), facilitating its catalytic mechanisms. Equally important, the folding of hexokinase to fit around the substrates (glucose and ATP) excludes water from the active site. This is essential, because if water were present, the

(A) Orientation

The two substrates are oriented so they can react.

Citrate synthase

Two substrates are bound next to one another at the active site of the enzyme citrate synthase.

(B) Physical strain

The enzyme strains the substrate.

Lysozyme

The active site of lysozyme strains and flattens its peptidoglycan substrate.

(C) Chemical charge

The enzyme adds charges to the substrate.

Chymotrypsin

Two amino acids at the active site of chymotrypsin become charged when in contact with the substrate.

Figure 8.11 Life at the Active Site   Enzymes use three basic mechanisms to cause their substrates to enter the transition state: (**A**) orientation, (**B**) physical strain, and (**C**) chemical charge. (A data from PDB 1AL6. B. Schwartz et al. 1997; B data from PDB 1BB6. V. B. Vollan et al. 1999. *Acta Crystallogr D Biol Crystallogr* 55: 60–66; C data from PDB 1AB9. N. H. Yennawar et al. 1994. *Biochemistry* 33: 7326–7366.)

Q: The enzyme chymotrypsin cleaves the peptide bonds of proteins after the amino acids tyrosine, phenylalanine, or tryptophan. Locations on the polypeptide chains with other amino acids are not cleaved by the enzyme. Looking at Table 3.2 (amino acids), can you explain the substrate specificity?

ATP could be hydrolyzed to ADP and P_i. But since water is absent, the transfer of a phosphate from ATP to glucose is favored.

Induced fit at least partly indicates what the role(s) of the rest of the protein may be:

- It provides a framework so that the amino acids of the active site are properly positioned in relation to the substrate(s).

- It participates in significant changes in protein shape and structure that result in induced fit.

- It provides binding sites for regulatory molecules (see Key Concept 8.5).

Empty active site

When the substrates bind to the active site, the two halves of the enzyme move together, changing the shape of the enzyme so that catalysis can take place.

Figure 8.12 Some Enzymes Change Shape When Substrate Binds to Them Shape changes result in an induced fit between enzyme and substrate, improving the catalytic ability of the enzyme. Induced fit can be observed in the enzyme hexokinase, seen here with and without its substrates, glucose (red) and ATP (yellow). (Data from PDB 1IG8. P. R. Kuser et al. 2000. *J Biol Chem* 275: 20814–20821 and PDB 1BDG. A. M. Mulichak et al. 1998. *Nat Struct Biol* 5: 555–560.)

Not all enzymes are proteins

Some RNA molecules can also act as biological catalysts; in these cases they are called **ribozymes**. As you saw in Figure 4.4, RNAs can fold into specific three-dimensional shapes that can bind substrates. Indeed, it takes only 25 bases in an RNA polymer to generate specific binding. The bases in RNA contain polar groups and hydrogen bonding possibilities with substrates. Some ribozymes act on themselves as self-cleaving RNAs; examples include RNAs in mitochondria and plastids. Other ribozymes act on chemically different substrates; the most notable among these is RNA in the ribosome that acts as a catalyst for peptide bond formation in protein synthesis. The catalytic ability of RNA is important evidence for the "RNA world" hypothesis, relating to the origin of life (see Key Concept 4.3).

Some enzymes require other molecules in order to function

Many enzymes require the presence of nonprotein chemical "partners" in order to function (**Table 8.2**):

- *Prosthetic groups* are distinct, non–amino acid atoms or molecular groupings that are permanently bound to their enzymes. An example is flavin adenine dinucleotide (FAD), which is bound to succinate dehydrogenase, an important enzyme in cellular respiration (see Key Concept 9.3).

- *Inorganic cofactors* include ions such as copper, zinc, and iron that are permanently bound to certain enzymes. For example, the enzyme alcohol dehydrogenase contains the cofactor zinc.

- A *coenzyme* is a nonprotein carbon-containing molecule that is required for the action of one or more enzymes. It is usually relatively small compared with the enzyme to which it binds.

A **coenzyme** moves from enzyme to enzyme, adding or removing chemical groups from the substrate. A coenzyme is like a substrate in that it does not permanently bind to the enzyme: it binds to the active site, changes chemically during the reaction, and then separates from the enzyme to participate in other reactions. There is actually no clear distinction between the functions of coenzymes and some substrates. For example, ATP and ADP have been described as coenzymes, even though they are really substrates that gain or lose phosphate groups during chemical reactions. The term "coenzyme" was coined before the functions of these molecules were fully understood. Biochemists continue to use the term, and for consistency with the field, we use it in this book.

Substrate concentration affects the reaction rate

For a chemical reaction of the type A → B, the rate of the uncatalyzed reaction is directly proportional to the concentration of the substrate, A. The higher the concentration of substrate, the faster the rate of the reaction. The appropriate enzyme not only speeds up the reaction; it also changes the shape of a plot of rate versus substrate concentration (**Figure 8.13**). For a given concentration of enzyme, the rate of the enzyme-catalyzed reaction initially increases as the substrate concentration increases from zero, but then it levels off. At some point, further increases in the substrate concentration do not significantly increase the reaction rate—the maximum rate has been reached.

The concentration of an enzyme is usually much lower than that of its substrate (e.g., in cells expressing the enzyme sucrase, there are far more molecules of sucrose than of the enzyme). As more and more substrate molecules bind to the available enzyme molecules, there is a saturation phenomenon like the one that occurs in facilitated diffusion (see Figure 6.12). When all the enzyme molecules are bound with substrate molecules, the enzyme is working as fast as it can—at its maximum rate. Nothing is gained by adding more substrate, because no free enzyme molecules are left to act as catalysts. Under these conditions the active sites are said to be saturated.

TABLE 8.2	Some Examples of Nonprotein "Partners" of Enzymes	
Type of molecule	**Role in catalyzed reactions**
PROSTHETIC GROUPS	
Heme	Binds ions, O_2, and electrons
FAD	Carries electrons/protons
Retinal	Converts light energy
INORGANIC COFACTORS	
Iron (Fe^{2+} or Fe^{3+})	Oxidation/reduction
Copper (Cu^+ or Cu^{2+})	Oxidation/reduction
Zinc (Zn^{2+})	Stabilizes DNA binding structure
COENZYMES	
Biotin	Carries —COO–
Coenzyme A	Carries —CO—CH_3
NAD	Carries electrons/protons
ATP	Provides/extracts energy

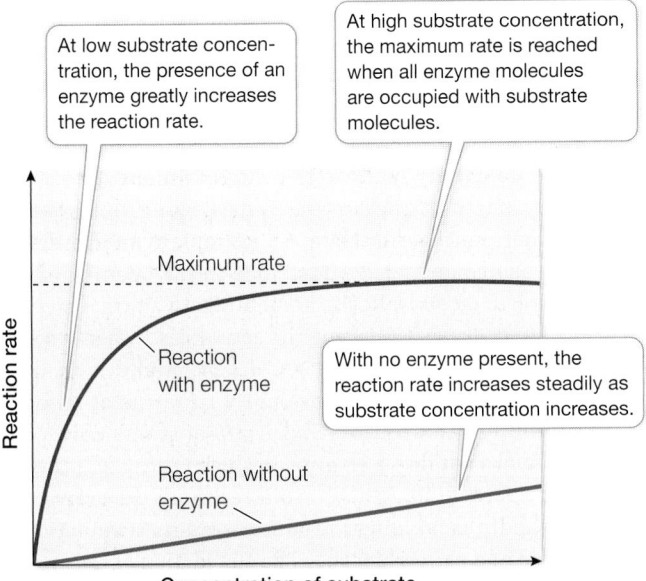

At low substrate concentration, the presence of an enzyme greatly increases the reaction rate.

At high substrate concentration, the maximum rate is reached when all enzyme molecules are occupied with substrate molecules.

Maximum rate

Reaction with enzyme

With no enzyme present, the reaction rate increases steadily as substrate concentration increases.

Reaction without enzyme

Reaction rate

Concentration of substrate

Figure 8.13 Catalyzed Reactions Reach a Maximum Rate
Because there is usually less enzyme than substrate present, the reaction rate levels off when the enzyme becomes saturated.

The maximum rate of a catalyzed reaction can be used to measure how efficient the enzyme is. The turnover number is the maximum number of substrate molecules that one enzyme molecule can convert to product per unit of time. This number ranges from 1 molecule every 2 seconds for lysozyme to an amazing 40 million molecules per second for the liver enzyme catalase.

8.4 Recap and Assess

Enzymes orient their substrates to bring together specific atoms so that bonds can form. An enzyme can participate in the reaction it catalyzes by temporarily changing shape or destabilizing the enzyme–substrate complex. Some enzymes require prosthetic groups, inorganic cofactors, or coenzymes in order to function.

1. The chemical composition of an enzyme before and after a catalyzed reaction is the same, but during the reaction an enzyme can change. How and why does this happen?

2. Compare enzymes and coenzymes with regard to chemical structure and function.

3. Plot reaction rate versus substrate concentration, and explain the shape of the curve.

You've seen in this key concept how individual enzymes work on their substrates. However, enzymes inside organisms don't operate in isolation—there may be thousands of different enzymes within a given cell. Let's see how all these different enzymes work together in a complex organism.

8.5 Enzyme Activities Can Be Regulated

Learning Objectives

8.5.1 Explain how metabolic pathways can shift in different directions.

8.5.2 Distinguish between different types of inhibitors.

8.5.3 Apply the concept of allosteric regulation to explain experimental results.

The chemical reactions in cells operate within metabolic pathways in which the product of one reaction is a reactant for the next. These pathways do not exist in isolation, but interact extensively, and each reaction in each pathway is catalyzed by a specific enzyme. Within a cell or organism, the presence and activity of enzymes determine the "flow" of chemicals through different metabolic pathways. The amount of enzyme activity, in turn, can be controlled in two ways:

1. *Regulation of gene expression.* The gene for an enzyme protein may be expressed more or less, resulting in more or fewer enzyme molecules in the cell. You learned in Chapter 7 that some signal transduction pathways result in changes in gene expression, and that often the genes that are switched on or off encode enzymes.

2. *Regulation of enzyme activity.* The enzyme may change its shape to hide its active site from the substrate, or a regulator molecule may prevent the substrate from reaching the active site. Blocking the activity of a single enzyme can affect an entire metabolic pathway.

The flow of molecules through interacting metabolic pathways can be studied, but this process quickly becomes complicated, because each pathway influences the others. Computer algorithms are used to model these pathways and show how they mesh in an interdependent system (**Figure 8.14**). Such models can help predict what will happen if the concentration of one molecule or another is altered. This field of biology is called **systems biology** and it has many applications.

In this key concept we will investigate the roles of enzymes in organizing and regulating metabolic pathways. We will also examine how the environment—particularly temperature and pH—affects enzyme activity.

 View in Achieve
Simulation 8.1 **Systems Biology**

Enzymes can be regulated by inhibitors

Chemical inhibitors can bind to enzymes, slowing down the rates of the reactions they catalyze. Some inhibitors occur naturally in cells; others are natural in the diet; still others are artificial. Naturally occurring inhibitors regulate metabolism; artificial ones can be used to treat disease, to kill pests, or to study how enzymes work. In some cases the inhibitor binds the enzyme irreversibly, and the enzyme becomes permanently inactivated. In other cases

Each circle represents a small molecule (metabolite).

Each line represents an enzyme-catalyzed metabolic reaction.

Metabolism of Cofactors and Vitamins

Nucleotide Metabolism

Carbohydrate Metabolism

Lipid Metabolism

Amino Acid Metabolism

ATP Production

Metabolism of Other Substances

The metabolites and reaction pathways overlap and intersect.

Figure 8.14 Metabolic Pathways The complex interactions of metabolic pathways can be modeled by the tools of systems biology. In cells, the main elements controlling these pathways are enzymes. (After KEGG: Kyoto Encyclopedia of Genes and Genomes. Map 01100 © 2004 Kanehisa Laboratories; M. Kanehisa et al. 2017. *Nucleic Acids Res* 45: D353–D361.)

the inhibitor has reversible effects; it can separate from the enzyme, allowing the enzyme to function fully as before. The removal of a natural reversible inhibitor increases an enzyme's rate of catalysis.

IRREVERSIBLE INHIBITION   If an inhibitor covalently binds to certain side chains at the active site of an enzyme, it will permanently inactivate the enzyme by destroying its capacity to interact with its normal substrate. An example of an irreversible inhibitor is aspirin, which we described in the opening of this chapter. Aspirin (acetylsalicylic acid) binds to a target enzyme called cyclooxygenase (COX) near its active site. When it binds, aspirin releases its acetyl group ($-CH_2CH_3$) and this group of atoms is transferred to bond covalently to serine at its polar hydroxyl group (**Figure 8.15**). The group of atoms now "coating" serine sticks out into a channel in the protein and prevents the substrate, arachidonic acid, from reaching the active site. So prostaglandin is no longer produced and its stimulation of inflammation and pain is blocked. The elucidation of the mechanism of aspirin's action as an inhibitor of a pathway involved in inflammation was a landmark in modern pharmacology, the study of drugs (**Investigating Life: How Do Anti-Inflammatory Drugs Work as Enzyme Inhibitors?**).

REVERSIBLE INHIBITION   In some cases an inhibitor is similar enough to a particular enzyme's natural substrate to bind non-covalently to its active site, yet different enough that the enzyme catalyzes no chemical reaction. While such a molecule is bound to the enzyme, the natural substrate cannot enter the active site and the enzyme is unable to function. Such a molecule is called a **competitive inhibitor** because it competes with the natural substrate for the active site (**Figure 8.16A,B**). In this case, the degree of inhibition depends on the relative concentrations of the substrate and the inhibitor: if the inhibitor concentration is higher, it is more likely to bind the active site of the enzyme than the substrate, and vice versa. The inhibition is reversible because if the concentration of substrate is increased or if the concentration

Figure 8.15 Irreversible Enzyme Inhibition
Aspirin transfers an acetyl group, which covalently bonds to a serine amino acid near the active site of its target enzyme. This permanent change prevents the substrate from binding. (Data from PDB 1PTH. P. J. Loll et al. 1995. *Nat Struct Biol* 2: 637–643.)

Q: What would be the chemical effects of adding an acetyl group ($-CO-CH_3$) to the active site serine?

Acetyl group

An acetyl group is transferred from aspirin to an amino acid in the active site.

Aspirin

Cyclooxygenase with aspirin in active site

Modified active site

▶InvestigatingLIFE How Do Anti-Inflammatory Drugs Work as Enzyme Inhibitors?

Experiment

Original Paper: J. R. Vane. 1971. Inhibition of prostaglandin synthesis as a mechanism of action of aspirin-like drugs. *Nature* 231: 232–235.

J. B. Smith and A. L Willis. 1971. Aspirin selectively inhibits prostaglandin production in human platelets. *Nature* 231: 235–238.

The opening story in this chapter describes how willow bark, the source of what became aspirin, is a centuries-old remedy for pain and inflammation. Until the late twentieth century, it was assumed that aspirin acted directly on the nervous system. Working at England's Royal College of Surgeons, a group led by John Vane showed that aspirin acts instead as an inhibitor of the enzymatic reaction that produces prostaglandin (PG), a fatty acid derivative important in inflammation.

HYPOTHESIS▶ Aspirin acts as an anti-inflammatory drug by inhibiting an enzyme that catalyzes prostaglandin synthesis.

METHOD▶

1a Obtain animal lungs.

1b Obtain human blood.

2a Break open cells to obtain homogenate.

2b Isolate platelets.

3 Add substrate, arachidonic acid, with and without aspirin, to cell extracts.

Arachidonic acid

Aspirin

Cell extracts

4 Measure amount of product, prostaglandin.

Prostaglandin

RESULTS▶

PG formed (ng) — Aspirin concentration (µg/mL)

CONCLUSION▶ In both animal and human cells, aspirin blocks the synthesis of the pro-inflammatory molecule, prostaglandin, in test tube experiments.

Work with the Data

For his discovery of the mechanism by which aspirin relieves pain, John Vane was awarded the Nobel Prize and knighted by Queen Elizabeth II. Key to the experiments was the assumption that enzyme activity and mechanism are the same outside the organism as they are inside. In the lab, if given its substrate and the same set of environmental conditions as in the cytoplasm, an enzyme will catalyze production of its product.

QUESTIONS▶

1. In the first set of experiments, lung tissue from guinea pigs was broken up to form a cell-free extract (homogenate). The substrate, arachidonic acid, was added to the extract, and after 30 minutes the amount of prostaglandin (PG) was measured. The results are shown in **Table A**. Plot PG synthesis versus aspirin concentration. What can you conclude?

2. A similar set of experiments was performed on human platelets (membrane-bound cell fragments derived from white blood cells). These cells are known to produce PG by the same enzyme mechanism as lung tissue under certain environmental conditions. The results are shown in **Table B**. What can you conclude from these results and about the generalizability of your conclusion from Question 1?

3. In a third set of experiments, platelets were isolated from human volunteers and their ability to make PG was measured (no aspirin present). Then these people were given a clinically effective dose of aspirin, and after a short period their platelets were isolated and PG synthesis measured (again, no aspirin in the test tube experiments). The results from three people are shown in **Table C**. How do these data either reinforce or refute your conclusion from Questions 1 and 2?

Table A

Aspirin concentration (µg/mL)	PG synthesis (ng)
0	220
1	172
2	136
10	99
50	33
80	0

Table B

Aspirin concentration (µg/mL)	PG synthesis (ng)
0	53
0.01	48
0.1	35
1	18
10	7

Table C

	Prostaglandin synthesis (ng)	
Individual	Before aspirin	After aspirin
1	160	16
2	168	5
3	103	20

Go to Achieve for a companion Data in Depth exercise.

(A) Normal enzyme–substrate binding

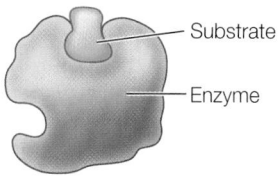

Normal substrate binding to enzyme active site.

(B) Competitive inhibition

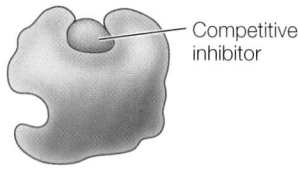

A competitive inhibitor binds to the active site, preventing substrate binding.

(C) Uncompetitive inhibition

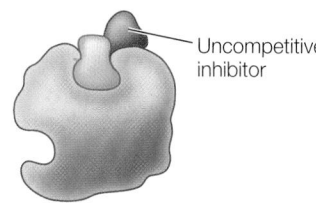

An uncompetitive inhibitor binds to the enzyme–substrate complex, preventing release of products.

(D) Noncompetitive inhibition

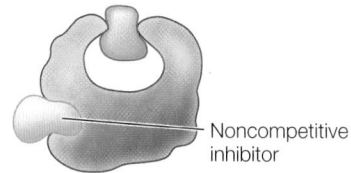

A noncompetitive inhibitor binds at a site other than the active site, changing enzyme structure so that normal substrate binding cannot occur.

Figure 8.16 Reversible Enzyme Inhibition There are several mechanisms of enzyme inhibition.

 View in Achieve
Animation 8.1 Enzyme Catalysis

of inhibitor is reduced, the substrate is more likely to bind, and the enzyme is active again.

An example of a competitive inhibitor is the drug methotrexate (**Figure 8.17**). An important coenzyme in the formation of purines (components of nucleic acids) is tetrahydrofolate, which is formed from dihydrofolate in a reaction catalyzed by dihydrofolate reductase (DHFR):

$$\text{Dihydrofolate} \xrightarrow{\text{DHFR}} \text{tetrahydrofolate}$$

When cancer cells reproduce, they need to replicate their DNA, and so they need to produce purines. This makes DHFR an ideal target for an anticancer drug. A team led by Sidney Farber at Harvard Medical School first showed that an analog of dihydrofolate could treat leukemia. The drug used by Farber (aminopterin) has since been replaced by a similar analog, methotrexate. This successful drug is used to treat inflammatory diseases such as psoriasis and rheumatoid arthritis, as well as cancer.

An **uncompetitive inhibitor** (**Figure 8.16C**) binds to the enzyme–substrate complex, preventing the complex from releasing products. Unlike competitive inhibition, uncompetitive inhibition cannot be overcome by adding more substrate.

A **noncompetitive inhibitor** binds to an unbound enzyme at a site distinct from the active site. Binding causes a change in the shape of the enzyme that alters its activity (**Figure 8.16D**). The active site may no longer bind the substrate, or if it does, the rate of product formation may be reduced. Like competitive inhibitors, noncompetitive inhibitors can become unbound, so their effects are reversible.

Allosteric enzymes are controlled via changes in shape

The change in enzyme shape that is due to noncompetitive inhibitor binding is an example of allostery (*allo*, "different," + *stereos*, "shape"). **Allosteric regulation** occurs when a non-substrate molecule binds to a site other than the active site of an enzyme, inducing the enzyme to change its shape. The change in shape alters the affinity of the active site for the substrate, and so the rate of the reaction is changed.

Often, an enzyme will exist in the cell in more than one possible shape (**Figure 8.18**):

- The *active form* of the enzyme has the proper shape for substrate binding.
- The *inactive form* of the enzyme has a shape that cannot bind the substrate.

Other non-substrate molecules can influence which form the enzyme takes:

- Binding of an *inhibitor* to a site other than the active site can stabilize the inactive form of the enzyme, making it less likely to convert to the active form.
- The active form can be stabilized by the binding of an *activator* to another site on the enzyme.

Both molecules bind to the active site of the enzyme dihydrofolate reductase. But methotrexate does not react and sits in the active site, blocking entry of dihydrofolate.

Dihydrofolate

Methotrexate

Figure 8.17 A Competitive Inhibitor to Treat Cancer Methotrexate has a structure similar to that of the substrate dihydrofolate, an enzyme important to cancer cell reproduction.

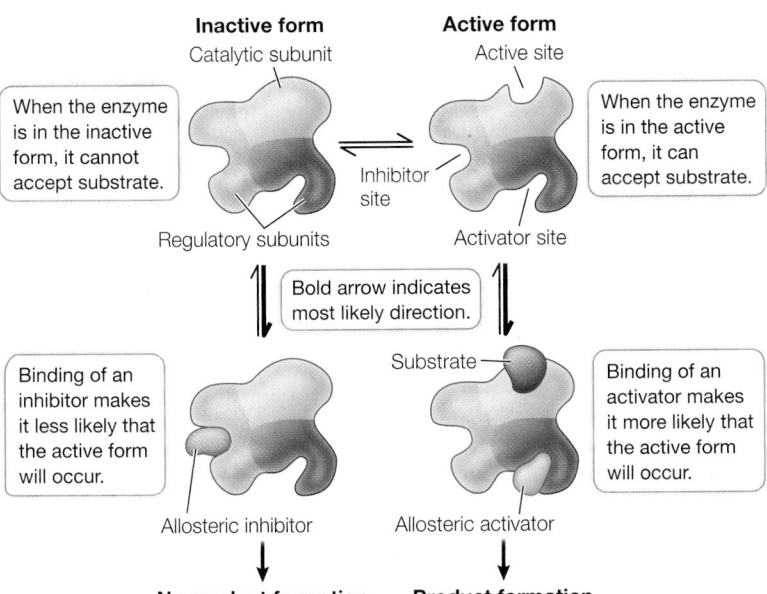

Inactive form
Catalytic subunit

Active form
Active site

When the enzyme is in the inactive form, it cannot accept substrate.

Inhibitor site

When the enzyme is in the active form, it can accept substrate.

Regulatory subunits

Activator site

Bold arrow indicates most likely direction.

Binding of an inhibitor makes it less likely that the active form will occur.

Substrate

Binding of an activator makes it more likely that the active form will occur.

Allosteric inhibitor

Allosteric activator

No product formation

Product formation

Figure 8.18 Allosteric Regulation of Enzymes Active and inactive forms of an enzyme can be interconverted, depending on the binding of non-substrate molecules at sites other than the active site. Binding an inhibitor stabilizes the inactive form, and binding an activator stabilizes the active form.

Q: Many enzymes with allosteric regulation have several polypeptide chains (quaternary structure). In some cases, the subunit with the binding site for the regulatory molecule is similar in several different enzymes. How would this be important in regulating biochemical pathways (see Figure 8.14)?

▶ **View in Achieve**
Animation 8.2 Allosteric Regulation of Enzymes

Like substrate binding, the binding of inhibitors and activators to their regulatory sites (also called allosteric sites) is highly specific. Most (but not all) enzymes that are allosterically regulated are proteins with quaternary structure; that is, they are made up of multiple polypeptide subunits. The polypeptide that has the active site is called the catalytic subunit. The allosteric sites are often located on different polypeptides, called the regulatory subunits (see Figure 8.18).

Some enzymes have multiple subunits containing active sites, and the binding of substrate to one of the active sites causes allosteric effects. When substrate binds to one subunit, there is a slight change in protein structure that influences the adjacent subunit. The slight change to the second subunit makes its active site more likely to bind to the substrate. So the reaction speeds up as the sites become sequentially activated.

As a result, an allosteric enzyme with multiple active sites and a non-allosteric enzyme with a single active site differ greatly in their reaction rates when the substrate concentration is low. Graphs of reaction rates plotted against substrate concentrations show this relationship (**Figure 8.19**):

- For a non-allosteric enzyme, the reaction rate first increases sharply with increasing substrate concentration, then tapers off to a constant maximum rate as the supply of enzyme becomes saturated.

- For a multisubunit allosteric enzyme, the reaction rate at first increases only gradually as substrate concentration increases. After the substrate binds to the first active site of the enzyme (the slowly increasing part of the curve), there is a change in the enzyme's quaternary structure such that the other sites become more likely to bind substrate, so the reaction speeds up (the rapidly increasing part of the curve). Once all sites are saturated with substrate, the reaction rate reaches a plateau (the upper, flat part of the curve). Within a certain range, the reaction rate is extremely sensitive to relatively small changes in substrate concentration. In addition, allosteric enzymes are very sensitive to low concentrations of inhibitors. Because of this sensitivity, allosteric enzymes are important in regulating entire metabolic pathways.

Allosteric effects regulate metabolic pathways

Metabolic pathways typically involve a starting material, various intermediate products, and an end product that is used for some purpose by the cell. In each pathway there are a number of reactions, each forming an intermediate product and each catalyzed by a different enzyme. The first step in a pathway is called the commitment step, meaning that once this enzyme-catalyzed reaction occurs, the "ball is rolling," and the other reactions happen in sequence, leading to the end product. But what if the cell has no requirement for that product—for example, if that product is available from the cell's environment in adequate amounts? It would be energetically wasteful for the cell to continue making something it does not need.

Connect the Concepts The number of molecules of a particular enzyme present in a cell at a given time is controlled in large part by the synthesis of that protein. See Key Concept 16.1 for a discussion of the regulation of protein synthesis.

One way to avoid this problem is to shut down the metabolic pathway by having the final product inhibit the enzyme that catalyzes the commitment step (**Figure 8.20**). Often this inhibition occurs allosterically. When the end product is present at a high concentration, some of it binds to an allosteric site on the commitment step enzyme, thereby causing it to become inactive. Thus the final product acts as a noncompetitive inhibitor (described earlier in this

(A) A non-allosteric enzyme

Reaction rate

Concentration of substrate

(B) An allosteric enzyme

Reaction rate

Concentration of substrate

Figure 8.19 Reactions of Non-Allosteric and Allosteric Enzymes Differ

(A) Feedback inhibition

(B) Gout

1 The first reaction is the commitment step.

2 Each of these reactions is catalyzed by a different enzyme, and each forms a different intermediate product.

Purine nucleotides: Adenine and guanine

Ribose 5-phosphate (starting material)

PRPP synthetase

5-phosphoribosyl-1-pyrophosphate (PRPP) (intermediate material)

3 Buildup of the end product allosterically inhibits the enzyme catalyzing the commitment step, thus shutting down its own production.

If the enzyme PRPP synthetase is genetically unable to bind purines for feedback inhibition, excess purines accumulate and lead to the formation of crystals in joints (gout).

© joloei/Shutterstock.com

Figure 8.20 Feedback Inhibition of Metabolic Pathways (A) The first reaction in a metabolic pathway is referred to as the commitment step. It is often catalyzed by an enzyme that can be allosterically inhibited by the end product of the pathway. The specific pathway shown here is the synthesis of purine nucleotides (ATP, GTP) from ribose 5-phosphate in humans. (B) Gout, an accumulation of crystals in joints caused by an excess of purines, can occur if there is a failure of feedback inhibition.

Q: The synthesis of cholesterol involves a biochemical pathway that begins with the enzyme HMG-CoA reductase. Statins are drugs that are widely used to inhibit cholesterol synthesis. How do you suppose statins work?

key concept) of the first enzyme in the pathway. This mechanism is known as feedback inhibition or end-product inhibition. We will describe many other examples of such inhibition in later chapters.

Many enzymes are regulated through reversible phosphorylation

Many enzymes involved in signal transduction are regulated via reversible phosphorylation (see Figure 7.14A). An enzyme can be activated by a protein kinase, which adds a phosphate from ATP to one or more specific amino acids. This results in a change in the shape of the enzyme, making it active. Such activation is reversible because another enzyme called a protein phosphatase can catalyze the hydrolysis and removal of phosphate groups, so that the enzyme becomes inactive again. In addition to the enzymes involved in signal transduction, many other enzymes and proteins in the cell (such as ion channels) are regulated via reversible phosphorylation. Reflecting the important role of protein phosphorylation in cell functions, the human genome contains more than 500 protein kinase genes: about 2% of all the protein-coding genes we have.

Enzymes are affected by their environment

Enzymes enable cells to perform chemical reactions and carry out complex processes rapidly without using the extremes of temperature and pH employed by chemists in the laboratory. However, because of their three-dimensional structures and the chemistry of the side chains in their active sites, enzymes (and their substrates) are highly sensitive to changes in temperature and pH. In Key Concept 3.2 we described the general effects of these environmental factors on proteins. Here we examine their effects on enzyme function (which, of course, depends on enzyme structure and chemistry).

pH AFFECTS ENZYME ACTIVITY The rates of most enzyme-catalyzed reactions depend on the pH of the solution in which they occur. While the water inside cells is generally at a neutral pH of 7, the presence of acids, bases, and buffers can alter this. Each

enzyme is most active at a particular pH; its activity decreases as the solution is made more acidic or more basic than the ideal (optimal) pH (**Figure 8.21**). As an example, consider the human digestive system (see Key Concept 49.3). The pH inside the human stomach is highly acidic, around pH 1.5. However, many enzymes that hydrolyze macromolecules in the intestines, such as proteases, have pH optima in the neutral range. So when food enters the small intestine, a buffer (bicarbonate) is secreted into the intestine to raise the pH to 6.5. This allows the hydrolytic enzymes to be active and digest the food.

An important factor in the effect of pH on enzyme function is ionization of the carboxyl, amino, and other groups on either the substrate or the enzyme. In neutral or basic solutions, carboxyl groups (—COOH) release H^+ to become negatively charged

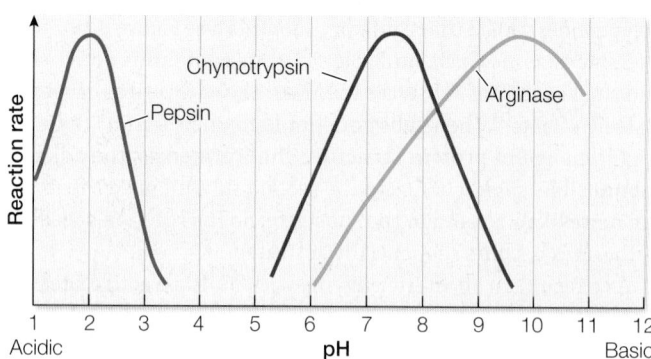

Figure 8.21 pH Affects Enzyme Activity An enzyme catalyzes its reaction at a maximum rate. The activity curve for each enzyme peaks at its optimal pH. For example, pepsin is active in the acidic environment of the stomach, whereas chymotrypsin is active in the small intestine.

Q: Inside the cell, the pH of the cytosol is typically 7.2, but inside the lysosome the pH is 4.8. A protease, which catalyzes the hydrolysis of proteins, is active within the lysosome but is inactive in the cytosol. How can this occur?

carboxylate groups ($-COO^-$). However, in neutral or acidic solutions, amino groups ($-NH_2$) accept H^+ to become positively charged $-NH_3^+$ groups (see the discussion of acids and bases in Key Concept 2.4). Thus in a neutral solution, an amino group is electrically attracted to a carboxyl group on another molecule or another part of the same molecule, because both groups are ionized and have opposite charges. If the pH changes, however, the ionization of these groups may change. For example, at a low pH (high H^+ concentration, such as the stomach contents where the enzyme pepsin is active), the excess H^+ may react with $-COO^-$ to form $-COOH$. If this happens, the group is no longer negatively charged and can no longer interact with positively charged groups in the protein, so the folding of the protein may be altered. If such a change occurs at the active site of an enzyme, the enzyme may no longer be able to bind to its substrate.

TEMPERATURE AFFECTS ENZYME ACTIVITY

In general, warming increases the rate of a chemical reaction because a greater proportion of the reactant molecules have enough kinetic energy to provide the activation energy for the reaction. Enzyme-catalyzed reactions are no different (**Figure 8.22**). However, temperatures that are too high inactivate enzymes, because at high temperatures enzyme molecules vibrate and twist so rapidly that some of their noncovalent interactions such as hydrogen bonds break. When an enzyme's tertiary structure is changed by heat it loses its function. Some enzymes denature at temperatures only slightly above that of the human body, but a few are stable even at the boiling point (or freezing point) of water. All enzymes, however, have an optimal temperature for activity.

In general, enzymes adapted to warm temperatures do not denature at those temperatures, because their tertiary structures are held together largely by covalent bonds and disulfide bridges, instead of the more heat-sensitive weak chemical interactions. Most enzymes in humans are more stable at high temperatures than are those of the bacteria that infect us, so that a moderate fever tends to denature bacterial enzymes, but not our own.

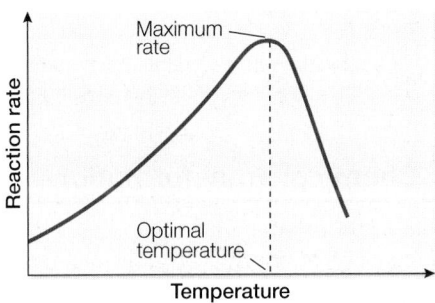

Figure 8.22 Temperature Affects Enzyme Activity   Each enzyme is most active at a particular optimal temperature. At higher temperatures the enzyme becomes denatured and inactive; this explains why the activity curve falls off abruptly at temperatures above the optimum.

KEY CONCEPT
8.5 Recap and Assess

The rates of most enzyme-catalyzed reactions are affected by interacting molecules (such as inhibitors and activators) and by environmental factors (such as temperature and pH). Reversible phosphorylation is another important mechanism for regulating enzyme activity.

1. What is feedback inhibition? How might the reactions shown in Figure 8.20A fit into a systems diagram such as the one shown in Figure 8.14?

2. Consider an enzyme that is subject to allosteric regulation. If a competitive inhibitor (not an allosteric inhibitor) is added to a solution containing such an enzyme, the ratio of enzyme molecules in the active form to those in the inactive form increases. Explain this observation.

3. In humans, hydrogen peroxide (H_2O_2) is a dangerous toxin produced as a by-product of several metabolic pathways. The accumulation of H_2O_2 is prevented by its conversion to harmless H_2O, a reaction catalyzed by the appropriately named enzyme catalase. Air pollutants can inhibit this enzyme and leave individuals susceptible to tissue damage by H_2O_2. How would you investigate whether catalase has an allosteric or a non-allosteric mechanism and whether the pollutants are acting as competitive or noncompetitive inhibitors?

▶Investigating LIFE

 How do anti-inflammatory drugs work as enzyme inhibitors?

Go into a drugstore or watch ads on TV, and it becomes obvious that there are many drugs that alleviate pain. Like aspirin, many of them target the prostaglandin pathway for inflammation. John Vane's research and later work showed that aspirin irreversibly inhibits the enzyme COX. But it turns out that there are two forms of COX, called COX-1 and COX-2, and there are several kinds of prostaglandins. COX-1 catalyzes the production of protective prostaglandins that are involved in blood clotting (which is why some people are advised to take aspirin to prevent blood clots after a heart attack) and the integrity of the lining of the stomach. COX-2 catalyzes production of prostaglandins involved with inflammation and associated pain. Aspirin inhibits both COX-1 and COX-2. So it is not surprising that people are advised to go easy on aspirin: it may block pain, but its use can lead to stomach upsets and an inability to clot blood after a wound. Knowledge of aspirin's limitations has led to a search for inhibitors of COX-2 only. Most of them are competitive inhibitors. How

would this affect how often you need to take the drug? Look up one of these drugs and read the description of how it works.

Future directions

As details at the atomic level of the binding of enzymes to substrates are worked out, biologists use the data to try to predict which substrates might bind to which enzymes. An important consideration in binding is ΔG; the less positive this parameter, the more likely binding will occur. Factors such as ionic bonds and van der Waals forces contribute to the ΔG of binding. These factors are also important in the binding of proteins to non-substrate molecules, including other proteins and RNA. Indeed, it is becoming apparent that in almost all cases a protein in the cell does not exist in isolation, but is bound to something(s) else. If the protein is an enzyme, its substrate binding must be its most preferred partner. Understanding all the possible molecular interactions will result in a deeper understanding of what really goes on at the chemical level inside the cell.

VISUAL SUMMARY 8

E. Stone. 1763. *Philos Trans R Soc Lond* 53: 195–200

You should be able to relate each summary to the adjacent figures. If you go to this visual summary in **Achieve**, you can follow links to figures, animations, activities, and simulations that will help you consolidate the material.

KEY CONCEPT

8.1 Chemical Transformations Involve Energy and Energy Transfers

- The **laws of thermodynamics** apply to living organisms. The first law states that **energy** cannot be created or destroyed. The second law states that energy transformations decrease the amount of energy available to do work (**free energy**, or **G**) and increase disorder.

- An **exergonic** reaction releases free energy and has a negative ΔG. An **endergonic** reaction consumes or requires free energy and has a positive ΔG.

Questions

1. The disaccharide sucrose is hydrolyzed into its component monosaccharides glucose and fructose:

    Sucrose + H_2O → glucose + fructose

    How does this conversion relate to the laws of thermodynamics?

2. Is the reaction in Question 1 exergonic or endergonic? Explain.

Figure 8.2

Figure 8.3

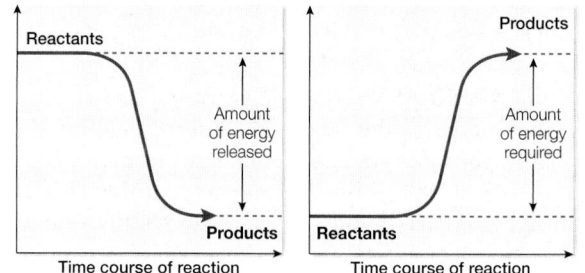

KEY CONCEPT

8.2 ATP Plays a Key Role in Biochemical Energetics

Go to Activity 8.1

- Adenosine triphosphate (ATP) serves as an energy currency in cells. Hydrolysis of ATP releases a relatively large amount of free energy.

- The ATP cycle couples exergonic and endergonic reactions, harvesting free energy from exergonic reactions, and providing free energy for endergonic reactions.

Questions

1. Are all exergonic reactions in the cell coupled to the formation of ATP from ADP? Explain.

2. Adenine, as part of adenosine monophosphate (AMP), is a nucleotide base in DNA. If DNA is hydrolyzed to nucleotides, can the AMP in DNA be used as a source of energy in coupled reactions?

Figure 8.6

KEY CONCEPT

8.3 Enzymes Speed Up Biochemical Transformations

Go to Activity 8.2

- The rate of a chemical reaction is independent of ΔG but is determined by the need for energy for the reactant(s) to reach a **transition state**.

- **Enzymes** are protein **catalysts** that affect the rates of biological reactions by supplying the **activation energy** (E_a) needed to initiate reactions.

Questions

1. Do the primary, secondary, or tertiary structures of an enzyme change during and after its catalyzed reaction?

2. In terms of energy, do enzymes catalyze exergonic but not endergonic reactions?

Figure 8.10

KEY CONCEPT

8.4 Enzymes Bring Substrates Together so Reactions Readily Occur

- At the active site, a substrate can be oriented correctly, chemically modified, or strained.

- Binding substrate causes many enzymes to change shape, exposing their active site(s) and allowing catalysis. The change in enzyme shape caused by substrate binding is known as **induced fit**.

- Substrate concentration affects the rate of an enzyme-catalyzed reaction.

Questions

1. Does a substrate need to fit exactly in the active site on an enzyme?

2. How do reaction rates for an enzyme-catalyzed reaction compare in the presence of the enzyme versus in the presence of an enzyme that has been placed in boiling water for 10 minutes prior to the reaction? See Figure 8.13.

Figure 8.11

Citrate synthase

Figure 8.13

KEY CONCEPT

8.5 Enzyme Activities Can Be Regulated

- Metabolism is organized into pathways in which the product of one enzyme-catalyzed reaction is a reactant for the next reaction.

- Enzyme activity is subject to regulation. Some inhibitors bind irreversibly to enzymes. Others bind reversibly.

- The end product of a metabolic pathway may inhibit an enzyme that catalyzes the commitment step of that pathway.

- Enzymes are sensitive to their environments. Both pH and temperature affect enzyme activity.

Questions

1. What is the difference between a competitive enzyme inhibitor and a noncompetitive inhibitor?

2. A cell can make the amino acid glutamine through an eight-step biochemical pathway, starting with glucose. The pathway is active when there is no glutamine in the environment, but shuts down when there is abundant glutamine in the environment. How might the shutdown occur?

Go to Animations 8.1 and 8.2 and Simulation 8.1

Figure 8.16

Figure 8.21

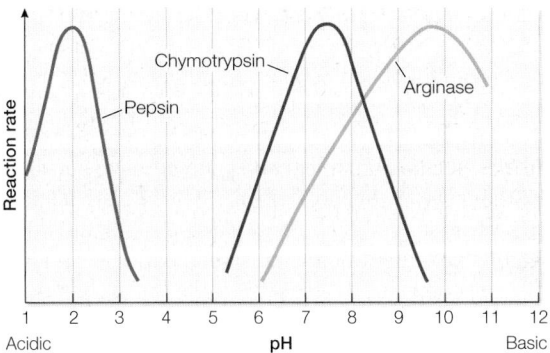

9 Pathways That Harvest Chemical Energy

KEY CONCEPTS

9.1 Cells Harvest Chemical Energy from Glucose Oxidation

9.2 In the Presence of Oxygen, Glucose Is Fully Oxidized

9.3 Oxidative Phosphorylation Forms ATP

9.4 In the Absence of Oxygen, Some Energy Is Harvested from Glucose

9.5 Metabolic Pathways Are Interrelated and Regulated

© 3d_mar/Shutterstock.com

Mitochondria are the powerhouses of the cell.

▶ InvestigatingLIFE

A Weighty Matter

With 40% of adults in the United States now described as obese, physicians have declared an "obesity epidemic." Dramatic increases in diseases associated with obesity—among them diabetes, heart disease, and cancer—have understandably alarmed the medical establishment.

While nutritional science has shown that not all foods affect all people in the same ways, in many cases the significant excess body weight of obese people can be prevented or reduced if they eat less. It is a matter of energy: if we eat more energy-yielding molecules than we need to build our bodies and to fuel activities such as brain functions and physical activity, we will store the unneeded energy as fat. There is an evolutionary advantage in storing fat: the energy in the C—C and C—H bonds in fat can be used later when food is scarce. But excess fat has adverse consequences.

Not all fat (adipose) tissues are the same. White adipose tissue (sometimes referred to simply as "white fat") is used primarily to store energy. Brown adipose tissue has high concentrations of mitochondria, which have iron-containing pigments. When energy-rich molecules in brown fat are catabolized, the stored energy is released not as chemical energy but as heat. The cells in brown fat make a protein called UCP1 (uncoupling

protein 1) that inserts into the inner membranes of mitochondria, making them permeable to protons (H^+). The general impermeability of these membranes to H^+ is key to coupling the catabolism of molecules such as fats to the release of their stored chemical-bond energy to make ATP. If the membranes become permeable to H^+, this coupling is lost and the stored energy is released as heat.

Human infants are born with a great deal of brown fat in their back and shoulders. Because infants have a high surface area-to-volume ratio, they tend to lose a lot of heat. One way they keep warm is to produce heat in their brown fat tissues. As a child grows up, the brown fat content of the body is reduced. Adults have mostly white fat, which has less UCP1 and generates less heat when the fat is catabolized. Biologists recently found brown fat in adults, particularly in the upper chest and neck, but also scattered elsewhere in the body, mixed in with much more prevalent white fat. The role of this tissue is under intense study.

 How are mitochondria related to obesity?
(Find the answer on page 192.)

KEY CONCEPT 9.1   Cells Harvest Chemical Energy from Glucose Oxidation

Learning Objectives

9.1.1   Describe the principles that govern metabolic pathways in cells.

9.1.2   Identify the change in energy that occurs during an oxidation–reduction reaction.

9.1.3   Describe the roles of electron acceptors and donors in biological redox reactions.

9.1.4   Analyze biological redox reactions to identify the oxidizing and reducing agents involved.

Energy is stored in the chemical bonds of molecules, and it can be released and transformed by the metabolic pathways of living cells. A **metabolic pathway** consists of a coordinated series of biochemical reactions that convert molecules into other molecules. As you read this chapter, keep in mind five principles that govern metabolic pathways:

1. A complex chemical transformation occurs in a series of separate reactions that form a metabolic pathway.

2. Each reaction is catalyzed by a specific enzyme.

3. Many metabolic pathways are similar in all organisms, from bacteria to humans.

4. In eukaryotes, many metabolic pathways are compartmentalized, with certain reactions occurring inside specific organelles, or even specific regions of an organelle.

5. Some key enzymes in each metabolic pathway can be inhibited or activated to alter the rate of the pathway.

Connect the Concepts The principles of energy transformations in living and nonliving systems are discussed in Key Concept 8.1.

Cells obtain energy from glucose

In cells, chemical energy released from bonds of molecules is used to make ATP (see Key Concept 8.2), which in turn drives endergonic reactions. Photosynthetic cells and organisms use energy from sunlight to synthesize their own energy-storing molecules, as we will describe in Chapter 10. While other carbohydrates, as well as lipids and proteins, can be used as energy sources, the most common chemical fuel in cells is the monosaccharide glucose. As you will see throughout this chapter, to release their energy to make ATP, the other molecules are converted into glucose or intermediate compounds that can enter into the various pathways of glucose metabolism.

As you saw in Key Concept 2.3, the familiar process of combustion (burning) is similar to the chemical processes that release energy in cells. If glucose is burned in a flame or is in a typical cell, it reacts with oxygen gas (O_2), forming carbon dioxide and water and releasing energy in the form of heat. The balanced equation for the complete reaction is

$$C_6H_{12}O_6 + 6\,O_2 \rightarrow 6\,CO_2 + 6\,H_2O + \text{free energy}$$
$$(\Delta G = -686 \text{ kcal/mol})$$

This is an oxidation–reduction reaction (more on this shortly), in which glucose loses electrons (becomes oxidized) and oxygen gains them (becomes reduced). The large free energy change (ΔG) is negative, indicating that the overall conversion is highly exergonic and can drive the endergonic formation of a lot of ATP from ADP and phosphate:

$$ADP + P_i + \text{free energy} \rightarrow ATP \ (\Delta G = +7.3 \text{ kcal/mol})$$

Three catabolic processes harvest the energy in the chemical bonds of glucose: glycolysis, cellular respiration, and fermentation (**Figure 9.1**). All three processes involve pathways made up of many distinct chemical reactions.

1. **Glycolysis** begins glucose catabolism. Through a series of chemical rearrangements, glucose is converted to two molecules of the three-carbon product **pyruvate**, and a small amount of energy is captured in usable forms. Glycolysis is an **anaerobic** process because it does not require O_2.

2. **Cellular respiration** uses O_2 from the environment and thus is **aerobic**. Each pyruvate molecule is completely converted into three molecules of CO_2 through a set of catabolic pathways including pyruvate oxidation, the citric acid cycle,

Figure 9.1 Energy for Life   Many prokaryotes and all eukaryotes obtain their energy from the molecules ultimately produced by photosynthesis, which converts solar energy into chemical-bond energy. Often, organisms convert molecules into glucose, which they metabolize to trap energy in ATP.

Q: Do all eukaryotes perform all the processes in the figure?

and an electron transport chain. In the process, a great deal of the energy stored in the covalent bonds of pyruvate is captured to form ATP.

3. **Fermentation** does not involve O_2 (it is anaerobic). With the exception of many microorganisms, fermentation converts pyruvate into lactic acid or ethyl alcohol (ethanol), both of which are still relatively energy-rich molecules. Because the breakdown of glucose is incomplete, much less energy is released when glycolysis is coupled to fermentation than when it is coupled to cellular respiration.

Redox reactions transfer electrons and energy

The release of energy from a molecule and the transfer of that energy to another molecule often involve the transfer of electrons. A reaction in which one substance transfers one or more electrons to another substance is called an **oxidation–reduction**, or **redox**, **reaction**.

- **Reduction** is the gain of one or more electrons by an atom, ion, or molecule.
- **Oxidation** is the loss of one or more electrons.

Oxidation and reduction *always occur together*: as one chemical is oxidized, the electrons it loses are transferred to another chemical, reducing it. In a redox reaction, we call the reactant that becomes reduced an oxidizing agent and the one that becomes oxidized a reducing agent (**Figure 9.2A**). A familiar

example is the formation of salt (NaCl) (see Figure 2.10), whereby Na transfers an electron to Cl, forming Na^+ and Cl^-. In terms of oxidation–reduction,

- Na gives up an electron, and so becomes oxidized. It is a reducing agent.
- Cl gains an electron, and so becomes reduced. It is an oxidizing agent.

You will see many examples of complete electron transfer in this and subsequent chapters, for example, the electron transport chain (see Key Concept 9.3).

Not all redox reactions involve a complete transfer of electrons (**Figure 9.2B**). Thanks to electronegativity and resulting polarity, many coupled reactions involve a degree of sharing of electrons between two atoms. To greatly simplify, consider the oxidation of glucose described in the equation in the previous section. In glucose, there are bonds between carbon atoms. The electrons in the C—C bond are shared equally. But in CO_2, the bonds are C=O, where the greater electronegativity of O results in a polar bond: electrons are shared unequally, spending more time near the O nucleus. Because there is movement of the shared electrons away from C, we can say that is has become oxidized. If the conversion of C—C to C=O is an oxidation, what is reduced? In an overall fashion, the oxidizing agent is oxygen. The electrons in the O=O bond are shared equally. But in H_2O, the O—H bond is polar, with the electrons spending more time near O (see Figure 2.9). Therefore O is reduced. In summary:

- Glucose is the reducing agent (electron donor) and becomes oxidized.
- O_2 is the oxidizing agent (electron acceptor) and becomes reduced.

Although oxidation and reduction are always defined in terms of electrons, it is often simpler to think in terms of the gain or loss of hydrogen atoms. The transfer of electrons is often associated with the transfer of hydrogen ions (a H atom contains $H^+ + e^-$). So when a molecule loses hydrogen atoms, it becomes oxidized.

The more reduced a molecule is, the more energy it has stored in its covalent bonds (**Figure 9.3**). In a redox reaction, some energy is transferred from the reducing agent to the reduced product.

(A) Complete transfer of electrons in a redox reaction

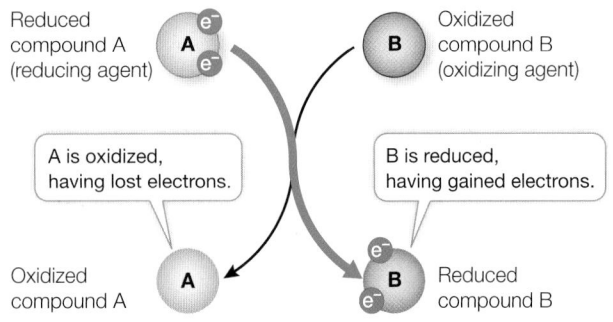

(B) Partial transfer of electrons in a redox reaction

Figure 9.2 Oxidation and Reduction (A) Electron transfer may be complete, such that one or more electrons move from one molecule to another (blue line), resulting in the donor molecule becoming less negatively charged, and the recipient molecule more negatively charged. (B) Electron transfer can be partial, so that electrons are not lost or gained, but an atom's share of electrons is changed (e.g., δ^+ is more oxidized than δ^-).

Q: In (B), which atom becomes oxidized and which becomes reduced?

H | H—C—H | H	H | H—C—OH | H	H | H—C=O	HO | H—C=O	O || C=O
Methane (CH_4)	Methanol (CH_3OH)	Formaldehyde (CH_2O)	Formic acid (HCOOH)	Carbon dioxide (CO_2)

Most reduced state   Most oxidized state
Highest free energy   Lowest free energy

Figure 9.3 Oxidation, Reduction, and Energy The more oxidized a carbon atom in a molecule is, the less stored free energy it has.

The rest remains in the reducing agent or is lost to entropy. As you will see, some of the key reactions of glycolysis and cellular respiration are highly exergonic redox reactions.

The coenzyme NAD⁺ is a key electron carrier in redox reactions

The coenzyme nicotinamide adenine dinucleotide (NAD⁺) acts as an electron carrier in redox reactions (**Figure 9.4A**). NAD⁺ exists in two chemically distinct forms, one oxidized (NAD⁺) and the other reduced (NADH) (**Figure 9.4B**). Both forms participate in redox reactions. The reduction reaction

$$NAD^+ + H^+ + 2\,e^- \rightarrow NADH$$

is actually the transfer of a proton (the hydrogen ion, H⁺) and two electrons, which are released by the accompanying oxidization reaction.

The electrons do not remain with the coenzyme. Oxygen is highly electronegative and readily accepts electrons from NADH. The oxidation of NADH by O_2 (which occurs in several steps)

$$NADH + H^+ + \tfrac{1}{2}\,O_2 \rightarrow NAD^+ + H_2O$$

is exergonic, with a standard free energy change at pH 7 (ΔG^0) of −52.4 kcal/mol (−219 kJ/mol). Note that the oxidizing agent appears here as "½ O_2" instead of "O." This notation emphasizes that it is molecular oxygen, O_2, that acts as the oxidizing agent.

Just as ATP can be thought of as a package of 7.3 kcal/mol (30.5 kJ/mol) of free energy, NADH can be thought of as a larger package of free energy (52.4 kcal/mol; see above). NAD⁺ is a common electron carrier in cells, but not the only one. Another carrier, flavin adenine dinucleotide (FAD), also transfers electrons during glucose metabolism.

Connect the Concepts Key Concept 8.4 describes the role of coenzymes, small molecules that assist in enzyme-catalyzed reactions. ADP acts as a coenzyme when it picks up energy released in an exergonic reaction and packages it to form ATP.

An overview: Harvesting energy from glucose

Both eukaryotic and prokaryotic cells can harvest energy from glucose using different combinations of the following metabolic pathways:

- Under aerobic conditions, when O_2 is available as the final electron acceptor, four pathways operate (**Figure 9.5A**).

(A)

(B)

Figure 9.4 **NAD⁺/NADH Is an Electron Carrier in Redox Reactions** **(A)** NAD⁺ is an important electron acceptor in redox reactions, and thus its reduced form, NADH, is an important energy intermediary in cells. The blue lines show the flow of electrons. **(B)** Most of the NAD⁺ molecule (left) remains unchanged by the redox reaction.

Glycolysis is followed by the three pathways of cellular respiration: pyruvate oxidation, the citric acid cycle (also called the Krebs cycle or the tricarboxylic acid cycle), and electron transport/ATP synthesis (also called oxidative phosphorylation).

- In eukaryotes and many prokaryotes, pyruvate oxidation, the citric acid cycle, and oxidative phosphorylation do not function under anaerobic conditions. The pyruvate produced by glycolysis is further metabolized by fermentation

(A) Glycolysis and cellular respiration

(B) Glycolysis and fermentation

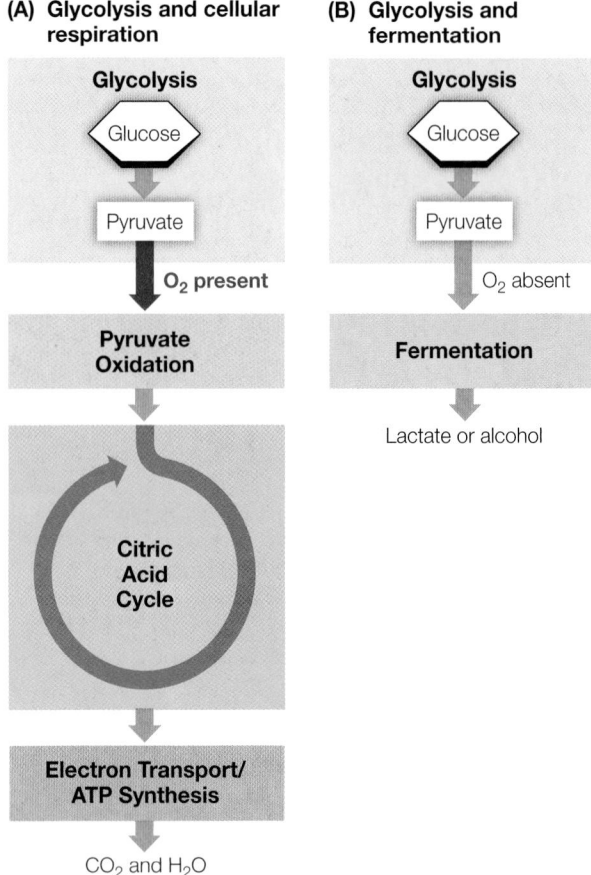

Figure 9.5 Energy-Yielding Metabolic Pathways Energy-yielding reactions can be grouped into five metabolic pathways: glycolysis, pyruvate oxidation, the citric acid cycle, the electron transport chain/ATP synthesis, and fermentation. **(A)** The three lower pathways occur only in the presence of O_2 and are collectively referred to as cellular respiration. **(B)** When O_2 is unavailable, glycolysis is followed by fermentation.

View in Achieve
Activity 9.1 Glycolysis and Fermentation

(Figure 9.5B). Some prokaryotes, however, are able to harvest energy in pathways involving oxidative phosphorylation even in the absence of oxygen (anaerobic respiration; see Key Concept 9.3).

The five pathways shown in Figure 9.5 occur in different locations in the cell (Table 9.1).

KEY CONCEPT
9.1 Recap and Assess

The free energy released from the oxidation of glucose is trapped in the form of ATP. In many prokaryotes and all eukaryotes, five major pathways combine in different ways to produce ATP, which supplies the energy for myriad other reactions in living cells.

1. What principles govern metabolic pathways in cells?
2. What are the roles of NAD^+ and O_2 with respect to electrons in a redox reaction?
3. The following reaction occurs in the citric acid cycle:

Succinate → Fumarate

Answer each of the following questions, and explain your answers:
a. Is this reaction an oxidation or a reduction?
b. Is the reaction exergonic or endergonic?
c. What kind of coenzyme does this reaction require?

Now that you have an overview of the metabolic pathways that harvest energy from glucose, let's take a closer look at the three pathways involved in aerobic glucose catabolism: glycolysis, pyruvate oxidation, and the citric acid cycle.

TABLE **9.1** | Cellular Locations for Major Energy Pathways in Eukaryotes and Prokaryotes

	Eukaryotes	Prokaryotes
	IN CYTOPLASM	**IN CYTOPLASM**
	Glycolysis	Glycolysis
	Fermentation	Fermentation
		Citric acid cycle
	INSIDE MITOCHONDRION	**ON CELL MEMBRANE**
	Matrix	Pyruvate oxidation
	Citric acid cycle	Respiratory chain
	Pyruvate oxidation	
	Inner membrane	
	Respiratory chain	

View in Achieve
Activity 9.2 Energy Pathways in Cells

One molecule of glucose

Step 1

Two of the first three steps are endergonic and require energy from ATP hydrolysis.

Step 2

Step 3

Fructose 1,6-bisphosphate

The six-carbon sugar is cleaved into two three-carbon sugars.

Step 4

Step 5

Two molecules of glyceraldehyde 3-phosphate

Step 6

Step 7

Step 8

Later steps are exergonic and release energy, forming ATP and NADH.

Step 9

Step 10

Two molecules of pyruvate

KEY CONCEPT 9.2   In the Presence of Oxygen, Glucose Is Fully Oxidized

Learning Objectives

9.2.1   Describe the energy inputs and outputs of glycolysis.

9.2.2   Explain how pyruvate oxidation connects the transformations of glycolysis and the citric acid cycle.

9.2.3   Compare and contrast glycolysis and the citric acid cycle.

In the presence of O_2 (aerobic), the pathways of glucose catabolism oxidize glucose completely to CO_2 and H_2O. Initially, the glycolysis reactions convert the six-carbon glucose molecule to two three-carbon pyruvate molecules (**Figure 9.6**). Pyruvate is then converted to CO_2 in a second series of reactions beginning with pyruvate oxidation and followed by the citric acid cycle. In addition to generating CO_2, the oxidation events are coupled with the reduction of electron carriers, mostly NAD^+. We will begin our consideration of the catabolism of glucose with a closer look at glycolysis.

In the glycolysis pathway, glucose is partially oxidized

Glycolysis takes place in the cytoplasm and involves ten enzyme-catalyzed reactions. During glycolysis, some of the covalent bonds between carbon and hydrogen atoms in the glucose molecule are oxidized, releasing some of the stored energy. The products are two molecules of pyruvate (pyruvic acid), two molecules of ATP, and two molecules of NADH. Glycolysis can be divided into two stages: the initial energy-investing reactions that consume ATP, and the energy-harvesting reactions that produce ATP and NADH (see Figure 9.6).

To help you understand the process without getting into extensive detail, we focus on two consecutive reactions in this pathway (**Figure 9.7**). Steps 6 and 7 are examples of two types of reactions that occur repeatedly in glycolysis and in many other metabolic pathways: oxidation–reduction, wherein energy released by glucose oxidation is trapped via the reduction of NAD^+ to NADH; and substrate-level phosphorylation, wherein energy released is sufficient to transfer a phosphate directly from the substrate to ADP, forming ATP.

The end product of glycolysis, pyruvate, is somewhat more oxidized than glucose. In the presence of O_2, further oxidation can occur. In prokaryotes these subsequent reactions take place in the cytoplasm, but in eukaryotes they take place in the mitochondrial matrix.

To summarize:

- The initial steps of glycolysis use the energy of hydrolysis of two ATP molecules per glucose molecule.

Figure 9.6 Glycolysis Converts Glucose into Pyruvate   Glucose is converted to pyruvate in ten enzyme-catalyzed steps. Along the way, two ATP are used (Steps 1 and 3), two NAD^+ are reduced to two NADH (Step 6), and four ATP are produced (Steps 7 and 10).

Step 6 / Step 7

	Step 6			**Step 7**	

Glyceraldehyde 3-phosphate dehydrogenase

CH_2O P
H—C—OH
C=O
H

P_i / NAD^+ → NADH

Glyceraldehyde 3-phosphate

Phosphoglycerate kinase

CH_2O P
H—C—OH
C=O
O P

ADP

1,3-Bisphosphoglycerate

ATP

CH_2O P
H—C—OH
C=O
O^-

3-Phosphoglycerate

Oxidation–reduction: This reaction is exergonic, and the energy released is trapped in the reduction of NAD^+ to NADH.

Substrate-level phosphorylation: This reaction is exergonic, but less energy is released than in Step 6, sufficient to be trapped in the conversion of ADP to ATP.

Figure 9.7 Glycolysis Close-Up Steps 6 and 7 in the glycolysis pathway (see Figure 9.6) illustrate the principles of molecular conversion and energy transfer.

Q: Which steps in glycolysis involve energy transfer with a coenzyme or carrier?

- The remaining steps produce four ATP molecules per glucose molecule, so the net production of ATP is two molecules.

- Glycolysis produces two molecules of NADH.

If O_2 is present, glycolysis is followed by the three stages of cellular respiration: pyruvate oxidation, the citric acid cycle, and the electron transport chain/ATP synthesis.

Pyruvate oxidation links glycolysis and the citric acid cycle

In eukaryotes, pyruvate is transported into the mitochondrial matrix (see Figure 5.13), where the next step in the aerobic catabolism of glucose occurs. This step involves the oxidation of pyruvate to a two-carbon acetate molecule and CO_2 (Figure 9.8A). The acetate is then bound to coenzyme A to form **acetyl coenzyme A**, or **acetyl CoA**. Acetyl CoA is used in various biochemical reactions as a carrier of the acetyl group (H_3C—C=O). Pyruvate is the link between glycolysis and further oxidative reactions (see Figure 9.5).

The formation of acetyl CoA is a multi-step reaction catalyzed by the pyruvate dehydrogenase complex (**Figure 9.8B**). The overall reaction is exergonic, in which one molecule of NAD^+ is reduced to NADH. However, the main role of acetyl CoA is to donate its acetyl group to the four-carbon compound oxaloacetate, forming the six-carbon molecule citrate. This initiates the citric acid cycle, one of life's most important energy-harvesting pathways.

The citric acid cycle completes the oxidation of glucose to CO_2

Acetyl CoA is the starting point for the citric acid cycle. This pathway of eight reactions completely oxidizes the two-carbon acetyl group to two molecules of CO_2. The free energy released from these reactions is captured by GDP (guanosine diphosphate) and the electron carriers NAD^+ and FAD (**Figure 9.9**). (Remember from Key Concept 7.2 that GDP is a nucleoside diphosphate like ADP.) This is a cycle because the starting material, oxaloacetate, is regenerated in the last step and is ready to accept another acetate group from acetyl CoA. The citric acid cycle operates twice for each glucose molecule that enters glycolysis (once for each pyruvate that enters the mitochondrion).

Let's focus on the final reaction of the cycle (see Step 8 in Figure 9.9), as an example of the kind of reaction that occurs (**Figure 9.10**). This oxidation reaction (see the carbon atom highlighted in blue) is exergonic, and the released energy is trapped by NAD^+, forming NADH. With four such reactions (the $FADH_2$ produced in Step 6 is a reduced coenzyme similar to NADH), the citric acid cycle harvests a great deal of chemical energy from the oxidation of acetyl CoA.

To summarize:

- The inputs to the citric acid cycle are acetate (in the form of acetyl CoA), water, GDP, and the oxidized electron carriers NAD^+ and FAD.

- The outputs are carbon dioxide, reduced electron carriers (NADH and $FADH_2$), and a small amount of GTP. The energy in the terminal phosphate of GTP is transferred to ATP:

$$GTP + ADP \rightarrow ATP + GDP$$

(A)

CH_3
C=O
C=O
O^-

Pyruvate

Coenzyme A

NAD^+ → NADH CO_2

CH_3
C=O
CoA

Acetyl CoA

(B)

Figure 9.8 Pyruvate Oxidation The pyruvate dehydrogenase complex is actually three enzymes that carry out three intermediate steps in the process. There are over 100 polypeptide chain subunits. (B after Mcn2k10/CC BY-SA 3.0.)

Q: Which atom or molecule becomes oxidized in this reaction and which becomes reduced?

Figure 9.9 The Citric Acid Cycle   The citric acid cycle has eight steps; in the last step, the starting material acceptor, oxaloacetate, is regenerated. Energy is released and captured by reducing NAD^+ or FAD, or by producing GTP. "6C," "5C," and so on indicate the number of carbon atoms in each intermediate in the cycle.

View in **Achieve**
Activity 9.3 **The Citric Acid Cycle**

Thus the citric acid cycle releases two carbons as CO_2 and produces four reduced electron carrier molecules.

Overall, for each molecule of glucose that is oxidized, two molecules of pyruvate are produced during glycolysis, and after oxidation these feed two turns of the citric acid cycle. So the oxidation of one glucose molecule yields:

- Six CO_2
- Ten NADH (two in glycolysis, two in pyruvate oxidation, and six in the citric acid cycle)
- Two $FADH_2$
- Four ATP

Pyruvate oxidation and the citric acid cycle are regulated by the concentrations of starting materials

You have now seen that pyruvate, a three-carbon molecule, is completely oxidized to CO_2 by pyruvate dehydrogenase and the citric acid cycle. For the cycle to continue, the starting molecules—acetyl CoA and oxidized electron carriers—must all be replenished. The electron carriers are reduced during the citric acid cycle and in Step 6 of glycolysis (see Figure 9.6), and they must be reoxidized:

$$NADH \rightarrow NAD^+ + H^+ + 2\ e^-$$
$$FADH_2 \rightarrow FAD + 2\ H^+ + 2\ e^-$$

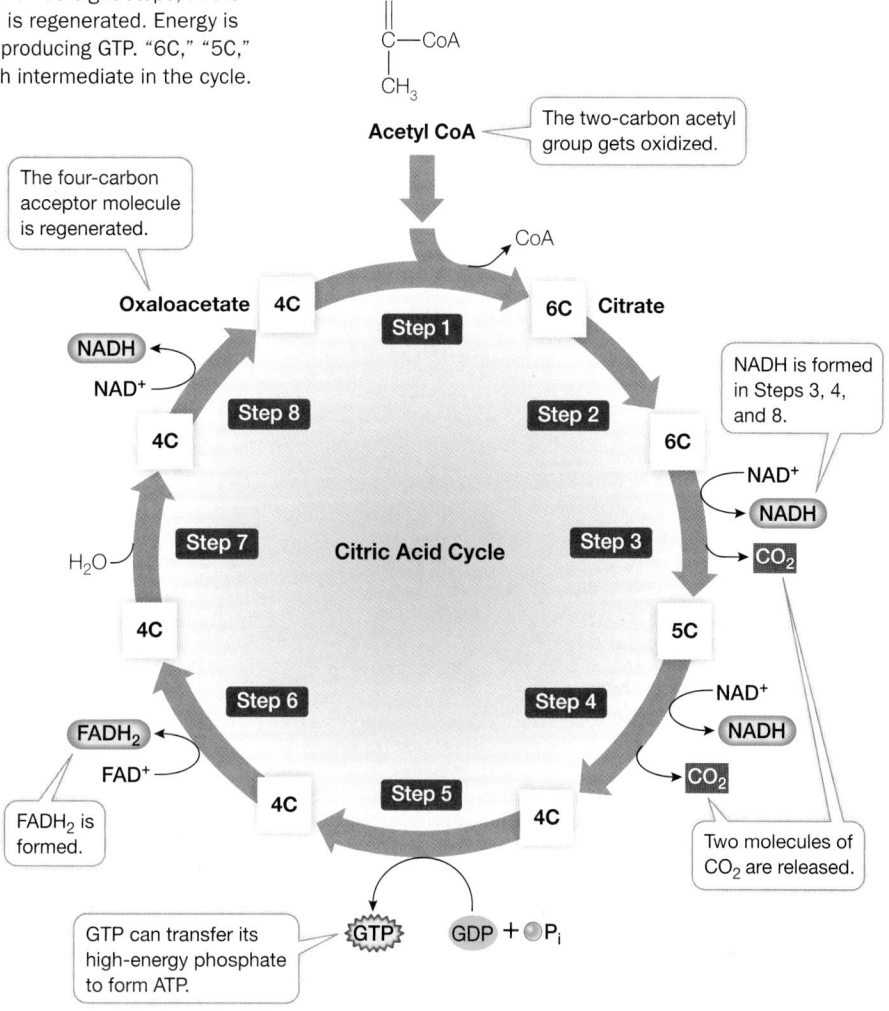

These oxidation reactions are coupled to reactions in which other molecules get reduced. When it is present, O_2 is the molecule that eventually accepts these electrons, and it is reduced to form H_2O (**Figure 9.11**).

Figure 9.10 Citric Acid Cycle Close-Up   Step 8 in the citric acid cycle (see Figure 9.9) illustrates the principles of molecular conversion and oxidation–reduction.

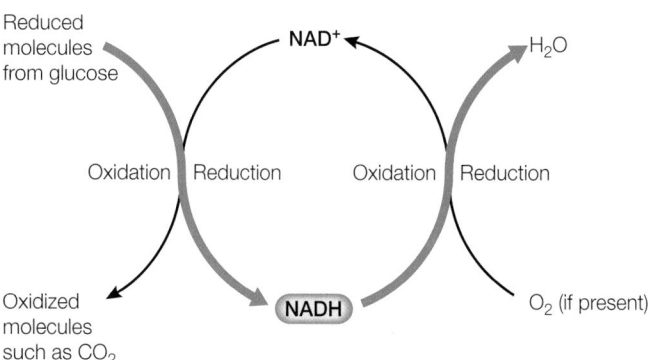

Figure 9.11 The Role of Oxygen: Overview   Oxygen (O_2) becomes reduced as NADH becomes oxidized, so that another molecule of glucose can be catabolized.

Q: Can you predict what would happen in the absence of O_2?

9.2 Recap and Assess

The oxidation of glucose in the presence of O_2 involves glycolysis, pyruvate oxidation, and the citric acid cycle. In glycolysis, glucose is converted to pyruvate with some chemical-bond energy capture. Pyruvate is oxidized first to acetyl CoA by pyruvate dehydrogenase, then completely to CO_2 by the citric acid cycle, releasing energy that is captured in the form of reduced electron carriers.

1. What is the net energy yield of glycolysis in terms of energy in ATP and reduced coenzymes invested and energy harvested?

2. What role does pyruvate oxidation play in relation to the citric acid cycle?

3. How is the citric acid cycle a "cycle" but glycolysis is not?

Pyruvate oxidation and the citric acid cycle cannot continue operating unless O_2 is available to receive electrons during the reoxidation of reduced electron carriers. However, these electrons are not passed directly to O_2, as you will learn next.

9.3 Oxidative Phosphorylation Forms ATP

Learning Objectives

9.3.1 Describe how the proton-motive force is established by the electron carriers and enzymes of the respiratory chain.

9.3.2 Analyze experimental results that relate to electron transport and chemiosmosis.

9.3.3 Predict results from experiments designed to explore aspects of electron transport and chemiosmosis.

In the presence of O_2, **oxidative phosphorylation** is a process of ATP synthesis resulting from the reoxidation of electron carriers in the presence of O_2. In this key concept we describe oxidative phosphorylation as it occurs in mitochondria in eukaryotes, but the same process occurs in prokaryotes (see Table 9.1).

There are two steps in oxidative phosphorylation

Two components can be distinguished in the process of oxidative phosphorylation:

1. *Electron transport.* The electrons from NADH and $FADH_2$ pass through the **respiratory chain**, a series of membrane-associated electron carriers. The flow of electrons along this pathway results in the active transport of protons out of the mitochondrial matrix and across the inner mitochondrial membrane, creating a proton concentration gradient.

2. *Chemiosmosis.* The protons diffuse back into the mitochondrial matrix through a channel protein, **ATP synthase**, which couples this diffusion to the synthesis of ATP. As we mentioned in the chapter opening, the inner mitochondrial membrane is normally impermeable to protons, so the only way for them to follow their concentration gradient is through the channel.

Before we proceed with the details of these pathways, let's consider an important question: Why should the respiratory chain be such a complex process? Why don't cells use the following single step?

$$2\,NADH + 2\,H^+ + O_2 \rightarrow 2\,NAD^+ + 2\,H_2O$$

The answer is that this reaction would simply release too much energy to be efficiently trapped to make ATP. Oxidizing NADH to NAD^+ is extremely exergonic—doing it in one step would be like setting off a stick of dynamite in the cell. There is no biochemical way to harvest that burst of energy efficiently and put it to physiological use (that is, no single metabolic reaction is so endergonic as to consume a significant fraction of that energy in a single step). To control the release of energy during the oxidation of glucose, cells have evolved a lengthy respiratory chain: a series of reactions, each of which releases a small amount of energy, one step at a time.

The respiratory chain transfers electrons and protons, and releases energy

The respiratory chain (an electron transport chain) is located in the inner mitochondrial membrane. Because of the extensive folding of the membrane, there is more room for the proteins involved in the chain than there would be in a membrane with less surface area. There are several interacting components, including large integral proteins, a small peripheral protein, and a small lipid molecule. **Figure 9.12** shows a plot that describes the free energy released as electrons are passed between the carriers.

- Four large protein complexes (I, II, III, and IV) contain electron carriers and associated enzymes. In eukaryotes they are integral proteins of the inner mitochondrial membrane, and three are transmembrane proteins.

- Cytochrome *c* is a small peripheral protein that lies in the intermembrane space. It is loosely attached to the outer surface of the inner mitochondrial membrane.

- Ubiquinone (often referred to as coenzyme Q10; abbreviated Q) is a small, nonpolar, lipid molecule that moves freely within the hydrophobic interior of the phospholipid bilayer of the inner mitochondrial membrane.

As illustrated in Figure 9.12, NADH passes electrons to protein complex I (called NADH-Q reductase), which in turn passes the electrons to Q. This electron transfer is accompanied by a large drop in free energy. Complex II (succinate dehydrogenase) passes electrons to Q from $FADH_2$, which was generated in Step 6 of the citric acid cycle (see Figure 9.9). These electrons enter the chain later than those from NADH and will ultimately produce less ATP.

Complex III (cytochrome *c* reductase) receives electrons from Q and passes them to cytochrome *c*. Complex IV (cytochrome *c* oxidase) receives electrons from cytochrome *c* and passes them to oxygen. Finally the reduction of oxygen to H_2O occurs:

$$O_2 + 4\,H^+ + 4\,e^- \rightarrow 2\,H_2O$$

Notice that four protons (H^+) are also consumed in this reaction. This contributes to the proton concentration gradient across the

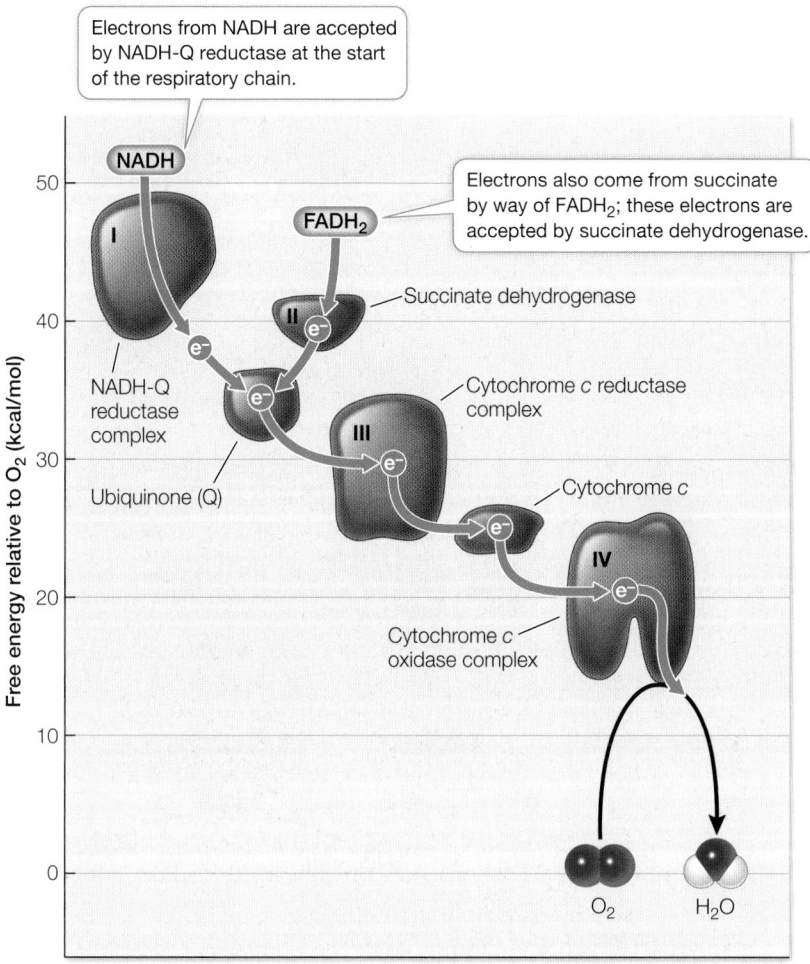

Electrons from NADH are accepted by NADH-Q reductase at the start of the respiratory chain.

Electrons also come from succinate by way of FADH$_2$; these electrons are accepted by succinate dehydrogenase.

Figure 9.12 The Oxidation of NADH and FADH$_2$ in the Respiratory Chain
Electrons from NADH and FADH$_2$ are passed along the respiratory chain, a series of protein complexes in the inner mitochondrial membrane containing electron carriers and enzymes. The carriers gain free energy when they become reduced and release free energy when they are oxidized. This illustration shows the standard free energy changes along the respiratory chain.

 View in Achieve
Activity 9.4 The Respiratory Chain

inner mitochondrial membrane by reducing the proton concentration in the mitochondrial matrix.

ATP is made through chemiosmosis

During electron transport, protons are also actively transported across the membrane: electron transport within each of the three transmembrane complexes (I, III, and IV) results in the transfer of protons from the matrix to the intermembrane space (**Figure 9.13**). Since the lipid bilayer does not allow charged H$^+$ to diffuse across it, transfer of H$^+$ across it through the electron transport chain sets up a gradient, with the concentration of H$^+$ in the intermembrane space higher than in the matrix. In addition, because H$^+$ carries a charge, there is more positive charge in the intermembrane space. About 20 H$^+$ are transported into the intermembrane space as four electrons are carried through the respiratory chain to O$_2$. These two gradients—of concentration

and charge—set up a **proton-motive force** which is a key factor in energy metabolism in cells: *The gradient of H$^+$ across the inner membrane is a source of potential energy.*

This energy is tapped for use by the cell by the membrane channel protein ATP synthase, which allows the H$^+$ to diffuse back into the matrix down its concentration gradient. In the process, potential energy is captured and used for the formation of ATP. The coupling of the proton-motive force and ATP synthesis is called the chemiosmotic mechanism—or **chemiosmosis**—and is found in all respiring cells.

To summarize, the energy originally contained in glucose and other fuel molecules is ultimately captured in the cellular energy currency, ATP. For each pair of electrons passed along the chain from NADH to oxygen, about 2.5 molecules of ATP are formed. FADH$_2$ oxidation produces about 1.5 ATP molecules because it enters the electron transport chain at a later step than NADH (see Figure 9.13).

ATP synthesis is a reversible reaction, and ATP synthase can also act as an ATPase, hydrolyzing ATP to ADP and P$_i$:

$$ATP \rightleftharpoons ADP + P_i + \text{free energy}$$

If the reaction goes to the right, free energy is released. In the mitochondrion, it is used to transfer H$^+$ out of the mitochondrial matrix—not the usual mode of operation. If the reaction goes to the left, it uses the free energy from H$^+$ diffusion into the matrix to make ATP. What makes it prefer ATP synthesis? There are two answers to this question:

1. ATP leaves the mitochondrial matrix for use elsewhere in the cell as soon as it is made, keeping the ATP concentration in the matrix low, and driving the reaction toward the left.

2. The H$^+$ gradient is maintained by electron and proton transport.

Every day a person hydrolyzes about 10^{25} ATP molecules to ADP. This amounts to 9 kg, a significant fraction of the person's entire body weight! The vast majority of this ADP is "recycled"—converted back to ATP—using free energy from the oxidation of glucose.

Experiments demonstrate chemiosmosis

Chemiosmosis has been tested in the lab. Let's look at two lines of evidence; first, a direct demonstration that a H$^+$ gradient can drive ATP synthesis, and second, disruption of the coupling of electron transport to ATP synthesis.

DIRECT DEMONSTRATION OF CHEMIOSMOSIS   The key experiment that demonstrated that a proton (H$^+$) gradient across a membrane could drive ATP synthesis was first performed using chloroplasts, the organelles in plants that convert the energy in sunlight into chemical energy (photosynthesis; see Chapter 10)

Cytoplasm

Outer mitochondrial membrane

Electron transport

ATP synthesis

Intermembrane space (high H⁺ concentration and positive charge)

NADH-Q reductase

Ubiquinone

Cytochrome c reductase

Cytochrome c

Cytochrome c oxidase

ATP synthase

I

II

III

IV

F_0 unit

Inner mitochondrial membrane

F_1 unit

NADH

NAD⁺ + H⁺

FADH₂

FAD⁺ + 2 H⁺

H⁺

H⁺

H₂O

2 H + ½ O₂

Matrix of mitochondrion (low H⁺ concentration and negative charge)

ADP + Pᵢ

H⁺

ATP

1 Electrons (carried by NADH and FADH₂) from glycolysis and the citric acid cycle "feed" the electron carriers of the inner mitochondrial membrane, which transfer protons (H⁺) out of the matrix to the intermembrane space.

2 Proton transfer creates an imbalance of H⁺—and thus a charge difference—between the intermembrane space and the matrix. This imbalance is the proton-motive force.

3 The proton-motive force drives protons back to the matrix through the H⁺ channel of ATP synthase (the F_0 unit). This movement of protons is coupled to the formation of ATP in the F_1 unit.

Figure 9.13 The Respiratory Chain and ATP Synthase Produce ATP by a Chemiosmotic Mechanism As electrons pass through the transmembrane protein complexes in the respiratory chain, protons are transferred from the mitochondrial matrix into the intermembrane space. As the protons return to the matrix through ATP synthase, ATP is formed.

View in **Achieve**
Animation 9.1 **Electron Transport and ATP Synthesis**

View in **Achieve**
Simulation 9.1 **Electron Transport**

(Figure 9.14). Soon thereafter, the same mechanism was shown to work in mitochondria.

View in **Achieve**
Animation 9.2 **Two Experiments Demonstrate the Chemiosmotic Mechanism**

UNCOUPLING ELECTRON TRANSPORT FROM ATP PRODUCTION
As you have seen, the coupling of electron transport (which generates the proton gradient) with chemiosmosis is vital for the capture of free energy in the form of ATP. Uncoupling protein 1 (UCP1), which is found in the mitochondria of brown fat cells (described in the chapter opening), demonstrates the importance of this coupling. By disrupting the gradient, UCP1 allows the energy released during electron transport to be in the form of heat, rather than chemical-bond energy trapped in ATP.

The relationship between UCP1 in brown fat and body weight has been investigated experimentally in a study of a genetic strain of mice that—unlike normal mice—do not get fat as they age (people tend to put on weight as they age, too). As **Investigating Life: Mitochondria, Genetics, and Obesity** reveals, it appears that the leaner mice make more UCP1 and oxidize (burn off) more fat than normal mice do. Might this observation point to ways to control weight gain in people? In a related study of obesity conducted in the 1930s, a chemical, dinitrophenol, was shown to uncouple oxidation and phosphorylation, just as UCP1 (which had not been discovered yet) does. Physicians got the idea that giving obese people the uncoupler would cause them to oxidize their fat. It worked, but since dinitrophenol acted on all mitochondria everywhere in the body, and not just in fat cells, severe side effects occurred as ATP production all over the body became critically low—in some

Experiment

Figure 9.14 An Experiment Demonstrates the Chemiosmotic Mechanism

Original Paper: A. T. Jagendorf and E. Uribe. 1966. ATP formation caused by acid-base transition of spinach chloroplasts. *Proc Natl Acad Sci USA* 55: 170–177.

The chemiosmosis hypothesis was a bold departure from the conventional scientific thinking of the time. It required an intact compartment enclosed by a membrane. Could a proton gradient drive the synthesis of ATP? The first experiments to answer this question used chloroplasts, plant organelles that use the same mechanism as mitochondria to synthesize ATP.

HYPOTHESIS▶ A H^+ gradient across a membrane that contains ATP synthase is sufficient to drive ATP synthesis.

METHOD▶

Chloroplasts are isolated from cells and broken to expose their thylakoids (internal compartments). The broken chloroplasts are preincubated in an acidic medium (pH 3.8).

pH 3.8 —Preincubation medium

—Thylakoid

The broken chloroplasts are moved quickly to an alkaline medium (pH 8). This lowers the H^+ concentration outside the thylakoids and creates a H^+ gradient across the thylakoid membrane (high inside, low outside).

RESULTS▶

ATP synthase reaction mixture

pH 8

H^+ movement out of the thylakoids drives the synthesis of ATP from ADP and P_i.

Reaction mixture

ADP + P_i H^+ ATP

Thylakoid membrane   **pH 8**

Inside thylakoid H^+ **pH 3.8**

CONCLUSION▶ A H^+ gradient across an ATP synthase–containing membrane is sufficient for ATP synthesis by organelles.

Go to **Achieve** for a companion Data in Depth exercise.

Intermembrane space

4 H^+

1 H^+ diffuses through this channel.

Inner mitochondrial membrane F_0

2 This subunit rotates.

Matrix

F_1

3 Rotation causes this subunit to change its three-dimensional shape to expose the active site for ATP synthesis.

4 H^+

ADP + P_i ATP

Figure 9.15 How ATP Is Made   Mitochondrial ATP synthase is a rotary motor.

▶ **Media Clip 9.1 ATP Synthase in Motion**
Life12e.com/mc9.1

9.15, are shared by living organisms as diverse as bacteria and humans. ATP synthase is a molecular motor composed of two parts: the F_0 unit, a transmembrane region that is the H^+ channel; and the F_1 unit, which contains the active sites for ATP synthesis. F_1 consists of six subunits (three each of two polypeptide chains), arranged like the segments of an orange around a central shaft-like polypeptide that interacts with the membrane-embedded F_0. Electron transport sets up an H^+ gradient across the membrane. This gradient has potential energy, and when H^+ diffuses through the channel, the potential energy is converted to kinetic energy, causing the central polypeptide to rotate. The energy is transmitted to the catalytic subunits of F_1, resulting in ATP synthesis. These molecular motors make ATP at rates up to 100 molecules per second.

Some microorganisms use non-O_2 electron acceptors

A general way to describe the last reaction in electron transport is:

$$X_{oxidized} + e^- \rightarrow X_{reduced}$$

Part of the amazing success of bacteria and archaea is that they have evolved biochemical pathways that allow them to exist in environments where O_2 is scarce or absent. As you will see in the next key concept, for most animals and plants, the anaerobic (no O_2) catabolism of glucose generally yields much less energy than aerobic catabolism. However, many bacteria and archaea exploit their environments to use alternative electron acceptors. This allows them to complete the electron transport chain and produce ATP even in the absence of O_2. **Table 9.2** summarizes some of these pathways, which are referred to as **anaerobic respiration**. Note that some of these microbes use ions as electron acceptors while others use small molecules.

cases too low for survival. So the idea of an artificial uncoupler for weight loss was dropped. However, stimulation of the natural uncoupler in brown fat is under study for obesity treatment.

HOW ATP SYNTHASE WORKS: A MOLECULAR MOTOR   The structure and mechanism of ATP synthase, illustrated in **Figure**

►Investigating LIFE   Mitochondria, Genetics, and Obesity

Experiment

Original Paper: X. L. Ma et al. 2011. Ablations of ghrelin and ghrelin receptor exhibit differential metabolic phenotypes and thermogenic capacity during aging. *PLOS ONE* 6: e16391.

As people (and mice) get older, they tend to accumulate fat. In the course of investigating a strain of mice genetically unable to make the receptor for a hormone called ghrelin that is involved in controlling appetite, Yuxiang Sun and her team at Baylor College of Medicine compared these mice with normal mice as they aged. They were surprised to find that the genetically changed mice did not put on as much weight as their normal counterparts. The researchers discovered that the genetic mutation in these mice caused uncoupling of oxidative phosphorylation and burning of body fat. Their experiment investigated whether levels of mitochondrial uncoupling protein 1 (UCP1) were different in the genetically changed mice than in normal mice.

HYPOTHESIS►   Mice that make more uncoupling protein (UCP1) burn more body fat.

METHOD►

Old (10–12 wk) genetically mutant mice

Old (10–12 wk) normal mice

Measure fat mass.

Measure body weight.

Measure mitochondrial UCP1.

RESULTS►

Fat mass is lower in mutant mice.

Body weight is lower in mutant mice.

UCP1 is higher in mutant mice.

CONCLUSION►   Increased UCP1 correlates with less fat and a lower body weight.

Work with the Data

In an effort to determine whether weight gain in normal mice might be due to inactivity or to eating too much (two of the well-known causes of weight gain), as opposed to a biochemical abnormality (such as unusual UCP1 levels), Sun and her team examined young (3–4 months old) and older (10–12 months old) mice of both strains. Error bars represent standard error of the mean. (Figures A–C after X. L. Ma et al. 2011. *PLOS ONE* 6: e16391. © 2011 Ma et al.; CC BY 4.0.)

QUESTIONS►

1. The researchers measured weight and body composition in terms of fat and lean body tissues. The results are shown in **Figure A**. Did the mutant mice and normal mice gain weight as they aged?

2. The researchers wondered whether the weight changes noted in Figure A were due to changes in eating patterns or exercising. So they measured how much food the mice ate per day and measured their movements over time in a special chamber. The results are shown in **Figure B**. What can you conclude about the role of food intake and exercise on the weight differences between the two strains of mice?

3. The uncoupling protein UCP1 found in the inner mitochondrial membrane of brown fat cells uncouples mitochondrial electron transport (oxidation) and ATP production (phosphorylation), so that instead of being trapped as chemical energy in the formation of ATP, the energy released by oxidation is released as heat. Sun and her team measured UCP1 levels in brown fat mitochondria of the two strains of mice. The results are shown in **Figure C**. What can you conclude about the role of UCP1 in the weight differences between the two strains of mice?

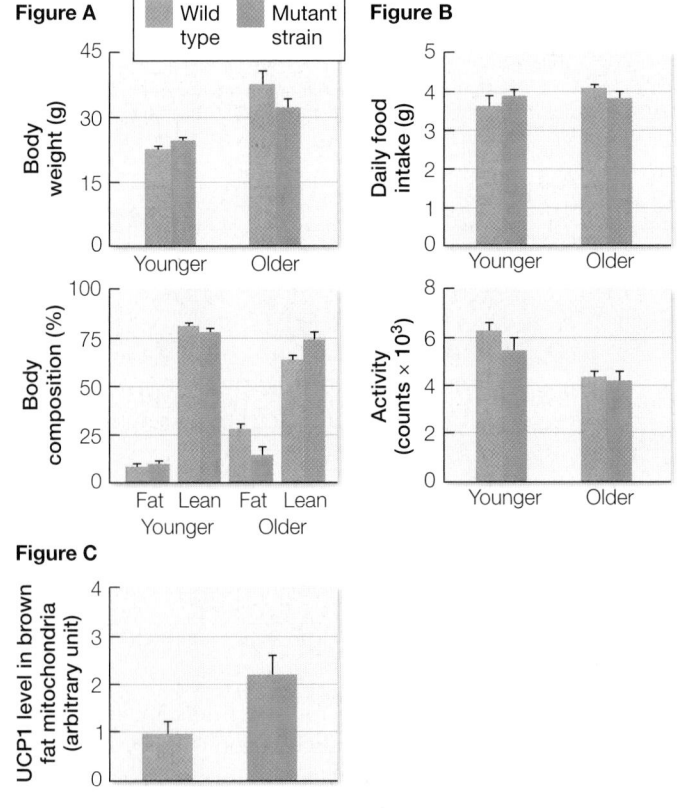

Go to Achieve for a companion Data in Depth exercise.

TABLE 9.2 | Electron Acceptors Used in the Respiratory Chain of Anaerobic Microbes

Terminal electron acceptor	Product formed	Organism
SO_4^{-2}	H_2S	*Desulfovibrio desulfuricans*
Fe^{3+}	Fe^{2+}	*Geobacter metallireducens*
NO_3^-	NO_2^-	*Escherichia coli*
CO_2	CH_4	*Methanosarcina barkeri*
CO_2	CH_3COO^-	*Clostridium aceticum*
Fumarate	Succinate	*Wolinella succinogenes*

Connect the Concepts The diversity of microbial metabolic pathways allows them to adapt to life in many environments. See Key Concept 24.2.

KEY CONCEPT
9.3 Recap and Assess

The oxidation of reduced electron carriers in the respiratory chain drives the active transport of protons across the inner mitochondrial membrane, generating a proton-motive force. Diffusion of protons down their electrochemical gradient through ATP synthase is coupled to the synthesis of ATP. Some bacteria and archaea can respire using alternative electron acceptors instead of O_2.

1. How are protons transported from the mitochondrial matrix to the intermembrane space during electron transport?

2. How does the experiment described in Figure 9.14 demonstrate the chemiosmotic mechanism?

3. Trace the sequence of changes in redox reactions that occur in mammalian tissue when the oxygen supply is cut off. The first change is that all of the cytochrome *c* becomes reduced, because electrons can still flow from cytochrome *c*, but there is no oxygen to accept electrons from cytochrome *c* oxidase. What happens after this?

4. The drug antimycin A blocks electron transport in mitochondria and chloroplasts. Explain what would happen if the experiment in Figure 9.14 were repeated in the presence of this drug.

Oxidative phosphorylation captures a great deal of energy in ATP. But it does not occur if O_2 is absent. We will turn now to the metabolism of glucose in anaerobic conditions.

KEY CONCEPT
9.4 In the Absence of Oxygen, Some Energy Is Harvested from Glucose

Learning Objectives

9.4.1 Describe the biochemical pathways of fermentation.

9.4.2 Explain why fermentation is necessary in anaerobic conditions.

In eukaryotes, in the absence of O_2 (anaerobic conditions), a small amount of ATP can be produced by glycolysis and fermentation. Like glycolysis, fermentation pathways occur in the cytoplasm. There are many different types of fermentation, but they all operate to regenerate NAD^+ so that the NAD^+-requiring reactions of glycolysis can continue. The two best-understood fermentation pathways are found in a wide variety of organisms, including eukaryotes:

- Lactic acid fermentation, the end product of which is lactic acid (lactate)
- Alcoholic fermentation, the end product of which is ethyl alcohol (ethanol)

Fermentation pathways allow glucose to be partially oxidized in the absence of oxygen

In **lactic acid fermentation**, pyruvate serves as the electron acceptor and lactate is the product (**Figure 9.16A**). This process takes place in many microorganisms and complex organisms, including higher plants and vertebrates. A notable example of lactic acid fermentation occurs in vertebrate muscle tissue. Usually, vertebrates get their energy for muscle contraction aerobically, with the circulatory system supplying O_2 to muscles. In small vertebrates, this is almost always adequate: for example, birds can fly long distances without resting. But in larger vertebrates such as humans, the circulatory system is not up to the task of delivering enough O_2 when the need is great, such as during intense activity. At this point, the muscle cells break down glycogen (a stored polysaccharide; see Figure 3.19) and undergo lactic acid fermentation.

Lactate buildup becomes a problem after prolonged periods of intense exercise because it is associated with an increase in the H^+ concentration in the cell, lowering the pH. This affects cellular activities, which return to normal upon resting. Lactate dehydrogenase, the enzyme that catalyzes the fermentation reaction, works in both directions. That is, when O_2 is available it can catalyze the oxidation of lactate to form pyruvate, which is then catabolized to CO_2 with concomitant energy release to form ATP. When lactate levels are decreased, muscle activity can resume.

Alcoholic fermentation takes place in certain yeasts (eukaryotic microbes) and some plant cells under anaerobic conditions. This process requires two enzymes, pyruvate decarboxylase and alcohol dehydrogenase, which metabolize pyruvate to ethanol (**Figure 9.16B**). As with lactic acid fermentation, the reactions are essentially reversible. For thousands of years, humans have used anaerobic fermentation by yeast cells to produce alcoholic beverages. The bubbles in beer and champagne are CO_2 from the action of pyruvate decarboxylase. The cells use sugars from plant sources (glucose from grapes or maltose from barley) to produce the end product, ethanol, in wine and beer.

By recycling NAD^+, fermentation allows glycolysis to continue, thus producing small amounts of ATP through substrate-level phosphorylation. The net yield of two ATPs per glucose molecule is much lower than the energy yield from cellular respiration. For this reason, most organisms existing in anaerobic environments are small microbes that grow relatively slowly.

Figure 9.16 Fermentation
Glycolysis produces pyruvate, ATP, and NADH from glucose. **(A)** Lactic acid fermentation uses NADH as a reducing agent to reduce pyruvate to lactate, thus regenerating NAD⁺ to keep glycolysis operating. **(B)** In alcoholic fermentation, pyruvate from glycolysis is converted into acetaldehyde, and CO_2 is released. NADH from glycolysis is used to reduce acetaldehyde to ethanol, thus regenerating NAD⁺ to keep glycolysis operating.

Q: Where do the bubbles in champagne and beer come from?

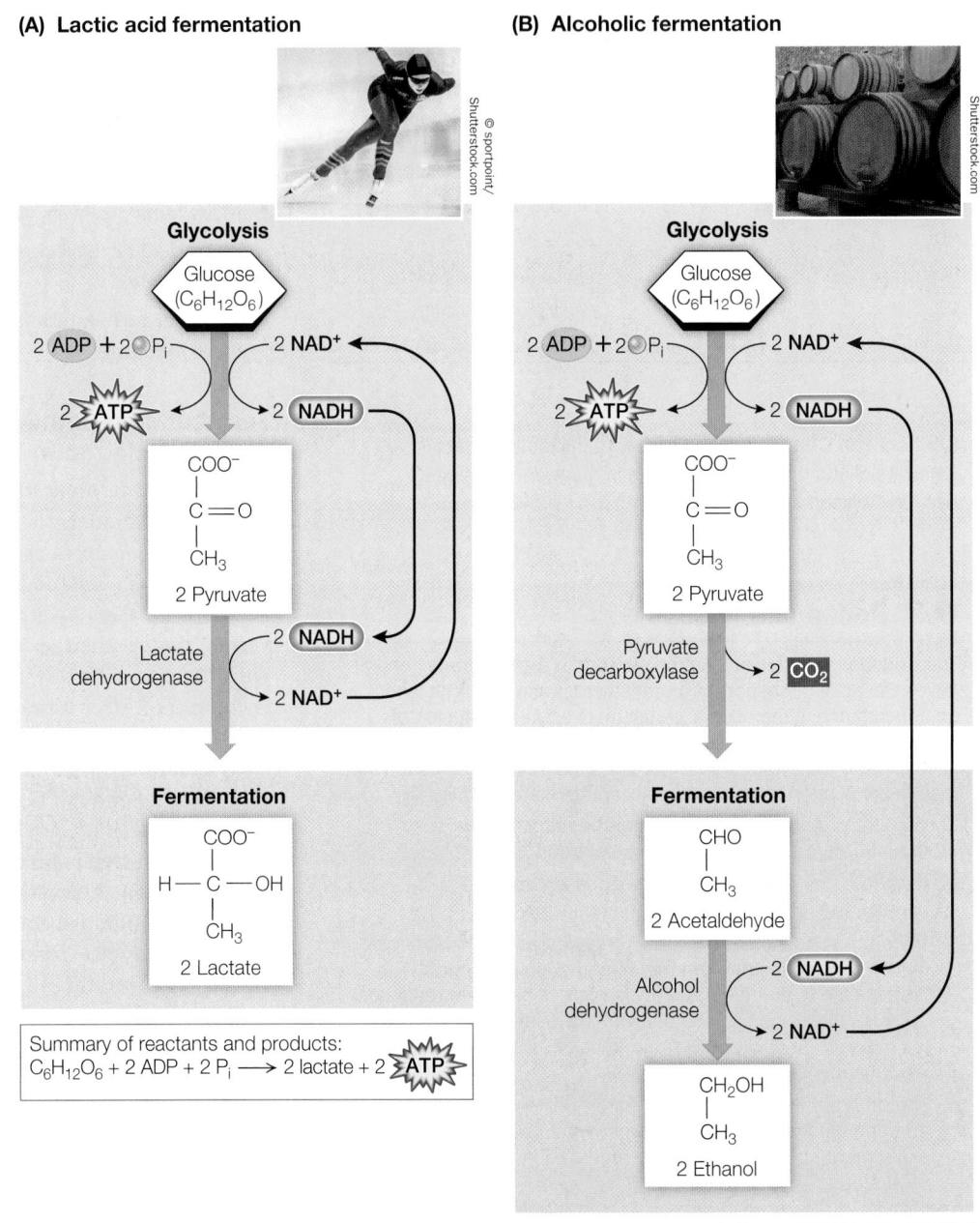

Cellular respiration yields much more energy than fermentation

The total net energy yield from glycolysis plus fermentation is two molecules of ATP per molecule of glucose oxidized. The maximum yield of ATP that can be harvested from a molecule of glucose through glycolysis followed by cellular respiration is much greater—about 32 molecules of ATP (**Figure 9.17**). (Review Figures 9.6, 9.7, 9.9, and 9.13 to see where all the ATP molecules come from.)

Why do the metabolic pathways that operate in aerobic environments produce so much more ATP? Glycolysis and fermentation only partially oxidize glucose. Much more energy remains in the end products of fermentation (lactic acid and ethanol)

than in CO_2, the end product of cellular respiration. In cellular respiration, carriers (mostly NAD⁺) are reduced during pyruvate oxidation and the citric acid cycle. Then the reduced carriers are oxidized by the respiratory chain, with the accompanying production of ATP by chemiosmosis (about 2.5 ATP for each NADH and 1.5 ATP for each $FADH_2$). In an aerobic environment, a cell or organism capable of aerobic metabolism will have the advantage over one that is limited to fermentation, in terms of its ability to harvest chemical energy. Two key events in the evolution of multicellular organisms were the rise in atmospheric O_2 levels (see Key Concept 24.2) and the development of metabolic pathways to use that O_2.

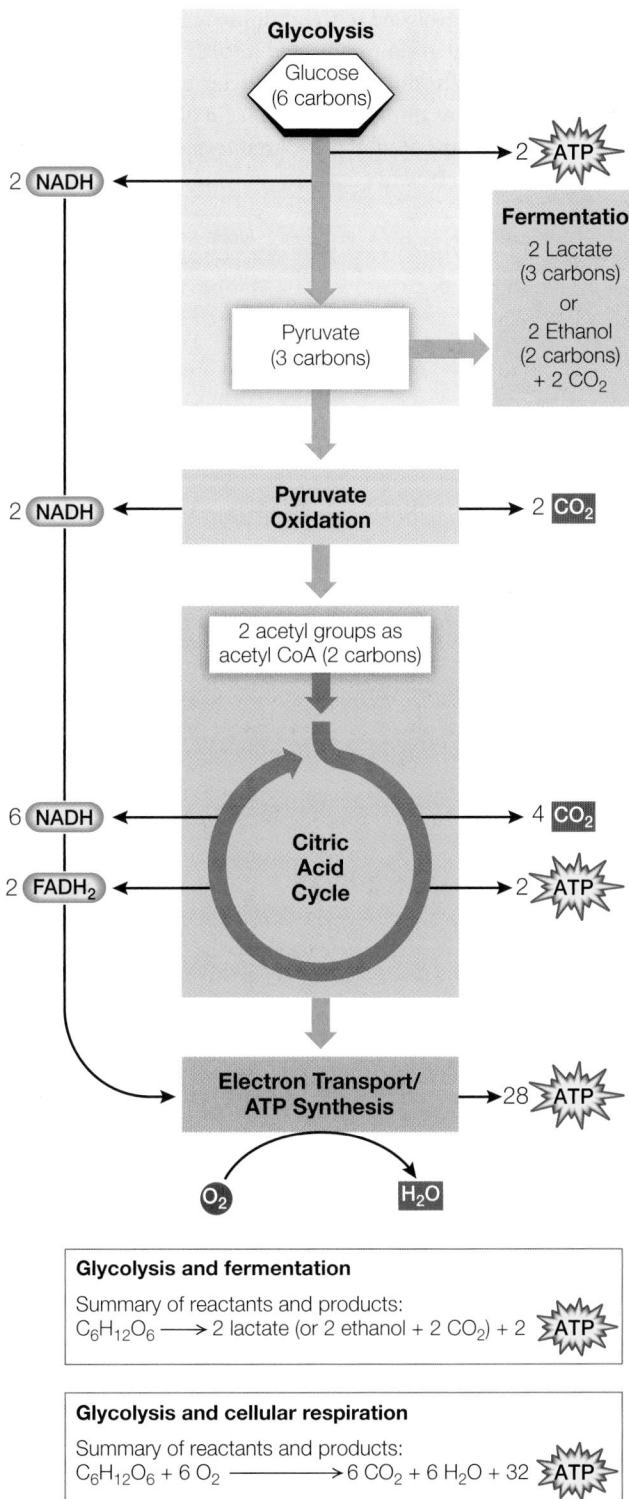

Figure 9.17 **Cellular Respiration Yields More Energy Than Fermentation** Electron carriers are reduced in pyruvate oxidation and the citric acid cycle, then oxidized by the respiratory chain. These reactions produce ATP via chemiosmosis.

 View in Achieve
Activity 9.5 **Energy Levels**

KEY CONCEPT
9.4 Recap and Assess

In the absence of O_2, fermentation pathways use NADH formed by glycolysis to reduce pyruvate and regenerate NAD^+. The energy yield of glycolysis coupled to fermentation is low because glucose is only partially oxidized. When O_2 is present, the electron carriers of cellular respiration allow for the full oxidation of glucose, so the energy yield from glucose is much higher.

1. Why is replenishing NAD^+ required to continue glycolysis in the absence of O_2?
2. How does fermentation replenish NAD^+?

Now that you've seen how cells harvest energy, let's see how that energy moves through other metabolic pathways in the cell.

KEY CONCEPT
9.5 Metabolic Pathways Are Interrelated and Regulated

Learning Objectives

9.5.1 Describe catabolic and anabolic pathways that link carbohydrate, lipid, and protein metabolism.

9.5.2 Trace the path of an atom as it moves through various metabolic pathways within a cell.

9.5.3 Explain how allosteric changes in an enzyme can be used to regulate flow through a metabolic pathway.

Glycolysis and the pathways of cellular respiration do not operate in isolation. Rather, there is an interchange of molecules into and out of these pathways, to and from the metabolic pathways for the synthesis and breakdown of amino acids, nucleotides, fatty acids, and other building blocks of life (see Figure 8.14). Carbon skeletons (i.e., the carbon backbones of organic molecules) can enter the catabolic pathways and be broken down to release their energy, or they can enter anabolic pathways to be used in the formation of the macromolecules that are the major constituents of the cell. These relationships are summarized in **Figure 9.18**. In this key concept we will explore how pathways are interrelated by the sharing of intermediate molecules, and we will see how pathways are regulated by the inhibitors of key enzymes.

Catabolism and anabolism are linked

A hamburger or veggie burger on a bun contains three major sources of carbon skeletons: carbohydrates, mostly in the form of starch (a polysaccharide); lipids, mostly as triglycerides (three fatty acids attached to glycerol); and proteins (polymers of amino acids). Look at Figure 9.18 to see how each of these three types of macromolecules can be hydrolyzed and used in catabolism or anabolism.

CATABOLIC INTERCONVERSIONS Polysaccharides, lipids, and proteins can all be broken down to provide energy:

• *Polysaccharides* are hydrolyzed to glucose. Glucose then passes through glycolysis and cellular respiration, where its energy is captured in ATP.

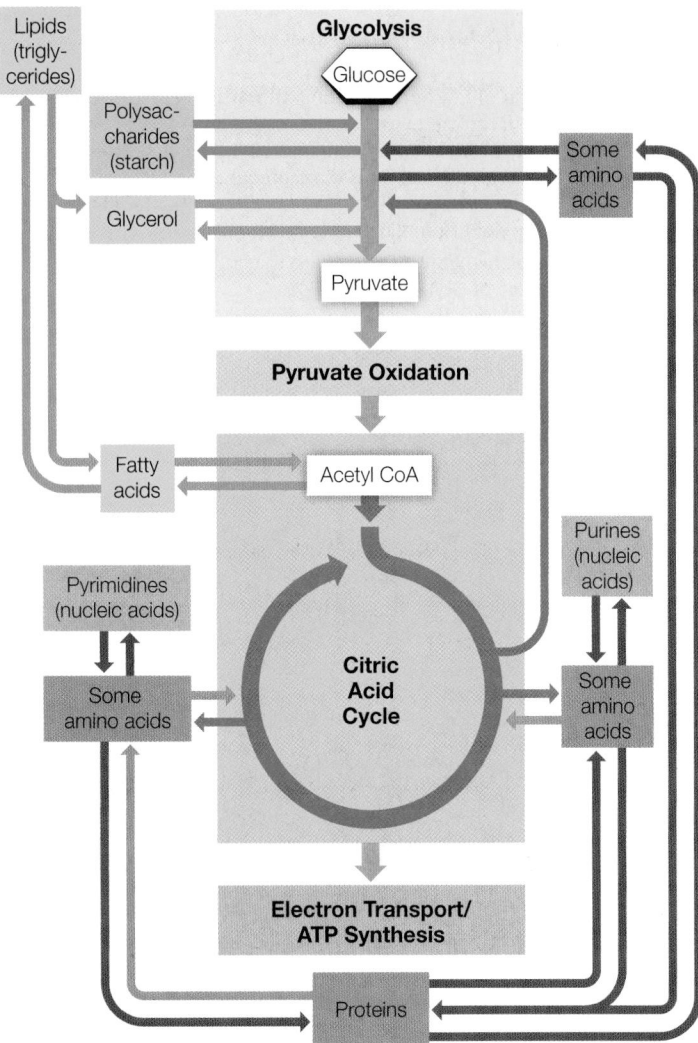

Figure 9.18 Relationships among the Major Metabolic Pathways of the Cell Note the central positions of glycolysis and the citric acid cycle in this network of metabolic pathways. Also note that many of the pathways can operate essentially in reverse.

Q: Can DNA be an energy source? Explain. Why do you think it is not usually employed in this way?

• *Lipids* are broken down into their constituents, glycerol and fatty acids. Glycerol is converted into dihydroxyacetone phosphate (DHAP), an intermediate in glycolysis. Fatty acids are highly reduced molecules that are converted to acetyl CoA inside the mitochondrion by a series of oxidation enzymes, in a process known as β-oxidation. For example, the β-oxidation of a 16-carbon (C_{16}) fatty acid occurs in several steps:

$$C_{16} \text{ fatty acid} + \text{CoA} \rightarrow C_{16} \text{ fatty acyl CoA}$$

$$C_{16} \text{ fatty acyl CoA} + \text{CoA} \rightarrow C_{14} \text{ fatty acyl CoA} + \text{acetyl CoA}$$

$$\text{Repeat 6 times} \rightarrow 8 \text{ acetyl CoA}$$

The acetyl CoA can then enter the citric acid cycle and be catabolized to CO_2.

• *Proteins* are hydrolyzed to their amino acid building blocks. The 20 different amino acids feed into glycolysis or the citric acid cycle at different points determined by their structures. For example, the amino acid glutamate is converted into α-ketoglutarate, an intermediate in the citric acid cycle (the five-carbon molecule in Figure 9.9):

Note that one of the products of this reaction is ammonia (NH_4^+), which is toxic to cells. If there is too much NH_4^+, the equilibrium point of the reaction will shift to the left, and the concentration of α-ketoglutarate, a citric acid cycle intermediate, will be reduced. The cycle can begin to shut down, with drastic effects on energy provision. Therefore excess NH_4^+ must be removed, and this is done by making urea: NH_2—CO—NH_2, a waste product excreted in urine.

ANABOLIC INTERCONVERSIONS   Many catabolic pathways can operate essentially in reverse, with some modifications. Glycolytic and citric acid cycle intermediates, instead of being oxidized to form CO_2, can be reduced and used to form glucose in a process called **gluconeogenesis** (which means "new formation of glucose"). Likewise, acetyl CoA can be used to form fatty acids. The most common fatty acids have even numbers of carbons: 14, 16, or 18. These are formed by the addition of two-carbon acetyl CoA "units" one at a time until the appropriate chain length is reached. Acetyl CoA is also a building block for various pigments, plant growth substances, rubber, steroid hormones, and other molecules.

Some intermediates in the citric acid cycle are reactants in pathways that synthesize important components of nucleic acids. For example, α-ketoglutarate is a starting point for purines, and oxaloacetate for pyrimidines. In addition, α-ketoglutarate is a starting point for the synthesis of chlorophyll (used in photosynthesis; see Chapter 10) and the amino acid glutamate (used in protein synthesis).

Catabolism and anabolism are integrated

A carbon atom from a protein in your burger can end up in DNA, fat, or CO_2, among other fates. How does the organism "decide" which metabolic pathways to follow, in which cells? With all of the possible interconversions, you might expect that cellular concentrations of various biochemical molecules would vary widely. Remarkably, the levels of these substances in what is called the metabolic pool—the sum total of all the biochemical molecules in a cell—are quite constant. Organisms regulate the enzymes in various cells in order to maintain a steady state between catabolism and anabolism.

> **Connect the Concepts** Control of metabolic pathways often rests with regulation of enzymes already present. Review the mechanisms of enzyme regulation in Key Concept 8.5.

The regulation of interconnecting biochemical pathways is a problem of systems biology, which seeks to understand how biochemical pathways interact (see Key Concept 8.5). It is a bit like trying to predict traffic patterns in a city: if an accident blocks traffic on a major road, drivers take alternate routes, where the traffic volume consequently changes.

Several mechanisms can be used to regulate the rate of each step in a biochemical pathway:

- *Changing the amount of active enzyme*: The cell can increase the expression of a gene encoding an enzyme.

- *Changing enzyme activity by covalent modifications*: Adding phosphate groups by protein kinase can alter the activity of an enzyme.

- *Feedback inhibition*: Allosteric changes in an enzyme due to binding of a product in a pathway can cause the entire pathway to shut down.

- *Substrate availability*: If the substrate of a particular enzyme is used up by another pathway, the first enzyme can no longer function and the pathway shuts down.

Consider what happens to the starch in your burger bun. In the digestive system, starch is hydrolyzed to glucose, which enters the blood for distribution to the rest of the body. But before the glucose is distributed, a regulatory check must be made: If there is already enough glucose in the blood to supply the body's needs, the excess glucose is converted into glycogen and stored in the liver and muscles. If not enough glucose is supplied by food, glycogen is broken down, or other molecules are used to make glucose by gluconeogenesis. The end result is that the level of glucose in the blood is remarkably constant. How does the body accomplish this?

Glycolysis and the citric acid cycle are subject to allosteric regulation (see Key Concept 8.5) of key enzymes involved. In a metabolic pathway, a high concentration of the final product can inhibit the action of an enzyme that catalyzes an earlier reaction (see Figure 8.20). Furthermore, an excess of the product of one pathway can activate an enzyme in another pathway, speeding up its reactions and diverting raw materials away from synthesis of the first product. These negative and positive feedback mechanisms are used at many points in the energy-harvesting pathways and are summarized in **Figure 9.19**.

- The main control point in glycolysis is the glycolytic enzyme phosphofructokinase, which catalyzes Step 3 in Figure 9.6. This enzyme is allosterically inhibited by ATP or citrate, and activated by ADP or AMP. Under anaerobic conditions, fermentation yields a relatively small amount of ATP, and phosphofructokinase operates at a high rate. However, when conditions are aerobic, respiration makes 16 times more ATP

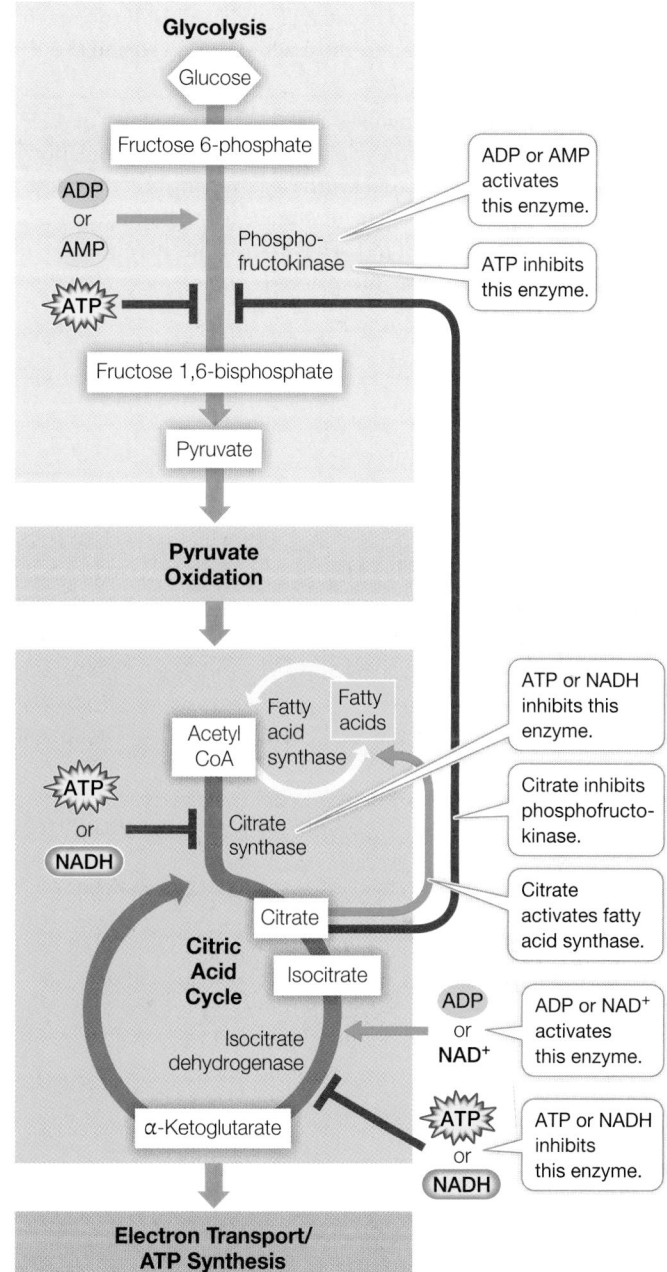

Figure 9.19 Allosteric Regulation of Glycolysis and the Citric Acid Cycle Allosteric regulation controls glycolysis and the citric acid cycle at crucial early steps, increasing their efficiency and preventing the excessive buildup of intermediates.

 View in Achieve
Activity 9.6 **Regulation of Energy Pathways**

than fermentation does, and the abundant ATP allosterically inhibits phosphofructokinase. So glycolysis slows down.

- The main control point in the citric acid cycle is the enzyme isocitrate dehydrogenase (which catalyzes Step 3 in Figure 9.9). This enzyme is activated by increases in substrate concentrations (ADP, NAD$^+$, and isocitrate) and is inhibited by products of the citric acid cycle: ATP and NADH. If too much ATP or NADH accumulates, the reaction is slowed and the citric acid cycle shuts down.

- Another control point involves acetyl CoA. If the level of ATP is high and the citric acid cycle shuts down, the accumulation of citrate activates fatty acid synthase, diverting acetyl CoA to the synthesis of fatty acids for storage (contributing to a person's accumulation of fat). These fatty acids may be metabolized later to produce more acetyl CoA.

KEY CONCEPT

9.5 Recap and Assess

Glucose can be made from intermediates in glycolysis and the citric acid cycle by gluconeogenesis. The metabolic pathways for the production and breakdown of lipids and amino acids are linked to those of glucose metabolism. Reaction products regulate key enzymes in the various pathways.

1. Give examples of the pathways relating to glycolysis and the citric acid cycle for catabolism of a lipid and the anabolism of a protein.

2. How does phosphofructokinase serve as a control point for glycolysis?

3. You eat a burger that contains polysaccharides, proteins, and lipids. How could carbon atoms in the proteins' amino acids and the glucose in the polysaccharides end up as fats?

▶Investigating LIFE

 How are mitochondria related to obesity?

Recall from the opening of this chapter that brown fat is adipose tissue with a high concentration of mitochondria, which have iron-containing pigments. The uncoupling protein UCP1, found in the inner membranes of mitochondria in brown fat cells, uncouples mitochondrial electron transport (oxidation) and ATP production (phosphorylation), so that instead of being trapped as chemical-bond energy in the formation of ATP, the energy released by oxidation is released as heat.

Hibernating animals take advantage of the heat emitted by the catabolism of energy-rich molecules in brown fat, especially when aroused. In hibernating animals, brown fat and UCP1 increase during the winter. It turns out that adult humans also experience a seasonal variation in brown fat, having more of it in the cooler months. Other factors such as diet and exercise being equal, increased fat catabolism occurs in the presence of UCP1 (as demonstrated by the experiment in **Investigating Life: Mitochondria, Genetics, and Obesity**).

Genetic studies confirm the role of UCP1 in fat breakdown as well. For example, some people have a genetically determined variant of UCP1 that has lower uncoupling activity than normal UCP1. As people with the variant get older, they accumulate more body fat than their peers with normal UCP1 do.

Future directions

Activating brown fat tissue may help in treating obesity. When brown fat is activated by cold temperature in animals, there is an increase in mitochondrial uncoupling, but also an increase in fatty acid breakdown (β-oxidation) and glucose uptake into cells to provide energy from a nonfat source (see Figure 9.18). This is accompanied by significant weight loss. Metabolic effects are seen throughout the body, especially in liver and muscle tissue. To get the message from brown fat cells to other tissues, the fat cells produce a protein called adiponectin. Amazingly, this protein is elevated in centenarians, many of whom are lean. In some centenarians, their genetic offspring also have elevated adiponectin, so the activation of brown fat may be inherited. Several drugs are being evaluated for their potential to activate brown fat.

VISUAL SUMMARY 9

© 3d_man/Shutterstock.com

You should be able to relate each summary to the adjacent figures. If you go to this visual summary in **Achieve**, you can follow links to figures, animations, activities, and simulations that will help you consolidate the material.

KEY CONCEPT

9.1   Cells Harvest Chemical Energy from Glucose Oxidation

Go to **Activities 9.1 and 9.2**

- The pathways of glucose catabolism are **glycolysis**, pyruvate oxidation, the citric acid cycle, and electron transport/ATP synthesis. Under **anaerobic** conditions, **fermentation** occurs.

- As glucose is **oxidized**, the electrons it loses are transferred or are part of a more electronegative bond in another material, which is thereby **reduced**.

- The coenzyme NAD^+ is a key electron carrier in biological **oxidation–reduction**, or **redox**, **reactions**. It exists in two forms, one oxidized (NAD^+) and the other reduced (NADH).

Questions

1. When glucose is oxidized, energy is trapped by ADP to make ATP. What is the source in nature of the energy in glucose?

2. Which is higher in free energy, NAD^+ or NADH, and why?

Figure 9.1

Figure 9.4

KEY CONCEPT

9.2   In the Presence of Oxygen, Glucose Is Fully Oxidized

Go to **Activity 9.3**

- Glycolysis consists of ten enzyme-catalyzed reactions that occur in the cell cytoplasm. The end products are two three-carbon molecules of pyruvate, two molecules of ATP, and two molecules of NADH. Energy is trapped in ATP and NADH.

- After pyruvate oxidation, the citric acid cycle fully oxidizes the glucose catabolites to CO_2.

Question

1. Why does glycolysis involve multiple steps, each catalyzed by a single enzyme?

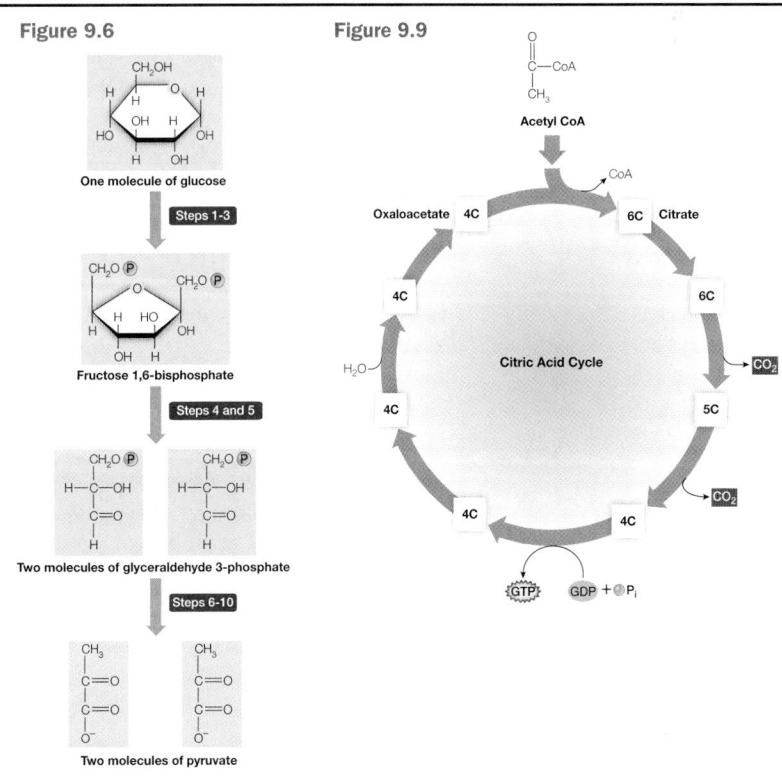

Figure 9.6

Figure 9.9

KEY CONCEPT

9.3 Oxidative Phosphorylation Forms ATP

Go to Activity 9.4,
Animations 9.1 and 9.2, and Simulation 9.1

- Oxidation of electron carriers in the presence of O_2 releases energy that can be used to form ATP in a process called **oxidative phosphorylation**.

- The NADH and $FADH_2$ produced in glycolysis, pyruvate oxidation, and the citric acid cycle are oxidized by the **respiratory chain**, regenerating NAD^+ and FAD. Oxygen (O_2) is the final acceptor of electrons and protons, forming water (H_2O).

- The respiratory chain transfers protons across the inner mitochondrial membrane, creating the **proton-motive force** that drives the synthesis of ATP from ADP by **chemiosmosis**.

Questions

1. Rotenone is an insecticide isolated from the roots of certain tropical plants. It inhibits NADH-Q reductase, which catalyzes the oxidation of NADH in the electron transport chain. How does rotenone kill cells?

2. What is the source of the electrons in the electron transport chain?

Figure 9.13

Figure 9.15

KEY CONCEPT

9.4 In the Absence of Oxygen, Some Energy Is Harvested from Glucose

Go to Activity 9.5

- In the absence of O_2, glycolysis is followed by fermentation. In the process, NAD^+ is regenerated from NADH so that glycolysis can continue, thus generating a small amount of ATP.

- For each molecule of glucose used, glycolysis plus fermentation yields two molecules of ATP In contrast, glycolysis operating with pyruvate oxidation, the citric acid cycle, and oxidative phosphorylation yields up to 32 molecules of ATP per molecule of glucose.

Questions

1. Why does the production of wine occur in sealed barrels or tanks?

2. In an initial attempt to run a marathon without training, a woman gets tired after a mile, with the pH in her muscle cells reduced. After rest, the pH is raised and her muscle function resumes. How do these events occur?

Figure 9.16

VISUAL SUMMARY 9

KEY CONCEPT

9.5 Metabolic Pathways Are Interrelated and Regulated

Go to Activity 9.6

- The catabolic pathways for the breakdown of carbohydrates, fats, and proteins feed into the energy-harvesting metabolic pathways.

- Anabolic pathways use intermediate components of the energy-harvesting pathways to synthesize fats, amino acids, and glucose.

- The rates of glycolysis and the citric acid cycle are controlled by allosteric regulation and by the diversion of excess acetyl CoA into fatty acid synthesis.

Questions

1. Before a race, some runners eat peanut butter, which contains abundant protein. How does protein provide energy?

2. Most biochemical pathways can operate essentially in both directions, and also can operate with increased or decreased rates. How does this regulation occur? Give an example.

Figure 9.18

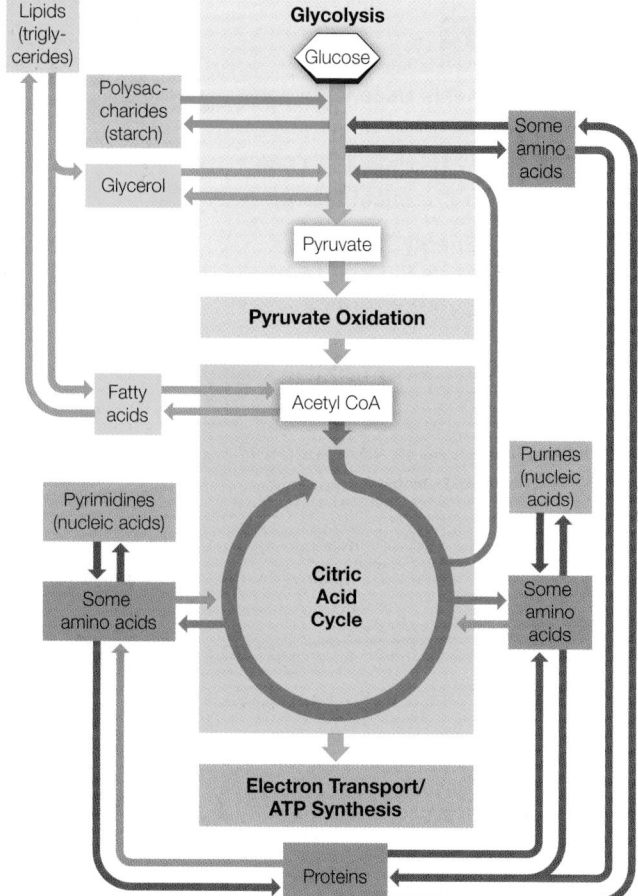

Go to **Achieve** for the eBook, **LearningCurve**, animations, activities, simulations, and additional resources and assignments.

10 Photosynthesis: Energy from Sunlight

KEY CONCEPTS

Michigan Technological University/US DOE

Photosynthesis and Rising CO_2 Experiments with pipes emitting CO_2 around crop plants are designed to predict the effects of rising atmospheric CO_2 on photosynthesis and crop productivity.

▶Investigating**LIFE**

Saving FACE

As human societies have become increasingly industrialized and dependent on energy to fuel vehicles, power plants, and factories, more and more fossil fuels have been combusted. As you know from Chapter 9, the combustion of hydrocarbons is exergonic, releasing not only energy but also CO_2. Because CO_2 is a "greenhouse gas" that traps heat in the atmosphere, the rising CO_2 level is already beginning to result in global climate change. However, the increased amount of CO_2 released has not all stayed in the atmosphere. About half of it has been absorbed by Earth's biological and chemical systems. To try to find out what is absorbing all this CO_2, a NASA satellite called the Orbiting Carbon Observatory is measuring not only the changing CO_2 in the air at various places but also the presence of the green plant pigment chlorophyll.

As you may know, green plants use the pigment chlorophyll in photosynthesis, which has the general equation

$$\text{CO}_2 + \text{H}_2\text{O} \xrightarrow{\text{Sunlight}} \text{carbohydrates} + \text{O}_2$$

Measurements by the orbiting satellite, as well as calculations from an interdisciplinary group of scientists called the Global Carbon Project, have found a significant role for green plant photosynthesis in reducing the effects of rising CO_2. Plants absorb

CO_2 in photosynthesis, but they also release it in cellular respiration (see Chapter 9):

$$\text{Carbohydrates} + \text{O}_2 \rightarrow \text{CO}_2 + \text{H}_2\text{O} + \text{energy}$$

The balance at present is tipped in favor of photosynthesis, and in an overall sense, plants absorb about half of the CO_2 emitted into the air by human activities. How this happens and how long it will last are key questions for biologists.

To begin to answer these questions, scientists developed a way to expose plants to high levels of CO_2 in the field. *Free-air concentration enrichment* (FACE) uses rings of pipes to release CO_2 into the air surrounding plants in fields or forests. Wind speed and direction are monitored by a computer, which constantly controls which pipes release CO_2. These experiments confirm that photosynthetic rates increase as the concentration of CO_2 rises, and indicate that as atmospheric CO_2 rises globally, there will be an increase in photosynthesis, and this may be reflected in more plant growth.

 What is the chemistry of photosynthesis, and how will it be affected by rising atmospheric CO_2?
(Find the answer on page 213.)

KEY CONCEPT 10.1 Photosynthesis Uses Light to Make Carbohydrates

Learning Objectives

10.1.1 Use experimental evidence to explain the source of the O_2 produced in oxygenic photosynthesis.

10.1.2 Describe the relationship between the light reactions and the carbon-fixation reactions of photosynthesis.

Catabolism—the breakdown of complex molecules into simpler units—is the reverse of anabolism—the construction of complex molecules from simpler units. Chapter 9 described several energy-releasing catabolic pathways. The energy stored in chemical bonds in almost all organisms (with the exception of those living near deep-sea vents) ultimately comes from the Sun. **Photosynthesis** (literally, "synthesis from light") is an anabolic process by which the energy of sunlight is captured and used to convert carbon dioxide (CO_2) into more complex carbon-containing compounds. Organism that carry out photosynthesis are **autotrophs** ("self-feeders"), able to use only water and CO_2 to essentially make their own "food"—carbohydrates—which can then be used directly or converted into other types of molecules for anabolic and catabolic processes. Autotrophs include plants, algae, and cyanobacteria. Other organisms, including animals, fungi, and most other bacteria, are **heterotrophs** ("other-feeders") that must consume other organisms, such as autotrophs or other heterotrophs, to obtain molecules for their activities.

Photosynthesis involves light and gas exchange

Plants, algae, and cyanobacteria live in aerobic environments and carry out oxygenic photosynthesis: the conversion of CO_2 and water (H_2O) into carbohydrates (which we will represent as a six-carbon sugar, $C_6H_{12}O_6$) and oxygen gas (O_2) (**Figure 10.1**).

$$6\ CO_2 + 6\ H_2O \rightarrow C_6H_{12}O_6 + 6\ O_2 \qquad (10.1)$$

Equation 10.1 describes an endergonic reaction. From experiments such as the ones described in the chapter-opening story using FACE, the role of CO_2 is well established. But while the equation is essentially correct, it is too general for a real understanding of the processes involved. Several questions arise: What are the precise chemical reactions of photosynthesis? What role does light play in these reactions? How do carbons become linked to form carbohydrates? What carbohydrates are formed? And does the oxygen gas come from CO_2 or H_2O?

Experiments with isotopes show that O_2 comes from H_2O in oxygenic photosynthesis

In 1941, Samuel Ruben and Martin Kamen at the University of California, Berkeley performed experiments using the isotopes ¹⁸O and ¹⁶O to identify the source of the O_2 produced during photosynthesis (**Investigating Life: What Is the Chemistry of Photosynthesis, and How Will Increasing CO_2 in the Atmosphere Affect It?**). Their results showed that all the oxygen gas produced during

Figure 10.1 The Ingredients for Photosynthesis A green plant uses light from the Sun, water from the soil, and carbon dioxide from the atmosphere to form organic compounds by photosynthesis.

photosynthesis comes from water, as is reflected in the revised balanced equation:

$$6\ CO_2 + 12\ H_2O \rightarrow C_6H_{12}O_6 + 6\ O_2 + 6\ H_2O \qquad (10.2)$$

Water appears on both sides of the equation because it is both used as a reactant (the 12 molecules on the left) and released as a product (the 6 new molecules on the right). This revised equation accounts for all the water molecules needed for all the oxygen gas produced.

The realization that water was the source of photosynthetic O_2 led to an understanding of photosynthesis in terms of oxidation and reduction. As you learned in Key Concept 9.1, oxidation–reduction (redox) reactions are coupled: when one molecule becomes oxidized in a reaction, another gets reduced. In this case, oxygen atoms in the reduced state in H_2O get oxidized to O_2:

$$12\ H_2O \rightarrow 24\ H^+ + 24\ e^- + 6\ O_2 \qquad (10.3)$$

while carbon atoms in the oxidized state in CO_2 get reduced to carbohydrate, with the simultaneous production of water:

$$6\ CO_2 + 24\ H^+ + 24\ e^- \rightarrow C_6H_{12}O_6 + 6\ H_2O \qquad (10.4)$$

Adding Equations 10.3 and 10.4 (chemistry students will recognize them as half-cell reactions) gives the overall Equation 10.2 shown earlier.

As just described, water is the donor of protons and electrons in oxygenic photosynthesis. Some bacteria live in anaerobic

▶InvestigatingLIFE   What Is the Chemistry of Photosynthesis, and How Will Increasing CO_2 in the Atmosphere Affect It?

Experiment

Original Paper: S. M. Ruben et al. 1941. Heavy oxygen (^{18}O) as a tracer in the study of photosynthesis. *J Am Chem Soc* 63: 877–879.

Understanding the chemical reactions of photosynthesis is key to understanding the effects of increasing atmospheric CO_2. In particular, the source of O_2 was not known. Two possibilities were the reactants, CO_2 and H_2O. In two separate experiments, Samuel Ruben and Martin Kamen labeled the oxygen in these molecules with the isotope ^{18}O, then tested the O_2 produced by a green plant to find out which molecules contributed the oxygen.

HYPOTHESIS▶ The oxygen released by photosynthesis comes from water rather than CO_2.

METHOD▶

Experiment 1

Give plants isotope-labeled water and unlabeled CO_2.

$H_2{}^{18}O$, CO_2

Experiment 2

H_2O, $C^{18}O_2$

Give plants isotope-labeled CO_2 and unlabeled water.

RESULTS▶

The oxygen released is labeled.

$^{18}O_2$

O_2

The oxygen released is unlabeled.

CONCLUSION▶ Water is the source of the oxygen atoms in the O_2 produced by photosynthesis.

Work with the Data

In the 1930s, Cornelius van Niel, then a graduate student at Stanford University, was the first to propose that the oxygen released during photosynthesis is not actually derived from carbon dioxide, but rather from the water molecules consumed in the reaction. This hypothesis was formed on the basis of the discovery that the anaerobic purple sulfur bacteria do not release oxygen during photosynthesis. Instead, these organisms convert hydrogen sulfide (H_2S) into elemental sulfur in their photosynthetic pathway (see Equation 10.5). This hypothesis was later confirmed by the experiment outlined above, which employed the "heavy" isotope of oxygen, ^{18}O, to trace the flow of oxygen in plants.

As part of the expanding research on radioisotopes during World War II, the U.S. government set up a radiation laboratory at the University of California, Berkeley. Out of this lab came key experiments that described the light-dependent and carbon-fixation pathways of photosynthesis. In this set of experiments, *Chlorella* algal cells

were exposed to water and CO_2, the latter coming from potassium carbonate (K_2CO_3) and potassium bicarbonate ($KHCO_3$), which dissolve in water to form CO_2. In Experiment 1, water had a higher isotope ratio of $^{18}O/^{16}O$ than CO_2; and in Experiment 2, CO_2 had a higher isotope ratio than water. A mass spectrometer was used to measure the isotope contents of the reactants and the O_2 produced, and the data were presented as the isotope ratio ($^{18}O/^{16}O$). These data are shown in the table.

QUESTIONS▶

1. In Experiment 1, was the isotope ratio of O_2 similar to that of H_2O or to that of CO_2? What about in Experiment 2?

2. What can you conclude from these data?

 View in Achieve
Animation 10.1 The Source of the Oxygen Produced by Photosynthesis

	Time before start of O_2 collection (min)	Time at end of O_2 collection (min)	$^{18}O/^{16}O$ (proportion ^{18}O in compound)		
			H_2O	$HCO_3^- + CO_3^{2-}$ (CO_2 sources)	O_2
Experiment 1: 0.09 M $KHCO_3$ + 0.09 M K_2CO_3 (^{18}O in H_2O)	0		0.85	0.20	
	45	110	0.85	0.41	0.84
	110	223	0.85	0.55	0.85
	225	350	0.85	0.61	0.86
Experiment 2: 0.14 M $KHCO_3$ + 0.06 M K_2CO_3 (^{18}O in CO_2)	0		0.20		
	40	110	0.20	0.50	0.20
	110	185	0.20	0.40	0.20

Source: S. M. Ruben et al. 1941. *J Am Chem Soc* 63: 877–879. Adapted with permission. © 1941 American Chemical Society.

Go to **Achieve** for a companion Data in Depth exercise.

environments and carry out non-oxygenic photosynthesis. In these cases, other molecules are used as electron donors in the reduction of CO_2 to carbohydrates. For example, purple sulfur bacteria use hydrogen sulfide (H_2S) as the electron donor:

$$12 \, H_2S + 6 \, CO_2 + \text{light} \rightarrow C_6H_{12}O_6 + 6 \, H_2O + 12 \, S \quad (10.5)$$

Green sulfur bacteria use sulfide ions, hydrogen, or ferrous iron as electron donors, whereas another group of bacteria uses compounds derived from arsenic. The remainder of this chapter will focus on oxygenic photosynthesis, which produces the vast majority of the organic carbon used by life on Earth today and replenishes the O_2 in our atmosphere.

Photosynthesis involves two pathways

Equation 10.2 summarized the overall process of photosynthesis, but not the steps by which it happens. **Figure 10.2** shows two related pathways (you will find similarities with the pathways involved in the catabolism of glucose described in Chapter 8):

1. The **light reactions** convert light energy into chemical energy in the form of ATP and the reduced electron carrier

Figure 10.2 An Overview of Photosynthesis Photosynthesis consists of two pathways: the light reactions and the carbon-fixation reactions. These reactions take place in the thylakoids and the stroma ("bed") of chloroplasts, respectively. See Figure 5.14 for more on the structure of chloroplasts.

Q: In the cell, where does the reduction of CO_2 occur, and what is the reducing agent?

NADPH. This molecule is similar to the coenzyme NADH (see Key Concept 9.1) but with an additional phosphate group attached to the sugar of its adenosine. In general, NADPH acts as a reducing agent in photosynthesis and other anabolic reactions.

2. The **carbon-fixation reactions** (also called light-independent reactions) do not use light directly, but instead use ATP, NADPH (made by the light reactions), and CO_2 to produce carbohydrate.

These pathways take place in chloroplasts, compartmentalized in different parts of the organelle (see Figure 10.2). As we describe these two series of reactions in more detail, you will see that they conform to the principles of biochemistry that we discussed in Chapters 8 and 9: energy transformations, oxidation–reduction, and the stepwise nature of biochemical pathways.

KEY CONCEPT
10.1 Recap and Assess

The light reactions of photosynthesis convert light energy into chemical energy. The carbon-fixation reactions use that chemical energy to reduce CO_2 to carbohydrates. While most photosynthetic organisms use water as the electron donor for reduction of CO_2, some use other molecules, such as hydrogen sulfide (H_2S).

1. What is the relationship between the light reactions and the carbon-fixation reactions of photosynthesis?

2. What is the experimental evidence that water is the source of the O_2 produced during photosynthesis?

We will describe the light reactions and the carbon-fixation reactions separately. We'll begin the next key concept by discussing the physical nature of light and the specific photosynthetic molecules that capture its energy.

KEY CONCEPT
10.2 Photosynthesis Converts Light Energy into Chemical Energy

Learning Objectives

10.2.1 Describe the transfer of energy within the reaction center of a light-harvesting complex.

10.2.2 Compare and contrast a pigment's absorption spectrum and its action spectrum.

10.2.3 Explain how ATP and NADPH are produced in a chloroplast.

Light is a form of energy, and it can be converted to other forms of energy such as heat or chemical energy. Our focus here is on light as the source of energy to drive the formation of ATP (from ADP and P_i) and NADPH (from $NADP^+$ and H^+).

Light energy is absorbed by pigments in photosynthesis

It is helpful here to discuss light in terms of its photochemistry and photobiology.

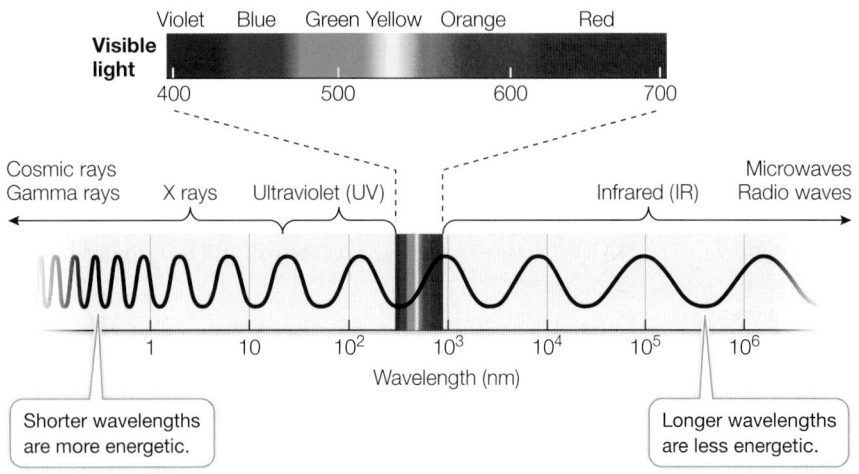

Figure 10.3 **The Electromagnetic Spectrum** The portion of the electromagnetic spectrum that is visible to humans (385–740 nm) is shown in detail at the top. (After S. Giannakis et al. 2016. *Appl Catal B*: *Environ* 199: 199–223.)

PHOTOCHEMISTRY Light is a form of **electromagnetic radiation**. Electromagnetic radiation is said to have a dual nature. Although it is propagated in waves, it also has particle-like behaviors. Particles of light can be described as packets of energy called **photons**, which have no mass. The amount of energy in electromagnetic radiation is inversely proportional to its **wavelength**—the shorter the wavelength, the greater the energy. The visible portion of the electromagnetic spectrum (**Figure 10.3**) encompasses a wide range of wavelengths and energy levels. In plants and other photosynthetic organisms, receptive molecules absorb photons and thereby harvest their energy for biological processes. These receptive molecules absorb only specific wavelengths of light—photons with specific amounts of energy.

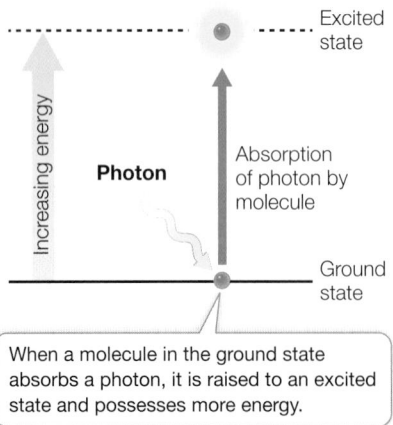

Figure 10.4 **Light and Chemical Energy** When light is absorbed by a molecule, it is raised to a higher energy level, as electrons are further away from the nucleus.

Q: In a compact fluorescent lightbulb, electric current is absorbed first by mercury vapor, which emits energy that is then absorbed by fluorescent coating, which emits light. What is the flow of energy in this system?

When a photon meets a molecule, one of three things can happen:

1. The photon may bounce off the molecule—it may be scattered or reflected.
2. The photon may pass through the molecule—it may be transmitted.
3. The photon may be absorbed by the molecule, adding energy to the molecule.

Neither of the first two outcomes causes any change in the molecule. However, in the case of absorption, the photon disappears and its energy is absorbed by the molecule. The photon's energy cannot disappear, because according to the first law of thermodynamics, energy is neither created nor destroyed. When the molecule acquires the energy of the photon, it is raised from a ground state (with lower energy) to an excited state, with higher energy (**Figure 10.4**). The difference in free energy between the molecule's excited state and its ground state is approximately equal to the free energy of the absorbed photon (a small amount of energy is lost to entropy, according to the second law of thermodynamics). The increase in energy boosts one of the electrons in the molecule into a shell farther from its nucleus; this electron is now held less firmly, making the molecule unstable and more chemically reactive.

Connect the Concepts As discussed in Key Concept 2.1, the electrons orbiting an atom are distributed in a series of electron shells, or energy levels, around the nucleus. The farther an electron is from the nucleus, the higher its energy level.

PHOTOBIOLOGY The specific wavelengths absorbed by a particular molecule are characteristic of that type of molecule. Molecules that absorb wavelengths in the visible spectrum are called **pigments**.

When a beam of white light (containing all the wavelengths of visible light) falls on a pigment, certain wavelengths are absorbed. The remaining wavelengths are scattered or transmitted and make the pigment appear to us as colored. For example, the pigment **chlorophyll** absorbs both blue and red light, and we see the remaining light, which is primarily green. If we plot light absorbed by a purified pigment against wavelength, the result is an **absorption spectrum** for that pigment.

In contrast to an absorption spectrum, an **action spectrum** is a plot of the rate of a biological activity carried out by an organism against the wavelengths of light to which it is exposed. An action spectrum for photosynthesis can be determined as follows:

1. Place the organism in a closed container.
2. Expose it to light of a certain wavelength for a period of time.
3. Measure the rate of photosynthesis by the amount of O_2 released.
4. Repeat with light of other wavelengths.

Figure 10.5 shows the absorption spectra of pigments in *Anacharis*, a common aquarium plant, and the action spectrum for photosynthesis by that plant. The two spectra can be compared to see which pigments in *Anacharis* contribute most to light harvesting

(A) The absorption spectra of *Anacharis*

(B) The action spectrum for *Anacharis*

Figure 10.5 **Absorption and Action Spectra**   **(A)** The three common photosynthetic pigments in plants have characteristic absorption spectra. These pigments are from the common aquarium plant *Anacharis*. **(B)** The peaks in the action spectrum for photosynthesis of *Anacharis* correspond to the peaks in the absorption spectrum of chlorophyll *a*.

Q: Phycobilins are pigments that absorb yellow light. These pigments can transfer their absorbed energy to chlorophyll. How does this occur, thermodynamically?

for photosynthesis. Looking at the graphs, you can see that the best wavelengths for photosynthesis in the action spectrum correspond to the wavelengths at which chlorophyll *a* absorbs the most light. This molecule has a complex ring structure (**Figure 10.6**), similar to that of the heme group of hemoglobin, with a magnesium ion at the center. A long hydrocarbon "tail" anchors the chlorophyll *a* molecule to a complex of proteins that span the thylakoid membrane. In addition to chlorophyll *a*, there are other hydrophobic pigments such as chlorophyll *b*, carotenoids, and phycobilins. The entire complex is, not surprisingly, called a **photosystem**.

Light absorption results in photochemical change

The pigment molecules in a photosystem are arranged in a specific orientation adjacent to one another. These are called **light-harvesting complexes**, or antenna systems. Their name gives away what they do: they absorb light, converting light energy into chemical energy. When a pigment molecule absorbs light, it enters an excited state (see Figure 10.4). This is an unstable situation, and the molecule rapidly returns to its ground state, releasing most of

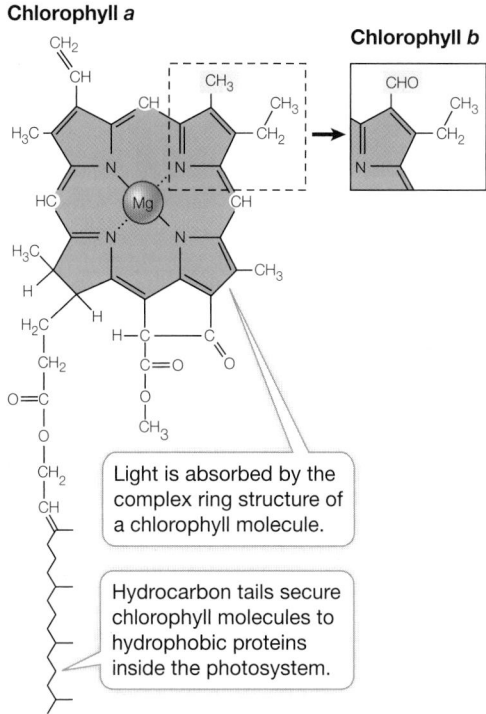

Figure 10.6 **Chlorophyll**   Chlorophyll consists of a complex ring structure (green) and a hydrocarbon tail that anchors it in the hydrophobic region of a membrane in the chloroplast thylakoid.

the absorbed energy. So rapid is this process that it is measured in picoseconds (trillionths of a second). Within the antenna systems of a photosystem, the energy released by a pigment molecule (for example, chlorophyll *b*) is absorbed by other, adjacent pigment molecules. The energy (not as electrons but in the form of chemical energy called resonance) is passed from molecule to molecule until it reaches a chlorophyll *a* molecule at the **reaction center** of the photosystem (**Figure 10.7**).

Before getting to what happens at the reaction center, let's pause and look at what happens with all the antenna pigments around it. Chlorophyll absorbs blue and red light, which are near the two ends of the visible spectrum (see Figure 10.3). The various accessory pigments absorb light in other parts of the spectrum and thus function to broaden the range of wavelengths that can be used for photosynthesis. You can see this in the action spectrum in Figure 10.5B: *Anacharis* is able to photosynthesize at wavelengths of light that chlorophyll *a* doesn't absorb but that other pigments absorb (e.g., 500 nanometers [nm]). Different photosynthetic organisms have different combinations of accessory pigments. Higher plants and green algae have chlorophyll *b* (with a structure and absorption spectrum very similar to that of chlorophyll *a*) and carotenoids such as β-carotene, which absorb photons in the blue and blue-green wavelengths. Phycobilins, which are found in red algae and cyanobacteria, absorb various yellow-green, yellow, and orange wavelengths.

Back to the reaction center: A ground-state chlorophyll *a* molecule (Chl) absorbs the energy from the adjacent chlorophylls and becomes excited (Chl*), but to return to the ground state this chlorophyll does not pass the energy to another pigment

Figure 10.7 Energy Transfer and Electron Transport Chlorophylls and carotenoids are embedded in membrane proteins to form light-harvesting complexes that, combined with other molecules such as electron carriers, form a photosystem. A pigment molecule absorbs a light photon and the energy is transferred in multiple steps to a reaction center chlorophyll a molecule. The excited chlorophyll a transfers its energy to an electron, converting it to chemical-bond energy, which is used to reduce an electron acceptor.

molecule—something very different occurs. *The reaction center converts the absorbed light energy into chemical energy* (see Figure 10.7). The chlorophyll molecule in the reaction center absorbs sufficient energy that it actually *gives up its excited electron to a chemical acceptor*:

$$Chl^* + acceptor \rightarrow Chl^+ + acceptor^- \qquad (10.6)$$

This, then, is the first consequence of light absorption by chlorophyll: *the reaction center chlorophyll (Chl*) loses its excited electron in a redox reaction and becomes Chl⁺.* As a result of this transfer of an electron, the chlorophyll gets oxidized, while the acceptor molecule gets reduced.

Reduction leads to ATP and NADPH formation

The electron acceptor that is reduced by Chl* is the first in a chain of electron carriers in the thylakoid membrane. Electrons are passed from one carrier to another in an energetically "downhill" series of reductions and oxidations. The final electron acceptor is $NADP^+$, which gets reduced:

$$NADP^+ + H^+ + 2\,e^- \rightarrow NADPH \qquad (10.7)$$

As in mitochondria, ATP is produced chemiosmotically in the thylakoid membrane during the process of photophosphorylation, which we will illustrate shortly. The overall process involves two electron transport processes, noncylic and cylic. The **noncyclic electron transport** reactions that use the energy from light to generate ATP and NADPH are illustrated in **Figure 10.8**.

Figure 10.8 Noncyclic Electron Transport Uses Two Photosystems Absorption of light energy by chlorophyll molecules in the reaction centers of photosystems I and II allows them to pass electrons into a series of redox reactions.

Q: An herbicide can act as an electron acceptor, becoming reduced by ferredoxin (Fd). What effect would this have on a plant?

Connect the Concepts The thylakoid membrane has an electron transport system similar to the respiratory chain of mitochondria (see Key Concept 9.3).

Two coordinated photosystems, each with its own reaction center, collaborate to produce ATP and NADPH. Each photosystem is associated with its own group of integral proteins embedded in the thylakoid membrane. To give you an idea of the complexity needed to carry out this function so vital to life on our planet, here is what photosystem II is made up of: 20 proteins + 50 chlorophyll *a* (only 2 are in the reaction center; the rest are in light-harvesting complexes) + 6 carotenoid molecules (light-harvesting complexes) + 2 plastoquinine molecules.

Let's look in more detail at what happens in these photosystems, beginning with photosystem II.

PHOTOSYSTEM II   Photosystem II has "P_{680}" chlorophylls at its reaction center—so named because they absorb light maximally at 680 nm. After an excited chlorophyll in the reaction center (Chl*) gives up its energetic electron to reduce a chemical acceptor molecule, the chlorophyll lacks an electron and is very unstable. It has a strong tendency to obtain an electron from another molecule to replace the one it lost—in chemical terms, it is a strong oxidizing agent. The replenishing electrons come from water, splitting the H—O—H bonds:

$$H_2O \rightarrow \tfrac{1}{2} O_2 + 2\,H^+ + 2\,e^- \qquad (10.8)$$

$$2\,e^- + 2\,Chl^+ \rightarrow 2\,Chl \qquad (10.9)$$

$$\text{Overall: } 2\,Chl^+ + H_2O \rightarrow 2\,Chl + 2\,H^+ + \tfrac{1}{2} O_2 \quad (10.10)$$

Notice that the source of O_2 in photosynthesis is H_2O (as demonstrated in Investigating Life: What Is the Chemistry of Photosynthesis, and How Will Increasing CO_2 in the Atmosphere Affect It?).

Back to the electron acceptor in the electron transport system: The energetic electrons are passed through a series of membrane-bound carriers to a final acceptor at a lower energy level. As in the mitochondrion, a proton gradient is generated and is used by ATP synthase to make ATP (see the next section).

PHOTOSYSTEM I   In photosystem I, which has "P_{700}" chlorophylls at its reaction center, an excited electron from the Chl* at the reaction center reduces an acceptor. The oxidized chlorophyll (Chl$^+$) now obtains an electron, but in this case the electron comes from the last carrier in the electron transport system. This links the two photosystems chemically. They are also linked spatially, with the two photosystems adjacent to one another in the thylakoid membrane. The energetic electrons from photosystem I pass through several molecules and end up reducing NADP$^+$ to NADPH.

Next in the process of harvesting light energy to produce carbohydrates is the series of carbon-fixation reactions. These reactions require more ATP than NADPH. If the pathway we just described—the linear or noncyclic pathway—were the only set of light reactions operating, there might not be sufficient ATP for carbon fixation. **Cyclic electron transport** makes up for this

1 The Chl* in the reaction center of photosystem I passes electrons to an electron carrier, ferredoxin (Fd), leaving positively charged chlorophyll (Chl$^+$).

2 The carriers of the electron transport system are in turn reduced.

Photosystem I

Fd

Electron transport

Energy of molecules

ATP

ADP + P_i

P_{700}

3 Energy from electron flow is captured for chemiosmotic synthesis of ATP.

4 The last reduced electron carrier passes electrons to electron-deficient chlorophyll, allowing the reactions to start again.

Figure 10.9 Cyclic Electron Transport Traps Light Energy as ATP

imbalance. This pathway uses photosystem I and the electron transport system to produce ATP but not NADPH; it is cyclic because an electron is passed from an excited chlorophyll and recycles back to the same chlorophyll (**Figure 10.9**).

Chemiosmosis is the source of the ATP produced in photophosphorylation

In Chapter 9 you learned about the chemiosmotic mechanism for ATP formation in the mitochondrion. A similar mechanism, called **photophosphorylation**, operates in the chloroplast, where electron transport is coupled to the transport of protons (H$^+$) across the thylakoid membrane, resulting in a proton gradient across the membrane (**Figure 10.10**).

The electron carriers in the thylakoid membrane are oriented so that protons are transferred from the stroma into the lumen of the thylakoid. Thus the lumen becomes more acidic (higher concentration of protons) compared with the stroma, resulting in an electrochemical gradient across the thylakoid membrane, whose bilayer is not permeable to H$^+$. Water oxidation creates more H$^+$ in the thylakoid lumen, and NADP$^+$ reduction removes H$^+$ in the stroma. Both reactions contribute to the H$^+$ gradient. The high concentration of H$^+$ in the thylakoid space drives the movement of H$^+$ back into the stroma through protein channels

Figure 10.10 Photophosphorylation   In the thylakoid membrane, electrons are passed from photosystem II to photosystem I via a series of electron carriers, including plastoquinone (PQ), cytochrome (Cyt), and plastocyanin (PC). From photosystem I the electrons are passed to ferredoxin (Fd) and then to NADP⁺ reductase. This process results in a proton gradient across the membrane, which drives ATP synthesis. Compare this illustration with Figure 9.13, where a similar process is depicted in mitochondria.

Q: An herbicide binds to plastoquinone and blocks electron transport in photosystem II. How does this kill a plant?

▶ **View in Achieve**
Animation 10.2 Photophosphorylation

▶ **Media Clip 10.1 Photosynthesis at Work**
Life12e.com/mc10.1

in the membrane. These channels are also enzymes—ATP synthases—that couple the movement of protons to the formation of ATP, as they do in mitochondria (see Figure 9.13). Indeed, the amino acid sequence of chloroplast ATP synthase is about 60% identical to that of human mitochondrial ATP synthase—a remarkable similarity, given that plants and animals had their most recent common ancestor more than a billion years ago. This is testimony to the evolutionary unity of life.

The mechanisms of the two enzymes are similar, but their orientations differ. In chloroplasts, protons flow through the ATP synthase out of the thylakoid lumen into the stroma (where the ATP is synthesized). In mitochondria, the protons flow out of the intermembrane space into the mitochondrial matrix.

KEY CONCEPT

10.2 Recap and Assess

Conversion of light energy into chemical energy occurs when photons are absorbed by chlorophylls and accessory pigments in the light-harvesting complex within the chloroplast. Light energy is used to drive a series of protein-associated redox reactions in the thylakoid membranes of the chloroplast. In the process of photophosphorylation, two linked photosystems establish a proton gradient across the membrane that drives ATP synthesis.

1. How can a pigment molecule lose the energy of an absorbed photon?

2. What is the difference between an absorption spectrum and an action spectrum?

3. How does cyclic electron transport in photosystem I result in the production of ATP?

You have seen how light energy drives the synthesis of ATP and NADPH in the stroma of chloroplasts. We will now turn to the carbon-fixation reactions of photosynthesis, which use energy-rich ATP and NADPH to reduce CO_2 and form carbohydrates.

KEY CONCEPT 10.3 Chemical Energy Trapped in Photosynthesis Is Used to Synthesize Carbohydrates

Learning Objectives

10.3.1 Describe the experiment that led to identification of the steps in the Calvin cycle.

10.3.2 Explain how light reactions stimulate the Calvin cycle.

Most of the enzymes that catalyze the reactions of CO_2 fixation are in the stroma of the chloroplast, where those reactions take place. These enzymes use the energy in ATP and NADPH, produced in the light reactions, to reduce CO_2 to carbohydrates. Therefore, with some exceptions, CO_2 fixation occurs only in the light.

Experiments elucidated the pathway of carbon fixation

To identify the reactions by which the carbon from CO_2 ends up in carbohydrates, scientists found a way to label CO_2 so they could isolate and identify the compounds formed from it during photosynthesis. In the 1950s, Melvin Calvin, Andrew Benson, and their colleagues used radioactively labeled CO_2 in which some of the carbon atoms were the radioisotope ^{14}C rather than the normal ^{12}C. They were able to trace the chemical pathway of CO_2 fixation (**Figure 10.11**). The first molecule that appeared in the pathway was a three-carbon sugar phosphate called 3-phosphoglycerate (3PG) (the ^{14}C is shown in red):

3-Phosphoglycerate (3PG)

Using successively longer exposures to $^{14}CO_2$, Calvin and his colleagues were able to trace the route of ^{14}C as it moved through a series of compounds, including monosaccharides and amino acids. It turned out the ^{14}C moved through a cyclical pathway. In this cycle, the CO_2 initially bonds covalently to a five-carbon acceptor molecule. The resulting six-carbon intermediate quickly breaks into two three-carbon molecules. As the cycle repeats, a carbohydrate is produced and the initial CO_2 acceptor is regenerated. This pathway was appropriately named the **Calvin cycle**.

The initial reaction in the Calvin cycle adds the one-carbon CO_2 to the five-carbon acceptor molecule ribulose 1,5-bisphosphate (RuBP). The product is an intermediate six-carbon compound, which quickly breaks down and forms two molecules of

Experiment

Figure 10.11A Tracing the Pathway of CO_2

Original Papers: Calvin and his colleagues described their experiments in a series of 26 papers titled "The Path of Carbon in Photosynthesis." Perhaps the most important was one that showed how labeled CO_2 could be used a tracer:

A. A. Benson et al. 1950. The path of carbon in photosynthesis. V. Paper chromatography and radioautography of the products. *J Am Chem Soc* 72: 1710–1718.

How is CO_2 incorporated into carbohydrate during photosynthesis? What is the first stable covalent linkage that forms with the carbon of CO_2? Melvin Calvin and his colleagues used short exposures to $^{14}CO_2$ to identify the first compound formed from CO_2.

HYPOTHESIS▶ The first product of CO_2 fixation is a three-carbon molecule.

METHOD▶

RESULTS▶

A chromatogram made after 3 seconds of exposure to $^{14}CO_2$ shows ^{14}C only in 3PG (3-phosphoglycerate).

A chromatogram made after 30 seconds of exposure to $^{14}CO_2$ shows ^{14}C in many molecules.

CONCLUSION▶ The initial product of CO_2 fixation is 3PG. Later, the carbon from CO_2 ends up in many molecules.

Figure 10.11B Work with the Data follows on next page.

Figure 10.11B Tracing the Pathway of CO_2

To elucidate the sequence of reactions that allow the carbon fixation, suspensions of the green alga *Chlorella* were exposed to $^{14}CO_2$ (see Figure 10.11A). After 3 seconds of photosynthesis, the ^{14}C from $^{14}CO_2$ was found only in 3-phosphoglycerate (3PG), but after 30 seconds many compounds were radioactive. These results could be expanded to determine the exact sequence of reactions and reaction intermediates in the Calvin cycle by exposing the cells to $^{14}CO_2$ for various periods of time.

The first reaction in CO_2 fixation can occur in the dark. To show this, *Chlorella* cells were exposed to $^{14}CO_2$ under bright lights for 20 minutes and the cells were harvested. The experiment was then repeated, but following the 20 minutes of light with varying periods of darkness (30 sec, 2 min, and 5 min). The cells were harvested and chromatograms were made to identify the labeled compounds, and a radioactivity detector was used to quantify the amount of ^{14}C in each compound. Typical data for such experiments are shown in the table.

Compound	Relative amount of radioactivity after:			
	20 min light	20 min light + 30 sec dark	20 min light + 2 min dark	20 min light + 5 min dark
3PG	6,200	12,500	12,100	6,100
RuBP	5,500	660	2,100	2,060
Sucrose	15,600	16,100	16,900	16,100

QUESTIONS▶

1. Plot radioactivity in 3PG versus time. What do the data show?

2. Why did the amount of radioactively labeled RuBP decline after 30 seconds in the dark?

 View in Achieve
Animation 10.3 Tracing the Pathway of CO_2

Go to **Achieve** for a companion Data in Depth exercise.

The Calvin cycle is made up of three processes

The Calvin cycle uses the ATP and NADPH made in the light to reduce CO_2 in the stroma to a carbohydrate. As in all biochemical pathways, each reaction is catalyzed by a specific enzyme. The cycle is composed of three distinct processes (**Figure 10.13**):

1. *Fixation* of CO_2. As we have seen, this reaction is catalyzed by rubisco, and its stable product is 3PG.

2. *Reduction* of 3PG to form glyceraldehyde 3-phosphate (G3P). This series of reactions involves a phosphorylation (using the ATP made in the light reactions) and a reduction (coupled to the oxidation of NADPH made in the light reactions).

3. *Regeneration* of the CO_2 acceptor, RuBP. Most of the G3P ends up as ribulose monophosphate (RuMP), and ATP is used to convert this compound into RuBP. So for every "turn" of the cycle, one CO_2 is fixed and one CO_2 acceptor is regenerated.

The product of this cycle is **glyceraldehyde 3-phosphate (G3P)**, which is a three-carbon sugar phosphate, also called triose phosphate:

$$
\begin{array}{c}
H \\
| \\
C = O \\
| \\
H - C - OH \\
| \\
H - C - O - \text{(P)} \\
| \\
H
\end{array}
$$

Glyceraldehyde 3-phosphate (G3P)

In a typical leaf, five-sixths of the G3P is recycled into RuBP. There are two fates for the remaining G3P, depending on the time of day and the needs of different parts of the plant:

1. Some of the G3P is *exported out of the chloroplast* to the cytoplasm, where it is converted to hexoses (glucose and fructose). These molecules may be used in glycolysis and mitochondrial respiration to power the activities of photosynthetic cells (see Chapter 9) or they may be converted into the disaccharide sucrose, which is transported out of the leaf to other organs in the plant. There the sucrose is hydrolyzed to its constituent

3PG (**Figure 10.12**). The intermediate compound is broken down so rapidly that Calvin did not observe radioactive carbon appearing in it first. The enzyme that catalyzes the reaction of CO_2 with RuBP, **ribulose bisphosphate carboxylase/oxygenase (rubisco)**, is the most abundant protein in the world! It constitutes up to 50% of all the protein in every plant leaf.

Figure 10.12 RuBP Is the Carbon Dioxide Acceptor In carbon fixation catalyzed by rubisco, CO_2 is added to a five-carbon compound, RuBP. The resulting six-carbon compound immediately splits into two molecules of 3PG.

The fate of the carbon atom in CO_2 is followed in red.

The enzyme rubisco catalyzes the reaction of CO_2 with RuBP.

The reaction intermediate splits into two molecules of 3-phosphoglycerate (3PG).

$$
CO_2 +
\begin{array}{c}
CH_2O\,\text{(P)} \\
| \\
C = O \\
| \\
H - C - OH \\
| \\
H - C - OH \\
| \\
CH_2O\,\text{(P)}
\end{array}
\xrightarrow{\textbf{Rubisco}}
\begin{array}{c}
C \\
| \\
\text{©} - C \\
| \\
C \\
| \\
C
\end{array}
\longrightarrow
\begin{array}{c}
CH_2O\,\text{(P)} \\
| \\
HO - C - H \\
| \\
\text{©}OO^-
\end{array}
+
\begin{array}{c}
COO^- \\
| \\
H - C - OH \\
| \\
CH_2O\,\text{(P)}
\end{array}
$$

Carbon dioxide

Ribulose 1,5-bisphosphate (RuBP)

Six-carbon skeleton of reaction intermediate

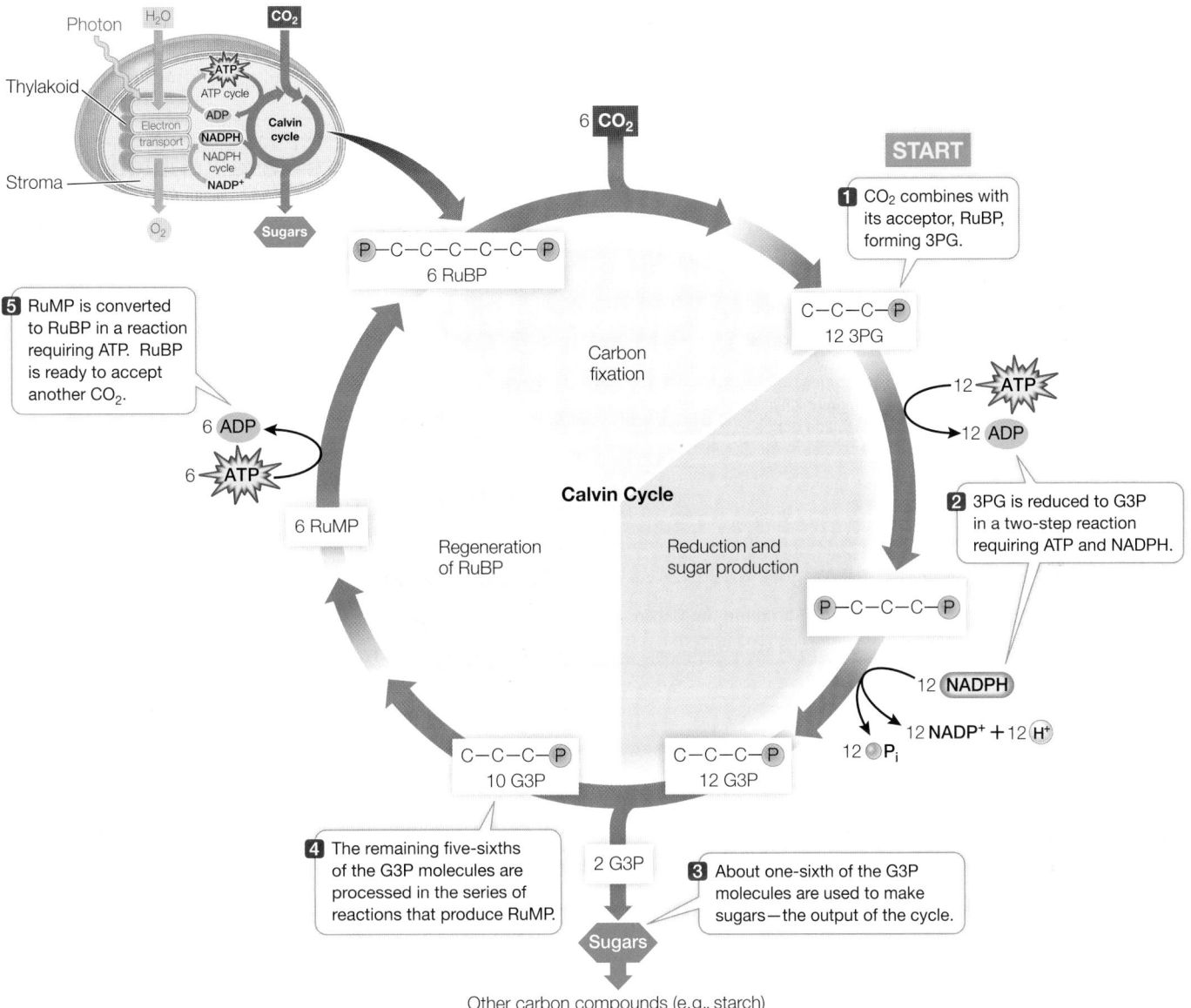

Figure 10.13 The Calvin Cycle   The Calvin cycle uses the ATP and NADPH generated in the light reactions and CO_2 to produce carbohydrate. Six turns of the cycle produce the equivalent of one molecule of glucose, a hexose sugar.

View in Achieve
Activity 10.1 The Calvin Cycle

monosaccharides, which can be used as sources of energy or as building blocks for other molecules.

2. Some of the G3P is used to *synthesize glucose* inside the chloroplast. As the day wears on, glucose molecules accumulate and are linked together to form the polysaccharide starch. This stored carbohydrate can then be drawn on during the night so that the photosynthetic tissues can continue to export sucrose to the rest of the plant, even when photosynthesis is not taking place. In addition, starch is abundant in nonphotosynthetic organs such as roots, underground stems, and seeds, where it provides glucose to fuel cellular activities, including plant growth.

The plant uses the carbohydrates produced in photosynthesis to make other molecules, including amino acids, lipids, and the building blocks of nucleic acids—in fact, all the organic molecules in the plant.

Light stimulates the Calvin cycle

As you have seen, the Calvin cycle uses NADPH and ATP, which are generated using energy from light. Two other processes connect the light reactions with this CO_2 fixation pathway. Both connections are indirect but significant:

1. *Light-induced pH changes in the stroma activate some Calvin cycle enzymes.* Proton transfer from the stroma into the thylakoid lumen causes an increase in the pH of the stroma

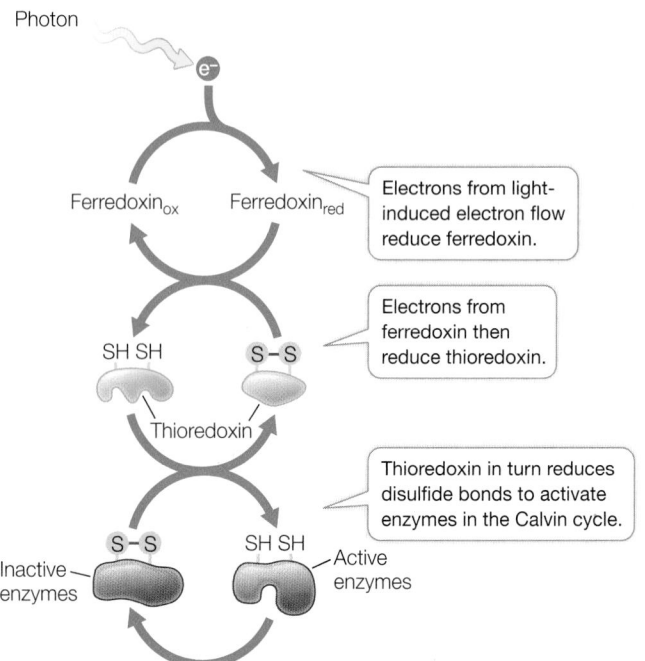

Figure 10.14 The Photochemical Reactions Stimulate the Calvin Cycle By reducing (breaking) disulfide bridges, electrons from the light reactions activate enzymes in CO_2 fixation.

from 7 to 8 (a tenfold decrease in H^+ concentration) that favors the activation of rubisco.

2. *Light-induced electron transport reduces disulfide bridges in four of the Calvin cycle enzymes, thereby activating them* (**Figure 10.14**). When ferredoxin is reduced in photosystem I (see Figure 10.8), it passes some electrons to a small, soluble protein called thioredoxin, and this protein passes electrons to four enzymes in the CO_2 fixation pathway. Reduction of the sulfurs in the disulfide bridges of these enzymes (see Figure 3.6) forms —SH groups and breaks the bridges. The resulting changes in their three-dimensional shapes activate the enzymes and increase the rate at which the Calvin cycle operates.

KEY CONCEPT
10.3 Recap and Assess

ATP and NADPH produced in the light reactions power the synthesis of carbohydrates by the Calvin cycle. This cycle fixes CO_2, reduces it, and regenerates the acceptor, RuBP, for further fixation.

1. What experiments led to the identification of 3PG as the initial product of carbon fixation?
2. In what ways does light stimulate the Calvin cycle?
3. Both photosynthetic electron transport and the Calvin cycle stop in the dark. Which specific reaction stops first? Which stops next? Continue answering the question "Which stops next?" until you have explained why both pathways have stopped.

Although all green plants carry out the Calvin cycle, some plants have evolved variations on, or additional steps in, the carbon-fixation reactions. These variations and additions have permitted plants to adapt to and thrive in certain environmental conditions. Let's look at these environmental limitations and the metabolic bypasses that have evolved to circumvent them.

KEY CONCEPT

10.4 Plants Have Adapted Photosynthesis to Environmental Conditions

Learning Objectives

10.4.1 Explain how and why C_4 plants maintain a high concentration of CO_2 around rubisco.

10.4.2 Explain how CAM plants carry out carbon fixation separately from Calvin cycle reactions.

In addition to fixing CO_2 during photosynthesis, rubisco can also react with O_2. This reaction, which leads to a process called photorespiration, lowers the overall rate of CO_2 fixation in some plants. After examining this problem, we'll look at some biochemical pathways and features of plant anatomy that compensate for the limitations of rubisco.

Photorespiration reduces overall CO_2 fixation

Rubisco is the key enzyme for life on Earth. Yet it is inefficient. Most enzymes catalyze hundreds to thousands of reactions per second (see Key Concept 8.3); rubisco catalyzes about three conversions of CO_2 per second. To satisfy the huge need for this reaction, plants make a lot of rubisco. Indeed, it constitutes up to half of the protein molecules in every leaf and is the single most abundant protein on Earth. Also, in addition to having binding sites for ribulose-1,5-bisphosphate and CO_2, there is a binding site on the enzyme for O_2. So rubisco is an **oxygenase** as well as a **carboxylase**:

- Rubisco is a carboxylase when it adds CO_2 to RuBP.
- Rubisco is an oxygenase when it adds O_2 to RuBP.

It is not clear why rubisco has oxygenase activity. One hypothesis is that since there was little or no O_2 in the ancient atmosphere when rubisco first appeared (see Key Concept 4.2), the active site did not need to be specific for CO_2. That means that the oxygenase activity is an evolutionary relic with no current role. In any case, binding of O_2 and catalysis result in the formation of a poison, phosphoglycolate:

$$RuBP + O_2 \rightarrow \text{phosphoglycolate} + \text{3-phosphoglycerate (3PG)} \quad (10.11)$$

The 3PG can enter the Calvin cycle. But phosphoglycolate, a two-carbon molecule, cannot—and moreover is an inhibitor of reactions in the Calvin cycle. So the plant cell has a pathway to get rid of phosphoglycolate and recover its carbons for entry into the Calvin cycle. Unfortunately, while the elimination of phosphoglycolate is efficient, recovery of the carbons is not and some is lost as CO_2. The phosphoglycolate is hydrolyzed to glycolate, which diffuses into peroxisomes (**Figure 10.15**). There, a series of reactions converts it into the amino acid glycine:

$$\text{Glycolate} + O_2 \rightarrow \text{glycine} \quad (10.12)$$

(A) The organelles of photorespiration

1 In the chloroplast stroma, RuBP reacts with O_2. Glycolate is formed.

2 Glycolate diffuses into a peroxisome, where it is converted to glycine.

Chloroplast

Peroxisome

3 Glycine moves to the mitochondrion and is converted to serine, releasing CO_2.

Mitochondrion

5 Glycerate moves to the chloroplast, where it is converted to 3PG and enters the Calvin cycle.

4 Serine moves back to the peroxisome and is converted to glycerate.

(B) Two catalytic activites of rubisco

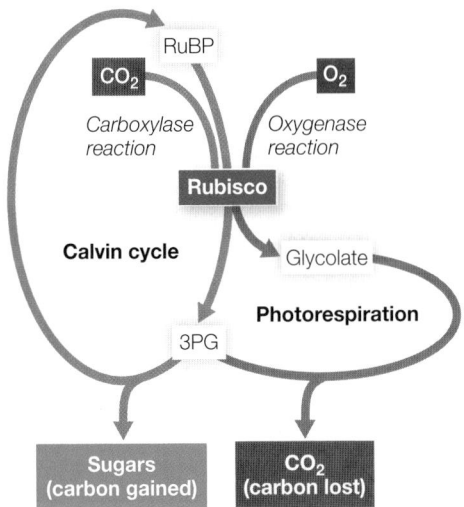

RuBP

CO_2 O_2

Carboxylase reaction   *Oxygenase reaction*

Rubisco

Calvin cycle   Glycolate

3PG   **Photorespiration**

Sugars (carbon gained)   **CO_2 (carbon lost)**

Figure 10.15 The Photorespiration Pathway   **(A)** The reactions of photorespiration take place in the chloroplasts, peroxisomes, and mitochondria. **(B)** Overall, photorespiration consumes O_2 and releases CO_2.

Q: Why is photorespiration considered a wasteful process in terms of plant growth?

Media Clip 10.2 Chloroplasts in Close-Up
Life12e.com/mc10.2

The glycine then diffuses into a mitochondrion, where two glycine molecules are converted in a series of reactions into the amino acid serine, releasing CO_2:

$$2 \text{ Glycine} \rightarrow \text{serine} + CO_2 \qquad (10.13)$$

The serine moves into the peroxisome, where it is converted to glycerate. The glycerate then moves into the chloroplast, where it is phosphorylated to make 3PG, which enters the Calvin cycle.

Note that it takes two phosphoglycolate molecules from Equation 10.11 to produce the two glycines used in Equation 10.13. So overall:

$$2 \text{ Phosphoglycolate (4 carbons)} + O_2 \rightarrow$$
$$3PG \text{ (3 carbons)} + CO_2 \qquad (10.14)$$

This pathway thus reclaims 75% of the carbons from phosphoglycolate for the Calvin cycle. In other words, the reaction of RuBP with O_2 instead of CO_2 *reduces the net carbon fixed by the Calvin cycle by 25%.*

What determines whether rubisco acts as an oxygenase or a carboxylase? In today's atmosphere the concentration of O_2 is 21% and that of CO_2 is 0.04%. You would think that if there were an "even competition" between CO_2 and O_2 for rubisco that O_2, with its higher concentration, would be favored. But such is not the case. It turns out that the affinity (binding) of rubisco for CO_2 is much stronger than it is for O_2, so in normal air inside a leaf, CO_2 fixation is favored even though the concentration of CO_2 in the air is far lower than that of O_2. It is when there is an even higher concentration of O_2 in the leaf relative to outside that O_2 competes with the CO_2, and rubisco combines RuBP with O_2 rather than with CO_2. This oxygenase activity reduces the overall amount of CO_2 that can be converted into carbohydrates, and may play a role in limiting plant growth.

- Relatively low O_2 and high CO_2 concentrations within the leaf favor carboxylase activity.

- Relatively high O_2 and low CO_2 concentrations within the leaf favor oxygenase activity.

Under what conditions inside the leaf does the air have higher O_2 and lower CO_2, favoring the oxygenase activity? On a hot, dry day, small pores in the leaf surface called **stomata** close to prevent water from evaporating from the leaf (see Figure 10.1). But stomata closure also prevents gases from entering and leaving the leaf. If stomata are closed, the CO_2 concentration in the leaf falls as CO_2 is used up in photosynthetic reactions, and the O_2 concentration rises because of these same reactions where water is used to form O_2 (see Investigating Life: What Is the Chemistry of Photosynthesis, and How Will Increasing CO_2 in the Atmosphere Affect It?). As the ratio of CO_2 to O_2 falls, the oxygenase activity of rubisco is favored. The pathway is called **photorespiration** because it consumes O_2 and releases CO_2 and because it occurs only in the light (mediated by the same enzyme activation processes that we mentioned earlier with regard to the Calvin cycle).

C_3 plants undergo photorespiration but C_4 plants do not

Plants differ in how they fix CO_2, and can be distinguished as C_3 or C_4 plants, based on whether the first product of CO_2 fixation is a three- or four-carbon molecule. In **C_3 plants** such as roses, wheat, and rice, the first product is the three-carbon molecule 3PG—as we have just described for the Calvin cycle. In these plants the cells of the mesophyll, which makes up the main body of the leaf, are full of chloroplasts containing rubisco (**Figure 10.16A**). On a hot day, these leaves close their stomata to conserve water, and as a result, rubisco acts as an oxygenase as well as a carboxylase, and photorespiration occurs.

(A) Arrangement of cells in a C$_3$ leaf

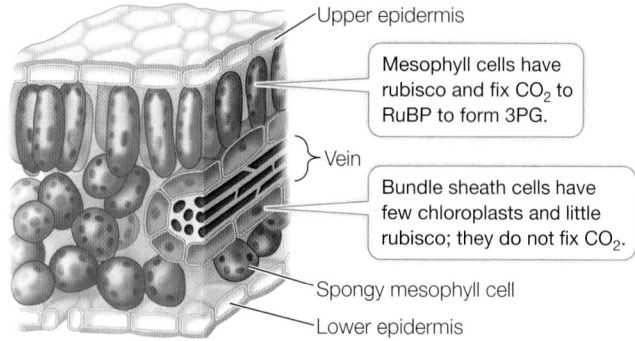

Upper epidermis

Mesophyll cells have rubisco and fix CO$_2$ to RuBP to form 3PG.

Vein

Bundle sheath cells have few chloroplasts and little rubisco; they do not fix CO$_2$.

Spongy mesophyll cell

Lower epidermis

(B) Arrangement of cells in a C$_4$ leaf

Mesophyll cells have the enzyme PEP carboxylase, which catalyzes the reaction of CO$_2$ and PEP to form the 4-carbon molecule oxaloacetate, which is converted to malate.

Bundle sheath cells have modified chloroplasts that concentrate CO$_2$ around rubisco.

Close proximity permits CO$_2$ "pumping" from mesophyll cells to bundle sheath cells.

Figure 10.16 Leaf Anatomy of C$_3$ and C$_4$ Plants   Carbon dioxide fixation occurs in different organelles and cells of the leaves in C$_3$ plants **(A)** and C$_4$ plants **(B)**. Cells that are tinted blue have rubisco.

 View in Achieve
Activity 10.2 **C$_3$ and C$_4$ Leaf Anatomy**

C$_4$ plants—8,000 species that include corn, sugarcane, and tropical grasses—make the four-carbon molecule **oxaloacetate** as the first product of CO$_2$ fixation (**Figure 10.16B**). On a hot day, they partially close their stomata to conserve water, but their rate of photosynthesis does not fall. What do they do differently?

C$_4$ plants have evolved a mechanism that increases the concentration of CO$_2$ around the rubisco enzyme while at the same time isolating the rubisco from atmospheric O$_2$. Thus in these plants the carboxylase reaction is favored over the oxygenase reaction; the Calvin cycle operates, but photorespiration does not occur. This mechanism involves the initial fixation of CO$_2$ in the mesophyll cells and then the transfer of the fixed carbon (as a four-carbon molecule) to the **bundle sheath cells**, where the fixed CO$_2$ is released for use in the Calvin cycle (**Figure 10.17A**). The bundle sheath cells are located in the interior of the leaf where less atmospheric O$_2$ can reach them than reaches cells near the surface of the leaf.

The first enzyme in the C$_4$ carbon fixation process, called **PEP carboxylase**, is present in the cytosol of mesophyll cells near the

(A) Carbon fixation by C$_4$ plants

Mesophyll cell

Cell membrane

Cell wall

CO$_2$

PEP

Carboxylation (carbon fixation)

C$_4$ cycle

ADP

ATP

Regeneration

1 Regeneration of the acceptor molecule requires energy from the hydrolysis of ATP.

4C compound   3C compound

Plasmodesmata

Bundle sheath cell

4C compound   3C compound

Decarboxylation

CO$_2$

2 Release of CO$_2$ maintains a locally high concentration, reducing photorespiration.

5C sugar   Carboxylation

Regeneration   **Calvin cycle**

Triose P   3C sugar

Reduction

(B) Carbon fixation by CAM plants

Sun   **Day**   **Night**

CO$_2$

CO$_2$

Calvin cycle

PEP

3C compound

4C compound

4C compound

4C compound   4C compound

Vacuole

Mesophyll cell

Figure 10.17 Adaptations for Efficiency in Photosynthesis   C$_4$ and CAM plants have different adaptations for fixing CO$_2$. 3C, 4C, and 5C indicate the number of carbon atoms in compounds. **(A)** In C$_4$ plants, CO$_2$ is fixed initially in the mesophyll cells but enters the Calvin cycle in the bundle sheath cells. **(B)** In CAM plants, CO$_2$ is initially fixed at night and then enters the Calvin cycle during the day. (B after Sabine Deviche, © Arizona Board of Regents/ASU Ask A Biologist; CC BY-SA 3.0. https://askabiologist. asu.edu/cam-plants)

Q: What is the major difference between C$_4$ plants and CAM plants in terms of CO$_2$ fixation and the Calvin cycle?

leaf's surface. This enzyme combines CO_2 with a three-carbon acceptor compound, **phosphoenolpyruvate** (**PEP**), to produce the four-carbon fixation product, oxaloacetate. PEP carboxylase has two advantages over rubisco:

1. It does not have oxygenase activity.

2. It fixes CO_2 even at very low CO_2 levels.

So even on a hot day when the stomata are partially closed and the ratio of O_2 to CO_2 rises, PEP carboxylase just keeps on fixing CO_2.

Oxaloacetate is converted to malate, which diffuses out of the mesophyll cells and into the bundle sheath cells (see Figure 10.16B). (Some C_4 plants convert the oxaloacetate to aspartate instead of malate, but we discuss only the malate pathway here.) The bundle sheath cells contain modified chloroplasts that are designed to concentrate CO_2 around the rubisco. There, the four-carbon malate loses one carbon (is decarboxylated), forming CO_2 and pyruvate. The latter moves back to the mesophyll cells where the three-carbon acceptor compound, PEP, is regenerated at the expense of ATP. So the "expenditure" of ATP in the mesophyll cell "pumps up" the CO_2 concentration around rubisco in the bundle sheath cell, ensuring that rubisco will function as a carboxylase and begin the Calvin cycle.

Under relatively cool or cloudy conditions, C_3 plants have an advantage over C_4 plants in that they don't expend energy to "pump up" the concentration of CO_2 near rubisco. But this advantage begins to be outweighed under conditions that favor photorespiration, such as warmer seasons and climates. Under these conditions C_4 plants have the advantage, especially if there is ample light to supply the extra ATP required for C_4 photosynthesis. For example, Kentucky bluegrass is a C_3 plant that thrives on lawns in April and May. But in the heat of summer it does not do as well, and Bermuda grass, a C_4 plant, takes over the lawn. The same is true on a global scale for crops: C_3 plants such as soybean, wheat, and barley have been adapted for human food production in temperate climates, whereas C_4 plants such as corn and sugarcane originated and are still grown in the tropics.

THE EVOLUTION OF CO_2 FIXATION PATHWAYS C_3 plants are more ancient than C_4 plants. Whereas C_3 photosynthesis appears to have begun about 2.5 billion years ago, C_4 plants appeared about 12 million years ago. A possible factor in the emergence of the C_4 pathway is the decline in atmospheric CO_2. When dinosaurs dominated Earth 100 million years ago, the concentration of CO_2 in the atmosphere was four times what it is now. As CO_2 levels declined thereafter, the C_4 plants would have gained an advantage over their C_3 counterparts in high-temperature, high-light environments.

CAM plants also use PEP carboxylase

Other plants besides the C_4 plants use PEP carboxylase to fix and accumulate CO_2. They include some water-storing plants (succulents) of the family Crassulaceae, many cacti, pineapples, and several other kinds of flowering plants. The CO_2 metabolism of these plants is called **crassulacean acid metabolism**, or **CAM**, after the family of succulents in which it was discovered. CAM is much like the metabolism of C_4 plants in that CO_2 is initially fixed into a four-carbon compound (**Figure 10.17B**). But in CAM plants the initial CO_2 fixation and the Calvin cycle are *separated in time rather than space*:

• At night, when it is cooler and water loss is minimized, the stomata open. CO_2 is fixed in mesophyll cells to form the four-carbon compound oxaloacetate, which is converted into malate and stored in the vacuole.

• During the day, when the stomata close to reduce water loss, the accumulated malate is shipped from the vacuole to the chloroplasts, where its decarboxylation supplies the CO_2 for the Calvin cycle, and the light reactions supply the necessary ATP and NADPH.

Table 10.1 compares photosynthesis in C_3, C_4, and CAM plants.

KEY CONCEPT
10.4 Recap and Assess

Rubisco catalyzes the carboxylation of RuBP to form two 3PGs, and the oxygenation of RuBP to form one 3PG and one phosphoglycolate. The diversion of rubisco to its oxygenase function decreases net CO_2 fixation. C_4 photosynthesis and CAM allow plants to fix CO_2 under warm, dry conditions when stomata are closed and CO_2 entry into the leaf is limited.

1. How do C_4 plants keep the concentration of CO_2 around rubisco high, and why?

2. Describe CAM plants and explain how they can temporally segregate CO_2 fixation from the Calvin cycle.

TABLE 10.1 | **Comparison of Photosynthesis in C_3, C_4, and CAM Plants**

	C_3 plants		C_4 plants		CAM plants	
Calvin cycle used?	Yes		Yes		Yes	
Primary CO_2 acceptor	RuBP		PEP		PEP	
Primary CO_2-fixing enzyme	Rubisco		PEP carboxylase		PEP carboxylase	
First product of CO_2 fixation	3PG (3-carbon)		Oxaloacetate (4-carbon)		Oxaloacetate (4-carbon)	
Affinity of primary fixing enzyme for CO_2	Moderate		High		High	
Photosynthetic cells of leaf	Mesophyll		Mesophyll and bundle sheath		Mesophyll with large vacuoles	
Photorespiration	Extensive		Minimal		Minimal	

© iStock.com/deIshana   © iStock.com/Gingima   © iStock.com/Dan Eckert

Now that you understand how photosynthesis produces carbohydrates, let's see how the pathways of photosynthesis are connected to other metabolic pathways.

KEY CONCEPT 10.5   Photosynthesis Is an Integral Part of Plant Metabolism

Learning Objectives

10.5.1 Identify the metabolic intermediates that link photosynthesis to other metabolic pathways.

10.5.2 Explain the efficiency of energy flow as it moves from the environment through living organisms on Earth.

Green plants are autotrophs and can synthesize all the molecules they need from simple starting materials: CO_2, H_2O, phosphate, sulfate, ammonium ions (NH_4^+), and small quantities of other mineral nutrients. Plants use the carbohydrates generated in photosynthesis to provide energy for processes such as active transport and anabolism. Both cellular respiration and fermentation can occur in plants, although the former is far more common. Unlike photosynthesis, plant cellular respiration occurs all the time in both the light and the dark.

Photosynthesis interacts with other metabolic pathways

Photosynthesis and respiration are closely linked through the Calvin cycle (**Figure 10.18**). The partitioning of G3P, the product of the Calvin cycle, is particularly important:

- Some G3P from the Calvin cycle enters glycolysis and is converted into pyruvate in the cytosol. This pyruvate can be used in cellular respiration for energy, or its carbon skeletons can be used in anabolic reactions to make lipids, proteins, and other carbohydrates (see Figure 9.18).

- Some G3P can enter a pathway that is the reverse of glycolysis (gluconeogenesis; see Key Concept 9.5). In this case, hexose phosphates (hexose P) and then sucrose are formed and transported to the nonphotosynthetic tissues of the plant (such as the root).

Energy flows from sunlight to reduced carbon in photosynthesis, then to ATP in respiration. Energy can also be stored in the bonds of macromolecules such as polysaccharides, lipids, and proteins. For a plant to grow, energy storage (as body structures) must exceed energy release; that is, overall carbon fixation by photosynthesis must exceed respiration. This principle is the basis of the ecological food chain, as you will see in later chapters.

Connect the Concepts Chapter 56 describes the sequence of energy flow through a community, including food chains and food webs.

Photosynthesis provides most of the energy that we need for life. Given the uncertainties about the future of photosynthesis (because of changes in CO_2 levels and climate change), it would be wise to seek ways to improve the efficiency of photosynthesis. **Figure 10.19** shows the various ways in which solar energy is used by plants or lost. In essence, only about 5% of the sunlight that reaches Earth is converted into plant growth. The inefficiencies of photosynthesis involve basic chemistry and physics (some light

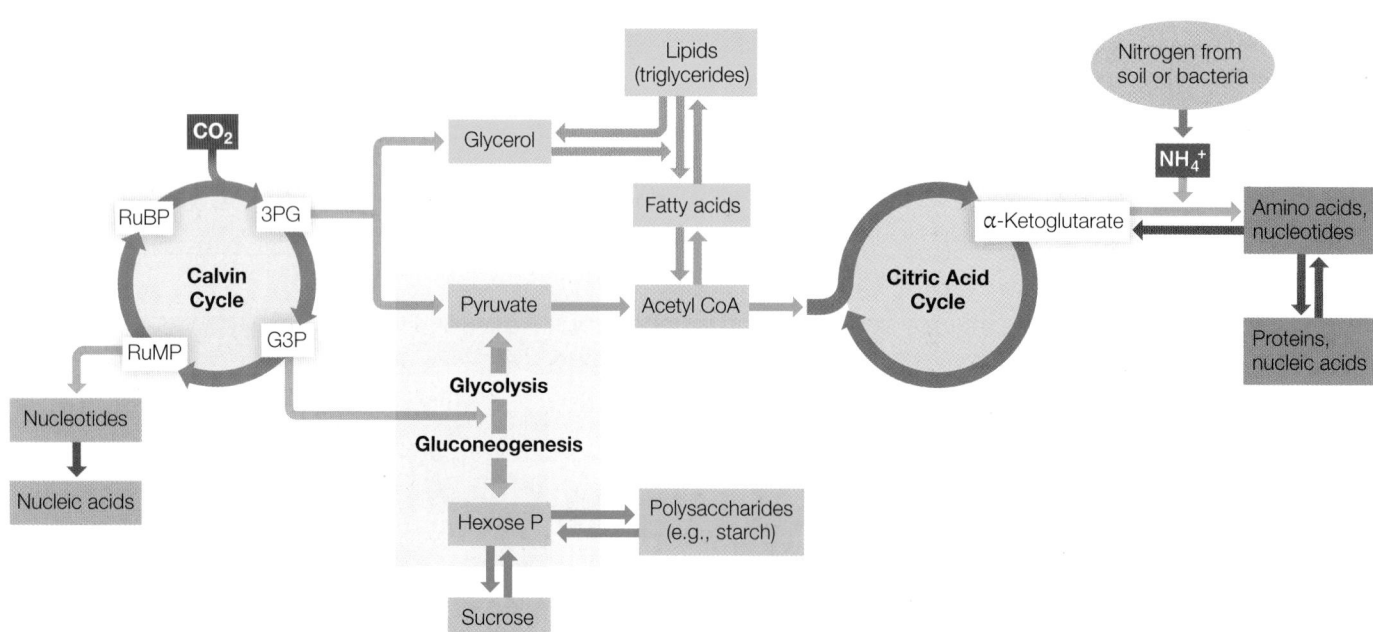

Figure 10.18 Metabolic Interactions in a Plant Cell   The products of the Calvin cycle are used in the reactions of cellular respiration (glycolysis and the citric acid cycle).

Q: What is the route of a carbon atom in CO_2 released in the air from the burning of fossil fuel by a gasoline-powered car to a protein in wheat bread?

100%
SUNLIGHT

ENERGY LOSS

50%

Wavelengths of light
not part of absorption
spectrum of photosynthetic
pigments (e.g., green light)

30%

Light energy not absorbed
due to plant structure
(e.g., leaves not properly
oriented to the Sun)

10%

Inefficiency of light
reactions converting
light to chemical-bond
energy

5%

Inefficiency of CO_2
fixation pathways

Wavelengths of light that
can be absorbed by
photosynthetic pigments,
and chemical-bond energy
available for CO_2 fixation.

5%
Chemical-bond
energy stored in
carbohydrates

© Aflo Foto Agency/Alamy Stock Photo

Figure 10.19 **Energy Losses in Photosynthesis**
Photosynthetic pathways preserve at most about 5% of the
Sun's energy input as chemical energy in carbohydrates.

energy is not absorbed by photosynthetic pigments) as well as
biology (plant anatomy and leaf exposure, the oxygenase reaction
of rubisco, and inefficiencies in metabolic pathways). While it is
hard to change chemistry and physics, biologists might be able
to use their knowledge of plants to improve on the basic biology
of photosynthesis. This could result in a more efficient use of
resources and better food production.

Connect the Concepts Plants have many anatomical and
physiological adaptations to improve the efficiency of photosynthesis.
See Chapter 37.

KEY CONCEPT
10.5 Recap and Assess

The products of photosynthesis are used in glycolysis and the citric acid cycle, as well as in the synthesis of lipids, proteins, and
other large molecules.

1. How do common intermediates link the pathways of glycolysis,
   the citric acid cycle, and photosynthesis?
2. Why is at most 5% of the solar radiation that reaches Earth
   converted to plant growth?

▶Investigating**LIFE**

Q and A **What is the chemistry of photosynthesis,
and how will it be affected by rising
atmospheric CO_2?**

The FACE experiments and other data point to several effects of
rising CO_2 on photosynthesis and plant biology. First, higher CO_2
levels generally lead to increased photosynthesis. This is especially true for C_3 plants such as wheat and rice, in which rubisco
is sensitive to the $CO_2:O_2$ ratio in the leaf. With more CO_2, this
ratio will favor the Calvin cycle and carbohydrate synthesis, as
opposed to the fixation of O_2, which results in photorespiration.
However, in the future this may be offset by climate change: the
rate of photorespiration increases with increased temperature,
so the greenhouse effect of CO_2 may counteract the photosynthetic effect. Second, increased photosynthesis results in more
root growth for the plants, which in turn improves their ability to
remove nitrogen and water from the soil. (You will learn more
about this in Chapter 35) This will stimulate plant growth in the
short term, but again, climate changes resulting in drought and
heat stress could counteract these beneficial effects. Third,
for unknown reasons, seeds and grains from plants grown in
elevated CO_2 have reduced contents of protein and iron. This
could have adverse effects on human nutrition.

Future directions

As the human population rises and land for farming is limited,
we are challenged to improve the productivity of crops. A significant increase in overall crop productivity would have global consequences. Increased atmospheric CO_2 will not have a great effect on C_4 plants. But the C_4 pathway accounts for about 25% of
all net carbon fixed. Some important species, such as corn, sorghum, and sugarcane, use the C_4 pathway, but the major grain
crops such as rice do not. An intensive research program is under way to understand the genetic control of the development of
the C_4 pathway, including not just the enzymes involved but also
how the distinctive leaf anatomy develops. This research may
lead to greater use of the C_4 pathway, and its related increase in
productivity in more plant species in a higher-CO_2 world.

You should be able to relate each summary to the adjacent figures. If you go to this visual summary in **Achieve**, you can follow links to figures, animations, activities, and simulations that will help you consolidate the material.

KEY CONCEPT

10.1 Photosynthesis Uses Light to Make Carbohydrates

Go to **Animation 10.1**

- In **photosynthesis**, the energy of sunlight is captured and used to convert CO_2 into more complex carbon-containing compounds.

- In the **light reactions**, light energy is converted into chemical-bond energy in the form of ATP and NADPH.

- In the **carbon-fixation reactions**, energy in ATP and NADPH is used to reduce CO_2, forming carbohydrates.

Questions

1. How is the chemical-bond energy different in ATP and NADPH?

2. The overall reaction of photosynthesis appears to be the reverse of the reactions of cellular respiration. Are they two sides of a reversible reaction?

Figure 10.2

KEY CONCEPT

10.2 Photosynthesis Converts Light Energy into Chemical Energy

Go to **Animation 10.2**

- Light is a form of **electromagnetic radiation**. It is emitted in particle-like packets called **photons** but has wavelike properties.

- Photosynthetic **pigments**, notably **chlorophylls** and **carotenoids**, embedded in chloroplast membrane proteins absorb light energy, which is transferred to a chlorophyll **reaction center** in a **photosystem**.

- Excited electrons in the reaction center are transferred to a molecule, reducing it.

- **Noncyclic electron transport** uses photosystems I and II to produce ATP, NADPH, and O_2. **Cyclic electron transport** uses only photosystem I and produces only ATP. Both systems generate ATP via the electron transport system.

Questions

1. If an electron acceptor was not present or able to be reduced in a photosystem, what would be the fate of the energy in excited chlorophyll after it absorbed light?

2. What is the difference between cyclic and noncyclic electron transport?

Figure 10.7

Figure 10.8

KEY CONCEPT
10.3 Chemical Energy Trapped in Photosynthesis Is Used to Synthesize Carbohydrates

Go to Activity 10.1 and Animation 10.3

- RuBP is the initial CO_2 acceptor, and 3PG is the first stable product of CO_2 fixation
- The **Calvin cycle** makes carbohydrates from CO_2. The cycle consists of three processes: fixation of CO_2, reduction and carbohydrate production, and regeneration of RuBP.

Questions

1. What are the roles of 3PG (3-phosphoglycerate) and G3P (glyceraldehyde 3-phosphate) in the carbon-fixation reactions of photosynthesis?

2. Is the carbon-fixation process of photosynthesis truly independent of light?

Figure 10.12

Carbon dioxide — Ribulose 1,5-bisphosphate (RuBP) — Six-carbon skeleton of reaction intermediate — 3-Phosphoglycerate

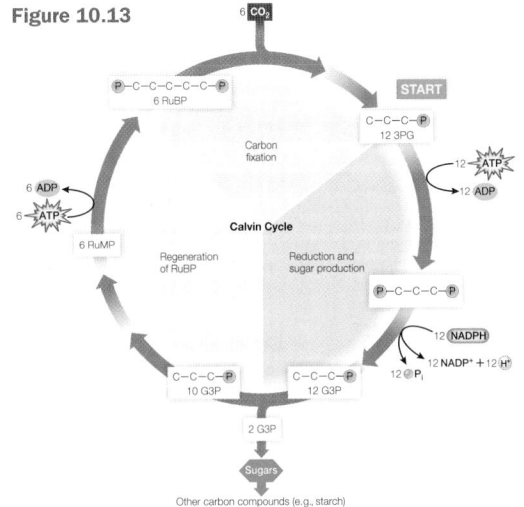

Figure 10.13

KEY CONCEPT
10.4 Plants Have Adapted Photosynthesis to Environmental Conditions

Go to Activity 10.2

- Rubisco can catalyze a reaction between O_2 and RuBP in addition to the reaction between CO_2 and RuBP. At high temperatures and low CO_2 concentrations, the **oxygenase** function of rubisco is favored over its **carboxylase** function.

- The oxygenase reaction is part of **photorespiration**, which reduces net carbon assimilation.

- In **C_4 plants**, CO_2 fixation is spatially separated from the Calvin cycle, whereas in **CAM** plants the processes are separated in time, with CO_2 fixation occurring during the night. Both processes increase photosynthetic efficiency.

Questions

1. In a hot, dry, environment, how are C_4 plants more productive in terms of carbon fixation than C_3 plants?

2. What are three major differences between the enzymes PEP carboxylase and rubisco?

Figure 10.15

Figure 10.17

KEY CONCEPT

10.5 Photosynthesis Is an Integral Part of Plant Metabolism

- Photosynthesis and cellular respiration are linked through the Calvin cycle, the citric acid cycle, and glycolysis.

- To survive, a plant must photosynthesize more than it respires.

- Photosynthesis uses only a small portion of the energy of sunlight.

Questions

1. What is the path of a carbon atom from the air inside a plant leaf to its release from the leaf into the atmosphere? Note the locations of the processes involved.

2. In a forest, trees grow as tall as possible, and leaves at the top spread out as a canopy. How is this advantageous for plant growth?

Figure 10.18

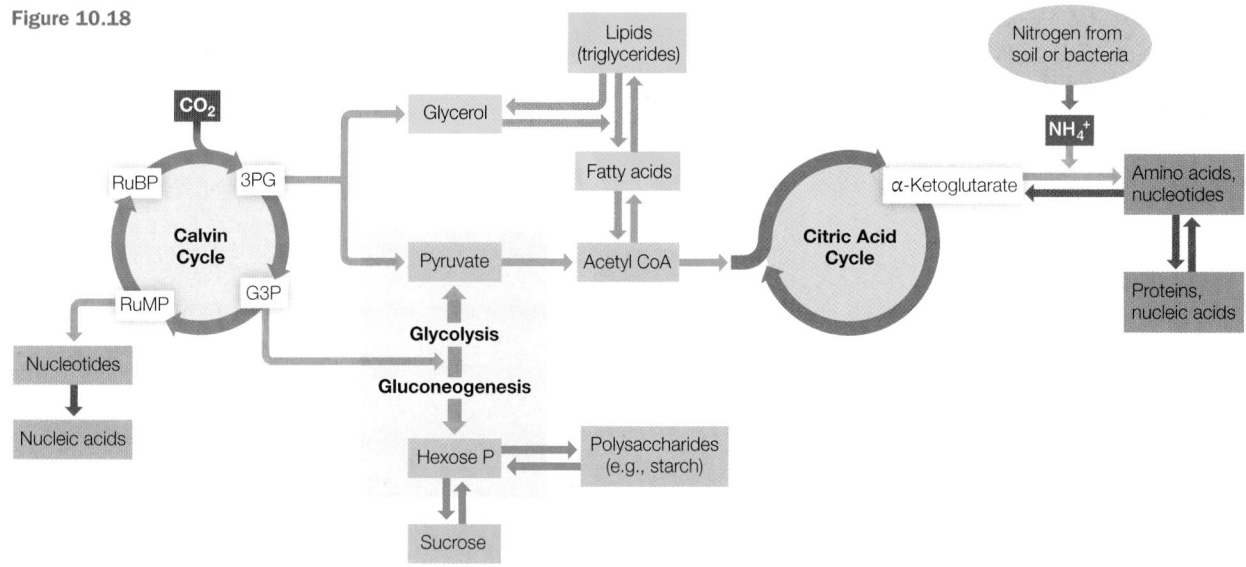

Go to **Achieve** for the eBook, **LearningCurve**, animations, activities, simulations, and additional resources and assignments.

The Cell Cycle and Cell Division 11

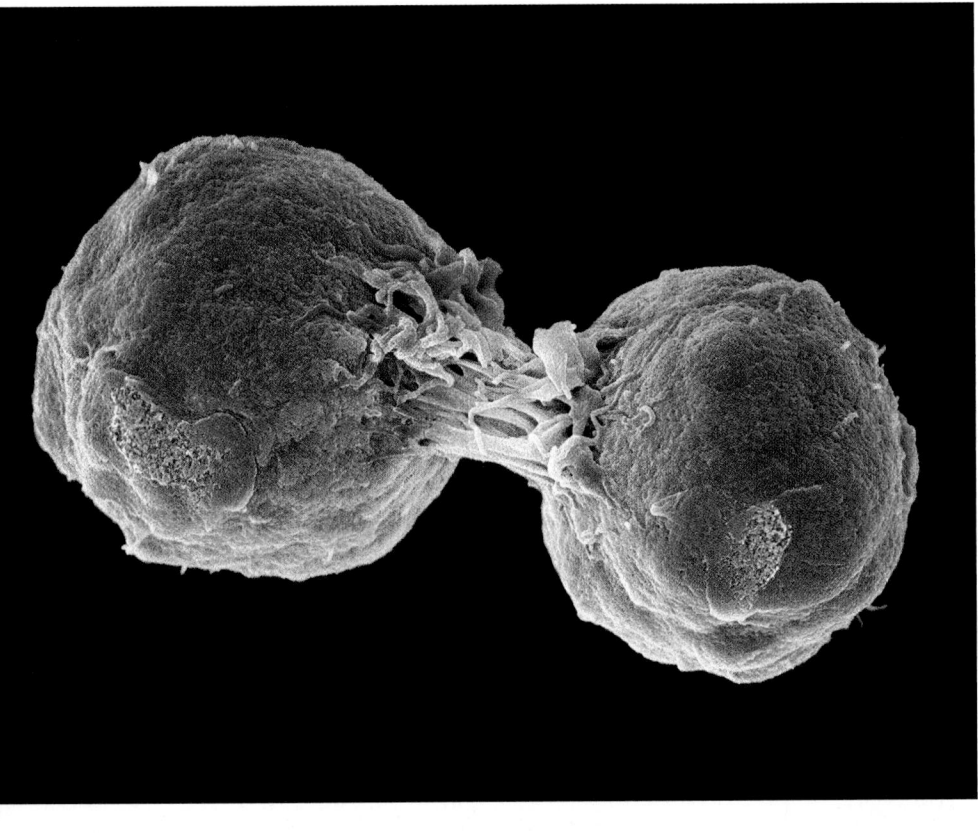

© Steve Gschmeissner/Science Source

KEY CONCEPTS

11.1 All Cells Derive from Other Cells

11.2 The Eukaryotic Cell Division Cycle Is Regulated

11.3 Eukaryotic Cells Divide by Mitosis

11.4 Cell Division Plays Important Roles in the Sexual Life Cycle

11.5 Meiosis Leads to the Formation of Gametes

11.6 Cell Death Is Important in Living Organisms

11.7 Unregulated Cell Division Can Lead to Cancer

Henrietta Lacks's tumor cells have far outlived her sad demise from cancer. They reproduce rapidly on the surface of a solid medium and have been grown in labs since her death in 1951.

▶Investigating LIFE

Immortal Cells

On January 29, 1951, 30-year-old Henrietta Lacks visited the nearby Johns Hopkins Hospital in Baltimore, Maryland, because she had been bleeding abnormally after the birth of her last child. The physician found the reason for the bleeding: a tumor the size of a quarter on her cervix. A piece of the tumor was sent to a pathologist in a clinical laboratory, who reported that the tumor was malignant.

A week later Ms. Lacks returned to the hospital, where physicians treated her tumor with radiation to try to kill it. But before the treatment began, they took a small sample of cells and sent them without her permission—a practice common then but not ethical today—to the research lab of George and Margaret Gey, two scientists at the hospital who had been trying for 20 years to coax human cells to live and multiply outside the body. If they could do so, they thought, they might find a cure for cancer. The Geys hit pay dirt with Lacks's cells; they grew and reproduced more vigorously than any cells they had ever seen and were given the name "HeLa cells." Unfortunately, they also grew fast in Lacks's body, and in a few months they had spread to almost all of her organs. Lacks died on October 4, 1951.

Because of their robust ability to reproduce, HeLa cells quickly became a staple of cell biology research. In controlled settings they could be infected with viruses, and they were instrumental in developing the supply of polioviruses that led to the first vaccine against that dread disease. HeLa cells have been used for important basic and applied research ever since, especially on the ways that human cells reproduce by cell division. Although Lacks had never been outside Virginia and Maryland, her cells have traveled all over the world and even into space on the space shuttle. Over the past 65 years, tens of thousands of research articles have been published using information obtained from Lacks's cells. You'll study one of them in this chapter.

Understanding the cell division cycle and its control is clearly an important subject for understanding cancer. But cell division is not just important in medicine. It underlies the growth, development, and reproduction of all organisms.

 What controls the reproduction of cancer cells?
(Find the answer on page 242.)

KEY CONCEPT 11.1 All Cells Derive from Other Cells

Learning Objectives

11.1.1 Describe the four events that characterize cell division.

11.1.2 Explain how replication and segregation co-occur during cell division in prokaryotes.

11.1.3 Explain how binary fission results in identical daughter cells.

11.1.4 State the two ways in which DNA replication differs in prokaryotes and eukaryotes.

The life cycle of an organism, from birth to death, is intimately linked to cell division. Cell division plays important roles in the development of an organism from a single cell, in the growth and repair of tissues in multicellular organisms, and in the reproduction of all organisms (Figure 11.1). Cell division in both prokaryotes and eukaryotes entails the following four events:

1. **Cell division signals**: One or more signals are required to initiate cell division. The signals may originate from either inside or outside the cell.

2. **DNA replication**: The dividing cell's genetic material (DNA) must be duplicated so that each of the two new cells will have a full complement of genetic information.

3. **DNA segregation**: The replicated DNA must be distributed appropriately to the two daughter cells, so that each receives a copy of every chromosome.

4. **Cytokinesis**: The cytoplasm must divide to form the two new cells, each surrounded by a cell membrane, and a cell wall in organisms that have one.

As you will see, these four events happen differently in prokaryotes and eukaryotes.

Prokaryotes divide by binary fission

In prokaryotes, cell division results in the reproduction of the entire single-celled organism. The cell grows in size, replicates its DNA, and then separates the cytoplasm and DNA into two new daughter cells in a process called **binary fission**.

CELL DIVISION SIGNALS External factors such as environmental conditions and nutrient concentrations are common signals for the initiation of cell division in prokaryotes. For example, the bacterium *Bacillus subtilis* can divide in under an hour if abundant sources of carbohydrate and mineral nutrients are available and if the pH and temperature are optimal. When nutrient levels are low, or the temperature is too hot or cold, or the pH too acidic or basic, the bacterium slows down its growth and eventually stops dividing. When conditions improve, growth and division resume. The bacterium *Escherichia coli*, which is widely used in genetic studies, can divide every 20 minutes under optimal conditions.

DNA REPLICATION As you saw in Key Concept 5.3, a **chromosome** consists of a long, thin DNA molecule that contains the genetic information for the organism, as well as various associated proteins. Most prokaryotes have just one main chromosome; when a cell divides, its chromosome must be replicated, and each of the two new daughter cells must receive a copy.

If the *E. coli* chromosome were spread out into a full circle, the circle would be about 500 micrometers (μm) in diameter, more than 200 times larger than the cell! To fit into the cell, bacterial DNA must be compacted. The DNA folds in on itself, and positively charged (basic) proteins bound to the negatively charged (acidic) DNA contribute to this folding.

Two regions of the prokaryotic chromosome play functional roles in cell reproduction:

1. *ori*: the site where replication of the circular chromosome starts (the *ori*gin of replication)

2. *ter*: the site where replication ends (the *ter*minus of replication)

(A) Reproduction

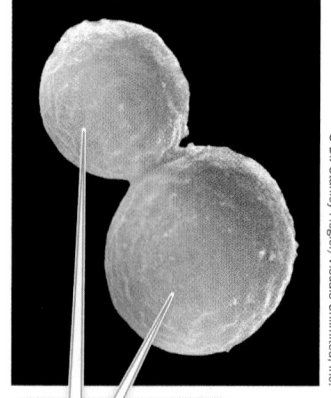

These eukaryotic yeast cells divide by budding.

© Dr. Stanley Flegler/Visuals Unlimited, Inc.

(B) Growth

Cell division contributes to the growth of this root tissue.

© Biodisc/Visuals Unlimited, Inc.

(C) Regeneration

Cell division contributes to the regeneration of a lizard's tail.

© Stefan Sollfors/Alamy Stock Photo

Figure 11.1 Important Consequences of Cell Division Cell division is the basis for **(A)** reproduction, **(B)** growth, and **(C)** repair and regeneration of tissues.

Chromosome replication takes place as the DNA is threaded through a replication complex of proteins near the center of the cell. Replication begins at the *ori* site and moves bidirectionally toward the *ter* site. While the DNA replicates, anabolic metabolism is active, resulting in cell growth. When replication is complete, the two daughter DNA molecules separate and segregate from one another at opposite ends of the cell. In rapidly dividing prokaryotes, DNA replication occupies the entire time between cell divisions.

DNA SEGREGATION   Replication begins near the center of the cell. Once replicated, the *ori* regions move toward opposite ends of the cell as replication of the rest of the parent molecule proceeds (**Figure 11.2A**). DNA sequences adjacent to each of the *ori* regions bind proteins that are essential for this segregation. This is an energy-requiring process, since the binding proteins hydrolyze ATP.

CYTOKINESIS   Immediately after chromosome replication is finished, cytokinesis begins. At first, the cell membrane pinches in to form a ring of fibers, termed the Z ring, similar to a purse string. The major component of these fibers is a protein called FtsZ that is related to eukaryotic tubulin (which makes up microtubules; see Figure 5.17). As the membrane pinches in, new cell wall materials are deposited, which finally separate the two cells (**Figure 11.2B**).

Eukaryotic cells divide by mitosis followed by cytokinesis

As in prokaryotes, cell reproduction in eukaryotes entails four events. The details, however, are quite different:

- *Cell division signals*: Like prokaryotes, single-celled eukaryotes often undergo cell division when environmental conditions are appropriate. For multicellular eukaryotes, the internal environmental conditions experienced by cells are often suitable for cell division, but this does not mean that cell division necessarily occurs. The reason is that cell division signals in multicellular eukaryotes are related to the function of the entire organism. For example, there is no need to produce additional liver cells when the liver has reached its optimal size. Once a cell is stimulated to begin dividing, internal signals come into play to ensure that cell division occurs correctly. We will discuss these signals in the next key concept.

- *DNA replication*: Eukaryotes have more DNA than prokaryotes, and it is contained in more than one chromosome (human cells, for example, have 46 chromosomes). While the mechanics of DNA replication are essentially the same in eukaryotes and prokaryotes, there are two major differences. First, eukaryotic DNA replication starts at numerous origins of replication, not at just one as in prokaryotes. Second, DNA replication in eukaryotes is usually limited to part of the period between cell divisions and does not overlap with the segregation of DNA into daughter cells.

- *DNA segregation*: Because eukaryotes have multiple chromosomes, segregation of the two sets of DNA molecules produced by replication is somewhat more complicated than it is in prokaryotes, and a mechanism called **mitosis** segregates them into two new nuclei. During mitosis, one copy of each chromosome

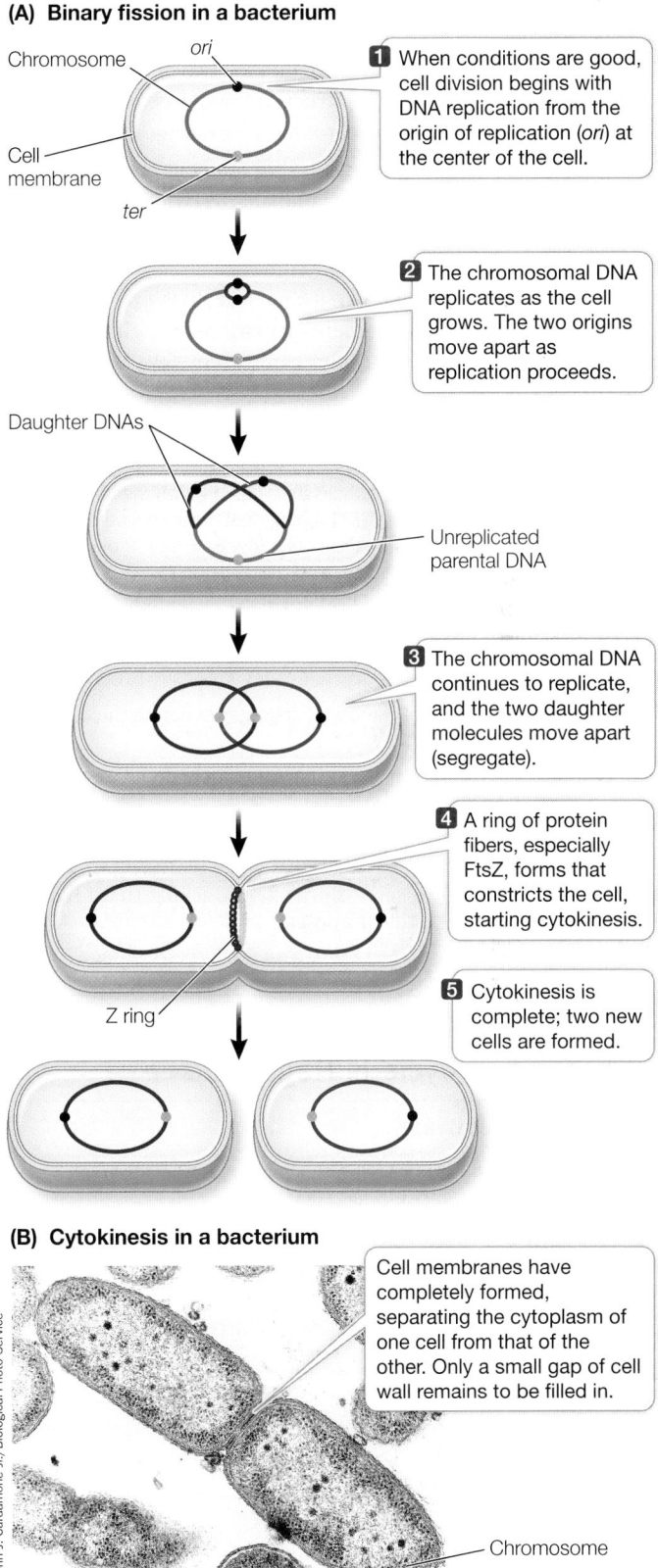

(A) Binary fission in a bacterium

Chromosome   *ori*

Cell membrane

ter

1 When conditions are good, cell division begins with DNA replication from the origin of replication (*ori*) at the center of the cell.

2 The chromosomal DNA replicates as the cell grows. The two origins move apart as replication proceeds.

Daughter DNAs

Unreplicated parental DNA

3 The chromosomal DNA continues to replicate, and the two daughter molecules move apart (segregate).

4 A ring of protein fibers, especially FtsZ, forms that constricts the cell, starting cytokinesis.

Z ring

5 Cytokinesis is complete; two new cells are formed.

(B) Cytokinesis in a bacterium

© John J. Cardamone Jr./Biological Photo Service

Cell membranes have completely formed, separating the cytoplasm of one cell from that of the other. Only a small gap of cell wall remains to be filled in.

Chromosome

Figure 11.2 Prokaryotic Cell Division   (A) DNA replication begins at the *ori* site and continues to the *ter* site, replicated DNA segregates to either end of the cell, and cytokinesis produces two cells. (B) Two identical daughter cells produced by binary fission. (A after K. Jonas. 2014. *Curr Opin Microbiol* 18: 54–60.)

in the parent cell ends up in each of the two new daughter cells. Chromosomes become highly condensed before they segregate, which makes them easier to move into the two new nuclei. The **spindle**, a special cytoskeletal structure composed of microtubules, is involved in moving chromosomes during segregation.

- *Cytokinesis*: Cytokinesis proceeds differently in plant cells (which have a cell wall) than in animal cells (which do not).

The cells resulting from mitosis are identical to the parent cell in the amount and kind of DNA they contain.

There is another mechanism for nuclear division called **meiosis**, which is involved in gamete formation. We will return to meiosis and describe differences with mitosis in Key Concept 11.5.

KEY CONCEPT

11.1 Recap and Assess

Four events are required for cell division: cell division signals, replication of the genetic material (DNA), segregation of replicated DNA, and separation of the two daughter cells (cytokinesis). Prokaryotes often have just one chromosome, and cell division can be rapid. Eukaryotes usually have multiple chromosomes, and the process of cell division is more intricate, involving either mitosis or meiosis.

1. What commonly controls whether a prokaryotic cell will begin binary fission?

2. Why must DNA be replicated and segregated before the cell can divide?

3. Why are DNA replication and cell division more complex in eukaryotes than in prokaryotes?

What determines whether a eukaryotic cell will divide? How does mitosis lead to identical cells? In the key concepts that follow, we will describe the details of mitosis.

KEY CONCEPT

11.2 The Eukaryotic Cell Division Cycle Is Regulated

Learning Objectives

11.2.1 Sketch and describe the four phases of the eukaryotic cell cycle.

11.2.2 Explain how the progress of a eukaryotic cell through the cell cycle is controlled by cyclin-dependent kinases.

11.2.3 Predict conditions under which external factors might stimulate the eukaryotic cell cycle.

As you will see throughout this book, different cells have different rates of cell division. Some cells, such as those in an early embryo, divide rapidly and continuously. Others, such as neurons in the brain, don't divide at all. This suggests that the signaling pathways for cells to divide are highly controlled.

In eukaryotes, the phases through which a single cell passes to produce daughter cells by cell division is known as the **cell cycle**. The cell cycle can be divided into four phases: G1, S, G2, and M. M phase includes mitosis and cytokinesis. The other three phases together make up interphase. During **interphase**, the cell nucleus is visible and typical cell functions occur, including DNA replication (during S phase) (**Figure 11.3**).

The duration of the cell cycle varies considerably in different cell types. In the early embryo the cell cycle may be as short as 30 minutes, whereas rapidly dividing cells in an adult human typically complete the cycle in about 24 hours. In general, cells spend most of their time in interphase. So if we take a snapshot through the microscope of a cell population, only a few cells will be in mitosis or cytokinesis at any given moment. In a cell cycle of 24 hours, the four phases would typically last for 11 hours (G1), 8 hours (S), 4 hours (G2), and 1 hour (M).

Here we describe the events of interphase, especially those that trigger mitosis.

- *G1 phase.* During **G1 phase**, each chromosome is a single, unreplicated DNA molecule with associated proteins. Variations in the duration of G1 account for most of the variability in the length of the cell cycle in different cell types. Some rapidly dividing embryonic cells dispense with it entirely, whereas other cells may remain in G1 for weeks or even years. G1 ends at the **G1-to-S transition**, when the commitment is made to DNA replication and subsequent cell division.

- *S phase.* DNA replication occurs during **S phase** (see Key Concept 13.3 for a detailed description of DNA replication). Each chromosome is duplicated and thereafter consists of two **sister chromatids** (the products of DNA replication). The sister chromatids remain joined together until mitosis, when they segregate into two daughter cells.

- *G2 phase.* During **G2 phase**, the cell makes preparations for mitosis—for example, by synthesizing and assembling

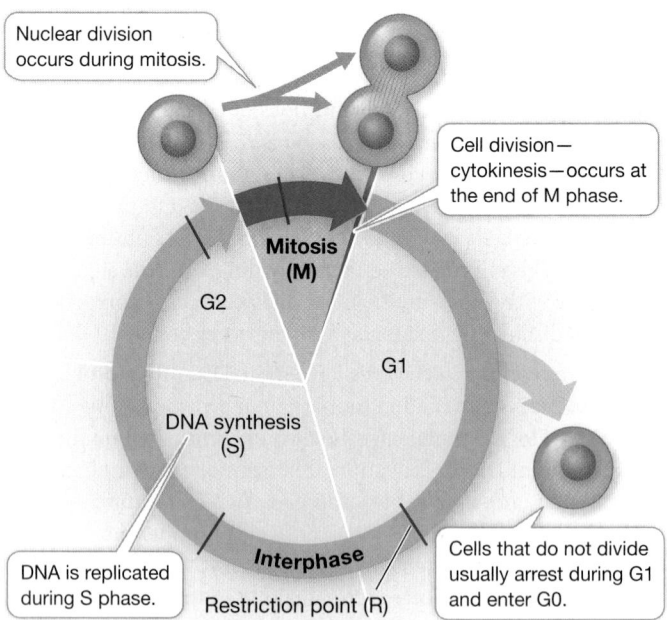

Figure 11.3 The Eukaryotic Cell Cycle The cell cycle consists of four phases: M, during which mitosis and cytokinesis take place, and G1, S, and G2, together termed interphase, during which cells grow and DNA replication occurs. Red lines indicate checkpoints for progression through the cell cycle.

Q: If the DNA content of a human skin cell at the beginning of mitosis is 12 picograms (1 pg = 10^{-12} g), what is the DNA content of a cell in G1?

the structures that move the chromatids to opposite ends of the dividing cell.

The initiation, termination, and operations of these phases are regulated by specific signals. Not all cells follow a continuous progression through the phases. Some cells in G1 enter an inactive resting phase of the cell cycle called **G0**. These cells sometimes return to G1 and the rest of the cell cycle under certain environmental conditions, such as an extracellular signal. Otherwise, cells may stay in G0; examples in humans are cells of the heart (cardiac muscle) and brain (neurons).

Specific internal signals trigger events in the cell cycle

Cell fusion experiments were used to reveal the existence of internal signals that control the transitions between stages of the cell cycle. For example, an experiment involving the fusion of HeLa cells (the cells described in the opening story) at different phases of the cell cycle showed that a cell in S phase produces a substance that activates DNA replication (Investigating Life: What Controls the Reproduction of Cancer Cells?). Similar experiments pointed to the existence of signals controlling entry into M phase.

▶Investigating**LIFE**   What Controls the Reproduction of Cancer Cells?

Experiment

Original Paper: P. N. Rao and R. T. Johnson. 1970. Mammalian cell fusion: Studies on the regulation of DNA synthesis and mitosis. *Nature* 225: 159–164.

Nuclei of cells in G1 do not undergo DNA replication, but nuclei in S phase do. Rao and Johnson wondered whether substances present in cells in S phase could be used to induce DNA replication in cells in G1.

HYPOTHESIS▶   A cell in S phase contains an activator of DNA replication.

METHOD▶

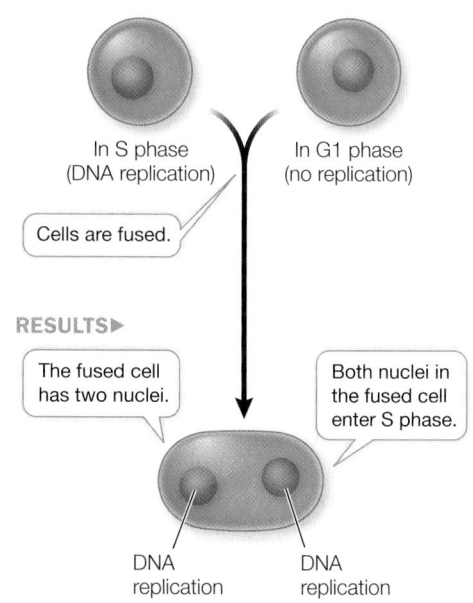

In S phase (DNA replication)   In G1 phase (no replication)

Cells are fused.

RESULTS▶

The fused cell has two nuclei.

Both nuclei in the fused cell enter S phase.

DNA replication   DNA replication

CONCLUSION▶   The S phase cell contains a substance that diffuses to the G1 nucleus and activates DNA replication.

Work with the Data

The fusion of cellular membranes is a natural process; it occurs during endocytosis and exocytosis, and in fertilization (the fusion of gametes). Membrane fusion also occurs when membrane-enclosed viruses infect their host cells. Occasionally these viruses also induce the fusion of adjacent host cells, creating a multinucleate cell. This observation led to the use of Sendai virus, a membrane-enclosed mouse respiratory virus, as a tool in the laboratory to fuse cells experimentally. Rao and Johnson used this strategy to study the regulation of the cell cycle.

In their experiment, Rao and Johnson used HeLa cells, which divide continuously (see the opening story of this chapter). First, they isolated cells in either G1 or S phase. Before fusion, the cells in S phase were exposed to a radioactively labeled component of DNA (thymidine). The radioactivity was incorporated into these cells' newly replicated DNA, labeling their nuclei. The S and G1 cells were then fused using Sendai virus (resulting in G1/S fusions) and again exposed to labeled thymidine. At various times after fusion, the scientists calculated the percent of previously unlabeled (G1) nuclei that had incorporated new label (i.e., had replicated their DNA) (**Figure A**). In a second series of experiments, S and G2 cells were fused in various combinations and then the numbers of cells in mitosis were counted and expressed as a percent of all cells in the population (**Figure B**).

Figure A   Figure B

QUESTIONS▶

1. According to Figure A, how long did it take for all the G1 nuclei in the G1/S cells to become labeled?

2. Examine the data for fused G1/G1 cells and unfused G1 cells in Figure A. Explain why these were appropriate controls for the experiment. When did these nuclei become labeled? Compare these times with each other and with that for the G1/S nuclei and discuss.

3. Examine the data in Figure B. Why did it take longer for the S phase cells to begin mitosis than the G2 cells?

4. According to Figure B, did fusion with G2 cells alter the timing of mitosis in the S cell nuclei? Explain what this means in terms of regulation of the cell cycle.

Go to Achieve for a companion Data in Depth exercise.

Progress through the cell cycle depends on the activities of **cyclin-dependent kinases,** or **CDKs.** Recall from Key Concept 7.2 that a protein kinase is an enzyme that catalyzes the transfer of a phosphate group from ATP to a target protein; this phosphate transfer is called phosphorylation. A particular CDK controls the G1-to-S transition, which is a control point in the cell cycle called the **restriction point (R)** (see Figure 11.3). Other CDKs control other parts of the cell cycle.

CDKs are not enzymatically active as protein kinases unless they are bound to another class of protein, the activators called **cyclins.** The binding of its cyclin—an example of allosteric regulation—activates the CDK by altering its shape and exposing its active site to substrates (**Figure 11.4**). The cyclin–CDK that controls passage from G1 to S phase is not the only such complex involved in regulating the eukaryotic cell cycle. There are different cyclin–CDK complexes, composed of particular cyclins and their associated CDKs, that act at different stages of the cycle. The details of how these complexes form and function vary among eukaryotic organisms, but we will focus here on the complexes found in mammalian cells. As an example, let's take a closer look at the cyclin–CDK complex that controls the G1-to-S transition.

Connect the Concepts As discussed in Key Concept 8.5, allosteric regulation occurs when another molecule induces a change in the three-dimensional structure of an enzyme. This changes the ability of the enzyme to bind its substrate, and so changes the rate of the reaction catalyzed by the enzyme.

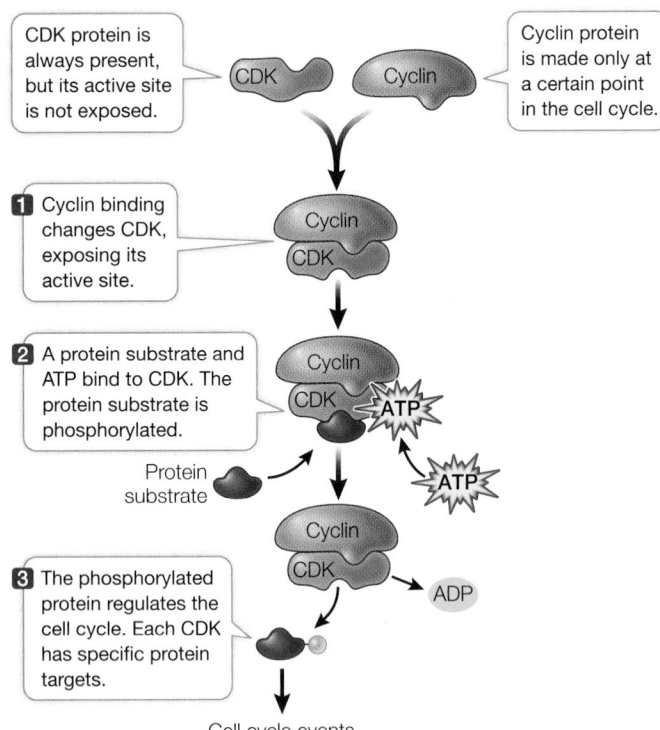

Figure 11.4 Cyclin Binding Activates CDK Binding of a cyclin changes the three-dimensional structure of an inactive CDK, making it an active protein kinase. Each cyclin–CDK complex phosphorylates a specific target protein in the cell cycle.

CDK protein is always present, but its active site is not exposed.

Cyclin protein is made only at a certain point in the cell cycle.

1 Cyclin binding changes CDK, exposing its active site.

2 A protein substrate and ATP bind to CDK. The protein substrate is phosphorylated.

Protein substrate

3 The phosphorylated protein regulates the cell cycle. Each CDK has specific protein targets.

Cell cycle events

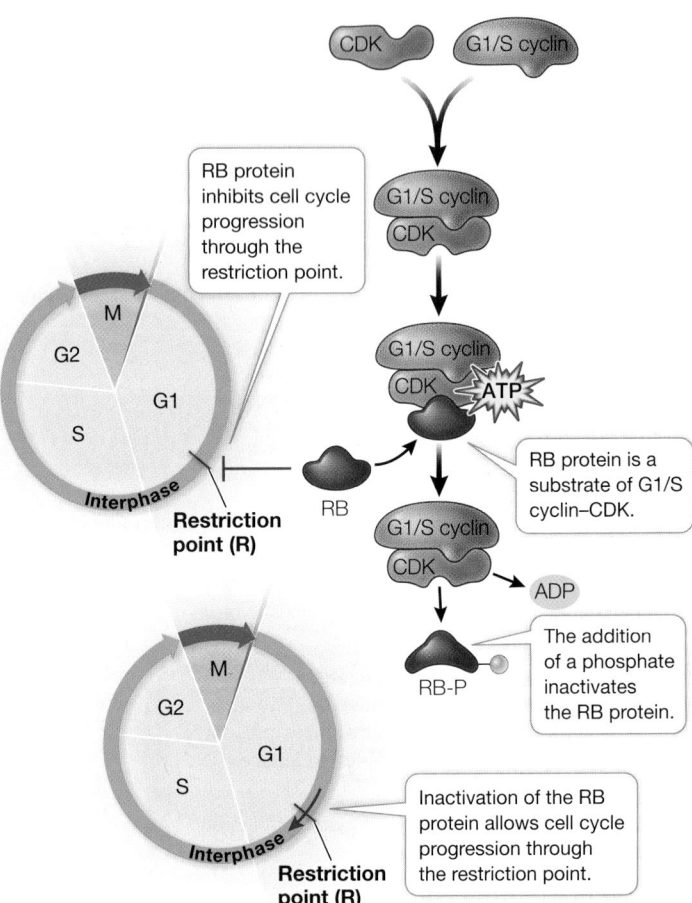

RB protein inhibits cell cycle progression through the restriction point.

Restriction point (R)

RB protein is a substrate of G1/S cyclin–CDK.

The addition of a phosphate inactivates the RB protein.

Inactivation of the RB protein allows cell cycle progression through the restriction point.

Restriction point (R)

Figure 11.5 Phosphorylation of RB Protein Controls Cell Cycle Progression The G1/S cyclin binds to and activates its CDK, which then phosphorylates the retinoblastoma protein (RB), inactivating it and allowing the cell cycle to progress from G1 to S

The G1/S cyclin–CDK catalyzes the phosphorylation of a protein called retinoblastoma protein (RB, named because of its role in cancer; see Key Concept 11.7). In many cells, RB acts as an inhibitor of the cell cycle at the restriction point (R). To begin S phase, a cell must get by the RB block. Here is where the G1/S cyclin–CDK comes in: it catalyzes the phosphorylation of RB molecules. This causes a change in the three-dimensional structure of RB, thereby inactivating it (**Figure 11.5**). With RB out of the way, the cell cycle can proceed.

Progress through the cell cycle is regulated by the activities of several CDKs, and so regulating *them* is a key to regulating cell division. An effective way to regulate CDKs is to regulate the presence or absence of cyclins (**Figure 11.6**). Simply put, if a cyclin is not present, its partner CDK is not active. As their name suggests, cyclins are present cyclically: they are made only at certain times in the cell cycle.

The different cyclin–CDKs act at **cell cycle checkpoints,** signaling pathways that regulate the cell cycle's progress. For example, if a cell's DNA is substantially damaged by radiation or toxic chemicals, the cell may be prevented from successfully completing a cell cycle. During interphase, there are three checkpoints, with a fourth during mitosis (see Figure 11.3). **Table 11.1**

Figure 11.6 Cyclins Are Transient in the Cell Cycle Cyclins are made at a particular time and then break down. **(A)** The G1/S cyclin is present during G1 and activates a CDK at that time. **(B)** Other cyclins control progression through other phases of the cell cycle. (B after WikiMiMa|Michael Matthes.)

lists some of the triggers that will cause the cell cycle to pause at each checkpoint.

As an example, let's consider the G1-to-S checkpoint (R). If DNA is damaged by radiation during G1, a signaling pathway results in the production of a protein called p21. (The *p* stands for "protein" and the *21* stands for its molecular weight—about 21,000 daltons.) The p21 protein binds to the G1/S CDK, preventing cyclin binding. This keeps the CDK in its inactive state, and the cell cycle pauses while repairs are made to the DNA (you will learn more about DNA repair in Key Concept 13.4). When the DNA damage pathway is no longer operating, p21 breaks down, allowing the cyclin–CDKs to function, and the cell cycle proceeds. If DNA damage is severe and cannot be repaired, the cell will undergo programmed cell death (apoptosis, which we will discuss later in this chapter). Such controls prevent defective cells from proliferating and potentially harming an organism.

Growth factors can stimulate cells to divide

Cyclin–CDKs provide cells with internal controls of their progress through the cell cycle. But the cell cycle is also influenced by external signals. Not all cells in an organism go through the cell cycle on a regular basis. Some cells either no longer go through the cell cycle and enter G0, or go through it slowly and divide infrequently. If such cells are to divide, they must be stimulated by external chemical signals called **growth factors**. Here are a few examples:

- If you cut yourself and bleed, specialized cell fragments called platelets gather at the wound to initiate blood clotting. The platelets produce and release a protein called platelet-derived growth factor which diffuses to the adjacent cells in the skin and stimulates them to divide and heal the wound.

- Red and white blood cells have limited lifetimes and must be replaced through the division of immature, unspecialized blood cell precursors in the bone marrow. Two types of growth factors, interleukins and erythropoietin, stimulate the division and specialization, respectively, of precursor cells of white blood cells and red blood cells.

Growth factors bind to specific receptors on target cells and activate signal transduction pathways (see Chapter 7) that end with cyclin synthesis, thereby activating CDKs and the cell cycle.

KEY CONCEPT
11.2 Recap and Assess

The eukaryotic cell cycle is under both external and internal control. CDKs control the eukaryotic cell cycle, and their activities are regulated by binding of cyclins. External signals such as growth factors can initiate the cell cycle.

1. Draw a cell cycle diagram with each of its phases.

2. How do cyclin–CDKs control the progress of the cell cycle?

3. What are growth factors, and how do they act to control the cell cycle?

4. The protein p16 acts on the cell cycle in a fashion similar to that of p21. Recently it was found that there is more p16 protein in the cells of older people than in younger people. What are the implications of this for aging?

TABLE 11.1 | Cell Cycle Checkpoints

Cell cycle phase	Checkpoint trigger
G1	DNA damage
S	Incomplete replication or DNA damage
G2	DNA damage
M	Chromosome unattached to spindle

Once the cell cycle is initiated and interphase is completed, the cell enters mitosis, where the replicated DNA is segregated into two daughter cells.

KEY CONCEPT 11.3   Eukaryotic Cells Divide by Mitosis

Learning Objectives

11.3.1 Describe DNA packaging and how it varies during the cell cycle.

11.3.2 List the five stages of mitosis and state what events occur in each.

11.3.3 Explain how the spindle is involved in segregation of sister chromatids.

11.3.4 Describe the differences between cytokinesis in animals and plants.

DNA is a very long polymer, up to several centimeters in length. At every stage of the cell cycle, these threads must be packaged into compact structures. A eukaryotic chromosome consists of one or two linear, double-stranded DNA molecules bound with many proteins (the complex of DNA and proteins is referred to as **chromatin**). Before S phase, each unreplicated chromosome contains only one double-stranded DNA molecule. After it replicates during S phase, however, there are two double-stranded DNA molecules: the sister chromatids (**Figure 11.7**). Throughout G2 the

sister chromatids are held together along most of their length by a protein complex called cohesin. At mitosis most of the cohesin is removed, except in a region called the **centromere**, where the chromatids remain held together. At the end of G2 and the beginning of mitosis, a second group of proteins called condensins coats the DNA molecules and makes them more compact.

If all of the DNA in a typical human cell were put end to end, it would be nearly 2 meters long. Yet the nucleus is only 5 μm (0.000005 meters) in diameter and therefore DNA must be extensively packaged in a highly organized way (**Figure 11.8**). This packing is achieved largely by proteins called histones (*histos*, "web" or "loom"), which are positively charged at cellular pH because of their high content of the basic amino acids lysine and arginine. The charged R groups on these amino acids bind to the negatively charged phosphate groups on DNA by ionic bonds. These DNA–histone interactions, as well as histone–histone interactions, result in the formation of beadlike units called **nucleosomes** (see Figure 11.8).

During interphase, the chromatin that makes up each chromosome consists of single DNA molecules wrapped around vast numbers of nucleosomes that resemble beads on a string. During this phase of the cell cycle, the DNA is accessible to proteins involved in replication and transcription. Once a mitotic chromosome is formed, its compact nature makes it inaccessible to replication and transcription factors, and so these processes cannot occur.

Mitosis during M phase of the cell cycle leads to the production of two nuclei that are genetically identical to each other and to the nucleus of the cell that entered the cell cycle in G1 (i.e., the parent cell). Mitosis ensures the accurate segregation of each copy

Figure 11.7 Chromosomes and Sister Chromatids DNA in the interphase nucleus is diffuse and becomes compacted as mitosis begins.

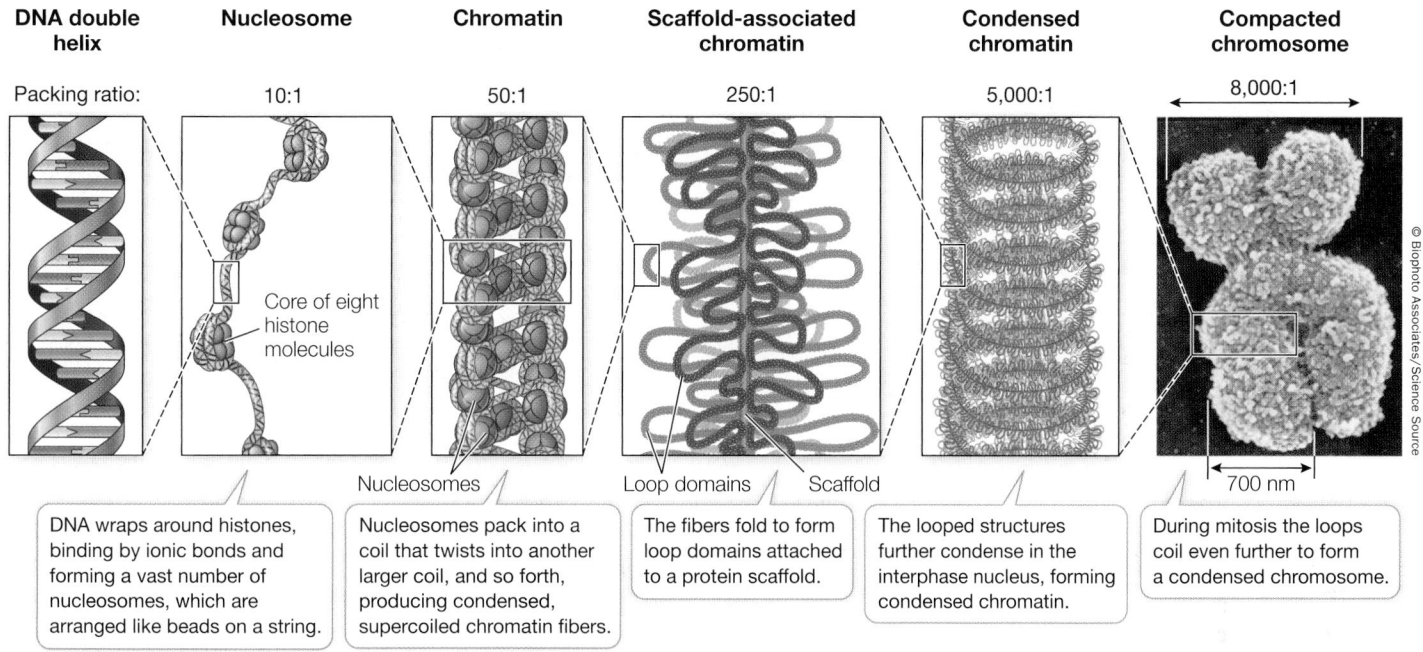

Figure 11.8 DNA Is Packed into a Mitotic Chromosome The nucleosome, formed by DNA and histones, is the essential building block in this highly compacted structure.

of a eukaryotic cell's multiple chromosomes into the daughter nuclei. While mitosis is a continuous process in which each event flows smoothly into the next, it is convenient to subdivide it into a series of stages: prophase, prometaphase, metaphase, anaphase, and telophase (Table 11.2, Figure 11.9).

Let's take a closer look at two cellular structures that contribute to the orderly segregation of the chromosomes during mitosis—the centrosomes and the spindle.

 View in Achieve
Animation 11.1 **Mitosis**

The centrosomes determine the plane of cell division

The spindle (also called the mitotic spindle or spindle apparatus) is a dynamic microtubule structure that moves sister chromatids

apart during mitosis. Before the spindle can form, its orientation is determined by the **centrosome** ("central body"), an organelle in the cytoplasm near the nucleus. In many organisms the centrosome consists of a pair of **centrioles**, each one a hollow tube formed by nine microtubule triplets. During S phase the centrosome duplicates, and at the beginning of prophase the two centrosomes separate from one another, moving to opposite ends of the nuclear envelope. These identify the "poles" toward which chromosomes move during anaphase. The cells of plants and fungi lack centrosomes, but distinct microtubule organizing centers at each end of the cell play the same role.

The positions of the centrosomes determine the plane where the animal cell will divide; therefore they determine the spatial relationship between the two new cells. This relationship may be of little consequence to single free-living cells such as yeasts, but it is important for cells in a multicellular organism. For example, during development from a fertilized egg to an embryo, the daughter cells from some divisions must be positioned correctly to receive signals to form new tissues.

The spindle begins to form during prophase

During interphase, only the nuclear envelope, the nucleoli (see Key Concept 5.3), and a barely discernible tangle of chromatin are visible under the light microscope. The appearance of the nucleus changes as the cell enters prophase. At this stage, most of the cohesin that has held the two products of DNA replication together since S phase is removed, so the individual chromatids become visible. They are still held together by a small amount of cohesin at the centromere. Late in prophase, specialized

TABLE **11.2**	Summary of Cell Cycle Events	
Phase	**Events**
G1	Growth
S	DNA replication
G2	Spindle synthesis begins; preparation for mitosis
M	
Mitosis	
Prophase	Condensation of chromosomes; spindle assembly
Prometaphase	Nuclear envelope breakdown; chromosome attachment to spindle
Metaphase	Alignment of chromosomes at metaphase plate
Anaphase	Separation of chromatids; migration to poles
Telophase	Chromosomes decondense; nuclear envelope re-forms
Cytokinesis	Cell separation; cell membrane and/or wall formation

Interphase	Prophase	Prometaphase

Nucleus
Centrosomes
Nucleolus

Nuclear
envelope

1 During S phase of interphase, the nucleus replicates its DNA and centrosomes.

Developing
spindle

Chromatids of
chromosome

2 The chromatin coils and supercoils, becoming more and more compact and condensing into visible chromosomes. The chromosomes consist of identical, paired sister chromatids formed in S phase. Centrosomes move to opposite poles.

Kinetochore
microtubules

Polar
microtubules

Kinetochore

3 The nuclear envelope breaks down. Kinetochore microtubules appear and connect the kinetochores to the poles.

Figure 11.9 **The Phases of Mitosis in an Animal Cell** Mitosis results in two new genetically identical nuclei, each one destined for one of the two daughter cells produced when a cell divides. In the micrographs, the green dye stains microtubules (and thus the spindle); the red dye stains the chromosomes. The chromosomes in the diagrams are stylized to emphasize the fates of the individual chromatids. For instructional purposes, the chromosomes from one parent are colored blue and those from the other parent are red.

View in **Achieve**
Activity 11.1 **Images of Mitosis**

structures called **kinetochores** develop in the centromere region, one on each chromatid. These structures will be important for chromosome movement.

Each of the two centrosomes, now on opposite sides of the nucleus, serves as a mitotic center, or pole, toward which the chromosomes will move (**Figure 11.10A**). During prophase and prometaphase, microtubules form between the poles and the chromosomes to make up the spindle. The spindle serves as a structure to which the chromosomes attach and as a framework keeping the two poles apart. Each half of the spindle develops as tubulin dimers aggregate from around the centrioles and form long fibers that extend into the middle region of the cell. The microtubules are initially unstable, constantly forming and falling apart, until they contact kinetochores or microtubules from the other half-spindle and become more stable.

There are two groups of microtubules in the spindle:

1. Polar microtubules form the framework of the spindle and run from one pole to the other.

2. Kinetochore microtubules, which form later, attach to the kinetochores on the chromosomes. The two sister chromatids in each replicated chromosome become attached to kinetochore microtubules from opposite poles (**Figure 11.10B**). This ensures that the two chromatids will eventually move to opposite poles.

Movement of the chromatids achieves the central goal of mitosis. It accomplishes the segregation of the genetic material that must occur before the cell can divide and complete the cell cycle. Prophase prepares for this movement, and the actual segregation takes place in the next three phases of mitosis.

Chromosome separation and movement are highly organized

During the next three phases of mitosis—prometaphase, metaphase, and anaphase—dramatic changes take place in the cell and the chromosomes (see Figure 11.9). During prometaphase, the nuclear envelope breaks down and spindle formation is completed. During metaphase, the chromosomes line up at the equatorial

| **Metaphase** | **Anaphase** | **Telophase** |

All photos © Nasser Rusan

Metaphase plate

Daughter chromosomes

4 The centromeres become aligned in a plane at the cell's equator.

5 The paired sister chromatids separate, and the new daughter chromosomes begin to move toward the poles.

6 The daughter chromosomes reach the poles. As telophase concludes, the nuclear envelopes and nucleoli re-form, the chromatin decondenses, and, after cytokinesis, the daughter cells enter interphase once again.

position (metaphase plate) of the cell. Now let's consider two key processes of anaphase: separation of the chromatids, and the mechanism of their actual movement toward the poles.

CHROMATID SEPARATION   The separation of chromatids occurs at the beginning of anaphase. It is controlled by an M phase cyclin–CDK, which activates another protein complex

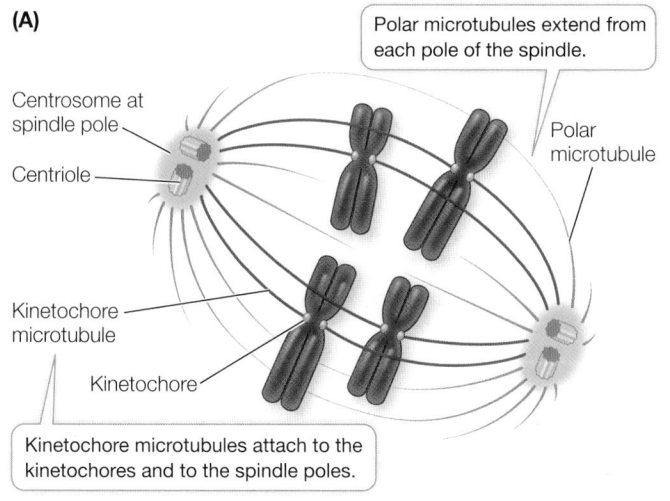

(A)

Polar microtubules extend from each pole of the spindle.

Centrosome at spindle pole

Centriole

Polar microtubule

Kinetochore microtubule

Kinetochore

Kinetochore microtubules attach to the kinetochores and to the spindle poles.

(B)

Kinetochore microtubules   Kinetochore

© Conly L. Rieder/Biological Photo Service

Figure 11.10 The Mitotic Spindle Consists of Microtubules (A) The spindle in an animal cell at metaphase. In plant cells, centrioles are not present. (B) An electron micrograph of metaphase, emphasizing the kinetochore microtubules.

▶ **View in Achieve** **Activity 11.2 The Mitotic Spindle** called the anaphase-promoting complex (APC). Separation occurs because one subunit of the cohesin protein holding the sister chromatids together is hydrolyzed by a specific protease, appropriately called separase (**Figure 11.11**). A cell cycle checkpoint, often called the spindle assembly checkpoint, occurs at the end of metaphase to inhibit the APC if one of the chromosomes is not attached properly to the spindle. When all chromosomes are attached, the APC is activated and the chromatids separate. After separation the chromatids are called **daughter chromosomes**. Note the difference between sister chromatids and daughter chromosomes:

- Sister chromatids share a centromere.
- Daughter chromosomes have their own centromere.

CHROMOSOME MOVEMENT   The migration of the two sets of daughter chromosomes to the poles of the cell is a highly organized, active process. Three mechanisms operate to move the chromosomes along. First, the kinetochores contain molecular motor proteins, including kinesins and cytosolic dynein (see Figures 5.20 and 5.21), which use energy from ATP hydrolysis to do the work of moving the chromosomes along the microtubules. Second, the kinetochore microtubules shorten, drawing the chromosomes toward them. Third, the centrosomes move apart, aiding in separation. The last stage of mitosis is telophase, when the spindle disappears and a nuclear envelope forms around each set of daughter chromosomes (see Figure 11.9). Finally, the cytoplasm divides to form the two daughter cells during cytokinesis: the last event in cell division.

 Media Clip 11.1 Mitosis: Live and Up Close
Life12e.com/mc11.1

Cytokinesis divides the cytoplasm

Cytokinesis divides the cell's cytoplasm after nuclear division in mitosis. There are substantial differences between the process in

(A) Cytokinesis of an animal cell

(B) Cytokinesis of a plant cell

Contractile ring

Cell plate

© Dr. David Phillips/Visuals Unlimited, Inc.

© B. A. Palevitz, E. H. Newcomb/Biological Photo Service

50 µm

10 µm

The contractile ring has completely separated the cytoplasms of these two daughter cells, although their surfaces remain in contact.

This row of vesicles will fuse to form a cell plate between the cell above and the cell below.

Figure 11.12 Cytokinesis Differs in Animal and Plant Cells (A) A sea urchin zygote (fertilized egg) that has just completed cytokinesis at the end of the first cell division of its development into an embryo. (B) A dividing plant cell in late telophase. Plant cells divide differently from animal cells because plant cells have cell walls.

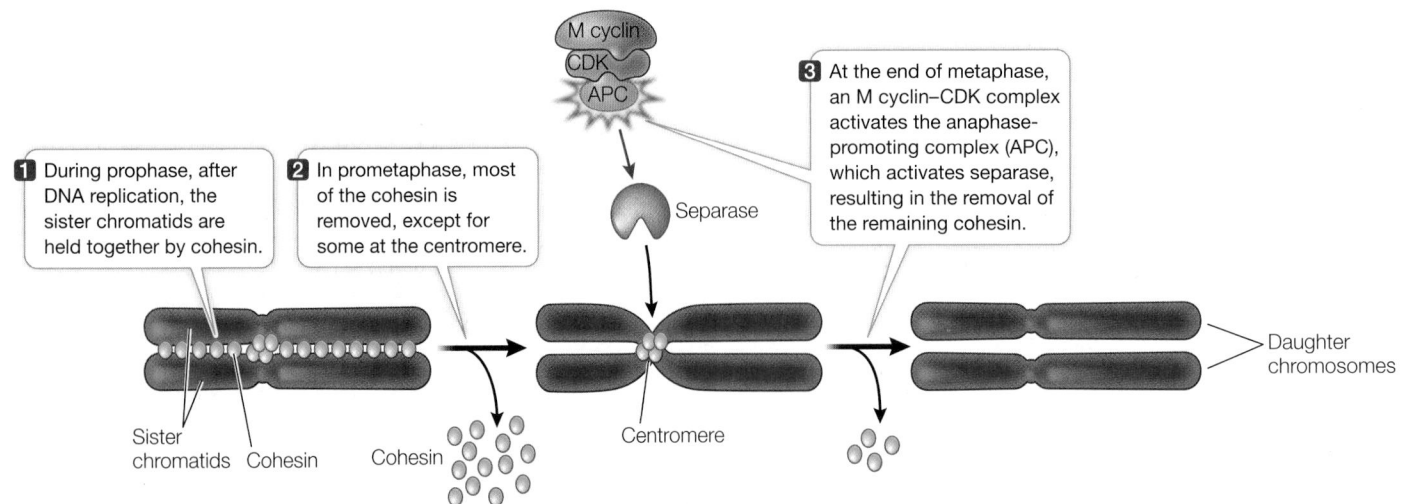

1 During prophase, after DNA replication, the sister chromatids are held together by cohesin.

2 In prometaphase, most of the cohesin is removed, except for some at the centromere.

M cyclin
CDK
APC

Separase

3 At the end of metaphase, an M cyclin–CDK complex activates the anaphase-promoting complex (APC), which activates separase, resulting in the removal of the remaining cohesin.

Sister chromatids   Cohesin

Cohesin

Centromere

Daughter chromosomes

Figure 11.11 Chromatid Attachment and Separation The cohesin protein complex holds sister chromatids together at the centromere. The enzyme separase hydrolyzes cohesin at the end of metaphase and beginning of anaphase, allowing the chromatids to separate into daughter chromosomes.

animal and plant cells. In animal cells, cytokinesis begins with a furrowing of the cell membrane, as if an invisible thread were cinching the cytoplasm between the two nuclei (**Figure 11.12A**). This contractile ring is composed of microfilaments of actin and associated myosin, which form a ring on the cytoplasmic surface of the cell membrane. These two proteins interact to produce a contraction, pinching the cell in two. The microfilaments assemble rapidly from actin monomers that are present in the interphase cytoskeleton.

The plant cell cytoplasm divides differently because plants have rigid cell walls. In plant cells, as the spindle breaks down after mitosis, membranous vesicles derived from the Golgi apparatus appear along the plane of cell division, roughly midway between the two daughter nuclei. The vesicles are propelled along microtubules by the motor protein kinesin, and fuse to form a new cell membrane. At the same time they contribute their contents to a cell plate, which is the beginning of a new cell wall (**Figure 11.12B**).

Following cytokinesis, each daughter cell contains all the components of a complete cell. A precise distribution of chromosomes is ensured by mitosis. In contrast, organelles such as ribosomes, mitochondria, and chloroplasts do not need to be distributed equally between daughter cells, as long as some of each are present in each cell. Accordingly, there is no mechanism with a precision comparable to that of mitosis to provide for their equal allocation to daughter cells.

KEY CONCEPT
11.3 Recap and Assess

Mitosis is the ordered division of a eukaryotic cell nucleus into two nuclei with identical sets of chromosomes. The process of mitosis, while continuous, can be viewed as a series of events (prophase, prometaphase, metaphase, anaphase, and telophase). Once two nuclei have formed, the cell divides into two cells by cytokinesis.

1. Describe the differences between a replicated and an unreplicated chromosome, and identify during what phases of the cell cycle each one is found.

2. What are the various levels of "packing" by which the genetic information contained in linear DNA is condensed during prophase?

3. Paclitaxel is an anticancer drug that binds to microtubules, preventing them from adding or removing subunits and causing them to form bundles. How do you think this drug works to stop cancer? Is Paclitaxel specific to cancer cells?

4. How does cytokinesis differ in plant and animal cells?

5. How would the cell cycle be affected if the cohesion protein was nonfunctional?

Mitosis results in two cells that are genetically identical. But there is another eukaryotic cell division process, meiosis, that results in genetic diversity. In the next key concept we will discuss the roles of mitosis and meiosis in sexual reproduction, and then turn to the details of meiosis in Key Concept 11.5.

KEY CONCEPT
11.4 Cell Division Plays Important Roles in the Sexual Life Cycle

Learning Objectives

11.4.1 Compare and contrast asexual and sexual reproduction.

11.4.2 Describe the roles of meiosis and fertilization in the sexual life cycle.

11.4.3 Differentiate between haploid and diploid cells and organisms.

11.4.4 Compare and contrast different sexual life cycles.

Repetition of the mitotic cell cycle allows a single cell to give rise to many cells that are genetically identical. Meiosis, by contrast, produces four daughter cells that are not genetically identical, with each carrying half the amount of DNA as the original G1 parent cell. Mitosis and meiosis are both involved in reproduction but in different ways: asexual reproduction involves only mitosis, whereas the sexual reproduction cycle involves both mitosis and meiosis.

Asexual reproduction is based on the mitotic division of the nucleus. An organism that reproduces asexually may be single-celled like yeast, reproducing itself with each cell cycle, or it may be multicellular like an aspen in a forest in the Wasatch Mountains of Utah (**Figure 11.13**). Aspen can reproduce sexually, with male and female plants, but in many aspen stands all the trees are the same sex, and DNA analyses have shown that they are **clones** of a single parent organism: the offspring are genetically identical to the parent. Any genetic variation among the trees is most likely due to a relatively small number of changes in the DNA that occur during DNA replication. As you will see, this small amount of variation contrasts with the extensive variation possible in sexually reproducing organisms.

© All Canada Photos/Alamy Stock Photo

Figure 11.13 Asexual Reproduction on a Large Scale In this forest, the aspen trees arose from a single tree by asexual reproduction. They are virtually identical genetically.

Connect the Concepts Asexual reproduction is common in land plants, and you can learn about this in Key Concept 36.3.

Unlike asexual reproduction, **sexual reproduction** results in an organism that is not identical to its parents. Sexual reproduction requires **gametes** created by meiosis; two parents each contribute one gamete to each of their offspring. Meiosis produces gametes—and thus offspring—that differ genetically from each other and from the parents. Because of this genetic variation, some offspring may be better adapted than others to survive and reproduce in a particular environment. While asexually reproducing organisms can have a small amount of genetic diversity, meiosis generates much more diversity, which is available for natural selection and evolution.

Sexual life cycles produce haploid and diploid cells

In most multicellular organisms, the body cells that are *not* specialized for reproduction, called **somatic cells**, each contain two sets of chromosomes, which are found in pairs. One chromosome of each pair comes from each of the organism's two parents; in humans, for example, 23 of the 46 chromosomes come from the biological mother and 23 from the biological father. The members of such a **homologous pair** are similar in size and appearance.

The two chromosomes in a homologous pair (called **homologs**) bear corresponding, though not identical, genetic information. For example, a homologous pair of chromosomes in a plant may carry different versions of a gene that controls seed shape. One homolog may carry the version for wrinkled seeds while the other may carry the version for smooth seeds. You'll see the seed-shape gene in Chapter 12.

There is no simple relationship between the size of an organism and the number of chromosomes in its genome. A housefly has 5 chromosome pairs and a horse has 32, but the smaller carp (a fish) has 52 pairs. Probably the highest number of chromosomes in any organism is in the fern *Ophioglossum reticulatum*, which has 1,260 (630 pairs)!

In contrast to somatic cells, gametes contain only a single set of chromosomes—that is, one homolog from each pair. The number of chromosomes in a gamete is denoted by n, and the cell is said to be **haploid**. During reproduction, two haploid gametes fuse to form a **zygote** in a process called **fertilization**. The zygote thus has two sets of chromosomes; its chromosome number is denoted by $2n$, and it is said to be **diploid**. Depending on the organism, the zygote may divide by either meiosis or mitosis. Either way, a new mature organism develops that is capable of sexual reproduction.

Fungus (*Rhizopus oligosporus*)
(haploid organism)

Fern (*Humata tyermanii*)
(diploid sporophyte)

Yellow-billed Stork (*Mycteria ibis*)
(diploid organism)

Haploid (*n*)
Diploid (*2n*)

Mature organism (*n*)

Spores (*n*)

Gametes
Male (*n*) Female (*n*)

Meiosis

Fertilization

Zygote (*2n*)

In the haplontic life cycle, the mature organism is haploid and the zygote is the only diploid stage.

Gametophyte (*n*)

Spore (*n*)

Meiosis

Gametes
Male (*n*) Female (*n*)

Fertilization

Zygote (*2n*)

Sporophyte (*2n*)

In the haplo-diplontic life cycle, the organism passes through haploid and diploid stages that are both multicellular.

Gametes
Male (*n*) Female (*n*)

Meiosis

Fertilization

Zygote (*2n*)

Mature organism (*2n*)

In the diplontic life cycle, the organism is diploid and the gametes are the only haploid stage.

Figure 11.14 Fertilization and Meiosis Alternate in Sexual Reproduction
In sexual reproduction, haploid (*n*) cells or organisms alternate with diploid (*2n*) cells or organisms.

View in **Achieve**
Activity 11.3 **Sexual Life Cycle**

All sexual life cycles involve meiosis to produce haploid cells and fertilization to produce a zygote. **Figure 11.14** presents three types of sexual life cycles. In some life cycles the products of meiosis undergo cell division, resulting in a mature organism with haploid cells. Specialized cells in these haploid organisms become gametes by mitosis. In other life cycles the gametes form directly from the products of meiosis. In all cases, gametes fuse to produce a zygote, beginning the diploid stage of the life cycle. Since the origin of sexual reproduction, evolution has generated many different versions of the sexual life cycle.

The essence of sexual reproduction is the *random selection of half of the diploid chromosome set*—one member of each genetically similar chromosome pair—to make a haploid gamete, followed by fusion of two haploid gametes to produce a diploid cell. Both of these steps contribute to a shuffling of genetic information in the population, so that no two individuals have exactly the same genetic makeup (unless they are identical twins). The diversity provided by sexual reproduction opens up enormous opportunities for evolution.

KEY CONCEPT
11.4 Recap and Assess

Sexual reproduction involves meiosis, which generates four haploid cells from a diploid parent cell, and fertilization, which produces a diploid cell from the fusion of two haploid cells. Sexual reproduction increases genetic diversity, the raw material of evolution by natural selection.

1. What general features do all sexual life cycles have in common?
2. You have a sample of a small green plant. How would you tell if it is haploid or diploid?
3. Diagram haplontic and diplontic life cycles, clearly showing the haploid and diploid phases of the life cycle.

Meiosis, unlike mitosis, results in daughter cells that differ genetically from the parent cell. We will now look at the details of meiosis to see how this genetic shuffling occurs.

KEY CONCEPT
11.5 Meiosis Leads to the Formation of Gametes

Learning Objectives

11.5.1 List the stages of meiosis and state what events occur in each.

11.5.2 Calculate the number of different gametes produced by independent assortment during meiosis.

11.5.3 Explain how crossing over during meiosis generates genetic diversity.

11.5.4 Explain how errors in mitosis or meiosis can lead to aneuploidy in cells.

11.5.5 Distinguish polyploidy from aneuploidy and explain how it occurs.

In the last key concept you learned about the role and importance of meiosis in sexual reproduction. Now you'll see how meiosis produces haploid cells. Unlike the products of mitosis, the

products of meiosis are genetically different from one another and from the parent cell.

Meiosis has three main effects:

1. It reduces the chromosome number from diploid ($2n$) to haploid (n).
2. It ensures that each of the haploid products has a complete set of chromosomes.
3. It generates genetic diversity among the products.

Meiosis reduces the chromosome number

Meiosis consists of *two* nuclear divisions that together reduce the number of chromosomes to the haploid number, in preparation for sexual reproduction. *Although the nucleus divides twice during meiosis, the DNA is replicated only once during the S phase that precedes it.* The events of meiosis are illustrated in **Figure 11.15**. You should refer to it often as you read about meiosis in detail. Two unique features characterize the first nuclear division, called **meiosis I**:

1. *Homologous chromosomes come together to pair* along their entire lengths. No such pairing occurs in mitosis.
2. *The homologous chromosome pairs separate*, but the individual chromosomes, each consisting of two sister chromatids, remain intact. (The chromatids will separate during meiosis II.)

Like mitosis, meiosis I is preceded by an interphase with an S phase, during which each chromosome is replicated. As a result, each chromosome consists of two sister chromatids, held together by cohesin proteins. Unlike mitosis, meiosis can occur only in diploid cells; haploid cells do not undergo meiosis. At the end of meiosis I, two haploid nuclei form, each with half of the original chromosomes (one member of each homologous pair). Since the centromeres did not separate, these replicated chromosomes are still composed of two sister chromatids. The sister chromatids are separated during **meiosis II** (similar to mitosis), which follows meiosis I. As a result, the products of the two divisions that make up meiosis are four cells, each containing the haploid number of unreplicated chromosomes. But these four cells are not genetically identical.

 View in Achieve
Animation 11.2 **Meiosis**

Chromatid exchanges during meiosis I generate genetic diversity

Meiosis I begins with a long prophase I (the first three panels of Figure 11.15), during which the chromosomes change markedly. The homologous replicated chromosomes pair by adhering along their lengths in a process called **synapsis**. (This does not happen in mitosis.) This pairing process lasts from prophase I to the end of metaphase I. Each synapsed pair of homologous chromosomes is called a bivalent. For example, in a human cell at the end of prophase I there are 23 bivalents, each consisting of two replicated homologs.

Throughout prophase I and metaphase I, the chromatin continues to coil and compact, so that the chromosomes appear ever thicker. At a certain point, the homologous chromosomes begin to

MEIOSIS I

Early prophase I

Mid-prophase I

Late prophase I–Prometaphase

Centrosomes

Pairs of homologs

Bivalent

Chiasma

1 The chromatin begins to condense following interphase.

2 Synapsis aligns homologs, and replicated chromosomes condense further.

3 The chromosomes continue to coil and shorten. The chiasmata reflect crossing over, the exchange of genetic material between nonsister chromatids in a homologous pair. In prometaphase the nuclear envelope breaks down.

MEIOSIS II

Prophase II

Metaphase II

Anaphase II

Metaphase II plate

7 The chromosomes condense again, following a brief interphase in which DNA does not replicate.

8 The centromeres of the paired chromatids line up across the metaphase II plate of each cell.

9 The sister chromatids separate and move to opposite poles. Independent alignment of homologous pairs at metaphase I and crossing over guarantee that each gamete will be different.

Metaphase I

Metaphase I plate

4 The homologous pairs of replicated chromosomes line up on the metaphase I plate.

Anaphase I

5 The homologous replicated chromosomes move to opposite poles of the cell.

Telophase I

6 The chromosomes gather into nuclei, and the original cell divides.

Telophase II

10 The chromosomes gather into nuclei, and the cells divide.

Products

11 Each of the four cells has a nucleus with a haploid number of unreplicated chromosomes.

All photos © C. A. Hasenkampf/Biological Photo Service

Figure 11.15 **Meiosis: Generating Haploid Cells**   In meiosis, four daughter nuclei are produced, each of which has half as many chromosomes as the original cell. Four haploid cells are the result of two successive nuclear divisions. The micrographs show meiosis in the male reproductive organ of a lily; the diagrams show the corresponding phases in an animal cell.

▶ **View in Achieve**
Activity 11.4 **Images of Meiosis**

(A)

Chiasmata

Homologous chromosomes

© Science VU/B. John/ Visuals Unlimited, Inc.

(B)

Chiasmata

Homologous chromosomes

Figure 11.16 Chiasmata: Evidence of Genetic Exchange between Chromatids **(A)** This micrograph shows a pair of homologous chromosomes, each with two chromatids, during prophase I of meiosis. Two chiasmata are visible. **(B)** Using colors to represent the two homologs emphasizes where they have undergone genetic exchange.

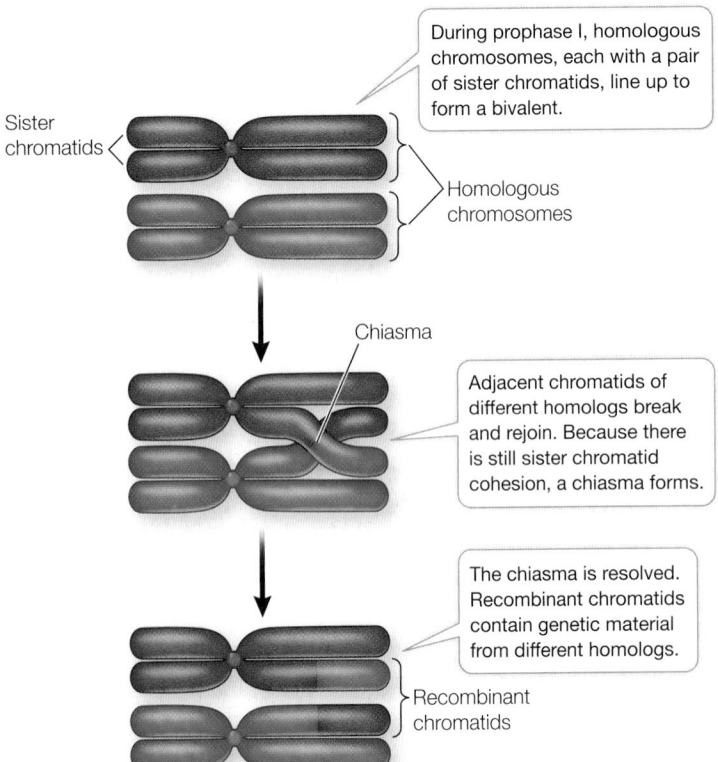

During prophase I, homologous chromosomes, each with a pair of sister chromatids, line up to form a bivalent.

Sister chromatids

Homologous chromosomes

Chiasma

Adjacent chromatids of different homologs break and rejoin. Because there is still sister chromatid cohesion, a chiasma forms.

The chiasma is resolved. Recombinant chromatids contain genetic material from different homologs.

Recombinant chromatids

Figure 11.17 Crossing Over Forms Genetically Diverse Chromosomes The exchange of genetic material by crossing over results in new combinations of genetic information on the recombinant chromosomes. The two different colors distinguish the chromosomes contributed by the male and female parents.

be pulled apart by spindle microtubules, especially near the centromeres, but they remain held together by physical attachments mediated by cohesins. Later in prophase I, regions having these attachments take on an X-shaped appearance (**Figure 11.16**) and are called **chiasmata** (singular *chiasma*, "cross").

A chiasma reflects an exchange of genetic material between nonsister chromatids on homologous replicated chromosomes—what geneticists call **crossing over** (**Figure 11.17**). The chromosomes usually begin exchanging material shortly after synapsis begins, but chiasmata do not become visible until later, when the homologs are beginning to separate. Crossing over results in **recombinant chromatids**, and it increases genetic variation among the products of meiosis by shuffling genetic information among the homologous pairs. In Chapter 12 we will explore further the genetic consequences of crossing over.

At this point, pause and think about what is going on at the molecular level: Each chromatid is a double-stranded DNA molecule, and the homologous chromatids therefore are homologous in DNA nucleotide sequence. Breakage and reunion of DNA molecules to form recombinant chromatids involve breakage of phosphodiester bonds that hold adjacent nucleotides on DNA together (see Figure 4.2) and formation of new bonds linking DNA molecules of two homologous, nonsister chromatids.

Mitosis seldom takes more than an hour or two, but meiosis can take much longer. In human males, the cells in the testis that undergo meiosis take about a week for prophase I and about a month for the entire meiotic cycle. In females, prophase I begins long before a woman's birth, during her early fetal development, resumes and proceeds to meiosis II as much as decades later, during the monthly ovarian cycle, and is completed only when fertilization occurs (see Key Concept 41.2).

During meiosis homologous chromosomes separate by independent assortment

A diploid organism has two sets of chromosomes ($2n$): one set derived from its male parent (the paternal set), and the other from its female parent (the maternal set). As the organism grows and develops, its cells undergo mitotic divisions. In mitosis, each chromosome behaves independently of its homolog, and its two sister chromatids are sent to opposite poles during anaphase. Each daughter nucleus ends up with $2n$ chromosomes, which are identical to those of the parent cell. In meiosis, things are very different. **Figure 11.18** compares the two processes.

Figure 11.18 Mitosis and Meiosis: A Comparison ▶ Meiosis I differs from mitosis chiefly by the pairing of homologs and by the continued association of sister chromatids during anaphase I, which results in a reduction in chromosome number (from $2n$ replicated chromosomes to n replicated chromosomes). Meiosis II and mitosis are essentially equivalent, with the sister chromatids of each chromosome ending up at opposite pole.

 View in Achieve
Simulation 11.1 Mitosis versus Meiosis

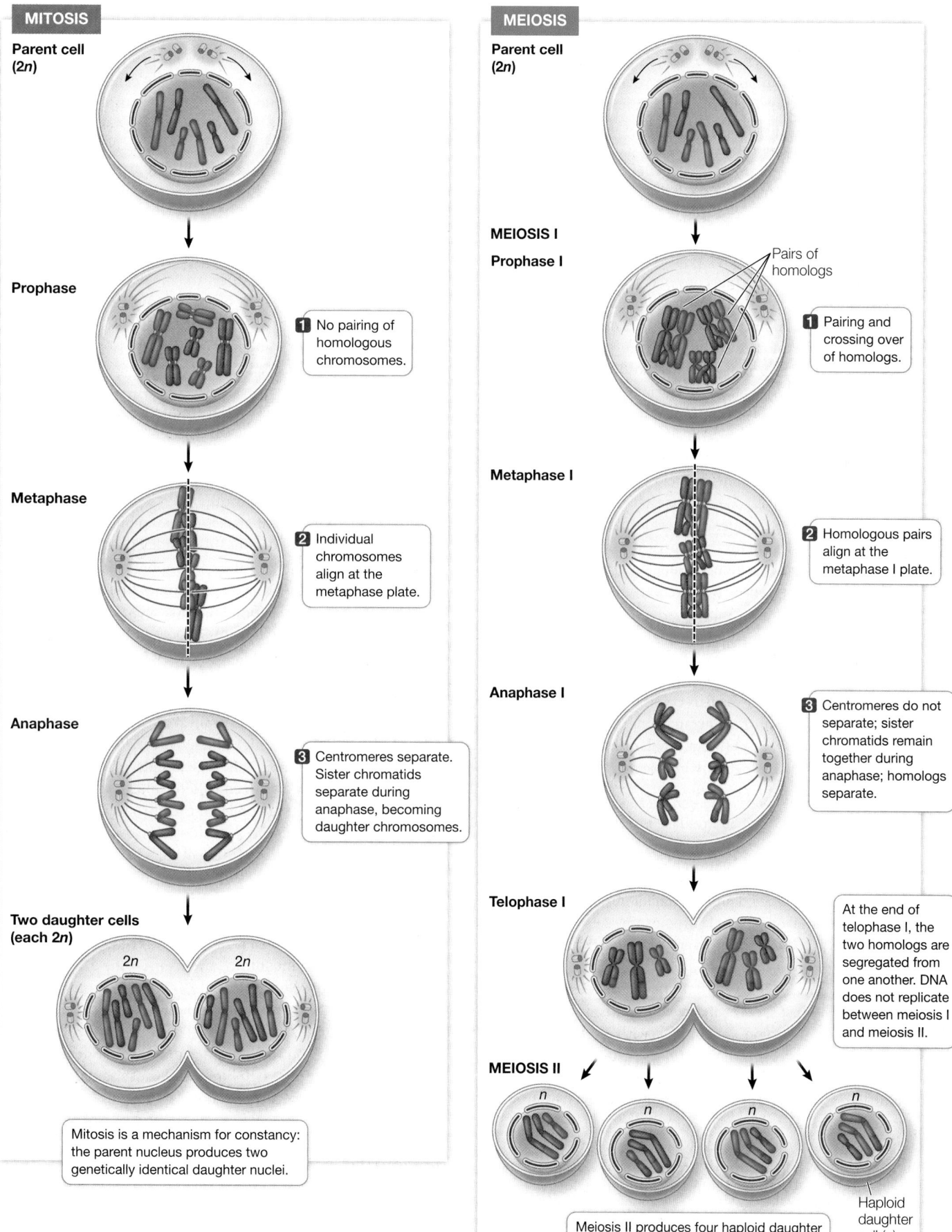

MITOSIS

Parent cell (2*n*)

Prophase

1 No pairing of homologous chromosomes.

Metaphase

2 Individual chromosomes align at the metaphase plate.

Anaphase

3 Centromeres separate. Sister chromatids separate during anaphase, becoming daughter chromosomes.

Two daughter cells (each 2*n*)

2*n*   2*n*

Mitosis is a mechanism for constancy: the parent nucleus produces two genetically identical daughter nuclei.

MEIOSIS

Parent cell (2*n*)

MEIOSIS I
Prophase I

Pairs of homologs

1 Pairing and crossing over of homologs.

Metaphase I

2 Homologous pairs align at the metaphase I plate.

Anaphase I

3 Centromeres do not separate; sister chromatids remain together during anaphase; homologs separate.

Telophase I

At the end of telophase I, the two homologs are segregated from one another. DNA does not replicate between meiosis I and meiosis II.

MEIOSIS II

n   *n*   *n*   *n*

Haploid daughter cell (*n*)

Meiosis II produces four haploid daughter cells that are genetically distinct.

In meiosis I, chromosomes of maternal origin pair with their paternal homologs during synapsis. To clarify, you have two copies of chromosome 1 of the human genome in your cells. Your maternal copy came from your biological mother and your paternal copy from your biological father. In meiosis I, your maternal and paternal chromosome 1's pair up. And so on with the other 22 pairs of chromosomes. *Pairing of maternal and paternal homologs does not occur in mitosis.* Segregation of the homologs during meiotic anaphase I ensures that each newly formed cell receives one member of each homologous pair (see steps 4–6 of Figure 11.15). Returning to the example of chromosome 1, at the end of meiosis I in your cells, each daughter nucleus contains one copy of chromosome 1 (either the maternal or paternal copy), whereas the diploid cell that began meiosis had two copies. Taking the other 22 pairs of chromosomes into account, at the end of meiosis I in humans, each of the two daughter cells has 23 of the original 46 chromosomes.

Recall that before meiosis begins each chromosome is duplicated in S phase of interphase. So the beginning cell of meiosis had two replicated copies of each chromosomal DNA molecule. After meiosis I each daughter cell therefore has one copy of each replicated chromosome. In meiosis II, each product of meiosis I divides further to form two haploid gametes, with one copy of each unreplicated chromosome. So the end product of meiosis II is four haploid gametes.

Crossing over is one reason for the genetic diversity among the products of meiosis; another is **independent assortment**, whereby each haploid cell receives an entire set of genes, but only one of each pair from each parent, from the diploid cell in a random fashion. It is a matter of chance which member of a homologous pair goes to which daughter cell at anaphase I. For example, imagine there are two homologous pairs of chromosomes in the diploid parent nucleus. A particular daughter nucleus could receive the paternal chromosome 1 and the maternal chromosome 2. Or it could get paternal 2 and maternal 1, or both maternal, or both paternal. It all depends on how the homologous pairs line up at metaphase I.

Connect the Concepts Mendel proposed the concept of independent assortment after he observed the results of genetic crosses with pea plants. See Key Concept 12.1.

Note that of the four possible chromosome combinations just described, only two produce daughter nuclei with full complements of either maternal or paternal chromosome sets (apart from the material exchanged by crossing over). *The greater the number of chromosomes, the less probable it is that the original parental combinations will be reestablished, and the greater the potential for genetic diversity.* Most species of diploid organisms have more than two pairs of chromosomes. In humans, with 23 chromosome pairs, 2^{23} (8,388,608) different combinations can be produced just by the mechanism of independent assortment. Taking the extra genetic shuffling afforded by crossing over into account, the number of possible combinations is very large indeed! Crossing over and independent assortment, along with the processes that result in mutations, provide the genetic diversity needed for the differential survival and reproduction of diverse individuals—the basis of evolution by natural selection.

You have seen how meiosis I is fundamentally different from mitosis. In contrast, meiosis II is similar to mitosis in that it involves the separation of sister chromatids into daughter nuclei (see steps 7–11 in Figure 11.15). However, because of crossing over during meiosis I, the sister chromatids are not necessarily identical to one another as they would be in mitosis. Chance assortment of the sister chromatids during meiosis II contributes further to the genetic diversity of the meiotic products. The final products of meiosis I and meiosis II are four haploid daughter cells, each with one set (*n*) of chromosomes, each of which is genetically unique.

Meiotic errors lead to abnormal chromosome structures and numbers

In the complex processes of mitosis and meiosis, things occasionally go wrong. In meiosis I, a pair of homologous chromosomes may fail to separate, and in mitosis or meiosis II, sister chromatids may fail to separate. Conversely, homologous chromosomes may fail to remain together during metaphase I of meiosis, and then both may migrate to the same pole in anaphase I. These are all examples of **nondisjunction**, which results in the production of aneuploid cells. **Aneuploidy** is a condition in which one or a few chromosomes are either lacking or present in excess. If nondisjunction occurs during meiosis, it can lead to offspring with either one too many, or one too few, chromosomes in all of their cells (**Figure 11.19**).

There are many different causes of aneuploidy, but one cause may be a breakdown in the cohesins that keep sister chromatids and bivalents joined together during prophase. These and other proteins ensure that when the chromosomes line up at the metaphase I plate, for example, one homolog will face one pole and the other homolog will face the other pole. If the cohesins break down at the wrong time, both homologs may go to the same pole.

Aneuploidy resulting from nondisjunction during meiosis is often lethal for the affected offspring. In a few cases, the affected offspring survive but may have certain abnormalities. An example in humans is Down syndrome, which occurs when a gamete has two copies of chromosome 21. If, for example, an egg with two of these chromosomes is fertilized by a normal sperm, the resulting zygote will have three copies of the chromosome: it will be **trisomic** for chromosome 21. A child with Down syndrome has mild to moderately impaired intellectual ability; characteristic abnormalities of the hands, tongue, and eyelids; and an increased susceptibility to cardiac abnormalities. About 1 child in 800 is born with Down syndrome. If an egg that did not receive chromosome 21 is fertilized by a normal sperm, the zygote will have only one copy: it will be **monosomic** for chromosome 21, and this is lethal during fetal development.

Trisomies and the corresponding monosomies are surprisingly common in human zygotes, with 10%–30% of all conceptions showing aneuploidy. But most of the embryos that develop from such zygotes do not survive to birth, and those that do often die before the age of 1 year (trisomies for chromosome 21 are the viable exception). At least one-fifth of all recognized pregnancies are spontaneously terminated (miscarried) during the first 2 months, largely because of trisomies and monosomies. The actual proportion of spontaneously terminated pregnancies is certainly higher, because the earliest ones often go unrecognized.

Other abnormal chromosomal events can also occur. In a process called **translocation**, a piece of a chromosome may break

(A) Nondisjunction during mitosis

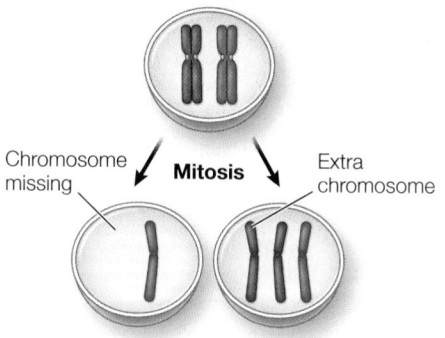

Figure 11.19 Nondisjunction Leads to Aneuploidy **(A)** In mitosis, nondisjunction results in both daughter cells being aneuploid: one cell has an extra copy of a chromosome and one cell lacks a copy. **(B)** Nondisjunction in meiosis I during sperm production results in four aneuploid gametes: two sperm have an extra copy of the chromosome and two sperm lack a copy. Fertilization of normal eggs produces aneuploid zygotes.

Q: What is the effect of meiosis II nondisjunction on gametes?

(B) Nondisjunction during meiosis I

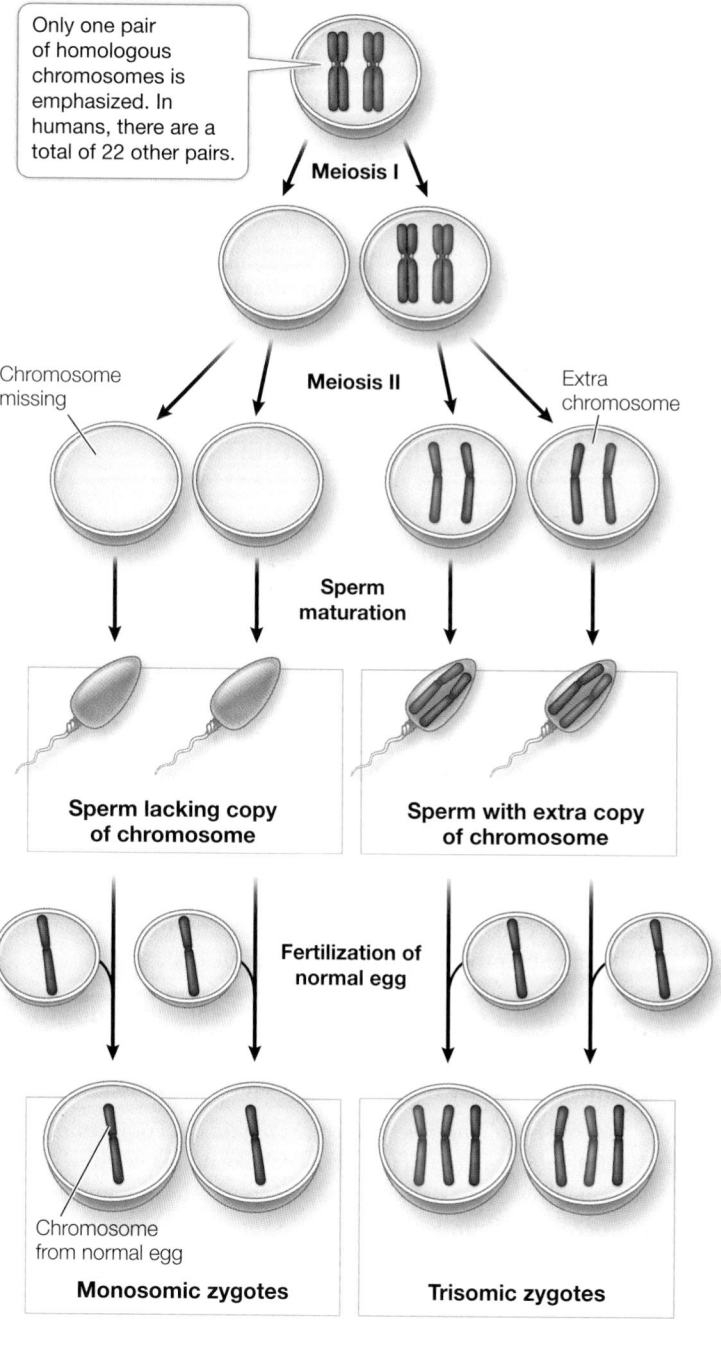

away and become attached to another chromosome. For example, a large part of one chromosome 21 may be translocated to another chromosome. Individuals who inherit this translocated piece along with two normal copies of chromosome 21 will also have Down syndrome.

The number, shapes, and sizes of the metaphase chromosomes constitute the karyotype

When cells are in metaphase of mitosis, it is often possible to count and characterize their individual chromosomes. If a photomicrograph of the entire set of chromosomes is made, the images of the individual chromosomes can be manipulated to pair them and place them in an orderly arrangement. Such a rearranged photomicrograph reveals the number, shapes, and sizes of the chromosomes in a cell, which together constitute its **karyotype** (Figure 11.20). In humans, karyotypes can aid in the diagnosis of chromosomal abnormalities such as trisomies or translocations, and this has led to an entire branch of medicine called cytogenetics. However, as you will see in Chapter 15, chromosome analysis with the microscope is replaced in some cases by direct analysis of DNA.

Polyploids have more than two complete sets of chromosomes

As mentioned in Key Concept 11.4, mature organisms are often either diploid (for example, most animals) or haploid (for example, most fungi). Under some circumstances, triploid (3*n*), tetraploid (4*n*), or higher-order **polyploid** nuclei may form. Each of these ploidy levels represents an increase in the number of complete chromosome sets present. If there is nondisjunction of all the chromosomes during meiosis I or II (see the earlier discussion), diploid gametes will form. Such an event might involve breakdown of the meiotic spindle so that anaphase I or II does not occur. A diploid gamete can lead to *auto*polyploidy after fertilization. Multiple fertilization (polyspermy) can also lead to autopolyploidy. Autotriploids and autotetraploids have been important in some cases in species formation. A diploid nucleus can undergo normal meiosis because there are two sets of chromosomes to make up homologous pairs, which separate during anaphase I. Similarly, a tetraploid nucleus has an even number of each kind of chromosome, so each chromosome can pair with its homolog. However, a triploid nucleus cannot undergo normal meiosis because one-third of the chromosomes would lack partners. As a result, triploid individuals are usually sterile.

Because polyploid nuclei have more chromosome sets, their cells tend to be larger. This has led to the use of polyploid plants

(A)

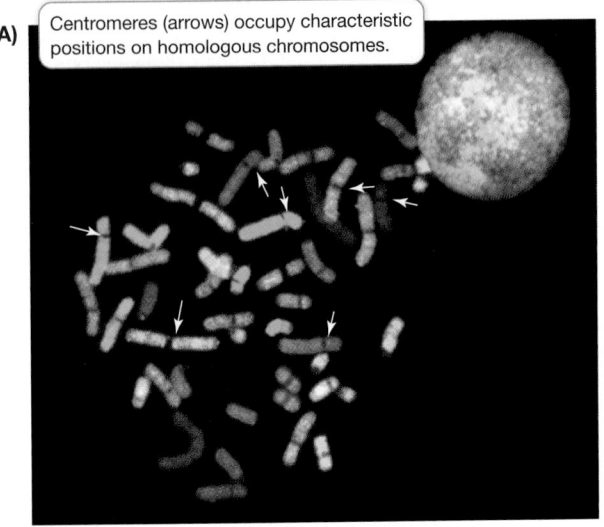

Centromeres (arrows) occupy characteristic positions on homologous chromosomes.

(B)

Human somatic cells are diploid with 23 pairs of chromosomes, including the sex chromosomes. This female's sex chromosomes are X and X; a male would have X and Y chromosomes.

Both photos courtesy of Dr. Thomas Ried and Dr. Evelin Schröck, NIH

Figure 11.20 The Human Karyotype **(A)** Chromosomes from a human cell in metaphase. The DNA of each chromosome pair has a specific nucleotide sequence that is stained by a particular colored dye, so that the chromosomes in a homologous pair share a distinctive color. Each chromosome at this stage is composed of two chromatids, but they cannot be distinguished. At the upper right is an interphase nucleus. **(B)** This karyogram, produced by computerized analysis of the image on the left, shows homologous pairs lined up together and numbered, clearly revealing the individual's karyotype.

in agriculture. Diploid bananas ($2n = 22$) are smaller and produce inedible seeds; triploid bananas ($3n = 33$) are larger and seedless. A similar phenomenon is seen in triploid seedless watermelon. Perhaps the best known, and certainly the most important, polyploid crop plant is wheat. In this case, hybridization occurred between species, forming new *allo*polyploid conditions:

- Haploid gametes from two species (A and B) mated and formed a diploid zygote (chromosomes AB).

- Nondisjunction of all chromosomes occurred during mitosis, resulting in tetraploid (AABB) cells, which then gave rise to fertile flowers (producing AB gametes).

Modern bread wheat is the result of two such events, which occurred about 8,000–10,000 years ago, resulting in an allohexaploid (AABBCC). Wheat's properties of grain formation and environmental adaptation thus come from three different ancestral species. Other allopolyploid crops include cotton, oats, and sugarcane.

KEY CONCEPT

11.5 Recap and Assess

Meiosis produces four daughter cells in which the chromosome number is reduced from diploid to haploid. Because of the independent assortment of chromosomes and the crossing over of homologous chromatids, the four products of meiosis are genetically distinct. Meiotic and mitotic errors, such as nondisjunction, can lead to abnormal numbers of chromosomes. Several important crop plants, such as wheat, are polyploid.

1. How do crossing over and independent assortment result in unique daughter nuclei?

2. Compare prophase I of meiosis with prophase of mitosis. Compare anaphase I of meiosis with anaphase of mitosis.

3. Rarely, a person is born with an extra X chromosome (XXY). How might this aneuploidy arise?

4. What is polyploidy, and how might it arise?

An essential role of cell division in complex eukaryotes is to replace dead cells. What causes cells to die?

KEY CONCEPT

11.6 Cell Death Is Important in Living Organisms

Learning Objectives

11.6.1 Compare and contrast necrosis and apoptosis.

11.6.2 Describe how apoptosis can aid an organism's survival.

11.6.3 Describe how apoptosis is regulated.

Cells within a living organism can die in one of two ways. **Necrosis** occurs when cells and tissues are damaged by mechanical means or toxins, or are starved of oxygen or nutrients. Necrotic cells often swell up and burst, releasing their contents into the extracellular environment and possibly causing inflammation (see Key Concept 40.2). **Apoptosis**, or programmed cell death, is a genetically determined series of events that occur during normal developmental processes and in adult tissues as well.

Programmed cell death removes cells that do not benefit the organism

In animals, there are two possible reasons for apoptosis:

1. *The cell is no longer needed by the organism.* For example, before birth, a human fetus has weblike hands, with connective tissue between the fingers. As development proceeds, this unneeded tissue disappears as the cells undergo apoptosis in response to specific signals.

Figure 11.21 Apoptosis: Programmed Cell Death **(A)** Many cells are programmed to "self-destruct" when they are no longer needed, or when they have lived long enough to accumulate a burden of DNA damage that might harm the organism. **(B)** Both external and internal signals stimulate caspases, the enzymes that break down specific cell constituents, resulting in apoptosis.

Q: Apoptosis occurs in most organisms, with a common molecular pathway. This indicates that apoptosis is important in terms of evolution. What might be a selective advantage for apoptosis?

2. *The longer cells live, the more prone they are to genetic damage that could lead to cancer.* This is especially true of epithelial cells on the surface of an organism, which may be exposed to radiation or toxic substances. Such cells normally die after only days or weeks and are replaced by new cells.

The events of apoptosis are similar in many organisms. The cell becomes detached from its neighbors and its chromatin is digested by enzymes that cut the DNA (between the nucleosomes) into fragments of about 180 base pairs. The cell forms membranous lobes, or "blebs," that break up into cell fragments (**Figure 11.21A**). In a remarkable example of the economy of nature, the surrounding, living cells usually ingest the remains of the dead cell by phagocytosis. Neighboring cells digest the apoptotic cell contents in their lysosomes, and the digested components are recycled.

Apoptosis is also used by plant cells in an important defense mechanism called the hypersensitive response. Plants can protect themselves from disease by undergoing apoptosis at the site of infection by a fungus or bacterium. With no living tissue to grow in, the invading organism is not able to spread to other parts of the plant. Because of their rigid cell walls, plant cells do not form blebs the way animal cells do. Instead, they digest their own cell contents in the vacuole and then release the digested components into the vascular system. You will learn more about this in Chapter 37.

A variety of signals, either external or from inside the cell, can lead to programmed cell death (**Figure 11.21B**). Such signals include hormones, growth factors, viral infection, certain toxins, or extensive DNA damage. These signals activate specific receptors, which in turn activate signal transduction pathways leading to apoptosis. Some apoptotic pathways target the mitochondria, for example, by increasing the permeability of mitochondrial membranes. The cell quickly dies if its mitochondria can't carry out cellular respiration. An important class of enzymes called **caspases**

are activated during apoptosis. These enzymes are proteases that hydrolyze target molecules in a cascade of events. The cell dies as the caspases hydrolyze proteins of the nuclear envelope, nucleosomes, cytoskeleton, and cell membrane.

KEY CONCEPT
11.6 Recap and Assess

Cell death can occur either by necrosis or by apoptosis. Apoptosis is governed by precise molecular controls.

1. What types of events initiate necrosis, and how do these events differ from those that initiate apoptosis?
2. In what situations is apoptosis necessary?
3. How is apoptosis regulated?

Mitosis adds cells to organisms, and apoptosis removes them. Under normal circumstances these processes are balanced so as to benefit the organism as a whole. In the next key concept we will examine what happens when this balance is disturbed and cell production runs out of control.

KEY CONCEPT
11.7 Unregulated Cell Division Can Lead to Cancer

Learning Objectives

11.7.1 Compare and contrast cancer cells and normal cells.

11.7.2 Explain how regulation of the cell cycle can become disrupted in cancer cells.

11.7.3 Justify the rationale for targeting events in the cell cycle as a means of treating cancer.

Perhaps no malady affecting people in the industrialized world instills more fear than cancer, and most people realize that it involves an inappropriate increase in cell numbers. One in three Americans will have some form of cancer in his or her lifetime, and at present, one in five will die of it. With 1.7 million new cases and 600,000 deaths in the United States annually, cancer ranks second only to heart disease as a killer.

Cancer cells differ from normal cells in important ways

Cancer cells differ from the normal cells from which they originate in two ways:

1. Cancer cells lose control over cell growth.

2. Cancer cells can migrate to other locations in the body.

Most cells in the body divide only if they are exposed to extracellular signals such as growth factors. Cancer cells do not respond to these controls, and instead divide more or less continuously, ultimately forming **tumors** (large masses of cells). By the time a physician can feel a tumor or see one on an X-ray film or CT scan, it already contains millions of cells. Tumors can be benign or malignant:

- **Benign** tumors resemble the tissue they came from, grow slowly, and remain localized where they develop. For example, a lipoma is a benign tumor of fat cells that may arise in the armpit and remain there. Benign tumors are not cancers, but they must be removed if they impinge on an organ, obstructing its function.

- **Malignant** tumors do not look like their parent tissue at all. A flat, specialized epithelial cell in the lung wall may turn into a relatively featureless, round, malignant lung cancer cell (**Figure 11.22**). Malignant cells often have irregular structures, such as variable nucleus sizes and shapes. This characteristic was used to identify the cells in Henrietta Lacks's tumor as malignant (see the opening investigation of this chapter).

© Dennis Kunkel Microscopy/Science Source

Figure 11.22 A Cancer Cell with Its Normal Neighbors This lung cancer cell (yellow-green) is quite different from the normal lung cells surrounding it. The cancer cell can divide more rapidly than its normal counterparts, and it can spread to other organs. This form of small-cell cancer is lethal, with a 5-year survival rate of only 10%. Most cases are caused by tobacco smoking.

The second and most fearsome characteristic of cancer cells is their ability to invade surrounding tissues and spread to other parts of the body by traveling through the bloodstream or lymphatic ducts. When malignant cells become lodged in some distant part of the body, they go on dividing and growing, establishing a tumor at that new site. This spreading of cancer, called **metastasis**, results in organ failures and makes the cancer very hard to treat.

Cancer cells lose control over the cell cycle and apoptosis

Earlier in this chapter you learned about proteins that regulate the progress of a eukaryotic cell through the cell cycle:

- Positive regulators such as growth factors stimulate the cell cycle: they are like "gas pedals."

- Negative regulators such as retinoblastoma protein (RB) inhibit the cell cycle: they are like "brakes."

Just as driving a car requires stepping on the gas pedal *and* releasing the brakes, a cell will go through a division cycle only if the positive regulators are active and the negative regulators are inactive.

In most cells, the two regulatory systems ensure that the cells divide only when needed. In cancer cells, these two processes are abnormal.

- **Oncogene** proteins are positive regulators in cancer cells. They are derived from normal positive regulators that have become mutated to be overly active or that are present in excess, and they stimulate the cancer cells to divide more often. Oncogene products could be growth factors, their receptors, or other components in the signal transduction pathways (see Chapter 7) that stimulate cell division. An example of an oncogene protein is a growth factor receptor in a breast cancer cell (**Figure 11.23A**). Normal breast cells have relatively low numbers of the human epidermal growth factor receptor HER2. So breast cells are not usually stimulated to multiply in the presence of this growth factor. In about 25% of breast cancers, a DNA change results in the increased production of the HER2 receptor. This results in positive stimulation of the cell cycle, and a rapid proliferation of cells with the altered DNA.

- **Tumor suppressors** are negative regulators in both cancer and normal cells, but in cancer cells they are inactive. An example is the RB protein, which when active acts at R (the restriction point) in G1 to block the cell cycle (see Figure 11.3). In some cancer cells RB is inactive, allowing the cell cycle to proceed. Some viral proteins can inactivate tumor suppressors. For example, the human papillomavirus infects cells of the cervix and produces a protein called E7. E7 binds to the RB protein and prevents it from inhibiting the cell cycle (**Figure 11.23B**). Another important tumor suppressor is p53, a transcription factor that is involved in cell cycle checkpoint pathways and apoptosis. The importance of p53 as a tumor suppressor is illustrated by the fact that more than 50% of human tumors have mutations in the gene that encodes p53.

(A)

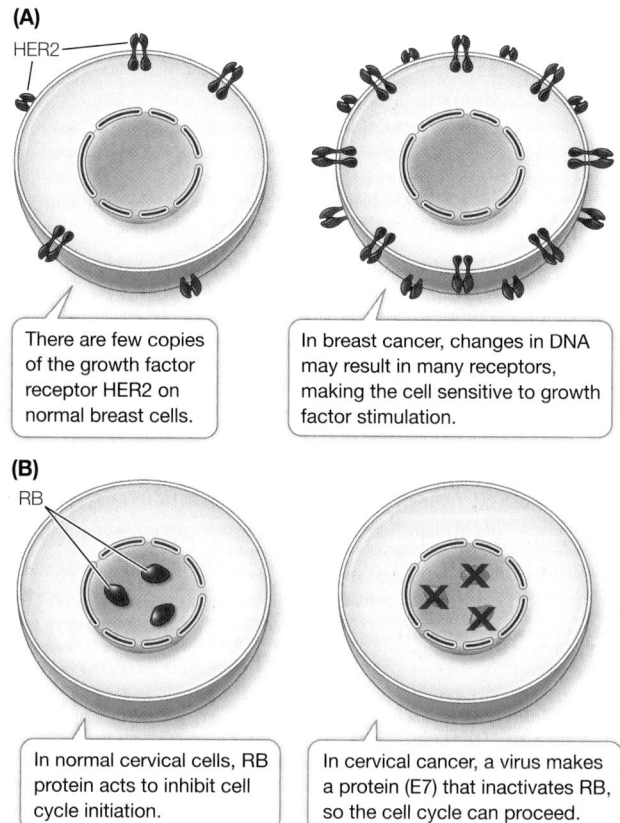

HER2

There are few copies of the growth factor receptor HER2 on normal breast cells.

In breast cancer, changes in DNA may result in many receptors, making the cell sensitive to growth factor stimulation.

(B)

RB

In normal cervical cells, RB protein acts to inhibit cell cycle initiation.

In cervical cancer, a virus makes a protein (E7) that inactivates RB, so the cell cycle can proceed.

Figure 11.23 Molecular Changes in Cancer Cells In cancer, oncogene proteins become active **(A)** and tumor suppressor proteins become inactive **(B)**.

With oncogenes (the gas pedal) and tumor suppressor genes (the brakes), it takes more than one protein to allow the cancer cell cycle to proceed. There may be several oncogenes and tumor suppressor genes involved in a single tumor. For example, two important oncogenes in mouse cells are *Myc*, whose expression stimulates the cell cycle and prevents apoptosis, and *Ras*, which encodes a signaling molecule you saw in Chapter 7 (see Figure 7.9). Experiments show that it takes the expression of both of these oncogenes to set the cell cycle in motion in mouse cells and convert them into tumor cells (**Figure 11.24**).

The discovery of apoptosis (see Key Concept 11.6) changed the way biologists think about cancer. In a population of cells, the net increase in cell numbers over time (the growth rate) is the difference between the rate at which cells are added (the rate of cell division) and the rate at which cells are lost (the rate of apoptosis):

Tumor growth rate = rate of cell division − rate of apoptosis

In normal nongrowing tissues, the rate of cell division equals the rate of apoptosis, so the cell population as a whole does not grow. Cancer cells are defective in their regulation of the cell cycle, resulting in increased rates of cell division. In addition, cancer cells can lose the ability to respond to positive regulators of apoptosis (see Figure 11.23B), and this results in lowered rates

Experiment

Figure 11.24 Does It Take Multiple Events to Trigger the Cancer Cell Cycle?

Original Papers: H. Land et al. 1983. Tumorigenic conversion of primary embryo fibroblasts required at least two cooperating oncogenes. *Nature* 304: 596–602.

E. Sinn et al. 1987. Coexpression of MMTV/v-Ha-*ras* and MMTV/c-*myc* genes in transgenic mice: Synergistic action of oncogenes in vivo. *Cell* 49: 465–475.

Experiments using mouse cells in the laboratory showed that the expression of more than one oncogene is required to transform a normal cell into a cancer cell.

HYPOTHESIS▶ The expression of both *Ras* and *Myc* oncogenes is needed to transform normal mouse cells into tumor cells.

METHOD▶

Normal cells

Normal mouse cells do not divide and form colonies in the lab dish, but tumor cells will divide.

Tumor cells

1 Prepare three sets of laboratory dishes containing equal numbers of normal mouse cells.

2 To one dish add DNA containing *Ras* genes, to the second dish add DNA containing *Ras* + *Myc* genes, and to the third dish add DNA containing only *Myc* genes.

Ras genes

Ras + *Myc* genes

Myc genes

RESULTS▶

Ras alone

Ras + *Myc*

Myc alone

CONCLUSION▶ The expression of both *Myc* and *Ras* oncogenes is required for tumor cell formation.

Go to **Achieve** for a companion **Data in Depth** exercise.

of cell death. Both of these defects lead to an increased growth rate of the cancer cell population.

Cancer treatments target the cell cycle

The most successful and widely used treatment for cancer is surgery. While physically removing a tumor is optimal, it is often difficult for a surgeon to get all of the tumor cells. (A tumor about 1 centimeter in diameter already has a billion cells!) Tumors are

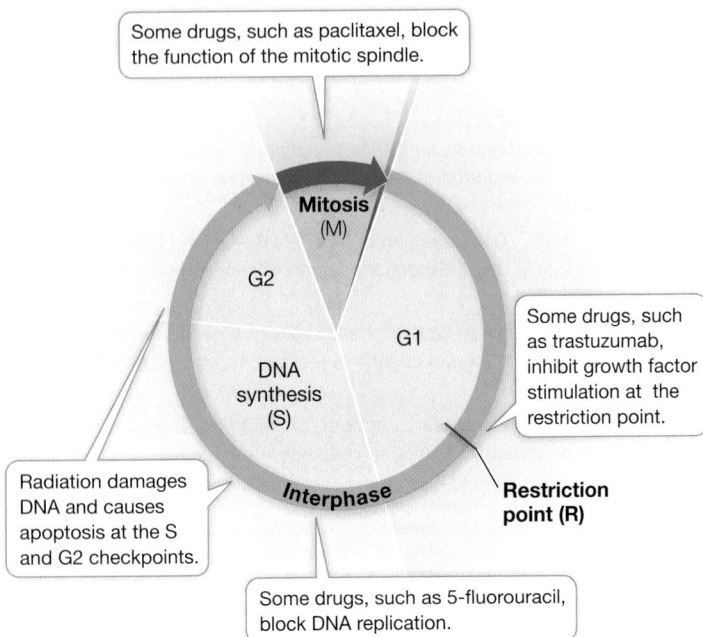

Some drugs, such as paclitaxel, block the function of the mitotic spindle.

Mitosis (M)

G2

G1

DNA synthesis (S)

Some drugs, such as trastuzumab, inhibit growth factor stimulation at the restriction point.

Radiation damages DNA and causes apoptosis at the S and G2 checkpoints.

Interphase

Restriction point (R)

Some drugs, such as 5-fluorouracil, block DNA replication.

Figure 11.25 Cancer Treatment and the Cell Cycle To prevent cancer cells from dividing, physicians use combinations of therapies that attack the cell cycle at different points.

Q: How do these treatments differ from treatments based on specific targets (see Figure 11.23)? Would the side effects of the two types of treatments be different?

generally embedded in normal tissues. Added to this is the probability that cells of the tumor may have broken off and spread to other organs. This makes it unlikely that localized surgery will be curative. So other approaches are taken to treat or cure cancer, and these generally target the cell cycle (**Figure 11.25**). The goal is to decrease the rate of cell division and/or increase the rate of apoptosis so that the cancer cell population decreases.

An example of a cancer drug that targets the cell cycle is 5-fluorouracil, which blocks the synthesis of thymine, one of the four bases in DNA. The drug paclitaxel prevents the functioning of microtubules in the mitotic spindle. Both drugs inhibit the cell cycle, and apoptosis causes tumor shrinkage. More dramatic is radiation treatment, in which a beam of high-energy radiation is focused on the tumor. DNA damage is extensive, and the cell cycle checkpoint for DNA repair is overwhelmed. As a result, the cell undergoes apoptosis. A major problem with these treatments is that they affect normal cells as well as the tumor cells. These treatments are toxic to tissues with large populations of normal dividing cells such as those in the intestine, skin, and bone marrow (where blood cells are produced).

A major effort in cancer research is to find treatments that target only cancer cells. A promising recent example is trastuzumab, which targets the HER2 growth factor receptor that occurs at high levels on the surfaces of some breast cancer cells (see Figure 11.23A). Trastuzumab binds specifically to the HER2 receptor but does not stimulate it. This prevents the natural growth factor from binding and stimulating cell division. Because cell division is blocked and the apoptosis rate remains the same, the tumor shrinks.

KEY CONCEPT
11.7 Recap and Assess

Cancer cells differ from normal cells in terms of their rapid cell division and their ability to spread (metastasis). Many proteins regulate the cell cycle, either positively (oncogenes) or negatively (tumor suppressors). In cancer, one or more of these proteins is altered in some way, making its activity abnormal. Radiation and many cancer drugs target genes and proteins involved in the cell cycle.

1. How do cells in normal tissue differ from those in benign and malignant tumors?
2. How are oncogene proteins and tumor suppressor proteins involved in cell cycle control in normal and cancer cells?
3. Cancer-treating drugs are usually given in combination to target several stages of the cell cycle. Why might this be a better approach than using a single drug?

We have now looked at the cell cycle and at cell division by binary fission, mitosis, and meiosis. We have described the normal cell cycle and how its regulation is disrupted in cancer. We have seen how meiosis produces haploid cells in sexual life cycles. In the coming chapters we will examine heredity, genes, and DNA.

▶Investigating LIFE

Q and A What controls the reproduction of cancer cells?

In normal tissues, the rate of cell division is offset by the rate of cell death. Unlike most normal cells, HeLa cells keep growing because they have a genetic imbalance that heavily favors cell reproduction over cell death. Henrietta Lacks was infected with the human papillomavirus, which stimulates cell division in cervical cells. In addition, an enzyme called telomerase, which keeps DNA intact and prevents cell death, is overexpressed in HeLa cells. This combination of traits—increased cell division plus decreased apoptosis—leads to the extraordinary growth rate of HeLa cells.

Because HeLa cells came from a tumor, you might expect that they are still cancer cells, and that they can form a tumor. But such is not the case. They are just cell division machines. What do you think they are missing that tumor cells have?

Future directions

Knowledge of which genes are abnormal in tumors has led to the development of drugs targeted to the specific proteins that are made from these genes. In some instances, such as breast cancers expressing HER2, the results in the clinic have been extraordinary. Patients are living longer, and even being cured by these targeted drugs. Less attention has been given to the other part of the cell population equation—cell death. Many of the widely used drugs that affect the cell cycle in general (see Figure 11.25) work not just by stopping the cell cycle but by damaging cells, triggering apoptosis. But as you may know, these drugs have widespread side effects, stopping cell division and triggering apoptosis in normal cells as well as tumor cells. We know about the molecular events in apoptosis. Perhaps targeted drugs that stimulate this process only in tumor cells could be effective.

You should be able to relate each summary to the adjacent figures. If you go to this visual summary in **Achieve**, you can follow links to figures, animations, activities, and simulations that will help you consolidate the material.

KEY CONCEPT

11.1   All Cells Derive from Other Cells

- Cell division involves **cell division signals**, **DNA replication**, **DNA segregation**, and **cytokinesis**.
- Prokaryotes reproduce by **binary fission**.

Questions

1. Briefly describe what happens in each of the four cell division events.

2. What are the functions of the *ori* and *ter* sequences on the bacterial chromosome?

Figure 11.2

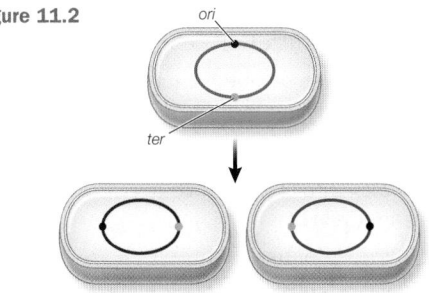

KEY CONCEPT

11.2   The Eukaryotic Cell Division Cycle Is Regulated

- The eukaryotic **cell cycle** has four phases: **G1**, **S** (DNA replication), **G2**, and M (mitosis and cytokinesis).
- Short-lived **cyclins** and their more permanent **CDKs** regulate the passage of cells through **cell cycle checkpoints.**

Questions

1. What events are occurring in the cell during each of the four phases of the eukaryotic cell cycle?

2. How are cyclins able to regulate movement through the cell cycle?

Figure 11.6

KEY CONCEPT

11.3   Eukaryotic Cells Divide by Mitosis

Go to **Activities 11.1 and 11.2 and Animation 11.1**

- DNA is packaged with proteins, especially histones, to form **chromatin**.
- Mitosis can be divided into prophase, prometaphase, metaphase, anaphase, and telophase and is followed by cytokinesis.
- During mitosis, sister chromatids separate, resulting in identical **daughter chromosomes**.

Questions

1. During mitosis, when do chromosomes align in the middle of the cell? When do sister chromatids move toward opposite poles? When do chromosomes become visible?

2. What is a nucleosome?

3. To what structures are the microtubules that move chromosomes attached?

Figure 11.8

Figure 11.9

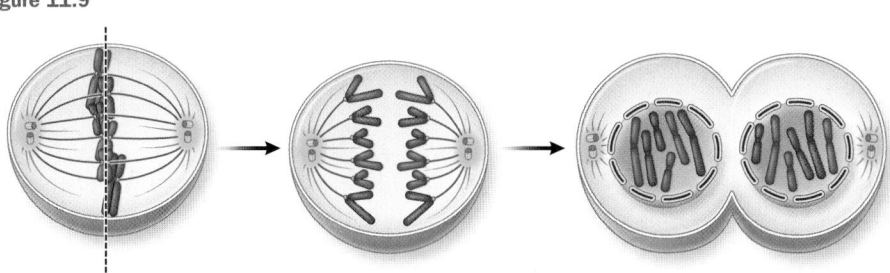

KEY CONCEPT

11.4 Cell Division Plays Important Roles in the Sexual Life Cycle

Go to Activity 11.3

- **Asexual reproduction** produces **clones**, new organisms that are genetically identical to the parent.
- The sexual life cycle involves meiosis and **fertilization**.
- Sexual life cycles can be haplontic, diplontic, or haplo-diplontic.

Questions

1. What two events characterize a sexual life cycle?

2. What is the difference between haplontic, diplontic, and haplo-diplontic life cycles?

Figure 11.14

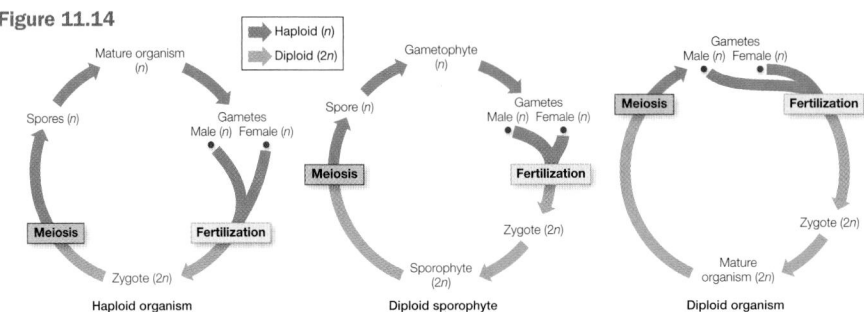

KEY CONCEPT

11.5 Meiosis Leads to the Formation of Gametes

Go to Activity 11.4, Animation 11.2, and Simulation 11.1

- Meiosis produces four genetically distinct haploid gametes from a diploid parent cell.
- Homologs pair during **synapsis** and exhibit **crossing over** during prophase I.
- **Meiosis I** differs from mitosis because homologs separate but sister chromatids remain together.
- **Nondisjunction** during mitosis or meiosis results in **aneuploidy**, or **polyploidy** if all chromosomes are involved.

Questions

1. Draw metaphase I in a diploid cell that has four chromosomes (two pairs of homologs).

2. Explain why mitosis, but not meiosis, can occur in a haploid organism.

Figure 11.18

Figure 11.19

KEY CONCEPT

11.6 Cell Death Is Important in Living Organisms

- A cell may die by **necrosis**, or it may self-destruct by genetically programmed **apoptosis**.
- Apoptosis is regulated by external and internal signals.

Questions

1. Some cells instigate apoptosis within a few minutes of being infected by a virus. Why might they do this?

2. During development, young healthy cells will sometimes undergo apoptosis. Why might they do this?

Figure 11.21

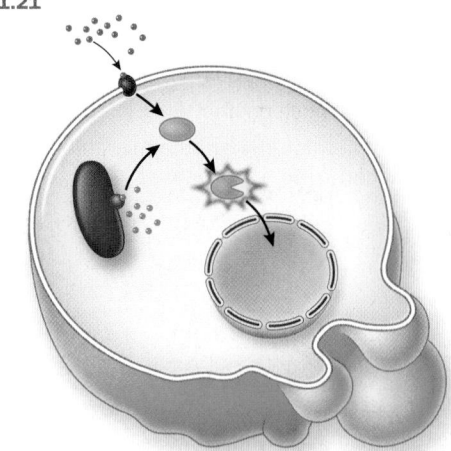

KEY CONCEPT

11.7 Unregulated Cell Division Can Lead to Cancer

- Cancer cells show uncontrolled cell division and **metastasis**.
- **Oncogenes** are activated and **tumor suppressors** are inhibited in cancer cells.
- Cancer treatment often targets the cell cycle in tumor cells.

Questions

1. What are two characteristic of cancer cells?

2. A misregulated oncogene is usually lethal when inherited in a gamete. In contrast, a misregulated tumor suppressor gene is often not lethal, though cancer rates tend to increase. Explain this difference.

Figure 11.23

Go to **Achieve** for the eBook, **LearningCurve**, animations, activities, simulations, and additional resources and assignments.

12 Inheritance, Genes, and Chromosomes

KEY CONCEPTS

12.1 Inheritance of Genes Follows Mendelian Laws

12.2 Alleles Can Produce Multiple Phenotypes

12.3 Genes Can Interact to Produce a Phenotype

12.4 Genes Are Carried on Chromosomes

12.5 Some Eukaryotic Genes Are Outside the Nucleus

12.6 Prokaryotes Can Transmit Genes by Mating

Red hair runs in families.

▶Investigating LIFE

What Are the Rules of Inheritance?

Red hair is the rarest natural hair color in humans, with a frequency of about 1%. It is most common in northern Europe, with Scotland leading at a frequency of about 15%. Throughout history people have attempted to find a correlation between red-headedness and other traits. Red hair and hot temper, for example, are often associated. A recent study by the Hamburg Research Institute in Germany on the sexual activity of hundreds of women came to the conclusion that redheads were having more sex than any other hair color group. Attempts have been made to prove that redheads have a lower tolerance to pain than do people with other hair colors.

Given the rarity of red hair, it is not surprising that it was an early subject of investigation in genetics, the science of heredity. As you will see in this chapter, the foundations of modern genetics were laid late in the nineteenth century through careful experimentation on pea plants by Gregor Mendel. By the early twentieth century, biologists examining human families noticed that red-haired children were usually born from (1) two red-haired parents, (2) one parent with dark hair and one with red, or (3) two dark-haired parents. This fit the pattern for recessive inheritance, in which the gene that determines red hair can be masked by a

dominant gene for dark hair. Exceptions were noted, however, and how red hair is inherited was uncertain until the late 1950s, when Brenda Ellis took a genetics course from Professor Ralph Singleton at Wake Forest University in North Carolina.

After hearing her professor discuss theories about the inheritance of red hair, Ellis investigated her family tree dating back six generations, noting which relatives had red hair. She surmised that all the redheads in her family were the offspring of either two dark-haired parents or one with dark hair and one with red hair. Each of the dark-haired people had a red-haired ancestor and were presumably carriers of a gene that determines red hair. The genetic explanation that Ellis and her professor gave for the striking pattern of recessive inheritance of red hair in her family has since become widely accepted.

Sometimes, however, red hair pops up in families with no genetic history of red hair. In this chapter we examine various patterns of inheritance and the genetic mechanisms by which they arise.

 How do inherited characteristics such as red hair skip generations? (Find the answer on page 270.)

12.1 Inheritance of Genes Follows Mendelian Laws

Learning Objectives

12.1.1 Explain how Mendel's crosses supported particulate inheritance but not blending inheritance.

12.1.2 Distinguish between a dominant and a recessive trait.

12.1.3 State Mendel's laws of inheritance and explain how meiosis can account for them.

12.1.4 Predict the results of a cross using a Punnett square.

12.1.5 Apply probability concepts to predict the results of crosses involving genes on different chromosomes.

12.1.6 Determine the inheritance of a trait using human pedigrees.

Genetics, the field of biology concerned with inheritance, has a long history. There is good evidence that people were deliberately breeding animals (horses) and plants (the date palm tree) for desirable characteristics as long as 5,000 years ago. The general idea was to examine the natural variation among the individuals of a species and "breed the best to the best and hope for the best." While this was a hit-or-miss method—sometimes the resulting offspring had all the good characteristics of the parents, but sometimes they did not—it was quite successful, resulting in many of the common domesticated plants and animals we see today.

By the mid-nineteenth century, two theories had emerged to explain the results of breeding experiments:

1. The hypothesis of *blending inheritance* proposed that gametes (sex cells such as eggs or sperm) contained hereditary determinants (what we now call genes) that blended when the gametes fused during fertilization. Like inks of different colors, the two different determinants lost their individuality after blending and could never be separated. For example, if a plant that made smooth, round seeds was crossed (bred) with a plant that made wrinkled seeds, the offspring would be intermediate between the two and the determinants for the two parental characteristics would be lost.

2. The hypothesis of *particulate inheritance* proposed that each determinant had a physically distinct nature; when gametes fused in fertilization, the determinants remained intact. According to this hypothesis, if a plant that made round seeds was crossed with a plant that made wrinkled seeds, the offspring (no matter the shape of their seeds) would still contain the determinants for the two characteristics.

The story of how these competing hypotheses were tested provides a striking example of how the scientific method can be used to support one theory and reject another. In the following sections we look in detail at experiments performed in the 1860s by an Austrian monk and scientist, Gregor Mendel, whose work clearly supported the particulate hypothesis.

Mendel's laws arose from controlled crosses of pea plants

After entering the priesthood at a monastery in Brno, in what is now the Czech Republic, Gregor Mendel was sent to the University of Vienna, where he studied biology, physics, and mathematics. He returned to the monastery in 1853 to teach. The abbot in charge had set up a small plot of land to do experiments with plants and encouraged Mendel to continue with the experiments. Over seven years, Mendel made crosses with many thousands of plants. Analysis of his meticulously gathered data suggested to him that inheritance was due to particulate factors.

Mendel presented his theories in two public lectures in 1865 and a detailed written publication in 1866, but his work was ignored by mainstream scientists until 1900. By that time, the discovery of chromosomes had suggested to biologists that genes might be carried on chromosomes. When they read Mendel's work on particulate inheritance, the biologists connected the dots between genes and chromosomes.

Mendel chose to study the common garden pea (*Pisum sativum*) because it has many features that make it ideal for addressing questions concerning inheritance, including (1) variability in one or more easily scorable characters, (2) large family sizes, (3) short generation times, (4) the ability to be grown easily and inexpensively, and (5) suitability for controlled matings. Pea flowers have both male and female sex organs: stamens and pistils, which produce gametes, sperm and eggs, that are contained within the pollen and ovules, respectively (**Figure 12.1**). Pea flowers normally self-fertilize. That is, male and female gametes on the same flower combine. However, the male organs can be removed from a flower so that it can be manually fertilized with pollen from a different flower. That's what Mendel did.

There are many varieties of pea plants with easily recognizable characteristics. A **character** is an observable physical feature, such as seed shape. A **trait** is a particular form of a character, such as round or wrinkled seeds. The traits expressed by an individual at one or more characters contribute to its **phenotype**—the observable properties of an individual resulting from both genetic and environmental factors. Mendel worked with varieties with contrasting traits for seven characters, such as seed shape, seed color, and flower color. These varieties were true-breeding: that is, when

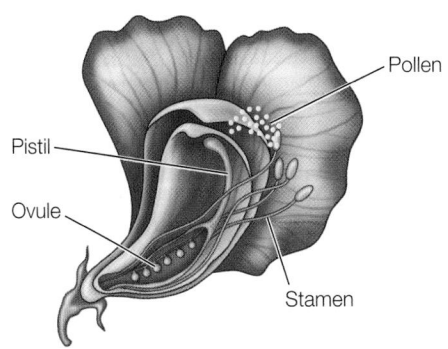

Figure 12.1 A Pea Flower Pea flowers have pollen-producing organs called stamens and an ovule-producing organ called the pistil.

Mendel crossed (moved pollen between) a plant that produced wrinkled seeds for example with another of the same variety, all of the offspring plants produced wrinkled seeds.

As you will see, Mendel proposed a set of hypotheses to explain the inheritance of particular pea traits, and then designed crossing experiments to test his hypotheses. He performed his crosses in the following manner:

- He removed the stamens (male parts) from flowers of one parental variety so that it couldn't self-fertilize. Then he collected pollen from another parental variety and placed it on the pistils of the emasculated flowers. The plants providing and receiving the pollen were the **parental generation**, designated **P**.

- In due course, seeds formed and were planted. The seeds and the resulting new plants constituted the **first filial generation**, or **F_1**. (The word "filial" refers to the relationship between offspring and parents, from the Latin *filius*, "son.") Mendel examined each F_1 plant to see which traits it bore and then recorded the number of F_1 plants expressing each trait.

- In some experiments the F_1 plants were allowed to self-pollinate and produce a **second filial generation**, or **F_2**. Again, each F_2 plant was characterized and counted.

Mendel's first experiments involved monohybrid crosses

When parents of different species or of different varieties of the same species are crossed, the resulting offspring are termed "hybrids." In Mendel's first experiments, he crossed parental (P) varieties with contrasting traits for a single character, producing monohybrids (from the Greek *monos*, "single") in the F_1 generation. He subsequently planted the F_1 seeds and allowed the

resulting plants to self-pollinate to produce the F_2 generation. This technique is referred to as a **monohybrid cross**.

Mendel performed the equivalent experiment for seven pea characters. You can follow his method in **Investigating Life: Mendel's Monohybrid Experiments**, using seed shape as an example. When he crossed a variety with round seeds to one with wrinkled seeds, all of the F_1 seeds were round—it was as if the wrinkled seed trait had disappeared completely. However, when F_1 plants were allowed to self-pollinate to produce F_2 seeds, about one-fourth of the seeds were wrinkled. These crosses were key to distinguishing the blending and particulate theories:

- The F_1 offspring were not a blend of the two traits of the parents. Only one of the traits was present (in this case, round seeds).

- Some F_2 offspring had wrinkled seeds. The trait had not disappeared because of blending.

These observations led to a rejection of the blending theory of inheritance and provided support for the particulate theory. We now know that hereditary determinants are not actually "particulate," but they *are* physically distinct entities: sequences of DNA carried on chromosomes, which we now call **genes**.

All seven crosses between varieties with contrasting traits gave the same pattern of data (**Table 12.1**). In the F_1 generation only one of the two traits was seen, but the other trait reappeared in about one-fourth of the offspring in the F_2 generation. Mendel called the trait that appeared in the F_1 and was more abundant in the F_2 the **dominant** trait, and the other trait **recessive**. In the F_2 generation, the *ratio* of plants exhibiting dominant versus recessive traits was about 3:1. (To calculate the ratios shown in Table 12.1, divide the number of F_2 plants with each trait by the number with the recessive trait.)

TABLE 12.1 | Mendel's Results from Monohybrid Crosses

Parental generation phenotypes			F_1 generation phenotypes	F_2 generation phenotypes			
	Dominant	Recessive		Dominant	Recessive	Total	Ratio
	Round seeds × Wrinkled seeds		Round	5,474	1,850	7,324	2.96:1
	Yellow seeds × Green seeds		Yellow	6,022	2,001	8,023	3.01:1
	Purple flowers × White flowers		Purple	705	224	929	3.15:1
	Inflated pods × Constricted pods		Inflated	882	299	1,181	2.95:1
	Green pods × Yellow pods		Green	428	152	580	2.82:1
	Axial flowers × Terminal flowers		Axial	651	207	858	3.14:1
	Tall stems × Dwarf stems (1 m) (0.3 m)		Tall	787	277	1,064	2.84:1

►Investigating**LIFE** Mendel's Monohybrid Experiments

Experiment

Original Paper: The original German version of Mendel's paper, *Versuche über Pflanzen-Hybriden*, with an English translation and extensive explanatory notes, is available online: mendelweb.org/Mendel.plain.html.

Mendel performed crosses with pea plants and carefully analyzed the outcomes to show that genetic determinants are particulate.

HYPOTHESIS► When two strains of peas with contrasting traits are bred, their characteristics are irreversibly blended in succeeding generations.

METHOD►

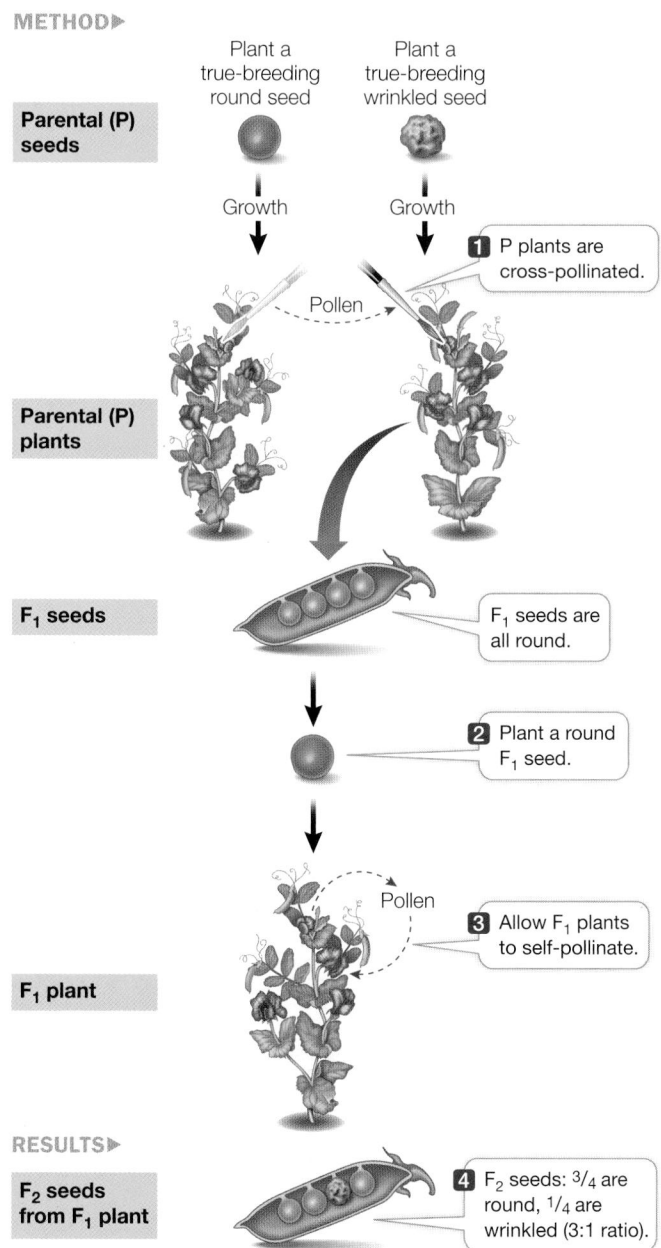

Plant a true-breeding round seed

Plant a true-breeding wrinkled seed

Parental (P) seeds

Growth

Growth

1 P plants are cross-pollinated.

Pollen

Parental (P) plants

F₁ seeds

F₁ seeds are all round.

2 Plant a round F₁ seed.

3 Allow F₁ plants to self-pollinate.

Pollen

F₁ plant

RESULTS►

F₂ seeds from F₁ plant

4 F₂ seeds: ³/₄ are round, ¹/₄ are wrinkled (3:1 ratio).

CONCLUSION► The hypothesis is rejected. There is no irreversible blending of characteristics, and a parental trait that was absent in the F₁ can reappear in succeeding generations.

Work with the Data

Mendel's monohybrid crosses were key to his rejection of the theory of blending inheritance. While the experiment at left illustrates a monohybrid cross with round and wrinkled seeds, another of his monohybrid crosses was between true-breeding green-seeded and yellow-seeded pea plants. All of the pea plants in the F₁ generation of this cross had yellow seeds. Mendel allowed the F₁ plants to self-pollinate and then analyzed the seed colors of the resulting F₂ generation. The table shows actual data from individual plants in the F₂ generation as reported in Mendel's paper. Mendel made mathematical calculations and presented the overall ratios for these two traits. He did not, however, perform a statistical analysis to determine whether the variations in the data reflected a general pattern of inheritance or were simply due to chance.

	Seed color	
Plant	**Yellow**	**Green**
1	25	11
2	32	7
3	14	5
4	70	27
5	24	13
6	20	6
7	32	13
8	44	9
9	50	14
10	44	18

QUESTIONS►

1. Use the hypothesis that the ratio of yellow to green seeds in the F₂ generation would be 3:1 and perform a chi-square test to analyze the results for each plant in the table (see Figure B12 in Appendix B for information about using the chi-square test). What can you conclude about this hypothesis from the individual plants? How many crosses have *P*-values > 0.05?

2. Now total the data from all the plants and rerun the chi-square analysis. Do your conclusions change? In terms of the expected phenotypic ratio, what does your analysis indicate about the need for using a large number of organisms in studies of genetics?

Go to Achieve for a companion Data in Depth exercise.

You can see in Table 12.1 that for each character, Mendel counted hundreds or even thousands of F_2 seeds or plants to see how many exhibited each trait. As we will discuss in more detail later in this key concept, the probability of a plant inheriting a particular trait is independent of the probability of another plant inheriting the same trait. If Mendel had looked at only a few F_2 progeny from the "round × round" cross, he might, by chance, have found only round seeds. Or he might have found a higher proportion of wrinkled seeds than he did. In order to discover underlying patterns and to develop his laws of inheritance, Mendel used very large numbers of plants.

Mendel went on to expand on the particulate theory. He proposed that hereditary determinants—which we will refer to as genes, although Mendel did not use that term—occur in pairs and segregate (separate) from one another during the formation of gametes. He concluded that each pea plant has two copies of the gene for each character (such as seed shape), one inherited from each parent. We now use the term **diploid** (**2n**) to describe the state of having two copies of each gene; **haploids** (*n*) have just a single copy. You saw these terms in Chapter 11 when you learned about the cell cycle and meiosis.

Mendel concluded that while each gamete contains one copy of each gene, the resulting zygote contains two copies, because it is produced by the fusion of two gametes. Furthermore, he surmised that different traits arise from different forms of a gene (now called **alleles**) for a particular character. For example, Mendel studied two alleles for seed shape: a dominant allele for round seeds and a recessive allele for wrinkled seeds.

- An organism that is **homozygous** for a gene has two alleles that are the same (for example, two copies of the allele for round seeds).

- An organism that is **heterozygous** for a gene has two different alleles (for example, one allele for round seeds and one allele for wrinkled seeds).

In a heterozygote, one of the two alleles may be dominant (such as round, *R*) and the other recessive (wrinkled, *r*). By convention, dominant alleles are designated with uppercase letters and recessive alleles with lowercase letters. Note that the terms dominant and recessive refer only to which phenotype is expressed when the two alleles are present together. They do not refer to which alleles are stronger, better, or more common.

Mendel proposed that an individual's phenotype is the result of its **genotype**, or genetic constitution. Round seeds and wrinkled seeds are two phenotypes resulting from three possible genotypes: the wrinkled seed phenotype is produced by the genotype *rr*, whereas the round seed phenotype is produced by either genotype *RR* or *Rr* (because the *R* allele determines the dominant round trait and the *r* allele determines the recessive wrinkled trait).

Mendel's first law states that the two copies of a gene segregate

How do Mendel's theories explain the proportions of traits seen in the F_1 and F_2 generations of his monohybrid crosses? Mendel's first law—the **law of segregation**—states that *when any individual produces gametes, the two copies of a gene separate, so that half of*

the gametes receive one copy and half receive the other copy. Thus gametes from a parent with the *RR* genotype will all carry the *R* allele; gametes from an *rr* parent will all carry the *r* allele. In an *Rr* individual, half the gametes will carry the *R* allele and the other half will carry *r*. What genotypes are produced when these gametes fuse to form the next generation? The allele combinations that will result from a cross can be predicted using a **Punnett square**. This device ensures that you consider all possible combinations of gametes when calculating expected genotype frequencies of the resulting offspring. A Punnett square is a simple grid with all possible male gamete (haploid sperm) genotypes shown along the top and all possible female gamete (haploid egg) genotypes along the left side. The grid is completed by filling in each square with the diploid genotype that is generated from each combination of gametes.

Let's use a Punnett square to derive the progeny of an *RR* × *rr* cross (**Figure 12.2**). To determine the genotypes in the F_1 generation, into each square we put an *R* from the male gamete (a sperm cell from the pollen tube) and an *r* from the female gamete (the egg cell). All the F_1 offspring of this cross (the F_1 generation) have the

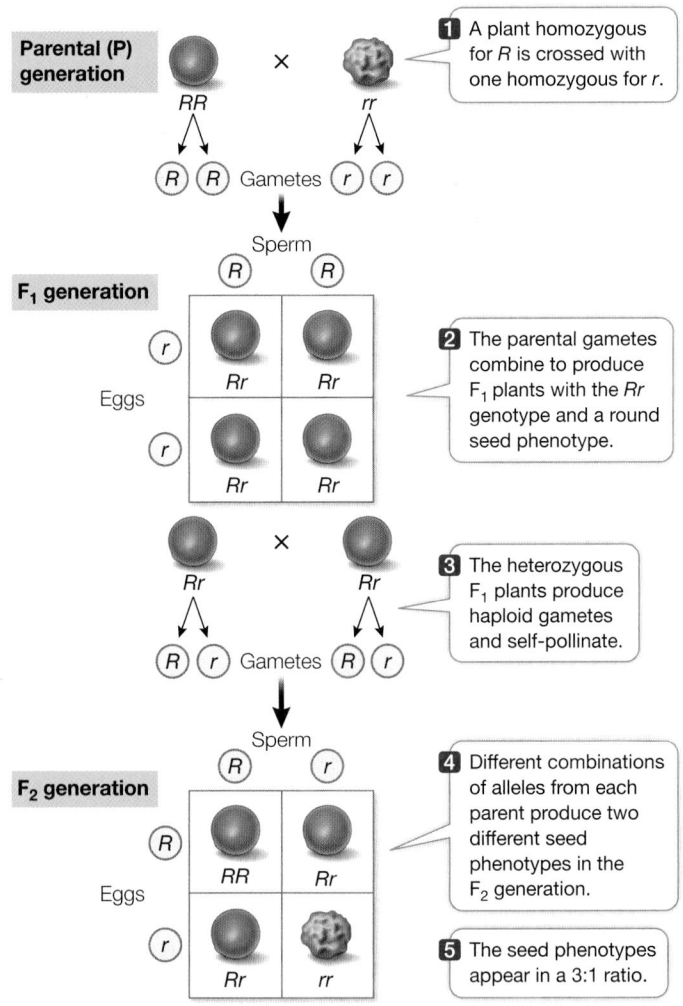

Figure 12.2 Mendel's Explanation of Inheritance Mendel concluded that inheritance depends on discrete factors from each parent that do not blend in the offspring.

Rr genotype, which produces seeds with a round phenotype. What happens when the F$_1$ generation are crossed among themselves to produce the F$_2$ generation? Once the Punnett square is filled in, we readily see that the four combinations of gametes give three possible genotypes (*RR*, *Rr*, and *rr*) in a 1:2:1 ratio if all combinations are equally likely. Since the *R* allele is dominant, such that *RR* and *Rr* both give round seeds, we predict a 3:1 ratio of the round and wrinkled phenotypes in the F$_2$ generation, which is remarkably close to the ratios Mendel found experimentally for all the traits he compared (see Table 12.1). Mendel's 3:1 ratio is thus explained by all four combinations in the Punnett square being equally likely, which requires that *R* and *r* are equally frequent in gametes of *Rr* individuals, which is equal segregation.

Mendel did not live to see his theories placed on a sound physical footing with the discoveries of chromosomes and DNA. Genes are now known to be sequences of DNA found on the much longer DNA molecules that make up chromosomes. With your knowledge of meiosis, you can envision the different alleles of a gene segregating as chromosomes separate during meiosis I (**Figure 12.3**). Since Mendel's first law is a result of events that occur during anaphase I of meiosis, it is perhaps not surprising that it has been found to hold in all meiotic organisms for almost every single gene.

We know now that genes determine phenotypes mostly by producing proteins with particular functions, such as enzymes. In many cases a dominant gene is expressed (transcribed and translated) to produce a functional protein, while a recessive gene is mutated so that it is no longer expressed, or it encodes a mutant protein that is nonfunctional. For example, the wrinkled seed phenotype of *rr* peas is caused by the absence of an enzyme called *starch branching enzyme 1* (SBE1), which is essential for starch synthesis. With less starch, the developing seed has more sucrose, and this causes an inflow of water by osmosis. When the seed matures and dries out, the water is lost, leaving a shrunken seed. A single copy of the *R* allele produces enough functional SBE1 to prevent the wrinkled phenotype, which accounts for the dominance of *R* over *r*.

Mendel verified his hypotheses by performing test crosses

Mendel arrived at his laws of inheritance by developing a series of hypotheses and then designing experiments to test them. One hypothesis was that there are two possible allele combinations (*RR* or *Rr*) for seeds with the round phenotype. Mendel verified this hypothesis by performing test crosses with F$_1$ seeds derived from a variety of other crosses. A **test cross** is used to determine whether an individual showing one or more dominant traits is homozygous or heterozygous for each gene. The individual in question is crossed with an individual that is homozygous for recessive alleles at each gene—easy to identify, because all individuals with the recessive phenotypes are homozygous for those traits.

The recessive homozygote for the seed shape gene has wrinkled seeds and the genotype *rr*. The round individual being tested may

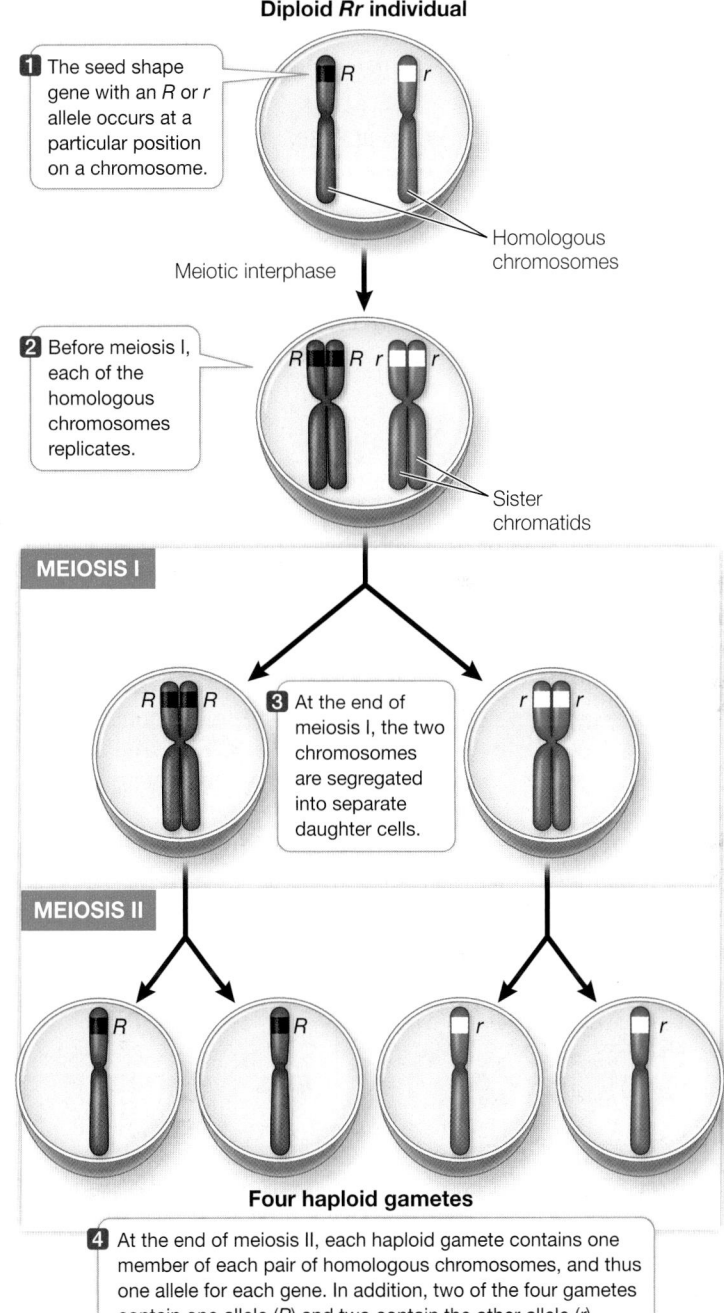

1 The seed shape gene with an *R* or *r* allele occurs at a particular position on a chromosome.

Homologous chromosomes

Meiotic interphase

2 Before meiosis I, each of the homologous chromosomes replicates.

Sister chromatids

MEIOSIS I

3 At the end of meiosis I, the two chromosomes are segregated into separate daughter cells.

MEIOSIS II

Four haploid gametes

4 At the end of meiosis II, each haploid gamete contains one member of each pair of homologous chromosomes, and thus one allele for each gene. In addition, two of the four gametes contain one allele (*R*) and two contain the other allele (*r*).

Figure 12.3 Meiosis Accounts for the Segregation of Alleles Although Mendel had no knowledge of chromosomes or meiosis, we now know that a pair of alleles resides on homologous chromosomes, and that those alleles segregate during meiosis.

Q: Cells in a pea leaf have 14 chromosomes. How many chromosomes are in each gamete?

be described initially as *R_* because we do not yet know the identity of the second allele. We can predict two possible results:

1. If the individual being tested is homozygous dominant (*RR*), all offspring of the test cross will be *Rr* and show the dominant trait (round seeds) (**Figure 12.4, left**).

Experiment

Figure 12.4 Homozygous or Heterozygous?

Original Paper: The original German version of Mendel's paper, *Versuche über Pflanzen-Hybriden*, with an English translation and extensive explanatory notes, is available online: mendelweb.org/Mendel.plain.html.

An individual with a dominant phenotype may have either a homozygous or a heterozygous genotype. The test cross determines genotype.

HYPOTHESIS▶ The progeny of a test cross can reveal whether an organism is homozygous or heterozygous.

METHOD▶

1a Test round peas of undetermined genotype... *R_* × *rr* **1b** ...by crossing them with wrinkled peas with a known genotype (homozygous recessive).

2a If the plant being tested is homozygous... *RR* × *rr* → R R | r r Gametes

2b If the plant being tested is heterozygous... *Rr* × *rr* → R r | r r Gametes

RESULTS▶

Sperm — *r* *r*

Eggs
	r	*r*
R	*Rr*	*Rr*
R	*Rr*	*Rr*

Sperm — *r* *r*

Eggs
	r	*r*
R	*Rr*	*Rr*
r	*rr*	*rr*

3a ...then all progeny will show the dominant phenotype (round).

3b ...then half the seeds from the cross will be wrinkled, and half will be round.

CONCLUSION▶ The plant being tested is likely homozygous.

CONCLUSION▶ The plant being tested is heterozygous.

▶ View in **Achieve**
Activity 12.1 **Homozygous or Heterozygous?**

Mendel's second law states that copies of different genes assort independently

Now let's consider inheritance patterns involving two different genes. Consider an organism that is heterozygous for genes for seed shape (round or wrinkled) and seed color (yellow or green). In our example, the dominant *R* and *Y* alleles came from one parent, and the recessive *r* and *y* alleles came from the other parent. When this organism produces gametes, do the *R* and *Y* alleles always go together in one gamete, and the *r* and *y* alleles in another? Or can a single gamete receive one recessive and one dominant allele (*R* and *y* or *r* and *Y*)?

Mendel performed another series of experiments to answer these questions. He began with peas that differed in *two* characters: seed shape and seed color. One parental variety produced only round, yellow seeds (*RRYY*), and the other produced only wrinkled, green ones (*rryy*). A cross between these two varieties, a **dihybrid cross**, produced an F$_1$ generation in which all the

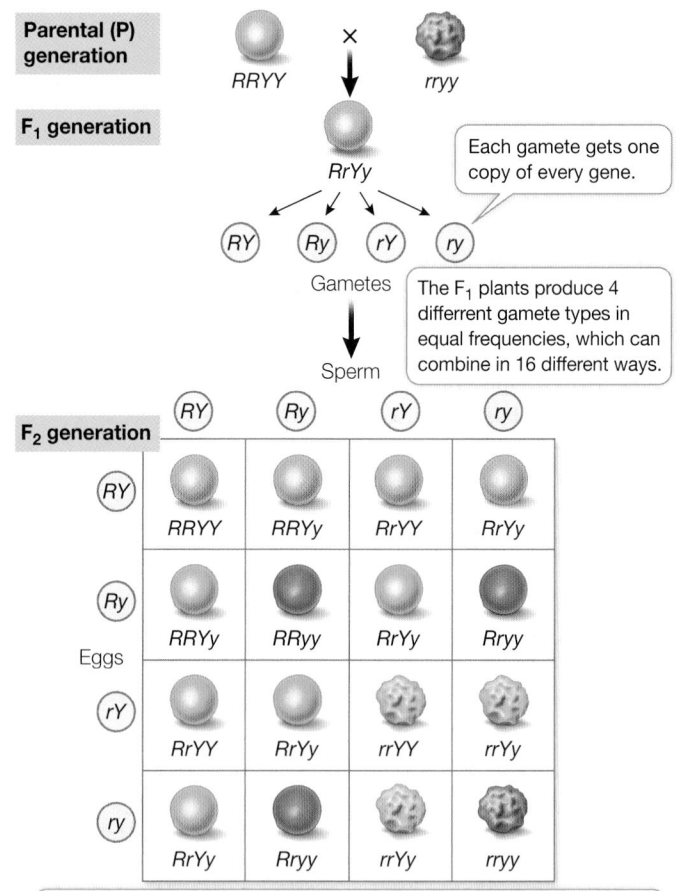

Parental (P) generation — *RRYY* × *rryy*

F$_1$ generation — *RrYy*

Each gamete gets one copy of every gene.

Gametes — *RY* *Ry* *rY* *ry*

The F$_1$ plants produce 4 different gamete types in equal frequencies, which can combine in 16 different ways.

F$_2$ generation

Sperm
	RY	*Ry*	*rY*	*ry*
RY	*RRYY*	*RRYy*	*RrYY*	*RrYy*
Ry	*RRYy*	*RRyy*	*RrYy*	*Rryy*
rY	*RrYY*	*RrYy*	*rrYY*	*rrYy*
ry	*RrYy*	*Rryy*	*rrYy*	*rryy*

Eggs

Results: When F$_1$ plants self-pollinate, the gametes combine randomly to produce an F$_2$ generation with four phenotypes in a 9:3:3:1 ratio.

Figure 12.5 Independent Assortment in a Dihybrid Cross The 16 possible combinations of gametes in the F$_1$ cross result in nine different F$_2$ genotypes. Because *R* and *Y* are dominant over *r* and *y*, respectively, the nine genotypes result in four phenotypes in a ratio of 9:3:3:1. These results show that the two genes segregate independently.

▶ Media Clip 12.1 **Mendel's Discoveries**
Life12e.com/mc12.1

2. If the individual being tested is heterozygous (*Rr*), then approximately half of the offspring of the test cross will be heterozygous (*Rr*) and show the dominant trait, and the other half will be homozygous for the recessive allele (*rr*) and show the recessive trait (**Figure 12.4, right**).

Mendel obtained results consistent with both of these predictions; thus his hypothesis accurately predicted the results of his test crosses.

plants were *RrYy*. Because the *R* and *Y* alleles were dominant, the F_1 seeds were all round and yellow.

Mendel continued this experiment into the F_2 generation by crossing F_1 individuals. In this case, he simply allowed the F_1 plants, which were all double heterozygotes, to self-pollinate. Depending on whether the alleles of the two genes are inherited together or separately, there are two possible outcomes:

1. *The alleles could maintain the associations they had in the parental generation—that is, the genes could be linked.* If this were the case, the F_1 plants would produce two types of gametes (*RY* and *ry*). The F_2 progeny resulting from self-pollination of these F_1 plants would consist of *two phenotypes*: round yellow and wrinkled green in a ratio of 3:1, just as in the monohybrid cross.

2. *The segregation of R from r could be independent of the segregation of Y from y—the two genes could be unlinked.* In this case, four kinds of gametes would be produced in equal numbers: *RY*, *Ry*, *rY*, and *ry*. When these gametes combine at random, they should produce an F_2 generation with *four phenotypes* (round yellow, round green, wrinkled yellow, and wrinkled green). Putting these possibilities into a Punnett square, we can predict that these four phenotypes would occur in a ratio of 9:3:3:1.

The results supported the second prediction: four different phenotypes appeared in the F_2 generation in a ratio of about 9:3:3:1 (**Figure 12.5**). On the basis of such experiments, Mendel proposed his second law—the **law of independent assortment**: *alleles of different genes assort independently of one another during gamete formation.* In the example just discussed, the segregation of the *R* and *r* alleles is independent of the segregation of the *Y* and *y* alleles. Mendel's second law is now understood in the context of meiosis (see Figure 11.15): *homologous chromosome pairs segregate independently of one another* during the formation of gametes, and so do any two genes located on different chromosome pairs (**Figure 12.6**). Since the explanation for Mendel's second law involves genes on different chromosomes, it is perhaps not surprising that gene pairs that are found close together on the same chromosome do not show inheritance patterns that are consistent with this law (see Key Concept 12.4).

Probability can be used to predict inheritance

One key to Mendel's success was his use of large numbers of plants. By counting many offspring from each cross, he observed clear patterns that allowed him to formulate his theories. After his work became widely recognized, geneticists began using simple probability calculations to predict the ratios of genotypes and phenotypes in the progeny of a given cross or mating. They use statistics

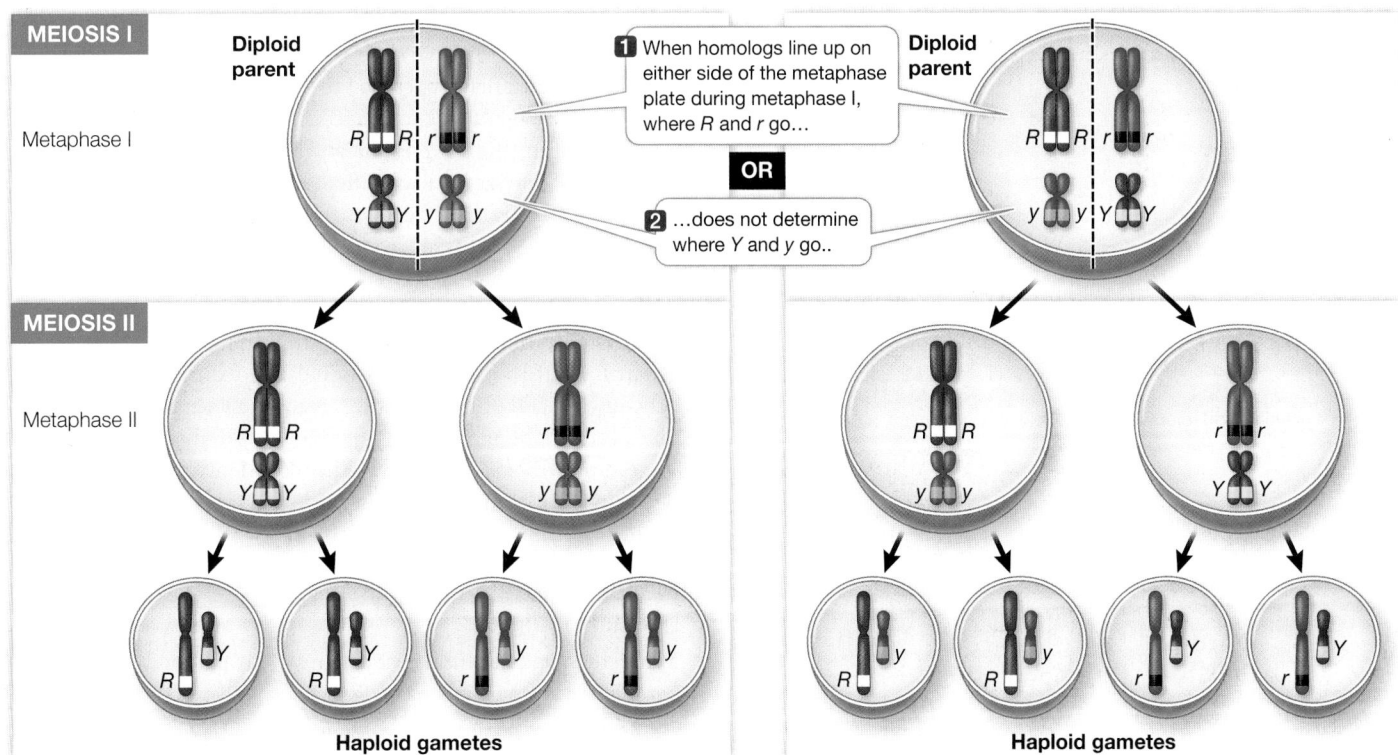

Figure 12.6 Meiosis Accounts for Independent Assortment of Alleles Independent assortment implies that a parent of genotype *RrYy* can form gametes with four different genotypes in equal proportions. This is explained by meiosis if the two possible alignments at metaphase I are equally likely.

View in Achieve
Animation 12.1 Independent Assortment of Alleles

Q: A diploid heterozygote for a single gene can produce haploid gametes of only two genetically distinct types. A double heterozygote can produce four genetically distinct types of gametes, as illustrated here. How many genetically distinct gametes could be produced by a quadruple heterozygote if the four genes assort independently? (Answer this without drawing a diagram!)

to determine whether the actual results match the prediction (as explored in the Work with the Data exercise on p. 263).

You can think of probabilities by considering a coin toss. The basic conventions of probability are simple:

- If an event is absolutely certain to happen, its probability is 1.
- If it cannot possibly happen, its probability is 0.
- All other events have a probability between 0 and 1.

There are two possible outcomes of a coin toss, and both are equally likely, so the probability of heads is ½—as is the probability of tails.

If two coins (say a penny and a dime) are tossed, each acts independently of the other (**Figure 12.7**). What is the probability of both coins coming up heads? In half of the tosses, the penny comes up heads, and in half of that fraction, the dime comes up heads. The probability of both coins coming up heads is ½ × ½ = ¼. In general, *the probability of two independent outcomes occurring together is found by multiplying the two individual probabilities* (the **multiplication rule**). The multiplication rule can be seen in the results of a monohybrid cross (see Figure 12.2). After the self-pollination of an *Rr* F_1 plant, the probability that an F_2 plant will have the genotype *RR* is ½ × ½ = ¼, because the chance that the sperm will have the genotype *R* is ½, and the chance that the egg will have the genotype *R* is also ½. Similarly, the probability of obtaining an *rr* offspring is also ¼.

Probability can also be used to predict the proportions of phenotypes in a dihybrid cross. Let's see how this works for the experiment shown in Figure 12.5. Using the principles we just described, you can calculate the probability of an F_2 seed being round. This is found by adding the probabilities of obtaining an *Rr* heterozygote from an *R* sperm and *r* egg (½ × ½ = ¼), an *Rr* heterozygote from an *r* sperm and *R* egg (½ × ½ = ¼), and an *RR* homozygote from an *R* sperm and *R* egg (½ × ½ = ¼): a total of ¾ (the **addition rule**). In general, *the probability of either of two independent outcomes occurring is found by adding the two probabilities of each outcome.* By the same reasoning, the probability that a seed will be yellow is also ¾. The two characters are determined by separate genes and are independent of each other, so:

- The joint probability for both round and yellow is ¾ × ¾ = ⁹⁄₁₆.

What is the probability of F_2 seeds being both wrinkled and yellow? The probability of being yellow is again ¾; the probability of being wrinkled is ½ × ½ = ¼, so:

- The joint probability for both wrinkled and yellow is ¼ × ¾ = ³⁄₁₆.

By the same reasoning:

- The joint probability for both round (¾) and green (¼) is also ³⁄₁₆.

Finally:

- The joint probability for both wrinkled and green is ¼ × ¼ = ¹⁄₁₆.

Looking at all four phenotypes, you can see that they are expected to occur in the ratio of 9:3:3:1.

A Punnett square or these simple probability calculations can be used to determine the *expected* proportions of offspring with particular phenotypes. In the dihybrid cross just discussed, about one-sixteenth of the F_2 seeds are expected to be wrinkled and green. But this does not mean that among 16 F_2 seeds there will always be exactly 1 wrinkled green seed. For any toss of a coin, the probability of heads is independent of what happened in all the previous tosses. Even if you get three heads in a row, the chance of a head in the next toss is still ½, and it is quite possible to toss a coin four times and get four heads. But if you toss the coin many times, you are highly likely to get heads in about half of the tosses. If Mendel had examined only a few progeny in each of his crosses, it is unlikely that he would have observed the phenotypic ratios that he did observe. It was his large sample sizes that allowed him to identify the underlying patterns of inheritance, and even these large sample sizes gave slight deviations from the expected ratios (see Table 12.1).

Mendel's laws can be observed in human pedigrees

Mendel worked out his laws by doing many planned crosses with pea plants and counting many offspring. Neither of these approaches is possible with humans, so human geneticists rely on **pedigrees**: family trees that show the occurrence of phenotypes (and alleles) in several generations of related individuals. You saw an example of this in the opening story of this chapter. The six-generation pedigree for red hair in Brenda Ellis's family is shown in **Figure 12.8**.

Because humans have small numbers of offspring, human pedigrees do not show the clear proportions of phenotypes that Mendel saw in his pea plants. For example, when a man and a woman who are both heterozygous for a recessive allele (say, *Aa*)

1 Two coin tosses are independent events, each with an outcome probability (*P*) of ¹⁄₂.

2 This outcome is the result of two independent events. The joint probability is ¹⁄₂ × ¹⁄₂ = ¹⁄₄ (multiplication rule).

P = ¹⁄₂   *P* = ¹⁄₂

Ⓡ   ⓡ

P = ¹⁄₂ Ⓡ

	R	R
R	¹⁄₂ × ¹⁄₂ = ¹⁄₄	¹⁄₂ × ¹⁄₂ = ¹⁄₄
r	¹⁄₂ × ¹⁄₂ = ¹⁄₄	¹⁄₂ × ¹⁄₂ = ¹⁄₄

Because there are two ways to arrive at a heterozygote, we add the probabilities of the two individual outcomes: ¹⁄₄ + ¹⁄₄ = ¹⁄₂ (addition rule).

Figure 12.7 Using Probability Calculations in Genetics As with the results of a coin toss, the probability of any given combination of alleles appearing in the offspring of a cross can be obtained by multiplying the probabilities of each event. Since a heterozygote can be formed in two ways, these two probabilities are added together.

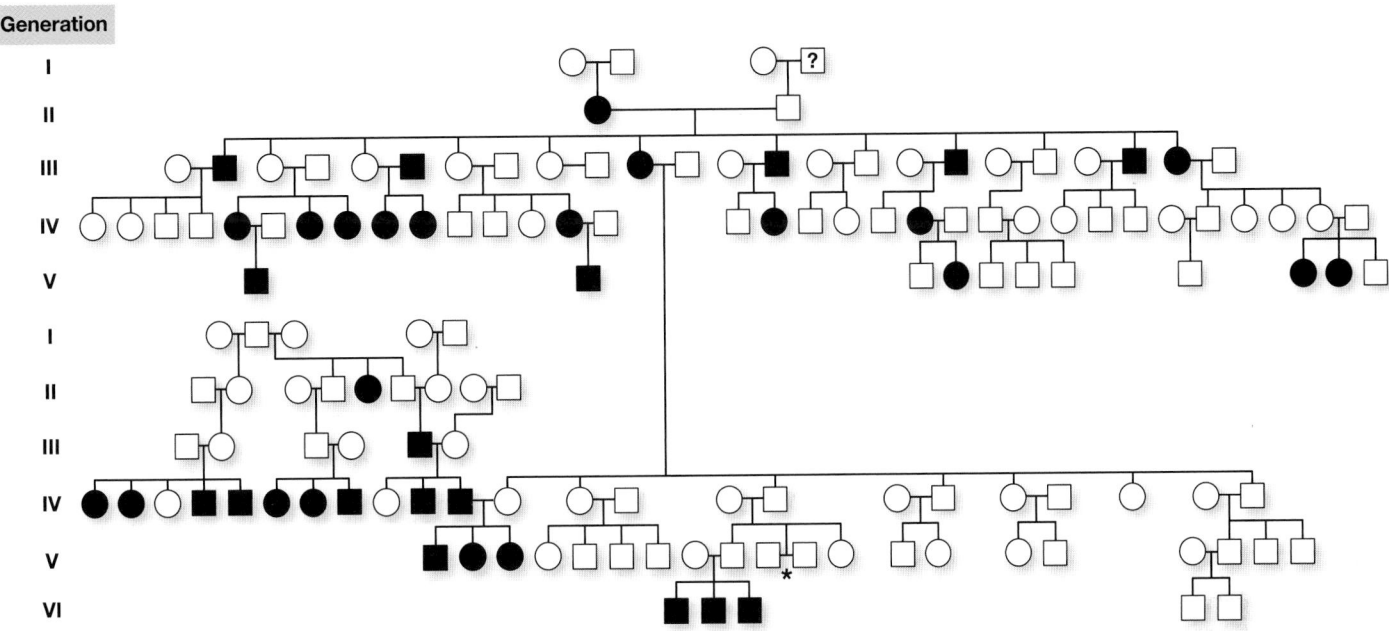

Figure 12.8 The Pedigree for Red Hair for Brenda Ellis's Family
The six-generation pedigree for red hair (filled circles and squares) allowed its inheritance to be determined. *Indicates twin relationship.

See Figure 12.9 for explanation of symbols. (After W. R. Singleton and B. Ellis. 1964. *J Hered* 55: 261, 266.)

have children together, each child has a ¼ probability of being a recessive homozygote (*aa*). If this couple were to have several dozen children, about one-fourth of them would be recessive homozygotes. But the offspring of a single couple are likely to be too few to show the exact one-fourth proportion. In a family

with only two children, for example, both children could easily be *aa* (or *Aa*, or *AA*).

Figure 12.9A is a pedigree showing the pattern of inheritance of a disease caused by a dominant allele. The following are the key features to look for in such a pedigree:

(A) Dominant inheritance

Generation I (parents)

Generation II

Generation III

Every affected individual has an affected parent.

Oldest Youngest

Siblings

About ½ of the offspring (of both sexes) of an affected parent are affected.

	Unaffected	Affected	Heterozygote (unaffected phenotype)
Female	○	●	◐
Male	□	■	◩
Mating	○—□	Mating between relatives	○═□

(B) Recessive inheritance

One parent is heterozygous…

…and the recessive allele is passed on to about ½ of the phenotypically unaffected offspring.

Generation I (parents)

Generation II

Generation III

Generation IV

Mating of heterozygous recessive parents may produce homozygous recessive (affected) offspring.

Figure 12.9 Pedigree Analysis and Inheritance (A) This pedigree represents a family affected by Huntington's disease, which results from a rare dominant allele. Everyone who inherits this allele is affected. (B) The family in this pedigree carries the allele for albinism, a recessive trait. Because the trait is recessive, heterozygotes do not have the albino phenotype, but they can pass the allele on to their offspring. In this family, in generation III the heterozygous parents are

cousins; however, the same result could occur if the parents were unrelated and both heterozygous.

Q: Looking back at Figure 12.8, is red hair a recessive or a dominant trait?

▶ **View in Achieve**
Simulation 12.1 Pedigree Analysis

- Every affected person has an affected parent; a dominant phenotype does not "skip generations" when looking back at ancestors.

- About half of the offspring with one affected parent are also affected. (This is easiest to observe among the 12 cousins in generation III.)

Compare this pattern with the one shown in **Figure 12.9B**, which is typical for the inheritance of a disease caused by a recessive allele:

- Affected people can have two parents who are not affected; a recessive disorder can skip generations when looking back at ancestors.

- Only a small proportion of people in the pedigree are affected: about one-fourth of children whose parents are both heterozygotes.

In the families of individuals who have a rare recessive phenotype, it is not uncommon to find a marriage of two relatives. This observation is a result of the rarity of recessive alleles that give rise to abnormal phenotypes. For two phenotypically normal parents to have a homozygous affected child (*aa*), the parents must both be heterozygous (*Aa*). If a particular recessive allele (*a*) is rare in the general population, the chance of two people mating to produce offspring who are both carrying that allele is quite low. However, if that allele is present in a family, two cousins might share it (see Figure 12.9B). For this reason, studies on populations that are isolated either culturally (by religion, as with the Amish in the United States) or geographically (as on islands) have been extremely valuable to human geneticists. People in these groups are more likely to marry relatives who may carry the same rare recessive alleles and to produce homozygous, affected offspring.

KEY CONCEPT
12.1 Recap and Assess

Mendel showed that genetic determinants are particulate and do not "blend" when the two gametes combine. Mendel's first law of inheritance states that two copies of a gene segregate during gamete formation. His second law states that genes assort independently during gamete formation. The frequencies with which different allele combinations will be expressed in offspring can be calculated with a Punnett square or using probability theory.

1. What results seen in the F_1 and F_2 generations of Mendel's monohybrid cross experiments refuted the blending theory of inheritance?

2. Diagram the processes of meiosis that underlie the laws of segregation and independent assortment.

3. In guinea pigs, black body color (*B*) is completely dominant over albino (*b*). For the crosses in the table, give the genotypes of the parents:

Parental phenotypes	Black offspring	Albino offspring	Parental genotypes?
Black × albino	12	0	
Albino × albino	0	12	
Black × albino	5	7	
Black × black	9	3	

4. The pedigree below shows the inheritance of a rare mutant phenotype in humans, congenital cataracts (black symbols).

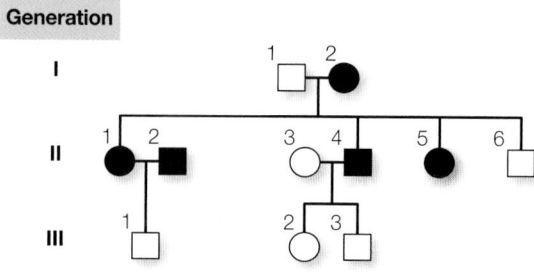

a. Are congenital cataracts inherited as a dominant or recessive trait?

b. Person #5 in the second generation mates with a man who does not have cataracts. Two of their four children, a boy and a girl, develop cataracts. What is the probability that their next child will be a girl with cataracts?

Mendel's laws of inheritance remain valid today; his discoveries laid the groundwork for all future studies of genetics. Inevitably, however, we have learned that things are more complicated than they seemed at first. Let's take a look at some of these complications, beginning with the interactions between alleles.

KEY CONCEPT
12.2 Alleles Can Produce Multiple Phenotypes

Learning Objectives

12.2.1 Recognize incomplete and codominance in a genetic cross.

12.2.2 Determine the possible blood types of an offspring when the blood types of the parents are known.

12.2.3 Define pleiotropy and give an example of an allele that is pleiotropic.

Over time genes accumulate changes, giving rise to new alleles. Thus there can be many alleles at a single gene that encode multiple traits for a single character. In addition, alleles do not always show simple dominant–recessive relationships. Furthermore, a single allele may have multiple phenotypic effects.

New alleles arise by mutation

Genes are subject to **mutations**, which are stable, inherited changes in the genetic material. In other words, an allele can mutate to become a different allele. For example, imagine that at one time all pea plants were tall, and that this trait was attributable to a height allele, *T*. At some point, a mutation occurred in *T* that resulted in a new allele, *t*, which causes short stature when homozygous. If this mutation were in a cell that underwent meiosis to form gametes, some of the resulting gametes would carry the *t* allele, and some offspring of this pea plant would carry the *t* allele. By creating variety, mutations provide the raw material for evolution.

Connect the Concepts Key Concept 14.1 describes a mutation as a change in the nucleotide sequence of DNA, and Key Concept 15.1 describes how various types of mutations affect phenotype in different ways.

Geneticists usually define one particular allele of a gene as the **wild type**; this allele is the one that is present in most individuals in nature ("the wild") and gives rise to an expected trait or phenotype. Other alleles of that gene, often called mutant alleles, may produce a different phenotype. A gene that has a wild-type allele less than 99% of the time (the rest of the alleles being mutant) is said to be **polymorphic** (Greek *poly*, "many," + *morph*, "form").

Many genes have multiple alleles

Because of random mutations, more than two alleles of a given gene may exist in a group of individuals. Any one individual has only two alleles—one from its biological mother and one from its biological father. But among multiple individuals there may be several different alleles. In fact, there are many examples of such multiple alleles, and they often show a hierarchy of dominance. An example is coat color in rabbits, determined by four alleles of the C gene:

1. C determines dark gray.
2. c^{chd} determines chinchilla, a lighter gray.
3. c^h determines Himalayan, where pigment is restricted to the extremities (point restricted).
4. c determines albino.

The hierarchy of dominance for these alleles is $C > c^{chd}, c^h > c$. Any rabbit with the C allele (paired with itself or any other allele) is dark gray, and a cc rabbit is albino. Intermediate colors result from different allele combinations, as shown in **Figure 12.10**. As this example illustrates, multiple alleles can increase the number of possible phenotypes. At the biochemical level, these alleles determine various amounts of a pigment because of an enzyme with various levels of activity.

A dramatic and serious example of multiple alleles involves the gene product targeted by certain widely used drugs designed to undermine the effects of the parasite that causes malaria in humans. There are numerous alleles of this parasite gene, some of which make the gene product insensitive to the drugs (they cannot bind to the target protein). Since the parasite is haploid, when a parasite has one of these resistance alleles and is in a human who is being treated with the drugs, that parasite will survive and reproduce while the vast majority of parasites with drug-sensitive wild-type alleles will be killed. Drug-resistant malaria causes great human suffering. The World Health Organization estimates that there are about 200 million new cases of malaria every year, more than half a million of them fatal.

Dominance is not always complete

In the pairs of alleles studied by Mendel, dominance is complete in heterozygous individuals. That is, an Rr individual always expresses the R phenotype. However, many genes have alleles that are not dominant or recessive to one another. Instead, the heterozygotes show an intermediate phenotype—at first glance, that appeared to support the old blending theory of inheritance. For example, if a true-breeding eggplant that produces the familiar purple fruit is crossed with a true-breeding white eggplant, all the F_1 plants produce violet fruit, an intermediate between the two parents. However, further crosses indicate that this apparent blending phenomenon can still be explained in terms of Mendelian genetics (**Figure 12.11**). The purple and white alleles have not disappeared, as those colors reappear when the F_1 plants are interbred.

When heterozygotes show a phenotype that is intermediate between those of the two homozygotes, the gene is said to be governed by **incomplete dominance**. In other words, neither of the two alleles is dominant over the other.

In codominance, both alleles at a gene are expressed

Sometimes the two alleles at a gene produce two different phenotypes that *both* appear in heterozygotes, a phenomenon called **codominance**. Note that this is different from incomplete dominance, where the phenotype of a heterozygote is an intermediate between the phenotypes of the parents. A good example of codominance is seen in the ABO blood group system in humans (this is also an example of multiple alleles and of complete dominance).

Early attempts at blood transfusion frequently killed the patient. Around 1900, the Austrian scientist Karl Landsteiner mixed blood cells and serum (blood from which cells have been removed) from different individuals. He found that only certain combinations of blood and serum are compatible. In other combinations, the red blood cells from one individual form clumps in the presence of serum from the other individual, a discovery that led to our ability to administer compatible blood transfusions that do not kill the recipient.

Clumps in mixed blood form as a consequence of mechanisms of the immune system that protect the body from invasion by "nonself" molecules or organisms. Specific proteins in human serum, called antibodies, react with foreign molecules or particles. The specific part of a molecule that is recognized by an antibody is called an antigen. Oligosaccharides on the surfaces of red blood cells can function as antigens. For example, people with type A blood

CC, Cc^{chd}, Cc^h, Cc	c^{chd}c^{chd}, c^{chd}c	c^hc^h, c^hc	cc
Dark gray	Chinchilla	Point restricted	Albino

Possible genotypes

Phenotypes

© iStock.com/Marina Golskaya · © iStock.com/purelook · David McIntyre · © ZTS/Shutterstock.com

Figure 12.10 Multiple Alleles for Coat Color in Rabbits These photographs show the phenotypes conferred by four alleles of the C gene for coat color in rabbits. Different combinations of two alleles give different coat colors and pigment distributions.

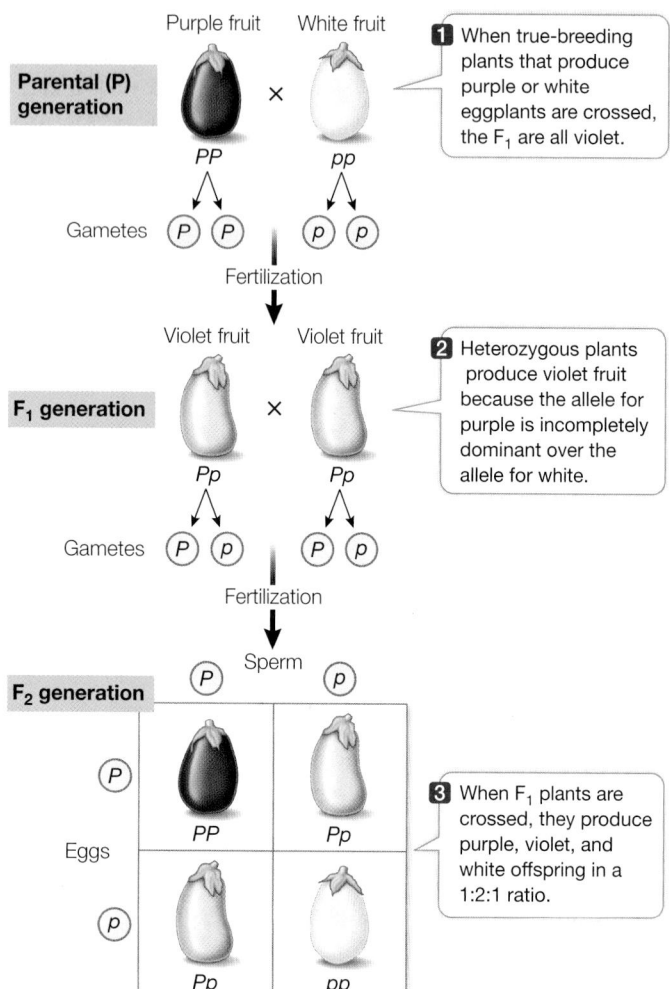

Parental (P) generation

Purple fruit × White fruit

PP pp

1 When true-breeding plants that produce purple or white eggplants are crossed, the F₁ are all violet.

Gametes (P) (P) (p) (p)

Fertilization

F₁ generation

Violet fruit × Violet fruit

Pp Pp

2 Heterozygous plants produce violet fruit because the allele for purple is incompletely dominant over the allele for white.

Gametes (P) (p) (P) (p)

Fertilization

F₂ generation

Sperm (P) (p)

Eggs (P) (p)

PP Pp

Pp pp

3 When F₁ plants are crossed, they produce purple, violet, and white offspring in a 1:2:1 ratio.

Figure 12.11 Incomplete Dominance Follows Mendel's Laws
An intermediate phenotype can occur in heterozygotes when neither allele is dominant. The heterozygous phenotype (here, violet fruit) may give the appearance of a blended trait, but the traits of the parental generation reappear in their original forms in succeeding generations, as predicted by Mendel's laws of inheritance.

make the A antigen but not the anti-A antibody, and those in the B group make the B antigen but not the anti-B antibody; A and B antigens are specific oligosaccharides on the surfaces of their red blood cells. If a person with type A blood is given a transfusion of type B or type AB blood, that individual's immune system will recognize the B antigen as nonself and its anti-B antibodies will react against it (**Figure 12.12**). Likewise, a person with type B blood has anti-A antibodies that will react with blood from an individual with the A antigen (type A or AB). However, someone with the codominant AB blood type makes *both* the A and the B antigens and does not make antibodies against either antigen. So a person with type AB blood can receive a transfusion from any of the blood groups. Individuals with type O blood make neither the A nor the B antigen and thus make anti-A and anti-B antibodies; as a result, they can receive blood only from a type O individual but can donate blood to individuals of any ABO blood group.

The oligosaccharides on the surfaces of red blood cells are made by enzymes that catalyze the formation of bonds between specific sugars. The ABO gene encodes one such enzyme and has three alleles, I^A, I^B, and i, each producing a different version of the enzyme. The product of the I^A allele adds N-acetylgalactosamine to the end of a preexisting oligosaccharide chain, resulting in the A antigen. The product of the I^B allele adds galactose to the same chain, making the B antigen. The i allele is fully recessive to the other two alleles and encodes a protein that has no enzymatic activity. The I^A and I^B alleles are codominant because a person with both alleles makes both the A and the B antigens, and both kinds of oligosaccharides occur on their red blood cells. You'll learn more about the functions of antibodies and antigens in Chapter 40.

Some alleles have multiple phenotypic effects

Mendel's principles were further extended when it was discovered that a single allele can influence more than one phenotype. In such a case, we say that the allele is **pleiotropic**. An example is the heritable human disease phenylketonuria, or PKU, which causes mental retardation and reduced hair and skin pigmentation. The disease occurs in people who have a mutation in the gene for a liver enzyme that converts the amino acid phenylalanine to tyrosine. Without a functional form of this enzyme, phenylalanine builds up in the body to toxic levels, and this affects development in a variety of ways. Given what we now know about genes and their functions, it is not surprising that a gene with such an important metabolic role should have pleiotropic effects. Other examples of pleiotropy include plant and animal genes whose products affect hormone levels, since many hormones play multiple roles in the body.

Blood type of cells	Geno-type	Blood types that body rejects	Blood type's reaction to added antibodies	
			Anti-A	Anti-B
A	$I^A I^A$ or $I^A i$	B and AB		
B	$I^B I^B$ or $I^B i$	A and AB		
AB	$I^A I^B$	None		
O	ii	A, B, and AB		

Red blood cells that do not react with antibody remain evenly dispersed.

Red blood cells that react with antibody clump together (speckled appearance).

Figure 12.12 ABO Blood Reactions Are Important in Transfusions
This table shows the results of mixing red blood cells of types A, B, AB, and O with serum containing anti-A or anti-B antibodies. As you look down the columns, note that each type, when mixed separately with anti-A and with anti-B, gives a unique pair of results; this is the basic method by which blood is typed. People with type O blood are the universal blood donors. People with type AB blood are good recipients, since they make neither type of antibody. When blood transfusions are incompatible, the reaction (clumping of red blood cells) can have severely adverse consequences for the recipient.

12.2 Recap and Assess

Genes are subject to random mutations that give rise to new alleles; thus many genes have more than two alleles within a population. Dominance is not necessarily an all-or-nothing phenomenon. Some genes have multiple effects on phenotype.

1. What is the difference between codominance and incomplete dominance?

2. A woman has blood type O and her biological mother has blood type B. What is the genotype of the mother? What are the possible blood types of the biological father?

3. In a particular plant species, two alleles control flower color, which can be yellow, green, or blue. Crosses of these plants produce the following offspring:

Parental phenotypes	Offspring phenotypes
Yellow × yellow	All yellow
Green × yellow	½ green and ½ yellow
Green × blue	½ blue and ½ green
Blue × blue	All blue

What will be the phenotypes, and ratio, of the offspring of a cross of green × green?

Thus far we have discussed phenotypic characters that are affected by single genes. In many cases, however, several genes interact to determine a phenotype. To complicate things further, the physical environment may influence which genes of an individual are expressed, meaning that phenotype is sometimes determined by both genes and the environment.

KEY CONCEPT
12.3 Genes Can Interact to Produce a Phenotype

Learning Objectives

12.3.1 Predict the phenotypes obtained in a cross involving two genes that show epistasis.

12.3.2 Determine from genotype and phenotype data whether a trait exhibits incomplete penetrance or variable expressivity.

12.3.3 Describe the difference between quantitative and qualitative (discrete) variation.

You have just seen how two alleles of the same gene can interact to produce a phenotype. Some phenotypes, such as human height, are influenced by the products of many genes, not just alleles of the same gene. We now turn to the genetics of such gene interactions.

Epistasis ("to stand on") occurs when the phenotypic expression of one gene is affected by another gene. For example, two genes (B and E) encode proteins that determine coat color in Labrador retrievers:

1. Allele B (black pigment) is dominant over b (brown, or chocolate).

2. Allele E (pigment deposition in hair) is dominant over e (no deposition, so hair is yellow).

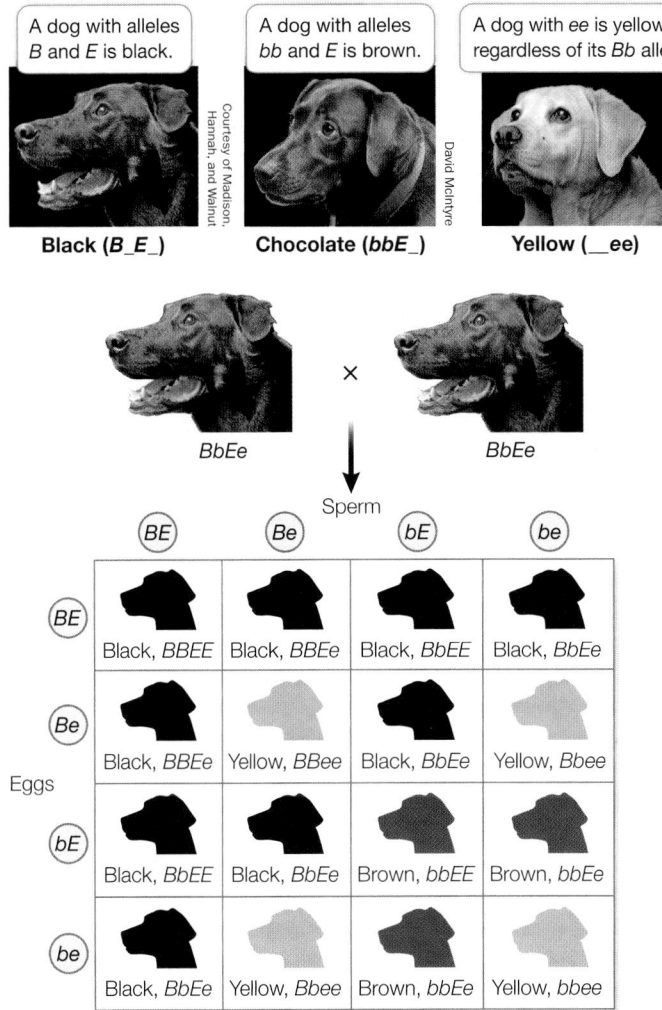

Figure 12.13 Genes May Interact Epistatically Epistasis occurs when one gene alters the phenotypic effect of another gene. In Labrador retrievers, the E gene controls whether or not pigment, determined by the B gene, is deposited into the coat.

Q: A mating of yellow and brown retrievers produced a black pup. What were the possible genotypes of the parents?

An EE or Ee dog with BB or Bb is black, and one with bb is brown. An ee dog is yellow regardless of the B gene alleles present (**Figure 12.13**). Because the product of the E allele is needed for the expression of both the B and the b alleles, E is said to be epistatic to B.

Hybrid vigor results from new gene combinations and interactions

In 1876, Charles Darwin reported that when he crossed two different true-breeding, homozygous genetic strains of corn, the offspring were 25% taller than either of the parent strains. Darwin's observation was largely ignored for the next 30 years. In 1908, George Shull "rediscovered" this idea, reporting that not just plant height but the weight of the corn grain produced was dramatically higher in the offspring (**Figure 12.14**). Agricultural scientists took note, and Shull's paper had a lasting impact on the field of applied genetics. The cultivation of hybrid corn spread rapidly in the United States

B73   Hybrid   Mo17

Courtesy of the Plant and Soil Sciences eLibrary, Dept. of Agronomy & Horticulture at the University of Nebraska-Lincoln

Figure 12.14 Hybrid Vigor in Corn Two parent lines of corn, B73 and Mo17, that are homozygous at most genes were crossed to produce the more vigorous hybrid line that is heterozygous at most genes.

and all over the world, quadrupling grain production. The practice of hybridization has spread to many other crops and animals used in agriculture. For example, beef cattle that are crossbred are larger and live longer than cattle bred within their own genetic strain.

Farmers have known for centuries that matings among close relatives (known as **inbreeding**) can result in **inbreeding depression**: reduced biological fitness arising from mating close relatives that tend to have the same recessive, sometimes deleterious, alleles. Inbreeding can produce offspring of smaller size and/or lower quality than matings between unrelated individuals. In contrast, superior qualities can arise from crossing inbred lines, a phenomenon called **hybrid vigor**, or **heterosis** (short for heterozygosis).

The mechanism by which heterosis arises is not known but is important to understand, given how agriculture relies on heterosis for improving food production. Two competing hypotheses have been proposed. The dominance hypothesis explains the extra growth in hybrids as an absence of inbreeding depression—by the assumption that hybrids are unlikely to be homozygous for deleterious recessive alleles. The overdominance hypothesis postulates that in hybrids, new combinations of alleles from the parental strains interact with one another, resulting in superior traits that did not occur in the parental lines. Recent studies suggest that both dominance and overdominance contribute to heterosis in specific characters.

The environment affects gene action

The phenotype of an individual does not result from its genotype alone. *Genotype and environment interact to determine the phenotype of an organism.* This is especially important to remember in the era of genome sequencing (covered in Chapter 17). When the sequence of the human genome was completed in 2003, it was hailed as the "book of life," and public expectations of the benefits gained from this knowledge were (and are) high. But this kind of "genetic determinism" is wrong. You already know that environmental variables such as light, temperature, and nutrition can affect the phenotypic expression of a genotype.

A familiar example of this phenomenon involves "point restriction" coat patterns found in Siamese cats and certain rabbit breeds (**Figure 12.15**). These animals carry a mutant allele of a gene that controls the growth of dark fur all over the body. As a result of this mutation, the enzyme encoded by the gene is inactive at temperatures above a certain point (usually around 35°C). The animals maintain a body temperature above this point, and so their fur is mostly light. However, the extremities—feet, ears, nose, and tail—are cooler, about 25°C, so the fur on these regions is dark. These animals are all white when they are born, because the extremities were kept warm in the mother's womb.

A simple experiment shows that the dark fur is temperature-dependent. If a patch of white fur on a point-restricted rabbit's back is shaved off and an ice pack is placed on the skin where the patch was, the fur that grows back will be dark. This indicates that although the gene for dark fur was expressed all along, the environment inhibited the activity of the mutant enzyme.

Two parameters describe the effects of genes and environment on the phenotype:

1. **Penetrance** is the proportion of individuals in a group with a given genotype that actually show the expected phenotype. For example, many people who inherit a mutant allele of the gene *BRCA1* develop breast cancer. But some people with the mutation do not. So the *BRCA1* allele is said to be incompletely penetrant.

2. **Expressivity** is the degree to which a genotype is expressed in an individual. For example, a woman with the mutant *BRCA1* allele may develop both breast and ovarian cancer as part of the phenotype, but another woman with the same mutation may develop only breast cancer. So the mutant allele is said to have variable expressivity.

The temperature of the extremities is lower and allows the enzyme that produces black coat color to be active.

The temperature of most of the body is too high to allow the enzyme that produces black coat color to be active.

© Mark Taylor/NPL/Minden Pictures

Figure 12.15 The Environment Influences Gene Expression This rabbit and cat express a coat pattern called "point restriction." Their genotypes specify dark fur, but the enzyme for dark color is inactive at normal body temperature, so only the extremities—the coolest regions of the body—express the dark fur phenotype.

Most complex phenotypes are determined by multiple genes and the environment

Certain simple characters, such as those that Mendel studied in peas, differ in discrete, **qualitative** ways, such as purple or white flowers, or round or wrinkled seeds. But many characters are complex, such as height in humans, with phenotypes that vary more or less continuously over a range. Some people are short, others are tall, and many are in between the two extremes. Such variation within a population is called **quantitative**, or continuous, variation (Figure 12.16).

In some cases the variation in quantitative characters results primarily from variation in genotypes across individuals within the population. For instance, much of human eye color is the result of several genes controlling the synthesis and distribution of dark melanin pigment. Dark eyes have a lot of it, brown eyes less, and green, gray, and blue eyes even less. In the latter cases, the distribution of other pigments in the eye is what determines light reflection and color.

In many cases, however, *quantitative variation is due to both genes and environment.* Height in humans certainly falls into this category. If you look at families, you often see that parents and their offspring all tend to be tall or short. However, nutrition also plays a role in height: American 18-year-olds today are about 6% taller than their great-grandparents were at the same age. Three generations are not enough time for mutations that would exert such a dramatic effect to spread throughout the general population, so the height difference must be due to environmental factors.

Geneticists call the chromosomal regions that together determine such complex characters **quantitative trait loci.** A **locus** (plural *loci*) is a specific position on a chromosome. A locus on a chromosome may be large or small (as small as a single base pair). A quantitative trait locus can contain one or several genes. Identifying quantitative trait loci is a major challenge, and an important one. For example, the amount of grain that a variety of rice produces in a growing season is determined by many interacting quantitative trait loci. Crop plant breeders have worked hard to identify these loci and the genes they contain in order to breed higher-yielding rice strains. In a similar way, human characteristics such as disease susceptibility and behavior are caused in part by quantitative trait loci. Some traits turn out to be affected by many loci in the genome. For example, there are about a thousand loci that contribute to the variation in human height, most of which have very small effect, usually less than a millimeter.

KEY CONCEPT
12.3 Recap and Assess

In epistasis, one gene affects the expression of another. Perhaps the most challenging problem for genetics is identifying the genes contributing to phenotypic variation for complex traits that are caused by many interacting genes and the environment.

1. An individual with three copies of chromosome 21 always has Down syndrome. However, some individuals are more severely affected than others. Does Down syndrome show incomplete penetrance? Variable expressivity?

2. In general, height is considered to be a quantitative trait. However, in Mendel's pea plants height is considered to be a qualitative trait. Explain why.

3. If the dominant allele *A* is necessary for hearing in humans, and another allele, *B*, located on a different chromosome, results in deafness no matter what other genes are present, what percentage of the offspring of a parental cross of *aaBb* × *Aabb* will be deaf?

Figure 12.16 Quantitative Variation   Quantitative variation is produced by the interaction of genes at multiple loci and the environment. These students (women [in white] are shorter; men [in blue] are taller) show continuous variation in height that is the result of interactions between many genes and the environment.

In the next key concept we'll see how the discovery that genes occupy specific positions on chromosomes enabled scientists who followed Mendel to provide a physical explanation for his model of inheritance, and to provide an explanation for those cases where Mendel's second law does not apply.

KEY CONCEPT
12.4
Genes Are Carried on Chromosomes

Learning Objectives

12.4.1 Describe evidence that two genes are genetically linked on the same chromosome.

12.4.2 Calculate the map distance between two genes using data from a test cross.

12.4.3 Predict the frequency of affected and unaffected offspring from a cross involving a sex-linked gene.

There are far more genes than chromosomes. Studies of different genes that are physically linked on the same chromosome reveal inheritance patterns that are not Mendelian. These patterns have been useful for identifying genes that are linked to one another, and for determining how far apart they are on the chromosome.

Soon after Mendel was rediscovered, dihybrid crosses that did not show 9:3:3:1 Mendelian F_2 ratios were discovered. Demonstrating that such violations of Mendel's law of independent assortment were caused by genetic linkage on chromosomes was first figured out in the fruit fly *Drosophila melanogaster*. Its small size, the ease with which it can be bred, its few chromosomes, and its short generation time make this animal an attractive experimental subject. Beginning in 1909, Thomas Hunt Morgan and his students at Columbia University pioneered the study of *Drosophila*, and today it remains an important model organism for studies of genetics.

 View in Achieve
Animation 12.2 **Alleles That Do Not Assort Independently**

Linked genes are inherited together

Some of the crosses Morgan performed with fruit flies yielded phenotypic ratios that were not in accordance with those predicted by Mendel's law of independent assortment. Morgan crossed *Drosophila* with known genotypes at two genes, *B* and *Vg*:

1. *B* (wild-type gray body) is dominant over *b* (black body).

2. *Vg* (wild-type wing) is dominant over *vg* (vestigial, a very small wing).

Morgan first showed that both of these genes followed Mendel's law of segregation. Then he performed a dihybrid cross, making an F_1 generation by crossing homozygous dominant *BBVgVg* flies with homozygous recessives (*bbvgvg*). He then test-crossed the F_1 flies: *BbVgvg × bbvgvg*. Morgan expected to see four phenotypes in a ratio of 1:1:1:1, but that is not what he observed. The body-color gene and the wing-size gene were not assorting independently; rather, particular alleles at these two genes were usually inherited together (**Figure 12.17**).

Experiment

Figure 12.17A   Some Alleles Do Not Assort Independently

Original Paper: T. H. Morgan. 1912. Complete linkage in the second chromosome of *Drosophila*. *Science* 36: 719–720.

Morgan's studies showed that the genes for body color and wing size in *Drosophila* are linked, so that their alleles do not assort independently.

HYPOTHESIS▶ Alleles at genes for different characters always assort independently.

METHOD▶

This heterozygous individual was produced from the cross *BBVgVg × bbvgvg*.

BbVgvg (gray body, normal wings) ♀   ×   *bbvgvg* (black body, vestigial wings) ♂

RESULTS▶

Genotypes	*BbVgvg* Gray, normal	*bbvgvg* Black, vestigial	*Bbvgvg* Gray, vestigial	*bbVgvg* Black, normal
Expected phenotypes if independent assortment occurs	575	575	575	575
Observed phenotypes (number of individuals)	965	944	206	185

These are the results expected from Mendel's second law (independent assortment)…

…but the actual results were inconsistent with the law.

Parental phenotypes   Recombinant phenotypes

CONCLUSION▶ The hypothesis is rejected. The alleles for these two genes do not assort independently, but are linked (on the same chromosome).

Morgan knew about chromosomes and meiosis. To explain the data, he proposed that the two *Drosophila* genes are on the same chromosome—that is, that they are physically linked. Suppose that the *B* and *Vg* genes are indeed located on the same chromosome. In that case, the F_1 flies would have one homolog containing the *B* and *Vg* alleles (from their homozygous *BBVgVg* parent) and the other homolog containing the *b* and *vg* alleles (from their homozygous *bbvgvg* parent). Why didn't all of Morgan's F_2 flies have the phenotypes that would result from them receiving either a *BVg* or a *bvg* gamete from the F_1 double heterozygous parent— that is, why didn't his cross result in gray flies with normal wings and black flies with vestigial wings, in a 1:1 ratio? If linkage were absolute—that is, if chromosomes always remained intact and unchanged—we would expect to see just those two types of progeny, resulting from the same two parental gametes that fused to create the F_1 parent. However, this does not always happen.

Work with the Data

Figure 12.17B   Some Alleles Do Not Assort Independently

Original Paper: T. H. Morgan. 1912. Complete linkage in the second chromosome of *Drosophila*. *Science* 36: 719–720.

Mendel's work was "rediscovered" 34 years after its publication. At that time, biologists began to find some exceptions to the rules of inheritance that Mendel had proposed. Thomas Hunt Morgan and his colleagues made dihybrid test crosses in fruit flies. They proposed that the clearest way to test for linkage was not to look at aberrations in the 9:3:3:1 phenotypic ratio expected from an $F_1 \times F_1$ cross, but to examine aberrations in the 1:1:1:1 ratio expected from an $F_1 \times$ homozygous recessive test cross (see Figure 12.4). Morgan's group then hypothesized that linkage had a physical basis, namely that genes are linked together on chromosomes and that rare crossing over during meiosis gives rise to the less frequent phenotypes. Examination of actual chromosomal events confirmed this.

QUESTIONS▸

1. Morgan first performed a dihybrid cross between black, normal-winged flies (*bbVgVg*) and gray, vestigial-winged flies (*BBvgvg*). The F_1 flies were interbred, yielding the F_2 phenotypes shown in the table (Experiment 1). Compare these data with the expected data in a 9:3:3:1 ratio by using the chi-square test (see Appendix B for information about the chi-square test). Are there differences, and are they significant?

2. To quantify linkage, Morgan crossed homozygous black, normal-winged females with homozygous gray, vestigial-winged males. He then crossed the F_1 females with black, vestigial-winged males. (Note that this is not the same F_1 used in the test cross as the one shown in the experiment in Figure 12.17A. In that case, the parents of the F_1 were *BBVgVg* and *bbvgvg*.) The results of this test cross are shown in the table (Experiment 2). Are these genes linked? If they are linked, what is the recombinant frequency between the genes (= the number of recombinant offspring divided by the total number of offspring)? Explain why these data are so different from the data shown in Figure 12.17A.

3. In a third experiment, Morgan crossed two genetic strains of flies that were homozygous for the body-color and wing-size genes. The F_1 flies were all gray and normal-winged, and these were interbred. The results are shown in the table (Experiment 3). What were the genotypes and phenotypes of the original parents that produced the F_1?

	Number of progeny showing each phenotype			
Experiment	Gray, normal	Black, normal	Gray, vestigial	Black, vestigial
1	2,316	1,146	737	0
2	578	1,413	1,117	307
3	246	9	65	18

Go to **Achieve** for a companion Data in Depth exercise.

Genes can be exchanged between chromatids and mapped

If physical linkage of genes meant that genetic linkage was absolute, then only parental-type gametes would be produced and Mendel's law of independent assortment would apply only to

genes on different chromosomes. Instead, alleles at different genes that are on the same chromosome *do* sometimes separate from one another during meiosis, resulting in recombinant gametes—gametes that differ from the parental-type gametes in terms of the alleles that they carry. Genes on the same chromosome may recombine to produce recombinant gametes when two homologous chromosomes physically exchange corresponding segments during prophase I of meiosis—that is, by crossing over (Figure 12.18). As discussed in Key Concept 11.2, DNA is replicated during S phase, so that by prophase I, when homologous

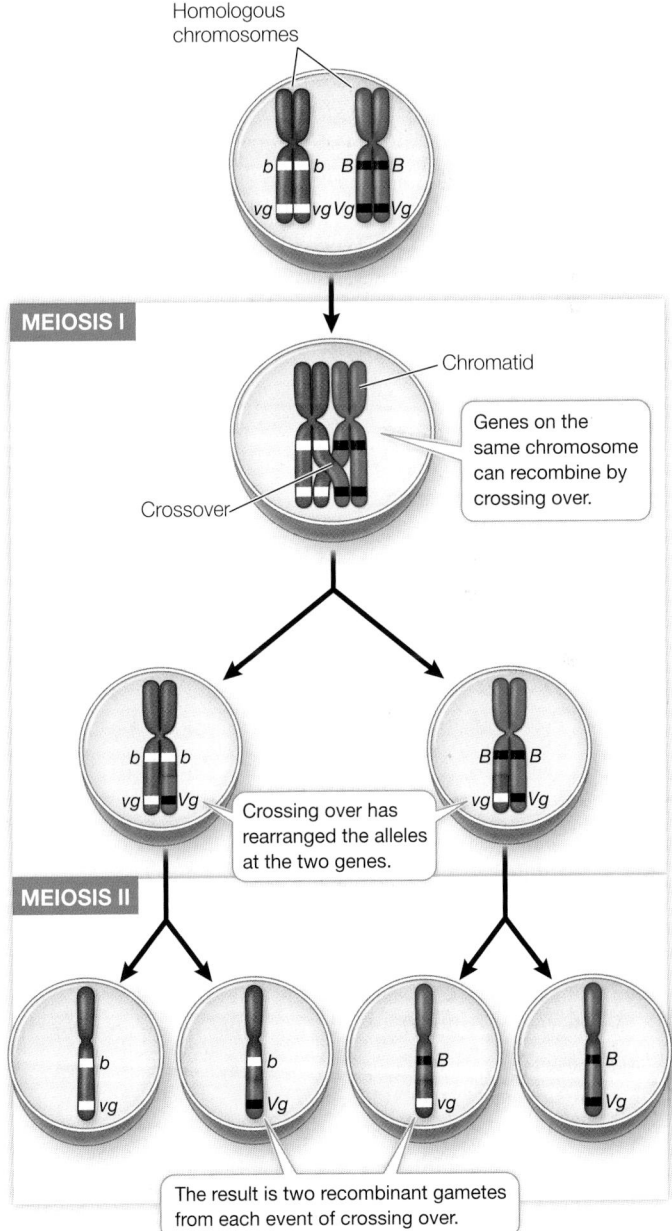

Figure 12.18 Crossing Over Results in Genetic Recombination Recombination accounts for why linked alleles are not always inherited together. Genes on the same chromosome can be recombined by crossing over, and linked alleles separated from one another. Such recombination occurs during prophase I of meiosis.

chromosome pairs come together, each chromosome consists of two sister chromatids.

Note that one exchange event involves *only two nonsister chromatids*, one from each member of the homologous pair, and can occur at any point along the length of the chromosome. The chromosome segments involved are exchanged reciprocally, so both chromatids involved in crossing over become recombinant (that is, each chromatid ends up with alleles from both of the organism's parents). Several exchange events can occur along the length of each homologous pair.

When crossing over takes place between two linked genes, not all the gametes will be parental types. Instead, recombinant gametes will appear as well, as they did in Morgan's test cross, producing recombinant offspring (see Figure 12.17). The frequency with which recombinant offspring are produced is called the **recombinant frequency**, which is calculated by dividing the number of recombinant offspring by the total number of offspring (**Figure 12.19**). Recombinant frequencies will be *greater for genes that are farther apart* on the chromosome than for genes that are closer together because an exchange event is more likely to occur between genes that are far apart. However, because of multiple crossovers, the recombinant frequency between two genes will never exceed 50%.

By calculating recombinant frequencies, geneticists can infer the locations of genes along a chromosome and generate a genetic map. **Figure 12.20** shows a map of five genes on a fruit fly chromosome constructed using the recombination frequencies generated by test crosses involving various pairs of genes. The recombination frequencies obtained in crosses involving two genes are converted to map units (also called centimorgans, cM); one map unit is equivalent to an average recombination frequency of 0.01 (1%). In the chromosome shown in Figure 12.20, the recombination frequency between the yellow body gene (*y*) and the white eye gene (*w*) is low, so they are close together on the map (1 map unit apart). Recombination between the yellow body gene (*y*) and the vermillion eye gene (*v*) is more frequent, so they are farther apart (31 map units).

Gene sequencing of DNA has allowed the relationship between genetic distance, in map units, and physical distance, in base pairs, to be determined. This relationship varies across regions of chromosomes and across organisms (in flies, 1 map unit is about 200–500,000 base pairs of DNA). While DNA sequencing has made genetic mapping of chromosomes using crosses less important in some areas of genetics research, it is still a way to verify that a particular DNA sequence corresponds with a particular phenotype. Linkage has allowed biologists to isolate genes and to identify genetic markers (a sequence of DNA that is easily scored) linked to important genes. This is important in breeding new crops and animals for agriculture, and for identifying people carrying medically significant mutations.

> **Connect the Concepts** As described in Key Concept 17.1, gene sequencing techniques reveal the nucleotide sequences of genes and identify where genes begin and end on the chromosome.

Sex linkage is revealed by studies of characters showing differences in reciprocal crosses

In his work, Mendel performed reciprocal crosses—for each cross he would use one parent as the pollen donor (male parent) and one as the pollen recipient (female parent) and vice-versa. Reciprocal crosses always gave similar results; it did not matter which individual was acting as the male, implying that traits are inherited identically through sperm and eggs. However, in species with separate sexes, reciprocal crosses sometimes give different results. For example, in humans a color-blind biological mother and a normal biological father always have color-blind sons and normal daughters, while a color-blind biological father and a normal biological mother have normal sons and daughters. To understand the types of inheritance in which reciprocal crosses give different results, we must consider the ways in which sex is determined in different species.

Recombinant frequency = $\dfrac{391 \text{ recombinants}}{2{,}300 \text{ total offspring}}$ = 0.17

Figure 12.19 Recombinant Frequencies The frequency of recombinant offspring, which are those produced by recombinant (nonparental) gametes, can be calculated.

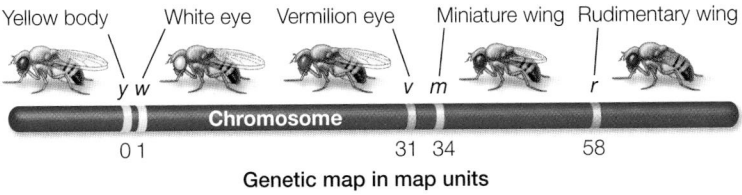

Figure 12.20 The Genetic Map of a Chromosome in Drosophila Showing the Positions of Five Genes The map distances between adjacent pairs of genes, obtained from genetic crosses, are used to generate a linear map (in map units) of the chromosome.

SEX DETERMINATION BY CHROMOSOMES   In corn, every diploid adult has both male and female reproductive structures. The tissues in these two types of structures are genetically identical, just as roots and leaves are genetically identical. Organisms such as corn, in which the same individual produces both male and female gametes, are said to be **monoecious** (Greek, "one house"). Other organisms, such as date palms and most animals, are **dioecious** ("two houses"), meaning that some individuals can produce only male gametes and others can produce only female gametes. In other words, in dioecious organisms the different sexes are different individuals.

In mammals and birds, sex is determined by differences in the chromosomes, but such determination operates in different ways in different groups of organisms. For example, in many animals, including mammals, sex is determined by a single pair of **sex chromosomes**, which are chromosomes that differ in copy number between males and females. The remaining chromosomes, called **autosomes**, occur in pairs in males and females. For example, in humans there are 22 pairs of autosomes in males and females, and 1 pair of sex chromosomes. The chromosomal bases for sex determination in various groups of animals are summarized in Table 12.2.

The sex chromosomes of female mammals consist of a pair of X chromosomes. Male mammals, by contrast, have one X chromosome and a sex chromosome that is not found in females, the Y chromosome. Females may be represented as XX (homogametic) and males as XY (heterogametic).

MALE MAMMALS PRODUCE TWO KINDS OF GAMETES   Each gamete produced by a male mammal has a complete set of autosomes, but just as each gamete carries one copy of each pair of autosomes, each carries one sex chromosome; half carry an X and the other half carry a Y. When an X-bearing sperm fertilizes an egg, the resulting XX zygote is female; when a Y-bearing sperm fertilizes an egg, the resulting XY zygote is male.

SEX CHROMOSOME ABNORMALITIES REVEALED THE GENE THAT DETERMINES SEX   Can we determine which chromosome, X or Y, carries the sex-determining gene, and can the gene be identified? One way to determine cause (e.g., the presence of a gene on the Y chromosome) and effect (e.g., maleness) is to look at cases of biological error, in which the expected outcome does not happen.

We can learn something about the functions of X and Y chromosomes from abnormal sex chromosome arrangements resulting from nondisjunction during meiosis or mitosis (see Key Concept 11.5). As you will recall, nondisjunction occurs when a pair of homologous chromosomes (in meiosis I) or sister chromatids (in mitosis or meiosis II) fails to separate. As a result, a gamete may have one too few or one too many chromosomes. If this gamete fuses with another gamete that has the full haploid chromosome set, the resulting offspring will be aneuploid, with fewer or more chromosomes than normal.

In humans, XO individuals sometimes appear. The O indicates that a chromosome is missing—that is, individuals who are XO have only one sex chromosome (an X). Human XO individuals are females who are moderately abnormal physically but normal mentally; usually they are also sterile. The XO condition in humans is called Turner syndrome. It is the only known case in which a person can survive with only one member of a chromosome pair (here, the XY pair), although most XO conceptions are spontaneously terminated early in development. XXY individuals also occur; this condition, which affects males, is called Klinefelter syndrome and results in overlong limbs and sterility.

These observations suggested that the gene controlling maleness is located on the Y chromosome. Observations of people with other types of chromosomal abnormalities helped researchers pinpoint the location of that gene:

- Some women are genetically XY but lack a small portion of the Y chromosome.

- Some men are genetically XX but have a small piece of the Y chromosome attached to another chromosome.

The Y fragments that are respectively missing and present in these two cases are the same and contain the maleness-determining gene, which was named *SRY* (sex-determining *r*egion on the *Y* chromosome).

The *SRY* gene encodes a protein involved in **primary sex determination**—that is, the determination of the kinds of gametes that an individual will produce and the organs that will make them (the male and female gonads). In the presence of the functional SRY protein, an embryo develops sperm-producing testes. If the embryo has no Y chromosome, the *SRY* gene is absent, and thus the SRY protein is not made. In the absence of the SRY protein, the embryo develops egg-producing ovaries. In this case, a gene on the X chromosome called *DAX1* produces an anti-testis factor. So the role of SRY in a male is to inhibit the maleness inhibitor encoded by *DAX1*. The SRY protein does this in male cells, but since it is not present in females, DAX1 can act to inhibit maleness.

One function of the gonads is to produce hormones (such as testosterone and estrogen) that send signals to the rest of the body and control the development of **secondary sex characteristics**.

TABLE **12.2**	Sex Determination in Animals	
Animal group	**Mechanism**
Bees	Males are haploid, females are diploid
Birds and butterflies	Males ZZ (homogametic), females ZW (heterogametic)
Mammals and flies	Males XY (heterogametic), females XX (homogametic)

These are outward manifestations of maleness and femaleness, such as differences in body type, breast development, body hair, and voice. Secondary sex characteristics distinguish males and females but are not directly part of the reproductive system.

SEX-LINKED INHERITANCE IN FRUIT FLIES   Like humans, fruit flies have an XY sex determination system, with males having one X and one Y, and females having two X chromosomes. However, in flies an XO individual is a male, not a female as in humans, and an XXY individual is a female, not a male as in humans. This indicates that in fruit flies it is the number of X chromosomes, not the presence of a Y chromosome, that determines sex. As in other organisms, the X and Y chromosomes are not complete homologs of one another: *many genes on the X chromosome are not present on the Y.* The X chromosome of *Drosophila* was one of the first to have specific genes assigned to it.

Thomas Morgan identified a **sex-linked** gene that controls eye color in *Drosophila*. The wild-type allele of the gene confers red eyes, whereas a recessive mutant allele confers white eyes. Morgan's experimental crosses demonstrated that this eye-color gene is on the X chromosome. If we abbreviate the eye-color alleles as *R* (red eyes) and *r* (white eyes), the presence of the alleles on the X chromosome is designated by X^R and X^r.

Morgan crossed a homozygous red-eyed female ($X^R X^R$) with a white-eyed male. The male is designated $X^r Y$ because the Y chromosome does not carry this gene. (Any gene that is present as a single copy in a diploid organism is called **hemizygous**.) All the sons and daughters from this cross had red eyes, because the red phenotype is dominant over white and all the progeny had inherited a wild-type X chromosome (X^R) from their mother (**Figure 12.21A**). This phenotypic outcome would have occurred even if the *R* gene had been present on an autosome rather than a sex chromosome. In that case, the male would have been homozygous recessive—*rr*.

When Morgan performed the reciprocal cross, in which a white-eyed female ($X^r X^r$) was mated with a red-eyed male ($X^R Y$), the results were unexpected: instead of all offspring being heterozygous with red eyes, *all the sons were white-eyed and all the daughters were red-eyed* (**Figure 12.21B**). The sons from the reciprocal cross inherited their only X chromosome from their white-eyed mother and were therefore hemizygous for the white allele. The daughters, however, got an X chromosome bearing the *r* allele from their mother and an X chromosome bearing the *R* allele from their father; therefore they were red-eyed heterozygotes. When these heterozygous females were mated with red-eyed males, half their sons had white eyes but all their daughters had red eyes. Together, these results showed that the eye color gene was present on the X chromosome and not on the Y.

These and other experiments led to the term **sex-linked inheritance**: inheritance of a gene that is carried on a sex chromo-

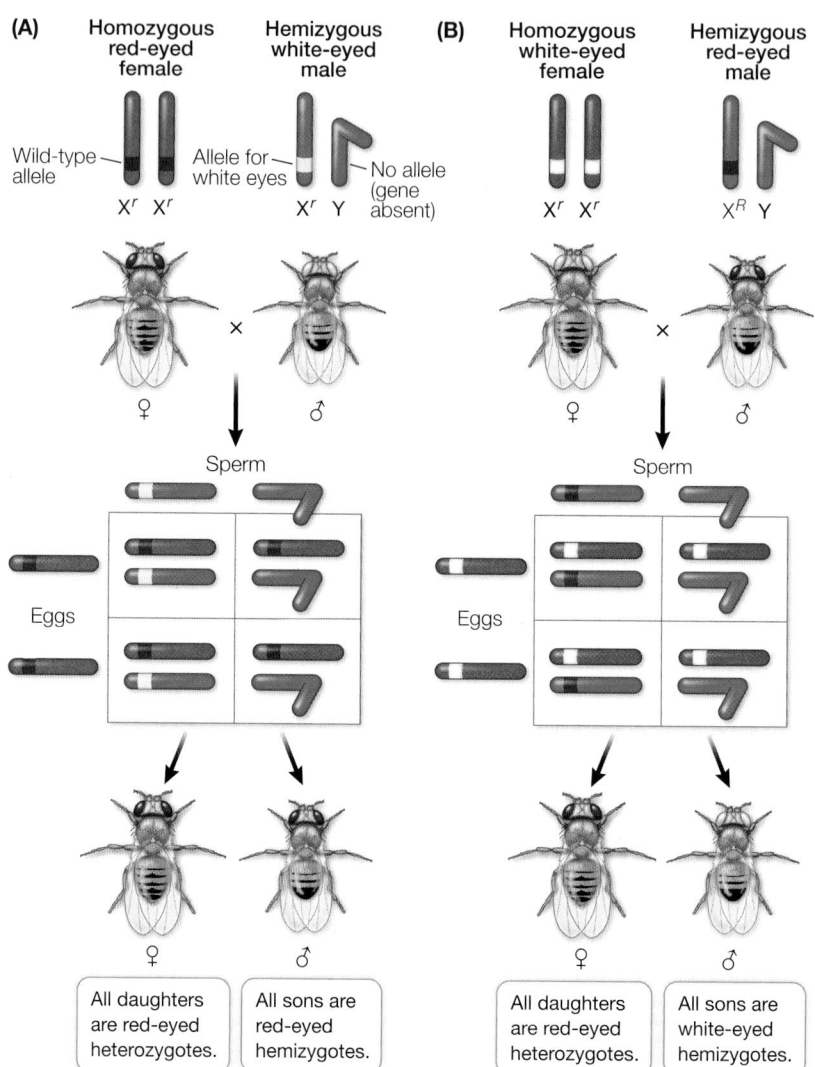

Figure 12.21 Eye Color Is a Sex-Linked Character in Drosophila   Morgan demonstrated that a mutant allele that causes white eyes in *Drosophila* is carried on the X chromosome. A cross in which the male had white eyes and the female red eyes **(A)** gave different results than the reciprocal cross **(B)**.

Q: If a red-eyed female was crossed with a white-eyed male and there were white-eyed males and females in the offspring, what was the genotype of the red-eyed female?

some. In mammals, the X chromosome is larger and carries many more genes than the Y. For this reason, most examples of sex-linked inheritance involve genes that are carried on the X chromosome. In humans, pedigree analyses of X-linked recessive phenotypes like the one in **Figure 12.22** reveal the following patterns (compare with the pedigrees of autosomal phenotypes in Figure 12.9):

- The phenotype appears much more often in males than in females, because only one copy of the rare allele is needed for its expression in males, whereas two copies must be present in females.

- A male with the mutation passes it on to all of his daughters; his sons get his Y chromosome.

Generation I (parents)

This man inherited the mutant X from his biological mother and expresses the mutant phenotype. He then passed the mutant X to his biological daughter, who passed it to her biological son, who is also affected.

A heterozygous carrier has a normal phenotype.

This woman inherited the mutant X from her biological mother.

Generation II

Generation III

Generation IV

Transmission from father to biological son or from grandfather to biological grandson through a son never occurs.

Two siblings inherited the mutant X from their biological mother. The son is red-green color-blind; his sister is a carrier.

- Heterozygous female (carrier)
- Affected male
- Unaffected male
- Unaffected female

Figure 12.22 Red-Green Color Blindness Is a Sex-Linked Trait in Humans The mutant allele for red-green color blindness is expressed as an X-linked recessive trait, and therefore is always expressed in males who carry that allele.

- Daughters who receive one X-linked mutation are heterozygous carriers. They are phenotypically normal but can pass the mutant allele to their sons (who will be affected) or daughters. On average, half their children will inherit the mutant allele since half of their X chromosomes carry the normal allele.

- As is true in autosomal recessive phenotypes, an X-linked recessive phenotype can skip a generation (looking backward)—affected individuals can have unaffected parents.

KEY CONCEPT
12.4 Recap and Assess

Simple Mendelian ratios are not observed when genes are linked on the same chromosome. Linkage results in atypical frequencies of phenotypes in the offspring from a test cross. Calculating recombination frequencies between genes can lead to a genetic map of the genes. Sex linkage refers to genes on one sex chromosome (usually the X) that have no counterpart on the other sex chromosome.

1. Describe the concept of genetic linkage and its implications in genetic crosses.

2. Explain why red-green color blindness is more common in males than in females and why all the sons of an affected female are affected.

3. Sometimes scientists get lucky. Peas have a haploid number of seven chromosomes, so many of their genes are linked. The genes underlying the seven characters studied by Mendel are on four chromosomes and two are close enough to show linkage in a genetic cross. Mendel got lucky in that he never performed a dihybrid cross using that pair of characters. Suppose pure breeding parents having round, yellow (*RRYY*) and wrinkled, green (*rryy*) seeds were crossed to give an F$_1$ pea plant that was heterozygous for both genes (*RrYy*). If this double heterozygote was test-crossed, and the genes were linked with a map distance of 10 units, what would the proportions of offspring phenotypes have been?

4. In *Drosophila*, three autosomal genes have alleles as follows:
   Gray body color (*B*) is dominant over black (*b*).
   Normal wing (*Vg*) is dominant over vestigial (*vg*).
   Red eye (*R*) is dominant over sepia (*r*).
   Two crosses were performed, with the following results:
   Cross I: Parents: heterozygous
   red eye, normal wing × sepia eye, vestigial wing
   Offspring: 131 red, normal
   120 sepia, vestigial
   122 red, vestigial
   127 sepia, normal
   Cross II: Parents: heterozygous
   gray body, normal wing × black body, vestigial wing
   Offspring: 236 gray, normal
   253 black, vestigial
   50 gray, vestigial
   61 black, normal
   Are any of the three genes linked on the same chromosome? If so, what is the distance between the linked genes (in map units)?

The genes we've discussed so far in this chapter are all in the cell nucleus. You might be surprised to learn that other organelles, including mitochondria and plastids, also carry genes. What are these genes, and how are they inherited?

KEY CONCEPT
12.5 Some Eukaryotic Genes Are Outside the Nucleus

Learning Objective

12.5.1 Predict inheritance patterns of genes present in organelles.

The nucleus is not the only organelle in a eukaryotic cell that carries genetic material. Mitochondria and plastids contain small numbers of genes in their circular DNA molecules. For example, in humans there are about 20,500 genes coding for proteins in the nuclear genome and 37 in the mitochondrial genome. Plastid genomes are about five times larger than those of mitochondria.

Connect the Concepts Key Concept 5.5 describes the endosymbiosis theory, which proposes that some organelles—particularly mitochondria and plastids—may be descended from prokaryotes that were engulfed by other, larger cells.

The inheritance of organelle genes differs from that of nuclear genes for several reasons:

- In most organisms, mitochondria and/or plastids are inherited only from the female. As you will learn in Chapter 42, eggs contain abundant cytoplasm and organelles, but the only part of the sperm that survives to take part in the union of haploid gametes is the nucleus. So you have inherited your biological mother's mitochondria (with their genes), but not your biological father's. This means that characters encoded on organelle genes show differences in reciprocal crosses.

- There may be hundreds of mitochondria and/or plastids in a cell. So a cell is not diploid for organelle genes.

- Organelle genes tend to mutate at much faster rates than nuclear genes.

Although most genes for organelle proteins are in the nucleus, several of the genes carried by cytoplasmic organelles are important for organelle assembly and function, and mutations of these genes can have profound effects on the organism. The phenotypes resulting from such mutations reflect the organelles' roles. For example, in plants and some photosynthetic protists, certain plastid gene mutations affect the proteins that assemble chlorophyll molecules into photosystems. These mutations result in a phenotype that is essentially white instead of green. A plant that inherits the white phenotype (from a flower on a white branch of a parent plant that is otherwise green) will die because it cannot synthesize carbohydrates. The inheritance of this phenotype follows a non-Mendelian, maternal pattern (**Figure 12.23**). Mitochondrial gene mutations that affect the respiratory chain result in reduced ATP production. In animals, these mutations have particularly noticeable effects in tissues with high energy requirements, such as the nervous system, muscles, and kidneys.

12.5 Recap and Assess

The genomes of organelles, specifically plastids and mitochondria, carry few genes, and they are usually inherited from the mother.

1. A disease called Leber's hereditary optic neuropathy is caused by a mutation in a gene carried on mitochondrial DNA. What would be the phenotype of their children if a man with this disease reproduced with a woman who did not have the disease? What would be the result if the woman had the disease and the man did not?

Mendel and those who followed him focused on eukaryotes, with diploid organisms and haploid gametes. A half-century after the rediscovery of Mendel's work, a process that allows genetic recombination was discovered in prokaryotes as well. We now turn to that process.

KEY CONCEPT
12.6 Prokaryotes Can Transmit Genes by Mating

Learning Objectives

12.6.1 Outline the steps involved in the transfer of genetic material from one cell to another by bacterial conjugation.

12.6.2 Explain the consequences of conjugation for prokaryotes.

As described in Chapter 5, prokaryotic cells lack nuclei; they contain their genetic material mostly as single chromosomes in central regions of their cells. Prokaryotes reproduce asexually by binary fission, a process that gives rise to progeny that are virtually identical genetically. That is, the offspring of cell reproduction in prokaryotes constitute a clone (see Chapter 11). You might expect, therefore, that there is no way for individuals of these organisms to exchange genes, as in sexual reproduction. But mutations do occur in prokaryotes just as they do in eukaryotes, and the resulting new alleles increase genetic diversity. In addition, it turns out that prokaryotes (both archaea and bacteria) do have a sexual process for transferring genes between cells. The process has been best studied in bacteria.

Bacteria exchange genes by conjugation

To illustrate the kind of experiment that led to the discovery of bacterial DNA transfer, consider two strains of the bacterium *E. coli* with different alleles for each of six genes. One strain carries the dominant (wild-type) alleles for three of the genes and the recessive (mutant) alleles for the other genes. This situation is reversed in the other strain. Simply put, the two strains have the following genotypes (remember that bacteria are haploid and thus have only one copy of each gene):

$$ABCdef \quad \text{and} \quad abcDEF$$

where capital letters indicate wild-type alleles and lowercase letters indicate mutant alleles.

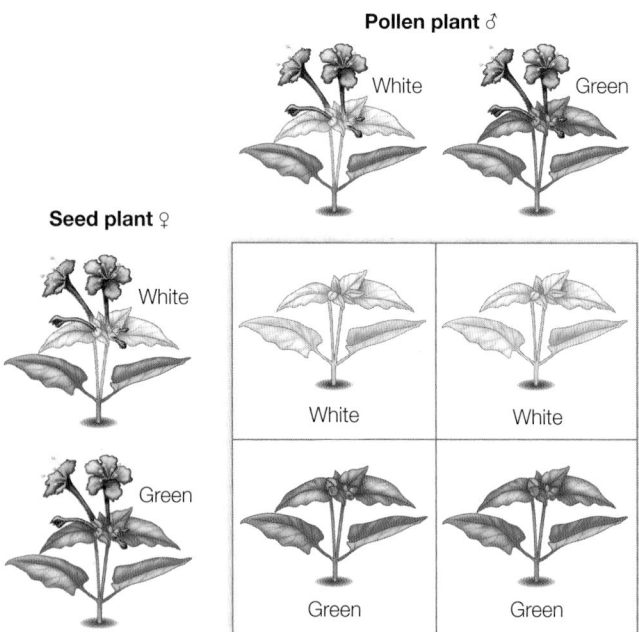

Figure 12.23 Cytoplasmic Inheritance In four o'clock plants, leaf color is inherited through the ovule only—the leaf color of the pollen parent does not matter. The white leaf color is caused by a chloroplast mutation.

When the two strains are grown together in the laboratory, most of the cells produce clones. That is, almost all of the cells that grow have the original genotypes. However, out of millions of bacteria, a few occur that have the genotype

ABCDEF

How could these completely wild-type bacteria arise? One possibility is mutation: in the *abcDEF* bacteria, the *a* allele could have mutated to *A*, the *b* allele to *B*, and the *c* allele to *C*. The problem with this explanation is that a mutation at any particular point in an organism's DNA sequence is a very rare event. The probability of all three events occurring in the same cell is extremely low—much lower than the actual rate of appearance of cells with the *ABCDEF* genotype. So the mutant cells must have acquired wild-type genes some other way—and this turns out to be the transfer of DNA between cells.

Electron microscopy shows that genetic transfers between bacteria can happen via physical contact between the cells (**Figure 12.24A**). Contact is initiated by a thin projection called a **sex pilus** (plural *pili*), which extends from one cell (the donor), attaches to another (the recipient), and draws the two cells together. Genetic material can then pass from the donor cell to the recipient through a thin cytoplasmic bridge called a conjugation tube. There is no reciprocal transfer of DNA from the recipient to the donor. This process is referred to as **bacterial conjugation**.

Once the donor DNA is inside the recipient cell, it can recombine with the recipient cell's genome. In much the same way that eukaryotic chromosomes pair up, gene for gene, in prophase I of meiosis, the donor DNA can line up beside its homologous sequences in the recipient, and crossing over can occur. Some of the genes from the donor can become integrated into the genome of the recipient, thus changing the recipient's genetic constitution (**Figure 12.24B**). When the recipient cells proliferate, the integrated donor genes are passed on to all progeny cells.

Bacterial conjugation is controlled by plasmids

In addition to their main chromosome, many bacteria harbor additional smaller, circular DNA molecules called **plasmids**, which replicate independently of the main chromosome. Plasmids typically contain at most a few dozen genes, which may fall into one of several categories:

- *Genes for unusual metabolic capabilities.* For example, bacteria carrying plasmids that confer the ability to break down hydrocarbons can be used to clean up oil spills.
- *Genes for antibiotic resistance.* Plasmids carrying genes for antibiotic resistance are called R factors, and since they can be transferred between bacteria via conjugation, they are a major threat to human health.
- *Genes that confer the ability to make a sex pilus.*

Connect the Concepts As discussed in Key Concept 18.2, biologists can use plasmids as vectors to carry new DNA into other cells. This recombinant DNA technique may be used to produce many copies of a gene of interest, either for analysis or to produce the gene's protein product in quantity.

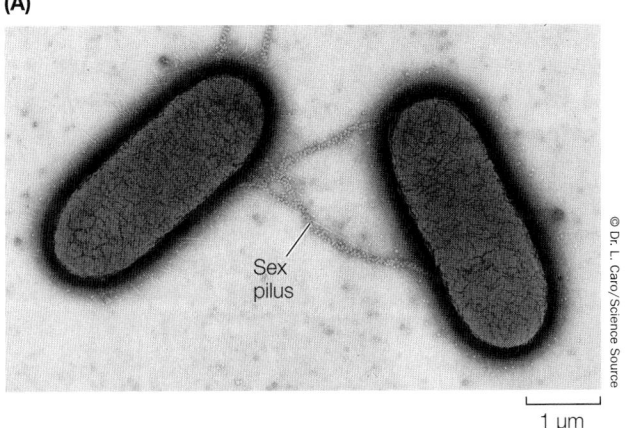

(A)

Sex pilus

1 μm

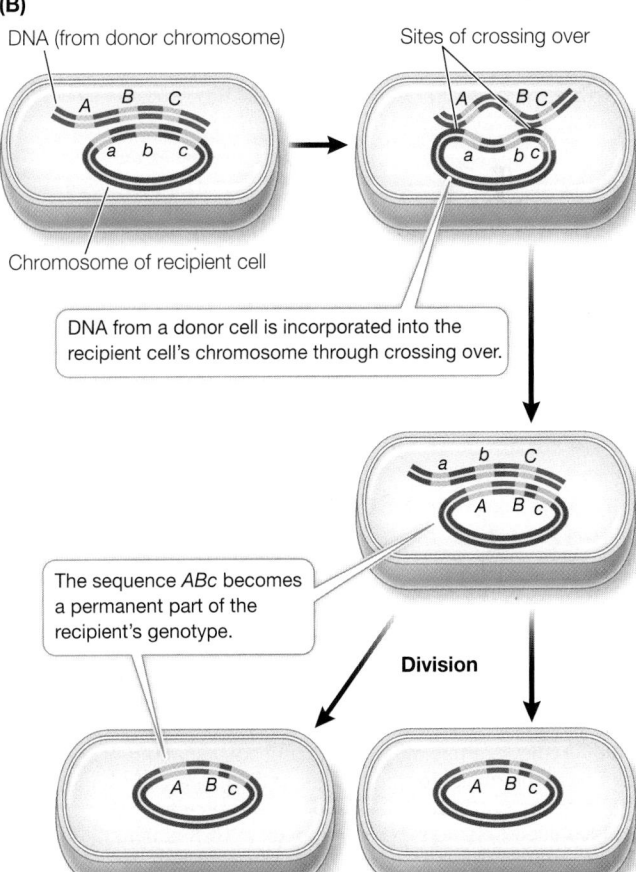

(B)

DNA (from donor chromosome)

Sites of crossing over

Chromosome of recipient cell

DNA from a donor cell is incorporated into the recipient cell's chromosome through crossing over.

The sequence *ABc* becomes a permanent part of the recipient's genotype.

Division

Figure 12.24 Bacterial Conjugation and Recombination   **(A)** Sex pili draw two bacteria into close contact, so that a cytoplasmic conjugation tube can form. DNA is transferred from one cell to the other via the conjugation tube. **(B)** DNA from a donor cell can become incorporated into a recipient cell's chromosome through two crossover events.

During bacterial conjugation it is usually plasmids that are transferred from one bacterium to another (**Figure 12.25**). A single strand of the donor plasmid is transferred to the recipient, and then synthesis of a complementary DNA strand results in two complete copies of the plasmid, one in the donor and one in the recipient.

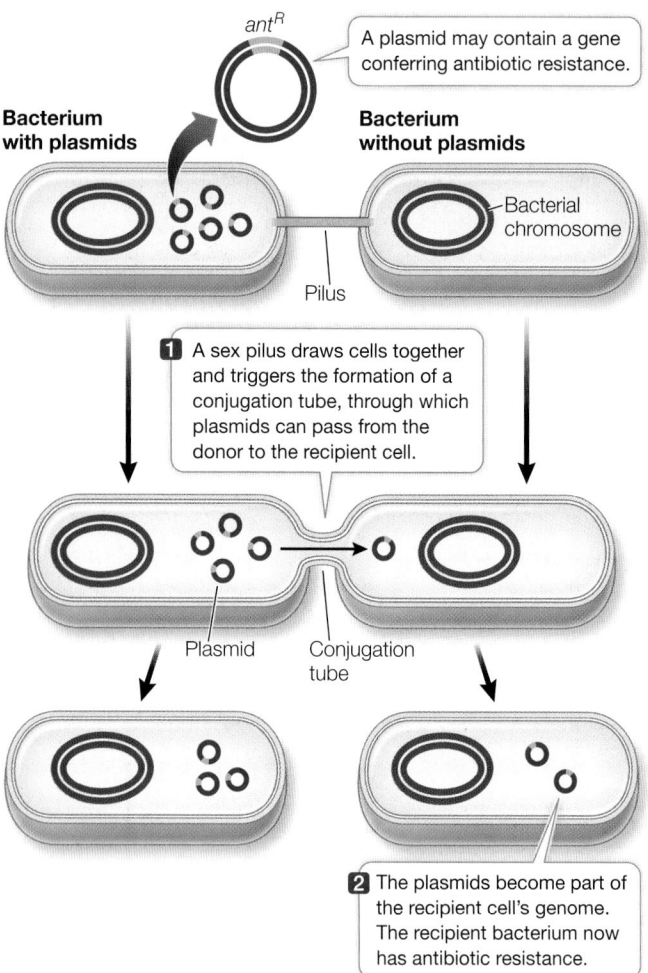

Figure 12.25 Gene Transfer by Plasmids When plasmids enter a cell via conjugation, their genes can be expressed in the recipient cell.

KEY CONCEPT
12.6 Recap and Assess

Although they are haploid and reproduce asexually, prokaryotes have the ability to transfer genes from one cell to another. These genes are usually carried on small, circular DNA molecules called plasmids, but chromosomal DNA is sometimes transferred as well.

1. Discuss the genetic significance of mating and recombination in bacteria.

2. What is the potential consequence of a plasmid being integrated into the main chromosome of a prokaryotic cell?

3. How does antibiotic resistance spread via plasmids?

 View in Achieve
Activity 12.2 **Concept Matching: Inheritance, Genes, and Chromosomes**

▶Investigating LIFE

Q and A **How do inherited characteristics such as red hair skip generations?**

Hair color is determined by the pigment melanin, which is synthesized from the amino acid tyrosine (see Table 3.2). There are two forms of this pigment, eumelanin (black or brown, depending on how much accumulates) and phaeomelanin (red or blond). Pigment production is an excellent example of intercellular signaling at work (see Chapter 7). Skin cells called melanocytes have a receptor, MC1R (*melanocortin 1 receptor*), for the signal melanocortin. Receptor binding sets off a signal transduction pathway that activates the cells to make much more eumelanin than phaeomelanin.

As is common with recessive traits, red hair results from a mutation in a gene, in this case a mutation in the *MC1R* gene, located on chromosome 16. As a recessive trait, it must be inherited from both parents to cause the hair to become red. The *MC1R* gene has multiple alleles: the wild type (*R*), which produces a normal receptor, and three recessive (*r*, mutated) alleles, each of which leads to red hair.

So what happens when a person inherits two of these recessive alleles? The wild-type MC1R protein is not expressed, so it does not bind the signal that would activate the eumelanin pathway, and phaeomelanin is made instead. If enough phaeomelanin accumulates, red hair results. The type of red hair that is inherited—fair, strawberry blonde, or auburn—depends on which recessive allele is inherited.

Future directions

As biologists learn more about individual genes and their alleles, they are beginning to make predictions about how gene products interact with one another and with factors in the environment. You probably know that smoking can cause lung cancer, yet there are some people who smoke a lot and don't get the disease. It turns out that these people often carry an allele that alleviates their encounter with the harmful substances in cigarette smoke. We all have genes whose products change environmental substances. In the case of cigarette smoke, the gene product of the typical allele turns the molecules in smoke into DNA-damaging, cancer-causing toxins. People who carry a mutant form of this gene are relatively resistant to getting lung cancer from smoking because the product of this mutant gene does not carry out the activation reactions. The genomes of all organisms carry such genes that are involved in environmental interaction. Describing these genes holds promise in understanding the relative contributions of environment and genetics to establishing a phenotype.

You should be able to relate each summary to the adjacent figures. If you go to this visual summary in **Achieve**, you can follow links to figures, animations, activities, and simulations that will help you consolidate the material.

KEY CONCEPT

12.1 Inheritance of Genes Follows Mendelian Laws

Go to Activity 12.1, Animation 12.1, and Simulation 12.1

- Mendel's **law of segregation** states that **alleles** at a gene segregate equally into gametes.

- Mendel's **law of independent assortment** states that alleles at different genes assort independently into gametes.

- Both of Mendel's laws can be explained by the behavior of chromosomes during meiosis.

- In **pedigrees, recessive** traits skip generations looking back to ancestors, whereas **dominant** traits do not.

Questions

1. A child is born with phenylketonuria, or PKU, a recessive disorder, but his parents are unaffected. What are their possible genotypes?

2. What are the expected gamete frequencies from a *TtPp* double heterozygote if the two genes are on different chromosomes?

3. A pea plant has the dominant phenotype for flower color (purple) and flower position (axial). What single cross would you perform to figure out its genotype at these two genes? Explain what the results of this cross could be.

Figure 12.6

Figure 12.9

KEY CONCEPT

12.2 Alleles Can Produce Multiple Phenotypes

- Genes often have multiple alleles.

- In **incomplete dominance**, neither of two alleles is dominant. The heterozygous phenotype is intermediate between the homozygous phenotypes.

- In **codominance**, the phenotypes of both homozygotes are expressed in the heterozygote.

- An allele that affects more than one trait is said to be **pleiotropic**.

Questions

1. A man with blood type AB marries a woman with blood type O. What are the possible blood types of their children?

Figure 12.10

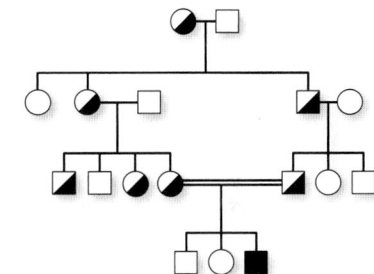

2. A homozygous red-flowered plant crossed with a homozygous white-flowered plant produces pink-flowered offspring. Assuming flower color is caused by a single gene, what color offspring would be produced by selfing the F₁ plants?

Figure 12.11

KEY CONCEPT

12.3 Genes Can Interact to Produce a Phenotype

- In **epistasis**, one gene affects the expression of another.
- Environmental conditions can affect the expression of a genotype, especially for **quantitative** characters.

Figure 12.13

Questions

1. A true-breeding chocolate lab is bred to a true-breeding yellow lab. What are the possible phenotypes of their puppies?

2. A homozygous recessive white-flowered strain of pea from Germany is crossed to a homozygous recessive white-flowered strain of pea from Australia, and all the offspring have purple flowers. How is this possible?

KEY CONCEPT

12.4 Genes Are Carried on Chromosomes

Go to Animation 12.2

- Genes on the same chromosome can recombine by crossing over.
- **Sex chromosomes** vary in copy number between the sexes and can cause differences in reciprocal crosses.

Figure 12.19

Questions

1. A test cross is made between a fly with straight-wings and an un-striped body, that is heterozygous for both genes underlying these characters (*CucuSrsr*), and a homozygous curled-wing, striped-body fly (*cucusrsr*), and the following offspring are obtained: 438 flies with straight wings and an unstriped body, 442 curled wings and striped body, 55 curled wings and unstriped body, and 65 straight wings and unstriped body. Are these genes on the same chromosome? If so, what is their map distance?

2. A cross between a true-breeding scalloped-winged male fly and a true-breeding normal-winged female fly produces all normal-winged offspring. However, the reciprocal cross produces normal-winged daughters and scalloped-winged sons. Explain these results.

KEY CONCEPT

12.5   Some Eukaryotic Genes Are Outside the Nucleus

■ Cytoplasmic organelles such as plastids and mitochondria are usually inherited from the biological mother.

Questions

1. A cross in the fungus *Neurospora* of a poky (slow growing) female with a normal male results in all the offspring being poky. A reciprocal cross results in all the offspring being normal. Explain the inheritance of the poky phenotype.

2. Is it possible for a single diploid cell that is not dividing to carry more than two alleles at a nuclear gene? What about at a mitochondrial gene?

Figure 12.23

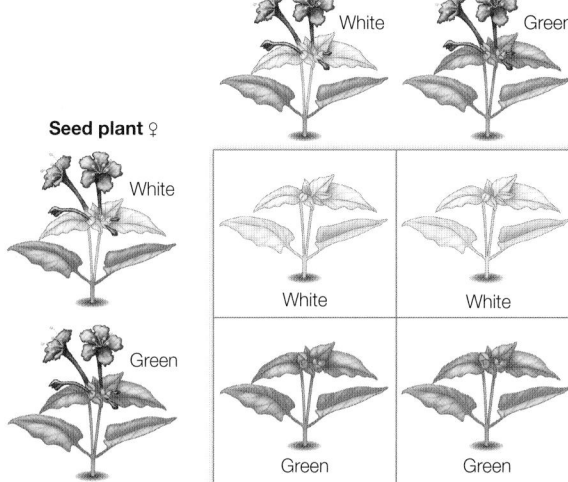

KEY CONCEPT

12.6   Prokaryotes Can Transmit Genes by Mating

Go to Activity 12.2

■ Prokaryotes can exchange chromosomal DNA, genes, and **plasmids** by **conjugation**.

Questions

1. Some bacterial cells are able to transmit genes to one another, while others are not. How might these two types of bacteria differ?

2. When an antibiotic resistance gene occurs on a plasmid, it is much more likely to be transmitted through a conjugation tube than when it is on the chromosome. Why is this the case?

Figure 12.25

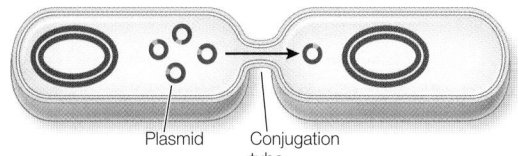

Go to **Achieve** for the eBook, **LearningCurve**, animations, activities, simulations, and additional resources and assignments.

13 DNA and Its Role in Heredity

KEY CONCEPTS

13.1 Experiments Revealed the Function of DNA as Genetic Material

13.2 DNA Has a Structure That Suits Its Function

13.3 DNA Is Replicated Semiconservatively

13.4 Errors in DNA Can Be Repaired

13.5 The Polymerase Chain Reaction Amplifies DNA

© Biology Pics/Science Source

A tiny virus, at center, burst, revealing its long thread of DNA.

▶ Investigating LIFE

Targeting DNA Replication in Cancer Therapy

Testicular cancer occurs with rapid cell divisions of germ cells and often spreads to other organs. It is the most common cancer in young men and is one of the few tumors of adults that is highly curable, due to a drug called cisplatin.

Dr. Barnett Rosenberg, a scientist at Michigan State University, was curious about how electric fields might affect cells. He put bacteria into a growth medium with platinum electrodes connected to a battery. The result was striking: the bacteria stopped dividing. To generalize the effect of electromagnetism on cells, Rosenberg tried the experiment again, this time using copper and zinc electrodes. This time the bacteria kept dividing. Only platinum electrodes inhibited cell division.

In light of the data, Rosenberg revised his hypothesis to propose that something leaked out of the platinum electrodes into the medium, and that this "something" blocked cell division. He confirmed his hypothesis by treating bacteria with the medium in which the platinum electrodes had been inserted; the bacteria did not divide. Realizing that cancer cells have uncontrolled cell division, he duplicated his experiments with tumor cells in a laboratory dish. His success at stopping tumor cell growth led to the isolation and development of cisplatin. The drug was so successful with testicular cancer that it has also been used with some success on other tumors. How does it work?

Cisplatin works by making the replication of DNA impossible. As you learned in Chapter 11, an essential event for cell division is the complete and precise duplication of the genetic material, DNA. The two strands of DNA unwind and separate, each strand acting as a template for the synthesis of a new strand. Strand separation is possible because the two strands are held together by weak forces, including hydrogen bonds. Cisplatin forms covalent bonds with nucleotides on opposite strands of the DNA, irreversibly cross-linking the two strands together. As a result, the DNA strands cannot separate for replication or expression. With such severe damage to its DNA, the cell then undergoes programmed cell death.

Dr. P. Marazzi/Science Source

Q and A What do we need to know about DNA replication to describe the mechanism of a drug that blocks it?

(Find the answer on page 294.)

Experiments Revealed the Function of DNA as Genetic Material

Learning Objectives

13.1.1 Describe how Griffith showed that a dead S strain could transform a living R strain of pneumococcal bacteria.

13.1.2 Explain how Avery's experiments using enzymes that break down different macromolecules indicated that DNA was the transforming agent in Griffith's experiment.

13.1.3 Explain why Hershey and Chase used radioactive sulfur and phosphorus and not nitrogen or carbon in their bacteriophage experiments to show that DNA, not protein, was the genetic material.

By the early twentieth century, geneticists had associated the presence of genes with chromosomes. Research began to focus on exactly which chemical component of chromosomes composed the genetic material.

Circumstantial evidence indicates that the genetic material is DNA

Scientists knew that chromosomes were made up of DNA and proteins. The development of a new dye that could bind specifically to DNA provided circumstantial evidence that DNA was the genetic material:

- *DNA was in the right place.* DNA was confirmed to be an important component of the nucleus and the chromosomes, which were known to carry genes.

- *DNA was present in the right amounts.* The amount of DNA in somatic cells (body cells not specialized for reproduction) was twice that in reproductive cells (eggs and sperm)—as might be expected for diploid and haploid cells, respectively.

- *DNA varied among species.* When cells from different species were stained with the dye and their color intensity measured, each species appeared to have its own specific amount of nuclear DNA.

You should already realize that circumstantial evidence is not a scientific demonstration of cause and effect. After all, proteins are also present in cell nuclei. Science relies on experiments to test hypotheses. The convincing demonstration that DNA is the genetic material came from two sets of experiments, one with bacteria and the other with viruses.

DNA from one type of bacterium genetically transforms another type

In the 1920s, English physician Frederick Griffith was studying the bacterium *Streptococcus pneumoniae*, or pneumococcus, one of the agents that cause pneumonia in humans (**Figure 13.1**). He was trying to develop a vaccine against this devastating illness (antibiotics had not yet been discovered). Griffith was working with two strains of pneumococcus:

1. Cells of the S strain produced colonies that looked smooth (S). Covered by a polysaccharide capsule, these cells were protected from attack by a host's immune system. When S cells were injected into mice, they reproduced and caused pneumonia, which killed the mice (the strain was virulent).

2. Cells of the R strain produced colonies that looked rough (R), lacked the protective capsule, and were not virulent, so the mice survived infection.

When Griffith injected mice with heat-killed S-type pneumococcus cells, the cells did not produce infection—dead bacteria don't kill mice. However, when he injected other mice with a mixture of living R-type cells and heat-killed S-type cells, to his astonishment, the mice died of pneumonia. When he examined blood from these mice, he found it full of living bacteria with characteristics of the virulent S strain! Griffith concluded that in the presence of the dead S-type pneumococcus cells, some of the living R-type cells had been transformed into virulent S cells, which then killed the mice. The fact that these S-type cells reproduced to make more S-type cells showed that the change from R-type to S-type was genetic.

Did this transformation of the bacteria need to occur in a mouse's body? No. The same transformation could be achieved in a test tube by mixing living R cells with heat-killed S cells, or even with a cell-free extract of the heat-killed S-type cells. (A cell-free extract contains all the contents of ruptured cells, but no intact cells.) These results demonstrated that some substance from the dead S pneumococcus cells could cause a heritable change in the living cells.

Oswald Avery and his colleagues at what is now The Rockefeller University identified the substance causing bacterial transformation in two ways:

1. *Eliminating other possibilities.* Cell-free extracts containing the transforming substance were treated with enzymes that destroyed candidates for the genetic material, such as proteins, RNA, and DNA. When the treated samples were tested, the ones treated with RNase and protease (which destroy RNA and proteins, respectively) were still able to transform R-type bacteria into the S-type. But the transforming activity was lost in the extract treated with DNase (which destroys DNA) (**Figure 13.2**).

2. *Positive experiment.* The researchers isolated virtually pure DNA from a cell-free extract containing the transforming substance. The DNA alone caused bacterial transformation.

We now know that the gene for the enzyme that catalyzes the synthesis of the polysaccharide capsule, which makes the bacterial colony look "smooth," was transferred into the R cells during transformation (recall Key Concept 12.6).

Viral infection experiments confirmed that DNA is the genetic material

Even with the bacterial transformation experiments, many biologists were still not convinced that DNA is the genetic material. One problem was that DNA, being made up of only four nucleotides (see Key Concept 4.1), seemed too uniform a substance to be able to confer instructions for all the functions and variety of life. The possibility remained that proteins, with all

Experiment

Figure 13.1 Genetic Transformation

Original Paper: F. Griffith. 1928. The significance of pneumococcal types. *Epidemiol Infect* 27: 113–159.

Griffith's experiments demonstrated that something in the virulent S strain of pneumococcus could transform nonvirulent R strain bacteria into a lethal form, even when the S strain bacteria had been killed by high temperatures.

HYPOTHESIS▶ Material in dead bacterial cells can genetically transform living bacterial cells.

METHOD▶

Kill the virulent S strain bacteria by heating.

Mix living, nonvirulent R strain bacteria with dead S strain cells.

1 Living S strain (virulent) — Injection

2 Living R strain (nonvirulent) — Injection

3 — Injection

4 — Injection

RESULTS▶

1 Mouse dies
Living S strain cells found in blood

2 Mouse healthy
No bacterial cells found in blood

3 Mouse healthy
No bacterial cells found in blood

4 Mouse dies
Living S strain cells found in blood

CONCLUSION▶ A chemical substance from one cell is capable of genetically transforming another cell.

their chemical and structural diversity (20 amino acids), fulfilled that role. Experiments with a virus were designed to distinguish between these alternatives.

Alfred Hershey and Martha Chase of the Cold Spring Harbor Laboratory in New York studied bacteriophage T2 (phage T2), which infects the bacterium *Escherichia coli*. Phage T2 consists of a DNA core packed inside a protein coat (**Figure 13.3**). When it attacks a bacterium, part (but not all) of the virus enters the bacterial cell. About 20 minutes later, the cell bursts, releasing dozens of virus particles that are copies of the infecting virus particle. Clearly the virus is somehow able to hijack the host cell's molecular machinery and convert it into a viral replication machine. Hershey and Chase set out to determine what part of the virus—DNA or protein—enters the host cell to bring about this genetic change. To trace the two components of the virus over its life cycle, the scientists labeled each component with a specific radioisotope:

• *Proteins were labeled with radioactive sulfur.* Proteins contain some sulfur (in the amino acids cysteine and methionine), but DNA does not. Sulfur has a radioactive isotope, ^{35}S. Hershey and Chase grew bacteriophage T2 in a bacterial culture in the presence of ^{35}S, so the proteins of the resulting viruses were labeled with (contained) the radioisotope.

• *DNA was labeled with radioactive phosphorus.* DNA contains a lot of phosphorus (in the deoxyribose–phosphate backbone; see Figure 4.5), whereas proteins contain little or none. Phosphorus also has a radioisotope, ^{32}P. The researchers grew another batch of T2 in a bacterial culture in the presence of ^{32}P, thus labeling the viral DNA with ^{32}P.

Hershey and Chase used these radioactively labeled viruses in their experiments (**Figure 13.4**). In one experiment, they allowed ^{32}P-labeled bacteriophage to infect bacteria; in the other, the bacteria were infected with ^{35}S-labeled bacteriophage. After a few minutes they agitated each mixture vigorously in a kitchen blender, stripping away the parts of the viruses that had not penetrated the bacteria, without bursting the bacteria. Then they separated the bacteria from the rest of the material (the remains of the viruses) from each experiment individually in a centrifuge. The result was that the bacterial cells in the centrifuge pellet contained most of the ^{32}P (and thus the viral DNA), and the supernatant fluid with the viral remains contained most of the ^{35}S (and thus the viral protein). These results indicated that it was the DNA that had been transferred into the bacteria, and that DNA was the molecule responsible for redirecting the genetic program of the bacterial cell.

 View in Achieve
Animation 13.1 The Hershey–Chase Experiment

Experiment

Figure 13.2 Genetic Transformation by DNA

Original Paper: O. T. Avery et al. 1944. Studies on the chemical nature of the substance inducing transformation of pneumococcal types. *J Exp Med* 79: 137–158.

Experiments by Avery and his colleagues showed that DNA from the virulent S strain of pneumococcus was responsible for the transformation in Griffith's experiments (see Figure 13.1).

HYPOTHESIS▶ The chemical nature of the transforming substance from pneumococcus is DNA.

METHOD▶

1 Heat kill virulent S strain bacteria, homogenize, and filter.

S strain (killed)

S strain (virulent) filtrate

2 Treat samples with enzymes that destroy RNA, proteins, or DNA.

RNase (destroys RNA) Protease (destroys proteins) DNase (destroys DNA)

3 Add the treated samples to cultures of R strain bacteria.

R strain (nonvirulent)

RESULTS▶

Virulent S strain and R strain bacteria

R strain bacteria only

4 Cultures treated with bacterial extracts treated with RNase or protease contain transformed S strain bacteria...

5 ...but the culture treated with DNase does not.

CONCLUSION▶ Because only DNase destroyed the transforming substance, the transforming substance must be DNA.

Bacteriophage T2

Protein coat

DNA

0.1 μm

1 Bacteriophage T2 attaches to the surface of a bacterium and injects its genetic material.

Bacterium

Phage genetic material

2 Viral genes take over the host's machinery, which synthesizes new viruses.

3 The bacterium bursts, releasing about 200 viruses.

Figure 13.3 Bacteriophage T2: Reproduction Cycle

Bacteriophage T2 is parasitic on *E. coli*, dependent on the bacterium to produce new viruses. The external structures of bacteriophage T2 consist entirely of protein, and the DNA is contained within the protein coat. When the virus infects an *E. coli* cell, its genetic material is injected into the host bacterium.

Eukaryotic cells can also be genetically transformed by DNA

The transformation of eukaryotic cells by DNA is often called **transfection**. Transfection can be demonstrated using a **genetic marker,** a gene whose presence in the recipient cells confers an observable phenotype. When transforming both prokaryotes and eukaryotes, researchers often use a genetically determined marker that can be easily selected—for example, antibiotic resistance or a nutritional requirement—and that permits the growth of transformed cells but not of nontransformed cells on a selective medium (for example, one that contains an antibiotic or that lacks a nutrient). A common marker in mammalian transfection experiments is a gene that confers resistance to the antibiotic neomycin, which kills nontransformed mammalian cells. Transfection is achieved by various methods, including chemical treatments that allow the DNA to be taken up by the cells. Any cell can be transfected, even an egg cell. In the latter case, a **transgenic organism** can result, which has every cell

Experiment

Figure 13.4 The Hershey–Chase Experiment

Original Paper: A. D. Hershey and M. Chase. 1952. Independent functions of viral protein and nucleic acid in growth of bacteriophage. *J Gen Physiol* 36: 39–56.

When Hershey and Chase infected bacterial cells with radioactively labeled bacteriophage T2, only labeled DNA was found in the bacteria. The infected cells were agitated to remove the viral coats from the bacteria and were then centrifuged to pellet the bacteria. The labeled protein remained in the supernatant. This showed that DNA, not protein, is the genetic material.

HYPOTHESIS▶ Either component of a bacteriophage—DNA or protein—might be the hereditary material that enters a bacterial cell to direct the assembly of new viruses.

METHOD▶

Experiment 1

1a Label phage. P is an element in DNA, but not in proteins.

DNA with ^{32}P   Bacteria

Experiment 2

1b Label phage. S is an element in proteins, but not in DNA.

Protein coat with ^{35}S   Bacteria

2 Infect bacteria with labeled viral coats.

3 Agitate in a blender to detach viruses from bacterial cells.

4 Centrifuge to force the bacterial cells to the bottom of the tube, forming a pellet. Supernatant fluid contains the viral coats.

RESULTS▶

5a Most of the ^{32}P is in the pellet with the bacteria.

Pellet

5b Most of the ^{35}S is in the supernatant fluid with the viral coats.

Supernatant fluid

CONCLUSION▶ DNA, not protein, enters bacterial cells and directs the assembly of new viruses.

Go to Achieve for a companion Data in Depth exercise.

---

genetically transformed. More detail on transforming eukaryotic cells is described in Chapter 18.

KEY CONCEPT
13.1 Recap and Assess

Experiments on bacteria and on viruses demonstrated that DNA is the genetic material. DNA from one genetic strain of bacteria was able to genetically transform another strain into the donor strain. Viral DNA was shown to be injected into a host cell and to genetically change that cell into a virus factory.

1. At the time of Griffith's experiments in the 1920s, what circumstantial evidence suggested to scientists that DNA might be the genetic material?

2. How did the experiments of Avery and his colleagues rule out protein as the genetic material?

3. What attributes of bacteriophage T2 were key to the Hershey–Chase experiments demonstrating that DNA, rather than protein, is the genetic material?

The transformation and viral infection experiments convinced biologists that the genetic material is DNA. It had been known for several decades that chemically, DNA is a polymer of nucleotides. Next, scientists turned to DNA's precise three-dimensional structure.

KEY CONCEPT
13.2 DNA Has a Structure That Suits Its Function

Learning Objectives

13.2.1 List the information that Watson and Crick used to develop their model of DNA structure.

13.2.2 Describe the structure of DNA and how it is consistent with Chargaff's rules.

13.2.3 Write down the sequence of the complementary strand of DNA if given the sequence of the other strand, indicating polarity.

13.2.4 Relate structural aspects of the DNA molecule to its biological functions.

Once it was known that DNA was the genetic material, scientists turned their attention to determining its structure. In doing so, they hoped to answer two questions: (1) how is DNA replicated between cell divisions, and (2) how does DNA direct the synthesis of specific proteins? DNA's structure was deciphered only after many types of experimental evidence were considered together in a theoretical framework.

Watson and Crick used chemical and physical evidence to deduce the structure of DNA

Data on the chemical makeup of DNA, coupled with X-ray diffraction data on the physical structure of the molecule, were used to solve DNA's structure.

CHEMICAL EVIDENCE FROM BASE COMPOSITION   Biochemists knew that DNA was a polymer of nucleotides. Each nucleotide consists of a molecule of the sugar deoxyribose, a phosphate group, and a nitrogen-containing base (see Figure 4.1). The only differences among the four nucleotides of DNA are their nitrogenous bases: the purines **adenine** (**A**) and **guanine** (**G**), and the pyrimidines **cytosine** (**C**) and **thymine** (**T**).

In the early 1950s, biochemist Erwin Chargaff and his colleagues at Columbia University reported that DNA from many different species exhibits certain regularities. This led to the following rule: in any DNA sample, the amount of adenine equals the amount of thymine (A = T), and the amount of guanine equals the amount of cytosine (G = C). This finding means that the total abundance of purines equals the total abundance of pyrimidines: A + G = T + C. While Chargaff and colleagues found that this rule held for every organism they examined, they noted that the relative abundances of A + T versus G + C vary among organisms. In human DNA, A and T each account for 27% of the nitrogenous bases present, while G and C each account for 23%. Put another way, in human DNA there is a ratio of 54% A + T to 46% C + G.

PHYSICAL EVIDENCE FROM X-RAY DIFFRACTION   Some chemical substances, when they are isolated and purified, can be made to form crystals. The positions of atoms in a crystallized substance can be inferred from the diffraction pattern of X-rays passing through the substance. In the early 1950s the New Zealand–born biophysicist Maurice Wilkins discovered a way to make highly ordered fibers of DNA that were suitable for X-ray diffraction studies. Images of his samples were made by Rosalind Franklin of Kings College, London (**Figure 13.5**) and were instrumental in deciphering the structure of DNA. Franklin's images suggested that DNA was a double (two-stranded) helix with ten nucleotides in each full turn, that each full turn was 3.4 nanometers (nm) in length, that the molecule had a constant diameter of 2 nm, and that phosphates were most likely on the outside of the helix.

WATSON AND CRICK'S MODEL   If you have taken chemistry courses, you may be familiar with model building, whereby balls (atoms) and sticks (bonds) are used to put together molecules based on known physical and chemical properties and bond angles. A physicist, Francis Crick, and a geneticist, James D. Watson

(**Figure 13.6A**), who were then at the Cavendish Laboratory at the University of Cambridge, used model building to solve the structure of DNA. They used the physical and chemical evidence we just described:

- To be consistent with Franklin's X-ray diffraction images, Watson and Crick's model had the nucleotide bases on the interior of the two strands, with a sugar–phosphate "backbone" on the outside. The backbone consisted of nucleotides attached via the deoxyribose sugar of one nucleotide and the phosphate of the next nucleotide. In addition, the two DNA strands ran in opposite directions, that is, they were **antiparallel**, meaning that the ribose of one strand was across from a phosphate of the other strand at each end of the molecule. The two strands would not fit together unless they were in an antiparallel configuration.

- To satisfy Chargaff's rule (A = T and G = C), Watson and Crick's model always paired a double-ring purine (A or G) on one strand with a single-ring pyrimidine (T or C) on the opposite strand. These **complementary base pairs** (A-T and G-C) have the same width down the double helix, a uniformity that was also confirmed by X-ray diffraction.

Crick and Watson built their model of DNA in late February 1953. This structure explained the known chemical properties of DNA, and it opened the door to understanding its biological functions.

Five key features define DNA structure

Five features summarize the molecular architecture of the DNA molecule (**Figure 13.6B**):

1. DNA is a *double-stranded helix*, with a sugar–phosphate backbone on the outside and base pairs lined up on the inside.

2. DNA is usually a *right-handed helix*. If you curl the fingers of your right hand and point your thumb upward, the curve of the helix follows the direction of your fingers, and it winds upward in the direction of your thumb. (See Figure 3.9, showing right- versus left-handed helices.)

3. DNA is *antiparallel* (the two strands run in opposite directions).

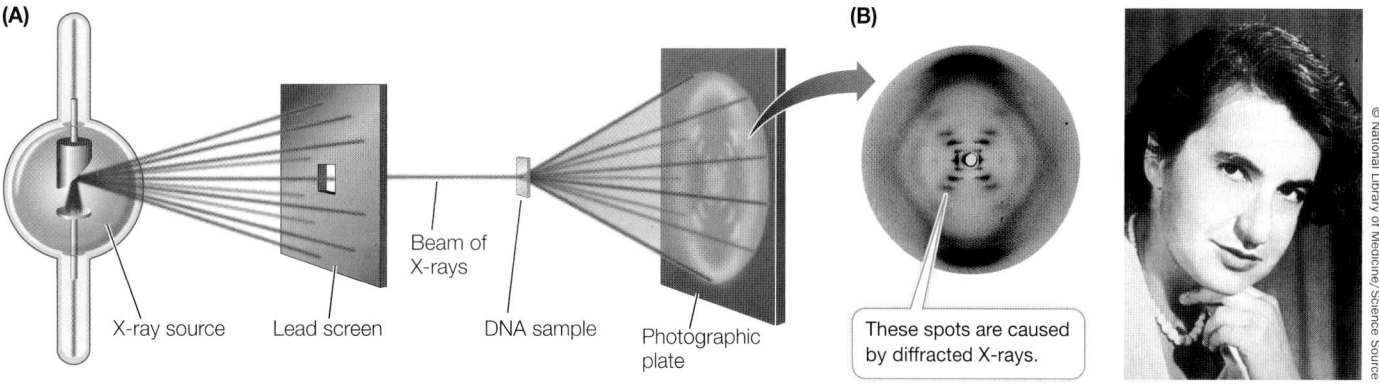

(A) X-ray source   Lead screen   Beam of X-rays   DNA sample   Photographic plate

These spots are caused by diffracted X-rays.

© National Library of Medicine/Science Source

Figure 13.5 **X-Ray Diffraction Helped Reveal the Structure of DNA** (A) The positions of atoms in a crystallized chemical substance can be inferred by the pattern of diffraction of X-rays passed through it.

The pattern of DNA is both highly regular and repetitive. (B) Rosalind Franklin's diffraction and her "photograph 51" (shown) helped scientists visualize the helical structure of the DNA molecule.

(A)

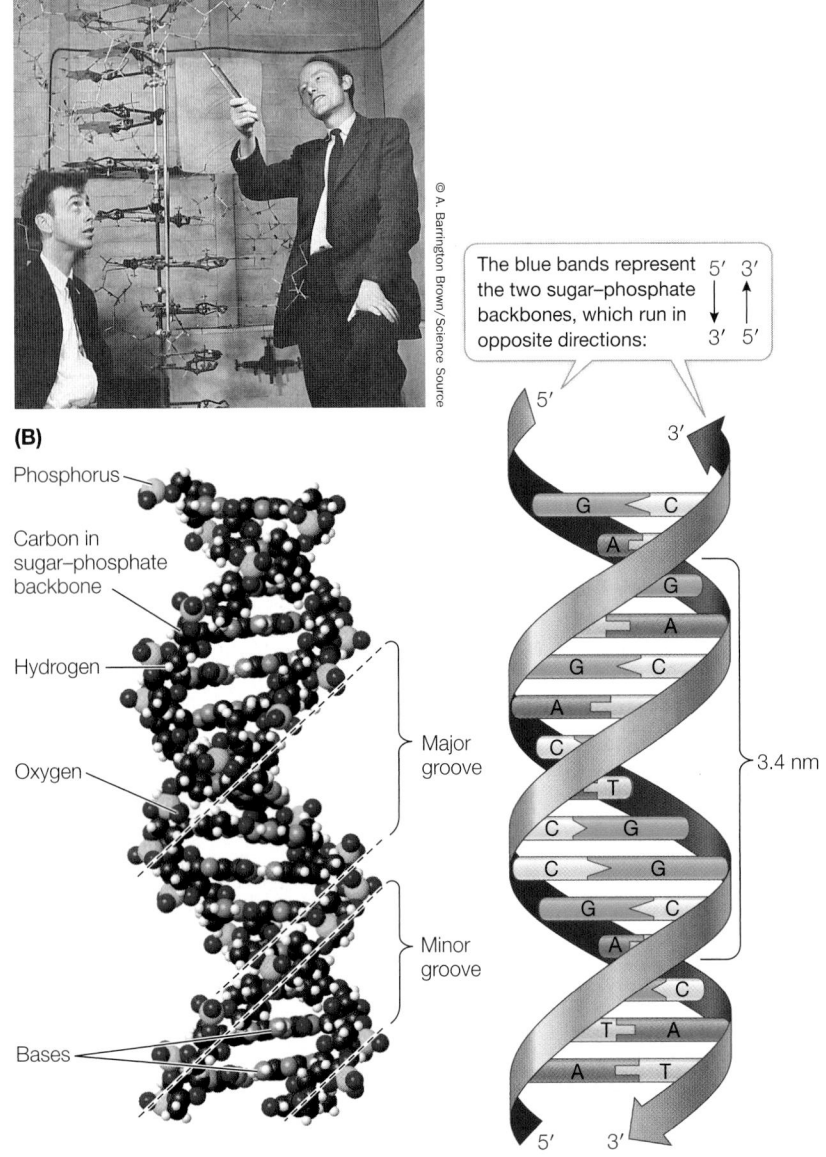

© A. Barrington Brown/Science Source

The blue bands represent the two sugar–phosphate backbones, which run in opposite directions:

(B)

Phosphorus

Carbon in sugar–phosphate backbone

Hydrogen

Oxygen

Bases

Major groove

Minor groove

3.4 nm

Figure 13.6 DNA Is a Double Helix **(A)** James Watson (left) and Francis Crick (right) proposed that the DNA molecule has a double-helical structure. **(B)** Biochemists can now pinpoint the position of every atom in a DNA molecule. To see that the essential features of the original Watson–Crick model have been verified, follow with your eyes the double-helical chains of sugar–phosphate groups and note the horizontal rungs of the bases. (B data from S. Arnott and D. W. Hukins. 1972. *Biochem Biophys Res Commun* 47: 1504–1509.)

Q: In DNA, where do the following chemical forces occur: hydrogen bonds, covalent bonds, and van der Waals forces?

 Media Clip 13.1 Discovery of the Double Helix
Life12e.com/mc13.1

4. DNA strands are held together by *complementary base pairing*, which involves hydrogen bonding between the bases on opposite strands. Base pairs are either an A purine with a T pyrimidine or a G purine with a C pyrimidine.

5. DNA has *major and minor grooves* in which the outer edges of the nitrogenous bases are exposed.

THE HELIX The sugar–phosphate backbones of the polynucleotide chains form a coil around the outside of the helix, and the nitrogenous bases point toward the center. In addition to the covalent bonds occurring between the atoms present in each of the strands, hydrogen bonds and van der Waals forces play important roles in the structure of DNA:

- *Hydrogen bonds* between complementary base pairs hold the two strands of the DNA helix together. Adenine (A) pairs with thymine (T) by forming two hydrogen bonds, and guanine (G) pairs with cytosine (C) by forming three hydrogen bonds (see Figure 13.7B).

- *van der Waals forces* occur between adjacent bases on the same strand. When the base rings come near one another, they tend to stack like poker chips because of these weak attractions.

ANTIPARALLEL STRANDS The backbone of each DNA strand contains repeating units of the five-carbon monosaccharide deoxyribose attached to a phosphate group (**Figure 13.7A**). The number followed by a prime (′) designates the position of a carbon atom in this sugar molecule. In a nucleotide, the phosphate ($-OPO_3^-$) is attached to the 5′ carbon of the deoxyribose. In the sugar–phosphate backbone of DNA, each 5′ phosphate group is connected to the 3′ carbon of the next deoxyribose, linking successive sugars together.

Thus the two ends of a polynucleotide chain differ. At one end of a chain is a free (not connected to another nucleotide) 5′ phosphate group; this is called the **5′ end**. At the other end is a free 3′ hydroxyl group (—OH); this is called the **3′ end**. In a DNA double helix, the 5′ end of one strand is paired with the 3′ end of the other strand, and vice versa. In other words, if you drew an arrow for each strand running from 5′ to 3′, the arrows would point in opposite directions (**Figure 13.7B**; see also Figure 4.5A).

BASE EXPOSURE IN THE GROOVES Look back at Figure 13.6B and note the major and minor grooves in the helix. These grooves exist because the backbones of the two strands are closer together on one side of the double helix (forming the minor groove) than on the other side (forming the major groove). **Figure 13.8** shows a "top-down" view of the four possible configurations of the flat, hydrogen-bonded base pairs in the major and minor grooves. The exposed outer edges of the base pairs are accessible for additional hydrogen bonding. Note that the arrangements of unpaired atoms and groups differ in A-T and G-C pairs. Thus the *surfaces of the A-T and C-G base pairs are chemically distinct*, allowing other molecules such as proteins to recognize specific base pair sequences and bind to them, which is crucial for DNA function. *The binding of proteins to specific base pair sequences*

Figure 13.7 **Each DNA Strand Consists of a Sugar–Phosphate Backbone** **(A)** The deoxyribose sugar has five carbons, numbered 1′ to 5′. The 5′ carbon is attached to a phosphate in a nucleotide. In a DNA molecule, each nucleotide in a strand has its 3′ carbon attached to the 5′ phosphate of the next nucleotide. **(B)** Each sugar–phosphate backbone has a free 5′ phosphate at one end and a free 3′ hydroxyl group at the other end, giving the backbone directionality. The two backbones run in opposite directions such that the 5′ end of one strand is opposite the 3′ end of the other strand, and vice versa.

(A) The phosphate group attaches to the 5′ carbon.

The next nucleotide's phosphate group attaches to the 3′ carbon.

The base attaches to the 1′ carbon.

(B)

Phosphate

Sugar

Base

is the key to protein–DNA interactions, which are necessary for the replication and expression of the genetic information in DNA.

The double-helical structure of DNA is essential to its function

The genetic material performs four important functions, and the DNA structure proposed by Watson and Crick was elegantly suited to three of them.

1. *The genetic material stores an organism's genetic information.* With its millions of nucleotides, the base sequence of a DNA molecule can encode and store an enormous amount of information. Variations in DNA sequences can account for species and individual differences. DNA fits this role nicely.

2. *The genetic material is susceptible to mutations* (permanent changes) *in the information it encodes.* For DNA, mutations might be simple changes in the linear sequence of base pairs.

The shaded atoms are available for hydrogen bonding to other molecules.

The sugar–phosphate backbone is on the outside of the double helix.

Figure 13.8 **Base Pairs in DNA Can Interact with Other Molecules** These diagrams show the four possible configurations of base pairs within the double helix. Atoms shaded in green are available for hydrogen bonding with other molecules, such as proteins.

3. *The genetic material is precisely replicated in the cell division cycle.* Replication could be accomplished using complementary base pairing, A with T and G with C. In the original publication of their findings in 1953, Watson and Crick coyly pointed out, "It has not escaped our notice that the specific pairing we have postulated immediately suggests a possible copying mechanism for the genetic material."

4. *The genetic material (the coded information in DNA) is expressed as the phenotype.* This function is not obvious in the structure of DNA. However, as we will see Chapter 14, the nucleotide sequence of DNA is copied into RNA, which uses the coded information to specify a linear sequence of amino acids—a protein. The folded forms of proteins determine many of the phenotypes of an organism.

KEY CONCEPT
13.2 Recap and Assess

DNA is a right-handed, double helix made up of two antiparallel polynucleotide chains. The two chains are held together by hydrogen bonds between the nucleotide bases, which exhibit complementary pairing: A with T, and G with C. Chemical groups on the bases that are exposed in the grooves of the helix are available for hydrogen bonding with other molecules, such as proteins.

1. Describe the evidence that Watson and Crick used to come up with the double helix model for DNA.

2. Speculate as to how the double-stranded structure of DNA relates to its functions.

3. A key to the function of DNA in directing information in the cell is the binding of other molecules such as proteins to the double helix at specific base sequences. Recalling the forces involved in protein interactions (see Figure 3.13) and the chemical groupings exposed in base pairs (see Figure 13.8), how do specific interactions between proteins and DNA occur?

Once the structure of DNA was understood, it was possible to investigate how DNA replicates itself. Next we examine the experiments that taught us how this elegant process works.

KEY CONCEPT
13.3 DNA Is Replicated Semiconservatively

Learning Objectives

13.3.1 Draw the results obtained in the Meselson–Stahl experiment that supported semiconservative replication, and explain what would have been found for conservative and dispersive replication.

13.3.2 Identify the function of each of the proteins involved in DNA replication.

13.3.3 Explain the end-replication problem and how it is solved by telomerase.

The mechanism of DNA replication that Watson and Crick proposed was soon confirmed. First, researchers showed that DNA could be replicated in a test tube containing simple substrates and an enzyme. A subsequent study showed that each of the two strands of the double helix can serve as a template for a new strand of DNA.

Test tube synthesis of DNA needed the following substances:

- The deoxyribonucleoside triphosphates dATP, dCTP, dGTP, and dTTP. These are the monomers from which the DNA polymers are synthesized.

- DNA molecules of a particular sequence that serve as **templates** to direct the sequence of nucleotides in the new molecules.

- A **DNA polymerase** enzyme to catalyze the polymerization reaction.

- Salts and a pH buffer, to create an appropriate chemical environment for the DNA polymerase.

The fact that DNA could be synthesized in a test tube confirmed that a DNA molecule contains the information needed for its own replication. The next challenge was to determine which of three possible replication patterns occurs during DNA replication:

1. *Semiconservative replication*, in which each parent strand serves as a template for a new strand, and the two new DNA molecules each have one original and one new strand (**Figure 13.9A**)

2. *Conservative replication*, in which the original double helix serves as a template for, but does not contribute to, a new double helix (**Figure 13.9B**)

3. *Dispersive replication*, in which fragments of the original DNA molecule serve as templates for assembling two new molecules, each containing original and new parts, perhaps at random (**Figure 13.9C**)

Watson and Crick's original paper suggested that DNA replication was semiconservative, but the test tube demonstration just described did not provide a basis for choosing among these three models.

 View in Achieve
Animation 13.2 DNA Replication and Polymerization

An elegant experiment demonstrated that DNA replication is semiconservative

In 1958 Matthew Meselson and Franklin Stahl at the California Institute of Technology convinced the scientific community that DNA is reproduced by **semiconservative replication**. They used density labeling to distinguish between parent strands of DNA and newly copied strands. Historians of science have called this one of the "most beautiful experiments" in biology. For that reason alone, as well as its results, it's worth taking a close look at it.

The key to the experiment was the use of a "heavy" isotope of nitrogen. Heavy nitrogen (^{15}N) is a rare, nonradioactive isotope that makes molecules containing it denser than chemically identical molecules containing the common isotope ^{14}N. Two cultures of the bacterium *E. coli* were grown for many generations, one in a medium containing ^{15}N and the other in a medium containing ^{14}N. When DNA extracts from the two cultures were combined and centrifuged in a solution of cesium chloride, which forms a density gradient under centrifugation,

Original DNA **Daughter molecules following replication**

(A)

Semiconservative replication would produce daughter molecules with both an original and a newly synthesized DNA strand.

(B)

Conservative replication would produce daughter molecules with either two original or two newly synthesized DNA strands.

(C)

Dispersive replication would produce daughter molecules with a mix of both original and newly synthesized DNA in each strand.

Figure 13.9 Three Models for DNA Replication In each model, the original DNA is shown in blue and the newly synthesized DNA in red.

two separate bands of DNA formed in the centrifugation tube. The DNA from the ^{15}N culture was heavier than the DNA from the ^{14}N culture, so it formed a band at a different position in the density gradient. Figure A in the Work with the Data portion of **Investigating Life: The Meselson–Stahl Experiment** shows a photo of the two bands.

Next, Meselson and Stahl grew another *E. coli* culture in ^{15}N medium, then transferred the bacteria to normal ^{14}N medium and allowed them to continue growing. The cells replicated their DNA and divided every 20 minutes. Meselson and Stahl collected some of the bacteria at time intervals and extracted DNA from the samples. You can follow their results for the first two generations in Investigating Life: The Meselson–Stahl Experiment. The results can be explained only by the semiconservative model of DNA replication. The crucial observations demonstrating this model were that all the DNA at the end of the first generation was of intermediate density, while at the end of the second generation there were two discrete bands: one of intermediate and one of light DNA. If the conservative model had been true, there would have been no intermediate density DNA. If the dispersive model were correct, then all of the replicated DNA would have been intermediate for the first few generations, with the single intermediate band becoming progressively lighter.

▶ **View in Achieve**
Animation 13.3 The Meselson–Stahl Experiment

There are three steps in DNA replication

Semiconservative DNA replication in the cell involves several different enzymes and other proteins. It takes place in three general steps:

1. Initiation: The DNA double helix is unwound to separate the two template strands and make them available for new base pairing. Each of the strands is then primed with RNA primers, as described in the next section, in preparation for template-dependent DNA synthesis.

2. Elongation: DNA synthesis occurs from the RNA primers with the addition of nucleotides that form complementary base pairs with template DNA. Incoming nucleotides are covalently linked together by phosphodiester bonds, forming a polymer whose base sequence is complementary to the bases in the template strand.

3. Termination: DNA synthesis ends when all of the DNA regions have been replicated.

The nucleotides that make up DNA are deoxyribonucleoside monophosphates (dNMPs) because they each contain deoxyribose and one phosphate group (see Figure 4.1). The four monomers that are used during DNA elongation are the deoxyribonucleoside triphosphates dATP, dTTP, dCTP, and dGTP, collectively referred to as dNTPs. They are triphosphates because each has three phosphate groups. The three phosphate groups are attached to the 5′ carbon on the deoxyribose sugar (as shown in the incoming nucleoside triphosphate in **Figure 13.10**).

Note that during DNA replication *nucleotides are added to the growing new strand at the 3′ end*—the end at which the DNA strand has a free hydroxyl (—OH) group on the 3′ carbon of its terminal deoxyribose. In the formation of the phosphodiester bond (a transesterification reaction), two of the phosphate groups on an incoming dNTP are removed (as pyrophosphate [PP$_i$]), and the remaining phosphate is bonded to the 3′ carbon on the terminal deoxyribose (see Figure 4.2). Just as energy is released when ATP is hydrolyzed to AMP (with subsequent hydrolysis of PP$_i$ to two phosphates), energy is released when dNTP releases PP$_i$ to form dNMP, and this energy is used to drive the transesterification reaction.

DNA polymerases add nucleotides to the growing chain

DNA replication begins with the binding of a large protein complex (the pre-replication complex) to a specific site on the DNA molecule. This complex contains several different proteins, including the enzyme DNA polymerase, which catalyzes the addition of nucleotides as the new DNA chain grows. All chromosomes have at least one region called the **origin of replication (ori)**, to which the pre-replication complex binds. Binding occurs when proteins in the complex recognize specific DNA sequences within the *ori*.

ORIGINS OF REPLICATION The single circular chromosome of the bacterium *E. coli* has 4×10^6 base pairs (bp) of DNA. The 245-bp *ori* sequence is at a particular location on the chromosome. Once the pre-replication complex binds to it, initiation begins with the local unwinding of the DNA and then replication proceeds in

▶Investigating LIFE   The Meselson–Stahl Experiment

Experiment

Original Paper: M. Meselson and F. Stahl. 1958. The replication of DNA in *Escherichia coli*. *Proc Natl Acad Sci USA* 44: 671–682.

A centrifuge was used to separate DNA molecules labeled with isotopes of different densities. This experiment revealed a pattern that supports the semiconservative model of DNA replication.

HYPOTHESIS▶ DNA replicates semiconservatively.

METHOD▶

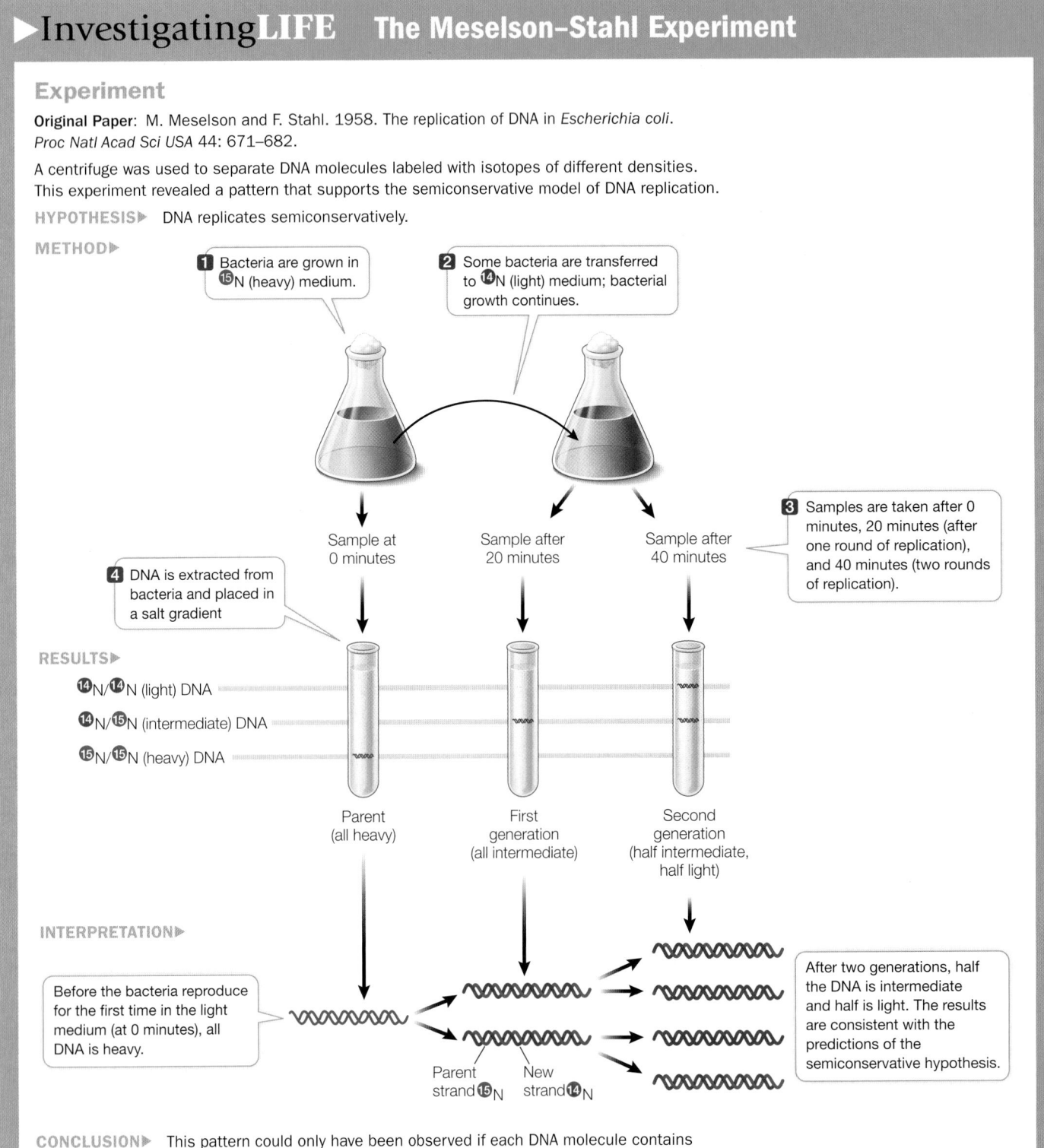

1 Bacteria are grown in ^{15}N (heavy) medium.

2 Some bacteria are transferred to ^{14}N (light) medium; bacterial growth continues.

3 Samples are taken after 0 minutes, 20 minutes (after one round of replication), and 40 minutes (two rounds of replication).

Sample at 0 minutes

Sample after 20 minutes

Sample after 40 minutes

4 DNA is extracted from bacteria and placed in a salt gradient

RESULTS▶

$^{14}N/^{14}N$ (light) DNA

$^{14}N/^{15}N$ (intermediate) DNA

$^{15}N/^{15}N$ (heavy) DNA

Parent (all heavy)

First generation (all intermediate)

Second generation (half intermediate, half light)

INTERPRETATION▶

Before the bacteria reproduce for the first time in the light medium (at 0 minutes), all DNA is heavy.

Parent strand ^{15}N New strand ^{14}N

After two generations, half the DNA is intermediate and half is light. The results are consistent with the predictions of the semiconservative hypothesis.

CONCLUSION▶ This pattern could only have been observed if each DNA molecule contains a template strand from the parental DNA; thus DNA replication is semiconservative.

Work with the Data

The Meselson–Stahl experiment has been called one of the "most beautiful experiments" in biology because of its essential simplicity. Meselson and Stahl used density gradients to examine how DNA molecules replicate, as illustrated in the experimental results shown in **Figure A**. The peaks on the drawing are proportional to the amount of DNA.

Figure B shows results of the experiment after each of four generations. Each sample contained the same number of bacteria, so the total amount of DNA in each panel was the same. (Both photos from M. Meselson and F. Stahl. 1958. *Proc Natl Acad Sci USA* 44: 671–682.)

QUESTIONS▶

1. Use the heights of the peaks to estimate the percent of total DNA that was heavy, intermediate, and light at each generation. Create a table summarizing these calculations and discuss whether they support the authors' conclusions.

2. What would the data look like if the bacteria had been allowed to divide for three more generations?

3. If Meselson and Stahl had done their experiment starting with light DNA and then added ^{15}N for succeeding generations, what would the bands look like?

4. What would the data look like if conservative replication were the correct model? What would the data look like if dispersive replication were correct?

Figure A

^{14}N ^{15}N **Position in tube**

Top   Bottom
of tube   of tube

Figure B

Go to **Achieve** for a companion
Data in Depth exercise.

Figure 13.10 Each New DNA Strand Grows from Its 5′ End to Its 3′ End   The DNA strand at the right (blue) is the template for the synthesis of the complementary strand that is growing at the left (orange). Here dCTP (circled) is about to react with the growing strand to add dCMP to the new strand, releasing pyrophosphate.

both directions around the circle, forming two **replication forks** (**Figure 13.11A**). The replication rate in *E. coli* is approximately 1,000 bp per second, so it takes about 40 minutes to fully replicate the chromosome (with two replication forks). Rapidly dividing *E. coli* cells divide every 20 minutes. In these cells, new rounds of replication begin at the *ori* of each new chromosome before the

first chromosome has fully replicated. In this way the cells can divide more frequently than the time needed to finish replicating the original chromosome!

Eukaryotic chromosomes are typically much longer than those of prokaryotes—up to 1 billion bp—and are linear, not circular. If replication occurred from a single *ori* with two forks

(A) A single *ori* in a prokaryotic chromosome

1 The *ori* sequence binds the pre-replication complex.

2 A replication bubble consists of two replication forks that move away from one another during elongation.

ori

ori

Pre-replication complex

Replication bubble

ori

Replication forks

ori

(B) Multiple *ori* in a eukaryotic chromosome

ori   *ori*   *ori*

There are multiple origins of replication.

Initiation of replication

Replication forks move away from each other during elongation.

Figure 13.11 The Origin of DNA Replication **(A)** Prokaryotic chromosomes usually have a single origin where DNA replication starts and proceeds in both directions. **(B)** The usually much larger eukaryotic chromosome typically has multiple replication origins.

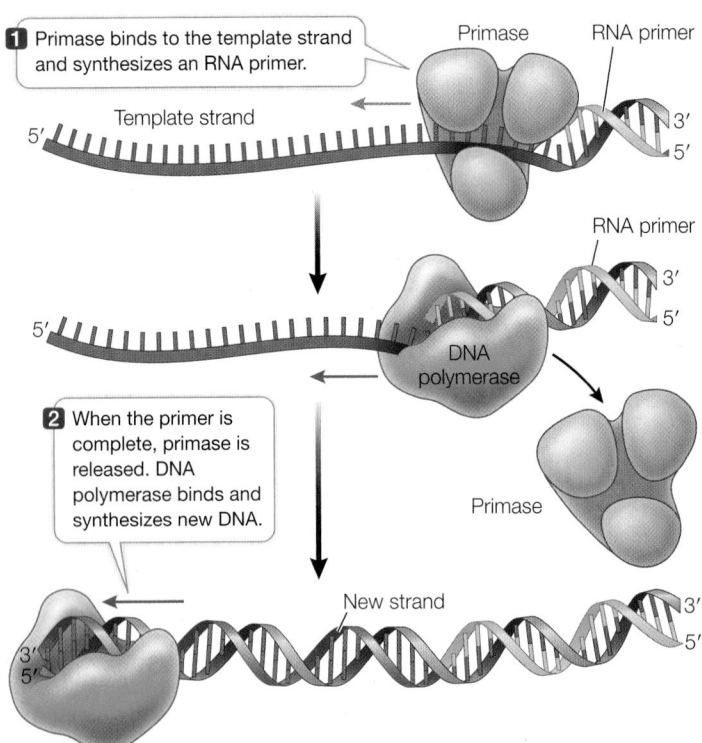

1 Primase binds to the template strand and synthesizes an RNA primer.

Primase

RNA primer

Template strand

5′

3′

5′

RNA primer

3′

5′

DNA polymerase

2 When the primer is complete, primase is released. DNA polymerase binds and synthesizes new DNA.

Primase

New strand

3′

5′

3′
5′

Figure 13.12 DNA Synthesis Requires a Primer DNA polymerases require a primer—a "starter" strand of RNA (or in some situations DNA; not shown) to which they can add new nucleotides.

growing away from each other, it would take weeks to fully replicate a chromosome. So eukaryotic chromosomes have multiple origins of replication, scattered at intervals of 10,000 to 40,000 bp (**Figure 13.11B**).

DNA REPLICATION BEGINS WITH A PRIMER   A DNA polymerase elongates a polynucleotide strand by covalently linking new nucleotides to a preexisting strand. However, it cannot start this process without a short "starter" strand, called a **primer**. In most organisms this primer is a short single strand of RNA (**Figure 13.12**), but in some organisms it is DNA. The RNA primer is complementary to the DNA template and is synthesized one nucleotide at a time by an enzyme called a **primase**. Once the primase has added a primer, the elongation phase of replication begins, with the DNA polymerase adding nucleotides to the 3′ end of the primer and continuing until replication of that section of DNA has been completed. The DNA polymerase continues to synthesize DNA until it runs out of template. Then the RNA primer is degraded, DNA is added in its place (by a different DNA polymerase), and the resulting DNA fragments are connected by the action of other enzymes. When DNA replication is complete, each new strand consists only of DNA.

DNA POLYMERASES ARE LARGE   DNA polymerases are much larger than their substrates (the dNTPs) and the template DNA, which is very thin. Molecular models of the

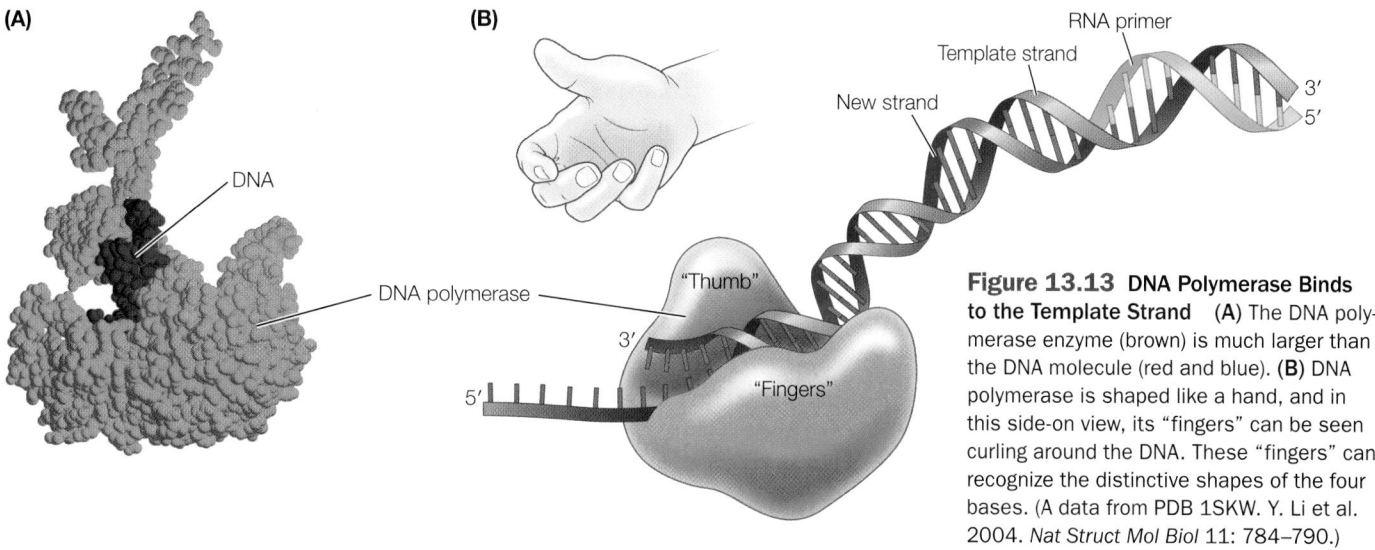

(A)

DNA

DNA polymerase

(B)

RNA primer

Template strand

New strand

3′
5′

"Thumb"

3′

"Fingers"

5′

Figure 13.13 DNA Polymerase Binds to the Template Strand **(A)** The DNA polymerase enzyme (brown) is much larger than the DNA molecule (red and blue). **(B)** DNA polymerase is shaped like a hand, and in this side-on view, its "fingers" can be seen curling around the DNA. These "fingers" can recognize the distinctive shapes of the four bases. (A data from PDB 1SKW. Y. Li et al. 2004. *Nat Struct Mol Biol* 11: 784–790.)

enzyme–substrate–template complex from bacteria show that the enzyme is shaped like an open right hand with a palm, a thumb, and fingers (**Figure 13.13**). Within the "palm" is the active site of the enzyme, which brings together each dNTP substrate and the template. The "finger" regions have precise shapes that can recognize the different shapes of the four nucleotide bases. They bind to the bases by hydrogen bonding and rotate inward. Most cells contain more than one kind of DNA polymerase, but only one of them is responsible for chromosomal DNA replication. The others are involved in primer removal and DNA repair. Fifteen DNA polymerases have been identified in humans, whereas the bacterium *E. coli* has five.

Many other proteins assist with DNA polymerization

Various other proteins play roles in other replication tasks; some of these are shown in **Figure 13.14**. The first event at the origin of replication is the localized unwinding and separation (denaturation) of the DNA strands. As we discussed in Key Concept 13.2, the two strands are held together by hydrogen bonds. An enzyme called **DNA helicase** uses energy from ATP hydrolysis to unwind and separate the strands, and **single-stranded binding proteins** bind to the unwound strands to keep them from reassociating into a double helix. This process makes each of the two template strands available for complementary base pairing.

DNA polymerase elongates both strands.

Single-stranded binding proteins keep the template strands separated.

Leading strand template

3′
5′

3′

Leading strand

Lagging strand

Okazaki fragment

RNA primer

3′
5′

5′3′

5′

Lagging strand template

DNA polymerase

Parent DNA

3′
5′

DNA helicase unwinds the double helix.

Primase synthesizes a primer.

Figure 13.14 Many Proteins Collaborate in the Pre-Replication Complex Several proteins in addition to DNA polymerase are involved in DNA replication. The two molecules of DNA polymerase shown here are actually part of the same complex.

Q: In bidirectional replication from a single origin point, with two replication forks moving in opposite directions, will the same DNA strands be leading and lagging on both forks?

▶ **View in Achieve**
Activity 13.1 The Pre-Replication Complex

The two DNA strands grow differently at the replication fork

The DNA at the replication fork—the site where DNA unwinds to expose the bases so that they can act as templates—opens up like a zipper in one direction. Study **Figure 13.15** and try to imagine what is happening over a short period of time. Remember that the two DNA strands are antiparallel; that is, the 3′ end of one strand is paired with the 5′ end of the other.

- One newly replicating strand (the **leading strand**) is oriented so that it can grow continuously at its 3′ end as the fork opens up.

- The other new strand (the **lagging strand**) is oriented so that as the fork opens up, its exposed 3′ end gets farther and farther away from the fork, and an unreplicated gap is formed. This gap would get bigger and bigger if there were not a special mechanism to overcome this problem.

Synthesis of the lagging strand requires the synthesis of relatively small, discontinuous stretches of DNA (100–200 nucleotides in eukaryotes; 1,000–2,000 nucleotides in prokaryotes). These discontinuous stretches are synthesized just as the leading strand is, by the addition of new nucleotides one at a time to the 3′ end

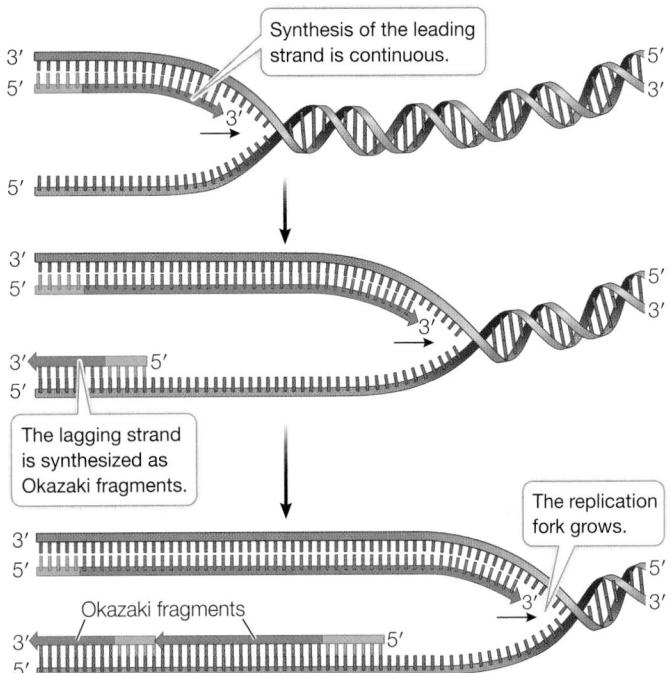

Figure 13.15 The Two New Strands Form in Different Ways
As the parent DNA unwinds, both new strands are synthesized in the 5′-to-3′ direction, although their template strands are antiparallel. The leading strand grows continuously forward, but the lagging strand grows in short discontinuous stretches called Okazaki fragments. Eukaryotic Okazaki fragments are hundreds of nucleotides long, with gaps between them.

View in Achieve
Animation 13.4 Leading and Lagging Strand Synthesis

of the new strand, but the synthesis of this new strand moves in the direction opposite to that in which the replication fork is moving. These stretches of new DNA are called **Okazaki fragments** (after their discoverer, the Japanese biochemist Reiji Okazaki). While the leading strand grows continuously "forward," the lagging strand grows in shorter, "backward" stretches with gaps between them.

A single primer is needed for synthesis of the leading strand, but each Okazaki fragment requires its own primer to be synthesized by the primase. In bacteria, priming is followed by DNA polymerase III synthesizing an Okazaki fragment by adding nucleotides to the primer until it reaches the primer of the previous fragment (**Figure 13.16**). At this point, DNA polymerase I replaces DNA polymerase III, and then removes the old primer and replaces it with DNA. Left behind is a tiny nick—the final phosphodiester bond between the adjacent Okazaki fragments is missing. The enzyme **DNA ligase** catalyzes the formation of that bond, linking the fragments and making the lagging strand whole.

DNA replication involves remarkable teamwork among various proteins that act on the DNA strands. Let's review the proteins involved in DNA replication in the order of their activity at the replication fork:

- *DNA helicase* unwinds the double helix and separates the two strands.

- *Single-stranded binding proteins* bind to separated strands and prevent them from re-forming the double helix.

- *DNA primase* makes RNA primers.

- *DNA polymerase* links new nucleotides to form the new DNA strands and removes the primers.

- *DNA ligase* connects Okazaki fragments made by DNA polymerase to one another.

Working together, these proteins make new DNA at a rate in excess of 1,000 base pairs per second.

A SLIDING CLAMP INCREASES THE RATE OF DNA REPLICATION
How do DNA polymerases work so fast? We saw in Key Concept 8.3 that an enzyme catalyzes a chemical reaction:

Substrate binds to enzyme → one product is formed → enzyme is released → cycle repeats

DNA replication would not proceed as rapidly as it does if it went through such a cycle for each nucleotide. Instead, DNA polymerases are **processive**—that is, they catalyze the formation of many phosphodiester bonds each time they bind to a DNA molecule:

Substrates bind to enzyme → many products are formed → enzyme is released → cycle repeats

The DNA polymerase–DNA complex is stabilized by a **sliding DNA clamp**, which has multiple identical subunits assembled into a doughnut shape (**Figure 13.17**). The doughnut's "hole" is just large enough to encircle the DNA double helix, along with a thin layer of water molecules for lubrication. The clamp binds to the DNA polymerase–DNA complex, keeping the enzyme and the

1 Primase forms an RNA primer.

2 DNA polymerase III adds nucleotides to the new Okazaki fragment only at the 3′ end, continuing until it encounters the primer on the previous Okazaki fragment.

3 DNA polymerase I hydrolyzes the primer and replaces it with DNA.

4 DNA ligase then catalyzes the formation of the phosphodiester bond that finally joins the two Okazaki fragments.

Figure 13.16 **The Lagging Strand Story**   In bacteria, DNA polymerase I and DNA ligase cooperate with DNA polymerase III to complete the complex task of synthesizing the lagging strand.

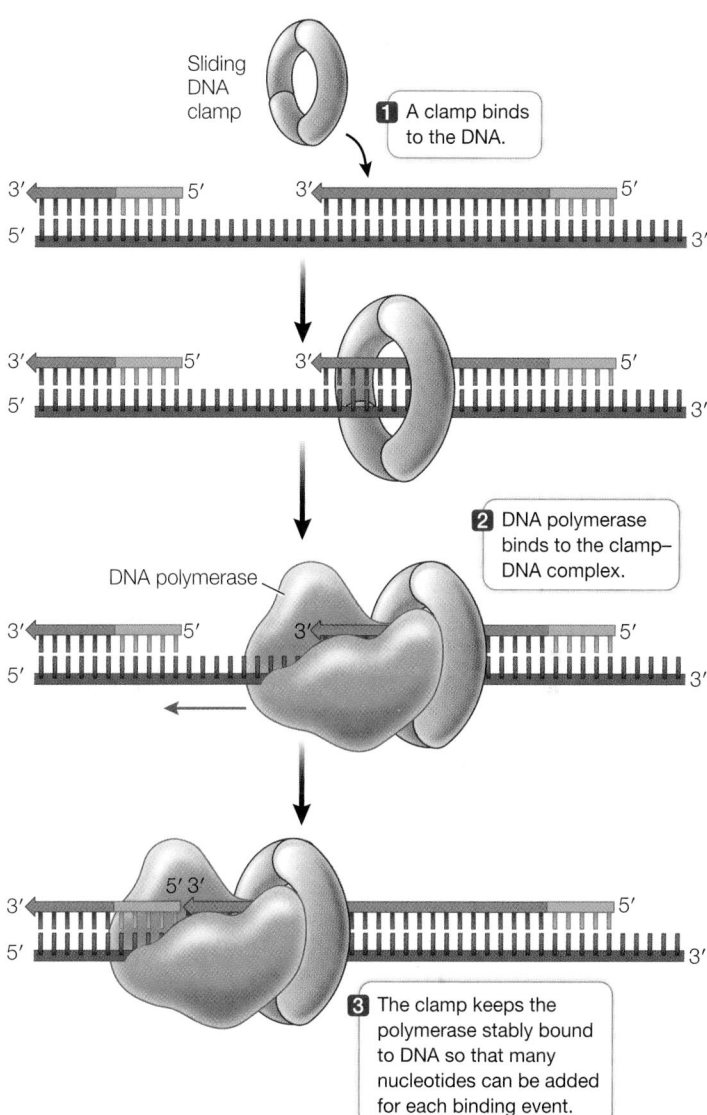

1 A clamp binds to the DNA.

2 DNA polymerase binds to the clamp–DNA complex.

3 The clamp keeps the polymerase stably bound to DNA so that many nucleotides can be added for each binding event.

Figure 13.17 **A Sliding DNA Clamp Increases the Efficiency of DNA Polymerization**   The clamp increases the efficiency of polymerization by keeping the enzyme bound to the substrate, so the enzyme does not have to repeatedly bind to template and substrate.

DNA associated tightly with each other. If the clamp is absent, DNA polymerase dissociates from DNA after forming 20 to 100 phosphodiester bonds. With the clamp, it can polymerize up to 50,000 nucleotides before it detaches.

DNA IS THREADED THROUGH A REPLICATION COMPLEX

From our discussion of the various enzymes involved in DNA replication, it is natural to think that the enzymes involved at different stages each move along the DNA templates separately. But this is not so. Instead, the enzymes used on both the leading and lagging strands are together, forming a large replication complex. Commonly in eukaryotes, the replication complexes seem to be stationary in the nucleus. It is the DNA that moves, essentially moving into the complex as a double stranded molecule and emerging as two double-stranded molecules.

Telomeres are not fully replicated and are prone to undergoing repair

As we discuss in Key Concept 13.4, DNA may be damaged by radiation or chemicals. When this happens, DNA repair mechanisms are activated, and breaks exposing free 3′ and 5′ groups in DNA are rejoined via a combination of DNA synthesis and DNA ligase activity. So the ends of chromosomes are a potential problem: the DNA repair system might recognize the ends as breaks, and join two chromosomes together. This would create havoc with genomic integrity.

In many eukaryotes, there are highly repetitive sequences at the ends of chromosomes called **telomeres**. In humans, the telomere sequence is TTAGGG-3′, and it is repeated about 2,500 times at each chromosome end. These repeats bind special proteins that prevent the DNA repair system from recognizing the chromosome ends as breaks. In addition, the repeats may form loops that have a similar protective role.

But there is another problem with chromosome ends. As you have seen, replication of the lagging strand occurs by the addition of Okazaki fragments to RNA primers. When the terminal RNA primer is removed on the lagging strand at the end of a chromosome, no DNA can be synthesized to replace it because there is no 3′ end to extend. In most cells, the short piece of single-stranded DNA at each end of the chromosome is removed. Thus the chromosome becomes slightly shorter with each cell division, an issue termed the "end-replication problem" (**Figure 13.18**).

Each human daughter chromosome can lose 50 to 200 base pairs of telomeric DNA from the end of what was the lagging strand after a round of DNA replication and cell division. After many cell divisions, the genes near the ends of the chromosomes can be lost, and the cell dies. This phenomenon explains, in part, why many cell lineages do not last the entire lifetime of the organism: their telomeres are lost. Continuously dividing cells, such as stem cells in somatic tissues and those producing gametes, have a special mechanism for maintaining their telomeric DNA. An enzyme called **telomerase** catalyzes the addition of any lost telomeric sequences in these cells (see Figure 13.18). Telomerase contains an RNA sequence that acts as a template for the synthesis of the telomeric DNA repeat sequence.

Telomerase is expressed in more than 90% of human cancers, and may be an important factor in the ability of cancer cells to divide continuously. Since most normal cells do not have this ability, telomerase is an attractive target for drugs designed to attack tumors specifically. There is also interest in telomerase and aging. When cultured human cells are transformed with a telomerase gene that is expressed at high levels, their telomeres do not shorten. Instead of living 20 to 30 cell generations and then dying, the cells become immortal. It remains to be seen how this finding relates to the aging of a whole organism.

In most cells the terminal nonreplicated nucleotides are removed and the chromosome is shortened.

In stem cells the enzyme telomerase uses an RNA template (made by primase) to extend the telomere.

Telomerase moves to the new end and DNA polymerase fills the gap. This process can be repeated multiple times to lengthen the telomere.

© Dr. Peter Lansdorp/Visuals Unlimited, Inc.

Figure 13.18 Telomeres and Telomerase   (A) In most cells, the chromosome shortens with each replication because the nonreplicated DNA at the 3′ end of the template DNA is removed. However, in stem cells (including gamete-forming stem cells) telomerase uses an RNA template to extend the telomere and prevent chromosome shortening. (B) Bright fluorescent staining marks the telomeric regions on these blue-stained human chromosomes.

Q: Why do the cells that form gametes express telomerase?

13.3 Recap and Assess

Meselson and Stahl showed that DNA replication is semiconservative: each parent DNA strand serves as a template for a new strand. Several proteins, most notably DNA polymerase, are involved in replication. New DNA is polymerized in one direction only. Since the two strands are antiparallel, one strand is made continuously and the other is synthesized in short Okazaki fragments that are eventually joined by DNA ligase, after primers are removed by DNA polymerase I.

1. How did the Meselson–Stahl experiment differentiate among the three models for DNA replication?

2. Name five proteins needed for DNA replication. What are their roles?

3. Why are there special sequences at the ends of chromosomes, and how are they replicated?

4. The drug dideoxycytidine, used to treat certain viral infections, is a nucleotide made with 2′,3′-dideoxyribose. This sugar lacks —OH groups at both the 2′ and the 3′ positions. Explain why dideoxycytidine stops the synthesis of DNA when it is added to the growing DNA chain.

Dideoxycytidine

The complex process of DNA replication is amazingly accurate, but it is not perfect. What happens when things go wrong?

13.4 Errors in DNA Can Be Repaired

Learning Objectives

13.4.1 Identify all the possible mismatches that can occur in a DNA molecule.

13.4.2 Explain how proofreading and mismatch repair act to reduce the rate of DNA replication errors.

13.4.3 Describe how excision repair acts on damaged nucleotides.

DNA must be accurately replicated and maintained. This is essential for the proper functioning of every cell, whether a prokaryote or a cell in a complex, multicellular organism. Yet the replication of DNA is not perfectly accurate, and DNA is subject to change by chemicals and other environmental agents. In the face of these threats, how has life gone on for so long?

Repair mechanisms preserve DNA

DNA polymerases make mistakes in assembling polynucleotide strands—typically about 1 wrong base is inserted per 100,000

replicated. While this may seem insignificant, consider the fact that every human cell has about 6 billion base pairs, so polymerases make about 60,000 mistakes (incorrect incorporations) in new strands every time a human cell divides. Such incorporation errors cause mismatches, in which the two bases across from each other in a DNA molecule are not complementary (for example, A across from C is a mismatch). It gets worse: bases can change spontaneously as well, and outside agents such as radiation can damage them. Mismatches and damaged bases can lead to mutations—permanent changes in the DNA sequence. Fortunately, all cells, including our own, have mechanisms for correcting mismatches and for repairing DNA containing damaged nucleotides. These mechanisms include the following:

- A **proofreading** mechanism corrects errors in replication as DNA polymerase makes them.

- A **mismatch repair** mechanism scans DNA immediately after it has been replicated and corrects any base-pairing mismatches.

- An **excision repair** mechanism removes damaged bases and replaces them with functional bases.

Most DNA polymerases perform a proofreading function each time they introduce a new nucleotide into a growing DNA strand (**Figure 13.19A**). When a DNA polymerase recognizes a mispairing of bases, it removes the improperly introduced nucleotide and tries again. (Other proteins in the replication complex also play roles in proofreading.) Proofreading catches 99% or more mismatches incorporated by the DNA polymerase, which lowers the overall error rate to about 1 error in every 10^7 nucleotides replicated.

After the DNA has been replicated, a second set of proteins surveys the newly replicated molecule and looks for mismatched base pairs that were missed in proofreading (**Figure 13.19B**). For example, this mismatch repair mechanism might detect an A-C base pair instead of an A-T pair. The repair system keeps track of the template versus newly synthesized strand and can recognize which of the two bases in the A-C pair is the wrong one. It then makes the appropriate repair. If the correct pair should be A-T, the repair system replaces C with T, restoring an A-T pair. Alternatively, if it recognizes that the correct pair should be C-G, it replaces A with G. After mismatch repair, the overall error rate of DNA replication falls to 1 error in 10^9 nucleotides replicated. When mismatch repair fails, more DNA mismatches escape repair and lead to mutations that alter DNA sequences. One form of colon cancer arises in part from a failure of mismatch repair.

DNA molecules can also be damaged during the life of a cell (e.g., when it is in G1 phase). High-energy radiation, chemicals from the environment, and spontaneous chemical changes can damage DNA. For example, when adjacent thymines on the same DNA strand absorb ultraviolet light (at about 260 nm), they form a covalent bond between the bases, making a thymine dimer. These dimers interfere with base pairing during replication, leading to random bases being inserted. This is the primary cause of skin cancer in humans. Excision repair mechanisms recognize damaged nucleotides and remove them (**Figure 13.19C**).

(A) DNA proofreading

DNA polymerase III

1 During DNA replication, an incorrect nucleotide may be added to the growing chain.

2 The proteins of the replication complex immediately excise the incorrect nucleotide.

3 DNA polymerase III adds the correct nucleotide and replication proceeds.

(B) Mismatch repair

DNA polymerase I

1 During DNA replication, a nucleotide was mispaired and missed in proofreading.

2 The mismatch repair proteins excise the mismatched nucleotide and some adjacent nucleotides.

3 DNA polymerase I adds the correct nucleotides.

4 DNA ligase repairs the remaining nick.

(C) Excision repair

1 A nucleotide in DNA is damaged.

2 The excision repair proteins excise the damaged nucleotide and some adjacent nucleotides.

3 DNA polymerase I adds the correct nucleotides.

4 DNA ligase repairs the remaining nick.

Figure 13.19 DNA Repair Mechanisms During replication, DNA polymerase III can detect and remove a mismatch when it is introduced (**A**), or mismatch repair can do so later (**B**), reducing the rate of errors in the replicated DNA. (**C**) Excision repair detects and repairs damage to existing DNA molecules.

KEY CONCEPT
13.4 Recap and Assess

DNA polymerases are not perfectly accurate. Although DNA polymerases make incorporation errors, proofreading and mismatch repair reduce the overall error rate of replication. In addition, excision repair mechanisms recognize and repair nucleotides altered or damaged by environmental factors.

1. From what you know about the role of DNA in the cell, what would be the genetic consequences of an unrepaired DNA mismatch in a G1 phase cell that then entered the cell cycle to give rise to gametes from meiosis?

2. One form of colon cancer is caused by a mutation in a gene encoding a protein involved in mismatch repair, so that it does not function correctly. Do you think this mutation is the one that leads to unregulated cell cycling? If not, what kind of gene might be affected? Recall cell cycle control genes involved in cancer formation (see Figure 11.24).

Understanding how DNA is replicated and repaired has allowed scientists to develop techniques for studying genes. We look next at one of the most widely used of these techniques.

KEY CONCEPT
13.5 The Polymerase Chain Reaction Amplifies DNA

Learning Objectives

13.5.1 Explain the purpose for each of the three steps in the PCR process.

13.5.2 Explain how PCR is targeted to particular DNA sequences.

The principles underlying DNA replication in cells have been used to develop an important laboratory technique that has been vital in analyzing genes and genomes. This technique allows researchers to make multiple copies of short DNA sequences.

The polymerase chain reaction can make multiple copies of a DNA sequence

In order to study DNA and perform genetic manipulations in the lab, it is often necessary to make multiple copies of a particular DNA sequence. While there are several methods for making multiple copies of a DNA sequence (see Chapter 18), one method, the **polymerase chain reaction (PCR)**, relies on characteristics of DNA polymerases.

The PCR is performed in a small tube that contains:

- A sample of double-stranded DNA from a biological sample, which contains the template sequence
- Two short, artificially synthesized primers that are complementary to the ends of the template sequence to be amplified
- The four dNTPs (dATP, dTTP, dCTP, and dGTP)
- A DNA polymerase that can tolerate high temperatures without losing function
- Salts and a buffer to maintain a near-neutral pH

PCR amplification is a cyclic process in which a sequence of steps is repeated over and over (**Figure 13.20**):

1. The first step involves heating the reaction mixture to near boiling point, to separate (denature) the two strands of the DNA template.
2. The reaction is then cooled to allow the primers to bind to their complementary sequences in the template strands.
3. Next, the reaction is warmed to an optimum temperature for the DNA polymerase to catalyze the production of the complementary new strands.

A single cycle takes a few minutes to produce two copies of the target DNA sequence, leaving the new DNA in the double-stranded state. Repeating the cycle many times leads to an exponential increase in the number of copies of the DNA sequence.

The PCR technique requires that the base sequences at the 3' end of each strand of the target DNA sequence be known, so that complementary primers, usually 15 to 30 bases long, can be made in the laboratory. Because of the uniqueness of DNA sequences, a pair of primers this length will usually bind to only a single region of DNA in an organism's genome. This specificity, despite the incredible diversity of DNA sequences, is a key to the power of PCR.

One initial problem with PCR was its temperature requirements. To denature DNA, it must be heated to more than 90°C—a temperature that destroys most DNA polymerases. When the PCR technique was first being developed, new enzyme had to be added after denaturation in each cycle, which made the technique impractical for widespread use. This problem was solved by nature: in the hot springs at Yellowstone National Park, as well as in other high-temperature locations, there lives a bacterium called, appropriately, *Thermus aquaticus* ("hot water"). The means by which this organism survives temperatures of up to 95°C was investigated by Thomas Brock and his colleagues at the University of Wisconsin, Madison. They discovered that *T. aquaticus* has metabolic machinery that is heat-resistant, including a DNA polymerase that does not denature at these high temperatures.

Scientists pondering the problem of copying DNA by PCR read Brock's basic research articles and got a clever idea: why not use

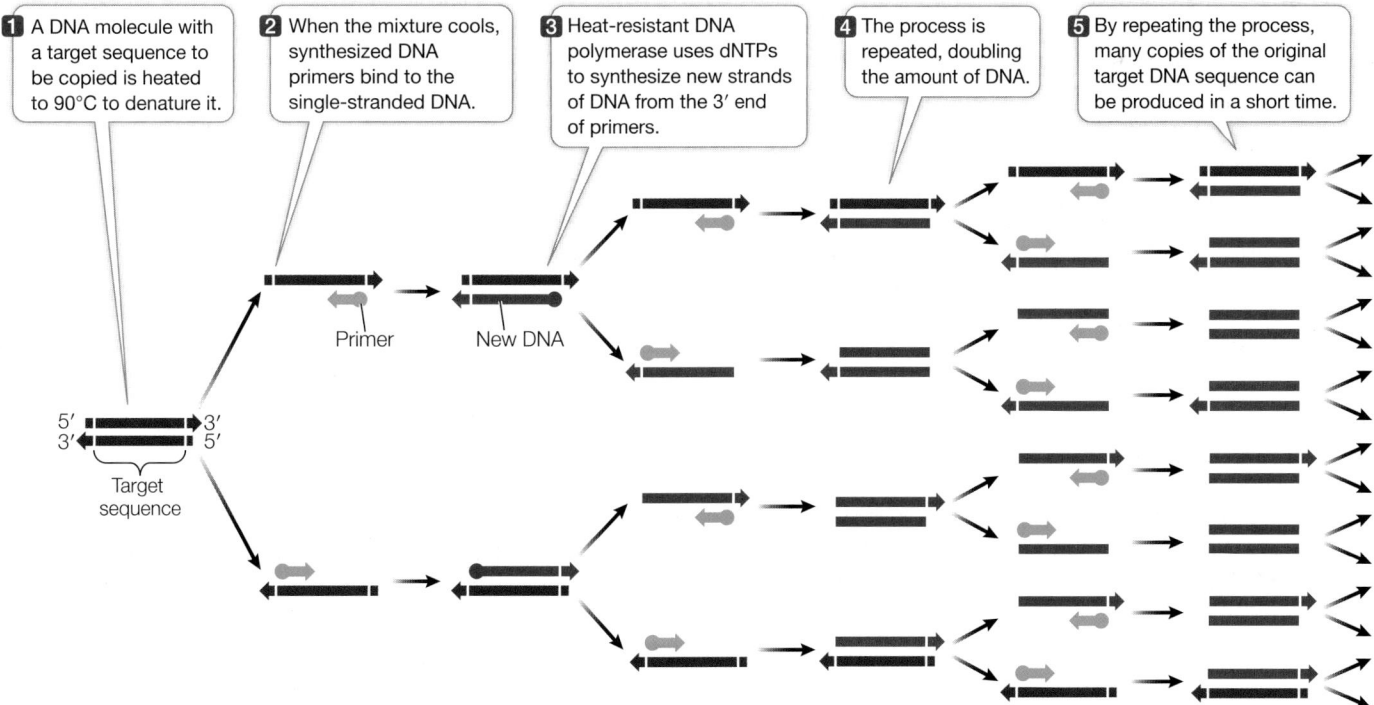

1 A DNA molecule with a target sequence to be copied is heated to 90°C to denature it.

2 When the mixture cools, synthesized DNA primers bind to the single-stranded DNA.

3 Heat-resistant DNA polymerase uses dNTPs to synthesize new strands of DNA from the 3' end of primers.

4 The process is repeated, doubling the amount of DNA.

5 By repeating the process, many copies of the original target DNA sequence can be produced in a short time.

Primer New DNA

Target sequence

Figure 13.20 The Polymerase Chain Reaction The steps in this cyclic process are repeated many times to produce multiple identical copies of a DNA fragment. This makes enough DNA for chemical analysis and genetic manipulations.

Q: How do PCR primers relate to DNA replication primers?

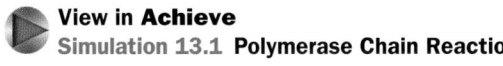 **View in Achieve**
Simulation 13.1 **Polymerase Chain Reaction**

T. aquaticus DNA polymerase in the PCR technique? It could withstand the 90°C denaturation temperature and would not have to be added during each cycle. The idea worked, and it earned biochemist Kary Mullis a Nobel prize. PCR has had an enormous impact on genetic research. Some of its most striking applications will be described in Chapters 15–18. These applications range from amplifying DNA in order to identify an individual person or organism, to detection of diseases.

KEY CONCEPT
13.5 Recap and Assess

Knowledge of the mechanisms of DNA replication led to the development of the PCR technique for making multiple copies of DNA sequences.

1. What is the role of primers in PCR?
2. One way to quickly identify an organism in the field is to use PCR: if there is amplification of a particular sequence, then the organism is identified. What is the basis for this test?

▶Investigating LIFE

 What do we need to know about DNA replication to describe the mechanism of a drug that blocks it?

Recall that the opening story in this chapter described the discovery that platinum electrodes inhibit cell division, which lead researchers to wonder if they could invent a drug containing platinum that might inhibit the uncontrolled growth of cancer cells. The drug that Dr. Barnett Rosenberg developed, cisplatin, was remarkably efficient at halting certain kinds of tumor growth. Understanding how cisplatin works came with an understanding of the chemistry of DNA and the mechanism by which it replicates.

Investigating Life: The Meselson–Stahl Experiment discusses the experiment that revealed that DNA replicates semiconservatively—that each strand of DNA serves as a template for a new strand. In the presence of cisplatin, DNA cannot denature to allow replication, suggesting that cisplatin interferes with strand separation. How is separation prevented, and what does it have to do with platinum?

Cisplatin contains a platinum atom bonded to two amino groups and two chlorine atoms (**Figure 13.21A**). In Rosenberg's experiments, this compound was formed when the platinum electrode reacted with salts in the surrounding solution. The bonds between the platinum atom and the chlorine atoms are weak, and the latter can be displaced by electron-rich substances (you may know from chemistry that these are called nucleophiles). In DNA, one of the nitrogen atoms of guanine (**Figure 13.21B**) displaces one of the chlorines, forming a strong covalent bond. If there is a nearby guanine on the opposite DNA strand, the other chlorine of the cisplatin molecule can be displaced as well, so that the cisplatin is effectively bonded to both of the DNA strands. In short, the DNA strands become cross-linked and cannot separate as needed for DNA replication (**Figure 13.21C**). Without replication, the cell cannot divide, and it undergoes apoptosis. The type of DNA lesion caused by cisplatin cannot be repaired by any of the cell's usual DNA repair mechanisms.

Future directions

Eukaryotic chromosomes have long strands of DNA, each with up to tens of millions of base pairs. During S phase of the cell cycle,

Cisplatin binds to two guanines, cross-linking the two strands of the DNA and distorting the double helix.

Figure 13.21 Cisplatin: A Small but Lethal Molecule

each chromosome must be replicated completely and only once. Since replication is bidirectional from an origin, and since S phase typically is not long enough to replicate an entire chromosome, there must be many starting points for replication. Understanding how these origins are recognized is a major challenge for biologists. A recent discovery may provide a clue as to how a DNA pre-replication complex arrives at each replication origin. While most RNA molecules transcribed from DNA leave their site of synthesis, some do not. These short RNAs, complementary to their DNA template, turn back instead and bind to the DNA by base pairing. Indeed, this rapid binding displaces the nontemplate strand of DNA, so it forms a loop. These loops of DNA cannot pair with their complementary strand, because that strand at that location is bound up with RNA. Emerging evidence suggests that the "R-loops," with their exposed DNA bases, act to recognize binding of the proteins of the DNA pre-replication complex.

© Biology Pics/Science Source

You should be able to relate each summary to the adjacent figures. If you go to this visual summary in **Achieve**, you can follow links to figures, animations, activities, and simulations that will help you consolidate the material.

KEY CONCEPT

13.1 Experiments Revealed the Function of DNA as Genetic Material   Go to **Animation 13.1**

- Bacterial transformation requires DNA.
- Bacteriophages inject DNA, not protein, into bacterial hosts.

Questions

1. How is a mixture of a dead S strain and a living R strain of pneumococcal bacteria able to kill a mouse?
2. Why did Hershey and Chase use sulfur and phosphorus to label proteins and DNA in bacteriophage?

Figure 13.2

KEY CONCEPT

13.2 DNA Has a Structure That Suits Its Function

- Chargaff showed that the amount of **adenine** (**A**) in DNA = the amount of **thymine** (**T**), and that the amount of **guanine** (**G**) = the amount of **cytosine** (**C**).
- Franklin determined many of the characteristics of DNA structure from her X-ray images.
- Watson and Crick proposed that DNA was a double-stranded molecule with each strand composed of a sugar–phosphate backbone with hydrogen bonding between **complementary base pairs**.

Questions

1. A sample of DNA from a rabbit consists of 24% adenine nucleotides. What are the frequencies of the other nucleotides?
2. One strand of a double-stranded DNA molecule has the sequence 5′ ACGGTTACC 3′. What is the sequence and polarity of the other strand?
3. How many different sequences are possible for a 10-base-pair DNA molecule?

Figure 13.6

KEY CONCEPT

13.3 DNA Is Replicated Semiconservatively   Go to **Activity 13.1** and **Animations 13.2–13.4**

- Meselson and Stahl used density labeling to show that DNA undergoes **semiconservative replication**. Each parent strand serves as a **template** for the synthesis of a new strand.
- **DNA polymerases**, which require **primers**, catalyze the addition of nucleotides to the 3′ end of each new strand.
- Replication begins at the **origins of replication** (**ori**) on both strands and proceeds in the 5′-to-3′ direction, forming **replication forks**, which have a **leading strand** and a **lagging strand**.
- **Telomerase** can extend **telomeres**, overcoming the chromosome shortening that occurs each time DNA is replicated.

Figure 13.15

Okazaki fragments

Questions

1. If replication was actually conservative, what results would Meselson and Stahl have obtained after one round of replication on light medium?

2. A replication fork is moving from left to right. If the top template strand is 5'-to-3' in the left-to-right direction, which strand is the leading and which is the lagging?

3. Many cancer cells express telomerase. Why does that make them more able to divide indefinitely?

Figure 13.18

KEY CONCEPT

13.4   Errors in DNA Can Be Repaired

- DNA polymerases occasionally incorporate the incorrect base in the new strand, which causes mismatches.

- Mismatches can be repaired by **proofreading** or **mismatch repair**.

- DNA damage is often repaired by **excision repair**.

Figure 13.19

Excision repair

Questions

1. An adenosine nucleotide is on the template strand of a DNA molecule. What are the possible mismatches that could be introduced by a DNA polymerase as it synthesizes the new strand?

2. How can the DNA replication error rate be lower than the DNA polymerase incorporation error rate?

KEY CONCEPT

13.5   The Polymerase Chain Reaction Amplifies DNA

Go to Simulation 13.1

- The **polymerase chain reaction** (**PCR**) allows amplification of a particular region of DNA.

Questions

1. What are the three steps of PCR?

2. Why is a heat-resistant DNA polymerase important for PCR?

Figure 13.20

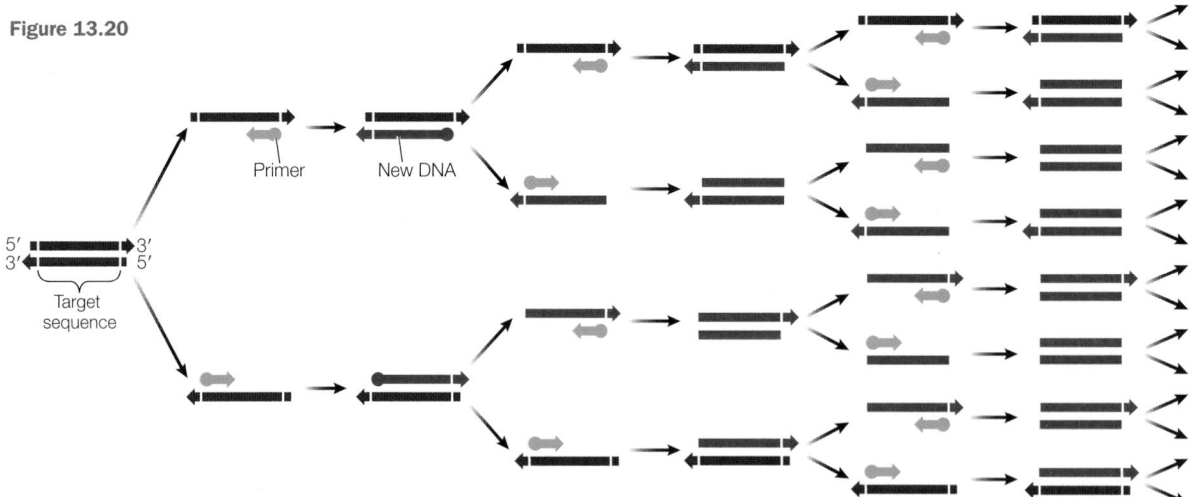

Primer   New DNA

Target sequence

Go to **Achieve** for the eBook, **LearningCurve**, animations, activities, simulations, and additional resources and assignments.

From DNA to Protein: Gene Expression 14

Courtesy of the National Institute of Allergy and Infectious Diseases (NIAID)

KEY CONCEPTS

14.1 Genes Code for Proteins

14.2 Information Flows from Genes to Proteins

14.3 DNA Is Transcribed to Produce RNA

14.4 Eukaryotic Pre-mRNA Transcripts Are Processed prior to Translation

14.5 The Genetic Code Determines the Protein Sequence Encoded by an mRNA

14.6 The Coding Sequence in mRNA Is Translated into Proteins by Ribosomes

14.7 Polypeptides Can Be Modified and Transported during or after Translation

Methicillin-resistant *Staphylococcus aureus*, a major cause of serious illness and death in the United States and Europe, is treated with antibiotics that target its gene expression.

▶Investigating LIFE

Employing the Genetic Code to Combat Superbugs

Staphylococcus aureus is among billions of bacteria that inhabit the human skin and nose, mostly with no ill effect. But sometimes, especially when the immune system has been weakened by age or disease, *S. aureus* can cause major skin infections and may enter the body through the nose or a wound site, causing serious and sometimes fatal infections of organs such as the heart and lungs.

Until recently, most *S. aureus* infections were successfully treated with penicillin and related drugs, including methicillin. These antibiotics bind and inactivate several related enzymes involved in the assembly of bacterial cell walls. New bacterial cells produced by cell division of antibiotic-treated bacteria do not survive.

Unfortunately, some *S. aureus* strains have acquired mutant versions of a penicillin-binding protein that are resistant to antibiotics—the mutant enzyme can catalyze the assembly of cell walls even in the presence of antibiotics. The mutant *mecA* allele that encodes this mutant protein can be passed from one bacterium to another by bacterial conjugation (see Key Concept 12.6).

What makes the mutant version of *mecA* different, and how does this difference lead to antibiotic resistance? Compared with the wild-type allele, the mutant *mecA* allele has a small change in its nucleotide sequence. This results in changes in the amino acid sequence of the expressed protein. This alteration in the protein's primary structure affects its secondary and tertiary structures: the protein folds into a shape that doesn't bind the antibiotics.

The fundamental lesson conveyed by this example is that *a gene is expressed as a protein*, and more specifically, that *the sequence of nucleotides in DNA is expressed as a sequence of amino acids in a protein*. Understanding how the nucleotide sequence of a gene produces a specific protein came with the discovery of the genetic code, a landmark in biological research.

Mutant bacterial strains that are stubbornly resistant to antibiotics are known as "superbugs." One greatly feared superbug is methicillin-resistant *S. aureus*, or MRSA. About 1 person in 50 carries MRSA, so it represents a real threat to public health. MRSA incidence is declining, thanks to careful monitoring and treatment in hospitals and nursing homes, where people are especially vulnerable. The infection is treated with a new class of antibiotics that target bacterial protein synthesis.

 How does knowledge of the genetic code help us understand the actions of some antibiotics?
(Find the answer on page 320.)

14.1 Genes Code for Proteins

Learning Objectives

14.1.1 Describe the attributes of model organisms used for genetic studies.

14.1.2 Determine the order of intermediates in a biosynthetic pathway, given growth data for various mutant strains on these intermediates.

14.1.3 Determine the locations of mutant enzymes in a biosynthetic pathway, given growth data for the mutant strains.

In Chapter 4 we introduced DNA and its role in gene expression. Then in Chapter 13 we presented evidence that DNA is the carrier of genetic information and described how DNA is replicated prior to cell division. Here we focus on the evidence that proteins are the major products of gene expression, and we describe how a gene is expressed as protein.

Scientists had a molecular understanding of phenotypes before it was known that DNA was the genetic material; they had studied the chemical differences between individuals carrying wild-type and mutant alleles in organisms as diverse as humans and bread molds and knew that the major phenotypic differences resulted from differences in specific proteins. But just *how* different proteins arise in different individuals was not understood.

Observations in humans led to the proposal that genes determine enzymes

The identification of a gene product as a protein began with a mutation. In the early twentieth century, English physician Archibald Garrod saw several children with a rare disease. One symptom of the disease was that the urine turned dark brown or black when exposed to air, which was especially noticeable on the infants' diapers. The disease was given the descriptive name alkaptonuria ("black urine") (**Figure 14.1A**).

Garrod noticed that the disease was most common in children whose parents were first cousins. Mendelian genetics had just been "rediscovered," and Garrod realized that because first cousins share on average one-eighth of their alleles, the children of first cousins might inherit a rare mutant allele from both parents. He proposed that alkaptonuria was a recessive phenotype caused by a mutant allele that causes the disease phenotype.

Garrod took the analysis further by identifying the biochemical abnormality in the affected children. He isolated from them an unusual substance, homogentisic acid, which accumulated in blood, joints (where it crystallized and caused severe pain), and urine (where it turned black). The chemical structure of homogentisic acid is similar to that of the amino acid tyrosine (**Figure 14.1B**).

The function of enzymes as biological catalysts had just been discovered. Garrod proposed that homogentisic acid was a breakdown product of tyrosine. He suggested that while homogentisic acid ordinarily would be converted to a harmless product, it was not being converted in children with alkaptonuria. Garrod further

(A)

Normal urine

Urine from an individual with alkaptonuria, after being exposed to air

(B)

Homogentisic acid

Tyrosine

(C)

A block at the first step of the pathway causes phenylketonuria (PKU).

Phenylalanine

Phenylalanine hydroxylase

Tyrosine

p-Hydroxyphenylpyruvic acid

Homogentisic acid

A block at this step causes alkaptonuria.

Homogentisic acid oxidase

Maleylacetoacetic acid

Figure 14.1 Alkaptonuria and Phenylketonuria **(A)** The physician Archibald Garrod showed that the accumulation of homogentisic acid in the urine of patients with alkaptonuria causes their urine to turn black when exposed to air. **(B)** Because the chemical structure of homogentisic acid is similar to that of the amino acid tyrosine, Garrod proposed that it was a breakdown product of the amino acid. **(C)** Both alkaptonuria and phenylketonuria are caused by mutations in specific enzymes in the pathway that breaks down phenylalanine.

hypothesized that the enzyme required for the breakdown of homogentisic acid was not being produced in these children. He suggested that a normal human allele (for the wild-type phenotype) was required for the synthesis of an enzyme that catalyzed this conversion. If the allele were mutated, the enzyme would be inactive and homogentisic acid would accumulate instead.

Garrod concluded that there must be *one gene to one enzyme* and coined the term "inborn error of metabolism" to describe this genetically determined biochemical disease. But his hypothesis was not confirmed until the enzyme and pathway were identified (**Figure 14.1C**). The enzyme, homogentisic acid oxidase, was identified as active in healthy people and inactive in alkaptonuria patients in 1958. The specific DNA mutation that caused the enzyme to be nonfunctional was not described until 1996. An enzyme that catalyzes another step in this pathway is nonfunctional in individuals who have phenylketonuria (PKU). From the pathway, you can see that PKU causes elevated levels of phenylalanine, and this leads to significant intellectual disability if untreated. Fortunately it is now routine to test for high phenylalanine levels in the blood of newborn infants, and if an affected child consumes a diet low in phenylalanine, intellectual disability is avoided.

To relate genes and enzymes more generally, biologists turned to simpler organisms that could be manipulated in the laboratory.

Experiments on bread mold established that genes determine enzymes

As they work to explain the principles that govern life, biologists often turn to organisms that are easy to manipulate experimentally. Such **model organisms** have certain characteristics that make them attractive experimental subjects. For example, model organisms (1) are easy to grow in the laboratory or greenhouse, (2) have short generation times, (3) often produce large numbers of progeny, and (4) are easy to manipulate genetically, by crossing or by other methods. Biologists use model organisms to discover principles that can then be applied to other organisms. You have encountered some model organisms in previous chapters, including the pea plants (*Pisa sativum*) used by Mendel (see Key Concept 12.1), the fruit flies (*Drosophila*) used by Morgan (see Key Concept 12.4), and the *E. coli* bacteria used by Meselson and Stahl (see Key Concept 13.3).

To this list we now add the bread mold *Neurospora*, a type of sac fungus (see Chapter 28). In addition to having the traits shared by other model organisms, this mold is haploid for most of its life cycle, so there are no issues with dominance of alleles: all alleles are expressed phenotypically and not masked by a heterozygous condition. Biologists at Stanford University led by George Beadle and Edward Tatum undertook studies to biochemically define the phenotypes in *Neurospora*.

Like Garrod, Beadle and Tatum hypothesized that the expression of a specific gene results in the activity of a specific enzyme. They set out to test this hypothesis directly. They grew *Neurospora* on a nutritional medium containing sucrose, minerals, and biotin, which is the only vitamin that wild-type *Neurospora* cannot synthesize itself. Using this minimal medium, the enzymes of wild-type *Neurospora* could catalyze all the metabolic reactions needed for growth.

The scientists then treated the wild-type *Neurospora* with X-rays, which function as a mutagen. A **mutagen** is something that damages DNA, causing **mutations**: heritable alterations in the DNA sequence. After the X-ray treatment, some *Neurospora* strains could no longer grow on the minimal medium. These mutant strains grew only if they were supplied with specific additional nutrients, such as particular vitamins. Beadle and Tatum hypothesized that these genetic strains had mutations in the genes that code for production of enzymes needed to synthesize the additional nutrients. For each mutant strain, the scientists were able to find a single compound that, when added to the minimal medium, supported the growth of that strain. These results suggested that mutations have simple effects, and that each mutation causes a defect in only one enzyme in a metabolic pathway. These conclusions confirmed Garrod's **one-gene, one-enzyme hypothesis**.

Mutations provide a powerful way to determine cause and effect in biology. Nowhere has this been more evident than in the elucidation of biochemical pathways. Such pathways consist of sequential steps (chemical reactions) in which each event is dependent on the occurrence of the preceding event. If each reaction is catalyzed by an enzyme, and each enzyme is encoded by a gene, then it should be possible to block a pathway at any step by knocking out (rendering nonfunctional) the gene encoding that enzyme by mutation. Strains with mutated genes will thus not be able to synthesize the final product of the pathway and will exhibit a mutant phenotype. Addition of a compound in the pathway that occurs before the step with the mutated enzyme will not allow the mutant strain to produce the final product of the pathway. In contrast, addition of a compound occurring after the step with the mutated enzyme will allow the mutant strain to produce the final product of the pathway.

Two colleagues of Beadle and Tatum, Adrian Srb and Norman Horowitz, used this reasoning to determine characteristics of the biosynthetic pathway for arginine. They isolated *Neurospora* mutants that could not survive without the amino acid arginine in their growth medium. By adding particular compounds hypothesized to be in the arginine biosynthetic pathway to the medium, Srb and Horowitz were able to identify a series of steps in the biochemical pathway leading to the synthesis of arginine (**Figure 14.2**).

One gene determines one polypeptide

The one-gene, one-enzyme relationship has undergone several modifications in light of our current knowledge of molecular biology. Many proteins, including many enzymes, are composed of more than one polypeptide chain, or subunit (recall quaternary protein structure from Key Concept 3.2). So it is more correct to speak of a **one-gene, one-polypeptide relationship**.

> **Connect the Concepts** Hemoglobin, illustrated in Figure 3.12 is an example of a protein composed of more than one polypeptide chain. Hemoglobin has four polypeptides—two α and two β subunits, and each kind of subunit is encoded by a separate gene.

So far we have seen that in terms of protein synthesis, the *function of a gene is to prescribe the production of a single, specific polypeptide*. But not all genes code for polypeptides. As we will see later in this chapter and in Chapter 16, many DNA sequences are transcribed to RNA molecules that are not translated into polypeptides, but instead have other functions.

Experiment

Figure 14.2A One Gene, One Enzyme

Original Paper: A. M. Srb and N. H. Horowitz. 1944. The ornithine cycle in *Neurospora* and its genetic control. *J Biol Chem* 154: 129–139.

Srb and Horowitz isolated several mutant strains of *Neurospora* that could not make arginine (arg). Several compounds, including ornithine and citrulline, are intermediates in the pathway for arginine synthesis. By systematically adding each of these molecules to the growth media for the mutant strains, the researchers deduced that each mutant strain was deficient in one enzyme along the arginine biosynthetic pathway.

HYPOTHESIS▶ Each gene determines an enzyme in a biochemical pathway.

METHOD▶ Place each *arg* mutant strain on a minimal nutritional medium with and without supplements.

RESULTS▶

Supplement added to minimal medium

| | | None | Ornithine | Citrulline | Arginine |

Neurospora growing on gel medium

This strain grows on *all* media; it can synthesize its own arginine. — **Wild type**

This strain grows only on arginine. It cannot convert either citrulline or ornithine to arginine. — **Mutant strain 1**

This strain grows on either arginine or citrulline. It can convert citrulline to arginine, but cannot convert ornithine to citrulline. — **Mutant strain 2**

This strain grows when any one of the three supplements is added. It can convert ornithine to citrulline and citrulline to arginine. — **Mutant strain 3**

INTERPRETATION▶

Gene *a* → Enzyme A
Gene *b* → Enzyme B
Gene *c* → Enzyme C

Precursor ⟶ Ornithine ⟶ Citrulline ⟶ Arginine

Strain 3 is blocked here. | **Strain 2 is blocked here.** | **Strain 1 is blocked here.**

If an organism cannot convert one particular compound to another, it presumably lacks an enzyme required for conversion, and the mutation is in the gene that codes for that enzyme.

CONCLUSION▶ Each gene specifies a particular enzyme.

Work with the Data

Figure 14.2B One Gene, One Enzyme

Original Paper: A. M. Srb and N. H. Horowitz. 1944. The ornithine cycle in *Neurospora* and its genetic control. *J Biol Chem* 154: 129–139.

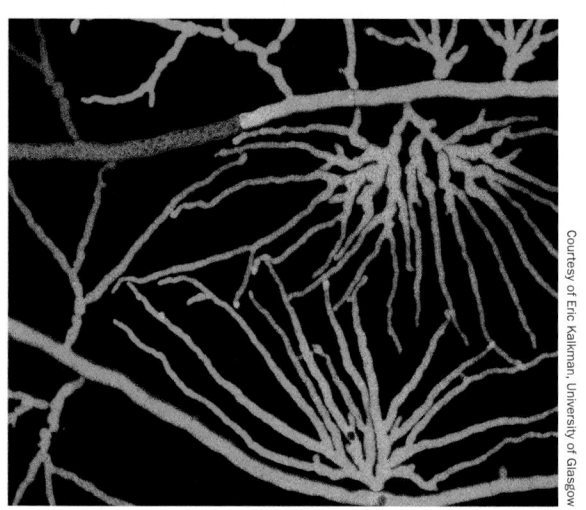

Courtesy of Eric Kalkman, University of Glasgow

Beadle and Tatum used X-rays to cause mutations in *Neurospora*. They isolated mutant strains that were unable to grow on minimal medium but were able to grow if the medium was supplemented with particular compounds. Their colleagues Adrian Srb and Norman Horowitz analyzed 15 mutant strains (the *arg* mutants) that could not synthesize arginine but could grow on medium supplemented with arginine. The scientists tested various compounds and found two, ornithine and citrulline, that could be used instead of arginine to support the growth of some of the mutant strains (as seen in Figure 14.2A). The results for three of the strains are shown in the table, with growth expressed as dry weight in milligrams of fungal material after growth for 5 days.

Strain	No addition	Ornithine added	Citrulline added	Arginine added
34105	1.1	25.5	30.0	33.2
33442	2.3	2.5	42.7	43.8
36703	0.0	0.0	0.0	20.4

QUESTIONS▶

1. Based on the biochemical pathway for arginine synthesis shown in Figure 14.2A, which gene (*a*, *b*, or *c*) was mutated in each strain?

2. Why was there some growth in strains 34105 and 33442 even when there were no additions to the growth medium?

3. Nineteen other amino acids were tested as substitutes for arginine in the three strains. In all cases, there was no growth. Explain these results.

Go to Achieve for a companion Data in Depth exercise.

14.1 Recap and Assess

Studies of mutations in humans and bread molds led to our understanding of the one-gene, one-polypeptide relationship. In most cases, the function of a gene is to code for a specific polypeptide.

1. What is a model organism, and why is *Neurospora* a good model for studying biochemical genetics?

2. How were the experiments on mutant strains of *Neurospora* set up to determine the order of steps in a biochemical pathway?

3. In bacteria, the biosynthesis of the amino acid tryptophan (T) from the precursor chorismate (C) involves four intermediate chemical compounds, which we will call D, E, F, and G. Here are the phenotypes of various mutant strains. Each strain has a mutation in a gene for a different enzyme; + means growth with the indicated compound added to the medium, and 0 means no growth. Based on these hypothetical data, order the compounds (C, D, E, F, G, and T) and enzymes (1, 2, 3, 4, and 5) in the tryptophan biosynthetic pathway.

	Addition to medium					
Mutant strain	**C**	**D**	**E**	**F**	**G**	**T**
1	0	0	0	0	+	+
2	0	+	+	0	+	+
3	0	+	0	0	+	+
4	0	+	+	+	+	+
5	0	0	0	0	0	+

Now that you have seen the evidence for the one-gene, one-polypeptide relationship, how does it work? That is, how is the information encoded in DNA used to produce a particular polypeptide?

14.2 Information Flows from Genes to Proteins

Learning Objective

14.2.1 Describe the central dogma of molecular biology and give examples of exceptions.

As we discussed in Chapter 13 and in Key Concept 14.1, DNA is the hereditary material and codes for RNAs and proteins. In the remainder of this chapter we focus on the processes that occur when a protein-coding gene is expressed. We briefly outlined gene expression in Key Concept 4.1. To review, this process occurs in two major steps:

1. During **transcription**, the information in a DNA sequence (a gene) is copied into a complementary RNA sequence.

2. During **translation**, this RNA sequence is used to create the amino acid sequence of a polypeptide.

The "**central dogma** of molecular biology" describes the primary ways in which information flows in a cell: from DNA to DNA, from DNA to RNA, and from RNA to protein (**Figure 14.3**). We have already discussed replication (see Key Concept 13.3) and now turn to transcription and translation.

Figure 14.3 The Central Dogma of Molecular Biology
The central dogma describes the primary ways in which information flows in the cell: from DNA to DNA, from DNA to RNA and from RNA to protein (solid lines). Information is stored in DNA and copied during replication. Certain DNA sequences are transcribed into RNA, and some RNA sequences are translated into amino acid sequences. Substantially less common, RNA replication (in some RNA viruses) and synthesis of DNA from RNA (reverse transcription) can occur (dashed lines). In no case is amino acid information used to synthesize RNA.

Q: Have you seen any examples in previous chapters where information flow does not follow the central dogma (dashed lines)?

Three types of RNA have roles in the information flow from DNA to protein

There are numerous types of RNA. Three of them have vital roles in gene expression and represent the most common RNAs in a typical cell.

MESSENGER RNA When a protein-coding gene is expressed, one of the two DNA strands in the gene is transcribed to produce a complementary RNA strand, which in eukaryotic cells is then processed to produce **messenger RNA (mRNA)**. In eukaryotic cells, the mRNA travels from the nucleus to the cytoplasm, where it is translated into a polypeptide (**Figure 14.4**). The nucleotide sequence of the mRNA determines the ordered sequence of amino acids in the polypeptide chain, which is synthesized by a ribosome. mRNAs represent about 5% of the RNA in a cell.

RIBOSOMAL RNA The **ribosome** is essentially a protein synthesis factory composed of multiple proteins and several **ribosomal RNAs (rRNAs)**. One of the rRNAs catalyzes peptide bond formation between amino acids, to form a polypeptide. rRNAs represent about 80% of the RNA in a cell.

TRANSFER RNA Another type of RNA called **transfer RNA (tRNA)** can both bind a specific amino acid and recognize specific sequences of nucleotides in mRNA. It is the tRNA that recognizes which amino acid should be added next to a growing polypeptide chain. tRNAs represent about 15% of the RNA in a cell.

 Media Clip 14.1 Protein Synthesis: An Epic on a Cellular Level Life12e.com/mc14.1

Figure 14.4 From Gene to Protein This diagram summarizes the processes of gene expression in eukaryotes. Note that the nucleus is typically about one-fourth the size shown here.

Q: In general, how would this diagram be different for a prokaryotic cell?

 View in Achieve
Activity 14.1 Eukaryotic Gene Expression

In some cases, RNA determines the sequence of RNA or DNA

While we have said that DNA is the genetic material, some viruses present exceptions to this aspect of the central dogma. As we saw in Key Concept 13.1, a virus is a non-cellular infectious particle that reproduces inside cells. Many viruses, such as the ones that cause influenza and polio, have RNA rather than DNA as their genetic material. That is, the nucleotide sequence of viral RNA acts as an information carrier and can be expressed as a protein. Because RNA is usually single-stranded, the question arises: how do these viruses replicate? More specifically, how do they duplicate their genetic material? Most viruses replicate by transcribing from RNA to RNA, making an RNA strand that is complementary to their genomes. This "opposite" strand is then used to make multiple copies of the viral genome.

Not all viruses whose genomes consist of RNA replicate by transcribing from RNA to RNA. Some, such as human immunodeficiency viruses (HIVs) and certain rare tumor viruses, make a DNA copy of their genome after infecting a host cell. This DNA copy is then incorporated into the host's genome. Synthesis of

DNA from RNA is called **reverse transcription**, and viruses that employ this kind of transcription are called **retroviruses**. Retroviruses rely on the host cell's transcription machinery to make more RNA. This RNA can either be translated to produce viral proteins, or incorporated as the viral genome into new viral particles. You might also recall that telomerase extends telomeres by synthesizing DNA from an RNA template and is thus another example of reverse transcription.

KEY CONCEPT
14.2 Recap and Assess

The expression of protein-coding genes can be broken down into two fundamental steps: transcription and translation. In transcription one strand of DNA is used to produce a complementary mRNA, whose sequence determines the mature mRNA transcript. The mRNA sequence determines the order of amino acids in a polypeptide. Translation is the process by which this information in mRNA is converted into a polypeptide chain.

1. What is the central dogma of molecular biology?
2. Do retroviruses violate the central dogma? Explain.

We will revisit viral genetics in later chapters (in Key Concepts 16.3 and 24.4). In the rest of this chapter we focus on gene expression in prokaryotes and eukaryotes. Understanding this process is essential for understanding how organisms function at the molecular level and is key to the application of biology to human welfare, in areas such as agriculture and medicine. We'll begin by describing how the information in DNA is transcribed to produce RNA.

KEY CONCEPT **DNA Is Transcribed to**
14.3 **Produce RNA**

Learning Objectives

14.3.1 Describe characteristics of RNA polymerases.
14.3.2 Describe the function of the promoter and terminator sequences in transcription.

The synthesis of RNA is directed by DNA. The base sequence of one strand of DNA is used as a template for RNA synthesis, so that the RNA made is complementary in sequence to that DNA strand, with the exception that in RNA there is uracil (U) instead of thymine (T) and in RNA the sugar is ribose instead of deoxyribose. It is important to realize that although the RNA made is a mirror image of its DNA template, the RNA has the same sequence as the other, non-template strand of DNA. So the information content of DNA is indeed preserved in RNA. Since the sequence of nucleotides in the non-template strand is the same as in the protein-coding RNA (except with Ts instead of Us) it is usually referred to as the coding strand.

Transcription—the formation of a specific RNA sequence from a specific DNA sequence—requires several components:

• A DNA template for complementary base pairing—one of the two strands of DNA

TABLE **14.1** Some RNAs in Eukaryotic Cells		
RNA type	Location of activity	Role
Ribosomal RNA (rRNA)	Cytoplasm (ribosome)	Component of ribosome, catalysis of peptide bond formation
Messenger RNA (mRNA)	Cytoplasm	Carrier of protein-coding sequence
Transfer RNA (tRNA)	Cytoplasm	Intermediary between mRNA and protein sequences
MicroRNA (miRNA)	Nucleus and cytoplasm	Regulates mRNA stability and translation
Small interfering RNA (siRNA)	Nucleus and cytoplasm	Regulates stability of other RNAs
Small nuclear RNA (snRNA)	Nucleus	Mediates mRNA processing

- The four ribonucleoside triphosphates ATP, GTP, CTP, and UTP, to act as substrates
- An RNA polymerase enzyme
- Salts and a pH buffer to create an appropriate chemical environment for RNA polymerase (if transcription is performed in a test tube)

Several kinds of RNA are made from DNA templates. The most important from a genetic point of view is mRNA. But transcription also produces tRNA and rRNA, whose roles in protein synthesis are described in Key Concept 14.6. Like polypeptides, these last two RNAs are encoded by specific genes. Eukaryotes also make many kinds of small RNAs, including small nuclear RNA (snRNA), microRNA (miRNA), and small interfering RNA (siRNA), which are also transcribed. Table 14.1 summarizes some of the RNAs found in eukaryotic cells. We will discuss the roles of miRNA and siRNA in Chapter 16.

RNA polymerases share common features

RNA polymerases from both prokaryotes and eukaryotes catalyze the synthesis of RNA from the DNA template. There is only one kind of RNA polymerase in bacteria, whereas there are several kinds in eukaryotes; however, they all share a common structure (**Figure 14.5**). Like DNA polymerases, RNA polymerases catalyze the addition of nucleotides in a 5′-to-3′ direction, but unlike DNA polymerases (see Figure 13.12), RNA polymerases *do not require a primer*.

Transcription occurs in three steps

Transcription can be divided into three distinct processes: (1) initiation, (2) elongation, and (3) termination. Follow these processes in **Figure 14.6**.

INITIATION Transcription begins when RNA polymerase binds to a special sequence of DNA called a **promoter** (see Figure 14.6A). Eukaryotic genes generally have one promoter each, whereas in prokaryotes and viruses, several genes often share one promoter. Promoters are important control sequences that "tell" the RNA polymerase two things:

1. Where to start transcription
2. Which strand of DNA to transcribe

A promoter has directionality, so the RNA polymerase is oriented to the appropriate strand to use as a template. The promoter also determines the **initiation site**, where transcription begins. Groups of nucleotides lying "upstream" from the initiation site (5′ on the coding strand and 3′ on the template strand) help the RNA polymerase bind. Other proteins, which can bind to specific DNA sequences and to RNA polymerase, help direct the polymerase onto the promoter. These proteins, which include **sigma factors** in prokaryotes and **transcription factors** in eukaryotes, help determine the specific genes that are expressed at a particular time in the cell.

Although every gene has a promoter, not all promoters are identical. Some are more effective at transcription initiation than others. Furthermore, there are differences between transcription initiation in prokaryotes and in eukaryotes. We will discuss promoters and their roles in regulating gene expression in Chapter 16.

ELONGATION After RNA polymerase has bound to the promoter, it begins the process of **elongation** (see Figure 14.6B). DNA unwinds about ten base pairs at a time, and RNA polymerase

RNA

Single-stranded DNA

RNA polymerase

Double-stranded DNA

This icon for RNA polymerase will be used in the figures that follow.

Figure 14.5 RNA Polymerase Interacting with DNA The RNA polymerase enzyme depicted (in yellow-brown) is from bacteriophage T7, but it is representative of most other RNA polymerases. The inset indicates how this enzyme will be represented in the figures that follow. (RNA polymerase by David McIntyre based on data from PDB ID: 1MSW. Y. W. Yin and T. A. Steitz. 2002. *Science* 298: 1387–1395.)

Figure 14.6 DNA Is Transcribed to Form RNA   DNA is locally unwound by RNA polymerase, and one strand then serves as a template for RNA synthesis. The RNA transcript is formed and then peels away, allowing the DNA that has already been transcribed to rewind into a double helix. Three distinct processes—initiation (**A**), elongation (**B**), and termination (**C**)—constitute transcription. RNA polymerase is larger in reality than indicated here (see Figure 14.5).

Q: Comparing RNA synthesis with DNA replication, what are the common features?

▶ **View in Achieve**
Animation 14.1 Transcription

1 RNA polymerase binds to the promoter and starts to unwind the DNA strands.

(A) Initiation

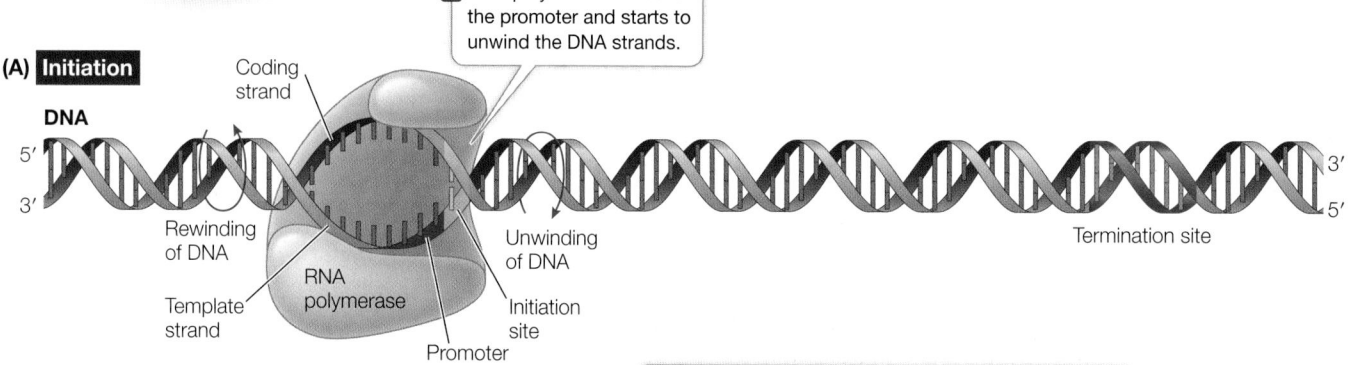

2 RNA polymerase moves along the DNA template strand from 3′ to 5′ and produces the RNA transcript by adding nucleotides complementary to the DNA template to the 3′ end of the growing RNA.

(B) Elongation

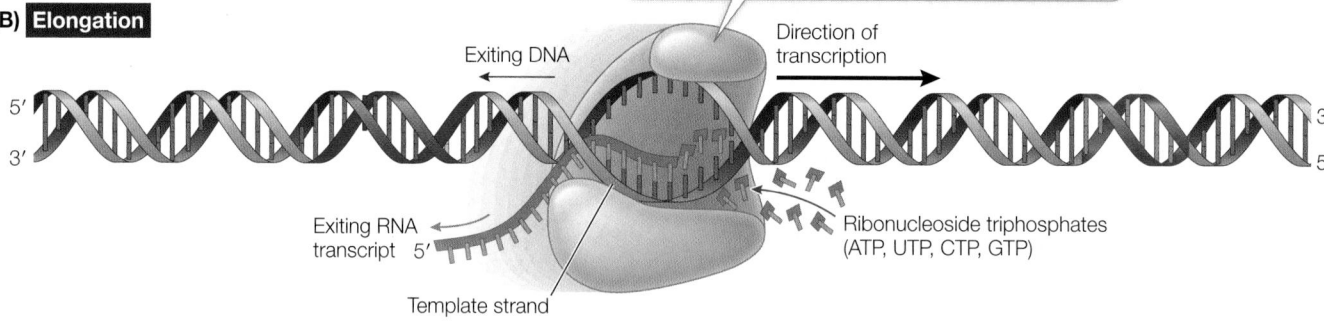

3 When RNA polymerase reaches the termination site, the RNA transcript and polymerase are released from the template.

(C) Termination

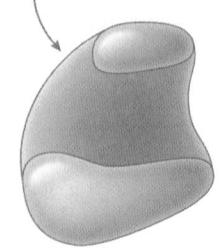

reads the template strand in the 3′-to-5′ direction. The first nucleotide in the new RNA forms its 5′ end, and subsequent nucleotides complementary to the DNA template are added to its 3′ end. Thus the RNA transcript is antiparallel to the DNA template strand.

You may recall from Key Concept 13.3 that DNA polymerase uses dNTPs (deoxyribonucleoside triphosphates) as substrates, and forms covalent bonds between each incoming dNTP and the 3′ end of the growing polynucleotide chain (see Figure 13.10). Energy released by the removal of two phosphate groups from the dNTP is used to drive the reaction. Similarly, RNA polymerase uses (ribo)nucleoside triphosphates (NTPs) as substrates, removing two phosphate groups from each substrate molecule and using the released energy to drive the polymerization reaction.

Because RNA polymerases do not proofread, transcription errors occur at a rate of one for every 10^4 to 10^5 bases. Because many copies of RNA are made, however, and because they often have only a relatively short life span, these errors are not as potentially harmful as mutations in DNA.

TERMINATION   Just as initiation sites in the DNA template strand specify the starting point for transcription, particular base sequences specify its **termination** (see Figure 14.6C). In prokaryotes there are two mechanisms for ending transcription. For some genes, the newly formed transcript folds back on itself and forms internal hydrogen bonds between bases. A loop forms, and this structure causes the transcript to fall away from the DNA template and the RNA polymerase. In other cases a protein binds to specific sequences on the transcript and causes the RNA to detach from the DNA template. Eukaryotes terminate transcription using methods that are similar to, but more complicated than, those found in prokaryotes.

KEY CONCEPT
14.3 Recap and Assess

Transcription, which is catalyzed by an RNA polymerase, proceeds in three steps: initiation, elongation, and termination.

1. Describe the actions of RNA polymerase during transcription.
2. Knocking out (rendering nonfunctional) a particular protein in a bacterium causes many, but not all, genes to produce longer mRNAs. Explain this result.
3. Errors in RNA transcription occur about 100,000 times more often than errors in DNA replication. Why can this higher rate be tolerated in RNA but not in DNA synthesis?

The general features of transcription that we have described were first elucidated in model prokaryotes, such as *E. coli*. Biologists then used the same methods to analyze this process in eukaryotes and found that there are some notable (and important) differences. We turn now to a more detailed description of eukaryotic gene expression.

KEY CONCEPT
14.4
Eukaryotic Pre-mRNA Transcripts Are Processed prior to Translation

Learning Objectives

14.4.1 Describe the mRNA processing steps in eukaryotes.

14.4.2 Predict the outcome of a defect in mRNA processing in a eukaryotic cell.

14.4.3 Compare the features of a eukaryotic gene with its mature mRNA transcript.

The process of gene expression from DNA to protein is essentially the same in eukaryotes as it is in prokaryotes. In the last key concept we described the basic features of transcription that are common to both. Here we focus on the differences, listed in **Table 14.2**, between prokaryotic and eukaryotic gene transcription.

In prokaryotes and eukaryotes, the sequence of an mRNA that reaches the ribosome is complementary to the sequence of a gene in the organism's DNA. One way to show this is by the technique of **nucleic acid hybridization**, shown in **Figure 14.7A**. This technique involves two steps:

1. A sample of chromosomal DNA containing the gene is denatured to break the hydrogen bonds between the base pairs and separate the two strands.
2. The single-stranded mRNA (called a **probe**) is incubated with the denatured DNA. If the probe has a base sequence complementary to the target DNA, a probe–target double helix forms by hydrogen bonding between the bases. Because the two strands are from different sources, the resulting double-stranded region is called a hybrid.

Hybridization experiments can be performed with various combinations of DNA and RNA (RNA as target and DNA as probe; DNA as both target and probe, etc.). In many hybridization experiments,

---

TABLE **14.2** | Differences between Prokaryotic and Eukaryotic Gene Expression		
Characteristic	**Prokaryotes**	**Eukaryotes**
Transcription and translation occurrence	At the same time, in the cytoplasm	Transcription in the nucleus, then translation in the cytoplasm
Gene structure	DNA sequence aligns perfectly with mRNA sequence	Regions of DNA in gene do not align with mature RNA (introns), and RNA 3′ region does not align with DNA (poly A tail)
Modification of mRNA after initial transcription but before translation	Usually none	Introns spliced out; 5′ end cap and 3′ poly A tail added

(A) The process of nucleic acid hybridization

(B) Hybridization experiments reveal noncoding introns in eukaryotic genes

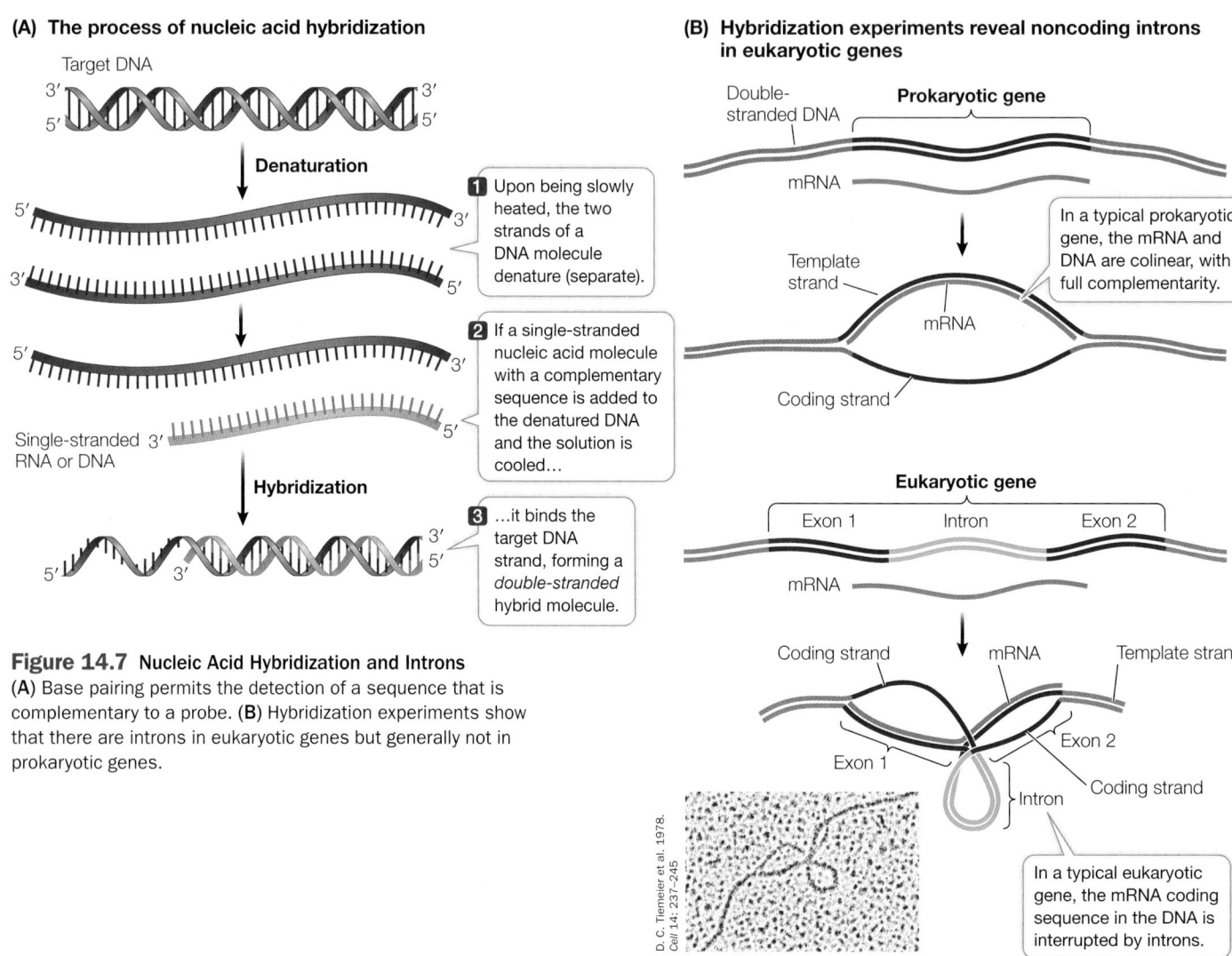

Figure 14.7 Nucleic Acid Hybridization and Introns
(A) Base pairing permits the detection of a sequence that is complementary to a probe. **(B)** Hybridization experiments show that there are introns in eukaryotic genes but generally not in prokaryotic genes.

the probe is labeled in some way so that its binding to a specific target sequence can be detected. The double-stranded hybrids can also be viewed by electron microscopy.

Noncoding sequences called introns often appear between genes in eukaryotic chromosomes

Differences between prokaryotic and eukaryotic transcription are revealed when mRNA probes from prokaryotes and eukaryotes are incubated with their respective chromosomal DNAs:

- In prokaryotes (**Figure 14.7B, top**) there is usually a 1:1 linear complementarity between the base sequence of the mRNA at the ribosome and that of the chromosomal DNA.

- In eukaryotes (**Figure 14.7B, bottom**) one or more non-hybridized DNA loops are often observed sticking out of the mRNA–DNA hybrid, indicating that there are stretches of DNA sequence that do not have a complementary sequence in the mRNA that is translated at the ribosome.

The discovery that some stretches of eukaryotic DNA sequence are not present in the mRNA that reaches the ribosome for translation

initiated the question of whether this "extra" DNA actually gets transcribed. Does transcription somehow skip these sequences, or are they transcribed and then edited out of the mRNA transcript before it arrives at the ribosome? To find out, an experiment can be conducted in which the initial mRNA transcript in the cell nucleus—the **precursor mRNA**, or **pre-mRNA** (see Figure 14.4)— is hybridized with chromosomal DNA. This experiment shows full, linear, loop-free hybridization between the pre-mRNA and the template DNA, allowing us to conclude that the noncoding, intervening regions of DNA, known as **introns**, do get transcribed but are then spliced out of the pre-mRNA in the nucleus. The remaining sequences (**exons**) make up the mRNA that reaches the ribosome. The step of splicing out the introns is one of the steps in **RNA processing** (Figure 14.8).

Introns *interrupt, but do not scramble*, the DNA sequence of a gene. The base sequences of the exons in the template strand, if joined and taken in order, form a continuous sequence that is complementary to that of the mature mRNA. In some cases the separated exons often encode different functional regions, or **domains**, of the protein. For example, the globin polypeptides that make up

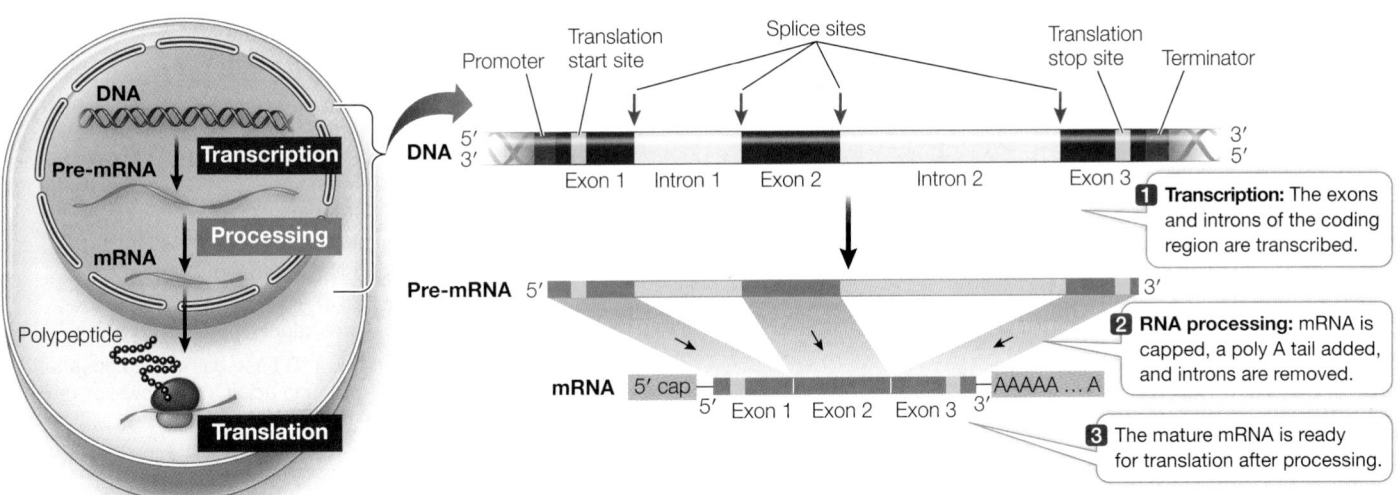

Figure 14.8 Transcription of a Eukaryotic Gene The β-globin gene diagrammed here is about 1,700 base pairs (bp) long. The three exons contain the sequence encoding 147 amino acids plus a signal (translation stop site) to terminate translation. The two introns—noncoding sequences of DNA containing almost 1,000 bp among them—are initially transcribed but are spliced out of the pre-mRNA transcript during processing.

hemoglobin each have two domains: one for binding to a nonprotein pigment called heme, and another for binding to the other globin subunits. These two domains are encoded by different exons in the globin genes. Most (but not all) eukaryotic genes contain introns, and in rare cases, introns are also found in prokaryotes. Introns can be numerous and large, though the average human gene has only eight, each with an average length of 3,300 bp. The largest human gene encodes a muscle protein called titin; it has 365 exons, which together code for 24,000–36,000 amino acids.

Pre-mRNA processing prepares the mRNA transcript for translation

The transcript of a eukaryotic gene is modified in several ways before it leaves the nucleus: both ends of the pre-mRNA are modified, and the introns are removed.

MODIFICATION AT BOTH ENDS Two steps in the processing of pre-mRNA take place in the nucleus, one at each end of the molecule (**Figure 14.9**):

1. A **5′ cap** is added to the 5′ end of the pre-mRNA as it is transcribed. The 5′ cap, which is a chemically modified molecule of guanosine triphosphate (GTP), facilitates the binding of mRNA to the ribosome for translation, and it protects the mRNA from being digested by ribonucleases that break down RNAs.

2. A **poly A tail** is added to the 3′ end of the pre-mRNA at the end of transcription. Transcription ends downstream of the protein-coding region in DNA. In eukaryotes there is usually a "polyadenylation" sequence (AAUAAA) near the 3′ end of the pre-mRNA,

downstream of the protein-coding region. This sequence acts as a signal for an enzyme to cut the pre-mRNA. Immediately after this cleavage, another enzyme adds 100 to 300 adenine nucleotides (the poly A tail) to the 3′ end of the pre-mRNA. This tail helps in the export of mature mRNA from the nucleus and is important for mRNA recognition and stability in the cytosol.

SPLICING TO REMOVE INTRONS Within the nucleus, a process called **RNA splicing** removes the introns and splices the exons together. You can follow the steps of this important process in **Figure 14.10**. There are specific sequences that are commonly found in introns (consensus sequences) that allow the splicing machinery to identify and precisely remove introns from pre-mRNAs. The splicing machinery includes proteins and RNA–protein complexes called small nuclear ribonucleoproteins (snRNPs) that together recognize and cut out each intron.

Molecular studies of human genetic diseases have provided insights into RNA splicing. For example, people with the genetic

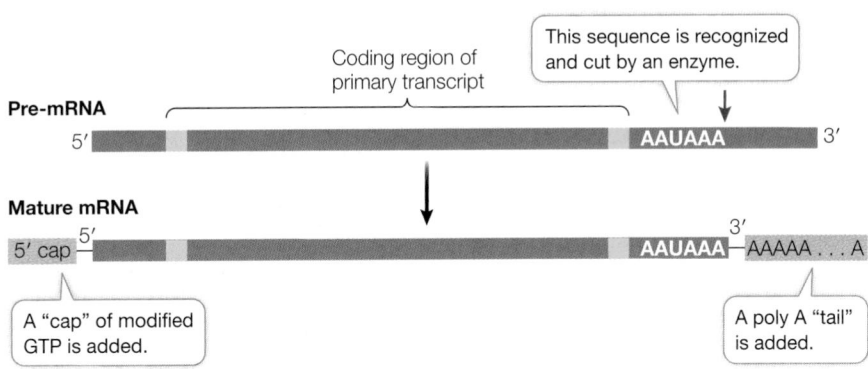

Figure 14.9 Processing the Ends of Eukaryotic Pre-mRNA Modifications at each end of the pre-mRNA transcript—the 5′ cap and the poly A tail—are important for mRNA function.

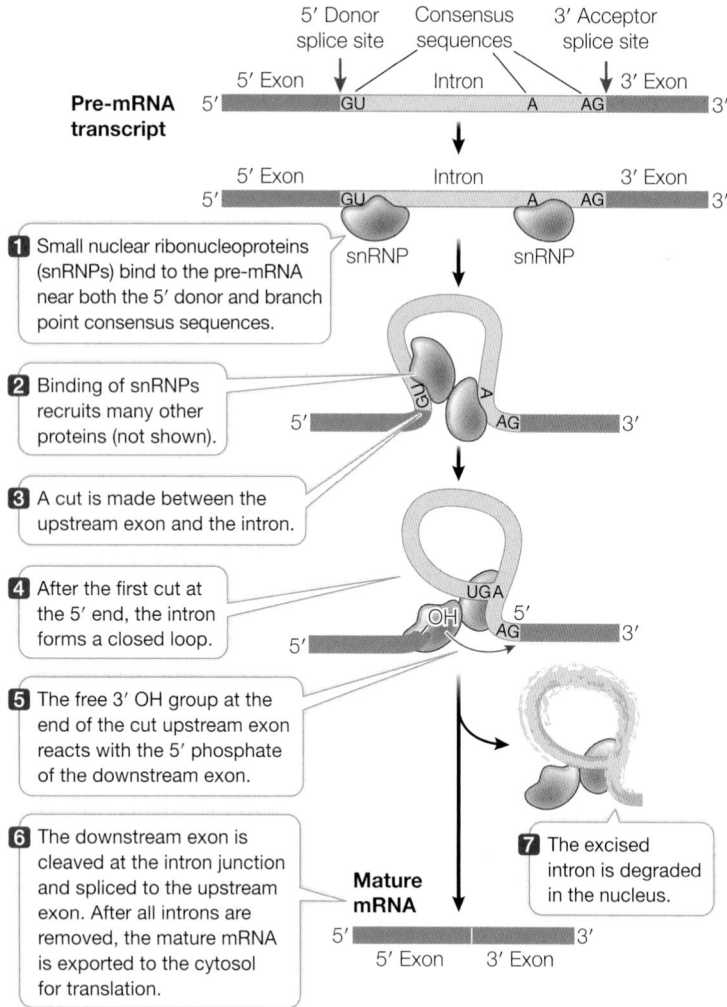

5′ Donor splice site   Consensus sequences   3′ Acceptor splice site

5′ Exon   Intron   3′ Exon

Pre-mRNA transcript   5′ —GU——A——AG— 3′

5′ Exon   Intron   3′ Exon

5′ —GU——A——AG— 3′

snRNP   snRNP

1 Small nuclear ribonucleoproteins (snRNPs) bind to the pre-mRNA near both the 5′ donor and branch point consensus sequences.

2 Binding of snRNPs recruits many other proteins (not shown).

3 A cut is made between the upstream exon and the intron.

4 After the first cut at the 5′ end, the intron forms a closed loop.

5 The free 3′ OH group at the end of the cut upstream exon reacts with the 5′ phosphate of the downstream exon.

6 The downstream exon is cleaved at the intron junction and spliced to the upstream exon. After all introns are removed, the mature mRNA is exported to the cytosol for translation.

7 The excised intron is degraded in the nucleus.

Mature mRNA

5′ —————— 3′
5′ Exon   3′ Exon

Figure 14.10 RNA Splicing The binding of snRNPs to consensus sequences bordering the introns on the pre-mRNA results in a series of proteins binding and cutting the pre-mRNA with great precision.

View in Achieve
Animation 14.2 RNA Splicing

disease beta thalassemia have a defect in the production of one of the hemoglobin subunits. These people suffer from severe anemia because they have an inadequate amount of hemoglobin in their red blood cells. In some cases, the genetic mutation that causes the disease occurs at an intron consensus sequence, where the splicing machinery binds to the RNA (see Figure 14.10, step 1) in the β-globin gene. Consequently, β-globin pre-mRNA is spliced incorrectly, and the resulting mRNA encodes a nonfunctional polypeptide.

After processing is completed in the nucleus, the mature mRNA has a polypeptide-coding region that will be translated by ribosomes, a 5′ untranslated region (upstream of the polypeptide-coding region), and a 3′ untranslated region (downstream of the polypeptide-coding region). The mature mRNA moves out into the cytosol through the nuclear pores. A protein bound to the 5′ nucleotide cap during processing is recognized by a receptor at the nuclear pore, stimulating export. Unprocessed or incompletely processed pre-mRNAs remain in the nucleus.

KEY CONCEPT
14.4 Recap and Assess

Most eukaryotic genes contain noncoding sequences called introns, which are removed from the pre-mRNA transcript in the nucleus. The mature mRNA transcript with 5′ cap and 3′ tail is then exported through a nuclear pore to ribosomes in the cytosol where translation takes place.

1. How and why is the pre-mRNA transcript modified at the 5′ and 3′ ends during mRNA processing?
2. Outline the steps involved in RNA splicing. What are the consequences if it does not happen correctly?
3. A eukaryotic gene that is 1,440 base pairs long codes for a polypeptide that is 192 amino acids long. However, only 576 base pairs encode the polypeptide. Discuss the discrepancy.

Transcription and posttranscriptional events produce an mRNA that is ready to be translated into a sequence of amino acids in a polypeptide. We turn now to the relationship between mRNA sequence and amino acid sequence.

KEY CONCEPT
14.5
The Genetic Code Determines the Protein Sequence Encoded by an mRNA

Learning Objectives

14.5.1 Use the genetic code table to determine the amino acid sequence encoded by an mRNA sequence.

14.5.2 Define redundancy in the genetic code.

14.5.3 Distinguish between sense and nonsense, or stop, codons.

The **genetic code** is the informational key by which a sequence of mRNA nucleotides corresponding to a gene is translated into the sequence of amino acids composing the protein expressed by that gene. That is, the genetic code specifies which amino acids will be used to build a protein. You can think of the code as consisting of a series of sequential, non-overlapping, three-letter "words." The three "letters" represent three adjacent nucleotide bases in the mRNA polynucleotide. Each three-letter "word" is called a **codon**, and each codon specifies a particular amino acid. Each codon is complementary to the corresponding triplet of bases in the DNA molecule from which it was transcribed. In short, the genetic code relates codons to their specifically encoded amino acids.

The genetic code is redundant but not ambiguous

Molecular biologists "broke" the genetic code in the early 1960s. The problem they addressed was perplexing: how could more than 20 "code words" be written with an "alphabet" consisting of only four "letters"? In other words, how could four bases (A, U, G, and C) code for 20 different amino acids?

A triplet code, based on three-letter codons, was considered likely. Since there are only four letters (A, G, C, and U), a one-letter code clearly could not unambiguously encode 20 amino acids; it could encode only four of them. A two-letter code could have only 4 × 4 = 16 unambiguous codons—still not enough. But a triplet code could have 4 × 4 × 4 = 64 codons, more than enough to encode the 20 amino acids.

Marshall W. Nirenberg and J. Heinrich Matthaei, at the U.S. National Institutes of Health, made the first decoding breakthrough in 1961 when they realized that the code would be easier to break if they were working with a very simple, known mRNA sequence rather than with a complex natural mRNA molecule. They set out to synthesize mRNA molecules consisting of just one type of nucleotide base; poly U mRNA, for example, consisted of just uracil nucleotides. Nirenberg and Matthaei's goal was to then identify, through a translation process conducted in a test tube, the polypeptide that the artificial messenger encoded. Their experiment, which is laid out in **Investigating Life: Deciphering the Genetic Code**, led to the identification of the first codons. Soon after this experiment, the rest of the code was identified. This was a major achievement, linking the information in DNA (the gene) to its expression in a protein (the phenotype). The understanding that the amino acids for each protein are spelled out via codons not only led to our understanding of the fundamentals of genetics and mutation, but to investigations into the genetic underpinnings of disease, such as the development of resistance in MRSA described in the opening of this chapter.

View in Achieve
Animation 14.3
Deciphering the Genetic Code

The complete genetic code is shown in **Figure 14.11**. Notice that there are many more codons than there are different amino acids in proteins. Proteins are built from just 20 amino acids, but all possible combinations of the four available "letters" (the bases) yield 64 (4^3) different three-letter codons. Why are there more codons than amino acids? One reason is that there is more than one codon for almost all amino acids. For example, leucine is represented by six different codons (see Figure 14.11). Only methionine and tryptophan are represented by just one codon each. Thus we say that the genetic code is redundant (or degenerate). Also, a few select codons serve functions other than coding for amino acids. AUG, for example, not only codes for methionine but is also the **start codon**, the initiation signal for translation. Sixty one codons encode amino acid information and are termed **sense codons**. Three codons (UAA, UAG, UGA) do not encode amino acid information and are termed **nonsense** or **stop codons**, as they act as termination signals for translation. When the translation machinery reaches one of these codons, translation stops and the polypeptide is released from the translation complex.

Don't confuse a *redundant* code with an *ambiguous* code. If the code were ambiguous, a single codon could specify two (or more) different amino acids, and there would be doubt about which amino acid should be incorporated into a growing polypeptide chain. Redundancy in the code simply means there is more than one clear way to say "Put leucine here." The genetic code is not ambiguous: a given amino acid may be encoded by more than one codon, but a codon can code for only one amino acid.

The genetic code is (nearly) universal

One of the most amazing discoveries following the deciphering of the genetic code in bacteria was that the genetic code is essentially identical across all the species on our planet. Thus the code must be an ancient one that has been maintained intact throughout the evolution of living organisms. Exceptions are known: for example, the code for mitochondrial DNA (see Key Concept 12.5) and for chloroplast DNA differs slightly from that used by prokaryotes and for the nuclear DNA of eukaryotic cells; and in one group of protists, UAA and UAG code for glutamine rather than for stop codons. The significance of these differences is not yet clear. What is clear is that the exceptions are exceedingly few, and involve only a few codons when present.

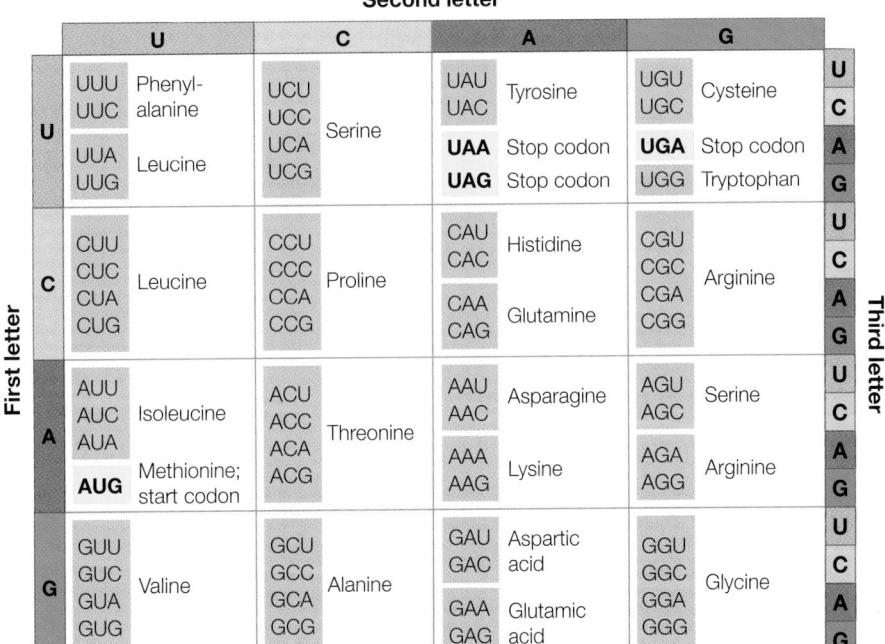

Figure 14.11 The Genetic Code Genetic information is encoded in mRNA in three-letter units—codons—made up of nucleoside monophosphates with the bases uracil (U), cytosine (C), adenine (A), and guanine (G) and is read in a 5′-to-3′ direction on mRNA. To decode a codon, find its first letter in the left column, then read across the top to its second letter, then read down the right column to its third letter. The amino acid the codon specifies is given in the corresponding row. For example, AUG codes for methionine, and GUA codes for valine.

View in Achieve
Activity 14.2 The Genetic Code

▶Investigating LIFE   Deciphering the Genetic Code

Experiment

Original Paper: M. Nirenberg and J. H. Matthaei. 1961. The dependence of cell-free protein synthesis in *E. coli* upon naturally occurring or synthetic polyribonucleotides. *Proc Natl Acad Sci USA* 47: 1588–1602.

Nirenberg and Matthaei used a test tube protein synthesis system to determine the amino acids specified by synthetic mRNAs of known compositions.

HYPOTHESIS▶ An artificial mRNA containing only one repeating base will direct the synthesis of a protein containing only one repeating amino acid.

METHOD▶

Prepare a bacterial extract containing all the components needed to make proteins except mRNA.

+ poly U ◁ Add an artificial mRNA containing only one repeating base. ▷ + poly C

U U U U U U U U U   C C C C C C C C C

RESULTS▶

Phe Phe Phe   Pro Pro Pro

The polypeptide produced contains a single amino acid.

CONCLUSION▶ Poly U contains codons for phenylalanine. Poly C contains codons for proline.

Work with the Data

After the relationship between DNA and proteins was established, genetic evidence pointed to triplets of nucleotides on RNA specifying each amino acid. The race was on to identify which triplet coded for which amino acid. Test tube systems were developed in which cell extracts were made and protein synthesis occurred. Marshall Nirenberg, a scientist at the U.S. National Institutes of Health, and J. Heinrich Matthaei, a postdoctoral fellow from Germany, made a synthetic RNA consisting of the base uracil only (called poly U, codon UUU) and tested it in 20 tubes. Each test tube was supplied with all 20 amino acids, but in each one a different amino acid was tagged with a radioactive marker. In each tube the same polypeptide was made: a protein consisting of the amino acid phenylalanine bonded repeatedly to itself. However, only in the test tube with radiolabeled phenylalanine was the resulting protein radioactive.

Go to **Achieve** for a companion Data in Depth exercise.

QUESTIONS▶

1. Poly U, an artificial mRNA, was added to a test tube with radio-labeled phenylalanine and all the other components for protein synthesis ("complete system"). Other test tubes differed from the complete system as indicated in the table. Samples were tested for incorporation of radioactivity into the resulting protein, with the results in **Table A**. Explain the results for each of the conditions.

Table A

Condition	Counts/minute (units of radioactivity)
Complete system	29,500
Minus poly U mRNA	70
Minus ribosomes	52
Minus ATP	83
Plus RNase (hydrolyzes RNA)	120
Plus DNase (hydrolyzes DNA)	27,600
Complete system minus all amino acids except radioactive phenylalanine	31,700

2. Poly U (red dots) was added to the test tubes and then samples were tested for protein synthesis by radioactive amino acid incorporation after various times (and were compared with results of a control run, in which no RNA was added, indicated by blue dots). The results are shown in the graph. What do these data show about the dependence of protein synthesis on added RNA?

3. The experiment described in Question 2 was repeated with different amino acids; the results are in **Table B**. Explain these results in terms of the codon specificity of poly U.

Table B

Radioactive amino acid(s)	Counts/minute/ mg protein (radioactivity level)
Phenylalanine	38,300
Glycine, alanine, serine, aspartic acid, glutamic acid	33
Leucine, isoleucine, threonine, methionine, arginine, histidine, valine, lysine, tyrosine, proline, tryptophan	899
Cysteine	113

Connect the Concepts As discussed in Key Concept 12.5, some cytoplasmic organelles, notably the mitochondria and chloroplasts, contain small numbers of genes that are remnants of the genomes of the prokaryotes that eventually gave rise to these organelles. The evolutionary process of endosymbiosis that is responsible for the assimilation of these organelles into eukaryotic cells is discussed in Key Concept 26.1.

A common genetic code suggests that it originated early in the evolution of life and is shared by descent from these early species. The common code has profound implications for genetic engineering, as we will see in Chapter 18, since it means that the code for a human gene is the same as that for a bacterial gene. It is therefore impressive, but not surprising, that a human gene can be quite easily expressed in *E. coli* via laboratory manipulations, since these cells speak the same "molecular language."

The codons illustrated in the Nirenberg and Matthaei experiment in Investigating Life: Deciphering the Genetic Code are mRNA codons. The base sequence of the template DNA strand that is transcribed to produce the mRNA is complementary and antiparallel to these codons. Thus, for example, 3'-AAA-5' in the template DNA strand corresponds to phenylalanine (which is encoded by the mRNA codon 5'-UUU-3'). In contrast, the coding strand of DNA has the same sequence as the mRNA (but with T's instead of U's). By convention, DNA sequences are usually shown beginning with the 5' end of the coding sequence.

You might be thinking that in a long DNA molecule with many protein-coding regions, one strand is the coding strand for all the genes and the other strand is the template strand. In fact, some genes are transcribed from one strand and some genes are transcribed from the other. There is strand switching along a long DNA molecule in terms of the roles of the two strands. So while it is incorrect to say that one strand is "the" coding strand for all genes in a particular DNA molecule, it is correct to say that for a given gene one strand is coding and the other is template.

KEY CONCEPT

14.5 Recap and Assess

The genetic code relates the information in mRNA (as a linear sequence of codons) to protein (a linear sequence of amino acids).

1. Explain why the genetic code has triplets (e.g., AUA) of nucleotides, rather than singlets (e.g., A) or doublets (e.g., AU).

2. Explain what it means to say the genetic code is redundant.

3. A short mRNA is translated into the following peptide: methionine-tryptophan-tryptophan-glycine-tryptophan. What are the possible sequences of mRNAs (from start to stop) that could encode this peptide?

Now that we understand the rules by which mRNA encodes protein information, let's see how the cell is able to synthesize proteins from mRNA molecules using the genetic code.

KEY CONCEPT **The Coding Sequence in**
14.6 **mRNA Is Translated into**
Proteins by Ribosomes

Learning Objectives

14.6.1 Describe initiation, elongation, and termination of translation.

14.6.2 Explain how tRNAs are able to translate mRNA codons into the corresponding amino acids.

14.6.3 Predict the consequences of an aminoacyl-tRNA synthetase attaching the wrong amino acid to a tRNA.

14.6.4 Describe each step experienced by a tRNA, starting with an uncharged tRNA in the cytosol and ending with the release of the uncharged tRNA from a ribosome.

14.6.5 Explain the biological significance of polysomes.

Transcription uses complementary base pairing to synthesize an mRNA molecule from a DNA template strand. The information in both molecules is equivalent—a sequence of nucleotides. In contrast, translation uses mRNA to synthesize a polypeptide; nucleotide information encodes amino acid information, as we showed with the genetic code. How is this translation accomplished? How is the genetic code "read" by the translation machinery? The answer is a special kind of RNA molecule called transfer RNA (tRNA) that can (1) read mRNA codons and (2) bring the corresponding amino acid to the ribosome.

Once the tRNAs "decode" the mRNA and deliver the appropriate amino acids, components of the ribosome catalyze the formation of peptide bonds between amino acids. Let's now look at how the tRNAs read codons and get the appropriate amino acids into the ribosome.

 View in Achieve
Animation 14.4 Translation

A transfer RNA carries a specific amino acid and binds to a specific mRNA codon

There is at least one specific tRNA molecule for each of the 20 amino acids. Each tRNA has three functions that are fulfilled by its structure and base sequence (**Figure 14.12**):

1. *tRNAs bind to particular amino acids.* Each tRNA binds to a specific enzyme that attaches it to only 1 of the 20 amino acids. The covalent attachment to an amino acid takes place at the 3' end of the tRNA. When it is carrying an amino acid, the tRNA is said to be "charged."

2. *tRNAs bind to mRNA.* At about the midpoint on the tRNA polynucleotide chain there is a triplet of bases called the **anticodon**, which is complementary to the mRNA codon for the particular amino acid that the tRNA carries. For example, the mRNA codon for arginine is 5'-CGG-3', and the complementary tRNA anticodon is 3'-GCC-5'. Like the

Figure 14.12 Transfer RNA The stem and loop structure of a tRNA molecule is well suited to its functions: binding to amino acids, binding to mRNA molecules, and interacting with ribosomes. ("Cloverleaf" model and three-dimensional representation after H. Shi and P. B. Moore. 2000. *RNA* 6: 1091–1105; tRNA space-filling representation by David McIntyre based on data from PDB ID: 1EHZ. H. Shi and P. B. Moore. 2000. *RNA* 6: 1091–1105.)

two strands of DNA, the codon and anticodon bind together via noncovalent hydrogen bonds.

3. *tRNAs interact with ribosomes.* The ribosome has several sites on its surface that just fit the three-dimensional structure of a tRNA molecule. Interaction between the ribosome and the tRNA is noncovalent.

Recall that 61 different codons encode the 20 amino acids in proteins (see Figure 14.11). Does this mean that the cell must produce 61 different tRNA species, each with a different anticodon? No. The cell gets by with about two-thirds of that number of tRNA species because the interaction between the bases at the third position of the codon–anticodon interaction, which is the 3′ end of the codon and the 5′ end of the anticodon, is not as specific as it is for other base pairs. This phenomenon is called wobble base pairing—base pairing that does not strictly follow the standard rules (i.e., A with U, and G with C). Wobble base pairing occurs only at the third position of the codon–anticodon interaction. Sometimes an unusual purine base, inosine (I), which can pair with A, C, and U, is found at the third position. For example, the presence of inosine in the tRNA with the anticodon 3′-UAI-5′ allows it to recognize and bind to the three isoleucine codons: AUU, AUC, and AUA. Wobble base pairing also occurs for some normal bases in the third position; for example, G in the third position of the anticodon can pair with C or U in the codon. Wobble base pairing explains many of the patterns observed in the genetic code (see Figure 14.11); you may have noticed that all codon pairs that start with the same two bases but end in C or U always code for the same amino acid—such codons can be read by tRNAs with a G in their third position. It is important to recognize that wobble base pairing allows fewer tRNAs to read the code than would be required with strict base pairing, but it does not allow the genetic code to be ambiguous. That is, *each mRNA codon can bind only to tRNAs that carry a specific amino acid.*

Each tRNA is specifically attached to an amino acid

The charging of each tRNA with its correct amino acid is achieved by a family of enzymes known as aminoacyl-tRNA synthetases. Each enzyme is specific for one amino acid and for its corresponding tRNA. The reaction uses ATP, forming a high-energy bond between the amino acid and the tRNAs (**Figure 14.13**). The energy in this bond is later used in the formation of peptide bonds between amino acids in a growing polypeptide chain.

The specificity between the tRNA and its corresponding amino acid is essential. For example, tRNAcys (with anticodon ACA), which is the tRNA that carries cysteine, always has cysteine added to it by its synthetase to form cys-tRNAcys. A clever experiment by Seymour Benzer and his colleagues at Purdue University demonstrated the importance of this specificity. They took the cys-tRNAcys molecule and chemically modified the cysteine, converting it into alanine (to form ala-tRNAcys). Which component—the amino acid or the tRNA—would be recognized when this hybrid charged tRNA was put into a protein synthesizing system? The answer was the tRNA. Everywhere in the synthesized protein where cysteine was supposed to be, alanine appeared instead. The cysteine-specific tRNA had delivered its cargo (alanine) to every mRNA codon for cysteine. This experiment showed that the protein synthesis machinery recognizes the anticodon of the charged tRNA, not the amino acid attached to it.

The ribosome is the workbench for translation

The ribosome is the molecular workbench where the task of translation is accomplished. Its structure enables it to hold mRNA

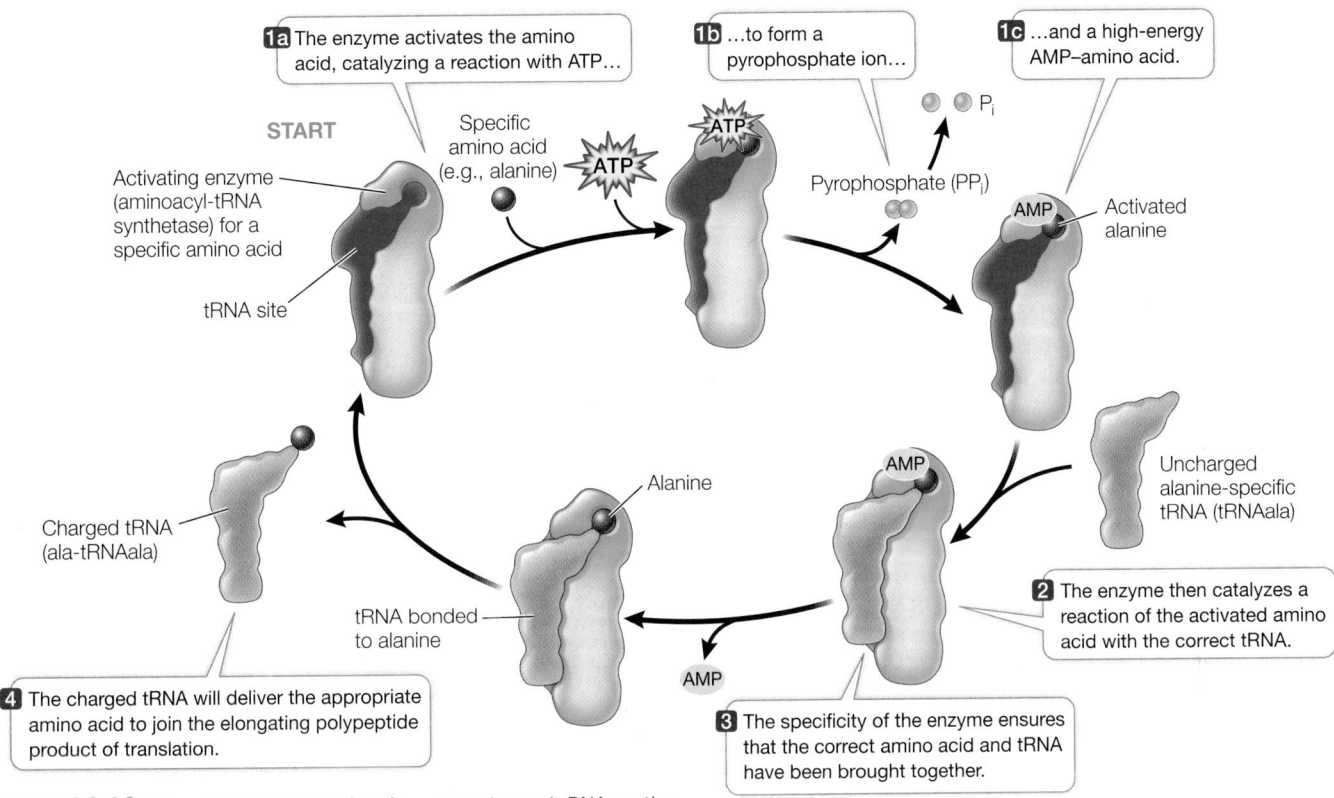

1a The enzyme activates the amino acid, catalyzing a reaction with ATP...

1b ...to form a pyrophosphate ion...

1c ...and a high-energy AMP–amino acid.

START

Specific amino acid (e.g., alanine)

ATP

Pyrophosphate (PP$_i$)

P$_i$

Activating enzyme (aminoacyl-tRNA synthetase) for a specific amino acid

tRNA site

AMP

Activated alanine

Charged tRNA (ala-tRNAala)

Alanine

AMP

Uncharged alanine-specific tRNA (tRNAala)

tRNA bonded to alanine

AMP

2 The enzyme then catalyzes a reaction of the activated amino acid with the correct tRNA.

4 The charged tRNA will deliver the appropriate amino acid to join the elongating polypeptide product of translation.

3 The specificity of the enzyme ensures that the correct amino acid and tRNA have been brought together.

Figure 14.13 Charging a tRNA Molecule   An aminoacyl-tRNA synthetase activates a specific amino acid and charges a specific tRNA with that amino acid.

and charged tRNAs in the correct positions, thus allowing a polypeptide chain to be assembled efficiently. A given ribosome does not specifically produce just one kind of protein. A ribosome can use any mRNA and all species of charged tRNAs, and thus can be used to make many different polypeptide products. Ribosomes can be used over and over again, and there are thousands of them in a typical cell.

Although ribosomes are small relative to other cellular structures, their mass of several million daltons makes them large in comparison with charged tRNAs. Each ribosome consists of two subunits, a large one and a small one (**Figure 14.14**). The two subunits and several dozen other molecules interact noncovalently. In fact, when hydrophobic interactions between the proteins and RNAs are disrupted, the ribosome falls apart. The two subunits separate and all the RNAs and proteins separate from one another. If the disrupting agent is removed, the complex structure self-assembles perfectly! This is amazing: think of throwing the pieces of a jigsaw puzzle up in the air and having them fit together when they land. The ribosome reflects the high specificity of molecular machines in a cell composed of many molecules.

Figure 14.14 Ribosome Structure
Each ribosome consists of a large and a small subunit. The subunits remain separate when they are not being used for protein synthesis. (Left by David McIntyre based on data from PDB 1GIX and 1G1Y. M. M. Yusupov et al. 2001. *Science* 292: 883–896.)

Q: The ribosome consists of several dozen proteins and several RNA molecules, held together noncovalently. What are the chemical forces involved? How can these forces be disrupted and the molecules separated from one another?

Large subunit

Small subunit

Ribosomes are irregularly shaped and composed of two subunits. Each subunit contains rRNA and numerous proteins.

E site   P site   A site

5′   AUG   Start codon   mRNA   3′

There are 3 sites for tRNA binding. Codon–anticodon interactions between tRNA and mRNA occur only at the P and A sites.

E   P   A

In eukaryotes, the large subunit consists of three different molecules of ribosomal RNA (rRNA) and about 45 different protein molecules, arranged in a precise configuration. The small subunit consists of 1 rRNA molecule and about 32 different protein molecules. The exact number of proteins present in each subunit varies a little across species. The ribosomes of prokaryotes are somewhat smaller than those of eukaryotes, and their ribosomal proteins and RNAs are different. Mitochondria and chloroplasts also contain ribosomes, which have features similar to those of prokaryotes (see Chapter 5).

There are three sites to which a tRNA can bind on the large subunit of the ribosome, designated A, P, and E (see Figure 14.14). The mRNA and ribosome move in relation to one another, and as they do so, an initially charged tRNA traverses these three sites in order:

1. The *A (aminoacyl-tRNA) site* is where the charged tRNA anticodon binds to the mRNA codon, thus lining up the correct amino acid to be added to the growing polypeptide chain.

2. The *P (peptidyl-tRNA) site* is where the tRNA carrying the growing peptide chain resides.

3. The *E (exit) site* is where the uncharged tRNA, having given up its amino acid, resides before being released from the ribosome into the cytosol to pick up another amino acid and begin the process again.

The ribosome has a fidelity function that ensures that the mRNA–tRNA interactions are accurate; that is, that a charged tRNA with the correct anticodon (e.g., 3'-UAC-5') forms hydrogen bonds with the appropriate codon in the mRNA (e.g., 5'-AUG-3'). The rRNA of the small ribosomal subunit plays a role in validating the three-base-pair match. If hydrogen bonds have not formed between all three base pairs, the tRNA must be the wrong one for that mRNA codon, and the incorrect tRNA is ejected from the A site of the ribosome.

Translation takes place in three steps

Translation is the process by which the information in mRNA (derived from DNA) is used to specify and link a specific sequence of amino acids, producing a polypeptide. Like transcription, translation occurs in three steps: initiation, elongation, and termination.

INITIATION   The translation of mRNA begins with the formation of an **initiation complex**, which consists of a charged tRNA and a small ribosomal subunit, both bound to the mRNA (**Figure 14.15**).

In prokaryotes, the rRNA of the small ribosomal subunit first binds to a complementary ribosome binding site (AGGAGG; known as the Shine–Dalgarno sequence) on the mRNA. This sequence is less than ten bases upstream of the actual start codon but lines up the start codon so that it is adjacent to the P site of the large subunit:

mRNA 5'.........A G G A G G......(start codon).....3'

rRNA 3'..........U C C U C C.........(P site)..........5'

Figure 14.15 The Initiation of Translation   Translation begins with the formation of an initiation complex. In prokaryotes, the small ribosomal subunit binds to the Shine–Dalgarno sequence to begin the process, whereas in eukaryotes it binds to the 5' cap.

Eukaryotes load the mRNA onto the ribosome somewhat differently: the small ribosomal subunit binds to the 5′ cap on the mRNA and then moves along the mRNA until it reaches the start codon.

Recall that the mRNA start codon in the genetic code is AUG (see Figure 14.11). The anticodon (UAC) of a methionine-charged tRNA binds to this start codon by complementary base pairing to complete the initiation complex. Thus the first amino acid in a polypeptide chain is always methionine. However, not all mature proteins have methionine as their N-terminal amino acid. In many cases, the initial methionine is removed by an enzyme after translation.

After the methionine-charged tRNA has bound to the mRNA, the large subunit of the ribosome joins the complex. The methionine-charged tRNA now lies in the P site of the ribosome, and the A site is aligned with the second mRNA codon. These ingredients—mRNA, two ribosomal subunits, and methionine-charged tRNA—are assembled by a group of proteins called initiation factors.

ELONGATION   A charged tRNA now enters the open A site of the large ribosomal subunit. If it does not have the correct anticodon, corresponding to the codon in the A site, it exits. At some point, a charged tRNA whose anticodon is complementary to the A site codon of the mRNA enters the A site (**Figure 14.16**). The large subunit then catalyzes two reactions:

1. It breaks the bond between the tRNA and its amino acid in the P site.

2. It catalyzes the formation of a peptide bond between the amino acid that has just been released from the P site tRNA and the one attached to the tRNA in the A site.

Because the large ribosomal subunit performs these two actions, it is said to have **peptidyl transferase** activity. In this way, methionine (the amino acid in the P site) becomes the N terminus of the new protein. The second amino acid is now bound to methionine but remains attached to its tRNA at the A site.

How does the large ribosomal subunit catalyze peptide bond formation? Harry Noller and his colleagues at the University of California at Santa Cruz did a series of experiments and found that:

• if they removed almost all of the proteins from the large subunit, it still catalyzed peptide bond formation.

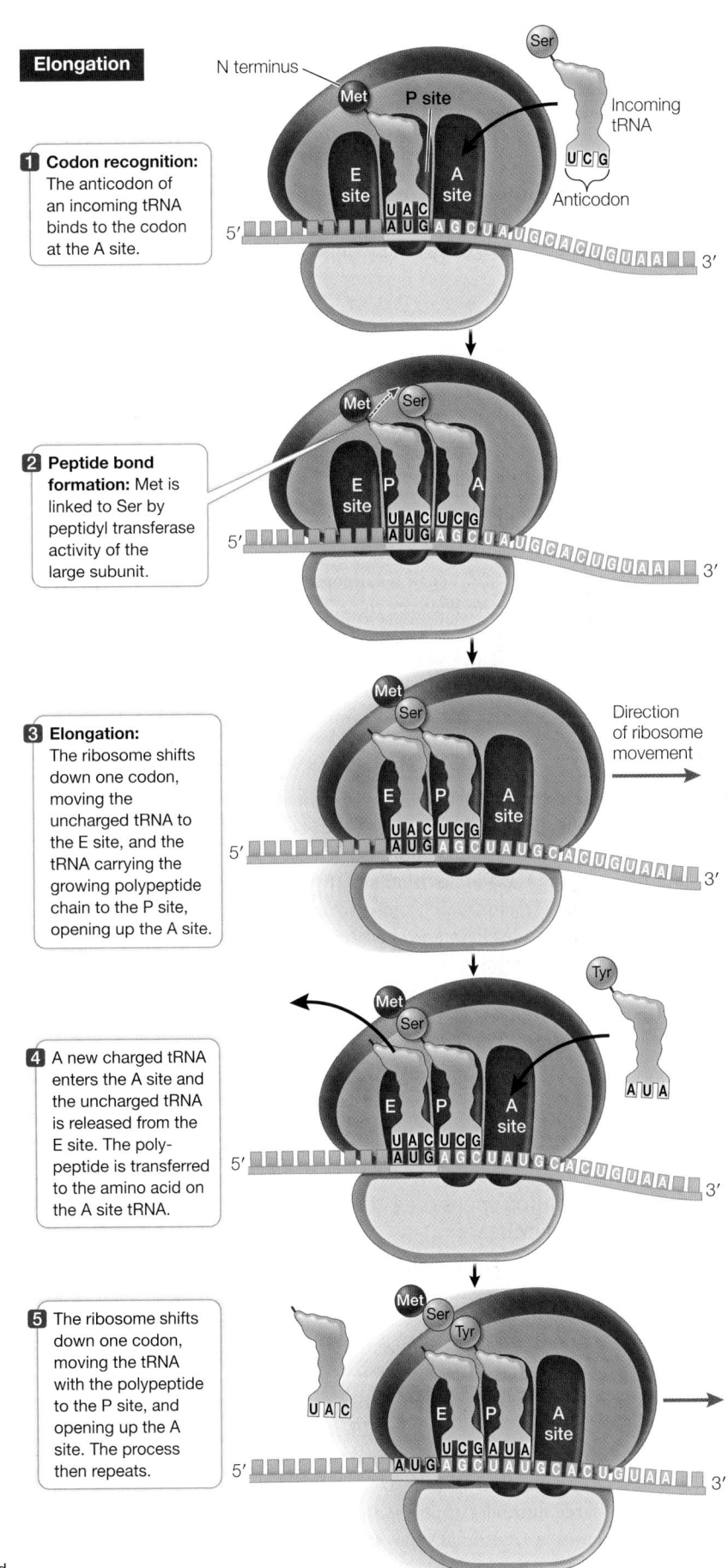

Figure 14.16 The Elongation of Translation
The polypeptide chain elongates as the mRNA is translated.

- if the rRNA was extensively modified, peptidyl transferase activity was destroyed.

The experiment showed that *rRNA is the catalyst*. The purification and crystallization of ribosomes have allowed scientists to examine ribosome structure in detail, and the catalytic role of rRNA in peptidyl transferase activity has been confirmed. These findings support the hypothesis that RNA, and catalytic RNA in particular, evolved before DNA (see Key Concept 4.3).

> **Connect the Concepts** As discussed in Key Concept 4.3, the folded, three-dimensional surface of an RNA molecule can be just as specific as that of a protein, and may thus take on a catalytic function. The "RNA world" hypothesis, which proposed that RNA serves as a catalyst for its own replication, was boosted by the discovery of ribozymes, catalytic RNAs that can speed up biological reactions, including those that involve their own nucleotides.

After the first tRNA releases its methionine, it moves to the E site and is then dissociated from the ribosome, returning to the cytosol to become charged with another methionine. The second tRNA, now bearing a dipeptide (a two-amino acid chain), is shifted to the P site as the ribosome moves one codon along the mRNA in the 5′-to-3′ direction. The elongation process continues, and the polypeptide chain grows, as these steps are repeated. Follow the process in Figure 14.16. All of these steps are assisted by ribosomal proteins called elongation factors.

TERMINATION   The elongation cycle ends, and translation is terminated, when a stop codon—UAA, UAG, or UGA—enters the A site (**Figure 14.17**). Stop codons do not correspond with any amino acids and thus do not bind any tRNAs. Rather, they bind a protein release factor, which allows hydrolysis of the bond between the polypeptide chain and the tRNA in the P site. The newly completed polypeptide thereupon separates from the ribosome. Its C terminus is the last amino acid to join the chain. Its N terminus, at least initially, is methionine, as a consequence of the AUG start codon. In its amino acid sequence, it contains information specifying its conformation, as well as its ultimate cellular destination.

Table 14.3 lists the nucleic acid signals for initiation and termination of transcription and translation.

Polysome formation increases the rate of protein synthesis

Several ribosomes can work simultaneously at translating a single mRNA molecule, producing multiple polypeptides at the same time. As soon as the first ribosome has moved far enough from the 5′ end of the mRNA, a second initiation complex can form, then a third, and so on. An assemblage consisting of a strand of mRNA with its beadlike ribosomes and their growing polypeptide chains is called a **polyribosome**, or **polysome** (**Figure 14.18**). Cells that are actively synthesizing proteins contain large numbers of polysomes and few free ribosomes or ribosomal subunits.

Termination

1. A release factor binds to the complex when a stop codon enters the A site.

2. The release factor disconnects the polypeptide from the tRNA in the P site.

3. The remaining components (mRNA and ribosomal subunits) separate.

Figure 14.17 The Termination of Translation   Translation terminates when the A site of the ribosome encounters a stop codon on the mRNA.

Q: What happens if there is not a stop codon in the mRNA?

TABLE **14.3**	Signals that Start and Stop Transcription and Translation	
	Transcription	**Translation**
Initiation	Promoter sequence in DNA	AUG start codon in the mRNA
Termination	Terminator sequence in DNA	UAA, UAG, or UGA in the mRNA

(A)

Figure 14.18 A Polysome **(A)** A polysome consists of multiple ribosomes and their growing polypeptide chains moving along an mRNA molecule. **(B)** An electron micrograph of a polysome.

KEY CONCEPT
14.6 Recap and Assess

A key step in protein synthesis is the attachment of an amino acid to its proper tRNA, which is facilitated by a family of specific activating enzymes called aminoacyl-tRNA synthetases. tRNAs are the molecules that read mRNA codons and bring the appropriate amino acid to the growing polypeptide. Translation of the genetic information from mRNA into protein occurs at the ribosome in three stages: initiation, elongation, and termination. Multiple ribosomes may act on a single mRNA to make multiple copies of the protein that it encodes.

1. What are the roles of rRNA molecules in the ribosome?
2. Suppose the following mature mRNA sequence encodes a single polypeptide:

   5′ cap-UCGAUCAUGCCCGGGUUAAGAUAUUUUAAAUAGAAUAAAAAA...AAA-3′

   a. Is this mRNA from a prokaryotic or a eukaryotic cell?
   b. Write out the sequence of the complementary DNA strand from which this mRNA was synthesized, assuming no introns were present.
   c. Write out the amino sequence of the translated polypeptide.
3. A charging enzyme inadvertently adds arginine to tRNAser. What will happen if this tRNA is used during translation?

The polypeptide chain that is released from the ribosome is not necessarily a functional protein. Let's look at some of the posttranslational changes that can affect the fate and function of a polypeptide.

KEY CONCEPT
Polypeptides Can Be Modified and Transported during or after Translation
14.7

Learning Objectives

14.7.1 Outline the steps by which a newly synthesized protein is moved into the nucleus or exported outside the cell.

14.7.2 Justify the claim that posttranslational modification of a protein is ultimately directed by the DNA sequence of the gene encoding the protein.

The site of a polypeptide's function may be far away from its point of synthesis. This is especially true for eukaryotes. The polypeptide may be moved into an organelle, or even out of the cell. In addition, polypeptides are often modified by the addition of new chemical groups that have functional significance. In this key concept we examine these posttranslational aspects of protein synthesis.

How are proteins directed to their cellular destinations?

As a polypeptide chain emerges from the ribosome it may simply fold into its three-dimensional shape and perform its cellular role locally in the cytosol. However, if a newly formed polypeptide is meant to do its work elsewhere, a **signal sequence** (or **signal peptide**)—a short stretch of amino acids attached to the polypeptide—will tell the polypeptide where in the cell it belongs. Proteins destined for different locations have different signals.

Protein synthesis always begins on free ribosomes, and the "default" location for a protein is the cytosol. In the absence of a signal sequence, the protein will remain in the same cellular compartment in which it was synthesized. Some proteins contain signal sequences that "target" them to the nucleus, mitochondria, plastids, or peroxisomes (**Figure 14.19**). A signal sequence binds to a specific receptor protein at the surface of the organelle. Once it has bound, the targeted protein moves into the organelle. For example, here is a nuclear localization signal (NLS):

-Pro-Pro-Lys-Lys-Lys-Arg-Lys-Val-

How do we know this signal sequence directs the protein to the nucleus? The function of this NLS peptide was established using experiments like the one illustrated in **Figure 14.20**. Proteins were made in the laboratory with or without the peptide, and then tested by injecting them into cells. Only proteins with the NLS were found in the nucleus.

If a polypeptide carries a signal of about 20 hydrophobic amino acids at its N terminus, it will be directed to the rough endoplasmic reticulum (RER) for further processing (see Figure 14.19). Note that this is not a specific sequence of amino acids, just a generally hydrophobic sequence at the N terminus that is first translated. Translation will pause, and the ribosome will bind to a receptor at the RER membrane. Once the polypeptide–ribosome complex is bound, translation will resume, and as elongation continues, the protein will traverse the RER membrane.

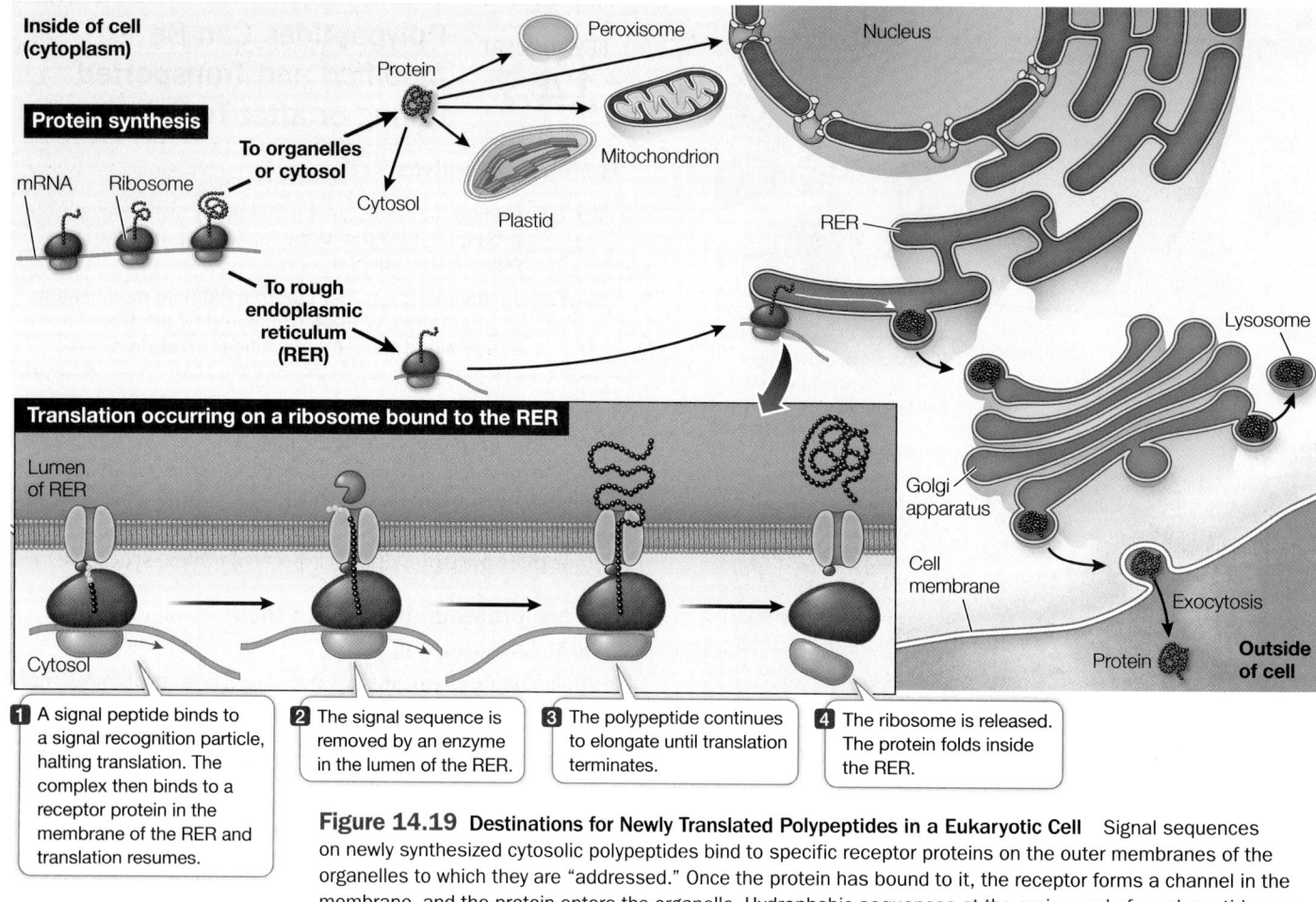

1 A signal peptide binds to a signal recognition particle, halting translation. The complex then binds to a receptor protein in the membrane of the RER and translation resumes.

2 The signal sequence is removed by an enzyme in the lumen of the RER.

3 The polypeptide continues to elongate until translation terminates.

4 The ribosome is released. The protein folds inside the RER.

Figure 14.19 Destinations for Newly Translated Polypeptides in a Eukaryotic Cell Signal sequences on newly synthesized cytosolic polypeptides bind to specific receptor proteins on the outer membranes of the organelles to which they are "addressed." Once the protein has bound to it, the receptor forms a channel in the membrane, and the protein enters the organelle. Hydrophobic sequences at the amino end of a polypeptide may halt translation, which then resumes after binding of the ribosome to the RER. The polypeptide either enters the membrane or the lumen of the RER.

Q: What happens to a protein that has no amino acid sequence "address"?

Such proteins may be retained in the lumen (the inside of the RER) or in the membrane of the RER, or they may move elsewhere within the endomembrane system (Golgi apparatus, lysosomes, and cell membrane). If the proteins lack specific signals or modifications (discussed shortly) that specify destinations within the endomembrane system, they are usually secreted from the cell via vesicles that fuse with the cell membrane.

The importance of signals is shown by Inclusion-cell (I-cell) disease, an inherited disease that causes death in early childhood. People with this disease have a mutation in the gene encoding a Golgi enzyme that adds specific sugars to proteins destined for the lysosomes. These sugars act like signal sequences; without them, enzymes that are essential for the hydrolysis of various macromolecules cannot reach the lysosomes, where the enzymes are normally active. Without these enzymes, the macromolecules accumulate in the lysosomes, and this lack of cellular recycling has drastic effects, resulting in early death.

Mitochondria and chloroplasts make some of their own proteins and import others

As you saw in Chapter 5, mitochondria and chloroplasts are semi-autonomous organelles, each having a small amount of DNA.

Both organelles contain the entire protein synthesis machinery, including a specific RNA polymerase, and their own specialized ribosomes that differ from the ones in the cytoplasm. The genetic coding capacity of the organelle DNA is small, however:

- Mitochondrial DNA encodes mitochondrial rRNAs, a few tRNAs, and 12 to 20 proteins, most of them involved in the respiratory chain.

- Chloroplast DNA encodes chloroplast rRNAs, some tRNAs, and about 40 proteins, many of which are involved in photosynthesis.

These organelles contain dozens more proteins, all of which are imported from the nuclear–cytoplasm protein synthesis system. In some cases (e.g., rubisco in the chloroplast) an organelle protein has several subunits, some of which are made locally inside the organelle and others of which are imported from the nucleus–cytoplasm system. As you can imagine, putting this together requires coordination between the two protein synthesis systems.

Many proteins are modified after translation

The amino acid sequences of most mature proteins are not identical to those in the polypeptide chains that are translated from

Experiment

Figure 14.20   Testing the Signal

Original Paper: C. Dingwall et al. 1988. The nucleoplasmin nuclear location sequence is larger and more complex than that of SV-40 large T antigen. *J Cell Biol* 107: 841–849.

A. Richardson and his colleagues performed a series of experiments to test whether the nuclear localization signal (NLS) is all that is needed to direct a protein to the nucleus.

HYPOTHESIS▶   An NLS is necessary for import of a protein into the nucleus.

METHOD▶

1 A protein labeled with a fluorescent dye is injected into the cytosol.

RESULTS▶

Injected protein:

Nucleoplasmin, a nuclear protein, with the NLS

Nucleoplasmin with the NLS removed

Pyruvate kinase, a cytosolic protein without the NLS

Pyruvate kinase, with attached NLS

NLS

2 The distribution of the protein in the cell is observed with a fluorescence microscope.

CONCLUSION▶   The NLS is essential for nuclear protein import and is sufficient to direct a normally cytosolic protein to the nucleus.

Translation

Posttranslational processing

| **Phosphorylation:** Added phosphate groups alter the shape of the protein. | **Glycosylation:** Adding sugars is important for targeting and recognition. | **Proteolysis:** Cleaving the polypeptide allows the fragments to fold into different shapes. |

Figure 14.21 Posttranslational Modifications of Proteins   Most polypeptides must be modified after translation in order to become functional proteins.

- **Glycosylation** is the addition of sugars to proteins to form glycoproteins. In both the RER and the Golgi apparatus, resident enzymes catalyze the addition of various sugars or short sugar chains to certain amino acid R groups on proteins. One such type of "sugar coating" is essential for directing proteins to lysosomes, as mentioned earlier. Other types are important in the conformation of proteins and their recognition functions at the cell surface (see Key Concept 6.2). Other attached sugars help stabilize extracellular proteins, or proteins stored in vacuoles in plant seeds.

- **Phosphorylation** is the addition of phosphate groups to proteins, and is catalyzed by protein kinases. The charged phosphate groups change the conformation of a protein, often exposing the active site of an enzyme or the binding site for another protein. We have seen the important role of phosphorylation in cell signaling (see Chapter 7) and the cell cycle (see Chapter 11).

KEY CONCEPT

14.7 Recap and Assess

Signal sequences in polypeptides direct them to their appropriate destinations inside or outside the cell. Many polypeptides are modified after translation.

1. How do signal sequences determine where a protein will go after it is made?

2. The genetic code determines the amino acid sequence of a protein. Is there a "code" that determines posttranslational modifications such as phosphorylation or glycosylation? How might this relate to the genetic code?

All of the processes we have just described result in a functional protein, but only if the amino acid sequence of that protein is correct. If the sequence is not correct, cellular dysfunction may result. Changes in the DNA—mutations—are a major source of errors in amino acid sequences. This is the subject of the next chapter.

mRNA on the ribosomes, because polypeptides are often modified in any of several ways after translation (**Figure 14.21**). These modifications are essential to the final functioning of the protein:

- **Proteolysis** is the cutting of a polypeptide chain, a reaction catalyzed by enzymes called proteases (also called peptidases or proteinases). Cleavage of the signal sequence from the growing polypeptide chain in the RER is an example of proteolysis (see Figure 14.19). Some proteins are actually made from polyproteins (long polypeptides) that are cut into final products by proteases. These proteases are essential to some viruses, including human immunodeficiency viruses (HIVs), because the large viral polyprotein cannot fold properly unless it is cut. Certain drugs used to treat acquired immune deficiency syndrome (AIDS) work by inhibiting the HIV protease, thereby preventing the formation of proteins needed for viral reproduction.

▶Investigating**LIFE**

Q and A **How does knowledge of the genetic code help us understand the actions of some antibiotics?**

MRSA can be treated if detected early. Sequencing the DNA of the bacteria can be used to detect mutations and predict the severity of the infection. Antibiotics such as tetracyclines, which target bacterial protein synthesis, are effective in some strains. Tetracyclines kill bacteria by interrupting translation, binding to the small subunit of bacterial ribosomes so that charged tRNA cannot bind to the A site on the ribosome. Tetracyclines do not kill eukaryotic cells, because eukaryotic ribosomes have different proteins and RNAs that do not offer a binding site for tetracyclines.

Whether tetracyclines will continue to offer a viable treatment for MRSA, however, is in doubt. Some strains of MRSA are already resistant to tetracyclines, having acquired genes that convey resistance through bacterial conjugation. The DNA of *S. aureus* has been altered through acquisition of genes from a plasmid so important that it has been given its own name, the resistome. As with methicillin resistance, the alleles of the resistome encode a ribosomal protein with an altered amino acid sequence that consequently does not bind the antibiotic.

Can you think of other ways to target protein synthesis in MRSA?

Future directions

While the expression of protein-coding genes has been well worked out, recent analyses of eukaryotic genomes show that a lot of transcription remains unaccounted for. International cooperation among laboratories in huge projects such as ENCODE (Encyclopedia of DNA Elements) has revealed, for example, that up to 70% of human DNA is transcribed at some point in some cells. With only 2% to 3% of DNA consisting of protein-coding genes, the question immediately arises as to what purpose the rest of the RNAs serve. A small fraction are tRNAs and rRNAs, and you will see in Chapter 16 that some of these noncoding RNAs are small (< 200 nucleotides) and have roles in regulating the expression of protein-coding genes. The roles of the longer RNAs (> 200 nucleotides) are much less clear. In humans, more than 25,000 of the longer RNAs have been identified. They have much in common with mRNAs: they are transcribed using the same RNA polymerase, undergoing poly A addition, capping at the 5′ and 3′ ends, and splicing. However, the longer RNAs are not as long as mRNAs and are not translated at the ribosome. Some never leave the nucleus, where they may be involved in pre-mRNA events such as transcription and splicing. Others actually arrive at the ribosome, where they may regulate the translation of particular mRNAs. These longer untranslated RNAs are found in many organisms, indicating that they must have important roles that have been selected for in evolution.

VISUAL SUMMARY 14

Courtesy of the National Institute of Allergy and Infectious Diseases (NIAID)

You should be able to relate each summary to the adjacent figures. If you go to this visual summary in **Achieve**, you can follow links to figures, animations, activities, and simulations that will help you consolidate the material.

KEY CONCEPT

14.1 Genes Code for Proteins

- **Model organisms** have characteristics that make them ideal for laboratory work.

- Experiments on metabolic enzymes led to the **one-gene, one-enzyme hypothesis**. We now know there is a **one-gene, one-polypeptide relationship**.

- A mutant that has a nonfunctional enzyme in a biosynthetic pathway can be rescued by adding pathway intermediates occurring after the blocked step.

Figure 14.2

Questions

1. List the characteristics of a model organism.

2. Individuals with PKU lack an enzyme that converts phenylalanine to tyrosine. Do you expect the levels of phenylalanine and tyrosine in individuals with PKU to be higher or lower than those in individuals without PKU? Why is the inability to synthesize tyrosine from phenylalanine not lethal in humans?

KEY CONCEPT

14.2 Information Flows from Genes to Proteins

Go to Activity 14.1

- The **central dogma** of molecular biology states how information usually flows in cells, from DNA to DNA, DNA to RNA and RNA to protein.

Questions

1. What three types of RNA molecules are involved in the flow of information from DNA to protein, and what are their primary functions?

2. Telomerase is an enzyme that uses an RNA template to synthesize DNA to extend telomeres. How does this enzyme fit into the central dogma?

Figure 14.3

KEY CONCEPT

14.3 DNA Is Transcribed to Produce RNA

Go to Animation 14.1

- **RNA polymerases** read in the 3′-to-5′ direction, synthesize in the 5′-to-3′ direction, and do not need a primer to begin synthesis.

- Transcription begins at a **promoter** sequence and ends at a terminator sequence.

Questions

1. What are the substrates for the RNA polymerase during transcription?

2. List the ways in which RNA polymerase differs from DNA polymerase.

Figure 14.6

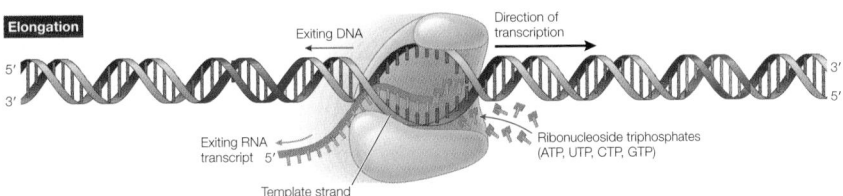

KEY CONCEPT

14.4 Eukaryotic Pre-mRNA Transcripts Are Processed prior to Translation

Go to Animation 14.2

- Prokaryotic mRNAs are not processed prior to being translated.

- Eukaryotic mRNAs have a **5′ cap** and a 3′ **poly A tail** added, and their **introns** are spliced out.

Questions

1. If a change in DNA sequence were to alter an intron splice site, what effect would that have on the resulting protein?

2. If an mRNA is not capped during processing, what are its possible fates?

3. When a cytosolic mRNA from a eukaryote is hybridized to nuclear DNA, in regions where the RNA hybridizes to the DNA, some loops appear that represent regions of DNA that do not pair with the mRNA. Explain the regions of the DNA sequence in the gene that do and do not hybridize to the mRNA.

Figure 14.8

KEY CONCEPT
14.5 The Genetic Code Determines the Protein Sequence Encoded by an mRNA

Go to **Activity 14.2** and **Animation 14.3**

- Coding sequence in mRNA is read as a series of **codons**, starting at the AUG **start codon**.

- The **genetic code** is nearly universal and specifies which amino acids will be included in the polypeptides encoded by mRNA.

Questions

1. Assuming that the ribosome starts translation at the start codon, write down the amino acid sequence of the protein that will be translated from the following mRNA: 5'-GCUUAGCAUGUUUCAAAGAGGUUGACUGAAU-AAAAAAAAAAAA-3'.

2. What is the difference between sense codons and stop (or nonsense) codons?

Figure 14.11

Second letter

	U	C	A	G	
U	UUU UUC Phenyl-alanine	UCU UCC UCA UCG Serine	UAU UAC Tyrosine	UGU UGC Cysteine	U C
	UUA UUG Leucine		**UAA** Stop codon **UAG** Stop codon	**UGA** Stop codon UGG Tryptophan	A G
C	CUU CUC CUA CUG Leucine	CCU CCC CCA CCG Proline	CAU CAC Histidine	CGU CGC CGA CGG Arginine	U C
			CAA CAG Glutamine		A G
A	AUU AUC AUA Isoleucine	ACU ACC ACA ACG Threonine	AAU AAC Asparagine	AGU AGC Serine	U C
	AUG Methionine; start codon		AAA AAG Lysine	AGA AGG Arginine	A G
G	GUU GUC GUA GUG Valine	GCU GCC GCA GCG Alanine	GAU GAC Aspartic acid	GGU GGC GGA GGG Glycine	U C
			GAA GAG Glutamic acid		A G

First letter (left) / *Third letter* (right)

KEY CONCEPT
14.6 The Coding Sequence in mRNA Is Translated into Proteins by Ribosomes

Go to **Animation 14.4**

- Each codon is translated into an amino acid by a specific tRNA by codon–**anticodon** base pairing.

- Translation initiates at the 5' end of the mRNA and begins at an AUG codon.

- Translation elongation involves the ribosome reading one codon at a time as it progresses down the mRNA.

- Charged tRNAs carrying a single amino acid enter the A site, then move to the P site, where they carry the entire polypeptide, then become uncharged and move to the E site, where finally they exit the ribosome.

- Termination occurs when the ribosome reaches a stop codon.

Questions

1. How is the genetic code "read" by a cell during translation?

2. When are the two subunits of a ribosome together?

3. Does a ribosome begin translation at the first nucleotide in an mRNA? If not, where does it begin?

Figure 14.16

KEY CONCEPT

14.7   Polypeptides Can Be Modified and Transported during or after Translation

- Some proteins have **signal sequences** that direct them to particular locations inside or outside the cell.

- Many proteins are modified post-translationally by mechanisms such as **proteolysis**, **glycosylation**, and **phosphorylation**.

Questions

1. What effect will removing a signal sequence have on a polypeptide?

2. Explain why polypeptides have a methionine amino acid at their amino end when they are first synthesized, but often have a different amino acid later on when they are fully functional.

Figure 14.19

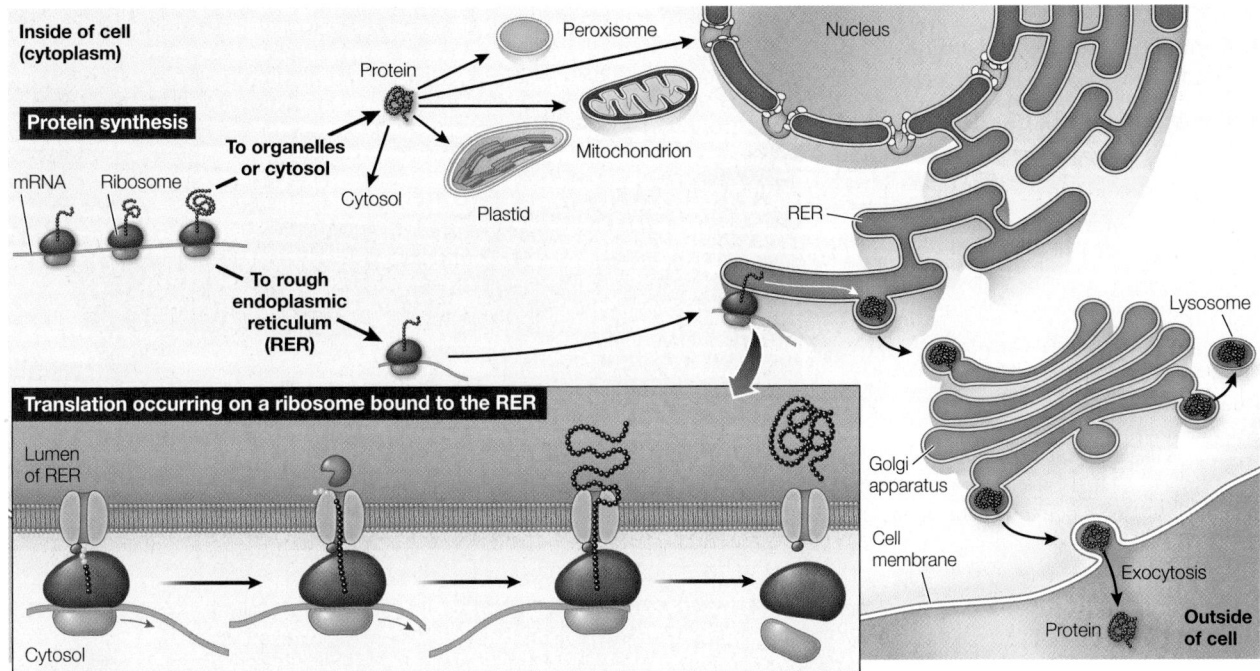

Go to **Achieve** for the eBook, **LearningCurve**, animations, activities, simulations, and additional resources and assignments.

15 Gene Mutation and Molecular Medicine

KEY CONCEPTS

15.1 Mutations Are Heritable Changes in DNA

15.2 Mutations in Humans Can Lead to Diseases

15.3 Mutations Can Be Detected and Analyzed

15.4 Genetic Screening Is Used to Detect Diseases

15.5 Genetic Diseases Can Be Treated

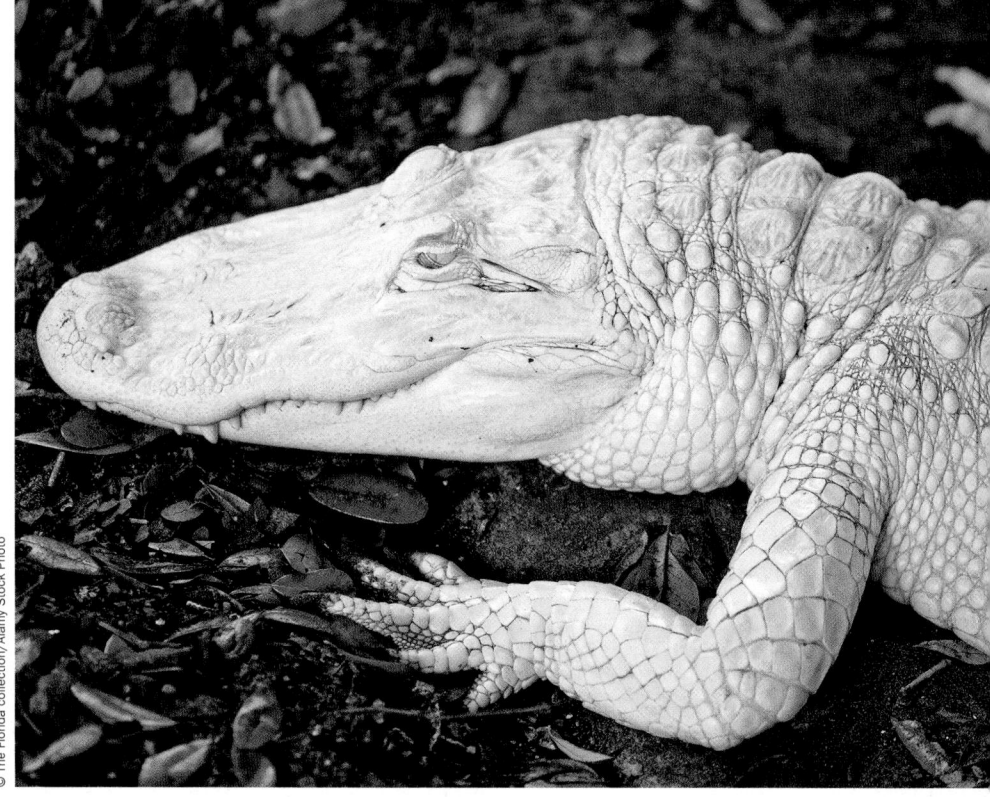

Albinism in this alligator is due to a mutation in both alleles of a single gene.

© The Florida collection/Alamy Stock Photo

▶Investigating LIFE

The Angelina Jolie Effect

The actress Angelina Jolie surprised many people by announcing that she had had both breasts removed upon learning that she carries a mutation in the "breast cancer gene." Her family history led to her being tested for the mutation. Her mother and grandmother both died of ovarian cancer and her aunt died of breast cancer. Ms. Jolie learned that a mutation in a gene called *BRCA1* increases the risk of breast and ovarian cancer. A woman with a harmful mutation in one allele of her *BRCA1* gene has an 80% chance of getting breast cancer by age 60, far in excess of the 8% likelihood for women without a mutation. Removal of breast tissue lowers this risk to 10%.

Ms. Jolie's announcement was widely praised by health-care professionals. Women at risk for carrying a *BRCA1* mutation have increasingly elected to be tested and, when found to be carriers, more often have preventative surgery.

The *BRCA1* mutation test is the culmination of research in the molecular genetics of cancer. As we discussed in Chapter 11, cancer can arise through mutations of either oncogenes (resulting in overstimulation of the cell cycle) or tumor suppressor genes (which would otherwise function to slow down the cell cycle). *BRCA1* is a tumor suppressor gene involved in DNA repair. Women who are at high risk for breast cancer inherit a mutated copy of this

© Pictorial Press Ltd/Alamy Stock Photo

gene, so that they have one wild-type allele and one mutated allele in every cell. If a certain mutation occurs in the wild-type allele in a cell then no functional protein can be made. *BRCA1* is not expressed in all tissues but in breast cells it is particularly important, and so the loss of functional *BRCA1* protein results in an increase in mutation rate in these cells. A higher mutation rate leads to accumulation of mutations in other genes, some of which may lead to improper activation of the cell cycle, resulting in uncontrolled cell division and other adverse effects of a growing tumor.

The precise description of mutations in genetically caused diseases exemplifies the emerging field of molecular medicine. Our ability to identify mutations is leading to more precise testing, diagnoses, and treatments for the diseases they cause.

 What is the breast cancer gene, and what are the issues with DNA testing for cancer? (Find the answer on page 347.)

15.1 Mutations Are Heritable Changes in DNA

Learning Objectives

15.1.1 Use a defined DNA sequence to distinguish among a transition, transversion, single base-pair insertion mutation, and single base-pair deletion mutation.

15.1.2 Using a normal and a mutant mRNA sequence, recognize silent, missense, nonsense, loss-of-stop, and frame-shift mutations.

15.1.3 Give examples of how a mutation in a noncoding region could cause a change in phenotype.

15.1.4 Describe what happens in the following chromosomal rearrangements: deletion, duplication, inversion, and translocation.

15.1.5 Compare and contrast spontaneous and induced mutations, and give examples of each.

15.1.6 Explain why some C-G base pairs in DNA are hot spots for mutation.

In Chapter 12 we defined mutations as stable, inherited changes in genes, and we saw that different alleles may produce different phenotypes (short pea plants versus tall, for example). In Chapters 13 and 14 we described the chemical nature of genes as DNA sequences, and how they are expressed as phenotypes (in particular, proteins). To reiterate, we can now define a **mutation** as a change in the nucleotide sequence of DNA that can be passed on from one cell, or organism, to another.

Mutations have different phenotypic effects

In organisms that have specialized cell lineages that give rise to gametes, a distinction is made between mutations that can be passed on to offspring and those that can't:

- **Somatic mutations** occur in somatic (non-gamete) cells. These mutations are passed on to the daughter cells during mitosis, and to the daughters of those cells in turn, but are not passed on to sexually produced offspring. For example, a mutation in a single human skin cell could result in a patch of skin cells that all have the same mutation, but it would not be passed on to the person's children.

- **Germ line mutations** occur in the cells of the germ line—the specialized cells that give rise to gametes. A gamete with the mutation passes it on to a new organism at fertilization. The new organism will have the mutation in every cell of its body and will be able to pass the mutation on to its offspring. The *BRCA1* mutation that Angelina Jolie, her aunt, and her mother inherited from Angelina's grandmother is a germ line mutation.

Does every mutation have a phenotypic effect? Not necessarily (**Figure 15.1**). Many mutations occur in a nonfunctional region of a DNA molecule, such that no gene product is affected. Alternatively, a mutation may occur in a gene but cause either no change in the gene product or a change that does not alter function (see Figure 15.1B). These cases result in no phenotypic change. For those mutations that do alter phenotype, we distinguish two main classes:

- A **loss-of-function mutation** may cause a gene to not be expressed at all, or the gene may be expressed but produces a dysfunctional RNA or a protein that can no longer play its cellular role, such as its catalytic function if it is an enzyme (see Figure 15.1C). Loss-of-function mutations almost always show recessive inheritance in diploid organisms, because the presence of one wild-type allele will usually result in sufficient functional RNA or protein for the cell. For example, recall from Key Concept 12.1 that the familiar wrinkled seed allele

Figure 15.1 Mutation and Protein Function
Mutations may or may not affect the protein phenotype.

Q: For a protein-coding gene, which of the three types of mutations will be most common, and why?

▶ **View in Achieve**
Simulation 15.1 Mutations and Function

(A) Normal allele: Codes for a functional protein

DNA

Transcription

mRNA

Translation

Functional protein

(B) Mutation with no phenotypic effect: Codes for a functional protein

Mutation

Transcription

Translation

Functional protein

(C) Loss-of-function mutation: Codes for a nonfunctional protein

Mutation

Transcription

Translation

Nonfunctional protein

(D) Gain-of-function mutation: Codes for a protein with a new function

Mutation

Transcription

Translation

Protein with new function

in pea plants, originally studied by Mendel, is due to a recessive loss-of-function mutation in the *SBE1* (*starch branching enzyme*) gene. The protein made by this gene catalyzes the branching of starch as seeds develop. In the homozygous mutant, the SBE1 protein is not functional, and that leads to osmotic changes, causing the wrinkled appearance. Complete loss-of-function mutations are often referred to as null alleles.

- A **gain-of-function mutation** leads to a gene product, usually a protein, with an altered function (see Figure 15.1D). A gain-of-function mutation usually shows dominant inheritance, because the presence of the wild-type allele does not prevent the mutant allele from functioning. This type of mutation is common in cancer. For example, there are mutations in oncogenes that result in proteins that constantly stimulate cell division.

Some mutations have effects on phenotype only under certain conditions. For example, a **conditional mutation** affects phenotype only under restrictive conditions and is not detectable under what are called permissive conditions. In Key Concept 14.1 we discussed arginine-requiring mutant strains of *Neurospora*. Such mutants grow normally when arginine is supplied to the medium but are unable to grow when arginine is not present in the medium, so their phenotype depends on the growth medium (see Figure 14.2). Some conditional mutations are temperature-sensitive, resulting in proteins with reduced stability at high temperatures. For example, the point restriction phenotype in rabbits and Siamese cats (see Figure 12.15) is due to a temperature-sensitive (conditional, loss-of-function) mutation in a coat color gene. At normal body temperature, the protein encoded by the gene is unstable and nonfunctional, so the animal's fur is not pigmented. However, in the body's cooler extremities, the protein is functional and dark fur results.

The effects of mutations on phenotype can be reversed, such that the phenotype reverts to wild type. **Reversion mutations** result when a gene is mutated a second time so that the DNA reverts to its original sequence or to a different sequence that results in the non-mutant phenotype.

Now let's look more closely at the DNA level to see how various kinds of mutations play out.

Point mutations are changes in single base pairs

A **point mutation** is the addition (insertion) or subtraction (deletion) of a single base pair, or the substitution of one base pair for another. There are two kinds of base substitutions (**Figure 15.2**). A **transition** occurs when the purine nucleotide in a base pair is replaced by the other purine (A replaces G or vice versa) and the pyrimidine is replaced by the other pyrimidine (T replaces C or vice versa). A **transversion** occurs when the purine nucleotide in a base pair is replaced by a pyrimidine (A or G replaces C or T) and the pyrimidine nucleotide is replaced by a purine (C or T replaces A or G).

What are the possible effects of a point mutation that occurs in the protein-coding region of a gene, such that the mature mRNA has a single nucleotide change? A silent mutation has no effect on the amino acid sequence of a protein, but missense, nonsense, loss-of-stop, and frame-shift mutations do result in changes in the protein, some of them drastic (**Figure 15.3**). Note that substitutions

(A) Transition

(B) Transversion

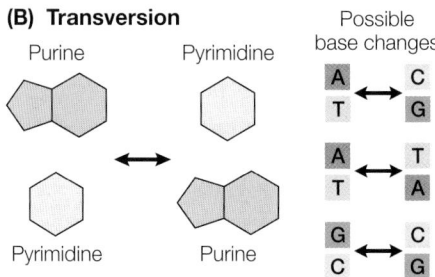

Figure 15.2 Two Types of Base Pair Substitutions A substitution mutation replaces one base pair with another. **(A)** In a transition, the purine in a base pair is replaced by the other purine, and the pyrimidine is replaced by the other pyrimidine. **(B)** In a transversion, the purine is replaced by a pyrimidine, and the pyrimidine is replaced by a purine.

alter only a single codon in the mRNA, while insertions and deletions generally alter many codons.

SILENT MUTATIONS   **Silent mutations** are DNA substitutions that result in a change of an mRNA sense codon (one that encodes an amino acid) into another sense codon that encodes the same amino acid (see Figure 15.3B). A change in a codon does not necessarily mean a change in the amino acid that gets translated, because of the redundancy of the genetic code (see Figure 14.11).

MISSENSE MUTATIONS   **Missense mutations** are DNA substitutions that change an mRNA sense codon into another sense codon that encodes a different amino acid, such that one amino acid substitutes for another in the encoded polypeptide (see Figure 15.3C). An example is the mutation that causes sickle-cell disease, a serious heritable blood disorder. The disease occurs in people who carry two copies of the sickle allele of the gene for β-globin—a subunit of hemoglobin, the protein in human blood that carries oxygen. The sickle allele differs from the wild-type allele by one base pair, resulting in a polypeptide that differs by one amino acid from the wild-type protein. Individuals who are homozygous for this recessive allele have defective, sickle-shaped red blood cells (**Figure 15.4**).

Connect the Concepts Many base substitution mutations result in changes in protein structure due to amino acid substitutions. Review the relationships between amino acid sequence and protein three-dimensional structure in Key Concept 3.2.

A missense mutation may result in a defective protein, but in many cases has no effect on the protein's function. For example, a hydrophilic amino acid may be substituted for another hydrophilic

(A) Wild type (normal)

(B) Silent mutation

(C) Missense mutation

(D) Nonsense mutation

(E) Loss-of-stop mutation

(F) Frame-shift mutation

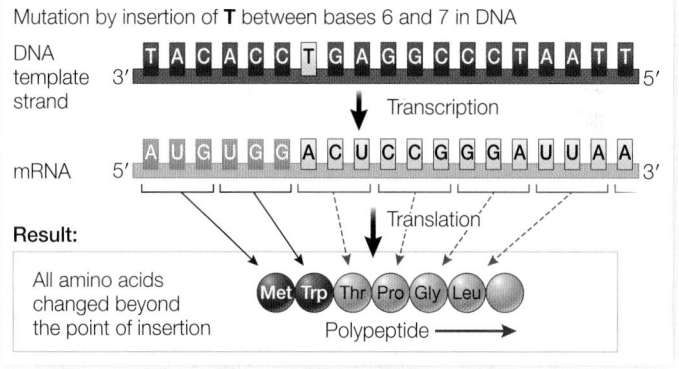

Figure 15.3 Point Mutations   When they occur in the coding region of a protein, single base pair changes, which cause single nucleotide changes in the mRNA, can cause silent, missense, nonsense, loss-of-stop, or frame-shift mutations.

View in Achieve
Simulation 15.2 Point Mutations

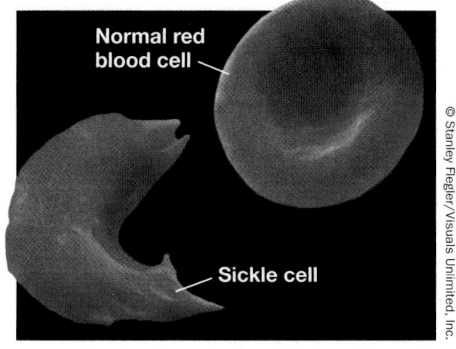

Figure 15.4 Sickle and Normal Red Blood Cell   The sickle cell anemia allele is a missense mutation that causes red blood cells to sickle when homozygous.

Media Clip 15.1 Sickle Cells: Deformed by a Mutation
Life12e.com/mc15.1

amino acid, so that the tertiary (and quaternary) structure of the protein is unchanged. In some cases a missense mutation reduces the functional efficiency of a protein rather than completely inactivating it. Therefore individuals homozygous for a missense mutation in a protein essential for life may survive if enough of the protein's function is retained.

In some cases, a gain-of-function missense mutation occurs, such that the mutated polypeptide has a novel function not exhibited by the wild-type polypeptide. An example is a mutation in the human *P53* gene, which codes for a tumor suppressor—a protein that inhibits the cell cycle (see Key Concept 11.7). Certain mutations of the *P53* gene cause this protein to both no longer inhibit cell division (an example of loss-of-function) and to promote cell division and prevent programmed cell death, which represent gain of function.

NONSENSE MUTATIONS   A **nonsense mutation** involves a base pair substitution that causes an mRNA sense codon to become a stop codon (see Figure 15.3D). A nonsense mutation results in a shortened protein, since translation does not proceed beyond the point where the mutation occurred. For example, a common mutation causing thalassemia (another blood disorder affecting hemoglobin) in Mediterranean populations is a nonsense mutation that drastically shortens the β-globin subunit. Shortened proteins usually are not functional; however, if the nonsense mutation occurs near the 3′ end of the gene, it may have little to no effect on function.

LOSS-OF-STOP MUTATIONS   A **loss-of-stop mutation** involves a base pair substitution that results in a change from an mRNA stop codon to a sense codon, causing additional amino acids to be added to the end of the polypeptide. For example, a substitution that converts UAA (stop) to UAC (tyrosine) allows the ribosome to continue translating (see Figure 15.3E). The effect of a loss-of-stop mutation depends on how many amino acids are added to the end of the polypeptide and how important that part of the polypeptide is to function.

FRAME-SHIFT MUTATIONS   Not all point mutations are base substitutions. A base pair may be inserted into, or deleted from, a sequence of DNA. Such changes in coding sequences are known as **frame-shift mutations** because they alter the mRNA reading frame (that is, consecutive triplets) in which the codons are read during translation (see Figure 15.3F). Think again of codons as three-letter words, each corresponding to a particular amino acid. Translation begins at a particular starting point (the AUG start codon) and proceeds three bases at a time—that is, codon by codon. If a nucleotide is inserted or deleted from a codon, then the three-letter "words" are shifted as translation proceeds beyond that point, and the result is a completely different amino acid sequence. Given this massive impact on polypeptide sequence, it is not surprising that frame-shift mutations almost always lead to the production of nonfunctional proteins.

MUTATIONS OUTSIDE THE CODING REGION   As we discuss in Chapter 17, in genomes such as ours, much of the DNA does not encode protein information. What happens if a point mutation occurs outside a protein-coding region, and thus does not alter a codon? In many such cases there is no effect on phenotype. For example, most of the positions in an intron are not required for intron splicing, and so most mutations in intron-coding regions do not alter phenotype. Similarly, intergenic regions—that is, regions that are found between genes—have many positions that have no function; mutations at these sequences have no effect on phenotype. However, while generally rare, mutations outside of coding regions may have significant effects. For example:

- Mutations in promoters or in other regulatory sequences may alter the rate of transcription of the gene.
- Mutations in DNA that alter RNA splicing sites may lead to incorrectly spliced mRNA and synthesis of an abnormal polypeptide.

Chromosomal rearrangements are extensive changes in the genetic material

Mutations can alter larger sequences of DNA than just a single base pair. In fact, some mutations are so large that they are visible at the chromosome level. You have already met one kind of chromosomal mutation, a change in chromosome number (see Key Concept 11.5). In aneuploidy an individual has an abnormal number of one or a few chromosomes. In polyploidy, an individual has more than two entire sets of chromosomes. In addition to undergoing changes in number, chromosomes (or more accurately, whole DNA molecules) can break and rejoin, grossly disrupting the sequence of genetic information. There are four types of such **chromosomal rearrangements**: deletions, duplications, inversions, and translocations. These mutations can be caused by double-strand breakage of chromosomes resulting from mutagens or by errors during crossing over.

- A **deletion** occurs by the removal of part of the genetic material and can happen if a chromosome breaks at two points and then rejoins, leaving out the DNA between the breaks (**Figure 15.5A**).
- A **duplication** can be produced at the same time as a deletion and can occur if homologous chromosomes break at different positions and then reconnect to the wrong partners (**Figure 15.5B**). Inappropriate alignment of homologs during prophase I followed by crossing over also causes this rearrangement. One of the two chromosomes ends up with a deleted segment, and the other has two copies (a duplication) of the same segment.
- An **inversion** can also result from the breaking and rejoining of a chromosome and can occur if a segment of DNA becomes "flipped," so that it runs in the opposite direction from its original orientation (**Figure 15.5C**).
- A **translocation** results when a segment of a chromosome breaks off and becomes attached to a different chromosome. As we mentioned in Key Concept 11.5, a translocation of a large segment of chromosome 21 is one cause of Down syndrome. Translocations often involve reciprocal exchanges of chromosome segments, as in **Figure 15.5D**.

Figure 15.5 Chromosomal Rearrangements Chromosomes may experience double-strand breaks or may exhibit incorrect crossing over during meiosis, resulting in the incorrect joining of chromosomal regions. This can result in deletions (**A, B**), duplications (**B**), inversions (**C**), or reciprocal translocations (**D**). Note that the letters on these illustrations represent large segments of the chromosomes. Because chromosomes contain regions of noncoding DNA, each segment may include anywhere from zero to hundreds or thousands of genes.

Q: How are chromosomal mutations detected?
Hint: See Figure 11.20.

Retroviruses and transposons can cause loss-of-function mutations or duplications

Key Concept 14.2 described how certain viruses called retroviruses can insert their genetic material into the host cell's genome. If such an insertion occurs within a gene, it usually causes a loss-of-function mutation in that gene. In many cases, the viral DNA remains in the host genome and is passed on from one generation to the next. When this happens the virus is called an endogenous retrovirus. Endogenous retroviruses are common—in fact, they make up 5% to 8% of the human genome.

Another form of DNA, called a transposon or transposable element, can also insert itself into the genome, causing insertion mutations. As you will see in Chapter 17, transposons are widespread in both prokaryotic and eukaryotic genomes. A transposon is a DNA sequence of a few hundred to a few thousand base

pairs that can move from one position in the genome to another. It usually carries genes that encode the enzymes needed for this movement. Some transposons remove themselves from their positions in the genome and then insert themselves into other sites (the "cut and paste" mode of transposition). These transposons do not always excise cleanly, but leave behind short sequences of a few base pairs that become permanent mutations in the affected genes. Other transposons first replicate themselves, and then the new copies are inserted into new sites in the genome (the "copy and paste" mode). A sequence of genomic DNA is sometimes carried along with the transposon DNA when it moves, and gene duplication occurs. As you'll see, gene duplication plays an important role in evolution.

Mutations can be spontaneous or induced

It is useful to distinguish between mutations that are spontaneous or induced, based on their causes. **Spontaneous mutations** are permanent changes in the genetic material that occur without any outside influence. The movement of transposons is an example of spontaneous mutation. Spontaneous mutations can also occur because cellular processes are imperfect, and may occur by several mechanisms (**Figure 15.6**):

- *Mistakes during replication.* As we discussed previously (in Key Concept 13.4), DNA polymerases sometimes incorporate the incorrect nucleotide into the growing strand, causing a mismatch. Incorporation errors occur rarely and are often caught by the proofreading function of the replication complex. However, they are more likely to occur and escape proofreading if the template base has undergone a spontaneous chemical rearrangement. Each base can exist in two different forms (called tautomers), one of which is common and one rare (see Figure 15.6A). When a base temporarily forms its rare tautomer, it can pair with the wrong base. For example, C normally pairs with G, but if C takes on the form of its rare tautomer at the time of DNA replication, it pairs with (and DNA polymerase will insert) an A. The result of such an incorporation error is a mismatch, which can be repaired to the correct base pair (see Figure 13.19). However, if the mismatch is repaired incorrectly (see Figure 15.6C), or if it is replicated before it is repaired (see Figure 15.6D), then a point mutation results. In this example, the A-C mismatch results in the original G-C base pair being replaced with an A-T base pair.

- *A chemical reaction may alter the structure and base-pairing properties of a DNA base.* For example, a spontaneous deamination reaction can result in loss of the amino group (NH_2) in cytosine, converting it to a uracil base (Figure 15.6B). If this occurs in a DNA molecule, the result is a mismatch that is usually repaired, because uracil should not be present in DNA and is preferentially removed during repair. However, since the repair mechanism is not perfect, the mismatch will sometimes remain when a cell undergoes replication. In these cases, DNA polymerase will add an A (which base-pairs with U on the template DNA) instead of a G (which normally pairs with C). This A-U mismatch will be repaired, or will undergo

(A) Tautomeric shift in a base

Cytosine
(common tautomer)

Cytosine
(rare tautomer)

(B) Deamination of a base

Deamination

Deaminated form
of cytosine (= **uracil**)

(C) Mismatch repair error

New strand

Mismatch repair

Template strand

A-C mismatch occurred from incorporation error by DNA polymerase during replication.

Mismatch repair incorrectly removed template strand and used new strand for repair.

Original G-C base pair has been replaced by A-T.

(D) Replication before mismatch repair

Replication before repair

Figure 15.6 Spontaneous Mutations Spontaneous mismatches, if not repaired, will lead to permanent point mutations in the DNA sequence following replication or incorrect repair. **(A)** All four nitrogenous bases in DNA exist in both a prevalent (common) form and a rare form. When a base spontaneously forms its rare tautomer, it can pair with a different base, causing a mismatch during replication. **(B)** Some bases can undergo other spontaneous chemical changes. In this example, spontaneous deamination results in loss of the amino group (NH_2) in cytosine, converting it to uracil, to give an A-G mismatch. **(C)** In some cases, mismatch repair incorrectly removes the template strand instead of the new strand, resulting in a base-pair substitution. **(D)** In other cases, the mismatch may not be repaired before the next round of replication, again resulting in a base-pair substitution.

replication to give an A-T base pair, which is a point mutation: G-C → A-T, or equivalently, C-G → T-A.

- *Meiotic errors.* Nondisjunction—the failure of homologous chromosomes to separate during meiosis—can occur, leading to one too many chromosomes or one too few (see Figure 11.19). Random chromosome breakage and rejoining, or crossing over between nonhomologous chromosomal regions, can produce deletions, duplications, inversions, or translocations.

Induced mutations occur when some agent from outside the cell—a **mutagen**—causes a change in DNA that leads to a mutation. As we mentioned earlier, retroviruses can function as mutagens. In addition, certain chemicals and radiation can cause mutations:

- *Some chemicals can alter nucleotide bases.* For example, nitrous acid (HNO_2) and similar molecules can react with cytosine

and convert it to uracil by deamination (see Figure 15.6B). This alteration has the same result as spontaneous deamination: instead of inserting a G, DNA polymerase inserts an A.

- *Some chemicals add groups to the bases.* For instance, benzopyrene, a component of cigarette smoke, adds a large chemical group to guanine, making it unavailable for base pairing. When DNA polymerase reaches such a modified guanine, replication stops. In some cases, replication is restarted by the incorporation of any one of the four bases at random into the new strand. Three-fourths of the time the inserted base is not cytosine, and a mismatch results, which may then lead to a mutation at the next round of replication.

- *Radiation damages the genetic material.* Radiation can damage DNA in two ways. First, ionizing radiation (including X-rays, gamma rays, and radiation from unstable isotopes) produces highly reactive chemicals called free radicals. Free radicals can change bases in DNA to forms that are not recognized by DNA polymerase. Ionizing radiation can also break the sugar–phosphate backbone of DNA, causing chromosomal rearrangements. Second, ultraviolet radiation (from the sun or a tanning lamp) is absorbed by thymine, causing it to form covalent bonds with adjacent thymine bases. Such thymine dimers, if unrepaired, block DNA replication, and the cell may respond by synthesizing a new strand that has a random sequence across from the block, increasing the likelihood of a mismatch and then a mutation.

Mutagens can be natural or artificial

Many people associate mutagens with materials made by humans, but many mutagenic substances are found in nature. An example of a naturally occurring mutagen is aflatoxin, which is made by the mold *Aspergillus*. When mammals ingest the mold, the aflatoxin is converted by the smooth endoplasmic reticulum (SER) in liver cells into a product that, like benzopyrene from cigarette smoke, binds to guanine; this also leads to mutations. Plants (and to a lesser extent animals) make thousands of small molecules with a variety of functions, some of which are mutagenic and potentially carcinogenic. Examples of human-made mutagens are nitrites, which are used to preserve meats. Once in mammals, nitrites get converted by the SER to nitrosamines, which are strongly mutagenic because they cause deamination of cytosine (see Figure 15.6B).

Radiation can also be human-made or natural. Some of the isotopes made in nuclear reactors and nuclear bomb explosions are certainly harmful. For example, extensive studies have shown increased mutations in the survivors of the atomic bombs dropped on Japan in 1945. As previously mentioned, natural ultraviolet radiation in sunlight also causes mutations.

By now, you may be getting worried about all the ways your DNA can be mutated. But for us, and for most organisms, DNA repair mechanisms have evolved so that most mismatches or damaged nucleotides in DNA do not get passed on to either the daughter cells or the next generation (see Figure 13.19). A large number of DNA damage occurs in the human genome under normal circumstances: among the diploid genome's 6.2 billion base pairs, there are tens of thousands of DNA-damaging events per cell per day. Of these, the vast majority affect only one strand and are repaired using the undamaged strand to give the correct DNA sequence, so that only a very small number become mutations.

Some base pairs are more vulnerable than others to mutation

In certain regions of DNA, many of the cytosine residues have methyl groups added at their 5 positions, forming 5-methylcytosine. Methylation plays an important role in gene regulation (discussed in Key Concept 16.4). DNA sequencing has revealed that mutation "hot spots" are often located where cytosines have been methylated. Figure 15.6 shows unmethylated cytosine, which can lose its amino group, either spontaneously or because of a chemical mutagen, to form uracil (see Figure 15.6B). This type of error is usually detected by the cell and repaired, because uracil is recognized as inappropriate for DNA. However, when 5-methylcytosine (methylated cytosine) loses its amino group, the product is thymine, a natural base for DNA. The DNA repair mechanism cannot distinguish which base, T or G, in the mismatch is incorrect and so half the time will repair the mismatch incorrectly (from T-G to T-A). In the absence of repair, the mismatch will segregate at replication and again result in a mutation in one of the daughter cells (**Figure 15.7**). Note that the reason that methylated C-G base pairs are hot spots for mutation does not imply that they deaminate at higher frequency than unmethylated C-G base pairs; instead, the resulting U-G mismatch from an unmethylated C deamination is more often correctly repaired because the repair machinery recognizes U as an incorrect base.

Mutations have both benefits and costs

As we will see in Part Six of this book, mutations are the raw material of evolution: they provide the genetic diversity that makes natural selection possible. This diversity can be beneficial in two ways. First, a mutation may benefit the organism immediately. Second, a mutation may have no immediate selective advantage to the organism, but it may cause a phenotypic change in the organism's offspring. The result will be a genetic variant in the population that may become advantageous if the environment changes in a later generation; the initially unselected mutation might thus be selected for under the new conditions.

We noted that gene duplication can arise through either chromosomal rearrangements or through the movements of

Figure 15.7 5-Methylcytosine in DNA Is a "Hot Spot" for Mutations If cytosine has been methylated to 5-methylcytosine, deamination results in a T-G mismatch that, if repaired incorrectly (by replacing the G nucleotide) or, if replicated (shown), will result in a C-G base pair being replaced by a T-A pair.

transposons. Gene duplication is an important source of genetic variation. In a duplicated pair of genes, one gene may continue to play its original role in the organism, while the other may acquire a gain-of-function mutation that produces a new phenotype. As with any other mutation, this may be of immediate benefit for the organism, or it may provide a later generation with a selective advantage.

By contrast, mutations in genes whose products are needed for normal cellular processes are often harmful, especially if they occur in germ line cells that produce eggs or sperm and thus are present in every cell in the body. In some cases, offspring can inherit harmful recessive alleles from both parents and have the homozygous condition. In their extreme form, such mutations produce phenotypes that are lethal, killing the organism during early development. Likewise, mutations in somatic cells can be harmful, as in the case of cancer. Think about what would happen if an oncogene that stimulates cell division in a colon cell had a gain-of-function mutation during development. The result would be the same as inheriting the mutant allele: a higher likelihood of developing colon cancer.

What can we do about mutation? While spontaneous mutagenesis is not in our control, we can certainly try to avoid mutagenic substances and radiation. Not surprisingly, many things that cause cancer (carcinogens) are also mutagens. A good example is benzopyrene (discussed earlier), which is found in coal tar, car exhaust fumes, charbroiled foods, and cigarette smoke. A major public-policy goal is to reduce the effects of both human-made and natural mutagens on human health. An example is the Montreal Protocol, an international environmental agreement signed and adhered to by all members of the United Nations. It bans chlorofluorocarbons and other substances that cause depletion of the ozone layer in the upper atmosphere of Earth. The thinning of the ozone layer can result in increased ultraviolet radiation reaching Earth's surface, which is implicated in somatic mutations that lead to skin cancer.

KEY CONCEPT
15.1 Recap and Assess

Mutations are permanent changes in the nucleotide sequence of DNA. Mutations can vary in magnitude from changes in single base pairs (point mutations) to extensive rearrangements of chromosomes or changes in the number of chromosomes. When mutations occur in somatic cells, they will be passed on to daughter cells; when they occur in germ line cells, they may be passed on to offspring.

1. Suppose a small polypeptide consists of five amino acids: methionine-threonine-glutamine-tryptophan-phenylalanine. If a point mutation occurred in the DNA that encoded the third mRNA codon (the one encoding glutamine), what would be the effects on the polypeptide sequence if the mutation was a silent, missense, nonsense, or frame-shift mutation?

2. What distinguishes the various kinds of chromosomal rearrangements: deletions, duplications, inversions, and translocations?

3. What are the differences between spontaneous and induced mutation? Give an example of each.

4. Why are some C-G base pairs prone to mutation?

You have seen that there are many different ways in which DNA can be altered, in terms of both the types of changes and the mechanisms by which they occur. We turn now to the ways in which mutations can cause disease.

KEY CONCEPT
15.2 Mutations in Humans Can Lead to Diseases

Learning Objectives

15.2.1 Give an example of an abnormal protein in humans that results from a genetic mutation and causes a disease.

15.2.2 Explain why point mutations, large deletions, and chromosomal abnormalities can all cause genetic disorders.

15.2.3 Describe what is meant by "expanding triplet repeats" in genetic disorders.

15.2.4 Justify the claim that many diseases arise from complex interactions between genetic and environmental factors.

The biochemistry that relates genotype (DNA) and phenotype (proteins) has been most completely described for model organisms, such as the prokaryote *E. coli* and the eukaryotes yeast and *Drosophila*. While the details vary, there is great similarity in the fundamental processes among these forms of life. These similarities have permitted the application of knowledge and methods discovered using these model organisms to the study of human biochemical genetics. Our focus in this chapter is mutations that affect human phenotypes, leading to diseases.

Disease-causing mutations may make proteins dysfunctional

Genetic mutations are often expressed phenotypically as proteins that differ from normal (wild-type) proteins. Abnormalities in enzymes, receptor proteins, transport proteins, structural proteins, and most of the other functional classes of proteins have all been implicated in genetic diseases.

LOSS OF ENZYME FUNCTION   In 1934, the urine of two intellectually disabled young siblings was found to contain phenylpyruvic acid, an unusual by-product of the metabolism of the amino acid phenylalanine. It took two decades for scientists to trace the complex clinical phenotype of the disease that afflicted these children, called phenylketonuria (PKU), back to its molecular cause. The disease results from an abnormality in a single enzyme, phenylalanine hydroxylase (PAH), which catalyzes the conversion of dietary phenylalanine to tyrosine (**Figure 15.8**). This enzyme is not active in the livers of PKU patients, leading to excesses of phenylalanine and phenylpyruvic acid in the blood. Since then, the nucleotide sequence of the *PAH* gene has been compared between healthy people and those with PKU, and more than 400 different disease-causing mutations have been found. The most common one is a missense mutation that results in tryptophan instead of

Figure 15.8 One Mutation Inactivates One Enzyme Phenylketonuria is caused by an abnormality in a specific enzyme that metabolizes the amino acid phenylalanine. Knowing the molecular causes of such single-gene, single-enzyme metabolic diseases can aid researchers in developing screening tests as well as treatments.

arginine at position 408 in the polypeptide chain (**Table 15.1**). As is often the case with loss-of-function mutations, the mutant alleles are recessive, because one functional allele is all that is needed to produce enough functional PAH to prevent the disease.

Hundreds of human genetic diseases that result from enzyme abnormalities have been discovered, some of which lead to intellectual disability and premature death. Most of these diseases are rare; PKU, for example, shows up in 1 out of every 10,000 newborns. As you by now realize, for any given gene there may be numerous alleles. Some alleles encode proteins that function normally, whereas others produce proteins that cause disease. Let's take a look at a gene whose alleles illustrate both of these circumstances—the gene for one of the polypeptide chains in hemoglobin.

ABNORMAL HEMOGLOBIN   As mentioned in Key Concept 15.1, sickle-cell disease is caused by a recessive, missense mutation. This blood disorder most often afflicts people whose ancestors came from the tropics or from the Mediterranean region.

Recall that human hemoglobin is composed of four globin subunits—two α-chains and two β-chains—as well as the pigment heme (see Figure 3.12). In the sickle-cell disease allele, one of the 146 amino acids in the β-globin polypeptide chain is abnormal: at position 6, glutamic acid is replaced by valine. This replacement changes the charge of the protein (glutamic acid is negatively charged and valine is uncharged), causing it to form long, needlelike aggregates in the red blood cells. The phenotypic result is sickle-shaped red blood cells and an impaired ability of the blood to carry oxygen. The sickled cells tend to block narrow blood capillaries, resulting in tissue damage and eventually death by organ failure.

Because hemoglobin is easy to isolate and study, its variations in the human population have been extensively documented (**Figure 15.9**). Hundreds of alleles caused by single amino acid alterations in β-globin, all due to mutations, have been reported. For example, at the same position that is mutated in sickle-cell disease (resulting in hemoglobin S), glutamic acid may be replaced by lysine, causing hemoglobin C disease. In this case, the resulting anemia is usually not severe. Many alleles that result in alterations of the amino acid sequence of hemoglobin do not affect its function. In fact, about 5% of us carry at least one missense point mutation in a β-globin allele.

Some of the more common examples of inherited diseases caused by specific protein defects are listed in **Table 15.2**. These mutations can be dominant, codominant, or recessive, and some are sex-linked.

Disease-causing mutations may involve any number of base pairs

Disease-causing mutations may involve a single base pair, a long stretch of DNA, multiple segments of DNA, or even entire chromosomes (as we saw for Down syndrome in Key Concept 11.5).

POINT MUTATIONS   Sickle-cell anemia is just one of many diseases caused by a point mutation. In some cases (sickle-cell anemia, for example), everyone with the disease has the same genetic mutation. In other cases, different loss-of-function point mutations in one gene can lead to the same disease. Think about it: the three-dimensional structure of an enzyme protein depends on its primary structure, so any change in the amino acid sequence of a protein has the potential to affect its structure, and consequently its function. For example, cystic fibrosis is a recessive disorder for which over 2,000 different causal mutant alleles have been identified.

TABLE **15.1**	Two Common Mutations That Cause Phenylketonuria				
	Codon 408 (20% of PKU cases)		**Codon 280 (2% of PKU cases)**		
	Normal	**Mutant**	**Normal**	**Mutant**	
Length of PAH protein	452 amino acids	452 amino acids	452 amino acids	452 amino acids	
DNA at codon	5'...CGG...3'	5'...TGG...3'	5'...GAA...3'	5'...AAA...3'	
	3'...GCC...5'	3'...ACC...5'	3'...CTT...5'	3'...TTT...5'	
mRNA at codon	...CGG...	...UGG...	...GAA...	...AAA...	
Amino acid at codon	Arginine	Tryptophan	Glutamic acid	Lysine	
Active PAH enzyme?	Yes	No	Yes	No	

Source: https://omim.org.

	Amino acid position (of 146)								
	2	6	7	16	24	26	56	63	95
A (wild type)	His	Glu	Glu	Gly	Gly	Glu	Gly	His	Lys
Tokuchi	Tyr								
S		Val							
C		Lys							
G			Gly						
J Baltimore				Asp					
Savannah					Val				
E						Lys			
Bangkok							Asp		
Zürich								Arg	
M Saskatoon								Tyr	
N Baltimore									Glu

Only three hemoglobin alleles (S, C, and E) lead to clinical problems.

Alleles of β-globin

Figure 15.9 Hemoglobin Polymorphism Each of these mutant alleles codes for a protein with a single amino acid change in the 146-amino acid chain of β-globin. Only three of the hundreds of known variants of β-globin, highlighted in yellow, are known to lead to clinical abnormalities. "S" is the sickle-cell anemia allele.

LARGE DELETIONS Larger mutations may involve many base pairs of DNA. For example, deletions in the X chromosome that include the gene for the protein dystrophin result in Duchenne muscular dystrophy. Dystrophin is important in organizing the structure of muscles, and people who have only the abnormal form have severe muscle weakness. Sometimes only part of the dystrophin gene is missing, leading to an incomplete but partly functional protein and a mild form of the disease. In other cases, deletions span the entire sequence of the gene, so that the protein is missing entirely, resulting in a severe form of the disease. In yet other cases, deletions involve millions of base pairs and cover not only the dystrophin gene but adjacent genes as well; the result may be several diseases in the same person.

CHROMOSOMAL ABNORMALITIES Chromosomal abnormalities also cause human diseases. Such abnormalities result from the gain or loss of complete chromosomes (aneuploidy) (see Figure 11.19), or from the gain or loss of chromosomal segments (see Figure 15.5). About 1 newborn in 200 has a chromosomal abnormality.

The constriction at the lower tip of this chromosome is the location of the fragile-X abnormality.

C. Harrison et al. 1983. *J Med Genet* 20: 280. With permission from BMJ Publishing Group Ltd.

Figure 15.10 A Fragile-X Chromosome at Metaphase The chromosomal abnormality associated with fragile-X syndrome shows up under the microscope as a constriction in the chromosome. This occurs during preparation of the chromosome for microscopy.

This may be inherited from a parent who also has the abnormality, or it may result from an error in meiosis during the formation of gametes in one of the parents. One example is fragile-X syndrome, which is a constriction in the tip of the X chromosome that can result in intellectual disability (**Figure 15.10**). About 1 male in 3,000 and 1 female in 7,000 are affected. Although the basic pattern of inheritance is that of an X-linked recessive trait, there are departures from this pattern. Not all people with the fragile-X chromosomal abnormality are intellectually disabled, as we will see.

Expanding triplet repeats demonstrate the fragility of some human genes

About one-fifth of all males who have the fragile-X chromosomal abnormality are phenotypically normal, as are most of their daughters. But many of those daughters' sons are intellectually disabled. In a family in which fragile-X syndrome appears, later generations tend to show earlier onset and more severe symptoms of the disease. It is almost as if the abnormal allele itself is changing—and getting worse. And that's exactly what is happening.

The gene associated with fragile-X syndrome (*FMR1*) contains a repeated triplet, CGG, at a certain point in the promoter region (**Figure 15.11**). In normal people, this triplet is repeated 6 to 54 times (the average is 29). In intellectually disabled people with fragile-X syndrome, the CGG sequence is repeated 200 to 2,000 times.

Males carrying a moderate number of repeats (55–199) show no symptoms and are called premutated. These repeats become more numerous as the daughters of these men pass the chromosome on

TABLE **15.2** Some Human Genetic Diseases			
Disease name	**Inheritance pattern; births frequency**	**Gene mutated; protein product**	**Clinical phenotype**
Marfan syndrome	Autosomal dominant; 1 in 5,000	*FBN1*; fibrillin-1	Weakened connective tissue, aortic aneurism, vision problems
Familial hypercholesterolemia	Autosomal codominant; 1 in 500 heterozygous	*LDLR*; low-density lipoprotein receptor	High blood cholesterol, heart disease
Cystic fibrosis	Autosomal recessive; 1 in 4,000	*CFTR*; chloride ion channel in membrane	Immune, digestive, and respiratory illness
Duchenne muscular dystrophy	Sex-linked recessive; 1 in 3,500 males	*DMD*; the muscle membrane protein dystrophin	Muscle weakness
Hemophilia A	Sex-linked recessive; 1 in 5,000 males	*HEMA*; factor VIII blood clotting protein	Inability to clot blood after injury, hemorrhage

Sources: H. Dietz. 2001. In GeneReviews®. www.ncbi.nlm.nih.gov/books/NBK1335/. Updated 2017 Oct 12; S. Singh and V. Bittner. 2015. *Curr Atheroscler Rep* 17: 3; https://omim.org/entry/219700; https://omim.org/entry/310200; https://rarediseases.org/rare-diseases/duchenne-muscular-dystrophy/; https://omim.org/entry/306700.

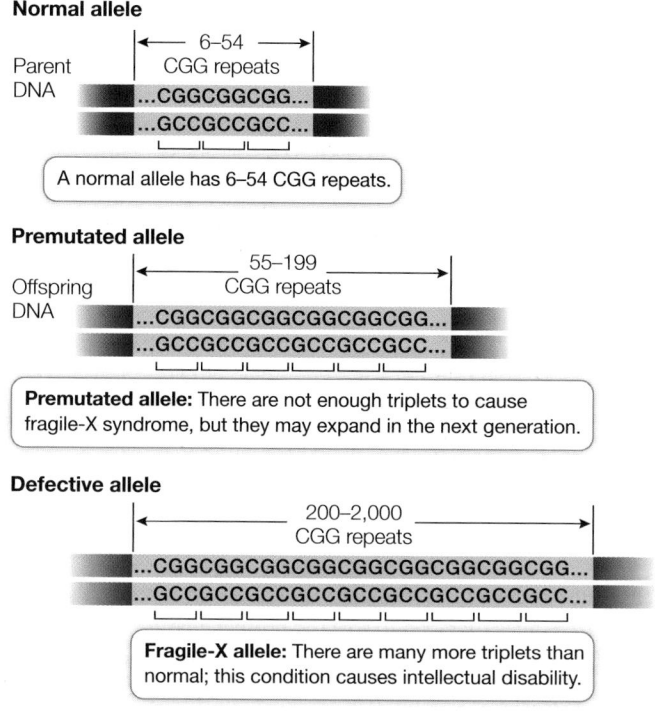

Normal allele

Parent DNA

6–54 CGG repeats

...CGGCGGCGG...
...GCCGCCGCC...

A normal allele has 6–54 CGG repeats.

Premutated allele

Offspring DNA

55–199 CGG repeats

...CGGCGGCGGCGGCGGCGG...
...GCCGCCGCCGCCGCCGCC...

Premutated allele: There are not enough triplets to cause fragile-X syndrome, but they may expand in the next generation.

Defective allele

200–2,000 CGG repeats

...CGGCGGCGGCGGCGGCGGCGGCGGCGG...
...GCCGCCGCCGCCGCCGCCGCCGCCGCC...

Fragile-X allele: There are many more triplets than normal; this condition causes intellectual disability.

Figure 15.11 The CGG Repeats in the FMR1 Gene Expand with Each Generation The genetic defect in fragile-X syndrome is caused by 200 or more repeats of the CGG triplet.

Q: Suppose an individual homozygous for 20 CGG repeats had a crossover during meiosis between homologous chromatids involving repeat number 8 in one chromatid and repeat number 12 in the other. What would the resulting repeat numbers be in each chromatid from this incorrect alignment during crossing over?

to their children. With 200 or more repeats, increased methylation of the cytosines in the CGG triplets is likely, which inhibits transcription of the *FMR1* gene (see Key Concept 16.4). The normal role of the protein product of this gene is to bind to mRNAs involved in neuron function and to regulate their translation at the ribosome. When the FMR1 protein is not made in adequate amounts, these mRNAs are not properly translated, and nerve cells die. Their loss often results in intellectual disability. The methylated cytosines bind proteins that cause the chromosome constriction and fragile appearance.

This phenomenon of **expanding triplet repeats** has been found in more than a dozen other diseases, such as myotonic dystrophy (involving repeated CTG triplets) and Huntington's disease (in which CAG is repeated). Such repeats, which may be found within a protein-coding region or outside it, appear to be present in many other genes without causing harm. How the repeats expand is not completely understood. One hypothesis is that DNA polymerase may slip after synthesizing a repeat and then fall back to copy it again; another is that incorrect alignment during crossing over in meiosis increases the copy number.

Cancer often involves somatic mutations

Many chromosomal and point mutations have been described in cancer cells. Such mutations affect oncogenes, whose products stimulate cell division, or tumor suppressor genes, whose products

(A) Colon cancer development

Section through colon (large intestine)

Normal cells

Loss of normal tumor suppressor gene *APC*

1 A polyp (small growth) forms on the colon wall.

2 A benign, precancerous tumor grows.

Activation of oncogene *RAS*

3 A class II adenoma (benign) grows.

Loss of tumor suppressor gene *DCC*

4 A class III adenoma (benign) grows.

Loss of tumor suppressor gene *P53*

5 A carcinoma (malignant tumor) develops.

(B) Normal versus cancerous colon

Both photos © David M. Martin, M.D./Science Source

Figure 15.12 Multiple Somatic Mutations Transform a Normal Colon Epithelial Cell into a Cancer Cell **(A)** At least four genes must be mutated in a single cell to produce metastatic colon cancer. **(B)** These images from a screening test reveal a normal colon (left) and colon cancer (right).

inhibit cell division (see Key Concept 11.7). More than two gene mutations are usually needed for full-blown cancer.

Because colon cancer progresses to full malignancy slowly, it has been possible to identify the gene mutations that lead to each stage. Figure 15.12 outlines the "molecular biography" of this form of cancer. At least three tumor suppressor genes and one oncogene must be mutated in sequence in a cell in the colon lining for cancer to develop.

Although the occurrence of all of these events in a single cell might seem unlikely, remember that the colon lining has millions of cells, that these cells arise from stem cells that are constantly dividing, and that these changes take place over many years of exposure to natural and synthetic substances in foods, some of which act as mutagens.

Many diseases are caused by multiple genes and environment

The example of cancer illustrates how many common phenotypes, including ones that cause disease, are **multifactorial**; that is, they are caused by the interactions of many genes and proteins with one or more factors in the environment. When studying genetics, we tend to call individuals either normal (wild type) or abnormal (mutant); however, in reality every individual contains thousands or millions of genetic variations that arose through mutations. Our susceptibility to disease is often determined by complex interactions between these genotypes and factors in the environment, such as the foods we eat or the pathogens we encounter. For example, a complex set of genotypes determines who among us can eat a high-fat diet and not experience a heart attack, or who will succumb to disease when exposed to infectious bacteria. Estimates suggest that up to 60% of all people are affected by diseases that are genetically influenced. Identifying these genetic influences is another major task of molecular medicine and human genome sequencing.

KEY CONCEPT
15.2 Recap and Assess

Many genetic mutations result in loss of protein function and cause a mutant phenotype (a genetic disease). Disease-causing mutations range from point mutations to chromosomal abnormalities. In expanding triplet repeat disease alleles are altered as they are passed down, such that repeat number can increase and give rise to a disease phenotype. Some genetic diseases are influenced by multiple genes and the environment.

1. Alkaptonuria is an inborn error of metabolism, caused by defects in an enzyme in the pathway that breaks down tyrosine (see Key Concept 14.1). Humans who are homozygous for one of these mutations make nonfunctional enzyme and accumulate the enzyme's substrate, homogentisic acid, which causes their disease symptoms. In 1996, researchers in Spain cloned and sequenced the gene for the enzyme and characterized several mutant alleles. Here is the wild-type coding strand sequence for part of the gene, with the amino acid sequence of the protein below:

    5'...TTG ATA CCC ATT GCC...3'

    ...Leu Ile Pro Ile Ala...

    Here is the sequence for one of the mutant alleles:

    5'...TTG ATA TCC ATT GCC...3'

    a. Use the genetic code table (see Figure 14.11) to determine the amino acid sequence produced by the mutant allele. What type of mutation is this: silent, nonsense, missense, loss-of-stop, or frame-shift?

    b. Why is this mutation likely to affect the function of the enzyme? (*Hint*: see Key Concept 3.2, especially Table 3.2.)

2. Not all women with a mutation in the *BRCA1* gene get early-onset breast cancer. Explain.

3. Why do some members of a family show symptoms of fragile-X syndrome and others do not?

In this key concept we described the ways in which mutations can lead to human disease. Let's turn now to the ways that biologists detect mutations in DNA.

KEY CONCEPT
15.3 Mutations Can Be Detected and Analyzed

Learning Objectives

15.3.1 Describe how restriction enzymes cut DNA.

15.3.2 Explain how gel electrophoresis separates DNA fragments based on their size.

15.3.3 Define DNA fingerprinting and explain how it works.

15.3.4 Describe how linkage to a genetic marker can be used to identify a disease-causing gene.

A challenge for biologists studying mutations is to precisely describe the DNA changes that lead to specific protein changes—an area of research called molecular genetics. Of course, the most direct and comprehensive way to analyze DNA is to determine its sequence of bases. DNA sequencing technologies are continually improving, and the entire genomes of many organisms have now been sequenced completely. Furthermore, the genomes of closely related organisms have been compared in order to identify mutations. We will discuss sequencing technology in Chapter 17. We are approaching the era where DNA sequencing will be the method of choice in searching for mutations. Whole genome DNA sequencing is not yet, however, in routine use in medicine. In this key concept we look at some of the techniques that are used in combination with DNA sequencing to study DNA, and to identify mutations that cause disease.

Cleavage of DNA by restriction enzymes can be used to rapidly detect mutations

All organisms, including bacteria, must have ways of dealing with their enemies. As we saw in Key Concept 13.1, bacteria can be attacked by viruses called bacteriophages. These viruses inject their genetic material into the host cell and turn it into a virus-producing factory, eventually killing the cell. Some bacteria defend themselves against such invasions by producing **restriction enzymes** (also known as restriction endonucleases), which cut double-stranded DNA molecules—such as those injected by bacteriophages—into smaller, noninfectious fragments (Figure 15.13). These enzymes break the bonds of the DNA backbone between the 3' hydroxyl group of one nucleotide and the 5' phosphate group of the next nucleotide. This cutting process is called **restriction digestion**.

There are many such restriction enzymes, each of which cleaves DNA at a specific sequence of bases called a **recognition sequence** or a **restriction site**. Most restriction sites are four to six base pairs long. Because each sequence of bases has a unique structure (see Key Concept 13.2), it can be specifically recognized by a particular restriction enzyme. Cells protect themselves from being digested by their own enzymes by either not having the particular restriction site in their genome, or by modifying their DNA, often with methyl groups, to prevent cutting by the restriction enzymes.

Figure 15.13 labels:

Virus —

1 A restriction enzyme cleaves the incoming viral DNA at restriction sites.

2 Other enzymes degrade the viral DNA into smaller fragments.

3 Methyl groups at the restriction sites block the restriction enzyme and protect the bacterial DNA from being cleaved.

Bacterial host cell

Host DNA

Figure 15.13 Bacteria Fight Invading Viruses by Making Restriction Enzymes

Restriction enzymes can be isolated from the cells that make them and used as biochemical reagents in the laboratory to give information about the nucleotide sequences of DNA molecules from other organisms. If DNA from any organism is incubated in a test tube with a restriction enzyme (along with buffers and salts that help the enzyme function), that DNA will be cut wherever the restriction site occurs. A specific sequence of bases defines each restriction site. For example, the enzyme *Eco*RI (named after its source strain of the bacterium *E. coli*) cuts DNA only where it encounters a specific six-base-pair sequence in the DNA double helix (**Figure 15.14A**). Note that the restriction site is palindromic, like the word "radar." This means that both strands have the same sequence when they are read from their 5′ (or their 3′) ends. The *Eco*RI enzyme has two identical active sites on its two subunits, which cleave the two strands simultaneously between the G and the A of each strand, resulting in a "staggered" cut that leaves identical 5′ overhangs (**Figure 15.14B**).

The *Eco*RI recognition sequence occurs, on average, about once in every 4,000 base pairs in a typical prokaryotic genome, or about once per four prokaryotic genes. So *Eco*RI can chop a large piece of DNA into smaller pieces containing, on average, just a few genes.

(A) The *Eco*RI restriction site

5′ . . . GAATTC . . . 3′
3′ . . . CTTAAG . . . 5′

(B) *Eco*RI makes a staggered double-stranded cut

5′ . . . GAATTC . . . 3′   ⟶   5′ . . . G   AATTC . . . 3′
3′ . . . CTTAAG . . . 5′   3′ . . . CTTAA   G . . . 5′

Figure 15.14 Restriction Enzymes Cut DNA at Specific Sequences (A) The restriction enzyme *Eco*RI recognizes a specific six-base-pair sequence in the DNA double helix. (B) When it makes a double-strand staggered cut, *Eco*RI generates identical 5′ overhangs (AATT).

Using *Eco*RI in the laboratory to cut small genomes, such as those of viruses that have tens of thousands of base pairs, may result in just a few fragments. For a huge eukaryotic chromosome with tens or hundreds of millions of base pairs, a very large number of fragments will be created.

Of course, "on average" does not mean that the enzyme cuts all stretches of DNA at regular intervals. For example, the *Eco*RI recognition sequence does not occur even once in the 40,000 base pairs of the bacteriophage T7 genome—a fact that is crucial to the survival of this virus, since its host is *E. coli*. Fortunately for *E. coli*, the *Eco*RI recognition sequence does appear in the DNA of other bacteriophages.

Gel electrophoresis separates DNA fragments

Restriction enzyme digestion is used to manipulate DNA in the laboratory so that mutations can be identified and analyzed. After a laboratory sample of DNA has been cut with one or more restriction enzymes, the DNA is in fragments, which must be separated to identify (map) where the cuts were made. Because the recognition sequence does not occur at regular intervals, the fragments are not all the same size, and these size differences can be used to separate the fragments from one another. Separating the fragments is necessary to determine the number and molecular sizes (in base pairs) of the fragments produced, or to identify and purify an individual fragment for further analysis or for use in an experiment.

Gel electrophoresis is a common and convenient technique for separating or purifying DNA fragments. Samples containing the fragments are placed in wells at one end of a semisolid gel (usually made of agarose or polyacrylamide), and an electric field is applied to the gel (**Figure 15.15**). Because of its phosphate groups, DNA is negatively charged at neutral pH; therefore, because opposite charges attract, the DNA fragments move through the gel toward the positive end of the field. Because the spaces between the polymers of the gel are small, small DNA molecules can move through the gel faster than larger ones. Thus DNA fragments of different sizes separate from one another, forming bands that can be detected with a dye. This provides three types of information:

1. *The number of fragments.* The number of fragments produced by digestion of a DNA sample with a given restriction enzyme depends on how many times that enzyme's recognition sequence occurs in the sample. Thus gel electrophoresis can provide some information about the presence of specific DNA sequences (the restriction sites) in the DNA sample.

2. *The sizes of the fragments.* DNA fragments of known size (size markers) are often placed in one well of the gel to provide a standard for comparison. The size markers are used to determine the sizes of the DNA fragments in samples in the other wells. By comparing the fragment sizes obtained with two or more restriction enzymes, the locations of their recognition sites relative to one another can be worked out (mapped).

3. *The relative abundance of a fragment.* In many experiments the investigator is interested in how much DNA is present. The relative intensity of a band produced by a specific fragment can indicate the amount of that fragment.

Research Tools

Figure 15.15 **Separating Fragments of DNA by Gel Electrophoresis** A mixture of DNA fragments is placed in a gel, and an electric field is applied across the gel. The negatively charged DNA moves toward the positive end of the field, with smaller molecules moving faster than larger ones. After minutes to hours for separation, the electric power is shut off and the separated fragments can be analyzed.

View in **Achieve**
Animation 15.1 Gel Electrophoresis

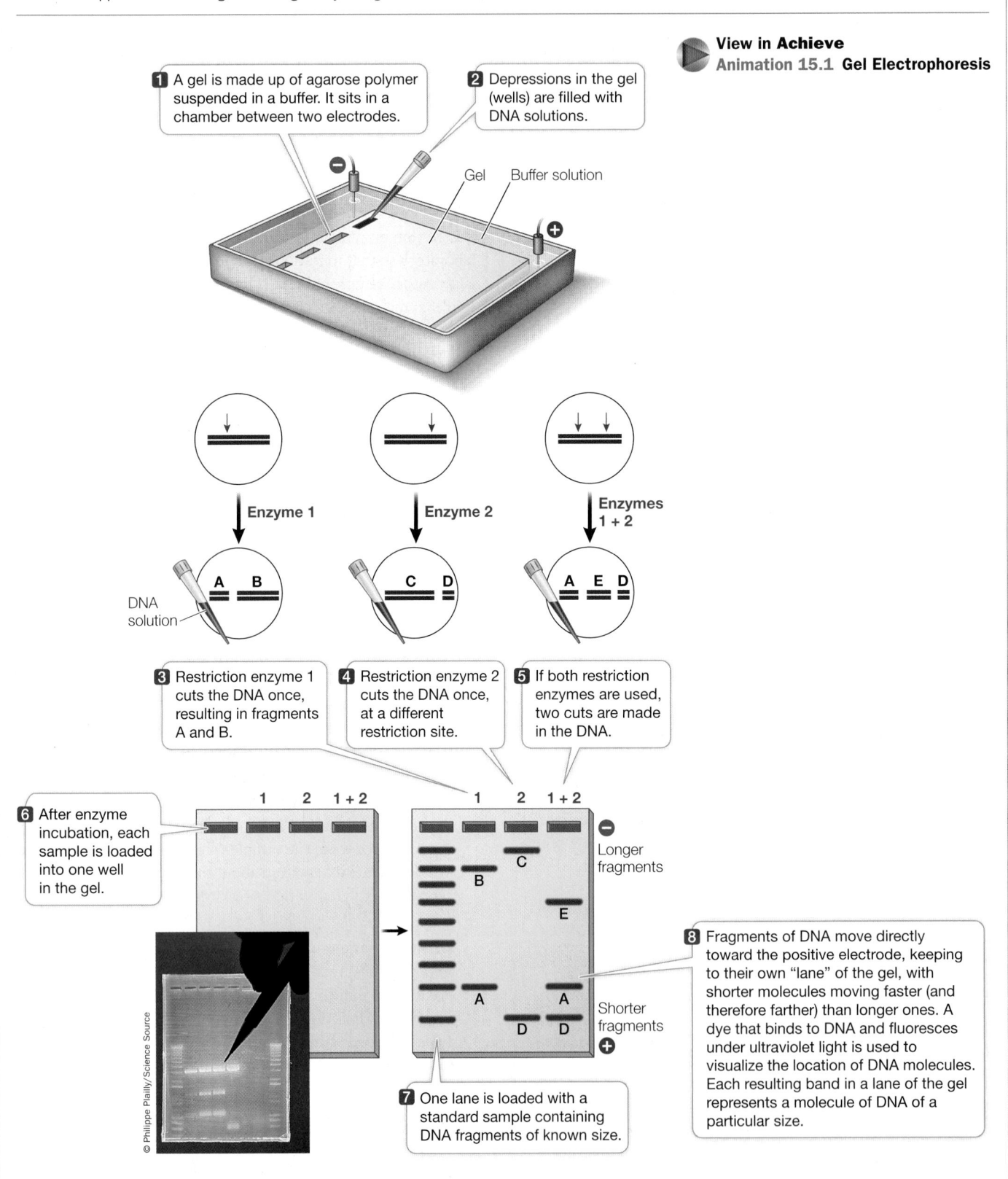

1 A gel is made up of agarose polymer suspended in a buffer. It sits in a chamber between two electrodes.

2 Depressions in the gel (wells) are filled with DNA solutions.

Gel   Buffer solution

Enzyme 1   **Enzyme 2**   **Enzymes 1 + 2**

DNA solution   A   B   C   D   A   E   D

3 Restriction enzyme 1 cuts the DNA once, resulting in fragments A and B.

4 Restriction enzyme 2 cuts the DNA once, at a different restriction site.

5 If both restriction enzymes are used, two cuts are made in the DNA.

6 After enzyme incubation, each sample is loaded into one well in the gel.

1   2   1 + 2   1   2   1 + 2

Longer fragments

C
B
E
A   A
D   D

Shorter fragments

© Philippe Plailly/Science Source

7 One lane is loaded with a standard sample containing DNA fragments of known size.

8 Fragments of DNA move directly toward the positive electrode, keeping to their own "lane" of the gel, with shorter molecules moving faster (and therefore farther) than longer ones. A dye that binds to DNA and fluoresces under ultraviolet light is used to visualize the location of DNA molecules. Each resulting band in a lane of the gel represents a molecule of DNA of a particular size.

DNA fingerprinting combines PCR with restriction analysis and electrophoresis

The methods we have just described are used in **DNA fingerprinting**, which identifies individuals based on differences in their DNA sequences. DNA fingerprinting works best with sequences that are highly polymorphic—that is, sequences that have multiple alleles (because of many mutations during the evolution of the organism) and are therefore likely to be different in different individuals. Two types of polymorphisms are especially informative:

1. **Single nucleotide polymorphisms (SNPs;** pronounced "snips") are nucleotide base pairs at which point mutations have become sufficiently frequent in a population to be readily detected. A polymorphic base pair is referred to as a SNP locus, or simply SNP, and the different base-pairs are termed SNP alleles. SNPs are numerous within genomes and have been mapped for many organisms. If one parent is homozygous for the A-T allele at a particular SNP locus in the genome, and the other parent is homozygous for G-C, the offspring will be heterozygous: one chromosome will have the A-T allele and the other will have the G-C allele. A SNP is often referred to with reference to only one of the two DNA strands—in this example in which one allele is A-T and the other G-C, the SNP is referred to as an A/G SNP or, equivalently, a T/C SNP. If a SNP occurs in a restriction enzyme recognition site, such that one variant is recognized by the enzyme and the other isn't, then individuals can be distinguished from one another very easily using the polymerase chain reaction (PCR; see Key Concept 13.5). A fragment containing the polymorphic sequence is amplified by PCR from samples of total DNA isolated from each individual. The fragments are then cut with the restriction enzyme and analyzed by gel electrophoresis.

   ▶ **View in Achieve**
   Activity 15.1 Allele-Specific Cleavage

2. **Short tandem repeats (STRs)** are short, repetitive DNA sequences that occur side by side (in tandem) on the chromosomes, usually in the noncoding regions. These repeat patterns, which contain one to five base pairs, are also inherited. For example, at a particular locus on chromosome 15 there may be an STR of "AGG." An individual may inherit an allele with six copies of the repeat (AGGAGGAGGAGGAGGAGG) from her mother and an allele with two copies (AGGAGG) from her father. Again, PCR is used to amplify DNA fragments containing these repeated sequences, and then the amplified fragments, which have different sizes because of the different numbers of the repeats, are distinguished by gel electrophoresis (Figure 15.16A).

(A) STR analysis compares sequence for specific loci from two or more DNA samples.

(B) DNA fingerprinting confirms individuals' identities

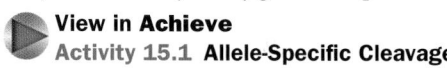

Figure 15.16 DNA Fingerprinting with Short Tandem Repeats **(A)** A particular STR locus can be analyzed to determine the number of repeat sequences that were inherited by an individual from each biological parent. The two alleles can be identified in an electrophoresis gel on the basis of their sizes. When several STR loci are analyzed, the pattern can constitute a definitive identification of an individual. **(B)** Remains of soldiers are positively identified by comparing their STR genotypes to relatives.

Q: Should everyone have their DNA fingerprinted at birth to create a "genetic ID" for use in screening for genetic diseases? What would be the advantages and disadvantages of this?

Connect the Concepts As described in Key Concept 13.5, PCR is a technique used to make multiple copies of a DNA sequence—that is, to amplify it. The process essentially automates DNA replication; over many cycles the amount of DNA can be increased exponentially.

The method of DNA fingerprinting used most commonly today relies on STR analysis. The Federal Bureau of Investigation in the United States currently uses 20 STR loci in its Combined DNA Index System (CODIS) database (Table 15.3). An analysis of these loci in your DNA would reveal your particular DNA fingerprint. Looking at Table 15.3, you might inherit:

- From your mother: allele 72 from chromosome 4; allele 23 from chromosome 7; allele 14 from chromosome 11; and allele 12 from chromosome 18

TABLE **15.3**	Four of the Genetic Loci Used for Identification in the CODIS Database		
Human chromosome	**Locus name**	**Repeated sequence**	**Number of alleles**
4	FGA	CTTT	98
7	D7S820	GATA	32
11	TH01	AATG	21
18	D18S51	AGAA	55

Source: https://strbase.nist.gov/fbicore.htm.

- From your father: allele 56 from chromosome 4; allele 22 from chromosome 7; allele 16 from chromosome 11; and allele 12 from chromosome 18

Note that in this case you are heterozygous for the alleles on three of the chromosomes and homozygous for the allele on chromosome 18. With the large number of alleles at each locus and 20 loci, the probability of two people sharing the same alleles across all the loci is very small. For example, if all 20 STR loci had 20 equally frequent alleles, the probability of two unrelated individuals showing an exact match would be about $(0.005)^{20}$, which is less than 1 in 10^{46}. So a DNA sample from a crime scene can be used to uniquely identify the individual who left the sample at the scene. This implies that a DNA sample can be used to uniquely identify an individual. This ability has been useful in criminal cases both to identify perpetrators and to exonerate previously convicted individuals, sometimes many years after their conviction. In addition, STR loci are often used to identify human remains. In these cases, identification involves comparing the STR fingerprint of the unknown individual to possible relatives, such as parents or siblings, who are expected to carry the same alleles (**Figure 15.16B**)

DNA analysis with genetic markers such as SNPs and STRs has applications throughout all areas of biological research. For example, these markers are used to analyze the organization of genomes, to identify species or individuals within species, to compare species or organisms to see how closely related they are, and to analyze particular genes and the phenotypes associated with them. In the remainder of this chapter we focus on the use of these markers and other technologies that are used to study and treat genetic diseases.

DNA analysis can be used to identify mutations that lead to disease

With diseases such as PKU and sickle-cell anemia, you have seen that the clinical phenotypes of inherited diseases could be traced to individual proteins, and that the genes could then be identified. For example, in sickle-cell anemia, the protein abnormality in hemoglobin was described first (a single amino acid change), and then the gene for β-globin was isolated and the DNA mutation was pinpointed:

Clinical phenotype → protein phenotype → gene

With the advent of new ways to identify DNA variations, a new pattern of human genetic analysis emerged. In these cases, the clinical phenotype is first related to a DNA variation, and then the gene and protein involved are identified. For cystic fibrosis (see Table 15.2), a mutant version of the gene *CFTR* was isolated first, and then the protein was characterized:

Clinical phenotype → gene → protein phenotype

Whichever approach is used, final identification of the protein(s) involved in a disease is important in designing specific therapies.

Genetic markers can be used to find disease-causing genes

Identifying a mutant gene requires finding a location on the chromosome that is closely linked to the gene of interest, a process called **linkage analysis**. The reference locations for gene isolation are **genetic markers**. Genetic markers such as STRs and SNPs can be used as landmarks to find a gene of interest, if the gene also has multiple alleles (for example, normal and disease-causing alleles). The key to this method is the well-established observation that if two genes are located near each other on the same chromosome, they are usually passed on together from parent to offspring (see Key Concept 12.4). The same holds true for any pair of DNA genetic markers. In the case of linkage analysis, the idea is to find markers that are progressively closer to the gene of interest.

As you have seen, SNPs and STRs are widespread in eukaryotic genomes. There is roughly one SNP for every 1,330 base pairs in the human genome, and any regions of the genome also contain repetitive DNA sequences such as those found in STRs. SNPs and STRs can be analyzed using the PCR techniques mentioned earlier. SNPs can also be detected using sophisticated chemical methods such as mass spectrometry.

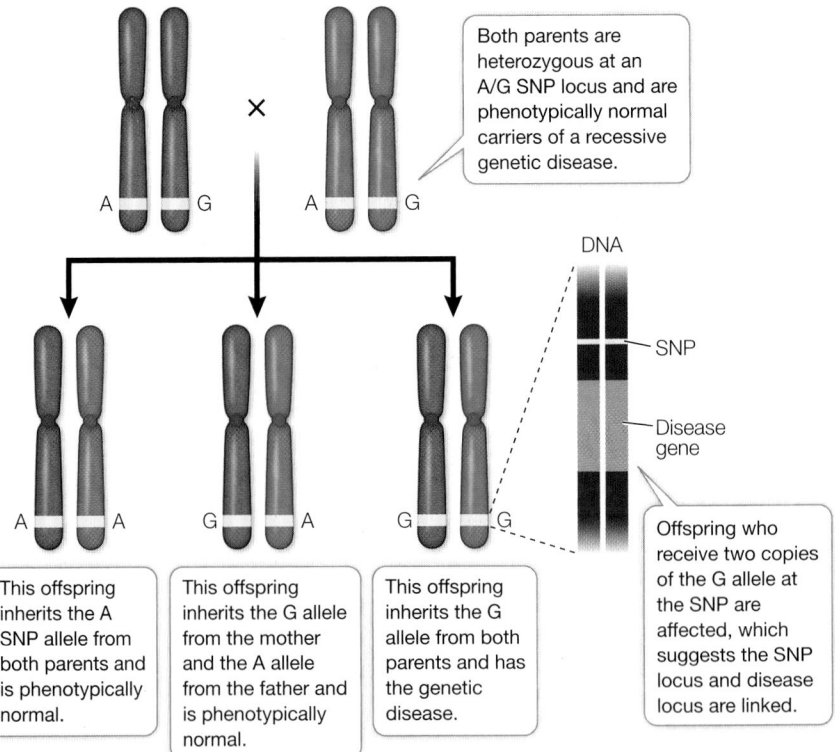

Figure 15.17 DNA Linkage Analysis   Linkage of an SNP to a disease-causing allele in many families narrows down the location of the defective gene, making its isolation and identification possible. In the example shown here, the disease locus is linked to an A/G SNP, with the disease-causing recessive allele linked to the G (or G-C base pair) SNP.

Q: In this example the G allele at this A/G SNP is associated with the disease-causing allele. Do you think this will also be the case in other families?

To narrow down the location of a gene, a scientist must find a genetic marker that is *always inherited with the gene*. To do this, family medical histories are taken and pedigrees are constructed. If a genetic marker and a genetic disease are inherited together in many families, then they must be near each other on the same chromosome (**Figure 15.17**). This situation recalls the conclusion reached in the classic studies of inheritance undertaken by Thomas Hunt Morgan and discussed in Key Concept 12.4: two genes do not always assort independently. Alleles at loci that are "linked" on the same chromosome will be more often inherited together—especially when the two loci are close to one another on the chromosome.

Linkage narrows down the position of a gene on a chromosome to a few hundred thousand base pairs. Once a linked DNA region is identified, many methods are available to identify the actual gene responsible for a genetic disease. The complete sequence of the region can be searched for candidate genes, using information available from databases of genome sequences. With luck a scientist can make an educated guess, based on biochemical or physiological information about the disease, along with information about the functions of candidate genes, as to which gene is responsible for the disease. The identification of DNA polymorphisms within candidate genes that correlate with the presence or absence of disease can also help narrow down the search. A variety of techniques, such as analyzing mRNA levels of candidate genes in diseased and healthy individuals, are used to confirm that the correct gene has been identified.

The isolation of the *BRCA1* gene that is involved in breast cancer (described in the chapter opening) offers a good illustration of molecular techniques used to identify genes associated with disease, and is described in **Investigating Life: How Was the *BRCA1* Gene Identified?** Analysis of the *BRCA1* mutations came after Mary-Claire King of the University of California at Berkeley

▶Investigating**LIFE**   How Was the *BRCA1* Gene Identified?

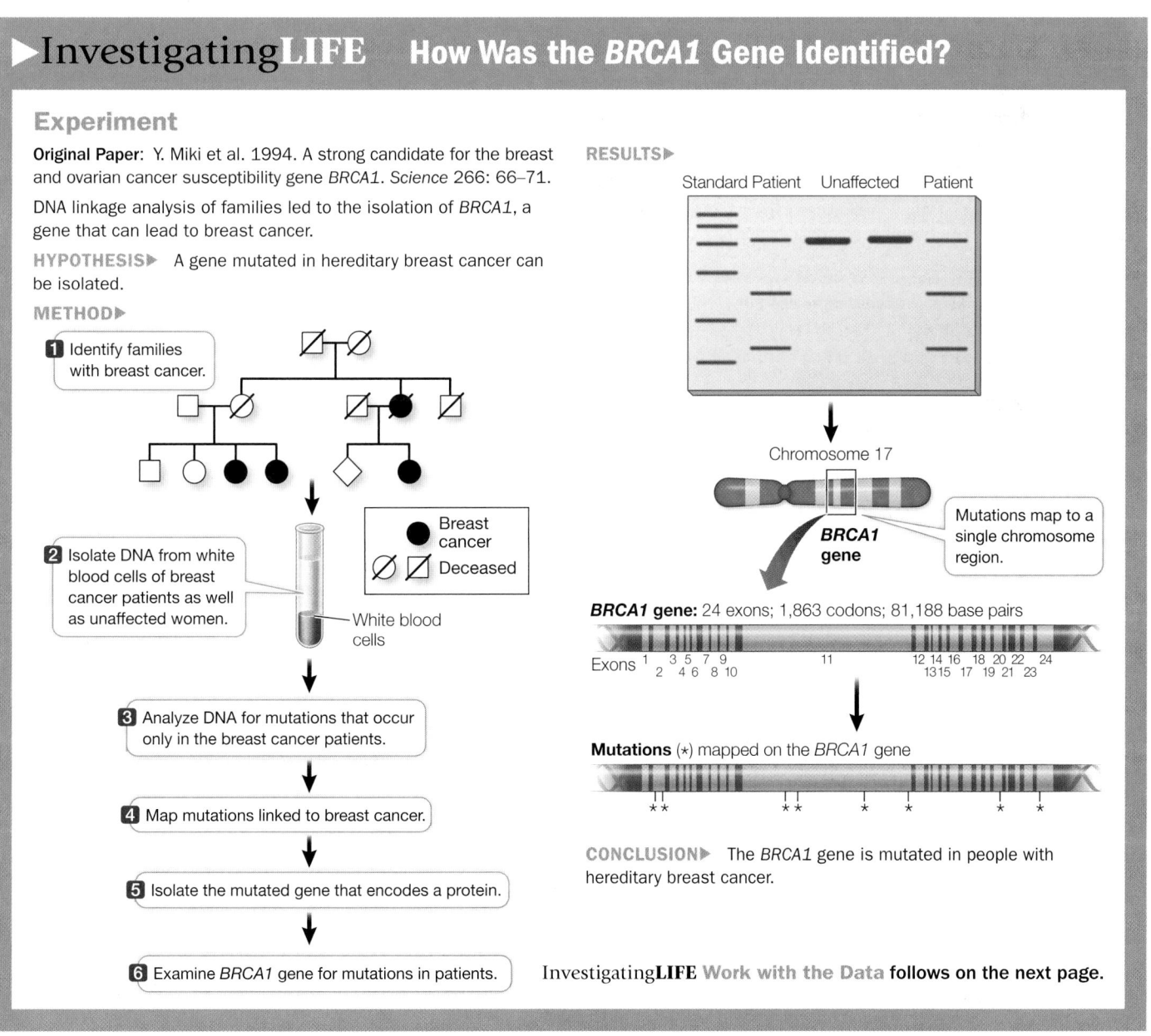

Experiment

Original Paper: Y. Miki et al. 1994. A strong candidate for the breast and ovarian cancer susceptibility gene *BRCA1*. *Science* 266: 66–71.

DNA linkage analysis of families led to the isolation of *BRCA1*, a gene that can lead to breast cancer.

HYPOTHESIS▶   A gene mutated in hereditary breast cancer can be isolated.

METHOD▶

1 Identify families with breast cancer.

2 Isolate DNA from white blood cells of breast cancer patients as well as unaffected women.

— White blood cells

● Breast cancer
⊘ ⊘ Deceased

3 Analyze DNA for mutations that occur only in the breast cancer patients.

4 Map mutations linked to breast cancer.

5 Isolate the mutated gene that encodes a protein.

6 Examine *BRCA1* gene for mutations in patients.

RESULTS▶

Standard Patient   Unaffected   Patient

Chromosome 17

BRCA1 gene

Mutations map to a single chromosome region.

BRCA1 gene: 24 exons; 1,863 codons; 81,188 base pairs

Exons   1 3 5 7 9   11   12 14 16 18 20 22 24
            2 4 6 8 10   13 15 17 19 21 23

Mutations (∗) mapped on the *BRCA1* gene

∗ ∗   ∗ ∗   ∗   ∗   ∗   ∗

CONCLUSION▶   The *BRCA1* gene is mutated in people with hereditary breast cancer.

Investigating**LIFE** **Work with the Data** follows on the next page.

Work with the Data

About one in ten cases of breast cancer is hereditary. That is, the cancer arises from a germ line mutation (meaning it occurs in all cells of the body) that is expressed in breast cells as cancer. The other nine in ten cases come about from somatic mutations in breast cells. The identification of a gene involved in hereditary breast cancer was made by DNA analysis. First, the location of the gene was narrowed down by analysis of SNPs in families in which several women had breast cancer (see the experiment). Then a team led by Mark Skolnick at the University of Utah and the company Myriad Genetics sequenced the DNA in the candidate region and looked for a sequence that had a promoter, transcription terminator, start and stop codons, and sequences at the ends of introns—in short, the sequences that mark a protein-coding gene. Once they found the candidate gene, they subjected it to a series of tests to see if it was the one associated with breast cancer.

QUESTIONS▶

1. Hereditary (as opposed to somatic) breast cancer is often suspected when the cancer develops relatively early in life. Hereditary cancers tend to arise earlier because they involve a germ line mutation present in all cells at birth, whereas a cancer due to a spontaneous somatic mutation in the DNA of a breast cell can happen any time (statistically, later). Skolnick's team examined the timing of breast cancer cases in families of patients who had different mutations in *BRCA1*. The results are shown in **Table A**. What conclusions can you draw concerning whether cancer was hereditary in these families?

Table A

Family	Total cases	Cases before age 50
A	31	20
B	22	14
C	10	7

2. DNA sequencing evaluated *BRCA1* in the cancer patients and their families, as well as in controls who did not have breast cancer themselves or in their family. The results are shown in **Table B**. Were the mutations in *BRCA1* present only in the breast cancer patients? What do you think the effects of the mutations were in each of the three families?

Table B

Family	Codon number in *BRCA1*	Change in patients	Change in controls?
A	1313	C → T	None (0/170)
B	1775	T → G	None (0/120)
C	24	Deletion 11 bp	None (0/180)

3. Human tissues from people without breast cancer were examined by nucleic acid hybridization (see Figure 14.7) for the level of *BRCA1* mRNA. The results are shown in **Table C**. What can you conclude about the kinds of cancer that might be caused by mutations in *BRCA1*?

Table C

Tissue	mRNA detected?
Breast	Yes
Colon	No
Intestine	No
Ovary	Yes
Prostate	No
Spleen	No
Testis	Yes
Thymus	Yes

Go to **Achieve** for a companion Data in Depth exercise.

---

worked with breast cancer patients and their families to identify SNPs closely linked to the breast cancer phenotype.

KEY CONCEPT
15.3 Recap and Assess

DNA molecules can be cut into fragments by restriction digestion and then sorted by gel electrophoresis. PCR is used to amplify sequences of interest from complex samples. These techniques are used in DNA fingerprinting to analyze DNA polymorphisms for the purpose of identifying individuals. Genes involved in disease can be identified by linkage analysis with markers, especially SNPs and STRs, to identify candidates, followed by confirmation using protein and expression differences between healthy and diseased individuals.

1. A DNA molecule is 100,000 base pairs in length. Assuming all four base pairs are equally frequent and the sequence is random, how many six-base-pair *Eco*RI restriction sites do you expect to be present?

2. Cystic fibrosis is an autosomal recessive disease in which thick mucus is produced in the lungs and airways. The gene responsible for this disease encodes a protein composed of 1,480 amino acids. In most patients with cystic fibrosis, the protein has 1,479 amino acids: a phenylalanine is missing at position 508. A baby is born with cystic fibrosis. He has an older brother who is not affected. How would you test the DNA of the older brother to determine whether he is a carrier for cystic fibrosis?

3. How can a gene mutation that causes a disease be mapped and detected before its protein product is known?

The determination of the precise molecular phenotypes and genotypes of various human genetic diseases has made it possible to diagnose these diseases even before symptoms appear. Let's take a detailed look at some of these genetic screening techniques.

KEY CONCEPT
15.4 Genetic Screening Is Used to Detect Diseases

Learning Objectives

15.4.1 Compare and contrast phenotypic and genotypic genetic screening.

15.4.2 Explain how DNA hybridization is used for genetic screening.

Genetic screening is the use of a test to identify people who have, are predisposed to, or are carriers of a genetic disease. It can be done at many times of life and used for many purposes:

- *Prenatal screening* can be used to identify an embryo or fetus with a disease so that medical intervention can be applied or decisions can be made about whether or not to continue the pregnancy.
- *Newborn babies* can be screened so that proper medical intervention can be initiated quickly for those babies who need it.
- *Asymptomatic people* who have relatives with a genetic disease can be screened to determine whether they are carriers of the disease-associated allele or are likely to develop the disease themselves.

Genetic screening can be done at the level of either the phenotype or the genotype.

Genetic screening can be done by examining the phenotype

Genetic screening can involve examining a protein or other chemical that is relevant to a phenotype associated with a particular disease. Perhaps the best example is the test for phenylketonuria (PKU), which has made it possible to identify the disease in newborns, so that treatment can be started immediately. It is very likely that you were screened as a newborn for PKU.

Newborn babies with PKU have a normal phenotype because phenylalanine is not yet elevated in their blood; before birth, excess phenylalanine in the fetal blood diffuses across the placenta and into the mother's circulatory system. Since the mother is almost always heterozygous, and therefore has adequate phenylalanine hydroxylase activity, her body metabolizes the excess phenylalanine from her fetus. After birth, however, phenylalanine begins to accumulate in the baby's blood. After a few days, the phenylalanine level may be ten times higher than normal. Within days, the developing brain is damaged, and untreated children with PKU become severely intellectually disabled. But if detected early, PKU can be treated with a special diet low in phenylalanine to avoid the brain damage that would otherwise result. Thus early detection is imperative.

Routine newborn screening for PKU and other diseases began in 1963 with the development of a simple, rapid test for the presence of excess phenylalanine in blood serum (**Figure 15.18**). This method uses drops of blood from newborn babies and can be automated so that a screening laboratory can process many samples in a day. Newborn babies' blood is now screened for up to 35 genetic diseases. Some are relatively common, such as congenital hypothyroidism, which occurs about once in 4,000 births and causes reduced growth and intellectual disability because of low levels of thyroid hormone. With early intervention, many of these infants can be successfully treated. So it is not surprising that newborn screening is required in many countries, including the United States and Canada. You were probably screened for several genetic diseases in the first days of your life. Ask your parents which ones!

DNA testing is the most accurate way to detect genetic disease

The level of phenylalanine in the blood is an indirect measure of phenylalanine hydroxylase activity in the liver. But how can we

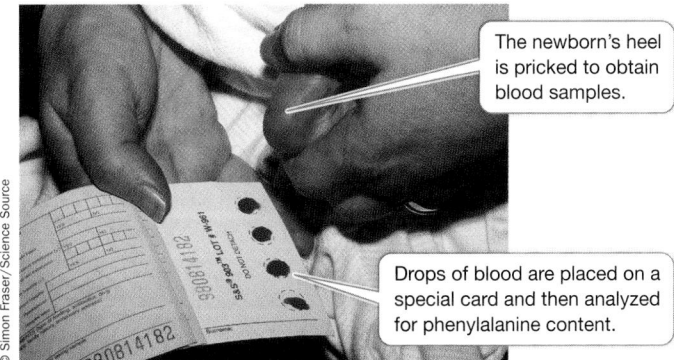

The newborn's heel is pricked to obtain blood samples.

Drops of blood are placed on a special card and then analyzed for phenylalanine content.

© Simon Fraser/Science Source

Figure 15.18 Phenotypic Screening of Newborns for Phenylketonuria   A blood test is used to screen newborns for phenylketonuria. Small samples of blood are taken from a newborn's heel. The samples are placed in a machine that measures the phenylalanine concentration in the blood. Early detection means that the symptoms of the condition can be prevented by putting the baby on a therapeutic diet.

screen for genetic diseases that are not detectable by blood tests? What if blood is difficult to obtain, as it is in a fetus? How are genetic abnormalities in heterozygotes, who express the normal protein at some level, identified?

> **Connect the Concepts** Genetic testing is a rapidly changing field, with tests being done at different stages of prenatal development. See Key Concept 42.2 for an overview of the stages of human development, to place the timing of genetic tests in perspective.

DNA testing is the direct analysis of DNA for a mutation, and it offers the most direct and accurate way of detecting an abnormal allele. Now that the mutations responsible for many human diseases have been identified, any cell in the body can be examined at any time of life for mutations. The amplification power of PCR means that only one or a few cells are needed for testing. These methods work best for diseases caused by only one or a few different mutations.

Consider, for example, two parents who are both heterozygous for the cystic fibrosis allele but who want to have a healthy child. If treated with the appropriate hormones, the mother can be induced to "superovulate," releasing several eggs. Eggs can be harvested and artificially inseminated. The fertilized eggs can be allowed to divide to the eight-cell stage. If one of these eight embryonic cells is removed, it can be tested for the presence of the cystic fibrosis allele. If the test is negative, the remaining seven-cell embryo can be implanted in the mother's womb, where it will develop normally.

Such preimplantation screening is performed only rarely. More typical are analyses of fetal cells after normal fertilization and implantation in the womb. Fetal cells or even DNA that has leaked out of dead cells can be analyzed at about the tenth week of pregnancy by a procedure termed chorionic villus sampling, or during the thirteenth to seventeenth weeks by amniocentesis. In either case, only a few fetal cells are necessary to perform DNA testing. Recently, very sensitive methods were developed so that DNA testing can be done with the few fetal cells that are released into the mother's blood. A 10-milliliter blood sample from a pregnant woman has enough fetal cells for the analysis of many disorders, including Down syndrome and cystic fibrosis. This relatively noninvasive procedure could replace amniocentesis and chorionic villus sampling—which both carry a slight risk of causing a miscarriage—in the near future.

DNA testing can also be performed with newborns. The blood samples used for screening for PKU and other disorders contain enough of the baby's blood cells to permit DNA analysis using PCR-based techniques. DNA analysis is now being used to screen for sickle-cell disease and cystic fibrosis; similar tests for other diseases will surely follow.

Among the numerous methods available for testing for a mutant sequence of DNA is DNA hybridization, and in particular allele-specific oligonucleotide hybridization. As you saw in Figure 14.7, nucleic acid hybridization can be used to detect the presence of a specific DNA sequence, such as a sequence containing a particular mutation. Samples of DNA are collected from people who may or may not carry the mutation, and PCR is used to amplify the region of DNA where the mutation may occur. Short synthetic DNA strands called oligonucleotide probes are hybridized with the denatured PCR products. The probe is labeled in some way (e.g., with radioactivity or a fluorescent dye) so that hybridization can be readily detected. This technique is illustrated in **Figure 15.19** using sickle-cell anemia as an example.

Detection of a mutation by DNA screening can be used for diagnosis of a genetic disease, so that appropriate treatment can begin. In addition, DNA screening provides a person with important information about his or her genome.

Research Tools

Figure 15.19 DNA Testing by Allele-Specific Oligonucleotide Hybridization
Testing of this family reveals that the two biological parents are heterozygous carriers of the sickle allele. The first child has inherited two normal alleles and is neither affected by the disease nor a carrier. The unborn fetus has inherited two mutant alleles and will be affected by sickle cell disease.

Spot containing DNA sample

1 DNA from individuals to be tested is dotted to filters and denatured.

Normal probe CCTGAGGAG   Sickle probe CCTGTGGAG

2 Single-stranded DNA is synthesized from the normal β-globin allele (A) and from the sickle allele (S).

3 The probes are labeled and hybridized to the DNA samples.

Probe CCTGAGGAG   CCTGTGGAG
DNA sample GGACTCCTC   GGACACCTC

4 The probes will hybridize to the DNA samples if complementary sequences are present.

Results: Mother Father Child Fetus

Probe for normal allele — The blue color indicates lack of hybridization.

Probe for sickle allele — The red color indicates hybridization.

(AS) (AS) (AA) (SS)

Genotypes of family members
(deduced from allele-specific hybridization)

View in Achieve
Animation 15.2 DNA Testing

KEY CONCEPT
15.4 Recap and Assess

Genetic screening can be used to identify people who have, are predisposed to, or are carriers of genetic diseases. Screening can be done at the phenotype level by identifying an abnormal protein such as an enzyme with altered activity. It can also be done at the genotype level by direct testing of DNA.

1. What is the advantage of screening for genetic mutations by allele-specific oligonucleotide hybridization relative to screening phenotype differences in enzyme activity?

2. Explain how allele-specific oligonucleotide hybridization could be used to perform genetic screening for sickle-cell anemia.

KEY CONCEPT
15.5 Genetic Diseases Can Be Treated

Learning Objectives

15.5.1 Explain how a genetic disease can be treated by modifying the disease phenotype.

15.5.2 Define gene therapy and compare ex vivo and in vivo approaches to gene therapy.

Ongoing research has resulted in the development of increasingly accurate diagnostic tests and a better understanding of various genetic diseases at the molecular level. This knowledge is now being applied to the development of new treatments for genetic diseases. In the next key concept we survey various approaches to treatment, including modifications of the mutant phenotype and gene therapy, in which the normal version of a mutant gene is supplied.

Most treatments for genetic diseases simply try to alleviate the patient's symptoms. But to effectively treat these diseases—whether they affect all cells, as in inherited disorders such as PKU, or only somatic cells, as in cancer—physicians must be able to diagnose the disease accurately, understand how the disease works at the molecular level, and intervene early, before the disease ravages or kills the individual. There are two main approaches to treating genetic diseases:

1. Modifying the disease phenotype
2. Replacing the defective gene (modifying the genotype)

Genetic diseases can be treated by modifying the phenotype

Altering the phenotype of a genetic disease so that it no longer harms an individual is commonly done in one of three ways: by restricting the substrate of a deficient enzyme, by inhibiting a harmful metabolic reaction, or by supplying a missing protein product (**Figure 15.20**).

RESTRICTING THE SUBSTRATE   Restricting the substrate of a deficient enzyme is the approach taken when a newborn is diagnosed with PKU. In this case, the deficient enzyme is phenylalanine hydroxylase, and the substrate is phenylalanine (see Figure 15.8). The infant's inability to break down phenylalanine in food leads to a buildup of the substrate, which causes the clinical symptoms. So the infant is immediately put on a special diet that contains only

enough phenylalanine for immediate use. Lofenalac*, a milk-based product that is low in phenylalanine, is fed to these infants just like formula. Later, certain fruits, vegetables, cereals, and noodles low in phenylalanine can be added to the diet. Meat, fish, eggs, dairy products, and bread, which contain high amounts of phenylalanine, must be avoided, especially during childhood, when brain development is most rapid. The artificial sweetener aspartame must also be avoided because it is made of two amino acids, one of which is phenylalanine.

People with PKU are generally advised to stay on a low-phenylalanine diet for life. Although maintaining these dietary restrictions may be difficult, it is effective. Numerous follow-up studies since newborn screening was initiated have shown that people with PKU who stay on the diet are no different from the rest of the population in terms of mental ability. This is an impressive achievement in public health, given the severity of intellectual disability in untreated patients.

METABOLIC INHIBITORS   In Key Concept 11.7 we described how drugs that are inhibitors of various cell cycle processes are used to treat cancer. Drugs are also used to treat the symptoms of many genetic diseases. As biologists have gained insight into the molecular characteristics of these diseases and the specific proteins involved, a more specific approach to treatment is taking shape. Targeted therapies are being developed, especially for cancer, and some have resulted in life-saving interventions. This is a major area of applied research.

SUPPLYING THE MISSING PROTEIN   An obvious way to treat a disease caused by the lack of a functional protein is to supply that protein. This approach is used to treat hemophilia A, a disease in which blood factor VIII is missing and blood clotting is impaired (see Table 15.2). In the past, the missing protein was obtained from blood. Sometimes, however, blood carries contaminants, such as viruses (e.g., HIV) or other pathogens that could harm the recipient. Now human clotting proteins are produced by recombinant DNA technology (see Chapter 18), making it possible to provide the protein in a much purer form.

Unfortunately, the phenotypes of many diseases caused by genetic mutations are very complex. In these cases, simple interventions like those we have just described do not work. Indeed, a recent survey of 351 diseases caused by single-gene mutations showed that current therapies increased patients' life spans by an average of only 15%.

Gene therapy offers the hope of specific treatments

If a cell lacks an allele that encodes a functional product, an optimal treatment would be to provide a functional allele. The objective of **gene therapy** is to add a new gene that will be expressed in appropriate cells in a patient. What cells should be targeted? There are two approaches:

1. **Germ line gene therapy**: The new gene is inserted into a gamete (usually an egg) or the fertilized egg. In this case, all cells of the adult will carry the new gene. Ethical considerations preclude the use of this method in humans.

Cause of disease

Normal
> Normally, a wild-type gene codes for a functional enzyme.

Disease
> In genetic disease, a mutant allele codes for a nonfunctional enzyme and the pileup of substrate leads to disease.

Treatment

> **Restriction of substrate:** Less substrate results in less severe disease symptoms.

> **Addition of metabolic inhibitor:** An inhibitor blocks the harmful effects of accumulated substrate.

> **Restoration of the missing enzyme:** The wild-type protein substitutes for the mutant enzyme.

Figure 15.20 Strategies for Treating Genetic Diseases

2. **Somatic cell gene therapy**: The new gene is inserted into somatic cells involved in the disease. This method is being tried for numerous diseases, ranging from inherited genetic disorders to cancer.

There are two approaches to somatic cell gene therapy:

1. **Ex vivo gene therapy**: Target cells are removed from the patient, given the new gene, and then reinserted into the patient. This approach is being used, for example, for diseases caused by defects in genes that are expressed in white blood cells.

2. **In vivo gene therapy**: The gene is inserted directly into a patient, targeted to the appropriate cells. An example is a treatment for lung cancer in which a solution with a therapeutic gene is squirted onto a tumor.

Armed with knowledge of how genes are expressed (see Chapter 14) and regulated (see Chapter 16), physicians can design a therapeutic gene that contains not only a normal protein-coding sequence but also other sequences—such as an appropriate promoter—required for the gene's expression in targeted cells.

A major challenge has been getting the therapeutic gene into cells. Uptake of DNA into eukaryotic cells is a rare event, and once the DNA is inside a cell, its entry into the nucleus and expression are rarer still. One solution to these problems is to insert the gene into a carrier virus (a viral vector) that can infect human cells but has been altered genetically to prevent viral replication. An example is the DNA virus called **adeno-associated virus**, which has been widely used in human gene therapy clinical trials. This virus has a small genome that can be spliced into a human gene; infects most human cells, including nondividing cells such as neurons; is harmless to humans; does not provoke rejection by the immune system; and enters the cell nucleus, where its DNA with the new gene can be expressed.

Adeno-associated virus has been used successfully in human gene therapy targeting Parkinson's disease (**Figure 15.21**). Parkinson's disease is a neurological condition that affects about 1 in 200 persons in their 60s, and 1 in 25 persons in their 80s. Its symptoms include muscle stiffness and shaking and—in about half of the patients—dementia. Patients with Parkinson's disease produce inadequate amounts of the neurotransmitter γ-aminobutyric acid (GABA) in a particular part of the brain due to degeneration of the neurons that normally produce GABA. Low GABA levels result in poor coordination of movement. Raising GABA levels would thus be a reasonable approach to treatment. Recognizing that synthesis of GABA is catalyzed by the enzyme glutamate decarboxylase, a team led by Dr. Andrew Feigin at the Feinstein Institute in New York packaged a glutamate decarboxylase gene into adeno-associated virus that was then injected into the affected part of the brain. After six months, the patients who received the virus-encapsulated gene had increased levels of GABA and significant improvement in their disease symptoms. Other diseases being treated with gene therapy using this virus include cystic fibrosis, hemophilia, and muscular dystrophy. While this looks exciting on paper, bear in mind that this type of therapy is very rare, at the frontier of medicine. It may be quite a while before we can go see our local gene therapist for a cure.

Experiment

Figure 15.21   Gene Therapy

Original Paper: P. A. LeWitt et al. 2011. AAV2-GAD gene therapy for advanced Parkinson's disease: A double-blind, sham-surgery controlled randomized trial. *Lancet Neurol* 10: 309–319.

Andrew Feigin and his colleagues showed that a virus can be used to insert a therapeutic gene into the brains of patients with Parkinson's disease.

HYPOTHESIS▶   Adding a gene for glutamate decarboxylase to brain cells can alleviate symptoms caused by GABA deficiency.

METHOD▶

1 A gene for glutamate decarboxylase is inserted into the genome of adeno-associated virus.

Gene for glutamate decarboxylase

DNA of virus

New gene in virus

2 The virus is injected into a patient's brain.

3 The virus carries the glutamate decarboxylase gene into the nuclei of brain cells, where it is expressed.

RESULTS▶   The patient's symptoms improved.

CONCLUSION▶   Gene therapy can relieve symptoms in a patient with a neurotransmitter deficiency.

Go to **Achieve** for a companion **Data in Depth** exercise.

KEY CONCEPT

15.5 Recap and Assess

Treatment of a human genetic disease may involve an attempt to modify the abnormal phenotype by restricting the substrate of a deficient enzyme, inhibiting a harmful metabolic reaction, or supplying a missing protein. By contrast, gene therapy aims to address a genetic defect by inserting a normal allele into a patient's cells.

1. How do metabolic inhibitors function in treating genetic diseases such as cancer?

2. How does in vivo gene therapy work? Can you give an example?

3. In the past, it was common for people with phenylketonuria (PKU) who were placed on a low-phenylalanine diet after birth to be allowed to return to a normal diet during their teenage years. Although the levels of phenylalanine in their blood were high, their brains were thought to be beyond the stage when they could be harmed. If a woman with PKU becomes pregnant, however, a problem arises. Typically, the fetus is heterozygous

but is unable, at early stages of development, to metabolize the high levels of phenylalanine that arrive from the mother's blood.

a. Why is the fetus likely to be heterozygous?

b. What do you think would happen to the fetus during this "maternal PKU" situation?

c. What would be your advice to a woman with PKU who wants to have a child?

In this chapter you have learned about mutations, focusing on DNA changes that affect phenotypes through specific protein products. But there is much more to molecular genetics than the sequences of genes and proteins. Determining which genes will be expressed when and where is a major function of the genome. In Chapter 16 we will turn to gene regulation.

▶Investigating**LIFE**

Q and A What is the breast cancer gene, and what are the issues with DNA testing for cancer?

Angelina Jolie's public announcement that she had elected to have her breasts removed in light of her cancer gene mutations attracted worldwide interest. In fact, the phrase "mutation" had never been so popular on internet search engines! Requests for *BRCA1* testing from worried women have increased dramatically. Two issues have arisen: who should be tested, and who should perform the test? Because breast cancer is relatively common (women have about a 10% lifetime chance of having it), having several relatives who have had the disease is not unusual. Medical geneticists have come up with several criteria for defining when *BRCA1* DNA analysis is warranted. These include having several close relatives who had or have the disease, with early onset (typically before age 50) and the presence of multiple tumors.

Even when a test shows no *BRCA1* mutations in a woman with a family history of breast or ovarian cancer, we cannot say that breast or ovarian cancer may not arise. It turns out that *BRCA1* mutations account for only about one in five cases of hereditary breast cancer. Other genes are involved; we just don't know what they are, so we can't analyze their DNA. Overall, hereditary breast cancer (a germ line mutation) accounts for only 10% of breast cancers. The other 90% arise from somatic mutation of breast cells.

As to who does the test, the *BRCA1* gene was isolated by a private company that patented the DNA sequence. Until recently, that company was the only lab that could do *BRCA1* analysis, and not surprisingly, the price was high. In 2013 the U.S. Supreme Court invalidated the patent, and now more labs can do it, and more cheaply.

Future directions

Are there genetic tests for other hereditary cancers? About 10% of all cancers are caused by inheritance of mutated oncogenes or tumor suppressor genes (as opposed to mutations that occur after birth). As with breast cancer, a person who inherits a cancer-causing mutation has a much higher chance of developing cancer than one who does not have that mutation. As whole genome DNA sequencing is developed (see Chapter 18), mutations involved with other types of hereditary cancers are being identified, and screening of relatives with a propensity for cancer is on the horizon.

VISUAL SUMMARY 15

© The Florida collection/Alamy Stock Photo

You should be able to relate each summary to the adjacent figures. If you go to this visual summary in **Achieve**, you can follow links to figures, animations, activities, and simulations that will help you consolidate the material.

KEY CONCEPT

15.1 Mutations Are Heritable Changes in DNA

Go to **Simulations 15.1 and 15.2**

- **Point mutations** can be **transitions**, **transversions**, or single base-pair insertions or deletions.

- Point mutations in codons cause **silent**, **missense**, **nonsense**, **loss-of-stop**, and **frame-shift mutations**.

- Point mutations in noncoding regions can have effects through changes in expression or splicing.

- Large **chromosomal rearrangements** include **deletions**, **duplications**, **inversions**, and **translocations**.

- **Mutations** are more likely in the presence of **mutagens** and can occur at hot spots.

Figure 15.3

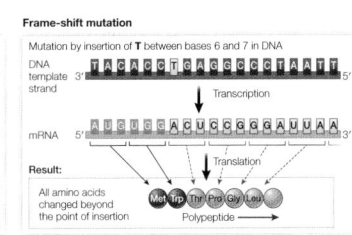

Questions

1. For each of the following point mutations in a protein-coding gene, indicate whether the mutation is a transition or transversion and whether it is a silent, missense, nonsense, or loss-of-stop mutation.

   Mutation 1: UCA → ACA

   Mutation 2: UCC → UCU

   Mutation 3: UGA → UGG

   Mutation 4: UGG → UGA

   Mutation 5: GGC → GGG

2. A cell culture is started from an organism possessing only two different chromosomes. Chromosome 1 contains eight regions, A—B—C—D—E—F—G—H, and chromosome 2 contains three regions, X—Y—Z. Over time, cells arise that carry different chromosomal rearrangements. Identify the type of chromosomal rearrangement for the following three cells: Cell 1: A—B—C—F—E—D—G—H and X—Y—Z; cell 2: X—D—E—F—G—H and A—B—C—Y—Z; cell 3: A—B—C—F—G—H and X—Y—Z.

Figure 15.5

KEY CONCEPT

15.2 Mutations in Humans Can Lead to Diseases

- Many genetic diseases are caused by point mutations that alter only a single amino acid and render a protein nonfunctional.

- Some genetic diseases involve large deletions or chromosomal abnormalities.

- **Multifactorial** diseases arise from complex interactions between multiple genes and the environment.

Questions

1. Explain why some missense mutations cause genetic disease whereas others do not.

2. Genotyping of breast cancer tumors in women indicates that some women have two mutated alleles of the *BRCA1* gene, even though there is no history of hereditary breast cancer in their families. How does this observation relate to *BRCA1* being a cause of higher rates of breast cancer in some families?

3. In expanding triplet repeat diseases, the incidence of the genetic disorder can increase over generations within a family. Why might this be the case?

Figure 15.9

	Amino acid position (of 146)								
	2	6	7	16	24	26	56	63	95
A (wild type)	His	Glu	Glu	Gly	Gly	Glu	Gly	His	Lys
Tokuchi	Tyr								
S		Val							
C		Lys							
G			Gly						
J Baltimore				Asp					
Savannah					Val				
E						Lys			
Bangkok							Asp		
Zürich								Arg	
M Saskatoon								Tyr	
N Baltimore									Glu

Alleles of β-globin

KEY CONCEPT

15.3 Mutations Can Be Detected and Analyzed   Go to Activity 15.1 and Animation 15.1

- **Restriction enzymes** are used to cut DNA into small fragments.
- Highly variable loci consisting of **short tandem repeats (STRs)** are used for **DNA fingerprinting**.
- A linked marker allows a disease-causing gene to be identified.

Figure 15.14

Questions

1. PCR is used to amplify a 10,000-base-pair linear sequence of DNA from an individual. When digested with *Eco*RI, the PCR product gives two DNA molecules: one 3,000 and one 7,000 base pairs in length.

   a. How many restriction sites are on the original amplified DNA molecule?

   b. The same PCR is performed on a sample from another individual and the 10,000-base-pair sequence subjected to *Eco*RI digestion. After digestion, a single 10,000-base-pair molecule is obtained. How many restriction sites are on the original DNA molecule that was amplified from this individual?

Figure 15.16

Mom   Dad   Offspring

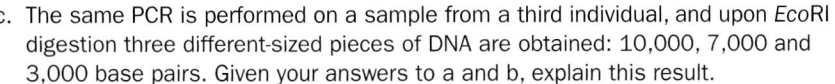

c. The same PCR is performed on a sample from a third individual, and upon *Eco*RI digestion three different-sized pieces of DNA are obtained: 10,000, 7,000 and 3,000 base pairs. Given your answers to a and b, explain this result.

2. DNA fingerprinting is often used in paternity cases. A man is trying to determine whether he is the father of a particular child. The genotypes for three STR loci are shown in the table. For each STR, the number of repeats in each allele is shown. Could the man be the father of the child?

Locus	Mother	Child	Man
FGA	28, 42	28, 40	31, 40
TPOX	9, 12	12, 15	13, 15
VWA	16, 22	16, 16	17, 18

KEY CONCEPT

15.4 Genetic Screening Is Used to Detect Diseases

Go to Animation 15.2

- **Genetic screening** for disorders can involve examination of a phenotype.
- Genetic screening for disorders can involve examination of a genotype using **DNA testing**.

Questions

1. What are the advantages of phenotypic versus genotypic screening for individuals who are heterozygous for a genetic disease?

2. Genotypic screening sometimes involves hybridization of an individual's DNA to allele-specific DNA sequences. DNA corresponding to both mutant and wild-type DNA is used. Why use both, rather than use just the mutant DNA sequence?

Figure 15.18

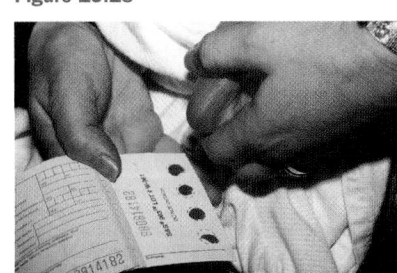

© Simon Fraser/Science Source

Figure 15.19

Results: Mother Father Child Fetus

Probe for normal allele

Probe for sickle allele

(AS) (AS) (AA) (SS)

KEY CONCEPT

15.5 Genetic Diseases Can Be Treated

- Some genetic disease can be treated by restricting a substrate, inhibiting an enzyme, or supplying a missing protein.
- The goal of **gene therapy** is to alter an individual's genotype in those cells where the expression of the mutant allele is causing problems.

Questions

1. Type I diabetes is caused by an inability to make insulin. How might such a disorder be treated? Would the same strategy work for type II diabetes (insulin insensitive)?

2. More genetic disorders of the bone marrow have been successfully treated using gene therapy than have disorders of other organs such as the lungs or liver. Why might that be the case?

Figure 15.20

Treatment

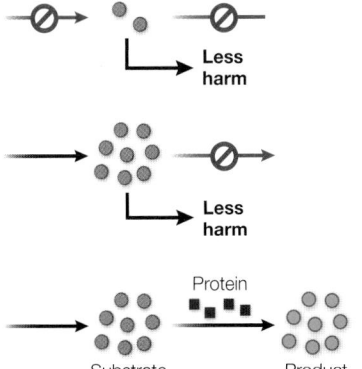

Less harm

Less harm

Protein

Substrate   Product

Figure 15.21

New gene in virus

16 Regulation of Gene Expression

KEY CONCEPTS

Worker bees care for a queen Gene expression differences underlie the differences in behavior of worker and queen bees.

▶ InvestigatingLIFE

Gene Expression and Behavior

Any teenager or parent of a teenager will tell you that those years can be rough. But some young people have a rougher time than others. Teens whose mothers were extremely stressed during pregnancy often have more behavioral problems than those whose mothers had calmer pregnancies. A recent study led by psychologist Thomas Elbert and evolutionary biologist Axel Meyer at the University of Konstanz in Germany suggests an underlying genetic cause for these behavioral differences. The study examined a gene for the glucocorticoid receptor, which is involved in regulating hormonal responses to stress. The researchers found that teenagers whose mothers had suffered physical abuse during pregnancy had higher rates of cytosine methylation in the promoter of this gene than did teenagers whose mothers had not suffered such abuse.

A major control point for gene expression is the promoter, a sequence of DNA adjacent to the coding region of a gene where proteins bind and control the rate of transcription. The ability of these proteins to bind to the promoter is affected by the level of DNA methylation in the promoter. As we mentioned in Key Concept 15.1, in certain regions of DNA many of the cytosine residues have methyl groups added at their 5 positions, forming 5-methylcytosine. If a gene promoter has a high degree of methylation, some proteins that promote transcription can't bind to it. Instead, other proteins bind to the methylated DNA and prevent

expression of the gene. DNA methylation plays an important role in gene regulation and is a normal part of development. But the level of methylation can change over time and can vary among individuals, as was the case for the teenagers in Elbert and Meyer's study. Their finding is interesting because it shows a correlation between maternal stress in humans and DNA methylation in their offspring.

Such studies have spawned the new field of behavioral epigenetics. Epigenetics is the study of heritable changes in gene expression that do not involve changes in the DNA sequence. These changes may underlie behaviors in other animals as well. A fascinating example is the well-known behavior of a queen bee, who "lords it over" her genetically identical worker sisters. Genes in the brains of these two types of bees have very different patterns of expression, and these in turn are caused by epigenetic changes.

Q&A **Can epigenetic changes be manipulated?**
(Find the answer on page 372.)

KEY CONCEPT 16.1 Prokaryotic Gene Expression Is Regulated in Operons

Learning Objectives

16.1.1 Describe the conditions that cause high expression of genes of the *lac* and *trp* operons.

16.1.2 Describe the roles of structural or regulatory DNA sequences in the *lac* and *trp* operons.

16.1.3 Determine how mutations in structural or regulatory genes of the *lac* or *trp* operons would alter the phenotype of a cell.

16.1.4 Explain how sigma factors and promoter sequences are involved in regulating classes of genes in prokaryotes.

Prokaryotes conserve energy and resources by making certain proteins only when they are needed. The protein content of a bacterium can change rapidly when conditions warrant. Based on what you learned about gene expression in Chapter 14, you might suggest several ways in which a prokaryotic cell could shut off the supply of an unneeded protein. The cell could:

- decrease the rate of transcription of mRNA for that protein;
- hydrolyze the mRNA after it is made, preventing translation;
- prevent translation of the mRNA at the ribosome;
- hydrolyze the protein after it is made; or
- temporarily inhibit the function of the protein in the cell.

Whichever mechanism is used, it must be both responsive to environmental signals and efficient. The earlier the cell intervenes in the process of protein synthesis, the less energy it wastes making an unneeded protein. Selective blocking of transcription is far more efficient than transcribing the gene, translating the message, and then degrading or inhibiting the protein. While all five mechanisms for regulating protein levels are found in nature, prokaryotes generally use the most efficient one: transcriptional regulation.

Gene expression begins at the promoter (see Key Concept 14.3), where RNA polymerase binds to initiate transcription. Note, however, that in a given cell at a given point in time, not all promoters are active. This observation suggests that gene transcription must be selective. The "decision" regarding which genes to activate involves two types of regulatory proteins that bind to DNA: repressor proteins and activator proteins. In both cases, these proteins bind to DNA to regulate the gene (**Figure 16.1**):

- In **negative regulation**, binding of a repressor protein prevents transcription.
- In **positive regulation**, an activator protein binds DNA to stimulate transcription.

Connect the Concepts A key DNA sequence involved in regulation is the promoter, where transcription begins and various regulatory proteins bind. Learn details about proteins at the promoter in Key Concept 14.3.

You will see examples of these mechanisms, or combinations of them, as we examine regulation in prokaryotes, eukaryotes,

(A) Negative regulation

(B) Positive regulation

Figure 16.1 Positive and Negative Regulation Proteins regulate gene expression by binding to DNA and preventing or allowing RNA polymerase to bind DNA at the promoter region to control transcription of the gene.

Q: Could a gene be under both positive and negative regulation?

and viruses. We'll focus first on a regulatory system for the use of the sugar lactose.

Regulating gene transcription conserves energy

As a normal inhabitant of the human intestine, *E. coli* must be able to adjust to sudden changes in its chemical environment. Its host may present it with one foodstuff one hour (e.g., glucose in fruit) and another the next (e.g., lactose in milk). Such changes in nutrients present the bacterium with a metabolic challenge. Glucose is the easiest sugar for the bacterium to metabolize, and is its preferred energy source. Lactose is a β-galactoside—a disaccharide containing galactose β-linked to glucose (see Key Concept 3.3). Three proteins are upregulated by *E. coli* in response to an increase in lactose:

1. β-Galactoside permease is a carrier protein in the bacterial cell membrane that transports the sugar into the cell.

2. β-Galactosidase is an enzyme that hydrolyses lactose to glucose and galactose.

3. β-Galactoside transacetylase transfers acetyl groups from acetyl CoA to certain β-galactosides. Its role in the metabolism of lactose is not clear.

When *E. coli* grows and reproduces in a lab medium that contains glucose but no lactose or other β-galactosides, the levels of these

Figure 16.2 Lactose Induces the Expression of a Gene for an Enzyme
(A) When the inducer lactose is added to the growth medium for the bacterium *E. coli*, the synthesis of β-galactosidase begins only after an initial lag period. **(B)** There is a lag period because the mRNA for β-galactosidase has to be made before the protein can be made. The amount of mRNA decreases rapidly after the lactose is removed, indicating that transcription is no longer occurring. These changes in mRNA levels indicate that the mechanism of induction by lactose is transcriptional regulation.

Q: Why doesn't the level of β-galactosidase drop following removal of the inducer, like the level of mRNA does?

(A) Lactose induces the synthesis of β-galactosidase

When lactose is added to the growth medium, an enzyme essential to the metabolism of lactose is made after a lag period.

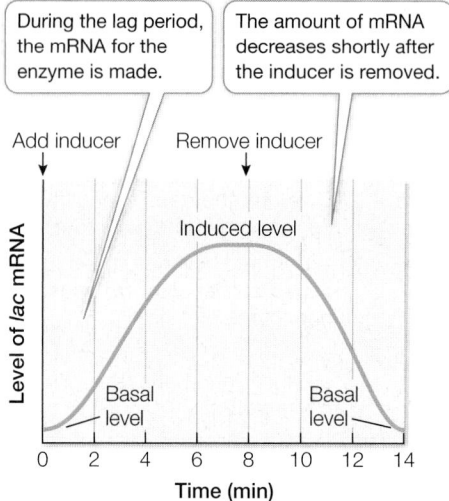

(B) Effect of inducer on mRNA level

During the lag period, the mRNA for the enzyme is made.

The amount of mRNA decreases shortly after the inducer is removed.

three proteins are extremely low—the cell does not waste energy and materials making the unneeded enzymes. But if the environment changes such that lactose is the predominant sugar available and very little glucose is present, the bacterium promptly begins making all three enzymes after a short lag period. While few molecules of β-galactosidase (and the other two enzymes) are present in an *E. coli* cell in the presence of glucose, in the absence of glucose the addition of lactose can induce the synthesis of about 1,500 times more molecules of β-galactosidase per cell (**Figure 16.2A**)!

What's behind this dramatic increase? An important clue comes from measuring the amount of mRNA for β-galactosidase. The mRNA level increases during the lag period after lactose is added to the medium, and this mRNA is translated into protein (**Figure 16.2B**). Moreover, the high mRNA level depends on the presence of lactose, because if the lactose is removed, the mRNA level goes down. *The response of the bacterial cell to lactose is clearly at the level of transcription.*

Compounds such as lactose that stimulate the synthesis of a protein are called **inducers**. The proteins that are produced are called **inducible proteins**, whereas proteins that are made all the time at a constant rate are called **constitutive proteins**.

We have now seen two basic ways of regulating the rate of a metabolic pathway. In Key Concept 8.5 we described the allosteric regulation of enzyme activity, which allows the rapid fine-tuning of metabolism. Regulation of protein synthesis—that is, regulation of the concentration of enzymes—is slower but results in greater savings of energy and resources. Protein synthesis is a highly endergonic process, since assembling mRNA, charging tRNA, and moving the ribosomes along mRNA all require the hydrolysis of nucleoside triphosphates such as ATP. **Figure 16.3** compares these two modes of regulation.

Operons are units of transcriptional regulation in prokaryotes

The genes in *E. coli* that encode the three enzymes for using lactose are structural genes; **structural genes** specify the primary structures (the amino acid sequences) of protein molecules that act as enzymes or cytoskeletal proteins. The three genes are adjacent to one another on the *E. coli* chromosome. This arrangement is no coincidence: the genes share a single promoter, and their DNA is transcribed into a single, continuous molecule of mRNA. Because this particular mRNA governs the synthesis of all three lactose-metabolizing enzymes, either all or none of these enzymes are made, depending on whether their common message—their mRNA—is present in the cell.

A cluster of genes with a single promoter is called an **operon**, and the operon that encodes the three lactose-metabolizing enzymes in *E. coli* is called the *lac* operon. The *lac* operon promoter

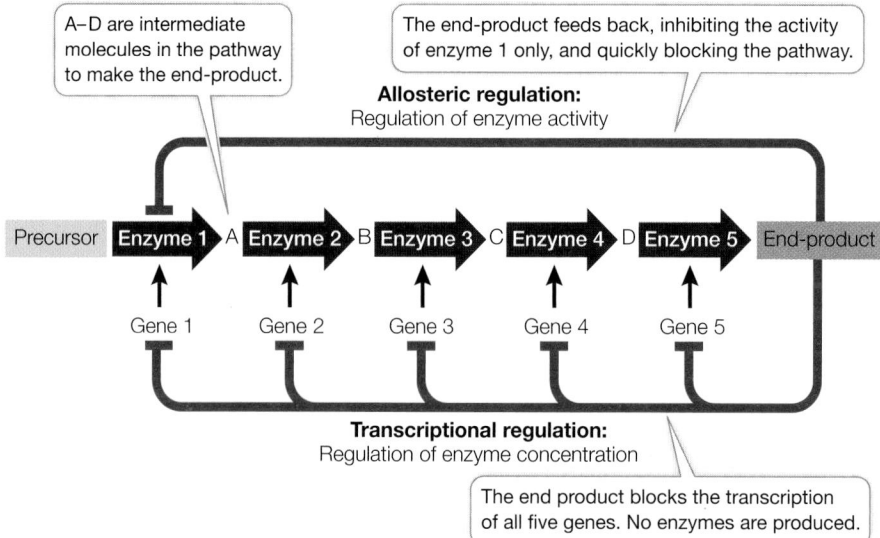

Figure 16.3 Two Ways to Regulate a Metabolic Pathway Feedback from the end-product of a metabolic pathway can block enzyme activity (allosteric regulation), or it can stop the transcription of genes that code for the enzymes in the pathway (transcriptional regulation).

Figure 16.4 The *lac* Operon of E. coli
The *lac* operon of E. coli is a segment of DNA that includes a promoter, an operator, and the three structural genes that code for lactose-metaboliz-ing enzymes.

β-Galactosidase, β-Galactoside permease, and β-Galactoside transacetylase are proteins needed for the metabolism of lactose.

can be very efficient (the maximum rate of mRNA synthesis can be high), but mRNA synthesis is very low when the enzymes are not needed. In addition to having a promoter, an operon has other **regulatory sequences** (DNA sequences to which the protein products of regulatory genes bind) that are not transcribed. A typical operon consists of a promoter, an operator, and two or more structural genes (**Figure 16.4**). The **operator** is a short stretch of DNA that lies between the promoter and the structural genes. It can bind very tightly with regulatory proteins that either activate or repress transcription.

There are numerous mechanisms to control the transcription of operons; we describe three examples:

1. An inducible operon regulated by a repressor protein
2. A repressible operon regulated by a repressor protein
3. An operon regulated by an activator protein

Operator–repressor interactions control transcription in the *lac* and *trp* operons

The *lac* operon contains a promoter, to which RNA polymerase binds to initiate transcription, and an operator, to which a **repressor** protein can bind. The gene that encodes this repressor is located near the *lac* operon on the E. coli chromosome. When the repressor is bound, transcription of the operon is blocked. This example of negative regulation was elegantly worked out by Nobel Prize winners François Jacob and Jacques Monod.

The repressor protein has two binding sites: one that binds to the operator DNA and the other that binds to the carbohydrate inducer. The environmental signal that induces the *lac* operon (for example, in the human digestive tract) is lactose, but the actual inducer is allolactose, a molecule that forms from lactose once it enters the cell. In the absence of the inducer, the repressor protein fits into the major groove of the operator DNA and recognizes and binds to a specific nucleotide base sequence. This prevents the binding of RNA polymerase to the promoter, and the operon is not transcribed (**Figure 16.5A**).

Figure 16.5 The *lac* Operon: An Inducible System (A) When lactose is absent, the synthesis of enzymes for its metabolism is inhibited. (B) Lactose leads to synthesis of the enzymes in the lactose-metabolizing pathway. The actual inducer is allolactose, which binds to the repressor protein and prevents its binding to the operator.

Q: If part B of this figure were not labeled "Lactose present," how could you determine that lactose is present?

View in Achieve
Animation 16.1 The *lac* Operon

(A) Lactose absent

1. The repressor protein encoded by gene *I* prevents transcription by binding to the operator.

2. The bound repressor prevents RNA polymerase from binding to the promoter; transcription is blocked.

DNA

P_I *I* P_{lac} O   Z   Y   A

Gene *I* constitutive promoter

mRNA

Active repressor

3. No mRNA is produced, so no Z, Y, or A proteins are produced.

(B) Lactose present

1. Allolactose induces transcription by binding to the repressor, which then cannot bind to the operator. RNA polymerase binds to the promoter and starts transcription of the operon.

Inducer (allolactose)

Inactive repressor

RNA polymerase

Direction of transcription

P_I *I* P_{lac} O   Z   Y   A

P_I *I* P_{lac} O   Z   Y   A

2. RNA polymerase transcribes the operon, producing an mRNA that is then translated to give the three structural proteins.

Transcription

mRNA transcript

Translation

Proteins of the lactose-metabolizing pathway

β-Galactosidase   β-Galactoside permease   β-Galactoside transacetylase

When the inducer is present, it binds to the repressor and changes the shape of the repressor. This change in three-dimensional structure (conformation) prevents the repressor from binding to the operator. As a result, RNA polymerase can bind to the promoter and start transcribing the structural genes of the *lac* operon (**Figure 16.5B**).

You can see from this example that a key to transcriptional control of gene expression is the presence of regulatory sequences that do not code for proteins but are binding sites for regulatory proteins and other proteins involved in transcription.

In contrast to the inducible system of the *lac* operon, other operons in *E. coli* are repressible; that is, they are usually expressed but can be repressed under specific conditions. In such a system, the repressor is not normally bound to the operator. But if another molecule called a **co-repressor** binds to the repressor, the repressor changes shape and binds to the operator, thereby inhibiting transcription. An example is the *trp* operon, whose five structural genes catalyze the synthesis of the amino acid tryptophan. When tryptophan is absent, the repressor does not bind to the operator and the structural genes are transcribed and translated (**Figure 16.6A**). However, if tryptophan is present in the cell, it is advantageous to stop making the enzymes for tryptophan synthesis. To do this, the repressor binds to tryptophan (the co-repressor) and then binds to the operator in the *trp* operon, shutting off transcription (**Figure 16.6B**).

Let's pause to summarize the differences between these two types of operons:

- In *inducible* systems, the substrate of a metabolic pathway (the inducer) interacts with a regulatory protein (the repressor), rendering the repressor incapable of binding to the operator and thus allowing transcription.

- In *repressible* systems, the product of a metabolic pathway (the co-repressor) binds to a regulatory protein (the repressor), which is then able to bind to the operator and block transcription.

Usually, inducible systems control catabolic pathways (which are turned on only when the substrate is available), whereas repressible systems control anabolic pathways (which are turned on until the concentration of the product becomes excessive). In both systems, the regulatory protein is a repressor that functions by binding to the operator. Next we consider an example of positive control involving an activator.

Connect the Concepts As discussed in Key Concept 8.1, there are two kinds of metabolism: Catabolic pathways break down complex molecules into simpler ones, releasing energy formerly stored in the chemical bonds. Anabolic pathways link simple molecules to form more complex molecules, a process that requires an input of energy.

 View in **Achieve**
Animation 16.2 **The *trp* Operon**

Protein synthesis can be controlled by increasing promoter efficiency

In negative control, transcription is *decreased* in the presence of a repressor protein. *E. coli* can also use positive control to *increase* transcription through the presence of an **activator** protein. For an

(A) Tryptophan absent

1. A regulatory gene (*trpR*) produces an inactive repressor, which cannot bind to the operator.

2. RNA polymerase transcribes the structural genes. Translation makes the enzymes of the tryptophan synthesis pathway.

(B) Tryptophan present

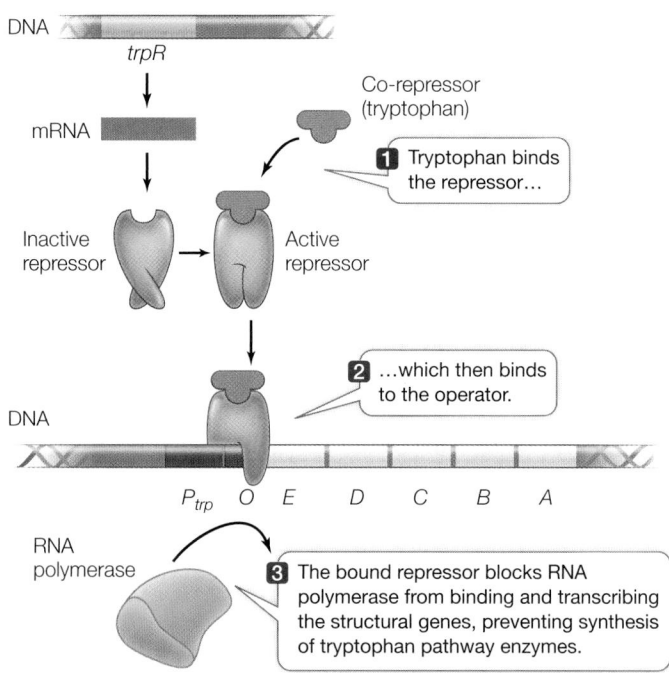

1. Tryptophan binds the repressor…

2. …which then binds to the operator.

3. The bound repressor blocks RNA polymerase from binding and transcribing the structural genes, preventing synthesis of tryptophan pathway enzymes.

Figure 16.6 The *trp* Operon   The tryptophan (*trp*) operon has a promoter, an operator, and five structural genes that encode the enzymes of the tryptophan synthesis pathway. A repressor protein, encoded by the *trpR* gene, produces an inactive repressor that becomes active when it binds to tryptophan and then is able to bind to the operator. The operon is thus transcribed when tryptophan is absent **(A)** but not when tryptophan is present **(B)**.

example we return to the *lac* operon, where the relative levels of glucose and lactose determine the amount of transcription. We have seen that in the presence of lactose the *lac* repressor is unable to bind to the *lac* operator to repress transcription (see Figure 16.5B). But glucose is the preferred source of energy for the cell, so if glucose and lactose levels are both high, the *lac* operon is still not transcribed efficiently. This is because efficient transcription of the *lac* operon requires binding of an activator protein to its promoter.

Low levels of glucose in the cell set off a signaling pathway that leads to increased levels of the second messenger cyclic AMP (cAMP) (see Key Concept 7.3). Cyclic AMP binds to an activator protein called *c*AMP *r*eceptor *p*rotein (CRP), producing a conformational change in CRP that allows it to bind to the *lac* promoter. CRP is an activator of transcription, because its binding results in more efficient binding of RNA polymerase to the promoter, and thus increased transcription of the structural genes (**Figure 16.7**). In the presence of abundant glucose, cAMP levels are low, CRP does not bind to the promoter, and the efficiency of transcription of the *lac* operon is reduced. This is an example of **catabolite repression**, a system of gene regulation in which the presence of the preferred energy source represses other catabolic pathways. The mechanisms controlling positive and negative regulation of the *lac* operon are summarized in **Table 16.1**.

RNA polymerases can be directed to particular classes of promoters

Thus far we have described a promoter as a specific DNA sequence located upstream of a transcription initiation site. The promoter binds RNA polymerase so that the enzyme can then catalyze the synthesis of RNA from a gene-coding region of DNA. The promoter also orients the polymerase so that it transcribes the correct one of the two DNA strands for that gene. Not all promoters are identical, but they all have similar sequences by which they are recognized by the RNA polymerase and other proteins. Prokaryotic promoters generally have two sites for these recognition sequences, which begin 10 and 35 base pairs upstream of the transcription start site (the –10 element and the –35 element). Different classes of promoters have different recognition sequences at these two sites. The largest class consists of promoters for "housekeeping genes," which are all the genes that are normally expressed in actively growing cells. In these genes, the –10 element is 5′-TATAAT-3′, and the –35 element is 5′-TTGACAT-3′ (N stands for any nucleotide):

(A) Low glucose, lactose present

1 When glucose levels are low, a regulatory protein (CRP) binds to cAMP and the CRP–cAMP complex binds to the promoter.

2 RNA polymerase then binds more efficiently to the promoter…

3 …and the *lac* operon—a set of genes encoding the lactose-metabolizing enzymes—is transcribed.

(B) High glucose, lactose present

1 When glucose levels are high, cAMP is low and CRP doesn't bind the promoter. RNA polymerase cannot bind efficiently.

2 Transcription of the structural genes for lactose-metabolizing enzymes is reduced.

Figure 16.7 Catabolite Repression Regulates the *lac* Operon **(A)** The promoter for the *lac* operon binds RNA polymerase more efficiently in the presence of cAMP, as occurs when glucose levels are low. **(B)** High glucose levels thus lead to low levels of transcription of the *lac* operon.

5′-NNNTTGACATNNNNNNNNNNNNNNNNNNNNNTATAATNNNN*NNNNNNNNNNNNN-3′
3′-NNNAACTGTANNNNNNNNNNNNNNNNNNNNNNATATTANNNN*NNNNNNNNNNNNN-5′

⎵_____⎵   ⎵_____⎵   ⎸
–35 Element   –10 Element   Transcription start site

Glucose	cAMP levels	CRP regulator	Lactose	*lac* Repressor	RNA polymerase binding?	Transcription of *lac* genes?	Lactose used by cells?
Present	Low	Not bound to promoter	Absent	Bound to operator	Absent	No	No
Present	Low	Not bound to promoter	Present	Not bound to operator	Present, not efficient	Low level	No
Absent	High	Bound to promoter	Absent	Bound to operator	Absent	No	No
Absent	High	Bound to promoter	Present	Not bound to operator	Present, very efficient	High level	Yes

TABLE 16.1 | Positive and Negative Regulation in the *lac* Operon

Other classes of genes have different recognition sequences at their −10 and −35 elements. Why do DNA recognition sequences differ in different classes of promoters? After all, they are all binding the same protein, RNA polymerase. The answer lies in the fact that these DNA sequences bind not just RNA polymerase but other proteins as well. And it is those other proteins that control how well RNA polymerase binds to certain promoter sequences, thereby giving the system the ability to regulate classes of genes together.

Sigma factors are the proteins in prokaryotic cells that bind to RNA polymerase and direct it to specific classes of promoters. The RNA polymerase must be bound to a sigma factor before it can recognize a promoter and begin transcription. For example, the sigma-70 factor is active most of the time and binds to the recognition sequences of housekeeping genes; other sigma factors are activated only under specific conditions and bind to other promoter sequences. For example, when *E. coli* cells experience conditions such as DNA damage or osmotic stress, the sigma-38 factor is activated, and it directs RNA polymerase to the promoters of various genes that are expressed under stress conditions. *E. coli* has seven sigma factors; this number varies in other prokaryotes.

Regulation of proteins directing RNA polymerase to certain promoters is not unusual. In fact, you'll see in the next key concept that it is also common in eukaryotes.

KEY CONCEPT
16.1 Recap and Assess

Gene expression in prokaryotes is most commonly regulated through control of transcription. An operon consists of two or more adjacent structural genes and a single set of regulatory sequences (promoter and operator) that control their transcription. Operons can be regulated by both negative and positive controls. Sigma factors control the expression of specific classes of prokaryotic genes that share recognition sequences in their promoters.

1. A prokaryotic cell can metabolize sugar "X," using the enzyme "Xase." When there is a low concentration of X in the environment, there is low activity of Xase in the cells; but when the X concentration is high, Xase activity is also high. What five mechanisms could the cell use to reduce the activity of Xase in the absence of X?

2. Assuming that glucose is absent, compare the *lac* operon promoter in the presence versus absence of lactose in terms of what proteins can and cannot bind.

3. How do sigma factors and recognition sequences act to affect the expression of classes of genes?

4. The repressor protein that acts on the *lac* operon of *E. coli* is encoded by a regulatory gene. Suppose that a mutation occurs in the regulatory gene that renders it unable to bind to DNA. What would the effect of such a mutation be on the regulation of the *lac* operon?

Studies of bacteria have provided a basic understanding of mechanisms that regulate gene expression and of the roles of regulatory proteins in both positive and negative regulation. You'll see these same types of mechanisms again as we now turn to the transcriptional control of gene expression in eukaryotes.

KEY CONCEPT
16.2 Eukaryotic Gene Expression Is Regulated by Transcription Factors

Learning Objectives

16.2.1 Distinguish between general and specific transcription factors.

16.2.2 Describe the function of mediator.

16.2.3 State the similarities and differences between enhancers and silencers.

16.2.4 Contrast coordinated regulation in prokaryotes and eukaryotes.

16.2.5 Give an example of a structural motif that is present in some transcription factors that allows them to recognize and bind specific regions of DNA.

For cell function in single-celled eukaryotes as well as the normal development of a multicellular organism from fertilized egg to adult, certain proteins must be made at just the right times and in just the right cells; these proteins must not be made at other times in other cells. Here are two examples from humans:

1. In human pancreatic exocrine cells, the digestive enzyme procarboxypeptidase A makes up 7.6% of all the protein in the cell; in other cell types it is usually undetectable.

2. In human breast duct cells, alpha-lactalbumin, a protein in breast milk, is made only late in pregnancy and during lactation. Alpha-lactalbumin is not made in any other cell types or at any other times.

Clearly the expression of eukaryotic genes is regulated.

As in prokaryotes, gene expression in eukaryotes can be regulated at several different points in the process of transcribing and translating the gene into a protein (**Figure 16.8**). In this key concept we describe the mechanisms that result in the selective transcription of specific genes. The mechanisms for regulating gene expression in eukaryotes have similar themes as in prokaryotes. Both types of cells use DNA–protein interactions and negative and positive regulation. However, there are many differences, some of them dictated by the presence in eukaryotes of a nucleus, which physically separates transcription and translation (**Table 16.2**). In the following discussion we restrict our attention to the initiation of transcription for protein-coding genes, which are transcribed by RNA polymerase II, one of the three RNA polymerases found in eukaryotes.

General transcription factors act at eukaryotic promoters

As in prokaryotes, a promoter in a eukaryotic gene is a sequence of DNA near the 5′ end of the coding region, where RNA polymerase binds and initiates transcription. Although eukaryotic promoters are more diverse than those of prokaryotes, many protein-coding genes contain a nucleotide sequence similar to the −10 element in prokaryotic promoters. This element is usually located close to the transcription start site and is called the **TATA box** because it is rich in A-T base pairs. When present, the TATA box is the site

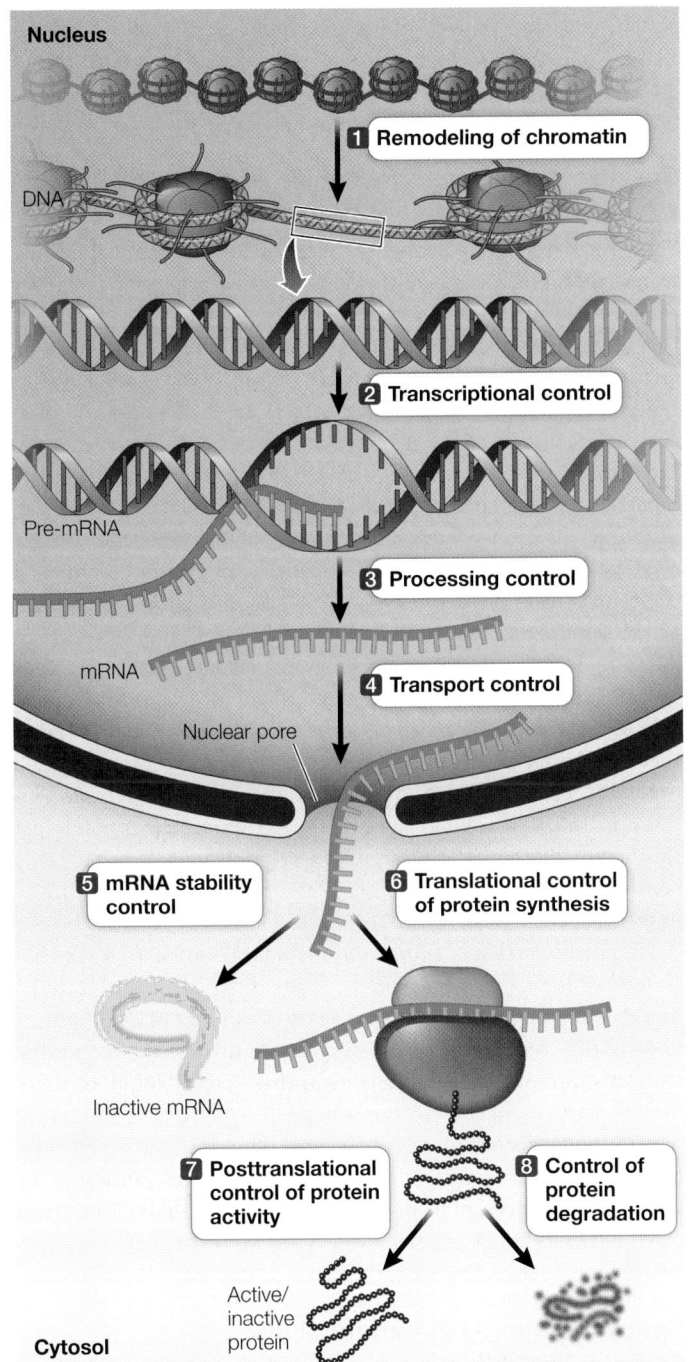

Figure 16.8 Potential Points for the Regulation of Gene Expression in Eukaryotes Gene expression can be regulated before transcription (1), during transcription (2), after transcription but before translation (3, 4, 5), at translation (6), or after translation (7, 8).

 Q: In prokaryotes, transcription and translation are often coupled in time and space, but in eukaryotes they are separated. What are the advantages of the nucleus as a compartment?

View in Achieve
Activity 16.1 Eukaryotic Gene Expression Control Points

where DNA begins to denature so that the template strand can be exposed. In addition to having a TATA box, eukaryotic promoters typically include multiple regulatory sequences that are recognized and bound by **transcription factors**: regulatory proteins that help control transcription.

Like the prokaryotic RNA polymerase, eukaryotic RNA polymerase II cannot simply bind to the promoter and initiate transcription. Rather, it does so only after various general transcription factors have assembled on the chromosome to form the basal transcription apparatus (**Figure 16.9**). **General transcription factors** are proteins that bind to most promoters and are distinct from **specific transcription factors** that act only at certain promoters or classes of promoters. First, the protein complex called TFIID ("TF" stands for transcription factor) binds to the TATA box. Binding of TFIID changes both its own shape and that of the DNA, presenting a new surface that attracts the binding of other general transcription factors to form a basal transcription apparatus, which is the minimal set of proteins needed to initiate transcription. RNA polymerase II binds only after several other proteins have bound to this apparatus.

Each general transcription factor has a role in gene expression:

- TFIIB binds both RNA polymerase II and TFIID and helps identify the transcription initiation site.

- TFIIF prevents nonspecific binding of the basal transcription apparatus to DNA and helps recruit RNA polymerase II; it is similar in function to a bacterial sigma factor.

- TFIIE binds to the promoter and stabilizes the denaturation of the DNA.

- TFIIH opens up the DNA for transcription.

Some regulatory DNA sequences, such as the TATA box, are common to the promoters of many eukaryotic genes and are

TABLE **16.2** | Transcription in Prokaryotes and Eukaryotes		
	Prokaryotes	**Eukaryotes**
Locations of functionally related genes	Often clustered in operons with one promoter	Often distant from one another with separate promoters
RNA polymerases	One	Three (RNA pol I, II, and III)
		I transcribes rRNA
		II transcribes mRNA
		III transcribes tRNA and small RNAs
Regulatory sequences besides promoter	Few	Many
Initiation of transcription	Binding of RNA polymerase to promoter	Binding of general and specific transcription factors, and of RNA polymerase

Promoter | Coding region

Initiation site for transcription

DNA — TATA box ↓

1 The first general transcription factor, TFIID, binds to the promoter at the TATA box...

2 ...and another general transcription factor joins it.

RNA polymerase II

3 RNA polymerase II binds only after several general transcription factors are already bound to DNA.

Basal transcription apparatus

4 More general transcription factors are added...

5 ...forming the basal transcription apparatus, and the RNA polymerase is ready to transcribe RNA.

Figure 16.9 The Initiation of Transcription in Eukaryotes Apart from TFIID, which binds to the TATA box, each general transcription factor in this basal transcription apparatus has binding sites only for the other proteins in the apparatus and does not bind directly to DNA. B, E, F, and H are general transcription factors.

▶ **View in Achieve**
Animation 16.3 **Initiation of Transcription**

recognized by general transcription factors that are found in all the cells of an organism. Other regulatory sequences are present in only a few genes and are recognized by specific transcription factors. These factors may be found only in certain types of cells or at certain stages of the cell cycle, or they may be activated by

signaling pathways in response to cellular or environmental signals (see Chapter 7). Once the basal transcription apparatus forms, transcription can begin. However, other transcription factors also play a role in regulating transcription.

Specific proteins can recognize and bind to DNA sequences and regulate transcription

Some regulatory DNA sequences are termed **enhancers**: they bind transcription factors that either activate transcription or increase the rate of transcription. Other regulatory elements are **silencers**: they bind factors that repress transcription. Binding of transcription factors to enhancers and silencers exemplifies positive and negative regulation respectively (see Figure 16.1). In eukaryotic microbes such as yeast, regulatory elements are almost always very close to the transcriptional start site. Similarly, most of the regulatory elements needed for correct expression of many vertebrate genes can be found within a few hundred base pairs of the transcription start site. For example, the mouse albumin gene promoter contains all the information needed for liver cell–specific expression within 170 base pairs upstream of the transcription start site. However, in many genes, regulatory elements may be located thousands or tens of thousands of base pairs away, and they may affect the expression of several nearby genes. Specific transcription factors bind to their regulatory elements and then bind to a protein complex called **mediator**, which facilitates the interaction with the basal transcription apparatus. In order for specific transcription factors to interact through mediator with the basal transcription apparatus, the DNA bends, bringing distant regulatory sequences into close proximity to the promoter (**Figure 16.10**).

The combination of transcription factors binding to a gene determines the rate of transcription. For example, the immature red blood cells in bone marrow make large amounts of β-globin. At least 13 different transcription factors are involved in regulating transcription of the β-globin gene in these cells. Not all of these factors are present or active in other cells, such as the immature white blood cells produced by the same bone marrow. As a result, the β-globin gene is not transcribed in those cells. So although the same genes are present in all cells, the fate of the cell is determined by which of its genes are expressed. How do transcription factors recognize specific DNA sequences?

Specific protein–DNA interactions underlie binding

As we have seen, transcription factors with specific DNA-binding domains are involved in the activation and inactivation of specific genes. There are several common structural themes in the protein domains that bind to DNA in both eukaryotes and prokaryotes. These themes, or **structural motifs**, consist of different combinations of structural elements (protein conformations) and may include special components such as zinc. One common structural motif is the helix-turn-helix, in which two α helices are connected via a non-helical turn. The interior-facing "recognition" helix interacts with the bases inside the DNA. The exterior-facing helix sits on the sugar–phosphate backbone, ensuring that the interior helix is presented to the bases in the correct configuration (**Figure 16.11**).

Figure 16.10 **Transcription Factors and Transcription Initiation**   The actions of many proteins determine whether and where RNA polymerase II will transcribe DNA. This example shows binding of two specific transcription factor activators, one at the regulatory promoter and one at an enhancer element.

Activator (specific transcription factor)

Sequences that bind specific transcription factors may be far from the transcription start site.

DNA

Enhancer

Basal transcription apparatus

Transcribed region

Regulatory protein binding

Transcription factor binding site

RNA polymerase II binding

Promoter

Mediator

Activator (specific transcription factor)

Mediator binds to the basal transcription apparatus.

Mediator binds specific transcription factors and the basal transcription apparatus to alter the rate of transcription.

DNA bending allows distantly bound transcription factors to interact with mediator.

Transcription

(A) The helix-turn-helix motif

α Helices

"Turn"

The helix-turn-helix motif is found in many DNA-binding proteins...

...and fits into the major groove of the DNA helix at specific DNA sequences.

(B) The *lac* repressor

Helix-turn-helix motif

lac repressor

DNA

The *lac* repressor is a dimer of two identical peptides, each with a helix-turn-helix motif.

Figure 16.11 **The Helix-Turn-Helix DNA-Binding Motif**   **(A)** The helix-turn-helix is one of several structural motifs seen in protein domains that bind to DNA. Such motifs facilitate recognition of, and binding to, specific DNA sequences. **(B)** The *lac* repressor binds to its operator using helix-turn-helix motifs. Data from PBD 2PE5. R. Daber et al. 2007. *J Mol Biol* 370: 609–619.

How does a protein recognize a sequence in DNA? As you learned in Key Concept 3.2, the complementary bases in DNA not only form hydrogen bonds with each other, but also can form additional hydrogen bonds with proteins, particularly at points exposed in the major and minor grooves. In this way, an intact DNA double helix can be recognized by a protein motif whose structure:

- fits into the major or minor groove;
- has amino acids that can project into the interior of the double helix; and
- has amino acids that can form hydrogen bonds with the interior bases.

Transcription factors underlie cell differentiation

During the development of a complex organism from fertilized egg to adult, cells become more and more differentiated (specialized). Since all differentiated cells contain the entire genome, their specific characteristics must arise from differential gene expression. Changes in gene expression result from the activation (and inactivation) of various transcription factors.

One well-studied example of cell differentiation is the conversion of undifferentiated muscle precursor cells into cells destined to form muscle (**Figure 16.12**). A key event in the commitment of these cells to become muscle is that they stop dividing. Indeed, during development, *cell division and cell differentiation are often mutually exclusive.* Cell signaling activates the gene for a transcription factor called MyoD (for *myoblast-determining* gene); this in turn activates the gene for p21, which is an inhibitor of the cyclin-dependent kinases (CDKs) that normally stimulate the cell cycle at G1 phase (see Figure 11.6). Expression of the *p21* gene causes the cell cycle to stop, and other transcription factors then enter the picture so that differentiation can proceed. Interestingly, MyoD is also activated in the stem cells that are present in adult muscle, indicating a role for this transcription factor in the repair of muscle tissue as it gets damaged and worn out.

Genes such as *myoD* that direct the most fundamental decisions in development (often by regulating other genes on other chromosomes) usually encode transcription factors. In some cases, a single transcription factor can cause a cell to differentiate in a certain way. In others, complex interactions between genes and proteins determine a sequence of transcriptional events that leads to differentiation.

The expression of sets of genes can be coordinately regulated by transcription factors

How do eukaryotic cells coordinate the regulation of several genes whose transcription must be turned on at the same time? Prokaryotes solve this problem by arranging multiple genes in an operon that is controlled by a single promoter, and by using

Figure 16.12 Transcription and Differentiation in the Formation of Muscle Cells Production of the transcription factor MyoD is important in muscle cell differentiation.

sigma factors to recognize particular classes of promoters. Most eukaryotic genes have their own separate promoters, and genes that are coordinately regulated may be far apart. In these cases, the expression of genes can be coordinated if they share regulatory sequences that bind the same transcription factors.

Shared regulatory sequences enable organisms to respond to stress—plants, for example, use shared regulatory sequences to respond to drought. Under conditions of drought stress, a plant must simultaneously synthesize several proteins whose genes are scattered throughout the genome. To coordinate expression of the stress response, each of the associated genes has a specific regulatory sequence near its promoter called the stress response element (SRE). A transcription factor binds to this element and stimulates mRNA synthesis (**Figure 16.13**). The stress response proteins not only help the plant conserve water, but also protect the plant against excess salt in the soil and freezing. This finding has considerable importance for agriculture because crops are often grown under less than optimal conditions or are affected by weather.

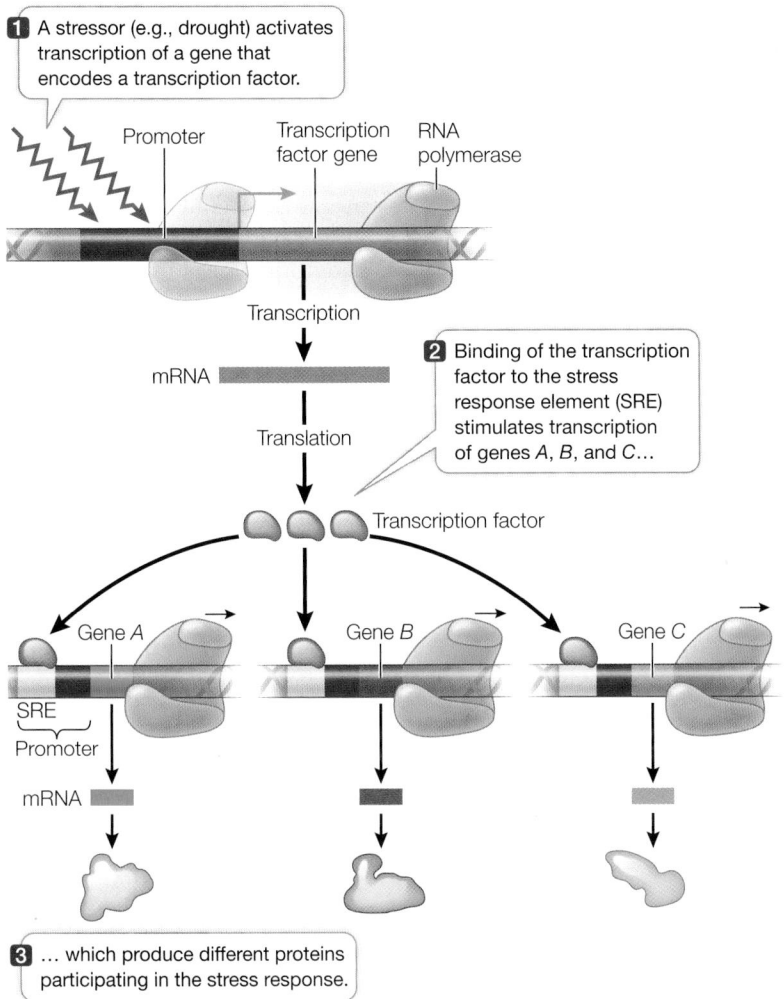

1 A stressor (e.g., drought) activates transcription of a gene that encodes a transcription factor.

Promoter

Transcription factor gene

RNA polymerase

Transcription

mRNA

2 Binding of the transcription factor to the stress response element (SRE) stimulates transcription of genes *A*, *B*, and *C*...

Translation

Transcription factor

Gene *A*

Gene *B*

Gene *C*

SRE

Promoter

mRNA

3 ... which produce different proteins participating in the stress response.

Figure 16.13 Coordinating Gene Expression A single environmental signal, such as drought stress, causes the synthesis of a transcription factor that acts on many genes.

KEY CONCEPT

16.2 Recap and Assess

Eukaryotes can increase or decrease transcription in various ways to help regulate gene expression. Several general transcription factors must bind to a eukaryotic promoter before RNA polymerase II will bind to it. Once the basal transcription apparatus forms, RNA polymerase II can begin transcription. Other, specific transcription factors bind to regulatory DNA sequences and interact with the basal transcription apparatus through mediator to control the level of gene expression. The regulation of gene expression determines cell differentiation, explaining why cells with the same DNA content can have different phenotypes.

1. How do specific and general transcription factors regulate the rate of gene transcription?

2. How do transcription factors recognize specific DNA sequences?

3. How can more than one gene show the same regulation in a eukaryote? How does this differ from coordinated gene regulation in prokaryotes?

We have seen how prokaryotes and eukaryotes regulate the transcription of their genes and operons. Next we will see how viruses can hijack prokaryotic and eukaryotic transcription mechanisms in order to complete their life cycles.

KEY CONCEPT **16.3**	**Viruses Regulate Their Gene Expression during the Reproductive Cycle**

Learning Objectives

16.3.1 Distinguish between the lytic and lysogenic cycles of a virus.

16.3.2 Explain the control of early versus late gene transcription during viral infection.

16.3.3 Give an example of how host transcription is turned off during viral infection.

16.3.4 Explain how expression of some HIV genes is regulated during the elongation stage of transcription.

16.3.5 Detail the steps at which different anti-HIV drugs work.

"A virus is a piece of bad news wrapped in protein." This quote from immunologist Sir Peter Medawar is certainly true for the cells that viruses infect. As we described in Chapter 13, a bacterial virus (**bacteriophage**) injects its genetic material into a host bacterium and turns that cell into a virus factory (see Figure 13.3). Other viruses enter cells intact and then shed their coats and take over the cell's replication machinery. Viral life cycles can be very efficient. An example is the poliovirus: a single poliovirus infecting a single mammalian cell can produce more than 100,000 new virus particles!

Understanding the reproductive cycle of a virus makes it possible to design therapeutic agents to fight infections by the virus. **Viruses** are small infective agents that make copies of themselves inside cellular organisms and that cannot reproduce outside host cells. Most virus particles, called **virions**, consist of only two or three components: the genetic material made up of DNA or RNA, a protein coat that protects the genetic material, and in some cases, an envelope of lipids that surrounds the protein coat. As we will see in this key concept, viral genomes include sequences that encode regulatory proteins. These proteins hijack the host cells' transcriptional machinery, allowing the viruses to complete their reproductive cycles.

Viruses undertake two kinds of reproductive cycles

After a virus infects a cell, typically it takes over the cell's molecular genetic machinery and begins the production of new virus. But in some cases there is an alternate series of events, in which the viral genome becomes integrated into the host genome.

LYTIC CYCLE   The Hershey–Chase experiment (see Figure 13.4) involved a typical **lytic** viral reproductive cycle, so named because soon after infection, the host cell bursts (lyses), releasing progeny viruses. In this cycle, the viral genome takes over the host's genetic machinery for its own reproduction immediately after infection. In the case of some bacteriophages, the process is extremely rapid—within 15 minutes, new phage particles appear in the bacterial cell. Ten minutes later, the "game is over," and these particles are released from the lysed cell. What happened?

At the molecular level, the reproductive cycle of a typical lytic virus has two stages: early and late, as illustrated in **Figure 16.14**. Follow along in the text and Figure 16.14 and you'll see examples of both stimulation and inhibition of host and viral gene expression:

- The viral genome contains a promoter that is recognized by a host RNA polymerase that is bound to the housekeeping sigma factor, sigma-70. As a result, in the early stage (1–2 min after phage DNA entry), viral genes that lie adjacent to this promoter are transcribed.

- These early genes often encode proteins that shut down host transcription. In some bacteriophages, one of these genes encodes a protein that binds to host sigma factors, especially sigma-70, inactivating them. In addition, proteins from the early genes stimulate viral genome replication and transcription of viral late genes. Three minutes after DNA entry, viral nuclease enzymes digest the host's chromosome, providing nucleotides for the synthesis of viral genomes.

- In the late stage, viral late genes are transcribed; they encode the proteins that make up the **capsid** (the outer shell of the virus) and other protein components of the virus and enzymes that lyse the host cell to release the new virions. This begins 9 minutes after DNA entry and 6 minutes before the first new phage particles appear.

The entire process—from binding and infection to release of new phage—takes about 30 minutes. During this period, the sequence of transcriptional events is carefully controlled to produce complete, infective virions.

LYSOGENIC CYCLE   Some viruses have evolved a more complex reproductive cycle that includes a process called **lysogeny**, which postpones the lytic cycle. In lysogeny, the viral DNA becomes

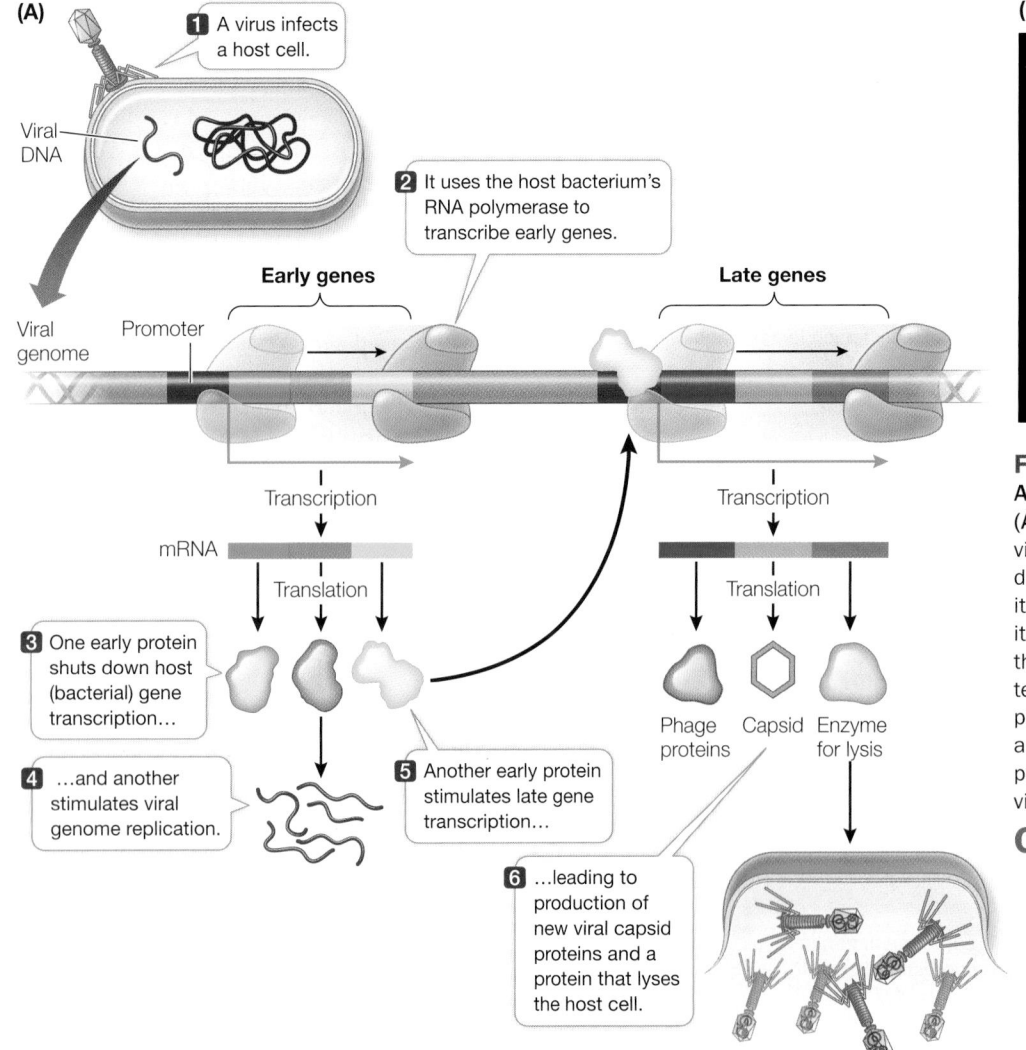

(A)

1 A virus infects a host cell.

Viral DNA

2 It uses the host bacterium's RNA polymerase to transcribe early genes.

Viral genome

Promoter

Early genes

Late genes

Transcription

Transcription

mRNA

Translation

Translation

3 One early protein shuts down host (bacterial) gene transcription…

4 …and another stimulates viral genome replication.

5 Another early protein stimulates late gene transcription…

Phage proteins   Capsid   Enzyme for lysis

6 …leading to production of new viral capsid proteins and a protein that lyses the host cell.

© Lee D. Simon/Science Source

Figure 16.14 The Lytic Cycle: A Strategy for Viral Reproduction
(A) In a host cell infected with a virus, the viral genome uses its early genes to shut down host transcription while it replicates itself. Once the viral genome is replicated, its late genes produce capsid proteins that package the genome and other proteins that lyse the host cell. **(B)** Bacteriophages have attached to this *E. coli* cell, and the reproductive cycle is underway, producing new phage particles. The cell is viewed in transverse section.

Q: How does the virus co-express early genes and then co-express late genes?

integrated into the host DNA and is not expressed. A bacteriophage genome that is inserted into the host genome and is not currently producing progeny phage is termed a **prophage** (Figure 16.15). As the host cell divides, the viral DNA gets replicated as part of the host chromosome. The prophage can remain inactive within the bacterial genome for thousands of generations, producing many copies of the original viral DNA, but no progeny bacteriophage.

However, under certain conditions, such as if the host cell is not growing well, the virus "cuts its losses." It switches to a lytic cycle, in which the prophage excises itself from the host chromosome and reproduces, producing progeny phage that lyse the cell. Lysogeny allows a virus to make copies of its genome without harming its host by inserting its DNA into the host chromosome, where it sits as a silent passenger until conditions are right for lysis.

Eukaryotic viruses can have complex life cycles

Eukaryotes are susceptible to infection by various kinds of viruses (see Key Concept 24.4), which can be broadly categorized based on whether their genome is single- or double-stranded DNA or RNA and how they replicate.

- *DNA viruses.* Some viruses contain double-stranded DNA genomes. Others have single-stranded DNA, and a complementary strand is made after the viral genome enters the host cell. Like some bacteriophages, DNA viruses that infect eukaryotes are capable of undergoing both lytic and lysogenic life cycles. Examples include the herpes viruses and papillomaviruses (which cause warts).

- *RNA viruses.* Most RNA virus genomes are single-stranded, though some are double-stranded. The RNA is translated by the host's machinery to produce viral proteins, some of which are involved in replication of the RNA genome. The influenza virus has an RNA genome.

- *Retroviruses.* As we described in Key Concept 14.2, a **retrovirus** is an RNA virus that carries a gene for **reverse transcriptase**, a protein that synthesizes DNA from an RNA template. The retrovirus uses this protein to make a DNA copy of its genome, which then becomes integrated into the host genome. The integrated DNA acts as a template for both mRNA and new viral genomes. HIV is a retrovirus that infects cells of the immune system and causes acquired immune deficiency syndrome (AIDS; see Key Concept 40.6).

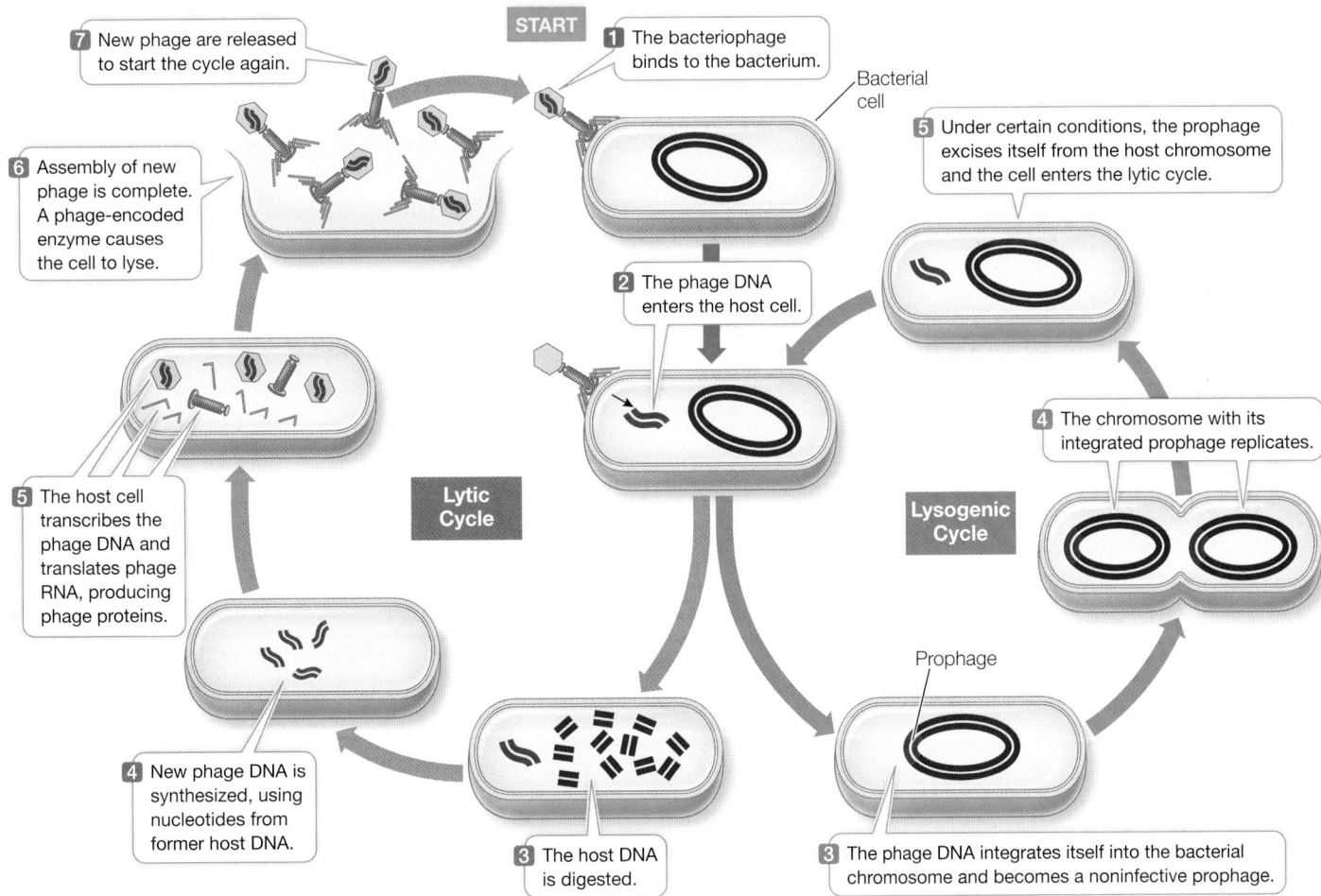

Figure 16.15 Some Bacteriophages Have Both Lytic and Lysogenic Cycles In the lytic cycle, infection of a bacterium by viral DNA leads directly to multiplication of the virus and lysis of the host cell. In the lysogenic cycle, an inactive prophage is integrated into the host DNA, where it is replicated during the bacterial life cycle.

Connect the Concepts Viral diversity is discussed in Key Concept 25.4, which explains why the genomes of some viruses consist of single-stranded RNA and how RNA retroviruses reproduce themselves by reverse transcription.

HIV gene regulation occurs at the level of transcription elongation

As we have discussed so far, many instances of gene regulation occur at the level of transcription *initiation*, involving both activator and repressor proteins that bind to the promoters of genes. However, studies of HIV and other viruses have revealed that transcription can also be controlled at the *elongation* stage.

HIV is an **enveloped virus**; it is enclosed within a phospholipid membrane derived from its host cells (a specific type of immune system cell) (**Figure 16.16**). During infection, proteins in this membrane interact with proteins on the host cell surface, and the viral envelope fuses with the host cell membrane. After the virus enters the cell, its capsid is broken down. The viral reverse transcriptase then uses the virus's RNA template to produce a complementary DNA (cDNA) strand, while at the same time degrading the viral RNA. The enzyme then makes a complementary copy of the cDNA, and the resulting double-stranded DNA is inserted into the host's chromosome by an enzyme appropriately named integrase. The integrated DNA is referred to as the **provirus**. Both the reverse transcriptase and the integrase are carried inside the HIV virion, along with other proteins needed at the very early stages of infection.

The HIV provirus resides permanently in the host chromosome and can remain in a latent (inactive) state for many years.

During this time transcription of the viral DNA is initiated, but host cell proteins prevent the RNA from elongating, and transcription is terminated prematurely. Under some circumstances, such as when the host immune cell is activated, the level of transcription initiation increases, and some viral RNA is made. One of these viral genes encodes a protein called tat (*trans*activator of *t*ranscription), which binds to a stem-and-loop structure at the 5′ end of the viral RNA. As a result of tat binding, the production of full-length viral RNA is dramatically increased, and the rest of the viral reproductive cycle is able to proceed. It was only after the discovery of this mechanism in HIV and similar viruses that researchers found that many eukaryotic genes are regulated at the level of transcription elongation.

Almost every step in the reproductive cycle of HIV is, in principle, a potential target for drugs to treat AIDS. The classes of anti-HIV drugs currently in use include:

- Inhibitors of virus binding to target cells (at step 1 in Figure 16.16)
- Inhibitors of internalization of virus following binding (at step 1)
- Reverse transcriptase inhibitors that block viral DNA synthesis from RNA (at step 2)
- Integrase inhibitors that block the incorporation of viral DNA into the host chromosome (at step 3)
- Protease inhibitors that block the posttranslational processing of viral proteins (at step 5)

Combinations of drugs from these classes have been spectacularly successful in treating HIV infection.

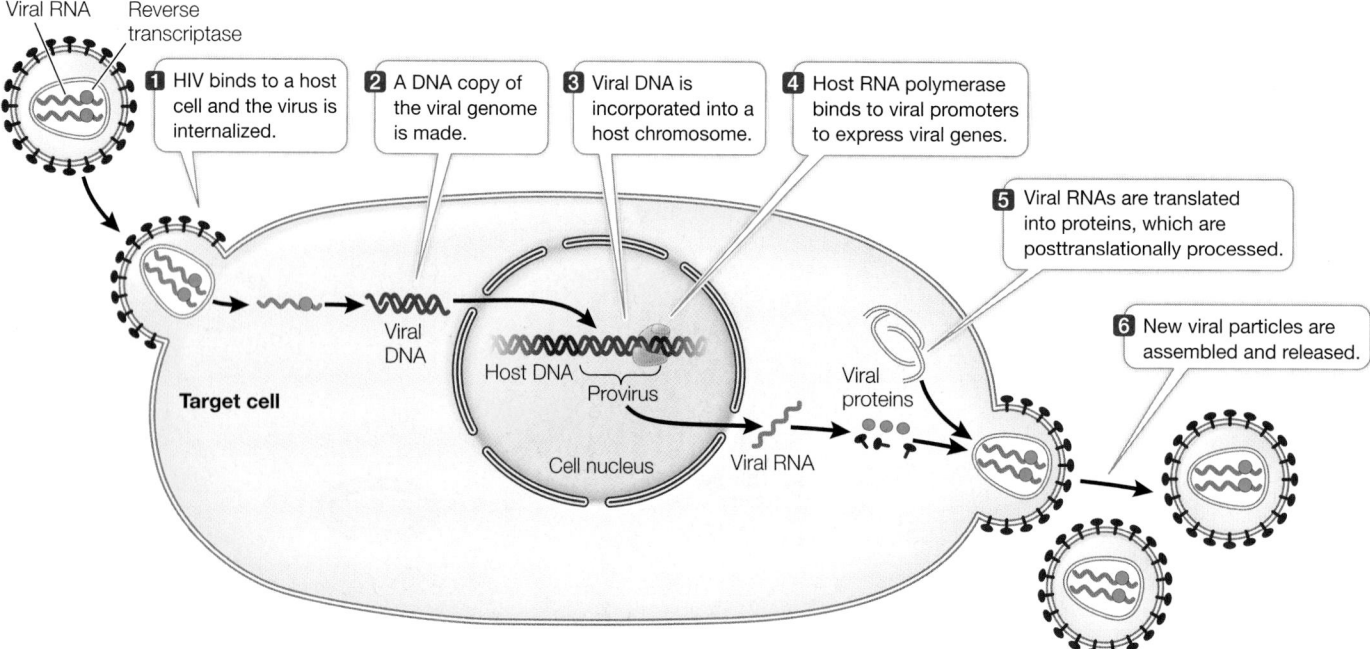

Figure 16.16 The Reproductive Cycle of HIV This retrovirus enters a host cell via fusion of its envelope with the host's cell membrane. Reverse transcription of retroviral RNA then produces a DNA provirus—a molecule of complementary DNA that inserts itself into the host's genome.

Q: Looking at Figures 16.15 and 16.16, would you classify HIV as a lytic or a lysogenic virus?

16.3 Recap and Assess

A virus consists of one or more nucleic acid molecules, a few proteins, and in some cases, a lipid envelope. Viruses require host cells to reproduce. Viral life cycles can include lytic and lysogenic stages. In the lytic life cycle, the cellular machinery is hijacked to synthesize new virions. In the lysogenic life cycle, the viral genome enters the host genome and is inactive until conditions become appropriate to become lytic. Studies of HIV revealed a new mechanism for gene regulation: the regulation of transcription elongation.

1. The sequence of the promoter for the early gene operon in a bacteriophage that infects *E. coli* is similar to the sequence of a housekeeping bacterial gene promoter. Why is this the case?

2. In some bacteriophages, one protein encoded by an early gene is a sigma factor. What does this viral sigma factor likely bind?

3. If the function of the protease that cuts HIV proteins was specifically blocked by a drug, what would be the effect on the HIV reproductive cycle?

So far we have discussed mechanisms that cells and viruses use to control gene transcription. These mechanisms usually involve the interaction of regulatory proteins with specific DNA sequences. However, as we discuss next, there are other mechanisms for controlling gene expression that do not depend on specific DNA sequences.

KEY CONCEPT
16.4 Epigenetic Changes Regulate Gene Expression

Learning Objectives

16.4.1 Define what is meant by CpG islands and describe their role in gene expression.

16.4.2 Explain how acetylation of histone proteins changes the structure of chromatin and affects the rate of transcription.

16.4.3 Draw and/or describe a methylated DNA molecule and follow it through replication, showing how inheritance of DNA methylation occurs.

16.4.4 Give an example that supports the claim that environmental effects have a role in epigenetic changes.

16.4.5 Describe how and where X chromosome inactivation occurs and explain why it is believed to occur.

In the mid-twentieth century, the developmental biologist Conrad Hal Waddington coined the term "epigenetics" and defined it as "that branch of biology which studies the causal interactions between genes and their products which bring the phenotype into being." Today **epigenetics** is defined more specifically, referring to the study of changes in gene expression not caused by changes in the DNA sequence.

Epigenetic changes are reversible but sometimes are stable and heritable. You saw an example of an epigenetic change in the opening story of this chapter, which described how genes inherited from mothers who had particularly stressful pregnancies were expressed at different levels than they were in children whose mothers had not suffered during pregnancy. In that example, stress—an environmental factor—prompted a higher degree of DNA **methylation**

(addition of a methyl group) in the promoter, reducing expression of a gene associated with behavior in teenagers. Here we examine more closely how epigenetic effects are caused either by DNA methylation or by alterations in chromosomal proteins.

DNA methylation occurs at the promoter and silences transcription

For those organisms in which DNA methylation occurs, from 1% to 5% of cytosine residues in the organism's DNA are chemically modified by the addition of a methyl group ($-CH_3$) to the 5-position carbon of the base, to form 5-methylcytosine (**Figure 16.17A**). This covalent addition is catalyzed by the enzyme **DNA methyltransferase** and,

(A) Reversible methylation of cytosine

Cytosine   5–Methylcytosine

(B) Inheritance of methylation and its effect on transcription

DNA methylase catalyzes the formation of 5-methylcytosine at CpG islands. Transcription is repressed.

After DNA replication, the cytosines on the new strand are unmethylated.

Maintenance methylase catalyzes cytosine methylation on the new strand.

Demethylase catalyzes removal of methyl groups. Transcription is activated.

Figure 16.17 DNA Methylation: An Epigenetic Change **(A)** The reversible formation of 5-methylcytosine in DNA. **(B)** DNA methylation can alter the rate of transcription: methylation of cytosine residues generally inhibits transcription, whereas demethylation generally activates transcription. A methylated region can be stably inherited when a maintenance methylase methylates the new strand following replication.

Q: Referring back to Figure 15.7, do you expect cytosines that are in CpG sites to have higher mutation rates than cytosines that are adjacent to one of the other bases?

in mammals, usually occurs in C residues that are adjacent to G residues. DNA regions rich in these doublets are called **CpG islands** and are especially abundant in promoters.

This covalent change in DNA is heritable: when DNA is replicated, a **maintenance methylase** catalyzes the formation of 5-methylcytosine in the new DNA strand. However, the pattern of cytosine methylation can also be altered, because methylation is reversible: a third enzyme, appropriately called **demethylase**, catalyzes the removal of the methyl group from cytosine (**Figure 16.17B**).

What is the effect of DNA methylation? During replication and transcription, 5-methylcytosine behaves just like plain cytosine: it base-pairs with guanine. But extra methyl groups in a promoter attract proteins that bind methylated DNA. These proteins are generally involved in the repression of gene transcription; thus heavily methylated genes tend to be inactive. Note that a gene that has CpG islands in its promoter region is not necessarily heavily methylated. Instead, it may be unmethylated in some tissues, or in some environments, and methylated in other tissues and environments. Methylation is thus a way to regulate gene expression across tissues and environments. *This form of regulation is epigenetic because it affects gene expression without altering the DNA sequence.*

DNA methylation is important in development from egg to embryo. For example, when a mammalian sperm enters an egg, many genes in first the male and then the female genome become demethylated. Thus many genes that are usually inactive are expressed during early development. As the embryo develops and its cells become more specialized, genes whose products are not needed in particular cell types become methylated. These methylated genes are "silenced"; their transcription is repressed. However, unusual or abnormal events can sometimes turn silent genes back on.

For example, DNA methylation may play roles in the genesis of some cancers. In cancer cells, oncogenes get activated and promote cell division, and tumor suppressor genes (which normally inhibit cell division) are turned off (see Chapter 11). This misregulation can occur when the promoters of oncogenes become demethylated while those of tumor suppressor genes become methylated, as is the case in colorectal cancer (see Figure 15.12).

Histone protein modifications affect transcription

Another mechanism for epigenetic gene regulation is the alteration of chromatin structure, or chromatin remodeling. As we saw in Chapter 11, DNA is packaged with histone proteins into nucleosomes (see Figure 11.8), which can make DNA physically inaccessible to RNA polymerase and the rest of the transcription apparatus. Each histone protein has a "tail" of approximately 20 amino acids at its N terminus that sticks out of the compact structure and contains certain positively charged amino acids (notably lysine). Ordinarily there is strong ionic bonding between the positively charged histone proteins and DNA, which is negatively charged because of its phosphate groups. However, enzymes called histone acetyltransferases can add acetyl groups to these positively charged amino acids, thus changing their charges (**Figure 16.18A**).

(A) Mechanism of acetylation

(B) Acetylation of histone tails

Figure 16.18 Epigenetic Remodeling of Chromatin for Transcription Initiation of transcription requires that nucleosomes change their structure, becoming less compact. (**A**) Histone acetyl transferase (HAT) adds an acetyl group to lysine residues. (**B**) Histone acetylation neutralizes the charge of positively charged lysines on histone proteins, weakening their binding to DNA, and making the DNA more accessible to bind general transcription factors (see Figure 16.9).

Reducing the positive charges of the histone tails reduces the affinity of the histones for DNA, opening up the compact nucleosome (**Figure 16.18B**). Additional chromatin remodeling proteins can bind to the loosened nucleosome–DNA complex, opening up the DNA for gene expression. Histone acetyltransferases can thus activate transcription.

Another kind of chromatin remodeling protein, histone deacetylase, can remove the acetyl groups from histones and thereby repress transcription. Histone deacetylases are targets for drug development to treat some forms of cancer. As noted earlier, certain genes block cell division in normal specialized tissues. In some cancers these genes are less active than in normal cells, and the histones near them show excessive levels of deacetylation. Theoretically, a drug acting as a histone deacetylase inhibitor could tip the balance toward acetylation, and this might activate genes that normally inhibit cell division.

Acetylation isn't the only type of histone modification that can affect gene activation and repression. For example, histone methylation (not to be confused with DNA methylation) is associated with gene inactivation, and histone phosphorylation also affects gene expression, the specific effects depending on which amino acids are modified. All of these effects are reversible, so the activity of a eukaryotic gene may be determined by very complex patterns of histone modification.

Epigenetic changes can be induced by the environment

Female honey bees all have the same genetic makeup. When they are in the immature stage called a larva, however, one female in the hive eats a protein-rich substance called royal jelly that dramatically alters the expression of many genes. The queen grows much larger than her peers, stays in the hive, and is tended to by the other bees. Above all, the queen lives up to several years and is fertile, laying the eggs that will produce more bees.

The multitudes of her female compatriot larvae express a different set of genes, becoming workers who build the honeycomb, forage for food, and tend to the queen for their short lives of a few weeks. All of these differences ultimately come from the environment, specifically the royal jelly diet. Recent investigations have shown that the differences in gene expression between these very different yet genetically identical bees are due to differences in DNA methylation (Investigating Life: Gene Expression and Behavior).

▶InvestigatingLIFE   Gene Expression and Behavior

Experiment

Original Paper: R. Kucharski et al. 2008. Nutritional control of reproductive status in honeybees via DNA methylation. *Science* 319: 1817–1830.

Most female honey bee larvae grow up to be workers; just a few eat royal jelly and become queens. To understand differences in gene expression in queen bees versus in their sisters with identical genomes, Ryszard Maleszka and colleagues at Australian National University developed an experiment to test for possible epigenetic effects.

The experiment involved injecting female honey bee larvae with a substance that inhibits expression of the enzyme DNA cytosine-5-methyltransferase (DNMT)—the enzyme that catalyzes the formation of 5-methylcytosine from cytosine in DNA. In a technique called RNAi, the scientists injected female larvae with a small RNA complementary to the mRNA for DNMT to specifically reduce mRNA levels of the DNMT gene.

HYPOTHESIS▶   DNA methylation underlies the developmental and behavioral differences between queen and worker honey bees.

METHOD▶

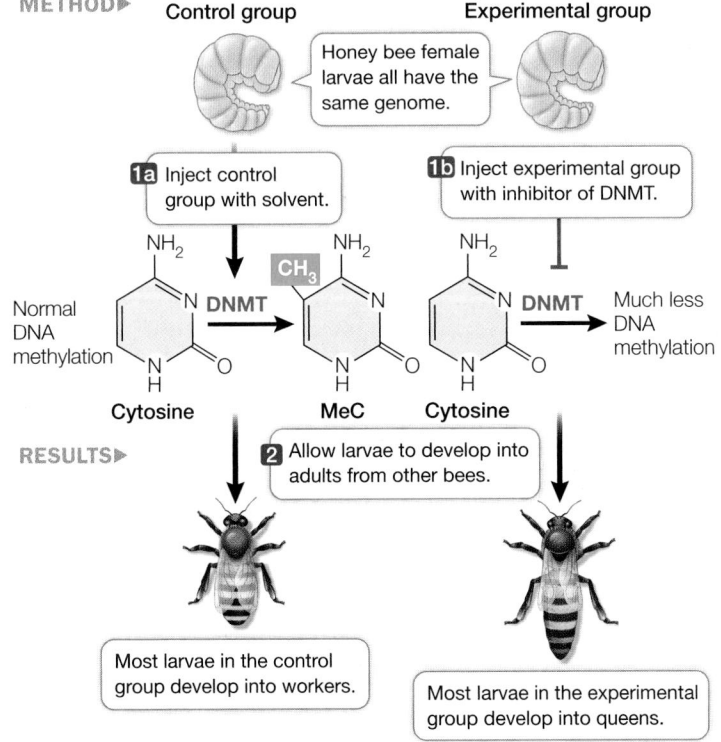

RESULTS▶

CONCLUSION▶   Decreasing DNA methylation mimics the effects of royal jelly, causing larvae destined to become worker bees to instead become queens.

Work with the Data

QUESTIONS▶

1. After injection with either an inhibitor of DNMT or a control, the level of DNMT mRNA was measured in the heads of the larvae and compared with the level of a control mRNA that is always expressed at a high level. The results are shown in Table A.

Table A

Time (h)	DNMT mRNA level compared with control (%)
23	105
48	41

   a. Why was mRNA measured in the heads of the larvae?

   b. What can you conclude about the effectiveness of the inhibition of DNMT expression?

2. The DNA of a gene that is normally expressed in the brain (head) of the larvae was sequenced and the percentage of 5-methylcytosine measured to determine the extent of cytosine methylation in CpG regions. Table B shows the results. What can you conclude about the effect of DNMT inhibition?

Table B

Condition	Percent 5-methylcytosine
Control	79
DNMT expression inhibited	63

3. Larvae that had been injected with the inhibitor for DNMT gene expression or a control were allowed to develop into adults. The phenotypes of the adults were evaluated, and categorized as workers, queens, or queen-like adults (intermediate). The data are shown in Table C. What do the data show about the effect of the inhibition of DNA methylation on the development of queens? Does the amount of DNA methylation strictly predict the extent of change in queen production?

Table C

Condition	Number of workers	Number of queen-like adults	Number of queens
Control	238	73	0
Inhibited	74	0	188

Go to **Achieve** for a companion
Data in Depth exercise.

Although they are reversible, many epigenetic changes such as DNA methylation and histone modification can permanently alter gene expression patterns in a cell. In a germ line cell that forms gametes, it might be possible for epigenetic changes to be passed on to the next generation. But what determines these epigenetic changes? A clue comes from a recent study of monozygotic (identical) twins. Monozygotic twins come from a single fertilized egg that divides to produce two separate cells; each of these goes on to develop into a separate individual. Monozygotic twins thus have identical genomes. But are they identical in their epigenomes? A comparison of DNA in hundreds of such twin pairs shows that in tissues of 3-year-olds, the DNA methylation patterns are virtually the same. But by age 50, by which time the twins have usually been living apart in different environments for decades, the patterns are quite different. This indicates that the *environment plays an important role in epigenetic modifications*, and thus in the regulation of genes that these modifications affect. Note, however, that epigenetic differences in somatic tissues do not mean there will also be differences in the germ line. In addition, in mammals, histone modifications and DNA methylation are mostly removed during gamete formation, meaning that epigenetic changes are reset, making epigenetic inheritance across generations unlikely in mammals.

 Media Clip 16.1
The Surprising Epigenetics of Identical Twins
Life12e.com/mc16.1

Global chromosome changes involve DNA methylation

Like single genes, large regions of chromosomes or even entire chromosomes can have distinct patterns of DNA methylation. Under a microscope, two kinds of chromatin can be distinguished in the stained interphase nucleus: **euchromatin** and **heterochromatin**. The euchromatin appears diffuse and stains lightly; it contains the DNA that is transcribed into mRNA. Heterochromatin

Figure 16.19 Chromatin in a Nucleus Highly condensed heterochromatin is darkly stained, while less condensed euchromatin is lightly stained.

is condensed and stains darkly; any genes it contains are generally not transcribed (**Figure 16.19**).

One of the most dramatic examples of heterochromatin is the inactive X chromosome in the nuclei of female mammals. A normal female mammal has two X chromosomes; a normal male has an X and a Y (see Key Concept 12.4). The X and Y chromosomes probably arose from a pair of autosomes (non–sex chromosomes) at least 180 million years ago. Over time, mutations caused the Y chromosome to gradually lose most of the genes it once shared with the X. As a result, females and males differ greatly in the "dosage" of X-linked genes. Each female cell has two copies of each gene on the X chromosome and therefore has the potential to produce twice as much of each protein product as a male with one X. Nevertheless, for over 75% of the genes on the X chromosome, transcription is essentially identical in males and females. How does this happen?

Figure 16.20 X Chromosome Inactivation (A) A Barr body and an active X chromosome in the nucleus of a human female cell. The X chromosomes are stained with a yellow-green fluorescent dye; the other chromosomes are stained with a red fluorescent dye. (B) A model for X chromosome inactivation.

During early embryonic development, one of the X chromosomes in each cell of a female is largely inactivated with regard to transcription. The same X chromosome remains inactive in all of that cell's descendants. In a given embryonic cell, the "choice" of which X in the pair to inactivate is random. Recall that one X in a female comes from her biological father and one from her biological mother. Thus in one embryonic cell the paternal X might be the one remaining transcriptionally active, but in a neighboring cell the maternal X might be active.

The inactivated X chromosome is identifiable within the nucleus because it is very compact, even during interphase. Typically, a nuclear structure called a Barr body (after its discoverer, Murray Barr) can be seen in human female cells under the light microscope (**Figure 16.20A**). This clump of heterochromatin, which is not present in XY males, is the inactivated X chromosome, and it consists of heavily methylated DNA. A normal XX female will have one Barr body in every somatic cell, whereas a rare XXX female will have two, and an XXXX female will have three. Interestingly, males that are XXY will have one Barr body, indicating that the process of inactivating X chromosomes when there is more than one in a nucleus works similarly in both sexes. These observations suggest that the interphase cells of each person, regardless of sex and of X chromosome copy number, have a single active X chromosome, and thus the same dosage of expressed X chromosome genes.

Condensation of the inactive X chromosome makes its DNA sequences physically unavailable to the transcriptional machinery. Most of the genes of the inactive X are heavily methylated. However, one gene, *Xist* (for *X* inactivation-specific transcript), is only lightly methylated and is transcriptionally active. On the active X chromosome, *Xist* is heavily methylated and not transcribed. The RNA transcribed from *Xist* binds to the X chromosome from which it is transcribed, and this binding leads to inactivation along the chromosome (**Figure 16.20B**).

KEY CONCEPT
16.4 Recap and Assess

Epigenetics describes stable changes in gene expression that do not involve changes in DNA sequences. These changes involve modifications of DNA (cytosine methylation) or of histone proteins bound to DNA and can be passed down through mitosis from a parent cell to daughter cells. Epigenetic changes can be affected by the environment. Large stretches of DNA can be epigenetically modified, leading to inactivation of many genes.

1. How do histone modifications affect transcription?
2. Give an example of evidence that epigenetic modifications affect behavior.
3. How does X chromosome inactivation occur, and why is it believed to occur?
4. In colorectal cancer, certain tumor suppressor genes are not active, and this results in uncontrolled cell division. Two possible explanations for the inactive genes are (a) mutations in the promoter or coding regions, resulting in reduced transcription or inactive proteins, respectively, and (b) epigenetic silencing at the promoters of the genes, resulting in reduced transcription. How would you investigate these two possibilities?

Gene expression involves transcription and then translation. So far we have described how gene expression is regulated at the transcriptional level. But as Figure 16.8 shows, there are many points at which regulation can occur after the initial gene transcript is made.

KEY CONCEPT
16.5
Eukaryotic Gene Expression Can Be Regulated after Transcription

Learning Objectives

16.5.1 Explain how the number of proteins produced by a cell can be greater than the number of protein-coding genes.

16.5.2 List three ways in which the relative amount of mRNA and its encoded protein can differ in a cell.

16.5.3 Describe how miRNAs and siRNAs reduce protein levels.

16.5.4 Predict whether a protein that is resistant to ubiquitination will tend to persist longer than a protein that is rapidly ubiquinated.

16.5.5 Describe the function of the proteasome in a cell.

Eukaryotic gene expression can be regulated both in the nucleus prior to mRNA export, and after the mRNA leaves the nucleus. This can happen in several ways.

RNA splicing can result in different mRNAs being made from the same gene

Most primary mRNA transcripts contain several introns (see Figure 14.8). Before the RNA is exported from the nucleus, a splicing mechanism recognizes the boundaries between exons and introns and converts pre-mRNA, which has the introns, into mature mRNA, which does not. For many genes, **alternative splicing** can occur, whereby some exons are spliced out along with the introns (**Figure 16.21**). This mechanism generates a family of different proteins, with different functions, from a single gene. Recent surveys show that over 90% of all human genes are alternatively spliced. Alternative splicing may be a key to the differences in levels of complexity among organisms. For example, although humans and chimpanzees have similar-sized genomes, there is more alternative splicing in the human brain than in the chimpanzee brain.

Alternative RNA splicing is controlled both by regulatory elements in the RNA sequence that bind specific proteins (similar to regulatory sequences in DNA) and by secondary RNA structures that form by hybridization between nucleotides in the single-stranded RNA molecule.

Small RNAs are important regulators of gene expression

As you'll see in Chapter 17, less than 5% of the genome in most plants and animals codes for proteins. Some of the genome encodes ribosomal RNA and transfer RNAs, but until recently biologists thought that the rest of the genome was not transcribed; some even called it "junk." Recent investigations, however, have

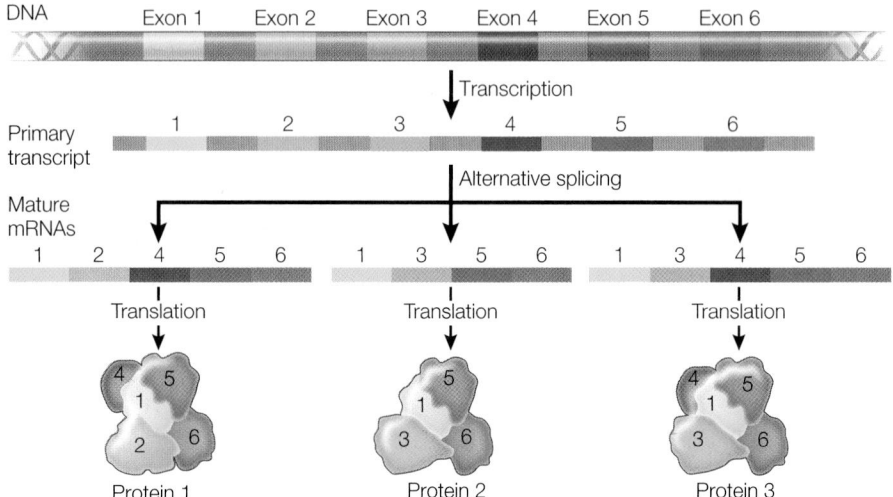

Figure 16.21 Alternative Splicing Results in Different Mature mRNAs and Proteins Pre-mRNA can be spliced differently in different tissues, resulting in different proteins.

Q: A protein-coding gene in a eukaryote has four introns. Assuming the first and last exons must remain in the mature mRNA, how many different proteins could be made by alternative splicing of the pre-mRNA from this gene?

shown that some of these noncoding regions are transcribed. The mature RNAs produced from these regions are often very small and therefore difficult to detect. In both prokaryotes and eukaryotes, these small RNA molecules are called **microRNA (miRNA)**.

There are more than 2,000 miRNAs encoded in the human genome. MicroRNAs are transcribed as longer precursors that fold into double-stranded RNA molecules and are then processed through a series of steps into single-stranded miRNAs. A mature miRNA is about 22 bases long. A protein complex called the RNA-induced silencing complex, or RISC, guides the miRNA to its target mRNA, to which it binds by base pairing and inhibits translation (**Figure 16.22A**). Each 22-bp miRNA often has dozens of mRNA targets because the base pairing between the miRNA and the target mRNA doesn't have to be perfect.

In addition to miRNAs, there is a similarly acting class of molecules called **small interfering RNAs (siRNAs)**, which use the same RNA-induced silencing complex. Small interfering RNAs often arise from viral infections, when two complementary strands of a viral genome are transcribed. Large double-stranded RNAs are formed, and as with miRNAs, these are converted into shorter single-stranded sequences; these bind to the target RNA and cause its degradation (**Figure 16.22B**). Small interfering RNAs are also derived from transposon sequences, which are widespread in eukaryotic genomes (see Key Concept 15.1). Therefore it is likely that gene silencing involving siRNAs evolved as a defense mechanism to prevent the translation of viral and transposon sequences. MicroRNAs and siRNAs are similar molecules that are processed by the same cellular enzymes. A major difference between them is that:

- miRNAs are synthesized from DNA sequences separate from their target, whereas

- siRNAs are targeted to their sequence of origin.

The remarkable conservation of the miRNA and siRNA gene-silencing mechanism across diverse organisms indicates that it is evolutionarily ancient and biologically important.

Translation of mRNA can be regulated by proteins

Is the amount of a protein in a cell determined only by the amount of its mRNA? The answer is no. For example, a survey of genes

Figure 16.22 mRNA Inhibition by RNAs MicroRNAs (**A**) and small interfering RNAs (**B**) can inhibit translation by binding to target mRNAs.

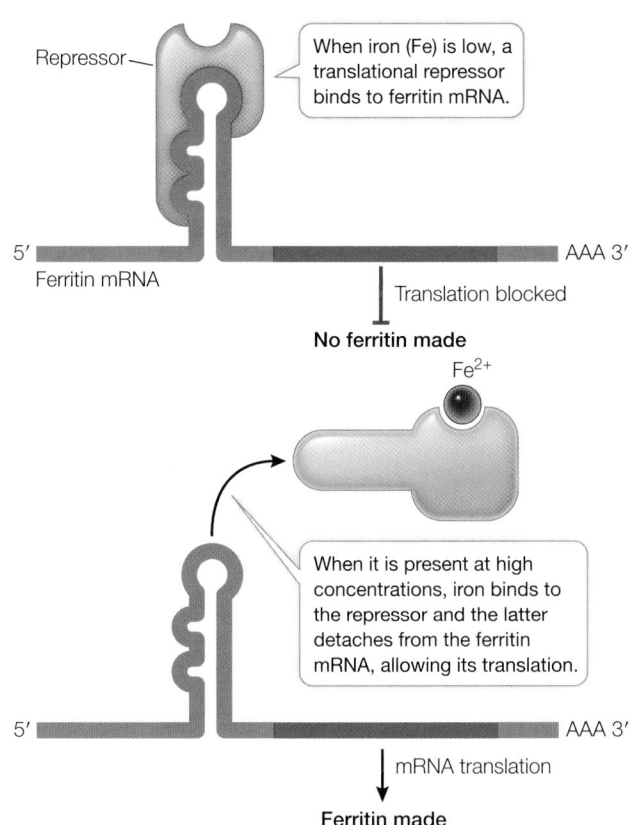

Figure 16.23 A Translational Repressor Can Repress Translation Binding of a protein to a target mRNA can inhibit its translation.

and their expression in yeast cells showed that for about one-third of the genes, there was a clear correlation between mRNA and protein: more mRNA led to more protein. But for two-thirds of the genes, there was no apparent relationship between the two: sometimes there was lots of mRNA and little or no protein, or lots of protein and little mRNA. Lots of protein when there is little mRNA can be explained by relatively short-lived mRNAs encoding long-lived proteins. But how to explain little protein when there is a lot of mRNA? The concentrations of these proteins must be determined by factors acting after the mRNA is made. Cells have two major ways to control the amount of a protein after transcription:

1. They can regulate translation of the protein's mRNA.

2. They can regulate how long a newly synthesized protein persists in the cell (protein longevity).

REGULATION OF TRANSLATION   There are a variety of ways in which the translation of mRNA can be regulated. One way, as we saw in the previous section, is to inhibit translation using the miRNA or siRNA pathway. A second way involves modification of the guanosine triphosphate (GTP) cap on the 5′ end of the mRNA (see Key Concept 14.4). An mRNA that is capped with an

unmodified GTP molecule is not translated. For example, stored mRNAs in the egg cells of the tobacco hornworm moth are capped with unmodified GTP molecules and are not translated. After the egg is fertilized, however, the caps are modified, allowing the mRNA to be translated to produce the proteins needed for early embryonic development.

In another system, repressor proteins directly block translation. For example, in mammalian cells the protein ferritin binds free iron ions (Fe^{2+}). When iron is present in excess, ferritin synthesis rises dramatically, but the amount of ferritin mRNA remains constant, indicating that the increase in ferritin synthesis is due to an increased rate of mRNA translation. Indeed, when the iron level in the cell is low, a translational repressor protein binds to the 5′ noncoding region of ferritin mRNA and prevents its translation by blocking its attachment to a ribosome. When the iron level rises, some of the excess Fe^{2+} ions bind to the repressor and alter its three-dimensional structure, causing the repressor to detach from the mRNA and allowing translation to proceed (**Figure 16.23**). The binding site for the translational repressor on mRNA is a stem-and-loop region with sufficient three-dimensional structure for recognition by a protein.

REGULATION OF PROTEIN LONGEVITY   The protein content of a cell at any given time is a function of both protein synthesis and protein degradation. Certain proteins can be targeted for destruction in a chain of events that begins when an enzyme attaches a 76-amino acid protein called **ubiquitin** (so named because it is ubiquitous, or widespread) to a lysine residue of the protein to be destroyed. Other ubiquitins then attach to the primary one, forming a polyubiquitin chain. The protein–polyubiquitin complex then binds to a huge protein complex called a **proteasome** (**Figure 16.24**). Upon entering the proteasome, the polyubiquitin is removed and ATP energy is used to unfold the target protein. Three different proteases then digest the protein into small peptides and amino acids.

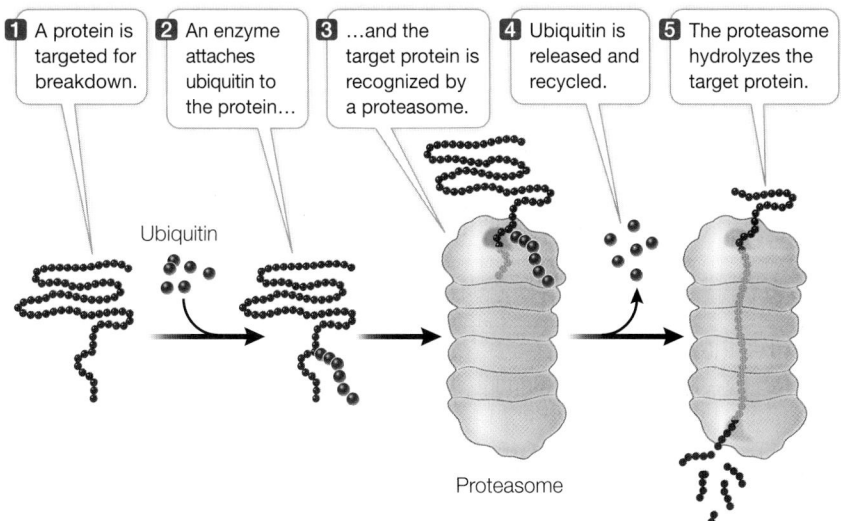

Figure 16.24 A Proteasome Breaks Down Proteins Proteins targeted for degradation are bound to ubiquitin, which then binds the targeted protein to a proteasome. The proteasome is a complex structure where proteins are digested by several powerful proteases.

You may recall from Key Concept 11.2 that cyclins are proteins that regulate the activities of key enzymes at specific points in the cell cycle. Cyclins must be broken down at just the right time, and this is done by attaching ubiquitin to them and degrading them in the proteasomes. Viruses can hijack this system. For example, some strains of the human papillomavirus (HPV) add ubiquitin to the p53 and retinoblastoma proteins, targeting them for proteasomal degradation. These proteins normally inhibit the cell cycle, so the result of this HPV activity is unregulated cell division (cancer).

KEY CONCEPT

16.5 Recap and Assess

One of the most important means of posttranscriptional regulation is alternative RNA splicing, which allows more than one protein to be made from a single gene. The stability of mRNA in the cytoplasm can also be regulated. MicroRNAs, siRNAs, mRNA modifications, and translational repressors can prevent mRNA translation. Proteins in the cell can be targeted for breakdown by ubiquitin and then hydrolyzed in proteasomes.

1. How do miRNAs and siRNAs regulate gene expression?

2. How does the three-dimensional structure of mRNA contribute to the regulation of its expression?

3. What is the role of the proteasome?

4. Before the human genome was sequenced, most scientists thought it contained 80,000 to 150,000 protein-coding genes. The actual sequence revealed only about 20,500. How can mRNA processing explain this discrepancy?

5. Pharmaceutical companies are interested in developing miRNA drugs. How might they work in cancer? (*Hint*: See Figure 11.23, about oncogene and tumor suppressor proteins.)

 View in Achieve
Activity 16.2 Concept Matching: Gene Expression

 ►InvestigatingLIFE

Qand**A** Can epigenetic changes be manipulated?

In the opening story you saw how epigenetic changes in cytosine methylation of a gene encoding a receptor resulted in behavioral changes in people's response to stress. In **Investigating Life: Gene Expression and Behavior**, you learned that epigenetic changes underlie the differences between worker and queen bees. Both examples involve changes in DNA that were triggered by the environment and resulted in altered gene expression.

As in bees, nutrients in the diets of mammals (including humans), such as folic acid and SAM-e (S-adenosyl methionine), contain methyl groups that can participate in reactions that modify DNA. Experiments with mice have shown that feeding young animals a diet enriched with these nutrients causes changes in epigenetic patterns and gene expression that remain throughout life. A new field called nutriepigenomics (could you have guessed the name?) has developed to investigate the possibility of altering gene expression in mammals by diet.

Future directions

In addition to investigating the possibility of altering DNA methylation by diet, researchers have developed specific drugs that target the enzymes involved in DNA methylation. In cancer, gene expression can be altered in many ways, such as by mutation (as you saw in Chapter 11). Cancer cells can alter gene expression though epigenetic mechanisms as well. For example, in some colon cancers, the expression of an important tumor suppressor gene involved in DNA repair is silenced by extensive DNA methylation at the promoter, resulting in uncontrolled cell division. The nucleotide analog 5′-azacytidine blocks DNA methyltransferase and can be employed to combat some cancers, by reducing DNA methylation and halting uncontrolled cell division. Other drugs are being used to block histone modifications that in the tumor cell result in gene expression changes.

 VISUAL SUMMARY 16

© imageBROKER/Alamy Stock Photo

You should be able to relate each summary to the adjacent figures. If you go to this visual summary in **Achieve**, you can follow links to figures, animations, activities, and simulations that will help you consolidate the material.

KEY CONCEPT

16.1 Prokaryotic Gene Expression Is Regulated in Operons

Go to **Animations 16.1 and 16.2**

- **Positive regulation** occurs when binding of an **activator** to DNA increases transcription. **Negative regulation** occurs when binding of a **repressor** to DNA decreases transcription.

- Expression of the *lac* **operon** requires high lactose (repressor not bound to the **operator**) and low glucose (cAMP–CRP bound to the promoter).

- The *lac* operon repressor is bound to its operator when lactose is absent; the *trp* operon repressor is bound to its operator when tryptophan is present.

Figure 16.5

Lactose present

- **Sigma factors** bind to RNA polymerase and direct it to specific classes of prokaryotic promoters.

Questions

1. Suppose a mutation occurs in the *lac* operon repressor gene so that the repressor can no longer bind its inducer (allolactose) but it can still bind DNA. What effect will this have on regulation of the *lac* operon?

2. Suppose a mutation occurs in the *trp* operon repressor gene such that the repressor can no longer bind its co-repressor (tryptophan) but it can still bind DNA. What effect will this have on regulation of the *trp* operon?

3. What would the effect of a mutation in sigma-70 that rendered it non-functional be on an *E. coli* cell?

Figure 16.7

Low glucose, lactose present

CRP cAMP RNA polymerase

Transcription

P_I I P_{lac} O Z Y A

KEY CONCEPT

16.2 Eukaryotic Gene Expression Is Regulated by Transcription Factors

Go to **Activity 16.1 and Animation 16.3**

- Protein **transcription factors** bind to **silencer** and **enhancer** sequences on DNA to regulate transcription in eukaryotes.

- **General transcription factors** are required for initiation of transcription at all eukaryotic protein-coding promoters.

- **Specific transcription factors** differ among genes and interact with the **basal transcription apparatus** through **mediator**.

- Transcription factors possess particular structural motifs that allow them to bind to particular DNA sequences.

- Transcription factors are responsible for differences in gene expression in cells that contain the same genome, and thus underlie cell differentiation.

Questions

1. What effects on gene expression and cell viability would occur if a general versus a specific transcription factor were knocked out (rendered nonfunctional)?

2. What effects on gene expression and cell viability would occur if a binding site for a general versus a specific transcription factor were knocked out (rendered unable to bind a transcription factor)?

3. What would be the effect of knocking out mediator in a cell?

4. How might a researcher prevent muscle precursor cells from differentiating into myoblasts (see Figure 16.12)?

Figure 16.10

Activator (specific transcription factor)

DNA

Enhancer

Basal transcription apparatus

Transcribed region

Regulatory protein binding | Transcription factor binding site | RNA polymerase II binding

Promoter

Mediator

Activator (specific transcription factor)

Transcription

KEY CONCEPT

16.3 Viruses Regulate Their Gene Expression during the Reproductive Cycle

- **Bacteriophages** are **viruses** that infect bacteria and can have **lytic** or lysogenic life cycles.

- Eukaryotic viruses include DNA, RNA, and **retroviruses**.

- Retroviruses such as HIV make a DNA copy of their genome that integrates into the host genome, and then transcription leads to production of new virus.

Questions

1. A bacterial strain that has been growing for many hours in a closed tube suddenly succumbs to bacteriophage infection. What do you think happened?

2. How might an early gene product turn off transcription of its bacterial host genes?

3. HIV may spend many years in the host genome before producing virions. Transcription initiation occurs during these years, but no viral proteins are made. Why not?

Figure 16.15

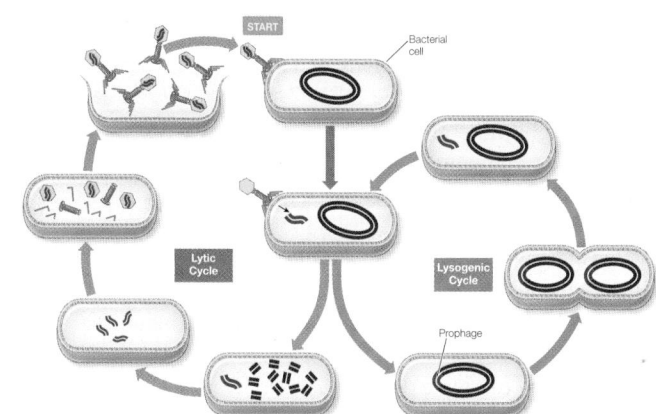

START

Bacterial cell

Lytic Cycle

Lysogenic Cycle

Prophage

KEY CONCEPT

16.4 Epigenetic Changes Regulate Gene Expression

- In many species, DNA **methylation** occurs at **CpG islands**, shutting down transcription.

- Histone deacetylation increases histone affinity for DNA, which reduces transcription.

- Epigenetic changes can be passed on through mitosis.

- X inactivation involves production of an *Xist* RNA, which coats the chromosome from which it was transcribed, causing it to become heterochromatic.

Questions

1. Some cytosine bases are never methylated. Why?

2. Explain why CpG methylation sites facilitate inheritance of methylation across cell division.

3. What would be the effect of deleting the *Xist* gene in a typical (XY) male mammal? In a typical (XX) female mammal?

Figure 16.17

Inheritance of methylation and its effect on transcription

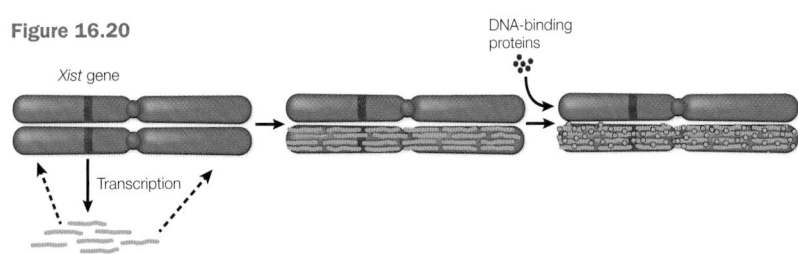

Figure 16.20

KEY CONCEPT

16.5 Eukaryotic Gene Expression Can Be Regulated after Transcription   Go to **Activity 16.2**

- **Alternative splicing** allows many different proteins to be produced from the same gene.

- mRNA levels can be uncorrelated with protein levels due to differences in stability and translational control of expression.

- The **microRNA** (**miRNA**) pathway inhibits translation; the similar **small interfering RNA** (**siRNA**) pathway degrades mRNAs.

- Protein stability is controlled by ubiquitination.

Questions

1. A gene encodes a four-exon pre-mRNA. Assuming that the first and last exons remain in the mature mRNA, how many different proteins can be produced by alternative splicing of the pre-mRNA?

2. Why might the abundance of a protein in a cell be quite low compared with its mRNA level?

3. A protein-coding gene experiences a missense mutation that changes a lysine to an arginine, both of which have positively charged side groups. This change substantially increases the stability of the protein. Why might this be the case?

Figure 16.21

Genomes 17

KEY CONCEPTS

17.1 Genomes Can Be Sequenced Rapidly

17.2 Prokaryotic Genomes Are Compact

17.3 Eukaryotic Genomes Contain Many Types of Sequences

17.4 Human Biology Is Revealed through the Genome

17.5 Proteomics and Metabolomics Can Provide Insights beyond the Genome

© Shotshop GmbH/Alamy Stock Photo

Genome sequencing has revealed insights into how size is controlled by genes.

▶Investigating LIFE

The Dog Genome Project

Canis lupus familiaris, the dog, was domesticated from gray wolves by humans thousands of years ago. Dogs and wolves are canids, a mammalian family that includes coyotes, foxes, jackals, and dingoes. Dogs show substantially more variation in size (and in several other characters) compared with other canids. The American Kennel Club recognizes about 195 different breeds, including the Chihuahua, with an adult weight of just 1.5 kilograms (3.3 pounds), and the Scottish deerhound, with an adult mass of 70 kilograms (154 pounds). In addition, there are hundreds of genetic diseases in dogs, many of which tend to be common in particular breeds and have counterparts in humans. To study the genes behind the enormous phenotypic variation, and to elucidate the relationships between genes and diseases, the Dog Genome Project was started in the late 1990s.

Two dogs—a boxer and a poodle—were the first to have their entire genomes sequenced. The dog genome contains 2.8 billion base pairs of DNA in 39 pairs of chromosomes. There are 19,000 protein-coding genes, most with close counterparts in other mammals, including humans. Given the whole genome sequence, researchers began to map genetic markers—specific nucleotides or short sequences of DNA—at particular locations on the genome that differ among individual dogs or breeds.

Genetic markers can be used to map the locations of (and thus identify) genes that control particular traits. For example, Dr. Elaine Ostrander and her colleagues at the National Institutes of Health studied Portuguese water dogs to identify genes that control size. Samples of cells for DNA isolation were obtained by sweeping a cotton swab over the inside of the cheek. It turned out that the gene for *insulin-like growth factor 1* (IGF-1) is important in determining size: large breeds have an allele that codes for an active IGF-1, and small breeds have a different allele that codes for a less active IGF-1.

Inevitably, some scientists set up companies to validate the "purebred" status of dogs, or determine the mix of breeds in mongrels, using DNA supplied by owners. Not to be outdone, cat fanciers have sequenced the genomes of domestic and wild cats. Identifying genetic differences across dog breeds and comparing them with phenotypic differences across breeds has allowed certain genes to be associated with certain phenotypes. As a result, genes for size, coat colors, behaviors, certain cancers, and other genetic diseases have been identified. Many of these genes cause similar phenotypes in other mammals, including humans.

 What have we learned from sequencing animal genomes? (Find the answer on page 396.)

KEY CONCEPT
17.1   Genomes Can Be Sequenced Rapidly

Learning Objectives

17.1.1 Arrange a series of overlapping DNA sequence reads to give a contiguous sequence of DNA.

17.1.2 Explain how RNA sequencing differs from genome sequencing.

17.1.3 Identify the characteristics of open reading frames.

17.1.4 Explain what is meant by genome annotation and why it is harder to do in eukaryotes than in prokaryotes.

17.1.5 Describe examples of comparative genomics.

Genome sequencing involves determining the nucleotide base sequence of the entire genome of an organism. For a prokaryotic organism with a single chromosome, the genome sequence is one continuous series of base pairs (bp). In the case of a diploid, sexually reproducing species with multiple autosomes and a pair of sex chromosomes (see Key Concept 12.4), the "sequenced genome" usually means the sequence of all the bases in one set of autosomes, in each of the two sex chromosomes, and in the mitochondrial (and other organelle) genomes.

With advances in the technology for DNA sequencing, there has been an explosion of genetic information that scientists can use in a variety of ways:

- The genomes of different species can be compared to find out how they differ at the DNA level, and this information can be used to trace evolutionary relationships.

- The sequences of individuals within a species can be compared to identify mutations that affect particular phenotypes.

- Sequence information can be used to identify genes for particular traits, such as genes associated with diseases.

The base sequence of a short DNA fragment can be determined quickly

The notion of sequencing the entire genome of a complex organism was not contemplated until 1986. The Nobel laureate Renato Dulbecco and others proposed at that time that the world scientific community be mobilized to undertake the sequencing of the entire human genome. One motive was to detect DNA damage in people who had survived the atomic bomb attacks and been exposed to radiation in Japan during World War II. But in order to detect changes in the human genome, scientists first needed to know its sequence.

The result was the publicly funded **Human Genome Project**, an enormous undertaking that was successfully completed in 2003. This effort was aided and complemented by privately funded groups. The genome project benefited from the development of many new methods that were first developed to sequence smaller genomes—those of prokaryotes and simple eukaryotes, the model organisms you have encountered in earlier chapters of this book. Many of these methods are still applied widely, and

powerful new methods for sequencing genomes have emerged. These methods are complemented by new ways to examine phenotypic diversity in a cell's proteins and in the metabolic products of the cell's enzymes.

Many prokaryotes have a single chromosome, whereas eukaryotes have many. Because of their differing sizes, chromosomes are easy to separate from one another. You might think that the straightforward way to sequence a chromosome would be to start at one end and simply sequence the DNA molecule one nucleotide at a time. But sequencing a DNA molecule millions of bp long from one end to the other is just not possible using current methods. At most, only a few thousand bp can be sequenced at a time, and the least expensive methods sequence only a few hundred bp at a time. To determine a genome sequence, long chromosomes must be broken into millions of smaller DNA fragments that are sequenced individually at the same time.

In the 1970s Frederick Sanger and his colleagues invented a way to sequence DNA by using chemically modified nucleotides that were originally developed to stop cell division in cancer. This method, or a variation of it, was used to obtain the first human genome sequence as well as those of several model organisms. However, it was relatively slow, very expensive at the genome scale, and labor-intensive. The first decade of the new millennium saw the development of faster and less expensive methods, often referred to under the general term **high-throughput sequencing**. These methods use miniaturization techniques first developed for the electronics industry, as well as the principles of DNA replication, often in combination with the polymerase chain reaction (PCR).

Connect the Concepts PCR can be automated and is a key to sequencing small amounts of DNA. Learn about PCR in Key Concept 13.5.

High-throughput sequencing methods are rapidly improving. Just one of the many approaches is outlined here and illustrated in **Figure 17.1**. First the DNA is prepared for sequencing by attaching it to a solid surface and amplifying the DNA by PCR (see Figure 17.1A):

1. A large molecule of DNA is cut into small fragments of a few hundred bp each. This can be done physically, using mechanical forces to shear (break up) the DNA, or by using enzymes that hydrolyze the phosphodiester bonds between nucleotides at intervals in the DNA backbone.

2. The DNA is denatured by heat, breaking the hydrogen bonds that hold the two strands together. Short, synthetic oligonucleotides (adapter sequences) are attached to each end of each single-stranded DNA fragment.

3. Single fragments are attached to the surface of a solid support, leaving a small amount of space between each molecule.

4. Each DNA fragment is amplified by PCR using primers complementary to the adapter sequences at the ends of each DNA fragment. The multiple (approximately 1,000) copies of the DNA at a single location allow for easy detection of added nucleotides during the sequencing steps.

(A) Amplification of DNA fragments by PCR

DNA

Fragmentation

1 A large molecule of DNA is cut into fragments.

Denaturing and addition of adapter

2 The fragments are denatured, and adapter sequences are added at each end of the fragments.

3 Single DNA fragments are attached to a solid surface.

Amplification

4 Each fragment is amplified in place by PCR.

Figure 17.1 High-Throughput DNA Sequencing (A) PCR amplification of individual single-stranded DNA fragments produces clusters of template molecules, half of which are identical and half of which are complementary to the original molecule. (B) The strand complementary to only one of the two templates is sequenced one color-labeled nucleotide at a time, and a microscopic camera detects the color (and hence the identity) of the added nucleotide. Each cluster produces a sequence that is 100–300 bp long.

▶ View in **Achieve**
Animation 17.1 **Sequencing the Genome**

▶ View in **Achieve**
Animation 17.2 **High-Throughput Sequencing**

(B) The DNA synthesis cycle

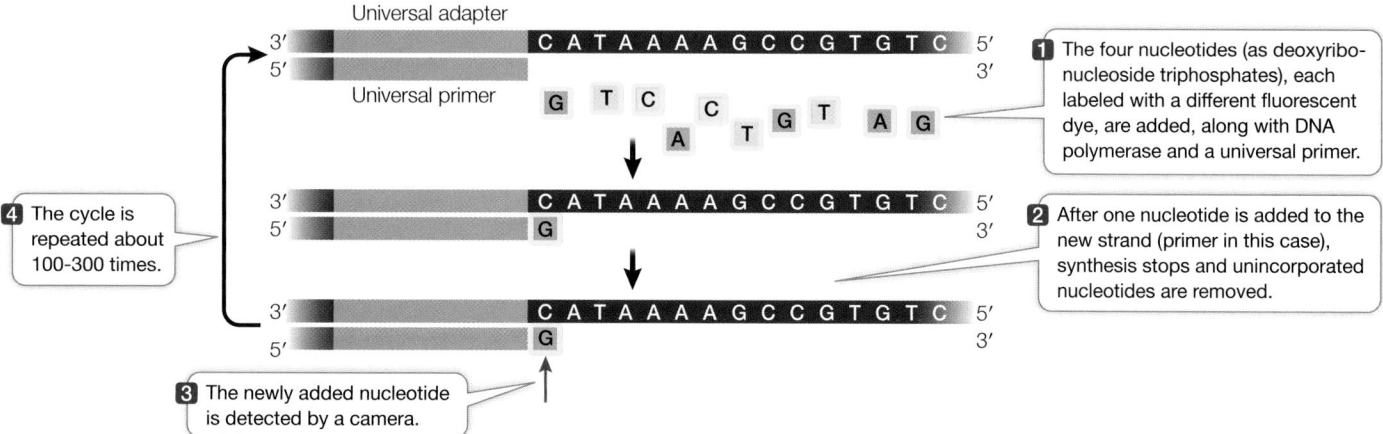

Universal adapter

3′ C A T A A A A G C C G T G T C 5′
5′ 3′

Universal primer

G T C   C   G T   A G
A   T   G   T   A   G

1 The four nucleotides (as deoxyribonucleoside triphosphates), each labeled with a different fluorescent dye, are added, along with DNA polymerase and a universal primer.

4 The cycle is repeated about 100-300 times.

3′ C A T A A A A G C C G T G T C 5′
5′ G 3′

2 After one nucleotide is added to the new strand (primer in this case), synthesis stops and unincorporated nucleotides are removed.

3′ C A T A A A A G C C G T G T C 5′
5′ G 3′

3 The newly added nucleotide is detected by a camera.

Once the DNA has been amplified, it is ready for sequencing. First, the fragments are heated to denature them and then a universal primer (complementary to one of the adapter sequences used for the PCR amplification step) is added. Then the DNA synthesis cycle begins (see Figure 17.1B):

1. At the beginning of each cycle, a solution containing DNA polymerase and the four deoxyribonucleoside triphosphates (dNTPs: dATP, dGTP, dCTP, and dTTP) is added to the DNA. Recall that dNTPs are the substrates that the DNA polymerase uses in DNA synthesis (see Key Concept 13.3).

Each of the four kinds of dNTPs is tagged with a different colored fluorescent dye.

2. The DNA synthesis reaction is set up so that only one nucleotide is added to the new DNA strand in each synthesis cycle. After each addition, the unincorporated dNTPs are removed.

3. The fluorescence of the new nucleotide at each location is detected with a camera. The color of the fluorescence indicates which of the four nucleotides was added.

4. The fluorescent tag is removed from the nucleotide that is already attached, and then the DNA synthesis cycle is repeated 100–300 times. Images are captured after each nucleotide is added. The series of colors at each location indicates the sequence of nucleotides in the growing DNA strand at that location.

The power of this method derives from the fact that:

• it is fully automated and miniaturized.

• millions of different fragments are sequenced at the same time.

• it is an inexpensive way to sequence large genomes. For example, at the time of this writing, a complete human genome can be sequenced in less than a day for less than $1,000. This is in stark contrast to the Human Genome Project, which took 13 years and $2.7 billion to sequence one genome!

Sequencing millions of short DNA fragments is only part of the process of constructing the genome. Once these fragments have been determined, they need to be put together in the correct order.

That is, they need to be arranged to reflect the contiguous sequence of the chromosomes from which they came. As shown in **Figure 17.2**, it is critical that the sequence fragments, or "reads," overlap one another; otherwise it would not be possible to align them. Of course, the problem of ordering hundreds of millions of fragments, each 100–300 bp long, from a human genome is more challenging than the 77 bp example in Figure 17.2! The field of **bioinformatics** was developed to analyze DNA sequences using sophisticated mathematics and computer programs to handle the large amounts of data generated in genome sequencing.

Transcriptomics identifies expressed genes

In addition to being able to sequence the entire genome of an organism, it is also possible to sequence the **transcriptome**, which is the subset of the genome that is expressed as RNA in a particular cell or tissue at a particular time. In many cases it is the transcriptome that is of most interest, because expressed genes are likely to affect phenotype. As we discussed in Chapter 16, the genomes of every somatic cell in the body are identical, but the DNA sequences that are expressed differ from cell to cell and from tissue to tissue. The determination of which genes are expressed in what amounts can be made by **RNA sequencing** (**RNA-seq**).

RNA sequencing is essentially the same as DNA sequencing except for the initial steps. With RNA, it is necessary first to synthesize DNA copies of the RNAs. As you might remember from Chapter 16, some RNA viruses possess a reverse transcriptase that they use to synthesize a double-stranded DNA molecule

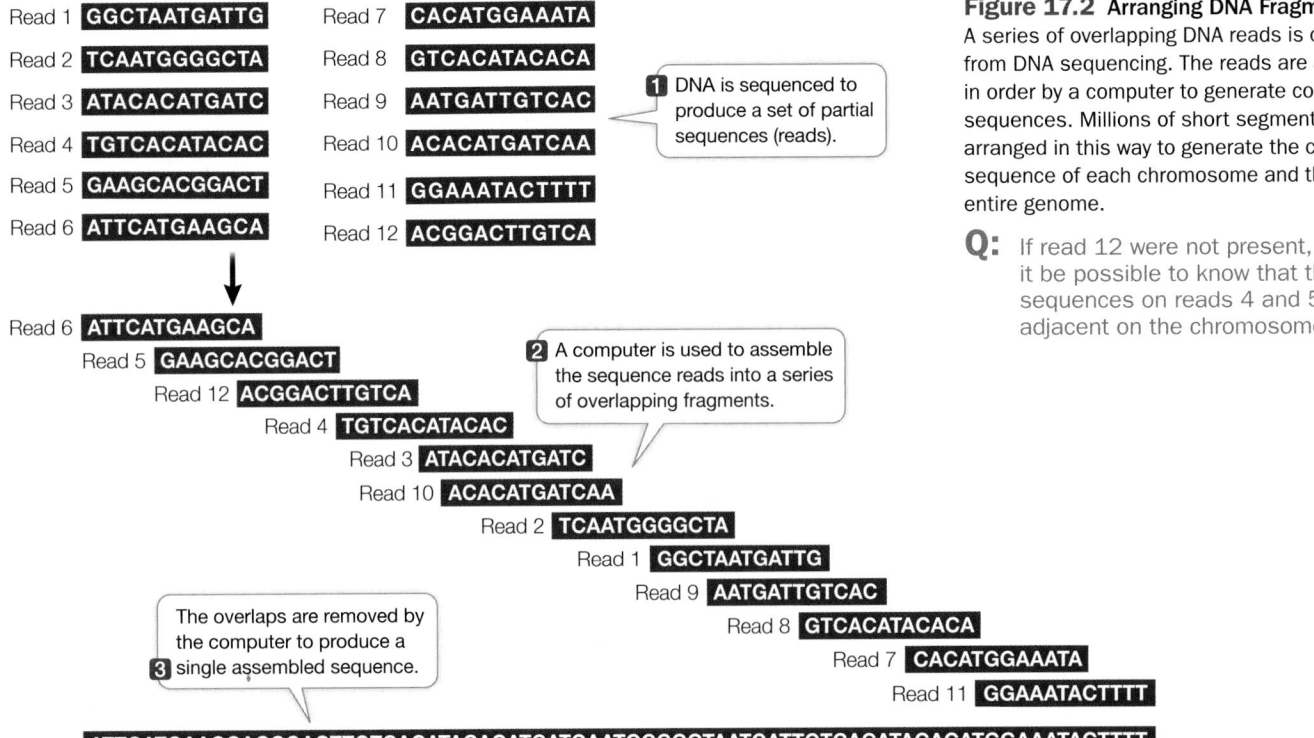

Figure 17.2 Arranging DNA Fragments
A series of overlapping DNA reads is obtained from DNA sequencing. The reads are arranged in order by a computer to generate contiguous sequences. Millions of short segments are arranged in this way to generate the complete sequence of each chromosome and thus the entire genome.

Q: If read 12 were not present, would it be possible to know that the sequences on reads 4 and 5 were adjacent on the chromosome?

RNA

Fragmentation

Fragmented RNA

1. RNA is cut into small similar-sized fragments.

Reverse transcription

cDNA

2. The fragments of RNA are reverse transcribed into cDNAs.

Sequencing and alignment

3. The cDNAs are sequenced, and the sequences are aligned with one another and to a known genome.

Genome

Figure 17.3 RNA Sequencing RNA is extracted from a sample, fragmented, and reverse transcribed into DNA, which is then sequenced. The sequences are aligned with one another and to a known genome if it is available. A gene with more fragments (per base) is expressed at a higher level than a gene with fewer fragments.

from an RNA molecule (see Figure 16.16). Biologists use this enzyme to generate DNA from fragmented cellular RNA, then sequence the complementary DNA (cDNA) using high-throughput sequencing. When these sequences are aligned with one another by computer (see Figure 17.2), each of the resulting contiguous sequences represents a single RNA molecule. In addition, the cDNA sequences can be aligned to the genome to determine which genomic regions are expressed (**Figure 17.3**). Comparing transcriptomes across cell types allows researchers to determine similarities and differences in the RNAs being expressed. If a genomic DNA sequence appears in a transcriptome (as RNA), it is substantially more likely to be functional than if it is seen only in the genome and not in the transcriptome.

Genome sequences yield several kinds of information

New genome sequences are being published at an accelerating pace, creating a torrent of biological information. This information is used in two related fields of research, both focused on studying genomes. In **functional genomics**, biologists use sequence information to identify various parts of genomes and their functions. In particular, biologists seek to identify all of the protein-coding genes, RNA genes, regulatory sequences, and other functional sequences such as telomeres and centromeres. Identifying the various functional regions of the genome is termed genome annotation. Finding these sequences can be challenging, since most genes in most genomes have never been studied. The search for

protein-coding genes leverages what is known about gene structure in prokaryotes and eukaryotes, the genetic code, and results from RNA sequencing.

To find a protein-coding gene, biologists look for **open reading frames**—sequences of DNA that encode a reasonably long sequence of amino acids before reaching a stop codon. Some open reading frames (essentially all in prokaryotes) represent the entire coding region for a gene, beginning with a start codon and ending with a stop codon. However, because of the widespread occurrence of introns, many open reading frames in eukaryotes represent only part of a protein coding region (an exon).

Once a protein-coding gene has been identified, the next step is to determine its function. Predicting the function of an encoded protein can be done using computational methods. Computer algorithms can scan the protein sequence and find motifs—regions of amino acids—that can be predicted to fold in certain ways or have enzyme activity. If a similar nucleotide or protein sequence has been discovered previously in another organism, it probably has a similar or identical function in the newly sequenced organism. For example, one might correctly guess that the RNA polymerase genes in humans and mice encode proteins with similar sequences and functions. An experimental approach to determine a gene's function is to insert it along with a promoter into a recipient cell or organism and look for a new phenotype. Conversely, knocking out the unidentified gene by mutation or deletion and looking for phenotypic changes may indicate the gene's normal function (see Chapter 18).

Regulatory sequences for genes, such as promoters and terminators for transcription, can be identified by characteristic consensus sequences (see Key Concept 14.4) in the vicinity of protein-coding regions. These regulatory regions are easier to find in prokaryotes because they occur in a more predictable location than in eukaryotes. Finding enhancers and silencers (see Key Concept 16.2) is especially difficult in eukaryotes because they may not be adjacent to the coding region of the gene.

In addition to functional genes, several other types of DNA sequences can be identified. These include centromere sequences (see Key Concept 11.3), telomere sequences (see Key Concept 13.3), transposons (see Key Concept 17.2), and other repetitive sequences.

Once genomes from different organisms were available, it allowed for development of the field of **comparative genomics**, which compares genomes both within and across species. Comparative genomics addresses several kinds of questions, including what genes are present in all species, how rapidly nucleotide and amino acid sequences change for different regions of the genome, how and how often new genes arise or old genes are lost from genomes, how gene order changes because of chromosomal rearrangements or other processes, and how species are related to one another. **Investigating Life: Comparative Analysis of the Tiger Genome** describes the recent sequencing of the tiger genome and how it relates to the genomes of other cats and other mammals.

Connect the Concepts The application of DNA sequencing to reconstructing phylogenies (evolutionary histories of organisms or their genes) is described in Chapter 20.

▶InvestigatingLIFE Comparative Analysis of the Tiger Genome

Experiment

Original Paper: Y. S. Cho et al. 2013. The tiger genome and comparative analysis with lion and snow leopard genomes. *Nat Commun* 4: 1–7.

Panthera tigris, the tiger, is possibly the most famous endangered species. Fewer than 4,000 individuals remain in the wild. While a century ago there were nine recognized genetically distinct subspecies, four have become extinct. The five extant subspecies include the Bengal tiger seen at zoos and the white Amur tiger that lives in snowy regions of Russia, China, and North Korea. While the genomes of other cats, such as the lion, snow leopard, and domestic cat, had already been sequenced, that of the tiger had not until this study.

HYPOTHESIS▶ Sequencing the genomes of big cats will reveal that the adaptive phenotypic variation seen among cats is due to genetic variation.

METHOD▶

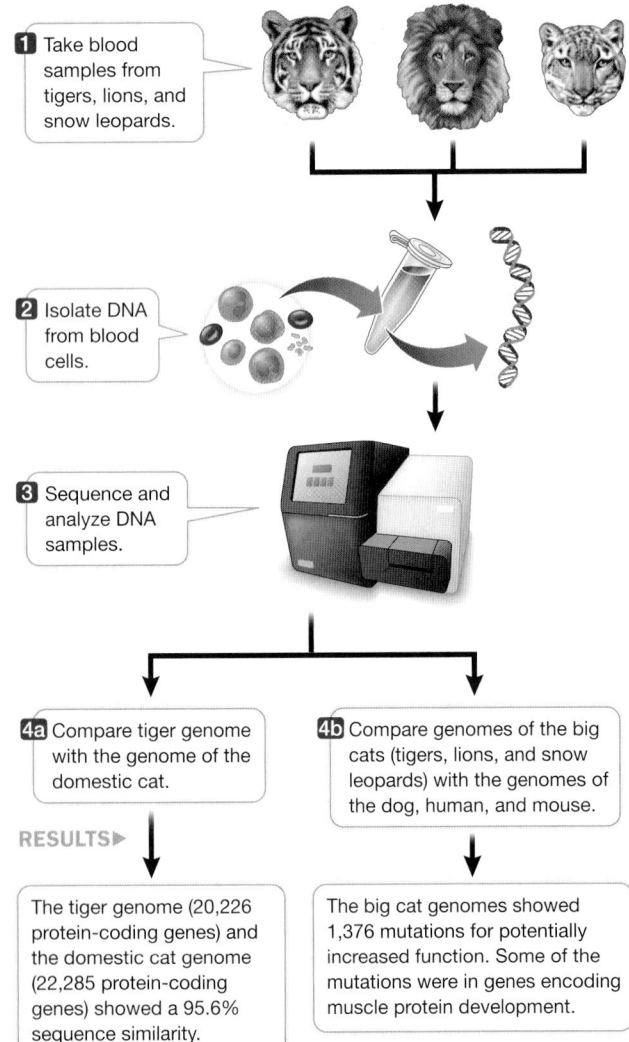

1 Take blood samples from tigers, lions, and snow leopards.

2 Isolate DNA from blood cells.

3 Sequence and analyze DNA samples.

4a Compare tiger genome with the genome of the domestic cat.

4b Compare genomes of the big cats (tigers, lions, and snow leopards) with the genomes of the dog, human, and mouse.

RESULTS▶

The tiger genome (20,226 protein-coding genes) and the domestic cat genome (22,285 protein-coding genes) showed a 95.6% sequence similarity.

The big cat genomes showed 1,376 mutations for potentially increased function. Some of the mutations were in genes encoding muscle protein development.

CONCLUSION▶ What would you conclude about the phenotype of big cats? Explore the possibilities in the following Work with the Data.

Work with the Data

An international team led by Jong Bhak at the Genome Research Foundation in Suwon, South Korea, determined the sequence of tiger DNA and compared it with lion and snow leopard DNA, as well as that of the domestic cat.

QUESTIONS▶

1. The overall sequence of tiger DNA was compared with that of the domestic cat. For reference, a comparison between the human and gorilla genomes was included. The time since the last common ancestor was also estimated. The results are shown in the table. What can you conclude about the rate of evolutionary change between the two cat genomes and between the human and gorilla genomes?

Comparison groups	Last common ancestor (millions of years ago)	Genome sequence similarity (%)
Domestic cat and tiger	10.8	95.6
Human and gorilla	8.8	94.8

2. While there are 20,226 protein-coding genes in the tiger genome, some of them are in gene families. That is, some genes are highly similar to one another and have the same function, and arose recently by gene duplication. Ignoring duplicates, there are 14,528 protein-coding genes in the tiger genome. The research team was interested in comparing the genomes of cats with those of other mammals. So they asked whether the gene families identified in the tiger and domestic cat genomes are also present in other mammals. Tigers and cats together have 16,417 protein-coding genes. The Venn diagram shows these and the 15,787 protein-coding genes in the opossum, the 16,515 in pandas and dogs, and the 16,798 in humans and mice. The number in an overlapping region represents the number of protein-coding genes shared with the overlapping genome(s). For example, the tiger and domestic cat genomes share 99 unique protein-coding genes with the opossum genome that are not found in the panda, dog, human, or mouse genomes.

   a. Looking at the Venn diagram, how many protein-coding genes are common to all of the mammalian genomes examined?

   b. How many protein-coding genes are found only in the tiger and domestic cat genomes? How many are found only in the human and mouse genomes?

   c. What do these data indicate about the basic mammalian genome?

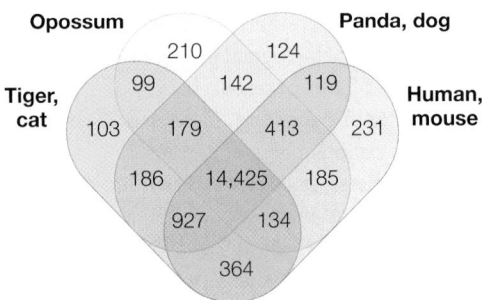

Go to **Achieve** for a companion Data in Depth exercise.

17.1 Recap and Assess

The sequencing of genomes involves randomly cutting chromosomes into short, overlapping fragments, sequencing 100–300 bp of each fragment, and then assembling the resulting overlapping reads into contiguous sequences for entire chromosomes. Current sequencing methods use miniaturization, automation, and powerful computers. Genome sequences are used in functional and comparative genomics.

1. When sequencing genomes, why are overlapping reads needed, and how are they arranged to produce the final sequence?

2. How are open reading frames recognized in a genome sequence? How can RNA sequencing data help identify open reading frames? What kind of information can be derived from an open reading frame?

3. What is comparative genomics? Give an example of how it is used.

The first genomes to be fully sequenced were those of viruses and prokaryotes. Next we discuss the information provided by the relatively simple prokaryotic genomes.

17.2 Prokaryotic Genomes Are Compact

Learning Objectives

17.2.1 Describe the characteristics of prokaryotic genomes.

17.2.2 Propose how one might determine the identity and abundance of microbes in a particular environment, such as the human gut.

17.2.3 Define a transposable element and describe how copy and paste transposition differs from cut and paste transposition.

In 1968 Robert W. Holley was awarded the Nobel Prize for the first sequencing of a nucleic acid—a tRNA with just 80 bases. It took Holley and his team 5 years to discover the sequence. A few years later the first genome was sequenced, that of a 5,386-bp bacteriophage. As methods gradually improved, the genome of a prokaryote was sequenced in the 1990s. With the new automated sequencing techniques we just described, we now have genome sequences for many prokaryotes, to the great benefit of microbiology and medicine.

Prokaryotic genomes have distinctive features

Bacterial and archaeal genomes have several notable features:

• *They are relatively small.* Prokaryotic genomes range from about 160,000 to 12 million bp and are usually organized into a single chromosome.

• *They are compact.* Typically, more than 85% of the DNA is in protein-coding sequences or RNA genes, with only short sequences between genes.

• *Prokaryotic gene sequences usually are not interrupted by introns.* An exception is the rRNA and tRNA genes of archaea, which frequently contain introns.

• *In addition to having a main chromosome, prokaryotes often have smaller, circular molecules of DNA called plasmids,* which may be transferred between cells (see Key Concept 12.6).

Beyond these similarities, there is great diversity among these single-celled organisms, reflecting the huge variety of environments in which they are found (described in Chapter 24). Let's examine prokaryotic genomes in terms of functional and comparative genomics.

FUNCTIONAL GENOMICS   As we described in Key Concept 17.1, functional genomics is the biological discipline that assigns functions to the products of gene sequences. You can see the various functions encoded by the protein-coding genes of three bacteria in Table 17.1. As an example, look at the first bacterial genome sequenced, that of *Haemophilus influenzae,* which lives in the human respiratory tract and can cause ear infections or, more seriously, meningitis in children. Its single, circular chromosome has 1,830,138 bp. In addition to its origin of replication and the genes coding for rRNAs and tRNAs, this bacterial chromosome has 1,656 protein-coding genes.

When the *H. influenzae* sequence was first announced 20 years ago, only 1,007 of the open reading frames coded for proteins with known functions. Since then, scientists have identified the functions of the rest of the encoded proteins. All of the major biochemical pathways and molecular functions are represented. For example, the genes that encode enzymes involved in glycolysis, fermentation, and electron transport have been identified. Gene sequences that code for membrane proteins have been identified as well, including those involved in active transport. An important

TABLE 17.1 | Functions of Protein-Coding Genes in Three Bacteria

Category	Number of genes in:		
	E. coli	H. influenzae	M. genitalium
Total protein-coding genes	4,140	1,656	483
Biosynthesis of amino acids	131	68	1
Biosynthesis of cofactors	103	54	5
Biosynthesis of nucleotides	58	53	19
Cell envelope proteins	237	84	17
Energy metabolism	243	112	31
Intermediary metabolism	188	30	6
Lipid metabolism	48	25	6
DNA replication, recombination, and repair	115	87	32
Protein folding	9	6	7
Regulatory proteins	178	64	7
Transcription	55	27	12
Translation	182	141	101
Uptake of molecules from the environment	427	123	34
Other functions (including unknown)	2,166	782	205

Source: Data from R. D. Fleischmann et al. 1995. *Science* 269: 496–512; C. M. Fraser et al. 1995. *Science* 270: 397–404; F. R. Blattner et al. 1997. *Science* 227: 1453–1462.

finding was that highly infective strains of *H. influenzae*—but not noninfective strains—have genes for surface proteins that attach the bacterium to the human respiratory tract. These surface proteins are now a focus of research on possible treatments for *H. influenzae* infections.

COMPARATIVE GENOMICS   Soon after the sequence of *H. influenzae* was announced, smaller (*Mycoplasma genitalium*: 580,073 bp) and larger (*E. coli*: 4,639,221 bp) bacterial sequences were completed. Thus began the era of comparative genomics. Scientists can identify genes that are present in one bacterium and missing in another, allowing them to relate these genes to bacterial function.

M. genitalium, for example, lacks enzymes needed to synthesize amino acids, whereas *E. coli* and *H. influenzae* both possess such enzymes. This finding reveals that *M. genitalium* must obtain all its amino acids from its environment (usually the human urogenital tract). Furthermore, *E. coli* has 55 genes that encode transcriptional activators, whereas *M. genitalium* has only 12. This relative lack of control over gene expression suggests that the biochemical flexibility of *M. genitalium* must be limited compared with that of *E. coli*.

The sequencing of prokaryotic and viral genomes has many potential benefits

Prokaryotic genome sequencing is providing insights into microorganisms that are important for agriculture and medicine. Scientists who analyze the sequences have discovered previously unknown genes and proteins that can be targeted for isolation and functional study. They have also discovered surprising relationships between some organisms, suggesting that genes may be transferred between different groups.

- *Rhizobium* species are bacteria that form symbiotic associations with plants, living inside the roots of legumes such as beans, peas, and clover. The bacteria fix atmospheric nitrogen from the air and convert it into forms usable by the plants, reducing the need for nitrogen-containing fertilizers. Genome sequences from several *Rhizobium* species have been used to identify the genes involved in successful symbiosis, and this knowledge is being used both to improve the efficiency of this process and to broaden the range of plants that can form these beneficial associations.

- *E. coli* strain O157:H7 causes illness (sometimes severe) in at least 70,000 people a year in the United States. Its genome has 5,416 genes, of which 1,387 are different from those in the familiar (and harmless) laboratory strains of this bacterium. Many of these unique genes are also present in other pathogenic bacteria, such as *Salmonella* and *Shigella*. This finding suggests that there is extensive genetic exchange among these species, and indeed, "superbugs" that have acquired multiple genes for antibiotic resistance are already a major problem. Sequencing of a particular strain of *E. coli* causing food-borne illness, and comparisons of that sequence with the bacterium in different lots of meat, for example, can allow scientists to pinpoint the processing plant or farm that is the source of the infection.

- Severe acute respiratory syndrome (SARS) was first detected in southern China in 2002 and rapidly spread in 2003. There is no effective treatment, and 10% of infected people die. Isolation of the causative agent, a virus, and the rapid sequencing of its genome revealed several novel proteins that are possible targets for antiviral drugs or vaccines. Research is under way on both fronts, since further outbreaks of this and other newly revealed pathogens are anticipated.

- Some archaea, such as *Methanobrevibacter*, produce methane gas (CH_4) in the stomachs of cows and other ruminants. By contrast, certain bacteria, such as *Methylococcus*, remove methane from the air and use it as an energy source. The genomes of both of these prokaryotes have been sequenced. Understanding the genes involved in methane production and consumption is stimulating thinking about ways to slow the progress of global warming, given that methane is the second most prevalent greenhouse gas emitted in the United States and a significant contributor to climate change (see Key Concept 52.2).

Metagenomics allows us to describe new organisms and ecosystems

If you take a microbiology laboratory course, you'll learn how to identify various prokaryotes on the basis of their growth on particular artificial media. For example, staphylococci are a group of bacteria that infect skin and nasal passages. When grown on a medium called blood agar, they form round, raised colonies. Microorganisms can also be identified by their nutritional requirements or the conditions under which they will grow (for example, aerobic vs. anaerobic). Such culture methods have been the mainstay of microbial identification for more than a century and are still useful and important. However, scientists can now use PCR and DNA sequencing to identify microbes without culturing them in the laboratory.

In 1985 Norman Pace, then at Indiana University, came up with the idea of isolating DNA directly from environmental samples. He used PCR to amplify specific rRNA-coding sequences from the samples to determine whether particular microbes were present. The PCR products were sequenced to explore their diversity. The term **metagenomics** was coined to describe this approach of analyzing genes without isolating the intact organism. It is now possible to sequence DNA samples from almost any environment. The sequences can be used to detect the presence of both known microbes and heretofore unidentified organisms (**Figure 17.4**). For example:

- Sequencing of DNA from 200 liters of seawater indicated that it contained 5,000 different viruses and 2,000 different bacteria, many of which had not been described previously.

- One kilogram of marine sediment contained 1 million different viruses, most of them new.

- Water runoff from a mine contained many previously unknown species of prokaryotes thriving in what was previously thought of as an inhospitable environment. Some of these

Figure 17.4 Metagenomics Microbial DNA extracted from the environment can be sequenced and analyzed. This has led to the description of many new genes, metabolic pathways, and species. (After X. C. Morgan and C. Huttenhower. 2012. *PLOS Comput Biol* 8: e1002808; X. C. Morgan et al. 2013. *Trends Genet* 29: 51–58.)

① Isolate microbial DNA from the environment.

② Sequence the DNA.

③ Determine the abundance of microbes present.

④ Identify metabolic pathways present in the sample.

Microbial species present

Metabolic pathways

Abundance

Abundance

organisms exhibited metabolic pathways that were previously unknown to biologists. These organisms may be useful in cleaning up pollutants from the water.

- Gut samples from 124 Europeans revealed that each person harbored at least 160 species of bacteria (making up their gut microflora, or **microbiome**). Many of these species were found in all individuals, but the presence of other bacteria varied from person to person. Such variations may be associated with obesity or with bowel diseases.

Connect the Concepts Learn more about how disruptions of the human gut microbiome are associated with various autoimmune diseases in Key Concept 24.3.

These and other discoveries are truly extraordinary and potentially very important. It is estimated that 90% of the microbial world has been invisible to biologists and is only now being revealed by metagenomics. Entirely new ecosystems of bacteria and viruses are being discovered in which, for example, one species produces a molecule that another species metabolizes. It is hard to overemphasize the importance of such an increase in our knowledge of the hidden world of microbes. This knowledge will help us understand natural ecological processes and has the potential to help us find better ways to manage environmental catastrophes such as oil spills, or to remove toxic heavy metals from soil.

Some sequences of DNA can move about the genome

As we mentioned in Key Concept 15.1, **transposable elements** (or **transposons**) are segments of DNA that can move from place to place in the genome. Genome sequencing has allowed scientists to study these elements more broadly, and they are now known to be widespread in both prokaryotes and especially eukaryotes. Prokaryotic transposable elements are often short sequences of 1,000–2,000 bp, and they can be found both in chromosomes and in plasmids. A transposable element might be at one location in the genome of one *E. coli* strain, and at a different location in another strain. The insertion of this movable DNA sequence from elsewhere in the genome into the middle of a protein-coding gene can disrupt that gene (**Figure 17.5A,B**). The mRNA transcribed from the disrupted gene will contain the extra sequence. In prokaryotes that lack introns the extra sequence will also be translated and the resulting protein will be substantially altered and almost certainly nonfunctional. Sometimes, two transposable elements located near one another (within a few thousand bp) will transpose together and carry the intervening DNA sequence with them, creating what is called a **composite transposon** (**Figure 17.5C**). Composite transposons have been important in spreading antibiotic resistance within and across prokaryotic species. Composite transposons carrying genes for antibiotic resistance can transpose from a chromosome to a plasmid that then moves between prokaryotic cells by conjugation (see Figure 12.25).

As you saw in Chapter 15, there are two ways in which different transposable elements move around the genome. A transposable element might splice out of one location and move to another location: the "cut and paste" mode (see Figure 17.5A). Or the element may be replicated, and the copy inserted into another site in the genome: the "copy and paste" mode (see Figure 17.5B). Transposable elements usually carry genes for enzymes such as transposases, which catalyze the reactions needed for transposition. Often

(A) Replicative transposition

If a transposon is copied and inserted into the middle of a gene, that gene is transcribed into an altered mRNA.

The original transposon remains in place.

(B) Nonreplicative transposition

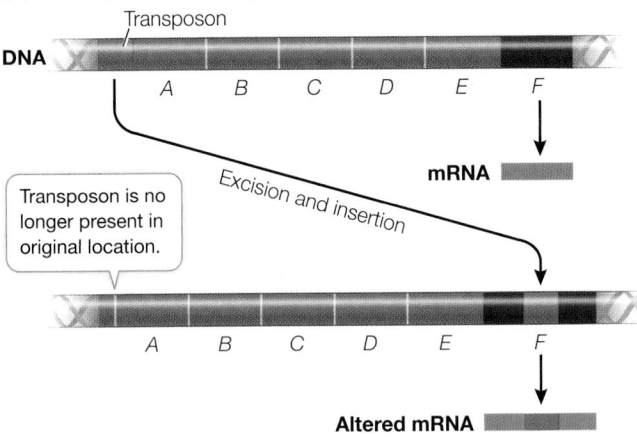

Transposon is no longer present in original location.

(C) A composite transposon

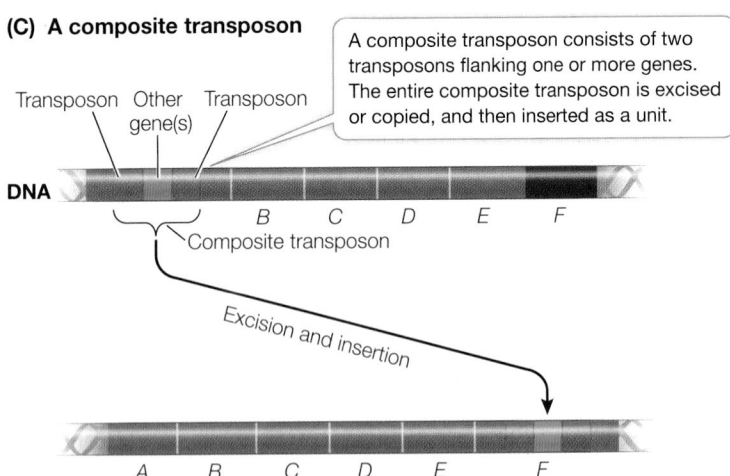

A composite transposon consists of two transposons flanking one or more genes. The entire composite transposon is excised or copied, and then inserted as a unit.

Figure 17.5 DNA Sequences That Move Transposable elements are DNA sequences that move from one location to another. **(A)** In the "copy and paste" method of transposition, the DNA sequence is replicated and the copy inserts elsewhere in the genome. **(B)** In the "cut and paste" method, the DNA sequence splices out of one location and inserts elsewhere in the genome. **(C)** Composite transposons contain one or more additional genes flanked by two transposable elements that move as a unit. Composite transposons can move either by the cut and paste method or by the copy and paste method.

Q: What type of movement is shown for the composite transposon in (C)?

the elements are flanked by inverted repeat DNA sequences that are recognized by these enzymes.

Will defining the genes required for cellular life lead to artificial life?

When we compare the genomes of prokaryotes and eukaryotes, a striking conclusion arises: certain genes are present in all organisms (universal genes). Not surprisingly, these include genes whose products are involved in DNA replication, transcription, and RNA translation to form proteins. There are also some (nearly) universal gene segments that are present in many genes in many organisms; for example, the sequence that codes for an ATP binding site in a protein. These findings suggest that there is some ancient, minimal set of DNA sequences that is common to all cells. One way to identify these sequences is to look for them in computer analyses of sequenced genomes.

Another way to begin to determine the minimal genome is to take an organism (preferably with a small genome) and deliberately mutate one gene at a time to identify essential genes. *M. genitalium* has one of the smallest known genomes—only 483 protein-coding genes. Even so, some of its genes are dispensable under some circumstances. For example, *M. genitalium* has genes for metabolizing both glucose and fructose, but it can survive in the laboratory on a medium containing only one of these sugars. Under such conditions it doesn't need the genes for metabolizing the other sugar.

What about other genes? A team led by Craig Venter has addressed this question with experiments involving the use of transposons as mutagens. When transposons in the bacterium are activated, they insert themselves into genes at random, mutating and inactivating them (**Figure 17.6**). The mutated bacteria are tested for growth and survival, and DNA from interesting mutants is sequenced to find out which genes contain transposons. Using this method, the team showed that only 382 genes are essential for growth of *M. genitalium* in the laboratory! The number of essential genes is not much greater in eukaryotic microbes: in yeast, only about 17% of the nearly 7,000 protein-coding genes are essential. Even in multicellular eukaryotes, the number of essential genes is a modest proportion of the total number of genes: about 30% of the 20,222 genes in the nematode *Caenorhabditis elegans* are essential for growth and reproduction.

One goal of identifying essential genes is to design new life forms with specific purposes, such as bacteria that will clean up oil spills. You'll learn about this approach, called synthetic genetics, in the next chapter.

Experiment

Figure 17.6 Using Transposon Mutagenesis to Determine the Minimal Genome

Original Papers: C. Hutchison et al. 1999. Global transposon mutagenesis and a minimal *Mycoplasma* genome. *Science* 286: 2165–2169.

J. Glass et al. 2006. Essential genes of a minimal bacterium. *Proc Natl Acad Sci USA* 103: 425–430. © 2006. National Academy of Sciences, U.S.A.

Mycoplasma genitalium has one of the smallest known genomes of any prokaryote. But are all of its genes essential to life? By inactivating the genes one by one, scientists determined which of them are essential for the cell's survival.

HYPOTHESIS▶ Only some of the genes in a bacterial genome are essential for cell survival.

METHOD▶

M. genitalium has 483 genes; only 2 are shown here.

A transposon inserts randomly into one gene, inactivating it.

Experiment 1

Experiment 2

A B

Inactive gene *A*

Inactive gene *B*

RESULTS▶

Each mutant is put into growth medium.

Growth means that gene *A* is not essential.

No growth means that gene *B* is essential.

CONCLUSION▶ If each gene is inactivated in turn, a "minimal essential genome" can be determined.

17.2 Recap and Assess

Comparative genomics of prokaryotes indicates that they have small, compact genomes, with genes that usually do not have introns, and sometimes they contain plasmids. Metagenomics involves sampling environmental DNA and has resulted in the identification of many new prokaryotic species, genes, and metabolic pathways. Transposable elements, including composite transposons, move from one place to another in the genome using either the cut and paste method or the copy and paste method. Identifying essential genes may lead to the creation of artificial species.

1. Prokaryotic genomes are often described as having a "need for speed," meaning fast replication. What characteristics of their genome make prokaryotes rapid replicators?

2. How do transposons move about the genome?

3. There are many bacterial species in your belly button. How would you use metagenomics to determine how many species are shared with other individuals and how many are unique to you?

Advances in DNA sequencing and sequence analysis have also led to sequencing of many eukaryotic genomes. We now look at some of the new insights that have come from these studies.

KEY CONCEPT
17.3 Eukaryotic Genomes Contain Many Types of Sequences

Learning Objectives

17.3.1 Explain why the genomes of eukaryotes are larger than those of prokaryotes.

17.3.2 Explain why larger eukaryotic genomes do not necessarily contain more protein-coding genes.

17.3.3 Provide an evolutionary explanation for how gene duplication might promote the evolution of new gene functions.

17.3.4 Summarize why the rRNA and tRNA genes involved in protein synthesis are present in multiple copies.

Eukaryotic and prokaryotic genomes differ in significant ways. Consider, for example, how the bacterial genomes in Table 17.2 compare with those of yeasts, plants, and animals—all eukaryotes. Key differences include the following:

- *Eukaryotic genomes are larger than prokaryotic genomes,* and they have more protein-coding genes. This difference is greatest for multicellular eukaryotes that have many cell types with specialized functions. As you can see in Table 17.2, the simple bacterium *Mycoplasma* has several hundred protein-coding genes in a genome of 0.58 million bp. A rice plant, in contrast, has almost 36,000 genes in a genome of 375 million bp!

TABLE 17.2 | Representative Sequenced Genomes

Organism	Haploid genome size (Mb)[a]	Number of protein-coding genes	Percent of genome that codes for proteins	Notable attributes
BACTERIA				
Mycoplasma genitalium	0.58	483	88	Minimal genome
Haemophilus influenzae	1.83	1,656	89	
Escherichia coli	4.6	4,140	88	Well-studied enteric bacterium
YEAST				
Saccharomyces cerevisiae	12.2	6,692	70	Protein targeting; cell organelles
PLANTS				Photosynthesis; cell walls
Arabidopsis thaliana	136	27,655	25	Small plant genome
Oryza sativa (rice)	375	35,825	12	Water tolerance for roots
Glycine max (soybean)	978	56,679	7	Lipid synthesis, storage
Zea mays (corn)	2,135	39,498	2.5	Transposable elements
ANIMALS				
Caenorhabditis elegans (nematode)	100	20,222	25	Tissue formation
Drosophila melanogaster (fruit fly)	144	13,931	13	Embryonic development
Homo sapiens (human)	3,100	20,454	1.2	Language

[a]Mb = Millions of base pairs.

Source: Data from Ensembl release 94 - October 2018. © EMBL-EBI and https://www.ncbi.nlm.nih.gov

- *Eukaryotic genomes have more regulatory sequences*—and encode many more regulatory proteins—than prokaryotic genomes. The greater complexity of eukaryotes requires much more regulation, which is evident in the many points of control associated with the expression of eukaryotic genes (see Key Concept 16.2 and Figure 16.8).

- *Much of eukaryotic DNA is noncoding.* Distributed throughout many eukaryotic genomes are various kinds of DNA sequences that are not transcribed into mature mRNAs, most notably introns and gene control sequences. As we discussed in Chapter 16, some noncoding sequences are transcribed into microRNAs. In addition, eukaryotic genomes contain various kinds of repeated sequences, sometimes in enormous abundance. Prokaryotes, in contrast, seldom contain long noncoding and repeated sequences.

- *Eukaryotes have multiple chromosomes*, whereas prokaryotes usually have a single, circular chromosome. As we have described in previous chapters, each eukaryotic chromosome has multiple origins of replication, a centromere region that holds the replicated chromosomes together and is the site of spindle attachment, and telomere sequences at each end of the chromosome that maintain chromosome integrity (**Figure 17.7**).

Genome sequences of model organisms provide important information

Most of our information about eukaryotic genomes has come from model organisms that have been studied extensively: the yeast *Saccharomyces cerevisiae*, the nematode (roundworm) *Caenorhabditis elegans*, the fruit fly *Drosophila melanogaster*, and the plant *Arabidopsis thaliana*. Model organisms have been chosen because they are relatively easy to grow and study in a laboratory, their genetics

are well studied, and they exhibit characteristics that represent a larger group of organisms.

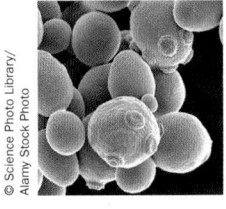

YEAST: THE BASIC EUKARYOTIC MODEL Yeasts are single-celled eukaryotes with a sexual life cycle that alternates between haploid and diploid stages. In nature they have a diplontic life cycle, while in the lab they have been mutated to become haplontic (see Figure 11.14). Like most eukaryotes, yeasts have membrane-enclosed organelles, such as the nucleus and endoplasmic reticulum. So it is not surprising that a single-celled yeast has a larger genome with more protein-coding genes than a single-celled bacterium (see Table 17.2). Gene inactivation studies similar to those carried out with *M. genitalium* (see Figure 17.6) indicate that only about 17% of the yeast's genes are essential for survival. The most striking difference between the yeast genome and that of *E. coli* is the number of genes for targeting proteins to organelles (**Table 17.3**). Both of these single-celled organisms appear to use about the same number of genes to perform the basic functions of cell survival. It is the compartmentalization of the eukaryotic yeast cell into organelles that requires it to have many more genes. This finding is direct, quantitative confirmation of something we have known for a century: the eukaryotic cell is structurally more complex than the prokaryotic cell.

THE NEMATODE: UNDERSTANDING EUKARYOTIC DEVELOPMENT A simple organism in which to study multicellularity is *Caenorhabditis elegans*, a 1-mm-long nematode (roundworm) that normally lives in the soil. It can also live in the laboratory, where

A chromosome as it appears in mitosis, with two duplicate DNA molecules (sister chromatids). Each molecule has specialized sequences for the initiation of replication (origins), for spindle interactions in mitosis (centromeres), and for maintaining the integrity of the ends (telomeres).

Chromosome (in mitosis)

Centromere sequences

Telomere sequences

DNA

Promoter containing regulatory sequences

Open reading frame (protein-coding sequence: exons)

Protein gene expression occurs at open reading frames, from which RNA polymerase II transcribes mRNAs that are translated to form polypeptides, which become functioning proteins. Genes contain DNA sequences for control of their expression.

mRNA

RNA polymerase II

Terminator of transcription

Some repetitive sequences are short, noncoding sequences that are repeated hundreds of times in tandem.

miRNA   tRNA gene   rRNA genes

RNA genes encode RNAs that are not translated into proteins. These RNAs include rRNA and tRNA, which are part of the protein translation machinery, and miRNAs involved in control of gene expression.

miRNA   tRNA   Ribosomes

Transposons

Some repetitive sequences are transposons that are dispersed across the genome.

Figure 17.7 Features of Eukaryotic Genomes Eukaryotic genome sequences contain many features, some of which are summarized in this overview. Sifting through all the information contained in a genome sequence can help us understand how an organism functions and what its evolutionary history might be.

Q: Does increasing genome size necessarily mean there are more protein-coding genes?

it has become a favorite model organism of developmental biologists. The nematode has a transparent body that develops over 3 days from a fertilized egg to an adult worm made up of nearly 1,000 cells. In spite of its small number of cells, the nematode has a nervous system, digests food, reproduces sexually, and ages. So it is not surprising that an intense effort was made to sequence the genome of this model organism.

The *C. elegans* genome (100 million bp) is eight times larger than that of the yeast *Saccharomyces cerevisiae* and has three times as many protein-coding genes (see Table 17.2). Gene inactivation studies have shown that only about 30% of these genes are essential for worm growth and reproduction. So the number of essential genes in the worm (about 6,000 genes) is about five times greater than in yeast (about 1,100 genes). Why are there so many more essential genes in the worm? All cells must have genes for survival, growth, and division. However, the cells of multicellular organisms must also have genes for holding cells together to form tissues, for cell differentiation, and for intercellular communication, all of which must occur correctly to produce a viable, fertile individual.

David McIntyre

DROSOPHILA MELANOGASTER: RELATING GENETICS TO GENOMICS The fruit fly *Drosophila melanogaster* is a famous model organism. Studies of fruit flies resulted in the formulation of many basic principles of genetics (see Key Concept 12.4). More than 2,500 genes of *D. melanogaster* had been characterized by the end

TABLE **17.3** | Comparison of the Genomes of *E. coli* and *S. cerevisiae*		
	E. coli	**Yeast**
GENOME LENGTH (bp)	4,640,000	12,157,000
NUMBER OF PROTEIN-CODING GENES	4,140	6,692
PROTEINS WITH ROLES IN:		
Metabolism	650	650
Energy production/storage	240	175
Membrane transport	280	250
DNA replication/repair/recombination	115	175
Transcription	55	400
Translation	182	350
Protein targeting/secretion	35	430
Cell structure	180	250

of the last century, and this fact alone was a good reason for sequencing the fruit fly's DNA. The fruit fly is a much larger organism than *C. elegans*, both in size (it has ten times more cells) and complexity, and it undergoes complicated developmental transformations from egg to larva to pupa to adult. **Figure 17.8** summarizes the functions of the *Drosophila* genes that have been characterized so far; this distribution is typical of complex eukaryotes.

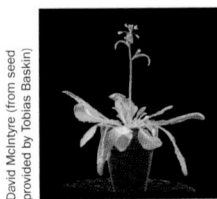

ARABIDOPSIS: STUDYING THE GENOMES OF PLANTS About 250,000 species of flowering plants dominate the land and fresh water. But in the context of the history of life, the flowering plants are fairly young, having evolved only about 200 million years ago. The genomes of some plants are huge—for example, the genome of corn is more than 2 billion bp, and that of wheat is 17 billion bp. Although we are naturally most interested in the genomes of plants we use as food and fiber, it is not surprising that scientists first chose to sequence a simpler flowering plant.

Arabidopsis thaliana is a member of the mustard family and has long been a favorite model organism of plant biologists. It is small (hundreds could grow and reproduce in the space occupied by this page), easy to manipulate, has a short generation time (about 2 months), and has a relatively small genome of 136 million bp. The *Arabidopsis* genome has almost 28,000 protein-coding genes (see Table 17.2), but remarkably, many of these genes are duplicates and probably originated by chromosomal rearrangements. When these duplicate genes are subtracted from the total, about 15,000 unique genes are left—similar to the number found in fruit flies. Indeed, many of the genes found in fruit flies have homologs (related genes) in *Arabidopsis* and other plants, suggesting that plants and animals have a common ancestor.

Arabidopsis does, of course, have some genes that distinguish it as a plant (**Table 17.4**). From what you know about plants, you can guess what these are: genes involved in photosynthesis, in the transport of water into the root and throughout the plant,

TABLE 17.4 | *Arabidopsis* Genes Unique to Plants

Function	Number of genes
Cell wall and growth	42
Water channels	300
Photosynthesis	139
Defense and metabolism	94

in the assembly of the cell wall, in the uptake and metabolism of inorganic substances from the environment, and in the synthesis of specific molecules used for defense against microbes and herbivores (organisms that eat plants). The plant-specific genes in *Arabidopsis* are also found in the genomes of other plants, including rice (*Oryza sativa*), the first major crop plant whose sequence was determined. Rice is the world's most important crop; it is a staple in the diet of 3 billion people. Despite its larger genome, rice has a set of genes remarkably similar to those of *Arabidopsis*. More recently the genome of the poplar tree *Populus trichocarpa* was sequenced. This rapidly growing tree is widely used for manufacturing paper and is a potential source of fixed carbon for making fuel. A comparison of the genomes of four flowering plants shows about 12,000 genes in common, comprising the minimal plant genome (**Figure 17.9**).

Eukaryotes have gene families

For about half of all eukaryotic protein-coding genes, only a single copy will be found in the haploid genome (two copies in somatic cells). But there are multiple copies of most other protein-coding genes, a phenomenon resulting from gene duplications. In some cases, over evolutionary time different copies of duplicated genes have undergone separate mutations, giving rise to groups of closely related genes, often with similar functions, called **gene**

Figure 17.8 Functions of a Typical Eukaryotic Genome
The distribution of gene functions in *Drosophila melanogaster* shows a pattern that is typical of many complex organisms. (After M. D. Adams et al. 2000. *Science* 287: 2185–2195.)

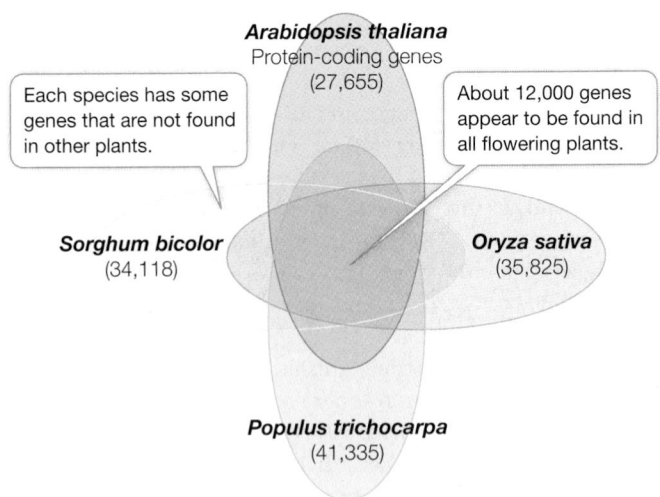

Figure 17.9 Plant Genomes The genomes of four flowering plants share a common set of approximately 12,000 genes that appear to comprise the minimal plant genome. (Data from Ensembl release 94 - October 2018. © EMBL-EBI.)

families. Some gene families, such as those encoding the globin proteins that make up hemoglobin, contain only a few members. Other families, such as the genes encoding the immunoglobulins that make up antibodies, have hundreds of members. In the human genome there are about 20,500 protein-coding genes, but 16,000 of these are members of gene families. So only about one-quarter of human genes are unique.

The DNA sequences in a gene family are usually different from one another. As long as at least one member encodes a functional protein, the other members may mutate in ways that change the functions of the proteins they encode. During evolution, the availability of multiple copies of a gene allows for selection of mutations that provide advantages under certain circumstances. If a mutated gene is useful, it may be selected for in succeeding generations. If the mutated gene is a total loss, the functional copy is still there to carry out its role.

Let's take a look at one gene family, the globin genes in vertebrates. The globins are components of hemoglobin and myoglobin (an oxygen-binding protein present in muscle). The globin genes all arose long ago from a single common ancestral gene. In humans there are three functional members of the α-globin cluster and five in the β-globin cluster (**Figure 17.10**). In adults, each hemoglobin molecule is a tetramer containing two identical α-globin subunits, two identical β-globin subunits, and four heme pigments (see Figure 3.12).

During human development, different members of the globin gene cluster are expressed at different times and in different tissues. This differential gene expression has great physiological significance. For example, hemoglobin that contains γ-globin, a subunit found in the hemoglobin of the human fetus, binds O_2 more tightly than adult hemoglobin does. This specialized form of hemoglobin ensures that in the placenta, O_2 is transferred from the mother's blood to the developing fetus's blood. Just before birth the liver stops synthesizing fetal hemoglobin and the bone marrow cells take over, making the adult form (two α and two β). Thus hemoglobins with different binding affinities for O_2 are provided at different stages of human development.

In addition to genes that encode proteins, many gene families include nonfunctional **pseudogenes**, which are designated with the Greek letter psi (ψ) (see Figure 17.10). Pseudogenes result from mutations that cause a loss of function rather than an enhanced or new function. The DNA sequence of a pseudogene may not differ greatly from that of other family members. It may simply lack a promoter, for example, and thus fail to be transcribed. Or it may lack a recognition site needed for the removal of an intron, so that the transcript it makes is not correctly processed into a useful mature mRNA. In some gene families pseudogenes outnumber functional genes. In such cases there appears to be no evolutionary advantage for the deletion of the pseudogenes, even though they have no apparent function.

Eukaryotic genomes contain repetitive sequences

In many eukaryotic genomes, the single-copy genes represent a small percentage of the DNA. Numerous repetitive DNA sequences that do not code for polypeptides make up the majority

Figure 17.10   The Globin Gene Family   The α-globin and β-globin clusters of the human globin gene family are located on different chromosomes. The genes of each cluster are separated by noncoding "spacer" DNA. The nonfunctional pseudogenes are indicated by the Greek letter psi (ψ). The γ gene has two variants, $A_γ$ and $G_γ$.

of the genome. These include highly repetitive sequences, and moderately repetitive sequences, including transposons. **Table 17.5** summarizes the types of sequences found in eukaryotes, including the major types of repetitive sequences.

Highly repetitive sequences are short (less than 100 bp) sequences that are repeated thousands of times in tandem (side-by-side) arrangements in the genome. They are not usually transcribed. Their proportion in eukaryotic genomes varies, from 10% in humans to about 50% in some species of fruit flies. Often they are associated with heterochromatin, the densely packed, transcriptionally inactive part of the genome. Other highly repetitive sequences are scattered around the genome. For example, short tandem repeats (STRs) of 1–5 bp can be repeated up to 100 times at a particular chromosomal location. The copy number of an STR at a particular location varies among individuals.

Connect the Concepts   Key Concept 15.3 described how STRs can be used in the identification of individuals (DNA fingerprinting).

Moderately repetitive sequences are repeated 10–1,000 times in eukaryotic genomes. These sequences include the genes that

TABLE **17.5** | Types of Sequences in Eukaryotic Genomes		
Category	**Transcribed**	**Translated**
SINGLE-COPY GENES		
Promoters and expression control sequences	No	No
Introns	Yes	No
Exons	Yes	Yes
MODERATELY REPETITIVE SEQUENCES		
rRNA and tRNA genes	Yes	No
Transposons		
I. Retrotransposons		
LTRs	Yes	No
SINEs	Yes	No
LINEs	Yes	Yes
II. DNA transposons	Yes	Yes
HIGHLY REPETITIVE SHORT SEQUENCES	No	No

are transcribed to produce tRNAs and rRNAs, which are used in protein synthesis. The cell makes tRNAs and rRNAs constantly, but even at the maximum rate of transcription, single copies of the tRNA and rRNA genes would be inadequate to supply the large amounts of these molecules needed by most cells. Thus the genome has multiple copies of these genes.

In mammals, four different rRNA molecules make up the ribosome: the 18S, 5.8S, 28S, and 5S rRNAs. (The S stands for Svedberg unit, which is a measure of size.) The 18S, 5.8S, and 28S rRNAs are transcribed together as a single precursor RNA molecule (**Figure 17.11**). As a result of several posttranscriptional steps, the precursor is cut into the final three rRNA products, and the noncoding "spacer" RNA is discarded. The sequence encoding these RNAs is moderately repetitive in humans: a total of 280 copies of the sequence are located in clusters on five different chromosomes.

Apart from the RNA genes, most moderately repetitive sequences are transposons, which, like the prokaryotic transposons we discussed earlier, can move about in the genome. Transposons make up more than 40% of the human genome and about 50% of the corn genome, but in many other eukaryotes the percentage is smaller (3%–10%).

Retrotransposons fall into three groups (see Table 17.5), based on the types of repetitive sequences they contain: long terminal repeats (LTRs), long interspersed elements (LINEs), and short interspersed elements (SINEs). Retrotransposons move about the genome in a distinctive way: they are transcribed into RNA, which then acts as a template for new DNA. The new DNA becomes inserted at a new location in the genome. This "copy and paste" method results in two copies of the transposon: one at the original location and the other at a new location. A single type of SINE retrotransposon, the 300-bp Alu element, accounts for 11% of the human genome; it is present in a million copies!

Transposons of the fourth type, the DNA transposons, do not use RNA intermediates. Like some prokaryotic transposable elements, they are excised from the original location and become inserted at a new location without being replicated (the "cut and paste" method).

What role do these moving sequences play in the cell? The best answer so far seems to be that transposons are simply molecular parasites that can be replicated. The insertion of a transposon at a new location can have important consequences. For example, the insertion of a transposon into the coding region of a gene results in a mutation (see Figure 17.6). This phenomenon accounts for rare forms of several genetic diseases in humans, including hemophilia and muscular dystrophy. If the insertion of a transposon takes place in the germ line, a gamete with a new mutation results. If the insertion takes place in a somatic cell, cancer may result.

(A) An rRNA gene

This rRNA gene is repeated many times (280 in humans).

DNA

13,000 bp
Transcribed region

30,000 bp
Nontranscribed spacer region

18S   5.8S   28S

Pre-rRNA transcript

Processing steps remove the spacers within the transcribed region.

rRNAs

18S   5.8S   28S

Figure 17.11 A Moderately Repetitive Sequence Codes for rRNA   **(A)** This rRNA gene, along with its nontranscribed spacer region, is repeated 280 times in the human genome, with clusters on five chromosomes. **(B)** This electron micrograph shows transcription of multiple rRNA genes.

Q: Are there similarities between the process depicted in the photo here and the process of translation via polysomes shown in Figure 14.18?

(B) Transcription of multiple rRNA genes

Strands of rRNA

Transcription begins here...

...the RNA elongates...

...and elongates until it is released here.

DNA

Many rRNA precursors are being transcribed from multiple rRNA genes.

Courtesy of O. L. Miller, Jr.

Sometimes an adjacent gene can be replicated along with a transposon, resulting in a gene duplication. A transposon can carry a gene, or a part of it, to a new location in the genome, shuffling the genetic material and creating new genes. Clearly, transposition stirs the genetic pot in eukaryotic genomes and thus contributes to genetic variation.

17.3 Recap and Assess

The genomes of eukaryotes contain many more genes than those of prokaryotes. Some of these "additional" genes encode functions associated with the compartmentalization of eukaryotic cells; others are needed to support multicellularity. The genome sequences of model organisms have been compared to identify common features of eukaryotic genomes, including the presence of abundant regulatory sequences, repetitive sequences, and noncoding DNA. Some eukaryotic genes make up gene families, which may include members that are mutated and nonfunctional. Many eukaryotic genomes contain enormous quantities of repetitive DNA and very little protein-coding DNA.

1. What kinds of genes found in *Caenorhabditis elegans* are expected to have few counterparts in yeasts?

2. What is the importance of gene duplication for evolution?

3. Why are there multiple copies of sequences coding for rRNA in the mammalian genome?

4. The genomes of rice, wheat, and corn are similar to one another and to that of *Arabidopsis*. What processes might explain why these four plants are nevertheless distinguished by unique proteins?

The analysis of eukaryotic genomes has resulted in an enormous amount of useful information, as we have seen. In the next key concept we look more closely at the human genome.

17.4 Human Biology Is Revealed through the Genome

Learning Objectives

17.4.1 Describe the characteristics of the human genome and its genes.

17.4.2 Use SNP genotype data to determine whether a SNP is associated with a phenotypic characteristic.

17.4.3 Explain how SNP genotypes are used to determine ancestry and identify individuals.

17.4.4 Explain how SNP genotypes are used in pharmacogenomics and personalized medicine.

Since the first human genome sequences were completed early in the first decade of this millennium, the genomes of many other individuals have been sequenced and published. With the rapid development of sequencing technologies, a human genome can be sequenced for less than $1,000.

The following are just some of the interesting facts that sequencing of the human genome has brought to light:

- The human genome contains about 20,500 protein-coding genes. About 40% of the genome is gene-related: 30% is introns, and 9% is regulatory or encodes functional RNAs that are not mRNAs. Of the 3.1 billion bp in the haploid genome, only an estimated 1.2% encodes proteins. The low number of protein-coding genes was a surprise. Before sequencing began, the diversity of human proteins suggested there might be 80,000–150,000 genes in the human genome. The actual number of genes—about the same as in the nematode *C. elegans*—means that posttranscriptional mechanisms (such as alternative splicing) must account for the observed number of proteins in humans. That is, the average human gene must code for several different proteins.

- The average human gene has 27,000 bp. Gene sizes vary greatly, from about 1,000 bp to 2.4 million bp. Some variation in gene size was expected given that human proteins (and their mRNAs) vary in size, from 100 to about 5,000 amino acids per polypeptide chain.

- Most human genes have many introns. The "average" human gene has eight of them, each with an average length of 3,300 bp.

- About half of the genome is made up of transposons (see Table 17.5) and other repetitive sequences.

- When the genomes of two unrelated individuals are compared, most of the sequence—about 99.9%—is identical. Before you jump to the conclusion that we are all the same, remember that we have 6.2 billion bp in our diploid genome, so that 0.1% difference represents 6.2 million bp that differ between you and an unrelated person! The main differences are in copy number variations of short repeated sequences and single base pair differences, termed single nucleotide polymorphisms (SNPs; see Key Concept 15.3). And don't forget epigenetic differences as well (see Key Concept 16.4).

- Protein-coding genes are not evenly distributed over the genome. Chromosome 19 is packed densely with genes (1 gene per 40 kb), whereas chromosome 18 has long stretches without coding regions (1 gene per 300 kb). The Y chromosome has the fewest genes (fewer than 100), and chromosome 1 has the most (about 2,000).

 Media Clip 17.1 A Big Surprise from Genomics
Life12e.com/mc17.1

Comparative genomics reveals the evolution of the human genome

Comparisons among sequenced genomes from prokaryotes and eukaryotes have revealed some of the evolutionary relationships among genes. About 20% of human genes are found across the tree of life, about 30% are shared by most eukaryotes but are absent in prokaryotes, about 25% are shared with most animals but are absent in single-celled eukaryotes, and about 25% are found only in vertebrates.

The genomes of various other primates, including all of the great apes, have now been sequenced. The search is on for a set of human genes that differ from those found in other primates and that make us unique. Chimpanzees are our closest living relatives, sharing about 96% of our DNA sequence, and for those sequences that are shared, they are nearly 99% identical. About 500 protein-coding genes have undergone accelerated evolution in humans and chimpanzees, including genes involved in hearing and brain development. Further analyses of these sequences may reveal genes that distinguish us from other apes, and that "make humans human."

> **Connect the Concepts** Key Concept 31.5 discusses how comparisons of human and other primate genomes have refined our understanding of human evolution.

Other clues about "human" genes have come from sequencing the genomes of ancient human relatives. An international team of scientists led by Svante Pääbo at the Max Planck Institute for Evolutionary Anthropology in Germany has extracted and sequenced DNA from the bones of Neanderthals, who lived in Europe until about 40,000 years ago. The entire Neanderthal genome has been sequenced. It is more than 99% identical to our human DNA, justifying the classification of Neanderthals as part of the same genus, *Homo*.

Comparisons of the human and Neanderthal genomes are ongoing and have already revealed several interesting facts:

- The gene *MC1R* is involved in skin and hair pigmentation. A point mutation found in Neanderthals but not in humans caused lower activity of the MC1R protein when it was introduced into cell cultures. Such lower activity of MC1R is known to result in fair skin and red hair in humans. So it appears that at least some Neanderthals may have had pale skin and red hair.

- The gene *FOXP2* is involved in vocalization in many organisms, including birds and mammals. In humans, mutations in this gene result in severe speech impairment. The Neanderthal *FOXP2* gene is identical to that of humans, whereas that of chimpanzees is slightly different. This has led to speculation that Neanderthals were capable of speech.

- While the human and Neanderthal genome sequences are very similar, there are differences in many point mutations and larger chromosomal arrangements. There are distinctive "human" DNA sequences and also distinctive "Neanderthal" sequences. Analysis of genomes from modern humans indicates that humans and Neanderthals interbred in the past, with transfer of DNA between the two species.

Human genomics can determine ancestry, identify individuals, and improve medicine

About 1 bp out of 1,330 in the human genome contains a SNP. For most SNPs, only two alleles are present in a population (G-C versus T-A, for example). When discussing SNP alleles, usually only one of the two nucleotide identities is written, so this SNP would be called a G/T (or a C/A) SNP (**Figure 17.12A**). At a G/T SNP, an individual could be a GG homozygote, a GT heterozygote, or a TT homozygote. SNP variation across individuals can be used in a variety of ways.

ANCESTRY AND IDENTIFICATION Some SNP alleles are common in certain human populations but rare in others, allowing

Figure 17.12 SNP Genotype and Phenotype **(A)** A single base-pair position in the genome that varies at the population level is a SNP. In this example we see a site that can be G-C or T-A, meaning it is a G/T, or equivalently a C/A, SNP. **(B)** The frequencies of two alleles (base pairs), shown using pie charts, at each of three SNPs in affected and unaffected individuals reveal that the G allele at SNP 2 is associated with the unaffected phenotype, whereas the G allele at SNPs 1 and 3 is not associated with either phenotype.

SNPs to be used to determine ancestry. For example, if an individual has alleles at several SNPs that are common only in East Asian populations, then that indicates the individual's ancestors are from that region. In addition, SNPs can be used to determine relatedness among people. Identical twins obviously will have identical SNP genotypes. However, other relatives, such as siblings or first cousins, will also have more similar SNP genotypes than expected for unrelated individuals. This allows relatives to be found simply by comparing SNP genotypes at many loci. It also means that if DNA is left at a crime scene, it can be genotyped at many SNP loci to identify the suspect who left the sample (an exact match) or a relative, who could then be used to help find the suspect.

COMPLEX TRAITS SNPs can also be used to determine genetic causes of quantitative traits, which has great potential in medicine. Quantitative traits are determined not by single genes but by multiple genes interacting with the environment (see Key Concept 12.3). Several common diseases such as diabetes, heart disease, and Alzheimer's disease are quantitative traits. A considerable amount of research involves attempting to identify the genes affecting such diseases. To find the causal genes, biologists genotype many SNPs across the genome and look for associations between the presence of a particular allele at a SNP and the disease. Examining multiple SNPs in multiple individuals, both with and without a disease of interest, to find an association between a particular SNP allele and the phenotype is termed a genome-wide association study (**Figure 17.12B**).

Association studies have revealed particular SNP alleles that are associated with increased risks for diseases. For example, a particular SNP allele on chromosome 10 is associated with a 65% increased risk for adult-onset diabetes when heterozygous, and an almost three-fold risk when homozygous. This information can have predictive value in counseling and treating patients. Private companies can now scan a human genome for these variants—and the price for this service keeps getting lower. However, at this point it is unclear what a person without symptoms should do with the information, since multiple genes and environmental influences contribute to the development of these diseases.

SNP GENOTYPING Given the usefulness of SNPs, being able to score an individual's genotype at multiple SNPs inexpensively is important. One approach that can target a few hundred thousand SNPs uses DNA microarrays. A **DNA microarray** is a grid of microscopic spots of different oligonucleotides (short single-stranded DNA sequences) arrayed on a solid surface. It can be "probed" with an individual's DNA (after denaturation) or RNA; if the individual's DNA contains a sequence that is complementary to one of the oligonucleotides, the sequence will hybridize to (base-pair with) the DNA at that spot, a process called nucleic acid hybridization (which you have already seen in Figures 14.7 and 15.19). Colored fluorescent dyes are used to detect spots that hybridize with a sequence in an individual's DNA. Often, adjacent spots have oligonucleotides that correspond to the two alleles at a particular SNP. For example, for an A/G SNP, one spot has the A allele oligonucleotide and the other has the G allele oligonucleotide. Extracting DNA from an individual, cutting it up, labeling it with a dye, and then hybridizing it to the microarray will yield different patterns depending on the genotype (**Figure 17.13**).

Of course, the most comprehensive way to analyze a person's genome is by actually sequencing it. As the cost of genome sequencing and analysis goes down, SNP microarrays will be superseded. In 2015 the U.S. government announced a plan to sequence the genomes of 1 million Americans and link the sequences to medical records. This approach is not new, but the large scale of it is. The goal is to relate genome changes to diseases such as cancer and diabetes, and to use these changes for diagnosis and, if they lead to changes in encoded proteins, to therapies targeted at the altered proteins.

PHARMACOGENOMICS Genetic variation can affect how an individual responds to a particular drug. For example, a drug may be chemically modified in the liver to make it more or less active. Consider an enzyme that catalyzes the following reaction:

$$\text{Active drug} \rightarrow \text{less active drug}$$

A mutation in the gene that encodes this enzyme may make the enzyme less active. For a given dose of the drug, a person with the mutation would have more active drug in the bloodstream than a person without the mutation. So the effective dose of the drug would be lower in the person with the mutation.

Now consider a different case, in which the liver enzyme is needed to make the drug active:

$$\text{Inactive drug} \rightarrow \text{active drug}$$

Figure 17.13 A DNA Microarray (A) A microarray chip contains hundreds of thousands of spots, each having a cluster of identical, single-stranded oligonucleotides. (B) For genotyping, two spots contain oligonucleotides that are identical, and complementary to the region of the genome containing the SNP, except at the location of the SNP, where each spot corresponds to one of the alleles (in reality, oligonucleotides are 25 bases in length). In this example, if DNA from an individual binds only to the left spot, that identifies the individual as a CC homozygote. If DNA binds only to the right spot, the individual is a TT homozygote. A heterozygous individual will have DNA binding equally to both spots.

A person carrying a mutation in the gene encoding this liver enzyme would not be affected by the drug, since the activating enzyme is not present.

The study of how an individual's genome affects his or her response to drugs or other outside agents is called **pharmacogenomics**. Just as it is possible to identify SNPs that are associated with particular disease susceptibilities, it is also possible to identify SNPs that are associated with specific drug responses. This type of analysis makes it possible to predict whether a drug will be effective. The objective is to personalize drug treatment so that a physician can know in advance whether an individual will benefit from a particular drug (**Figure 17.14**). This approach might also be used to reduce the incidence of adverse drug reactions by identifying individuals who will metabolize a drug slowly, which can lead to a dangerously high level of the drug in the body.

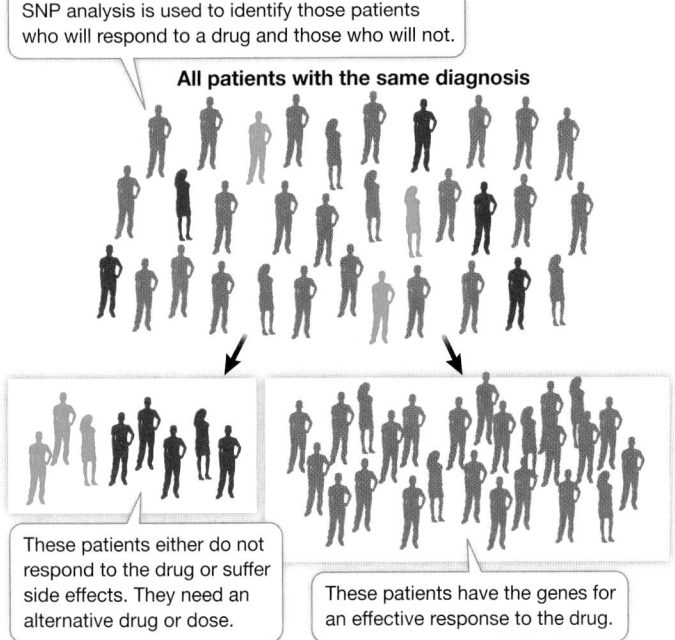

SNP analysis is used to identify those patients who will respond to a drug and those who will not.

All patients with the same diagnosis

These patients either do not respond to the drug or suffer side effects. They need an alternative drug or dose.

These patients have the genes for an effective response to the drug.

Figure 17.14 Pharmacogenomics Correlations between SNP genotypes (indicated by different colors) and responses to drugs help physicians develop personalized medical care. (After J. A. Johnson. 2003. *Trends Genet* 19: 660–666.)

KEY CONCEPT
17.4 Recap and Assess

The haploid human genome has 3.1 billion bp, about 40% of which is gene-related sequence, though only about 1.2% codes for proteins. Most of the 20,500 human genes are subject to alternative splicing, which in part explains why there are many more different proteins than protein-coding genes. SNP genotyping is used to determine ancestry, identify individuals, and find correlations between specific SNPs and disease and drug susceptibility. These efforts hold promise for understanding disease risk and appropriate treatment options at the individual level—the beginning of personalized medicine.

1. How do human cells express a larger number of proteins than is accounted for by the number of protein-coding genes in the human genome?

2. Only 1.2% of the human genome encodes proteins. Does this imply that only a small percentage of the genome encodes genes?

3. A thousand affected and 1,000 unaffected individuals for a disorder are genotyped at three SNPs, and the frequency of each allele is determined. The following data are obtained:

	Frequencies at SNP 1		Frequencies at SNP 2		Frequencies at SNP 3	
	Allele A	Allele C	Allele G	Allele A	Allele T	Allele C
Affected	0.22	0.78	0.61	0.39	0.74	0.26
Unaffected	0.21	0.79	0.59	0.41	0.22	0.78

Are any of the alleles at these SNPs associated with the disorder?

Genome sequencing has advanced our understanding of biology enormously. High-throughput technologies are now being applied to other components of the cell: proteins and metabolites. We now turn to the results of these studies.

KEY CONCEPT
17.5 Proteomics and Metabolomics Can Provide Insights beyond the Genome

Learning Objectives

17.5.1 Explain why the proteome differs in different conditions.

17.5.2 Summarize why the number of proteins in the proteome is often substantially larger than the number of protein-coding genes that are expressed.

17.5.3 Define the metabolome and provide examples of applications of metabolomic data for human health.

Statements such as "The human genome is the book of life" were commonly made at the time the human genome sequence was first revealed, reflecting a belief in "genetic determinism"—that a person's phenotype is determined primarily by his or her genotype. But as we have repeatedly stressed, an organism is not just a product of the alleles that it carries at its genes. In addition, both the current environment and past environments experienced by an organism play a role. For example, one cannot predict levels of gene expression in a particular organism from its genotype alone. To understand the relationship between genotype and phenotype, researchers have begun to focus on the proteins and the small molecules present in an organism. The hope is that, with genomics, the fields of proteomics and metabolomics will provide a more complete understanding of the relationship between genotype and phenotype.

The proteome is the complete set of proteins in a cell, tissue, or organism at a given time

As we have mentioned earlier, many genes encode more than a single protein (**Figure 17.15**). Alternative splicing of a given gene can allow different combinations of exons to be transcribed into the mature mRNAs. Posttranslational modifications also increase the number of protein variants that can be derived from one gene. It should also be noted that in a multicellular organism many proteins are produced only by certain cells and only under specific conditions. Even single-celled organisms express only a subset of their genes at any particular time. The **proteome** is the sum total of the proteins produced by a cell, tissue, or organism at a given time, under defined conditions.

Connect the Concepts Recall from Key Concept 16.5 that different mRNAs can be made from the same gene by alternative splicing, resulting in a family of different proteins, with different functions, from a single gene. Recall also that proteins can be modified in posttranslational processes such as proteolysis, glycosylation, and phosphorylation (see Figure 14.21).

The proteome is analyzed by mass spectrometry, a technique that uses electromagnets to identify proteins by their mass. The ultimate aim of proteomics is just as ambitious as that of genomics. Whereas genomics seeks to describe the genome and its expression, proteomics seeks to identify and characterize all of the expressed proteins.

Figure 17.15 Proteomics A single gene can code for multiple proteins.

Comparisons of the proteomes of humans and other eukaryotic organisms have revealed a common set of proteins that can be categorized into groups with similar amino acid sequences and similar functions. When considered on a whole-organism basis, 45% of the yeast proteome, 23% of the nematode proteome, and 35% of the fruit fly proteome are shared by the human proteome. Functional analyses indicate that a set of 2,100 proteins provides the basic metabolic functions of a eukaryotic cell, such as glycolysis, the citric acid cycle, membrane transport, protein synthesis, DNA replication, and so on (Figure 17.16).

There are, of course, many uniquely human proteins in addition to those we share with other eukaryotic organisms. As we have mentioned before, proteins have different functional regions called domains (for example, a domain for binding a substrate, or a domain for spanning a membrane). While a particular organism may have many unique proteins, those proteins are often just unique combinations of domains that exist in other organisms. *This reshuffling of the genetic deck is a key to evolution.*

Proteins seldom exist in isolation. Most interact with other molecules, such as nucleic acids (e.g., transcription factors and DNA), other proteins (e.g., the respiratory chain complexes in mitochondria), and lipids (receptors in the cell membrane). A major task of proteomics is analyzing these interactions.

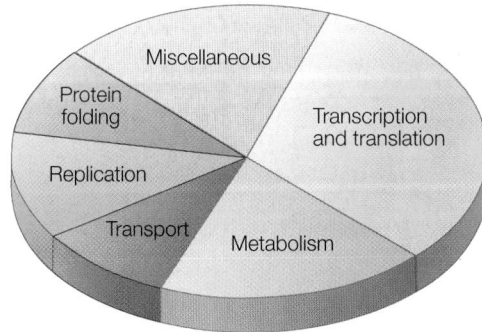

Figure 17.16 Proteins of the Eukaryotic Proteome About 1,300 proteins are common to all eukaryotes and fall into these categories. Although their amino acid sequences may differ to a limited extent, the proteins perform the same essential functions in all eukaryotes. (After E. V. Koonin et al. 2004. *Genome Biol* 5:R7)

Metabolomics is the study of chemical phenotype

Studying genes and proteins gives a limited picture of what is going on in a cell. As we have seen, both gene function and protein function are affected by the internal and external environments of the cell. Many proteins are enzymes, and their activities affect the concentrations of their substrates and products. So as the proteome changes, so do the abundances of small molecules called metabolites. The **metabolome** is the complete set of small molecules present in a cell, tissue, or organism under defined conditions. These include:

- *Primary metabolites* involved in normal processes, such as intermediates in pathways such as glycolysis. This category also includes hormones and other signaling molecules.

- *Secondary metabolites*, which are often unique to particular organisms or groups of organisms. They are often involved in special responses to the environment. Examples are antibiotics made by microbes, and the many chemicals made by plants that are used in defense against pathogens and herbivores.

Not surprisingly, measuring metabolites involves sophisticated analytical instruments. If you have studied organic or analytical chemistry, you may be familiar with gas chromatography and high-performance liquid chromatography, which separate molecules, and with mass spectrometry and nuclear magnetic resonance spectroscopy, which are used to identify them. These measurements result in "chemical snapshots" of cells or organisms, which can be related to physiological states.

There has been some progress in defining the human metabolome. A database created by David Wishart and colleagues at the University of Alberta contains more than 100,000 metabolite entries. The challenge now is to relate levels of these substances to physiology. For example, you probably know that high levels of glucose in the blood are associated with diabetes. But what about the early stages of heart disease? There may be a pattern of metabolites that is diagnostic of this disease. This could aid in early diagnosis and treatment.

Plant biologists are ahead of medical researchers in the field of metabolomics. Over the years, tens of thousands of secondary metabolites have been identified in plants, many of them made in response to environmental challenges. Some of these will be discussed in Chapter 37. The metabolome of the model organism *Arabidopsis thaliana* is being described and will give insight into how a plant copes with stresses such as drought or pathogen attack. This knowledge could be helpful in optimizing plant growth for agriculture.

KEY CONCEPT
17.5 Recap and Assess

The proteome is the set of all proteins produced by a cell, tissue, or organism under specific conditions. The metabolome is the total content of small molecules, such as intermediates in primary metabolism, hormones, and secondary metabolites. The proteome and the metabolome can be analyzed using chemical methods that separate and identify molecules.

1. Why is the proteome often larger than the number of genes that are expressed?

2. Why would it be useful to have a database of primary and secondary metabolites involved in human metabolism?

 View in Achieve
Activity 17.1 Concept Matching: Genomes

▶InvestigatingLIFE

Q and A   What have we learned from sequencing animal genomes?

In certain dog breeds, such as whippets, the muscles of some individuals can be much bulkier than is normal. Genome analyses have shown that the gene for myostatin, a protein that inhibits muscle growth, is mutated in whippets that have bulky muscles. When the myostatin gene is mutated, the protein that inhibits muscle growth is dysfunctional (**Figure 17.17**). Comparative genomics reveals that the myostatin gene is also mutated in certain breeds of cattle and sheep that are noted for overdeveloped muscles.

With the knowledge that myostatin affects muscle development, some consideration has been given to the possibility of manipulating myostatin in humans to treat muscle-wasting diseases such as muscular dystrophy. As you might expect, athletes anxious to have bulkier muscles are also very interested in this gene and its protein product.

Future directions

Few scientific endeavors have received as much hype and hope as genome sequencing. A major effort is under way to sequence the genomes of tumors in as many people as possible, to screen for mutations. When the *BRCA1* gene was identified as mutated in breast cancer (see Chapter 15), some medical scientists hoped that cancer would be like other genetic diseases such as sickle-cell anemia—caused by a single mutation in a single gene. So far, the lessons learned from cancer genomes include that there are many mutations in a tumor, and that some of them drive the tumor formation while others do not; that the mutations in one person's tumor of a particular type may differ from those in the same tumor in

© kostudio/Shutterstock.com

© Bruce Stotesbury/PostMedia News/Zuma Press

Figure 17.17 Muscular Gene   These dogs are both whippets, but the muscle-bound dog (right) has a mutation in the myostatin gene.

someone else; and that tumor genomes evolve over time as the tumor grows and spreads. Understanding tumor genomes is not straightforward. Nevertheless, the goal is to study genomes to determine how gene products and the environment interact to form the tumor phenotype, and to design therapy for that tumor in individual people. This is called precision medicine, and it is in the future. It is a model for a goal of genomics: to determine the relationship among genotype, the environment, and phenotype.

VISUAL SUMMARY 17

© Shotshop GmbH/Alamy Stock Photo

You should be able to relate each summary to the adjacent figures. If you go to this visual summary in **Achieve**, you can follow links to figures, animations, activities, and simulations that will help you consolidate the material.

KEY CONCEPT

17.1   Genomes Can Be Sequenced Rapidly

Go to Animations 17.1 and 17.2

- **High-throughput sequencing** generates millions of overlapping reads that can be assembled into contiguous DNA sequences.

- In **RNA sequencing** (**RNA-seq**), DNA copies of RNAs are sequenced to determine the kinds and numbers of RNAs being expressed.

- **Functional genomics** includes genome annotation, which identifies the functional parts of the genome such as **open reading frames**.

- **Comparative genomics** provides insights into the evolution of particular genes and organisms.

Figure 17.2

Read 1 GGCTAATGATTG
Read 9 AATGATTGTCAC
Read 8 GTCACATACACA
Read 7 CACATGGAAATA
Read 11 GGAAATACTTTT

GGCTAATGATTGTCACATACACATGGAAATACTTTT

Questions

1. Arrange the following seven reads into a contiguous DNA sequence: 1. CCATGGTCAA, 2. GTCAAATGCC, 3. ACGGCTTTAT, 4. ATGCCGATTG, 5. TTTATATCGT, 6. ATCGTCCATG, 7. GATTGCGCGG.

2. In eukaryotes, RNA sequencing often begins with a step that captures RNAs with a poly A tail, so that only the mRNA is sequenced. What are the advantages of examining only the mRNA?

3. Why is it harder to identify open reading frames in eukaryotic genomes than in prokaryotic genomes?

KEY CONCEPT

17.2 Prokaryotic Genomes Are Compact

- Prokaryotic genomes are small and compact, usually lack introns, and sometimes contain plasmids.

- **Metagenomics** involves sampling an environment and then sequencing the DNA to identify the organisms that are found there.

- **Transposable elements**, or **transposons**, use either the copy and paste method or the cut and paste method to move in the genome. In either case, they can take host genes with them.

Questions

1. You have sequenced a microbe with a small genome. What features would suggest the genome is from a prokaryote rather than a eukaryote?

2. Why does metagenomics identify more bacterial species in an environment than standard lab culturing methods do?

3. Some transposons move by first making RNA copies that are then reverse transcribed into DNA. Do such transposons use cut and paste transposition or copy and paste transposition?

Figure 17.5

KEY CONCEPT

17.3 Eukaryotic Genomes Contain Many Types of Sequences

- Eukaryotic genomes are often large, with numerous introns and repetitive sequences.

- Large genomes do not necessarily have more protein-coding genes; instead, variation is often due to differences in repetitive DNA.

- Some eukaryotic genes are members of **gene families** and have similar functions. Some members of gene families are nonfunctional **pseudogenes**.

- One method for increasing gene expression is gene duplication, which creates new gene copies that are then able to diverge in function.

Figure 17.7

Questions

1. Eukaryotic microbes such as yeasts have genomes that are not much larger than prokaryotic genomes. What would you predict about the makeup of these genomes compared with those of multicellular eukaryotes?

2. A large part of multicellular eukaryotic genomes has been called "junk DNA." Why do you think this is said?

3. What are the two most likely fates of a new gene duplicate?

KEY CONCEPT

17.4 Human Biology Is Revealed through the Genome

- The human genome is large, with over 50% repetitive DNA and only 1.2% encoding proteins.

- The human genome contains about 20,500 protein-coding genes—substantially fewer than was expected, given that the genome encodes tens of thousands of proteins, which is due in part to alternative splicing.

- SNPs occur about every 1,330 bp and are used to determine ancestry, identify individuals, and find associations between genetic diseases and drug responses (**pharmacogenomics**).

Questions

1. About half the human genome is repetitive DNA. What kinds of repetitive DNA are most common in the genome?

2. A patient is prescribed a drug whose metabolism in the body is under the control of known genes and alleles. How could SNP genotyping be used to get information on whether this drug would be effective in this patient?

Figure 17.12

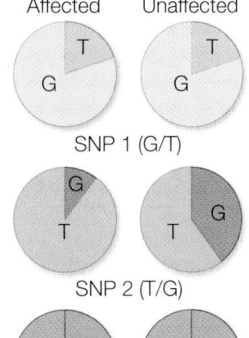

KEY CONCEPT

17.5 Proteomics and Metabolomics Can Provide Insights beyond the Genome

Go to Activity 17.1

- The **proteome** is the complete set of proteins in a cell, tissue or organisms at a given time.

- The number of proteins in the proteome is substantially larger than the number of protein-coding genes.

- The **metabolome** consists of all the small molecules in a cell, tissue, or organism under defined conditions.

Questions

1. Even in single-cell eukaryotes containing few introns, the number of proteins in the proteome is much larger than the number of protein-coding genes. Why?

2. Why might the proteome differ in different tissues?

3. Metabolite profiles can be used to determine whether certain pathways in a cell, tissue or organism are functioning correctly. Why might this ability be useful for medicine?

Figure 17.15

Go to **Achieve** for the eBook, **LearningCurve**, animations, activities, simulations, and additional resources and assignments.

Recombinant DNA and Biotechnology 18

KEY CONCEPTS

18.1 DNA from Different Sources Forms Recombinant DNA

18.2 There Are Several Ways to Insert DNA into Cells

18.3 DNA for Study Is Obtained in a Variety of Ways

18.4 Several Tools Are Used to Study the Function of DNA

18.5 DNA Can Be Manipulated for Commercial Use

Nucleic acids and proteins can be analyzed and changed in small volumes, in this case far less than 1 milliliter.

© Erik Isakson/Getty Images

▶ Investigating LIFE

DNA Technology Meets Medicine

Janet was arriving at her office when she first felt numb on the left side of her face. She became confused and had difficulty finding her office. After a passerby called 911, an emergency response team transported Janet to a nearby hospital. She had had a stroke, but amazingly, she was back at work and fully functional two days later.

A stroke can occur when a large blood vessel that supplies the brain with oxygen and nutrients is blocked. Blockage is often associated with the formation of a blood clot on a plaque – a fat deposit on the inner walls of a blood vessel. Within minutes of blockage, cellular respiration in affected brain cells is reduced, and within minutes to hours, the cells die. Nerves controlling muscles in Janet's face were affected first, followed by brain regions involved in cognitive processes.

Janet was treated with tissue plasminogen activator, or TPA, a protein involved in dissolving blood clots. Your body produces TPA when you have a cut; its action is seen when the clot "goes away" a few days later. Janet's cells would have gradually made TPA to slowly dissolve the clot blocking the vessel to her brain, but in the meantime her brain cells would have died. To speed up the process, Janet was injected with TPA right around the clot.

Where did the TPA used in Janet's treatment come from? TPA is a protein made in tiny amounts by blood vessel cells. Extracting enough TPA from tissues is impractical; recombinant DNA technology is required to get enough of it for therapeutic injection into a bloodstream. As you will learn in Investigating Life: Producing TPA, the process involves inserting the gene that encodes TPA into living bacterial cells in the lab. These cells are then biochemically coaxed into expressing TPA protein in quantity. The production of TPA is but one example of how knowledge of molecular biology and advances in biotechnology have transformed biological research and launched new industries that employ microbes to produce proteins and other useful chemicals.

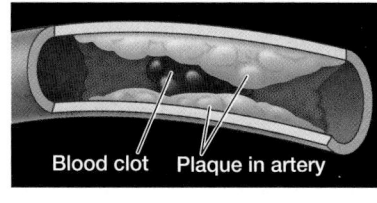

Blood clot   Plaque in artery

 How is biotechnology changing medicine?
(Find the answer on page 418.)

18.1 DNA from Different Sources Forms Recombinant DNA

Learning Objectives

18.1.1 Describe how staggered cuts made in DNA by restriction enzymes create sticky ends.

18.1.2 Explain why DNA ligase is used in addition to restriction enzymes to make recombinant DNA.

18.1.3 Summarize the Cohen and Boyer experiments on creating recombinant DNA.

Recombinant DNA is a DNA molecule that has been made in the laboratory using at least two different sources of DNA. The DNAs used for recombination can be from the same organism (e.g., from different chromosomes), from different members of the same species, or from entirely different organisms.

In Chapter 15 you learned that restriction enzymes are able to cleave double-stranded DNA at particular palindromic recognition sequences (restriction sites). When restriction enzymes cut at their restriction sites, they can create either blunt ends or complementary overhangs (short sequences of single-stranded DNA) termed **sticky ends** (Figure 18.1). Hundreds of restriction enzymes are known, many of which create their own unique sticky ends.

Any two DNA molecules with sticky ends that are complementary can form hydrogen bonds with one another. The sticky ends of the original molecule may bond (anneal), or two different fragments may bond. Indeed, a fragment from one source, such as a human, can bond to a fragment from any other source, such as a bacterium, as long as the ends are complementary. The fragments are initially held together by only a few weak hydrogen bonds, since there is a missing phosphodiester bond (a "nick") in each strand of the double helix. However, the nicks can be sealed by adding the enzyme DNA ligase to catalyze the formation of the strong, covalent, phosphodiester bonds between adjacent nucleotides in each of the strands, joining them to form a single, larger molecule (Figure 18.2).

Figure 18.2 Cutting, Splicing, and Joining DNA *Eco*RI can be used to cut two different DNA molecules (blue and orange). The resulting sticky ends can hydrogen-bond with complementary exposed bases on other DNA fragments, which can then be covalently joined using DNA ligase to form the missing phosphodiester bonds in each strand of the DNA backbone, creating a recombinant molecule.

Q: If two DNA molecules were digested with *Eco*RI and *Kpn*I restriction enzymes, respectively, and then mixed together with DNA ligase, would you expect recombinant molecules between them to be produced?

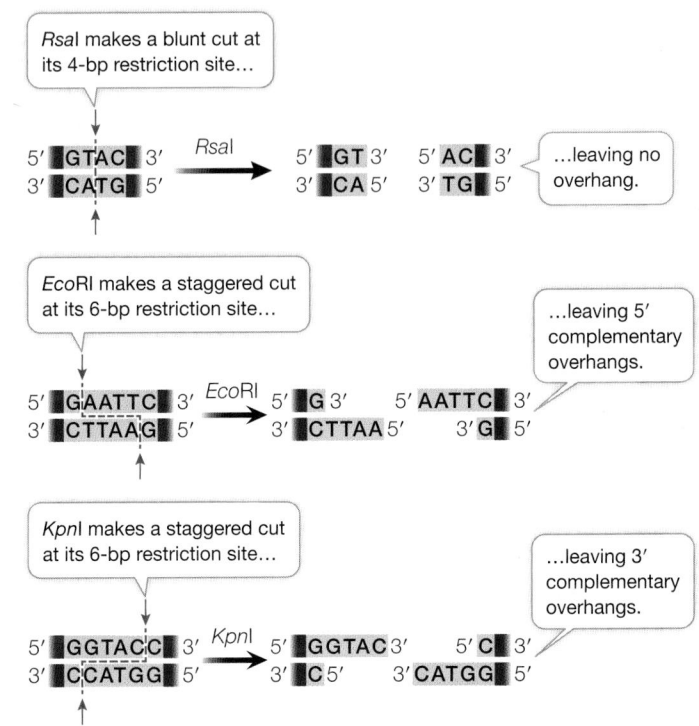

Figure 18.1 Restriction Enzymes Cut at Restriction Sites Some restriction enzymes cut the two strands of DNA at sites that are directly opposite one another, resulting in blunt-ended fragments. Other enzymes make cuts that are offset from one another, which results in staggered ends that have a 5′ or 3′ overhang. These are referred to as "sticky ends" because they are able to form hydrogen bonds with (that is, "stick to") complementary sequences on other DNA molecules. The names of the enzymes reflect their organism of origin. *Eco*RI, for example, was found in *E. coli*.

With these tools—restriction enzymes and DNA ligase—scientists are able to create recombinant DNA and have been doing so since 1973. In that year, Stanley Cohen at Stanford University, Herbert Boyer at the University of California, and their colleagues created recombinant bacterial plasmids. As illustrated in **Figure 18.3**, they isolated two different plasmids (small circular DNA molecules that replicate independently of the main chromosome; see Figure 12.25) from *Escherichia coli*. Each of the two plasmids contained a different antibiotic resistance gene. The scientists cut the two plasmids with restriction enzymes, mixed the fragments together, and then used DNA ligase to rejoin DNA molecules, creating recombinant plasmids. The recombinant plasmids of this ligation reaction were then inserted into new *E. coli* cells, and the cells were grown in the presence of both antibiotics. A few of the transformed bacteria could grow on the medium, and the researchers were able to show that a single recombinant plasmid containing the genes for resistance to both antibiotics explained this result. With this experiment, recombinant DNA technology was born.

Recently, new tools have been developed for making recombinant DNA. Methods based on the polymerase chain reaction (PCR) allow the joining of any two DNA molecules without the need for conveniently placed restriction enzyme sites. Despite these advances, restriction enzymes and DNA ligase are still used routinely for recombinant DNA construction in biology labs.

Experiment

Figure 18.3   Can DNA from Two Different Sources Be Recombined into a Single Functional DNA Molecule?

Original Paper: S. N. Cohen et al. 1973. Construction of biologically functional bacterial plasmids in vitro. *Proc Natl Acad Sci USA* 70: 3240–3244.

With the discovery of restriction enzymes and DNA ligase, it became possible to combine DNA fragments from different sources in the laboratory. But would such "recombinant DNA" be functional when inserted into a living cell? The results of this experiment by Stanley Cohen and Herbert Boyer completely changed the scope of genetic research, increasing our knowledge of gene structure and function and ushering in the new field of biotechnology.

HYPOTHESIS▶ Biologically functional recombinant plasmids can be made in the laboratory.

METHOD▶   *E. coli* plasmids carrying a gene for resistance to either the antibiotic kanamycin (K) or tetracycline (T) are cut with the *Eco*RI restriction enzyme. *Eco*RI cuts the kanamycin-resistant plasmid in three locations and the tetracycline-resistant plasmid in a single location.

Experimental group

Plasmids are cut.

K^r   T^r

E. coli plasmid

Cut with *Eco*RI

The cut plasmids are mixed with DNA ligase; and some recombinant molecules are produced.

Transform and select

RESULTS▶   Sensitive *E. coli*   *E. coli* resistant to both antibiotics

CONCLUSION▶ Two DNA fragments with different genes can be joined to make a functional recombinant DNA molecule.

 Media Clip 18.1 Striking Views of Recombinant DNA Being Made
Life12e.com/mc18.1

Go to **Achieve** for a companion Data in Depth exercise.

KEY CONCEPT
18.1 Recap and Assess

DNA fragments from different sources can be joined together to make recombinant DNA. DNA can be cut with a restriction enzyme and then rejoined with DNA ligase. There are many different restriction enzymes, each with its own recognition sequence. Several restriction enzymes produce sticky ends, which facilitate the production of recombinant DNA.

1. The following is the sequence of one strand of the restriction site for the *Hind*III restriction enzyme: 5′ … AAGCTT … 3′. What is the sequence of the other strand? If this enzyme results in a four-nucleotide 5′ overhang, where are the cut sites?

2. How did Cohen and Boyer make the first recombinant DNA molecule and confirm that they had done so?

Recombinant DNA has no biological significance until it is inserted inside a living cell, which can replicate and transcribe the transplanted genetic information. How can recombinant DNA made in the laboratory be inserted and expressed in living cells?

KEY CONCEPT   There Are Several Ways
18.2   to Insert DNA into Cells

Learning Objectives

18.2.1 List the three requirements of a bacterial plasmid cloning vector and describe the reason each is required.

18.2.2 Explain how a reporter gene such as *GFP* allows for easy screening for recombinant plasmids in bacterial cloning.

18.2.3 Outline the steps involved in transforming a multicellular organism using zygotic injection of foreign DNA.

18.2.4 Outline the steps involved in transforming a multicellular organism using injection of transformed, cultured cells during early development.

One reason for making recombinant DNA is to **clone**—that is, to produce many identical copies of—a particular gene or other DNA sequence. We have seen the term "clone" used in the context of whole cells or organisms (see Chapters 11 and 12) that are genetically identical to one another. The easiest way to clone a piece of DNA is to use an organism that can make clones of itself. For example, a gene can be cloned by inserting it into a bacterial cell such as *E. coli*. If a new piece of DNA is inserted and the bacterium is allowed to reproduce, it will produce millions of identical cells, all carrying identical copies of the piece of DNA. Cloning might be done to get enough DNA for sequencing and subsequent analysis, to produce a protein product in quantity, or as a step toward creating an organism with a new phenotype.

In single-celled organisms such as *E. coli* that are able to make identical copies of themselves, the primary challenge is getting the foreign DNA into the cell. Recombinant DNA is cloned by inserting it into host cells in a process known as **transformation**—or **transfection** if the host cells are derived from an animal. A host cell or organism that contains recombinant DNA is referred to as a **transgenic** cell or organism, and the non-native DNA is called a transgene. Later in this chapter we will encounter many examples of transgenic organisms, including yeast, rice plants, and even cattle.

Selectable genetic markers are used to identify host cells containing recombinant DNA

Various methods are used to create transgenic cells. Generally these methods are inefficient in that only a few of the cells that are exposed to the recombinant DNA actually become transformed with it. In order to isolate and reproduce only transgenic cells, **selectable marker** genes, such as genes that confer resistance to antibiotics, are often included as part of the recombinant DNA molecule. When an antibiotic resistance gene is used as the selectable marker, the cells from the transformation experiment are grown in the presence of the antibiotic; the antibiotic kills all nontransgenic cells, leaving only the transgenic cells. Antibiotic resistance genes were the selectable markers used in Cohen and Boyer's experiment (see Figure 18.3).

Genes can be inserted into prokaryotic or eukaryotic cells

In theory, any cell or organism can act as a host for the introduction of recombinant DNA. For single-celled organisms such as bacteria and yeasts, creating a single transgenic cell results in a transgenic organism. Both bacteria and yeasts have been heavily used as research organisms:

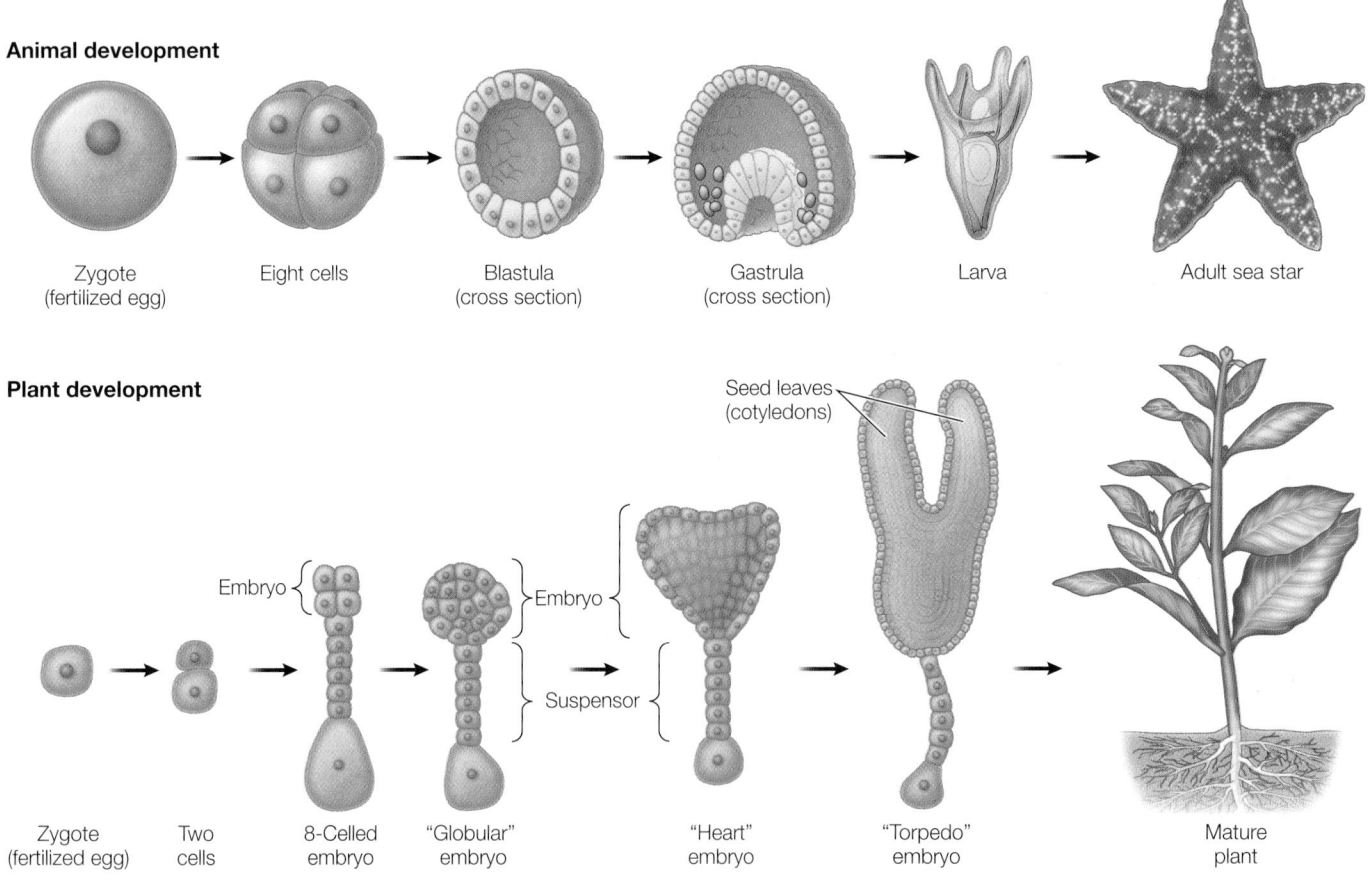

Animal development

Zygote (fertilized egg)   Eight cells   Blastula (cross section)   Gastrula (cross section)   Larva   Adult sea star

Plant development

Seed leaves (cotyledons)

Embryo   Embryo   Suspensor

Zygote (fertilized egg)   Two cells   8-Celled embryo   "Globular" embryo   "Heart" embryo   "Torpedo" embryo   Mature plant

Figure 18.4 From Fertilized Egg to Adult The stages of development from a single-celled zygote to a mature organism containing millions or trillions of cells are shown for an animal and for a plant.

▶ **View in Achieve**
Activity 18.1 Stages of Development

- *Bacteria* are easily grown and manipulated in the laboratory. Much of their molecular biology is known, especially for well-studied bacteria such as *E. coli.* Furthermore, bacteria contain plasmids, which are easily manipulated to carry recombinant DNA into the cell. While bacteria have been extremely useful for cloning pieces of DNA, they are not always well suited as hosts for expressing eukaryotic genes because they differ in the details of transcription, RNA processing, translation, and posttranslational modification (see Chapter 14).

- *Yeasts* such as *Saccharomyces cerevisiae* are commonly used as eukaryotic hosts for recombinant DNA studies. The advantages of using yeasts include their rapid cell division (less than 2 hours to proceed through the cell cycle), ease of growth in the laboratory, and relatively small genome size (see Table 17.2). In addition, yeast cells have most of the characteristics of other eukaryotic cells, with a notable exception being those associated with multicellularity.

For multicellular organisms, it is also possible to produce a transgenic organism by transforming a single cell. Multicellular sexual organisms pass through a single-celled zygote stage (see Figure 11.14) that develops into an adult organism containing many thousands to many trillions of cells (**Figure 18.4**). One method for creating transgenic individuals involves creating transgenic zygotes by injecting fertilized eggs with a transgene. The transgenic zygotes then develop into transgenic organisms, with every cell transgenic (**Figure 18.5**).

An alternative method for obtaining a transgenic multicellular organism is to use cell culture. The cultured cells must be **totipotent stem cells**—cells that have the ability to develop into any other cell type. Transformation is performed in culture, and transgenic cells are selected and allowed to produce large numbers of daughter cells. In plants, once cells are transformed in cell culture, they can be coaxed to develop into a mature plant (see Figure 35.4). This is not possible in an animal. Instead, transgenic cells are injected into a developing animal, usually at a very early stage of development such as the blastula (see Figure 18.4). The result of injecting transgenic cells is an embryo that is a mixture of original cells and transgenic cells (**Figure 18.6**). If transgenic cells give rise to gametes in the adult animal, then the resulting zygotes will have the transgene and will develop into offspring that have the transgene in all of their cells.

Inserted DNA is usually integrated into the host chromosome

Some prokaryotic cells can take up intact DNA molecules from the environment, which makes transformation quite easy; recall the bacterium *Streptococcus pneumonia* in which the R strain can be transformed by DNA of the S strain present in

1 Donor ewes are treated with hormones to achieve superovulation. After insemination, fertilized eggs are collected.

2 Foreign DNA is injected into the fertilized eggs.

3 Eggs are transferred to recipient ewes.

4 Transgenic lambs carrying the foreign DNA are identified.

Figure 18.5 Transforming a Zygote to Make a Transgenic Organism One method for obtaining a transgenic multicellular organism is to transform a zygote (fertilized egg) by injecting it with foreign DNA and then screening for transgenic offspring that carry the foreign DNA incorporated into their genome.

1 Mouse totipotent stem cells are grown in lab culture.

2 Cells are transfected with a transgene.

3 Transgenic cells are selected.

4 Transgenic cells are injected into an early mouse embryo.

Blastocyst

Development of embryo and birth

5 The resulting mouse is a mixture of original and transgenic cells.

6 If transgenic cells give rise to gametes, the resulting offspring will have the transgene in every cell.

Figure 18.6 Injecting Transgenic Cells to Make a Transgenic Organism One method for obtaining a transgenic multicellular organism is to transform cells in culture and inject them into an early developmental stage, thereby creating an embryo that is a mixture of original cells and transgenic cells. If any of the transgenic cells give rise to gametes in the adult animal, the resulting zygotes will have the transgene and will develop into offspring that have the transgene in all of their cells.

the environment (see Figure 13.2). However, most cells cannot do this, and so various laboratory methods have been devised to get DNA into cells. Cells can be chemically treated to make their outer membranes more permeable, and then mixed with the DNA so that it can diffuse into the cells. Another approach is called electroporation: a short electric shock is used to create temporary holes in the membranes through which the DNA can diffuse into the cell. Viruses can be altered so that they carry recombinant DNA into cells. A common method for transforming plants involves a specific bacterium that inserts DNA into plant cells. Transgenic animals can be produced by injecting recombinant DNA into the nuclei of fertilized eggs (see Figure 18.5). There are even "gene guns" that "shoot" the host cells with tiny metal particles coated with the DNA.

The challenge of inserting new DNA into a cell lies not only in getting it into the host cell, but also in getting it to replicate as the host cell divides. As you saw in Key Concept 13.3, DNA polymerase does not bind to and copy just any sequence. If the new DNA is to be replicated, it must become part of a segment of DNA that contains an origin of replication. Such a DNA molecule is called a **replicon**, or replication unit.

There are two general ways in which the newly introduced DNA can become part of a replicon within the host cell:

1. It can be spliced into a host chromosome directly.

2. It can enter the host cell as part of a carrier DNA sequence, called a **vector**, and can then either integrate into a host chromosome or be replicated from its own origin of replication.

Several types of vectors are used to get DNA into cells, some of which we now describe in more detail.

PLASMIDS AS VECTORS   As we described in Chapter 12, plasmids are generally small, circular DNA molecules that replicate autonomously in many prokaryotic cells. Several characteristics make plasmids useful as transformation vectors:

- Plasmids are relatively small (an *E. coli* plasmid is usually 2,000–6,000 bp) and are therefore easy to manipulate in the laboratory.

- A plasmid often has one or more restriction enzyme recognition sequences that each occur only once in the plasmid sequence. This makes it easy to insert new DNA into the prokaryotic plasmid before it is used to transform host cells.

- Many plasmids contain genes that confer resistance to antibiotics, which can serve as selectable markers.

- Plasmids have a bacterial origin of replication (*ori*) and can replicate independently of the host chromosome. It is not uncommon for a bacterial cell to contain hundreds of copies of a recombinant plasmid. For this reason, the power of bacterial transformation to amplify a gene is extraordinary. A 1-liter culture of bacteria harboring the human β-globin gene in a typical plasmid has as many copies of that gene as there are cells in a typical adult human (10^{14}).

A plasmid used as a vector in the laboratory has been extensively altered to include convenient features (**Figure 18.7A**):

- Multiple unique restriction sites for cloning purposes (see *Eco*RV, *Bam*HI, *Sal*I, and *Pst*I in Figure 18.7A)

- An origin of replication that will function in a particular type of host cell (see *ori* in Figure 18.7A)

- One or more selectable markers (see ampicillin resistance and tetracycline resistance in Figure 18.7A)

PLASMID VECTORS FOR PLANTS   An important vector for carrying new DNA into many types of plants is a plasmid found in the bacterium *Agrobacterium tumefaciens*. This bacterium lives in the soil, infects plants, and causes a disease called crown gall, which is characterized by the presence of growths (or tumors) on the plant. *Agrobacterium* contains a large plasmid called Ti (for *tumor-inducing*) (**Figure 18.7B**). When the bacterium infects a plant cell, a region of the Ti plasmid called the T DNA is inserted into the host plant cell, where it becomes incorporated into one of the plant's chromosomes. The Ti plasmid carries the genes needed for this transfer and incorporation of the T DNA. The T DNA carries genes that are then expressed by the host cell, causing the growth of tumors and the production of specific sugars that the bacterium uses as sources of energy. Scientists have exploited this remarkable natural "genetic engineer" to insert foreign DNA into the genomes of plants.

When the *Agrobacterium* Ti plasmid is used as a vector for plant transformation, the tumor-inducing and sugar-producing genes on the T DNA are removed and replaced with foreign DNA.

(A)
Plasmid pBR322; 4,361 bp
Host; *E. coli*

(B)
Ti plasmid; 200,000 bp
Hosts: *Agrobacterium tumefaciens*
(entire plasmid) and infected plants (T DNA only)

Figure 18.7 Plasmid Vectors   (A) *E. coli* cloning plasmids contain one or more selectable markers to identify transgenic cells, an origin of replication, and one or more restriction sites for inserting foreign DNA. (B) *Agrobacterium* injects the T DNA region of its Ti plasmid during infection. When the Ti plasmid is used as a vector for plant transformation, genes on the T DNA are removed and replaced with foreign DNA. The creation of recombinant Ti plasmids allows for the transformation of many different host plant species.

The recombinant Ti plasmids are first used to transform *Agrobacterium* cells from which the original Ti plasmids have been removed. Then the *Agrobacterium* cells are used to infect plant cells and transfer the T DNA, now containing genes placed there by the researcher, to the host cell chromosomes.

VIRUSES AS VECTORS   As a DNA molecule becomes larger than about 10,000 base pairs, it becomes challenging to get it across a cell membrane using chemical or electrical methods. However, in some cases the goal is to clone or transform with a larger DNA molecule. Although many prokaryotic genes are smaller than 10,000 base pairs, most eukaryotic genes—with their introns and extensive flanking sequences—are bigger. A vector that accommodates larger DNA inserts is needed for these genes.

Both prokaryotic and eukaryotic viruses are used as vectors for eukaryotic DNA. Bacteriophage λ, which infects *E. coli*, has a DNA genome of about 45,000 base pairs, all of which are injected into a host cell during infection. About 20,000 base pairs are not necessary for the bacteriophage to complete the lytic part of its life cycle (see Figure 16.15). These 20,000 base pairs can be deleted and replaced with DNA from another organism, which then gets replicated along with the virus DNA. Alternatively, essentially the entire phage genome can be replaced with DNA from another organism and packaged into phage heads. These phage heads are able to inject the DNA into the host bacterial cell exactly as they would inject their own genome. Once inside the cell, the DNA either circularizes to form a large plasmid or becomes incorporated into the genome.

Reporter genes help select or identify host cells containing recombinant DNA

Transformation is inefficient; only a very small percentage of a population of cells will be successfully transformed. Furthermore, the process of making recombinant DNA is far from perfect. During a ligation reaction, DNA molecules can combine in various ways, many of which do not produce the desired recombinant molecule (see Figures 18.2 and 18.3). Methods have been developed to improve the chance that a desired combination will occur. A simple approach is to cut the vector with two different restriction enzymes that have sites near each other. This produces a molecule with incompatible sticky ends, which is much less likely to simply recircularize during the ligation reaction. The desired insert molecule is cut with the same two enzymes, so that theoretically a functional circular plasmid can be produced only if the vector and insert ligate with one another. Even so, it is often the case that only a small proportion of the ligation products have the desired recombinant sequence.

How can we identify or select the host cells that contain the desired sequence? One way is to use selectable markers, such as those for antibiotic resistance used in early experiments with recombinant DNA (see Figure 18.3). Selectable markers are one type of **reporter gene**, which is any gene whose expression is easily observed. Here are several types of reporter genes:

- As described earlier, an antibiotic resistance gene in a plasmid or other vector allows the detection of transformed host cells grown in the presence of the selected antibiotic. If the host cells are normally sensitive to the antibiotic, they will grow on medium containing the antibiotic only if they have been transformed by the vector. This approach is used in the selection of transgenic prokaryotic and eukaryotic cells, including those of plants and animals. In some cases a plasmid contains two antibiotic resistance genes and one of them is used for cloning. For example, suppose the plasmid in Figure 18.7A was used to clone a piece of foreign DNA at the *Bam*HI site. Transformation could be selected for using ampicillin. The resulting bacteria could then be tested (screened) for resistance to tetracycline. Bacteria that were resistant to ampicillin and sensitive to tetracycline would have the plasmid containing a piece of foreign DNA.

- The β-galactosidase (*lacZ*) gene in the *E. coli lac* operon (see Figure 16.4) codes for an enzyme that can convert the artificial substrate X-Gal into a bright blue product. Many plasmids include the *lacZ* gene with multiple unique restriction sites where target DNA sequences can be inserted within its sequence. These plasmids also carry genes for antibiotic resistance. Bacterial colonies containing the plasmid are selected on a solid medium containing the antibiotic. X-Gal is also included in the medium. If a bacterial colony contains a recombinant plasmid that carries the foreign DNA inserted into the *lacZ* gene, it will not make β-galactosidase and the colony will be white. Clones that contain the original plasmid with no insert express the *lacZ* gene and make blue colonies (**Figure 18.8**). The *lacZ* gene can thus be used to screen transformed colonies to see if their plasmid contains an inserted fragment of foreign DNA.

- Green fluorescent protein (GFP), which normally occurs in the jellyfish *Aequorea victoria*, emits visible green light when exposed to ultraviolet light. The gene for this protein has been isolated and incorporated into vectors and can be used similarly to *lacZ* to screen for recombinant plasmids containing foreign DNA (see Figure 18.8). GFP has also been modified to emit other colors when exposed to ultraviolet light, allowing multiple reporters to be used at the same time.

- Both *lacZ* and GFP are widely used as reporter genes in other situations besides cloning. The protein-coding sequence of one of these reporter genes can be attached to promoters or other regulatory sequences from other genes to study how these sequences regulate gene expression under different conditions or in different tissues of a transgenic multicellular organism (**Figure 18.9A**). The coding sequence of a reporter gene can also be added to the amino or carboxyl end of another protein-coding gene to "tag" the protein produced by that gene. For example, GFP can be used to study how and where a protein is localized in eukaryotic cells (**Figure 18.9B**).

How are numerous transgenic individuals produced from one?

When a researcher goes to the effort of making a transgenic organism, the goal is to produce numerous transgenic individuals, not just one. With single-celled organisms, one transgenic individual can easily be cloned by normal, asexual cell division (binary fission in prokaryotes or mitosis in eukaryotes) into numerous identical

Research Tools

Figure 18.8 Selection for Recombinant Plasmids Selectable marker (reporter) genes are used by biologists to select for bacteria that have taken up a plasmid and check for foreign DNA. In a typical experiment, most of the bacteria will not take up any DNA. Of those that do, only a small fraction will take up a recombinant plasmid containing foreign DNA.

1 A plasmid has genes for ampicillin resistance (*amp*ʳ) and β-galactosidase (*lacZ*).

2 A restriction enzyme cuts the plasmid in the *lacZ* gene.

*amp*ʳ

lacZ

ori

Ligation

3 The foreign DNA has sticky ends that are compatible with the cut DNA.

4 Ligation of the plasmid and foreign DNA results in a recombinant plasmid with an insert that inactivates the *lacZ* gene.

Transformation

5 Host cells are transformed and grown on medium with ampicillin and the substrate for β-galactosidase.

6 Blue colonies have the intact *lacZ* gene.

7 White colonies have the inactivated *lacZ* gene, indicating that they carry the recombinant plasmid containing foreign DNA.

© Dr. Jack Bostrack/Visuals Unlimited, Inc.

Only cells that are ampicillin-resistant and white carry the recombinant plasmid containing foreign DNA.

DNA taken up by ampicillin-sensitive *E. coli* lacking *lacZ* enzyme	Phenotype for ampicillin	Phenotype for *lacZ*
None	Sensitive	Not applicable (no growth)
Foreign DNA	Sensitive	Not applicable (no growth)
Plasmid with no insert	Resistant	Blue
Recombinant plasmid containing foreign DNA	Resistant	White

(A)

The regulatory region causes GFP expression in nervous tissue.

From Z. Yang et al. 2007. *BMC Dev Bio* 7: 97. CC BY 2.0

150 μm

Recombinant DNA structure:

GATA2 upstream regulatory region

GFP

GFP protein-coding region

(B)

The GFP-tagged protein binds to microtubules of the cytoskeleton.

From I. Lang et al. 2014. *Plants* 3: 583–593. CC BY 4.0

10 μm

Recombinant DNA structure:

GFP	*MAP4*

GFP protein-coding region

MAP4 protein-coding region

Figure 18.9 Green Fluorescent Protein as a Reporter Gene **(A)** Expression of GFP protein in a transgenic zebrafish (*Danio rerio*) 24 hours after fertilization. The recombinant DNA consists of 7.3 kilobase pairs (kbp) of the upstream region of a transcription factor gene (*GATA2*) joined to the coding sequence of GFP. The GFP fluorescence is strongest in neuronal cells (in the brain) of the embryo, indicating that this is where the GATA2 transcription factor is normally expressed. **(B)** GFP-tagged MAP4 protein expressed in *Arabidopsis thaliana* shoot tissue. Because MAP4 binds to microtubules, the GFP fluorescence shows the structure of the cytoskeleton in the cells.

Q: Are cells killed during GFP visualization? Why is this important?

transgenic individuals (see Key Concept 11.4). In sexual eukaryotes, cloning a single individual is not as easy. The first cloned mammal, a sheep, was produced in 1996 by Ian Wilmut and his colleagues at the Roslin Institute in Edinburgh. The method involved the fusion of a somatic (nonreproductive) cell from an adult animal, containing the donor nucleus, with an enucleated egg. After the fused cell underwent several cell divisions, the resulting early embryo was transplanted into the womb of a surrogate mother. Eventually a lamb named Dolly was born (**Figure 18.10**). Dolly carried the same genetic material as the nuclear donor and thus was a clone of that donor. Although this process has been repeated with more than 20

Research Tools

Figure 18.10 Cloning a Mammal   The experimental proce-dure described here produced the first cloned mammal, a sheep named Dolly (shown on the left in the photo). As an adult, Dolly mated and subsequently gave birth to a normal offspring, thus showing that a cloned mammal is fully functional.

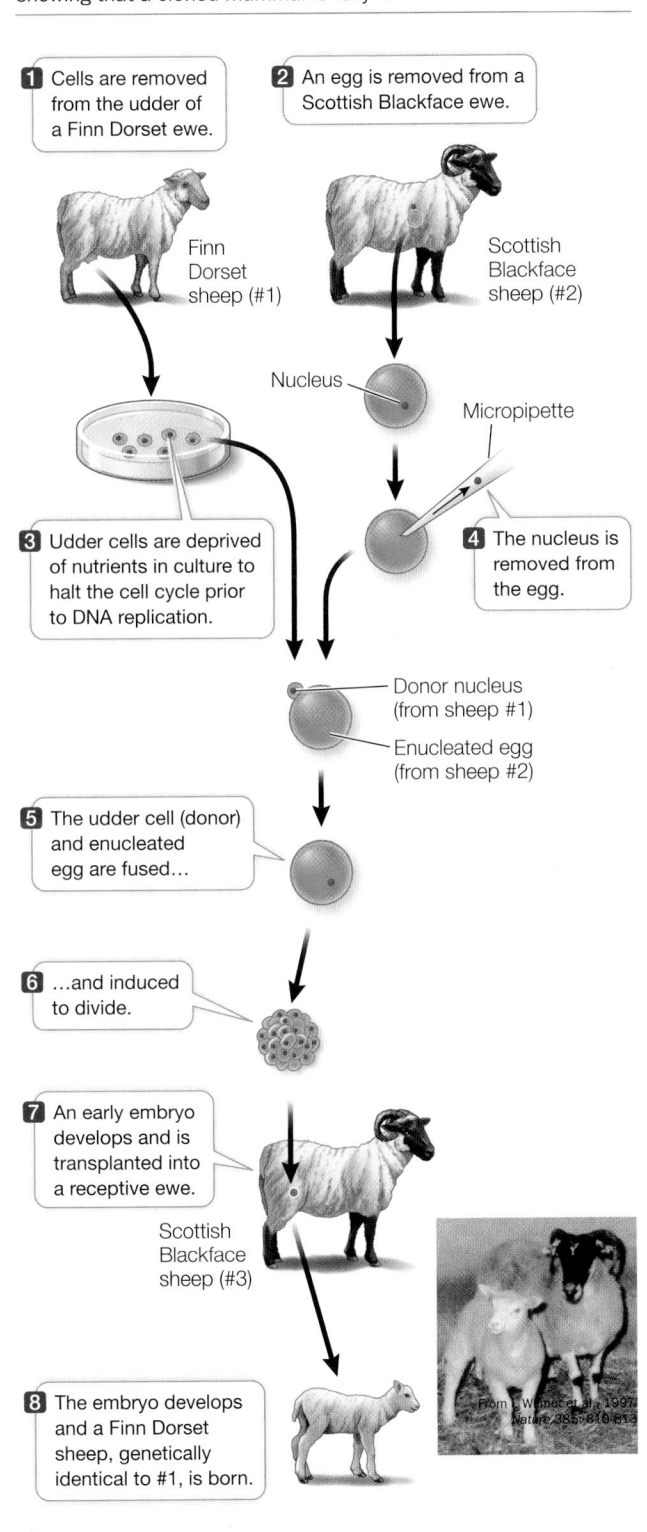

1 Cells are removed from the udder of a Finn Dorset ewe.

2 An egg is removed from a Scottish Blackface ewe.

Finn Dorset sheep (#1)

Scottish Blackface sheep (#2)

Nucleus

Micropipette

3 Udder cells are deprived of nutrients in culture to halt the cell cycle prior to DNA replication.

4 The nucleus is removed from the egg.

Donor nucleus (from sheep #1)

Enucleated egg (from sheep #2)

5 The udder cell (donor) and enucleated egg are fused...

6 ...and induced to divide.

7 An early embryo develops and is transplanted into a receptive ewe.

Scottish Blackface sheep (#3)

From I. Wilmut et al., 1997. Nature 385:810-813.

8 The embryo develops and a Finn Dorset sheep, genetically identical to #1, is born.

Go to **Achieve** for a companion **Data in Depth** exercise.

mammal species, including cats, deer, dogs, horses, pigs, rabbits, and mice, it is expensive and not practical for producing large numbers of clones. How, then, to produce numerous, genetically identical transgenic individuals?

The technique that is used most often is to transform a ge-netically uniform (true-breeding) strain that has been obtained from many generations of inbreeding (see Key Concept 12.3). Such inbred strains are homozygous at most genes. Once a trans-genic individual is obtained using one of the methods described earlier (see Figures 18.5 and 18.6), it is bred to a nontransgenic individual to produce offspring, some of which are heterozygous for the transgene. Heterozygotes are then interbred to produce individuals homozygous for the transgene. Although they are not technically clones, the resulting homozygotes are geneti-cally uniform and can be interbred to make additional transgenic individuals of essentially identical genotype.

KEY CONCEPT
18.2 Recap and Assess

Recombinant DNA can be cloned by using a vector to insert it into a suitable host cell. Plasmid vectors contain a selectable marker; an origin of replication; and a cloning site, which may reside in a reporter gene. In multicellular eukaryotes, transfor-mation involves zygotic transformation or transformation in cell culture. Once a transgenic individual is produced, asexual repro-duction can be used to produce multiple clones. Although cloning is possible, copying a transgenic animal most often involves crossing genetically identical individuals that are homozygous for the transgene. Reporter genes can be used to check for a DNA insertion in cloning vectors or to show when a protein is being expressed or where it is localized.

1. Assume you are using a plasmid vector that contains genes encoding ampicillin resistance and GFP, with a restriction site in the latter gene only. Arrange a–e below to reflect the sequence of steps for inserting a piece of foreign DNA into this plasmid, introducing the recombinant plasmid into bacteria, and verifying that the plasmid and the foreign gene are both present in the bacteria.
   a. Transform host cells.
   b. Put cells on medium containing antibiotic and grow resis-tant colonies.
   c. Select colonies that do not fluoresce under ultraviolet light.
   d. Digest vector and foreign DNA with a restriction enzyme.
   e. Ligate the digested plasmid together with the foreign DNA.

2. Compare the use of a plasmid whose coding site is in a GFP gene versus a plasmid whose coding site is in a streptomycin resistance gene in terms of detecting cells containing a recombinant plasmid carrying foreign DNA.

3. When transforming mice, transgenic cells originally derived from a brown mouse are often injected into an early developmental stage of a white mouse. Assuming white is recessive to brown coat color, how might mice carrying transgenic cells be identified following the injections and how might mice containing the transgene in every cell be produced?

We have described how DNA can be cut with restriction enzymes, inserted into a vector, and introduced into host cells. We have also seen how host cells carrying recombinant DNA can be identified. Now let's consider where the genes or DNA fragments used in these procedures come from.

KEY CONCEPT
18.3   DNA for Study Is Obtained in a Variety of Ways

Learning Objectives

18.3.1 Describe the differences between genomic and cDNA libraries.

18.3.2 Explain why genomic libraries do not differ across tissues but cDNA libraries do.

18.3.3 Explain how RT-PCR is used to amplify a specific gene sequence.

18.3.4 Describe what is meant by synthetic DNA and give examples of its use.

A major goal of molecular biology is to learn the functions of particular DNA sequences and the proteins they encode. DNA sequences for study are obtained from several sources that we describe in this key concept: random fragments of chromosomes that are maintained as gene libraries, complementary DNA obtained by reverse transcription from mRNA, products of the polymerase chain reaction (PCR), and artificially synthesized or mutated DNA.

DNA for study can come from a library

DNA is contained in chromosomes, of which there are usually many in a cell. And chromosomes can be enormous, containing millions to billions of base pairs and hundreds to thousands of genes. Intact genomic DNA is too large to be introduced into host cells. How, then, are single genes, containing only thousands of base pairs, isolated from such large molecules? One method is to first break chromosomes into smaller DNA molecules, clone each molecule, and then find the gene of interest among the clones.

A **genomic library** is a collection of DNA fragments that make up the entire genome of an organism. Restriction enzyme digestion or other means, such as mechanical shearing, can be used to break chromosomes into small pieces. Each fragment is then cloned by inserting it into a vector, which is then taken up by a host cell. Proliferation of a single such transformed cell produces a colony of cells, each of which harbors many copies of the same fragment of DNA (**Figure 18.11A**). Many clones are required to make a genomic library for an entire genome.

If a plasmid vector is used, about 700,000 separate clones are required to make a library of the human genome. By using bacteriophage λ, which can carry about four times as much DNA as a typical plasmid, the number of clones in the library can be reduced

to about 160,000. Although this still seems like a large number, a single petri plate can hold thousands of phage colonies, or plaques, which are easily screened for the presence of a particular DNA sequence by hybridization to an appropriate nucleic acid probe.

Connect the Concepts The technique of nucleic acid hybridization, illustrated in Figure 14.7, involves using a single-stranded nucleic acid probe with a complementary sequence to the target DNA. If the probe forms a double-stranded hybrid molecule, the target DNA fragment has been identified.

cDNA is made from mRNA transcripts

In many cases scientists are interested in protein-coding regions of DNA, which represent a very small fraction of some eukaryotic genomes (see Key Concept 17.3). To find these genes, a much smaller DNA library—one that includes only the genes transcribed in a particular tissue at a particular point in time—can be made from **complementary DNA**, or **cDNA** (**Figure 18.11B**). Making cDNA involves isolating mRNA from cells, then making cDNA

Research Tools

Figure 18.11 Constructing Libraries   (A) A genomic library can be made by breaking the DNA into small fragments, incorporating the fragments into a vector, and then transforming host cells with the recombinant vectors. Each colony of cells contains many copies of a small part of the genome. (B) The many mRNAs in a cell can be copied into cDNAs and a library made from them.

(A) Genomic DNA library construction

(B) cDNA library construction

Q: What attribute of eukaryotic mRNAs might be used to isolate them from other RNAs in a cell?

copies of that mRNA by complementary base pairing in a process called **reverse transcription**. Reverse transcription is catalyzed by the enzyme **reverse transcriptase.**

A collection of cDNAs from a particular tissue at a particular time in the life cycle of an organism is called a **cDNA library**. Because mRNAs do not last long in the cytoplasm, the types and amounts of mRNAs present in a cell are a good representation of the transcription rates of all the genes in that cell. So a cDNA library is a "snapshot" that captures the transcription pattern of a set of cells at a given point in time. cDNA libraries have been invaluable for comparing gene expression in different tissues at different stages of development. For example, researchers have found that up to one-third of all the genes of an animal are expressed only during development. cDNA is also a good starting point for cloning eukaryotic genes, because the clones contain only the coding sequences of the genes (the introns having been spliced out; see Figure 14.8). Also, if a eukaryotic gene is highly expressed in a particular tissue, a cDNA library made from that tissue will be enriched for the gene, making it easier to identify and clone the gene.

DNA can be amplified using PCR or can be synthesized artificially

When the DNA sequence surrounding a region of interest is known, a DNA library is not needed. Instead, PCR can be used to amplify the target sequence. PCR can begin with as little as 10^{-12} g of DNA (a picogram). Any fragment of DNA can be amplified by PCR as long as appropriate primers are available, which requires knowing the DNA sequence surrounding the target. If the appropriate primers (two are needed—one for each strand of DNA) are added to template DNA in a PCR reaction, millions of copies of the DNA sequence between the primers can be produced in just a few hours. This amplified DNA can then be inserted into a vector and cloned in host cells.

> **Connect the Concepts** As illustrated in Figure 13.20, the polymerase chain reaction (PCR) automates replication of a DNA fragment in a test tube. Also called DNA amplification, the process involves repeatedly synthesizing DNA complementary to a target sequence to make enough DNA for chemical analysis and genetic manipulations.

PCR can also be used to amplify a specific cDNA sequence. In this case, mRNA is isolated from an organism or tissue, and reverse transcriptase is used to make cDNA from the mRNA. Then PCR is used to amplify a specific sequence directly from the sample of cDNA. This procedure, called **RT-PCR**, has become an invaluable tool for studying the expression of particular genes in cells and organisms.

Artificial DNA can be synthesized using organic chemistry to link nucleotides together in a specified sequence. This process is now fully automated, and a laboratory can make large numbers of short- to medium-length sequences overnight. PCR primers, for example, are made in this way. The synthesis of artificial DNA does not require a template, so DNA with any sequence can be made. This flexibility is useful for creating DNA fragments with desirable characteristics, such as convenient restriction sites or specific mutations. Longer synthetic sequences can be pieced together to construct completely artificial genes that have been designed for specific purposes.

For example, a gene might be designed to be highly expressed in a particular cell type, or to encode a highly active enzyme.

> **Connect the Concepts** Plasmids containing synthetic transposon DNA have been used to transfect host cells to inactivate genes one by one and give insight into the minimal genome. See Key Concept 17.2.

KEY CONCEPT
18.3 Recap and Assess

DNA for study can be obtained from genomic libraries, cDNA libraries, and PCR, or it can be artificially synthesized.

1. What type of approach would you use for analyzing each of the following, and why?
   a. The expression of a gene encoding amylase, a starch hydrolyzing enzyme, in seeds as they germinate
   b. The sequence of the amylase gene in two different genetic strains of corn
2. How could RT-PCR be used to compare the expression of a particular gene in muscle versus liver tissues?
3. Describe some uses for synthetic DNA.

We've explored the various sources of DNA that can be used to make recombinant DNA molecules, and how organisms are transformed with recombinant DNA. We now turn to some of the ways that recombinant DNA and transformation methods can be used to study the functions of genes and proteins.

KEY CONCEPT
18.4   Several Tools Are Used to Study the Function of DNA

Learning Objectives

18.4.1 Give examples of ways in which particular genes are chosen for study.

18.4.2 Describe how DNA microarrays are used to examine patterns of gene expression.

18.4.3 Outline how RNA interference can be used to reduce expression of a particular gene.

18.4.4 Explain how CRISPR can be used to knock down, knock out, or replace a specific gene.

So far in this chapter we have seen how recombinant DNA is made and how organisms are transformed with recombinant DNA. In this key concept we examine some of the ways in which genes of interest are identified and describe several techniques for studying the functions of genes.

Genes of interest can be identified by genetic mapping or by studying gene expression

There are many thousands of genes in a genome (see Chapter 17). Many of these genes function in multiple tissues or at different times of development. How does a scientist decide which among these genes to study? In some cases a gene can be identified by genetic mapping of a Mendelian disorder in a pedigree (see Figure 15.17). Many genes have been identified in this way. For example, the gene that causes cystic fibrosis was identified in the late 1980s using this method and has been under intense study ever since. In other cases gene expression can be used to find a gene to study. A researcher might be interested in a gene that is expressed in a particular tissue or stage of development, or that is misexpressed in diseased individuals. For example, embryonic cells that will eventually give rise to skin cells, normal adult skin cells, and skin cancer cells all express a unique set of genes. A developmental biologist might be interested in the genes uniquely expressed in the embryonic cells, while an oncologist might be interested in those uniquely expressed in the cancer cells.

To identify distinct patterns of gene expression, scientists could isolate mRNA from cells and measure the amount of each gene's mRNA one gene at a time by hybridization or RT-PCR. But that would be expensive and time-consuming. It is far simpler to do these hybridizations for every gene in a single step, and that is made possible with **DNA microarray** technology.

DNA microarrays ("gene chips") contain a series of DNA sequences attached to a glass slide in a precise order. In Chapter 17 we discussed the use of DNA microarrays for single nucleotide polymorphism (SNP) genotyping (see Figure 17.13). For RNA expression, each microscopic spot contains thousands of copies of a particular oligonucleotide of 20 or more bases that is the sequence of an exon from a protein-coding gene in the genome. Each oligonucleotide can hybridize with only one RNA sequence and thus is a unique identifier of expression of that gene. If a gene is highly expressed, there will be many RNA molecules in the sample to hybridize to the corresponding spot on the microarray. Alternatively, spots representing genes that are not expressed will show no hybridization. Gene microarrays are usually used to examine differential expression; gene expression in one sample is often compared with that in another sample. In the field of oncology, for example, patterns of gene expression provide invaluable information to clinicians trying to characterize patients' tumors. To do this, RNAs are extracted from tumor and normal tissues, labeled with different fluorescent colors (e.g., red and green), and then RNAs from both tissues are hybridized to the microarray. After hybridization, spots of a single color (red or green) represent genes expressed more highly in one tissue, while spots with both colors (yellow) represent genes with similar expression in both tissues (**Figure 18.12**).

The function of a gene can be determined by modifying its expression post-transcriptionally

Once a gene has been identified, there are many questions that can be addressed to determine its function. Where and when in the organism is the gene expressed? Where is the protein produced by the gene localized? What happens when the gene is knocked down (has its expression reduced) or is knocked out (eliminated), such that a functional protein is not made?

Where and when a gene is expressed and the localization of the protein product can be examined using reporter genes; the regulatory region for a gene can be placed upstream of a reporter to determine expression pattern, or a coding sequence can be added to a gene to determine where the protein localizes (see Figure 18.9). But how do we knock down or knock out a gene?

One way to reduce expression is by blocking the translation of a gene's mRNA. The process developed for blocking translation is

1 RNAs from tumor and normal tissue are labeled with different fluorescent dyes and combined.

2 The samples are hybridized to a microarray. Each spot corresponds to a particular gene.

3 The color of a spot indicates the relative level of expression of the gene in the tumor tissue compared with normal tissue.

Samples from patient

Tumor RNA   Normal RNA

Green spot indicates higher expression in normal tissue.

Red spot indicates higher expression in tumor tissue.

Yellow spot indicates similar expression in both tissues.

Figure 18.12 Using DNA Microarrays for Clinical Decision-Making The pattern of expression of a group of genes in tumor tissues (the pattern of colored spots) helps clinicians decide on the optimal treatment for a patient. Actual arrays have more spots than shown here.

 View in Achieve
Animation 18.1 **DNA Microarray Technology**

yet another example of scientists imitating nature. As described in Key Concept 16.5, gene expression is sometimes regulated by the production of double-stranded RNA molecules that are processed to produce short, single-stranded microRNAs (miRNAs) and small interfering RNAs (siRNAs). These miRNAs and siRNAs are complementary to specific mRNA sequences and combine with proteins to form an RNA-induced silencing complex (RISC). When miRNAs and siRNAs are hybridized (bound) to their target mRNAs, the RISC inhibits translation (miRNAs) or causes degradation (siRNAs) of the mRNA (see Figure 16.22). Scientists use RNA-induced silencing for blocking the expression of particular genes post-transcriptionally. An organism can be transformed to produce miRNAs or siRNAs that are complementary to and thus bind to specific endogenous mRNAs (**Figure 18.13A,B**). A related method uses synthetic single-stranded RNA sequences complementary to target mRNAs that prevent translation by hybridizing to the mRNA. The synthetic RNA is called **antisense RNA** because it binds by base pairing to the "sense" bases on the mRNA (**Figure 18.13C**). Both methods of knocking down expression of a gene have been widely used to test cause-and-effect relationships in biological research.

It may be possible to make drugs that treat diseases by reducing gene expression post-transcriptionally. For example, people with the genetic disease familial hypercholesterolemia are unable to break down cholesterol in their blood and thus accumulate fat deposits in their blood vessels (as was the case with Janet, whose story opened this chapter). This excess cholesterol is transported in blood as part of a lipoprotein. Mipomersen is an antisense RNA drug directed against the translation of the mRNA for the "protein" part of this

(A) Normal translation

(B) miRNAs and siRNAs prevent translation

(C) Antisense RNA binds to mRNA and prevents translation

Figure 18.13 Using RNA-Induced Silencing and Antisense RNA to Block Translation of mRNA **(A)** Normally an mRNA is translated to produce a protein. Translation of a target mRNA can be prevented with **(B)** RNA-induced silencing using miRNA or siRNA, or with **(C)** antisense RNA that is complementary to the target mRNA.

lipoprotein. When people who have hypercholesterolemia take mipomersen, the level of the lipoprotein is reduced and so is the level of cholesterol in their bloodstream. Fat accumulation in their blood vessels is lowered. An siRNA-based therapy has been developed to treat macular degeneration, an eye disease that results in near-blindness when blood vessels proliferate in the eye. The signaling molecule that stimulates vessel proliferation is a growth factor. An siRNA that targets this growth factor's mRNA shows promise in stopping and even reversing the progress of the disease.

Genes can be inactivated and altered using CRISPR technology

Mutations that occur in nature have been important in demonstrating cause-and-effect relationships for specific genes. However, mutations in nature are rare events, and they occur at random locations in genes. DNA technology allows us to inactivate a particular gene in a specific manner to gain insight into its normal function. In addition, DNA technology allows us to explore the consequences of various specific mutations by creating them artificially. Synthetic DNA can be made with any desired sequence and used to replace the wild-type sequence, and its effect on the organism can be observed when the mutant DNA is expressed in host cells. Several methods can be used to knock out specific genes and replace wild-type sequences with particular mutant sequences (or vice versa). One method that has become widespread in recent years involves CRISPR.

CRISPR technology offers a powerful approach for "gene editing" (adding, disrupting, or changing the sequence of specific genes) and for altering gene regulation (**Figure 18.14**). As with many other tools of biotechnology, the method emulates a mechanism found in nature, one that some bacteria and many archaea use to defend themselves against viral infections. The genomes of these species have many short (24–48 bp) palindromic sequences of DNA (see Key Concept 18.1), with unique 24-base-pair spacer DNA in between, which are known by the acronym **CRISPR** (clustered regularly interspaced short palindromic repeat sequences). While the CRISPR sequence is the same for each repeating unit, the spacers are different. Each spacer is a fragment of DNA from a virus that previously infected the cell but did not end up killing its host. The spacer sequences thus provide "genetic mug shots" that inform the cell carrying them what viruses to look out for. When a virus carrying a sequence similar to the spacer DNA injects its DNA into the cell, the unit—CRISPR and spacer—is transcribed into RNA, to which a second short RNA attaches. This RNA complex then performs the following two functions:

1. Because the spacer sequence is complementary to part of the viral genome, it attaches to it by base pairing.

2. The complex binds a protein called CAS9, which is a nuclease that creates a double-strand break of the invading virus DNA at the recognized sequence, destroying its ability to produce new viruses and thereby protecting the host cell.

Therefore any cell that was once infected by a virus has the "memory" of that infection encoded in its genome, and those of all cells that are produced from it.

Once this natural immune system was described, it occurred to Emmanuelle Charpentier at Umeå University in Sweden and Jennifer Doudna at the University of California, Berkeley that it might be adapted to cut any DNA at a specific location: all that was needed was the RNA complementary to the target (a "guide" RNA) and the CAS9 enzyme. It is possible to synthesize a guide RNA that is complementary to any sequence in a genome. This means that transformation of a cell with the CAS9 gene and the appropriate guide RNA can be used to cut host DNA at any site of one's choosing.

What happens once the DNA has been cut? In a living cell, a double-strand break causes repair pathways to be activated to

Research Tools

Figure 18.14 Inactivating or Mutating a Gene by CRISPR
A molecular system used by bacteria to combat invading viruses (**A**) has been adapted to inactivate or mutate any gene (**B**).

(A) In prokaryotes, CRISPR prevents infection by prior viruses

Bacterial genome

Spacer: unique   CRISPR: repeat

Bacterial RNA

RNA

CAS9 nuclease

Unique sequence

Virus DNA

1 Bacteria and archaea have many CRISPR sequences separated by unique spacers that are remnants of prior virus invaders.

2 When a virus with a target unique sequence invades the cell, an RNA is made that includes the CRISPR sequence. Another RNA is added. CAS9, a nuclease, binds to the RNA.

3 The complex binds to the unique target on the invading viral genome. The nuclease cuts the virus DNA, inactivating it.

Cut

4 The nuclease cuts the virus DNA, inactivating it and preventing viral reproduction in the bacterial cell.

(B) In the lab, CRISPR can cut DNA at any sequence

Lab RNA

1 An RNA can be made in the lab that has any desired target sequence and the CAS9 binding sequence, so any gene can be inactivated.

Target DNA in cell

Target cut

NHEJ

Repair sequence

Imperfect repair

Repaired target

2 Imperfect repair by non-homologous end joining (NHEJ) results in a gene knockout (left), while repair using a complementary sequence containing a specific alteration introduces a specific mutation (right).

▶ **View in Achieve**
Simulation 18.1 CRISPR

fix the break. One pathway, called non-homologous end joining (NHEJ), simply ligates the two broken ends back together. NHEJ is error-prone, meaning that repair is imperfect and so mutations are often present after ligation (see Figure 18.14B). If the cut was in a protein-coding gene, then repair by NHEJ can lead to missense, nonsense, or frameshift mutations, potentially rendering the protein nonfunctional.

The simplicity of CRISPR technology to inactivate genes holds great promise. To give just one example, a fungal disease called powdery mildew can devastate a wheat crop. Many wheat varieties have a gene whose expression inhibits wheat's natural defenses against this disease, so the only way to control the disease is through heavy application of fungicides. Scientists in China used CRISPR technology to inactivate this gene, so that natural resistance is favored.

CRISPR technology can also be used to create specific mutations. Biologists can specify the mutation by synthesizing a short DNA sequence complementary to the region at the break. Then, when CAS9 cuts the DNA molecule, a repair pathway that uses complementary DNA may use the introduced DNA to make the repair so that the new sequence will have a specific alteration (see Figure 18.14B).

Perhaps more dramatic than the ability to induce mutations is the possibility of correcting mutations, particularly those that cause disease. In these cases CAS9 cuts the mutated gene in the host chromosome and then repair uses a complementary DNA with the wild-type sequence. For example, the disease cystic fibrosis is caused by mutation of a membrane transport protein. Scientists in the Netherlands have used CRISPR to correct the mutation in cells from patients with this disease. While this is not a cure (the corrected gene would have to function in many tissues), the possibility arises that the mutated gene could be corrected in germ line cells, such as those of an early embryo. The ease with which the human germ line genome can be altered using CRISPR technology has elicited numerous ethical and legal concerns.

CRISPR can also be used to knock down expression of a gene. This approach uses a CAS9 that has been modified so that it can no longer cut DNA. The inactivated CAS9 binds both the guide RNA and DNA and can thus be directed to a gene. Once bound, the inactivated CAS9 physically prevents transcription of the gene, even though it does not cut the DNA.

KEY CONCEPT

18.4 Recap and Assess

Researchers identify genes to study by genetic mapping or by analyzing gene expression, often using DNA microarrays. Gene function can be studied by examining the phenotype following reduction in expression or inactivation of the gene. miRNAs, siRNAs, and antisense RNAs can be used to reduce gene expression by selectively blocking mRNA translation. CRISPR technology allows selective inactivation, alteration, or reduced expression of particular genes.

1. In some bladder cancers, the gene for the cell signaling protein, *RAS*, is mutated, resulting in an altered protein that stimulates cell division. How might RNA-induced silencing be used to develop an RNA drug to treat this disease? Would the drug be specific for the cancer?

2. As pea seeds germinate, the embryo changes which genes are expressed. How would you use microarrays to analyze this?

3. Both antisense RNA and CRISPR technology can be used to block the expression of specific genes. What additional advantage does CRISPR have?

Now that you've seen how DNA can be fragmented, recombined, manipulated, and put back into living organisms, let's see some examples of how these techniques are used to make useful products.

KEY CONCEPT 18.5 DNA Can Be Manipulated for Commercial Use

Learning Objectives

18.5.1 Describe the essential features of bacterial expression vectors.

18.5.2 Summarize the advantages of modern recombinant DNA technology over selective breeding in agriculture.

18.5.3 Evaluate the ethical and environmental concerns posed by specific uses of biotechnology, taking into account the risks and rewards that would likely come from their use.

Biotechnology is the use of cells or whole living organisms to produce materials useful to people, such as foods, medicines, and chemicals. People have been using various forms of biotechnology for a long time. For example, the use of yeasts to brew beer and wine dates back at least 8,000 years, and the use of bacterial cultures to make cheese and yogurt is a technique many centuries old. For a long time people exploited these biochemical transformations without being aware of the organisms and genes involved. Today, with recombinant DNA techniques, almost any gene can be inserted into bacteria, yeasts, mammalian cells, plant cells, or even whole organisms, inducing them to make a gene product in large amounts.

Cells can be turned into factories for a desired protein

If a eukaryotic gene is inserted into a typical bacterial plasmid and used to transform *E. coli*, none of the gene product will be made unless other key prokaryotic DNA sequences are included with the gene so that it is expressed. Chapter 14 described the characteristics of a bacterial gene, all of which are required for expression of a transgene. A bacterial promoter, a transcription termination signal, and a sequence for binding of bacterial ribosomes to the mRNA (the Shine–Dalgarno sequence) must all be included in the transformation vector if the transgene is to be transcribed and translated in a bacterial cell.

To ensure expression of foreign genes by host cells, scientists make **expression vectors** having not only the characteristics of cloning vectors, but the extra sequences needed for the transgene to be expressed in the host cell. The insertion of an expression vector for a bacterial host is illustrated in **Figure 18.15**. An expression vector for a eukaryotic host would require the poly A–addition

Figure 18.15 Expression of a Transgene in a Host Cell Produces Large Amounts of Its Protein Product To be expressed in *E. coli*, a gene derived from a eukaryote requires bacterial sequences for transcription initiation (promoter), transcription termination, and ribosome binding. Expression vectors contain these additional sequences, enabling the eukaryotic protein to be synthesized in the prokaryotic cell.

Q: Would a eukaryotic gene obtained from a genomic library produce a functional protein if expressed in a bacterial expression plasmid?

▶ **View in Achieve**
Activity 18.2 Expression Vectors

sequence for mRNA stability and a promoter that contains all the elements needed for expression in a eukaryotic cell.

An expression vector can be designed to deliver transgenes to any class of prokaryotic or eukaryotic host and may include additional features:

- An *inducible promoter*, which responds to a specific signal, can be included. For example, a promoter that responds to hormonal stimulation can be used so that the transgene will be expressed at high levels only when the hormone is added.

- A *tissue-specific promoter*, which is expressed only in a certain tissue at a certain time, can be used if localized expression is desired. For example, many seed proteins are expressed only in the plant embryo. Coupling a transgene to a seed-specific promoter will allow the gene to be expressed only in seeds.

- *Signal sequences* can be added so that the gene product is directed to an appropriate destination. For example, when a protein is made by yeast or bacterial cells in a liquid medium, it is economical to include a signal directing the protein to be secreted into the extracellular medium for easier recovery.

TABLE 18.1 | Some Medically Useful Products of Biotechnology

Product	Use
Colony-stimulating factor	Stimulates production of white blood cells in patients with cancer and AIDS
Erythropoietin	Prevents anemia in patients undergoing kidney dialysis and cancer therapy
Factor VIII	Replaces clotting factor missing in patients with hemophilia A
Growth hormone	Replaces missing hormone in people of short stature
Insulin	Stimulates glucose uptake from blood in people with insulin-dependent (type I) diabetes
Platelet-derived growth factor	Stimulates wound healing
Tissue plasminogen activator	Dissolves blood clots after heart attacks and strokes
Vaccine proteins: hepatitis B, herpes, influenza, Lyme disease, meningitis, pertussis, etc.	Prevent and treat infectious diseases

Medically useful proteins can be made using biotechnology

Biotechnology produces many medically useful products (**Table 18.1**), and more are in various stages of development. A good illustration of a medical application of biotechnology is the manufacture of tissue plasminogen activator (TPA), discussed in the opening of this chapter. As noted there, TPA is a human protein involved in hydrolysis of blood clots and can be used to remove clots that block blood flow in a stroke.

To make TPA in amounts needed for clinical use, scientists first isolated the *TPA* gene by taking the mRNA for *TPA* and making a cDNA copy in the lab. The cDNA was then inserted into an expression vector and used to transform mammalian cells (**Investigating Life: Producing TPA**). The transgenic cells made the protein in quantity, and it soon became available commercially. As you saw at the start of the chapter, the drug has been a success in treating strokes.

Another way of making medically useful products in large amounts is **pharming**: the production of pharmaceuticals in farm animals or plants. For example, a gene encoding a useful protein might be placed next to the promoter of the gene that encodes lactoglobulin, an abundant milk protein. Transgenic animals carrying this recombinant DNA will secrete large amounts of the foreign protein into their milk. These natural "bioreactors" can produce abundant supplies of the protein, which can be separated easily from the other components of the milk (**Figure 18.16**).

DNA manipulation is changing agriculture

The cultivation of plants and the husbandry of animals provide the world's oldest examples of manipulating genetics for human use, dating back more than 10,000 years. Over the centuries, people have adapted crops and farm animals to their needs, producing organisms with desirable characteristics such as large seeds, high fat content in milk, or resistance to disease.

Until recently, the most common way to improve crop plants and farm animals was to identify individuals with desirable phenotypes that existed as a result of natural variation. Through many deliberate crosses—a process called selective breeding—the genes responsible for the desirable trait could be introduced into a widely used variety or breed of that organism.

> **Connect the Concepts** In genetics experiments, typically only a few genes and alleles are involved. But crop plants have phenotypes determined by many genes and alleles. This makes selecting genetically stable, desirable offspring from crosses between two varieties challenging. See Key Concepts 12.2 and 12.3.

Despite some spectacular successes—among them the breeding of high-yielding varieties of wheat, rice, and hybrid corn—such deliberate crossing can be a hit-or-miss affair. Many desirable traits are controlled by multiple genes, and it is hard to predict the results of a cross or to maintain a prized combination as a true-breeding variety year after year, especially because in sexual reproduction combinations of desirable genes are quickly separated by meiosis. Furthermore, traditional breeding takes a long time: many plants and animals take years to reach maturity and then can reproduce only once or twice a year—a far cry from the rapid reproduction of bacteria.

Here are just some of the advantages that modern recombinant DNA technology offers over traditional methods of breeding:

- *The ability to identify specific genes.* The development of genetic markers allows breeders to select for specific desirable genes, making the breeding process more precise and rapid.

- *The ability to introduce any gene from any organism into a plant or animal species.* This ability, combined with mutagenesis techniques, vastly expands the range of possible new traits.

- *The ability to generate new organisms quickly.* Manipulating cells in the laboratory and regenerating a whole plant or animal by cloning is much faster than traditional breeding.

Consequently, recombinant DNA technology has found many applications in agriculture (**Table 18.2**). Here we describe a few examples to demonstrate the approaches that plant scientists have used to improve crop plants.

PLANTS THAT MAKE THEIR OWN INSECTICIDES   Plants are subject to infections by viruses, bacteria, and fungi, but probably the most important crop pests are herbivorous insects. From the locusts

TABLE 18.2 | Agricultural Applications of Biotechnology under Development

Goal	Technology/genes
Improving the environmental adaptations of plants	Genes for drought tolerance, salt tolerance
Improving nutritional traits	High-lysine seeds; β-carotene in rice
Improving crops after harvest	Delay of fruit ripening; sweeter vegetables
Using plants as bioreactors	Plastics, oils, and drugs produced in plants

►Investigating LIFE   Producing TPA

Experiment

Original Paper: D. Collen et al. 1984. Biological properties of human tissue-type plasminogen activator obtained by expression of recombinant DNA in mammalian cells. *J Pharmacol Exp Ther* 231: 146–152.

For a protein such as TPA to become useful in the clinic, the expression of recombinant DNA (in this case, the *TPA* gene coupled to an active promoter) in cells must result in the production of a large amount of the protein. The protein is then purified and used to treat patients with a stroke, by catalyzing the dissolution of a blood clot in an artery leading to the brain.

HYPOTHESIS► A clinically useful TPA can be made by recombinant DNA technology.

METHOD►

mRNA for *TPA*

Reverse transcription

cDNA for *TPA*

1 Isolate mRNA for the *TPA* gene.

2 Using reverse transcription, copy mRNA for the *TPA* gene into cDNA.

Expression vector for mammalian cell

3 Create an expression vector suitable for a mammalian host.

◄ *Bam*HI

4 Insert the *TPA* gene into the expression vector.

TPA gene

RESULTS►

Mammalian cell

DNA

TPA

5 The transformed cell produces TPA in large amounts.

6 TPA is harvested, purified, and injected into a stroke patient to dissolve the blood clot.

CONCLUSION► TPA made by biotechnology can be used to treat patients.

Work with the Data

It is essential that a purified molecule made by biotechnology have the desired biological properties. In the case of TPA, the goal was to mimic the properties of the natural clot-dissolving molecule. Désiré Collen, a physician–scientist in Belgium, led an international team that compared laboratory-made TPA with the natural molecule made by human cells. They performed two types of experiments, one on clots suspended in human blood in the lab, and the other on clots that had developed in rabbits. The team also investigated the time course of clot dissolution and the dose of TPA needed for the effect.

QUESTIONS►

1. Human blood clots were prepared in the lab using a radioactively labeled clotting molecule. Dissolution of the clot resulted in the radioactive molecules becoming hydrolysis products (monomers), so comparing soluble to insoluble radioactivity was a measure of clot dissolution. **Table A** shows the results of clot dissolution over time after injection with natural TPA, TPA made by biotechnology, and a control injection without TPA. Plot the data in a graph of percent clot dissolution over time. What can you conclude about the experiment?

2. To determine whether lab-made TPA could dissolve clots in the mammalian blood system, clots were induced in a large vein in rabbits. After 20 hours, either natural or lab-made TPA was injected at the clot region, and the dissolution of the clot was measured 4 hours later. The results are shown in **Table B**. What can you conclude about this experiment? The results show the SEM (standard error of the mean) for the data. How would you use a statistical test to examine the difference, if any, between the two treatment groups and compare them with the control?

Table A

	Percent clot dissolution		
Time (hr)	No TPA (control)	Natural TPA	Lab-made TPA
1	0	4	5
2	0	10	20
3	1	20	35
4	1	35	55
5	2	50	65

Table B

	Percent clot dissolution (SEM)	
Dose of TPA (units)	Natural TPA	Lab-made TPA
0 (control)	14.3 (1.4)	14.3 (1.4)
12,000	19.8 (5.4)	22.3 (6.0)
24,000	24.5 (7.9)	30.6 (0.8)
48,000	38.9 (4.8)	49.3 (9.7)
96,000	66.0 (6.3)	75.4 (3.9)

Go to **Achieve** for a companion
Data in Depth exercise.

1 Lambs containing a human transgene are identified and grown to adulthood (see Figure 18.5).

2 Adult transgenic ewes produce the human protein in their milk.

3 The human protein is extracted from the milk.

4 The therapeutic protein is administered to human patients.

Figure 18.16 Pharming A eukaryotic expression vector carrying a human gene is used to produce transgenic offspring. As adults, these transgenic offspring express the human protein in their milk. The milk is easily harvested and the protein isolated, purified, and made clinically available to patients.

of biblical (and modern) times to the cotton boll weevil (*Anthonomus grandis*), insects have continually eaten the crops people grow.

The development of insecticides has improved the situation, but insecticides have their own problems. Many, including the organophosphates, are relatively nonspecific and kill beneficial insects in the broader ecosystem as well as crop pests. Some pesticides even have toxic effects on other groups of organisms, including people. What's more, many insecticides persist in the environment for a long time.

Some bacteria produce proteins that can kill insects. For example, the bacterium *Bacillus thuringiensis* produces a protein that is toxic to the larvae of several species of insects, but not to mammals or birds. The toxicity of this protein to insects is 80,000 times greater than that of a typical commercial insecticide. When an unlucky larva eats the bacteria, the toxin becomes activated and binds specifically to the insect's gut, producing holes and killing the insect. Dried preparations of *B. thuringiensis* have been sold for decades as safe insecticides that break down rapidly in the environment. But the biodegradation of these preparations is their limitation, because it means that the dried bacteria must be applied repeatedly during the growing season.

A longer-acting approach is to have the crop plants themselves make the toxin, and this is exactly what plant scientists have done. The toxin gene from *B. thuringiensis* has been isolated, cloned, and extensively modified by the addition of a plant promoter and other regulatory sequences. Transgenic corn, cotton, soybeans, tomatoes, and other crops are now being grown successfully with this added gene. Farmers growing these transgenic crops use less of other pesticides.

CROPS THAT ARE RESISTANT TO HERBICIDES Herbivorous insects are not the only threat to agriculture. Weeds may grow in fields and compete with crop plants for water and soil nutrients. Glyphosate is a widely used and effective herbicide, or weed killer, that works only on plants. It inhibits an enzyme system in the chloroplast that is involved in the synthesis of amino acids. Glyphosate is a broad-spectrum herbicide that kills most weeds, but unfortunately it also kills crop plants. One solution to this problem is to use it to rid a field of weeds before the crop plants start to grow. But as any gardener knows, when the crop begins to grow, the weeds reappear. If the crop were not affected by the herbicide, the herbicide could be applied to the field at any time without harming the crop.

Scientists have used expression vectors to make plants that synthesize a different form of the target enzyme for glyphosate that is unaffected by the herbicide. The gene for this enzyme has been inserted into corn, cotton, and soybean plants, making them resistant to glyphosate. The herbicide can then be sprayed on fields in which the resistant crop plants are actively growing, killing only the weeds. This technology has expanded rapidly, and a large proportion of cotton and soybean plants now carry this gene.

GRAINS WITH IMPROVED NUTRITIONAL CHARACTERISTICS

To remain healthy, humans must consume adequate amounts of β-carotene, which the body converts into vitamin A. About 400 million people worldwide suffer from vitamin A deficiency, which makes them susceptible to infections and blindness. One reason is that rice grains, which do not contain β-carotene, make up a large part of their diets. Rice grains lack the two-enzyme biochemical pathway that synthesizes β-carotene.

Plant biologists Ingo Potrykus and Peter Beyer isolated one of the genes for the β-carotene pathway from the bacterium *Erwinia uredovora* and the other from daffodil plants. They added a promoter and other signals for expression in the developing rice grain and then transformed rice plants with the two genes. The resulting rice plants produce grains that look yellow because of their high β-carotene content. A newer variety with a corn gene replacing the one from daffodils makes even more β-carotene and is golden in color (**Figure 18.17**). A daily intake of about 150 grams of this cooked rice can supply all the β-carotene a person needs. This new transgenic strain has been crossed with strains adapted for various local environments, in the hope of improving the diets of millions of people.

Wild-type rice   Golden rice 1   Golden rice 2

Courtesy of the Golden Rice Humanitarian Board, www.goldenrice.org

Figure 18.17 Transgenic Rice Rich in β-Carotene Middle and right: The grains from these transgenic rice strains are colored because they make the pigment β-carotene, which is converted to vitamin A in the human body. Left: Wild-type rice grains do not contain β-carotene.

CROPS THAT ADAPT TO THE ENVIRONMENT   Agriculture depends on ecological management—tailoring the environment to the needs of crop plants and animals. A farm field is an un-natural, human-designed system that must be carefully managed to maintain optimal conditions for crop growth. For example, excessive irrigation can cause increases in soil salinity. The Fertile Crescent, the region between the Tigris and Euphrates rivers in the Middle East where agriculture probably originated 10,000 years ago, is no longer fertile. It is now a desert, largely because the soil has a high salt concentration. Few plants can grow on salty soils, partly because of osmotic effects that result in wilting, and partly because excess salt ions are toxic to plant cells.

> Connect the Concepts   Learn about the effects of salt on plants in Key Concept 37.1.

Some plants can tolerate salty soils because they have a protein that transports Na^+ ions out of the cytoplasm and into the vacuole, where the ions can accumulate without harming plant growth (see Key Concept 5.3 for a description of the plant vacuole). Scientists developed a highly active version of the gene for this transporter protein and used it to transform crop plants that are less tolerant to salt, including rapeseed, wheat, and tomatoes. When this gene was added to tomato plants, they grew in water that was four times as salty as the typical lethal level (**Figure 18.18**). This finding raises the prospect of growing crops on what were previously unproductive soils.

Perhaps the most spectacular transgenic crop developed so far is a strain of rice that is resistant to both salt stress (using the gene just mentioned) and drought stress (using a gene from a bacterium) and has the ability to grow on nitrogen-deficient soils (using a gene from barley). This triply-tolerant rice is undergoing field tests.

These examples illustrate what could become a fundamental shift in the relationship between crop plants and the environment. *Instead of manipulating the environment to suit the plant,*

(A)

(B)

Courtesy of Eduardo Blumwald

Figure 18.18 Salt-Tolerant Tomato Plants   Transgenic plants containing a gene for salt tolerance thrive in salty water **(A)**, whereas plants without the transgene die **(B)**. This technology may allow crops to be grown on salty soils.

Courtesy of Tom Deerinck and Mark Ellisman of the National Center for Microscopy and Imaging Research at the University of California at San Diego

Figure 18.19 Synthetic Cells   These cells of *Mycoplasma mycoides* contain a synthetic genome.

Q: What are some potential uses of synthetic cells?

biotechnology may allow us to adapt the plant to the environment. As a result, some of the negative effects of agriculture, such as water pollution, could be lessened.

Synthetic biology can create living factories for new products

In Key Concept 17.2 you learned how inactivating genes one at a time can help define which genes are necessary for life in a particular organism and which ones confer special properties to the organism. One goal of this research is to design new life forms with specific purposes. That is, new genes could be added to the minimal genome. An important step toward this goal has been the laboratory synthesis of an artificial genome and its insertion into bacterial cells. This was first done using the bacterium *Mycoplasma mycoides*. The artificial genome was then inserted into empty cells of a related species, *Mycoplasma capricolum*, whose own DNA had been hydro-lyzed. The new DNA directed the cell to perform the biochemical functions of life, including reproduction (**Figure 18.19**).

The aims of synthetic biology are bold: to create bacteria or other organisms with new functions, such as producing hydrocarbons for fuel, new drugs for medicine, bacteria that make or break down plastics and other polymers, and so on. But before these functions can be added to the genome, the genes involved must be clearly described, including regulatory genes and sequences such as promoters that function in host cells. Thousands of such genes and chemicals that regulate their expression have now been associated with many known gene functions. For example, a single function—bacteria making ammonium sulfate that could be used for fertilizer in farming—requires more than 70 genes.

There is public concern about biotechnology

Concerns have been raised about the wisdom and safety of genetically modifying crops and other organisms. These concerns are centered on three claims:

1. Genetic manipulation is an unnatural interference with nature.

2. Genetically altered foods are unsafe to eat.

3. Genetically altered crop plants are dangerous to the environment.

Advocates of biotechnology tend to agree with the first claim. However, they point out that all crops are unnatural in the sense that they come from artificially bred plants growing in a manipulated environment (a farmer's field). Recombinant DNA technology just adds another level of sophistication to these technologies. Synthetic biology, however, takes genetic manipulation dramatically further.

To counter concern about whether genetically engineered crops are safe for human consumption, biotechnology advocates point out that only single genes are added and that these genes are specific for plant function. For example, the *B. thuringiensis* toxin produced by transgenic plants has no effect on people. However, as plant biotechnology moves from adding genes that improve plant growth to adding genes that affect human biology, such concerns will become more pressing.

Various negative environmental impacts have been envisaged. The concern has been raised, for example, about the possible "escape" of transgenes from crops to other species. If the gene for herbicide resistance, for example, were inadvertently transferred from a crop plant to a closely related weed, that weed could thrive in herbicide-treated areas. Increased use of herbicides has already resulted in the selection of weeds with naturally occurring mutations that make them resistant to that herbicide. Widespread use of glyphosate on fields of glyphosate-resistant crops, for example, has resulted in the selection of rare mutations in weeds that make

them resistant to glyphosate. Field-evolved resistance now occurs in half the major weed species examined. In addition, herbicides may cause harm either when consumed or to other non-target organisms present in the environment. For example, glyphosate use has been implicated in changes in the gut microbiome (see Key Concept 24.3) of honey bees, and is listed by the World Health Organization as a probable human carcinogen.

Because of the potential benefits of biotechnology, scientists believe that it is wise to proceed, albeit with caution.

KEY CONCEPT
18.5 Recap and Assess

Expression vectors allow the expression of transgenes in host cells. Biotechnology has been used to produce medicines and to develop transgenic plants with improved agricultural and nutritional characteristics.

1. What are the similarities and differences between a cloning vector and an expression vector?

2. Compared with traditional methods, what are the advantages of using biotechnology for plant breeding?

3. After Cohen and Boyer did their experiment (see Key Concept 18.1), a group of scientists, public health officials, and bioethicists held a conference and agreed to a temporary moratorium on most recombinant DNA research. What do you think were the concerns that led to the moratorium? How was safety assured so that the moratorium was lifted?

▶Investigating LIFE

 How is biotechnology changing medicine?

What are the limitations of treating patients with the clot-busting drug TPA, made by biotechnology? We opened this chapter with the story of Janet's stroke, pointing out how important it is to treat stroke patients quickly. An analysis published in 2014 of many studies done in the 20 years since TPA was first clinically used showed that the probability of having no significant disability is 75% higher in people who get TPA within 3 hours of stoke onset compared with people who don't get TPA. This benefit is reduced if a patient gets the drug later and is almost nonexistent at 6 hours poststroke.

One of the problems that arose when TPA treatments were initially administered was that the drug tended to break down rapidly in the bloodstream after injection. Biotechnologists solved this problem by altering the *TPA* gene slightly so that the protein gets glycosylated (adding sugars), which leads to a longer lifetime in the bloodstream. As other drugs are developed by biotechnology, the TPA story is being repeated: initial success, problems with the chemistry, and then modification.

While the commercial production of drugs by DNA biotechnology has had some successes, the examples are relatively limited and certainly not as notable as those in traditional biotechnology, where bacteria and other microbes are manipulated by their environment to make large amounts of molecules, such as antibiotics. However, as we described, DNA manipulation technologies, especially CRISPR, hold great promise to profoundly change medical diagnosis and treatment.

Future directions

A striking example of "old" biotechnology (in which a microorganism is coaxed into making a valuable product) merging with "new" biotechnology (which uses recombinant DNA) is the emerging field of cyanobacteria-produced plant secondary metabolites. Plants make these small-molecule metabolites to protect themselves against infections, injuries, and environmental factors. Many of the metabolites are strong antioxidants that react with and eliminate harmful oxidants such as oxygen atoms with unpaired electrons (superoxides) in cells under stress. Because human cells in disease states produce such oxidants that harm tissues, there is intense interest in using certain secondary metabolites that plants produce as drugs. Unfortunately, it takes a huge quantity of plants to obtain enough of a given antioxidant for clinical use.

This is where cyanobacteria come in. Cyanobacteria (sometimes incorrectly called blue-green algae) are photosynthetic single-celled organisms that grow well under light conditions in ponds or vats in the lab. Although they are not plants, cyanobacteria have genes encoding some of the enzymes involved with secondary metabolite production. Using recombinant DNA technology, genes from plants that encode other needed compounds in the pathway of certain antioxidants (specifically, phenylpropanoids) have been inserted into cyanobacteria, turning these organisms into factories that produce plant metabolites for clinical use.

You should be able to relate each summary to the adjacent figures. If you go to this visual summary in **Achieve**, you can follow links to figures, animations, activities, and simulations that will help you consolidate the material.

KEY CONCEPT

18.1   DNA from Different Sources Forms Recombinant DNA

■ Restriction enzymes make blunt or staggered cuts in DNA at specific palindromic sequences. Staggered cuts generate fragments with **sticky ends**.

■ DNA ligase is used to join DNA from different sources.

■ The first **recombinant DNA** molecules combined parts of two different bacterial plasmids.

Questions

1. The restriction enzyme *Rsa*I has a four-base-pair recognition site. Assuming all four base pairs are equally frequent, how many *Rsa*I cut sites would you expect there to be in a 5,000-base-pair plasmid?

2. Why are restriction enzymes that make staggered cuts, rather than those that make blunt cuts, preferred for making recombinant DNA?

Figure 18.1

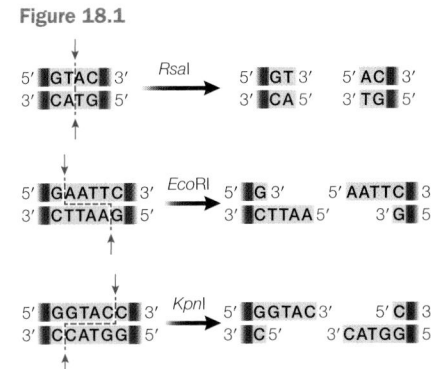

KEY CONCEPT

18.2   There Are Several Ways to Insert DNA into Cells

Go to Activity 18.1

■ Single-celled organisms are often used for **transformation** because a **transgenic** individual is easily made and cloned.

■ Transforming multicellular organisms involves transforming zygotes or cells in culture.

■ Cloning **vectors** contain a cloning site (a restriction enzyme recognition sequence), an origin of replication, and a **selectable marker**.

■ **Reporter genes** such as *lacZ* and *GFP* can be used to screen for an insert in a cloning vector, measure expression, or determine protein location.

■ Producing numerous **clones** of multicellular, sexual organisms involves producing inbred, genetically uniform individuals that are homozygous for the transgene.

Questions

1. What are the functions of each of the required attributes of a cloning vector?

2. How can a multicellular transgenic animal be produced by transforming a single cell?

3. What is the difference between a genetically uniform transgenic strain of yeast and a transgenic strain of mouse?

Figure 18.8

© Dr. Jack Bostrack/Visuals Unlimited, Inc.

KEY CONCEPT

18.3   DNA for Study Is Obtained in a Variety of Ways

■ DNA libraries consist of thousands to millions of hosts (often bacterial or viral) carrying foreign DNA in cloning vectors.

■ **Genomic libraries** are created by inserting DNA fragments from a genome into host cells; **cDNA libraries** are created by **reverse transcription** of mRNA from a particular tissue and developmental stage.

■ DNA or cDNA sequences can be amplified by PCR for cloning or for measuring gene expression.

■ Synthetic DNA can be used as PCR primers, to make probes for hybridization to identify genotypes, and to make custom genes with particular sequences.

Questions

1. A bacterial plasmid can comfortably handle a foreign DNA insert of up to 5,000 base pairs. Approximately how many bacterial clones (each containing a single plasmid) would be needed to make a genomic library for yeast, with a haploid genome of 12 million base pairs?

Figure 18.11

2. Explain how a cDNA library constructed from human brain tissue is likely to be similar to and different from a cDNA library constructed from human pancreatic tissue.

3. Explain how a genomic DNA library constructed from human brain tissue is likely to be similar to and different from a genomic library constructed from human pancreatic tissue.

KEY CONCEPT

18.4 Several Tools Are Used to Study the Function of DNA

Go to Animation 18.1 and Simulation 18.1

- Scientists often study genes that are responsible for genetic diseases or for desirable traits in crop species, or that are expressed at particular times or locations.

- **DNA microarrays** are used to examine expression of all the genes in the entire genome in a particular tissue, or tissues.

- The function a gene can studied by using posttranscriptional RNA interference to reduce or eliminate its expression.

- **CRISPR** allows a gene to be knocked out, knocked down, or altered.

Figure 18.12

Samples from patient

Tumor RNA   Normal RNA

Figure 18.14

In the lab, CRISPR can cut DNA at any sequence

Lab RNA

Target DNA in cell

Target cut

NHEJ

Repair sequence

Imperfect repair

Repaired target

Questions

1. A scientist wishes to study genes involved in early eye development in squid. How might she go about finding such genes?

2. After isolating a candidate gene involved in eye development, a researcher decides to try reducing its expression using RNA interference and scoring the effect on eye development. Outline the general steps to do this.

3. Suppose miRNA targeting of the candidate squid gene causes a subtle change in eye phenotype. The researcher now wishes to knock out the gene. How might she accomplish this using CRISPR?

KEY CONCEPT

18.5 DNA Can Be Manipulated for Commercial Use

Go to Activity 18.2

- A bacterial **expression vector** has all three characteristics of a cloning vector (cloning site, selectable marker, and origin of replication) as well as a promoter, transcriptional termination sequence, ribosome binding site (for prokaryotic hosts), and poly A sequence (for eukaryotic hosts).

- Modern recombinant technology allows the introduction of specific foreign genes into a species.

- Transgenic plants often have a much higher yield because of reduced levels of pathogen attack (using pesticide genes), less competition (using herbicide-resistant genes), and increased ability to grow well in poor conditions.

Figure 18.5

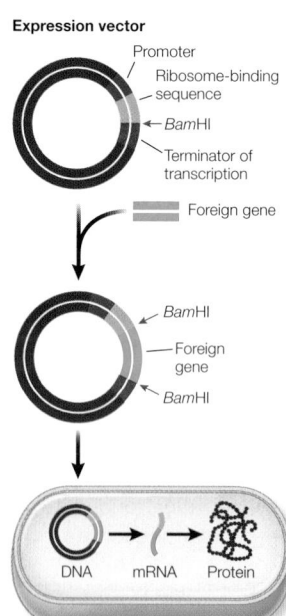

Expression vector

Promoter
Ribosome-binding sequence
BamHI
Terminator of transcription

Foreign gene

BamHI
Foreign gene
BamHI

DNA   mRNA   Protein

Questions

1. Inserting a eukaryotic gene into a bacterial expression vector and obtaining a functional protein can be challenging. Even when a gene is inserted into the vector, the resulting protein may be substantially different from the normal protein. Why might this be the case?

2. Sometimes a human protein-coding gene is placed under the control of a milk protein promoter and then a strain of sheep carrying the transgene is produced. What is the advantage of such a transgene?

3. Transgenic plants carrying the *Bacillus thuringiensis* toxin gene show high yields. Why is this the case?

Go to **Achieve** for the eBook, **LearningCurve**, animations, activities, simulations, and additional resources and assignments.

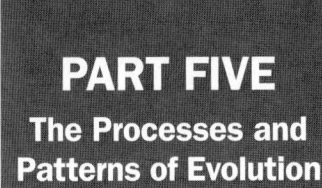

PART FIVE
The Processes and Patterns of Evolution

Processes of Evolution 19

KEY CONCEPTS

19.1 Evolution Is Both Factual and the Basis of Broader Theory

19.2 Mutation, Selection, Gene Flow, Genetic Drift, and Nonrandom Mating Result in Evolution

19.3 Evolution Can Be Measured by Changes in Allele Frequencies

19.4 Selection Can Be Stabilizing, Directional, or Disruptive

19.5 Selection Can Maintain Variation within and among Populations

19.6 Evolution Is Constrained by History and Trade-Offs

© blickwinkel/Alamy Stock Photo

Mexican free-tailed bats (*Tadarida brasiliensis*) taking flight from a bridge in Austin, Texas.

▶Investigating**LIFE**

An Evolutionary Arms Race between Bats and Moths

Many species of bats roost by day and fly out as night approaches. The mass exodus of thousands or even millions of bats from a roost is an impressive sight, often attracting crowds of human bat-watchers. In urban areas, the cavities under bridges can attract enormous colonies of bats. People once feared these urban bat colonies, but we now know that many species of bats prey on night-flying insects, including mosquitoes and agricultural pests. Each bat can consume a third of its weight in insects per night, so just 1,000 bats consume about 4 tons of insects every year.

Most bats catch insects in flight at night. About 50 million years ago, bats evolved the ability to echolocate, which allows them to detect flying insects (such as moths) in darkness. The bats produce ultrasonic sounds, and compare these outgoing sound pulses with the returning echoes of the pulses that bounce off the flying insects. Because bats are among the greatest threats to night-flying insects, any insect that can escape detection by bats is much more likely to survive and reproduce. Inherited traits that lead to greater survival increase in the population over time as surviving insects pass these traits on to their offspring.

Many groups of night-flying insects, including several groups of moths, have evolved the ability to detect the ultrasonic sounds of bats. When such a moth hears a bat, it flies away from the

source of the sound. If the bat is too close, the moth may dive rapidly to avoid capture. The moths in each generation that are better able to detect and avoid bats leave more offspring, so moths gradually evolve more effective escape mechanisms.

As moths get better at avoiding bats, why don't the bats starve? Because populations of bats are evolving too. In each generation, the individual bats best able to detect and capture flying insects get the most food, which allows them to put the most effort into reproduction. Their offspring inherit their prey-detection capabilities, so populations of bats evolve more efficient insect-catching abilities, even as the moth populations evolve better escape strategies. This gradual change in both moth and bat populations is known as evolution by natural selection—a process that is constantly shaping and changing all species of life on our planet.

© Michael Durham/Minden Pictures

 How do complex traits such as echolocation, or the ability to avoid detection by echolocation, evolve in the first place? (Find the answer on page 441.)

KEY CONCEPT
19.1
Evolution Is Both Factual and the Basis of Broader Theory

Learning Objectives

19.1.1 Differentiate between the everyday use of the word "theory" and a scientific theory.

19.1.2 Compare and contrast natural selection with the selection by human breeders for specific traits in domestic plants and animals.

19.1.3 Apply the principles of natural selection to predict and explain evolutionary outcomes.

All biological populations change in their genetic makeup over time. Change in the genetic composition of populations over time is called **evolution**. We can, and do, observe evolutionary change on a regular basis, both in laboratory experiments and in natural populations. We measure the rate at which new mutations arise, observe the spread of new genetic variants through a population, and see the effects of genetic change on the form and function of organisms. In the fossil record, we observe the long-term morphological changes (which are the result of underlying genetic changes) that have occurred among living organisms. These underlying changes in the genetic makeup of populations drive the origin and extinction of species and fuel the diversification of life.

Since we can directly observe evolution, why do we speak of "evolutionary theory"?

In addition to observing and recording physical changes over evolutionary time, biologists have accumulated a large body of evidence about *how* these changes occur, and about *what* evolutionary changes have occurred in the past. The resulting understanding of the processes of evolutionary change is known as **evolutionary theory**.

Evolutionary theory has many useful applications. We constantly apply it, for example, to the study and treatment of diseases. Evolutionary theory is critical to the improvement of agricultural crops and practices, and to the development of industrial processes that produce new molecules with useful properties. At a more basic level, knowledge of evolutionary theory allows biologists to understand how life diversified. It also helps us make predictions about the biological world.

In everyday speech, people tend to use the word "theory" to mean an untested hypothesis, or even a guess. But evolutionary theory does not refer to any single hypothesis, and it certainly is not guesswork. A vast and rich array of geological, morphological, behavioral, and molecular data supports the factual basis of evolution. Observations of fossils and natural populations are supported by experiments that demonstrate the basic operation of evolutionary processes.

When we refer to evolutionary theory, we are referring to our understanding of the processes that result in genetic changes in populations over time. We then apply that understanding to interpret the changes we observe in natural populations. We can directly observe the evolution of many living organisms. We can observe the yearly changes in the viruses that give us the flu, but it is evolutionary theory that allows us to apply our observations to the task of developing more effective vaccines against flu viruses.

Several processes of evolutionary change are recognized, and the scientific community is continually using evolutionary theory to expand its understanding of how and when these processes apply to particular biological problems.

 Media Clip 19.1 Watching Evolution in Real Time
Life12e.com/mc19.1

Darwin and Wallace introduced the idea of evolution by natural selection

In the early 1800s, it was not yet evident to many people that populations of living organisms evolve. But several biologists had suggested that the species living on Earth had changed over time—that is, that evolution had taken place. Jean-Baptiste Lamarck, for one, presented strong evidence for the fact of evolution in 1809, but his ideas about *how* it occurred were not convincing. At that time, no one had yet envisioned a viable process for evolution.

In the 1820s, a young Charles Darwin became passionately interested in the subjects of geology (with its new sense of Earth's great age) and natural history (the scientific study of how different organisms function and carry out their lives in nature). Despite these interests, he planned, at his father's behest, to become a doctor. But surgery conducted without anesthesia nauseated Darwin, and he gave up medicine to study at Cambridge University for a career as a clergyman in the Church of England. Always more interested in science than in theology, he gravitated toward scientists on the faculty, especially the botanist John Henslow. In 1831, Henslow recommended Darwin for a position on HMS *Beagle*, a Royal Navy vessel that was preparing for a survey voyage around the world (**Figure 19.1**).

Whenever possible during the five-year voyage, Darwin went ashore to study rocks and to observe and collect plants and animals. He noticed striking differences between the species he saw in South America and those of Europe. He observed that the species of the temperate regions of South America (Argentina and Chile) were more similar to those of tropical South America (Brazil) than they were to temperate European species. When he explored the islands of the Galápagos archipelago, west of Ecuador, he noted that most of the animals were endemic to the islands (meaning they were unique and found nowhere else), although they were similar to animals found on the mainland of South America. Darwin also observed that the fauna of the Galápagos differed from island to island. He postulated that some animals had come to the archipelago from mainland South America and had subsequently undergone different changes on each of the islands. He wondered what might account for these changes.

When he returned to England in 1836, Darwin continued to ponder his observations. His thoughts were strongly influenced by the geologist Charles Lyell, who had recently popularized the idea that Earth had been shaped by slow-acting forces that are still at work today. Darwin reasoned that similar thinking could be applied to the living world. Within a decade, he had developed the framework of an explanatory theory for evolutionary change based on three major propositions:

1. Species are not immutable; they change over time.

2. Divergent species share a common ancestor and have diverged from one another gradually over time—a concept Darwin termed **descent with modification**.

Charles Robert Darwin

Figure 19.1 Darwin and the Voyage of the *Beagle* The mission of HMS *Beagle* was to chart the oceans and collect oceanographic and biological information from around the world. The world map indicates the ship's path; the inset map shows the Galápagos archipelago, whose organisms were an important source of Darwin's ideas on natural selection. The portrait is of Charles Darwin at age 27, shortly after the *Beagle* returned to England.

▶ **View in Achieve**
Activity 19.1 Darwin's Voyage

3. Changes in species over time can be explained by **natural selection**: the increased survival and reproduction of some individuals compared with others, based on differences in their traits.

The first of these propositions was not unique to Darwin; several earlier authors had argued for the fact of evolution. A more revolutionary idea was his second proposition, that divergent species are related to one another through common descent. But Darwin is probably best known for his third proposition, that of natural selection.

Darwin realized that many more individuals of most species are born than survive to reproduce. He also knew that, although offspring usually resemble their parents, offspring are not identical to one another or to either parent. Finally, he was well aware that human breeders of plants and animals often selected their breeding stock based on the occurrence of particular traits that they found desirable. Over time, this selection by breeders resulted in dramatic changes in the appearance of the descendants of those plants or animals. In natural populations, wouldn't the individuals with traits that provided the best chances of survival and reproduction be the ones most likely to pass their traits on to the next generation? Darwin called this process natural selection, to emphasize that the "selection" in nature was based on traits that increased survival and reproduction of organisms. In essence, nature, rather than a human, was doing the "selection" for which organisms would contribute the most to the next generation. To emphasize this distinction, Darwin called the selective breeding process by humans **artificial selection**, and emphasized that humans often selected traits in breeding stock that would confer disadvantages to reproduction or longevity in nature.

In 1844, Darwin wrote a long essay describing the role of natural selection as a process of evolution. But he was reluctant to publish it, preferring to assemble more evidence first. Darwin's hand was forced in 1858, when he received a letter and manuscript from another traveling English naturalist, Alfred Russel Wallace, who was studying the plants and animals of the Malay Archipelago. Wallace asked Darwin to evaluate his manuscript, which included an explanation of natural selection almost identical to Darwin's. Darwin was at first dismayed, believing Wallace to have preempted his idea. Parts of Darwin's 1844 essay, together with Wallace's manuscript, were presented to the Linnean Society of London on July 1, 1858, thereby crediting both men for the idea of natural selection. Darwin then worked quickly to finish his full-length book, *On the Origin of Species*, which was published the following year.

 View in Achieve
Animation 19.1 Natural Selection

Although Darwin and Wallace independently articulated the concept of natural selection, Darwin developed his ideas first. Furthermore, *On the Origin of Species* proved to be a stunning work of scholarship that provided exhaustive evidence from many fields supporting both the premise of evolution itself and the understanding of natural selection as a process of evolution. Thus both concepts are more closely associated with Darwin than with Wallace.

The publication of *On the Origin of Species* in 1859 stirred considerable interest (and controversy) among scientists and the public alike. Scientists spent much of the rest of the nineteenth century amassing biological and paleontological data to test evolutionary ideas and document the history of life on Earth. By 1900, the fact of biological evolution (defined at that time as change in the physical characteristics of populations over time) was established beyond any reasonable doubt. As biologists discovered the details of genetic inheritance in the twentieth century, the genetic mechanisms of evolution became clear. The development of methods for sequencing DNA in the late 1970s allowed biologists to document evolutionary changes within and between species with great precision. This technology led to explosive growth in the field of evolutionary biology. In the past four decades, well over a quarter of a million scientific papers on evolutionary observations, experiments, and theory have been published.

KEY CONCEPT
19.1 Recap and Assess

Evolution, or changes in the genetic composition of biological populations over time, is directly observable. Natural selection occurs when specific genetic changes increase the rates of survival or reproduction of individuals in a population relative to individuals that do not possess those changes. Under such conditions, the frequency of the favored genetic change increases in the population from one generation to the next.

1. Why do biologists speak of "evolutionary theory" if the facts of evolution are not in doubt?

2. Antibiotics are drugs that kill most bacteria, but genetic mutations can allow some individual bacteria to survive short-term exposure to these drugs. How would you expect the frequency of resistant bacteria to change over time in populations of bacteria that were exposed to an antibiotic drug on a regular basis? Why do you think antibiotics come with a warning to take the full course of the treatment, rather than stopping after you begin to feel better?

3. In what ways does selection by humans in breeding agricultural crops differ from natural selection? Give an example of a trait that might be favored by artificial selection in agriculture, but selected against by natural selection in a wild population.

4. Natural selection cannot adapt populations to conditions they have not experienced. Yet many organisms appear to respond to natural events before they happen. For example, many mammals go into hibernation while it is still quite warm. Similarly, many birds leave the temperate zone for their southern wintering grounds long before winter has arrived. How do you think such "anticipatory" behaviors evolve?

5. As more humans live longer, many people face degenerative conditions such as Alzheimer's disease that (in most cases) are linked to advancing age. Assuming that some individuals may be genetically predisposed to successfully combat these conditions, is it likely that natural selection alone would act to favor such a predisposition in human populations? Why or why not?

Although the importance of natural selection to evolution has been confirmed in many thousands of scientific studies, it is not the only process that drives evolution. In the next key concept we'll consider a more complete view of evolutionary processes and how they operate.

KEY CONCEPT
19.2 Mutation, Selection, Gene Flow, Genetic Drift, and Nonrandom Mating Result in Evolution

Learning Objectives

19.2.1 Distinguish between the everyday and scientific uses of the terms "adapt" and "evolve."

19.2.2 Describe how each of the five processes of evolution can result in changes in gene frequencies across generations of a population.

The word "evolution" is often used in a general sense to mean simply "change," but in a biological context "evolution" refers specifically to change in the genetic makeup of populations over time. Developmental changes that occur in a single individual over the course of the life cycle are not the result of evolutionary change. Evolution is genetic change across generations of a **population**—a group of individuals of a single species that live and interbreed in a particular geographic area at the same time. It is important to remember that *individuals do not evolve; populations do*.

The premise of natural selection was one of Darwin's principal insights and has been demonstrated to be an important process of evolution, but natural selection does not act alone. Four additional processes—mutation, gene flow, genetic drift, and nonrandom mating—affect the genetic makeup of populations over time. Before we consider how the other processes can change the frequencies of gene variants in a population, we need to understand how mutation brings such variants into existence.

Mutation generates genetic variation

The origin of genetic variation is mutation. As described in Key Concept 15.1, a mutation is any change in the nucleotide sequences of an organism's DNA. The process of DNA replication is not perfect, and some changes appear almost every time a genome is replicated. Mutations occur randomly with respect to an organism's needs; it is natural selection acting on this random variation that results in adaptation. Most mutations are either harmful to their bearers (deleterious mutations) or have no effect (neutral mutations). But a few mutations are beneficial, and even previously deleterious or neutral alleles may become advantageous if environmental conditions change. In addition, mutation can restore genetic variation that other evolutionary processes have removed. Thus mutation both creates and helps maintain genetic variation in populations.

Mutation rates can be high, especially in viruses and bacteria, which explains the rapid evolution of many pathogens. But in many protein-coding genes of multicellular organisms, the mutation rate is very low (on the order of 10^{-8} to 10^{-9} changes per base pair of DNA per generation). Even low overall mutation rates, however, create considerable genetic variation, because each of a large number of genes may change, and populations often contain large numbers of individuals. For example, if the probability of a point mutation (an addition, deletion, or substitution of a single base) were 10^{-9} per base pair per generation, then each human gamete—the DNA of which contains 3×10^9 base pairs—would average three new point mutations ($3 \times 10^9 \times 10^{-9} = 3$), and each zygote would carry an average of six new mutations. The current human population of about 7 billion people would thus be expected to carry about 42 billion new mutations (i.e., changes in the nucleotide sequences of their DNA that were not present one generation earlier). So even though the mutation rate in humans is low, human populations still contain enormous genetic variation on which other evolutionary processes can act.

As a result of mutation, different forms of a gene, known as **alleles**, may exist at a particular chromosomal locus (see Key Concept 12.1). At any particular locus, a single diploid individual has no more than two of the alleles found in the population to which it belongs. The sum of all copies of all alleles at all loci found in a population constitutes that population's **gene pool** (**Figure 19.2**). (We can also refer to the gene pool for a particular chromosomal locus or loci.) The gene pool is the sum of the genetic variation in the population. The proportion of each allele in the gene pool is the allele frequency. Likewise, the proportion of each genotype among individuals in the population is the genotype frequency.

A simple experiment demonstrates how mutations accumulate in populations in a continual, almost constant fashion over time (**Figure 19.3**). Lines of the bacterium *E. coli* were grown in the laboratory for 20,000 generations, and the genomes were sequenced from individuals in the experimental lines at least once every 5,000 generations. Over the experiment, the lines accumulated about 45 changes to their genomes, and these changes appeared at a fairly constant rate over time. Populations of all living organisms experience a similar accumulation of mutations over time (although the rate of change differs among species), and these changes provide the raw material for evolution.

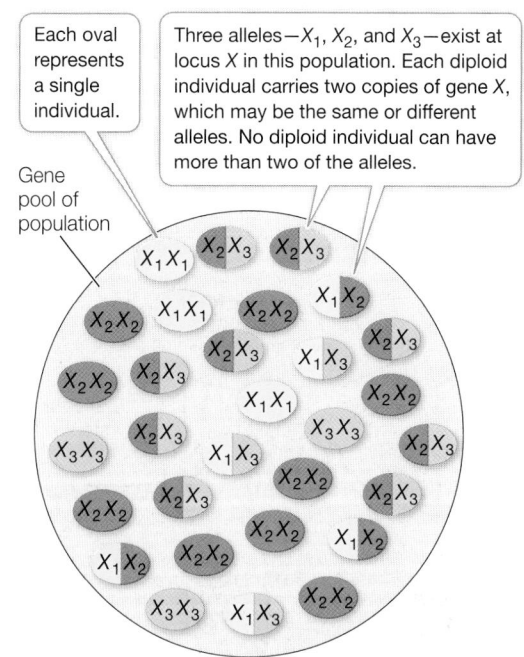

Figure 19.2 A Gene Pool   A gene pool is the sum of all the alleles found in a population or at a particular locus in that population. This figure shows the gene pool for one locus, *X*, in a population of diploid organisms. The allele frequencies in this case are 0.20 for X_1, 0.50 for X_2, and 0.30 for X_3 (see Figure 19.10).

Connect the Concepts   As discussed in Key Concept 12.1, alleles of different genes assort independently in meiosis. The frequencies with which different allele combinations will be expressed in offspring can be calculated using a Punnett square or probability theory.

Figure 19.3 Mutations Accumulate Continually   An experimental lineage of the bacterium *Escherichia coli* was propagated in the laboratory for 20,000 generations. Genomes were sequenced from individuals sampled at various points during the experiment and were compared with the genome of the ancestral clone. Note that mutations accumulated at a relatively constant rate throughout the experiment. (After J. E. Barrick et al. 2009. *Nature* 461: 1245–1247.)

Selection for terminal buds

Cabbage

Selection for flower clusters

Cauliflower

Brassica oleracea
(a common wild mustard)

Selection for lateral buds

Selection for stems and flowers

Brussels sprouts

Broccoli

Selection for stem

Selection for leaves

Kohlrabi

Kale

Figure 19.4 Many Vegetables from One Species   All the crop plants shown here derive from a single wild mustard species. European agriculturalists produced these cultivars by selecting and breeding plants with unusually large buds, stems, leaves, or flowers. The results substantiate the vast amount of variation present in the gene pool of the ancestral species.

Selection acting on genetic variation leads to new phenotypes

As a result of mutation, the gene pools of nearly all populations contain variation for many traits. Selection that favors different traits can lead to distinctively different lineages that descend from the same ancestor. For example, artificial selection for different traits in a single European species of wild mustard produced many important crop plants (**Figure 19.4**). Agriculturalists were able to achieve these results because the original mustard population had genetic variation for the characters of interest (such as stem thickness or number of leaves).

Darwin compared artificial selection, which was commonly practiced by animal and plant breeders, with natural selection that occurred in natural populations. Many of Darwin's observations on the nature of variation and selection came from domesticated plants and animals. Darwin bred pigeons and thus knew firsthand the astonishing diversity in color, size, form, and behavior that breeders could achieve (**Figure 19.5**). He recognized close parallels between selection by breeders and selection in nature. Whereas artificial selection resulted in traits that were preferred by the human breeders, natural selection resulted in traits that helped organisms survive and reproduce more effectively. In both cases, selection simply increased the frequency of the favored trait from one generation to the next.

Laboratory experiments also demonstrate the existence of considerable genetic variation in populations, and show how this variation can lead to evolution through selection. In one such experiment, investigators bred populations of the fruit fly *Drosophila melanogaster* with high or low numbers of bristles on their abdomens from an initial population with intermediate numbers of bristles. After 35 generations, all flies in both the high- and low-bristle lineages had bristle numbers that fell well outside the range found in the original population (**Figure 19.6**). Selection for high and low bristle numbers resulted in new combinations of the many different genes that were present in the original population, so that the phenotypic variation seen in subsequent generations fell outside the phenotypic variation seen in the original population.

Figure 19.5 Artificial Selection   Charles Darwin, who raised pigeons as a hobby, noted similar forces at work in artificial and natural selection. The "fancy" pigeons shown here represent 3 of the more than 300 varieties derived from the wild Rock Pigeon (*Columba livia*; far left) by artificial selection on characters such as color and feather distribution.

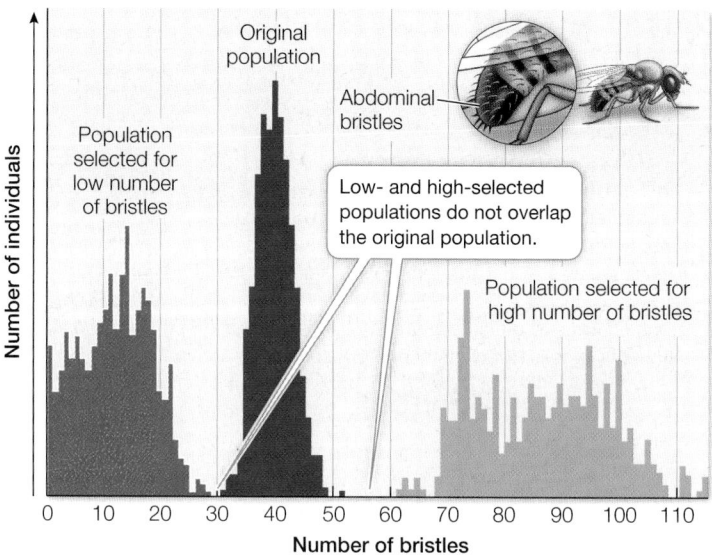

Figure 19.6 Artificial Selection Reveals Genetic Variation
When investigators subjected *Drosophila melanogaster* to artificial selection for abdominal bristle number, that character evolved rapidly. The graph
shows the number of flies with different numbers of bristles in the original
population and after 35 generations of artificial selection for low and for
high bristle numbers. (After G. A. Clayton et al. 1956. *J Genet* 55: 131–151.)

Q: How did flies in the selected populations end up with fewer
or more bristles than were observed in any of the flies in the
original population?

Natural selection increases the frequency of beneficial mutations in populations

Darwin knew that far more individuals of most species are born
than survive to reproduce. He also knew that, although offspring
tend to resemble their parents, the offspring of most organisms
are not identical either to their parents or to one another. He suggested that slight differences among individuals affect the chance
that a given individual will survive and reproduce, which increases
the frequency of the favored trait in the next generation. A favored
trait that spreads through a population by natural selection is
known as an **adaptation**; this word is used to describe both the
trait itself and the process that produces the trait.

Biologists regard an organism as being adapted to a particular
environment when they can demonstrate that a slightly different
organism reproduces and survives less well in that environment.
To understand adaptation, biologists compare the performances
of individuals that differ in their traits.

In the story that opens this chapter, we learned that many groups
of moths have evolved the ability to detect ultrasounds of bats, which
allows the moths to fly away from the bats or use evasive flight behavior to avoid predation. But many species of moths are unable to
hear bats, so these moths have to rely on other strategies to avoid bat
detection. As described in **Investigating Life: Do Long Wing Tails
Help Moths Escape Bat Predation?**, Jesse Barber and his colleagues
noticed that several groups of non-hearing moths have long extensions of their wings ("wing tails"), and they wondered if these structures might serve to distract echolating bats and allow the moths
to escape. To find out, the researchers cut the wing tails off some

individual moths and compared the rates of bat predation, and
flight performance, in the moths with and without wing tails.
They found that the wing tails had very little effect on a moth's
flying efficiency, but conveyed a huge advantage in reducing bat
predation. The wing tails flutter as the moths fly, and the echolocation system of the bats is more likely to locate the fluttering
nonessential wing tail than the body of the moth, thereby allowing a moth to survive a bat attack. Thus the wing tails appear to
be an adaptation that helps moths avoid bat predation.

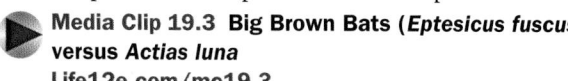   **Media Clip 19.3 Big Brown Bats (*Eptesicus fuscus*)
versus *Actias luna***
Life12e.com/mc19.3

▶ **View in Achieve**
Simulation 19.1 Natural Selection

Gene flow may change allele frequencies

Few populations are completely isolated from other populations
of the same species. Migration of individuals and movements of
gametes (in pollen, for example) between populations—a phenomenon called **gene flow**—can change allele frequencies in
a population. If the arriving individuals survive and reproduce
in their new location, they may add new alleles to the population's gene pool, or they may change the frequencies of alleles
present in the original population.

   View in Achieve
Simulation 19.2 Diversity

Connect the Concepts If gene flow between two populations
stops, those populations may diverge and become different species;
see Key Concept 22.2.

Genetic drift may cause large changes in small populations

In small populations, **genetic drift**—random changes in allele
frequencies from one generation to the next—may produce large
changes in allele frequencies over time. Harmful alleles may increase in frequency, and rare advantageous alleles may be lost.
Even in large populations, genetic drift can influence the frequencies of neutral alleles (which do not affect the survival and reproductive rates of their bearers).

   View in Achieve
Simulation 19.3 Genetic Drift

To illustrate the effects of genetic drift, suppose there are only
two females in a small population of normally brown mice, and
one of these females carries a newly arisen dominant allele that
produces black fur. Even in the absence of any selection, it is unlikely that the two females will produce exactly the same number of offspring. Even if they do produce identical litter sizes and
identical numbers of litters, chance events that have nothing to
do with genetic characteristics are likely to result in differential
mortality among their offspring. If each female produces one litter, but a flood envelops the black female's nest and kills all of her
offspring, the novel allele could be lost from the population in just
one generation. In contrast, if the brown female's litter is lost, then
the frequency of the newly arisen allele (and phenotype) for black
fur will rise dramatically in just one generation.

▶InvestigatingLIFE   Do Long Wing Tails Help Moths Escape Bat Predation?

Experiment

Original Paper: J. R. Barber et al. 2015. Moth tails divert bat attack: Evolution of acoustic deflection. *Proc Nat Acad Sci USA* 112: 2812–2816.

Many groups of moths have evolved the ability to hear the ultrasounds that bats produce for echolocation. These moths can then use evasive behavior to avoid predation by the bats. But almost half of all moths lack ears to hear the sounds produced by bats. Jesse Barber and his colleagues noticed that many non-hearing moths have long, posterior wing extensions ("wing tails"), and wondered if these wing tails might serve to deflect attacks by echolocating bats.

HYPOTHESIS▶ As the long tails on moth wings flutter in flight, they serve to deflect the attacks of echolocating bats.

METHOD▶

1. Remove the wing tails from an experimental group of luna moths (*Actias luna*).

2. In an experimental setting, compare the capture rate by big brown bats (*Eptesicus fuscus*) of moths with and without wing tails.

3. Control for the effects of wing tail size by conducting comparable experiments on moths with various wing tail sizes, in species that naturally lack wing tails.

4. Compare the flying efficiency of luna moths with and without wing tails, to test the possibility that wing tails improve flying performance.

RESULTS▶ The successful capture rate by bats of luna moths was much higher in moths that had their wing tails removed. Large wing tail size does seem to have an effect on reducing successful preda-

tion as well, but the long wing tails of luna moths provide a much greater benefit to predation avoidance than predicted by the increase in wing tail size alone. The removal of wing tails from luna moths had no significant effect on the flight performance of the moths. The graph shows successful capture rate by bats of luna moths with and without wing tails. Brackets show 95% confidence intervals.

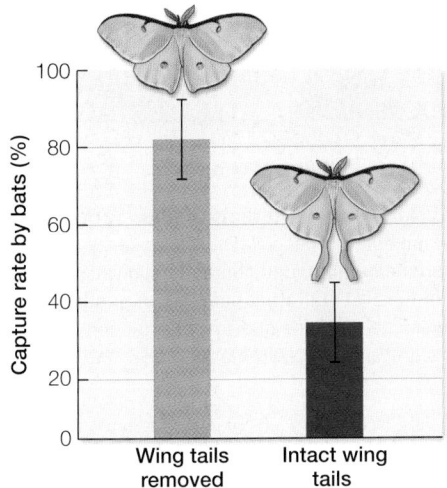

CONCLUSION▶ The tail extensions on the wings of luna moths reduce the rate of successful bat attacks on the moths. Bats attack the fluttering wing tails of luna moths rather than their bodies, allowing the moths to escape. The wing tails do not provide improvements in flight performance, but rather in predation avoidance.

Genetic drift is especially potent when a population is reduced dramatically in size. Even populations that are normally large may occasionally pass through environmental events that only a small number of individuals survive, a situation known as a **population bottleneck**. The effect of genetic drift in such a situation is illustrated in **Figure 19.7**, in which red and yellow beans represent two alleles of a gene. Most of the beans in the small sample of the "population" that "survives" the bottleneck event are, just by chance, red, so the new population has a much higher frequency of red beans than the previous generation had. In a real population, the red and yellow allele frequencies would be described as having "drifted."

A population forced through a bottleneck is likely to lose much of its genetic variation. For example, when Europeans first arrived in North America, millions of Greater Prairie-Chickens

Figure 19.7 A Population Bottleneck Population bottlenecks occur when only a few individuals survive a random event. The result may be a change in allele frequencies within the population.

1 The original population has approximately equal frequencies of red and yellow alleles.

2 A chance environmental event greatly reduces the population size.

3 The allele frequencies in the surviving population differ from those of the original population.

4 As the population grows following the bottleneck event, its allele frequencies reflect the surviving population (more red than yellow alleles).

Work with the Data

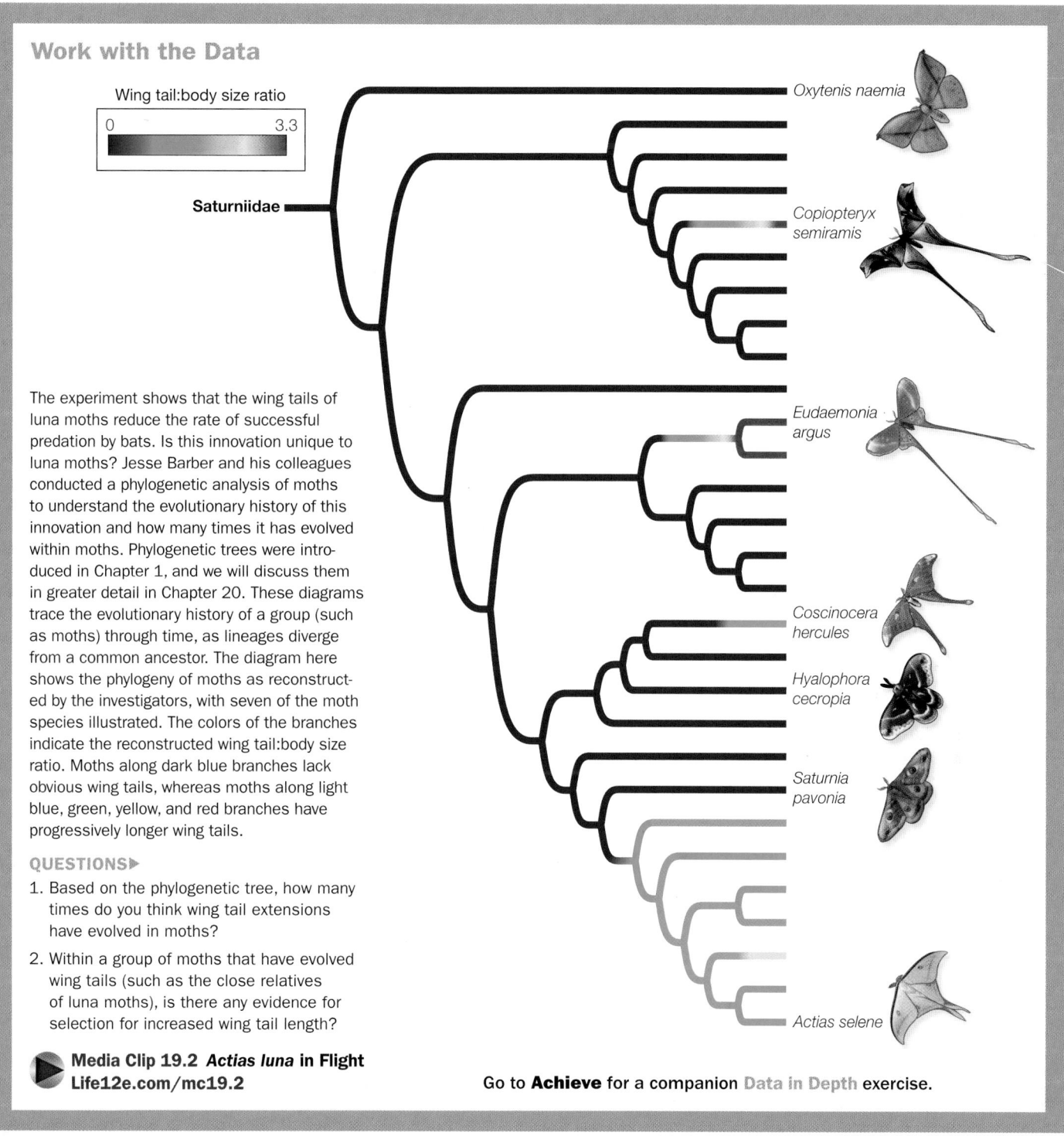

Wing tail:body size ratio

0   3.3

Saturniidae

The experiment shows that the wing tails of luna moths reduce the rate of successful predation by bats. Is this innovation unique to luna moths? Jesse Barber and his colleagues conducted a phylogenetic analysis of moths to understand the evolutionary history of this innovation and how many times it has evolved within moths. Phylogenetic trees were introduced in Chapter 1, and we will discuss them in greater detail in Chapter 20. These diagrams trace the evolutionary history of a group (such as moths) through time, as lineages diverge from a common ancestor. The diagram here shows the phylogeny of moths as reconstructed by the investigators, with seven of the moth species illustrated. The colors of the branches indicate the reconstructed wing tail:body size ratio. Moths along dark blue branches lack obvious wing tails, whereas moths along light blue, green, yellow, and red branches have progressively longer wing tails.

Oxytenis naemia

Copiopteryx semiramis

Eudaemonia argus

Coscinocera hercules

Hyalophora cecropia

Saturnia pavonia

Actias selene

QUESTIONS▶

1. Based on the phylogenetic tree, how many times do you think wing tail extensions have evolved in moths?

2. Within a group of moths that have evolved wing tails (such as the close relatives of luna moths), is there any evidence for selection for increased wing tail length?

▶ **Media Clip 19.2 *Actias luna* in Flight**
Life12e.com/mc19.2

Go to **Achieve** for a companion Data in Depth exercise.

(*Tympanuchus cupido*) inhabited the midwestern prairies. As a result of hunting and habitat destruction by the new settlers, the Illinois population of this species plummeted from about 100 million birds in 1900 to fewer than 50 individuals in the 1990s. A comparison of DNA from birds collected in Illinois during the middle of the twentieth century with DNA from the surviving population in the 1990s showed that Illinois prairie-chickens have lost most of their genetic diversity. Loss of genetic variation in small populations is one of the problems facing biologists who attempt to protect endangered species.

Genetic drift can have similar effects when a few pioneering individuals colonize a new region. Because of its small size, the colonizing population is unlikely to possess all of the alleles found in the gene pool of its source population. The resulting change in genetic variation, called a **founder effect**, is equivalent to that in a large population reduced by a bottleneck.

Nonrandom mating can change genotype or allele frequencies

Mating patterns often alter genotype frequencies because the individuals in a population do not choose mates at random. For example, self-fertilization is common in many groups of organisms, especially plants. Any time individuals mate preferentially with other individuals of the same genotype (including themselves), homozygous genotypes will increase in frequency and heterozygous genotypes will decrease in frequency over time. The opposite effect (more heterozygotes, fewer homozygotes) is expected when individuals mate primarily or exclusively with individuals of different genotypes.

Many nonrandom mating systems produce changes in genotype frequencies but not in allele frequencies, and thus do not, by themselves, result in evolutionary change in a population. However, nonrandom mating systems that result in different reproductive success among individuals do produce allele frequency changes from one generation to the next. One such process, **sexual selection**, occurs when individuals of one sex mate preferentially with particular individuals of the opposite sex rather than at random.

Sexual selection was first suggested by Charles Darwin, who developed the idea to explain the evolution of conspicuous traits that would appear to inhibit survival, such as bright colors and elaborate courtship displays in males of many species. He hypothesized that these features either improved the ability of their bearers to compete for access to mates (intrasexual selection) or made their bearers more attractive to members of the opposite sex (intersexual selection).

Darwin argued that while natural selection typically favors traits that enhance the survival of their bearers or their bearers' descendants, sexual selection is primarily about successful reproduction. An animal that survives but fails to reproduce makes no contribution to the next generation. Thus sexual selection may favor traits that enhance an individual's chances of reproduction even when these traits reduce its chances of survival. For example, females may be more likely to see or hear males with a given trait (and thus be more likely to mate with those males), even though the favored trait also increases the chances that the male will be seen or heard by a predator.

One example of a trait that Darwin attributed to sexual selection is the remarkable tail of the male African Long-tailed Widowbird (*Euplectes progne*), which is longer than the bird's head and body combined (**Figure 19.8**). Male widowbirds normally select, and defend from other males, a territory where they perform courtship displays to attract females. To investigate whether sexual selection drove the evolution of widowbird tails, a biologist clipped the tails of some captured male widowbirds and lengthened the tails of others by gluing on additional feathers. He then cut and reglued the tail feathers of still other males, which served as controls. Both short- and long-tailed males successfully defended their display territories, indicating that a long tail does not confer an advantage in male–male competition. However, males with artificially elongated tails attracted about four times more females than did males with shortened tails (**Figure 19.9**). Thus males with long tails pass on their genes to more offspring than do males with short tails, which leads to the evolution of this unusual trait.

Euplectes progne

Figure 19.8 What Is the Advantage? The extensive tail of the male African Long-tailed Widowbird inhibits its ability to fly. Darwin attributed the evolution of this seemingly nonadaptive trait to sexual selection.

Experiment

Figure 19.9 Sexual Selection in Action

Original Paper: M. Andersson. 1982. Female choice selects for extreme tail length in a widowbird. *Nature* 299: 818–820.

Behavioral ecologist Malte Andersson tested Darwin's hypothesis that excessively long tails evolved in male widowbirds because female preference for longer-tailed males increased their mating and reproductive success.

HYPOTHESIS▶ Female widowbirds prefer to mate with the male that displays the longest tail; longer-tailed males thus are favored by sexual selection because they will father more offspring.

METHOD▶

1. Capture males and artificially lengthen or shorten tails by cutting or gluing on feathers. In a control group, cut and replace tails to their normal length (to control for the effects of tail cutting).

2. Release the males to establish their territories and mate.

3. Count the nests with eggs or young on each male's territory.

RESULTS▶ Male widowbirds with artificially shortened tails established and defended display sites successfully but fathered fewer offspring than did control or unmanipulated males. Males with artificially lengthened tails fathered the most offspring.

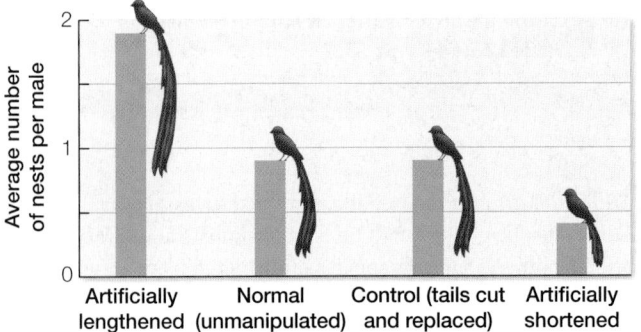

CONCLUSION▶ Sexual selection in widowbirds has favored the evolution of long tails in the males.

19.2 Recap and Assess

Evolutionary processes change the genetic structure of a population from one generation to the next. These processes include mutation, natural selection, gene flow, genetic drift, and nonrandom mating.

1. In everyday language, we speak of individuals "evolving" over their lifetime (if, for example, they change their opinion about an issue). This sense of "evolving" is clearly very different than what biologists mean when they refer to biological evolution. Explain why changes within an individual's lifetime are not examples of biological evolution.

2. How is mutation a necessary component of the evolutionary processes?

3. What kinds of traits would be more likely to evolve by genetic drift than by natural selection?

4. Describe conditions in which nonrandom mating does and does not lead to evolution.

5. Why might gene flow slow the evolution of a population?

The processes of mutation, natural selection, gene flow, genetic drift, and nonrandom mating can all result in evolutionary change. We will consider next how evolutionary change that results from these processes is measured.

19.3 Evolution Can Be Measured by Changes in Allele Frequencies

Learning Objectives

19.3.1 Calculate the allele frequencies for two alleles at a given locus in a diploid population.

19.3.2 Calculate observed and expected genotype frequencies from allele frequencies based on the principles of Hardy–Weinberg equilibrium.

19.3.3 Interpret data and formulate hypotheses to explain deviations from Hardy–Weinberg expectations in observed genotype frequencies.

Much of evolution occurs through gradual changes in the relative frequencies of different alleles in a population from one generation to the next. Major genetic changes can also be sudden, as happens when two formerly separated populations merge and hybridize, or when genes within a population are duplicated within the genome. But in most cases, we measure evolution by looking at changes in allele and genotype frequencies in populations over time.

A population's genetic structure can be described by frequencies of alleles and genotypes

To measure allele frequencies in a population precisely, we would need to count every allele at every locus in every individual in the population. Fortunately, we do not need to make such complete measurements because we can reliably estimate allele frequencies for a given locus by counting alleles in a reasonably sized sample of individuals from the population. The sum of all allele frequencies at a locus is equal to 1, so measures of allele frequency range from 0 to 1.

An allele's frequency is calculated using the following formula:

$$p = \frac{\text{number of copies of the allele in the population}}{\text{total number of copies of all alleles in the population}}$$

If only two alleles (we'll call them A and a) for a given locus are found among the members of a diploid population, those alleles can combine to form three different genotypes: AA, Aa, and aa. A population with more than one allele at a locus is said to be polymorphic ("many forms") at that locus. Applying the formula just mentioned, as shown in **Figure 19.10**, we can calculate the relative frequencies of alleles A and a in a population of N individuals as follows:

- Let N_{AA} be the number that are homozygous for the A allele (AA).

- Let N_{Aa} be the number that are heterozygous (Aa).

- Let N_{aa} be the number that are homozygous for the a allele (aa).

Research Tools

Figure 19.10 Calculating Allele and Genotype Frequencies Allele and genotype frequencies for a gene locus with two alleles in the population can be calculated using the equations in panel 1. When the equations are applied to two populations (panel 2), we find that the *frequencies of alleles A and a in the two populations are the same, but the alleles are distributed differently between heterozygous and homozygous genotypes.*

1 In any population, where N is the total number of individuals in the population:

$$\text{Frequency of allele } A = p = \frac{2N_{AA} + N_{Aa}}{2N} \qquad \text{Frequency of allele } a = q = \frac{2N_{aa} + N_{Aa}}{2N}$$

Frequency of genotype $AA = N_{AA}/N$
Frequency of genotype $Aa = N_{Aa}/N$
Frequency of genotype $aa = N_{aa}/N$

2 Compute the allele and genotype frequencies for two separate populations of $N = 200$:

Population 1 (mostly homozygotes)	Population 2 (mostly heterozygotes)
$N_{AA} = 90$, $N_{Aa} = 40$, and $N_{aa} = 70$	$N_{AA} = 45$, $N_{Aa} = 130$, and $N_{aa} = 25$
$p = \dfrac{180 + 40}{400} = 0.55$	$p = \dfrac{90 + 130}{400} = 0.55$
$q = \dfrac{140 + 40}{400} = 0.45$	$q = \dfrac{50 + 130}{400} = 0.45$
Freq. $AA = 90/200 = 0.45$ Freq. $Aa = 40/200 = 0.20$ Freq. $aa = 70/200 = 0.35$	Freq. $AA = 45/200 = 0.225$ Freq. $Aa = 130/200 = 0.65$ Freq. $aa = 25/200 = 0.125$

Note that $N_{AA} + N_{Aa} + N_{aa} = N$, the total number of individuals in the population, and that the total number of copies of both alleles present in the population is $2N$, because each individual is diploid. Each AA individual has two copies of the A allele, and each Aa individual has one copy of the A allele. Therefore the total number of A alleles in the population is $2N_{AA} + N_{Aa}$. Similarly, the total number of a alleles in the population is $2N_{aa} + N_{Aa}$. If p represents the frequency of A, and q represents the frequency of a, then

$$q = \frac{2N_{aa} + N_{Aa}}{2N}$$

and

$$p = \frac{2N_{AA} + N_{Aa}}{2N}$$

The calculations in Figure 19.10 demonstrate two important points. First, notice that for each population, $p + q = 1$, which means that $q = 1 - p$. So when there are only two alleles at a given locus in a population, we can calculate the frequency of one allele and obtain the second allele's frequency by subtraction. If there is only one allele at a given locus in a population, its frequency is 1: the population is then monomorphic at that locus, and the allele is said to be **fixed**.

Second, notice that population 1 (consisting mostly of homozygotes) and population 2 (consisting mostly of heterozygotes) have the same allele frequencies for A and a. Thus they have the same gene pool for this locus. Because the alleles in the gene pool are distributed differently among individuals, however, the genotype frequencies of the two populations differ.

The frequencies of the different alleles at each locus and the frequencies of the different genotypes in a population describe that population's **genetic structure**. Allele frequencies measure the amount of genetic variation in a population, whereas genotype frequencies show how a population's genetic variation is distributed among its members. Other measures, such as the proportion of loci that are polymorphic, are also used to measure variation in populations. With these measurements, it becomes possible to consider how the genetic structure of a population changes or remains the same over generations—that is, to measure evolutionary change.

Evolution will occur unless certain restrictive conditions exist

In 1908, the British mathematician Godfrey Hardy and the German physician Wilhelm Weinberg independently deduced the conditions that must prevail if the genetic structure of a population is to remain the same over time. If the conditions they identified do not exist, then evolution will occur. The resulting principle is known as **Hardy–Weinberg equilibrium**. Hardy–Weinberg equilibrium describes a model in which allele frequencies do not change across generations and genotype frequencies can be predicted from allele frequencies (**Figure 19.11**). The principles of Hardy–Weinberg equilibrium apply only to sexually reproducing organisms. Several conditions must be met for a population to be at Hardy–Weinberg equilibrium. Note that the following

conditions correspond inversely to the five principal processes of evolution (discussed in Key Concept 19.2):

- *There is no mutation.* The alleles present in the population do not change, and no new alleles are added to the gene pool.
- *There is no selection among genotypes.* Individuals with different genotypes have equal probabilities of survival and equal rates of reproduction.

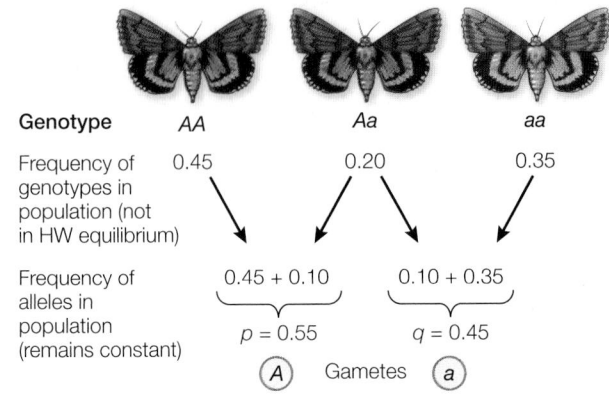

Generation I (Founder population)

Genotype	AA	Aa	aa
Frequency of genotypes in population (not in HW equilibrium)	0.45	0.20	0.35

Frequency of alleles in population (remains constant)

0.45 + 0.10 → $p = 0.55$ 0.10 + 0.35 → $q = 0.45$

Ⓐ   Gametes   ⓐ

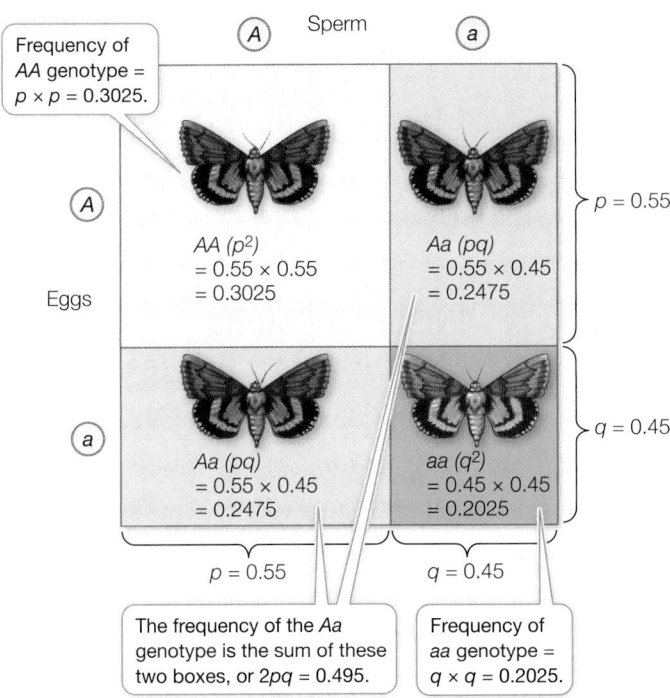

Generation II (Hardy–Weinberg equilibrium restored)

Sperm Ⓐ   ⓐ

Frequency of AA genotype = $p \times p = 0.3025$.

Eggs

Ⓐ | AA (p^2) = 0.55 × 0.55 = 0.3025 | Aa (pq) = 0.55 × 0.45 = 0.2475 | $p = 0.55$

ⓐ | Aa (pq) = 0.55 × 0.45 = 0.2475 | aa (q^2) = 0.45 × 0.45 = 0.2025 | $q = 0.45$

$p = 0.55$ $q = 0.45$

The frequency of the Aa genotype is the sum of these two boxes, or $2pq = 0.495$.

Frequency of aa genotype = $q \times q = 0.2025$.

Figure 19.11 One Generation of Random Mating Restores Hardy–Weinberg Equilibrium   Generation I of this population is made up of migrants from several source populations and so is not initially in Hardy–Weinberg equilibrium. After one generation of random mating, the allele frequencies are unchanged, and the genotype frequencies return to Hardy–Weinberg expectations. The lengths of the sides of each rectangle are proportional to the allele frequencies in the population; the areas of the rectangles are proportional to genotype frequencies.

- *There is no gene flow.* There is no movement of individuals into or out of the population or reproductive contact with other populations.

- *Population size is infinite.* The larger a population, the smaller will be the effect of genetic drift.

- *Mating is random.* Individuals do not preferentially choose mates with certain genotypes.

If these idealized conditions hold, two major consequences follow. First, the frequencies of alleles at a locus remain constant from generation to generation. Second, following one generation of random mating, the genotype frequencies occur in the following proportions:

Genotype	AA	Aa	aa
Frequency	p^2	$2pq$	q^2

To understand why these consequences are important, start by considering a population that is *not* in Hardy–Weinberg equilibrium, such as generation I in Figure 19.11. This could occur, for example, if the initial population is founded by migrants from several other populations, thus violating the Hardy–Weinberg assumption of no gene flow. In this example, generation I has more homozygous individuals and fewer heterozygous individuals than would be expected under Hardy–Weinberg equilibrium (a condition known as heterozygote deficiency).

Even with a starting population that is not in Hardy–Weinberg equilibrium, we can predict that after a single generation of random mating, and if the other Hardy–Weinberg assumptions are not violated, the allele frequencies will remain unchanged, but the genotype frequencies will return to Hardy–Weinberg expectations. Let's explore why this is true.

In generation I of Figure 19.11, the frequency of the *A* allele (*p*) is 0.55. Because we assume that individuals select mates at random, without regard to their genotype, gametes carrying *A* or *a* combine at random—that is, as predicted by the allele frequencies *p* and *q*. Thus in this example the probability that a particular sperm or egg will bear an *A* allele is 0.55. In other words, 55 out of 100 randomly sampled sperm or eggs will bear an *A* allele. Because *q* = 1 − *p*, the probability that a sperm or egg will bear an *a* allele is 1 − 0.55 = 0.45.

To obtain the probability of two *A*-bearing gametes coming together at fertilization, we multiply the two independent probabilities of their occurrence:

$$p \times p = p^2 = (0.55)^2 = 0.3025$$

Therefore 0.3025, or 30.25%, of the offspring in generation II will have homozygous genotype *AA*. Similarly, the probability of two *a*-bearing gametes coming together is

$$q \times q = q^2 = (0.45)^2 = 0.2025$$

which means that 19.25% of generation II will have the *aa* genotype.

There are two ways of producing a heterozygote: an *A* sperm may combine with an *a* egg, the probability of which is *p* × *q*; or an *a* sperm may combine with an *A* egg, the probability of which

is *q* × *p*. Consequently, the overall probability of obtaining a heterozygote is 2*pq*, or 0.495. The frequencies of the *AA*, *Aa*, and *aa* genotypes in generation II of Figure 19.11 now meet Hardy–Weinberg expectations, and the frequencies of the two alleles (*p* and *q*) have not changed from generation I.

Under the assumptions of Hardy–Weinberg equilibrium, allele frequencies *p* and *q* remain constant from generation to generation. If Hardy–Weinberg assumptions are violated and the genotype frequencies in the parental generation are altered (say, by the loss of a large number of *AA* individuals from the population), then the allele frequencies in the next generation will be altered. However, based on the new allele frequencies, another generation of random mating will be sufficient to restore the genotype frequencies to Hardy–Weinberg equilibrium.

 View in Achieve
Simulation 19.4 **Hardy–Weinberg Equilibrium**

Deviations from Hardy–Weinberg equilibrium show that evolution is occurring

You probably have realized that populations in nature never meet the stringent conditions necessary to be at Hardy–Weinberg equilibrium—which explains why all biological populations evolve. Why, then, is this model considered so important for the study of evolution? There are two reasons. First, the equation is useful for predicting the approximate genotype frequencies of a population from its allele frequencies. Second—and crucially—the model allows biologists to evaluate which processes are acting on the evolution of a particular population. The specific patterns of deviation from Hardy–Weinberg equilibrium can help us identify the various processes of evolutionary change.

KEY CONCEPT
19.3 Recap and Assess

Hardy–Weinberg equilibrium describes the theoretical conditions required for evolution *not* to occur. Deviations from Hardy–Weinberg expectations provide information about how evolution *is* occurring in a given population.

1. The following sample lists the genotype at locus *A* for 10 individuals in a diploid population: *AA*, *AA*, *Aa*, *Aa*, *Aa*, *Aa*, *aa*, *aa*, *aa*, *aa*.

   a. Based on this sample, what is the observed frequency of allele *a*? The observed frequency of allele *A*?

   b. What are the observed frequencies of genotypes *aa*, *Aa*, and *AA*?

   c. After one generation of random mating, what would be the Hardy–Weinberg expectations for the frequencies of genotypes *aa*, *Aa*, and *AA*?

2. In a population of toads, allele *A* is present at a frequency of 0.2, and allele *a* is present at a frequency of 0.8. Based on Hardy–Weinberg expectations, what is the expected frequency of the genotype *Aa* in the population?

3. Assume that the observed frequency of the genotype *Aa* in the toad population in Question 2 is 0.15, rather than the expected frequency you calculated. What are some possible explanations?

Our discussion so far has focused on changes in allele frequencies at a single gene locus. Genes do not exist in isolation, however, but interact with one another (and with the environment) to produce an organism's phenotype. What effects can these interactions have on selection?

KEY CONCEPT 19.4 Selection Can Be Stabilizing, Directional, or Disruptive

Learning Objectives

19.4.1 Describe the effect of each type of selection (stabilizing, directional, and disruptive) on phenotype evolution.

19.4.2 Distinguish conditions in which selection is likely to be stabilizing, directional, or disruptive.

Although evolution is defined as changes in the genetic makeup of a population from one generation to the next, natural selection acts directly on the phenotype—that is, on the physical features expressed by an organism with a given genotype—and therefore acts only indirectly on the genotype. The reproductive contribution of a phenotype to subsequent generations relative to the contributions of other phenotypes is called its **fitness**.

Changes in reproductive rate do not necessarily change the genetic structure of a population. For example, if all individuals in a population experience the same increase in reproductive rate (during an environmentally favorable year, for instance), the genetic structure of the population will not change. Changes in numbers of offspring are responsible for increases and decreases in the *size* of a population, but only changes in the *relative* success of different phenotypes in a population will lead to changes in allele frequencies from one generation to the next. The fitness of individuals of a particular phenotype is a function of the probability of those individuals surviving multiplied by the average number of offspring they produce over their lifetimes. In other words, the *fitness of a phenotype is determined by the relative rates of survival and reproduction of individuals with that phenotype.*

Until now, we have only discussed traits influenced by alleles at a single locus. Such traits are often distinguished by discrete qualities (black versus white, or smooth versus wrinkled) and so are called **qualitative traits**. Many traits, however, are influenced by alleles at more than one locus. Such traits are likely to show *continuous* quantitative variation rather than *discrete* qualitative variation, and so are known as **quantitative traits**. For example, body size is a continuous variable; the distribution of body sizes of individuals in a population, a trait that is influenced by genes at many loci as well as by the environment, is likely to resemble a continuous bell-shaped curve.

Natural selection can act on characters with quantitative variation in any one of several different ways, producing quite different results (Figure 19.12):

- **Stabilizing selection** preserves the average characteristics of a population by favoring average individuals.

Figure 19.12 Natural Selection Can Operate in Several Ways The graphs in the left-hand column show the fitness of individuals with different phenotypes for the same character. The right-hand graphs show the distribution of the phenotypes in the population before (dashed line) and after (solid line) the influence of selection.

Q: Why might selection for a trait in a population shift from directional to stabilizing selection over time, even if the optimal value for the trait stays constant?

- **Directional selection** changes the characteristics of a population by favoring individuals that vary in one direction from the mean of the population.

- **Disruptive selection** changes the characteristics of a population by favoring individuals that vary in both directions from the mean of the population.

Stabilizing selection reduces variation in populations

If the smallest and largest individuals in a population contribute fewer offspring to the next generation than do individuals closer to the average size, then stabilizing selection is operating on body size (see Figure 19.12A). Stabilizing selection reduces variation in populations, but it does not change the mean. Natural selection frequently acts in this way, countering increases in variation brought about by sexual recombination, mutation, or gene flow. Rates of phenotypic change in many species are slow because natural selection is often stabilizing. Stabilizing selection operates, for example, on human birth weight. Babies who are lighter or heavier at birth than the population mean die at higher rates than babies whose weights are close to the mean (**Figure 19.13**). In discussions of specific genes, stabilizing selection is often called **purifying selection** because there is selection against any deleterious mutations to the usual gene sequence.

Directional selection favors one extreme

Directional selection is operating when individuals at one extreme of a character distribution contribute more offspring to the next generation than other individuals do, shifting the average value of that character in the population toward that extreme. The opening story in this chapter describes directional selection for improved echolocation abilities in bats over time, and also directional selection for improved ultrasound hearing in their prey.

In the case of a single gene locus, directional selection may result in favoring a particular genetic variant—referred to as **positive selection** for that variant. By favoring one phenotype over another, directional selection results in an increase in the frequencies of alleles that produce the favored phenotype.

Figure 19.14 **A Result of Directional Selection** In the American Southwest, long horns were advantageous for defending calves from attacks by predators, so cows with longer horns were more likely to raise calves successfully. As a result, horn length in feral herds of cattle increased between the early 1500s and the 1860s, leading to the Texas Longhorn breed. This evolutionary trend has been maintained by modern ranchers practicing artificial selection.

Courtesy of David Hillis

If directional selection operates over many generations, an evolutionary trend is seen in the population (see Figure 19.12B). Evolutionary trends often continue for many generations, but they can be reversed if the environment changes and different phenotypes are favored, or halted when an optimal phenotype is reached or trade-offs between different adaptational advantages oppose further change. The character then undergoes stabilizing selection.

The long horns of Texas Longhorn cattle (**Figure 19.14**) are an example of a trait that has evolved through directional selection. Texas Longhorns are descendants of cattle brought to the New World by Christopher Columbus, who picked up a few cattle in the Canary Islands and brought them to the island of Hispaniola in 1493. The cattle multiplied, and their descendants were taken to the mainland of Mexico. Spaniards exploring what would become Texas and the southwestern United States brought these cattle with them, and some of them escaped and formed feral herds. Populations of feral cattle increased greatly over the next few hundred years, but there was heavy predation from bears, mountain lions, and wolves, especially on the young calves. Cows with longer horns were more successful in protecting their calves against attacks, and over a few hundred years the average horn length in the feral herds increased considerably. In addition, the cattle evolved resistance to endemic diseases of the Southwest, as well as higher fecundity and longevity. Texas Longhorns often live and produce calves well into their twenties—about twice as long as many breeds of cattle that have been artificially selected by humans for traits such as high fat content or high milk production (which are examples of artificial directional selection).

Disruptive selection favors extremes over the mean

When disruptive selection operates, individuals at opposite extremes of a character distribution contribute more offspring to the next generation than do individuals close to the mean, which increases variation in the population (see Figure 19.12C).

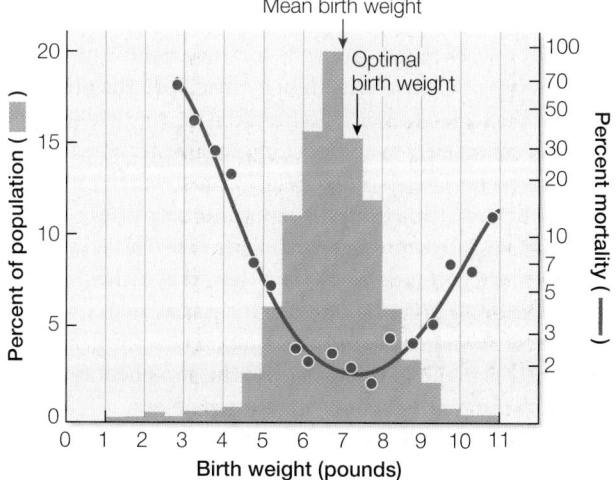

Figure 19.13 **Human Birth Weight Is Influenced by Stabilizing Selection** Babies that weigh more or less than average are more likely to die soon after birth than are babies with weights closer to the population mean. (After L. L Cavalli-Sforza and W. F. Bodmer. 1971. *The Genetics of Human Populations*. W. H. Freeman and Company: San Francisco.)

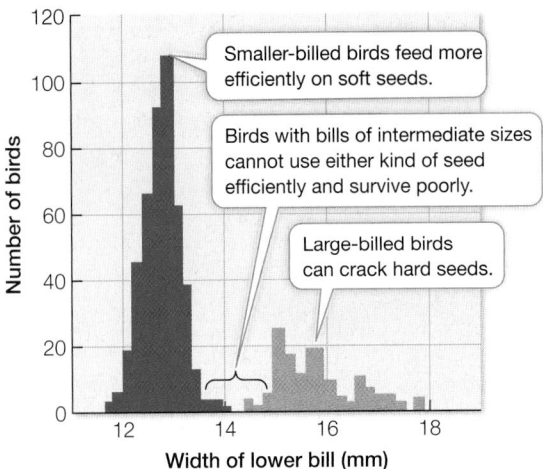

Figure 19.15 Disruptive Selection Results in a Bimodal Character Distribution The bimodal distribution of bill size in the black-bellied seedcracker (*Pyrenestes ostrinus*) of West Africa is a result of disruptive selection, which favors individuals with larger and smaller bill sizes over individuals with intermediate-sized bills. (After T. B. Smith. 1993. *Nature* 363: 618–620.)

The strikingly bimodal (two-peaked) distribution of bill size in the Black-bellied Seedcracker (*Pyrenestes ostrinus*), a West African finch (**Figure 19.15**), illustrates how disruptive selection can influence populations in nature. The seeds of two types of sedges (marsh plants) are the most abundant food source for these finches during part of the year. Birds with large bills can readily crack the hard seeds of the sedge *Scleria verrucosa*. Birds with small bills can crack *S. verrucosa* seeds only with difficulty; however, they feed more efficiently on the soft seeds of *S. goossensii* than do birds with larger bills. Young finches whose bills deviate markedly from the two predominant bill sizes do not survive as well as finches whose bills are close to one of the two sizes represented by the distribution peaks. Because there are few abundant food sources in the finches' environment, and because the seeds of the two sedges do not overlap in hardness, birds with intermediate-sized bills are less efficient in using either one of the species' principal food sources. Disruptive selection therefore maintains a bimodal bill size distribution.

KEY CONCEPT
19.4 Recap and Assess

Natural selection can both change and stabilize phenotypes within populations. Directional selection can result in continuous change to phenotypes; stabilizing selection slows change from a favored phenotype; and disruptive selection can result in one population that exhibits multiple distinct phenotypes.

1. Describe the different expected outcomes of stabilizing, directional, and disruptive selection.
2. Why would you expect selection on human birth weight to be stabilizing rather than directional?
3. Offer some examples of extreme phenotypes in animal or plant populations that could be explained by directional selection.

Genetic drift, stabilizing selection, and directional selection all tend to reduce genetic variation within populations. Nevertheless, as we

have seen, most populations harbor considerable genetic variation. What processes maintain genetic variation within populations?

KEY CONCEPT 19.5
Selection Can Maintain Variation within and among Populations

Learning Objectives

19.5.1 Explain how genetic variation is useful for a species in the face of environmental variability.

19.5.2 Describe how clinal variation within a species may be maintained through different selection pressures across the range of the species.

Genetic variation is the raw material on which mechanisms of evolution act. But if favored alleles increase in frequency in populations, then why aren't other alleles always lost from the population? In this key concept we discuss some factors that affect how genetic variation is maintained within populations.

Frequency-dependent selection maintains genetic variation within populations

Natural selection often preserves variation as a polymorphism (the presence of two or more variants of a character in the same population). When the fitness of a given phenotype depends on its frequency in a population, a polymorphism may be maintained by a process known as **frequency-dependent selection**. *Perissodus microlepis*, a small fish that lives in Lake Tanganyika in East Africa, provides an example of frequency-dependent selection.

P. microlepis feeds on the scales of other fishes, approaching its prey from behind and dashing in to bite off several scales from the prey's flank. Because of an asymmetrical jaw joint, the mouth of this scale-eating species opens either to the right or to the left; the direction is genetically determined (**Figure 19.16**). "Right-mouthed" individuals always attack from the victim's left, and "left-mouthed" individuals always attack from the victim's right. The distorted mouth enlarges the area of teeth in contact with the prey's flank, but only if the scale-eater attacks from the appropriate side.

Prey fishes are alert to approaching scale-eaters, so attacks are more likely to be successful if the prey must watch both flanks. Vigilance by prey thus favors equal numbers of right- and left-mouthed scale-eaters in a population, because if attacks from one side were more common than the other, prey fishes would pay more attention to potential attacks from that side. Over an 11-year study of *P. microlepis* in Lake Tanganyika, the genetic polymorphism was found to be stable, and the two phenotypes of the scale-eaters remained at about equal frequencies.

Heterozygote advantage maintains polymorphic loci

In many cases, different alleles of a particular gene are advantageous under different environmental conditions. Most organisms experience a wide variety of environmental conditions over time. A night is dramatically different from the preceding day. A cold, cloudy day differs from a clear, hot one. Day length and temperature change

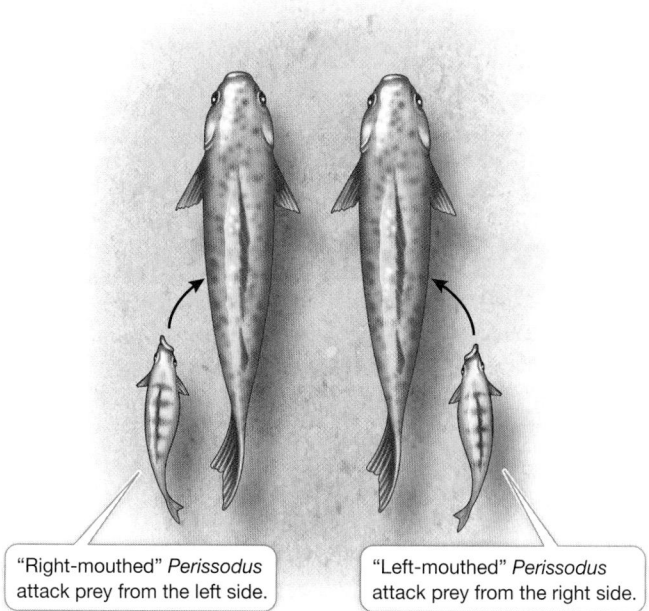

"Right-mouthed" *Perissodus* attack prey from the left side.

"Left-mouthed" *Perissodus* attack prey from the right side.

Figure 19.16 A Stable Polymorphism   Frequency-dependent selection maintains equal proportions of left- and right-mouthed individuals of the scale-eating fish *Perissodus microlepis*.

seasonally. For many genes, a single allele is unlikely to perform well under all these conditions. In such cases, heterozygous individuals (with two different alleles) are likely to outperform homozygous individuals (with only one of those two alleles).

Colias butterflies of the Rocky Mountains live in environments where dawn temperatures are often too cold, and afternoon temperatures too hot, for the butterflies to fly. Populations of these butterflies are polymorphic for a gene that encodes the enzyme phosphoglucose isomerase (PGI), which influences how well a butterfly flies at different temperatures. Butterflies with certain PGI genotypes can fly better during the cold hours of early morning; others perform better during midday heat. The optimal body temperature for flight is 35°C–39°C, but some butterflies can fly with body temperatures as low as 29°C or as high as 40°C. During spells of unusually hot weather, heat-tolerant genotypes are favored; during spells of unusually cool weather, cold-tolerant genotypes are favored.

Heterozygous *Colias* butterflies can fly over a greater range of temperatures than homozygous individuals, which should give them an advantage in foraging and finding mates. A test of this prediction found that heterozygous males did indeed have a mating advantage, and further, that this advantage maintains the polymorphism in the population (**Figure 19.17**). Of course, the heterozygous genotype can never become fixed in the population, because the offspring of two heterozygotes will always include both classes of homozygotes in addition to heterozygotes.

Genetic variation within species is maintained in geographically distinct populations

Much of the genetic variation within species is preserved as differences among members living in different places (populations). Populations often vary genetically because they are subjected to different selective pressures in different environments. Environmental conditions may vary significantly even over short

Experiment

Figure 19.17A   A Heterozygote Mating Advantage

Original Papers: W. B. Watt et al. 1986. Females' choice of "good genotypes" as mates is promoted by an insect mating system. *Science* 12: 1187–1190.

W. B. Watt et al. 1985. Adaptation at specific loci. IV. Differential mating success among glycolytic allozyme genotypes of Colias butterflies. *Genetics* 109: 157–175.

Among butterflies of the genus *Colias*, males that are heterozygous for two alleles of the PGI enzyme can fly farther under a broader range of temperatures than males that are homozygous for either allele. Does this ability give heterozygous males a mating advantage?

HYPOTHESIS▶   Heterozygous male *Colias* will have proportionally greater mating success than homozygous males.

METHOD▶

1. For each of two *Colias* species, capture mated female butterflies in the field. In the laboratory, allow them to lay eggs.

2. Determine the genotypes of the females and their offspring, and thus the genotypes of the fathers.

3. Compare the frequency of heterozygotes among successfully mating males with the frequency of heterozygotes among all viable males (i.e., males captured flying with females).

RESULTS▶   For both species, the proportion of heterozygotes among the males that mated successfully was higher than the proportion of heterozygotes among all viable males.

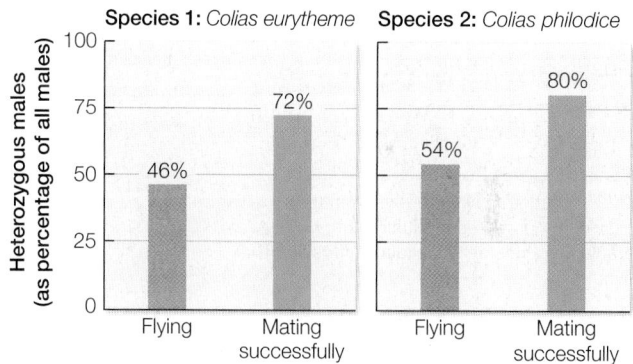

Species 1: *Colias eurytheme*   Species 2: *Colias philodice*

Heterozygous males (as percentage of all males)

Species 1: 46% Flying, 72% Mating successfully
Species 2: 54% Flying, 80% Mating successfully

CONCLUSION▶   Heterozygous *Colias* males have a mating advantage over homozygous males.

Figure 19.17B Work with the Data follows on next page.

distances. For example, in the Northern Hemisphere, temperature and soil moisture differ dramatically between north- and south-facing mountain slopes. In the Rocky Mountains of Colorado, the proportion of ponderosa pines (*Pinus ponderosa*) that are heterozygous for a particular peroxidase enzyme is particularly high on south-facing slopes, where temperatures fluctuate dramatically, often on a daily basis. This heterozygous genotype performs well over a broad range of temperatures. On north-facing slopes and at higher elevations, where temperatures are cooler and fluctuate less strikingly, a peroxidase homozygote, which has a lower optimal temperature, is much more frequent.

Plant species may also vary geographically in the chemicals they synthesize to defend themselves against herbivores. Some individuals of the white clover (*Trifolium repens*) produce the

Work with the Data

Figure 19.17B A Heterozygote Mating Advantage

Original Paper: W. B. Watt et al. 1985. Adaptation at specific loci. IV. Differential mating success among glycolytic allozyme genotypes of Colias butterflies. *Genetics* 109: 157–175.

Ward Watt and his colleagues tested the hypothesis that males with two different alleles for the PGI enzyme (heterozygotes) were more likely to mate successfully with females than were homozygous males. They reasoned that the heterozygous males could fly farther under a broader range of temperatures than could homozygous males, and that this ability would give heterozygous males greater access to receptive females. To test this hypothesis, they needed to know the frequency of heterozygotes among successfully mating males, and they needed to compare that frequency with the frequency of heterozygotes among males in the general population (i.e., all the potential mates available to females). To estimate the frequency of heterozygotes among mating males, Watt and his colleagues collected mated female butterflies in the field and allowed them to lay eggs in the laboratory. They hatched the eggs and determined the genotypes of the offspring, as well as the genotypes of the females. Using this information, they could determine the genotypes of the males that fathered the larvae. They then compared the estimated frequency of heterozygotes among the successful fathers with the frequency of heterozygotes among all viable males in the population. Samples of their data are given in the table.

Species	All viable males[a]		Mating males	
	Heterozygous/ total	Percent heterozygous	Heterozygous/ total	Percent heterozygous
C. philodice	32/74	43.2	31/50	62
C. eurytheme	44/92	47.8	45/59	76.3

[a]"Viable males" are males captured flying with females (hence the potential to mate).

QUESTIONS▸

1. If we assume that the proportions of each genotype among mating males should be the same as the proportions seen among all viable males, what is the number of *mating males* expected to be heterozygous and homozygous in each sample?

2. Use a chi-square test (see Appendix B) to evaluate the significance of the difference in the observed and expected numbers of heterozygous and homozygous individuals among the mating males. The critical value ($P = 0.05$) of the chi-square distribution with one degree of freedom is 3.841. Are the observed numbers of genotypes among mating males significantly different ($P < 0.05$) from the expected numbers in these samples?

3. The investigators determined the genotypes of enough larvae from each batch of eggs to judge the genotype of the father with 99% certainty. How many larvae did they need to measure to achieve that level of certainty?

   Hint: If the female is homozygous—say, genotype *ii*—the number needed is small. However, if a female is heterozygous—say, genotype *ij*—and only *ii* and *ij* progeny are found among her offspring, more larvae need to be genotyped. In this particular case, the father can be only *ii* or *ij*. If he were *ij*, the probability that any one offspring is not *ij* = 0.75, so the chance of getting only *ii* and *ij* among *N* offspring is 0.75^N. What value of *N* is required to reduce the probability of error in determining the father's genotype to 0.01?

Go to Achieve for a companion
Data in Depth exercise.

The proportion of cyanide-producing individuals increases gradually along a gradient from colder to milder winters. −13.3°C

Blue lines (isotherms) connect points with equal January mean temperatures.

4.4°C   −8.9°C   0°C   2.0°C   −4.4°C   8.0°C

Plants produce cyanide — Plants do not produce cyanide

Figure 19.18 Geographic Variation in a Defensive Chemical
The proportion of cyanide-producing individuals in European populations of white clover (*Trifolium repens*) depends on winter temperatures. (After H. Daday. 1956. *Heredity* 8: 61–78.)

poisonous chemical cyanide. Poisonous individuals are less appealing to herbivores—particularly mice and slugs—than are non-poisonous individuals. However, clover plants that produce cyanide are more likely to be killed by frost, because freezing damages cell membranes and releases cyanide into the plant's own tissues.

In European populations of *Trifolium repens*, the frequency of cyanide-producing individuals increases gradually from north to south and from east to west (**Figure 19.18**). A pattern of gradual change in phenotype across a geographic gradient is known as **clinal variation**. In the white clover cline, poisonous plants make up a large proportion of populations only in areas where winters are mild. Cyanide-producing individuals are rare where winters are cold, even though herbivores graze clovers heavily in those areas.

KEY CONCEPT

19.5 Recap and Assess

Frequency-dependent selection and heterozygote advantage act to maintain considerable genetic variation in most populations. Variation within species is also maintained among geographically distinct populations.

1. Human populations in central Africa have a high frequency of sickle-cell anemia, a genetic disorder that occurs in individuals who are homozygous for a particular allele of the hemoglobin gene. Despite strong selection against the homozygous sickle-cell condition, the sickle allele is maintained in relatively high frequencies in human populations that live in areas where malaria was historically common (compare the maps here;

figure source: F. B. Piel et al. 2010. *Nat Commun* 1: 104). Formulate a hypothesis that explains how this deleterious allele could be maintained in the population, even though individuals who are homozygous for the sickle allele are strongly disadvantaged.

Historic range of malaria in human populations

Distribution of sickle-cell allele

2. How could you test the hypothesis that you formulated in your answer to Question 1?

3. How could the presence of a great deal of genetic variation within a population increase the chances that some members of the population would survive an unprecedented environmental change? Why is there no guarantee that this would be the case?

The mechanisms of evolution have produced a remarkable variety of organisms. There are organisms that have adapted to nearly every environment on Earth. This natural variation, along with the success of breeders attempting to produce desired traits in domesticated plants and animals, suggests that evolution can produce a wide variety of adaptive traits. But are there limits to the adaptations evolution can produce?

KEY CONCEPT 19.6 Evolution Is Constrained by History and Trade-Offs

Learning Objectives

19.6.1 Describe how a preexisting trait or set of traits can limit the outcome of selection.

19.6.2 Give an example of an evolutionary trade-off.

19.6.3 Describe why short-term evolutionary outcomes may differ from long-term evolutionary outcomes.

We would be mistaken to assume that evolutionary mechanisms can produce any trait we might imagine. Evolution is constrained

in many ways. Lack of appropriate genetic variation, for example, prevents the development of many potentially favorable traits. If the allele for a given trait does not exist in a population, that trait cannot evolve, even if it would be highly favored by natural selection. Most possible combinations of genes and genotypes have never existed in any population and so have never been tested under natural selection.

In addition, constraints are imposed on organisms by the dictates of physics and chemistry. The size of cells, for example, is constrained by the stringencies of surface area-to-volume ratios (see Figure 5.2). The ways in which proteins can fold are limited by the bonding capacities of their constituent molecules (see Key Concept 3.2). And the energy transfers that fuel life must operate within the laws of thermodynamics (see Key Concept 8.1). Keep in mind that evolution works within the boundaries of these universal constraints as well as the constraints described in this key concept.

Preexisting traits may constrain evolution

Evolutionary outcomes are often constrained *because all evolutionary innovations are modifications of previously existing structures*. Human engineers seeking to power an airplane can start "from scratch" to design a completely new type of engine (powered by jet propulsion) to replace the previous type (powered by propellers). Evolutionary changes, however, cannot happen in this way. Current phenotypes of organisms are constrained by historical conditions and past selective pressures.

A striking example of an evolutionary constraint is provided by the evolution of fishes that spend most of their time on the sea bottom, where a ventrally flattened body is advantageous. One such lineage, the bottom-dwelling skates and rays, shares a common ancestor with sharks, whose bodies are already somewhat ventrally flattened and whose skeletal frame is made of flexible cartilage. Skates and rays evolved a body type that further flattened their bellies, allowing them to swim along the ocean floor (**Figure 19.19A**).

By contrast, plaice, sole, and flounder are bottom-dwelling descendants of deep-bellied, laterally flattened ancestors with bony skeletons. The only way these fishes can lie flat is to flop over on their sides. Their ability to swim is thus curtailed, but their bodies can lie still and are well camouflaged. During development, one eye of these flatfishes moves so that both eyes are positioned on the same side of the body (**Figure 19.19B**). Such shifts in eye position have evolved several times, and shifts have happened in both directions (that is, both left- and right-eyed flatfishes have evolved independently). Small shifts in the position of one eye probably helped ancestral flatfishes see better, resulting in the body forms found today. This path to producing a flattened body may not be optimal, but the fishes' developmental capabilities constrain the pathways that evolution can take.

Trade-offs balance costs and benefits

Adaptations frequently impose both costs and benefits. For an adaptation to be favored, the fitness benefits it confers must exceed the fitness costs it imposes—in other words, the **trade-off** must be worthwhile. For example, there are metabolic costs associated with developing and maintaining certain conspicuous features (such as antlers or horns) that males use to compete with

(A) *Taeniura lymma*

(B) *Bothus lunatus*

Figure 19.19 Two Solutions to a Single Problem **(A)** This stingray, whose ancestors were dorsoventrally flattened, lies on its belly. Stingrays' bodies are symmetrical around the dorsal backbone.

(B) This flounder, whose ancestors were laterally flattened, lies on its side. (The backbone of this individual is at the left.) Flounders' eyes migrate during development so that both are on the same side of the body.

other males for access to females. The fact that these features are common in many species suggests that the benefits derived from possessing them must outweigh the costs.

As a result of trade-offs, many traits that are adaptive in one context may be maladaptive in another. Consider the rough-skinned newt and one of its predators, the common garter snake (**Figure 19.20A**). The newt sequesters a potent neurotoxin called tetrodotoxin (TTX) in its skin. TTX paralyzes nerves and muscles by blocking sodium channels (see Key Concept 43.2). Most vertebrates—including many garter snakes—will die if they eat a rough-skinned newt. But some garter snakes can eat rough-skinned

newts and survive: TTX-resistant sodium channels have evolved in the nerves and muscles of such individuals. However, for several hours after eating a newt, TTX-resistant snakes can move only slowly, and they never move as fast as nonresistant snakes. Resistant snakes are thus more vulnerable to their own predators than are TTX-sensitive snakes. This vulnerability leads to selection *against* TTX-resistant sodium channels in garter snake populations that occur outside the range of rough-skinned newts, even though there is selection *for* TTX resistance in many areas where newts are present (**Figure 19.20B**).

▶ **View in Achieve**
Animation 19.2 Assessing the Costs of Adaptation

(A)

(B)

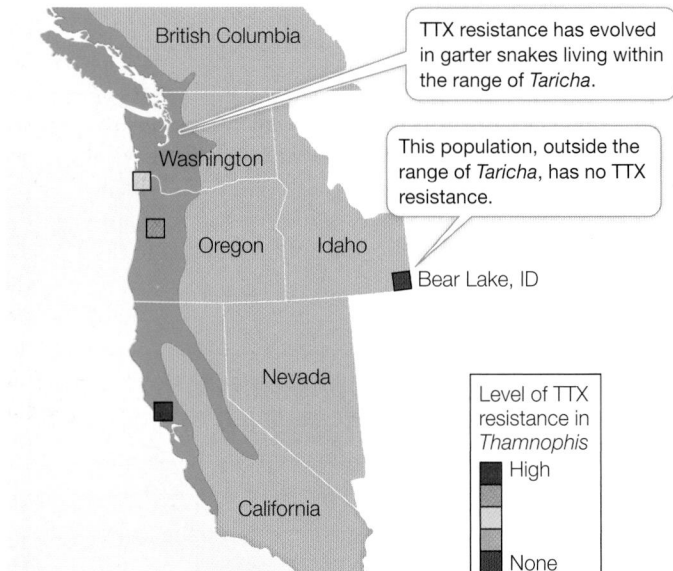

TTX resistance has evolved in garter snakes living within the range of *Taricha*.

This population, outside the range of *Taricha*, has no TTX resistance.

British Columbia

Washington

Oregon   Idaho

Bear Lake, ID

Nevada

Level of TTX resistance in *Thamnophis*

High

None

California

Figure 19.20 Resistance to a Toxin Comes at a Cost
(A) Garter snakes (*Thamnophis sirtalis*) prey on rough-skinned newts (*Taricha granulosa*). Rough-skinned newts defend themselves by sequestering a neurotoxin, TTX, in their skin. In turn, TTX-resistant sodium channels have evolved in some snake populations, allowing the snakes to eat toxic newts but resulting in slower movement by the

snakes. **(B)** High TTX resistance in garter snakes is found only in regions where snake and newt populations overlap (bright green area). (B after E. D. Brodie, III and E. D. Brodie, Jr. 1990. *Evolution* 44: 651–659.)

Q: Why doesn't TTX resistance spread throughout the range of the garter snake?

Short-term and long-term evolutionary outcomes sometimes differ

The short-term changes in allele frequencies within populations that we have emphasized in this chapter, often termed **microevolutionary** changes, are an important focus of study for evolutionary biologists. These changes can be observed directly, they can be manipulated experimentally, and they demonstrate the actual processes by which evolution occurs.

Long-term patterns of **macroevolutionary** change can also be strongly influenced by events that occur so infrequently (such as a meteorite impact) or so slowly (such as continental drift) that they are unlikely to be observed during short-term studies. The evolutionary mechanisms at work may change over time with changing environmental conditions. Even among the descendants of a single ancestral species, different lineages may evolve in different directions. Additional types of evidence—evidence demonstrating the effects of rare and unusual events on trends in the fossil record—must be gathered if we wish to understand the course of evolution over billions of years. We will consider these long-term aspects of evolution in the remaining chapters of Part 5.

KEY CONCEPT

19.6 Recap and Assess

Evolution is often constrained because all evolutionary innovations are modifications of previously existing structures. An adaptation can evolve only if the fitness benefits it confers exceed the fitness costs it imposes. The outcomes of short-term selection can be dramatically altered by events that occur over much longer periods of time.

1. The largest living adult insects weigh less than 75 g (less than a relatively small songbird, such as a starling). Many flying birds are much larger than any insect, so clearly flight alone does not constrain the current size of insects. Formulate a hypothesis for why there are no giant insects presently roaming Earth.

2. Natural selection results in gradual changes *within species* over long periods of time. Describe an event that could result in significant and sudden changes across many species simultaneously.

▶Investigating**LIFE**

How do complex traits such as echolocation, or the ability to avoid detection from echolocation, evolve in the first place?

In the opening story of this chapter, we discussed the evolutionary arms race between echolocating bats and the moths that evolved the ability to detect bat ultrasounds, and then avoid the predators. Moths are not the only potential bat prey that have evolved the ability to hear ultrasounds. Many other groups of insects can hear the sounds produced by bats, and act to avoid these predators. In many cases, the insects can already hear, as they have evolved complex communication systems to attract mates. This produces the natural variation in the trait (hearing) that is needed for natural selection to act.

As we learned in the experiment discussed in **Investigating Life: Do Long Wing Tails Help Moths Escape Bat Predation?**, many non-hearing insects have evolved other strategies for confusing or avoiding echolocating bats. Several species of moths have evolved long extensions of their wings, called wing tails. The wing tails flutter as the moths fly, and the fluttering wing tails serve to distract the echolocating bats. A bat that attacks the long wing tail of a moth may get nothing but a tiny piece of moth wing, while the moth survives the attack.

Some bats locate their prey using the sounds produced by the prey themselves. There are species of bats that locate prey by the sound of calling frogs, insects, or even the ripples made by fishes on the surface of the water. These prey species often must limit or modify the sounds they produce to balance the benefits of producing a sound with the costs associated with bat predation.

Species rarely evolve to a state of perfection and then stop evolving. Prey species are constantly evolving new ways to avoid predation, so predator species must evolve improved means of capturing prey. Although there are often historical, physiological, or mechanical limits to what can evolve, species are constantly changing in response to changes in their physical environment and species interactions. This constant selection for change, over millions or even billions of years, has produced the enormous diversity of life we see on Earth.

Future directions

Bats are not the only animals that have evolved the ability to echolocate. Toothed whales and dolphins, as well as some burrowing shrews and cave-dwelling birds, also use echolocation to "see" their environment with sound. So echolocation has evolved repeatedly in species that live in environments in which sight is limited. But how does a trait like echolocation first begin to evolve in a species? Some rudimentary form of the trait has to be present before selection can act to refine this sensory mode. Often, species co-opt a trait that evolved for other purposes, and then selection refines it over time for a new purpose.

Most humans do not use echolocation. We rely heavily on sight, and most of us feel awkward moving around unfamiliar spaces in the dark. But what would happen if humans were forced to live in an environment where we could not see? We already hear, of course, so we have a system that could be co-opted for echolocation. We are also capable of making sounds. Echolocation simply requires the production of sounds, the ability to detect the reflected sounds, and the ability to process the information appropriately. Indeed, some blind humans have trained themselves to use echolocation to sense their environment (see Media Clip 19.4). An individual learning a behavior is not the same as evolution of a behavior within a species, however. Before natural selection can act, there has to be genetic variation in the population for the trait in question. The fact that a few humans are able to use simple forms of echolocation shows that variation for this trait is already present in our species. The same is true for many species, which is why it is not surprising that echolocation has evolved multiple times in species that live or feed in the dark.

Media Clip 19.4 Human Echolocation
Life12e.com/mc19.4

© blickwinkel/Alamy Stock Photo

VISUAL SUMMARY 19

You should be able to relate each summary to the adjacent figures. If you go to this visual summary in **Achieve**, you can follow links to figures, animations, activities, and simulations that will help you consolidate the material.

KEY CONCEPT
19.1 Evolution Is Both Factual and the Basis of Broader Theory

Go to Activity 19.1 and Animation 19.1

- **Evolution** is genetic change in populations over time. Evolution can be observed directly in living populations as well as in the fossil record of life.

- **Evolutionary theory** refers to our understanding of the mechanisms of evolutionary change.

- Charles Darwin is best known for his ideas on the common ancestry of divergent species and on **natural selection** (the differential survival and reproduction of individuals based on variation in their traits) as a mechanism of evolution.

Questions

1. Explain the difference between "the fact of evolution" and what scientists mean by "evolutionary theory."

2. What did Darwin mean by "descent with modification"?

3. How did Darwin suggest that biological evolution could occur?

KEY CONCEPT
19.2 Mutation, Selection, Gene Flow, Genetic Drift, and Nonrandom Mating Result in Evolution

Go to Simulations 19.1–19.3

- Mutation is the source of the genetic variation on which the mechanisms of evolution act.

- Within **populations**, selection acts to increase the frequency of beneficial **alleles** and to decrease the frequency of deleterious alleles.

- **Gene flow**, **genetic drift**, and nonrandom mating (as arises from **sexual selection**) can also result in the evolution of populations.

Questions

1. How does artificial selection differ from natural selection?

2. How can genetic drift oppose the forces of natural selection?

3. Why did Darwin distinguish the special case of sexual selection?

Figure 19.6

Figure 19.8

Euplectes progne

© Eleanor H Hattingh/Shutterstock.com

KEY CONCEPT

19.3 Evolution Can Be Measured by Changes in Allele Frequencies

Go to Simulation 19.4

- Allele frequencies measure the amount of genetic variation in a population. Genotype frequencies show how a population's genetic variation is distributed among its members. Together, allele and genotype frequencies describe a population's **genetic structure**.

- **Hardy–Weinberg equilibrium** predicts genotype frequencies from allele frequencies in the absence of evolution. Deviation from these frequencies indicates that evolutionary mechanisms are at work.

Questions

1. How many generations of random mating are required to achieve Hardy–Weinberg equilibrium expectations?

2. How do the assumptions of Hardy–Weinberg equilibrium correspond to the five principal processes of evolution?

Figure 19.11

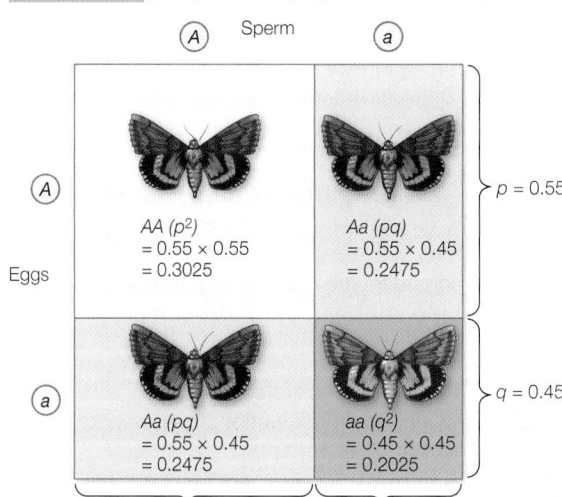

Generation II (Hardy–Weinberg equilibrium restored)

KEY CONCEPT

19.4 Selection Can Be Stabilizing, Directional, or Disruptive

- **Stabilizing selection** reduces variation without changing the mean value of a trait.

- **Directional selection** shifts the mean value of a trait toward one extreme.

- **Disruptive selection** favors both extremes of a trait value, resulting in a bimodal character distribution.

Question

1. Which of the three types of selection (stabilizing, directional, or disruptive) does each of the following cases represent?

   a. Higher survival and reproduction of giraffes with longer necks compared with those with shorter necks.

   b. Higher survival and reproduction of cattle with intermediate calf weights compared with those with high or low calf weights.

   c. Higher survival and reproduction of grasshoppers with either small or large mouthparts, compared with those with intermediate-sized mouthparts.

Figure 19.12

Stabilizing selection

Directional selection

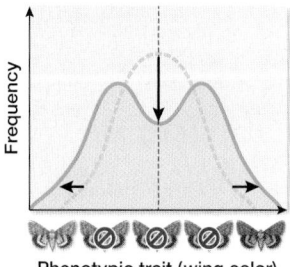

Disruptive selection

Phenotypic trait (wing color)

KEY CONCEPT

19.5 Selection Can Maintain Variation within and among Populations

■ A polymorphism may be maintained by **frequency-dependent selection** when the fitness of a genotype depends on its frequency in a population.

■ A polymorphism may also be maintained by heterozygote advantage when the fitness of the heterozygote exceeds the fitness of either homozygote.

■ Genetic variation within species may be maintained by the existence of genetically distinct populations over geographic space. A gradual change in phenotype across a geographic gradient is known as **clinal variation**.

Question

1. Which of the following are examples of frequency-dependent selection, heterozygote advantage, or clinal variation?

   a. Increased sprinting performance of individuals with two different alleles of an actin gene, compared with individuals with two copies of just one of the alleles.

   b. Increased survival of individuals with rare color

Figure 19.16

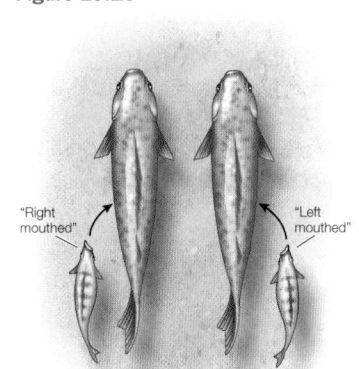

"Right mouthed"   "Left mouthed"

Figure 19.18

Plants produce cyanide   Plants do not produce cyanide

patterns, compared with those with common color patterns.

   c. Geographic variation in the size of deer from northern to southern latitudes.

KEY CONCEPT

19.6 Evolution Is Constrained by History and Trade-Offs

Go to Animation 19.2

■ Evolutionary outcomes are often constrained because all evolutionary innovations are modifications of previously existing structures.

■ Most adaptations impose costs as well as benefits. An adaptation can evolve only if the benefits it confers exceed the costs it imposes.

Questions

1. Why is flight more likely to evolve in some groups than in others? For example, why do you think there are no flying turtles?

2. Why don't all snakes that could potentially eat poisonous newts evolve resistance to their toxins?

Figure 19.19

Taeniura lymma

© age fotostock/Alamy Stock Photo

Bothus lunatus

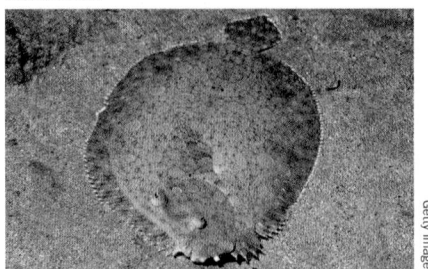

© Oliver Lucanus/NIS/Minden Pictures/Getty Images

Figure 19.20

British Columbia

Washington

Oregon   Idaho

Bear Lake, ID

Nevada

Level of TTX resistance in *Thamnophis*
- High
- None

California

Reconstructing and Using Phylogenies 20

KEY CONCEPTS

20.1 All of Life Is Connected through Its Evolutionary History

20.2 Phylogeny Can Be Reconstructed from Traits of Organisms

20.3 Phylogeny Makes Biology Comparative and Predictive

20.4 Phylogeny Is the Basis of Biological Classification

Phylogenies allow us to understand the evolution of diversity, as within this single genus of South African plants (*Protea*).

▶ Investigating LIFE

Using Phylogeny to Improve a Genetic Tool

Green fluorescent protein (GFP) was discovered in 1962 when Osamu Shimomura led a team that was able to purify the protein from the tissues of the bioluminescent jellyfish *Aequorea victoria*. Some 30 years after GFP's initial discovery, Martin Chalfie had the idea (and the technology) to link the gene for GFP to other protein-coding genes so that the expression of specific genes of interest could be visualized in glowing green within cells and tissues of living organisms (see Figure 18.9). This work was extended by Roger Tsien, who changed some of the amino acids within GFP to create fluorescent proteins of several distinct colors. Different-colored fluorescent proteins meant that the expression of several different proteins could be visualized and studied in the same organism at the same time. These three scientists were awarded the 2008 Nobel Prize in Chemistry for the isolation and development of GFP for visualizing gene expression.

Tsien was able to produce different-colored proteins, but he could not produce a *red* protein. This was frustrating; a red fluorescent protein would be particularly useful to biologists because red light penetrates tissues more easily than do other colors. Tsien's work stimulated Mikhail Matz to look for new fluorescent proteins in corals. Among the different coral species he studied, Matz found coral proteins that fluoresced in various shades of green, cyan (blue-green)—and red.

How had fluorescent red pigments evolved among the corals, given that the necessary molecular changes had eluded Tsien? To answer this question, Matz sequenced the genes of the fluorescent proteins and used these sequences to reconstruct the evolutionary history of the amino acid changes that produced different colors in different species of corals.

Matz's work showed that the ancestral fluorescent protein in corals was green, and that red fluorescent proteins evolved in a series of gradual steps. His analysis of evolutionary relationships allowed him to retrace these steps. Such an evolutionary history, as depicted in a tree of relationships among lineages, is called a phylogeny.

The evolution of many aspects of an organism's biology can be studied using phylogenetic methods. This information is used in all fields of biology to understand the structure, function, and behavior of organisms.

 How are phylogenetic methods used to resurrect protein sequences from extinct organisms?
(Find the answer on page 462.)

Learning Objectives

20.1.1 Draw and label the parts of a phylogenetic tree and explain the biological interpretation of each part.

20.1.2 Use a phylogenetic tree to determine relationships and infer character changes among species.

20.1.3 Explain how homoplasies (convergences and reversals of characters) are accounted for when constructing phylogenetic relationships.

The sequencing of complete genomes from many diverse species has confirmed what biologists have long suspected: all of life is related through a common ancestor. The common ancestry of life explains why the general principles of biology apply to all organisms. Thus we can learn much about how the human genome works by studying the biology of model organisms because we share a common evolutionary history with those organisms. The evolutionary history of these relationships is known as **phylogeny**, and a **phylogenetic tree** is a diagrammatic reconstruction of that history.

Phylogenetic trees depict evolutionary relationships among lineages

Phylogenetic trees are commonly used to depict the evolutionary history of species, populations, and genes. For many years such trees have been constructed based on physical structures, behaviors, and biochemical attributes of related organisms. Now, as genomes are sequenced for more and more organisms, biologists are able to reconstruct the history of life in ever greater detail.

In Chapter 19 we discussed why we expect populations of organisms to evolve over time. We call a series of ancestor and descendant populations a **lineage**, which we can depict as a line drawn on a time axis, as shown in **Figure 20.1**. What happens when a single lineage divides into two? For example, a geographic barrier may divide an ancestral population into two descendant populations that no longer interbreed with one another. We depict such an event as a split, or **node**, in a phylogenetic tree (see Figure 20.1). Each of the descendant populations gives rise to a new lineage, and as these independent lineages evolve, new traits arise in each. As the lineages continue to split over time, this history can be represented in the form of a branching tree that can be used to trace the evolutionary relationships from the ancient common ancestor of a group of species, through the various lineage splits, up to the present populations of the organisms.

A phylogenetic tree may portray the evolutionary history of all life forms. Phylogenetic trees can also depict the history of a major evolutionary group (such as the insects) or of a much smaller group of closely related species. In some cases, phylogenetic trees are used to show the history of individuals, populations, or genes within a species. The common ancestor of all the organisms in the tree forms the **root** of the tree.

The depictions of phylogenetic trees in this book are rooted at the left, with time flowing from left (earliest) to right (most recent) (**Figure 20.2A**). The timing of splitting events in lineages is shown by the position of nodes on a time axis. These splits represent events where one lineage diverged into two, such as a speciation event (for a tree of species), a gene duplication event (for a tree of genes), or a transmission event (for a tree of viral lineages transmitted through a host population). The time axis may have an explicit scale, or it may simply show the relative timing of divergence events.

In this book's illustrations, the order in which nodes are placed along the horizontal (time) axis has meaning, but the vertical distance between the branches does not. Vertical distances have been adjusted for legibility and clarity of presentation; they do not correlate with the degree of similarity or difference among groups. Note too that lineages can be rotated around nodes in the tree, so the vertical order of lineages is also largely arbitrary (**Figure 20.2B**). The important information in the tree is the branching order along the time axis, as this indicates when the various lineages last shared a common ancestor.

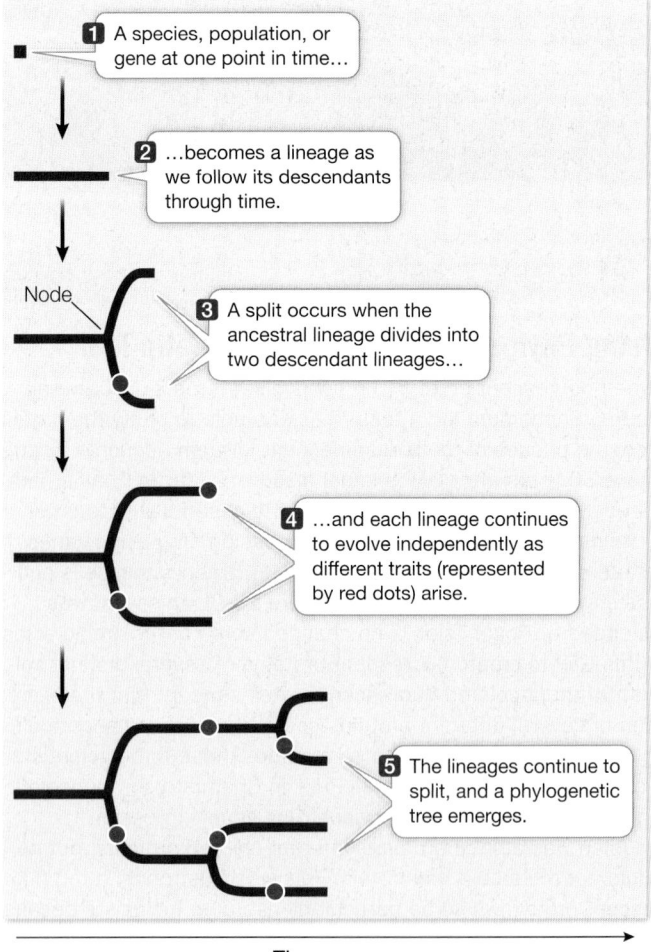

1 A species, population, or gene at one point in time…

2 …becomes a lineage as we follow its descendants through time.

Node

3 A split occurs when the ancestral lineage divides into two descendant lineages…

4 …and each lineage continues to evolve independently as different traits (represented by red dots) arise.

5 The lineages continue to split, and a phylogenetic tree emerges.

Time

Figure 20.1 The Components of a Phylogenetic Tree Evolutionary relationships among organisms can be represented in a treelike diagram.

(A)

In this book, all phylogenetic trees show the common ancestor for the group on the left; this is called the root of the tree.

The splits in branches are called nodes and indicate a division of one lineage into two.

The positions of the nodes on the time scale (if present) indicate the times of the corresponding speciation events.

Figure 20.2 How to Read a Phylogenetic Tree   (A) Phylogenetic trees can be produced with time scales, as shown here, or with no indication of time. If no time scale is shown, then the trees are meant to depict only the relative order of divergence events.
(B) Lineages can be rotated around a given node, so the vertical order of taxa is largely arbitrary.

(B)

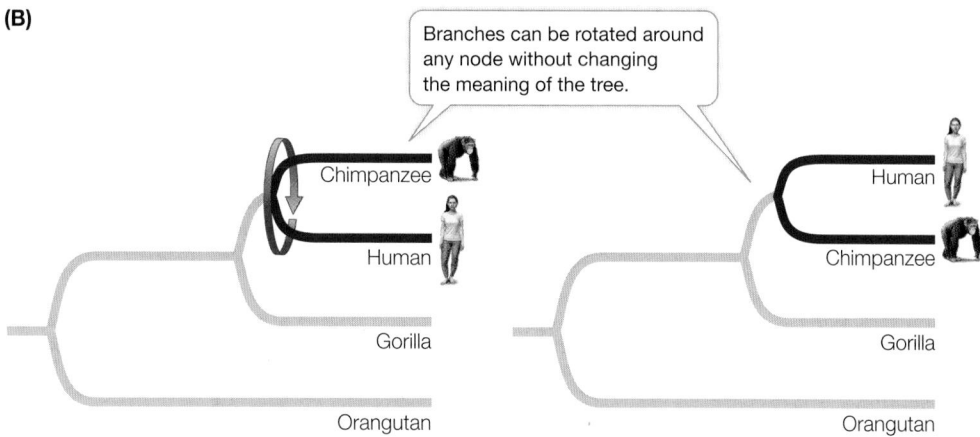

Branches can be rotated around any node without changing the meaning of the tree.

Any group of species that we designate with a name is a **taxon** (plural *taxa*). Examples of familiar taxa include humans, primates, mammals, and vertebrates; in this series, each taxon is also a member of the next, more inclusive taxon. Any taxon that consists of all the evolutionary descendants of a common ancestor is called a **clade**. Clades can be identified by picking any point on a phylogenetic tree and from that point tracing all the descendant lineages to the tips of the terminal branches (**Figure 20.3**). Two species that are each other's closest relatives are called **sister species**. Similarly, any two clades that are each other's closest relatives are called **sister clades**.

Before the 1980s, phylogenetic trees tended to be seen only in the literature on evolutionary biology, especially in the area of **systematics**—the study and classification of biodiversity. But almost every journal in the life sciences published over the past few decades contains phylogenetic trees. Trees are widely used in

molecular biology, biomedicine, physiology, behavior, ecology, and virtually all other fields of biology. Why have phylogenetic studies become so widespread?

Phylogenetic trees are the basis of comparative biology

In biology we study life at all levels of organization—from genes, cells, organisms, populations, and species to the major divisions of life. In most cases, however, no individual gene or organism (or other unit of study) is exactly like any other gene or organism that we investigate.

Consider the individuals in your biology class. We recognize each person as an individual human, but we know that no two are exactly alike. If we knew everyone's family tree in detail, the genetic similarity of any pair of students would be more predictable. We would find that more closely related students have many more

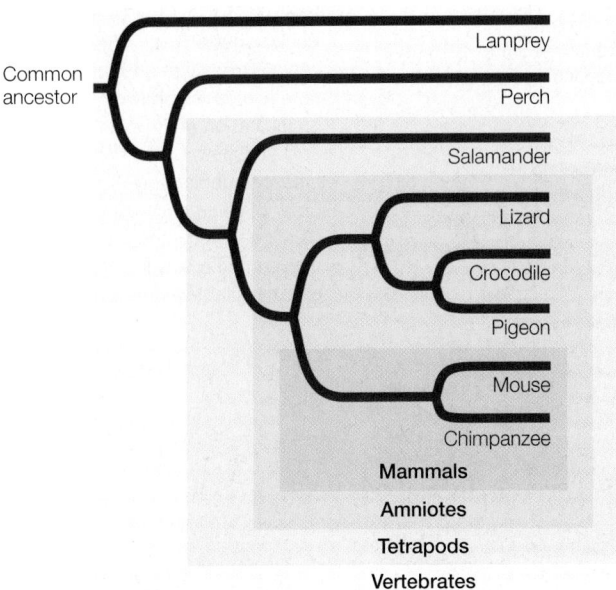

Figure 20.3 Clades Represent an Ancestor and All of Its Evolutionary Descendants   All clades are subsets of larger clades, with all of life as the most inclusive taxon. In this example, the groups called mammals, amniotes, tetrapods, and vertebrates represent successively larger clades. Only a few species within each clade are represented on the tree.

traits in common (from the color of their hair to their susceptibility or resistance to diseases). Likewise, biologists use phylogenies to make comparisons and predictions about shared traits across genes, populations, and species.

The evolutionary relationships among species, as represented in the **tree of life**, form the basis for biological classification. Biologists estimate that there are tens of millions of species on Earth. So far, however, only about 1.8 million species have been classified—that is, formally described and named. New species are being discovered all the time and phylogenetic analyses are constantly reviewed and revised, so our knowledge of the tree of life is far from complete. Yet knowledge of evolutionary relationships is essential for making comparisons in biology, so biologists build phylogenies for groups of interest as more data become available. The tree of life's evolutionary framework allows us to make many predictions about the behavior, ecology, physiology, genetics, and morphology of species that have not yet been studied in detail.

When biologists compare species, they observe traits that differ within the group of interest and try to understand when these traits evolved. In many cases, investigators are interested in how the evolution of a trait relates to environmental conditions or selective pressures. For instance, scientists have used phylogenetic analyses to discover changes in the genome of human immunodeficiency viruses (HIVs) that result in resistance to particular drug treatments. The association of a particular genetic change in HIV with a particular treatment provides a hypothesis about the evolution of resistance that can be tested experimentally.

Any features shared by two or more species that have been inherited from a common ancestor are said to be **homologous**.

Homologous features may be any heritable traits, including DNA sequences, protein structures, anatomical structures, and even some behavior patterns. For example, all living vertebrates have a vertebral column, as did the ancestral vertebrate. Therefore the vertebral column is judged to be homologous in all vertebrates.

Derived traits provide evidence of evolutionary relationships

In tracing the evolution of a character, biologists distinguish between ancestral and derived traits. Each character of an organism evolves from one condition (the **ancestral trait**) to another condition (the **derived trait**). Derived traits that are shared among a group of organisms and are also viewed as evidence of the common ancestry of the group are called **synapomorphies** (*syn*, "shared," + *apo*, "derived," + *morph*, "form," referring to the "form" of a trait). Thus the vertebral column is considered a synapomorphy—a shared, derived trait—of the vertebrates. (The ancestral trait was an undivided supporting rod as still occurs in some close relatives of vertebrates.)

Not all similar traits are evidence of relatedness. Similar traits in unrelated groups of organisms can develop for either of the following reasons:

- Superficially similar traits may evolve independently in different lineages, a phenomenon called **convergent evolution**. For example, although the *forelimb bones* of bats and birds are homologous, having been inherited from a common tetrapod ancestor, the *wings* of bats and birds are not homologous because they evolved independently from the forelimbs of different nonflying ancestors (**Figure 20.4**). Functionally similar structures that have independent evolutionary origins are called **analogous** characters.

- A character may revert from a derived state back to an ancestral state in an event called an **evolutionary reversal**. For example, the derived limbs of terrestrial tetrapods evolved from the ancestral fins of their aquatic ancestors. Then, within the mammals, the ancestors of modern cetaceans (whales and dolphins) returned to the ocean, and cetacean limbs evolved to once again resemble their ancestral state—fins. The superficial similarity of cetacean and fish fins does not suggest a close relationship between these groups. Instead, the similarity arises from evolutionary reversal.

Similar traits generated by convergent evolution and evolutionary reversals are called homoplastic traits or **homoplasies**.

 Media Clip 20.1 Morphing Arachnids
Life12e.com/mc20.1

A particular trait may be ancestral or derived, depending on our point of reference. For example, all birds have feathers. We infer from this that feathers (which are highly modified scales) were present in the common ancestor of modern birds. Therefore we consider the presence of feathers to be an ancestral trait for any particular group of modern birds, such as the songbirds. However, feathers are not present in any other living animals. In reconstructing a phylogeny of all living vertebrates, the presence of feathers is a derived trait found only among birds, and thus is a synapomorphy of the birds.

Bat wing

Bird wing

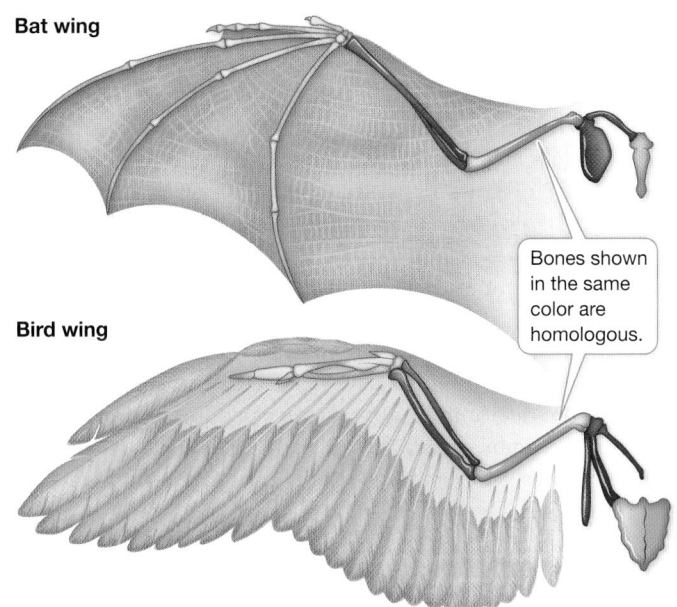

Bones shown in the same color are homologous.

Figure 20.4 The Bones Are Homologous, the Wings Are Not
The supporting bone structures of both bat wings and bird wings are derived from a common four-limbed ancestor and are thus homologous. However, the wings themselves—an adaptation for flight—evolved independently in the two groups.

KEY CONCEPT
20.1 Recap and Assess

A phylogenetic tree is a description of evolutionary relationships among organisms or their genes. All living organisms share a common ancestor and are related through the phylogenetic tree of life. Groups of related species that are descended from the same common ancestor are known as clades. Shared derived traits (known as synapomorphies) provide evidence for evolutionary relationships among species.

1. What biological processes are represented in phylogenetic trees?

2. Why is it important to consider only homologous characters in constructing phylogenetic trees?

3. Why might similar traits arise independently in species that are only distantly related? Can you think of examples among familiar organisms? How do biologists account for these homoplasies in reconstructing phylogenies?

Phylogenetic analyses have become increasingly important to many types of biological research in recent years, and they are the basis for the comparative nature of biology. For the most part, however, evolutionary history cannot be observed directly. How, then, do biologists reconstruct the past? One way is by using phylogenetic analyses to construct a tree.

KEY CONCEPT
20.2 Phylogeny Can Be Reconstructed from Traits of Organisms

Learning Objectives

20.2.1 Analyze a phylogenetic tree to identify synapomorphies, homoplasies, and relationships among taxa.

20.2.2 Construct a phylogenetic tree from a data matrix of characters.

To illustrate how a phylogenetic tree is constructed, consider the eight vertebrate animals listed in **Table 20.1**: lamprey, perch, salamander, lizard, crocodile, pigeon, mouse, and chimpanzee. We will initially assume that any given derived trait arose only once during the evolution of these animals (that is, there has been no convergent evolution), and that no derived traits were lost from any of the descendant groups (there has been no evolutionary reversal). For simplicity, we have selected traits that are either present (+) or absent (−).

Shared traits reflect common ancestry

In a phylogenetic study, the group of organisms of primary interest is called the **ingroup**. As a point of reference, an ingroup is compared with an **outgroup**: a species or group that is closely related to the ingroup but is known to be phylogenetically outside it. In other words, the root of the tree is located between the ingroup and the outgroup. Any trait that is present in both the ingroup and the outgroup must have evolved before the origin of the ingroup and thus must be ancestral for the ingroup. In contrast, traits that are present in only some members of the ingroup must be derived traits within that ingroup. As we will see in Chapter 31, a group of jawless fishes called the lampreys is thought to have separated from the lineage leading to the other vertebrates before the jaw

TABLE **20.1** | **Eight Vertebrates and the Presence or Absence of Some Shared Derived Traits**

Taxon	Jaws	Lungs	Claws or nails	Gizzard	Feathers	Fur	Mammary glands	Keratinous scales
Lamprey (outgroup)	−	−	−	−	−	−	−	−
Perch	+	−	−	−	−	−	−	−
Salamander	+	+	−	−	−	−	−	−
Lizard	+	+	+	−	−	−	−	+
Crocodile	+	+	+	+	−	−	−	+
Pigeon	+	+	+	+	+	−	−	+
Mouse	+	+	+	−	−	+	+	−
Chimpanzee	+	+	+	−	−	+	+	−

arose. Therefore we have included the lamprey as the outgroup for our analysis. Because derived traits are traits acquired by other members of the vertebrate lineage *after* they diverged from the outgroup, any trait that is present in both the lamprey and the other vertebrates is judged to be ancestral.

We begin by noting that the chimpanzee and mouse share two traits—mammary glands and fur—that are absent in both the outgroup and in the other species of the ingroup. Therefore we infer that mammary glands and fur are derived traits that evolved in a common ancestor of chimpanzees and mice after that lineage separated from the lineages leading to the other vertebrates. These characters are synapomorphies that unite chimpanzees and mice (as well as all other mammals, although we have not included other mammalian species in this example). By the same reasoning, we can infer that the other shared derived traits are synapomorphies for the various groups in which they are expressed. For instance, keratinous scales are a synapomorphy of the lizard, crocodile, and pigeon.

Table 20.1 also tells us that, among the animals in our ingroup, the pigeon has a unique trait: feathers. Feathers are a synapomorphy of birds and their extinct relatives. However, because we have only one bird in this example, the presence of feathers provides no clues concerning relationships among these eight species of vertebrates. However, gizzards are found in both birds and crocodiles, so this trait is evidence of a close relationship between birds and crocodilians.

By combining information about the various synapomorphies, we can construct a phylogenetic tree. We infer from our information that mice and chimpanzees—the only two animals that share

fur and mammary glands—share a more recent common ancestor with each other than they do with pigeons and crocodiles. Otherwise we would need to assume that the ancestors of pigeons and crocodiles also had fur and mammary glands but subsequently lost them. There is no basis for making these additional assumptions.

Figure 20.5 shows a phylogenetic tree for the vertebrates in Table 20.1, based on the shared derived traits we examined. This particular tree was easy to construct because it is based on a very small sample of traits, and the derived traits we examined evolved only once and were never lost after they appeared. Had we included a snake in the group, our analysis would not have been as straightforward. We would have needed to examine additional characters to determine that snakes evolved from a group of lizards that had limbs. In fact, the analysis of many characters shows that snakes evolved from burrowing lizards that became adapted to a subterranean existence.

Parsimony provides the simplest explanation for phylogenetic data

The phylogenetic tree shown in Figure 20.5 is based on only a very small sample of traits. Typically, biologists construct phylogenetic trees using hundreds or thousands of traits. With larger data sets, we would expect to observe traits that have changed more than once, and thus would expect to see convergence and evolutionary reversal. How do we determine which traits are synapomorphies and which are homoplasies? One way is to invoke the principle of parsimony.

View in Achieve
Simulation 20.1 **Phylogeny and Molecular Evolution**

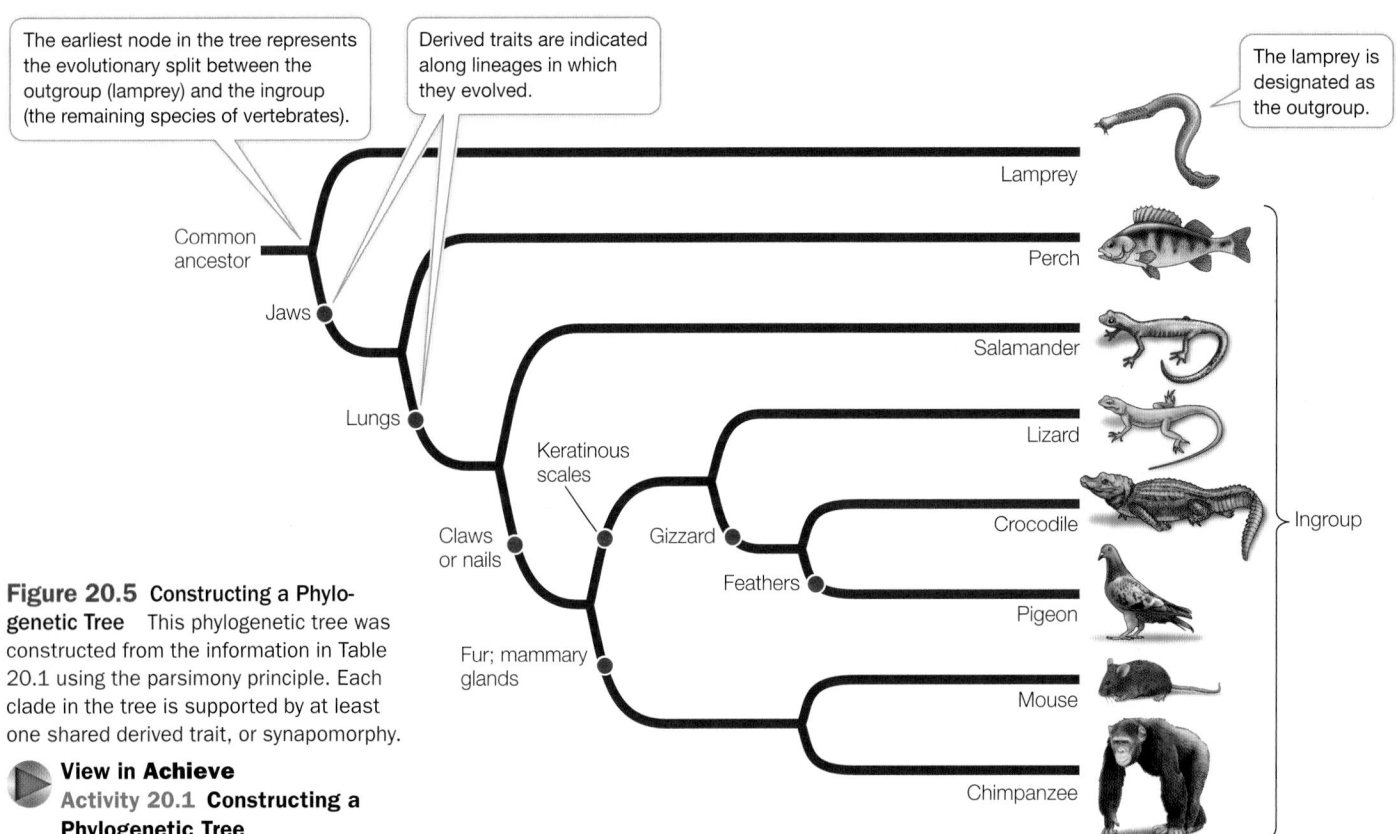

The earliest node in the tree represents the evolutionary split between the outgroup (lamprey) and the ingroup (the remaining species of vertebrates).

Derived traits are indicated along lineages in which they evolved.

The lamprey is designated as the outgroup.

Common ancestor

Jaws

Lungs

Keratinous scales

Claws or nails

Gizzard

Feathers

Fur; mammary glands

Lamprey

Perch

Salamander

Lizard

Crocodile

Pigeon

Mouse

Chimpanzee

Ingroup

Figure 20.5 Constructing a Phylogenetic Tree   This phylogenetic tree was constructed from the information in Table 20.1 using the parsimony principle. Each clade in the tree is supported by at least one shared derived trait, or synapomorphy.

View in Achieve
Activity 20.1 Constructing a Phylogenetic Tree

In its most general form, the **parsimony principle** states that the preferred explanation of observed data is the simplest explanation. Applying the principle of parsimony to the reconstruction of phylogenies entails minimizing the number of evolutionary changes that need to be assumed over all characters in all groups in the tree. In other words, the best hypothesis under the parsimony principle is one that requires the fewest homoplasies. This application of parsimony is a specific case of a general principle of reasoning called Occam's razor: the best explanation is the one that best fits the data while making the fewest assumptions. More complicated explanations are accepted only when the evidence requires them. Phylogenetic trees represent our best estimates about evolutionary relationships, given our current knowledge. They are continually modified as additional evidence becomes available.

Phylogenies are reconstructed from many sources of data

Naturalists have constructed various forms of phylogenetic trees for more than 150 years. In fact, the only figure in the first edition of *On the Origin of Species* was a phylogenetic tree. Tree construction has been revolutionized, however, by the advent of computer software that allows us to consider far more data and analyze far more traits than could ever before be processed. Combining these advances in methodology with the massive comparative data sets being generated through studies of genomes, biologists are learning details about the tree of life at a remarkable pace (see Appendix A: The Tree of Life).

Any trait that is genetically determined, and therefore heritable, can be used in a phylogenetic analysis. Evolutionary relationships can be revealed through studies of morphology, development, the fossil record, behavioral traits, and molecular traits such as DNA and protein sequences. Let's take a closer look at the types of data used in modern phylogenetic analyses.

MORPHOLOGY   An important source of phylogenetic information is **morphology**: the presence, size, shape, and other attributes of body parts. Since living organisms have been observed, depicted, collected, and studied for millennia, we have a wealth of recorded morphological data as well as extensive museum and herbarium collections of organisms whose traits can be measured. New technological tools, such as the electron microscope and computed tomography (CT) scans, enable systematists to examine and analyze the structures of organisms at much finer scales than was formerly possible.

Most species are described and known primarily by their morphology, and morphology still provides the most comprehensive data set available for many taxa. The morphological features that are important for phylogenetic analysis are often specific to a particular group. For example, the presence, development, shape, and size of various features of the skeletal system are important in vertebrate phylogeny, whereas floral structures are important for studying the relationships among flowering plants.

Morphological approaches to phylogenetic analysis have some limitations, however. Some taxa exhibit little morphological diversity, despite great species diversity. For example, the phylogeny of the leopard frogs of North and Central America would be difficult to infer from morphological differences alone, because the many species look very similar, despite important differences in their behavior and physiology. At the other extreme, few morphological traits can be compared across distantly related species (earthworms and mammals, for example). Furthermore, some morphological variation has an environmental (rather than a genetic) basis and so must be excluded from phylogenetic analyses. An accurate phylogenetic analysis often requires information beyond that supplied by morphology.

DEVELOPMENT   Similarities in developmental patterns may reveal evolutionary relationships. Some organisms exhibit similarities only in early developmental stages. The larvae of marine creatures called sea squirts, for example, have a flexible gelatinous rod in the back—the notochord—that disappears as the larvae develop into adults. All vertebrate animals also have a notochord at some time during their development (**Figure 20.6**). This shared structure is one of the reasons for inferring that sea squirts are more closely related to vertebrates than would be suspected if only adult sea squirts were examined.

> **Connect the Concepts**   Evolutionary developmental biology, discussed in Chapter 21, compares the developmental processes of different organisms to determine the ancestral relationship between them, and to discover how developmental processes evolved. Genetic toolkit genes are expressed in different ways in different species, resulting in major morphological differences among species. The existence of highly conserved genes involved in development makes it likely that similar traits will evolve repeatedly.

PALEONTOLOGY   The fossil record is another important source of information on evolutionary history. Fossils show us where and when organisms lived in the past and give us an idea of what they looked like. Fossils provide important evidence that helps us distinguish ancestral from derived traits. The fossil record can also reveal when lineages diverged and began their independent evolutionary histories. Furthermore, in groups with few species that have survived to the present, information on extinct species is often critical to an understanding of the large divergences among the surviving species. The fossil record has limitations, however. Few or no fossils have been found for some groups, and the fossil record for many groups is fragmentary.

BEHAVIOR   Some behavioral traits are culturally transmitted and others are genetically inherited. If a particular behavior is culturally transmitted, it may not accurately reflect evolutionary relationships (but may nonetheless reflect cultural connections). Many bird songs, for instance, are learned and may be inappropriate traits for phylogenetic analysis. Frog calls, however, are genetically determined and appear to be acceptable sources of information for reconstructing phylogenies.

MOLECULAR DATA   All heritable variation is encoded in DNA, and so the complete genome of an organism contains an enormous set of traits (the individual nucleotide bases of DNA) that can be used in phylogenetic analyses. In recent years, DNA sequences have become among the most widely used sources of data for constructing phylogenetic trees. Comparisons of nucleotide sequences are not limited to the DNA in the cell nucleus. Eukaryotes have genes

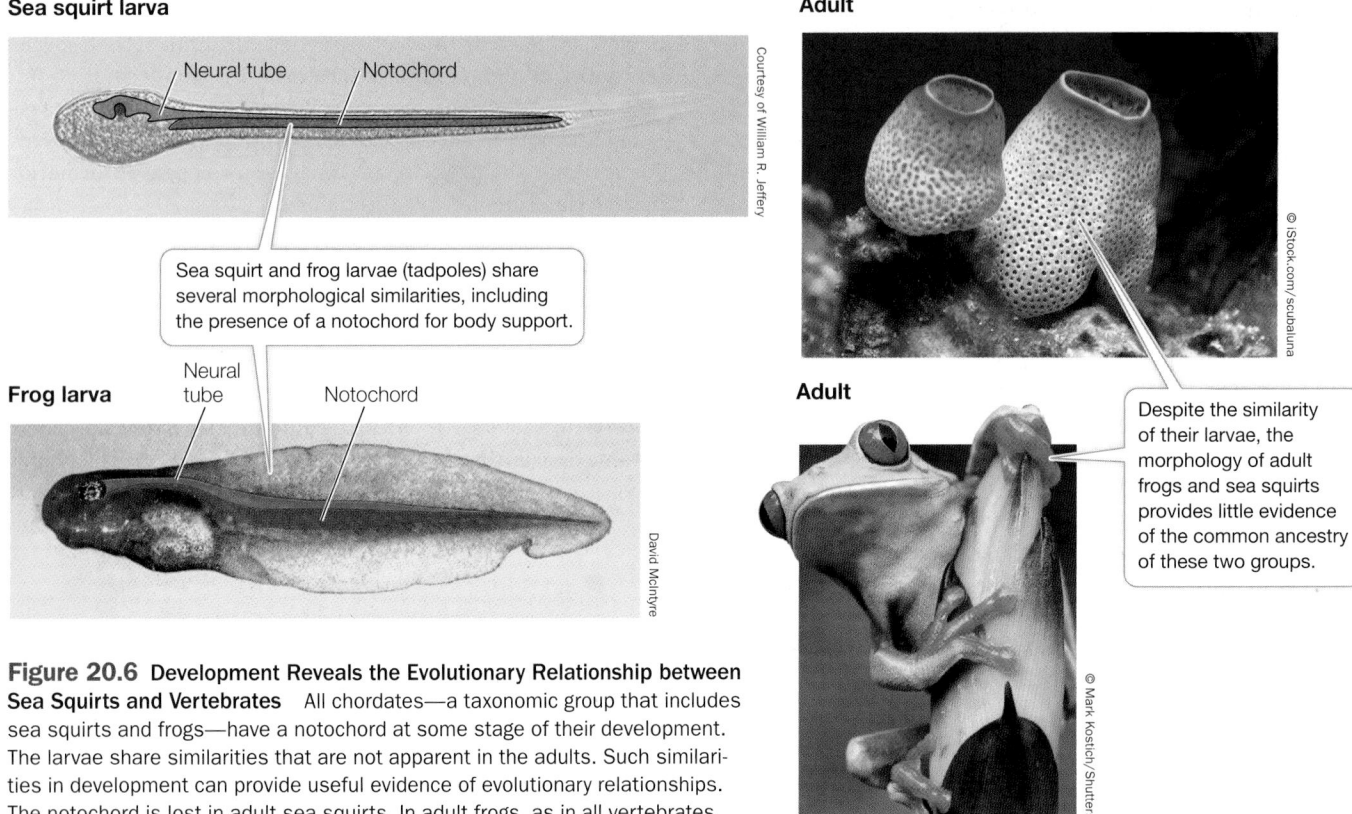

Sea squirt larva

Neural tube   Notochord

Sea squirt and frog larvae (tadpoles) share several morphological similarities, including the presence of a notochord for body support.

Frog larva

Neural tube   Notochord

Adult

Adult

Despite the similarity of their larvae, the morphology of adult frogs and sea squirts provides little evidence of the common ancestry of these two groups.

Courtesy of William R. Jeffery

David McIntyre

© iStock.com/scubaluna

© Mark Kostich/Shutterstock

Figure 20.6 Development Reveals the Evolutionary Relationship between Sea Squirts and Vertebrates All chordates—a taxonomic group that includes sea squirts and frogs—have a notochord at some stage of their development. The larvae share similarities that are not apparent in the adults. Such similarities in development can provide useful evidence of evolutionary relationships. The notochord is lost in adult sea squirts. In adult frogs, as in all vertebrates, the vertebral column replaces the notochord as the support structure.

in their mitochondria as well as in their nuclei. Plant cells also have genes in their chloroplasts. The chloroplast genome (cpDNA), which is used extensively in phylogenetic studies of plants, has changed slowly over evolutionary time, so it is often used to study relatively ancient phylogenetic relationships. Most animal mitochondrial DNA (mtDNA) has changed more rapidly, so mitochondrial genes are used to study evolutionary relationships among closely related animal species (the mitochondrial genes of plants evolve more slowly). Many nuclear gene sequences are also commonly analyzed, and now that entire genomes have been sequenced from many species, they too are used to construct phylogenetic trees. Information on gene products (such as the amino acid sequences of proteins) is also widely used for phylogenetic analyses.

Mathematical models expand the power of phylogenetic reconstruction

As biologists began to use DNA sequences to infer phylogenies in the 1970s and 1980s, they developed explicit mathematical models describing how DNA sequences change over time. These models account for multiple changes at a given position in a DNA sequence. They also take into account different rates of change at different positions in a gene, at different positions in a codon, and among different nucleotides. For example, nucleotide transitions (changes between two purines or between two pyrimidines) usually occur more often than transversions (changes between a purine and pyrimidine).

Mathematical models can be used to compute how a tree might evolve given the observed data. A **maximum likelihood** method will identify the tree that most likely produced the observed data, given the assumed model of evolutionary change. Maximum likelihood methods can be used for any kind of data, but they are most often used with molecular data, for which explicit mathematical models of evolutionary change are easier to develop. The principal advantages of maximum likelihood analyses are that they incorporate more information about evolutionary change than do parsimony methods, and they are easier to treat in a statistical framework. The principal disadvantages are that they are computationally intensive and require explicit models of evolutionary change (which may not be available for some kinds of character changes).

The accuracy of phylogenetic methods can be tested

If phylogenetic trees represent reconstructions of past events, and if many of these events occurred before any humans were around to witness them, how can we test the accuracy of phylogenetic methods? Biologists have conducted experiments both in living organisms and with computer simulations that have demonstrated the effectiveness and accuracy of phylogenetic methods.

In one experiment designed to test the accuracy of phylogenetic analysis, a single viral culture of bacteriophage T7 was used as a starting point, and lineages were allowed to evolve from this ancestral virus in the laboratory (**Investigating Life: Testing the Accuracy of Phylogenetic Analysis**). The initial culture was split into two separate lineages, one of which became the ingroup for analysis and the other of which became the outgroup for rooting the tree. The lineages in the ingroup were split in two after every 400 generations,

▶InvestigatingLIFE   Testing the Accuracy of Phylogenetic Analysis

Experiment

Original Paper: D. M. Hillis et al. 1992. Experimental phylogenetics: Generation of a known phylogeny. *Science* 255: 589–592.

To test whether analysis of gene sequences can accurately reconstruct evolutionary phylogeny, we must have an unambiguously known phylogeny to compare against the reconstruction. Will the observed phylogeny match the reconstruction?

HYPOTHESIS▶   A phylogeny reconstructed by analyzing the DNA sequences of living organisms can accurately match the known evolutionary history of the organisms.

METHOD▶   In the laboratory, researchers produced an unambiguous phylogeny of nine viral lineages, enhancing the mutation rate to increase variation among the lineages.

Viral sequences from the end points of each lineage (blue dots) were subjected to phylogenetic analysis by investigators who were unaware of the history of the lineages or the gene sequences of the ancestral viruses. These investigators reconstructed the phylogeny and ancestral DNA sequences based solely on their analyses of the descendants' genomes.

RESULTS▶   The true phylogeny and ancestral DNA sequences were accurately reconstructed solely from the DNA sequences of the viruses at the tips of the tree branches.

CONCLUSION▶   Phylogenetic analysis of DNA sequences can accurately reconstruct evolutionary history.

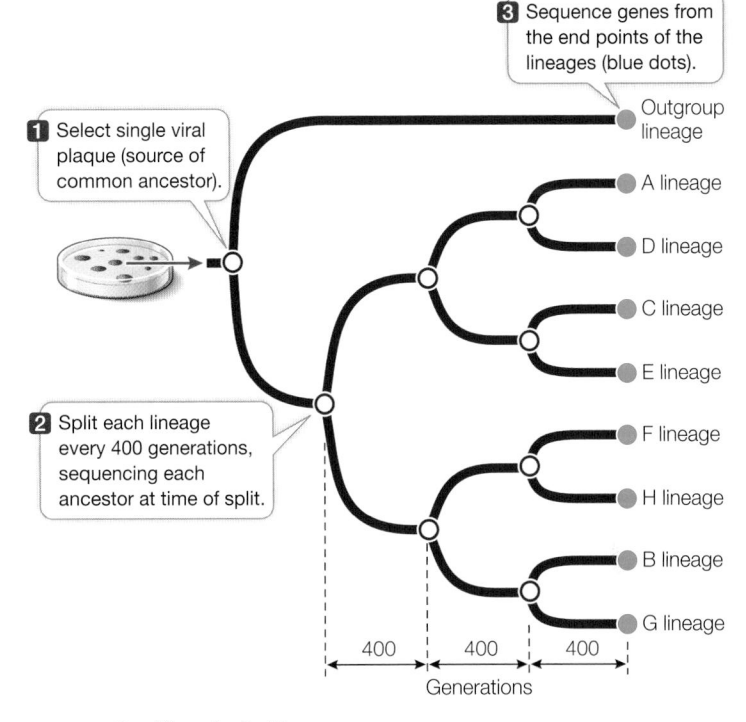

▶ **1** Select single viral plaque (source of common ancestor).

▶ **2** Split each lineage every 400 generations, sequencing each ancestor at time of split.

▶ **3** Sequence genes from the end points of the lineages (blue dots).

Outgroup lineage
A lineage
D lineage
C lineage
E lineage
F lineage
H lineage
B lineage
G lineage

400   400   400
Generations

▶ View in **Achieve**
Animation 20.1 Using Phylogenetic Analysis to Reconstruct Evolutionary History

Work with the Data

Original Paper: J. J. Bull et al. 1993. Experimental molecular evolution of bacteriophage T7. *Evolution* 47: 993–1007.

The full DNA sequences for the viral lineages produced in this experiment are thousands of nucleotides long. However, 23 of the nucleotide positions are shown in the table below, and you can use these data to repeat the researchers' analysis. Each nucleotide position represents a separate character.

QUESTIONS▶

1. Construct a phylogenetic tree from the nucleotide positions using the parsimony principle (see Key Concept 20.2 and the examples in Table 20.1 and Figure 20.5). Use the outgroup to root your tree. Assume that all changes among nucleotides are equally likely.

2. Using your tree from Question 1, reconstruct the DNA sequences of the ancestral lineages.

3. Transitions are mutations that change one purine to the other (G ↔ A) or one pyrimidine to the other (C ↔ T), whereas transversions exchange a purine for a pyrimidine or vice versa (e.g., A → C or T; C → A or G). Which kind of mutation predominates in this phylogeny? Why might this be the case?

Go to **Achieve** for a companion
Data in Depth exercise.

Lineage	Character at position																						
	1	2	3	4	5	6	7	8	9	10	11	12	13	14	15	16	17	18	19	20	21	22	23
A	T	C	G	G	G	C	C	C	C	C	C	C	A	A	C	C	G	A	T	A	C	A	A
B	C	C	G	G	G	T	C	C	C	T	C	C	G	A	T	T	A	G	C	G	T	G	G
C	C	C	G	G	G	C	C	C	T	C	C	T	A	A	C	C	G	G	T	A	C	A	A
D	T	C	A	G	G	C	C	C	C	C	C	C	A	A	C	C	G	A	T	A	C	A	A
E	C	T	G	G	G	C	C	C	C	C	C	T	A	A	C	C	G	G	T	A	C	A	A
F	C	T	G	A	A	C	C	C	C	C	C	C	G	A	C	T	G	G	C	G	C	G	G
G	C	C	G	G	G	T	T	C	C	T	C	C	G	A	T	T	A	G	C	G	C	G	G
H	C	C	G	G	A	C	C	C	C	C	C	C	G	C	C	T	G	G	C	G	C	G	G
Outgroup	C	C	G	G	G	C	C	T	C	C	T	C	G	A	C	C	G	G	C	A	C	G	G

and samples of the virus were saved for analysis at each branching point. The lineages were allowed to evolve until there were eight lineages in the ingroup. Mutagens were added to the viral cultures to increase the mutation rate so that the amount of change and the degree of homoplasy would be typical of the organisms analyzed in average phylogenetic analyses. The investigators then sequenced samples from the end points of the eight ingroups and one outgroup lineages, as well as from the ancestors at the branching points. They then gave the sequences from the end points of the lineages to other investigators to analyze, without revealing the known history of the lineages or the sequences of the ancestral viruses.

After the phylogenetic analysis was completed, the investigators asked two questions. Did phylogenetic methods reconstruct the known history correctly? And were the sequences of the ancestral viruses reconstructed accurately? The answer in both cases was yes. The branching order of the lineages was reconstructed exactly as it had occurred, more than 98% of the nucleotide positions of the ancestral viruses were reconstructed correctly, and 100% of the amino acid changes in the viral proteins were reconstructed correctly.

The experiment shown in Investigating Life: Testing the Accuracy of Phylogenetic Analysis demonstrated that phylogenetic analysis was accurate under the conditions tested, but it did not examine all possible conditions. Other experimental studies have taken other factors into account, such as the sensitivity of phylogenetic analysis to convergent environments and highly variable rates of evolutionary change. In addition, computer simulations based on evolutionary models have been used extensively to study the effectiveness of phylogenetic analysis. These studies have also confirmed the accuracy of phylogenetic methods and have been used to refine those methods and extend them to new applications.

KEY CONCEPT
20.2 Recap and Assess

Using the parsimony principle, phylogenetic trees are constructed to find the simplest explanation for evolutionary changes in traits among a set of organisms. Maximum likelihood methods incorporate more explicit mathematical models of evolutionary change to reconstruct evolutionary history. Laboratory tests and simulations have confirmed the general accuracy of phylogenetic methods.

The matrix below supplies data for seven land plants and an outgroup: an aquatic plant known as a stonewort. Each trait is scored as either present (+) or absent (–) in each of the plants.

	Trait						
Taxon	Protected embryos	True roots	Persistently green sporophyte	Vascular cells	Stomata	True leaves	Seeds
Stonewort (outgroup)	–	–	–	–	–	–	–
Liverwort	+	–	–	–	–	–	–
Pine tree	+	+	+	+	+	+	+
Bracken fern	+	+	+	+	+	+	–
Club moss	+	+	+	+	+	–	–
Sphagnum moss	+	–	–	–	+	–	–
Hornwort	+	–	+	–	+	–	–
Sunflower	+	+	+	+	+	+	+

1. Use the data matrix to reconstruct the phylogeny of land plants.
2. Which two of these taxa are most closely related?
3. Plants that produce seeds are known as seed plants. What is the sister group to the seed plants among these taxa?
4. Which two traits evolved along the same branch of your reconstructed phylogeny?
5. Are there any homoplasies in your reconstructed phylogeny?

Why do biologists expend the time and effort necessary to reconstruct phylogenies? Information about the evolutionary relationships among organisms is a useful source of data for scientists investigating a wide variety of biological questions. Next we will describe how phylogenetic trees are used to answer questions about the past, and to predict and compare traits of organisms in the present.

KEY CONCEPT
20.3 Phylogeny Makes Biology Comparative and Predictive

Learning Objectives

20.3.1 Formulate a hypothesis about the origin of an epidemic using a phylogenetic tree.

20.3.2 Calculate the rate of a molecular clock from a graph that shows changes over time.

Once a phylogeny is reconstructed, what do we do with it? What else, beyond an understanding of evolutionary history, does phylogeny offer us?

Phylogenetic trees can be used to reconstruct past events

Reconstructing past events is important for understanding many biological processes. In the case of zoonotic diseases (diseases caused by infectious organisms transmitted to humans from another animal host), it is important to understand when, where, and how the disease first entered a human population. Human immunodeficiency virus (HIV) is the cause of such a zoonotic disease, acquired immunodeficiency syndrome, or AIDS. Phylogenetic analyses have become important for studying the transmission of viruses such as HIV. Phylogenies are also important for understanding the present global diversity of HIV and for determining the virus's origins in human populations. A broader phylogenetic analysis of immunodeficiency viruses shows that humans acquired these viruses from two different hosts: HIV-1 from common chimpanzees (*Pan troglodytes*), and HIV-2 from sooty mangabeys (*Cercocebus atys*) (**Figure 20.7**).

HIV-1 is the common form of the virus in human populations in central Africa, where chimpanzees are hunted for food, and HIV-2 is the common form in human populations in western Africa, where sooty mangabeys are hunted for food. Thus it seems likely that these viruses entered human populations through hunters who cut themselves while skinning chimpanzees and

Figure 20.7 **Phylogenetic Tree of Immunodeficiency Viruses**
The evolutionary relationships of immunodeficiency viruses show that these viruses have been transmitted to humans from two different simian hosts: HIV-1 from common chimpanzees and HIV-2 from sooty mangabeys. (SIV stands for simian immunodeficiency virus.) (After B. Hahn et al. 2000. *Science* 287: 607–614.)

Phylogenies allow us to compare and contrast living organisms

Male swordtails—a group of fishes in the genus *Xiphophorus*—have a long, colorful tail extension, and their reproductive success is closely associated with this appendage. Males with a long sword are more likely to mate successfully than are males with a short sword (an example of sexual selection; see Key Concept 19.2). Several explanations have been advanced for the evolution of this structure, including the hypothesis that the sword simply exploits a preexisting bias in the sensory system of the females. This sensory exploitation hypothesis suggests that female swordtails had a preference for males with long tails even before the tails evolved (perhaps because females assess the size of males by their total body length—including the tail—and prefer larger males).

sooty mangabeys. The global pandemic of AIDS occurred when these infections in local African populations rapidly spread through human populations around the world.

In recent years, phylogenetic analysis has become important in forensic investigations that involve viral transmission events. For example, phylogenetic analysis was critical for a criminal investigation of a physician who was accused of purposefully injecting blood from one of his HIV-positive patients into his former girlfriend in an attempt to kill her. The phylogenetic analysis revealed that the HIV strains present in the girlfriend were a subset of those present in the physician's patient (**Figure 20.8**). Other evidence was needed, of course, to connect the physician to this purposeful transmission event, but the phylogenetic analysis was important to support the viral transmission event from the patient to the victim.

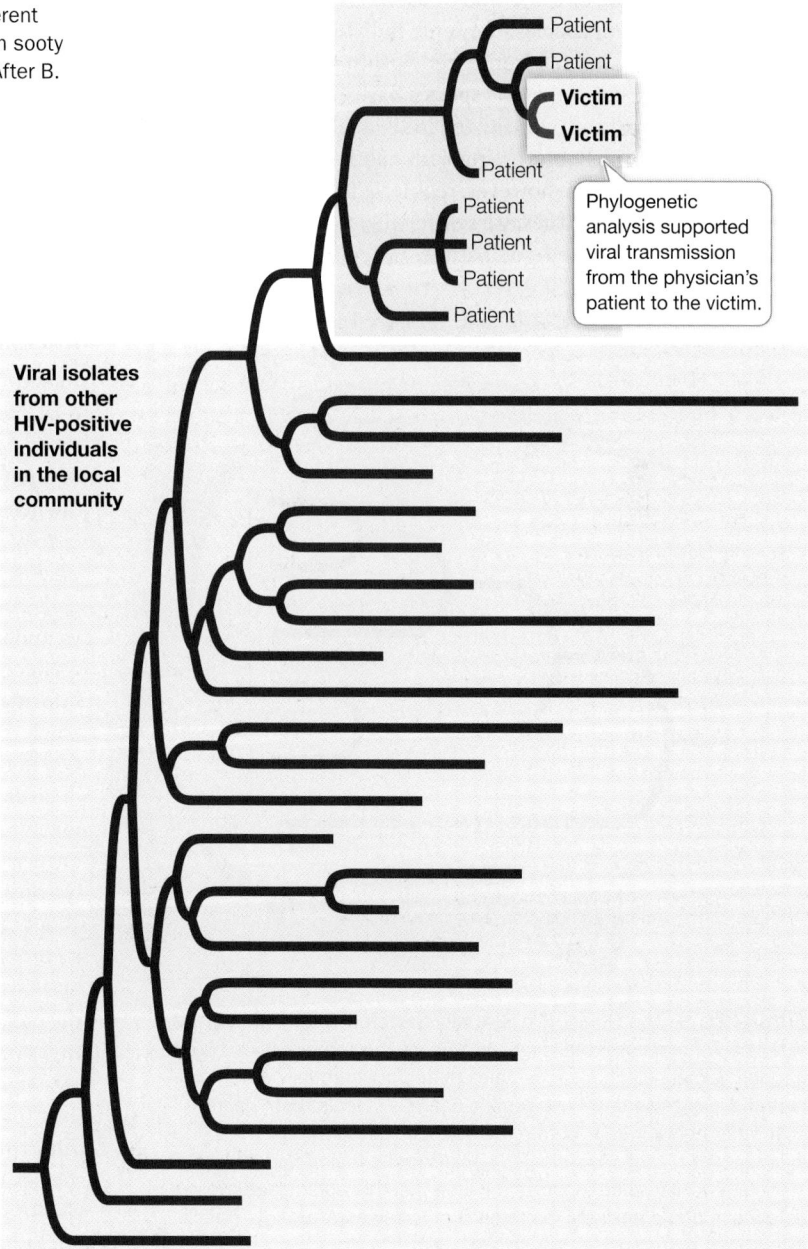

Figure 20.8 **A Forensic Application of Phylogenetic Analysis**   This phylogenetic analysis demonstrated that strains of HIV present in a victim (shown in red) were a phylogenetic subset of viruses isolated from a physician's patient (shown in blue). This analysis was part of the evidence used to show that the physician drew blood from his HIV-positive patient and injected it into the victim in an attempt to kill her. A jury found the physician guilty of attempted murder. (After M. Metzker et al. 2002. *Proc Natl Acad Sci USA* 99: 14292–14297. © 2002 National Academy of Sciences, U.S.A.)

Q: What hypothetical phylogenetic results could have exonerated the physician?

To test the sensory exploitation hypothesis, phylogenetic analysis was used to identify the relatives of swordtails that had split most recently from their lineage before the evolution of swords. These closest relatives turned out to be fishes in the genus *Priapella*. Even though male *Priapella* do not normally have swords, when researchers attached artificial swordlike structures to the tails of male *Priapella*, female *Priapella* preferred those males. This result provided support for the hypothesis that female *Xiphophorus* had a preexisting sensory bias favoring tail extensions even before the trait evolved (**Figure 20.9**). Thus a long tail became a sexually selected trait because of the preexisting preference of the females. The phylogeny allows us to understand when the trait evolved relative to the change in female preference.

Phylogenies can reveal convergent evolution

Like most animals, flowering plants (angiosperms) often reproduce by mating with another individual of the same species. But in many angiosperm species, the same individual produces both male and female gametes (contained within pollen and ovules, respectively). Self-incompatible species have mechanisms to prevent fertilization of the ovule by the individual's own pollen, and so must reproduce by outcrossing with another individual. Individuals of some species, however, regularly fertilize their ovules using their own pollen; they are self-fertilizing or selfing species, and their gametes are self-compatible.

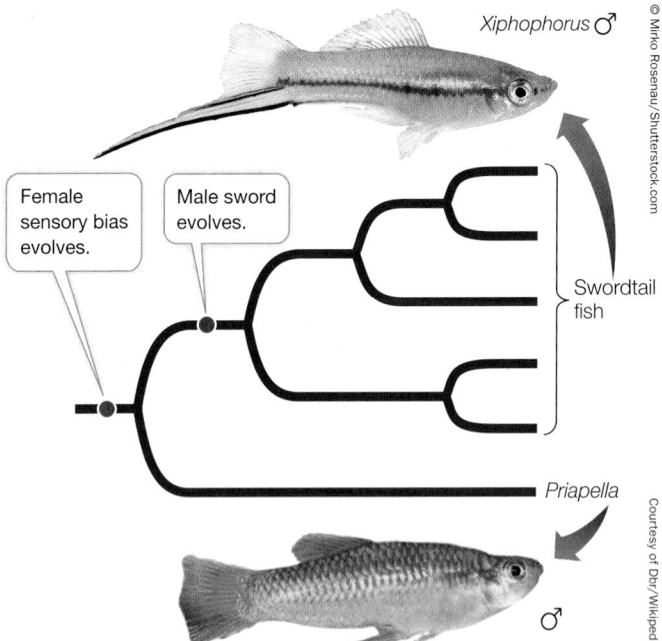

Figure 20.9 The Origin of a Sexually Selected Trait The tail extension of male swordtails (genus *Xiphophorus*) apparently evolved through sexual selection, as females mated preferentially with males that had long "swords." Phylogenetic analysis reveals that *Priapella* split from the swordtails before the evolution of the sword. The independent finding that female *Priapella* prefer male *Priapella* with an artificial sword further supports the idea that this appendage evolved as a result of a preexisting preference in females. (After A. L. Basolo. 1995. *Proc R Soc Lond B Biol Sci* 259: 307–311.)

Connect the Concepts Self-incompatibility in plants depends on a plant's ability to determine whether pollen is genetically different than its own pollen. How a plant does this is discussed in Key Concept 36.1.

The evolution of angiosperm fertilization mechanisms was examined in *Leptosiphon*, a genus in the phlox family that exhibits a diversity of mating systems and pollination mechanisms. The self-incompatible (outcrossing) species of *Leptosiphon* have long petals and are pollinated by long-tongued flies. In contrast, self-pollinating species have short petals and do not require insect pollinators to reproduce successfully. Using ribosomal DNA sequences, investigators reconstructed a phylogeny of this genus (**Figure 20.10**). They then determined whether each species was self-compatible by artificially pollinating flowers with the plant's own pollen or with pollen from other individuals and observing whether viable seeds formed.

The reconstructed phylogeny suggests that self-incompatibility is the ancestral state and that self-compatibility evolved three times within this group of *Leptosiphon*. The change to self-compatibility eliminated the plants' dependence on an outside pollinator and has been accompanied by the evolution of reduced petal size. Indeed, the striking morphological similarity of the flowers in the self-compatible groups once led to their being classified as members of a single species (*L. bicolor*). Phylogenetic analysis, however, shows them to be members of three distinct lineages. From this information we can infer that self-compatibility and its associated floral structure are convergent in the three independent lineages that had been called *L. bicolor*.

Ancestral states can be reconstructed

In addition to using phylogenetic methods to infer evolutionary relationships, biologists can use these techniques to reconstruct the morphology, behavior, or nucleotide and amino acid sequences of ancestral species (as was demonstrated for the ancestral sequence of bacteriophage T7 in Investigating Life: Testing the Accuracy of Phylogenetic Analysis). In the opening of this chapter, we described how Mikhail Matz used phylogenetic analysis to reconstruct the sequence of changes in fluorescent proteins of corals to understand how red fluorescent proteins could be produced.

Reconstruction of ancient DNA sequences can also provide information about the biology of long-extinct organisms. For example, phylogenetic analysis was used to reconstruct an opsin protein in the ancestral archosaur (the most recent common ancestor of birds, dinosaurs, and crocodiles). Opsins are pigment proteins involved in vision; different opsins (with different amino acid sequences) are excited by different wavelengths of light. Knowledge of the opsin sequence in the ancestral archosaur would provide clues about the animal's visual capabilities and therefore about some of its probable behaviors. Investigators used phylogenetic analysis of opsin from living vertebrates to estimate the amino acid sequence of the pigment that existed in the ancestral archosaur. A protein with this same sequence was then constructed in the laboratory. The investigators tested the reconstructed opsin and found a significant shift toward the red end of the spectrum in the light sensitivity of this protein compared with that of most modern opsins. Modern species that exhibit similar sensitivity are adapted for nocturnal vision, so the investigators inferred that the ancestral archosaur might have been active at night. Thus, reminiscent of the movies

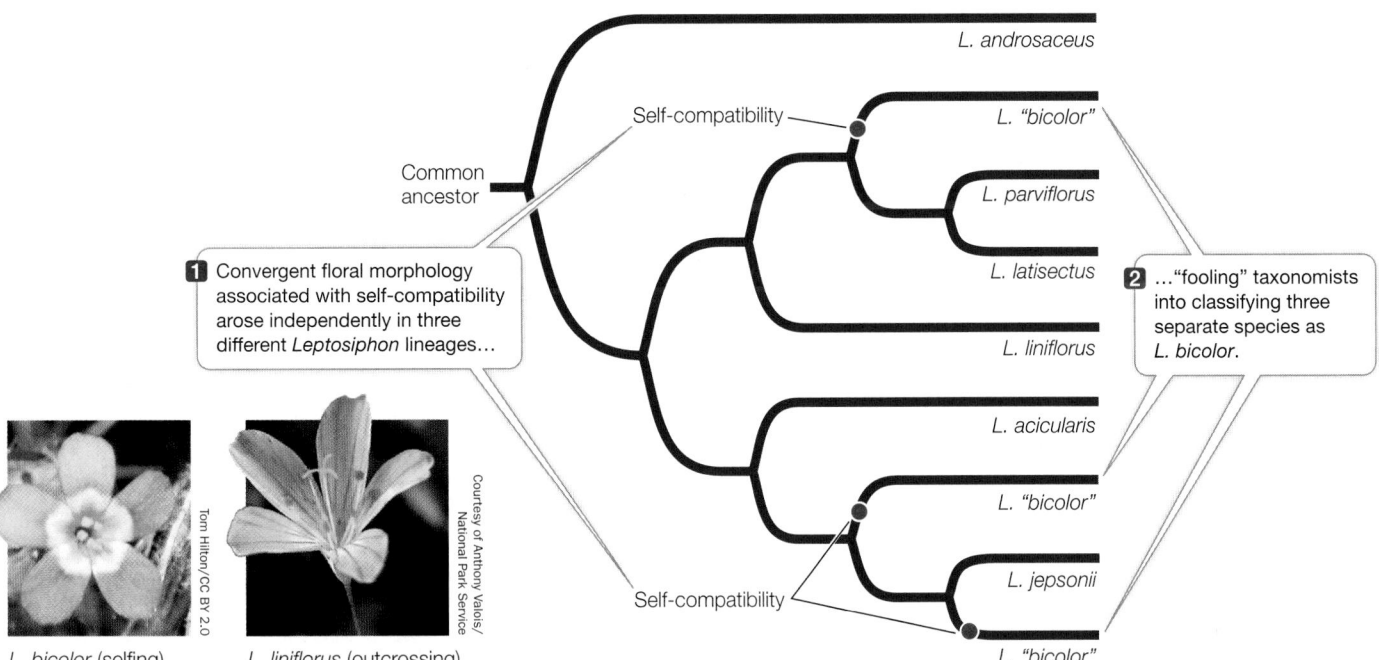

1 Convergent floral morphology associated with self-compatibility arose independently in three different *Leptosiphon* lineages...

2 ..."fooling" taxonomists into classifying three separate species as *L. bicolor.*

L. bicolor (selfing)   *L. liniflorus* (outcrossing)

Figure 20.10 Phylogeny Reveals Convergent Evolution
Self-compatibility apparently evolved independently three times among these species of the plant genus *Leptosiphon*. Because the appearance and structure of the flowers converged in the three selfing lineages, taxonomists mistakenly thought they were varieties of the same species. (After K. E. Holsinger. 2000. *Proc Natl Acad Sci USA* 97: 7037–7042. © 2000 National Academy of Sciences, U.S.A.)

Jurassic Park and *Jurassic World*, phylogenetic analyses are being used to reconstruct extinct species, one protein at a time.

Molecular clocks help date evolutionary events

For many applications, biologists want to know not only the order in which evolutionary lineages split but also the timing of those splits. In 1965, Emile Zuckerkandl and Linus Pauling hypothesized that rates of molecular change were constant enough that they could be used to predict evolutionary divergence times—an idea that has become known as the **molecular clock** hypothesis.

Of course, different genes evolve at different rates, and there are also differences in evolutionary rates among species associated with differing generation times, environments, efficiencies of DNA repair systems, and other biological factors. Nonetheless, among closely related species, a given gene usually evolves at a reasonably constant rate. Therefore the protein encoded by the gene accumulates amino acid replacements at a relatively constant rate (**Figure 20.11**). A molecular clock uses the average rate at which a given gene or protein accumulates changes to gauge the time of divergence for a particular split in the phylogeny. Molecular clocks must be calibrated using independent data, such as the fossil record, known times of divergence, or biogeographic dates (e.g., the time of separations of continents). Using such calibrations, times of divergence have been estimated for many groups of species that have diverged over millions of years.

Molecular clocks are not only used to date ancient events; they are also used to study the timing of comparatively recent events. Most samples of HIV-1 have been collected from humans only since the early 1980s, although a few isolates from medical biopsies

are available from as early as the 1950s. Biologists can use the observed changes in HIV-1 over the past several decades to project back to the common ancestor of all HIV-1 isolates, and estimate

The slope represents an average rate of change in amino acid sequences (the molecular clock).

Figure 20.11 A Molecular Clock for the Protein Hemoglobin
Amino acid replacements in hemoglobin have occurred at a relatively constant rate over nearly 500 million years of evolution. The graph shows the relationship between the time of divergence and the proportion of amino acids that have changed for 13 pairs of vertebrate hemoglobin proteins. The average rate of change represents the molecular clock for hemoglobin in vertebrates. (After R. E. Dickerson. 1971. *J Mol Evol* 1: 26–45.)

(A) Tree of HIV-1 samples plotted on a divergence axis

(B) Plot of average rate of divergence (the molecular clock)

(C) Extrapolation: Origin of 1959 sample

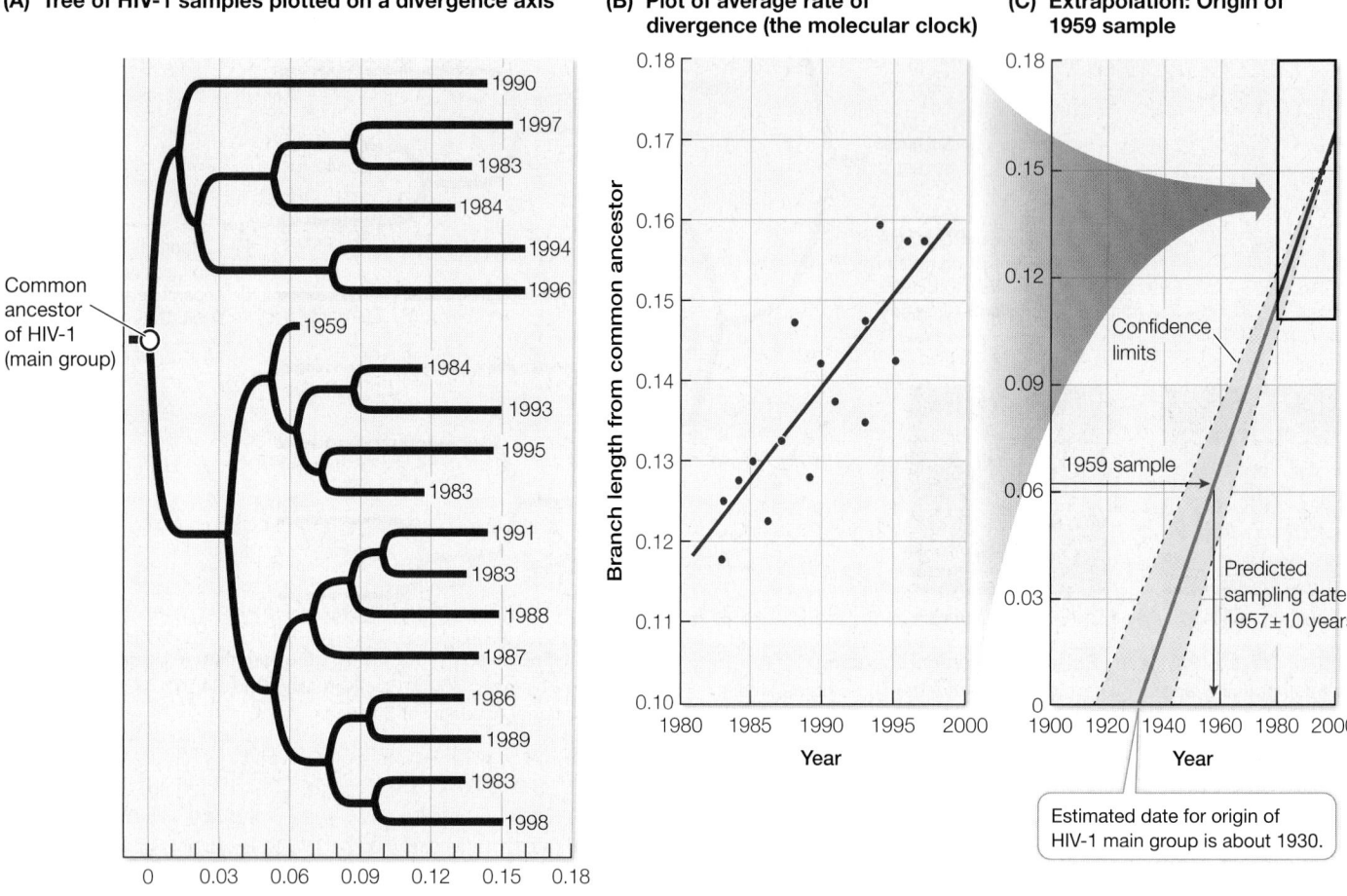

Common ancestor of HIV-1 (main group)

Branch length (substitutions/site) from common ancestor

Branch length from common ancestor

Year

Confidence limits

1959 sample

Predicted sampling date 1957±10 years

Estimated date for origin of HIV-1 main group is about 1930.

Figure 20.12 Dating the Origin of HIV-1 in Human Populations
(A) A phylogenetic tree for samples of the main group of HIV-1 virus. The dates indicate the years in which the samples were taken. (For clarity, only a small fraction of the samples that were examined in the original study are shown.) **(B)** A plot of sample year versus genetic divergence from the common ancestor provided an average rate of divergence, or a molecular clock. **(C)** The molecular clock was used to date a sample taken in 1959 (as a test of the clock) and to estimate the date of origin

of the HIV-1 main group (about 1930). Branch length from a common ancestor represents the average number of substitutions per nucleotide; the blue shaded region indicates the 95% confidence limits of the molecular clock predictions. (After B. Korber et al. 2000. *Science* 288: 1789–1796.)

Q: What would be the expected branch length from the common ancestor of an HIV isolate from 1970?

when HIV-1 first entered human populations from chimpanzees (**Figure 20.12**). This molecular clock was calibrated using the samples from the 1980s and 1990s, and then tested using the samples from the 1950s. As shown in Figure 20.12C, a sample from a 1959 biopsy is dated by molecular clock analysis at 1957 ± 10 years. Extrapolation back to the common ancestor of the samples suggested a date of origin for this group of viruses of about 1930. Although AIDS was unknown to Western medicine until the 1980s, this analysis shows that HIV-1 was present (probably at a very low frequency) in human populations in Africa for at least a half-century before its emergence as a global pandemic. Biologists have used similar analyses to conclude that immunodeficiency viruses have been transmitted repeatedly into human populations from multiple primates for more than a century (see also Figure 20.7).

KEY CONCEPT
20.3 Recap and Assess

Phylogenetic trees are used to reconstruct the evolutionary history of lineages, to determine when and where traits arose, and to make biological comparisons among genes, populations, and species. They can also be used to reconstruct ancestral traits and to estimate the timing of evolutionary events.

1. West Nile virus kills birds of many species and can cause fatal encephalitis (inflammation of the brain) in humans and horses. In the 1930s the virus was first isolated in Africa, where it is thought to be endemic. By the 1990s it had been found throughout much of Eurasia. West Nile virus was not found in North America until 1999, when it was first detected in New York, but since that time it has spread rapidly across most of the United States. Use the phylogenetic tree of West

Nile virus isolates shown here to construct a hypothesis about the origin of the virus lineage that was introduced into the United States (*figure source*: R. S. Lanciotti et al. 1999. *Science* 1286: 2333–2337). The isolates are identified by their place and date of isolation.

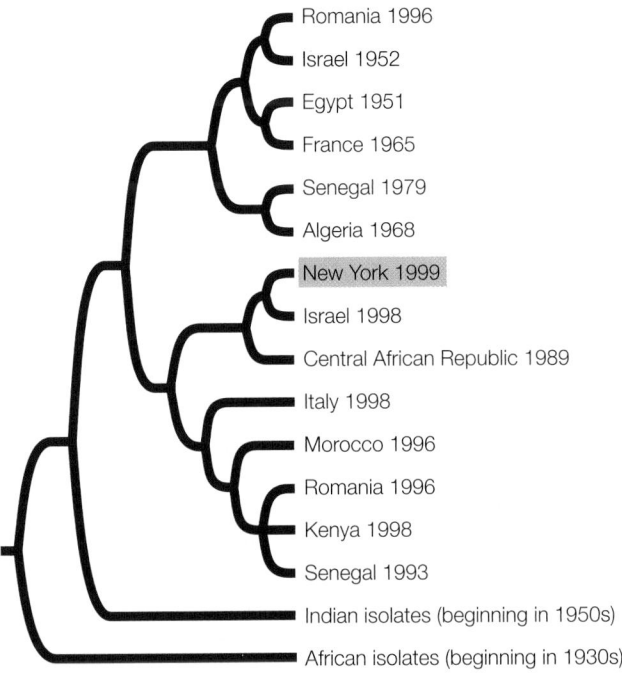

2. Researchers examined the molecular divergence of a mitochondrial DNA gene (*cyt b*) among sister species of birds called honeycreepers on different islands of Hawaii. They then plotted the measured molecular divergence against the estimated dates for separation of the islands (*figure source*: R. C. Fleischer et al. 1998. *Mol Ecol* 7: 533–545; bars represent 95% confidence limits for the estimated molecular divergences). Calculate the average rate of change in *cyt b* (the molecular clock) from the graph.

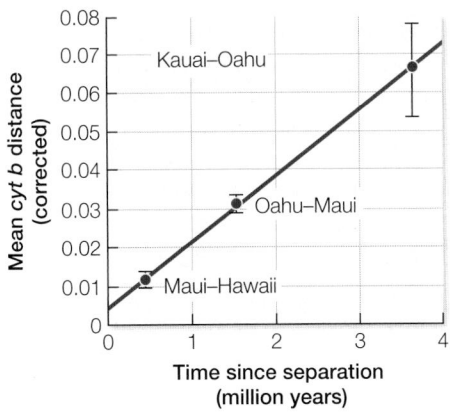

All of life is connected through evolutionary history, and the relationships among organisms provide a natural basis for making biological comparisons. For these reasons, biologists use phylogenetic relationships as the basis for organizing life into a coherent classification system.

Phylogeny Is the Basis of Biological Classification

Learning Objectives

20.4.1 Use a phylogeny to classify a group of organisms.

20.4.2 Analyze a phylogenetic tree to identify monophyletic, polyphyletic, and paraphyletic groups.

The biological classification system in widespread use today is derived from a system developed by the Swedish biologist Carolus Linnaeus in the mid-1700s. Linnaeus developed a naming system called **binomial nomenclature** that has allowed scientists throughout the world to refer unambiguously to the same organisms by the same names.

Linnaean classification is based on standard taxon ranks

Linnaeus gave each species a two-part name, one part identifying the species itself and the other the genus to which it belongs. A **genus** (plural *genera*) is a group of closely related species. Optionally, the name of the taxonomist who first proposed the species name may be added at the end. Thus *Homo sapiens* Linnaeus is the name of the modern human species. *Homo* is the genus to which the species belongs, and *sapiens* identifies the particular species in the genus *Homo*; Linnaeus proposed the species name *Homo sapiens*.

You can think of *Homo* as equivalent to your surname and *sapiens* as equivalent to your first name. The first letter of the genus name is capitalized, and the specific name is lowercase. Both of these formal designations are italicized. Rather than repeating the name of a genus when it is used several times in the same discussion, biologists often spell it out only once and abbreviate it with the initial letter thereafter (e.g., *D. melanogaster* rather than *Drosophila melanogaster*).

As we noted earlier, any group of organisms that is treated as a unit in a biological classification system, such as all species in the genus *Drosophila*, or all insects, or all arthropods, is called a taxon. In the Linnaean system, species and genera are further grouped into a hierarchical system of higher taxonomic categories. The taxon above the genus in the Linnaean system is the family. The names of animal families end in the suffix "-idae." Thus Formicidae is the family that contains all ant species, and the family Hominidae contains humans and our recent fossil relatives, as well as orangutans, gorillas, and our closest living relatives, the chimpanzees. Family names are based on the name of a member genus; Formicidae is based on the genus *Formica*, and Hominidae is based on *Homo*. The same rules are used in classifying plants, except that the suffix "-aceae" is used for plant family names instead of "-idae." Thus Rosaceae is the family that includes the genus *Rosa* (roses) and its relatives.

In the Linnaean system, families are grouped into orders, orders into classes, classes into phyla (singular *phylum*), and phyla into kingdoms. However, the ranking of taxa within Linnaean classification is subjective. Whether a particular taxon is considered, say, an order or a class is informative only with respect to the *relative* ranking of other related taxa. Although families are always grouped within orders, orders within classes, and so forth, there is nothing that makes a "family" in one group equivalent (in number of genera or in evolutionary age, for instance) to a "family" in another group.

Linnaeus recognized the overarching hierarchy of life, but he developed his system before evolutionary thought had become widespread. Biologists today recognize the tree of life as the basis for biological classification and often name taxa without placing them into the various Linnaean ranks.

Evolutionary history is the basis for modern biological classification

Today's biological classifications express the evolutionary relationships of organisms. Taxa are expected to be **monophyletic**, meaning that the taxon contains an ancestor and all descendants of that ancestor, and no other organisms. In other words, a monophyletic taxon is a historical group of related species, or a complete branch on the tree of life. As noted earlier, this is also the definition of a clade. A true monophyletic group can be removed from a phylogenetic tree by a single "cut" in the tree, as shown in **Figure 20.13**.

Note that there are many monophyletic groups on any phylogenetic tree, and that these groups are successively smaller subsets of larger monophyletic groups. This hierarchy of biological taxa, with all of life as the most inclusive taxon and many smaller taxa within larger taxa, down to the individual species, is the modern basis for biological classification.

Although biologists seek to describe and name only monophyletic taxa, the detailed phylogenetic information needed to do so is not always available. A group that does not include its common ancestor is **polyphyletic**. A group that does not include all the descendants of a common ancestor is referred to as **paraphyletic** (see Figure 20.13). Virtually all taxonomists now agree that polyphyletic and paraphyletic groups are inappropriate as taxonomic units because they do not correctly reflect evolutionary history. Some classifications still contain such groups because some organisms have not been evaluated phylogenetically. As mistakes in prior classifications are detected, taxonomic names are revised and polyphyletic and paraphyletic groups are eliminated from the classifications.

Several codes of biological nomenclature govern the use of scientific names

Several sets of explicit rules govern the use of scientific names. Biologists around the world follow these rules voluntarily to facilitate communication and dialogue. There may be dozens of common names for an organism in many different languages, and the same common name may refer to more than one species (**Figure 20.14**). The rules of biological nomenclature are designed so that there is only one correct scientific name for any single recognized taxon, and (ideally) a given scientific name applies only to a single taxon (that is, each scientific name is unique). Sometimes the same species is named more than once (when more than one taxonomist has taken up the task). In these cases, the rules specify that the valid name is the first name that was proposed. If the same name is inadvertently given to two different species, then the species that was named second must be given a new name.

Because of the historical separation of the fields of zoology, botany (which originally included mycology, the study of fungi), and microbiology, different sets of taxonomic rules were developed for each of these groups. Yet another set of rules emerged later for classifying viruses. This separation of fields resulted in duplicated taxon names in groups governed by the different sets of rules. *Drosophila*, for example, is both a genus of fruit flies and a genus of fungi, and some species in both groups have identical names. Until recently these duplicated names caused little confusion, since traditionally biologists who studied fruit flies were unlikely to read the literature on fungi (and vice versa). Today, given the prevalence of large, universal biological databases (such as GenBank, which includes DNA sequences from across all life), it is increasingly important that each taxon have a unique and unambiguous name. Biologists are working on a universal code of nomenclature that can be applied to all organisms, so that every species will have a unique identifying name or registration number. This will assist efforts to build an online Encyclopedia of Life (eol.org) that links all the information for all the world's species.

Phylogenetic methods are used by biologists to compare the evolutionary relationships across all of life and to study many evolutionary processes. In Chapter 21 we will use phylogenies as one of several tools to understand evolution at the level of genes and genomes.

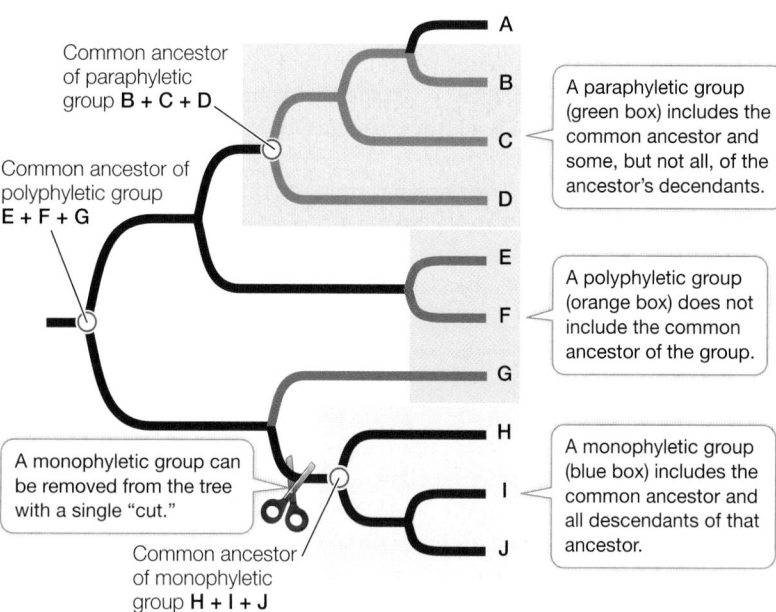

Figure 20.13 Monophyletic, Polyphyletic, and Paraphyletic Groups Monophyletic groups are the basis of taxa in modern biological classifications. Polyphyletic and paraphyletic groups are not appropriate for use in classifications because they do not accurately reflect evolutionary history.

View in Achieve
Activity 20.2 Types of Taxa

(A) *Asclepias tuberosa*

(B) *Castilleja coccinea*

(C) *Hieracium aurantiacum*

Figure 20.14 Same Common Name, Not the Same Species
All three of these distinct plant species are called "Indian paint-brush." Binomial nomenclature allows us to avoid the ambiguity of such common names and communicate exactly what is being described. **(A)** *Asclepias tuberosa* is a perennial milkweed native to eastern North America. **(B)** *Castilleja coccinea* is also native to eastern North America, but is a member of a very different group of plants called scrophs. **(C)** *Hieracium aurantiacum* is a European species of aster that has been widely introduced into North America.

KEY CONCEPT
20.4 Recap and Assess

Biologists organize and classify life by identifying and naming mono phyletic groups. Several sets of rules govern the use of scientific names so that each species and higher taxon can be identified and named unambiguously.

Consider the phylogeny and three possible classifications shown here.

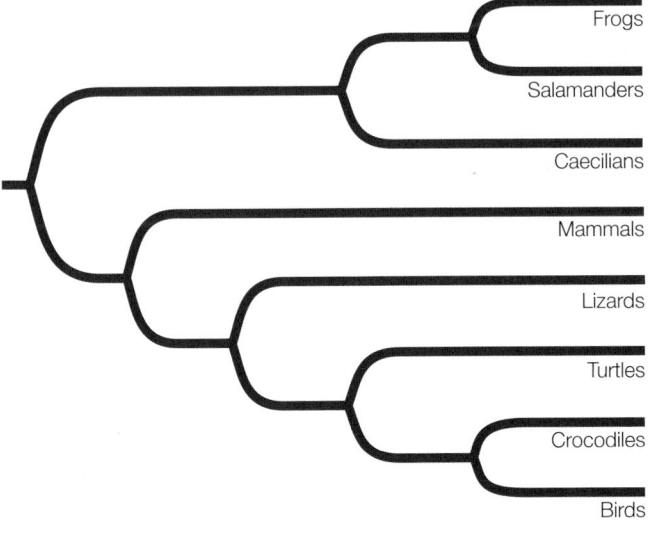

Classification one:

Named group	Included taxa
Amphibia	Frogs, salamanders, and caecilians
Mammalia	Mammals
Reptilia	Lizards, turtles, and crocodiles
Aves	Birds

Classification two:

Named group	Included taxa
Amphibia	Frogs, salamanders, and caecilians
Mammalia	Mammals
Reptilia	Lizards, turtles, crocodiles, and birds

Classification three:

Named group	Included taxa
Amphibia	Frogs, salamanders, and caecilians
Homothermia	Mammals and birds
Reptilia	Lizards, turtles, and crocodiles

1. Which of these classifications contains a paraphyletic group?

2. Which of these classifications contains a polyphyletic group?

3. Which of these classifications is consistent with the goal of including only monophyletic groups in a biological classification?

InvestigatingLIFE

Q and A **How are phylogenetic methods used to resurrect protein sequences from extinct organisms?**

Most genes and proteins of organisms that lived millions of years ago have decomposed in the fossil remains of these species. Nonetheless, the sequences of many ancient genes and proteins can be reconstructed by the methods described in this chapter. As we saw in **Investigating Life: Testing the Accuracy of Phylogenetic Analysis**, we can reconstruct ancestral DNA sequences—if we have enough information about the genomes of their descendants. Biologists have reconstructed gene sequences from species that have been extinct for millions of years. Using this information, a laboratory can reconstruct real proteins that correspond to those gene sequences. This is how Mikhail Matz and his colleagues were able to resurrect fluorescent proteins from the extinct ancestors of modern corals, then visualize the colors produced by these proteins in the laboratory (**Figure 20.15**).

Future directions

Biologists are now using phylogenetic analysis to reconstruct many ancient protein sequences. These reconstructed protein sequences are then made into actual proteins in the laboratory. For example, when biologists measured the temperature optima for resurrected proteins that were present in the common ancestor of all life, they found that the proteins functioned best in the range of 55°C–65°C. This result is consistent with hypotheses that life evolved in a high-temperature environment.

To reconstruct protein sequences from species that have been extinct for millions or even billions of years, biologists use detailed mathematical models that take into account much of what we have learned about molecular evolution, as described in Key Concept 20.2. These models incorporate information on rates of replacement among different amino acids in proteins, information on

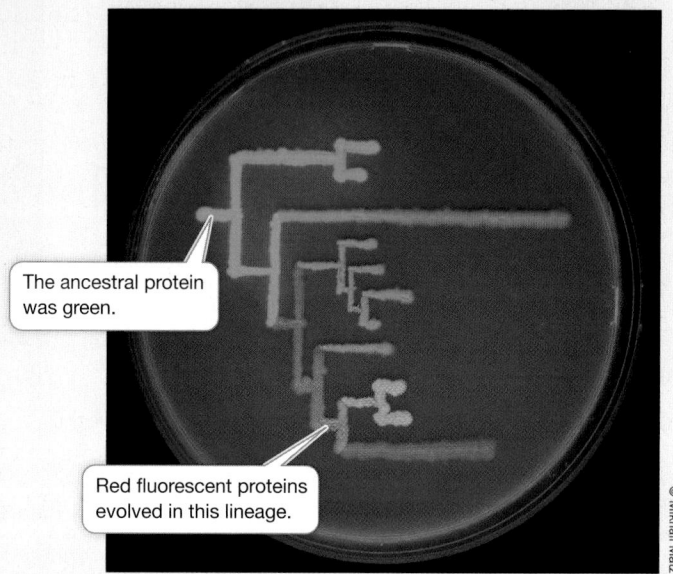

The ancestral protein was green.

Red fluorescent proteins evolved in this lineage.

Figure 20.15 Evolution of Fluorescent Proteins of Corals
Mikhail Matz and his colleagues used phylogenetic analysis to reconstruct the sequences of fluorescent proteins that were present in the extinct ancestors of modern corals. They then expressed these proteins in bacteria and plated the bacteria in the form of a phylogenetic tree to show how the colors evolved over time.

different substitution rates among nucleotides, and changes in the rate of molecular evolution among the major lineages of life. These studies are opening up opportunities to see how proteins have evolved through time and how extinct species once functioned.

You should be able to relate each summary to the adjacent figures. If you go to this visual summary in **Achieve**, you can follow links to figures, animations, activities, and simulations that will help you consolidate the material.

KEY CONCEPT

20.1 All of Life Is Connected through Its Evolutionary History

- **Phylogeny** is the history of evolutionary relationships among organisms or their genes. Groups of evolutionarily related species are represented as branches in a **phylogenetic tree**.

- Named species and groups of species are called **taxa**. A taxon that consists of an ancestor and all of its evolutionary descendants is called a **clade**. **Homologies** are similar traits that have been inherited from a common ancestor.

- A **derived trait** that is shared by two or more taxa and is inherited from their common ancestor is called a **synapomorphy**. Distantly related species may show similar traits that do not result from common ancestry. **Convergent evolution** and **evolutionary reversals** can give rise to such traits, which are called **homoplasies**.

Questions

1. Draw a phylogenetic tree of humans, chimpanzees, gorillas, and orangutans. Label the root and nodes.

2. What does the root of the tree represent?

3. What do the nodes represent?

Figure 20.1

Figure 20.4

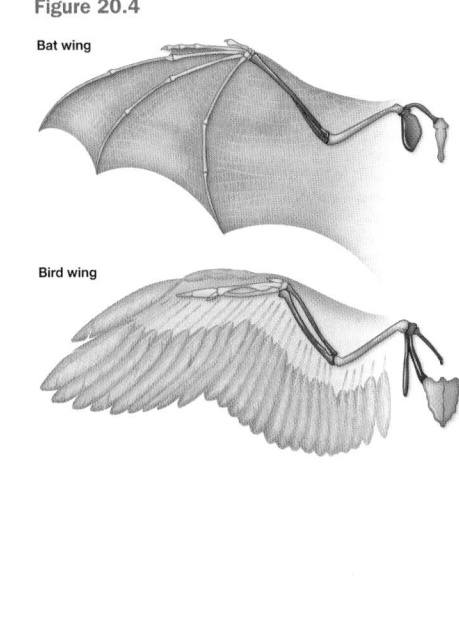

Bat wing

Bird wing

KEY CONCEPT

20.2 Phylogeny Can Be Reconstructed from Traits of Organisms

Go to **Activity 20.1, Animation 20.1,** and **Simulation 20.1**

- Phylogenetic trees can be constructed from synapomorphies using the **parsimony principle**.

- Phylogenetic trees can also be constructed using **maximum likelihood** methods, which find the tree most likely to have generated the observed data under a specific model of evolution.

- Phylogenetic methods have been tested in both experimental and simulation studies, and have been shown to be accurate under a wide variety of conditions.

Questions

1. What does the parsimony method minimize?

2. What is an example of a synapomorphy?

3. Why is it important that phylogenetic characters are genetically determined, rather than being influenced by the organism's environment?

Figure 20.5

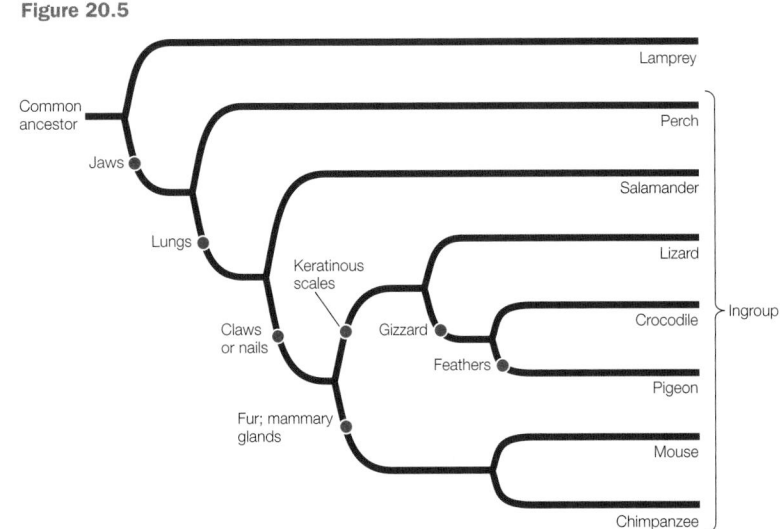

KEY CONCEPT

20.3 Phylogeny Makes Biology Comparative and Predictive

- Phylogenetic trees are used to make comparisons among living organisms.

- Phylogenetic trees are used to reconstruct the past and to understand the origin of traits.

- Phylogenetic trees may include estimates of divergence times of lineages determined by **molecular clock** analysis.

Questions

1. Draw a phylogenetic tree of HIV-1, HIV-2, and related SIVs from other primates.

2. Use the tree of HIVs and SIVs to explain the multiple origins of HIV in human populations.

3. How can phylogenetic trees be used to date at least one origin of HIV in humans?

Figure 20.9

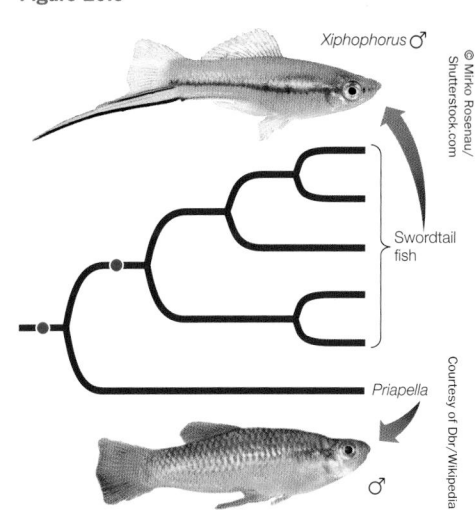

Xiphophorus ♂

© Mirko Rosenau/Shutterstock.com

Swordtail fish

Priapella

Courtesy of Dor/Wikipedia

♂

Figure 20.11

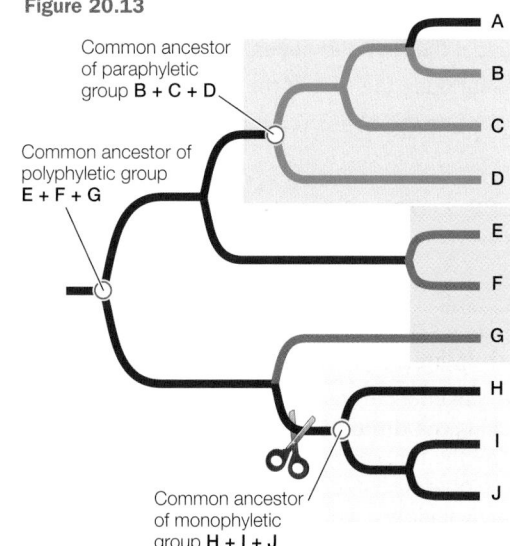

KEY CONCEPT

20.4 Phylogeny Is the Basis of Biological Classification

Go to Activity 20.2

- Biologists use phylogenetic relationships to organize life into a coherent classification system.

- Taxa in modern classifications are expected to be **monophyletic** groups. **Paraphyletic** and **polyphyletic** groups are not considered appropriate taxonomic units.

- Several sets of rules govern the use of scientific names, with the goal of providing unique and universal names for taxa.

Questions

1. Draw a phylogenetic tree, with taxon labels A–F.

2. Label a monophyletic group and a paraphyletic group on the tree.

3. What are the advantages of scientific names for taxa, as compared with common names?

Figure 20.13

Common ancestor of paraphyletic group B + C + D

Common ancestor of polyphyletic group E + F + G

Common ancestor of monophyletic group H + I + J

A
B
C
D
E
F
G
H
I
J

Evolution of Genes and Genomes

Courtesy of Dan Higgins and Douglas Jordan/CDC

KEY CONCEPTS

21.1 DNA Sequences Record the History of Gene Evolution

21.2 Genomes Reveal Both Neutral and Selective Processes of Evolution

21.3 Changes in the Size and Arrangement of Genomes Can Result in New Features

21.4 Changes in Gene Expression Often Shape Evolution

21.5 Molecular Evolution Has Many Practical Applications

An artist's view of an influenza virus The spikes on the surface represent proteins that elicit an immune response in humans.

Courtesy of the Office of the Public Health Service Historian

▶Investigating LIFE

Evolutionary Theory Helps Us Make Better Flu Vaccines

Combat in World War I ended in November 1918. But the death toll from four years of war was soon surpassed by the casualties of a massive influenza epidemic that killed more than 50 million people worldwide—more than twice the number of World War I combat deaths.

The 1918–1919 pandemic was noteworthy because the death rate among young adults—who are usually less likely to die from influenza than are the elderly or the very young—was 20 times higher than in flu epidemics before or since. Why was that particular virus so deadly, especially to typically hardy individuals? The 1918 flu strain triggered an especially intense reaction in the human immune system. This overreaction meant that people with strong immune systems were likely to be more severely affected.

Usually we can count on our immune system to fight viruses, and the immune response is the basis of vaccination. Since 1945, programs to administer flu vaccines have helped keep the number and severity of influenza outbreaks in check. Last year's vaccine, however, will probably not be effective against this year's virus. New strains of flu virus are evolving continuously, producing genetic variation in the population. If these viruses did not evolve, we would become resistant to them and annual vaccination would become unnecessary. But because the viruses do evolve, biologists

must develop a new and different flu vaccine each year.

The vertebrate immune response is initiated when the immune system recognizes proteins on the viral surface. Changes in viral surface proteins can allow the virus to escape immune detection. Virus strains with the greatest number of changes to their surface proteins are most likely to avoid detection and infect their hosts, and thus have an advantage over other strains. Biologists observe evolution in action by following changes in influenza virus proteins from year to year, and with this knowledge can produce more effective vaccines.

We learn a great deal about the molecular basis of evolution by examining rapidly evolving organisms such as viruses. Molecular studies of evolution, in turn, are put to practical uses, such as the development of better strategies for combating deadly diseases.

Q and A **Why was the 1918–1919 flu pandemic worse than any before or since?** (Find the answer on page 490.)

<table>
<tr><td>

KEY CONCEPT 21.1 DNA Sequences Record the History of Gene Evolution

</td></tr>
</table>

Learning Objectives

21.1.1 Analyze and compare DNA and protein sequences across species by using matrices of similarities and differences.

21.1.2 Explain why counts of nucleotide or amino acid differences between two sequences often underestimate the actual number of changes that have occurred between the sequences.

An organism's **genome** is the full set of genes it contains, as well as any noncoding regions of the DNA (or in the case of some viruses, RNA). Most of the genes of eukaryotic organisms are found on chromosomes in the nucleus, but genes are also present in chloroplasts and mitochondria. In organisms that reproduce sexually, both males and females contribute nuclear genes, but mitochondrial and chloroplast genes are usually transmitted only via the cytoplasm of one of the two gametes (often from the female parent).

Evolution results from changes to gene sequences, location, and expression

Genomes must be replicated to be transmitted from parents to offspring. DNA replication does not occur without error, however. Mistakes in DNA replication—mutations—provide much of the raw material for evolutionary change. Even though the replication error rate per nucleotide is very small, most genomes are so large that a few errors are usually made every time a genome is replicated. These errors are actually essential for the long-term survival of life, because mutations are the initial source of the genetic variation that permits species to evolve in response to changes in their environment.

A particular allele of a gene will not be passed on to successive generations unless an individual carrying that allele survives and reproduces. The allele must function in combination with many other genes in the genome or it will quickly be selected against. Moreover, the degree and timing of a gene's expression are affected by its location in the genome. Evolutionary changes result from mutations to gene sequences, from gene duplications and rearrangements, and from changes in the timing, degree, and location of gene expression.

A genome, then, is not simply a random collection of genes in a random order along chromosomes. Rather, it is a complex set of integrated genes, regulatory sequences, and structural elements, interspersed with vast stretches of noncoding DNA that may have little direct function. The sequences of genes, as well as their location and expression, are subject to evolutionary change, as are the extent and location of noncoding DNA. All of these changes can affect the phenotype of an organism.

Biologists have now sequenced the complete genomes of a large number of organisms, including humans. The information in these sequences is helping us understand how and why organisms differ, how they function, and how they have evolved.

Evolution of genomes results in biological diversity

The field of **molecular evolution** investigates the mechanisms and consequences of the evolution of macromolecules—particularly nucleic acids (DNA and RNA) and proteins. Molecular evolutionists study relationships between the structures of genes and proteins and the functions of organisms. They also examine molecular variation to reconstruct evolutionary history and to study the mechanisms and consequences of evolution. Students of this field ask questions such as: What does molecular variation tell us about a gene's function? Why do the genomes of different organisms vary in size? What evolutionary forces shape patterns of variation among genomes? And a crucial question from an evolutionary perspective: How do genomes acquire new functions? Investigations into the evolution of particular nucleic acids and proteins are instrumental in reconstructing the evolutionary histories of genes. Ultimately, molecular evolutionary biologists hope to explain the molecular basis of biological diversity.

The evolution of nucleic acids and proteins depends on genetic variation introduced by mutations. One of several ways genes evolve is by means of nucleotide substitutions (the incorporation of point mutations in populations). In genes that encode proteins, nucleotide substitutions sometimes result in amino acid replacements that can change the charge, the structure, and other chemical and physical properties of the encoded protein. These changes in a protein molecule often affect the way that protein functions in the organism.

Evolutionary changes in genes and proteins can be identified by comparing nucleotide or amino acid sequences from different organisms. The longer two sequences have been evolving separately, the more differences they accumulate (bearing in mind that different genes in the same species evolve at different rates). Determining how long ago changes in nucleotide or amino acid sequences occurred is a useful step toward inferring their causes. Knowledge of the pattern and rate of evolutionary change in a given macromolecule is useful in reconstructing the evolutionary history of groups of organisms.

To compare genes or proteins from different organisms, biologists need a way to identify homologous parts of macromolecules. (Recall from Key Concept 20.1 that homologous features are those shared by two or more species that have been inherited from a common ancestor.) Homologous parts of a protein can be identified by their homologous amino acid sequences. And since nucleotide sequences encode amino acid sequences, the concept of homology extends down to the level of individual nucleotide positions. Therefore one of the first steps in studying the evolution of genes or proteins is to align homologous positions in the amino acid or nucleotide sequence of interest.

Genes and proteins are compared through sequence alignment

Once the nucleotide or amino acid sequences of molecules from different organisms have been determined, they can be compared. Homologous positions can be identified only if we first pinpoint the locations of deletions and insertions that have occurred in the molecules of interest in the time since the organisms diverged from a common ancestor. A simple hypothetical example illustrates this **sequence alignment** technique. In **Figure 21.1** we

Figure 21.1 Amino Acid Sequence Alignment Amino acid sequence alignment is a way of arranging protein sequences to identify regions of homology between the sequences. Gaps are inserted between the amino acid residues to align similar residues in columns. Differences (number of amino acid differences plus insertion or deletion events) and similarities (number of identical amino acids) between each pair of aligned sequences are then summarized in a similarity matrix. Homologous DNA sequences can be aligned in a similar manner.

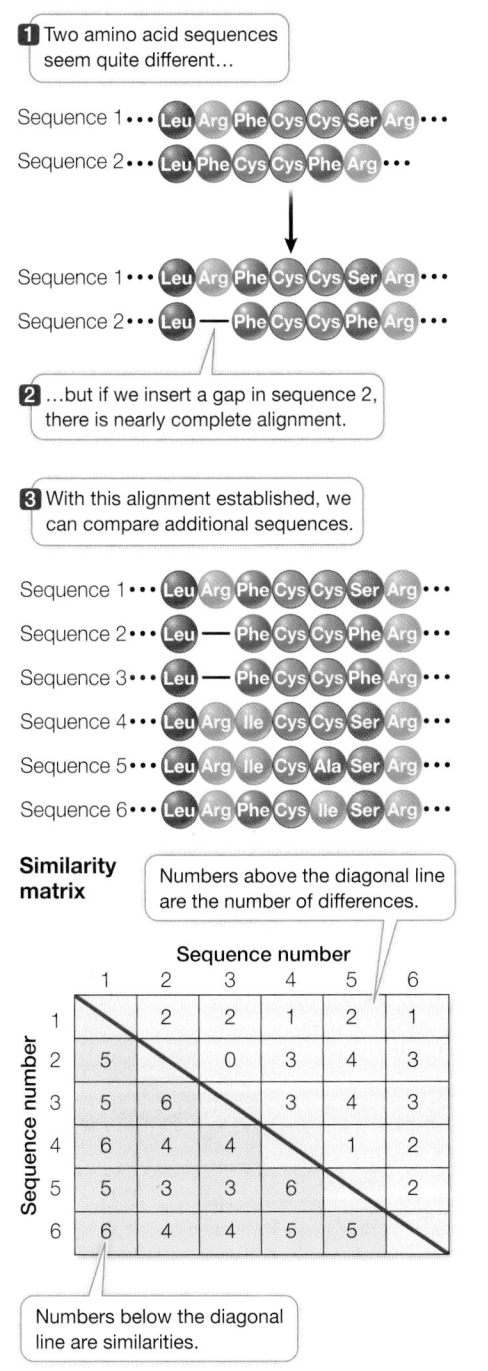

compare two amino acid sequences from homologous proteins in different organisms. The two sequences at first appear to differ in both the number and identity of their amino acids. If we insert a gap after the first amino acid in sequence 2 (after leucine), however, the similarities in the two sequences become obvious. This gap represents the occurrence of one of two evolutionary events: an insertion of an amino acid in the longer protein or a deletion of an amino acid in the shorter protein. Having adjusted for this insertion or deletion event, we can see that the two sequences differ by only one amino acid at position 6 (serine or phenylalanine).

 View in Achieve
Activity 21.1 Amino Acid Sequence Alignment

Adding a single gap—that is, identifying a deletion or an insertion—aligns the two sequences in Figure 21.1. Additional sequences can now be added to the alignment in a similar manner. Longer amino acid sequences, and those that have diverged more extensively, require more elaborate adjustments. Explicit models (incorporated into computer algorithms) have been developed to account for the relative probabilities of deletions, insertions, and particular amino acid replacements.

Having aligned the sequences, we can compare them by counting the number of nucleotides or amino acids that differ between them. Summing the numbers of the same and different amino acids in each pair of sequences allows us to construct a **similarity matrix**, which gives us a measure of the minimum number of changes that have occurred since the divergence of each pair of organisms (see Figure 21.1).

 View in Achieve
Activity 21.2 Similarity Matrix Construction

Models of sequence evolution are used to calculate evolutionary divergence

The sequence comparison procedure illustrated in Figure 21.1 gives a simple count of the number of similarities and differences between the proteins of two species. In the context of two aligned DNA sequences, we can count the number of differences at homologous nucleotide positions, and this count indicates the minimum number of nucleotide changes that must have occurred since the two sequences diverged from a common ancestral sequence.

Although it is useful in determining a *minimum* number of changes between two DNA sequences, the count provided by sequence alignment almost certainly underestimates the *actual* number of changes that have occurred since the sequences diverged. Any given change counted in a similarity matrix of DNA sequences may result from multiple substitution events that occurred at a given nucleotide position over time. As illustrated in **Figure 21.2**, any of the following events may have occurred at a given nucleotide position that would not be revealed by a simple count of similarities and differences between two DNA sequences:

- *Multiple substitutions.* More than one change has occurred at a given position between the ancestral sequence and at least one of the observed sequences.

- *Coincident substitutions.* At a given position, different substitutions have occurred between the ancestral sequence and each observed sequence.

Observed sequence 1	Ancestral sequence	Observed sequence 2	
A	A	A	
C	C	→ T	Single substitution
G	G	G	
G	G	G	
T	T → C →	G	Multiple substitutions
A	A	A	
T	T	T	
T	T	T	
G ←	A	→ T	Coincident substitutions
C	C	C	
C ←	G	→ C	Parallel substitutions
G	G	G	
G	G	G	
C	C	C	
T	T	T	
A	A → G * →	A	*Back substitution (reversion)
T	T	T	
A	A	A	

Figure 21.2 Multiple Substitutions Are Not Reflected in Pairwise Sequence Comparisons   Two observed sequences descended from a common ancestral sequence (center) have undergone a series of substitutions. Although the two observed sequences differ by only three nucleotides (colored letters), these three differences result from a total of nine substitutions (arrows).

- *Parallel substitutions.* The same substitution has occurred independently between the ancestral sequence and each observed sequence.
- *Back substitutions* (also called reversions). In a variation on multiple substitutions, after a change at a given position, a subsequent substitution has changed the position back to the ancestral state.

To correct for undercounting of substitutions, molecular evolutionists have developed mathematical models that describe how DNA (and protein) sequences evolve. These models take into account the relative rates of change from one nucleotide to another. For

Tuna

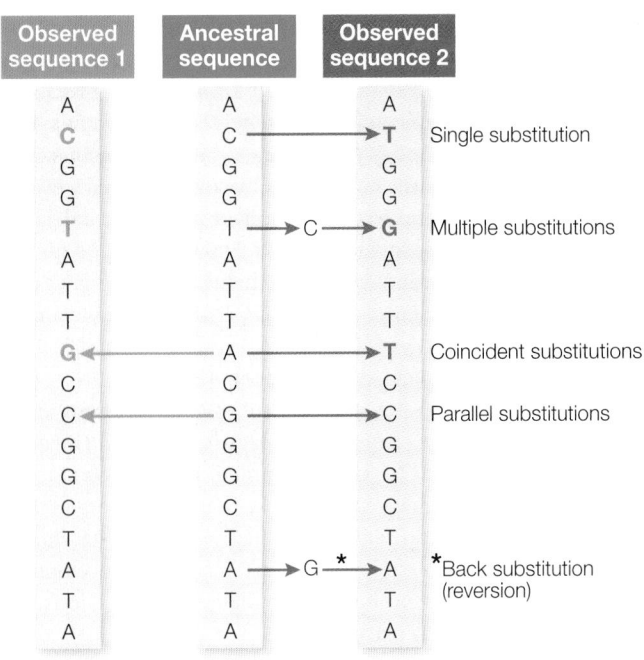

Data from PDB 5CYT, T. Takano, 1984

Rice

Data from PDB 1CCR, H. Ochi et al., 1983. *J Mol Biol* 166: 407

Acidic side chains
D Aspartic acid
E Glutamic acid

Basic side chains
H Histidine
K Lysine
R Arginine

Hydrophobic side chains
F Phenylalanine
I Isoleucine
L Leucine
M Methionine

V Valine
Y Tyrosine
W Tryptophan
A Alanine

Other
C Cysteine
P Proline
Q Glutamine
N Asparagine
S Serine
T Threonine
G Glycine

The number 1 indicates an invariant position in the cytochrome *c* molecule (i.e., all the organisms have the same amino acid in this position). Such a position is probably under strong purifying selection.

Amino acids at positions marked by red arrowheads have side chains that interact with the heme group.

Position in sequence   1   5   10   15   20   25   30
Number of amino acids at the position   1 3 5 5 5 1 3 3 4 1 4 3 2 1 3 3 1 1 2 4 3 4 2 3 4 2 1 4 1 1 2 1 5 1

Human, chimpanzee	G D V E K G K K I F I M K C S Q C H T V E K G G K H K T G P N L H G
Rhesus monkey	G D V E K G K K I F I M K C S Q C H T V E K G G K H K T G P N L H G
Horse	G D V E K G K K I F V Q K C A Q C H T V E K G G K H K T G P N L H G
Donkey	G D V E K G K K I F V Q K C A Q C H T V E K G G K H K T G P N L H G
Cow, pig, sheep	G D V E K G K K I F V Q K C A Q C H T V E K G G K H K T G P N L H G
Dog	G D V E K G K K I F V Q K C A Q C H T V E K G G K H K T G P N L H G
Rabbit	G D V E K G K K I F V Q K C A Q C H T V E K G G K H K T G P N L H G
Gray whale	G D V E K G K K I F V Q K C A Q C H T V E K G G K H K T G P N L H G
Gray kangaroo	G D V E K G K K I F V Q K C A Q C H T V E K G G K H K T G P N L N G
Chicken, turkey	G D I E K G K K I F V Q K C S Q C H T V E K G G K H K T G P N L H G
Pigeon	G D I E K G K K I F V Q K C S Q C H T V E K G G K H K T G P N L H G
Pekin duck	G D V E K G K K I F V Q K C S Q C H T V E K G G K H K T G P N L H G
Snapping turtle	G D V E K G K K I F V Q K C A Q C H T V E K G G K H K T G P N L N G
Rattlesnake	G D V E K G K K I F T M K C S Q C H T V E K G G K H K T G P N L H G
Bullfrog	G D V E K G K K I F V Q K C A Q C H T C E K G G K H K V G P N L Y G
Tuna	G D V A K G K K T F V Q K C A Q C H T V E N G G K H K V G P N L W G
Dogfish	G D V E K G K K V F V Q K C A Q C H T V E N G G K H K T G P N L S G
Samia cynthia (moth)	G N A E N G K K I F V Q R C A Q C H T V E A G G K H K V G P N L H G
Tobacco hornworm moth	G N A D N G K K I F V Q R C A Q C H T V E A G G K H K V G P N L H G
Screwworm fly	G D V E K G K K I F V Q R C A Q C H T V E A G G K H K V G P N L H G
Drosophila (fruit fly)	G D V E K G K K L F V Q R C A Q C H T V E A G G K H K V G P N L H G
Baker's yeast	G S A K K G A T L F K T R C E L C H T V E K G G P H K V G P N L H G
Candida krusei (yeast)	G S A K K G A T L F K T R C A E C H T I E A G G P H K V G P N L H G
Neurospora crassa (mold)	G D S K K G A N L F K T R C A E C H – – E – N L T Q K I G P A L H G
Wheat	G N P D A G A K I F K T K C A Q C H T V D A G A – H K Q G P N L H G
Sunflower	G D P T T G A K I F K T K C A Q C H T V E K G A – H K Q G P N L H G
Mung bean	G D S K S G E K I F K T K C A Q C H T V D K G A – H K Q G P N L N G
Rice	G N P K A G E K I F K T K C A Q C H T V D K G A – H K Q G P N L N G
Sesame	G D V K S G E K I F K T K C A Q C H T V D K G A – H K Q G P N L N G

Gaps indicate insertion and/or deletion events.

example, *transitions* (changes between the two purines, A ↔ G, or between the pyrimidines, C ↔ T) are typically more frequent than *transversions* (a purine is replaced by a pyrimidine, or vice versa). These models also include parameters such as the different rates of substitution across different parts of a gene and the proportions of each nucleotide present in a given sequence. Once such parameters have been estimated, the model is used to correct for multiple substitutions, coincident substitutions, parallel substitutions, and back substitutions. The revised estimate accounts for the *total* number of substitutions likely to have occurred between two sequences, which is almost always greater than the observed number of differences.

As sequence information becomes available for more and more genes in an ever-expanding database, sequence alignments can be extended across multiple homologous sequences, and the minimum number of insertions, deletions, and substitutions can be summed across homologous genes of an entire group of organisms. Similar databases have been constructed for homologous proteins. **Figure 21.3** shows aligned data for cytochrome *c* protein sequences in 33 species of animals, plants, and fungi. Such information is used extensively in determining evolutionary relationships among species.

Experimental studies examine molecular evolution directly

Although molecular evolutionists are often interested in naturally evolved genes and proteins, molecular evolution can also

Figure 21.3 Amino Acid Sequences of Cytochrome c   The amino acid sequences shown in the table were obtained from analyses of the enzyme cytochrome *c* from 33 species of plants, fungi, and animals. Note the lack of variation across the sequences at positions 70–80, suggesting that this region is under strong purifying selection and that changing its amino acid sequence would impair the protein's function. The molecular models at the upper left are created from these sequences and show the three-dimensional structures of tuna and rice cytochrome *c*. Alpha helixes are in red, and the molecule's heme group is shown in yellow. (Based on table by Graphic Presentation Services, Inc. in R. E. Dickerson. 1972. *Sci Am* 226: 58–72.)

▶ **Media Clip 21.1 The Ubiquitous Protein**
Life12e.com/mc21.1

> Multiple amino acids at a position indicate a great deal of change. The alternative residues may be functionally equivalent, or are selected for different functions.

Invariant

| 35 | 40 | 45 | 50 | 55 | 60 | 65 | 70 | 75 | 80 | 85 | 90 | 95 | 100 | 104 |

3 3 2 1 3 2 1 3 3 6 1 2 3 1 2 5 1 2 2 5 3 3 2 5 1 5 4 5 2 2 5 3 1 1 3 1 1 1 1 1 1 1 1 1 1 1 1 1 3 1 5 1 2 2 1 6 9 2 1 7 2 2 2 3 2 2 2 6 4 4 5 4

```
LFGRKTGQAPGYSYTAANKNKGIIWGEDTLMEYLENPKKYIPGTKMIFVGIKKKEERADLIAYLKKATNE
LFGRKTGQAPGYSYTAANKNKGIIWGEDTLMEYLENPKKYIPGTKMIFVGIKKKEERADLIAYLKKATNE
LFGRKTGQAPGFTYTDANKNKGITWKEETLMEYLENPKKYIPGTKMIFAGIKKKTEREDLIAYLKKATNE
LFGRKTGQAPGFSYTDANKNKGITWKEETLMEYLENPKKYIPGTKMIFAGIKKKTEREDLIAYLKKATNE
LFGRKTGQAPGFSYTDANKNKGITWGEETLMEYLENPKKYIPGTKMIFAGIKKKGEREDLIAYLKKATNE
LFGRKTGQAPGFSYTDANKNKGITWGEETLMEYLENPKKYIPGTKMIFAGIKKTGERADLIAYLKKATKE
LFGRKTGQAVGFSYTDANKNKGITWGEDTLMEYLENPKKYIPGTKMIFAGIKKKDERADLIAYLKKATNE
LFGRKTGQAVGFSYTDANKNKGITWGEETLMEYLENPKKYIPGTKMIFAGIKKKGERADLIAYLKKATNE
LFGRKTGQAPGFTYTDANKNKGIIWGEDTLMEYLENPKKYIPGTKMIFAGIKKKGERADLIAYLKKATNE

LFGRKTGQAEGFSYTDANKNKGITWGEDTLMEYLENPKKYIPGTKMIFAGIKKKSERVDLIAYLKDATSK
LFGRKTGQAEGFSYTDANKNKGITWGEDTLMEYLENPKKYIPGTKMIFAGIKKKAERADLIAYLKQATAK
LFGRKTGQAEGFSYTDANKNKGITWGEDTLMEYLENPKKYIPGTKMIFAGIKKKSERADLIAYLKDATAK
LIGRKTGQAEGFSYTEANKNKGITWGEETLMEYLENPKKYIPGTKMIFAGIKKKAERADLIAYLKDATSK
LFGRKTGQAVGYSYTAANKNKGIIWGDDTLMEYLENPKKYIPGTKMVFTGLSKKKERTNLIAYLKEKTAA
LIGRKTGQAAGFSYTDANKNKGITWGEDTLMEYLENPKKYIPGTKMIFAGIKKKGERQDLIAYLKSACSK
LFGRKTGQAEGYSYTDASKNKGIVWNNDTLMEYLENPKKYIPGTKMIFAGIKKKGERQDLVAYLKSATS
LFGRKTGQAQGFSYTDASKNKGITWQQETLRIYLENPKKYIPGTKMIFAGLKKKSERQDLIAYLKKTAAS

FYGRKTGQAPGFSYSNANKAKGITWGDDTLFEYLENPKKYIPGTKMVFAGLKKANERADLIAYLKESTK
FFGRKTGQAPGFSYSNANKAKGITWQDDTLFEYLENPKKYIPGTKMVFAGLKKANERADLIAYLKQATK
LFGRKTGQAAGFAYTNANKAKGITWQDDTLFEYLENPKKYIPGTKMIFAGLKKPNERGDLIAYLKSATK
LIGRKTGQAAGFAYTNANKAKGITWQDDTLFEYLENPKKYIPGTKMIFAGLKKPNERGDLIAYLKSATK
IFGRHSGQAQGYSYTDANIKKNVLWDENNMSEYLTNPKKYIPGTKMAFGGLKKEKDRNDLITYLKKACE
IFSRHSGQAQGYSYTDANKRAGVEWAEPTMSDYLENPKKYIPGTKMAFGGLKKAKDRNDLVTYMLEASK
LFGRKTGQADGYAYTDANKQKGITWDENTLFEYLENPKKYIPGTKMAFGGLKKDKDRNDIITFMKEATA
LFGRQSGSTAGYSYSAANKNKAVEWEENTLYDYLLNPKKYIPGTKMVFPGLKKPQDRADLIAYLKKATSS
LFGRQSGTTAGYSYSAANKNMAVIWEENTLYDYLLNPKKYIPGTKMVFPGLKKPQERADLIAYLKTSTA
LFGRQSGTTAGYSYSTANKNMAVIWEEKTLYDYLLNPKKYIPGTKMVFPGLKKPQERADLIAYLKESTA
LFGRQSGTTPGYSYSTADKNMAVIWEENTLYDYLLNPKKYIPGTKMVFPGLKKPQERADLISYLKEATS
LFGRQSGTTPGYSYSAANKNMAVIWGENTLYDYLLNPKKYIPGTKMVFPGLKKPQDRADLIAYLKEATA
```

be observed directly in the laboratory. Increasingly, evolutionary biologists are studying evolution experimentally. Because substitution rates are related to generation time rather than to absolute time, most of these experiments use unicellular organisms or viruses with short generations. Viruses, bacteria, and unicellular eukaryotes (such as the yeasts) can be cultured in large populations in the laboratory, and many of these organisms can evolve rapidly. In the case of some RNA viruses, the natural substitution rate may be as high as 1 substitution per 1,000 nucleotides per generation. Therefore in a virus of a few thousand nucleotides, one or more substitutions are expected (on average) every generation, and these changes can easily be determined by sequencing the entire viral genome (because of its small size). Generation time may be only tens of minutes (rather than years or decades, as in many animals), so biologists can directly observe substantial molecular evolution in a controlled population over the course of days, weeks, or months.

Experimental molecular evolutionary studies are used for a wide variety of purposes and have greatly expanded the ability of evolutionary biologists to test evolutionary concepts and principles. Biologists now routinely study evolution in the laboratory, and as we will see later in this chapter, they can use in vitro evolutionary techniques to produce novel molecules that perform new functions with industrial and pharmaceutical uses.

KEY CONCEPT
21.1 Recap and Assess

The genomes of all organisms evolve over time. Evolutionary changes can be detected by aligning and then comparing the nucleic acid and protein sequences of different species. Experimental studies of molecular evolution under controlled conditions allow biologists to study many processes of evolution directly.

1. Align the following sequences. Then create a matrix that compares both the number of identical nucleotides and the number of differences (including insertion and deletion events).

   Sequence *a*: AATGCAGGGTATACG

   Sequence *b*: ATTCAGGGTATACC

   Sequence *c*: ATTGCAGCGTATAACC

   Sequence *d*: ATTGCAGGGTATACG

2. Explain why a simple count of nucleotide differences between two sequences often underestimates the actual number of nucleotide substitutions since the sequences diverged. Use an example based on the comparison of your alignment of Sequences *a* and *b* from Question 1.

We have seen that molecular evolutionists can directly observe the evolution of genomes over time, compare the genomes of different organisms, and reconstruct the changes that have occurred during their evolution. Let's turn now to the question of how genomes change, and examine some of the consequences of those changes.

KEY CONCEPT
21.2 Genomes Reveal Both Neutral and Selective Processes of Evolution

Learning Objectives

21.2.1 Explain how substitutions may be neutral or selective in a given organism.

21.2.2 Provide a mathematical explanation for why the rate of evolution of neutral mutations is independent of population size.

21.2.3 Evaluate gene sequences of protein-coding genes to identify positions that are evolving under purifying versus positive selection, and apply this knowledge to a biological problem.

Most natural populations harbor far more genetic variation than we would expect to find if genetic variation were influenced by natural selection alone. This discovery, combined with the knowledge that many mutations do not change molecular function, stimulated the development of the neutral theory of molecular evolution.

Much of molecular evolution is neutral

To discuss the evolution of genes, we need to consider the specific types of mutations that are possible. A nucleotide substitution is a change in a single nucleotide in a DNA sequence (a type of point mutation; see Key Concept 15.1). Many nucleotide substitutions have no effect on phenotype, even if the change occurs in a gene that encodes a protein, because most amino acids are specified by more than one codon. A substitution that does not change the encoded amino acid is known as a **synonymous substitution** (also called a **silent substitution**) (**Figure 21.4A**). Synonymous

(A) Synonymous substitutions

Leu (UUA) → UUG Leu

Thr (ACU) → ACA Thr

Leu (UUA) → CUA Leu

(B) Nonsynonymous substitutions

Leu (UUA) → UUC Phe

Trp (UGG) → UGA Stop translation

Gly (GGA) → AGA Arg

This nonsense substitution would result in an incomplete protein.

Figure 21.4 When One Nucleotide Changes (A) Synonymous substitutions do not change the amino acid specified and do not affect protein function. Such substitutions are less likely than other substitutions to be influenced by natural selection, although they contribute greatly to the buildup of neutral genetic variation in a population. (B) Nonsynonymous substitutions do change the amino acid sequence and are likely to have an effect (often deleterious, but sometimes beneficial) on protein function. Such nucleotide substitutions are targets for natural selection.

substitutions do not affect the functioning of a protein (although they may have other effects, such as changes in mRNA stability or translation rates) and are therefore less likely than other types of substitutions to be influenced by natural selection.

A nucleotide substitution that does change the amino acid sequence encoded by a gene is known as a **nonsynonymous substitution** (a **missense substitution** changes an amino acid, and a **nonsense substitution** produces a new stop codon) (**Figure 21.4B**). In general, nonsynonymous substitutions are likely to be deleterious to the organism. But not every amino acid replacement alters a protein's shape and charge (and hence its functional properties). Therefore some nonsynonymous substitutions are selectively neutral, or nearly so. Another possibility is that a nonsynonymous substitution alters a protein in a way that confers an advantage to the organism and is therefore favored by natural selection.

Synonymous substitutions accumulate over time in protein-coding genes at a much higher rate than nonsynonymous substitutions do. This is true even though the underlying mutation rates for both types of substitutions are equal (or at least similar). The reason is simple: as most nonsynonymous substitutions are harmful to the function of a gene, they are removed from the population over time through natural selection. Therefore substitution rates are higher at nucleotide positions that do not change the amino acid being expressed (**Figure 21.5**). The rate of substitution is even higher in **pseudogenes**, which are copies of genes that are no longer functional (and so are not subject to strong selection).

Insertions, deletions, and rearrangements of DNA sequences are all mutations that may affect a larger portion of the gene or genome than do point mutations. Insertions and deletions of nucleotides in a protein-coding sequence interrupt its reading frame, unless they occur in multiples of three nucleotides (the length of one codon). Rearrangements may merely change the order of whole genes along chromosomes, or they may rearrange functional domains among individual genes.

When biologists began to examine the details of genetic variation of populations, they soon discovered many gene variants that had little or no effect on function. This gave rise to new ideas about how these neutral variants arise and spread in populations. Motoo Kimura proposed the **neutral theory** in 1968. He suggested that, at the molecular level, the majority of variants found in most populations are selectively neutral. That is, most gene variants confer neither an advantage nor a disadvantage on their bearers. Therefore these neutral variants must accumulate through genetic drift rather than through positive selection.

We saw in Key Concept 19.2 that genetic drift of existing gene variants tends to be greatest in small populations. However, the rate of fixation of *new* neutral mutations by genetic drift is independent of population size. To see why this is so, consider a population of size N and a neutral mutation rate of μ (mu) per gamete per generation at a particular locus. The number of new mutations would be, on average, $\mu \times 2N$, because $2N$ gene copies are available to mutate in a population of diploid organisms. The probability that a given mutation will be fixed by drift alone is its frequency, which equals $1/(2N)$ for a newly arisen mutation. We can multiply these two terms to get the rate of fixation of neutral mutations (m) in a given population of N individuals:

$$m = 2N\mu \frac{1}{2N}$$

But notice that the two effects of population size (N) cancel one another out:

$$m = \cancel{2N}\mu \frac{1}{\cancel{2N}}$$

Therefore the rate of fixation of neutral mutations m depends only on the neutral mutation rate μ and is independent of population size. Any given mutation is more likely to appear in a large population than in a small one, but any mutation that does appear is more likely to become fixed in a small population. The rate of fixation of neutral mutations is thus equal to the mutation rate in populations of any size (i.e., $m = \mu$).

As long as the underlying mutation rate is constant, genes and proteins evolving in different populations should diverge from one another in neutral changes at a constant rate. The rate of evolution of particular genes and proteins is indeed often relatively constant over time, and therefore can be used as a molecular clock to calculate evolutionary divergence times between species (see Key Concept 20.3).

Neutral theory does not imply that most mutations have no effect on the individual organism, even though much of the genetic variation present in a population is the result of neutral evolution. Many mutations are rarely or never observed in populations because they are lethal or strongly detrimental, and the individuals that carry them are quickly removed from the population through natural selection. Similarly, because mutations that confer a selective advantage tend to be quickly fixed in populations, they also do not result in significant variation at the population level. Nonetheless, if we compare homologous

Figure 21.5 Rates of Substitution Differ Rates of nonsynonymous substitution are typically much lower than rates of synonymous substitution, and much lower than substitution rates in pseudogenes. This pattern reflects stronger stabilizing selection in functional genes than in pseudogenes.

proteins from *different* populations or species, some amino acid positions will remain constant under purifying selection, others will vary through neutral genetic drift, and still others will differ as a result of positive selection for change. How can these evolutionary processes be distinguished?

Positive and purifying selection can be detected in the genome

As we have just seen, substitutions in a protein-coding gene can be either synonymous or nonsynonymous, depending on whether or not they change the resulting amino acid sequence of the protein. The relative rates of synonymous and nonsynonymous substitutions are expected to differ in regions of genes that are evolving neutrally, or evolving under positive selection for change, or staying unchanged under purifying selection.

- If a given amino acid in a protein can be one of many alternatives (without changing the protein's function), then an amino acid replacement is neutral with respect to the fitness of an organism. In this case, the rates of synonymous and nonsynonymous substitutions in the corresponding DNA sequences are expected to be very similar, so the ratio of the two rates should be close to 1.

- If a given amino acid position is under **positive selection** for change, the observed rate of nonsynonymous substitutions is expected to exceed the rate of synonymous substitutions in the corresponding DNA sequences.

- If a given amino acid position is under **purifying selection**, then the observed rate of synonymous substitutions is expected to be much higher than the rate of nonsynonymous substitutions in the corresponding DNA sequences.

The evolution of lysozyme illustrates how and why particular codons in a gene sequence might be under different modes of selection. The enzyme lysozyme is found in almost all animals. It is produced in the tears, saliva, and milk of mammals and in the albumen (whites) of bird eggs. Lysozyme digests the cell walls of bacteria, rupturing and killing them. As a result, it plays an important role as a first line of defense against invading bacteria. Most animals defend themselves against bacteria by digesting them, which is probably why most animals have lysozyme. Some animals also use lysozyme in the digestion of food.

Among mammals, a mode of digestion called foregut fermentation has evolved twice. In mammals with this mode of digestion, the foregut—consisting of part of the esophagus and/or stomach—has been converted into a chamber in which bacteria break down ingested plant matter by fermentation. Foregut fermenters can obtain nutrients from the otherwise indigestible cellulose that makes up a large proportion of plant tissue. Foregut fermentation evolved independently in ruminants (a group of hoofed mammals that includes cattle) and in certain leaf-eating monkeys, such as langurs. We know that these evolutionary events were independent because both langurs and ruminants have close relatives that are not foregut fermenters.

In both mammalian foregut-fermenting lineages, lysozyme has been modified to play a new, nondefensive role. The modified lysozyme enzyme ruptures some of the bacteria that live in the foregut,

releasing nutrients metabolized by the bacteria, which the mammal then absorbs. How many changes in the lysozyme molecule were needed to allow it to perform this function amid the digestive enzymes and acidic conditions of the mammalian foregut? To answer this question, Caro-Beth Stewart and her colleagues compared the lysozyme-coding sequences in foregut fermenters with those in several of their nonfermenting relatives. They determined which amino acids differed and which were shared among the species (**Figure 21.6**), as well as the rates of synonymous and nonsynonymous substitutions in lysozyme genes across the evolutionary history of the sampled species.

For many of the amino acid positions of lysozyme, the rate of synonymous substitution in the corresponding gene sequence was much higher than the rate of nonsynonymous substitution. This observation indicates that many of the amino acids that make up lysozyme are evolving under purifying selection. In other words, there is selection against change in the lysozyme protein at these positions, and the encoded amino acids must therefore be critical for lysozyme function. At other positions, several different amino acids function equally well, and the corresponding codons have similar rates of synonymous and nonsynonymous substitutions.

The most striking finding was that amino acid replacements in lysozyme happened at a much higher rate in the lineage leading to langurs than in any other primate lineage. The high rate of nonsynonymous substitution in the langur lysozyme gene shows that lysozyme went through a period of rapid change in adapting to the foreguts of langurs. Moreover, the lysozymes of langurs and cattle exhibit five instances of convergent evolution, a process whereby organisms that are not closely related independently evolve similar traits as a result of having to adapt to similar environments or ecological niches. More specifically, the lysozymes of langurs and cattle share five convergent amino acid replacements, all of which lie on the surface of the lysozyme molecule, well away from the enzyme's active site. Two of these shared replacements are changes from arginine to lysine, which make the protein more resistant to degradation by the stomach enzyme pepsin. By understanding the functional significance of amino acid replacements, biologists can explain the observed changes in amino acid sequences in terms of changes in the functioning of the protein.

Connect the Concepts As explained in Key Concept 20.1, not all similar traits are evidence of relatedness. Similar traits may evolve independently in different lineages through the phenomenon of convergent evolution.

A large body of fossil, morphological, and molecular evidence shows that langurs and cattle do not share a recent common ancestor. However, langur and ruminant lysozymes share several amino acids that neither mammal shares with the lysozymes of its own closer relatives. The lysozymes of these two mammals have converged on some of the same amino acids despite their very different ancestry. The amino acids they share give these lysozymes the ability to lyse the bacteria that ferment plant material in the foregut.

The ability to test for positive, purifying, and neutral selection has allowed biologists to distinguish functional from nonfunctional genes, and to understand how genes are evolving within given species.

Experiment

Figure 21.6A   Convergent Molecular Evolution

Original Paper: C.-B. Stewart et al. 1987. Adaptive evolution in the stomach lysozymes of foregut fermenters. *Nature* 330: 401–404.

Langurs (a group of monkeys) and cattle are only distantly related but both have evolved foregut fermentation. They uniquely express the enzyme lysozyme in their stomachs (foreguts) to aid in breaking down bacteria that are involved in fermentation. Stewart and colleagues compared the gene sequences of lysozyme in mammals with and without foregut fermentation to see if there is convergence in the independently evolved amino acid sequences of lysozyme in langurs and cattle.

HYPOTHESIS▶   Similar selective conditions in distantly related mammals have resulted in convergence of adaptations for foregut fermentation in the amino acid sequences of lysozyme.

METHOD▶

1. Isolate and sequence lysozyme from two distantly related mammal species with foregut fermentation (langur and cattle) as well as other mammals that are more closely related to either langurs or to cattle but lack foregut fermentation.

2. Tabulate the pairwise differences in the amino acid sequences. Plot the amino acid changes on the phylogenetic tree and count the number of convergent similarities between each pair of species. The results can then be plotted as a matrix.

RESULTS▶   The matrix shows the number of all pairwise amino acid differences above the diagonal and the number of convergent similarities below the diagonal.

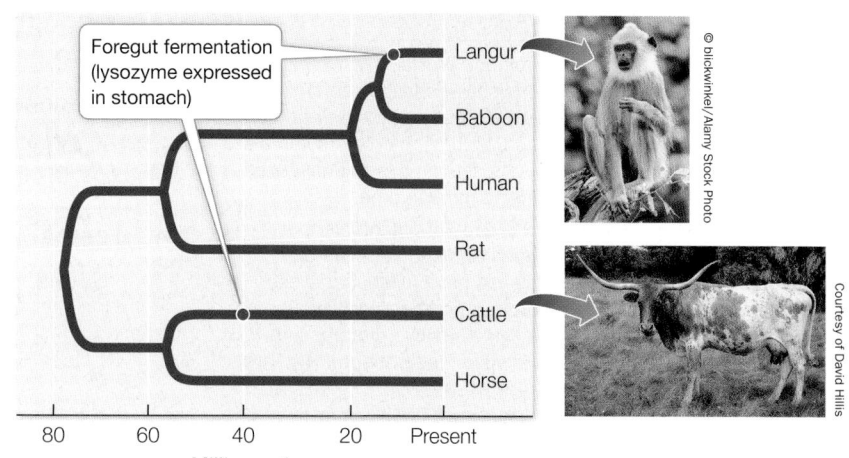

Foregut fermentation (lysozyme expressed in stomach)

Millions of years ago

The lysozymes of langurs and cattle are convergent for 5 amino acids.

	Langur	Baboon	Human	Rat	Cattle	Horse
Langur		14	18	38	32	65
Baboon	0		14	33	39	65
Human	0	1		37	41	64
Rat	0	1	0		55	64
Cattle	5	0	0	0		71
Horse	0	0	0	0	1	

CONCLUSION▶   The lysozyme sequences of the two species with foregut fermentation account for the majority of the convergent amino acid replacements observed among these species, demonstrating molecular convergence associated with the independent evolution of foregut fermentation.

Work with the Data

Figure 21.6B   Convergent Molecular Evolution

Original Papers: C.-B. Stewart et al. 1987. *Nature* 330: 401–404.

After C.-B. Stewart et al. 1987. Adaptive evolution in the stomach lysozymes of foregut fermenters. *Nature* 330: 401–404

W. Messier and C.-B. Stewart. 1997. Episodic adaptive evolution of primate lysozymes. *Nature* 385: 151–154.

Caro-Beth Stewart and her colleagues collected lysozyme sequences from six species of mammals. A small sample of their data is shown in the table. The phylogeny of these six species is well supported from analysis of many genes and much morphological data.

QUESTIONS▶

1. Using the phylogenetic tree (see Figure 21.6), plot the amino acid changes across the phylogeny of the six mammals. Assume that the ancestral state is the amino acid present at the base of the tree.

2. Which amino acid positions show unique convergence between the langur and cattle lineages (i.e., the derived state is found *only* in cattle and langurs)?

3. Which additional position is convergent between cattle and the ancestor of langurs and baboons?

4. Did you detect any other convergent amino acid changes between any other pair of lineages? What does this suggest about the convergent changes you observed between cattle and langurs?

Go to **Achieve** for a companion Data in Depth exercise.

Amino acid position											
Species	**2**	**14**	**17**	**21**	**50**	**63**	**75**	**87**	**117**	**118**	**130**
Langur	I	K	L	K	E	Y	D	N	Q	N	V
Baboon	I	R	L	R	Q	Y	N	D	Q	N	V
Human	V	R	M	R	R	Y	N	D	Q	N	V
Rat	T	R	M	Y	Q	Y	N	D	K	N	V
Cattle	V	K	L	K	E	W	D	N	R	D	L
Horse	V	A	M	G	G	W	N	E	K	D	L
Ancestral state	V	R	M	R	Q	W	N	D	K	N	V

21.2 Recap and Assess

The neutral theory of molecular evolution provides an explanation for the relatively constant rate of molecular change seen in many species. By examining the relative rates of synonymous and non-synonymous substitutions in genes over time, bio-logists can distinguish the evolutionary mechanisms acting on individual genes, and understand how they are changing through time.

1. Over evolutionary history, many groups of organisms that inhabit caves have lost the organs of sight. For example, although surface-dwelling crayfishes have functional eyes, several crayfish species that are restricted to underground habitats lack eyes. Opsins are light-sensitive proteins known to have an important function in vision (see Chapter 44), and opsin genes are expressed in eye tissues. Opsin genes are present in the genomes of eyeless, cave-dwelling crayfishes. Two alternative hypotheses that might explain the presence of opsin genes in an eyeless organism are (a) the genes were inherited from an eyed ancestor but are no longer functional; or (b) the genes have a new function other than vision. How would you investigate these two hypotheses using the sequences of the opsin genes in various species of crayfishes?

2. Why is the rate of fixation of neutral mutations independent of population size? Use mathematical expressions to demonstrate why this is true.

3. An investigator compared many gene sequences encoding surface proteins from influenza viruses sampled over time and collected the data shown in the table.

Codon position	Synonymous substitutions	Nonsynonymous substitutions
12	0	7
15	1	9
61	0	12
80	7	0
137	12	1
156	24	2
165	3	4
226	38	3

a. Which positions encode amino acids that are likely to have changed as a result of positive selection? Explain your answer.

b. Which positions encode amino acids that are likely to have changed as a result of purifying selection? Explain your answer.

(Hint: To calculate rates of each substitution type, consider the number of synonymous and nonsynonymous substitutions present relative to the number of possible substitutions of each type. There are approximately three times as many possible nonsynonymous substitutions as there are synonymous substitutions.)

Based on data in GenBank under accession numbers AF008656 to AF008909, as analyzed in W. M. Fitch et al. 1997. *Proc Natl Acad Sci* U.S.A. 94: 7712–7718 © 1997. National Academy of Sciences, U.S.A.; R. M. Bush et al. 1999. *Science* 286: 1921–1925.

Although nucleotide substitutions within coding sequences result in many important changes to organisms, genomes evolve through many additional processes. In particular, additions and deletions of

noncoding sequences, gene duplications, and movement of genes between genomes can have major evolutionary consequences.

21.3 Changes in the Size and Arrangement of Genomes Can Result in New Features

Learning Objectives

21.3.1 Explain the role of noncoding DNA in the evolution of genome size.

21.3.2 Compare and contrast the evolutionary advantages and disadvantages of sexual reproduction.

21.3.3 Describe how genes can move among different lineages via lateral gene transfer.

21.3.4 Using a phylogenetic tree of a gene family, identify gene duplications across the history of a group of species.

21.3.5 Describe how a duplicated gene provides opportunities for the evolution of new functions.

Several evolutionary processes result in changes to the size and organization of genomes, which can lead to acquisition of major new characteristics in populations. These genome-scale processes often result in larger and more rapid evolutionary changes than do single point mutations.

Genome sizes among organisms differ by orders of magnitude

We know that genome size varies tremendously among organisms. Across broad taxonomic categories, there is some correlation between genome size and organismal complexity. The genome of the tiny bacterium *Mycoplasma genitalium* has only 470 genes. *Homo sapiens*, by contrast, has about 20,500 protein-coding genes. **Figure 21.7** shows the number of genes from a sample of organisms whose genomes have been fully sequenced, arranged by their evolutionary relationships. As this figure reveals, however, a larger genome does not always indicate greater complexity (compare rice with the other plants, for example). It is not surprising that more complex genetic instructions are needed for building and maintaining a large multicellular organism than a small single-celled bacterium. What is surprising is that some organisms, such as lungfishes, some salamanders, and lilies, have about 40 times as much DNA as humans do (**Figure 21.8**). Structurally, a lungfish or a lily is not 40 times more complex than a human. So why does genome size vary so much?

Differences in genome size are not so great if we take into account only the portion of DNA that actually encodes proteins. The organisms with the largest total amounts of nuclear DNA (some ferns and flowering plants) have 80,000 times as much DNA as do the bacteria with the smallest genomes, but no species has more than about 100 times as many protein-coding genes as a bacterium. Therefore much of the variation in genome size lies not in the number of functional genes, but in the amount of noncoding DNA (see Figure 21.8).

Why do the cells of most eukaryotic organisms have so much noncoding DNA? Does this noncoding DNA have a function? Although it does not encode proteins, noncoding DNA can alter

Figure 21.7 **Evolution of Gene Number**   This figure shows the number of genes from a sample of organisms whose genomes have been fully sequenced, arranged by their evolutionary relationships. Bacteria and archaea (purple branches) typically have fewer genes than most eukaryotes. Among eukaryotes, multicellular organisms with tissue organization (plants and animals; dark green and blue branches, respectively) have more genes than single-celled organisms (aqua branches) or multicellular organisms that lack pronounced tissue organization (yellow branches). (Data from T. R. Gregory et al. 2007. *Nucleic Acids Res* 35 [Database issue]: D332–D338.)

the expression of the genes surrounding it. The degree or timing of gene expression can vary dramatically depending on a gene's location relative to noncoding sequences that regulate gene expression. Other regions of noncoding DNA consist of pseudogenes (nonfunctional copies of former genes). Pseudogenes are often carried in the genome because the cost of doing so is very small. Occasionally these pseudogenes become the raw material for the evolution of new genes with novel functions. Other noncoding sequences function in maintaining chromosomal structure. Still others consist of transposable elements (also called transposons; see Key Concept 17.2) that spread through populations because they reproduce faster than the host genome.

Figure 21.8 **A Large Proportion of DNA Is Noncoding**   Most of the DNA of bacteria and yeasts encodes RNAs or proteins, whereas a large percentage of the DNA of multicellular species is noncoding. (Data from T. R. Gregory et al. 2007. *Nucleic Acids Res* 35 [Database issue]: D332–D338.)

It may be that the proportion of noncoding DNA is related primarily to population size. Noncoding sequences that are only slightly deleterious to the organism are likely to be purged by selection most efficiently in species with large population sizes. In species with small populations, the effects of genetic drift can overwhelm selection against noncoding sequences that have small deleterious consequences. Therefore selection against the accumulation of noncoding sequences is most effective in species with large populations, and thus species such as bacteria and yeasts have relatively little noncoding DNA compared with species with small populations (see Figure 21.8).

Sex results in the recombination of genomes

In asexually reproducing organisms, each new individual is genetically identical to its parent unless there has been a mutation. When organisms reproduce sexually, however, offspring differ from their parents because of crossing over and independent assortment of chromosomes during meiosis, as well as the combination of genetic material from two different gametes, as described in Key Concept 12.4. Sexual recombination generates an endless variety of genotype combinations that increase the evolutionary potential of populations—a long-term advantage of sex. Although some species may reproduce asexually most of the time, most asexual species have some means of achieving genetic recombination.

The evolution of meiosis and sexual recombination was a crucial event in the history of life. Exactly how these processes arose is puzzling, however, because in the short term, sex has at least three striking disadvantages:

1. Recombination breaks up adaptive combinations of genes.
2. Sex reduces the rate at which females pass genes on to their offspring.
3. Dividing offspring into separate genders greatly reduces the overall reproductive rate.

To see why this last disadvantage exists, consider an asexual female that produces the same number of offspring as a sexual female. Let's assume that both females produce two offspring, but that 50% of the sexual female's offspring will be males (and thus contribute only sperm). In this next (F_1) generation, both asexual females will produce two more offspring each, but there is only one sexual F_1 female to produce offspring. Thus the effective reproductive rate of the asexual lineage is twice that of the sexual lineage.

The evolutionary problem is to identify the advantages of sex that can overcome short-term disadvantages. Several hypotheses have been proposed to explain the existence of sex, none of which is mutually exclusive. One hypothesis is that sexual recombination facilitates repair of damaged DNA, because breaks and other errors in DNA on one chromosome can be repaired by copying the intact sequence from the homologous chromosome.

Another advantage of sexual reproduction is that it permits the elimination of deleterious mutations. As explained in Key Concept 13.4, DNA replication is not perfect. Errors are introduced in every generation, and most of these errors result in lower fitness. Asexual organisms have no mechanism to eliminate deleterious mutations. Hermann J. Muller noted that the accumulation of deleterious mutations in a nonrecombining genome is like a genetic ratchet.

The mutations accumulate—"ratchet up"—at each replication. A mutation occurs and is passed on when the genome replicates, then two new mutations occur in the next replication, so three mutations are passed on, and so on. Over time, the least-mutated class of individuals is lost from the population as new mutations occur. Deleterious mutations cannot be eliminated except by the death of the lineage or a rare back mutation. The accumulation of deleterious mutations in lineages that lack genetic recombination is known as **Muller's ratchet**. In sexual species, by contrast, genetic recombination produces some individuals with more of these deleterious mutations and some with fewer. The individuals with fewer deleterious mutations are more likely to survive. Thus sexual reproduction allows natural selection to eliminate particular deleterious mutations from the population over time.

Still another advantage of sex is the great variety of genetic combinations it creates in each generation. Sexual recombination does not directly influence the frequencies of alleles; rather, *it generates new combinations of alleles on which natural selection can act*. It expands variation in a character influenced by alleles at many loci by creating new genotypes. For example, genetic variation can be a defense against pathogens and parasites. Most pathogens and parasites have much shorter life cycles than their hosts and can rapidly evolve counteradaptations to host defenses. Sexual recombination can give the host's defenses a chance to keep up.

Lateral gene transfer can result in the gain of new functions

The tree of life is usually visualized as a branching diagram, with each lineage diverging into two (or more) lineages over time, from one common ancestor to the millions of species that are alive today. Ancestral lineages divide into descendant lineages, resulting in speciation events that are diagrammed on the tree of life. Species' genomes are altered as well by processes that result in **lateral gene transfer**—the horizontal movement of individual genes, organelles, or fragments of genomes from one lineage to another. Some species may pick up fragments of DNA directly from the environment. A virus may pick up some genes from one host and transfer them to a new host when the virus becomes integrated into the new host's genome. Hybridization between species also results in the lateral transfer of large numbers of genes.

Lateral gene transfer can be highly advantageous to a species that incorporates novel genes from a distant relative. Genes that confer antibiotic resistance, for example, are commonly transferred among different species of bacteria. Lateral gene transfer is another way, in addition to mutation and recombination, in which species can increase their genetic variation. That genetic variation then provides the raw material on which selection acts, resulting in evolution.

A phylogenetic tree constructed from a single laterally transferred genome fragment is likely to reflect only the evolutionary history of that fragment, rather than the overall organismal phylogeny (see Key Concept 20.1). Most biologists prefer to build trees from large samples of genes or their products, so that the underlying species tree (as well as any lateral gene transfer events) can be reconstructed. Depictions of lateral gene transfer events on the underlying species tree are known as **reticulations**.

The degree to which lateral gene transfer events occur in various parts of the tree of life is a matter of considerable current investigation and debate. Lateral gene transfer appears to be relatively uncommon among most eukaryotic lineages, although the two major endosymbioses that gave rise to mitochondria and chloroplasts can be viewed as lateral transfers of entire bacterial genomes to the eukaryotic lineage. Some groups of eukaryotes, most notably some plants, are subject to relatively high levels of hybridization among closely related species. Hybridization leads to the exchange of many genes among recently separated lineages of plants. The greatest degree of lateral transfer, however, appears to occur among bacteria. Many bacterial genes have been transferred repeatedly among lineages of bacteria, to the point that relationships among bacterial species are often hard to decipher. Nonetheless, the broad relationships of the major groups of bacteria can still be determined (as we will discuss in Part Six of this book). Lateral transfer of genes also makes it difficult to identify the boundaries of bacterial species, which is one reason why fewer bacterial species have been named than are known to exist.

Many new functions arise following gene duplication

Gene duplication is yet another way in which genomes can acquire new functions. When a gene is duplicated, one copy of that gene is potentially freed from having to perform its original function. The initially identical copies of a duplicated gene can have any one of four subsequent fates:

1. Both copies of the gene may retain their original function (which can result in a change in the amount of gene product that is produced by the organism).

2. Both copies of the gene may retain the ability to produce the original gene product, but the expression of the genes may diverge in different tissues or at different times in development.

3. One copy of the gene may be incapacitated by the accumulation of deleterious substitutions and become a nonfunctional pseudogene, or may be eliminated from the genome altogether.

4. One copy of the gene may retain its original function while the second copy accumulates enough substitutions that it can perform a different function.

How often do gene duplications arise, and which of these four outcomes is most likely? Investigators have found that rates of gene duplication are fast enough for a yeast or *Drosophila* population to acquire several hundred duplicate genes over the course of a million years. They have also found that most of the duplicated genes in these organisms are very young. Many extra genes are lost from a genome within 10 million years (which is rapid on an evolutionary time scale).

Some genes may be duplicated many times, resulting in large numbers of related pseudogenes scattered throughout the genome. In the human genome, the functional copy of the ribosomal protein gene *RPL21* is located on chromosome pair 13, but pseudogenes derived from it are found on most of the other chromosome pairs (**Figure 21.9**). Although not all genes are represented by pseudogenes, there are nearly as many known pseudogenes in the human genome as there are functional protein-coding genes.

Although many extra genes disappear rapidly, some duplication events lead to the evolution of genes with new functions. Several successive rounds of duplication and mutation may result in a **gene family**: a group of homologous genes with related functions, often arrayed in tandem along a chromosome. An example of this process is provided by the globin gene family (**Figure 21.10**). The globins were among the first proteins to be sequenced and compared. Comparisons of their amino acid sequences strongly suggest that the different globins arose via gene duplications. These comparisons also allow us to estimate how long the globins have been evolving separately, because differences among these proteins have accumulated with time.

(A) Duplications of *RPL21* gene on the human chromosomes

1 2 3 4 5 6 7 8 9 10 11 12 13 14 15 16 17 18 19 20 21 22 X Y

The functional copy of the *RPL21* gene

(B) Ratio of functional genes to pseudogenes in the human genome

21,000   19,000

Genes   Pseudogenes

Figure 21.9 Some Functional Genes Are Duplicated Many Times as Nonfunctional Pseudogenes (A) The functional gene that encodes ribosomal protein RPL21 is located on human chromosome 13 (indicated in orange). In addition, there are many nonfunctional pseudogenes of *RPL21* in the human genome, produced through repeated duplication events (indicated in blue). (B) Although *RPL21* represents a relatively extreme example of pseudogene duplication, there are almost as many known pseudogenes in the human genome as there are functional genes. (After M. Gerstein and D. Zheng. 2006. *Sci Am* 295: 48–55; Courtesy of Lucy Reading-Ikkanda.)

Figure 21.10 **A Globin Family Gene Tree**   This gene tree suggests that the α-globin (blue) and β-globin (green) gene clusters diverged about 450 million years ago (mya) (open circle), soon after the origin of vertebrates. (After W-H Li and D. Graur. 1991. *Fundamentals of Molecular Evolution.* Sinauer Associates: Sunderland, MA.)

Q: When did the gene duplication event that gave rise to the delta and beta chains occur?

 View in Achieve
Activity 21.3 Gene Tree Construction

Hemoglobin, a tetramer (four-subunit molecule) consisting of two α-globin and two β-globin polypeptide chains, carries oxygen in blood. Myoglobin, a monomer, is the primary O_2 storage protein in muscle. Myoglobin's affinity for O_2 is much higher than that of hemoglobin, but hemoglobin has evolved to be more diversified in its roles. Hemoglobin binds O_2 in the lungs or gills, where the O_2 concentration is relatively high, transports it to deep body tissues, where the O_2 concentration is low, and releases it in those tissues. With its more complex tetrameric structure, hemoglobin is able to carry four molecules of O_2, as well as hydrogen ions and carbon dioxide, in the blood.

To estimate the time of the globin gene duplication that gave rise to the α- and β-globin gene clusters, we can create a **gene tree**—a phylogenetic tree that describes the evolutionary history of particular genes or gene families, in this case the gene sequences that encode the various globins (see Figure 21.10). The rate of molecular evolution of globin genes has been estimated from other studies, using the divergence times of groups of vertebrates that are well documented in the fossil record. These studies indicate an average rate of divergence for globin genes of about 1 nucleotide substitution every 2 million years. By applying this rate to the globin gene tree, we can estimate the divergence time of the two globin gene clusters at about 450 million years ago.

Many gene duplications affect only one or a few genes at a time, but entire genomes are duplicated in polyploid organisms (which include many plants). When all the genes are duplicated, there are massive opportunities for new functions to evolve. That is exactly what appears to have happened in the evolution of vertebrates. The genomes of the jawed vertebrates appear to have four diploid sets of many major genes, which led biologists to conclude that two genome-wide duplication events occurred in the ancestor of these species. These duplications have allowed considerable specialization of individual vertebrate genes, many of which are now highly tissue-specific in their expression.

Some gene families evolve through concerted evolution

Although the members of the globin gene family have diversified in form and function, the members of many other gene families do not evolve independently of one another. For instance, almost all organisms have many copies (up to thousands) of the ribosomal RNA genes. Ribosomal RNA (rRNA) is the principal structural element of ribosomes and, as such, has a primary role in protein synthesis. Every living species needs to synthesize proteins, often in large amounts (especially during early development). Having many copies of the rRNA genes ensures that organisms can rapidly produce many ribosomes and thereby maintain a high rate of protein synthesis.

Like all portions of the genome, ribosomal RNA genes evolve, and differences accumulate in the rRNA genes of different species. But within any one species, the multiple copies of the rRNA genes are very similar, both structurally and functionally. This similarity makes sense because, ideally, every ribosome in a species should synthesize proteins in the same way. In other words, within a given species, the multiple copies of these rRNA genes are evolving in concert with one another, a phenomenon called **concerted evolution**.

 View in Achieve
Animation 21.1 Concerted Evolution

How does concerted evolution occur? Two different mechanisms appear to be responsible. The first of these is **unequal crossing over**. When DNA is replicated during meiosis in a diploid species, the homologous chromosome pairs align and recombine by crossing over (see Key Concept 11.5). In the case of highly repeated genes, however, it is easy for genes to become displaced in alignment, since so many copies of the same genes are present on the chromosomes

(Figure 21.11A). The end result is that one chromosome may gain extra copies of the repeat and the other chromosome may have fewer copies of the repeat. If a new substitution arises in one copy of the repeat, it can spread to new copies (or be eliminated) through unequal crossing over. Thus over time, a novel substitution will either become fixed or it will be lost entirely. In either case, all copies of the repeat will remain very similar to one another.

The second mechanism that produces concerted evolution is **biased gene conversion**. This mechanism can be much faster than unequal crossing over and has been shown to be the primary mechanism for concerted evolution of rRNA genes. DNA strands are frequently broken and repaired (see Key Concept 13.4). At many times during the cell cycle, the genes for ribosomal RNA are clustered close together. If damage occurs to one of the genes, a copy of the rRNA gene on another chromosome may be used to repair the damaged copy, and the sequence that is used as a template can thereby replace the original sequence (Figure 21.11B). In many cases, this repair

system appears to be biased in favor of using particular sequences as templates for repair, and thus the favored sequence rapidly spreads across all copies of the gene. In this way, changes may appear in a single copy and then rapidly spread to all the other copies.

Regardless of the mechanism responsible, the net result of concerted evolution is that the copies of a highly repeated gene do not evolve independently of one another. Mutations still occur, but once they arise in one copy, they either spread rapidly across all the copies or are lost from the genome completely. This process allows the products of each copy to remain similar over time in both sequence and function.

KEY CONCEPT
21.3 Recap and Assess

The noncoding portion of eukaryotic genomes is more variable in size across species than is the coding portion. Sexual recombination produces new combinations of genes and facilitates the elimination of deleterious mutations from populations. Lateral gene transfer can result in the transfer of genetic functions between distantly related species, whereas duplication can lead to the evolution of new functions. Some highly repeated genes undergo concerted evolution, which maintains uniform functionality.

1. Suggest and contrast two hypotheses for the wide diversity of genome sizes among different organisms.

2. Contrast three disadvantages and three advantages of sexual reproduction compared with asexual reproduction. Why do you think that most species have some means of achieving genetic recombination among individuals?

3. What are some potential advantages of lateral gene transfer to the organisms that gain new genes by this mechanism?

4. Consider the following tree of a gene family sampled from the complete genomes of humans, chimpanzees, and gorillas. All members of the gene family are included in the tree. How many gene duplications and losses are likely to have occurred in the history of this gene family? Diagram their locations on the tree.

(A) Unequal crossing over

(B) Biased gene conversion

Figure 21.11 Concerted Evolution   Two mechanisms can produce concerted evolution of highly repeated genes. **(A)** Unequal crossing over results in deletions and duplications of a repeated gene. **(B)** Biased gene conversion can rapidly spread a new variant across multiple copies of a repeated gene.

5. Why is gene duplication considered important for long-term evolutionary change?

6. Describe the pattern of concerted evolution among highly repeated genes, and diagram the processes that lead to concerted evolution.

We have considered how changes in gene structure and number can produce evolutionary change. We will next consider how phenotypic transformations can also be produced by changes in the amount, timing, and location of gene expression during development.

KEY CONCEPT 21.4 **Changes in Gene Expression Often Shape Evolution**

Learning Objectives

21.4.1 Describe factors that determine cell fate during development, using body segmentation in animals as an example.

21.4.2 Defend the claim "Genes controlling development are highly conserved across animals," using a specific example.

21.4.3 Provide examples of morphological differences among species that result from changes in the amount, timing, and location of gene expression.

21.4.4 Summarize how a mutation in a developmental gene led to a reduction in leg number in insects compared with other arthropods.

Although a genome contains all of the genes needed to form a complete organism, these genes need to be expressed at specific times and in specific tissues. Given that every cell in the body contains the same genetic information, how are the right genes turned on to form a head at the anterior end of an animal, or a tail at the posterior end? Why don't heads or tails form elsewhere in the developing embryo? How do insects develop antennae on their head, but legs on their thorax? As biologists began to study and answer these questions, they realized that changes in gene expression might account for much of the evolution of diverse body forms we observe across living organisms. Thus was born the science of evo-devo, or evolutionary developmental biology.

A cascade of transcription factors establishes body segmentation in animals

Before we examine how changes in gene expression can account for evolution of body forms, we need to consider how body axis orientation and segmentation are controlled during development. This has been especially well studied in the fruit fly *Drosophila melanogaster*, but many of the genes that control developmental processes are conserved across a diversity of organisms, including ourselves.

The insect body is made up of segments that differ from one another. The adult fly has an anterior head (composed of several fused segments), three different thoracic segments, and eight abdominal segments at the posterior end. Each segment gives rise to different body parts: for example, antennae and eyes develop from head segments, wings from the thorax, and so on.

The life cycle of *Drosophila* from fertilized egg to adult takes about 2 weeks. The egg hatches into a larva, which then forms a pupa, which finally is transformed into the adult fly. By the time a larva appears—about 24 hours after fertilization—there are recognizable segments. Although the thoracic and abdominal segments all look similar, the fates of the cells to become different adult segments are already determined.

As in other organisms, fertilization in *Drosophila* leads to a rapid series of mitoses. However, the first 12 nuclear divisions do not result in the formation of new cells. A multinucleate embryo forms instead of a multicellular embryo. With no cell membranes to cross, gene inducers known as **morphogens** can diffuse easily within the embryo. Many of these morphogens affect transcription in the cell nuclei.

Genetic studies of *Drosophila* revealed a sequential pattern (cascade) of gene expression that results in the determination of each segment within 24 hours after fertilization. Three classes of genes are involved:

1. **Maternal effect genes** set up the major axes (anterior–posterior and dorsal–ventral) of the embryo.

2. **Segmentation genes** determine the boundaries and polarity of each of the segments.

3. **Hox genes** determine what organ will be made at a given location.

MATERNAL EFFECT GENES   Like the eggs and early embryos of many other organisms, *Drosophila* eggs and larvae are characterized by unevenly distributed mRNAs and proteins, which are the products of specific maternal effect genes. These genes are transcribed in the cells of the mother's ovary, and the mRNAs are passed to the egg. These mRNAs and proteins establish the anterior–posterior axis and the dorsal–ventral axis of the developing embryo. Where some of these proteins are in highest concentrations in the embryo, transcription of additional genes is stimulated. For example, products of maternal effect genes stimulate the *hunchback* gene to be transcribed in the anterior end of the embryo, and the resulting gradient of Hunchback protein (itself a transcription factor) establishes the head region. A gradient of other proteins concentrated in the posterior region of the embryo establishes the anterior–posterior axis of the developing embryo.

The events that involve maternal effect genes begin before fertilization and continue after it, during the multinucleate stage, which lasts a few hours. At this stage the embryo looks like a bunch of indistinguishable nuclei under the light microscope. But the fates of the individual nuclei and the cells they will occupy have already begun to be determined. After the anterior and posterior ends have been established, the next step in pattern formation in fruit flies is the determination of segment number and locations.

SEGMENTATION GENES   The number, boundaries, and polarity of the *Drosophila* larval segments are determined by proteins encoded by the segmentation genes. These genes are expressed when there are about 6,000 nuclei in the embryo (about 3 hours after fertilization). Three classes of segmentation genes act one after the other to regulate finer and finer details of the segmentation pattern:

1. **Gap genes** organize broad areas along the anterior–posterior axis. Mutations in gap genes result in gaps in the body plan—the omission of several consecutive larval segments.

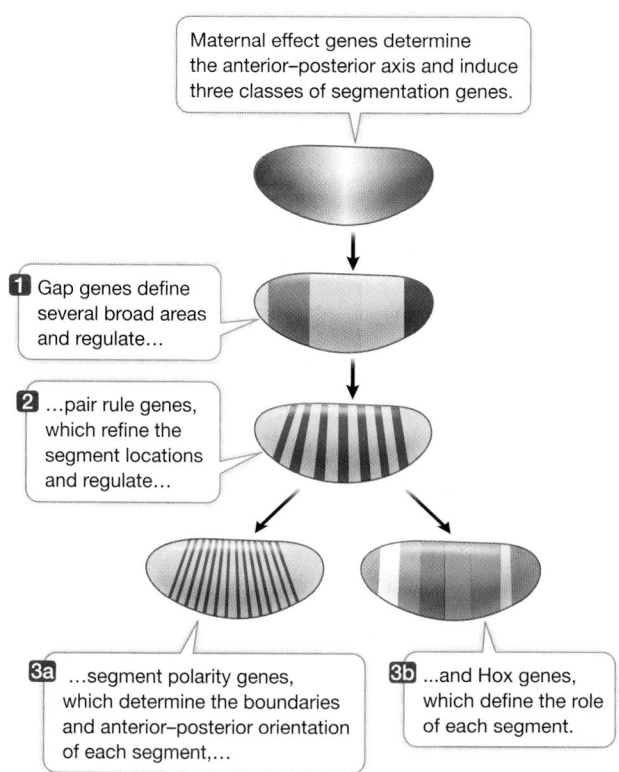

Figure 21.12 A Gene Cascade Controls Pattern Formation in the *Drosophila* Embryo Maternal effect genes induce gap, pair rule, and segment polarity genes. Hox genes then define the role of each segment. By the end of this cascade, a group of nuclei at the anterior of the embryo, for example, is determined to become the first head segment in the adult fly.

2. **Pair rule genes** divide the embryo into units of two segments each. Mutations in pair rule genes result in embryos missing every other segment.

3. **Segment polarity genes** determine the boundaries and anterior–posterior organization of the individual segments. Mutations in segment polarity genes can result in segments in which posterior structures are replaced by reversed (mirror-image) anterior structures.

The expression of the genes is sequential (**Figure 21.12**). The products of the gap genes active pair rule genes, and the pair rule gene products activate segment polarity genes. By the end of this part of the cascade, nuclei throughout the embryo "know" which segment they will be part of in the adult fly. The next set of genes in the cascade determines the form and function of each segment.

> ▶ **View in Achieve**
> **Animation 21.2 Pattern Formation in the *Drosophila* Embryo**
>
> ▶ **Media Clip 21.2 Spectacular Fly Development in 3D**
> Life12e.com/mc21.2

HOX GENES Hox genes encode a family of transcription factors that are expressed in different combinations along the length of the embryo, and help determine cell fates within each segment. Expression of certain Hox genes leads to the development of antennae in the head segment, whereas other Hox genes are expressed in the thorax to make wings, and so on. The *Drosophila* Hox genes occur in two clusters in the genome, in the same order as the segments whose function they determine (**Figure 21.13**). Hox genes are shared by all animals, and mutations in these genes have been linked to major changes in body structure among different animal groups.

How do we know that the Hox genes determine segment identity, and what structures are expressed in each segment? A clue comes from **homeotic mutations**—mutations that result in the replacement of one organ by another. For example, a mutation in the Hox gene *Antennapedia* causes legs to grow on the head of *Drosophila* in place of antennae (**Figure 21.14**). When another Hox gene, *bithorax*, is mutated, an extra pair of wings grows in a thoracic segment where wings do not normally occur. So the normal (wild-type) functions of the Hox genes must be to "tell" a segment what organ to form. Hox genes encode transcription factors and have a conserved 180-base-pair sequence called the **homeobox** (from which the genes get their name). The homeobox encodes a 60-amino acid sequence called the **homeodomain**. The homeodomain recognizes and binds to a specific DNA sequence in the promoters of its target genes, "turning on" the formation of specific structures.

> **Connect the Concepts** As discussed in Key Concept 16.2, cell differentiation often is mediated by changes in gene expression resulting from the activation or deactivation of various transcription factors.

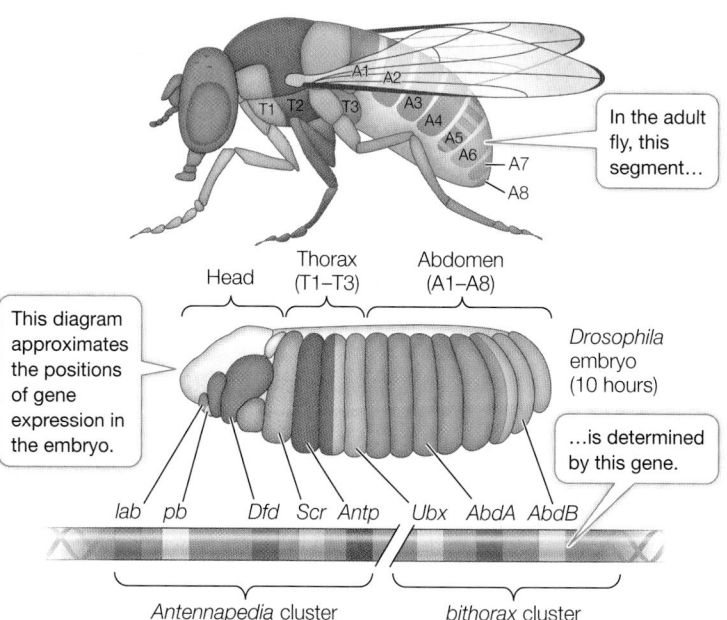

Figure 21.13 Hox Genes in *Drosophila* Determine Segment Identity Two clusters of Hox genes on chromosome 3 (bottom) determine segment function in the adult fly (top). These genes are expressed in the embryo (center) long before the structures of the segments actually appear. (Top after M. Peifer et al. 1987. *Genes Dev* 1: 891–898; bottom after S. D. Hueber et al. 2010. *PLOS ONE* 5: e10820. doi:10.1371/journal.pone.0010820.)

(A)

(B)

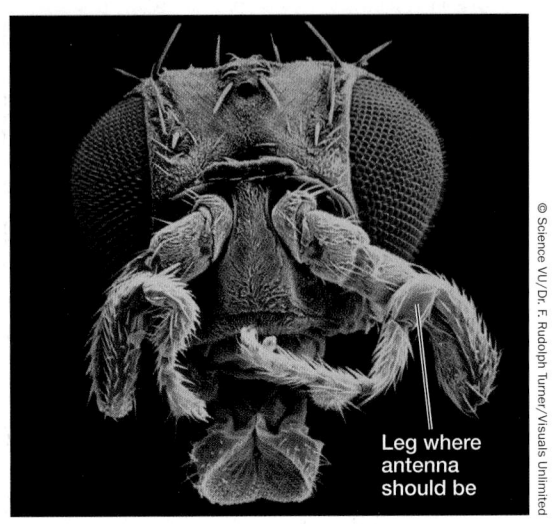

Figure 21.14 A Homeotic Mutation Replaces One Structure with Another (A) Normal development of antennae on the head of a fruit fly. (B) A homeotic mutation of the Hox gene *Antennapedia*, which controls formation of legs during development, causes legs, rather than antennae, to grow on the head.

A common "toolkit" of genetic mechanisms controls gene expression in development

About a dozen major kinds of eyes are found among animals, including the camera-like eyes of humans and the compound eyes of insects. Although the eyes of insects and vertebrates evolved independently, a remarkable discovery showed that common developmental pathways are involved in the embryonic formation of eyes in both groups.

More than a century ago, a mutation was described in *Drosophila* called *eyeless*, with a phenotype of—you guessed it—no eyes. This mutation remained a laboratory curiosity for many decades until its molecular nature was elucidated in the 1990s. Biologists isolated the protein product of the wild-type version of the *eyeless* gene, which they determined was a transcription factor that controls the expression of genes responsible for eye development. How did they know this? By making recombinant DNA constructs that allowed the wild-type *eyeless* gene to be expressed in different embryonic tissues of transgenic flies, the biologists were able to produce flies with extra eyes on various body parts such as the legs, the antennae, and under the wings.

The big surprise came when the biologists sequenced the *eyeless* gene and used computers to query a database of genes with known sequences. The *eyeless* gene sequence was similar to that of the *Pax6* gene in mice; *Pax6*, when mutated, leads to the development of abnormally small eyes. Could the extremely different eyes of flies and mice be variations on a common developmental theme? To test for functional similarity between the insect and mammalian genes, the biologists repeated their experiments on flies, but using the mouse *Pax6* gene instead of the fly *eyeless* gene. Once again, eyes developed at various sites on the transgenic flies. Thus a gene whose expression normally leads to the development of a mammalian eye now led to the development of the very different insect eye.

Fruit flies and mice last shared a common ancestor more than a half-billion years ago. Yet the *eyeless* and *Pax6* genes contain sequences that are highly conserved, not only in these two species but in others as well. Biologists call such genes **homologous**, meaning that they evolved from a gene present in a common ancestor (see Key Concept 20.1).

In recent years a large number of homologous genes (the regulatory "toolkit") have been shown to control development in distantly related species. For example, the fruit fly homeotic genes such as *Antennapedia* and *bithorax* are similar to mouse (and human) genes that play similar developmental roles. This discovery indicates that the positional information controlled by these genes has been conserved, even as the structures formed at each position have changed. Remarkably, these genes are arranged along a chromosome in both fruit fly and mouse in the same order as they are expressed along the anterior–posterior axis of the embryos (**Figure 21.15**). These and other examples have led biologists to the idea that certain developmental mechanisms are controlled by specific sequences composing a **genetic toolkit**, the contents of which have been changed and reshuffled over the course of evolutionary time to produce the amazing diversity of plants, animals, and other organisms that we see today.

Developmental modules based on a common set of genetic instructions can evolve separately within a species because **genetic switches** control how the toolkit is used. These switches turn genes on or off, or regulate the degree and timing of gene expression. Multiple switches control each gene, creating different expression patterns in different locations. In this way, elements of the genetic toolkit can be involved in multiple developmental processes and still allow individual modules to develop and evolve independently.

During evolution, changes in the functions of genetic switches have led to changes in the forms and functions of organisms. To illustrate this, let's look at the development of wings in *Drosophila* and other insects. *Drosophila* species are members of the insect group Diptera, which means "two wings"—that is,

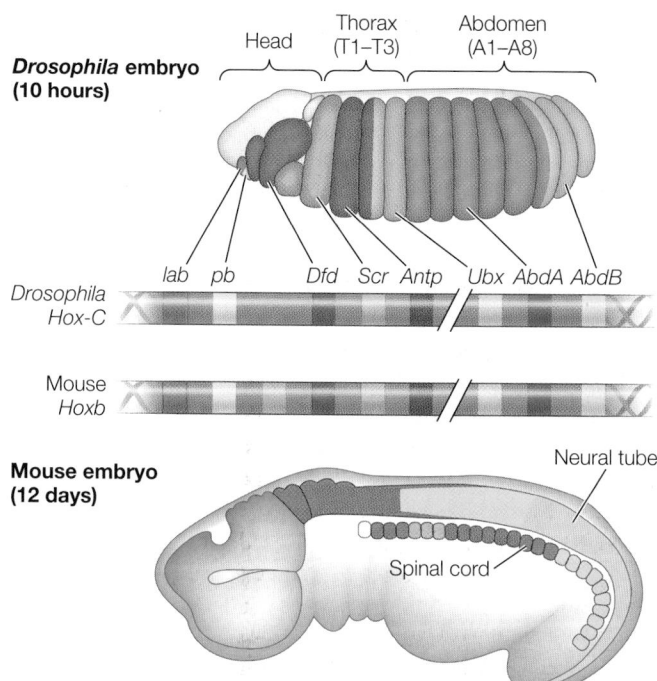

Figure 21.15 Regulatory Genes Show Similar Expression Patterns Homologous genes encoding similar transcription factors are expressed in similar patterns along the anterior–posterior axes of both insects and vertebrates. The mouse (and human) Hox genes are present in multiple copies; this prevents a single mutation from having drastic effects. (Top after S. D. Hueber et al. 2010 *PLOS ONE* 5: e10820. doi:10.1371/journal.pone.0010820; bottom after S. B. Carroll. 1995. *Nature* 376: 479–485.)

they have a single pair of wings, whereas most insects have two pairs of wings (i.e., four wings). The single pair of wings of dipterans develops on the second thoracic segment, where the Hox gene *Antennapedia* (*Antp*) is expressed. *Antp* is also expressed in the third thoracic segment, but in that segment a pair of balancing organs called halteres develops in dipterans. A critical difference between thoracic segments 2 and 3 is that another Hox gene, *Ultrabithorax* (*Ubx*), is expressed along with *Antp* in segment 3 (**Figure 21.16**). *Ubx* represses *Antp* function in dipterans. If *Ubx* is inactivated by mutation, a second pair of wings forms in thoracic segment 3, as is typical of many other insect groups. Thus some major morphological differences among groups of animals can result from relatively small changes in gene expression.

▶ **View in Achieve**
Animation 21.3 Modularity

The amount, timing, and location of gene expression control many morphological features

The modularity of development means that the molecular pathways for developmental processes such as organ formation operate independently of one another. For instance, the *Antennapedia* mutant fly shown in Figure 21.14 grew legs where antennae should be, but the rest of the segments formed structures

normally. Modularity allows the timing and location of a developmental process to change without changing the whole organism. Major changes can result from differences in the amount, timing, and location of gene expression.

HETEROMETRY   A striking example of **heterometry** ("different measure") is seen in beak development in Darwin's finches, in which the beaks of some species are large and robust for cracking seeds and in other species are thin and long for probing for food (see Figure 22.8). When he visited the Galápagos archipelago, Charles Darwin wrote that "seeing this gradation and diversity of structure in one small intimately related group of birds, one might really fancy that from an original paucity of birds in this archipelago, one species had been taken and modified for different ends."

Darwin had no idea of the genetic basis for such modification. Now we do. Beak shapes are evident when birds hatch from their eggs, so they must be determined during development. The beak develops from tissues at the anterior of the embryo that will form the facial bones. Cell divisions in this embryonic tissue are controlled by signaling proteins, one of which is called bone morphogenetic protein 4 (BMP4); another is the protein calmodulin. If BMP4 is present early and in large amounts, the

Figure 21.16 Segments Differentiate under Control of Genetic Switches The binding of a single protein, Ultrabithorax (Ubx), determines whether a thoracic segment produces full wings or halteres. (After S. D. Hueber et al. 2010. *PLOS ONE* 5: e10820. doi:10.1371/journal.pone.0010820.)

Q: What would happen if a butterfly embryo were genetically engineered so that *Ubx* was expressed in all its thoracic segments?

(A)

(B) Mixed diet of seeds and insects

Ancestral sharp-beaked finch

Low BMP4: low beak depth/width

Low CaM: short beak

Probing cactus flowers and fruit

Low BMP4: low beak depth/width

High CaM: elongated beak

Common Cactus-Finch (*G. scandens*)

Probing cactus flowers and fruit

Low–moderate BMP4: moderate beak depth/width

High CaM: elongated beak

Large Cactus-Finch (*G. conirostris*)

Crushing seeds

Moderate BMP4: moderate beak depth/width

Low CaM: short beak

Medium Ground-Finch (*G. fortis*)

Crushing hard/large seeds

Early/high BMP4: high beak depth/width

Low CaM: short beak

Large Ground-Finch (*G. magnirostris*)

Figure 21.17 Heterometry and the Beaks of Finches (A) Bird beaks can be measured in three dimensions (length, width, and depth) for the purpose of comparing different species. (B) Among Darwin's finches, mutations resulting in different patterns of BMP4 and calmodulin (CaM) expression may be responsible for the different species' beak sizes and shapes, which are suited for exploiting different types of food. The four species shown here are all in the genus *Geospiza*. (After A. Abzhanov et al. 2004. *Science* 305: 1462–1465.)

beak becomes broad and deep. If calmodulin is present early and in large amounts, the beak grows longer and thinner (**Figure 21.17**). Thus beak structure is affected by changes in protein production.

HETEROCHRONY   The evolution of the giraffe neck provides an example of **heterochrony** ("different time"). Giraffes, like most mammals, have seven cervical (neck) vertebrae. So giraffes did not get longer necks by adding more vertebrae. Instead, the cervical vertebrae of giraffes are much longer than those of other mammals (**Figure 21.18**).

Bone growth in mammals is the result of the proliferation of cartilage-producing cells called chondrocytes. Bone growth is stopped by a genetic signal that results in apoptosis, or cell death, of chondrocytes and calcification of the bone matrix. In giraffes this signaling process is delayed in the cervical vertebrae, so these vertebrae grow longer. Thus the evolution of longer necks resulted from changes in the timing of expression of the genes that control bone formation.

HETEROTOPY   Spatial differences in the expression of a developmental gene are known as **heterotopy** ("different place"), exemplified by the different development of feet in ducks and chickens. The feet of all bird embryos have webs of skin that connect the toes. This webbing is retained in adult ducks (and other aquatic birds) but not in adult chickens (and other nonaquatic birds). The loss of webbing is controlled by the BMP4 signaling protein, which we noted is also

(A) Giraffe

(B) Human

Both photos © Bone Clones. www.boneclones.com

Figure 21.18 Heterochrony in the Development of a Longer Neck There are seven vertebrae in the neck of a giraffe (A) and human (B) (not to scale). But the vertebrae of the giraffe are much longer (25 cm vs. 1.5 cm in the human) because during development, growth continues for a longer period of time. This timing difference is called heterochrony.

involved in beak development (another example of use of a common genetic toolkit to produce different kinds of change).

BMP4 protein induces the cells that produce webbing to undergo apoptosis and thus eliminate the webbing between the toes. The hindlimbs of both duck and chicken embryos express the *BMP4* gene in the webbing between the toes. However, duck and chicken embryos differ in expression of the *Gremlin* gene, which encodes a protein that inhibits *BMP4* expression (**Figure 21.19**). In ducks, but not in chickens, *Gremlin* is expressed in the webbing cells and Gremlin protein inhibits *BMP4* expression. With no BMP4 protein to stimulate apoptosis, a webbed foot develops. If chick hindlimbs are experimentally exposed to Gremlin during development, the adult chicken will have ducklike webbed feet.

Mutations in developmental genes can cause major morphological changes

Sometimes a major developmental change is caused by an alteration in the regulatory molecule itself rather than by a change in where, when, or how much it is expressed. The gene that controls the number of legs in arthropods offers an excellent example. Arthropods all have head, thoracic, and abdominal regions with variable numbers of segments. Insects, such as *Drosophila*, have three pairs of legs on their three thoracic segments, whereas centipedes have many legs on both thoracic and abdominal segments. All arthropods express a gene called *Distal-less* (*Dll*) that controls segmental leg development. In insects, *Dll* expression is repressed in abdominal segments by the Hox gene *Ultrabithorax* (*Ubx*). *Ubx* is expressed in the abdominal segments of all arthropods, but it has different effects in different species. In centipedes, *Ubx* is co-expressed with *Dll* to promote the formation of legs. During the evolution of insects, a mutation in the *Ubx* gene sequence resulted in a modified Ubx protein that represses *Dll* expression in abdominal segments (**Figure 21.20**). A phylogenetic tree of

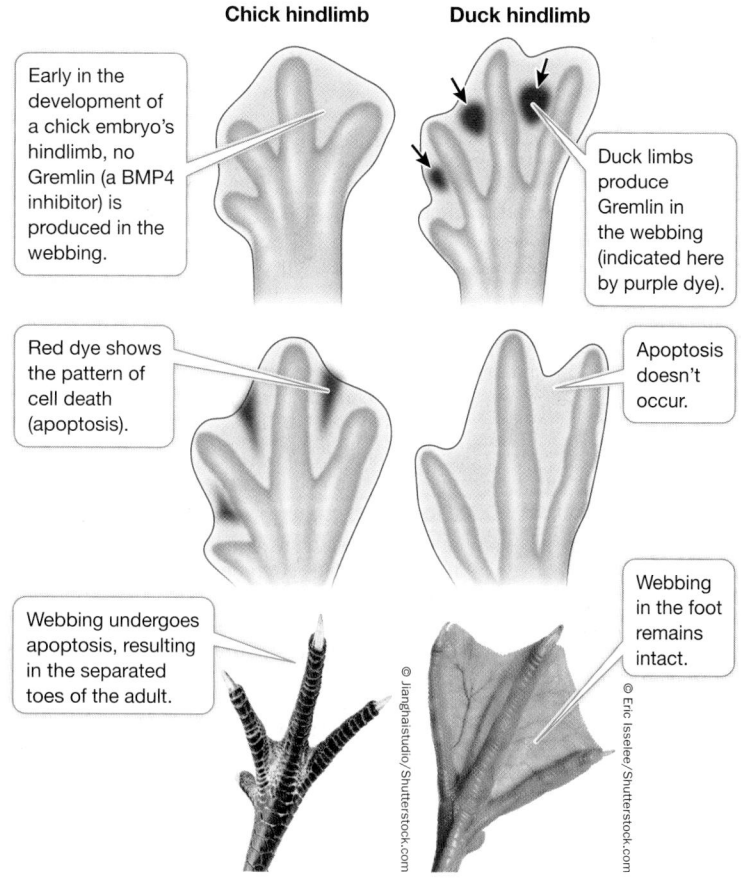

Figure 21.19 Heterotopy in Gremlin Expression Correlates with Changes in Hindlimb Structure The left column shows foot development in a chicken; the right column shows foot development in a duck. Gremlin protein in the webbing of the duck foot inhibits BMP4 signaling, thus preventing the embryonic webbing from undergoing apoptosis.

Q: What do you predict would happen if you blocked the expression of *Gremlin* in the feet of duck embryos?

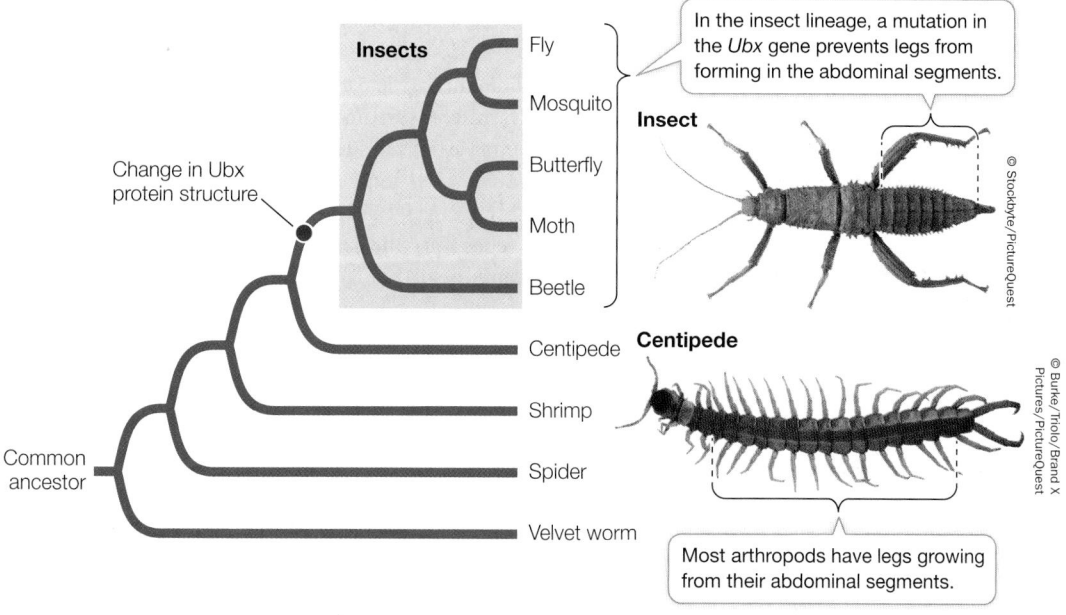

Figure 21.20 A Mutation in a Hox Gene Changed the Number of Legs in Insects In the insect lineage (blue box) of the arthropods, a change to the *Ubx* gene resulted in a protein that inhibits the *Dll* gene, which is required for legs to form. Because insects express this modified *Ubx* gene in their abdominal segments, no legs grow from these segments. Other arthropods, such as centipedes, produce an unmodified Ubx protein and do grow legs from their abdominal segments. (After R. Galant and S. Carroll. 2002. *Nature* 415: 910–913.)

arthropods shows that this change in *Ubx* occurred in the ancestor of insects, at the same time that abdominal legs were lost.

21.4 Recap and Assess

A genetic toolkit consisting of highly conserved regulatory genes governs pattern formation in multicellular organisms. Genetic toolkit genes act independently among modules of a developing embryo. The expression of these developmental genes can differ among species in various ways, often resulting in major morphological differences. They can differ in amount of expression (heterometry), in the timing of expression (heterochrony), or in the location of expression (heterotopy). A mutation in a gene controlling a developmental pathway can result in major changes in morphology.

1. Using the story of the eye-determining genes *Pax6* and *eyeless*, support the claim that genes controlling development are highly conserved.

2. In a series of experiments on chick embryos, researchers applied different concentrations of BMP4 to the embryos' beak growth region. They measured the size of the beak cartilage at a later stage of development. Based on the data in the table, what can you conclude about the role of BMP4 in beak growth?

Amount of BMP4	Cartilage diameter (mm)
None (control)	0.5
0.1 unit	0.7
0.3 unit	1.0
1.0 unit	1.8

Data from P. Wu et al. 2004. *Science* 305: 1465–1466.

3. How have diverse body forms in arthropods evolved by means of mutations in developmental genes?

Our understanding of molecular evolution has many practical applications across biology, and new ones are being developed every day. We now consider a few of these applications to medicine and industry.

21.5 Molecular Evolution Has Many Practical Applications

Learning Objectives

21.5.1 Describe how studies of molecular evolution are used to understand protein function.

21.5.2 Explain how the methods of in vitro evolution correspond to natural evolutionary processes.

21.5.3 Evaluate evolutionary relationships among viral sequences to understand the transmission of a viral disease.

Studies of molecular evolution have practical applications throughout biology, from understanding basic aspects of biological function to studies of human health.

Molecular sequence data are used to determine the evolutionary history of genes

A gene tree can show the evolutionary relationships of a single gene in different species, or it can trace the evolution of members of a gene family (as in Figure 21.10). The methods for constructing a gene tree are the same as those we described in Key Concept 20.2 for building phylogenetic trees of species. The process involves identifying differences between genes and using those differences to reconstruct the evolutionary history of the genes. Gene trees are often used to construct phylogenetic trees of species, but the two types of trees are not necessarily equivalent. Processes such as gene duplication can give rise to differences between the phylogenetic trees of genes and species. From a gene tree, biologists can reconstruct the history and timing of gene duplication events and learn how gene diversification has resulted in the evolution of new protein functions.

All the genes of a particular gene family have similar sequences because they have a common ancestry. As we discussed in Key Concept 20.1, features that are similar as a result of common ancestry are said to be homologous. When discussing gene trees, however, we usually need to distinguish between two forms of homology. Homologous genes that are found in different species and whose divergence we can trace to the speciation events that gave rise to those species are called **orthologs**. Homologous genes in the same or different species that are related through gene duplication events are called **paralogs**. When we examine a gene tree, the questions we wish to address determine whether we should compare orthologous or paralogous genes. If we wish to reconstruct the evolutionary history of the species that contain the genes, then our comparison should be restricted to orthologs (because they will reflect the history of speciation events). If we are interested in the changes in function that have resulted from gene duplication events, however, then the appropriate comparison is among paralogs (because they will reflect the history of gene duplication events). If our focus is on the diversification of a gene family through both processes, then we will want to include both paralogs and orthologs in our analysis.

Figure 21.21 depicts a gene tree for the members of a gene family called *engrailed* (its members encode transcription factors that regulate development). At least three gene duplications have occurred in this family, resulting in up to four different *engrailed* genes (*En*) in some vertebrate species (such as the zebrafish, *Danio rerio*). All of the *engrailed* genes are homologs because they have a common ancestor. Gene duplication events have generated paralogous *engrailed* genes (*En1* and *En2*) in some lineages of vertebrates. We could compare the orthologous sequences of the *En1* group of genes to reconstruct the history of the bony vertebrates (i.e., all the vertebrate species in Figure 21.21 except the lamprey), or we could use the orthologous sequences of the *En2* group of genes and expect the same answer (because there is only one history of the underlying speciation events). All bony vertebrates have both groups of *engrailed* genes because the two groups arose from a gene duplication event in the common ancestor of bony vertebrates. If we wanted to focus on the diversification that occurred as a result of this duplication, then the appropriate comparison would be between the paralogous genes of the *En1* versus *En2* groups.

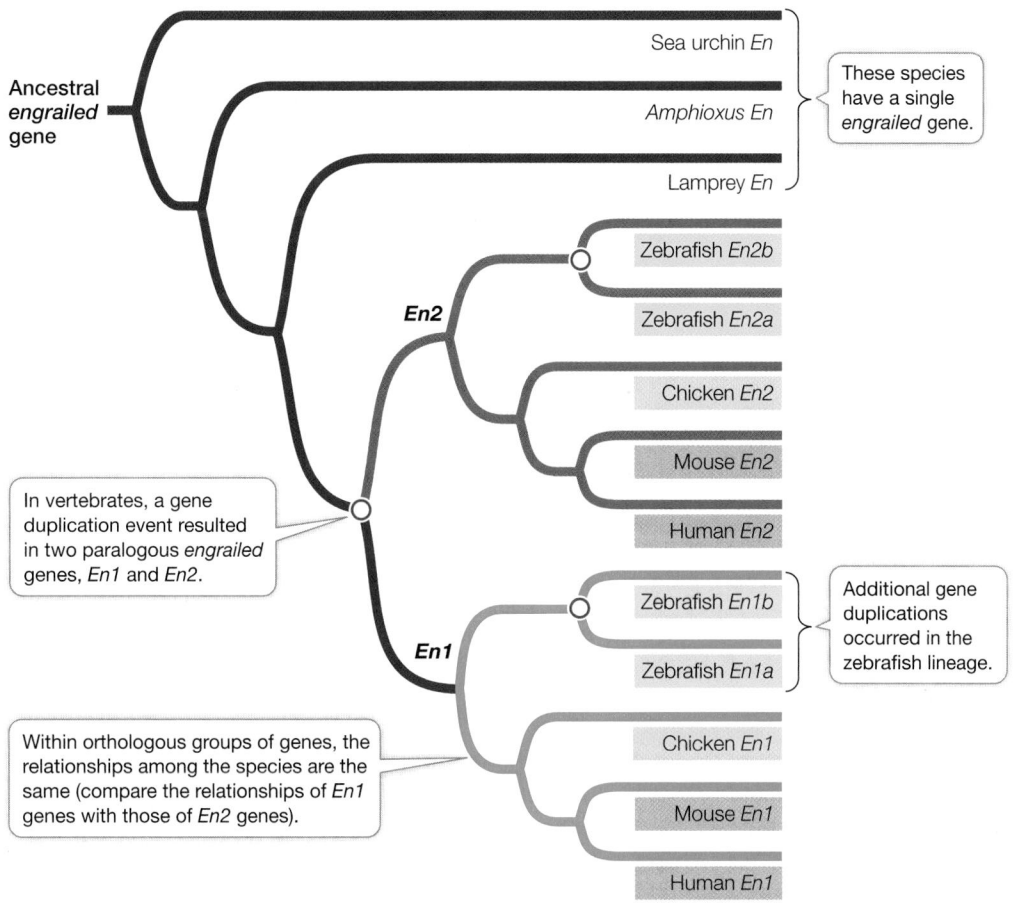

In vertebrates, a gene duplication event resulted in two paralogous *engrailed* genes, *En1* and *En2*.

These species have a single *engrailed* gene.

Additional gene duplications occurred in the zebrafish lineage.

Within orthologous groups of genes, the relationships among the species are the same (compare the relationships of *En1* genes with those of *En2* genes).

Figure 21.21 Phylogeny of the engrailed Genes The *engrailed* genes are homologous because they share a common ancestor. Speciation events have generated orthologous *engrailed* genes, and gene duplication events (open circles) have generated paralogous *engrailed* genes among bony vertebrates. (After A. Force et al. 1999. *Genetics* 151: 1531–1545.)

Q: How many gene duplication events occurred just within the zebrafish lineage?

Gene evolution is used to study protein function

Earlier in this chapter we discussed the ways in which biologists can detect regions of genes that are under positive selection for change. What are the practical uses of this information? Consider the evolution of the family of genes encoding voltage-gated sodium channels. Sodium channels have many functions, including the control of muscle contractions as well as nerve impulses in the nervous system. Sodium channels can be blocked by various toxins, such as tetrodotoxin (TTX), a neurotoxin present in the tissues of some puffer fishes and several other animals. A human who eats those tissues of a puffer fish that contain TTX can become paralyzed and die because the toxin blocks sodium channels and prevents muscles and nerves from functioning.

Connect the Concepts As described in detail in Key Concept 43.2, voltage-gated ion channels are stimulated to open or close by a change in the electric charge difference across a cell membrane, and thus let various ions into or out of cells.

But puffer fishes have sodium channels too, so why doesn't the TTX cause paralysis in the puffer fishes themselves? The sodium channels of puffer fishes (and of other animals that sequester TTX, such as the rough-skinned newt shown in Figure 19.20) have evolved to become resistant to the toxin. Nucleotide substitutions in the puffer fish genome have resulted in changes in the proteins

that make up the sodium channels, and those changes prevent TTX from binding to the sodium channel pore.

Several different substitutions that result in TTX resistance have evolved in the various duplicated sodium channel genes of the many species of puffer fishes. Many other changes that have nothing to do with the evolution of TTX resistance have occurred in these genes as well. Biologists who study the function of sodium channels can learn a great deal about how the channels work (and about neurological diseases that are caused by mutations in the sodium channel genes) by understanding which changes have been selected for TTX resistance. They do this by comparing the rates of synonymous and nonsynonymous substitutions across the genes in various lineages that have evolved TTX resistance. In a similar manner, molecular evolutionary principles are used to understand function and diversification of function in many other proteins.

In vitro evolution is used to produce new molecules

As biologists studied the relationships among selection, evolution, and function in macromolecules, they realized that molecular evolution could be employed in a controlled laboratory environment to produce new molecules with novel and useful functions. Thus were born the applications of **in vitro evolution**.

Living organisms produce thousands of compounds that humans have found useful. The search for such naturally occurring compounds, which can be used for pharmaceutical, agricultural, or industrial purposes, has been termed "bioprospecting." These compounds are the result of millions of years of molecular evolution across millions of species of living organisms. Biologists can imagine molecules that *could* have evolved but, lacking the right combination of selection pressures and opportunities, have not. For instance, we might want to have a molecule that binds a particular environmental contaminant so that the contaminant can be isolated and extracted from the environment. But if the contaminant is synthetic (i.e., not produced naturally), it is unlikely that any living organism will have evolved a molecule with the function we desire. This problem was the inspiration for the field of in vitro evolution.

The principles of in vitro evolution are based on the principles of molecular evolution that we have learned from the natural world. Consider the evolution of a new RNA molecule that was produced in the laboratory using the principles of mutation and selection. This molecule's intended function was to join two other RNA molecules. That is, the lab created a ribozyme—an RNA molecule capable of catalyzing a biochemical reaction. The process started with a large pool of random RNA sequences (10^{15} different sequences, each about 300 nucleotides long), which were then selected for any ligase activity (**Figure 21.22**). None were very effective ligases, but some were slightly better than others. The best of the ribozymes were selected and reverse-transcribed into cDNA (using the enzyme reverse transcriptase). The cDNA molecules were then amplified using the polymerase chain reaction (PCR; see Figure 13.20).

> **Connect the Concepts** Key Concept 17.1 describes how complementary DNA (cDNA) is made by complementary base-pairing to mRNA isolated from cells.

PCR amplification is not perfect, and it introduced many new mutations into the pool of sequences. These sequences were then transcribed back into RNA molecules using RNA polymerase II, and the process was repeated. The ligase activity of the RNAs evolved quickly; after ten rounds of in vitro evolution, it had increased by about 7 million times. Similar techniques have since been used to create a wide variety of molecules with novel enzymatic and binding functions.

Molecular evolution is used to study and combat diseases

Many of the most problematic human diseases are caused by living, evolving organisms that present a moving target for modern medicine. Historically, viral diseases such as influenza have been among the greatest factors in human mortality, and new viral diseases are constantly emerging in human populations, such as the human immunodeficiency virus (HIV) that causes AIDS. The control of these and many other human diseases depends on techniques that can track the evolution of pathogenic organisms over time.

Advances in transportation over the past century have allowed humans to move around the world with unprecedented speed and frequency. Unfortunately, this mobility has allowed pathogens to be transmitted among human populations, and between humans and other animals, at increasing rates. Cross-species

Figure 21.22 **In Vitro Evolution** Starting with a large pool of random RNA sequences, David Bartel and Jack Szostak of Massachusetts General Hospital produced a new ribozyme through rounds of mutation and selection for the ability to ligate (join) RNA sequences. (After D. P. Bartel and J. W. Szostak. 1993. *Science* 261: 1411–1418.)

transmission of viruses has led to the global emergence of many "new" diseases.

In the opening of this chapter we described the devastating influenza pandemic of 1918–1919. Michael Worobey and his colleagues used evolutionary analyses of influenza genomes to explore the reasons why this particular flu epidemic was so much more severe than any before or since (**Investigating Life: Why Was the 1918–1919 Influenza Pandemic So Severe?**). They reconstructed the evolutionary history of influenza viruses in birds, pigs, horses, and humans and found that influenza viruses have repeatedly been transferred from birds to the various mammals. Most cross-species transfers have been accompanied by a major epidemic in the new host. The 1918–1919 epidemic occurred immediately after such a transfer between hosts. Human

▶InvestigatingLIFE Why Was the 1918–1919 Influenza Pandemic So Severe?

Experiment

Original Paper: T. M. Tumpey et al. 2005. Characterization of the reconstructed 1918 Spanish influenza pandemic virus. *Science* 310: 77–80.

M. Worobey et al. 2014. A synchronized global sweep of the internal genes of modern avian influenza virus. *Nature* 508: 254–257.

As conveyed in the story that opens this chapter, the 1918–1919 influenza pandemic killed more than 50 million people worldwide— many more than the number of World War I–related combat deaths. Unlike flu epidemics before or since, the flu viruses that circulated in the 1918–1919 epidemic triggered an especially intense reaction in the human immune system. What was different about the flu viruses circulating at that time?

Terrence Tumpey and his colleagues at the Centers for Disease Control and Prevention isolated and sequenced a complete flu virus from biopsies of 1918 victims of the pandemic. Michael Worobey of the University of Arizona and his colleagues then analyzed and compared the genomes of flu viruses that have been collected from 1918 to the present, from birds, pigs, horses, and humans. The viruses are largely transmitted within each of these host groups, but rarely jump between host groups. Worobey and his colleagues reconstructed the phylogeny of the viruses to determine if the 1918 virus had recently "jumped" into human populations from another species.

HYPOTHESIS▶ The 1918–1919 influenza epidemic was so severe because the 1918 virus had recently moved into human populations from another species.

METHOD▶

1. Sequence the genomes of influenza viruses isolated from samples of birds, pigs, horses, and humans throughout the past century.

2. Reconstruct a phylogenetic tree based on sequences of the polymerase protein PA from the influenza virus genomes. Repeat this analysis for each of the genes in the genome. (Note that only the results based on PA are shown here.)

3. Determine the rate of evolution of the influenza viruses in each species, and use this information to conduct a molecular clock analysis to date the origins of each cross-species transmission.

RESULTS▶ Species-specific rates of the polymerase protein PA from the genome of influenza viruses in each host species:

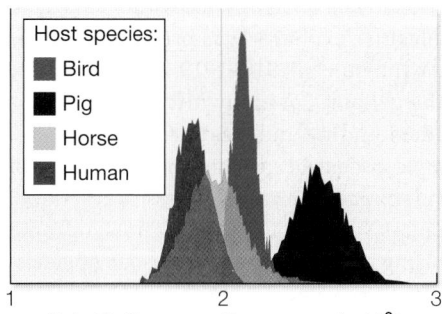

Time-calibrated phylogeny of the PA gene from influenza:

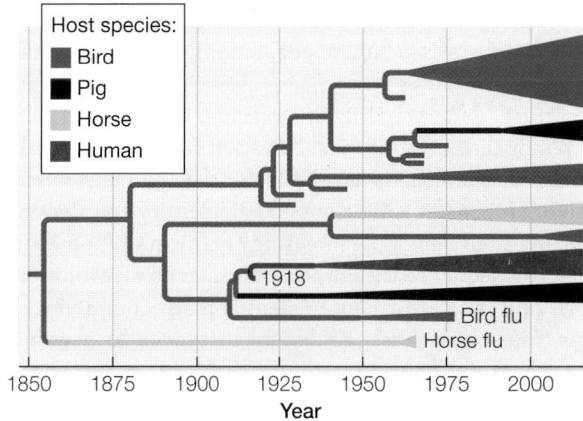

Viruses represented by blue lineages were isolated from birds; green lineages from pigs; orange lineages from horses; and red lineages from humans. The triangles represent many closely related sequences sampled from the respective species in the time period indicated; the width of the triangle is proportional to the number of sequences analyzed. The 1918 human influenza virus is labeled "1918."

CONCLUSION▶ What would you conclude about the 1918–1919 influenza pandemic from these results? Explore the possibilities in the following Work with the Data.

Work with the Data

Michael Worobey and his colleagues were able to reconstruct many of the cross-species transmissions of influenza virus that have occurred over the past 150 years, and to determine a likely reason that the 1918–1919 pandemic in humans was so severe. Can you replicate their conclusions?

QUESTIONS▶

1. All the influenza viruses shown in the tree in the experiment are thought to have arisen in one group of host animals. Which group of animals do you think is the original source of the virus, and why?

2. How many cross-species transmissions are shown on the tree? What hosts were involved (as source and recipient) of each transmission event?

3. What do you think is a likely explanation for the severity of the 1918–1919 influenza pandemic in humans?

4. Influenza was known in humans well before the 1918–1919 pandemic. Why do you think that no human influenza viruses are indicated on the tree before about 1918?

Go to **Achieve** for a companion Data in Depth exercise.

immune systems had no experience with the newly acquired virus, and the strong resulting reaction caused many of the strongest symptoms and deaths. Now that cross-species transmission has been associated with major flu epidemics, health workers around the world are constantly monitoring flu cases for indications of new cross-species transmissions. When emerging viruses are identified early on, efforts to control and eradicate them have a good chance of being successful. So far, our understanding of molecular evolution has prevented a repeat of the devastating flu pandemic of 1918–1919.

Studies of the genomes of many infectious agents have advanced our understanding and treatment of the diseases they cause. For example, rodent-borne hantaviruses were identified as the source of widespread respiratory illnesses, and the virus (and its host) that causes severe acute respiratory syndrome (SARS) was identified using evolutionary comparisons of genes. Studies of the origins, the timing of emergence, and the global diversity of many human pathogens depend on the principles of molecular evolution, as do the efforts to develop and use effective vaccines against these pathogens. For example, the techniques used to develop modern polio vaccines, as well as the methods used to track their effectiveness in human populations, rely on molecular evolutionary approaches.

In the future, understanding of molecular evolution will become even more critical to the identification of human (and other) diseases. Once biologists have collected data on the genomes of enough organisms, it will be possible to identify an infection by sequencing a portion of the infecting organism's genome and comparing this sequence with other sequences on an evolutionary tree. At present it is difficult to identify many common viral infections (those that cause "colds," for instance). As genomic databases and evolutionary trees increase, however, automated methods of sequencing and rapid phylogenetic comparison of the sequences will allow us to identify and treat a much wider array of human illnesses.

KEY CONCEPT

21.5 Recap and Assess

Studies of molecular evolution have provided biologists with new tools for understanding the functions of macromolecules and how those functions can change over time. These tools can be used to develop synthetic molecules and to identify and combat human diseases.

1. Describe a specific example of how gene evolution can be used to study protein function.
2. List the key elements of in vitro evolution. How do these elements correspond to natural evolutionary processes?
3. How are principles of evolutionary biology used to identify emerging diseases?

Now that we have discussed how organisms and biological molecules evolve, we are ready to consider the process of speciation. Speciation is what leads to the branching events on the tree of life, and is the process that results in the millions of species that constitute biodiversity.

▶Investigating LIFE

Q and A **Why was the 1918–1919 flu pandemic worse than any before or since?**

Many different strains of influenza virus circulate among human populations and other vertebrate hosts each year, but only a few of those strains survive and produce descendants. One of the ways in which influenza strains differ is in the configuration of proteins on their surface. These surface proteins are the targets of recognition by the host immune system. When changes occur in the surface proteins of an influenza virus, the host immune system may no longer recognize the invading virus, so that virus is more likely to replicate successfully. Those virus strains with the greatest number of changes to their surface proteins are most likely to escape detection by the host immune system, and are therefore most likely to spread among the host population and result in future flu epidemics. In other words, there is positive selection for change in the surface proteins of influenza viruses.

As demonstrated by data presented in **Investigating Life: Why Was the 1918–1919 Influenza Pandemic So Severe?**, the 1918–1919 flu epidemic occurred shortly after the cross-species transfer of an avian flu virus into human populations. For humans, this was a new virus, different than any influenza viruses that had circulated before in human populations. As human immune systems had no previous exposure to this virus, they had not yet developed effective immune defenses. The virus overstimulated human immune systems, which led to secondary complications and death. Today investigators carefully monitor influenza viruses circulating in human populations around the world. Early detection of new cross-species transmissions from birds or pigs into human populations is the key to their elimination before they can result in new global human influenza pandemics.

Future directions

By comparing the survival and proliferation rates of influenza virus strains that have different gene sequences coding for surface proteins, biologists can study the adaptation of the viruses over time. If biologists can predict which of the currently circulating flu virus strains are most likely to escape host detection, they can then identify the strains that are most likely to be involved in upcoming influenza epidemics and can target those strains for vaccine production.

How can biologists make such predictions? By determining the ratio of synonymous to nonsynonymous substitutions in genes that encode viral surface proteins, biologists can detect which codon changes (i.e., mutations) are under positive selection. They can then assess which of the currently circulating flu strains show the greatest number of changes in these positively selected codons. It is these flu strains that are most likely to survive, proliferate, and lead to the flu epidemics of the future, so they are the logical targets for new vaccines. This practical application of evolutionary theory leads to more effective flu vaccines—and thus fewer illnesses and influenza-related deaths each year.

You should be able to relate each summary to the adjacent figures. If you go to this visual summary in **Achieve**, you can follow links to figures, animations, activities, and simulations that will help you consolidate the material.

KEY CONCEPT

21.1   DNA Sequences Record the History of Gene Evolution   Go to Activities 21.1 and 21.2

■ **Sequence alignments** of proteins or nucleic acids from different organisms allow us to compare the sequences and identify homologous positions.

■ The minimum number of changes between sequences can be calculated from a **similarity matrix**.

■ Models of sequence evolution can be used to account for changes that cannot be observed directly.

Figure 21.1

Questions

1. What biological processes might lead us to hypothesize a gap in a set of aligned gene sequences?

2. What are four types of nucleotide substitutions that might lead us to underestimate the total number of changes between two sequences that are compared in a similarity matrix?

KEY CONCEPT

21.2   Genomes Reveal Both Neutral and Selective Processes of Evolution

■ **Nonsynonymous substitutions** of nucleotides result in amino acid replacements in proteins, whereas **synonymous substitutions** do not. Rates of synonymous substitution are typically higher than rates of nonsynonymous substitution in protein-coding genes (a result of stabilizing selection).

■ Much of the change in nucleotide sequences over time is a result of neutral evolution. The rate of fixation of neutral mutations is independent of population size and is equal to the mutation rate. Specific codons within a given gene sequence can be under different modes of selection.

■ **Positive selection** for change in a protein-coding gene may be detected by a higher rate of nonsynonymous than synonymous substitutions. The reverse is true of **purifying selection**.

■ Common selective constraints can lead to convergent evolution of amino acid sequences in distantly related species.

Figure 21.4

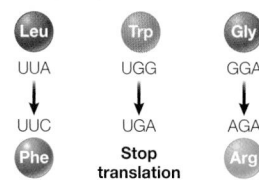

Questions

1. Why do we expect stabilizing selection to result in higher rates of synonymous than nonsynonymous substitutions?

2. How can biologists distinguish protein-coding genes that are evolving under positive selection from those evolving under stabilizing selection?

3. Which position in codons (first, second, or third) would you expect to evolve the fastest? Why?

Figure 21.6

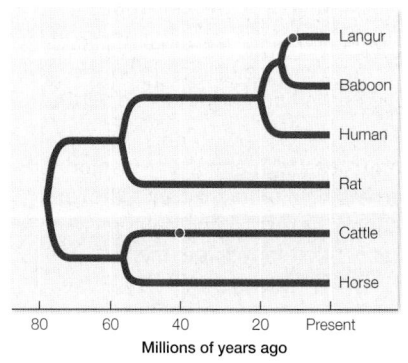

	Langur	Baboon	Human	Rat	Cattle	Horse
Langur		14	18	38	32	65
Baboon	0		14	33	39	65
Human	0	1		37	41	64
Rat	0	1	0		55	64
Cattle	5	0	0	0		71
Horse	0	0	0	0	1	

The lysozymes of langurs and cattle are convergent for 5 amino acids.

KEY CONCEPT
21.3 Changes in the Size and Arrangement of Genomes Can Result in New Features

Go to Activity 21.3 and Animation 21.1

- The total size of genomes varies much more widely across multicellular organisms than does the number of functional genes.

- Despite its short-term disadvantages, sexual reproduction generates countless genotype combinations that increase genetic variation in populations. In the absence of genetic recombination (as in some asexual organisms), deleterious mutations accumulate with each replication—a phenomenon known as **Muller's ratchet**.

- **Lateral gene transfer** can result in the rapid acquisition of new functions from distantly related species.

- **Gene duplications** can result in increased production of the gene's product, in divergence of the duplicated gene's expression, in pseudogenes, or in new gene functions. Several rounds of gene duplication can give rise to multiple genes with related functions, known as a **gene family**.

- Some highly repeated genes undergo **concerted evolution**, in which the multiple copies within the genome maintain their similarity, even as the genes diverge among species.

Figure 21.8

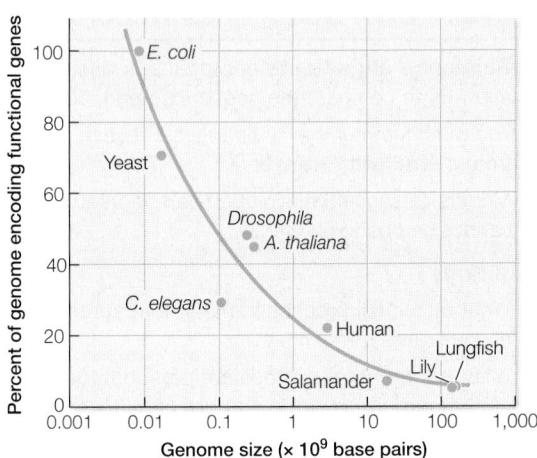

Questions

1. How would you support the statement that large genomes do not necessarily result in more complex organisms?

2. How does sexual recombination help keep deleterious mutations from accumulating in a population?

3. In what organisms is lateral gene transfer most common?

4. What is an example of a new function that arose following gene duplication?

KEY CONCEPT
21.4 Changes in Gene Expression Often Shape Evolution

Go to Animations 21.2 and 21.3

- A cascade of transcriptional activation sets up the axes of the embryo, the development of the body segments, and the determination of cell fate in each segment. **Hox genes** help determine cell fate in the embryos of animals.

- Genes encoding transcription factors and other regulatory proteins that govern pattern formation in the developing bodies of multicellular organisms compose what is called a **genetic toolkit**. These regulatory genes have been highly conserved throughout evolution.

- Developmental genes can be expressed in a modular fashion in different amounts (**heterometry**), in different timing (**heterochrony**), or in different locations (**heterotopy**). Mutations to genes that regulate development often result in major morphological changes.

Figure 21.15

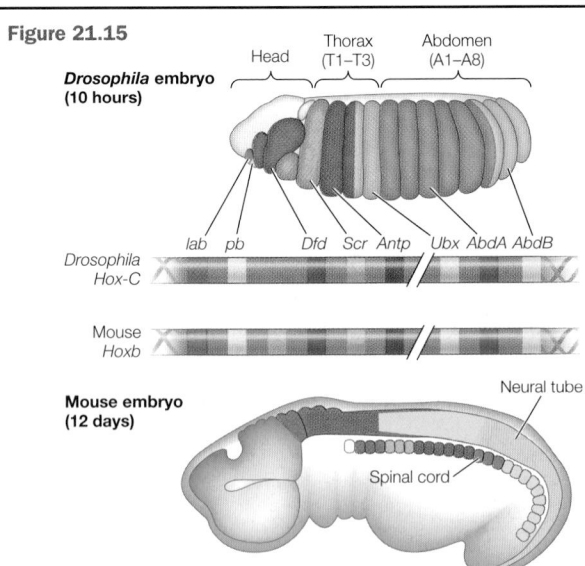

Questions

1. What is an example of a homeotic mutation?

2. Give examples of heterometry, heterochrony, and heterotopy.

3. How have changes in body segment development been important in the evolution of arthropod appendages?

Figure 21.20

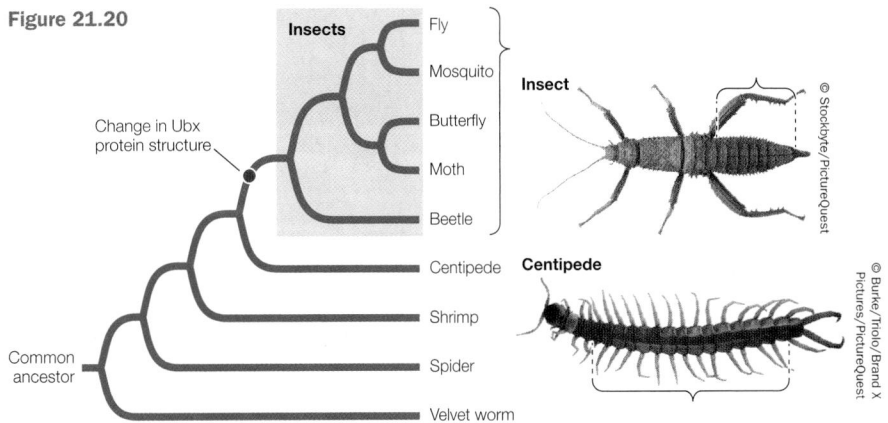

KEY CONCEPT

21.5 Molecular Evolution Has Many Practical Applications

- Protein function can be studied by examining gene evolution. Detection of positive selection can be used to identify molecular changes that have resulted in functional changes.

- **In vitro evolution** is used to produce synthetic molecules with particular desired functions.

- Many diseases are identified, studied, and combated through molecular evolutionary investigations.

Questions

1. Why is positive selection associated with functional change?

2. What are the similarities and differences between in vitro evolution and natural selection?

Figure 21.22

22 Speciation

KEY CONCEPTS

22.1 Species Are Reproductively Isolated Lineages on the Tree of Life

22.2 Speciation Is a Natural Consequence of Population Subdivision

22.3 Speciation May Occur through Geographic Isolation or in Sympatry

22.4 Reproductive Isolation Is Reinforced When Diverging Species Come into Contact

22.5 Speciation Rates Are Highly Variable across Life

Photos by David McIntyre (courtesy of Exotic Fish and Pet World, Southampton, MA) and ©Nantawat Chotsuwan/Shutterstock, Andreas Gradin, Mikola Gyorgy, Grigorev Mikhail, Vladimir Wrangel/Shutterstock.com, © iStock.com/Vladimir Wrangel

This composite photograph shows a few of the nearly 1,000 species of haplochromine cichlids that are endemic to Lake Malawi, all of which are from a single founder species.

▶ Investigating LIFE

Rapid Speciation in African Lake Cichlids

Not quite 2 million years ago, a tectonic split in the Great Rift Valley of East Africa led to the formation of Lake Malawi, which lies between the modern countries of Malawi, Tanzania, and Mozambique. A few fish species entered the new lake, including a type known as a haplochromine cichlid. Today the descendants of this early invader include nearly 1,000 species of haplochromine cichlids. All of them are endemic to Lake Malawi—they are found nowhere else. This vast array of cichlid species makes this the most diverse lake in the world in terms of its fish fauna. How did so many different species arise from a single ancestral species in less than 2 million years?

By studying the history and timing of speciation events in Lake Malawi, biologists have pieced together some of the processes that led to so many cichlid species. The earliest haplochromine cichlids to enter the new lake encountered diverse habitats in Lake Malawi, as some shores were rocky and others were sandy. Cichlid populations quickly adapted to these distinct habitat types. Fish in rocky habitats adapted to breeding and living in rocky conditions, and those in sandy habitats evolved specializations for life over sand. These changes resulted in an early speciation event.

Within each of these major habitat types, there were numerous opportunities for diet specialization. Various populations

of cichlids became rock scrapers, bottom feeders, fish predators, scale biters, pelagic zooplankton eaters, or plant specialists. Each of these feeding specializations requires a different mouth morphology. The offspring of fish that bred with fish of similar morphology were more likely to survive than were fish with two very different parents. These differences in fitness led to the formation of many more new species, each adapted to a different feeding mode.

The Lake Malawi cichlids continued to diverge and form new species. Male cichlids compete for the attention of females through their bright body colors. Diversification of the body colors of males, and of the preferences of females for different body colors, led to many more new species of cichlids, each isolated from the other by its sexual preferences. Now biologists are studying the genomes of these Lake Malawi cichlids to understand the details of the genetic changes that have given rise to so many species over so little time.

 If speciation typically takes thousands to millions of years, how do biologists conduct experiments to study this process? (Find the answer on page 510.)

Species Are Reproductively Isolated Lineages on the Tree of Life

Learning Objectives

22.1.1 Explain how biologists define species using morphology, reproduction, and evolutionary history.

22.1.2 Describe how reproductive isolation plays a role in each species concept.

Biological diversity does not vary in a smooth, continuous way. People have long recognized groups of similar organisms that mate with one another, and they have noticed that there are usually distinct morphological breaks between these groups. Groups of organisms that share a suite of genetic and morphological attributes, and are reproductively isolated from other such groups, are known as **species** (note that this is both the plural and singular form of the word). Species are the result of the process of **speciation**: the divergence of biological lineages and the emergence of reproductive isolation between lineages.

Although "species" is a useful and common term, its usage varies among biologists who are interested in different aspects of speciation. Different biologists think about species differently because they ask different questions: How can we recognize and identify species? How do new species arise? How do different species remain separate? Why do rates of speciation differ among groups of organisms? In answering these questions, biologists focus on different attributes of species, leading to several different ways of thinking about what species are and how they form. Most of the various **species concepts** proposed by biologists are simply different ways of approaching the question "What are species?" Let's compare three major classes of species concepts to contrast the ways that biologists think about species.

We can recognize many species by their appearance

Someone who is knowledgeable about a group of organisms, such as birds or flowering plants, can usually distinguish the different species found in a particular area simply by looking at them. Standard field guides to birds, mammals, insects, and wildflowers are possible only because many species change little in appearance over large geographic distances (**Figure 22.1A**).

More than 250 years ago, Carolus Linnaeus developed the system of binomial nomenclature by which species are named today (see Key Concept 20.4). Linnaeus described and named thousands of species, but because he knew nothing about the genetics and little of the mating behavior of the organisms he was naming, he classified them on the basis of their appearance alone. In other words, Linnaeus used a **morphological species concept**, a construct that assumes that a species comprises individuals that "look alike" and that individuals that do not look alike belong to different species. Although Linnaeus could not have known it, the members of most of the groups he classified as species look alike because they share many alleles of the genes that code for their morphological features.

Using morphology to define species is practical and useful, but it also has limitations. Members of the same species do not always look alike. For example, males, females, and young individuals do not always resemble one another closely (**Figure 22.1B**). Furthermore, morphology is of little use in the case of cryptic species—instances in which two or more species are morphologically indistinguishable but do not interbreed (**Figure 22.2**). Biologists therefore cannot rely on appearance alone in determining whether individual organisms are members of the same or different species. Today biologists use several additional types of information—especially behavioral and genetic data—to differentiate species.

Reproductive isolation is a key aspect of most species concepts

The most important factor in the divergence of sexually reproducing lineages from one another is the development of **reproductive isolation**, a state in which two groups of organisms can no longer exchange genes. If individuals of group A mate and reproduce only with one another, then group A constitutes a distinct species within which genes recombine. In other words, group A is an independent evolutionary lineage—a separate branch on the tree of life.

(A)

Dolichonyx oryzivorus
Male, Pennsylvania

CheepShot/CC BY 2.0

Dolichonyx oryzivorus
Male, Illinois

Kelly Colgan Azar/CC BY-ND 2.0

(B)

Dolichonyx oryzivorus
Female

Mike's Birds/CC BY-SA 2.0

Figure 22.1 Not All Members of the Same Species Look Alike
(A) It is easy to identify these two male Bobolinks (*Dolichonyx oryzivorus*) as members of the same species, even though they were photographed hundreds of miles apart in Pennsylvania and Illinois, respectively.

Despite their geographic separation, the two individuals are morphologically very similar. **(B)** Bobolinks are sexually dimorphic, which means the female's appearance is quite different from that of the male.

(A) *Hyla versicolor*

(B) *Hyla chrysoscelis*

Figure 22.2 Cryptic Species Look Alike but Do Not Interbreed
These two species of gray tree frogs cannot be distinguished by their external morphology, but they do not interbreed even when they occupy the same geographic range. *Hyla versicolor* **(A)** is a tetraploid species (four sets of chromosomes), whereas *H. chrysoscelis* **(B)** is diploid (two sets of chromosomes). And although they look alike, the males have distinctive mating calls; female frogs recognize and mate with males of their own species based on these calls.

To emphasize the importance of reproductive isolation in maintaining species, evolutionary biologist Ernst Mayr proposed the **biological species concept:** *"Species are groups of actually or potentially interbreeding natural populations which are reproductively isolated from other such groups."* The phrase "actually or potentially" is an important element of this definition. "Actually" says that the individuals live in the same area and interbreed with one another. "Potentially" says that even though the individuals do not live in the same area, and therefore do not interbreed, other information suggests that they *would* do so if they were able to get together. This widely used species concept is not sufficient for all purposes, however. For example, it does not apply to organisms that reproduce asexually, and it is limited to a single point in evolutionary time.

The lineage approach to understanding species takes a long-term view

Evolutionary biologists often think of species as branches on the tree of life, an idea that articulates a **lineage species concept**. In this framework for thinking about species, one species splits into two descendant species, which thereafter evolve as distinct lineages. A lineage species concept allows biologists to consider species over evolutionary time.

A **lineage** is an ancestor–descendant series of populations followed over time. Each species has a history that starts with a speciation event (at which one lineage on the tree is split into two) and ends either at extinction or at another speciation event (at which the species produces two daughter species). The process of lineage splitting may be gradual, taking thousands of generations to complete. At the other extreme, an ancestral lineage may be split in two within a few generations (as happens with polyploidy, which we discuss in Key Concept 22.3). The gradual nature of some splitting events means that at a single point in time, the final outcome of the process may not be clear. In these cases it may be difficult to predict whether the incipient species will continue to diverge and become fully isolated from their sibling species, or if they will merge again in the future.

The different species concepts are not mutually exclusive

Many named variants of these three major classes of species concepts exist. These various concepts are not incompatible; they simply emphasize different aspects of species or speciation. The morphological species concept emphasizes the practical aspects of recognizing species visually, although it sometimes results in underestimation or overestimation of the actual number of species. Mayr's biological species concept emphasizes that reproductive isolation is what allows sexual species to evolve independently of one another. The lineage species concept embraces the idea that sexual species are maintained by reproductive isolation, but extends the concept of a species as a lineage over evolutionary time. The species-as-lineage concept also accommodates species that reproduce asexually.

Virtually all species exhibit some degree of genetic recombination among individuals, even if recombination events are relatively rare and not associated with sexual reproduction. Significant reproductive isolation between species is therefore necessary for lineages to remain distinct over evolutionary time. Furthermore, reproductive isolation is responsible for the morphological distinctiveness of most species, because mutations that result in morphological changes cannot spread between reproductively isolated species. Therefore no matter which species concept we emphasize, the evolution of reproductive isolation is important for understanding the origin of species.

KEY CONCEPT
22.1 Recap and Assess

Species are distinct lineages on the tree of life. Speciation is usually a gradual process as one lineage divides into two. Over time, lineages of sexual species remain distinct from one another because they have become reproductively isolated.

1. Why do different biologists emphasize different attributes of species in formulating species concepts?

2. What makes reproductive isolation such an important component of each of the species concepts discussed here?

3. Why is the biological species concept not applicable to asexually reproducing organisms? Do you think this limits its applicability?

Although Charles Darwin titled his groundbreaking book *On the Origin of Species*, in fact it included very little discussion of speciation as we understand it today. Darwin devoted most of his attention to demonstrating that individual species are altered over time by natural selection. The remaining sections of this chapter discuss the many aspects of speciation that biologists have learned about since Darwin's time.

Figure 22.3 **The Dobzhansky–Muller Model**   In this simple two-locus version of the model, two lineages from the same ancestral population become physically separated from each other and evolve independently. A new allele becomes fixed in each descendant lineage, but at a different locus. Neither of the new alleles is incompatible with the ancestral alleles, but the two new alleles in the two different genes are incompatible with each other. Thus the two descendant lineages are reproductively incompatible.

 View in Achieve
Simulation 22.1 **Speciation**

KEY CONCEPT 22.2 Speciation Is a Natural Consequence of Population Subdivision

Learning Objectives

22.2.1 Describe the Dobzhansky–Muller model of speciation and explain how genetic differences between species are correlated with reproductive isolation.

22.2.2 Evaluate data from two populations to determine if they are reproductively isolated.

Not all evolutionary changes result in new species. A single lineage may change over time without giving rise to a new species. Speciation requires the interruption of gene flow within a species whose members formerly exchanged genes. But if a genetic change prevents reproduction between individuals of a species, how can such a change spread through a species in the first place?

Incompatibilities between genes can result in reproductive isolation

If a new allele that causes reproductive incompatibility arises in a population, it cannot spread through the population because no other individuals will be reproductively compatible with the individual that carries the new allele. So how can one reproductively cohesive lineage ever split into two reproductively isolated species? Several early geneticists, including Theodosius Dobzhansky and Hermann Joseph Muller, developed a genetic model to explain this apparent conundrum (**Figure 22.3**).

The **Dobzhansky–Muller model** is quite simple. First, assume that a single ancestral population is subdivided into two daughter populations (by the formation of a new mountain range, for instance), which then evolve as independent lineages. In one of the descendant lineages, a new allele (*A*) arises and becomes fixed (see Figure 22.3). In the other lineage, another new allele (*B*) becomes fixed *at a different gene locus*. Neither new allele at either locus results in any loss of reproductive compatibility by itself. However, the two new forms of these two different genes have never occurred together in the same individual or population. Recall that the products of many genes must work together in an organism. It is possible

that the new proteins encoded by the two new alleles will not be compatible with each other. If individuals from the two lineages come back together after these genetic changes, they may still be able to interbreed. However, the hybrid offspring will have a new combination of genes that may be functionally inferior or even lethal (the combination of alleles *A* and *B* at the two loci in this example). This will not happen with all new combinations of genes, but over time, isolated lineages will accumulate many allele differences at many gene loci. Some combinations of these differentiated genes will not function well together in hybrids. Thus genetic incompatibility between the two isolated lineages will develop over time.

Many empirical and experimental examples support the Dobzhansky–Muller model. This model works not only for pairs of individual genes but also for some kinds of chromosomal rearrangements. Bats of the genus *Rhogeessa*, for example, exhibit considerable variation in centric fusions of their chromosomes. In other words, the chromosomes of the various species contain the same basic chromosomal arms, but in some species two acrocentric (one-armed) chromosomes have fused at the centromere to form larger, metacentric (two-armed) chromosomes. A polymorphism in centric fusion causes few, if any, problems in meiosis because the respective chromosomes can still align and assort normally. Therefore a given centric fusion can become fixed in a lineage. However, if a *different* centric fusion becomes fixed in a second lineage, then hybrids between individuals of each lineage will not be able to produce normal gametes in meiosis (**Figure 22.4**). Most of the closely related species of *Rhogeessa* display different combinations of these centric fusions and are thereby reproductively isolated from one another.

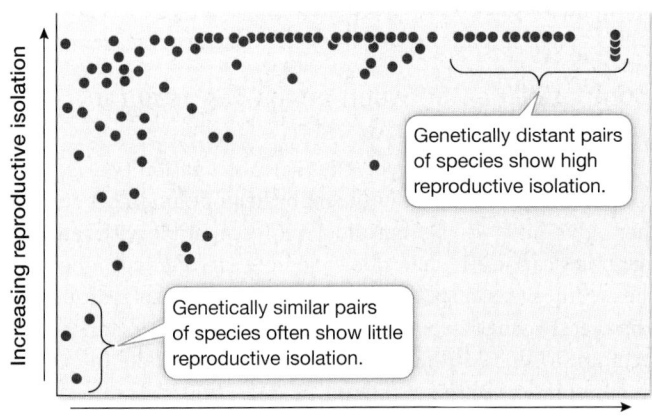

Rhogeessa tumida

The original lineage has 3 one-armed chromosomes.

The ancestral population separates into two independent lineages.

Centric fusion between chromosomes 1 and 2 creates a new, two-armed chromosome but does not disrupt chromosome pairing during meiosis.

Fusion of 1 + 2 becomes fixed.

Normal pairing of chromosomes cannot occur in hybrids.

A different centric fusion between chromosomes 2 and 3 also does not disrupt chromosome pairing.

Fusion of 2 + 3 becomes fixed.

Figure 22.4 **Speciation by Centric Fusion** In this chromosomal version of the Dobzhansky–Muller model, two independent centric fusions of one-armed chromosomes occur in two sister lineages. Neither centric fusion by itself results in difficulties at meiosis, whether the fusion is found in just one or in both pairs of chromosomes. After fixation of the different fusions in each lineage, however, F_1 hybrids between the two lineages are sterile, because the three different chromosomes involved in these centric fusions cannot pair normally at meiosis in hybrids. Most of the species in the bat genus *Rhogeessa* differ from one another by such centric fusions.

Reproductive isolation develops with increasing genetic divergence

As pairs of species diverge genetically, they become increasingly reproductively isolated (**Figure 22.5**). Both the rate at which reproductive isolation develops and the mechanisms that produce it vary from group to group. Reproductive incompatibility has been shown to develop gradually in many groups of plants, animals, and fungi, reflecting the slow pace at which incompatible genes accumulate in each lineage. In some cases, complete reproductive isolation may take millions of years. In other cases (as with the chromosomal fusions of *Rhogeessa* just described), reproductive isolation can develop over just a few generations.

Partial reproductive isolation (reduced reproductive compatibility) has evolved in many strains of plants that have been artificially isolated by humans. In 1835, Thomas Drummond collected seeds of a newly discovered species of phlox in Texas and distributed them to nurseries in Europe. The European nurseries established more than 200 true-breeding strains of Drummond's phlox (*Phlox drummondii*) that differ in flower size, flower color, and plant growth form. The breeders did not select directly for reproductive incompatibility between strains, but in subsequent experiments in which strains were crossed and seed production was measured and compared, biologists found that reproductive compatibility between strains had been reduced by 14% to 50%,

Genetically distant pairs of species show high reproductive isolation.

Genetically similar pairs of species often show little reproductive isolation.

Increasing reproductive isolation

Increasing genetic divergence

Figure 22.5 **Reproductive Isolation Increases with Genetic Divergence** Among pairs of *Drosophila* species, the more the species differ genetically (*x* axis), the greater their reproductive isolation from each other (*y* axis). Each dot represents a comparison of one species pair. Such positive relationships between genetic distance and reproductive isolation have been observed in many groups of plants, animals, and fungi. (After J. A. Coyne and H. A. Orr. 1989. *Evolution* 43: 362–381.)

Q: Why might some genetically similar species pairs exhibit high levels of reproductive isolation?

depending on the cross—even though the strains had been isolated from one another for less than two centuries.

KEY CONCEPT
22.2 Recap and Assess

When two parts of a population become isolated from each other by some barrier to gene flow, they begin to diverge genetically. The Dobzhansky–Muller model describes how new alleles or chromosomal arrangements that arise in the two descendent lineages can lead to genetic incompatibility, and hence reproductive isolation, of the two lineages.

1. The Dobzhansky–Muller model suggests that divergence among alleles at different gene loci leads to genetic incompatibility between species. Why is genetic incompatibility between two alleles at the same locus considered less likely?

2. Why do some combinations of chromosomal centric fusions cause problems in meiosis? Can you diagram what would happen at meiosis in a hybrid of the divergent lineages shown in Figure 22.4?

3. Assume that the reproductive isolation seen in *Phlox drummondii* strains results from lethal combinations of incompatible alleles at several loci among the various strains. Given this assumption, why might the reproductive isolation seen among these strains be partial rather than complete?

We have now seen how the splitting of an ancestral population leads to genetic divergence and reproductive incompatibility in the two descendant lineages. Next we consider ways in which the descendant lineages could have become separated in the first place.

KEY CONCEPT
22.3 Speciation May Occur through Geographic Isolation or in Sympatry

Learning Objectives

22.3.1 Compare and contrast allopatric and sympatric speciation, and recognize examples of speciation as being one or the other.

22.3.2 Diagram the relationship between geographic isolation and speciation, and interpret data to make and support predictions.

Many biologists who study speciation have concentrated on geographic processes that can result in the division of an ancestral species. Splitting of the geographic range of a species is one obvious way of achieving such a division, but it is not the only way.

Physical barriers give rise to allopatric speciation

Speciation that results when a population is divided by a physical barrier is known as **allopatric speciation** (Greek *allos*, "other," + *patria*, "homeland"). Allopatric speciation is thought to be the dominant mode of speciation in most groups of organisms. The physical barrier that divides the range of a species may be a body of water or a mountain range for terrestrial organisms, or dry land for aquatic organisms—in other words, any type of habitat that is inhospitable to the species. Such barriers can form when

continents drift, sea levels rise or fall, glaciers advance or retreat, or climates change. The populations separated by such barriers are often, but not always, initially large. The lineages that descend from these founding populations evolve differences for a variety of reasons, including mutation, genetic drift, and adaptation to different environments in the two areas. As a result, many pairs of closely related **sister species**—species that are each other's closest relatives—may exist on either side of the geographic barrier. An example of a physical geographic barrier that produced many pairs of sister species was the Pleistocene glaciation that isolated freshwater streams in the eastern highlands of the Appalachian Mountains from streams in the Ozark and Ouachita Mountains (**Figure 22.6**). This splitting event resulted in many parallel speciation events among isolated lineages of stream-dwelling organisms.

Allopatric speciation may also result when some members of a population cross an existing barrier and establish a new, isolated population. Many of the more than 800 species of *Drosophila* found in the Hawaiian Islands are restricted to a single island. We know that these species are the descendants of new populations founded by individuals dispersing among the islands when we find that the closest relative of a species on one island is a species on a neighboring island rather than a species on the same island. Biologists who have studied the chromosomes of these fruit flies estimate that speciation in this group of *Drosophila* has resulted from at least 45 such founder events (**Figure 22.7**).

The species of finches found on the islands of the Galápagos archipelago, some 1,000 kilometers off the coast of Ecuador, are among the most famous examples of allopatric speciation. Darwin's finches (as they are usually called, because Darwin was the first scientist to study them) arose in the Galápagos from a single South American finch species that colonized the islands. Today the Galápagos species differ strikingly not only from their closest mainland relative, but also from one another (**Figure 22.8**). The islands are sufficiently far apart that the birds move among them only infrequently. In addition, environmental conditions differ widely from island to island. Some islands are relatively flat and arid; others have forested mountain slopes. Sister lineages on different islands have diverged over hundreds of thousands of years, and several feeding specializations have arisen on different islands with different environments. Although finches occasionally fly between islands, an immigrant finch population is not likely to become established unless the new environment is appropriate for its feeding specialization, and no other similar species are already present on the island. Each island now has from 1 to 4 species of finches, and biologists recognize between 14 and 18 species across the archipelago.

Sympatric speciation occurs without physical barriers

Geographic isolation is usually required for speciation, but under some circumstances speciation can occur in the absence of a physical barrier. Speciation without physical isolation is called **sympatric speciation** (Greek *sym*, "together with"). But how can such speciation happen? Given that speciation is usually a gradual process, how can reproductive isolation develop when individuals have frequent opportunities to mate with one another?

(A) Distribution of freshwater stream fishes in the Pliocene

Prior to glaciation, the ancestors of each pair of species (A, B, C, D) were distributed throughout the central highlands.

Central highlands

(B) Distribution of freshwater stream fishes in the Pleistocene

Glaciation split the central highlands and divided many populations.

Maximum glacial advance

Ozarks

Ouachitas

Eastern highlands

A₁ Missouri saddled darter
Etheostoma tetrazonum

A₂ Variegated darter
E. variatum

B₁ Bleeding shiner
Luxilus zonatus

B₂ Warpaint shiner
L. coccogenis

C₁ Ozark minnow
Notropis nubilus

C₂ Tennessee shiner
N. leuciodus

D₁ Ozark madtom
Noturus albater

D₂ Elegant madtom
N. elegans

▶ View in **Achieve**
Animation 22.1 **Speciation Mechanisms**

◀ **Figure 22.6 Allopatric Speciation** Allopatric speciation may result when an ancestral population is divided into two separate populations by a physical barrier and those populations then diverge. **(A)** Many species of freshwater stream fishes were distributed throughout the central highlands of North America in the Pliocene (about 5.3–2.6 million years ago). **(B)** During the Pleistocene (about 2.6 million years ago–10,000 years ago), glaciers advanced and isolated fish populations in the Ozark and Ouachita Mountains to the west from fish populations in the highlands of the Appalachian Mountains to the east. Numerous species diverged as a result of this separation, including the ancestors of the four pairs of sister species shown here. (After R. L. Mayden. 1985. *Southwest Nat* 30: 195–211; R. L. Mayden. 1987. In *Quarternary Environments of Kansas. Kansas Geol Surv Guidebook Series 5*, W. C. Johnson (ed.), pp. 141–151. University of Kansas: Lawrence, Kansas.)

Q: After the retreat of the glaciers, why did the fish species in the Ozarks and Ouachitas remain reproductively isolated from those in the Appalachians to the east?

DISRUPTIVE SELECTION Sympatric speciation may occur with some forms of disruptive selection (see Key Concept 19.4) in which individuals with certain genotypes have a preference for distinct microhabitats where mating takes place. For example, sympatric speciation via disruptive selection appears to be taking place in the Apple Maggot Fly (*Rhagoletis pomonella*) of eastern North America. Until the mid-1800s, *Rhagoletis* flies courted, mated, and deposited their eggs only on hawthorn fruits. Then, some flies began to lay their eggs on apples, which European immigrants had introduced into eastern North America. Apple trees are closely

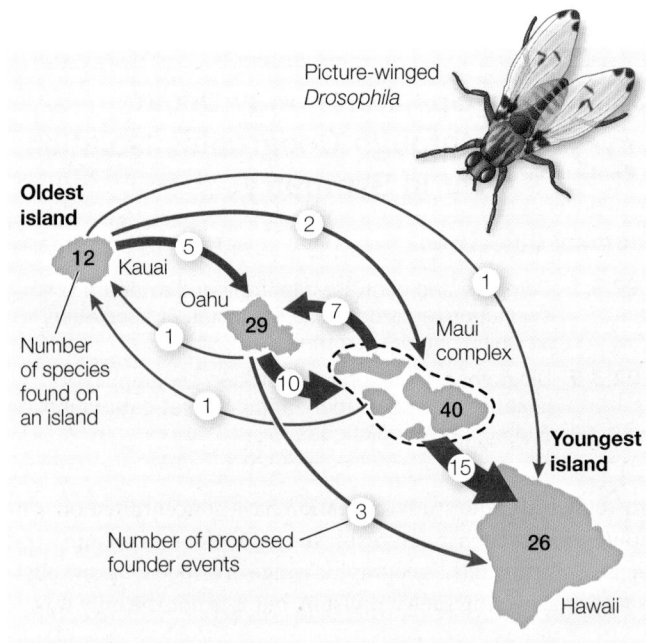

Picture-winged *Drosophila*

Oldest island

12 Kauai

5

2

Oahu

29

1

7

1

10

1

Maui complex

40

15

3

Youngest island

26

Hawaii

Number of species found on an island

Number of proposed founder events

Figure 22.7 Founder Events Lead to Allopatric Speciation The large number of species of picture-winged *Drosophila* in the Hawaiian Islands is the result of founder events: the founding of new populations by individuals dispersing among the islands. The islands, which were formed in sequence as Earth's crust moved over a volcanic "hot spot," vary in age. (After H. L. Carson and A. R. Templeton. 1984. *Annu Rev Ecol Syst* 15: 97–131.)

▶ View in **Achieve**
Animation 22.2 **Founder Events and Allopatric Speciation**

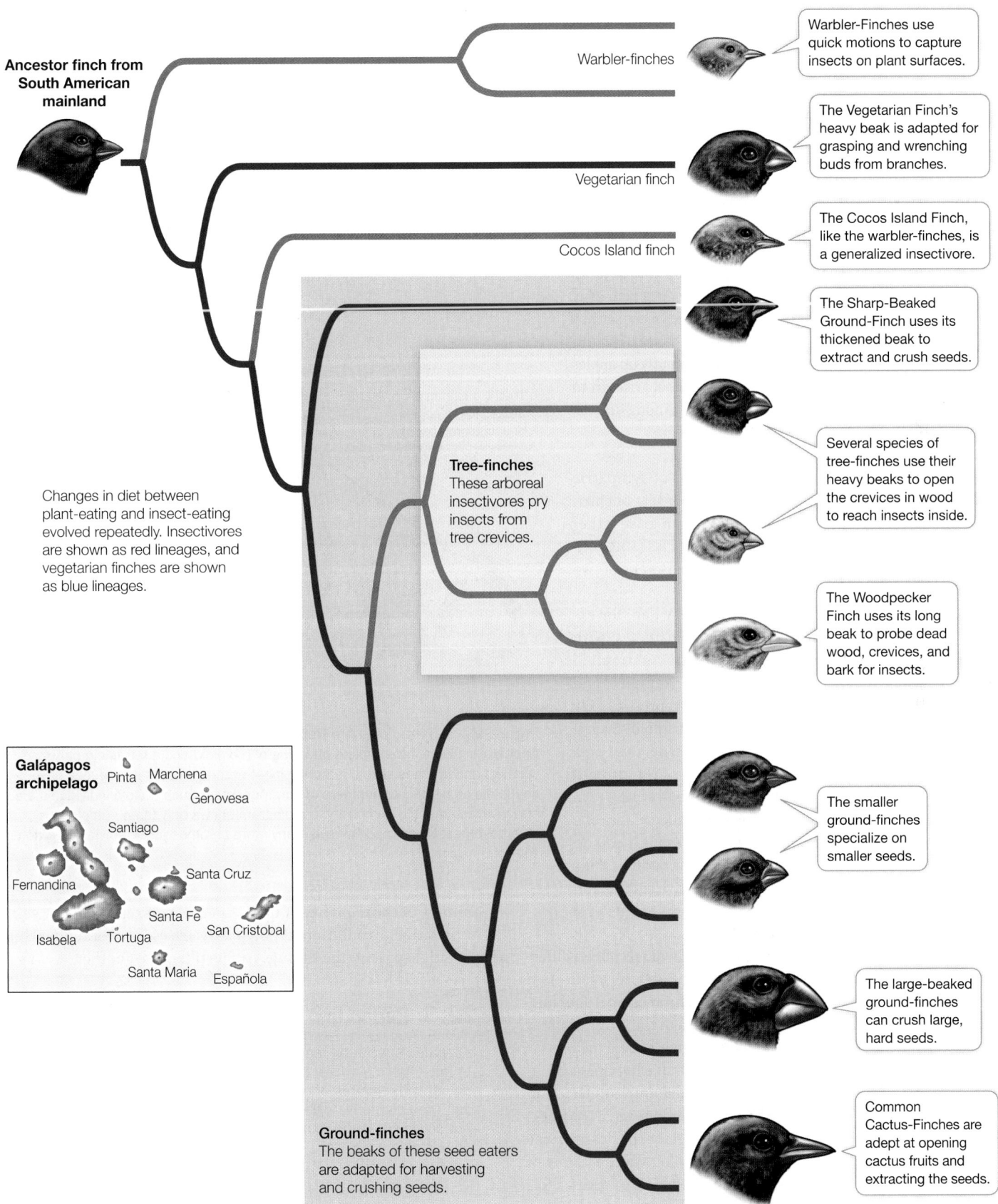

Ancestor finch from South American mainland

Warbler-finches

> Warbler-Finches use quick motions to capture insects on plant surfaces.

Vegetarian finch

> The Vegetarian Finch's heavy beak is adapted for grasping and wrenching buds from branches.

Cocos Island finch

> The Cocos Island Finch, like the warbler-finches, is a generalized insectivore.

> The Sharp-Beaked Ground-Finch uses its thickened beak to extract and crush seeds.

Tree-finches
These arboreal insectivores pry insects from tree crevices.

> Several species of tree-finches use their heavy beaks to open the crevices in wood to reach insects inside.

> The Woodpecker Finch uses its long beak to probe dead wood, crevices, and bark for insects.

Changes in diet between plant-eating and insect-eating evolved repeatedly. Insectivores are shown as red lineages, and vegetarian finches are shown as blue lineages.

> The smaller ground-finches specialize on smaller seeds.

> The large-beaked ground-finches can crush large, hard seeds.

> Common Cactus-Finches are adept at opening cactus fruits and extracting the seeds.

Galápagos archipelago
Pinta   Marchena
Genovesa
Santiago
Santa Cruz
Fernandina
Santa Fe
Isabela   Tortuga   San Cristobal
Santa Maria   Española

Ground-finches
The beaks of these seed eaters are adapted for harvesting and crushing seeds.

Figure 22.8 Allopatric Speciation among Darwin's Finches
The descendants of the ancestral finch that colonized the Galápagos archipelago several million years ago evolved into many different species whose beaks are variously adapted to feed on buds, seeds, or insects. (After S. Lamichhaney et al. 2015. *Nature* 518: 371–375.)

related to hawthorns, but the smell of the fruits differs, and the apple fruits appear earlier than those of hawthorns. Some early-emerging female *Rhagoletis* laid their eggs on apples, and over time, a genetic preference for the smell of apples evolved among early-emerging insects. When the offspring of these flies sought out apple trees for mating and egg deposition, they mated with other flies reared on apples, which shared the same preferences.

Today the two groups of *Rhagoletis pomonella* in the eastern United States appear to be on the way to becoming distinct species. One group mates and lays eggs primarily on hawthorn fruits, the other on apples. The incipient species are partially reproductively isolated because they mate primarily with individuals raised on the same fruit and because they emerge from their pupae at different times of the year. In addition, the apple-feeding flies now grow more rapidly on apples than they originally did. Sympatric speciation that arises from such host-plant specificity may be widespread among insects, many of which feed on only a single plant species.

POLYPLOIDY   The most common means of sympatric speciation is **polyploidy**, or the duplication of sets of chromosomes within individuals. Polyploidy can arise either from chromosome duplication in a single species (**autopolyploidy**) or from the combining of the chromosomes of two different species (**allopolyploidy**).

An autopolyploid individual originates when, for example, two accidentally unreduced diploid gametes (with two sets of chromosomes) combine to form a tetraploid individual (with four sets of chromosomes). Tetraploid and diploid individuals of the same species are reproductively isolated because their hybrid offspring are triploid. Even if these offspring survive, they are usually sterile; they cannot produce normal gametes because their chromosomes do not segregate evenly during meiosis (**Figure 22.9**). So a tetraploid individual usually cannot produce viable offspring by mating with a diploid individual—but it *can* do so if it self-fertilizes or mates with another tetraploid. Thus polyploidy can result in complete reproductive isolation in two generations—an important exception to the general rule that speciation is a gradual process.

Allopolyploids may be produced when individuals of two different (but closely related) species interbreed. Such hybridization often disrupts normal meiosis, which can result in chromosomal doubling. Allopolyploids are often fertile because each of the chromosomes has a nearly identical partner with which to pair during meiosis.

Speciation by polyploidy has been particularly important in the evolution of plants, although it has contributed to speciation in animals as well (such as the tree frogs in Figure 22.2). Botanists estimate that about 70% of flowering plant species and 95% of fern species are the result of recent polyploidization. Some of these species arose from hybridization between two species followed by chromosomal duplication and self-fertilization. Other species diverged from polyploid ancestors, so that the new species shared their ancestors' duplicated sets of chromosomes. New species arise by polyploidy more easily among plants than among

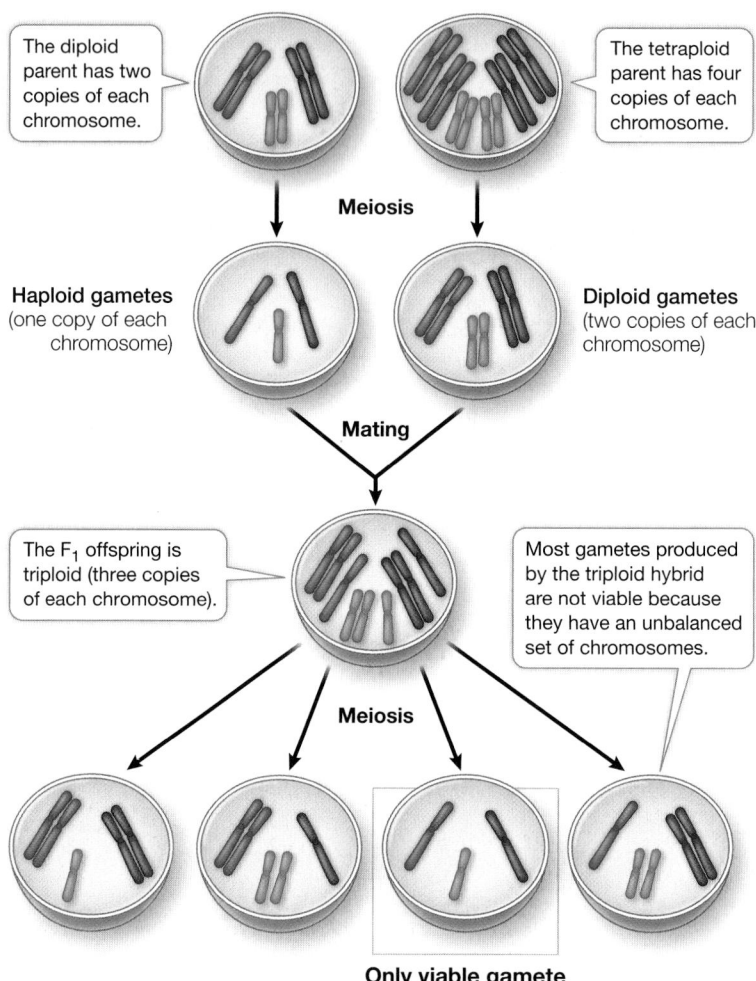

Figure 22.9 Tetraploids Are Reproductively Isolated from Their Diploid Ancestors Even if the triploid offspring of a diploid and a tetraploid parent survives and reaches sexual maturity, most of the gametes it produces have aneuploid (unbalanced) numbers of chromosomes. Such triploid individuals are effectively sterile. (For simplicity, the diagram shows only three homologous chromosomes. Most species have many more chromosomes, so viable gametes are extremely rare.)

animals because plants of many species can reproduce by self-fertilization. In addition, if polyploidy arises in several offspring of a single parent, the siblings can fertilize one another.

KEY CONCEPT
22.3 Recap and Assess

Allopatric speciation results from the separation of populations by geographic barriers; it is the dominant mode of speciation among most groups of organisms. Sympatric speciation may result from disruptive selection that results in ecological isolation, but polyploidy is the most common cause of sympatric speciation among plants.

1. Explain how speciation via polyploidy can happen in only two generations.
2. If allopatric speciation is the most prevalent mode of speciation, what do you predict about the geographic distributions of many closely related species? Does your answer differ for species that are sedentary versus highly mobile?

3. The species of Darwin's finches shown in the phylogeny in Figure 22.8 have all evolved on islands of the Galápagos archipelago within the past 3 million years. Molecular clock analysis (see Key Concept 20.3) has been used to determine the dates of the various speciation events in that phylogeny. Geological techniques for dating rock samples (see Key Concept 23.1) have been used to determine the ages of the various Galápagos islands. The table shows the number of species of Darwin's finches and the number of islands that have existed in the archipelago at several times during the past 4 million years (Data from P. R. Grant. 2001. *Oikos* 92: 385–403).

Time (millions of years ago)	Number of islands	Number of finch species
0.25	18	14
0.50	18	9
0.75	9	7
1.00	6	5
2.00	4	3
3.00	4	1
4.00	3	0

a. Plot the number of species of Darwin's finches and the number of islands in the Galápagos archipelago (dependent variables) against time (independent variable).

b. Are the data consistent with the hypothesis that isolation of populations on newly formed islands is related to speciation in this group of birds? Why or why not?

c. If no more islands form in the Galápagos archipelago, do you think that speciation by geographic isolation will continue to occur among Darwin's finches? Why or why not? What additional data could you collect to test your hypothesis (without waiting to see if speciation occurs)?

Most populations separated by a physical barrier become reproductively isolated only slowly and gradually. If two incipient species once again come into contact with each other, what keeps them from merging back into a single species?

KEY CONCEPT 22.4 Reproductive Isolation Is Reinforced When Diverging Species Come into Contact

Learning Objectives

22.4.1 Create graphical representations of hybridization frequencies and analyze data to develop hypotheses about postzygotic isolation.

22.4.2 Compare and contrast prezygotic and postzygotic isolating mechanisms.

22.4.3 Relate the width of a hybrid zone to the fitness of hybrid offspring.

As we discussed in Key Concept 22.2, once a barrier to gene flow is established, reproductive isolation will begin to develop through genetic divergence. Over many generations, differences accumulate in the isolated lineages, reducing the probability that individuals from each lineage will mate successfully with individuals in the other lineage when they come back into contact. In this way, reproductive isolation can evolve as a by-product of the genetic changes in the two diverging lineages.

If reproductive isolation is incomplete when incipient species come back into contact, some hybridization is likely to occur. If hybrid individuals are less fit than non-hybrids, selection will favor parents that do not produce hybrid offspring. Under these conditions, selection will result in the strengthening, or **reinforcement**, of mechanisms that prevent hybridization.

Mechanisms that prevent hybridization from occurring are called **prezygotic isolating mechanisms**. Mechanisms that reduce the fitness of hybrid offspring are called **postzygotic isolating mechanisms**. Postzygotic isolating mechanisms result in selection against hybridization, which in turn leads to the reinforcement of prezygotic isolating mechanisms.

Prezygotic isolating mechanisms prevent hybridization

Prezygotic isolating mechanisms, which come into play before fertilization, can prevent hybridization in several ways.

MECHANICAL ISOLATION   Differences in the sizes and shapes of reproductive organs may prevent the union of gametes from different species. With animals, the shapes of the reproductive organs of males and females of the same species often match, so that reproduction between individuals with mismatched reproductive structures is not physically possible. In plants, mechanical isolation may involve a pollinator. For example, some orchid species produce flowers that look and smell like the females of a particular species of bee or wasp (**Figure 22.10**). When a male bee

Ophrys apifera

Bombus lucorum

Figure 22.10 Mechanical Isolation through Mimicry   Many orchid species maintain reproductive isolation by means of flowers that look and smell like females of one—and only one—bee or wasp species. A male insect of the correct species must land on the flower and attempt to mate with it; only males of this particular species are physically configured to collect and transfer the orchid's pollen. The constraints of this method of pollen transfer reproductively isolate the plant from related orchid species that attract different insect pollinators. The species shown here are the two players in one such interspecific relationship.

or wasp visits and attempts to mate with the flower (thinking it is a female of his species), his mating behavior results in the transfer of pollen to and from his body by appropriately configured anthers and stigmas on the flower. Insects that visit the flower but do not attempt to mate with it do not trigger the transfer of pollen between the insect and the flower.

TEMPORAL ISOLATION Many organisms have distinct mating seasons. If two closely related species breed at different times of the year (or different times of day), they may never have an opportunity to hybridize. For example, in sympatric populations of three closely related leopard frog species, each species breeds at a different time of year (**Figure 22.11**). Although there is some overlap in the breeding seasons, the opportunities for hybridization are minimized.

BEHAVIORAL ISOLATION Individuals may reject, or fail to recognize, individuals of other species as potential mating partners. For example, the mating calls of male frogs of related species

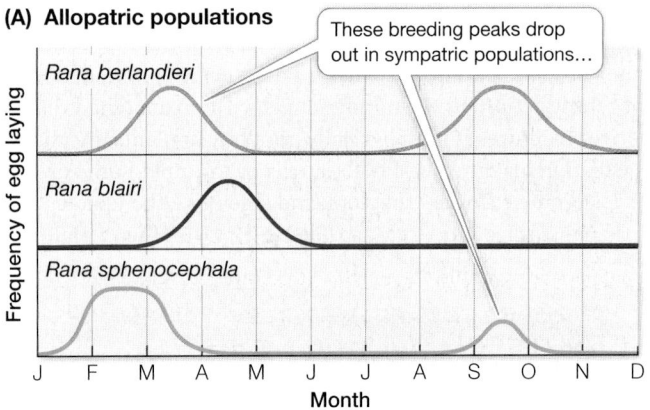

(A) Allopatric populations

These breeding peaks drop out in sympatric populations...

Rana berlandieri

Rana blairi

Rana sphenocephala

Frequency of egg laying

J F M A M J J A S O N D
Month

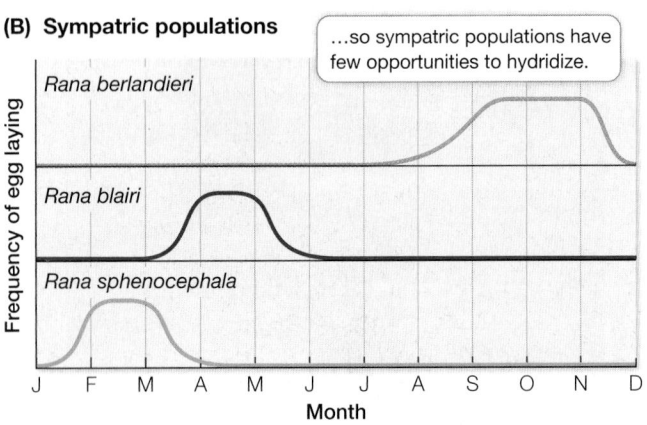

(B) Sympatric populations

...so sympatric populations have few opportunities to hydridize.

Rana berlandieri

Rana blairi

Rana sphenocephala

Frequency of egg laying

J F M A M J J A S O N D
Month

Figure 22.11 Temporal Isolation of Breeding Seasons (A) The peak breeding seasons of three species of leopard frogs (*Rana*) overlap when the species are physically separated (allopatry). (B) Where two or more species of *Rana* live together (sympatry), overlap between their peak breeding seasons is greatly reduced or eliminated. (After D. M. Hillis. 1981. *Copeia* 1981: 312–319.)

Q: What means of selection helps reinforce this prezygotic isolating mechanism in areas of sympatry?

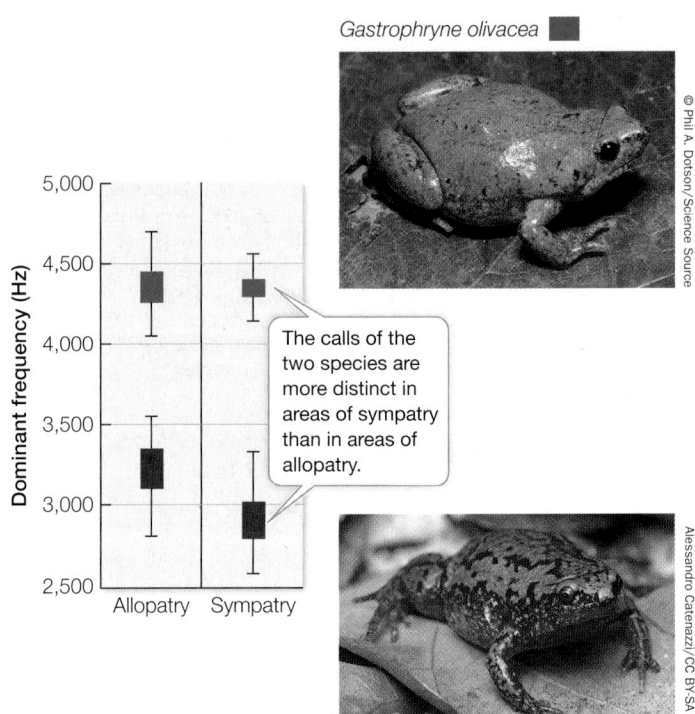

Gastrophryne olivacea ■

© Phil A. Dotson/Science Source

Dominant frequency (Hz)

5,000

4,500

4,000

3,500

3,000

2,500

Allopatry   Sympatry

The calls of the two species are more distinct in areas of sympatry than in areas of allopatry.

Alessandro Catenazzi/CC BY-SA 2.5

Gastrophryne carolinensis ■

Figure 22.12 Behavioral Isolation in Mating Calls The males of most frog species produce species-specific calls. The calls of the two closely related frog species shown here differ in their dominant frequency (a high-frequency sound wave results in a high-pitched sound; a low frequency results in a low-pitched sound). Female frogs are attracted to the calls of males of their own species. Bars indicate 95% confidence limits for the mean frequencies of the calls. (After J. J. Loftus-Hills and M. J. Littlejohn. 1992. *Evolution* 46: 896–906.)

 Media Clip 22.1 Narrowmouth Toads Calling for Mates
Life12e.com/mc22.1

diverge quickly (**Figure 22.12**). Female frogs respond to mating calls from males of their own species but ignore the calls of other species, even closely related ones. The evolution of female preferences for certain male coloration patterns among the cichlids of Lake Malawi, described in the opening story of this chapter, is another example of behavioral isolation.

Sometimes the mate choice of one species is mediated by the behavior of individuals of other species. For example, whether or not two plant species hybridize may depend on the food preferences of their pollinators. The floral traits of plants, including their color and shape, can enhance reproductive isolation either by influencing which pollinators are attracted to the flowers or by altering where pollen is deposited on the bodies of pollinators. A plant whose flowers are pendant will be pollinated by an animal with different physical characteristics than will a plant in which the flowers grow upright (**Figure 22.13A,B**). Because each pollinator prefers (and is adapted to) a different type of flower, pollinators will rarely transfer pollen from one plant species to the other. Such isolation by pollinator behavior is seen in the mountains of California in two sympatric species of columbines (*Aquilegia*) that have diverged in flower color, structure, and orientation.

(A)

(B)

(C) *Aquilegia formosa*

(D) *Aquilegia pubescens*

Figure 22.13 Reproductive Isolating Mechanisms May Be Mediated by Species Interactions **(A)** This hummingbird's morphology and behavior are adapted for feeding on nectar from pendant flowers. **(B)** The nectar-extracting proboscis of this hawk moth is adapted to flowers that grow upright. **(C)** *Aquilegia formosa* flowers are normally pendant and are pollinated by hummingbirds. **(D)** Flowers of *A. pubescens* are normally upright and are pollinated by hawk moths. In addition, their long floral spurs appear to restrict access by some other potential pollinators.

A. formosa (**Figure 22.13C**) has pendant flowers with short spurs (spikelike, nectar-containing structures) and is pollinated by hummingbirds. *A. pubescens* (**Figure 22.13D**) has upright, lighter-colored flowers with long spurs and is pollinated by hawk moths. The difference in pollinators means that these two species are effectively reproductively isolated even though they populate the same geographic range.

> **Connect the Concepts** Some plants and their pollinators become so tightly adapted to each other that they develop mutually dependent relationships, as described in Key Concept 27.3.

HABITAT ISOLATION When two closely related species evolve preferences for living or mating in different habitats, they may never come into contact during their respective mating periods. The *Rhagoletis* flies discussed in Key Concept 22.3 experienced such habitat isolation, as did the cichlid fishes that first adapted to rocky or sandy habitats upon entering Lake Malawi, as described in the opening of this chapter.

GAMETIC ISOLATION The sperm of one species may not attach to the eggs of another species because the eggs do not release the appropriate attractive chemicals, or the sperm may be unable to penetrate the egg because the two gametes are chemically incompatible. Thus even though the gametes of two species may come into contact, the gametes never fuse into a zygote.

Gametic isolation is extremely important for many aquatic species that spawn (release their gametes directly into the environment). For example, gametic isolation has been extensively studied in spawning sea urchins. A protein known as bindin is found in sea urchin sperm and functions in attaching ("binding") the sperm to eggs. All sea urchin species studied produce this egg-recognition protein, but the bindin gene sequence diverges so rapidly that it becomes species-specific. Since sperm can attach only to eggs of the same species, no interspecific hybridization occurs.

Postzygotic isolating mechanisms result in selection against hybridization

Genetic differences that accumulate between two diverging lineages may reduce the survival and reproductive rates of hybrid offspring in any of three ways:

1. *Low hybrid zygote viability*. Hybrid zygotes may fail to mature normally, either dying during development or developing phenotypic abnormalities that prevent them from becoming reproductively capable adults.

2. *Low hybrid adult viability*. Hybrid offspring may have lower survivorship than non-hybrid offspring.

3. *Hybrid infertility*. Hybrids may mature into infertile adults. For example, the offspring of matings between horses and donkeys—mules—are typically sterile. Although otherwise healthy, sterile mules produce no descendants.

Natural selection does not directly favor the evolution of postzygotic isolating mechanisms. But if hybrids are less fit, individuals that breed only within their own species will leave more surviving offspring than will individuals that interbreed with another species. Therefore individuals that can avoid interbreeding with members of other species will have a selective advantage, and any trait that contributes to such avoidance will be favored.

Donald Levin of the University of Texas has studied reinforcement of prezygotic isolating mechanisms in flowers of the genus *Phlox*. Levin noticed that most individuals of *P. drummondii* in most of the range of the species in Texas have pink flowers. However, where *P. drummondii* is sympatric with its close relative, the pink-flowered *P. cuspidata*, most *P. drummondii* have red flowers. No other *Phlox* species has red flowers. The results of an experiment that Levin performed showed that reinforcement may explain why red flowers are favored where the two species are sympatric (**Investigating Life: Flower Color Reinforces a Reproductive Barrier in *Phlox***).

▶Investigating**LIFE** Flower Color Reinforces a Reproductive Barrier in *Phlox*

Experiment

Original Paper: D. A. Levin. 1985. Reproductive character displacement in *Phlox. Evolution* 39: 1275–1281.

Most *Phlox drummondii* flowers are pink, but in regions where they are sympatric with *P. cuspidata*—which is always pink—most *P. drummondii* individuals are red. Most pollinators preferentially visit flowers of one color or the other. In this experiment, Donald Levin explored whether flower color reinforces a prezygotic reproductive barrier, lessening the chances of interspecific hybridization.

HYPOTHESIS▶ Red-flowered *P. drummondii* are less likely to hybridize with *P. cuspidata* than are pink-flowered *P. drummondii*

METHOD▶

1. Introduce equal numbers of red- and pink-flowered *P. drummondii* individuals into an area with many pink-flowered *P. cuspidata*.

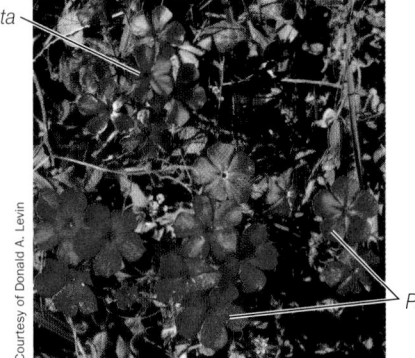

P. cuspidata

P. drummondii

2. After the flowering season ends, measure hybridization by assessing the genetic composition of the seeds produced by *P. drummondii* plants of both colors.

RESULTS▶ Of the seeds produced by pink-flowered *P. drummondii*, 38% were hybrids with *P. cuspidata*. Only 13% of the seeds produced by red-flowered individuals were genetic hybrids. Bars indicate 95% confidence intervals for the mean percent of hybrid seeds.

Phlox drummondii

CONCLUSION▶ *P. drummondii* and *P. cuspidata* are less likely to hybridize if the flowers of the two species differ in color.

Work with the Data

Donald Levin of the University of Texas proposed that *Phlox drummondii* has red flowers only in locations where it is sympatric with pink-flowered *P. cuspidata* because having red flowers decreases interspecific hybridization. To test this hypothesis, Levin introduced equal numbers of red- and pink-flowered *P. drummondii* individuals into an area with many pink-flowered *P. cuspidata*. At the end of the flowering season, he assessed the genetic composition of the seeds produced by *P. drummondii*. The results are shown in the table.

Morph (flower color)	Number of seeds (progeny)		
	P. drummondii	Hybrid	Total
Red	181 (87%)	27 (13%)	208
Pink	86 (62%)	53 (38%)	139

QUESTIONS▶

1. Check the 95% confidence intervals for the proportion of hybrid seeds in red- and pink-flowered *P. drummondii* in the graph in the Results of the experiment. There are many websites available for calculating confidence intervals; a good one is the Vassar College statistical computation site, VassarStats.

net. You can go to this site and select "Proportions" from the left-hand menu, then select "The Confidence Interval of a Proportion." What are the numerical values of the 95% confidence intervals?

2. Notice that the proportions of hybrids among the seeds of red- versus pink-flowered samples are significantly different, because the 95% confidence intervals do not overlap. To quantify the significance of this difference, use the website suggested in Question 1, but select "Significance of the Difference Between Two Independent Proportions" from the "Proportions" menu. What null hypothesis are you testing in this case? (See Appendix B if you need help.) What is the *P*-value of getting results at least as different as these two samples if your null hypothesis is true?

3. How would you extend or improve the experimental design of this study? What kinds of additional test sites or conditions would you want to examine? How might replicate or control sites make the study more convincing?

Go to **Achieve** for a companion
Data in Depth exercise.

Likely cases of reinforcement are often detected by comparing sympatric and allopatric populations of potentially hybridizing species, as in the case of *Phlox*. If reinforcement is occurring, then sympatric populations of closely related species are expected to evolve more effective prezygotic reproductive barriers than do allopatric populations of the same species. As Figure 22.11 shows, the breeding seasons of sympatric populations of different leopard frog species overlap much less than do those of allopatric populations. Similarly, the frequencies of the frog mating calls illustrated in Figure 22.12 are more divergent in sympatric populations than in allopatric populations. In both cases, there appears to have been natural selection against hybridization in areas of sympatry.

Hybrid zones may form if reproductive isolation is incomplete

Unless reproductive isolation is complete, closely related species may hybridize in areas where their ranges overlap, resulting in the formation of a **hybrid zone**. When a hybrid zone first forms, most hybrids are offspring of crosses between individuals of the two hybridizing species. However, subsequent generations include a variety of individuals with varying proportions of their genes derived from the original two species, so hybrid zones often contain recombinant individuals resulting from many generations of hybridization.

Detailed genetic studies can tell us why narrow hybrid zones may persist for long periods between the ranges of two species.

Figure 22.14 A Hybrid Zone   The narrow zone (shown in red) in which fire-bellied toads meet and hybridize with yellow-bellied toads has been stable for hundreds of years. (After J. Vörös et al. 2006. *Mol Phylogenet Evol* 38: 705–718.)

The fire-bellied toad (*Bombina bombina*) lives in eastern Europe; the closely related yellow-bellied toad (*B. variegata*) lives in western and southern Europe. The ranges of the two species overlap in a long but narrow zone stretching 4,800 kilometers from eastern Germany to the Black Sea (**Figure 22.14**). Hybrids between the two species suffer from a range of defects, many of which are lethal. Those hybrids that survive often have skeletal abnormalities, such as a misshapen mouth, ribs that are fused to vertebrae, and a reduced number of vertebrae. By following the fates of thousands of toads from the hybrid zone, investigators found that a hybrid toad, on average, is only half as fit as an individual of either species. The hybrid zone remains narrow because there is strong selection against hybrids and because adult toads do not move over long distances. The zone has persisted for hundreds of years, however, because individuals of both species continue to move short distances into it, continually replenishing the hybrid population.

KEY CONCEPT
22.4 Recap and Assess

Reproductive isolation may result from prezygotic or postzygotic isolating mechanisms. Lower fitness of hybrids can lead to the reinforcement of prezygotic isolating mechanisms.

1. As shown in Figure 22.11, the leopard frogs *Rana berlandieri* and *R. sphenocephala* usually have non-overlapping breeding seasons in areas of sympatry, but where they are allopatric, both species breed in both spring and fall. When new ponds are created where the ranges of the two species come close together, frogs from previously allopatric populations may colonize the new ponds and hybridize during their overlapping breeding seasons.

Imagine you have collected and tabulated data on hybridization between these two frog species. You have sampled various life stages of frogs and their tadpoles for 2 years after an initial spring breeding season at a newly established pond. Use the data in the table to answer the following questions.

Life stage	R. berlandieri	R. sphenocephala	F₁ hybrids
Recently hatched tadpoles (spring, year 1)	155	125	238
Late-stage tadpoles (summer, year 1)	45	55	64
Newly metamorphosed froglets (fall, year 1)	32	42	15
Adult frogs (year 2)	10	15	1

a. Create four pie charts (one for each life stage) showing the proportions of each species and of hybrids at each stage.

b. Offer possible reasons for the differences in the proportion of hybrids found at each life stage. Suggest some postzygotic isolating mechanisms that are consistent with your data.

c. Over time, what changes might you expect in the breeding seasons of the two species at this particular pond, and why? How would future pie charts differ from those you created here, if your predictions about breeding seasons are correct?

2. In each of the columbine (*Aquilegia*) species shown in Figure 22.13, the orientation of the flowers and the length of the flower spurs are associated with a particular type of pollinator (hummingbirds or hawk moths). Columbine flowers vary in other ways as well—for example, in color and probably in fragrance. What experiments could you design to determine the traits that various pollinators use to distinguish among the flowers of different columbine species?

3. Why don't most narrow hybrid zones, such as the one between *Bombina bombina* and *B. variegata* shown in Figure 22.14, get wider over time?

Some groups of organisms have many species, others only a few. Hundreds of species of *Drosophila* evolved in the small area of the Hawaiian Islands over about 20 million years. In contrast, there are only a few species of horseshoe crabs in the world, and only one species of ginkgo tree (*Ginkgo biloba*), even though these latter groups have persisted for hundreds of millions of years. Why do different groups of organisms have such different rates of speciation?

KEY CONCEPT 22.5 Speciation Rates Are Highly Variable across Life

Learning Objectives

22.5.1 List four factors that commonly affect speciation rates.

22.5.2 Describe the conditions that favor adaptive radiation.

Many factors influence the likelihood that a lineage will split to form two or more species. Therefore rates of speciation (the proportion of existing species that split to form new species over a given period) vary greatly among groups of organisms. What are some of the factors that influence the probability of a given lineage splitting into two?

Several ecological and behavioral factors influence speciation rates

Many factors can influence rates of speciation across groups, including the diet, behavioral complexity, and dispersal abilities of the respective species.

DIET SPECIALIZATION   Populations of species that have specialized diets may be more likely to diverge than those with more generalized diets. To investigate the effects of diet specialization on rates of speciation, Charles Mitter and colleagues compared species richness in some closely related groups of true bugs (hemipterans). The common ancestor of these groups was a predator that fed on other insects, but a dietary shift to herbivory (eating plants) evolved at least twice in the groups under study. Herbivorous bugs typically specialize on one or a few closely related species of plants, whereas predatory bugs tend to feed on many different species of insects. A high diversity of host-plant species can lead to a correspondingly high species diversity among herbivorous specialists. The study by Mitter and his colleagues showed that among these insects, the herbivorous groups do indeed contain many more species than do the related predatory groups (**Figure 22.15**).

POLLINATION   Speciation rates are faster in animal-pollinated than in wind-pollinated plants. Animal-pollinated groups have,

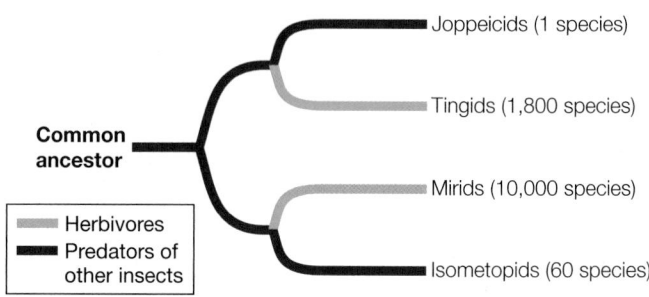

Figure 22.15 Dietary Shifts Can Promote Speciation
Herbivorous groups of hemipteran insects have speciated several times faster than closely related predatory groups. (After C. Mitter et al. 1988. *Am Nat* 132: 107–128.)

---

on average, 2.4 times as many species as related groups pollinated by wind. Among animal-pollinated plants, speciation rates are correlated with pollinator specialization. In columbines (*Aquilegia*), the rate of evolution of new species has been about three times faster in lineages that have long nectar spurs than in lineages that lack spurs. Why do nectar spurs increase the speciation rate? Apparently it is because spurs restrict the number of pollinator species that visit the flowers, thus increasing opportunities for reproductive isolation (see Figure 22.13).

SEXUAL SELECTION   It appears that the mechanisms of sexual selection (see Key Concept 19.2) result in high rates of speciation, as we saw in the case of the cichlids of Lake Malawi. Some of the most striking examples of sexual selection are found in birds with polygynous mating systems (meaning one male may attract and mate with many different females). Birdwatchers travel thousands of miles to Papua New Guinea to witness the mating displays of male birds of paradise, which have brightly colored plumage (**Figure 22.16A**) and look distinctly different from females of their species—a phenomenon called sexual dimorphism. Males assemble at display grounds called leks, and females come there to choose a mate. After mating, the females leave the display grounds, build their nests, lay their eggs, and feed their offspring with no help from the males. The males remain at the lek to court more females.

The closest relatives of the birds of paradise are the manucodes (**Figure 22.16B**). Male and female manucodes differ only slightly in size and plumage (they are sexually monomorphic). They form monogamous pair bonds, and both sexes contribute to raising the young. There are only 5 species of manucodes, compared with 33 species of birds of paradise. By itself, this one comparison would not be convincing evidence that sexually dimorphic clades have higher rates of speciation than do monomorphic clades. However, when biologists examined all the examples of birds in which one clade is sexually dimorphic and the most closely related clade is sexually monomorphic, the sexually dimorphic clades were significantly more likely to contain more species. But why would sexual dimorphism be associated with a higher rate of speciation?

Animals with complex sexually selected behaviors are likely to form new species at a high rate because they make sophisticated discriminations among potential mating partners. They distinguish members of their own species from members of other species, and

(A) *Seleucidis melanoleuca*

Figure 22.16 Sexual Selection Can Lead to Higher Speciation Rates Birds of paradise (the brightly colored male is above the female on the branch) **(A)** and manucodes **(B)** are closely related bird groups of the South Pacific. Speciation rates are much higher among the sexually dimorphic, polygynous birds of paradise (33 species) than among the sexually monomorphic, monogamous manucodes (5 species).

(B) *Manucodia comrii*

they make subtle discriminations among members of their own species on the basis of size, shape, appearance, and behavior. Such discriminations can greatly influence which individuals are most successful in mating and producing offspring, so they may lead to rapid evolution of behavioral isolating mechanisms among populations.

DISPERSAL ABILITY   Speciation rates are usually higher in groups with poor dispersal abilities than in groups with good dispersal abilities because even narrow barriers can be effective in dividing a species whose members are highly sedentary. Until recently, the Hawaiian Islands had about 1,000 species of land snails, many of which were restricted to a single valley. Because snails move only short distances, the high ridges that separate the valleys were effective barriers to their dispersal. Unfortunately, introductions of other

species and changes in habitat have resulted in the recent extinction of most of these unique Hawaiian land snails.

Rapid speciation can lead to adaptive radiation

The rapid proliferation of a large number of descendant species from a single ancestor species is called an **evolutionary radiation**. Evolutionary radiations often occur when a species colonizes a new area, such as an island archipelago that contains no other closely related species, because of the large number of open ecological niches. If such a rapid proliferation of species results in an array of species that live in a variety of environments and differ in the characteristics they use to exploit those environments, it is referred to as an **adaptive radiation**.

Several remarkable adaptive radiations have occurred in the Hawaiian Islands. In addition to its 1,000 species of land snails, the native Hawaiian biota includes 1,000 species of flowering plants, 10,000 species of insects, and more than 100 bird species. However, there were no amphibians, no terrestrial reptiles, and only one native terrestrial mammal (a bat) on the islands until humans introduced additional species. The 10,000 known native species of insects on Hawaii are believed to have evolved from about 400 immigrant species; only 7 immigrant species are believed to account for all the native Hawaiian land birds. Similarly, as we saw earlier in this chapter, an adaptive radiation in the Galápagos archipelago resulted in the many species of Darwin's finches, which differ strikingly in the size and shape of their bills and, accordingly, in the food resources they use (see Figure 22.8).

The 28 species of Hawaiian sunflowers called silverswords are an impressive example of an adaptive radiation in plants (**Figure 22.17**).

Madia sativa (tarweed)

Argyroxiphium sandwicense

Wilkesia gymnoxiphium

Dubautia menziesii

Figure 22.17 Rapid Evolution among Hawaiian Silverswords
The Hawaiian silverswords, three closely related genera of the sunflower family, are believed to have descended from a single common ancestor (a plant similar to the tarweed *Madia sativa*) that colonized Hawaii from the Pacific coast of North America. The four plants shown here are more closely related than they appear to be based on their morphology.

DNA sequences show that these species share a relatively recent common ancestor with a species of tarweed from the Pacific coast of North America. Whereas all mainland tarweeds are small, upright herbs (nonwoody plants such as *Madia sativa*; see Figure 22.17), the silverswords include shrubs, trees, and vines as well as both upright and ground-hugging herbs. Silversword species occupy nearly all the habitats of the Hawaiian Islands, from sea level to above the timberline in the mountains. Despite their extraordinary morphological diversification, all silverswords are genetically very similar.

The Hawaiian silverswords are more diverse in size and shape than the mainland tarweeds because their tarweed ancestors first arrived on islands that harbored very few plant species. In particular, there were few trees and shrubs because such large-seeded plants rarely disperse to oceanic islands. Trees and shrubs have evolved from nonwoody ancestors on many oceanic islands. On the mainland, however, tarweeds live in ecological communities that contain many tree and shrub species in lineages with long evolutionary histories. In those environments, opportunities to exploit the "tree" way of life have already been preempted.

22.5 Recap and Assess

Dietary specialization, pollinator specialization, sexual selection, and poor dispersal abilities are correlated with high rates of speciation. Open ecological niches present opportunities for adaptive radiations.

1. How can pollinator specialization in plants and sexual selection in animals increase rates of speciation?

2. Why do adaptive radiations often occur when a founder species invades an isolated geographic area?

The result of 3.8 billion of years of evolution has been many millions of species, each adapted to live in a particular environment and to use environmental resources in a particular way. In Chapter 23 we will consider the broader evolutionary history of life on Earth and examine the long-term evolutionary changes that have given rise to all of life's diversity.

 View in Achieve
Activity 22.1 **Concept Review: Speciation**

Investigating LIFE

Q and A **If speciation typically takes thousands to millions of years, how do biologists conduct experiments to study this process?**

Although speciation usually takes thousands to millions of years, and is typically studied in natural settings such as Lake Malawi or in field experiments like the one described in **Investigating Life: Flower Color Reinforces a Reproductive Barrier in Phlox**, some aspects of speciation can be studied and observed in controlled laboratory experiments. Most such experiments use organisms with short generation times, in which evolution is expected to be relatively rapid.

William Rice and George Salt conducted an experiment in which fruit flies (*Drosophila melanogaster*) were allowed to choose food sources in different habitats. The habitats—where mating also took place—were vials in different parts of an experimental cage (**Figure 22.18**). The vials differed in three environmental factors: (1) light; (2) the direction (up or down) in which the fruit flies had to move to reach food; and (3) the concentrations of two aromatic chemicals, ethanol and acetaldehyde. In just 35 generations, the two groups of flies that chose the most divergent habitats had become reproductively isolated from each other, having evolved distinct preferences for the different habitats.

The experiment by Rice and Salt (1988. *Am Nat* 131: 911–917) demonstrated an example of habitat isolation as a prezygotic isolating mechanism. Even though the different habitats were in the same cage, and individual fruit flies were capable of flying from one habitat to the other, habitat preferences were inherited by offspring from their parents, and populations from the two divergent habitats did not interbreed. Similar habitat isolation is thought to have resulted in the early split between cichlids that preferred the rocky versus the sandy shores of Lake Malawi. In controlled experiments like this one, biologists can observe many aspects of the process of speciation directly.

Figure 22.18 Evolution in the Laboratory For their experiments on the evolution of prezygotic isolating mechanisms in *Drosophila melanogaster*, Rice and Salt built an elaborate system of varying habitats contained within vials inside a large fly enclosure. Some groups of flies developed preferences for widely divergent habitats and became reproductively isolated within 35 generations.

Future directions

Biologists can now sequence entire genomes of organisms, which allows them to compare divergent genes in pairs of recently divergent species, and to identify the genes responsible for prezygotic and postzygotic isolation. These same techniques also allow researchers to detect any level of hybridization between species. Thus we are now able to determine the genetic basis of reproductive isolation, and measure the rate at which diverging species become isolated from one another. With these advances, biologists can now appreciate the details and genetic basis for the origin of species.

You should be able to relate each summary to the adjacent figures. If you go to this visual summary in **Achieve**, you can follow links to figures, animations, activities, and simulations that will help you consolidate the material.

KEY CONCEPT

22.1 Species Are Reproductively Isolated Lineages on the Tree of Life

- **Speciation** is the process by which one **species** splits into two or more daughter species, which thereafter evolve as distinct **lineages**.

- The **morphological species concept** distinguishes species on the basis of physical similarities; it often underestimates or overestimates the actual number of reproductively isolated species.

- The **biological species concept** distinguishes species on the basis of **reproductive isolation**.

- The **lineage species concept** recognizes independent evolutionary lineages as species and allows biologists to consider species over evolutionary time.

Photos by David McIntyre (courtesy of Exotic Fish and Pet World, Southampton, MA) and ©Nantawat Chotsuwan/Shutterstock, Andreas Gradin, Mikola Gyorgy, Grigorev Mikhail, Vladimir Wrangel/Shutterstock.com, © iStock.com/ Vladimir Wrange

Questions

1. What species concept(s) would paleontologists likely use to group fossil remains into species?

2. How is reproductive isolation, the core of the biological species concept, also related to morphological and lineage species concepts?

KEY CONCEPT

22.2 Speciation Is a Natural Consequence of Population Subdivision

Go to Simulation 22.1

- Genetic divergence results from the interruption of gene flow within a population.

- The **Dobzhansky-Muller model** describes how reproductive isolation between two physically isolated populations can develop through the accumulation of incompatible genes or chromosomal arrangements.

- Reproductive isolation increases with increasing genetic divergence between populations.

Figure 22.3

Genotype of ancestral population

Locus 1 Locus 2

Questions

1. Why does the Dobzhansky–Muller model involve changes at multiple gene loci?

2. What kinds of chromosomal rearrangements work particularly well with the Dobzhansky–Muller model? Why?

Figure 22.5

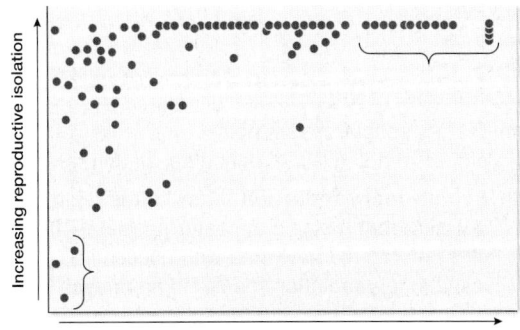

Increasing reproductive isolation

Increasing genetic divergence

KEY CONCEPT
22.3 Speciation May Occur through Geographic Isolation or in Sympatry

Go to Animations 22.1 and 22.2

- **Allopatric speciation**, which results when populations are separated by a physical barrier, is the dominant mode of speciation. This type of speciation may follow founder events, in which some members of a population cross a barrier and found a new, isolated population.

- **Sympatric speciation** results when the genomes of two groups diverge in the absence of physical isolation. It can result from disruptive selection in two or more distinct microhabitats.

- Sympatric speciation can occur within two generations via **polyploidy**, an increase in the number of chromosomes sets. Polyploidy may arise from chromosome duplications within a species (**autopolyploidy**) or from hybridization that results in combining the chromosomes of two species (**allopolyploidy**).

Questions

1. What types of geographic events are likely to give rise to many species (in different groups) simultaneously via allopatric speciation?

2. How does speciation occur so quickly through polyploidy?

Figure 22.6

Distribution of freshwater stream fishes in the Pliocene

Central highlands

Distribution of freshwater stream fishes in the Pleistocene

Maximum glacial advance

Ozarks
Ouachitas
Eastern highlands

KEY CONCEPT
22.4 Reproductive Isolation Is Reinforced When Diverging Species Come into Contact

- **Prezygotic isolating mechanisms** prevent hybridization; **postzygotic isolating mechanisms** reduce the fitness of hybrids.

- Postzygotic isolating mechanisms lead to **reinforcement** of prezygotic isolating mechanisms by natural selection.

- **Hybrid zones** may form and persist if reproductive isolation between species is incomplete.

Figure 22.11

Allopatric populations

Frequency of egg laying

Rana berlandieri

Rana blairi

Rana sphenocephala

J F M A M J J A S O N D
Month

Sympatric populations

Frequency of egg laying

Rana berlandieri

Rana blairi

Rana sphenocephala

J F M A M J J A S O N D
Month

Questions

1. What are five major types of prezygotic isolating mechanisms?

2. What are three major types of postzygotic isolating mechanisms?

KEY CONCEPT
22.5 Speciation Rates Are Highly Variable across Life

Go to Activity 22.1

- Dietary specialization, pollinator specialization, sexual selection, and dispersal ability all influence speciation rates.

- **Evolutionary radiation** refers to the rapid proliferation of descendant species from a single ancestor species. This often occurs when a species colonizes a new area with unoccupied ecological niches. If evolutionary radiation results in an array of species that live in a variety of environments and differ in the characteristics they use to exploit those environments, it is referred to as **adaptive radiation**.

Figure 22.15

Common ancestor

Herbivores
Predators of other insects

Joppeicids (1 species)

Tingids (1,800 species)

Mirids (10,000 species)

Isometopids (60 species)

Questions

1. Why are speciation rates often higher among herbivorous insects than among carnivorous insects?

2. How does dispersal ability affect speciation rates?

3. What biogeographic event often precedes an evolutionary radiation?

Go to **Achieve** for the eBook, **LearningCurve**, animations, activities, simulations, and additional resources and assignments.

The History of Life on Earth 23

Layers of rocks in the Grand Canyon reveal almost 2 billion years of Earth's history.

© Michael Matti/Alamy Stock Photo

KEY CONCEPTS

23.1 Events in Earth's History Can Be Dated

23.2 Changes in Earth's Physical Environment Have Affected the Evolution of Life

23.3 Major Events in the Evolution of Life Can Be Read in the Fossil Record

▶Investigating LIFE

When Giant Insects Ruled the Skies

The largest dragonflies alive today have wingspans that can be covered by a human hand. Three hundred million years ago (mya), however, dragonflies such as *Meganeuropsis permiana* had wingspans of more than 70 centimeters—well over 2 feet, matching or exceeding the wingspans of many modern birds of prey. These dragonflies were the largest flying predators of their time. Shown here is an artist's reconstruction of *M. permiana* is shown at the same scale as a modern dragonfly.

No flying insects alive today are anywhere near this size. But during the Carboniferous and Permian geological periods, 350 to 250 mya, many groups of flying insects contained gigantic species. *Meganeuropsis* probably ate huge mayflies and other giant flying insects that shared its home in the Permian swamps. These enormous insects were themselves eaten by giant amphibians. None of these insects or amphibians would be able to survive on Earth today. The oxygen concentrations in Earth's atmosphere were about 50% higher then than they are now, and those high oxygen concentrations are thought to have been necessary to support giant insects and their huge amphibian predators.

Paleontologists have uncovered fossils of *Meganeuropsis permiana* in the rocks of Kansas. How do we know the age of these fossils, and how can we know how much oxygen that long-vanished

atmosphere contained? The layering of rocks allows us to tell their ages relative to one another, but it does not by itself indicate a given layer's absolute age.

© iStock.com/Natasha Litova

© Mark Turner/Alamy Stock Photo

Scientists have developed sophisticated techniques that use the decay rates of radioisotopes, the ratios of certain molecules in rocks, and changes in Earth's magnetic field to infer conditions and events in the remote past and to date them accurately. It is those methods that allow us to age the fossils of *Meganeuropsis* and to calculate the concentration of oxygen in Earth's atmosphere at the time.

Earth is about 4.5 billion years old, and life has existed on it for about 3.8 billion of those years. That means human civilizations have occupied Earth for less than 0.0003% of the history of life. Discovering what happened before humans were around is an ongoing and exciting area of science.

 How can modern experiments test hypotheses about the evolutionary impact of ancient environmental changes?
(Find the answer on page 532.)

23.1 Events in Earth's History Can Be Dated

Learning Objectives

23.1.1 Construct a geological map indicating the ages of exposed rocks and use the map to search for fossils of a given age.

23.1.2 Select appropriate methods for dating fossils and rocks from different geological time periods.

23.1.3 Place important events in biological history onto a time line of Earth's history.

Some evolutionary changes happen rapidly enough to be studied directly and manipulated experimentally. Plant and animal breeding by agriculturalists and the evolution of surface proteins in influenza viruses are examples of rapid, short-term evolution that we have discussed in previous chapters. Such changes can take place in months, years, decades, or centuries. Other evolutionary changes, such as the appearance of new species and major evolutionary lineages, usually take place over much longer time scales.

To understand long-term patterns of evolutionary change, we must not only think in time scales spanning many millions of years, but also consider events and conditions very different from those we observe today. Earth of the distant past was so unlike our present Earth that it would seem like a foreign planet inhabited by strange organisms. The continents were not where they are now, and climates were sometimes dramatically different from those of today. We know this because much of Earth's history is recorded in its rocks.

Geological strata tell us the relative ages of rocks

We cannot tell the ages of rocks just by looking at them, but we can visually determine the ages of rocks *relative to one another*. The first person to formally recognize this fact was the seventeenth-century Danish physician Nicolaus Steno. Steno realized that in undisturbed **sedimentary rocks** (rocks formed by the accumulation of sediments), the oldest layers of rock, or **strata** (singular *stratum*), lie at the bottom, and successively higher strata are progressively younger.

Geologists subsequently combined Steno's insight with their observations of fossils contained in sedimentary rocks. They developed the following principles of **stratigraphy** (the study of geological strata):

- Fossils of similar organisms are found in widely separated places on Earth.

- Certain fossils are always found in younger strata, and certain other fossils are always found in older strata.

- Fossilized organisms found in younger strata are more similar to modern organisms than are those found in older strata.

These patterns revealed much about the relative ages of sedimentary rocks and the fossils they contain, as well as patterns in the evolution of life. But geologists still could not tell the actual, as opposed to the relative, ages of rocks. A method for absolute dating of rocks—that is, determining their actual age rather than just their age relative to one another—did not become available

until after radioactivity was discovered at the beginning of the twentieth century.

Radioisotopes provide a way to date fossils and rocks

Radioactive isotopes of atoms—radioisotopes—decay in a predictable pattern over long periods. Over a specific time interval, known as a **half-life**, half of the atoms in a radioisotope decay to become a different isotope (**Figure 23.1A**). The use of this knowledge to date fossils and rocks is known as **radiometric dating**.

> **Connect the Concepts** As noted in Key Concept 2.1, stable isotopes of the same element have the same number of protons but different numbers of neutrons. Radioisotopes, however, are not stable; they spontaneously give off energy in the form of alpha, beta, or gamma radiation, which transforms the original atom.

To use a radioisotope to date a past event, we must know or estimate the concentration of that isotope at the time of that event, and we must know the radioisotope's half-life. In the case of carbon-14 (^{14}C), a radioisotope of carbon, the production of new ^{14}C in the upper atmosphere—by the reaction of neutrons with nitrogen-14 (^{14}N, a stable isotope of nitrogen)—just balances the natural radioactive decay of ^{14}C into ^{14}N. Therefore the ratio of ^{14}C to the more common stable isotope of carbon, carbon-12 (^{12}C), is relatively constant in living organisms and in their environment. As

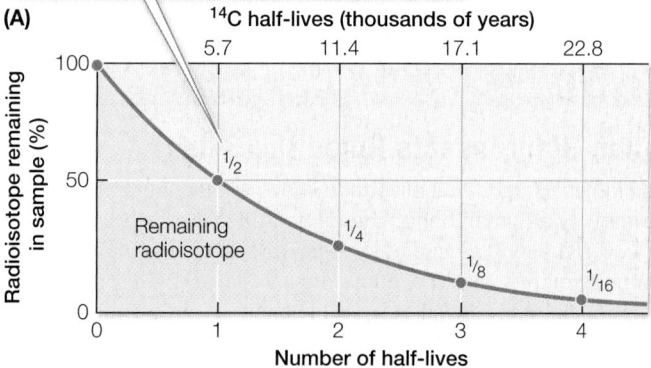

Radioisotope	Decay product	Half-life (years)	Useful dating range (years)
Carbon-14 (^{14}C)	Nitrogen-14 (^{14}N)	5,700	100–60,000
Uranium-234 (^{234}U)	Thorium-230 (^{230}Th)	80,000	10,000–500,000
Uranium-235 (^{235}U)	Lead-207 (^{207}Pb)	704 million	200,000–4.5 billion
Potassium-40 (^{40}K)	Argon-40 (^{40}Ar)	1.3 billion	10 million–4.5 billion

Figure 23.1 Radioactive Isotopes Allow Us to Date Ancient Rocks The decay of radioactive isotopes into stable isotopes happens at a steady rate. A half-life is the time it takes for half of the remaining atoms to decay in this way. **(A)** The graph demonstrates the principle of half-life using carbon-14 (^{14}C) as an example. The half-life of ^{14}C is 5,700 years. **(B)** Different radioisotopes have different characteristic half-lives that allow us to estimate the ages of many rocks.

soon as an organism dies, however, it ceases to exchange carbon compounds with its environment. Its decaying ^{14}C is no longer replenished, and the ratio of ^{14}C to ^{12}C in its remains decreases over time. Paleontologists can use the ratio of ^{14}C to ^{12}C in fossil material to date fossils that are 60,000 years old or younger (and thus the sedimentary rocks that contain those fossils). If fossils are older than that, so little ^{14}C remains that the limits of detection using this particular isotope are reached.

Radiometric dating methods have been expanded and refined

Sedimentary rocks are formed from materials that existed for varying lengths of time before being weathered, fragmented, and transported, sometimes over long distances, to the site of their deposition. Therefore the radioisotopes in sedimentary rock do not contain reliable information about the date of its formation. Radiometric dating of rocks older than 60,000 years requires estimating radioisotope concentrations in **igneous rocks**, which are formed when molten material cools. To date sedimentary strata, geologists search for places where volcanic ash or lava flows have intruded into the sedimentary rock.

A preliminary estimate of the age of an igneous rock determines which radioisotopes can be used to date it (**Figure 23.1B**). The decay of potassium-40 (which has a half-life of 1.3 billion years) to argon-40, for example, has been used to date many of the ancient events in the evolution of life. Fossils in the adjacent sedimentary rock that are similar to those in other rocks of known ages provide additional clues to the rock's age.

Scientists have used several methods to construct a geological time scale

Radiometric dating of rocks, combined with fossil analysis, is the most powerful method of determining geological age. But in places where sedimentary rocks do not contain suitable igneous intrusions and few fossils are present, paleontologists turn to other dating methods.

One method, known as paleomagnetic dating, relates the ages of rocks to patterns in Earth's magnetism, which change over time. Earth's magnetic poles move and occasionally reverse themselves. Both sedimentary and igneous rocks preserve a record of Earth's magnetic field at the time they were formed, and that record can be used to determine the ages of those rocks. Other dating methods use information about continental drift, information about sea level changes, and molecular clocks.

Connect the Concepts As Key Concept 20.3 explains, a molecular clock measures the average rate at which a given gene or protein product accumulates changes, and this rate of change can be used to deduce the geological time when two biological lineages diverged from one another.

Using all of these methods, geologists developed the geological time scale (**Table 23.1**). They divided the broad history of life into four eons. The Hadean refers to the time on Earth before life evolved. The early history of life occurred in the Archean, which ended about the time that photosynthetic organisms first appeared on Earth. Prokaryotic life diversified rapidly in the Proterozoic,

and the first eukaryotes in the fossil record date from this time. These three eons are sometimes referred to collectively as Precambrian time, or simply the **Precambrian**. The Precambrian lasted for approximately 4 billion years and thus accounts for the vast majority of geological time. It was in the Phanerozoic, however—a mere 542-million-year time span—that multicellular eukaryotes rapidly diversified. To emphasize the events of the Phanerozoic, Table 23.1 shows the subdivision of this eon into eras and periods. The boundaries between these divisions of time are based largely on the striking differences geologists observe in the assemblages of fossil organisms contained in successive strata. This geological record of life reveals a remarkable story of a world in which the continents and biological communities are constantly changing.

KEY CONCEPT
23.1 Recap and Assess

The layering of sedimentary rock strata enables geologists to determine the relative ages of fossils. Assigning actual ages to these strata requires analysis of radioactive decay, paleomagnetic dating, and fossil comparisons across strata. Geologists divide the history of life into eons, eras, and periods based on assemblages of fossil organisms found in successive layers of rocks.

Imagine you have been assigned the job of producing a geological map of rocks that were formed between 600 and 400 mya. You collect a sample from each of ten sites (1–10 on the map), determine the ratio of lead-206 (^{206}Pb) to uranium-238 (^{238}U) for each sample, and use these ratios to estimate the ages of the rock samples. Your results are shown in the table.

Site	^{206}Pb/^{238}U ratio	Estimated age (mya)
1	0.076	474
2	0.077	479
3	0.069	431
4	0.081	505
5	0.076	474
6	0.070	435
7	0.089	550
8	0.080	500
9	0.079	495
10	0.077	479

1. Use this table and Table 23.1 to assign each sample to a geological period.

(Key Concept 23.1 Recap and Assess continues on page 517)

TABLE 23.1 | Earth's Geological History

Eon	Era	Period	Onset[a]	Major physical changes on Earth	Major events in the history of life
Phanerozoic (~0.5 billion years long)	Cenozoic	Quaternary (Q)	2.6 mya	Cold/dry climate; repeated glaciations	Humans evolve; many large mammals become extinct
		Neogene (N)[b]	23.0 mya	Continents near current positions; North and South America become connected	Considerable movement of plants and animals between North and South America through the Isthmus of Panama
		Paleogene (Pg)[b]	65.5 mya	Climate warms, then cools in response to changing CO_2 levels in Earth's atmosphere	Diversification of major vertebrate groups, flowering plants, and insects following the mass extinction at the end of the Cretaceous
	Mesozoic	Cretaceous (K)	145.5 mya	Laurasian continents attached to one another; Gondwana begins to drift apart; meteorite strikes near current Yucatán Peninsula at end of period	Dinosaurs continue to diversify; mass extinction at end of period (~76% of species lost)
		Jurassic (J)	201.6 mya	Two large continents form: Laurasia (north) and Gondwana (south); warm climate	Diverse dinosaurs; radiation of ray-finned fishes; first fossils of flowering plants
		Triassic (Tr)	251.0 mya	Pangaea begins to drift apart; hot/humid climate	Early dinosaurs; first mammals; marine invertebrates diversify; mass extinction at end of period (~65% of species lost)
	Paleozoic	Permian (P)	299 mya	Extensive lowland swamps; O_2 levels 50% higher than present; by end of period continents aggregate to form Pangaea, and O_2 levels drop rapidly	Reptiles diversify; giant amphibians and flying insects present; mass extinction at end of period (~96% of species lost)
		Carboniferous (C)	359 mya	Climate cools; marked latitudinal climate gradients	Extensive fern/horsetail/giant club moss forests; first reptiles; insects diversify
		Devonian (D)	416 mya	Continents collide at end of period; giant meteorite probably strikes Earth	Jawed fishes diversify; first insects and amphibians; mass extinction at end of period (~75% of marine species lost)
		Silurian (S)	444 mya	Sea levels rise; two large land masses emerge; hot/humid climate	Jawless fishes diversify; first ray-finned fishes; plants and animals colonize land
		Ordovician (O)	488 mya	Massive glaciation; sea level drops 50 meters	Mass extinction at end of period (~75% of species lost)
		Cambrian (Є)	542 mya	Atmospheric O_2 levels approach current levels	Rapid diversification of multicellular animals; diverse photosynthetic protists
Proterozoic	Collectively called the Precambrian (~4 billion years long)		2.5 bya	Atmospheric O_2 levels increase from negligible to about 18%; "snowball Earth" from about 750 to 580 mya	Origin of photosynthesis, multicellular organisms, and eukaryotes
Archean			3.8 bya	Earth accumulates more atmosphere (still almost no O_2); meteorite impacts greatly reduced	Origin of life; prokaryotes flourish
Hadean			4.6–4.5 bya	Formation of Earth; cooling of Earth's surface; atmosphere contains almost no free O_2; oceans form; Earth under almost continual bombardment from meteorites	Life not yet present

[a]mya, million years ago; bya, billion years ago.

[b]The Neogene and Paleogene are often referred to as the Tertiary when discussed together.

Media Clip 23.1 The Age of Earth
Life12e.com/mc23.1

(Key Concept 23.1 Recap and Assess continued)

2. Use the estimated ages and geological periods of the ten samples to mark rough boundaries of the geological periods on the site map.

3. If you wanted to refine the boundary between the Ordovician and Silurian on your map, which of three new sampling sites—*x*, *y*, or *z*—would you add to your analysis next?

4. If you were interested in finding fossils of terrestrial plants or animals, where on this map would you concentrate your searches?

As geologists began to develop accurate ways to measure the age of Earth, they began to understand that Earth is far older than anyone had previously understood. During its 4.5-billion-year history, Earth has undergone massive physical changes. These changes have influenced the evolution of life, and life, in turn, has influenced Earth's physical environment.

KEY CONCEPT 23.2
Changes in Earth's Physical Environment Have Affected the Evolution of Life

Learning Objectives

23.2.1 Characterize the relative impact of weather events and climate changes on Earth's physical conditions.

23.2.2 Explain how the production of atmospheric oxygen has affected Earth and its living organisms.

23.2.3 Analyze the connections between a specific geological event or environmental change (e.g., fluctuations in ocean currents or sea levels, volcanic eruptions, meteorite strikes) and an evolutionary trend among living organisms.

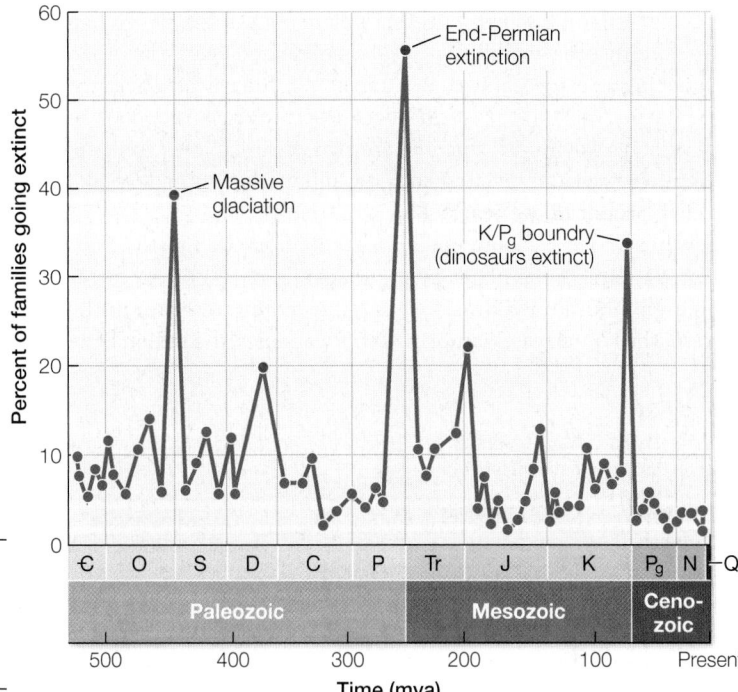

Figure 23.2 Periodic Mass Extinctions Mark Many Geologic Boundaries   Five sharp rises (marked by red dots) above the background extinction rate have occurred throughout the Phanerozoic. The most sweeping of these events, the end-Permian extinction, was associated with dramatic drops in sea level (see Figure 23.4), global temperature, and atmospheric oxygen level (see Figure 23.8). (Data from D. M. Raup and J. J. Sepkoski, Jr. 1982. *Science* 215: 1501–1503.)

As we saw in Key Concept 23.1, the Phanerozoic is notable for the rapid diversification of multicellular eukaryotes. The diversity of multicellular organisms has not, however, simply increased steadily through time. Throughout the history of life, new species have arisen while other species have become extinct. In the absence of major, rapid environmental changes, the average rate of extinction is known as the background extinction rate. But there have been times during which extinction rates have increased dramatically over the background levels (**Figure 23.2**). These **mass extinction events**, during which a large proportion of the species living at the time disappeared, are the cause of some of the striking differences in fossil assemblages that geologists use to divide the Phanerozoic into eras and periods. After each mass extinction, the diversity of life rebounded, although recovery took millions of years. Here we consider some of the physical changes on Earth that have resulted in dramatic changes in life's diversity.

Earth's continents have not always been where they are today

The globes and maps that adorn our walls, shelves, and books give an impression of a static Earth. It would be easy for us to assume

that the continents have always been where they are. But we would be wrong. The idea that Earth's land masses have changed their positions over the millennia, and that they continue to do so, was first put forth in 1912 by the German meteorologist and geophysicist Alfred Wegener. His idea, known as **continental drift**, was initially met with skepticism and resistance. By the 1960s, however, physical evidence and increased understanding of **plate tectonics**—the geophysics of the movement of major land masses—had convinced virtually all geologists of the reality of Wegener's vision. Plate tectonics provided the geological mechanism that explained Wegener's hypothesis of continental drift.

Earth's crust consists of several solid plates, which collectively make up the solid **lithosphere** ("stone sphere"). Thick continental and thinner oceanic lithospheric plates overlie a more malleable layer of Earth's mantle, known as the **asthenosphere** ("weak sphere"). Heat produced by radioactive decay deep in Earth's core sets up large-scale convection currents in the mantle. New crust is formed as mantle material rises between diverging plates, pushing them apart.

Where oceanic plates and continental plates converge, the thinner oceanic plate is forced underneath the thicker continental plate, a process known as **subduction**. Subduction results in volcanism and mountain building on the continental boundary (**Figure 23.3A**). For example, in the Pacific Northwest of North America, a series of volcanoes formed the Cascade mountain range as the Juan de Fuca oceanic plate has been subducted beneath a portion of the continental North American Plate (**Figure 23.3B**). When two oceanic plates collide, one is also subducted below the other, producing a deep oceanic trench and associated volcanic activity. The deepest part of the world's oceans—the Mariana Trench in the western Pacific—formed where two oceanic plates collided. Volcanic activity associated with the subduction at the Mariana Trench produced the nearby Mariana Islands.

When two thick continental plates collide, neither plate is subducted. Instead, the plates push up against one another, forming high mountain chains. The highest mountain chain in the world, the Himalayas, was formed this way when the Indian Plate collided with the Eurasian Plate. When continental plates diverge, new crust forms in the intervening spaces, resulting in deep clefts called rift valleys in which large freshwater lakes typically form. The Great Rift Valley lakes of eastern Africa, including Lake Malawi (discussed at the opening of Chapter 22), were formed in this way. Two plates can also slide past one another, forming a transform fault boundary (such as the San Andreas Fault that produces violent seismic activity in parts of California).

Many physical conditions on Earth have oscillated in response to plate tectonic processes. We now know that the movement of the plates has sometimes brought continents together and at other times has pushed them apart, as seen in the maps across the top of Figure 23.14. The positions and sizes of the continents influence oceanic circulation patterns, global climates, and sea levels. Sea levels are influenced directly by plate tectonic processes (which can influence the depth of ocean basins) and indirectly by oceanic circulation patterns, which affect patterns of glaciation. As climates cool, glaciers form and tie up water over land masses; as climates warm, glaciers melt and release water.

▶ View in **Achieve**
Animation 23.1
Movement of the Continents

Earth's climate has shifted between hot and cold conditions

Through much of Earth's history, the climate was considerably warmer than it is today, and temperatures decreased more gradually toward the poles. At other times, Earth was colder than it is today. Rapid drops in sea levels throughout the history of Earth have resulted mainly from increased global glaciation (**Figure 23.4**). Many of these drops in sea level were accompanied by mass extinctions—particularly of marine organisms, which could not survive the disappearance of the shallow seas that covered vast areas of the continental shelves.

Earth's cold periods were separated by long periods of milder climates. Because we are living in one of the colder periods, it is difficult for us to imagine the mild climates that were found at high latitudes in the past. The Quaternary, which began 2.6 mya and extends to the present, has been marked by a series of glacial advances, interspersed with warmer interglacial intervals during which the glaciers retreated.

"Weather" refers to the daily events at a given location, such as individual storms and the high and low temperatures on a given day. "Climate" refers to long-term average expectations over the various seasons at a given location. Weather often changes rapidly, whereas climates typically

(A) Cooling mantle material forms lithospheric crust.

At spreading zones, convection currents bring mantle material to the surface, where it forms new lithospheric crust as it cools.

Oceanic plate

Asthenosphere

Mantle

Where an oceanic plate meets a continental plate, the thinner oceanic plate is subducted under the thicker continental plate, resulting in volcanic activity and mountain building.

Continental plate

(B)

puuikibeach/CC BY 2.0

Figure 23.3 Plate Tectonics and Continental Drift (A) The heat of Earth's core generates convection currents in the viscous mantle material underlying the oceanic and continental plates. Those currents push the continental plates, along with the land masses they carry, together or apart. Where plates collide, one may slide under the other, creating mountain ranges and often volcanoes. (B) The Cascade Range of the Pacific Northwest of North America is an example of a mountain chain produced by subduction of an oceanic plate under a continental plate.

Q: Why are both shores of the Pacific Ocean ringed with volcanic mountain ranges?

▶ **Media Clip 23.2 Lava Flows and Magma Explosions**
Life12e.com/mc23.2

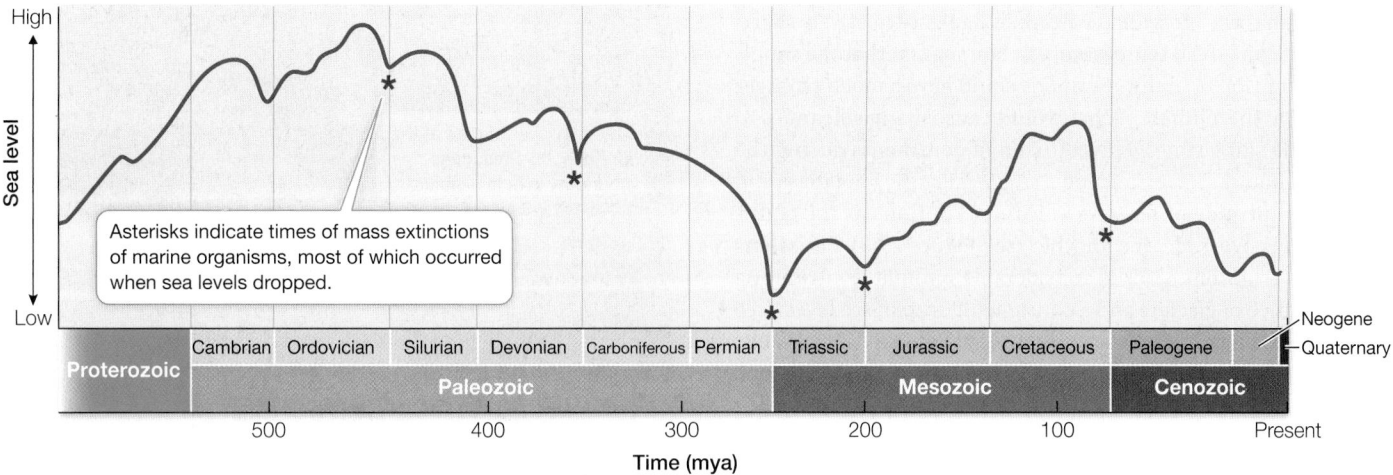

Figure 23.4 Sea Levels Have Changed Repeatedly   Rapid drops in sea level are associated with periods of globally cooler temperatures and increased glaciation. Most mass extinctions of marine organisms have coincided with low sea levels. (After A. Hallum. 1984. *Annu Rev Earth Planet Sci* 12: 205–243.)

Q: Why do cooler global temperatures result in lower sea levels?

change slowly. However, major climate shifts have taken place over periods as short as 5,000 to 10,000 years, primarily as a result of changes in Earth's orbit around the Sun. A few climate shifts have been even more rapid. For example, during one Quaternary interglacial period, the ice-locked Antarctic Ocean became nearly ice-free in less than 100 years. Some climate changes have been so rapid that the extinctions caused by them appear to be nearly instantaneous in the fossil record. Such rapid changes are usually caused by sudden shifts in ocean currents.

We are currently living in a time of rapid climate change caused largely by a buildup of atmospheric CO_2, primarily from the burning of fossil fuels by human populations. We are reversing the energy transformations accrued in the burial and decomposition of organic material that occurred (especially) in the Carboniferous, Permian, and Triassic, which gave rise to the fossil fuels we are using today. But we are burning these fuels over a few hundred years, rather than the many millions of years over which those deposits accumulated. The current rate of increase of atmospheric CO_2 is unprecedented in Earth's history. A doubling of the atmospheric CO_2 concentration—which may happen during the current century—is expected to increase the average temperature of Earth, change rainfall patterns, melt glaciers and ice caps, and raise sea levels.

Connect the Concepts Today's rapid climate changes are having an enormous effect on populations of many living organisms, as discussed in Key Concept 57.2.

Volcanoes have occasionally changed the history of life

Most volcanic eruptions produce only local or short-lived effects, but a few large volcanic eruptions have had major consequences for life. When Krakatau (a volcanic island in the Sunda Strait off Indonesia) erupted in 1883, it ejected more than 25 cubic kilometers of ash and rock as well as large quantities of sulfur dioxide gas (SO_2). The SO_2 was ejected into the stratosphere and carried by high-altitude winds around the planet. Its presence led to high concentrations of sulfurous acid (H_2SO_3) in high-altitude clouds, creating a "parasol effect" that resulted in less sunlight reaching Earth's surface. Global temperatures dropped by 1.2 degrees Celsius in the year following the eruption, and global weather patterns showed strong effects for another 5 years. More recently, the eruption of Mount Pinatubo in the Philippines in 1991 (**Figure 23.5**) temporarily reduced global temperatures by about 0.5 degrees Celsius.

Figure 23.5 Volcanic Eruptions Can Cool Global Temperatures When Mount Pinatubo erupted in 1991, it increased the concentrations of sulfurous acid in high-altitude clouds, which temporarily lowered global temperatures by about 0.5 degrees Celsius.

Although these individual volcanoes had only relatively short-term effects on global temperatures, they suggest that the simultaneous eruption of many volcanoes could have a much stronger effect on Earth's climate. What would cause many volcanoes to erupt at the same time? The collision of continents during the Permian, about 275 mya, formed a single, gigantic land mass and caused a multitude of massive volcanic eruptions as the continental plates overrode one another (see Figure 23.3). Emissions from these eruptions blocked considerable sunlight, contributing to the advance of glaciers and a consequent drop in sea levels (see Figure 23.4). Thus volcanic eruptions were probably responsible, at least in part, for the greatest mass extinction in Earth's history.

Extraterrestrial events have triggered changes on Earth

Asteroids are large rocky bodies in orbit around the Sun. If an asteroid, or even a rock too small to be called an asteroid, collides with Earth and survives its passage through our atmosphere to hit the surface, then it is called a meteorite. At least 30 meteorites of sizes between tennis and soccer balls strike Earth each year. Collisions of larger meteorites or comets are rare, but such collisions have probably been responsible for several mass extinctions. Several types of evidence tell us about these collisions. Their craters, and the dramatically disfigured rocks that result from their impact, are found in many places. Geologists have discovered compounds in these rocks that contain helium and argon with isotope ratios characteristic of meteorites, which are very different from the ratios found elsewhere on Earth.

A meteorite impact from the Chicxulub asteroid, which was 10–15 kilometers in diameter, caused or contributed to a mass extinction at the end of the Cretaceous (about 65.5 mya). The first clue that a meteorite was responsible came from the abnormally high concentrations of the element iridium found in a thin layer separating rocks deposited during the Cretaceous from rocks deposited during the Paleogene (**Figure 23.6**). Iridium is abundant in some meteorites, but it is exceedingly rare on Earth's surface. When scientists then discovered a circular crater 180 kilometers in diameter buried beneath the northern coast of the Yucatán Peninsula of Mexico, they constructed the following scenario. When it collided with Earth, the meteorite released energy equivalent to that of 100 million megatons of high explosives, creating great tsunamis. A massive plume of debris rose into the atmosphere, spread around Earth, and descended. The descending debris heated the atmosphere to several hundred degrees and ignited massive fires. It also blocked the Sun, preventing plants from photosynthesizing. The settling debris formed the iridium-rich layer. About a billion tons of soot with a composition matching that of smoke from forest fires was also deposited. These events had devastating effects on biodiversity. Many fossil species (including non-avian dinosaurs) that are found in Cretaceous rocks are not found in the overlying Paleogene rocks.

Oxygen concentrations in Earth's atmosphere have changed over time

As the continents have moved over Earth's surface, the world has experienced other physical changes, including large increases and decreases in atmospheric oxygen concentrations. The atmosphere

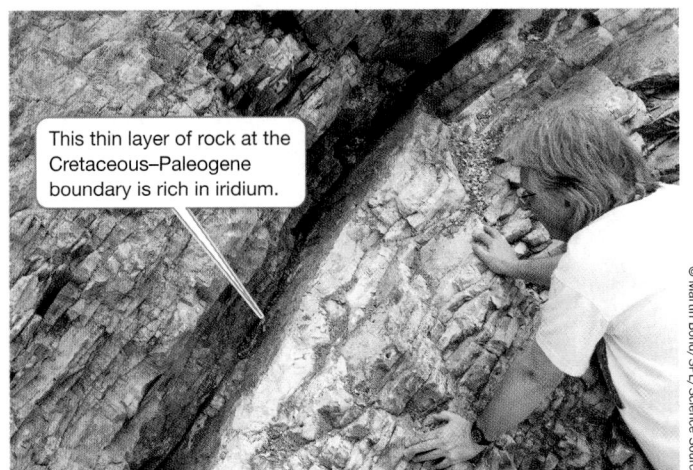

This thin layer of rock at the Cretaceous–Paleogene boundary is rich in iridium.

© Martin Bond/SPL/Science Source

Figure 23.6 Evidence of a Meteorite Impact The white layers of rock are Cretaceous in age, whereas the layers at the upper left were deposited in the Paleogene. Between the two is a thin, dark layer of clay that contains large amounts of iridium, a metal common in some meteorites but rare on Earth. Its high concentration in this sediment layer, deposited about 65.5 million years ago, suggests the impact of a large meteorite at that time.

of early Earth probably contained little or no free oxygen gas (O_2). The increase in atmospheric O_2 came in two big steps more than a billion years apart.

Oxygenation of Earth's atmosphere began about 2.5 billion years ago (bya), when the ancestors of modern cyanobacteria evolved the ability to use water as the source of hydrogen ions for photosynthesis. By chemically splitting H_2O, these bacteria generated O_2 as a waste product. They also made electrons available for reducing

David McIntyre

5 cm

Figure 23.7 Banded Iron Formations Indicate Early Photosynthesis The alternating red and dark layers in this 2.25-billion-year-old sedimentary rock formation from Lake Superior resulted from a reaction between dissolved iron and the atmospheric oxygen produced by Earth's first photosynthetic organisms. The chemical reaction produced nearly pure iron oxide, or hematite, which forms the gray, metallic layers in this sample. The red bands are jasper tinged with much smaller amounts of iron oxide.

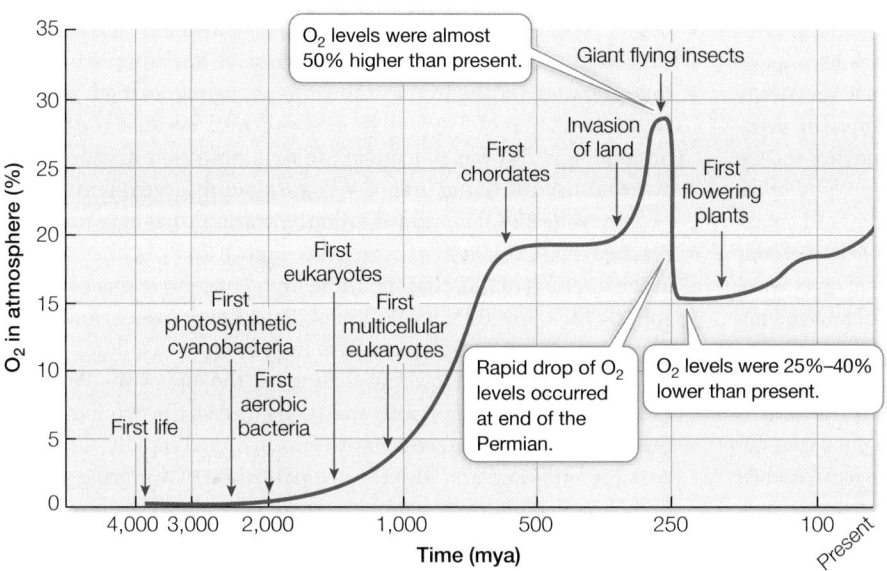

Figure 23.8 Atmospheric Oxygen Concentrations Have Changed over Time   Changes in atmospheric oxygen concentrations have strongly influenced, and have been influenced by, the evolution of life. (Note that the horizontal axis of the graph is on a logarithmic scale.) (Data from R. A. Berner. 2006. *Geochimica et Cosmochimica Acta* 70: 5653–5664; R. Frei et al. 2009. *Nature* 461: 250–253.)

Q: Why did oxygen levels decrease at the end of the Permian?

CO_2 to form the carbohydrate end-products of photosynthesis (see Key Concept 10.3). The O_2 they produced dissolved in water and reacted with dissolved iron. The reaction product then precipitated as iron oxide, which accumulated in alternating layers of red and dark rock known as banded iron formations (**Figure 23.7**). These formations provide evidence for the earliest photosynthetic organisms.

As photosynthetic organisms continued to release O_2, oxygen gas began to accumulate in the atmosphere.

The second step occurred about a billion years later, when some of these photosynthetic bacteria became symbiotic within eukaryotic cells, leading to the evolution of chloroplasts in photosynthetic plants and other eukaryotes. This change resulted in continued accumulation of O_2 in Earth's atmosphere (**Figure 23.8**).

One group of O_2-generating bacteria, the cyanobacteria, were a major component of complex communities that formed rocklike structures called stromatolites, which are abundantly preserved in the fossil record. To this day, cyanobacteria still form stromatolites in a few very salty places (**Figure 23.9**). Cyanobacteria liberated enough O_2 to open the way for the evolution of oxidation reactions as the energy source for the synthesis of ATP.

As oxygen increased in the atmosphere, ultraviolet radiation from the Sun began to produce increased concentrations of ozone (O_3) in the stratosphere, 20–30 kilometers above Earth's surface. This ozone layer absorbs much of the Sun's damaging ultraviolet radiation and prevents it from reaching Earth's surface, which allowed expansion of life on land.

Thus the evolution of life irrevocably changed the physical nature of Earth. Those physical changes, in turn, influenced the evolution of life. When it first appeared in the atmosphere, O_2 was toxic to most of the anaerobic prokaryotes that inhabited Earth at the time.

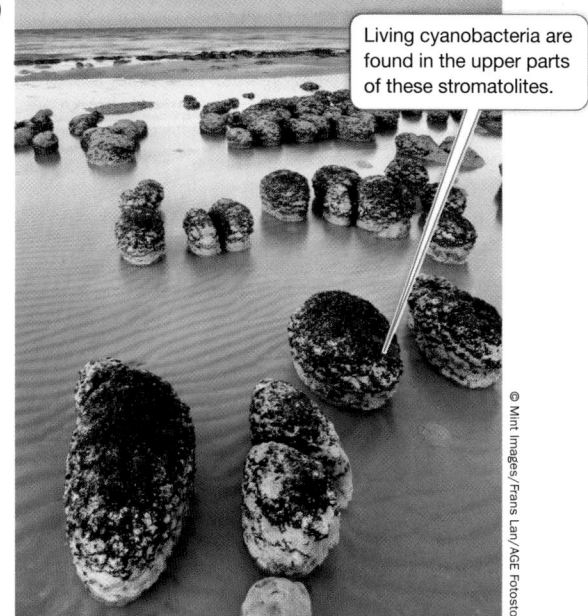

Figure 23.9 Stromatolites   **(A)** A vertical section through a fossil stromatolite. **(B)** These rocklike structures are living stromatolites that thrive in the very salty waters of Shark Bay in Western Australia.

Over millennia, however, prokaryotes that evolved the ability to tolerate and use O_2 not only survived but gained the advantage. Aerobic metabolism proceeds more rapidly, and harvests energy more efficiently, than anaerobic metabolism. Organisms with aerobic metabolism replaced anaerobes in most of Earth's environments.

An atmosphere rich in O_2 also made possible larger and more complex organisms. Small single-celled aquatic organisms can obtain enough oxygen by simple diffusion even when dissolved oxygen concentrations in the water are very low. Larger single-celled organisms, however, have lower surface area-to-volume ratios. To obtain enough oxygen by simple diffusion, larger organisms must live in an environment with a relatively high oxygen concentration. Bacteria can thrive at 1% of the current oxygen concentration, but eukaryotic cells require levels that are at least 2%–3% of the current concentration. For concentrations of dissolved oxygen in the oceans to have reached these levels, much higher atmospheric concentrations were needed.

Probably because it took many millions of years for Earth to develop an oxygenated atmosphere, only single-celled prokaryotes lived on Earth for more than 2 billion years. About 1.5 billion years ago, atmospheric O_2 concentrations became high enough for larger eukaryotic cells to flourish (see Figure 23.8). Further increases in atmospheric O_2 concentrations in the late Precambrian enabled several groups of multicellular eukaryotes to evolve and diversify.

Oxygen concentrations increased again during the Carboniferous and Permian because of the evolution of large vascular plants. These plants lived in the expansive lowland swamps that existed at the time (see Table 23.1). Massive amounts of organic material were buried in these swamps as the plants died, leading to the formation of Earth's vast coal deposits. Because the buried organic material was not subject to oxidation as it decomposed, and because the living plants were producing large quantities of O_2, atmospheric O_2 increased to concentrations that have not been reached again in Earth's history (see Figure 23.8). As mentioned at the opening of this chapter, these high concentrations of atmospheric O_2 allowed the evolution of giant flying insects and large amphibians that could not survive in today's atmosphere.

The drying of the lowland swamps at the end of the Permian reduced the burial of organic matter as well as the production of O_2, so atmospheric O_2 concentrations dropped rapidly. Over the past 200 million years, with the diversification of flowering plants, O_2 concentrations have again increased, but not to the levels that characterized the Carboniferous and Permian.

Biologists have conducted experiments that demonstrate the changing selection pressures that can accompany changes in atmospheric O_2 concentrations. When fruit flies (*Drosophila melanogaster*) are raised in hyperoxic conditions (i.e., with artificially increased atmospheric concentrations of O_2), they evolve larger body sizes in just a few generations (**Investigating Life: The Relationship between Atmospheric Oxygen Concentration and Body Size in Insects**). The present atmospheric O_2 concentrations

---

▶Investigating LIFE   The Relationship between Atmospheric Oxygen Concentration and Body Size in Insects

Experiment

Original Paper: C. J. Klok et al. 2009. Single and multigenerational responses of body mass to atmospheric oxygen concentration in *Drosophila melanogaster*: Evidence for roles of plasticity and evolution. *J Evol Biol* 22: 2496–2504.

C. Jaco Klok and his colleagues asked whether insects raised in hyperoxic conditions (i.e., in an atmosphere having a higher partial pressure of oxygen than is normal today) would evolve to be larger than their counterparts raised under today's atmospheric conditions. They raised strains of fruit flies (*Drosophila melanogaster*) under both conditions to test the effects of increased O_2 concentrations on the evolution of body size.

HYPOTHESIS▶ In hyperoxic conditions, increased partial pressure of oxygen results in evolution of increased body size in flying insects.

METHOD▶

1. Separate a population of fruit flies into multiple lineages.

2. Raise half the lineages in current atmospheric (control) conditions; raise the other lineages in hyperoxic (experimental) conditions. Continue all lineages for seven generations.

3. Raise the F_8 individuals of all lineages under identical (current) atmospheric conditions.

4. Weigh 50 flies from each of the replicate lineages and test for statistical differences in body weight.

RESULTS▶ The average body mass of F_8 individuals of both sexes raised under hyperoxic conditions was significantly ($P < 0.001$) greater than that of individuals in the control lineages. Error bars indicate 95% confidence limits.

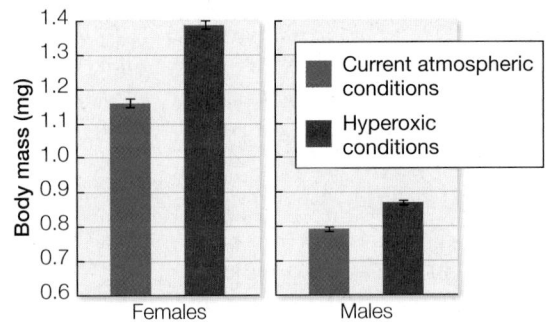

CONCLUSION▶ Increased O_2 concentrations led to evolution of larger body size in fruit flies, consistent with the trends seen among other flying insects in the fossil record.

appear to constrain body size in these flying insects, whereas increases in O_2 appear to relax those constraints. This experiment demonstrates that the stabilizing selection on body size at present O_2 concentrations can quickly switch to directional selection for a change in body size in response to a change in O_2 concentrations.

Connect the Concepts Stabilizing selection resists change from a current state, whereas directional selection results in change away from the current state (see Key Concept 19.4).

Extinction happens continuously, but mass extinctions result from sudden environmental changes

The physical and biological components of Earth's environment are constantly changing. As we saw in Chapter 22, new species are constantly being generated. At the same time, some species decline to the point that they can no longer maintain viable populations and become extinct. Both speciation and extinction have been occurring throughout the history of life. Why do species become extinct? Short-term or long-term environmental fluctuations can make growth or reproduction difficult. As new species arise, they may outcompete existing species for food, space, or other resources. If a prey species becomes extinct, predators that depend on the prey may decline or disappear as well.

As population sizes decrease, the probability of extinction accelerates. At any population size, there is variation in reproductive success, and a particular individual may fail to reproduce successfully. When population sizes are very small, such variation has a bigger influence. Low reproduction by a few individuals in a small population is likely to lead to loss of the population. The smaller the population, the larger the role that chance plays. Variation in reproductive rates is less likely to lead to extinction in large populations, where chance effects play a much smaller role.

Smaller populations can also have density-dependent disadvantages compared with larger populations—a phenomenon known as the **Allee effect**. Allee effects can occur, for example, from the inability of a small group to defend itself against predators, or from a decline in the ability of individuals to find mates. Small populations can also decline from the negative effects of inbreeding depression and genetic drift (see Chapter 19). These processes can result in loss of genetic variation, uncovering of deleterious alleles, and loss of beneficial alleles.

An experiment on sea palms (a species of kelp) illustrates the relative influence of various factors on extinction probability as it relates to population size (**Figure 23.10**). Biologists experimentally established isolated populations of sea palms on intertidal rocky shores and examined their survivorship through time. At small population sizes, random demographic factors were most likely to lead to local extinction, whereas environmental fluctuations were much more likely to cause the extinction of larger populations.

The five mass extinction events shown in Figure 23.2 are notable because they suddenly increased the extinction rate and affected a large percentage of living organisms at the same time. In each case, rapid and extreme environmental changes caused many species to become extinct simultaneously.

Work with the Data

Original Papers: J. F. Harrison and G. G. Haddad. 2011. Effects of oxygen on growth and size: Synthesis of molecular, organismal and evolutionary studies with *Drosophila melanogaster*. *Annu Rev Physiol* 73: 13.1–13.9.

J. F. Harrison et al. 2010. Atmospheric oxygen level and the evolution of insect body size. *Proc R Soc Lond B Biol Sci* 277: 1937–1946.

The data in the bar graphs show that the body mass of individuals in the experimental populations of *Drosophila* increased, on average, about 2% per generation under hyperoxic conditions (although the rate of increase was not constant over the experiment). Here you will extrapolate from Harrison et al.'s study to determine whether the observed rate of increase in body mass per generation that these researchers observed in *Drosophila* is sufficient to account for the giant dragonflies of the Permian.

QUESTIONS▶

1. Suppose that the average rate of increase in dragonfly size during the Permian was much slower than the rate observed in the experiment. For this exercise, assume that the actual rate of increase for dragonflies was just 0.01% per generation, rather than the 2% observed over a few generations for *Drosophila*. Also assume that dragonflies complete only 1 generation per year (as opposed to 40 or more generations for *Drosophila*). Starting with an average body mass of 1 gram, calculate the projected increase in dragonfly body mass over 50,000 years. This calculation is similar to computing compound interest for a savings account. Use the formula $W = S(1 + R)^N$ where W = the final mass, S = the starting mass, R = the rate of increase per generation (0.0001 in this case), and N = the number of generations.

2. What percent of the Permian does 50,000 years represent? Use Table 23.1 for your calculation.

3. Given your calculations, do you think that increased O_2 concentrations during the Permian were sufficient to account for the evolution of giant dragonflies? Why or why not?

Go to Achieve for a companion Data in Depth exercise.

Experiment

Figure 23.10A What Factors Influence Extinction in Small Populations?

Original Paper: J. T. Wootton and C. A. Pfister. 2013. Experimental separation of genetic and demographic factors on extinction risk in wild populations. *Ecology* 94: 2117–2123.

J. Timothy Wootton and Catherine Pfister established new, isolated populations of sea palms (a species of kelp, *Postelsia palmaeformis*) on exposed rocky shores of the northwestern United States. They then studied the probability of population extinction as a function of genetic structure and population size.

HYPOTHESIS▶ Random variation in demographic events (individual births and deaths) will overwhelm genetic factors as contributions to short-term extinction probabilities in small populations. Extinction in larger populations will occur primarily from environmental fluctuation.

METHOD▶

1. Establish new isolated populations of *Postelsia palmaeformis* on rocky shorelines.

   Establish three types of populations:

Photo by C. A. Pfister, from J. T. Wootton and C. A. Pfister. 2013. Ecology 94: 2117

   a. Inbred populations (populations derived from a single individual)

   b. Control populations (populations established from multiple individuals from the same source population)

   c. Outbred populations (populations established from multiple individuals from different source populations)

2. After populations are established, thin populations to small (*N* = 20) or large (*N* = 50) size. Follow the populations through time, recording population size each spring.

RESULTS▶ In the smallest populations, random variation in births and deaths was by far the largest contributing factor to population extinction. Genetic effects had very little contribution to short-term extinction rates in this species. Allee effects were most evident in populations of 1–10 individuals. Above *N* = 10, almost all population extinction resulted from environmental fluctuations.

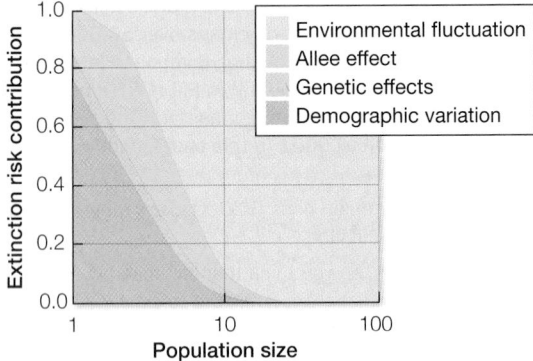

Legend:
- Environmental fluctuation
- Allee effect
- Genetic effects
- Demographic variation

y-axis: Extinction risk contribution (0.0 to 1.0)
x-axis: Population size (1, 10, 100)

CONCLUSION▶ Chance variation in births and deaths has the highest effect on extinction at the smallest population sizes. At larger population sizes, most local extinction results from fluctuation in the environment.

Work with the Data

Figure 23.10B What Factors Influence Extinction in Small Populations?

Original Paper: J. T. Wootton and C. A. Pfister. 2013. Experimental separation of genetic and demographic factors on extinction risk in wild populations. *Ecology* 94: 2117–2123.

After establishing the experimental populations, the researchers counted the number of individuals present in each population each spring. They then recorded which populations were extant (still existing) or extinct in the following year. The table shows data for a few of the population sizes they examined:

Population size in previous year	Number of populations extant in following year	Number of populations extinct in following year
1–5	2	13
20	13	13
50	19	5
100–1,000	24	0

QUESTIONS▶

1. Draw a graph showing probability of extinction (*y* axis) as a function of population size (*x* axis) based on the data in the table. Use a log scale for the *x* axis. Draw a curve to approximate the relationship between probability of extinction and population size.

2. The graph you produced in Question 1 shows the extinction probability of a population after 1 year. If you started a population with 20 individuals, how likely do you think it would be to survive for 2 years? What additional data could you collect after 1 year to help answer this question?

Go to Achieve for a companion Data in Depth exercise.

KEY CONCEPT

23.2 Recap and Assess

Physical conditions on Earth have changed dramatically over time. Changes in Earth's climate and sea levels have had major effects on biological evolution. Continental drift, volcanic eruptions, and large meteorite strikes have contributed to major climate changes during Earth's history, and many of these climate shifts have resulted in mass extinction events. Changes in atmospheric concentrations of O_2 have also influenced the evolution of life, and the evolution of life has, in turn, affected the physical nature of the planet.

1. Explain why an occasional major winter blizzard is irrelevant to discussions of global climate warming.

2. Describe changes in the environment that may have favored the evolution of groups of multicellular organisms near the end of the Precambrian.

The many dramatic physical events in Earth's history have influenced the nature and timing of evolutionary changes among Earth's living organisms. Next we look more closely at some of the major events that characterize the history of life on Earth.

<table>
<tr><td>

KEY CONCEPT
23.3

</td><td>

Major Events in the Evolution of Life Can Be Read in the Fossil Record

</td></tr>
</table>

Learning Objectives

23.3.1 List four major environmental changes in Earth's history and explain how they have affected biodiversity.

23.3.2 Explain what is meant by the "Cambrian explosion" and identify the factors that enabled rapid diversification of multicellular organisms.

How do we know about the physical changes in Earth's environment and their effects on the evolution of life? To reconstruct life's history, scientists rely heavily on the fossil record. As we have seen, geologists divided Earth's history into eons, eras, and periods based on their distinct fossil assemblages (see Table 23.1). Biologists refer to the assemblage of all organisms of all kinds living at a particular time or place as a **biota**. All of the plants living at a particular time or place are its **flora**; all of the animals are its **fauna**.

About 300,000 species of fossil organisms have been described and named, and the number steadily grows. The number of named species, however, is only a tiny fraction of the species that have ever lived. We do not know how many species lived in the past, but we have ways of making reasonable estimates. Of the present-day biota, about 1.8 million species have been named. The actual number of living species is probably well over 10 million, and possibly much higher, because many species have not yet been discovered and described by biologists. So the number of described fossil species is only about 3% of the estimated minimum number of living species. Life has existed on Earth for about 3.8 billion years. Many species last only a few million years before undergoing speciation or becoming extinct. From this we know that Earth's biota must have turned over many times during geological history. So the total number of species that have lived over evolutionary time must vastly exceed the number living today. Why have only about 300,000 of these tens of millions of species been described from fossils to date?

Several factors contribute to the paucity of fossils

Only a tiny fraction of organisms ever become fossils, and only a tiny fraction of fossils are ever discovered by paleontologists. Most organisms live and die in oxygen-rich environments, in which they quickly decompose. Organisms are not likely to become fossils unless they are transported by wind or water to sites that lack oxygen, where decomposition proceeds slowly. Furthermore, geological processes transform many rocks, destroying the fossils they contain, and many fossil-bearing rocks are deeply buried and inaccessible. Paleontologists have studied only a tiny fraction of the sites that contain fossils, although they find and describe many new ones every year.

The fossil record is most complete for marine animals that had hard skeletons (which resist decomposition). Among the nine major animal groups with hard-shelled members, approximately

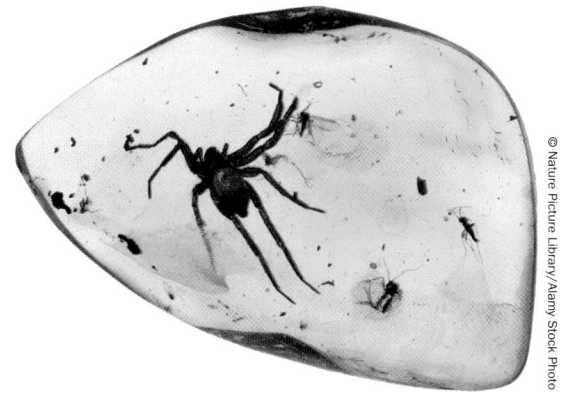

Figure 23.11 Fossils in Amber Chunks of amber—fossilized tree resin—often contain detailed fossils such as this spider, which was preserved when it became trapped in the sticky resin.

200,000 species have been described from fossils—roughly twice the number of living marine species in these same groups. Paleontologists lean heavily on these groups in their interpretations of the evolution of life. Insects and arachnids are also relatively well represented in the fossil record because they are numerically abundant and have hard exoskeletons (**Figure 23.11**). The fossil record, though incomplete, is good enough to document clearly the factual history of the evolution of life.

By combining information about physical changes during Earth's history with evidence from the fossil record, scientists have composed portraits of what Earth and its inhabitants may have looked like at different times. We know in general where the continents were and how life changed over time, but many of the details are poorly known, especially for events in the more remote past.

Precambrian life was small and aquatic

Life first appeared on Earth about 3.8 billion years ago (**Figure 23.12**). The fossil record of organisms that lived prior to the Phanerozoic is fragmentary, but it is good enough to establish that diversity of multicellular organisms increased dramatically in the late Precambrian.

For most of its history, life was confined to the oceans, and all organisms were small. For more than 3 billion years, all organisms lived in shallow seas. These seas slowly began to teem with microscopic prokaryotes. After the first eukaryotes appeared during the Proterozoic, they began to feed on the much smaller prokaryotes. As eukaryotes diversified, small floating organisms, known collectively as **plankton**, were strained from the water and eaten by larger filter-feeding eukaryotes. Other eukaryotes ingested sediments on the seafloor and digested the remains of organisms within them. But it still took about a billion years for eukaryotes to begin diversifying rapidly into the many different multicellular groups that we know today.

What limited the diversity of multicellular eukaryotes (in terms of their size and shape) for much of their early existence? It is likely that a combination of factors was responsible. We have already noted that oxygen levels increased throughout the Proterozoic, and it is likely that high atmospheric and dissolved oxygen concentrations were needed to support large multicellular

Figure 23.12 A Sense of Life's Time The top time line shows the 4.5-billion-year history of Earth. Most of this history is accounted for by the Precambrian, a 4-billion-year time span that saw the origin of life and organisms. The most recent 600 million years are expanded in the bottom time line and detailed in Figure 23.14.

organisms. In addition, geological evidence points to a series of intensely cold periods during the late Proterozoic, which would have resulted in seas that were largely covered by ice and continents that were covered by glaciers. The "snowball Earth" hypothesis suggests that cold conditions confined life to warm places such as hot springs, deep thermal vents, and perhaps a few equatorial oceans that avoided ice cover. The last of these Proterozoic glaciations ended about 580 million years ago, just before several major radiations of multicellular eukaryotes appear in the fossil record (**Figure 23.13**). Many of the multicellular organisms known from the late Proterozoic and early Phanerozoic were very different from any animals living today and may be members of groups that left no living descendants.

Life expanded rapidly during the Cambrian

The Cambrian (542–488 mya) marks the beginning of the Paleozoic, the first era of the Phanerozoic. The O_2 concentration in the Cambrian atmosphere was approaching its current level, and the glaciations of the late Proterozoic had ended nearly 40 million years earlier. A geologically rapid diversification of life took place that is often called the **Cambrian explosion**. This name is somewhat misleading, as the series of radiations it refers to actually began before the start of the Cambrian and continued for about 60 million years into the early Cambrian (see Figure 23.13). Nonetheless, 60 million years represents a relatively short amount of time, especially considering that the first eukaryotes had appeared about a billion (= 1,000 million) years earlier. Many of the major animal groups represented by species alive today first appeared during these evolutionary radiations. **Figure 23.14** provides an overview of the numerous continental and biotic innovations that have characterized the Phanerozoic.

For the most part, fossils tell us only about the hard parts of organisms, but in some well-studied Cambrian fossil beds the soft parts of many animals were preserved. Multicellular life was largely or completely aquatic during the Cambrian. If there was life on land at this time, it was probably restricted to microorganisms.

Figure 23.13 Diversification of Multicellular Organisms: The Cambrian Explosion Shortly after the end of Proterozoic glaciations (about 580 mya), several major radiations of multicellular organisms appear in the fossil record. (**A**) These microscopic fossils from the Doushantuo rock formation of China are the remains of tiny four- and eight-celled stages of multicellular organisms. (**B**) Unusual soft-bodied marine invertebrates, unlike any animals alive at present, characterize the fossilized fauna preserved at Ediacara in southern Australia. (**C**) By the early Phanerozoic, fossilized faunas such as those preserved in Canada's Burgess Shale include extinct representatives of some of the major animal groups alive today.

(C) Burgess Shale fossils

(A) Doushantuo fossils

(B) Ediacaran fossils

Rapid increase of multicellular organisms (Cambrian explosion)

Major radiation of several marine groups

First vascular plants and terrestrial arthropods evolve; first jawed fishes

Many animal groups radiate; forests appear on land

| Proterozoic | Cambrian | Ordovician | Silurian | Devonian |

Paleozoic

Millions of years ago

500

75% of all animals go extinct as sea levels drop by 50 meters

400

75% of marine species go extinct

Cambrian

Devonian

Marrella splendens

Ottoia sp.

Anomalocaris canadensis (claw only)

Archaeopteris

Eusthenopteron foordi

Beneski Museum of Natural History, Amherst College, courtesy of The Trustees of Amherst College

© John Sibbick/Science Source

© Alan Sirulnikoff/Science Source

© Kevin Schafer/Alamy Stock Photo

© John Cancalosi/Getty Images

© National Geographic Image Collection/Alamy Stock Photo

© Gerald & Buff Corsi/Visuals Unlimited, Inc.

Figure 23.14 A Brief History of Multicellular Life on Earth The geologically rapid "explosion" of life shortly before and during the Cambrian saw the rise of many major animal groups that have representatives surviving today. The following three pages depict life's history through the Phanerozoic. The movements of the major continents during the past half-billion years are shown in the maps of Earth, and associated biotas for each time period are depicted. The artists' reconstructions are based on fossils such as those shown in the photographs. (After R. S. Dietz and J. C. Holden. 1970. *J Geophys Res* 75: 4939–4956; R. S. Dietz and J. C. Holden. 1970. *Sci Am* 223: 30–41.)

Extensive swamp forests produce coal; origin of amniotes; great increase in terrestrial animal diversity

Giant amphibians and flying insects; ray-finned fishes abundant in fresh water

On land, conifers become dominant plants; frogs and reptiles begin to diversify

First mammals appear

Dinosaurs, pterosaurs, ray-finned fishes diversify

First known flowering plant fossils

Carboniferous	Permian	Triassic	Jurassic

Paleozoic	Mesozoic

300

Extinction of 96% of Earth's species; oxygen levels drop rapidly

200

Mass extinction event, including about 65% of all species

Pangaea

Laurasia

Gondwana

Permian

© John Sibbick/Science Source

Jurassic

© Sergey Krasovskiy/Stocktrek Images/Corbis

© Biophoto Associates/Science Source

Europasaurus holgeri

Courtesy of Gondwana Studios

Estemmenosuchus sp.

© John Cancalosi/Alamy Stock Photo

Equisetum sp.

Ginkgo sp.

dpa picture alliance archive/Alamy Stock Photo

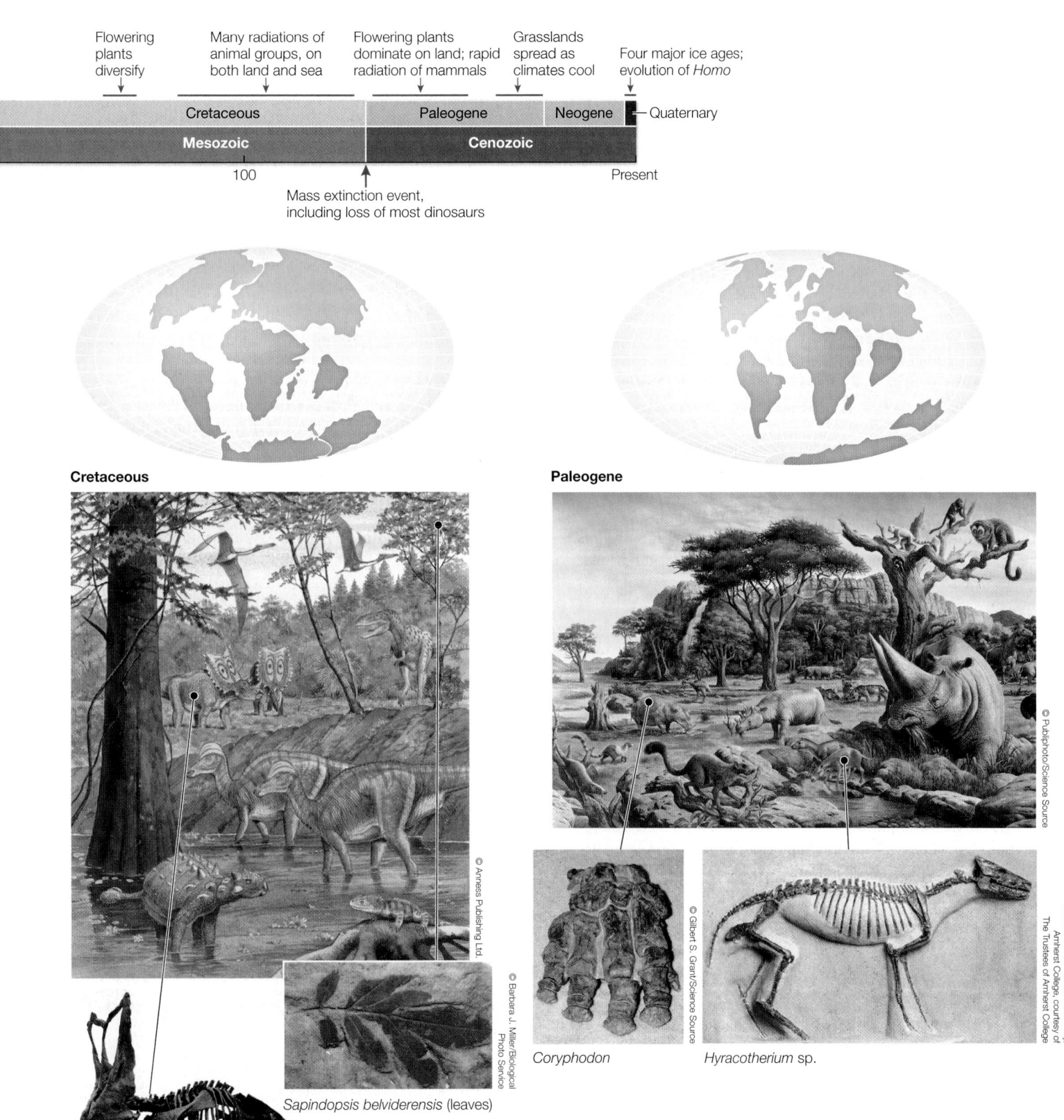

Flowering plants diversify

Many radiations of animal groups, on both land and sea

Flowering plants dominate on land; rapid radiation of mammals

Grasslands spread as climates cool

Four major ice ages; evolution of *Homo*

| Cretaceous | Paleogene | Neogene | Quaternary |

Mesozoic | **Cenozoic**

100   Present

Mass extinction event, including loss of most dinosaurs

Cretaceous

Paleogene

© Arness Publishing Ltd.

© Pubiphoto/Science Source

Sapindopsis belviderensis (leaves)

© Barbara J. Miller/Biological Photo Service

Coryphodon

© Gilbert S. Grant/Science Source

Hyracotherium sp.

Beneski Museum of Natural History, Amherst College, courtesy of The Trustees of Amherst College

Chasmosaurus belli

© Oleksiy Maksymenko /Alamy Stock Photo

Many groups of organisms that arose during the Cambrian later diversified

Geologists divide the remainder of the Paleozoic into the Ordovician, Silurian, Devonian, Carboniferous, and Permian periods. Each period is characterized by the diversification of specific groups of organisms. Mass extinctions marked the ends of the Ordovician, Devonian, and Permian.

THE ORDOVICIAN (488–444 MYA) During the Ordovician, the continents, which were located primarily in the Southern Hemisphere, still lacked multicellular life. Evolutionary radiation of marine organisms, however, was spectacular during the early Ordovician, especially among animals, such as brachiopods and mollusks, that lived on the seafloor and filtered small prey from the water. At the end of the Ordovician, as massive glaciers formed over the southern continents, sea levels dropped about 50 meters, and ocean temperatures dropped. About 75% of all animal species became extinct, probably because of these major environmental changes.

THE SILURIAN (444–416 MYA) During the Silurian, the continents began to merge together. Marine life rebounded from the mass extinction at the end of the Ordovician. Animals able to swim in open water and feed above the ocean floor appeared for the first time. Fishes diversified as bony armor gave way to the less rigid scales of modern fishes, and the first jawed fishes and the first fishes with supporting rays in their fins appeared. The tropical sea was uninterrupted by land barriers, and most marine organisms were widely distributed. On land, the first vascular plants evolved late in the Silurian (about 420 mya). The first terrestrial arthropods—scorpions and millipedes—evolved at about the same time.

THE DEVONIAN (416–359 MYA) Rates of evolutionary change accelerated in many groups of organisms during the Devonian. The major land masses continued to move slowly toward each other. In the oceans there were great evolutionary radiations of corals and of shelled, squid-like cephalopod mollusks.

Terrestrial communities changed dramatically during the Devonian. Club mosses, horsetails, and tree ferns became common, and some attained the size of large trees. Their roots accelerated the weathering of rocks, resulting in the development of the first forest soils. The first plants to produce seeds appeared in the Devonian. The earliest fossil centipedes, spiders, mites, and insects date to this period, as do the earliest terrestrial vertebrates.

A mass extinction of about 75% of all marine species marked the end of the Devonian. Paleontologists are uncertain about its cause, but two large meteorites collided with Earth at about that time and may have been responsible, or at least a contributing factor. The continued merging of the continents, with the corresponding reduction in the area of continental shelves, also may have contributed to this mass extinction.

THE CARBONIFEROUS (359–299 MYA) Large glaciers formed over high-latitude portions of the southern land masses during the Carboniferous, but extensive swamp forests grew on the tropical continents. These forests were dominated by giant tree ferns and horsetails with small leaves. Their fossilized remains formed the coal we now mine for energy. In the seas, crinoids (a group of echinoderms, related to sea stars and sea urchins) reached their greatest diversity, forming "meadows" on the seafloor.

The diversity of terrestrial animals increased greatly during the Carboniferous. Snails, scorpions, centipedes, and insects were abundant and diverse. Insects evolved wings, becoming the first animals to fly. Flight gave herbivorous insects easy access to tall plants, and plant fossils from this period show evidence of chewing by insects (**Figure 23.15**). The terrestrial vertebrates split into two lineages. The amphibians became larger and better adapted to terrestrial existence, while the sister lineage led to the amniotes—vertebrates with well-protected eggs that can be laid in dry places.

THE PERMIAN (299–251 MYA) During the Permian, the continents merged into a single supercontinent called Pangaea. Permian rocks contain representatives of many of the major groups of insects we know today. By the end of the period the amniotes had split into two lineages: the reptiles, and a second lineage that would lead to the mammals. Ray-finned fishes became common in the fresh waters of Pangaea.

Toward the end of the Permian, conditions for life deteriorated. Massive volcanic eruptions resulted in outpourings of lava that covered large areas of Earth. The ash and gases produced by the volcanoes blocked sunlight and cooled the climate. The death and decay of the massive Permian forests rapidly used up atmospheric oxygen, and the loss of photosynthetic organisms meant that relatively little new atmospheric oxygen was produced. In addition, much of Pangaea was located close to the South Pole by the end of the Permian. All of these factors combined to produce the most extensive continental glaciers since the snowball Earth times of the late Proterozoic. Atmospheric oxygen concentrations gradually dropped from about 30% to 15%. At such low concentrations, most animals would have been unable to survive at elevations above 500 meters, so about half of the land area would have been uninhabitable at the end of the Permian. The combination of these changes resulted in the most drastic mass extinction in Earth's history. Scientists estimate that about 96% of all multicellular species became extinct at the end of the Permian.

Figure 23.15 Evidence of Insect Diversification The margins of this fossil fern leaf from the Carboniferous have been chewed by insects.

Geographic differentiation increased during the Mesozoic

The few organisms that survived the Permian mass extinction found themselves in a relatively empty world at the start of the Mesozoic Era (251 mya). As Pangaea slowly began to break apart in the Mesozoic, the biotas of the newly separated continents began to diverge. The oceans rose and once again flooded the continental shelves, forming huge, shallow inland seas. Atmospheric oxygen concentrations gradually rose as photosynthesis increased. Life once again proliferated and diversified, but different groups of organisms came to the fore. The three groups of phytoplankton (floating photosynthetic organisms) that dominate today's oceans—dinoflagellates, coccolithophores, and diatoms—became ecologically important at this time, and their remains are the primary origin of the world's oil deposits. Seed-bearing plants replaced the trees that had ruled the Permian forests.

The Mesozoic is divided into three periods: the Triassic, Jurassic, and Cretaceous. The Triassic and Cretaceous were terminated by mass extinctions, probably caused by meteorite impacts.

THE TRIASSIC (251–201.6 MYA)   Pangaea remained largely intact through the Triassic. Many invertebrate groups diversified, and many burrowing animals evolved from groups living on the surfaces of seafloor sediments. On land, conifers and seed ferns were the dominant trees. The first frogs and turtles appeared. A great radiation of reptiles began, which eventually gave rise to crocodilians and dinosaurs (including birds). The first mammals appeared. The end of the Triassic was marked by a mass extinction that eliminated about 65% of the species on Earth.

THE JURASSIC (201.6–145.5 MYA)   Late in the Jurassic, Pangaea became fully divided into two large continents: **Laurasia**, which drifted northward, and **Gondwana** in the south. Ray-finned fishes rapidly diversified in the oceans. The first lizards appeared, and flying reptiles (pterosaurs) evolved. Most of the large terrestrial predators and herbivores of the period were dinosaurs. Several groups of mammals made their first appearance, and the earliest known fossils of flowering plants are from late in this period.

THE CRETACEOUS (145.5–65.5 MYA)   By the mid-Cretaceous, Gondwana had largely broken apart into the southern continents we know today (although the Indian subcontinent was still separated from Asia). A continuous sea encircled the tropics. Sea levels were high, and Earth was warm and humid. Life proliferated both on land and in the oceans. Marine invertebrates increased in diversity. On land, the reptile radiation continued as dinosaurs diversified further and the first snakes appeared. Early in the Cretaceous, flowering plants began the radiation that led to their current dominance of the land. By the end of the period, many groups of mammals had appeared.

As described in Key Concept 23.2, another meteorite-caused mass extinction took place at the end of the Cretaceous. In the seas, many planktonic organisms and bottom-dwelling invertebrates became extinct. On land, almost all animals larger than about 25 kilograms in body mass became extinct. Many species of insects died out, perhaps because the growth of the plants they fed on was greatly reduced following the impact. Some species in northern North America and Eurasia survived in areas that were not subjected to the devastating fires that engulfed most low-latitude regions.

Modern biotas evolved during the Cenozoic

By the early Cenozoic Era (65.5 mya), the positions of the continents were getting closer to their present positions, but the Indian subcontinent was still separated from Asia, and the Atlantic Ocean was much narrower. The early Cenozoic was characterized by extensive radiations of amphibians, reptiles, and mammals, but other groups were also undergoing important changes.

Flowering plants diversified extensively and came to dominate world forests except in the coolest regions, where the forests were composed primarily of gymnosperms. Novel changes in one group of plants (the legumes) allowed them to use atmospheric nitrogen directly by forming symbioses with a few species of nitrogen-fixing bacteria. The evolution of this symbiosis was the first "green" revolution and dramatically increased the amount of nitrogen available for terrestrial plant growth. This symbiosis remains fundamental to the ecological base of life as we know it today.

The Cenozoic is divided into the Paleogene, Neogene, and Quaternary periods, which are commonly subdivided into epochs (**Table 23.2**). The Paleogene and Neogene are often referred to as the Tertiary when they are discussed together, especially in the older literature.

THE PALEOGENE (65.5–23.0 MYA)   During the Paleogene, the Indian subcontinent continued its northward drift. By about 55 mya it made initial contact with parts of southeastern Asia. By about 35 mya, the Indian Plate ran fully into the Eurasian Plate, and the Himalayas began to be pushed up as a result.

The early Paleogene was a hot and humid time, as CO_2 levels in Earth's atmosphere were high, which produced a greenhouse effect. The tropics were probably too hot to support rainforest vegetation and instead were clothed in low-lying vegetation. By late in the Paleogene, however, increased plankton growth in the oceans, combined with the eventual burial of plankton in oceanic sediments, led to the removal of considerable CO_2 from Earth's atmosphere, and the climate became considerably cooler and drier. Many lineages of flowering plants evolved herbaceous (nonwoody) forms, and grasslands spread over much of Earth.

Amphibians, snakes, lizards, birds, and mammals all underwent extensive radiations during the Paleogene. The first of several waves

TABLE **23.2** | Subdivisions of the Cenozoic Era

Period	Epoch	Onset (mya)
Quaternary	Holocene (Recent)	0.01 (~10,000 years ago)
	Pleistocene	2.6
Neogene	Pliocene	5.3
	Miocene	23
Paleogene	Oligocene	34
	Eocene	55.8
	Paleocene	65.5

of plants and terrestrial animals dispersed between Asia and North America across one of the several land bridges that have intermittently connected the two continents during the past 55 million years.

THE NEOGENE (23.0–2.6 MYA) During the Neogene, the continents began to take their current positions. North and South America became connected by the Isthmus of Panama, which resulted in considerable interchange of plants and terrestrial animals between the two continents. For the same reason, the tropical areas of the Atlantic and Pacific oceans became isolated from one another, which resulted in divergence of the respective marine faunas of these oceans. Diversification of major plant and animal groups continued, as the biotas of the continents began to resemble those we see today.

THE QUATERNARY (2.6 MYA TO PRESENT) We are living in the Quaternary. It is subdivided into two epochs, the Pleistocene and the Holocene (the Holocene is also known as the Recent).

The Pleistocene was a time of drastic cooling and climate fluctuations. During 4 major and about 20 minor ice ages, massive glaciers spread across the continents, and the ranges of animal and plant populations shifted toward the equator. The last of these glaciers retreated from temperate latitudes less than 15,000 years ago. Organisms are still adjusting to this change. Many high-latitude ecological communities have occupied their current locations for no more than a few thousand years.

It was during the Pleistocene that divergence within one group of mammals, the primates, resulted in the evolution of the hominoid lineage. Subsequent hominoid radiation eventually led to the species *Homo sapiens*—modern humans. Many large bird and mammal species became extinct in Australia and in the Americas after *H. sapiens* arrived on those continents about 45,000 and 15,000 years ago, respectively. Many paleontologists believe at least some of these extinctions were the result of hunting and other influences of humans.

Connect the Concepts The evolution of modern humans and their close relatives during the Pleistocene is discussed in Key Concept 31.5.

The tree of life is used to reconstruct evolutionary events

The fossil record reveals broad patterns in life's evolution. To reconstruct major events in the history of life, biologists also rely on the phylogenetic information in the tree of life (see Appendix A). We can use phylogeny, in combination with the fossil record, to reconstruct the timing of such major events as the acquisition of mitochondria in the ancestral eukaryotic cell, the several independent origins of multicellular organisms, and the movement of life onto dry land. We can also follow major changes in the genomes of organisms, and we can even reconstruct many gene sequences of species that are long extinct.

Connect the Concepts Key Concept 20.3 describes how biologists reconstruct the gene sequences of extinct organisms.

Changes in Earth's physical environment have clearly influenced the diversity of organisms we see on the planet today. To study the evolution of that diversity, biologists examine the evolutionary relationships among species. Deciphering phylogenetic

relationships is an important step in understanding how life has diversified on Earth. The next part of this book will explore the major groups of life and the different solutions these groups have evolved to meet major challenges such as reproduction, energy acquisition, dispersal, and escape from predation.

KEY CONCEPT
23.3 Recap and Assess

Life evolved in the oceans about 3.8 billion years ago. The evolution of photosynthesis resulted in increased concentrations of atmospheric oxygen, which facilitated both the evolution of multicellular organisms and the invasion of life onto land. Numerous climate changes and rearrangements of the continents, as well as meteorite impacts, contributed to five major mass extinctions.

1. Give a likely reason for the "green" revolution of the Cenozoic, and explain why it enabled flowering plants to diversify.

2. Compare the tree of life in Appendix A (see Figures A1 and A2) with the chronology of major events in Table 23.1. To represent the diversity of life in one figure, the tree in the appendix is not drawn proportionally in relation to time. Which geological eon, era, or period seems most compressed on the tree, and why?

 View in Achieve
Activity 23.1 Concept Matching: The History of Life on Earth

Investigating LIFE

Q and A   **How can modern experiments test hypotheses about the evolutionary impact of ancient environmental changes?**

Several experiments have been conducted to test the link between O_2 concentrations and evolution of body size in flying insects (one of these is discussed in **Investigating Life: The Relationship between Atmospheric Oxygen Concentration and Body Size in Insects**). Results of these experiments are consistent with the evolution of larger body size in flying insects in hyperoxic (high-oxygen) environments. Experiments have also been conducted under hypoxic (low-oxygen) conditions, such as existed at the end of the Permian. Results of these experiments suggest that the evolution of body size is constrained under hypoxic conditions, even under strong artificial selection for larger body size. These latter results are consistent with the extinction of many of the large flying insects at the end of the Permian, the result of rapidly decreasing O_2 concentrations. Giant flying insects simply could not have survived the lower O_2 concentrations that existed at that time. The mass extinction at the end of the Permian is the only known mass extinction that involved considerable loss of insect diversity.

Future directions

Experiments with living organisms are providing information about how quickly various groups of organisms evolve. They also inform us about the factors involved in extinction of species (as in the example in Figure 23.10). As human activities affect the climate of Earth, experimental approaches will be important to help us predict how our actions may affect future directions of evolution and extinction.

You should be able to relate each summary to the adjacent figures. If you go to this visual summary in **Achieve**, you can follow links to figures, animations, activities, and simulations that will help you consolidate the material.

KEY CONCEPT

23.1 Events in Earth's History Can Be Dated

- The relative ages of organisms can be determined by the dating of fossils and the **strata** of **sedimentary rocks** in which they are found.

- **Radiometric dating** techniques use a variety of radioisotopes with different **half-lives** to date events in the remote past.

- Geologists divide the history of life into eons, eras, and periods based on major differences in the fossil assemblages found in successive strata.

Figure 23.1

^{14}C half-lives (thousands of years)

| | 5.7 | 11.4 | 17.1 | 22.8 |

Radioisotope remaining in sample (%)

100 — Remaining radioisotope — 1/2 — 1/4 — 1/8 — 1/16 — 50 — 0

Number of half-lives: 0 1 2 3 4

Radioisotope	Decay product	Half-life (years)	Useful dating range (years)
Carbon-14 (^{14}C)	Nitrogen-14 (^{14}N)	5,700	100–60,000
Uranium-234 (^{234}U)	Thorium-230 (^{230}Th)	80,000	10,000–500,000
Uranium-235 (^{235}U)	Lead-207 (^{207}Pb)	704 million	200,000–4.5 billion
Potassium-40 (^{40}K)	Argon-40 (^{40}Ar)	1.3 billion	10 million–4.5 billion

Questions

1. How much of the evolutionary history of life was exclusively aquatic? When did plants and animals first colonize the continental land masses?

2. Why is carbon-14 dating limited to approximately the past 60,000 years?

3. What radioisotopes can be used to date much older rocks, up to the age of Earth?

4. How much of Earth's history does the Phanerozoic represent?

TABLE **23.1** | Earth's Geological History

Eon	Era	Period	Onset
Phanerozoic (~0.5 billion years long)	Cenozoic	Quaternary (Q)	2.6 mya
		Neogene (N)	23.0 mya
		Paleogene (Pg)	65.5 mya
	Mesozoic	Cretaceous (K)	145.5 mya
		Jurassic (J)	201.6 mya
		Triassic (Tr)	251.0 mya
	Paleozoic	Permian (P)	299 mya
		Carboniferous (C)	359 mya
		Devonian (D)	416 mya
		Silurian (S)	444 mya
		Ordovician (O)	488 mya
		Cambrian (E)	542 mya
Proterozoic			2.5 bya
Archean	Collectively called the Precambrian (~4 billion years long)		3.8 bya
Hadean			4.6–4.5 bya

KEY CONCEPT

23.2 Changes in Earth's Physical Environment Have Affected the Evolution of Life

Go to Animation 23.1

- Earth's crust consists of solid plates that move across the underlying mantle. **Continental drift** is caused by convection currents in the mantle, which move the plates and the continents that lie on top of them.

- Major physical events on Earth, such as continental collisions and volcanic eruptions, have affected Earth's climate, atmosphere, and sea levels. In addition, extraterrestrial events such as meteorite strikes have created sudden and dramatic environmental shifts and led to **mass extinction events**.

- Oxygen-generating cyanobacteria liberated enough O_2 to open the door to oxidation reactions in metabolic pathways. Aerobic prokaryotes were able to harvest more energy than anaerobic organisms and began to proliferate. Increases in atmospheric O_2 concentrations supported the evolution of large eukaryotic cells and, eventually, multicellular organisms.

Figure 23.4

Sea level — High / Low

| Proterozoic | Cambrian | Ordovician | Silurian | Devonian | Carboniferous | Permian | Triassic | Jurassic | Cretaceous | Paleogene | Neogene / Quaternary |

Paleozoic — Mesozoic — Cenozoic

Time (mya): 500 400 300 200 100 Present

Figure 23.8

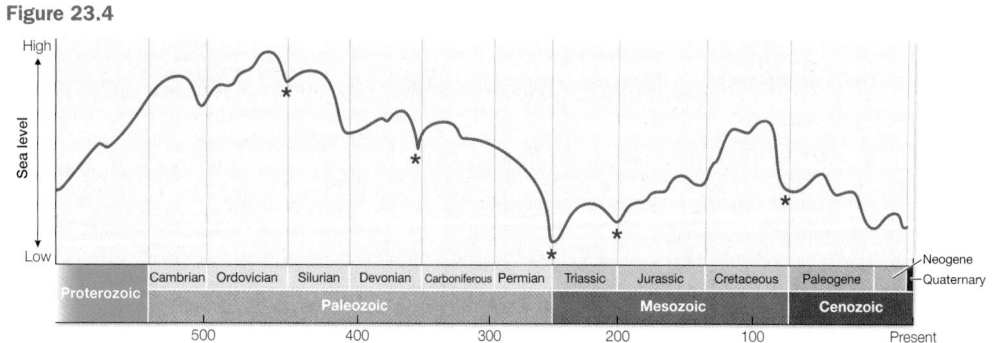

O_2 in atmosphere (%): 35, 30, 25, 20, 15, 10, 5, 0

Labels: First life; First photosynthetic cyanobacteria; First aerobic bacteria; First eukaryotes; First multicellular eukaryotes; First chordates; Invasion of land; Giant flying insects; First flowering plants

Time (mya): 4,000 3,000 2,000 1,000 500 250 100 Present

Questions

1. Explain how changes in atmospheric oxygen enabled the evolution of multicellular life.

2. What environmental changes resulted in the sudden drop in atmospheric oxygen at the end of the Permian?

3. Describe the relationship between global temperature change and sea level fluctuations.

4. How can volcanic eruptions change the global climate?

KEY CONCEPT 23.3 Major Events in the Evolution of Life Can Be Read in the Fossil Record

Go to **Activity 23.1**

- Paleontologists use fossils and evidence of geological changes to determine what Earth and its **biota** may have looked like at different times.

- Before the Phanerozoic, life was almost completely confined to the oceans. Multicellular life diversified extensively during the **Cambrian explosion**, a prime example of an evolutionary radiation.

- The periods of the Paleozoic were each characterized by the diversification of specific groups of organisms. During the Mesozoic, distinct terrestrial biotas evolved on each continent.

- The Cenozoic is divided into the Paleogene, Neogene, and Quaternary periods, which in turn are subdivided into epochs. The Cenozoic saw the emergence of the modern biotas as vertebrates radiated extensively and flowering plants became dominant.

- The tree of life can be used to reconstruct the timing of evolutionary events.

Questions

1. Why are the evolutionary changes in faunas near the beginning of the Cambrian sometimes described as an "explosion"?

2. What were two major causes of mass extinction events in Earth's history?

3. When did snowball Earth exist, and why might it be important in understanding the Cambrian explosion?

4. Describe the relationship of the modern continents to Gondwana, Laurasia, and Pangaea.

Figure 23.12

Figure 23.13

Doushantuo fossils

Ediacaran fossils

Burgess Shale fossils

Bacteria, Archaea, and Viruses 24

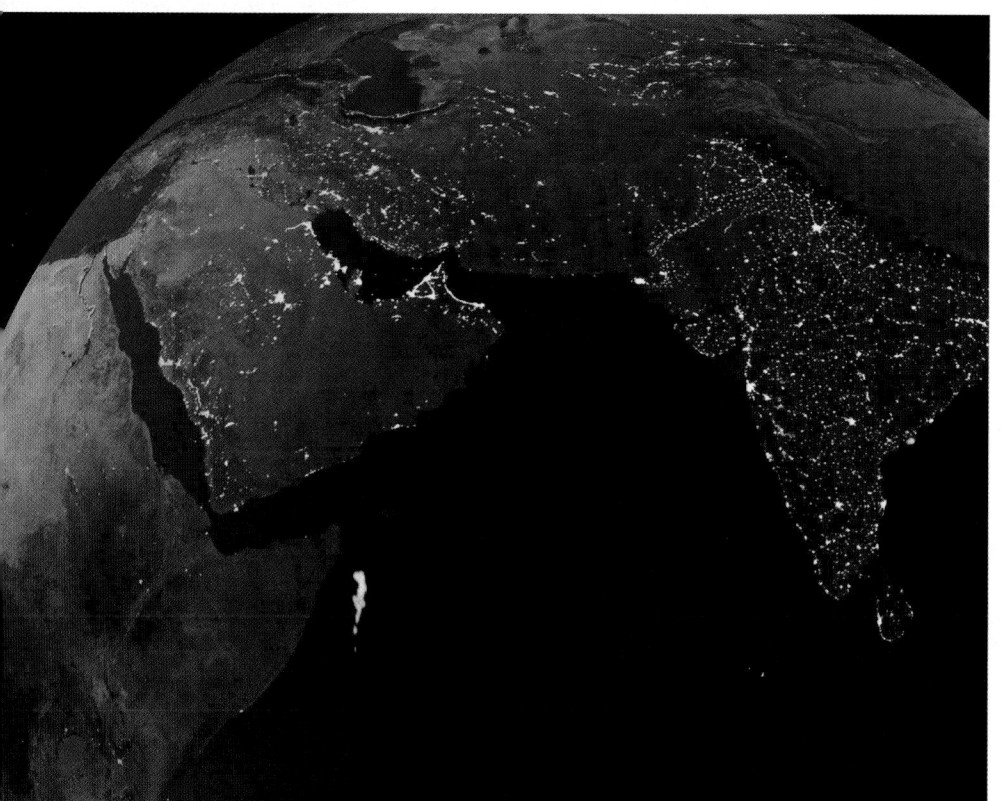

"Milky seas" data prepared by Steven Miller of the Naval Research Laboratory, Monterey, CA. Background data (Earth at Night image) courtesy Marc Imhoff (NASA/GSFC) and Christopher Elvidge (NOAA/NGDC); image by Craig Mayhew (NASA/GSFC) and Robert Simmon (NASA/GSFC)

KEY CONCEPTS

24.1 Bacteria and Archaea Represent the First Split in the Tree of Life

24.2 Prokaryotic Diversity Reflects the Ancient Origins of Life

24.3 Ecological Communities Depend on Prokaryotes

24.4 Viruses Have Multiple Evolutionary Origins

The milky blue area near the Horn of Africa represents a large, bioluminescent bloom of bacteria, as seen from space.

▶Investigating LIFE

Bacteria Light Up the Sea

One night in January of 1995, the British merchant vessel *Lima* was off the coast of Somalia, near the Horn of Africa. This area is infamous for bands of pirates, so the crew was keeping a watchful eye on the seas when they spotted an eerie, whitish glow on the horizon. It was directly in their path, and there was no way to avoid it. Was this strange sight the result of some strange trick of piracy?

Within 15 minutes of first sighting the glow, the *Lima* was surrounded by shining waters for as far as her crew could see. The ship's log recorded that "it appeared as though the ship was sailing over a field of snow or gliding over the clouds." Fortunately for the crew, the glow had nothing to do with pirates.

For centuries, mariners in this part of the world had reported occasional "milky seas" in which the sea surface produced a strange glow at night, extending from horizon to horizon. Scientists up to that point had never been able to confirm the reality or the cause of such phenomena. It was well established, however, that many organisms emit light by bioluminescence, a complex, enzyme-catalyzed biochemical reaction that emits light but not heat.

What kind of organism could cause the vast expanse of bioluminescence observed by the *Lima*? Some marine organisms emit flashes of light when they are disturbed, but they could not have produced the sustained and uniform glow seen in milky seas. The only organisms known to produce the level of sustained bioluminescence consistent with milky seas are certain prokaryotes, such as bacteria of the genus *Vibrio*. Using information supplied by the *Lima*, biologists scanned satellite images of the Indian Ocean for the specific light wavelengths emitted by *Vibrio*. The satellite images clearly identified thousands of square kilometers of *Vibrio*-produced milky seas.

Vibrio's bioluminescence requires a critical concentration of a specific chemical signal produced by the bacteria, so at low densities, free-living *Vibrio* populations do not glow. But as a colony establishes itself on phytoplankton, the bacteria's population density increases and concentrations of the luminescence signal build up. Eventually bacterial density becomes high enough for the huge colony to produce visible light. Such chemical-induced action among bacterial cells is referred to as quorum sensing.

 How and why do bacteria communicate with one another to assess their density?
(Find the answer on page 557.)

Learning Objectives

24.1.1 Compare and contrast the features of bacteria, archaea, and eukaryotes.

24.1.2 Describe how archaea and bacteria each contributed to the evolution of eukaryotes.

24.1.3 Draw a phylogenetic tree demonstrating the effects of lateral gene transfer.

You may think that you have little in common with a bacterium. But all multicellular eukaryotes, including you, share many attributes with the **prokaryotes**—organisms that lack a nucleus (see Key Concept 5.1). For example, all organisms, whether eukaryotes or prokaryotes,

- have cell membranes and ribosomes (see Chapter 5 and 6).
- have a common set of metabolic pathways, such as glycolysis (see Chapter 9).
- replicate DNA semiconservatively (see Chapter 13).
- use DNA as the genetic material to encode proteins, and use similar genetic codes to produce those proteins by transcription and translation (see Chapter 14).

These shared features support the hypothesis that all living organisms share a common ancestor. If life had multiple origins, there would be little reason to expect all organisms to use overwhelmingly similar genetic codes or to share structures as distinctive as ribosomes. Furthermore, similarities in the DNA sequences of genes that are shared by all organisms confirm the monophyly of life.

The earliest split in the tree of life gave rise to Bacteria and Archaea

Although all living things share many features, major differences have evolved across the diversity of life. Biologists have now sequenced the genomes of many living organisms, and these genomes allow us to reconstruct the details of evolutionary history. These studies clarify that the earliest split in the tree of life resulted in two major groups: Bacteria and Archaea (**Figure 24.1**).

Although the earliest division of life gave rise to two major lineages, biologists usually refer to *three* major **domains** of life: Bacteria, Archaea, and Eukarya (which includes all plants, animals, and fungi). But if you examine Figure 24.1, you will see that the third domain, Eukarya, arose through phylogenetic contributions from both bacteria and archaea. (Note that we use lowercase when referring to members of these domains and initial capitals when referring to the domains themselves.) Most genes of eukaryotes are more closely related to those of archaea, but several endosymbiotic events involving bacteria also contributed to making eukaryotes a distinctive new lineage. So biologists are beginning to view eukaryotes as a specialized group of archaea that developed some important new features (including a cell nucleus and mitochondria, at least partly through contributions from bacteria). We call all

the organisms that lack these specializations prokaryotes (Greek, "before the kernel," or before the evolution of a cellular nucleus).

In Chapter 20 we discussed the concept of monophyly (a group that includes an ancestor and all of its descendants) and the importance of monophyly in biological taxonomy. However, the reticulations of bacterial and archaeal lineages near the base of the tree of life make the recognition of strictly monophyletic groups of life's primary domains impractical. Prokaryotes are clearly not a monophyletic group (because the group excludes some of their descendants—the eukaryotes), but the name "prokaryotes" is nonetheless a useful way of talking about all organisms that are not eukaryotes. In a similar manner, when biologists talk about "archaea" or "bacteria," they are typically excluding their eukaryotic descendants, so neither of those groups are strictly monophyletic either. These complications in our taxonomic terminology are unavoidable, given the reticulations that occur among the major lineages near the base of the tree of life. We will use "bacteria" and "archaea" to refer to the two major groups of prokaryotes, and "eukaryotes" to refer to the lineage that emerged from combinations of some specific bacteria and archaea.

All prokaryotic organisms are unicellular, although they may form large, coordinated colonies or communities consisting of many individuals. Eukaryotes, by contrast, include both unicellular as well as many multicellular life forms. As we saw in Chapter 5, prokaryotic cells differ from eukaryotic cells in some important ways:

- *Prokaryotic cells do not divide by mitosis.* Instead, after replicating their DNA, prokaryotic cells divide by their own method, binary fission (see Key Concept 11.1).

- *The organization of the genetic material differs.* The DNA of the prokaryotic cell is not organized within a membrane-enclosed nucleus. DNA molecules in prokaryotes are often circular. Many (but not all) prokaryotes have only one main chromosome and are effectively haploid, although many have additional smaller DNA molecules, called plasmids (see Key Concept 12.6).

- *Prokaryotes have none of the membrane-enclosed cytoplasmic organelles that are found in most eukaryotes.* However, the cytoplasm of a prokaryotic cell may contain a variety of infoldings of the cell membrane and photosynthetic membrane systems that are not found in eukaryotes.

Although the study and classification of eukaryotic organisms go back centuries, much of our knowledge of the evolutionary relationships of prokaryotes is extremely recent. Not until the final quarter of the twentieth century did advances in molecular genetics and biochemistry enable the research that revealed the deep-seated distinctions between archaea and bacteria.

The two prokaryotic groups differ in significant ways

A glance at **Table 24.1** will show you that there are major differences (most of which cannot be seen even under an electron microscope) between archaea and bacteria. Archaea share several features with eukaryotes, but they also retain some ancestral similarities with bacteria. The basic unit of an archaeon (the term for a single archaeal organism) or bacterium (a single bacterial

Figure 24.1 The Major Groups of the Living World   This phylogenetic tree of Bacteria and Archaea shows their relationships to each other and to their descendants, Eukarya. The relationships among the many clades of bacteria, most of which are not shown here, are incompletely resolved at this time.

▶ **View in Achieve**
Animation 24.1 The Primary Divisions of Life

TABLE 24.1 | Characteristics of Bacteria, Archaea, and Eukarya

Characteristic	Bacteria	Archaea	Eukarya
Membrane-enclosed nucleus	Absent	Absent	Present
Membrane-enclosed organelles	Few	Absent	Many
Peptidoglycan in cell wall	Present	Absent	Absent
Membrane lipids	Ester-linked Unbranched	Ether-linked Branched	Ester-linked Unbranched
Ribosomes[a]	70S	70S	80S
Initiator tRNA	Formylmethionine	Methionine	Methionine
Operons	Yes	Yes	Rare
Plasmids	Yes	Yes	Rare
Number of RNA polymerases[b]	One	One	Three
Ribosomes sensitive to chloramphenicol and streptomycin	Yes	No	No
Ribosomes sensitive to diphtheria toxin	No	Yes	Yes

[a]70S ribosomes are smaller than 80S ribosomes.

[b]The structure of archaeal RNA polymerase is similar to that of eukaryotic polymerases.

organism) is the prokaryotic cell. Each single-celled prokaryote contains a full complement of genetic and protein-synthesizing systems, including DNA, RNA, and all the enzymes needed to transcribe and translate genetic information into proteins. The prokaryotic cell also contains at least one system for generating the ATP it needs.

Genetic studies clearly indicate that all forms of life share a single common ancestor. As we noted earlier, most of the eukaryotic genome shares a more recent common ancestor with certain groups of archaea than with bacteria (see Figure 24.1). However, the mitochondria of eukaryotes and the chloroplasts of photosynthetic eukaryotes (such as plants) originated through endosymbioses with bacteria. Some biologists prefer to view the origin of eukaryotes as a fusion of two equal partners (one ancestor that was related to modern archaea and another that was more closely related to modern bacteria). Others view the divergence of the early eukaryotes from specific groups of archaea as an event separate from the later endosymbioses. In either case, most eukaryotic genes are more closely related to those of specific groups of archaea, whereas other genes (especially genes related to mitochondria and chloroplasts) are most closely related to those of bacteria.

Connect the Concepts The origin of mitochondria and chloroplasts by endosymbiosis is described in Key Concepts 5.5 and 26.1.

Biologists estimate that the last common ancestor of all living organisms lived about 3 billion years ago. We can deduce that it had DNA as its genetic material, and that its machinery for transcription and translation produced RNAs and proteins, respectively. This ancestor likely had a circular chromosome. All living organisms are the products of billions of years of mutation, natural selection, and genetic drift, and they are all well adapted to present-day environments. The earliest prokaryotic fossils, which date back at least 3.5 billion years, indicate that there was considerable diversity among the prokaryotes even during those earliest days of life.

The small size of prokaryotes has hindered our study of their evolutionary relationships

Until about 300 years ago, nobody had even *seen* an individual prokaryote. Most prokaryotes remained invisible to humans until the invention of the first simple microscope. Prokaryotes are so small, however, that even the best light microscopes don't reveal much about them. It took advanced microscopic equipment and modern molecular techniques to open up the microbial world. (Microscopic organisms—both prokaryotes and eukaryotes—are often collectively referred to as "microbes.")

Before DNA sequencing became practical, taxonomists based prokaryote classification on observable phenotypic characters such as shape, color, motility, nutritional requirements, and sensitivity to antibiotics. One of the characters most widely used to classify prokaryotes is the structure of their cell walls.

The cell walls of almost all bacteria contain **peptidoglycan**, a cross-linked polymer of amino sugars that produces a firm, protective, meshlike structure around the cell. Peptidoglycan is a substance unique to bacteria; its absence from the cell walls of archaea is a key difference between the two prokaryotic domains. Peptidoglycan is also an excellent target for combating pathogenic (disease-causing) bacteria because it has no counterpart in eukaryotic cells. Antibiotics such as penicillin and ampicillin, as well as other agents that specifically interfere with the synthesis of peptidoglycan-containing cell walls, tend to have little, if any, effect on the cells of humans and other eukaryotes.

The **Gram stain** is a technique that can be used to separate most types of bacteria into two distinct groups. A smear of bacterial cells on a microscope slide is soaked in a violet dye and treated with iodine; it is then washed with alcohol and counterstained with a red dye called safranin. **Gram-positive bacteria** retain the violet dye and appear blue to purple (**Figure 24.2A**). The alcohol washes the violet stain out of **Gram-negative bacteria**, which then pick up the safranin counterstain and appear pink to red (**Figure 24.2B**). For most bacteria, the effect of the Gram stain is determined by the chemical structure of the cell wall:

- A *Gram-negative cell wall* usually has a thin peptidoglycan layer, which is surrounded by a second, outer membrane quite distinct in chemical makeup from the cell membrane (see Figure 24.2B). Together the cell wall and the outer membrane are called the cell envelope. The space between the cell membrane and the outer membrane (known as the periplasmic space) contains proteins that are important in digesting some materials, transporting others, and detecting chemical gradients in the environment.

- A *Gram-positive cell wall* usually has about five times as much peptidoglycan as a Gram-negative cell wall. Its thick peptidoglycan layer is a meshwork that may serve some of the same purposes as the periplasmic space of the Gram-negative cell envelope.

Shape is another phenotypic character that is useful for the basic identification of bacteria. The three most common shapes are spheres, rods, and spiral forms (**Figure 24.3**). Many bacterial

(A) Gram-positive bacteria have a uniformly dense cell wall consisting primarily of peptidoglycan.

Outside of cell

Cell wall (peptidoglycan)

Cell membrane

Inside of cell

(B) Gram-negative bacteria have a very thin peptidoglycan layer and an outer membrane, which together make up the cell envelope.

Outside of cell

Outer membrane of cell envelope

Periplasmic space

Cell envelope

Peptidoglycan layer

Periplasmic space

Cell membrane

Inside of cell

Figure 24.2 The Gram Stain and the Bacterial Cell Wall When treated with Gram-staining reagents, the cell walls of bacteria react in one of two ways. **(A)** Gram-positive bacteria have a thick peptidoglycan cell wall that retains the violet dye and appears deep blue or purple. **(B)** Gram-negative bacteria have a thin peptidoglycan layer that does not retain the violet dye, but picks up the counterstain and appears pink to red.

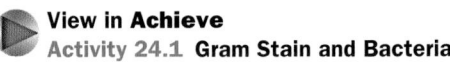

View in **Achieve**
Activity 24.1 **Gram Stain and Bacteria**

names are based on these shapes. A spherical bacterium is called a **coccus** (plural *cocci*). Cocci may live singly or may associate in two- or three-dimensional arrays such as chains, plates, blocks, or clusters of cells. A rod-shaped bacterium is called a **bacillus** (plural *bacilli*). A spiral bacterium (shaped like a corkscrew) is called a **spirillum** (plural *spirilla*). Bacilli and spirilla may be single, form chains, or gather in regular clusters. Among the other bacterial shapes are long filaments and branched filaments.

Less is known about the shapes of archaea because many of these organisms have never been seen. Many archaea are known only from samples of DNA from the environment. However, the species whose morphologies are known include cocci, bacilli, and even triangular and square species. Some flattened species grow on surfaces, arranged like sheets of postage stamps.

Cocci Bacilli Spirilla

0.50 μm   2 μm   0.50 μm

Left and middle photo courtesy of Janice Haney Carr/CDC; right photo courtesy of Rob Weyant/CDC

Figure 24.3 Bacterial Cell Shapes This composite, colorized micrograph shows the three most common bacterial shapes. Spherical cells are called cocci; those pictured are a species of *Enterococcus* from the mammalian gut. Rod-shaped cells are called bacilli; these *Escherichia coli* also reside in the gut. The helix-shaped spirilla are *Leptospira interrogans*, a human pathogen.

The nucleotide sequences of prokaryotes reveal their evolutionary relationships

Analyses of the nucleotide sequences of ribosomal RNA (rRNA) genes provided the first comprehensive evidence of evolutionary relationships among prokaryotes. Comparisons of rRNA genes are often used to identify microbes. For several reasons, rRNA is particularly useful for phylogenetic studies and identification purposes:

- rRNA was present in the common ancestor of all life and is therefore evolutionarily ancient.

- No free-living organism lacks rRNA, so rRNA genes can be compared across the tree of life.

- rRNA plays a critical role in translation in all organisms, so lateral transfer of rRNA genes among distantly related species is unlikely.

- rRNA has evolved slowly enough that gene sequences from even distantly related species can be aligned and analyzed.

Although studies of rRNA genes reveal much about the evolutionary relationships of prokaryotes, they don't always reveal the entire evolutionary history of these organisms. In some groups of prokaryotes, analyses of multiple gene sequences have suggested several different phylogenetic patterns. How could such differences among different gene sequences arise? Studies of whole prokaryotic genomes have revealed that even distantly related prokaryotes sometimes exchange genetic material.

Lateral gene transfer can lead to discordant gene trees

As noted earlier, prokaryotes reproduce by binary fission. If we could follow these divisions back through evolutionary time, we would be tracing the complete tree of life. At a much broader scale, these divisions of organisms lead to splits among the major

evolutionary lineages, or species of life (represented in highly abbreviated form in Appendix A). Because binary fission is an asexual process that replicates whole genomes, we would expect phylogenetic trees of prokaryotes constructed from most gene sequences (see Chapter 21) to reflect these same relationships.

Even though binary fission is an asexual process, there are other processes—including transformation, conjugation, and transduction—that allow the transfer of genetic information between some prokaryotes without reproduction. Thus prokaryotes can transfer and recombine their DNA with that of other individuals (this is sex in the genetic sense of the word), but this genetic exchange is not directly linked to reproduction, as it is in most eukaryotes.

Connect the Concepts Prokaryotic exchange of genetic material by conjugation and transformation is described in Key Concept 12.6 and Chapter 18, respectively.

From early in evolution to the present day, some genes have been moving "sideways" from one prokaryotic species to another, a phenomenon known as **lateral gene transfer** (sometimes called horizontal gene transfer). Lateral gene transfers are well documented among closely related species, and some have been documented even across the domains of life.

Consider, for example, the genome of *Thermotoga maritima*, a bacterium that can survive extremely high temperatures. By comparing the 1,869 gene sequences of *T. maritima* with sequences encoding the same proteins in other species, investigators found that some of this bacterium's genes have their closest relationships not with the genes of other bacterial species, but with the genes of archaea that live in similar extreme environments.

When genes involved in lateral transfer events are sequenced and analyzed, the resulting **gene trees** will not match the organismal tree in every respect (**Figure 24.4**). The individual gene trees will vary because the history of lateral transfer events is different for each gene. Biologists can reconstruct the underlying organismal phylogeny by comparing multiple genes (to produce a consensus tree) or by concentrating on genes that are unlikely to be involved in lateral gene transfer events. For example, genes that are involved in fundamental cellular processes (such as the rRNA genes discussed in the previous section) are unlikely to be replaced by the same genes from other species because functional, locally adapted copies of these genes are already present.

What kinds of genes are most likely to be involved in lateral gene transfer? Genes that result in a new adaptation that confers higher fitness on a recipient species are most likely to be transferred repeatedly among species. For example, genes that produce antibiotic resistance are often transferred among bacterial species on plasmids, especially under the strong selection pressure such as that imposed by modern antibiotic medications. Improper or overly frequent use of antibiotics can select for resistant strains of bacteria that are much harder to treat. This selection for antibiotic resistance explains why informed physicians have become more careful in prescribing antibiotics.

It is debatable whether lateral gene transfer has seriously complicated our attempts to resolve the tree of prokaryotic life. Recent work suggests that it has not. Lateral gene transfer rarely creates problems at higher taxonomic levels, even though it may

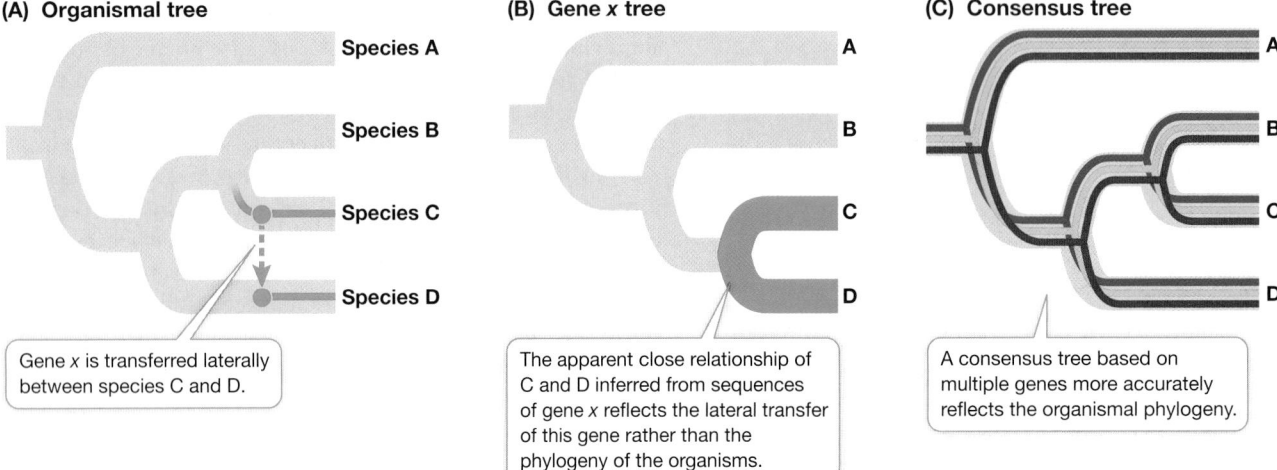

(A) Organismal tree

Species A
Species B
Species C
Species D

Gene *x* is transferred laterally between species C and D.

(B) Gene *x* tree

A
B
C
D

The apparent close relationship of C and D inferred from sequences of gene *x* reflects the lateral transfer of this gene rather than the phylogeny of the organisms.

(C) Consensus tree

A
B
C
D

A consensus tree based on multiple genes more accurately reflects the organismal phylogeny.

Figure 24.4 Lateral Gene Transfer Complicates Phylogenetic Relationships   (A) The phylogeny of four hypothetical prokaryotic species, two of which have been involved in a lateral transfer of gene *x*. (B) A tree based only on gene *x* shows the phylogeny of the laterally transferred gene, rather than the organismal phylogeny. (C) A consensus tree based on multiple genes is more likely to reflect the true organismal phylogeny, especially if those genes come from a stable core of genes involved in fundamental processes.

Q: Why are multiple lateral gene transfers between the same two branches on a phylogeny expected to be rare, at least compared with similarities inherited through the stable core?

complicate our understanding of the relationships among individual species. Some species clearly obtain some of their genes from otherwise distantly related species, so evolutionary histories of individual genes may differ within a single organism. But it is now possible to make nucleotide sequence comparisons involving entire genomes, and these studies are revealing a stable core of crucial genes that are uncomplicated by lateral gene transfer. Gene trees based on this stable core more accurately reveal the organismal phylogeny (see Figure 24.4). The problem remains, however, that only a very small proportion of the prokaryotic world has been described and studied.

The great majority of prokaryotic species have never been studied

Most prokaryotes have defied all attempts to grow them in pure culture, causing biologists to wonder how many species, and possibly even major clades, we might be missing. A window onto this problem was opened with the introduction of a new way of examining nucleic acid sequences. When biologists are unable to work with the whole genome of a single prokaryotic species, they can instead examine genomes collected from an environmental sample (such as a scoop of sediment from the seafloor). This technique is known as **environmental genomics**.

Biologists now routinely isolate gene sequences, or even whole genomes, from environmental samples such as soil and seawater. Comparing such sequences with previously known ones has revealed that an extraordinary number of the sequences represent new, previously unrecognized species. Biologists have described only about 10,000 species of bacteria and only a few hundred species of archaea (see Figure 1.12). The results of some environmental genomic studies suggest that there may be millions—perhaps hundreds of millions—of prokaryotic species. Other biologists put the estimate much lower, arguing that the high dispersal ability of many bacterial species greatly reduces endemism (i.e., the number of species restricted to a particular geographic area). Only the magnitude of these estimates differs, however; all sides agree that we have just begun to uncover Earth's prokaryotic diversity.

KEY CONCEPT
24.1 Recap and Assess

Bacteria and archaea are the two major lineages that arose from the first split in the tree of life. Eukaryotes evolved from a group of archaea that captured and incorporated bacteria through endosymbiosis. Mitochondria and chloroplasts are among the cellular structures of eukaryotes that are derived from endosymbiosis of bacteria. Although only about 10,000 species of bacteria and a few hundred species of archaea have been formally described, genetic evidence suggest there are many millions of species.

1. What findings support the separation of Bacteria and Archaea into separate domains?

2. The figure below shows an organismal tree in which gene *x* has undergone a lateral transfer event. Draw the phylogenetic tree you would expect based on gene *x*, as well as the phylogenetic tree you would expect based on a consensus of non-transferred genes.

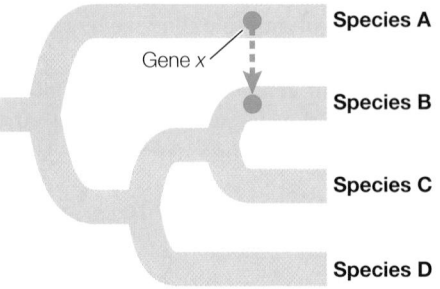

Gene *x*

Species A
Species B
Species C
Species D

3. How did eukaryotes arise through evolutionary contributions from both archaea and bacteria?

Despite the challenges of reconstructing prokaryotic phylogeny, taxonomists are starting to establish evolutionary classification systems for these organisms. With a full understanding that new information requires periodic revisions in these classifications, we next apply a current system of classification to organize our survey of prokaryotic diversity.

KEY CONCEPT 24.2 Prokaryotic Diversity Reflects the Ancient Origins of Life

Learning Objectives

24.2.1 Interpret a phylogenetic tree of major lineages of bacteria and archaea and use it to explain the origins of eukaryotes.

24.2.2 Discuss two lines of evidence that support the origin of life in a high-temperature environment.

24.2.3 Explain the role of bacteria in changing the oxygen content of Earth's atmosphere.

The prokaryotes were alone on Earth for a very long time, adapting to new environments and to changes in existing environments. They have survived to this day, in massive numbers and incredible diversity, and they are found nearly everywhere. In numbers of individuals, prokaryotes are far more abundant than eukaryotes. Individual prokaryotes in the oceans number more than 3×10^{28}— more than the number of stars in the universe. Closer to home, the individual bacteria living in your intestinal tract outnumber all the humans who have ever lived.

Given our still-fragmentary knowledge of prokaryotic diversity, it is not surprising that there are many different hypotheses about the relationships of the major groups of prokaryotes. In this book we use a classification system that is supported by nucleotide sequence data. We discuss a few of the major bacterial groups that have the broadest phylogenetic support and have received the most study, including hadobacteria, hyperthermophilic bacteria, firmicutes, actinobacteria, cyanobacteria, spirochetes, chlamydias, and proteobacteria (see Figure 24.1). Many other major groups of bacteria are known but are less thoroughly studied. We then describe the archaea, whose great diversity is just beginning to be fully understood and appreciated.

Two early-branching lineages of bacteria live at very high temperatures

Several lineages of bacteria and archaea are **extremophiles**: they thrive under extreme conditions that would kill most other organisms. The **hadobacteria**, for example, are thermophiles (Greek, "heat lovers"). The group's name is derived from Hades, the ancient Greek name for the underworld. Hadobacteria of the genus *Deinococcus* are resistant to radiation and can degrade nuclear waste and other toxic materials. They can also survive extremes of cold as well as hot temperatures. Another hadobacterium, *Thermus aquaticus*, was the source of the thermally stable DNA polymerase that was critical for the development of the polymerase chain reaction. *Thermus aquaticus* was originally isolated from a hot spring,

but it can be found wherever hot water occurs (including in many residential hot-water heaters).

The **hyperthermophilic bacteria** are another major group of extremophiles. Genera such as *Aquifex* live near volcanic vents and in hot springs, sometimes at temperatures near the boiling point of water. Some species of *Aquifex* need only hydrogen, oxygen, carbon dioxide, and mineral salts to live and grow. Species of the genus *Thermotoga* live deep underground in oil reservoirs as well as in other high-temperature environments.

Biologists have hypothesized that high temperatures characterized the ancestral conditions for life, given that most environments on early Earth were much hotter than those of today. Reconstructions of ancestral bacterial genes have supported this hypothesis by showing that the ancestral sequences functioned best at elevated temperatures. The presence of multiple lineages of extremophiles at the base of the bacterial tree (see Figure 24.1) also provides support for the origin of life in a high-temperature environment.

Firmicutes include some of the smallest cellular organisms

The **firmicutes** are also known as low-GC Gram-positive bacteria. The first part of this description (low-GC) derives from the relatively low ratio of G-C to A-T nucleotide base pairs in their DNA. The second part (Gram-positive) is less accurate: some of the firmicutes are in fact Gram-negative, and some have no cell wall at all. Despite these differences, phylogenetic analyses of DNA sequences support the monophyly of this bacterial group.

One group of firmicutes can produce resting structures called **endospores** (**Figure 24.5**). When a key nutrient such as nitrogen or carbon becomes scarce, the bacterium replicates its DNA and encapsulates one copy, along with some of its cytoplasm, in a

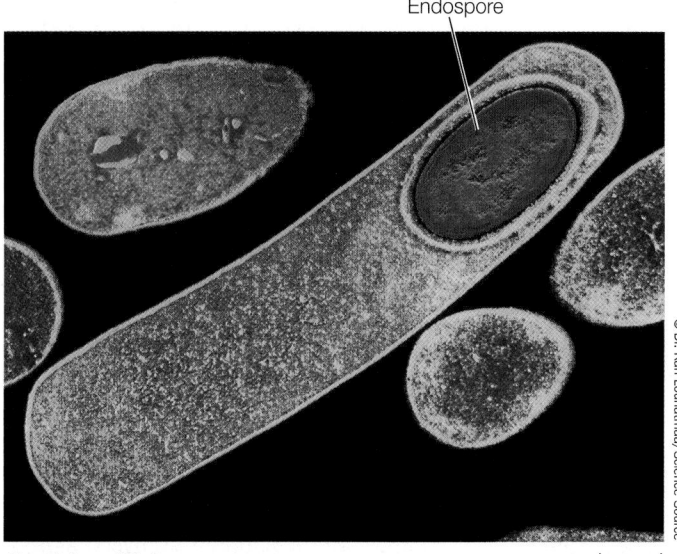

Endospore

Clostridium difficile

0.3 μm

© Dr. Kari Lounatmaa/Science Source

Figure 24.5 A Structure for Waiting Out Bad Times Under harsh conditions, some firmicutes can replicate their DNA and encase it in an endospore. The parent cell then breaks down, and the endospore survives in a dormant state until conditions improve.

Staphylococcus aureus   1 μm

© Eye of Science/Science Source

Figure 24.6 **Staphylococci**   "Grape clusters" are the usual arrangement of these firmicutes, which are often the cause of skin or wound infections.

Mycoplasma sp.   0.7 μm

© Don W. Fawcett/Science Source

Figure 24.7 **Tiny Cells**   With about one-fifth as much DNA as *E. coli* has, mycoplasmas are among the smallest known bacteria.

tough endospore wall heavily thickened with peptidoglycan and surrounded by a spore coat. The parent cell then breaks down, releasing the endospore. Endospore production is not a reproductive process, as the endospore merely replaces the parent cell. The endospore, however, can survive harsh environmental conditions that would kill the parent cell, such as high or low temperatures or drought, because it is dormant—its normal metabolic activity is suspended. Later, if it encounters favorable conditions, the endospore becomes metabolically active and divides, forming new cells that are like the parent cell. Members of this endospore-forming group include the many species of *Clostridium* and *Bacillus*. Some of their endospores can be reactivated after more than 1,000 years of dormancy. There are even credible claims of reactivation of *Bacillus* endospores that are millions of years old.

Endospores of *Bacillus anthracis* are the cause of anthrax. Anthrax is primarily a disease of cattle and sheep, but it can be fatal in humans. When the endospores sense macrophage (a type of white blood cell that digests cellular debris and foreign substances in mammalian blood), they reactivate and release toxins into the bloodstream. *Bacillus anthracis* has been used as a bioterrorism agent because it is relatively easy to transport large quantities of its endospores and release them among human populations, where they may be inhaled or ingested.

Members of the genus *Staphylococcus*—the **staphylococci** (**Figure 24.6**)—are abundant on the human body surface; they are responsible for boils and many other skin problems. *Staphylococcus aureus* is the best-known human pathogen in this genus; it is present in 20% to 40% of normal adults (and in 50%–70% of hospitalized adults). In addition to causing skin diseases, *S. aureus* can cause respiratory, intestinal, and wound infections.

Another interesting group of firmicutes, the **mycoplasmas**, lack cell walls, although some have a stiffening material outside the cell membrane. The mycoplasmas are among the smallest cellular organisms known (**Figure 24.7**). The smallest mycoplasmas have a diameter of about 0.2 μm. They are small in another crucial sense as well: they have less than half as much DNA as

most other prokaryotes. It has been speculated that the DNA in a mycoplasma, which codes for fewer than 500 proteins, may be close to the minimum amount required to encode the essential properties of a living cell.

Actinobacteria include major pathogens as well as valuable sources of antibiotics

Actinobacteria, also known as high-GC Gram-positive bacteria, have a higher ratio of G-C to A-T nucleotide base pairs than do the firmicutes (low-GC Gram-positives). These bacteria develop an elaborately branched system of filaments (**Figure 24.8**) that resembles the filamentous growth habit of fungi, albeit at a smaller scale. Some actinobacteria reproduce by forming chains of spores at the tips of the filaments. In species that do not form spores, the

Branch point

Actinomyces sp.   2 μm

© David M. Phillips/Science Source

Figure 24.8 **Actinobacteria Often Produce Branching Filaments** The tangled, branching filaments seen in this scanning electron micrograph are typical of this medically important bacterial group.

branched, filamentous growth ceases and the structure breaks up into typical cocci or bacilli, which then reproduce by binary fission.

The actinobacteria include several medically important bacteria. *Mycobacterium tuberculosis* causes tuberculosis, which kills 2 million people each year. Genetic data suggest that this bacterium may have been infecting our ancestors for almost 3 million years, making it the oldest known human bacterial pathogen. The genus *Streptomyces* produces streptomycin as well as hundreds of other antibiotics. We derive most of our antibiotics from actinobacteria.

Cyanobacteria were the first photosynthesizers

Cyanobacteria, sometimes called blue-green bacteria because of their pigmentation, are photosynthetic. They use chlorophyll *a* for photosynthesis and release oxygen gas (O_2); many species also fix nitrogen (discussed in Key Concept 24.3). The production of oxygen by these bacteria transformed the atmosphere of early Earth, eventually leading to the oxygen-rich atmosphere we know today.

Cyanobacteria carry out the same type of photosynthesis that is characteristic of eukaryotic photosynthesizers. They contain elaborate and highly organized internal membrane systems called **photosynthetic lamellae**. As mentioned in Key Concept 24.1, the chloroplasts of photosynthetic eukaryotes are derived from an endosymbiotic cyanobacterium. So all photosynthesis is either directly from cyanobacteria, or from eukaryotes with chloroplasts that are derived from cyanobacteria.

Cyanobacteria may live free as single cells or associate in multicellular colonies. Depending on the species and on growth conditions, these colonies may range from flat sheets one cell thick to filaments to spherical balls of cells. Some filamentous colonies of cyanobacteria differentiate into three specialized cell types: vegetative cells, spores, and heterocysts (**Figure 24.9**). **Vegetative cells** photosynthesize, **spores** are resting stages that can

survive harsh environmental conditions and eventually develop into new filaments, and **heterocysts** are cells specialized for nitrogen fixation. All of the known cyanobacteria with heterocysts fix nitrogen. Heterocysts also have a role in reproduction: when filaments break apart to reproduce, the heterocyst may serve as a breaking point.

Spirochetes move by means of axial filaments

Spirochetes are Gram-negative, motile bacteria characterized by a unique structure known as an axial filament, which is composed of multiple internal flagella running through the periplasmic space (**Figure 24.10A**). The cell body is a long cylinder coiled into a helix. The internal flagella begin at either end of the cell and overlap in the middle. Motor proteins connect the axial filament to the cell wall, enabling the corkscrew-like movement of the bacterium. Many spirochetes are parasites of humans; a few are pathogens, including those that cause syphilis (**Figure 24.10B**) and Lyme disease. Others live free in mud or water.

Chlamydias are extremely small parasites

Chlamydias are among the smaller bacteria (0.2–1.5 μm in diameter). They are obligate parasites—that is, they can live only as parasites in the cells of other organisms. It was once believed that their obligate parasitism resulted from an inability to produce ATP—that chlamydias were "energy parasites." However, genome sequencing indicates that chlamydias have the genetic capacity to produce at least some ATP. They can augment this capacity by using an enzyme called a translocase, which allows them to take up ATP from the cytoplasm of their host in exchange for ADP from their own cells.

These tiny, Gram-negative cocci are unique among prokaryotes because of a complex life cycle that involves two different

(A) *Anabaena* sp.
Heterocyst
Spore
Vegetative cells

(B) *Nostoc punctiforme*
Vegetative cells

0.4 μm

0.4 μm

A thick wall separates the cytoplasm of the nitrogen-fixing heterocyst from the surrounding environment.

Figure 24.9 Cyanobacteria **(A)** Some cyanobacteria form filamentous colonies containing three cell types. **(B)** Heterocysts are specialized for nitrogen fixation and may serve as a breaking point when filaments reproduce. **(C)** This pond in Canada has experienced eutrophication: phosphorus and other nutrients generated by human activity have accumulated, feeding an immense green mat (commonly referred to as "pond scum") that is made up of several species of free-living cyanobacteria.

Media Clip 24.1 Cyanobacteria
Life12e.com/mc24.1

(A)

Internal flagella

Cell wall

Outer
membook

50 nm

© J. A. Breznak & H. S. Pankratz/Biological Photo Service

(B)

Treponema pallidum

2 μm

© Paul W. Johnson/Biological Photo Service

Figure 24.10 Spirochetes Get Their Shape from Axial Filaments
(A) A spirochete from the gut of a termite, seen in cross section, shows the internal flagella that compose the axial filament, which these helical prokaryotes use to produce a corkscrew-like movement. (B) This spirochete species causes syphilis in humans.

forms of cells, elementary bodies and reticulate bodies (**Figure 24.11**). Various strains of chlamydias cause eye infections (especially trachoma), sexually transmitted diseases, and some forms of pneumonia in humans.

The proteobacteria are a large and diverse group

By far the largest bacterial group, in terms of numbers of described species, is the **proteobacteria**. The proteobacteria include many species of Gram-negative photoautotrophs (see Key Concept 24.3) that use light-driven reactions to metabolize sulfur, as well as dramatically diverse bacteria that bear no phenotypic resemblance to the photoautotrophic species. Genetic and morphological evidence indicates that the mitochondria of eukaryotes were derived from a proteobacterium by endosymbiosis.

Among the proteobacteria are some nitrogen-fixing genera, such as *Rhizobium*, and other bacteria that contribute to the global nitrogen and sulfur cycles. *Escherichia coli*, one of the most studied organisms on Earth, is a proteobacterium. So, too, are many of the most famous human pathogens, such as *Yersinia pestis* (which causes bubonic plague), *Vibrio cholerae* (cholera), and *Salmonella typhimurium* (gastrointestinal disease) (**Figure 24.12**).

The bioluminescent *Vibrio* shown at the opening of this chapter are also members of this group. There are many potential applications of the genes that encode bioluminescent proteins in

1 Elementary bodies are taken into a eukaryotic cell by phagocytosis...

2 ...where they develop into thin-walled reticulate bodies, which grow and divide.

Chlamydia psittaci   Host cell membrane

0.2 μm

Courtesy of Randall C. Cutlip

3 Reticulate bodies reorganize into elementary bodies, which are liberated by the rupture of the host cell.

Figure 24.11 Chlamydias Change Form Elementary bodies and reticulate bodies are the two cell forms of the chlamydia life cycle.

Salmonella typhimurium

0.5 μm

© CNRI/Science Source

Figure 24.12 Proteobacteria Include Many Familiar Bacteria
These conjugating (see Key Concept 12.6) cells of *Salmonella typhimurium* are exchanging genetic material. This pathogen causes a wide range of gastrointestinal illnesses in humans.

Media Clip 24.2 A Swarm of *Salmonella*
Life12e.com/mc24.2

Euonymus sp.

Figure 24.13 Crown Gall Crown gall, a type of tumor shown here growing on the stem of a *Euonymus* shrub, is caused by the proteobacterium *Agrobacterium tumefaciens*.

bacteria. Already, these genes are being inserted into the genomes of other species in which the resulting bioluminescence is used as a marker of gene expression. Futuristic proposals for making use of bioluminescence in bioengineered organisms include crop plants that glow when they become water-stressed and need to be irrigated, and glowing trees that could light highways at night in place of electric lights.

Although fungi cause most plant diseases, and viruses cause others, about 200 known plant diseases are of bacterial origin. Crown gall, with its characteristic tumors (**Figure 24.13**), is one of the most striking. The causal agent of crown gall is *Agrobacterium tumefaciens*, a proteobacterium that harbors a plasmid used in recombinant DNA studies as a vehicle for inserting genes into new plant hosts.

Gene sequencing enabled biologists to differentiate Archaea from Bacteria

The original identification of Archaea as a group distinct from Bacteria was based on phylogenetic relationships determined from rRNA gene sequences. This separation was supported when biologists sequenced the first complete archaeal genome, which consisted of 1,738 genes—more than half of which were unlike any genes ever found in Bacteria.

Archaea are known for living in extreme habitats such as those with high salinity (salt content), low oxygen concentrations, high temperatures, or high or low pH (**Figure 24.14**). Many archaea are not extremophiles, however—they are common in soil, in many aquatic environments, and in the guts of animals, for example.

Recent studies are revealing many new lineages of archaea, a few of which are shown in Figure 24.1: **Euryarchaeota**, **Crenarchaeota**, **Thaumarchaeota**, **Korarchaeota**, and **Lokiarchaeota**.

Experiment

Figure 24.14A What Is the Highest Temperature Compatible with Life?

Original Paper: K. Kashefi and D. R. Lovley. 2003. Extending the upper temperature limit for life. *Science* 301: 934.

Can any organism thrive at temperatures above 120°C? This is the temperature used for sterilization, known to destroy all previously described organisms. Kazem Kashefi and Derek Lovley isolated an unidentified prokaryote from water samples taken near a hydrothermal vent and found it survived and even multiplied at 121°C. The organism was dubbed "Strain 121," and its gene sequencing results indicate that it is an archaeal species.

HYPOTHESIS▶ Some prokaryotes can survive at temperatures above 120°C.

METHOD▶

1. Seal samples of unidentified, iron-reducing, thermal vent prokaryotes in tubes with a medium containing Fe^{3+} as an electron acceptor. Control tubes contain Fe^{3+} but no organisms.

2. Hold both tubes in a sterilizer at 121°C for 10 hours. If the iron-reducing organisms are metabolically active, they will reduce the Fe^{3+} to Fe^{2+} (as magnetite, which can be detected with a magnet).

RESULTS▶

The solids are attracted to the magnet, indicating that the organisms in this solution are alive and engaged in iron-reducing biochemical reactions.

Heating to 121°C sterilizes the control solution.

From K. Kashefi and D. R. Lovley. 2003. *Science* 301: 934. Courtesy of Kazem Kashefi.

CONCLUSION▶ Archaea of Strain 121 can survive at temperatures above the previously defined sterilization limit.

Figure 24.14B Work with the Data follows on next page.

The Lokiarchaeota were the first discovered members of the **Asgard archaea**—a group of particular interest because recent studies of their genomes show that they include the closest known prokaryotic relatives of eukaryotes.

Two characteristics shared by all archaea are the absence of peptidoglycan in their cell walls and the presence of lipids of distinctive composition in their cell membranes (see Table 24.1). The unusual lipids in the membranes of archaea are found in no bacteria or eukaryotes. Most lipids in bacterial and eukaryotic membranes contain unbranched long-chain fatty acids connected to glycerol molecules by **ester linkages**:

Work with the Data

FIGURE 24.14B What Is the Highest Temperature Compatible with Life?

Original Paper: K. Kashefi and D. R. Lovley. 2003. Extending the upper temperature limit for life. *Science* 301: 934.

After Kashefi and Lovley isolated Strain 121, they examined its growth at various temperatures. The table shows generation time (time between cell divisions) at nine temperatures.

Temperature (°C)	Generation time (hr)
85	10
90	4
95	3
100	2.5
105	2
110	4
115	6
120	20
130	No growth, but cells not killed

QUESTIONS▶

1. Make a graph from these data showing generation time as a function of temperature.

2. Which temperature appears to be closest to the optimum for the growth of Strain 121?

3. Note that no growth occurred at 130°C, but that the cells were not killed. How would you demonstrate that these cells were still alive?

Go to **Achieve** for a companion **Data in Depth** exercise.

In contrast, some lipids in membranes of archaea contain long-chain hydrocarbons connected to glycerol molecules by **ether linkages**:

$$\begin{array}{c} H \quad\quad H \\ | \quad\quad\quad | \\ -C-O-C- \\ | \quad\quad\quad | \\ H \quad\quad H \end{array}$$

In addition, the long hydrocarbon chains in the lipids of archaea are branched. One class of archaeal lipids contains glycerol at *both* ends of the hydrocarbons (**Figure 24.15**). These lipids form a lipid monolayer structure that is unique to archaea. They still fit into a biological membrane because they are twice as long as the typical lipids in the bilayers of other membranes. Lipid monolayers and bilayers are both found among the archaea.

Archaea live in extremely diverse environments

Most known crenarchaeotes are either thermophilic, acidophilic (acid loving), or both. Members of the genus *Sulfolobus* live in hot sulfur springs at temperatures of 70°C to 75°C. They become metabolically inactive at 55°C (131°F). Hot sulfur springs are also extremely acidic. *Sulfolobus* grows best in the range from pH 2 to pH 3, but some members of this genus readily tolerate pH values as low as 0.9. Most acidophilic thermophiles maintain an internal

Some archaea have long-chain hydrocarbons that span the membrane (a lipid monolayer).

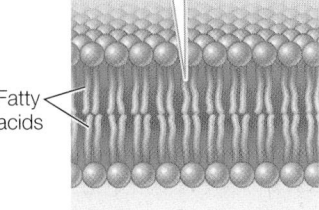

Other archaeal hydrocarbons fit the same template as those of bacteria and eukaryotes (a lipid bilayer).

Fatty acids

Figure 24.15 Membrane Architecture in Archaea   The long-chain hydrocarbons of many archaeal lipids have glycerol molecules at both ends, so that the membranes they form consist of a lipid monolayer. In contrast, the membranes of other archaea, bacteria, and eukaryotes consist of a lipid bilayer.

pH of 5.5 to 7 (close to neutral) in spite of their acidic environment. These and other crenarchaeotes thrive where very few other organisms can even survive (**Figure 24.16**).

Some species of euryarchaeotes are **methanogens**: they produce methane (CH_4) by reducing carbon dioxide as the key step in their energy metabolism. All of the methanogens are obligate anaerobes (see Key Concept 24.3). Comparison of their rRNA gene sequences has revealed a close evolutionary relationship among these methanogenic species, which were previously assigned to several different groups of bacteria.

Methanogenic euryarchaeotes release approximately 2 billion tons of methane gas into Earth's atmosphere each year, accounting for 80% to 90% of the methane that enters the atmosphere, including that produced in many animal digestive systems (including our own). Approximately one-third of this methane comes from methanogens living in the guts of ruminants such as cattle, sheep, and deer, and another large fraction comes from methanogens living

© Poul Riishede/Shutterstock.com

Figure 24.16 Some Crenarchaeotes Like It Hot   Thermophilic crenarchaeotes can thrive in the intense heat of volcanic hot sulfur springs such as these in Yellowstone National Park.

in the guts of termites and cockroaches. Methane is increasing in Earth's atmosphere by about 1% per year and contributes to the greenhouse effect. Part of that increase is due to increases in cattle and rice production and the methanogens associated with both.

Another group of euryarchaeotes, the **extreme halophiles** (salt lovers), live exclusively in very salty environments. Because they contain pink carotenoid pigments, these archaea are sometimes easy to see (**Figure 24.17**). Extreme halophiles grow in the Dead Sea and in brines of all types. The reddish pink spots that can occur on pickled fishes are colonies of halophilic archaea. Few other organisms can live in the saltiest homes that the extreme halophiles occupy—most would "dry" to death, losing too much water to the hypertonic environment. Extreme halophiles have been found in lakes with pH values as high as 11.5. These are the most alkaline environments inhabited by living organisms, and almost as alkaline as household ammonia.

Some of the extreme halophiles have a unique system for trapping light energy and using it to form ATP—without using any form of chlorophyll—when oxygen is in short supply. They use the pigment retinal (also found in the vertebrate eye) combined with a protein to form a light-absorbing molecule called bacteriorhodopsin.

Another member of Euryarchaeota, *Thermoplasma*, has no cell wall. It is thermophilic and acidophilic, its metabolism is aerobic, and it lives in coal deposits. Its genome of 1,100,000 base pairs is among the smallest (along with that of the mycoplasmas) found in any free-living organism, although some parasitic organisms have even smaller genomes.

Many of the known archaea are crenarchaeotes or euryarchaeotes, but studies of extreme environments have identified several lineages that are not closely related to either of these major groups. For example, the korarchaeotes are known only from DNA isolated directly from hot environments. The thaumarchaeotes were originally found in hot environments as well but have since been found to be common in marine surface waters, where they oxidize ammonia and appear to play an important role in the nitrogen cycle.

The lokiarchaeotes were discovered in 2015 by sequencing environmental samples from near a hydrothermal vent called Loki's Castle deep in the Arctic Ocean. An organism's genome was detected and sequenced from this deep-sea sample. Sequence analysis revealed that the organism was a distinct lineage of archaea, which was named *Lokiarchaeum*. Of particular interest was the finding that the *Lokiarchaeum* genome contains a large number of genes with cell membrane–related functions—genes and functions that had previously been known to occur only in eukaryotes.

After the discovery of *Lokiarchaeum*, biologists began to look for related archaea in other aquatic environments (both marine and freshwater) and discovered many new lineages of archaea with affinities to eukaryotes. Together, these close relatives of eukaryotes are known as the Asgard archaea (named after Asgard, one of the nine worlds of Norse mythology). The genomes of the Asgard archaea include many additional genes that were formerly thought to be restricted to eukaryotes, including genes that function in eukaryotes in controlling cell shape and cytoskeleton formation. These findings suggest that some of the properties that have long been associated exclusively with eukaryotes probably first arose within the Asgard archaea.

Figure 24.17 Extreme Halophiles Highly saline environments such as these commercial seawater evaporating ponds in San Francisco Bay are home to extreme halophiles. The archaea are easily visible here because of the rich red coloration of their carotenoid pigments.

KEY CONCEPT
24.2 Recap and Assess

Bacteria and archaea are highly diverse groups that survive in almost every imaginable habitat on Earth. Many prokaryotes can survive and even thrive in habitats where no eukaryotes can live, including extremely hot, acidic, or saline conditions. Eukaryotes are most closely related to the Asgard archaea, although endosymbioses of bacteria within eukaryotic cells contributed to the evolution of eukaryotic organelles.

1. Consider the differences between prokaryotes and eukaryotes shown in Table 24.1. Why might eukaryotes be more like archaea in some features and more like bacteria in others?

2. Given that all species of life have evolved for the same amount of time since their common origin, how would you respond to someone who characterizes prokaryotes as "primitive"? Include at least two examples of major groups of prokaryotes to support your answer.

3. How have bacteria changed Earth's atmosphere over the past 3 billion years?

4. What two lines of evidence can you use to support the idea that eukaryotes evolved from a lineage of the Asgard archaea?

Prokaryotes are found almost everywhere on Earth and live in a wide variety of ecosystems. In the next key concept we examine the contributions of prokaryotes to the functioning of those ecosystems.

KEY CONCEPT   **Ecological Communities**
24.3   Depend on Prokaryotes

Learning Objectives

24.3.1 Describe what biofilms are, how they are formed, and why they present problems for humans.

24.3.2 Explain how bacteria communicate through quorum sensing.

24.3.3 Explain the critical role of prokaryotes in the nitrogen cycle.

(A) Recruitment of organisms for biofilm community

(B) Dental plaque: a living biofilm community

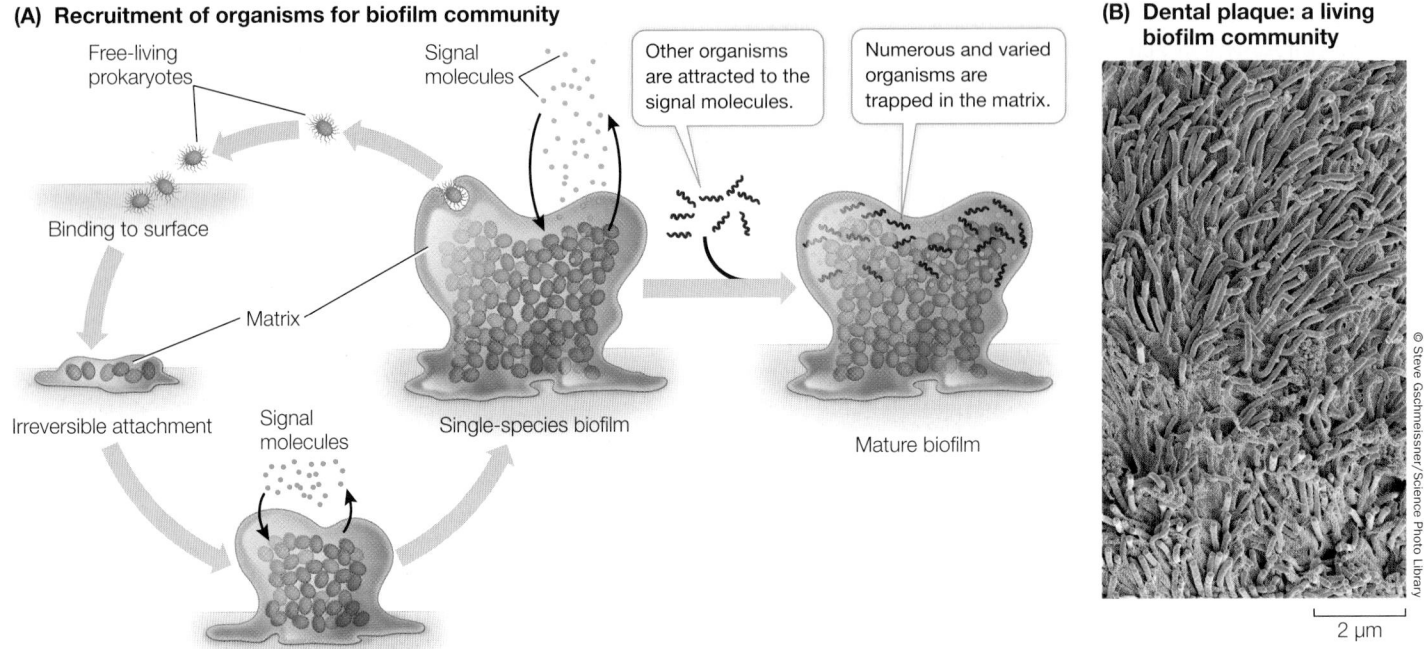

Figure 24.18 Forming a Biofilm **(A)** Free-living prokaryotes readily attach themselves to surfaces and form films that are stabilized and protected by a surrounding matrix. Once the population is large enough, the developing biofilm can send out chemical signals that attract other microorganisms. **(B)** Scanning electron micrography reveals a biofilm of dental plaque. The bacteria (red) are embedded in a matrix consisting of proteins from both bacterial secretions and saliva. (A after D. Monroe. 2007. *PLOS Biol* 5: e307.)

Prokaryotic cells do not usually live in isolation. Rather, they live in communities of many different species, often including microscopic eukaryotes. Whereas some microbial communities are harmful to humans, others provide important services. They help us digest our food, break down municipal waste, and recycle organic matter and chemical elements in the environment.

Many prokaryotes form complex communities

Some microbial communities form layers in sediments, and others form clumps a meter or more in diameter. Many microbial communities tend to form dense **biofilms**. Upon contacting a solid surface, the cells bind to that surface and secrete a sticky, gel-like polysaccharide matrix that traps other cells (**Figure 24.18**). Once a biofilm forms, the cells become more difficult to kill.

Biofilms are found in many places, and in some of those places they cause problems for humans. The material on our teeth that we call dental plaque is a biofilm. Pathogenic bacteria are difficult for the immune system—and modern medicine—to combat once they form a biofilm, which may be impermeable to antibiotics. Biofilms may form on just about any available surface, including contact lenses and artificial joint replacements. They foul metal pipes and cause corrosion, a major problem in steam-driven electricity generation plants. Fossil stromatolites—large, rocky structures made up of alternating layers of fossilized biofilm and calcium carbonate—are among the oldest remnants of life on Earth (see Figure 23.9A).

Some biologists are studying the chemical signals that prokaryotes use to communicate with one another and that trigger density-linked activities such as biofilm formation. One example of this type of communication—called **quorum sensing**—is found in the bioluminescent *Vibrio* that are shown in the opening photo of this chapter. How does quorum sensing work? As demonstrated in **Investigating Life: How Do Bacteria Communicate with One Another?**, individual *Vibrio* bacteria can excrete a signal that is detected by other individuals, and this signal then functions to turn on the genes that produce luciferase—an enzyme that produces bioluminescence when it is active.

Microbiomes are critical to the health of many eukaryotes

Although only a few bacterial species are pathogens, popular notions of bacteria as "germs" and fear of the consequences of infection cause many people to assume that most bacteria are harmful. Increasingly, however, biologists are discovering that the health of humans (as well as that of most other eukaryotes) depends in large part on the health of our **microbiomes**: the communities of bacteria and archaea that live in and on our bodies. Other communities of microbes live in close association with other multicellular organisms.

Every surface of your body is covered with diverse communities of bacteria (**Figure 24.19**). A recent study identified more than 1,000 species of bacteria that live on human skin. Inside your body, your digestive system teems with bacteria. When these communities are disrupted, they must be restored before the body can function normally.

Biologists are discovering that many complex health problems are linked to the disruption of our microbiomes. These diverse

▶Investigating LIFE   How Do Bacteria Communicate with One Another?

Experiment

Original Paper: M. B. Miller and B. L. Bassler. 2001. Quorum sensing in bacteria. *Annu Rev Microbiol* 55: 165–199.

Bonnie Bassler and her colleagues at Princeton University investigated how *Vibrio fischeri* bacteria communicate with one another. These bacteria produce bioluminescence when they are present in sufficiently high densities. In a normal *V. fischeri* bacterium, the following pathway produces bioluminescence when a bacterial colony becomes dense enough to produce sufficient signal:

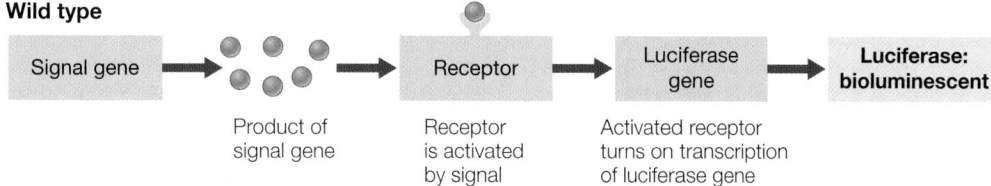

Wild type

Signal gene → Product of signal gene → Receptor (Receptor is activated by signal) → Luciferase gene (Activated receptor turns on transcription of luciferase gene) → **Luciferase: bioluminescent**

The fact that the bacteria emit light only when they are present in high densities suggests that the signal is used to communicate among nearby bacteria, alerting one another to their presence. But how can we tell that the signal produced by one bacterium is being received by another?

HYPOTHESIS▶ *V. fischeri* can transmit the signal molecule from one individual to another, thus communicating about the presence of other nearby bacteria.

METHOD▶

1. Select two mutant strains of *V. fischeri* incapable of emitting light on their own. In strain A, a mutation for the signal receptor renders the bacteria unable to detect the signal molecule, so they do not bioluminesce:

Strain A

Signal gene → Product of signal gene → Receptor (Receptor unable to detect signal) → Luciferase gene (Luciferase gene present but not transcribed) → **No luciferase produced; no bioluminescence**

2. Strain B bacteria have a mutated signal gene, so they do not produce a signal molecule, although the receptor and the luciferase gene are normal:

Strain B

Signal gene → No signal produced   Receptor (Receptor not activated) → Luciferase gene (Luciferase gene present but not transcribed) → **No luciferase produced; no bioluminescence**

3. Incubate samples of *V. fischeri* on agar petri plates, as follows:
    Plate 1: Strain A only
    Plate 2: Strain B only
    Plate 3: Half of plate with strain A, half with strain B

RESULTS▶

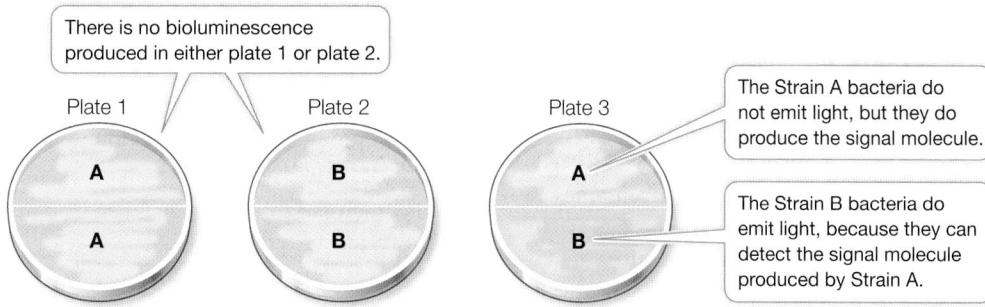

There is no bioluminescence produced in either plate 1 or plate 2.

Plate 1 — A / A

Plate 2 — B / B

Plate 3 — A / B

The Strain A bacteria do not emit light, but they do produce the signal molecule.

The Strain B bacteria do emit light, because they can detect the signal molecule produced by Strain A.

CONCLUSION▶ *Vibrio* bacteria can detect the signal molecule produced by other nearby bacteria *and* use this information to detect the presence of other bacteria.

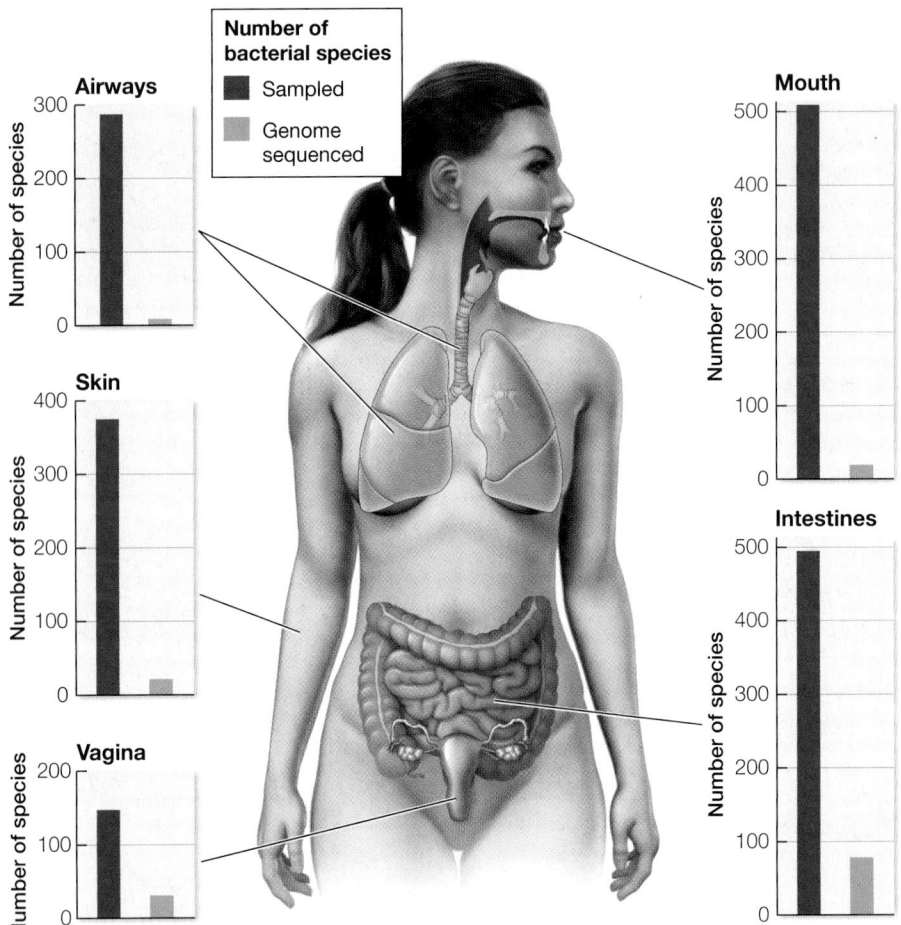

Figure 24.19 The Body's Microbiome Is Critical to the Maintenance of Health Surveys of the human microbiome have shown that this community includes thousands of diverse bacterial species that are adapted to grow in or on various parts of the body. Although we now know that the composition of this microbiome is closely associated with many aspects of human health, most of the component species are poorly characterized and remain largely unstudied by biologists. What has become clear is that, although the "subcommunities" in different parts of the body share similarities, each is a site-specific assemblage of many distinct species. (After Y. K. Lee and S. K. Mazmanian. 2010. *Science* 330: 1768–1773.)

microbes from a wider variety of sources. Many of the bacteria acquired in this way are not well suited for human health. Biologists have discovered that the incidence of many autoimmune diseases is much higher in people who were born by cesarean section and in those who were fed on formula as infants, compared with individuals who were born vaginally and breast-fed as infants. The difference appears to be related to the composition of the individual's original microbiome.

Humans use some of the metabolic products—especially vitamins B_{12} and K—produced by the microbiome living in the large intestine. Communities of bacteria line our intestines with a dense biofilm that is in intimate contact with the mucosal lining of the gut. This biofilm facilitates nutrient transfer from the intestine into the body, functioning like a specialized "tissue" that is essential to our health. This biofilm has a complex ecology that scientists have just begun to explore in detail—including the possibility that the species composition of an individual's gut microbiome may contribute to obesity.

Animals harbor a variety of microbes in their digestive tracts, many of which play important roles in digestion. Cattle depend on prokaryotes to break down plant material. Like most animals, cattle cannot produce cellulase, the enzyme needed to start the digestion of the cellulose that makes up the bulk of their plant food. However, bacteria living in a special section of the gut, called the rumen, produce enough cellulase to process the daily diet for the cattle.

microbial communities affect the expression of our genes and play a critical role in the development and maintenance of a healthy immune system. When our microbiomes contain an appropriate community of beneficial species, our bodies function normally. But these communities are strongly affected by our life experiences, by the food we eat, by the medicines we take, and by our exposure to various environmental toxins. The recent rapid increase in the rate of autoimmune diseases in humans—diseases in which the immune system begins to attack the body—has been linked to the changing diversity and composition of our microbiomes.

The early acquisition of an appropriate microbiome is critical for lifelong health. Normally, a human infant acquires much of its microbiome at birth, from the microbiome in its mother's vagina. Other components of the microbiome are also acquired from the mother, especially through breast feeding. Recent studies have shown that babies born by cesarean section, as well as babies that are bottle-fed on artificial milk formula, typically acquire

A small minority of bacteria are pathogens

The late nineteenth century was a productive era in the history of medicine—a time when bacteriologists, chemists, and physicians proved that many diseases are caused by microbial agents. During this time, the German physician Robert Koch laid down a set of four rules for establishing that a particular microorganism causes a particular disease:

1. The microorganism is always found in individuals with the disease.

2. The microorganism can be taken from the host and grown in pure culture.

3. A sample of the culture produces the same disease when injected into a new, healthy host.

4. The newly infected host yields a new, pure culture of microorganisms identical to those obtained in the second step.

These rules, called **Koch's postulates**, were important tools in a time when it was not widely understood that microorganisms cause disease. Although modern medical science has more powerful diagnostic tools, Koch's postulates remain useful. For example, physicians were taken aback in the 1980s when stomach ulcers—long accepted and treated as the result of excess stomach acid—were shown by Koch's postulates to be caused by the bacterium *Helicobacter pylori* (**Figure 24.20**).

For an organism to be a successful pathogen, it must:

- arrive at the body surface of a potential host;
- enter the host's body;
- evade the host's defenses;
- reproduce inside the host; and
- infect a new host.

Failure to complete any of these steps ends the disease cycle of a pathogenic organism. Yet in spite of the many defenses available to potential hosts, some bacteria are very successful pathogens. Pathogenic bacteria are often surprisingly difficult to combat, even with today's arsenal of antibiotics. One source of this difficulty is their ability to form biofilms.

For the host, the consequences of a bacterial infection depend on several factors. One is the invasiveness of the pathogen: its ability to multiply in the host's body. Another is its toxigenicity: its ability to produce toxins (chemical substances that are harmful to the host's tissues). *Corynebacterium diphtheriae*, the agent that causes diphtheria, has low invasiveness and multiplies only in the throat, but its toxigenicity is so great that the entire body is affected. In contrast, *Bacillus anthracis*, which causes anthrax, has low toxigenicity but is so invasive that the entire bloodstream ultimately teems with the bacteria.

There are two general types of bacterial toxins: exotoxins and endotoxins. **Endotoxins** are released when certain bacteria grow or lyse (burst). Endotoxins are lipopolysaccharides (complexes consisting of a polysaccharide and a lipid component) that form part of the outer bacterial membrane. Endotoxins are rarely fatal to the host; they normally cause fever, vomiting, and diarrhea. Among the endotoxin producers are some strains of the proteobacteria *Salmonella* and *Escherichia*.

Exotoxins are soluble proteins released by living, multiplying bacteria. They are highly toxic—often fatal—to the host. Human diseases induced by bacterial exotoxins include tetanus (*Clostridium tetani*), cholera (*Vibrio cholerae*), and bubonic plague (*Yersinia pestis*). Anthrax is caused by three exotoxins produced by *Bacillus anthracis*. Botulism is caused by exotoxins produced by *Clostridium botulinum*; these exotoxins are among the most poisonous ever discovered. The lethal dose for humans of one exotoxin of *C. botulinum* is about one-millionth of a gram. Nonetheless, much smaller doses of this exotoxin, marketed under various trade names (e.g., Botox®), are used to treat muscle spasms and for cosmetic purposes (temporary wrinkle reduction in the skin).

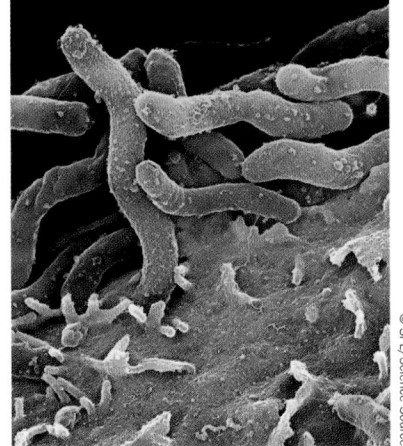

Helicobacter pylori

2 µm

© SPL/Science Source

Marshall and Warren set out to satisfy Koch's postulates:

Test 1

The microorganism must be present in every case of the disease.

Results: Biopsies from the stomachs of many patients revealed that the bacterium was always present if the stomach was inflamed or ulcerated.

Test 2

The microorganism must be cultured from a sick host.

Results: The bacterium was isolated from biopsy material and eventually grown in culture media in the laboratory.

Test 3

The isolated and cultured bacteria must be able to induce the disease.

Results: Marshall was examined and found to be free of bacteria and inflammation in his stomach. After drinking a pure culture of the bacterium, he developed stomach inflammation (gastritis).

Test 4

The bacteria must be recoverable from newly infected individuals.

Results: Biopsy of Marshall's stomach 2 weeks after he ingested the bacteria revealed the presence of the bacterium, now christened *Helicobacter pylori*, in the inflamed tissue.

Conclusion

Antibiotic treatment eliminated the bacteria and the inflammation in Marshall's stomach. The experiment was repeated on healthy volunteers, and many patients with gastric ulcers were cured with antibiotics. Thus Marshall and Warren demonstrated that the stomach inflammation leading to ulcers is caused by *H. pylori* infections in the stomach.

Figure 24.20 Satisfying Koch's Postulates Robin Warren and Barry Marshall of the University of Western Australia won the 2005 Nobel Prize in Physiology or Medicine for showing that ulcers are caused not by the action of stomach acid but by infection with the bacterium *Helicobacter pylori*. (After B. J. Marshall and J. R. Warren. 1983. *Lancet* 321: 1273–1275; B. J. Marshall et al. 1985. *Med J Aust* 142: 436–439.)

Prokaryotes have amazingly diverse metabolic pathways

Archaea and bacteria outdo the eukaryotes in terms of metabolic diversity. Although they are much more diverse in size and shape, eukaryotes draw on fewer metabolic mechanisms for their energy needs. In fact, much of the eukaryotes' energy metabolism is carried out in organelles—mitochondria and chloroplasts—that are endosymbiotic descendants of bacteria. The long evolutionary history of prokaryotes, during which they have had time to explore a wide variety of habitats, has led to the extraordinary diversity of their metabolic "lifestyles"—their use or nonuse of oxygen, their energy sources, their sources of carbon atoms, and the materials they release as waste products.

ANAEROBIC VERSUS AEROBIC METABOLISM   Some prokaryotes can live only by anaerobic metabolism because oxygen is poisonous to them. These oxygen-sensitive organisms are called **obligate anaerobes**. By definition, an anaerobe does not use oxygen as an electron acceptor for its respiration. Other prokaryotes, called **facultative anaerobes**, can alternate between an anaerobic mode of metabolism (such as fermentation) and an aerobic mode (such as cellular respiration) as conditions dictate. **Aerotolerant anaerobes** cannot conduct cellular respiration, but they are not damaged by oxygen when it is present. At the other extreme from the obligate anaerobes, some prokaryotes are **obligate aerobes**, unable to survive for extended periods in the *absence* of oxygen. Obligate aerobes require oxygen for cellular respiration.

NUTRITIONAL CATEGORIES   All living organisms face the same nutritional challenges: they must synthesize energy-rich compounds such as ATP to power their life-sustaining metabolic reactions, and they must obtain carbon atoms to build their own organic molecules. Biologists recognize four broad nutritional categories of organisms: photoautotrophs, photoheterotrophs, chemoautotrophs, and chemoheterotrophs. Prokaryotes are represented in all four groups (Table 24.2).

Photoautotrophs perform photosynthesis. They use light as their energy source and carbon dioxide (CO_2) as their carbon source. The cyanobacteria, like green plants and other photosynthetic eukaryotes, use chlorophyll *a* as their key photosynthetic pigment and produce oxygen gas (O_2) as a by-product of noncyclic electron transport.

There are other photoautotrophs among the bacteria, but these organisms use bacteriochlorophyll as their key photosynthetic pigment, and they do not produce O_2. Instead, some of these photosynthesizers produce particles of pure sulfur, because hydrogen sulfide (H_2S), rather than H_2O, is their electron donor for photophosphorylation. Many proteobacteria fit into this category. Bacteriochlorophyll molecules absorb light of longer wavelengths than the chlorophyll molecules used by other photosynthesizing organisms. As a result, bacteria using this pigment can grow in water under fairly dense layers of algae, using light of wavelengths that are not absorbed by the algae (**Figure 24.21**).

Photoheterotrophs use light as their energy source but must obtain their carbon atoms from organic compounds made by other organisms. Their "food" consists of organic compounds such as carbohydrates, fatty acids, and alcohols. For example, compounds released from plant roots (as in rice paddies) or from decomposing photosynthetic bacteria in hot springs are taken up by photoheterotrophs and metabolized to form building blocks for other compounds. Sunlight provides the ATP necessary for metabolism through photophosphorylation.

Chemoautotrophs obtain their energy by oxidizing inorganic substances, and they use some of that energy to fix carbon (convert inorganic carbon into organic carbon-based molecules). Some chemoautotrophs use reactions identical to those of the typical photosynthetic cycle, but others use alternative pathways for carbon fixation. Some bacteria oxidize ammonia or nitrite ions to form nitrate ions. Others oxidize hydrogen gas, hydrogen sulfide, sulfur, and other materials. Many archaea are chemoautotrophs.

Finally, **chemoheterotrophs** obtain both energy and carbon atoms from one or more complex organic compounds that have been synthesized by other organisms. Most known bacteria and archaea are chemoheterotrophs—as are all animals and fungi and many protists.

Although most chemoheterotrophs rely on the breakdown of organic compounds for energy, some chemoheterotrophic prokaryotes obtain their energy by breaking down inorganic substances. Organisms that obtain energy from oxidizing inorganic substances (both chemoautotrophs as well as some chemoheterotrophs) are also known as lithotrophs (Greek, "rock consumers").

Prokaryotes play important roles in element cycling

The metabolic diversity of the prokaryotes makes them key players in the cycles that keep elements moving through ecosystems.

Many prokaryotes are decomposers: organisms that metabolize organic compounds in dead organic material and return the products to the environment as inorganic substances. Prokaryotes, along with fungi, return tremendous quantities of carbon to the atmosphere as carbon dioxide, thus carrying out a key step in the carbon cycle.

The key metabolic reactions of many prokaryotes involve nitrogen or sulfur. For example, some bacteria carry out respiratory electron transport without using oxygen as an electron acceptor. These organisms use oxidized inorganic ions such as nitrate, nitrite, or sulfate as electron acceptors.

TABLE 24.2 | How Organisms Obtain Their Energy and Carbon

Nutritional category	Energy source	Carbon source
Photoautotrophs (some bacteria, some eukaryotes)	Light	Carbon dioxide
Photoheterotrophs (some bacteria)	Light	Organic compounds
Chemoautotrophs (some bacteria, many archaea)	Inorganic substances	Carbon dioxide
Chemoheterotrophs (some bacteria, some archaea, most eukaryotes)	Usually organic compounds; sometimes inorganic substances	Organic compounds

Figure 24.21 Bacteriochlorophyll Absorbs Long-Wavelength Light   The green alga *Ulva* contains chlorophyll, which absorbs no light of wavelengths longer than 750 nanometers (nm). Purple sulfur bacteria, which contain bacteriochlorophyll, can conduct photosynthesis using longer infrared wavelengths. As a result, these bacteria can grow under layers of algae. (After F. Haxo and L. R. Blinks. 1950. *J Gen Physiol* 33: 389–422; S. Mehrabi et al. 2001. *Biomol Eng* 18: 49–56.)

Algae contain chlorophyll *a*, which absorbs light of red and blue wavelengths.

Bacteria with bacteriochlorophyll can use long-wavelength (infrared) light, which the algae do not absorb, for their photosynthesis.

Examples include the **denitrifiers**, which release nitrogen to the atmosphere as nitrogen gas (N_2). These normally aerobic bacteria, mostly species of the genera *Bacillus* and *Pseudomonas*, use nitrate (NO_3^-) as an electron acceptor in place of oxygen if they are kept under anaerobic conditions:

$$2\,NO_3^- + 10\,e^- + 12\,H^+ \rightarrow N_2 + 6\,H_2O$$

Denitrifiers play a key role in the cycling of nitrogen through ecosystems. Without denitrifiers, which convert nitrate ions back into nitrogen gas, all forms of nitrogen would leach from the soil and end up in lakes and oceans, making life on land much more difficult.

Nitrogen fixers convert atmospheric nitrogen gas into a chemical form (ammonia) that is usable by the nitrogen fixers themselves as well as by other organisms:

$$N_2 + 6\,H \rightarrow 2\,NH_3$$

All organisms require nitrogen in order to build proteins, nucleic acids, and other important compounds. Nitrogen fixation is thus vital to life as we know it. This all-important biochemical process is carried out by a wide variety of archaea and bacteria (including cyanobacteria) but by no eukaryotes, so we depend on these prokaryotes for our very existence.

Connect the Concepts   For descriptions of the role of nitrogen in plant nutrition and in the global nitrogen cycle, see Key Concepts 34.3 and 56.4.

Ammonia is oxidized to nitrate in soil and in seawater by chemoautotrophic bacteria called **nitrifiers**. Bacteria of two genera, *Nitrosomonas* and *Nitrosococcus*, convert ammonia (NH_3) to nitrite ions (NO_2^-), and *Nitrobacter* oxidizes nitrite to nitrate (NO_3^-), the form of nitrogen most easily used by many plants. What do the nitrifiers get out of these reactions? Their metabolism is powered by the energy released by the oxidation of ammonia or nitrite. For example, by passing the electrons from nitrite through an electron transport system, *Nitrobacter* can make ATP and, using some of this ATP, can also make NADH. With this ATP and NADH, the bacterium can convert CO_2 and H_2O into glucose.

We have already seen the importance of the cyanobacteria in the cycling of oxygen: in ancient times, the oxygen generated by their photosynthesis converted Earth's atmosphere from an anaerobic to an aerobic environment (see Key Concept 23.2). Other prokaryotes—both bacteria and archaea—contribute to the cycling of sulfur. Deep-sea hydrothermal vent ecosystems depend on chemoautotrophic prokaryotes that are incorporated into large communities of crabs, mollusks, and giant worms, all living at a depth of 2,500 meters—below any hint of sunlight. These bacteria obtain energy by oxidizing hydrogen sulfide and other substances released in the near-boiling water flowing from volcanic vents in the ocean floor.

KEY CONCEPT
24.3 Recap and Assess

Many prokaryotes are beneficial and even necessary to other forms of life. Most animals, including humans, depend on a complex community of prokaryotes—a microbiome—to maintain health, especially of the immune and digestive systems. Prokaryotes play critical roles in cycling many elements through Earth's ecosystems, including carbon, nitrogen, and oxygen. Some bacteria are pathogenic—the direct causes of diseases. Finding cures for pathogenic diseases entails understanding how pathogens enter and reproduce in the body.

1. How do biofilms form, and why are they of special interest to researchers?

2. Why would elimination of all bacteria from a human gut be problematic from a health standpoint?

3. Why is nitrogen metabolism in prokaryotes vital to other organisms?

Before moving on to discuss the diversity of eukaryotic life, it is appropriate to consider another category of life that includes some pathogens: the viruses. Although they are not cellular, viruses are numerically among the most abundant forms of life on Earth. Their effects on other organisms are enormous. Where did viruses come from, and how do they fit into the tree of life? Biologists are still working to answer these questions.

24.4 Viruses Have Multiple Evolutionary Origins

Learning Objectives

24.4.1 Explain why viruses are difficult to place within the tree of life.

24.4.2 Contrast the "escaped component" and "reduced parasite" hypotheses for the origin of viruses, and name major groups of viruses that best support each hypothesis.

24.4.3 Explain why phage therapy is an active area of research.

Some biologists do not think of viruses as living organisms, primarily because they are not cellular and must depend on cellular organisms for basic life functions such as replication and metabolism. But viruses are derived from the cells of living organisms. They use the same essential forms of genetic information storage and transmission as do cellular organisms. Viruses infect all cellular forms of life—both prokaryotes and eukaryotes. They replicate, mutate, evolve, and interact with other organisms, often causing serious diseases in their hosts. Finally, viruses clearly evolve independently of other organisms, so it is almost impossible not to treat them as a part of life.

Viruses are abundant in many environments. In some freshwater and marine ecosystems, they can occur at densities of up to 10 million viruses per milliliter of water. Biologists estimate that there are approximately 10^{31} individual virus particles on Earth—about 1,000 times the number of cellular organisms on the planet. Viruses have an enormous effect on the ecology of the oceans. Every day, about one-half of the bacteria in the oceans are killed by viruses. Huge marine blooms of bacteria, such as the *Vibrio* bloom shown in the opening of this chapter, do not last for long because viral blooms soon follow the initial bacterial bloom. As the viruses increase, they begin to kill bacteria faster than the bacteria can reproduce.

Although viruses are found nearly everywhere on Earth and play an important role in many ecosystems, many aspects of their ecology and evolution are still poorly known. For example, several factors make virus phylogeny difficult to resolve. The tiny size of many virus genomes restricts the phylogenetic analyses that can be conducted to relate viruses to cellular organisms. Their rapid mutation rate, which results in rapid evolution of virus genomes, tends to cloud evolutionary relationships over long periods. There are no known fossil viruses (viruses are too small and delicate to fossilize), so the paleontological record offers no clues to virus origins. Finally, viruses are highly diverse (**Figure 24.22**). Several lines of evidence support the hypothesis that viruses have evolved repeatedly within each of the major groups of life. The difficulty in resolving deep evolutionary relationships of viruses makes a phylogeny-based classification difficult. Instead, viruses are placed in one of several functionally similar groups on the basis of the structure of their genomes (for example, whether the genomes are composed of RNA or DNA, and are double- or single-stranded). Most of these defined groups are not thought to represent monophyletic taxa, however.

Many RNA viruses probably represent escaped genomic components of cellular life

Although viruses are now obligate parasites of cellular species, many viruses may once have been cellular components involved in basic cellular functions—that is, they may be "escaped" components of cellular life that now evolve independently of their hosts.

NEGATIVE-SENSE SINGLE-STRANDED RNA VIRUSES   An example of a likely "escaped" biochemical function comes from viruses with genomes composed of single-stranded **negative-sense RNA**: RNA that is the complement of the mRNA needed for protein translation. Many of these negative-sense single-stranded RNA viruses have only a few genes, including one for an RNA-dependent RNA polymerase that allows them to make mRNA from their negative-sense RNA genome. Modern cellular organisms cannot generate mRNA in this manner (at least in the absence of viral infections), but scientists speculate that single-stranded RNA genomes may have been common in the distant past, before DNA became the primary molecule for genetic information storage.

A self-replicating RNA polymerase gene that began to replicate independently of a cellular genome could conceivably acquire a few additional protein-coding genes through recombination with its host's DNA. If one or more of these genes were to foster the development of a protein coat, the virus might then survive outside the host and infect new hosts. It is believed that this scenario has been repeated many times independently across the tree of life, given that many of the negative-sense single-stranded RNA viruses that infect organisms from bacteria to humans are not closely related to one another. In other words, negative-sense single-stranded RNA viruses do not represent a distinct taxonomic group, but rather exemplify a particular process of cellular escape that probably happened many different times.

Familiar examples of negative-sense single-stranded RNA viruses include the viruses that cause measles, mumps, rabies, and influenza (see Figure 24.22A).

POSITIVE-SENSE SINGLE-STRANDED RNA VIRUSES   The genome of another type of single-stranded RNA virus is composed of positive-sense RNA. Positive-sense genomes are already set for translation; no replication of the genome to form a complement strand is needed before protein translation can take place. Positive-sense single-stranded RNA viruses (see Figure 24.22B) are the most abundant and diverse class of viruses. Most of the viruses that cause diseases in crop plants are members of this group. These viruses kill patches of cells in the leaves or stems of plants, leaving live cells amid a patchwork of discolored dead tissue (giving them the name of mosaic, or mottle, viruses) (**Figure 24.23**). Other viruses in this group infect bacteria, fungi, and animals. Human diseases caused by positive-sense single-stranded RNA viruses include polio, hepatitis C, and the common cold. As is true of the other functionally defined groups of viruses, these viruses appear to have evolved multiple times across the tree of life from different groups of cellular ancestors.

RNA RETROVIRUSES   The RNA retroviruses are best known as the group that includes the human immunodeficiency viruses

(A)

50 nm

© Chris Bjornberg/Science Source

A negative-sense single-stranded RNA virus: The influenza A virus. This virus is responsible for seasonal influenza epidemics in humans. Surface view.

(B)

40 nm

© Dr. Linda M. Stannard, University of Cape Town/Science Source

A positive-sense single-stranded RNA virus: Coronavirus of a type thought to be responsible for severe acute respiratory syndrome (SARS). Surface view.

(C)

20 nm

© Dr. Hans Gelderblom/Visuals Unlimited, Inc.

An RNA retrovirus: One of the human immunodeficiency viruses (HIVs) that causes AIDS. Cutaway view.

(D)

20 nm

© BSIP SA/Alamy Stock Photo

A double-stranded DNA virus: One of the many herpes viruses (Herpesviridae). Different herpes viruses are responsible for many human infections, including chicken pox, shingles, cold sores, and genital herpes (HSV1/2). Surface view.

(E)

80 nm

© Dr. Harold Fisher/Visuals Unlimited, Inc.

A double-stranded DNA virus: Bacteriophage T4. Viruses that infect bacteria are referred to as bacteriophage (or simply phage). T4 attaches leglike fibers to the outside of its host cell and injects its DNA into the cytoplasm through its "tail" (pink structure in this rendition).

(F)

210 nm

© Dr. Raoult/Science Source

A double-stranded DNA mimivirus: This *Acanthamoeba polyphaga* mimivirus (APMV) has a genome larger than some prokaryotic genomes. Cutaway view.

Figure 24.22 Viruses Are Diverse Relatively small genomes and rapid evolutionary rates make it difficult to reconstruct phylogenetic relationships among viruses. Instead, viruses are classified largely by general characteristics of their genomes. The images here are computer artists' reconstructions based on cryoelectron micrographs.

Yellow areas are dead leaf cells, killed by a mosaic virus.

© Nigel Cattlin/Alamy Stock Photo

Figure 24.23 Mosaic Viruses Are a Problem for Agriculture Mosaic, or mottle, viruses are the most diverse class of viruses. This leaf is from an apple tree infected with a mosaic virus.

(HIVs; see Figure 24.22C). Like the previous two categories of viruses, RNA retroviruses have genomes composed of single-stranded RNA and probably evolved as escaped cellular components.

Retroviruses are so named because reverse transcription (see Key Concept 14.2) is a necessary component of their reproduction. When the retrovirus enters the nucleus of its vertebrate host, viral reverse transcriptase produces complementary DNA (cDNA) from the viral RNA genome and then replicates the single-stranded cDNA to produce double-stranded DNA. Another virally encoded enzyme called integrase catalyzes the integration of the new piece of double-stranded viral DNA into the host's genome. The viral genome is then replicated along with the host cell's DNA. The integrated retroviral DNA is known as a **provirus**.

Retroviruses are only known to infect vertebrates, although genomic elements that resemble portions of these viruses are a component of the genomes of a wide variety of organisms, including bacteria, plants, and many animals. Several retroviruses are associated with the development of various forms of cancer, as cells infected with these viruses are likely to undergo uncontrolled replication.

As retroviruses become incorporated into the genomes of their hosts, many become nonfunctional copies that are no longer expressed as functional viruses. These sequences may provide a record of ancient viral infections that plagued our ancestors. Humans, for example, carry about 100,000 fragments of **endogenous retroviruses** in our genome. These fragments make up about 8% of our DNA—a considerably larger fraction of our genome than the fraction that comprises all of our protein-coding genes (about 1.2% of our genome).

DOUBLE-STRANDED RNA VIRUSES   Double-stranded RNA viruses may have evolved repeatedly from single-stranded RNA ancestors—or perhaps vice versa. These viruses, which are not closely related to one another, infect organisms from throughout the tree of life. Many plant diseases are caused by double-stranded RNA viruses. Other viruses of this type cause many cases of infant diarrhea in humans.

Some DNA viruses may have evolved from reduced cellular organisms

Another class of viruses has a double-stranded DNA genome (see Figure 24.22D–F). This group is also almost certainly polyphyletic (with many independent origins). Many of the common phage that infect bacteria are double-stranded DNA viruses, as are the viruses that cause smallpox and herpes in humans.

Some biologists think that at least some of the DNA viruses may represent highly reduced parasitic organisms that have lost their cellular structure as well as their ability to survive as free-living species. For example, the mimiviruses, which are some of the largest DNA viruses (see Figure 24.22F), have a genome in excess of a million base pairs of DNA that encode more than 900 proteins. This genome is similar in size to the genomes of many parasitic bacteria and about twice as large as the genome of the smallest bacteria (**Figure 24.24**). Phylogenetic analyses of these DNA viruses suggest that they have evolved repeatedly from cellular organisms. Furthermore, recombination among different viruses may have allowed the exchange of various genetic modules, further complicating the history and origins of these viruses.

Viruses can be used to fight bacterial infections

Although some viruses cause devastating diseases, other viruses have been used to fight disease. Most bacterial diseases are treated today with antibiotics. Antibiotics were first discovered in the 1930s, but they were not widely used to treat bacterial diseases until the 1940s. So antibiotics were not yet available during World War I, when bacterial infections plagued the battlefields. Battlefield wounds were often infected by bacteria, and in the absence of antibiotics, these infections often led to

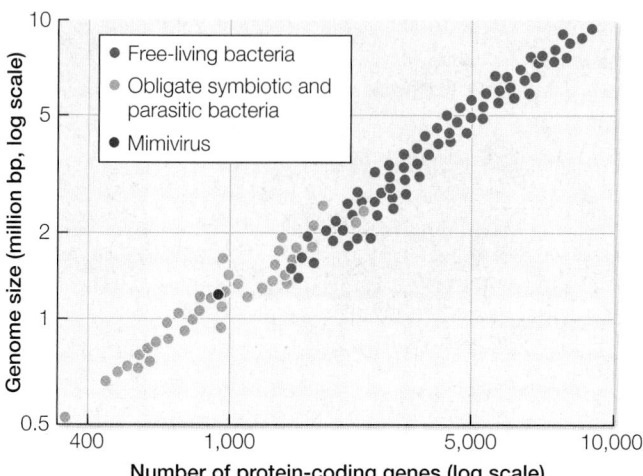

Figure 24.24 Mimiviruses Have Genomes Similar in Size to Those of Many Parasitic Bacteria   The genome of *Acanthamoeba polyphaga* mimivirus contains 1,181,404 base pairs and encompasses 911 protein-coding genes. This observation is consistent with the hypothesis that this virus evolved from a parasitic bacterium. (After S. J. Giovannoni et al. 2005. *Science* 309: 1242–1245.)

Q: Why do parasitic bacteria generally have smaller genomes and fewer protein-coding genes than do free-living bacteria?

the loss of limbs and lives. While trying to find a way to combat this problem, a physician named Felix d'Herelle discovered the first evidence of viruses that attack bacteria. He named these viruses bacteriophage, or "eaters of bacteria." Herelle extracted bacteriophage from the stool of infected patients. He then used these extracts to treat patients with deadly bacterial infections, including dysentery, cholera, and bubonic plague. This practice became known as **phage therapy**. After the war, phage therapy was widely used among the general public to treat bacterial infections of the skin and intestines.

▶ Media Clip 24.3 **Bacteriophage Attack *E. coli***
Life12e.com/mc24.3

Phage therapy was mostly replaced by the use of antibiotics in the 1930s and 1940s as physicians grew concerned about treating patients with live viruses. Phage therapy continued to be used in the Soviet Union but largely disappeared from western medical practice. Today, however, many antibiotics are losing their effectiveness as bacterial pathogens evolve resistance to these drugs. Phage therapy is once again an active area of research, and it is likely that bacteriophage will become increasingly important as weapons against bacterial diseases. One advantage that bacteriophage may have over antibiotics is that, like bacteria, bacteriophage can evolve. As bacteria evolve resistance to a strain of bacteriophage, biologists can select for new strains of bacteriophage that retain their effectiveness against the pathogens. In this way, biologists are using their understanding of evolution to combat the problem of antibiotic-resistant bacteria.

It appears that the enormous diversity of viruses is, at least in part, a result of their multiple origins from many different cellular organisms. It may be best to view viruses as spin-offs from the various branches on the tree of life—sometimes evolving independently of cellular genomes, sometimes recombining with them. One way to think of viruses is as the "bark" on the tree of life: certainly an important component all across the tree, but not quite like the main branches.

KEY CONCEPT
24.4 Recap and Assess

Viruses are highly diverse cellular forms of life that appear to have evolved independently from many different cellular organisms. Major groups of viruses are characterized by the nature of their genomes. Some viruses appear to have evolved from escaped components of cellular organisms, whereas other viruses may have evolved from parasitic cellular ancestors. Although some viruses are responsible for serious diseases, other viruses can be used to combat bacterial infections.

1. How does the size of viral genomes limit phylogenetic analyses of viruses?

2. What are the two main hypotheses of viral origins?

3. How can viruses be used to treat some human diseases?

InvestigatingLIFE

Q and A How and why do bacteria communicate with one another to assess their density?

As we explored in **Investigating Life: How Do Bacteria Communicate with One Another?**, *Vibrio* bacteria send a chemical signal that is received by other bacteria. This signal is needed to produce bioluminescence. As *Vibrio* populations increase in density, the bioluminescence becomes strong enough to be visible to humans and other animals. But how is bioluminescence an advantage to the bacteria? What is its function?

Although marine *Vibrio* are able to live independently, they truly thrive inside the guts of fishes and other marine animals. Inside a fish, *Vibrio* cells attach themselves to food particles, including phytoplankton, and are often expelled into the ocean as waste. How can they get back into their preferred environment? The bioluminescent glow produced by a dense colony of free-living *Vibrio* growing on phytoplankton attracts fishes, which consume the phytoplankton and thus ingest the bacteria—which gets the bacteria into a new host fish.

The bioluminescent *Vibrio* described in **Investigating Life: How Do Bacteria Communicate with One Another?**, *V. fischeri*, have evolved a symbiotic relationship with the Hawaiian bobtail squid (*Euprymna scolopes*). Chemicals produced by a developing squid embryo specifically "recruit" *V. fischeri* from the surrounding seawater. The bacteria then preferentially migrate to specific tissues that develop into a bioluminescent "light organ" in the belly of the adult squid (**Figure 24.25**). The tiny (about 3 cm long) adult squid feed while floating near the sea surface at night. The soft glow produced by the bioluminescent bacteria mimics the moonlight above, so the squid are less visible to potential predators coming at them from below.

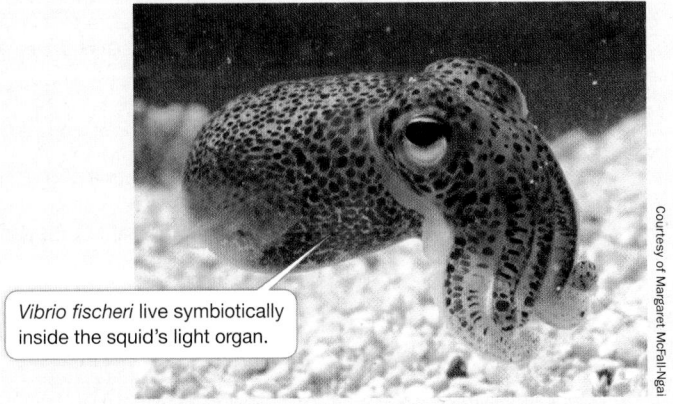

Vibrio fischeri live symbiotically inside the squid's light organ.

Figure 24.25 Bioluminescent Bacterial Symbionts
Vibrio bacteria within the light organ emit bioluminescence downward as the Hawaiian bobtail squid floats near the ocean surface to feed. At night, this allows the squid to blend in with the moonlight or starlight rather than becoming a target for a predator from below.

Future directions

Research that helps biologists understand how bacteria communicate, and allows us to disrupt or change communication signals among bacteria, is critical for developing treatment strategies against persistent bacterial infections. In the case of health-threatening bacteria that produce problematic biofilms, researchers hope to find ways to block the quorum-sensing signals that lead to the production of the matrix polysaccharides, thus preventing pathogenic biofilms from forming.

VISUAL SUMMARY 24

Steven Miller, Naval Research Laboratory, Monterey, CA

You should be able to relate each summary to the adjacent figures. If you go to this visual summary in **Achieve**, you can follow links to figures, animations, activities, and simulations that will help you consolidate the material.

KEY CONCEPT 24.1 Bacteria and Archaea Represent the First Split in the Tree of Life

Go to **Animation 24.1** and **Activity 24.1**

- The earliest split in the tree of life is between Bacteria and Archaea. Eukarya branched off from Archaea, having evolved specializations (such as a nucleus and organelles, some of which resulted from endosymbiosis with bacteria) that differentiate the eukaryotes from the **prokaryotes**.

- Bacteria and archaea can be differentiated by their cell walls. The cells walls of bacteria contain **peptidoglycan**, which is a target for the action of many antibiotics.

- Although **lateral gene transfer** sometimes complicates

our understanding of prokaryotic evolutionary history, prokaryotes are now principally classified by the nucleotide sequences of their genomes.

Questions

1. What evidence links the origin of eukaryotes more strongly with archaea than with bacteria?

2. How is peptidoglycan relevant to the function of antibiotics?

3. How does lateral gene transfer complicate the study of bacterial phylogeny?

Figure 24.4

KEY CONCEPT 24.2 Prokaryotic Diversity Reflects the Ancient Origins of Life

- Prokaryotes are the most numerous organisms on Earth, but only a small fraction of prokaryotic diversity has been characterized to date.

- Life on Earth likely originated in a high-temperature environment.

- Biotic communities depend on the actions of bacteria, which provide such important ecological services such as nitrogen fixation and oxygen production through photosynthesis.

- Archaea live in highly diverse environments and include many **extremophiles** and **methanogens**.

Questions

1. What lines of evidence support the origin of life in a hot environment?

2. How have cyanobacteria been critical in changing Earth's environment over the past 3 billion years?

3. What genes present in Asgard archaea were formerly thought to be found only in eukaryotic genomes?

Figure 24.16

© Poul Riishede/Shutterstock.com

KEY CONCEPT

24.3 Ecological Communities Depend on Prokaryotes

- **Microbiomes** are communities of prokaryotes that live in and on the bodies of multicellular organisms and are often important to the health of the hosts. Bacteria use processes such as **quorum sensing** to recruit members to their communities.

- **Koch's postulates** establish the criteria by which an organism may be classified as a pathogen. Relatively few bacteria—and no archaea—are known to be pathogens.

- Prokaryotic metabolism is diverse. Prokaryotes fall into four broad nutritional categories: **photoautotrophs, photoheterotrophs, chemoautotrophs,** and **chemoheterotrophs**.

- Prokaryotes play key roles in the cycling of elements such as nitrogen, oxygen, sulfur, and carbon.

Questions

1. How are biofilms important to human health?
2. When and where do newborn humans typically acquire their microbiomes?
3. Which group—bacteria, archaea, or eukaryotes—contains no organisms that use light as an energy source?

Figure 24.18

Recruitment of organisms for biofilm community

Free-living prokaryotes

Binding to surface

Matrix

Irreversible attachment

Signal molecules

Single-species biofilm

Growth and division, formation of matrix

Signal molecules

Mature biofilm

Dental plaque: a living biofilm community

© Steve Gschmeissner/Science Photo Library

2 μm

KEY CONCEPT

24.4 Viruses Have Multiple Evolutionary Origins

- Viruses have evolved many times from many different groups of cellular organisms. They are placed in groups according to the structure of their genomes, but these groups are not thought to represent monophyletic taxa.

- Viruses manipulate host genetic mechanisms in various ways to replicate themselves. **Retroviruses**, for example, use reverse transcriptase to produce complementary DNA from their viral RNA genome and then insert their genetic material into the host's genome.

- Some viruses cause serious diseases in cellular organisms, but bacteriophage can be used to treat bacterial infections, in a process known as **phage therapy**.

Questions

1. What molecules encode viral genomes?
2. How did endogenous retroviruses end up in vertebrate genomes?
3. Why did phage therapy fall out of use, and why is it once again of interest?

Figure 24.24

- Free-living bacteria
- Obligate symbiotic and parasitic bacteria
- Mimivirus

Genome size (million bp, log scale)

Number of protein-coding genes (log scale)

25 The Origin and Diversification of Eukaryotes

KEY CONCEPTS

25.1 Eukaryotes Acquired Features from Both Archaea and Bacteria

25.2 Major Lineages of Eukaryotes Diversified in the Precambrian

25.3 Protists Reproduce Sexually and Asexually

25.4 Protists Are Critical Components of Many Ecosystems

A bloom of dinoflagellates of the genus *Noctiluca* was responsible for this red tide in Puget Sound in the U.S. state of Washington.

© Don Paulson/PureStock/AGE Fotostock

▶Investigating LIFE

Predicting Toxic Red Tides

In summer 2005, a devastating red tide crippled the shellfish industry along the Atlantic coast of North America from Canada to Massachusetts. This red tide was produced by a bloom of dinoflagellates of the genus *Alexandrium*. These protists produce a powerful toxin that accumulates in clams, mussels, and oysters. A person who eats a mollusk contaminated with the toxin can experience a syndrome known as paralytic shellfish poisoning. Many people were sickened by eating mollusks that were harvested before the problem was diagnosed, and losses to the shellfish industry in 2005 were estimated at $50 million.

Several species of dinoflagellates produce toxic red tides in many parts of the world. Along the Gulf of Mexico, red tides caused by dinoflagellates of the genus *Karenia* produce a neurotoxin that affects the central nervous systems of fishes, which become paralyzed and cannot respire effectively. Huge numbers of dead fishes wash up on Gulf Coast beaches during a *Karenia* red tide. In addition, wave action can produce aerosols of the *Karenia* toxin, and these aerosols often cause asthma-like symptoms in humans on shore.

After the losses that resulted from the 2005 red tide, biologists at the Woods Hole Oceanographic Institution (WHOI) on Cape Cod began to monitor and model dinoflagellate populations off the New England coast. If biologists could accurately forecast future blooms, people in the area could be made aware of the problem in advance and adjust the shellfish harvest (and their eating habits) accordingly.

Biologists from WHOI monitored counts of dinoflagellates in the water and in seafloor sediments. They also monitored river runoff, water currents, water temperature and salinity, winds, and tides. An additional environmental factor was the "nor'easter" storms common along the New England coast. By correlating their measurements of these environmental factors with dinoflagellate counts, biologists produced a model that predicted growth of dinoflagellate populations.

In spring 2008, the WHOI team determined that all the factors were in place to produce another red tide like the one of 2005—if a nor'easter occurred to blow the dinoflagellates toward the coast. A nor'easter did occur at just the wrong time, and another red tide materialized in summer 2008, just as predicted. But this time, people were warned. Shellfish harvesters adjusted their harvest, and many fewer people were harmed by eating toxic mollusks.

 Red tides are harmful, but how are dinoflagellates beneficial to marine ecosystems? (Find the answer on page 578.)

Eukaryotes Acquired Features from Both Archaea and Bacteria

Learning Objectives

25.1.1 Explain the use of the term "protist" and describe the relationships of major protist groups to other eukaryotes.

25.1.2 List the five key events that led to the evolution of eukaryotes from a prokaryotic ancestor, and know how these events allowed for the establishment of unique cellular functions.

25.1.3 Explain how major changes in Earth's environment affected the evolution of the eukaryotic cell.

25.1.4 Classify the history of genes in a eukaryotic cell based on whether their origins are nuclear, mitochondrial, or chloroplastic.

We easily recognize trees, mushrooms, and insects as plants, fungi, and animals, respectively. But there is a dazzling assortment of other eukaryotic organisms—many microscopic, but some, like kelp, which grow very large—that do not fit into these three groups. Eukaryotes that are not plants, animals, or fungi have traditionally been called **protists**. But phylogenetic analyses reveal that many of the groups we commonly refer to as protists are not, in fact, closely related. Thus the term "protist" does not describe a monophyletic group, but is a term of convenience for "all the eukaryotes that are not plants, animals, or fungi."

The unique characteristics of the eukaryotic cell lead scientists to conclude that the eukaryotes are monophyletic, and that a single eukaryotic ancestor diversified into the many different protist lineages as well as giving rise to the plants, fungi, and animals. As we saw in Key Concept 24.1, eukaryotes are a specialized group of archaea that acquired a cell nucleus. The mitochondria and chloroplasts of eukaryotes, however, are clearly derived from bacterial lineages (see Figure 24.1).

Biologists have hypothesized that the origin of eukaryotes from a specialized archaeal ancestor was followed by the endosymbioses with bacterial lineages that led to the origin of mitochondria and chloroplasts. Some biologists prefer to view the origin of eukaryotes as the fusion of lineages from the two prokaryotic groups. This difference is largely a semantic one that hinges on the subjective point at which we deem the eukaryotic lineage to have become definitively "eukaryotic." In either case, we can make some reasonable inferences about the events that led to the evolution of a new cell type, bearing in mind that the environment underwent an enormous change—from low to high availability of free atmospheric oxygen (O_2)—during the course of these events.

The modern eukaryotic cell arose in several steps

Several events were important in the origin of the modern eukaryotic cell (**Figure 25.1**):

- The origin of a flexible cell surface
- The origin of a cytoskeleton

- The origin of a nuclear envelope, which enclosed a genome organized into chromosomes
- The appearance of digestive vacuoles
- The acquisition of mitochondria and chloroplasts via endosymbiosis

FLEXIBLE CELL SURFACE   We presume that ancient prokaryotic organisms, like most present-day prokaryotic cells, had firm cell walls. The first step toward the eukaryotic condition was the loss of the cell wall by an archaean. This wall-less condition occurs in some present-day prokaryotes.

Consider the possibilities open to a flexible cell without a firm wall, starting with cell size. As a cell grows larger, its surface area-to-volume ratio decreases (see Figure 5.2). Unless the surface area can be increased, the cell volume will reach an upper limit. If the cell's surface is flexible, however, it can fold inward and become more elaborate, creating more surface area for gas and nutrient exchange. With a surface flexible enough to allow infolding, the cell can exchange materials with its environment rapidly enough to sustain a larger volume and more rapid metabolism (see Figure 25.1, steps 1–2). Furthermore, a flexible surface can pinch off bits of the environment, bringing them into the cell by endocytosis. These infoldings of the cell surface, which also exist in some modern prokaryotes, were important for the evolution of large eukaryotic cells.

CHANGES IN CELL STRUCTURE AND FUNCTION   Other early steps that were important for the evolution of the eukaryotic cell involved increased compartmentalization and complexity of the cell (see Figure 25.1, steps 3–7):

- The development of a more complex cytoskeleton
- The formation of ribosome-studded internal membranes, some of which surrounded the DNA
- The enclosure of the cell's DNA in a nucleus
- The formation of a flagellum from microtubules of the cytoskeleton
- The evolution of digestive vacuoles

Until a few years ago, biologists thought that cytoskeletons were restricted to eukaryotes. Improved imaging technology and molecular analyses have now revealed homologs of many cytoskeletal proteins in prokaryotes, so simple cytoskeletons evolved before the origin of eukaryotes. The cytoskeleton of a eukaryote, however, is much more developed and complex than that of a prokaryote. This greater development of microfilaments and microtubules supports the eukaryotic cell and allows it to manage changes in shape, to distribute daughter chromosomes, and to move materials from one part of its larger cell to other parts. In addition, the presence of microtubules in the cytoskeleton allowed some cells to develop the characteristic eukaryotic flagellum.

The DNA of a prokaryotic cell is attached to a site on its cell membrane. If that region of the cell membrane were to fold into the cell, the first step would be taken toward the evolution of a nucleus, a primary feature of the eukaryotic cell. The nuclear envelope appeared early in the eukaryotic lineage. The next step was probably phagocytosis—the ability to engulf and digest other cells.

1 The protective cell wall was lost.

Cell wall

DNA

2 Infolding of the cell membrane added surface area without increasing the cell's volume.

3 Cytoskeleton (microfilament and microtubules) increased in complexity.

4 Internal membranes studded with ribosomes formed.

5 As regions of the infolded cell membrane enclosed the cell's DNA, a precursor of a nucleus formed.

6 Microtubules from the cytoskeleton formed the eukaryotic flagellum, enabling propulsion.

7 Early digestive vacuoles evolved into lysosomes using enzymes from the early endoplasmic reticulum.

8 Mitochondria formed through endosymbiosis with a proteobacterium.

9 Endosymbiosis with cyanobacteria led to the development of chloroplasts.

Flagellum

Mitochondrion

Chloroplast

Nucleus

Figure 25.1 Evolution of the Eukaryotic Cell   The loss of a firm cell wall allowed the cell membrane to fold inward and create more surface area, which facilitated the evolution of larger cells. As cells grew larger, cytoskeletal complexity increased, and the cell became increasingly compartmentalized. Endosymbioses involving bacteria gave rise to mitochondria and (in photosynthetic eukaryotes) to chloroplasts.

Q: How could you use DNA sequencing and phylogenetic analysis to test the endosymbiotic origins hypothesis for mitochondria and chloroplasts?

ENDOSYMBIOSIS   At the same time the processes we have just outlined were taking place, cyanobacteria were generating oxygen as a product of photosynthesis. The increasing concentrations of oxygen in the oceans, and eventually in the atmosphere, had disastrous consequences for most organisms of the time, which were unable to tolerate the newly oxidizing environment. But some prokaryotes evolved strategies to use the increasing oxygen, and—fortunately for us—so did some of the new phagocytic eukaryotes.

At about this time, endosymbiosis began to play a role in eukaryotic evolution (see Figure 25.1, steps 8–9). The theory of endosymbiosis proposes that certain organelles are the descendants of prokaryotes engulfed, but not digested, by ancient eukaryotic cells. One crucial event in the history of eukaryotes was the incorporation of a proteobacterium that evolved into the mitochondrion. Initially the new organelle's primary function was probably to detoxify O_2 by reducing it to water. Later this reduction became coupled with the formation of ATP in cellular respiration. After this step, the essential eukaryotic cell was complete.

> **Connect the Concepts** You may wish to review the reactions of cellular respiration in Key Concept 5.3.

Photosynthetic eukaryotes are the result of yet another endosymbiotic step: the incorporation of a prokaryote related to today's cyanobacteria, which became the chloroplast.

Chloroplasts have been transferred among eukaryotes several times

Eukaryotes in several different groups possess chloroplasts, and groups with chloroplasts appear in several distantly related eukaryotic clades. Some of these groups differ in the photosynthetic pigments their chloroplasts contain. And not all chloroplasts are limited to a pair of surrounding membranes—in some microbial eukaryotes, chloroplasts are surrounded by three or more membranes. We now view these observations as evidence of a remarkable series of endosymbioses. This conclusion is supported by extensive evidence from electron microscopy and nucleic acid sequence comparisons.

All chloroplasts trace their ancestry back to the engulfment of one cyanobacterium by a larger eukaryotic cell. This event, the step that first gave rise to the photosynthetic eukaryotes, is known as **primary endosymbiosis (Figure 25.2A)**. The cyanobacterium, a Gram-negative bacterium,

(A) Primary endosymbiosis

Eukaryote

Cyanobacterium

Peptidoglycan

Cyanobacterium outer membrane

Cyanobacterium inner membrane

Host cell membrane

Over evolutionary history, one of these three membranes was lost.

Host cell nucleus

Chloroplast

Peptidoglycan has been lost except in glaucophytes.

(B) Secondary endosymbiosis

Host eukaryotic cell

Chloroplast-containing eukaryotic cell

Host membrane (from endocytosis) encloses the engulfed cell.

A trace of the engulfed cell's nucleus is retained in some groups.

The inner of these two membranes has been lost in euglenids and dinoflagellates.

Figure 25.2 Endosymbiotic Events in the Evolution of Chloroplasts
(A) A single instance of primary endosymbiosis ultimately gave rise to all of today's chloroplasts. **(B)** Secondary endosymbiosis—the uptake and retention of a chloroplast-containing cell by another eukaryotic cell—took place several times, independently.

▶ View in **Achieve**
Animation 25.1 **Family Tree of Chloroplasts**

had both an inner and an outer membrane (see Figure 24.2B). Thus the original chloroplasts had two surrounding membranes: the inner and outer membranes of the cyanobacterium. Remnants of the peptidoglycan-containing cell wall of the bacterium are present in the form of a bit of peptidoglycan between the chloroplast membranes of glaucophytes, the first eukaryotic group to branch off

following primary endosymbiosis (as we will see in Chapter 26). Primary endosymbiosis also gave rise to the chloroplasts of the red algae, green algae, and land plants. The red algal chloroplast retains certain pigments of the original cyanobacterial endosymbiont that are absent in green algal chloroplasts.

Almost all remaining photosynthetic eukaryotes are the result of additional rounds of endosymbiosis. For example, the photosynthetic euglenids derived their chloroplasts from **secondary endosymbiosis (Figure 25.2B)**. Their ancestor took up a unicellular green alga, retaining its chloroplast and eventually losing the rest of the constituents of the alga. This history explains why the photosynthetic euglenids have the same photosynthetic pigments as the green algae and land plants. It also accounts for the third membrane of the euglenoid chloroplast, which is derived from the euglenid's cell membrane (as a result of endocytosis). An additional round of endosymbiosis—**tertiary endosymbiosis**—occurred when a dinoflagellate apparently lost its chloroplast and took up another protist that had acquired its chloroplast through secondary endosymbiosis.

KEY CONCEPT
25.1 Recap and Assess

The modern eukaryotic cell probably arose from an ancestral prokaryotic archaean in several steps, including the origin of a flexible cell surface and the enclosure of the genetic material in a nucleus. Later, endosymbioses of proteobacteria and cyanobacteria led to the origins of mitochondria and chloroplasts, respectively.

1. Why was the development of a flexible cell surface a key event for eukaryotic evolution?

2. Explain how increased availability of atmospheric oxygen (O_2) could have influenced the evolution of the eukaryotic cell.

Background for Questions 3–4: Ribosomal RNA (rRNA) genes are present in the nuclear genome of eukaryotes. There are also rRNA genes in the genomes of mitochondria and chloroplasts. Therefore photosynthetic eukaryotes have three different sets of rRNA genes, which encode the structural RNA of three separate sets of ribosomes. The gene tree below shows the evolutionary relationships among rRNA gene sequences isolated from the nuclear genomes of humans, yeast, and corn; from a prokaryotic archaean (*Halobacterium*), a proteobacterium (*E. coli*), and a cyanobacterium (*Chlorobium*); and from the mitochondrial and chloroplast genomes of corn.

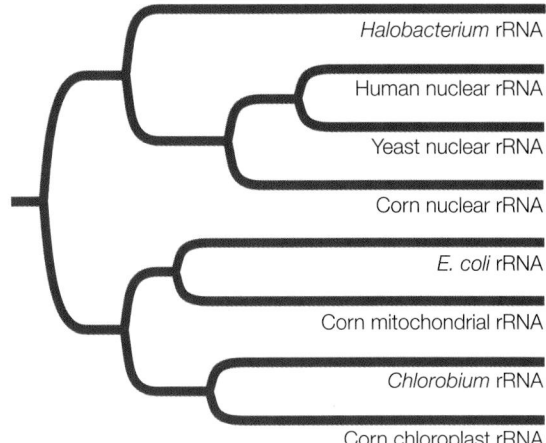

Halobacterium rRNA

Human nuclear rRNA

Yeast nuclear rRNA

Corn nuclear rRNA

E. coli rRNA

Corn mitochondrial rRNA

Chlorobium rRNA

Corn chloroplast rRNA

3. Why are the three rRNA genes of corn *not* one another's closest relatives?

4. How would you explain the closer relationship of the mitochondrial rRNA gene of corn to the rRNA gene of *E. coli* than to the nuclear rRNA genes of other eukaryotes? Can you explain the relationship of the rRNA gene from the chloroplast of corn to the rRNA gene of the cyanobacterium?

5. Explain why the term "protists" does not refer to a formal taxonomic group.

The features that eukaryotes gained from prokaryotic archaea and bacteria have allowed them to exploit many different environments. This led to the evolution of great diversity among eukaryotes, beginning with a radiation that started in the Precambrian.

KEY CONCEPT 25.2 Major Lineages of Eukaryotes Diversified in the Precambrian

Learning Objectives

25.2.1 Distinguish among the major groups of microbial eukaryotes (alveolates, stramenopiles, rhizarians, excavates, and amoebozoans).

25.2.2 Justify the position that it is relatively easy for multicellularity to evolve.

25.2.3 Elaborate on why protists are important to our medical and economic concerns.

Most eukaryotes can be placed in one of eight major clades that began to diversify about 1.5 billion years ago: alveolates, stramenopiles, rhizarians, excavates, plants, amoebozoans, fungi, and animals (**Figure 25.3**). Plants, fungi, and animals each have close protist relatives (such as the choanoflagellate relatives of animals), which we will discuss along with those major multicellular eukaryotic groups in Chapters 26–31.

Each of the five major groups of protist eukaryotes covered in this chapter consists of organisms with enormously diverse body forms and nutritional lifestyles. Some protists are motile, whereas others do not move. Some protists are photosynthetic, whereas others are heterotrophic. Most protists are unicellular, but some are multicellular. Most protists are microscopic, but a few are huge (giant kelps, for example, can grow to half the length of a football field). We refer to the unicellular species of protists as **microbial eukaryotes**, but keep in mind that there are large, multicellular protists as well.

Multicellularity has arisen dozens of times across the evolutionary history of eukaryotes. Four of the origins of multicellularity resulted in large organisms that are familiar to most people: plants, animals, fungi, and brown algae (the last are a group of stramenopiles). In addition, there are dozens of smaller and less familiar groups among the eukaryotes that include multicellular species. Recent experimental studies have shown that artificial selection for multicellularity can produce repeated, convergent evolution of multicellular forms over just a few months in some normally unicellular eukaryotic species. In addition, many unicellular species retain individual identities but nonetheless associate in large multicellular colonies. There is a near-continuum between fully integrated, multicellular organisms on the one hand and loosely integrated multicellular colonies of cells on the other. Biologists do not always agree on where to draw the line between the two.

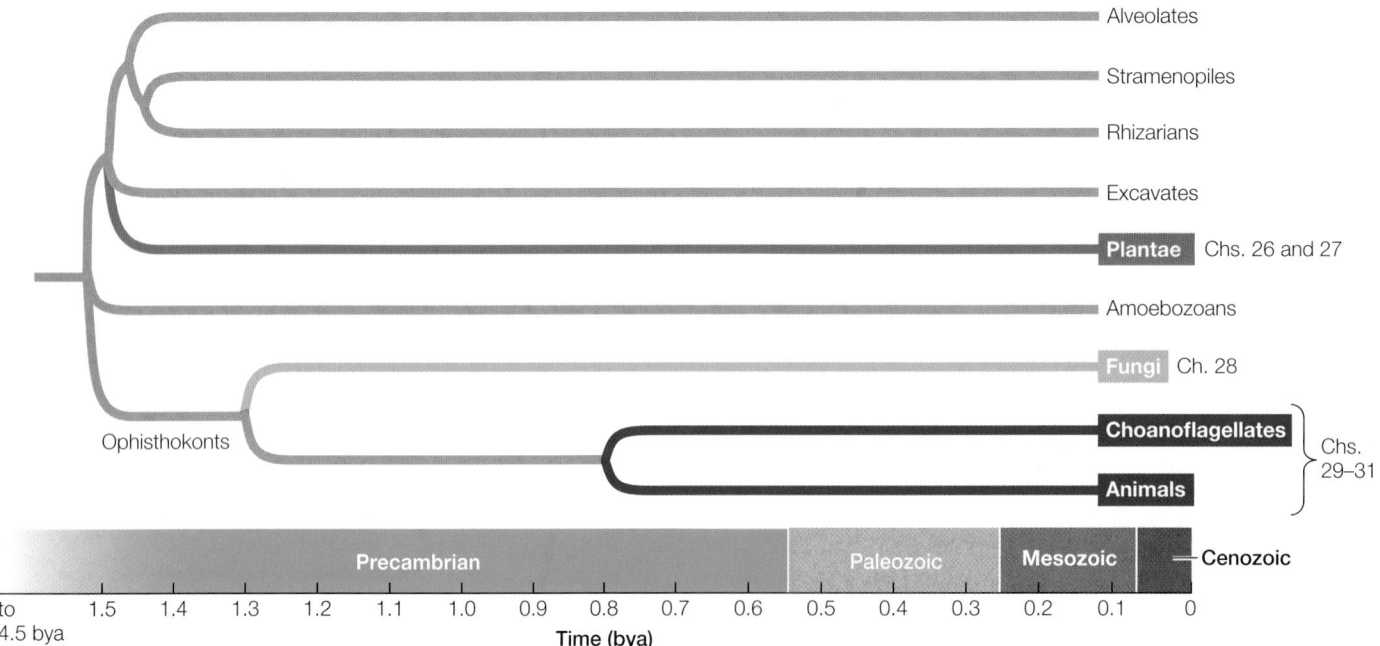

Figure 25.3 Precambrian Divergence of Major Eukaryotic Groups A phylogenetic tree shows a current hypothesis and estimated time line for the origin of the major groups of eukaryotes. The rapid divergence of major lineages between 1.5 and 1.4 billion years ago (bya) makes reconstruction of their precise relationships difficult. The major multicellular groups (tinted boxes) will be covered in subsequent chapters.

Biologists used to classify protists largely on the basis of their life histories and reproductive features. In recent years, however, electron microscopy and gene sequencing have revealed many new patterns of evolutionary relatedness among these groups. Analyses of slowly evolving gene sequences are making it possible to explore evolutionary relationships among eukaryotes in ever greater detail and with greater confidence. Nonetheless, some substantial areas of uncertainty remain, and lateral gene transfer may complicate efforts to reconstruct the evolutionary history of protists (as was also true for prokaryotes; see Key Concept 24.1). Today we recognize great diversity among the many distantly related protist clades.

Alveolates have sacs under their cell membranes

Alveolates are so named because they possess sacs, called alveoli, just beneath their cell membranes, which may play a role in supporting the cell surface. All alveolates are unicellular, and most are photosynthetic, but they are diverse in body form. The alveolate groups we consider in detail here are the dinoflagellates, apicomplexans, and ciliates.

DINOFLAGELLATES   Most **dinoflagellates** are marine and photosynthetic; they are important primary producers of organic matter in the oceans. Although fewer *species* of dinoflagellates live in fresh water, individuals can be abundant in freshwater environments. The dinoflagellates are of great ecological, evolutionary, and morphological interest. A distinctive mixture of photosynthetic and accessory pigments gives their chloroplasts a golden brown color. Some dinoflagellate species cause red tides, as discussed at the start of this chapter. Other species are photosynthetic endosymbionts that live within the cells of other organisms, including invertebrate animals (such as corals; see Investigating Life: Can Corals Reacquire Dinoflagellate Endosymbionts Lost to Bleaching?) and other marine protists (see Figure 25.12A). Still others are nonphotosynthetic and live as parasites within other marine organisms.

Dinoflagellates have a distinctive appearance. They generally have two flagella, one in an equatorial groove around the cell, the other starting near the same point as the first and passing down a longitudinal groove before extending into the surrounding medium (**Figure 25.4**). Some dinoflagellates can take on different forms, including amoeboid ones, depending on environmental conditions. It has been claimed that the dinoflagellate *Pfiesteria piscicida* can occur in at least two dozen distinct forms, although this claim is highly controversial. In any case, this remarkable dinoflagellate, when present in large enough numbers, is harmful to fishes and can both stun and feed on them.

APICOMPLEXANS   The exclusively parasitic **apicomplexans** derive their name from the apical complex, a mass of organelles contained in the apical end (the tip) of the cell. These organelles help the apicomplexan invade its host's tissues. For example,

Amphidiniopsis kofoidii

Equatorial groove   Flagellum   Longitudinal groove   20 μm

Figure 25.4 A Dinoflagellate   The presence of two flagella is characteristic of many dinoflagellates, although these appendages are contained within deep grooves and thus are seldom visible. One flagellum lies within the equatorial groove and provides forward thrust and spin to the organism. The second flagellum originates in the longitudinal groove and acts like the rudder of a boat.

 Media Clip 25.1 A Dinoflagellate Shows Off Its Flagellum
Life12e.com/mc25.1

the apical complex enables *Plasmodium*, the causative agent of malaria, to enter its target cells in the human body after transmission by a mosquito.

Like many obligate parasites, apicomplexans have elaborate life cycles featuring asexual and sexual reproduction through a series of very dissimilar life stages (see Figure 25.20). In many species, these life stages are associated with two different types of host organisms, as is the case with *Plasmodium*. Another apicomplexan, *Toxoplasma*, alternates between cats and rats to complete its life cycle. A rat infected with *Toxoplasma* loses its fear of cats, which makes it more likely to be eaten by, and thus transfer the parasite to, a cat.

CILIATES   The **ciliates** are named for their numerous hairlike cilia, which are shorter than, but otherwise identical to, eukaryotic flagella. The ciliates are much more complex in body form than are most other unicellular eukaryotes (**Figure 25.5**). Their definitive characteristic is the possession of two types of nuclei (whose roles we describe in Key Concept 25.3 when we discuss protist reproduction). Almost all ciliates are heterotrophic, although a few contain photosynthetic endosymbionts.

Paramecium, a frequently studied ciliate genus, exemplifies the complex structure and behavior of ciliates (**Figure 25.6**). The slipper-shaped cell is covered by an elaborate pellicle, a structure composed principally of an outer membrane and an inner layer of closely packed, membrane-enclosed sacs (the alveoli) that surround the bases of the cilia. Defensive organelles called trichocysts are also present in the pellicle. In response to

(A) *Paramecium* sp. **(B)** *Didinium nasutum* **(C)** *Trichodina* sp.

Cilia 10 μm

Bands of cilia 7 μm

Oral surface

Cilia

15 μm

Figure 25.5 Diversity among the Ciliates **(A)** A free-swimming organism, this *Paramecium* belongs to a ciliate group whose members have many cilia of uniform length. **(B)** The barrel-shaped *Didinium*

nasutum feeds on other ciliates, including *Paramecium*. Its cilia occur in two separate bands. **(C)** The parasite *Trichodina* creates suction with its ring of cilia that help attach it to the surface of a fish host.

a threat, a microscopic explosion expels the trichocysts in a few milliseconds, and they emerge as sharp darts, driven forward at the tip of a long, expanding filament.

The cilia provide *Paramecium* with a form of locomotion that is generally more precise than locomotion by flagella. A *Paramecium* can coordinate the beating of its cilia to propel itself either forward or backward in a spiraling manner. It can also back off swiftly when it encounters a barrier or a negative stimulus. The coordination of ciliary beating is probably the result of a differential distribution of ion channels in the cell membrane near the two ends of the cell.

Organisms living in fresh water are hypertonic to their environment. Many freshwater protists, including *Paramecium*, address this problem by means of specialized **contractile vacuoles** that excrete the excess water the organisms constantly take in by osmosis. The excess water collects in the contractile vacuoles, which then contract and expel the water from the cell.

Paramecium and many other protists engulf solid food by endocytosis, forming a **digestive vacuole** within which the food is digested (**Figure 25.7**). Smaller vesicles containing digested food pinch away from the digestive vacuole and enter the cytosol. These tiny vesicles provide a large surface area across which the products of digestion can be absorbed by the rest of the cell.

▶ **View in Achieve**
Animation 25.2 Digestive Vacuoles

Stramenopiles typically have two unequal flagella, one with hairs

A morphological synapomorphy of most **stramenopiles** is the possession of rows of tubular hairs on the longer of their two flagella. Some stramenopiles lack flagella, but they are descended from ancestors that possessed flagella. The stramenopiles include the diatoms and the brown algae, which are photosynthetic, and the oomycetes, which are not.

DIATOMS   All of the **diatoms** are unicellular, although some species associate in filaments. Many have sufficient carotenoids in their chloroplasts to give them a yellow or brownish color. All of them synthesize carbohydrates and oils as photosynthetic storage products. Diatoms lack flagella except in male gametes.

Architectural magnificence on a microscopic scale is the hallmark of the diatoms. Almost all diatoms deposit silica (hydrated silicon dioxide) in their cell walls. The cell wall of a diatom is constructed in two pieces, with the top overlapping the bottom like the top of a petri dish. The silica-impregnated walls have

Micronuclei function in genetic recombination.

The macronucleus controls the cell's activities.

Contractile vacuole

Alveoli

Cilia

Digestive vacuole

Oral groove

Anal pore

Pellicle

Trichocyst

Fibrils

Alveolus

Cilium

Figure 25.6 Anatomy of *Paramecium* *Paramecium*, with its many specialized organelles, exemplifies the complex body form of ciliates.

▶ **View in Achieve**
Activity 25.1 Anatomy of *Paramecium*

Experiment

Figure 25.7   The Role of Vacuoles in Ciliate Digestion

Original Paper: S. O. Mast. 1947. The food-vacuole in *Paramecium*. *Biol Bull* 92: 31–72.

An acidic environment is known to aid digestion in many multicellular organisms. Do ciliates also use acid to obtain nutrients?

HYPOTHESIS▶   The digestive vacuoles of *Paramecium* produce an acidic environment that allows the organism to digest food particles.

METHOD▶

1. Feed *Paramecium* yeast cells stained with Congo red, a dye that is red at neutral or basic pH but turns green at acidic pH.

2. Under a light microscope, observe the formation and degradation of digestive vacuoles within the *Paramecium*. Note time and sequence of color (i.e., acid level) changes.

RESULTS▶

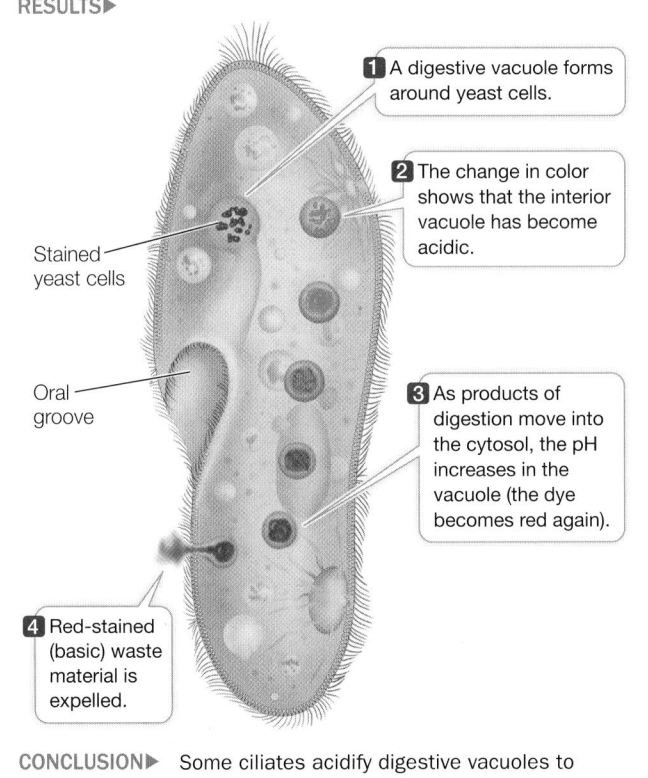

Stained yeast cells

Oral groove

1 A digestive vacuole forms around yeast cells.

2 The change in color shows that the interior vacuole has become acidic.

3 As products of digestion move into the cytosol, the pH increases in the vacuole (the dye becomes red again).

4 Red-stained (basic) waste material is expelled.

CONCLUSION▶   Some ciliates acidify digestive vacuoles to assist in the breakdown of food.

© James Solliday/Biological Photo Service

Diatoms display either radial (circular) symmetry…

…or bilateral (left–right) symmetry.

25 µm

Figure 25.8 **Diatom Diversity**   This bright-field micrograph illustrates the variety of species-specific forms found among the diatoms.

▶ **Media Clip 25.2 Diatoms in Action**
Life12e.com/mc25.2

fuse. The resulting zygote then grows substantially in size before a new cell wall is laid down.

Diatoms are found in all the oceans and are frequently present in great numbers. They are major photosynthetic producers in coastal waters (see Key Concept 25.4) and are among the dominant organisms in the dense "blooms" of phytoplankton that occasionally appear in the open ocean. Diatoms are also common in fresh water and even occur on the wet surfaces of terrestrial mosses.

BROWN ALGAE   The **brown algae** obtain their namesake color from the carotenoid fucoxanthin, which is abundant in their chloroplasts. The combination of this yellow-orange pigment with the green of chlorophylls *a* and *c* yields a brownish tinge. All brown algae are multicellular, and some are extremely large. Giant kelps such as those of the genus *Macrocystis* may be up to 60 meters long.

▶ **Media Clip 25.3 A Kelp Forest**
Life12e.com/mc25.3

The brown algae are almost exclusively marine. They are composed either of branched filaments (**Figure 25.9A**) or of leaflike growths (**Figure 25.9B**). Some float in the open ocean; the most famous example is the genus *Sargassum*, which forms dense mats in the Sargasso Sea in the mid-Atlantic. Most brown algae, however, attach themselves to rocks near the shore. A few thrive only where they are regularly exposed to heavy surf. All of the attached forms develop a specialized structure, called a holdfast, that literally glues them to the rocks. The "glue" of the holdfast is alginic acid, a gummy polymer found in the walls of many brown algal cells. In addition to its function in holdfasts, alginic acid cements algal cells and filaments together. It is harvested and used by humans as an emulsifier in ice cream, cosmetics, and other products.

intricate patterns unique to each species (**Figure 25.8**). Despite their remarkable morphological diversity, all diatoms are symmetrical—either bilaterally (with "right" and "left" halves) or radially (with the type of symmetry possessed by a circle).

Diatoms reproduce both sexually and asexually. Asexual reproduction by binary fission is somewhat constrained by the stiff cell wall. Both the top and bottom of the "petri dish" become tops of new "dishes" without changing appreciably in size. As a result, the new cell made from the former bottom is smaller than the parent cell. If this process continued indefinitely, one cell line would simply vanish, but sexual reproduction largely solves this potential problem. Gametes are formed, shed their cell walls, and

(A) Filamentous growth pattern   **(B) Leaf-like growth pattern**

Himanthalia elongata   *Postelsia palmaeformis*   Holdfasts

Figure 25.9 Brown Algae   (A) This seaweed illustrates the filamentous growth form of the brown algae. **(B)** Sea palms exemplify the leaflike growth form of brown algae. Sea palms and many other brown algal species are "glued" to the rocks by tough, branched structures called holdfasts that can withstand the pounding of the surf.

OOMYCETES   The **oomycetes** are the water molds and their terrestrial relatives. Water molds are filamentous and stationary. They are **absorptive heterotrophs**—that is, they secrete enzymes that digest large food molecules into smaller molecules that they can absorb. They are all aquatic and **saprobic**—meaning they feed on dead organic matter. If you have seen a whitish, cottony mold growing on dead fishes or dead insects in water, it was probably a water mold of the common genus *Saprolegnia* (**Figure 25.10**).

Some other oomycetes, such as the downy mildews, are terrestrial. Although most of the terrestrial oomycetes are harmless or helpful decomposers of dead matter, a few are plant parasites that attack crops such as avocados, grapes, and potatoes.

Oomycetes were once classified as fungi. However, we now know that their similarity to fungi is only superficial, and that the oomycetes are more distantly related to the fungi than are many other eukaryotic groups, including humans (see Figure 25.3). For example, the cell walls of oomycetes are typically made of cellulose, whereas those of fungi are made of chitin.

Rhizarians typically have long, thin pseudopods

The three primary groups of **rhizarians**—cercozoans, foraminiferans, and radiolarians—are unicellular and mostly aquatic. The rhizarians have contributed their shells to ocean sediments, some of which have become terrestrial features over the course of geological history.

CERCOZOANS   The **cercozoans** are a diverse group with many forms and habitats. Some are aquatic; others live in soil. One group of cercozoans possesses chloroplasts derived from a green alga by secondary endosymbiosis, and those chloroplasts contain a trace of the alga's nucleus.

FORAMINIFERANS   Some **foraminiferans** secrete external shells of calcium carbonate (**Figure 25.11**). These shells have accumulated over time to produce much of the world's limestone. Some foraminiferans live as plankton; others live on the seafloor. Living

Saprolegnia sp.

3 mm

Figure 25.10 An Oomycete   The filaments of a water mold radiate from the carcass of a beetle.

1 mm

Figure 25.11 Building Blocks of Limestone   Some foraminiferans secrete calcium carbonate to form shells. The shells of different species have distinctive shapes. Over millions of years, the shells of foraminiferans have accumulated to form limestone deposits.

(A) *Amphilonche heteracantha*

(B) *Thyrsocyrtis* sp.

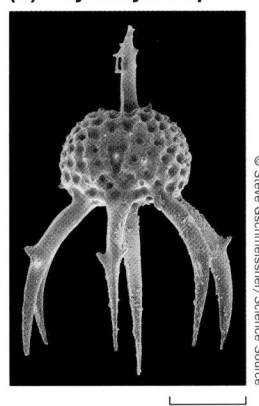

© Larry Jon Friesen

© Steve Gschmeissner/Science Source

50 μm

100 μm

Figure 25.12 Radiolarians Exhibit Distinctive Pseudopods and Radial Symmetry **(A)** The radiolarians are distinguished by their thin, stiff pseudopods and by their radial symmetry. The pigmentation seen at the center of this radiolarian's glassy endoskeleton is imparted by endosymbiotic dinoflagellates. **(B)** The endoskeleton secreted by a radiolarian.

foraminiferans have been found 10,896 meters down in the western Pacific's Challenger Deep—the deepest point in the world's oceans. At that depth, however, they cannot secrete normal shells because the surrounding water is too poor in calcium carbonate.

In living planktonic foraminiferans, long, threadlike, branched pseudopods extend through numerous microscopic apertures in the shell and interconnect to create a sticky, reticulated net, which the foraminiferans use to catch smaller plankton. In some foraminiferan species, the pseudopods provide locomotion.

RADIOLARIANS **Radiolarians** are recognizable by their thin, stiff pseudopods, which are reinforced by microtubules (**Figure 25.12A**). These pseudopods greatly increase the surface area of the cell, and they help the cell stay afloat in its marine environment.

Radiolarians also are immediately recognizable by their distinctive radial symmetry. Almost all radiolarian species secrete glassy endoskeletons (internal skeletons). The skeletons of the different species are as varied as snowflakes, and many have elaborate geometric designs (**Figure 25.12B**). A few radiolarians are among the largest of the unicellular eukaryotes, measuring several millimeters across.

Excavates began to diversify about 1.5 billion years ago

The **excavates** include several diverse groups that began to split from one another soon after the origin of eukaryotes. Several groups of excavates lack mitochondria, an absence that once led to the view that these groups might represent early-diverging eukaryotes that diversified before the evolution of mitochondria. However, the discovery of genes in the nucleus that are normally associated with mitochondria suggests that the absence of mitochondria is a derived condition in these organisms. In other words, ancestors of these excavate groups probably possessed

Excavates
— Diplomonads
— Parabasalids
— Heteroloboseans
— Euglenids
— Kinetoplastids

mitochondria that were lost or reduced over the course of evolution. The existence of these organisms today shows that eukaryotic life is possible without mitochondria, at least among parasitic species.

DIPLOMONADS AND PARABASALIDS The **diplomonads** and the **parabasalids** are unicellular and lack mitochondria (although they have reduced organelles that are derived from mitochondria). The parasitic *Giardia lamblia*, a diplomonad, causes the intestinal disease giardiasis. *Giardia* infections may result from contact with contaminated water. In the United States, such infections are common among hikers and campers using spring or stream water in recreational areas, as well as among children kept in close quarters (as in day-care centers). The tiny *Giardia* contain two nuclei bounded by nuclear envelopes and have a cytoskeleton and multiple flagella (**Figure 25.13A**).

In addition to flagella and a cytoskeleton, the parabasalids have undulating membranes that also contribute to the cell's locomotion. *Trichomonas vaginalis* (**Figure 25.13B**) is a parabasalid responsible for a sexually transmitted disease in humans. Infection of the male urethra, where it may occur without symptoms, is less common than infection of the vagina.

(A) *Giardia muris*

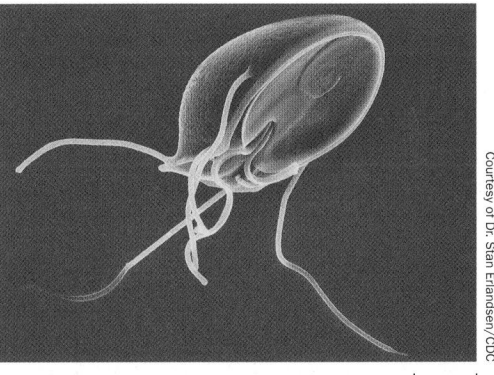

Courtesy of Dr. Stan Erlandsen/CDC

2 μm

(B) *Trichomonas vaginalis*

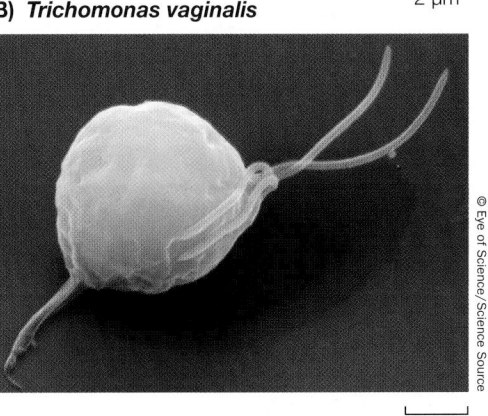

© Eye of Science/Science Source

2 μm

Figure 25.13 Some Excavate Groups Lack Mitochondria **(A)** *Giardia*, a diplomonad, has flagella and two nuclei. **(B)** *Trichomonas*, a parabasalid, has flagella and undulating membranes. Neither of these organisms possess mitochondria.

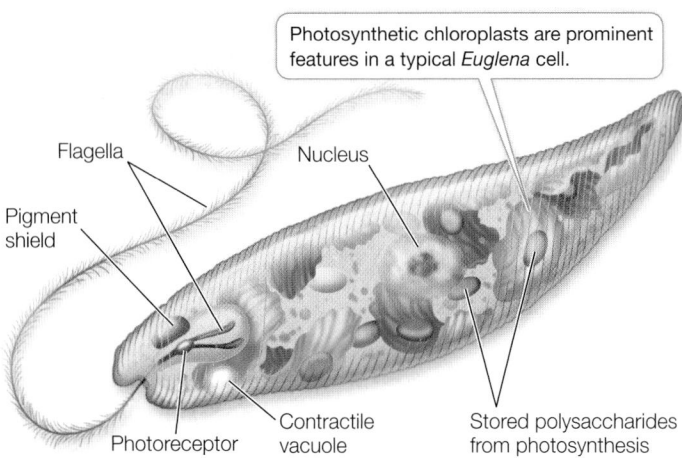

Figure 25.14 A Photosynthetic Euglenid In the *Euglena* species illustrated in this drawing, the second flagellum is rudimentary. Note that the primary flagellum originates at the anterior of the organism and trails toward its posterior.

HETEROLOBOSEANS

The amoeboid body form appears in several protist groups that are only distantly related to one another. The body forms of **heteroloboseans**, for example, resemble those of loboseans, an amoebozoan group that is not at all closely related to heteroloboseans (see the next section). Amoebas of the free-living heterolobosean genus *Naegleria*, some of which can enter the human body and cause a fatal disease of the nervous system, usually have a two-stage life cycle, in which one stage has amoeboid cells and the other flagellated cells.

EUGLENIDS AND KINETOPLASTIDS

The **euglenids** and **kinetoplastids** together constitute a clade of unicellular excavates with flagella. Their mitochondria contain distinctive disc-shaped cristae, and their flagella contain a crystalline rod not found in other organisms. They reproduce primarily asexually by binary fission.

The flagella of euglenids arise from a pocket at the anterior end of the cell. Spiraling strips of proteins under the cell membrane control the cell's shape. Some euglenids are photosynthetic. **Figure 25.14** depicts a typical cell of the genus *Euglena*. Like most other euglenids, this common freshwater organism has a complex cell structure. It propels itself through the water with the longer of its two flagella, which may also serve as an anchor to hold the organism in place. The second flagellum is often rudimentary.

Media Clip 25.4 Euglenids
Life12e.com/mc25.4

The euglenids have diverse nutritional requirements. Many species are always heterotrophic. Other species, including species of *Euglena*, are fully autotrophic in sunlight, using chloroplasts to synthesize organic compounds through photosynthesis. When kept in the dark, these euglenids lose their

photosynthetic pigment and begin to feed exclusively on dissolved organic material in the water around them. A "bleached" *Euglena* resynthesizes its photosynthetic pigment when it is returned to the light and becomes autotrophic again. But *Euglena* cells treated with certain antibiotics or mutagens lose their photosynthetic pigment completely; neither they nor their descendants are ever autotrophs again. However, those descendants function well as heterotrophs.

The kinetoplastids are unicellular parasites with two flagella and a single, large mitochondrion. The mitochondrion contains a kinetoplast, a unique structure housing multiple circular DNA molecules and associated proteins. Some of these DNA molecules encode "guide proteins" that edit mRNA within the mitochondrion.

The kinetoplastids include several medically important species of pathogenic trypanosomes (**Table 25.1**). Some of these organisms are able to change their cell surface recognition molecules frequently, allowing them to evade our best attempts to kill them and thus eradicate the diseases they cause.

Amoebozoans use lobe-shaped pseudopods for locomotion

Amoebozoans appear to have diverged from other eukaryotes about 1.5 billion years ago (see Figure 25.3). It is not yet clear whether they are more closely related to opisthokonts (which include fungi and animals) or to other major groups of eukaryotes.

The lobe-shaped pseudopods of amoebozoans (**Figure 25.15**) are a hallmark of the amoeboid body form. Amoebozoan pseudopods differ in form and function from the slender pseudopods of rhizarians. We consider three amoebozoan groups here: the loboseans and two groups known as slime molds.

LOBOSEANS

Loboseans are small amoebozoans that feed on other small organisms and particles of organic matter by phagocytosis, engulfing them with pseudopods. Many loboseans are adapted for life on the bottoms of lakes, ponds, and other bodies of water. Their creeping locomotion and their manner of engulfing food particles fit them for life close to a relatively rich supply of sedentary organisms or organic particles. Most loboseans exist as predators, parasites, or scavengers. Members of one group of loboseans, the testate amoebas, live inside shells. Some of

TABLE 25.1	Three Pathogenic Trypanosomes		
	Trypanosoma brucei	***Trypanosoma cruzi***	***Leishmania major***
Human disease	Sleeping sickness	Chagas disease	Leishmaniasis
Insect vector	Tsetse fly	Assassin bugs (many species)	Sand fly
Vaccine or effective cure	None	None	None
Strategy for survival	Changes surface recognition molecules frequently	Causes changes in surface recognition molecules on host cell	Reduces effectiveness of macrophage hosts
Site in human body	Bloodstream; in final stages, attacks nerve tissue	Enters cells, especially muscle cells	Enters cells, primarily macrophages
Approximate number of deaths per year	7,000	11,000	63,000

Amoeba proteus

Pseudopods

120 μm

Figure 25.15 An Amoeba in Motion   The flowing pseudopods of this "chaos amoeba" (a lobosean) are constantly changing shape as the amoeba moves and feeds.

▶ **Media Clip 25.5 Amoeboid Movement**
Life12e.com/mc25.5

Nebela collaris

Shell (test)
made of
sand grains

Cell
membrane
of amoeba

Pseudopods
of amoeba

18 μm

Figure 25.16 Life in a Glass House   This testate amoeba has built a lightbulb-shaped shell, or test, by gluing sand grains together. Its pseudopods extend through the single aperture in the test.

these amoebas produce casings by gluing sand grains together (**Figure 25.16**). Other testate amoebas have shells secreted by the organism itself.

PLASMODIAL SLIME MOLDS   If the nucleus of an amoeba began rapid mitotic division, accompanied by a tremendous increase in cytoplasm and organelles but no cytokinesis, the resulting organism would resemble the multinucleate mass of a **plasmodial slime mold**. During its vegetative (feeding, nonreproductive) stage, a plasmodial slime mold is a wall-less mass of cytoplasm with numerous diploid nuclei. This mass streams very slowly over its substrate in a remarkable network of strands called a plasmodium (**Figure 25.17A**). The plasmodium is an example of a **coenocyte**: many nuclei enclosed in a single cell membrane. The outer cytoplasm of the plasmodium (closest to the environment) is normally less fluid than the interior cytoplasm and thus provides some structural rigidity.

Plasmodial slime molds provide a dramatic example of movement by **cytoplasmic streaming**. The outer cytoplasm of the plasmodium becomes more fluid in places, and cytoplasm rushes into those areas, stretching the plasmodium. This streaming reverses its direction every few minutes as cytoplasm rushes into a new area and drains away from a previous one, moving the plasmodium over its substrate. Sometimes an entire wave of plasmodium moves across a surface, leaving strands behind. Microfilaments and a contractile protein called myxomyosin interact to produce the streaming movement. As it moves, the plasmodium engulfs food particles by endocytosis—predominantly bacteria, yeasts, spores of fungi, and other small organisms as well as decaying animal and plant remains.

A plasmodial slime mold can grow almost indefinitely in its plasmodial stage as long as the food supply is adequate and other conditions, such as moisture and pH, are favorable. If conditions become unfavorable, however, one of two things can happen. First, the plasmodium can form an irregular mass of hardened cell-like components. This resting structure rapidly becomes a plasmodium again when favorable conditions are restored.

Alternatively, the plasmodium can transform itself into spore-bearing fruiting structures (**Figure 25.17B**). These stalked or branched structures rise from heaped masses of plasmodium. They derive their rigidity from walls that form and thicken between their nuclei. The diploid nuclei of the plasmodium divide by meiosis as the fruiting structure develops. One or more knobs, called sporangia, develop on the end of the stalk. Within a sporangium, haploid nuclei become surrounded by walls to form spores. Eventually, as the fruiting structure dries, it sheds its spores.

The spores germinate into wall-less, haploid cells called swarm cells, which can either divide mitotically to produce more haploid swarm cells or function as gametes. Swarm cells can live as separate individual cells that move by means of flagella or pseudopods, or they can become walled and resistant resting cysts when conditions are unfavorable; when conditions improve again, the cysts release swarm cells. Two swarm cells can also fuse to form a diploid zygote, which divides by mitosis (but without a wall forming between the nuclei) and thus forms a new coenocytic plasmodium.

(A) A plasmodium

30 mm

(B) Fruiting structures of a plasmodial slime mold

1.5 mm

Figure 25.17 A Plasmodial Slime Mold (A) The plasmodial form of the slime mold *Hemitrichia serpula* covers rocks, decaying logs, and other objects as it engulfs bacteria and other food items; it is also responsible for the organism's common name of "pretzel mold." (B) Fruiting structures of *Leocarpus fragilis*.

 Media Clip 25.6 Plasmodial Slime Mold Growth
Life12e.com/mc25.6

CELLULAR SLIME MOLDS Whereas the plasmodium is the basic vegetative unit of the plasmodial slime molds, a single amoeboid cell is the vegetative unit of the **cellular slime molds** (**Figure 25.18**). Cells called **myxamoebas**, which have single haploid nuclei, swarm together as they engulf bacteria and other food particles by endocytosis and reproduce by mitosis and fission. This simple life cycle stage, consisting of swarms of independent, isolated cells, can persist indefinitely as long as food and moisture are available.

When conditions become unfavorable, the cellular slime molds form fruiting structures, as do their plasmodial counterparts. The individual myxamoebas aggregate into a mass called a slug or **pseudoplasmodium**. Unlike the true plasmodium of the plasmodial slime molds, this structure is not simply a giant sheet of cytoplasm with many nuclei; the individual myxamoebas within the slug retain their cell membranes and therefore their identity.

A slug may migrate over a substrate for several hours before becoming motionless and reorganizing to construct a delicate, stalked fruiting structure. Cells at the top of the fruiting structure develop into thick-walled spores, which are eventually released. Later, under favorable conditions, the spores germinate, releasing myxamoebas.

The cycle from myxamoebas through slug and spores to new myxamoebas is asexual. Cellular slime molds also have a sexual cycle, in which two myxamoebas fuse. The product of this fusion develops into a spherical structure that ultimately germinates, releasing new haploid myxamoebas.

KEY CONCEPT
25.2 Recap and Assess

The major lineages of eukaryotes began to diverge about 1.5 billion years ago. Major groups of eukaryotes are highly diverse in their habitat, nutrition, locomotion, and body form. Many protists are photosynthetic autotrophs, but heterotrophic lineages have evolved repeatedly. Although most protists are unicellular, multicellularity has arisen independently many times.

1. For each pair of groups below, describe how you could recognize members of the two groups and differentiate them from one another. Then describe features that the two groups in each pair share.
   a. Foraminiferans and radiolarians
   b. Ciliates and dinoflagellates
   c. Diatoms and brown algae
   d. Plasmodial slime molds and cellular slime molds

2. The fossil record of eukaryotes from the Precambrian is poor compared with that from the Cambrian and later geological periods, even though eukaryotes were diversifying for the last billion years of the Precambrian. Can you think of some reasons why the eukaryotic fossil record became more extensive in the Cambrian?

3. Give examples of alveolates, stramenopiles, and excavates that are important for medical or culinary reasons.

4. The red tides produced by some dinoflagellates are not produced by other alveolates. But similar red tides are produced by some diatoms, which are distantly related to dinoflagellates. Thus the production of red tides is convergent in dinoflagellates and diatoms. Describe another example from the text of convergent evolution in protists but outside alveolates.

Dictyostelium discoideum

The sporangium of the mature fruiting structure will release spores.

Fruiting structure (various stages)

Slug

0.25 mm

Figure 25.18 A Cellular Slime Mold This composite micrograph shows the life cycle of a *Dictyostelium* slime mold.

Media Clip 25.7 Cellular Slime Mold Aggregation
Life12e.com/mc25.7

The ancient origins of the major eukaryotic lineages and the adaptation of these lineages to a wide variety of lifestyles and environments resulted in enormous protist diversity. It is not surprising, then, that reproductive modes among protists are also highly diverse.

KEY CONCEPT 25.3 Protists Reproduce Sexually and Asexually

Learning Objectives

25.3.1 Distinguish between sex (in the sense of exchange of genes leading to genetic recombination) and reproduction.

25.3.2 Predict the evolutionary consequences of reproduction without sex for many generations.

Although most protists engage in both asexual and sexual reproduction, sexual reproduction has yet to be observed in some groups. In some protists, as in all prokaryotes, the acts of sex and reproduction are not directly linked.

Several asexual reproductive processes have been observed among the protists:

- The equal splitting of one cell into two by mitosis followed by cytokinesis

- The splitting of one cell into multiple (i.e., more than two) cells

- The outgrowth of a new cell from the surface of an old one (known as **budding**)

- The formation of specialized cells (spores) that are capable of developing into new individuals (known as **sporulation**)

Asexual reproduction results in offspring that are genetically nearly identical to their parents (they differ only by new mutations that may arise during DNA replication). Such asexually reproduced groups of nearly identical organisms are known as **clonal lineages**.

Sexual reproduction among the protists takes various forms. In some protists, as in animals, the gametes are the only haploid cells. In others, the zygote is the only diploid cell. In still others, both diploid and haploid cells undergo mitosis, giving rise to alternating multicellular diploid and haploid life stages.

Some protists reproduce without sex and have sex without reproduction

As we noted in Key Concept 25.2, members of the genus *Paramecium* are ciliates, which commonly have two types of nuclei in a single cell (one macronucleus and from one to several micronuclei; see Figure 25.6). The micronuclei are typical eukaryotic nuclei and are essential for genetic recombination. Each macronucleus contains many copies of the genetic information, packaged in units containing only a few genes each. The macronuclear DNA is transcribed and translated to regulate the life of the cell.

When paramecia reproduce asexually, all of the nuclei are copied before the cell divides. Paramecia (and many other protists) also have an elaborate sexual behavior called **conjugation**, in which two individuals line up tightly against each other and fuse in the oral groove region of the body. Nuclear material is extensively reorganized and exchanged over the next several hours (**Figure 25.19**). Each cell ends up with two haploid micronuclei, one of its own and one from the other cell, which fuse to form a new diploid micronucleus. A new macronucleus develops from that micronucleus through a series of dramatic chromosomal rearrangements. The exchange of nuclei is fully reciprocal: each of the two paramecia gives and receives an equal amount of DNA. The two organisms then separate and go their own ways, each equipped with new combinations of alleles.

Conjugation in *Paramecium* is a sexual process of genetic recombination, but it is not a reproductive process. Two cells begin

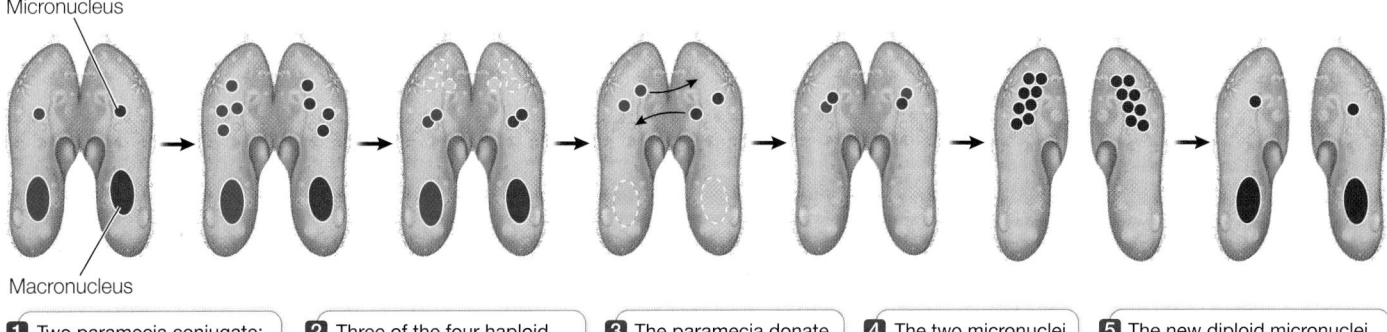

Micronucleus

Macronucleus

1 Two paramecia conjugate; all but one micronucleus in each cell disintegrate. The remaining micronucleus undergoes meiosis.

2 Three of the four haploid micronuclei disintegrate; the remaining micronucleus undergoes mitosis.

3 The paramecia donate micronuclei to each other. The macronuclei disintegrate.

4 The two micronuclei in each cell—each genetically different—fuse.

5 The new diploid micronuclei divide mitotically, eventually giving rise to a macronucleus and the appropriate number of micronuclei.

Figure 25.19 Conjugation in Paramecia The exchange of micronuclei by two conjugating *Paramecium* individuals results in genetic recombination. After conjugation, the cells separate and continue their lives as two individuals.

Q: Why is conjugation considered sex without reproduction?

conjugation and two cells are there at the end, so no new cells are created. As a rule, each asexual clone of paramecia must conjugate periodically. Experiments have shown that if some species are not permitted to conjugate, the clones can live through only about 350 cell divisions before dying out.

Some protist life cycles feature alternation of generations

Alternation of generations is a type of life cycle found in many multicellular protists, all land plants, and some fungi (see Figure 26.6). A multicellular, diploid, spore-producing organism gives rise to a multicellular, haploid, gamete-producing organism. When two haploid gametes fuse, a diploid organism is produced. The haploid organism, the diploid organism, or both may also reproduce asexually. Note that alternation of generations is distinct from the familiar reproductive system of animals, in which the only haploid stages are unicellular gametes produced by multicellular, diploid adults.

The two alternating (spore-producing and gamete-producing) generations differ genetically (one has diploid cells, the other haploid cells), but they may or may not differ morphologically. In **heteromorphic** alternation of generations, the two generations differ morphologically; in **isomorphic** alternation of generations, they do not. Examples of both heteromorphic and isomorphic alternation of generations are found among the brown algae.

The gamete-producing generation does not produce gametes by meiosis because the gamete-producing organism is already haploid. Instead, specialized cells of the diploid spore-producing organism, called **sporocytes**, divide meiotically to produce four haploid spores. The spores may eventually germinate and divide mitotically to produce the multicellular haploid generation, which then produces gametes by mitosis and cytokinesis.

Gametes, unlike spores, can produce new organisms only by fusing with other gametes. The fusion of two gametes produces a diploid zygote, which then undergoes mitotic divisions to produce a diploid organism. The diploid organism's sporocytes then undergo meiosis and produce haploid spores, starting the cycle anew.

25.3 Recap and Assess

Protists reproduce both asexually and sexually, although sex occurs independently of reproduction in some species. Some multicellular protists exhibit alternation of generations, alternating between multicellular haploid and diploid life stages.

1. Why is conjugation between paramecia considered a sexual process but not a reproductive process?

2. Why do you think paramecia that are not allowed to conjugate begin to die out after about 350 rounds of asexual reproduction?

3. Although most diploid animals have haploid stages (e.g., eggs and sperm), their life cycles are not considered examples of alternation of generations. Why not?

Given the diversity of protists and of the environments in which they live, it is not surprising that they influence their environments in numerous ways.

KEY CONCEPT
25.4 Protists Are Critical Components of Many Ecosystems

Learning Objectives

25.4.1 Illustrate and/or describe the complex life cycle of a parasite that involves multiple hosts.

25.4.2 Summarize the consequences of overproduction of some diatoms and dinoflagellates.

25.4.3 Describe some of the beneficial and harmful interactions that protists have with other species.

25.4.4 Provide two examples of how protists are important to humans.

Some protists are food for marine animals, while others poison those animals. Some are packaged as nutritional supplements for humans, and some are human pathogens. The remains of some form the sands of many modern beaches, and others are a major source of the oil that sometimes fouls those beaches.

Phytoplankton are primary producers

A single protist clade, the diatoms, performs about one-fifth of all photosynthetic carbon fixation on Earth—about the same amount as all of Earth's rainforests. These spectacular unicellular organisms (see Figure 25.8) are the predominant component of the oceanic phytoplankton, but the phytoplankton include many other protists that also contribute heavily to global photosynthesis. Like green plants on land, these "floating photosynthesizers" are the gateway for energy from the Sun into the rest of the living world; in other words, they are **primary producers**. These autotrophs are eaten by heterotrophs, including animals and many other protists. Those consumers are, in turn, eaten by other consumers. Most aquatic heterotrophs (with the exception of some species in the deep sea) depend on photosynthesis performed by phytoplankton.

Some microbial eukaryotes are deadly

Some microbial eukaryotes are pathogens that cause serious diseases in humans and other vertebrates. The best-known pathogenic protists are members of the genus *Plasmodium*, a highly specialized group of apicomplexans that spend part of their life cycle as parasites in human red blood cells, where they are the cause of malaria. In terms of the number of people affected, malaria is one of the world's three most serious infectious diseases: it infects more than 215 million people, and kills nearly half a million people, each year. On average, about two people die from malaria every minute of every day—most of them in sub-Saharan Africa, although malaria occurs in more than 90 countries.

Mosquitoes of the genus *Anopheles* transmit *Plasmodium* to humans. The parasites enter the human circulatory system when an infected female *Anopheles* mosquito penetrates the skin in search of blood. The parasites find their way to cells in the liver and the lymphatic system, change their form, multiply, and reenter the bloodstream, where they invade red blood cells.

The parasites multiply inside the red blood cells, which then lyse (burst), releasing new swarms of parasites. These episodes of bursting red blood cells coincide with the primary symptoms of malaria, which include fever, shivering, vomiting, joint pains, and convulsions. If another *Anopheles* bites the victim, the mosquito takes in *Plasmodium* cells along with blood. Some of the ingested cells develop into gametes that unite in the mosquito,

forming zygotes. The zygotes lodge in the mosquito's gut, divide several times, and move into its salivary glands, from which they can be passed on to another human host. Thus *Plasmodium* is an extracellular parasite in the mosquito vector and an intracellular parasite in the human host (**Figure 25.20**). Such an organism—that is, a parasite that requires more than one host—is said to have a **complex life cycle**.

Plasmodium has proved to be a singularly difficult pathogen to attack. The complex *Plasmodium* life cycle is best broken by the removal of stagnant water, in which mosquitoes breed. Using insecticides to reduce the *Anopheles* population can also be effective,

(A)

1 A blood-feeding female mosquito ingests the *Plasmodium* gametocytes.

2 Within the mosquito, male and female gametocytes develop into gametes, which fuse.

Male gamete

Female gamete

3 The resulting zygote enters the mosquito's gut wall and forms a cyst.

8 Eventually, some merozoites develop into male and female gametocytes.

Mosquito's gut wall

7b ...grow and divide, and lyse the cells. They can reinfect the liver, producing new generations.

➡ Events in mosquito
➡ Events in human

4 The zygote gives rise to sporozoites that invade the salivary gland.

Red blood cell

Mosquito's salivary gland

7a Merozoites also invade red blood cells,...

5 The mosquito injects sporozoites into a human's blood when it feeds. The sporozoites then take up residence in the liver.

Human liver cell

6 Sporozoites penetrate liver cells and develop into merozoites.

(B)

Cysts

Mosquito's gut wall

170 μm

© London School of Hygiene/SPL/Science Source

Figure 25.20 **Life Cycle of the Malarial Parasite** **(A)** Like many parasitic species, the apicomplexan *Plasmodium falciparum* has a complex life cycle, part of which is spent in mosquitoes of the genus *Anopheles* and part in humans. The sexual phase (gamete fusion) of this life cycle takes place in the insect, and the zygote is the only diploid stage. **(B)** Encysted *Plasmodium* zygotes (artificially colored blue) cover the stomach wall of a mosquito. Invasive sporozoites will hatch from the cysts and be transmitted to a human, in whom the parasite causes malaria.

 View in Achieve
Animation 25.3 **Life Cycle of the Malarial Parasite**

but the benefits must be weighed against the ecological, economic, and health risks posed by the insecticides themselves.

Even some of the phytoplankton that are such important primary producers can be deadly, as described in this chapter's opening story. Some diatoms and dinoflagellates reproduce in enormous numbers when environmental conditions are favorable for their growth. In the resulting red tides, the concentration of dinoflagellates may reach 60 million per liter of ocean water and produce potent nerve toxins that harm or kill many vertebrates, especially fishes.

Some microbial eukaryotes are endosymbionts

Endosymbiosis is common among the microbial eukaryotes, many of which live within the cells of animals. Many radiolarians harbor photosynthetic endosymbionts (see Figure 25.12A). As a result, these radiolarians, which are not photosynthetic themselves, appear greenish or golden, depending on the type of endosymbiont they contain. This arrangement is often mutually beneficial: the radiolarian can make use of the carbon compounds produced by its photosynthetic guest, and the guest may in turn make use of metabolites made by the host or receive physical protection. In some cases, the guest is exploited for its photosynthetic products while receiving little or no benefit itself.

Dinoflagellates are also common endosymbionts and can be found in both animals and other protists. Most, but not all, dinoflagellate endosymbionts are photosynthetic. Some dinoflagellates live endosymbiotically in the cells of corals, contributing the products of their photosynthesis to the partnership. Their importance to the corals is demonstrated when the dinoflagellates die or are expelled by the corals as a result of changing environmental conditions such as rising water temperatures or increased water turbidity. This phenomenon is known as **coral bleaching**. Unless the corals can acquire new endosymbionts, they are ultimately damaged or destroyed as a result of their reduced food supply (Investigating Life: Can Corals Reacquire Dinoflagellate Endosymbionts Lost to Bleaching?).

▶Investigating LIFE   Can Corals Reacquire Dinoflagellate Endosymbionts Lost to Bleaching?

Experiment

Original Paper: C. L. Lewis and M. A. Coffroth. 2004. The acquisition of exogenous algal symbionts by an octocoral after bleaching. *Science* 304: 1490–1492.

Some corals lose their chief nutritional source when their photosynthetic endosymbionts die, often as a result of changing environmental conditions. This experiment by Cynthia Lewis and Mary Alice Coffroth investigated the ability of corals to acquire new endosymbionts after bleaching.

HYPOTHESIS▶ Bleached corals can acquire new photo-synthetic endosymbionts from their environment.

METHOD▶

1. Count numbers of *Symbiodinium*, a photosynthetic dinoflagellate, living symbiotically in samples of a coral (*Briareum* sp.).

2. Stimulate bleaching by maintaining all *Briareum* colonies in darkness for 12 weeks.

3. After 12 weeks of darkness, count numbers of *Symbiodinium* in the coral samples; then return all colonies to light.

4. In some of the bleached colonies (the experimental group), introduce *Symbiodinium* strain B211— dinoflagellates that contain a unique molecular marker. Do not expose the others (the control group) to strain B211. Maintain both groups in the light for 6 weeks.

RESULTS▶ Error bars show 95% confidence limits for the means.

Six weeks after return to light, both groups showed increases in number of symbionts present. DNA analysis showed that strain B211 symbionts were present in the experimental group.

After 12 weeks in dark, 0%–1% of the photosynthetic endosymbionts remained.

Pre-bleach

Post-bleach

Both photos courtesy of M. A. Coffroth and C. Lewis, University at Buffalo

CONCLUSION▶ Corals can acquire new endosymbionts from their environment following bleaching.

We rely on the remains of ancient marine protists

Diatoms are lovely to look at, but their importance to us goes far beyond aesthetics, and even beyond their role as primary producers. Diatoms store oil as an energy reserve and to keep themselves afloat at the correct depth in the ocean. Over millions of years, diatoms have died and sunk to the ocean floor, where they have undergone chemical changes. In this way, they have become a major source of petroleum and natural gas, two of our most important energy supplies and political concerns.

Because the silica-containing cell walls of dead diatoms resist decomposition, some sedimentary rocks are composed almost entirely of diatom skeletons that sank to the seafloor over time. Diatomaceous earth, which is obtained from such rocks, has many industrial uses, such as insulation, filtration, and metal polishing. It has also been used as an "Earth-friendly" insecticide that clogs the tracheae (breathing structures) of insects.

Other ancient marine protists have also contributed to today's world. Some foraminiferans, as we have seen, secrete shells of calcium carbonate. After they reproduce (by mitosis and cytokinesis), the daughter cells abandon the parent shell and make new shells of their own. The discarded shells of ancient foraminiferans make up extensive limestone deposits in various parts of the world, forming a layer hundreds to thousands of meters deep over millions of square kilometers of ocean bottom. Foraminiferan shells also make up much of the sand of some beaches. A single gram of such sand may contain as many as 50,000 foraminiferan shells and shell fragments.

The shells of individual foraminiferans are easily preserved as fossils in marine sediments. Each geological period has a distinctive assemblage of foraminiferan species. Because the shells of foraminiferan species have distinctive shapes (see Figure 25.11) and because they are so abundant, the remains of foraminiferans are especially valuable in classifying and dating sedimentary rocks. In addition, analyses of the chemical makeup of foraminiferan shells can be used to estimate the global temperatures prevalent at the time when the shells were formed.

KEY CONCEPT
25.4 Recap and Assess

Protists have many effects, both positive and negative, on their environment. Some species are important primary producers, many are endosymbionts, and some are pathogens. Protists are among the most important producers of fossil fuels, and they are important components of sedimentary rocks.

1. What is the role of female *Anopheles* mosquitoes in the transmission of malaria?
2. Explain the roles of dinoflagellates in the two very different phenomena of coral bleaching and red tides.
3. What are two ways in which diatoms are important to human society?

The next six chapters will explore the major evolutionary radiations of multicellular eukaryotes, along with the protist ancestors from which they arose. Chapters 26 and 27 will describe the origin and diversification of plants, Chapter 28 will present the fungi, and Chapters 29–31 will provide a brief overview of the animals.

Work with the Data

The data in the table below come from DNA analyses of *Symbiodinium* strains found in the experimental and control colonies of corals (*Briareum*) before and after bleaching. *Symbiodinium* strain B211 (which was not present before bleaching) was introduced to the experimental colonies after bleaching. Use these data to answer the questions below.

	Symbiodinium strain present (% of colonies)			
	Non-B211	**B211**	**None**[a]	**Colony died**
EXPERIMENTAL COLONIES (STRAIN B211 ADDED)				
Pre-bleach	100	0	0	0
Post-bleach	58	0	42	0
Week 3	0	92	0	8
Week 6	8	58	8	25
CONTROL COLONIES (NO STRAIN B211)				
Pre-bleach	100	0	0	0
Post-bleach	67	0	33	0
Week 3	67	0	33	0
Week 6	67	0	17	17

[a]Colonies remained alive, but no *Symbiodinium* were detected.

QUESTIONS▶

1. Are new strains of *Symbiodinium* taken up only by coral colonies that have lost all their original endosymbionts?

2. Does the acquisition of a new *Symbiodinium* strain always result in survival of a recovering *Briareum* colony?

3. In week 3, only strain B211 was detected in the experimental colonies, but in week 6, non-B211 *Symbiodinium* were detected in 8% of the experimental colonies. Can you suggest an explanation for this observation?

Go to **Achieve** for a companion
Data in Depth exercise.

InvestigatingLIFE

Q and A   **Red tides are harmful, but how are dinoflagellates beneficial to marine ecosystems?**

The opening of this chapter discussed harmful red tides, or blooms of dinoflagellates. But not all dinoflagellate blooms produce problems for other species. Dinoflagellates are important components of many ecosystems, as we have seen throughout this chapter. Photosynthetic dinoflagellates also produce much of the atmospheric oxygen that most animals need to survive.

As we saw in **Investigating Life: Can Corals Reacquire Dinoflagellate Endosymbionts Lost to Bleaching?**, corals and many other species depend on symbiotic dinoflagellates for food. In addition, as photosynthetic organisms, free-living planktonic dinoflagellates are among the most important primary producers in aquatic food webs. They are a major component of the phytoplankton and provide an important food source for many species.

Future directions

Some dinoflagellates produce a beautiful bioluminescence (**Figure 25.21**). Unlike the bioluminescent bacteria described at the start of Chapter 24, however, dinoflagellates cannot generate a steady bioluminescence, but instead produce bright flashes of light when disturbed, as people who swim in the ocean at night in certain regions often observe. What function do these flashes serve? Many light-emitting dinoflagellates are preyed on by other species, such as small crustaceans. When the dinoflagellates produce a bright flash, it functions like a "burglar alarm," and attracts secondary predators of the crustaceans. Experiments have shown that crustaceans reduce their feeding on dinoflagellates when they flash this

© Per-Andre Hoffmann/Alamy Stock Photo

Figure 25.21 **Light Up the Sea**   Bioluminescent dinoflagellates flash as an outrigger disturbs the ocean surface off the island of Bali.

signal. However, recent research shows another function of bioluminescence in toxic species of dinoflagellates. These toxic species produce a much lower intensity bioluminescence which may function as a warning of their toxicity to potential predators. So depending on the intensity and other details of the flash in different species, the bioluminescence can serve either to attract secondary predators or to warn off primary predators. Research on communication by bioluminescence continues as a rich field of investigation.

▶ **Media Clip 25.8** **Flashing Dinoflagellate**
Life12e.com/mc25.8

VISUAL SUMMARY 25

© Don Paulson/PureStock/AGE Fotostock

You should be able to relate each summary to the adjacent figures. If you go to this visual summary in **Achieve**, you can follow links to figures, animations, activities, and simulations that will help you consolidate the material.

KEY CONCEPT

25.1   Eukaryotes Acquired Features from Both Archaea and Bacteria   Go to **Animation 25.1**

- The term **protist** does not describe a formal taxonomic group. It is shorthand for "all eukaryotes that are not plants, animals, or fungi."

- Early events in the evolution of the eukaryotic cell included the loss of the firm cell wall and infolding of the cell membrane. Such infolding led to segregation of the genetic material in a membrane-enclosed nucleus.

- Mitochondria evolved by endosymbiosis with a proteobacterium.

- **Primary endosymbiosis** of a eukaryote and a cyanobacterium gave rise to the first chloroplasts. **Secondary endosymbiosis** and **tertiary endosymbiosis** between chloroplast-containing eukaryotes and other eukaryotes gave rise to the distinctive chloroplasts of euglenids, dinoflagellates, and other groups.

Questions

1. Are all protists small in size (microbial)?
2. What is the phylogenetic evidence that mitochondria and chloroplasts arose through endosymbiosis?

Figure 25.1

Figure 25.2

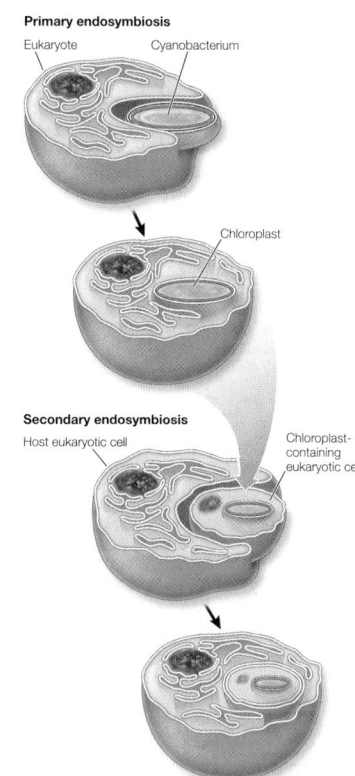

Primary endosymbiosis

Secondary endosymbiosis

KEY CONCEPT
25.2 Major Lineages of Eukaryotes Diversified in the Precambrian

Go to Activity 25.1 and Animation 25.2

- Most eukaryotes can be placed in one of eight major clades that diverged about 1.5 billion years ago: alveolates, stramenopiles, rhizarians, excavates, plants, amoebozoans, fungi, and animals.

- **Alveolates** are unicellular organisms with sacs (alveoli) beneath their cell membranes. Alveolate clades include the marine **dinoflagellates**, the parasitic **apicomplexans**, and the diverse, highly motile **ciliates**.

- **Stramenopiles** typically have two flagella of unequal length, the longer one bearing rows of tubular hairs. Among the stramenopiles are the unicellular **diatoms**; the multicellular **brown algae**; and the nonphotosynthetic **oomycetes**, many of which are **saprobic**.

- **Rhizarians** are unicellular and aquatic. They include the **cercozoans**; the **foraminiferans**, which secrete shells of calcium carbonate; and the **radiolarians**, which have thin, stiff pseudopods and glassy endoskeletons.

- The unicellular **excavates** include parasitic as well as free-living species, some of which have lost typical mitochondria.

- The **amoebozoans** move by means of lobe-shaped pseudopods and include both unicellular and multicellular members; examples are the **plasmodial slime molds** and **cellular slime molds**.

Questions

1. Name five of the major groups of eukaryotes in which multicellularity has arisen independently.
2. Which five of the major groups of eukaryotes contain numerous photosynthetic species?

Figure 25.3

KEY CONCEPT

25.3 Protists Reproduce Sexually and Asexually

- Asexual reproduction gives rise to **clonal lineages** of organisms.

- **Conjugation** in *Paramecium* is a sexual process but not a reproductive one.

- **Alternation of generations**, which involves cycles between a multicellular diploid stage and a multicellular haploid stage, is a feature of many multicellular protist life cycles (as well as those of some fungi and all land plants).

The alternating generations may be **heteromorphic** or **isomorphic**.

Questions

1. Explain how some species can recombine their genomes sexually, yet reproduce asexually.

2. Why is animal reproduction, which involves haploid gametes produced by diploid organisms, not considered alternation of generations?

Figure 25.19

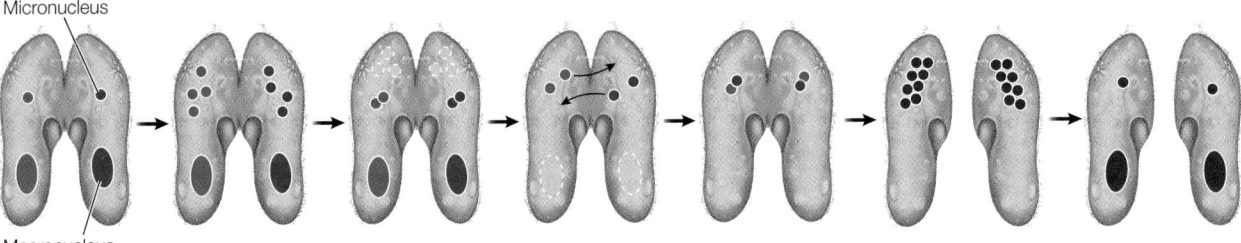

Micronucleus

Macronucleus

KEY CONCEPT

25.4 Protists Are Critical Components of Many Ecosystems

Go to Animation 25.3

- Diatoms are responsible for about one-fifth of the photosynthetic carbon fixation on Earth. They and other members of the phytoplankton are important **primary producers** in the marine environment. Ancient diatoms are a major source of today's petroleum and natural gas deposits.

- Some protists are pathogens of humans and other vertebrates.

- Endosymbiotic relationships are common among microbial protists and often benefit both the endosymbionts and their protist or animal partners.

Questions

1. Describe two distinct problems for human populations that are caused by protists.

2. What are two important benefits to humans from protists?

Figure 25.20

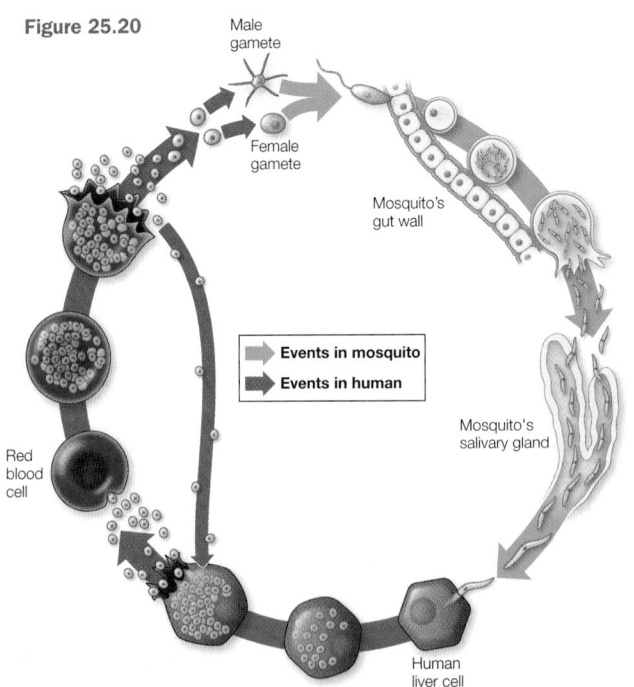

Male gamete

Female gamete

Mosquito's gut wall

Events in mosquito
Events in human

Mosquito's salivary gland

Red blood cell

Human liver cell

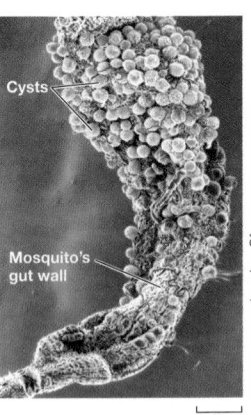

Cysts

Mosquito's gut wall

170 μm

Go to **Achieve** for the eBook, **LearningCurve**, animations, activities, simulations, and additional resources and assignments.

Plants without Seeds: From Water to Land

KEY CONCEPTS

26.1 Primary Endosymbiosis Produced the First Photosynthetic Eukaryotes

26.2 Key Adaptations Permitted Plants to Colonize Land

26.3 Vascular Tissues Led to Rapid Diversification of Land Plants

Courtesy of the U.S. Coast Guard

An explosive blowout of the drilling rig **Deepwater Horizon** in April 2010 resulted in almost 5 million barrels of oil spilling into the Gulf of Mexico. This oil was the product of ancient photosynthesis of marine algae, whose remains were trapped beneath the ocean floor.

▶Investigating LIFE

A Planet Powered by Photosynthesis, Past and Present

The living world depends largely on energy from the Sun, which drives photosynthesis. Using sunlight, plants convert water and carbon dioxide (CO_2) into carbohydrates and produce atmospheric oxygen (O_2) as a by-product. Life on Earth as we know it today depends on the carbohydrates and O_2 produced by plants.

Today there is great interest in using solar power to help meet human energy needs. But unicellular eukaryotes capitalized on this process first, and long ago. Single-celled eukaryotes incorporated tiny solar energy converters into their cells more than 1.5 billion years ago, when they formed partnerships with photosynthetic cyanobacteria. These endosymbionts—which over time would become the chloroplasts of modern plants—allowed many eukaryotes to use solar energy to drive the reactions that convert water and CO_2 into organic carbon compounds. Fossil fuels such as coal, natural gas, and petroleum are the remains of carbon compounds produced by ancient organisms using photosynthesis. Hence fossil fuels were produced using solar energy captured by photosynthetic organisms millions of years ago.

If fossil fuels were produced using solar energy, then why is the burning of fossil fuels so problematic? The problem is that the CO_2 used to produce these fossil fuels was drawn by plants from Earth's atmosphere over many hundreds of millions of years. In contrast, we are now burning these fuels, and thus releasing trapped CO_2 back into the atmosphere, over the course of just a few centuries. This has resulted in a rapid increase in concentrations of CO_2 (and other carbon compounds, such as methane) in Earth's atmosphere. The increased concentrations of carbon compounds increase the ability of Earth's atmosphere to trap heat from the Sun, thus warming the overall climate of Earth. Although many changes in Earth's climate have occurred in the past, the burning of fossil fuels by humans is resulting in perhaps the fastest increases in global temperature in Earth's history. This rapid rise in global temperature has enormous consequences for life on Earth—hence our need to develop renewable, sustainable sources of energy that don't depend on burning fossil fuels.

Can we grow new biofuels that capture carbon from Earth's atmosphere?

(Find the answer on page 598.)

KEY CONCEPT
26.1
Primary Endosymbiosis Produced the First Photosynthetic Eukaryotes

Learning Objectives

26.1.1 Identify the common evolutionary origin of chloroplasts on the tree of life and explain the meaning of primary endosymbiosis.

26.1.2 Describe the ten major clades of Plantae and their evolutionary relationships to one another.

Photosynthesis is critical to life as we know it. As detailed in Chapter 10, photosynthesis uses energy from sunlight to convert carbon dioxide and water into carbohydrates and oxygen. The reverse process, known as catabolism, provides organisms with the energy they need to function, grow, and reproduce. So almost all living organisms depend on the carbohydrates and oxygen produced by photosynthesis.

More than a billion and a half years ago, when a cyanobacterium was first engulfed by an early eukaryote, the history of life was altered radically. The chloroplasts that resulted from primary endosymbiosis of this cyanobacterium (see Figure 25.2) were obviously important for the evolution of plants and other photosynthetic

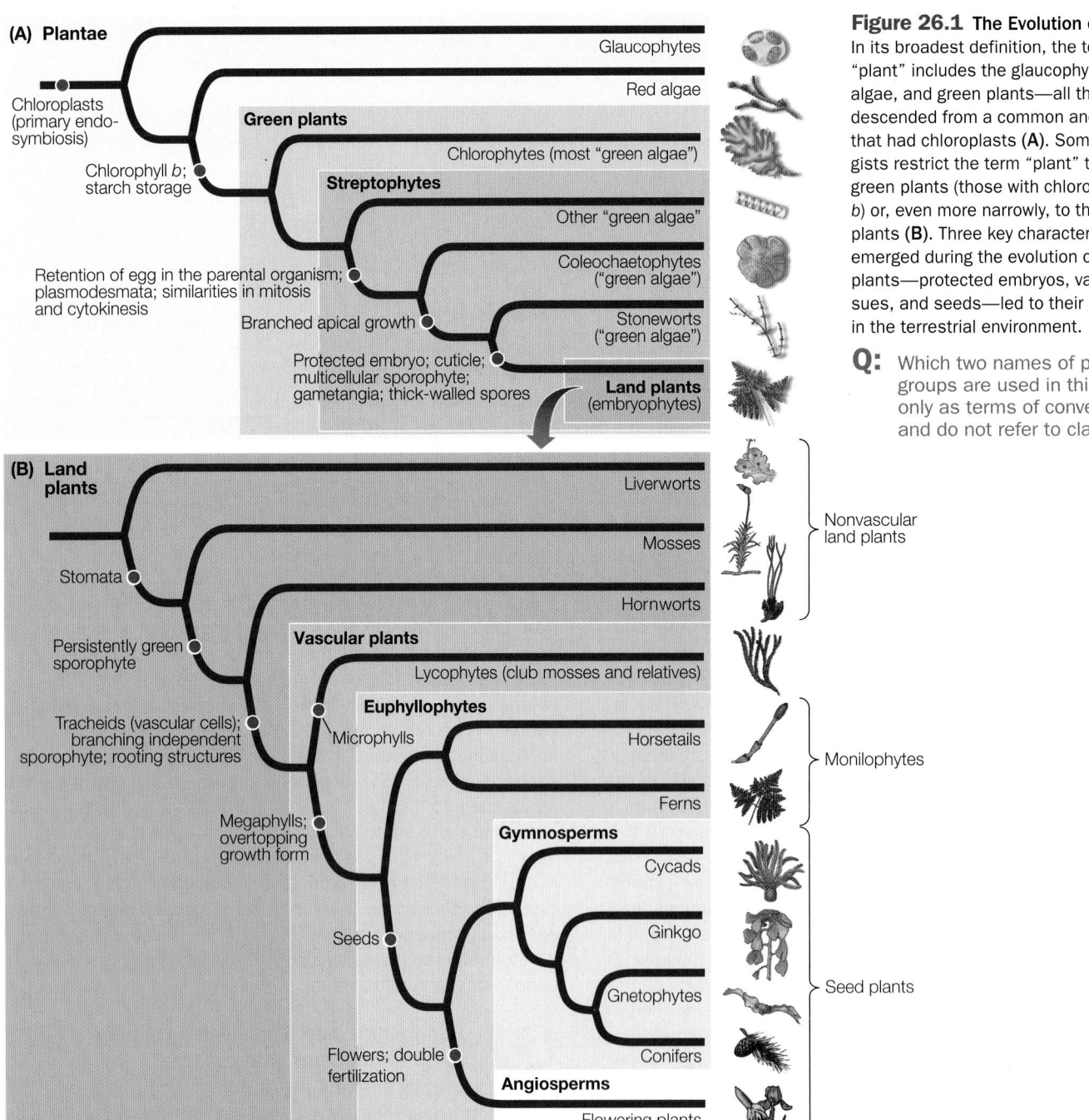

Figure 26.1 The Evolution of Plants In its broadest definition, the term "plant" includes the glaucophytes, red algae, and green plants—all the groups descended from a common ancestor that had chloroplasts (**A**). Some biologists restrict the term "plant" to the green plants (those with chlorophyll *b*) or, even more narrowly, to the land plants (**B**). Three key characteristics that emerged during the evolution of land plants—protected embryos, vascular tissues, and seeds—led to their success in the terrestrial environment.

Q: Which two names of plant groups are used in this figure only as terms of convenience, and do not refer to clades?

Work with the Data

The Phylogeny of Land Plants

Original Paper: Y.-L. Qiu et al. 2006. The deepest divergences in land plants inferred from phylogenomic evidence. *Proc Natl Acad Sci USA* 103: 15511–15516. © 2006 National Academy of Sciences, U.S.A.

In addition to the morphological characters of land plants shown on the phylogeny in Figure 26.1, DNA sequences are widely used to study and reconstruct the evolutionary history of plants. These sequences are many tens of thousands of nucleotides long and have been collected from a large number of species. The full data set used by Yin-Long Qiu and his colleagues (available at treebase.org) includes DNA sequences from 67 genes. The table below provides sample sequences from a chloroplast gene that has been used to reconstruct the relationships of representative plant species; the table shows 27 nucleotide positions for 10 species.

QUESTIONS▶

1. Construct a phylogenetic tree of these 10 species using the parsimony method (see Key Concept 20.2 and the examples in Table 20.1 and Figure 20.5 for instructions). Use the outgroup to root your tree. Assume that all changes among nucleotides are equally likely.

2. How many changes (from one nucleotide to another) occur along each branch on your tree?

3. Which nucleotide positions (i.e., which character states) exhibit homoplasy (convergence or reversal of the character state)?

4. Which group on your tree represents the streptophytes? The land plants? The vascular plants? The euphyllophytes? The seed plants? The angiosperms?

Go to Achieve for a companion Data in Depth exercise.

Species	\multicolumn{27}{c}{Nucleotide position (character state)}
	1	2	3	4	5	6	7	8	9	10	11	12	13	14	15	16	17	18	19	20	21	22	23	24	25	26	27
Outgroup (chlorophyte alga)	T	A	T	T	A	T	G	A	T	T	C	C	A	A	A	T	A	T	T	A	T	A	A	T	C	T	A
Stonewort	T	A	T	T	T	A	A	A	T	T	A	C	T	A	A	T	A	A	T	A	T	A	A	T	C	T	A
Liverwort	A	C	T	T	T	T	A	A	T	G	A	T	T	C	A	G	A	A	T	A	T	A	A	T	C	T	A
Moss	A	C	T	T	T	T	A	A	T	A	T	T	T	T	A	A	T	A	T	A	A	A	A	T	C	T	T
Hornwort	A	C	T	T	T	T	A	A	T	G	T	T	T	T	A	A	T	A	C	A	G	A	A	A	C	T	T
Lycophyte	A	C	T	C	C	C	G	G	T	G	T	T	C	T	G	A	T	A	C	A	A	G	G	A	C	C	T
Fern	C	C	T	C	C	G	A	G	C	G	T	T	C	T	T	A	G	A	T	A	A	G	G	A	C	C	T
Pine tree	A	C	C	C	C	G	C	G	C	G	T	T	C	T	G	A	T	G	C	G	A	G	G	A	T	C	T
Rice	A	C	C	C	C	G	C	G	C	G	T	T	C	T	G	A	T	G	C	G	A	G	G	A	T	A	T
Tobacco	A	C	C	A	C	G	C	G	C	G	T	T	C	T	G	A	T	G	C	G	A	G	G	A	T	A	T

eukaryotes, but they were also critical to the evolution of all life on land. Until photosynthetic plants were able to move onto land, there was very little on land to support multicellular animals or fungi, and almost all life was restricted to the oceans and fresh waters.

Primary endosymbiosis is a shared derived trait—a synapomorphy—of the group known as **Plantae** (Figure 26.1). Although *Plantae* is Latin for "plants," in everyday language—and throughout this book—the unmodified common name "plants" is usually used to refer only to the land plants. However, the first several clades to branch off the tree of life after primary endosymbiosis are all aquatic. Most aquatic photosynthetic eukaryotes (other than those secondarily derived from land plants) are known by the common name **algae**. This name, however, is just a convenient way to refer to these groups, which are not all closely related. Many of the photosynthetic groups we discussed in Chapter 25 (which acquired chloroplasts through secondary endosymbiosis) are also commonly called algae.

Connect the Concepts As noted in Key Concept 20.1, derived traits shared by a group of organisms that offer evidence of their common ancestry are called synapomorphies.

Several distinct clades of algae were among the first photosynthetic eukaryotes

The ancestor of Plantae was unicellular and may have been similar in general form to the modern **glaucophytes** (Figure 26.2). These microscopic freshwater algae are thought to be the sister group to the rest of Plantae (see Figure 26.1A). The chloroplast of glaucophytes is unique in containing a small amount of peptidoglycan between its inner and outer membranes—the same arrangement

Glaucocystis   Chloroplasts

20 μm

© Dr. Peter Siver/Visuals Unlimited, Inc.

Figure 26.2 Glaucophytes May Resemble Some of the Earliest Plantae The large chloroplasts of unicellular glaucophytes differ from chloroplasts of other Plantae in retaining a layer of peptidoglycan. This feature is thought to have been retained from the endosymbiotic cyanobacteria that gave rise to the chloroplasts of Plantae. The photograph shows a colony of four individuals, each with many chloroplasts.

(A) *Rhodymenia* sp.   **(B)** *Calliarthron* sp.

1 cm   3 mm

Figure 26.3 Red Algae Contain a Red Accessory Photosynthetic Pigment **(A)** The rich red color of red algae is a result of the pigment phycoerythrin. **(B)** Coralline red alga is named for its coral-like appearance.

found in cyanobacteria. Peptidoglycan has been lost from the remaining photosynthetic eukaryotes.

In contrast to the glaucophytes, almost all **red algae** are multicellular (**Figure 26.3**). Their characteristic color is a result of the accessory photosynthetic pigment **phycoerythrin**, which is found in relatively large amounts in the chloroplasts of many red algae. In addition to phycoerythrin, red algal chloroplasts contain chlorophyll *a* as well as several other accessory pigments.

The red algae include species that grow in the shallowest tidal pools as well as the photosynthesizers found deepest in the ocean (as deep as 260 meters if nutrient conditions are right and the water is clear enough to permit light to penetrate). A few red algae inhabit fresh water. Most grow attached to a substrate by a structure known as a holdfast.

Despite their name, red algae don't always appear red in color. The ratio of two pigments—phycoerythrin (red) and chlorophyll *a* (green)—depends largely on the intensity of light that reaches the alga. In deep water, where light is dim, algae accumulate large amounts of phycoerythrin (which absorbs light at short wavelengths) and appear red. But many species growing near the surface contain a higher concentration of chlorophyll *a* and thus appear bright green.

The remaining algal groups in Plantae are the various "green algae." Like land plants, the green algae contain both chlorophylls *a* and *b* and store their reserve of photosynthetic products as starch in chloroplasts. All the groups that share these features are commonly called **green plants** because both of their photosynthetic pigments are green.

The largest clade of "green algae" is the **chlorophytes**. There are more than 17,000 species of chlorophytes, most of which are aquatic (some are marine, though more are freshwater forms), although there are a few terrestrial forms that live in moist environments. Chlorophytes range in size from microscopic unicellular forms to multicellular forms many centimeters long and display an incredible variety of shapes and body forms. Surprisingly large and well-formed colonies of cells are found in some unicellular freshwater groups, such as the genus *Volvox* (**Figure 26.4A**). Certain cells in these colonies are specialized for reproduction. The cells in these colonies are not differentiated into specialized tissues and organs, as in land plants and animals, but they show vividly how the preliminary step of this great evolutionary innovation might have been taken.

Volvox is a colonial unicellular chlorophyte, but there are also many true multicellular species of chlorophytes. Some of these are filamentous. Others, like species in the genus *Ulva* (**Figure 26.4B**), grow into thin, membranous sheets up to 30 centimeters wide.

Biologists are exploring mass production of several species of chlorophytes as a source of biofuels. One of the biggest limitations in using algae for biofuels relates to the cost of providing an appropriate growth medium for the algae. Growth media typically require fresh water and abundant sources of carbon, nitrogen, and

(A) *Volvox* sp.   **(B)** *Ulva lactuca*

Daughter colonies produced   Somatic   Parent
by reproductive cells   cells   colony

120 μm

Figure 26.4 Chlorophytes Display a Wide Diversity of Forms
(A) *Volvox* colonies are precisely spaced arrangements of individual cells. Specialized reproductive cells produce daughter colonies, which will eventually release new individuals. **(B)** Sea lettuce grows in marine waters and intertidal areas.

phosphorus. These nutrients are already present in most municipal wastewater supplies, and the removal of these nutrients by growing algae would help clean the water supply. Investigating Life: Can Chlorella Algae Be Grown in Municipal Sewage Wastewater for Biofuel Production? explores the potential of municipal wastewater as a growth medium for algae used in biofuel production.

▶Investigating LIFE Can Chlorella Algae Be Grown in Municipal Sewage Wastewater for Biofuel Production?

Experiment

Original Paper: A. M. Bhatnagar et al. 2010. *Chlorella minutissima—A promising fuel alga for cultivation in municipal wastewaters. Appl Biochem Biotechnol* 161: 523–536.

Growing algae for use in biofuel production requires an abundant source of fresh water that contains appropriate nutrients. Appropriate nutrients for growing algae are present in municipal wastewater, but other contaminants of wastewater (such as salts and detergents) could diminish algal growth. Ashish Bhatnagar and his colleagues at the University of Georgia conducted an experiment to see if *Chlorella minutissima* algae could be grown successfully in municipal wastewater.

HYPOTHESIS▶ *Chlorella minutissima* algae can be grown successfully in municipal wastewater, either with or without dilution from traditional growth medium.

METHOD▶

1. Grow replicate cultures of a standard inoculate of *Chlorella minutissima* algae in growth medium, as well as in 25%, 50%, 75%, and 100% municipal wastewater.

2. Control temperature and light conditions for all cultures.

3. Measure growth of the algae after 15 days by measuring the concentration of chlorophyll *a* present in each culture.

RESULTS▶ Errors bars indicate ±1 standard deviation.

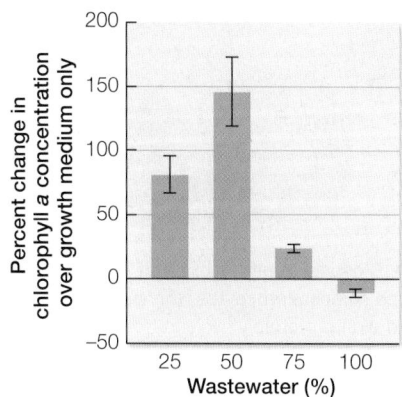

CONCLUSION▶ *Chlorella minutissima* algae can be grown effectively in municipal wastewater, and growth may even exceed production in standard growth medium.

Q: At what tested concentration of wastewater do the algae grow best?

Work with the Data

After determining that municipal wastewater could be used to grow *Chlorella minutissima* for biofuel production, Ashish Bhatnagar and his colleagues explored the effects on *Chlorella* growth of various sources of carbon that were present in the wastewater. The table below shows three measures of algal growth in standard growth medium, as well as in the medium with added sources of carbon. Use these data to answer the following questions.

QUESTIONS▶

1. Calculate 95% confidence intervals for mean measures of chlorophyll *a* concentration in the various growth media (see Appendix B for directions on calculating confidence intervals from standard errors). Which carbon source additives result in significantly higher or lower chlorophyll *a* concentrations (based on non-overlapping confidence intervals) compared with the growth medium only?

2. Plot the measures for chlorophyll *a* concentration, biomass, and cell count for each growth condition. Which two measures appear to be most strongly correlated? Can you think of reasons why the uncorrelated measure might show a different trend than the two correlated measures?

Go to Achieve for a companion Data in Depth exercise.

Measurement[a]	Growth medium only	Growth medium + propionate	Growth medium + acetate	Growth medium + citrate	Growth medium + sucrose	Growth medium + glucose
Chlorophyll a concentration (mg/L)	13.41	1.72	9.4	15.26	17.63	37.21
	(1.24)	(0.03)	(0.82)	(0.59)	(0.86)	(3.76)
Biomass (mg/L)	899	120	630	1,007	1,164	2,456
	(27.6)	(12.6)	(35.1)	(110.4)	(87.9)	(297.7)
Cell count (per 10^{-5} mL)	2.01	0.51	1.89	1.50	1.93	1.76
	(0.17)	(0.02)	(0.08)	(0.07)	(0.17)	(0.18)

[a]Measures are means, with standard errors of mean shown in parentheses.

(A) *Coleochaete* sp.

(B) *Chara rusbyana* (stonewort)

150 μm

Figure 26.5 The Closest Relatives of Land Plants **(A)** This species is a representative of the coleochaetophytes, the sister clade of stoneworts plus land plants. **(B)** The land plants probably evolved from a common ancestor shared with the stoneworts, an abundant group of multicellular green algae often found in freshwater pools and lakes (although a few species are found in marine environments). A species in the common genus *Chara* is shown here.

▶ **Media Clip 26.1 Reproductive Structures of Stoneworts**
Life12e.com/mc26.1

Two groups of green algae are the closest relatives of land plants

All green algae other than the chlorophytes form a group together with the land plants known as **streptophytes** (see Figure 26.1A). Several microscopic structural features, backed by clear evidence from molecular studies, indicate that the closest relatives of the land plants are two groups of aquatic green algae, the **coleochaetophytes** (Figure 26.5A) and the **stoneworts** (Figure 26.5B). Both of these multicellular algal groups retain their eggs in the parental organism, as land plants do. As in land plants, the cytoplasm of adjacent cells in these algal groups is connected through structures called plasmodesmata; they also share similarities in the details of mitosis and cytokinesis. Of these two groups, stoneworts are thought to be the sister group of land plants (see Figure 26.1A). The growth form of stoneworts is branching and apical (new growth occurs at the tips of branches), as in most land plants. Phylogenetic analysis of gene sequences has confirmed the close relationships of coleochaetophytes and stoneworts to the land plants.

There are ten major groups of land plants

One of the key synapomorphies of the **land plants** is development from an embryo that is protected by tissues of the parent plant. For this reason, land plants are sometimes called **embryophytes** (*phyton*, "plant"). The green plants, the streptophytes, and the land plants have each been called "the plant kingdom" by different authorities; others take an even broader view and include red algae and glaucophytes as "plants." To avoid confusion in this chapter, we use modifying terms (e.g., "land plants" or "green plants") to refer to the various clades of Plantae shown in Figure 26.1.

The land plants that exist today fall naturally into ten major clades (listed by their common names in the center column of Table 26.1). Members of seven of those clades possess well-developed vascular systems that transport materials throughout the plant body. We call these seven groups, collectively, the **vascular plants**, or **tracheophytes**, because they all possess fluid-conducting cells called **tracheids** (discussed in more detail in Chapter 32). The remaining three clades (liverworts, mosses, and hornworts) lack tracheids and are referred to collectively as **nonvascular land plants**. Note, however, that the three groups of nonvascular land plants do *not* form a clade (unlike the vascular plants, which *are* a clade).

TABLE 26.1 | Classification of Land Plants

Group	Common name	Characteristics
NONVASCULAR LAND PLANTS		
Hepatophyta	Liverworts	No stomata; gametophyte flat or leafy
Bryophyta	Mosses	Filamentous stage; gametophyte leafy; sporophyte grows apically (at the tip)
Anthocerophyta	Hornworts	Embedded archegonia; sporophyte grows basally (i.e., from the ground)
VASCULAR PLANTS		
Lycopodiophyta	Lycophytes: club mosses and allies	Microphylls in spirals; sporangia in leaf axils
Monilophyta	Horsetails and ferns	Simple leaves in whorls or frondlike compound leaves
SEED PLANTS		
Gymnosperms		
Cycadophyta	Cycads	Compound leaves; swimming sperm; seeds on modified leaves
Ginkgophyta	Ginkgo	Deciduous; fan-shaped leaves; swimming sperm
Gnetophyta	Gnetophytes	Vessels in vascular tissue; opposite, simple leaves
Coniferophyta	Conifers	Seeds in cones; needle- or scalelike leaves
Angiosperms	Flowering plants	Endosperm; carpels; gametophytes much reduced; seeds contained within fruits

26.1 Recap and Assess

Primary endosymbiosis is a synapomorphy of Plantae. The glaucophytes, the sister clade of the other Plantae, are unicellular algae that are similar to some of the earliest photosynthetic eukaryotes. The green plants contain chlorophyll *b* in addition to the chlorophyll *a* found in all Plantae.

1. Explain the different possible uses of the term "plant."
2. Why doesn't the term "algae" designate a formal taxonomic group?
3. What are some of the key differences among glaucophytes, red algae, and the various clades of green algae?
4. What evidence supports the phylogenetic relationship between land plants and the various groups of aquatic green algae?

The green algal ancestors of the land plants lived at the margins of ponds or marshes, ringing them with a mat of dense green. It was from such a marginal habitat, which was sometimes wet and sometimes dry, that early plants made the transition onto land.

KEY CONCEPT
26.2 Key Adaptations Permitted Plants to Colonize Land

Learning Objectives

26.2.1 Describe one or more key innovations in land plants that were most important to their transition to a terrestrial environment, and justify your choice(s).

26.2.2 Distinguish alternation of generations in plants from the life cycles of animals.

How did the land plants arise? To address this question, we can compare land plants with their closest relatives among the green algae. The features that differ between the two groups include the adaptations that allowed the first land plants to survive in the terrestrial environment.

Adaptations to life on land distinguish land plants from green algae

Land plants first appeared in the terrestrial environment between 500 and 450 million years ago (mya). How did they survive in an environment that differed so dramatically from the aquatic environment of their ancestors? While the water essential for life is everywhere in the aquatic environment, water is difficult to obtain and retain in the terrestrial environment.

No longer bathed in fluid, organisms on land faced potentially lethal desiccation (drying). Large terrestrial organisms had to develop ways to transport water to body parts distant from the source of the water. And whereas water provides aquatic organisms with support against gravity, a plant living on land must either have some other support system or sprawl unsupported on the ground. A land plant must also use different mechanisms for dispersing its gametes and progeny than its aquatic relatives, which can simply release them into the water.

Survival on land was facilitated by the evolution among plants of numerous adaptations, including:

- The *cuticle*, a coating of waxy lipids that retards water loss
- *Stomata*, small closable openings in leaves and stems that are used to regulate gas exchange and water loss
- *Gametangia*, multicellular organs that enclose plant gametes and prevent them from drying out
- *Embryos*, young plants contained within a protective structure
- Certain *pigments* that afford protection against the mutagenic ultraviolet radiation that bathes the terrestrial environment
- Thick *spore walls* containing a polymer that protects the spores from desiccation and resists decay
- A *mutually beneficial association with fungi* (mycorrhizae) that promotes nutrient uptake from the soil

The cuticle may be the most important—and the earliest—of these features. Composed of several unique waxy lipids that coat the leaves and stems of land plants, the cuticle has several functions, the most obvious and important of which is to keep water from evaporating from the plant body.

As ancient plants colonized the land, they not only adapted to the terrestrial environment, they also modified it by contributing to the formation of soil. Acids secreted by plants help break down rock, and the organic compounds produced by the breakdown of dead plants contribute nutrients to the soil. Such effects are repeated today as plants colonize and grow in new areas.

Life cycles of land plants feature alternation of generations

A universal feature of the life cycles of land plants is alternation of generations. Recall from Key Concept 25.3 the two hallmarks of alternation of generations:

1. The life cycle includes both a multicellular diploid stage and a multicellular haploid stage.
2. Gametes are produced by mitosis, not by meiosis. Meiosis produces **spores** that develop into multicellular haploid organisms.

If we begin looking at the land plant life cycle at the single-cell stage—the diploid zygote—then the first phase of the cycle is the formation, by mitosis and cytokinesis, of a multicellular **embryo**, which eventually grows into a mature diploid plant. This multicellular diploid plant is called the **sporophyte** ("spore plant").

Cells contained within specialized reproductive organs of the sporophyte, called **sporangia** (singular *sporangium*), undergo meiosis to produce haploid, unicellular spores. By mitosis and cytokinesis, a spore develops into a haploid plant. This multicellular haploid plant, called the **gametophyte** ("gamete plant"), produces haploid gametes by mitosis. The fusion of two gametes (fertilization) forms a single diploid cell—the zygote—and the cycle is repeated (**Figure 26.6**).

The sporophyte generation extends from the zygote through the adult multicellular diploid plant and sporangium formation. In contrast, the gametophyte generation extends from the spore

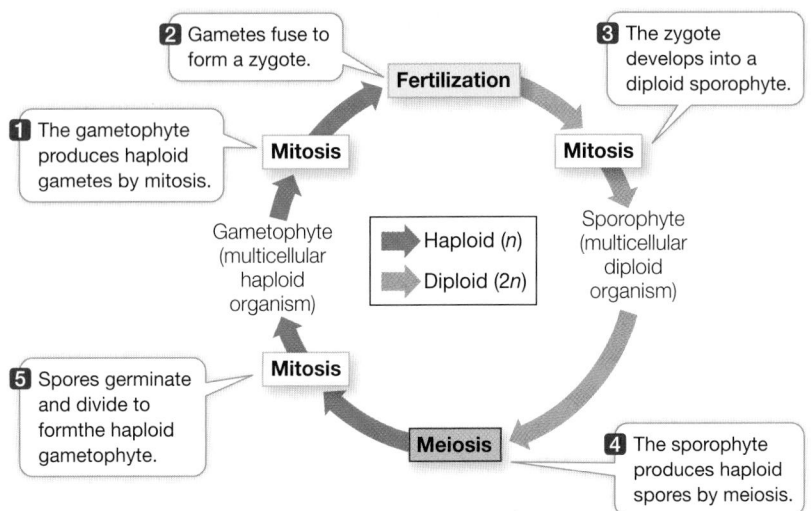

Figure 26.6 Alternation of Generations in Land Plants A multicellular diploid sporophyte generation that produces spores by meiosis alternates with a multicellular haploid gametophyte generation that produces gametes by mitosis.

Q: What is a major difference in the haploid portion of the life cycle of plants and animals?

through the adult multicellular haploid plant to the gametes. The transitions between the generations are accomplished by fertilization and by meiosis. In all land plants, the sporophyte and the gametophyte differ genetically: the sporophyte has diploid cells, and the gametophyte has haploid cells.

There is a trend toward reduction of the gametophyte generation in plant evolution. In the nonvascular land plants, the gametophyte is larger, longer-lived, and more self-sufficient than the sporophyte. In those groups that appeared later in plant evolution, however, the sporophyte is the larger, more conspicuous, longer-lived, and more self-sufficient generation.

Nonvascular land plants live where water is readily available

The living species of nonvascular land plants are the liverworts, mosses, and hornworts. These three groups are thought to be similar in many ways to the earliest land plants. Most of these plants grow in dense mats, usually in moist habitats. Even the largest of these species are only about half a meter tall, and most are only a few centimeters tall or long. Why have they not evolved to be taller? The probable answer is that they lack an efficient vascular system for transporting water and minerals from the soil to distant parts of the plant body.

The nonvascular land plants lack the true leaves, stems, and roots that characterize the vascular plants, although they have structures analogous to each. Their growth form allows water to move through the mats of plants by capillary action. They have leaflike structures that readily catch and hold any water that splashes onto them. They are small enough that minerals can be distributed throughout their bodies by diffusion. As in most land plants, layers of maternal tissue protect their embryos from desiccation. Nonvascular land plants also have a cuticle,

although it is often very thin (or even absent in some species) and thus is not highly effective in retarding water loss.

Most nonvascular land plants live on the soil or on vascular plants, but some grow on bare rock, on dead and fallen tree trunks, and even on buildings. Their ability to grow on such marginal surfaces results from a mutualistic association with fungi. The earliest association of land plants with fungi dates back at least 460 million years. This mutualism probably facilitated the absorption of water and minerals, especially phosphorus, from the first soils.

> **Connect the Concepts** Land plants of many groups have mutualistic associations with fungi, as described in Key Concept 28.2.

Nonvascular land plants are widely distributed over six continents and even exist (albeit very locally) on the coast of the seventh, Antarctica. Most are terrestrial. Although a few species live in fresh water, these aquatic species are descended from terrestrial ones. None live in the oceans.

The sporophytes of nonvascular land plants are dependent on the gametophytes

In the nonvascular land plants, the conspicuous green structure visible to the naked eye is the gametophyte. The gametophyte is photosynthetic and is therefore nutritionally independent; the sporophyte may or may not be photosynthetic, but it is always nutritionally dependent on the gametophyte and remains permanently attached to it.

Figure 26.7 illustrates a moss life cycle that is typical of the life cycles of nonvascular land plants. A sporophyte produces unicellular haploid spores as products of meiosis within a sporangium. When a spore germinates, it gives rise to a multicellular haploid gametophyte whose cells contain chloroplasts and are thus photosynthetic. Eventually gametes form within specialized sex organs, called the **gametangia**. The **archegonium** is a multicellular, flask-shaped female sex organ that produces a single egg. The **antheridium** is a male sex organ in which sperm, each bearing two flagella, are produced in large numbers. Both archegonia and antheridia are produced on the same individual in many species, so each individual has both male and female reproductive structures. Adjacent individuals often fertilize one another's gametes, however, which helps maintain genetic diversity in the population.

Once released from the antheridium, the sperm must swim or be splashed by raindrops to a nearby archegonium on the same or a neighboring plant—a constraint that reflects the aquatic origins of the nonvascular land plants' ancestors. The sperm are aided on their journey by chemical attractants released by the egg or the archegonium. Before sperm can enter the archegonium, however, certain cells in the neck of the archegonium must break down, leaving a water-filled canal through which the sperm can swim to complete their journey. Notice that *all of these events require liquid water.*

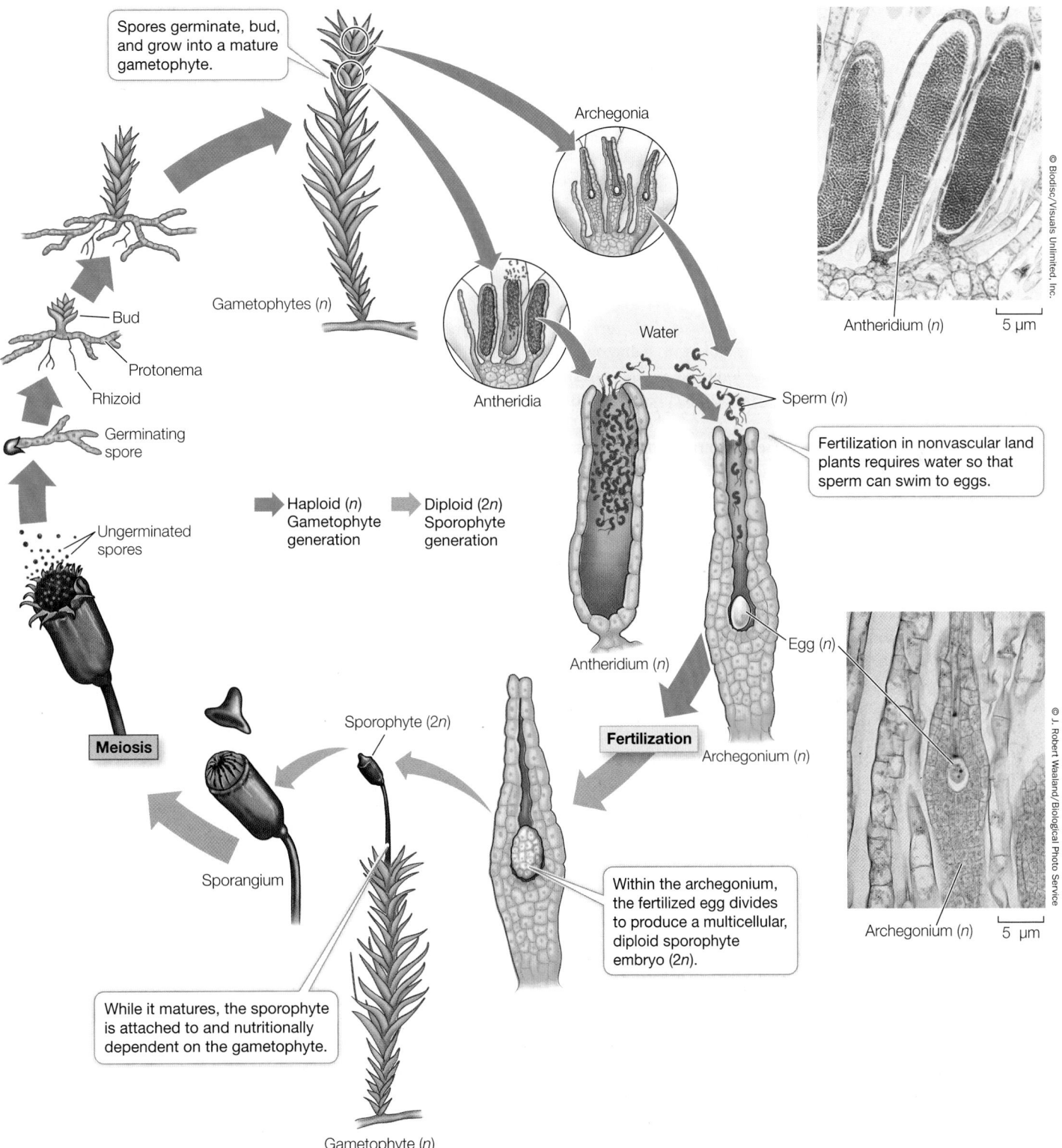

Spores germinate, bud, and grow into a mature gametophyte.

Archegonia

Gametophytes (n)

Antheridia

Bud

Protonema

Rhizoid

Germinating spore

Ungerminated spores

Haploid (n) Gametophyte generation

Diploid (2n) Sporophyte generation

Water

Antheridium (n)   5 μm

© Biodisc/Visuals Unlimited, Inc.

Sperm (n)

Fertilization in nonvascular land plants requires water so that sperm can swim to eggs.

Egg (n)

Antheridium (n)

Fertilization

Archegonium (n)

Meiosis

Sporophyte (2n)

Sporangium

Within the archegonium, the fertilized egg divides to produce a multicellular, diploid sporophyte embryo (2n).

Archegonium (n)   5 μm

© J. Robert Waaland/Biological Photo Service

While it matures, the sporophyte is attached to and nutritionally dependent on the gametophyte.

Gametophyte (n)

Figure 26.7 A Life Cycle Dependent on Water   The life cycles of nonvascular land plants, exemplified here by that of a moss, are dependent on an external source of liquid water. The visible green structure of such plants is the gametophyte, which contains haploid archegonia and antheridia. Water carries sperm from the antheridia into an archegonium, inside which an egg is fertilized and grows into a multicellular, diploid sporangium.

View in **Achieve**
Animation 26.1 Life Cycle of a Moss

Media Clip 26.2 Nonvascular Plant Reproduction
Life12e.com/mc26.2

Once sperm arrive at an egg, the nucleus of a sperm fuses with the egg nucleus to form a diploid zygote. Mitotic divisions of the zygote produce a multicellular, diploid sporophyte embryo. The sporophyte matures and produces a single sporangium, within which meiotic divisions produce spores and thus the next gametophyte generation.

Liverworts are the sister clade of the remaining land plants

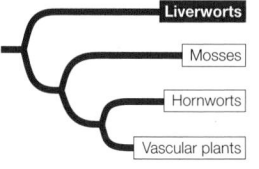

There are about 9,000 species of **liverworts**. Most liverworts have leafy gametophytes (**Figure 26.8A**). Some have thalloid gametophytes: green, leaflike layers that lie flat on the ground (**Figure 26.8B,C**). The simplest liverwort gametophytes are flat plates of cells, a centimeter or so long, that produce antheridia or archegonia on their upper surfaces and rhizoids (rootlike filaments) on their lower surfaces.

Liverwort sporophytes are shorter than those of mosses and hornworts, rarely exceeding a few millimeters. The liverwort sporophyte has a stalk that raises the sporangium above the gametophyte. In most species, the stalk elongates by expansion of cells throughout its length. This elongation raises the sporangium above ground level, allowing the spores to be dispersed more widely. The sporangia of liverworts are simple: a globular sporangium wall surrounds a mass of spores. In some species of liverworts, spores are not released by the sporophyte until the surrounding sporangium wall rots. In other liverworts, however, the spores are thrown from the sporangium by structures that shorten and compress as they dry out. When the stress becomes sufficient, the compressed structure snaps back to its resting position, throwing spores in all directions.

Among the most familiar thalloid liverworts are species of the genus *Marchantia*. *Marchantia* is easily recognized by the characteristic structures on which its male and female gametophytes bear their antheridia and archegonia (see Figure 26.8C). Like most liverworts, *Marchantia* also reproduces asexually by simple

fragmentation of the gametophyte. In addition, *Marchantia* and some other liverworts and mosses reproduce asexually by means of gemmae (singular *gemma*), which are lens-shaped clumps of cells (see Figure 26.8B). In a few liverworts, the gemmae are held in structures called gemmae cups, which promote dispersal of the gemmae by raindrops.

▶ **Media Clip 26.3 Liverwort Life Cycle**
Life12e.com/mc26.3

Water and sugar transport mechanisms emerged in the mosses

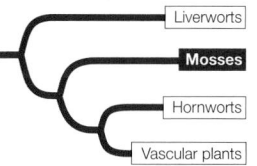

The most familiar of the nonvascular land plants are the **mosses**. These hardy little plants, of which there are about 15,000 species, are found in almost every terrestrial environment. They are often found on damp, cool ground, where they form thick mats (**Figure 26.9**). The mosses are the sister clade of the vascular plants plus the hornworts (see Figure 26.1B).

The mosses, along with the hornworts and vascular plants, share an advance over the liverworts in their adaptation to life on land: they have openings called **stomata**, which allow CO_2 to enter the plant body and allow water and O_2 to leave it. Stomata are a synapomorphy of mosses and all other land plants except liverworts.

In mosses, the gametophyte begins its development following spore germination as a branched, filamentous structure called a protonema (see Figure 26.7). Although the protonema looks a bit like a filamentous green alga, this structure is unique to the mosses. Some of the filaments contain chloroplasts and are photosynthetic; others, called rhizoids, are nonphotosynthetic and anchor the protonema to the substrate. After a period of linear growth, cells close to the tips of the photosynthetic filaments divide rapidly in three dimensions to form buds. The buds eventually develop a distinct tip, or apex, and produce the familiar leafy moss shoot with leaflike structures arranged spirally. These leafy shoots produce antheridia or archegonia (see Figure 26.7).

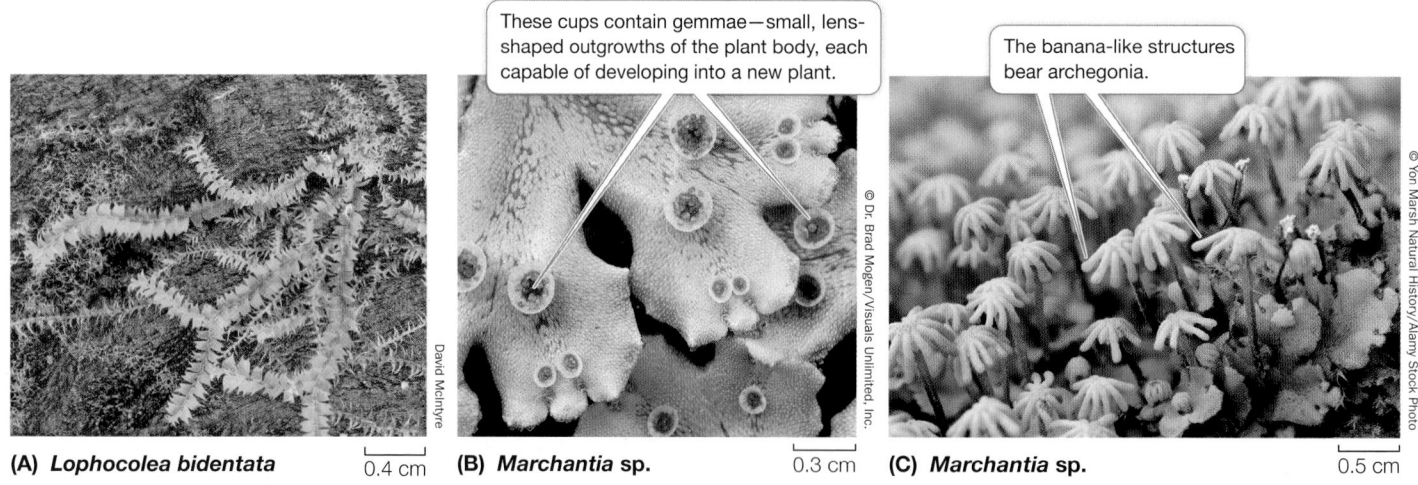

These cups contain gemmae—small, lens-shaped outgrowths of the plant body, each capable of developing into a new plant.

The banana-like structures bear archegonia.

(A) *Lophocolea bidentata* — 0.4 cm   **(B)** *Marchantia* sp. — 0.3 cm   **(C)** *Marchantia* sp. — 0.5 cm

Figure 26.8 Liverwort Diversity **(A)** The gametophyte of a leafy liverwort. **(B)** The gametophytes of the thalloid liverwort *Marchantia* lie flat on the ground. **(C)** *Marchantia* gametophytes bearing archegonia.

Figure 26.9 Mosses Often Cover the Ground in Dense Mats
(A) Dense layers of moss carpet a field of solidified volcanic lava in Iceland. (B) A close-up view of moss.

Q: When you see a growing moss, are you more likely to see the haploid or the diploid multicellular stage? Is your answer the same for a fern and for a flowering plant?

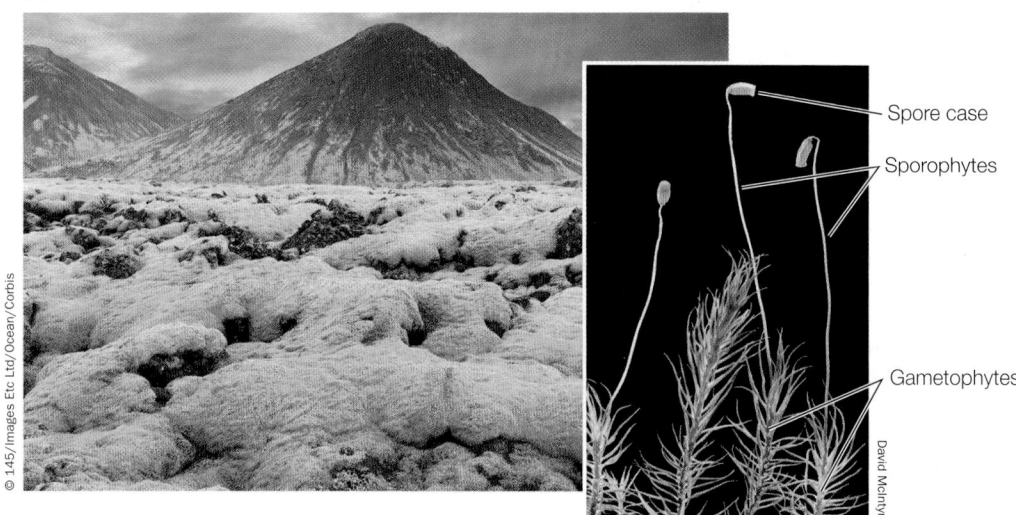

(A)

Spore case
Sporophytes
Gametophytes

(B) *Polytrichum commune*

Some moss gametophytes are too large to transport enough water through their bodies solely by diffusion. Gametophytes and sporophytes of many mosses contain a type of cell called a hydroid, which dies and leaves a tiny channel through which water can travel. The hydroid is functionally similar to the tracheid, the characteristic water-conducting cell of the vascular plants, but it lacks lignin and the cell wall structure found in tracheids. The possession of hydroids and of a limited system for transport of sugar in some mosses shows that the term "nonvascular plant" is somewhat misleading when applied to these plants. Despite their simple system of internal transport, however, the mosses are not considered vascular plants because they lack tracheids or other components of xylem and phloem.

Mosses of the genus *Sphagnum* (**Figure 26.10A**) often grow in cool, swampy places, where the plants begin to decompose in water after they die. Rapidly growing upper layers of moss

compress the deeper-lying, decomposing layers. Partially decomposed plant matter is called **peat**. In some parts of the world, people derive the majority of their fuel from peat bogs (**Figure 26.10B**). *Sphagnum*-dominated peatlands cover a total area approximately half the size of the United States—more than 1% of Earth's surface. Millions of years ago, continued compression of peat composed primarily of other seedless plants gave rise to coal.

Hornworts have distinctive chloroplasts and stalkless sporophytes

Liverworts
Mosses
Hornworts
Vascular plants

The approximately 100 species of **hornworts** are so named because their sporophytes look like little horns (**Figure 26.11**). Hornworts appear at first glance to be liverworts with

(A) *Sphagnum* sp.

Sporophyte
Gametophyte

(B) A peat bog

Figure 26.10 Sphagnum Moss   (A) *Sphagnum* bogs are extremely dense growths of the moss shown here in a close-up view. (B) Workers mine a bog for peat, a fossil fuel formed from decomposing *Sphagnum* mosses.

The sporophytes of hornworts can reach 20 cm in height.

Gametophytes are flat plates a few cells thick.

© Daniel Vega/AGE Fotostock

Anthoceros sp.

Figure 26.11 Hornworts Get Their Name from Their Hornlike Sporophytes Unlike liverworts and mosses, hornworts have sporophytes that are persistently green. The hornworts share this trait with the vascular plants.

very simple gametophytes. Their gametophytes are flat plates of cells a few cells thick.

Hornworts have several characteristics that distinguish them from liverworts and mosses. First, the cells of hornworts each contain a single large, platelike chloroplast, whereas the cells of the other two groups contain numerous small, lens-shaped chloroplasts. Second, of the sporophytes in all three groups, those of the hornworts come closest to being capable of growth without a set limit. Liverwort and moss sporophytes have a stalk that stops growing as the sporangium matures, so elongation of the sporophyte is strictly limited. The hornwort sporophyte, however, has no stalk, and it is persistently green (a trait shared with vascular plants). A basal region of the sporangium remains capable of indefinite cell division, continuously producing new spore-bearing tissue above. The sporophytes of some hornworts growing in mild and continuously moist conditions can become as tall as 20 centimeters. Eventually, however, the sporophyte's growth is limited by its simple transport system.

Hornworts have a symbiotic relationship with cyanobacteria that promotes their growth by providing them with access to nitrogen, which is often a limiting resource. Internal cavities of hornworts that are filled with mucilage can dry out, forming air-filled cavities through which cyanobacteria can enter. Cyanobacteria such as *Nostoc* convert atmospheric nitrogen gas into a form usable by their host plant; in return, the hornwort provides the symbiont with carbohydrates.

KEY CONCEPT
26.2 Recap and Assess

The transition of plants to land required numerous adaptations, including the cuticle, stomata, gametangia, protected embryos, pigments, thick spore walls, and mutually beneficial associations with fungi. Nonvascular land plants rely on liquid water for reproduction.

1. Explain what is meant by "alternation of generations." Why do we not use this phrase for humans?
2. Describe key adaptations of plants to the terrestrial environment, and describe the distribution of those adaptations among the liverworts, mosses, and hornworts.

New features appeared in plants as they continued to adapt to the terrestrial environment. One of the most important of these was vascular tissues, the characteristic that defines the vascular plants.

KEY CONCEPT
26.3 Vascular Tissues Led to Rapid Diversification of Land Plants

Learning Objectives

26.3.1 Detail the differences among tracheids, xylem, and phloem.

26.3.2 List five important structures in vascular plants that probably first arose in lycophytes.

26.3.3 Discuss the possible selective advantages of heterospory over homospory.

The first plants possessing vascular tissues did not arise until tens of millions of years after the earliest nonvascular plants had colonized the land. But once vascular tissues arose, their ability to transport water and food throughout the plant body allowed the vascular plants to spread to new terrestrial environments and to diversify rapidly.

Vascular tissues transport water and dissolved materials

The key synapomorphy of the vascular plants is a well-developed vascular system containing two types of tissues that are specialized for the transport of materials from one part of the plant to another. One type of vascular tissue, the **xylem**, conducts water and minerals from the soil to aerial parts of the plant. Because some of its cell walls contain a stiffening substance called lignin, xylem also provides support against gravity in the terrestrial environment. The other type of vascular tissue, the **phloem**, conducts the products of photosynthesis from sites where they are produced or released to sites where they are used or stored.

Connect the Concepts The vascular tissues of plants are described in detail in Chapters 32 and 33.

Although the vascular plants are an extraordinarily large and diverse group, one particular event was critical to their evolution. Sometime during the Paleozoic, probably in the mid-Silurian (430 mya), a new cell type—the tracheid—evolved in sporophytes of the earliest vascular plants. The tracheid is the principal water-conducting element of the xylem in all vascular plants except the angiosperms (flowering plants) and gnetophytes—and tracheids persist even in these groups, along with a more specialized and efficient system derived from them.

The evolution of tracheids set the stage for the complete and permanent invasion of land by plants. First, these cells provided

Figure 26.12 Artist's Reconstruction of an Ancient Forest
Forests of the Carboniferous were characterized by abundant vascular plants such as club mosses, ferns, and horsetails, some of which reached heights of 40 meters. Huge flying insects (see the opening of Chapter 23) thrived in these forests, which are the source of modern coal deposits.

a pathway for the transport of water and mineral nutrients from a source of supply to regions of need in the plant body. Second, the cell walls of tracheids, stiffened by lignin, provided rigid structural support. This support is a crucial factor in a terrestrial environment because it allows plants to grow upward and thus compete for sunlight. A taller plant can intercept more direct sunlight (and thus conduct photosynthesis more readily) than a shorter plant, which may be shaded by the taller one. Increased height also improves the dispersal of spores.

The vascular plants featured another evolutionary novelty: a branching, independent sporophyte. A branching sporophyte body can produce more spores than an unbranched body, and it can develop in complex ways. The sporophyte of a vascular plant is nutritionally independent of the gametophyte at maturity. Among the vascular plants, the sporophyte is the large and obvious plant that one normally pays attention to in nature, in contrast to the relatively small, dependent sporophytes typical of most nonvascular land plants.

Diversification of vascular plants made land more suitable for animals

The initial absence of herbivores (plant-eating animals) on land helped make the first vascular plants successful. By the late Silurian (about 425 mya), the proliferation of land plants made the terrestrial environment more hospitable to animals. Arthropods, vertebrates, and other animals moved onto land only after vascular plants became established there.

Trees of various kinds appeared in the Devonian and dominated the landscape of the Carboniferous (359–299 mya). Forests of lycophytes (club mosses) up to 40 meters tall, along with horsetails and tree ferns, flourished in the tropical swamps of what would become North America and Europe (**Figure 26.12**). Plant parts from those forests sank into the swamps and were gradually covered by layers of sediment. Over millions of years, as the buried plant material was subjected to intense pressure and elevated temperatures, it was transformed into coal. Today that coal powers nearly 40% of the world's electricity generation. The world's coal deposits, although huge, are not infinite, and humans are burning coal deposits at a far faster rate than they were produced.

In the subsequent Permian, when the continents came together to form Pangaea, the continental interior became warmer and drier. The 200-million-year reign of the lycophyte–fern forests came to an end as they were replaced by forests of early gymnosperms.

The closest relatives of vascular plants lacked roots

The closest relatives of living vascular plants belonged to several extinct groups called **rhyniophytes** (**Figure 26.13**). The rhyniophytes were among a very few types of land plants in the Silurian. The landscape at that time probably consisted mostly of bare

Figure 26.13 An Ancient Relative of the Vascular Plants
The extinct rhyniophyte *Aglaophyton major* lacked roots and leaves. It had a central column of xylem running through its stems but no true tracheids. A horizontal underground stem called a rhizome anchored the plant. The dichotomously branching aerial stems were less than 50 centimeters tall. Some stems were topped by sporangia.

ground, with mats of nonvascular plants and stands of rhyniophytes in low-lying moist areas. Early versions of the structural features of the vascular plant groups appeared in the rhyniophytes of that time. These shared features strengthen the case for the origin of all vascular plants from a common nonvascular land plant ancestor.

Rhyniophytes did not have roots. They were apparently anchored in the soil by horizontal portions of stem called **rhizomes**, which bore water-absorbing unicellular filaments called **rhizoids**. These plants also bore aerial branches, and sporangia—homologous to the sporangia of mosses—were found at the tips of those branches. The branching pattern of rhyniophytes was **dichotomous**; that is, the apex (tip) of the shoot divided to produce two equivalent new branches, with each pair of branches diverging at approximately the same angle from the original stem.

Lycophytes are sister to the other vascular plants

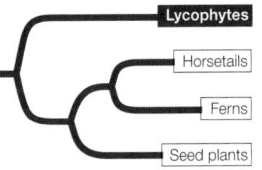

The club mosses and their relatives, the spike mosses and quillworts, are collectively called **lycophytes**. The lycophytes are the sister group to the remaining vascular plants (see Figure 26.1B). There are relatively few (just over 1,200) surviving species of lycophytes.

The lycophytes have true roots that branch dichotomously. The arrangement of vascular tissue in their stems is simpler than that in other vascular plants. They bear simple leaflike structures called **microphylls**, which are arranged spirally on the stem (**Figure 26.14A**). Growth in lycophytes comes entirely from apical cell division. Branching in the stems, which is also dichotomous, occurs by division of an apical cluster of dividing cells.

The sporangia of many club mosses are aggregated in conelike structures called **strobili** (singular *strobilus*) (see Figure 26.14A), which are clusters of spore-bearing microphylls attached to the end of the stem. Other club mosses lack strobili and bear their sporangia on (or adjacent to) the upper surfaces of specialized microphylls.

Horsetails and ferns constitute a clade

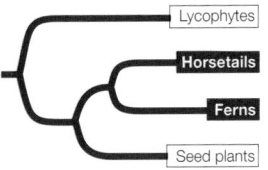

The horsetails and ferns were once thought to be only distantly related. As a result of genomic analyses, we now know that they form a clade, the **monilophytes**. In the monilophytes—as in the seed plants, to which they are the sister group (see Figure 26.1B)—there is differentiation between a main stem and side branches (including the leaves derived from these branches). This pattern contrasts with the dichotomous branching characteristic of the lycophytes and rhyniophytes, in which each split gives rise to two branches of similar size.

Today there are only about 15 species of **horsetails**, all in the genus *Equisetum*. The horsetails have reduced true leaves that form in distinct whorls (circles) around the stem (**Figure 26.14B**). Horsetails are sometimes called "scouring rushes" because rough silica deposits found in their cell walls once made them useful for cleaning. They have true roots that branch irregularly. Horsetails have a large sporophyte and a small gametophyte, each independent of the other.

The first ferns appeared during the Devonian. Today this group comprises more than 12,000 species. Analyses of gene sequences indicate that a few species traditionally allied with ferns may in fact be more closely related to horsetails than to ferns. Nonetheless, the majority of ferns form a monophyletic group.

(A) *Lycopodium digitatum*   (B) *Equisetum sylvaticum*   (C) *Marsilea mutica*   (D) *Dicksonia* sp.

Figure 26.14 Lycophytes and Monilophytes   (A) Club mosses have microphylls arranged spirally on their stems. Strobili are visible at the tips of these stems. (B) Horsetails have a distinctive growth pattern in which the stem grows in segments above each whorl of leaves. These are fertile shoots with sporangia-bearing structures at the apex. (C) The floating leaves of a water fern. (D) Tree ferns dominate this forest in Oparara Basin Kahurangi National Park in New Zealand.

Although most ferns are terrestrial, a few species live in shallow fresh water (**Figure 26.14C**). Terrestrial ferns are characterized by large leaves with branching vascular strands (**Figure 26.14D**). Some fern leaves become climbing organs and may grow to be as long as 30 meters.

In the alternating generations of a fern, the gametophyte is small, delicate, and short-lived, but the sporophyte can be very large and can sometimes survive for hundreds of years (**Figure 26.15**). Ferns require liquid water for the transport of the male gametes to the female gametes, so most ferns inhabit shaded, moist woodlands and swamps. The sporangia of ferns typically are borne on a stalk in clusters called **sori** (singular *sorus*). The

sori are found on the undersurfaces of the leaves, sometimes covering the entire undersurface and sometimes located at the edges.

Vascular plants branched out

Several features that were new to the vascular plants evolved in lycophytes and monilophytes. Roots probably had their evolutionary origins as a branch, either of a rhizome or of the aboveground portion of a stem. These branches presumably penetrated the soil and branched further. The underground portion could anchor the plant firmly, and even in this primitive condition it could absorb water and minerals.

Figure 26.15 Life Cycle of a Fern
The most conspicuous stage in the fern life cycle is the mature diploid sporophyte, shown at the bottom of this diagram. The inset shows sori on the underside of a fern leaf. Each sorus contains many spore-producing sporangia.

▶ View in **Achieve**
Activity 26.1 The Fern Life Cycle

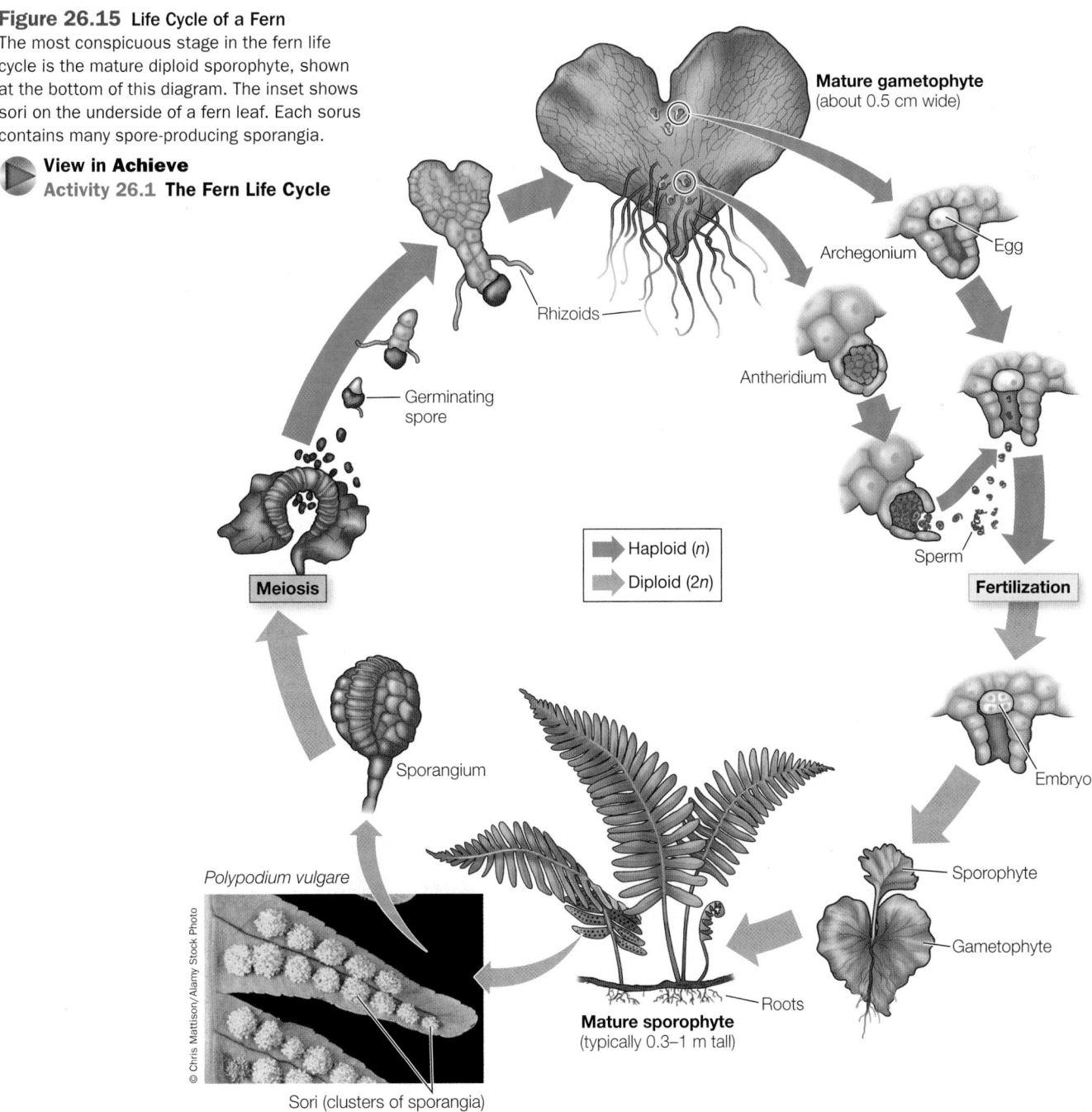

Mature gametophyte
(about 0.5 cm wide)

Archegonium — Egg

Antheridium

Sperm

Rhizoids

Germinating spore

Haploid (*n*)
Diploid (2*n*)

Meiosis

Fertilization

Sporangium

Embryo

Sporophyte

Gametophyte

Roots

Mature sporophyte
(typically 0.3–1 m tall)

Polypodium vulgare

© Chris Mattison/Alamy Stock Photo

Sori (clusters of sporangia)

(A) Microphylls

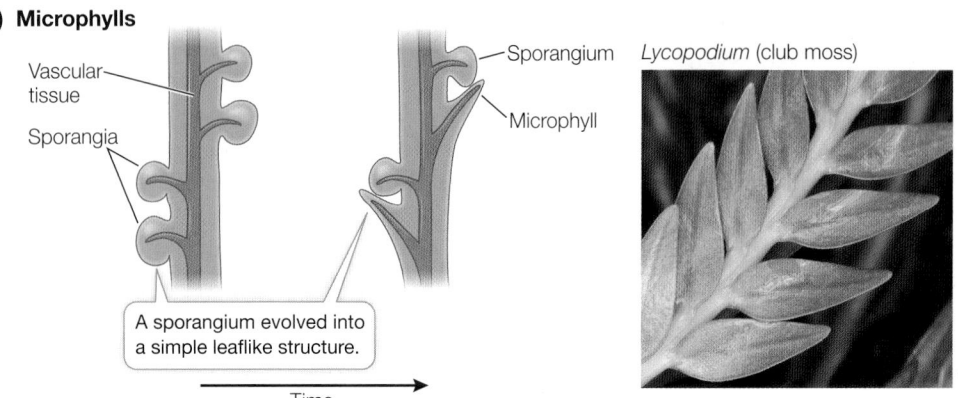

Lycopodium (club moss)

Figure 26.16 Evolution of Leaves
(A) Microphylls are thought to have evolved from sterile sporangia. **(B)** The megaphylls of monilophytes and seed plants may have arisen as photosynthetic tissue developed between branch pairs that were "left behind" as dominant branches overtopped them.

(B) Megaphylls

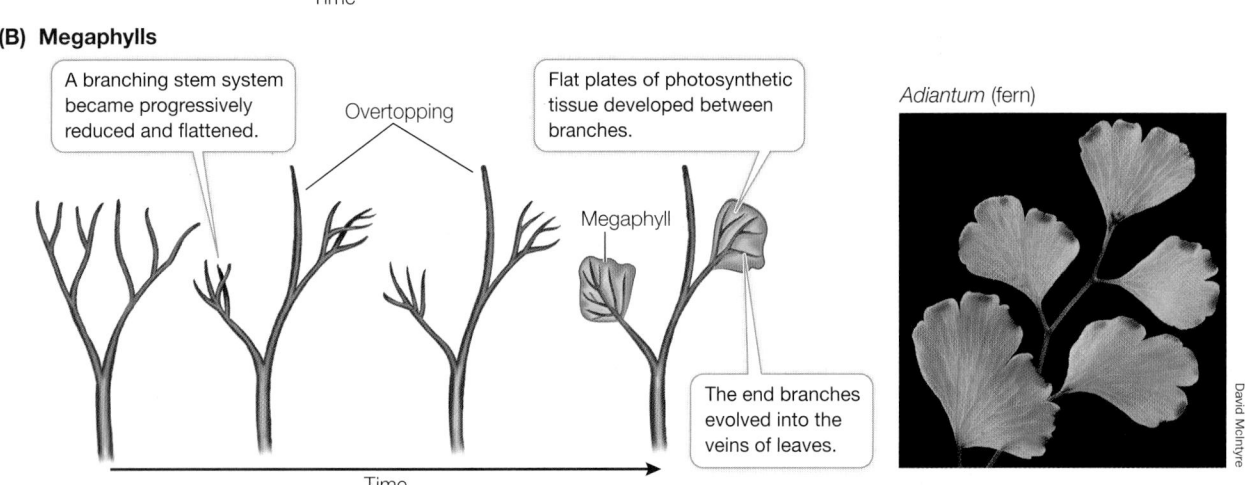

Adiantum (fern)

The microphylls of lycophytes were probably the first leaflike structures to evolve among the vascular plants. Microphylls are usually small and only rarely have more than a single vascular strand, at least in existing species. Some biologists believe that microphylls had their evolutionary origins as sterile sporangia (**Figure 26.16A**). The principle characteristic of a microphyll is a vascular strand that departs from the vascular system of the stem in such a way that the structure of the stem's vascular system is scarcely disturbed. This pattern was evident even in the lycophyte trees of the Carboniferous, many of which had microphylls many centimeters long.

The monilophytes and seed plants constitute a clade called the **euphyllophytes** (*eu*, "true," + *phyllos*, "leaf"). An important synapomorphy of the euphyllophytes is **overtopping**, a growth pattern in which one branch differentiates from and grows beyond the others (**Figure 26.16B**). Overtopping would have given these plants an advantage in the competition for light, enabling them to shade their dichotomously branching competitors. The overtopping growth of the euphyllophytes also allowed a new type of leaflike structure to evolve. This larger, more complex leaf is called a **megaphyll**. The megaphyll is thought to have arisen from the flattening of a portion of a branching stem system that exhibited overtopping growth. This change was followed by the development of photosynthetic tissue between the members of overtopped groups of branches, which had the advantage of increasing the photosynthetic surface area of those branches.

The first megaphylls, which were very small, appeared in the Devonian. We might expect that evolution should have led swiftly to the appearance of more and larger megaphylls because of their greater photosynthetic capacity. However, it took some 50 million years, until the Carboniferous, for large megaphylls to become common. Why should this have been so, especially given that other advances in plant structure were taking place during that time?

According to one theory, the high concentration of CO_2 in the atmosphere during the Devonian reduced selection for the stomata that allow a leaf to take up CO_2 for use in photosynthesis. With more CO_2 available, fewer stomata were needed. In the Devonian, larger leaves with a limited number of stomata would have absorbed heat from sunlight, but they would have been unable to lose heat fast enough by evaporation of water through their stomata. The resulting overheating would have been lethal. Recent research has supported this hypothesis, indicating that larger megaphylls evolved only as CO_2 concentrations dropped over millions of years (**Figure 26.17**).

Connect the Concepts As explained in Key Concept 33.3, stomata are pores in the epidermis of plants that open and close to regulate uptake of CO_2 into the plant and guard against excessive diffusion of water out of the plant. Various environmental factors trigger the opening and closing of stomata, including light, the CO_2 level in photosynthetic cells of the plant, and water availability.

Experiment

Figure 26.17 Atmospheric CO_2 Concentrations and the Evolution of Megaphylls

Original Paper: C. P. Osborne et al. 2004. Biophysical constraints on the origin of leaves inferred from the fossil record. *Proc Natl Acad Sci USA* 101: 10360–10362. © 2004. National Academy of Sciences, U.S.A.

High concentrations of atmospheric CO_2 during the first part of the Devonian may have limited the evolution of leaf size. C. P. Osborne and colleagues compared the leaf sizes of fossil plants against estimates of CO_2 concentrations in the atmosphere at the time the plants were alive.

HYPOTHESIS▶ High atmospheric CO_2 concentrations during the early Devonian, and the resulting lack of selection for more stomata, kept leaf sizes small.

METHOD▶

1. Analyze 300 plant fossils from the Devonian and Carboniferous and measure the sizes of their leaves.

2. Compare the pattern of change in leaf size with that of the estimated change in atmospheric CO_2 concentrations over the same time span.

RESULTS▶

Among these fossils, increasing leaf sizes generally followed declining levels of atmospheric CO_2.

CONCLUSION▶ Leaf size increased as levels of CO_2 in the atmosphere decreased.

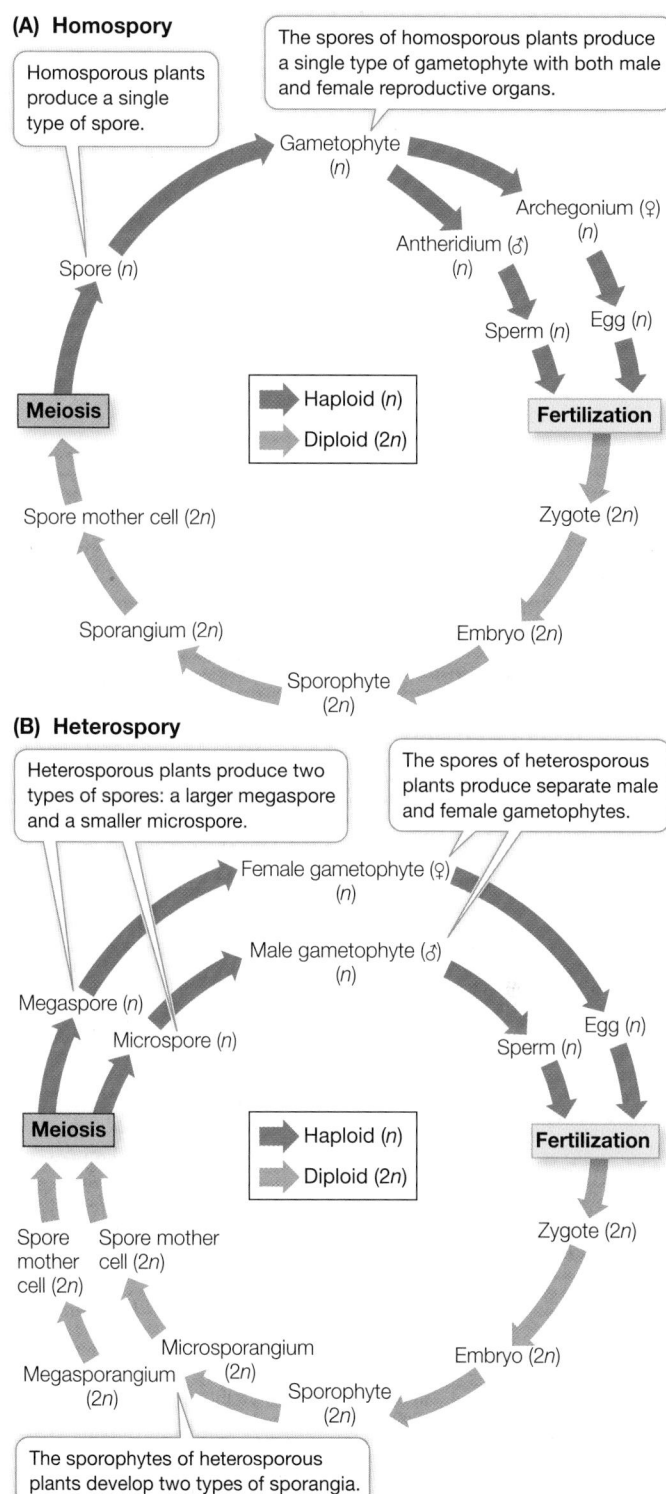

Figure 26.18 Homospory and Heterospory **(A)** Homosporous plants bear a single type of spore. Each gametophyte has two types of sex organs, antheridia (male) and archegonia (female). **(B)** Heterosporous plants bear two types of spores that develop into distinctly male and female gametophytes.

 View in Achieve
Activity 26.2 **Homospory**

View in Achieve
Activity 26.3 **Heterospory**

Heterospory appeared among the vascular plants

In the lineages of present-day, seedless vascular plants that are most similar to their ancestors, the gametophyte and the sporophyte are independent, and both are usually photosynthetic. The spores produced by the sporophyte are of a single type and develop into a single type of gametophyte that bears both female and male reproductive organs (see Figure 26.15). Such plants, which bear a single type of spore, are said to be **homosporous** (Figure 26.18A).

A system with two distinct types of spores evolved somewhat later. Plants of this type are said to be **heterosporous**

(Figure 26.18B). In heterospory, one type of spore—the **mega-spore**—develops into a specifically **female gametophyte** (or megagametophyte) that produces only eggs. The other type, the **microspore**, is smaller and develops into a **male gametophyte** (or microgametophyte) that produces only sperm. The sporophyte produces megaspores in small numbers in **megasporangia** and microspores in large numbers in **microsporangia**. Heterospory affects not only the spores and the gametophytes but also the sporophyte plant itself, which must develop two types of sporangia.

The earliest vascular plants were all homosporous, but heterospory evidently evolved several times independently among later groups of vascular plants. The fact that heterospory evolved repeatedly suggests that it affords selective advantages. What advantages does heterospory provide? Heterospory allows the production of many small microspores, which are easily transported from plant to plant. Heterospory also results in the production of a few large megaspores in large megasporangia, which can provide nutrition and protection for the developing embryo. With this division, plants can increase the opportunities for long-distance cross-fertilization, and at the same time increase the chances for survival of the developing embryo.

KEY CONCEPT

26.3 Recap and Assess

Vascular plants are characterized by a vascular system specialized for the transport of materials from one part of the plant to another. A new type of cell, the tracheid, marked the origin of this group. Later evolutionary events included the appearance of roots, leaves, and heterospory.

1. How do the vascular tissues xylem and phloem serve the vascular plants?

2. Describe the evolution and distribution of different kinds of leaves and roots among the vascular plants.

3. Explain the concept of heterospory. How does heterospory provide selective advantages over homospory?

All of the vascular plant groups we have discussed thus far disperse by means of spores. The embryos of these seedless vascular plants develop directly into sporophytes, which either survive or die, depending on environmental conditions. The spores of some seedless plants may remain dormant and viable for long periods, but the embryos of seedless plants are relatively unprotected. Greater protection of the embryo evolved in the seed plants, which we will consider in the next chapter.

▶Investigating LIFE

 Can we grow new biofuels that capture carbon from Earth's atmosphere?

Before we consider the practicality of biofuel production, let's look at how much carbon is tied up in all the major groups of life on Earth (Figure 26.19). In 2018, biologists estimated the gigatons of carbon (GtC) that are incorporated into each major group. All of life represents about 500 GtC. Of the total, about 90% of carbon (450 GtC) is in plants, and most of the biomass of plants is present on land. The uncertainty of the estimate is relatively low for plants (the 95% confidence limits are within 1.2-fold of the estimate, or 375–540 GtC), but the uncertainty of the estimates for the other groups is higher, especially for bacteria and archaea. Despite the broad confidence limits in these estimates, it is clear that most life on Earth is green, and that it is this plant life that sustains (directly or indirectly) almost all other life on Earth. Some plants (such as corn) are currently grown for biofuel (ethanol) production, but the input of fossil fuels in corn agriculture is very high. Are there more practical and sustainable sources of biofuels?

Future directions

What if we could grow biofuels that captured carbon from the atmosphere, while using minimal fossil fuels to grow the plants? Algae appear to provide the most likely source for such sustainable biofuels. The primary commercial limitations to growing algae for biofuels include the need to establish efficient growing facilities, water needs, costs of fertilizers, costs and difficulties associated with harvest and refining, and labor expenses. As we explored in **Investigating Life: Can Chlorella Algae Be Grown in Municipal Sewage Wastewater for Biofuel Production?**, considerable research is being conducted on ways to reduce these costs, such as growing algae for biofuels in municipal wastewater. Many new methods for growing and harvesting algae are being developed (**Figure 26.20**). Once some of the technical difficulties have been overcome, it is possible that commercial production of biofuels from algae will provide a significant, sustainable source of energy for humans.

- Plants (90% ± 1.2-fold)
- Bacteria (5% ± 10-fold)
- Fungi (2.4% ± 3-fold)
- Archaea (0.8% ± 13-fold)
- Protists (0.8% ± 4-fold)
- Animals (0.4% ± 5-fold)

Figure 26.19 Most Life on Earth Is Green   This pie chart shows the estimated percentages of carbon found in the major groups of living organisms on Earth; 95% confidence limits are shown as x-fold of the estimates. (After Y. M. Bar-On et al. 2018. *Proc Natl Acad Sci USA* 115: 6506–6511; with updates from Y. M. Bar-On and R. Milo. 2019. *Nat Rev Microbiol* 17: 199–200.)

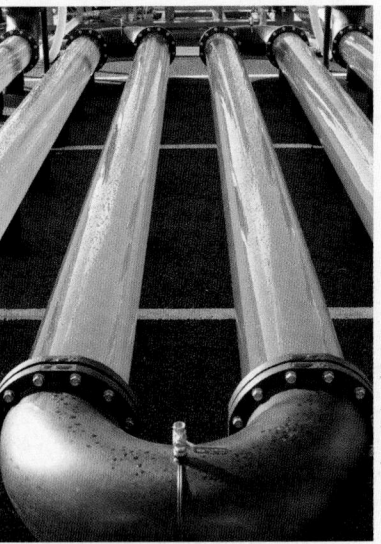

Figure 26.20 Biodiesel from Algae In this algal cultivation system for biofuel production, algae are grown in tubes of clear plastic.

Courtesy of the U.S. Coast Guard

You should be able to relate each summary to the adjacent figures. If you go to this visual summary in **Achieve**, you can follow links to figures, animations, activities, and simulations that will help you consolidate the material.

KEY CONCEPT

26.1 Primary Endosymbiosis Produced the First Photosynthetic Eukaryotes

- Primary endosymbiosis gave rise to chloroplasts and the subsequent diversification of **Plantae**. The descendants of the first photosynthetic eukaryote include **glaucophytes**, **red algae**, several groups of green algae, and **land plants**, all of which contain chlorophyll *a*.

- **Streptophytes** include the land plants and two groups of green algae. **Green plants**, which in-clude the streptophytes and the remaining green algae, are characterized by the presence of chlorophyll *b* (in addition to chlorophyll *a*).

- Land plants, also known as **embryophytes**, arose from an aquatic green algal ancestor related to today's **stoneworts**. Land plants develop from embryos that are protected by parental tissue.

Figure 26.1

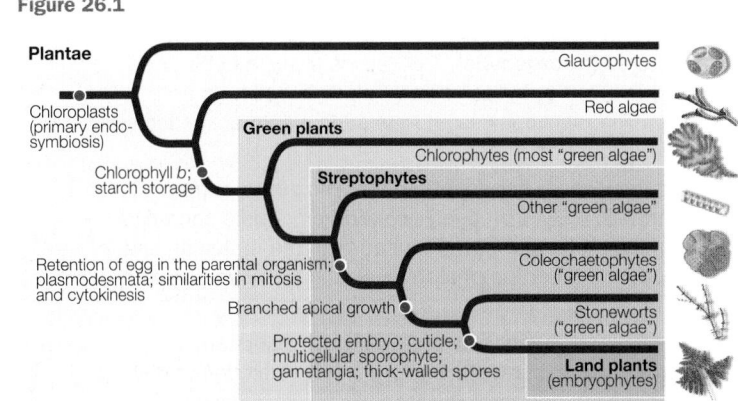

Questions

1. What kind of organism became endosymbiotic in plants and gave rise to chloroplasts?

2. Photosynthesis uses energy to convert carbon dioxide and water into carbohydrates and oxygen. What is the reverse of this process called?

KEY CONCEPT

26.2 Key Adaptations Permitted Plants to Colonize Land

Go to Animation 26.1

- The acquisition of a cuticle, stomata, **gametangia**, a protected **embryo**, protec-tive pigments, thick spore walls with a protective polymer, and a mutualistic association with fungi were all adaptations of land plants to terrestrial life.

- All land plant life cycles feature alternation of gen-erations, in which a multi-cellular diploid **sporophyte** alternates with a multicellular haploid **gametophyte**.

- The nonvascular land plants comprise the **liverworts**, **mosses**, and **hornworts**. These groups lack specialized vascular tissues for the conduction of water or nutrients through the plant body, and their life cycles depend on liquid water.

Figure 26.6

Figure 26.7

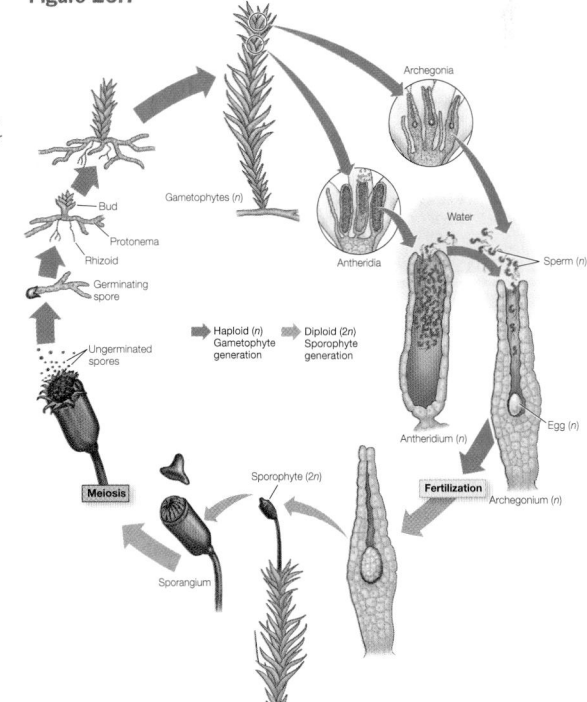

Questions

1. How do each of the adaptations to terrestrial life that we have just listed convey an advantage to life on land?

2. When you look at a moss, which is most obvious—the haploid gametophyte generation, or the diploid sporophyte generation?

3. What part of the moss is the diploid sporophyte generation?

KEY CONCEPT

26.3 Vascular Tissues Led to Rapid Diversification of Land Plants

Go to **Activities 26.1–26.3**

- The vascular plants have a vascular system consisting of **xylem** and **phloem** that conducts water, minerals, and products of photosynthesis through the plant body.

- Among living vascular plant groups, the **lycophytes** (club mosses and relatives) have only small, simple leaflike structures (**microphylls**). True leaves (**megaphylls**) are found in **monilophytes** (which include **horsetails** and ferns). The monilophytes and the seed plants are collectively called **euphyllophytes**.

- Roots may have evolved either from **rhizomes** or from stems. Microphylls probably evolved from sterile sporangia, and megaphylls may have resulted from the flattening and reduction of a portion of a stem system with **overtopping** growth.

- The earliest-diverging groups of vascular plants are **homosporous**, but **heterospory**—the production of distinct **megaspores** and **microspores**—has evolved several times.

Questions

1. In the late Paleozoic, forests of giant club mosses, ferns, and horsetails covered large areas of land. What are these groups like today? Why do you think this is the case?

2. What is the advantage of heterospory over homospory that has facilitated heterospory's repeated evolution?

3. How is a fern gametophyte different from the gametophyte of a seed plant?

Figure 26.16

Microphylls

Megaphylls

Figure 26.18

Homospory

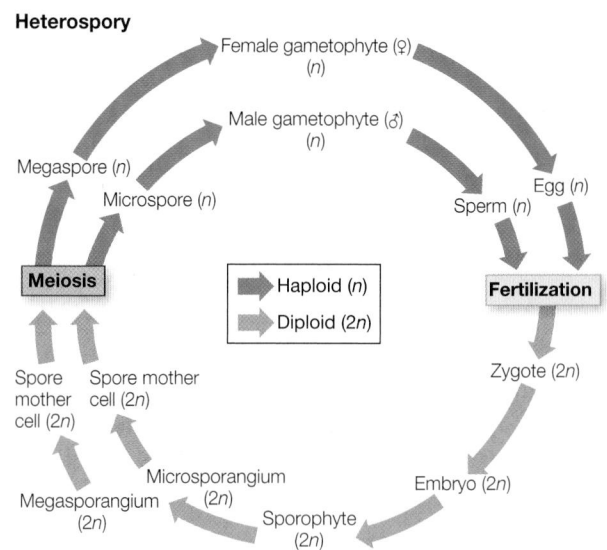

Heterospory

Go to **Achieve** for the eBook, **LearningCurve**, animations, activities, simulations, and additional resources and assignments.

The Evolution of Seed Plants 27

Phoenix dactylifera, the date palm, is widely cultivated for its edible fruit.

KEY CONCEPTS

27.1 Pollen, Seeds, and Wood Contributed to the Success of Seed Plants

27.2 Once Dominant Gymnosperms Still Thrive in Some Environments

27.3 Flowers and Fruits Led to Increased Diversification of Angiosperms

27.4 Plants Play Critical Roles in Terrestrial Ecosystems

© Zvonimir Atletić/Alamy Stock Photo

▶ InvestigatingLIFE

Brought Back from Extinction by a Seed

The Judean date is a fruit that was once much prized, admired for its nutritional and medicinal properties. This fruit was the source of the "honey" in the biblical "land of milk and honey." Today that ancient strain of date is gone. Or is it?

About 2,000 years ago, a seed developed in a fruit on a Judean date palm. The fruit that contained that seed found its way to a storeroom in the fortress Masada in Judea. In 73 CE a band of Jewish zealots involved in a revolt against Rome fled to this refuge with their families and provisions. The fortress was eventually sacked and left in ruins.

Twenty centuries later, archeologists working in Masada discovered the date seed that was long ago stored in the Masada fortress and confirmed its age. The previous record for seed survival and germination was 1,300 years, held by lotus seeds that recently germinated under the care of scientists in China. But botanist Elaine Solowey succeeded in making the 2,000-year-old date seed germinate! For 10 years the seedling has thrived, and is now mature and producing pollen.

Seeds are important structures for the evolutionary survival of plants. Each seed protects an enclosed plant embryo from

environmental extremes through what may be a very long and stressful resting period—in the case of the Judean date, many centuries in a harsh desert. Such hardiness has contributed to making seed plants the predominant plants on Earth. All of today's forests are dominated by seed plants.

So will the resurrected palm serve as the parent of a new population of Judean dates, thus bringing that genotype back from extinction? Unfortunately, it cannot do so alone, because date palms have separate sexes, and the single known individual is a male that can produce only pollen. However, the search is on for other ancient seeds of Judean dates from archeological sites, and it is hoped that one of those will grow into a female plant that can produce new fruit and seeds. Even if a female Judean date seed cannot be found, the male Judean date's pollen can be used to introduce valuable genes back into other, still living, strains of dates.

 How long can most seeds survive, and why is seed dormancy important?
(Find the answer on page 620.)

KEY CONCEPT 27.1 Pollen, Seeds, and Wood Contributed to the Success of Seed Plants

Learning Objectives

27.1.1 Explain how the evolution of pollen enabled seed plants to thrive in terrestrial environments.

27.1.2 List three major advantages of having seeds.

27.1.3 Describe the earliest group of woody plants and list two advantages of woody plants.

By the late Devonian, more than 360 million years ago, Earth was home to a great variety of land plants, many of which we discussed in Chapter 26. The land plants shared the hot, humid terrestrial environment with insects, spiders, centipedes, and early tetrapods. These plants and animals evolved together, each acting as agents of natural selection on the other. In the Devonian, a new innovation appeared when some plants developed extensively thickened woody stems. Among the first plants with this adaptation were seedless vascular plants called **progymnosperms**, all

species of which are now extinct. The progymnosperms included many large trees.

Two other innovations, **pollen** and **seeds**, arose in the seed plants. Pollen increases reproductive opportunities in a terrestrial environment, and seeds provide a secure and lasting structure that protects the dormant stage of the embryo. A plant embryo may safely wait within its seed (in some cases for many years, or even centuries) until conditions are right for germination.

The earliest fossil evidence of seed plants is found in late Devonian rocks. Like the progymnosperms, these now-extinct **seed ferns** were woody. They possessed fernlike foliage but had seeds attached to their leaves. By the end of the Permian, other groups of seed plants had become dominant (**Figure 27.1**). Today's living seed plants fall into two major groups, the **gymnosperms** (such as pines and cycads) and the hugely diverse group known as the **angiosperms** (flowering plants).

Features of the seed plant life cycle protect gametes and embryos

In Key Concept 26.2 we described a major trend in land plant evolution: the sporophyte became less dependent on the gametophyte, which became smaller in relation to the sporophyte.

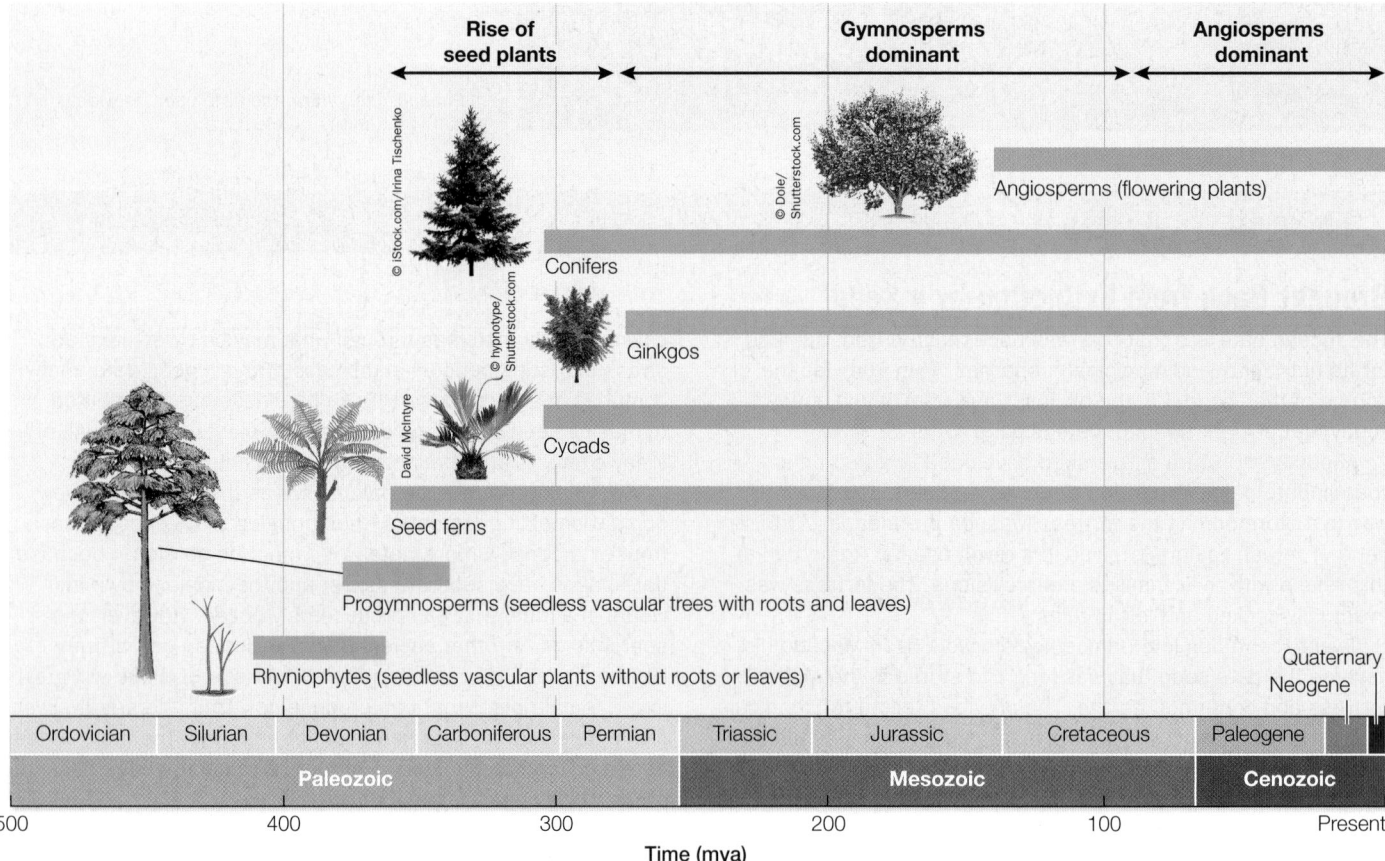

Figure 27.1 The Fossil Record of Seed Plant Evolution
Woody growth evolved in the seedless progymnosperms. The now-extinct seed ferns had woody growth, fernlike foliage, and seeds attached to their leaves. New lineages of seed plants arose during the Carboniferous, but the earliest known fossils of flowering plants are from near the Jurassic–Cretaceous boundary. The flowering plants have dominated most terrestrial environments through the Cenozoic. (mya, millions of years ago.)

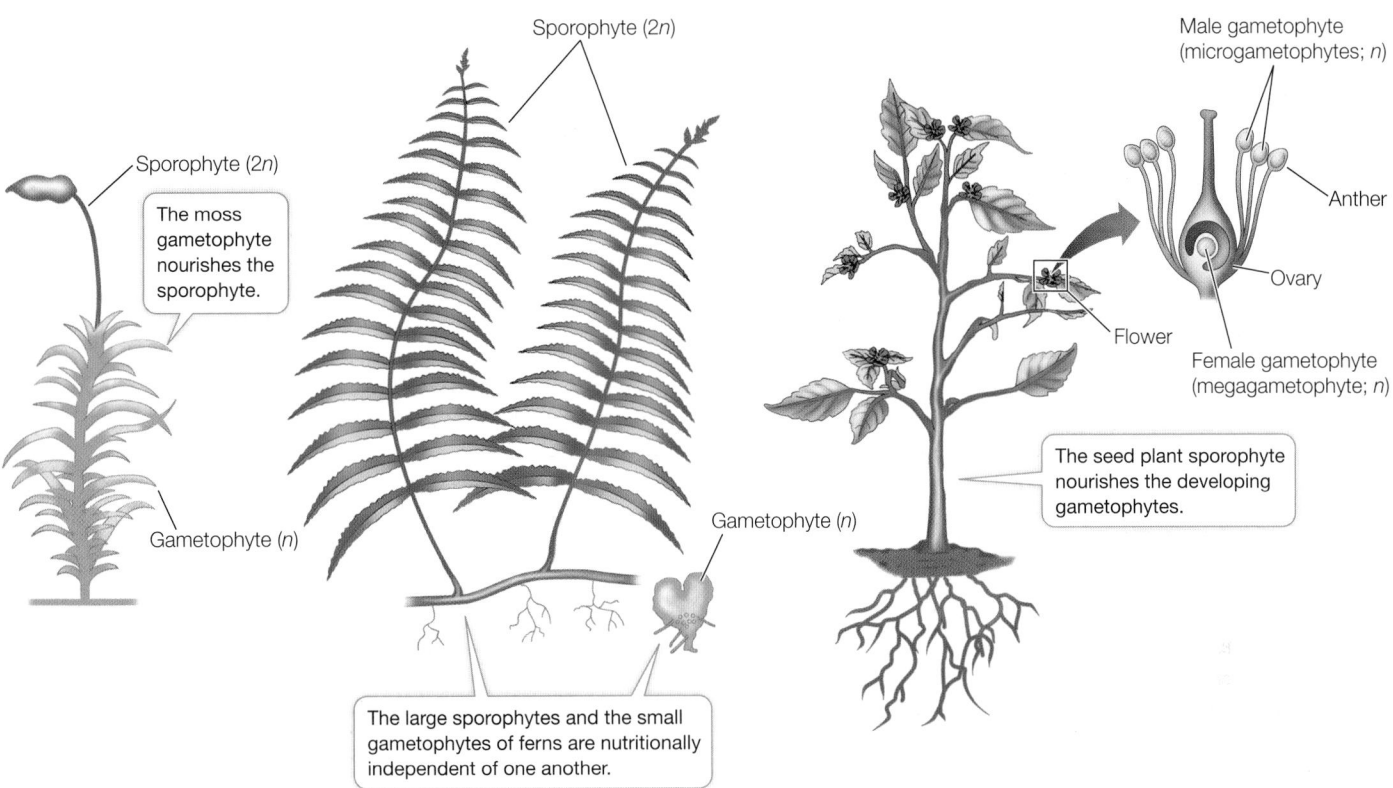

Figure 27.2 The Relationship between Sporophyte and Gametophyte In the course of plant evolution, the gametophyte (brown) has been reduced and the sporophyte (blue) has become more prominent.

This trend continued with the seed plants, whose gametophyte generation is reduced even further than it is in the ferns (**Figure 27.2**). The haploid seed plant gametophyte develops partly or entirely while attached to and nutritionally dependent on the diploid sporophyte.

Among the seed plants, only the earliest-diverging groups of gymnosperms (including modern cycads and ginkgos) have swimming sperm. Even in these groups, sperm is transferred via pollen grains, so fertilization does not require liquid water outside the plant body. The evolution of pollen, along with the advent of seeds, gave seed plants the opportunity to colonize drier areas and spread over the terrestrial environment.

Seed plants are heterosporous (see Figure 26.18B)—that is, they produce two types of spores, one that becomes a male gametophyte (microgametophyte) and one that becomes a female gametophyte (macrogametophyte). They form separate microsporangia and megasporangia on structures that are grouped on short stems, such as the stamens and carpels of an angiosperm flower.

Within the microsporangium, the meiotic products are microspores. Within its spore wall, a microspore divides mitotically one or a few times to form a multicellular male gametophyte, also known as a single grain of pollen. Pollen grains are released from the microsporangium to be distributed by wind or by an animal pollinator (**Figure 27.3**). As in seedless land plants, the spore wall that surrounds the pollen grain contains a substance called sporopollenin, the most chemically resistant biological compound known. Sporopollenin protects the pollen grain against

Corylus avellana

Figure 27.3 Blown on the Wind Pollen grains are the male gametophytes of seed plants. The male flowers of this hazel tree release pollen-containing spores that are dispersed by the wind and may land near female gametophytes of other hazel plants.

▶ **Media Clip 27.1 Pollen Transfer by Wind**
Life12e.com/mc27.1

dehydration and chemical damage—another advantage in terms of survival in the terrestrial environment.

In contrast to the microspores, the megaspores of seed plants are not shed. Instead, they develop into female gametophytes within the megasporangia. These female gametophytes are dependent on the sporophyte for food and water.

In most seed plant species, only one of the meiotic products in a megasporangium survives. The surviving haploid nucleus divides mitotically, and the resulting cells divide again to produce a multicellular female gametophyte. The megasporangium is surrounded by sterile sporophytic structures, which form an **integument** that protects the megasporangium and its contents. Together, the megasporangium and integument constitute the **ovule**, which will develop into a seed after fertilization.

The arrival of a pollen grain at an appropriate landing point, close to a female gametophyte on a sporophyte of the same species, is called **pollination**. A pollen grain that reaches this point develops further. It produces a slender **pollen tube** that elongates

and digests its way toward the female gametophyte (**Figure 27.4**). When the tip of the pollen tube reaches the female gametophyte, sperm are released from the tube and fertilization occurs.

The resulting diploid zygote divides repeatedly, forming an embryonic sporophyte. After a period of embryonic development, growth is temporarily suspended (the embryo enters a dormant stage). The end product at this stage is the multicellular seed.

The seed is a complex, well-protected package

A seed contains tissues from three generations (**Figure 27.5**). A seed coat develops from the integument—the tissues of the diploid sporophyte parent that surround the megasporangium. Within the megasporangium is haploid tissue from the female gametophyte, which contains a supply of nutrients for the developing embryo. (This tissue is fairly extensive in most gymnosperm seeds. In angiosperm seeds it is greatly reduced, and nutrition for the embryo is supplied instead by a tissue called endosperm.) In the center of the seed is the third generation, the embryo of the new diploid sporophyte.

(A) A growing pollen tube

Pollen grains

The pollen tube elongates on its way to the female gametophyte.

(B) The process of pollination

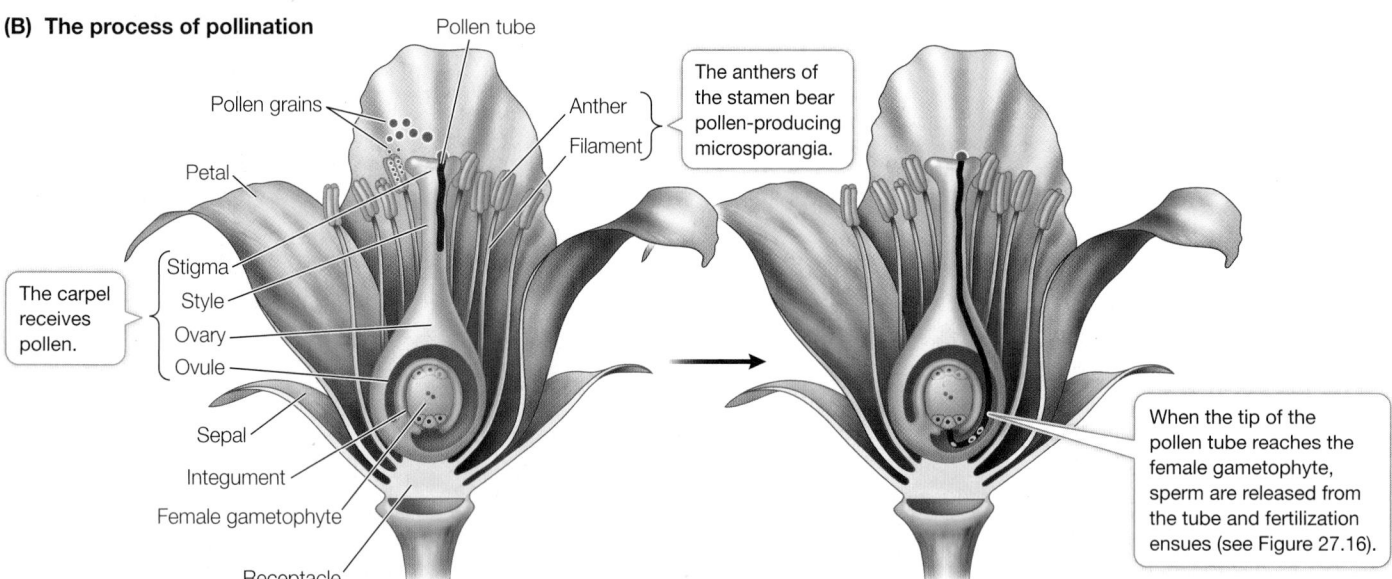

Pollen tube

Pollen grains

Petal

Anther

Filament

The anthers of the stamen bear pollen-producing microsporangia.

Stigma

Style

Ovary

Ovule

The carpel receives pollen.

Sepal

Integument

Female gametophyte

Receptacle

When the tip of the pollen tube reaches the female gametophyte, sperm are released from the tube and fertilization ensues (see Figure 27.16).

Figure 27.4 Pollination Is a Hallmark of the Seed Plants   In most seed plants, a pollen tube grows from the pollen grain to the female gametophyte, where sperm are released and fertilize the egg within the ovule. Once fertilization takes place, the ovule can develop into a seed (see Figure 27.5). **(A)** Scanning electron micrograph of a pollen tube growing in the flower of an angiosperm, the prairie gentian. **(B)** The process of pollination is diagrammed for a generalized angiosperm flower.

 View in Achieve
Activity 27.1 Flower Morphology

(A) Unfertilized ovule

1 The fleshy megasporangium (*2n*) is protected by the integument.

(B) Fertilized ovule

2 The megaspore grows into a multicellular, haploid female gametophyte (*n*).

(C) Seed

Seed coat (derived from integument; parental sporophyte tissue)

Immature female pine cone (cross section)

Integument

Megaspore (*n*)

Egg nucleus (*n*)

Germinated pollen grain (*n*)

Micropyle

Pollen grain (*n*)

Food supply (female gametophyte tissue; *n*)

Embryo (new sporophyte; *2n*)

3 A pollen grain (*n*) enters through the micropyle and develops a pollen tube (germinates).

4 The germinated pollen grain releases a sperm nucleus, fertilizing the egg nucleus and initiating seed formation.

Figure 27.5 **A Seed Develops**   These cross sections diagram the development of the ovule into a seed in a gymnosperm (*Pinus* sp.). Angiosperm seed development has differences (e.g., angiosperm integuments have two layers rather than one, and the angiosperm embryo is nourished by specialized tissue called endosperm) but follows the same principle (compare Figures 27.8 and 27.16). **(A)** The haploid megaspore is nourished by tissues of the parental sporophyte (the diploid megasporangium). **(B)** The mature megaspore is fertilized by a pollen grain that penetrates the integument, germinates (grows a pollen tube; see Figure 27.4A), and releases a sperm nucleus. **(C)** Fertilization initiates production of a seed. A mature seed contains three generations: a diploid embryo (the new sporophyte), which is surrounded by haploid female gametophyte tissue that supplies nutrition, which is in turn surrounded by the seed coat (diploid parental sporophyte tissue).

The seed is a well-protected resting stage. As we discussed in the opening of this chapter, the seeds of some species may remain dormant but stay viable (capable of growth and development) for many years, germinating only when conditions are favorable for the growth of the sporophyte. During the dormant stage, the seed coat protects the embryo from excessive drying and may also protect it against potential predators that would otherwise consume the embryo and its nutrient reserves. Many seeds have structural adaptations or are contained in fruits that promote their dispersal by wind or, more often, by animals. When the young sporophyte resumes growth, it draws on the food reserves in the seed. The possession of seeds is a major reason for the enormous evolutionary success of the seed plants, which are the dominant life forms of most modern terrestrial floras.

The germination of the Judean date described in the opening story is an extreme example of seed dormancy. How do we know how long most seeds remain viable? To find out, William J. Beal, a biologist at Michigan State University, decided to begin an experiment in 1879 that he could not hope to finish in his lifetime (**Investigating Life: William Beal's Seed Viability Study**). He prepared 20 lots of seeds for long-term storage. Each lot consisted of 50 seeds from each of 23 species of plants. He mixed each lot of seeds with sand and placed the mixture in an uncapped bottle, then buried all the bottles upside down (so they would stay dry) on a sandy knoll. The seeds experienced normal temperature fluctuations for Michigan. At regular intervals ever since, other biologists have excavated a bottle and checked the viability of the seeds it contained. The seeds of most species remained viable for decades, whereas others have remained viable for more than a century.

A change in stem anatomy enabled seed plants to grow to great heights

Fossils of the closest relatives of seed plants (progymnosperms) and the earliest seed plants (seed ferns) are found in late Devonian rocks (see Figure 27.1). These plants had thickened woody stems, developed through the proliferation of xylem. This type of growth, which increases the diameter of stems and roots in many modern seed plants, is called **secondary growth**. Its product is secondary xylem, or wood.

The younger portion of the wood produced by secondary growth is well adapted for water transport, but older wood becomes clogged with resins or other materials. Although no longer functional in transport, the older wood continues to provide support for the plant. This support allows woody plants to grow taller than other plants around them and thus capture more light for photosynthesis.

Not all seed plants are woody. In the course of seed plant evolution, many groups lost the woody growth habit; however, other advantageous attributes helped them become established in an astonishing variety of places.

▶InvestigatingLIFE William Beal's Seed Viability Study

Experiment

Original Papers: W. J. Beal. 1884. The vitality of seeds. *Proc Soc Prom Agr Sci* 5: 44–46.

H. T. Darlington. 1941. The sixty-year period for Dr. Beal's seed viability. *Am J Bot* 28: 271–273.

A. Kivilaan and R. S. Bandurski. 1981. The one hundred–year period for Dr. Beal's seed viability experiment. *Am J Bot* 68: 1290–1292.

F. W. Telewski and J. Zeevaart. 2002. The 120-year period for Dr. Beal's seed viability study. *Am J Bot* 89: 1285–1288.

William Beal began an experiment in 1879 to measure the long-term viability of seeds of several common plants. This ongoing experiment has been continued by biologists for well over a century. For the first 40 years of the experiment, Beal checked seed viability every 5 years. H. T. Darlington took over the experiment in 1915 and extended the sampling period to 10-year intervals beginning in 1920. R. S. Bandurski took over the experiment when Darlington retired, and extended the sampling period to 20 years in 1980, a century after the experiment began.

QUESTION▶ How long do seeds of common plants remain viable?

METHOD▶

1. Collect 1,000 seeds of each of 23 species of plants.

2. Divide the seeds into 20 lots of 50 seeds of each of the 23 species.

3. Mix each of the lots of seeds with sand, and place the mixtures in uncapped bottles.

4. Bury the bottles upside down (to prevent the entry of water) on a marked, sandy knoll.

5. At regular intervals, excavate a bottle and check the viability of its contents.

RESULTS▶ The table shows the number of germinating seeds (of the original 50) from three of the species in years 50–100 of this ongoing experiment.

Species	Years after burial					
	50	**60**	**70**	**80**	**90**	**100**
Oenothera biennis (evening primrose)	19	12	7	5	0	0
Rumex crispus (curly dock)	26	2	7	1	0	0
Verbascum blattaria (moth mullein)	31	34	37	35	10	21

Source: F. W. Telewski and J. Zeevaart. 2002. *Am J Bot* 89: 1285–1288.

CONCLUSION▶ Biologists have used this and similar experiments to estimate the maximum viability of seeds of many species of plants under near-natural environmental conditions. Explore how these data can be used to make predictions about seed viability in the Work with the Data exercise.

M. H. Siddall

Work with the Data

The data presented in this experiment can be used to make predictions about seed viability. Use the data to answer the following questions.

1. Calculate the percent of viable seeds for these three species in years 50–100 and graph seed survivorship as a function of time buried.

2. No seeds of the first two species were viable after 90 years of the experiment. Assume 100% seed viability at the start of the experiment (year 0), and predict from your graph the approximate year when you think the last *Verbascum blattaria* seeds will germinate.

3. What factors do you think might influence the differences among the species in long-term seed viability?

Go to Achieve for a companion Data in Depth exercise.

KEY CONCEPT

27.1 Recap and Assess

Today's living seed plants fall into two major groups, the gymnosperms and the angiosperms. Pollen grains, seeds, and wood are major evolutionary innovations of the seed plants. Protection of embryos is a hallmark of seed plants.

1. Explain the importance of pollen in freeing seed plants from dependence on liquid water.

2. How do seeds and seed dormancy help plants survive in highly seasonal environments?

3. What part did the evolution of wood play in changing the terrestrial landscape?

The seed ferns have long been extinct, but the surviving seed plants have been remarkable successes. After the seed ferns, the gymnosperms were the next group of plants to dominate terrestrial environments.

27.2 Once Dominant Gymnosperms Still Thrive in Some Environments

Learning Objectives

27.2.1 Describe and contrast the roles of male and female gametophytes in reproduction.

27.2.2 Summarize the functions of cones in conifers.

27.2.3 Describe the role of fire in the life history of the lodgepole pine.

The gymnosperms are seed plants that do not form flowers or fruits. Gymnosperms (which means "naked-seeded") are so named because their ovules and seeds, unlike those of angiosperms, are not protected by ovary or fruit tissue.

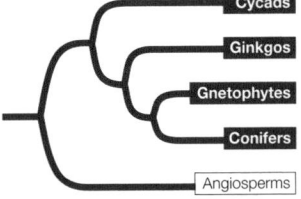

Gymnosperms dominated the terrestrial world through the Mesozoic but were replaced across large areas of Earth by flowering plants during the Cenozoic (see Figure 27.1). Although they now number fewer than 1,200 living species, gymnosperms are second only to the angiosperms in their dominance of the terrestrial environment.

There are four major groups of living gymnosperms

The living gymnosperms can be divided into four major groups:

1. **Cycads** are palmlike plants of the tropics and subtropics (**Figure 27.6A**). Of the present-day gymnosperms, the cycads are probably the earliest-diverging clade. There are about 300 species, some of which grow as tall as 20 meters. The tissues of many species are highly toxic to humans if ingested.

2. **Ginkgos**, common during the Mesozoic, are represented today by a single species, *Ginkgo biloba*, the maidenhair tree (**Figure 27.6B**). There are both male (microsporangiate) and female (megasporangiate) maidenhair trees. The difference is determined by X and Y sex chromosomes, as in humans. Few other plants have distinct sex chromosomes.

3. **Gnetophytes** number about 90 species in three very different genera, which share certain characteristics analogous to ones found in the angiosperms. One of the gnetophytes is *Welwitschia mirabilis* (**Figure 27.6C**), a long-lived desert

(A) *Encephalartos* sp.

(B) *Ginkgo biloba*

(C) *Welwitschia mirabilis*

(D) *Pinus longaeva*

Figure 27.6 Diversity among the Gymnosperms (A) Many cycads have growth forms that resemble those of both ferns and palms, although cycads are not closely related to either group. (B) The characteristic broad leaves of the maidenhair tree. (C) The two permanent straplike leaves of *Welwitschia mirabilis*, a gnetophyte, grow throughout the life of the plant, breaking and splitting as they grow. (D) Conifers dominate many types of landscapes in the Northern Hemisphere. Bristlecone pines such as these are the longest-lived individual trees known.

plant with just two permanent straplike leaves, which split into many pieces that sprawl across the sand.

4. **Conifers** are by far the most abundant of the gymnosperms. There are about 700 species of these cone-bearing plants, including the pines, spruces, and redwoods (**Figure 27.6D**).

With the exception of the gnetophytes, the living gymnosperm groups have only tracheids as water-conducting and support cells in the xylem. Most gymnosperms lack the vessel elements and fibers (cells specialized for water conduction and support, respectively) that are found in angiosperms. While the gymnosperm water-transport and support system may thus seem somewhat less efficient than that of the angiosperms, it serves some of the largest trees known. The coastal redwoods of California are the tallest gymnosperms, with some individuals growing to well over 100 meters tall.

During the Permian, as environments became warmer and dryer, the conifers and cycads flourished. Gymnosperm forests changed over time as the gymnosperm groups evolved. Gymnosperms dominated the Mesozoic, during which the continents drifted apart and large dinosaurs lived. Gymnosperms were the principal trees in all forests until about 65 million years ago, and even today conifers are the dominant trees in many forests, especially at high latitudes and elevations. The oldest living single organism on Earth today is a gymnosperm in California—a bristlecone pine (*Pinus longaeva*) that germinated about 5,000 years ago, at about the time the ancient Egyptians were starting to develop writing.

Conifers have cones and lack swimming sperm

The great Douglas fir and cedar forests found in the northwestern United States and the massive boreal forests of pine, fir, and spruce of northern Eurasia and North America, as well as on the upper slopes of mountain ranges elsewhere, rank among the great forests of the world. All these trees belong to one group of gymnosperms: the conifers, or cone-bearers.

Male and female **cones** contain the reproductive structures of conifers. The female (seed-bearing) cone is known as a **megastrobilus** (plural *megastrobili*). An example of a familiar megastrobilus is the woody cone of pine trees. The seeds in a megastrobilus are protected by a tight cluster of woody scales, which are modifications of branches extending from a central axis (**Figure 27.7A**). The typically much smaller male (pollen-bearing) cone is known as a **microstrobilus**. The microstrobilus is typically herbaceous rather than woody, as its scales are composed of modified leaves, beneath which are the pollen-bearing microsporangia (**Figure 27.7B**).

The life cycle of a pine illustrates reproduction in gymnosperms (**Figure 27.8**). As in other seed plants, conifers have male gametophytes in the form of pollen grains, which frees the plant completely from its dependence on liquid water for fertilization. Wind, rather than water, assists conifer pollen grains in their first stage of travel from the microstrobilus to the female gametophyte inside a cone. A pollen tube provides the sperm with the means for the last stage of travel by elongating through maternal sporophytic tissue. When the pollen tube reaches the female gametophyte, it releases two sperm, one of which degenerates after the other unites with an egg. Union of sperm and egg results in a zygote. Mitotic divisions and further development of the zygote result in an embryo.

The megasporangium, in which the female gametophyte will form, is enclosed in a layer of sporophytic tissue—the integument—that will eventually develop into the seed coat that protects the embryo. The integument, the megasporangium inside it, and the tissue attaching it to the maternal sporophyte constitute the ovule. The pollen grain enters through a small opening in the integument at the tip of the ovule, the **micropyle**.

(A) Female cones (megastrobili) in *Pinus contorta*

Cross section of a megastrobilus

Woody scale

Seed

Central axis

© Scenics & Science/Alamy Stock Photo

Female cones, or megastrobili

© Fritz Pölking/Blickwinkel/AGE Fotostock

(B) Male cones (microstrobili) in *Pinus contorta*

Cross section of a microstrobilus

Herbaceous scale

Pollen-containing microspores

Central axis

© Scenics & Science/Alamy Stock Photo

Male cones, or microstrobili

© Gunter Marx/Alamy Stock Photo

Figure 27.7 Female and Male Cones   **(A)** The woody scales of female cones (megastrobili) are modified branches. **(B)** The herbaceous scales of male cones (microstrobili) are modified leaves.

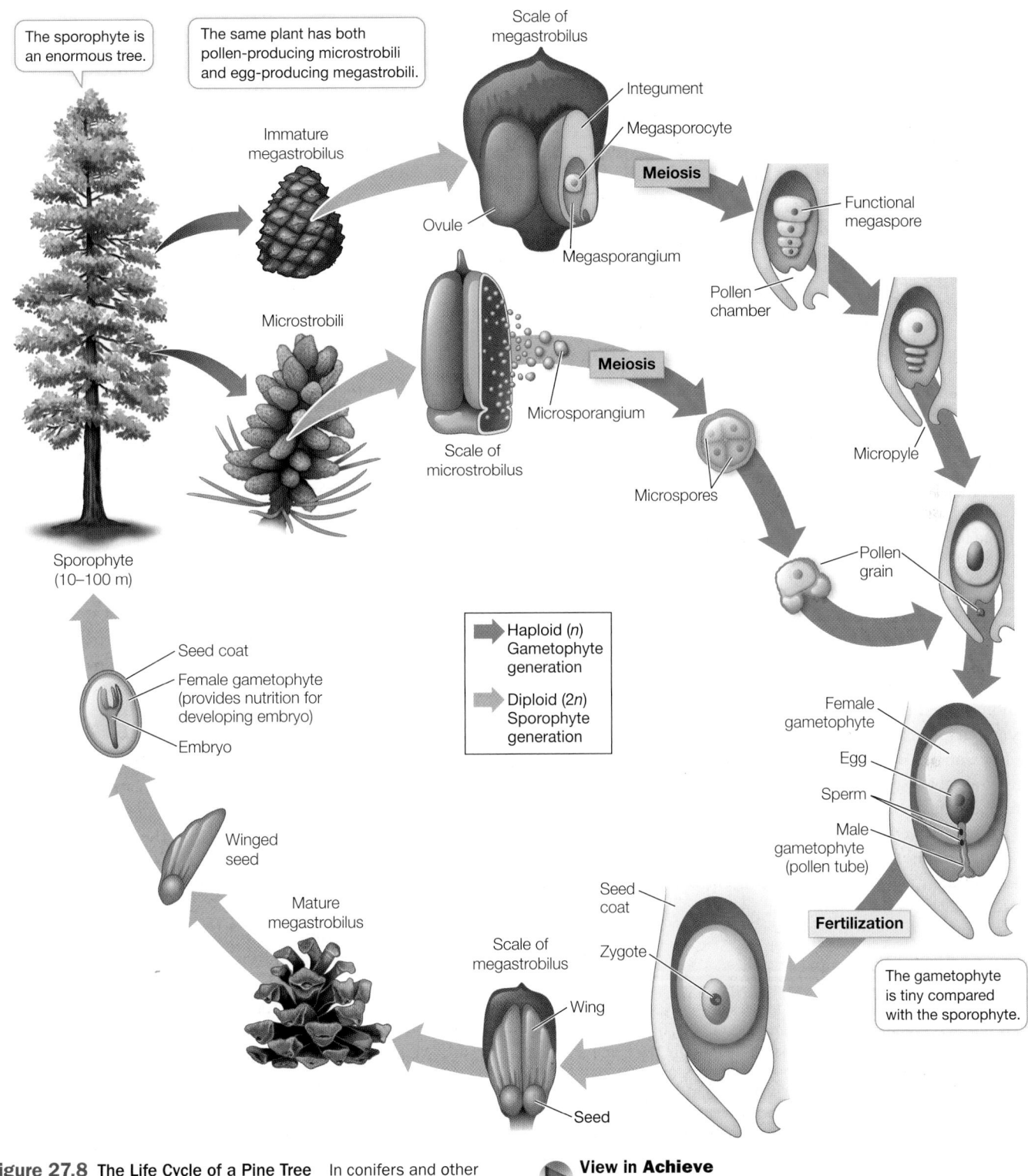

Figure 27.8 The Life Cycle of a Pine Tree In conifers and other gymnosperms, the gametophytes are small and nutritionally dependent on the sporophyte generation.

View in **Achieve**
Animation 27.1 Life Cycle of a Conifer

View in **Achieve**
Activity 27.2 Life Cycle of a Conifer

Most conifer ovules (which will develop into seeds after fertilization) are borne exposed on the upper surfaces of the scales of the cone (megastrobilus). The only protection of the ovules comes from the scales, which are tightly pressed against one another within the cone. Some pines, such as the lodgepole pine (*Pinus contorta*), have such tightly closed cones that only fire suffices to split them open and release the seeds. These species are said to be fire-adapted, and fire is essential to their reproduction. A fire

Figure 27.9 From Devastation, New Life A stand of lodgepole pines in Yellowstone National Park. The mature trees were destroyed by a forest fire in 1988. However, the fire released large numbers of seeds from cones, and now many young lodgepole pine trees are growing in the burn area.

devastated lodgepole pine forests in Yellowstone National Park in 1988, but also released large numbers of seeds from cones. As a result, large numbers of lodgepole pine seedlings are now emerging in the burn area (Figure 27.9).

About half of all conifer species have soft, fleshy modifications of the cones that envelop their seeds. Some of these modified tissues are fleshy, fruitlike cones, as in junipers. Others are fruitlike extensions of the seeds, called arils, as in yews. These tissues, although often mistaken for "berries," are not true fruits. As you will see in Key Concept 27.3, true fruits are the plant's ripened ovaries, which are absent in gymnosperms. Nonetheless, the fleshy tissues that surround many conifer seeds serve a similar purpose as that of the fruits of flowering plants, acting as an enticement for seed-dispersing animals. Animals eat these fleshy tissues and disperse the seeds in their feces, often depositing the seeds considerable distances away from the parent plant.

KEY CONCEPT
27.2 Recap and Assess

Living gymnosperms can be divided into four major groups: cycads, ginkgos, gnetophytes, and conifers. Although they have declined since the Mesozoic, gymnosperms are still the dominant trees in some areas, especially at high elevations and latitudes. All gymnosperms are woody and have seeds that are not protected by ovaries, although some have fleshy, fruitlike cones or extensions of seeds that entice animals to disperse the seeds.

1. Why is fire necessary for the survival of some gymnosperms?
2. Distinguish between the roles of the female gametophyte and the pollen grain in the life cycle of a conifer.
3. What is the function of the fleshy cones that surround the seeds of many gymnosperms?

Although gymnosperms still dominate the terrestrial landscape in some environments, angiosperms (the flowering plants) have become the dominant land plants across much of Earth.

KEY CONCEPT
27.3 Flowers and Fruits Led to Increased Diversification of Angiosperms

Learning Objectives

27.3.1 Distinguish between the two different roles of sperm in angiosperm double fertilization.
27.3.2 Explain the difference between pollination and fertilization.
27.3.3 Predict the likely modes of seed dispersal based on the type of fruit a plant produces.
27.3.4 Outline the functions of flowers, fruits, and seeds.

The most obvious feature defining the angiosperms is the **flower**, which is their sexual structure. Production of **fruits** is also a synapomorphy (shared derived trait) of angiosperms. After fertilization, the ovary of a flower (together with the seeds it contains) develops into a fruit that protects the seeds and can promote seed dispersal. As we will see, both flowers and fruits afford major reproductive advantages to angiosperms. These advantages led to the dominance of the terrestrial environment by angiosperms in the Cenozoic (see Figure 27.1).

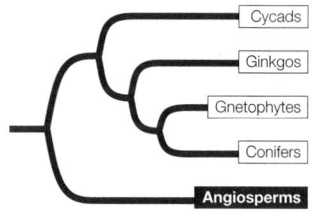

Angiosperms have many shared derived traits

The name *angiosperm* ("enclosed seed") is derived from another distinctive trait of flowering plants that is related to the formation of fruits: the ovules and seeds are enclosed in a modified leaf called a **carpel**. Besides protecting the ovules and seeds, the carpel often interacts with incoming pollen to prevent self-fertilization, thus favoring cross-fertilization and increasing genetic diversity.

The female gametophyte of the angiosperms is even more reduced than that of the gymnosperms, usually consisting of only seven cells (see Figure 27.16). Thus the angiosperms represent the current extreme of the trend we have traced throughout the evolution of the vascular plants: the sporophyte generation becomes larger and more independent of the gametophyte, while the gametophyte generation becomes smaller and more dependent on the sporophyte.

The xylem of most angiosperms is distinguished by the presence of specialized water-transporting cells called **vessel elements**. These cells are larger in diameter than tracheids and connect with one another without obstruction, allowing easy water movement. A second distinctive cell type in angiosperm xylem is the **fiber**, which plays an important role in supporting the plant body. Angiosperm phloem possesses another unique cell type, called a companion cell. Like the gymnosperms, woody angiosperms show secondary growth, increasing in diameter by producing secondary xylem and secondary phloem.

A more comprehensive list of angiosperm synapomorphies, then, includes the following (some of these traits will be discussed later in this chapter):

- Flowers
- Fruits
- Ovules and seeds enclosed in a carpel
- Highly reduced gametophytes
- Germination of pollen on a stigma
- Double fertilization
- Endosperm (nutritive tissue for the embryo)
- Phloem with companion cells

The majority of these traits bear directly on angiosperm reproduction, which is a large factor in the success of this dominant plant group.

The sexual structures of angiosperms are flowers

Flowers come in an astonishing variety of forms—just think of some of the flowers you recognize. Flowers may be single, or they may be grouped together to form an **inflorescence**. Different families of flowering plants have characteristic types of inflorescences, such as the compound umbels of the carrot family (**Figure 27.10A**), the heads of the aster family (**Figure 27.10B**), and the spikes of many grasses (**Figure 27.10C**).

If you examine any familiar flower, you will notice that the outer parts look somewhat like leaves. In fact, all the parts of a flower *are* modified leaves. The diagram in Figure 27.4B represents a generalized flower (for which there is no exact counterpart in nature). The structures bearing microsporangia are called **stamens**. Each stamen is composed of a **filament** bearing an **anther** that contains the pollen-producing microsporangia. The structures bearing megasporangia are called carpels. The swollen base of the carpel, containing one or more ovules (each containing a megasporangium surrounded by two protective

integuments), is called the **ovary**. The stalk at the top of the carpel is the **style**, and the terminal surface that receives pollen grains is the **stigma**. Two or more fused carpels, or a single carpel if only one is present, are also called a **pistil**.

In addition, many flowers have specialized sterile (non-spore-bearing) leaves. The inner ones are called **petals** (collectively, the **corolla**) and the outer ones **sepals** (collectively, the calyx). The corolla and calyx can be quite showy and often play roles in attracting animal pollinators to the flower. The calyx more commonly protects the immature flower in bud. From base to apex, these floral organs—sepals, petals, stamens, and carpels—are usually positioned in circular arrangements or whorls and attached to a central stalk.

The generalized flower in Figure 27.4B has both functional megasporangia and functional microsporangia. Such flowers are referred to as **perfect** (or hermaphroditic). Many angiosperms produce two types of flowers, one with only megasporangia and the other with only microsporangia. Consequently, either the stamens or the carpels are nonfunctional or absent in a given flower, and the flower is referred to as **imperfect**.

Species such as corn or birch, in which both megasporangiate (female) and microsporangiate (male) flowers occur on the same plant, are said to be **monoecious** ("one-housed"—but, it must be added, one house with separate rooms). Complete separation of imperfect flowers occurs in some other angiosperm species, such as willows and date palms; in these species, an individual plant produces either flowers with stamens or flowers with carpels, but never both. Such species are said to be **dioecious** ("two-housed").

Flower structure has evolved over time

The flowers of the earliest-diverging clades of angiosperms have a large and variable number of tepals (undifferentiated sepals and petals), carpels, and stamens (**Figure 27.11A**). Evolutionary change within the angiosperms has included some striking modifications of this early condition: reductions in the number of each type of

(A) *Heracleum mantegazzianum*   **(B)** *Zinnia elegans*   **(C)** *Sorghum halepense*

Flowers · Umbel · Compound umbel · Ray flowers · Disc flowers · Anthers of spikelet · Stigma of spikelet

© Colin Underhill/Alamy Stock Photo · © John N. A. Lott/Biological Photo Service · © Nigel Cattlin/Alamy Stock Photo

Figure 27.10 Inflorescences **(A)** The inflorescence of the giant hogweed, a member of the carrot family, is a compound umbel. Each umbel bears flowers on stalks that arise from a common center. **(B)** Zinnias are members of the aster family; their inflorescence is a head. Within the head, each of the long, petal-like structures is a ray flower; the central portion of the head consists of dozens to hundreds of disc flowers. **(C)** Some grasses, such as Johnson grass, have inflorescences called spikes, which are composed of many smaller groups of flowers, or spikelets.

(A) *Nymphaea* sp.

(B) *Paphiopedilum* sp.

Figure 27.11 Flower Form and Evolution **(A)** A water lily shows the major features of early flowers: it is radially symmetrical, and the individual tepals, stamens, and carpels are separate, numerous, and attached at their bases. **(B)** Orchids such as this Venus slipper have a bilaterally symmetrical structure that evolved much later than radial flower symmetry.

(A) Carpel evolution

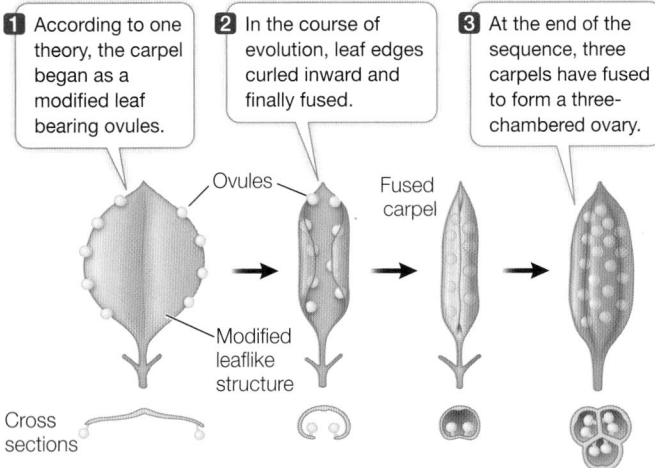

1 According to one theory, the carpel began as a modified leaf bearing ovules.

2 In the course of evolution, leaf edges curled inward and finally fused.

3 At the end of the sequence, three carpels have fused to form a three-chambered ovary.

Ovules

Fused carpel

Modified leaflike structure

Cross sections

(B) Stamen evolution

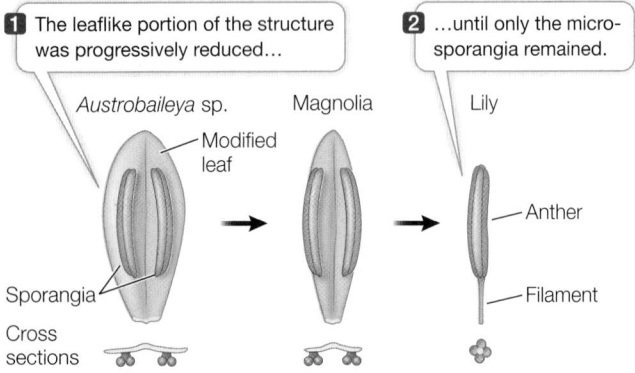

1 The leaflike portion of the structure was progressively reduced…

2 …until only the microsporangia remained.

Austrobaileya sp. Magnolia Lily

Modified leaf

Anther

Sporangia

Filament

Cross sections

Figure 27.12 Carpels and Stamens Evolved from Leaflike Structures **(A)** Possible stages in the evolution of a carpel from a more leaflike structure. **(B)** The stamens of three modern plants show three possible stages in the evolution of that organ. (It is *not* implied that these species evolved from one another; their structures simply illustrate the possible stages.)

floral organ to a fixed number, differentiation of petals from sepals, and changes in symmetry from radial (as in a lily or magnolia) to bilateral (as in a sweet pea or orchid), often accompanied by an extensive fusion of parts (**Figure 27.11B**).

According to one hypothesis, the first carpels to evolve were leaves with marginal sporangia, folded but incompletely closed. Early in angiosperm evolution, the carpels fused with one another, forming a single, multichambered ovary (**Figure 27.12A**). In some flowers, the other floral organs are attached at the top of the ovary rather than at the bottom as in Figure 27.4B. The stamens of the most ancient flowers may have been leaflike (**Figure 27.12B**), with little resemblance to the stamens of the generalized flower seen in Figure 27.4B.

Why do so many flowers have carpels with long styles and anthers with long filaments? Natural selection has favored length in both of these floral organs, probably because length increases the likelihood of successful pollination. Long filaments may bring the anthers into contact with insect bodies, or they may place the anthers in a better position to catch the wind. Similar arguments apply to long styles.

A perfect flower represents a compromise of sorts. On the one hand, by attracting a pollinating bird or insect, the plant is attending to both its female and male functions with a single flower type, whereas plants with imperfect flowers must create that attraction twice—once for each type of flower. On the other hand, the perfect flower can favor self-pollination, which is usually disadvantageous. Another potential problem is that the female and male functions might interfere with each other—for example, the stigma might be so placed as to make it difficult for pollinators to reach the anthers, thus reducing the export of pollen to other flowers.

Might there be a way around these problems? One solution is seen in the bush monkeyflower (*Mimulus aurantiacus*), which is pollinated by hummingbirds. Its flower has a stigma that initially serves as a screen, hiding the anthers (**Figure 27.13**). Once a hummingbird touches the stigma, however, one of the stigma's two lobes is retracted, so that subsequent hummingbird visitors pick up pollen from the previously screened anthers. Thus the first

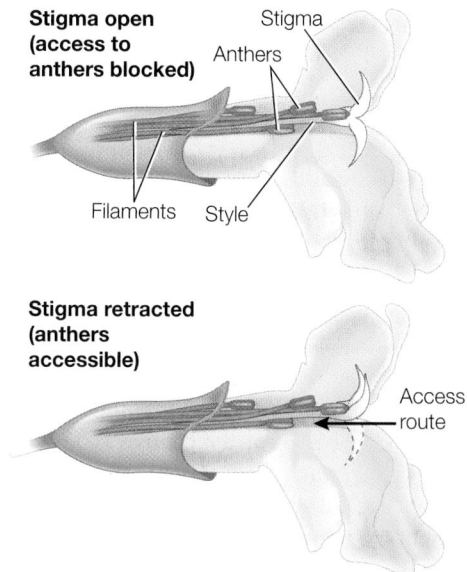

Stigma open (access to anthers blocked)

Stigma

Anthers

Filaments Style

Stigma retracted (anthers accessible)

Access route

Figure 27.13 An Unusual Way to Prevent Selfing Both long stamens and long styles facilitate cross-pollination, but if these male and female structures are too close to each other, the likelihood of (disadvantageous) self-pollination increases. In *Mimulus aurantiacus*, the stigma is initially open, blocking access to the anthers. A hummingbird's touch as it deposits pollen on the stigma causes one lobe of the stigma to retract, creating a path to the anthers and allowing pollen dispersal by subsequent hummingbird visitors. (After A. E. Fetscher. 2001. *Proc R Soc Lond B Biol Sci* 268: 525–529.)

bird to visit the flower transfers pollen from another plant to the stigma, eventually leading to fertilization. Later visitors pick up pollen from the now-accessible anthers, fulfilling the flower's male function. **Figure 27.14** describes the experiment that revealed the function of this mechanism.

Angiosperms have coevolved with animals

Whereas most gymnosperms are pollinated by wind, most angiosperms are pollinated by animals. The many different mutualistic pollination relationships between plants and animals are vital to both parties.

Connect the Concepts Mutualisms benefit both partners in a relationship, as described in Chapter 54.

Many flowers entice animals to visit them by providing food rewards. Pollen grains themselves sometimes serve as food for animals. In addition, some flowers produce a sugary fluid called nectar as a pollinator attractant, and some of these flowers have specialized structures to store and distribute it. In the process of visiting flowers to obtain nectar or pollen, animals often carry pollen from one flower to another or from one plant to another. Thus, in their quest for food, the animals contribute to the genetic diversity of the plant population. Insects, especially bees, are among the most important pollinators. Other major pollinators include some species of birds and bats.

 Media Clip 27.2 Pollen Transfer by a Bat
Life12e.com/mc27.2

Experiment

Figure 27.14 The Effect of Stigma Retraction in Monkeyflowers

Original Paper: A. E. Fetscher. 2001. Resolution of male-female conflict in an hermaphroditic flower. *Proc R Soc Lond B Biol Sci* 268: 525–527.

Elizabeth Fetscher's experiments showed that the unusual stigma retraction response to pollination in monkeyflowers (illustrated in Figure 27.13) enhances the dispersal of pollen to other monkeyflowers.

HYPOTHESIS▶ The stigma-retraction response in *Mimulus aurantiacus* increases the likelihood that an individual flower's pollen will be exported to another flower once pollen from another flower has been deposited on its stigma.

METHOD▶

1. Set up three groups of monkeyflower arrays. Each array consists of one pollen-donor flower and multiple pollen-recipient flowers (with the anthers removed to prevent pollen donation).

2. In control arrays, the stigma of the pollen donor is allowed to function normally.

3. In one group of experimental arrays, the stigma of the pollen donor is permanently propped open (blocking access to the anthers).

4. In a second group of experimental arrays, the stigma of the pollen donor is artificially sealed closed (allowing access to the anthers).

5. Allow hummingbirds to visit the arrays, then count the pollen grains transferred from each donor flower to the recipient flowers in the same array.

RESULTS▶ Error bars indicate standard error of the mean; the three groups are significantly different at $P<0.05$.

Almost twice as much pollen was exported from control flowers as from flowers with stigmas propped open.

Experimentally sealing stigmas in the closed position resulted in greater pollen dispersal.

Number of pollen grains deposited on recipients

350
300
250
200
150
100
50
0

Controls   Stigmas propped open   Stigmas sealed closed

CONCLUSION▶ The stigma-retraction response enhances the male function of the flower (dispersal of pollen) once the female function (receipt of pollen) has been performed.

For more than 150 million years, angiosperms and their animal pollinators have coevolved in the terrestrial environment. The animals have affected the evolution of the plants, and the plants have affected the evolution of the animals. Flower structure has become incredibly diverse under these selection pressures. Some of the products of coevolution are highly specific. For example, the flowers of some yucca species are pollinated by only one species of yucca moth, and that moth may exclusively pollinate just one species of yucca. Such specific relationships provide plants with a reliable mechanism for transferring pollen only to members of their own species.

Most plant–pollinator interactions are much less specific. In most cases, many different animal species pollinate the same plant species, and the same animal species pollinates many different plant species. However, even these less specific interactions have developed some specialization. Bird-pollinated flowers are often red and odorless. Many insect-pollinated flowers have characteristic odors. Bee-pollinated flowers may have conspicuous markings, called nectar guides, that are conspicuous only to animals, such as bees, that can see colors in the ultraviolet region of the spectrum (**Figure 27.15**).

The fruits of some plants that are still around today originally evolved to attract large frugivorous animals—many of which went extinct in the Pleistocene. For example, the large round fruits of the osage orange tree attracted wooly mammoths, which ate the fruits and dispersed the seeds. After the extinction of the mammoths, osage orange trees survived in large part because early humans used the wood of this species for making bows for hunting, dispersing the fruits to new areas in the process. Some other species that depended on now-extinct mammals to disperse their seeds, however, may be slowly declining toward extinction.

The angiosperm life cycle produces diploid zygotes nourished by triploid endosperms

Like all seed plants, angiosperms are heterosporous. As you have seen, their ovules are contained within carpels rather than being exposed on the surfaces of scales, as in most gymnosperms. The male gametophytes, as in the gymnosperms, are pollen grains.

Pollination in the angiosperms consists of the arrival of a male gametophyte—a pollen grain—on a receptive surface in a flower (the stigma). As in the gymnosperms, pollination is the first in a series of events that results in the formation of a seed. The next event is the growth of a pollen tube extending to the female gametophyte. The third event is a fertilization process that, in detail, is unique to the angiosperms (**Figure 27.16**).

In nearly all angiosperms, *two* male gametes, contained in a single male gametophyte, participate in fertilization. The nucleus of one sperm combines with that of the egg to produce a diploid zygote, the first cell of the sporophyte generation. In most angiosperms, the other sperm nucleus combines with two other haploid nuclei of the female gametophyte to form a cell with a *triploid* (3n) nucleus. That cell, in turn, gives rise to triploid tissue, the **endosperm**, which nourishes the embryonic sporophyte during its early development. This process, in which two fertilization events take place, is known as **double fertilization**. In some angiosperms, additional haploid nuclei are incorporated to form even higher ploidy levels in the endosperm, or the second sperm fuses with only one haploid nucleus, resulting in diploid endosperm.

As Figure 27.16 shows, the zygote develops into an embryo, which consists of an embryonic axis (the "backbone" that will become a stem and a root) and one or two **cotyledons**, or "seed leaves." The cotyledons have different fates in different plants. In many, they serve as absorptive organs that take up and digest the endosperm. In others, they enlarge and become photosynthetic when the seed germinates. Often they play both roles.

The ovule develops into a seed containing the products of the double fertilization that characterizes angiosperms: a diploid zygote and a triploid endosperm (see Figure 27.16). The endosperm serves as storage tissue for starch or lipids, proteins, and other substances that will be needed by the developing embryo.

Fruits aid angiosperm seed dispersal

Fruits typically aid in seed dispersal. Fruits may attach to or be eaten by an animal. The animal is then likely to move, after which the seeds may fall off or be defecated. Fruits are not necessarily fleshy. Fruits can also be hard and woody, or small and have modified structures that allow the seeds to be dispersed by wind or water (**Figure 27.17**).

A fruit may consist of only the mature ovary and its seeds, or it may include other parts of the flower or structures associated

Argentina anserina

Both photos © Bjorn Rorslett/Science Source

Figure 27.15 See Like a Bee To normal human vision, the petals of silverweed appear solid yellow. Ultraviolet photography reveals patterns that attract bees to the central region, where pollen and nectar are located.

Flower of mature sporophyte

Anther

Seedling

Seed

Cotyledons

Double fertilization results in a 2n zygote and 3n endosperm.

Endosperm

Embryo

Endosperm nucleus (3n)

Zygote (2n)

Double Fertilization

Ovary

Ovule

Megasporocyte (2n)

Megasporangium

Anther

Microsporocyte

Diploid (2n)

Haploid (n)

Meiosis

Pollen grain (male gametophyte, n)

Microspores (4)

Pollen grain

Pollen tube

Surviving megaspore (n)

Three of the four megaspores that result from meiosis degenerate.

Sperm

Polar nuclei (2)

The typical angiosperm female gametophyte (n) consists of seven cells.

Egg

Figure 27.16 The Life Cycle of an Angiosperm   Double fertilization results in triploid endosperm in most species of angiosperms. One sperm nucleus fertilizes the egg to form the zygote, while the other combines with the two polar nuclei to form the endosperm.

View in Achieve
Animation 27.2 Life Cycle of an Angiosperm

with it. A **simple fruit** is one that develops from a single carpel or several fused carpels, such as a plum or cherry. A raspberry is an example of an **aggregate fruit**—one that develops from several separate carpels of a single flower. Pineapples and figs are examples of **multiple fruits**, formed from a cluster of flowers (an inflorescence). Fruits derived from parts in addition to the carpel and seeds are called **accessory fruits**—examples are apples, pears, and strawberries.

Media Clip 27.3 Flower and Fruit Formation
Life12e.com/mc27.3

Figure 27.17 Fruits Come in Many Forms (A) The single seeds inside the simple fruits of Bing cherries are dispersed by animals. (B) Each seed of the horse chestnut is covered by a hard, woody fruit that allows it to survive drought. Although such fruits are commonly called "nuts," this is a culinary rather than a biological term. (C) The highly reduced simple fruits of dandelions are dispersed by wind. (D) A multiple fruit, the pineapple (*Ananas comosus*), has become one of the most economically significant fruit crops of the tropics. (E) An aggregate fruit (blackberry). (F) An accessory fruit (pear).

Q: The large incisors of rodents help these animals penetrate the shells of woody nuts, which they consume as food. But unlike many animals that eat fruits without digesting the seeds, rodents destroy the seeds when they eat them. So how do rodents aid in dispersing the seeds of nut-bearing plants?

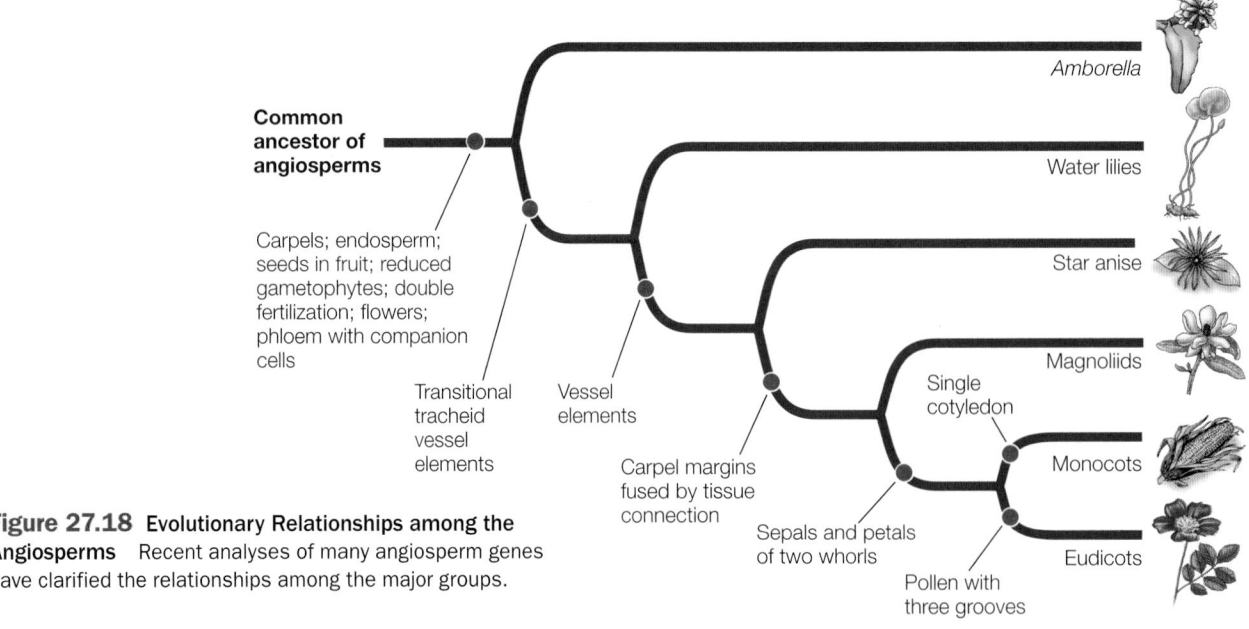

Figure 27.18 Evolutionary Relationships among the Angiosperms Recent analyses of many angiosperm genes have clarified the relationships among the major groups.

(A) *Amborella trichopoda*

Sterile stamens

(B) *Nymphaea sp.*

(C) *Illicium floridanum*

(D) *Magnolia* sp.

(E) *Aristolochia ringens*

Figure 27.19 Monocots and Eudicots Are Not the Only Surviving Angiosperms   **(A)** *Amborella*, a shrub, is sister to the remaining extant angiosperms. Notice the sterile stamens on this female flower, which may serve to lure insects that are searching for pollen. **(B)** The water lily clade was the next to diverge after *Amborella*. **(C)** Star anise and its relatives belong to another early-diverging angiosperm clade. **(D, E)** The largest clade other than the monocots and eudicots is the magnoliid complex, which includes magnolias and the group known as "Dutchman's pipe."

Recent analyses have revealed the phylogenetic relationships of angiosperms

Figure 27.18 shows the relationships among the major angiosperm clades. Recent molecular and morphological analyses have supported the hypothesis that the sister group of remaining flowering plants is a single species of the genus *Amborella* (**Figure 27.19A**). This woody shrub with cream-colored flowers lives only on New Caledonia, an island in the South Pacific. Other early-branching angiosperm groups include the water lilies (**Figure 27.19B**),

star anise and its relatives (**Figure 27.19C**), and the **magnoliids** (**Figure 27.19D,E**). The magnoliids include many familiar and useful plants, such as avocados, cinnamon, black pepper, and magnolias.

The two largest clades—the **monocots** and the **eudicots**—include the great majority of angiosperm species. The monocots are so called because they have a single embryonic cotyledon, whereas the eudicots have two.

Representatives of the two largest angiosperm clades are everywhere. The monocots (**Figure 27.20**) include grasses, cattails, lilies,

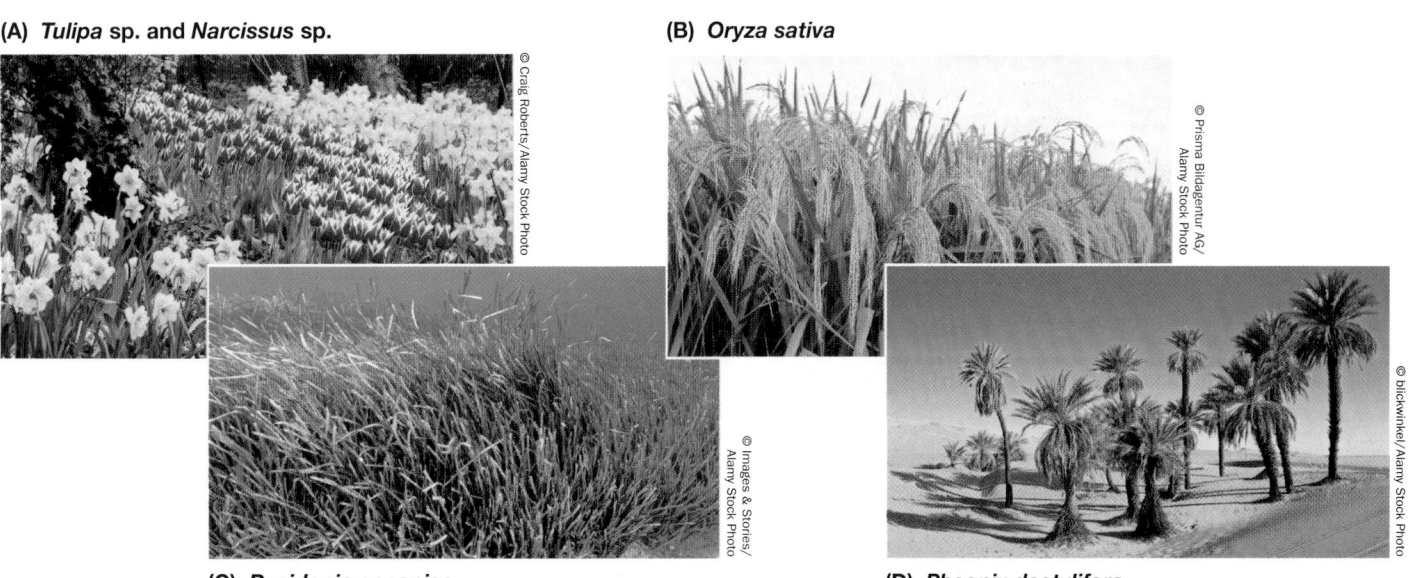

(A) *Tulipa* sp. and *Narcissus* sp.

(B) *Oryza sativa*

(C) *Posidonia oceanica*

(D) *Phoenix dactylifera*

Figure 27.20 Monocots   **(A)** Monocots include many popular garden flowers such as these tulips (pink and white) and daffodils (yellow). **(B)** Monocot grasses such as rice feed the world; wheat, sugarcane, and corn (maize) are also grasses. **(C)** Seagrasses such as this Neptune's grass form "meadows" in the shallow, sunlit waters of the world's oceans. **(D)** Palms are among the few monocot trees. Date palms like these are a major food source in some areas of the world.

(A) *Malus* sp.

(B) *Banksia coccinea*

(C) *Escobaria vivipara*

(D) *Rafflesia arnoldii*

Figure 27.21 Eudicots **(A)** Eudicots include many trees, such as this crabapple tree. **(B)** Scarlet Banksia is a species of an Australian genus of eudicots that attracts a wide diversity of pollinators by producing large quantities of nectar. **(C)** Cacti comprise a large group of eudicots, with about 1,500 species in the Americas. Many, such as this spinystar cactus, bear large flowers for a brief period of each year. **(D)** *Rafflesia arnoldii*, found in the rainforests of Indonesia, bears the largest flower in the world. The flower lives as a parasite on tropical vines and has lost its leaf, stem, and even root structures. It smells like decaying meat, which attracts its fly pollinators.

orchids, and palms. The eudicots (**Figure 27.21**) include the vast majority of familiar seed plants, including most herbs (i.e., nonwoody plants), vines, trees, and shrubs. Among the eudicots are such diverse plants as oaks, willows, beans, snapdragons, roses, and sunflowers.

KEY CONCEPT
27.3 Recap and Assess

Angiosperms are the dominant terrestrial plants of the Cenozoic. The synapomorphies of angiosperms include flowers, fruit, carpels, double fertilization, and endosperm. Most angiosperms also possess distinctive cells in the xylem and phloem. The largest angiosperm clades are the monocots and the eudicots.

1. What are the respective roles of the two sperm in double fertilization in angiosperms?

2. Explain the difference between pollination and fertilization.

3. What are some of the differences between fruits that are dispersed by attracting animals to a food resource and those that are dispersed by attaching themselves to animals? Give examples of each.

4. What are the different functions of flowers, fruits, and seeds?

5. Many fleshy fruits attract animals, which eat the fruit and then disperse the seeds in their feces. If all other factors are equal, large seeds have a better chance of producing a successful seedling than small seeds. So why isn't there selection for larger seeds in the fruits of all plants? In one study in Peru, the feces of the spider monkey *Ateles paniscus* were found to contain seeds from 71 species of plants. After eating fruit, the monkeys usually travel some distance before defecating, thus dispersing any undigested seeds. If monkey feces are left undisturbed on the forest floor, rodents eat and destroy the vast majority of the seeds in the feces. To germinate successfully, the seeds in spider monkey feces need to be buried by dung beetles, which makes the discovery and destruction of seeds by rodents much less likely.

Ellen Andresen hypothesized that dung beetles were more likely to remove larger than smaller seeds from spider monkey dung before burying the dung. She added plastic beads of various diameters to spider monkey dung (to simulate seeds) and measured the percentage of beads buried with the dung by the beetles. Use her data to answer the questions below.

Bead diameter (mm)	2	4	6	8	10	12
Percent buried	100	76	52	39	20	4

Source: E. Andresen. 1999. *Biotropica* 31: 145–158.

a. Plot bead size (the independent variable) versus percent of beads buried by dung beetles (the dependent variable).

b. Calculate a regression line for the relationship shown in your graph (see Appendix B). Approximately what percent of beads with a diameter of 5 mm would you predict would be buried by the beetles? What about beads 14 mm in diameter?

c. What other factors besides size might influence the probability of seed burial by dung beetles? Can you design an experiment to test your hypotheses?

d. Describe how changes in the population sizes of spider monkeys, rodents, and dung beetles would affect the reproductive success of various plant species.

The remarkable diversity of the seed plants has been shaped by both biotic and abiotic components of the environments to which they have adapted. In turn, land plants—and seed plants in particular—shape their environments.

KEY CONCEPT 27.4 Plants Play Critical Roles in Terrestrial Ecosystems

Learning Objectives

27.4.1 Describe how seed plants have been used for medicinal purposes.

27.4.2 Summarize the ecological services that angiosperms perform.

27.4.3 Summarize the main plants that humans use for food.

Plants make profound contributions to ecosystem services—processes by which the environment maintains resources that benefit human society. Once life moved onto land, it was largely plants that shaped the terrestrial environment.

Plants produce oxygen and remove carbon dioxide from the atmosphere, and they play important roles in forming soils and renewing soil fertility. Plant roots help hold soil in place, providing protection against erosion by wind and water (**Figure 27.22**). Plants also moderate the local climate in various ways, such as by increasing humidity, providing shade, and blocking wind. All of these ecosystem services permit a great diversity of fungi and animals to exist on land.

Seed plants have been sources of medicine since ancient times

Although we also use medicines derived from fungi, lichens, and actinobacteria, seed plants are the source of many of our medications. A few examples of medicines derived from plants are shown in **Table 27.1**. Even in synthetic pharmaceuticals, the chemical structures of the active ingredients are often based on the biochemistry of substances isolated from plants.

How are plant-based medicines discovered? Many were discovered over the millennia by people who lived alongside useful plants and discovered the properties of the plants through trial and error. Some plant-based medicines have come into widespread use through the work of ethnobotanists, who study how people use and view plants in their local environments. This work proceeds all over the globe today. An older example of this approach is the discovery of quinine as a treatment for malaria. In the sixteenth

© Calvin Chan/Alamy Stock Photo

Figure 27.22 Plants Prevent Erosion   When forest vegetation was cleared on these hillsides in Malaysia, landslides and extensive soil erosion quickly followed. Adjacent forested areas did not have landslides.

century, Spanish priests in Peru became aware that the native population used the bark of local *Cinchona* trees to treat fevers. The priests successfully used the bark to treat malaria. Word of the medicine spread to Europe, where it was put into use as early as 1631. The active ingredient of *Cinchona* bark—quinine—was identified in 1820, and quinine remained the standard malarial remedy well into the twentieth century.

Since the mid-1900s, many plant-based medicines have been found by systematic testing of plants from all over the world. One example of a medicine discovered in this way is Taxol®, an important anticancer drug. Among the myriad plant samples that had been tested by 1962, extracts of the bark of the Pacific yew (*Taxus brevifolia*) showed anti-tumor activity in tests against rodent tumors. The active ingredient, paclitaxel, was isolated in 1971 and tested against human cancers in 1977. After another 16 years, the U.S. Food and Drug Administration approved it for human use, and Taxol® is now widely used in treating breast and ovarian cancers as well as several other types of cancers.

Seed plants are our primary food source

Plants are primary producers. They trap energy and carbon by means of photosynthesis, making those resources available not only for their own needs, but also for the herbivores and omnivores that consume them, for the carnivores and omnivores that eat the herbivores, and for the prokaryotes and fungi that complete food webs. The earliest steps in human civilization involved cultivating angiosperms to provide a reliable food supply.

Today, twelve species of seed plants account for most of the food eaten by humans: rice, coconut, wheat, corn (maize), potato, sweet potato, cassava (also called tapioca or manioc), sugarcane, sugar beet, soybean, common bean (*Phaseolus vulgaris*), and banana. Hundreds of other seed plants are cultivated for food, but none rank with these twelve in importance. Indeed, more than half of the world's human population derives the bulk of its food energy from the seeds of a single plant, *Oryza sativa*, better known as rice. Rice is particularly important in eastern Asia, where it has been cultivated for more than 8,000 years (**Figure 27.23**).

TABLE 27.1 | Some Medicinal Plants and Their Products

Plant	Product	Medical application
Belladonna	Atropine	Dilate pupils for eye examination
Pineapple stem	Bromelain	Control tissue inflammation
Foxglove	Digitalin	Strengthen heart muscle contraction
Ephedra	Ephedrine	Ease nasal congestion
Japanese mint	Menthol	Relieve coughing
Opium poppy	Morphine	Relieve pain
Pacific yew	Paclitaxel	Treat ovarian and breast cancers
Cinchona bark	Quinine	Treat malaria
Curare plant	Tubocurarine	Muscle relaxant (used in surgery)
Periwinkle	Vincristine	Treat leukemia and lymphoma

Figure 27.23 Rice Feeds Much of the World's Human Population
These rice fields, or "paddies," are in south China. Rice has been cultivated in this manner for thousands of years.

In addition to providing food directly for human consumption, plants also provide feed for agricultural production of animals. In particular, the grasses that grow in the world's rangelands are the primary forage for the grazing animals that humans use for meat and dairy products.

KEY CONCEPT

27.4 Recap and Assess

Terrestrial ecosystems could not function without the foods and habitats provided by plants. Plants produce oxygen and remove carbon dioxide from the atmosphere, help form soils, and hold soils in place against erosion by wind and water. Plants also provide us with many important medicines and are the basis (directly or indirectly) of virtually all of our food.

1. Name three plants that are used in medicine for humans, and give an example of how each is used.

2. A parcel of agricultural land that has been used to produce corn for decades no longer produces healthy crops. Tests indicate that the soil is depleted of nitrogen and organic matter. A farm extension agent recommends that the farmer grow soybeans and then rotate this crop with corn in future years. She also recommends that the farmer till the stubble from the crops after harvest into the soil. Why are these practices expected to help crop production?

3. What major group of plants provides (either directly or indirectly) the majority of calories consumed by humans? Explain your answer.

As you will see in the coming chapters, the transformation of the terrestrial environment by plants was critical to the terrestrial invasion by fungi and animals.

▶ Investigating LIFE

Q and A How long can most seeds survive, and why is seed dormancy important?

As you saw in **Investigating Life: William Beale's Seed Viability Study** and in the opening of this chapter, seeds of some plants can remain dormant but viable for decades, centuries, or in extreme cases, even millennia. Seed dormancy is especially important for the long-term survival of plant species that grow in unpredictable or highly fluctuating environments. If the appropriate conditions for seed growth and seedling maturation occur only rarely, then seeds need to be able to remain dormant in the soil until those favorable conditions occur. Biologists refer to dormant seeds in a given area as the "seed bank." What conditions will cause the seeds to break their dormancy and sprout? Fire, heavy rain, appropriate temperatures, or disturbance by animals are some of the more common stimulants for breaking seed dormancy. Many seeds need to be consumed by an animal and to pass through the acidic conditions of the animal's digestive system before the seeds will sprout. As anyone who has planted a new garden will know, soil disturbance will often produce the conditions needed for many dormant seeds to start growing. A new garden often requires persistent weeding to remove all the unwanted (by the gardener) plants that have been "awakened" from the seed bank.

Future directions

We've noted that humans depend on a relatively small number of plants for the majority of our food needs, although many more species of plants are grown and eaten for food. Traditionally, different locally adapted strains of crop plants have been grown by different farmers in different regions of the world. Agricultural companies now produce new varieties of crops that increase agricultural production. Unfortunately, a downside to these new strains is that farmers across the world have switched to growing relatively few varieties of important crop plants, which increases our global risk to disease and pests. If all farmers

Office and handling area · Airlock doors · Sleeve to protect tunnel from erosion and climatic changes · Tunnel entrance · Bridge · Seed vaults

Figure 27.24 The Global Seed Vault This vault is located more than 100 meters inside a sandstone mountain on the Norwegian island of Spitsbergen, about 1,000 kilometers from the North Pole. The location was chosen for secure, long-term storage of seeds because the surrounding ground was expected to remain perpetually frozen and the site is secure against earthquakes, floods, and other natural disasters. However, global warming now threatens the surrounding permafrost.

grow the same strain of wheat, for example, and that strain is susceptible to a particular pathogen or insect pest, what happens when the pathogen or pest spreads and all the susceptible wheat is lost?

To guard against devastating losses of important plants, many nations around the world have collaborated to develop a secure seed vault, which stores and protects the genetic diversity of crop plants (**Figure 27.24**). This seed vault is built into a sandstone mountain, which has long been surrounded by permafrost on the Arctic island of Spitsbergen, Norway (although the permafrost is now threatened by global warming). It is situated at a high enough elevation that it will remain above sea level even if all the polar ice caps were melted by global warming. Cooling systems maintain the vault at −18°C, and even if these systems fail, insulation and local cold weather would protect the seeds inside and maximize their viability. This seed vault complements several shorter-term seed depositories that are maintained in individual countries. Such seed depositories are used by biologists to develop new varieties of plant crops and to research the genetic variation of plant species from around the world.

You should be able to relate each summary to the adjacent figures. If you go to this visual summary in **Achieve**, you can follow links to figures, animations, activities, and simulations that will help you consolidate the material.

KEY CONCEPT 27.1

Pollen, Seeds, and Wood Contributed to the Success of Seed Plants

Go to **Activity 27.1**

- The two major groups of living seed plants are the **gymnosperms** and **angiosperms**, both of which include many woody species.

- Seed plants do not require liquid water for fertilization. **Pollen** grains, the male gametophytes of seed plants, are carried to a female gametophyte by wind or by animals.

- Following **pollination**, a **pollen tube** emerges from the pollen grain and elongates to deliver gametes to the female gametophyte.

- An **ovule** consists of the seed plant female gametophyte and the **integument** of sporophytic tissue that protects it. The ovule develops into a **seed**.

Figure 27.4

A growing pollen tube

Pollen grains

© Dr. Jeremy Burgess/Science Source

Questions

1. What is the difference between pollen and sperm?

2. When you look at a seed plant, which is most obvious—the haploid gametophyte generation or the diploid sporophyte generation?

3. Which parts of a seed plant constitute the gametophyte generation?

Figure 27.5

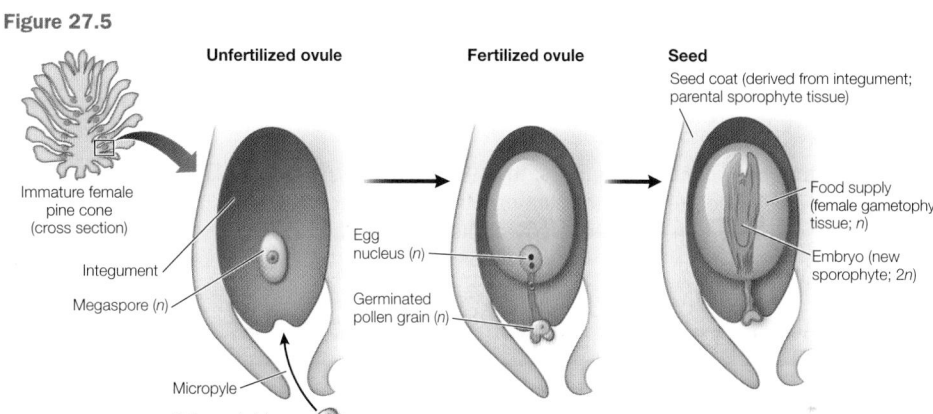

Immature female pine cone (cross section)

Unfertilized ovule

Integument
Megaspore (n)
Micropyle
Pollen grain (n)

Fertilized ovule

Egg nucleus (n)
Germinated pollen grain (n)

Seed

Seed coat (derived from integument; parental sporophyte tissue)
Food supply (female gametophyte tissue; n)
Embryo (new sporophyte; $2n$)

KEY CONCEPT 27.2

Once Dominant Gymnosperms Still Thrive in Some Environments

Go to **Activity 27.2 and Animation 27.1**

- The gymnosperms produce ovules and seeds that are not protected by ovary or fruit tissues.

- The major gymnosperm groups are the **cycads**, **ginkgos**, **gnetophytes**, and **conifers**.

Questions

1. Why are forest fires often necessary for the long-term survival of some gymnosperm forests?

2. If gymnosperm seeds are not protected by fruits, then what are the red "berries" on a juniper tree?

Figure 27.7

Female cones (megastrobili) in *Pinus contorta*

Cross section of a megastrobilus

Woody scale
Seed
Central axis

© Scenics & Science/ Alamy Stock Photo

Female cones, or megastrobili

© Fritz Pölking/ Blickwinkel/AGE Fotostock

Male cones (microstrobili) in *Pinus contorta*

Cross section of a microstrobilus

Herbaceous scale
Pollen-containing microspores
Central axis

© Scenics & Science/Alamy Stock Photo

Male cones, or microstrobili

© Gunter Marx/Alamy Stock Photo

KEY CONCEPT
27.3 Flowers and Fruits Led to Increased Diversification of Angiosperms

Go to Animation 27.2

- **Flowers** and **fruits** are unique to the angiosperms, distinguishing them from the gymnosperms.

- The floral organs, from the base to the apex of the flower, are the **sepals**, **petals**, **stamens**, and one or more **carpels**. Stamens bear microsporangia in **anthers**. The carpel includes an **ovary** containing ovules and a receptive surface called the **stigma**.

- Flowers may be pollinated by wind or by animals. Many angiosperms have coevolved with their animal pollinators.

- The **magnoliids** are the sister group to the **monocots** and **eudicots** (the most species-rich angiosperm clades).

Figure 27.18

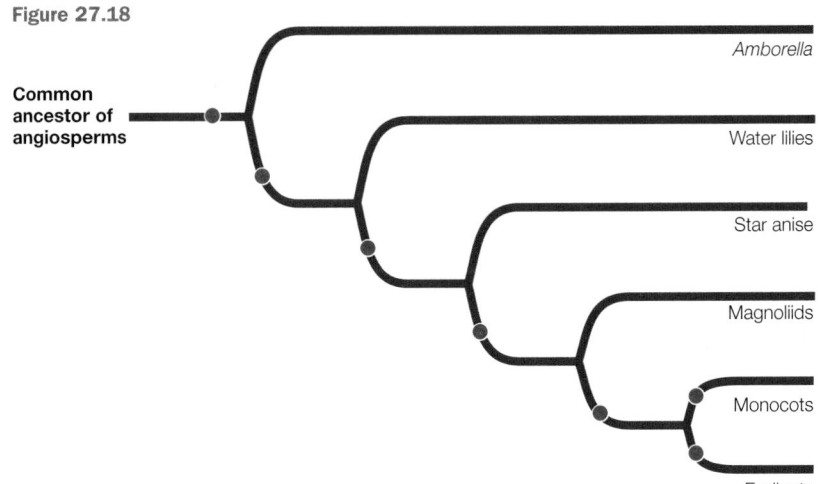

Common ancestor of angiosperms

- Amborella
- Water lilies
- Star anise
- Magnoliids
- Monocots
- Eudicots

Questions

1. What are three ways that different flowers attract insect pollinators?

2. Which of the following are true fruits: the parachute-like structures on a mature dandelion head; the acorns on an oak tree; a pineapple?

KEY CONCEPT
27.4 Plants Play Critical Roles in Terrestrial Ecosystems

- Plants provide critical ecosystem services that affect soil, water, air quality, and climate.

- Plants provide humans with many important medicinal products.

- Plants are primary producers and as such are the foundation of terrestrial food webs.

Questions

1. What plant produces paclitaxel, an important drug for the treatment of ovarian and breast cancers?

2. What single plant produces the majority of food energy for more than half the world's human population?

Figure 27.22

© Calvin Chan/Alamy Stock Photo

Figure 27.23

© Xinhua/Alamy Stock Photo

Go to **Achieve** for the eBook, **LearningCurve**, animations, activities, simulations, and additional resources and assignments.

The Evolution and Diversity of Fungi 28

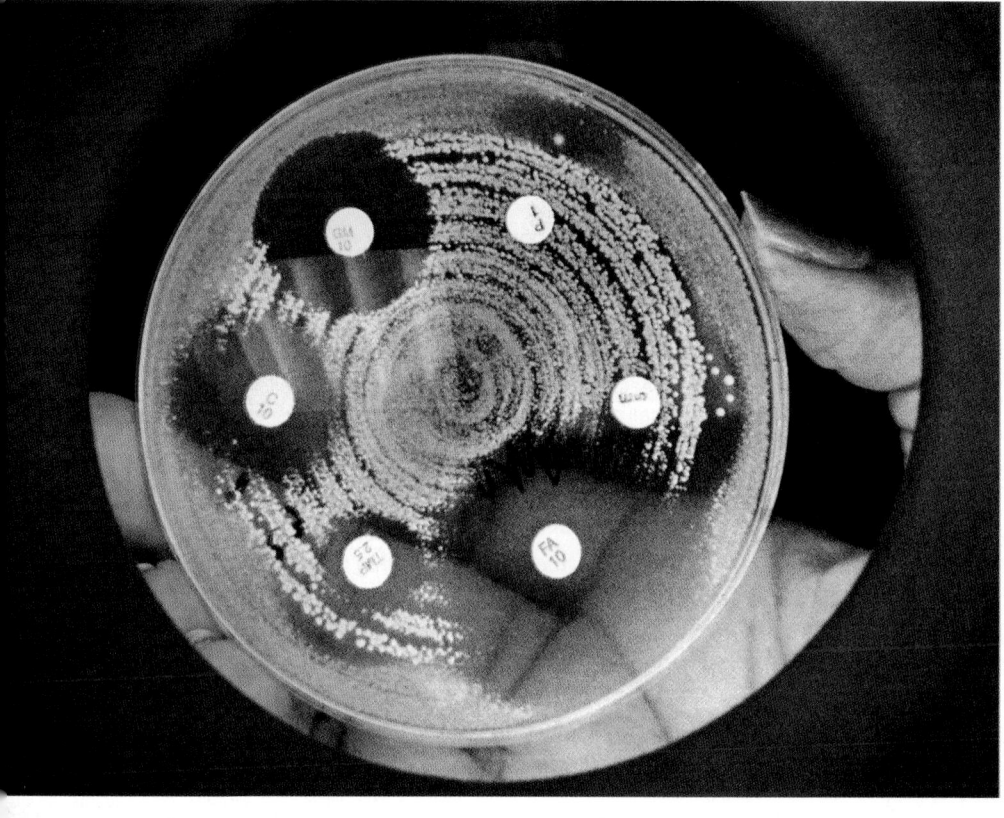

Six antibiotics (contained on white disks) are tested for their effectiveness against a bacterium (background of yellow-green colonies). The larger zones of growth inhibition (clear areas around white disks) indicate higher antibiotic effectiveness.

© Sotiris Zafeiris/Science Source

KEY CONCEPTS

28.1 Fungi Digest Food Outside Their Bodies

28.2 Fungi Are Decomposers, Parasites, Predators, or Mutualists

28.3 Sex in Fungi Involves Multiple Mating Types

28.4 Fungi Have Many Practical Uses

▶ InvestigatingLIFE

The Accidental Discovery of Antibiotics

Alexander Fleming was already a famous scientist in 1928, but his laboratory was often a mess. That year he was studying the properties of *Staphylococcus* bacteria, the agents of dangerous staph infections. In August he took a long vacation with his family. When he returned in early September, he found that some of his petri dishes of *Staphylococcus* had become infested with a fungus that killed many of the bacteria.

Many scientists would have sighed at the loss, thrown out the petri dishes, and started new cultures of bacteria. But when Fleming looked at the dishes, he saw something exciting. Around each colony of fungi was a ring within which all the bacteria were dead.

Fleming hypothesized that the bacteria-free rings around the fungal colonies were produced by a substance excreted from the fungi, which he initially called "mould juice." He identified the fungi as members of the genus *Penicillium* and eventually named the antibacterial substance they produced "penicillin." Fleming published his discovery in 1929, but initially it received very little attention.

Over the next decade, Fleming produced small quantities of penicillin for testing as an antibacterial agent. Some of the tests showed promise, but many were inconclusive, and eventually Fleming gave up on the research. But his tests had shown enough

promise to attract the attention of several chemists, who worked out the practical problems of producing a stable form of the substance. Clinical trials of this stable form of penicillin were extremely successful, and by 1945 it was being produced and distributed as an antibiotic on a large scale. That same year, Fleming and two of the chemists, Howard Florey and Ernst Chain, received the Nobel Prize in Physiology or Medicine for their work on penicillin.

The development of penicillin was one of the most important achievements in modern medicine. Until the introduction of modern antibiotics, the most widespread agents of human death included bacterial infections such as gangrene, tuberculosis, and syphilis. Penicillin proved to be highly effective in curing such infections, and its success led to the creation of the modern pharmaceutical industry. Soon many additional antibiotic compounds were isolated from other fungi or synthesized in the laboratory, leading to a "golden age" of human health.

 Why are the regions of inhibited bacterial growth around the various antibiotics so different in size, and how is that relevant to human health care? (Find the answer on page 642.)

KEY CONCEPT 28.1 Fungi Digest Food Outside Their Bodies

Learning Objectives

28.1.1 Explain how the structure of fungi facilitates their ability to decompose and consume other organisms.

28.1.2 Assess the ability of fungi to exist in different environments.

Fungi are distinctive in the way they digest their food. They secrete digestive enzymes to break down large food molecules in the environment, then absorb the breakdown products through their cell membranes in a process known as **absorptive heterotrophy**. This mode of nutrition allows them to be successful in a wide variety of environments. Many fungi are **saprobes**, meaning they absorb nutrients from dead organic matter. Others are parasites or predators, feeding on or consuming other living organisms. Still others are mutualists, living in intimate associations with other organisms that benefit both partners.

Modern fungi evolved from a unicellular protist ancestor that had a flagellum, although most fungi are not motile and have now lost this structure. The probable common ancestor of the animals was also a flagellated protist much like the living choanoflagellates (see Figure 29.2). Current evidence, including the sequences of many genes, suggests that the fungi, choanoflagellates, and animals share a common ancestor not shared by other eukaryotes. These three lineages form a group known as the **opisthokonts** (**Figure 28.1**). A synapomorphy (shared derived trait) of the opisthokonts is a flagellum that, if present, is posterior, as in animal sperm. The flagella of all other eukaryotes attach at the front or sides of the cell, rather than at the rear.

Synapomorphies that distinguish the fungi as a group among the opisthokonts include absorptive heterotrophy and the presence of **chitin**, a nitrogen-containing structural polysaccharide, in their cell walls. The fungi represent one of the four independent evolutionary origins of large multicellular organisms (plants, brown algae, and animals are the other three).

Saccharomyces cerevisiae

New cells have broken off from each of these yellow areas.

5 μm

Figure 28.2 Yeasts Unicellular, free-living fungi are known as yeasts. Many yeasts reproduce by budding—mitosis followed by asymmetrical cell division—as illustrated here.

Yeasts are unicellular, free-living fungi

Most fungi are multicellular, but single-celled species are found in most fungal groups. Unicellular, free-living fungi are referred to as **yeasts** (**Figure 28.2**). Some fungi have both a yeast life stage and a multicellular life stage. Thus the term "yeast" does not refer to a single taxonomic group, but rather to a lifestyle that has evolved multiple times. Yeasts live in liquid or moist environments and absorb nutrients directly across their cell surfaces.

The ease with which many yeasts can be cultured, combined with their rapid growth rates, has made them ideal model organisms for study in the laboratory. They present many of the same advantages to laboratory investigators as do many bacteria, but because they are eukaryotes, their genome structures and cells are much more like those of humans and other eukaryotes than are those of bacteria.

Connect the Concepts Why we select and study a variety of model organisms is discussed in Key Concept 17.3. Each model organism has distinctive advantages and disadvantages. The features of yeasts make them ideal for some investigations but impractical for others.

Multicellular fungi use hyphae to absorb nutrients

The body of a multicellular fungus is called a **mycelium** (plural *mycelia*). A mycelium is composed of a branching mass of individual tubular filaments called **hyphae** (singular *hypha*; **Figure 28.3A**), in which absorption of nutrients takes place primarily at each tip. The cell walls of the hyphae are greatly strengthened by microscopic fibrils of chitin. In some species of fungi, the hyphae are subdivided into cell-like compartments by incomplete crosswalls called **septa** (singular *septum*). These subdivided hyphae are referred to as **septate**. Septa do not completely close off compartments in the hyphae. Pores at the centers of the septa allow cytoplasm and organelles—sometimes even nuclei—to move in a controlled way between compartments (**Figure 28.3B**). In other species of fungi, the hyphae lack septa but may contain hundreds of nuclei. These multinucleate, undivided hyphae are referred to as **coenocytic**. The coenocytic condition results from repeated nuclear divisions without cytokinesis.

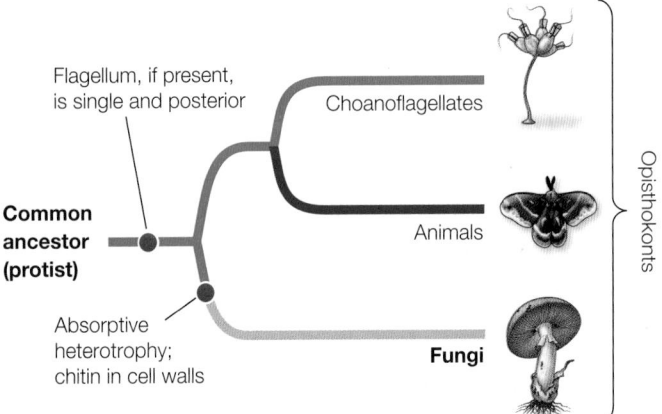

Flagellum, if present, is single and posterior

Choanoflagellates

Common ancestor (protist)

Animals

Absorptive heterotrophy; chitin in cell walls

Fungi

Opisthokonts

Figure 28.1 Fungi in Evolutionary Context Absorptive heterotrophy and the presence of chitin in their cell walls distinguish the fungi from other opisthokonts.

(A) Fungal hyphae in dry rot

Vessel in xylem   Fungal hyphae

© Dr. Jeremy Burgess/Science Source

10 μm

(B) Anatomy of hyphae

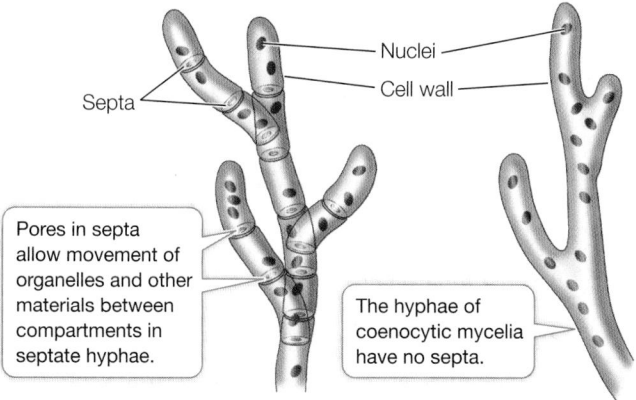

Nuclei

Cell wall

Septa

Pores in septa allow movement of organelles and other materials between compartments in septate hyphae.

The hyphae of coenocytic mycelia have no septa.

(C) The mycelium of a club fungus

The aboveground mushroom represents the fruiting structure produced from the mycelia of two combined, mating individuals.

The main (vegetative) portion of each mycelium is typically much more extensive than the fruiting structure (only a small portion is shown in this figure).

Figure 28.3 Mycelia Are Made Up of Hyphae   (A) The minute individual hyphae of fungal mycelia can penetrate small spaces. In this artificially colored micrograph, hyphae (yellow structures) of a dry-rot fungus are penetrating the xylem tissues of a log. (B) The hyphae of septate fungal species are divided into organelle-containing compartments by porous septa. The hyphae of coenocytic fungal species have no septa. (C) The fruiting structure of a club fungus is short-lived, but the filamentous, nutrient-absorbing mycelium can be long-lived and cover large areas.

Certain modified hyphae, called **rhizoids**, anchor some fungi to their substrate (i.e., the dead organism or other matter on which they grow). These rhizoids are not homologous to the rhizoids of plants, and they are not specialized to absorb nutrients and water.

Fungi can grow very rapidly when conditions are favorable. In some species, the total hyphal growth of a fungal mycelium (not the growth of an individual hypha) may exceed 1 kilometer a day! The hyphae may be widely dispersed to forage for nutrients over a large area, or they may clump together in a cottony mass to exploit a rich nutrient source. The familiar mushrooms you may notice growing in moist areas are spore-producing fruiting structures (**Figure 28.3C**). In the fungal species that produce these structures, the mycelial mass is often far larger than the visible mushroom. The mycelium of one individual fungus discovered in Oregon covers almost 900 hectares underground and weighs considerably more than a blue whale (the largest animal). Aboveground, this individual is evident only as isolated clumps of mushrooms.

Fungi are in intimate contact with their environment

The filamentous hyphae of a fungus give it a unique relationship with its physical environment. The fungal mycelium has an enormous surface area-to-volume ratio compared with that of most large multicellular organisms. This large ratio allows the fungus to take in a great deal of water and mineral nutrients when soil moisture is high, which allows rapid growth in moist environments. The downside of the large surface area-to-volume ratio of the mycelium is its tendency to lose water rapidly in a dry environment. Thus fungi are most common in moist environments. You have probably observed the tendency of molds, toadstools, and other fungi to appear in damp places.

Another characteristic of some fungi is a tolerance for highly hypertonic environments (those with a solute concentration higher than their own; see Key Concept 6.3). Many fungi are more resilient than bacteria in hypertonic surroundings. Jelly, for example, does not support bacterial growth because its high sugar content makes it too hypertonic to those organisms, but it may eventually harbor mold colonies. Mold in the refrigerator illustrates yet another trait of many fungi: tolerance of temperature extremes. Many fungi grow in temperatures as low as −6°C, and some can tolerate temperatures higher than 50°C.

KEY CONCEPT
28.1 Recap and Assess

Fungi, like animals, are opisthokonts. Fungi are distinguished from other opisthokonts by absorptive heterotrophy and by the presence of chitin in their cell walls. Unicellular fungi called yeasts absorb nutrients directly across their cell surfaces. The body form of multicellular fungi—a mycelium made up of rapidly growing hyphae—allows them to practice absorptive heterotrophy efficiently in a variety of moist environments.

1. How does fungal structure facilitate absorptive heterotrophy?

2. What are the advantages and disadvantages to multicellular fungi of the large surface area-to-volume ratio of the mycelium? How does the mycelium restrict the types of environments in which fungi are generally found?

Fungi are important components of healthy ecosystems. They interact with other organisms in many ways, some of which are harmful and some beneficial to those other organisms.

KEY CONCEPT 28.2

Fungi Are Decomposers, Parasites, Predators, or Mutualists

Learning Objectives

28.2.1 Explain how saprobic fungi are critical to Earth's carbon cycle.

28.2.2 Describe the relationship and summarize the benefits to each partner in a lichen association.

28.2.3 Describe the specific benefits that mycorrhizal interactions provide for fungi and their associated partner organisms.

Without the fungi, our planet would be very different. Picture Earth with only a few stunted plants and watery environments choked with the remains of dead organisms. Fungi do much of Earth's garbage disposal. Fungi not only help clean up the landscape and form soil, but also play a key role in recycling mineral nutrients. Furthermore, the colonization of the terrestrial environment was made possible in large part by associations that fungi formed with land plants and other organisms.

Saprobic fungi are critical to the planetary carbon cycle

Saprobic fungi, along with bacteria, are the major decomposers on Earth, contributing to the decay of nonliving organic matter and thus to recycling of the elements used by living things. In forests, for example, the mycelia of fungi secrete extracellular enzymes that degrade plant materials into simpler compounds that are then absorbed. Fungi are the principal decomposers of cellulose and lignin, the main components of plant cell walls (most bacteria cannot break down these materials). Other fungi produce enzymes that decompose keratin and thus break down animal structures such as hair and nails.

Were it not for the fungal decomposers, Earth's carbon cycle would fail. Great quantities of carbon atoms would remain trapped forever on forest floors and elsewhere. Instead, those carbon atoms are returned to the atmosphere in the form of CO_2 by fungal respiration, where they are again available for photosynthesis by plants.

> **Connect the Concepts** Earth's carbon cycle is discussed in detail in Key Concept 56.4. Fungi play a critical role in this cycle by decomposing other organisms and releasing carbon dioxide.

There was a time in Earth's history when populations of saprobic fungi declined dramatically. Vast tropical swamps existed during the Carboniferous and much of the Permian, as you saw in Chapter 23. When plants in these swamps died, they began to form peat. Peat formation led to acidification of the swamps. That acidity, in turn, drastically reduced the fungal population. The result? With the decomposers largely absent, large quantities of peat remained on the swamp floor and over time were converted into coal.

In contrast to their decline during the Carboniferous and much of the Permian, fungi did very well at the end of the Permian, a quarter of a billion years ago, when the aggregation of continents produced volcanic eruptions that triggered a global mass extinction. The fossil record shows that even as the majority of all multicellular species became extinct, fungi flourished—demonstrating both their hardiness and their role in recycling the elements in dead plants and animals.

Simple sugars and the breakdown products of complex polysaccharides are the favored sources of carbon for saprobic fungi. Most fungi obtain nitrogen from proteins or the products of protein breakdown. Many fungi can use nitrate (NO_3^-) or ammonium (NH_4^+) ions as their sole source of nitrogen. No known fungus can get its nitrogen directly from inorganic nitrogen gas, however, as can some free-living and plant-associated bacteria (that is, fungi cannot fix nitrogen; see Key Concept 24.3).

What happens when a fungus faces a dwindling food supply? A common strategy is to reproduce rapidly and abundantly. When conditions are good, fungi produce great quantities of spores, but the rate of spore production is commonly even higher when nutrient supplies go down. The spores may then remain dormant until conditions improve, or they may be dispersed to areas where nutrient supplies are higher.

Not only are fungal spores abundant in number, but they are extremely tiny and easily spread by wind or water (Figure 28.4). These attributes virtually ensure that the spores will be scattered over great distances and that at least some of them will find conditions suitable for growth. The air we breathe contains as many as 10,000 fungal spores per cubic meter. No wonder we find fungi just about everywhere.

 Media Clip 28.1 Fungal Decomposers
Life12e.com/mc28.1

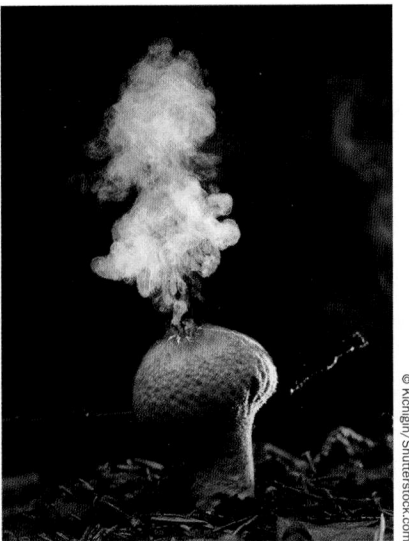

Lycoperdon perlatum

Figure 28.4 Spores Galore Puffballs (a type of club fungus) disperse trillions of spores in great bursts. Few of the spores travel very far, however; some 99% of them fall within 100 meters of the parent puffball.

Some fungi engage in parasitic or predatory interactions

Whereas saprobic fungi obtain their energy, carbon, and nitrogen directly from dead organic matter, other species of fungi obtain their nutrition from parasitic—and even predatory—interactions.

PARASITIC FUNGI **Mycologists** (biologists who study fungi) distinguish between two classes of parasitic fungi based on their degree of dependence on their host. **Facultative parasites** can grow on living organisms but can also grow independently (including on artificial media). **Obligate parasites** can grow only on a specific, living host. The fact that their growth depends on a living host shows that obligate parasites have specialized nutritional requirements.

Plants and insects are the most common hosts of parasitic fungi. The filamentous structure of fungal hyphae is especially well suited to a life of absorbing nutrients from living plants. The slender hyphae of a parasitic fungus can invade a plant through stomata, through wounds, or in some cases, by direct penetration of epidermal cell walls (**Figure 28.5A**). Once inside the plant, the hyphae branch out to expand the mycelium. Some hyphae produce **haustoria**, branching projections that push through cell walls into living plant cells, absorbing the nutrients within those cells. The haustoria do not break through the cell membranes inside the cell walls, but instead invaginate into the membranes, so that the cell membrane fits them like a glove (**Figure 28.5B**). Fruiting structures may form, either within the plant body or on its surface.

Some parasitic fungi live in a close physical (symbiotic) relationship with a plant host that is usually not lethal to the plant.

Others are *pathogenic*, weakening or even killing the host from which they derive nutrition.

 Media Clip 28.2 Mind-Control Killer Fungi
Life12e.com/mc28.2

PATHOGENIC FUNGI Although most human diseases are caused by bacteria or viruses, fungal pathogens are a major cause of death among people with compromised immune systems. Many people with AIDS die of fungal diseases, such as the pneumonia caused by *Pneumocystis jirovecii*. Even *Candida albicans* and certain other yeasts that are normally part of a healthy microbiome can cause severe diseases, such as esophagitis (which impairs swallowing), in individuals with AIDS and in individuals taking immunosuppressive drugs. Various fungi cause other, less threatening human diseases, such as ringworm and athlete's foot. The relatively close relationship between fungi and animals makes it difficult to find drugs that target unique features of fungal metabolism without harming human patients. As a result, fungal diseases are a growing international health problem.

The worldwide decline of amphibian species has been linked to the spread of a chytrid fungus, *Batrachochytrium dendrobatidis* (or *Bd* for simplicity). In some areas of the world where this fungus has been present for millennia, amphibian populations appear to be tolerant of *Bd* and it does not cause widespread die-offs. But a pathogenic strain known as the global pandemic lineage of *Bd* appears to have been introduced around the world in recent decades, likely through commercial trade of amphibians. These introductions of the global pandemic lineage of *Bd* are implicated in the loss or decline of many frog and salamander populations, and even the extinction of entire species.

(A) Parasitic mildew

Hyphae of fungal mycelium

This hypha is penetrating the leaf's interior through a stoma.

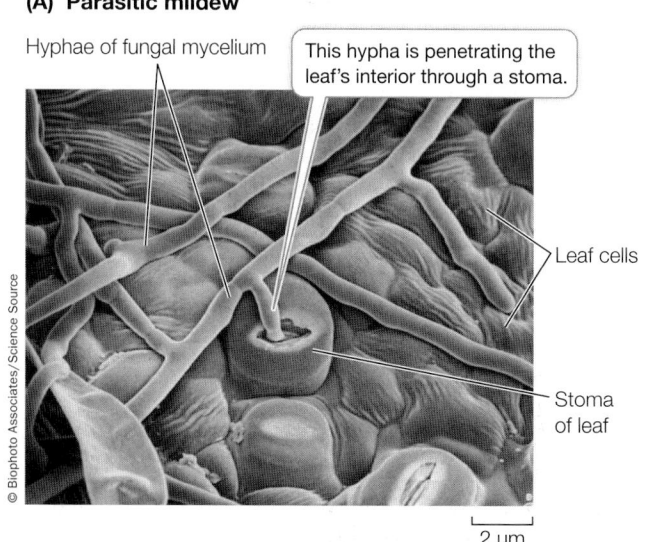

Leaf cells

Stoma of leaf

2 µm

Figure 28.5 Invading a Leaf **(A)** Hyphae of the mildew *Phyllactinia guttata* growing on the surface of a hazel leaf. **(B)** Haustoria are fungal hyphae that push into the living cells of plants, from which they absorb nutrients.

(B) The parasitic action of haustoria

The haustorium penetrates the cell wall but not the cell membrane.

Cell membrane

3 Some hyphae penetrate cells within the leaf.

Stoma

1 Fungal spores germinate on the lower surface of the leaf.

2 Elongating hyphae pass through stomata into the interior of the leaf.

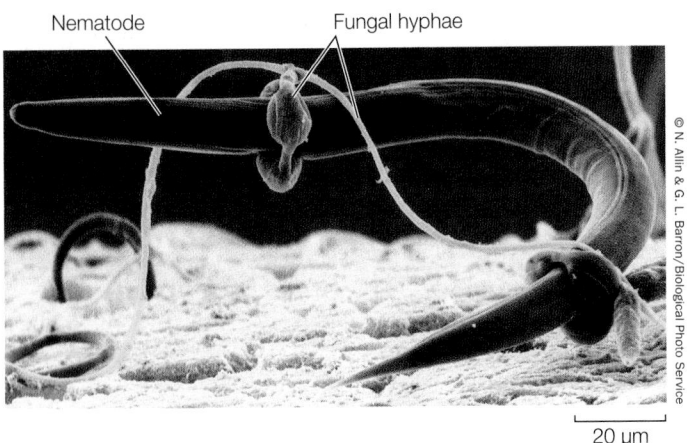

Figure 28.6 **Fungus as Predator** A nematode is trapped by hyphal rings of the soil-dwelling fungus *Arthrobotrys dactyloides*.

Fungi are by far the most important plant pathogens, causing annual crop losses amounting to billions of dollars. Major fungal diseases of crop plants include black stem rust of wheat and other diseases of wheat, corn, and oats. The agent of black stem rust is *Puccinia graminis*, which has a complicated life cycle that involves two plant hosts (wheat and barberry). In an epidemic in 1935, *P. graminis* was responsible for the loss of about one-fourth of the wheat crop in Canada and the United States.

PREDATORY FUNGI   Some fungi have adaptations that enable them to function as active predators, trapping nearby microscopic protists or animals. This feeding strategy is especially important in environments with lots of available carbon but little nitrogen, such as wood. The most common predatory strategy seen in fungi is to secrete sticky substances from the hyphae so that passing organisms stick to them. The hyphae then quickly invade the trapped prey, growing and branching within it, spreading through its body, absorbing nutrients, and eventually killing it.

A more dramatic adaptation for predation is the constricting ring formed by some species of soil fungi (**Figure 28.6**). When nematodes (tiny roundworms) are present in the soil, these fungi form three-celled rings with a diameter that just fits a nematode. A nematode crawling through one of these rings stimulates the fungus, causing the cells of the ring to swell and trap the worm. Fungal hyphae quickly invade and digest the unlucky victim.

Mutualistic fungi engage in relationships that benefit both partners

Certain relationships between fungi and other organisms have nutritional consequences for both partners. Two relationships of this type are **symbiotic** (the partners live in close, permanent contact with each other) as well as **mutualistic** (the relationship benefits both partners).

LICHENS   A **lichen** is not a single organism, but rather a meshwork of at least two radically different species: a fungus and a photosynthetic alga or cyanobacterium. Recent studies suggest that an additional fungal species (a unicellular yeast) is also usually involved in this mutualism. Together the organisms that constitute a lichen can survive some of the harshest environments on Earth (although they are sensitive to poor air quality; see Key Concept 28.4). The biota of Antarctica, for example, features more than 100 times as many kinds of lichens as of plants. Relatively little experimental work has focused on lichens, perhaps because they grow so slowly—typically less than 1 centimeter in a year.

There are nearly 30,000 described "species" of lichens, each of which is assigned the name of its multicellular fungal component. These fungal components may constitute as many as 20% of all fungal species. Most of them are sac fungi (Ascomycota). Some of them are able to grow independently without a photosynthetic partner, but most have never been observed in nature other than in a lichen association. The photosynthetic component of a lichen is most often a unicellular green alga, but it can be a cyanobacterium, or may even include both.

Lichens are found in all sorts of exposed habitats: on tree bark, on open soil, and on bare rock. Reindeer moss (not a moss at all, but the lichen *Cladonia subtenuis*) covers vast areas in Arctic, sub-Arctic, and boreal regions, where it is an important part of the diets of caribou and other large mammals.

The body forms of lichens fall into three principal categories. **Crustose** (crustlike) lichens adhere tightly to their substrate (**Figure 28.7A**). **Fruticose** lichens are highly branched and can grow upward like shrubs, or hang in long strands from tree branches or

(A) Crustose lichen

(B) Fruticose lichen

(C) Foliose lichen

Figure 28.7 **Lichen Body Forms** The body forms of lichens fall into three principal categories. **(A)** Two crustose lichen species are growing together on this exposed rock surface. **(B)** The light green "shrubby" growth is a fruticose lichen. **(C)** Foliose lichens have a leafy appearance.

A soredium consists of one or a few photosynthetic cells surrounded by fungal hyphae.

Soredia detach from the parent lichen and travel in air currents, founding new lichens when they settle in a suitable environment.

Upper layer of hyphae

Photosynthetic cell layer

Loose layer of hyphae

Lower level of hyphal rhizoids

Figure 28.8 Lichen Anatomy Cross section showing the layers of a foliose lichen and the release of soredia.

rocks (**Figure 28.7B**). **Foliose** (leafy) lichens are loosely attached and grow parallel to their substrate (**Figure 28.7C**).

A cross section of a typical foliose lichen reveals a tight upper region of fungal hyphae, a layer of photosynthetic cyanobacteria or algae, a looser hyphal layer, and finally hyphal rhizoids that attach the entire structure to its substrate (**Figure 28.8**). The meshwork of fungal hyphae takes up mineral nutrients needed by the photosynthetic cells and also holds water tenaciously, providing a suitably moist environment. The fungus obtains fixed carbon from the photosynthetic products of the algal or cyanobacterial cells.

Within the lichen, fungal hyphae are tightly pressed against the photosynthetic cells and sometimes invade them without breaching the cell membrane (similar to the haustoria in parasitic fungi; see Figure 28.5). The photosynthetic cells not only survive these intrusions but continue to grow. Algal cells in a lichen "leak" photosynthetic products at a greater rate than do similar cells growing on their own, and photosynthetic cells taken from lichens grow more rapidly on their own than when associated with a fungus. On the basis of these observations, we could consider lichen fungi to be parasitic on their photosynthetic partners. In many places where lichens grow, however, the photosynthetic cells could not grow at all on their own.

Lichens can reproduce simply by fragmentation of the vegetative body (the **thallus**) or by means of specialized structures called **soredia** (singular *soredium*). Soredia consist of one or a few photosynthetic cells bound by fungal hyphae. They become detached from the lichen, are dispersed by air currents, and upon arriving at a favorable location, develop into a new lichen thallus (see Figure 28.8). Alternatively, the fungal partner may go through its sexual reproductive cycle, producing haploid spores. When these spores are discharged, however, they disperse alone, unaccompanied by the photosynthetic partner.

Lichens are often the first colonists on new areas of bare rock. They get most of the mineral nutrients they need from the air

and rainwater, augmented by minerals absorbed from dust. A lichen begins to grow shortly after a rain, as it begins to dry. As it grows, the lichen acidifies its environment slightly, and this acidity contributes to the slow breakdown of rocks, an early step in soil formation. With further drying, the lichen's photosynthesis ceases. The water content of the lichen may drop to less than 10% of its dry weight, at which point the lichen becomes highly insensitive to extremes of temperature.

MYCORRHIZAE   Many vascular plants depend on a symbiotic association with fungi. This ancient association between plants and fungi was critical to the successful exploitation of the terrestrial environment by plants. Unassisted, the root hairs of many plants often do not take up enough water or minerals to sustain growth. However, the roots of such plants usually do become infected with fungi, forming an association called a **mycorrhiza** (plural *mycorrhizae*). There are two types of mycorrhizae, distinguished by whether or not the fungal hyphae penetrate the plant cell walls.

In **ectomycorrhizae**, the fungus wraps around the root tip, and its mass is often as great as that of the root itself (**Figure 28.9A**). The fungal hyphae penetrate the root and wrap around individual root cells but do not penetrate the cell walls. An extensive web of hyphae penetrates the soil in the area around the root, so that up to 25% of the volume near the root may be fungal hyphae. The hyphae attached to the root increase the surface area for the absorption of water and minerals, and the mass of hyphae in the soil acts like a sponge to hold water in the neighborhood of the root. Infected roots are short, swollen, and club-shaped, and they lack root hairs.

(A) An ectomycorrhizal fungus

(B) An arbuscular mycorrhizal fungus

Root cell walls

200 μm

© R. L. Peterson/Biological Photo Service

Hyphae of the fungus *Pisolithus tinctorius* cover a eucalyptus root.

Arbuscule

5 μm

© Carolina Biological Supply Co./Visuals Unlimited, Inc.

Figure 28.9 Mycorrhizal Associations   (A) Ectomycorrhizal fungi wrap themselves around a plant root, increasing the area available for absorption of water and minerals. (B) Hyphae of arbuscular mycorrhizal fungi infect the root internally and penetrate the root cell walls, branching within the cells and forming a treelike structure, the arbuscule. (The cell cytoplasm has been removed to better visualize the arbuscule.)

The fungal hyphae of **arbuscular mycorrhizae** enter the root and penetrate the cell walls of the root cells, forming arbuscular (treelike) structures inside the cell wall but outside the cell membrane. These structures, like the haustoria of parasitic fungi and the contact regions of fungal hyphae and photosynthetic cells in lichens, become the primary site of exchange between plant and fungus (**Figure 28.9B**). As in the ectomycorrhizae, the fungus forms a vast web of hyphae leading from the root surface into the surrounding soil.

Connect the Concepts Mycorrhizae can vastly increase the root surface area in contact with essential nutrients in the soil. The importance of arbuscular mycorrhizae in plant nutrition is described in detail in Key Concept 34.3.

The mycorrhizal association is important to both partners. The fungus obtains needed organic compounds, such as sugars and amino acids, from the plant. In return, the fungus, because of its very high surface area-to-volume ratio and its ability to penetrate the fine structure of the soil, greatly increases the plant's ability to absorb water and minerals (especially phosphorus). The fungus may also provide the plant with certain growth hormones and may protect it against attack by disease-causing microorganisms.

Plants that have active arbuscular mycorrhizae typically are a deeper green and may resist drought and temperature extremes better than plants of the same species that have little mycorrhizal development. Attempts to introduce some plant species to new areas have failed until some of the soil from the native area (presumably containing the fungus necessary to establish mycorrhizae) was provided. Trees without ectomycorrhizae do not grow well in the absence of abundant nutrients and water, so the health of our forests depends on the presence of ectomycorrhizal fungi. Many agricultural crops require inoculation of seeds with appropriate mycorrhizal fungi prior to planting. Without these fungi, the plants are unlikely to grow well, or in some cases at all. Certain plants that live in nitrogen-poor habitats, such as cranberry bushes and orchids, invariably have mycorrhizae. Orchid seeds will not germinate in nature unless they are already infected by the fungus that will form their mycorrhizae. Plants that lack chlorophyll always have mycorrhizae, which they often share with the roots of green, photosynthetic plants. In effect, these plants without chlorophyll are feeding on nearby green plants, using the fungus as a bridge.

Endophytic fungi protect some plants from pathogens, herbivores, and stress

In a tropical rainforest, 10,000 or more fungal spores may land on a single leaf each day. Some are plant pathogens, some do not affect the plant at all, and some invade the plant in a beneficial way. Fungi that live within aboveground parts of plants without causing obvious deleterious symptoms are called **endophytic fungi**. Recent research has shown that endophytic fungi are abundant in plants in all terrestrial environments.

Among the grasses, individual plants with endophytic fungi are more resistant to pathogens and to insect and mammalian herbivores than are plants lacking endophytes. The fungi produce alkaloids (nitrogen-containing compounds) that are toxic to animals. The alkaloids do not harm the host plant. In fact, some plants produce alkaloids (such as nicotine) themselves. The fungal alkaloids also increase the ability of grasses to resist stress of various types, including drought (water shortage) and salty soils. Such resistance is beneficial for some crops, although it can produce toxicity for grazing animals.

The role, if any, of endophytic fungi in most broad-leaved plants is unclear. They may convey protection against pathogens, or they may simply occupy space within leaves without conferring any benefit, but also without doing harm. The benefit, in fact, might be all for the fungus.

KEY CONCEPT
28.2 Recap and Assess

Fungi interact with other organisms in many ways, both harmful and beneficial. Saprobic fungi play critical roles in the recycling of elements required by living organisms. Lichens are mutualistic associations of fungi with algae or cyanobacteria. Mycorrhizae are associations of fungi and the roots of plants; they are essential for the survival of most plant species.

1. What is the role of fungi in Earth's carbon cycle?
2. Describe the nature and benefits of the lichen association.
3. How does the mycorrhizal association benefit both the plant and the fungus?

Before molecular techniques were widely used to study the phylogenetic relationships of fungi, one criterion used for assigning fungi to taxonomic groups was the nature of their life cycles—including the types of fruiting structures they produce. Next we take a closer look at life cycles in the major groups of fungi.

KEY CONCEPT
28.3 Sex in Fungi Involves Multiple Mating Types

Learning Objectives

28.3.1 Compare and contrast sexual reproduction in fungi with that in plants and animals.

28.3.2 Describe the dikaryotic stage of the fungal life cycle, distinguish which major fungal groups include a dikaryotic stage, and explain how the dikaryotic stage differs from the haploid and diploid stages.

28.3.3 Compare and contrast the life cycles of zygospore fungi, sac fungi, and club fungi.

Although fungal life cycles are even more diverse than was once realized, specific types of life cycles generally distinguish five major groups of fungi: chytrids (Chytridiomycota and Blastocladiomycota), zygospore fungi (Zoopagomycota), arbuscular mycorrhizal fungi (Glomeromycotina), sac fungi (Ascomycota), and club fungi (Basidiomycota). In addition, a reduced parasitic group, microsporidia, is usually considered to be related to fungi, although the exact relationships of microsporidia within eukaryotes are

Figure 28.10 A Phylogeny of the Fungi   Microsporidia are reduced parasites that are thought to be related to fungi, although their relationships are still debated. The dashed lines indicate that chytrids and zygospore fungi are possibly paraphyletic (see Table 28.1). The sac fungi and club fungi together form the clade Dikarya.

▶ **View in Achieve**
Activity 28.1 Fungal Phylogeny

debated. **Figure 28.10** diagrams the evolutionary relationships of these groups as they are understood today.

Chytrids and the zygospore fungi may not represent monophyletic groups, as they each consist of several distantly related lineages that retain some ancestral features. The clades that are thought to be monophyletic within these two informal groupings are listed in **Table 28.1**. Most recent evidence from DNA analyses has supported the relationship of the microsporidia to fungi, the possible paraphyly of the chytrids and the zygospore fungi, and the monophyly of sac fungi and club fungi.

Fungi reproduce both sexually and asexually

Both asexual and sexual reproduction occur among the fungi (**Figure 28.11**). Asexual reproduction takes several forms:

- The production of (usually) haploid spores within sporangia
- The production of haploid spores (not enclosed in sporangia) at the tips of hyphae; in sac fungi, such spores are called **conidia** (Greek *konis*, "dust")
- Cell division by unicellular fungi—either a relatively equal division of one cell into two (*fission*) or an asymmetrical division in which a smaller daughter cell is produced (*budding*)
- Mitotic growth and fragmentation of the mycelium

Sexual reproduction is rare (or even unknown) in some groups of fungi but common in others. Sexual reproduction may not occur in some species, or it may occur so rarely that biologists have never observed it. Species in which no sexual stage has been observed were once placed in a separate taxonomic group because knowledge of the sexual life cycle was considered necessary for classifying fungi. Now, however, these species can be related to other species of fungi through analysis of their DNA sequences.

Fungi mate in the most interesting of ways. They don't limit themselves to the confines of "males" and "females," but rather have many different **mating types**, any two of which can reproduce. And when they mate, they don't merely pass a few gamete cells between individuals like plants or animals do; instead, they fuse their bodies to become one and then exchange their nuclei. After fusing, many mating pairs remain fused for some time (a mushroom is basically two fused fungi getting it on), and the sexual act can thus last for weeks or months at a time. Eventually the nuclei fuse and recombine, and "genetic sex" finally takes place. After making millions of offspring, the exhausted fungi disintegrate their combined bodies and never text each other again.

TABLE **28.1**	Classification of the Fungi		
Group	**Common name**	**Features**	
Microsporidia	Microsporidia	Intracellular parasites of animals; greatly reduced, among smallest eukaryotes known; polar tube used to infect hosts; placement among fungi is debated	
Chytridiomycota and Blastocladiomycota	Chytrids[a]	Mostly aquatic and microscopic; in some species, zoospores and gametes have flagella	
Zoopagomycota	Zygospore fungi[b]	Reproductive structure is a unicellular zygospore with many diploid nuclei; hyphae coenocytic; no fleshy fruiting body	
Glomeromycotina	Arbuscular mycorrhizal fungi	Form arbuscular mycorrhizae in plant roots; often reproduce asexually, but recent studies show sexual reproduction as well	
Ascomycota	Sac fungi	Sexual reproductive saclike structure known as an ascus, which contains haploid ascospores; hyphae septate; dikaryon	
Basidiomycota	Club fungi	Sexual reproductive structure is a basidium, a swollen cell at the tip of a specialized hypha that supports haploid basidiospores; hyphae septate; dikaryon	

[a]The relationships between Chytridiomycota and Blastocladiomycota, both treated as chytrids here, are not yet well resolved.
[b]Two small groups traditionally considered zygospore fungi now appear to be more closely related to arbuscular mycorrhizal fungi.

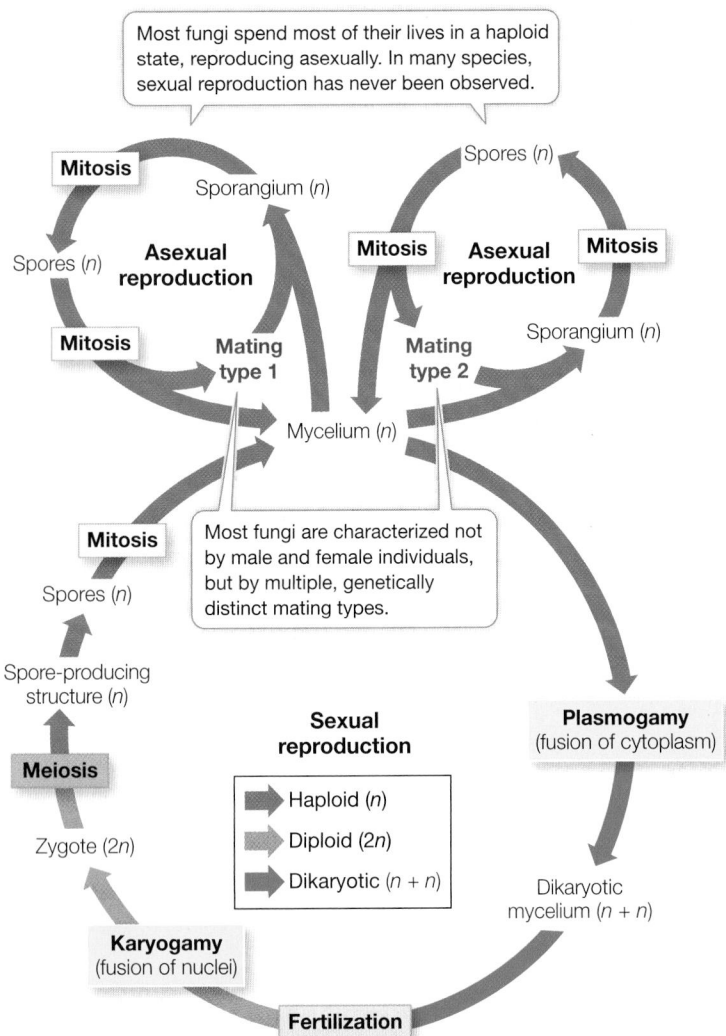

Figure 28.11 A Generalized Fungal Life Cycle Environmental conditions may determine which mode of reproduction—sexual or asexual—takes place at a given time.

Major groups of fungi differ in the details of when and how the nuclei from two individuals fuse and recombine, and in whether they produce a fleshy fruiting structure, as we discuss later in this key concept.

Microsporidia may be highly reduced, parasitic fungi

Microsporidia are highly reduced, unicellular parasites. They are among the smallest eukaryotes known, with infective spores that are only 1–40 micrometers (μm) in diameter. About 1,500 species have been described, but many more species are thought to exist. Their relationships among the eukaryotes have puzzled biologists for many decades, although the sequences of several microsporidian genes suggest a close relationship to fungi.

Microsporidia lack true mitochondria, although they have reduced structures, known as **mitosomes**, that are derived from mitochondria. Unlike mitochondria, however, mitosomes contain no DNA—the mitochondrial genome has been completely transferred to the nucleus. Because microsporidia lack mitochondria, biologists initially suspected that they represented an early lineage of eukaryotes that diverged before the endosymbiotic event from which mitochondria evolved. The presence of mitosomes, however, indicates that this hypothesis is incorrect. DNA sequence analysis, along with the fact that their cell walls contain chitin, has suggested that microsporidia may be highly reduced, parasitic fungi, although their exact relationship to fungi is still being investigated.

Microsporidia are obligate intracellular parasites of animals, especially of insects, crustaceans, and fishes. Some species are known to infect mammals, including humans. Most infections by microsporidia cause chronic disease in the host, with effects that include weight loss, reduced fertility, and a shortened life span. The host cell is penetrated by a polar tube that grows from the microsporidian spore. The function of the polar tube is to inject the contents of the spore, the sporoplasm, into the host (**Figure 28.12**). The sporoplasm then replicates within the host cell and produces new infective spores. The life cycle of some species is complex and involves multiple hosts, whereas other species infect a single host. In some insects, parasitic microsporidia are transmitted vertically (i.e., from parent to offspring). Only asexual reproduction is known for some microsporidia, but other species appear to have both asexual and sexual cycles.

Most chytrids are aquatic

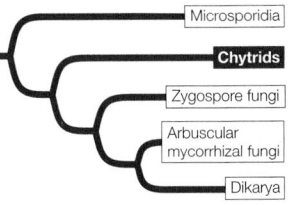

The **chytrids** (**Figure 28.13**) include several distinct lineages of mostly aquatic microorganisms once classified with the protists. However, morphological evidence (cell walls that consist primarily of chitin) and molecular evidence support their classification

Tubulinosema ratisbonensis

Figure 28.12 Invasion of the Microsporidia The spores of microsporidia grow polar tubes that transfer the contents of the spores into the host's cells. The species shown here infects many animals, including humans.

Chytriomyces hyalinus

25 μm

Figure 28.13 A Chytrid   Branched rhizoids emerge from the sporangium of a mature chytrid.

as early-diverging fungi. In this book we use the term "chytrid" to refer to both of the formally named clades listed as chytrids in Table 28.1, but some mycologists use this term to refer to only the Chytridiomycota. There are fewer than 1,000 described species among these two groups of chytrids.

Chytrids reproduce both sexually and asexually. Unlike other fungi, some chytrids that reproduce sexually possess flagellated gametes (similar to sperm in animals, except that both male and female gametes are flagellated in chytrids). The spores (called zoospores) are also flagellated (**Figure 28.14A**). Chytrids are the only fungi that include species with flagella at any life cycle stage. The retention of flagella reflects the aquatic environment in which fungi first evolved. As one type of gamete is larger than the other, the gametes can be distinguished as male (small gametes) and female (large gametes; see Figure 28.14A). Except for size, however, the two gametes are very similar.

The chytrids are diverse in form. Some are unicellular, others have rhizoids, and still others have coenocytic hyphae. They may be parasitic (on organisms such as algae, mosquito larvae, nematodes, and amphibians) or saprobic. Some have complex mutualistic relationships with foregut-fermenting animals such as cattle and deer. Many chytrids live in freshwater habitats or in moist soil, but some are marine.

Most fungal life cycles feature separate fusion of cytoplasms and nuclei

Most members of the remaining four groups of fungi are terrestrial. Although the terrestrial fungi grow in moist places, they do not have motile gametes, so liquid water is not required for fertilization. Instead, the cytoplasms of two individuals of different mating types fuse (a process called **plasmogamy**) before their nuclei fuse (a process called **karyogamy**; see Figure 28.11). Terrestrial zygospore fungi, arbuscular mycorrhizal fungi, sac fungi, and club fungi all include some sexual species.

Zygospore fungi reproduce sexually when adjacent hyphae of two different mating types release chemical signals that cause them to grow toward each other. These hyphae produce gametangia, which are specialized cells for reproduction that are retained as part of the hyphae. In the gametangia, nuclei replicate without cell division, resulting in multiple haploid nuclei in both gametangia. The two gametangia then fuse to form a unicellular zygosporangium that contains many haploid nuclei of each mating type (**Figure 28.14B**). These haploid nuclei quickly pair up to form multiple diploid nuclei within the zygosporangium. A thick, multilayered cell wall develops around the zygosporangium to form a well-protected resting stage that can remain dormant for months. In harsh environmental conditions, this resting stage may be the only cell that survives as the surrounding cells of the hyphae die. At this stage the single surviving cell is known as a **zygospore**, which is the basis of the name of the zygospore fungi. When environmental conditions improve, the nuclei within the zygospore undergo meiosis and one or more stalked **sporangiophores** sprout, each bearing a sporangium. Each sporangium contains the products of meiosis: haploid nuclei that are incorporated into spores. These spores disperse and germinate to form a new generation of haploid hyphae.

The zygospore fungi have traditionally included five major lineages of terrestrial fungi that live on soil as saprobes, as parasites of insects and spiders, or as mutualists of other fungi and invertebrate animals. However, recent genome analyses suggest that two of these lineages may be more closely related to the arbuscular mycorrhizal fungi. Zygospore fungi produce no cells with flagella, and only one diploid cell—the zygospore—appears in the entire life cycle. Their hyphae are coenocytic. Most species do not form a fleshy fruiting structure. Instead, the hyphae spread in a radial pattern from the spore, with occasional stalked sporangiophores reaching up into the air (**Figure 28.15**).

More than 1,000 species of zygospore fungi have been described. One species you may have seen is *Rhizopus stolonifer*, the black bread mold. *Rhizopus* produces many stalked sporangiophores, each bearing a single sporangium containing hundreds of minute spores (see Figure 28.14B).

Arbuscular mycorrhizal fungi form symbioses with plants

Arbuscular mycorrhizal fungi (Glomeromycotina) are terrestrial fungi that associate with plant roots in a symbiotic, mutualistic relationship (see Figure 28.9B). Only a few hundred species have been formally described, but 80% to 90% of all plants have associations with arbuscular mycorrhizal fungi, and most of the diversity of the group remains to be discovered.

The hyphae of arbuscular mycorrhizal fungi are coenocytic. These fungi use glucose from their plant partners as their primary energy source, converting it into other, fungus-specific sugars that cannot return to the plant. Until recently, arbuscular mycorrhizal fungi were known to reproduce only asexually, but recent studies demonstrate that they can undergo meiosis and genetic recombination.

(A) Sexual life cycle of the chytrids

Unlike other fungi, some chytrids produce flagellated male and female gametes from a multicellular haploid stage.

Haploid zoospores (*n*)

Sporangium

Multicellular haploid chytrid (*n*)

Allomyces sp.

Female gametangium

Male gametangium

© J. Robert Waaland/Biological Photo Service

30 μm

Meiosis

Haploid (*n*)
Diploid (2*n*)

Multicellular diploid chytrid (2*n*)

Female gamete (*n*)

Male gamete (*n*)

Zygote (2*n*)

Fertilization Karyogamy

(B) Sexual life cycle of the zygospore fungi

The single-celled zygospore is the only diploid cell in the life cycle of zygospore fungi.

© Dr. Jeremy Burgess/Science Source

Rhizopus stolonifer   25 μm

Each spore germinates to produce a new mycelium.

Spores

Sporangium

Sporangiophore

Hypha of − mating type

Hypha of + mating type

Gametangia (*n*)

Sporangiophore

Haploid (*n*)
Diploid (2*n*)
Dikaryotic (*n* + *n*)

Plasmogamy

Meiosis

After the surrounding cells of the hyphae die, this dormant unicellular stage, with multiple diploid nuclei, is called the zygospore.

Zygospore

Zygosporangium

Fertilization Karyogamy

Multiple diploid nuclei form within the zygosporangium.

A zygosporangium of *Rhizopus stolonifer*

© Dr. Merton Brown/Visuals Unlimited, Inc.

Figure 28.14 Sexual Life Cycles of Chytrids and Zygospore Fungi (A) Chytrids are the only fungi that possess flagella at any stage of the life cycle. (B) The unicellular zygospore, which contains multiple diploid nuclei, is a resting structure unique to the zygospore fungi.

Q: How is one chytrid gamete identified as male and the other as female?

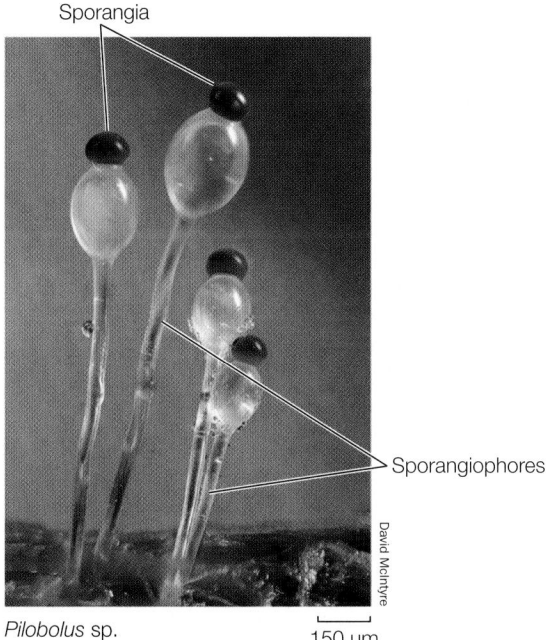

Sporangia

Sporangiophores

David McIntyre

Pilobolus sp.   150 µm

Figure 28.15 Zygospore Fungi Produce Sporangiophores
These transparent structures are sporangiophores produced by a
zygospore fungus growing on decomposing animal dung. The sporangiophores grow toward the light and end in tiny sporangia, which the
stalked sporangiophores can eject as far as 2 meters. Animals ingest
sporangia and then disseminate the spores in their feces.

▶ View in **Achieve**
Animation 28.1 Life Cycle of a Zygospore Fungus

The dikaryotic condition is a synapomorphy of sac fungi and club fungi

In the two remaining groups
of fungi—the sac fungi and the
club fungi—some stages have a
nuclear configuration other than the familiar haploid or diploid
states (**Figure 28.16**). In these fungi, karyogamy (fusion of nuclei)
occurs long after plasmogamy (fusion of cytoplasm), so that *two
genetically different haploid nuclei coexist and divide within each
cell of the multicellular fruiting body*. This stage of the life cycle
is called a **dikaryon** ("two nuclei"), and its ploidy is indicated as
$n + n$. The dikaryon is a synapomorphy of the sac fungi and club
fungi, which are placed together in a clade called **Dikarya**.

Eventually, specialized cells form on the fruiting body, within
which pairs of genetically dissimilar nuclei—one from each parent—fuse, giving rise to zygotes long after the original "mating."
The diploid zygote nucleus then undergoes meiosis, producing four
haploid nuclei. The mitotic descendants of those nuclei become
spores, which germinate to give rise to the next haploid generation.

A life cycle with a dikaryotic stage has several unusual features.
First, there are no gamete *cells*, only gamete *nuclei*. Second, the
only true diploid structure is the zygote, although for a long period
the genes of both parents are present in the dikaryon and can
be expressed. In effect, the dikaryon is neither diploid ($2n$) nor
haploid (n). Rather, it is dikaryotic ($n + n$). Therefore a harmful

recessive mutation in one nucleus may be compensated for by a
normal allele on the same chromosome in the other nucleus, and
dikaryotic hyphae often have characteristics that are different
from their n or $2n$ products. The dikaryotic condition is perhaps
the most distinctive of the genetic peculiarities of the fungi.

The sexual reproductive structure of sac fungi is the ascus

The **sac fungi** (Ascomycota) are a large and diverse group of fungi
found in marine, freshwater, and terrestrial habitats. There are
approximately 64,000 known species, nearly half of which are the
fungal partners in lichens. The hyphae of sac fungi are segmented
by more or less regularly spaced septa. A pore in each septum permits extensive movement of cytoplasm and organelles (including
nuclei) from one segment to the next.

Sac fungi are distinguished by the production of sacs called
asci (singular *ascus*), which at maturity contain sexually produced
haploid **ascospores** (see Figure 28.16A). The ascus is the characteristic sexual reproductive structure of the sac fungi. In the past,
the sac fungi were classified on the basis of whether or not the asci
are contained within a specialized fruiting structure known as an
ascoma (plural *ascomata*) and on differences in the morphology
of that fruiting structure. DNA sequence analyses have resulted
in a revision of these traditional groupings, however.

SAC FUNGUS YEASTS   Some species of sac fungi are unicellular
yeasts. The 1,000 or so species in this group are among the most
important domesticated fungi. Perhaps the best known is baker's,
or brewer's, yeast (*Saccharomyces cerevisiae*; see Figure 28.2 and
Key Concept 28.4), which catabolizes glucose obtained from its
environment into ethanol and carbon dioxide by fermentation.
Other sac fungus yeasts live on fruits such as figs and grapes and
play an important role in the making of wine. Many others are
associated with insects. In the guts of some insects, they provide
enzymes that break down materials that are otherwise difficult
for the insects to digest, especially cellulose.

Sac fungus yeasts reproduce asexually by budding. Sexual reproduction takes place when two adjacent haploid cells of dissimilar mating types fuse. In some species, the resulting zygote buds
to form a diploid cell population. In others, the zygote nucleus
undergoes meiosis immediately. When this happens, the entire
cell becomes an ascus. Depending on whether the products of
meiosis then undergo mitosis, a yeast ascus contains either eight
or four ascospores, which germinate to become haploid cells. The
sac fungus yeasts have lost the dikaryotic stage.

FILAMENTOUS SAC FUNGI   Most sac fungi are filamentous
species, such as the cup fungi (**Figure 28.17A**), in which the ascomata are cup-shaped and can be as large as several centimeters
across (although most are much smaller). The inner surfaces of
the ascomata, which are covered with a mixture of specialized
hyphae and asci, produce huge numbers of spores. The edible
ascomata of some species, including morels (**Figure 28.17B**) and
truffles, are regarded by humans as gourmet delicacies (and can
sell at prices higher than gold). The underground ascomata of
truffles have a strong odor that attracts mammals such as pigs,

(A) Sexual life cycle of the sac fungi

In sac fungi, the products of meiosis are borne in a microscopic sac called an ascus. The fleshy fruiting bodies consist of both dikaryotic and haploid hyphae.

Hyphae of – mating type

Mating structure

Germinating ascospores (n)

Ascospores (n)

Hyphae of + mating type

Ascospores

Ascus

© Dr. Cecil H. Fox/Science Source

Ascus   40 μm

Mitosis

Haploid (n)
Diploid (2n)
Dikaryotic (n + n)

Plasmogamy

Dikaryotic mycelium (n + n)

Haploid hyphae (n)

Meiosis

Fused nuclei (zygote)

Dikaryotic asci (n + n)

Fertilization Karyogamy

Ascoma (fruiting structure)

(B) Sexual life cycle of the club fungi

In club fungi, the products of meiosis are borne on the surface of the gills on specialized hyphal tips called basidia. Fruiting bodies consist solely of dikaryotic hyphae, and the dikaryotic phase can last a long time.

Mating type 1

Mating type 2

Mycelial hyphae

Plasmogamy

Populations of club fungi may produce dozens to hundreds of different mating types.

Dikaryotic mycelium (n + n)

Basidiospores

Basidium

Haploid (n)
Diploid (2n)
Dikaryotic (n + n)

Gills

Gills lined with basidia

Basidioma (fruiting structure)

© Biophoto Associates/Science Source

Basidium   50 μm

Meiosis

Fused nuclei (zygote)

Nuclei

Developing basidium (n + n)

Fertilization Karyogamy

Figure 28.16 Sexual Life Cycles among the Dikarya **(A)** In sac fungi, the products of meiosis are borne in a microscopic sac called an ascus. The fleshy fruiting structure, the ascoma, consists of both dikaryotic and haploid hyphae. **(B)** The basidium is the characteristic sexual reproductive structure of the club fungi. The fruiting structures, called basidiomata, consist solely of dikaryotic hyphae, and the dikaryotic phase can last a long time.

Q: How does the dikaryotic condition differ from diploidy?

View in Achieve
Activity 28.2 Life Cycle of a Dikaryotic Fungus

Figure 28.17 Sac Fungi **(A)** These brilliant red cups are the ascomata of a cup fungus. **(B)** Morels, which have a spongelike ascoma and a subtle flavor, are considered a culinary delicacy by humans.

(A) *Cookeina tricholoma*

(B) *Morchella esculenta*

which then eat the fungi and disperse the spores. Humans sometimes take advantage of pigs' attraction to truffles and use pigs to locate truffles for human consumption.

The sexual reproductive cycle of filamentous sac fungi includes the formation of a dikaryon, although this stage is relatively brief compared with that in club fungi. Many filamentous sac fungi form multinucleate mating structures (see Figure 28.16A). Mating structures of two different mating types fuse and produce a dikaryotic mycelium, containing nuclei from both mating types. The dikaryotic mycelium often forms a cup-shaped ascoma, which bears the asci. Only after the formation of asci do the nuclei from the two mating types finally fuse. Both nuclear fusion and the subsequent meiosis that produces haploid ascospores take place within individual asci. The ascospores are ultimately released (sometimes shot off forcefully) by the ascus to begin the new haploid generation.

The sac fungi also include many of the filamentous fungi known as molds. **Molds** consist of filamentous hyphae that do not form large ascomata, although they can still produce asci and ascospores. Many molds are parasites of flowering plants. Chestnut blight and Dutch elm disease are both caused by molds. The chestnut blight fungus, which was introduced to the United States in the 1890s, had destroyed the American chestnut as a commercial species by 1940. Before the blight, this species accounted for more than half the trees in the eastern North American forests. Another familiar story is that of the American elm. Sometime before 1930, the Dutch elm disease fungus (first discovered in the Netherlands but native to Asia) was introduced into the United States on infected elm logs from Europe. Spreading rapidly—especially via bark beetles—the fungus destroyed great numbers of American elm trees.

Other plant pathogens among the sac fungi include the powdery mildews that infect cereal crops, lilacs, and roses, among many other plants. Mildews can be a serious problem for farmers and gardeners, and a great deal of research has focused on ways to control these agricultural pests.

The filamentous sac fungi can also reproduce asexually by means of conidia that form at the tips of specialized hyphae (**Figure 28.18**). Small chains of conidia are produced by the millions and can survive for weeks in nature. The conidia are often what give molds their characteristic colors.

The basidium is the sexual reproductive structure of club fungi

Club fungi (Basidiomycota) produce some of the most spectacular fruiting structures found among the fungi. These fruiting structures, called **basidiomata** (singular *basidioma*), include mushrooms of all kinds, puffballs (see Figure 28.4), and the bracket fungi often encountered on trees and fallen logs in a damp forest. About 30,000 species of club fungi have been described. They include about 4,000 species of mushrooms, including both poisonous (**Figure 28.19A**) and edible species. Bracket fungi (**Figure 28.19B**) play an important role in the carbon cycle by breaking down wood. They also do great damage to both cut lumber and timber stands. Some of the most economically damaging plant pathogens are club fungi, including the rust fungi and smut fungi that parasitize cereal grains. In contrast, other club fungi contribute to the survival of plants as fungal partners in ectomycorrhizae.

The hyphae of club fungi characteristically have septa with small, distinctive pores. As they grow, haploid hyphae of different mating types meet and fuse, forming dikaryotic hyphae, each cell

Penicillium notatum

5 μm

Figure 28.18 Conidia Chains of conidia (yellow) are developing at the tips of specialized hyphae arising from a *Penicillium notatum* mold. This species is used to produce the antibiotic penicillin.

Figure 28.19 Club Fungus Basidiomata
(A) The fly agaric is a poisonous mushroom that contains hallucinogenic compounds.
(B) A bracket fungus growing parasitically on a tree. Although this particular species is occasionally eaten when young, many similar-appearing bracket fungi are poisonous.

(A) *Amanita muscaria*   **(B) *Laetiporus sulphureus***

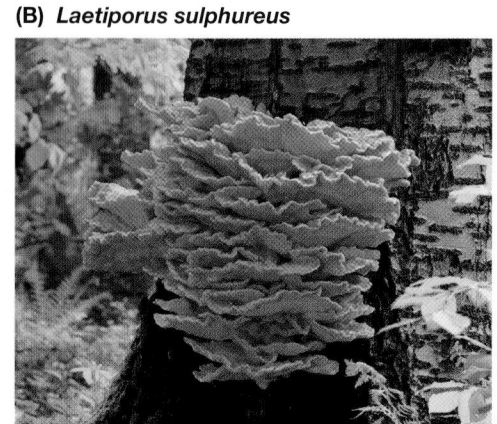

of which contains two nuclei, one from each parent hypha. The dikaryotic mycelium grows and eventually, when triggered by rain or another environmental cue, produces a basidioma. The dikaryotic stage may persist for years, or even centuries. This pattern contrasts with the life cycle of the sac fungi, in which the dikaryon is found only in the stages leading up to formation of the asci.

The **basidium** (plural *basidia*), a swollen cell at the tip of a specialized hypha, is the characteristic sexual reproductive structure of the club fungi (see Figure 28.16B). In mushroom-forming club fungi, the basidia typically form on specialized structures of the basidiomata known as gills. The basidium is the site of nuclear fusion and meiosis and thus plays the same role in the club fungi as the ascus does in the sac fungi and the zygosporangium does in the zygospore fungi.

After nuclei fuse in the basidium, the resulting diploid nucleus undergoes meiosis, and the four resulting haploid nuclei are incorporated into haploid **basidiospores**, which form on tiny stalks on the outside of the basidium. A single basidioma of the common bracket fungus *Ganoderma applanatum* can produce as many as 4.5 *trillion* basidiospores in one growing season. Basidiospores typically are forcibly discharged from their basidia and then germinate, and give rise to hyphae with haploid nuclei.

KEY CONCEPT
28.3 Recap and Assess

Sexual reproduction is common in some groups of fungi but has never been observed in others. Many fungal species have two or more genetically distinct but visually indistinguishable mating types. To mate, individuals of most sac fungi and club fungi fuse to produce dikaryotic fruiting bodies, in which two genetically different haploid nuclei coexist in each cell of the multicellular structure.

1. Explain the concept of mating types. How are they different from male and female sexes?
2. Describe how microsporidia infect the cells of their animal hosts.
3. What feature of the chytrids suggests that the fungi had an aquatic ancestor?
4. What is the role of the zygospore in the life cycle of zygospore fungi?
5. What distinguishes the fruiting bodies of sac fungi from those of club fungi?

Fungi are of special interest to biologists because of the roles they play in interactions with other organisms, including humans. But they are also useful as tools for studying many kinds of biological problems and for finding solutions to those problems.

KEY CONCEPT
28.4 Fungi Have Many Practical Uses

Learning Objectives

28.4.1 Describe four ways that fungi are used to produce food and drink for humans.

28.4.2 Provide an example of how fungi can be used for medical purposes.

28.4.3 Explain two ways that fungi can be used as bioindicators of environmental health.

We've briefly noted the important part that fungi play in the production of human foods and beverages. We have also described the diverse roles that fungi play in natural ecosystems, from decomposers to pathogens to mutalistic partners. These diverse ecological roles have led to the use of fungi in studies of environmental change and in remediation of environmental pollution. Many fungi are also important model organisms for laboratory investigations of basic biological process. Others, as you saw at the opening of this chapter, have given us treatments for human diseases.

Fungi are important in producing food and drink

Grains from grasses provide most of the world's food supply for humans. But in most cases, we do not eat these grains directly as they are produced by the plants. Instead, we use them as a source of starch. To make the starch more pleasing and digestible for human consumption, we usually convert it to more complex and tasty forms of food and drink, often with the help of fungi.

Baker's (or brewer's) yeast (*Saccharomyces cerevisiae*) converts the starch from grain into ethanol. This process also forms carbon dioxide bubbles in bread dough, causing it to rise, which gives baked bread its light texture. The ethanol and carbon dioxide are baked away in bread making (which produces the pleasant aroma of baking bread). In contrast, the ethanol and carbon dioxide are retained when yeast is used to ferment grain into beer. The carbon dioxide gives beer its fizz, and the alcohol and yeast contribute to the taste and appeal of beer to those who enjoy it. Sugars, especially from fruit such as grapes, are also converted into alcohol and carbon dioxide by yeasts in the production of wine (although the carbon dioxide is not retained in most finished wine, as it is in beer). Many different strains of *S. cerevisiae* are used in wine production, which contributes to the distinctive nature of wine from different regions and wineries. Many other species of local, native yeasts are also used in producing distinctive local wines and beers. For example, fission yeast (*Schizosaccharomyces pombe*) was first isolated from African millet beer. Fission yeast takes its specific name (*pombe*) from the Swahili word for beer.

▶ **Media Clip 28.3 Time Lapse of Beer Fermentation**
Life12e.com/mc28.3

Brown molds of the genus *Aspergillus* are important in some human diets. *Aspergillus tamarii* acts on soybeans in the production of soy sauce, and *A. oryzae* is used in brewing the Japanese alcoholic beverage sake from rice. *Aspergillus niger* is the source of most commercial citric acid production. Citric acid gives food and soft drinks a tart taste and is also used as a food preservative. But some species of *Aspergillus* that grow on grains and on nuts such as peanuts and pecans produce extremely carcinogenic (cancer-inducing) compounds called aflatoxins. Aflatoxins can occur in high concentrations in foods such as peanut butter. In the United States and most other industrialized countries, moldy grain infected with *Aspergillus* is typically thrown out. In Africa, where food is scarcer, the grain is often eaten, moldy or not, and causes severe health problems, including high levels of certain cancers.

Penicillium is a genus of green molds, of which some species produce the antibiotic penicillin, as described in the beginning of this chapter. But several species of *Penicillium* are important for food production as well. For example, *P. camemberti* and *P. roqueforti* are the organisms responsible for the characteristic strong flavors of Camembert and Roquefort cheeses, respectively.

Many fungi serve directly as a human food source. Mushroom enthusiasts seek out the delicious fruiting structures of a wide variety of edible sac and club fungi. In the United States, relatively few species of mushrooms are grown commercially, and wild mushrooms are collected mostly for personal consumption. But in many parts of the world, a wide variety of wild mushrooms are collected for sale and consumption. Fungi used for food are not limited to fruiting bodies such as mushrooms, however. Various species of lichens are eaten in Arctic regions as well as in parts of North America and Asia. In southwestern China, for example, several species of lichens are used as a primary ingredient in cooking (**Figure 28.20**).

Fungi provide important weapons against diseases and pests

We started this chapter with the story of the discovery of penicillin. The discovery of antibiotics produced by fungi revolutionized medical treatment of bacterial diseases in humans and their domestic animals. Live strains of fungi are also used to combat various pest species of plants and animals.

Figure 28.20 Some Lichens Are Edible In southwestern China, several species of lichens that grow on tree bark serve as a primary ingredient in the local cuisine.

In Africa, the parasitic plant witchweed (*Striga*) causes crop losses of about U.S.$7 billion every year. A group of Canadian biologists discovered that a strain of the mold *Fusarium oxysporum* could be applied to crops to control witchweed without harming the crop plants (**Figure 28.21**). Other strains of *Fusarium* that preferentially attack coca plants, the source of cocaine, have been proposed to combat illicit drug production. Still other fungi are used to attack various animal pests, such as termites and aphids, and even malaria-carrying mosquitoes.

Figure 28.21 A Pathogenic Fungus Attacks a Parasitic Plant The fungus *Fusarium oxysporum* is a potent pathogen of witchweed (*Striga*), a parasitic plant that attacks crops. The fungal spores are shown in blue; fungal filaments are in tan. Both colors were added to enhance this scanning electron micrograph.

Lichen diversity and abundance are indicators of air quality

Lichens can live in many harsh environments where few other species can survive, as you saw in Key Concept 28.2. In spite of their hardiness, however, lichens are highly sensitive to air pollution because they are unable to excrete any toxic substances they absorb. This sensitivity means that lichens are good biological indicators of air pollution levels. It also explains why they are not commonly found in heavily industrialized regions or in large cities.

Monitoring the diversity and abundance of lichens growing on trees is a practical and inexpensive system for gauging air quality around cities. Maps of lichen diversity provide environmental biologists with a tool for tracking the distribution of air pollutants and their effects. Sensitive biological indicators of pollution, such as lichen growth, allow biologists to monitor air quality without the use of specialized equipment. Lichens are naturally distributed across the environment, and they can also provide a long-term measure of the effects of air pollution across many seasons and years.

Fungi record and help remediate environmental pollution

Each year, biologists deposit samples of many groups of organisms in the collections of natural history museums. These museum collections serve many purposes, one of which is to document changes in the biota of our planet over time.

Collections of fungi made over many decades or centuries provide a record of the environmental pollutants that were present when the fungi were growing. Biologists can analyze these historical samples to see how different sources of pollutants were affecting our environment before anyone thought to take direct measurements (**Investigating Life: Using Fungi to Study Environmental Contamination**). These long-term records are also useful for analyzing the effectiveness of cleanup efforts and regulatory programs for controlling environmental pollutants.

You have already seen that fungi are critical to the planetary carbon cycle because of their role in breaking down dead organic matter. Fungi are also used in remediation efforts to help clean up sites that have been polluted by oil spills or contaminated with toxic petroleum-derived hydrocarbons. Many herbicides, pesticides, and other synthetic hydrocarbons are broken down primarily through the action of fungi.

Reforestation may depend on mycorrhizal fungi

When a forest is cut down, it is not just the trees that are lost. A forest is an ecosystem that depends on the interaction of many species. As we have discussed, many plants depend on close relationships with mycorrhizal fungal partners. When trees are removed

---

Investigating LIFE   Using Fungi to Study Environmental Contamination

Experiment

Original Paper: A. R. Flegal et al. 2010. Declining—but persistent—atmospheric contamination in central California from the resuspension of historic leaded gasoline emissions as recorded in the lace lichen (*Ramalina menziesii* Taylor) from 1892 to 2006. *Environ Sci Technol* 44: 5613–5618.

A. Russell Flegal and his colleagues analyzed museum samples of lace lichens (*Ramalina menziesii*) collected between 1892 and 2006 near San Francisco, California. Their goals were to determine the sources of lead contamination and to evaluate the effectiveness of efforts to reduce this contamination.

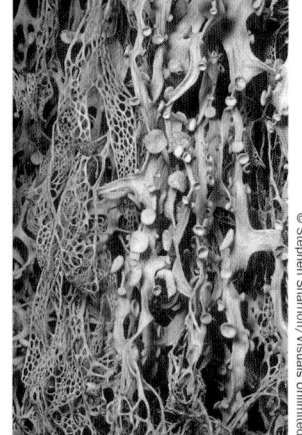

© Stephen Sharnoff/Visuals Unlimited, Inc.

QUESTION▶ Is environmental lead contamination through time consistent with known sources of pollution, and have efforts to reduce lead pollution been effective?

METHOD▶

1. Obtain museum samples of lace lichen (*Ramalina menziesii*) collected near San Francisco.

2. Measure concentrations of lead (Pb) as well as the ratios of two lead isotopes, ^{206}Pb and ^{207}Pb.

3. Compare the ratio of the two isotopes in the lichen samples with that of the possible sources:

    a. Lead smelter, in operation from 1885 to 1971: $^{206}Pb/^{207}Pb$ ratio of 1.15–1.17

    b. Leaded gasoline, in use from 1930s to early 1980s: $^{206}Pb/^{207}Pb$ ratio of 1.18–1.23

    c. Resuspension of historic lead contamination as atmospheric aerosols in recent decades: $^{206}Pb/^{207}Pb$ ratio of 1.16–1.19

RESULTS▶ Peak environmental lead contamination occurred in the 1960s to 1980s, with a rapid drop in the early 1980s after the closure of the smelter and the elimination of leaded gasoline. Average $^{206}Pb/^{207}Pb$ ratios of lead were below 1.17 before the 1930s, between 1.18 and 1.19 in the 1940s and 1950s, and >1.22 in the early 1980s. The ratios have declined since then.

CONCLUSION▶

1. The levels of environmental lead contamination, and ratios of lead isotopes, are consistent with the identified sources.

2. The closure of the lead smelter and elimination of leaded gasoline have significantly reduced environmental lead contamination.

from a site, the populations of mycorrhizal fungi there decline rapidly. If we wish to restore the forest on the site, we cannot simply replant it with trees and other plants and expect them to survive. The mycorrhizal fungal community must be reestablished as well. For large forest restoration projects, a planned succession of plant growth and soil improvement is often necessary before forest trees can be replanted. As the community of soil fungi gradually recovers, trees that have been inoculated with appropriate mycorrhizal fungi in tree nurseries can be planted to reintroduce greater diversity to the soil fungal community.

Fungi are used as model organisms in laboratory studies

Much of what we know about many basic aspects of cell and molecular biology comes from the study of model organisms. Among the eukaryotes, some fungi have numerous advantages over model plant and animal systems for laboratory investigations.

Of particular importance as model organisms are several species of sac fungi: *Aspergillus nidulans* (a brown mold), *Neurospora crassa* (a red bread mold), *Saccharomyces cerevisiae* (baker's, or brewer's, yeast), and *Schizosaccharomyces pombe* (fission yeast). These species can be cultured in large numbers in small spaces, and they have short generation times, so that genetic investigations can be conducted in days rather than years. Furthermore, their genomes are relatively small and encode relatively few genes compared with those of most plants and animals, so it is easier to elucidate the functions of the fungal genes responsible for basic biological functions.

KEY CONCEPT
28.4 Recap and Assess

Fungi are important to humans in many ways. Some species are consumed directly as food, while others are important in food production. Fungi serve as important indicators of ecosystem health and are critical in reforestation and in pollution remediation efforts. Several species are important model organisms for studies of eukaryotic cell and molecular biology. Fungi are widely used to combat diseases and pests.

1. What are some of the ways in which fungi or fungal products contribute to the human food supply?

2. What are some advantages of using surveys of lichen diversity and museum collections of lichens to measure long-term changes in air quality, compared with direct measurements of atmospheric pollutants?

3. Can you develop a strategy for tree harvest that would ease the difficulty and expense of reforestation projects by retaining viable communities of mycorrhizal fungi?

4. Consider the following data or lichens at five survey sites. Predict the relative order of the sites with respect to their distance from the center of a large city. Other factors (besides distance to city center, such as prevailing wind direction) might affect your prediction. Can you think of two other major factors that might influence these results?

Site number	Number of lichen species	Tree branches covered in lichens (%)
1	5	38
2	1	2
3	3	15
4	8	75
5	13	100

Work with the Data

The study by Flegal and his colleagues resulted in the following data:

Sample	Year collected	Lead concentration (μg of Pb/g lichen)	^{206}Pb/^{207}Pb ratio
1	1892	11.9	1.165
2	1894	4.0	1.155
3	1906	13.7	1.154
4	1907	22.9	1.157
5	1945	49.9	1.187
6	1957	34.2	1.185
7	1978	50.9	1.221
8	1982	10.0	1.215
9	1983	4.6	1.224
10	1987	1.0	1.198
11	1988	1.3	1.199
12	1995	1.9	1.202
13	2000	0.4	1.184
14	2006	1.8	1.184

Data from A. R. Flegal et al. 2010. *Environ Sci Technol* 44: 5613–5618.

QUESTIONS▶

1. Using the data in the table, plot lead concentration in the lichen samples against year of sample collection. Make a second plot, this one of ^{206}Pb/^{207}Pb ratio against year of sample collection. Calculate trend lines for your plots by plotting the average for each adjacent pair of observations, from 1892 to 2006. (In other words, plot the average for samples 1 and 2, then the average for samples 2 and 3, and so on, to produce a trend line for the data.)

2. Do your analyses support the conclusions of the study? How do you think you could improve the analysis?

Go to Achieve for a companion
Data in Depth exercise.

Q and A **Why are the regions of inhibited bacterial growth around the various antibiotics so different in size, and how is that relevant to human health care?**

The variable regions of inhibited growth that surround the various antibiotic samples reflect the differential effectiveness of antibiotics to a particular bacterium. Physicians who treat a bacterial infection need to know which antibiotic will be most effective for clearing that infection. An antibiotic that might work well to fight one infection might work poorly to fight another. Experiments like the one shown identify which antibiotics are best at inhibiting growth of a tested bacterium. Bigger zones of inhibited growth indicate more effective antibiotics.

Beginning in the 1940s, antibiotics derived from fungi ushered in a "golden age" of freedom from bacterial infections. Today, however, many of these antibiotics are losing their effectiveness as pathogenic bacteria evolve resistance to them (Figure 28.22).

Most medical antibiotics are chemically modified forms of substances that are found naturally in fungi and other organisms. Fungi naturally produce antibiotic compounds to defend themselves against bacterial growth and to reduce competition from bacteria for nutritional resources. These naturally occurring compounds are usually chemically modified to increase their stability, improve their effectiveness, and facilitate synthetic production. From the late 1950s to the late 1990s, no new major classes of antibiotics were discovered. In recent years, however, three new classes of antibiotics have been synthesized based on information learned from naturally occurring, fungally derived antibiotics, leading to improved treatment of some formerly resistant strains of bacteria.

Penicillium notatum

The top three bacterial strains fail to grow in the "zone of inhibition" surrounding the mold.

This bacterial strain is resistant to the antibiotic produced by *P. notatum*.

© Biophoto Associates/Science Source

Figure 28.22 Penicillin Resistance In a petri dish similar to those in Alexander Fleming's lab, four strains of a pathogenic bacterium have been cultured along with *Penicillium* mold. One strain is resistant to the mold's antibiotic substance, as is evidenced by its growth up to the mold.

Future directions

Biologists are developing applications to use fungi to combat nonbacterial diseases. One of the more unusual applications of fungi is in the war against malaria. Biologists have discovered that two species of fungi, *Beauveria bassiana* and *Metarhizium anisopliae*, can kill malaria-causing mosquitoes when applied to mosquito netting. Mosquitoes have not yet shown evidence of developing resistance to these biological pathogens.

 VISUAL SUMMARY 28

© Sotiris Zafeiris/Science Source

You should be able to relate each summary to the adjacent figures. If you go to this visual summary in **Achieve**, you can follow links to figures, animations, activities, and simulations that will help you consolidate the material.

KEY CONCEPT

28.1 Fungi Digest Food Outside Their Bodies

- Fungi are distinguished from other **opisthokonts** by **absorptive heterotrophy** and by the presence of **chitin** in their cell walls.

- Some fungi are **saprobes**, others are parasites or predators, and some are mutualists.

- **Yeasts** are unicellular, free-living fungi.

- The body of a multicellular fungus is a **mycelium**— a meshwork of filaments called **hyphae**. Hyphae may be **septate** (having septa) or **coenocytic** (multinucleate).

Figure 28.3

Anatomy of hyphae

The mycelium of a club fungus

Nuclei
Septa
Cell wall

Questions

1. What is a fundamental difference in the way that fungi obtain their nutrition, as compared with plants and animals?

2. How do some fungi blur the distinctions between unicellularity and multicellularity?

KEY CONCEPT

28.2 Fungi Are Decomposers, Parasites, Predators, or Mutualists

- Saprobic fungi, which act as decomposers, make crucial contributions to the recycling of elements, especially carbon.

- Many fungi are parasites, harvesting nutrients from host cells by means of **haustoria**.

- Some fungi associate with unicellular green algae, cyanobacteria, or both to form **lichens**, which live on exposed surfaces of rocks, trees, and soil.

- **Mycorrhizae** are mutualistic associations of fungi with plant roots. They improve a plant's ability to take up nutrients and water. **Endophytic fungi** live within plants and may provide their hosts with protection against herbivores and pathogens.

Figure 28.5

Parasitic mildew
Hyphae of fungal mycelium
© Biophoto Associates/Science Source
Leaf cells
Stoma of leaf
2 μm

The parasitic action of haustoria
Cell membrane
Stoma

Figure 28.8

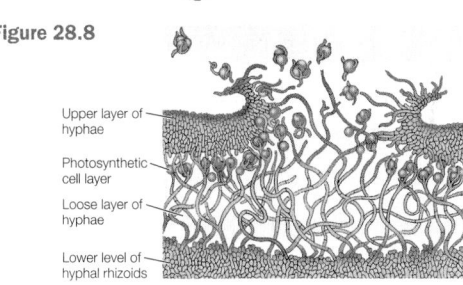

Upper layer of hyphae
Photosynthetic cell layer
Loose layer of hyphae
Lower level of hyphal rhizoids

Questions

1. How would life on Earth be fundamentally different without fungi?

2. What are two distinct kinds of mycorrhizal mutualisms that form with plants?

KEY CONCEPT

28.3 Sex in Fungi Involves Multiple Mating Types

Go to Activities 28.1 and 28.2 and Animation 28.1

- The **microsporidia** and **chytrids** diversified early in fungal evolution. The zygospore fungi, arbuscular mycorrhizal fungi, sac fungi, and club fungi form a monophyletic group, and the latter two groups form the clade **Dikarya**.

- Many species of fungi reproduce both sexually and asexually. In many fungi, sexual reproduction occurs between individuals of different **mating types**.

- In the sexual reproduction of terrestrial fungi, **plasmogamy** (fusion of cytoplasm) precedes **karyogamy** (fusion of nuclei).

- **Zygospore fungi** have a resting stage known as a **zygospore**, which contains many diploid nuclei.

- **Arbuscular mycorrhizal fungi** form symbiotic, mutualistic associations with plant roots; 80%–90% of all plants have associations with arbuscular mycorrhizal fungi.

- In **sac fungi** and **club fungi**, a mycelium containing two genetically different haploid nuclei, called a **dikaryon**, is formed. The dikaryotic ($n + n$) condition is unique to the fungi.

Figure 28.11

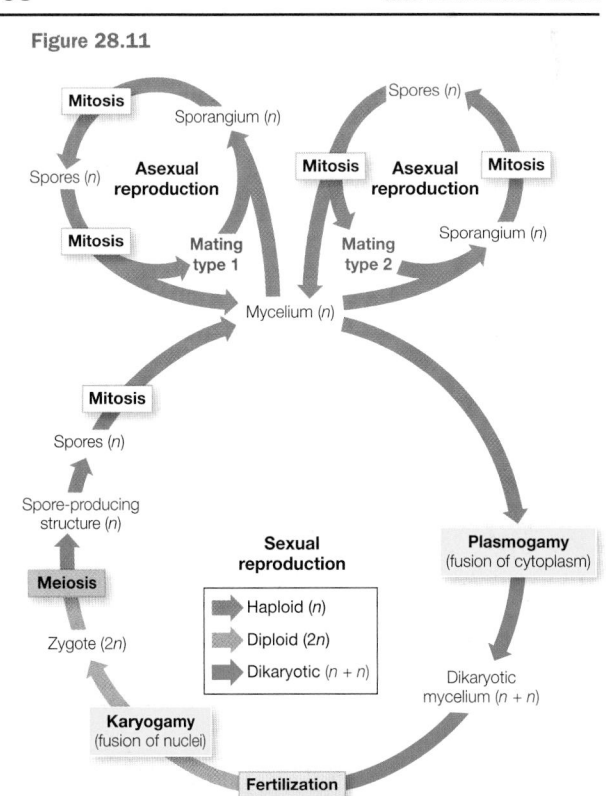

Mitosis
Sporangium (n)
Spores (n)
Asexual reproduction
Mitosis
Mating type 1
Spores (n)
Mitosis
Asexual reproduction
Mitosis
Sporangium (n)
Mating type 2
Mycelium (n)

Mitosis
Spores (n)
Spore-producing structure (n)
Meiosis
Zygote ($2n$)

Sexual reproduction

Haploid (n)
Diploid ($2n$)
Dikaryotic ($n + n$)

Plasmogamy (fusion of cytoplasm)
Dikaryotic mycelium ($n + n$)
Karyogamy (fusion of nuclei)
Fertilization

Questions

1. How is the dikaryotic condition different from the haploid and diploid states?

2. Why are mating types in most fungi not identified as male and female?

KEY CONCEPT

28.4 Fungi Have Many Practical Uses

- Some fungi are consumed as food by humans; other fungi are critical in baking, fermentation, and flavoring food.

- Fungi play important roles in cleaning up environmental pollutants such as synthetic petroleum-derived hydrocarbons. The diversity and abundance of lichen growth on trees are sensitive indicators of air quality.

- Reforestation projects require restoration of the mycorrhizal fungal community.

- Fungi provide important weapons against diseases and pests.

Questions

1. What critical function do fungi play in baking and brewing?

2. Why are lichens particularly useful as indicators of environmental pollution?

Figure 28.20

Courtesy of David Hillis

Figure 28.21

© Dr. Gary Gaugler/Visuals Unlimited, Inc.

Go to **Achieve** for the eBook, **LearningCurve**, animations, activities, simulations, and additional resources and assignments.

Animal Origins and the Evolution of Body Plans

29

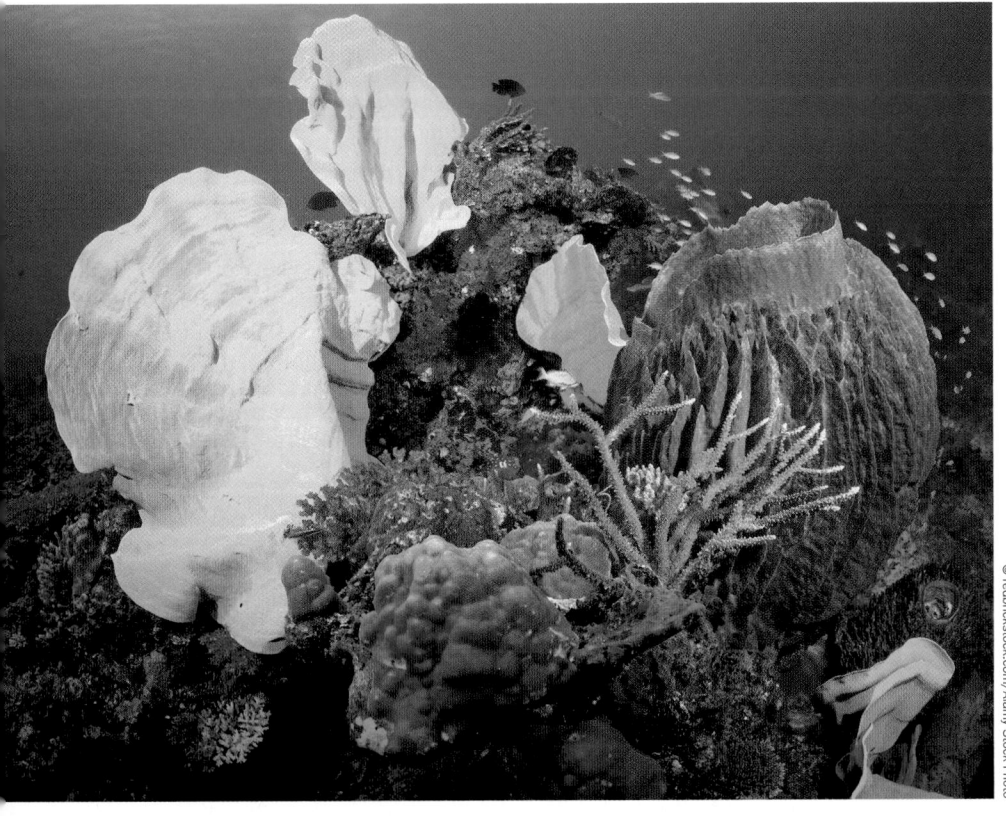

© redbrickstock.com/Alamy Stock Photo

Many of the major animal lineages, including sponges, cnidarians, and chordates, can be seen together in this coral reef.

KEY CONCEPTS

29.1 Diverse Body Plans Allow Animals to Move and Feed in Many Ways

29.2 Animal Life Cycles Involve Trade-Offs

29.3 The Root of the Animal Tree Provides Clues to Early Animal Diversification

▶Investigating LIFE

A Mysterious Animal Discovered in an Aquarium

In 1883 the zoologist Franz Schulze noticed something unusual in his Austrian laboratory: transparent, flattened organisms were crawling on the sides of his saltwater aquarium. These organisms, which Schulze had collected accidentally along with the sponges that were his primary interest, appeared to be animals, but they were unlike any animals previously described—especially since they continually changed shape as they moved.

Further examination revealed that the new organisms were indeed animals. Structurally, however, they were among the simplest animals that Schulze—or anyone else—had ever observed, being made up of only four types of cells. He named the new species *Trichoplax adhaerens*, which means "sticky hairy plate." For decades, however, most biologists dismissed Schulze's findings, insisting that the transparent organisms must be larval forms of other, well-known animals.

In the 1960s more detailed studies confirmed the distinctive nature of *Trichoplax*. Even then, this odd animal continued to be known almost exclusively from aquariums. Finally, in the early 2000s biologists located natural populations of *T. adhaerens* growing on hard surfaces in tropical and subtropical coastal regions. A few additional closely related species have been discovered (although most have not yet been formally named). Collectively, these species are known as placozoans (Greek, "flat animals").

The more biologists have studied *Trichoplax*, the odder this animal appears. It has the smallest genome of any animal studied to date. The mature stages lack body symmetry and have no mouth, gut, or nervous system. Is *Trichoplax* a relict representative of a group of animals that appeared early in animal evolution?

Which groups of organisms are at the root of the animal tree has been a subject of considerable investigation and debate. Several possible hypotheses of relationships have been explored with genomic analyses. The structural simplicity of *Trichoplax* is now considered by most biologists to be an evolutionary reversal from a more complex body form. Most genomic studies point to other groups of animals as forming the earliest split with the remaining species.

This chapter explores the earliest branches on the animal tree and shows how a few fundamental "body plans" have been modified to yield the remarkable variety of animal forms described in this and the following two chapters.

 Which animal groups are involved in the earliest split in the animal tree?
(Find the answer on page 665.)

KEY CONCEPT 29.1 Diverse Body Plans Allow Animals to Move and Feed in Many Ways

Learning Objectives

29.1.1 Explain how differences in body symmetry, body cavities, segmentation, appendages, and nervous systems are functionally related to movement and feeding in animals.

29.1.2 Describe two important functions of nervous systems that allow many animals to have better control over mobility in the water, land, and air.

How do we recognize an organism as an animal? The answer may seem obvious for many familiar animals, but less so for groups such as sponges, which were once thought to be plants.

Some of the general characteristics we associate with animals include:

- *Multicellularity.* In contrast to the bacteria, archaea, and most protists (see Chapters 24 and 25), all animals are multicellular. Animal life cycles feature complex patterns of development from a single-celled zygote into a multicellular adult.

- *Heterotrophic metabolism.* In contrast to most plants, all animals are heterotrophs. Animals are able to synthesize very few organic molecules from inorganic chemicals, so they must obtain the necessary organic molecules from their environment.

- *Internal digestion.* Although the fungi are also heterotrophs (see Chapter 28), animals and fungi digest their food differently. Whereas fungi digest food outside their bodies, most animals use internal processes to break down materials from their environment into the organic molecules they need. Most animals

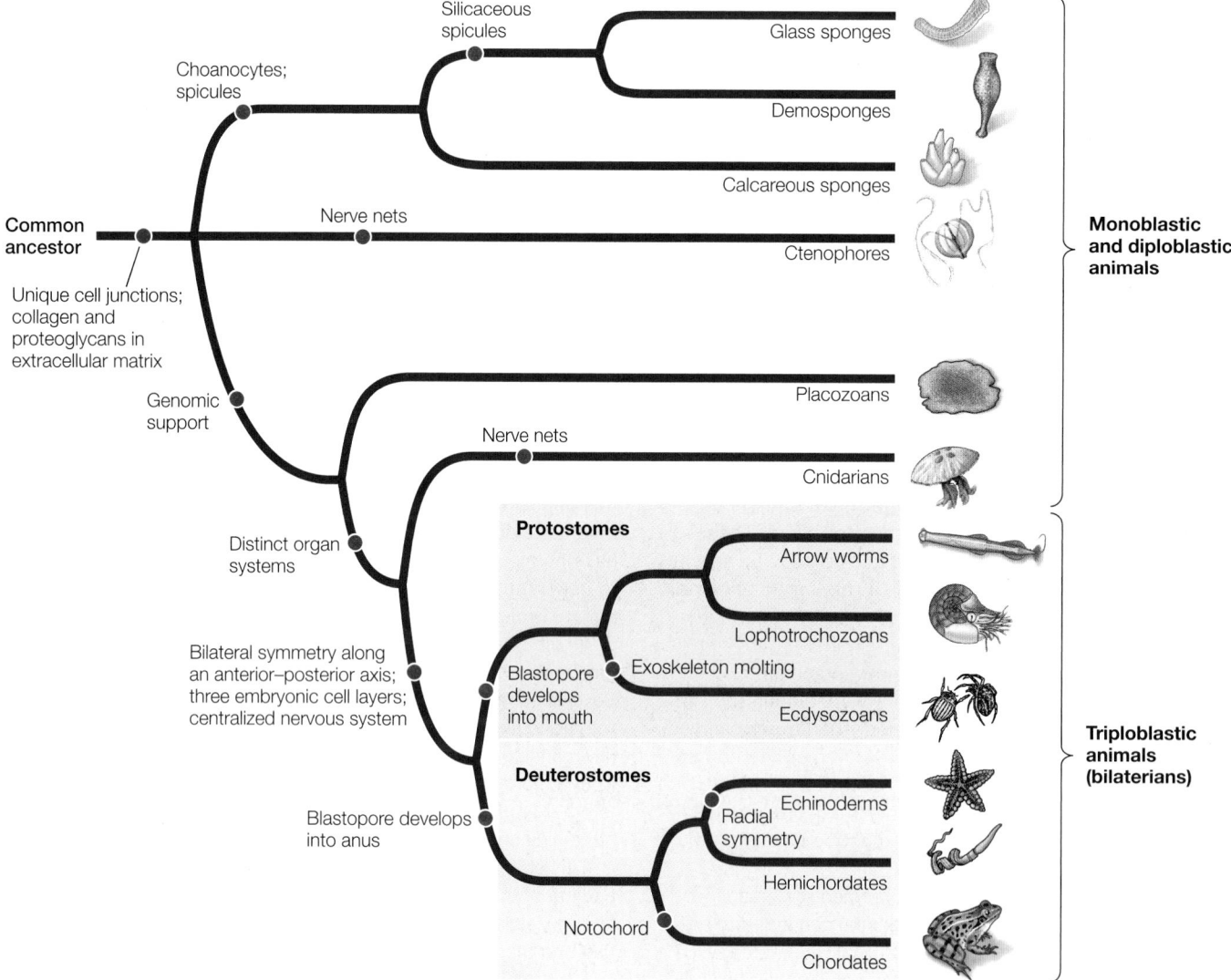

Figure 29.1 A Phylogenetic Tree of the Animals This tree presents the best-supported current hypotheses of the evolutionary relationships among major groups of animals. The traits highlighted by red circles are explained in this and the following two chapters.

Q: Based on this tree, which of the depicted traits evolved multiple times among animals, and in which lineages?

ingest food into an internal **gut** that is continuous with the outside environment and in which digestion takes place.

• *Movement and nervous systems.* In contrast to the majority of plants and fungi, most animals can move their bodies. This movement is often coordinated through a well-developed nervous system, which also typically functions as a sensory system. Animals must move to find food or bring food to them. Muscle tissue and nervous systems are unique to animals, and many animal body plans are specialized for movement and detection of prey.

Although these general features help us recognize animals, none is diagnostic for all animals. Some animals do not move, at least during certain life stages, and some plants and fungi do have limited movement. Some animals lack a nervous system, and the diffuse nerve nets (which lack a coordinating brain) of ctenophores and cnidarians are distinct and independently evolved from the **central nervous systems** (which have a coordinating brain) of bilaterians. Some animals lack a gut, and many multicellular organisms are not animals. So on what basis do we group all animals together in a single clade?

Animal monophyly is supported by gene sequences and cellular morphology

The most convincing evidence that all the organisms considered to be animals share a common ancestor comes from phylogenetic analyses of their gene sequences. Many complete animal genomes are now available, and more are being sequenced each year. Analyses of these genomes and of many individual gene sequences have shown that the animals are indeed monophyletic. The best-supported phylogenetic tree for the major animal groups is shown in **Figure 29.1**.

Surprisingly few morphological features are shared across all animal species. The morphological synapomorphies (shared, derived traits) that are present are evident primarily at the cellular level. They include a common set of extracellular matrix molecules, including collagen and proteoglycans, and several unique features of the junctions between animal cells. Although some animals in a few groups lack one of these cellular characteristics, it is believed that these traits were possessed by the ancestor of all animals and were subsequently lost in those groups.

Similarities in the organization and function of Hox and other developmental genes provide additional evidence of developmental mechanisms shared by a common animal ancestor. The Hox genes specify body pattern and axis formation, leading to developmental similarities across animals.

Connect the Concepts Hox genes and their role in animal development and evolution are discussed in Chapter 21.

The common ancestor of animals may have been a colonial flagellated protist similar to existing colonial choanoflagellates (**Figure 29.2A**), which have similarities to the multicellular sponges (**Figure 29.2B**). Why did these early animal ancestors

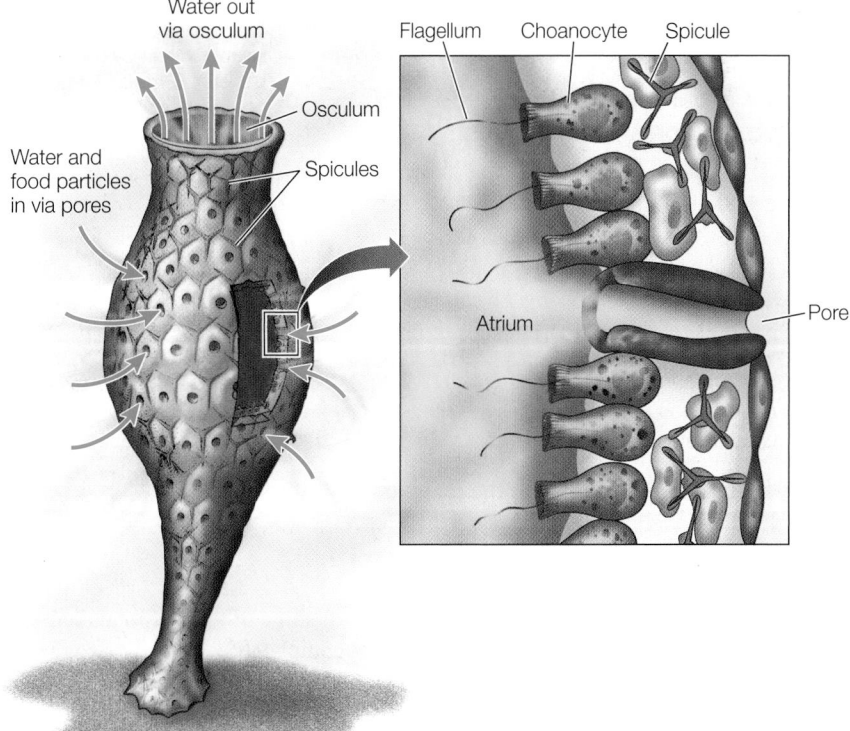

(A) Colony of choanoflagellate protists

Flagellum

Individual choanoflagellates form colonies that are attached to a single stalk.

Single cell

Stalk

(B) Structure and function of sponge choanocytes

Water out via osculum

Osculum

Water and food particles in via pores

Spicules

Flagellum   Choanocyte   Spicule

Atrium

Pore

Figure 29.2 Choanocytes in Sponges Resemble Choanoflagellate Protists (A) The similarity of choanoflagellate protist colonies to sponge choanocytes supports an evolutionary link between this protist lineage and the animals. **(B)** A sponge moves food-containing water through its body by beating the flagella of its choanocytes. Water enters the sponge through small pores and passes into water canals or an open atrium, where the choanocytes capture food particles from the water. The spicules are supportive, skeletal structures.

begin to form multicellular colonies? One hypothesis is that multicellular colonies are more efficient than are single cells at capturing their prey. Experiments with living species of choanoflagellates show that they spontaneously form multicellular colonies in response to signaling compounds that are found on certain species of planktonic bacteria they eat (Figure 29.3).

Once multicellular colonies were formed in early animal lineages, it is likely that certain cells in the colony began to be specialized—some for movement, others for nutrition, others for reproduction, and so on. Once this functional specialization had begun, cells could continue to differentiate. Coordination among groups of cells could have improved by means of specific regulatory and signaling molecules that guided differentiation and migration of cells in developing embryos. Such coordinated groups of cells eventually evolved into the larger and more complex organisms that we call animals.

Nearly 80% of the 1.8 million named species of living organisms are animals, and millions of additional animal species await discovery. Evidence about the evolutionary relationships among animal groups can be found in fossils, in patterns of embryonic development, in the morphology and physiology of living animals, in the structure of animal proteins, and in gene sequences. Increasingly, studies of higher-level relationships have come to depend on genomic sequence comparisons, as genomes are ultimately the source of all inherited trait information.

A few basic developmental patterns differentiate major animal groups

The early cell divisions of an embryo are known as **cleavage**. Several different patterns of cleavage exist among animals. Although these patterns can be useful for characterizing major animal groups, genomic analyses have shown that many changes have occurred in cleavage patterns throughout animal evolution.

> **Connect the Concepts** The various patterns of embryonic cleavage and animal development are described in more detail in Key Concept 42.1.

Cleavage patterns are influenced by the configuration of the yolk, the acellular nutritive material that nourishes the growing embryo. The eggs of many animal groups contain a small amount of yolk that is evenly distributed throughout the egg cytoplasm. In some of these groups, the zygote and its descendant cells divide completely and evenly in a pattern known as **radial cleavage**. Radial cleavage is thought to be the ancestral condition for the bilaterian animals, as it is widely distributed among the major lineages. **Spiral cleavage**—a complicated permutation of radial cleavage—is found among many lophotrochozoans (a group that includes earthworms and clams). Lophotrochozoans with spiral cleavage

are thus sometimes known as spiralians. The early branches of the ecdysozoans (molting animals, such as insects and nematodes) have radial cleavage, but most ecdysozoans have an idiosyncratic cleavage pattern that is neither radial nor spiral in organization.

Distinct layers of cells form during the early development of most animals. These cell layers differentiate into specific organs and organ systems as development continues. The embryos of **diploblastic** animals have two cell layers: an outer **ectoderm** and

---

Experiment

Figure 29.3   What Induces Choanoflagellates to Form Multicellular Colonies?

Original Paper: R. A. Alegado et al. 2012. A bacterial sulfonolipid triggers multicellular development in the closest living relatives of animals. *eLife* 1: e00013.

The choanoflagellate *Salpingoeca rosetta* forms multicellular, rose-shaped colonies (rosettes) at low frequencies in natural conditions. The rosette colonies are more efficient than are single cells at capturing some prey species of planktonic bacteria. Rosanna Alegado and her collaborators investigated the chemical signals that induce the choanoflagellates to form multicellular colonies when environmental conditions favor the rosette formations.

HYPOTHESIS▶   Multicellular colonies of *S. rosetta* are induced by chemical compounds found on specific species of planktonic bacteria.

METHOD▶

1. Isolate individual species of bacteria from an environmental sample of *S. rosetta* and its associated bacterial community.

2. Use a combination of antibiotics to produce a bacteria-reduced culture line of *S. rosetta* that does not spontaneously form rosette colonies (the RCA line, for "rosette colonies absent").

3. Feed the RCA line with each of the isolated species of bacteria from step 1. Record any rosette colony formation.

4. Isolate compounds that induce multicellular colony formation from rosette-producing bacteria identified in step 3.

RESULTS▶   Alegado and colleagues tested various compounds from planktonic bacteria in the genus *Algoriphagus* and found that RIF-1, a sulfonolipid produced by the bacteria, is the signal that induces formation of multicellular colonies in *S. rosetta*.

In an environmental sample with many diverse bacteria, *S. rosetta* forms occasional multicellular colonies.

After treatment with antibiotics, no multicellular colonies are produced.

The addition of high concentrations of planktonic bacteria in the genus *Algoriphagus* induces the *S. rosetta* to form multicellular colonies.

From R. A. Alegado et al. 2012, *eLife* 1:e00013/CC BY 4.0

CONCLUSION▶   A chemical signal (RIF-1) from a particular genus of prey bacteria can induce the formation of multicellular colonies in some species of choanoflagellates.

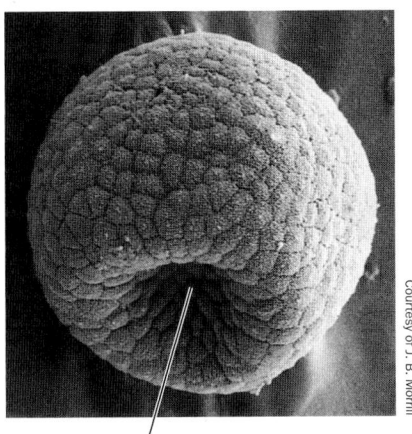

Blastopore

Figure 29.4 Gastrulation Illuminates Evolutionary Relationships The blastopore is clear in this scanning electron micrograph of a sea urchin gastrula. Because sea urchins (echinoderms) are deuterostomes, this blastopore will eventually become the anal end of the animal's gut.

an inner **endoderm**. Embryos of **triploblastic** animals have, in addition to ectoderm and endoderm, a third distinct cell layer, **mesoderm**, which lies between the ectoderm and the endoderm. The existence of three cell layers in embryos is a synapomorphy of the triploblastic animals (which form a clade), whereas the diploblastic animals (ctenophores, placozoans, and cnidarians, which are not a clade) exhibit the ancestral condition (see Figure 29.1). Some biologists also consider sponges to be diploblastic, but since they do not have clearly differentiated tissue types or embryonic cell layers, they are usually considered to be **monoblastic.**

During early development in many animals, in a process known as gastrulation, a hollow ball one cell thick indents to form a cup-shaped structure. The opening of the cavity formed by this indentation is called the blastopore (**Figure 29.4**). The overall pattern of gastrulation immediately after formation of the blastopore divides the triploblastic animals into two major groups:

1. In the **protostomes** (Greek, "mouth first"), the mouth arises from the blastopore, and the anus forms later.

2. In the **deuterostomes** ("mouth second"), the blastopore becomes the anus, and the mouth forms later.

Although the developmental patterns of animals are more varied than suggested by this simple dichotomy, sequencing data indicate that the protostomes and deuterostomes represent distinct animal clades. Together these two groups are known as the **bilaterians** (named for their usual bilateral symmetry), and they account for the vast majority of animal species.

The general structure of an animal, the arrangement of its organ systems, and the integrated functioning of its parts are referred to as its **body plan**. As we discussed in Chapter 21, the regulatory and signaling genes that govern many major aspects of development (including body symmetry, body cavities, segmentation, and appendages) are widely shared among the different animal groups. Although the myriad animal body plans cover a wide range of morphologies, they can be seen as variations on five key features:

1. The *symmetry* of the body
2. The structure of the *body cavity*
3. The *segmentation* of the body
4. The existence and location of *external appendages* that are used for sensing, feeding, locomotion, mating, and other functions
5. The development of the *nervous system*

Each of these features affects how an animal interacts with its environment.

Most animals are symmetrical

The overall shape of an animal can be described by its **symmetry.** An animal is said to be symmetrical if it can be divided along at least one plane into similar halves. Animals that have no plane of symmetry are said to be asymmetrical. Placozoans and many sponges are asymmetrical, but most other animals have some kind of symmetry, which is governed by the expression of regulatory genes during development.

In animals with **radial symmetry**, body parts are arranged around one main axis at the body's center (**Figure 29.5A**). Ctenophores (comb jellies) and many cnidarians (such as sea anemones and jellyfishes) are radially symmetrical, as are adult echinoderms. A perfectly radially symmetrical animal can be divided into similar halves by any plane that contains the main axis. However, most radially symmetrical animals—including the adults of echinoderms such as sea stars—are slightly modified, so that only some planes can divide them into identical halves. Some radially symmetrical animals are sessile (they remain fixed in one place) or drift with

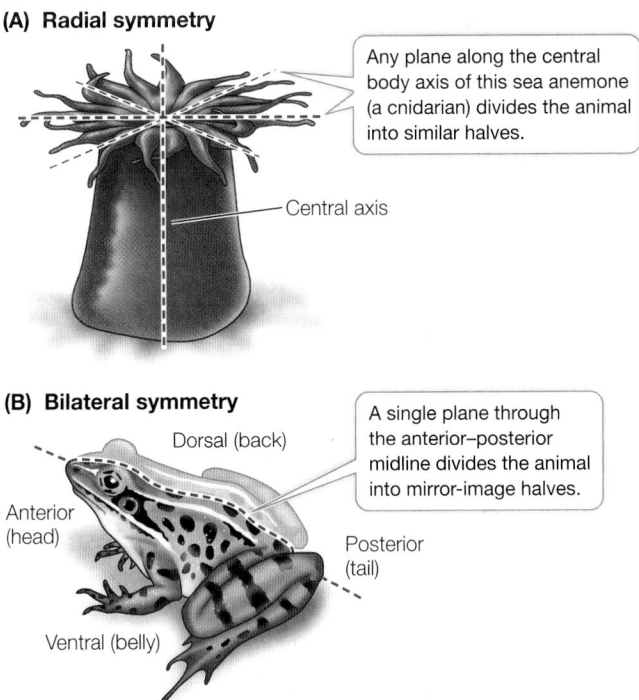

(A) Radial symmetry

Any plane along the central body axis of this sea anemone (a cnidarian) divides the animal into similar halves.

Central axis

(B) Bilateral symmetry

A single plane through the anterior–posterior midline divides the animal into mirror-image halves.

Dorsal (back)

Anterior (head)

Posterior (tail)

Ventral (belly)

Figure 29.5 Body Symmetry   Most animals are either **(A)** radially symmetrical or **(B)** bilaterally symmetrical.

water currents. Others move about slowly but can move equally well in any direction.

Bilateral symmetry is characteristic of animals that have a distinct front end, which typically precedes the rest of the body as the animal moves. A bilaterally symmetrical animal can be divided into mirror-image (left and right) halves by a single plane that passes through the midline of its body. This plane runs from the front, or **anterior**, end of the body, to the rear, or **posterior**, end (**Figure 29.5B**). A plane at right angles to the midline divides the body into two dissimilar sides. The back of a bilaterally symmetrical animal is its **dorsal** surface; the underside is its **ventral** surface.

Bilateral symmetry is strongly correlated with **cephalization** (Greek *kephalos*, "head"), which is the concentration of sensory organs and nervous tissues at the anterior end of the animal. Cephalization has been favored by natural selection because the anterior end of a bilaterally symmetrical animal typically encounters new environments first.

The structure of the body cavity influences movement

The body plans of triploblastic animals can be divided into three types based on the presence and structure of an internal, fluid-filled **body cavity**:

1. **Acoelomate** animals such as flatworms lack an enclosed, fluid-filled body cavity. Instead, the space between the gut (derived from endoderm) and the muscular body wall (derived from mesoderm) is filled with masses of cells called mesenchyme (**Figure 29.6A**). These animals typically move by beating cilia.

2. **Pseudocoelomate** animals have a body cavity called a pseudocoel, a fluid-filled space in which many of the internal organs are suspended. A pseudocoel is enclosed by muscles (mesoderm) only on its outside; there is no inner layer of mesoderm surrounding the internal organs (**Figure 29.6B**).

3. **Coelomate** animals have a body cavity, the coelom, that develops within the mesoderm. It is lined with a layer of muscular tissue called the peritoneum, which also surrounds the internal organs. The coelom is thus enclosed on both the inside and the outside by mesoderm (**Figure 29.6C**).

The structure of an animal's body cavity strongly influences the ways in which it can move. The body cavities of many animals function as **hydrostatic skeletons**. Fluids are relatively incompressible, so when the muscles surrounding a fluid-filled body cavity contract, fluids shift to another part of the cavity. If the body tissues around the cavity are flexible, fluids squeezed out of one region can cause another region to expand. The moving fluids can thus move specific body parts. (You can see how a hydrostatic skeleton works by watching a snail emerge from its shell.) A coelomate animal has better control over the movement of the fluids in its body cavity than a pseudocoelomate animal does. An animal that has longitudinal muscles (running along the length of

(A) Acoelomate (flatworm)

(B) Pseudocoelomate (roundworm)

(C) Coelomate (earthworm)

Figure 29.6 Animal Body Cavities   **(A)** Acoelomates do not have an enclosed body cavity. **(B)** Pseudocoelomates have a body cavity enclosed by mesoderm only on its outside. **(C)** Coelomates have a body cavity that is enclosed by mesoderm on both its inside and its outside.

 View in Achieve
Activity 29.1 Animal Body Cavities

the body) as well as circular muscles (encircling the body cavity) has even greater control over its movement.

In terrestrial environments, the hydrostatic function of fluid-filled body cavities applies mostly to relatively small, soft-bodied organisms. Most larger animals (as well as many smaller ones) have hard skeletons that provide protection and facilitate movement. Muscles are attached to those firm structures, which may be inside the animal or on its outer surface (in the form of a shell or cuticle).

Segmentation facilitates specialization

Segmentation—the division of the body into segments—is seen in many animal groups. Segmentation facilitates specialization of different body regions. It also allows an animal to alter the shape of its body in complex ways and to control its movements precisely. If an animal's body is segmented, muscles in each individual segment can change the shape of that segment independently of the others. In only a few segmented animals is the body cavity separated into discrete compartments, but even partly separated compartments allow better control of movement. Segmentation occurs in several groups of protostomes and deuterostomes.

In some animals, such as annelids (earthworms and their relatives), similar body segments are repeated many times (**Figure 29.7A**). In other animals, including most arthropods, segments differ strikingly from one another (**Figure 29.7B**). The dramatic evolutionary radiation of the arthropods (including the insects, spiders, centipedes, and crustaceans) was based on changes in a segmented body plan that features muscles attached to the inner surface of an external skeleton, including a variety of external appendages that move these animals. In some animals, distinct body segments are not apparent externally—for example, the segmented vertebrae of vertebrates, including humans. Nonetheless, muscular segmentation is clearly visible in humans with well-defined, muscular bodies (**Figure 29.7C**).

Appendages have many uses

Getting around under their own power allows animals to obtain food, to avoid predators, and to find mates. Even some sedentary species, such as sea anemones, have larval stages that use cilia to swim, thus increasing the animal's chances of finding a suitable habitat.

Appendages that project externally from the body greatly enhance an animal's ability to move around. Many echinoderms, including sea urchins and sea stars, have large numbers of tube feet that allow them to move slowly across the substrate. Animals whose appendages have become modified into limbs are capable of highly controlled, more rapid movement. The presence of jointed limbs has been a prominent factor in the evolutionary success of the arthropods and the vertebrates. In four independent instances—among the arthropod insects and among the vertebrate pterosaurs, birds, and bats—body plans emerged in which limbs were modified into wings, allowing these animals to use powered flight.

Appendages also include many structures that are not used for locomotion. Many animals have antennae, which are specialized appendages used for sensing the environment. Other appendages (such as claws and the mouthparts of many arthropods) are adaptations for capturing prey or chewing food. In some species, appendages are used for reproductive purposes, such as sperm transfer or egg incubation.

Nervous systems coordinate movement and allow sensory processing

The bilaterian animals have a well-coordinated central nervous system. More diffuse nervous systems, called nerve nets, are present in some other animals, such as ctenophores and cnidarians.

(A) *Hermodice carunculata*

All of the segments of this marine annelid are similar.

Setae

Tail segments are modified for hunting and defense.

Abdominal segments are modified for digestion and reproduction.

Anterior segments have fused and bear appendages for locomotion and feeding.

(B) *Hadrurus arizonensis*

(C) *Homo sapiens*

The muscles of the human abdomen are segmented.

Figure 29.7 Segmentation   **(A)** All of the segments of this marine fireworm, an annelid, are similar. Its appendages are tipped with bristles (setae) that are used for locomotion and (in this species) for protection—the setae contain a noxious toxin. **(B)** Segmentation allows the evolution of differentiation among the segments. The segments of this scorpion, an arthropod, differ in their form, their function, and the appendages they bear. **(C)** Muscular segmentation is clearly visible in the abdomen of this body builder.

Nervous systems appear to be completely absent in a few animal groups, such as sponges and placozoans.

The central nervous system of bilaterians coordinates the actions of muscles, which allows coordinated movement of appendages and body parts. This coordination of muscles permits highly effective and efficient movement on land, in water, or through the air. The central nervous system is also essential for processing the sensory information gathered from a wide variety of sensory systems. Many animals have sensory systems for detecting light, for forming images of their environment (sight), for mechanical touch, for detecting movement, for detecting sounds (hearing), for detecting electrical fields, and for chemical detection (e.g., taste and smell). These sensory systems allow animals to find food, and the ability of animals to move allows them to capture or collect food from their environment. These same abilities also allow most animals to move to avoid potential predators or to search for suitable mates. Most animals can also assess the suitability of different environments and move appropriately in response to that information.

 Media Clip 29.1
Nervous Systems Lead to Efficient Predators
Life12e.com/mc29.1

Animals use diverse forms of movement to feed

As we have already noted, animals are heterotrophs, or "other-feeders." Although some animals rely on photosynthetic endosymbionts to nourish them (see Investigating Life: Can Corals Reacquire Dinoflagellate Endosymbionts Lost to Bleaching? in Chapter 25), most animals must expend energy to obtain an outside source of nutrition, otherwise known as food.

The need to locate food has favored the evolution of sensory structures that provide animals with detailed information about their environment as well as nervous systems that can receive, process, and coordinate that information. Furthermore, in order to acquire food, animals must either move through the environment to where food is located, or move the environment and the food it contains to them. Animals that move from one place to another are **motile**; animals that stay in one place are **sessile**.

The principal feeding strategies that animals use fall into five broad categories:

1. **Filter feeders** (or **suspension feeders**) strain small organisms from their environment.

2. **Herbivores** eat plants or parts of plants.

3. **Predators** capture and eat other animals.

4. **Parasites** live in or on other, generally much larger, organisms, from which they obtain energy and nutrients.

5. **Detritivores** feed on dead organic material.

Each of these strategies can be found in many different animal groups, and none of them is limited to a single group. Individuals of some species employ more than one of these feeding strategies, and some animals employ different feeding strategies at different stages of their life cycle. The constant and ongoing need to obtain food, the variety of nutrient sources available in a given environment, and the necessity of competing with other animals to obtain food mean that a variety of feeding strategies can be found among all the major animal groups.

Filter feeders capture small prey

Air and water often contain small organisms and organic molecules that are potential food for animals. Moving air and water may carry those items to an animal that positions itself in a good location. Other animals can move through the environment, filtering out prey items as they move. In either case, filter feeders use some kind of straining device to filter the food from the environment.

(A) *Spirobranchus giganteus*

(B) *Eubalaena australis*

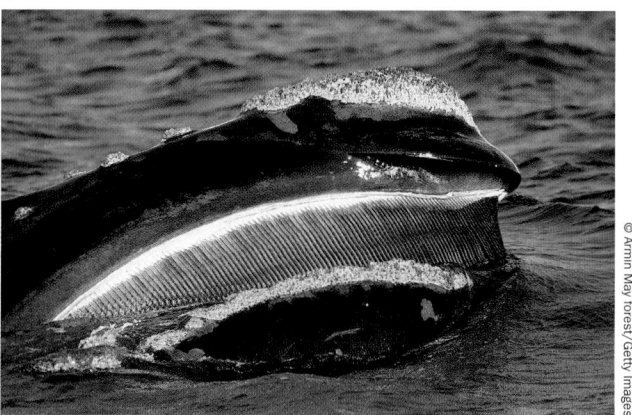

Figure 29.8 Filter-Feeding Strategies **(A)** Sessile marine filter feeders such as this Christmas tree worm, a polychaete (annelid), allow the ocean currents to bring their food—plankton—to them. **(B)** The southern right whale is a motile filter feeder that strains small crustaceans such as krill from the oceans for its food.

Many sessile aquatic animals rely on water currents to bring prey to them (**Figure 29.8A**). Some sessile filter feeders (such as sponges; see Figure 29.2B) expend energy to move water past their food-capturing devices. Motile filter feeders move their bodies to the nutrient source. Flamingos, for example, use their serrated beaks to filter small organisms out of the muddy mixture they pick up as they wade through shallow water. Baleen whales—the largest animals that have ever lived—are filter feeders that strain tiny crustaceans from the water column as they swim (**Figure 29.8B**).

 Media Clip 29.2 Filter Feeders
Life12e.com/mc29.2

Herbivores eat plants

An individual plant has many different structures—leaves, wood, roots, sap, flowers, fruits, nectar, and seeds—that animals can consume. Not surprisingly, then, many different kinds of herbivores—animals that feed only on plants—may feed on a single kind of plant, consuming different parts of the plant or feeding on the

(A)

(B)

Figure 29.9 Active and Sit-and-Wait Predators   **(A)** The appendages (legs and wings) of the Merlin (*Falco columbarius*), along with its strong beak, are adaptations to the life of an active predatory hunter.

(B) A crocodile typically sits motionless in the water, waiting in one spot for unsuspecting prey to walk within striking range.

same part in different ways. Whereas an individual animal that is captured by a predator is likely to die, herbivores often feed on plants without killing them.

Animals do not need to expend energy subduing and killing plants in order to feed on them. However, plant matter can be difficult to digest and can pose special challenges to terrestrial herbivores because the dominant land plants tend to have several different kinds of tissues, many of which are tough or fibrous. Herbivorous animals typically have long, complex guts to accomplish the tasks involved in digesting plants. Animals also must expend energy to detoxify plants' defensive chemicals.

Connect the Concepts   The structure and function of animal guts, including the differences in the guts of herbivores and carnivores, are explained in Key Concept 49.3.

Predators and omnivores capture and subdue prey

Predators possess features that enable them to capture and subdue other animals (referred to as their **prey**). Many vertebrate predators have sensitive sensory organs that enable them to locate prey, as well as sharp teeth or claws that allow them to capture and subdue prey (**Figure 29.9**). Predators may stalk and pursue their prey or wait (often camouflaged) for their prey to come to them.

Omnivores ("all-devouring") are animals, such as raccoons and humans, that eat both plants and other animals. The diets of some omnivores differ at different life stages; many songbirds, for example, eat fruit or seeds as adults but feed insects to their young.

Parasites live in or on other organisms

Parasites obtain nutrients from another organism—a **host**—by living on or within the host. Some animal parasites consume parts of the host itself (such as ticks that suck body fluids); others highjack nutrients the host would otherwise consume (such as tapeworms

that may live in the intestines of mammals). Most animal parasites are much smaller than their hosts, and many parasites can consume parts of their host without killing it. To set up residence within a host, a parasite must first overcome the host's defenses. Parasites often have complex life cycles that rely on multiple hosts, as you will see in Key Concept 29.2.

Parasites that live inside their hosts are called endoparasites, and these are often morphologically very simple. Endoparasites often function without a digestive system, absorbing their food directly from the host's gut or body tissues. Many flatworms are endoparasites of humans and other mammals, as we will describe in Chapter 30.

Parasites that live outside their hosts are called ectoparasites; they are generally more complex morphologically than endoparasites. Ectoparasites have digestive tracts and mouthparts that enable them to pierce the host's tissues or suck on the host's body fluids. Fleas and ticks are ectoparasitic arthropods that feed on many vertebrates, including humans.

Detritivores live on the remains of other organisms

Detritivores feed on the dead bodies or waste products of other organisms, organic matter known as **detritus**. Detritivores (sometimes called decomposers) perform an important ecosystem function by breaking down dead organic matter and returning the nutrients it contains to the environment in a form that can be used by other organisms. Detritivores are common in any soil with high organic content, as well as on the ocean floor. Well-known detritivores include earthworms and other annelids, millipedes, and many insects and crustaceans.

 Media Clip 29.3 Detritivores
Life12e.com/mc29.3

Variations in body symmetry, body cavity structure, life cycles, patterns of development, and survival strategies differentiate the many animal species. **Table 29.1** summarizes the living members of the major animal groups.

TABLE **29.1** | **Summary of Living Members of the Major Animal Groups**		
Group	**Approximate number of living species described**	**Major subgroups, other names, and notes**
Sponges	8,500	Demosponges, glass sponges, calcareous sponges
Ctenophores	250	Comb jellies
Placozoans	2	Additional species have been discovered but not yet formally named
Cnidarians	12,500	Anthozoans: Corals, sea anemones, sea pens Hydrozoans: Hydras, hydroids Scyphozoans: Jellyfishes
Orthonectids	45	Microscopic wormlike parasites of marine invertebrates; relationships uncertain
Rhombozoans	125	Tiny (0.5–7 mm) parasites of cephalopods; relationships uncertain
PROTOSTOMES		
Arrow worms	180	Glass worms
LOPHOTROCHOZOANS		
Bryozoans	5,500	Moss animals
Flatworms	30,000	Free-living flatworms; flukes and tapeworms (all parasitic); monogeneans (ectoparasites of fishes)
Gastrotrichs	800	"Hairy backs"
Rotifers and relatives	3,800	Rotifers, spiny-headed worms, jaw worms
Ribbon worms	1,200	Proboscis worms
Brachiopods	450	Lampshells
Phoronids	10	Sessile marine filter feeders
Annelids	19,000	Polychaetes (generally marine; may not be monophyletic) Clitellates: earthworms, freshwater worms, leeches
Mollusks	117,000	Chitons Bivalves: Clams, oysters, mussels Gastropods: Snails, slugs, limpets Cephalopods: Squid, octopuses, nautiloids
ECDYSOZOANS		
Nematodes	25,000	Roundworms
Horsehair worms	350	Gordian worms
Kinorhynchs	180	Mud dragons
Loriciferans	30	Brush heads
Priapulids	20	Penis worms
Onychophorans	180	Velvet worms
Tardigrades	1,200	Water bears
ARTHROPODS		
Chelicerates	114,000	Horseshoe crabs, sea spiders, arachnids (scorpions, harvestmen, spiders, mites, ticks)
Myriapods	12,000	Millipedes, centipedes
Crustaceans	67,000	Crabs, shrimps, lobsters and crayfishes, barnacles, copepods
Hexapods	1,056,000	Insects, springtails, two-pronged bristletails, proturans
DEUTEROSTOMES		
Xenoturbellids	5	Secondarily simple marine worms; relationships uncertain
Acoels	400	Very small (mostly <2 mm) flattened marine worms; relationships uncertain
Echinoderms	7,500	Crinoids (sea lilies, feather stars), brittle stars, sea stars, sea daisies, sea urchins, sea cucumbers
Hemichordates	120	Acorn worms, pterobranchs
CHORDATES		
Tunicates	2,800	Sea squirts (ascidians), thaliaceans, larvaceans
Lancelets	35	Cephalochordates
Vertebrates	71,000	Hagfishes, lampreys, cartilaginous fishes, ray-finned fishes, coelacanths, lungfishes, amphibians, reptiles (including birds), mammals

29.1 Recap and Assess

We generally recognize animals as multicellular heterotrophs with internal digestion, muscular systems that allow movement, and nervous systems. Animals are thought to be monophyletic because they share several derived traits, especially among their gene sequences. Major developmental differences also provide evidence of their evolutionary relationships. The body plans of animals are variations on patterns of symmetry, body cavity structure, segmentation, appendages, and nervous systems. Most animals either move through the environment to where food is located or move the environment and the food it contains to them.

1. What general features distinguish animals from other major groups of living organisms?
2. Differentiate among the members of each of the following sets of related terms:
   a. radial symmetry/bilateral symmetry
   b. protostome/deuterostome
   c. diploblastic/triploblastic
3. Why is bilateral symmetry strongly associated with cephalization, the concentration of sensory organs in an anterior head?
4. Explain several ways in which body cavities, segmentation, and centralized nervous systems improve control over movement.
5. How can you distinguish among filter feeders, predators, and parasites—all of which may feed on other animals?
6. What adaptations are necessary for animals that eat plants? What adaptations are needed for a predatory lifestyle?

As an animal grows from a single-celled zygote into a larger, more complex adult, its body structure, its diet, and the environment in which it lives may all change. In the next key concept we describe some animal life cycles and discuss why they are so varied.

29.2 Animal Life Cycles Involve Trade-Offs

Learning Objectives

29.2.1 Formulate a hypothesis that accounts for animal species that lose metamorphosis and evolve direct development.
29.2.2 Distinguish the similarities and differences between coloniality and multicellularity.
29.2.3 Explain the concept of "trade-offs" by comparing two distinct life cycles of animal species.

The life cycle of an animal encompasses its embryonic development, birth, growth to maturity, reproduction, and death. During its life an individual animal ingests food, grows, interacts with other individuals of the same and other species, and reproduces.

Many animal life cycles feature specialized life stages

In some groups of animals, newborns look much like miniature versions of the adults (a pattern called **direct development**). Newborns of most animal species, however, differ dramatically from

adults. Many animal species have a life stage called a **larva** (plural *larvae*), which is an immature form that the animal takes early in its life before assuming an adult form. Some of the most striking life cycle changes are found among insects such as beetles, flies, moths, butterflies, and bees, which undergo radical change (called **complete metamorphosis**) between their larval and adult stages (Figure 29.10). In these animals, one stage may be specialized for feeding and the other for reproduction. Adults of many moth species, for example, do not eat. In some animal species, individuals eat during all life cycle stages, but what they eat changes with the stage. For example, butterfly larvae (known as caterpillars) eat leaves and flowers, whereas most adult butterflies eat only nectar. Having different life cycle stages that are specialized for different activities may increase the efficiency with which an animal performs those activities and reduce the competition for food between juveniles and adults.

(A) Larva

(B) Pupa

(C) Adult

Figure 29.10 A Life Cycle with Complete Metamorphosis
(A) The larval stage (caterpillar) of the cecropia moth (*Hyalophora cecropia*) is specialized for feeding. (B) The pupa is the stage during which the transformation to the adult form occurs. (C) The adult moth is specialized for dispersal and reproduction and does not feed.

Most animal life cycles have at least one dispersal stage

At some time during their lives, most animals move, or are moved, so few animals die exactly where they were born. Movement of organisms away from a parent organism or from an existing population is called **dispersal**.

Animals that are sessile as adults typically disperse as eggs or larvae. Most sessile marine animals discharge their eggs and sperm into the water, where fertilization takes place. A larva soon hatches and floats freely in the plankton, where it filters small food items from the water. Many animals that live on the seafloor, including polychaete worms and mollusks, have a radially symmetrical larval form known as a **trochophore** (Figure 29.11A). Other animals, such as crustaceans, have a bilaterally symmetrical larval form called a **nauplius** (Figure 29.11B). Both types of larvae feed for some time in the plankton and may travel long distances before settling on the ocean floor and transforming into adults.

Other animal species that are motile as adults disperse when they are mature. A caterpillar, for example, may spend its entire larval stage feeding on a single plant, but after it metamorphoses into a flying adult—a butterfly or moth—it may fly to and lay eggs on other plants located far from the one where it spent its caterpillar days. In some species, individuals disperse during several different life cycle stages.

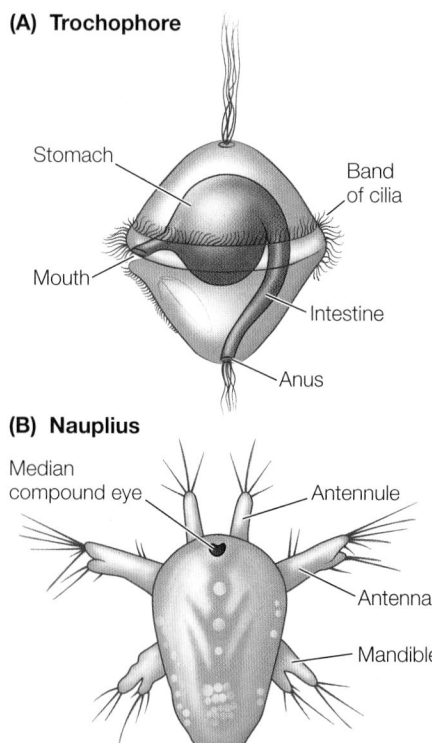

(A) Trochophore

Stomach
Band of cilia
Mouth
Intestine
Anus

(B) Nauplius

Median compound eye
Antennule
Antenna
Mandible

Figure 29.11 Planktonic Larval Forms of Marine Animals
(A) The trochophore ("wheel-bearer") is a distinctive larval form found in several marine animal clades with spiral cleavage, most notably the polychaete worms and the mollusks. (B) This nauplius larva will mature into a crustacean with a segmented body and jointed appendages.

Parasite life cycles facilitate dispersal and overcome host defenses

Animals that live as endoparasites are bathed in the nutritious tissues of their host or in the digested food that fills their host's digestive tract. Thus they may not need to exert much energy to obtain food, but to survive they must overcome the host's defenses. Furthermore, either they or their offspring must disperse to new hosts while their host is still living, because they die when their host dies.

The fertilized eggs of some parasites are voided with the host's feces and later ingested directly by other host individuals. Most parasite species, however, have complex life cycles involving one or more intermediate hosts and several larval stages (Figure 29.12). Some intermediate hosts transport individual parasites directly between other host species. Others house and support the parasite until another host ingests them. Complex life cycles may thus facilitate the transfer of individual parasites among hosts.

Some animals form colonies of genetically identical, physiologically integrated individuals

Most people tend to view the distinction between individuals and populations as clear-cut. In several groups of animals, however, asexual reproduction without fission leads to the formation of colonies composed of many physiologically integrated individuals. At first appearance, these colonies may look much like a single integrated organism. The individuals in the colony are clonal copies of one another, so they are genetically homogeneous.

Coloniality has arisen several times among animal groups, with widely varying levels of integration and specialization among the individuals. In some species, colonies are composed of loosely connected but integrated individuals that all function alike (Figure 29.13). In other colonial species, the individuals may become specialized for different functions, just as different cell types in multicellular organisms do. The Portuguese man-of-war (a cnidarian; see Figure 29.20) is an example of such a colonial animal, as it is composed of many individuals of four different specialized body forms, all integrated and functioning together. The individuals in the colony are themselves multicellular, however, unlike the cells of a single multicellular organism.

No life cycle can maximize all benefits

A common saying, "a jack-of-all-trades is master of none," suggests why there are constraints on the evolution of life cycles. The characteristics an animal has in any one life cycle stage may improve its performance in one activity but reduce its performance in another—a situation known as a trade-off. An animal that is good at filtering small food items from the water, for example, is unlikely to be good at capturing large prey. Similarly, energy devoted to building protective structures such as shells cannot be used for growth.

Some major trade-offs can be seen in animal reproduction. Some animals produce large numbers of small eggs, each with a small energy store (Figure 29.14A). Other animals produce a small number of large eggs, each with a large energy store (Figure 29.14B).

Figure 29.12 Reaching a New Host by a Complex Route The broad fish tapeworm *Diphyllobothrium latum* must pass through the bodies of a copepod (a type of crustacean) and at least one fish before it can reinfect its primary host, a mammal. Such complex life cycles assist the parasite's colonization of new host individuals, but they also provide opportunities for humans to break the cycle with hygienic measures (such as thoroughly cooking food to kill the parasites).

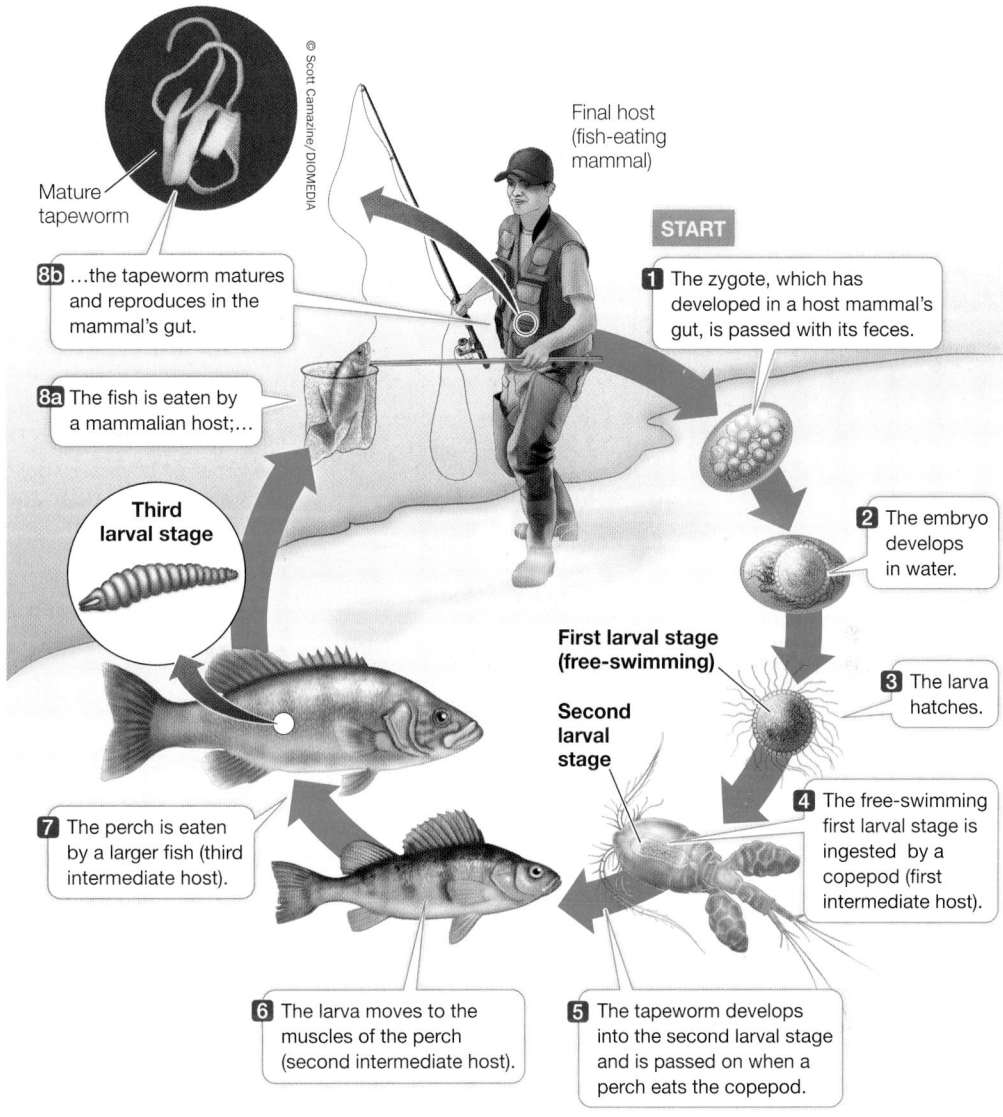

Mature tapeworm

© Scott Camazine/DIOMEDIA

Final host (fish-eating mammal)

START

8b ...the tapeworm matures and reproduces in the mammal's gut.

8a The fish is eaten by a mammalian host;...

1 The zygote, which has developed in a host mammal's gut, is passed with its feces.

2 The embryo develops in water.

Third larval stage

First larval stage (free-swimming)

Second larval stage

3 The larva hatches.

7 The perch is eaten by a larger fish (third intermediate host).

4 The free-swimming first larval stage is ingested by a copepod (first intermediate host).

6 The larva moves to the muscles of the perch (second intermediate host).

5 The tapeworm develops into the second larval stage and is passed on when a perch eats the copepod.

Reteporella couchii

© Borut Furlan/Getty Images

Figure 29.13 Colonial Animals This bryozoan colony consists of many asexually reproducing, genetically homogeneous, physiologically interacting individuals. The colony looks much like a single individual with many parts, but in fact is a group of individuals acting together.

With a fixed amount of energy available for reproduction, a female animal can produce many small eggs or a few large eggs, but she cannot produce many large eggs. Thus there is a trade-off between the number of offspring produced and the energy resources each offspring receives from its mother.

The larger the energy store in an egg, the longer an offspring can develop before it must either find its own food or be fed by its parents. Birds of all species lay relatively small numbers of relatively large eggs, but incubation periods vary. In some species, eggs hatch when the young are still helpless (**Figure 29.15A**). Such **altricial** young must be fed and cared for until they can feed themselves; parents can provide for only a small number of altricial offspring. In contrast, some bird species incubate their eggs longer, and the hatchlings are developed to the point that they are able to forage for themselves almost immediately (**Figure 29.15B**). The young of such species are called **precocial**.

(A) *Rana temporaria*

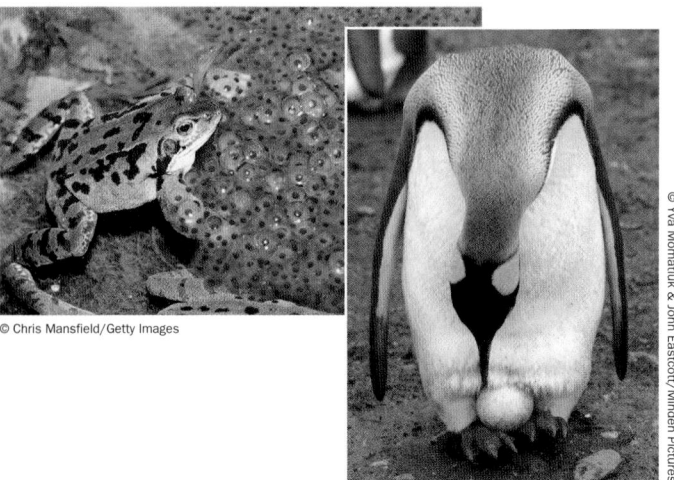

© Chris Mansfield/Getty Images

© Yva Momatiuk & John Eastcott/Minden Pictures

(B) *Aptenodytes patagonicus*

Figure 29.14 Many Small or Few Large Allocation of energy to eggs requires trade-offs. **(A)** This European common frog has divided her reproductive energy among a large number of small eggs. **(B)** This King Penguin has invested all of her reproductive energy in one large egg.

Q: What are the respective advantages and disadvantages of these two reproductive strategies?

(A) *Turdus migratorius*

© By Laura Zenker/SinglEye Photography/Getty Images

(B) *Anser anser*

© F.lonline digitale Bildagentur GmbH/Alamy Stock Photo

Figure 29.15 Helpless or Independent **(A)** The altricial young of the American Robin are essentially helpless when they hatch. Their parents feed and care for them for several weeks. **(B)** Graylag Goose hatchlings are precocial, ready to swim and feed independently almost immediately after hatching.

29.2 Recap and Assess

Many animals have life cycle stages that differ from one another morphologically. In some animals, the larval form is a dispersal stage; in other animals, the adults are more likely to disperse than are larvae. In several groups of organisms, asexual reproduction without fission leads to coloniality.

1. Why can't a life cycle evolve that maximizes all aspects of feeding and reproduction simultaneously?

2. How does a colony of unicellular animals differ from a multicellular animal?

In the remainder of this chapter and in Chapters 30 and 31, we will become acquainted with the major animal groups and learn how the general characteristics of body form and life history strategies we have just described apply to each of them.

KEY CONCEPT 29.3 The Root of the Animal Tree Provides Clues to Early Animal Diversification

Learning Objectives

29.3.1 Apply knowledge of phylogenetic relationships among major groups of animals to describe the evolution and loss of major structural features.

29.3.2 Compare the life histories of sponges, ctenophores, placozoans, and cnidarians and discuss their similarities and differences.

Looking at Figure 29.1, you can see that the protostome and deuterostome animals together comprise a monophyletic group known as Bilateria. Some major traits that support the monophyly of bilaterians (in addition to genomic analyses) are strong bilateral symmetry, the presence of three distinct cell layers in embryos (triploblasty), and a centralized nervous system. There are, however, four animal groups—the sponges, ctenophores, placozoans, and cnidarians—that are not bilaterians.

The root of the animal tree is still debated

Biologists have proposed at least three different lineages as sister group of the remaining animals. Traditionally, sponges have been considered the sister group of other animals, based in large part on the similarity of some sponges to choanoflagellates (see Figure 29.2) and on the fact that sponges lack a nervous system. Placozoans also have very few tissue types, and also have no nervous system, so they have also been placed by most biologists as branching off near the base of the animal tree. However, as we explore in **Investigating Life: Reconstructing Animal Phylogeny from Protein-Coding Genes**, some recent genomic studies suggest that the first split in the animal tree may have been between the lineage that leads to ctenophores and the rest of the animals.

Recent studies of the many genes that encode nervous systems indicate that these genes were duplicated and specialized separately in ctenophores, cnidarians, and bilaterians. This finding suggests

▶Investigating LIFE   Reconstructing Animal Phylogeny from Protein-Coding Genes

Experiment

Original Paper: C. W. Dunn et al. 2008. Broad phylogenomic sampling improves resolution of the Animal Tree of Life. *Nature* 452: 745–749.

Several breakthroughs in our understanding of animal phylogeny have occurred in recent years as the sequences of genes and proteins have been compared across species. Casey Dunn and his colleagues compared sequences from many different proteins across a wide variety of animal groups to reconstruct their phylogeny.

QUESTIONS▶ What was the earliest split in the animal tree? Are ctenophores, sponges, or placozoans the sister group of other animals?

METHOD▶

1. Collect mRNA from major groups of animals and choano-flagellate outgroups.

2. Reverse transcribe the mRNA into cDNA.

3. Sequence the cDNA, translate the genes into the amino acid sequences of the proteins, and align sequences of homologous proteins.

4. Reconstruct the phylogeny of the animal groups from the aligned protein sequences.

RESULTS▶ The tree below represents just a sample of the major lineages examined by Dunn and colleagues.

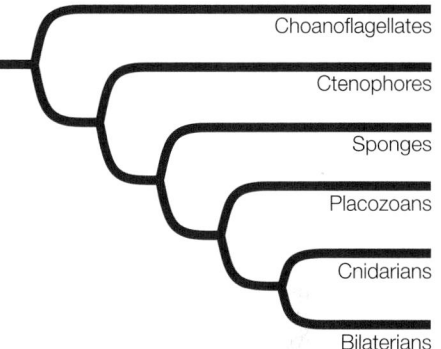

CONCLUSION▶ According to this data set, the earliest split in the animal tree was between ctenophores and the remaining animals.

Work with the Data

The table below includes a small sample of the data collected and analyzed by Dunn and his colleagues. Use these representative data to reconstruct a tree of the represented species. In the original paper, Dunn and colleagues reported on 11,234 amino acid positions among 77 species of animals. Twenty-seven of these amino acid positions for 11 of those species are shown in the table. (See Table 3.2 for the one-letter amino acid abbreviations.)

QUESTIONS▶

1. Construct a phylogenetic tree of these 11 species using the parsimony method. Use the outgroup (a choanoflagellate) to root your tree. Assume that all changes from one amino acid to another are equally likely. See Key Concept 20.2 for a review of the parsimony method of reconstructing phylogenetic trees.

2. How many character state changes (i.e., changes from one amino acid to another) occur along each branch on your tree?

3. Which characters support the ctenophores as the sister group of the remaining animals?

4. Which group on your tree represents the bilaterian animals? The protostomes? The deuterostomes?

Species	1	2	3	4	5	6	7	8	9	10	11	12	13	14	15	16	17	18	19	20	21	22	23	24	25	26	27
Clam	Y	S	T	G	L	H	E	N	Y	A	R	A	M	R	I	A	L	T	I	V	K	L	S	I	V	I	L
Earthworm	Y	A	T	G	L	H	E	N	Y	P	H	A	M	R	I	A	L	T	I	V	K	L	S	I	V	M	L
Tardigrade	Y	A	T	G	L	H	E	H	Y	K	R	A	M	R	V	A	T	S	I	V	R	L	N	L	V	L	L
Fruit fly	F	A	T	G	L	H	E	N	Y	K	R	A	M	R	I	A	L	S	I	V	S	L	D	L	V	L	L
Sea urchin	Y	A	T	G	L	L	E	N	Y	P	N	A	M	R	I	A	L	T	V	I	R	Q	N	L	T	V	K
Human	W	A	A	G	L	R	E	H	Y	P	K	A	I	R	I	S	V	T	V	I	R	Q	N	L	T	V	K
Chicken	W	A	A	G	L	R	E	H	Y	P	R	A	I	R	I	A	V	T	V	I	R	Q	N	L	T	V	K
Lancelet	Y	A	T	G	L	R	E	H	Y	P	K	A	M	R	I	A	V	T	V	I	R	L	N	L	T	V	K
Sponge	Y	G	L	S	L	R	P	N	F	P	K	S	M	S	V	A	L	T	V	I	R	Q	N	L	V	I	L
Ctenophore	Y	G	L	G	Q	D	P	N	F	P	K	S	M	S	V	A	L	T	V	I	R	Q	N	L	V	I	L
Choanoflagellate (outgroup)	Y	G	L	G	Q	D	P	N	F	P	K	S	F	S	V	A	L	T	V	I	R	Q	N	L	V	I	L

Character state (amino acid at position)

Go to **Achieve** for a companion Data in Depth exercise.

that nervous systems evolved independently in these three groups in response to similar selection pressures associated with multicellularity, movement, and prey capture. Therefore the nervous systems of these groups are no longer considered homologous, or as evidence for a close evolutionary relationship. Most biologists now agree that the sponges and ctenophores were the first two lineages to split from the remaining animals, although there is still disagreement about which of these two lineages split first. The placozoans were then the next group to split from the remaining animals, followed by the split that gave rise to the cnidarians (see Figure 29.1).

Whichever of these groups was first to diverge, biologists think that the common ancestor of animals was very different from all animals that are alive today. An early split on the animal tree does not imply that sponges or ctenophores look anything like the ancestral animal. For example, all living ctenophores are quite closely related to one another, and they have been evolving for as long as all other animal lineages—ever since animals last shared a common ancestor more than 700 million years ago. Thus many traits of modern ctenophores (as well as modern sponges) are highly derived and specialized.

Molecular analyses of genomes place the earliest splits in animal phylogeny at more than 700 million years ago, well before the first large multicellular animals appear in the fossil record about 565 million years ago (see Figure 23.12). The first animals are thought to have had relatively few cells and to have been quite small. Then large multicellular animals, along with some of their characteristics (such as nervous systems), appear to have evolved several times in different animal lineages. As Earth warmed and oxygen concentrations increased in the oceans near the beginning of the Cambrian, several groups of animals evolved larger bodies and greater tissue complexity.

Sponges are loosely organized animals

Although they have some specialized cells, **sponges** have no distinct embryonic cell layers and no true organs. Early naturalists classified sponges as plants because they were sessile and lacked body symmetry.

Sponges have hard skeletal elements called **spicules**, which may be small and simple or large and complex. Three major groups of sponges, which separated soon after the split between sponges and the rest of the animals, are distinguished by their spicules. Members of two groups (demosponges and glass sponges) have skeletons composed of siliceous spicules made of hydrated silicon dioxide (**Figure 29.16A,B**). These spicules have greater flexibility and toughness than synthetic glass rods of similar length. Members of the third group, the calcareous sponges, take their name from their calcium carbonate spicules (**Figure 29.16C**).

The body plan of all sponges—even large ones, which may reach a meter or more in length—is an aggregation of cells built around a water canal system. Sponges bring water into their bodies by beating the flagella of their specialized feeding cells, the **choanocytes** (see Figure 29.2B). Water, along with any food

(A) *Xestospongia* sp.

(B) *Euplectella aspergillum*

(C) *Sycon* sp.

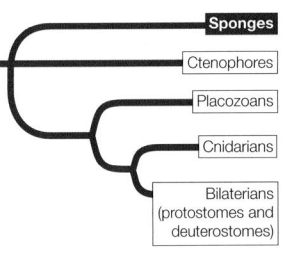

Spicules

Figure 29.16 Sponge Diversity **(A)** The majority of sponge species are demosponges, such as this barrel sponge. The system of pores and water canals (see Figure 29.2B) that is typical of the sponge body plan is apparent in this photograph. **(B)** The supporting structures of both demosponges and glass sponges are siliceous spicules, seen here in the skeleton of a glass sponge. **(C)** The spicules of calcareous sponges are made of calcium carbonate.

particles it contains, enters the sponge by way of small pores and passes into the water canals or a central atrium, where choanocytes capture food particles.

A skeleton of simple or branching spicules, often combined with a complex network of elastic fibers, supports the body of most sponges. Sponges also have an extracellular matrix, composed of collagen, adhesive glycoproteins, and other molecules, that holds the cells together. Most sponges are filter feeders. A few species are carnivores that trap prey on hook-shaped spicules that protrude from the body surface.

Most of the 8,500 species of sponges are marine animals. Only about 50 species of sponges live in fresh water. Sponges come in a wide variety of sizes and shapes that are adapted to different movement patterns of water. Sponges living in intertidal or shallow subtidal environments are subject to strong wave action and attach firmly to the substrate. Most sponges that live in slowly flowing water are flattened and are oriented at right angles to the

(A) Generalized anatomy of a ctenophore

Tentacle

Gut

Tentacle sheath

Ctenes

Pharynx

Mouth

Prey adhere to the sticky cells that cover the tentacles.

(B) Mnemiopsis leidyi

© Larry Jon Friesen

2.5 cm

Figure 29.17 Comb Jellies Feed with Tentacles (A) The body plan of a typical ctenophore. The long, sticky tentacles sweep through the water, efficiently harvesting small prey. (B) This comb jelly, photographed in Sydney Harbor, Australia, has short tentacles. Comb jellies get their name from the ctenes—rows or "combs" of cilia used for movement.

Ctenophores move by beating cilia rather than by muscular contractions. Most of the 250 known species have eight comblike rows of cilia-bearing plates, called **ctenes** (Figure 29.17). The feeding tentacles of ctenophores are covered with cells that discharge adhesive material when they contact prey. After capturing its prey, a ctenophore retracts its tentacles to bring the food to its mouth. In some species, the entire surface of the body is coated with sticky mucus that captures prey. Most ctenophores eat small planktonic organisms, although some eat other ctenophores. Ctenophores are common in open seas and can become abundant in protected bodies of water, where large populations may inhibit the growth of other organisms.

Ctenophore life cycles are uncomplicated. Gametes are released into the body cavity and then discharged through the mouth or the anal pores. Fertilization takes place in open seawater. In nearly all species, the fertilized egg develops directly into a miniature ctenophore, which gradually grows into an adult.

Media Clip 29.4 Ctenophores
Life12e.com/mc29.4

direction of current flow, allowing them to intercept water and the food it contains as it flows past them.

Sponges reproduce both sexually and asexually. In most species, a single individual produces both eggs and sperm, but individuals do not self-fertilize. Water currents carry sperm from one individual to another. Sponges also reproduce asexually by budding and fragmentation.

View in Achieve
Activity 29.2 **Sponge and Diploblast Classification**

Ctenophores are radially symmetrical and diploblastic

Ctenophores, also known as comb jellies, were until recently thought to be most closely related to the cnidarians (jellyfishes, corals, and their relatives). But ctenophores lack most of the Hox genes found in cnidarians and bilaterians, and recent studies of their genomes have indicated that ctenophores were among the earliest lineages to split from the remaining animals (see Investigating Life: Reconstructing Animal Phylogeny from Protein-Coding Genes).

Ctenophores have a radially symmetrical, diploblastic body plan. The two cell layers are separated by an inert, gelatinous extracellular matrix called **mesoglea**. Ctenophores, unlike sponges, have a complete gut, meaning they have different openings for food entry and waste elimination. Food enters through a mouth, and wastes are eliminated through two anal pores.

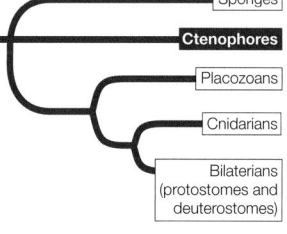

Sponges
Ctenophores
Placozoans
Cnidarians
Bilaterians (protostomes and deuterostomes)

Placozoans are abundant but rarely observed

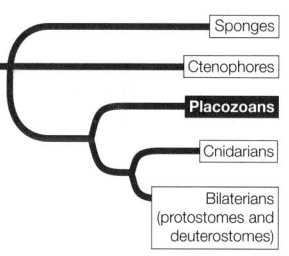

Sponges
Ctenophores
Placozoans
Cnidarians
Bilaterians (protostomes and deuterostomes)

As we discussed in the opening of this chapter, **placozoans** are (like sponges) structurally very simple animals with only four distinct cell types (Figure 29.18A). Individuals in the mature, asymmetrical life stage are usually observed adhering to surfaces (such as the glass of aquariums, where they were first discovered, or to rocks and other hard substrates in nature). Their structural simplicity—they have no mouth, gut, or nervous system—initially led biologists to suspect they might be the sister group of all other animals. Most phylogenetic analyses have not supported this hypothesis, however, and some aspects of the placozoans' structural simplicity may be secondarily derived. They are generally considered to have a diploblastic body plan, with upper and lower epithelial (surface) layers that sandwich a layer of contractile fiber cells.

Recent studies have found that placozoans have a pelagic (open-ocean) life stage that is capable of swimming (Figure 29.18B), but the life history of placozoans is incompletely known. Most studies have focused on the larger adherent stages that can be found in aquariums, where they appear after being inadvertently collected with other marine organisms. The transparent nature and small size of placozoans make them very difficult to observe in nature. Nonetheless, it is known that placozoans can reproduce both asexually as well as sexually, although the details of their sexual reproduction

(A)

(B)

Courtesy of Wim van Egmond

Figure 29.18 Placozoan Simplicity **(A)** As seen in this artist's rendition, adult placozoans are tiny (1–2 mm across), flattened, asymmetrical animals. **(B)** Recent studies have found a symmetrical, weakly swimming pelagic stage of placozoan to be abundant in many warm tropical and subtropical seas. (B after V. B. Pearse and O. Voigt. 2007. *Integr Comp Biol* 47(5): 677–692. Drawing by J. Keller and C. Patton, based on observations by V.B.P.)

Figure 29.19 The Life Cycle of Most Cnidarians Has Two Stages The life cycle of a scyphozoan (jellyfish) exemplifies the typical cnidarian body forms: the sessile, asexual polyp and the motile, sexual medusa. Some species of cnidarians have life cycles that lack polyps or medusae. (Adapted from F. M. Bayer and H. B. Owre. 1968. *The Free-Living Lower Invertebrates*, Macmillan Publishing Co.: New York.)

View in Achieve
Animation 29.1 Life Cycle of a Cnidarian

are poorly understood. They are found in warm coastal seas around the world.

Cnidarians are specialized carnivores

The **cnidarians** (jellyfishes, sea anemones, sea pens, corals, and hydrozoans) make up the largest and most diverse group of non-bilaterian animals. The mouth of a cnidarian is connected to a blind sac called the **gastrovascular cavity** (a cnidarian thus does not have a complete gut). The gastrovascular cavity functions in digestion, circulation, and gas exchange, and it also acts as a hydrostatic skeleton. The single opening serves as both mouth and anus.

The life cycle of many cnidarians has two distinct stages, one sessile and the other motile (**Figure 29.19**), although one or the other of these stages is absent in some groups. In the sessile **polyp** stage, a cylindrical stalk is attached to the substrate. The motile **medusa** (plural *medusae*) is a free-swimming stage shaped like a bell or an umbrella. It typically floats with its mouth and feeding tentacles facing downward.

Mature polyps produce medusae by asexual budding. Medusae then reproduce sexually, producing eggs or sperm by meiosis and releasing the gametes into the water. A fertilized egg develops into a free-swimming, ciliated larva called a **planula**, which eventually settles to the bottom and develops into a polyp.

Cnidarians are specialized predators adapted for capturing and subduing relatively large and complex prey. As we noted at the start of this key concept, recent genomic studies suggest that the nerve nets found in cnidarians are largely independently derived from those found in ctenophores, as well as from the nervous systems found in bilaterians. The tentacles of cnidarians are covered with specialized cells that contain stinging organelles called **nematocysts**, which inject toxins into their prey (**Figure 29.20**). Some cnidarians, including many corals and anemones, gain additional nutrition from photosynthetic endosymbionts that live in their tissues.

Cnidarians have cells containing muscle fibers whose contractions enable the animals to move, as well as simple nerve nets that integrate the body's activities. Their bodies also contain specialized structural molecules (collagen, actin, and myosin). Yet cnidarians, like ctenophores, are largely made up of inert mesoglea. Most species

(A) Portuguese man-of-war (*Physalia physalis*)

(B)

Once discharged, stylets and spines on the nematocyst anchor it to the prey.

Cnidocytes

Nucleus | Empty nematocyst capsule | Everted shaft | Stylet (barb) | Spines | Base of tube | Uncoiled nematocyst tube

Cnidocyte | **Nematocyst**

Figure 29.20 Nematocysts Are Potent Weapons **(A)** The tentacles of the Portuguese man-of-war, a hydrozoan, are rife with specialized cells called cnidocytes. These cells contain stinging organelles called nematocysts, which inject toxins into their prey. The Portuguese man-of-war is a colonial organism, composed of many physiologically integrated individuals with specialized functions. **(B)** Nematocysts of the Portuguese man-of-war cause painful reactions when they come into contact with human skin.

▶ **Media Clip 29.5 Stunning Siphonophore: Colonial Hydrozoans**
Life12e.com/mc29.5

have low metabolic rates and can survive in environments where they encounter prey only infrequently.

Of the roughly 12,500 living cnidarian species, all but a few live in the oceans (**Figure 29.21**). The smallest cnidarians can barely be seen without a microscope. One small group, known as myxozoans, consists of tiny parasites, usually with a two-host life cycle that includes a fish and an annelid worm or a bryozoan. The largest known jellyfish is 2.5 meters in diameter, and some colonial hydrozoans (which include the Portuguese man-of-war; see Figure 29.20) can reach lengths in excess of 30 meters. Here we describe the three clades of cnidarians that contain the most species: anthozoans, scyphozoans, and hydrozoans.

ANTHOZOANS   Members of the **anthozoan** clade include sea anemones, sea pens, and corals. Sea anemones (see Figure 29.21A), all of which are solitary, are widespread in both warm and cold ocean waters. Sea pens (see Figure 29.21B), by contrast, are colonial. Each colony consists of two or more different kinds of polyps. The primary polyp has a lower portion

(A) *Urticina crassicornis*

© blickwinkel/Alamy Stock Photo

(B) *Virgularia gustaviana*

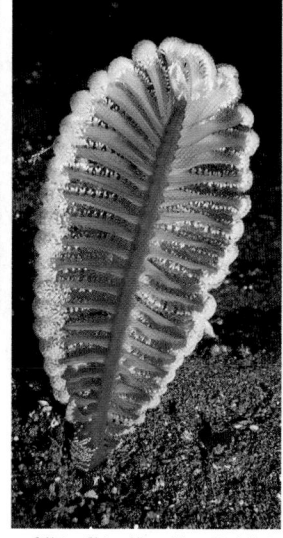

© Nature Picture Library/Alamy Stock Photo

(C) *Netrostoma setouchina*

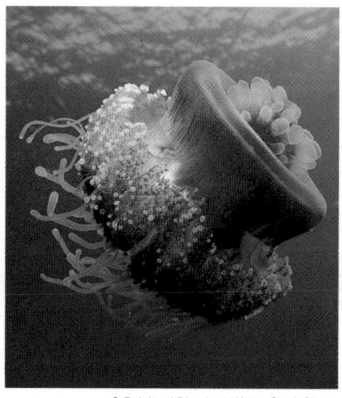

© Reinhard Dirscherl/Alamy Stock Photo

(D) *Obelia* sp.

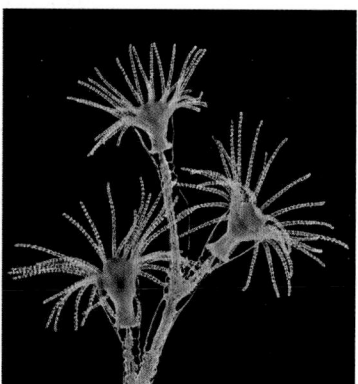

© Larry Jon Friesen

Figure 29.21 Diversity among Cnidarians **(A)** Sea anemones are sessile, living attached to marine substrates. Water currents carry prey into the nematocyst-studded tentacles. **(B)** The sea pen is a colonial cnidarian that lives in soft bottom sediments and projects polyps above the substrate. **(C)** This jellyfish illustrates the complexity of a scyphozoan medusa. **(D)** Polyp colonies of this hydrozoan grow on rocks of intertidal pools.

(A) *Symphyllia* sp.

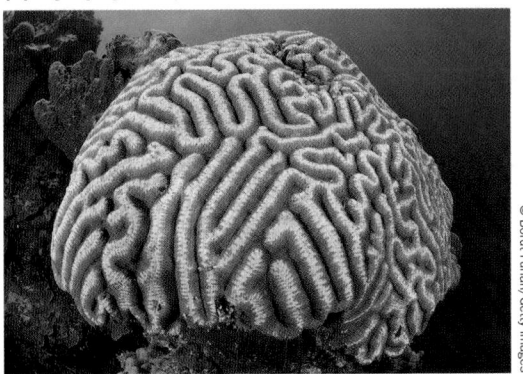

© Borut Furlan/Getty Images

(B)

© Travelscape Images/Alamy Stock Photo

Figure 29.22 Corals **(A)** The descriptive common name of this Caribbean coral is "brain coral." **(B)** Many different coral species form the Great Barrier Reef off the coast of Australia.

anchored in the bottom sediment and a branched upper portion that projects above the substrate. Along the upper portion, the primary polyp produces smaller secondary polyps by budding. Some of these secondary polyps differentiate into feeding polyps; in some species, other secondary polyps differentiate to circulate water through the colony.

The common names of coral groups—brain corals, staghorn corals, and organ pipe corals, among others—often describe their appearance (**Figure 29.22A**). Corals are sessile and colonial. The polyps of most species form a skeleton by secreting a matrix of organic molecules on which they then deposit calcium carbonate. As the colony grows, old polyps die, but their calcium carbonate skeletons remain. Living corals form a layer on top of a growing bank of skeletal remains, eventually forming chains of islands and reefs. The Great Barrier Reef along the northeastern coast of Australia is a system of coral formations more than 2,000 kilometers long, which is about the distance from New York City to St. Louis (**Figure 29.22B**). A single coral reef in the Red Sea has been calculated to contain more material than all the buildings in the major cities of North America combined.

Corals flourish at shallow depths in clear, nutrient-poor tropical waters. They grow well in such environments because unicellular photosynthetic dinoflagellates live endosymbiotically within their cells. These dinoflagellates provide the corals with products of photosynthesis; the corals, in turn, provide the dinoflagellates with nutrients and a place to live. This endosymbiotic relationship explains why reef-forming corals are restricted to

clear surface waters, where light levels are high enough to support photosynthesis.

Coral reefs throughout the world are threatened by rising CO_2 levels (which result in increased ocean temperatures and acidification of ocean waters through the formation of carbonic acid). Polluted runoff from development on adjacent shorelines is an additional threat to corals. Warmer temperatures lead to the loss of coral endosymbionts (known as coral bleaching), and acidification can cause coral skeletons to dissolve. An overabundance of nitrogen from fertilizer in runoff is advantageous to algae, which overgrow and eventually smother the corals.

Connect the Concepts Investigating Life: Can Corals Reacquire Dinoflagellate Endosymbionts Lost to Bleaching? in Chapter 25 describes an experiment in which coral endosymbionts were lost and replaced by new endosymbionts in response to changing environmental conditions.

SCYPHOZOANS   The several hundred species of **scyphozoans** are all marine. The mesoglea of their medusae is thick and firm, giving rise to their common name of jellyfishes (or sea jellies). The medusa rather than the polyp dominates the life cycle of scyphozoans. An individual medusa is male or female, releasing eggs or sperm into the open sea. A fertilized egg develops into a small planula larva that quickly settles on a substrate and develops into a small polyp. This polyp feeds and grows and may produce additional polyps by budding. After a period of growth, the polyp begins to bud off small medusae, which feed, grow, and transform into adult medusae (see Figures 29.19 and 29.21C).

HYDROZOANS   The polyp typically dominates the life cycle of **hydrozoans**, but some species have only medusae and others have only polyps. Most hydrozoans are colonial. A single planula larva eventually gives rise to a colony of many polyps, all interconnected and sharing a continuous gastrovascular cavity (**Figure 29.23**). Within such a colony, some polyps have tentacles with many nematocysts; they capture prey for the colony. Other individuals lack tentacles and are unable to feed, but are specialized for the asexual production of medusae. Still others are fingerlike and defend the colony with their nematocysts.

Some small groups of parasitic animals may be the closest relatives of bilaterians

Two small groups of tiny marine parasites are listed in Table 29.1 but are not depicted in the phylogeny in Figure 29.1: the orthonectids and the rhombozoans. Recent genomic analyses suggest that these groups may be among the closest surviving relatives of the bilaterians, although their exact phylogenetic placement is uncertain. Both groups are highly reduced parasites that lack many of the structures that traditionally have been used to study animal relationships. As their genomes become more completely known, the relationships of these two groups to other animals should become clearer. Two other small groups (also listed in Table 29.1 but not shown in Figure 29.1) have been proposed as also falling just outside the bilaterians: the xenoturbellids and acoels. Some genomic analyses, however, suggest that these animals are actually highly specialized deuterostomes.

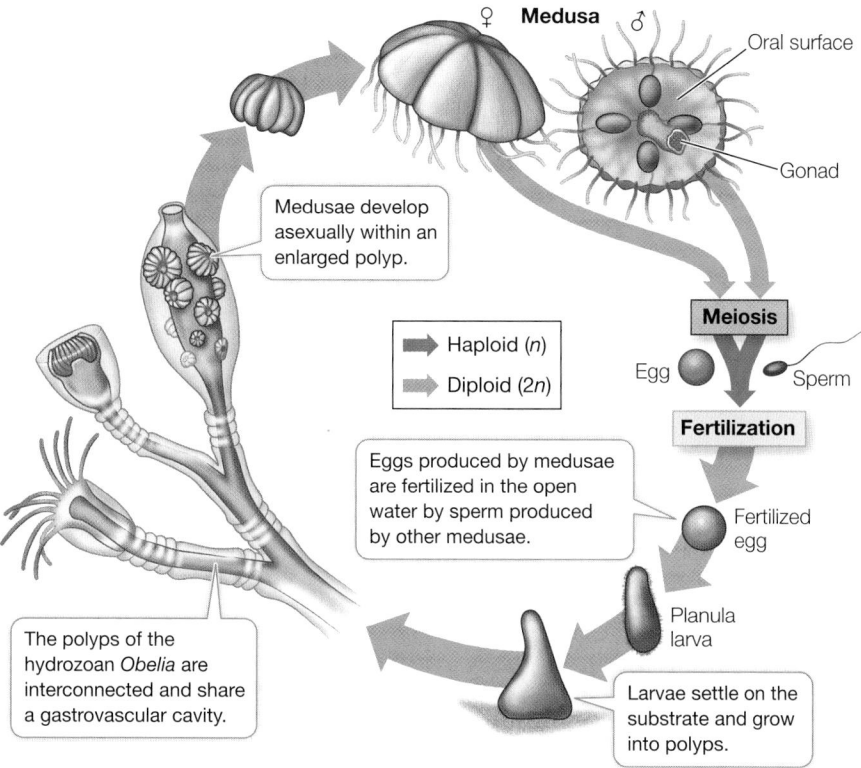

Medusae develop asexually within an enlarged polyp.

The polyps of the hydrozoan *Obelia* are interconnected and share a gastrovascular cavity.

Haploid (*n*)

Diploid (2*n*)

Meiosis

Egg   Sperm

Fertilization

Eggs produced by medusae are fertilized in the open water by sperm produced by other medusae.

Fertilized egg

Planula larva

Larvae settle on the substrate and grow into polyps.

Figure 29.23 Many Hydrozoans Are Colonial   The polyps in a hydrozoan colony may differentiate to perform specialized tasks. In the species whose life cycle is diagrammed here, the medusa is the sexual reproductive stage, producing eggs and sperm in organs called gonads. (Adapted from F. M. Bayer and H. B. Owre. 1968. *The Free-Living Lower Invertebrates*, Macmillan Publishing Co.: New York.)

KEY CONCEPT
29.3 Recap and Assess

Early animal diversification led to five major lineages: sponges, ctenophores, placozoans, cnidarians, and bilaterians. Sponges and ctenophores split first from the remaining animals, followed closely by the placozoans. The earliest animals are thought to have been small and to have consisted of relatively few cells per individual. Large multicellular animals, with greater tissue differentiation, arose independently several times, giving rise to the five major groups of modern animals. Major components of nervous systems arose independently in three of these lineages (ctenophores, cnidarians, and bilaterians).

1. What is the basis for the claim that animal nervous systems evolved independently in ctenophores, cnidarians, and bilaterians?

2. Why are sponges and placozoans considered to be animals even though they lack the complex body structures found in most other animal groups?

3. The discoveries that placozoans in their pelagic stages are abundant in warm seas and that the mature stage settles on smooth surfaces suggest how these organisms might be collected and surveyed. What sampling procedures might you use to discover whether placozoans occur at a particular location along a coast?

▶ **View in Achieve**
Simulation 29.1 Diversity

▶Investigating**LIFE**

Q and A   **Which animal groups are involved in the earliest split in the animal tree?**

Three major hypotheses have been proposed in recent decades about the earliest split in the animal tree. Given the structural simplicity of sponges and their similarity to some animal outgroups (especially choanoflagellates), for many years biologists considered sponges to form the sister group of all other animals. When placozoans were first described, their structural simplicity also led other biologists to suspect that they, rather than sponges, were the sister group of other animals. In contrast, the ctenophores share some superficial similarities with cnidarians and were traditionally considered to be more closely related to them, rather than splitting earlier at the base of the animal tree. However, as biologists collected complete genomes from all these lineages, it became clearer that the simplicity of placozoans derives from a mix of ancestral retained features and secondarily derived losses of complexity. For example, although placozoans, with only four cell types and no true organs, are structurally less complex than ctenophores, this structural simplicity is now thought to represent an evolutionary reversal in the placozoan lineage. In contrast, some of the "advanced" features of ctenophores (such as their nervous systems) were gained through independent gene duplications and specializations compared with the nervous systems of cnidarians and bilaterians. As we explored in **Investigating Life: Reconstructing Animal Phylogeny from Protein-Coding Genes**, phylogenetic analyses of many genes suggest that ctenophores are the sister group of all other animals; other analyses of large numbers of genes support the sponges as the sister group of all other animals. Which answer is correct should become clearer as additional complete genomes are collected from sponges and ctenophores.

Future directions

As biologists collect more genomes from new species of animals, it is becoming possible to reconstruct the various gene duplications and changes that have led to the major structural and functional differences among animal groups. Whether sponges or ctenophores are the sister group of other animals, it is clear that there have been multiple independent origins of animal nervous systems. Having several independent origins of nervous systems is a boon for understanding how nervous systems arise and evolve. The understanding and study of these genomes are just beginning, but already complete genomes are shedding considerable light on the origins of animal complexity.

© redbrickstock.com/Alamy Stock Photo

You should be able to relate each summary to the adjacent figures. If you go to this visual summary in **Achieve**, you can follow links to figures, animations, activities, and simulations that will help you consolidate the material.

KEY CONCEPT
29.1 Diverse Body Plans Allow Animals to Move and Feed in Many Ways

Go to Activity 29.1

- Differences in their patterns of early development characterize two major clades of **triploblastic** animals, the **protostomes** and the **deuterostomes**.

- Animal **body plans** can be described in terms of **symmetry**, **body cavity** structure, **segmentation**, type of appendages, and type of nervous system.

- On the basis of their body cavity structure, animals can be described as **acoelomates**, **pseudocoelomates**, or **coelomates**.

- Segmentation takes many forms and improves control of movement, especially if the animal also has appendages.

Questions

1. What major difference in early development distinguishes protostomes from deuterostomes?

2. Which major groups of animals exhibit radial symmetry?

3. How do body cavities differ in acoelomates, pseudocoelomates, and coelomates?

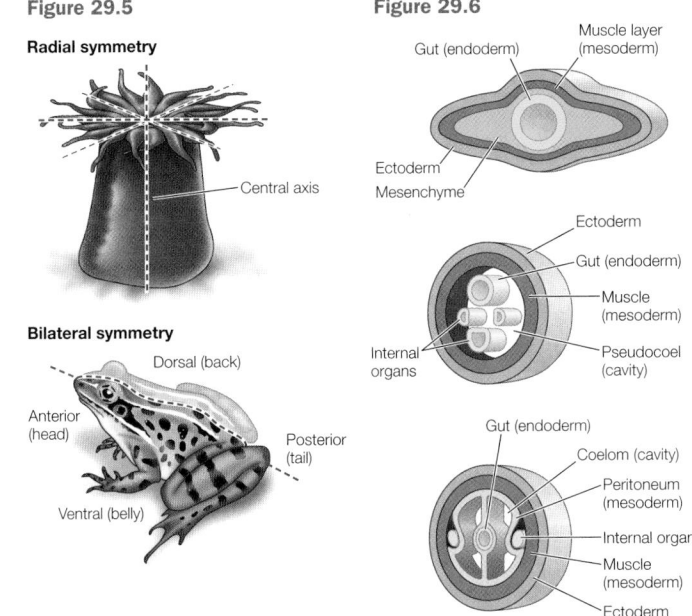

Figure 29.5

Radial symmetry

Central axis

Bilateral symmetry

Dorsal (back)

Anterior (head)

Posterior (tail)

Ventral (belly)

Figure 29.6

Gut (endoderm)
Muscle layer (mesoderm)
Ectoderm
Mesenchyme

Ectoderm
Gut (endoderm)
Muscle (mesoderm)
Internal organs
Pseudocoel (cavity)

Gut (endoderm)
Coelom (cavity)
Peritoneum (mesoderm)
Internal organ
Muscle (mesoderm)
Ectoderm

KEY CONCEPT
29.2 Animal Life Cycles Involve Trade-Offs

- The stages of an animal's life cycle may be specialized for different activities. An immature stage whose morphology is dramatically different from that of the adult stage is called a **larva**.

- Most animal life cycles have at least one **dispersal** stage.

- A characteristic of an animal or a life cycle stage may improve the animal's performance in one activity but reduce its performance in another, a situation known as a **trade-off**.

- Parasites have complex life cycles that may involve one or more hosts and several larval stages.

- In some groups of animals, asexual reproduction without fission leads to the formation of colonies composed of many genetically homogeneous, physiologically integrated individuals.

Questions

1. How can specialized stages of life cycles facilitate dispersal?

2. How might specialized stages of life cycles allow animals to reduce competition between juveniles and adults?

3. How can complex life cycles with specialized stages help parasites move among multiple hosts?

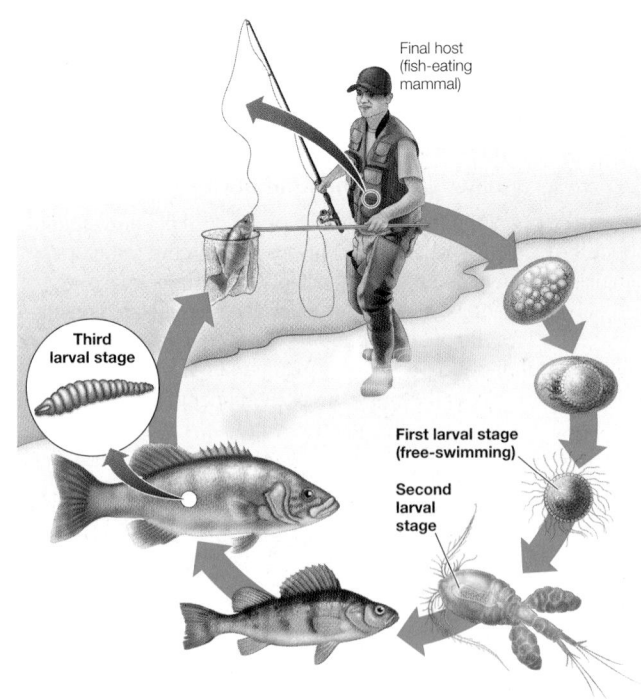

Figure 29.12

Final host (fish-eating mammal)

Third larval stage

First larval stage (free-swimming)

Second larval stage

KEY CONCEPT
29.3
The Root of the Animal Tree Provides Clues to Early Animal Diversification

Go to Activity 29.2, Animation 29.1, and Simulation 29.1

- Several large, multicellular groups diverged early in animal evolution, including **sponges**, **ctenophores**, **placozoans**, **cnidarians**, and bilaterians. The ancestral animal was unlike any of the modern groups and was likely small and composed of relatively few cells and no differentiated tissues.

- Complex nervous systems developed several times in animals, including in ctenophores, cnidarians, and bilaterians.

- The life cycle of most cnidarians has two distinct stages: a sessile **polyp** stage and a motile **medusa**. A fertilized egg develops into a free-swimming larval **planula**, which settles to the bottom and develops into a polyp.

Questions

1. Which two groups are considered the most likely candidates to be the sister group of the remaining animals?

2. Which animal groups lack a nervous system?

Figure 29.19

Go to **Achieve** for the eBook, **LearningCurve**, animations, activities, simulations, and additional resources and assignments.

30 Protostome Animals

KEY CONCEPTS

30.1 Protostomes Account for More Than Half of All Described Species

30.2 Many Lophotrochozoans Have Ciliated Feeding Structures or Life Stages

30.3 Ecdysozoans Grow by Shedding Their Cuticles

30.4 Arthropods Are the Most Abundant and Diverse Group of Animals

The majority of described species of life are protostomes, largely because of the enormous diversity of insects. Beetles alone account for almost one-fourth of all described species.

© pixelprof / Getty Images

▶ Investigating LIFE

Exploring the Diversity of Life on Earth

Of the 1.8 million species of life that have been discovered and named by biologists, a large majority are protostomes. One group of protostomes, the insects, accounts for more than 1 million of these species, or more than half of all known species of living organisms. Although these numbers may seem incredibly large, they represent a relatively small fraction of the total protostome diversity that is thought to exist on Earth.

As recently as the 1980s, many biologists thought that about half of existing insect species had been described, but today they think that the number of described insect species may be a much smaller fraction of the total number of living species. Why did they change their minds?

A simple but important field study suggested that the number of existing insect species had been significantly underestimated. Knowing that the insects of tropical rainforests—the most species-rich habitat on Earth—were poorly known, entomologist Terry Erwin made a comprehensive sample of one group of insects, the beetles, in the canopies of a single species of tropical forest tree, *Luehea seemannii*, in Panama. Erwin fogged the canopies of large *L. seemannii* trees with an insecticide and collected the insects that fell from the trees in collection nets.

He collected about 1,200 species of beetles—many of them previously undescribed—from this one species of tree.

Erwin then used a set of assumptions to estimate the total number of insect species in tropical rainforests. His assumptions included estimates of the number of species of trees in these forests; the proportion of beetles that specialize on a specific species of host tree; the relative proportion of beetles to other insect groups; and the proportion of beetles that live in trees versus those that live in leaf litter on the ground. From this and similar studies, Erwin estimated that there may be 30 million or more species of insects on Earth. Although recent tests of Erwin's assumptions suggest that 30 million was an overestimate, it is clear that the vast majority of insect species remain to be discovered.

Erwin's pioneering study highlighted the fact that we live on a poorly known planet, most of whose species have yet to be named and described. Much of that undiscovered diversity occurs among several groups of protostomes.

 Which groups of protostomes are thought to contain the most undiscovered species?
(Find the answer on page 692.)

Protostomes Account for More Than Half of All Described Species

30.1

Learning Objectives

30.1.1 Contrast the advantages of having a hard body covering versus a soft body in different habitats.

30.1.2 Associate major evolutionary innovations among the protostomes with life in aquatic versus terrestrial environments.

You may recall that the embryos of diploblastic animals (the ctenophores, placozoans, and cnidarians, which we discussed in Chapter 29) have two cell layers: an outer ectoderm and an inner endoderm (see Key Concept 29.1). Sometime after the origin of the diploblastic animals, a third embryonic cell layer evolved: the mesoderm, which lies between the ectoderm and the endoderm. Mesoderm is found in the two major triploblastic animal clades, the protostomes and the deuterostomes. If we were to judge solely on the basis of numbers, both of species and of individuals, the protostomes would emerge as by far the more successful of the two groups.

As noted in Key Concept 29.1, the name "protostome" means "mouth first." In protostomes, the embryonic blastopore becomes the mouth as the animal develops. In contrast, in deuterostomes ("mouth second"), the blastopore becomes the anal opening of the gut. The protostomes are extremely varied, but they are all bilaterally symmetrical animals whose bodies exhibit two major derived traits:

1. An anterior brain that surrounds the entrance to the digestive tract

2. A ventral nervous system consisting of paired or fused longitudinal nerve cords

Other aspects of protostome body organization differ widely from group to group (**Table 30.1**). Before gene sequences were available for phylogenetic analysis, biologists considered the structure of the body cavity to be a critical feature in animal classification. But the results of genetic analyses have shown that body cavity forms have undergone considerable convergence in the course of protostome evolution. Although the common ancestor of the protostomes had a coelom, subsequent modifications of the coelom distinguish many protostome lineages. In some lineages (such as the flatworms and entoprocts), the coelom has been lost (that is, these groups reverted to an acoelomate state). Some lineages are characterized by a pseudocoel, a body cavity lined with mesoderm in which the internal organs are suspended (see Figure 29.6B). In two of the most prominent protostome clades, the coelom has been highly modified:

- Arthropods lost the ancestral condition of the coelom over the course of evolution. Their internal body cavity has become a **hemocoel**, or "blood chamber," in which fluid from an open circulatory system bathes the internal organs before returning to blood vessels.

TABLE 30.1 | Anatomical Characteristics of Some Major Protostome Groups

Group	Body cavity	Digestive tract	Circulatory system
ARROW WORMS	Coelom	Complete	None
LOPHOTROCHOZOANS			
Bryozoans	Coelom	Complete	None
Entoprocts	None	Complete	None
Flatworms	None	Blind gut	None
Rotifers	Pseudocoel	Complete	None
Gastrotrichs	Pseudocoel	Complete	None
Ribbon worms	Coelom	Complete	Closed
Brachiopods	Coelom	Complete in most	Open
Phoronids	Coelom	Complete	Closed
Annelids	Coelom	Complete	Closed or open
Mollusks	Reduced coelom	Complete	Open except in cephalopods
ECDYSOZOANS			
Nematodes	Pseudocoel	Complete	None
Horsehair worms	Pseudocoel	Greatly reduced	None
Arthropods	Hemocoel	Complete	Open

- Most mollusks have an open circulatory system with some of the attributes of the hemocoel, but they retain vestiges of an enclosed coelom around their major organs.

The protostomes can be divided into two major clades—the lophotrochozoans and the ecdysozoans—largely on the basis of DNA sequence analysis (**Figure 30.1**).

 View in Achieve
Activity 30.1 Features of the Protostomes

Cilia-bearing lophophores and trochophores evolved among the lophotrochozoans

Lophotrochozoans derive their name from two different ciliated features: a feeding structure known as a lophophore and a free-living larval form known as a trochophore. Neither the lophophore nor the trochophore is universal to all lophotrochozoans, however.

Several distantly related groups of lophotrochozoans (including bryozoans, entoprocts, brachiopods, and phoronids) have a **lophophore**, a circular or U-shaped ring of ciliated, hollow tentacles around the mouth (**Figure 30.2**). This complex organ is used for both food collection and gas exchange. Biologists once grouped taxa that have lophophores together as "lophophorates," but it is now clear that they are not one another's closest relatives. The lophophore appears to have evolved independently at least twice, or else it is an ancestral feature of lophotrochozoans and has been lost in many groups. Nearly all animals with a lophophore are sessile as adults. They use the tentacles and cilia of the lophophore to capture small floating organisms from the water. Other sessile lophotrochozoans have less well-developed tentacles that they use for the same purpose.

 Media Clip 30.1 Feeding with a Lophophore
Life12e.com/mc30.1

Figure 30.1 Phylogenetic Tree of
Protostomes Two major lineages, the
lophotrochozoans and the ecdysozoans,
dominate the protostome tree. Some small
groups are not included in this tree. The
phylogenetic relationships shown here are
supported mainly by genomic sequence
data. Although genomic studies are contributing greatly to our knowledge of animal
phylogeny, most species of protostomes
have yet to be studied in detail.

▶ View in **Achieve**
Activity 30.2
Protostome Classification

Some lophotrochozoans, especially in their larval form, use cilia
for locomotion. The larval form known as a **trochophore** moves by
beating a band of cilia (see Figure 29.11A). This movement of cilia
also brings plankton closer to the larva, where it can capture and
ingest them (its cilia are therefore similar in function to the cilia
of the lophophore). Trochophore larvae are found among many of
the major groups of lophotrochozoans, including the mollusks, annelids, ribbon worms, entoprocts, and bryozoans. This larval form
was probably present in the common ancestor of lophotrochozoans
but has been subsequently lost in several lineages.

Some lophotrochozoans (including flatworms, ribbon worms,
annelids, and mollusks) exhibit spiral cleavage in early development, in which layers of new cells spiral obliquely around the axis
of the animal–vegetal pole of the early embyro. Some biologists
group these taxa together as "spiralians," although phylogenetic
analyses of gene sequences do not support monophyly of taxa with
spiralian cleavage. Nonetheless, spiral cleavage may have been
present in the lophotrochozoan ancestor and subsequently lost
in several descendant lineages.

Connect the Concepts As described in Key Concept 42.2,
cleavage is the sequence of early cell divisions that transforms the
diploid zygote into a mass of undifferentiated cells that will develop
into the embryo. Different patterns of cleavage result in differential
distributions of nutrients and cytoplasmic determinants within the
egg cytoplasm.

Plumatella repens

Bryozoans can oscillate, rotate, and retract their lophophore tentacles.

1 mm

Figure 30.2 Bryozoans Use the Lophophore to Feed The extended lophophore dominates the anatomy of the colonial bryozoans. This species inhabits fresh water, although most bryozoans are marine.

Many lineages of lophotrochozoans have a wormlike body form, which means that they are bilaterally symmetrical, legless, soft-bodied, and at least several times longer than they are wide. A wormlike body form enables animals to burrow efficiently through marine sediment or soil. However, as you will see in Key Concept 30.2, the mollusks—the most familiar of the lophotrochozoans to many people—have a very different body organization.

Ecdysozoans must shed their cuticles

Ecdysozoans have an external covering, or **cuticle**, that is secreted by the underlying epidermis (the outermost cell layer). The cuticle provides these animals with both protection and support. Once formed, however, the cuticle cannot grow. How, then, can ecdysozoans increase in size? They do so by shedding, or **molting**, the cuticle and replacing it with a new, larger one.

▶ **Media Clip 30.2 Molting a Cuticle**
Life12e.com/mc30.2

A fossil Cambrian arthropod preserved in the process of molting shows that molting evolved more than 500 million years ago (**Figure 30.3A**). An increasingly rich array of molecular and genetic evidence, including a set of Hox genes shared by all ecdysozoans, suggests they have a single common ancestor. Thus molting of a cuticle is a trait that may have evolved only once during animal evolution.

Before an ecdysozoan molts, a new cuticle is already forming underneath the old one. Once the old cuticle is shed, the new one expands and hardens. Until it has hardened, though, the animal is vulnerable to its enemies, both because its outer surface is easy to penetrate and because an individual with a soft cuticle can move only slowly or not at all (**Figure 30.3B**).

The cuticles of some ecdysozoans, mainly arthropods, function as external skeletons, or **exoskeletons**. These exoskeletons are thickened by layers of protein and a strong, waterproof

(A) Fossil evidence of molting

Molted exoskeleton

Emerging animal

(B) Whip scorpion (*Heterophrynus batesii*) undergoing molting

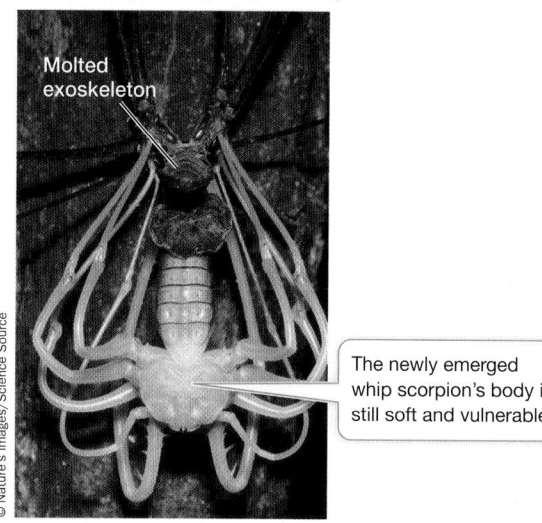

Molted exoskeleton

The newly emerged whip scorpion's body is still soft and vulnerable.

Figure 30.3 Molting: Past and Present **(A)** This 500-million-year-old fossil from the Cambrian, an individual of a long-extinct arthropod species captured in the process of molting, shows that the molting process is an evolutionarily ancient trait. **(B)** This tail-less whip scorpion has just emerged from its discarded exoskeleton. It will be highly vulnerable until its new cuticle has hardened.

polysaccharide called **chitin**. An animal with a rigid, chitin-reinforced exoskeleton can neither move in a wormlike manner nor use cilia for locomotion. A hard exoskeleton also impedes the passage of oxygen and nutrients into the animal, presenting new challenges in other areas besides growth. Thus new mechanisms of locomotion and gas exchange evolved in those ecdysozoans with hard exoskeletons.

To move rapidly, an animal with a rigid exoskeleton must have body extensions that can be manipulated by muscles. Such appendages evolved in the late Precambrian, leading to the **arthropod** ("jointed foot") clade. Arthropod appendages exist in an amazing variety of forms. They serve many functions, including walking and swimming, gas exchange, food capture and manipulation, copulation, and sensory perception. Arthropods grasp food with

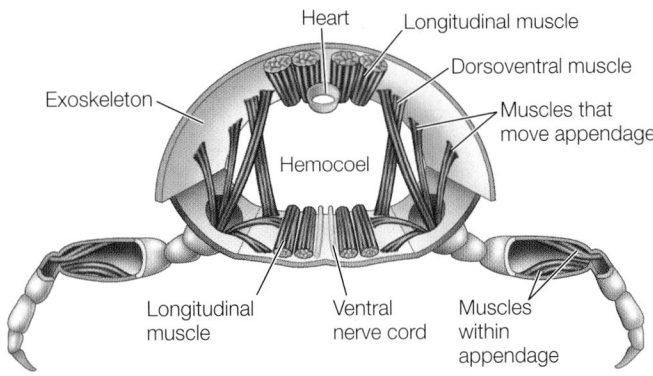

Figure 30.4 Arthropod Skeletons Are Rigid and Jointed This cross section through a thoracic segment of a generalized arthropod illustrates the arthropod body plan, which is characterized by a rigid exoskeleton with jointed appendages.

their mouth and associated appendages and digest it internally. Their muscles are attached to the inside of the exoskeleton. Each segment has muscles that operate that segment and the appendages attached to it (**Figure 30.4**).

The arthropod exoskeleton has had a profound influence on the evolution of these animals. Encasement within a rigid body covering provides support for walking on dry land, and the waterproofing provided by chitin keeps the animal from dehydrating in dry air. Thus aquatic arthropods were, in short, excellent candidates to invade terrestrial environments. As you will see, they did so several times.

Arrow worms retain some ancestral developmental features

Nearly all triploblastic animal groups can be readily classified as either protostomes or deuterostomes, but the evolutionary relationships of one small group, the **arrow worms**, were debated for many years. The blastopore of arrow worms develops into an anus (as in deuterostomes), but they have ventral nerve cords and spiral cleavage (as in many protostomes). Recent studies of gene sequences, however, clearly identify arrow worms as protostomes. There is still some question as to whether they are the closest relatives of the lophotrochozoans (as shown in Figure 30.1) or possibly the sister group of all other protostomes.

The arrow worm body is divided into three compartments: head, trunk, and tail (**Figure 30.5**). The body is transparent or translucent. Most arrow worms swim in the open sea. A few species live on the seafloor. Their abundance as fossils indicates that they were common more than 500 million years ago. The 180 or so known living species of arrow worms are small enough—ranging from 3 millimeters to 12 centimeters in length—that their gas exchange and waste excretion requirements are met by diffusion through the body surface. They lack a circulatory system; wastes and nutrients are moved around the body in the coelomic fluid, which is propelled by cilia that line the coelom.

Arrow worms are hermaphroditic; that is, each individual produces both male and female gametes. In most species, eggs are fertilized internally following elaborate courtship between

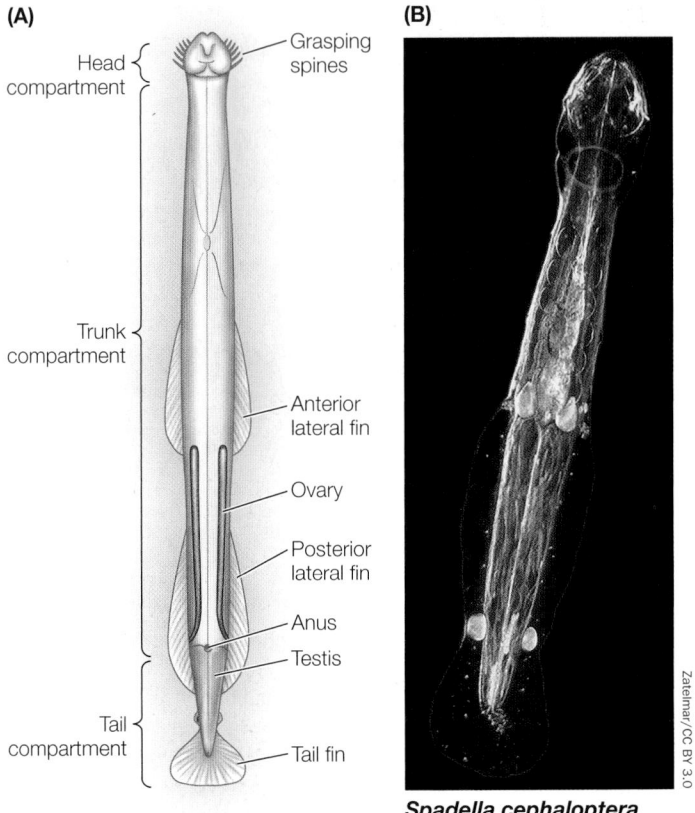

Spadella cephaloptera

Figure 30.5 An Arrow Worm Arrow worms have a three-part body organization. Their fins and grasping spines are adaptations for a predatory lifestyle. Individuals are hermaphroditic, producing both eggs in an ovary and sperm in a testis.

two individuals, although some species can self-fertilize. Miniature adults hatch directly from the eggs; these animals have no distinct larval stage.

Arrow worms are stabilized in the water by means of one or two pairs of lateral fins and a tail fin. They are major predators of planktonic organisms in the open ocean, ranging in size from small protists to young fishes as large as the arrow worms themselves. An arrow worm typically lies motionless in the water until water movement signals the approach of prey. The arrow worm then darts forward and uses the stiff spines adjacent to its mouth to grasp its prey.

KEY CONCEPT
30.1 Recap and Assess

The shared derived traits of protostomes include a blastopore that develops into a mouth (except in arrow worms), an anterior brain, and a ventral nervous system. Several lophotrochozoan groups are characterized by a filter-feeding ciliated structure known as a lophophore or by cilia-bearing larvae known as trochophores. Ecdysozoans, which have a body covering known as a cuticle, must molt periodically in order to grow.

1. How does an animal's body covering influence the way it exchanges gases, feeds, and moves?

2. What features make arthropods well adapted for colonizing terrestrial environments?

In the next key concept we continue our survey of the protostomes with a more detailed look at the major groups of lophotrochozoans and the diverse body forms that are found among them.

KEY CONCEPT 30.2 Many Lophotrochozoans Have Ciliated Feeding Structures or Life Stages

Learning Objectives

30.2.1 Associate major morphological features of protostomes with the environment and life history of the respective organisms.

30.2.2 Provide examples demonstrating how modifications of existing structures can lead to increases is species diversity.

Lophotrochozoans come in a variety of sizes and shapes, ranging from relatively simple animals with a blind gut (that is, a gut with only one opening) and no internal transport system to animals with a complete gut (having separate entrance and exit openings) and a complex internal transport system. They include some species-rich groups, such as flatworms, annelids, and mollusks. Several of these groups have wormlike bodies, but the lophotrochozoans encompass a wide variety of morphologies, including a few groups with external shells. Some lophotrochozoan groups have only recently been discovered by biologists.

Most bryozoans and entoprocts live in colonies

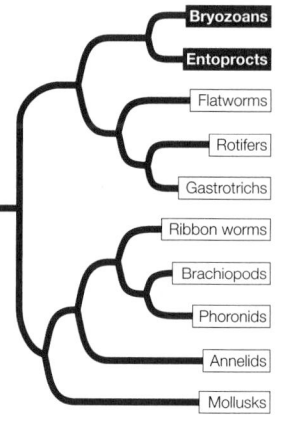

Most of the 5,500 known species of **bryozoans** ("moss animals") and 170 known species of **entoprocts** (meaning "anus inside") are colonial animals that live in a "house" made of material secreted by the external body wall. The colonial species are sessile, but the few solitary species can slowly move around in their environment. Almost all bryozoans and entoprocts are marine, although a few species occur in fresh or brackish water.

A bryozoan colony consists of many small (1–2 mm) individuals connected by strands of tissue along which nutrients can be moved. Bryozoan colonies can grow to contain more than 2 million individuals, all stemming from the asexual reproduction of the colony's founder. Rocks in coastal regions in many parts of the world are covered with luxuriant growths of bryozoans. Some bryozoans create miniature reefs in shallow waters. In some species, the individual colony members are differentially specialized for feeding, reproduction, defense, or support. Individual bryozoans in a colony are able to oscillate their lophophore to increase contact with prey. They can also retract it into their "house" (see Figure 30.2).

Bryozoans can also reproduce sexually. Sperm are released into the water, which carries the sperm to other individuals. Eggs are fertilized internally; developing embryos are brooded before they exit as larvae to seek suitable sites for attachment to the substrate. Entoprocts can also reproduce asexually. Some species of entoprocts release unfertilized eggs into the water for fertilization, whereas other species brood their developing young as bryozoans do.

Bryozoans and entoprocts differ in the placement of the anus. In bryozoans the anus is located outside the ring of tentacles that make up the lophophore, whereas the anus of entoprocts is located in the center of this ring. The lophophores of the two groups also function differently: food particles are carried from the tips to the bases of the tentacles in bryozoans, but from the bases to the tips of the tentacles in entoprocts. Entoprocts lack a coelom, whereas bryozoans have a three-part coelom.

Flatworms, rotifers, and gastrotrichs are structurally diverse relatives

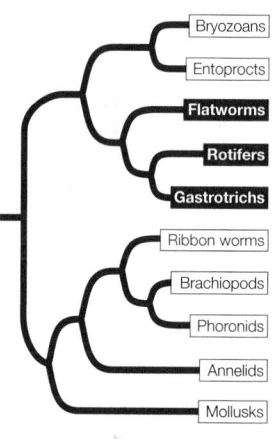

Flatworms, rotifers, gastrotrichs, and their close relatives are a structurally diverse group of organisms whose relationships to one another have been hypothesized only recently. Recent genomic studies show that this monophyletic lophotrochozoan group includes both acoelomate subgroups (e.g., the flatworms) and pseudocoelomate subgroups (e.g., the rotifers and gastrotrichs), and yet the closest relatives of this group—the bryozoans and entoprocts—are coelomate and acoelomate, respectively. Thus this group provides an example of the evolutionary convergence in body cavity form that we described in Key Concept 30.1.

FLATWORMS   **Flatworms** lack specialized organs for transporting oxygen to their internal tissues. In the absence of a gas transport system, each cell must be near a body surface, a requirement met by the dorsoventrally flattened body form that gives these animals their common name. The digestive tract of a free-living flatworm consists of a mouth opening into a blind gut. The gut is often highly branched, forming intricate patterns that increase the surface area available for the absorption of nutrients. Some small free-living flatworms are cephalized, with a head bearing chemoreceptor organs, two simple eyes, and a tiny brain composed of anterior thickenings of the longitudinal nerve cords. Free-living flatworms glide over surfaces on a layer of mucus, powered by broad bands of cilia (**Figure 30.6A**).

Although many flatworms are free-living, most flatworm species are parasites. Of the parasitic species, most are endoparasites. There are also flatworms that feed externally on animal tissues (living or dead), and some graze on plants. A likely evolutionary transition was from feeding on dead organisms to feeding on the body surfaces of dying hosts to invading and consuming parts of healthy hosts.

(A) *Eurylepta californica*, **a free-living flatworm**

© Larry Jon Friesen

(B) **Diagram of a typical parasitic flatworm**

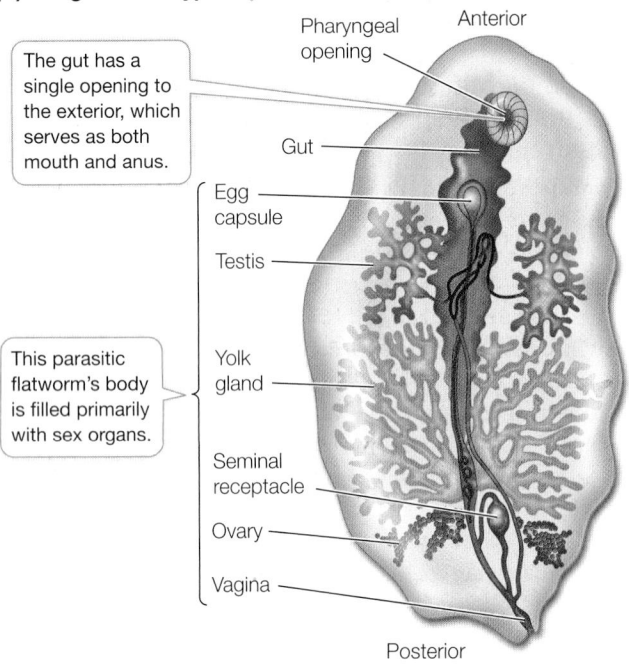

The gut has a single opening to the exterior, which serves as both mouth and anus.

This parasitic flatworm's body is filled primarily with sex organs.

Pharyngeal opening

Anterior

Gut

Egg capsule

Testis

Yolk gland

Seminal receptacle

Ovary

Vagina

Posterior

Figure 30.6 **Flatworms Include Both Parasites and Free-Living Forms** **(A)** Some flatworm species, such as this Pacific marine flatworm, are free-living. **(B)** The fluke diagrammed here lives endoparasitically in the gut of sea urchins and is typical of endoparasitic flatworms. Because their hosts provide all the nutrition they need, these internal parasites do not require elaborate feeding or digestive organs and can devote most of their body to reproduction.

Most of the 30,000 known species of living flatworms are tapeworms and flukes; members of these two groups are endoparasites, particularly of vertebrates (**Figure 30.6B**). Because they absorb digested food from the digestive tracts of their hosts, many endoparasitic flatworms lack digestive tracts of their own. Some cause serious human diseases, such as schistosomiasis, which is common in parts of Asia, Africa, and South America. The species that causes this devastating disease has a complex life cycle involving both freshwater snails and mammals as hosts. Members of another flatworm group, the monogeneans, are ectoparasites of fishes and other aquatic vertebrates. The turbellarians include most of the free-living species.

ROTIFERS   Most species of **rotifers** are tiny (50–500 μm long)—smaller than some ciliate protists—but they have specialized internal organs (**Figure 30.7A,B**). A complete gut passes from an anterior mouth to a posterior anus; the body cavity is a pseudocoel that functions as a hydrostatic skeleton. Rotifers typically propel themselves through the water by means of rapidly beating cilia rather than by muscular contraction.

▶ **Media Clip 30.3 Rotifer Feeding**
Life12e.com/mc30.3

The most distinctive organ of rotifers is a conspicuous ciliated organ called the corona, which surmounts the head of many species. Coordinated beating of the cilia sweeps particles of organic matter from the water into the animal's mouth and down to a complicated structure called the mastax, in which food is ground into small pieces. By contracting muscles around the pseudocoel, a few rotifer species that prey on protists and small animals can protrude the mastax through the mouth and seize small objects with it.

Most of the known species of rotifers live in fresh water. Some species rest on the surfaces of mosses or lichens in a desiccated, inactive state until it rains. When rain falls, they absorb water and become mobile, feeding in the films of water that temporarily cover the plants. Most rotifers live no longer than a few weeks.

Both males and females are found in some species of rotifers, but only females are known among the bdelloid rotifers (the *b* in "bdelloid" is silent). Biologists have concluded that the bdelloid rotifers may have existed for tens of millions of years without regular sexual reproduction. Lack of genetic recombination generally leads to the buildup of deleterious mutations, so long-term asexual reproduction typically leads to extinction. Recent studies, however, have indicated that bdelloid rotifers may avoid this problem by picking up fragments of genes from their environment during the desiccation–rehydration cycle, which allows genetic recombination among individuals in the absence of direct sexual exchange.

Connect the Concepts The consequences of asexual reproduction, and the reasons that it commonly leads to a buildup of deleterious mutations, are discussed in Key Concept 21.3.

A few highly reduced lineages appear to have descended from the free-living rotifers. The spiny-headed worms are parasites with complex life cycles, often parasitizing several animal hosts (**Figure 30.7C**). The jaw worms are tiny marine organisms that glide between sand grains in shallow marine environments. Although spiny-headed worms and jaw worms are structurally quite distinct, molecular analyses have revealed that both groups are essentially highly modified rotifers.

GASTROTRICHS   The 800 known species of **gastrotrichs** (also called "hairy-backs") are abundant, tiny (0.05–3 mm) animals that live in marine sediments, in fresh waters, and in the water films that surround grains of soil. Their transparent bodies have a flat ventral surface that is covered with cilia (**Figure 30.7D**). Most species are simultaneous hermaphrodites, with both male and female reproductive organs, although the male organs have been greatly reduced or lost in some species that reproduce asexually.

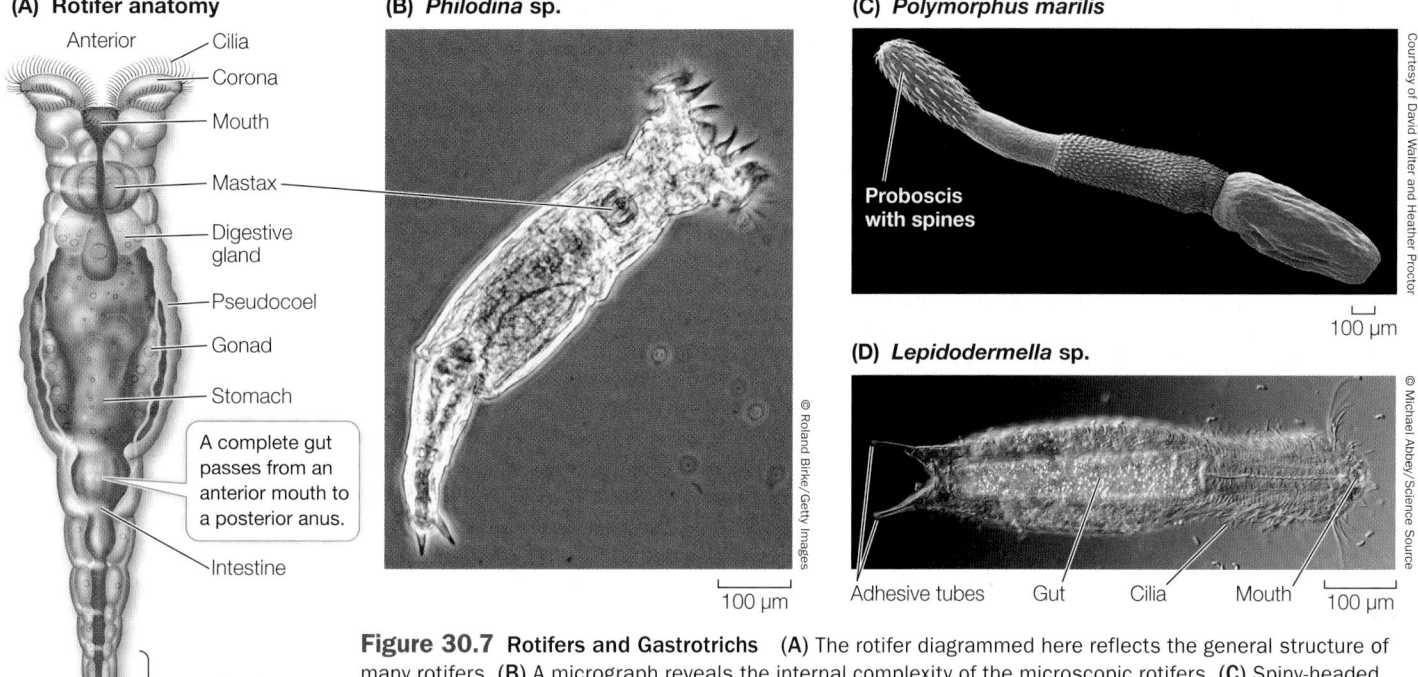

(A) Rotifer anatomy

Anterior
Cilia
Corona
Mouth
Mastax
Digestive gland
Pseudocoel
Gonad
Stomach

A complete gut passes from an anterior mouth to a posterior anus.

Intestine
"Foot" with "toes"
Anus
Posterior

(B) *Philodina* sp.

100 μm

(C) *Polymorphus marilis*

Proboscis with spines

100 μm

(D) *Lepidodermella* sp.

Adhesive tubes   Gut   Cilia   Mouth

100 μm

Figure 30.7 Rotifers and Gastrotrichs (**A**) The rotifer diagrammed here reflects the general structure of many rotifers. (**B**) A micrograph reveals the internal complexity of the microscopic rotifers. (**C**) Spiny-headed worms are parasitic rotifer relatives. The spines of the proboscis anchor the animal to the organs of its host. (**D**) Gastrotrichs superficially resemble rotifers but have flattened ventral surfaces covered with cilia, as flatworms do.

Ribbon worms have a long, protrusible feeding organ

Ribbon worms (or proboscis worms) have simple nervous and excretory systems similar to those of flatworms. Unlike flatworms, however, they have a closed circulatory system and a complete digestive tract with a mouth at one end and an anus at the other. Small ribbon worms move slowly by beating their cilia. Larger ones employ waves of muscle contraction to move over the surface of sediments or to burrow into them.

Within the body of nearly all of the 1,200 known species of ribbon worms is a fluid-filled cavity called the rhynchocoel, within which lies a hollow, muscular **proboscis**. The proboscis, which is the worm's feeding organ, may extend much of the length of the body. Contraction of the muscles surrounding the rhynchocoel causes the proboscis to evert explosively through an anterior pore (**Figure 30.8A**). The proboscis may be armed with sharp stylets that pierce prey and discharge paralysis-causing toxins into the wound.

▶ **Media Clip 30.4**
Explosive Extrusion of Ribbon Worm Proboscis
Life12e.com/mc30.4

Most ribbon worm species are marine, although there are species that live in fresh water or on land. Most species are less than 20 centimeters long, but individuals of some species reach 20

Bryozoans
Entoprocts
Flatworms
Rotifers
Gastrotrichs
Ribbon worms
Brachiopods
Phoronids
Annelids
Mollusks

(A)

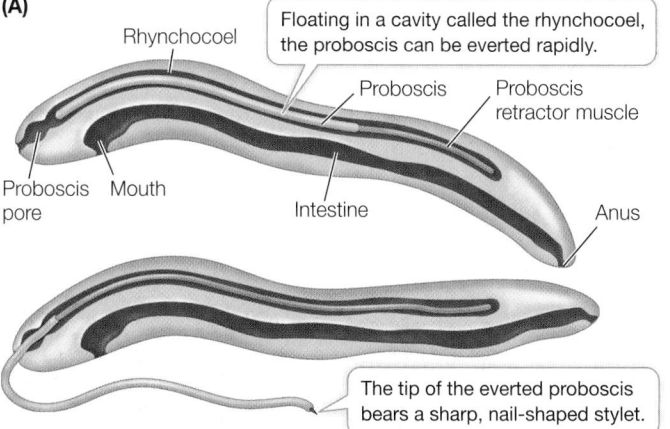

Rhynchocoel

Floating in a cavity called the rhynchocoel, the proboscis can be everted rapidly.

Proboscis   Proboscis retractor muscle

Proboscis pore   Mouth

Intestine   Anus

The tip of the everted proboscis bears a sharp, nail-shaped stylet.

(B) *Baseodiscus cingulatus*

Figure 30.8 Ribbon Worms (**A**) The proboscis is the ribbon worm's feeding organ. (**B**) Although most ribbon worms are small, some marine species such as this one can reach several meters in length.

meters or more. Some genera feature species that are conspicuous and brightly colored (**Figure 30.8B**). Recent molecular analyses suggest that ribbon worms may be most closely related to the brachiopods and phoronids.

Brachiopods and phoronids use lophophores to extract food from the water

Recall that the bryozoans and entoprocts use a lophophore to feed. Brachiopods and phoronids also feed using a lophophore, but this structure may have evolved separately in these groups. Although neither the brachiopods nor the phoronids are represented by many living species, the brachiopods (which have hard external shells and thus leave an excellent fossil record) are known to have been much more abundant in the past.

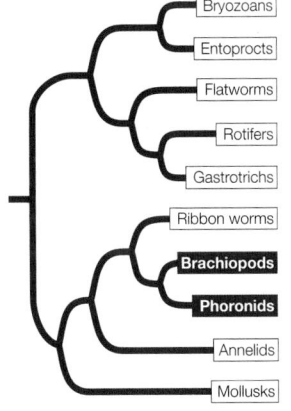

BRACHIOPODS Brachiopods (lampshells) are solitary marine animals. They have a rigid shell that is divided into two parts connected by a ligament (**Figure 30.9**). The two halves can be pulled shut to protect the soft body. Brachiopods superficially resemble bivalve mollusks, but shells have evolved independently in the two groups. The two halves of the brachiopod shell are dorsal and ventral, rather than lateral as in bivalves. The lophophore is located within the shell. The beating of cilia on the lophophore draws water into the slightly opened shell. Food is trapped in the lophophore and directed to a ridge, along which it is transferred to the mouth.

Most brachiopods are 4 to 6 centimeters long. They live attached to a solid substrate or embedded in soft sediments. Most species are attached by means of a short, flexible stalk that holds the animal above the substrate. Gases are exchanged across body surfaces, especially the tentacles of the lophophore. Most brachiopods release their gametes into the water, where they are fertilized. The larvae remain among the plankton for only a few days before they settle and develop into adults.

Laqueus sp.

Figure 30.9 A Brachiopod's Lophophore The lophophore of this North Pacific brachiopod can be seen between the valves of its shell.

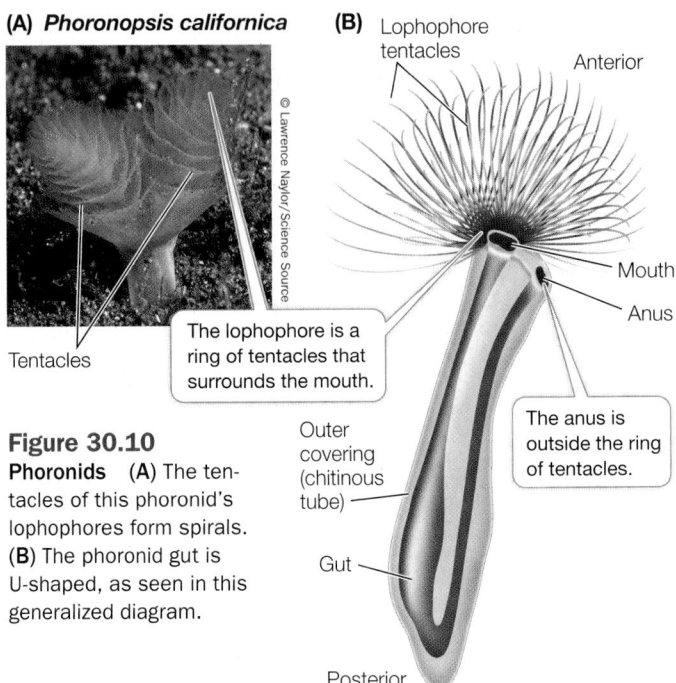

(A) *Phoronopsis californica* **(B)**

The lophophore is a ring of tentacles that surrounds the mouth.

The anus is outside the ring of tentacles.

Figure 30.10
Phoronids **(A)** The tentacles of this phoronid's lophophores form spirals. **(B)** The phoronid gut is U-shaped, as seen in this generalized diagram.

Brachiopods reached their peak abundance and diversity in Paleozoic and Mesozoic times. More than 26,000 fossil species have been described. Only about 450 species are known to survive, but they remain common in some marine environments.

PHORONIDS The ten known species of **phoronids** are small (5–25 cm long), sessile worms that live in muddy or sandy sediments or attached to rocky substrates. Phoronids are found in marine waters from the intertidal zone to about 400 meters deep. They secrete tubes made of chitin, within which they live, and have a U-shaped gut with the anus located outside the lophophore (**Figure 30.10**). Their cilia drive water into the top of the lophophore, and the water exits through the narrow spaces between the tentacles. Suspended food particles are caught and transported to the mouth by ciliary action. Some species release eggs into the water, where they are fertilized, but other species produce large eggs that are fertilized internally and retained in the parent's body, where they are brooded until they hatch.

Annelids have segmented bodies

The wormlike bodies of **annelids** are clearly segmented. As described in Key Concept 29.1, segmentation allows an animal to move different parts of its body independently, giving it much better control of its movement. The earliest segmented worms, preserved as fossils from the middle Cambrian, were burrowing marine annelids.

In most large annelids, the coelom in each segment is isolated

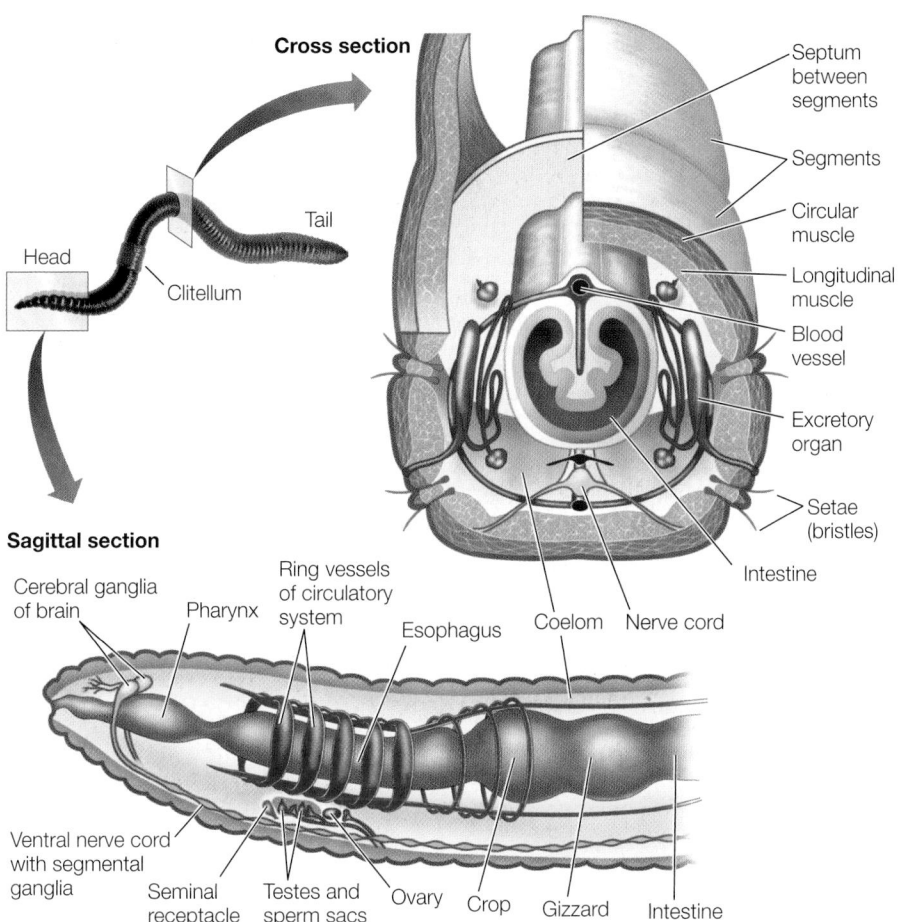

Figure 30.11 Annelids Have Many Body Segments   The segmented structure of annelids such as this earthworm is apparent both externally and internally. Many organs are repeated serially.

from those in other segments (**Figure 30.11**). A separate nerve center called a ganglion (plural ganglia) controls each segment; nerve cords that connect the ganglia coordinate their functioning. Most annelids lack a rigid external protective covering; instead they have a thin, permeable body wall that serves as a general surface for gas exchange. Most annelids are thus restricted to moist environments because they lose body water rapidly in dry air. The approximately 19,000 described species live in marine, freshwater, and moist terrestrial environments.

POLYCHAETES   More than half of all annelid species are commonly known as **polychaetes** ("many hairs"), although this is a descriptive term rather than the name of a single clade. Recent molecular studies indicate that polychaetes are paraphyletic with respect to the remaining annelids. Most polychaetes are marine, and many live in burrows in soft sediments. Most of them have one or more pairs of eyes and one or more pairs of tentacles, with which they capture prey or filter food from the surrounding water, at the anterior end of the body (**Figure 30.12A**; see also Figure 29.7A). In some species, the body wall of most segments extends laterally as a series of thin outgrowths called parapodia. The parapodia function in gas exchange, and some species use them to move. Stiff bristles called setae protrude from each parapodium, forming temporary

contact with the substrate and preventing the animal from slipping backward when its muscles contract.

Members of one polychaete clade, the **pogonophorans**, secrete tubes made of chitin and other substances, in which they live (**Figure 30.12B**). Pogonophorans have lost their digestive tract (they have no mouth or gut). So how do they obtain nutrition? Part of the answer is that pogonophorans can take up dissolved organic matter directly from the sediments in which they live or from the surrounding water. Much of their nutrition, however, is provided by endosymbiotic bacteria that the pogonophorans house in a specialized organ known as the trophosome. These bacteria oxidize hydrogen sulfide and other sulfur-containing compounds, fixing carbon from methane in the process. Uptake of the hydrogen sulfide, methane, and oxygen used by the bacteria is facilitated by hemoglobin in the pogonophorans' tentacles. It is this hemoglobin that gives the tentacles their red coloration.

Pogonophorans were not discovered until early in the twentieth century, when the first species were discovered on the seafloor at depths of up to a few hundred meters. In recent decades, deep-sea explorers have found them living many thousands of meters below the ocean surface. In these deep oceanic sediments, they may reach densities of many thousands per square meter. About 160 species have been described. The largest and most remarkable pogonophorans are 2 meters or more in length and live near deep-sea hydrothermal vents—volcanic openings in the seafloor through which hot, sulfide-rich water pours. The methane and hydrogen sulfide from these vents provide the raw materials for carbon fixation by the pogonophorans' endosymbiotic bacteria.

CLITELLATES   The approximately 3,000 described species of **clitellates**, which form a well-supported clade within the annelids, are found in freshwater, marine, and terrestrial environments. The clitellates appear to be phylogenetically nested among various groups of polychaetes, although the exact relationships are not yet clear. There are two major groups of clitellates, the oligochaetes and the leeches.

Oligochaetes ("few hairs") have no parapodia, eyes, or anterior tentacles, and they have only four pairs of setae bundles per segment. Earthworms—the most familiar oligochaetes—burrow in and ingest soil, from which they extract food particles. All oligochaetes are hermaphroditic. Sperm are exchanged simultaneously between two copulating individuals (**Figure 30.12C**). Eggs and sperm are deposited in a cocoon outside the adult's body. Fertilization occurs within the cocoon after it is shed, and when development is complete, miniature worms emerge and immediately begin independent life.

(A) *Spirographis spallanzanii*

(B) *Riftia* sp.

(C) *Lumbricus terrestris*

(D) *Hirudo medicinalis*

Figure 30.12 Diversity among the Annelids **(A)** Fan worms, or "feather duster worms," are sessile marine polychaetes that grow in masses, filtering food from the water with their tentacles. This individual has been removed from its chitinous tube. **(B)** Pogonophorans live around hydrothermal vents deep in the ocean. Their tentacles can be seen protruding from their chitinous tubes. **(C)** Earthworms, like all oligochaetes, are hermaphroditic; when they copulate, each individual donates and receives sperm. **(D)** The medicinal leech has been a tool of physicians and healers for centuries. Even today, leeches have uses in clinical practice.

Leeches, like oligochaetes, lack parapodia and tentacles. The coelom of leeches is not divided into compartments; the coelomic space is largely filled with undifferentiated tissue. Groups of segments at each end of the body are modified to form suckers, which serve as temporary anchors that aid the leech in its movement. With its posterior sucker attached to a substrate, the leech extends its body by contracting its circular muscles. The anterior sucker is then attached, the posterior one detached, and the leech shortens itself by contracting its longitudinal muscles. Leeches live in freshwater or terrestrial habitats.

Most leeches are ectoparasites that feed by making an incision in a host, from which blood flows. A leech can ingest so much blood in a single feeding that its body may enlarge severalfold. The leech secretes an anticoagulant into the wound that keeps the host's blood flowing. For centuries, medical practitioners employed leeches to draw blood to treat diseases they believed were caused by an excess of blood or by "bad blood." Although most leeching practices (such as inserting a leech in a person's throat to alleviate swollen tonsils) have been abandoned, *Hirudo medicinalis* (the medicinal leech; **Figure 30.12D**) is used today to reduce fluid pressure and prevent blood clotting in damaged tissues, to eliminate pools of coagulated blood, and to prevent scarring. The anticoagulants of certain other leech species also contain anesthetics and blood vessel dilators and are being studied for possible medical uses.

Media Clip 30.5 Leeches Feeding on Blood
Life12e.com/mc30.5

Mollusks have undergone a dramatic evolutionary radiation

Mollusks are the most diverse group of lophotrochozoans, both in numbers of species and in the environments they occupy. Although the major groups of mollusks differ dramatically in morphology, they all share the same three major body components: a foot, a visceral mass, and a mantle (**Figure 30.13A**).

1. The molluscan foot is a large, muscular structure that originally was both an organ of locomotion and a support for the internal organs. In squid and octopuses, the foot has been modified to form arms and tentacles borne on a head with complex sensory organs. In other groups, such as clams, the foot is a burrowing organ. In some groups the foot is greatly reduced.

2. The heart and the digestive, excretory, and reproductive organs are concentrated in a centralized, internal **visceral mass**.

3. The **mantle** is a fold of tissue that covers the organs of the visceral mass. The mantle secretes the hard, calcareous shell that is typical of many mollusks.

In most mollusks, the mantle extends beyond the visceral mass to form a mantle cavity. Within this cavity lie gills that are used

Bryozoans
Entoprocts
Flatworms
Rotifers
Gastrotrichs
Ribbon worms
Brachiopods
Phoronids
Annelids
Mollusks

(A) Generalized molluscan body plan

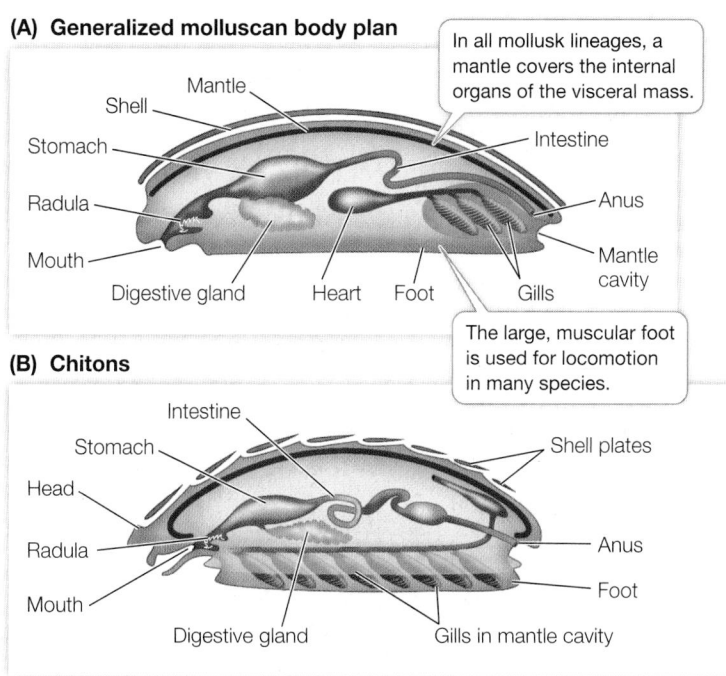

In all mollusk lineages, a mantle covers the internal organs of the visceral mass.

Labels: Mantle, Shell, Stomach, Radula, Mouth, Digestive gland, Heart, Foot, Gills, Intestine, Anus, Mantle cavity

The large, muscular foot is used for locomotion in many species.

Figure 30.13 Organization and Diversity of Molluscan Bodies (A) The major molluscan groups display different variations on a body plan that includes three major components: a foot, a visceral mass of internal organs, and a mantle. In many species, the mantle secretes a calcareous shell. (B) Chitons have eight overlapping calcareous plates surrounded by a girdle. (C) Most gastropods have a single dorsal shell, into which they can retreat for protection. (D) Bivalves get their name from their two hinged shells, which can be tightly closed. (E) Cephalopods are active predators; they use their arms and tentacles to capture prey. This squid has an internal shell but no external shell.

(B) Chitons

Labels: Intestine, Stomach, Head, Radula, Mouth, Digestive gland, Shell plates, Anus, Foot, Gills in mantle cavity

Tonicella lineata

© Larry Jon Friesen

(C) Gastropods

Labels: Intestine, Mantle, Gill, Anus, Siphon, Cephalic tentacles, Head, Mouth, Mantle cavity, Shell, Heart, Digestive gland, Stomach, Foot

The radula is a unique molluscan feeding structure modified for scraping.

Helix sp.

© Dimitri Vervitsiotis/Getty Images

(D) Bivalves

Labels: Digestive gland, Stomach, Mouth, Mantle (covers inside of shell), Foot, Shell, Heart, Intestine, Anus, Siphons, Gill, Mantle of lower shell

Argopecten irradians

© Stephen Frink/Getty Images

(E) Cephalopods

Labels: Arms, Beak, Head, Intestine, Shell, Stomach, Mantle, Tentacle, Radula, Siphon, Mantle cavity, Gill, Heart, Digestive gland

In cephalopod mollusks, the foot is modified into arms and tentacles.

Sepioteuthis lessoniana

© Jones/Shimlock-Secret Sea Visions/Getty Images

for gas exchange. When cilia on the gills beat, they create a current of water. The tissue of the gills, which is highly vascularized (contains many blood vessels), takes up oxygen from the water and releases carbon dioxide. Many mollusk species use their gills as filter-feeding devices, whereas others feed using a rasping structure known as a **radula** to scrape algae from rocks. In some mollusks, such as the marine cone snails, the radula has been modified into a drill or poison dart.

In all mollusks except cephalopods, the blood vessels do not form a closed system. Blood and other fluids empty into a large, fluid-filled hemocoel, through which fluids move and deliver oxygen to the internal organs. Eventually the fluids reenter the blood vessels and are moved by a heart.

Monoplacophorans were the most abundant mollusks during the Cambrian, 500 million years ago, but only a few species survive today. In monoplacophorans, in contrast to all other living mollusks, the gas exchange organs, muscles, and excretory pores are repeated over the length of the body.

The four major clades of living mollusks are the chitons, gastropods, bivalves, and cephalopods. Each of these groups is readily identifiable and distinct, even though they share variations on a common body plan.

CHITONS   Eight overlapping calcareous plates, surrounded by a structure known as the girdle, protect the internal organs and muscular foot of **chitons** (Figure 30.13B). The chiton body is bilaterally symmetrical, and the internal organs, particularly the digestive and nervous systems, are relatively simple. Most chitons are marine omnivores that scrape algae, bryozoans, and other organisms from rocks with a sharp radula. An adult chiton spends most of its life clinging tightly to rock surfaces with its large, muscular, mucus-covered foot. It moves slowly by means of rippling waves of muscular contraction in the foot. Fertilization in most chitons takes place in the water, but in a few species fertilization is internal and embryos are brooded within the body. There are approximately 1,000 living species of chitons known.

GASTROPODS   **Gastropods** (Figure 30.13C) are the most species-rich and widely distributed mollusks, with about 85,000 known living species. Snails, whelks, limpets, slugs, nudibranchs (sea slugs), and abalones are all gastropods. Most species move by gliding on the muscular foot, but in a few species—the sea butterflies and heteropods—the foot is a swimming organ with which the animal moves through open ocean waters.

Marine nudibranchs and terrestrial slugs are gastropods that have lost their protective shell over the course of evolution (Figure 30.14). Without a shell, these groups rely on other forms of protection from predation. The coloration of many nudibranchs is aposematic, meaning that it serves to warn potential predators of toxicity. Other nudibranch species and most terrestrial slugs exhibit camouflaged coloration.

Shelled gastropods have one-piece shells. The only mollusks that live in terrestrial environments—land snails and slugs—are gastropods. In these terrestrial species, the mantle tissue is modified into a highly vascularized lung.

(A) *Chromodoris kuniei*

(B) *Deroceras* sp.

(C) *Octopus bimaculoides*

Figure 30.14 Mollusks in Some Groups Have Lost Their Shells
(A) Nudibranchs ("naked gills"), also called sea slugs, are shell-less gastropods. This species is brightly colored, alerting potential predators of its toxicity. **(B)** Slugs are terrestrial, shell-less gastropods that feed on decomposing vegetation on the damp forest floor. **(C)** Octopuses have neither an external nor an internal shell, which allows these cephalopods to squeeze through tight spaces.

 Media Clip 30.6 Octopuses Can Pass through Small Openings
Life12e.com/mc30.6

BIVALVES   Clams, oysters, scallops, and mussels are all familiar **bivalves**. The approximately 30,000 known species are found in both marine and freshwater environments. Bivalves have a hinged, two-part shell that extends over the sides of the body as well as the top (Figure 30.13D). Many clams use the foot to burrow into mud and sand. Bivalves feed by taking in water through an opening called an incurrent siphon and filtering food from the water with their large gills, which are also the main sites of gas exchange.

Water and gametes exit through the excurrent siphon. Fertilization takes place in open water in most species.

CEPHALOPODS The **cephalopods**— squid, cuttlefishes, octopuses, and nautiluses—first appeared near the beginning of the Cambrian. By the Ordovician a variety of types were present. Today there are about 800 described living species. In these mollusks the excurrent siphon is modified to allow the animal to control the volume of the mantle cavity and thereby bring in or expel water (**Figure 30.13E**). The modification of the mantle into a device for forcibly ejecting water from the cavity through the siphon enables these animals to move rapidly through the water by "jet propulsion." With their greatly enhanced mobility, cephalopods became the major predators in the open waters of the Devonian oceans. They remain important marine predators today.

As is typical of active, rapidly moving predators, cephalopods have a head with complex sensory organs—most notably eyes that are comparable to those of vertebrates in their ability to resolve images. The head is closely associated with a large, branched foot that bears the arms and/or tentacles and a siphon. Arms are distinguished by the presence of suckers along most of their length. Tentacles, in contrast, have suckers only near the tips or lack suckers altogether. Octopuses typically have eight arms and no tentacles, whereas squid and cuttlefishes have eight arms plus two tentacles. Cephalopods use their arms and tentacles to capture and subdue prey; octopuses also use their arms to move over the substrate. The large, muscular mantle provides a solid external supporting structure. The gills hang in the mantle cavity.

Many early cephalopods had an external chambered shell divided by partitions. The only surviving cephalopods with such shells are the nautiluses (genus *Nautilus*). The chambers inside nautilus shells are connected by a strand of tissue that runs through ducts in the partitions. Blood in this tissue carries water *from* the chambers and gases *into* the chambers, thus providing buoyancy. Most cephalopods retain an internal shell that functions for internal support and, in some species, is also chambered and buoyant. Octopuses have completely lost their shells, which allows them to compress their bodies through very small openings.

KEY CONCEPT
30.2 Recap and Assess

Lophotrochozoans include animals with diverse body types. Wormlike forms include some flatworms, ribbon worms, phoronids, and annelids. There has been convergent evolution of lophophores (in bryozoans and entoprocts versus brachiopods and phoronids) and of external two-part shell coverings (in brachiopods versus bivalve mollusks).

1. How do flatworms survive without an internal transport system?

2. Why are most annelids restricted to moist environments?

3. Mollusks have evolved a great diversity of body plans. Provide some examples that demonstrate how the basic body organization of mollusks has been modified to yield this diversity.

The second of the two major protostome clades, the ecdysozoans, contains the vast majority of Earth's animal species. What evolutionary innovations led to this massive diversity?

KEY CONCEPT
30.3 Ecdysozoans Grow by Shedding Their Cuticles

Learning Objectives

30.3.1 Compare cuticle thickness in the different ecdysozoans and explain the consequences of such variation.

30.3.2 Explain why the nematode *Caenorhabditis elegans* is a widely used model system in laboratory research.

30.3.3 Explain why nematode diversity is important to global ecosystems.

30.3.4 Provide examples of nematodes that are human parasites.

Many ecdysozoans are wormlike in form, although others—the arthropods, velvet worms (onychophorans), and tardigrades—have limbs. In this key concept we look at the two clades of wormlike ecdysozoans: the priapulids, kinorhynchs, and loriciferans in one clade and the nematodes and horsehair worms in the other. Key Concept 30.4 is devoted to the most diverse ecdysozoans—the arthropods and their relatives—and the many forms their appendages take.

As we noted in Key Concept 30.1, ecdysozoans can be identified by the presence of a body covering known as a cuticle, which provides these animals with both protection and support. The name of the group, Ecdysozoa, is derived from the Greek *ecdysis* ("to get out of") plus *zoa* ("animals"). Periodic shedding of the cuticle is necessary so that ecdysozoans can grow. In many ecdysozoans that have wormlike bodies, the cuticle is relatively thin and flexible; it offers the animal some protection but provides only modest body support. A thin cuticle allows the exchange of gases, minerals, and water across the body surface, but it restricts the animal to moist habitats. Many species of ecdysozoans with thin cuticles live in marine sediments from which they obtain food, either by ingesting sediments and extracting organic material from them or by capturing larger prey using a toothed **pharynx** (a muscular organ at the anterior end of the digestive tract). Some freshwater species absorb nutrients directly through their thin cuticles, as do parasitic species that live within their hosts (endoparasites). Many wormlike ecdysozoans are predators, eating protists and small animals.

Several marine ecdysozoan groups have relatively few species

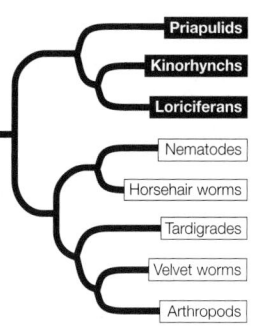

Members of three species-poor groups of wormlike marine ecdysozoans—the priapulids, kinorhynchs, and loriciferans—have relatively thin cuticles that are molted periodically as the animals grow to full size. Embryos of a fossil species related to these ecdysozoans have been discovered in sediments laid down in China about 500 million years ago. This remarkable discovery shows that the ancestors of these animals developed directly from an egg to the adult form, as most of their modern descendants do.

The 20 known species of **priapulids** are cylindrical, unsegmented, wormlike animals with a three-part body plan consisting of a proboscis, trunk, and caudal appendage ("tail"). It should be clear from their appearance why they were named after the Greek fertility god Priapus (**Figure 30.15A**). Priapulids range in length from 0.5 millimeters to 20 centimeters. They live in burrows in fine marine sediments and prey on soft-bodied invertebrates such as polychaetes, which they capture with a toothed, muscular pharynx that they evert through the mouth and then withdraw into the body together with the grasped prey. Fertilization is external, and most species have a larval form that also lives in the mud.

About 180 species of **kinorhynchs** have been described. They live in marine sands and muds and are virtually microscopic; no kinorhynchs are longer than 1 millimeter. Their bodies are divided into 13 segments, each covered with a separate cuticular plate (**Figure 30.15B**). These plates are periodically molted during growth. Kinorhynchs feed by ingesting sediments through a retractable proboscis (the group name means "movable snout"). They then digest the organic material found in the sediment, which may include living algae as well as dead matter. Kinorhynchs have no distinct larval stage; fertilized eggs develop directly into juveniles, which emerge from their egg cases with 11 of the 13 body segments already formed.

Loriciferans are also minute animals less than 1 millimeter long. They were not discovered until 1983. About 100 living species are known to exist, although only about 30 of these have been formally described to date. The body is divided into a head, neck, thorax, and abdomen and is covered by six plates, from which the loriciferans get their name (Latin *lorica*, "corset"). The plates around the base of the neck bear anterior-directed spines of unknown function (**Figure 30.15C**). Loriciferans live in coarse marine sediments. Little is known about what they eat, but some species apparently eat bacteria.

Nematodes and their relatives are abundant and diverse

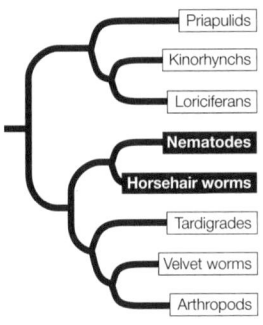

Nematodes (roundworms) have a thick, multilayered cuticle that gives their unsegmented body its shape (**Figure 30.16**). As a nematode grows, it sheds its cuticle four times. Nematodes exchange oxygen and nutrients with their environment through both the cuticle and the gut wall, which is only one cell layer thick. Materials are moved through the gut by rhythmic contraction of a highly muscular pharynx. Nematodes move by contracting their longitudinal muscles.

Nematodes are probably the most abundant and universally distributed of all animal groups. Many nematodes are microscopic; the largest known nematode, which reaches a length of 9 meters, is a parasite in the placentas of sperm whales (*Physeter macrocephalus*). About 25,000 species have been described, but the actual number of living species may be more than 1 million. Countless nematodes live as scavengers in the upper layers of the soil, on the bottoms of lakes and streams, and in marine sediments. The topsoil of rich farmland may contain contain over 20 billion nematodes per hectare. A single rotting apple may contain as many as 90,000 individuals.

(A) *Priapulus caudatus* Proboscis
Trunk
Caudal appendage ("tail")
Courtesy of Jen Grenier and Sean Carroll, U. Wisconsin

(B) *Pycnophyes kielensis*
Cuticular plates
G. E. Budd. 2004. *Nature* 427: 205–207. Courtesy of Graham Budd

(C) *Nanaloricus mysticus*
Proboscis
Spines
Cuticular plates
Courtesy of Reinhardt Møbjerg Kristensen

Figure 30.15 Wormlike Marine Ecdysozoans Members of three ecdysozoan groups are marine bottom-dwellers. **(A)** Most priapulid species live in burrows on the ocean floor, extending the proboscis to feed. **(B)** Kinorhynchs are virtually microscopic. The cuticular plates that cover their bodies are molted periodically. **(C)** Six cuticular plates form a "corset" around the minute loriciferan body.

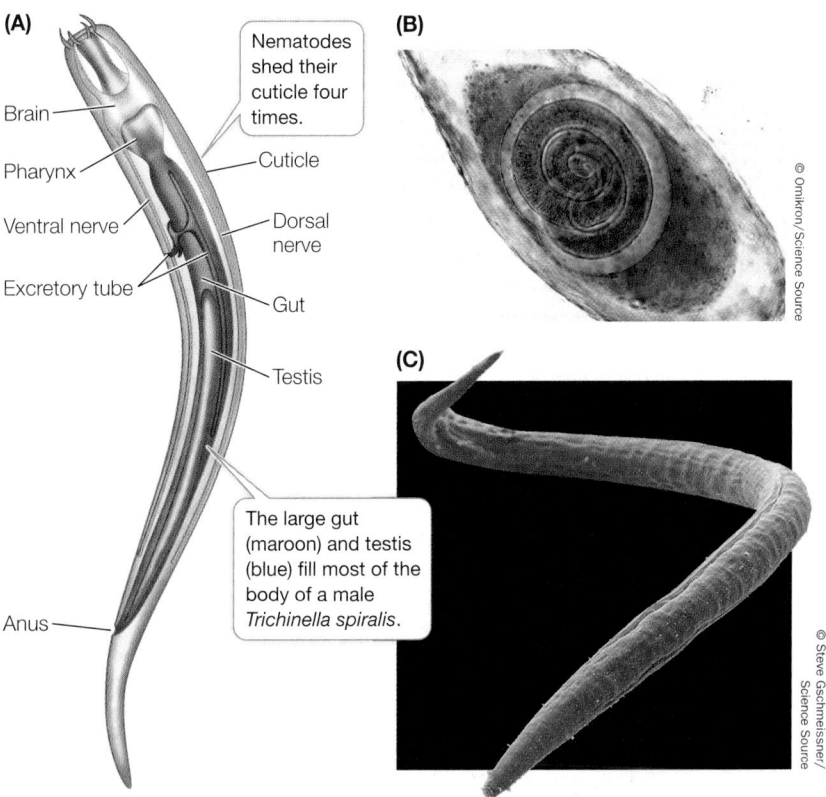

Figure 30.16 Nematodes **(A)** The body plan of *Trichinella spiralis*, which causes trichinosis, is typical of parasitic nematodes. **(B)** This polarized light micrograph shows a cyst of *T. spiralis* in the muscle tissue of a host. **(C)** This free-living nematode lives in freshwater environments.

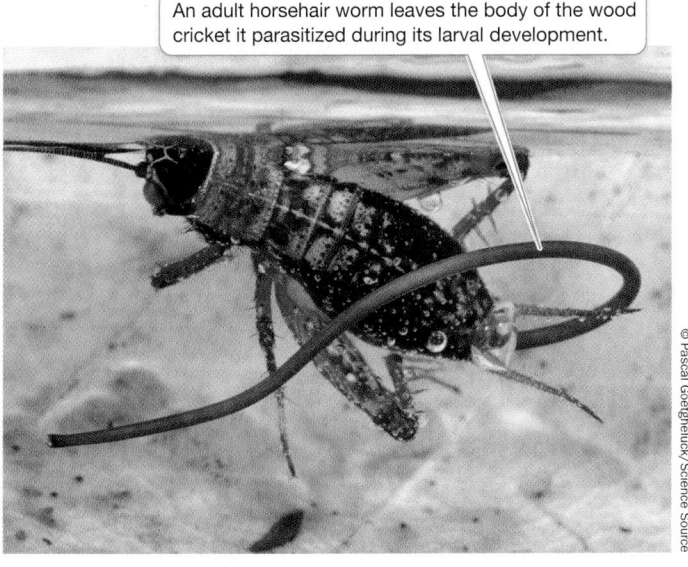

Figure 30.17 Horsehair Worm Larvae Are Parasitic The larva of this horsehair worm (*Paragordius tricuspidatus*) can manipulate its host's behavior. The hatching worm causes the cricket to jump into water, where the worm emerges from the insect's body to continue its life cycle as a free-living adult. The cricket, having delivered its parasitic burden, drowns.

One soil-inhabiting nematode, *Caenorhabditis elegans*, serves as a model organism in the laboratories of geneticists and developmental biologists. It is ideal for such research because it is easy to cultivate, matures in 3 days, and has a fixed number of body cells. Its genome has been completely sequenced.

Many nematodes are predators, feeding on protists and small animals (including other roundworms). Most significant to humans, however, are the many species that parasitize plants and animals. The nematodes that parasitize humans (causing serious diseases such as trichinosis and elephantiasis), domestic animals, and economically important plants have been studied intensively in an effort to find ways of controlling them.

The structure of parasitic nematodes is similar to that of free-living species, but the life cycles of many parasitic species have special stages that facilitate the transfer of individuals among hosts. *Trichinella spiralis*, the species that causes the human disease trichinosis, has a relatively simple life cycle. A person may become infected by eating the flesh of an animal (usually a pig) that has *Trichinella* larvae encysted in its muscles (see Figure 30.16B). The larvae are activated in the person's digestive tract, emerge from their cysts, and attach to the intestinal wall, where they feed. Later they bore through the intestinal wall and are carried in the bloodstream to muscles, where they form new cysts. If present in great numbers, these cysts can cause severe pain or death.

About 350 species of the unsegmented **horsehair worms** have been described. As their name implies, these animals are extremely thin in diameter; horsehair worms range from a few millimeters up to 1 meter in length. Most adult worms live in fresh water, among leaf litter and algal mats near the edges of streams and ponds. A few species live in damp soil.

Horsehair worm larvae are endoparasites of freshwater crayfishes and of terrestrial and aquatic insects (**Figure 30.17**). An adult horsehair worm has no mouth, and its gut is greatly reduced and probably nonfunctional. Some species may feed only as larvae, absorbing nutrients from their hosts across the body wall. But other species continue to shed their cuticles and grow after they have left their hosts, suggesting that adult worms may also absorb nutrients from their environment.

KEY CONCEPT
30.3 Recap and Assess

Priapulids, kinorhynchs, and loriciferans are relatively small, poorly known groups of wormlike marine ecdysozoans. Nematodes and horsehair worms have unsegmented wormlike bodies. Nematodes are among the most abundant and widely distributed animal groups.

1. How and why does cuticle thickness vary among the ecdysozoans?

2. Describe at least three ways in which nematodes have significant impacts on humans.

We turn next to the animals that not only dominate the ecdysozoan clade but also constitute the most diverse group of animals on Earth.

KEY CONCEPT

KEY CONCEPT 30.4 Arthropods Are the Most Abundant and Diverse Group of Animals

Learning Objectives

30.4.1 Describe morphological innovations of arthropods and their effects on arthropod diversity.

30.4.2 Distinguish among the two different forms of metamorphosis in arthropods.

30.4.3 Explain how the evolutionary innovations among arthropods are related to the habitats in which they live.

Arthropods and their relatives are ecdysozoans with paired appendages. Arthropods are the most diverse group of animals in numbers of species (more than 1.2 million have been described, and many more remain to be discovered). Furthermore, the number of individual arthropods alive at any one time is estimated to be about 10^{18}, or 1 billion billion. Among the animals, only the nematodes are thought to exist in greater numbers.

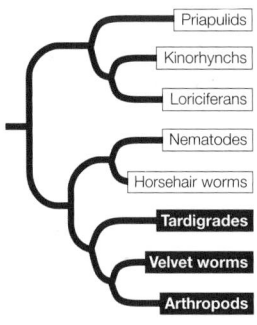

Priapulids
Kinorhynchs
Loriciferans
Nematodes
Horsehair worms
Tardigrades
Velvet worms
Arthropods

Several key features have contributed to the success of the arthropods. As you have seen, their muscles are attached to the inside of their rigid exoskeletons. Their bodies are segmented, and each segment has muscles that operate that segment and the jointed appendages attached to it (see Figure 30.4). Jointed appendages permit complex movements, and different appendages are specialized for different functions. Encasement of the body within a rigid exoskeleton provides the animal with support for walking in the water or on dry land and provides some protection against predators. The waterproofing provided by chitin keeps the animal from dehydrating in dry air.

The four major arthropod groups living today are all species-rich: chelicerates (including the arachnids—spiders, scorpions, mites, and their relatives), myriapods (millipedes and centipedes), crustaceans (including shrimps, crabs, and barnacles), and hexapods (insects and their wingless relatives). The latter three groups are together known as mandibulates.

The jointed appendages of arthropods gave the clade its name, from the Greek words *arthron*, "joint," and *podos*, "foot" or "limb." Arthropods evolved from ancestors with simple, unjointed appendages. The exact forms of those ancestors are unknown, but some arthropod relatives with segmented bodies and unjointed appendages survive today. Before we describe the modern arthropods, we discuss those arthropod relatives, as well as an early clade that went extinct but left an important fossil record.

Arthropod relatives have fleshy, unjointed appendages

The two living groups most closely related to the arthropods provide us with clues about the likely appearance of ancestral arthropod appendages. **Tardigrades** (water bears) have fleshy, unjointed legs and use their fluid-filled body cavity as a hydrostatic skeleton (**Figure 30.18A**). Tardigrades are tiny (0.5–1.5 mm long) and lack both a circulatory system and gas exchange organs. The 1,200 known extant species live in marine sands and on temporary water films on plants. When these films dry out, the animals also lose water and shrink to small, barrel-shaped objects that can survive for at least a decade in a dormant state. Tardigrades have been found at densities as high as 2 million per square meter of moss.

Until fairly recently, biologists debated whether the **velvet worms** (onychophorans) were more closely related to annelids or to arthropods, but molecular evidence clearly links them to the latter. Indeed, with their soft, fleshy, unjointed, claw-bearing legs and elongated bodies, velvet worms may be similar in appearance to the ancestors of arthropods (**Figure 30.18B**). The 180 known

(A) *Macrobiotus sapiens*

© Eye of Science/Science Source

(B) *Macroperipatus torquatus*

© George Grall/National Geographic Creative/Alamy Stock Photo

Figure 30.18 Arthropod Relatives with Unjointed Appendages **(A)** Tardigrades (water bears) can be abundant on the wet surfaces of mosses and plants and in temporary pools of water. **(B)** Velvet worms have unjointed legs and use the body cavity as a hydrostatic skeleton. They are sometimes referred to as "living fossils," meaning they are an ancient group that has changed very little over millennia.

Cheirurus ingricus

Figure 30.19 A Trilobite Fossil The relatively simple, repetitive segments of the now-extinct trilobites are illustrated by a fossil trilobite from the shallow seas of the Ordovician, some 450 million years ago.

species of velvet worms live in leaf litter in humid tropical environments. They have soft, segmented bodies that are covered by a thin, flexible cuticle that contains chitin. Like the tardigrades, velvet worms use their fluid-filled cavity as a hydrostatic skeleton. Fertilization is internal, and the large, yolky eggs are brooded within the body of the female.

Jointed appendages appeared in the trilobites

The **trilobites** flourished in Cambrian and Ordovician seas, but they disappeared in the great Permian extinction at the close of the Paleozoic (251 million years ago). Because they had heavy exoskeletons that readily fossilized, they left behind an abundant record of their existence (**Figure 30.19**). About 10,000 species have been described.

The trilobites are the earliest known arthropods to have had jointed appendages. The body segmentation and appendages of trilobites followed a relatively simple, repetitive plan, but some of their appendages were modified for different functions. This specialization of appendages is a theme in the continuing evolution of the arthropods.

Chelicerates have pointed, nonchewing mouthparts

In the **chelicerates**, the head bears two pairs of pointed appendages modified to form mouthparts, called chelicerae, that are used to grasp (rather than chew) prey. Chelicerates typically have a two-part body plan, with anterior segments fused to form a cephalothorax, and rear segments fused to form an abdomen. In some groups, such as mites and ticks, there is no clear distinction between these two body parts. Most chelicerates have four pairs of walking legs. The 114,000 described species are grouped into three major clades: sea spiders (pycnogonids), horseshoe crabs, and arachnids.

The sea spiders, make up a poorly known group of about 1,000 marine species (**Figure 30.20A**). Most are small, with leg spans less than 1 centimeter, but some deep-sea species have leg spans up to 60 centimeters. A few sea spiders eat algae, but most are carnivorous, eating a variety of small invertebrates.

There are only four living species of horseshoe crabs, but many close relatives are known from fossils. Horseshoe crabs, which have changed very little morphologically over their long history, have a large horseshoe-shaped covering over most of the body. They are common in shallow waters along the eastern coast of North America and the southern and eastern coasts of Asia, where they scavenge and prey on bottom-dwelling animals. Periodically they crawl into the intertidal zone in large numbers to mate and lay eggs (**Figure 30.20B**).

Arachnids are abundant in terrestrial environments. Most arachnids have a simple life cycle in which miniature adults hatch from internally fertilized eggs and begin independent lives almost immediately. Some arachnids retain their eggs during development and give birth to live young.

The most species-rich and abundant arachnids are the spiders, scorpions, harvestmen, mites, and ticks (**Figure 30.21**). More than 60,000 described species of mites and ticks live in soil, leaf litter, mosses, and lichens, under bark, and as parasites of plants and animals. Mites are vectors for wheat and rye mosaic viruses; they cause mange in domestic animals and skin irritation in humans.

Spiders, of which about 50,000 species have been described, are important terrestrial predators with hollow chelicerae, which they use to inject venom into their prey. Some have excellent vision that enables them to chase and seize their prey. Others spin elaborate webs made of protein threads in which they snare prey. The threads are produced by modified abdominal appendages connected to internal glands that secrete the proteins, which solidify on contact with air. The webs of different groups of spiders are strikingly varied, and this variation enables the spiders to position their snares in many different environments for many different types of prey.

(A) *Pseudopallene* sp.

(B) *Limulus polyphemus*

Figure 30.20 Two Small Chelicerate Groups **(A)** Although they are not spiders, it is easy to see how sea spiders got their common name. **(B)** A spawning aggregation of horseshoe crabs. Horseshoe crabs, like the velvet worms (see Figure 30.18B), are an example of "living fossils."

(A) *Simaetha* sp.

(B) *Androctonus* sp.

(C) *Leiobunum rotundum*

(D) *Brevipalpus phoenicis*

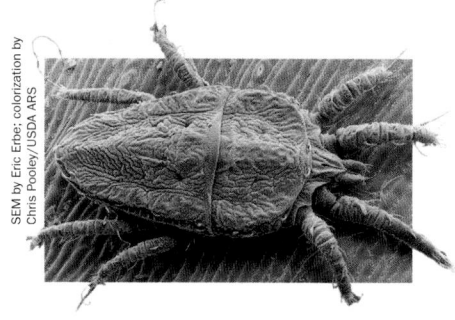

Figure 30.21 Arachnid Diversity **(A)** Jumping spiders are active, visually oriented, diurnal predators of insects. **(B)** Scorpions are nocturnal predators of small animals. **(C)** Harvestmen, also called daddy longlegs, are scavengers. **(D)** Mites include many free-living species as well as blood-sucking ectoparasites.

(A) *Scolopendra hardwickei*

(B) *Polydesmus* sp.

Figure 30.22 Myriapods **(A)** Centipedes have modified appendages that function as poisonous fangs for capturing active prey. They have one pair of legs per segment. **(B)** Millipedes are scavengers and plant eaters; they have smaller jaws and legs than centipedes do, and they have two pairs of legs per segment.

Mandibles and antennae characterize the remaining arthropod groups

The remaining three arthropod groups—the myriapods, crustaceans, and hexapods—have mouthparts that are mandibles, rather than chelicerae, so they are collectively called **mandibulates**. Mandibles can be used for chewing as well as for biting and holding food. Another distinctive characteristic of the mandibulates is the presence of sensory antennae on the head.

MYRIAPODS   The **myriapods** comprise the centipedes, millipedes, and their close relatives. Centipedes and millipedes have a well-formed head that bears the mandibles and antennae characteristic of mandibulates. Their distinguishing feature is a long, flexible, segmented trunk that bears many pairs of legs. Centipedes, which have one pair of legs per segment (**Figure 30.22A**), prey on insects and other small animals. In millipedes, two adjacent segments are fused so that each fused segment has two pairs of legs (**Figure 30.22B**). Millipedes scavenge and eat plants. More than 3,000 species of centipedes and 9,000 species of millipedes have been described; many more species probably remain unknown. Although most myriapods are less than a few centimeters long, some tropical species are ten times that size.

CRUSTACEANS   **Crustaceans** are the dominant marine arthropods today, and they are also common in fresh water and some terrestrial environments. The most familiar crustaceans are the shrimps, lobsters, crayfishes, and crabs (all decapods; **Figure 30.23A**) and the sow bugs (isopods; **Figure 30.23B**). Additional species-rich groups include the amphipods, ostracods, branchiopods (**Figure 30.23C**), and copepods (**Figure 30.23D**), all of which are found in freshwater and marine environments.

Barnacles are unusual crustaceans that are sessile as adults (**Figure 30.23E**). Adult barnacles look more like mollusks than like other crustaceans, but as the zoologist Louis Agassiz remarked more than a century ago, a barnacle is "nothing more than a little shrimp-like animal, standing on its head in a limestone house and kicking food into its mouth."

▶ **Media Clip 30.7 Barnacles Feeding**
Life12e.com/mc30.7

Most of the 67,000 described species of crustaceans have a body that is divided into three regions: head, thorax, and abdomen (**Figure 30.24**). The segments of the head are fused together, and the head bears five pairs of appendages. Each of the multiple thoracic and abdominal segments usually bears one pair of appendages. The appendages on different parts of the body are specialized for different functions, such as gas exchange, chewing, capturing food, sensing, walking, and swimming. In

(A) *Grapsus grapsus*

(B) *Armadillidium vulgare*

(C) *Triops longicaudatus*

(D) *Cyclops strenuus*

(E) *Lepas anatifera*

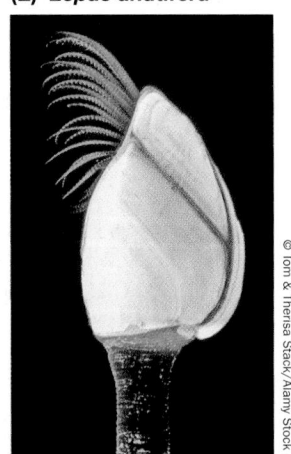

Figure 30.23 Crustacean Diversity **(A)** This decapod crustacean is a "Sally Lightfoot" crab from the Galápagos. **(B)** This pillbug, a terrestrial isopod, can roll into a tight ball when threatened. **(C)** Tadpole shrimp are branchiopods, not to be confused with the decapod crustaceans commonly called shrimp, or with the brachiopods (see Figure 30.9). **(D)** Minute copepods such as this one are an important link in aquatic food chains. **(E)** Barnacles are sessile as adults, attaching to a substrate by their muscular stalks and feeding with retractable feeding appendages (the delicate, tentacle-like structures seen here).

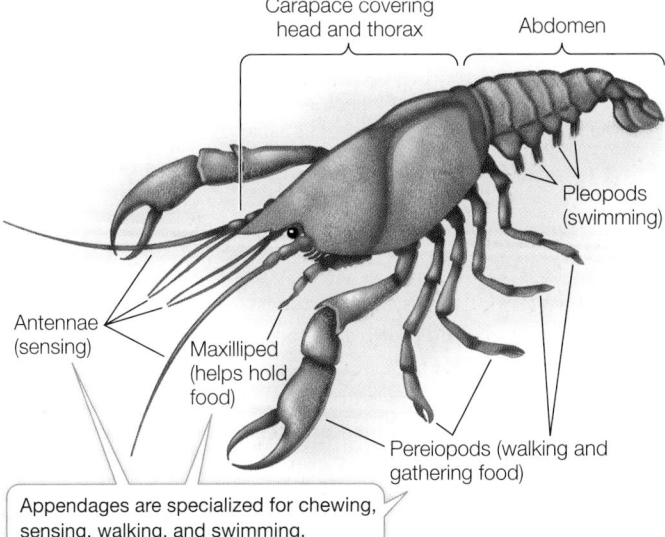

Carapace covering head and thorax

Abdomen

Pleopods (swimming)

Antennae (sensing)

Maxilliped (helps hold food)

Pereiopods (walking and gathering food)

Appendages are specialized for chewing, sensing, walking, and swimming.

Figure 30.24 Crustacean Body Plan The bodies of crustaceans are divided into three regions: the head, thorax, and abdomen. Each body region bears specialized appendages. A shell-like carapace covers the head and thorax.

Q: In what ways is the crustacean body plan similar to and different from the insect body plan shown in Figure 30.26?

many species, a fold of the exoskeleton, the carapace, extends dorsally and laterally back from the head to cover and protect some of the other segments.

The fertilized eggs of most crustacean species are attached to the outside of the female's body, where they remain during their early development (see Figure 30.23D). At hatching, the young of some species are released as larvae; those of other species are released as juveniles that are similar in form to the adults. Still other species release eggs into the water or attach them to an object in the environment.

More than half of all described species are insects

During the Devonian, more than 400 million years ago, some mandibulates colonized terrestrial environments. Of the several groups (including some crustacean isopods and decapods) that successfully colonized the land, none is more prominent today than the six-legged **hexapods**, which include the **insects** and their wingless relatives.

As you saw at the opening of this chapter, more than 1 million of the 1.8 million described living species on Earth are insects, but that is a small fraction of the number of species of insects that are thought to exist on Earth. One of Terry Erwin's experiments is shown in more detail in **Investigating Life: How Many Unknown Species?** This and similar experiments show that we have much to learn about the biodiversity of our own planet.

►Investigating LIFE   How Many Unknown Species?

Experiment

Original Papers: T. L. Erwin. 1988. In *Biodiversity*, E. O. Wilson (ed.), pp. 123–129. National Academy Press: Washington, D.C.

T. L. Erwin. 1997. In *Biodiversity II*, M. L. Reaka-Kudla et al. (eds.), pp. 27–40. Joseph Henry Press: Washington, D.C.

Entomologist Terry Erwin decided to estimate the number of undescribed species of insects. He devised and executed the following experiment in the forests of Panama.

QUESTION►   How many species of insects exist on Earth?

METHOD►

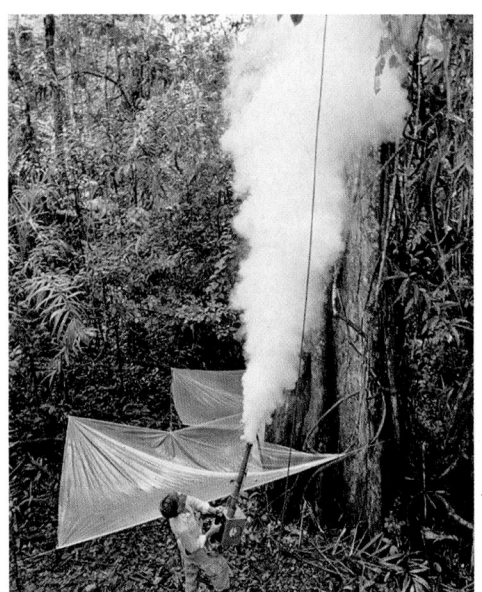

© Mark Moffett/Minden Pictures

1. Use insecticide fog to collect all beetles from *Luehea seemannii* trees.

2. Sort beetles into species based on morphological differences.

3. Calculate the number of host-specific species (those restricted to *L. seemannii*) and the number of generalists.

4. Estimate the number of tree species per hectare of Panamanian forest.

5. Calculate the percent of tree-dwelling versus ground-dwelling beetles.

6. Calculate the percent of beetles among all insect species.

7. Use the calculations above to extrapolate the total number of insect species on Earth.

RESULTS►   Erwin estimated that there are more than 30 million insect species on Earth (only about 1 million of which have been described).

CONCLUSION►   Insect diversity is far greater than indicated by the known number of species, and the number of undescribed insect species far exceeds the total number of described species on Earth.

Work with the Data

The data in the table were used by entomologist Terry Erwin to estimate the undescribed diversity of insects. Review the design of Erwin's experiment in the accompanying box and in the opening story of this chapter. Then use Erwin's data to answer the questions.

Approximate number of beetle species collected from *Luehea seemannii* trees	1,200
Estimated number of host-specific beetle species in this sample	163
Number of species of canopy trees per hectare of forest	70
Percent of beetle species living in canopy (as opposed to ground-dwelling species)	75%
Percent of beetles among all insect species	40%

Source: T. L. Erwin. 1982. *The Coleopterists Bulletin* 36: 74–75.

QUESTIONS►

1. From the data in the table, estimate the number of insect species in an average hectare of Panamanian forest. Assume that the data for beetles on *L. seemannii* are representative of the other tree species, and that all the species of beetles that are not host-specific were collected in the original sample. Remember to sum your estimates of the number of (a) host-specific beetle species in the forest canopy; (b) non-host-specific beetle species in the forest canopy; (c) beetle species on the forest floor; and (d) species of all insects other than beetles.

2. There are about 50,000 species of tropical forest trees. Assume that the data for beetles on *L. seemannii* are representative of other species of tropical trees and calculate the number of host-specific beetle species found on these trees. Add an estimated 1 million species of non-host-specific beetles that are expected across different species of trees (including those in temperate regions). Estimate the number of ground-dwelling beetle species based on the percent used in Question 1. Now use this information to estimate the number of insect species on Earth, based on the percent of beetles among all insect species.

Go to Achieve for a companion
Data in Depth exercise.

The wingless relatives of the insects—the springtails, two-pronged bristletails, and proturans—are probably the most similar of living forms to insect ancestors (**Figure 30.25**). These hexapods have a simple life cycle: they hatch from eggs as miniature adults. They differ from insects in having internal mouthparts. Springtails can be extremely abundant (up to 200,000 per m^2) in soil, leaf litter, and on vegetation and are the most abundant hexapods in the world in terms of number of individuals (as opposed to number of species).

Like crustaceans, insects have a body with three regions: head, thorax, and abdomen. They have a single pair of antennae on the head and three pairs of legs attached to the thorax. In most groups of insects, the thorax also bears two pairs of wings. Unlike other arthropods, insects have no appendages growing from their abdominal segments (**Figure 30.26**). Insects

Tomocerus minor

0.5 mm

Figure 30.25 Wingless Hexapods The wingless hexapods, such as this springtail, have a simple life cycle. They hatch looking like miniature adults, then grow by successive molts of the cuticle.

are distinguished from springtails and other hexapods by their external mouthparts and by antennae that contain a motion-sensitive receptor called Johnston's organ. In addition, insects have a derived mechanism for gas exchange in air: a system of air sacs and tubular channels called tracheae (singular trachea) that extend from external openings called spiracles inward to tissues throughout the body (see Figure 47.4).

Table 30.2 lists the major insect groups. Two groups—the jumping bristletails and silverfishes—are wingless and have simple life cycles, like the springtails and other non-insect hexapods. The remaining groups are all pterygote insects. **Pterygotes** have two pairs of wings, except in some groups in which one or both pairs of wings have been secondarily lost. These secondarily wingless

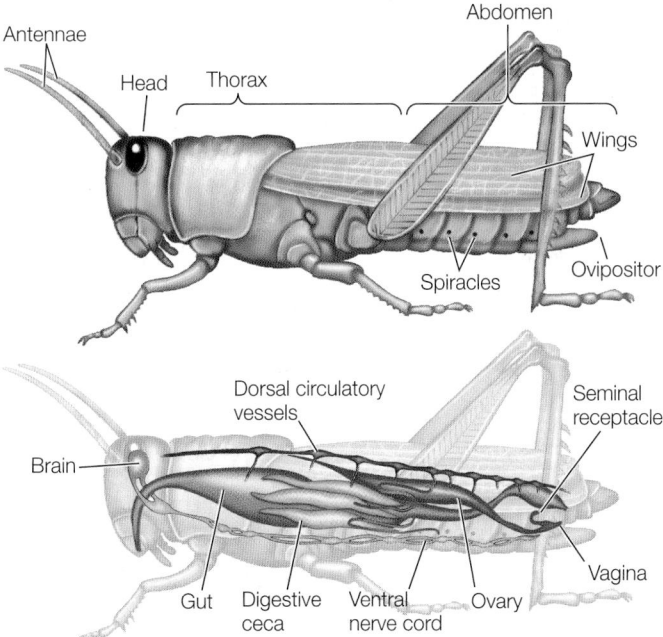

Figure 30.26 Insect Body Plan Like those of crustaceans, the bodies of insects are divided into three regions: head, thorax, and abdomen. In insects, however, the thorax bears three pairs of legs and, in most groups, two pairs of wings. Unlike other arthropods, insects have no appendages growing from their abdominal segments.

groups include the parasitic lice and fleas, some beetles, and the worker individuals of many ant species.

Hatchling pterygotes do not look like adults; they undergo substantial changes at each molt. The immature stages of insects between molts are called **instars**. A substantial change that occurs between one developmental stage and another is called **metamorphosis**. If the changes between stages are gradual, an insect is

TABLE **30.2** | The Major Insect Groups[a]

Group	Approximate number of described living species
Jumping bristletails (Archaeognatha)	560
Silverfishes (Thysanura)	580
PTERYGOTE (WINGED) INSECTS (PTERYGOTA)	
Mayflies (Ephemeroptera)	3,250
Dragonflies and damselflies (Odonata)	6,000
NEOPTERANS (NEOPTERA)[b]	
Ice-crawlers (Grylloblattodea)	35
Gladiators (Mantophasmatodea)	15
Stoneflies (Plecoptera)	3,800
Webspinners (Embioptera)	500
Angel insects (Zoraptera)	40
Earwigs (Dermaptera)	2,000
Grasshoppers and crickets (Orthoptera)	24,000
Stick insects (Phasmida)	3,000
Cockroaches (Blattodea)	4,500
Termites (Isoptera)	3,000
Mantids (Mantodea)	2,500
Booklice and barklice (Psocoptera)	5,800
Thrips (Thysanoptera)	6,000
Lice (Phthiraptera)	5,000
True bugs, cicadas, aphids, leafhoppers (Hemiptera)	105,000
HOLOMETABOLOUS NEOPTERANS (HOLOMETABOLA)[c]	
Ants, bees, wasps (Hymenoptera)	150,000
Beetles (Coleoptera)	400,000
Twisted-wing parasites (Strepsiptera)	650
Lacewings, ant lions, mantidflies (Neuropterida)	6,000
Dobsonflies, alderflies, fishflies (Megaloptera)	350
Snakeflies (Raphidioptera)	250
Scorpionflies (Mecoptera)	800
Fleas (Siphonaptera)	2,000
True flies (Diptera)	125,000
Caddisflies (Trichoptera)	12,000
Butterflies and moths (Lepidoptera)	180,000

[a]The hexapod relatives of insects include the springtails (Collembola; 3,000 spp.), two-pronged bristletails (Diplura; 600 spp.), and proturans (Protura; 10 spp.). All are wingless and have internal mouthparts.

[b]Neopteran insects can tuck their wings close to their body.

[c]Holometabolous insects are neopterans that undergo complete metamorphosis.

said to have **incomplete metamorphosis**. If the change between at least some stages is dramatic, an insect is said to have **complete metamorphosis** (see Figure 29.10). In many insects with complete metamorphosis, different stages are specialized for different functions and use different food sources. In many species the larvae are specialized for feeding and growing, whereas the adults are specialized for reproduction and dispersal.

▶ **Media Clip 30.8 Complete Metamorphosis**
Life12e.com/mc30.8

The adults of most flying insects have two pairs of stiff, membranous wings attached to the thorax. True flies, however, have one pair of wings and a pair of stabilizers called halteres (which are derived from the second pair of wings). In winged beetles, one pair of wings—the forewings—forms heavy, hardened wing covers.

Two groups of pterygotes, the mayflies and dragonflies (**Figure 30.27A**), cannot fold their wings against their body. This is the ancestral condition for pterygote insects, and the mayflies and dragonflies are not closely related to one another. Members of both groups have predatory or herbivorous aquatic larvae that transform into flying adults after they crawl out of the water. Dragonflies (and their relatives the damselflies) are active predators as adults. In contrast, adult mayflies lack functional digestive tracts. Adult mayflies live only about a day, just long enough to mate and lay eggs.

All other pterygote insects—the **neopterans**—can tuck their wings out of the way upon landing and crawl into crevices and other tight places. Some neopteran groups undergo incomplete metamorphosis, so hatchlings of these insects are sufficiently similar in form to adults to be recognizable. Examples include the grasshoppers (**Figure 30.27B**), roaches, mantids, stick insects, termites, stoneflies, earwigs, thrips, true bugs (**Figure 30.27C**), aphids, cicadas, and leafhoppers. These groups acquire adult organ systems, such as wings and compound eyes, gradually through several juvenile instars.

More than 80% of all insects belong to a subgroup of the neopterans called the **holometabolous** insects (see Table 30.2),

(A) *Libellula depressa,* Odonata

(B) *Brachystola magna,* Orthoptera

(C) *Graphosoma lineatum,* Hemiptera

(D) *Cetonia aurata,* Coleoptera

(E) *Gumaga* sp., Trichoptera

(F) *Papilio machaon,* Lepidoptera

Figure 30.27 Diverse Pterygotes **(A)** Unlike most flying insects, a dragonfly cannot fold its wings over its back. **(B)** Orthopteran insects such as grasshoppers undergo several larval molts (instars), but the juveniles resemble small adults (incomplete metamorphosis). **(C)** Hemipterans are "true" bugs. **(D–H)** Holometabolous insects undergo complete metamorphosis. **(D)** Coleoptera is the largest insect group; beetles such as this rose chafer account for more than half of all holometabolous species. **(E)** A larval caddisfly emerges from its case constructed from silk and sand. **(F)** The swallowtail butterfly is found in most parts of North America. **(G)** Blowflies are among the "true" flies, the Dipterans. Adult blowflies feed on pollen or nectar but lay their eggs on carrion, upon which the larvae feed. **(H)** This western paper wasp is a hymenopteran, a group in which most members display social behaviors.

(G) *Delia* sp., Diptera

(H) *Mischocyttarus flavitarsis,* Hymenoptera

which undergo complete metamorphosis (see Figure 30.27D-H). The many species of beetles account for almost half of this group (**Figure 30.27D**). Also included are lacewings and their relatives; caddisflies (**Figure 30.27E**); butterflies and moths (**Figure 30.27F**); true flies (**Figure 30.27G**); and bees, wasps, and ants, some species of which display unique and highly specialized social behaviors (**Figure 30.27H**).

Molecular data suggest that insects began to diversify over 400 million years ago, soon after the appearance of the first land plants. These early hexapods evolved in a terrestrial environment that lacked any other similar organisms, which in part accounts for their remarkable success. But the success of the insects is also due to their wings. Pterygote insects were the first animals in evolutionary history to achieve the ability to fly. Homologous genes control the development of insect wings and crustacean appendages, suggesting that the insect wing evolved from a dorsal branch of a crustacean-like limb (**Figure 30.28**). The dorsal limb branch of crustaceans is used for gas exchange. Thus the insect wing probably evolved from a gill-like structure that had a gas exchange function.

Flight opened up many new lifestyles and feeding opportunities that only the insects could exploit, such as pollination of (and coevolution with) flowering plants. Flight is almost certainly one of the reasons for the remarkable numbers of both insect species and individual insects, and for their unparalleled evolutionary success.

Figure 30.28 The Origin of Insect Wings?   Insect wings may be derived from an ancestral appendage similar to that of modern crustaceans. (**A**) A diagram of the ancestral, multibranched arthropod limb. The uppermost dorsal branch may have been used for gas exchange. (**B, C**) The *pdm* gene, a Hox gene, is expressed throughout the dorsal limb segment of the thoracic limb of a crayfish (**B**) and in the wings of *Drosophila* (**C**).

Q: If the hypothesized origin of insect wings is correct, then what was a possible function of the structure that would become a wing in flying insects?

KEY CONCEPT
30.4 Recap and Assess

All arthropods have segmented bodies. Muscles in each segment operate that segment and the appendages attached to it. Jointed, specialized appendages permit complex patterns of movement, including, in insects, the ability to fly. With flight, insects took advantage of new feeding and lifestyle opportunities, which contributed to the unparalleled evolutionary success of this group.

1. What features have contributed to making arthropods among the most abundant animals on Earth, both in number of species and in number of individuals?

2. Describe the difference between incomplete and complete metamorphosis.

3. There are more described and named species of insects than of all other species on Earth combined. However, only a very few insect species live in marine environments, and those species are restricted to the intertidal zone or the ocean surface. What factors may have contributed to the insects' lack of success in the oceans?

Key Features of Protostome Evolution

The protostomes encompass a staggering number of different body forms and lifestyles. The following aspects of protostome evolution have contributed to this enormous diversity:

• The evolution of *segmentation* permitted some groups of protostomes to move different parts of the body independently of one another. Species in some groups gradually evolved the ability to move rapidly over and through the substrate, through water, and through air.

• *Complex life cycles* with dramatic changes in form between one stage and another allow individuals of different stages to specialize on different resources.

• *Parasitism* has evolved repeatedly, and many protostome groups parasitize plants and animals.

• The evolution of *diverse feeding structures* allowed protostomes to specialize on many different food sources. Specialization on food sources undoubtedly contributed to reproductive isolation and further diversification.

• Predation was a major selection pressure favoring the development of *hard external body coverings* (exoskeletons and shells). Such coverings evolved independently in many lophotrochozoan and ecdysozoan groups. In addition to providing protection, these coverings became key elements in the development of new systems of locomotion.

• *Better locomotion* permitted prey to escape from predators, but also allowed predators to pursue their prey more effectively. Thus the evolution of animals has been, and continues to be, a complex "arms race" among predators and prey.

 View in Achieve
Animation 30.1 **An Overview of the Protostomes**

Many major evolutionary trends among the protostomes are shared by the deuterostomes, which include the chordates, the group to which humans belong. We will turn to the deuterostomes in the next chapter.

►InvestigatingLIFE

Q and A **Which groups of protostomes are thought to contain the most undiscovered species?**

It is perhaps easier to list the groups of protostomes for which a nearly complete inventory of living species has been done than to list all the groups for which many new species remain to be described. Among the insects, the best-studied group, in terms of species, is the butterflies, which are widely collected and studied. There are still many species of other lepidopterans (such as moths), however, remaining to be discovered. As we explored in **Investigating Life: How Many Unknown Species?**, some other major insect groups, such as beetles, contain many undescribed species.

New species discovery and description rates remain high for almost all other major groups of protostomes. Second to the insects, and perhaps even rivaling the insects in undiscovered diversity, are the nematodes. Although known nematode diversity is only about one-fortieth of known insect diversity (in terms of number of described species), the taxonomy of nematodes has been much more poorly studied than that of insects. Some biologists think there are likely to be species-specific parasitic nematodes specializing on most other species of multicellular organisms. If so, then there may be as many species of nematodes as there are of plants, fungi, and other animals combined.

Most of the other diverse groups of protostomes also contain many as yet undetected species, judging from the rate of new species descriptions. In particular, flatworms (especially the parasitic flukes and tapeworms), marine annelids, mollusks, crustaceans, myriapods, and chelicerates all contain large numbers of undescribed species.

Future directions

Biologists have now placed almost all known species into a comprehensive tree of life (see Appendix A). This achievement allows the development of new technology for automated species discovery and identification. Once we can identify an organism, it is then possible to connect it to all the known information about that species. It should soon be possible to construct a hand-held device that will isolate DNA from any sample, and then to sequence a series of target genes that can be used to place an unknown sample within the tree of life. This process results in either identification of a known species, or placement of an undescribed species with its closest relatives in the tree. This technology is expected to revolutionize the study of biodiversity and its applications.

 VISUAL SUMMARY 30

© pixelprof/Getty Images

You should be able to relate each summary to the adjacent figures. If you go to this visual summary in **Achieve**, you can follow links to figures, animations, activities, and simulations that will help you consolidate the material.

KEY CONCEPT
30.1 **Protostomes Account for More Than Half of All Described Species**

Go to Activities 30.1 and 30.2

- Protostomes ("mouth first") are bilaterally symmetrical animals that have an anterior brain surrounding the entrance to the digestive tract and a ventral nervous system. Protostomes comprise two major clades, the lophotrochozoans and the ecdysozoans.

- **Lophotrochozoans** include a wide diversity of animals. Within this group evolved **lophophores** (a complex organ for food collection and gas exchange) and free-living **trochophore** larvae.

- **Ecdysozoans** have a **cuticle** covering their body, which they must **molt** in order to grow. Some ecdysozoans, notably the **arthropods**, have a rigid cuticle reinforced with **chitin** that functions as an **exoskeleton**.

Figure 30.2 *Plumatella repens*

© Gerd Guenther/Science Source

1 mm

Questions

1. What developmental trait distinguishes most protostomes from other animals?

2. Give examples of familiar lophotrochoans and ecdysozoans.

3. What are some lophotrochozoans and ecdysozoans that are commonly consumed by many humans?

Figure 30.3 Whip scorpion (*Heterophrynus batesii*) undergoing molting

Molted exoskeleton

© Nature's Images/Science Source

KEY CONCEPT

30.2 Many Lophotrochozoans Have Ciliated Feeding Structures or Life Stages

■ Lophotrochozoans range from animals with a blind gut and no internal transport system to animals with a complete digestive tract and a complex internal transport system.

■ Most species of **bryozoans** and **entoprocts** live in colonies produced through asexual reproduction.

■ **Ribbon worms** feed using a long, protrusible **proboscis**.

■ The shelled **brachiopods** and worm-like **phoronids** use a lophophore to feed; this lophophore may have evolved independently of the lophophore in bryozoans and entoprocts.

■ The most species-rich groups of lophotrochozoans are the **flatworms**, **annelids**, and **mollusks**.

Questions

1. If the lophophores of brachiopods, phoronids, bryozoans, and entoprocts did not evolve independently in these groups, what is an alternative explanation for its presence in these relatively distantly related lophotrochozoans?

2. Paired, hinged shells that completely enclose the body evolved independently in which two major groups of lophotrochozoans?

Figure 30.1 (top)

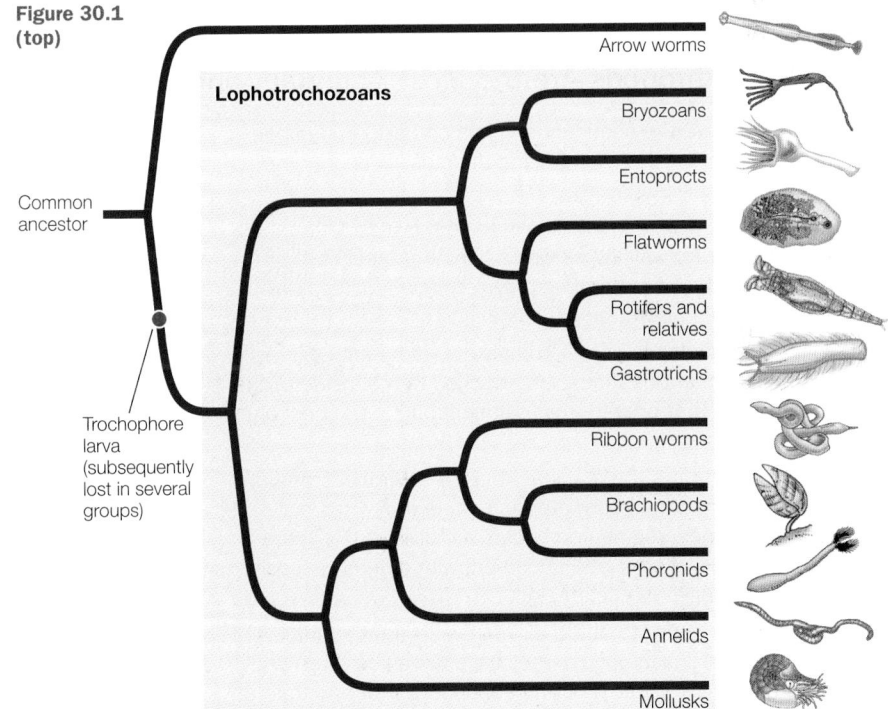

Common ancestor

Trochophore larva (subsequently lost in several groups)

Lophotrochozoans

Arrow worms
Bryozoans
Entoprocts
Flatworms
Rotifers and relatives
Gastrotrichs
Ribbon worms
Brachiopods
Phoronids
Annelids
Mollusks

KEY CONCEPT

30.3 Ecdysozoans Grow by Shedding Their Cuticles

- Ecdysozoans include the most diverse groups of animals, including **nematodes** and arthropods.

- Several species-poor groups of wormlike marine ecdysozoans—**priapulids, kinorhynchs**, and **loriciferans**—have thin cuticles.

- **Horsehair worms** are extremely thin; many are endoparasites as larvae.

Questions

1. What are the primary functions of the cuticle in ecdysozoans?

2. What attributes make the nematode *Caenorhabditis elegans* ideal for use as a model organism in the laboratories of many geneticists and developmental biologists?

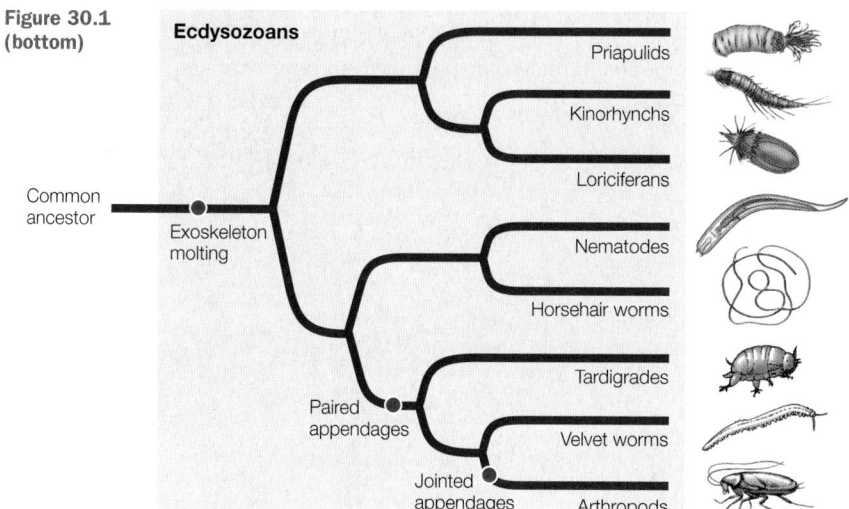

Figure 30.1 (bottom)

KEY CONCEPT

30.4 Arthropods Are the Most Abundant and Diverse Group of Animals   Go to Animation 30.1

- Arthropods are the dominant animals on Earth in number of described species, and among the most abundant in number of individuals.

- Encasement within a rigid exoskeleton provides arthropods with support for walking as well as some protection from predators. The waterproofing provided by chitin keeps arthropods from dehydrating in dry air.

- Jointed appendages permit complex movements. Each arthropod segment has muscles attached to the inside of the exoskeleton that operate that segment and the appendages attached to it.

- **Crustaceans** are the dominant marine arthropods and are also found in many freshwater and some terrestrial environments. Their segmented bodies are divided into three regions (head, thorax, and abdomen) with different, specialized appendages in each region.

- **Hexapods**—**insects** and their relatives—are the dominant terrestrial arthropods. They have the same three body regions as crustaceans, but no appendages form in their abdominal segments. Wings and the ability to fly first evolved among the insects, allowing them to exploit new lifestyles.

Questions

1. What are the other major groups of living arthropods, besides the crustaceans and hexapods?

2. What was the likely original function of the organ from which insect wings evolved?

Figure 30.24

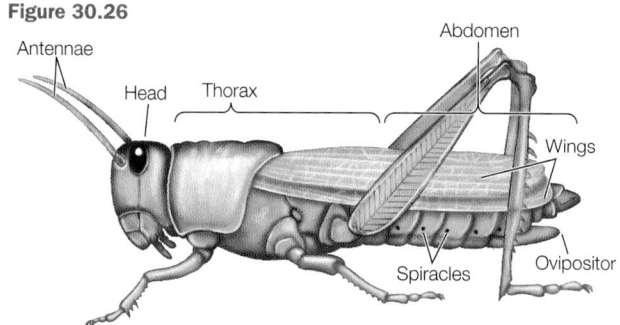

Figure 30.26

Deuterostome Animals 31

© Sylvain Cordier/Getty Images

KEY CONCEPTS

Grass snake (*Natrix natrix*) with eggs Shelled eggs facilitated the colonization of drier terrestrial environments by deuterostomes.

▶Investigating LIFE

Which Came First, the Chicken or the Egg?

When people ponder the chicken and egg problem, it is supposedly a riddle without an answer. The first chicken must have hatched from an egg, but then didn't another chicken have to lay that egg? But if you understand evolutionary biology, then the answer to the question of whether the chicken or the egg came first is obvious, and it isn't even close. Shelled eggs originated hundreds of millions of years before the first chicken walked on Earth.

The lineage of birds that we now know as chickens is only a few million years old. If we followed that lineage back through time, the birds in it would look less like modern chickens with each preceding generation. But all birds lay shelled eggs (a phenomenon called oviparity, or "egg birth"), so we can logically infer that eggs existed long before the first chicken did. Birds are the only living group of dinosaurs, but fossil eggs for many groups of extinct dinosaurs have been discovered. The closest living relatives of birds are the crocodilians, and they also lay shelled eggs, as do turtles. Many (but not all) lizards and snakes also lay shelled eggs, and so do the earliest branching lineages of mammals, including the echidnas and duck-billed platypus. Other mammals modify the shelled egg into structures that allow the embryo to develop within the mother, so that the young are born after "hatching" inside the mother (viviparity, or "live birth").

By comparing reproductive biology across species, biologists can trace the origin of the shelled egg to the origin of amniotes. Amniotes include all living mammals and reptiles (including birds). The group derives its name from the amnion, one of four membranes that surround the embryo within the shelled egg of amniotes.

Most amphibians also lay eggs, but their eggs have no shell. The soft, jellylike coating of amphibian eggs can easily dry, threatening the developing embryo. So amphibian eggs need to be deposited in water, or at least in moist places where desiccation is not a problem. This limitation kept the earliest terrestrial tetrapods from fully exploiting drier terrestrial environments. The shelled egg was thus an important evolutionary innovation that resulted in a great terrestrial explosion of the amniotes.

 What are the advantages and disadvantages of egg laying versus live birth?

(Find the answer on page 723.)

KEY CONCEPT
31.1

Deuterostomes Include Echinoderms, Hemichordates, and Chordates

Learning Objectives

31.1.1 Summarize the developmental and molecular characteristics that distinguish deuterostomes.

31.1.2 Identify the major deuterostome clades and give examples of each.

It may surprise you to learn that both you and a sea urchin are deuterostomes. Adult sea stars, sea urchins, and sea cucumbers—the most familiar echinoderms—look so different from adult vertebrates (fishes, frogs, lizards, birds, and mammals) that it may be difficult to believe all these animals are closely related. The evidence that all deuterostomes share a common ancestor that is not shared with the protostomes includes early developmental patterns and phylogenetic analysis of gene sequences, factors that are not apparent in the forms of the adult animals.

Deuterostomes share early developmental patterns

Historically, the deuterostomes were distinguished by three early developmental patterns:

1. Radial cleavage

2. Development of the blastopore into the anus and formation of the mouth at the opposite end of the embryo from the blastopore (the pattern that gives the deuterostomes their name)

3. Development of a coelom from mesodermal pockets that bud off from the cavity of the gastrula rather than by splitting of the mesoderm, as occurs among protostomes

These distinctions, however, are not the strongest evidence for the monophyly of the deuterostomes. Radial cleavage is not exclusive to deuterostomes, and it is now thought to be the ancestral condition for all bilaterians. In fact, some of the groups now known to be protostomes were once thought to be deuterostomes because their developmental patterns are similar to those of echinoderms and chordates. The development of the blastopore into an anus does characterize the deuterostomes, but it may be the ancestral condition for bilaterians rather than a derived feature of deuterostomes. Today the strongest support for the shared evolutionary relationships of the deuterostomes comes from phylogenetic analyses of DNA sequences of many different genes.

There are three major deuterostome clades

All deuterostomes are triploblastic, coelomate animals (see Figure 29.6C). Skeletal elements, where present, are internal rather than external. Some species have segmented bodies, but the segments are less obvious than those of annelids and arthropods. Although there are far fewer species of deuterostomes than of protostomes (see Table 29.1), we have a special interest in deuterostomes because we are members of that clade. The deuterostomes are also of interest because they include many large animals that strongly influence the characteristics of ecosystems. Many deuterostome species have been intensively studied in all fields of biology. Complex social behaviors are well developed among some deuterostomes (especially among the vertebrates).

The major groups of living deuterostomes comprise three distinct clades (**Figure 31.1**):

1. **Echinoderms**: sea stars (starfishes), sea urchins, and their relatives

2. **Hemichordates**: acorn worms and pterobranchs

3. **Chordates**: tunicates, lancelets, and vertebrates

In addition, some recent genomic analyses suggest that two poorly known groups, the xenoturbellids and the acoels, may also be deuterostomes, although the exact position of these groups among animals remains controversial.

 View in Achieve
Animation 31.1 An Overview of the Deuterostomes

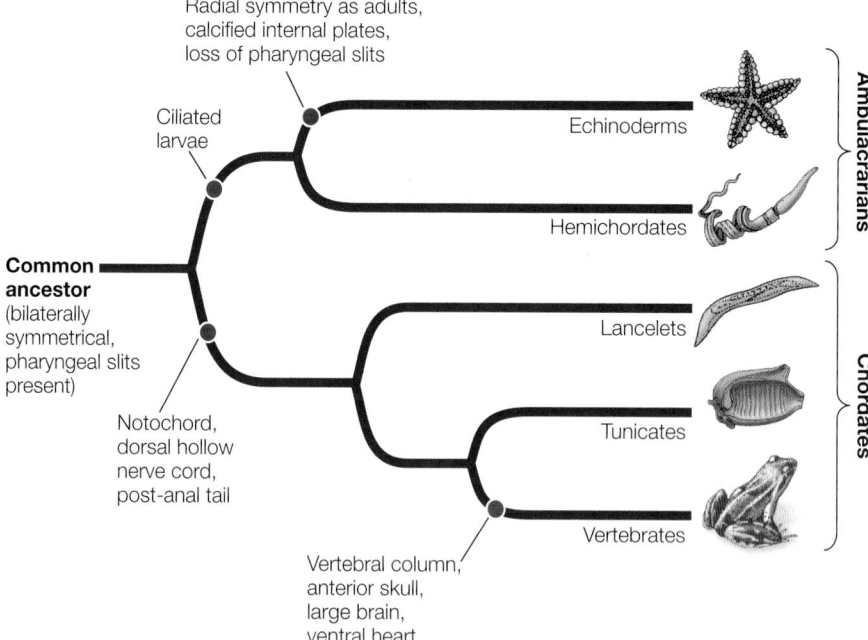

Figure 31.1 Phylogeny of the Deuterostomes The three principal groups of deuterostomes are the echinoderms, the hemichordates, and the chordates, the last of which includes the lancelets, tunicates, and vertebrates. The echinoderms and the vertebrates contain most of the described species.

 View in Achieve
Activity 31.1 Deuterostome Phylogeny

Yunnanozoon lividum

Mouth   Esophagus   External gills   Segments

Figure 31.2 Ancestral Deuterostomes Had External Gills The extinct yunnanozoans may be ancestral deuterostomes. This fossil, which dates from the Cambrian, shows the six pairs of external gills and segmented posterior body that characterized these animals.

Fossils shed light on deuterostome ancestors

Scientists are learning much about the ancestors of modern deuterostomes from fossils discovered in 520-million-year-old rocks in China. Some of these early deuterostomes had skeletons similar to those of echinoderms, but unlike modern adult echinoderms, they had bilateral symmetry and a pharynx with slits through which water flowed. Another early deuterostome group, the yunnanozoans, was discovered in China's Yunnan Province. The well-preserved fossils reveal animals that had a large mouth, six pairs of external gills, and a segmented posterior body section bearing a light cuticle (**Figure 31.2**). The features of these fossil animals, together with findings from phylogenetic analyses of living species, show that the earliest deuterostomes were bilaterally symmetrical, segmented animals with pharyngeal slits. The adult forms of the living echinoderms with their unique symmetry (in which the body parts are arranged along five radial axes) evolved much later. Other deuterostomes retained the ancestral bilateral symmetry.

KEY CONCEPT
31.1 Recap and Assess

The three major clades of deuterostomes are the echinoderms, the hemichordates, and the chordates. The common ancestry of these groups is supported by early developmental similarities and by phylogenetic analyses of DNA sequences.

1. What three developmental traits do all deuterostomes have in common? Why are some of these traits no longer considered to be strong evidence for the monophyly of deuterostomes?

2. What evidence provides strong support for the monophyly of deuterostomes?

3. What are the three major groups of deuterostomes? Place each of the following in the appropriate group: humans, acorn worms, rattlesnakes, tunas, sea squirts, and sea stars.

We begin our survey of the deuterostomes with the echinoderms and hemichordates, the most distant of our relatives among the deuterostomes.

KEY CONCEPT
31.2 Echinoderms and Hemichordates Are Restricted to Marine Environments

Learning Objectives

31.2.1 Compare the body plans of larval and adult echinoderms.

31.2.2 Summarize the ways that various echinoderms use their tube feet to feed.

31.2.3 Contrast the ways that echinoderms and hemichordates feed.

About 13,000 species of echinoderms in 23 major groups have been described from their fossil remains. They are probably only a small fraction of the echinoderm species that have ever lived. Only 6 of the 23 major groups known from fossils are represented by species that survive today; many clades were lost during the periodic mass extinctions that have occurred throughout Earth's history. All of the 7,500 extant species of echinoderms and 120 species of hemichordates live in marine environments.

The echinoderms and hemichordates (together known as **ambulacrarians**) have a bilaterally symmetrical, ciliated larva (**Figure 31.3A**). Adult hemichordates are also bilaterally symmetrical. Echinoderms, however, undergo a radical change in form as they develop into adults (**Figure 31.3B**), changing from a bilaterally symmetrical larva into an adult with **pentaradial symmetry** (symmetry in five or multiples of five). As is typical of animals with radial symmetry, echinoderms have no head, and most species move equally well in many directions. Rather than having an anterior–posterior (head–tail) and dorsal–ventral (back–belly) body organization, most echinoderms have an **oral** side containing the mouth and an opposite **aboral** side containing the anus.

Some recent genomic analyses suggest that two groups of small, highly reduced, soft-bodied marine organisms, the xenoturbellids and the acoels, may be the sister group of the ambulacrarians, although other studies suggest that they are the sister group of all the other bilaterians. The five known species of **xenoturbellids** are wormlike organisms up to 20 centimeters long that feed on or parasitize marine mollusks. They have a very simple body plan, with almost no well-defined organ systems. The mostly tiny (<2 mm) **acoels** are also highly reduced, wormlike organisms that live as plankton, between grains of sediment, or on other organisms such as corals (**Figure 31.4**). They are among the simplest of bilaterian animals, with no gut, circulatory system, respiratory system, or excretory system. They feed through a mouth and form a vacuole around tiny food items. They are hermaphrodites, and their sperm form between the epidermis and digestive structure. There are about 400 known species of acoels.

From S. Bengtson. 2000. *Palaeontol Electronica* 3: 1-14

(A) Sea star larva
(bilateral symmetry)

(B) Adult sea star
(pentaradial symmetry)

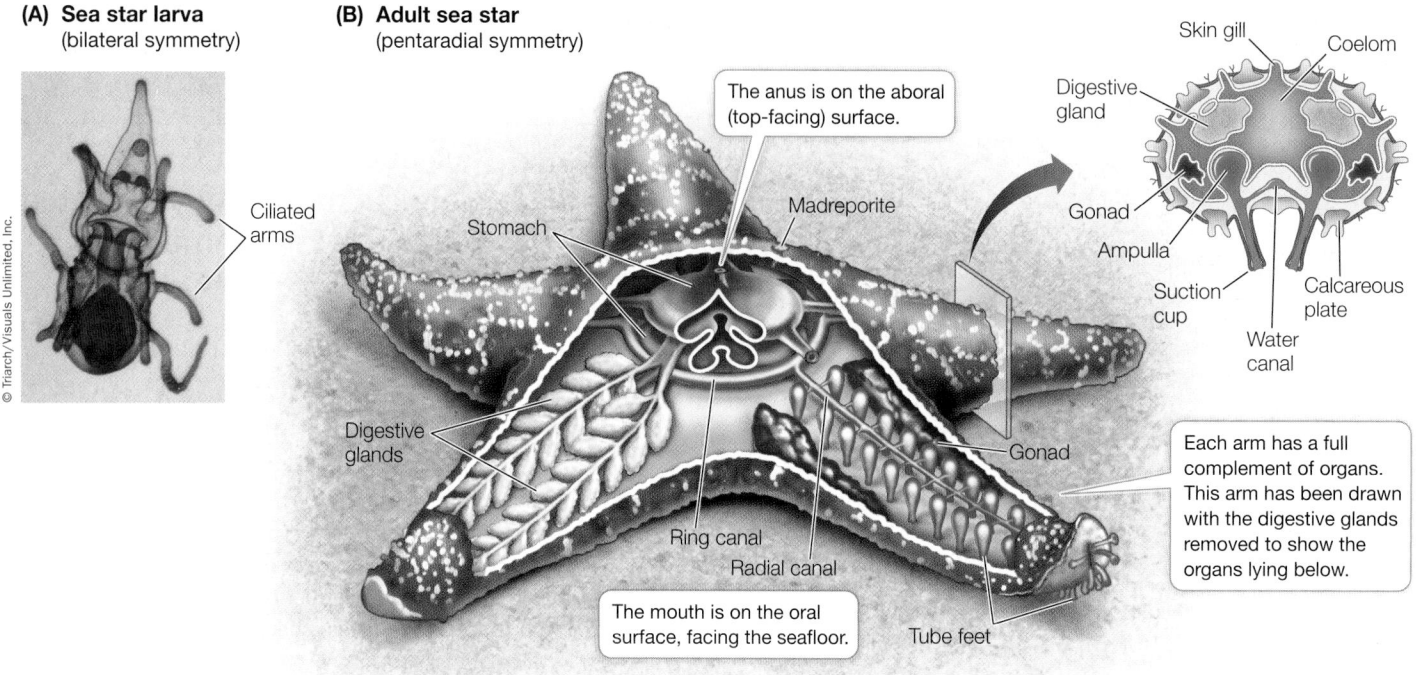

Figure 31.3 caption labels: Ciliated arms; The anus is on the aboral (top-facing) surface.; Stomach; Madreporite; Skin gill; Coelom; Digestive gland; Gonad; Ampulla; Suction cup; Calcareous plate; Water canal; Digestive glands; Each arm has a full complement of organs. This arm has been drawn with the digestive glands removed to show the organs lying below.; Ring canal; Radial canal; Gonad; The mouth is on the oral surface, facing the seafloor.; Tube feet

Figure 31.3 Echinoderms Are Bilaterally Symmetrical as Larvae but Radially Symmetrical as Adults (A) The ciliated larva of a sea star has bilateral symmetry. Hemichordates have a similar larval form. (B) An adult sea star displays the pentaradial symmetry of adult echinoderms. The canals and tube feet of the water vascular system, as well as the calcified internal skeleton, are shown in this diagram. The body's orientation is oral–aboral rather than anterior–posterior.

Echinoderms have unique structural features

In addition to pentaradial symmetry, adult echinoderms have two unique structural features. One is a system of calcified internal plates covered by thin layers of skin and some muscles. The calcified plates of most

Waminoa sp.

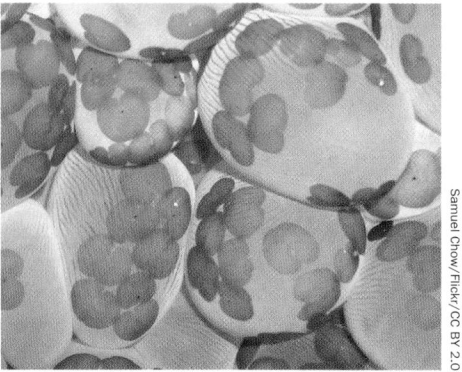

Figure 31.4 Highly Reduced Acoels May Be Relatives of the Ambulacrarians Acoels (yellow) are seen here living on bubble coral (white). Acoels ("without coelom") feed by enveloping food particles in a vacuole within which nutrients are digested. These hermaphroditic animals can reproduce rapidly and may become problematic in saltwater aquariums.

echinoderms are thick, and they fuse inside the entire body, forming an **internal skeleton**. The other unique feature of this group is a **water vascular system**, a network of water-filled canals leading to extensions called **tube feet** (see Figure 31.3B). This system functions in gas exchange, locomotion, and feeding. Seawater enters the system through a perforated structure called a madreporite. A calcified canal leads from the madreporite to the ring canal, which surrounds the esophagus (the tube leading from the mouth to the stomach). Radial canals branch off from the ring canal, extending through the arms (in species that have arms) and connecting with the tube feet. These structural innovations have been modified in many ways, resulting in a striking array of very different animals.

Members of one major extant echinoderm clade, the crinoids (sea lilies and feather stars), were more abundant and species-rich 500–300 million years ago than they are today. There are some 80 described living sea lily species, most of which are sessile organisms attached to the substrate by a stalk. Feather stars (**Figure 31.5A**) grasp the substrate with specialized flexible appendages that allow for limited movement. About 600 living species of feather stars have been described.

Although some crinoids are sessile, most surviving echinoderms are motile. The two main groups of motile echinoderms are the echinozoans (sea urchins and sea cucumbers) and the asterozoans (sea stars and brittle stars). Sea urchins are hemispherical in shape and lack arms (**Figure 31.5B**). They are covered with spines that are attached to the underlying skeleton with ball-and-socket joints. These joints enable the spines to be moved so they can

(A) *Comanthina schlegeli*

(B) *Strongylocentrotus purpuratus*

(C) *Pseudocolochirus* sp.

(D) *Asterias rubens*

(E) *Ophiothrix spiculata*

Figure 31.5 Echinoderm Diversity   **(A)** The flexible arms of this variable bushy feather star (a crinoid) are clearly visible. **(B)** Sea urchins are important grazers on algae in the intertidal zones of the world's oceans. **(C)** This sea cucumber has expelled a portion of its viscera as a sticky defense against a potential predator. **(D)** Sea stars are important predators on bivalve mollusks such as mussels and clams. Suction tips on its tube feet allow a sea star to grasp both shells of a bivalve and pull them open. **(E)** The arms of a brittle star are composed of hard but jointed plates.

converge toward a point that has been touched. The spines, which vary among species in size and shape, can be used for locomotion; a few produce toxic substances. They provide effective protection for the urchin, as many a scuba diver has found out the hard way. Sand dollars are flattened, disc-shaped relatives of sea urchins.

Sea cucumbers also lack arms, and their bodies are oriented in an atypical manner for an echinoderm (**Figure 31.5C**). The mouth is anterior and the anus is posterior (front and rear), in contrast to the oral–aboral (top and bottom) orientation of other echinoderms. Sea cucumbers can use most of their tube feet to move, but they use them primarily for attaching to the substrate.

Sea stars, popularly called starfishes, are the most familiar echinoderms (**Figure 31.5D**). Their gonads and digestive organs are located in the arms, as seen in Figure 31.3B. Their tube feet serve as organs of locomotion, gas exchange, and attachment. Each tube foot of a sea star consists of an internal ampulla connected by a muscular tube to an external suction cup that can stick to the substrate. The tube foot is moved by expansion and contraction of the circular and longitudinal muscles of the tube. Brittle stars are similar in structure to sea stars, but their flexible arms are composed of jointed, hard plates (**Figure 31.5E**), their gonads and viscera are contained in the central disc, and their tube feet lack suction cups or ampullae.

Echinoderms use their tube feet in a great variety of ways to capture prey. Sea lilies, for example, feed by orienting their arms in passing water currents. Food particles then strike and stick to the tube feet, which are covered with mucus-secreting glands. The tube feet transfer these particles to grooves in the arms, where ciliary action carries the food to the mouth.

Most sea urchins capture phytoplankton with their tube feet or scrape algae from rocks with a complex rasping structure. Sea cucumbers capture food with their anterior tube feet, which are modified into large, feathery, sticky tentacles that can be protruded from the mouth. Periodically a sea cucumber withdraws the tentacles, wipes off the material that has adhered to them, and digests it.

Many sea stars use their tube feet to capture large prey such as polychaetes, gastropod and bivalve mollusks, small crustaceans such as crabs, and fishes. With hundreds of tube feet acting simultaneously, a sea star can grasp a bivalve in its arms, anchor the arms with its tube feet, and by steady contraction of the muscles in its arms, gradually exhaust the muscles the bivalve uses to keep its shell closed (see Figure 31.5D). To feed on the bivalve, the sea star can push its stomach out through its mouth and then through the narrow space between the two halves of the bivalve's shell. The sea star's stomach then secretes enzymes that digest the prey.

 Media Clip 31.1 Sea Star Hunting Bivalves
Life12e.com/mc31.1

Most of the 2,000 species of brittle stars ingest particles from the upper layers of sediments and assimilate the organic material from them, although some species filter suspended food particles from the water, and others capture small animals.

Hemichordates are wormlike marine deuterostomes

Hemichordates—acorn worms and ptero-branchs—have a bilaterally symmetrical, wormlike body organized in three major parts: a proboscis, a collar (which bears the mouth), and a trunk (which contains the other body parts). The 90 known species of acorn worms range up to 2 meters long (**Figure 31.6A**). They live in burrows in muddy and sandy marine sediments. The digestive tract of an acorn worm consists of a mouth behind which are a muscular pharynx and an intestine. The pharynx opens to the outside through several pharyngeal slits through which water can exit. Highly vascularized tissue surrounding the pharyngeal slits serves as a gas exchange

(A) *Saccoglossus kowalevskii*

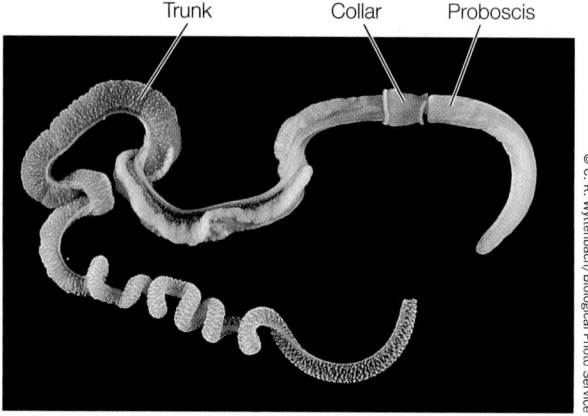

Trunk Collar Proboscis

© C. R. Wyttenbach/Biological Photo Service

(B)

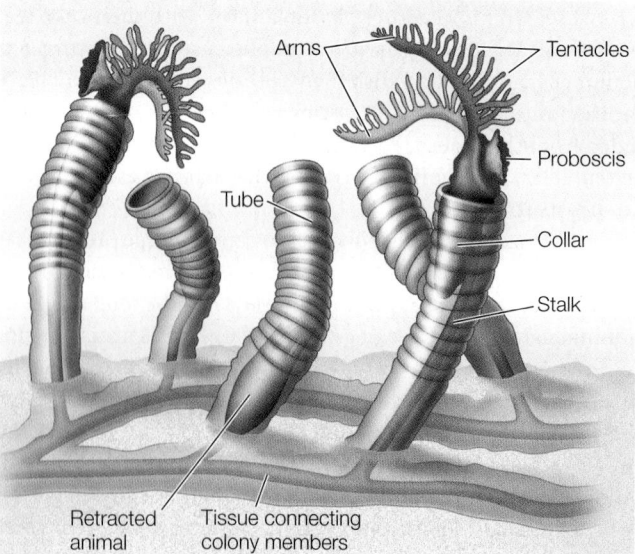

Arms Tentacles
Proboscis
Tube
Collar
Stalk
Retracted animal Tissue connecting colony members

Figure 31.6 Hemichordates **(A)** The proboscis of an acorn worm is modified for burrowing. **(B)** Some pterobranch species form colonies.

apparatus. Acorn worms respire by pumping water into the mouth and out through the pharyngeal slits. They capture prey with the large proboscis, which is coated with sticky mucus to which small organisms in the sediment stick. The mucus and its attached prey are conveyed by cilia to the mouth. In the esophagus, the food-laden mucus is compacted into a ropelike mass that is moved through the digestive tract by ciliary action.

The 30 living species of pterobranchs are sedentary marine animals up to 12 millimeters long that live in a tube secreted by the proboscis. Some species are solitary; others form colonies of individuals joined together (**Figure 31.6B**). Behind the proboscis is a collar with anywhere from one to nine pairs of arms. The arms bear long tentacles that capture prey and function in gas exchange.

KEY CONCEPT
31.2 Recap and Assess

Adult echinoderms are characterized by pentaradial symmetry, an internal skeleton of calcified plates, and a unique water vascular system. Hemichordates have a bilaterally symmetrical body divided into three parts: proboscis, collar, and trunk. Both groups are restricted to marine environments.

1. How does the body form of echinoderm larvae differ from that of echinoderm adults?

2. Describe some of the ways that echinoderms use their tube feet to obtain food, and contrast this with the feeding mechanism of hemichordates.

Having described the deuterostome groups that are most distantly related to us, we next turn our attention to the unique features that evolved in the chordates, a clade dominated by the vertebrates.

KEY CONCEPT
31.3 More Than Half of Chordates Are Also Aquatic

Learning Objectives

31.3.1 Identify chordates and vertebrates, and distinguish them from other animals.

31.3.2 Compare and contrast hagfishes and lampreys, and explain why hagfishes are not considered vertebrates by all biologists.

31.3.3 Describe how changes in appendages, jaws, teeth, and swim bladders led to new foraging opportunities for vertebrates.

There are three principal chordate clades: the **lancelets** (also called cephalochordates), the **tunicates** (also called urochordates), and the **vertebrates** (see Figure 31.1). Like the echinoderms and hemichordates that we discussed in Key Concept 31.1, all lancelets and tunicates are marine. The earliest vertebrates also diversified in marine environments, and then moved into fresh waters. From there, the **tetrapods** (four-legged vertebrates and their descendants) invaded terrestrial environments. Today fishes make up a little more than half of vertebrate species. Note that we use the word "fishes" to refer to all the aquatic vertebrates that are not tetrapods. (Also note that the plural "fishes" is used to refer to multiple species of fishes, whereas the plural "fish" is used to refer to many individuals of the same species of fish.) Fishes are not a monophyletic group of vertebrates (some fishes are more closely related to tetrapods than they are to other groups of fishes), which is why we do not recognize fishes as a formal taxon.

As you have seen, it is not obvious from examining adult animals that echinoderms, hemichordates, and chordates share a common ancestor. The evolutionary relationships among some chordate groups are not immediately apparent either. The features that reveal all of these evolutionary relationships are seen primarily in the larvae—in other words, it is during the early developmental stages that these evolutionary relationships are evident. Adult chordates vary greatly in form, but all chordates display the following derived structures at some stage in their development (**Figure 31.7**):

- A *dorsal hollow nerve cord*
- A *tail* that extends beyond the anus
- A dorsal supporting rod, the *notochord*

The **notochord** is the most distinctive derived chordate trait. It is composed of a core of large cells with turgid fluid-filled vacuoles, which make it rigid but flexible. In the tunicates the notochord is lost during metamorphosis to the adult stage. In most vertebrate species it is replaced during development by skeletal structures that provide support for the body.

The pharyngeal slits found in the common ancestor of deuterostomes are present at some developmental stage in all chordates but are often lost or greatly modified in adults. In chordates, the pharyngeal slits are separated and supported by structural elements called pharyngeal arches. In tunicates and lancelets, the pharynx functions as a straining device to filter small food particles. In fishes and larval amphibians, some of the pharyngeal arches develop into gill arches, which support the respiratory gills and are often used as feeding structures as well. Developmentally, some pharyngeal arches also develop into elements of the vertebrate jaw, as well as parts of the tongue, larynx, trachea, and middle ear of tetrapods. Some of the pharyngeal slits are modified in tetrapods to form the eustachian tube and middle ear chamber.

(A)

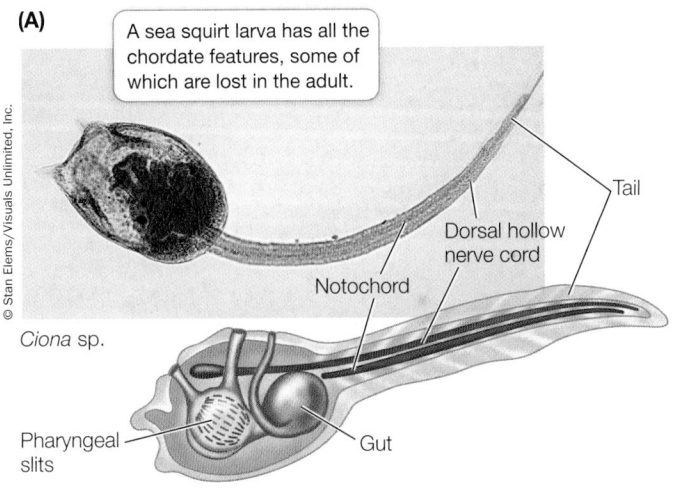

A sea squirt larva has all the chordate features, some of which are lost in the adult.

© Stan Elems/Visuals Unlimited, Inc.

Ciona sp.

Tail

Dorsal hollow nerve cord

Notochord

Pharyngeal slits

Gut

(B)

David McIntyre

An adult lancelet retains all the chordate features and also has a much enlarged pharyngeal basket.

Pharyngeal slits

Notochord

Dorsal hollow nerve cord

Gut

Branchiostoma lanceolatum

Anus

Tail

Figure 31.7 Key Features May Be Most Apparent in Early Development (A) The sea squirt larva (but not the adult) has all three key features of chordates: a dorsal hollow nerve cord, a post-anal tail, and a notochord. (B) All three chordate synapomorphies are retained in the adult lancelet.

Adults of most lancelets and tunicates are sessile

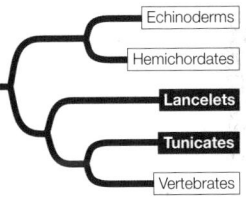

The 35 species of lancelets are small animals that rarely exceed 5 centimeters in length. The notochord, which provides body support, extends the entire length of the body throughout the animal's life (see Figure 31.7B). Lancelets are found in shallow marine and brackish waters worldwide. Most of the time they lie covered in sand with their head protruding above the sediment, but they can swim. The pharynx has been enlarged and modified to form a structure called a pharyngeal basket, with which the lancelet filters prey from the water. During the reproductive season, the gonads of males and females enlarge greatly. At spawning, the walls of the gonads rupture, releasing eggs and sperm into the water column, where fertilization takes place.

All members of the three major tunicate groups—the sea squirts, thaliaceans, and larvaceans—are marine animals. More than 90% of the 2,800 known species of tunicates are sea squirts (also called ascidians). Individual sea squirts range in length from less than 1 millimeter to 60 centimeters. Some sea squirts form colonies by asexual budding from a single founder. Colonies may measure several meters across. The baglike body of an adult sea squirt is enclosed in a tough tunic, which is the basis for the name "tunicate" (**Figure 31.8A**). The tunic is composed of proteins and a complex polysaccharide secreted by epidermal cells. The sea squirt pharynx is enlarged into a pharyngeal basket that filters prey from the water passing through it.

Figure 31.8 Adult Tunicates
(A) The transparent tunic and the pharyngeal basket are clearly visible in this sea squirt.
(B) A chainlike colony of thaliaceans (salps) floats in tropical waters.

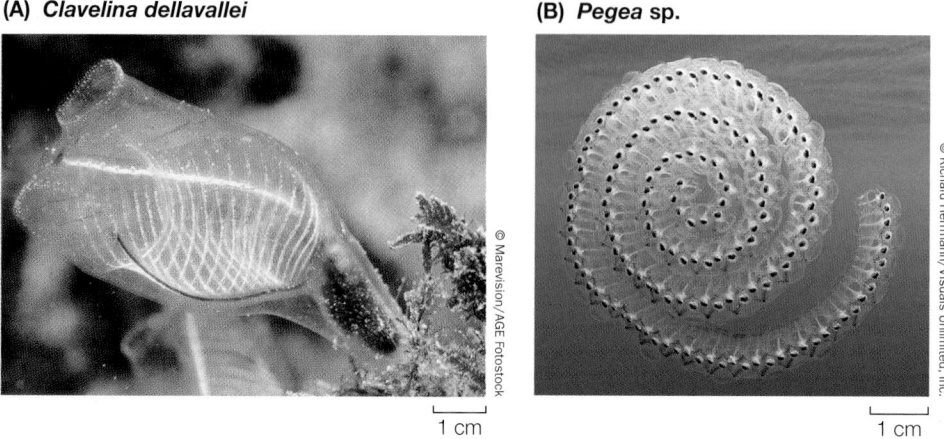

(A) *Clavelina dellavallei*

(B) *Pegea* sp.

1 cm

1 cm

In addition to its pharyngeal slits, a sea squirt larva has a dorsal hollow nerve cord and a notochord that is restricted mostly to the tail region (see Figure 31.7A). Bands of muscle surround the notochord, which provide support for the body. After a short time swimming in the plankton, the larvae of most species settle on the seafloor and transform into sessile adults. The swimming, tadpolelike larvae suggest a close evolutionary relationship between tunicates and vertebrates (see Figure 20.6).

Thaliaceans (salps and their relatives) are tunicates that can live singly or in chainlike colonies up to several meters long (**Figure 31.8B**). They float in tropical and subtropical oceans at depths down to 1,500 meters. Larvaceans are solitary planktonic animals that retain the notochord and dorsal hollow nerve cord throughout their lives. Most larvaceans are less than 5 millimeters long, but some species that live near the bottom of deep ocean waters build delicate casings of mucus that may be more than a meter wide. They snare sinking organic particles (their primary food source) with elaborate filters built into their mucus "houses." When the old "house" gets clogged with excess debris, the animal builds a new one.

A dorsal supporting structure replaces the notochord in vertebrates

In one chordate group, the vertebrates, a new dorsal supporting structure evolved. This group takes its name from the jointed, dorsal **vertebral column** that typically replaces the notochord during early development as the primary supporting structure. The individual elements in the vertebral column are called vertebrae. Four other key features characterize the vertebrates as well (**Figure 31.9**):

- An anterior *skull* enclosing a large brain
- A rigid internal *skeleton* supported by the vertebral column
- Internal organs *suspended in a coelom*
- A well-developed *circulatory system*, driven by contractions of a ventral heart

These structural features can support large, active animals. The internal skeleton provides support for an extensive

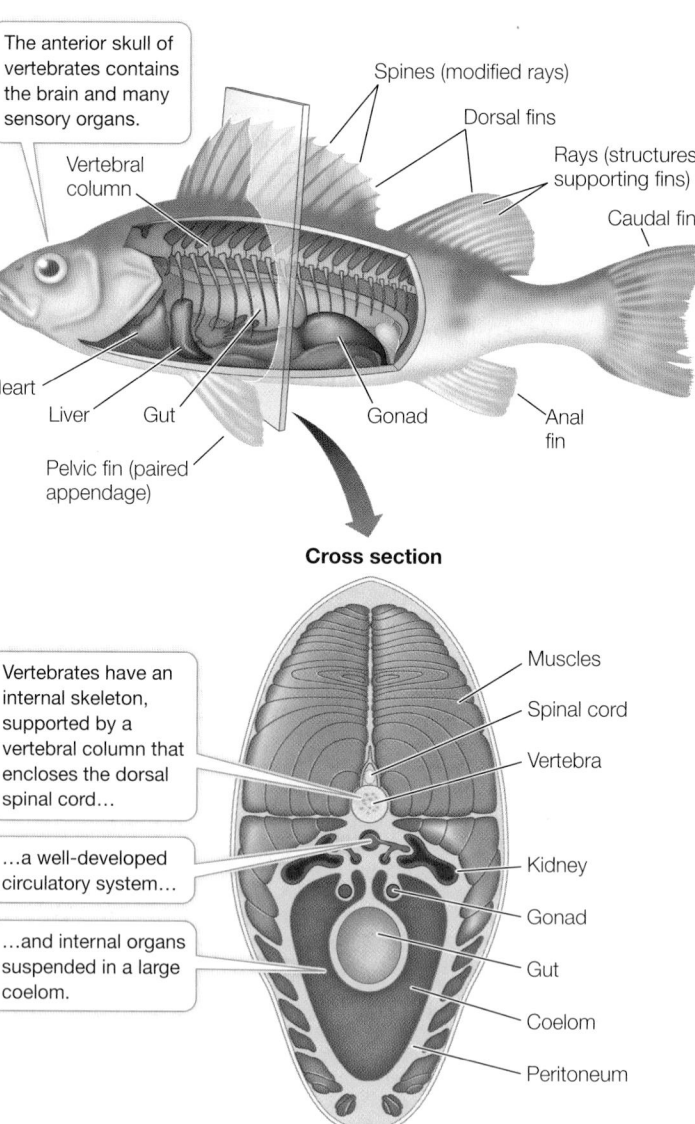

The anterior skull of vertebrates contains the brain and many sensory organs.

Spines (modified rays)

Dorsal fins

Rays (structures supporting fins)

Caudal fin

Vertebral column

Heart

Liver Gut

Gonad

Anal fin

Pelvic fin (paired appendage)

Cross section

Vertebrates have an internal skeleton, supported by a vertebral column that encloses the dorsal spinal cord...

...a well-developed circulatory system...

...and internal organs suspended in a large coelom.

Muscles

Spinal cord

Vertebra

Kidney

Gonad

Gut

Coelom

Peritoneum

Figure 31.9 The Vertebrate Body Plan A ray-finned fish is used here to illustrate some of the structural elements common to all vertebrates. In addition to the paired pelvic fins, these fishes have paired pectoral fins on the sides of the body (not seen in this cutaway view).

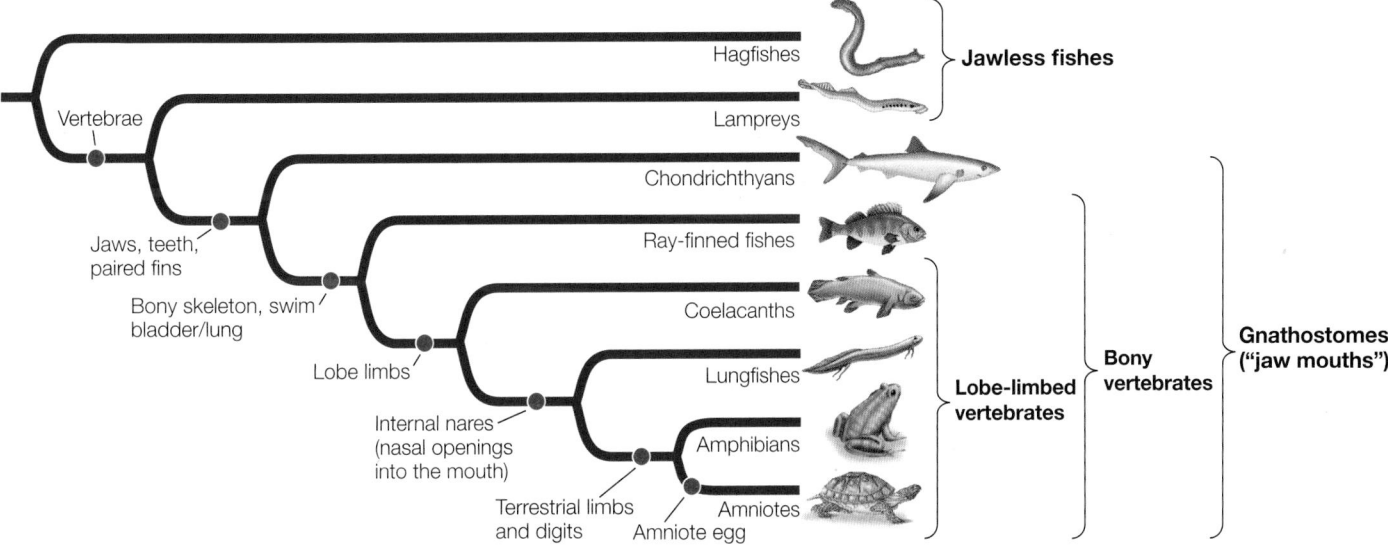

Figure 31.10 Phylogeny of the Living Vertebrates This phylogenetic tree shows the evolution of some of the key innovations among the major groups of vertebrates. Note that several recent analyses favor a closer relationship of hagfishes to lampreys (which together form the taxon cyclostomes). If the cyclostomes are a monophyletic group, then hagfishes may have secondarily lost some distinctive features of the other vertebrates, including vertebrae.

muscular system, which receives oxygen from the circulatory system and is controlled by the central nervous system. The evolution of these features allowed many vertebrates to become large, active predators, which in turn allowed the vertebrates to diversify widely (**Figure 31.10**).

All of the nonvertebrate deuterostomes live in marine environments. The lineage that led to the vertebrates is also thought to have evolved in the oceans, although probably in an estuarine environment (where fresh water meets salt water). The first vertebrates appeared in the Cambrian; since then they have radiated into marine, freshwater, terrestrial, and aerial environments worldwide. There are about 71,000 species of living vertebrates.

The phylogenetic relationships of jawless fishes are uncertain

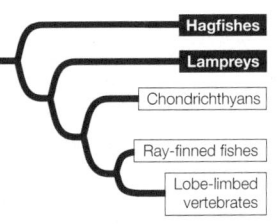

The **hagfishes** are thought by some biologists to be the sister group of the remaining vertebrates (see Figure 31.10). Hagfishes (**Figure 31.11A**) have a weak circulatory system with three small accessory hearts (rather than a single, large heart); a partial cranium, or skull (containing a brain with no cerebrum or cerebellum, two main regions that characterize the brains of other vertebrates); and no jaws or stomach. They also lack separate, jointed vertebrae and have a skeleton composed of a firm but pliable material called cartilage. Thus some biologists do not consider hagfishes to be vertebrates and instead use the term "craniates" to refer collectively to the hagfishes and the vertebrates. Recent analyses of gene sequences and recently discovered fossils suggest, however, that hagfishes may be the sister group of the **lampreys** (**Figure 31.11B**); in this phylogenetic arrangement, the hagfishes and the lampreys are collectively called the cyclostomes ("circle mouths"). If in fact the

(A) *Eptatretus stoutii*

(B) *Lampetra fluviatilis*

Figure 31.11 Modern Jawless Fishes (A) Hagfishes burrow in the ocean mud, from which they extract small prey. They also scavenge on dead or dying fishes. Hagfishes have degenerate eyes, which has led to their being called (inaccurately) "blind eels." (B) Many species of lampreys are ectoparasites that attach to the bodies of living fishes and use their large, jawless mouth to suck blood and flesh. This species lives in freshwater rivers, but some lampreys can live in marine environments.

hagfishes and lampreys do form a monophyletic group, then hagfishes must have secondarily lost many of the major vertebrate morphological features during their evolution.

The 80 known species of hagfishes are unusual marine animals that produce copious quantities of mucus as a defense. They are virtually blind and rely largely on the four pairs of sensory tentacles around the mouth to detect food. Although they have no jaws, hagfishes have a tonguelike structure equipped with toothlike rasps that they use to tear apart dead organisms and to capture their principal prey, polychaete worms. Hagfishes have direct development (no larvae), and individuals may actually change sex from year to year (from male to female and vice versa).

▶ **Media Clip 31.2 Hagfish Slime**
Life12e.com/mc31.2

Although the lampreys and hagfishes may look superficially similar (with elongated eel-like bodies and no paired fins), they differ greatly in their biology. Lampreys have a complete skull and distinct and separate (although rudimentary) vertebrae, all cartilaginous rather than bony. Lampreys undergo a complete metamorphosis from filter-feeding larvae, known as ammocoetes, which are morphologically similar to adult lancelets. The adults of many species of lampreys are parasitic, although several lineages of lampreys evolved to become nonfeeding as adults. These nonfeeding adults survive for only a few weeks after metamorphosis—just long enough to breed. In the species that are parasitic as adults, the round mouth is a rasping and sucking organ that is used to attach to prey and rasp at the flesh (see Figure 31.11B).

The nearly 50 species of lampreys either live permanently in fresh water or are anadromous—meaning they live in coastal salt water and move into fresh water to breed. Some species of lampreys are critically endangered because of recent habitat changes and losses.

Jaws and teeth improved feeding efficiency

Many kinds of jawless fishes were found in the seas, estuaries, and fresh waters of the Devonian, but hagfishes and lampreys are the only jawless fishes that survived beyond the Devonian. Late in the Ordovician, some fishes evolved jaws via modifications of the skeletal arches that supported the gills (**Figure 31.12A**). Those fishes and their descendants are referred to as **gnathostomes** (Greek, "jaw mouths"). Jaws greatly improved feeding efficiency, as an animal with jaws can grasp, subdue, and swallow large prey. Jawed fishes rapidly diversified during the Devonian, eventually replacing the jawless fishes in dominance of the seas.

The earliest jaws were simple, but the evolution of teeth made feeding even more efficient (**Figure 31.12B**). In predators, teeth function crucially both in grasping and in breaking up prey. In both predators and herbivores, teeth enable an animal to chew both soft and hard body parts of their food organisms. Chewing also aids chemical digestion and improves an animal's ability to extract nutrients from its food. Vertebrates are remarkable in the diversity of their jaws and teeth, and in their physiological adaptations for digestion of a wide variety of food items.

Connect the Concepts The many physiological adaptations of vertebrates for digesting plants and animals are described in detail in Chapter 49.

Fins and swim bladders improved stability and control over locomotion

Most jawed fishes have a pair of pectoral fins just behind the gill slits and a pair of pelvic fins anterior to the anus (see Figures 31.9 and 31.13A). These paired fins stabilize the fish's position in water

(A)

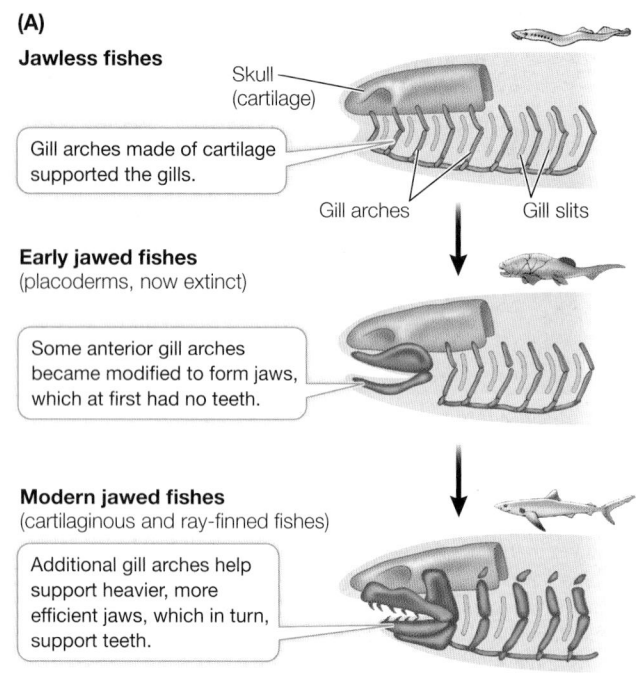

Jawless fishes

Skull (cartilage)

Gill arches made of cartilage supported the gills.

Gill arches   Gill slits

Early jawed fishes (placoderms, now extinct)

Some anterior gill arches became modified to form jaws, which at first had no teeth.

Modern jawed fishes (cartilaginous and ray-finned fishes)

Additional gill arches help support heavier, more efficient jaws, which in turn, support teeth.

(B)

© Ethan Miller/Getty Images

Figure 31.12 Jaws and Teeth Increased Feeding Efficiency
(**A**) These diagrams illustrate one probable scenario for the evolution of jaws from the anterior gill arches of jawless fishes. (**B**) Jaws of the extinct giant shark *Carcharodon megalodon* display the teeth that indicate an extreme predatory lifestyle.

(A) *Carcharodon carcharias*

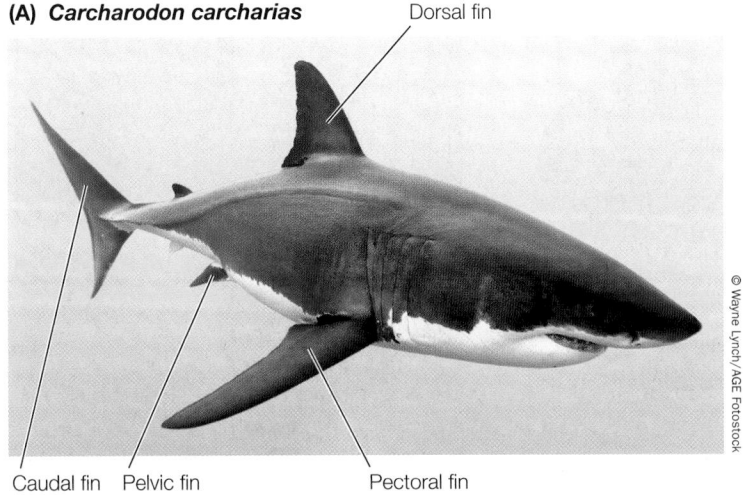

Dorsal fin

© Wayne Lynch/AGE Fotostock

Caudal fin Pelvic fin Pectoral fin

(B) *Taeniura lymma*

© blickwinkel/Alamy Stock Photo

The pectoral fins of rays are modified for propulsion; their other fins are greatly reduced.

(C) *Hydrolagus colliei*

© RGB Ventures LLC dba SuperStock/Alamy Stock Photo

Figure 31.13 Chondrichthyans **(A)** Most sharks are active marine predators, as epitomized by the great white shark seen here. **(B)** Skates and rays, represented here by a blue spotted fantail ray, feed on the ocean bottom. **(C)** A chimaera, or ratfish. Many of these deep-sea fishes possess modified dorsal fins that contain toxins.

(and in some cases, help propel it). Median dorsal and anal fins also stabilize the fish, or may be used for propulsion in some species. In many fishes, the caudal (tail) fin helps propel the animal and enables it to turn rapidly.

Several groups of jawed fishes became abundant during the Devonian. Among them were the **chondrichthyans**—sharks, skates, and rays (about 1,000 living species) and chimaeras (40 living species). Like hagfishes and lampreys, these fishes have a skeleton composed entirely of cartilage. Their skin is flexible and leathery, sometimes bearing scales that give it the consistency of sandpaper. Sharks move forward by means of lateral (side-to-side) undulations of the body and caudal fin (**Figure 31.13A**). Skates and rays propel themselves by means of vertical undulating movements of their greatly enlarged pectoral fins (**Figure 31.13B**).

Most sharks are predators, but some feed by straining plankton from the water. Most skates and rays live on the ocean floor, where they feed on mollusks and other animals buried in the sediments. Nearly all chondrichthyans live in the oceans, but a few are estuarine or migrate into lakes and rivers. One group of rays is found in river systems of South America. The less familiar chimaeras (**Figure 31.13C**) live in deep-sea or cold waters.

One lineage of aquatic gnathostomes gave rise to the bony vertebrates, which soon split into two main lineages—the **ray-finned fishes** and the **lobe-limbed vertebrates**. Bony vertebrates have internal skeletons of calcified, rigid bone rather than flexible cartilage. In early bony vertebrates, gas-filled sacs supplemented the

gas exchange function of the gills by giving the animals access to atmospheric oxygen. These features enabled these fishes to live where oxygen was periodically in short supply, as it often is in freshwater environments. In the ray-finned fishes, these lunglike sacs evolved into **swim bladders**, which are organs of buoyancy. By adjusting the amount of gas in its swim bladder, a ray-finned fish can control the depth at which it remains suspended in the water while expending very little energy to maintain its position.

The outer body surface of most species of ray-finned fishes is covered with thin, flat, lightweight scales that provide protection or enhance movement through the water. The gills open into a single chamber covered by a hard flap, called an operculum. Movement of the operculum increases the flow of water over the gills, where gas exchange takes place.

Ray-finned fishes began to diversify during the Mesozoic and continued to radiate extensively throughout the Paleogene and Neogene. Today there are about 35,000 known living species, encompassing a remarkable variety of sizes, shapes, and lifestyles (**Figure 31.14**). The smallest are less than 1 centimeter long; the largest weigh as much as 900 kilograms. Ray-finned fishes exploit nearly all types of aquatic food sources. In the oceans they filter plankton from the water, rasp algae from rocks, eat corals and other soft-bodied colonial animals, dig animals from soft sediments, and prey on virtually all kinds of other fishes. In fresh water they eat plankton, devour insects, eat fruits that fall into the water, and prey on other aquatic vertebrates and, occasionally,

Figure 31.14 Diversity among the Ray-Finned Fishes **(A)** The brightly colored regal angelfish lives around Indo-Pacific coral reefs. Its deep, laterally compressed body and enlarged dorsal and anal fins increase its apparent size. **(B)** This slow-moving weedy seadragon relies on its highly modified body and fins to provide camouflage in swaying seaweed. **(C)** This spotted boxfish is a member of another large ray-fin clade, the serranids, which also includes the sea basses and groupers. **(D)** Deep-sea angler-fishes live below the level of light penetration. The large fish shown here is a female; the two smaller fish are males, which fuse to the female for life.

(A) *Pygoplites diacanthus*

(B) *Phyllopteryx taeniolatus*

(C) *Ostracion meleagris*

(D) *Edriolychnus schmidti*

terrestrial vertebrates. Many ray-finned fishes are solitary, but in open water others form large aggregations called schools. Many species perform complicated behaviors to maintain schools, build nests, court mates, and care for their young.

Although ray-finned fishes can readily control their position in open water using their fins and swim bladder, their eggs tend to sink. Some species produce small eggs that are buoyant enough to complete their development in open water, but many marine fishes move to food-rich shallow waters to lay their eggs. That is why coastal waters and estuaries are so important in the life cycles of many marine fishes. Some ray-finned fishes, such as salmon, are anadromous, moving from the ocean to the fresh waters in which they breed.

KEY CONCEPT
31.3 Recap and Assess

Chordates are characterized by a dorsal hollow nerve chord, a post-anal tail, and a dorsal supporting rod called a notochord at some point during the life cycle. Specialized structures for support (a vertebral column), locomotion (such as fins), and feeding (jaws and teeth) evolved among aquatic vertebrates.

1. Describe the synapomorphies that characterize the chordates and the vertebrates, respectively.

2. How do the hagfishes differ from the lampreys in morphology? Why do some biologists contend that hagfishes are not vertebrates?

3. The body plan of most vertebrates is based on four appendages. What are the varied forms that these appendages take, and how are they used? In which lineages have two or more of these appendages been lost?

In the lobe-limbed vertebrates, the gas-filled sacs that gave rise to swim bladders in ray-finned fishes became specialized for another purpose: breathing air. That adaptation set the stage for the vertebrates to move onto the land.

KEY CONCEPT
31.4 Tetrapods Diversified Rapidly in Terrestrial Environments

Learning Objectives

31.4.1 Explain how features of amphibians can make them especially vulnerable to environmental change.

31.4.2 Summarize the evidence for the phylogenetic position of birds among the reptiles.

31.4.3 Describe how a mass extinction affected the diversification of mammals.

31.4.4 Trace the evolution of endothermy, hair, and feathers across the phylogeny of amniotes.

The evolution of lunglike sacs in fishes set the stage for the vertebrate invasion of the land. Some early ray-finned fishes probably used those sacs to supplement their gills when oxygen levels in the water were low, as many groups of ray-finned fishes do today. But with their unjointed fins, those fishes could only flop around when out of water. Changes in the structure of the fins first allowed lobe-limbed vertebrates to support themselves better in shallow water, and later to move better on land.

Jointed limbs enhanced support and locomotion on land

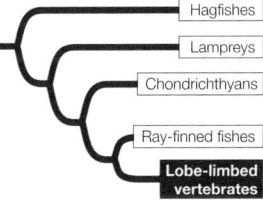

In the lobe-limbed vertebrates, the paired pelvic and pectoral fins developed into more muscular fins that were joined to the body by a single enlarged bone. The modern representatives of these lobe-limbed vertebrates include the coelacanths, lungfishes, and tetrapods.

The coelacanths flourished from the Devonian until about 65 million years ago, when they were thought to have become extinct. However, in 1938 a commercial fisherman caught a living coelacanth off South Africa. Since that time, hundreds of individuals of this extraordinary fish, *Latimeria chalumnae*, have been collected (**Figure 31.15A**). A second species, *L. menadoensis*, was discovered in 1998 off the Indonesian island of Sulawesi. *Latimeria*, a predator of other fishes, reaches a length of about 1.8 meters and weighs up to 82 kilograms. Its skeleton is composed mostly of cartilage, not bone. The cartilaginous skeleton is a derived feature in this clade because it had bony ancestors.

 Media Clip 31.3 Coelacanths in the Deep Seas
Life12e.com/mc31.3

Lungfishes were important predators in shallow-water habitats in the Devonian, but most lineages died out. The six surviving species live in stagnant swamps and muddy waters in South America, Africa, and Australia (**Figure 31.15B**). Lungfishes have lungs derived from the lunglike sacs of their ancestors as well as gills. When ponds dry up, individuals of most species can burrow deep into the mud and survive for many months in an inactive state while breathing air.

It is believed that some early aquatic lobe-limbed vertebrates began to use terrestrial food sources, became more fully adapted to life on land, and eventually evolved to become ancestral tetrapods ("four legs"). How was this transition from an animal that swam in water to one that walked on land accomplished? Early in 2006, scientists reported the discovery of a Devonian fossil lobe-limbed vertebrate, since then named Tiktaalik, which possessed appendages intermediate between the fins of fishes and the limbs of terrestrial tetrapods (**Figure 31.15C**). It appears that limbs capable of propping up a large fish and making the front-to-rear movements necessary for walking evolved while these animals still lived in water. These limbs appear to have functioned in holding the animals upright in shallow water, perhaps even allowing them to hold their head above the water's surface. These same structures were then co-opted for movement on land, at first probably for foraging on brief trips out of water.

Among the lobe-limbed vertebrates, limbs capable of movement on land evolved from the short, muscular fins of aquatic ancestors (**Figure 31.16**). The resulting four terrestrial limbs give the tetrapods their name. The basic skeletal elements of those limbs can be traced through major changes in limb form and function among the terrestrial vertebrates.

An early split in the tetrapod tree (see Figure 31.10) led to two main groups of terrestrial vertebrates: **amphibians**, most of which

(A) *Latimeria chalumnae*

(B) *Protopterus annectens*

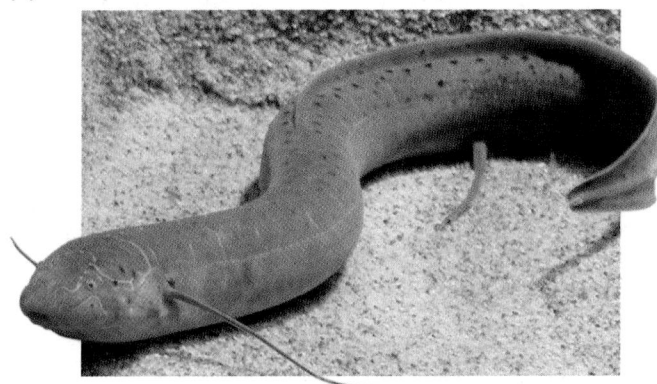

(C) *Tiktaalik roseae*

Tiktaalik's pectoral fins show some of the skeletal structures of tetrapod limbs.

Figure 31.15 The Closest Relatives of Tetrapods (A) The African coelacanth, discovered in deep waters of the Indian Ocean off the coast of South Africa, represents one of two surviving species of a group that was once thought to be extinct. (B) All surviving lungfish species, such as this African lungfish, live in the Southern Hemisphere. (C) *Tiktaalik*, a fossil lobe-limbed vertebrate from the Devonian, is believed to represent a transitional species intermediate between the finned fishes and the limbed tetrapods.

remained tied to moist environments, and the **amniotes**, many of which adapted to much drier conditions.

Amphibians adapted to life on land

Most modern amphibians are confined to moist environments because they lose water rapidly through the skin when exposed to dry

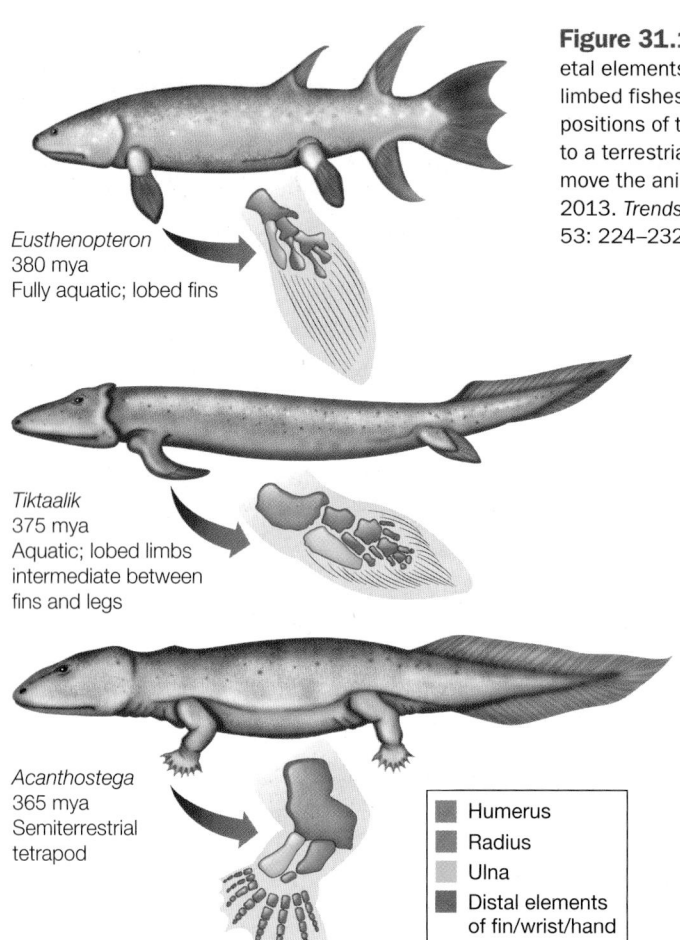

Eusthenopteron
380 mya
Fully aquatic; lobed fins

Tiktaalik
375 mya
Aquatic; lobed limbs
intermediate between
fins and legs

Acanthostega
365 mya
Semiterrestrial
tetrapod

Humerus
Radius
Ulna
Distal elements
of fin/wrist/hand

Figure 31.16 Tetrapod Limbs Are Modified Fins The major skeletal elements of the tetrapod limb were already present in aquatic lobe-limbed fishes some 380 million years ago (mya). The relative sizes and positions of these elements changed as lobe-limbed vertebrates moved to a terrestrial environment, where limbs were needed to support and move the animal's body on land. (After I. Schneider and N. H. Shubin. 2013. *Trends Genet* 29: 419–426; M. C. Davis. 2013. *Integr Comp Biol* 53: 224–232.)

air. In addition, their eggs are enclosed within delicate gelatinous envelopes that cannot prevent water loss in dry conditions. In some amphibian species, adults live mostly on land but return to fresh water to lay and fertilize their eggs (**Figure 31.17**). The fertilized eggs give rise to larvae that live in water until they undergo metamorphosis to become terrestrial adults. However, many amphibians (especially those in tropical and subtropical areas) have evolved a wide variety of additional reproductive modes and types of parental care. Internal fertilization, for example, evolved several times among amphibian species. Many species develop directly into adultlike forms from fertilized eggs laid on land or carried by the parents. Other species of amphibians are entirely aquatic, never leaving the water at any stage of their lives, and many of these species retain a larval-like morphology.

The more than 8,000 known species of amphibians living today belong to three major groups: the wormlike, limbless, tropical, burrowing, or aquatic caecilians (**Figure 31.18A**), the tail-less frogs and toads (collectively called anurans) (**Figure 31.18B**), and the tailed salamanders (**Figure 31.18C,D**).

Anurans are most diverse in wet tropical and warm temperate regions, although a few are found at very high latitudes. There are

Figure 31.17 In and Out of the Water Many amphibian species have life cycles like the one diagrammed here, in which the early stages take place in water and the aquatic tadpole transforms into a terrestrial adult through metamorphosis. Some species of amphibians, however, have direct development (with no aquatic larval stage), and others are aquatic throughout life.

Q: What is a potential advantage of maintaining an aquatic tadpole stage, even though the adults are terrestrial?

▶ **View in Achieve**
Animation 31.2
Life Cycle of a Frog

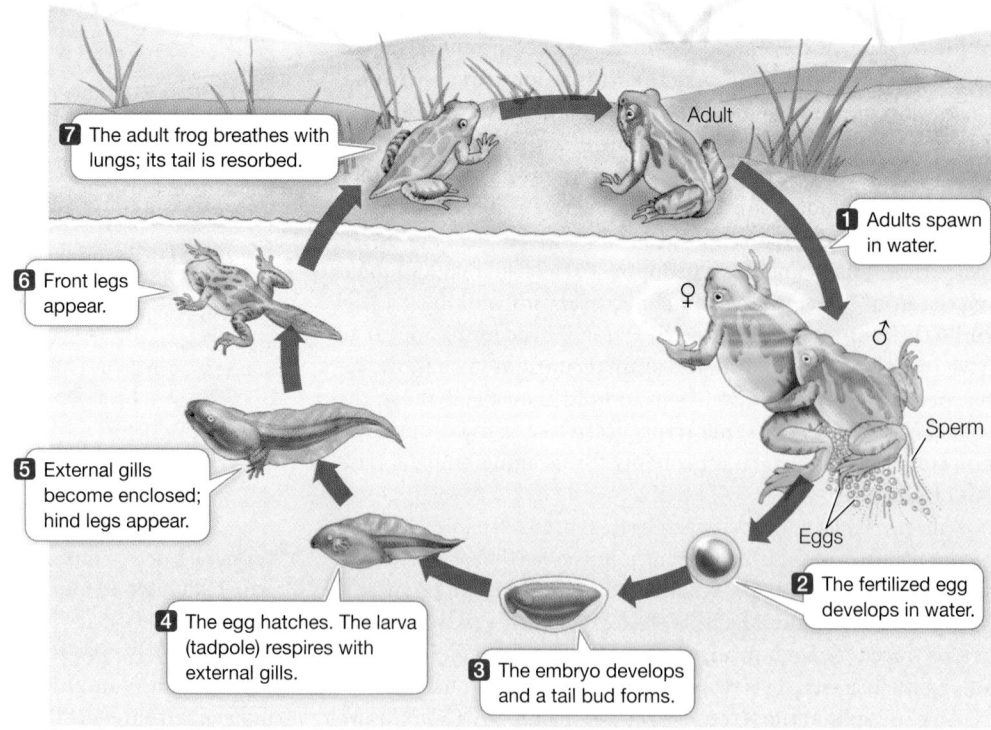

7 The adult frog breathes with lungs; its tail is resorbed.

Adult

1 Adults spawn in water.

6 Front legs appear.

♀

♂

Sperm

5 External gills become enclosed; hind legs appear.

Eggs

4 The egg hatches. The larva (tadpole) respires with external gills.

3 The embryo develops and a tail bud forms.

2 The fertilized egg develops in water.

(A) *Siphonops annulatus*

(B) *Incilius periglenes*

(C) *Salamandra salamandra*

(D) *Eurycea waterlooensis*

Figure 31.18 Diversity among the Amphibians **(A)** Burrowing caecilians superficially look more like worms than like amphibians. They have internal fertilization, and many species are viviparous. **(B)** A golden toad pair in Costa Rica; the male is on top. This is one of many amphibian species that has been lost to extinction in the past few decades. **(C)** A European fire salamander. **(D)** This Austin blind salamander's life cycle is completely aquatic; it has no terrestrial stage. The eyes of this cave dweller are greatly reduced.

far more anurans than any other amphibians, with well over 7,000 described species and more being discovered every year. Some anurans have tough skins and other adaptations that enable them to live for long periods in deserts, whereas others live in moist terrestrial and arboreal environments. Some species are completely aquatic as adults. All anurans have a short vertebral column and a pelvic region that is modified for leaping, hopping, or propelling the body through water by kicking the hind legs.

The more than 700 described species of salamanders are most diverse in temperate regions of the Northern Hemisphere and in cool, moist environments in the mountains of Central America, although a few species penetrate into tropical regions. Many salamanders live in rotting logs or moist soil. One major group has lost the lungs, and these species exchange gases entirely through the skin and mouth lining—body parts that all amphibians use, in addition to their lungs, for gas exchange. A completely aquatic lifestyle has evolved several times among the salamanders (see Figure 31.18D). These aquatic species have arisen through a developmental process known as **neoteny**, or the retention of juvenile traits (in this case, gills) by delayed somatic development. Most species of salamanders have internal fertilization, which is usually achieved through the transfer of a small, jellylike, sperm-embedded capsule called a spermatophore.

Many amphibians have complex social behaviors. Most male anurans utter loud, species-specific calls to attract females of their own species (and sometimes to defend breeding territories), and they compete for access to females that arrive at the breeding sites. Many amphibians lay large numbers of eggs, which they abandon once they are deposited and fertilized. Other amphibians lay only a few eggs, which are fertilized and then cared for. A few species of frogs, salamanders, and caecilians are viviparous, meaning they give birth to well-developed young that have received nutrition from the female during gestation.

▶ **Media Clip 31.4 Answering a Mating Call**
Life12e.com/mc31.4

Amphibians are the focus of much attention today because populations of many species are declining rapidly, especially in mountainous regions of western North America, Central and South America, and northeastern Australia. Worldwide, about one-third of amphibian species are now threatened with extinction or have disappeared completely in the last few decades. Scientists are investigating several hypotheses to account for these amphibian declines.

Connect the Concepts One of the major factors associated with amphibian declines is the global spread of a pathogenic chytrid fungus, as discussed in Key Concept 28.2.

Amniotes colonized dry environments

Several key innovations for conserving water contributed to the ability of the amniotes to exploit a wide range of terrestrial habitats. The **amniote egg** (which gives the group its name) is relatively impermeable to water and allows the embryo to develop in a contained aqueous environment (**Figure 31.19A**). Its leathery or brittle, calcium-impregnated shell retards evaporation of the fluids inside but permits passage of oxygen and carbon dioxide. The amniote egg also stores large quantities of food in the form of **yolk**, allowing the embryo to attain a relatively advanced state of development before it hatches. Within the shell are **extraembryonic membranes** that protect the embryo from desiccation and assist it with gas exchange and excretion of nitrogenous waste products of metabolism.

As we described in the opening of this chapter, modifications of the amniote egg in several different groups of amniotes allowed the embryo to develop inside (and exchange nutrients and wastes with) its mother's body (**Figure 31.19B**). For example, in most mammals the egg lost its shell entirely while the functions of the extraembryonic membranes were retained and expanded, giving rise to viviparity. Viviparity appears to have evolved many times among lizards and snakes. In **Investigating Life: Have Shelled Eggs Re-Evolved among Viviparous Reptile Lineages?**, we explore the possibility that shelled eggs may have re-evolved in some lizards and snakes.

Other innovations evolved in the organs of terrestrial adults. A tough, impermeable skin, covered with scales or modifications of scales such as hair or feathers, greatly reduced water loss. Adaptations of the kidneys (the vertebrate excretory organs) allowed amniotes to excrete concentrated urine, ridding the body of nitrogenous wastes without losing a large amount of water in the process (see Chapter 50).

(A)

Extraembryonic
membranes:

Yolk sac

Chorion

Allantois

Amnion

Shell

Amniotic cavity   Embryo

(B)

Maternal portion of placenta

Fetal portion
of placenta

Umbilical
cord

Embryo

Amniotic cavity

Human embryo and placenta

© Pr. M. Forest, CNRI/Science Source

Figure 31.19 The Amniote Egg (A) The evolution of the amniote egg, with its water-retaining shell, four extraembryonic membranes, and embryo-nourishing yolk, was a major step in adaptation to the terrestrial environment. A chicken egg is shown here. (B) In most mammals, the developing embryo is retained inside the mother's body, with which the embryo exchanges nutrients and wastes via the placenta.

Q: How were the various membranes in the amniote egg modified in mammals to support viviparity?

▶ **View in Achieve**
Activity 31.2 The Amniote Egg

▶Investigating LIFE   Have Shelled Eggs Re-Evolved among Viviparous Reptile Lineages?

Experiment

Original Papers: R. A. Pyron and F. T. Burbrink. 2014. Early origin of viviparity and multiple reversions to oviparity in squamate reptiles. *Ecol Lett* 17: 13–21.

A. M. Wright et al. 2015. Which came first: The lizard or the egg? Robustness in phylogenetic reconstruction of ancestral states. *J Exp Zool B (Mol Dev Evol)* 324B: 504–516.

The shelled amniote egg is a complex structure, and the transition from oviparity to viviparity requires extensive changes in reproductive morphology and physiology. For example, oviparous species have uterine shell glands that secrete calcium for eggshell construction. These shell glands are modified in viviparous species to provide calcium to the developing embryo. Viviparity is thought to have evolved from oviparity more than 100 times among lizards and snakes, but biologists wondered if the process can be reversed: does egg laying ever re-evolve in live-bearing lineages?

QUESTION▶ Can complex traits such as shelled eggs re-evolve once they have been lost?

METHOD▶

1. Reconstruct the phylogeny of lizards and snakes (squamates).

2. Collect data on the reproductive mode of more than 8,000 species of lizards and snakes.

3. Reconstruct the evolution of transitions between oviparity and viviparity on the phylogeny.

RESULTS▶ The number of reversals from viviparity to oviparity depends on the model of character change, but there is support for the re-evolution of egg laying from live birth in one group of lizards and in two groups of snakes.

CONCLUSION▶ Although transitions from oviparity to viviparity are much more common than the reverse, egg laying may have re-evolved in a few lineages of squamates.

Oviparous: Pueblan milk snake (*Lampropeltis polyzona campbelli*)

© FLPA/Alamy Stock Photo

Viviparous: Blotched blue-tongue lizard (*Tiliqua nigrolutea*)

© Saeed Khan/AFP/Getty Images

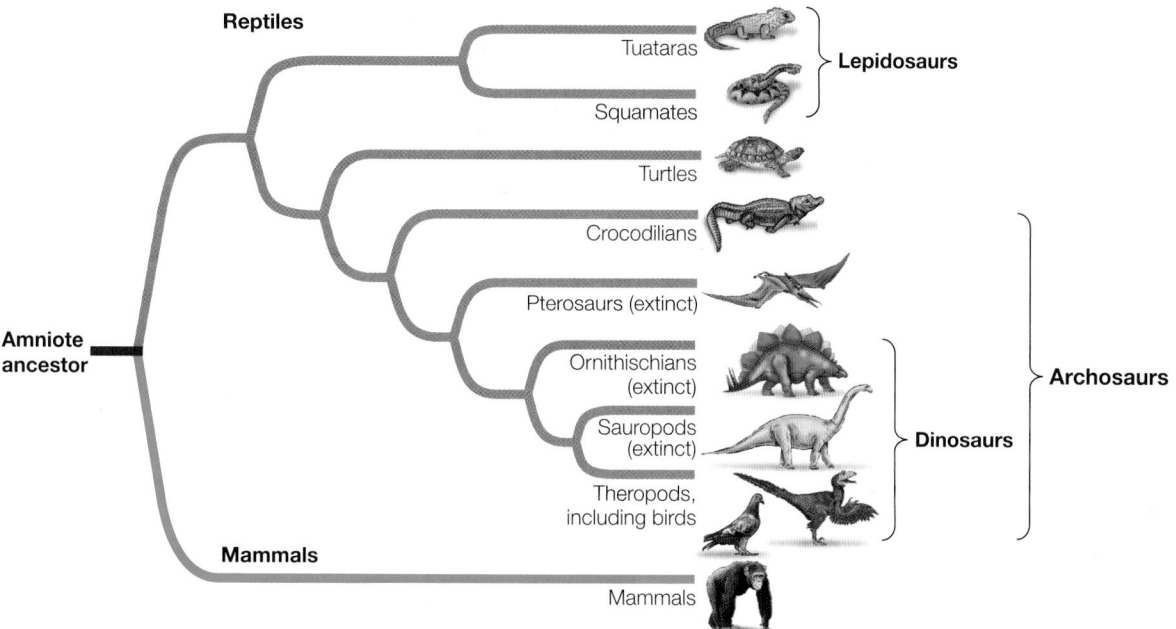

Figure 31.20 Phylogeny of Amniotes   This tree of amniote relationships shows the primary split between mammals and reptiles. The reptile portion of the tree shows that one lineage led to the lepidosaurs (snakes, lizards, and tuataras), another to the turtles, and a third to the archosaurs (the crocodilians, several extinct groups, and the birds).

Work with the Data

Original Paper: A. M. Fenwick et al. 2012. The serpent and the egg: Unidirectional evolution of reproductive mode in vipers? *J Zool Syst Evol Res* 50: 59–66.

The tree below shows a small portion of the phylogeny and reproductive data collected for squamates, from the New World pit vipers. Use this data sample to answer the questions.

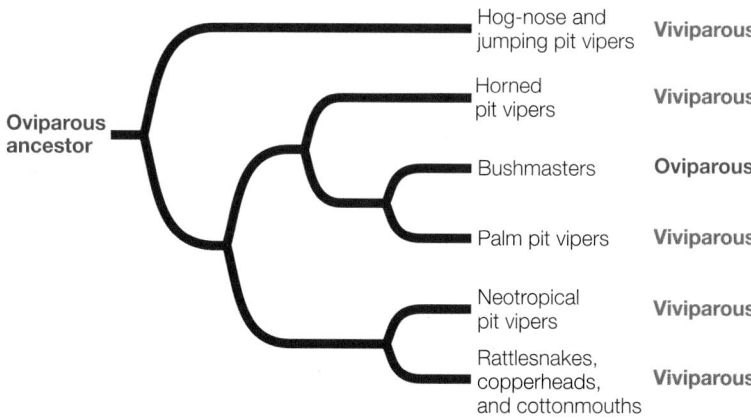

QUESTIONS▶

1. Starting with a root state of oviparity, plot the minimum number of changes between oviparity and viviparity (in either direction) that is necessary to explain the distribution of reproductive states on the tree. What is the minimum number of changes required on this tree? Does that number include any reversals to oviparity?

2. Assume that the only changes that can occur are changes from oviparity to viviparity (do not allow any changes in the opposite direction). How many additional transitions in reproductive mode are necessary under this assumption compared with the result you obtained in Question 1?

Go to Achieve for a companion *Data in Depth* exercise.

During the Carboniferous, the amniotes split into two major groups: the **reptiles** and the lineage that eventually led to the **mammals** (**Figure 31.20**).

Reptiles adapted to life in many habitats

The lineage leading to modern reptiles began to diverge from other amniotes more than 300 million years ago. More than 19,000 species of reptiles exist today, more than half of which are birds. Birds are the only living representatives of the otherwise extinct dinosaurs, the dominant terrestrial vertebrates of the Mesozoic.

The **lepidosaurs** constitute the second most species-rich clade of living reptiles. This group is composed of the **squamates** (lizards, snakes, and amphisbaenians—the last a group of mostly legless, wormlike, burrowing reptiles with greatly reduced eyes) and the **tuataras**, which superficially resemble lizards but differ from them in possessing more rigid skulls and other anatomical features. Many species related to the tuataras lived during the Mesozoic, but today only a single species survives (**Figure 31.21A**), and is restricted to a few islands off New Zealand.

The skin of a lepidosaur is covered with horny scales that greatly reduce loss of water from the body surface. These scales, however, make the skin unavailable as an organ of gas exchange. Gases are exchanged almost entirely via the lungs, which are proportionally much larger in surface area than those of amphibians.

(A) *Sphenodon punctatus*

(B) *Trioceros jacksonii*

(C) *Diadophis punctatus*

(D) *Chelonoidis nigra abingdonii*

Figure 31.21 Reptilian Diversity **(A)** This tuatara represents the only surviving species in its lineage. **(B)** The Jackson's chameleon is native to eastern Africa but was introduced to Hawaii in 1972. **(C)** The ringneck snake of North America is harmless to humans. It coils its tail to reveal a bright orange underbelly, which distracts potential predators from the vital head region. **(D)** Galápagos tortoises (there are several closely related species) are the largest turtles and among the largest reptiles. They have been documented to live for more than 100 years in the wild.

A lepidosaur forces air into and out of its lungs by bellows-like movements of its ribs. The three-chambered lepidosaur heart partially separates oxygenated blood from the lungs from deoxygenated blood returning from the body. With this type of heart, lepidosaurs can generate high blood pressure and can sustain a relatively high metabolism.

Most lizards are insectivores, although some are herbivores and a few prey on other vertebrates. Most lizards walk on four limbs (**Figure 31.21B**), although limblessness has evolved repeatedly among the lizards, especially in burrowing and grassland species. The largest lizard is the predaceous Komodo dragon (*Varanus komodoensis*) of the East Indies, which grows as long as 3 meters and can weigh more than 150 kilograms.

▶ **Media Clip 31.5 Komodo Dragons Bring Down Prey**
Life12e.com/mc31.5

The major group of limbless squamates is the snakes (**Figure 31.21C**). All snakes are carnivores, and many can swallow objects much larger than themselves. Several snake groups possess venom glands and the ability to inject venom rapidly into their prey.

The **turtles** comprise a reptilian group that has changed relatively little in basic body form since the early Mesozoic. In these reptiles, dorsal and ventral bony plates form a shell into which the head and limbs can be withdrawn in many species (**Figure 31.21D**). The dorsal shell is a modification of the ribs. It is notable that pectoral girdles are inside the ribs of turtles, making them unlike any other vertebrates. Most turtles live in aquatic environments, but several groups, such as tortoises and box turtles, are terrestrial. Sea turtles spend their entire lives at sea except when they come ashore to lay eggs. Human exploitation of sea turtles and their eggs has resulted in worldwide declines of these species, all of which are now endangered. A few species of turtles are strict herbivores or carnivores, but most species are omnivores that eat a variety of aquatic and terrestrial plants and animals.

Crocodilians and birds share their ancestry with the dinosaurs

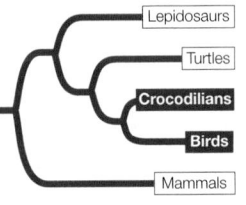

Another reptilian clade, the **archosaurs**, includes the crocodilians, pterosaurs, non-avian dinosaurs, and birds. Only the crocodilians and birds are represented by living species today. Modern **crocodilians**—crocodiles, caimans, gharials, and alligators—are confined to tropical and warm temperate environments (**Figure 31.22A**). All crocodilians are carnivorous; they eat vertebrates of all kinds, including large mammals. Crocodilians spend much of their time in water, but

(A) *Caiman crocodilus*

(B) *Struthio camelus*

Figure 31.22 Archosaurs The two surviving groups of archosaurs are very different. **(A)** The crocodilians live in tropical and warm temperate climates. The spectacled caiman is the most common crocodilian throughout much of tropical Central and South America. **(B)** Birds are the other living archosaur group. This Common Ostrich is a palaeognath, a group that includes several flightless and weakly flying birds of the Southern Hemisphere. Flightless members of this early-diverging group lack the sternum keel structure that anchors the flight muscles of other bird groups.

they lay their eggs in nests they build on land or on floating piles of vegetation. The eggs are warmed by heat generated by decaying organic matter that the female places in the nest. The female provides other forms of parental care as well: typically she guards the eggs until they hatch, and in some species she continues to guard and communicate with her offspring after they hatch.

Dinosaurs rose to prominence about 215 million years ago and dominated terrestrial environments for about 150 million years. However, only one group of dinosaurs, the **birds**, survived the mass extinction at the end of the Cretaceous. During the Mesozoic, most terrestrial animals more than a meter long were dinosaurs. Many were agile and could run rapidly; they had special muscles that enabled the lungs to be filled and emptied while the limbs moved. We can infer the existence of such muscles in dinosaurs from the structure of the vertebral column in fossils. Some of the largest dinosaurs weighed as much as 70,000 kilograms.

Biologists have long accepted the phylogenetic position of birds among the reptiles, although birds clearly have many unique, derived morphological features. In addition to the strong morphological evidence for this placement, fossil and molecular data emerging over the last few decades have provided definitive supporting evidence. Birds are a specialized group of **theropods**, a clade of predatory dinosaurs that shared such traits as a bipedal stance, hollow bones, a furcula ("wishbone"), elongated metatarsals with three-fingered feet, elongated forelimbs with three fingers, and a pelvis that points backward. Modern birds are endothermic, meaning that they regulate their body temperature by producing and retaining metabolic heat, rather than by absorbing heat from their external environment (see Key Concept 38.4). Although we cannot directly assess this physiological trait in extinct species, many fossil theropods share morphological traits that suggest they may have been endothermic as well.

The living bird species fall into two major groups that diverged about 90–80 million years ago from a flying ancestor. The few modern descendants of one lineage include a group of secondarily flightless and weakly flying birds, some of which are very large. This group, called the palaeognaths, includes the South and Central American tinamous and several large flightless birds of the southern continents—the rheas, Emu (*Dromaius novaehollandiae*), kiwis, cassowaries, and the world's largest birds, the ostriches (**Figure 31.22B**). The second lineage, the neognaths, has left a much larger number of descendants, most of which have retained the ability to fly.

Feathers allowed birds to fly

Fossil theropods discovered in early Cretaceous deposits in Liaoning Province, in northeastern China, show that the scales of some small predatory dinosaurs were highly modified to form **feathers**. Initially these feathers were simply a body covering that probably provided insulation and enhanced coloration. But the feathers of some later dinosaurs, such as *Microraptor gui*, were structurally similar to those of modern birds (**Figure 31.23A**).

Another theropod that was even more closely related to modern birds, *Archaeopteryx*, lived about 150 million years ago. *Archaeopteryx* had teeth (unlike modern birds), but it was covered with feathers that are virtually identical to those of birds (**Figure 31.23B**). It also had well-developed wings, a long tail, and a furcula to which some of the flight muscles were probably attached. *Archaeopteryx* had clawed fingers on its forelimbs, but it also had typical perching bird claws on its hindlimbs. It probably lived in trees and shrubs and used the fingers to assist it in clambering over branches. It probably glided or flew weakly. The descendants of *Archaeopteryx* and similar Mesozoic theropods were the modern birds, most of which are accomplished fliers.

▶ Media Clip 31.6 Falcons in Flight
Life12e.com/mc31.6

The evolution and specialization of feathers were a major force for diversification. Feathers are lightweight, but they are strong and structurally complex (**Figure 31.24**). The stiff central shaft of the flight feathers on a bird's wings arises from the skin of the forelimbs to create the flying surfaces. Other strong feathers sprout like a fan from the shortened tail and serve as stabilizers during

(A)

(B)

Impressions of feathers can be seen around the fossilized skeletons.

From X. Xu et al. 2003. Nature 421: 335-340. Reprinted by permission from Springer Nature

© James L. Amos/Science Source

Figure 31.23 Mesozoic Bird Relatives Fossils support the evolution of birds from other theropods. **(A)** *Microraptor gui* was a feathered theropod from the early Cretaceous (about 140 mya). **(B)** *Archaeopteryx* was even more closely related to modern birds.

flight. The feathers that cover the body, along with an underlying layer of down feathers, provide birds with insulation that helps them survive in virtually all of Earth's climates.

The bones of theropod dinosaurs, including birds, are hollow with internal struts that increase their strength. Hollow bones would have made early theropods lighter and more mobile; later they facilitated the evolution of flight. The sternum (breastbone) of flying birds forms a large, vertical keel to which the flight muscles are attached.

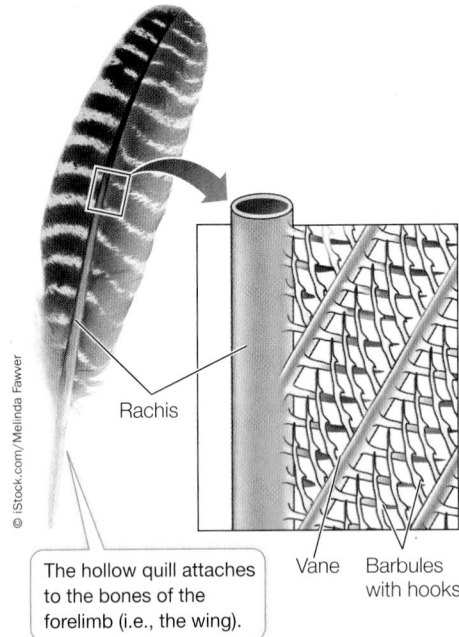

© iStock.com/Melinda Fawver

Rachis

The hollow quill attaches to the bones of the forelimb (i.e., the wing).

Vane   Barbules with hooks

Figure 31.24 Feather Anatomy The flight feathers of birds are attached to the wing's skin by the hollow portion, or quill, of a stiff central shaft. The rachis is the solid portion of the shaft from which radiate fine branches (vanes) with interlocking hooks and barbules. Overall, this structure represents a major evolutionary innovation: a strong, lightweight surface that enables flight.

Flight is metabolically expensive. A flying bird consumes energy at a rate about 15–20 times faster than a running lizard of the same weight. Because birds have such high metabolic rates, they generate large amounts of heat. They control the rate of heat loss using their feathers, which may be held close to the body or elevated to alter the amount of insulation they provide. The lungs of birds allow air to flow through unidirectionally rather than pumping air in and out (see Key Concept 47.2). This flow-through structure of the lungs increases the efficiency of gas exchange and thereby supports a high metabolic rate.

There are about 10,000 species of living birds, which range in size from the 150-kilogram ostriches to a tiny hummingbird weighing only 2 grams (**Figure 31.25**). The teeth so prominent among other dinosaurs were secondarily lost in the ancestral birds, but birds nonetheless eat almost all types of animal and plant material. Insects and fruits are the most important dietary items for terrestrial species. Birds also eat seeds, nectar and pollen, leaves and buds, carrion, and other vertebrates. By eating the fruits and seeds of plants, birds serve as major agents of seed dispersal.

Mammals radiated after the extinction of non-avian dinosaurs

Reptiles

Prototherians

Marsupials

Eutherians

Small and medium-sized mammals coexisted with the large dinosaurs throughout most of the Mesozoic, and most of the major groups of mammals that are alive today arose in the Cretaceous. After the non-avian dinosaurs disappeared during the mass extinction at the end of the Cretaceous, mammals increased dramatically in numbers, diversity, and size. Today mammals range in size from tiny shrews and bats weighing only about 2 grams to the blue whale (*Balaenoptera musculus*), the largest animal on Earth, which measures up to 32 meters long and can weigh as much as 160,000 kilograms. Mammals have far fewer, but more highly differentiated, teeth than do fishes, amphibians, or reptiles. Differences among mammals in the number, type, and arrangement of teeth reflect their varied diets (see Figure 49.6).

(A) *Sialia mexicana*

© Larry Jon Friesen

(B) *Trichoglossus haematodus*

© Lorraine Harris/ Getty Images

(C) *Bubo virginianus*

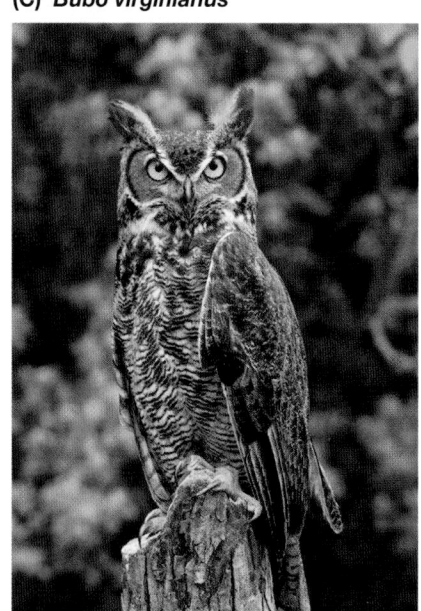

© DnDavis/Shutterstock.com

Figure 31.25 Diversity among the Birds **(A)** Perching, or passeriform, birds such as this Western Bluebird constitute the most species-rich of all bird groups. **(B)** Some 375 species of parrots, macaws, parakeets, and lorikeets such as the one shown here are another large bird group. **(C)** The Great Horned Owl is a nighttime predator that can find prey using its sensitive auditory "sonar" system. **(D)** The Long-billed Curlew of North America is one of many species of wading birds.

(D) *Numenius americanus*

© Larry Jon Friesen

Four key features distinguish the mammals:

1. *Sweat glands*, which secrete sweat that evaporates and thereby cools an animal

2. *Mammary glands*, which in females secrete a nutritive fluid (milk) on which newborn individuals feed

3. *Hair*, which provides a protective and insulating covering

4. A *four-chambered heart* that completely separates the oxygenated blood coming from the lungs from the deoxygenated blood returning from the body (this last characteristic is convergent with the archosaurs, including modern birds and crocodilians)

Mammalian eggs are fertilized within the female's body, and in nearly all mammalian groups the resulting embryos undergo a period of development inside the female's body in an organ called the uterus. In the uterus, the embryo is contained in an amniotic sac that is homologous with one of the four membranes found in the amniote egg (see Figure 31.19). The embryo is connected to the wall of the uterus by an organ called a placenta. The placenta allows for nutrient and gas exchange, as well as waste elimination from the developing embryo, via the female's circulatory system. Most mammals develop a covering of hair (fur), which is luxuriant in some species but has been greatly reduced in others, including cetaceans (whales and dolphins) and humans. Thick layers of insulating fat (blubber) replace hair as a heat-retention mechanism in the cetaceans. Humans learned to use clothing for this purpose when they dispersed from warm tropical areas.

The approximately 5,700 species of living mammals are divided into two primary groups: the **prototherians** and the **therians** (Table 31.1). Members of the therian clade are further divided into the **marsupials** and the **eutherians**.

PROTOTHERIANS   Only five species of living prototherians are known, and they are found only in Australia and New Guinea. These mammals, the duck-billed platypus and four species of echidnas, differ from other mammals in laying shelled eggs and having sprawling legs (Figure 31.26). Prototherians supply milk for their

(A) *Tachyglossus aculeatus*

© Tier Und Naturfotografie J und C Sohns/Getty Images

(B) *Ornithorhynchus anatinus*

© Dave Watts/Alamy Stock Photo

Figure 31.26 Prototherians **(A)** The short-beaked echidna is one of four surviving species of echidnas. **(B)** The duck-billed platypus lives in freshwater streams in eastern Australia.

TABLE 31.1 | Major Groups of Living Mammals

Group	Number of described species	Examples
PROTOTHERIANS		
Monotremes (Monotremata)	5	Echidnas, duck-billed platypus
THERIANS		
MARSUPIALS		
Diprotodonts (Diprotodontia)	146	Kangaroos, wallabies, possums, koala, wombats
New World opossums (Didelphimorphia)	93	Opossums
Carnivorous marsupials (Dasyuromorphia)	75	Quolls, dunnarts, numbat, Tasmanian devil
Omnivorous marsupials (Peramelemorphia)	24	Bandicoots and bilbies
Shrew opossums (Paucituberculata)	7	Andean rat opossums
Marsupial moles (Notoryctemorphia)	2	Southern and northern marsupial moles
Microbiothere (Microbiotherea)	1	Monito del monte
EUTHERIANS		
Rodents (Rodentia)	2,337	Rats, mice, squirrels, woodchucks, ground squirrels, beavers, capybara
Bats (Chiroptera)	1,171	Fruit bats, echolocating bats
Even-toed hoofed mammals and cetaceans (Cetartiodactyla)	469	Deer, sheep, goats, cattle, antelopes, giraffes, camels, swine, hippopotamuses, whales, dolphins
Shrews, moles, and relatives (Soricomorpha)	428	Shrews, moles, solenodons
Primates (Primates)	396	Lemurs, monkeys, apes, humans
Carnivores (Carnivora)	284	Wolves, dogs, bears, cats, weasels, pinnipeds (seals, sea lions, walruses)
Rabbits and relatives (Lagomorpha)	92	Rabbits, hares, pikas
African insectivores (Afrosoricida)	50	Tenrecs, golden moles
Spiny insectivores (Erinaceomorpha)	24	Hedgehogs
Armadillos (Cingulata)	21	Armadillos
Tree shrews (Scandentia)	20	Tree shrews
Odd-toed hoofed mammals (Perissodactyla)	16	Horses, zebras, tapirs, rhinoceroses
Long-nosed insectivores (Macroscelidea)	15	Elephant shrews
Anteaters and sloths (Pilosa)	10	Anteaters, tamanduas, sloths
Pangolins (Pholidota)	8	Asian and African pangolins
Hyraxes and relatives (Hyracoidea)	5	Hyraxes, dassies
Sirenians (Sirenia)	4	Manatees, dugongs
Elephants (Proboscidea)	3	African and Indian elephants
Colugos (Dermoptera)	2	Flying lemurs
Aardvark (Tubulidentata)	1	Aardvark

young, but they have no nipples on their mammary glands; the milk simply oozes out and is lapped off the fur by the offspring.

MARSUPIALS Females of most marsupial species have a ventral pouch in which they carry and feed their offspring (see Figure 31.27A). Gestation (pregnancy) in marsupials is brief; the young are born tiny but with well-developed forelimbs, with which they climb to the pouch. They attach to a nipple but cannot suck. The mother ejects milk into the tiny offspring until it grows large enough to suckle. Once her offspring have left the uterus, a female marsupial may become sexually receptive again. She can then carry fertilized eggs that are capable of initiating development to replace the offspring in her pouch should something happen to them.

At one time marsupials were found on all continents, but the approximately 350 living species are now restricted to Australasia (**Figure 31.27A,B**) and the Americas (especially South America) (**Figure 31.27C**). Of the seven major groups of marsupials shown in Table 31.1, only the New World opossums, the shrew opossums, and the diminutive monito del monte are found in the Americas. Only one species, the Virginia opossum, is found in North America north of Mexico. Marsupials radiated to become herbivores, insectivores, and carnivores, but no marsupials live in the oceans. None can fly, although some arboreal (tree-dwelling) marsupials are gliders. The largest living marsupials are the kangaroos of Australia, which can weigh up to 90 kilograms. Much larger marsupials existed in Australia until humans exterminated them soon after reaching that continent about 45,000 years ago.

EUTHERIANS The majority of mammals are eutherians ("true" therians). Eutherians are sometimes called placental mammals, but this name is inappropriate because marsupials also have placentas, although they are not as well developed as in eutherians. Eutherians are more developed at birth than are marsupials; no external pouch houses them after they are born.

The more than 5,300 species of living eutherians are divided into 20 major groups (see Table 31.1). The relationships of these groups to one another have been difficult to determine because most of the major groups diverged within a short time during an explosive adaptive radiation. Modern genomic analyses have elucidated these relationships, however (**Figure 31.28**). These studies have revealed that the major early splits in eutherian lineages are closely associated with the breakup of the continents during the Mesozoic (see Figure 23.14), after which the major groups of mammals radiated independently in Laurasia, Africa, and South America. The reconnection of South America and North America via the Isthmus of Panama about 3 million years ago resulted in a huge faunal exchange between those continents, which is particularly evident among the mammals. South American groups such as armadillos moved north into North America, and Laurasian groups such as carnivores and odd- and even-toed hoofed animals moved south into South America.

Eutherians are extremely varied in their form and ecology (**Figure 31.29**). The extinction of the non-avian dinosaurs at the end of the Cretaceous may have made it possible for eutherians to diversify and radiate into a large range of ecological niches.

Many eutherian species grew large, and some assumed the roles of dominant terrestrial predators previously occupied by the large dinosaurs. Among these predators, social hunting behavior evolved in several species, including members of the carnivore and primate clades.

The two most diverse groups of eutherians are the rodents and the bats, which together account for about two-thirds of the species. Rodents are traditionally defined by the unique morphology of their teeth, which are adapted for gnawing through substances such as wood. The bats probably owe much of their success to the evolution of flight, which allows them to exploit a variety of food sources and colonize remote locations with relative ease.

▶ **Media Clip 31.7 Bats Feeding in Flight**
Life12e.com/mc31.7

Grazing and browsing by members of several eutherian groups helped transform the terrestrial landscape. Herds of grazing herbivores fed on open grasslands, whereas browsers fed on shrubs and trees. The effects of these herbivores on plant life favored the evolution of the spines, tough leaves, and difficult-to-eat growth forms found in many plants. In turn, adaptations in the teeth and digestive systems of many herbivore lineages allowed these species to consume many plants despite such defenses—a striking example of coevolution. A large animal can survive on food of lower quality than a small animal can, and large size evolved in several groups of grazing and browsing mammals (see Figure 31.29C). The evolution of large herbivores, in turn, favored the evolution of large carnivores able to attack and overpower them.

Several lineages of terrestrial eutherians subsequently returned to the aquatic environments their ancestors had left behind (see Figure 31.29D). The completely aquatic cetaceans—whales and dolphins—evolved from even-toed hoofed ancestors (cetaceans are closely related to the hippopotamuses). The seals,

(A) *Macropus giganteus*

(B) *Myrmecobius fasciatus*

(C) *Didelphis virginiana*

Figure 31.27 Diversity among the Marsupials **(A)** Australia's eastern gray kangaroo is among the largest living marsupials. This female carries her young offspring in the characteristic marsupial pouch. **(B)** The diet of the banded anteater of western Australia consists almost entirely of termites. **(C)** The Virginia opossum is the only marsupial found north of Mexico.

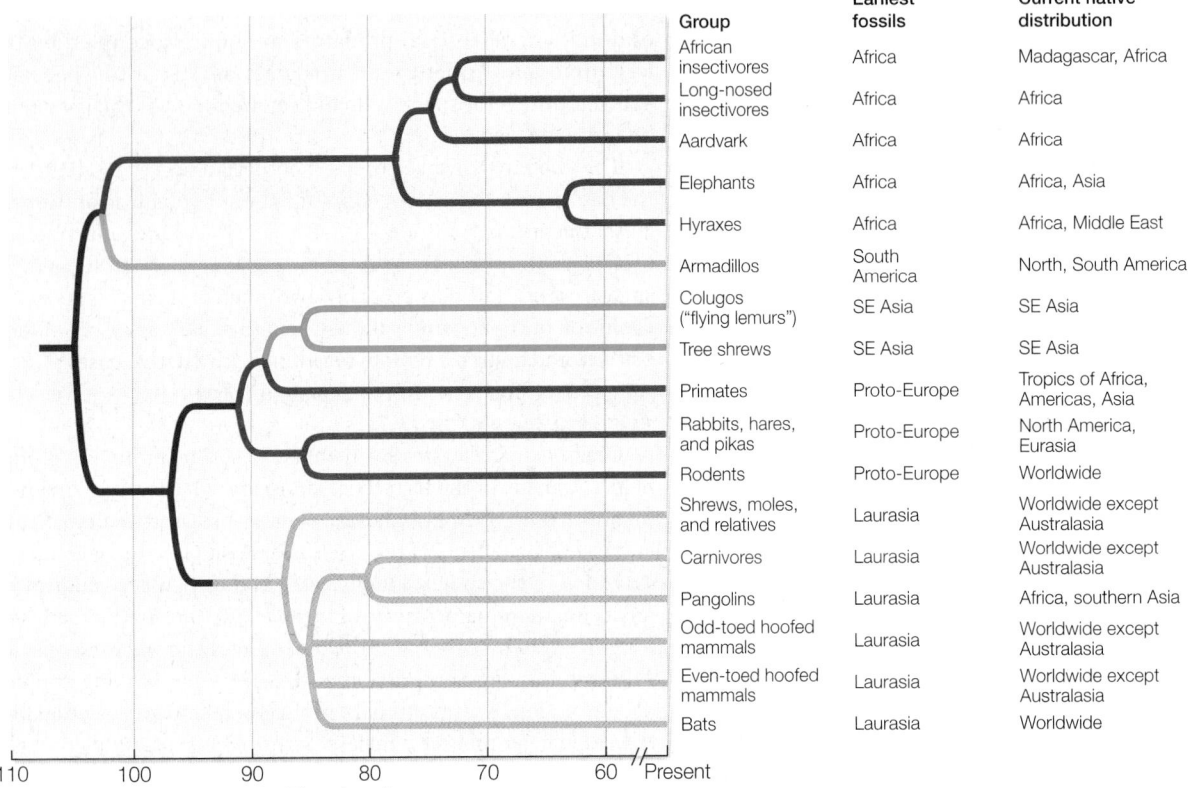

Group	Earliest fossils	Current native distribution
African insectivores	Africa	Madagascar, Africa
Long-nosed insectivores	Africa	Africa
Aardvark	Africa	Africa
Elephants	Africa	Africa, Asia
Hyraxes	Africa	Africa, Middle East
Armadillos	South America	North, South America
Colugos ("flying lemurs")	SE Asia	SE Asia
Tree shrews	SE Asia	SE Asia
Primates	Proto-Europe	Tropics of Africa, Americas, Asia
Rabbits, hares, and pikas	Proto-Europe	North America, Eurasia
Rodents	Proto-Europe	Worldwide
Shrews, moles, and relatives	Laurasia	Worldwide except Australasia
Carnivores	Laurasia	Worldwide except Australasia
Pangolins	Laurasia	Africa, southern Asia
Odd-toed hoofed mammals	Laurasia	Worldwide except Australasia
Even-toed hoofed mammals	Laurasia	Worldwide except Australasia
Bats	Laurasia	Worldwide

110   100   90   80   70   60 // Present
Time (mya)

Figure 31.28 Major Groups of Eutherians Diversified as the Continents Drifted Apart This phylogenetic tree shows the relationships among most of the major terrestrial eutherian groups, the location of the earliest fossils found for each group (also indicated in the color distinctions of the various branches), and the current distributions of the groups. The major splits in eutherian evolution correspond in large degree to the tectonic history of the major continents (see Figures 23.14 and 52.14).

(A) *Castor canadensis*

(B) *Plecotus townsendii*

(D) *Tursiops truncates*

(C)

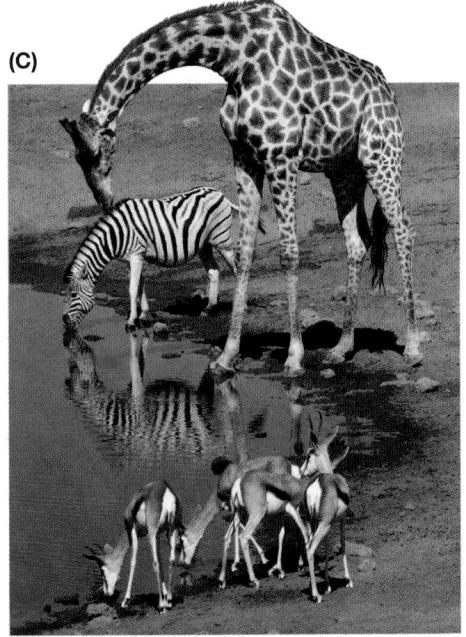

Figure 31.29 Diversity among the Eutherians **(A)** The North American beaver exhibits the gnawing teeth that characterize rodents. Almost half of all eutherians are rodents. **(B)** Flight evolved in the ancestor of bats. This Townsend's big-eared bat uses its enlarged ears to detect insect prey by echolocation. **(C)** Large hoofed mammals such as giraffes, zebras, and springboks are major herbivores of grasslands and savannas. **(D)** Bottlenosed dolphins are cetaceans, a cetartiodactyl group that returned to the marine environment.

sea lions, and walruses also returned to the marine environment, and their limbs became modified into flippers. Weasel-like otters retain their limbs but have also returned to aquatic environments, colonizing both fresh and salt water. The manatees and dugongs colonized estuaries and shallow seas.

KEY CONCEPT
31.4 Recap and Assess

The initial vertebrate colonization of dry land was facilitated by the evolution of lunglike sacs and jointed limbs. The amniotes also evolved impermeable body coverings, efficient kidneys, and the amniote egg, which resists desiccation.

1. Amphibians have survived and prospered for millions of years, but today many species are disappearing and populations of others are in serious decline. What features of their life histories might make amphibians especially vulnerable to the kinds of environmental changes now happening on Earth?

2. How has the diversification of mammals been influenced by mass extinction events and continental drift?

3. In the not-too-distant past, the idea that birds were reptiles met with skepticism. Explain how fossils, morphology, and molecular evidence now support the position of birds among the reptiles.

4. Consider the phylogeny of the amniotes and the evolution of endothermy, hair, and feathers. Which of these traits likely evolved convergently in more than one lineage? What is a likely functional relationship among these traits? What are some reasons why many paleontologists think that several extinct theropods were endothermic?

Figure 31.30 **Phylogeny of the Primates**   The phylogeny of primates is among the best studied of any major group of mammals. This tree is based on evidence from many genes, morphology, and fossils.

The biology of one eutherian group—the primates—has been the subject of extensive research. The behavior, ecology, physiology, and molecular biology of the primates are of special interest to us because this lineage includes humans.

KEY CONCEPT
31.5 Humans Evolved among the Primates

Learning Objectives

31.5.1 Summarize the diversity within the primates.

31.5.2 Articulate the relationship between bigger brains, smaller jaws, and neoteny.

One lineage of small, arboreal, insectivorous eutherians underwent extensive evolutionary radiation to become the **primates** (**Figure 31.30**). Grasping limbs with opposable digits, an adaptation to arboreal life, is one of the major features that distinguish primates from other mammals.

Two major lineages of primates split late in the Cretaceous

About 90 million years ago, late in the Cretaceous, the primates split into two clades: the wet-nosed primates (strepsirrhines) and the dry-nosed primates (haplorhines). **Wet-nosed primates**—lemurs, lorises, and galagos—once lived on all continents, but today they are restricted to Africa, Madagascar, and tropical Asia. All mainland wet-nosed primate species are arboreal and nocturnal. On the island of Madagascar, however, the site of a remarkable radiation of lemurs, there are also diurnal and terrestrial species (**Figure 31.31**). Tarsiers were once considered a part of this lineage as well, although today we know that they are more closely related to **simians**—monkeys and apes—than to lemurs, lorises, and galagos.

The second primate lineage, the **dry-nosed primates**—tarsiers, New World monkeys, Old World monkeys, and apes—began to diversify shortly after the mass extinction event at the end of the Cretaceous, in Africa or Asia. New World monkeys diverged from Old World monkeys and apes slightly later, but early enough that they may have originated in Africa and reached South America when those two continents were still close to each other. New

Varecia variegata

Figure 31.31 **A Wet-Nosed Primate** The black-and-white ruffed lemur is one of the many lemur species found in Madagascar, where it is part of a unique assemblage of endemic plants and animals. Lemurs live in groups of up to a dozen animals and defend their territories.

World monkeys now live only in South and Central America, and all of them are arboreal (**Figure 31.32A**). Many of them have a long, prehensile tail with which they can grasp branches. Many Old World monkeys are arboreal as well, but several species are terrestrial (**Figure 31.32B**). No Old World monkey has a prehensile tail.

About 35 million years ago, a lineage that led to the modern apes separated from the Old World monkeys. Between 22 and 5.5 million

(A) *Ateles geoffroyi*

(B) *Mandrillus sphinx*

Figure 31.32 **Monkeys** **(A)** The spider monkeys of Central America are typical of the New World monkeys, all of which are arboreal. Note the prehensile (gripping) tail. **(B)** Although many Old World monkeys are arboreal, none has a prehensile tail. Many Old World monkey species, like this mandrill, are thoroughly terrestrial.

years ago, dozens of species of apes lived in Europe, Asia, and Africa. The Asian apes—gibbons and orangutans (**Figure 31.33A,B**)—descended from two of these ape lineages. Orangutans are the closest living sister group of the modern African apes: gorillas (**Figure 31.33C**), chimpanzees (**Figure 31.33D**), and humans.

Bipedal locomotion evolved in human ancestors

About 6 million years ago in Africa, a lineage split occurred that would lead to the chimpanzees on the one hand and to the **hominin** clade, which includes modern humans and their extinct close relatives, on the other.

The earliest protohominins, known as ardipithecines, had distinct morphological adaptations for **bipedal locomotion** (walking on two legs). Bipedal locomotion frees the forelimbs to manipulate objects and to carry them while walking. It also elevates the eyes, enabling the animal to see over tall vegetation to spot predators and prey. Bipedal locomotion is also energetically more economical than quadrupedal locomotion (walking on four legs). All three advantages were probably important for the ardipithecines and their descendants, the australopithecines (**Figure 31.34**).

The first australopithecine skull was found in South Africa in 1924. Since then australopithecine fossils have been found at many sites in Africa. The most complete fossil skeleton yet found was discovered in Ethiopia in 1974. The skeleton, approximately 3.5 million years old, was that of a young female who has since become known to the world as "Lucy." Lucy was assigned to the species *Australopithecus afarensis*. Fossil remains of more than 100 *A. afarensis* individuals have since been discovered, and there have been recent discoveries of fossils of other australopithecine species that lived in Africa 5–4 million years ago.

Experts disagree over how many species are represented by australopithecine fossils, but it is clear that multiple species of hominins lived together over much of eastern Africa several million years ago. A lineage of larger species (weighing about 40 kg) is represented by *Paranthropus robustus* and *P. boisei*, both of which died out between 1 and 1.5 million years ago. A lineage of smaller australopithecines gave rise to the genus *Homo*.

Early members of the genus *Homo* lived contemporaneously with *Paranthropus* in Africa for about a million years. Some 2-million-year-old fossils of an extinct species called *H. habilis* were discovered in the Olduvai Gorge, Tanzania. Other fossils of *H. habilis* have been found in Kenya and Ethiopia. Associated with these fossils were tools that these early hominins used to obtain food.

Another extinct hominin species, *Homo erectus*, arose in Africa about 1.6 million years ago. Soon thereafter it had spread as far as eastern Asia, becoming the first hominin to leave Africa. Members of *H. erectus* were nearly as large as modern people, but their brains were smaller and they had comparatively thick skulls. The cranium, which had thick, bony walls, may have been an adaptation to protect the brain, ears, and eyes from impacts caused by a fall or a blow from

(A) *Hylobates lar*

(B) *Pongo pygmaeus*

(C) *Gorilla gorilla*

(D) *Pan troglodytes*

Figure 31.33 Apes **(A)** The several genera of gibbons are all smaller in size than the other apes. Gibbons are found throughout Southeast Asia. **(B)** Orangutans are also native to Asia, living in the forests of Sumatra and Borneo. **(C)** Gorillas—the largest apes—are restricted to humid African forests. This male is a lowland gorilla. **(D)** Chimpanzees, our closest relatives, are found in forested regions of Africa.

Figure 31.34 A Phylogenetic Tree of Hominins At times in the past, more than one hominin species lived on Earth at the same time. Originating in Africa, hominins spread to Europe and Asia multiple times. All but one of those species are now extinct, but that one species, modern *Homo sapiens*, has colonized nearly every corner of the planet.

Australopithecus afarensis (Lucy)

Australopithecus africanus

Ardipithecine ancestors

Paranthropus robustus

Paranthropus boisei

The *Paranthropus* lineages coexisted with species of *Homo* and *Australopithecus* in Africa.

No fossils are known of this lineage until about 500,000 years ago.

Homo floresiensis (extinct 12,000 years ago)

Homo erectus (extinct 250,000 years ago)

Homo neanderthalensis (extinct 28,000 years ago)

Homo sapiens (now worldwide)

Several species of *Homo* co-existed in Africa, Asia, and Europe until recently.

- Africa only
- Expansion out of Africa

Homo habilis

Expansion from Africa occurred 70,000–60,000 years ago.

Expansion into the New World occurred about 15,000 years ago.

4   3   2   1   Present

Time (mya)

a blunt object. What would have been the source of such blows? Fighting with other *H. erectus* individuals is a possible answer.

Homo erectus used fire for cooking and for hunting large animals, and made characteristic stone tools that have been found in many parts of Africa and Asia. Populations of *H. erectus* survived until at least 250,000 years ago, although more recent fossils may also be attributable to this species. In 2004 some 18,000-year-old fossil remains of a small *Homo* were found on the island of Flores in Indonesia. Since then, numerous additional fossils of this diminutive hominin have been found on Flores, dating from about 500,000 to 12,000 years ago, when a major volcanic eruption on Flores likely led to their extinction. Many anthropologists think that this small species, named *H. floresiensis*, was most closely related to *H. erectus*.

Human brains became larger as jaws became smaller

In another hominin lineage that diverged from *H. erectus* and *H. floresiensis*, the brain increased rapidly in size, and the jaw muscles, which were large and powerful in earlier hominins, dramatically decreased in size. These two changes were simultaneous, which suggests that they might have been developmentally linked. These changes are another example of evolution by neoteny (which, you may recall from our discussion of amphibians, is the retention of juvenile traits through delayed somatic development). Human and chimpanzee skulls are similar in shape at birth, but chimpanzee skulls undergo a dramatic change in shape as the animals mature (**Figure 31.35**). In particular, the jaw grows considerably in relation to the brain case. As human skulls grow, relative proportions much closer to those of the juvenile skull are retained, which results in a large brain case and small jaw compared with those of chimpanzees. A mutation in a regulatory gene that is expressed only in the head may have removed a barrier that had previously prevented this remodeling of the human cranium.

The striking enlargement of the brain relative to body size in the hominin lineage was probably favored by an increasingly complex social life. Any features that allowed group members to communicate more effectively with one another would have been valuable in cooperative hunting and gathering as well as for improving one's status in the complex social interactions that must have characterized early human societies, just as they do ours today.

Several *Homo* species coexisted during the mid-Pleistocene, from about 1.5 million to about 250,000 years ago. All were skilled hunters of large mammals, but plants were important components of their diets as well. During this period another distinctly human trait emerged: rituals and a concept of life after death. Deceased individuals were buried with tools and clothing, supplies for their presumed existence in the next world.

One species, *Homo neanderthalensis*, was widespread in Europe and Asia between about 500,000 and 28,000 years ago. Neanderthals were short, stocky, and powerfully built. Their massive skull housed a brain somewhat larger than our own. They manufactured a variety of tools and hunted large mammals, which they probably ambushed and subdued in close combat. A closely related lineage, the Denisovans, is known from less complete fossils, primarily from Asian caves.

Recently, biologists have been able to extract DNA from the bones of Neanderthals and Denisovans, and have compared the genomes of these species with those of modern humans. Early modern humans (*H. sapiens*) expanded out of Africa between 70,000 and 60,000 years ago. Then, about 35,000 years ago, *H. sapiens* moved into the range of *H. neanderthalensis* in Europe and western Asia, and into the range of the Denisovans in eastern Asia. Neanderthals abruptly disappeared about 28,000 years ago. Many anthropologists believe that Neanderthals and Denisovans were exterminated by those early modern humans. But comparisons of Neanderthal, Denisovan, and modern human genomes indicate

Figure 31.35 Neoteny in the Evolution of Humans The skulls and heads of juvenile chimpanzees and humans start out relatively similar in shape. The grid over the skulls shows how the various bony elements change in their relative proportions over the course of maturation. The adult human skull retains a shape closer to its juvenile shape, resulting in a brain that is much larger relative to other parts of the skull (notably the jaw).

The skulls of juvenile chimpanzees and humans are quite similar to each other.

Pan   *Homo*

The chimp skull undergoes much more dramatic change in development than does the human skull.

that there was some limited interbreeding among these groups while they occupied the same range. In humans with Eurasian ancestry, 1%–4% of the genes in their genomes may be derived from Neanderthal ancestors. The genomes of some modern native people of Southeast Asia, Melanesia, and Australia contain even higher proportions of Denisovan genes. So all three of these lineages contributed in some degree to modern humans.

Early modern humans made and used a variety of sophisticated tools. They created the remarkable paintings of large mammals, many of them showing scenes of hunting, found in European caves. The animals they depicted were characteristic of the cold steppes and grasslands that occupied much of Europe during periods of glacial expansion. Early modern humans also spread across Asia, reaching North America about 15,000 years ago (although some scholars argue for an even earlier date of arrival in the Americas). Within a few thousand years, they had spread southward through North America to the southern tip of South America.

Humans developed complex language and culture

As our ancestors evolved larger brains, their behavioral capabilities increased, especially the capacity for language. Most animal communication consists of a limited number of signals, which refer mostly to immediate circumstances and are each used in a specific context. Human language is far richer in its symbolic character than other animal vocalizations. Our words can refer to past and future times and to distant places. We are capable of learning thousands of words, many of them referring to abstract concepts. We can rearrange words to form sentences with complex meanings.

The expanded mental abilities of humans enabled the development of a complex culture, in which knowledge and traditions are passed along from one generation to the next by teaching and observation. Cultures can change rapidly because genetic changes are not necessary for a cultural trait to spread through a population. Cultural norms, however, are not transferred automatically and must be deliberately taught to each generation.

Cultural transmission greatly facilitated the domestication of plants and animals and the resultant conversion of most human societies from ones in which food was obtained by hunting and gathering to ones in which pastoralism (herding large animals) and agriculture provided most of the food. The development of agriculture led to an increasingly sedentary life, the growth of cities, greatly expanded food supplies, rapid increases in the human population, and the appearance of occupational specializations, such as artisans, shamans, and teachers.

KEY CONCEPT
31.5 Recap and Assess

Grasping limbs with opposable digits distinguish primates from other mammals. Bipedal locomotion and large brains evolved in the primate ancestors that led to humans, which facilitated the development of complex language and culture.

1. Describe the differences between Old World and New World monkeys.

2. Explain how neoteny resulted in the development of humans with relatively large brains and small jaws.

 View in **Achieve**
Activity 32.3 **Deuterostome Classification**

 View in **Achieve**
Activity 32.4 **The Major Groups of Organisms**

 ▶Investigating**LIFE**

Q and A What are the advantages and disadvantages of egg laying versus live birth?

Oviparity and viviparity involve some trade-offs of parental resources. In egg-laying species, all the nutrition for the developing embryo is supplied in the yolk. This means there is no continuing drain of parental resources as the embryo develops. One advantage of oviparity is that a female can often produce more offspring (since she devotes fewer resources to each one). Clutch size is often larger in oviparous species of lizards and snakes than in closely related viviparous species, although there are exceptions. Because each offspring in oviparous species receives a smaller parental investment compared with offspring of viviparous species, hatchlings tend to be smaller than the offspring of viviparous species.

Why is it sometimes advantageous for a species to commit more resources to fewer offspring? Developing embryos are retained in females in viviparous species, so females can control the temperature of development by behavioral thermoregulation. In high elevation and other cool environments, for example, females can bask in the sun during the day, and then retreat to cover at night. In addition, sometimes survival of offspring may depend on larger size and more parental investment. For example, in areas with short growing seasons and relatively cold temperatures, producing a few large offspring may yield significantly more descendants than producing a large number

of small offspring that are less likely to survive. In contrast, in a favorable environment with abundant resources, producing many smaller offspring is likely to produce the most descendants. Indeed, there is a correlation between reproductive mode and elevational range in many groups of squamates, with oviparous species occurring at lower elevations and viviparous species at higher elevations.

Future directions

It is comparatively easy, from evolutionary and physiological points of view, for viviparity to evolve from oviparity in squamates. The membranes of the amniote egg can be modified to provide maternal nutrition, as well as gas and waste exchange (see Figure 31.19). Evolutionary reversal—from viviparity to oviparity—has been thought to be more difficult, since complex modifications for shell deposition, independent growth, and hatching from the shell need to re-evolve. But recent investigations have shown that many of these evolutionary changes can be accomplished by simple shifts in the timing and amount of gene expression, rather than through changes in the underlying genes themselves. A few candidate squamate lineages (including the huge venomous bushmasters of Central and South America) have been identified in which such reversals appear to have occurred. Biologists are now focusing on these exceptional reversals to learn how lineages may redevelop structures and physiological processes that were lost in ancestors that lived millions of years earlier.

You should be able to relate each summary to the adjacent figures. If you go to this visual summary in **Achieve**, you can follow links to figures, animations, activities, and simulations that will help you consolidate the material.

KEY CONCEPT
31.1 Deuterostomes Include Echinoderms, Hemichordates, and Chordates

Go to Activity 31.1 and Animation 31.1

- Deuterostomes vary greatly in adult form, but based on the distinctive patterns of early development they share and on phylogenetic analyses of their gene sequences, they are thought to be monophyletic.

- There are far fewer species of deuterostomes than of protostomes, but many deuterostomes are large and ecologically important.

- The deuterostomes comprise three major clades: the **echinoderms**, **hemichordates**, and **chordates**.

Questions

1. Draw a phylogenetic tree that depicts the relationships among the following animals: humans, sea squirts, sea stars, sharks, crinoids, and acorn worms.

2. Based on phylogenetic and fossil evidence, how would you describe the earliest deuterostomes?

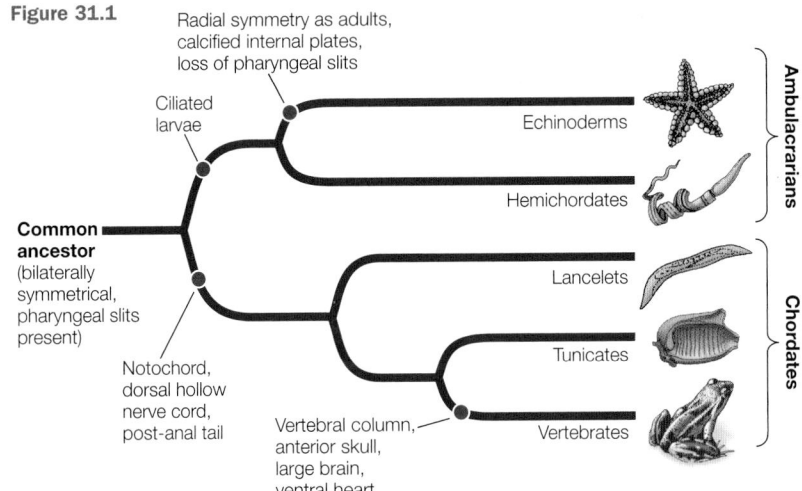

Figure 31.1

KEY CONCEPT
31.2 Echinoderms and Hemichordates Are Restricted to Marine Environments

- Echinoderms and hemichordates both have bilaterally symmetrical, ciliated larvae.

- Most adult echinoderms have **pentaradial symmetry**. Echinoderms have an **internal skeleton** of calcified plates and a unique **water vascular system** connected to extensions called **tube feet**.

- Hemichordates are bilaterally symmetrical and have a three-part body divided into a proboscis, collar, and trunk.

Questions

1. What evidence can you offer that the pentaradial symmetry of adult echinoderms is a derived (rather than ancestral) condition within the ambulacrarians?

2. What two additional marine groups may be related to echinoderms and hemichordates (although their relationships are still debated)?

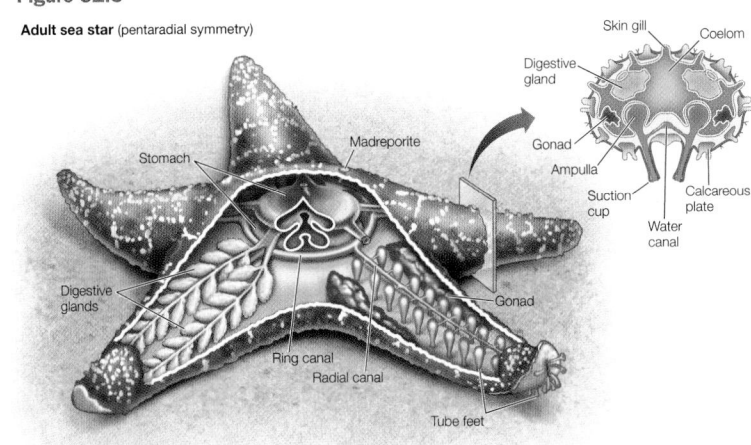

Figure 31.3

Adult sea star (pentaradial symmetry)

Figure 31.6

KEY CONCEPT

31.3   More Than Half of Chordates are Also Aquatic

- Chordates fall into three principal subgroups: **lancelets, tunicates**, and **vertebrates**. At some stage in their development, all chordates have a dorsal hollow nerve cord, a post-anal tail, and a **notochord**.

- The vertebrate body is characterized by a rigid internal skeleton, which is supported by a **vertebral column** that replaces the notochord, internal organs suspended in a coelom, a ventral heart, and an anterior skull with a large brain.

- The evolution of jaws from gill arches enabled individuals to grasp large prey and, together with teeth, cut them into small pieces.

Questions

1. Draw the phylogenetic relationships among the following animals: hagfishes, lampreys, sharks, ray-finned fishes, coelacanths, lungfishes, frogs, and turtles.

2. Name a shared morphological character that supports each of your groups in the tree from Question 1.

Figure 31.7

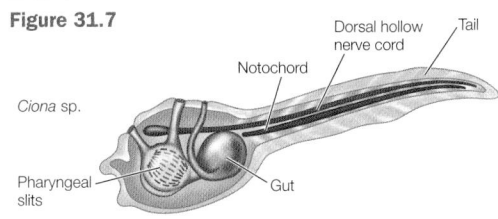

Ciona sp.

Dorsal hollow nerve cord · Tail · Notochord · Pharyngeal slits · Gut

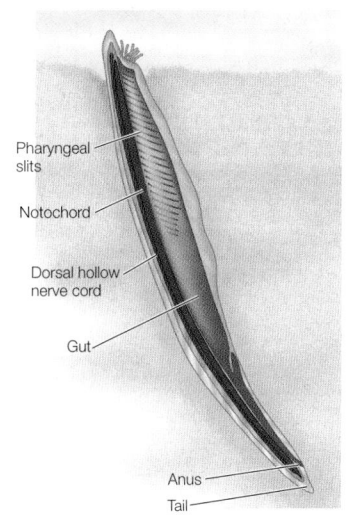

Branchiostoma lanceolatum

Pharyngeal slits · Notochord · Dorsal hollow nerve cord · Gut · Anus · Tail

Figure 31.9

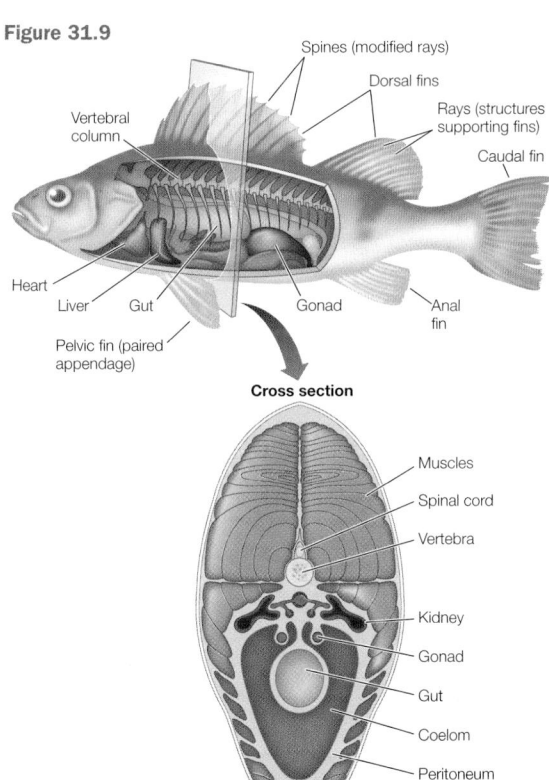

Spines (modified rays) · Dorsal fins · Rays (structures supporting fins) · Caudal fin · Vertebral column · Heart · Liver · Gut · Gonad · Anal fin · Pelvic fin (paired appendage)

Cross section

Muscles · Spinal cord · Vertebra · Kidney · Gonad · Gut · Coelom · Peritoneum

Figure 31.12

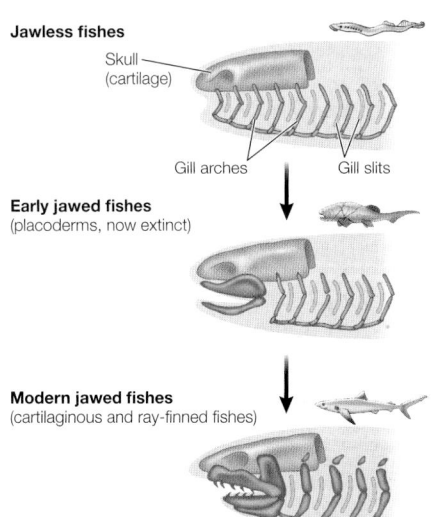

Jawless fishes

Skull (cartilage) · Gill arches · Gill slits

Early jawed fishes
(placoderms, now extinct)

Modern jawed fishes
(cartilaginous and ray-finned fishes)

KEY CONCEPT
31.4 Tetrapods Diversified Rapidly in Terrestrial Environments

Go to Activity 31.2 and Animation 31.2

- Lungs and jointed appendages enabled one lineage of lobe-limbed vertebrates to colonize the land. This lineage gave rise to the tetrapods.
- The earliest split in the tetrapod tree is between the **amphibians** and the **amniotes** (**reptiles** and **mammals**).
- Most modern amphibians are confined to moist environments because they and their eggs lose water rapidly.
- An impermeable skin, efficient kidneys, and an egg that could resist desiccation evolved in the amniotes.

Questions

1. What are two examples of aquatic lobe-limbed vertebrates that are not tetrapods?

2. What are the two major groups of tetrapods that independently evolved the ability to maintain a relatively constant body temperature?

3. Which group of living tetrapods is most closely related to the extinct non-avian dinosaurs?

Figure 31.16

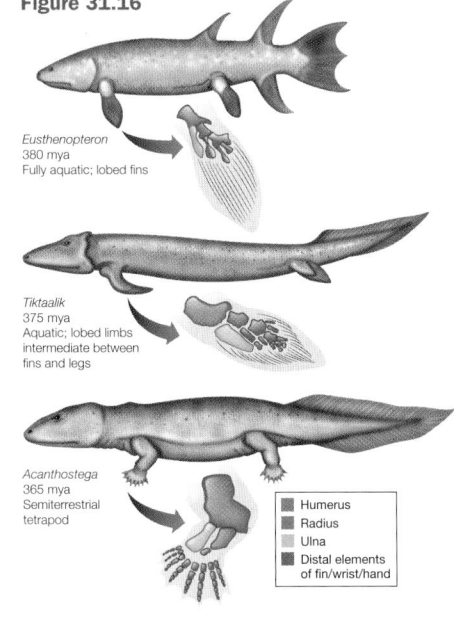

Eusthenopteron
380 mya
Fully aquatic; lobed fins

Tiktaalik
375 mya
Aquatic; lobed limbs intermediate between fins and legs

Acanthostega
365 mya
Semiterrestrial tetrapod

- ■ Humerus
- ■ Radius
- ■ Ulna
- ■ Distal elements of fin/wrist/hand

Figure 31.19

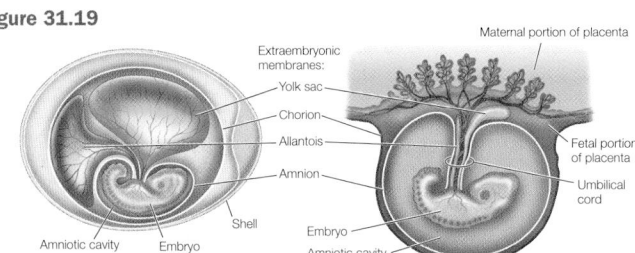

Extraembryonic membranes:
- Yolk sac
- Chorion
- Allantois
- Amnion
- Shell
- Amniotic cavity
- Embryo

Maternal portion of placenta
Fetal portion of placenta
Umbilical cord
Embryo
Amniotic cavity

KEY CONCEPT
31.5 Humans Evolved among the Primates

Go to Activities 31.3 and 31.4

- Grasping limbs with opposable digits distinguish **primates** from other mammals. The **wet-nosed primates** include the lemurs, lorises, and galagos; the **dry-nosed primates** include tarsiers, New World monkeys, Old World monkeys, and apes (including humans).
- **Hominin** ancestors developed efficient **bipedal locomotion**. Several species of *Homo* coexisted in parts of the world until recently.
- Within the *Homo* lineage, brains became larger as jaws became smaller. The two events appear to be developmentally linked and are an example of evolution via neoteny.

Questions

1. Several species of *Homo* are thought to have lived together on Earth until recently. Why is *Homo sapiens* thought to be the only species alive today?

2. What evidence suggests that *Homo sapiens* interbred to some extent with other *Homo* species in the past?

Figure 31.35

Pan   *Homo*

The Plant Body 32

© MisoKnitl/Getty Images

Plants such as this old tree have roots, stems, and leaves that perform the functions of the organism.

KEY CONCEPTS

32.1 The Plant Body Is Organized in a Distinctive Way

32.2 Plant Organs Are Made Up of Cells Organized into Three Types of Tissues

32.3 Meristems Build a Continuously Growing Plant

32.4 Domestication Has Altered Plant Form

▶Investigating LIFE

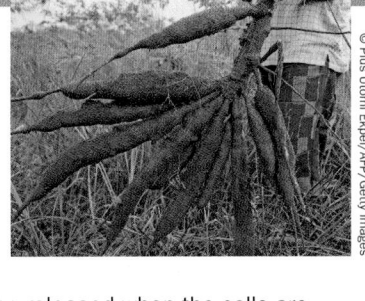

© Pius Utomi Ekpei/AFP/Getty Images

Bread of the Tropics

To North Americans and Europeans, it is tapioca. To Central and South Americans, it is yuca. To Africans, it is manioc or bananku. The roots of the cassava plant, *Manihot esculenta*, are important in the diets of more than 800 million people. Cassava is grown mostly by family farmers for their own consumption. The root of the plant is a store of starch, which can be hydrolyzed and used by the plant as the stems and leaves grow. Other crop plants such as rice and wheat apportion about 35% of the total carbon fixed in photosynthesis into their storage organs (the grains), whereas cassava apportions an astounding 80% into the root, as starch. For humans, this is a convenient and concentrated source of food energy. Indeed, cassava has been nicknamed the "bread of the tropics" because, just as wheat bread is the major starchy food in the Western world, cassava supplies the starch in tropical areas.

Most cassava plants are clones. The plants have wide adaptability and grow well in dry soils, in both hot and cool climates. Typically, the farmer breaks off some pieces of stem and plants them. Because most plant cells are totipotent (see Key Concept 18.2), some of the stem cells redifferentiate and form roots, while others become growing shoots. A whole new plant develops, and the roots are ready to eat 6 months to 2 years later.

There are countless recipes for preparing cassava as food, but it is nutritionally incomplete. Although rich in carbohydrates,

cassava is a relatively poor source of protein, a requirement for the human diet. Eating cassava presents other difficulties. Cassava roots and leaves contain cyanogenic compounds, which are converted to cyanide by enzymes released when the cells are broken open. Cyanide is highly toxic and potentially lethal because it blocks electron transport in the mitochondria. Therefore it is essential to soak, cook, or ferment cassava, to break down the cyanogenic compounds and eliminate the cyanide, before it can be eaten safely. In all probability, the plant uses cyanide production as a protection against predators that eat it.

We open with the topic of cassava because it offers a preview of a wide range of studies embraced by the discipline of plant physiology. Plant physiology is a broad subject, covering photosynthesis, transport, plant nutrition, regulation of growth and development, reproduction, and the interactions between plants and their environments.

 How might plant biologists improve the cassava plant for human use? (Find the answer on page 745.)

32.1 The Plant Body Is Organized in a Distinctive Way

Learning Objectives

32.1.1 Describe the overall structure of a flowering plant in terms of its major systems and axes.

32.1.2 Identify ways in which meristem-based growth overcomes some of the problems posed by scarce resources and an inability to move.

32.1.3 List criteria that distinguish monocots and eudicots.

32.1.4 Explain the process by which a zygote develops into an embryo.

Despite their obvious differences in size and form, all vascular plants have essentially the same simple structural organization. This chapter describes the basic architecture of the largest group of vascular plants, the angiosperms (flowering plants), and shows how so much diversity can literally grow out of such a simple, basic form. There are more than 300,000 angiosperm species. A major distinguishing feature of angiosperms is flowers, which consist of modified leaves and stems and carry the organs for sexual reproduction. We will examine the structures and functions of flowers in detail in Chapter 37.

Vegetative (nonsexual) plant organs are organized into two systems (**Figure 32.1**):

1. The **root system** anchors the plant in place, absorbs water and dissolved minerals, and stores the products of photosynthesis from the shoot system. The extreme branching of plant roots and their high surface area-to-volume ratios allow them to absorb water and mineral nutrients from the soil efficiently.

2. The **shoot system** consists of the stems, leaves, and flowers. Broadly speaking, the **leaves** are the chief organs of photosynthesis. The **stems** hold and display the leaves to the Sun and provide connections for the transport of materials between roots and leaves. **Axillary buds** form in the angle (axil) where a leaf meets the stem. A **bud** is an undeveloped shoot that can develop further. If an axillary bud becomes active, it can develop into a new branch, which is an extension of the shoot system.

Most angiosperms are either monocots or eudicots

As you saw in Key Concept 27.3, most angiosperms belong to one of two major clades. *Monocots* are generally narrow-leaved flowering plants such as grasses, lilies, and orchids. *Eudicots* are broad-leaved flowering plants such as soybeans, roses, sunflowers, and maples. These two clades, which account for 97% of flowering plant species, are named for the number of **cotyledons**, leaf-like organs, that are present in a mature seed. However, monocots (with one cotyledon) and eudicots (with two cotyledons) differ in several basic characteristics, as shown in **Figure 32.2**. We'll provide more detailed comparisons between these clades throughout the chapter.

Meristems generate the plant body

Plants harvest energy from sunlight and collect water and mineral nutrients from the atmosphere and the soil. Because these resources are sometimes limited, plants must collect them from large areas, both above and below the ground. Plants are further challenged by their inability to walk; a plant cannot, for example, relocate from a dry, shady location to one that is wet and sunny. The plant body plan responds to these challenges in two ways:

1. Stems, leaves, and roots enable a plant anchored to one spot to capture scarce resources effectively, both above and below the ground.

2. Plants can grow throughout their lifetimes, enabling them to respond to environmental cues. A plant can redirect its growth to exploit opportunities in its immediate environment; for example, it can extend its roots toward a water supply.

The ability of plants to grow new body parts throughout their lifetime distinguishes plants from most animals. Most animals stop growing when they reach the adult state, a growth pattern referred to as **determinate**. In

Figure 32.1 Vegetative Plant Organs and Systems The basic plant body plan, showing the root and shoot systems and the principal vegetative organs, of (**A**) a eudicot and (**B**) a monocot.

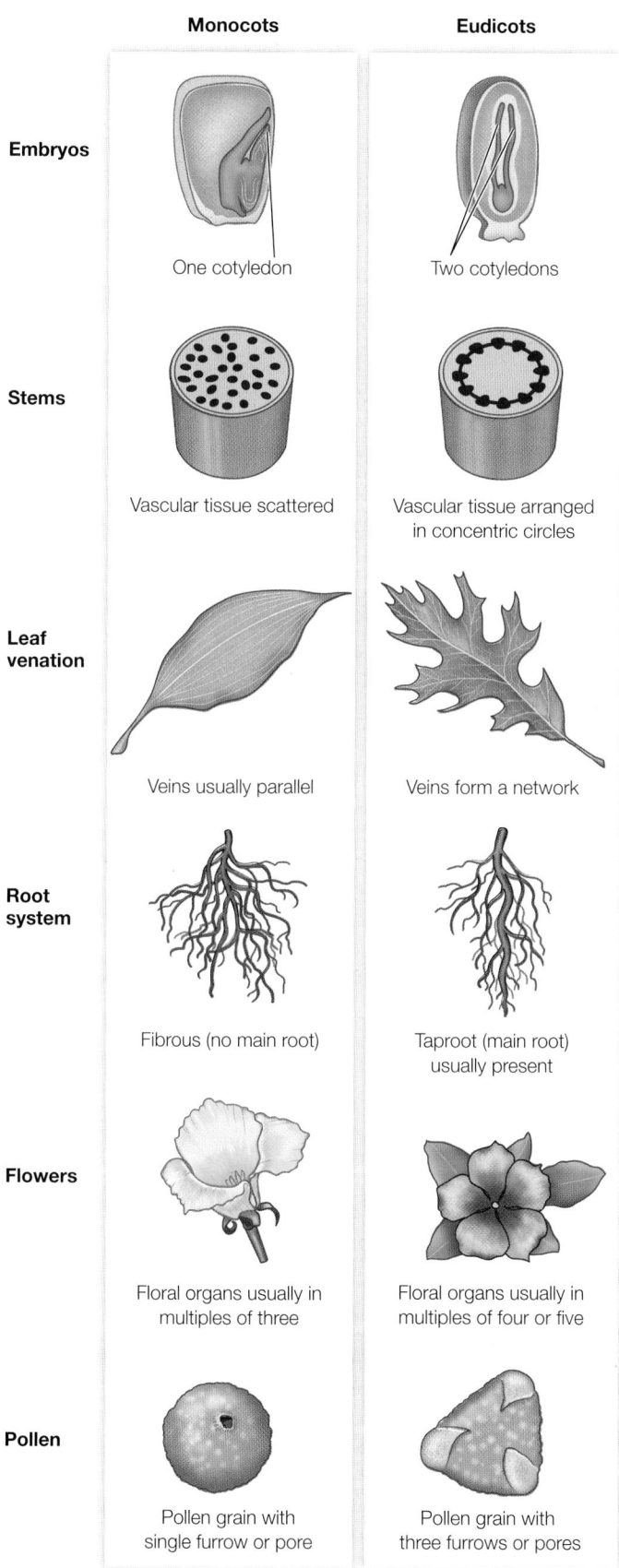

	Monocots	Eudicots
Embryos	One cotyledon	Two cotyledons
Stems	Vascular tissue scattered	Vascular tissue arranged in concentric circles
Leaf venation	Veins usually parallel	Veins form a network
Root system	Fibrous (no main root)	Taproot (main root) usually present
Flowers	Floral organs usually in multiples of three	Floral organs usually in multiples of four or five
Pollen	Pollen grain with single furrow or pore	Pollen grain with three furrows or pores

Figure 32.2 Comparing the Two Major Angiosperm Clades
There are several structural differences between monocots and eudicots.

contrast, the open-ended growth of plants is **indeterminate**. The number of branches they will produce depends on the environment; it is not specified when a seedling starts growing. Indeterminate growth of the shoot and root systems is made possible by meristems. Meristems are localized regions of undifferentiated cells that are the sources of all new growth in the adult plant. Even before seed germination, the plant embryo has two **apical meristems**: a **shoot apical meristem** near the end of the embryonic shoot, and a **root apical meristem** at the end of the embryonic root.

Meristematic cells are small and closely packed. The cells that perpetuate the meristems, called **initials**, are comparable to animal stem cells (discussed in Key Concept 18.2). When the initials divide, some of the daughter cells develop into new initials, and some differentiate into more specialized cells.

Two types of meristems contribute to the growth and development of the adult plant (**Figure 32.3**):

1. The apical meristems in the root and shoot orchestrate primary growth (the growth of shoots and roots), ultimately giving rise to every cell in the primary plant body, directly or through the formation of additional meristems.

2. **Lateral meristems** orchestrate growth in thickness and facilitate branching of roots or shoots. Two lateral meristems (also called secondary meristems), vascular cambium and cork cambium, contribute to the secondary plant body (the bark and wood).

Apical–basal polarity and radial symmetry are characteristics of the plant body

Two basic patterns are established early in plant embryogenesis (embryo formation) (**Figure 32.4**). The apical–basal axis, the ends of which are defined by the shoot and root meristems, is the plant's central axis. The radial axis is the concentric arrangement of the tissue systems (discussed in Key Concept 32.2). We will focus here on how these axes develop in a model eudicot, *Arabidopsis thaliana*, that has been studied extensively by plant physiologists and geneticists. You can follow the steps that occur during *A. thaliana* embryogenesis in **Figure 32.5**.

The first step in the formation of an *A. thaliana* embryo is a mitotic division of the zygote that gives rise to two daughter cells, an apical daughter cell and a basal daughter cell (see Figure 32.5, Step 1). An asymmetrical plane of cell division results in an uneven distribution of cytoplasm between these two cells, and this determines their different fates. Signals in the smaller, apical daughter cell induce it to produce the embryo proper, while the larger basal daughter cell produces the **suspensor**, which forms a stalk under the embryo (see Figure 32.5, Step 2). This division not only establishes the apical–basal axis of the new plant but also determines its polarity (which end is the tip, or apex, and which is the base). The end of the embryo attached to the suspensor forms the root. A long, thin suspensor and a more spherical or globular embryo are distinguishable after just four mitotic divisions. The suspensor soon ceases to elongate.

In eudicots such as *A. thaliana*, the initially globular embryo develops into the characteristic heart stage as the cotyledons

Each terminal bud contains a shoot apical meristem.

In woody plants the vascular cambium and cork cambium thicken the stem and root.

Terminal bud

Axillary bud

Terminal bud

Lateral meristems:

Cork cambium

Vascular cambium

© Ed Reschke/Getty Images

Shoot apical meristem

Leaf primordia

Axillary bud primordium

100 μm

Root apical meristem

Root cap

© James Solliday/Biological Photo Service

50 μm

Figure 32.3 Apical and Lateral Meristems Root and shoot apical meristems produce the primary plant body, lengthening it; lateral meristems produce the secondary plant body, thickening it.

Media Clip 32.1 Rapid Growth of Brambles
Life12e.com/mc32.1

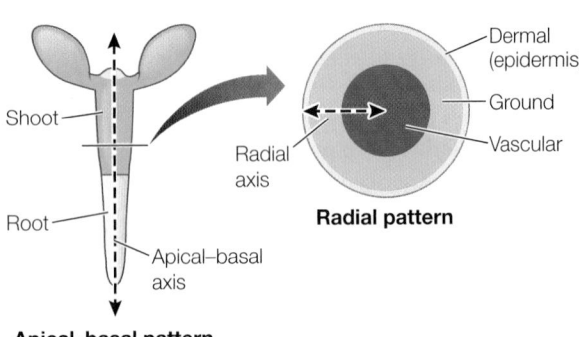

Shoot

Root

Apical–basal axis

Radial axis

Radial pattern

Dermal (epidermis)

Ground

Vascular

Apical–basal pattern

Figure 32.4 Two Patterns for Plant Morphogenesis The apical–basal pattern is the arrangement of cells and tissues along a main axis from root to shoot. The radial pattern determines the concentric arrangement of tissues as organs grow in thickness.

start to grow (see Figure 32.5, Step 3). Further elongation of the cotyledons and of the main axis of the embryo gives rise to the torpedo stage, during which some of the internal tissues begin to differentiate (see Figure 32.5, Step 4). Between the cotyledons is the shoot apical meristem; at the other end of the axis is the root apical meristem. Each of these meristems contains undifferentiated cells that will continue to divide to give rise to the organs that will develop during the life of the plant.

As shown in Step 2 of Figure 32.5, the plant embryo is first a sphere and later a cylinder. The root and stem retain this cylindrical shape throughout the plant's life. You can see this most easily in the trunk (mature stem) of a tree. By the end of embryogenesis, the radial symmetry of the plant has been established (see Figure 32.4). The embryonic plant contains three tissue types, arranged concentrically, which will give rise to the tissues of the adult plant body.

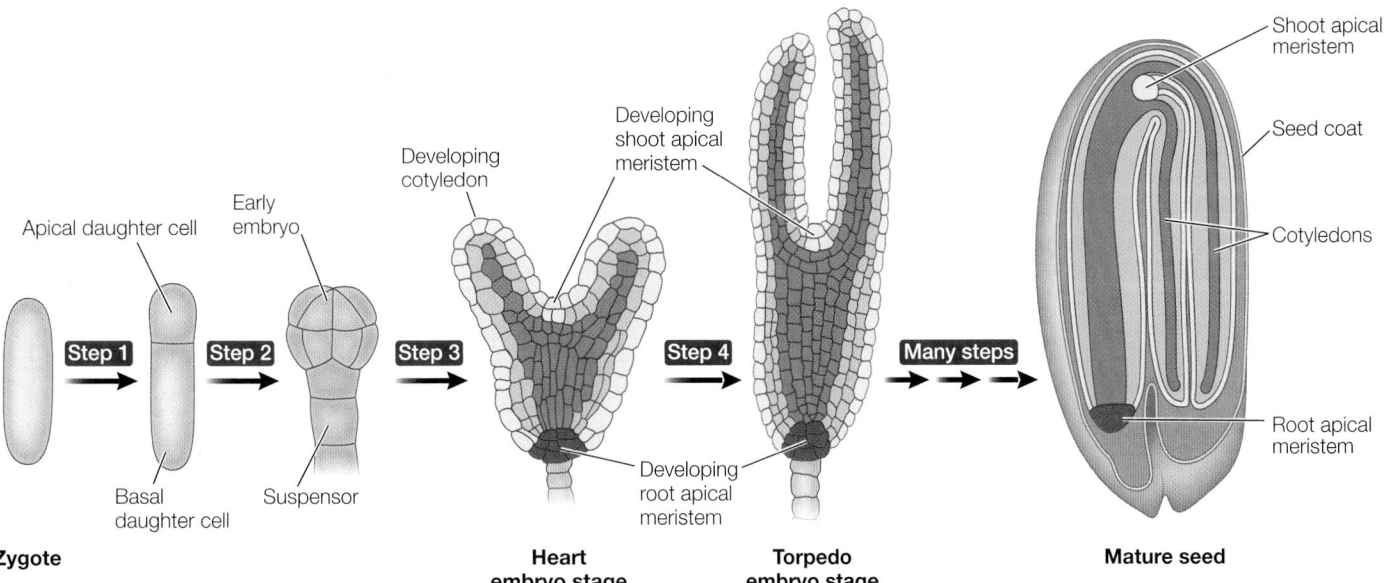

Figure 32.5 Plant Embryogenesis The basic body plan of the model eudicot *Arabidopsis thaliana* is established in several steps. By the heart stage, three tissue types—dermal (tan), ground (light green), and vascular (blue)—are established. These tissue types are shown in the mature seed, which develops after many more stages.

Q: How do you think the differences between the apical and basal daughter cells are established?

KEY CONCEPT
32.1 Recap and Assess

The vegetative plant body consists of a root system and a shoot system. Most angiosperms are either monocots or eudicots, which differ in several basic ways. Plants are distinct from most animals in that they grow from meristems, a feature that makes plant growth indeterminate and allows plants to adapt their bodies to the changing environment. The tissues of the plant body develop along two axes: the apical–basal axis (which establishes a polar pattern from root to shoot) and the radial axis (which establishes a concentric pattern of vascular, ground, and dermal tissue systems).

1. How do plants explore their environment for resources even though they are rooted in place?

2. Describe one primary way in which plant development differs from animal development.

3. Describe the initial step during embryogenesis that leads to the apical–basal pattern.

4. What would you expect a mutant strain of *A. thaliana* that lacks apical–basal polarity in the embryo to look like when it matures?

In Key Concept 32.2 we will look more closely at the types of cells that plants contain and the tissue systems that are formed from them.

KEY CONCEPT
32.2 Plant Organs Are Made Up of Cells Organized into Three Types of Tissues

Learning Objectives

32.2.1 Explain how primary and secondary cell walls differ in terms of their location, structure, and when they are produced.

32.2.2 Compare and contrast parenchyma, collenchyma, and sclerenchyma cells.

32.2.3 Describe the three tissue systems in terms of their origin and location in the plant.

32.2.4 Describe the water-conducting elements in plants, and compare these elements in gymnosperms and angiosperms.

By the end of embryogenesis, both the apical–basal and radial axes have been established. Unlike complex animals that can have dozens of different tissues (humans, for example, have three kinds of muscle tissue alone), plants have just three major tissue systems, each of which has specialized cells.

Unlike animals, plant cells have walls made out of cellulose (a polysaccharide). This wall is interrupted by membrane-lined cytoplasmic channels called plasmodesmata (see Key Concept 5.4). As plants have neither an internal skeleton nor a hard exoskeleton, their cell walls serve the important structural function of holding the plant upright. However, this rigid extracellular matrix makes it impossible for cells to move from place to place,

As the cell expands, the primary cell wall thins.

When expansion stops, the cells may deposit secondary walls.

Secondary wall

Figure 32.6 Primary and Secondary Cell Walls

as they do in animal development. Furthermore, overly strong walls can prevent cell elongation.

The wall of a growing plant cell is called the **primary cell wall**. When cell expansion stops, some types of plant cells deposit one or more additional cellulosic layers to form a thick, rigid **secondary cell wall** that is internal to the primary cell wall (**Figure 32.6**).

Secondary cell walls cannot expand. Instead they provide the mechanical support that allows some plants to produce large stems. The secondary wall contains layers of ordered cellulose microfibrils embedded in a remarkable substance called **lignin**. Lignin is a major component of wood; it is a complex, carbon-containing polymer.

This matrix is strong, waterproof, and resistant to digestion by animals. After cellulose, lignin is the most abundant biological polymer on Earth, accounting for 20%–35% of the dry weight of wood.

Three types of plant cells have distinct cell wall properties

Each species must strike a compositional balance between thin cell walls, which permit growth, provide flexibility, and conserve resources, and thicker cell walls that provide more mechanical support. Different plants take different approaches to this challenge, involving three types of cells: parenchyma, collenchyma, and sclerenchyma (**Figure 32.7**).

1. **Parenchyma** cells are the most abundant cells in plants. They have large vacuoles and relatively thin walls (see Figure 32.7A). They perform a wide variety of functions, including photosynthesis (in the shoot), transport, synthesis and secretion of metabolites, and storage of protein in seeds and of starch in roots. Because their walls are thin, the firmness of parenchyma cells depends on their water content: they are firm when they are **turgid** (full of water), somewhat like a water balloon. Parenchyma cells have only primary cell walls, meaning that cell wall material is added only while the cell is expanding. Many retain the capacity to divide, as when a wound results in cell proliferation.

(A) Parenchyma

Parenchyma cells   Primary cell walls

David McIntyre

50 μm

(B) Collenchyma

Collenchyma cells   Primary cell walls

© Ed Reschke/Getty Images

50 μm

(C) Sclerenchyma

Fibers   Secondary cell walls

© Biophoto Associates/Science Source

50 μm

Sclereids   Secondary cell walls

David McIntyre

50 μm

Figure 32.7 Plant Cell Types **(A)** Parenchyma cells in the petiole of *Coleus*. Note the thin, uniform cell walls. **(B)** Collenchyma cells make up the outer cell layers of this spinach leaf vein. Their walls are thick at the corners of the cells and thin elsewhere. **(C)** Two types of sclerenchyma cells. Left: Fibers in a sunflower stem (*Helianthus*). The thick secondary walls are stained red. Right: Sclereids. The extremely thick secondary walls of sclereids are laid down in layers. They provide support and a hard texture to structures such as nuts and seeds.

2. **Collenchyma** cells are firm enough to provide support for growing tissues such as stems, yet flexible enough to permit growth. They are generally elongated, and their primary walls are characteristically thicker at the corners of the cells due to the deposition of pectins (see Figure 32.7B). When a plant becomes dry, cells lose their turgor and wilting occurs in portions of the plant (generally the growing tips) that are composed of parenchyma and collenchyma. Collenchyma cells provide support to leaf petioles, nonwoody stems, and growing organs. The familiar "strings" in celery stalks consist primarily of collenchyma. Like parenchyma cells, collenchyma cells have only primary cell walls.

3. **Sclerenchyma** cells have very thick walls reinforced with lignin. They form a primary cell wall when they are elongating, and then, after cell elongation stops, they add additional layers of material to the wall, forming a secondary cell wall (see Figure 32.7C). Most sclerenchyma cells then undergo programmed cell death (apoptosis; see Key Concept 11.6), but their strong cell walls remain and provide support for the plant even when the cells are not turgid. Sclerenchyma cells come in several types. **Fibers** are often organized into bundles and provide relatively rigid support to wood, bark, and other parts of the plant. **Sclereids** may pack together densely, as in a nut's shell or in some seed coats. Isolated clumps of sclereids, called stone cells, occur in pears and some other fruits and give them their characteristic gritty texture.

These three cell types are distributed across the three tissue types described below.

Plants are composed of three main tissues

Plant cells are organized into three tissue types: dermal, ground, and vascular (**Figure 32.8**). These tissues first arise in the embryo and persist throughout the life of the plant. In the shoot meristem, cell division frequently takes place such that the newly generated cells sit side by side. Over time, this pattern of cell division generates three distinct layers within the meristem (**Figure 32.9**). The outermost layer produces the dermal layer. Layer two produces ground tissue. Vascular tissue arises from the third layer.

The **dermal tissue** forms the outer covering of the plant. The aboveground epidermal cells secrete a protective extracellular layer called a **cuticle**. The cuticle is made up of cutin (a polymer composed of long chains of fatty acids), a complex mixture of waxes, and cell wall polysaccharides. The cuticle limits water loss, reflects potentially damaging solar radiation, and serves as a barrier against pathogens. Some epidermal cells differentiate to form:

- Stomatal guard cells, which form stomata (pores) for gas exchange in leaves

- Trichomes, or leaf hairs, which provide protection against insects and damaging solar radiation, as well as secrete oils (such as those produced by mints)

- Root hairs, which greatly increase root surface area, thus providing more surface for the uptake of water and mineral nutrients

- The stems and roots of woody plants develop a dermal tissue called periderm (discussed in Key Concept 32.3).

The **ground tissue** comprises most of the tissue between the dermal tissue and the vascular tissue and thus makes up most of the plant body. Cells in this tissue may play important roles in photosynthesis or storage of carbohydrates, fats, or in succulent plants, water.

The **vascular tissue** is the plant's plumbing, or transport system. Its presence is the distinguishing feature of vascular plants. Its two constituent tissues, the xylem and phloem, distribute materials throughout the plant. The **xylem** distributes water and

Dermal tissue
Ground tissue
Vascular tissue

The **dermal tissue** forms the outer covering of the plant.

The **ground tissue** carries out photosynthesis, stores photosynthetic products, and helps support the plant.

The **vascular tissue** conducts water and solutes throughout the plant.

Figure 32.8 Three Tissue Types Extend throughout the Plant Body The arrangement shown here is typical of eudicots, but the three tissue types are continuous in the bodies of all vascular plants.

Q: What is a major difference between cells in the ground tissue in the leaf compared with the root?

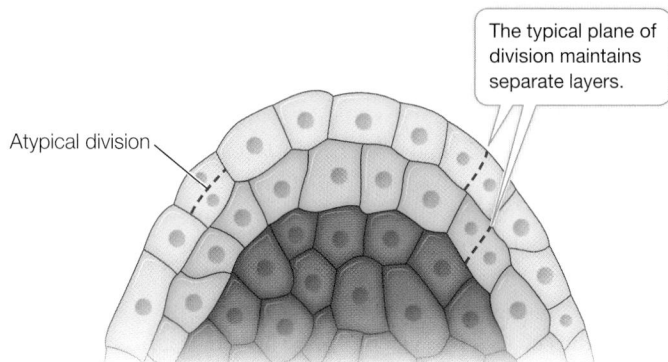

The typical plane of division maintains separate layers.

Atypical division

Figure 32.9 The Shoot Apical Meristem Is Composed of Three Layers of Cells Cells in each layer typically divide in a plane that maintains the separate layers. Occasional atypical divisions in other planes can result in cells originally of one layer "invading" the next layer, as shown.

mineral ions taken up by the roots to all the cells of the stems and leaves. The **phloem** performs a variety of functions, including transport, support, and storage. It plays a particularly critical role in supplying the energy-rich molecules and chemical building blocks needed by all living cells of the plant body. The phloem transports carbohydrates away from the sites of production, which are called **sources** (primarily leaves), and delivers them to sites of utilization or storage, called **sinks**. Sinks include growing tissues, storage organs, and developing flowers.

Let's take a closer look at the structures of the diverse cell types that make up these vascular tissues. In Chapter 33 you'll see how they transport water and materials throughout the plant body.

XYLEM TISSUE   Xylem tissue contains conducting cells called **tracheary elements**, which have secondary cell walls and undergo

apoptosis before assuming their function of transporting water and dissolved minerals. There are two types of tracheary elements: tracheids and vessel elements. The spindle-shaped **tracheids (Figure 32.10A)** are evolutionarily more ancient than vessel elements and are the major cell type in the wood of gymnosperms (major groups of gymnosperms are covered in Key Concept 27.2). When tracheids die, their internal components disintegrate and pits remain between the cells. Pits are cavities in secondary walls, arranged such that pits of adjacent cells are situated across from each other. Water and minerals move rapidly from one cell to another because these substances need to cross only one thin extracellular barrier, the primary cell wall.

Flowering plants have evolved a water-conducting system made up of vessels that are formed from individual cells called **vessel elements**. These cells are laid down end-to-end. Like tracheids, vessel elements have pits in their cell walls, but their pits are generally larger in diameter than those of tracheids. Before they undergo apoptosis, the end walls of vessel elements partially break down, forming a continuous hollow tube that functions as an open pipeline for water conduction (**Figure 32.10B**). In the course of angiosperm evolution, vessel elements have become shorter and wider, and their end walls have become less oblique and less obstructed. These adaptations have presumably increased the efficiency of water transport through the vessels. The xylem of many angiosperms includes both tracheids and vessels.

PHLOEM TISSUE   The transport cells of the phloem, unlike those of the mature xylem, are living cells. In flowering plants the characteristic cells of the phloem are called **sieve tube elements** (**Figure 32.10C**). Like vessel elements, these cells meet end-to-end. They form long sieve tubes, which transport carbohydrates and many other materials from their sources (usually leaves) to tissues that consume or store them (for example, roots).

(A) Tracheids

50 μm

© John D. Cunningham/Visuals Unlimited, Inc.

(B) Vessel elements

Vessel elements

Secondary cell walls

50 μm

© J. Robert Waaland/Biological Photo Service

(C) Sieve tube elements

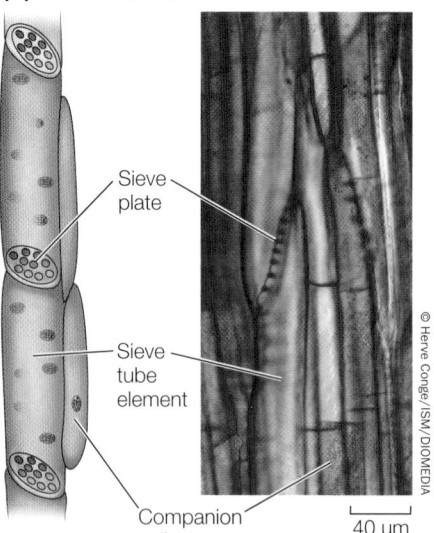

Sieve plate

Sieve tube element

Companion cell

40 μm

© Herve Conge/ISM/DIOMEDIA

Figure 32.10 Vascular Tissue Cell Types (A, B) Tracheary elements: (A) Tracheids in pinewood. The thick secondary walls are stained dark red. (B) Vessel elements in the stem of a squash. The secondary walls are stained red; note the different patterns of thickening, including rings and spirals. (C) Sieve tube elements and companion cells in the stem of a cucumber.

Whereas the end walls of vessel elements break down to facilitate flow through the vessels, the end walls of sieve tube elements form tunnels through which carbohydrates and other needed substances flow. The end walls of sieve tube elements are called sieve plates. Although the sieve tube elements remain alive, some of their components, including the nucleus, ribosomes, and vacuole, break down during development. The sieve tube elements are, however, closely connected via plasmodesmata to **companion cells**—specialized parenchyma cells that retain all their organelles and function as "life support systems" for the sieve tube elements.

KEY CONCEPT
32.2 Recap and Assess

The plant body is composed of cells that can be divided into three classes based on the properties of their cell walls: the thin-walled parenchyma cells; collenchyma cells, which provide more rigid support without preventing growth; and sclerenchyma cells, whose secondary cell walls can support plants even when the cells are not turgid. The three concentric tissue types in the plant embryo—dermal, ground, and vascular—give rise to the tissues and organs of the adult plant. These tissues have unique combinations of specialized cells that carry out the various functions necessary for plant life.

1. Create a table comparing the three cell types in terms of their structure and function.

2. What structural differences make tissues consisting of collenchyma cells more flexible than those consisting primarily of sclerenchyma cells?

3. Describe the differences between tracheids and vessel elements.

In Key Concept 32.3 we will see how the tissues are established by the meristems and how they contribute to the overall structure of the plant.

KEY CONCEPT
32.3 Meristems Build a Continuously Growing Plant

Learning Objectives

32.3.1 Explain the function of meristems in plant growth, including the types of cells and organs that are produced by the root and shoot apical meristems.

32.3.2 Draw a longitudinal section of the developing root, from the tip upward, indicating the names and activities of the zones.

32.3.3 Explain how the vascular cambium increases the width of a woody plant.

Plants and animals develop and function differently. While animals use their mobility to look for food, plants are sessile (rooted in one place) and instead grow toward scarce resources, both aboveground (shoots toward sunlight) and belowground (roots toward water and minerals). This open-ended growth can occur in either of two ways: **Primary growth** is characterized by cell division followed by cell enlargement. Primary growth results in the proliferation and lengthening of shoots and roots. All

seed plants have a primary plant body, which consists of all the nonwoody parts of the plant. Many herbaceous plants consist entirely of a primary plant body. **Secondary growth** increases plant thickness. Woody plants, such as trees and shrubs, have a secondary plant body consisting of wood and bark. As the tissues of the secondary plant body are laid down, the stems and roots thicken.

Indeterminate primary growth originates in apical meristems

Because apical meristems can perpetuate themselves indefinitely, a stem or root can continue to lengthen and grow indefinitely; in other words, growth of the plant body as a whole is indeterminate. All plant organs arise ultimately from cell divisions in apical meristems, followed by cell expansion and differentiation. Several types of apical meristems play roles in organ formation:

- Shoot apical meristems supply the cells for new leaves and stems. The shoot apical meristem also retains some cells as initials, which allows the meristem to be maintained. In addition to the main stem of the plant, each branch has its own shoot apical meristem. Shoot apical meristems are also called **vegetative meristems** because they give rise to vegetative tissues (leaves, stems, and roots).

- When the plant is ready to flower, one or more of its shoot apical meristems are transformed into **inflorescence meristems**, and these in turn develop **floral meristems**. (Chapter 36 is dedicated to the reproduction of flowering plants; inflorescence and floral meristems are discussed in Key Concept 36.2.)

- Root apical meristems supply the cells that extend roots, enabling the plant to penetrate and explore the soil for water and minerals. Like the shoot apical meristem, the root apical meristem retains some cells as initials. Each type of root (i.e., the taproot, a lateral root, or an adventitious root; see below) has its own meristem.

Because meristems can continue to produce new organs throughout the lifetime of the plant, the plant body is much more variable in form than the typical animal body, which produces each organ only once.

Let's look more closely at how the root apical meristem produces the root system.

The root apical meristem gives rise to the root cap and the primary root

The root apical meristem produces all the cells that contribute to the growth and development of the root (**Figure 32.11**). Some of the daughter cells from the apical (tip) end of the root apical meristem contribute to a **root cap**, which protects the delicate growing region of the root as it pushes through the soil. The root cap secretes a mucopolysaccharide (slime) that acts as a lubricant. Even so, the cells of the root cap are often damaged or scraped away and must therefore be replaced constantly. The root cap is also the structure that detects the pull of gravity and thus controls the downward growth of roots.

In the middle of the root apical meristem is a quiescent center, in which cell divisions are rare. The quiescent center cells

(A) Root anatomy

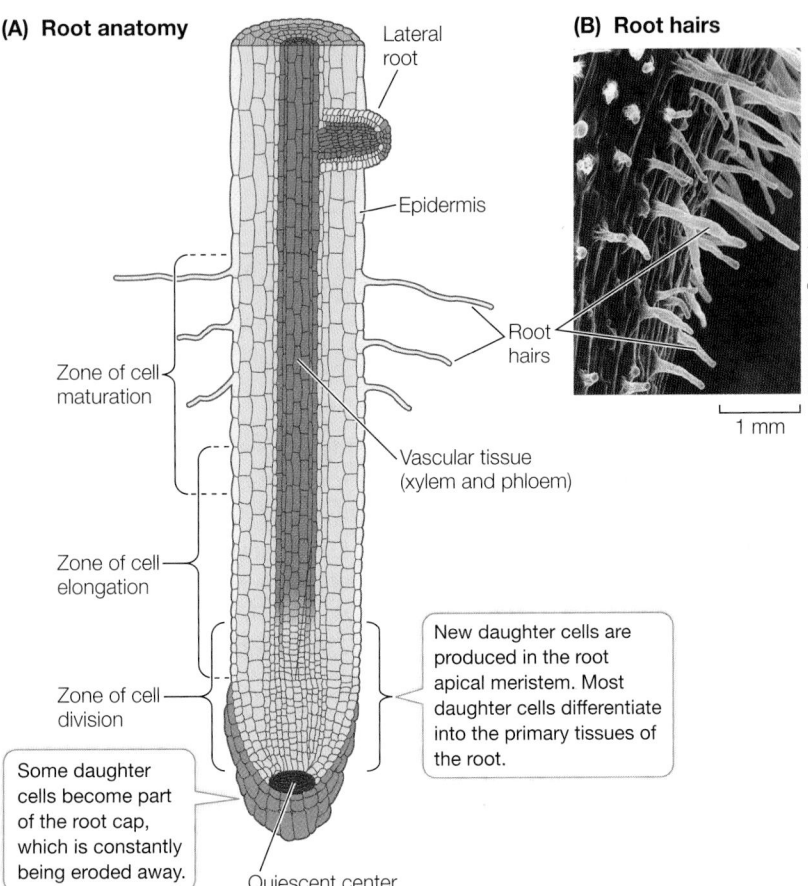

Lateral root

Epidermis

Root hairs

Zone of cell maturation

Vascular tissue (xylem and phloem)

Zone of cell elongation

Zone of cell division

New daughter cells are produced in the root apical meristem. Most daughter cells differentiate into the primary tissues of the root.

Some daughter cells become part of the root cap, which is constantly being eroded away.

Quiescent center

(B) Root hairs

Root hairs

© John N. A. Lott/Biological Photo Service

1 mm

Figure 32.11 **Tissues and Regions of the Root Tip** **(A)** Extensive cell division creates the complex structure of the root. **(B)** Root hairs, seen with a scanning electron microscope.

 Media Clip 32.2 Cell Expansion in Root Hairs Life12e.com/mc32.2

The root apical meristem produces cells that make up the root tissues

While the longitudinal axis of a root can be described in terms of the zones it contains, the radial axis can be described in terms of the differing cell types that make up the different portions of the root. In flowering plants, the cells that make up the root are similar in that they contain the three tissue types described above, however, the differing arrangement of tissues in the roots of eudicots and monocots is one of the ways in which the two clades are distinguished (**Figure 32.12**). Some commonalities in the cell types that comprise the radial structure are as follows:

- The epidermis is the outer layer of cells that is adapted for protection of the root and absorption of mineral ions and water. Many of the epidermal cells produce long, delicate **root hairs**, which vastly increase the surface area of the root (see Figure 32.11B). Root hairs grow out among the

may be in G1 phase of the cell cycle for 10 days. The quiescent center influences the cells around it such that they retain the character of initial cells rather than differentiating. The daughter cells produced above the quiescent center (that is, on the shootward side away from the root cap) form the main body of the root.

Because plant cells do not move past one another, the distance between a cell and the quiescent center is related to the length of time since the cell was created. This leads to several distinct zones in the root. The meristem is close to the root tip and includes both the initial cells that surround the quiescent center and the **zone of cell division**. Just shootward of this is the **zone of cell elongation**, where the newly formed cells elongate and thus push the root tip farther into the soil. Shootward of that zone is the **zone of cell differentiation** (also called the maturation zone), where the cells take on their mature forms.

Figure 32.12 **Products of the Root Meristem** The arrangement of tissues in the stele differs in the roots of eudicots **(A)** and monocots **(B)**. The photomicrographs show cross sections of the stele of a representative eudicot (a buttercup, *Ranunculus*) and a representative monocot (corn, *Zea mays*), showing the arrangement of the primary root tissues.

 View in **Achieve** Activity 32.1 **Eudicot Root** View in **Achieve** Activity 32.2 **Monocot Root**

(A) Eudicot root

Stele

(B) Monocot root

Stele

Pith
Xylem
Phloem
Pericycle
Endodermis
Cortex
Epidermis

Endodermis   Pericycle   Cortex

Phloem   Xylem   60 μm

© Ed Reschke/Getty Images

Endodermis   Phloem   Xylem

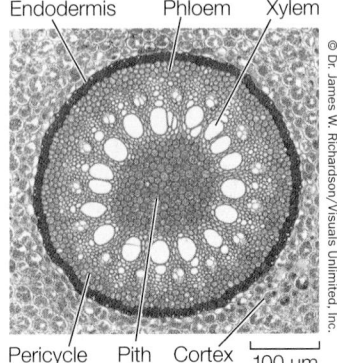

Pericycle   Pith   Cortex   100 μm

© Dr. James W. Richardson/Visuals Unlimited, Inc.

Developing lateral root   Epidermis

Figure 32.13 **Lateral Root Anatomy**   Scanning electron micrograph of the tip of a lateral root in a willow tree. Cells in the pericycle divide and the products differentiate, forming the tissues of a lateral root.

Figure 32.14 Egyptian Papyrus Depicting the Weighing of Souls from the Book of the Dead

soil particles, probing nooks and crannies and taking up water and minerals.

- The **cortex** is a region of ground tissue produced internal to the epidermis. The cells of the multilayered cortex have various functions, including storage.

- The **endodermis** is the innermost layer of the cortex. Unlike other cortical cells, the endodermal cells contain a waterproof substance called suberin in their primary cell walls. The suberin forms a cylindrical ring around the inside of the endodermis, which allows the endodermal cells to control the movement of water and dissolved mineral ions into and out of the vascular tissue system.

- Interior to the endodermis is the vascular cylinder, or **stele**. The stele consists of the pericycle, xylem tissue, and phloem tissue. The **pericycle** consists of one or more layers of cells with flexible developmental potential. It has three important functions: (1) It is the tissue within which lateral roots arise (**Figure 32.13**). (2) It can contribute to secondary growth by giving rise to lateral meristems that thicken the root. (3) Its cells contain membrane transport proteins that export nutrient ions into the cells of the xylem.

At the very center of the root of a eudicot lies the xylem. Seen in cross section, it typically has the shape of a star with a variable number of points (see Figure 32.12A). Between the points are bundles of phloem. In monocots, a region of parenchyma cells called the **pith** typically lies in the center of the root, surrounded by xylem and phloem (see Figure 32.12B). Pith, which often stores carbohydrate reserves, is also found in the stems of both eudicots and monocots. Strips of pith of the stem of the papyrus plant *Cyperus papyrus* can be glued together and used to make a paperlike substance called by its species name. Papyrus dates from earlier than 2500 BCE in Egypt, and was the writing surface of choice until about 300 CE, when parchment from animal skins replaced it (**Figure 32.14**).

The root system anchors the plant and takes up water and dissolved minerals

Water and minerals enter most plants through the root system, which is located in the soil. Because light does not penetrate the

soil, roots typically lack the capacity for photosynthesis. Although hidden from view, the root system is often larger than the visible shoot system. For example, the root system of a 4-month-old winter rye plant (*Secale cereale*) was found to be 130 times longer in total than the shoot system, with almost 13 million branches that had a cumulative length of more than 500 kilometers!

Angiosperm root systems develop from the embryonic root, called the **radicle**. From this common starting point, the root systems of monocots and eudicots develop differently. Following seed germination, the radicle of most eudicots develops as a primary root called the **taproot**, which extends downward by tip growth and outward by initiating **lateral roots**. The taproot and the lateral roots form a **taproot system**, which can take a variety of forms. For example, the taproot itself often functions as a nutrient storage organ, as in carrots (*Daucus carota*), sugar beets (*Beta vulgaris*), and sweet potato (*Ipomoea batatas*) (**Figure 32.15A**).

In contrast, the primary root of monocots (and some eudicots) is short-lived. Because they originate from the stem at ground level or just below, the roots of a typical monocot are called **adventitious** ("arriving from outside") **roots**, and they form a **fibrous root system** composed of numerous thin roots that are all roughly equal in length (**Figure 32.15B**). Many fibrous root systems have large surface areas for the absorption of water and minerals. A fibrous root system clings to soil very well. The fibrous root systems of grasses, for example, may protect steep hillsides where runoff from rain would otherwise cause erosion.

In some plants—corn, banyan, and pandanus trees, for example—adventitious roots grow down from above the ground and function as props to help support the shoot system (**Figure 32.15C**). These **prop roots** have evolved for different reasons in different species. For example, some monocots may develop prop roots because they are unable to support aboveground growth through the thickening of their stems. Pandanus trees often grow near coastal beaches, where their prop roots help provide support in very sandy soils. Banyans begin life as epiphytes (plants that grow on other plants) and then develop woody prop roots, which enable them to grow into huge trees.

(A) Taproots

© iStock.com/modesigns58

(B) Fibrous root system

© zkruger/Getty Images

(C) Prop roots

David McIntyre

Figure 32.15 Root Systems of Eudicots and Monocots **(A)** The taproot systems of eudicots, such as carrots and sugar beets, contrast with **(B)** the fibrous root system of a leek and **(C)** the adventitious prop roots of corn.

The products of the shoot apical meristem form the shoot system

Now let's turn to the shoot, which comprises the stem and leaves. Shoots are composed of repeating modules called phytomers (**Figure 32.16**). A phytomer in the shoot system consists of a node with its attached leaf or leaves, the internode below the node, and axillary buds, each of which forms in the angle between a leaf and the stem. Shoots grow by adding new phytomers. The new phytomers originate from cells in the shoot apical meristem, which is present

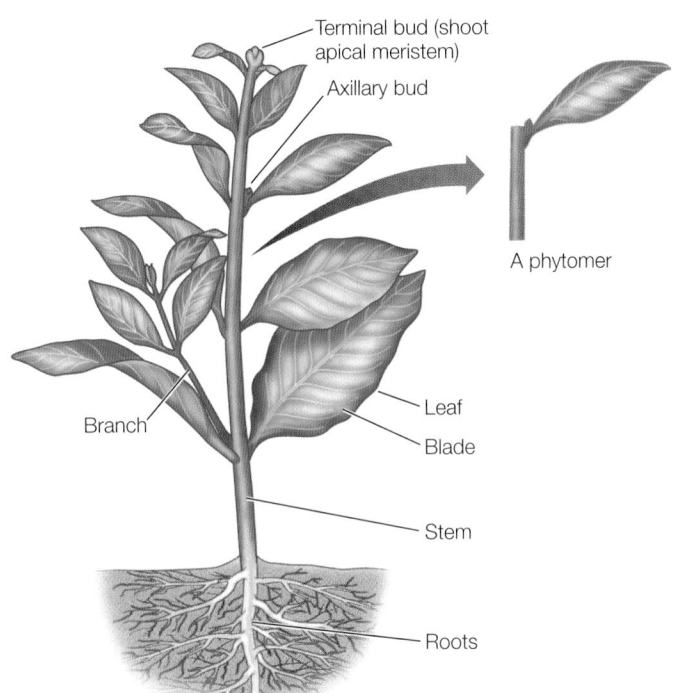

Terminal bud (shoot apical meristem)

Axillary bud

A phytomer

Branch

Leaf

Blade

Stem

Roots

Figure 32.16 The Shoot Is Built of Repeating Units Called **Phytomers** Each phytomer consists of an internode (stem), leaf, and axillary bud.

at the apex of the main stem, and from meristems that are located at the tip of each branch.

As the shoot grows and extends, bulges called **leaf primordia** develop on the sides of the shoot apical meristem at regular intervals (see Figure 32.3). Each primordium can develop into a mature leaf. In addition, axillary buds form at the bases of the leaf primordia. These have the potential to grow out and form a new shoot (branch) with a meristem at its tip. The sites where leaf primordia form become nodes on the developing stem. The regions between the nodes (the internodes) lengthen initially via cell division and later by cell elongation. The growing stem has no protective structure analogous to the root cap, but the leaf primordia can act as a protective covering for the shoot apical meristem.

The vascular systems of stems differ from those of roots. In a root, the vascular tissue lies deep in the interior, with the xylem at or near the center (see Figure 32.12). The vascular tissue of a young stem, however, is divided into discrete **vascular bundles** (**Figure 32.17**). Each vascular bundle contains both xylem and phloem. In eudicots the vascular bundles generally form a ring, whereas in monocots they are scattered throughout the stem.

In addition to the vascular tissues, the stem contains other important storage and supportive tissues. In eudicots the pith lies inside the ring of vascular bundles and also extends between them, forming regions called pith rays. To the outside lies the cortex, which may contain supportive collenchyma cells with thickened walls. The pith and cortex constitute the ground tissue system of the stem. The outermost cell layer of the young stem is the epidermis.

The stem supports leaves and flowers but can have other roles

The main role of stems is to elevate and support the photosynthetic organs (leaves) as well as the reproductive organs (flowers). But in some plants the stem does other things for the plant. For instance, the potato tuber that we eat comes from the ground but is not a root; it's an underground stem that acts as a storage organ for the plant. The "eyes" of a potato are depressions containing axillary

(A) Eudicot vascular bundles

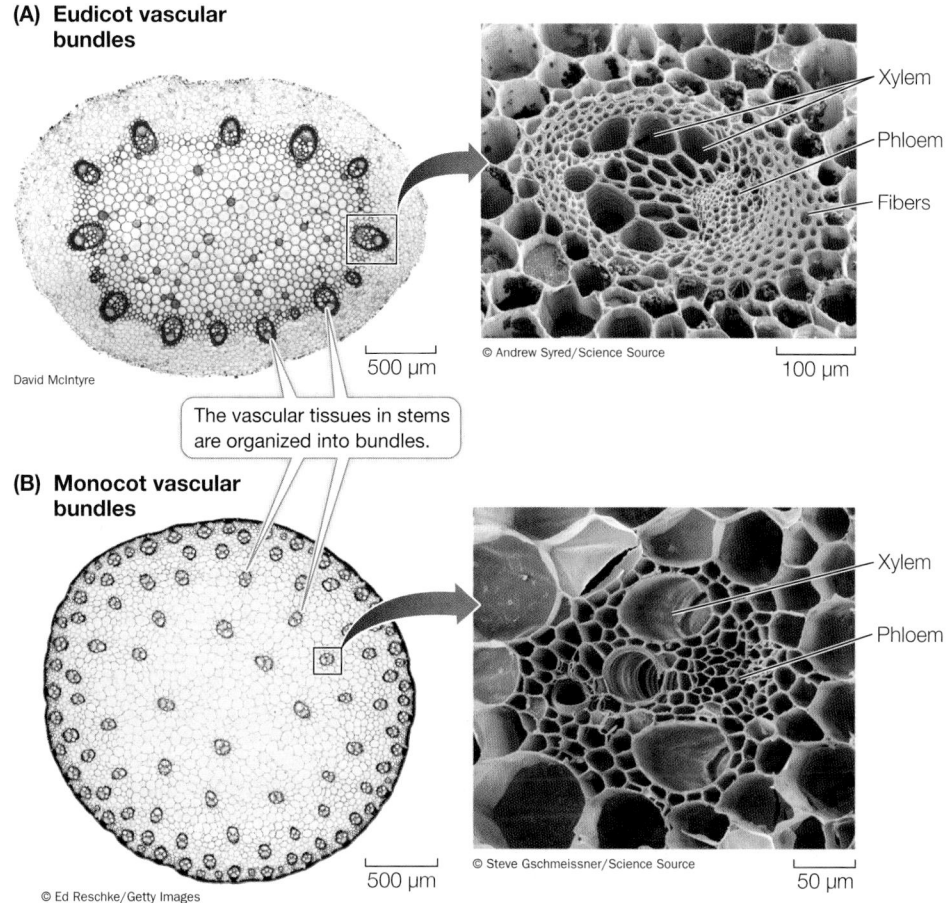

The vascular tissues in stems are organized into bundles.

(B) Monocot vascular bundles

David McIntyre

500 μm

© Andrew Syred/Science Source

100 μm

Xylem

Phloem

Fibers

© Ed Reschke/Getty Images

500 μm

© Steve Gschmeissner/Science Source

50 μm

Xylem

Phloem

Figure 32.17 Vascular Bundles in Stems (**A**) In herbaceous eudicot stems, the vascular bundles are arranged in a cylinder, with pith in the center and the cortex outside the cylinder. (**B**) A scattered arrangement of vascular bundles is typical of monocot stems.

▶ View in **Achieve** Activity 32.3 **Eudicot Stem**
▶ View in **Achieve** Activity 32.4 **Monocot Stem**

buds—in other words, a sprouting potato is just a branching stem (**Figure 32.18A**). Many desert plants have enlarged, water-retaining stems (**Figure 32.18B**). The runners of strawberry plants are horizontal stems that develop adventitious roots some distance from the main stem (**Figure 32.18C**); if the links between the rooted portions are broken, independent plants can develop on each side of the break—a form of vegetative (asexual) reproduction (see Key Concept 36.3).

Leaves are determinate organs produced by shoot apical meristems

For most of its life, a plant produces leaves from apical meristems. Leaves originate from the edges of the apical meristem as initial cells that differentiate into leaf primordia. Leaves differ from stems in two important ways:

1. Unlike the growth of the stem, which is indeterminate, the growth of a leaf is determinate.

2. Whereas the tissues of the stem are arranged in a radial pattern, the leaf, as a flat organ, has a distinct top side and bottom side.

Connect the Concepts The leaf is elegantly structured for the reactions of photosynthesis. For more detail on photosynthesis and the role of leaf tissues, see Key Concepts 10.1 and 10.4.

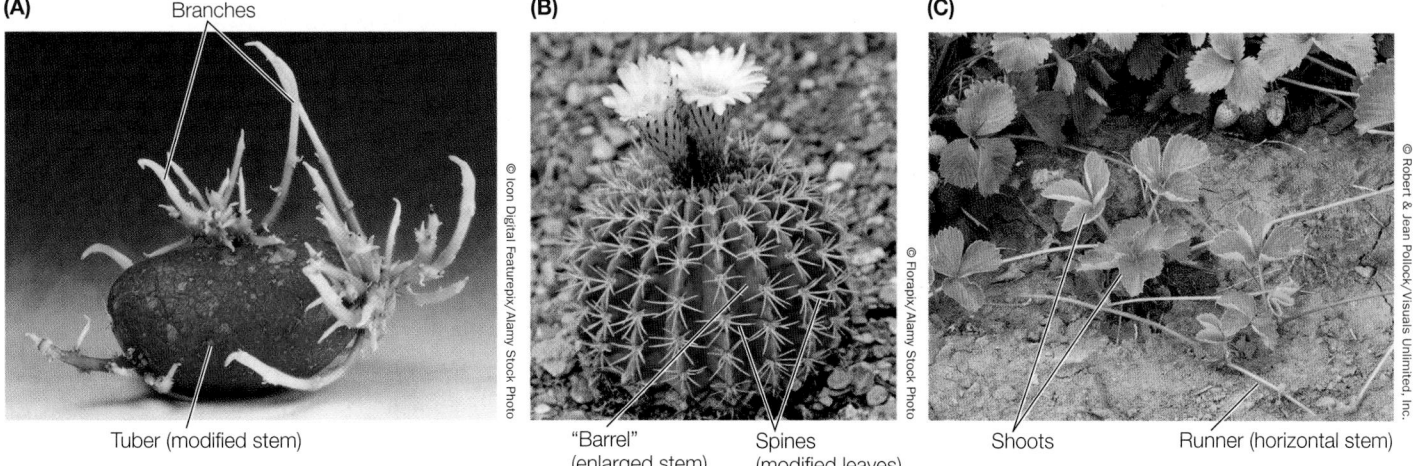

(A) Branches

Tuber (modified stem)

© Icon Digital Featurepix/Alamy Stock Photo

(B)

"Barrel" (enlarged stem)

Spines (modified leaves)

© Florapix/Alamy Stock Photo

(C)

Shoots

Runner (horizontal stem)

© Robert & Jean Pollock/Visuals Unlimited, Inc.

Figure 32.18 Modified Stems (**A**) A potato is a modified stem called a tuber; the sprouts that grow from its "eyes" are shoots, not roots. (**B**) The stem of this barrel cactus is enlarged to store water. Its highly modified leaves serve as thorny spines. Most of this plant's photosynthesis occurs in the stem. (**C**) The runners of strawberry are horizontal stems that produce roots and shoots at intervals. Rooted portions of the plant can live independently if the runner is cut.

Leaf anatomy is beautifully adapted to carry out photosynthesis, and to support that process by exchanging the gases O_2 and CO_2 with the environment, while at the same time limiting evaporative water loss (**Figure 32.19**). Its extensive vascular system supplies the leaf with water and mineral nutrients and exports the products of photosynthesis to the rest of the plant. Figure 32.19A shows a typical eudicot leaf in three dimensions. The photosynthetic parenchyma tissue in leaves is the **mesophyll** (which means "middle of the leaf"). Most eudicot leaves have two zones of mesophyll: an upper layer of elongated cells called the palisade mesophyll, and a lower layer of irregularly shaped cells called the spongy mesophyll. Within the spongy mesophyll is a great deal of air space through which CO_2 can diffuse to photosynthesizing cells.

Vascular tissue branches extensively throughout the leaf, forming a network of veins (see Figure 32.19B). Veins extend to within a few cell diameters of all the cells of the leaf by the xylem, ensuring that the mesophyll cells are well supplied with water and minerals. The products of photosynthesis are loaded into the veins for export to the rest of the plant. In addition to photosynthetic products, leaves make defensive molecules such as the ones in cassava that you learned about in the chapter opener. **Investigating Life: Understanding the Synthesis and Transport of Cyanogenic Glycosides** describes how it was determined that cassava leaves produce these chemicals.

The epidermis covers the entire surface of the leaf. The epidermal cells secrete a waxy cuticle that is impermeable to water. Although this impermeability prevents excessive water loss, it also

poses a problem: while the epidermis keeps water in the leaf, it also keeps out CO_2—the other raw material of photosynthesis.

The problem of balancing water retention and CO_2 availability is solved by guard cells, a system we'll examine in detail in Key Concept 33.3. Stomatal guard cells are modified epidermal cells that can change their shape, thereby opening or closing pores called **stomata** (singular *stoma*). The stomata serve as passageways between the environment and the leaf's interior (see Figure 32.19C). When the stomata are open, CO_2 can enter and O_2 can leave, but water can also be lost.

Many stems and roots undergo secondary growth

As you have seen, the roots and stems of some eudicots develop a secondary plant body, the tissues of which include wood and bark. These tissues are derived by secondary growth from the two lateral meristems:

- The **vascular cambium** is a cylindrical layer of tissue consisting predominantly of elongated cells that divide frequently. It supplies the cells of the secondary xylem and secondary phloem, which eventually become wood and bark, respectively.

- The **cork cambium** produces mainly waxy-walled protective cells. It supplies some of the cells that become bark.

In cold parts of the world, each year deciduous trees lose their leaves and have bare branches and twigs over the winter. The apical meristems of the twigs are enclosed in buds protected by bud scales. When the buds begin to grow in spring, the scales fall away, leaving scars that show where the bud was. These scars

Figure 32.19 The Eudicot Leaf (**A**) This three-dimensional diagram shows a section of a eudicot leaf. (**B**) The network of fine veins in this maple leaf carries water to the mesophyll cells and carries photosynthetic products away from them. (**C**) Carbon dioxide enters the leaf through stomata like this one on the epidermis of a eudicot leaf.

Trichomes are epidermal hairs that can break up airflow, reducing water loss from the leaf. In some species, including the marjoram shown here, modified epidermal hairs serve as oil glands.

View in Achieve
Activity 32.5 Eudicot Leaf

▶Investigating LIFE Understanding the Synthesis and Transport of Cyanogenic Glycosides

Experiment

Original Paper: K. Jørgensen et al. 2005. Cassava plants with a depleted cyanogenic glycoside content in leaves and tubers. Distribution of cyanogenic glycosides, their site of synthesis and transport and blockage of biosynthesis by RNA interference technology. *Plant Physiol* 139: 363–374.

As described in the chapter opener, cassava is the most important root crop in the world. Its use as food is challenging, however, because the plant produces molecules that can be transformed into toxic cyanide when the tissues are disrupted. These cyanogenic glycosides (CGs) are important in defending the plant against animals that eat it, including humans. For the millions of people who eat cassava, careful processing is needed to avoid poisoning. Unfortunately, the processing methods lower the overall nutritional value of the food. Understanding how CGs are made and end up in the fleshy root is an important step in possibly using genetics to produce a crop that does not make CGs. At the Royal Veterinary and Agricultural University in Copenhagen, a team led by Birger Møller investigated the synthesis and transport of CGs in cassava plants.

HYPOTHESIS▶ Molecules that produce cyanide in the cassava are made in the leaves and transported to the underground root.

METHOD▶

Cassava plant

First petiole — 1, 2
Shoot apex
3
Third petiole
4
5
6   7

1 Leave stem intact and measure CG in plant shoot regions.

2 Remove phloem from stem below fifth leaf and then measure CG in plant parts.

RESULTS▶

Region	Relative CG concentration
Shoot apex	Moderate
First petiole	High
Third leaf	Low
Third petiole	Low

Region	Relative CG concentration
Fifth leaf	High
Stem above cut	Moderate
Stem below cut	Very Low

CONCLUSION▶ Cyanogenic glycosides are made in leaves and are transported through petioles to the stem, from which they are transported to the root.

Work with the Data

QUESTIONS▶

1. Cyanogenic glycosides in plant organs were measured in an intact stem of a cassava plant and in one in which the phloem had been cut below the fifth leaf. The results are shown in the graphs. What can you conclude about the source of CGs?

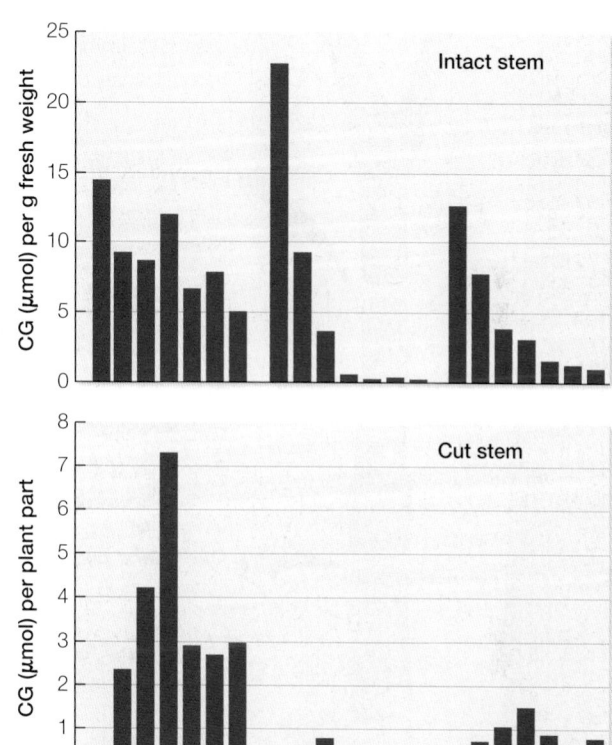

2. When a stem is girdled, it is cut carefully so that the epidermal, cortical, and outer vascular tissues (phloem) are removed. Using intact plants, the biologists girdled the stem of a cassava plant. After 2 days, they measured CGs in various regions on the stem. The results for CG levels after girdling between the fifth and sixth nodes are shown in the table. What can you conclude about the source and transport of CGs? Why was the level in the sixth leaf (below the girdle) so high?

Region	CG level (μmol)
Fifth leaf	59
Stem above cut	15
Stem below cut	0.2
Sixth leaf	55

Go to Achieve for a companion Data in Depth exercise.

Epidermis   Cortex

Terminal bud — — Bud scale

Axillary bud

Primary growth   *Growth*

Ray initials

Pith

Primary xylem

Vascular cambium

Primary phloem

Cortex   Epidermis

Secondary growth   *Growth*   Phloem ray

Xylem ray

Primary xylem

Secondary xylem

Vascular cambium

Secondary phloem

Primary phloem   Cork cambium

Two years' growth   *Growth*

— Leaf scar

Secondary xylem (two years of production)

Vascular cambium

Secondary phloem

Primary phloem   Cork cambium   Cork

Pith
Primary xylem
Secondary xylem
Vascular cambium
Secondary phloem
Primary phloem
Cork cambium
Cork

Figure 32.20 A Woody Twig Has Both Primary and Secondary Growth The apical meristems in this dormant twig will produce primary growth in spring. Lateral meristems are responsible for secondary growth. When the vascular cambium divides parallel to the outside of the stem, it forms a new ring of cells. New layers of cells on the interior side of the vascular cambium add to the xylem, while those exterior to the vascular cambium add to the phloem.

secondary phloem cells toward the outside. In the stem, cells in the pith rays between the vascular bundles also divide, forming a continuous cylinder of vascular cambium running the length of the stem. This cylinder, in turn, gives rise to complete cylinders of secondary xylem (the **wood**) and secondary phloem, which contributes to the bark. It also produces vascular rays for lateral transport, a structure not found in primary xylem and phloem. Therefore the vascular cambium produces vessel elements, tracheids, parenchyma cells, and supportive fibers in the secondary xylem; and sieve tube elements, companion cells, fibers, and parenchyma cells in the secondary phloem.

▶ **View in Achieve**
Animation 32.1 Secondary Growth: The Vascular Cambium

As secondary growth of stems or roots continues, the expanding vascular tissue stretches and breaks the epidermis and the outer layers of the cortex, which ultimately flake away. Before these dermal tissues are broken away, cells lying near the surface of the secondary phloem begin to divide, forming a cork cambium. This meristematic tissue produces layers of cork, a protective tissue composed of cells with thick walls waterproofed with suberin. The cork soon becomes the outermost tissue of the stem or root (see Figure 32.20). Without the activity of the cork cambium, the sloughing off of the outer primary tissues would expose the plant to potential damage, such as excessive water loss or invasion by microorganisms. Sometimes the cork cambium produces cells toward the inside as well as the outside; these cells constitute a tissue known as the phelloderm.

The cork cambium, cork, and phelloderm constitute the secondary dermal tissue called periderm. As the vascular cambium continues to produce secondary vascular tissue, these corky layers are lost, but the continuous formation of new cork cambia in the underlying secondary phloem gives rise to new corky layers. The periderm and the secondary phloem—that is, all the tissues external to the vascular cambium—constitute the **bark**.

When periderm forms on stems or roots, the underlying tissues still need to release CO_2 and take up O_2 for cellular respiration. Spongy regions in the periderm called **lenticels** can allow such gas exchange (**Figure 32.21**).

You may be curious about cork, which is used as stoppers in wine bottles and in flasks in the chemistry lab. Cork is harvested from the cork oak tree (*Quercus suber*) (**Figure 32.22**), which is grown for that purpose mainly in Portugal. The tree lives more than 100 years, and cork is first harvested when the tree is 25

allow us to identify the parts of the twig from each year's growth. The dormant twig shown in **Figure 32.20** is the product of both primary and secondary growth. The buds consist entirely of primary tissues.

The vascular cambium is initially a single layer of cells lying between the primary xylem and the primary phloem within the vascular bundles. The root or stem increases in diameter when the cells of the vascular cambium divide, producing secondary xylem cells toward the inside of the root or stem and producing

Figure 32.21 Lenticels Allow Gas Exchange through the Periderm
The region of periderm that appears to be broken open is a lenticel in a year-old elderberry (*Sambucus*) twig,

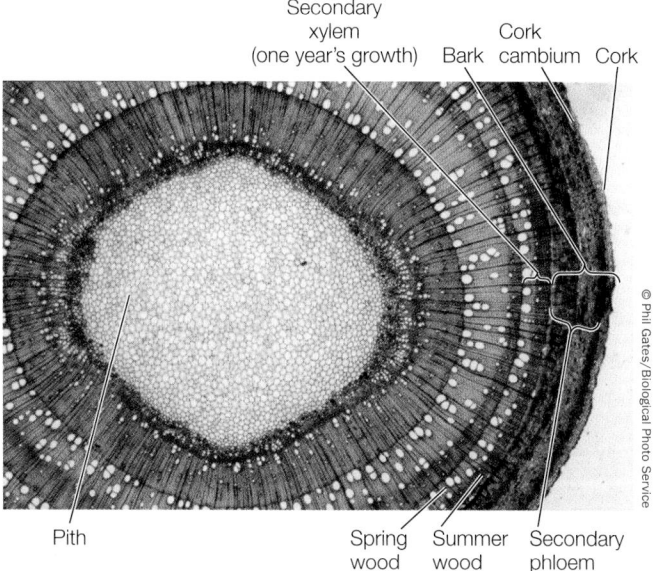

Figure 32.23 Annual Rings Rings of secondary xylem are the most noticeable feature of this cross section from a tree trunk

years old. The outer bark is removed first, carefully exposing the cork layers, which are then removed without damaging the living tissues. The cork cambium then produces more cork, so a tree can be harvested every 10 years.

Cross sections of most tree trunks (stems) in temperate-zone forests show annual rings of wood (**Figure 32.23**), which result from seasonal environmental conditions. In spring, when water is relatively plentiful, the tracheids or vessel elements produced by the vascular cambium tend to be large in diameter and relatively thin-walled. Such wood is well adapted for transporting water and minerals. As water becomes less available during the summer, narrower cells with thicker walls are produced, making this summer wood darker and perhaps more dense than the wood formed in spring. Thus each growing season is usually recorded in a tree trunk by a clearly visible annual ring. Trees in the moist tropics do not undergo seasonal growth, so they do not lay down such obvious regular rings. Variations in temperature or water supply can lead to the formation of more than one ring in a single year,

but most commonly a single annual ring is formed. Next time you are in the woods and see a fallen tree, try to count the annual rings to gauge the age of the tree.

Only eudicots and other non-monocot angiosperms, along with many gymnosperms, have a vascular cambium and a cork cambium and thus undergo secondary growth. The few monocots that form thickened stems—palms, for example—do so without secondary growth. Palms have a very wide apical meristem that produces a wide stem, and dead leaf bases add to the diameter of the stem. All monocots grow in essentially this way, as do other angiosperms that lack secondary growth.

KEY CONCEPT
32.3 Recap and Assess

Meristems are localized regions of cell division that are the sources of all new organs in the adult plant. Initial cells within the root apical meristem divide to form the root cap and the cells of the primary root. The cells do not move past one another so the zones of cell division, elongation and maturation in the primary root are located at increasing distances from the initial cells. Root branching can occur when new meristems arise from pericycle cells within the root. The shoot apical meristem gives rise to the cells that comprise the shoot system, including the branches which arise from meristems that form the axils of leaves. The vascular cambium increases plant thickness and forms wood and bark in many eudicots.

1. How can an apical meristem be maintained for years while continuing to form leaves?

2. Identify the meristems of the plant that are responsible for primary growth and indicate how tissues and organs are formed from them.

3. What cells are derived from the root apical meristem, and what is the general process of root growth?

4. Compare and contrast the vascular cambium and the shoot apical meristem. What aspects of the vascular cambium define it as a meristem?

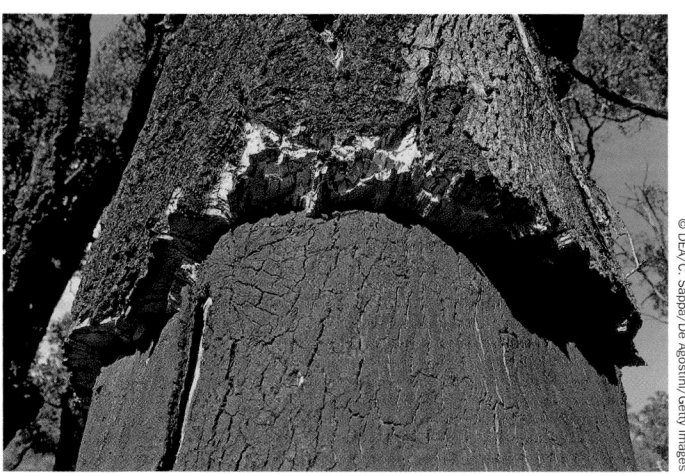

Figure 32.22 Cork Grows from the Cork Cambium of the Cork Oak (*Quercus suber*)

The building of the plant body by meristems allows a plant to respond to its environment by redirecting its growth. Thus individual plants of the same species can vary greatly in form. What underlies this variation, and how have we humans used it to our advantage?

KEY CONCEPT
32.4
Domestication Has Altered Plant Form

Learning Objectives

32.4.1 Explain how the simple, repeating units that make up a plant can be modified to generate a wide variety of plant architectures.

32.4.2 Explain why the seeds from wild relatives of crop plants are valuable.

You have seen in this chapter that a simple, modular plant body plan underlies the remarkable diversity of the flowering plants that cover our planet. Differences in plant form among species are not surprising, given the high levels of genetic diversity among plant species. However, members of the same species can also show remarkable diversity in form. From a genetic perspective, this suggests that minor differences in gene content or gene regulation can underlie dramatic differences in plant form.

It is hard to believe that modern corn was domesticated from the wild grass teosinte, which still grows in the hills of Mexico (**Figure 32.24**). One of the most conspicuous differences is that teosinte, like other wild grasses, is highly branched, whereas domesticated corn has a single shoot. This morphological difference is due in large part to the activity of a single gene called *TEOSINTE BRANCHED 1* (*TB1*). The protein product of *TB1* regulates the growth of axillary buds (see Figure 32.1). The allele of *tb1* in domesticated corn represses branching, whereas the allele in teosinte permits branching.

Even harder to believe is that a single species, *Brassica oleracea* (wild mustard), is the ancestor of many familiar and morphologically diverse crops, including kale, broccoli, brussels sprouts, and cabbage.

Connect the Concepts The diversity of plants derived from wild mustard illustrated in Figure 19.4 demonstrates how artificial selection—the purposeful selection of specific phenotypes by humans—can produce rapid evolutionary change.

Each of these familiar vegetable crops has the same basic body plan. Starting with morphologically diverse populations of the wild ancestor, humans selected and planted the seeds of variants with traits they found desirable. For example, brussels sprout plants were selected for their enlarged axillary buds, cabbage plants for their enlarged terminal buds and short internodes, and broccoli and cauliflower plants for their large clusters of flower buds. Such selection is really an act of genetic engineering because in selecting plants that have some particular trait one is choosing those plants that have a collection of genes that allow the trait to be expressed or formed. Many generations of such artificial selection produced the crops that fill the produce section of supermarkets and the stands of farmers' markets.

Figure 32.24 Modern Corn Was Domesticated from the Wild Grass Teosinte   Each teosinte plant has multiple branches. Beginning more than 8,000 years ago in Mexico, farmers favored plants with minimal branching. Reducing the number of branches results in fewer ears per plant but allows each ear to grow larger and produce more seeds.

Teosinte   Corn

Just as they were for ancient farmers, the genomes of plants are priceless resources today. The genetic variation in crop plants and their wild relatives includes DNA sequences that are adapted to different conditions than those found in current farm fields, often including resistance to a wider range of pests. These genomes can be used to improve our crop plants or adapt them to changing conditions. The improvement of crop plants is a work in progress that is being carried out in plant breeding programs worldwide. These programs are now more important than ever. Increased human activity is dramatically changing our planet and leading to the extinction of more and more plant species. For this reason, various organizations around the world have developed seed banks, where seeds of diverse species, and variants within species, are stored. As the climate continues to change, new varieties of old crops and new crops that are better adapted to a warmer climate with more extreme fluctuations in water availability will be needed.

KEY CONCEPT
32.4 Recap and Assess

Crop domestication involves artificial selection of certain desirable traits found in wild plant populations. By understanding the basic body plan of plants, one can more easily understand the morphological relationship between a crop plant and its wild relatives.

1. Why are the seeds from wild relatives of crop plants valuable?

▶Investigating LIFE

Q and A How might plant biologists improve the cassava plant for human use?

Many people depend on cassava roots for food. Unfortunately, the roots must undergo processing to remove sources of toxic cyanide before they are eaten. As you saw in Investigating Life: Understanding the Synthesis and Transport of Cyanogenic Glycosides, cyanide-forming molecules are formed in leaves and then transported to the roots through the vascular system. Molecular biologists have described the details of organ-specific synthesis of the machinery responsible for a major cyanogenic molecule. RNA interference (see Key Concept 18.4) has been used to block cassava leaves from making the toxic precursor, and as a result its concentration in the edible roots goes down by 99% compared with untreated plants. This is a promising way to reduce the requirements for processing of the crop.

Future directions

An international group of plant biologists and agricultural scientists has been set up to stimulate research on cassava. The Bio-Cassava Plus Consortium has not only found ways to improve the nutritional quality of cassava, but has also sought ways to improve the plant's ability to grow in drought conditions. Cassava has been crossed with a treelike relative, *Manihot glaziovii*, and the resulting plants produce roots that are not only fleshy and edible but that grow deep into the soil, where they can tap into water supplies far below the surface in dry climates. The hope is that this new crop variant will improve conditions for people in drought-prone places such as sub-Saharan Africa, where tens of millions of people routinely experience famine.

VISUAL SUMMARY 32

© MisoKnitl/Getty Images

You should be able to relate each summary to the adjacent figures. If you go to this visual summary in **Achieve**, you can follow links to figures, animations, activities, and simulations that will help you consolidate the material.

KEY CONCEPT

32.1   The Plant Body Is Organized in a Distinctive Way

- Angiosperms (flowering plants) are grouped in two major clades: monocots and eudicots.

- Plant growth is **indeterminate**: the number of organs depends on the environment.

- Groups of cells called meristems give rise to the post-embryonic plant body.

- The apical–basal and radial axes are established during embryogenesis.

Questions

1. How does the meristematic nature of plant growth minimize the negative effects of being anchored in one place?

2. Iris plants generally have narrow leaves with parallel veins and flowers that contain six petal-like organs: an outer set of three organs that hang downward, and an inner set of three organs that are more vertically oriented. Are irises monocots or eudicots?

3. Draw a picture of a eudicot embryo at the heart stage. Do the cotyledons begin to form before or after the shoot apical meristem is mature?

Figure 32.3

Shoot apical meristem

Lateral meristems:
Cork cambium
Vascular cambium

Root apical meristem

KEY CONCEPT

32.2 Plant Organs Are Made Up of Cells Organized into Three Types of Tissues

- Three types of plant cells can be classified based primarily on the properties of their cell walls: **parenchyma**, **collenchyma**, and **sclerenchyma**.

- The planes of division within the shoot apical meristem give rise to separate layers of cells that form the tissues.

- Plant structures are built from three types of tissue: **dermal**, **ground**, and **vascular tissue**.

Questions

1. The cells that make up a plant stem are produced in the shoot apical meristem by cell division that results in small cells. Many mature sclerenchyma cells are quite long, yet their walls are reinforced in a way that does not permit them to expand. Explain how both of these statements can be true.

2. Why are the growing tips of a plant more likely to wilt than more mature parts of a plant? Your answer should reference specific types of cells.

3. In which tissue can cutin and trichomes be found?

4. How do the conducting cells of xylem differ in gymnosperms and angiosperms?

Figure 32.8

Dermal tissue
Ground tissue
Vascular tissue

Figure 32.9

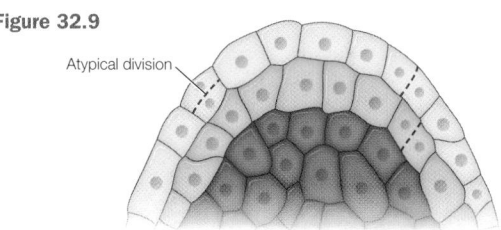

Atypical division

KEY CONCEPT

Go to Activities 32.1–32.5 and Animation 32.1

32.3 Meristems Build a Continuously Growing Plant

- The shoot apical meristem gives rise to the leaves and stem. Branches form indirectly from axillary buds.

- The root apical meristem gives rise to the root, which forms **lateral roots** through division of internal cells.

- Tree stems grow thicker through the action of the **vascular cambium**, which can divide to create a new ring of cells. One ring remains vascular cambium; the other ring becomes secondary xylem (if produced toward the interior) or secondary phloem (if produced toward the exterior.)

Questions

1. How does the existence of meristems contribute to the indeterminate nature of plant growth?

2. In which longitudinal zone of the root are the initial cells located?

3. In what tissue are the palisade mesophyll cells (a type of parenchyma cell) in a leaf located?

4. In what ways are the activities of the shoot and root apical meristems similar to that of the vascular cambium? In what ways are they different?

Figure 32.20

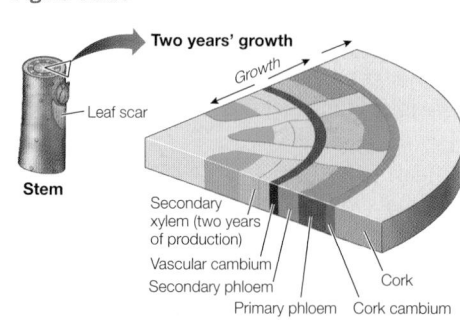

Two years' growth

Growth

Leaf scar

Stem

Secondary xylem (two years of production)

Vascular cambium

Secondary phloem

Primary phloem

Cork

Cork cambium

Figure 32.11

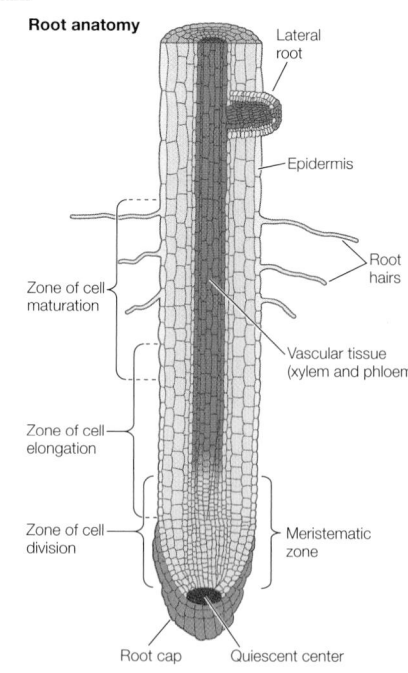

Root anatomy

Lateral root

Epidermis

Root hairs

Zone of cell maturation

Vascular tissue (xylem and phloem)

Zone of cell elongation

Zone of cell division

Meristematic zone

Root cap

Quiescent center

KEY CONCEPT

32.4 Domestication Has Altered Plant Form

- The plant body plan is simple, yet it can be changed dramatically by minor differences in genes, as evidenced by the natural diversity of wild plants.

- Crop domestication involves artificial selection of certain desirable traits found in wild populations.

Questions

1. Changes in the proportions of different plant organs generate great diversity in plant architecture. What anatomical part of the plant are brussels sprouts and garlic cloves?

2. How can you tell that the anatomical part of an onion that people generally eat is not a root?

3. Why is it that selecting plants with desirable traits can be considered a form of genetic engineering?

Figure 32.24

Teosinte   Corn

Go to **Achieve** for the eBook, **LearningCurve**, animations, activities, simulations, and additional resources and assignments.

33 Transport in Plants

KEY CONCEPTS

33.1 Plants Acquire Water and Minerals from the Soil

33.2 Water and Minerals Are Transported in the Xylem

33.3 Stomata Control the Loss of Water and the Uptake of CO_2

33.4 Solutes Are Transported in the Phloem

Cultivation of rice, the most important food crop in Asia, requires large quantities of water.

© Izzet Keribar/Getty Images

▶ InvestigatingLIFE

Thirsty Rice

Plants need a lot of water to grow. Crop plant cultivation consumes far more water than all other human activities combined. Meeting the demand is especially challenging in drought-prone regions, compelling us to understand how plants use water so that we can select or breed plants that use it more efficiently. Much of the mass that plants acquire as they grow is due to their net fixation of atmospheric CO_2 into carbohydrates through photosynthesis. As the CO_2 used in photosynthesis enters the plant, generally through open stomata in the leaves, water is lost to the atmosphere. The ratio of carbon fixed to water lost is known as a plant's water-use efficiency.

One of the least water-efficient of all crop plants is, unfortunately, one of our most important: rice. Rice plants use up to three times more water per unit of growth than crops such as wheat and corn. The precariousness of heavily water-dependent rice farming was dramatically demonstrated in eastern India between 1997 and 2003, when drought reduced rice production by more than 5 million tons—some farmers lost up to 50% of their crops.

A strain of rice requiring less water yet producing the same amount of grain would both make the world supply of rice less vulnerable to drought and help conserve water for other uses. A team of scientists began the quest for such a strain by studying the model organism *Arabidopsis thaliana*. They searched for mutations of *A. thaliana* that had superior water-use efficiency. One genetic variant they studied has an extensive root system (indicating higher capacity for water uptake) and thick leaves with abundant photosynthetic tissue (indicating prolific photosynthesis). Molecular and physiological characterization linked the improved water usage of this *A. thaliana* strain to a mutation in a single gene that codes for a transcription factor that the scientists called HARDY. This protein turns out to be a member of a family of transcription factors that plants use to regulate genes in response to biotic and abiotic stress. When biotechnologists isolated this gene (*HARDY*) and put it into rice plants, the transformed rice plants not only had higher water-use efficiency than wild-type rice plants but were more tolerant of dry soil as well.

Laboratories around the world are using *A. thaliana* to isolate genes involved in water usage and other important physiological processes. The knowledge gained from these studies may lead to various improvements of crop plants.

 What methods are used to reduce water loss in agriculture? (Find the answer on page 760.)

33.1 Plants Acquire Water and Minerals from the Soil

Learning Objectives

33.1.1 Describe how solute potential and pressure potential affect the movement of water across the plant cell membrane.

33.1.2 Describe how aquaporins, ion channels, and ion pumps affect the movement of water and solutes across the plant cell membrane.

33.1.3 Using the terms "apoplast" and "symplast," describe the role of the Casparian strip in regulating the movement of water and ions from the soil to the xylem.

Terrestrial plants must obtain both water and mineral nutrients from the soil, through their roots, and the water is transported through the plant in xylem tissue. Carbohydrates and other important materials mostly originate in leaves and circulate through the phloem (**Figure 33.1**). Water is required for photosynthesis in the leaves (see Key Concept 10.1), for transporting solutes between plant organs, for cooling the plant, and for developing the internal pressure that supports the plant body.

The minerals that a plant needs are transported along with the water. Several steps in water and mineral transport are considered in this chapter. In this key concept we focus on the first part of the journey—the uptake of water and minerals into the roots and their transport into the xylem.

CO$_2$ (reactant of photosynthesis)

O$_2$ (product of photosynthesis)

H$_2$O (transpiration)

Sucrose

CO$_2$ enters and O$_2$ and H$_2$O exit the leaves via the stomata (see Figure 33.8).

H$_2$O

H$_2$O enters through the roots.

Figure 33.1 The Pathways of Water and Solutes in a Plant
Water travels from the soil to the atmosphere, with only a small fraction used within the plant.

Water potential differences govern the direction of water movement

Water moves into and out of plant cells. The direction of water movement from cell to cell is determined by **water potential (ψ, psi)**, defined as the tendency of water molecules to move in response to forces such as pressure and solute concentration gradients. Water tends to move away from regions of high pressure and toward regions of high solute concentration.

How does a high solute concentration affect the tendency of water to move across a cell membrane? The explanations traditionally given in introductory biology textbooks and on the internet are now considered to be misconceptions. A more current explanation in line with physicists' understanding is as follows: While water molecules are able to diffuse across a semipermeable membrane in both directions, solute molecules cannot cross the membrane. As a result, the movement of solute molecules that contact a semipermeable membrane is redirected away from the membrane, much as a ball bounces off a wall. This movement of the solute particles away from the membrane impacts the solvent as well, with the result that the solvent (water) is also directed away from the membrane. Therefore a higher solute concentration decreases the effective pressure of free water on the membrane, allowing more water to enter.

In the case of plant roots in soil water, whenever water moves across a selectively permeable membrane by osmosis, it moves toward the region of lower (more negative) water potential (**Figure 33.2A, left**). We measure water potential in megapascals (MPa), a unit of pressure. Atmospheric pressure, 1 atmosphere, is about 0.1 MPa, or 14.7 pounds per square inch; a typical pressure in an automobile tire is about 0.2 MPa.

> **Connect the Concepts** The key to water movement is osmosis. You can review the process of osmosis and the role of the cell membrane in Key Concept 6.3.

Water potential has two major components:

1. **Solute potential (ψ_s):** As solutes are added to pure water, the tendency to take up water increases, and water potential decreases.

2. **Pressure potential (ψ_p):** As plant cells take up water, they tend to swell. The result is an increase in pressure inside the cell (**turgor pressure**), which decreases the tendency of the cell to take up more water (increases the water potential) (**Figure 33.2A, right**).

A solution's water potential is the sum of its (usually negative) solute potential (ψ_s) and its (usually positive) pressure potential (ψ_p):

$$\psi = \psi_s + \psi_p$$

By definition, the solute potential of pure water is zero (no solutes); because added solutes decrease water potential, solute potential is usually negative. Pressure potential is defined as zero when it equals atmospheric pressure. Pressure potential less than atmospheric pressure is negative; pressure potential greater than atmospheric pressure is positive.

To see how these relationships affect cell expansion, consider what happens if a plant cell is immersed in a beaker of pure water

(A) A theoretical illustration of water potential

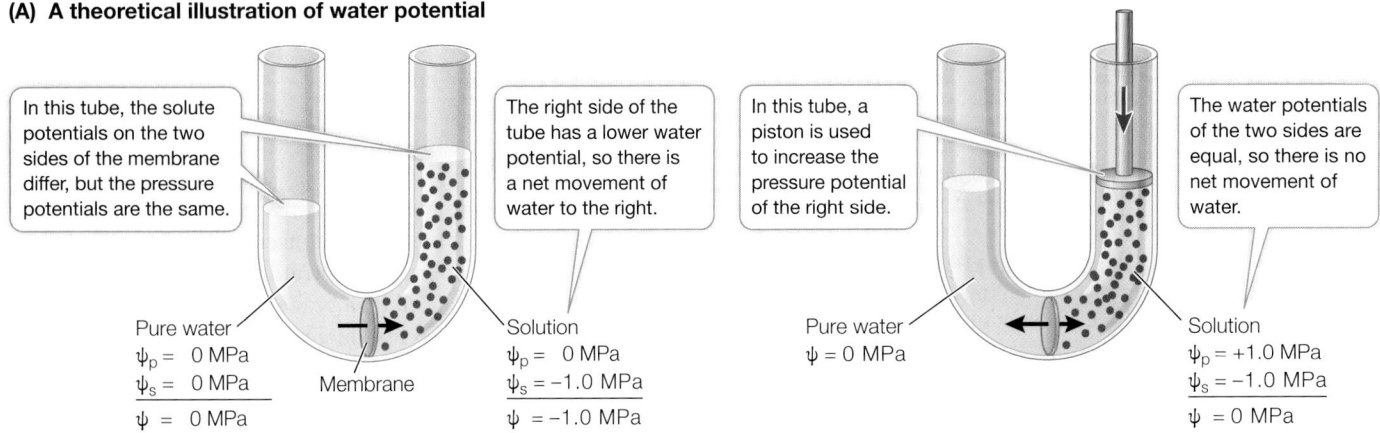

In this tube, the solute potentials on the two sides of the membrane differ, but the pressure potentials are the same.

The right side of the tube has a lower water potential, so there is a net movement of water to the right.

In this tube, a piston is used to increase the pressure potential of the right side.

The water potentials of the two sides are equal, so there is no net movement of water.

Pure water
$\psi_p =$ 0 MPa
$\psi_s =$ 0 MPa
$\psi =$ 0 MPa

Membrane

Solution
$\psi_p =$ 0 MPa
$\psi_s = -1.0$ MPa
$\psi = -1.0$ MPa

Pure water
$\psi =$ 0 MPa

Solution
$\psi_p = +1.0$ MPa
$\psi_s = -1.0$ MPa
$\psi =$ 0 MPa

(B) The effect of differences in water potential on a plant cell

The inside of the cell has a lower solute potential than the surrounding water. In this example, the cell has a pressure potential of zero.

The cell has a lower water potential than the water outside, so there is net movement of water into the cell.

The cell has a negative solute potential, but has a positive pressure potential.

The pressure potential of the cell balances its solute potential, so the cell's water potential is zero. There is no net movement of water.

Pure water
$\psi =$ 0 MPa

Flaccid cell
$\psi_p =$ 0 MPa
$\psi_s = -1.0$ MPa
$\psi = -1.0$ MPa

Pure water
$\psi =$ 0 MPa

Turgid cell
$\psi_p = +1.0$ MPa
$\psi_s = -1.0$ MPa
$\psi =$ 0 MPa

Figure 33.2 Water Potential, Solute Potential, and Pressure Potential

View in Achieve
Simulation 33.1 **Water Uptake in Plants**

(**Figure 33.2B**). If the cell is initially flaccid (i.e., the internal pressure is equal to atmospheric pressure), then the solutes in the cell will cause water to enter by osmosis until the pressure potential exactly balances the solute potential and the water potential is zero. At this point the cell is **turgid**—that is, it has a significantly positive pressure potential. Plant cells are surrounded by water with dissolved solutes rather than pure water, and their water potential is dependent on the water potential in the soil. But because turgid cells have a positive pressure potential, there is no net movement of water into them. The physical structures of many plants are maintained by the positive pressure potential of the water in their cells. If the pressure potential drops (for example, if the plant does not have enough water), the plant wilts (**Figure 33.3**).

Water and ions move across the root cell's cell membrane

Now that you've seen how water can move into plant cells by osmosis, what about ions? The movement of water and mineral ions across a root cell membrane can be impeded for two reasons:

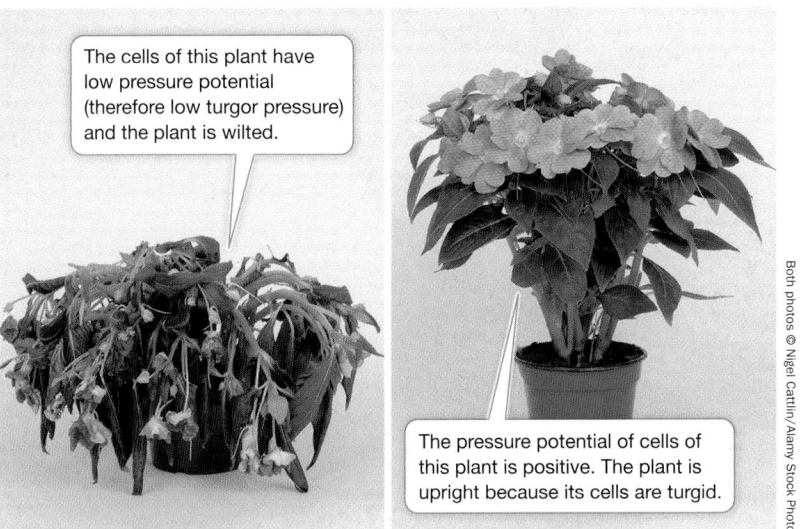

The cells of this plant have low pressure potential (therefore low turgor pressure) and the plant is wilted.

The pressure potential of cells of this plant is positive. The plant is upright because its cells are turgid.

Figure 33.3 A Wilted Plant A plant wilts when the pressure potential in its cells (and therefore the turgor pressure) is low.

Q: Sometimes a plant will wilt even if it is adequately watered, because of an excess of fertilizer (dissolved ions in the soil). Why?

1. The interior of the membrane is hydrophobic, whereas water and mineral ions are polar.
2. Some mineral ions must be moved against their concentration gradients.

However, as you saw in Chapter 6, membrane proteins assist with the movement of materials across membranes:

- *Aquaporins.* Aquaporins (see Key Concept 6.3) are located in both the cell membrane and the tonoplast (vacuolar membrane) of a plant cell. Aquaporins allow water to diffuse rapidly across these membranes. The number of aquaporins in a particular cell varies by cell type, and can vary with environmental conditions. The permeability of some aquaporins also can be regulated. Alterations in aquaporin abundance and permeability change the *rate* of osmosis across the membrane. Note that water movement through aquaporins is always passive: from a region of higher water potential to one of lower water potential.

- *Ion channels and pumps.* When the concentration of a charged ion in the soil is greater than that in the plant, transport proteins can move the ions into the plant by facilitated diffusion, which is a passive process (see Key Concept 6.3). The concentrations of most ions in the soil solution, however, are lower than those inside the plant. In these cases the plant must actively take up ions *against* their concentration gradients—a process that requires energy (see Key Concept 6.4).

Electric charge differences also play a role in the uptake of mineral ions. For example, a negatively charged ion that moves into a negatively charged compartment is moving against an *electrical gradient*, and this requires energy. Concentration and electrical gradients combine to form an electrochemical gradient. Uptake against an electrochemical gradient involves active transport, which requires energy and specific transport proteins.

Connect the Concepts Electrochemical gradients are important in many biological systems. Learn more about electrochemical gradients, and their role in the animal nervous system, in Key Concept 43.2.

Active transport in plants is frequently driven by a **proton pump**, which uses energy obtained from ATP to move protons out of the cell against a proton concentration gradient (**Figure 33.4, step 1**). Because protons (H^+) are positively charged, their accumulation outside the cell has two results:

1. An electrical gradient is created, with the region outside the cell more positively charged than the inside.
2. A proton concentration gradient develops, with more protons outside the cell than inside.

Both the electrical gradient and the concentration gradient affect the movement of other ions. The balance between the electrical and concentration gradients is such that cations (positively charged ions) such as potassium (K^+) can move into the cell by facilitated diffusion through specific membrane channels (**Figure 33.4, step 2**). In addition, the proton concentration gradient can be harnessed to drive secondary active transport, in which the energy released when H^+ ions move back into the cell is coupled to movement of another ion against its electrochemical gradient. For example, symport proteins

Figure 33.4 The Proton Pump in Transport of K^+ and Cl^- The active transport of hydrogen ions (H^+) out of the cell by the proton pump (1) drives the movement of both cations (2) and anions (3) into the cell.

couple the movement of chloride (Cl^-) against the electrochemical gradient with that of H^+ (**Figure 33.4, step 3**).

Water and ions pass to the xylem by way of the apoplast and symplast

The journey from the soil through the roots to the xylem occurs primarily by one of two pathways, either separately or simultaneously: the fast lane (called the apoplast) and the slow(er) lane (called the symplast) (**Figure 33.5**):

- The **apoplast** (Greek *apo*, "away from," + *plast*, "living material") consists of the cell walls, which lie outside the cell membranes, and the intercellular spaces (spaces between cells) that are common in many plant tissues. Typically, the apoplast occupies 5%–20% of plant tissues by volume. The apoplast is a continuous meshwork through which water and

Figure 33.5 Apoplast and Symplast Plant cell walls and intercellular spaces constitute the apoplast. The symplast comprises the living cells connected by plasmodesmata. To enter the symplast, water and solutes must pass through a cell membrane. No such selective barrier limits movement through the apoplast.

dissolved substances can flow without ever having to cross a membrane. Movement of materials through the apoplast is thus unregulated and rapid.

• The **symplast** (Greek *sym*, "together with") is all the other parts of the cells, the fluid part of which is connected by plasmodesmata (see Figure 7.16B). Secretory cells such as those in flowers that make nectar have a lot of plasmodesmata. So do cells in the root tip, where the selectively permeable cell membranes of the root cells control access to the symplast. Movement of water and dissolved substances into the symplast is tightly regulated.

Water and minerals that pass from the soil solution through the apoplast can travel as far as the endodermis, the innermost layer of the root cortex (**Figure 33.6**; see Key Concept 32.3). The cell wall of the endodermis is distinguished from the rest of the ground tissue by the presence of a lignin-rich strip of material that is surrounded by a waxy layer of suberin (a hydrophobic substance composed largely of fatty acids). Called the **Casparian strip**, this region acts as a seal that prevents water and ions from moving through apoplastic spaces between the endodermal cells. Therefore all water and ions must enter the symplast in order to cross the endodermis into the stele, which contains the vascular tissues of the root. The materials pass from the endodermal cells to cells in the stele via plasmodesmata.

Once they have passed the endodermal barrier, water and minerals remain in the symplast until they reach parenchyma cells in the pericycle or xylem. These cells then actively export mineral ions into the apoplast of the stele. As the concentrations of mineral ions in the apoplast increase, its water potential becomes more negative. Consequently, water moves out of the cells and into the apoplast by osmosis. In other words, ions are transported actively, and water follows passively. The end result of transport is that water and minerals end up in the xylem, where they constitute the **xylem sap. Table 33.1** shows the composition of xylem sap.

Plants regulate the type and number of nutrient transporters in response to nutrient levels.

Transporter

Epidermal cell Cortical cell

Soil

Root hair

Epidermis

Cortex

Endodermis

Pericycle

Xylem

Vascular tissue

Epidermis Cortex Endodermis Vascular tissue

Soil solution

Apoplast

Symplast

Plasmodesmata

Pericycle

Water and solutes that pass the endodermis can enter the vascular tissue. Once there, they can be transported to the rest of the plant.

At the Casparian strip, water and solutes in the apoplast must enter the symplast to cross the endodermis.

Water and solutes travel through the symplast or apoplast until they reach the endodermis.

Figure 33.6 Pathways to the Root Xylem Water and solutes can move into the root through the symplast or the apoplast until they reach the endodermis (shown in dark green); there the water and solutes must enter the symplast to bypass the Casparian strip (dark blue), a region of the endodermal cell wall that contains lignin and is impregnated with the water-repelling substance suberin. Inside the vascular tissue, the water and solutes enter the xylem (light blue).

Q: What type of animal cell junction is best compared with the Casparian strip? See Figure 6.6.

View in Achieve
Activity 33.1 Apoplast and Symplast of the Root

TABLE **33.1**	Composition of Xylem and Phloem Fluids	
Substance	Xylem	Phloem
Ions, minerals (g/L)	0.2–4	1–5
Amino acids (g/L)	0.1–1	5–40
Sugars (g/L)	0	100–300
Solute potential, Ψ_s (MPa)	–0.02 to –0.2	–0.6 to –3

KEY CONCEPT
33.1 Recap and Assess

Differences in water potential govern the osmotic flow of water from the soil into the plant stele; this is a passive process. Uptake of minerals from the soil that occurs along an electrochemical gradient is an active process requiring energy and membrane transport proteins. Water and minerals can move toward the root vascular tissue through either the apoplast or the symplast, but cannot reach the xylem without crossing a cell membrane.

1. Consider two cells, A and B:

Cell A	Cell B
ψ_p = 0.32 MPa	ψ_p = 0.40 MPa
ψ_s = –0.90 MPa	ψ_s = –0.95 MPa

   Assuming the cells are sitting next to one another, which way will the water flow: toward cell A or toward cell B? Explain your answer.

2. What is the role of the cell wall in determining the direction of water movement and plant form?

3. A major component of root growth is osmotically driven cell expansion, which is achieved by the formation and swelling of the central vacuole. What role would you predict the presence and abundance of aquaporins to play in this cell expansion?

So far we've described the movement of water and minerals into plant roots and their entry into the root xylem. How does the xylem sap move once it is in the xylem?

KEY CONCEPT
33.2 Water and Minerals Are Transported in the Xylem

Learning Objectives

33.2.1 Solve problems relating to the transport of water by the xylem when given information on water potential.

33.2.2 Discuss the interaction of the processes of transpiration, cohesion, and tension in the movement of water through the xylem.

33.2.3 Provide evidence for the importance of each of the processes of transpiration, cohesion, and tension in the movement of water through the xylem.

Once water has arrived in the xylem, it is all "uphill" from there. Before considering the ascent of water and minerals to the leaves, reacquaint yourself with the cells in the xylem through which water and minerals are transported: the tracheids and vessel elements (see Figure 32.10A,B). Recall that these xylem cells are dead and lack all cell contents. When fused end-to-end, they form long tubular "straws" of lignified cell walls called **xylem vessels**. These

vessels provide both structural support and the rigidity needed to maintain a gradient of pressure.

Consider the magnitude of what the xylem accomplishes. A single maple tree 15 meters tall was estimated to have some 177,000 leaves, with a total leaf surface area of 675 square meters—about one and a half times the area of a basketball court. During a summer day, that tree loses 220 liters of water *per hour* to the atmosphere by evaporation from the leaves. So to prevent wilting, the xylem needs to transport 220 liters of water up to 15 meters from the roots to the leaves every hour. (By comparison, a 50-gallon drum holds 189 liters.)

Connect the Concepts As you learn about water movement in the xylem, keep in mind the properties of water described in Key Concept 2.4.

Various hypotheses have proposed how water moves in the xylem

Until the twentieth century, two mechanisms for moving water to the top of a tree through the xylem were under consideration: upward pressure by living cells and capillary action. Both of these possibilities were largely ruled out by experiments:

- A simple experiment in 1893 ruled out the hypothesis that root cells might initiate a *pumping mechanism* to propel water upward. A tree was cut at its base and the sawed-off part was placed in a vat containing a solution of poison that killed living cells. The poison rose up the trunk, killing any living cells it encountered along the way. The experiment demonstrated that a living pump in the root is not necessary to push the xylem sap up a tree. Because the roots were absent, it was clear that they were not involved in this movement through the xylem. Furthermore, when the poison sap reached the leaves, they died and all upward movement of the solution stopped, showing that living leaves are necessary for water to move in the xylem.

- Because of its surface tension (see Key Concept 2.4) and adhesive forces between water and its container, water will move up a narrow column by a mechanism called *capillary action*. You've seen this when you put a straw into a cup of water. Capillary action was ruled out as a primary mechanism for upward xylem sap transport when calculations showed that xylem vessels (at 100 micrometers [μm] in diameter) are too wide to get water to the top of a 15-meter tree in this fashion. In fact, the maximum height for a water column raised by capillary action alone in a 100-μm tube would be only 0.15 meters.

The transpiration–cohesion–tension mechanism accounts for xylem transport

The current model of xylem transport involves three processes (**Figure 33.7**):

1. *Transpiration* of water molecules from the leaves by evaporation

2. *Tension* (negative pressure) in the xylem sap resulting from transpiration from the leaves

3. *Cohesion* of water molecules in the xylem sap, from the leaves to the roots

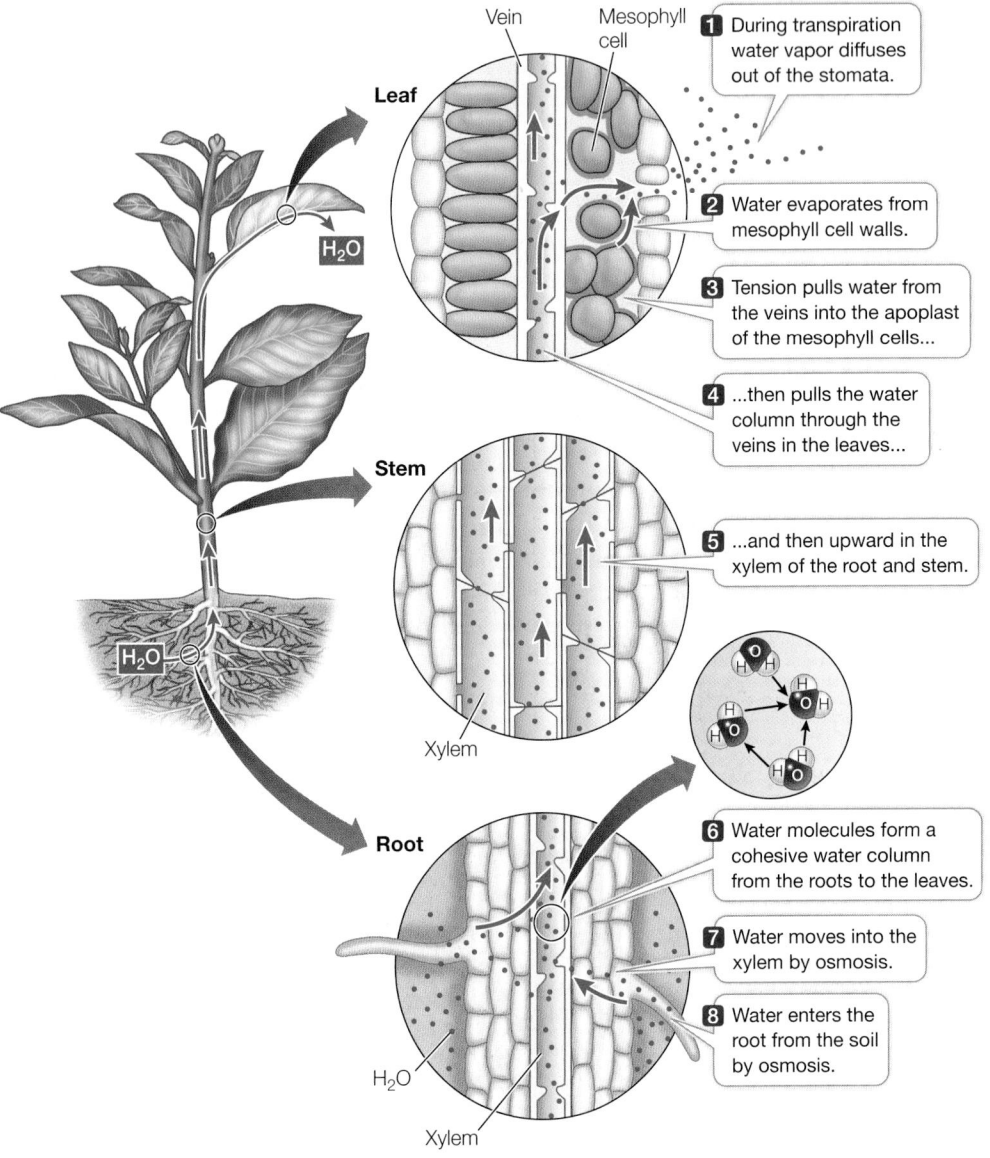

Leaf

Vein

Mesophyll cell

1 During transpiration water vapor diffuses out of the stomata.

2 Water evaporates from mesophyll cell walls.

3 Tension pulls water from the veins into the apoplast of the mesophyll cells...

4 ...then pulls the water column through the veins in the leaves...

Stem

5 ...and then upward in the xylem of the root and stem.

Xylem

Root

6 Water molecules form a cohesive water column from the roots to the leaves.

7 Water moves into the xylem by osmosis.

8 Water enters the root from the soil by osmosis.

H₂O

Xylem

Figure 33.7 **The Transpiration–Cohesion–Tension Mechanism**
Transpiration causes evaporation from mesophyll cell walls, generating tension on the xylem. Cohesion among water molecules in the xylem transmits the tension from the leaf to the root, causing water to flow in the xylem from the roots to the atmosphere.

Q: What would be the effect of high relative humidity in the air around the leaves on root uptake of water? Explain.

Media Clip 33.1 Inside the Xylem
Life12e.com/mc33.1

View in Achieve
Animation 33.1 Xylem Transport

Each part of this theory is supported by evidence:

- The difference in water potential between the soil solution and the air is huge, on the order of −100 MPa. This difference should generate more than enough tension to pull a water column up a tree.

- There is a continuous column of water in the xylem, which is made possible by the cohesive forces holding water molecules together.

- Actual measurements of xylem pressures in cut stems show negative pressure potentials, indicating considerable tension in the xylem.

The concentration of water vapor in the atmosphere is lower than that in the air spaces inside the leaf. Because of this difference, water vapor diffuses from the intercellular spaces of the leaf to the outside air, in a process called **transpiration**. Within the leaf, water evaporates from the moist walls of the mesophyll cells and enters the intercellular spaces. As water evaporates from the aqueous film coating each cell, the film shrinks back into tiny spaces in the cell walls, increasing the curvature of the water surface and thus increasing its surface tension. This increased *tension* (negative pressure potential) in the surface film draws more water into the walls from the cells, replacing that which was lost. The resulting tension in the mesophyll draws water from the xylem of the nearest vein into the apoplast surrounding the mesophyll cells. The removal of water from the veins, in turn, establishes tension on the entire column of water contained in the xylem. *Cohesion* between water molecules in the column prevents the column from breaking. So these three forces—transpiration, tension, and cohesion—operate together to draw water up the xylem, all the way from the roots to the leaves.

The transpiration–cohesion–tension mechanism accounts for the movement of water through the xylem. Dissolved mineral ions are carried along with the water to all of the plant's living tissues, where the ions are used for various cellular processes. In addition to promoting the transport of minerals, transpiration has an added benefit of cooling a plant's leaves. The evaporation of water from mesophyll cells consumes heat, thereby decreasing the leaf temperature. A farmer can hold a leaf between thumb and forefinger to estimate its temperature; if the leaf doesn't feel cool, that means transpiration is not occurring and it must be time to water.

As you saw in the opening investigation of this chapter, farmers strive to improve the water-use efficiency of their crops. The roles of the root system and transpiration are important. A gene from the model plant *Arabidopsis thaliana* has been shown to improve water-use efficiency by encoding a transcription factor that regulates the expression of other genes that affect this trait (**Investigating Life: Improving Water-Use Efficiency in Rice**).

▶Investigating LIFE   Improving Water-Use Efficiency in Rice

Experiment

Original Paper: A. Karaba et al. 2007. Improvement of water use efficiency in rice by expression of *HARDY*, an *Arabidopsis* drought and salt resistance gene. *Proc Natl Acad Sci USA* 104: 15270–15275.

The objective of improving rice production involves cultivating a large amount of plant material (biomass)—meaning a large amount of grain—while using less water. The relationship between biomass produced and water consumed is called water-use efficiency. A team at Virginia Polytechnic University led by Andrew Pereira approached this problem by isolating a gene that confers drought resistance

from the model plant *Arabidopisis thaliana*. This gene, called *HARDY*, encodes a transcription factor in the AP/ERF family that activates transcription of genes involved in the plant's response to stresses. The team showed that *A. thaliana* strains that expressed the HARDY transcription factor were much more resistant to drought and to an environment high in dissolved salts. They then inserted the *HARDY* gene into a high-expressing vector and made transgenic rice plants. Initial studies showed that the plants were drought-resistant. (Photos from A. Karaba et al. © 2007. National Academy of Sciences U.S.A.)

HYPOTHESIS▶ A gene from *A. thaliana* confers drought resistance and improves water-use efficiency.

METHOD▶

CONCLUSION▶ High expression of the *A. thaliana* gene *HARDY* in rice plants confers drought resistance and improved water-use efficiency.

1 Isolate DNA sequences associated with the transcription and translation of the *HARDY* gene from *A. thaliana* plants.

2 Link *HARDY* to active promoter in an expression vector.

3 Transform rice plant seedlings.

4a Water to 100% soil saturation (control).

4b Water to 70% soil saturation (drought).

5 Observe plant phenotype and measure water-use efficiency.

RESULTS▶

Control		Drought	
HARDY	Wild type	HARDY	Wild type

Water-use efficiency (g carbon fixed/kg water used)			
3.1	1.5	3.0	1.9

Work with the Data

The investigators measured several parameters in both wild-type and transgenic *HARDY* rice:

- Water-use efficiency: g carbon fixed/kg water used
- Transpiration rate: water lost in g/cm^2 plant area/day
- Carbon fixation rate: g/cm^2 plant area/day
- Biomass accumulation: g in root + shoot

Results are shown in the table and expressed as mean ± SD (standard deviation; see Appendix B for explanation of SD).

Parameter	Wild type	*HARDY*
Water-use efficiency	1.5 ± 0.06	3.0 ± 0.5
Transpiration rate	5.2 ± 0.2	4.0 ± 0.4
Carbon fixation rate	0.7 ± 0.06	1.3 ± 0.06
Biomass accumulation	7.5 ± 0.5	13.0 ± 0.6

QUESTIONS▶

1. Explain the origin of changes in water-use efficiency.
2. What statistical test would you use to evaluate the significance of any differences found?

Go to **Achieve** for a companion
Data in Depth exercise.

33.2 Recap and Assess

The transpiration–cohesion–tension mechanism explains the ascent of xylem sap. Transpiration draws water out of leaves, resulting in tension that pulls water from the xylem. Because of cohesion between water molecules, water is pulled passively through the xylem vessels in continuous columns, always toward a region with lower pressure potential.

1. What experiment ruled out the role of pressure from the roots in the upward flow of water in the xylem?

2. The table at right shows measurements of water potential (Ψ) in a 100-meter-tall tree and its surroundings:

   Gravity exerts a force of -0.01 MPa per meter of height above ground.

Region	Ψ (MPa)
Soil water	-0.3
Xylem of root	-0.6
Xylem of trunk	-1.2
Inside of leaf	-2.0
Outside air	-58.5

   a. Is the water potential in the leaf sufficiently low to draw water to the top of the tree?

   b. Would transpiration continue if soil water potential suddenly decreased to -1.0 MPa?

   c. What would you expect to happen to the xylem water potential if all of the stomata closed?

3. Explain why all three parts of the transpiration–cohesion–tension mechanism are necessary for water transfer through the xylem.

4. What types of evidence provide support for the transpiration–cohesion–tension mechanism of water transport through the xylem?

Although transpiration provides the driving force for the transport of water and minerals in the xylem, it also results in the loss of tremendous quantities of water from the plant. How plants control this loss will be the subject of the next key concept.

33.3 Stomata Control the Loss of Water and the Uptake of CO_2

Learning Objectives

33.3.1 Analyze reasons why stomata do not always remain open, considering the processes of both photosynthesis and water conservation.

33.3.2 Discuss the importance of the proton pump and K^+ ions in the actions of stomata, and list environmental changes that trigger the opening and closing of stomata.

The epidermis of leaves and stems secretes a waxy cuticle, which is impermeable to water and thus helps minimize the loss of water from transpiration. However, the cuticle is also impermeable to CO_2. The cuticle poses a dilemma: how can the plant balance its need to retain water with its need to obtain CO_2 for photosynthesis?

Stomata control water loss and gas exchange

An elegant compromise has evolved in plants in the form of pores called **stomata** (singular *stoma*) in the epidermis of their leaves.

A pair of specialized epidermal cells, called **guard cells**, controls the opening and closing of each stoma (**Figure 33.8A**). When the stomata are open, CO_2 can enter the leaf by diffusion—but water vapor diffuses out of the leaf at the same time. Closed stomata prevent water loss but also exclude CO_2 from the leaf.

Most plants open their stomata only when the light intensity is sufficient to maintain a moderate rate of photosynthesis. At night, when darkness precludes photosynthesis, their stomata are closed; no CO_2 is needed, and water is conserved. Even during the day, the stomata close if water is being lost at too rapid a rate.

Stomata are ancient structures; they have been found in plant fossils that are more than 400 million years old. For this reason they are thought to predate the evolution of leaves. Stomata are found in all vascular plants and in many nonvascular plants, including mosses (but not liverworts; see Chapter 26).

The stoma and guard cells seen in Figure 33.8A are typical of eudicots. Monocots typically have specialized epidermal cells associated with their guard cells. However, the principle of operation, which we will now describe in more detail, is the same for both monocot and eudicot stomata.

The guard cells control the size of the stomatal opening

The opening and closing of stomata are regulated by several environmental factors, including light, CO_2 levels, temperature, and water availability. Plants can also change the total number of stomata in response to longer-term changes in environmental conditions.

LIGHT AND CO_2 CONCENTRATION Guard cells can respond to changes in light and CO_2 concentration in a matter of minutes by changing their solute potential. The absorption of light by a pigment in the guard cell's cell membrane activates a proton pump (see Figure 33.4), which actively transports H^+ out of the guard cells and into the apoplast of the surrounding epidermis. The resulting electrochemical gradient drives K^+ into the guard cells, where it accumulates (**Figure 33.8B**). Negatively charged chloride (Cl^-) ions and organic ions also move into and out of the guard cells along with the K^+ ions, maintaining electrical balance. The increased concentration of K^+ and other solutes inside the guard cells makes the solute potential of the guard cells more negative. Water then enters by osmosis, increasing the turgor pressure of the guard cells. The guard cells change their shape, becoming more turgid in response to the increase in pressure potential, so that a space—the stoma—appears between them. This structural change is similar to what happens when air is pumped into a bicycle inner tube; sides that originally lay flat against one another are pushed apart, creating an opening in the center. The stoma closes in the absence of light: the proton pump becomes less active, K^+ ions diffuse passively out of the guard cells, water follows by osmosis, the pressure potential decreases, and the guard cells sag together and seal off the stoma. Guard cell membranes are particularly rich in aquaporins, making guard cells well adapted for the rapid water movements involved in stomatal responses.

WATER Stomata also respond to water availability. Water stress is a common problem for plants, especially on a hot, windy day,

(A) An open stoma

(B) Ion concentration effects on stomatal opening

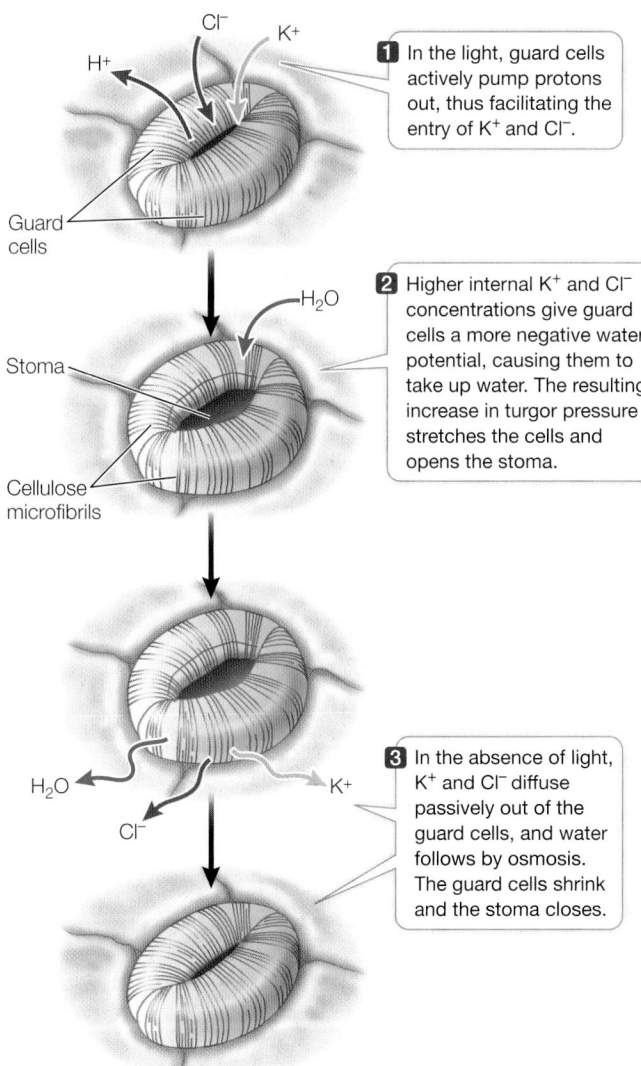

1 In the light, guard cells actively pump protons out, thus facilitating the entry of K^+ and Cl^-.

2 Higher internal K^+ and Cl^- concentrations give guard cells a more negative water potential, causing them to take up water. The resulting increase in turgor pressure stretches the cells and opens the stoma.

3 In the absence of light, K^+ and Cl^- diffuse passively out of the guard cells, and water follows by osmosis. The guard cells shrink and the stoma closes.

Figure 33.8 Stomata **(A)** Scanning electron micrograph of an open stoma formed by two sausage-shaped guard cells. **(B)** Potassium ion concentrations affect the water potential of the guard cells, controlling the opening and closing of stomata. Negatively charged ions (e.g., Cl^-) that accompany K^+ maintain electrical balance and contribute to the changes in water potential that open and close the stomata.

when plants might close their stomata even when the Sun is shining. When the water potential of the plant declines, the concentration of the hormone abscisic acid increases in the vicinity of the guard cells, causing the stomata to close.

STOMATA NUMBER   A plant can regulate water loss not just by the opening or closing of stomata, but by changing the number of stomata. The process of controlling the number of stomata takes place over days or weeks. Trees, for example, can reduce stomata numbers by shedding leaves, or by making new leaves that have few stomata.

KEY CONCEPT
33.3 Recap and Assess

CO_2, which is needed for photosynthesis, enters leaves via tiny pores called stomata. Stomata also permit the loss of water by transpiration. Guard cells open or close stomata in response to a variety of environmental cues. Plants control their total numbers of stomata by shedding leaves or by altering the density of stomata on new leaves.

1. What is the role of K^+ ions in the functioning of guard cells?
2. Describe how water availability can affect stomatal function.

Stomata are normally open during daylight hours, allowing photosynthesis—the production of carbohydrates from CO_2 and water. In the next key concept we'll discuss how the products of photosynthesis are delivered to other parts of the plant, supporting plant growth.

KEY CONCEPT   **Solutes Are Transported**
33.4   **in the Phloem**

Learning Objectives

33.4.1 Identify and define sources and sinks in plants as they relate to the products of photosynthesis.

33.4.2 Explain why energy and active transport are required to transport phloem sap and how the pressure flow model makes phloem sap flow possible.

33.4.3 Define and compare the processes of loading and unloading in phloem sap transport.

Photosynthesis occurs primarily in the leaf (see Figure 10.1). The carbohydrate products of photosynthesis (mainly sucrose) diffuse to the nearest small vein (composed of xylem and phloem), where they are actively transported into sieve tube elements of the phloem. The movement of carbohydrates and other solutes through the phloem is called **translocation**.

The products of photosynthesis are called **photosynthates**, and the content of the phloem is called the **phloem sap** (see Table 33.1). Phloem sap is translocated throughout the plant from sources to sinks:

• A **source** is an organ (such as a mature leaf or a storage root) that *produces*, by photosynthesis or by digestion of stored reserves, more sugars than it requires.

- A **sink** is an organ (such as a root, flower, developing fruit, or immature leaf) that *consumes* sugars for its own growth and storage needs of the plant.

Sources and sinks can change roles. For example, the storage roots of cassava (see Chapter 32) are sinks when they accumulate carbohydrates but are sources when their stored carbohydrates are mobilized to nourish other organs when the plant grows.

Sucrose and other solutes are carried in the phloem

Evidence that the phloem carries sugar and other solutes was first obtained in the 1600s when the Italian scientist Marcello Malpighi removed a ring of bark from the trunk of a tree—that is, he "girdled" the tree. The bark contained the phloem, while the xylem in the underlying wood remained intact. Over time, the bark in the region above the girdle swelled (**Figure 33.9**).

Malpighi correctly concluded that a solution coming from the leaves above the girdle was trapped in the bark. Later the bark below the girdle died, presumably because it no longer received nutrients from the leaves. Eventually the roots, and then the entire tree, died—suggesting that sugar transport might occur in the phloem.

The cells that make up the phloem's conducting tubes are sieve tube elements (see Figure 32.10C). Like the vessel elements in the xylem, sieve tube elements meet end-to-end. However, unlike vessel elements, whose end walls are broken down as they mature, sieve tube elements retain their end walls. Communication between sieve tube elements is achieved by plasmodesmata in their end walls. During sieve tube development, the diameter of these plasmodesmata increases 10- to 100-fold, resulting in pores that allow the flow of phloem sap between neighboring cells. Because the end walls of sieve tube elements look and function like sieves, they are called **sieve plates** (**Figure 33.10**).

What happens next is truly remarkable and makes sieve tube elements among the most unusual cell types in nature. As the holes in the sieve plates expand, most of the cell contents are lost, including the nucleus, Golgi apparatus, and most of the ribosomes and cytoskeleton. Despite this, sieve tube elements live for an entire growing season in deciduous trees, and for decades in some other plants. How can sieve tube elements live for so long with no nucleus? The answer is that each sieve tube element has one or more **companion cells** (see Figure 33.10). Companion cells are produced as daughter cells along with the sieve tube elements when parent cells divide. Numerous plasmodesmata link a companion cell with its neighboring sieve tube element. Companion cells retain all their organelles and provide all the components needed to maintain the sieve tube elements—they may be thought of as the "life support systems" of the sieve tube elements.

Plant biologists have used aphids to precisely analyze the contents of the phloem. Aphids are insects that feed on plants by drilling into sieve tube elements with a specialized organ, the stylet. After a stylet is inserted into a plant, the contents of the phloem are forced through the stylet into the aphid's digestive tract because the pressure potential in the sieve tube is higher than that outside the plant. So great is the pressure that some

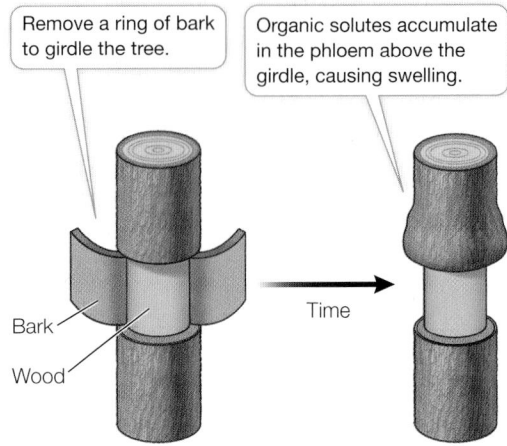

Figure 33.9 Girdling a Tree Disrupts Phloem Transport

of the liquid is forced through the insect's body and out its anus (**Figure 33.11**).

If an aphid is frozen in the act of feeding, its body can be chopped off the plant stem, leaving the stylet intact. Phloem sap continues to flow from the stylet for hours, and can be collected

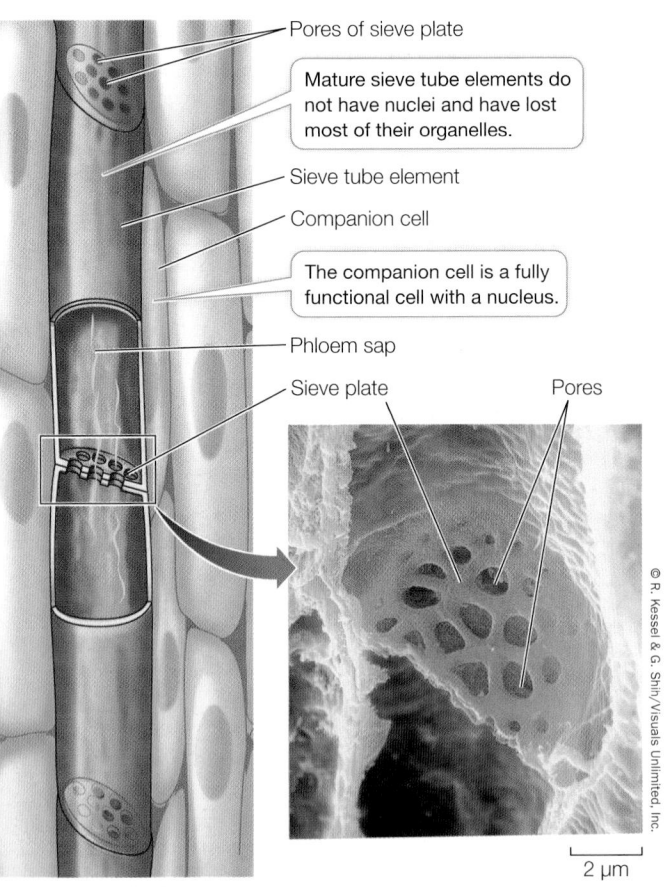

Figure 33.10 **Sieve Tubes** Individual sieve tube elements join together to form long tubes that transport carbohydrates and other nutrient molecules throughout the plant body in the phloem. Sieve plates form at the ends of each sieve tube element, and phloem sap passes through the pores in the sieve plate.

Figure 33.11 Aphid Inserting its Stylet into the Phloem   Aphids' ability to tap into phloem allows them to feed on phloem sap. Researchers have used inserted stylets to collect and examine the contents of the phloem.

for analysis. These and other experiments led to several important observations:

- Sucrose makes up 90% of the phloem sap solutes. The phloem sap also contains hormones, proteins, small molecules such as amino acids, mineral nutrients, and viruses.

- The flow rate can be very high, as much as 150 centimeters per hour.

- Different sieve tube elements conduct their contents in different directions—for example, up or down the stem. Therefore the overall movement in the phloem is bidirectional.

- The movement of phloem sap requires living cells, in contrast to movement in the xylem.

The pressure flow model accounts for translocation in the phloem

The observations we just described have led to the **pressure flow model** as an explanation for translocation in the phloem (**Figure 33.12**). According to this model, sucrose is actively transported at a source into companion cells, from which it flows through plasmodesmata into the sieve tube elements. This gives those cells a higher sucrose concentration than the surrounding cells (a more negative solute potential), and water therefore enters the sieve tube elements from the xylem by osmosis. The entry of this water increases turgor pressure (causes a more positive pressure potential) at the source end of the sieve tube, so that the entire fluid content of the sieve tube is pushed toward the sink end of the tube—in other words, the sap moves in response to a pressure gradient. Pressure-driven flow is called **bulk flow**. In the sink, the sucrose is unloaded both passively and by active transport, and water moves back into the xylem. In this way, the gradient of solute potential and pressure potential needed for the movement of phloem sap (translocation) is maintained.

Two steps in phloem translocation require metabolic energy:

1. **Loading**: Transport of sucrose and other solutes from sources into companion cells and then into the sieve tubes

2. **Unloading**: Transport of solutes from the sieve tubes into sinks

The need for metabolic energy is the reason why phloem transport, unlike xylem transport, requires living cells.

Connect the Concepts Interactions among biochemical pathways (such as photosynthesis, cellular respiration, and the Calvin cycle) that produce carbohydrates that fuel processes such as translocation are discussed in Key Concept 10.5.

Sucrose and other solutes can move from the mesophyll cells into the phloem by either an apoplastic pathway or a symplastic pathway. In the apoplastic pathway, sucrose and other solutes leave the mesophyll cells and enter the apoplast before they reach the sieve tube elements. Specific sugars and amino acids are then actively transported into cells of the phloem. Because the solutes cross at least one selectively permeable membrane in the apoplastic pathway, selective transport can be used to regulate which specific substances enter the phloem. In the symplastic pathway, the solutes remain within the symplast all the way from the mesophyll cells to the sieve tube elements.

In sink regions, the solutes are transported *out* of the sieve tube elements and into the surrounding tissues. This unloading serves several purposes: it helps maintain the gradient of solute potential, and hence of pressure potential, in the sieve tubes; it

Figure 33.12 The Pressure Flow Model   Water potential differences produce a pressure gradient that drives bulk flow of phloem sap from sources to sinks.

View in Achieve
Animation 33.2 The Pressure Flow Model

TABLE 33.2 | Mechanisms of Sap Flow in Plant Vascular Tissues

	Xylem	Phloem
Driving force for flow	Transpiration from leaves	Active transport of sucrose
Site of flow	Nonliving vessel elements and tracheids	Living sieve tube elements
Pressure potential in sap	Negative (pull from top; tension)	Positive (push from source; pressure)

helps build up high concentrations of carbohydrates in storage organs, such as developing fruits and seeds; and it moves nutrients to parts of the plant that are growing rapidly, such as shoots that form after the winter.

Table 33.2 contrasts the pressure flow model of translocation in the phloem with the transpiration–cohesion–tension model of xylem transport.

The control of phloem sap travel from source to sink has great importance for people. The parts of plants that we use for food, such as seeds (e.g., the rice in the opening story), fruits, and storage organs, are mostly sinks. Increasing the flow of sucrose into these organs as they develop can increase food production in crop plants.

KEY CONCEPT
33.4 Recap and Assess

Carbohydrates produced by photosynthesis are translocated from source to sink through the phloem by a pressure flow mechanism.

1. Explain the difference between a source and a sink.
2. How does loading of sucrose at the source result in bulk flow toward the sink?

 Investigating LIFE

Q and A **What methods are used to reduce water loss in agriculture?**

Ensuring the availability of water and its dissolved nutrients is a challenge to growing our crops. Historically, the approach of farmers has been to grow crops adapted to the local environment (e.g., rice in areas of heavy rainfall) or adapt the environment for the plant (irrigation). With our changing climate resulting in droughts, a new approach—adapting the plant's genetic ability to the environment—has begun. The *HARDY* gene, described in Investigating Life: Improving Water-Use Efficiency in Rice, confers adaptation to drought in rice plants by upregulating the expression of clusters of genes involved in water-use efficiency, the ratio of plant biomass produced to water transpired. This is largely achieved through increased leaf thickness, with more mesophyll cells resulting in increased photosynthesis, as well as increased root growth, for greater uptake of water from the soil. The *HARDY* gene acts during development of leaves and roots, which you will recall happens throughout the life of the plant.

Future directions

Sorghum bicolor (Figure 33.13) is an important grain crop worldwide, grown for human food, animal feed, and as a source for biofuels. It is especially valuable because it is both drought- and heat-tolerant, and so is important in hot, dry regions in Africa and South America. At the University of Illinois, scientists are trying to improve the water-use efficiency of sorghum by reducing transpiration in two ways: reduction of leaf stomata and shifting more photosynthesis to lower leaves, which are nearer to the ground and thus surrounded by humid air. Thousands of varieties of sorghum are stored in "seed banks." Samples of these seeds will be germinated and grown in the search for the two desired phenotypes. In addition, a deliberate molecular approach using transgenic plants will be attempted. It is hoped that the result will be a crop even better adapted to make the best use of limited water.

© BLUR LIFE 1975/Shutterstock.com

Figure 33.13 *Sorghum bicolor*

You should be able to relate each summary to the adjacent figures. If you go to this visual summary in **Achieve**, you can follow links to figures, animations, activities, and simulations that will help you consolidate the material.

KEY CONCEPT

33.1 Plants Acquire Water and Minerals from the Soil

Go to Activity 33.1 **and** Simulation 33.1

- **Water potential** (ψ) = **solute potential** (ψ_s) + **pressure potential** (ψ_p). Water tends to move toward regions with high concentrations of solutes and away from regions with high pressure.

- The **Casparian strip** blocks movement of water and minerals through the **apoplast**.

- Uptake of many mineral nutrients is regulated by the abundance and activity of specific transport proteins.

Figure 33.2

Pure water
$\psi = 0$ MPa

Turgid cell
$\psi_p = +1.0$ MPa
$\psi_s = -1.0$ MPa
$\psi = 0$ MPa

Questions

1. A cell with a high concentration of solutes has a more negative solute potential than does a cell with a lower concentration of solutes (e.g., a cell with $\Psi_s = -1$ MPa has a higher concentration of solutes than a cell with $\Psi_s = -0.8$ MPa). Explain how assigning a more negative number to these values makes sense in the context of the water potential equation.

2. Because the Casparian strip exists, most molecules can't reach the vascular tissues without passing through a cell membrane. How might this protect plants from toxic compounds present in the soil water? How might this allow cells to regulate the concentration of beneficial molecules?

Figure 33.6

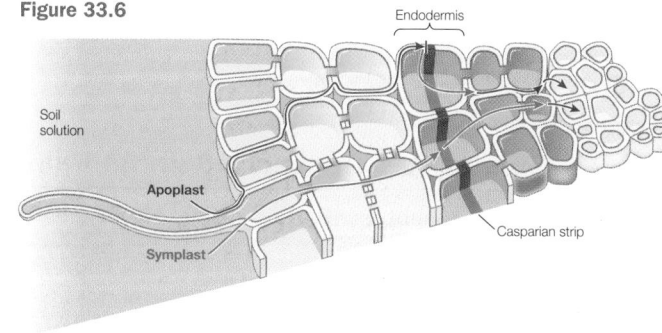

Endodermis

Soil solution

Apoplast

Symplast

Casparian strip

3. Consider a simple model of a plant cell in which the cell wall is represented by a cardboard box and the cell membrane is represented by a tightly sealed plastic bag inside the box. If you placed this model cell in a mud puddle, which part would get wet? Does that part represent the apoplast or the symplast?

KEY CONCEPT

33.2 Water and Minerals Are Transported in the Xylem

Go to Animation 33.1

- Loss of water from leaves creates tension (negative pressure) that pulls a column of water through the xylem tissue. This is called the transpiration–cohesion–tension mechanism for movement of xylem sap.

Questions

1. Is the pressure potential (Ψ_p) in vessel elements through which water is actively moving upward positive or negative?

2. A common misconception is that water is pushed up a tree by a positive pressure from the roots. What experimental evidence indicates that this is not required to raise water to the top of a tall tree?

Figure 33.7

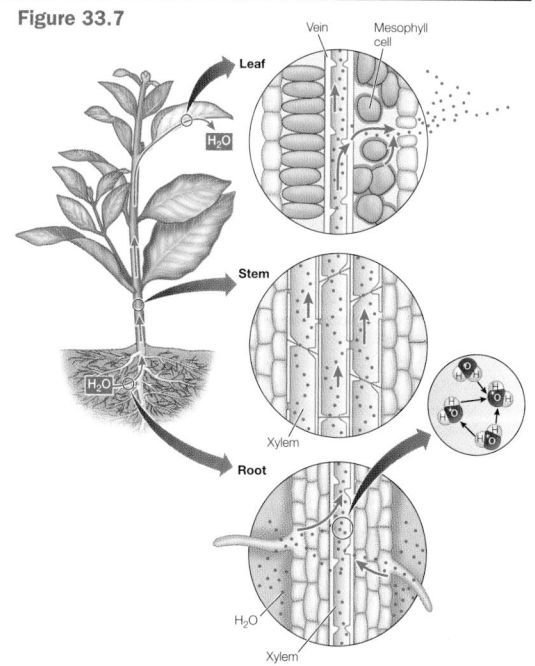

Leaf

H_2O

Vein

Mesophyll cell

Stem

Root

H_2O

Xylem

H_2O

Xylem

KEY CONCEPT

33.3 Stomata Control the Loss of Water and the Uptake of CO_2

- **Stomata** open to allow for CO_2 intake and close to prevent excessive water loss.

- Stomata open when K^+ ions enter the **guard cells**. Water follows osmotically, swelling the guard cells and pushing them apart.

- The hormone abscisic acid can trigger stomatal closure.

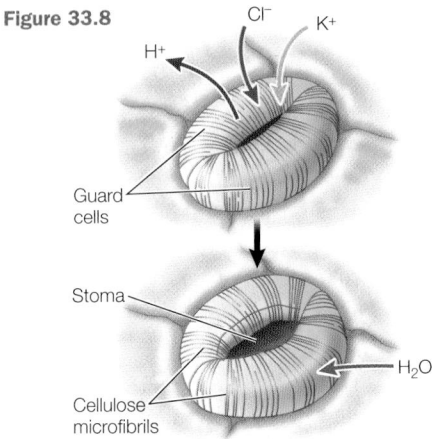

Figure 33.8

Questions

1. Explain how light-activation of a proton pump can lead to an influx of K^+ ions into the guard cells.

2. How can an influx of water into guard cells cause the stomatal pore to open?

3. Given the manner in which light regulates stomatal opening, when is the pressure in the conducting cells of the xylem likely to be higher: just before dawn or about an hour after dawn?

KEY CONCEPT

33.4 Solutes Are Transported in the Phloem

Go to Animation 33.2

- The phloem carries **photosynthate** and other solutes from **source** to **sink** via **bulk flow**.

- According to the **pressure flow model**:

  - High concentrations of solutes at the source draw water into the phloem, increasing pressure that pushes the fluid and its contents toward the sink.

  - As solutes are unloaded at sinks, water moves out and the pressure drops.

Figure 33.12

Questions

1. Very young leaves are sinks, whereas the same leaves, when older, may be sources. Explain what happens to drive the conversion from sink to source.

2. It takes energy to move fluids around. The human circulatory system is driven by a large pump (the heart). What energy-requiring pump or pumps drive water transport in the phloem? *Hint*: How is the pressure that drives bulk flow generated?

3. What parts of phloem transport rely on the presence of cell membranes within the phloem tissue?

Go to **Achieve** for the eBook, **LearningCurve**, animations, activities, simulations, and additional resources and assignments.

Plant Nutrition 34

Corn plants, such as those being fertilized here, extract a lot of nitrogen compounds from the soil. Excess nitrogen that the corn plants do not take up gets left behind in the soil, where it can be a pollutant.

▶Investigating LIFE

Improving Plant Nutrition to Feed the World

Crops such as rice, wheat, and corn supply more than half of the human diet. Plants require good nutrition in order to grow, and one of the nutrients often in short supply in soils is nitrogen. Organic farmers traditionally supply nitrogen by spreading animal waste (manure) over the field; as nature takes its course, the complex macromolecules in manure are broken down to ammonium (NH_4^+).

In 1917, Fritz Haber and Carl Bosch invented a way to make ammonia in the factory, revolutionizing crop plant nutrition. The Haber–Bosch process has been called one of the most important scientific feats of the twentieth century. Chemical fertilizer in the form of ammonium salts led to spectacular increases in food production. But nitrogen fertilizer is expensive in two ways. First, the Haber–Bosch process of manufacturing ammonium from hydrogen and nitrogen gases is very energy intensive and costly. Second, nitrogen fertilizer is also environmentally expensive.

Nitrogen fertilizer contributes to global warming through the burning of fossil fuels in its production and application. Furthermore, some is converted to nitrous oxide gas (N_2O) in the soil. Nitrous oxide is a potent contributor to global warming, and its release can be especially significant when fertilizer is overapplied. In addition, rain can cause nitrogen fertilizer to be lost from farm fields and end up in lakes, rivers, or groundwater. When nitrogen-laden rivers enter the sea, excessive growth of marine algae is likely to result. Eventually the algae die, and the organisms that decompose the algae use up so much oxygen in the water that there is not enough left to support marine life. Nitrogen fertilizer runoff has resulted in vast "dead zones" in waters near the mouths of major rivers, including the Mississippi River Delta in the Gulf of Mexico.

Scientists are working on several strategies by which nitrogen fertilizer might be used more efficiently. One strategy is to improve farming practices, by applying optimal rates of nitrogen to crops while reducing losses to the environment. The other strategy is to alter the genetics of crop plants to improve their uptake and assimilation of nitrogen. Many processes are involved in a plant's use of nitrogen from the soil, such as uptake into the roots, transport to other organs in the vascular system, and incorporation of nitrogen into organic molecules such as amino acids and nucleotides. Each process involves many genes, underscoring the complexity of inheritance.

 How can nitrogen-use efficiency be improved? (Find the answer on page 776.)

34.1 Plants Require Nutrients

Learning Objectives

34.1.1 Identify nutrient deficiencies based on observations.

34.1.2 Explain difficulties involved in testing nutrient requirements for plant growth.

Every living thing—and a plant is no exception—must obtain raw materials from its environment. These **nutrients** include the major ingredients of macromolecules: carbon, hydrogen, oxygen, and nitrogen. A common misconception is that plants receive most of their mass from the soil. This is correct only to the extent that water is concerned. The elements that contribute most to the dry weight (weight after water is removed) of a plant are carbon and oxygen—meaning that most of the mass of a plant comes from the air. Plants are autotrophs, and obtain both carbon and oxygen from the atmosphere through the reactions of photosynthesis and cellular respiration (see Chapters 9 and 10). In addition to serving as a source of energy, the fixed carbon molecules from photosynthesis form the physical building blocks from which the plant body is constructed. Hydrogen comes mainly from water, so it is plentiful when there is an adequate water supply. Nitrogen,

as you will see later in this chapter, enters most plants from the soil. The activities of microorganisms are important in converting organic nitrogen and nitrogen gas into inorganic forms that are usable by plants.

Plants require nutrients in different amounts

In addition to nitrogen, organisms require other **mineral nutrients**: inorganic elements that are used for various cellular processes. For example, proteins contain sulfur (S), nucleic acids contain phosphorus (P), chlorophyll contains magnesium (Mg), cytochromes contain iron (Fe), and cellular signaling can involve calcium (Ca). Most plants obtain these nutrients from the soil. Within the soil, minerals dissolve in water as ions, forming a solution—called the **soil solution**—that contacts the roots of plants.

A plant nutrient is called an **essential element** if the plant fails to complete its life cycle or grows abnormally when the element is absent or insufficient. Essential elements (**Table 34.1**) fall roughly into two categories—macronutrients and micronutrients—based on the amounts required by plants.

- A plant needs **macronutrients** in concentrations of at least 1 gram per kilogram of the plant's dry matter.

- A plant needs **micronutrients** in concentrations of less than 100 milligrams per kilogram of the plant's dry matter.

How do we know if a plant is getting enough of a particular nutrient?

TABLE 34.1 | Mineral Elements Required by Plants

Element (abbreviation; absorbed form)	Typical amount in plant (g/kg dry wt)	Major functions	Deficiency symptoms
MACRONUTRIENTS			
Nitrogen ($N; NO_3^-$ and NH_4^+)	15	In proteins, nucleic acids	Oldest leaves turn yellow and die prematurely; plant is stunted
Phosphorus ($P; H_2PO_4^-$ and HPO_4^{2-})	2	In nucleic acids, ATP, phospholipids, and phosphoproteins	Plant is dark green with purple veins and is stunted
Potassium ($K; K^+$)	10	Enzyme activation; water balance; ion balance; stomatal opening	Older leaves have dead edges
Sulfur ($S; SO_2^{4-}$)	1	In proteins and coenzymes	Young leaves are yellow to white with yellow veins
Calcium ($Ca; Ca^{2+}$)	5	Affects the cytoskeleton, membranes, and many enzymes; second messenger	Growing points die back; young leaves are yellow and crinkly
Magnesium ($Mg; Mg^{2+}$)	2	In chlorophyll; required by many enzymes; stabilizes ribosomes	Older leaves have yellow stripes between veins
MICRONUTRIENTS			
Iron ($Fe; Fe^{2+}$ and Fe^{3+})	0.1	In active site of many redox enzymes and electron carriers; chlorophyll synthesis	Young leaves are white or yellow
Chlorine ($Cl; Cl^-$)	0.1	Photosynthesis; ion balance	Leaf tips wilt; leaves turn yellow and die
Manganese ($Mn; Mn^{2+}$)	0.05	Cofactor for many enzymes	Younger leaves are pale with green veins
Boron [$B; B(OH)_3$]	0.02	Required for proper cell wall formation and expansion	Poor growth of leaves and roots
Zinc ($Zn; Zn^{2+}$)	0.02	Enzyme activation; auxin synthesis	Young leaves are abnormally small; older leaves have many dead spots
Copper ($Cu; Cu^{2+}$)	0.006	Cofactor for some redox enzymes and electron carriers	New leaves are dark green, may have dead spots
Nickel ($Ni; Ni^{2+}$)	0.001	Activation of the enzyme urease	Leaf tips die; deficiency is rare
Molybdenum ($Mo; MoO_4^{2-}$)	0.0001	Cofactor of enzymes involved in nitrogen reduction	Leaves turn yellow between veins; older leaves die

Deficiency symptoms reveal inadequate nutrition

When a plant is deficient in an essential element, it displays characteristic **deficiency symptoms**. Table 34.1 and **Figure 34.1** describe some of the symptoms that help growers diagnose mineral nutrient deficiencies in plants. With proper diagnosis, the missing nutrient(s) can be provided in the form of a **fertilizer** (an added source of mineral nutrients).

Hydroponic experiments identified essential elements

The essential elements for plants were identified by growing plants **hydroponically**—that is, with their roots suspended in nutrient solutions instead of soil (**Figure 34.2**). Growing plants in this manner allows for greater control of nutrient availability than is possible in a complex medium such as soil.

In the first experiments of this type, performed more than a century and a half ago, plants seemed to grow normally in solutions containing only calcium nitrate $[Ca(NO_3)_2]$, magnesium sulfate $(MgSO_4)$, and potassium phosphate (KH_2PO_4). A solution missing any of these compounds could not support normal growth. Tests with other compounds that included various combinations of these elements soon established the existence of six essential elements: calcium, nitrogen, magnesium, sulfur, potassium, and phosphorus. These are now known as the essential mineral macronutrients.

Figure 34.2 Hydroponic Systems Provide Control over the Nutrients to which the Roots Are Exposed

Iron was the first micronutrient to be clearly established as essential, in the 1840s. The most recent micronutrient to be listed as essential was nickel, in 1983. Identifying essential micronutrients proved to be more difficult than identifying macronutrients because of the small amounts involved. Sufficient amounts of micronutrients can be present in the environment used to grow plants or in the plants themselves. A seed may contain enough of a micronutrient to supply the embryo and the entire plant throughout its lifetime. There might even be enough left over to pass on to third-generation plants. Because of such difficulties, nutrition experiments must be performed in tightly controlled laboratories with special air filters that exclude microscopic salt particles in the air, and must use only the purest available chemicals.

KEY CONCEPT
34.1 Recap and Assess

Plants are autotrophs that obtain carbon and oxygen by photosynthesis, and mineral nutrients and water from the soil. Nutrients required by plants are classified as macronutrients or micronutrients depending on the amount needed. Micronutrients are often needed in such minute amounts that only sophisticated chemical experiments can determine their essentiality.

1. Methods for determining whether a particular element is essential for plant growth were established more than a century and a half ago, yet the essentiality of some elements was discovered only recently. Why?

2. If the young leaves of a plant are yellow, what nutrient deficiencies may be suspected? What if the yellow leaves are the oldest ones?

You have seen that plants require a specific set of nutrients in large and small amounts for optimal growth and development. Let's look at how a plant finds and takes up these nutrients from its environment.

Calcium: New leaves are misshapen or stunted. Existing leaves remain green.

Iron: Young leaves are yellow/white with green veins. Mature leaves are normal.

Nitrogen: Upper leaves are light green. Lower leaves are yellow. Bottom (older) leaves are yellow and shriveled.

Potassium: Yellowing tips and edges, especially in young leaves. Dead or yellow patches or spots develop on leaves.

Manganese: Yellow spots and/or elongated holes between veins.

Zinc: Chlorosis between veins. Yellowing tips and margins. Spreading gray-brown spots.

Magnesium: Lower leaves turn yellow from edge inward. Veins remain green.

Phosphorus: Leaves are darker than normal. Loss of leaves.

Figure 34.1 Mineral Nutrient Deficiency Symptoms Deficiencies of several nutrients are depicted in this diagram. Of course, it is very unlikely that a single plant would show all of these symptoms.

 View in **Achieve**
Animation 34.1 Nitrogen and Iron Deficiencies

KEY CONCEPT
34.2

Plants Acquire Nutrients from the Soil

Learning Objectives

34.2.1 Explain how root growth affects the acquisition of soil nutrients.

34.2.2 Describe ways in which a plant is able to control the rate of movement of nutrients into a cell.

34.2.3 Detail how soil fertility is influenced by the process of cation exchange.

34.2.4 Explain how soil fertility is affected by changing land use patterns, including applications of different types of fertilizers.

We can move from place to place to find the nutrients we need. But a plant cannot change its location (it is sessile), and so must obtain nutrients from its immediate environment. With the exception of carbon and oxygen, a plant's supply of nutrients is strictly local, and a plant may use up the water and mineral nutrients in its local environment as it grows. How does a plant cope with the problem of scarce nutrient supplies?

Plants rely on growth to find nutrients

As you learned in Chapter 32, plants differ fundamentally from animals in that plants grow throughout their lifetimes. In fact, growth is a plant's version of movement. For example, roots obtain most of the mineral nutrients plants need. By growing through the soil, roots mine it for new sources of mineral nutrients and water. The growth of stems and leaves helps a plant secure light and carbon dioxide, which in turn allows the roots to continue their growth through the soil. Deficiencies in water or specific mineral nutrients can stimulate plants to grow more roots, to improve the plants' chances of finding the nutrients they need.

As it grows, a plant—or even a single root—must deal with a variable environment. Animal droppings create high local concentrations of nitrogen. A particle of calcium carbonate may make a tiny area of the soil alkaline, while dead organic matter may make a nearby area acidic. Such microenvironments encourage or discourage the proliferation of a root system and help direct its growth. For example, phosphate has low mobility in the soil and is found primarily in the topsoil, along with the bulk of the organic matter. When *Arabidopsis thaliana* plants are grown on a controlled medium that is deficient in phosphorus, they produce many lateral roots, as well as more and longer root hairs, but this growth is limited to the upper portions of the root system (**Figure 34.3A**). Collectively, these changes in the root system promote foraging for nutrients in the topsoil.

In contrast, the form of nitrogen most commonly taken up by plants, nitrate (NO_3^-), is relatively mobile in soil and is more prevalent in lower regions of the soil. When *A. thaliana* plants are grown on a uniform medium that contains moderately low levels of nitrogen, the primary root is longer than that of plants grown with higher concentrations of nitrogen, and the lateral roots are more vertically oriented (**Figure 34.3B**). In other words, low nitrogen levels can cause the root system to grow deeper into

(A) Effect of varying phosphorus supply

Phosphorus added (μM)

625   100   0

(B) Effect of varying nitrogen supply

Nitrogen added (μM)

11,400   550   110

]1 cm

Figure 34.3 Plants Alter the Architecture of Their Root Systems in Response to Soil Nutrients   Plants shown here were grown on media with uniformly low levels of either phosphorus (**A**) or nitrogen (**B**). (After B. D. Gruber et al. 2013. *Plant Physiol* 163: 161–179.)

the soil where the likelihood of reaching nitrate-rich patches of soil may increase.

Nutrient uptake and assimilation are regulated

Nutrients must cross the cell membranes of cells in order to be used in the cell or be incorporated into larger molecules. Polar molecules, including mineral ions, cross the membrane via specialized transport systems. In Chapter 33 you saw how water and ions move into plant roots by way of the apoplast (through cell walls and intercellular spaces) or symplast (directly through cells). The Casparian strip prevents water and ions from entering the xylem tissues of the roots without first entering the symplast (see Key Concept 33.1). In most cases, ions are actively transported across the cell membrane of epidermal cells into the symplast because their concentrations in the soil solution are generally lower than their concentrations inside cells. These active transporters therefore serve as gatekeepers that affect which nutrients will be transported to the xylem and thus the rest of the plant.

Plants have specialized transport systems for the uptake of specific ions (**Figure 34.4**). For example, *A. thaliana* has more than 50 genes that encode nitrate (NO_3^-) transporters, 6 genes encoding ammonium (NH_4^+) transporters, and at least 4 genes for phosphate (PO_4^{3-}) transporters. Nutrient uptake is highly regulated because the levels of ions inside cells must be maintained at constant levels. The genes for ion transporters are regulated at the transcriptional level by the amounts of each nutrient inside cells: low nutrient levels stimulate transcription, whereas high levels repress transcription. In addition, the transporter proteins themselves are regulated (for example, by phosphorylation) to control their ion transport activity.

The incorporation of nutrients into more complex molecules is also regulated according to the plant's needs. The enzymes involved in incorporating nitrate and ammonium into amino acids are regulated at the transcriptional and posttranscriptional levels to increase assimilation when available nitrogen is abundant. The uptake and assimilation of nitrogen are also stimulated by photosynthesis, and this ensures that the nitrogen status in the plant is coordinated with its carbon status.

The types and numbers of nutrient transporters in epidermal cell membranes are regulated by nutrient concentrations inside and outside the cell.

Regulation by transporters

Soil

Epidermal cell

Cortical cell

Regulation by growth Nutrients Root tip

Soil

Roots grow toward a high concentration of a mineral nutrient.

Figure 34.4 Plants Regulate Their Nutrition Plant roots branch and grow toward nutrients. Nutrients are taken up by transport proteins in the cell membrane. The number of transporters for a given nutrient can be regulated in response to nutrient availability.

Soil provides anchorage and nutrients for plants

Most terrestrial plants grow in soil. Soils provide:

- mechanical support.
- mineral nutrients and water from the soil solution.
- O_2 for root respiration.

Soils have living and nonliving components (**Figure 34.5**). The living components include plant roots as well as populations of

bacteria, fungi, protists, and animals such as earthworms and insects. The nonliving portion of the soil includes rock fragments ranging in size from large stones to sand to silt, and finally to tiny particles of clay that are 2 micrometers (μm) or less in diameter. Soil also contains water and dissolved mineral nutrients, air spaces, and dead organic matter. The air spaces in soil contain O_2. Typical percentages of these components are:

Particles: 45%   Water: 25%   Air: 25%   Organisms: 5%

Although soils vary greatly, almost all of them have a soil profile consisting of several recognizable horizontal layers, called **horizons**, lying on top of one another. Soil scientists recognize three major horizons—termed A, B, and C—in the profile of a typical soil (**Figure 34.6**):

- The **A horizon** is the **topsoil** that supports the plant's nutrient needs. It contains most of the soil's living and dead organic matter.
- The **B horizon** is the **subsoil**, which accumulates materials from the topsoil above it and from the parent rock below.
- The **C horizon** is the **parent rock**, also called bedrock, which is in the process of breaking down to form soil.

Soil fertility is a soil's ability to support plant growth. A topsoil's fertility is determined by several factors. Topsoils vary greatly in their proportions of sand, silt, and clay, and this influences their ability to support plant growth. For example, mineral nutrients tend to be **leached** from the upper soil horizons—dissolved in rain or irrigation water and carried to deeper horizons, where they are unavailable to plant roots. Dissolved minerals are readily leached from sandy soil because sand particles are relatively large and

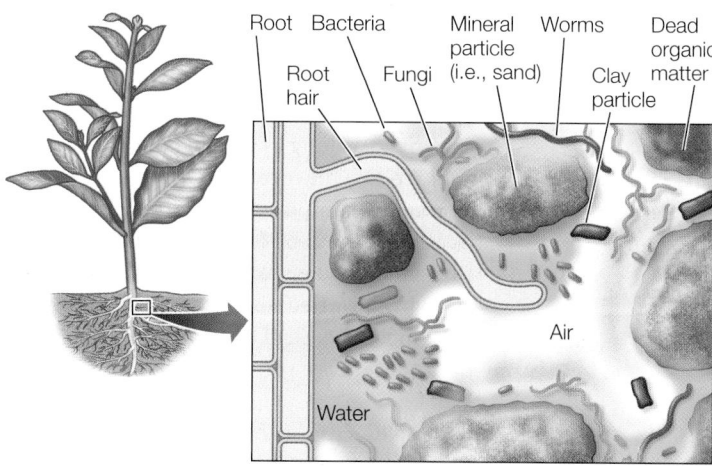

Root Bacteria Mineral particle (i.e., sand) Worms Dead organic matter

Root hair Fungi Clay particle

Air

Water

Figure 34.5 The Complexity of Soil Soils favorable for plant growth contain both clay and larger mineral particles, as well as water, air, and organic matter. Other organisms are also present.

A horizon Topsoil

B horizon Subsoil

C horizon Weathering parent rock

David McIntyre

Figure 34.6 A Soil Profile The A, B, and C horizons can sometimes be seen at construction sites such as this one in Massachusetts. The upper layer (the A horizon) is home to most of the living organisms in the soil.

cannot hold water. Clay, by contrast, binds more water than sand does, and the charged surfaces of clay particles bind mineral ions that plant roots ultimately take up. But clay particles are tiny and pack tightly together, leaving little space for air. A **loam** is a soil that is an optimal mixture of sand, silt, and clay and thus has sufficient levels of air, water, and available nutrients for plants. Loams also usually contain organic matter. Most of the best topsoils for agriculture are loams.

In addition to mineral particles, soils contain dead organic matter, largely from plants. Soil organisms break down dead leaves and other plant organs on the ground into a substance called **humus**. This material is used as a food source by microbes that break down complex organic molecules and release simpler molecules into the soil solution. Humus also provides air spaces that increase O_2 availability to plant roots.

Soils are the source of plant nutrition

Humus and clay particles often carry negative charges. These particles form ionic bonds (see Key Concept 2.2) with the positively charged ions (cations) of many minerals that are important for plant nutrition, such as potassium (K^+), magnesium (Mg^{2+}), and calcium (Ca^{2+}). To become available to plants or other organisms, these cations must be detached from the clay particles. How can this breakage of ionic bonds happen?

Recall that the root surface is covered with root hairs (see Figure 32.11). Transporters in the cell membranes of the root hairs actively pump protons (H^+) out of the cell. In addition, cellular respiration in the roots releases CO_2, which dissolves in the soil water and reacts with it to form carbonic acid. This acid ionizes to form bicarbonate and free protons:

$$CO_2 + H_2O \rightleftharpoons H_2CO_3 \rightleftharpoons H^+ + HCO_3^-$$

Proton-pumping by the root and ionization of carbonic acid both act to increase the proton concentration (lower the pH) in the soil surrounding the root. The protons bind more strongly to clay particles than do mineral cations; in essence, they trade places with the cations in a process called **cation exchange** (Figure 34.7). Cation exchange releases important cations into the soil solution, where they are available to be taken up by the roots. Soil fertility is determined in part by the soil's ability to provide nutrients in this manner.

Some soil particles, such as ones containing oxides of iron or aluminum, are positively charged under acid conditions and can exchange anions (Cl^-, for example) in a process similar to cation exchange. However, soil pH is rarely low enough for anion exchange to occur. As a result, important anions such as nitrate (NO_3^-) and sulfate (SO_4^{2-})—direct sources of nitrogen and sulfur, respectively—may leach rapidly from the A horizon.

As you've seen, soil fertility is affected by soil pH. The H^+ concentration affects the binding of cations and anions to soil particles, and can affect the solubility of other nutrients, such as iron. In addition, soil pH affects the absorption of nutrients by plant roots. The pH level of a soil depends on its mineral and organic contents and can be altered by various factors, including rainfall, weathering (the breakdown of rock into soil particles), plant growth, and fertilizer applications. The optimal soil pH for most plants is in the range 6–7.5, but some plants, such as blueberries and cranberries, prefer pH levels of 4.5–5.

Fertilizers add nutrients to soil

Leaching and the harvesting of crops can deplete a soil of its nutrients, so that new crops grow poorly on that soil. Soil fertility can be restored or increased in various ways, including shifting agriculture to another location or applying organic or chemical fertilizers.

SHIFTING AGRICULTURE   In the past, when the soil could no longer support a level of plant growth sufficient for agricultural purposes, people simply moved to another location. The nutrients in the soil of a field allowed to lie fallow will be replenished gradually through the addition of organic matter from the growth and death of plants naturally present, and by the weathering of the parent rock. Both processes take a long time, which is not a problem as long as a lot of land is available. Today, however, the food needs of a large human population are too great to allow land to be left vacant for a long time, and people are disinclined to move away from settled homesteads. As a consequence, chemical fertilizers are often used to improve soil fertility.

ORGANIC FERTILIZERS   Microorganisms in the soil break down organic molecules into smaller, simpler molecules. These simpler molecules can dissolve in

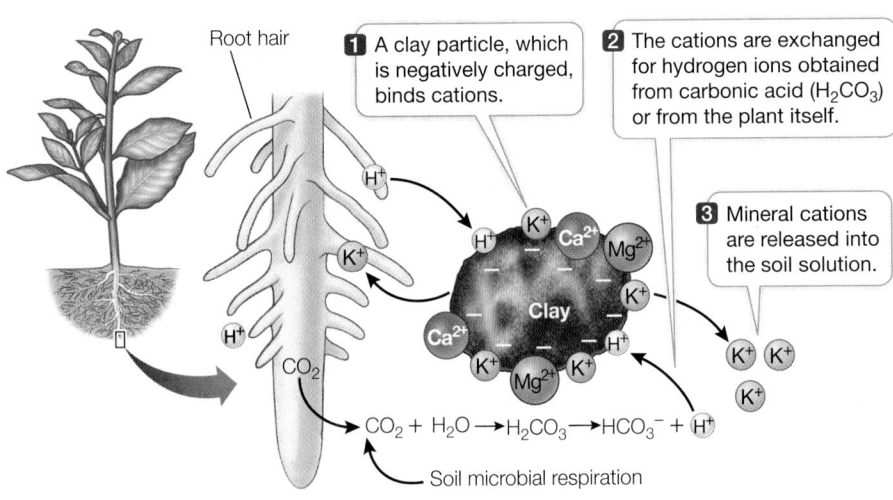

Figure 34.7 Cation Exchange   Plants obtain mineral nutrients from the soil primarily in the form of positive ions; potassium (K^+) is the example shown here.

Q: Do negatively charged ions behave differently?

soil water and enter plant roots. For example, soil bacteria break down the proteins in dead leaves and produce ammonium ions (NH_4^+), which in turn are converted into nitrate (NO_3^-). Both ammonium and nitrate can be taken up and used by plants:

$$\text{Proteins in leaves} \xrightarrow{\text{Bacteria}} NH_4^+ \xrightarrow{\text{Bacteria}} NO_3^-$$

Farmers can increase the nutrient content of soil by adding organic materials such as compost (partially decomposed plant materials) or manure (waste from farm animals). Manure is a particularly good source of nitrogen. In either case, the addition of these **organic fertilizers** adds nutrients to the soil much more rapidly than weathering or the gradual addition of organic matter from natural vegetation. Organic fertilizers allow for a slow release of ions as the materials decompose.

INORGANIC FERTILIZERS   **Inorganic fertilizers** supply mineral nutrients in forms that can be taken up immediately by plants or that are rapidly converted to usable forms in the soil. Inorganic fertilizers are easily transported and handled, and allow farmers to control the amount of a particular nutrient that is supplied to each crop. Particular fertilizers are used in varying amounts, depending on the needs of the crop and the type of soil. For example, much higher amounts of nitrogen are applied to cornfields than to soybean fields. Inorganic fertilizers come in many forms. Common ones include ammonia (NH_3), urea (NH_2—CO—NH_2), and salts formed from positive and negative ions such as ammonium (NH_4^+), potassium (K^+), nitrate (NO_3^-), phosphate (PO_4^{3-}), and sulfate (SO_4^{2-}).

KEY CONCEPT
34.2 Recap and Assess

Land plants live anchored in the soil and obtain water and mineral nutrients from it. Both the uptake and assimilation of nutrients are regulated according to a plant's needs, through coordinated changes in growth and production of transport proteins. Soils are complex in structure and vary in fertility. Farmers can add fertilizers to improve the nutrient contents of soils.

1. How do plants control the uptake and assimilation of mineral nutrients?

2. Soils are dynamic systems. What changes might result when land is subjected to heavy irrigation for agriculture after being relatively dry for many years?

3. How does the process of cation exchange enhance soil fertility?

Thus far we have focused on the uptake of nutrients in the soil by plant roots. An understanding of how plants acquire nutrients from the soil would be incomplete, however, without taking into account the involvement of soil microbes, including fungi and bacteria. In the next key concept we will focus on the intimate interactions of plants with these organisms, which are essential to the success of most terrestrial plants.

KEY CONCEPT
34.3 Soil Organisms Increase Nutrient Uptake by Plant Roots

Learning Objectives

34.3.1 Describe the process by which plants establish mutualistic relationships with fungi and bacteria, and the benefits derived from these relationships.

34.3.2 Explain the role of nitrogen-fixing organisms in supporting life on Earth.

34.3.3 Describe crop rotation and explain how it relates to plant nutrition.

One gram of soil can contain 6,000–50,000 bacterial *species* and up to 200 *meters* of fungal hyphae (the long branching cells of fungi), although both are largely invisible to the naked eye. Plants spend a significant amount of their photosynthate to produce and exude (secrete) a wide range of compounds from their roots into this complex environment, and as a result, plants influence the type and abundance of the organisms that live near their roots. These secretions are called **exudates**, and the region of soil close enough to a root to be affected by them is called the **rhizosphere**. The composition of the rhizosphere changes over time depending on the environment and the state of the plant. When plants are attacked, their roots may secrete molecules that increase the abundance of beneficial bacteria. Some of these bacteria prime a plant's defenses, helping protect it against future attacks. Other secretions can attract symbiotic partners or can poison competitors. The existence of a dynamic bacterial community in the rhizosphere has led to comparisons between the bacteria in the rhizosphere and the bacterial communities in the human gut.

Plants send signals to soil organisms

In Chapter 28 we described mycorrhizae, the association of fungi with plant roots—an interaction that occurs in more than 90% of terrestrial plants. Our example in Chapter 28 was ectomycorrhizal fungi, which wrap themselves around a plant root (see Figure 28.10). In this chapter we examine arbuscular mycorrhizae, in which fungal hyphae penetrate root cells. We also describe here the close association between the roots of some plants and rhizobia, a group of nitrogen-fixing bacteria (bacteria that convert atmospheric N_2 into a more biologically useful form). You will see that mycorrhizal and rhizobial associations are both initiated by signals sent by plant roots that attract the soil organisms, and that the development of these associations involves similar genes and cellular pathways.

Connect the Concepts Mycorrhizal and rhizobial associations are examples of mutualism, one of the major types of interactions discussed in Key Concept 54.1.

FORMATION OF MYCORRHIZAL ASSOCIATIONS   You can follow the events in the formation of arbuscular mycorrhizae in **Figure 34.8A**. Plant roots produce molecules called **strigolactones** that stimulate rapid growth of fungal hyphae toward the root. In

Figure 34.8 Roots Send Signals for Colonization Plant roots send chemical signals to arbuscular mycorrhizal fungi **(A)** and nitrogen-fixing bacteria **(B)** to stimulate colonization. (PAM = periarbuscular membrane.)

(A) Formation of arbuscular mycorrhizal fungi

Cortical cells   Epidermis   Strigolactones   Spore

1 Plant roots produce strigolactones that stimulate rapid growth of fungal hyphae toward the root.

Hypha

Fungal signal

2 Fungal signal stimulates plant to produce a pre-penetration apparatus (PPA).

PPA

3 Fungal hypha enters the PPA and is guided to the root cortex through the apoplast.

4 Fungus grows along the root length.

PAM

5 Hyphae induce formation of new PPA structures inside cortical cells.

6 Hyphae enter PPAs and branch to form arbuscules, where nutrients are exchanged.

(B) Formation of a nitrogen-fixing root nodule

Cortical cells   Root hair

Rhizobia

1 Root hairs release flavonoids and other chemical signals that attract rhizobia.

Infection thread

2 Rhizobia proliferate and cause a root hair to curl and an infection thread to form.

3 Stimulated by Nod factors secreted by bacteria, root cells begin to divide.

4 The infection thread grows into the cortex of the root.

5 The infection thread releases bacterial cells, which become bacteroids in the root cells.

Bacteroids   Nodule meristem

6 The nodule forms as plant cells continue to divide and become infected with bacteria.

response, the fungi produce signals that stimulate expression of genes that promote symbioses with other organisms. The products of some of these genes give rise to the prepenetration apparatus (PPA), which guides the growth of the fungal hyphae into the root cortex. The sites of nutrient exchange between fungus and plant are the arbuscules, which form within root cortical cells. Despite the intimacy of this association, the plant and fungal cytosols never mix—they are separated by two membranes, the fungal cell membrane and the periarbuscular membrane (PAM), which is continuous with the plant cell membrane.

FORMATION OF NITROGEN-FIXING NODULES A group of plants called legumes (members of the plant family Fabaceae) can form symbioses with soil bacteria in several genera collectively known as rhizobia. The legume roots release flavonoids and other chemical signals that attract the rhizobia to the vicinity of the roots (**Figure 34.8B**). The flavonoids also trigger the transcription of bacterial *nod* genes, the products of which synthesize Nod (nodulation) factors. These and other factors, when secreted by the bacteria, cause cells in the root cortex to divide, leading to the formation of a primary nodule meristem. This meristem gives rise to the plant tissue that constitutes the **root nodule**. Bacteria enter the root via an infection thread, analogous to the PPA in mycorrhizal associations, and eventually reach cells inside the root nodule. There the bacteria are internalized by nodule cells, enclosed in membrane vesicles similar to the PAM. Inside the vesicles, the bacteria differentiate into **bacteroids**—the form of the bacteria that can fix nitrogen.

A COMMON MECHANISM   Mycorrhizal associations are not only common, they are ancient. Fossils of some of the earliest land plants (circa 400 million years ago) contain structures that look similar to modern arbuscules. Strikingly, the appearance of arbuscules in these plants predates the evolution of roots. The accumulated evidence strongly suggests that fungal associations coevolved with land plants.

Nodule formation depends on some of the same genes and mechanisms that allow mycorrhizae to develop. For example, both processes involve folding in of the cell membrane to allow entry of the fungal hyphae or rhizobia. The similarities in the structures formed during the development of mycorrhizae and nodules are especially striking, considering that the symbioses involve members of two different kingdoms (fungi and bacteria) (**Figure 34.9**).

Mycorrhizae expand the root system

In many cases the roots of vascular plants cannot nutritionally support plant growth alone—they simply cannot reach all the nutrients available in the soil. Mycorrhizae expand the root surface area 10- to 1,000-fold, increasing the amount of soil that can be mined for nutrients. In addition, because fungal hyphae are much finer than root hairs, they can get into pores in the soil that are inaccessible to roots. In this way, mycorrhizae probe a vast quantity of soil for nutrients and deliver them into root cortical cells.

The primary nutrient that the plant obtains from a mycorrhizal interaction is phosphorus. In exchange, the fungus obtains an energy source: the products of photosynthesis. In fact, up to 20% of the photosynthate of terrestrial plants is directed to and consumed by arbuscular mycorrhizal fungi. Such associations are excellent examples of mutualism, an interaction between two species in which both species benefit. Mutualism is a type of symbiosis, in which two different species live in close contact for a significant portion of their life cycles. As is demonstrated in **Investigating Life: Mycorrhizal Fungi Can Replace Fertilizer in Cassava Cultivation**, the relationship between mycorrhizae and plant roots can be exploited by increasing the fungal population. Many species of fungus invade roots. Identification and genetic improvement of these species is now possible, which holds great promise for improving phosphorus nutrition in important crops.

Soil bacteria are essential in getting nitrogen from air to plant cells

The essential mineral nutrient most commonly in short supply, in both natural and agricultural situations, is nitrogen. This is surprising because elemental nitrogen (N_2) makes up almost four-fifths of Earth's atmosphere. However, plants cannot use N_2 directly as a nutrient. The triple bond linking the two nitrogen atoms is extremely stable, and a great deal of energy is required to break it; thus N_2 is a highly unreactive substance.

Some prokaryotes have an enzyme that enables them to convert N_2 into a more reactive and biologically useful form by a process called **nitrogen fixation**:

$$N_2 + 6 H^+ + 6 e^- \rightarrow 2 NH_3$$

This equation is simplified: actually, H_2 gas is a byproduct. **Nitrogen fixers**, including those present in root nodules, fix approximately 170 million metric tons of nitrogen per year. Humans use industrial methods to fix about 80 million metric tons per year. In addition, about 20 million metric tons per year are fixed in the atmosphere by nonbiological means such as lightning, volcanic eruptions, and forest fires. Rain brings these atmospherically formed products to the ground.

Two types of organisms can fix nitrogen:

1. Free-living organisms living in soil and water (e.g., *Azotobacter* bacteria and *Nostoc* cyanobacteria [the latter sometimes called blue-green algae])

Mycorrhizal infection

Plant cell wall

Plant cell membrane

Periarbuscular membrane

Vacuole

Vacuole

Fungal cell wall

Fungal cell membrane

Nucleus

In both types of infections, a strand of plant cytoplasm forms in the next cell to be crossed, ahead of the hypha or infection thread.

A plant membrane separates the fungus and rhizobia from the rest of the plant cell.

Rhizobial infection

Infection thread membrane

Rhizobia

Preinfection thread

Figure 34.9 Intracellular Structures in Plant–Fungus and Plant–Rhizobia Symbioses Several steps in the development of mycorrhizae and nodules involve similar structures.

▶Investigating LIFE — Mycorrhizal Fungi Can Replace Fertilizer in Cassava Cultivation

Experiment

Original Paper: I. Ceballos et al. 2013. The *in vitro* mass-produced model mycorrhizal fungus, *Rhizophagus irregularis*, significantly increases yields of the globally important food security crop cassava. *PLOS ONE* 8: e70633.

Phosphorus is a plant macronutrient obtained from the soil. Unfortunately, in many tropical regions the phosphate level in the soil is inadequate to support the needs of crop production, forcing farmers to use inorganic phosphate fertilizer, which is a finite and expensive resource. The need for phosphate fertilizer poses an especially acute problem for farmers in poor, tropical regions of the world.

Mycorrhizal fungi very efficiently absorb phosphate ions from the soil. Plant roots with a symbiotic relationship with mycorrhizae obtain phosphorus, while the fungi obtain photosynthate (products of photosynthesis) from the plant. Ian Sanders and his team at the University of Lausanne in Switzerland, in collaboration with Alia Rodriguez and her team at the National University of Colombia in Bogota, investigated whether production of cassava could be increased by adding concentrated spores of mycorrhizae, thus lowering the need for phosphate fertilizer.

HYPOTHESIS▶ Adding arbuscular mycorrhizae to the soil can replace the need for phosphate fertilizer and increase food production in cassava.

METHOD▶

1 Grow cassava in a field.

2 Remove a sample of soil and purify mycorrhizal fungi (MF).

3 Grow fungal spores in the lab, and put spores in gel for transport.

4a **Field 1:** Apply MF only to planted cassava stems (no phosphate fertilizer).

4b **Field 2:** Apply phosphate fertilizer only to planted cassava stems (no MF).

4c **Field 3:** No additions.

5 Allow plants to grow for 14 months and harvest roots (food).

Work with the Data

QUESTIONS▶

1. Concentrated spores of the mycorrhizal fungus *Rhizophagus irregularis* were added to fields of cassava stems tied to stakes. Control fields did not receive the spores. The experiments took place at Yopal, Colombia, in a tropical region. At various times, developing roots were examined microscopically for the presence of fungal hyphae. The results are shown in **Table A**. Storage roots were harvested after 400 days.

Table A

Days after spores were added	Percent colonization
45	40
90	45
135	47
180	49
225	40
270	62
315	82

Plot the data as percent colonization versus time (days after spores added). When did the colonization of fungi increase? Why do you think there was a lag time?

2. In a large field experiment, plots of 300 plants each were treated either with or without fungal spores, and with or without phosphate fertilizer in an amount usually needed for optimal growth (100%) or half of that (50%). The results are shown in **Table B**, as fresh weight (g) of cassava roots, the crop (±SEM, standard error of the mean; see Appendix B for an explanation of SEM).

Table B

	No fertilizer	50% fertilizer	100% fertilizer
Fungal spores	38 (2)	40 (1)	43 (2)
No fungal spores	28 (2)	36 (3)	35 (2)

a. Did the addition of mycorrhizal spores affect the cassava production? What is the evidence for your answer?

b. What statistical test would you use to test for significance of the effects of fertilizer and added mycorrhizae?

Go to Achieve for a companion **Data in Depth** exercise.

RESULTS▶

CONCLUSION▶ Adding purified mycorrhizal spores increases cassava production and reduces the need for phosphate fertilizer.

2. Symbiotic organisms living in other organisms (e.g., rhizobia in roots of legumes, and *Anabaena* cyanobacteria in aquatic ferns)

Nitrogenase catalyzes nitrogen fixation

Nitrogen fixation is the reduction (see Key Concept 9.1) of nitrogen gas. It proceeds by the stepwise addition of three pairs of hydrogen atoms to N_2 (**Figure 34.10**). In addition to N_2, these reactions require three things:

1. A strong reducing agent (e.g., ferredoxin) to transfer hydrogen atoms (protons and electrons) to N_2 and to the intermediate products of the reaction

2. A great deal of energy, which is supplied by ATP

3. The enzyme **nitrogenase**, which catalyzes the reaction

Nitrogenase is strongly inhibited by oxygen, and many nitrogen fixers are anaerobes that live in environments with little or no O_2. But rhizobia are *aerobic* and fix nitrogen in aerobic plant roots. How can nitrogenase function under these circumstances?

Plants typically house nitrogen-fixing bacteria in root nodules. Within a nodule, O_2 is maintained at a low level that is sufficient to support respiration, but not so high as to inactivate nitrogenase. This is possible because the cytoplasm of nodule cells contains a plant-produced protein called **leghemoglobin**, which is an O_2 carrier. Leghemoglobin is a close relative of hemoglobin, the red, oxygen-carrying pigment of animals, and is thus an evolutionarily ancient molecule. Some plant nodules contain enough of it to be bright pink inside. Leghemoglobin, with its iron-containing heme groups, transports enough oxygen to the nitrogen-fixing bacteria to support their respiration, while keeping free oxygen concentrations low enough to protect nitrogenase.

Biological nitrogen fixation does not always meet agricultural needs

Crop rotation systems have been used for hundreds or thousands of years by many human civilizations. In these systems, each field is used to grow different crops in different years, with legumes (such as alfalfa, clover, peas, and beans) included in the rotation. The rotation may also include periods of grazing by farm animals.

Because of their association with nitrogen-fixing bacteria, legumes can replace all or some of the nitrogen removed by grain crops such as wheat and corn. Even with these systems, however, bacterial nitrogen fixation is not always sufficient to support the needs of agriculture. Some traditional farmers used to plant dead fish along with corn; the decaying fish released nitrogen that the developing corn could use. Today farmers use inorganic nitrogen fertilizers produced through industrial nitrogen fixation to meet the food needs of a rapidly expanding human population.

Connect the Concepts The importance of nitrogen fixation in the ecological nitrogen cycle is discussed in Key Concept 56.4.

Ammonia formation is the first step in nitrogen assimilation by plants

Nitrogen fixation by free-living bacteria in the soil results in the formation of ammonia (NH_3), and most of it is rapidly ionized to form ammonium (NH_4^+). The latter can be taken up by plant roots and is then used as a source of amino groups ($-NH_2$) in the formation of such molecules are amino acids and nucleotides. Soil bacteria called **nitrifiers** oxidize ammonia to nitrate ions (NO_3^-)—another form that plants can take up—by the process of **nitrification**. Soil pH affects which form of nitrogen is taken up by plants: nitrate ions are taken up preferentially under more basic conditions, and ammonium ions under more acidic ones. To use nitrate that has entered the roots, the plant must reduce it to ammonium in a process called **nitrate reduction**, which occurs in two enzyme-catalyzed steps. First, nitrate is converted to nitrite (NO_2^-) in the cytosol, and then nitrite is converted to ammonium in the plastids.

KEY CONCEPT
34.3 Recap and Assess

Two mutualistic interactions with soil microbes are critical to the success of terrestrial plants. Fungi and plants form mycorrhizae, which greatly increase the soil volume that roots can scavenge for nutrients. Bacteria in soils and root nodules fix atmospheric nitrogen into forms that plants and ultimately animals can use.

1 The enzyme nitrogenase binds a molecule of nitrogen gas.

2 A reducing agent transfers three successive pairs of hydrogen atoms to N_2.

3 The final products—two molecules of ammonia—are released, freeing the nitrogenase to bind another N_2 molecule.

Substrate:
Nitrogen gas (N_2)

Enzyme: Nitrogenase

Enzyme binds substrate

Reduction   Reduction   Reduction

Product: Ammonia (NH_3)

Nitrogenase

Figure 34.10 Nitrogenase Fixes Nitrogen Throughout the chemical reactions of nitrogen fixation, the reactants are bound to the enzyme nitrogenase. A reducing agent transfers hydrogen atoms to nitrogen, and eventually the final product—ammonia—is released.

This reaction requires a large input of energy: about 16 ATPs are consumed per reaction.

Q: Why does O_2 inhibit this reaction?

1. What is exchanged between plants and fungi in mycorrhizae? Between leguminous plants and bacteria in nodules?

2. Earth's biosphere as we know it depends on the existence of a few species of nitrogen-fixing prokaryotes. What do you think might happen if one of these species were to become extinct? If all of them were to disappear?

3. A common cropping method is crop rotation, with corn or soybeans being rotated on a given plot of land. Explain this in terms of plant nutrition, especially available nitrogen in the soil.

4. Researchers grew lemon seedlings in soils that contained phosphate fertilizer, arbuscular mycorrhizal fungi, or both. The table shows the mean dry weight of the seedlings after 6 months. What do these results tell us about the role of phosphate fertilizer in the growth of lemon plants?

Phosphate fertilizer added (g)	Mycorrhizae present	Seedling dry weight (g)
0	No	1
0	Yes	10
12	No	28
12	Yes	166
24	No	20
24	Yes	210

Let's turn now to some special mechanisms for obtaining nutrients that have evolved in plant species with unusual lifestyles.

KEY CONCEPT

34.4 Carnivorous and Parasitic Plants Obtain Nutrients in Unique Ways

Learning Objectives

34.4.1 Explain how carnivorous plants use nutrients from insects.

34.4.2 Create a hypothesis to explain the evolution of a parasitic plant species.

34.4.3 Analyze evidence that chemical signals involved in plant–bacteria and plant–fungi interactions represent an ancient process.

Most plants obtain their mineral nutrients from the soil solution. Carnivorous and parasitic plants are examples of plants that obtain nutrients from other sources.

Carnivorous plants supplement their mineral nutrition

Some plants augment their nitrogen supply by capturing and digesting flies and other insects. There are about 500 of these **carnivorous plant** species, the best known of which are Venus flytraps (genus *Dionaea*) (**Figure 34.11A**), sundews (genus *Drosera*) (**Figure 34.11B**), and pitcher plants (genus *Sarracenia*).

Carnivorous plants are typically found in boggy habitats that are acidic and nutrient-deficient. To obtain extra nitrogen, these plants capture animals, digest their proteins, and absorb the amino acids. Pitcher plants have pitcher-shaped leaves that collect small

(A) *Dionaea muscipula*

(B) *Drosera scorpioides*

Figure 34.11 Carnivorous Plants Some plants have adapted to nitrogen-poor environments by becoming carnivorous. **(A)** The Venus flytrap obtains nitrogen from the bodies of insects trapped inside the plant when its hinges snap shut. **(B)** Sundews trap insects on sticky hairs. Secreted enzymes will digest the carcass externally.

amounts of rainwater. Insects and even small rodents are lured into the pitchers by bright colors or attractive scents and are prevented from leaving by stiff, downward-pointing hairs. The animals eventually die and are digested by a combination of plant enzymes and bacteria in the water. Sundews have leaves covered with hairs that secrete a sticky, sugary liquid. Insects become stuck to these hairs, and more hairs curve over to further entrap them. Enzymes secreted by the plant digest the insects. Venus flytraps have specialized leaves with two halves that fold together. When an insect touches special hairs called trigger hairs on the leaf, its two halves snap together. The spiny margins interlock and imprison the insect before it can escape. The leaf then secretes enzymes that digest its prey.

The closing of the Venus flytrap's leaf is one of the fastest movements in the plant world, requiring only 0.1 seconds. To find out how this happens, Dr. Lakshminarayanan Mahadevan and colleagues at Harvard University painted fluorescent dots on the surface of the flytrap's leaf surface and used high-speed cameras to record the trap snapping shut when its trigger hairs were touched. They then used computer analysis of the recorded dot movements to generate a mathematical model to help explain the movement. The researchers found that the first step is the osmosis-driven elongation of cells on the outer surface of the leaf. The expansion of only one side of the leaf causes it to snap from a convex into a concave shape, much like a contact lens flipping inside out.

Carnivorous plants photosynthesize and extract soil nutrients just like other plants, but eating insects helps them grow faster in their natural habitats. They use the additional nitrogen from the insects to make more proteins, chlorophyll, and other nitrogen-containing compounds.

Parasitic plants take advantage of other plants

Approximately 1% of flowering plant species derive some or all of their water, mineral nutrients, and sometimes even photosynthate from other plants. These **parasitic plants** have evolved absorptive organs called **haustoria**, which invade the host and tap into the vascular tissues in the root or stem.

Parasitic plants are divided into two broad classes based on their nutritional interactions with their hosts. **Hemiparasites** can still photosynthesize but derive water and mineral nutrients from the living bodies of other plants. Perhaps the most familiar hemiparasites are the several genera of mistletoes. Mistletoes are green and carry on some photosynthesis, but they parasitize other plants for water and mineral nutrients and may derive photosynthetic products from them as well. Dwarf mistletoe (*Arceuthobium americanum*) is a serious parasite in forests of the western United States, destroying more than 3 billion board feet of lumber per year.

Holoparasites are completely parasitic and do not perform photosynthesis. They are taxonomically and morphologically diverse. Some, such as members of the dodder family, are plantlike in appearance, with small leaf remnants and flowers (**Figure 34.12**). Some holoparasites do not have leaves or stems because they spend most of their life cycle underground and only break the surface to flower.

Several parasitic plant species lack many of the genes normally present in the chloroplast genome (which in turn is only a remnant of the genome of the original endosymbiont from which the chloroplast evolved; see Key Concepts 5.5 and 25.1). These genes, which are needed for photosynthesis, have been lost because there is no evolutionary pressure to retain them. Thus while the parasitic lifestyle can be viewed as a free ride, for some plants it is also a one-way ticket, with no possibility of return to self-sufficiency.

The plant–parasite relationship is similar to plant–fungus and plant–bacteria associations

Plant–bacteria and plant–fungus associations both involve reciprocal signaling between the two species (see Figure 34.8). Parasitic plants also need to detect signals from nearby plants so they can grow toward them and obtain their nutrients, but obviously this is to the disadvantage of the potential host plant. In one interesting case, a parasitic plant has evolved the ability to recognize the chemical signals produced by plants to attract beneficial fungi.

The holoparasite *Striga* (witchweed) is a serious pest of cereal crops in Africa. Key Concept 34.3 described how arbuscular fungi are attracted to plant roots by compounds called strigolactones. One of these same molecules induces the seed germination of some parasitic plants, including *Striga*. Scientists strongly suspect that this is no coincidence. The mycorrhizal interaction is ancient (more than 400 million years old) and predates the evolution of parasitic plants. For this reason scientists hypothesize that a mechanism evolved in the ancestors of modern *Striga* to recognize a compound that was already produced by plants to attract soil microbes.

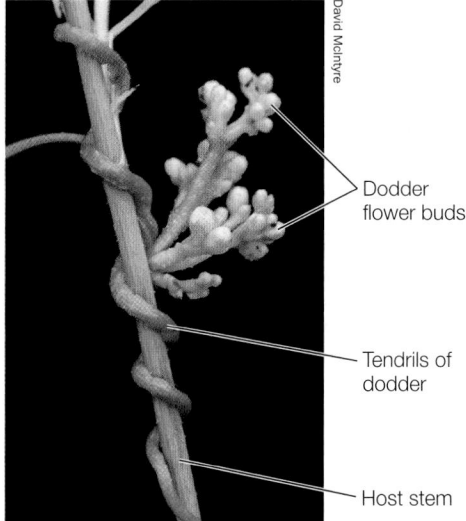

Figure 34.12 A Parasitic Plant Tendrils of dodder (genus *Cuscuta*) wrap around a mugwort (genus *Artemisia*). The parasitic dodder obtains water, sugars, and other nutrients through tiny, rootlike protuberances that penetrate the surface of the host plant.

 Media Clip 34.1 A Venus Flytrap "Snaps to It"
Life12e.com/mc34.1

In *Striga* we thus find an example of "opportunistic evolution"—that is, the repurposing of preexisting processes rather than the development of new processes. This is not the first time you have encountered this phenomenon in this chapter. Recall that the formation of nodules by rhizobia uses some of the same mechanisms used by arbuscular fungi to establish residence inside plant cells (see Figure 34.8). This implies an evolutionary connection between the two symbioses.

KEY CONCEPT
34.4 Recap and Assess

Carnivorous plants supplement their nutrition by extracting materials from animals. Rapid reflexes have evolved in some of these plants for trapping their prey. Parasitic plants, by contrast, get some or all of their sustenance from other plants. Holoparasites cannot function as autotrophs, having lost chloroplast genes that code for photosynthetic machinery.

1. Describe the process by which carnivorous plants get nutrients from their prey. What is the primary nutrient they acquire?

2. Some mutant *Arabidopsis thaliana* plants that are very bushy (their shoots are more highly branched than wild-type plants) cannot make strigolactones because of a mutation in a gene necessary for strigolactone biosynthesis. If an investigator applies strigolactones to the plants, they grow normally. What does this experiment suggest about the role of strigolactones in plant growth? How does this add to the story of strigolactones as signals for arbuscules and parasitic plants?

3. Holoparasitic plants have lost many of the morphological and genetic traits necessary for an autotrophic lifestyle. From an evolutionary standpoint, how do you think this happened? (*Hint*: Think about selection pressures.)

 View in Achieve
Activity 34.1 Concept Matching: Plant Nutrition

▶Investigating**LIFE**

Q and A   How can nitrogen-use efficiency be improved?

We described in the opening of this chapter and in **Investigating Life: Mycorrhizal Fungi Can Replace Fertilizer in Cassava Cultivation** the possibility of improving plant nitrogen nutrition by manipulating the environment around the plant, in particular by adding fertilizers and mycorrhizae to the soil. Negative environmental effects of fertilizer addition can be minimized by using farm machinery that determines the exact amount of fertilizer to apply in each section of a field. Smallholder rice farmers can compare the leaves of their crop with a leaf color chart that is calibrated to determine when application of additional nitrogen fertilizer may be effective. Another approach is to use conventional plant breeding (genetics) and biotechnology to improve the plant's ability to use nitrogen. Publication of the corn genome sequence has provided useful information about genes involved in nitrogen use. For example, the seed company Pioneer Hi-Bred developed a strain of corn that produces a more efficient version of the enzyme glutamine synthetase (GS). GS adds ammonia to glutamate to form glutamine, and therefore plays an important role in nitrogen assimilation in plants. The new corn strain uses up to 20% less nitrogen fertilizer to produce the same yields as other corn varieties.

Future directions

As we pointed out at the beginning of the chapter, the manufacture of nitrogen fertilizer by the Haber–Bosch process is expensive, in terms of energy needed, greenhouse gases released, and economic costs. For too many farmers, nitrogen deficiency limits the growth of their crops. Efforts are under way to discover alternative ways of producing NH_3. One ambitious goal is to transfer a suite of genes from nitrogen-fixing prokaryotes into plants such that the plants acquire the ability to fix nitrogen. While long-standing efforts in this direction have not yet succeeded, the technology for transferring genes has been established and the ability to target proteins to parts of the cell, such as mitochondria or other organelles where oxygen levels may be controlled, makes the idea seem less far-fetched than it was in the past. Another option is to devise a less energy intensive method for industrial fixation of nitrogen by finding a new catalyst that would allow the reaction to proceed with a lower energy input. The search for a new catalyst is currently an active area of research.

VISUAL SUMMARY 34

© Russ Munn/AgStock Images/AGE Fotostock

You should be able to relate each summary to the adjacent figures. If you go to this visual summary in **Achieve**, you can follow links to figures, animations, activities, and simulations that will help you consolidate the material.

KEY CONCEPT

34.1   Plants Require Nutrients

Go to Animation 34.1

- Plants are photosynthetic autotrophs that can produce all their organic molecules from carbon dioxide, water, and minerals, including a nitrogen source. **Mineral nutrients** are obtained from the **soil solution**.

- Plants require **essential elements**: six **macronutrients** and eight **micronutrients**.

- **Deficiency symptoms** suggest what essential element(s) a plant lacks.

Questions

1. One of the most pervasive misconceptions about plants is that they obtain most of their dry mass from the soil. Where does the largest fraction of a plant's dry mass come from?

2. Cooked spinach is often said to be a good source of iron. Is the idea that dark leafy greens are high in iron consistent with the appearance of the young leaves on an iron-deficient plant?

3. How might you identify a nutrient deficiency in a plant?

Figure 34.1

KEY CONCEPT

34.2 Plants Acquire Nutrients from the Soil

- **Soils** contain living and nonliving components.

- Plants can regulate the uptake of nutrients by altering their root architecture and by increasing the number or activity of transport proteins.

- **Cation exchange** occurs when plants pump H⁺ into the soil, liberating cations that plants can then take up.

Questions

1. How is a plant's ability to take in nutrients affected by its ability to regulate gene expression in response to environmental conditions?

2. How might a plant with a deficiency of a particular cation increase its uptake of that cation? What is the cost associated with this strategy?

3. What changes in the soil might result when a deciduous forest is cut down and replaced by crops that are harvested each year?

Figure 34.7

KEY CONCEPT

34.3 Soil Organisms Increase Nutrient Uptake by Plant Roots

- Plants send signals that affect organisms living in the **rhizosphere**.

- Plant secretion of **strigolactones** can promote associations with mycorrhizal fungi that promote uptake of minerals such as phosphate.

- Legumes can promote nodulation by secreting flavonoids. **Nitrogen fixation** occurs in **root nodules** with the aid of bacteria that produce the enzyme **nitrogenase**.

Questions

1. How do mycorrhizal associations increase nutrient uptake?

2. What properties of root nodules promote nitrogen fixation?

3. In what ways might the root–soil interface be similar to the interior of the human gut?

Figure 34.8

KEY CONCEPT

34.4 Carnivorous and Parasitic Plants Obtain Nutrients in Unique Ways   Go to Activity 34.1

- **Carnivorous plants** are autotrophs that supplement a low nitrogen supply by feeding on insects or other small animals.

- **Parasitic plants** draw on other plants to meet their needs. **Hemiparasites**, such as mistletoes, gain water from their hosts but still photosynthesize. **Holoparasites** are completely dependent on their hosts.

Questions

1. Venus flytrap plants have green leaves. What function do the green leaves serve? Would the plants survive without these?

2. Indian pipes (*Monotropa uniflora*), also called ghost plants, are totally white and live in dark forests. Which type of parasitic plants are these?

Figure 34.11   *Dionaea muscipula*

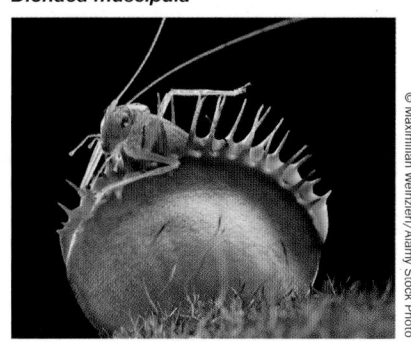

© Maximilian Wenzler/Alamy Stock Photo

Go to **Achieve** for the eBook, **LearningCurve**, animations, activities, simulations, and additional resources and assignments.

35 Regulation of Plant Growth

KEY CONCEPTS

35.1 Plant Development Occurs Progressively as Plants Mature

35.2 Gibberellins and Auxin Have Diverse Effects but a Generally Similar Mechanism of Action

35.3 Other Plant Hormones Have Diverse Effects

35.4 Photoreceptors Initiate Developmental Responses to Light

The root, stem, and leaf develop from a plant embryo within a seed. Here, two seedlings are shown opening their first leaves.

© Tim Gainey/Alamy Stock Photo

▶ Investigating LIFE

A Nobel Prize for a Plant Biologist

© Micheline Pelletier Decaux/Getty Images

In their constant search for ways to help farmers produce more food for a growing population, biologists have developed cereal crops whose physiology allows them to produce more grain per plant (resulting in higher yields). The drawback of this approach is that the sheer weight of the load of seeds may cause the stem to bend over. The problem is made worse when fertilizer added to the soil stimulates plants to grow taller. Harvesting seeds on the ground is very difficult; think of how hard it would be to pick up seeds one by one, when some have already sprouted.

During World War II, Japan, an island nation with a limited amount of land suitable for farming, was blockaded and could not import food or other supplies. Food was rationed and many people were hungry, but there were no major famines in Japan during that period. How were the Japanese able to produce enough grain to feed their population? The answer to this question lay in the fields: the Japanese had bred genetic strains of rice and wheat with short, strong stems, growing in thickness rather than height, that could bear high yields of grain without bending over. An agricultural advisor to the American army that temporarily occupied Japan in 1945 sent samples of the grains to the United States.

A decade later, the American plant geneticist Norman Borlaug, who was working in Mexico at the time, began making genetic crosses between the Japanese wheat and other varieties that had genes conferring rapid growth, adaptability to varying climates, and resistance to fungal diseases. The results were "semi-dwarf" wheat varieties that gave record yields. The varieties were grown first in Mexico, and later in India and Pakistan during the 1960s. At about the same time and using a similar strategy, scientists in the Philippines developed semi-dwarf rice with equally spectacular results. People who had lived on the edge of starvation now produced enough food. Countries that had relied on food from other countries were now able to grow more than enough grain, and export the surplus. The development of these semi-dwarf grains began what was called the "green revolution." Borlaug was awarded the Nobel Peace Prize for his research on wheat, which is estimated to have saved a billion lives.

 How is plant growth controlled, and what changes in growth patterns made the new strains of wheat and rice successful? (Find the answer on page 799.)

Plant Development Occurs Progressively as Plants Mature

Learning Objectives

35.1.1 Describe how plant cells increase in size by taking in water.

35.1.2 Explain how expression of a transcription factor can establish the identity of a cell.

35.1.3 Hypothesize as to why retaining the ability to undergo redifferentiation is advantageous to plants.

35.1.4 List the ways a seed can maintain dormancy, and describe with examples how each method might be overcome to achieve germination.

35.1.5 Construct a diagram that shows how a genetic screen can be used to identify the genes in the development of plant signal transduction pathways.

As organisms move through their life cycles, they change continually. A gardener who plants a seed may talk about the resulting plant as if it were a single thing, but the size and structure of the seed, seedling, leafy plant, and fruit-bearing plant are always different. **Development** is the term used to describe the process by which a plant or other organism changes, taking on the successive forms that characterize its life cycle. Plant development occurs through a combination of **growth**, an increase in size of the body and its organs, and **differentiation**, the process by which cells become different from one another. Because plants are rooted in place, their survival depends on their ability to cope with the environment around them. They can't run away or put on a coat as we can. Their remarkable ability to produce new organs and reshape their bodies throughout their lives plays a significant role in their ability to thrive in a variety of environmental circumstances.

Cell expansion increases the size of a plant cell and gives it shape

The size of a plant increases when cells expand. Cell expansion often leads to cell division, which partitions the existing material into smaller units, so increases in size and cell number are highly correlated. Plant cells increase in size by taking in water in what is called the **stress–relaxation cycle** (Figure 35.1). The cycle begins when pressure from the cell contents (turgor pressure) acts on the cell wall. This physical stress alters the structure of the material that makes up the cell wall. Some of the changes that occur in the cell wall are reversed when the pressure decreases, but some of the changes are not reversible—much as when someone pulls on a swimsuit that is too small and the material becomes permanently stretched out. Once the structure of the cell wall changes, the wall "relaxes." Relaxation of the wall causes the internal turgor pressure to fall—because the forces between the cell and its wall are equal and opposite. Having a lower internal pressure can result in more water entering the cell, continuing the cycle.

The rate of cell wall expansion can be regulated by changing the chemical composition of the wall. Some plant hormones increase the rate of cell expansion by making the wall easier to extend ("looser"). That is, they change the composition of the wall such that a given amount of pressure results in a larger expansion of the cell. These hormones promote growth.

Growing plant cells must synthesize new wall material that adds to the thickness of their walls; otherwise their walls would continually become thinner. Most plant cell walls are composed of long filaments called cellulose microfibrils that are embedded in a network of polysaccharides and proteins. Cellulose is a polymer composed of repeating glucose units joined in a straight chain

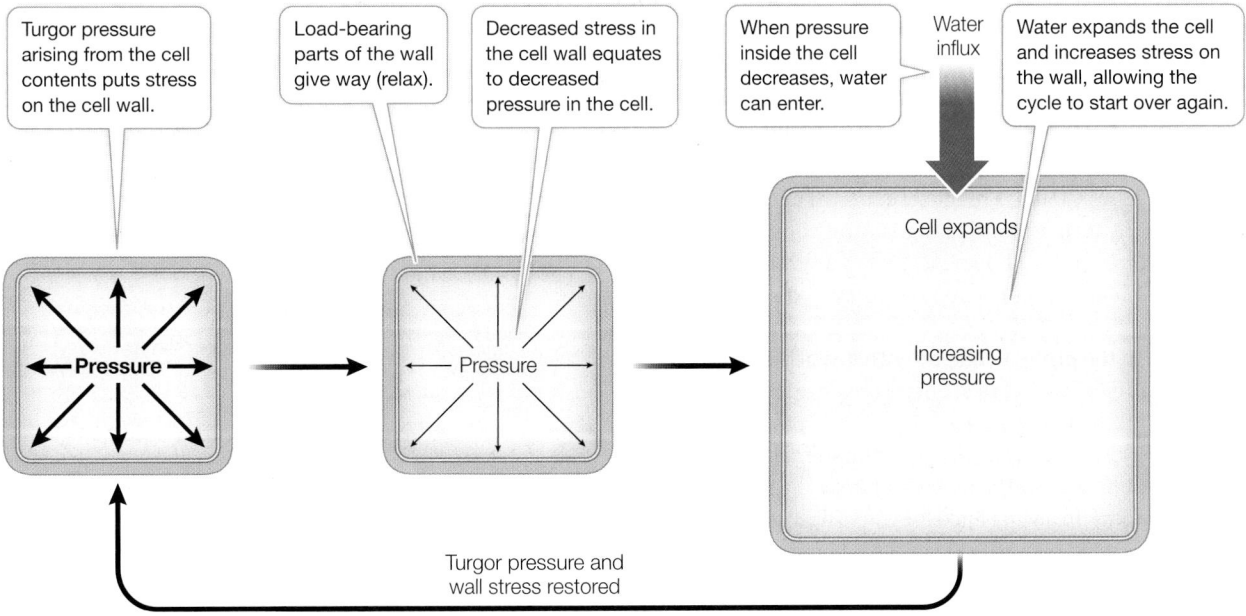

Figure 35.1 Plant Cell Expansion Occurs via the Stress–Relaxation Cycle
(After D. J. Cosgrove. 2015. *J Exp Bot* 67: 463–476.)

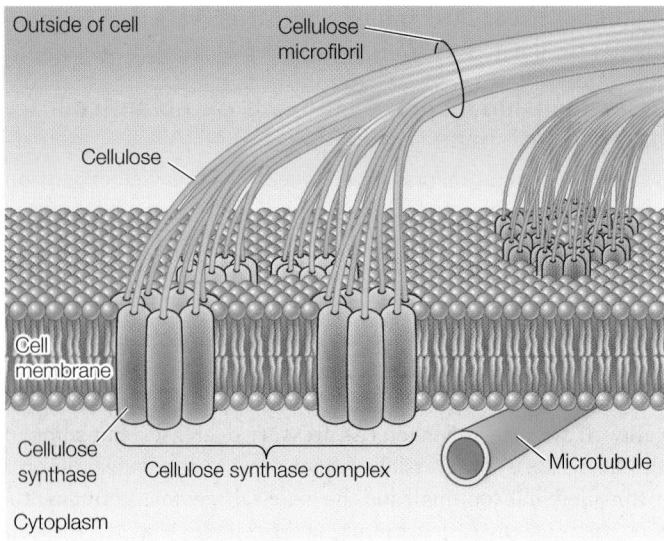

Figure 35.2 Cellulose Synthase Complexes   Cellulose synthase complexes form chains of glucose (glucan) that come together in the cell wall space to form cellulose microfibrils.

(see Figure 3.19). Cellulose microfibrils are synthesized by protein complexes called cellulose synthases that sit in the cell membrane, receiving subunits from the cytoplasm and releasing microfibril chains toward the cell wall (**Figure 35.2**). The cellulose synthase complexes synthesize multiple chains at a time, and these chains pack together to form a single microfibril. Cellulose microfibrils provide strength and rigidity to the wall.

If plant cells lacked a stiff restraint, they would grow as spheres and plants might resemble beach balls. Neither plants nor plant cells are entirely spherical, however. Epidermal cells on the leaf can be shaped like pieces of a jigsaw puzzle, while cells in an elongating stem are often cylindrical. Nonspherical shapes arise because the plant has the ability to regulate the extent of growth in one area versus another. Typically, the wall in one part of a cell is softer or easier to loosen than the wall in other parts of the cell. These differences give an asymmetry to cell expansion that affects the overall shape of a plant.

Whether a cell continues to expand in the same manner or changes its direction of expansion is of central importance to the development of the organism. Changes in the direction of expansion are responsible for the formation of branches and complex shapes. The direction of maximal cell expansion usually can be predicted by the arrangement of cortical microtubules, cytoskeletal proteins that are anchored to the cell membrane. Cortical microtubules are linked to the protein complexes that synthesize cellulose, and the orientation of the cortical microtubules appears to direct the orientation in which cellulose microfibrils are laid down in the cell wall. For elongated cells in a growing stem, both the microtubules and cellulose microfibrils wrap around the narrow axis of the cell, like hoops in a wine barrel (**Figure 35.3**). Cellulose microfibrils resist expansion, resulting in there being more growth in length than in width. The orientation of microtubules is highly regulated by the proteins that bind to them and gives the plant a mechanism for controlling the shape of its body.

Cell fates become progressively more restricted during development

As plants mature, cells not only get larger, but also acquire different characteristics. A zygote is a single cell that gives rise to an embryo and, from that, an organism. The cells of an early embryo are totipotent (*toti*, "all," + *potent*, "capable"), meaning they have the potential to differentiate into any cell type, including more embryonic cells. As the embryos of many organisms mature, cells become progressively restricted in their potential, eventually being limited to producing just one cell type. When a cell has taken on the characteristics of a single specific cell type, we say that it has differentiated. That differentiated state reflects the cell fate.

While plant cells undergo progressive changes in their identity as the plant develops, plant cells are remarkable in the extent to which they remain capable of redifferentiation. It is possible to cut sections of mature leaves or roots and grow them in culture. Culturing plant cells causes them to lose their prior differentiated state and form a callus (plural *calli*)—a cluster of dividing cells. Given appropriate hormonal treatments, callus cells can redifferentiate to form a whole new plant. In 1958 Frederick Steward at Cornell University showed that if he isolated cells from a carrot root and maintained them in a suitable nutrient medium, he could induce them to divide and give rise to masses of calli, which no longer had the cell-type characteristics that they started with. These callus cells could be maintained in culture indefinitely. Furthermore, if the callus cells were provided with the right chemical cues, they could develop into embryos and eventually into complete new plants (**Figure 35.4**). The new plants in Steward's experiments were genetically identical to the cells from which they came—that is, they were clones of the original carrot plant. The ability to produce clones is evidence that the somatic cells in a plant have all the genetic information needed to become any cell in the plant. The next section explores the mechanisms by which distinct cell fates are specified.

Changes in gene expression underlie cell fate determination and differentiation

A central component of development is the ability to form distinct cell types. The cells in human eyes contain proteins that allow us to see light, while intestinal cells produce digestive enzymes; if eyes produced digestive enzymes, they would not work

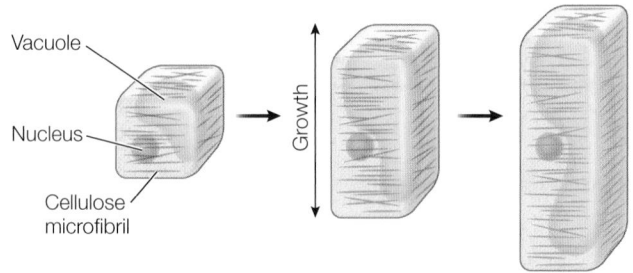

Figure 35.3 The Orientation of Cellulose Microfibrils Affects the Direction of Cell Expansion   Transverse cellulose microfibrils restrict lateral expansion, resulting in an elongated shape.

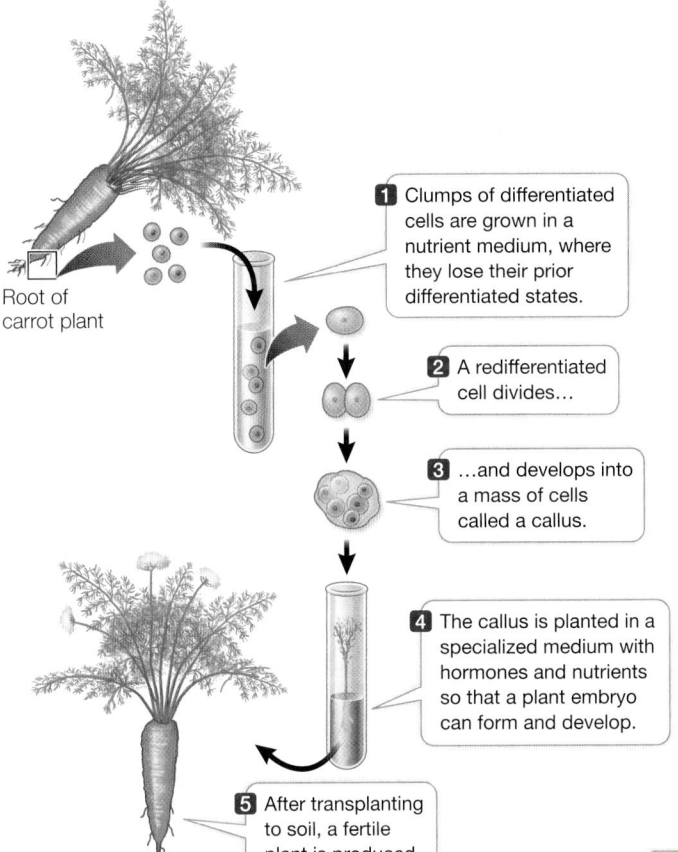

1 Clumps of differentiated cells are grown in a nutrient medium, where they lose their prior differentiated states.

2 A redifferentiated cell divides...

3 ...and develops into a mass of cells called a callus.

4 The callus is planted in a specialized medium with hormones and nutrients so that a plant embryo can form and develop.

5 After transplanting to soil, a fertile plant is produced.

Root of carrot plant

Figure 35.4 Differentiated Plant Cells Can Be Totipotent When differentiated plant cells are removed from the plant and placed in medium with nutrients and specific growth hormones, they can redifferentiate into callus and then be induced to generate an entire new plant. (After F. C. Steward. 1958. *Am J Bot* 45: 705–709.)

very well! The same is true for plants. Epidermal cells in the root contain proteins that span the cell membrane and promote uptake of nutrients from the soil, while leaves contain proteins that promote photosynthesis. Given that each cell in a multicellular organism generally contains the same genes, how do the differences between cell types arise? The answer is that the distinction between cells largely arises from the proteins they contain.

Transcription factors, a class of proteins that bind to regulatory sequences in DNA, play a central role in regulating gene expression (**Figure 35.5**). If a transcription factor affects the expression of other transcription factors, a cascade is generated, amplifying the effect. Some transcription factors that sit at the head of such cascades are called master regulators because their expression can cause a cell to produce or repress so many proteins that the cell takes on a new cell fate. Development can thus be seen as a question of how cells come to express different transcription factors, particularly the master regulators that cause a cell to differentiate into its final cell fate.

An example of plant transcription factors that act to specify cell fate is found in the PLETHORA (PLT) family. Stem cells are cells that both maintain themselves and give rise to the cells that produce differentiated cell types. In plants, stem cells can be found in the meristems: think of the vascular cambium that maintains itself while producing cells that form the xylem and phloem, or of the divisions that take place in the center of the shoot apical meristem that give rise to the cells that form the stem and leaves. In the root meristem, stem cells surround the quiescent center, a small group of cells that rarely divide (**Figure 35.6A**). If the root meristem did not contain stem cells, the cell production that leads to regular growth of the root would stop. *PLETHORA* genes encode transcription factors that are required for the formation and maintenance of stem cells. Experiments examining mutant plants that have lost the function of multiple PLETHORA proteins have demonstrated that PLETHORA proteins confer the stem cell identity. Plants lacking functional copies of *PLT1* and *PLT2* have short roots, while embryos lacking *PLT1*, *PLT2*, and *PLT3* form no root at all (**Figure 35.6B**). In contrast, when high levels of PLT2 protein are induced in the shoot apical meristem, the meristem gives rise to a structure that resembles a root (**Figure 35.6C**)! A mutation in which one type of organ is replaced by another is called a homeotic mutation.

1 Transcription of a gene that encodes a master regulator is initiated by a signal.

Promoter   Transcription factor gene   RNA polymerase II

Transcription

2 The protein produced is a transcription factor that can bind to DNA elements in the promoters of other genes, stimulating or repressing transcription of genes *A*, *B*, and *C*...

mRNA

Translation

Transcription factor

Gene *A*   Gene *B*   Gene *C*

Promoter

mRNA

3 ... which produce different proteins that contribute to the identity of the cell.

Figure 35.5 Coordinating Gene Expression A single signal causes the synthesis of a transcription factor that acts on many genes.

(A)

Stem cells

Rootlike structure

(C)

(B)

B and C from C. Galinha et al. 2007. *Nature* 449: 1053–1057

Figure 35.6 *PLETHORA* **Expression Maintains Root Stem Cells**
Loss of *PLETHORA* (*PLT*) function results in failure to maintain the stem cells in the root. **(A)** Diagram showing the stem cells and the quiescent center in the root meristem. **(B)** A wild-type root is shown on the left; a *plt1,plt2* double mutant in the center; and a *plt1,plt2,plt3* triple mutant on the right. When stem cells are not maintained, the root in the mutant plants does not continue to elongate. (Wild-type plant gene names are written in uppercase, mutant gene names in lowercase.) **(C)** Inducing expression of *PLETHORA 2* in the shoot apical meristem results in the formation of a rootlike structure there.

Genetic screens have increased our understanding of molecular pathways that regulate development

A method that has been particularly helpful in identifying factors that regulate development is called a **genetic screen**. If a mutation in a specific gene disrupts a developmental process, then the product of that gene must be involved in that process. In a similar way, genetic studies can be used to analyze signal transduction pathways in plants: if proper signaling does not occur in a mutant plant, then the mutant gene must be involved in the signal transduction process. Mapping the mutant gene and identifying its function is a starting point for understanding the signaling pathway. *Arabidopsis thaliana* has been a major model organism for plant biologists investigating signal transduction.

One technique for identifying the genes involved in a plant signal transduction pathway is illustrated in **Figure 35.7**. This genetic screen involves creating a large, random collection of mutant plants and identifying those individuals that are likely to have a defect in the pathway of interest. Plant genes can be randomly mutated in a variety of ways, including treatment with a chemical mutagen or the random insertion of transposons (see Key Concept 17.2) in the genome. After treatment, the plants are grown and then examined for a specific phenotype, usually a characteristic that is influenced by the pathway of interest. Once mutant plants have been selected, their genotypes are compared with those of wild-type plants. *A. thaliana* mutants with altered developmental patterns have provided a wealth of new information about the mechanisms of hormone and receptor action.

Research Tools

Figure 35.7 A Genetic Screen Genetics of the model plant *Arabidopsis thaliana* can be used to identify the steps of a signal transduction pathway. If a mutant strain does not respond to a hormone (in this case, ethylene), the corresponding wild-type gene must be essential for the pathway (in this case, ethylene response). This method has been instrumental to scientists in understanding plant growth regulation. (All photos from J. M. Alonso and J. R. Ecker. 2006. *Nat Rev Genet* 7: 524–536.)

Q: In undertaking a search for *natural* mutant strains for ethylene response, how would you modify the procedure?

1 A phenotype of interest is chosen, in this case response to ethylene. Growth of wild-type seedlings in the dark is altered by ethylene (right).

No ethylene added   Ethylene added

2 Seeds are treated with a mutagen and then planted.

Many seeds suspended in a mutagen solution in a test tube

3 The treated plants are grown in the dark and then screened. One mutant shows insensitivity to the hormone (uninhibited growth).

Ethylene-insensitive mutant

Ethylene-sensitive (wild-type) plants

4 The gene involved in ethylene signaling is mapped, cloned, and studied.

Gene required for ethylene response

In early development, the seed germinates and forms a growing seedling

To see how some of the factors discussed so far come together, let's consider the first stages of plant development, beginning with the seed. The events of plant reproduction and development that lead to the formation of seeds are discussed in Chapter 36. A seed is the structure that contains the early embryo. Unlike most animal embryos, plant seeds may be held in "suspended animation," with the development of the embryo halted, for long periods. If development stops even when external conditions (such as water supply) are adequate for development, the seed is said to be **dormant**.

DORMANCY   Seed dormancy may last for weeks, months, or years. Plants use several mechanisms to maintain dormancy:

- *Exclusion of water or oxygen* from the embryo by an impermeable seed coat
- *Mechanical restraint* of the embryo by a tough seed coat
- *Chemical inhibition* of germination by growth regulators
- *Photodormancy*: some seeds need a period of light or dark before they can germinate
- *Thermodormancy*: some seeds need high or low temperatures to germinate

Dormancy can be broken by conditions that overcome these mechanisms. For example, the seed coat may be damaged by passage through an animal's digestive system, or heavy rains may wash away chemical inhibitors. There are some unusual methods to overcome dormancy. One example is the breaking of dormancy by components of smoke. *Emmenanthe penduliflora* is a common plant in dry chaparral of the southwestern United States, an area that is prone to wildfires. These plants germinate rapidly after a fire. Jon Keeley of Occidental College in Los Angeles found that dormancy in seeds of this plant is broken not by heat but by smoke—in particular, by the nitrogen oxides found in smoke. Other molecules in smoke have been identified that regulate seed germination.

Plant biologists distinguish between seed *dormancy*, which prevents germination under conditions that are suitable for plant growth, and seed *quiescence*, which occurs when a seed fails to germinate because conditions are unfavorable for growth. Some seeds may remain quiescent, yet viable, for centuries; botanists have germinated a 1,300-year-old lotus seed recovered from a dry lake bed in China.

Seed dormancy and quiescence are common, so they must provide selective advantages for plants. Dormancy ensures that the seed will germinate at a time suitable for the plant to complete its life cycle. For example, some seeds require exposure to a long cold period (winter) before they germinate in the spring; this ensures that the plant has the entire growing season to mature and set new seeds. Dormancy and quiescence also help seeds survive droughts or long-distance dispersal, allowing plants to colonize new territory.

GERMINATION   Seeds begin to **germinate**, or sprout, when dormancy is broken and environmental conditions are satisfactory. The first step in germination is the uptake of water, called **imbibition** (from *imbibe*, "to drink in"). Before germination, a seed contains very little water: only 5%–15% of its weight is water, compared with 80%–95% in most other plant parts. Seeds also contain polar macromolecules, such as cellulose and starch, which attract and bind water molecules. Consequently a seed has a very negative water potential (see Chapter 33) and will take up water if the seed coat is permeable to water. The force exerted by imbibing seeds, which expand several-fold in volume, demonstrates the magnitude of their water potential; for example, imbibing cocklebur seeds can exert a pressure of up to 1,000 atmospheres.

As a seed takes up water, it undergoes metabolic changes: enzymes are activated upon hydration, RNA and then proteins are synthesized, the rate of cellular respiration increases, and other metabolic pathways are activated. In many seeds, cell division is not initiated during the early stages of germination. Instead, growth results solely from the expansion of small, preformed cells.

As germination proceeds, starch, proteins, and lipids that are stored in the seed are hydrolyzed to provide metabolic energy and chemical building blocks—carbohydrates, amino acids, and lipid monomers—for the growing embryo. These reserves are stored in the **cotyledons** (the first leaf or leaves of the embryo) or in the endosperm (the non-embryonic storage tissue of the seed). Germination is completed when the **radicle** (embryonic root) emerges from the seed coat. The plant is then called a **seedling**.

If the seed germinates underground, the new seedling must elongate rapidly (in the right direction!) and cope with a period of life in darkness or dim light. Photoreceptors that sense light and specialized cells that sense gravity direct this stage of development and prepare the seedling for growth in the light.

The pattern of early shoot development varies among the flowering plants. **Figure 35.8** shows the shoot development patterns of monocots and eudicots. In monocots, the growing shoot is protected by a sheath of cells called the **coleoptile** as it pushes its way through the soil. In eudicots, the shoot is protected by the cotyledons.

Several hormones and photoreceptors help regulate plant growth

The description just provided of the early stages of plant development illustrates some of the environmental cues that influence plant growth. When part of a plant, such as a leaf cell, senses a change in its environment, signal transduction pathways that result in the synthesis and activation of specific plant hormones may be stimulated. The resulting hormones function as signals that can act locally or, in many cases, travel to other parts of the plant where they can trigger pathways that affect plant growth. In most cases these changes involve alterations in the expression of specific genes.

Perhaps the most important environmental cue for a plant is light: the source of energy for photosynthesis. Plants have an abundance of **photoreceptors** that detect changes in the quality and direction of light as well as the timing of light availability (day length). Photoreceptors are often proteins associated with pigments. Light acts directly on photoreceptors, which in turn regulate developmental processes that need to be responsive to light, such as the many changes that occur as a seedling emerges from the soil.

(A) Monocot shoot development (corn)

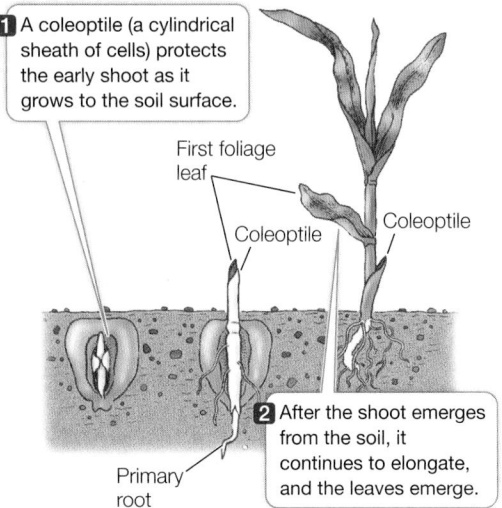

1 A coleoptile (a cylindrical sheath of cells) protects the early shoot as it grows to the soil surface.

First foliage leaf

Coleoptile

Coleoptile

2 After the shoot emerges from the soil, it continues to elongate, and the leaves emerge.

Primary root

(B) Eudicot shoot development (bean)

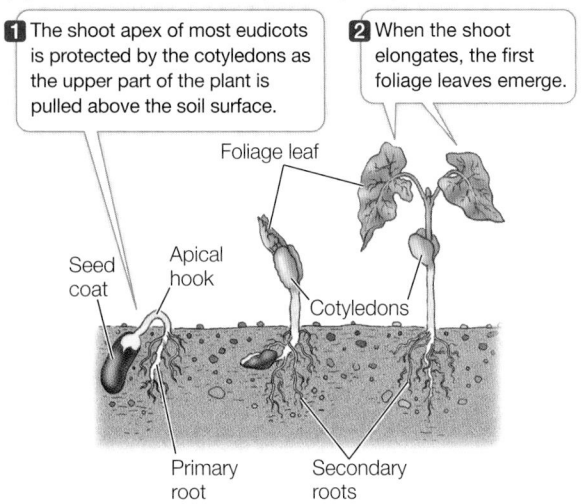

1 The shoot apex of most eudicots is protected by the cotyledons as the upper part of the plant is pulled above the soil surface.

2 When the shoot elongates, the first foliage leaves emerge.

Foliage leaf

Seed coat

Apical hook

Cotyledons

Primary root

Secondary roots

Figure 35.8 Patterns of Early Shoot Development **(A)** In grasses and some other monocots, growing shoots are protected by a coleoptile until they reach the soil surface. **(B)** In most eudicots, the growing point of the shoot is protected within the cotyledons.

 View in Achieve
Activity 35.1 Monocot Shoot Development

 View in Achieve
Activity 35.2 Eudicot Shoot Development

KEY CONCEPT
35.1 Recap and Assess

Plants grow and produce new organs throughout their lives, a feature that allows them to acclimate to changing environmental conditions. Cell expansion occurs when the internal pressure of the cell leads to structural changes in the wall that reduce that pressure, allowing more water to enter. Cells differentiate into distinct cell types largely as a result of changes in gene expression. Early embryonic development in many plants occurs within seeds, which may remain dormant for a long period. Water uptake (imbibition) and germination occur when external cues in the environment are present.

1. Describe how cell expansion occurs in the context of the stress–relaxation cycle.

2. Explain how the activity of a transcription factor can determine cell type. What is it that the transcription factor does?

3. Under what conditions would it be advantageous for a species to have seed dormancy broken by fire?

4. How would a genetic screen be used to identify a plant gene involved in seed dormancy?

You have now seen the early stages of plant growth and development, and how the environment influences these processes. We turn now to the subject of plant hormones, which are central to the internal regulation of development.

KEY CONCEPT
35.2 Gibberellins and Auxin Have Diverse Effects but a Generally Similar Mechanism of Action

Learning Objectives

35.2.1 Provide evidence for the role of gibberellins in various plant growth processes.

35.2.2 Provide evidence for the role of auxin in plant growth and development.

35.2.3 Explain the mechanisms that result in shoots growing toward the light.

Hormones are chemical signals that act at very low concentrations at target sites often distant from where they are produced. Most plant hormones differ from their counterparts in animals in that each plant hormone plays multiple regulatory roles (**Table 35.1**). Several plant hormones regulate the growth and development of plants from seedling to adult (**Table 35.2**). Other hormones (for example, jasmonic acid and salicylic acid) are involved in plant defenses against herbivores and microorganisms, as we will discuss in Chapter 37.

Early in the twentieth century, two plant hormones were discovered: **gibberellins** (there are several active forms) and **auxin** (there are several forms, but one predominates). Initially, the discoveries came from observations of natural phenomena:

• *Gibberellins*: In rice plants, a disease caused by the fungus *Gibberella fujikuroi* resulted in plants that grew overly tall and spindly.

TABLE **35.1**	Comparison of Plant and Animal Hormones	
Characteristic	**Plant hormones**	**Animal hormones**
Size, chemistry	Peptides, small organic molecules	Peptides, proteins, small molecules
Site of synthesis	Usually at many locations	Specialized glands or cells
Site of action	Local or distant	Usually distant, transported
Effects	Often diverse	Often specific
Regulation	By biochemical feedback	By central nervous system, ions, or feedback

TABLE 35.2 | Plant Growth Hormones

Hormone	Structure	Typical activities
Abscisic acid*		Maintains seed dormancy; closes stomata; can affect growth of the root system
Auxins (mainly indole-3-acetic acid)		Promote stem elongation, adventitious and lateral root initiation, lateral root emergence, xylem formation, and fruit growth; inhibit axillary bud outgrowth, leaf abscission, and root elongation
Brassinosteroids		Promote growth, stem and pollen tube elongation, tolerance to some stresses; affect light-regulated seedling growth and act as an important component in cross-talk with many other hormones
Cytokinins		Inhibit leaf senescence; promote cell division and axillary bud outgrowth; affect root growth
Ethylene		Promotes fruit ripening, leaf abscission, and senescence; inhibits stem elongation and gravitropism
Gibberellins (e.g., gibberellic acid)		Promote seed germination, stem growth, and ovule and fruit development; break winter dormancy; mobilize nutrient reserves in grass seeds

*See Chapter 36.

- *Auxin*: Biologists (including Charles and Francis Darwin) and indoor gardeners noted that seedlings would bend toward the light when placed near a light source.

A chemical substance was then isolated that could cause each phenomenon:

- Gibberellic acid (see Table 35.2) made by the *G. fujikuroi* fungus caused rice plants to overgrow. In addition, the short (dwarf) pea plants that Gregor Mendel worked with during his groundbreaking discoveries on the nature of inheritance (see Chapter 12) were found to carry a loss-of-function mutation in a gene that encodes an enzyme involved in gibberellin biosynthesis (**Figure 35.9A**). Wild-type plants that do not have this mutation make more gibberellin and grow taller.

- Indole-3-acetic acid (auxin, see Table 35.2) applied asymmetrically to the growing tips of seedlings caused cell elongation

on the side away from the light, which resulted in the shoot bending toward the light. Furthermore, the appearance of mutant plants that do not make auxin could be restored to that of wild-type plants by adding auxin. *Arabidopsis thaliana* plants that do not make auxin are short (and have smaller leaves and other defects); supplying them with auxin reverses those characteristics and restores a wild-type appearance (**Figure 35.9B**).

Note that the phenotype involved—short stature, or dwarfism—is similar in both mutant plants even though different hormones are involved.

The approaches we have outlined—observation, hormone isolation, hormone treatment, and analysis of mutant plants—are just some of the methods used to identify plant hormones and understand their roles in plant development. Plant biologists have also studied hormones using chemical inhibitors and using

(A) Effect of gibberellin

(B) Treatment with auxin

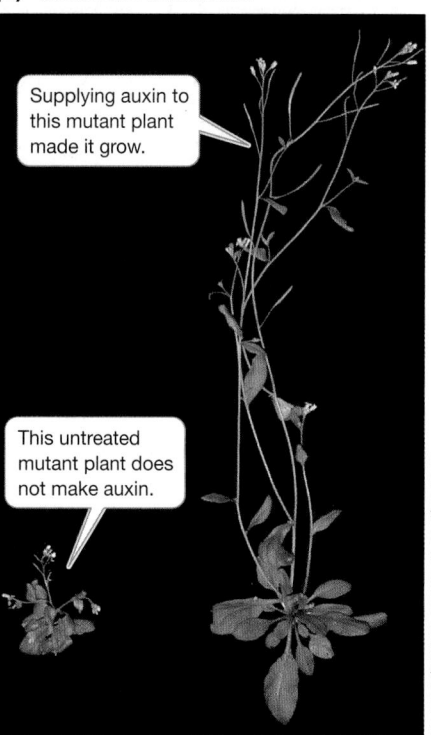

Figure 35.9 Hormones Reverse a Mutant Phenotype **(A)** The short (dwarf, left) pea plants that Mendel studied are now thought to have arisen because of a loss-of-function mutation in a gene that encodes an enzyme involved in gibberellin synthesis. **(B)** The short phenotype of this *Arabidopsis thaliana* mutant was reversed in the plant on the right by supplying auxin.

plant transformation experiments that alter hormone levels or the plants' responses to hormones.

Gibberellins have many effects on plant growth and development

The functions of gibberellins can be inferred from the effects of experimentally decreasing gibberellins or blocking their action at various points in plant development. Such experiments reveal that gibberellins have multiple roles in regulating plant growth.

STEM ELONGATION   The effects of gibberellins on wild-type plants are not as dramatic as those seen on dwarf plants. However, gibberellins are indeed active in wild-type plants, because inhibitors of gibberellin synthesis cause a reduction in stem elongation. Such inhibitors can be put to practical uses. For example, plants such as chrysanthemums that are grown in greenhouses tend to get tall, but leggy plants do not appeal to consumers. Flower growers spray such plants with gibberellin synthesis inhibitors to control their height. Some wheat crops are similarly sprayed to keep them short, so they do not fall over when they produce grain; the result is chemically produced semi-dwarfs similar to the genetically produced varieties described in the opening story of this chapter. In some plants, such as cabbage, the normal growth habit is to be a squat, leafy head near the ground. When environmental

signals are right, however, the plant "bolts," quickly producing a tall stem with flowers—a response that can be mediated by gibberellins.

FRUIT GROWTH   Gibberellins and other hormones regulate the growth of fruits. Grapevines that produce seedless grapes develop smaller fruits than varieties that produce seed-bearing grapes. Biologists wanting to explain this phenomenon removed seeds from immature seeded grapes and found that this prevented normal fruit growth, suggesting that the seeds are sources of a growth regulator. Biochemical studies showed that developing seeds produce gibberellins, which diffuse into the immature fruit tissue. Spraying young seedless grapes with a gibberellin solution causes them to grow as large as seeded ones, and this is now a standard commercial practice (**Figure 35.10**).

MOBILIZATION OF SEED RESERVES   Early in seed germination, hydrolytic enzymes are produced to break down stored reserves of starch, proteins, and lipids. Just after imbibition in germinating seeds of barley and other cereals, the embryo secretes gibberellins. The hormones diffuse through the endosperm to a surrounding tissue called the **aleurone layer**, which lies underneath the seed coat. The gibberellins trigger a cascade of events in the aleurone layer, causing it to synthesize and secrete enzymes that hydrolyze proteins and starch stored in the endosperm (**Figure 35.11**).

Figure 35.10 Gibberellins and Fruit Growth   Spraying developing seedless grapes with gibberellins (right) increases their size compared with untreated fruit (left).

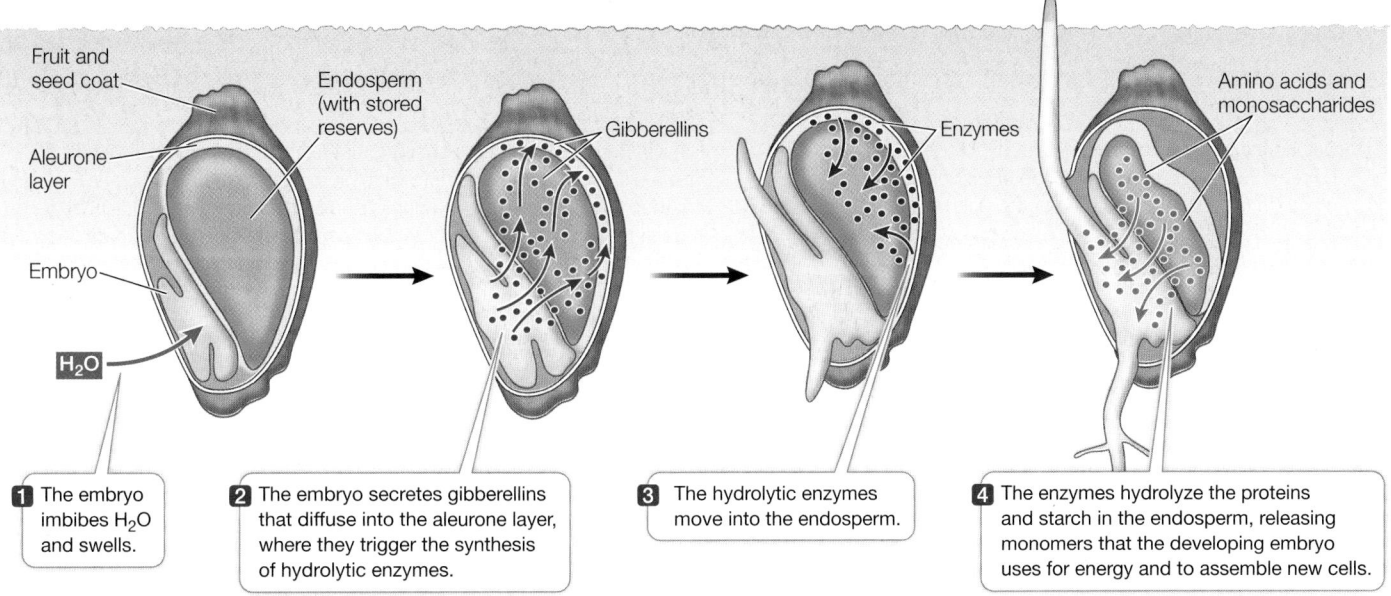

1 The embryo imbibes H_2O and swells.

2 The embryo secretes gibberellins that diffuse into the aleurone layer, where they trigger the synthesis of hydrolytic enzymes.

3 The hydrolytic enzymes move into the endosperm.

4 The enzymes hydrolyze the proteins and starch in the endosperm, releasing monomers that the developing embryo uses for energy and to assemble new cells.

Figure 35.11 Embryos Mobilize Their Reserves   During seed germination in cereal grasses, gibberellins trigger a cascade of events that result in the conversion of starch and protein reserves into monomers that can be used by the developing embryo.

Q: In brewing beer, stored starch in barley seeds is converted to maltose. How do you think this is done in the brewery?

▶ **View in Achieve**
Activity 35.3 Events of Seed Germination

These observations have practical importance: in the beer brewing industry, gibberellins are used to enhance the "malting" (germination) of barley and the breakdown of its endosperm, producing sugar that is fermented to alcohol.

Another hormone, abscisic acid (ABA) (see Table 35.2) plays an antagonistic role with gibberellins in seed dormancy and germination. ABA levels are high in dormant seeds and fall off during germination. Thus ABA plays a role in maintaining seed dormancy, whereas gibberellins function to break dormancy and promote germination.

Auxin plays a role in differential plant growth

Auxin was first discovered for its role in the bending of plants toward light. Subsequent research has shown that auxin is involved in many other aspects of plant growth and development.

IDENTIFYING AUXIN AND ITS TRANSPORT   Auxin (from the Greek "to increase") was discovered in the context of **phototropism**: a response to light in which plant stems bend toward a light source. This was a familiar observation by biologists and home gardeners when the ever-curious Charles Darwin and his son Francis investigated this phenomenon and concluded that a signal was made in the shoot apex and diffused down the shoot in a polar (unidirectional) fashion, stimulating cell elongation.

▶ **View in Achieve**
Animation 35.1 Tropisms

The Darwins worked with canarygrass (*Phalaris canariensis*) seedlings grown in the dark. While underground, a young grass seedling is protected by a coleoptile (see Figure 35.8). The coleoptiles of grasses are phototropic—they grow toward the

light (**Figure 35.12**). To find the light-receptive region of the coleoptile, the Darwins "blindfolded" the coleoptiles of dark-grown canarygrass seedlings in various places and then illuminated them from one side (**Investigating Life: The Darwins' Phototropism Experiment**). The coleoptile grew toward the light whenever its tip was exposed. If the top millimeter or more of the coleoptile was covered, however, the coleoptile showed no phototropic response. The Darwins concluded that the tip contains the photoreceptor that responds to light. The actual bending toward the light, however, takes place in a growing region a few millimeters below the tip. Therefore, the Darwins reasoned, *some type of signal must travel from the tip of the coleoptile to the growing region.*

Light

Figure 35.12 Phototropism   Plants grow toward the light by elongating more on the side away from the light, and less on the side toward to the light. This difference in elongation generates a curve.

▶Investigating LIFE   The Darwins' Phototropism Experiment

Experiment

Original Paper: C. R. Darwin assisted by F. Darwin. 1880. *The Power of Movement in Plants*. Chapter IX: Sensitiveness of plants to light: Its transmitted effects. John Murray: London.

Charles Darwin and his son Francis wanted to know how plants bend toward the light. They grew canarygrass seedlings (coleoptiles) in the dark. To discover what part of the coleoptile responds to light, they covered up ("blindfolded") different regions of each coleoptile and then exposed the seedlings to light from one side. The Darwins discovered that the tip of the seedling senses the light and that growth occurs below the tip. Their observations led them to hypothesize the existence of a growth-promoting signal produced by the coleoptile tip.

HYPOTHESIS▶   Only part of the coleoptile senses the light that triggers phototropism.

METHOD▶

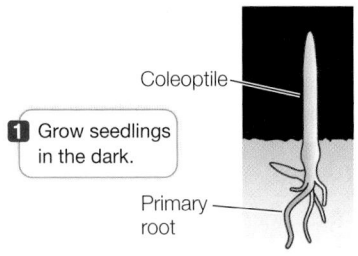

Coleoptile

1 Grow seedlings in the dark.

Primary root

2 "Blindfold" the seedlings in different places and expose to light on one side.

Blindfold

Light

RESULTS▶

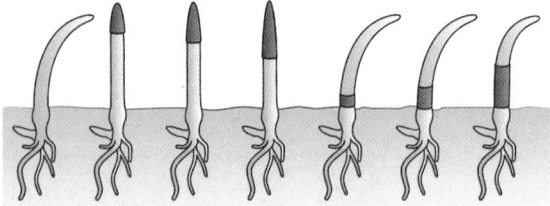

Coleoptiles responded to light only when the tip was exposed.

CONCLUSION▶   The coleoptile tip senses light and then transmits a growth signal to the tissue away from the light source.

Work with the Data

Fascinated by experiments showing that light induces plants to bend toward it and that this is due to increased growth on the "dark side" of the stem, Charles Darwin and his son Francis performed additional experiments on canarygrass (*Phalaris canariensis*) seedlings grown in the dark to learn more about how the seed germinates in the soil. Their conclusion that the light-sensing mechanism might reside in the coleoptile was validated when they repeated their experiments with the coleoptile tip cut off: bending did not occur. Because it was possible that the cut plants did not bend because they had been irreversibly damaged in some way, the Darwins repeated their initial experiment with undamaged seedlings whose coleoptile tips had been covered with a thin glass tube cap that was blacked out with India ink. In this case the plants did not bend. The Darwins' conclusion that the tip of the coloptile senses the light and transmits a message to tissue below the tip to grow was initially controversial but ultimately led to the identification of auxin, the first plant growth hormone.

QUESTIONS▶

1. The figure shows a drawing by the Darwins of the bending of coleoptiles after 8 hours of light exposure. From which direction was the light shone?

Fig. 181

2. The Darwins reported:

   "Seven cotyledons [Note: The Darwins used the term "cotyledon" for what is now called a coleoptile.] had their tips cut off for lengths varying between 0.1 and 0.16 of an inch, and these, when left exposed all day to a lateral light, remained upright. In another set of 7 cotyledons, the tips were cut off for a length of only about 0.05 of an inch (1.27 mm) and these became bowed towards a lateral light, but not nearly so much as the many other seedlings in the same pots."

   What do these data indicate about the possible role of the tip and about the possibility that injury in cutting blocks the bending response?

3. The Darwins described their further experiments:

   "The summits of nine cotyledons, differing somewhat in height, were enclosed for rather less than half their lengths in uncoloured or transparent tubes; and these were then exposed before a south-west window on a bright day for 8 h. All of them became strongly curved towards the light, in the same degree as the many other free seedlings in the same pots; so that the glass-tubes certainly did not prevent the cotyledons from bending towards the light. Nineteen other cotyledons were, at the same time, similarly enclosed in tubes thickly painted with Indian ink. On five of them, the paint, to our surprise, contracted after exposure to the sunlight, and very narrow cracks were formed, through which a little light entered; and these five cases were rejected. Of the remaining 14 cotyledons, the lower halves of which had been fully exposed to the light for the whole time, 7 continued quite straight and upright; 1 was considerably bowed to the light, and 6 were slightly bowed, but with the exposed bases of most of them almost or quite straight."

   What do these data indicate about the role of the tip? Can you explain why there was slight bending in six of the coleoptiles that were covered with painted tubes?

   Go to **Achieve** for a companion Data in Depth exercise.

Others showed that placing the coleoptile tip (the source of the growth signal) on a decapitated coleoptile led to bending, even when a block of gelatin separated the tip and coleoptile:

| Tip removed | Gelatin between tip and coleoptile stump | Normal phototropic curvature remains possible |

In these experiments, the soluble growth signal moved from the coleoptile tip into the gelatin and then down into the decapitated coleoptile; later the growth signal was isolated from such gelatin blocks and identified as indole-3-acetic acid (see Table 35.2), the major form of auxin.

 View in Achieve
Animation 35.2 Went's Experiment

MECHANISM OF AUXIN TRANSPORT   The movement of auxin down a coleoptile is an example of polar (directional) transport. Polar transport of auxin (**Figure 35.13**) depends on four biochemical processes:

1. *Diffusion across a cell membrane.* Polar molecules (in the chemical sense) diffuse across cell membranes less readily than nonpolar molecules (see Key Concept 6.3).

2. *Membrane protein asymmetry.* Some proteins that transport auxin are located in specific portions of the cell membrane (see Key Concept 6.4 for a discussion of transport proteins). In the stem, most of the transport proteins that allow auxin to efflux (move out of the cell) are located at the basal (bottom) end of the cell.

3. *Proton pumping/chemiosmosis.* A proton pump (see Figure 33.4) moves H^+ from the cytoplasm to the cell wall, thereby increasing the intracellular pH and decreasing the pH in the cell wall. Proton pumping also sets up an electrochemical gradient (see Key Concept 9.3), which provides potential energy to drive the transport of auxin by the carriers just mentioned.

4. *Ionization of a weak acid.* The main form of auxin, indole-3-acetic acid, is a weak acid (see Key Concept 2.4):

$$A^- + H^+ \rightleftharpoons HA$$

When the pH is low, this reaction is driven to the right, and HA (non-ionized auxin) is the predominant form. When the pH is higher, there is more A^- (ionized auxin).

The polar auxin transporters are distributed such that the hormone predominately moves down along the *longitudinal* (up and down) axis of the shoot. However, *lateral* (side-to-side) redistribution of auxin occurs and is responsible for directional plant

1 Auxin enters the cell by passive diffusion as an uncharged acid or through auxin import proteins (AUX/LAX), symported with H^+.

2 Proton pumps in the cell membrane maintain the cell wall at an acidic pH and set up a chemiosmotic gradient to drive the transport of auxin.

3 Auxin$^-$ predominates in the cytosol, which has a neutral pH.

4 Auxin$^-$ exits the cell via auxin anion efflux carriers (PIN) that are concentrated at the basal end of each cell.

5 In the cell wall, the lower pH causes auxin$^-$ to become auxin, which can diffuse into the next cell or enter through an auxin-H^+ symporter.

Figure 35.13 Polar Transport of Auxin   Proton pumps set up a chemiosmotic gradient directing ionized auxin (A^-) toward the basally placed active transport carriers for auxin, which leads to a net movement of auxin in a basal direction.

growth. This was shown in early experiments that followed the Darwins' when a coleoptile tip containing the growth hormone was placed asymmetrically on the decapitated coleoptile. The asymmetrical distribution of growth hormone down the coleoptile resulted in excess growth on that side, and bending away from it, even in the absence of light:

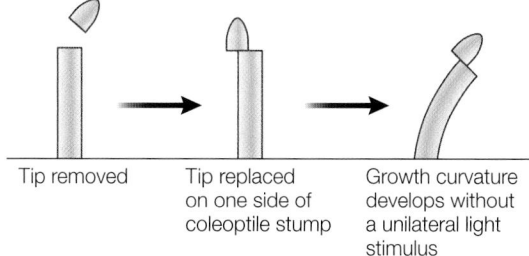

| Tip removed | Tip replaced on one side of coleoptile stump | Growth curvature develops without a unilateral light stimulus |

Movement of auxin to the shaded side of the plant could be explained if auxin transporters on the lit side relocate within cells such that auxin exits the cells laterally (sideways, toward the shaded side). There is evidence that supports this hypothesis.

This lateral movement of auxin explains the bending of canarygrass seedlings toward light that the Darwins observed. When light strikes a canarygrass coleoptile on one side, auxin at the tip moves laterally toward the shaded side. The asymmetry is maintained as auxin moves down the coleoptile, so that in the growing region below, the auxin concentration is highest on the

(A) Phototropism

1 Auxin moves to the shaded side within the tip.

2 The redistributed auxin moves down the coleoptile.

3 A higher auxin concentration causes more rapid growth by cell expansion on the shaded side. The tip curves toward the light.

Light

Coleoptile

Auxin

The cells on the shaded side expand more than those on the other side.

(B) Negative gravitropism of shoot

1 Auxin is preferentially transported from the tip to the lower side of the shoot in response to gravity.

2 A higher auxin concentration causes more rapid growth on the lower side. The tip curves upward.

Figure 35.14 Plants Respond to Light and Gravity Phototropism (**A**) and gravitropism (**B**) occur in shoot apices in response to a redistribution of auxin.

shaded side. Cell elongation is thus stimulated on the shaded side, causing the coleoptile to grow toward the light (**Figure 35.14A**).

Light is not the only signal that can cause the redistribution of auxin. Auxin moves to the lower side of a shoot that has been tipped sideways, causing more rapid growth in the lower side and hence an upward bending of the shoot. Such growth in a direction determined by gravity is called **gravitropism** (**Figure 35.14B**). The upward gravitropic response of shoots is defined as negative gravitropism; that of roots, which bend downward, is positive gravitropism. Gravitropism in roots also involves differential growth caused by lateral movement of auxin, but the details of the mechanism differ between the root and the shoot.

Auxin affects plant growth in several ways

Like the gibberellins, auxin has many roles in plant development. Auxin affects the vegetative and reproductive growth of plants in several ways.

ROOT INITIATION Cuttings from the shoots of some plants can produce roots and develop into entire new plants. For this to occur, parenchyma cells in the interior of the shoot must redifferentiate and form an apical meristem of a new root. These changes are similar to those that take place in the pericycle of a root when a lateral root forms (see Figure 32.12). Shoot cuttings of many species can be made to develop roots by dipping the cut surfaces into an auxin solution. These observations together with data from plants carrying mutations that affect auxin synthesis, auxin receptors, or downstream factors in auxin response pathways support the idea that the plant's own auxin plays a role in the initiation of lateral roots. Commercial preparations that enhance the rooting of plant cuttings typically contain synthetic auxins.

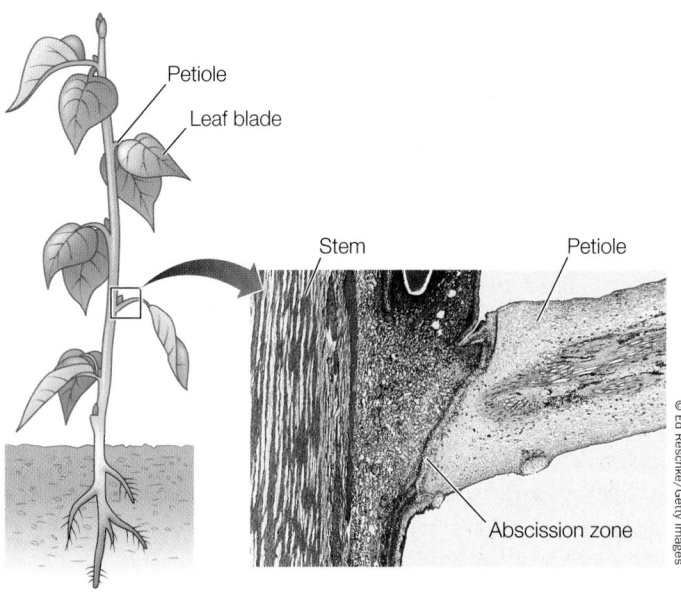

Petiole

Leaf blade

Stem

Petiole

Abscission zone

© Ed Reschke/Getty Images

Figure 35.15 Changes Occur When a Leaf Is about to Fall The breakdown of cells in the abscission zone of the petiole causes the leaf to fall.

LEAF ABSCISSION Auxin inhibits the detachment of old leaves from stems. This detachment process, called **abscission**, is the cause of leaves falling from some trees in the autumn. Many leaves consist of a blade and a petiole that attaches the blade to the stem. Abscission results from the breakdown of a specific part of the petiole, the abscission zone (**Figure 35.15**). If the blade of a leaf is cut off, the petiole falls from the plant more rapidly than if the leaf had remained intact. If the cut surface is treated with an auxin solution, however, the petiole remains attached to the plant, often longer than an intact leaf would have. The timing of leaf abscission in nature appears to be determined in part by a decrease in the movement through the petiole of auxin produced in the blade.

APICAL DOMINANCE   Auxin helps maintain **apical dominance**, a phenomenon in which apical (terminal) buds inhibit the growth of axillary buds (see Figure 32.1), resulting in the growth of a single main stem with minimal branching. Apical dominance can be demonstrated by an experiment with a young seedling. If the plant remains intact, the stem elongates and the axillary buds remain inactive. Removal of the apical bud—the major site of auxin production—results in growth of the axillary buds. If the cut surface of the stem is treated with auxin, however, the axillary buds do not grow. The apical buds of branches also exert apical dominance: the axillary buds on the branch are inactive unless the apex of the branch is removed. That is why gardeners prune shrubs to encourage branching.

FRUIT DEVELOPMENT   Fruit development normally depends on prior fertilization of the ovule (egg), but in many species treatment of an unfertilized ovary with auxin or gibberellins causes **parthenocarpy**—fruit formation without fertilization. Parthenocarpic fruits form spontaneously in some cultivated varieties of plants, including seedless grapes, bananas, and some cucumbers.

CELL EXPANSION   Cell expansion causes plant growth. As discussed in Key Concept 35.1, the cell wall plays a key role in controlling the rate and direction of plant cell growth. Auxin acts on cell walls to regulate this process.

Cell expansion is driven mostly by the uptake of water, which enters the cytoplasm of the cell and accumulates in its central vacuole (**Figure 35.16**). Growth of the vacuole accounts for most of the increase in volume of a growing cell, and the vacuole often makes up more than 90% of the volume of a mature cell. As the vacuole expands, it presses the cytoplasm against the cell wall, and the wall resists this force (the basis of turgor pressure). The cell wall is an extensively cross-linked network of polysaccharides and proteins, dominated by cellulose microfibrils. If the cell is to expand, some adjustments must be made in the wall structure to allow the wall to "give" under turgor pressure. Think of a balloon (the cell surrounded by a membrane) inside a box (the cell wall). How does the cell wall "box" loosen to allow expansion?

The **acid growth hypothesis** explains auxin-induced cell expansion (see Figure 35.16). The hypothesis holds that auxin increases the pumping of protons (H⁺) from the cytoplasm into the cell wall, lowering the pH of the wall and activating enzymes called expansins. Expansins cause polysaccharides in the cell wall to adhere less strongly to the cellulose microfibrils, allowing the microfibrils to slip past one another. Expansins loosen the cell wall, making it easier to stretch as the cell expands. Several lines of evidence support the acid growth hypothesis. For example, adding acid to the cell wall to lower the pH stimulates cell expansion even in the absence of auxin. Conversely, when a buffer is used to prevent the wall from becoming more acidic, auxin-induced cell expansion is blocked. The acid growth hypothesis applies to most species; in some plants, auxin stimulates secretion of new cell wall components quickly enough to account for even rapid changes in growth rate.

Figure 35.16 Auxin Increases Cell Expansion   The plant cell wall is an extensive network of cross-linked polymers. Auxin induces wall loosening by activating a proton pump that reduces pH in the cell wall.

Q: Where else in the plant cell are proton pumps important?

View in Achieve
Animation 35.3 Auxin Affects Cell Walls

Auxin and gibberellins trigger the destruction of specific target proteins

The molecular mechanisms underlying both auxin and gibberellin action have been worked out with the help of genetic screens (see Figure 35.7). Biologists started by identifying mutant plants whose growth and development are insensitive to the hormones—that is, plants that are *not* affected by added hormone. Such mutant plants fall into two general categories:

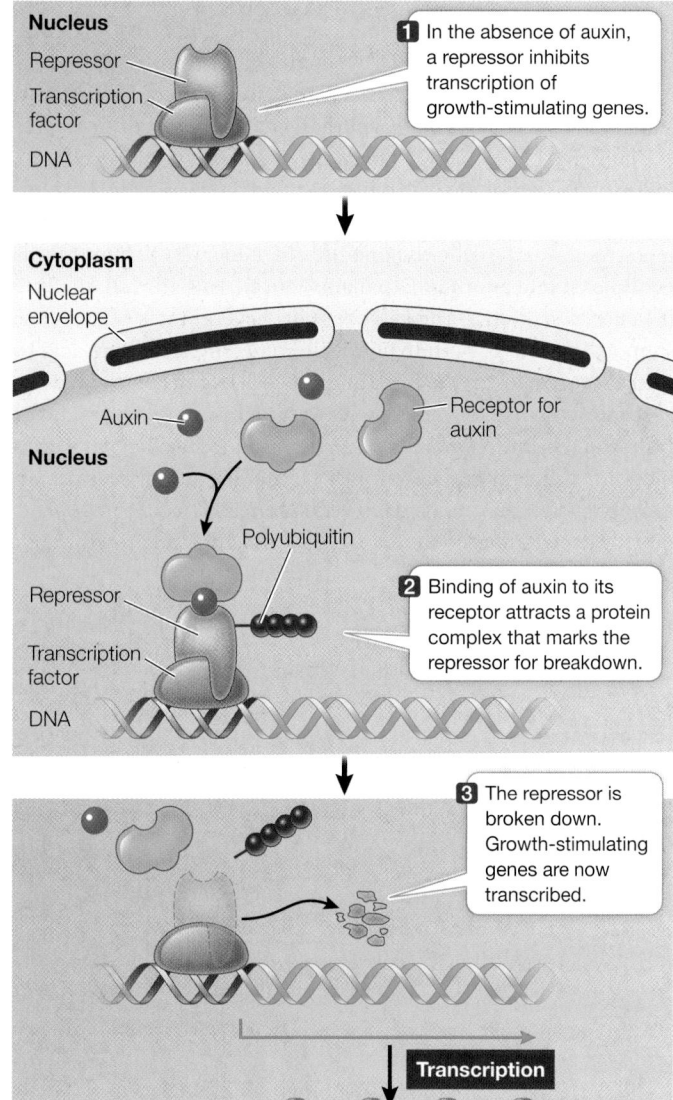

Nucleus
Repressor
Transcription factor
DNA

1 In the absence of auxin, a repressor inhibits transcription of growth-stimulating genes.

Cytoplasm
Nuclear envelope
Auxin
Nucleus
Receptor for auxin
Polyubiquitin
Repressor
Transcription factor
DNA

2 Binding of auxin to its receptor attracts a protein complex that marks the repressor for breakdown.

3 The repressor is broken down. Growth-stimulating genes are now transcribed.

Transcription

mRNA

Figure 35.17 Auxin Causes Proteins to be Marked for Degradation The auxin signal transduction pathway shown here is similar to that of gibberellins in that both hormones affect transcription by causing proteins that regulate transcription to be degraded.

Q: Are the molecules (receptor, repressor, transcription factor, ubiquitin, proteasome) the same or different in auxin versus gibberellin signaling?

Media Clip 35.1 Gibberellin Binding to Its Receptor
Life12e.com/mc35.1

1. *Excessively tall plants.* These plants resemble wild-type plants given an excess of hormone and grow no taller when given extra hormone. They grow tall even when treated with inhibitors of hormone synthesis. Their hormone response is always "on," even in the absence of the hormone. In such cases, it is presumed that the normal allele for the mutant gene codes for an inhibitor of the hormone signal transduction pathway. In wild-type plants that pathway is "off," but in the mutant plants the pathway is "on" and the plant grows tall.

2. *Dwarf plants.* These plants resemble dwarf plants that are deficient in hormone synthesis (see Figure 35.9), but they do not respond to added hormone. In these mutant plants the hormone response is always "off," regardless of the presence of the hormone.

By examining the proteins that were affected by these mutations, the steps leading from hormone receptor to response were worked out (**Figure 35.17**).

Both auxin and gibberellins act by removing a repressor protein (here called a target protein) that affects transcription of some genes. The specific target proteins that are degraded vary between the two hormones. As the concentration of hormone within a cell increases, the hormone promotes formation of a large protein complex that includes the hormone, the hormone receptor, the target protein that will be broken down, and an enzyme complex that adds a label (polyubiquitin) to the target protein. Addition of polyubiquitin to a target protein results in the marked protein being broken down in the proteasome (see Figure 16.24). The part of this complex that recognizes (binds to) the target protein is called an F-box protein. Whereas animal genomes have few F-box-containing proteins, plant genomes have hundreds, an indication that this type of gene regulation is common in plants.

KEY CONCEPT
35.2 Recap and Assess

Gibberellins are plant hormones that affect stem growth, fruit size, seed germination, and many other aspects of plant development; the effects vary from species to species. Auxin regulates cell expansion and thus mediates phototropism and gravitropism; it also plays roles in apical dominance, leaf abscission, fruit development, and root initiation. The molecular mechanisms by which gibberellins and auxin convey their effects on plants are similar: both hormones affect gene transcription by causing specific proteins that regulate transcription to be degraded.

1. What would the result be, in terms of the synthesis of hydrolytic enzymes, if germinating barley seeds were treated with an inhibitor of mRNA translation? What would the result be if the seeds were treated with an inhibitor of proteasome function? What would the result be if the two inhibitors were applied to coleoptiles treated with auxin?

2. Explain why, even though auxin moves away from the lighted side of a coleoptile tip, the coleoptile grows toward the light.

3. Corn stunt spiroplasma (a bacterium) causes a significant reduction in the growth rate of infected corn plants. Diseased plants take on a dwarfed form. Since their appearance is reminiscent of a genetically dwarfed corn, you suspect that the bacterium may inhibit the synthesis of gibberellins by corn plants. Describe two experiments you might conduct to test this hypothesis, only one of which requires chemical measurement.

As you have seen, auxin and gibberellin can lead to the degradation of transcriptional regulators, with the specific proteins that are degraded varying depending on the type of cell. Thus a single hormone can have many different effects. In the next key concept, you will learn about other important plant hormones that also have multiple effects.

KEY CONCEPT 35.3 Other Plant Hormones Have Diverse Effects

Learning Objectives

35.3.1 Use information on the functions of cytokinins to predict how different aspects of plant growth will be affected by cytokinins and by various combinations of cytokinins and auxin.

35.3.2 Describe the function of ethylene in fruit ripening, and explain its importance in the cut-flower and food-production industries.

35.3.3 Identify some effects of brassinosteroids on plant growth.

The discoveries of gibberellins and auxin led to the isolation of additional classes of plant hormones (see Table 35.2). These hormones have multiple effects, and in many cases they interact with one another.

Cytokinins are active from seed to senescence

Like bacteria and yeasts, plant cells such as parenchyma cells can be grown in a liquid or solidified growth medium containing sugars and salts. The cells will divide continuously until they run out of nutrients. In the early days of plant cell culturing, scientists experimented with many supplements to determine the optimal chemical environment for growth. The best supplement was coconut milk, the fluid that surrounds the developing embryo in coconut fruit. Investigators suspected that a molecule in the fluid must stimulate plant cell division.

A clue to the identity of the molecule came when Folke Skoog at the University of Wisconsin tested various pure substances that might substitute for coconut milk. DNA was among the substances tested, and it did not work; however, heating DNA at high pressure in an autoclave produced a mixture that strongly promoted plant cell division. A derivative of adenine called kinetin was identified as the active ingredient. Because it stimulated cell division (cytokinesis), it was called a **cytokinin**.

Kinetin does not exist in cells, but it gave scientists a hint as to what type of molecule might be the active ingredient in coconut milk. An adenine derivative called **zeatin** was extracted from corn endosperm, and since then more than 150 different cytokinins have been isolated, and most are derivatives of adenine.

Cytokinins (see Table 35.2) have several different effects, in many cases interacting with auxin:

- Adding an appropriate combination of auxin and cytokinins to a growth medium induces rapid proliferation of cultured plant cells.

- Cytokinins can cause certain light-requiring seeds to germinate even when kept in constant darkness.

- In plant cell cultures, a high cytokinin-to-auxin ratio promotes the formation of shoots; a low ratio promotes the formation of roots.

- Cytokinins usually inhibit the elongation of stems, but they cause lateral swelling of stems and roots (the fleshy roots of radishes are an extreme example).

- Cytokinins stimulate axillary buds to grow into branches; the auxin-to-cytokinin ratio controls the extent of branching (bushiness) of a plant. A lower ratio promotes more branching.

- Cytokinins delay the senescence of leaves. If leaf blades are detached from a plant and placed in water or a nutrient solution, they quickly turn yellow and show other signs of senescence. If instead they are placed in a solution containing a cytokinin, they remain green and senesce much more slowly. Roots contain abundant cytokinins, and cytokinin transport to the leaves delays senescence (**Figure 35.18**).

Ethylene is a gaseous hormone that hastens leaf senescence and fruit ripening

Whereas the cytokinins delay senescence, another plant hormone promotes it: the gas **ethylene** (see Table 35.2), which is sometimes called the senescence hormone. Ethylene can be produced by all parts of the plant, and like all plant hormones, it has several effects.

Back when streets were lit by gas rather than by electricity, leaves on trees near street lamps dropped earlier than those on trees farther from the lamps. We now know why: ethylene, a combustion product of the illuminating gas, caused the early abscission. Whereas auxin delays leaf abscission, ethylene strongly promotes it; thus the balance of auxin and ethylene controls abscission.

FRUIT RIPENING   By promoting senescence, ethylene also speeds the ripening of fruit. As a fruit ripens, it loses chlorophyll and its cell walls break down; ethylene promotes both of these processes. Ethylene also causes an increase in its own production. Thus once ripening begins, more and more ethylene forms, and because it is a gas, it diffuses readily throughout the fruit and even to neighboring fruits on the same or other plants. The old saying "one rotten apple spoils the barrel" is true. That rotten apple is a rich source of ethylene, which speeds the ripening and subsequent rotting of the other fruit in a barrel or other confined space.

This leaf was not treated.

This leaf was treated with cytokinin, which delays senescence.

Figure 35.18 Cytokinin Delays Leaf Senescence

(A) Fruit ripening

These tomatoes were not treated with ethylene.

These stored tomatoes were treated with ethylene to promote ripening.

Photo by Adel A. Kader © 1997 Regents of the University of California. Used by permission

(B) Apical hook formation

Apical hook

Figure 35.19 Ethylene Promotes Fruit Ripening and Formation of an Apical Hook (A) Tomato fruits ripen when gassed with ethylene. (B) Formation of an apical hook gives a seedling a firm structure that can push up through the soil. The hook opens after the seedling reaches the surface of the soil.

Farmers used to poke holes in developing figs to make them ripen faster. We now know that wounding causes an increase in ethylene production by the fruit, and that the raised ethylene level promotes ripening in many fruits, including apples, bananas, melons, apricots, and tomatoes (**Figure 35.19A**). Today commercial shippers and storers of such fruit hasten ripening by adding ethylene to storage chambers. This use of ethylene is the single most important use of a natural plant hormone in agriculture and commerce. Ripening can also be delayed by the use of "scrubbers" and adsorbents that remove ethylene from the atmosphere in fruit storage chambers.

As flowers senesce, their petals may abscise, decreasing their value in the cut-flower industry. Growers and florists often immerse the cut stems of ethylene-sensitive flowers in dilute solutions of silver thiosulfate before sale. Silver salts inhibit ethylene action by interacting directly with the ethylene receptor—thus they delay senescence, keeping flowers "fresh" for longer. An alternative product, used to delay fruit ripening and preserve cut flowers, is 1-methylcyclopropene, a gas that also binds to ethylene receptors and blocks their function.

STEM GROWTH   Ethylene is active at other stages of plant development as well. In some species, including deepwater rice, higher concentrations of ethylene build up around the stems of plants that are submerged in water, promoting rapid elongation of those stems. Increased levels of ethylene may arise because the rate of diffusion of this gas is slower in water than in air, because of changes in the rate of ethylene synthesis, or a combination of the two.

The effects of ethylene on seedling development illustrate the interactions that occur among plant hormones. The hypocotyl of many eudicot seedlings forms an **apical hook** that protects the delicate shoot apex while the stem grows through the soil (**Figure 35.19B**). As in phototropic and gravitropic responses, the apical hook is maintained through an auxin gradient, which promotes the elongation of cells on the outer surface of the hook. Once the

seedling breaks through the soil surface and is exposed to light, the auxin level on the inside of the hook increases and the hook unfolds, raising the shoot apex and the expanding leaves into the sunlight.

There is evidence that ethylene controls the formation of the auxin gradient during seedling development. Treatment of dark-grown seedlings of some species with ethylene results in what is called the "triple response": an exaggeration of the apical hook and a thickening and shortening of the hypocotyl and root (this response was exploited in a genetic screen for ethylene-response mutant plants; see Figure 35.7). It has been shown that ethylene affects both auxin synthesis and transport during apical hook development.

Brassinosteroids are plant steroid hormones

In animals, steroid hormones such as cortisol and estrogen are formed from cholesterol (see Figure 39.2B). Initially, biologists isolated a plant steroid hormone from the pollen of rape, a member of the Brassicaceae (mustard family). When applied to various plant tissues, this **brassinosteroid** (see Table 35.2) stimulated cell elongation, pollen tube elongation, and vascular tissue differentiation, but it inhibited root elongation. Since then, dozens of chemically related, growth-affecting brassinosteroids have been found in most plants.

Mutant plants that either do not make brassinosteroids or have defects in brassinosteroid reception and signal transduction are usually dwarf, infertile, and slow to develop (**Figure 35.20**). These effects can be reversed by adding small amounts of brassinosteroids, indicating that brassinosteroids are true hormones. These hormones have diverse effects, which vary among plants. Brassinosteroids can:

- promote xylem differentiation.
- promote growth of pollen tubes during reproduction.
- promote seed germination.
- promote apical dominance and leaf senescence.
- enhance cell elongation and cell division in shoots.

The signaling pathway for these plant steroids differs sharply from those for steroid hormones in animals. In animals, steroids diffuse through the cell membrane and bind to receptors in the cytoplasm. In contrast, the receptor for brassinosteroids is an integral protein in the cell membrane.

Mutant

Wild type

A defect in the brassinosteroid signaling pathway results in stunted growth of this *Arabidopsis thaliana* mutant.

Courtesy of Eugenia Russinova, VIB Department of Plant Systems Biology, Ghent University, Belgium

Figure 35.20 Brassinosteroids Promote Growth

35.3 Recap and Assess

Cytokinins, ethylene, and brassinosteroids are hormones that work in concert with auxin and gibberellins to mediate plant development. They have various effects on different plants, ranging from stem growth to fruit ripening. They also interact in their effects with other hormones. Ethylene is remarkable in that it is a gas.

1. A plant has an extremely bushy growth habit. What can you say about the likely auxin-to-cytokinin ratio in this plant?

2. Some supermarkets sell plastic bags that are impregnated with activated charcoal, which binds gases. The bags are designed to keep fruit fresh. How do they work?

3. A plant shows rapid leaf senescence. Which hormone or hormones are most likely active in this plant? Which are most likely inactive?

A plant's response to light—the energy source for photosynthesis—is crucial to its survival. You saw how the Darwins' pioneering investigations of phototropism led to the discovery of auxin. Let's now look more closely at how plants sense and respond to light.

KEY CONCEPT
35.4 Photoreceptors Initiate Developmental Responses to Light

Learning Objectives

35.4.1 Describe and evaluate evidence for the existence of blue-light receptors in plants.

35.4.2 Explain the process and conditions under which conversion of the P_r and P_{fr} forms of phytochrome occur.

35.4.3 Explain how a photoreceptor works by describing which part interacts with light and how that interaction leads to a change in cell signaling.

Light is possibly the most important of the many environmental cues to which plants respond. Much has been learned about the receptors that plants use to sense light, and we focus on those receptors here.

What are plant photoreceptors?

Plants respond to two aspects of light: (1) its *quality*—that is, the wavelengths of light that can be absorbed by molecules in the plant; and (2) its *quantity*—that is, the intensity and duration of light exposure.

In Chapter 10 you learned about the role of light in photosynthesis: how chlorophyll and other pigments absorb light at certain wavelengths (quality), and how light intensity affects photosynthetic rate (quantity). Here we discuss how light affects plant development. Earlier in this chapter we described phototropism and how auxin mediates a plant stem's bending toward light. In addition to phototropism, light influences seed germination, shoot elongation, the initiation of flowering, and many other important aspects of plant development. Several photoreceptors take part in these processes. **Blue-light receptors** such as cryptochromes and

phototropins mediate the effects of higher-intensity blue light, and phytochrome mediates the effects of red light.

Phototropins and cryptochromes are blue-light receptors

Charles and Francis Darwin showed that the apical tip of a growing coleoptile receives light as a signal and then redistributes auxin to stimulate cell elongation below the tip on the shaded side. You may recall from Chapter 10 that an action spectrum involves exposing plants to different wavelengths of light to determine which wavelengths are most effective in driving a given process (e.g., photosynthesis). For photosynthesis, such studies showed that the most effective wavelengths are those absorbed by chlorophylls (see Figure 10.5). When an action spectrum was obtained for phototropism of coleoptiles, blue light (peak 436 nanometers [nm]) was found to be the most effective at inducing the coleoptile to curve (**Figure 35.21**). What is the blue-light-absorbing receptor/pigment? Biologists have used a genetic approach to answer this question, once again employing the model plant *Arabidopsis thaliana*.

Researchers recovered blue-light-insensitive mutant *A. thaliana* plants from a genetic screen and identified the gene for a blue-light receptor protein located in the cell membrane called **phototropin**. Phototropin protein has a flavin mononucleotide

(A) Absorption spectrum of phototropin

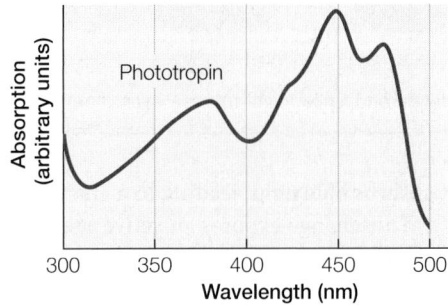

(B) Action spectrum for phototropism

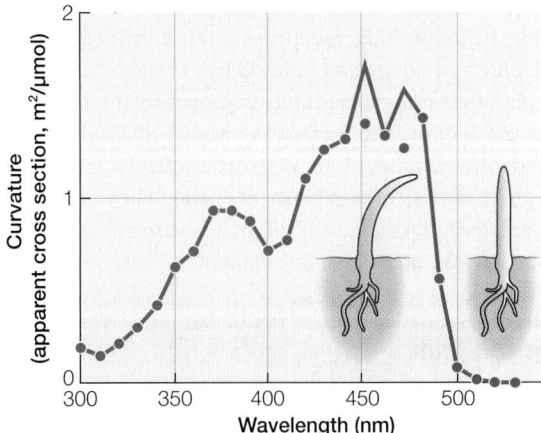

Figure 35.21 Action Spectrum for Phototropism The absorption spectrum for phototropin (**A**) is similar to the action spectrum for the bending of a coleoptile toward light (**B**). Maximum bending occurs when coleoptiles are exposed to blue light. (A after W. R. Briggs and J. M. Christie. 2002. *Trends Plant Sci* 7: 204–210; B after T. Baskin and M. Iino. 1987. *Photochem Photobiol* 46: 127–136.)

Experiment

Figure 35.22A   Sensitivity of Seeds to Red and Far-Red Light

Original Paper: H. A. Borthwick et al. 1952. A reversible photoreaction controlling seed germination. *Proc Natl Acad Sci USA* 38: 662–666.

Lettuce seeds will germinate if exposed to a brief period of light. An action spectrum indicated that red light was most effective in promoting germination, but far-red light would reverse the stimulation if presented right after the red light flash. Harry Borthwick and his colleagues asked what would be the effect of repeated alternating flashes of red and far-red light. In each case, the final exposure determined the germination response. This observation led to the conclusion that a single, photoreversible molecule was involved. That molecule turned out to be phytochrome.

HYPOTHESIS▶   The effects of red and far-red light on lettuce seed germination are mutually reversible.

METHOD▶

Expose lettuce seeds to alternate periods of red light **R** for 1 minute and far-red light **FR** for 4 minutes.

RESULTS▶

Most germinate   Few germinate   Most germinate   Few germinate

CONCLUSION▶   Red light and far-red light reverse each other's effects.

associated with it that absorbs blue light, leading to a change in the shape of the protein. This change exposes an active site for a protein kinase, which in turn initiates a signal transduction cascade that ultimately results in the stimulation of cell elongation by auxin. Phototropin is also involved in chloroplast movements in relation to light, and in the light-induced opening of stomata.

Another class of blue-light receptors is the **cryptochromes**, which absorb blue and ultraviolet light. When activated by light, these yellow pigments induce seedlings to grow shorter hypocotyls and larger cotyledons, and increase synthesis of a red-purple pigment called anthocyanin, along with other effects. Like phototropin, cryptochromes contain pigments called chromophores (see the next section) that can absorb light, resulting in a conformational change in the photoreceptor protein.

Phytochromes mediate the effects of red and far-red light

Photomorphogenesis refers to several physiological and developmental events in plants that are controlled by light. For example:

- A bean seedling germinating belowground has an elongated stem, a pale yellow, folded leaf, and a hook that protects the first leaves (see Figures 35.8 and 35.19B)—it is **etiolated**. As the seedling reaches the surface of the soil, it undergoes several light-induced changes: the apical hook straightens, the

rudimentary leaves unfold, and chlorophyll is made, so that photosynthesis can begin. Even very dim light will induce these changes.

- Lettuce seeds spread on the soil will germinate only in response to light. Even just a flash of dim light will suffice.

- Adult cocklebur plants flower when they are exposed to long nights. If there is a brief light flash in the middle of the night, they do not flower.

Action spectra of these processes show that they are induced by light with wavelengths in the range of 650–680 nm, which we see as red light. This indicates that plants must have a photoreceptor pigment that absorbs this part of the red light spectrum and initiates photomorphogenesis.

What is especially remarkable about these red light responses is that *they are reversible by far-red light* (710–740 nm). For example, if lettuce seeds are exposed to brief, alternating periods of red and far-red light in close succession, they respond only to the final exposure. If it is red, they germinate; if it is far-red, they remain dormant (**Figure 35.22**). This reversibility of the effects of red and far-red light regulates many other aspects of plant development, including flowering and seedling growth.

The basis for the effects of red and far-red light resides in the photoreceptor pigment protein in the cytoplasm of plants called **phytochrome**. Phytochrome exists in two interconvertible "isoforms," or states. The molecule undergoes a conformational change upon absorbing light at particular wavelengths. The default or "ground" state, which absorbs principally red light, is called P_r. When P_r absorbs a photon of red light it is converted into P_{fr}. P_{fr} is the active form of phytochrome—the form that triggers important biological processes in various plants (**Figure 35.23**).

The part of phytochrome that absorbs red and far-red light is a covalently attached pigment called a chromophore (**Figure 35.24A**). The chromophore of P_r preferentially absorbs red light; when it does so, it changes conformation and the phytochrome is converted to the P_{fr} form. When the chromophore of P_{fr} absorbs far-red light, the phytochrome is converted back to the P_r form. If you know organic chemistry, this reaction is a familiar *cis-trans* isomerization. In addition to being affected by these rapid

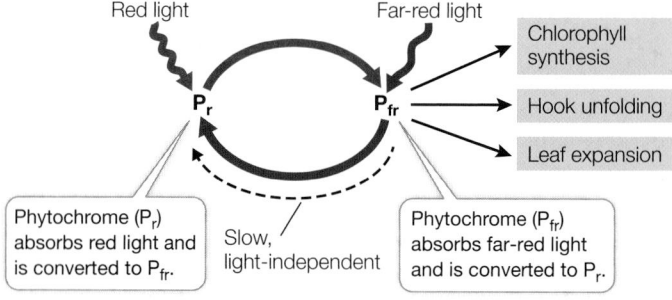

Figure 35.23 Phytochrome Is a Photoreceptor Pigment Protein

Work with the Data

Figure 35.22B Sensitivity of Seeds to Red and Far-Red Light

Original Paper: H. A. Borthwick et al. 1952. A reversible photo-reaction controlling seed germination. *Proc Natl Acad Sci USA* 38: 662–666.

Harry Borthwick, Sterling Hendricks, and colleagues at the U.S. Department of Agriculture performed a series of landmark experiments that suggested the existence of a receptor for red light that determined seed germination. After it was discovered that plants responded to the length of day (photoperiodism; see Chapter 36), the importance of nonphotosynthetic responses to light as a developmental signal became a hot topic of research. For over a century, it was known that lettuce seeds required light to germinate. By placing lettuce seeds in an environment where other environmental variables such as temperature were controlled, Borthwick's group tested the light signaling on germination.

QUESTIONS▶

1. An action spectrum (see Figure 10.5) for seed germination was obtained by first soaking the seeds on wet filter paper in the dark for 16 hours for imbibition, and then exposing them to different wavelengths of light for 1 minute. Having been exposed to a possible germination signal, the seeds were returned to the dark and tested for germination after 2 days. The results are shown in **Table A** in terms of energy efficiency (how much light energy was required for 50% seed germination).

   a. Explain the energy efficiency measurement: what do high and low numbers mean?

   b. Plot the data as energy efficiency versus wavelength. What can you conclude about the most efficient wavelengths of light for germination?

2. There was evidence from other light signaling responses in plants that the light effects were reversible by exposure to different wavelengths of light. After the data in Table A were obtained, Borthwick's team decided to first expose groups of 200 seeds to light at 660

nm (red, R) for 1 minute, and then some batches to light at 700 nm (far-red, FR) for 4 minutes. The seeds were returned to the dark and germination evaluated after 2 days. **Table B** shows the results.

   a. What can you conclude about the nature of the light signal responder?

   b. Why was there some germination in the "None" condition?

Table A

Wavelength (nm)	Energy required for 50% seed germination (joules × 10^{-3}/cm^2)
560	35
570	25
580	15
590	10
600	8
620	6
640	4
660	3
680	4
690	45
700	80

Table B

Wavelengths used	Percent germination
None	8.5
R	98
FR	54
R then FR then R	100
R then FR then R then FR	43
R then FR then R then FR then R	99

Go to **Achieve** for a companion **Data in Depth** exercise.

---

light-mediated changes, the P_{fr} form can also slowly revert to the P_r form, an event that typically occurs gradually. Because this reversion does not require light, it is called dark reversion.

The absorption spectra for P_r and P_{fr} (**Figure 35.24B**) correlate with their action spectra. As you have seen, phytochrome affects seed germination, shoot development after etiolation, and flowering. In *A. thaliana* there is a gene family that encodes five slightly different phytochromes, each functioning in different photomorphogenic responses.

For a plant in nature, the ratio of red to far-red light determines whether a phytochrome-mediated response will occur:

- In daylight the ratio is about 1.2:1; because there is more red than far-red light, the P_{fr} form predominates.

- In the shade of other plants, the ratio is as low as 0.13:1, and phytochrome is mostly in the P_r form. The low ratio of red to far-red light in the shade results from absorption of red light by chlorophyll in the leaves overhead, so less of the red light gets through to the plants below.

For some plants growing in the shade, the low ratio stimulates cell elongation and the plants grow upward toward the sunlight. The shade cast by other plants also prevents germination of seeds that require red light to germinate. The reflective properties of the soil

can also affect the red to far-red ratio—and thus plant behavior. For example, cotton seedlings grow more slowly on soils (such as clay) that reflect more red than far-red light.

Phytochrome stimulates gene transcription

How does phytochrome, or more specifically P_{fr}, work? Phytochrome has two subunits (**Figure 35.25**), each composed of a protein chain and a chromophore. Gene transcription is stimulated when P_r is converted to the P_{fr} isoform. When P_r absorbs red light, the chromophore changes shape, causing change in the conformation of the protein itself, from the P_r form to the P_{fr} form. Conversion to the P_{fr} form (see Figure 14.18) results in movement of P_{fr} from the cytoplasm to the nucleus. Once in the nucleus, P_{fr} binds to some transcription factors and induces their degradation. This action can stimulate expression of genes that were formerly repressed, and repress expression of genes that were formerly stimulated. The effect is quite large: in *A. thaliana*, phytochrome affects an amazing 2,500 genes (10% of the entire genome!) by either increasing or decreasing their expression. Some of these genes are related to hormones. For example, when P_{fr} is formed in seed germination, genes for gibberellin synthesis are activated and genes for gibberellin breakdown are repressed. As a result, gibberellins accumulate and seed reserves are mobilized.

(A) The *cis* and *trans* isomers of the chromophore pigment in phytochrome

(B) Absorption spectra of P_r and P_{fr}

The P_r form of phytochrome absorbs red light.

The P_{fr} form of phytochrome absorbs far-red light.

Figure 35.24 Phytochrome Exists in Two Forms Absorption spectra of phytochrome reveal two interconvertible forms, corresponding to the *cis* and *trans* isomers of phytochrome's chromophore. The P_r form absorbs red light; the P_{fr} form absorbs far-red light.

Figure 35.25 Phytochrome Stimulates Gene Transcription Phytochrome is composed of two polypeptide chains, each with a chromophore. This pair of polypeptides undergoes a conformational change upon absorbing light. When phytochrome absorbs red light, it converts to the P_{fr} form, which activates transcription of phytochrome-responsive genes.

Circadian rhythms are entrained by light reception

The timing and duration of biological activities in living organisms are governed in all eukaryotes and some prokaryotes by what is commonly called a "biological clock"—an oscillator within cells that alternates back and forth between two states at roughly 12-hour intervals. The major outward manifestations of this clock are known as **circadian rhythms** (Latin *circa*, "about," + *dies*, "day"). Think of your own life: in all probability you sleep at night and are awake during the day. The circadian rhythms of animals are discussed in Key Concept 51.2. In plants, circadian rhythms influence, for example, the opening (during the day) and closing (at night) of stomata in *A. thaliana*, and the raising toward sunlight (during the day) and lowering (at night) of leaves in bean plants. From these two examples, it is obvious that circadian rhythms are ecologically useful adaptations, in that they relate the plant's physiology to its environment.

Two qualities characterize circadian rhythms, as well as other regular biological cycles: the **period** is the length of one cycle, and the **amplitude** is the magnitude of the change over the course of a cycle. The circadian rhythms of plants have several noteworthy characteristics:

- The period of a circadian rhythm is remarkably insensitive to temperature, although lowering the temperature may drastically reduce the amplitude.

- Circadian rhythms are highly persistent; they may continue for days, even in the absence of environmental cues, such as light–dark periods.

- Circadian rhythms can be entrained, within limits, by light–dark cycles that do not exactly correspond to

24 hours. That is, the period of a rhythm can be made to coincide (within limits) with that of the light–dark cycle to which the organism is exposed.

Consider what happens when a person abruptly moves across many time zones: what was the night becomes the day, and gradually the person's sleep–wakefulness circadian rhythm entrains to the new environmental cues. Similar entrainment occurs in plants adapting to day length as the seasons progress during the year. The action spectrum for plant entrainment indicates that phytochrome (and to a lesser extent, blue-light receptors) is very likely involved. At sundown phytochrome is mostly in the active P_{fr} form. But as the night progresses, P_{fr} gradually gets converted back to the inactive P_r form. By dawn phytochrome is mostly in the P_r state, but as daylight begins, it rapidly converts to P_{fr}. The switch to the P_{fr} state resets the plant's biological clock. However long the night, the clock is still reset at dawn every day. Thus while the total period measured by the clock is consistent, the clock adjusts to changes in day length over the course of the year.

KEY CONCEPT
35.4 Recap and Assess

Light controls several physiological and developmental events in plants, a process called photomorphogenesis. Pigment photoreceptors such as phototropin, cryptochromes, and phytochrome mediate the effects of light on plant growth and development. Phytochrome exists in two interconvertible states; conversion from one state to the other is controlled by the ratio of red to far-red light. Circadian rhythms are influenced by light reception.

1. What is the evidence for blue-light receptors in plants?

2. Why does red light affect seed germination differently than far-red light does?

▶Investigating LIFE

Q and A How is plant growth controlled, and what changes in growth patterns made the new strains of wheat and rice successful?

In normal wheat plants, gibberellins stimulate stem elongation. But in the semi-dwarf plants, a mutation affects the signal transduction mechanism for gibberellins so that the stem cells do not respond to it and growth is reduced. In rice, the mutation is in the gene for an enzyme in the biochemical pathway for the synthesis of gibberellins. Without the hormone, the stem does not elongate. The lives of countless people have been saved by intentional disruptions of hormone signaling. These high-yielding crops respond to added fertilizer with greatly increased growth and production of grain compared with conventional varieties of wheat and rice.

Future directions

Unlike animal hormones, which are made in one tissue and often have specific effects on a limited range of targets, plant hormones are widespread in their sites of synthesis and their effects. It is not surprising that with several hormones in a given tissue at a particular time, they interact to produce a physiological effect, a phenomenon called crosstalk. For example, as a seed germinates underground, the growth of the embryonic stem, or hypocotyl (see Figure 35.19B), is stimulated by auxin and gibberellins, and inhibited by ethylene and brassinosteroids. Studies on model plants such as *Arabidopsis thaliana* are revealing proteins common to the signaling pathways of these hormones that have a role in their interacting effects.

VISUAL SUMMARY 35

© Tim Gainey/Alamy Stock Photo

You should be able to relate each summary to the adjacent figures. If you go to this visual summary in **Achieve**, you can follow links to figures, animations, activities, and simulations that will help you consolidate the material.

KEY CONCEPT
35.1 Plant Development Occurs Progressively as Plants Mature   Go to Activities 35.1 and 35.2

■ Plants respond to their environments by changing their patterns of **growth** and **development**. Unlike most animals, plants create new organs throughout their life cycle.

■ Plant cells expand via the **stress–relaxation cycle**, in which the internal pressure of a cell acts on the cell wall, loosening (relaxing) the wall. This lowers the internal pressure in the cell, allowing water to enter.

■ Transcription factors called master regulators cause cells to differentiate into distinct types.

Figure 35.4

Root of carrot plant

■ **Genetic screens** can be used to identify the factors that carry out specific processes in plants.

Figure 35.5

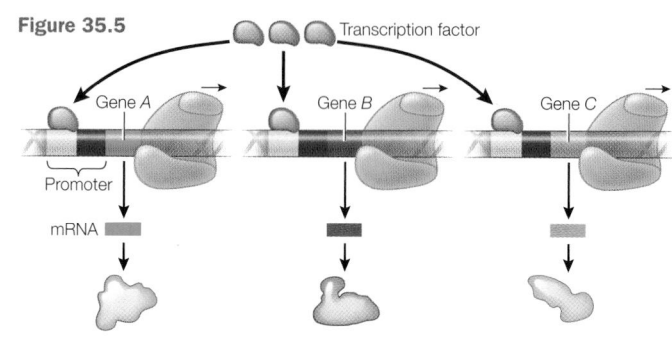

Questions

1. What anatomical feature of plants allows them to create new organs continually throughout their lives?

2. How is the identity of a cell determined?

3. Why might the remarkable degree of developmental flexibility that plant cells exhibit be particularly advantageous?

4. Construct a flow chart that illustrates how a genetic screen can be used to identify the genes involved in the development of plant signal transduction pathways.

KEY CONCEPT
35.2 Gibberellins and Auxin Have Diverse Effects but a Similar Mechanism of Action

Go to Activity 35.3 **and** Animations 35.1–35.3

■ The location of **auxin** transport proteins in cells results in directional movement of auxin called polar auxin transport.

■ **Phototropism** occurs when perception of light leads to lateral redistribution of auxin. More auxin on the shaded sided leads to more elongation on that side, causing the plant to grow toward the light.

■ **Gibberellins** have many effects, including cell elongation, fruit growth, and mobilization of seed storage polymers during germination.

■ Both auxin and gibberellins affect gene expression by causing proteins that affect transcription of specific genes to be marked for degradation.

Figure 35.13

Questions

1. An experiment has been performed in which a section of a stem is removed from a plant, a block of agar containing auxin is placed on the top side, and a block of agar that does not contain auxin is placed on the bottom of the stem segment. In this case, the auxin moves from the top to the bottom. If the same experiment is performed, but the piece of stem tissue is inverted such that the side that grew closer to the roots is on top, auxin that is applied to the top of the system does not move down. Explain these results.

2. Construct a flow diagram showing the steps by which gibberellins promote seed germination.

3. The effect that many plant hormones have on a cell varies depending on the type of cell. Keeping in mind that there are many different F-box proteins in plants, and that each F-box protein targets a different subset of target proteins for degradation, come up with a hypothesis as to how auxin can have different effects on different types of cells.

Investigating Life: The Darwins' Phototropism Experiment

Light

KEY CONCEPT
35.3 Other Plant Hormones Have Diverse Effects

■ **Cytokinins** promote plant cell division and delay leaf senescence, among other effects. Cytokinins often work in opposition to auxin, particularly when controlling the formation of shoots versus roots.

■ **Ethylene** is a gaseous plant hormone. Ethylene stimulates its own production, resulting in an autocatalytic cycle that causes fruit to ripen all at once.

■ **Brassinosteroids** are plant steroid hormones. Among the responses they affect are cell elongation, pollen tube elongation, vascular tissue differentiation, and root elongation.

Figure 35.18

Questions

1. Plants can often be regenerated from callus tissue by placing the callus first on media containing auxin, and then on media rich in cytokinins. What happens at each stage of this process to allow formation of a complete plant?

2. Explain why one rotten apple spoils the whole barrel.

Figure 35.19

Fruit ripening

Apical hook formation

Apical hook

© Nigel Cattlin/ Alamy Stock Photo

Photo by Adel A. Kader © 1997 Regents of the University of California. Used by permission.

KEY CONCEPT

35.4 Photoreceptors Initiate Developmental Responses to Light

■ Photoreceptors such as **phototropin** and **phytochrome** are proteins that contain small organic molecules called chromophores that can absorb photons of particular wavelengths. Absorbing light results in a change in the conformation of the protein.

■ Phytochrome is a photoreceptor that has two interconvertible states, P_r and P_{fr}. The fraction that is in the active (P_{fr}) state depends on the ratio of red to far-red light to which the plant is exposed.

■ When the chromophore of phytochrome absorbs red light, the conformation of the photoreceptor changes to the active P_{fr} form, which moves to the nucleus and influences transcriptional activity affecting many genes.

Questions

1. Beronda Montgomery and colleagues conducted experiments with plant lines in which the chromophore of phytochrome was rapidly degraded.

    a. What types of changes would you expect to see in such plants?

    b. What might you learn if a chromophore-degrading enzyme were expressed just in one cell type, or one layer of a leaf?

2. Imagine that you are trying to identify the photoreceptor for a newly discovered light response that occurs in plants. Compare and contrast the type of information one learns from (a) comparing the action spectrum for a response to the absorption spectrum of a potential photoreceptor and (b) the results of a genetic screen in which mutagenized plants that fail to respond to a light stimulus are identified. What does each type of data provide? Is one more important than the other?

Figure 35.23

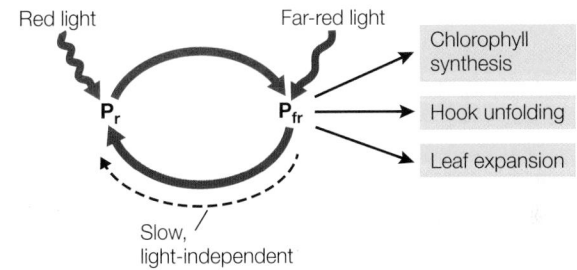

Red light   Far-red light

P_r P_{fr}

Chlorophyll synthesis

Hook unfolding

Leaf expansion

Slow, light-independent

Figure 35.24

Visible spectrum

Go to **Achieve** for the eBook, **LearningCurve**, animations, activities, simulations, and additional resources and assignments.

36 Reproduction in Flowering Plants

KEY CONCEPTS

36.1 Most Angiosperms Reproduce Sexually

36.2 Hormones and Signaling Determine the Transition from the Vegetative to the Reproductive State

36.3 Angiosperms Can Reproduce Asexually

The poinsettia is a popular Christmas flower. But the red "flowers" are not flowers at all; instead, they are leaves (bracts).

© Geoffrey Robinson/Alamy Stock Photo

▶Investigating LIFE

What Signals Flowering?

Dairy farmer Albert Ecke was fascinated by the red and green shrubs that grew all over southern California and were used by Mexican-Americans for red dye. The shrub, *Euphorbia pulcherrima*, got the name "poinsettia" from the man who first brought it to the United States: the first U.S. ambassador to Mexico, Joel Roberts Poinsett. In the early 1900s, Ecke started selling the plants at his farm in Hollywood. But two challenges stood in the way of his making this plant a commercial success.

First, although poinsettias generally bloomed in the fall and early winter in the mild climate of southern California, when Ecke grew them in fields in Hollywood, the formation of flowers was unreliable. Biologists later found that the flowering of poinsettias required at least a 14-hour night for several weeks. Any interruption in the long night—by passing cars or street lamps or lighting from nearby movie sets, for example—inhibited flowering. So Ecke's son Paul moved the growing operation south, to isolated fields far from Los Angeles. A second challenge was that the plants were tall and gangly. Although pretty, they were hard to transport and not attractive indoors. Paul Ecke found a variety of poinsettia that was much more compact. He propagated this variety and eventually developed it into the short potted plant that is so popular today. The Eckes decided that the time of flowering was just right for making the poinsettia a "Christmas flower," so

they promoted this now portable plant as a holiday decoration, blanketing live television shows with free plants between Thanksgiving and Christmas. The campaign was successful: more than 100 million poinsettias are now sold in the United States during the Christmas season every year, making it the nation's best-selling potted plant.

© alisbalb/Getty Images

Breeding more attractive flowering plants that are easier to grow is an ongoing part of floriculture, the industry involved with the production of floral crops. You may be surprised to learn that the brightly colored "flowers" of poinsettias are not flowers at all. The red parts of the plant that we most notice and appreciate are actually specialized leaves called bracts. The flowers are grouped in small clusters in the center of the plant alongside yellow nectar-producing glands.

 How did an understanding of angiosperm reproduction allow floriculturists to develop a commercially successful poinsettia?
(Find the answer on page 819.)

KEY CONCEPT
36.1
Most Angiosperms Reproduce Sexually

Learning Objectives

36.1.1 Outline the life cycle of a flowering plant, including the steps that give rise to the haploid and diploid stages.

36.1.2 Describe two methods for preventing self-fertilization in angiosperms.

36.1.3 Describe the relationship among fertilization, seed development, and fruit development.

Most angiosperms (flowering plants) have evolved to reproduce sexually because this strategy has the selective advantage of producing the genetic diversity that is the raw material for evolution. Sexual reproduction in angiosperms involves mitosis, meiosis, and the alternation of haploid and diploid generations (see Figure 11.14).

There are several important differences between sexual reproduction in angiosperms and vertebrate animals:

- In animals, the germ line cells are determined before birth. In angiosperms, the cells that will form gametes are determined in the adult organism, usually in response to environmental conditions.

- In animals, meiosis usually produces gametes directly. In plants, meiosis produces spores. After the spores germinate, they undergo mitosis, forming a multicellular but haploid stage that then produces gametes.

- In animals, there is no multicellular haploid stage. The existence of multicellular diploid (sporophyte) and haploid (gametophyte) life stages in most angiosperms is called the alternation of generations.

How does the flower function as a structure for sexual reproduction?

The plant life cycle typically involves the alternation of haploid and diploid generations (**Figure 36.1**) (see Key Concept 11.4). In angiosperms, the adult plant is a diploid sporophyte, and the male and/or

female haploid gametophytes (structures that produce gametes) are contained in the flowers (see Key Concepts 27.1 and 27.3 for a description of flower parts and floral evolution). A complete flower consists of four concentric groups of organs arising from modified leaves: the carpels, stamens, petals, and sepals (**Figure 36.2A**).

- The carpels are the female sex organs that contain the developing female gametophytes.

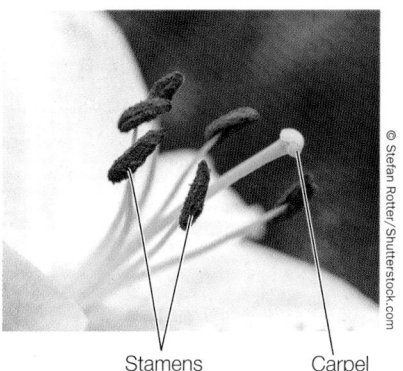

(A) Organs of a flower

(B) Perfect: lily (*Lilium* sp.)

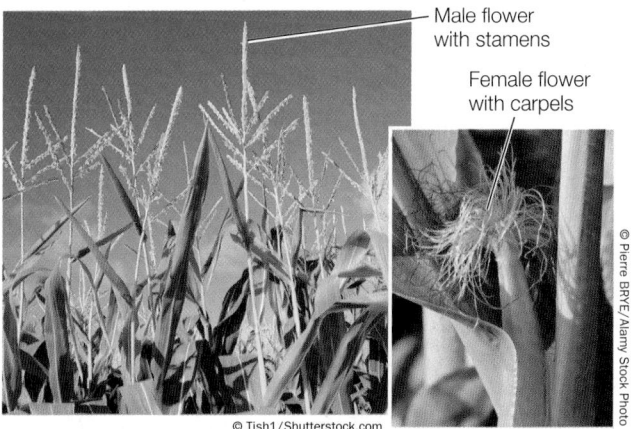

(C) Imperfect monoecious: corn (*Zea mays*)

Male flower with stamens

Female flower with carpels

(D) Imperfect dioecious: American holly (*Ilex opaca*)

Female flower with carpels

Male flower with stamens

Both photos © Bill Beatty/Visuals Unlimited, Inc.

Figure 36.2 Perfect and Imperfect Flowers (A) The organs of a complete flower are sepals, petals, stamen, and carpels (B) A lily is an example of a perfect flower, meaning one that has both male and female sex organs. (C) Imperfect flowers are either male or female. Corn is a monoecious species: both types of imperfect flowers are borne on the same plant. (D) American holly is a dioecious species; some American holly plants bear male imperfect flowers whereas others bear female imperfect flowers.

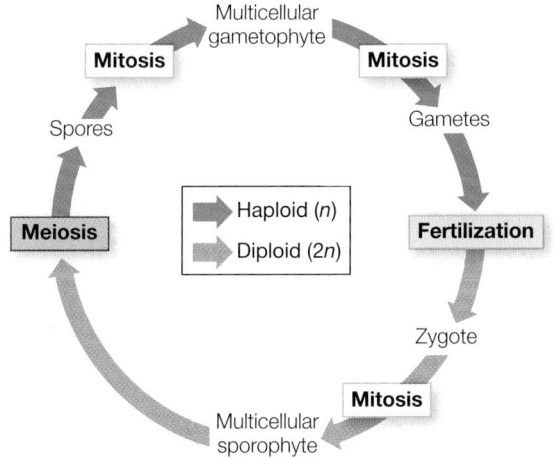

Figure 36.1 Alternation of Generations Unlike vertebrate animals, flowering plants have a life cycle that includes a multicellular haploid phase. This haploid generation gives rise to the gametes.

- The stamens are the male sex organs that contain the developing male gametophytes.

Most angiosperms have flowers with both stamens and carpels; such flowers are termed "perfect" (**Figure 36.2B**). "Imperfect" flowers, by contrast, are those with only male or only female sex organs. Male flowers have stamens but not carpels, and female flowers have carpels but not stamens. Some plants, such as corn, bear both male and female flowers on an individual plant; such species are called **monoecious** ("one house") (**Figure 36.2C**). In **dioecious** species, individual plants bear either male-only or female-only flowers; an example is holly (**Figure 36.2D**).

Flowering plants have microscopic gametophytes

You can follow the roles of male and female gametophytes in angiosperm reproduction in **Figure 36.3**. The gametophytes develop from haploid spores in the flower:

- Each female gametophyte (megagametophyte) is called an **embryo sac**, and it develops inside an ovule. One or more ovules are contained within the ovary, which is the lower part of the carpel.

- Male gametophytes (microgametophytes), which are called **pollen grains**, develop inside the anther, which is part of the stamen.

FEMALE GAMETOPHYTE   Of the four haploid megaspores resulting from meiosis, three undergo apoptosis (programmed cell death). The remaining megaspore undergoes three mitotic divisions without cytokinesis, producing eight haploid nuclei, all initially contained within a single cell—three nuclei at one end, three at the other, and two in the middle. Subsequent cell wall formation leads to an elliptical, seven-celled female gametophyte with a total of eight nuclei:

Male gametophytes

4 The microspore undergoes mitosis, forming a tube cell and a generative cell.

5 The pollen grain is transferred to the stigma (pollination).

Pollen grains (n)

Microspores (n)

Meiosis   Mitosis

Microsporocyte (2n)   Tube cell nucleus   Generative cell

6 The pollen tube grows toward the embryo sac (the female gametophyte).

Anther ♂

Flower of mature sporophyte

Petal

Stigma

Style

Carpel

Anther

Ovary

Ovule

Sepal   Filament   Stamen

Receptacle

Pollen tube

3 The embryo sac is the female gametophyte. After three mitotic divisions, it contains eight haploid nuclei, partitioned into seven cells.

1 Meiosis produces four megaspores.

Surviving megaspore

Antipodal cells

Three mitoses

♀ Ovule

Meiosis

Megasporocyte (2n)   Megaspores (n)   Microphyle

Synergids   Egg cell

Polar nuclei

Tube cell nucleus   Sperm (2)   Endosperm nucleus (3n)   Zygote (2n)

7 Double fertilization results in a 2n zygote (from egg and sperm) and 3n endosperm (from the two polar nuclei and second sperm).

2 Three of the megaspores undergo programmed cell death.

Female gametophyte

Figure 36.3 Sexual Reproduction in Angiosperms   The embryo sac is the female gametophyte; the pollen grain is the male gametophyte. The male and female gametes meet and fuse in the embryo sac. Flowering plants have double fertilization, in which a zygote and an endosperm nucleus form from separate fusion events. The zygote forms by the fusion of one sperm cell with the egg cell. The endosperm forms after the other sperm cell fuses with the central cell, which contains two nuclei. The thee nuclei fuse, forming a diploid cell.

Q: Considering the way in which the cells of the female gametophyte form, how similar or different would you predict the DNA content of the two polar nuclei to be?

View in Achieve
Activity 36.1 Sexual Reproduction in Angiosperms

- At one end of the female gametophyte are three small cells: the egg cell and two cells called synergids. The egg cell is the female gamete, and the synergids participate in fertilization by attracting the pollen tube. The pollen tube enters one of the synergids before the sperm cells are released for fertilization.

- At the opposite end of the female gametophyte are three antipodal cells, which eventually degenerate.

- In the large central cell are two **polar nuclei**.

The female gametophyte, or embryo sac, is the entire seven-cell, eight-nucleus structure.

MALE GAMETOPHYTE   The four haploid products of meiosis (the microspores) each develop a cell wall and undergo a single mitotic division, usually producing four two-celled pollen grains that are released into the environment. The two cells in a pollen grain have different roles:

- After **pollination** (the transfer of a pollen grain to a stigma, part of the female reproductive organ), the generative cell divides by mitosis to form two sperm cells that participate in fertilization.

- The tube cell forms the elongating pollen tube that delivers the sperm to the embryo sac.

Connect the Concepts   Flower structure evolved over time. Natural selection has favored floral features that have increased the likelihood of successful pollination. Key Concepts 27.3 and 55.3 describe how angiosperms coevolved with animal pollinators and how ecological communities are formed through interactions among plant and animal species.

A pollen tube delivers sperm cells to the embryo sac

When a functional pollen grain lands on a compatible stigma, it germinates. A key event is water uptake by pollen from the stigma: pollen loses most of its water as it matures. Germination involves the development of a **pollen tube** (**Figure 36.4**). The pollen tube either traverses the tissue of the style (part of the carpel; see Figure 36.3) or, if the style is hollow, grows on the inner surface of the style until it reaches an ovule. The growth rate of the pollen tube varies greatly among species, but it can be as fast as 1 centimeter an hour.

The growth of the pollen tube is guided in part by a chemical signal in the form of a small protein produced by the synergids within the ovule. If one synergid is destroyed, the ovule still attracts pollen tubes, but destruction of both synergids renders the ovule unable to attract pollen tubes, and fertilization does not occur.

Genetic screens (see Figure 35.7) of mutants in *Arabidopsis thaliana* have revealed several genes whose expression in synergids is needed for guiding the pollen tube. There is evidence that a small molecule made by the embryo sac—γ-aminobutyric acid, or GABA—is an attractant for pollen tube growth. This would be an amazing coincidence, since this molecule is also a signal in the vertebrate nervous system.

© Christian Gautier/Biosphoto/Minden Pictures

Pollen grains on stigmas

Styles

Pollen tube

Figure 36.4 Pollen Tubes Begin to Grow   Staining pollen with a dye allows it to be seen through a microscope. These pollen grains have landed on the stigmas of a crocus.

 Media Clip 36.1 Pollen Germination in Real Time
Life12e.com/mc36.1

Many flowering plants control pollination or pollen tube growth to prevent inbreeding

You'll recall from discussions of Mendel's work (see Key Concept 12.1) that some plants can reproduce sexually by both cross-pollination and self-pollination. Self-pollination increases the chances of successful pollination but leads to homozygosity, which reduces genetic diversity. Because diversity is the raw material of evolution by natural selection, homozygosity can be selectively disadvantageous. Most plants have evolved mechanisms that prevent self-fertilization. Angiosperms prevent self-fertilization in two main ways: (1) physical separation of male and female gametophytes and (2) genetic self-incompatibility.

Connect the Concepts   As described in Key Concept 27.3, flowers known as perfect flowers have functioning megasporangia and microsporangia. Perfect flowers are thus capable of self-pollination, which is usually disadvantageous. Various mechanisms have evolved in perfect flowers to prevent "selfing"; one is described in Figure 27.13.

SEPARATION OF MALE AND FEMALE GAMETOPHYTES   Self-fertilization is prevented in dioecious species, which bear only male or female flowers on a particular plant. Pollination in dioecious species is accomplished only when one plant pollinates another. In monoecious plants, which bear both male and female flowers on the same plant, the physical separation of the male and female flowers is often sufficient to prevent self-fertilization. Some monoecious species prevent self-fertilization by staggering the development of male and female flowers so they do not bloom at the same time, making these species functionally dioecious.

GENETIC SELF-INCOMPATIBILITY   A pollen grain that lands on the stigma of the same plant will fertilize the female gamete *only if the plant is self-compatible*, meaning capable of self-pollination. To prevent self-fertilization, many plants are genetically self-incompatible. **Self-incompatibility** depends on the ability of a plant to determine whether pollen is genetically similar or genetically different from itself. Rejection of "same-as-self" pollen prevents self-fertilization. How does it occur?

Self-incompatibility in many flowering plants is controlled by a cluster of tightly linked genes called the *S* locus (for *self-incompatibility*). The *S* locus encodes proteins in the pollen and style that interact during the recognition process. A self-incompatible species typically has many alleles of the *S* locus. The pollen phenotype may be determined by its own haploid genotype or by the diploid genotype of its parent plant. In either case, if the pollen expresses an allele that matches either of the alleles expressed in the recipient pistil, the pollen is rejected. Depending on the type of self-incompatibility system, the rejected pollen either fails to germinate or is prevented from growing through the style (**Figure 36.5**); either way, self-fertilization is prevented.

Angiosperms perform double fertilization

In most angiosperm species, the mature pollen grain consists of two cells: a large tube cell enclosing a much smaller generative cell. When a compatible pollen grain lands on the stigma of a plant of the same species, it germinates, and the pollen tube grows through the style tissue to the embryo sac (**Figure 36.6, step 1**). During this process, the generative cell undergoes one mitotic division and cytokinesis to produce two haploid **sperm cells** (**Figure 36.6, step 2**).

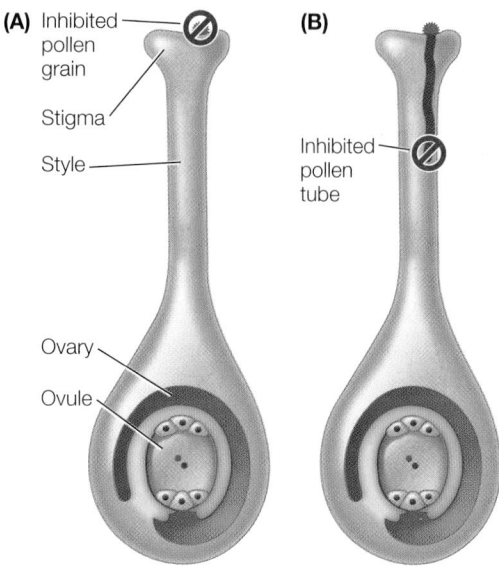

Figure 36.5 Self-Incompatibility   In a self-incompatible plant, pollen is rejected if it expresses an S allele that matches one of the S alleles of the stigma and style. Self pollen may fail to germinate (**A**) or its pollen tube may die before reaching an ovule (**B**). In either case, the egg cannot be fertilized by a sperm from the same plant.

Two fertilization events now occur. One of the two synergids degenerates when the pollen tube arrives and the two sperm cells are released into its remains (**Figure 36.6, step 3**). Each sperm cell then fuses with a different cell of the embryo sac. One sperm cell fuses with the egg cell, and the two nuclei fuse, producing the diploid zygote; the other sperm cell fuses with the central cell, and its

Figure 36.6 Double Fertilization   Two sperm are involved in two cell fusion events, hence the term "double fertilization." One sperm is involved in the formation of the diploid zygote, and the other results in the formation of the triploid endosperm cell that divides to form endosperm. Double fertilization is a characteristic feature of angiosperm reproduction.

▶ **View in Achieve**
Animation 36.1 Double Fertilization

nucleus fuses with the two polar nuclei, forming a **triploid (3*n*) cell** (Figure 36.6, steps 4 and 5). Immediately after fertilization the triploid nucleus undergoes rapid mitotic divisions to form a specialized nutritive tissue, the **endosperm**. In most species the endosperm nucleus initially divides without cytokinesis, forming a large, multinucleate cell, and cell walls form later between the nuclei. After the endosperm begins developing, the zygote undergoes mitotic division to form the new sporophyte embryo. The developing embryo uses the endosperm tissue as a source of nutrients, energy, and carbon-based anabolic building blocks. In some cases the endosperm persists until germination and is used as a source of nutrients by the developing seedling; this is prevalent in grains such as corn, wheat, and rice. The source of nutrients is important because the seedling often begins its development underground and cannot perform photosynthesis right away.

The remaining cells of the male and female gametophytes—the antipodal cells, the remaining synergid, and the pollen tube nucleus—degenerate as the embryo begins to develop.

Double fertilization, a hallmark of angiosperms, is so named because it involves two cell fusion events:

- One sperm cell fuses with the egg cell.
- The other sperm cell fuses with the central cell.

The fusion of a sperm cell with the central cell to form the triploid endosperm nucleus is one of the defining characteristics of angiosperms.

Embryos develop within seeds contained in fruits

Fertilization initiates the highly coordinated growth and development of the embryo, endosperm, integuments, and carpel. The integuments—protective tissue layers surrounding the ovule—develop into the seed coat, and the ovary wall becomes the outer layers of the fruit that encloses the seed (see Figure 36.7A).

In Chapter 35 you learned about the events in plant embryonic development and its hormonal control. As seeds develop, they prepare for dispersal and dormancy by losing up to 95% of their water content. You can see this desiccation by comparing corn grains (e.g., popcorn) with ripe corn from the cob. A dry seed is still alive; it has protective proteins that keep its cells in a living state.

In angiosperms, the ovary—together with the seeds it contains—develops into a fruit after fertilization has occurred. Fruits have two main functions:

1. They aid in seed dispersal.
2. They protect the seed from damage by animals and infection by microbial pathogens.

A **fruit** may consist of only the mature ovary and seeds, or it may include other parts of the flower. Some species produce fleshy, edible fruits, such as peaches and tomatoes, whereas the fruits of other species are dry (Figure 36.7).

The diverse forms of fruits reflect the varied strategies plants use to disperse their progeny. Because plants cannot move, their progeny need some mechanism for separating themselves from their parents. Wide dispersal of progeny may not always be advantageous, however. If a plant has successfully grown and reproduced, its location is likely to be favorable for the next generation

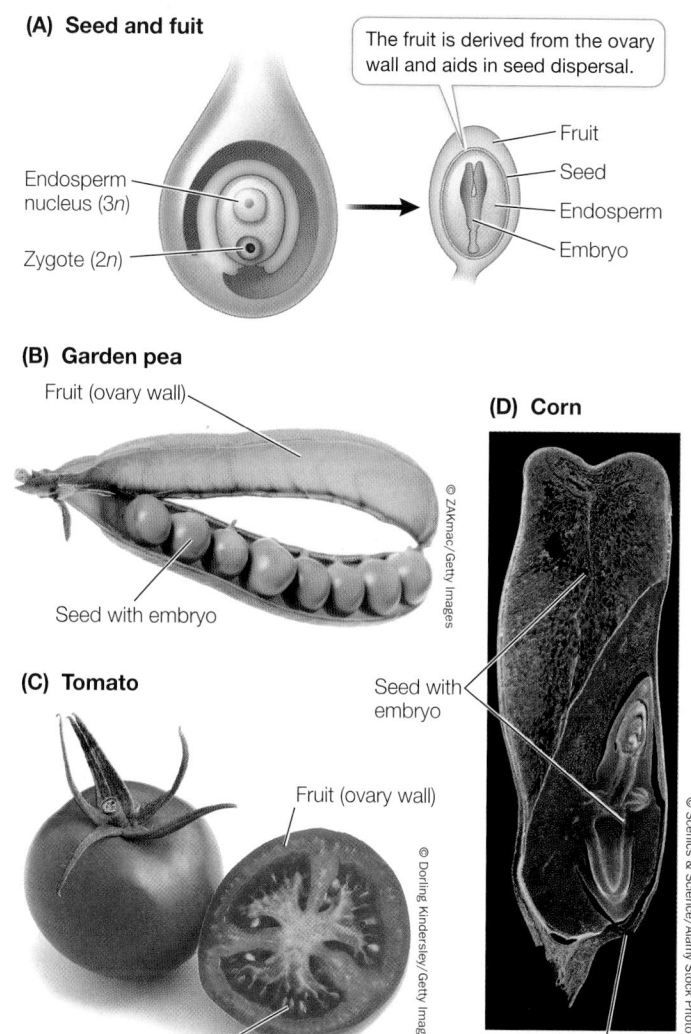

(A) Seed and fruit

The fruit is derived from the ovary wall and aids in seed dispersal.

Endosperm nucleus (3*n*)

Zygote (2*n*)

Fruit
Seed
Endosperm
Embryo

(B) Garden pea

Fruit (ovary wall)

Seed with embryo

(D) Corn

Seed with embryo

Fruit (ovary wall)

(C) Tomato

Fruit (ovary wall)

Seed with embryo

© ZAKmac/Getty Images

© Dorling Kindersley/Getty Images

© Scenics & Science/Alamy Stock Photo

Figure 36.7 Angiosperm Fruits   There are a variety of fruits, but all have a seed containing the embryo, surrounded by a fruit that comes from the wall of the ovary.

too. Some offspring do indeed stay near their parents. This is the case in many tree species, whose seeds simply fall to the ground. However, this strategy has several potential disadvantages. If the species is a perennial, the offspring that germinate near their parents will be competing with their parents for resources, which may be too limited to support a dense population. Furthermore, even though local conditions were good enough for the parent to produce at least some seeds, there is no guarantee that conditions will still be good the next year, or that they won't be better elsewhere. Thus in many cases seed dispersal is vital to a species' survival.

Many fruits help disperse seeds over substantial distances, increasing the probability that at least a few of the seeds will find suitable conditions for germination and growth to sexual maturity. Some wind-dispersed seeds have fruits with "wings," like those of the familiar maple. In other cases, the fruits and seeds are tiny, and they include feathery structures, such as in thistle. Other fruits, such as burs, attach themselves to animals or to your clothes and shoes. Water disperses some fruits; coconuts have been known to float thousands of miles between islands. Seeds swallowed whole by an animal along with fruits such as berries travel through the animal's digestive tract and are deposited some distance from the parent plant.

Biologists are beginning to understand the relationships between seed development (from ovules) and fruit development (from carpels). Some seedless fruits, such as varieties of watermelons and grapes, develop when fertilization occurs, but the embryo then aborts. In other cases, such as bananas, the fruit develops without fertilization. In most cases, however, fruit development does not occur in the absence of fertilization. Several years ago a farmer in Spain who grows sugar apples (*Annona squamosa*) noticed a seedless fruit and brought it to the attention of scientists. A single gene was subsequently identified whose mutated form results in this seedless phenotype. The wild-type version of this gene encodes a transcription factor important to the development of the outer tissues of the ovule. The gene is present in the genomes of all angiosperms examined. In the future, therefore, it may be possible to produce other seedless fruits by engineering mutations in this gene.

Seed development is under hormonal control

Chapter 35 described the role of the gibberellin hormones in the mobilization of stored macromolecules in the seed endosperm during germination. The development of seeds is under the control of a different hormone, **abscisic acid (ABA)**. (Unfortunately, its name is misleading, because it does not directly control leaf abscission.) Most plant tissues make ABA, and like other plant hormones, it has multiple effects (see Table 35.2). During early seed development the ABA level is usually low, and it rises as the seed matures. This increase stimulates the endosperm to synthesize seed storage proteins. It also stimulates the synthesis of proteins that prevent cell death as the seeds dry.

ABA also keeps the developing seed from germinating on the plant before it dries. Premature germination, termed **vivipary**, is undesirable in seed crops (such as wheat) because the grain is damaged if it starts to sprout. Viviparous seedlings are also unlikely to survive if they remain attached to the parent plant and are unable to establish themselves in the soil. Mutant strains of corn that are insensitive to ABA have viviparous seeds, indicating the importance of ABA in preventing precocious germination.

The general effect of ABA in preventing germination extends to seed dormancy. Seeds tend to stay dormant if their ABA levels are high and germinate when the levels go down. This usually occurs as dormancy is broken.

KEY CONCEPT
36.1 Recap and Assess

Flowers contain the organs for sexual reproduction in angiosperms. Unlike animals, in which meiosis leads directly to gametes (egg and sperm), plants have a multicellular haploid generation. In angiosperms, meiosis forms two types of spores. The male spores (microspores) give rise to a haploid pollen tube that goes on to form the sperm. The female spores (megaspores) give rise to a haploid female gametophyte that contains the egg. After fertilization, the flower develops into seed(s) and fruit. The selective advantages of seeds and fruits include long-term viability and multiple modes of dispersal.

1. How would plant reproduction be affected if the pollen tube failed to grow and develop properly?

2. What two fertilization events occur during double fertilization? Name the products of fertilization.

3. What might happen if the haploid polar nuclei contained a loss-of-function allele for a gene whose activity was required for endosperm formation? What advantage results from the formation of a triploid endosperm?

4. What part of the flower develops into the seed? Into the fruit?

We have now traced the sexual life cycle of angiosperms from the flower to the gametophytes, pollination, fertilization, and the dispersal of seeds. We discussed seed germination and seedling development in Chapter 35, and vegetative plant growth in Chapter 32. Next we look at the rest of the angiosperm life cycle—the transition from the vegetative to the flowering state—and how this transition is regulated.

KEY CONCEPT
36.2 Hormones and Signaling Determine the Transition from the Vegetative to the Reproductive State

Learning Objectives

36.2.1 Relate the type of meristem a plant has to the type of organs it produces.

36.2.2 Explain how floral organs are specified.

36.2.3 Explain how flowering is triggered in a plant that is sensitive to day length.

Flowering is one of the major events in a plant's life. Flowering requires a reallocation of energy and materials away from making more nonreproductive plant parts (vegetative growth) to making flowers and gametes (reproductive growth). Once a plant is old enough, it can respond to internal or external signals to initiate reproduction. Flowering can happen right at maturity as part of a predetermined developmental program or in response to environmental cues such as light or temperature.

Flowering occurs at specific places and specific times

Plants fall into three categories depending on when they mature and initiate flowering, and what happens after they flower:

1. **Annuals** complete their lives in one year. This class includes many crops important to the human diet, such as corn, wheat, rice, and soybean. When the environment is suitable, these plants grow rapidly, with little or no secondary growth. After flowering, they use most of their materials and energy to develop seeds and fruits, and the rest of the plant withers away.

2. **Biennials** take 2 years to complete their lives. These are much less common than annuals and include carrots, cabbage, and onions. Typically, biennials produce only vegetative growth during the first year and store carbohydrates in underground

roots (carrot) and stems (celery). In the second year they use most of the stored carbohydrates to produce flowers and seeds rather than vegetative growth, and the plant dies after seeds form.

3. **Perennials** live 3 or more—sometimes many more—years. Maple trees can live up to 400 years. Perennials include many trees and shrubs, as well as wildflowers. Typically these plants flower every year but stay alive and keep growing for another season; the reproductive cycle repeats each year. However, some perennials (e.g., century plant) grow vegetatively for many years, flower once, and die.

No matter what type of life cycle they have, angiosperms all make the transition to flowering. The first visible sign of a transition to the flowering state may be a change in one or more apical meristems in the shoot system. As you saw in Chapter 32, meristems have a pool of undetermined cells. During vegetative growth, a shoot apical meristem continually produces leaves, axillary buds, and stem tissues (**Figure 36.8A**) in a kind of unrestricted growth called indeterminate growth (see Key Concept 32.1).

Flowers may appear singly or in an orderly cluster that constitutes an **inflorescence**. If a vegetative apical meristem becomes an **inflorescence meristem**, it stops making leaves and axillary buds and produces other structures: smaller leafy structures called bracts, as well as new meristems in the angles between the bracts and the stem (**Figure 36.8B**). These new meristems may also be inflorescence meristems, or they may be **floral meristems**, each of which gives rise to a flower. Conversion of an apical meristem to an inflorescence meristem occurs as a result of a change in the set of genes that are expressed in the meristematic cells.

Figure 36.8 Flowering and the Apical Meristem A vegetative apical meristem **(A)** grows without producing flowers. Once the transition to the flowering state is made **(B)**, inflorescence meristems give rise to bracts and to floral meristems **(C)**, which become the flowers.

Once the shoot apical meristem has been converted into an inflorescence meristem, it may begin producing flowers. Each floral meristem typically produces four consecutive whorls or spirals of organs—the sepals, petals, stamens, and carpels discussed earlier in the chapter—separated by very short internodes, keeping the flower compact (**Figure 36.8C**). (As noted in Key Concept 36.1, flowers that contain both stamens and carpels are called perfect flowers.) In contrast to vegetative apical meristems and some inflorescence meristems, floral meristems are responsible for determinate growth—growth of limited duration.

Floral organ identity genes

The type of organ that will be produced in each of the whorls is determined by the transcription factors that are expressed in those cells. In the model plant *Arabidopsis thaliana*, each flower begins as a floral meristem of about 700 cells arranged in a dome, and the four whorls develop from this meristem. The organs that make up the flower are evolutionarily derived from leaves. Their identity is determined by three classes of **organ identity genes**—classes A, B, and C—that encode transcription factors (**Figure 36.9**). These proteins act in combination to specify the type of organ that will be produced. For example, a combination of transcription factors that gives rise to purple petals would do so in part by leading to the expression of enzymes required for synthesis of purple pigment. Expression of class A genes alone gives rise to sepals, a combination of class A and class B genes gives rise to petals, a combination of class B and class C genes gives rise to stamens, and class C genes alone give rise to carpels. The genes that are expressed in a whorl (see Figure 36.9) generate that whorl's specific organ identity.

(A) The four organs of a flower

Mature flower

Whorl 1: sepal   Whorl 2: petal   Whorl 3: stamen   Whorl 4: carpel

Early flower differentiation (meristems)

Arabidopsis thaliana flower

David McIntyre

A flower contains four whorls of organs. Each whorl is produced by a distinct group of cells whose identity is determined by the transcription factors present.

Sepals
Petals
Stamens
Carpels

(B) Floral organ identity genes

| A | B | C |

Three classes of organ identity genes, A, B, and C, code for polypeptides that combine to make transcription factors.

Transcription factor

DNA

Promoter

In this case, the combination AB stimulates transcription of genes for petal formation.

Petal

(C) Expression of identity genes

The combinations of AA, AB, BC, and CC each act to stimulate expression of genes for a particular organ.

	Whorl 1	Whorl 2	Whorl 3	Whorl 4
Organ identity genes expressed		B	B	
	A	A	C	C
Transcription factor	AA	AB	BC	CC
Flower structure	Sepal	Petal	Stamen	Carpel

Figure 36.9 **ABC Model for Flower Formation**   **(A)** The four organs of a flower—sepals (pink), petals (purple), stamens (green), and carpels (yellow)—grow in whorls that develop from the floral meristem. **(B)** Floral organs are determined by three classes of organ identity genes, the polypeptide products of which combine to form transcription factors. **(C)** Combinations of polypeptide subunits in transcription factors activate expression of specific genes.

▶ **View in Achieve**
Simulation 36.1 Genes and Development

Modifications of this basic structure can result in great diversity. For example, expression of class B genes in the outermost whorl as well as in whorls 2 and 3 causes what would have been sepals to look like petals. This explains how tulip flowers arise (Figure 36.10). The multiple petals in cultivated roses are derived from wild relatives with one whorl of five petals and many stamens. A simple conversion of stamens to petals can be achieved by changing the boundary of class A gene expression.

Orchids can be particularly remarkable in having multiple types of unusually shaped petals. These appear to have arisen through diversification of the organ identity genes, creating a situation in which individual orchid petals express different versions of the identity genes. Flowers that lack specific organs, such as flowers that are all male or all female, can arise through selective abortion of particular whorls.

Floral organ identity genes often become activated in response to external cues (day length, temperature) or internal cues (hormones). We begin with day length, or photoperiod.

Photoperiodic cues can initiate flowering

The study of how light affects the transition to flowering began with two observations in the early twentieth century:

- Normally, tobacco grows to about 1.5 meters tall before flowering in the summer, but a variety called Maryland Mammoth grows to an amazing 5 meters. Farmers in Virginia were frustrated because they could not easily get seeds from this luxuriant plant for successive crops. Instead of flowering, it continued to grow until the late fall frost killed it.

- Because of improvements in agricultural techniques, soybean yields became so great that it was hard for farmers to harvest all the plants at once. Hoping to stagger the harvests, farmers tried planting the seeds in groups several weeks apart, but all resulting plants nevertheless formed flowers and seeds at the same time.

© Wildlife GmbH/Alamy Stock Photo

Figure 36.10 Anatomy of a Tulip Flower

Figure 36.11 Day Length and Flowering   Flowering of Maryland Mammoth tobacco is initiated when the days become shorter than a critical length. Maryland Mammoth tobacco is thus called a short-day plant. Henbane, a long-day plant, shows an inverse pattern of flowering. (After W. W. Garner and H. A. Allard. 1921. In *Yearbook 1920*, USDA, pp. 377–400. U.S. Government Printing Office: Washington, D.C.)

The explanation for both of these observations was the same: the signal that set the plants' shoot apical meristems on the path to flowering was the length of daylight, or **photoperiod**. When soybeans experience days of a certain length, they flower, regardless of how "old" they are. Maryland Mammoth tobacco *can* flower, but it doesn't do so in Virginia because it dies when the weather there gets cold. Maryland Mammoth is now grown commercially in Florida. You saw another example of the role of photoperiod in the opening investigation of this chapter, dealing with poinsettias.

Scientists used greenhouse experiments to measure the day length required for different plant species to flower. Maryland Mammoth tobacco did not flower if exposed to more than 14 hours of light per day; flowering was only initiated once day length became shorter than 14 hours, as it does in December. Other plants (such as soybean and henbane) flowered only when the days were long (**Figure 36.11**). Control of an organism's responses by the length of day or night is called **photoperiodism**.

Plants vary in their responses to photoperiodic cues

Plants that flower in response to photoperiodic stimuli fall into two main classes:

1. **Short-day plants** (**SDPs**) flower only when the day is shorter than a critical maximum. They include coffee, morning glory, Maryland Mammoth tobacco, poinsettias, and chrysanthemums. Thus, for example, you see chrysanthemums in nurseries in the fall and poinsettias in winter.

2. **Long-day plants** (**LDPs**) flower only when the day is longer than a critical minimum. Spinach, lettuce, and clover are examples of LDPs. For example, spinach tends to flower in the summer, so for harvesting leaves, it is planted in early spring.

While there are variations on these two patterns, photoperiodic control of flowering serves an important role: it synchronizes the flowering of plants of the same species in a local population, and this promotes cross-pollination and successful reproduction.

Night length is a key photoperiodic cue that determines flowering

The terms "short-day plant" and "long-day plant" imply that *day length* is the environmental cue that triggers flowering. Actually, the important cue is *night length*, as a series of greenhouse experiments confirmed (**Figure 36.12**). In a greenhouse, the overall length of a day or night can be varied, irrespective of the 24-hour natural cycle. For example, if cocklebur, an SDP, is exposed to several long periods of light (16 hours each), it will still flower as long as the dark period between them is 9 hours or longer. This 9-hour inductive dark period also induces flowering even if the light period varies from 8 hours to 12 hours.

Biologists noticed that when the inductive dark period was interrupted by a brief period of light, the flowering signal generated by the long night disappeared. It took several days of long nights for the plant to recover and initiate flowering. Interrupting the day with a dark period had no effect on flowering. A clue as to what occurred in the plant when the flash of light was given came when biologists determined the action spectrum for the wavelengths of light that were effective. As with lettuce seed germination (see Figure 35.22), red light was most effective at breaking the "night" stimulus, and its effect was reversible by far-red light (**Investigating Life: The Flowering Signal**). Later, the photoreceptor involved was identified as a phytochrome.

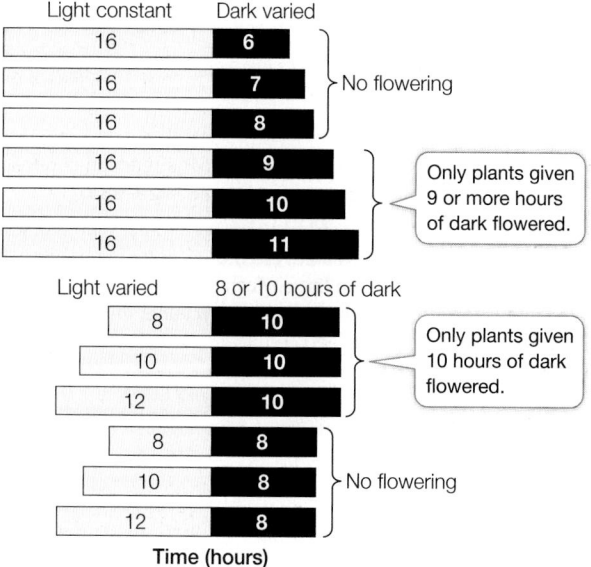

Figure 36.12 Night Length and Flowering   Greenhouse experiments using cocklebur, a short-day plant, showed that night length, not day length, is the environmental cue that initiates flowering.

▶InvestigatingLIFE The Flowering Signal

Experiment

Original Paper: S. B. Hendricks and H. W. Siegelman. 1967. Phytochrome and photoperiodism in plants. In *Photobiology, Ionizing Radiations*, M. Florkin and E. H. Stotz (Eds.), pp. 211–235. Elsevier: New York.

Knowing that plants measure night duration, the question became whether the dark hours to which a plant is exposed must be continuous. Using SDPs and LDPs as test subjects, Karl Hamner and James Bonner demonstrated that this was the case by interrupting the night with short bursts of light. Sterling Hendricks and William Siegelman repeated the experiments using light of different wavelengths to gain information about the photoreceptor involved.

HYPOTHESIS▶ Red light participates in the photoperiodic timing mechanism.

METHOD▶ Grow plants under short-day conditions, but interrupt the night with light of different wavelengths.

CONCLUSION▶ When plants are exposed to red (R) and far-red (FR) light in alternation, the final treatment determines the effect. Phytochrome is the photoreceptor.

 View in Achieve
Simulation 36.2 **Flowering and Day Length**

Work with the Data

Original Paper: H. A. Borthwick et al. 1952. The reaction controlling floral initiation. *Proc Natl Acad Sci USA* 38: 929–934.

After it was established that the length of night, rather than day, was critical for flowering in some plants, the U.S. Department of Agriculture group that had worked on the phytochrome response of lettuce seed germination (see Figure 35.22) asked whether the signaling system that initiated lettuce seed germination was the same as that involved in flowering.

QUESTIONS▶

1. Cocklebur plants, which are SDPs that flower when exposed to long nights, were grown in conditions that could induce flowering, except that the nights were interrupted by a flash of light such that flowering was prevented. Following that nighttime flash, some of the plants were exposed to a second light. Plants were then allowed to grow for some days in short-night conditions that would not induce flowering, and the number of plants that contained a floral meristem was examined by dissection. **Table A** shows the results.

Table A

Wavelength (nm)	Number of plants with a floral meristem after exposure to second light			
	16 min	8 min	4 min	2 min
680	0	0	0	0
700	1	3	0	0
720	3	3	3	1

  a. Why were the plants grown in short-night conditions after the light flashes, prior to evaluation of flowering?

  b. What can you conclude from the data in terms of the receptor and time needed?

2. Groups of four plants were exposed to red, far-red, or no light at the beginning of the dark period (extending the day). Following this, the plants were given a dark period of the length indicated. The results are shown in **Table B**. Explain the changes in the critical night length required for flowering in terms of the phytochrome system.

Table B

Length of dark period (h)	Number of plants with a floral meristem		
	No light	660 nm	720 nm
7.0	—	—	4
7.5	—	—	4
8.0	0	0	4
8.5	4	0	4
9.0	4	4	—
9.5	4	4	—

Go to Achieve for a companion
Data in Depth **exercise.**

As described in Key Concept 35.4, phytochromes and a blue-light receptor function together to "entrain" a circadian rhythm in plants. These photoreceptors cycle through active and inactive phases over repeated 24-hour periods. One gene whose expression follows a circadian rhythm is *CONSTANS (CO)*, which

encodes a transcriptional regulator that controls the expression of flowering genes.

Experiments with *Arabidopsis thaliana*, an LDP, have shown that photoperiodic flowering times are determined by interactions between photoreceptors and the CO protein. *CO* gene expression goes through regular 24-hour cycles with peak expression occurring in the afternoon. On long days, the peak of *CO* mRNA production coincides with a period of daylight, whereas on short days it occurs after dark. The coincidence of light and *CO* mRNA levels affects the plant because CO protein is stabilized by light in the afternoon, so CO protein builds up only during long days. Accumulation of CO protein does not occur on short days.

 View in Achieve
Animation 36.2 The Effect of Interrupted Days and Nights

The flowering stimulus originates in a leaf

Early experiments indicated that reception of the photoperiodic stimulus occurs within the leaf. For example, in the LDP spinach, flowering occurred if the leaves were exposed to long-day periods of light, while the shoot apical meristem was masked to simulate short days. Flowering could not occur when the leaves were masked to simulate short days, while the bud was exposed to long-day periods of light.

These "masking" experiments were extended to SDPs as well (**Figure 36.13**). Because the receptor of the stimulus (in the leaf) is physically separated from the tissue on which the stimulus acts (the bud meristem), the inference can be drawn that a systemic signal travels from the leaf through the plant's tissues to the bud meristem. Other evidence that a diffusible chemical travels from the leaf to the bud meristem signal includes the following:

- If a photoperiodically induced leaf is immediately removed from a plant after the inductive dark period, the plant does not flower. If, however, the induced leaf remains attached to the plant for several hours, the plant will flower. This result suggests that something is synthesized in the leaf in response to the inductive dark period, and then moves out of the leaf to induce flowering.

- If two cocklebur plants are grafted together, and if only one of the plants is exposed to inductive long nights, both plants flower.

- In several species, if an induced leaf from one species is grafted onto another, noninduced plant of a different species, the recipient plant flowers.

The transmissible signal was given a name, **florigen** ("flower inducing"), in 1937, but its chemical nature was not described until 2008.

Florigen is a small protein

The characterization of florigen was made possible by genetic and molecular studies of the model plant *Arabidopsis thaliana*. Three genes are involved in the signaling response for flowering (**Figure 36.14**):

1. *FT* (***FLOWERING LOCUS T***) codes for florigen. FT is a small (20 kilodalton [kDa]) protein that can travel through plasmodesmata. FT is synthesized in the phloem companion cells of the leaf and then diffuses into the adjacent sieve tube elements. It then is carried through the phloem to the apical meristem. If the protein-coding region of the *FT* gene is coupled to an active promoter and expressed at high levels in the shoot meristem, flowering is induced even in the absence of an appropriate photoperiodic stimulus.

Experiment

Figure 36.13A The Flowering Signal Moves from Leaf to Bud

Original Paper: K. C. Hamner and J. Bonner. 1938. Photoperiodism in relation to hormones as factors in floral initiation and development. *Bot Gaz* 100: 388–431.

The receptors for photoperiod are in the leaf, but the transition to flowering occurs in the shoot apical meristem. To investigate whether there is a diffusible substance that travels from leaf to bud, Hamner and Bonner exposed only the leaf to the photoperiodic stimulus.

HYPOTHESIS▶ The leaves measure the photoperiod.

METHOD▶ Grow cocklebur plants (short-day) under long days and short nights. Mask a leaf on some plants and see if flowering occurs.

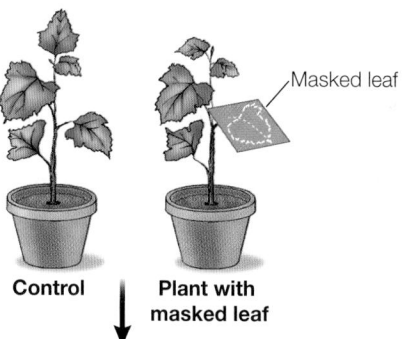

Control   **Plant with masked leaf**

RESULTS▶ If even one leaf is masked for part of the day—thus shifting that leaf to short days and long nights—the plant will flower.

CONCLUSION▶ The leaves measure the photoperiod. Therefore some signal must move from the induced leaf to the flowering parts of the plant.

Figure 36.13B Work with the Data follows on next page.

---

2. *CO* (***CONSTANS***) codes for the transcription factor that activates the synthesis of FT. As described earlier in this key concept, *CO* expression follows a circadian rhythm, and stabilization of the CO protein occurs when the protein is produced in the light, allowing it to accumulate in long days. Like *FT*, *CO* is expressed in leaf companion cells. If *CO* is experimentally overexpressed in the leaf, flowering is induced. However, if *CO* is overexpressed in the apical meristem, flowering is not induced, indicating that *CO* functions in the leaf.

Work with the Data

Figure 36.13B   The Flowering Signal Moves from Leaf to Bud

Original Paper: K. C. Hamner and J. Bonner. 1938. Photoperiodism in relation to hormones as factors in floral initiation and development. *Bot Gaz* 100: 388–431.

In 1938 Karl Hamner at the University of Chicago was working on the role of plant nutrition in flowering. The plant he studied, cocklebur, is a short-day plant that requires 16 hours of darkness to flower. When the plants were kept in 6 hours darkness (16 hours light) in a greenhouse, they did not flower. One day Hamner came to the lab to find all the plants flowering. It turned out that there had been a power outage, and the plants had received a single inductive short day (long night). Realizing that this provided a simple system to study flowering, Hamner invited a major scientist in the field, James Bonner from Caltech, to join him for the summer. The two biologists carried out a series of experiments using the single inductive period that showed that flowering is induced by night length as opposed to day length (see Figure 36.12) and that the flowering signal is received by the leaf, from which it travels to a bud, inducing flowering. A Russian plant physiologist, Mikhail Chailakhyan, named this signal florigen. More recently, the molecular nature of this signal was described.

QUESTIONS▶

1. Intact cocklebur plants (6) or plants with their leaves removed (6) were placed in the inductive (short-day) photoperiod. After 14 days, the researchers obtained the results in **Table A**. Based on these data, which part of the plant senses the photoperiod?

Table A

Treatment	Number of plants that flowered
No inductive period, intact plant	0
Inductive period, intact plant	6
Inductive period, leaves removed	0

2. Cocklebur plants were treated so that a single leaf was exposed to the inductive (short) photoperiod while the rest of the plant received the long photoperiod. The results obtained after 18 days are shown in **Table B**. What do these results indicate about the location of the receptor for flowering?

Table B

Treatment	Number of plants	Result
Untreated	6	Vegetative
Treated, one leaf	32	Flower

3. What do the data tell you about the signal that is generated by the plant in response to photoperiod and that induces flowering in the apical meristem?

Go to Achieve for a companion Data in Depth exercise.

1 An inductive photoperiod stabilizes CO, which acts as a transcription factor.

Photoperiodic stimulus

CO

DNA

Transcription

Companion cell

FT

Sieve tube element

FT

2 FT is made and enters sieve tube elements through plasmodesmata.

3 FT is transported through the phloem up to the apical bud.

5 Floral meristems that give rise to flowers arise after the apical meristem is respecified as an inflorescence meristem.

Apical meristem

AP1

DNA (FT) (FD)

Transcription

4 FT combines with FD, and the complex induces transcription of several mRNAs (*LFY, SOC1, AP1*), the protein products of which further activate one another's expression.

CO	CONSTANS protein
FT	FLOWERING LOCUS T protein (florigen)
FD	FLOWERING LOCUS D protein
AP1	APETALA1 protein

Figure 36.14 Florigen and Its Molecular Biology Florigen is a protein (FT) made in the phloem companion cells. It travels in the sieve tube elements from the leaf to the bud meristem. There, florigen combines with another protein to stimulate transcription of genes that initiate flower formation.

3. **FD** (**FLOWERING LOCUS D**) encodes a protein that binds to FT protein when it arrives in the apical meristem. The FD protein is a transcription factor that, when bound to FT, initiates transcription of a set of genes that code for other transcription factors, including the class A floral organ identity gene *APETALA1* (*AP1*) (see Figure 36.9). The small group of transcription factors that is upregulated by FT–FD creates a positive feedback loop, as several of the proteins upregulate expression of other proteins in the group. Having a positive feedback loop at the center of a developmental transition is advantageous because it can act as a switch between two distinct programs. The meristem is either vegetative, producing leaves, or the positive feedback loop has been activated and the meristem is reprogrammed such that it gives rise to flowers. There is little chance of an in-between state.

Before FT was isolated, grafting experiments indicated that many different plant species could be induced to flower by the same chemical signal. Results of molecular experiments confirmed that the *FT* gene is involved in photoperiod signaling in many species:

- Transgenic plants (e.g., tobacco and tomato) that express the *A. thaliana FT* gene at high levels flower regardless of day length.

- Transgenic *A. thaliana* plants that express *FT* homologs from other plants (e.g., rice and tomato) flower regardless of day length.

The manner in which light affects the degradation of CO protein is complex. One system that leads to the ubiquitination and then degradation of CO protein is inhibited by several light-activated receptors, resulting in stabilization of CO in the light. Additionally, the amount of active phytochrome B (phyB) present in the morning affects the rate of CO degradation. Recall that phytochrome exists in two forms, P_r and P_{fr}. At night, the P_{fr} form gradually is converted back to P_r. So long nights result in more P_{fr} being converted back to P_r. A low level of P_{fr} in the morning results in less breakdown of CO protein. A high level of CO results in the transcription of genes for flowering, such as *FT*. To summarize:

Low P_{fr} → more CO → more transcription of *FT* → flowering

We have considered the photoperiodic regulation of flowering, from photoreceptors in the leaf to florigen that travels from the induced leaf to the sites of flower formation. In some plants, however, flowering is induced by other stimuli. These additional stimuli can function with photoperiodism or independently of it.

Flowering can be induced by temperature or gibberellin

Whereas some plants use the environmental cue of day length to induce flowering, other plants use different mechanisms. These include temperature (another environmental cue) and gibberellin (an internal, hormonal cue).

TEMPERATURE   In some plant species, notably certain cereal grains, the environmental signal for flowering is cold temperature, a phenomenon called **vernalization** (Latin *vernus*, "spring"). In both wheat and rye, we distinguish two categories of flowering

Winter-annual *Arabidopsis* without vernalization

Winter-annual *Arabidopsis* with vernalization

Figure 36.15 Vernalization   A genetic strain of *Arabidopsis thaliana* (winter-annual *A. thaliana*) requires vernalization for flowering. Without it, the plant is large and vegetative (left), but with the cold period it is smaller and flowers (right).

behavior. Spring wheat, for example, is a typical annual plant: it is sown in the spring and flowers in the same year. Winter wheat is sown in the fall, grows to a seedling, overwinters (often covered by snow), and flowers the following summer. If winter wheat is not exposed to cold in its first year, it will not flower normally the next year.

Studies of *A. thaliana* have shown how vernalization leads to flowering (Figure 36.15). In some strains of *A. thaliana* a gene called *FLC* (*FLOWERING LOCUS C*) encodes a transcription factor that blocks the FT–FD florigen pathway (see Figure 36.14) by inhibiting expression of FT and FD. Cold temperature inhibits the synthesis of FLC protein, allowing the FT and FD proteins to be expressed, and flowering to proceed. Similar proteins control some steps in vernalization in cereals.

Epigenetics plays an important role in the inhibition of *FLC* gene expression by cold temperature. Before vernalization, the chromatin at the promoter of the *FLC* gene is in a relaxed configuration, with histone protein acetylation lowering the ionic attraction of these proteins for DNA, which allows transcription (**Figure 36.16A**). During vernalization, a gene is expressed whose protein product is involved in the deacetylation of histones on the *FLC* gene. Deacetylation causes the chromatin to be more compact, which blocks *FLC* gene expression (**Figure 36.16B**).

 Media Clip 36.2 How Plants Remember
Life12e.com/mc36.2

Connect the Concepts   As described in Key Concept 16.4, epigenetic remodeling of chromatin involves loosening the nucleosome–DNA complex, opening up DNA for gene transcription. See Figure 16.18.

GIBBERELLIN   *A. thaliana* plants do not flower if they are genetically deficient in the hormone gibberellin, or if they are treated with an inhibitor of gibberellin synthesis. These observations implicate gibberellins in flowering. Direct application of gibberellins to *A. thaliana* buds results in activation of the meristem identity gene *LEAFY,* which in turn promotes the transition to flowering.

(A) Chromatin relaxed

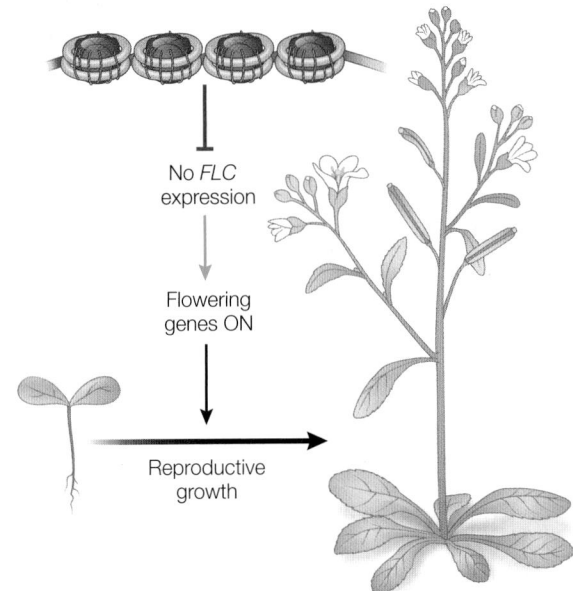

(B) Chromatin compact (prolonged cold winter)

Figure 36.16 Chromatin Remodeling during Vernalization
(A) In the absence of vernalization, *FLOWERING LOCUS C* (*FLC*) is expressed and flowering is repressed. **(B)** Prolonged cold weather leads to chromatin remodeling that represses expression of *FLC*. The absence of FLC protein allows flowering genes to be expressed.

Figure 36.17 Induction of Flowering   Multiple factors that promote flowering affect the expression of the same small group of genes.

Some plants do not require an environmental cue to flower

Several plant species and strains do not require a photoperiod or vernalization to flower, but instead flower on cue from an "internal clock." For example, flowering in some strains of tobacco will be initiated in the terminal bud when the stem has grown four phytomers in length (recall that stems are composed of repeating units called phytomers; see Figure 32.16). If such a bud with a single adjacent phytomer is removed and planted, the cutting will flower because the bud has already received the cue for flowering. But the rest of the shoot below the bud that has been removed will not flower because it is only three phytomers long. After it grows an additional phytomer, it will flower. These results suggest that there is something about the *position* of the bud (atop four phytomers of stem) that determines its transition to flowering.

The bud might "know" its position by the concentration of some substance that forms a positional gradient along the length of the plant. Such a gradient could be formed if the root makes a diffusible inhibitor of flowering whose concentration diminishes with plant height. When the plant reaches a certain height, the concentration of the inhibitor would become sufficiently low at the tip of the shoot to allow flowering. What this inhibitor might be is unclear, but there is evidence that it acts by decreasing the amount of FLC, allowing the FT–FD pathway to proceed (just as cold acts on FLC in vernalization). A positional gradient that acts on FLC would be consistent with other mechanisms affecting flowering, which all converge on *LEAFY* and *APETALA1* (Figure 36.17).

KEY CONCEPT
36.2 Recap and Assess

Angiosperms begin flowering after the apical meristem starts expressing a specific set of genes that convert the meristem to an inflorescence meristem. As flowers form, the combination of transcription factors expressed in each of the four whorls of the flower specifies what type of organ (sepal, petal, stamen, or carpel) will be produced. In some angiosperms, the transition to the flowering (reproductive) state is controlled by night length, a phenomenon called photoperiodism. The photoperiodic flowering stimulus originates in the leaf, and a signaling pathway ends in the expression of floral organ identity genes in the bud. In other angiosperms, other cues can drive the transition to flowering.

1. Construct a diagram showing how a tulip flower that has two outer whorls, both of which look like petals, could arise by expanding the location in which particular organ identity genes are expressed.

2. A horticulturist provides cut flowers for many occasions and often requires large numbers of flowers all blooming at the same time. Many of her flowers are normally summer-blooming, or long-day plants. How might she force these flowers to bloom during the winter?

3. Describe the proteins and mutations that could be involved in the following observations:

   a. A mutant plant flowers without its normal inductive dark period. When a leaf from the mutant plant is grafted onto an unexposed wild-type plant, the recipient plant flowers.

   b. A mutant plant does not flower when exposed to the normal inductive dark period. When a leaf from a mutant plant that has been exposed to the inductive dark period is grafted onto an unexposed wild-type plant, the recipient plant flowers.

c. A plant flowers only after exposure to cold.

d. If a gene is experimentally overexpressed in the leaf, flowering is induced. Overexpression of the gene in the shoot apical meristem, however, does not induce flowering.

You have seen how environmental factors interact with genes to control flowering in angiosperms. The function of flowers is sexual reproduction, which maintains beneficial genetic variation in a population. Many angiosperms, however, also benefit from being able to reproduce asexually.

KEY CONCEPT 36.3 Angiosperms Can Reproduce Asexually

Learning Objectives

36.3.1 Compare and contrast sexual and asexual reproduction in plants, including both the end result and the advantages and disadvantages.

36.3.2 List types of locations where vegetatively reproducing plants might occur, and give reasons for their occurrence in these locations.

36.3.3 Describe how apomixis occurs and how this might be useful in agriculture.

Although sexual reproduction takes up most of the space in this chapter, asexual reproduction accounts for many of the individual plants present on Earth. This fact suggests that in some circumstances asexual reproduction must be advantageous. In fact, many plants reproduce both asexually and sexually. For example, irises (*Iris* spp.), have beautiful flowers for sexual reproduction but also a rhizome (an underground stem) from which new plants can arise asexually (**Figure 36.18**).

We have noted that genetic recombination is one of the advantages of sexual reproduction. Self-fertilization is a form of sexual reproduction, but offers fewer opportunities for genetic recombination than does cross-fertilization. A diploid, self-fertilizing plant that is heterozygous for a certain locus can produce both kinds of homozygotes for that locus plus the heterozygote among its progeny, but it cannot produce any progeny carrying alleles that it does not itself possess. Nevertheless many self-fertilizing plant species produce viable and vigorous offspring.

Asexual reproduction eliminates genetic recombination altogether. A plant that reproduces asexually produces progeny genetically identical to the parent. What, then, is the advantage of asexual reproduction? If a plant is well adapted to its environment, asexual reproduction allows it to pass on to all its progeny a superior combination of alleles, which might otherwise be separated by sexual recombination.

Plants reproduce asexually by several methods

Stems, leaves, and roots are considered vegetative organs and are distinguished from flowers, the reproductive parts of the plant. Asexual reproduction is often accomplished through the modification of a vegetative organ, which is why the term **vegetative reproduction** is sometimes used to describe asexual reproduction in plants. Often the stem is the organ that is modified for vegetative reproduction. Strawberries, for example, produce horizontal stems, called stolons or runners, which grow along the soil surface, form roots at intervals, and establish potentially independent plants (**Figure 36.19A**). Asexual reproduction by shoot tips is accomplished when the tips of upright branches sag to the ground and develop roots, as in blackberry and forsythia.

Some plants, such as potatoes, form enlarged fleshy tips of underground stems, called tubers, that can produce new plants from the "eyes." Rhizomes are horizontal underground stems that can give rise to new shoots. Bamboo is a striking example of a plant that reproduces vegetatively by means of rhizomes. A single bamboo plant can give rise to a stand—even a forest—of plants constituting a single, physically connected entity.

Whereas stolons and rhizomes are horizontal stems, bulbs and corms are short, vertical, underground stems. Lilies and garlic form bulbs (**Figure 36.19B**), short stems with many fleshy, highly modified leaves that store nutrients. These storage leaves make up most of the bulb. They can give rise to new plants by dividing or by producing new bulbs from axillary buds. Crocuses, gladioli, and many other plants produce corms, underground stems that function very much as bulbs do. Corms are disclike and consist primarily of stem tissue; they lack the fleshy modified leaves that are characteristic of bulbs.

Stems are not the only vegetative organs modified for asexual reproduction. Leaves may also be the source of new plantlets, as in some succulent plants called mother of thousands (genus *Kalanchoe*) (**Figure 36.19C**). Many kinds of angiosperms, ranging from grasses to trees such as aspen and poplars, form interconnected, genetically homogeneous populations by means of suckers—shoots produced by roots. What appears to be a whole stand of aspen trees, for example, may be a clone derived from a single tree by suckers (see Figure 11.13). This is why the leaves of a whole stand of aspen typically turn yellow at the same time.

Plants that reproduce vegetatively often grow in physically unstable soils such as eroding hillsides. Plants with stolons or rhizomes, such as beach grasses, rushes, and sand verbena, are

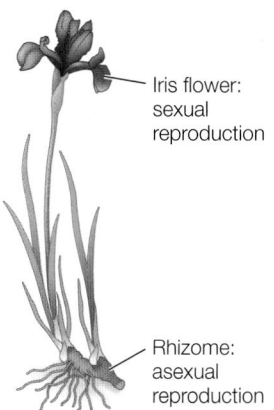

Iris flower: sexual reproduction

Rhizome: asexual reproduction

Figure 36.18 Sexual and Asexual Reproduction in Irises

(A) Stolons

Horizontal stems (or runners) of the strawberry plant can take root and form new plants.

© Robert & Jean Pollock/Visuals Unlimited, Inc.

(B) Bulbs

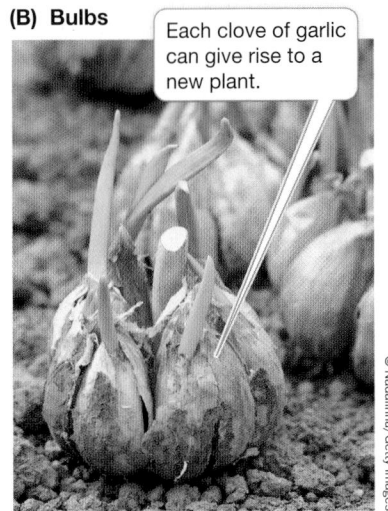

Each clove of garlic can give rise to a new plant.

© Nadalinna/Getty Images

(C) Plantlets

The plantlets forming on the margin of this mother of thousands leaf will fall to the ground and become independent plants.

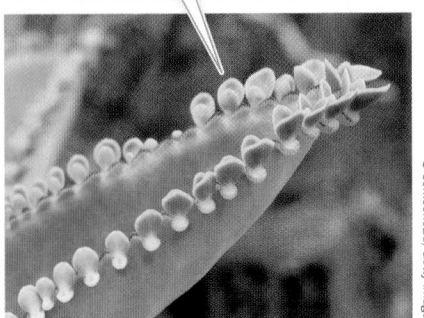

© someone25/Getty Images

Figure 36.19 Vegetative Organs Modified for Reproduction

common pioneers on coastal sand dunes. Rapid vegetative reproduction enables these plants, once introduced, not only to multiply but also to survive burial by the shifting sand; in addition, the dunes are stabilized by the extensive network of rhizomes or stolons that develops. Vegetative reproduction is also common in some deserts, where the environment is often not suitable for seed germination and the establishment of seedlings.

Vegetative reproduction has a disadvantage

Vegetative reproduction is highly efficient in an environment that is stable over the long term. A change in the environment, however, can leave an asexually reproducing species at a disadvantage. A striking example is provided by the demise of the English elm (*Ulmus procera*), which was apparently introduced into England as a clone by the ancient Romans. This tree reproduces asexually by suckers and is incapable of sexual reproduction. In 1967 Dutch elm disease first struck the English elms. After two millennia of clonal growth, the population lacked genetic diversity, and no individuals carried genes that would protect them against the disease. Today the English elm is all but gone from England.

Vegetative reproduction is important in agriculture

One of the oldest methods of vegetative reproduction used in agriculture consists of simply making cuttings of stems, inserting them in soil, and waiting for them to form roots and become autonomous plants. The cuttings are usually encouraged to root by treatment with auxin, a plant hormone.

Woody plants can be propagated asexually by **grafting**: attaching a bud or a piece of stem from one plant to a root or root-bearing stem of another plant. The part of the resulting plant that comes from the root-bearing "host" is called the **stock**; the part grafted on is the **scion** (Figure 36.20). The vascular cambium of the scion associates with that of the stock, forming a continuous cambium that produces xylem and phloem. The cambium allows the transport of water and minerals to the scion and of photosynthate to

the stock. Much of the fruit grown for market in the United States is produced on grafted trees, as are wine grapes.

Another method widely used for asexual plant propagation is **meristem culture**, in which pieces of shoot apical meristem are cultured on growth media to generate plantlets, which can then be planted in the field. This strategy is vital when uniformity is desired, as in forestry, or when virus-free plants are the goal, as with strawberries and potatoes.

In apomixis, flowers are used in asexual reproduction

Some plants produce flowers but use them to reproduce asexually rather than sexually. Dandelions, blackberries, some citrus trees, and some other plants reproduce by the asexual production of seeds, which is called **apomixis**. In sexual reproduction, seeds form from the union of haploid gametes in the embryo sac. But in apomixis, reproduction occurs differently. For example:

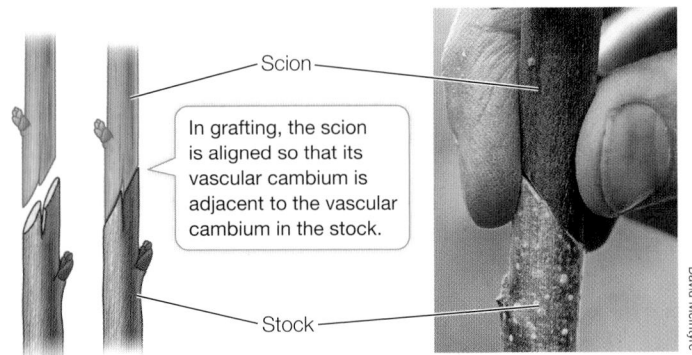

Scion

In grafting, the scion is aligned so that its vascular cambium is adjacent to the vascular cambium in the stock.

Stock

David McIntyre

Figure 36.20 Grafting Grafting—attaching a piece of a plant to the root or root-bearing stem of another plant—is a common horticultural technique. The "host" root or stem is the stock; the upper grafted piece is the scion. In the photo, a scion of one apple variety is being grafted onto a stock of another variety.

- The megasporocyte in the ovule that is supposed to undergo meiosis fails to do so, resulting in a diploid egg cell, which then goes on to form an embryo and seed.

- Diploid cells from the integument surrounding the embryo sac form a diploid embryo sac, and the sac goes on to form an embryo and seed.

In both cases, seed and fruit development proceed normally. But the genetic consequences are profound: *apomixis produces clones.*

Some agriculturally important plants are hybrids that are derived by crossing two genetically different varieties. Because these hybrids have two sets of chromosomes that are not homologous to one another, they cannot undergo meiosis and are sterile. This means they cannot form the seeds and fruits that are desired by people. In citrus, apomixis occurs naturally, which gets around this problem. Kentucky bluegrass, a mainstay of lawns, reproduces in this manner as well.

Many important crops, such as corn, are grown as hybrids because the progeny of a cross between two inbred, homozygous genetic strains are often superior to either of their parents, a phenomenon called hybrid vigor (see Key Concept 12.3). Unfortunately, once farmers have obtained a hybrid with desirable characteristics, they cannot use those plants to create similar seed for the next year. You can imagine the genetic chaos when a hybrid, which is heterozygous at many of its loci (e.g., *AaBbCcDdEe*, etc.), is crossed with itself: there will be many new combinations of alleles (e.g., *AabbCCDdee*, etc.), resulting in highly variable progeny. The only way to reliably reproduce the hybrid is to maintain populations of the original parents to cross again each year. That is exactly what seed companies do. For farmers, it means buying new seeds every year—an expensive proposition.

If a hybrid carried a gene for apomixis, however, it could reproduce asexually, and its offspring would be genetically identical to itself. New hybrids could be developed that would be adapted to specific environments and could be propagated by the farmers on the spot. So an intensive search is on for genes for apomixis that could be introduced into desirable crops and allow them to be propagated indefinitely. Such a gene has been identified in corn, but the yield of the variety that contains it is low.

KEY CONCEPT
36.3 Recap and Assess

Angiosperms may reproduce asexually by means of modified stems, roots, or leaves. Asexual reproduction is advantageous when a plant has a superior genotype well adapted to its environment, but it can decrease the genetic diversity of plant populations. Seeds and fruits, normally the result of sexual reproduction, can form asexually through apomixis.

1. What are the advantages and disadvantages of asexual reproduction in plants? What are the advantages and disadvantages of sexual reproduction?

2. In what types of situations might asexual reproduction in plants be adaptive?

3. Thompson Seedless® grapes are produced from triploid plants. Explain why these grapes are seedless. Describe the role played by the flower in fruit formation when no seeds are being formed.

4. Most of the navel orange trees that once grew all over southern California were derived by grafting and apomixis from a single tree that still exists in Riverside, California. How would you prove this?

You have seen how angiosperms reproduce sexually and asexually. A disadvantage of asexual reproduction is that its genetic inflexibility may leave a population unable to cope with new challenges. In the next chapter we will focus on the mechanisms that have evolved in plants to cope with biological and physical challenges in their environment.

▶Investigating LIFE

Q and A — How did an understanding of angiosperm reproduction allow floriculturists to develop a commercially successful poinsettia?

Poinsettias are short-day plants, using the long nights of winter as a signal for flowering. In fact, the poinsettia's inductive dark period of 14 hours was among the first described in a flowering plant. To control photoperiod, the plants are grown in greenhouses, where the photoperiod is carefully regulated.

Another important factor in the poinsettia's commercial success was the plant's growth habit. In Mexico, the wild relatives of cultivated varieties grow up to 3 meters tall, with few branches (compare the plants shown in the opening question with the commercial variety in the chapter-opening photo). Paul Ecke found a variety that was much shorter and formed an attractive branching plant with axillary shoots. These compact poinsettias were initially propagated asexually by grafting to native plants.

Many new varieties of poinsettias have been generated by conventional sexual reproduction. You can look for the phenotypes of these varieties next holiday season. They include stiff stems, new colors (such as white), and longer lifetimes for the colorful bracts. How do you think these characteristics have been introduced into the cultivated varieties?

Future directions

Sequencing of the genomes of agriculturally important plants and genetic screening of mutant strains have led to an accumulation of knowledge of genes controlling the transition to flowering. Efforts are under way to use this understanding to breed crops that produce more seeds more often, by conventional means or biotechnology. This has enormous potential for human welfare. Consider legumes, which are in two general clades, most represented by peas and soybeans. The former is a long-day plant that responds to cold (vernalization), while the latter is more acclimated to warm climes and responds to short days to flower. Genes for the photoperiodic response and signal transduction for flowering have been identified for both species. For example, genetic changes in signaling could allow the plants to have more vegetative growth prior to flowering, which might lead to more floral meristems, more flowers, and more seeds.

You should be able to relate each summary to the adjacent figures. If you go to this visual summary in **Achieve**, you can follow links to figures, animations, activities, and simulations that will help you consolidate the material.

KEY CONCEPT

36.1 Most Angiosperms Reproduce Sexually

Go to **Activity 36.1** and **Animation 36.1**

- The life cycle of flowering plants has two stages: a haploid gametophyte and a diploid sporophyte.

- Gametophytes produce gametes (eggs and sperm), and sporophytes produce spores.

- In **double fertilization**, one sperm fertilizes an egg, forming the 2n zygote, and the other sperm fertilizes the **polar nuclei**, forming the 3n **endosperm**.

Figure 36.3

Questions

1. How do female gametophytes and male gametophytes differ, and how are these differences important to sexual reproduction?

2. In the human life cycle, single-celled gametes (eggs and sperm) are produced directly by meiosis of the diploid organism. Which stage of the plant life cycle do humans lack?

3. Name one physical and one genetic method that can prevent inbreeding.

KEY CONCEPT

36.2 Hormones and Signaling Determine the Transition from the Vegetative to the Reproductive State

Go to **Animation 36.2** and **Simulations 36.1** and **36.2**

- **Florigen**, the hormone that induces a vegetative meristem to be converted to an **inflorescence** (reproductive) **meristem**, is produced in leaves in response to an inductive night length.

- An inflorescence meristem can produce floral primordia. Within a floral primordium, the expression of class A, B, and C **organ identity genes** determines which type of organ (sepal, petal, stamen, or carpel) is produced in each of the four whorls of the flower.

- Many plants use the photoreceptor phytochrome to perceive day-length. **Short-day plants (SDPs)** bloom when the night is longer than some critical value; **long-day plants (LDPs)** bloom when the night is shorter than some critical value.

Figure 36.9

	Whorl 1	Whorl 2	Whorl 3	Whorl 4
Organ identity genes expressed		B	B	
	A	A	C	C
Transcription factor	AA	AB	BC	CC
Flower structure	Sepal	Petal	Stamen	Carpel

Figure 36.14

Questions

1. Explain how expression of a transcription factor can affect the identity of a developing organ.

2. Explain how the co-occurrence of CO expression and a period of afternoon light affects flowering.

3. Give at least two pieces of evidence supporting the presence of a transmissible substance that moves from leaves to bud meristems to initiate flowering.

KEY CONCEPT

36.3 Angiosperms Can Reproduce Asexually

- Asexual reproduction allows rapid multiplication of organisms that are well suited to their environment.

- **Vegetative reproduction** occurs when vegetative organs—such as the stem—are used for reproduction.

- **Apomixis** is a form of reproduction in which seeds form without fertilization.

Questions

1. What form of reproduction (sexual or asexual) might be most advantageous in the face of global climate change?

2. Give an example of a habitat where vegetatively reproducing plants might occur, and give reasons for their occurrence in that location.

3. How can a failure to undergo meiosis lead to apomixis?

Figure 36.19

© Robert & Jean Pollock/Visuals Unlimited, Inc.

Figure 36.20

Scion

Stock

David McIntyre

Go to **Achieve** for the eBook, **LearningCurve**, animations, activities, simulations, and additional resources and assignments.

37 Plant Responses to Environmental Challenges

KEY CONCEPTS

37.1 Plants Can Sense and Respond to Environmental Stresses

37.2 Plants Respond to Pathogens with Constitutive and Induced Responses

37.3 Plants Have Mechanical and Chemical Defenses against Herbivores

Global climate change is increasing the frequency of severe weather, including droughts and floods. Spring floods can delay or even prevent planting and so decrease agricultural yield.

© Ken Schulze/Shutterstock.com

▶ Investigating LIFE

How Does Global Climate Change Impact Plant Growth?

Global climate change encompasses a wide range of environmental factors, including increases in atmospheric carbon dioxide, temperature, the severity of storms, and the incidence of drought. All of these can impact plant growth. Increased levels of CO_2 boost the amount of substrate available for photosynthesis and thus can have a fertilizing effect on plant growth. However, this effect can be outweighed by the negative effects of high temperature and changes in precipitation. In addition, if changes in climate affect the timing of plant and pathogen life cycles in an asynchronous manner, plant–pathogen interactions can be strongly affected. Climatic conditions can also affect the extent of an interaction when it does occur. For example, hot, humid conditions that tend to increase stomatal opening can favor infection by fungi, such as the wheat rust shown here, that enter leaves through open stomata. In addition, warmer winter temperatures increase both the percentage of pathogens overwintering and their metabolic rates, which can translate to an increase in plant predation. Models predict that an increase in average global temperature of about 2 degrees Celsius over preindustrial levels would increase the damage done by pests by close to 50% for wheat and about 30% for corn. While the future impact of climate change on agricultural production will depend on the extent of warming and the degree to which people are able to select the most appropriate crops, climate change has already had negative effects on agriculture in some regions, particularly for corn and wheat.

© Nigel Cattlin/Alamy Stock Photo

 How can plants respond to the environmental challenges posed by global climate change? (Find the answer on page 838.)

Plants Can Sense and Respond to Environmental Stresses

Learning Objectives

37.1.1 Describe what types of sensors plants use to perceive their environment.

37.1.2 Distinguish between the response (acclimation) an individual plant may have to an environmental condition and an adaptation to that environment.

37.1.3 Outline the signaling pathway that allows plants to respond to low soil moisture.

37.1.4 Assess how well the rate of dark reversion of phytochrome fits the criteria of what a temperature sensor should be.

37.1.5 Describe ways in which plants respond to extremes of soil moisture content or temperature to minimize their harmful effects.

Plants are threatened by many aspects of the physical environment, such as drought, waterlogged soils, and extreme temperatures (Table 37.1). Plants cope with environmental stresses through adaptation or acclimation.

- **Adaptation** is a genetically encoded strategy for maximizing survival and reproduction in a particular environment. A plant may have structures or biochemical properties that aid in its survival in the face of environmental challenges. Adaptations are the result of evolution by natural selection.

- **Acclimation** is increased tolerance for environmental extremes following exposure to them. An individual plant previously exposed to cold, for example, may be more likely to survive the subsequent winter.

Before a plant can acclimate to a particular environmental challenge, the plant must sense that aspect of the environment. Although plants do not have eyes, they do have photoreceptors that allow them to sense the intensity and wavelengths (color) of light. Plant root systems are able to sense levels of dissolved nutrients, and leaves can detect levels of volatile (gaseous) compounds in the air around them—capacities that share something with our own senses of taste and smell. Plants can also sense attack by pests and pathogens. Once a threat has been perceived, plants have an opportunity to mount appropriate responses. The following sections describe some of the ways in which plants sense and respond to their environment.

Plant growth is limited by water availability

Inadequate water supply is one of the primary factors that limits plant growth. In the future, water resources are predicted to become more scarce. Additionally, global climate change is expected to increase the extent of water limitation on plant growth through increased temperatures, which promote evaporation, and through an increase in drought, particularly in regions that already tend to be dry.

When the weather is abnormally dry, the water potential (see Key Concept 33.1) of the soil declines (becomes more negative). Water moves to the region with the lowest water potential, so a low water potential in the soil makes it more difficult for a plant to take in water. If a plant's roots cannot take up water from the soil, the plant cannot grow. Water is needed to keep cells hydrated, to drive the transport of nutrients and sugars through the plant, and to produce the turgor pressure that drives cell expansion. Extreme water deficits in plant cells also reduce membrane integrity as the polar–nonpolar forces that orient the lipid bilayer are reduced, and lead to changes in the three-dimensional structures of proteins. In some cases, the changes cause proteins to form nonfunctional aggregates (clumps). A plant can suffer irreversible damage when the structure of its cells is compromised in these ways.

Hormonal signaling promotes response to drought stress

When plants sense water deficit, a signaling pathway is set in motion that initiates several measures to conserve water and maintain cellular integrity. This pathway begins with the production of the hormone abscisic acid (ABA) in leaves and roots (Figure 37.1). ABA affects the cells that it reaches by binding to a soluble protein receptor, thereby setting off a series of reactions that end up (a) affecting the opening and closing of specific ion channels and (b) regulating the expression of specific genes. The signal transduction cascade that leads to these changes is initiated when ABA binding to its receptor causes the conformation (shape) of the receptor to change. In this new conformation, the ABA receptor can bind to and inactivate a protein phosphatase (an enzyme that removes phosphate groups from other proteins). Inactivation of this protein phosphatase affects the structure and activity of many proteins, and thus affects the activities of the cell. In the end, high levels of ABA promote stomatal closure and, in some cases, increase the resistance to water flow through the rest of the plant. As a result, the amount of water lost via transpiration decreases. ABA also affects root growth such that mild drought often results in an increase in root biomass.

| TABLE **37.1**   Environmental Stresses on Plants ||
Condition	**Effect on plants**
Drought	Reduced water potential, dehydration
Flooding	Reduced O_2 and respiration
High temperature	Changes in membrane fluidity and in proteins
Low temperature	Changes in membrane fluidity, damage by ice crystals
Salinity	Reduced water potential, dehydration
Metal element toxicity	Disruption of metabolism

2 Binding of a protein phosphatase to the ABA–receptor complex inactivates the phosphatase. Target proteins of the phosphatase now remain phosphorylated.

3a ABA causes the stomata to close, conserving water in leaves.

1 Drought stress causes an increase in ABA in leaves and roots.

3b Abscisic acid affects growth of the root system.

Figure 37.1 Plants Respond to Water Stress by Producing the Hormone Abscisic Acid (ABA) ABA protects plants against water stress by closing stomata, changing gene expression, and altering root architecture.

Many plant genes whose expression is altered by drought stress have been identified, largely through research using DNA microarrays, proteomics, and other molecular approaches. One group of proteins in which production is upregulated during drought stress is the *l*ate *e*mbryogenesis *a*bundant (LEA; pronounced "lee-yuh") proteins (see Figure 37.1). These hydrophobic proteins also accumulate in maturing seeds as they dry out (hence their name). The LEA proteins bind to membrane proteins and other cellular proteins to stabilize them, preventing them from clumping together and losing function as seeds dry out.

Some species concentrate CO_2 in specialized cells called bundle sheath cells. This takes energy but may give plants an advantage when CO_2 levels in the leaf would otherwise fall due to rapid photosynthesis.

Vascular bundle

Mesophyll cell

Bundle sheath cell

Hot, dry conditions promote stomatal closure. As photosynthesis continues, CO_2 levels in the leaf fall.

© Carolina Biological Supply/
Visuals Unlimited, Inc.

Figure 37.2 C$_4$ Photosynthesis Many plants adapted for C_4 photosynthesis have altered leaf anatomy, allowing CO_2 to be concentrated in specialized cells called bundle sheath cells.

Some plants have special adaptations for life in very dry conditions

In contrast to short-term acclimation to the environment that occurs via induced responses during the life of an individual plant, some plant species have evolved constitutive adaptations—defenses that are always present—that allow them to survive in low-water environments. Many of these adaptations prevent or reduce the inevitable water loss through transpiration that occurs during active photosynthesis. Other adaptations help plants tolerate the high levels of light and heat that are often found in deserts. Understanding the constitutive adaptions present in plants that grow in dry environments is of particular interest to scientists who want to increase the drought resistance of crop plants in hopes of better suiting them to present and future climatic conditions. This remains a challenging goal, however, as adaptations that improve drought tolerance often decrease plant yield. Understanding plant adaptations is also valuable in adding to a general appreciation of how plants survive. Here we describe several examples of constitutive adaptations of **xerophytes** (Greek *xeros*, "dry," + *phyte*, "plant")—plants adapted to dry environments.

ADAPTATIONS FOR PHOTOSYNTHESIS   The primary photosynthetic pathway described in Chapter 10 is called C_3 photosynthesis. Some plants, including some xerophytes that are adapted to life in hot climates, have an adaptation called C_4 photosynthesis that allows them to bind CO_2 in cells located near the stomata and then release it in cells surrounding the vasculature—the bundle sheath cells that exist in plants that employ this photosynthetic strategy (**Figure 37.2**; see also Figure 10.17A). Because this system concentrates CO_2 in the inner cells, it requires some energy, but it avoids some of the added costs incurred when stomatal closure causes CO_2 levels in the leaf to fall. C_4 photosynthesis reduces the amount of water lost for each molecule of CO_2 fixed. Other plants, generally succulents, employ crassulacean acid metabolism (CAM) for photosynthesis, which allows them to open their stomata only at night when it is cooler (see Figure 10.17B). CO_2 taken in during the night is incorporated into an organic acid and stored until daylight when it is re-released in chloroplasts undergoing the light reactions. The amount of CO_2 taken up by this mechanism is reduced, so CAM plants grow more slowly, but because the amount of water lost during CAM is drastically reduced, it can be advantageous in areas such as deserts where growth would otherwise not occur.

LEAF STRUCTURES   Additional structural adaptations found in the leaves of many xerophytes include a thick cuticle and a profusion of trichomes (leaf hairs) over the leaf epidermis, which

Stomata

A section through a leaf's surface shows a crypt lined with stomata and protected by trichomes.

Trichomes (protective hairs)

Cuticle on the lower surface of leaf

© Dr. Jack Bostrack/Visuals Unlimited, Inc.

Figure 37.3 Stomatal Crypts Stomata in the leaves of some xerophytes are located in sunken cavities called stomatal crypts. This close-up of a single crypt shows the sunken stomata and the trichomes (hairs) that surround them and cover the entrance to the crypt. The trichomes trap moist air. Note also the thick cuticle that prevents water loss from the leaf.

retard water loss by trapping moist air next to stomatal openings. Trichomes can also diffract and diffuse sunlight, thereby decreasing the intensity of light impinging on the leaves and the risk of damage to the photosynthetic apparatus by excess light.

In some xerophytes the stomata are located in sunken cavities below the leaf surface, known as **stomatal crypts**, where they are sheltered from the drying effects of air currents (**Figure 37.3**). Trichomes surrounding the stomata slow air currents further. Cacti

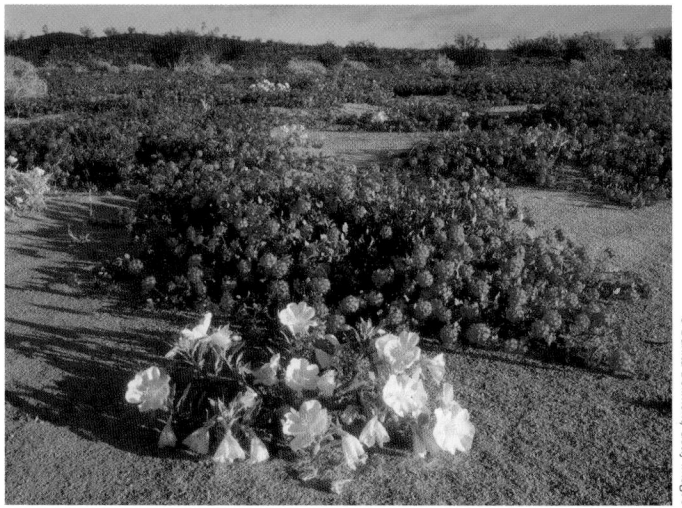

© Danita Delimont/Getty Images

Figure 37.4 Desert Annuals Escape Drought The seeds of many desert annuals lie dormant for long periods, awaiting conditions appropriate for germination. When they do receive enough moisture to germinate, they grow and reproduce rapidly before the short wet season ends. During the long dry spells, only dormant seeds remain alive.

and similar plants have spines rather than typical leaves, and photosynthesis is confined to the fleshy stems. The spines may help the plants cope with desert conditions by reflecting solar radiation or by dissipating heat. Spines also deter herbivores.

ADAPTATIONS FOR OBTAINING AND STORING WATER Xerophytes and other plants that must cope with inadequate water supplies may modify their root structures. Cacti have shallow but extensive fibrous root systems that effectively intercept water at the soil surface following even light rains. Mesquite (*Prosopis*), common in the arid southwestern United States and Mexico, obtains water through taproots that grow to great depths, reaching water supplies far underground, as well as from condensation on its leaves. **Succulence**—the possession of fleshy, water-storing leaves or stems—allows plants to take up large amounts of water when it is available (such as after a brief thunderstorm) and then draw on the stored water during subsequent dry periods. Cacti are an example of succulent plants. Succulents can also have a reduced number of stomata, which further reduces water loss. Some species of plants accumulate high concentrations of the amino acid proline or of secondary metabolites in their vacuoles. This **solute accumulation** lowers the water potential in a plant's cells below that in the soil, which allows the roots to take up water via osmosis. Some plants also accumulate solutes in response to current environmental conditions, as described in the section on saline environments.

DROUGHT ESCAPE Some desert plants have no special structural adaptations for water conservation. Instead, these desert annuals, called drought escapers, simply evade periods of drought. Drought escapers carry out their entire life cycle—from seed to seed—rapidly to exploit the brief period in which rainfall makes the surrounding desert soil sufficiently moist for growth and reproduction (**Figure 37.4**). A different strategy is seen in some deciduous perennial plants, particularly in Africa and South America, that reduce their surface area by shedding their leaves in response to drought, and so conserve water. These plants remain dormant until conditions are again favorable for growth.

Plants can acclimate to salty soil

Salty, or saline, environments (high in Na^+, K^+, Ca^{2+}, and Cl^-) are found in nature in diverse locales, from hot, dry deserts to moist, cool coastal marshes. Rising sea levels and storm surges bring salty water to coastal plant communities. In addition, agricultural land can become increasingly saline as a result of irrigation as sodium that is dissolved in the irrigation water is left behind when the water evaporates. In ancient times, the region between the Tigris and Euphrates Rivers (in what is now Iraq) was once highly fertile, but extensive irrigation canals brought salts that accumulated and raised the water table, which was salty. Ancient records show a shift in production from salt-sensitive to salt-resistant crops and a decline in yield. Salinization, which can eventually make land unsuitable for farming, continues to be a problem worldwide today (**Figure 37.5**).

Because of its high salt concentration, a saline environment has a very negative water potential. To obtain water from such an environment, a plant must have an even more negative water potential; otherwise water will move out of its cells, and the plant

Figure 37.5 Salty Soil Accumulation of salt from irrigation water with inadequate drainage has caused this soil in central California to become unsuitable for most plant growth.

will wilt and die. Plants can attain water potentials that are lower than the surrounding soil by accumulating solutes in their cells. Because sodium at high levels can inhibit enzymes and protein synthesis, plants accumulate solutes other than sodium. Accumulation of the amino acid proline is a common response.

Plants are not simply inhibited by salt. They actively perceive and respond to it. The sensor(s) that allow plants to perceive water potential and sodium levels are still the subject of debate. Because exposure to low water potentials will decrease the turgor pressure inside cells, proteins in the cell membrane that are sensitive to how stretched the membrane is or that measure the distance between the membrane and the cell wall are possible options for sensors. Whatever the sensor, ABA levels often increase in response to salty soils and can have species-specific effects on root architecture. Plants can also respond to increasing concentrations of salt

Figure 37.6 Excreting Salt This saltwater mangrove plant has special salt glands that excrete salt, which appears here as crystals on the leaves.

by growing away from them, a process called **halotropism** (*halo*, "salt"). Halotropism is mediated by auxin. Auxin becomes redistributed in the root such that roots grow away from the region of highest salt concentration.

Plants that are adapted for survival in saline soils are called **halophytes**. Most halophytes take up Na⁺, and many take up Cl⁻, into their roots and transport those ions to their leaves, where they accumulate in the central vacuoles of leaf cells, away from more sensitive parts of the cells. The accumulated salts in the tissues of halophytes make their water potential more negative than that in the soil solution and allow them to take up water from their saline environment. Some halophytes have **salt glands** in their leaves that excrete salt, which collects on the leaf surface until it is removed by rain or wind (**Figure 37.6**). This adaptation, which reduces the danger of poisoning by accumulated salt, is also found in some desert plants. The negative water potential in the salt-laden leaves also promotes water flow from the roots up through the xylem by the transpiration–cohesion–tension mechanism (see Key Concept 33.2).

Some plants grow in saturated soils

For some plants, the environmental challenge is too much water, the opposite of that faced by xerophytes. Some plants live in environments so wet that the diffusion of oxygen to their roots is severely limited. These plants have shallow root systems that grow slowly; oxygen levels are likely to be highest near the surface of the soil, and slow growth decreases the roots' need for oxygen.

The root systems of some plants adapted to swampy environments, such as cypresses and some plants that grow in coastal mangrove habitats, have **pneumatophores**, which are extensions that grow out of the water and up into the air (**Figure 37.7A**). Pneumatophores contain lenticels (openings; see Figure 32.21) that allow oxygen to diffuse through them, aerating the submerged parts of the root system.

Many submerged or partly submerged aquatic plants have large air spaces in the leaf and stem parenchyma and in the petioles. Tissue containing such air spaces is called **aerenchyma** (**Figure 37.7B**). Aerenchyma stores oxygen produced by photosynthesis and permits its ready diffusion to parts of the plant where it is needed for cellular respiration. Aerenchyma also imparts buoyancy. Furthermore, because aerenchyma contains far fewer cells than most other plant tissues, metabolism in aerenchyma proceeds at a lower rate, so the need for oxygen is much reduced.

You may be familiar with rice paddies, where rice grows in a flooded environment. The strains of rice that thrive there—and provide food for millions—have hollow stems like straws, so that air can be supplied to submerged parts of the plant. Remarkably, these strains also have genes that respond to flooding due to heavy rains, by stimulating the plant to grow faster and keep the leaves above the water surface. These genes, appropriately called *SNORKEL-1* and *SNORKEL-2*, encode transcription factors that stimulate the expression of genes involved in cell elongation.

Plants can cope with temperature extremes

Plant growth and development are highly responsive to temperature. In many species, warm temperatures can increase the rate

(A)

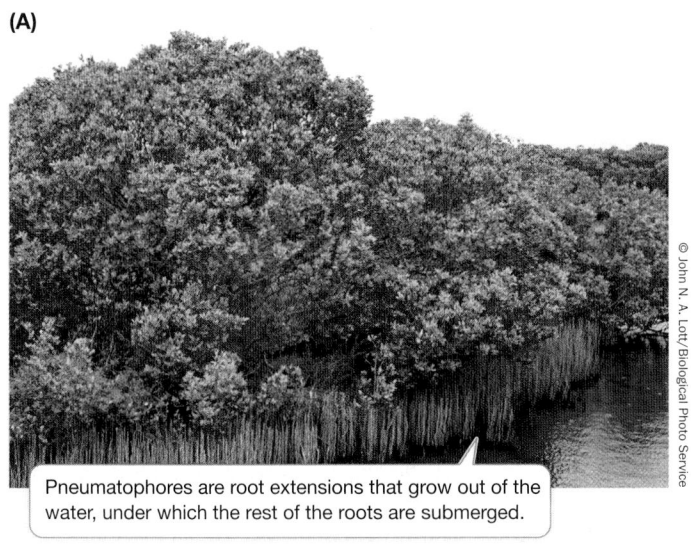

Pneumatophores are root extensions that grow out of the water, under which the rest of the roots are submerged.

© John N. A. Lott/Biological Photo Service

(B)

Open channel

Cells obtain oxygen through the open channels of air-filled aerenchyma tissue.

Vascular bundle

75 µm

© John N. A. Lott/Biological Photo Service

Figure 37.7 Coming Up for Air **(A)** The roots of these mangroves obtain oxygen through pneumatophores. **(B)** This scanning electron micrograph of a cross section of a petiole of the yellow water lily shows the structure of the air-filled channels that make up aerenchyma tissue.

of stem elongation. In many spring-blooming species, warm temperatures can promote early flowering. More rapid flowering and stem elongation are not simply passive accelerations of processes that were occurring at lower temperatures—they are active cellular responses that involve changes in gene expression. A signal can only induce a response if it is perceived, so the existence of temperature responses means that plants must have a receptor that allows them to perceive the current temperature. When plants receive a signal in the form of a soluble molecule such as ABA, auxin, or nitrate, binding of the signal molecule to its receptor changes the conformation and chemistry of the receptor in ways that affect its interaction with other molecules. When the signal is light, photoreceptors—proteins that contain pigments that absorb photons—similarly change their conformation and set off signal transduction pathways. What happens when the signal is temperature? What sort of a receptor can detect a change in temperature?

Dark reversion of phytochrome may serve as a temperature sensor

Exciting new data suggest that phytochrome may act as a temperature sensor as well as a light sensor. The amount of active phytochrome (P_{fr}) in a plant depends on the intensity and wavelengths of light to which it is exposed (**Figure 37.8**), and on the rate at which the active P_{fr} reverts to the inactive P_r state. This is like saying that the amount of water in a bathtub depends on the rate at which water flows into it and the rate at which the tub drains. Reversion

Figure 37.8 Dark Reversion of Phytochrome Is Temperature-Sensitive **(A)** The P_{fr} form of phytochrome can revert to the P_r form by exposure to far-red light or by a light-independent process called dark reversion. **(B)** The total amount of P_{fr} phytochrome present when continually illuminated with dim red light depends on the temperature, as would be expected if the rate of dark reversion is temperature-dependent. (B after M. Legris et al. 2016. *Science* 354: 897–900.)

(A)

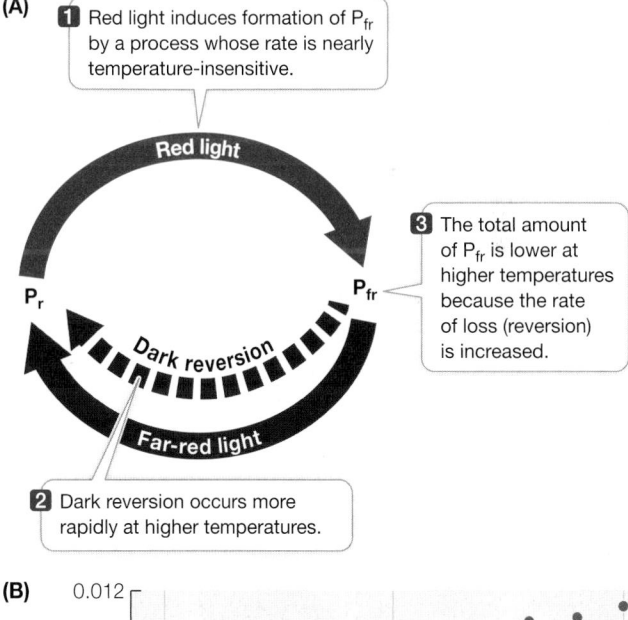

1 Red light induces formation of P_{fr} by a process whose rate is nearly temperature-insensitive.

Red light

P_r

P_{fr}

Dark reversion

Far-red light

3 The total amount of P_{fr} is lower at higher temperatures because the rate of loss (reversion) is increased.

2 Dark reversion occurs more rapidly at higher temperatures.

(B)

Absorbance at 725 nm

Time (min)

- 10°C
- 20°C
- 25°C
- 30°C

of the active P_{fr} to the inactive P_r (draining of the tub) can occur if the plant is exposed to far-red light. In addition, P_{fr} can revert to P_r on its own without the addition of far-red light; this process is called dark reversion because it does not require light. However, dark reversion actually occurs both in the light and the dark. If the rate at which P_{fr} dark-reverts to P_r speeds up as the temperature rises, then the amount of P_{fr} in a plant will decline, even if the light exposure stays the same. This idea was tested by exposing plants to continuous red light, which produces the active P_{fr} at a constant rate (e.g., the rate at which the tub filled was held constant). When this experiment was done at different temperatures, higher temperatures resulted in lower amounts of P_{fr} (e.g., higher temperatures must have increased the rate at which the tub drained) (see Figure 37.8B). Might the rate at which phytochrome dark-reverts from the active to the inactive state convey information about temperature to the plant and thus serve as a temperature sensor?

To determine whether phytochrome has a causal effect on plant response to temperature, researchers compared the ability of normal (wild-type) plants to respond to temperature with that of plants in which phytochrome was disrupted. Two responses that plants have to temperature were observed:

1. In wild-type plants, stem elongation occurs more rapidly in warm temperatures than in cold temperatures. In plants that lack functional phytochrome, this temperature response is disrupted. Stems of phytochrome mutants grown in cold temperatures are longer than normal, indicating that the presence of phytochrome represses stem elongation (**Figure 37.9**).

2. Wild-type plants also respond to warm temperatures by increasing the expression of some genes during the night. Might phytochrome, which can act as a transcription factor, be responsible for some of the temperature-dependent changes in gene expression that occur during the night? When the phytochrome gene is mutated such that P_{fr} forms but can never dark-revert to P_r (e.g., such that phytochrome is always active), the temperature-responsive expression of many genes is lost.

Figure 37.9 **Temperature-Dependent Stem Elongation Requires Phytochrome**   An *Arabidopsis thaliana* quintuple mutant that does not make functional phytochrome, *phyABCDE*, does not exhibit the temperature-dependent elongation response seen in wild-type plants.

Q: Are the mutants that lack phytochrome shorter or taller than wild-type plants when grown in the cold? Does phytochrome promote or inhibit stem elongation?

Together, these data suggest that phytochrome may serve as a temperature sensor in plants—a separate, second function for this remarkable protein.

Plants respond to temperature in many ways

Plants expand the range of temperatures that they can survive by mounting specific responses to temperature. As discussed earlier, cold temperatures generally repress growth. On a subcellular scale, temperature can affect membrane fluidity and alter membrane permeability to solutes. High temperatures cause membranes to become more fluid, while low temperatures cause membranes to become less fluid. These changes have strong effects on cellular function: imagine the impact on cell activity if the ATP-generating enzyme ATP synthase could not move rapidly in the membrane! Many plant species can adjust to cold temperatures through a process called **cold-hardening**, which requires repeated exposure to moderately cool temperatures over many days. A key change during cold-hardening is an increase in the proportion of unsaturated fatty acids in cell membranes, which allows them to retain their fluidity and function normally at cooler temperatures. Plants have a greater ability to modify the degree of saturation of their membrane lipids than animals do. In addition, low temperatures induce the formation of proteins that protect against chilling injury.

If ice crystals form within plant cells, they can kill the cells by puncturing organelles and cell membranes. Furthermore, the growth of ice crystals outside the cells can draw water from the cells and dehydrate them. Freeze-tolerant plants have a variety of adaptations to cope with these problems, including the production of antifreeze proteins that slow the growth of ice crystals.

Plants have inducible responses to hot temperatures

Plant species differ in their sensitivity to temperature, but all plants have their limits. High temperatures destabilize membranes and denature many proteins, especially some of the enzymes of photosynthesis. Heat stress can also have a strongly negative effect on pollination. The plant inducible response to heat stress is similar to the response to drought stress in that new proteins are made, often under the direction of an abscisic acid–mediated signaling pathway. Within minutes of experimental exposure to raised temperatures (typically an increase of 5–10 degrees Celsius), plants synthesize several kinds of **heat shock proteins**. Some heat shock proteins (called chaperonins) help maintain the activities of the cytoplasm by assisting other proteins in maintaining their folded structure. Threshold temperatures for the production of heat shock proteins vary, but 39°C is sufficient to induce them in most plants.

KEY CONCEPT
37.1 Recap and Assess

Among the many environmental challenges that plants face are those of drought, saline soils, and extreme temperatures. Plants survive these through a combination of structural adaptations and physiological responses. Plant scientists are working to discover the various sensors that permit plants to perceive a wide variety of stimuli. Mechanisms that protect plants from drought stress are initiated by a signaling pathway involving abscisic acid.

Halophytes have several adaptations to saline habitats, many of which involve mechanisms that lower their water potential. Recent evidence suggests that phytochrome may act as a temperature sensor, because the rate of dark reversion is temperature-sensitive. This would be a second function for phytochrome (light perception being the first).

1. Colleagues in plant physiologist José Dinneny's laboratory discovered that when *Arabidopsis thaliana* roots were exposed to two different environments, one wet and one dry, lateral roots formed preferentially on the wet side. They termed this process hydropatterning. Is hydropatterning an example of an adaptation or an acclimation?

2. If an inhibitor of ABA synthesis was sprayed on a plant and the plant was exposed to drought conditions, what would happen?

3. In the coming decades, climate change will impact the growth and productivity of plants, including the crops on which we depend for our food. For each of the environmental conditions given here, describe the types of physiological stress plants may undergo and give examples of possible responses that plants may mount to reduce the effects of those stresses.

   a. In Pakistan, reduced rainfall causes a reduction in wheat yields.

   b. In the Mekong Delta of Vietnam, rising sea level inundates rice fields, causing a drastic reduction in yields.

4. What attributes does something need to have in order to qualify as a receptor? To what extent does the dark reversion of phytochrome meet those standards?

The ability of plants to persist in the natural world requires not only that they deal successfully with challenges such as heat and drought that are part of the abiotic environment; plants also need to fend off biotic threats—the pests and pathogens that attack them. In the next key concept we describe plant responses to pathogens (organisms that can infect plants).

Figure 37.10 Diseases of Tomato Plants A wide variety of disease agents cause a variety of symptoms.

Q: As in animals, diseases in plants are caused by a wide variety of organisms. Can you name human diseases caused by the four types of agents described in this figure?

KEY CONCEPT
37.2
Plants Respond to Pathogens with Constitutive and Induced Responses

Learning Objectives

37.2.1 Compare and contrast general immunity and specific immunity.

37.2.2 Apply the concept of the genetic "arms race" between plants and their pathogens to the evolution of *R* (resistance) genes and *Avr* (avirulence) genes.

37.2.3 Describe and discuss the types of responses that plants have to pathogen attack: gene-for-gene resistance, the hypersensitive response, systemic acquired resistance, and production of siRNAs.

It is remarkable that plants, which are composed largely of edible material and are unable to get up and run away, survive given all the living organisms that might benefit from attacking them. Thousands of diseases affect plants, each caused by a different strain of pathogen. Plant pathogens include bacteria, fungi, protists, nematodes, and viruses. For example, many pathogens affect tomato plants, some of which may be familiar to you from growing tomatoes in your backyard or finding spoiled tomatoes in a neglected area of your kitchen (**Figure 37.10**).

Many plant diseases are named for the symptoms rather than the agent that causes them. For example, the condition called "blight," characterized by browning and death of plant tissues, can be caused by bacteria, fungi, or oomycetes. Successful infection by a pathogen can have significant effects on a plant, reducing photosynthesis and causing massive cell and tissue death. Plants are able to persist because they have a wide variety of systems for recognizing and fighting off disease. Plants and pathogens have evolved together in a continuing "arms race": pathogens have evolved ways to attack plants, and plants have evolved ways to defend themselves against those attacks.

What determines the outcome of a battle between a plant and a pathogen? The key to success for the plant is to respond to information from the pathogen quickly and massively. Plants use both mechanical and chemical defenses in this effort. These defenses can either be:

- **Constitutive**, always present in the plant, or

- **Induced**, produced in reaction to damage or stress

Physical barriers can be constitutive or induced defenses

A plant's first line of defense is its outer surfaces, which can prevent the entry of pathogens. As Chapter 32 described, the organs of a growing plant that are exposed to the outside environment are largely covered with cutin, suberin, and waxes. These constitutive defenses not only prevent water loss by evaporation but can also prevent fungal spores and bacteria from entering the underlying tissues. Some fungi get around this defense by secreting enzymes that hydrolyze these substances, breaking them down to gain entry.

Another way in which plants can use physical barriers to limit infection is by the rapid deposition of additional polymers on the inside of the cell wall. This is an example of an induced response because it occurs only after an infection has begun. The newly deposited macromolecules not only reinforce the mechanical barrier formed by the cell wall, but also block the plasmodesmata, limiting the ability of viral pathogens to move from cell to cell. The polysaccharides also serve as a base on which lignin, a polymer that provides strength and rigidity, may be laid down. Lignin enhances the mechanical barrier, and the toxicity of lignin precursor chemicals makes the cell inhospitable to some pathogens.

Induced responses are triggered by elicitors

Before a plant can mount an induced response to a pathogen, the plant must sense that an infection is occurring. A wide range of molecules called **elicitors** have been identified that trigger plant defenses. These molecules vary in character, from peptides made by bacteria to cell wall fragments from fungi. Elicitors can also be derived from fragments of plant cell wall components broken down by pathogens.

The responses of plants to elicitors can be described in terms of the "plant immune system." Two forms of immunity are recognized (**Figure 37.11**):

1. *General immunity* is triggered by general elicitors called pathogen associated molecular patterns (PAMPs). PAMPs are usually molecules that are produced by entire classes of pathogens, such as flagellin (found in bacterial flagella) or chitin (found in fungal cell walls). Thus general immunity is an overall response rather than a response that is triggered by a specific pathogen in a particular plant. PAMPs are recognized by transmembrane receptors called **pattern recognition receptors** (**PRRs**), which activate signaling pathways that lead to general immunity.

2. *Specific immunity* is triggered by specific elicitors called **effectors**. Effectors include a wide variety of specific pathogen-produced molecules. Effectors bind to plant

Figure 37.11 Signaling between Plants and Pathogens Molecular interactions between plants and pathogens are highly coevolved. The presence of a pathogen stimulates the plant to produce defensive molecules that work in many different ways.

Q: Would you expect these defensive molecules to be expressed in the cells of roots or leaves, or in both?

View in Achieve
Animation 37.1 Signaling between Plants and Pathogens

receptors called R proteins (discussed in more detail in the next section) that trigger the specific immunity response.

Many of the signaling pathways associated with general and specific immunity are the same, although the signals that induce them are different. Both forms of immunity involve signaling pathways that are triggered by binding between the elicitors (either PAMPs or effectors) and their receptors. These pathways lead to various responses:

- *Formation of NO and reactive oxygen*: Receptor binding triggers the rapid production of nitric oxide (NO) and reactive oxygen species such as superoxide and hydrogen peroxide. These reactive molecules are toxic to some pathogens, and they are components of signal transduction pathways leading to local and systemic (plantwide) defenses.

- *Callose deposition*: The β-1,3-glucan polymer callose is deposited on the inside of the cell wall to strengthen the wall and seal off the cell.

- *Hormonal signaling*: Some pathways result in the production of plant hormones, including salicylic acid and jasmonic acid. We describe the roles of these hormones in plant immunity later in the chapter.

- *Changes in gene expression*: Signal transduction cascades lead to changes in gene expression. The upregulated genes include **pathogenesis-related (PR) genes** and genes encoding the production of antimicrobial substances called **phytoalexins**.

Plants produce several types of pathogenesis-related (PR) proteins. Some are enzymes that break down the cell walls of pathogens. Chitinase, for example, is a PR protein that breaks down chitin, which is found in many fungal cell walls. In some cases the breakdown products of the pathogen cell walls serve as elicitors that trigger further defensive responses.

Another class of PR proteins are the plant defensins, which are similar to defensins produced by animals (see Key Concept 40.2). These small peptides bind to fungal membranes and are toxic to a wide range of fungal targets, but they are not toxic to plant or animal cells. Other PR proteins may serve as alarm signals to plant cells that have not yet been attacked. In general, PR proteins appear not to be rapid-response weapons; rather, they act more slowly, perhaps after other, faster responses have blunted the pathogen's attack.

Phytoalexins are antibiotics produced by infected plants and are toxic to many fungi and bacteria. Most are small molecules, and each is made by only a few plant species. They are elicited by effectors of pathogenic bacteria and fungi and are made within hours of the onset of infection. Because their antimicrobial activity is nonspecific, phytoalexins can destroy many species of fungi and bacteria in addition to the one that originally triggered their production. Some phytoalexins can also kill the plant cells that produced them, thus sealing off the infection site (the hypersensitive response, discussed shortly).

An example of a phytoalexin is camalexin, made by the model organism *Arabidopsis thaliana*. Its production is induced by a conserved protein kinase cascade that is triggered by receptor binding in either general

Figure 37.12 Production of camalexin, a phytoalexin, from tryptophan is induced by many pathogens.

or specific immunity. This protein kinase cascade results in the upregulation of genes encoding enzymes that convert the amino acid tryptophan to camalexin (**Figure 37.12**). Camalexin appears to work by disrupting the cell membranes of invading pathogens.

> **Connect the Concepts** Protein kinase cascades are common in signal transduction. See Key Concept 7.3.

Specific immunity is genetically determined

When pathogens attack, they come in contact with plant cells. If the plant does not have a receptor that can recognize infection by a particular species or strain of pathogen, the plant will not turn on specific inducible defenses.

Receptors that reside in the cytoplasm of plant cells that are resistant to infection are called **R (resistance) proteins**. R proteins interact with the product of a pathogen-encoded factor called an **avirulence (Avr) factor**. There are hundreds of Avr factors, which vary among pathogen species and strains. There are also hundreds of plant R proteins that recognize the presence of Avr factors. Recognition can be direct, as when a plant R protein binds to an Avr factor, or indirect, meaning a third protein is involved (**Figure 37.13**). In all cases, however, a single R protein, encoded by a

(A) Direct interaction

Sometimes direct interaction of an R protein (from the plant) and a corresponding Avr factor (from the invader) leads to a defense response.

Avr factor

R protein

Defense response

(B) Indirect interaction

Defenses triggered by indirect interactions involve an R protein that is normally blocked by a second plant factor. An Avr factor removes or inactivates this second plant protein, allowing the R protein to initiate a defense response.

Second plant protein

Avr factor

R protein

R protein

Defense response

Figure 37.13 Gene-for-Gene Resistance If a gene in a pathogen that codes for an elicitor "matches" a gene in a plant that codes for a receptor, the receptor binds the elicitor, and a defensive response results. (After J. L. M. Soosaar et al. 2005. *Nat Rev Microbiol* 3: 789–798.)

plant **R** (resistance) **gene** must in some way interact with the product of a pathogen-encoded factor. While the direct method requires that the pathogen produce one particular protein in order to be recognized, the indirect method has the potential to increase the range of pathogens that can be detected. Imagine, for example, that a third (intermediate) protein that is part of the plant's constitutive defensive response is bound by the plant R protein. Any infection that results in enzymatic modification of this intermediate protein such that the plant R protein no longer binds to it will liberate the R protein, setting in motion a signal transduction pathway that triggers the plant's specific immunity. This type of resistance, whether direct or indirect, is called **gene-for-gene resistance** because it involves a recognition event between two specific molecules: one determined by an *Avr* gene in the pathogen and the other determined by an *R* gene in the plant.

The lack of an appropriate R protein receptor makes the plant especially susceptible to that pathogen. A major goal of plant breeders for the past 50 years has been to identify *R* and *Avr* genes and to breed new *R* genes into crops to make them more resistant to pathogens. Comparative genomics can be used: if a gene that confers resistance is found in one species, it may exist in close relatives, and may even be used to create a transgenic crop that is resistant to the pathogen. An example is described in **Investigating Life: A Gene for Resistance to Wheat Rust.**

Specific immunity usually leads to the hypersensitive response

Once a pathogenic infection is recognized, the plant mounts a response. One common response is surprising: rather than minimizing damage to an infected cell, the plant cells around the site of infection undergo a **hypersensitive response** entailing programmed cell death. The hypersensitive response leads to the sacrifice of a few cells to protect the rest of the plant, resulting in necrotic lesions (**Figure 37.14**). This strategy is particularly effective against viruses because viral replication does not take place without the proteins and metabolic products of a living plant cell. Viruses are typically carried to a plant by insects (often aphids), but extensive infection requires that the virus spread from cell to cell within the plant. Death of a small group of infected cells can help seal off the site of infection, preventing spread of the pathogen. Surrounding (still living) cells that

▶Investigating LIFE
A Gene for Resistance to Wheat Rust

Experiment

Original Papers: S. Periyannan et al. 2013. The gene *Sr33*, an ortholog of barley *Mla* genes, encodes resistance to wheat stem rust race Ug99. *Science* 341: 786–788.

A. Saintenac et al. 2013. Identification of wheat gene *Sr35* that confers resistance to Ug99 stem rust race group. *Science* 341: 783–786.

Wheat rust, particularly a new strain called Ug99 (so named because it was first identified in Uganda in 1999), is a major pathogen of wheat that can cause significant reduction in grain production. Cultivated wheat is not resistant to this pathogen strain. But *Aegilops tauschii*, a species of goatgrass that grows in the wild and is a genetic relative of cultivated wheat, is resistant. An international research team isolated a gene called *Sr33* that was responsible for this resistance. The gene encodes a cytoplasmic receptor. Meanwhile, Eduard Akhunov at Kansas State University studied another primitive relative of bread wheat called *Triticum monococcum*, which also is resistant to wheat rust. His team isolated another gene for resistance, called *Sr35*.

HYPOTHESIS▶ A wild relative of wheat carries a gene for resistance to the wheat rust pathogen.

METHOD▶

1. Compare genomes of two barley strains, one susceptible to the mildew fungus and one that is resistant to it.

Susceptible   Resistant

Sr33

2. Isolate barley gene for resistance (*Sr33*) to mildew fungus.

3. Using barley gene as a probe, isolate a homologous gene in goatgrass, a wild relative of wheat that is resistant to wheat rust.

4. Insert high-expressing resistance gene into bread wheat.

5. Test bread wheat for resistance to wheat rust pathogen infection.

RESULTS▶

Wild-type wheat is infected.

Transgenic wheat is resistant.

CONCLUSION▶ A gene from a wild relative of wheat can confer resistance to wheat rust in bread wheat.

Work with the Data

A series of mutations in *Sr33* was generated by mutagenesis and a genetic screen was performed for susceptibility to wheat rust infection (**Figure A**). The white segment on bar 5 indicates the deleted DNA, and the map location of the *Sr33* gene is indicated by the bottom bracket.

QUESTIONS▶

1. The results for the wild-type *Sr33* and mutant E5–E9 *Sr33* are shown in **Figure B**. What can you conclude about the role of *Sr33* in rust resistance?

2. The bread wheat strain called Fielder was made transgenic for a high-expressing *Sr33* gene. It was then exposed to wheat rust. The results are shown in **Figure C**. What does this transgenic approach indicate about the role of *Sr33* in rust resistance? Compare your conclusion with that of Question 1.

3. *Triticum monococcum* with wild-type *Sr35* (**Figure D**, left) was compared with two strains of wheat with mutated *Sr35* genes (**Figure D**, center and right) with regard to infection by wheat rust. What can you conclude about the role of *Sr35* in resistance?

4. Cultivated Fielder bread wheat was made transgenic for a high-expressing *Sr35* gene. It was then exposed to the Ug99 strain of wheat rust. The results are shown in **Figure E**. What does this indicate about the *Sr35* gene?

Figure A

E5 — Deletion mutant of *Sr33*

E6
E7 ⎫ Point mutations
E8 ⎬ of *Sr33*
E9 ⎭

Wild-type *Sr33*

Sr33

Figure B

Wild-type *Sr33*   E5   E6   E7   E8   E9

Figure C

Fielder   Fielder + *Sr33*

Figure D

Two strains with mutated *Sr35* gene

Wild-type *Sr35*

Figure E

Sr35 transgenic   Fielder control

Go to **Achieve** for a companion Data in Depth exercise.

Figures A-C from S. Periyannan et al. 2013. Science 341: 786–788; Figures D and E from C. Saintenac et al. 2013. Science 341: 783–786

---

produce cell wall polysaccharides assist by sealing off plasmodesmata. Some of the responding cells also produce toxic chemicals, including phytoalexins, before they die. The resulting necrotic lesion contains and isolates what is left of the infection. The rest of the plant remains free of the infecting pathogen.

Systemic acquired resistance is a form of long-term immunity

Thus far we have described the events that occur in plant cells at or near the site of invasion by a pathogen. In both general and specific immunity, the infected cells also send hormonal signals to the rest of the plant, stimulating a systemic response. **Systemic acquired resistance** is a general increase in the resistance of the entire plant to a wide range of pathogens. It is not limited to the pathogen that originally triggered it, or to the site of the original infection, and its effect may last as long as an entire growing season.

This defensive response is initiated by the plant hormone salicylic acid. Salicylic acid production is triggered by receptor binding in both general and specific immunity. Salicylic acid then functions as a signal that triggers the production of reactive oxygen species and the induction of genes that encode PR proteins. There are many classes of PR proteins, which function in various ways to protect plants against insect attack and against invasion by fungi, bacteria, viruses, and nematodes.

These responses occur at the site of infection and, to a lesser extent, throughout the plant. A derivative of salicylic acid can form a gas that can travel through the air, carrying the defense signal not only to other parts of the same plant but to other nearby plants. Plant-to-plant signaling is also done through mycorrhizae associated with roots. These beneficial fungi (see Key Concept 34.3) form a network that appears to transmit signals from an infected plant to its neighbors.

Another type of systemic acquired resistance is a more specific defense against viruses with RNA genomes. Viruses that infect

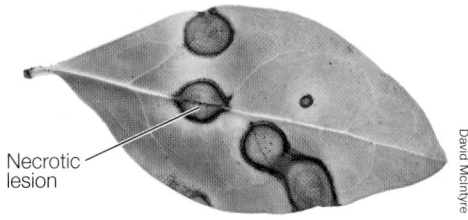

Necrotic lesion

David McIntyre

Figure 37.14 The Hypersensitive Response Results in Necrotic Lesions Death of a small region of plant cells can prevent the spread of viruses which require living cells.

plants are generally nothing more than RNA or DNA (the viral genome) wrapped in a protein coat. Once viral RNA or DNA enters a plant cell, the plants own enzymes act on it, resulting in production of more copies of the viral genome and the viral coat protein, which self-assemble into new viruses. How can a plant protect against viral replication if the viral genome is the only part of the process that belongs specifically to the virus? Many plants have a mechanism that specifically recognizes and destroys virally-encoded mRNA.

Replication of some viruses includes a phase in which double stranded RNA (dsRNA) is produced (**Figure 37.15**). In many plants, a plant-encoded enzyme called Dicer binds to this double stranded RNA and cuts it into short segments called small interfering RNA (siRNAs). These siRNAs interact with another cellular component called the RNA-induced silencing complex (RISC). When an siRNA associated with RISC binds to complementary regions on other segments of virally-encoded mRNA, the viral mRNA is destroyed. Destruction of the virally-encoded mRNA blocks viral replication. The siRNAs spread quickly throughout the entire plant through plasmodesmata, providing systemic resistance.

Figure 37.15 Production of Small Interfering RNAs Can Protect Plants by Blocking Translation of Virally Encoded mRNAs Many plants defend themselves against viral replication by producing siRNAs that specifically recognize virally-encoded mRNAs. Once virally-encoded mRNAs are recognized, they are degraded. This system blocks viral replication without blocking the production of plant-encoded proteins.

KEY CONCEPT
37.2 Recap and Assess

Plants have both constitutive and induced defense mechanisms to protect themselves against pathogens. General and specific immunity involve several common signaling pathways, but specific immunity is a stronger response that usually leads to the hypersensitive response and cell death. Specific immunity involves reactions between genetically determined molecules of the pathogen(s) and host plant. Systemic acquired resistance provides a longer-lasting, more general immunity throughout the plant.

1. A tomato plant can be infected with the fungus *Cladosporium*. The host plant and pathogen can have various genes involved in the hypersensitive response. Complete the table below to show the effects of each fungal strain on tomato leaves:

Cladosporium genotype	Tomato genotype		
	R1R2	R3R4	R1R4
Avr1Avr2			
Avr2Avr3			
Avr1Avr4			

2. Describe how a researcher could determine whether an induced response in a plant cell represents general immunity or specific immunity.

3. A researcher makes a small incision in a leaf of a healthy plant and applies salicylic acid to the cut. How might the researcher expect the plant to respond?

Not all biological threats to plants come from pathogens. Another threat comes from the many animals that eat plants.

KEY CONCEPT
37.3 Plants Have Mechanical and Chemical Defenses against Herbivores

Learning Objectives

37.3.1 Describe physical methods plants use to defend themselves against herbivores.

37.3.2 Discuss the range of effects that secondary metabolites might have on organisms attacking plants.

37.3.3 Describe the key components of signal transduction pathways that are activated by herbivory or wounding.

Herbivores—animals that eat plants—depend on plants for energy and nutrients. Their foraging activities cause physical damage to plants, and they often spread disease among plants as well. While the majority of herbivores are insects (**Figure 37.16**), every major

(A) *Locusta migratoria*

© Arco Images GmbH/
Alamy Stock Photo

(B) *Manduca sexta*

© Jeffdongphotography/Shutterstock.com

Figure 37.16 Insect Herbivores   The great majority of herbivores are insects. **(A)** Some herbivores, such as this locust, are generalists that will attack nearly any plant. **(B)** Others are specialists, like this tobacco hornworm, which feeds only on tobacco and related plants.

class of vertebrates includes at least a few herbivores. Plants cannot evade their consumers by running away, but they have many other ways of protecting themselves against herbivory.

Plants have mechanical defenses against herbivores

Plants have both constitutive and induced mechanical defenses against herbivores. Constitutive anatomical barriers include trichomes (specialized hairs; see Figure 37.2) and thorns, spines that are specialized for defense. An example of an induced

mechanical defense is the production of latex. Some plants, such as *Euphorbia* species, produce a thick, white aqueous suspension of cellular debris, oils, and resins called latex when they are injured by an herbivore. Insects trapped by this sticky substance starve to death.

Connect the Concepts   In this chapter we discuss herbivory in the context of how a plant's physiology is affected by an herbivore. See also Key Concept 54.2, which discusses herbivory in the ecological context of species interactions.

Plants produce constitutive chemical defenses against herbivores

Plants attract, resist, and inhibit other organisms with a wide range of chemicals known as secondary metabolites. Primary metabolites are substances such as proteins, nucleic acids, carbohydrates, lipids, and their building blocks, which are produced and used by all living organisms, including plants. Primary metabolites are used in basic cellular processes such as photosynthesis, respiration, and nutrient uptake. **Secondary metabolites** are substances that are not used for basic cellular processes. Each is found in only certain organisms or groups of organisms.

The more than 10,000 known plant secondary metabolites range in molecular mass from about 70 to more than 380,000 daltons, but most have a low molecular mass (**Table 37.2**). The

TABLE 37.2 | Secondary Metabolites Used in Defense

Class	Type	Role	Example
Nitrogen-containing	Alkaloids	Neurotoxin	Nicotine in tobacco
	Glycosides	Inhibit electron transport	Dhurrin in sorghum
	Nonprotein amino acids	Disrupt protein structure	Canavanine in jack bean
Nitrogen–sulfur-containing	Glucosinolates	Inhibit respiration	Methylglucosinolate in cabbage
Phenolics	Coumarins	Block cell division	Umbelliferone in carrots
	Flavonoids	Phytoalexins	Capsidol in peppers
	Tannins	Inhibit enzymes	Gallotannin in oak trees
Terpenes	Monoterpenes	Neurotoxins	Pyrethrin in chrysanthemums
	Diterpenes	Disrupt reproduction and muscle function	Gossypol in cotton
	Triterpenes	Inhibit transport	Digitalis in foxglove
	Sterols	Block animal hormones	Spinasterol in spinach
	Polyterpenes	Deter feeding	Latex in *Euphorbia*

Ephedrine (an alkaloid)

Methylglucosinolide

Umbelliferone

Pyrethrin

effects of defensive secondary metabolites on animals are diverse. Some act on the nervous systems of herbivorous insects, mollusks, or mammals. Others damage the digestive tracts of herbivores. Some secondary metabolites are toxic to fungal or bacterial pathogens. Secondary metabolites are not only used for defense; some have other roles in the plant. For instance, phenolic compounds called anthocyanins are toxic to insects and bacteria. But they also are pigmented and aid in attracting pollinators, accumulate in vacuoles and thus contribute to osmotic pressure in cells, and even regulate dormancy in some plants.

Canavanine is a secondary metabolite that has a defensive effect. Canavanine is an amino acid that is not normally found in proteins, but it is very similar to the amino acid arginine, which is found in almost all proteins (**Figure 37.17**). When an insect larva consumes canavanine-containing plant tissue, the canavanine is incorporated into the insect's proteins in some of the places where the mRNA codes for arginine, because the enzyme that charges the tRNA specific for arginine fails to discriminate accurately between the two amino acids (see Key Concept 14.5). The structure of canavanine, however, is different enough from that of arginine that some of the resulting proteins end up with a modified tertiary structure, and hence reduced biological activity. These defects in protein structure and function lead to developmental abnormalities that kill the insect.

Taking cues from nature, we have practical uses for many plant secondary metabolites or molecules made from them in the lab. Throughout human history, these have formed the basis of herbal medicine as plant extracts are used. As knowledge of chemistry accumulated, people purified the active ingredients of these plants. For instance, the foxglove plant gave us the cardiac drug digitalis. Some wild animals also seek out specific plants when they have infections, gastric issues, or are bothered by pests such as biting insects. Eloy Rodriguez and colleagues isolated compounds from some plants that are sought out by animals suffering from particular issues, and found that the plants contained specific compounds with medicinal properties.

Figure 37.17 Canavanine Can Protect Plants Against Herbivory When insect larva eat leaves that contain canavanine, the insects incorporate this atypical amino acid into their proteins, resulting in proteins with reduced activity.

Plants respond to herbivory with induced defenses

In Key Concept 37.2 we described the defenses that are induced in plants in response to pathogen attack. Plants also respond to wounding and herbivory with induced defenses involving signal transduction pathways. Less is known about the elicitors and receptors involved in these responses, but several classes of chemical elicitors have been identified. These elicitors are either derived from the herbivores themselves or are products of the digestion of plant tissues. For example, the enzymes that insects use to digest plant carbohydrates and lipids can elicit defensive responses. Some elicitors are produced when plant material passes through an herbivore's digestive tract; these elicitors are composed of a fatty acid derived from the plant and an amino acid derived from the insect gut. One such elicitor, produced by insects feeding on corn plants, has been named volicitin for its ability to induce production of volatile signals that can travel to other plant parts—and to neighboring corn plants—and stimulate their defense responses. In addition, many herbivorous insects lay their eggs on plants, and some components of the fluids secreted during egg laying have been identified as elicitors.

The signal transduction pathways that are activated by herbivory or wounding involve several key components, some of which are shared by the pathways that are induced by pathogens:

- *Membrane signaling*: The cell membrane is the part of the plant cell that is in contact with the environment. Within the first minute after an herbivore strikes, changes in the electric potential of the cell membrane occur in the damaged area. As we will describe in our chapter on the animal nervous system (see Key Concept 43.2), such changes can be rapidly transmitted as a signal along the cell membrane. In the case of plants responding to herbivory, the continuity of the symplast (see Figure 33.6) ensures that the signal travels over much of the plant within 10 minutes.

- *Reactive oxygen species*: Both wounding and herbivory trigger the production of reactive oxygen species (such as superoxide and hydrogen peroxide), which act as signaling molecules in pathways that lead to changes in gene expression.

- *Hormonal signaling*: Herbivory induces the production of several hormones that stimulate various plant responses. The most important of these is **jasmonic acid (jasmonate)**, which triggers systemic defenses against herbivores.

 Media Clip 37.1 Plants Can Hear Danger Life12e.com/mc37.1

Jasmonates trigger a range of responses to wounding and herbivory

When the plant senses an herbivore-produced elicitor, it makes jasmonate (the ionized form of jasmonic acid) and a variety of jasmonate derivatives. These molecules trigger many plant defenses both at the site of herbivore attack and throughout the plant. When caterpillars (small herbivores) chew on a plant, substances in the insect's saliva and the physical wounding of the plant cells serve as signals to which the plant can respond (**Figure 37.18**). A derivative of jasmonate in which jasmonic acid is bound to the amino acid Ile (JA-Ile) induces changes in gene expression

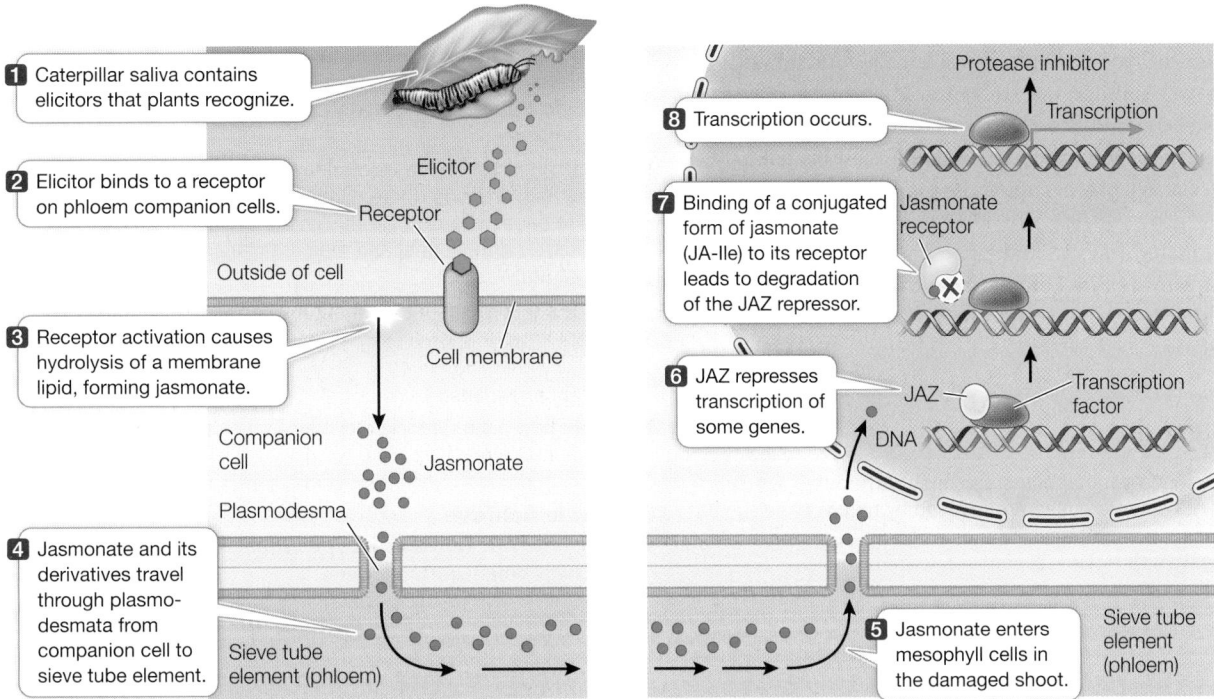

1 Caterpillar saliva contains elicitors that plants recognize.

2 Elicitor binds to a receptor on phloem companion cells.

Elicitor

Receptor

Outside of cell

3 Receptor activation causes hydrolysis of a membrane lipid, forming jasmonate.

Cell membrane

Companion cell

Jasmonate

Plasmodesma

4 Jasmonate and its derivatives travel through plasmo-desmata from companion cell to sieve tube element.

Sieve tube element (phloem)

Protease inhibitor

Transcription

8 Transcription occurs.

7 Binding of a conjugated form of jasmonate (JA-Ile) to its receptor leads to degradation of the JAZ repressor.

Jasmonate receptor

X

6 JAZ represses transcription of some genes.

JAZ

Transcription factor

DNA

5 Jasmonate enters mesophyll cells in the damaged shoot.

Sieve tube element (phloem)

Figure 37.18 Response to Caterpillar Attack   Herbivory initiates a chain of events that leads to the production of defensive chemicals. Hormones produced at the site of attack can set off a series of reactions resulting in synthesis of defensive compounds throughout the plant.

▶ **View in Achieve**
Simulation 37.1 Plant Defenses

by binding to a receptor. The bound receptor complex targets a transcriptional inhibitor called a JAZ protein for degradation. Once the JAZ protein is degraded, genes that were previously inhibited can be transcribed and expressed. An important group of plant proteins that are expressed in response to insect attack are protease inhibitors. Once inside an insect's gut, protease inhibitors interfere with proteases (enzymes that degrade proteins) that are part of the insect's digestive system. The resulting disruption of the caterpillar's ability to digest the plant material it eats stunts the growth of the caterpillar.

Jasmonates can also be part of a "call for help" by triggering the formation of volatile compounds that attract insects that prey on herbivores attacking the plant. When corn is attacked by one particular moth larva, for example, the plant produces volatile compounds that attract wasps that parasitize herbivorous caterpillars.

Why don't the defensive chemicals that are so toxic to herbivores and pathogens kill the plants that produce them? In some cases the defensive chemicals are directed at organs or systems that are not found in plants, such as the nervous, digestive, or endocrine systems of animals. In addition, plants that produce toxic defensive chemicals sequester them in vacuoles or store them as harmless precursors until used.

Plants don't always win the arms race

Milkweeds such as *Asclepias syriaca* store their defensive chemicals in latex in specialized tubes called **laticifers**, which run alongside the veins in the leaves. When damaged, a milkweed releases copious amounts of toxic latex from its laticifers. Field studies have shown that most insects that feed on neighboring plants of other species do not attack laticiferous plants, but there

are exceptions. One population of beetles that feeds on *A. syriaca* exhibits a remarkable prefeeding behavior: these beetles cut a few veins in the leaves before settling down to dine. Cutting the veins causes massive latex leakage from the adjacent laticifers and interrupts the latex supply to a downstream portion of the leaf. The beetles then move to the relatively latex-free portion and eat their fill (**Figure 37.19A**).

(A)

(B)

Courtesy of Thomas Eisner, Cornell U

© iStock.com/Chaiababa

Figure 37.19 Disarming a Plant's Defense and Applying It
(A) This beetle is inactivating a milkweed's defense system by cutting its laticifer supply lines. **(B)** Collecting latex from a rubber tree in the Philippines.

When latex dries, it becomes rubbery. That's a good adjective, because we have exploited the sticky, moldy properties of dry latex from the tree *Hevea brasiliensis* to turn it into rubber for tires, shoes, adhesives, and condoms, to name a few products (**Figure 37.19B**). Because Japan occupied the regions of the world where rubber trees grow, during World War II U.S. and British chemists investigated ways to make synthetic rubber. They analyzed latex, determined its composition of hydrocarbons, and then made rubber in the lab. Today, half of the rubber used worldwide is synthetic.

KEY CONCEPT
37.3 Recap and Assess

Many plants use secondary metabolites as constitutive defenses against herbivory. Other defenses are induced by herbivory through signal transduction pathways. The plant hormone jasmonate stimulates local and systemic responses to herbivores.

1. Tobacco plants produce nicotine as a secondary metabolite. The plants also have induced defenses against herbivores. How would these defenses work together to protect the plant from herbivores?

2. Armyworm larvae feed on corn leaves. They deposit their frass, or waste, in crevices where corn leaves meet stalks. The frass releases chemicals that signal the plant that it is being attacked by armyworms, and the corn plant mounts a defense against armyworms.

   a. Does this represent a constitutive or an induced defense? Explain your answer.

   b. How would chemicals in armyworm frass affect the corn plant's response?

3. Explain how plants attacked by herbivores can use jasmonate to "call for help."

 View in Achieve
Activity 37.1 **Concept Review: Plant Responses to Environmental Challenges**

 ▶InvestigatingLIFE

Q and A How can plants respond to the environmental challenges posed by global climate change?

A common misconception is that because plants do not have the same sensory organs that people do, plants are not aware of their environments. However, the ability of plants to detect and respond to stimuli is not all that different from our own. We see light, taste chemical compounds, smell volatile molecules, detect temperature, and respond to mechanical pressure. Plants also sense and respond to all these types of stimuli. Like animals, plants have receptor proteins that interact with the signals being perceived and activate signal transduction pathways that lead to responses, often including changes in gene expression. In many cases, plants go so far as to change the number and location of their organs so as to best fit their current environments; the architecture of their bodies is determined in response to the conditions they experience. This ability to sense and respond gives plants improved opportunities for survival in the face of changing environmental conditions.

Plants are well suited to deal with many of the environmental changes associated with global climate change because they already have receptors that allow them to sense relevant environmental factors. For example, drought, which can severely limit plant growth, is expected to increase in frequency, but plants can reduce its impact through ABA-mediated responses. Likewise, plants can detect many pests and pathogens and mount responses to them. However, these responses require energy, and energy spent on defense is not available for growth. Increased levels of CO_2 do supply more substrate for photosynthesis, which could lead to an increase in plant growth. To see how all these

factors may play out, experiments were run in which plants were grown in natural environments to which additional CO_2 was added. The results of several such experiments showed that plant growth did not increase as much as was expected from the increase in CO_2 alone. In many cases, growth became limited by water and nutrients. High temperatures can also be detrimental to growth and reproduction. The limits of what some species can withstand are already being seen in some regions, where the ranges of some plants have shifted toward higher latitudes.

Future directions

The rapid pace of climate change is expected to make production of crops sufficient to feed the world significantly more challenging. Growing a more diverse set of crop species may buffer the system against year-to-year variation in severe weather and provide some improvement in pest management. Another approach that may mitigate the effects of climate change is to understand and then reengineer plants so that they will be able to maintain yields under less than optimal conditions. Production of drought-tolerant plants (discussed in the opening to Chapter 33) and of plants with enhanced disease resistance are areas of particular interest. So too is the idea of enhancing the efficiency of photosynthesis. Because a substantial amount of energy is lost through photorespiration (a detrimental interaction that happens when rubisco interacts with oxygen), many projects focus on finding a way to reduce its cost. One bold project aims to increase the yield of rice, a C_3 plant, by introducing C_4-like photosynthetic systems that are expected to decrease the frequency of photorespiration and improve water use efficiency.

© Ken Schulze/Shutterstock.com

You should be able to relate each summary to the adjacent figures. If you go to this visual summary in **Achieve**, you can follow links to figures, animations, activities, and simulations that will help you consolidate the material.

KEY CONCEPT

37.1 Plants Can Sense and Respond to Environmental Stresses

- Plants sense their environment by monitoring changes in signal receptors and employ signal transduction pathways to initiate responses.

- Plants respond to water stress by producing the hormone abscisic acid (ABA), which leads to stomatal closure as well as to changes in gene expression and root formation.

- Phytochrome appears to be a temperature sensor as well as a light receptor.

Questions

1. Plants can perceive ABA because they have a receptor for it. What type of molecule serves as an ABA receptor? How does binding to ABA change such a receptor?

2. What is the trade-off between having stomata open and closed?

3. Provide evidence to support the claim that phytochrome is a temperature sensor. Indicate which part of the requirements for a receptor (or sensor) each piece of evidence fills.

4. A phytochrome mutant that can form P_{fr} but does not undergo dark reversion has been identified. Make a diagram indicating the extent of stem elongation expected for wild-type plants and for plants carrying this non-reverting phytochrome mutation.

Figure 37.1

Figure 37.9

From J. H. Jung et al. 2016. Science 354: 886–889.

KEY CONCEPT

37.2 Plants Respond to Pathogens with Constitutive and Induced Responses

Go to **Animation 37.1**

- Plants and pathogens have evolved together in a continuing "arms race."

- Plants respond to broad classes of organisms with general immunity responses and to particular pathogens with specific immunity.

- **Gene-for-gene resistance** depends on a match between a plant's **R** (**resistance**) **genes** and a pathogen's **Avr** (**avirulence**) **genes**.

- In **systemic acquired resistance**, salicylic acid activates synthesis of defensive compounds throughout the plant.

- Plants use small interfering RNAs (siRNAs) to develop immunity to invading RNA viruses.

Questions

1. What is the advantage of having chemical defenses that are inducible rather than constitutive?

2. Outline a pathway from signal to response that leads to a hypersensitive response.

3. Explain how the production of siRNAs can defend a plant against viral infection.

Figure 37.13

Direct interaction

Indirect interaction

Figure 37.14

Necrotic lesion

KEY CONCEPT
37.3 Plants Have Mechanical and Chemical Defenses against Herbivores

Go to Activity 37.1 and Simulation 37.1

■ Plants produce a wide range of **secondary metabolites**, some of which provide defenses against herbivores.

■ Hormones, including **jasmonic acid (jasmonate)** and its derivatives, induce defense responses at the site of attack and throughout the plant.

■ Production of protease inhibitors can be an effective defense against attack by hungry caterpillars.

Questions

1. Formulate a hypothesis as to why mechanical defenses are typically constitutive but some chemical defenses are inducible.

2. Plants that produce canavanine are not as strongly affected by this compound as their would-be attackers are, even when the plant aminoacyl-tRNA synthetases are exposed to canavanine. Speculate as to what molecular-level change could make the plants resistant to canavanine.

3. Explain how the production of protease inhibitors can protect plants from herbivory by caterpillars.

Figure 37.18

Go to **Achieve** for the eBook, **LearningCurve**, animations, activities, simulations, and additional resources and assignments.

Physiology, Homeostasis, and Temperature Regulation

38

KEY CONCEPTS

38.1 Animals Are Composed of Organs Built from Four Types of Tissues

38.2 Physiological Systems Maintain Homeostasis of the Internal Environment

38.3 Biological Processes Are Temperature-Sensitive

38.4 Body Temperature Depends on the Balance between Heat In and Heat Out of the Body

38.5 Body Temperature Is Regulated through Adaptations for Heat Production and Heat Loss

Human epidemics of Ebola have occurred numerous times in sub-Saharan Africa, and usually in hot humid climates. Ebola is highly contagious, so patients must be quarantined, and health care workers must be protected by complete encapsulation in personal protective equipment (PPE). PPE prevents heat loss from the body, so these workers can take care of patients for only a short time before they have to leave the quarantined ward and shed their PPE to avoid hyperthermia.

▶Investigating LIFE

Heat Limits Physical Performance and Can Kill

When a person's internal body temperature rises above 40°C, major organs begin to fail, a condition known as heat stroke. Every year some athletes suffer heat stroke, which frequently leads to death if whole body cooling is not done expeditiously. Other individuals such as soldiers, firefighters, and construction workers work in hot environments while being dressed in heavy protective equipment. They must take precautions to avoid heat stroke. A special case is health care workers in Ebola outbreak areas in hot West Africa. Frequently they cannot work for more than 20 or 30 minutes in the isolation wards with infected patients.

Activity increases the danger of heat stroke because working muscles generate heat. Circulating blood carries heat out of working muscles and distributes it throughout the body, raising the temperature of the body's internal organs. Some of the heated blood flows to the skin and is lost to the environment. Humans are subject to the heat-loss problems faced by all mammals. First, mammals have high rates of metabolic heat production. Second, their normal internal temperatures are not far from those that cause heat stroke, so they don't have much

of a safety zone. And third, most mammals have fur—great for conserving body heat in cold environments, but an impediment to heat loss in warm ones. Humans don't have fur, but our skin is still a good insulator.

The evolution of heat-loss adaptations has been important for mammals. You know about sweating and panting, but another important mechanism was discovered recently. To increase the heat-loss potential of non-hairy skin areas, mammals have evolved special, gated blood vessels that can open to bring lots of blood, and therefore heat, to these areas. In furred mammals, these areas may include the nose, tongue, ears, face, and foot-pads. Humans are not furred, but our ancestors were, and we retain these mammalian blood vessel adaptations in our hands, feet, and face (which is why we can tell a person's thermal state by shaking hands).

 How can we increase heat loss from the body to protect against heat stress?
(Find the answer on page 860.)

38.1 Animals Are Composed of Organs Built from Four Types of Tissues

Learning Objectives

38.1.1 Identify factors that limit cell size.

38.1.2 Explain the advantages of multicellularity.

38.1.3 Describe the characteristic features of the four tissue types.

Animals are amazing in all they do to survive, thrive, and propagate. They live in environments that could not support single cells, they extract energy from the environment, they build complex molecules and structures, they alter their environments, and they reproduce. All of these feats and more depend on complex body components and physiological systems that have evolved since the first appearance of multicellular organisms on this planet. What does it take to be an animal?

How would you build a multicellular animal?

This might seem like a silly question; even bioengineers don't build animals. But as you begin to study animal form and function, or animal physiology, it is instructive to think of all of the problems animals must solve to survive. For example they must:

- extract energy and nutrients from the environment.

- build all of the internal structures they need.

- eliminate toxins and metabolic waste products.

- sense the environment and respond to it in various ways, including movement.

- maintain constant conditions in their internal environments.

- reproduce.

Single- and multicellular organisms have evolved to conquer these challenges. In fact, single-celled organisms are remarkably abundant and thrive in widely diverse environments. Multicellular organisms have evolved complex body systems to conquer the same challenges. Given the success of single-celled organisms, why have multicellular animals evolved? How is it advantageous to be multicellular? Multicellularity confers two advantages—large size and the opportunity for cells to specialize.

There are advantages and challenges to getting bigger

Advantages to being bigger include being able to prey on other organisms and also being able to resist or work against forces in the environment, such as wave forces in reefs. There is a problem, however, that single-celled organisms must overcome as they get bigger. Exchanges with the environment, such as uptake of oxygen and nutrients as well as elimination of wastes, occur across the cell membrane, so the extent of these exchanges is limited by the surface area of the cell membrane. For simple globular-shaped cells, their cell surface area increases with the square of the linear dimension of the cell, but the needs of the cell increase as a function of the volume of the cell, which is a function of the cube of the linear dimension.

Of course there are adaptations to get around this problem, including being flat and thin or having lots of projections and indentations in the surface, but in general the surface area-to-volume relationship is a challenge for growing bigger.

> **Connect the Concepts** Figure 5.2 illustrates how cell volume grows faster than cell surface area as cells get bigger.

Cell specialization is essential for multicellular animals to grow bigger. If a multicellular animal consists of only a few layers of cells, those cells can carry out their own exchanges directly with the environment. A good example is a sponge (**Figure 38.1**). Bigger organisms have cells that are not in contact with the external environment. The needs of those cells must be supplied by an *internal* environment—extracellular fluid that bathes all the cells of the animal's body. Different cells and groups of cells must be specialized to contribute to the maintenance of that internal environment. Thus each cell contributes to the internal environment, and each cell is supported by that internal environment.

Cell specializations have tremendous adaptive value for even the simplest multicellular animals. Some cells can be specialized for movement, some for intake of food, and some for reproduction. But evolving a specialized function for a cell type usually comes at the expense of other cellular functions, which may be lost or at least compromised. The specialized cells of an organism thus engage in a kind of collaborative enterprise by providing a particular service for all of the cells of the organism while benefiting from different services provided by those other cells. Thus the cells specialized for movement do not have to also capture and process food, and the reproductive cells do not have to move the whole animal to find a mate.

There are four tissue types

Specialized cells rarely function alone, but rather as groups of similar cells called **tissues**. There are many different kinds of cells, but they are all classified as one of four tissue types: epithelial, muscle, connective, or nervous (**Figure 38.2**):

Figure 38.1 No Cell Too Far The sponge *Leucosolenia* consists of tubes about 2 centimeters long with an outer and an inner layer of cells and a jellylike matrix. There are pores between the cells of the tube. The inner cells have flagella that create a current of water that flows in through the pores and out through the opening at the top. The individual cells of this animal can obtain nutrients and oxygen directly from the seawater.

Creating Compartments: Epithelial Tissues

Stratified squamous epithelium: The outer layers of skin (epidermis) separate internal from external environment and protect the body.

40 µm

© Ed Reschke/Getty Images

Cubodial epithelium: Makes up tubules and ducts and can have secretory and absorptive functions.

25 µm

© Ed Reschke/Getty Images

Cubodial epithelial cells

Cilia

Columnar epithelium: Lines many internal organs such as the airways of the lungs and the small intestine. Can have secretory and absorptive functions. Enables movements of substances between body compartments.

20 µm

© Carolina Biological Supply, Co/Visuals Unlimited, Inc.

Secretory cells: The stomach lining includes epithelial cells that secrete digestive juices and acid. Other secretory epithelial cells are found in the salivary, sweat, and mammary glands, and in the pancreas and anterior pituitary.

© Biophoto Associates/Science Source

Generating Forces: Muscle Tissues

Cardiac muscle: Responsible for contractions of the heart.

15 µm

© Ed Reschke/Getty Images

Smooth muscle: Provides motility to internal organs such as the digestive tract. Controls diameter of blood vessels.

30 µm

© SPL/Science Source

Skeletal muscle: Responsible for voluntary movements of the body.

15 µm

© Ed Reschke/Getty Images

(Continued)

Figure 38.2 How to Build an Animal
Tissues are the building blocks.

Q: If we consider the functions of skeletal muscle in running, what are roles played by the three other tissue types in this process?

Figure 38.2 (continued)

Providing Support: Connective Tissues

Layers of bone cells in mineralized matrix

M. H. Ross et al. 2009. Atlas of Descriptive Histology. Sinauer Associates: Sunderland, MA

Bones: Provide support structures for the body that make it possible for muscles to generate movements.

250 μm

Brown fat   80 μm   White fat   80 μm

M. H. Ross et al. 2009. Atlas of Descriptive Histology. Sinauer Associates: Sunderland, MA

Adipose tissue: White fat cushions and supports organs, provides thermal insulation, and stores energy. Brown fat produces heat.

White blood cell   Red blood cells

© Dr. Thomas Deerinck/Visuals Unlimited, Inc.

Blood cells: Red blood cells carry respiratory gases. White blood cells protect against foreign substances and microorganisms invading the body.

15 μm

Collagen fibers

© Biology Pics/Science Source

Ligaments and tendons: Connect bones to bones and muscles to bones.

Processing Information: Nervous Tissues

© Dr. John D. Cunningham/Visuals Unlimited, Inc.

Sensors: These cells of the retina encode information about the external environment.

Cell body of neuron   **Axon**

© James Cavallini/Science Source

Neurons: Communicate information from sensors to the central nervous system, store and integrate information, communicate commands to muscles and glands.

20 μm

Neurons

Astrocytes

© Ralph C. Eagle, Jr./Science Source

Glia: Support neurons in many ways and modulate their signaling; insulate neuronal processes; provide immune functions for the central nervous system.

60 μm

1. **Epithelial tissues** are sheets of cells that create barriers between different compartments and frequently have secretory functions.

2. **Muscle tissues** contract to generate forces and movement.

3. **Connective tissues** provide structure and support.

4. **Nervous tissues** convey and process information.

These are very general groupings that reflect developmental origins, but within each group there are various specializations that accommodate different functions. For example, connective tissue includes bones, cartilage, fat, and blood. Epithelial tissue includes the outer layers of skin (epidermis) and many types of secretory cells that produce and release substances internally, such as hormones, and externally, such as sweat and digestive juices. You might think of digestive juices as being secreted internally, but the lumen of the digestive tract is continuous with the external environment. You will learn a lot about the diversity of functions accomplished through specializations of these four tissue types in the chapters that follow.

Organs are built from multiple tissues

Organs are internal structures that carry out specific functions. An organ is composed of an outer covering, or epithelium, and one or more other kinds of tissues. Indeed, most organs include all four tissue types. The gut (digestive tract) is a good example (**Figure 38.3**). Its inner surface is lined with a sheet of columnar epithelial cells. Different types of epithelial cells in this lining secrete hormones or digestive juices or absorb nutrients from the gut. Beneath the epithelial lining is a layer of connective tissue called the mucosa. Within this connective tissue are blood vessels, neurons, and glands (clusters of secretory epithelial cells). Concentric layers of smooth muscle tissue enable the gut to contract to mix food with digestive juices. A network of neurons between the muscle layers controls these movements.

An individual organ is usually part of an **organ system**, a group of organs that work together to carry out certain functions. The stomach, small intestine, liver, and pancreas, for example, are parts of the digestive system. The structure of an animal involves an organizational hierarchy. Cells form tissues, tissues form organs, organs work together as organ systems, and all work together as a multicellular organism.

KEY CONCEPT
38.1 Recap and Assess

There are limits to how large cells can be because metabolic needs are related to cell volume, and abilities to satisfy those needs are determined by cell surface area. Cell volume grows faster than cell surface area. Multicellularity and cell specialization enabled organisms to grow larger. Groups of similar cells form tissues, and multicellular animals are composed of four tissue types: epithelial, connective, nervous, and muscle. Individual organs include multiple tissue types and are part of organ systems.

1. For single-celled organisms, why does increased size create a problem with obtaining oxygen, and what adaptations could reduce this problem?

2. What are the advantages of being a multicellular organism rather than a single-celled organism?

3. Provide an example of how multiple tissue types are involved in the construction of an organ. What does each tissue type contribute to the function of that organ?

Subsequent chapters will describe each of the organ systems in much greater detail. The remainder of this chapter focuses on the mechanisms of control and regulation of the internal environment, using temperature as the example.

KEY CONCEPT
38.2 Physiological Systems Maintain Homeostasis of the Internal Environment

Learning Objectives

38.2.1 Explain why homeostasis of the internal environment in a multicellular animal is critical to the animal's survival.

38.2.2 Discuss the relationships between the fluid compartments in the human body.

38.2.3 Differentiate among negative feedback, positive feedback, and feedforward control mechanisms, and give examples.

The evolution of multicellularity made it possible to enclose and therefore create an internal fluid environment that bathes all cells

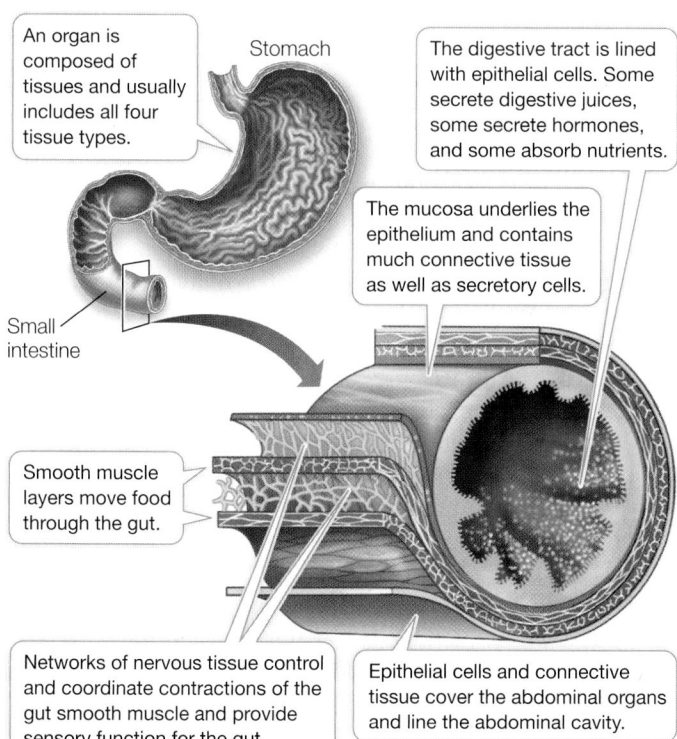

An organ is composed of tissues and usually includes all four tissue types.

Stomach

The digestive tract is lined with epithelial cells. Some secrete digestive juices, some secrete hormones, and some absorb nutrients.

The mucosa underlies the epithelium and contains much connective tissue as well as secretory cells.

Small intestine

Smooth muscle layers move food through the gut.

Networks of nervous tissue control and coordinate contractions of the gut smooth muscle and provide sensory function for the gut.

Epithelial cells and connective tissue cover the abdominal organs and line the abdominal cavity.

Figure 38.3 Tissues Form Organs The organs of the human digestive system, such as the stomach and small intestine, are made up of all four tissue types.

View in Achieve
Activity 38.1 Tissues and Cell Types

of the organism. Since that internal environment provided for all of the needs of the individual cells, individual cell lines could become specialized as to what they contributed to the internal environment. Specialization in one function usually goes hand in hand with losses in other functions. But those functional losses in each cell line were compensated for by the constancy of the internal environment. The evolution of organs composed of multiple tissues and the evolution of informational systems to control organ activities improved the abilities of animals to maintain a constant internal environment. In essence, the evolution of physiological systems to maintain various aspects of the internal environment made it possible for multicellular animals to become larger, and more complex, and allowed them to occupy many different environments.

The internal environment is the extracellular fluid that serves all the needs of the cells of the body

Individual cells get their nutrients from the surrounding extracellular fluid (ECF) and dump their waste products into it. A human is about 60% water. Two-thirds of that water is intracellular fluid and one-third is the ECF. About 20% of the ECF (about 3 liters) is the **blood plasma** that circulates in our blood vessels. The remaining 80% (about 11 liters) is the **interstitial fluid** that bathes every cell of the body (**Figure 38.4**). Water and small molecules freely exchange between the interstitial fluid and the blood plasma. Thus nutrients move into the interstitial fluid from the blood plasma, and wastes move into the blood plasma from the interstitial fluid. As long as the composition and physical conditions of the interstitial fluid are held within certain limits, cells are protected from the changes and harsh conditions of the external environment. A stable internal environment makes it possible for an animal to occupy habitats that would kill its cells if they were directly exposed to the external conditions. How is the internal environment kept constant?

The constant composition of the internal environment is always being challenged by the external environment and by the metabolic

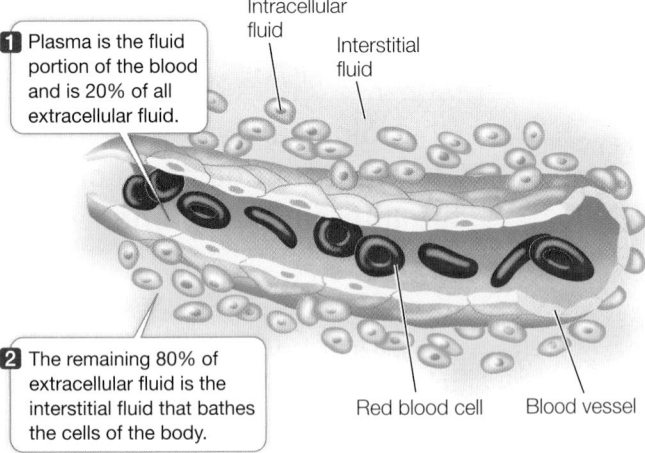

1 Plasma is the fluid portion of the blood and is 20% of all extracellular fluid.

Intracellular fluid

Interstitial fluid

2 The remaining 80% of extracellular fluid is the interstitial fluid that bathes the cells of the body.

Red blood cell   Blood vessel

Figure 38.4 The Internal Environment The extracellular fluid (ECF) is the "internal environment," and it is about one-third of total body water. The ECF is about 20% blood plasma and 80% interstitial fluid. The composition and physiological state of the ECF must remain stable within narrow limits, and maintaining that stability is the job of the body's organ systems.

activities of the cells of the body. Organisms must maintain their internal environment in a state of **homeostasis**—a narrow range of stable and optimal physical and biochemical conditions. If a physiological system fails to function properly, homeostasis is compromised, and cells are damaged and can die. To avoid the loss of homeostasis, organ systems are controlled and regulated in response to changes in both the external and internal environments. The maintenance of homeostasis is a central theme of physiology.

Physiological systems are regulated to maintain homeostasis

The activities of physiological systems are *controlled*—speeded up or slowed down—by actions of the nervous and endocrine systems. But to *regulate* these systems and maintain homeostasis, information is required. As an analogy, think of the thermostat that controls the furnace and air conditioner to regulate the temperature of a house (**Figure 38.5**). The desired temperature is a **set point**, or reference point on the thermostat. The thermostat acts as a **comparator** by sensing the current temperature in the house and comparing that value to the set point. Thus the sensing of the air temperature is **feedback** information. Any difference between the set point and feedback information results in an **error signal**. The error signal is converted into commands to the furnace or air conditioner, turning them on or off.

Regulatory systems such as a building thermostat or a physiological regulatory system obtain, process, and integrate information. Regulatory systems use that information to issue commands to **effectors** such as muscles or glands that effect changes in the internal environment. Effectors are also called **controlled systems** because their activities are controlled by the neural or hormonal signals from their respective regulatory systems. Important components of any regulatory system are the sensors such as light-, temperature-, and pressure-sensitive cells that provide feedback information to be compared with internal set points.

Negative feedback is information used to counteract the influence that created an error signal. Whatever force is pushing the system away from its set point must be "negated." In our thermostat analogy, an air temperature below the set point causes the furnace to be turned on, which then reverses the direction of change in the air temperature.

Although not as common as negative feedback, **positive feedback** also exists in physiological systems. Rather than returning a system to a set point, positive feedback amplifies a response (i.e., it increases the deviation from the set point). An example is sexual behavior, in which a little stimulation causes more behavior, which causes more stimulation, and so on. Positive feedback responses tend to reach a limit and terminate rapidly. The birth process is a good example. Contractions of the uterus push the baby into the birth canal, and stretching of the birth canal stimulates more and stronger contractions until the baby is delivered, at which time contractions cease.

Feedforward information is a feature of regulatory systems that changes the set point in anticipation of a change in conditions. The timer on a thermostat provides feedforward information by changing the system's temperature set point, usually lowering it in the evening and raising it in the morning. Hearing

A clock provides feedforward information, changing the set point at different times of day.

The set point of the thermostat indicates desired temperature.

The sensor measures room temperature and provides feedback to the thermostat.

The thermostat compares sensor feedback to the set point and generates commands to the controlled systems.

Set point

16° 18° 20° 22° 24°

Sensor

Regulatory system (thermostat)

Furnace **Controlled systems** Air conditioner

Figure 38.5 A Thermostat Regulates Temperature A thermostat regulates the temperature of a room by turning the furnace or air conditioner on or off in response to the difference between feedback information (room temperature) and set points that are programmed into the thermostat.

the words "on your mark" before a race is feedforward information that raises your heart rate in anticipation of running. Feedforward information anticipates a change in the internal environment before that change occurs.

 View in Achieve
Simulation 38.1 Temperature Regulation System

KEY CONCEPT
38.2 Recap and Assess

The internal environment provides for the needs of all the cells that make up a complex multicellular animal. The internal environment is the extracellular fluid compartments of the body. Organs and organ systems control the chemical and physical composition of the extracellular fluids to maintain homeostasis. The activities of organs and organ systems are regulated. Regulation requires information about optimal conditions (set points) and existing conditions (feedback) to create commands to effector cells and organs.

1. What are the relationships between the extracellular fluid of the body, the organ systems, and homeostasis?

2. Based on your body mass, estimate how much water is in your body. What is your intracellular fluid volume, your extracellular fluid volume, your blood plasma volume, and your interstitial fluid volume?

3. Explain the differences between negative and positive feedback and feedforward control mechanisms.

Principles of control and regulation help organize our thinking about physiological systems. Once we understand how a system works, we can then ask how it is regulated. Part Eight of this book

describes various physiological systems, how they function, and how they are regulated. We'll begin by extending our example of a house thermoregulatory system to that of the mammalian body.

KEY CONCEPT
38.3 Biological Processes Are Temperature-Sensitive

Learning Objectives

38.3.1 Discuss the effects of temperature on living systems.

38.3.2 Describe the Q_{10} concept.

38.3.3 Explain how isozymes are involved in seasonal temperature acclimatization.

Temperatures of environments where organisms live vary enormously, from the boiling hot springs of Yellowstone National Park to the interior of Antarctica, where the temperature can fall below −80°C. But in general, cells can function over only a narrow range of temperatures. The evolution of thermoregulatory adaptations enables maintenance of suitable thermal conditions in the internal environment.

Temperature affects living systems

If cells cool below their freezing point, ice crystals form and damage cell structures. Some animals have adaptations, such as antifreeze molecules in their blood that help them resist freezing; others can survive freezing (**Figure 38.6**). Generally, however, cells must remain above freezing to stay alive. The upper temperature limit for survival in most cells is below 45°C because of protein denaturation. Some specialized algae, however, can grow in hot springs at 70°C, and some archaea live at near 100°C.

Rana sylvatica

Figure 38.6 Frozen Frogs Wood frogs live in the northeastern United States, across most of Canada, and up into northern Alaska. They freeze solid in the winter and survive. During the fall and early winter, urea and glucose accumulate in the frogs' cells and act as intracellular cryoprotectants (like antifreeze in your car radiator). Also, much intracellular water is redistributed to the extracellular fluid, which can freeze without damaging cells.

Connect the Concepts Protein denaturation by heat is due to effects on secondary and tertiary structure of the protein, as described in Key Concept 3.2.

One adaptation cells have to survive episodes of exposure to high temperatures is **heat shock proteins** (**HSPs**). HSPs are chaperone proteins that protect other proteins from denaturation, and they are found in organisms ranging from bacteria to humans (see Key Concept 3.2 and Figure 3.15). Sudden heating induces the expression of HSPs, which act to stabilize proteins and prevent or reverse errors in protein folding.

Although the survival limits for most cells fall in the range of 0°C–40°C, most species have much narrower thermal limits for optimal function. To stay within those limits in spite of environmental conditions, animals have **thermoregulatory adaptations** that enable them to tolerate extreme conditions or to control their body temperatures in spite of environmental conditions. These adaptations may determine the thermal tolerances of species and thereby determine their geographic ranges. When environments change rapidly, as is happening globally at present, animals may find themselves in situations that exceed their thermal tolerances. A good example is the reef-building corals discussed in the opening of Chapter 1.

Q_{10} is a measure of temperature sensitivity

Even between 0°C and 40°C, changes in body temperature can create problems for animals. Most biochemical reactions and the physiological processes they are involved in are temperature-sensitive, going faster at higher temperatures. The temperature sensitivity of a reaction or process can be described in terms of Q_{10}, a factor calculated by dividing the rate of a process or reaction at a certain temperature, R_T, by the rate of that same process or reaction at a temperature 10 degrees Celsius lower, R_{T-10}:

$$Q_{10} = \frac{R_T}{R_{T-10}}$$

Connect the Concepts As discussed in Key Concept 8.5, increases in temperature increase reaction rates because reactant molecules have more kinetic energy. Enzymes that control rates of biochemical reactions in metabolic pathways are influenced by temperature as well.

Q_{10} can be measured for a simple biochemical reaction or for a complex physiological process, such as rate of oxygen consumption. If a reaction or process is not temperature-sensitive, it has a Q_{10} of 1. Most biological Q_{10} values are between 2 and 3. A Q_{10} of 2 means that the reaction rate doubles as temperature increases by 10 degrees Celsius, and a Q_{10} of 3 indicates a tripling of the rate as temperature increases by 10 degrees Celsius (**Figure 38.7**).

Notice that the Q_{10} values (except for Q_{10} = 1) plotted in Figure 38.7 produce curves rather than straight lines. This is because temperature increases in additive intervals (10, 20, 30, etc.) but reaction rates increase in a multiplicative fashion (2, 4, 8, 16, 32, etc.). Such curvilinear plots are common in biological data.

Changes in body temperature can disrupt an animal's physiology because not all of the biochemical reactions that constitute the metabolism of an animal have the same Q_{10}. These biochemical

Figure 38.7 Q_{10} **and Reaction Rate** The larger the Q_{10} of a reaction or process, the faster its rate rises in response to an increase in temperature.

reactions are linked together in complex networks: the products of one reaction are the reactants for other reactions. Because different reactions have different Q_{10}'s, changes in tissue temperature will shift the rates of some reactions more than others, disrupting the overall network. To maintain homeostasis, organisms compensate for or prevent changes in body temperature.

Animals acclimatize to seasonal temperatures

The body temperatures of some animals (especially aquatic animals) are coupled to environmental temperature. The body temperature of a fish in a pond, for example, is the same as the water temperature, which might range from 4°C in winter to 24°C in summer. If we bring that fish into the laboratory in the summer and measure the rates of any of its physiological or biochemical processes such as oxygen consumption at different water temperatures, we will demonstrate a Q_{10} relationship. On the basis of the Q_{10} relationship, we would predict that the fish's oxygen consumption—a measure of its metabolic rate—would be much lower in the winter pond because the water temperature is lower. However, if we bring that fish back into the laboratory in the winter and measure its metabolic rate at winter pond temperature, we find that rate to be higher than we predicted. The fish's biochemistry and physiology will have **acclimatized** to the seasonal change in water temperature so that it can remain active at winter temperatures. What could be the mechanism of this acclimatization? Many organisms express multiple forms of enzymes (**isozymes**) that may have different temperature optima. In winter, organisms express the forms that show maximum substrate affinity at low temperatures, and in summer they express the forms that have maximum substrate affinity at high temperature. Another mechanism of temperature acclimatization is a change in the composition of cell membranes designed to maintain optimum fluidity despite changes in temperature (see

Key Concept 6.1). Acclimatization in animals essentially means that their metabolic functions are less sensitive to long-term changes in their environment than to short-term changes.

Small changes in temperature can have large physiological effects

The story opening this chapter described how heavy exercise, exposure to hot environments, or being clad in insulative protective gear can rapidly elevate a person's body temperature to a dangerously high level. Our ability to function physically or mentally is rapidly compromised by hyperthermia, and sustained hyperthermia of only a few degrees can lead to death. To avoid the serious consequences of hyperthermia, it is important to reduce heat-generating muscular work and to increase heat loss from the body as soon as possible. The body has protective fail-safe mechanisms, one of which is heat-induced cramps. Ask any athlete whether or not a cramp makes them stop exercising. Another fail-safe mechanism is to deprive the muscle of energy, causing muscle failure. Pyruvate kinase is an enzyme critical for production of ATP in muscles; it catalyzes the last step in glycolysis, producing pyruvate molecules that can enter the mitochondria and be metabolized to produce ATP (see Figure 9.17). Without ATP, muscles fatigue and can't do work. Muscle pyruvate kinase inactivates at high temperatures, which shuts off muscle function and thereby prevents thermal damage to the muscle. Pyruvate kinase is reactivated when the muscle cools, and the muscle can resume work. You may wonder, if we could protect athletes and emergency workers from hyperthermia by enhancing extraction of heat from their muscles, could we increase their performances and capacity to work in the heat? We consider this question in Investigating Life: Can the Work Capacity of Workers in PPE be Extended by Extracting Heat from the Palms of the Hands?

▶Investigating LIFE Can the Work Capacity of Workers in PPE Be Extended by Extracting Heat from the Palms of the Hands?

Experiment

Original Paper: D. A. Grahn et al. 2018. A method to reduce heat strain while clad in encapsulating outerwear. *J Occup Environ Hyg* 15: 573–579.

In the opening story of this chapter you learned that mammals have evolved special heat-dissipation adaptations underlying their non-hairy skin. These skin areas are small, but their adaptation is high-volume blood vessels that can rapidly transfer heat from the body core to the skin. Humans don't have fur, but they do have these same blood vessel adaptations. In this experiment, individuals clad in personal protective equipment (PPE) were exposed to a hot ambient temperature (45°C) for 60 minutes, with or without a cooling system worn under their PPE that cooled the palms of their hands. The outcome measure was esophageal temperature measured at the level of the heart so as to obtain the best average body core temperature.

J Occup Environ Hyg 15: 573–579
D. A. Grahn et al. 2018.

HYPOTHESIS▶ Extracting heat from the palms of the hands will extend dwell time in the heat for a worker in PPE.

METHOD▶

1. Recruit 10 healthy individuals between the ages of 19 and 23 years old.

2. Fully encapsulate the subjects in Tyvek® PPE (DuPont Corporation) and have each subject self-insert a thermocouple (Mallinckrodt Medical Inc.) down his or her esophagus to the level of the heart.

3. In randomized fashion, have each subject rest in an environmental chamber at 45°C with or without a wearable palmar cooling system under their PPE.

4. Terminate exposures at 60 minutes or when esophageal temperature reaches 39°C.

RESULTS▶ For all 10 subjects, their esophageal temperatures (T_{es}) measured at 5-minute intervals were averaged and the standard deviations (SD) calculated.

Time (min)	T_{es}, mean (SD)	
	Control, no cooling	**Palm Cooling**
0	36.85 (0.18)	36.65 (0.30)
5	36.86 (0.21)	36.67 (0.33)
10	36.93 (0.20)	36.72 (0.28)
15	37.05 (0.19)	36.76 (0.27)
20	37.15 (0.29)	36.79 (0.26)
25	37.34 (0.26)	36.86 (0.28)
30	37.55 (0.26)	36.95 (0.29)
35	37.76 (0.23)	37.05 (0.29)
40	37.99 (0.22)	37.14 (0.30)
45	38.20 (0.20)	37.24 (0.30)
50	38.40 (0.18)	37.32 (0.29)
55	38.60 (0.17)	37.40 (0.32)
60	38.80 (0.16)	37.49 (0.32)

CONCLUSION▶ By analyzing these data, you will be able to conclude whether the hypothesis is supported or not supported by this experiment.

Investigating**LIFE** Work with the Data follows on the next page.

Work with the Data

This experiment involves a simple outcome measure: esophageal temperature at 5-minute intervals during exposure to 45°C while fully encapsulated in PPE, as an Ebola health care worker would experience. The experimental manipulation is heat extraction from the palms by a portable cooling system worn under the PPE.

QUESTIONS▶

1. Plot the data with time on the x axis and T_{es} on the y axis. Using the t-test formula in Figure B11 in Appendix B, test which of the pairs of data at each temperature are statistically different. That formula will give you a t-value, and knowing that your sample size is 10, you can refer to a t-statistic table to find the probability that

the values are significantly different. You can also use an online statistics program to perform paired t-tests on the data.

2. Using the linear parts of the curves (after 20 minutes), what are the rates of T_{es} increase with and without cooling?

3. Is the hypothesis supported or disproven? Explain.

4. Assuming that a core temperature of 39°C is the point at which a worker must leave the "hot zone," how much longer can the work session be with palmar cooling?

5. The subjects in this experiment rested in the heat. How would you expect the data to differ if subjects sustained a modest workload?

Go to **Achieve** for a companion Data in Depth exercise.

KEY CONCEPT
38.3 Recap and Assess

Cells can survive only within a narrow range of temperatures, but even changes within that range can be disruptive because different physiological processes have different temperature sensitivities.

1. How can fluctuations in body temperature disrupt complex physiological processes?

2. Plot a Q_{10} = 2.5 curve for a physiological process using arbitrary units as measures of that process.

3. What characteristic of isozymes might explain their role in metabolic seasonal temperature acclimatization?

Now that you know how animals are affected by temperature, we'll look next at the adaptations that allow animals to survive wide ranges of thermal environments and wide ranges of metabolic activities.

KEY CONCEPT
38.4 Body Temperature Depends on the Balance between Heat In and Heat Out of the Body

Learning Objectives

38.4.1 Give examples of an ectotherm, an endotherm, and a heterotherm, and explain their responses to changes in environmental temperature.

38.4.2 Describe the paths of heat exchange between an animal and its environment.

38.4.3 Explain why "hot fishes" such as great white sharks can maintain a core body temperature above that of the sea while most other fishes cannot.

Body temperature is a measure of the heat content of the body. Animals produce heat internally through their metabolism, and they continuously exchange heat with their environment. The balance between heat gain and heat loss determines the animal's body temperature. Thermoregulatory adaptations enable animals

to modulate the various paths of heat exchange between themselves and their environment.

Animals can be classified by their thermoregulatory characteristics

One way of classifying animals is according to the constancy of their body temperatures. Animals that maintain a constant body temperature are called **homeotherms**, and animals that experience a fluctuating body temperature are called **poikilotherms**. Another classification is based on the source of heat that predominantly determines body temperature. **Endotherms** such as birds and mammals have the ability to vary their metabolic heat production to compensate for the loss of heat to the environment. **Ectotherms** such as invertebrates, fishes, amphibians, and non-avian reptiles are largely dependent on environmental sources of heat. We use the terminology of ectotherm and endotherm in this book, but no classification scheme is perfect. Many ectotherms can generate considerable internal heat to raise their body temperature, and endotherms that hibernate can periodically appear to give up the ability to generate internal heat. To accommodate these departures from a strict dichotomy, we add the term **heterotherms**—organisms that act like ectotherms some of the time and like endotherms at other times.

Endotherms produce substantial amounts of metabolic heat

Transfers of energy in biological systems are inefficient. In both ectotherms and endotherms, in every transfer of energy—from food molecules to ATP, from ATP to biological work—some of the energy is lost as heat. Working muscles produce heat, as do all of the metabolic activities of all tissues.

> **Connect the Concepts** As discussed in Key Concept 8.1, transfers of energy are governed by the first and second laws of thermodynamics, which explain why heat is always a by-product of metabolism.

Why do endotherms produce more heat than ectotherms? The surprising answer is that the cells of endotherms are less efficient at using energy than are the cells of ectotherms. The cells of endotherms are more "leaky" to ions than are the cells of ectotherms. Therefore Na^+ ions are constantly diffusing into the cells, and K^+ ions are constantly diffusing out. Even an endotherm at rest must spend considerable amounts of energy to transport Na⁺ out of the cells and transport K⁺ back in. Because of their constant need to actively transport ions, endotherms expend more energy than do ectotherms just to maintain the ion concentration gradients across their cell membranes. This situation is analogous to a leaky boat: the faster water comes in (i.e., the faster ions diffuse down their concentration gradients), the more metabolic energy has to be expended to bail the water out (i.e., pump ions back up their concentration gradients). Since endotherms expend more energy than ectotherms do to maintain ion concentration gradients, they produce more internal heat.

We can speculate that a mutation resulting in seemingly faulty or leaky ion channels might underlie the evolution of endothermy. Such a mutation in a small ectotherm would have increased its energy expenditure and therefore its heat production. Increased heat production would have enabled the animal to be active earlier in the morning or for a longer time after sunset. Being active in twilight, and eventually at night, would open up a new world of ecological opportunities—a world in which there was less competition from similar-sized ectotherms and less danger of predation.

Two major differences between endotherms and ectotherms are (1) their resting metabolic rates—the sum total of all energy expenditures in their bodies when at rest—and (2) their responses to changes in environmental temperature.

Ectotherms and endotherms respond differently to changes in environmental temperature

How do similar-sized ectotherms and endotherms respond to changes in environmental temperature? Let's compare a lizard and a mouse. We put each animal in a closed chamber and measure its

body temperature and its resting metabolic rate as we set the temperature of the chamber at different levels between 0°C and 40°C. The body temperature of the lizard equilibrates with that of the chamber, whereas the body temperature of the mouse remains stable over most of this range (**Figure 38.8A**). The metabolic rate of the lizard (already much lower than that of the mouse when both are at the same body temperature) decreases as the temperature drops (**Figure 38.8B**). In contrast, the mouse's metabolic rate increases as the chamber temperature falls below 25°C. This increase in metabolism produces enough heat to prevent the mouse's body temperature from falling. In other words, the mouse can regulate its body temperature by increasing its metabolic rate and thereby maintaining its physiological functions at an optimal level; the lizard cannot.

This experiment might lead us to conclude that the ectotherm cannot regulate its body temperature, but observations of the lizard in nature do not support this conclusion. In nature, the lizard can regulate its body temperature quite well. It does so by behavioral mechanisms rather than by altering its internal metabolic heat production. Air temperature in the desert can fluctuate by 40 degrees Celsius or more in a few hours; the lizard, however, can limit its variation in body temperature and even maintain a fairly stable body temperature by using behavior to alter its heat exchange with the environment. Its behavioral strategies include spending time in a burrow, basking in the sun, seeking shade, climbing vegetation, and changing its orientation with respect to the Sun (**Figure 38.9**).

Endotherms also use behavior as a first line of defense against thermal stress. They select the most comfortable thermal environment possible. They change posture or their orientation to the Sun, move between sunshine and shade, and move between still air and moving air. Examples of more complex thermoregulatory

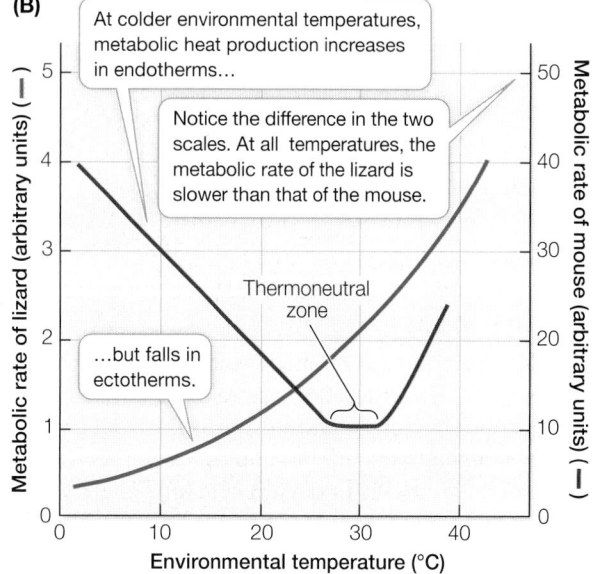

Figure 38.8 **Ectotherms and Endotherms React Differently to Environmental Temperatures** (A) At the same environmental temperature, an ectotherm and an endotherm of approximately the same body size (here, a lizard and a mouse) have different body temperatures. (B) The metabolic rates of the lizard and mouse react in opposite ways to cooler temperatures.

Q: In the plot of body temperature versus environmental temperature, why does the mouse curve fall on the far left side and rise on the far right side? In the plot of metabolic rate versus environmental temperature, why does the mouse's metabolic rate rise at higher temperatures?

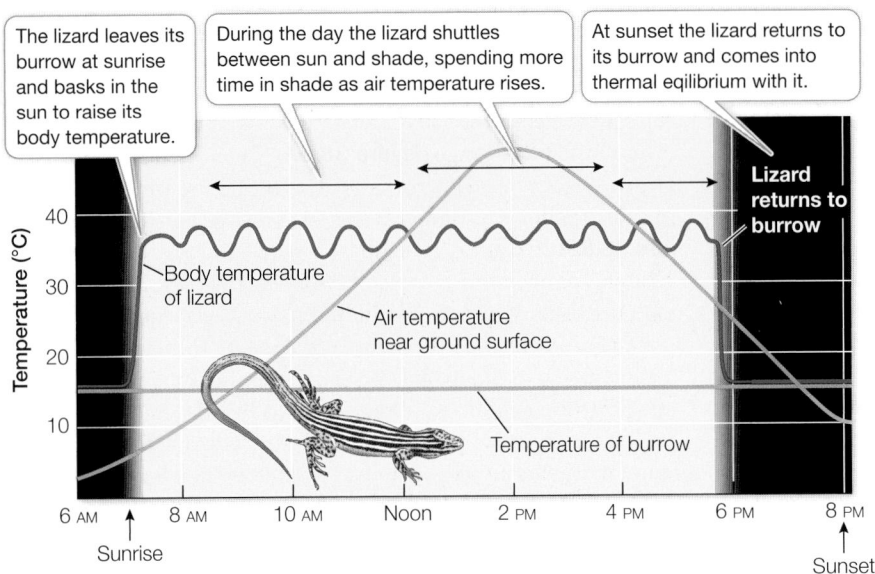

The lizard leaves its burrow at sunrise and basks in the sun to raise its body temperature.

During the day the lizard shuttles between sun and shade, spending more time in shade as air temperature rises.

At sunset the lizard returns to its burrow and comes into thermal eqilibrium with it.

Lizard returns to burrow

Body temperature of lizard

Air temperature near ground surface

Temperature of burrow

6 AM   8 AM   10 AM   Noon   2 PM   4 PM   6 PM   8 PM

Sunrise

Sunset

Figure 38.9 Using Behavior to Regulate Body Temperature The body temperature of an ectotherm such as a lizard depends on environmental heat, but the lizard can regulate its temperature by moving from place to place.

behaviors include nest construction and social behaviors such as huddling. Humans put on or remove clothing and burn fossil fuels to generate the energy to heat or cool buildings. Large mammals such as elephants and water buffalo (*Bubalus bubalis*) may wallow in water when the environment is hot.

Energy budgets reflect adaptations for regulating body temperature

Both ectotherms and endotherms influence their body temperatures by altering four avenues of heat exchange between their bodies and the environment (**Figure 38.10**):

1. **Radiation** Heat moves from warmer objects to cooler ones via the exchange of infrared radiation (what you feel when you stand in front of a fire).

2. **Convection** Heat exchanges with a surrounding medium such as air or water that flows over a surface (the wind-chill factor).

3. **Conduction** Heat flows directly between two objects at different temperatures when they come into contact (e.g., an icepack on a sprained ankle).

4. **Evaporation** Heat is transferred away from a surface when water evaporates on that surface (the effect of sweating).

The total balance of heat production and heat exchange can be expressed as an **energy budget**, based on the simple fact that if the body temperature of an animal is to remain constant, the heat entering the animal must equal the heat leaving it. The heat coming in is usually from metabolism and radiation (R_{abs}, for radiation absorbed). Heat leaves the body via the four mechanisms listed above—radiation emitted (R_{out}), convection, conduction, and evaporation. The energy budget takes the mathematical form

$$\underbrace{\text{heat}_{in}}_{\text{metabolism} + R_{abs}} = \underbrace{\text{heat}_{out}}_{R_{out} + \text{convection} + \text{conduction} + \text{evaporation}}$$

The energy budget is a useful concept because any adaptation that influences the ability of an animal to control its temperature must affect one or more components of the energy budget. The energy budget gives us the ability to quantify and compare the thermal adaptations of animals. One interesting observation is that all of the components on the right side of the energy budget equation—that is, the heat-loss side—depend on the surface temperature of the animal. In fact, if the environmental temperature is above skin surface temperature, convection and conduction are avenues of heat gain rather than loss. One way surface temperature can be controlled is by altering the flow of blood to the skin.

Both ectotherms and endotherms control blood flow to the skin

Heat is mostly moved around the internal environment by blood flow. Heat produced in muscles during exercise is transported out of the muscle and to the heart in the blood. That

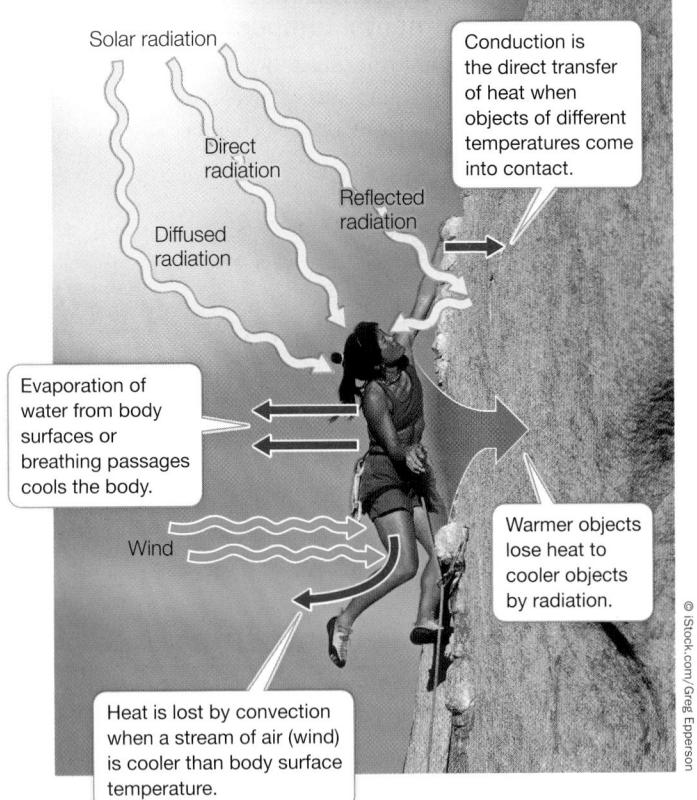

Solar radiation

Direct radiation

Diffused radiation

Reflected radiation

Conduction is the direct transfer of heat when objects of different temperatures come into contact.

Evaporation of water from body surfaces or breathing passages cools the body.

Wind

Warmer objects lose heat to cooler objects by radiation.

Heat is lost by convection when a stream of air (wind) is cooler than body surface temperature.

© iStock.com/Greg Epperson

Figure 38.10 Avenues of Heat Exchange between an Animal and Its Environment An animal's body temperature is determined by the balance between internal heat production and four avenues of heat exchange with the environment: radiation, convection, conduction, and evaporation.

heat is then distributed around the body by the blood, raising body temperature. Blood flow to the skin enables internal heat to be lost to the environment through radiation, convection, conduction, and evaporation, thus bringing the body temperature back toward normal. When body temperature is too low or the environment is too cold, the blood vessels supplying the skin constrict, reducing heat loss to the environment.

The ability to control blood flow to the skin can be an important adaptation for an ectotherm such as the marine iguana (a reptile) of the Galápagos archipelago (**Figure 38.11**). The Galápagos are volcanic islands that lie on the equator but are bathed by cold ocean currents. Iguanas bask in the sunshine on hot black lava rocks on the shore, and periodically enter the cold ocean water to feed on seaweed. While the iguanas are feeding, they lose heat to the cold ocean water. This cooling lowers their metabolism, making them slower, more vulnerable to predators, and incapable of efficient digestion. The iguanas therefore alternate between feeding in the cold seawater and basking on the hot rocks. It is advantageous for iguanas to retain body heat as long as possible while swimming and to warm up as fast as possible when basking. They accomplish these results by changing their heart rate and the rate of blood flow to their skin and around their bodies.

What about furred mammals? Fur acts as insulation to keep body heat in, making it possible for mammals to function in cold environments. When they are active, however, mammals must get rid of excess heat, and it does little good to transport that heat to the skin under the fur. Thus as mentioned at the opening of this chapter, mammals have specialized blood vessels for transporting heat to their hairless skin surfaces. Heat loss from these areas is tightly controlled by the opening and closing of these blood vessels. When you are cold, the blood flow to your hands and feet decreases and they feel cold, but when you exercise, the blood vessels serving these skin areas dilate, increasing the blood flow and therefore the heat dissipation.

Media Clip 38.1
Thermoregulation in Animals
Life12e.com/mc38.1

Some fishes conserve metabolic heat

The muscles of active fishes produce substantial amounts of metabolic heat, but most fishes cannot retain that heat. Blood pumped from the fish heart goes directly to the gills, where it comes very close to the surrounding water to exchange oxygen and carbon dioxide. Any heat the blood picks up from metabolically active muscles is lost to the water flowing across its gills. It is therefore surprising that some large, rapidly swimming fishes, such as giant bluefin tuna (*Thunnus thynnus*) (see Figure 1.16A) and great white sharks (*Carcharodon carcharias*), can maintain swimming muscle temperatures

10–15 degrees Celsius higher than the surrounding water. The heat comes from their powerful swimming muscles, and the ability of these "hot" fishes to conserve that heat is based on the remarkable arrangement of their blood vessels.

In the typical ("cold") fish circulatory system, oxygenated blood from the gills collects in a large blood vessel, the **aorta**, that runs through the center of the fish, distributing blood to all organs and muscles (**Figure 38.12A**). "Hot" fishes have a small aorta running down their body, and most of their oxygenated blood is transported in large side vessels just under the skin (**Figure 38.12B**). The cold blood leaving the gills is therefore kept close to the surface of the "hot" fishes as it flows posteriorly to the swimming muscles. The cold blood flows into the muscle mass through small vessels branching off the large side vessels. These many small vessels run parallel to the vessels bringing oxygen-depleted but warm blood out of the swimming muscles and back toward the heart. Because the vessels carrying the cold blood into the muscles are in close contact with the vessels carrying warm blood out of the muscles, heat flows from the warm to the cold blood by conduction. Therefore the heat produced by the active muscles is retained in the muscle mass.

Because heat is exchanged between blood vessels carrying blood in opposite directions, this adaptation is called

Figure 38.11 Some Ectotherms Regulate Blood Flow to the Skin Galápagos marine iguanas control blood flow to the skin to alter their heating and cooling rates. (Graph after G. A. Bartholomew and R. C. Lasiewski. 1965. *Comp Biochem Physiol* 16: 573–582.)

(A) "Cold" fishes

1 In the gills, blood is oxygenated and cooled to seawater temperature.

2 Cold blood flows through the center of the fish in the large dorsal aorta.

Heart

5 The heart pumps blood to the gills.

4 Veins return blood to the heart.

3 Arteries carry blood to the tissues.

(B) "Hot" fishes

1 Blood is oxygenated in the gills.

2 Cold blood flows from the gills to the body in arteries just under the skin.

5 The heart pumps blood to the gills.

4 Veins under the skin return blood to the heart.

3 In the countercurrent heat exchangers, arterial blood flowing into the muscle is warmed by venous blood flowing out of the muscle.

(C) The countercurrent heat exchanger in fish

The major vein and artery just under the skin are at the same cool temperature.

Vein Artery

Capillary bed (muscles generate heat)

Countercurrent heat exchanger

Figure 38.12 "Cold" and "Hot" Fishes (A) Blood flowing through fish gills comes into temperature equilibrium with water temperature. In most fish species, this oxygenated but cool blood flows through a large dorsal aorta to the rest of the body. Thus it is an internal cooling source. (B) The anatomy of "hot" fish species circulates most of the cool, oxygenated blood to the body through large peripheral arteries rather than through a central aorta. As this cool arterial blood flows into the swimming muscle, it is warmed by heat being carried out of the swimming muscle by the veins. Thus the heat generated by the swimming muscles is conserved in the muscle mass. (C) The close, parallel arrangement of the arteries carrying blood into the muscles and the veins carrying blood out of the muscle makes efficient countercurrent heat exchange possible.

countercurrent heat exchange (Figure 38.12C). By keeping heat within the muscles, these fishes can maintain an internal body temperature considerably higher than the water temperature. Each 10-degree Celsius rise in muscle temperature increases a "hot" fish's power output almost threefold, giving it a faster and more powerful swimming capability.

Some ectotherms regulate metabolic heat production

By definition, ectotherms are largely dependent on environmental sources of heat for thermoregulation, but some ectotherms raise their body temperature by producing excess metabolic heat. For example, the powerful flight muscles of many insects must reach 35°C–40°C before the insects can fly, and they must maintain these high temperatures during flight. Such insects warm up to fly by contracting their flight muscles isometrically in a manner similar to shivering in mammals. The heat-producing ability of insect muscle can be quite remarkable. An impressive case is a species of scarab beetles that live mostly underground in mountains north of Los Angeles, California. The males come aboveground to mate and fly in search of females. They undertake this mating ritual at night, in winter, during snowstorms.

Honey bees regulate temperature as a group. They live in large colonies consisting mostly of female worker bees that maintain

the hive and rear the larval offspring of the single queen bee. During winter, worker bees cluster around the brood (eggs and larvae). They adjust their individual metabolic heat production and density of clustering so that the brood temperature remains remarkably constant, at about 34°C, even as the outside air temperature drops below freezing.

KEY CONCEPT
38.4 Recap and Assess

Endotherms use metabolic heat production to maintain constant high body temperatures. Body temperatures of ectotherms are more dependent on environmental heat sources. Both ectotherms and endotherms use behavior to control their body temperature. Heat exchange between an animal and its environment occurs via radiation, convection, conduction, and evaporation, all of which depend on body surface temperature. Some ectotherms use metabolic heat production episodically to raise body temperature.

1. Why is the body temperature of an ectotherm that is exposed to variations in environmental temperature more constant in nature than in the laboratory?

2. For each path of heat exchange, what determines whether heat is gained or lost by the animal?

3. Explain the circulatory system adaptations that allow "hot" fishes, unlike most other ("cold") fishes, to raise the temperature of their swimming muscles.

Endotherms respond to changes in environmental temperature by changing their rates of metabolic heat production. They also have other adaptations for controlling their rates of heat exchange with their environments. How do they regulate these various avenues of heat exchange to achieve a constant internal body temperature?

KEY CONCEPT 38.5

Body Temperature Is Regulated through Adaptations for Heat Production and Heat Loss

---

Learning Objectives

38.5.1 Describe and interpret a plot of metabolic rate versus environmental temperature for an endotherm.

38.5.2 Discuss how differences in physical features of endotherms of the same or similar species relate to the selective pressures of the climates in which they live.

38.5.3 Explain how the mammalian brain thermostat uses feedback and feedforward information to regulate body temperature.

38.5.4 Describe the unique thermoregulatory abilities of hibernators.

As explained in Key Concept 38.2, there is a difference between control and regulation. Think of driving your car. You control the speed of the car with the accelerator and the brake, but you regulate the speed of your car by comparing the speed limit (set point) with your speedometer (feedback) to generate command signals to your foot that is operating the accelerator and brake. For understanding how body temperature is regulated, you must understand the adaptations for heat production and heat loss, how they are controlled, and what information is used to modulate the control signals to achieve a regulated body temperature.

Basal heat production rates of endotherms correlate with body size

Physiologists can determine an animal's metabolic rate and therefore its rate of heat production by measuring its consumption of O_2 or production of CO_2. Within a narrow range of environmental temperatures, called the **thermoneutral zone** (see Figure 38.8B), the metabolic rates of endotherms (birds and mammals) are at low levels and independent of environmental temperature. The metabolic rate of a resting endotherm at a temperature within its thermoneutral zone is its **basal metabolic rate (BMR)**. BMR is usually measured in animals that are quiet but awake and not using energy for digestion, reproduction, or growth. Thus BMR is the rate at which a resting animal is consuming just enough energy to carry out its minimal body functions.

As you might expect, the BMR of an elephant is greater than that of a mouse. After all, the elephant is more than 100,000 times larger than the mouse. However, the BMR of the elephant is only

about 7,000 times greater than that of the mouse. That means that a gram of mouse tissue uses energy at a rate 15 times greater than a gram of elephant tissue (**Figure 38.13**). Across all of the endotherms, BMR per gram of tissue increases as animals get smaller.

Why should this disproportionate difference exist? There are several possible reasons. As animals get bigger, they have a smaller surface area-to-volume ratio (see Figure 5.2). Since heat production is related to the volume (i.e., mass) of the animal, but its capacity to dissipate heat is related to its surface area, it has been reasoned that larger animals evolved lower metabolic rates to avoid overheating. However, this explanation alone is insufficient because the relationship between body mass and metabolic rate holds for even very small organisms and for ectotherms, in which overheating is not a problem. Other hypotheses have also been proposed. For example, a larger animal has a greater proportion of support tissues (e.g., skin and bone), which are not as metabolically active as other tissue types. The real explanation is probably a mixture of different factors, but the relationship holds over a very broad range of species.

For an endotherm, a metabolic rate versus environmental temperature curve represents the integrated response of all the animal's thermoregulatory adaptations (**Figure 38.14**). The thermoneutral zone is bounded by a **lower critical temperature** and an **upper critical temperature**. When the environmental temperature is within the thermoneutral zone, an endotherm's thermoregulatory responses do not require much energy and could be considered passive; such responses include changing posture, fluffing fur or feathers, and altering blood flow to the skin. When an endotherm is outside its thermoneutral zone, however, its thermoregulatory responses are active and require metabolic energy.

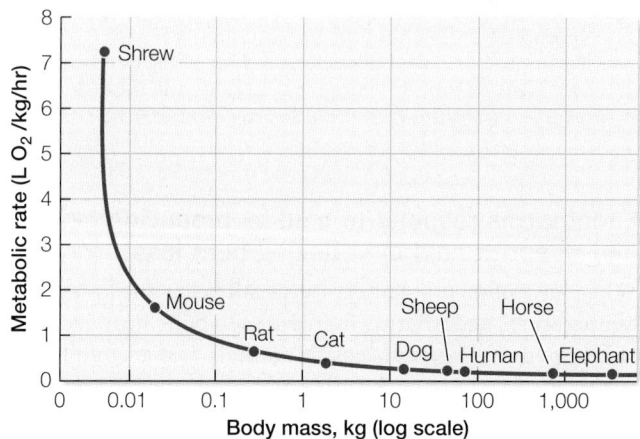

Figure 38.13 The Mouse-to-Elephant Curve On a weight-specific basis, the basal metabolic rate of small endotherms is much greater than that of larger endotherms. This classic illustration, originally published in the 1930s, plots O_2 consumption per kilogram of body mass (a measure of metabolic rate) against a logarithmic plot of body mass.

Q: Only nine species are shown on this curve, but hundreds of species from the tropics to the Arctic fit on this curve as well. What does that fact allow you to conclude about whether or not basal metabolic rate is an adaptation to climate?

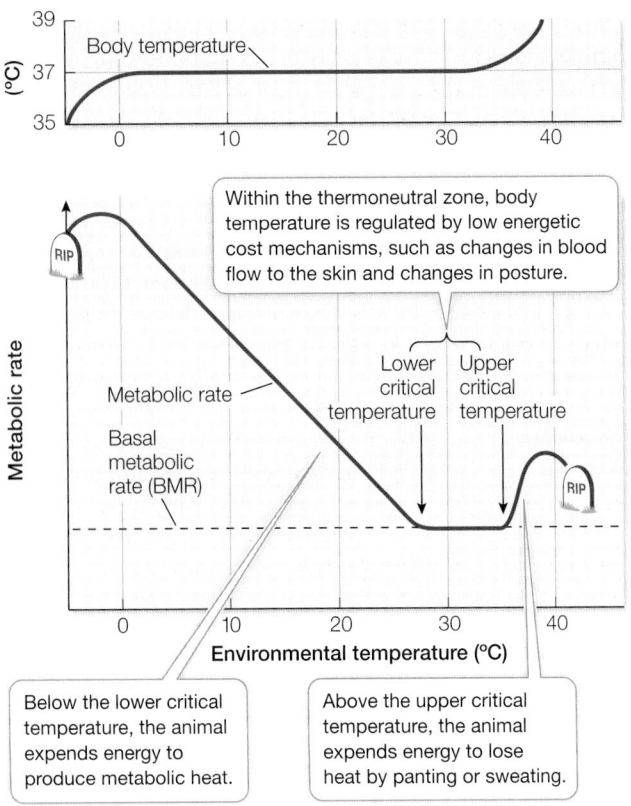

Figure 38.14 Environmental Temperature and Mammalian Metabolic Rates A plot of an endotherm's metabolic rate versus environmental temperature represents the integrated response of all of its thermoregulatory mechanisms. Outside the thermoneutral zone, maintaining a constant body temperature requires expending energy. Outside extreme limits (0°C and 40°C in this instance), the animal cannot maintain its body temperature and dies.

Q: The segment of the curve below the lower critical temperature can be described by the equation $MR = K(T_b − T_a)$. In this equation, what does K stand for? Why does this equation predict that the curve it describes will meet the x axis at a temperature that equals body temperature?

Endotherms respond to cold by producing heat and adapt to cold by reducing heat loss

When environmental temperatures fall below the lower critical temperature, endotherms increase metabolic heat production to compensate for heat loss. Mammals can accomplish this by shivering and/or nonshivering heat production. Birds use only shivering heat production. Shivering uses the contractions of skeletal muscles to convert ATP to ADP, with the energy from this process released as heat. Shivering muscles pull against each other so that little movement other than a tremor results. "Shivering heat production" is perhaps too narrow a term, however; increased muscle tone and increased body movements also contribute to increased heat production in cold environments.

Most nonshivering heat production occurs in specialized adipose tissue called **brown fat**. This tissue looks brown because of its abundant mitochondria and rich blood supply (see Figure

38.2). In brown fat cells, a protein called **thermogenin** uncouples proton movement from ATP production, allowing protons to leak across the inner mitochondrial membrane rather than having to pass through the ATP synthase and generate ATP (review the discussion of brown fat and the chemiosmotic mechanism in Key Concept 9.3). In nonshivering thermogenesis, metabolic fuels are consumed without producing ATP, but heat is still released.

Pads of brown fat are found in newborns of many mammalian species. Brown fat is also commonly found in adult mammals that are small and acclimatized to cold, and in mammals that hibernate. Recently it has been discovered that adult humans have small amounts of brown fat distributed around the body and that its metabolic activity is stimulated by cold exposure. One study found less brown fat activity in obese than in lean individuals, leading to the hypothesis that individual differences in propensity for weight gain may be related to the amount of brown fat in an individual, as described in the opening stories of Chapters 9 and 39.

In addition to their ability to produce heat, endotherms that live in cold climates have evolved adaptations to reduce their heat loss. Heat is lost from the body surface, and cold-climate species have anatomical adaptations that give them smaller surface area-to-volume ratios than their warm-climate relatives (**Figure 38.15**). These adaptations include rounder body shapes and shorter appendages.

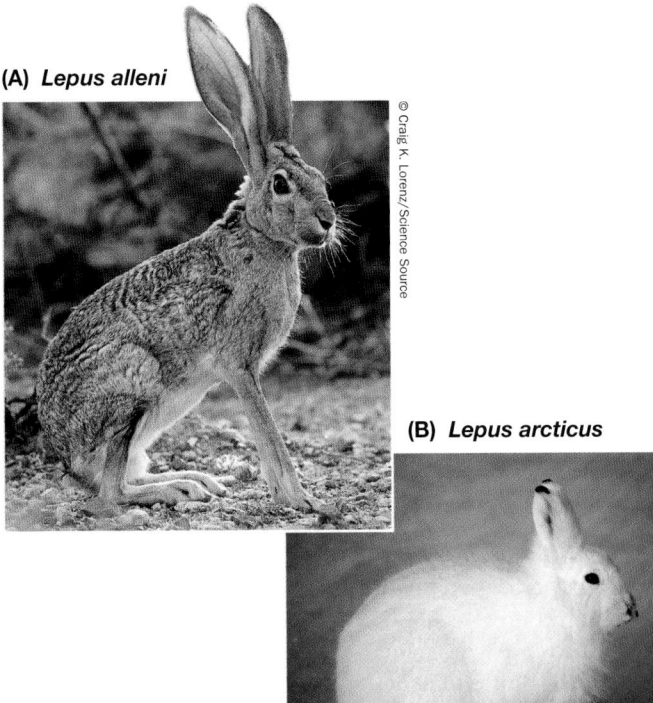

Figure 38.15 Adaptations to Cold and Hot Climates **(A)** The antelope jackrabbit is found in the Sonoran Desert of Arizona. Its large ears serve as heat exchangers, passing heat from the animal's blood to the surrounding air. **(B)** The thick fur of the Arctic hare provides insulation, and its rounded body shape lowers its surface area-to-volume ratio. The ears and extremities are smaller than those of its warm-climate relatives, so less heat is lost to the environment.

The most common and important means of decreasing heat loss is to increase thermal insulation. Animals adapted to cold climates have much thicker layers of fur, feathers, and/or fat than do their warm-climate relatives. Fur and feathers are good insulators because they trap a layer of still, warm air close to the skin surface. If that air is displaced by water, insulation is drastically reduced. In many species, oil secretions spread through fur or feathers by grooming are critical for resisting wetting and maintaining a high level of insulation. In terms of the energy budget equation presented in Key Concept 38.4, remember that heat exchange between the animal and its environment is a function of the animal's surface temperature. For a body area covered by fur or feathers, surface temperature is that of the outer surface of the fur or feathers.

The ability to decrease blood flow to the noninsulated skin is an important thermoregulatory adaptation for cold-climate endotherms. Constriction of blood vessels in the skin, and especially in the appendages, greatly improves an animal's ability to conserve heat. Countercurrent heat exchange like that you saw in "hot" fishes is also an important adaptation in the appendages of endotherms. Warm blood flowing out to the paw of a wolf, the hoof of a caribou, or the foot of a bird parallels the flow of the cooler blood returning to the body core. Heat is transferred from the outgoing to the returning blood, thus retaining heat in the animal's core.

 View in Achieve
Activity 38.2 Thermoregulation in an Endotherm

Evaporation of water dissipates heat, but at a cost

At the upper end of the thermoneutral zone, an endotherm dissipates heat through adaptations that don't require much energy: increasing blood flow to the skin, seeking shade and cool breezes, and decreasing activity. But when the environmental temperature exceeds the upper critical temperature, these adaptations are not sufficient and overheating becomes a problem. For exercising animals (including athletes), overheating can occur even at low environmental temperatures. Large mammals, especially those in hot habitats such as elephants, rhinoceroses, and water buffaloes, have little or no insulating fur and seek out water to wallow in when the air temperature is high. Having water in contact with the skin greatly increases heat loss because the heat-absorbing capacity of water is much greater than that of air.

Evaporation from external or internal body surfaces through sweating or panting can also cool an endotherm. A gram of water absorbs about 580 calories of heat when it evaporates. If this evaporation occurs on the skin, most of the heat comes from the skin. However, sweat or saliva that falls off the body provides no cooling. Thus when the need for heat loss is greatest, water from the internal environment can be squandered with no cooling benefit. Water is heavy, so animals do not carry an excess supply of it, and many hot environments are also arid. In habitats that are both hot and dry, sweating and panting are cooling adaptations of last resort.

Sweating and panting are *active* processes that require expending metabolic energy. That is why the metabolic rate increases when the upper critical temperature is exceeded (see Figure 38.14). A sweating or panting animal is generating heat in the process of dissipating heat, which can be a losing battle.

The mammalian thermostat uses feedback information

The thermoregulatory mechanisms and adaptations of endotherms are controlled by neural regulatory systems that integrate information from environmental and internal sources and then issue commands to the effectors that alter the heat content of the body. These regulatory systems are similar in principle in birds and mammals but differ in many details. Here we focus on the nervous system thermostats of mammals.

The major thermoregulatory integrative center of mammals is at the base of the brain in a structure called the **hypothalamus** (**Figure 38.16**). The hypothalamus is a key player in many regulatory systems of vertebrates. Experiments demonstrating its role have shown that slight cooling of the hypothalamus stimulates constriction of skin blood vessels and that stronger cooling increases metabolic heat production. As a result, cooling of the

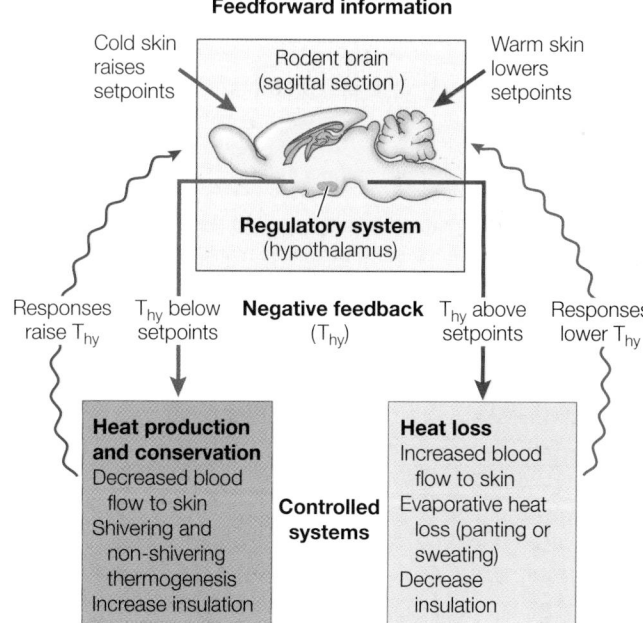

Figure 38.16 The Mammalian Thermostat Like the home thermostat in Figure 38.5, the mammalian hypothalamus is the regulatory system that controls the body's heating and cooling responses by integrating thermosensory and other information and generating command signals to those mechanisms. The hypothalamus generates set points for activating these responses and the hypothalamic temperature (T_{hy}) is the negative feedback information. Set points are raised or lowered by feedforward information such as skin temperature, time of day, sleep, and exercise.

 View in Achieve
Animation 38.1 The Hypothalamus

hypothalamus in an unchanging, thermoneutral environment will cause body temperature to rise. Conversely, hypothalamic heating causes the overall body temperature to fall (**Figure 38.17**).

Experiment

Figure 38.17   The Hypothalamus Regulates Body Temperature

Original Paper: H. C. Heller et al. 1974. CNS regulation of body temperature in euthermic hibernators. *Am J Physiol* 227: 576–582.

A mammal's hypothalamus was subjected directly to temperature manipulation. The body's responses to the manipulations were as expected if the hypothalamus is the mammalian "thermostat."

HYPOTHESIS▶ Heating or cooling the mammalian hypothalamus results in predictable changes in body temperature.

METHOD▶

1. Implant a probe into the hypothalamus of a living ground squirrel's brain. Use the probe to heat or cool the hypothalamus directly (i.e., without affecting the ambient temperature).

2. Manipulate the hypothalamic temperature T_H.

3. Measure the animal's metabolic rate and body temperature throughout the period of hypothalamic manipulation.

RESULTS▶

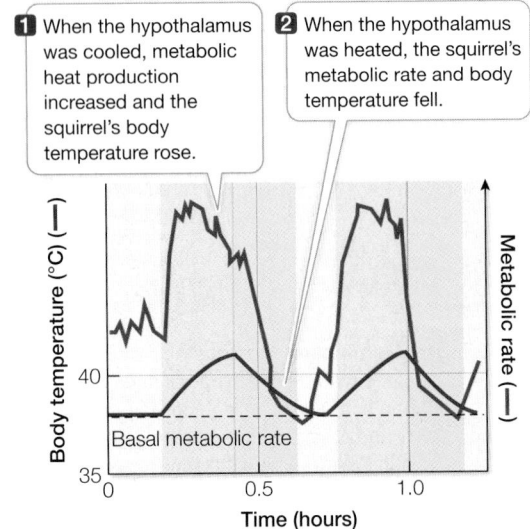

1 When the hypothalamus was cooled, metabolic heat production increased and the squirrel's body temperature rose.

2 When the hypothalamus was heated, the squirrel's metabolic rate and body temperature fell.

CONCLUSION▶ The ground squirrel's hypothalamus acts as a thermostat. When cooled, it activates metabolic heat production; when warmed, it suppresses metabolic heat production and favors heat loss.

In mammals, the temperature of the hypothalamus itself is the major feedback signal. The hypothalamus generates set points for various thermoregulatory responses. When the temperature of the hypothalamus exceeds or drops below those set points, thermoregulatory responses are controlled to reverse the direction of temperature change (see Figure 38.16). The system integrates other sources of information in addition to hypothalamic temperature. For example, temperature sensors in the skin register environmental temperature. A change in skin temperature is feedforward information that shifts hypothalamic set points; the set point for metabolic heat production is higher when the skin is cold and lower when the skin is warm.

Hypothalamic set points are higher during wakefulness than during sleep, and they are higher during the active part of the daily cycle than the inactive part, even if the animal is awake at both times. Even when an endotherm is kept under constant environmental conditions, its body temperature displays a daily cycle of changes in set point. This kind of cycle, a circadian rhythm, is controlled by an internal biological clock.

Connect the Concepts Key Concept 51.5 explains how a region of the hypothalamus called the suprachiasmatic nucleus generates endogenous daily cycles called circadian rhythms that influence many physiological processes, including temperature regulation.

Some animals conserve energy by turning down the thermostat

Hypothermia is a below-normal body temperature. It can result from starvation (lack of metabolic fuel), exposure to extreme cold, serious illness, or anesthesia. In each of these cases, the drop in body temperature is *unregulated*. However, many birds and mammals undergo *regulated* hypothermia to survive periods of cold and food scarcity.

Hummingbirds, for example, are very small endotherms with a high metabolic rate, and going even a single day without food could exhaust their metabolic reserves. Hummingbirds and other small endotherms extend the period over which they can survive without food by dropping their body temperature by 10–20 degrees Celsius during the portion of the day when they are normally inactive, thus lowering their metabolic rate and conserving energy. Daily bouts of regulated hypothermia are called **daily torpor**.

Regulated hypothermia that lasts for days or even weeks, during which the body temperature falls close to environmental temperature, is called **hibernation** (**Figure 38.18**). Many species of mammals, including bats, bears, marmots, and ground squirrels, hibernate, but only one species of bird (the Common Poorwill, *Phalaenoptilus nuttallii*) has been shown to hibernate. The metabolic rate needed to sustain a hibernating animal may be only one-fiftieth its basal metabolic rate, and many hibernating animals maintain body temperatures close to freezing. Arousal from hibernation occurs when the hypothalamic set point returns to the normal level. The ability of animals to enter daily torpor or deep hibernation to reduce their thermoregulatory set point so dramatically probably evolved as an extension of the set point decrease that accompanies sleep in all mammals and birds.

(A)

1 During more than half the year, a ground squirrel regulates its body temperature near 37°C.

2 During winter months, bouts of hibernation are interrupted by brief returns to normal body temperature.

(B)

3 Entrance into hibernation begins with a drop in metabolic rate followed by a drop in body temperature.

4 Arousal from hibernation begins with a large rise in metabolic heat production, followed by body warming.

Awake ground squirrel

Hibernating ground squirrel

Figure 38.18 Hibernation Patterns in a Ground Squirrel   **(A)** During most of the year, the ground squirrel regulates its body temperature around 37°C. During winter months, however, these animals hibernate in underground burrows, living off stored fuel (in the form of either fat or cached food). **(B)** The metabolic demands for these stored fuels are decreased by bouts of torpor, during which body temperature drops close to that of the environment for long periods of time.

38.5 Recap and Assess

Within the thermoneutral zone, an endotherm controls its body temperature by passive means. Above or below the thermoneutral zone, an endotherm must expend considerable metabolic energy to control body temperature. Thermoregulatory responses in mammals are regulated by the hypothalamus.

1. What determines the upper and lower boundaries of the thermoneutral zone?

2. Explain why arctic species of mammals tend to be bigger and stockier than closely related species in warmer environments.

3. What is the role of feedforward information in the mammalian thermoregulatory system?

4. Explain why the mammalian thermoregulatory system has been described as a proportional thermostat with an adjustable set point.

Q and A How can we increase heat loss from the body to protect against heat stress?

In the opening story to this chapter you saw that intense physical work or high ambient temperatures can rapidly cause a human to become hyperthermic. Even within a safe zone, body temperature is a critical factor in limiting physical performance. A working body has to dissipate heat to the environment, and that requires a difference in temperature between the body surface and the environment. This is why the fastest marathon times occur when ambient temperatures are between 10°C and 16°C. The relevant body surface temperature for furred mammals is mostly the surface of the fur. For us it is mostly the surface of our clothing. We can take off our clothes, but furred mammals cannot take off their fur. Mammals have evolved special blood vessel adaptations in their non-hairy skin that can accommodate large volumes of blood and therefore support high levels of heat loss. The experiment in **Investigating Life: Can the Work Capacity of Workers in PPE Be Extended by Extracting Heat from the Palms of the Hands?** used a technology to extract heat from the palms, which are non-hairy skin, and showed that it decreased the rate of rise of core body temperature in workers dressed in PPE. How does this heat-loss adaptation, and the technology designed to amplify it, work?

Blood flows from the heart through large arteries, then through small arteries, and then through the tiny capillaries where the blood delivers nutients and carries away waste products of metabolism, and then into veins that carry the blood back to the heart. The circulatory adaptations of the "heat portals" in non-hairy mammalian skin are an exception to this pattern. In the non-hairy skin, gated shunts deliver arterial blood directly to veins, bypassing the capillaries. These veins in non-hairy skin form networks that can accommodate a large volume of blood when the shunts are open. Based on this knowledge, biologists at Stanford University developed the "rapid-cooling" technology used in the Investigating Life experiment. The palms are placed in contact with pads containing circulating cool water. When this device is used, body temperature rises more slowly during exercise or exposure to heat, even for workers clad in PPE.

Future directions

In this chapter you learned that virtually all biological processes are affected by temperature. Therefore if we have a new technology that can rapidly and efficiently alter the heat content of the body, we should find many applications for it. What could some of those applications be? One that has been recognized is improving athletic performance. Endurance is extended, and when used in a conditioning routine, the number of exercises that can be done increases, resulting in huge conditioning gains. There are also medical applications. Active thermoregulatory responses such as vasoconstriction and shivering are inactivated by anesthesia, and patients can become seriously hypothermic. Their body temperatures can be stabilized by heat exchange through their natural heat portals. Some medical conditions render patients temperature-sensitive. An example is multiple sclerosis (MS). Individuals with MS can suffer serious increases in their symptoms if their body temperature rises even a little bit. They may lose their vision, balance, ability to walk, or ability to think clearly. They can be protected from these effects of heat by cooling their natural heat portals. Evidence suggests that some cancer treatments could be augmented by the induction of hyperthermia and that the consequences of stroke or heart attack could be lessened by timely induction of hypothermia. There can be many benefits from improved abilities to control human body temperature.

VISUAL SUMMARY 38

© dpa picture alliance/Alamy Stock Photo

You should be able to relate each summary to the adjacent figures. If you go to this visual summary in **Achieve**, you can follow links to figures, animations, activities, and simulations that will help you consolidate the material.

KEY CONCEPT

38.1 Animals Are Composed of Organs Built from Four Types of Tissues   Go to **Activity 38.1**

- Multicellularity makes it possible for animals to grow big and for cells to become specialized for specific functions.

- Specialized cells compose four types of **tissues—epithelial, muscle, connective,** and **nervous**—that constitute the **organs** of an animal.

- **Organ systems** carry out specific essential functions that benefit all the cells of the body.

Questions

1. What is the relationship between volume and surface area as cells get bigger?

2. Give an example of each of the four tissue types and its function.

3. Why is cell specialization important for multicellular animals?

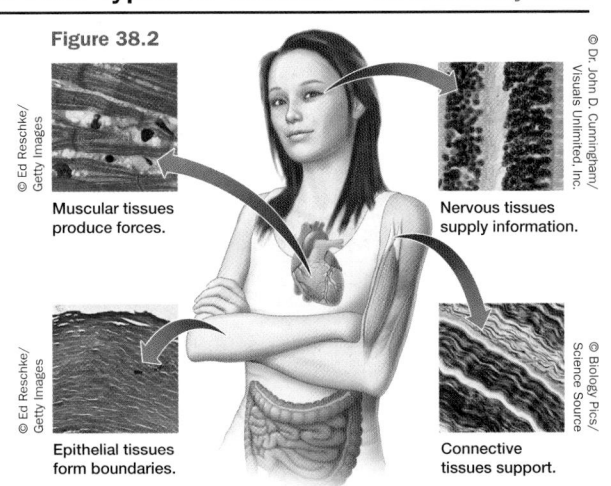

Figure 38.2

Muscular tissues produce forces.
© Ed Reschke/Getty Images

Nervous tissues supply information.
© Dr. John D. Cunningham/Visuals Unlimited, Inc.

Epithelial tissues form boundaries.
© Ed Reschke/Getty Images

Connective tissues support.
© Biology Pics/Science Source

KEY CONCEPT
38.2 Physiological Systems Maintain Homeostasis of the Internal Environment

Go to Simulation 38.1

- The internal environment consists of extracellular fluid, which comprises **blood plasma** and **interstitial fluid**.

- **Homeostasis** is the maintenance of constancy of the internal environment. To maintain homeostasis, physiological **regulatory systems** compare **feedback** information to **set points** to generate command signals to **effectors**.

- **Negative feedback** brings a function back to the set point, **positive feedback** moves the function farther from the set point, and **feedforward information** changes the set point.

Questions

1. What is the distribution of water in the human body?

2. Compare the functions of negative, positive, and feedforward information, and give an example of each.

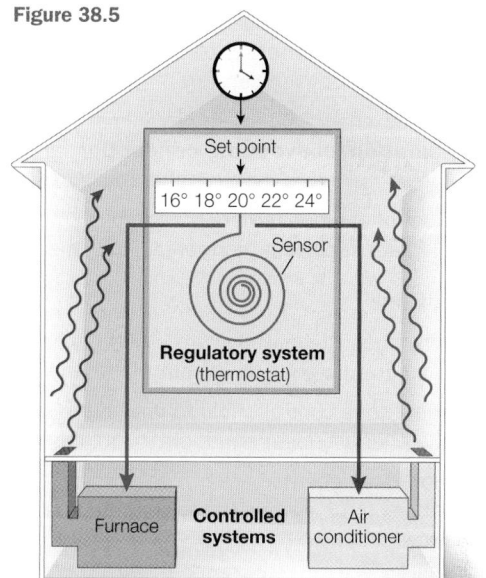

Figure 38.5

KEY CONCEPT
38.3 Biological Processes Are Temperature-Sensitive

- For most living organisms, internal temperature must be within the range of 0°C–40°C.

- The **Q_{10}** concept describes the effect of temperature on biochemical and living systems.

- **Thermoregulatory adaptations** enable animals to maintain optimal internal temperature despite external conditions.

- Animals can adjust to seasonal changes through mechanisms of **acclimatization**.

Questions

1. What dangers do extreme temperatures pose for living organisms?

2. If the rate of a chemical reaction doubles over a 10-degree-Celsius rise in temperature, what is its Q_{10}?

3. What adaptations might a fish have for surviving seasonal temperature changes and for surviving acute temperature changes?

Figure 38.7

$$Q_{10} = \frac{R_T}{R_{T-10}}$$

KEY CONCEPT
38.4 Body Temperature Depends on the Balance between Heat In and Heat Out of the Body

- Thermoregulatory adaptations of **ectotherms** are mostly behavioral, whereas **endotherms** also have physiological means of maintaining a constant body temperature.

- Heat exchanges between an animal and its environment occur via **radiation**, **convection**, **conduction**, and **evaporation**, and along with metabolism they make up the **energy budget** of an animal.

- Control of blood temperature through metabolism and blood flow to the skin are important thermoregulatory mechanisms.

Questions

1. Why does the metabolic rate of the mammal go up as environmental temperature goes down, but that of the lizard goes down?

2. How does control of blood flow to the skin influence the components of the energy budget equation?

3. How does countercurrent heat exchange enable a giant tuna to maintain a body temperature above sea temperature?

Figure 38.8

KEY CONCEPT
38.5 Body Temperature Is Regulated through Adaptations for Heat Production and Heat Loss

Go to **Activity 38.2** and **Animation 38.1**

- The **basal metabolic rates** (**BMRs**) of endotherms are measured within their **thermoneutral zones**, and when divided by body mass, they are lower as species get bigger.

- When an animal is outside its thermoneutral zone, heat loss and heat production responses require energy expenditure.

- **Brown fat** is a tissue that produces heat by uncoupling oxidative phosphorylation from ATP production.

- The mammalian thermoregulatory system resides in the **hypothalamus**, which generates set points for thermoregulatory responses and uses its own temperature as negative feedback and skin temperature as well as other variables as feedforward information.

- Mammalian **hibernation** is regulated **hypothermia**.

Figure 38.16

Questions

1. Describe the mouse-to-elephant curve.

2. What is meant by upper and lower critical temperatures?

3. Why is the mammalian thermoregulatory system called a proportional thermostat with adjustable set points?

KEY CONCEPTS

39.1 Hormones Circulate around the Body and Affect Cells That Have Receptors

39.2 The Endocrine and Nervous Systems Work Together

39.3 Hormones Play Important Roles in Development

39.4 Hormones Regulate Metabolism and the Internal Environment

Sex hormones are responsible for the dramatic differences between male and female red deer (*Cervus elaphus*).

▶Investigating LIFE

The Smart and Healthy Hormone

Exercise, especially aerobic exercise, benefits many aspects of health, such as cardiovascular fitness, body weight management, and improved sleep. Improved cognition has been added recently to the list of benefits. How can exercise improve so many functions of the body, and even the brain? One mechanism for stimulating diverse cellular functions all over the body is hormonal communication. Hormones are signaling molecules that are produced and secreted by certain cells, diffuse into the blood, and circulate throughout the entire body. These signals have effects on any cells that have receptors for them, but the resulting actions depend on the nature of the receiving cells.

An interesting, new hormone discovered at Harvard University in 2012 could be the "exercise hormone." It is a small protein of 112 amino acids that is released from exercising muscle into the extracellular fluid. Since this molecule was thought to have a signaling function, it was named irisin. Iris is the messenger of the Greek gods, and she travels the world with the speed of the wind. Irisin was shown to have several actions supporting physical activity. White fat is normally not a metabolically active tissue, but irisin transforms it to be more like brown fat (see Key Concept 38.5), which has more mitochondria, more blood flow, and greater ability to mobilize lipids. Irisin causes the "browning" of white fat and improves glucose metabolism and bone remodeling. Irisin seems to be the muscle's way of telling other tissues to "shape up."

Could irisin also be the signal that mediates the effects of exercise on brain function? One important factor that increases in the brain with regular exercise is BDNF (brain-derived neurotrophic factor). The benefits of increasing BDNF in the brain might not just help athletes play smarter, but BDNF could have huge impacts in aging populations by contributing to improvements in depression, epilepsy, stroke, Alzheimer's disease, and Parkinson's disease. What links does BDNF production have to exercise? Does the brain just "know" when we are exercising, or could irisin from the muscle be communicating that information? Normally proteins do not cross the blood–brain barrier, so is irisin produced in the brain during exercise, or is the brain receiving this exercise signal from the muscle in the blood?

 Q and A In what ways does irisin mediate the health and cognitive benefits of exercise?
(Find the answer on page 883.)

KEY CONCEPT 39.1   Hormones Circulate around the Body and Affect Cells That Have Receptors

Learning Objectives

39.1.1 Describe the structural feature of hormones that determines whether they act on cell surface or cytoplasmic receptors.

39.1.2 Explain how different target cells in the body can respond differently to the same hormone.

39.1.3 Discuss scientific thinking about the evolutionary history of hormones in multicellular animals.

In multicellular animals, physiological regulatory systems require information and cell-to-cell communication. Most intercellular communication is by means of chemical signals that bind to receptors, as described in Chapter 7. Some types of chemical signals discussed in other chapters include growth factors, morphogens, and cytokines. In subsequent chapters you will learn about chemical signals used by the nervous system called neurotransmitters. Each of these examples involves a chemical message secreted by cells and received by other cells (target cells) that have appropriate receptors. These four groups of chemical signals are named according to the types of actions they have: growth factors influence cell division, morphogens influence developmental processes, cytokines control immune system cells, and neurotransmitters enable nerve cells to communicate with each other and with target cells such as muscles. In this chapter we cover another broad class of chemical signals called **endocrines**. These chemical signals are secreted by epithelial cells directly into the extracellular fluid (ECF; see Key Concept 38.2). From the ECF, endocrines can diffuse locally and also into the blood, which distributes them throughout the body.

There are multiple chemical communication systems in the body

Some analogies might help differentiate how chemical signaling in the immune, nervous, and endocrine information systems works. The immune system (the topic of Chapter 40) operates like an army of private security guards. Immune system cells make their rounds of the body, and if they detect a security breach, they sound their alarms—cytokines—which activate the body's defenses. The nervous system (see Chapters 43–45) operates like a landline telephone system: a central integration and command center receives incoming calls and sends signals along specific wires to specific receivers. The endocrine system is more like a radio, television, or cell-phone system, broadcasting signals that can be picked up by anyone who has an appropriate receiver that is turned on and tuned in. Some endocrine signals are weak, like those of a walkie-talkie, and are picked up only locally, but others are strong, like those of a major broadcast station, and reach distant parts of the body. In all cases, the signals are received only by cells that have appropriate receptors, and the responses of those cells are determined by the cells' internal signal transduction machinery.

Endocrine signaling can act locally or at a distance

Endocrine signals that enter the blood are called **hormones** (from a Greek word meaning to excite, arouse, or stimulate). Hormones activate target cells wherever they occur in the body (**Figure 39.1A**). You probably are familiar with several hormones, such as testosterone, estrogen, insulin, and norepinephrine. Those molecules are well known, as are their sites of release and their actions.

Some endocrine signals are released in such tiny quantities, or are so rapidly inactivated by enzymes or taken up so efficiently by local cells, that they never diffuse into the blood in sufficient amounts to act on distant cells (**Figure 39.1B**). Because these signals affect only target cells near their release site, they are called **paracrines** (*para*, "near"). An example of a paracrine signal is histamine, one of the mediators of inflammation. The most local action an endocrine signal can have is when it binds to receptors on or in the same cell that secreted it. An **autocrine** signal is so

(A) Signals that act at a distance

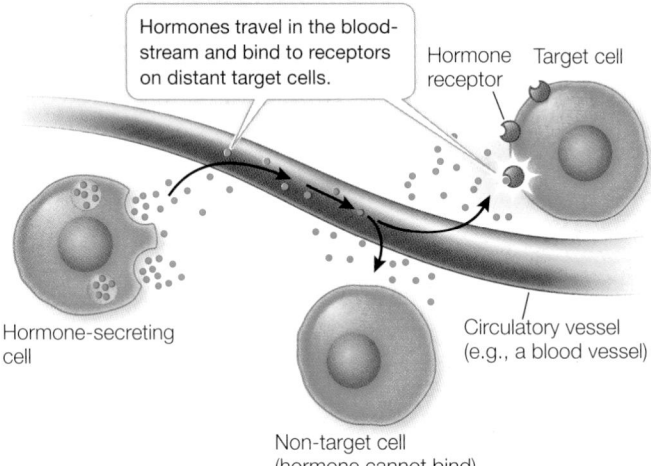

Hormones travel in the bloodstream and bind to receptors on distant target cells.

Hormone receptor   Target cell

Hormone-secreting cell

Circulatory vessel (e.g., a blood vessel)

Non-target cell (hormone cannot bind)

(B) Signals that act locally

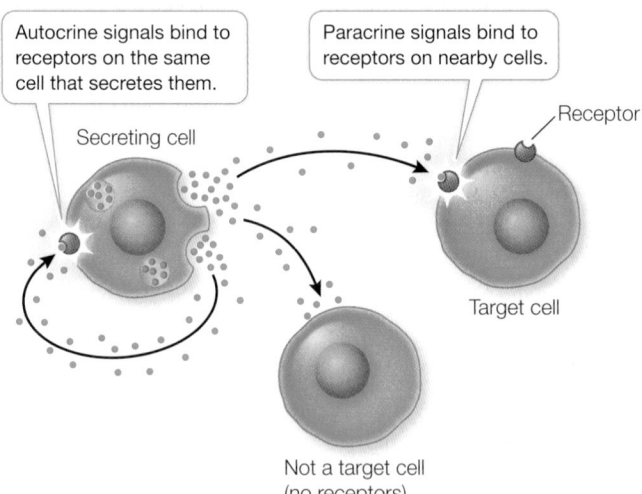

Autocrine signals bind to receptors on the same cell that secretes them.

Paracrine signals bind to receptors on nearby cells.

Secreting cell

Receptor

Target cell

Not a target cell (no receptors)

Figure 39.1 Chemical Signaling Systems (A) Hormones are distributed throughout the body in the bloodstream. (B) Paracrines and autocrines diffuse locally in the extracellular fluid. Paracrines influence nearby cells, and autocrines influence the same cells that release them.

named because it influences the cell that secreted it. Hormones and paracrines can have autocrine functions as a means of providing negative feedback to control their own rates of secretion.

Some endocrine cells exist as single cells within a tissue. Hormones of the digestive tract, for example, are secreted by isolated endocrine cells in the walls of the stomach and small intestine. Many hormones are secreted by aggregations of endocrine cells called **endocrine glands**. A single endocrine gland may secrete multiple hormones. Be sure you don't confuse endocrine glands with **exocrine glands**. Endocrine glands secrete hormones within the body, whereas exocrine glands secrete substances through ducts to the outside of the body (sweat glands and salivary glands are examples).

Two other categories of chemical signals are neuroendocrines, or **neurohormones**, which are secreted by nerve cells and enter the circulation, and **pheromones**, which are released from the body of an animal to influence the behavior and physiology of other animals in its vicinity. We discuss pheromones in Chapter 51.

There are three chemical groups of hormones

The chemical structures of hormones are diverse, but they can be classified into three groups:

1. **Peptide** and **protein hormones** are the majority of hormones. A peptide consists of 2 or more amino acids, and a protein is defined as having 50 or more amino acids. Insulin is therefore a small protein hormone (**Figure 39.2A**). Peptide and protein hormones are water-soluble and thus easily transported in the blood. Peptide and protein hormones are frequently packaged in vesicles within the cells that make them, and then released by exocytosis.

2. **Steroid hormones** (such as estrogen and testosterone) are synthesized from cholesterol (**Figure 39.2B**), are lipid-soluble, and pass easily through cell membranes. Steroid hormones diffuse out of the cells that make them and are usually bound to carrier molecules in the blood.

3. **Amine hormones** are mostly synthesized from the amino acid tyrosine (the thyroid hormone thyroxine is one example; **Figure 39.2C**). Some amine hormones are water-soluble and others are lipid-soluble; their modes of release differ accordingly.

Figure 39.2 Three Classes of Hormones
(**A**) The largest hormone molecules are peptides and proteins. An example of a protein hormone is the pancreatic hormone insulin. (**B**) Steroid hormones are modified from cholesterol molecules. They include the corticosteroids produced by the adrenal gland and the sex steroids produced primarily by the gonads. (**C**) Amine hormones are tiny molecules synthesized from a single amino acid. Both epinephrine and thyroxine are synthesized from tyrosine units, but thyroxine is lipid-soluble and epinephrine is water-soluble. Their modes of release and transport and the locations of their receptors differ accordingly.

Hormone action is mediated by receptors on or within their target cells

Water-soluble hormones cannot pass readily through cell membranes; instead they bind to receptors on the surfaces of target cells. These receptors are large transmembrane glycoprotein complexes with three domains:

1. A binding domain that projects outside the cell membrane

2. A transmembrane domain that anchors the receptor in the membrane

3. A cytoplasmic domain that extends into the cytoplasm of the cell

When a hormone binds to the binding domain, the cytoplasmic domain initiates the target cell's response, usually through second messengers. Second messengers activate cascades of intracellular events, eventually activating protein kinases or protein phosphatases (see Figures 7.6 and 7.7). In most cases these protein kinases and phosphatases activate or inactivate enzymes in the cytoplasm that lead to the cell's response, but the signaling cascade initiated by the receptor can also generate signals that enter the nucleus and alter gene expression (see Figure 7.10).

Lipid-soluble hormones can diffuse through cell membranes, and therefore their receptors are usually inside cells, in either the cytoplasm or the nucleus. There are also some membrane-bound receptors for lipid-soluble hormones, but they are the exception rather than the rule. In most cases, the complexes formed by the lipid-soluble hormones and their receptors act by altering gene expression in the cell's nucleus (see Figure 7.8).

Hormone action depends on the nature of the target cell and its receptors

Wherever a hormone encounters a cell with an appropriate receptor, it can bind to that receptor and trigger a response. The nature of the response depends on the signal transduction pathways of the responding cell. Therefore the same hormone can cause different responses in different types of cells.

Consider the amine hormone **epinephrine**, and the closely related amine hormone and neurotransmitter **norepinephrine**. Both of these molecules are involved in the **fight-or-flight response** (**Figure 39.3**). Suppose you are walking in the forest and almost step on a rattlesnake. You jump back, your heart starts to thump, and protective reactions are set in motion. The jump and the heart thumping are driven by almost instantaneous activation of your sympathetic nervous system (see Figure 45.8), which uses norepinephrine to signal target cells. Your sympathetic nervous system also stimulates endocrine cells in the adrenal glands located just above your kidneys. The adrenal glands secrete both epinephrine and norepinephrine, which diffuse rapidly into your blood, circulate around your body, and activate the many components of the fight-or-flight response.

1 The brain detects danger and signals the leg muscles to jump back…

2 …and signals the adrenal glands to release epinephrine and norepinephrine into the blood, triggering a number of effects.

The liver breaks down glycogen to supply glucose (fuel) to the blood.

The heart beats faster and stronger. Blood pressure rises.

Adrenal gland

Fat cells release fatty acids (fuel) to the blood.

Blood vessels to the gut and skin constrict, shunting more blood to the muscles.

Figure 39.3 The Fight-or-Flight Response The brain of a person suddenly faced with a threatening situation sends a signal to the adrenal glands, which almost instantaneously release the hormones epinephrine and norepinephrine. Epinephrine and norepinephrine circulate around the body and induce the various components of the fight-or-flight response in different tissues.

Epinephrine and norepinephrine bind to receptors in your heart, causing a faster and stronger heartbeat. Your heart is now pumping more blood. Epinephrine also binds to receptors in certain blood vessels. By causing constriction of blood vessels supplying your skin, kidneys, and digestive tract—tissues not essential for immediate survival—epinephrine results in more blood being available for the muscles needed for your escape from danger.

Epinephrine binds to cells in the liver, stimulating them to break down glycogen and release glucose into the blood as a quick energy supply (see Figure 7.15). In fatty tissue, epinephrine stimulates the breakdown of fats to yield fatty acids—another source of energy. These are just some of the actions triggered by one hormone. In each case the cellular response depends on the cell's receptors, its associated intracellular signaling cascade, and the mechanisms activated by that signaling cascade.

Hormone structure is conserved through evolution, but functions change

Intercellular chemical signaling was critical for the evolution of multicellularity, so hormones have a long evolutionary history. The least complex multicellular animals—the sponges—do not have nervous systems, but they do have intercellular chemical communication. Studying the evolution of hormonal signaling reveals an interesting generalization: the signal molecules themselves are highly conserved. The amino acid sequence of the hormone irisin discussed in the chapter opener is 100% identical in mice and humans. We find the same chemical compounds over broad groups of organisms, although their functions may differ. As organisms have evolved to occupy different environments and have different lifestyles, the same hormone–receptor systems have diversified to serve different functions. A good example of this evolutionary diversification is the hormone prolactin (**Figure 39.4**). The name prolactin reflects the role this hormone plays in mammals to stimulate the growth of mammary glands and the production of milk. Mammary glands are unique to mammals, but we find prolactin in all vertebrate groups—and in all cases it is involved in some way in reproduction.

The list of hormones known to exist is long and growing longer (as shown by the recent discovery of irisin). To make the subject manageable, we focus primarily on the endocrine system of mammals. **Figure 39.5** presents the human endocrine glands and most of the hormones that are discussed in this and subsequent chapters.

Fishes
Prolactin is required for osmoregulation in freshwater species. In saltwater species that return to fresh water to spawn (e.g., salmon), prolactin production in adults may play a role in generating the drive to return to natal streams.

Amphibians
In some species, prolactin creates a "water drive" that returns adults to breeding locations. It stimulates oviduct development and production of egg jelly in females. In some species, it controls development of sexual characteristics.

Mammals
In females, prolactin stimulates growth of the mammary glands and milk production. In humans, it is responsible for the sensation of sexual gratification as well as the male refractory period following sexual intercourse.

Birds
In some species, prolactin stimulates nesting activity, incubation behavior, and parental care in both sexes. In pigeons and doves it stimulates production of crop milk to nurture the young nestlings.

Figure 39.4 Prolactin's Structure Is Conserved, but Its Functions Have Evolved   The hormone prolactin is found in all vertebrate groups and has a long evolutionary history. Its probable function in early vertebrates was in regulating the body's salt and water balance (osmoregulation). It maintains this function in some species, and has evolved in others to control several physiological processes, most of which are associated with reproduction.

Pineal gland
Melatonin: helps regulate daily rhythms

Thyroid gland (see Figures 39.12 and 39.15)
Thyroxine (T_3 and T_4): increases cell metabolism; essential for growth and neural development
Calcitonin: stimulates incorporation of calcium into bone

Parathyroid glands (on posterior surface of thyroid; see Figure 39.15)
Parathyroid hormone (PTH): stimulates release of calcium from bone and absorption of calcium by gut and kidney

Adrenal gland (see Figure 39.18)
Cortex
Cortisol: mediates metabolic responses to stress
Aldosterone: involved in salt and water balance
Sex steroids: in small amounts

Medulla
Epinephrine (adrenaline) and *norepinephrine* (noradrenaline): stimulate immediate fight-or-flight reactions

Gonads (see Chapter 41)
Testes (male)
Testosterone: development and maintenance of male sexual characteristics

Ovaries (female)
Estrogens: development and maintenance of female sexual characteristics
Progesterone: supports pregnancy

Hypothalamus (see Figure 39.6)
Release and release-inhibiting neuro-hormones control the anterior pituitary; *ADH* and *oxytocin* are transported to and released from the posterior pituitary

Anterior pituitary (see Figure 39.7)
Thyrotropin (TSH): activates the thyroid gland
Follicle-stimulating hormone (FSH): in females, stimulates maturation of ovarian follicles; in males, stimulates spermatogenesis
Luteinizing hormone (LH): in females, triggers ovulation and ovarian production of estrogens and progesterone; in males, stimulates production of testosterone
Adrenocorticotropic hormone (ACTH): stimulates adrenal cortex to secrete cortisol
Growth hormone (GH): stimulates protein synthesis and growth
Prolactin: stimulates milk production
Melanocyte-stimulating hormone (MSH): stimulates production of the pigment melanin
Endorphins and enkephalins: pain control

Posterior pituitary (see Figure 39.6)
Receives and releases two hypothalamic hormones:
Oxytocin: stimulates contraction of uterus, flow of milk, interindividual bonding
Antidiuretic hormone (ADH; also known as vasopressin): promotes water conservation by kidneys

Thymus (diminishes in adults)
Thymosin: activates immune system T cells

Pancreas (islets of Langerhans)
Insulin: stimulates cells to take up and use glucose
Glucagon: stimulates liver to release glucose
Somatostatin: slows release of insulin and glucagon and digestive tract functions

Other organs include cells that produce and secrete hormones

Organ	Hormone
Adipose tissue	Leptin
Heart	Atrial natriuretic peptide
Kidney	Erythropoietin
Stomach	Gastrin, ghrelin
Intestine	Secretin, cholecystokinin
Liver	Somatomedins, insulin-like growth factors
Skeletal muscle	Irisin

Figure 39.5 The Endocrine System of Humans Cells that produce and secrete hormones may be organized into discrete endocrine glands, or they may be embedded in the tissues of other organs, such as the digestive tract or kidneys. The hypothalamus is part of the brain, but it includes cells that secrete neurohormones into the extracellular fluid.

 View in Achieve
Activity 39.1 The Human Endocrine Glands

KEY CONCEPT
39.1 Recap and Assess

Endocrine signals initiate responses in target cells that vary depending on the signal transduction pathways of the responding cells. Autocrines and paracrines act locally. Hormones are chemical signals released by endocrine cells into the extracellular fluid, where they diffuse into the blood and travel to distant target cells. The receptors for water-soluble hormones are on the surfaces of target cells; the receptors for most lipid-soluble hormones are inside the target cells. The responses activated by a hormone depend on the nature of the target cell, thus one hormone can have many functions. The chemical structures of signal molecules have been highly conserved over evolutionary time, but the same molecules can serve different functions in different organisms.

1. Why are the effects of epinephrine more rapid than the effects of estrogen?

2. Why is the presence of a particular hormone in two species not an indication of the closeness of their evolutionary relationship?

3. How can a single hormone have two different effects in the same species?

The endocrine system and the nervous system are both information systems, but a major difference between them is their speed of communication. As we will see in Chapter 44, neural signals are very fast and reach distant parts of the body in hundredths or thousandths of a second. Neural signals are also fast to disappear and therefore can rapidly communicate complex information such as that necessary to type on a laptop. Endocrine signals have to be secreted and then have to diffuse and circulate, and they frequently act through intracellular mechanisms such as protein synthesis that take time. Thus the nervous system is good at generating complex rapid responses, and the endocrine system at generating sustained responses. The different characteristics of the two information systems make it advantageous for them to work together.

KEY CONCEPT 39.2 The Endocrine and Nervous Systems Work Together

Learning Objectives

39.2.1 Describe the developmental origins of the anterior pituitary and the posterior pituitary.

39.2.2 Diagram the anatomical and signaling relationships among the hypothalamus, the pituitary gland, and a peripheral endocrine gland.

39.2.3 Using an example, explain how a negative-feedback loop controls hormone secretion.

The nervous system and the endocrine system control and regulate virtually all physiological and behavioral mechanisms that contribute to homeostasis, survival, and reproductive success. Challenges to an organism usually trigger both physiological and behavioral responses, as we saw with respect to thermoregulation in Chapter 38 and also with the fight-or-flight reactions shown in Figure 39.3. Therefore the endocrine and nervous systems must work together in an integrated fashion, and indeed they do. The nervous system receives and integrates an enormous amount of information from the body and from the environment. The nervous system uses that information to control many tissue and organ functions as well as behavior. It is therefore not surprising that the nervous system regulates many endocrine functions. Conversely, hormones circulate to the nervous system, providing feedback information used in regulation. Hormones reaching the brain also stimulate behaviors that contribute to the health and well-being of an organism.

The pituitary is an interface between the nervous and endocrine systems

The **pituitary gland** sits in a depression at the bottom of the skull, just over the back of the roof of the mouth (**Figure 39.6**). It is attached by a stalk to the hypothalamus, a part of the brain involved in many physiological regulatory systems such as that of thermoregulation (see Key Concept 38.5). Through its close connection with the hypothalamus, the pituitary serves as the interface between the nervous system and the endocrine system and is involved in the hormonal control of many physiological processes.

The pituitary has two parts with different developmental origins. The **anterior pituitary** originates as an outpocketing of the roof of the embryonic mouth cavity. The **posterior pituitary** originates as an outpocketing of the floor of the developing brain. Thus the anterior pituitary originates from gut epithelial tissue and the posterior pituitary from neural tissue. Both parts interact with

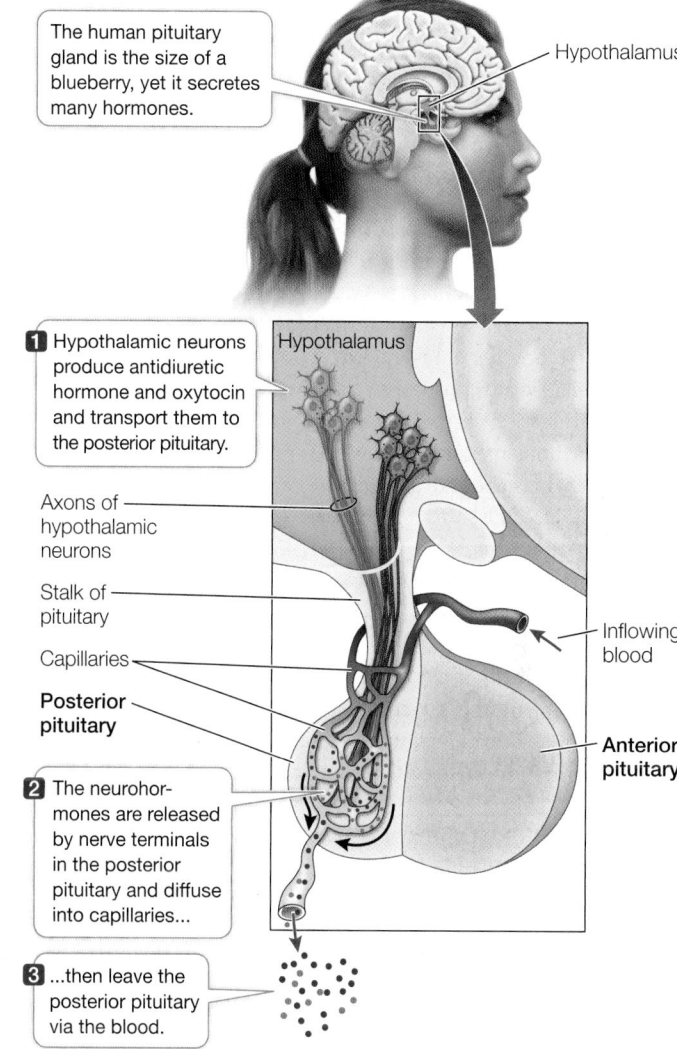

1 Hypothalamic neurons produce antidiuretic hormone and oxytocin and transport them to the posterior pituitary.

2 The neurohormones are released by nerve terminals in the posterior pituitary and diffuse into capillaries...

3 ...then leave the posterior pituitary via the blood.

Figure 39.6 The Posterior Pituitary Releases Neurohormones Neurons in the hypothalamus produce two peptide neurohormones— antidiuretic hormone and oxytocin—which are stored in and released by nerve endings in the posterior pituitary.

the nervous system but in different ways. The anterior pituitary is controlled by hypothalamic neurohormones that reach the anterior pituitary via the blood. The posterior pituitary contains long extensions of hypothalamic neurons that release their neurohormones in the posterior pituitary.

 View in Achieve
Animation 39.1 The Hypothalamic–Pituitary– Endocrine Axis

THE POSTERIOR PITUITARY   The long extensions of hypothalamic neurons into the posterior pituitary are called **axons**. The terminals of these axons in the posterior pituitary contain vesicles of neurohormones—either antidiuretic hormone or oxytocin. When these hypothalamic neurons are activated, they fire electrical signals (action potentials) that travel down their axons and cause the release of the neurohormones (see Figure 39.6).

Connect the Concepts As described in Key Concept 44.2, action potentials are sudden and transient electrical signals generated by voltage-gated ion channels in the cell membrane of the axon. These signals travel rapidly along axons, and their arrival at the axon terminals initiates the release of neurotransmitters.

The main action of **antidiuretic hormone (ADH)** in mammals and birds is to increase the amount of water conserved by the kidneys. When ADH secretion is high, the kidneys produce only a small volume of highly concentrated urine. When ADH secretion is low, the kidneys produce a large volume of dilute urine. The posterior pituitary increases its release of ADH when blood pressure falls or the blood becomes too salty. ADH is also known as **vasopressin** because at high concentrations it causes the constriction of peripheral blood vessels as a means of elevating blood pressure.

The hormone **oxytocin** is released from the posterior pituitary when a woman is about to give birth. Oxytocin stimulates contractions of the uterine muscles, which pushes the baby against the opening of the uterus, the cervix. Stretching of the cervix stimulates more oxytocin release, resulting in the delivery of the baby. Oxytocin also brings about the flow of milk from the mother's breasts. The baby's suckling stimulates neurons in the mother's brain that cause the secretion of oxytocin. Even the crying of her baby can cause a nursing mother to secrete oxytocin, resulting in the release of breast milk—a good example of how the nervous system integrates information that regulates hormonally mediated processes.

THE ANTERIOR PITUITARY   The anterior pituitary produces and releases into the circulation four peptide and protein hormones that act as **tropic hormones**, meaning they control the activities of other endocrine glands. These four tropic hormones are thyrotropin (thyroid-stimulating hormone), luteinizing hormone (LH), follicle-stimulating hormone (FSH), and adrenocorticotropic hormone (ACTH). Each is produced by a different type of pituitary cell. We discuss these tropic hormones later in this chapter and in Chapter 41 when we describe their target glands—the thyroid, testes, ovaries, and adrenal cortex. Other peptide and protein hormones produced by the anterior pituitary are prolactin (see Figure 39.4), growth hormone, enkephalins and endorphins, and melanocyte-stimulating hormone (MSH).

Growth hormone (GH) acts on a wide variety of tissues to promote growth and development. One of its important effects is to stimulate cells to take up amino acids. Growth hormone also promotes growth by stimulating the liver to produce somatomedins that stimulate the growth of bone and cartilage and other cells and tissues. Overproduction of GH in children causes gigantism; affected individuals may grow to nearly 8 feet tall. Underproduction of GH results in pituitary dwarfism, in which individuals fail to reach normal adult height.

Endorphins and **enkephalins** are the body's natural painkillers. In the brain, these molecules act as neurotransmitters in pathways that control pain. Their production in the anterior pituitary is normally quite small and probably has little significant effect.

Melanocyte-stimulating hormone (MSH) stimulates the production of the pigment melanin in skin and hair. MSH is produced by a thin layer of cells between the anterior and posterior pituitary that is sometimes called the intermediate lobe of the pituitary.

Hypothalamic neurohormones control the anterior pituitary

Hypothalamic neurons do not extend into the anterior pituitary as they do into the posterior pituitary. So how do the neurohormones produced by hypothalamic neurons reach the anterior pituitary cells they control? The pituitary is connected to the brain by the pituitary stalk (**Figure 39.7**). Within that stalk are hypothalamic–pituitary **portal blood vessels** (blood vessels that begin and end in capillary beds). The hypothalamic cells secrete neurohormones at the bottom of the hypothalamus where the stalk begins. The neurohormones diffuse into the portal blood vessels that begin there, and are carried in the blood to where the portal vessels end in the anterior pituitary. Hypothalamic neurohormones are released in such tiny amounts that they were only hypothesized to exist before the technology was developed to isolate and characterize their structure.

In the 1960s two large teams of scientists led by Roger Guillemin at the Salk Institute and Andrew Schally at Baylor University initiated the search for these hypothalamic secretions. Massive numbers of hypothalami from pigs and sheep were collected from slaughterhouses and shipped to their laboratories. One extraction effort began with the hypothalami from 270,000 sheep and yielded only 1 milligram of purified **thyrotropin-releasing hormone (TRH)**—the first hypothalamic release-stimulating hormone to be isolated and characterized. TRH turned out to be a simple tripeptide consisting of glutamine, histidine, and proline. It causes certain anterior pituitary cells to release the tropic hormone thyrotropin, which in turn stimulates the activity of the thyroid gland.

Soon after discovering TRH, Guillemin's and Schally's teams identified **gonadotropin-releasing hormone (GnRH)**, which stimulates certain anterior pituitary cells to release the tropic hormones that control the activity of the gonads (the ovaries and the testes). For these discoveries, Guillemin and Schally shared the 1977 Nobel Prize in Physiology or Medicine with Rosalyn Yalow, who invented the technique of radioimmunoassay, which made possible the measurement of miniscule amounts of specific molecules such as releasing hormones.

Many other hypothalamic neurohormones, including both releasing and release-inhibiting hormones, are now known. The major hypothalamic neurohormones that control anterior pituitary function are listed in Figure 39.7.

Negative-feedback loops regulate hormone secretion

In addition to being controlled by hypothalamic releasing and release-inhibiting hormones, the endocrine cells of the anterior pituitary are also under direct and indirect negative-feedback control by the hormones of the target glands they stimulate (see Figure 39.7). For example, cortisol, produced by the adrenal gland in response to ACTH secreted by the anterior pituitary, reaches the pituitary in the circulating blood and inhibits further release of ACTH. Cortisol also acts as a negative-feedback signal to the hypothalamus, inhibiting the release of corticotropin-releasing hormone (CRH). Because cortisol is the final hormone released in this chain of interacting structures called the hypothalamic–pituitary–adrenal axis, its feedback actions are called long-loop

(A)

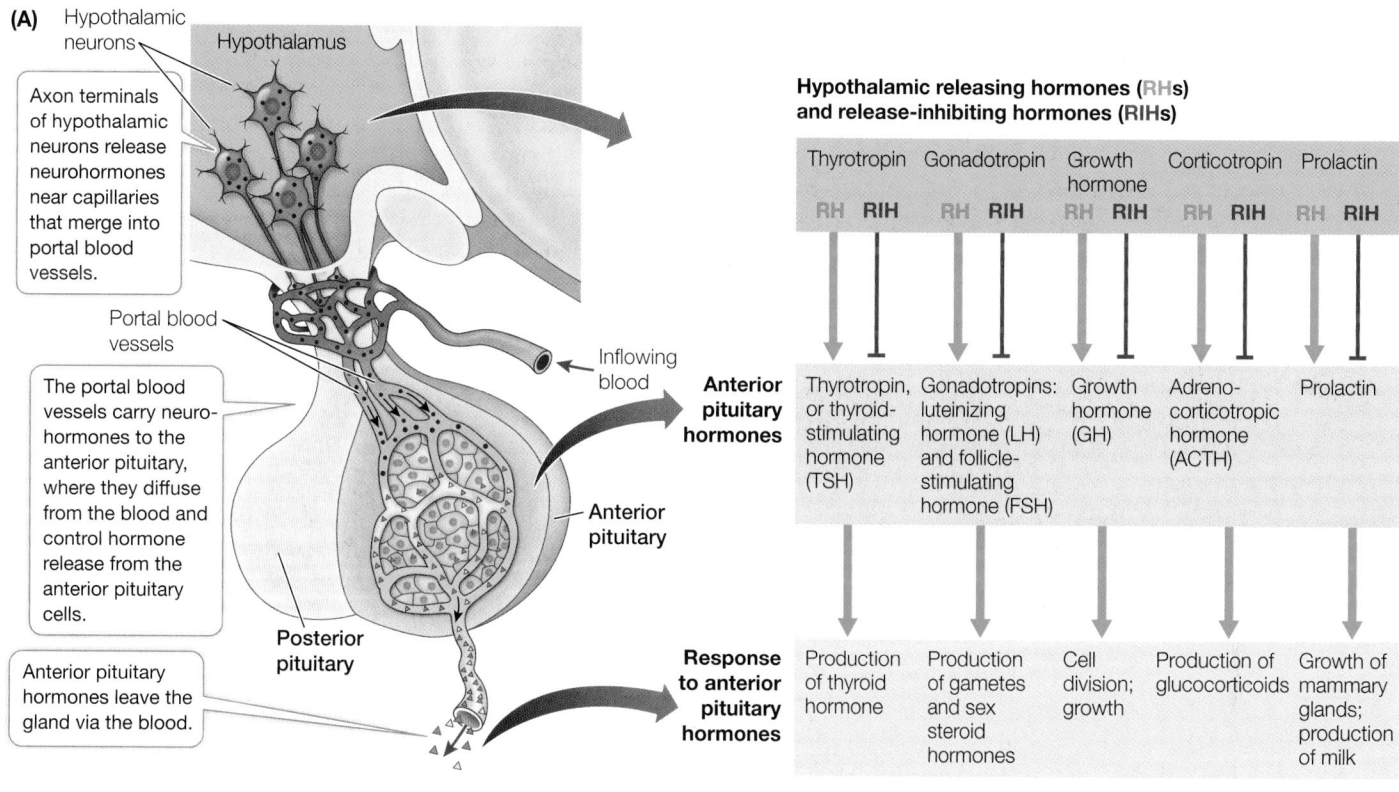

Hypothalamic neurons

Hypothalamus

Axon terminals of hypothalamic neurons release neurohormones near capillaries that merge into portal blood vessels.

Portal blood vessels

The portal blood vessels carry neurohormones to the anterior pituitary, where they diffuse from the blood and control hormone release from the anterior pituitary cells.

Anterior pituitary hormones leave the gland via the blood.

Posterior pituitary

Inflowing blood

Anterior pituitary

Hypothalamic releasing hormones (RHs) and release-inhibiting hormones (RIHs)

	Thyrotropin		Gonadotropin		Growth hormone		Corticotropin		Prolactin	
	RH	RIH	RH	RIH	RH	RIH	RH	RIH	RH	RIH
Anterior pituitary hormones	Thyrotropin, or thyroid-stimulating hormone (TSH)		Gonadotropins: luteinizing hormone (LH) and follicle-stimulating hormone (FSH)		Growth hormone (GH)		Adreno-corticotropic hormone (ACTH)		Prolactin	
Response to anterior pituitary hormones	Production of thyroid hormone		Production of gametes and sex steroid hormones		Cell division; growth		Production of glucocorticoids		Growth of mammary glands; production of milk	

(B)

External or internal conditions

→ Stimulation
⊣ Inhibition

or

Hypothalamus

Releasing or release-inhibiting hormone

"Short-loop" negative feedback

"Long-loop" negative feedback

Anterior pituitary

Tropic hormone

Endocrine gland

Hormone

negative feedback. In this system, the tropic hormone ACTH also exerts negative-feedback control on the hypothalamic cells that produce the corresponding releasing hormone (CRH). This action is called short-loop negative feedback because of the proximity of the pituitary and the hypothalamus.

Figure 39.7 The Anterior Pituitary Is Controlled by the Hypothalamus Cells of the anterior pituitary produce tropic hormones that control other endocrine glands, as well as several other peptide and protein hormones. These cells are controlled by neurohormones produced in the hypothalamus and are called releasing or release-inhibiting hormones. These neurohormones are delivered through portal blood vessels that run between the hypothalamus and the anterior pituitary through the pituitary stalk.

Q: Melanocyte-stimulating hormone (MSH) is an anterior pituitary hormone (not shown in Figure 39.7A). When anterior pituitary cells are grown in culture, they release MSH into the medium. If extracts of the hypothalamus are added to the medium, the release of MSH decreases. What do these results tell you about the hypothalamic control over MSH-producing cells?

Hormones influence the nervous system

Hormones have more influences on the nervous system than simply being negative-feedback signals controlling their own secretion. For example, the posterior pituitary hormone oxytocin, which plays a role in the birth process and in stimulating the flow of milk from the breasts, also has a strong behavioral effect in promoting bonding (see the story that opens Chapter 7). If oxytocin release is experimentally blocked, mammalian mothers, from rats to sheep, will reject their newborn offspring, but if a virgin rat is given a dose of oxytocin, she will adopt strange pups as if they were her own. Oxytocin promotes pair bonding in a variety of animals. In humans, oxytocin secretion rises with intimate sexual contact, and it has been nicknamed the "cuddle hormone." Experiments using games involving financial exchanges have shown that puffs of oxytocin applied to the nostrils raise the level of trust between players. Thus circulating hormones can have a strong influence on behavior. Another example is the effects of sex hormones, which we will discuss in Key Concept 51.3.

The effects of hormones on the brain that we have been discussing here are mostly activation effects—they influence the likelihood that the organism will act in a particular way. The hormone irisin that we presented at the beginning of this chapter plays a broader and more general role in brain function by improving the cognitive ability of the brain. Thus this hormone is not influencing a specific behavior, but it is promoting the higher functions of the brain in processing and integrating information.

These effects are apparently mediated by BDNF and include the production of new brain cells, increased blood flow, and changes in the structures supporting communication between brain cells. Irisin may play a very important role in maintaining brain health, and therefore it is important to understand how exercise influences the release of BDNF in the brain. **Investigating Life: How Could Irisin Mediate the Benefits of Exercise on Cognition?** explores this interesting question.

▶InvestigatingLIFE How Could Irisin Mediate the Benefits of Exercise on Cognition?

Experiment

Original Paper: C. D. Wrann et al. 2013. Exercise induces hippocampal BDNF through a PGC-1α/FNDC5 pathway. *Cell Metab* 18: 649–659.

Irisin secreted by exercising muscle is cleaved from a protein called FNDC5, and FNDC5 expression is controlled by the transcription factor PGC-1α. Irisin then circulates in the blood, but because of the blood–brain barrier (see Key Concept 43.1), it is unlikely to reach brain structures such as the hippocampus where it could enhance cognition. However, could irisin also be expressed in the brain? If so, exercise should result in similar changes in expression of FNDC5 and its transcription factor PGC-1α in the hippocampus as it does in skeletal muscle. First, we need to show in our experimental system and with our assays that exercise induces expression of PGC-1α and FNDC5 in exercising muscle. Then we can use the same experimental system to investigate expression in the hippocampus.

HYPOTHESIS▶ Endurance exercise results in increased expression of PGC-1α and FNDC5 in skeletal muscle.

METHOD▶

1. Have one group of mice exercise daily on running wheels for 30 days and a control group that does not. *N* = 10 for each group.

2. At the end of 30 days, measure PGC-1α and FNDC5 mRNA levels in leg muscle of both groups of mice.

3. Plot the data for each variable (FNDC5 and PGC-1α) for the exercised and control mice, and use an unpaired *t*-test (see Appendix B) to evaluate the significance of the results.

RESULTS▶ Error bars indicate ± 1 standard deviation.

CONCLUSION▶ Relative levels of FNDC5 mRNA were significantly higher in the exercised than in the non-exercised mice ($P < 0.001$). Relative levels of PGC-1α mRNA also were significantly higher in the exercised than in the non-exercised mice ($P < 0.01$).

Work with the Data

Similar measurements of expression of FNDC5 and PGC-1α mRNAs were made from the hippocampus of the exercised and the non-exercised mice. Again, *N* = 10 for each group. The results are shown in the table.

FNDC5		PGC-1α	
Control	**Exercised**	**Control**	**Exercised**
1.02	1.33	1.22	1.23
1.10	1.24	0.84	1.09
0.92	1.68	1.06	1.35
0.93	1.30	1.26	1.18
1.21	1.34	1.04	1.40
0.93	1.33	1.12	1.18
0.96	1.50	1.04	1.46
1.01	1.29	1.09	1.19
1.00	1.44	1.02	1.54
0.97	1.41	0.54	1.16

QUESTIONS▶

1. Plot the data as was done for the leg skeletal muscle results. Then you can apply the same analysis methods to these data that were applied to the leg muscle data in the preceding experiment. Did exercise have a significant effect on FNDC5 and PGC-1α expression in the hippocampus?

2. The neurotrophic factor BDNF is a secreted protein that plays important roles in neural changes associated with learning and memory. How would you determine if the exercise protocol induced a significant increase in BDNF expression in the hippocampus, assuming you have an assay for BDNF?

3. How could you determine if a noted increase in the expression of FNDC5 in the hippocampus is sufficient for an increased expression of BDNF in the hippocampus? Assume you can culture hippocampal neurons so that the expression of FNDC5 is stimulated or suppressed.

Go to Achieve for a companion
Data in Depth exercise.

KEY CONCEPT
39.2 Recap and Assess

The pituitary is the interface between the nervous system and the endocrine system. The posterior pituitary releases two neurohormones, antidiuretic hormone (ADH) and oxytocin. The anterior pituitary, under the control of other neurohormones from the hypothalamus, releases four tropic hormones that control other endocrine glands. In addition, the anterior pituitary produces and releases five other hormones that act directly on non-endocrine tissues. The hypothalamus and pituitary are under negative-feedback control by the hormones of their target glands.

1. Explain how the control of oxytocin release involves positive feedback control, whereas the control of ADH release involves negative feedback control.

2. How do hypothalamic neurons control the release of hormones from the anterior pituitary?

3. Explain what is meant by long-loop and short-loop negative feedback in the hypothalamic control of endocrine function.

The hypothalamic and pituitary hormones and some of the endocrine glands they control are easy to conceptualize because they share common features in how they are organized and function. But the entire list of hormones is diverse, making generalizations difficult. We cannot consider all of the hormones in this chapter. Instead, we focus on hormones that have some common functions—one of which is the coordination of developmental processes.

KEY CONCEPT
39.3 Hormones Play Important Roles in Development

Learning Objectives

39.3.1 Describe how hormones control complete and incomplete metamorphosis of arthropods.

39.3.2 Explain how an individual can have a male genotype but female body characteristics and genitalia.

39.3.3 Explain the role of negative feedback in the timing of puberty in humans.

The development of an animal from a fertilized egg requires the coordination of processes throughout the body. Imagine the problems that would arise if growth of the body were not symmetrical, or if the growth of organ systems did not match the demands placed on them by the growing body. Because hormones circulate in the blood to all parts of the body, they are ideal signals for integrating and coordinating the many diverse processes involved in development.

Insect development consists of either complete or incomplete metamorphosis

The changes that occur in a developing insect can be dramatic and involve major changes in body form. Insects such as bees and butterflies undergo a developmental process called **complete metamorphosis**. Starting out as a caterpillar (a larva), a butterfly feeds voraciously and goes through a series of growth stages called **instars** that are separated by molts. The last instar builds a cocoon and enters into a quiescent, transformative state called a pupa. The tissues of the pupa are extensively remodeled to form the adult body,

which is entirely different from that of the larva. The larval butterfly crawls and eats vegetation; the adult butterfly flies and consumes flower nectar. Many other species of insects undergo **incomplete metamorphosis**, which involves less extreme changes of body form. These insects also go through a series of instars, getting bigger with each molt, but the last juvenile instar simply molts into the adult form with all of the essential adult body parts. Molting involves shedding the skin, or in many cases the rigid exoskeleton, and therefore requires coordination of cellular processes in the entire epidermis of the animal. Both complete and incomplete metamorphosis require integrated processes in all parts of the insect body.

Connect the Concepts Insect metamorphosis is described in more detail in Key Concept 30.4.

Experiments on insect development revealed hormonal signaling systems

Pioneering experiments of hormonal action and control in insects were done on the bloodsucking bug *Rhodnius prolixus*, which undergoes incomplete metamorphosis. Newly hatched *Rhodnius* lack certain adult features and molt five times before developing into a mature adult. A blood meal triggers each episode of molting and growth. *Rhodnius* is an amazingly hardy experimental animal—it survives for quite a long time after its head is cut off. If decapitated within an hour after a blood meal, *Rhodnius* can survive for up to a year, but it never molts. If decapitated a week after its blood meal, however, it does molt, but into an adult (**Figure 39.8A**).

(A)

Juvenile *Rhodnius*   *Rhodnius* decapitated 1 hour after meal (remains a juvenile)   *Rhodnius* decapitated 1 week after meal (molts into adult)

(B)

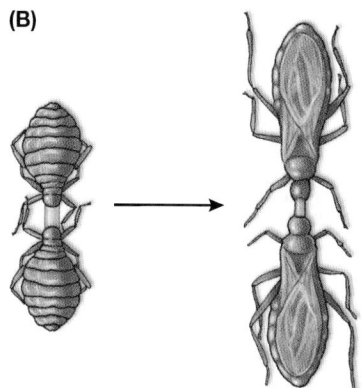

Figure 39.8 Diffusible Substance Controls Molting in a Bloodsucking Bug (A) Stimulation of molting in *Rhodnius prolixus* depends on signals coming from the head following a blood meal. (B) By connecting two bugs together with a glass tube, the experimenter showed that the molting signal was a diffusible substance.

This observation suggested that molting is triggered by some substance slowly diffusing from the head. To test this hypothesis, two decapitated bugs—one decapitated soon after a blood meal and one a week after a blood meal—were connected together with a glass tube that allowed body fluids to cross between the two bugs. Both molted into adults, proving that a diffusible substance from the bug's head triggered molting (**Figure 39.8B**). Since those pioneering experiments on *Rhodnius*, the diffusible substances (hormones) controlling molting in arthropods have been identified chemically and their functions have been described.

Three hormones regulate molting and maturation in arthropods

An arthropod's nervous system receives various types of information about the environment (e.g., day length, temperature, social cues, nutrition) that help determine the optimal timing for the stages of growth and development. When conditions are right, the brain signals the **prothoracic gland** to produce the hormones that orchestrate physiological processes involved in development and molting.

Two hormones, **prothoracicotropic hormone** (**PTTH**) and **ecdysone**, work in sequence to regulate molting in arthropods. Cells in the brain produce PTTH, which is why it has also been called "brain hormone." PTTH is transported to and stored in paired structures called the **corpora cardiaca** attached to the brain (**Figure 39.9**). After appropriate stimulation (which for *Rhodnius* is a blood meal), PTTH is released and diffuses through the extracellular fluid to an endocrine gland, the prothoracic gland. PTTH stimulates the prothoracic gland to secrete the hormone ecdysone. Ecdysone diffuses to target tissues and stimulates molting.

Ecdysone is a steroid hormone (see Figure 39.2B) and thus is related to the vertebrate hormones estrogen and testosterone (which also play roles in controlling growth and development). Ecdysone is lipid-soluble and readily passes through the cell membrane of its target cells (mostly cells of the epidermis). In the target cells, ecdysone binds to a receptor that induces expression of genes encoding enzymes involved in digesting the old cuticle and secreting a new one.

What determines whether an instar molts into another juvenile form or matures into an adult? **Juvenile hormone** is a molecule that is released continuously from the **corpora allata** (structures that are attached to the corpora cardiaca, which release PTTH). As long as juvenile hormone is present, *Rhodnius* molts into another juvenile instar. Normally *Rhodnius* stops producing juvenile hormone during the fifth instar and then molts into an adult.

The role of juvenile hormone is more complex in insects that undergo complete metamorphosis. An example of complete metamorphosis is provided by the silkworm moth *Hyalophora cecropia* (see Figure 39.9). As long as juvenile hormone is present in high concentrations, larvae molt into larger larvae. When the level of juvenile hormone falls, larvae spin cocoons and molt into pupae. Because no juvenile hormone is produced in pupae, they molt into adults. Many modern pesticides use juvenile hormone analogs to prevent larvae developing into adults.

These cases of insect development show how just a few hormones can coordinate major developmental effects that involve

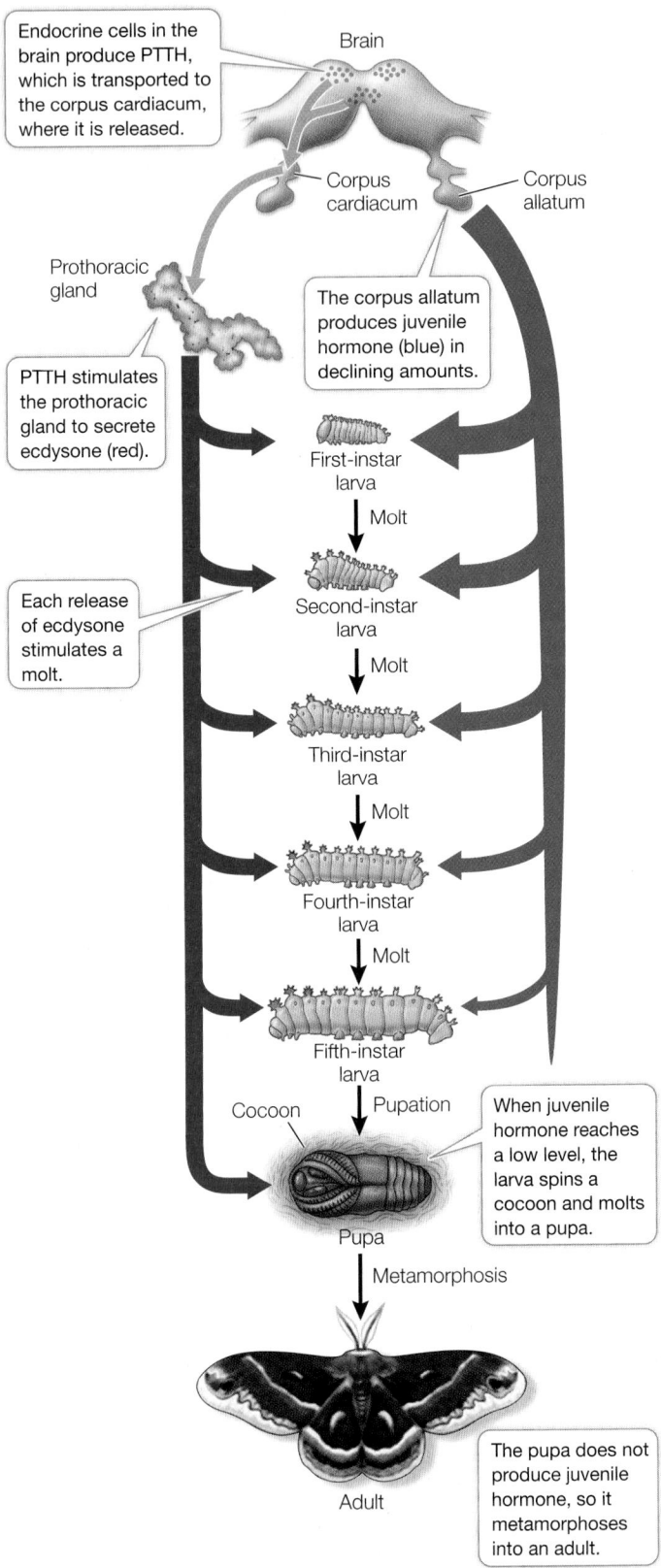

Figure 39.9 Hormonal Control of Metamorphosis   Three hormones control molting and metamorphosis in the silkworm moth *Hyalophora cecropia*. (After C. M. Williams. 1952. *Biol Bull* 103: 120–138.)

View in Achieve
Animation 39.2 Complete Metamorphosis

different cell types and tissues in the body. The hormonal signals reach all parts of the body simultaneously, and depending on the receptors on different cell types and the internal mechanisms driven by those receptors, the developmental processes are orchestrated.

Sex steroids control vertebrate sexual development

Hormones control many developmental processes in vertebrates. One example already mentioned in Key Concept 39.2 is the influence that the anterior pituitary growth hormone has on growth. Other examples are the hormones involved in sex development. The **gonads**—the testes of the male and the ovaries of the female—produce hormones as well as sperm and ova. The male steroid hormones are collectively called **androgens**, and the dominant hormone is testosterone. The female steroids are **estrogens** and **progesterone**. The dominant estrogen is estradiol, which is synthesized from testosterone. Males and females both synthesize testosterone, but females have an enzyme (aromatase) that converts testosterone to estradiol.

▶ **Media Clip 39.1 The Testosterone Factor**
Life12e.com/mc39.1

The sex steroids determine whether a mammalian embryo develops into a phenotypic female or male. In humans, the gonads of an early embryo are undifferentiated. Beginning in about the seventh week of development, the expression of genes on the Y chromosome of an XY individual normally causes the undifferentiated gonads to produce androgens. In response to androgens, the reproductive system develops the male phenotype. If no Y chromosome is present (i.e., the individual is genotype XX), androgens are not produced at this time and female structures develop (**Figure 39.10**). After birth, the sex steroids control the maturation of the reproductive organs and the development and maintenance of secondary sexual characteristics, such as breasts and facial hair.

Phenotypic sex determination provides a good example of the importance of receptors in hormonal control mechanisms. XY individuals are occasionally born who because of a mutation do not have functional androgen receptors—a condition called androgen insensitivity syndrome. These individuals have an XY genotype and internal testes, but they develop the external body form and genitalia of a female.

Puberty is the transition from juvenile body form and sexual functions to those of the adult. In juvenile humans, sex steroids are produced at low levels. At puberty (around age 12 or 13), sex steroid production increases rapidly, stimulating maturation of the secondary sexual characteristics (body forms, structures, and behavior). Why does this sudden increase occur? In both juvenile and adult humans, the activities of the gonads are controlled by the anterior pituitary tropic hormones **luteinizing hormone** (**LH**) and **follicle-stimulating hormone** (**FSH**), which together are the **gonadotropins**. The production of gonadotropins by the anterior pituitary is under the control of gonadotropin-releasing hormone (GnRH) produced by the hypothalamus (**Figure 39.11**). The production of GnRH is controlled by negative feedback from circulating sex steroids. Before puberty the circulating levels of sex steroids are low, but the

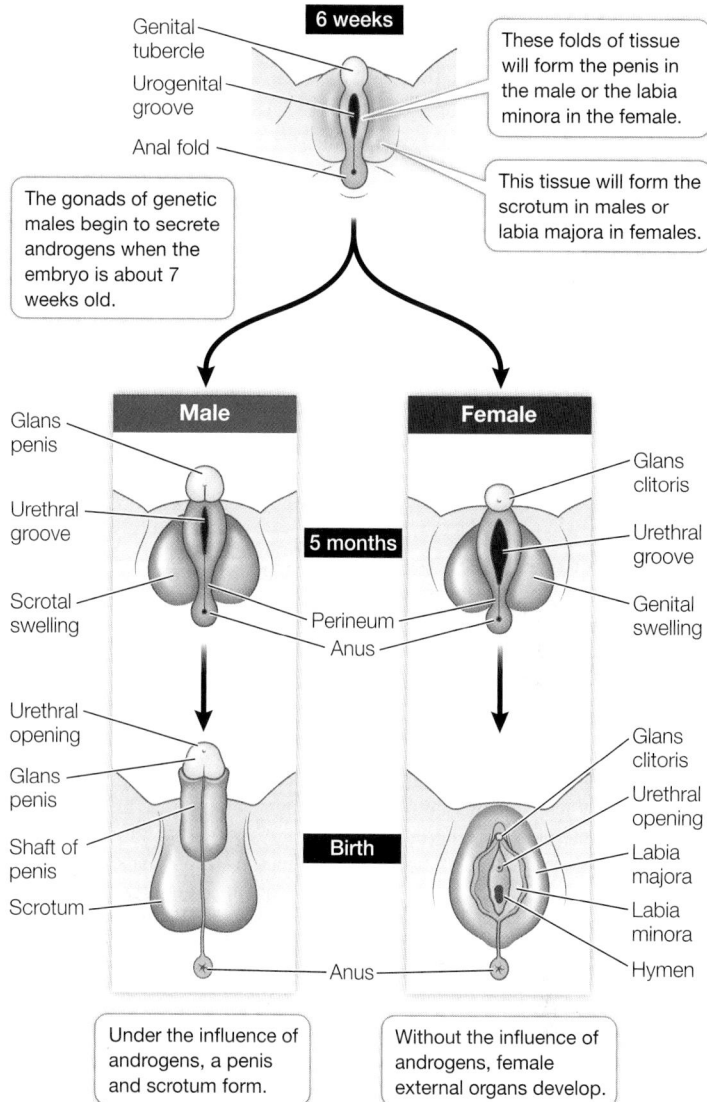

Figure 39.10 Sex Steroids Direct the Development of Human Sex Organs The external sex organs of early human embryos are undifferentiated. Androgens promote the development of male sex organs. In the absence of androgens, female sex organs form.

Q: What do you think the effect of a mutation that results in nonfunctional androgen receptors would be?

hypothalamus is highly sensitive to that negative-feedback signal. As a result, only low levels of GnRH are released. Puberty is initiated by a reduction in the sensitivity of hypothalamic GnRH-producing cells to negative feedback. As a result, GnRH production increases, stimulating increased production of gonadotropins and hence increased production of sex steroids.

In females, increasing levels of LH and FSH at puberty stimulate the ovaries to increase their production of the female sex hormones. The increased circulating levels of these hormones stimulate the development of the traits of a sexually mature woman: enlarged breasts, vagina, and uterus; broadened hips; increased subcutaneous fat; pubic hair; onset of menstrual and ovarian cycles (see Figure 41.14); and behavioral changes. In males,

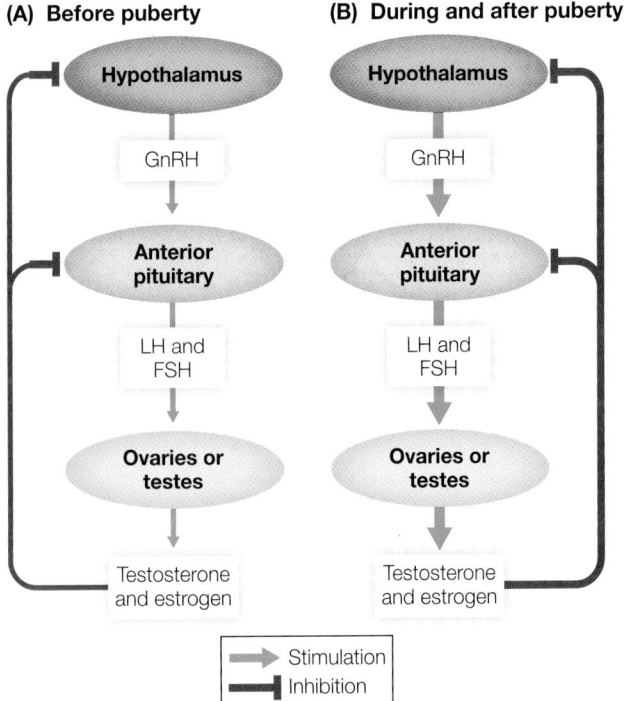

(A) Before puberty **(B)** During and after puberty

Stimulation
Inhibition

Figure 39.11 The Trigger for Puberty (A) In a prepubertal individual, the gonads produce sex steroids in small quantities, and because the hypothalamus is highly sensitive to the negative-feedback effects of those sex steroids, GnRH production is suppressed. (B) A sudden decrease in the sensitivity of the hypothalamus to this feedback causes increased production of GnRH and the onset of puberty.

an increasing level of LH stimulates groups of cells in the testes to increase their synthesis of testosterone, which in turn initiates the physiological, anatomical, and behavioral changes associated with adolescence. The voice deepens, hair begins to grow on the face and body, and the testes and penis grow larger. Testosterone also stimulates bone and skeletal muscle growth. FSH in males stimulates production of sperm.

The roles that sex steroids play in adult sexual behavior and reproduction as well as the control and regulation of these hormones will be described in more detail in Chapter 41.

39.3 Recap and Assess

Hormones play major roles in development. Because they circulate throughout the body, they can simultaneously affect many cells and tissues, but in different ways depending on the receptors and intracellular pathways in those cells. Thus hormones can coordinate the complex sets of responses involved in development. Arthropod development involves complete or incomplete metamorphosis controlled by ecdysone, juvenile hormone, and prothoracicotropic hormone (PTTH). Human gonadal and phenotypic sex development is controlled by steroid hormones.

1. Why did decapitation of *Rhodnius* prevent molting when done 1 hour after feeding but not when done 1 week after feeding?

2. How can a person with an XY genotype develop with the phenotype of a female?

3. What is the role of negative feedback in the timing of puberty?

A common feature of the roles of hormones in development is that they coordinate the execution of events programmed into the genome. These functions have evolved to be rather stable in the face of changes in the internal and external environments. In contrast, hormonal systems involved in maintaining homeostasis of the internal environment have evolved to be very sensitive to changes in the internal or external environment that could compromise homeostasis. We look at some of these hormonal regulatory mechanisms in the next key concept.

KEY CONCEPT
39.4 Hormones Regulate Metabolism and the Internal Environment

Learning Objectives

39.4.1 Explain how both hyperthyroidism and hypothyroidism cause goiter.

39.4.2 Explain how the concentration of calcium in the blood is regulated.

39.4.3 Describe how insulin and glucagon regulate blood sugar levels.

39.4.4 Apply concepts about hormonal control of stress to explain why prolonged stress can have negative effects on the body.

Hormones participate in regulating all physiological systems. In this key concept we examine a few examples of hormonal actions that are critical in regulating the internal environment. For simplicity we focus on humans, but these systems are similar in all mammals.

Thyroxine stimulates many metabolic processes

Thyroxine is a crucial signal in the regulation of cellular energy metabolism, and it is produced and secreted by the **thyroid gland**. This gland wraps around the front of the windpipe (trachea) and expands into a lobe on either side (see Figures 39.5 and 39.15). There are two cell types in the thyroid gland, and they produce different hormones. Thyroxine is produced by epithelial cells that make up spherical, colloid-containing structures called follicles (**Figure 39.12A**). Between the follicles are cells that produce **calcitonin**, which is involved in regulating blood calcium, as we will describe shortly.

Follicle cells synthesize the glycoprotein thyroglobulin in the endoplasmic reticulum and package it in secretory vesicles in the Golgi apparatus (**Figure 39.12B**). Thyroglobulin is a polymer of the amino acid tyrosine. Follicle cells also take up iodide from the blood using Na^+ cotransport and move it into the follicle lumen. The thyroglobulin vesicles are secreted into the lumen along with an enzyme that oxidizes the iodide to iodine. Iodine is highly reactive and combines with the tyrosine units of the thyroglobulin. When the thyroid gland is stimulated to release thyroxine, the follicle cells take up thyroglobulin from the lumen of the follicle by endocytosis. These bits of thyroglobulin are then cleaved to form smaller molecules consisting of only two tyrosine units, and these molecules leave the follicle cells and enter the blood (**Figure 39.13**).

(A) Cross section of a thyroid gland

Calcitonin-producing cells

Follicle

Colloid in follicle lumen

Epithelial cells of follicles

© Biophoto Associates/Science Source

Figure 39.12 The Thyroid Gland Consists of Many Follicles **(A)** Cross section through a thyroid gland, showing numerous follicles bounded by epithelial cells. Calcitonin-secreting cells are located in the spaces between the follicles. **(B)** The epithelial cells of the follicle synthesize thyroglobulin and secrete it into the lumen of the follicle, where it is iodinated and stored until it is processed by the epithelial cells to generate T_3 and T_4.

(B) Production of T_3 and T_4 hormones by the thyroid gland

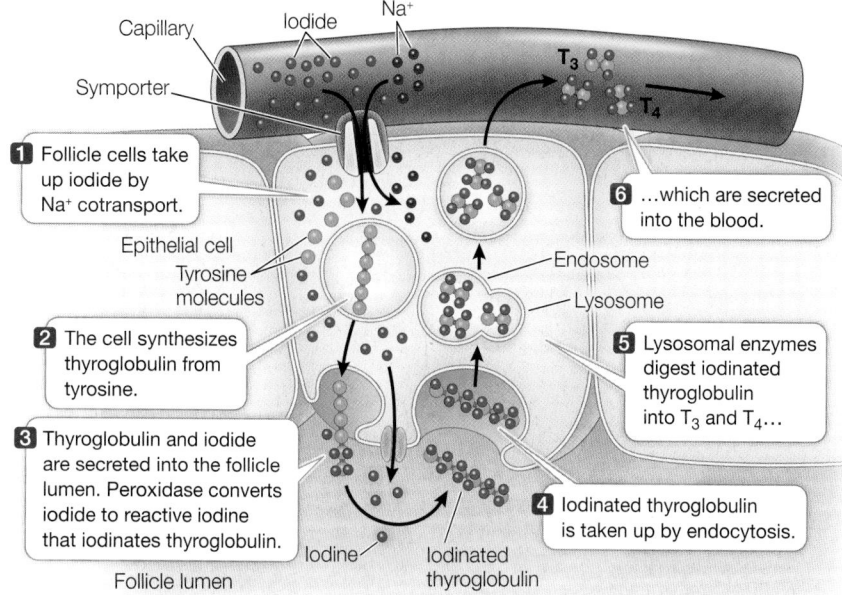

Capillary

Iodide   Na+

Symporter

T_3

T_4

1 Follicle cells take up iodide by Na+ cotransport.

6 ...which are secreted into the blood.

Epithelial cell

Tyrosine molecules

Endosome

Lysosome

2 The cell synthesizes thyroglobulin from tyrosine.

5 Lysosomal enzymes digest iodinated thyroglobulin into T_3 and T_4...

3 Thyroglobulin and iodide are secreted into the follicle lumen. Peroxidase converts iodide to reactive iodine that iodinates thyroglobulin.

4 Iodinated thyroglobulin is taken up by endocytosis.

Iodine   Iodinated thyroglobulin

Follicle lumen

The thyroid usually releases about ten times as much T_4 as T_3. However, T_3 is a more active hormone than T_4, so when you read about the effects of thyroxine, keep in mind that the actions discussed are primarily those of T_3. The difference in the activities of T_3 and T_4 makes it possible to control the effects of thyroxine in different tissues. Within target cells, T_4 can be converted to T_3 by an enzyme called deiodinase. A different deiodinase can convert T_4 into an inactive hormone called reverse T_3. Deiodinase can also inactivate T_3 by converting it into T_2 or T_1. Thus each target cell can have a unique sensitivity to thyroid hormones using these enzymes to control the conversion of T_4 to T_3 or to reverse T_3, T_2, or T_1.

THE PRODUCTION AND RELEASE OF THYROXINE ARE REGULATED BY TSH AND TRH The tropic hormone **thyroid-stimulating hormone** (**TSH**, also known as **thyrotropin**) is produced by the anterior pituitary. TSH activates the thyroxine-producing follicle cells in the thyroid. Thyrotropin-releasing hormone (TRH), produced in the hypothalamus and transported to the anterior

pituitary through the portal blood vessels, activates the TSH-producing pituitary cells. The hypothalamus uses environmental information, such as temperature or day length, to determine whether to increase or decrease its secretion of TRH. This sequence of steps is regulated by a negative-feedback loop (see Figure 39.7B). Circulating thyroxine inhibits the response of pituitary cells to TRH, so less TSH is released when thyroxine levels are high, and more TSH is released when thyroxine levels are low. Circulating thyroxine also exerts negative feedback on the production and release of TRH by the hypothalamus.

Because thyroxine is lipid-soluble, it enters cells readily and binds to receptors in the nucleus. When bound to thyroxine, these receptors, which are found in most cells of the body, are transcription factors. They move to the nucleus and stimulate the transcription of numerous genes whose products are transport proteins, structural proteins, and enzymes involved in metabolic pathways; thus thyroxine elevates the metabolic rates of most cells and tissues. Exposure to cold for several days leads to an increased release of thyroxine, an increased conversion of T_4 to T_3, and therefore an increased basal metabolic rate (see Key Concept 38.5).

During development and growth, thyroxine promotes amino acid uptake and protein synthesis. Insufficient thyroxine in a human fetus or growing child greatly retards physical and mental development, resulting in a condition known as cretinism.

GOITER An enlarged thyroid gland is called a **goiter** (**Figure 39.14**). A goiter can be caused by either hyperthyroidism (excess production of thyroxine) or hypothyroidism (thyroxine deficiency). The negative-feedback loop whereby thyroxine controls TSH release explains how two seemingly opposite conditions result in the same symptom.

1. The most common cause of *hyperthyroid* goiter is Graves' disease, an autoimmune disease involving an

(A) T_4

HO — ⬡ — O — ⬡ — CH_2 — CH — C — OH
                                           | ||
                                          NH_2 O

(B) T_3

HO — ⬡ — O — ⬡ — CH_2 — CH — C — OH
                                           | ||
                                          NH_2 O

Figure 39.13 Cleavage of Thyroglobulin Yields Two Active Hormones **(A)** Tetraiodothyronine (T_4) is iodinated at four locations. **(B)** Triiodothyronine (T_3) is iodinated at only three locations.

© Scott Camazine/Science Source

Figure 39.14 **A Hypothyroid Goiter** In this condition, dietary iodide deficiency leads to a lack of functional thyroxine, resulting in the oversynthesis of thyroglobulin and subsequent enlarged follicles.

antibody to the TSH receptor. This antibody binds to and activates the TSH receptors on the follicle cells, causing uncontrolled production and release of thyroxine. Blood levels of TSH are low due to negative feedback from high levels of thyroxine, but the thyroid remains maximally stimulated and grows bigger. People with hyperthyroidism have high metabolic rates, usually feel hot, and may develop a buildup of fat behind the eyeballs that causes their eyes to bulge.

2. *Hypothyroid* goiter results when there is not enough circulating thyroxine to turn off TSH production. A common cause is deficiency of dietary iodide, without which the follicle cells cannot make active thyroxine (T_3 or T_4). Without negative feedback from thyroxine, TSH levels remain high and the thyroid continues to produce thyroglobulin. Because sufficient iodine is not available, however, the thyroglobulin is poorly iodinated. When it is broken down by the follicle cells, it produces little functional T_3 or T_4. As a result, TSH levels remain high and stimulate more and more synthesis of thyroglobulin, and the thyroid gets bigger. The symptoms of hypothyroidism are low metabolism, intolerance of cold, and general physical and mental sluggishness.

Goiter affects about 5% of the world's population. The addition of iodide to table salt has greatly reduced the incidence of hypothyroid goiter in industrialized nations, but the condition is still common in other parts of the world and is a leading cause of intellectual impairment.

Three hormones regulate blood calcium concentrations

Blood calcium must be regulated within a narrow range or serious problems occur. If blood calcium falls below this range, the nervous system becomes overly excited, resulting in muscle spasms and even seizures. If blood calcium rises above this range, the nervous system becomes depressed and muscles—including the heart—weaken. Regulation of blood calcium is difficult because only about 0.1% of the calcium in the body is located in the extracellular fluid. About 1% is in cells, and almost 99% is in the bones. Therefore the body must maintain a tiny pool of calcium in the blood at a precise concentration, and that tiny pool can be influenced greatly by relatively small shifts in the much larger pools of calcium in the cells and bones.

The body has multiple mechanisms for changing blood calcium levels, including:

• Deposition or resorption of bone

• Excretion or retention of calcium by the kidneys

• Absorption of calcium from the digestive tract

These mechanisms are controlled by three hormones: calcitonin, parathyroid hormone, and calcitriol (synthesized from vitamin D).

 View in Achieve
Animation 39.3 **Hormonal Regulation of Calcium**

CALCITONIN REDUCES BLOOD CALCIUM Remember that calcitonin is produced by cells in the thyroid gland. These cells are stimulated to release their hormone when blood calcium rises. Calcitonin acts to lower the concentration of calcium in the blood, mainly by stimulating calcium uptake by bone-forming cells (**Figure 39.15**). Bone is continuously remodeled through a dynamic process that involves both resorption of old bone and synthesis of new bone, as we will discuss in Key Concept 46.3. Cells called osteoclasts break down bone and release calcium into the blood, and cells called osteoblasts take up calcium from the blood and deposit it in new bone. Calcitonin decreases the activity of osteoclasts and thereby favors removal of calcium from the blood and its deposition in bone by osteoblasts. The turnover of bone in adult humans is not very high, so calcitonin does not play a major role in calcium homeostasis in adults. It is probably more important in young individuals whose bones are actively growing.

PARATHYROID HORMONE INCREASES BLOOD CALCIUM The **parathyroid glands** are four tiny structures embedded in the posterior surface of the thyroid gland (see Figure 39.15). Their single hormone product, **parathyroid hormone** (**PTH**, also called parathormone), is the most important hormone in the regulation of blood calcium levels. Circulating calcium activates receptors in the cell membrane of the parathyroid cells. When these receptors are activated, they inhibit the synthesis and release of PTH. A fall in blood calcium removes this inhibition and triggers the synthesis and release of PTH. PTH stimulates bone turnover by actions on both osteoclasts and osteoblasts. The end result of these actions of PTH is a net increase of calcium in the blood. PTH also maintains blood concentration of calcium by stimulating the kidneys to reabsorb it rather than excrete it in the urine.

CALCITRIOL INCREASES BLOOD CALCIUM In the past, fragile bones were common among people living at high latitudes, where winter days are short and the winter diet often lacks fish,

Figure 39.15 Hormonal Regulation of Calcium Calcitonin, parathyroid hormone (PTH), and calcitriol (the active form of calciferol, or vitamin D) regulate Ca^{2+} levels in the blood.

Normal blood concentrations of calcium and phosphate are just below the levels at which they precipitate out of solution as calcium phosphate salts. Even a small rise in concentrations may cause precipitation that leads to maladies such as kidney stones and calcium deposits in the arteries (hardening of the arteries). To reduce this risk, PTH acts on the kidneys to increase the elimination of phosphate via the urine.

Insulin and glucagon regulate blood glucose concentrations

Before the 1920s, the disease **diabetes mellitus** was fatal. The name diabetes refers to excessive urine production, and the name mellitus refers to the fact that the urine is sweet. These symptoms are both due to the large amounts of glucose in the blood and therefore in the urine. Other characteristics of the disease are weakness, lethargy, and a dramatic loss of body mass. Even before the discovery of hormones, diabetes was known to be connected with abnormal glucose metabolism and with the pancreas—a large gland located just below the stomach (see Figure 39.5). The exact links, however, were not clear. Today we recognize two forms of diabetes. The form that was mostly seen prior to the 1920s usually occurred in young people and was called juvenile diabetes. We now call it type I diabetes, and it is caused by a lack of the protein hormone **insulin**, which is produced and secreted by cells in the pancreas called β cells.

Glucose enters cells by diffusion, but cell membranes are not very permeable to glucose. Glucose transporter proteins in cell membranes facilitate the movement of glucose into cells, and the glucose transporters called GLUT4 that are most common in muscle and adipose tissue are controlled by insulin. When insulin binds to its receptor on the cell membrane, it causes these glucose transporters to move from cytoplasmic vesicles to the cell membrane, thus making the cell more permeable to glucose (**Figure 39.16**). When insulin is not present, these transporters are returned to the cytoplasmic pool through endocytosis.

Another form of diabetes, called adult onset or type II diabetes, is in epidemic proportions in the United States today. Type II diabetes is associated with high carbohydrate consumption, obesity, and lack of exercise. It is caused either by low production of insulin or by insensitivity to insulin. More than 90% of diabetes cases seen in the United States today are type II diabetes, and the numbers are rising alarmingly. Statistics from the Centers for Disease Control and Prevention show that the number of new cases of type II diabetes reported in the United States in 1991 was less than 600,000 and had been fairly stable since 1980. Between 1991 and 2012, the annual number of new cases tripled. Today the incidence of diabetes in the United States is over 30 million, more than 9% of the population. Diabetes is currently the seventh leading cause of death in the United States, and it is a common contributor to blindness, kidney failure, stroke, heart disease, and amputations resulting from ulcerations. This disease is largely preventable and even reversible with lifestyle changes.

dairy products, and fresh vegetables. Since the condition could be reversed by taking cod-liver oil, it was assumed that a vitamin deficiency was involved. That vitamin was named **vitamin D**, but when its chemical identity was established, this molecule turned out not to be a vitamin at all.

A vitamin is a substance that the body requires in small quantities but cannot synthesize for itself and must therefore obtain from food (or from supplements such as vitamin pills). However, vitamin D—more accurately named calciferol—is synthesized naturally from cholesterol when skin cells receive ultraviolet light. Calciferol is not an active hormone, but through actions of enzymes in the liver and kidneys it is converted into the active form called **calcitriol**, which circulates in the blood and acts on distant cells (and therefore *is* a hormone). The conversion of calciferol to calcitriol is activated by PTH. Calcitriol promotes the absorption of calcium from food in the gut. Thus the combined actions of PTH and calcitriol raise blood calcium levels.

PTH lowers blood phosphate levels

Bones are made of phosphate as well as calcium. When PTH stimulates the release of calcium from bone, it also releases phosphate.

Figure 39.16 Glucose Transporters Are Controlled by Insulin Most tissues of the body depend on insulin to promote the uptake of glucose into cells. Glucose enters cells by diffusion, but that diffusion is facilitated by passive glucose transporters. When insulin binds to receptors on the cell surface, it stimulates the transfer of one type of glucose transporter (GLUT4) from intracellular sequestration to the cell membranes. When insulin levels fall, the glucose transporters are again sequestered intracellularly.

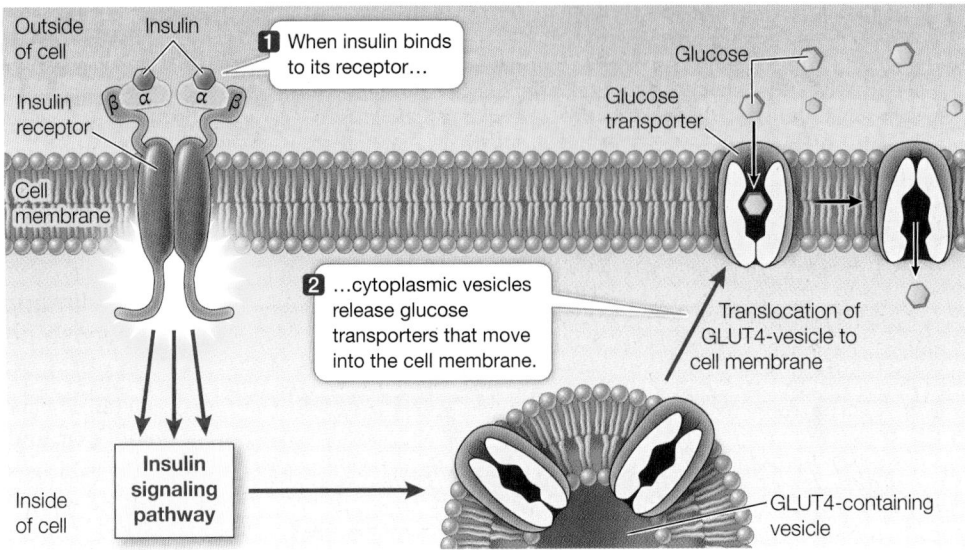

In both type I and type II diabetes, glucose entry into cells is impaired, resulting in so much glucose accumulating in the blood that it starts to spill over into the urine. A high concentration of glucose in the blood increases urine output by two mechanisms. First, it causes water to move from cells into the blood by osmosis, and this increase in blood volume results in increased urine production. Second, the increased glucose in the tubules of the kidneys pulls more water into the urine by osmosis. Diabetic individuals lose their metabolic fuel in their urine, and they can become dehydrated. Because glucose uptake by muscle and adipose tissue is impaired in the absence of insulin, muscle cells must depend on fat and protein for fuel, and adipose tissue cannot replenish its stores of triglycerides. The body wastes away if the condition is not treated.

For centuries, the prospects for people suffering with type I diabetes were bleak. A change came almost overnight in 1921, when the physician Frederick Banting and medical student Charles Best at the University of Toronto discovered they could reduce the symptoms of diabetes by injecting an extract prepared from pancreatic tissue. The active component of this extract was found to be insulin, a small protein consisting of just 51 amino acids. In the United States today, insulin replacement therapy using manufactured insulin allows more than 1.5 million people with type I diabetes to lead almost normal lives.

Much evidence now shows that type II diabetes can be treated with a combination of dietary changes and weight loss. **Figure 39.17** looks at the intriguing question of whether the hormone irisin (introduced in the opening of this chapter) can mediate the beneficial effects of exercise on glucose metabolism in type II diabetes patients.

ISLETS OF LANGERHANS   The pancreas is mostly an exocrine gland that produces digestive enzymes and secretes them through ducts into the gut (see Figure 49.13). But within the pancreas are clusters of endocrine cells called **islets of Langerhans**, after the German medical student who discovered them. They contain three types of cells, each of which produces a specific hormone:

1. Beta (β) cells produce and secrete insulin.
2. Alpha (α) cells produce and secrete **glucagon**, a hormone that has effects mostly opposite from those of insulin.
3. Delta (δ) cells produce the hormone **somatostatin**.

After a meal, the concentration of glucose in the blood rises, stimulating the β cells of the islets to release insulin. Insulin causes target cells throughout the body to use circulating glucose as fuel and convert it into storage products such as glycogen and fat. When the gut is empty of food, blood glucose concentration falls and the islets stop releasing insulin. As a result, most cells shift to using glycogen and fat rather than glucose as fuel. If blood glucose concentration falls substantially below normal, the islet α cells release glucagon, which stimulates the liver to break down stored glycogen and release glucose into the blood. We will discuss these actions in greater detail in Key Concept 49.4.

SOMATOSTATIN   Somatostatin is released from the δ cells of the pancreas in response to rapid increases of glucose and amino acids in the blood. This hormone has paracrine functions within the islets, where it inhibits the release of both insulin and glucagon. Outside the pancreas it acts as a hormone, slowing the digestive activities of the gut and extending the period during which nutrients are absorbed. Somatostatin is also produced in very small amounts by cells in the hypothalamus. Hypothalamic somatostatin, also called **growth hormone–inhibiting hormone (GHIH)**, is transported in the portal blood vessels to the anterior pituitary, where it inhibits the release of growth hormone and thyrotropin.

The adrenal gland is two glands in one

An **adrenal gland** sits above each kidney, just below the middle of your back. Functionally and anatomically, each adrenal gland consists of a gland within a gland (**Figure 39.18**). The core, or **adrenal medulla**, produces epinephrine (adrenalin) and, to a lesser degree, norepinephrine (noradrenalin). The medulla develops

Experiment

Figure 39.17A Effects of Exercise on Glucose Metabolism

Original Paper: Y. Zhang et al. 2014. Irisin stimulates browning of white adipocytes through mitogen-activated protein kinase p38 MAP kinase and ERK MAP kinase signaling. *Diabetes* 63: 514–525.

Exercise has been shown to have benefits for individuals with type II diabetes and for obese individuals. Imaging studies have revealed an inverse correlation between brown fat abundance and body mass—lean people have more brown fat and obese people have less. Given that irisin has been shown to have a "browning" effect on white fat, making it more metabolically active, might irisin mediate the beneficial effects of exercise on glucose metabolism and body mass?

HYPOTHESIS▶ Irisin can mediate exercise-induced improvements in glucose metabolism.

METHOD▶

1. For 2 weeks, treat mice with daily injections of irisin (experimentals) to simulate effects of exercise. Treat control mice with injections of saline.

2. After 2 weeks, sacrifice mice and collect fat tissues to analyze for expression of genes for uncoupling protein (UCP1, an indication of irisin's "browning" effect) and betatrophin (βt, a peptide that stimulates proliferation of insulin-secreting cells in the pancreas).

3. Determine the average expression for the two genes under control and experimental conditions. Determine the standard deviations.

Do t-tests to determine if the treatment (irisin injections) had a significant effect on the expression of genes for UCP1 and for βt.

RESULTS▶ The table shows gene expression (in arbitrary units) in white adipose tissue (simulated data based on published means and SDs). The bar graph shows the mean expression levels of the two genes ± 1 SD.

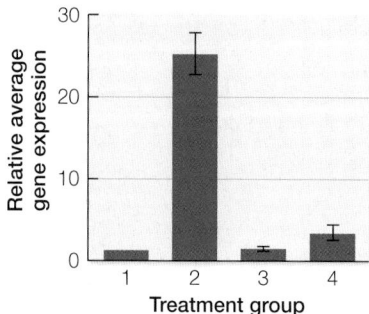

CONCLUSION▶

1. The treatment with irisin resulted in a significant increase ($P < 0.001$) in expression of UCP1 in the white fat, demonstrating the known effect of irisin.

2. The treatment with irisin also resulted in a significant increase in the expression of βt ($P < 0.001$), which could stimulate insulin production in the pancreas.

		Relative gene expression of individual									
Gene	**Treatment group**	**1**	**2**	**3**	**4**	**5**	**6**	**7**	**8**	**Mean**	**SD**
UCP1	Control (1)	1.42	1.42	1.40	1.42	1.38	1.41	1.40	1.41	1.41	0.01
UCP1	Experimental (2)	23.46	21.68	28.2	26.36	25.77	22.99	28.72	26.13	25.41	2.50
βt	Control (3)	1.36	1.30	1.33	1.40	2.01	1.43	1.46	1.55	1.48	0.23
βt	Experimental (4)	3.62	3.56	3.40	3.03	3.56	4.65	3.41	1.83	3.38	0.78

Work with the Data

Figure 39.17B Effects of Exercise on Glucose Metabolism

Original Paper: Y. Zhang et al. 2014. Irisin stimulates browning of white adipocytes through mitogen-activated protein kinase p38 MAP kinase and ERK MAP kinase signaling. *Diabetes* 63: 514–525.

Figure 39.17A showed that elevated irisin levels could stimulate pancreatic function in ways that could benefit individuals with type II diabetes. Betatrophin had been shown to stimulate proliferation of insulin-producing cells in the pancreas, increase release of insulin, and improve the ability of individuals to process glucose from dietary sources. The question then arose whether these health benefits associated with betatrophin could be stimulated by irisin treatment. Additional experiments were done to investigate this question. Researchers kept mice on a high-fat diet for 10 weeks and then treated half of the mice with daily injections of irisin for 2 weeks while the other half received daily saline injections (control). $N = 8$ for both groups. The table shows body mass before and after the 2-week injection treatment, fasting insulin levels, and blood glucose levels. All values are means ± 1 standard deviation. Use an unpaired t-test to compare the body mass and fasting insulin of the two groups.

Group	Body mass (g) before	Body mass (g) after	Fasting insulin (ng/mL)	Blood glucose (mg/dL)
Control	40.1 ± 4.4	40.9 ± 4.8	4.3 ± 1.0	150 ± 5
Irisin treated	43.7 ± 2.7	40.2 ± 2.8	2.1 ± 0.5	130 ± 7

QUESTIONS▶

1. In the first experiment, why was it important to measure a known marker of brown fat function, namely UCP1, in the same experiment in which the expression of a new candidate gene, namely βt, was being measured as a response to irisin treatment?

2. In the second experiment, why were the mice first placed on a high-fat diet?

3. Type II diabetes is frequently associated with obesity and is characterized by insulin resistance. As a result, insulin levels can be high while glucose metabolism is still impaired. What evidence was produced supporting the hypothesis that elevated irisin levels could benefit obese individuals or individuals with type II diabetes?

Go to **Achieve** for a companion **Data in Depth** exercise.

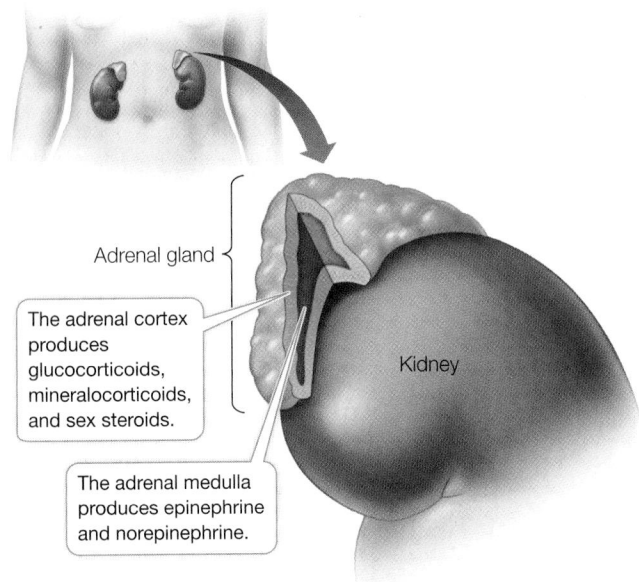

Figure 39.18 The Adrenal Is Really Two Glands An adrenal gland, consisting of an outer cortex and an inner medulla, sits above each kidney. The medulla and the cortex produce different hormones.

from nervous tissue and is under the control of the nervous system. Surrounding the medulla is the **adrenal cortex**, which produces steroid hormones. The cortex is under hormonal control by a tropic hormone produced by cells in the anterior pituitary.

THE ADRENAL CORTEX The cells of the adrenal cortex use cholesterol to produce three classes of steroid hormones (see Figure 39.2B), collectively called **corticosteroids**:

1. *Mineralocorticoids* influence the salt and water balance of the extracellular fluid.

2. *Glucocorticoids* influence blood glucose concentrations as well as other aspects of fat, protein, and carbohydrate metabolism.

3. *Sex steroids* play roles in sexual development, sexual behavior, and anabolism (tissue building).

In adult humans, the adrenal cortex secretes only negligible amounts of sex steroids. The major producers of sex steroids are the gonads, as we saw in Key Concept 39.3.

Aldosterone, the primary mineralocorticoid, stimulates the kidneys to conserve sodium and excrete potassium, as we will discuss in Chapter 50. If the adrenal glands are removed from an animal, sodium must be added to its diet, or its sodium will be depleted and it will die.

The main glucocorticoid in humans is **cortisol**, which is critical for mediating the body's metabolic responses to stress. Within minutes of a stressful stimulus (one provoking fear or anger, for example), blood cortisol levels begin to rise. This response is much slower than the neurally mediated epinephrine and norepinephrine response to stress, but it lasts longer. Whereas epinephrine and norepinephrine cause sudden increases in blood pressure, cortisol causes a sustained increase in blood pressure. Cortisol stimulates tissues that are not critical for escaping the danger or

threat to switch from using blood glucose for energy to using fats and proteins. This action preserves circulating glucose to fuel the actions of the nervous system and skeletal muscles necessary to meet the threat. Cortisol's elevation of blood pressure increases delivery of oxygen to the muscles, preparing them for flight or fight. Cortisol also inhibits the immune system. Dealing with the immediate stressor is more important than feeling sick, having allergic reactions, or healing wounds. This explains why cortisol and drugs that mimic its actions are useful for reducing inflammation and allergic responses. Cortisol decreases activity of the gut and reproductive systems—you can digest lunch and reproduce later if you escape the threat. The actions of cortisol are adaptive in responding to acute stress, but they can cause problems if sustained over time, as sometimes occurs in modern society due to social, economic, and job-related stressors.

Cortisol release is controlled by **adrenocorticotropic hormone** (**ACTH**) from the anterior pituitary. ACTH release is controlled in turn by **corticotropin-releasing hormone** (**CRH**) from the hypothalamus (see Figure 39.7). The action of ACTH on the adrenal cortex is to stimulate the synthesis of cortisol. Like other steroid hormones, cortisol is not stored in vesicles and therefore is available for immediate release. As cortisol or other steroid hormones diffuse into the blood, they combine with carrier proteins, and their release from these proteins can have a long time course, thus stretching out their actions. Also, many of their actions stimulate gene expression in target cells, which takes time but has a long-lasting effect.

Turning off the stress responses activated by cortisol is as important as turning them on. A study of stress in rats showed that old rats could turn on these stress responses as effectively as young rats, but they lost the ability to turn them off as rapidly. As a result, they suffered from the well-known consequences of stress seen in humans: digestive system problems, cardiovascular problems, strokes, impaired immune system function, and increased susceptibility to cancers and other diseases. Acute stress responses are turned off by negative feedback from cortisol on both the ACTH-secreting cells of the anterior pituitary and the CRH-secreting cells of the hypothalamus. With chronic or prolonged stress, these control mechanisms become insufficient and cortisol exerts negative feedback through another brain region, the hippocampus. Prolonged exposure to cortisol, however, causes trauma to and loss of hippocampal cells, resulting in the decreased ability to turn off the stress response.

Loss of adrenal cortical function results in Addison's disease, characterized by fatigue, muscle weakness, digestive problems, low blood sodium (hyponatremia), low blood pressure, and salt hunger. Without replacement hormone treatment, death is likely. An interesting symptom of Addison's disease is darkening of many skin areas that normally are not exposed to the sun—for instance, the lining of the cheeks. You can understand the cause of this symptom by thinking about the source of ACTH and the control of its secretion. In the hypothalamic–pituitary–adrenal axis (see Figure 39.7), an end hormone (in this case cortisol) frequently serves as a negative-feedback signal to the pituitary and also the hypothalamus. If the hormones of the adrenal cortex are absent, that negative feedback is gone, and the system will call for more ACTH. The production of ACTH by pituitary cells involves the expression of a polypeptide called proopiomelanocortin which is then cleaved to produce multiple peptide hormones. These include ACTH, MSH, endorphins, and enkephalins. The excess production of MSH is the cause of the skin darkening in Addison's disease.

THE ADRENAL MEDULLA   Stress causes the adrenal medulla to release epinephrine and norepinephrine, which arouse the body to action. As we saw earlier in this chapter, epinephrine and norepinephrine increase heart rate and blood pressure and divert blood flow to active muscles and away from the gut and skin. Only about one-fifth as much norepinephrine is secreted from the adrenal medulla as epinephrine, but it has similar functions. Norepinephrine is also used by the nervous system as a neurotransmitter, and it is involved in controlling many physiological processes.

Epinephrine and norepinephrine are both water-soluble, and both bind to the same set of receptors on the surfaces of target cells. These **adrenergic receptors** are of two general types, α-adrenergic and β-adrenergic. The α-adrenergic receptors respond more strongly to norepinephrine than to epinephrine, whereas β-adrenergic receptors respond about equally to both epinephrine and norepinephrine. Because of this difference in receptor affinities, it is possible for drugs to blunt the flight-or-fight responses without disrupting physiological regulatory processes. Such drugs are called "beta blockers" because, by inhibiting β-adrenergic receptors, they can reduce the fight-or-flight response to epinephrine without disrupting the physiological regulatory functions of norepinephrine mediated through the α-adrenergic receptors. Beta blockers are commonly prescribed to reduce symptoms of anxiety such as dry mouth and elevated heart rate (palpitations).

Many chemicals may act as hormones

We have discussed the major mammalian endocrine glands and their hormones in this chapter, but many more hormones exist. As we discuss the organ systems of the body in the chapters that follow, we will frequently describe hormones that their tissues produce as well as hormones that control their functions.

The pineal gland has a daily cycle of melatonin release

Humans, like most vertebrate species, have a **pineal gland** located between the cerebral hemispheres. The pineal has a daily rhythm of production and secretion of the hormone **melatonin**. The functions of the pineal and melatonin have to do with coordinating daily rhythms of physiological functions and, in many species, seasonal changes such as reproduction timing, migration, and preparations for environmental stress such as cold weather.

KEY CONCEPT
39.4 Recap and Assess

The major endocrine glands of mammals include the hypothalamus, pituitary gland, thyroid gland, parathyroid glands, pancreas, adrenal glands, gonads, and pineal gland. Each of these glands secretes and responds to hormones that play crucial roles in controlling physiology and development. Thyroxine is a lipid-soluble hormone that influences the expression of genes involved in regulating cell metabolism. Calcitonin and parathyroid hormone (PTH) regulate blood calcium levels, mainly by regulating the remodeling of bone. Blood glucose levels are controlled by insulin. When blood glucose levels rise, insulin is released and promotes uptake of glucose by cells. When blood glucose levels fall, the lack

of insulin decreases uptake of glucose by most cells. Glucagon is released in the event of serious hypoglycemia, and it stimulates breakdown of glycogen to raise blood glucose levels. The adrenal cortex produces steroid hormones, the most important of which is cortisol, which is involved in stress responses. The adrenal medulla produces and releases epinephrine and norepinephrine.

1. If you analyzed the chemical composition of thyroglobulin from a hyper- and a hypothyroid patient, how would the two samples differ?

2. Two symptoms of type II diabetes are insulin insensitivity and poor glucose tolerance (slow clearance of glucose from the blood). Explain the likely causes of these symptoms.

3. Osteoporosis is a weakening of the bones due to an imbalance between bone resorption and bone formation. Explain why liver and kidney disease are associated with a higher risk of osteoporosis.

4. Explain how chronic stress can lead to stress-related diseases.

 View in Achieve
Activity 39.2 Concept Review: Vertebrate Hormones

 InvestigatingLIFE

Q**and**A   **In what ways could irisin mediate the health benefits of exercise?**

The initial discovery of irisin and its functions revealed that it induces brown fat–like changes in white fat, including expression of the gene that codes for uncoupling protein (UCP1), which enables brown fat cells to metabolize lipids without producing ATP. As a result, metabolism in the brown fat cells is not inhibited by the buildup of ATP or the lack of ADP, and the brown fat can simply metabolize excess energy and generate heat.

Exercise does more than promote weight loss and toned muscles. It also improves cognition and glucose metabolism. Improving glucose metabolism can help reverse the changes associated with type II diabetes—elevated blood glucose, elevated blood insulin, loss of sensitivity of the pancreas to glucose, and loss of sensitivity of body tissues to insulin. **Investigating Life: How Could Irisin Mediate the Benefits of Exercise on Cognition?** and Figure 39.17 present experiments showing that irisin is a mediator of benefits of exercise on cognition and glucose metabolism. It seems likely that irisin is a major integrating factor in a large suite of healthful benefits of exercise.

Future directions

The experiments explored in **Investigating Life: How Could Irisin Mediate the Benefits of Exercise on Cognition?** and Figure 39.17 suggest the interesting possibility that irisin could be developed as a therapeutic that might be useful in treating the national epidemic of obesity and type II diabetes. It might also prove to be beneficial in cognitive declines due to conditions such as stroke and Alzheimer's disease. Before such treatments can be developed, however, research is needed on such questions as: Are there potential negative side effects of abnormal elevations of irisin? Is there the potential for abuse of irisin, similar to what has been seen with other growth-promoting agents such as growth hormone and testosterone? It would seem that the safest way to benefit from the actions of irisin would be to use the natural approach of regular exercise to promote its normal production and release.

© Tierfotoagentur/Alamy Stock Photo

You should be able to relate each summary to the adjacent figures. If you go to this visual summary in **Achieve**, you can follow links to figures, animations, activities, and simulations that will help you consolidate the material.

KEY CONCEPT
39.1 Hormones Circulate around the Body and Affect Cells That Have Receptors

Go to Activity 39.1

- Endocrine cells secrete chemical signals that induce responses in other cells that have receptors for those molecules.

- **Hormones** are endocrine signals that circulate in the blood and activate distant target cells.

- **Protein** and **peptide hormones** are water-soluble and have cell surface receptors. **Steroid hormones** are lipid-soluble and have cytoplasmic receptors. Some **amine hormones** are water-soluble and some are lipid-soluble. The same hormone can cause different responses in different target cells.

- Chemical structures of hormones are highly conserved, but functions change.

Figure 39.1

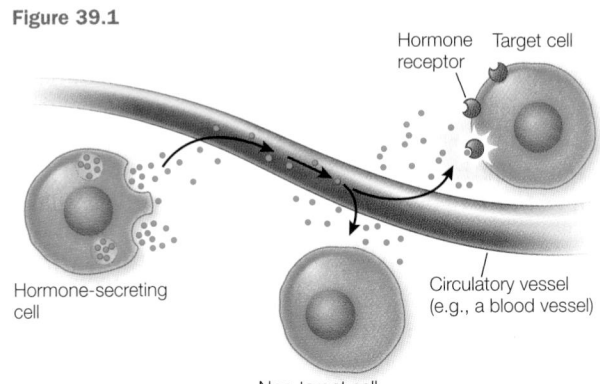

Questions

1. What are the functional consequences of insulin being water-soluble and estrogen being lipid-soluble?

2. How and why does epinephrine cause glycogen to be broken down in the liver, but also cause decreased activity in the gut?

KEY CONCEPT
39.2 The Endocrine and Nervous Systems Work Together

Go to Animation 39.1

- The **pituitary gland** is the interface between the nervous and endocrine systems.

- The **posterior pituitary** secretes **antidiuretic hormone** (**ADH**) and **oxytocin**. The **anterior pituitary** secretes four **tropic hormones**, as well as **growth hormone** (**GH**), **prolactin, endorphins, enkephalins**, and **melanocyte-stimulating hormone** (**MSH**).

- The anterior pituitary is controlled by hypothalamic neurohormones.

- Hormone release is controlled by negative-feedback loops.

Figure 39.7

Questions

1. If a young woman had an accident that destroyed her pituitary, what effects would you expect to see on her metabolic rate, menstrual cycle, and urine production, and why?

2. ADH acts on the kidney and on blood vessels. How do these two different actions contribute to the same physiological effect?

KEY CONCEPT

39.3 Hormones Play Important Roles in Development

Go to **Animation 39.2**

- **Prothoracicotropic hormone** (**PTTH**) and **ecdysone** control molting in arthropods, and **juvenile hormone** prevents maturation.

- In mammals, **androgens**, **estrogens**, and **progesterone** control sexual development, secondary sexual characteristics, and reproductive functions.

Questions

1. Why do many insecticides contain analogs of juvenile hormone?

2. If you injected the gonadotropins LH and FSH into a juvenile mammal, would you expect to see responses in the testes and ovaries? Why or why not?

Figure 39.11

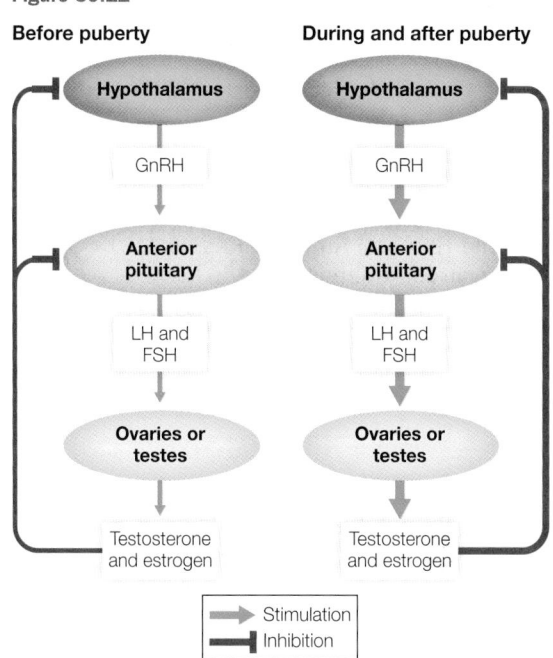

KEY CONCEPT

39.4 Hormones Regulate Metabolism and the Internal Environment

Go to **Activity 39.2** and **Animation 39.3**

- The **thyroid gland** produces and secretes T_3 and T_4, which control many aspects of cell metabolism.

- Blood calcium is regulated by three hormones: **calcitonin**, **parathyroid hormone** (**PTH**), and **calcitriol**.

- Three hormones secreted by the pancreas—**insulin**, **glucagon**, and **somatostatin**—regulate blood glucose.

- The **adrenal medulla** produces and releases epinephrine and norepinephrine.

- The **adrenal cortex** produces **aldosterone**, which stimulates the kidneys to conserve sodium and excrete potassium; **cortisol**, which mediates stress responses; and small amounts of sex steroids.

- The **pineal gland** releases **melatonin**, a hormone involved in controlling biological rhythms.

Questions

1. Why are thyroid hormones well suited for mediating seasonal adaptations?

2. Why is PTH considered to be the most important regulator of blood calcium?

3. Why are β-adrenergic blockers rather than α-adrenergic blockers used to control anxiety?

4. Why is it adaptive that muscle and fat require insulin for adequate uptake of glucose, but the brain does not?

Figure 39.15

Go to **Achieve** for the eBook, **LearningCurve**, animations, activities, simulations, and additional resources and assignments.

40 Immunology: Animal Defense Systems

KEY CONCEPTS

40.1 Animals Use Innate and Adaptive Mechanisms for Defense

40.2 Innate Defenses Are Nonspecific

40.3 Adaptive Defenses Are Specific

40.4 The Humoral Adaptive Response Involves Antibodies

40.5 The Cellular Adaptive Response Involves T Cells and Receptors

40.6 Malfunctions in Immunity Can Be Harmful

Soldiers being vaccinated against smallpox in the nineteenth century. Using vaccines continues to be important in protecting an army as it is exposed to pathogens in the environment.

© Universal History Archive/UIG/Getty Images

▶Investigating LIFE

Vaccines and Immunity

Vials in two deep freezers, one in Atlanta, Georgia, and one in Siberia, are all that is left of the smallpox virus. Smallpox killed as many as 500 million people in the twentieth century, but the disease made its last appearance in 1978 and was declared eradicated in 1980, thanks to vaccination. A vaccine is usually an inactive form of a pathogen or toxin that provokes the immune system to produce antibodies: specific proteins directed against the target. The immune system destroys whatever is bound to the antibodies.

The eradication of smallpox was a spectacular international accomplishment. So why hasn't vaccination for other potentially lethal diseases such as the flu (influenza) been widely accepted by the public? More than one-third of Americans refuse flu shots, and a significant number of parents refuse vaccination for their children.

Unfortunately, those who refuse vaccination may harm people other than themselves. A vaccination program can control or eradicate a disease only if a high percentage (typically above 80%) of people are vaccinated, thus disrupting the chain of infection from person to person. A high level of vaccination results in "herd immunity," a state in which even those who cannot be vaccinated or who have weak immune systems are protected from infection. This protection is lost if the vaccination rate falls below the level needed for herd immunity. The elderly or sick, and infants with their immature immune systems, are most at risk.

The best way to develop herd immunity in a population is compulsory vaccination. In many countries, vaccination is a prerequisite for school enrollment and military enlistment and is required during epidemics. For example, during the periodic smallpox epidemics in the twentieth century in the United States, doctors accompanied by police would go into neighborhoods where the disease raged, vaccinating all those who were uninfected and removing infected people to quarantine. You can imagine the reaction of parents whose children were taken away, often to die. Henning Jacobson was arrested when he refused vaccination during a smallpox epidemic. He took his case to the U.S. Supreme Court, which ruled in 1905 that each state is entitled to protect its citizens. This provided a legal framework for compulsory vaccination that continues to this day. But opposition and court challenges continue.

 What are the mechanisms and implications of long-lasting immunity? (Find the answer on page 909.)

40.1 Animals Use Innate and Adaptive Mechanisms for Defense

Learning Objectives

40.1.1 Describe the three phases of an internal response to a pathogen.

40.1.2 Distinguish between innate and adaptive immunity.

40.1.3 Describe how the Toll-like receptor (TLR) pathway is activated in innate immunity.

40.1.4 List the three categories of white blood cells and gives examples of each.

Animals have several ways of defending themselves against **pathogens**—harmful organisms and viruses that can cause disease. Once a pathogen breaches the physical defenses designed to keep it out, internal defense systems are activated. These internal systems are based on differences between *self* and *nonself*, or foreign, molecules. The internal defensive response involves three phases:

1. *Recognition phase.* The organism recognizes the pathogen as foreign because it can discriminate between self and nonself.

2. *Activation phase.* The recognition event leads to a mobilization of cells and molecules to fight the invader.

3. *Effector phase.* The mobilized cells and molecules destroy the invader.

There are two general types of defense mechanisms:

1. **Innate defenses**, *or nonspecific defenses, are mechanisms that provide the first line of defense against pathogens.* Innate defenses typically act very rapidly and include physical barriers such as the skin, molecules that are toxic to invaders, and phagocytic cells that ingest invaders. (Recall from Key Concept 6.5 that phagocytosis is a form of endocytosis, in which a cell engulfs a large particle or another cell.) The innate immune system recognizes broad classes of organisms and molecules, such as viruses, bacteria, fungi, protists, parasitic worms, and various toxins.

2. **Adaptive defenses** *are aimed at specific pathogens and are activated by cells in the innate immune system.* For example, the adaptive immune system can make an antibody protein that will recognize, bind to, and aid in the destruction of a specific pathogen, if that specific pathogen ever enters the body. Adaptive defenses are typically slower to develop than innate defenses and longer-lasting.

An organism that is able to avoid the detrimental effects of attack by a pathogen is said to have immunity to that pathogen.

Innate defenses evolved before adaptive defenses

All animals have innate defenses against their enemies. For example, horseshoe crabs first appeared in the fossil record about 400 million years ago. These arthropods, represented today by four living species, rely only on innate defenses. These defenses include barriers, defensive cells, and defensive molecules (**Figure 40.1**):

- Barriers include physical mechanisms for resisting infections. The hard exoskeleton that is characteristic of arthropods prevents pathogens from getting inside horseshoe crabs.

- Defensive cells include those that bind to microbial pathogens, ingest them by endocytosis, and destroy them by hydrolysis. Amebocytes in the blood of horseshoe crabs fulfill this defensive role.

- Horseshoe crabs have a wide array of defensive molecules that are released from cells in their blood and are toxic to invading pathogens. These molecules include peptides that disrupt bacterial cell membranes, rendering them permeable; and peptides that bind to bacterial surfaces and cross-link them.

(A) An Atlantic horseshoe crab (*Limulus polyphemus*)

A barrier is the first line of innate defense.

© iStock.com/LagunaticPhoto

(B) Amebocytes

Amebocytes recognize and ingest pathogen cells.

From P. Armstrong and M. Conrad. 2008. Blood Collection from the American Horseshoe Crab, *Limulus Polyphemus*. *J Vis Exp* 20: e958, doi:10.3791/958

(C) Blood cell

Granules in blood cell contain defensive molecules.

T. Shigenaga et al. 1993. *J Biochem* 114: 307–316

Figure 40.1 Innate Defenses in Horseshoe Crabs (**A**) A hard, impermeable exoskeleton acts as a barrier against pathogens. (**B**) Phagocytic amebocytes ingest and hydrolyze invading pathogens. (**C**) Blood cells release chemicals harmful to invading pathogens.

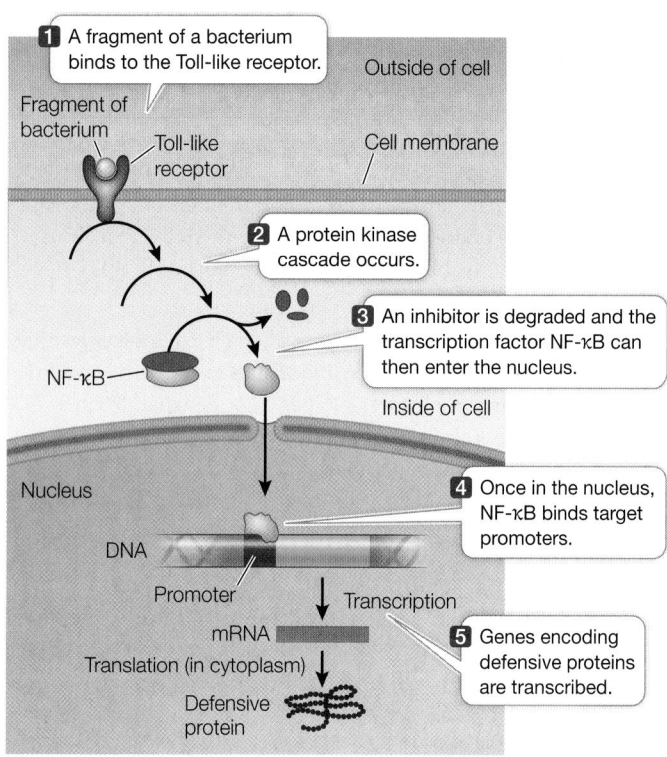

1 A fragment of a bacterium binds to the Toll-like receptor.

Outside of cell

Fragment of bacterium

Toll-like receptor

Cell membrane

2 A protein kinase cascade occurs.

3 An inhibitor is degraded and the transcription factor NF-κB can then enter the nucleus.

NF-κB

Inside of cell

Nucleus

4 Once in the nucleus, NF-κB binds target promoters.

DNA

Promoter

Transcription

mRNA

Translation (in cytoplasm)

Defensive protein

5 Genes encoding defensive proteins are transcribed.

Figure 40.2 Cell Signaling and Defense Binding of a pathogenic molecule or fragment to the Toll-like receptor initiates a signal transduction pathway that results in the transcription of genes whose products are involved in innate defenses.

Studies of internal innate immune defenses, along with genome sequencing, have revealed that the recognition and activation phases evolved very early in animals. For example, animals as diverse as humans and fruit flies share a class of receptors called **Toll-like receptors** (**TLRs**) that participate in innate defense responses. These receptors recognize foreign molecules called pathogen-associated molecular patterns (PAMPs). In vertebrates, each TLR recognizes and binds to a specific molecule that is found in a broad class of pathogens, such as a component of the bacterial cell wall. Binding triggers a signal transduction pathway that ends with the expression of genes for anti-pathogen molecules (**Figure 40.2**). This pathway exists in some form in many animal groups, including humans.

Connect the Concepts The recognition of PAMPs is widespread in immunity and is therefore an evolutionarily ancient mechanism. Plants have an immune response to invading pathogens that also involves PAMPs; see Key Concept 37.2.

Mammals have both innate and adaptive defenses

Mammals, like other vertebrates, have both kinds of defense mechanisms, and these mechanisms are the focus of this chapter. In mammals, the innate and adaptive mechanisms operate together as a coordinated defense system. Table 40.1 gives an overview of these defenses. Innate immunity is the body's first line of defense, because the adaptive defenses often require days or even weeks to become effective.

TABLE 40.1 | Innate and Adaptive Immune Responses to an Infection

Role	System	Mechanisms
Prevent invasion	Innate, nonspecific (first line)	Physical barrier (skin and lining of organs)
		Dryness, low pH
		Mucus
		Lysozyme, defensins
Early response to invasion (< 96 hr)	Innate, nonspecific (second line)	Inflammation
		Phagocytosis
		Natural killer cells
		Complement system
		Interferons
Late response to invasion (> 96 hr)	Adaptive, specific	Humoral immunity (antibodies from B cells)
		Cellular immunity (T cells)

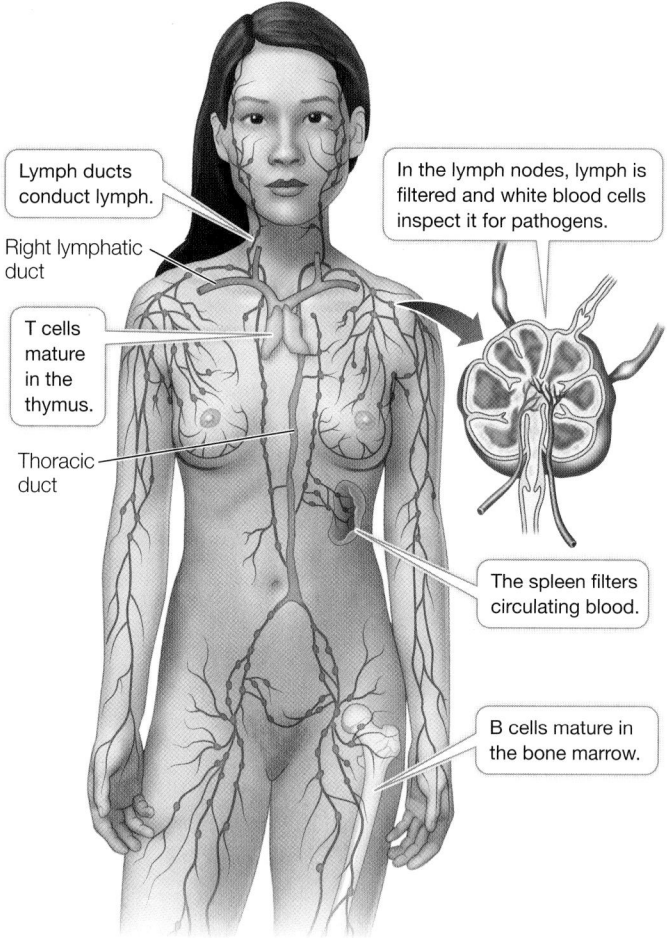

Lymph ducts conduct lymph.

Right lymphatic duct

T cells mature in the thymus.

Thoracic duct

In the lymph nodes, lymph is filtered and white blood cells inspect it for pathogens.

The spleen filters circulating blood.

B cells mature in the bone marrow.

Figure 40.3 The Human Lymphatic System A network of ducts and vessels collects lymph from body tissues and carries it toward the heart, where it mixes with blood to be pumped back to the tissues. Other lymphoid tissues, including the lymph nodes, thymus, spleen, and bone marrow, are also essential to the body's defense system.

 View in Achieve
Activity 40.1 The Human Defense System

Blood and lymph tissues play important roles in defense

The components of the mammalian defense system are dispersed throughout the body and interact with almost all of its other tissues and organs. The lymphatic system is an essential part of the immune system and includes the thymus, bone marrow, spleen, lymph nodes, lymphatic vessels, and lymph (**Figure 40.3**). The lymphatic system functions in partnership with the circulatory system, which includes the heart and blood vessels. Blood and lymph have nondefensive functions that will be discussed in Chapter 48. They each have central roles in defense as well.

Blood and lymph both consist of liquids in which cells are suspended:

- **Blood plasma** is a yellowish solution containing ions, small molecule solutes, and soluble proteins. Suspended in the plasma are red blood cells, white blood cells, and platelets (cell fragments essential to blood clotting). Whereas red blood cells are normally confined to the closed circulatory system (the heart, arteries, capillaries, and veins), white blood cells and platelets are also found in the lymph.

- **Lymph** is a fluid that is derived from the blood (but lacking red blood cells) and other tissues that accumulates in intercellular spaces throughout the body. From these spaces, the lymph moves slowly into the vessels of the lymphatic system. Tiny lymph capillaries conduct this fluid to larger ducts that eventually join together, forming two large vessels, the thoracic duct and right lymphatic duct, which join a major vein (the left subclavian vein) near the heart. By this system of vessels, the lymph is eventually returned to the blood and the circulatory system.

At many sites along the lymph vessels are small, roundish structures called **lymph nodes**, which contain large numbers of a type of white blood cell called **lymphocytes**. As lymph passes through a lymph node, the lymphocytes encounter foreign cells and molecules that have entered the body, and if they are recognized as foreign, an immune response is initiated.

White blood cells play many defensive roles

One milliliter of human blood typically contains about *5 billion* red blood cells and *7 million* of the larger **white blood cells** (also called leukocytes). All of these cells originate from multipotent stem cells (constantly dividing undifferentiated cells that can form several different cell types) in the bone marrow. There

are three major groups of white blood cells: granulocytes, monocyte-derived cells, and lymphocytes (**Figure 40.4**). Granulocytes include basophils, eosinophils, and neutrophils, all of which circulate in the blood, and the mast cells, which are found in various tissues around the body. Monocyte-derived cells include monocytes and the macrophages and dendritic cells that monocytes can develop into. Macrophages and dendritic cells are both found in tissues and play important roles in stimulating an adaptive immune response (after traveling to lymph nodes). Lymphocytes include the B cells and T cells, which are the workhorses of the adaptive immune response and reside primarily in the lymph nodes, and the natural killer cells, which are found in various tissues and are responsible for attacking virus-infected and tumor cells. Neutrophils, monocytes, macrophages, and dendritic cells are all able to phagocytose microbial particles. Both defensive and cell signal proteins play fundamental roles in the interactions and functioning of these cells.

Cell category		Maturation location	Primary site of function	Function
Granulocytes				
	Basophils (I, A)	Bone marrow	Blood	Release histamine
	Eosinophils (A)	Bone marrow	Blood	Kill antibody-coated parasites
	Neutrophils (I)	Bone marrow	Blood	Stimulate inflammation; phagocytosis
	Mast cells (I)	Tissues	Tissues	Release histamine when damaged
Monocyte-derived				
	Monocytes (I, A)	Blood	Blood and lymph	Phagocytosis; antigen presentation; develop into macrophages and dendritic cells
	Macrophages (I, A)	Tissues	Tissues and lymph	Phagocytosis; antigen presentation
	Dendritic cells (I, A)	Tissues	Tissues and lymph	Phagocytosis; antigen presentation
Lymphocytes				
	B cells (A)	Bone marrow	Lymph	Differentiate to form antibody-producing cells and memory cells; antigen presentation
	T cells (A)	Thymus	Lymph	Kill virus-infected cells and cancer cells; regulate activities of other white blood cells
	Natural killer cells (I)	Lymph nodes	Tissues	Attack and lyse virus-infected and cancer cells

Figure 40.4 **White Blood Cells**   White blood cells have key roles in both innate (I) and adaptive (A) immunity.

View in Achieve
Animation 40.1 **Cells of the Immune System**

Immune system proteins bind pathogens or signal other cells

The cells that defend mammalian bodies work together, interacting with one another and with the cells of invading pathogens. These cell–cell interactions are accomplished by a variety of key proteins, including receptors, other cell surface proteins, and signal molecules. Four of the major players are listed here and are discussed in more detail later in the chapter.

1. **Antibodies** are proteins that bind specifically to certain substances identified by the immune system as being foreign. The specific molecules that bind to antibodies are called **antigens**. Antibodies are produced by B cells.

2. **Major histocompatibility complex (MHC)** proteins are used to display antigens on the surfaces of self cells, so that the antigens can be detected by the T cells of the immune system. MHC proteins also function as important self-identifying labels.

3. **T cell receptors** are integral membrane proteins on the surfaces of T cells. They recognize and bind to antigens presented by the MHC proteins on the surfaces of other cells.

4. **Cytokines** are soluble signal proteins released by many cell types. They bind to cell surface receptors and alter the behavior of their target cells.

KEY CONCEPT
40.1 Recap and Assess

All animals have innate defenses against pathogens, and vertebrates have innate and adaptive defenses. Both kinds of mechanisms are based on the ability to differentiate self from nonself. Innate defenses target a broad range of foreign molecules and organisms, whereas adaptive defenses target specific molecules and pathogens. Both innate and adaptive defenses involve specialized white blood cells.

1. Describe three characteristics of innate immunity and adaptive immunity that distinguish them from each other.

2. Some people have a rare genetic disease that results in defective signaling in the TLR pathway. What would be the phenotype of such individuals?

3. If you compared the genomes of an insect and a human with regard to the presence of genes involved in immunity, what might you find?

The outcome of an infectious disease—the life or death of the host—often depends on the success of both rapid, innate responses and long-lasting, adaptive responses to invading pathogens. We turn now to the innate defenses that protect vertebrates from disease.

KEY CONCEPT
40.2 Innate Defenses Are Nonspecific

Learning Objectives

40.2.1 Summarize the various mechanisms for preventing entry into the body by a pathogen.

40.2.2 Explain how the innate defense system defends against a pathogen once it has entered the body.

40.2.3 List the steps in the inflammatory response.

Innate defenses are general protection mechanisms that attempt to stop pathogens from entering the body or to quickly eliminate those that do manage to enter. They are "innate," meaning no previous experience with the pathogen is required, and are thus "ready to go," in contrast to adaptive responses, which take time to develop after a pathogen or toxin has been encountered and recognized as being foreign.

Innate immunity is sometimes described as nonspecific immunity because it is applied indiscriminately to any potentially harmful invader. There are two lines of innate defense (**Figure 40.5**). The first line of innate defense is encountered by a potential pathogen as soon as it lands on the surface of an animal.

Preventing invasion is the first line of defense

A pathogen that cannot enter the body can do little harm. Regions where the body is in contact with the environment are areas where innate defenses are deployed to prevent invasion. Consider the formidable challenges that a pathogenic bacterium faces to invade the body:

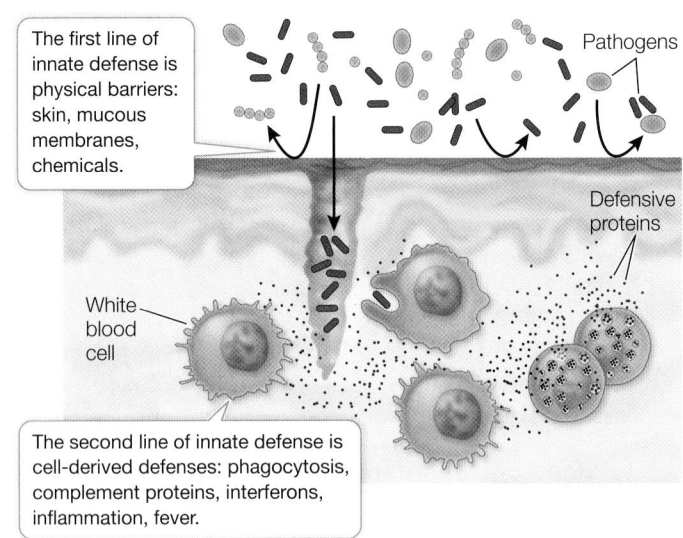

The first line of innate defense is physical barriers: skin, mucous membranes, chemicals.

Pathogens

Defensive proteins

White blood cell

The second line of innate defense is cell-derived defenses: phagocytosis, complement proteins, interferons, inflammation, fever.

Figure 40.5 Innate Immunity Several innate factors act to prevent invasion. If pathogens do enter the body, other innate factors quickly provide nonspecific defenses against them.

 Media Clip 40.1 The Chase Is On: Phagocyte versus Bacteria
Life12e.com/mc40.1

- The *physical barrier*: A bacterium has to penetrate a tissue in order to invade the body. Cells in tissues that are at body surfaces in contact with the environment, such as gut cells, are held together by tight junctions, making entry difficult. Skin is about 30 cell layers thick, making it especially difficult to penetrate; it also sheds constantly and is salty and dry—conditions that inhibit microbial growth. For a bacterium to penetrate the skin, a break is usually required, which is why cuts and scrapes increase the risk of infection.

- The *presence of mucus*: **Mucus** is a slippery secretion produced by mucous membranes found on the surfaces of many internal epithelial tissues in contact with the external environment, such as in the digestive, respiratory, and urogenital systems (see Key Concept 38.1). Mucus traps microorganisms so they can be removed by the beating of cilia (see Figure 5.19), which continuously move the mucus and its trapped debris away.

- The *presence of lysozyme*: **Lysozyme** is an enzyme made by cells of the mucous membranes that is secreted into mucus and attacks the cell walls of many bacteria, causing them to lyse (burst open).

- The *presence of defensins*: **Defensins**, also made by mucous membranes, are peptides of 18–45 amino acids that contain hydrophobic domains. They are toxic to a wide range of pathogens, including bacteria, microbial eukaryotes, and enveloped viruses. Defensins insert themselves into the cell membranes of these organisms and make the membranes permeable, thus killing the invaders. Defensins are also produced in phagocytes, where they kill pathogens ingested by phagocytosis. Plants also produce defensins in response to pathogen exposure.

- The *presence of extreme conditions*: Harsh conditions in the gut can also kill pathogens. For example, gastric juice in the stomach is a deadly environment for many bacteria because of the hydrochloric acid and proteases that are secreted into it.

- The *presence of normal flora*: Bacteria and fungi that normally live and reproduce in great numbers on our body surfaces without causing disease will compete with pathogens for space and nutrients.

Connect the Concepts Key Concept 37.2 describes constitutive and induced responses to pathogens in plants. Among the latter are the pathogenesis-related (PR) proteins, which are similar to defensins produced by animals. These small peptides bind to fungal membranes and are toxic to a wide range of fungal targets, but they are not toxic to plant or animal cells. Other PR proteins may serve as alarm signals to plant cells that have not yet been attacked.

Recognition and response involve a variety of cells and proteins

The second line of innate defense involves recognition of a pathogen or damage. Several types of white blood cells, including neutrophils, monocyte-derived cells, and mast cells (see Figure 40.4), express receptors that give them the ability to recognize molecules associated with pathogens or with cell damage (as might be produced with trauma). Natural killer cells also have the ability to

recognize self cells that are expressing abnormal proteins on their cell surface, as might occur when the cells are infected by a bacterium or exhibiting a cancer phenotype. The response to recognition varies depending on the cell type but often involves a variety of proteins, including complement proteins and interferons.

PHAGOCYTES   Some phagocytes, such as neutrophils and monocytes, travel freely in the circulatory and lymphatic systems; others, such as macrophages and dendritic cells, move out of blood vessels and adhere to certain tissues. When these cells recognize a pathogenic cell, virus, pathogen molecule, or molecule produced by cell damage, they ingest it by phagocytosis (**Figure 40.6A**). Inside the phagocyte the phagosome (vesicle with ingested particle) fuses with a lysosome to form a phagolysosome (or secondary lysosome), which results in the digestion of the ingested pathogen (**Figure 40.6B**; see also Figure 5.12). In addition, phagocytes may release cytokines to recruit other phagocytes. Finally, several phagocytes, especially monocyte-derived dendritic cells, are antigen-presenting cells that travel to the lymph nodes to initiate an adaptive immune response. Dendritic cells act as messengers

(A)

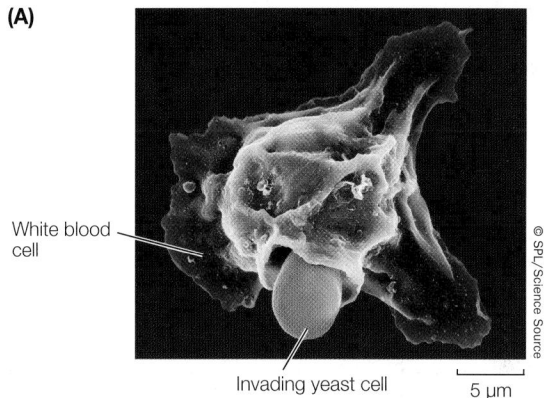

White blood cell

Invading yeast cell

© SPL/Science Source

5 µm

(B)

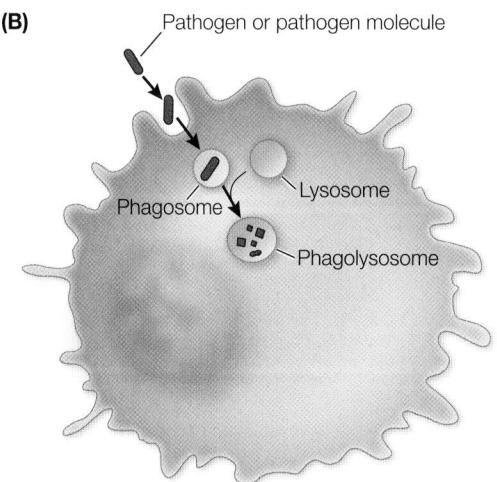

Pathogen or pathogen molecule

Lysosome

Phagosome

Phagolysosome

Figure 40.6 **Phagocytes Endocytose Pathogens and Related Molecules**   Several types of white blood cells are phagocytic and will endocytose cells, viruses, and various molecules as part of an immune response. (**A**) A white blood cell in the process of ingesting an invading yeast cell. (**B**) Once ingested in a vesicle (phagosome), fusion with a lysosome causes degradation of the invading pathogen.

between the innate and adaptive immune systems. The dendritic cell "presents" an antigenic fragment from an ingested pathogen on its surface, along with class II MHC proteins, to T cells (see Key Concept 40.5). The dendritic cell also secretes signals that activate other cells of the adaptive immune system.

NATURAL KILLER CELLS   One type of lymphocyte, the **natural killer cells**, can distinguish virus-infected cells and some tumor cells from their normal counterparts and initiate apoptosis (programmed cell death) of these target cells. In addition to exhibiting this innate defense action, natural killer cells interact with the adaptive immune system by lysing antibody-labeled target cells.

MAST CELLS   **Mast cells** are found predominantly in peripheral tissues in contact with the environment. They are stimulated by pathogens or injury. One of their functions is to initiate the inflammatory response by releasing cytokines and other chemical signals (see the next section). Mast cells also interact with the adaptive immune system and are able to respond to particular antigens after they bind a specific class of antibodies (IgE; see Key Concept 40.4) produced during an adaptive response.

COMPLEMENT PROTEINS   Vertebrate blood contains more than 20 different proteins that make up the antimicrobial complement system. This system can be activated by various mechanisms, including both innate and adaptive defense responses. The proteins act in a characteristic sequence, or cascade, with each protein activating the next:

1. First, the proteins attach to specific components on the surface of a microbe or to an antibody that has already bound to the microbe's surface. In either case, binding helps phagocytes recognize and destroy the microbe.

2. Then, complement proteins activate the inflammatory response (see Figure 40.7) and attract phagocytes to the site of infection.

3. Finally, complement proteins lyse invading cells (such as bacteria).

INTERFERONS   When a cell is infected by a pathogen, it produces small amounts of signal proteins called **interferons** that increase the resistance of neighboring cells to infection. Interferons are a class of cytokines and have been found in many vertebrates. Various molecules, including double-stranded (virus) RNA, induce the production of interferons. Thus interferons are particularly important as a defense against viruses. Interferons bind to receptors on the cell membranes of uninfected cells, stimulating a signaling pathway that inhibits virus reproduction if the cells are

Figure 40.7 Interactions of Cells and Chemical Signals Result in Inflammation   Histamine and other signals are released from mast cells to initiate the inflammatory response. The chemical signals associated with inflammation attract phagocytes, which digest the pathogens and damaged cells.

Q: Antihistamines are a class of drugs widely used to treat people with inflammation. How do you think they work?

 View in Achieve
Activity 40.2 Inflammatory Response

subsequently infected. In addition, interferons stimulate the cells to hydrolyze bacterial or virus proteins to peptides, an initial step in adaptive immunity (see Key Concept 40.3).

Inflammation is a coordinated innate response to infection or injury

When mammalian tissue is damaged because of infection or injury, the body responds with **inflammation**. This response can happen almost anywhere in the body, internally as well as on the surface. Inflammation is an important phenomenon: it isolates the damaged area to stop the spread of the damage; it recruits cells and molecules to the damaged location to kill potential invaders; and it promotes healing. The first responders to tissue damage are mast cells, which adhere to the skin and the linings of organs and release numerous chemical signals, including:

- **Tumor necrosis factor**, a cytokine protein that kills target cells and activates immune cells.

- **Prostaglandins**, fatty acid derivatives involved in various responses, including the widening of blood vessels. Prostaglandins interact with nerve endings and are partly responsible for the pain caused by inflammation.

- **Histamine**, an amino acid derivative that leads to the important process of dilation and leakiness of blood vessels. When released in excess, as in some allergic reactions, histamines cause itchy, watery eyes and rashes.

The redness and heat of inflammation result from the dilation and leakiness of blood vessels in the infected or injured area (**Figure 40.7**). Phagocytes, especially neutrophils, which are abundant in the blood, enter the inflamed area, where they engulf the invaders and dead tissue cells. Phagocytes are responsible for most of the healing associated with inflammation. They produce several cytokines, which (among other functions) can signal the brain to produce a fever. This rise in body temperature accelerates B and T cell production and phagocytosis, thereby speeding the immune response. In some cases, pathogens are temperature-sensitive and their growth is inhibited. The pain of inflammation results from increased pressure due to swelling, the action of leaked enzymes on nerve endings, and the action of prostaglandins, which increase the sensitivity of the nerve endings to pain.

Following inflammation, pus may accumulate. Pus is a mixture of leaked fluid and dead cells: bacteria, neutrophils (the most abundant white blood cells), and damaged body cells. Pus is a normal result of inflammation and is gradually consumed and further digested by macrophages.

KEY CONCEPT
40.2 Recap and Assess

Innate immunity is the first line of defense against pathogens. Innate immunity includes barriers to prevent invasion, such as skin, mucus, enzymes, and chemicals, and after invasion, cellular responses involving the recognition of various molecules. Recognition by white blood cells of molecules produced by pathogens or cell trauma leads to coordinated responses such as the production of defensive proteins and inflammation.

1. A pathogenic bacterium lands on a cell in one of your nasal sinuses. Outline the innate defenses that come into play.

2. Your immune system does not mount an innate defense response to a speck of dust that lands in your eye, but it may mount an innate response to a bacterium. Why?

3. When a splinter of wood permeates the skin, the skin swells up. Outline the events by which this occurs.

Often the innate immune system, with its nonspecific defenses, is adequate to prevent or fight off a pathogenic infection. But in many cases this system works together with adaptive immunity, which detects and responds to specific pathogens. We now turn to the development and functioning of adaptive immunity.

KEY CONCEPT
40.3   Adaptive Defenses Are Specific

Learning Objectives

40.3.1 Distinguish between the recognition, activation, and effector phases in adaptive immunity.

40.3.2 Explain the function of antigen-presenting, T-helper, cytotoxic T, and B cells in an adaptive immune response.

40.3.3 Summarize how vaccines provide long-lasting immunity to pathogens.

More than a century ago, experiments showed that guinea pigs that had recovered from a bacterial infection that causes diphtheria produced a substance in their blood that could protect other guinea pigs from infection with lethal doses of the diphtheria bacterium. This observation led to the concept of adaptive immunity and to the understanding that factors promoting immunity are found in blood.

In this key concept we outline the main features of the adaptive immune system. We consider the two major types of adaptive responses: the humoral immune response, which produces antibodies against pathogen antigens that are not associated with particular cells; and the cellular immune response, which produces a response against antigens present on cells that are infected. These two responses work in concert.

What are the key features of adaptive immunity?

Four important features of the adaptive immune system are:

1. Specificity

2. The ability to distinguish self from nonself

3. The ability to respond to an enormous diversity of foreign molecules

4. Immunological memory

SPECIFICITY   The B and T cell lymphocytes are crucial components of adaptive immunity. T cell receptors and the antibodies produced by B cells recognize and bind to specific foreign substances (antigens), and this interaction initiates an adaptive immune response. The specific sites on antigens that the immune system recognizes are called **antigenic determinants**,

Figure 40.8 Antibodies Bind Particular Parts of Antigens
Antibodies bind to a small region of an antigen called an antigenic
determinant, or epitope. A single antigen has numerous potential
epitopes and can thus be recognized by more than one antibody.

or **epitopes** (**Figure 40.8**). An antigenic determinant is a specific portion of a large molecule, such as a certain sequence of amino acids that may be present in a protein. Antigens are usually proteins or polysaccharides, and there can be multiple antigens on a single invading bacterium. A single antigenic molecule can have multiple, different antigenic determinants. The host animal responds to the presence of an antigen with highly specific defenses involving T cell receptors and antibodies. These receptors and soluble proteins bind to the antigenic determinants. Each T cell and each antibody is specific for a single antigenic determinant.

DISTINGUISHING SELF FROM NONSELF   You have seen how the innate immune system identifies foreign molecules and thus distinguishes between self and nonself. The adaptive immune system has a different set of mechanisms for distinguishing self from nonself. The human body contains tens of thousands of different molecules, each with a specific three-dimensional structure capable of generating immune responses. Thus every cell in the body has a tremendous number of antigens. A crucial requirement of an individual's adaptive immune system is that it recognizes the body's own antigens and does not attack them.

DIVERSITY   Challenges to the immune system are numerous. Pathogens take many forms: viruses, bacteria, protists, fungi, and multicellular parasites. Furthermore, each pathogenic species usually exists as many subtly different genetic strains, and each strain possesses multiple surface features. Estimates vary, but a reasonable guess is that a single person can respond specifically to 10 million different antigens. Upon recognizing an antigen, the adaptive immune system responds by activating B and T cell lymphocytes of the appropriate specificity.

IMMUNOLOGICAL MEMORY   After the adaptive immune system responds to a particular type of pathogen once, the adaptive immune system "remembers" that pathogen and can usually respond more rapidly and powerfully to the same threat in the future. This **immunological memory** usually saves us from repeats of childhood diseases such as chicken pox and is the basis for protection using vaccination.

All four of these features of adaptive immune defense characterize both the humoral immune response and the cellular immune response.

Monocyte-derived cells play a key role in activating the adaptive immune system

As you have seen, one way to eliminate pathogens with the innate immune system is phagocytosis. After ingesting a pathogenic organism or infected host cell, monocyte-derived cells display fragments of the pathogen on their cell surfaces. These fragments function as antigens, and **antigen presentation** is one way that components of the innate immune system communicate with the adaptive immune system. Monocyte-derived cells play a key role in activating the adaptive immune system. After engulfing pathogens or infected host cells, these cells migrate to lymph nodes, where they present antigen to immature (previously unexposed) T cells. In addition, the antigen-presenting cells secrete cytokines and other signals that stimulate the activation and differentiation of the T cells.

Two types of adaptive immune responses interact

The adaptive immune system mounts two types of responses against invaders: the humoral immune response and the cellular immune response. These two responses work simultaneously and cooperatively, sharing many mechanisms. In particular, a robust B cell response cannot happen without T cells. We will use the example of a viral infection in an overview of these two types of responses (**Figure 40.9**). These responses also occur when bacteria or other pathogens invade the body and grow inside cells.

B cells that make antibodies are the workhorses of the **humoral immune response**, and **cytotoxic T (T_C) cells** that bind and cause the death of antigen-expressing cells are the workhorses of the **cellular immune response**. There are three phases in both types of adaptive immune responses:

1. *Recognition phase*: In both cellular and humoral immunity, recognition occurs when an antigen is inserted into the cell membrane of an antigen-presenting cell, with the unique antigen structure protruding from the cell membrane. The antigen-presenting white blood cells denoted in Figure 40.4 are particularly good at presenting antigens to **T-helper (T_H) cells**. However, many different cell types, when infected, can present antigens to T_C cells. A virus-infected host cell may present antigen to a T_C cell or it may be phagocytosed by an antigen-presenting white blood cell. Free virus particles or molecules may also be phagocytosed. Antigen-presenting cells partially degrade pathogen molecules, leaving smaller antigens, which are often oligopeptides of about ten amino acids that are directed to the external surface of the cell membrane. Several different antigens from a virus may be presented on the surface of an antigen-presenting cell. Each antigen is recognized by a T_H cell or a T_C cell bearing a T cell receptor protein that is able to recognize (bind) the antigen. In both humoral and cellular immunity, binding initiates the activation phase.

2. *Activation phase*: When the T_H cell recognizes an antigen on an antigen-presenting cell, it propagates and releases

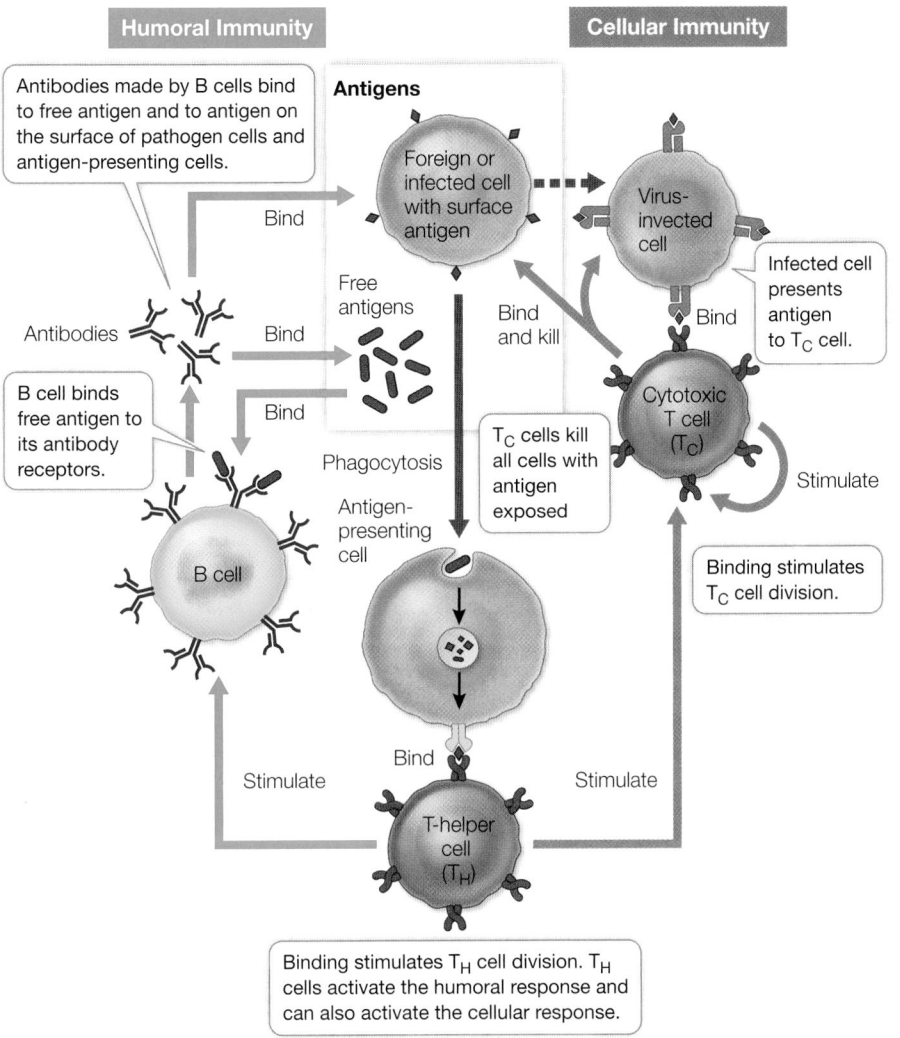

Figure 40.9 **The Adaptive Immune System**   Humoral immunity involves the production of antibodies by B cells. Cellular immunity involves the activation of cytotoxic T cells that bind to cells expressing the antigen. Both antibodies and T cell receptors are specific for a particular antigen. For further details, see Figure 40.18.

Q: In AIDS, a virus infects T$_H$ cells and kills them. What would be the effects on adaptive immunity?

View in Achieve
Animation 40.2 **Pregnancy Test**

Adaptive immunity develops as a result of clonal selection

Before the humoral and cellular immune responses can take place, the body needs to generate a vast diversity of B and T cells that have the ability to bind different antigens. How does this tremendous diversity arise? As we will discuss in Key Concept 40.4, this diversity is generated primarily by DNA changes—chromosomal rearrangements and other mutations—that occur shortly after the B and T cells are formed in the bone marrow. Millions of different B cells develop, each of which can produce only one kind of antibody. Similarly, there are millions of different T cells, each with one specific kind of T cell receptor. Thus the adaptive immune system is "predeveloped"—*all of the machinery available to respond to an immense diversity of antigens is already there, even before the antigens are ever encountered.*

As we have described, when a pathogen enters the vertebrate body it stimulates the innate immune system. In addition to triggering its own defensive responses, the innate immune system triggers adaptive defensive responses via specific antigens that are presented on the surfaces of antigen-presenting cells, particularly dendritic cells. This triggers the proliferation of B and T cells that are specific for those particular antigens. How does this proliferation occur? The answer lies in the process of **clonal selection**: *antigen binding "selects" a particular B or T cell for proliferation.* When an antigen fits the surface receptor on a B or T cell and binds to it, that cell is activated. It divides to form a clone of cells (a genetically identical group derived from a single cell), all of which recognize and react to the same antigen. This process is illustrated for B cells in **Figure 40.10**. Binding and activation select a particular B or T cell, while proliferation generates the clone, hence the term "clonal selection."

Clonal deletion helps the immune system distinguish self from nonself

Normally the body is tolerant of its own molecules. One way that the immune system does this is through the process of **clonal deletion**. This occurs during the early differentiation of T and B cells, when these cells encounter self antigens. There are mature cells expressing self antigens in the areas where T and B cells develop. The presence of self antigens allows developing B and T cells to be tested for binding to self antigens early in their development. Any immature B or T cell that expresses an antibody or T cell receptor that can bind to a self antigen undergoes apoptosis within a short time and is removed from the lymphocyte pool (see Figure 40.10).

cytokines that stimulate B cells and T$_C$ cells bearing receptors that can bind the same antigen to divide. The result is a clone of B cells that function in humoral immunity and a clone of T$_C$ cells that function in cellular immunity. T$_C$ cells can also be directly stimulated upon binding to an antigen-presenting cell; no involvement of T$_H$ cells is needed in this case.

3. *Effector phase*: In the humoral immune response, cells of the B clone produce antibodies that bind to virus particles or virus-infected cells. The bound antibodies attract phagocytes and complement proteins that engulf and destroy the virus and the virus-infected cells. In cellular immunity, cells of the T$_C$ clone bind to virus-infected cells and cause their death, often by stimulating apoptosis.

Figure 40.10 Clonal Selection and Deletion in B Cells   Left side: The binding of a foreign antigen to a specific receptor on the surface of a B cell stimulates that cell to divide, producing a clone of genetically identical cells to fight that invader. Most cells of the clone are plasma cells containing extensive rough endoplasmic reticulum for synthesizing antibodies. Some cells become long-lived memory cells that can last for years or decades in the lymph system (especially in the spleen). Right side: The binding of a self antigen on a B cell leads to apoptosis and loss of the cell.

Q: You may never have been exposed to Ebola virus. Do you have cells that make antibodies against this virus? Explain.

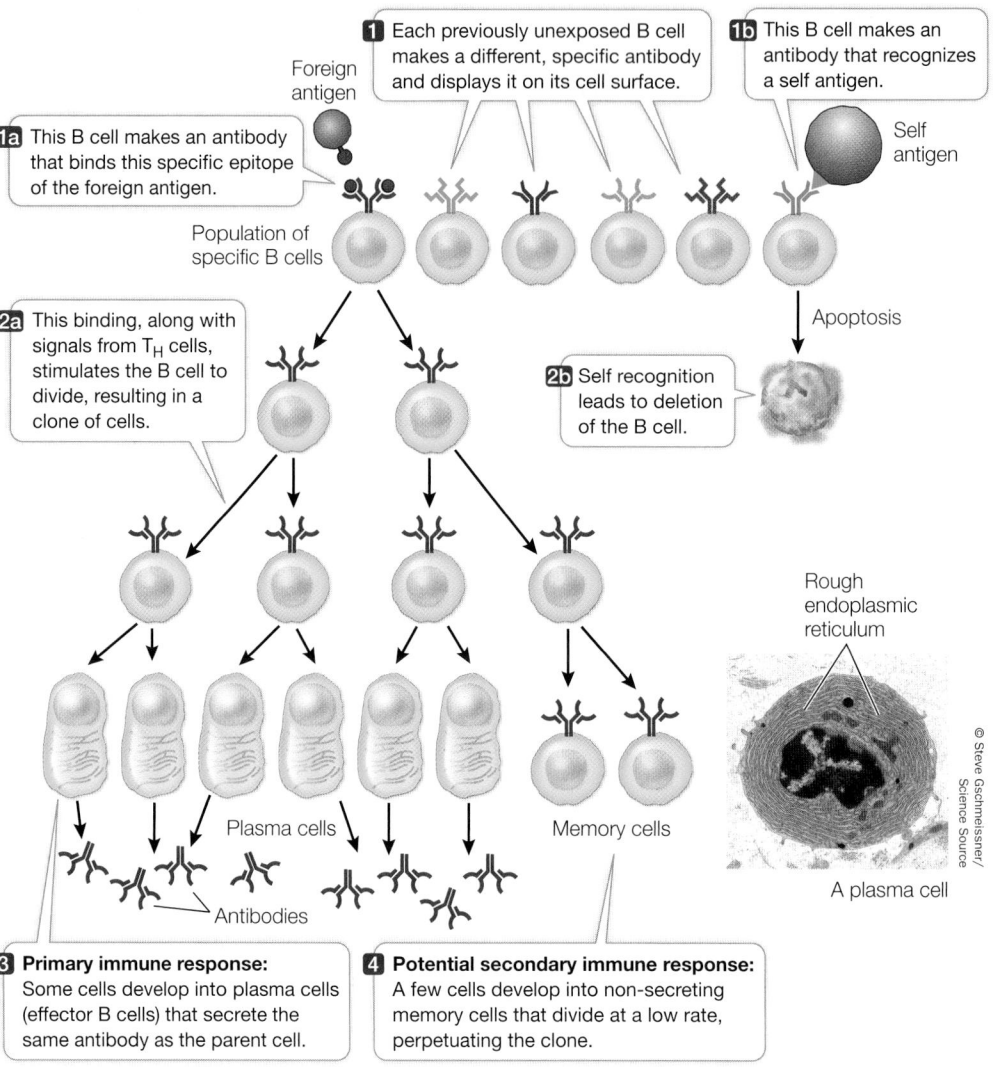

1 Each previously unexposed B cell makes a different, specific antibody and displays it on its cell surface.

1b This B cell makes an antibody that recognizes a self antigen.

Foreign antigen

1a This B cell makes an antibody that binds this specific epitope of the foreign antigen.

Self antigen

Population of specific B cells

2a This binding, along with signals from T$_H$ cells, stimulates the B cell to divide, resulting in a clone of cells.

Apoptosis

2b Self recognition leads to deletion of the B cell.

Rough endoplasmic reticulum

Plasma cells

Memory cells

Antibodies

A plasma cell

© Steve Gschmeissner/ Science Source

3 Primary immune response: Some cells develop into plasma cells (effector B cells) that secrete the same antibody as the parent cell.

4 Potential secondary immune response: A few cells develop into non-secreting memory cells that divide at a low rate, perpetuating the clone.

Immunological memory results in a secondary immune response

The first time a vertebrate animal is exposed to a particular antigen there is a time lag (usually several days) before the B cell–produced antibody molecules and T cells specific to that antigen slowly increase. But for years afterward—sometimes for life—the immune system "remembers" that particular antigen, allowing the body to mount a faster response the next time it encounters the antigen. How does this happen?

The answer lies in the fact that activated B and T cells divide and differentiate to produce *two types* of daughter cells: effector cells and memory cells.

1. **Effector cells** carry out the attack on the antigen. Effector B cells, called **plasma cells**, secrete antibodies. Effector T cells release cytokines and other molecules that initiate reactions that destroy nonself or altered cells. Effector cells live only a few days.

2. **Memory cells** (see Figure 40.10) are long-lived cells that retain the ability to start dividing on short notice to produce more effector and more memory cells. Memory B and T cells may survive in the body for decades, rarely dividing.

Effector cells and memory cells can respond to an antigen in two different ways:

1. When the body first encounters a particular antigen, a **primary immune response** is activated, in which the previously unexposed B and T cells that recognize that antigen proliferate to produce clones of effector and memory cells.

2. After a primary immune response to a particular antigen, subsequent encounters with the same antigen will trigger a much more rapid and powerful **secondary immune response**. The memory cells that bind with that antigen proliferate, launching a huge army of plasma cells and effector T cells. The secondary immune response is more rapid because memory cells are present in higher concentration than are naive B and T cells that have never been activated.

Vaccines are an application of immunological memory

Thanks to immunological memory, exposure to many diseases (including childhood diseases such as chicken pox) provides a natural immunity to those diseases. Furthermore, it is possible to provide artificial immunity against many life-threatening diseases by **vaccination**: the introduction of antigen into the body in a form that does not cause disease.

Vaccination initiates a primary immune response, generating memory cells without making the person ill. Later, if a pathogen carrying the same antigen attacks, specific memory cells already exist. They recognize the antigen and quickly overwhelm the invaders with a massive production of B and T cells and antibodies (Figure 40.11). The success of vaccines at reducing the frequency of many infectious diseases cannot be overstated; several pathogens that used to cause common childhood or adult illnesses—many of them deadly—have become minimal public health issues thanks to vaccination.

Because of mutation, an antigenic determinant on a pathogen can change over time. If the change is significant in terms of three-dimensional structure, a primary immune response directed against an antigen may not result in a secondary immune response with an altered antigen. For pathogens that have rapidly evolving antigens, vaccination will be less effective. You are familiar with this with regard to influenza. More often than not, the annual flu season features a genetic strain of the flu virus that is not sufficiently related to the previous season's vaccine; so a new vaccine, which selects new B cell clones, must be made. A remarkable recent finding is that memory cells can last a long time and help in a response to new, related antigens. People who were exposed to a particular strain of flu retain antibody-making memory cells against that strain for decades and develop a rapid immune

Figure 40.11 The Timing and Magnitude of an Adaptive Immune Response   The primary immune response, initiated by pathogen invasion or by vaccination, leads to a moderate response that may take days to weeks. Reinfection by a pathogen expressing the same antigens results in a much more robust and rapid response that prevents disease.

response to a new, genetically different strain that appears years later. In the case of flu, the memory cells are making antibodies that bind to not just the first strain of flu they responded to, but to later ones as well. Characterizing these antibodies may provide a clue to developing a vaccine that is broadly effective and obviates the need to develop new ones (Investigating Life: What Are the Mechanisms and Implications of Long-Lasting Immunity?).

▶Investigating LIFE   What Are the Mechanisms and Implications of Long-Lasting Immunity?

Experiment

Original Paper: M. Miller et al. 2013. Neutralizing antibodies against previously encountered influenza virus strains increase over time: A longitudinal analysis. *Sci Transl Med* 5: 1–9.

The Framingham Heart Study was begun in 1948 with the objective of finding out the causes of heart disease and stroke. About 5,000 people ages 30–62 and living in the town Framingham, Massachusetts, have been subjected every 2 years to extensive medical exams in an attempt to relate lifestyle factors to heart disease. Subsequent generations have been added to the study ever since. Not only has this study led to major findings about the causes of heart disease, but it has provided a wealth of data on other medical conditions as well. Peter Palese of the Icahn School of Medicine at Mount Sinai Hospital in New York City measured antibodies in blood to flu virus strains from 40 people in the Framingham study, born between 1917 and 1952. They had been exposed to major flu outbreaks in 1957, 1968, and 1977, as well as to the typical flu that comes up every year. Blood samples were examined between 1987 and 2008 to see if these people still had antibodies against the three major flu outbreak strains, and whether these antibody amounts increased over time as people fought off the new, less virulent strains that arise every year.

HYPOTHESIS▶   Exposure to new strains of flu stimulates antibody production against strains to which an individual was exposed previously.

METHOD▶   **1** Obtain blood samples from people born between 1917 and 1952 who had been exposed to Asian flu (1957), Hong Kong flu (1968), and Russian flu (1977).

2 Measure antibodies against the three strains in blood samples taken between 1987 and 2008.

RESULTS▶

Asian flu, 1957
Hong Kong flu, 1968
Russian flu, 1977
Concentration of antibodies to flu strain
1987   2008
Year blood sample taken

CONCLUSION▶   People exposed to flu virus develop long-lasting memory cells that make antibodies that have broad specificity to other flu strains.

Investigating LIFE Work with the Data follows on the next page.

Work with the Data

QUESTIONS▶

1. Blood samples were taken from 1987 to 2008, and the people's reactivity against various flu strains was tested. **Figure A** shows the results for antibodies against the Russian flu strain of 1977 in numerous individuals. The black points, connected by black lines, are the means for each sample period. Note that these people were exposed to many flu strains after 1977. The data shown are typical for the way specific immune reactions are measured. The titer is presented as a reciprocal. For example, a titer of 2 means that undiluted serum sample gave an antibody reaction (titer 1), and so did a dilution of 1 part serum and 1 part water (dilution of 1/2, reciprocal = 2). If the sample was diluted to a titer of 4 (1 part serum, 3 parts water), there was no reaction because the concentration of antibody was too low. The higher the titer number, the more the blood serum could be diluted to still react with the antigen; that is, a higher titer number means there were more antibodies in the original serum sample. What can you conclude about the titer of anti-Russian flu strain over the years 1987–2008?

2. The flu virus mutates rapidly. In contrast, another virus to which people are exposed, cytomegalovirus (CMV), does not mutate rapidly. Antibody titers against CMV were measured, and the data are shown in **Figure B**. The blue points, connected by blue lines, are the means for each sample period. What can you conclude from these data? Compare the antibody response to CMV over time with that against the Russian flu virus strain and comment.

3. A protein on the surface of the flu virus called hemagglutinin (HA) is exposed to the immune system because of its prominent location (**Figure C**). When the flu virus genes mutate, the "head" of the protein tends to accumulate more changes than the stalk. Thus the amino acid sequences of stalk regions of various flu strains are similar. The investigators measured antibodies to the stalk region that were either broadly reactive to various flu strains, or not broadly reactive. The results are shown in the table. What can you conclude about the broadly reactive antibodies? How does this provide a guide for the development of a broadly based flu vaccine?

Types of antibodies to stalk region	Titer
Broadly reactive	4,080
Not broadly reactive	1,024

Go to **Achieve** for a companion Data in Depth exercise.

Figure A

Figure B

Figure C

Head-reactive antibodies are virus strain–specific.

Stalk-reactive antibodies are more general to many virus strains.

KEY CONCEPT

40.3 Recap and Assess

The adaptive immune system reacts against foreign antigens—parts of molecules that can bind antibodies or T cell receptors. An amazing diversity of both antibodies (produced by B cells) and of T cell receptors are produced, resulting in a huge variety of antigens that can be bound. In the primary immune response, B cells and T cells that recognize a particular antigen proliferate by clonal selection. Immunological memory prepares the body for a much stronger secondary immune response.

1. A fellow passenger sneezes on the train and the common cold virus enters your nose and infects cells lining your nasal passage. Outline how your body responds, noting the type and stages of the adaptive immune response.

2. In 2009 the H1N1 strain of influenza spread around the world. People who had been alive at the time of the 1918 epidemic had fewer symptoms. Explain this in terms of immunological memory.

3. How do vaccines make use of immunological memory?

The general features of the adaptive system are that it is premade to respond specifically to virtually any antigen, and it involves an initial primary response to the antigen and a more powerful secondary response when the same antigen is encountered in the future. As we noted, the adaptive system has a humoral response with B cells making antibodies and a cellular response with T cells expressing specific receptors. We now turn to these two types of adaptive responses, beginning with the humoral system.

KEY CONCEPT 40.4   The Humoral Adaptive Response Involves Antibodies

Learning Objectives

40.4.1 Compare the antigen-binding site of an antibody with other proteins such as enzymes that bind other molecules.

40.4.2 Describe the processes that give rise to antibody diversity.

40.4.3 Compare the diversity of specific antibodies in an individual with the diversity of other biological molecules.

Every day in the human body, billions of B cells survive the test of clonal deletion and are released from the bone marrow into the circulatory system and the lymphatic system. B cells are the basis for the humoral immune response.

A B cell begins as an unexposed B cell with a receptor protein on its cell surface that is specific for a particular antigen. The cell is activated by antigen binding to this receptor, and after stimulation by a T_H cell, it gives rise to a clone of plasma cells that make antibodies as well as to a smaller number of memory cells (see Figure 40.10). The stimulation occurs after the B cell presents antigen to a T_H cell expressing a receptor that can recognize the antigen. The T_H cell then secretes cytokines that stimulate the B cell to divide.

Activated plasma cells (effector B cells) can synthesize and secrete large amounts of antibody proteins—up to 2,000 molecules per second! *All the plasma cells arising from a given B cell produce antibodies that are specific for the antigen that originally bound to the parent B cell.* Thus antibody specificity is maintained as B cells proliferate.

 View in Achieve
Animation 40.3 Humoral Immune Response

Antibody protein structure reflects function

Antibodies belong to a class of proteins called **immunoglobulins**. There are several types of immunoglobulins, but all contain a tetramer consisting of four polypeptide chains: two "heavy chains" and two "light chains" (**Figure 40.12**). In each immunoglobulin molecule, the two light chains are identical, and the two heavy chains are identical. Disulfide bonds hold the chains together, characteristically in a Y-like shape.

Each of the four polypeptide chains has a constant region and a variable region (see Figure 40.12A):

- The amino acid sequences of the **constant regions** are similar among the immunoglobulins. They determine the destination and function—the class—of each immunoglobulin.

- The amino acid sequences of the **variable regions** are different for each specific immunoglobulin. Their three-dimensional antigen-binding sites are determined by their amino acid sequences and are responsible for antibody specificity.

Antigen–antibody binding is noncovalent. The attractive forces involved in holding antigen and antibody together include hydrogen bonds, ionic bonds, hydrophobic interactions, and van der Waals forces (see Key Concept 2.2). These attractive forces are generated from particular amino acids at the binding site on both molecules. So for an antibody protein, the sequence of amino acids at the binding site is crucial to its specificity. Generating antibody diversity is thus a molecular genetics challenge, as we will soon discuss.

(A) General structure of an immunoglobulin

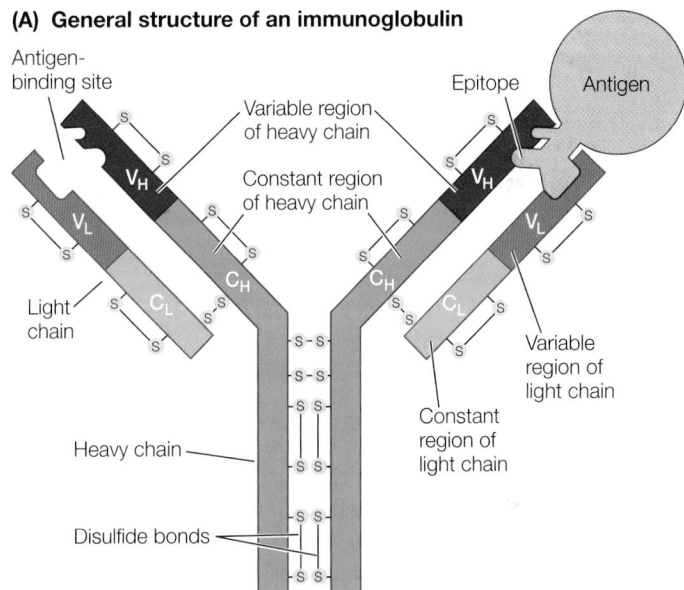

(B) Space-filling model of an immunoglobulin

Figure 40.12 The Structure of an Immunoglobulin
Four polypeptide chains (two light, two heavy) make up an immunoglobulin molecule. Both diagrammatic (**A**) and space-filling (**B**) representations of immunoglobulin are shown here.

 View in Achieve
Activity 40.3 Immunoglobulin Structure

The two antigen-binding sites on each immunoglobulin molecule are identical, making the antibody bivalent (*bi*, "two," + *valent*, "binding"), meaning the molecule can bind two antigen molecules at once. Bivalency, in addition to the presence of multiple epitopes on the surfaces of many antigens (including large proteins, viruses, and bacteria, as you saw in the case of the influenza virus explored in Investigating Life: What Are the Mechanisms and Implications of Long-Lasting Immunity?), permits antibodies to form large complexes with the antigens. These complexes are easy targets for ingestion and breakdown by phagocytes (**Figure 40.13**).

There are five classes of immunoglobulins

While the variable regions are responsible for the specificity of an immunoglobulin, the constant regions of the heavy chain determine the class of the immunoglobulin. **Table 40.2** describes the five classes of immunoglobulins and their functions. The most abundant class in the circulatory system is IgG; these soluble antibody proteins make up about 80% of the total immunoglobulin content of the bloodstream. They are made in greatest quantity during a secondary immune response. IgG molecules defend the body in several ways. For example, after some IgG molecules bind to antigens, they become attached by their heavy chains to phagocytes. This attachment permits the phagocytes to destroy the antigens by phagocytosis (see Figure 40.13B).

Immunoglobulin diversity results from DNA rearrangements and other mutations

Each mature B cell makes antibodies targeted to only one single antigen. And there are millions of possible antigens to which an individual can be exposed. How can the genome encode enough different antibodies to protect the body against all the possible pathogens? Although a single individual makes millions of immunoglobulins that differ in their amino acid sequences, there are not millions of different immunoglobulin genes. It turns out that instead of a single gene encoding each complete immunoglobulin, the genome of the differentiating B cell has multiple different coding regions for each domain of the protein, and diversity is generated by putting together different combinations of these regions. Shuffling of this genetic deck generates the enormous immunological diversity that characterizes each individual mammal.

This shuffling may remind you of the alternative splicing that occurs during RNA processing (see Key Concept 16.5). However, the difference with immunoglobulins is that shuffling to generate antibody diversity occurs at the DNA level: every B cell clone produces a different antibody sequence because it has a different DNA sequence at its heavy and light antibody genes. Given that

every cell in the body begins with essentially identical DNA sequences, how do these DNA sequence differences arise?

Each gene encoding an immunoglobulin chain is in reality a "supergene" assembled by means of genetic recombination from several

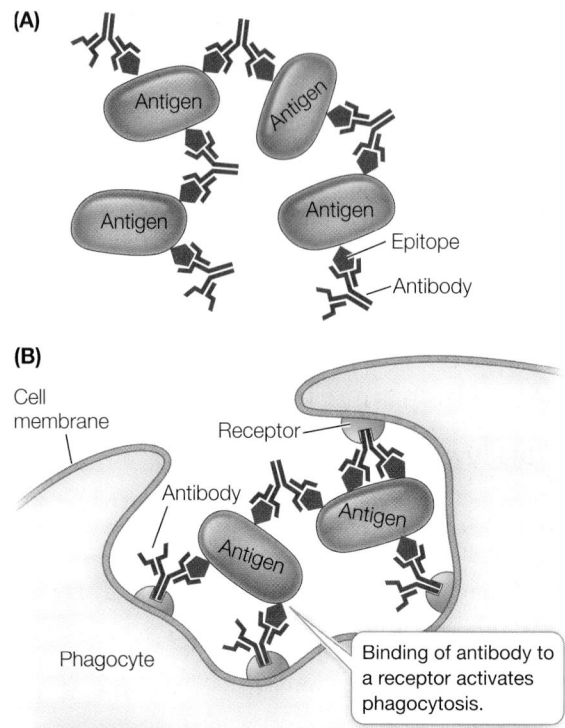

Figure 40.13 Antibodies Cause Aggregation of Antigenic Targets Because antibodies are bivalent, each one can bind to two antigen molecules at once, aggregating them (**A**) and making them easy targets for phagocytes (**B**).

TABLE 40.2 | Immunoglobulin Classes

Class	General structure		Location	Function
IgG	Monomer		Free in blood plasma; about 80% of circulating antibodies	Most abundant antibody in primary and secondary immune responses; crosses placenta and provides immunity to fetus
IgM	Pentamer		Surface of B cell; free in blood plasma	Antigen receptor on B cell membrane; first class of antibodies released by B cells during primary response
IgD	Monomer		Surface of B cell	Cell surface receptor of mature B cell; important in B cell activation
IgA	Dimer		Saliva, tears, breast milk, and other body secretions	Protects mucosal surfaces; prevents attachment of pathogens to epithelial cells
IgE	Monomer		Secreted by plasma cells in skin and tissues lining gastrointestinal and respiratory tracts	Binds to mast cells and basophils to sensitize them to subsequent binding of antigen, which triggers release of histamine that contributes to inflammation and some allergic responses

Figure 40.14 Antibody Supergene
Human immunoglobulin heavy chains
have four domains, each of which is
coded for by one of several possible
genes selected from a cluster of similar
genes. Each immunoglobulin heavy-
chain protein has one gene from each of
the four clusters (V, D, J and constant).

clusters of smaller genes scattered along part of a chromosome (**Figure 40.14**). Every cell in the body has tens of immunoglobulin genes located in separate clusters that are potentially capable of participating in the synthesis of both the variable and constant regions of immunoglobulin chains. In most body cells and tissues, these genes remain intact and separated from one another. But during B cell development, these genes are cut out, rearranged, and joined together in DNA recombination events. One gene from each cluster is chosen randomly for joining, and the others are deleted. In the case of one multigene set, the J genes, some of the extra sequences are removed by RNA splicing (**Figure 40.15**).

In this manner, a unique immunoglobulin supergene is assembled from randomly selected "parts." Each B cell precursor assembles two supergenes, one for a specific heavy chain and the other, assembled independently, for a specific light chain. Each B cell also rearranges, and expresses, genes from a single chromosome for each chain—the other chromosome is not rearranged unless the process fails for the first chromosome. This remarkable example of genetic differentiation generates an enormous diversity of immunoglobulins from the same genome. It is a major exception to the generalization that all somatic cells derived from the fertilized egg have essentially identical DNA sequence.

(A) DNA rearrangement

Variable region

Constant region

V segments   D segments   J segments   C segments

Embryonic DNA

VDJ joining

(B) Transcription and RNA splicing

B cell DNA

V D J   μ

Transcription

After V, D, J, and C DNA segments have been joined, the resulting functional supergene is transcribed.

Primary RNA transcript

μ

Splicing

Splicing of the primary RNA transcript removes any introns and extra J regions.

mRNA

V D J   μ

Translation

Light chain

Heavy chain

Figure 40.15 Heavy-Chain Gene Recombination and RNA Splicing Two types of rearrangements in the heavy-chain gene clusters are required for antibody formation. **(A)** Prior to transcription, DNA is rearranged to join one each of the V, D, and J genes into a variable region supergene. **(B)** After transcription, RNA splicing joins the VDJ region to the constant region and removes extra J regions, if present.

Assembly and display

B cell

Figure 40.14 illustrates the gene families that encode the constant and variable regions of the heavy chain in humans. Multiple genes encode each of the three parts of the variable region: 65 *V*, 27 *D*, and 6 *J* genes, though these numbers can vary across chromosomes. In addition, the sequences of the *V*, *D*, and *J* regions on one copy of a chromosome are likely to differ from those on the other copy because there is a lot of allelic diversity at these genes. Each B cell randomly selects one gene from each of these gene clusters in one of the two chromosome copies to make the final coding sequence (*VDJ*) of the heavy-chain variable region. So the number of different heavy chains that can be made through this random recombination process is quite large:

$$65\ V \times 27\ D \times 6\ J \times 2 \text{ copies of the supergene} = 21,060$$
$$\text{possible combinations}$$

Now consider that the light chains are similarly constructed, although they differ in that there are two supergenes (on different chromosomes), either of which can be used, and the *D* part of the variable region is not present in the light chain. The two supergenes have 40 *V* and 5 *J* and 30 *V* and 4 *J* genes respectively, yielding [(40 × 5) + (30 × 4)] x 2 copies of each supergene = 640 possible combinations. The number of possible combinations of light- and heavy-chain variable regions is thus:

$$21,060 \text{ different heavy chains} \times 640 \text{ different light chains} = 13.5$$
$$\text{million possibilities!}$$

Other mechanisms generate even more diversity:

• When the DNA sequences that encode the *V*, *D*, and *J* regions are rearranged so that they are next to one another, the recombination event is not precise, and errors occur at the junctions. This imprecise recombination can create codon deletions, codon insertions, and frame-shift mutations, with resulting amino acid changes.

• After the DNA sequences are cut and before they are rejoined, the enzyme terminal transferase often adds some nucleotides to the free ends of the DNA pieces. These additional bases create insertion mutations.

• There is a very high spontaneous somatic mutation rate in immunoglobulin genes, 10,000-fold higher than for other genes. Once again, this process creates many new alleles and adds to antibody diversity.

Connect the Concepts When they occur in the coding regions of proteins, point mutations can cause silent, missense, nonsense, loss-of-stop, or frame-shift mutations (see Figure 15.3).

When we include these possibilities with the millions of combinations that can be made by random DNA rearrangements, it is not surprising that the immune system can mount a response to almost any natural or artificial substance.

Once the DNA rearrangements are completed, each supergene is transcribed and then translated to produce an immunoglobulin light chain or heavy chain. These chains combine to form an active immunoglobulin protein. Importantly, each B cell produces a single heavy and light chain so that all of its antibodies bind the same antigen.

DNA rearrangements in B cells occur in the bone marrow, where they are synthesized. In contrast, DNA changes in T cells occur in the thymus, which is where T cell precursors travel after synthesis in the bone marrow. During your lifetime, you continue to synthesize functional B cells in your bone marrow. However, because your thymus rapidly diminishes in size after puberty, you make substantially fewer T cells once you reach adulthood. The repertoire of T cells available at puberty represents the ones you will have at your disposal to mount an immune response for the rest of your life.

 View in Achieve
Animation 40.4 **A B Cell Builds an Antibody**

The constant region is involved in immunoglobulin class switching

Generally, a B cell makes only one class of immunoglobulin at a time. But **class switching** can occur, in which a B cell changes the immunoglobulin class it synthesizes.

Early in its life, a B cell makes IgM and IgD antibodies. The pre-mRNA that the B cell synthesizes for the heavy chain contains the constant regions for both of these antibodies (the μ and δ genes in Figure 40.14), and alternative splicing generates mature mRNAs with either the IgM or IgD constant region. If the B cell later becomes a plasma cell during a humoral immune response, a rearrangement occurs in the cell's DNA, positioning the variable region genes (consisting of the same *V*, *D*, and *J* genes) next to a constant region gene farther away on the original DNA molecule. Such a DNA deletion results in the production of a new immunoglobulin with a different constant region of the heavy chain, and therefore a different function (see Table 40.2). However, this immunoglobulin has the same variable regions—and therefore the same antigen specificity—as the IgM and IgD produced by the parent B cell. The new immunoglobulin protein falls into one of the other three classes (IgA, IgE, or IgG), depending on which of the constant region genes is placed adjacent to the variable region genes.

KEY CONCEPT
40.4 Recap and Assess

The humoral immune response is based on the synthesis by B cells of specific immunoglobulins. The specificity of an immunoglobulin derives from the amino acid sequence of its variable regions on the light and heavy chains. B cells can make millions of immunoglobulins with different specificities through DNA rearrangement of the *V*, *D*, and *J* genes, imprecise recombination, addition of nucleotides, and high mutation rates. The particular class of immunoglobulin produced by a B cell is determined by its constant region.

1. Describe the part of an antibody molecule that interacts with an antigen. How is it similar to the active site of an enzyme? How does it differ?

2. Why don't B cells use alternative RNA splicing to generate antibody diversity?

3. Discuss the diversity of antibody specificities in an individual in relation to the diversity of enzymes. Does every cell in an animal contain genetic information for all of that organism's enzymes? For all of the immunoglobulins? Explain your answer.

By making antibodies, B cells are the major players in the humoral immune response. We now turn to the cellular immune response, and the T cells responsible for it.

The Cellular Adaptive Response Involves T Cells and Receptors

Learning Objectives

40.5.1 Summarize the role of MHC proteins in the activation of T cells.

40.5.2 Explain how T-helper cells are involved in activating the humoral immune response.

40.5.3 Explain how cytotoxic T cells kill virus-infected cells.

40.5.4 Describe how Tregs suppress some cellular and humoral immune responses.

Two types of effector T cells (T-helper cells and cytotoxic T cells) are involved in the cellular immune response. They work along with proteins of the major histocompatibility complex (the MHC proteins), which present antigens on the surfaces of cells and contribute to the immune system's tolerance for the body's own cells.

Like B cells, T cells possess specific membrane receptors. The T cell receptor is not an immunoglobulin, but a glycoprotein with a molecular weight of about half that of an IgG. It is made up of two polypeptide chains, each encoded by a separate gene (**Figure 40.16**). The two chains have distinct regions with constant and variable amino acid sequences. The variable regions consist of 42 *V* and 61 *J* regions for one polypeptide and 48 *V*, 3 *D*, and 7 *J* regions for the other chain, yielding 2,562 possible combinations from one chromosome and 1,008 from the other. Thus the T cell receptor dimer can produce more than 5 million (2,562 x 1008 x 2 copies of each chromosome) different amino acid sequences from recombination alone. In addition, as with B cell antibodies, the recombination process is error-prone and terminal transferases add base pairs during recombination. Together, these processes massively increase the number of possible T cell receptors, but unlike B cell antibodies, T cell receptors do not exhibit somatic hypermutation

to further increase diversity. As in the immunoglobulins, the variable regions provide the site for specific binding to antigens. But there is one major difference: whereas an antibody can bind to an antigen whether it is present on the surface of a cell or not, a T cell receptor binds only to an antigen displayed by an MHC protein on the surface of an antigen-presenting or target cell.

When a T cell is activated by contact with a specific antigen, it proliferates and forms a clone. Its descendants form clones of two types of effector T cells (see Figure 40.9):

1. T-helper (T_H) cells assist both the cellular and the humoral immune responses.

2. Cytotoxic T (T_C) cells recognize virus-infected or mutated cells and kill them by inducing lysis.

 View in Achieve
Animation 40.5 Cellular Immune Response

MHC proteins present antigen to T cells, causing recognition

Both T_H and T_C cells express T cell receptors that bind to antigen on the cell surface. But the response of each cell type to binding is quite different. T_H binding results in activation of the adaptive immune response, whereas T_C binding results in death of the cell carrying the antigen. MHC proteins form complexes with antigens on cell surfaces and assist with recognition by the T cells, so that the appropriate type of T cell binds.

The MHC proteins are cell membrane glycoproteins. Two types of MHC proteins function to present antigens to the two different types of T cells:

1. **Class I MHC proteins** are present on the surface of every nucleated cell in the mammalian body. These proteins are used to present antigens to T_C cells. Thus, any nucleated cell can potentially present antigen to a T_C cell. The antigens can be cytosolic fragments of virus proteins in virus-infected cells or abnormal proteins made by cancer cells as a result of somatic mutations. A T_C cell with the appropriate T cell receptor binds to the antigen–MHC complex. To ensure binding, the T_C cell also has a cell surface receptor protein called CD8 that recognizes and binds to MHC I.

2. **Class II MHC proteins** are on the surfaces of antigen-presenting monocyte-derived cells and B cells. They present antigens to T_H cells. Unlike cells that present antigens using class I MHC proteins, antigen presentation by these cells is one of their primary functions. These cells ingest antigens and break them down in the phagolysosome (see Figure 40.6B); one of the resulting fragments then binds to MHC II for presentation (**Figure 40.17**). A T_H cell with the appropriate T cell receptor binds to the antigen–MHC complex. To ensure binding, the T_H cell also has a cell surface receptor protein called CD4 that recognizes and binds to MHC II.

T cells are synthesized in the bone marrow but mature in the thymus, where all of the gene rearrangements occur. During maturation, it is important that the T cells end up with either a CD8 or CD4 receptor, for recognizing MHC I and II respectively, and that the T cell receptor does not recognize self antigens. Most

Figure 40.16 A T Cell Receptor   The receptors on T cells are smaller than those on B cells. The two polypeptides on the T cell receptor contain both variable and constant regions. The constant regions fix the receptor in the cell membrane, while the variable regions establish the specificity for binding to antigen.

1 The antigen-presenting cell takes up an antigen by phagocytosis.

2 The cell breaks down the antigen into fragments in the phagolysosome.

3 A class II MHC protein binds an antigen fragment.

4 The MHC presents the antigen to a T_H cell.

Antigen — Class II MHC protein

Lysosome

Phagosome

Antigen-presenting cell

Phagolysosome

CD4 — T cell receptor

T_H cell

Figure 40.17 Monocyte-Derived Cells and B Cells Are Antigen-Presenting Cells A monocyte-derived cell or B cell endocytoses an antigen, breaks it into fragments, and then displays one of the fragments on an MHC II protein at the cell surface. T cell receptors, with their CD4 cell surface receptor proteins, on a specific T_H cell can then bind to and interact further with the antigen–MHC II complex.

immature T cells that enter the thymus are lost during this process of "thymic selection" for cells expressing the appropriate receptors that are unable to recognize self antigens as foreign.

In humans there are three genetic loci for class I MHC proteins and three for class II MHC proteins. Each of these six loci has as many as 100 different alleles in the human population. With so many alleles, the number of possible genotypes is enormous; it is not surprising that different people are likely to have different MHC genotypes. This is why it can be difficult to find a good "match" for organ donations; a donor MHC genotype that does not match the recipient's MHC genotype will be recognized as foreign and stimulate an immune response. To accomplish its role in antigen presentation, an MHC protein has an antigen-binding site that can hold a peptide of about 10–20 amino acids.

Information on MHC proteins, the cellular origins of antigens, and T cells is summarized in Table 40.3.

T-helper cells and MHC II proteins contribute to the humoral immune response

When a T_H cell that has survived the selection processes in the thymus binds to an antigen-presenting cell, it releases cytokines

that cause the T_H cell to proliferate (an autocrine signal; see Key Concept 7.1), producing a clone of T_H cells with the same specificity. The steps to this point constitute the activation phase of the humoral immune response, and they occur in the lymphoid tissues. Next comes the effector phase, in which the T_H cells activate previously unexposed B cells with the same specificity to produce antibodies.

As noted earlier, B cells are also antigen-presenting cells. B cells take up antigens bound to their surface immunoglobulin receptors by endocytosis, break them down, and display antigenic fragments on class II MHC proteins. When a T_H cell binds to the displayed antigen–MHC II complex, it releases cytokines that cause the B cell to produce a clone of plasma cells and memory cells (**Figure 40.18A**). Finally, the plasma cells secrete antibodies, completing the effector phase of the humoral immune response. A humoral immune response thus requires that an antigen be recognized by a T_H cell and a B cell. Without recognition by both, an effective response will not occur.

Cytotoxic T cells and MHC I proteins contribute to the cellular immune response

Class I MHC proteins play a role in the cellular immune response that is similar to the role played by class II MHC proteins in the humoral immune response. In a virus-infected or mutated cell, foreign or abnormal proteins or peptide fragments in the cytosol are carried to the ER where they combine with class I MHC molecules. The resulting complex is displayed on the cell surface and presented to T_C cells. When a T_C cell recognizes and binds to this antigen–MHC I complex, the T_C cell is activated to proliferate (**Figure 40.18B**). In some cases a T_H cell that binds the same antigen-presenting cell is needed to activate T_C cell proliferation.

In the effector phase of the cellular immune response, T_C cells recognize and bind to cells bearing the same antigen–MHC I complex. These bound T_C cells produce a substance called perforin, which ultimately results in apoptosis of the bound target cell. In addition, the T_C cells can bind to a specific receptor (called Fas) on the target cell that initiates apoptosis in that cell. These two mechanisms work in concert to eliminate the antigen-containing host cell. Because T_C cells recognize MHC proteins complexed with nonself antigens, they help rid the body of its own virus-infected or cancer cells.

Regulatory T cells suppress the humoral and cellular immune responses

A third class of T cells called **regulatory T cells** (**Tregs**) ensures that the immune system does not attack self cells and molecules indiscriminately. Tregs are similar to other T cells: they mature in the thymus gland, carry CD4 receptors, and become activated if they bind to antigen–MHC complexes. But Tregs differ in one

TABLE **40.3**	The Interaction between T Cells and Antigen-Presenting Cells				
Presenting cell type	**Antigen presented**	**MHC class**	**T cell type**	**T cell surface protein**
Any nucleated cell	Cytosolic protein fragment	Class I	Cytotoxic T (T_C) cell	CD8
Monocyte-derived cells and B cells	Fragments from phagocytosed proteins	Class II	T-helper (T_H) cell	CD4

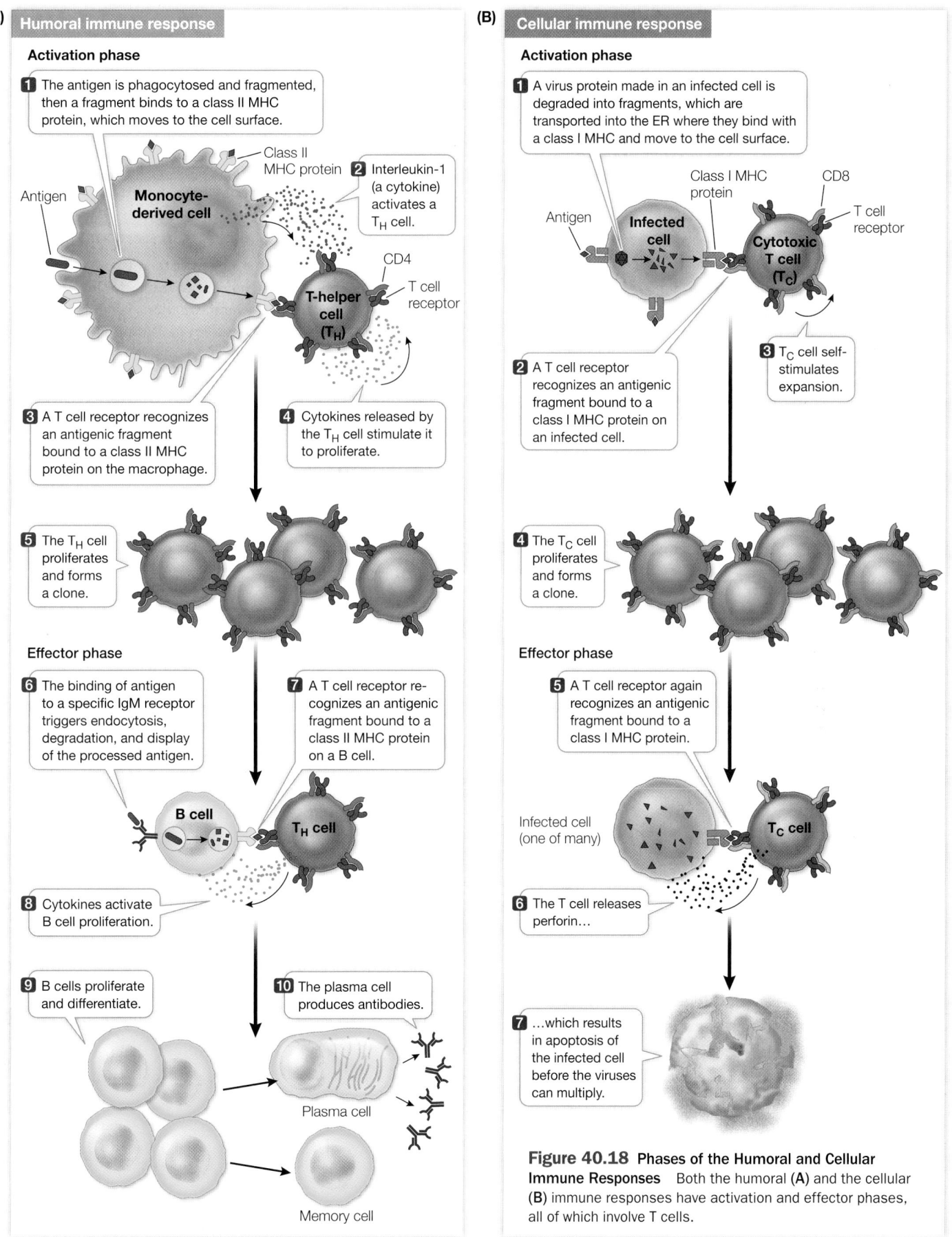

(A) Humoral immune response

Activation phase

1 The antigen is phagocytosed and fragmented, then a fragment binds to a class II MHC protein, which moves to the cell surface.

Class II MHC protein

Antigen

Monocyte-derived cell

2 Interleukin-1 (a cytokine) activates a T_H cell.

CD4

T cell receptor

T-helper cell (T_H)

3 A T cell receptor recognizes an antigenic fragment bound to a class II MHC protein on the macrophage.

4 Cytokines released by the T_H cell stimulate it to proliferate.

5 The T_H cell proliferates and forms a clone.

Effector phase

6 The binding of antigen to a specific IgM receptor triggers endocytosis, degradation, and display of the processed antigen.

7 A T cell receptor recognizes an antigenic fragment bound to a class II MHC protein on a B cell.

B cell

T_H cell

8 Cytokines activate B cell proliferation.

9 B cells proliferate and differentiate.

10 The plasma cell produces antibodies.

Plasma cell

Memory cell

(B) Cellular immune response

Activation phase

1 A virus protein made in an infected cell is degraded into fragments, which are transported into the ER where they bind with a class I MHC and move to the cell surface.

Class I MHC protein

CD8

Antigen

Infected cell

Cytotoxic T cell (T_C)

T cell receptor

2 A T cell receptor recognizes an antigenic fragment bound to a class I MHC protein on an infected cell.

3 T_C cell self-stimulates expansion.

4 The T_C cell proliferates and forms a clone.

Effector phase

5 A T cell receptor again recognizes an antigenic fragment bound to a class I MHC protein.

Infected cell (one of many)

T_C cell

6 The T cell releases perforin…

7 …which results in apoptosis of the infected cell before the viruses can multiply.

Figure 40.18 Phases of the Humoral and Cellular Immune Responses   Both the humoral (**A**) and the cellular (**B**) immune responses have activation and effector phases, all of which involve T cells.

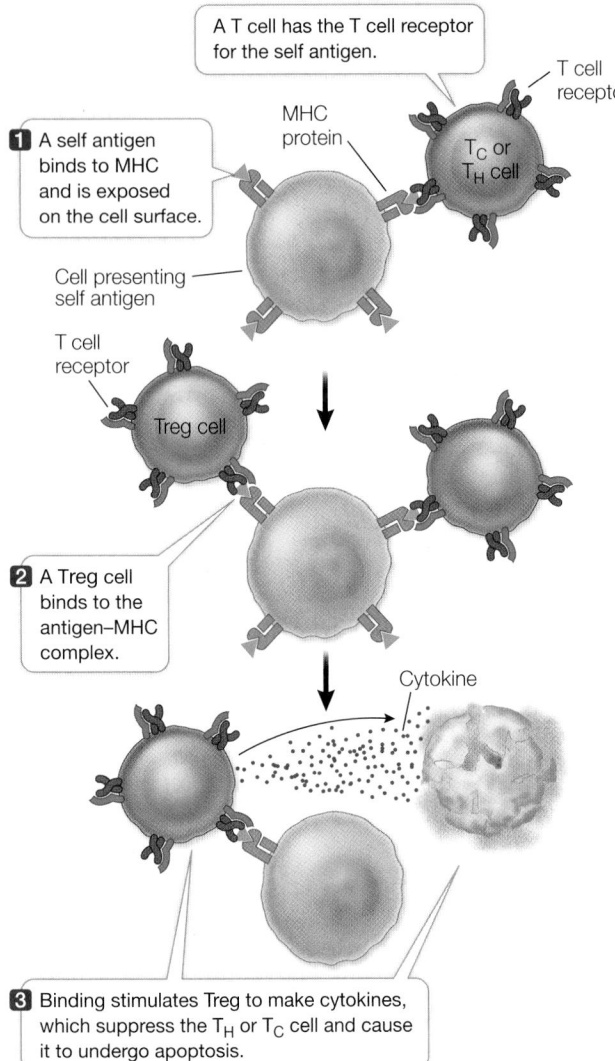

A T cell has the T cell receptor for the self antigen.

T cell receptor

MHC protein

T_C or T_H cell

1 A self antigen binds to MHC and is exposed on the cell surface.

Cell presenting self antigen

T cell receptor

Treg cell

2 A Treg cell binds to the antigen–MHC complex.

Cytokine

3 Binding stimulates Treg to make cytokines, which suppress the T_H or T_C cell and cause it to undergo apoptosis.

Figure 40.19 Tregs and Tolerance A special class of T cells called regulatory T cells (Tregs) inhibits the activation of the immune system in response to self antigens.

important way: the antigens that Tregs recognize are *self antigens*. The activation of Tregs causes them to secrete cytokines, which block the activation of T cells that are bound to the same antigen-presenting cell (**Figure 40.19**). Thus Tregs constitute another mechanism for distinguishing self from nonself.

KEY CONCEPT
40.5 Recap and Assess

The cellular immune response acts against pathogen-infected or mutated body cells. Specific receptors on T cells bind to antigen–MHC complexes displayed on cell surfaces. T-helper cells bind antigens presented on MHC II proteins by monocyte-derived and B cells and contribute to the humoral immune response. Cytotoxic T cells bind to antigens presented on MHC I proteins by any nucleated cell and contribute to the cellular immune response. Tregs suppress immune responses to self antigens.

1. MHC proteins almost always differ among unrelated people, so organ transplants usually provoke a cellular immune response by the host, causing rejection. People receiving transplants

are given a drug called cyclosporine, which inhibits cytokine release by T cells. Why do you think cytokine inhibition by cyclosporine reduces rejection?

2. When a virus infects a cell, the immune system mounts an adaptive response to this infection. What are the roles of the T cell receptor and MHC protein in this response?

3. Cancer cells often express proteins that the body has never seen, so they are targeted by the cellular adaptive immune system. In some cancers, however, Tregs increase in numbers and activity. Why would this indicate a poor prognosis?

Given the numerous and complex cellular interactions that activate the immune system and generate antibody diversity, you may have perceived many points at which the immune system could fail. We now turn to several situations in which one or more components of this complex system malfunction.

KEY CONCEPT
40.6 Malfunctions in Immunity Can Be Harmful

Learning Objectives

40.6.1 Summarize the responses that occur during immediate and delayed hypersensitivity.

40.6.2 Describe how desensitization can be used to minimize allergic reactions.

40.6.3 Summarize the hypotheses that explain how autoimmunity can occur.

40.6.4 Explain how HIV infection causes immune deficiency.

Sometimes the immune system overreacts, as in an allergic response. Sometimes it attacks self antigens, as in autoimmune disease. And sometimes it fails to act, or acts weakly, as in immune deficiency disease.

The immune system mounts an excessive response in allergic reactions

An **allergic reaction** arises when the human immune system overreacts to (is hypersensitive to) a dose of antigen. Although the antigen itself may present no danger to the host, the inappropriate immune response may produce inflammation and other symptoms, which can cause serious illness or even death. Allergic reactions are the most familiar examples of this phenomenon. Allergic reactions may involve immediate hypersensitivity or delayed hypersensitivity.

IMMEDIATE HYPERSENSITIVITY **Immediate hypersensitivity** arises when an allergic individual is exposed to an antigen (in this case referred to as an allergen) from the environment, such as a food, pollen, or the venom of an insect. In response to the allergen, the individual makes large amounts of IgE. When this happens, mast cells in tissues and basophils in the blood bind the constant end of the IgE. If that individual is exposed to the same allergen again, binding of the allergen to the IgE causes the mast cells and basophils to rapidly release a large amount of histamine (**Figure 40.20**). This results in symptoms such as dilation of blood vessels, inflammation, and difficulty breathing. If not treated with antihistamines, a

Initial response: sensitization

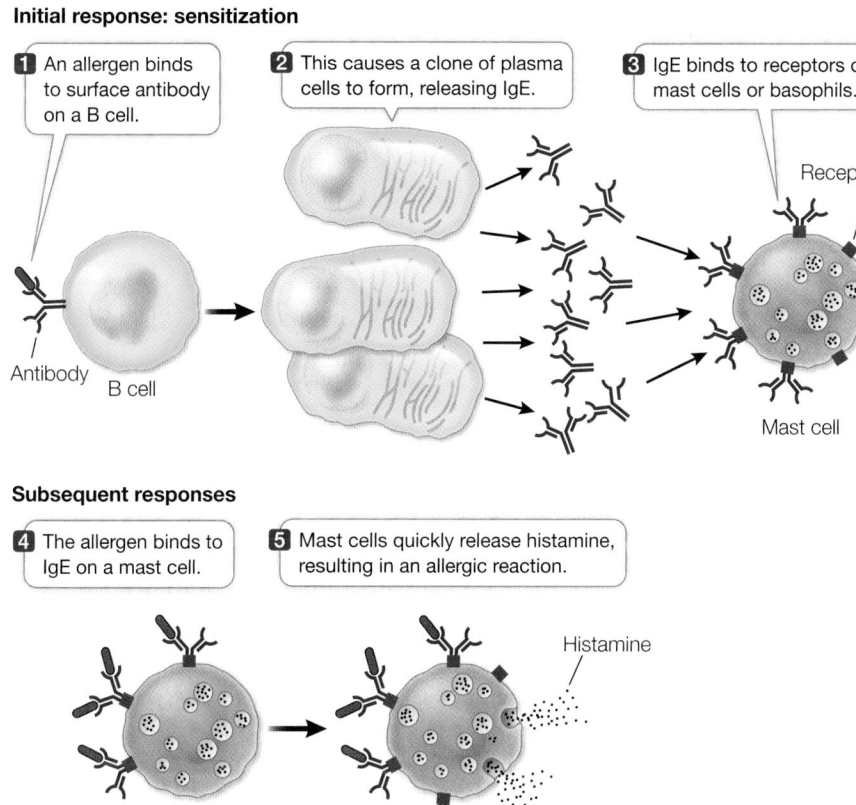

1 An allergen binds to surface antibody on a B cell.

2 This causes a clone of plasma cells to form, releasing IgE.

3 IgE binds to receptors on mast cells or basophils.

Receptor

Antibody
B cell

Mast cell

Subsequent responses

4 The allergen binds to IgE on a mast cell.

5 Mast cells quickly release histamine, resulting in an allergic reaction.

Histamine

Figure 40.20 An Allergic Reaction An allergen is an antigen that stimulates B cells to make large amounts of IgE antibodies, which bind to mast cells and basophils. When the body encounters the allergen again, these cells produce large amounts of histamine, which has harmful physiological effects.

severe allergic reaction can lead to death. It is not known why some people produce excessive amounts of IgE in response to allergens. There is some evidence for genetic factors predisposing people to allergic responses.

Allergy to pollen can be treated using a process called desensitization. The process involves injecting small amounts of the allergen (typically just an extract of the offending plant tissue) into the skin—enough to stimulate IgG production but not enough to stimulate IgE production. The next time the person is exposed to the allergen, IgG binds to it, tying it up before IgE can bind it and stimulate mast cells to release histamine.

Desensitization does not work well for food allergens because the IgE response to those substances is so strong that even a small amount of antigen provokes it. The best approach for those with food allergies is to avoid foods containing the allergens. This can be difficult, but food labels listing all the ingredients are helpful. Molecular biologists are beginning to identify the antigens that act as allergens, with the hope of developing vaccines or genetically modified foods that lack the allergenic epitopes.

DELAYED HYPERSENSITIVITY **Delayed hypersensitivity** is an allergic reaction that does not begin until hours after exposure to an antigen. In this case the antigen is taken up by antigen-presenting cells, and a T cell response is initiated. A T_H cell

produces a clone of cells that secrete various cytokines, which cause such reactions as inflammation and rash. These events take time (hence the term "delayed"). An example is the rash that develops after exposure to poison ivy.

Autoimmune diseases are caused by reactions against self antigens

Errors in the selection of T cells in the thymus can result in T cells that bind to antigen–MHC complexes that carry self antigens. Although the precise origin of **autoimmunity** is not known, there are at least two hypotheses:

- *Failure of clonal deletion*. B or T cells that recognize self antigens and should have been destroyed by clonal deletion are not destroyed.
- *Molecular mimicry*. T cells that recognize a nonself antigen, such as a virus, also recognize something on a self antigen that has a similar structure.

Autoimmunity does not always result in disease, but several autoimmune diseases are common:

- People with *systemic lupus erythematosus* (SLE) have antibodies to many cellular components, including DNA and nuclear proteins released from dying cells. These antinuclear antibodies can cause serious damage when they bind to normal tissue antigens and form large circulating antigen–antibody complexes, which become stuck in tissues and provoke inflammation.
- People with *rheumatoid arthritis* have difficulty in shutting down a T cell response to self antigens. These patients may have low activity of CTLA4, an inhibitory protein that blocks T cells from reacting to self antigens. This results in inflammation of the joints and other tissue damage.
- *Hashimoto's thyroiditis* is the most common autoimmune disease in women over 50. Immune cells attack thyroid tissue, resulting in fatigue, depression, weight gain, and other symptoms.
- *Insulin-dependent diabetes mellitus*, or type I diabetes, occurs most often in children. It is caused by an immune reaction against several proteins in the cells of the pancreas that manufacture the protein hormone insulin. This reaction kills the insulin-producing cells, so people with type I diabetes must take insulin daily in order to survive.

AIDS is an immune deficiency disorder

There are several inherited and acquired immune deficiency disorders. In some individuals, T or B cells never form; in others, B cells lose the ability to give rise to plasma cells. In either case, the affected individual is unable to mount an adaptive immune response and thus lacks a major line of defense against pathogens.

The T_H cell is perhaps the most central component of the immune system because of its essential roles in both the humoral and cellular immune responses (see Figure 40.9). This cell is the target of **human immunodeficiency virus** (**HIV**), the retrovirus that results in **acquired immune deficiency syndrome** (**AIDS**).

HIV can be transmitted from person to person in body fluids containing the virus (such as blood, semen, or vaginal fluid). The recipient tissue is either blood (by transfusion) or a mucous membrane lining an organ (the mucus contains a high concentration of B and T cells). HIV initially infects macrophages, T_H cells, and antigen-presenting dendritic cells in the blood and tissues. At first there is an immune response to the viral infection, and T_H cells are activated. But because HIV infects the T_H cells, they are killed both by HIV itself and by T_C cells that lyse infected T_H cells. Consequently T_H cell numbers decline after the first month or so of infection. Meanwhile, the extensive production of HIV by infected cells activates the humoral immune system. Antibodies bind to HIV, and the complexes are removed by phagocytes. The HIV level in blood goes down. There is still a low level of infection, however, because of the depletion of T_H cells (**Figure 40.21**). This process reaches a low, steady-state level called the "set point." This point varies among individuals and is a strong predictor of the rate of progression of the disease. For most people it takes 8–10 years without treatment for the more severe manifestations of AIDS to develop. In some it can take as little as a year; in others, 20 years.

During this dormant period, people carrying HIV generally feel fine, and their T_H cell levels are adequate for them to mount immune responses. Eventually, however, as the virus continues to destroy the T_H cells, their numbers fall to the point where the infected person is susceptible to infections that the T_H cells would normally eliminate. These infections result in conditions such as Kaposi's sarcoma, a skin tumor caused by a herpes virus; pneumonia caused by the fungus *Pneumocystis jirovecii*; and lymphoma tumors caused by the Epstein–Barr virus. These conditions result from opportunistic infections because the pathogens take advantage of the crippled immune system of the host. They lead to death within a year or two.

HIV has been intensively studied. This has resulted in the development of drugs targeted to HIV proteins, such as the reverse transcriptase that makes cDNA from the virus RNA, and the virus protease that cuts the large precursor virus protein into its final active proteins. Treatment with combinations of such drugs has had spectacular success. Before the 1990s, getting AIDS was a death sentence, with few sufferers surviving beyond a year or two. Today the survival of a treated, infected person is decades longer. Unfortunately, like many medical treatments, HIV drugs are not available to all who need them—particularly in poor regions of the world where AIDS is prevalent. Since AIDS is caused by a viral infection, a vaccine would seem an appropriate preventive agent. Unfortunately, despite a huge international effort that is ongoing, a vaccine against HIV has not been developed, probably because the virus "hides out" inside immune cells and is prone to a high mutation rate. There are about 1.2 million deaths per year worldwide from AIDS.

KEY CONCEPT
40.6 Recap and Assess

Failures of the immune system include allergic reactions (caused by hypersensitivity to antigens), autoimmune diseases (caused by reactions against self antigens), and immune deficiency disorders.

1. Some people are allergic to bee stings. Outline the events that characterize the immune reactions involved.

2. There has been recent progress in treating bee sting allergy by desensitization. How does this work?

3. A new cancer treatment involves promoting autoimmunity by designing a drug to inhibit CTLA4, a protein on T cells that normally blocks them from mounting an autoimmune response. How does this treatment work? What might be its side effects?

1 Soon after the initial HIV infection, the immune system destroys most of the virus.

2 The T_H cell concentration gradually falls and the HIV concentration rises.

3 As T_H cells are further reduced, immune function is impaired and opportunistic infections occur.

4 Almost all natural immunity is lost.

T_H cell concentration

HIV concentration

This is the set point of low-level HIV production.

Figure 40.21 The Course of an HIV Infection An HIV infection may be carried, unsuspected, for many years before the onset of symptoms. (After M. Kogan and J. Rappaport. 2011. *Retrovirology* 8:25. doi:10.1186/1742-4690-8-25.)

▶ Investigating LIFE

Q and A — What are the mechanisms and implications of long-lasting immunity?

You have seen in this chapter that lasting immunity against a pathogen can be achieved in two ways, both of which involve exposure to an antigen associated with the pathogen and the resulting production of memory cells. The first way is natural: in **Investigating Life: What Are the Mechanisms and Implications of Long Lasting Immunity?**, we showed that people exposed to virulent strains of flu viruses retain their immunity, and even increase it when exposed to less harmful flu strains. The second way is artificial: as we described in the opening story, vaccines have been spectacularly successful at inducing lasting immunity and even eradicating diseases when enough people are vaccinated. Why, then, do people refuse vaccination? There appear to be several reasons. One is complacency—the threat of disease may seem remote. For example, measles, which used to kill thousands of children every year in the United States and still does in poor countries, is no longer a highly visible threat. Second, some people believe that vaccines, although exhaustively tested and proven safe, are unsafe and cause disease. The internet is full of such incorrect assertions. Third, false alarms have led people to dismiss vaccination advisories. The discovery of the H1N1 flu virus (swine flu) in Mexico in 2009 led to a high alert and a mass vaccination program that turned out not to be

necessary. In addition, some people are suspicious of governmental programs in general. Vaccination is a scientific success in terms of bolstering immunity and eradicating disease. But like any technology, its acceptance is a political issue.

Future directions

Following activation of the immune system, many effector cells are mobilized. Most eventually die, but some survive as memory cells. Researchers are investigating how this happens. At the University of Wisconsin, Marulasiddappa Suresh and his colleagues have shown that a single transcription factor called FoxO1 plays an important role in the effector-to-memory-cell transition. This molecule is not needed for the production of effector cells, but if it is not there, memory cells do not form. The genes regulated by FoxO1 are being characterized and may hold the key to the memory cell. Meanwhile, at Yale University, Susan Kaech and her colleagues have shown that an intercellular signal molecule, interleukin-7 (IL-7), binds to effector cells and results in changes that may allow memory cell survival. Specifically, the target cells produce a membrane channel that allows rapid uptake of glycerol, the backbone of fats. Production of fats in the memory cell may provide the energy needed for long-term survival. Understanding how memory cells form and survive may provide valuable information for the production of better vaccines.

VISUAL SUMMARY 40

© Universal History Archive/UIG/Getty Images

You should be able to relate each summary to the adjacent figures. If you go to this visual summary in **Achieve**, you can follow links to figures, animations, activities, and simulations that will help you consolidate the material.

KEY CONCEPT

40.1 Animals Use Innate and Adaptive Mechanisms for Defense

Go to Activity 40.1 and Animation 40.1

- **Innate defenses** are present in all animals and respond to a broad range of **pathogens**.

- **Adaptive defenses** are present in vertebrates and target specific pathogens.

- A variety of **white blood cell** types and their receptors are involved in both responses.

Questions

1. When a pathogen enters the body, it triggers an internal response. What are the three phases of this response?

2. Several Toll-like receptors (TLRs) are found in the genome. What would be the effect of knocking out (rendering nonfunctional) both alleles of (a) a gene encoding a TLR or (b) the gene encoding the Nf-κB transcription factor, which is one of the main targets of the TLR signal transduction pathway?

Figure 40.1

Granulocytes

 Basophils

 Eosinophils

 Neutrophils

 Mast cells

Monocyte-derived

 Monocytes

  Macrophages

 Dendritic cells

Lymphocytes

 B cells

 T cells

 Natural killer cells

KEY CONCEPT

40.2   Innate Defenses Are Nonspecific

Go to **Activity 40.2**

- Organisms use a variety of physical, chemical, and enzyme barriers and the host microbiome to prevent pathogen entry.

- A pathogen that enters the body is recognized by the foreign macromolecules it expresses.

- Innate responses to pathogens include phagocytosis and the release of complement proteins and cytokines.

- **Inflammation** causes **mast cells** to release chemicals that recruit phagocytes.

Questions

1. Why is lysozyme concentration high in tears? Do you think it is also high in breast milk?

2. When an invader is recognized as foreign, how might a white blood cell first respond to it?

3. When you cut yourself, the wound often swells up. What has happened to cause this?

Figure 40.5

KEY CONCEPT

40.3   Adaptive Defenses Are Specific

Go to **Animation 40.2**

- An enormous diversity of receptors able to bind specific antigens are produced by B and T cells; cells expressing self-recognizing receptors are deleted.

- Initiating an adaptive immune response requires antigen binding and often involves antigen-presenting cells.

- An adaptive immune response can be humoral or cellular.

- **Clonal selection** produces **effector cells** that respond to the current infection and **memory cells** ready to respond to a re-peated infection by the same pathogen.

Questions

1. What is the difference between clonal dele-tion and clonal selection? When does each of these events happen?

2. B cells can bind antigen. Why must T-helper cells recognize the same antigen to get a humoral response?

3. Vaccination requires the development of memory cells. Why do you think some vaccines require "boosters"?

Figure 40.10

KEY CONCEPT

40.4 The Humoral Adaptive Response Involves Antibodies

Go to Activity 40.3 and
Animations 40.3 and 40.4

- Immunoglobulins come in five classes and may be B cell membrane receptors or secreted from B cells. **Class switching** involves DNA rearrangements.

- Immunoglobulins show enormous diversity in the amino acid sequences of their **variable regions** due to rearrangements of the V, D, and J genes.

Questions

1. Suppose a mammal possesses 50 V, 20 D, and 5 J genes for its heavy chain and 50 V and 5 J genes for its light chain. How many possible antibodies can it make from rearranging these genes?

2. The number of antibodies actually produced by the mammal in question 1 is greater than 50 million. Where does this additional diversity come from?

3. A B cell that never undergoes class switching produces both IgM and IgD antibodies. How is it able to produce two classes of antibodies?

Figure 40.12

General structure of an immunoglobulin

KEY CONCEPT

40.5 The Cellular Adaptive Response Involves T Cells and Receptors

Go to Animation 40.5

- T cell receptor proteins have extreme diversity due to rearrangements of the V, D, and J genes in their variable regions.

- **Class I** and **II MHC proteins** present antigens to CD8-expressing cytotoxic T cells and CD4-expressing T-helper cells respectively and are thus involved in both the humoral and cellular immune responses.

- In humans, MHC proteins are encoded at six genes, each of which is quite variable due to allelic variation (more than 100 alleles in the human population).

- **Regulatory T cells** (**Tregs**) destroy other T cells expressing self antigens.

Questions

1. Why is a CD4 or CD8 receptor required for T cell activation?

2. What are the similarities and difference in generating diversity in T cell receptors and B cell receptors (antibodies)?

3. Antigen presentation can occur to either T_H or a T_C cells. Outline the similarities and differences of antigen presentation and the responses obtained by each of these cell types.

Figure 40.17

KEY CONCEPT

40.6 Malfunctions in Immunity Can Be Harmful

- **Immediate hypersensitivity** is due to a rapid and substantial release of histamines from mast cells that are bound to an IgE antibody that recognizes the allergen (antigen).

- **Delayed hypersensitivity** is due to a T-helper cell response that release cytokines.

- Desensitization leads to the increase in circulating IgG antibodies that bind an allergen before it can bind to IgE on mast cells.

- **Autoimmunity** occurs when T or B cells recognize self antigens.

- **Human immunodeficiency virus** (**HIV**) targets T-helper cells, weakening the immune system, and if untreated eventually leads to **acquired immune deficiency syndrome** (**AIDS**).

Figure 40.21

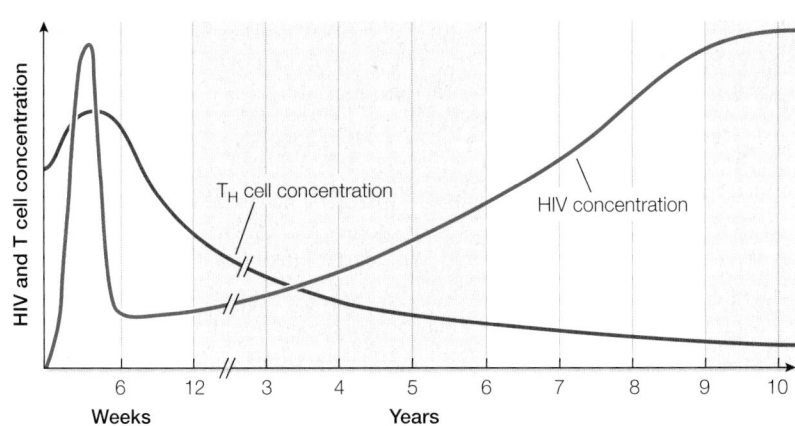

Questions

1. Why do some individuals show more extreme allergic reactions with every exposure to an allergen?

2. Allergic reactions often involve the release of large amounts of histamine. How might antihistamines work to reduce an allergic reaction?

3. HIV is particularly effective at disrupting an individual's ability to mount an immune response. Why is this the case?

Go to **Achieve** for the eBook, **LearningCurve**, animations, activities, simulations, and additional resources and assignments.

Animal Reproduction

This Blue-footed Booby (*Sula nebouxii*) pair is in a courtship dance.

▶Investigating LIFE

No Time to Waste

Female tammar wallabies (*Macropus eugenii*) become sexually receptive and mate soon after they give birth. The resulting embryo can be born any time from a month to a year later. Humans have a set 9-month pregnancy, so this highly variable duration of pregnancy seems unusual and leads to questions of "why" and "how." Knowing more about the development of the young wallaby, called a joey, helps. The joey is very immature when born. It crawls into its mother's pouch (the marsupium) where it suckles and grows for up to 10 months when it is weaned.

Answering the "why" question is not difficult. Reproductive success is the currency of evolution. Reproductive success depends on how many offspring a female can produce and on the chances that those offspring survive, reproduce, and pass on their genes to the following generation. Mating soon after giving birth (as the wallaby does) can maximize the number of offspring a female produces, but it does not necessarily maximize the survival and success of those offspring. Survival of offspring in many species depends on the ability of the mother to provide maternal care. Mammalian mothers produce milk to nourish their young, and that has an enormous energy cost. Therefore the females of many mammalian species do not become fertile and sexually receptive again until they have weaned their young. But this is not true for the tammar wallaby.

The large energy investment that a tammar wallaby mother makes to successfully rear a single offspring means that giving birth while still having one joey in the pouch lowers the chances of having either of those young survive. The adaptation of this species is developmental arrest, or diapause. The fertilized egg begins to develop into an embryo, but at an early stage of development its cell divisions cease, its metabolism decreases, and it remains in the uterus without implanting in the uterine lining as long as the previous offspring is suckling. If that offspring dies or is weaned, the quiescent embryo in the uterus is activated, implants in the uterine lining, and continues its development. Having an embryo ready to go when conditions are right is a way of maximizing reproductive success, but the "how" question remains.

 What signal controls the breaking of diapause in the tammar wallaby? (Find the answer on page 936.)

KEY CONCEPT 41.1 Asexual Reproduction Is Efficient but Limits Genetic Variability

Learning Objectives

41.1.1 Describe circumstances that make asexual reproduction advantageous or disadvantageous.

41.1.2 Describe the characteristics of the different types of asexual reproduction.

41.1.3 Explain conditions that would favor parthenogenesis over other forms of asexual reproduction.

When we think of reproduction, we think of sex, but many species can reproduce asexually—the offspring are exact genetic copies of the parents. Most of the animal species that reproduce asexually are invertebrates living in rather constant environments. However, examples of asexual reproduction do occur in vertebrates. Reproduction by female sharks living in aquariums with no males has been reported. The natural habitat of these fishes is the open ocean where potential mates might not be readily available. Asexual reproduction is efficient because no time or energy is wasted on mating and every member of the population can convert resources into offspring.

You can demonstrate to yourself the efficiency of asexual reproduction with a thought exercise. Start with two females, one reproducing sexually and one asexually. Assume that each can have two offspring, but in the case of the sexually reproducing female, one will be a male. Also assume that in each subsequent generation all of the females (mothers and daughters) will have two offspring each. In the first generation, the asexually reproducing female will have two daughters. Thus in the next generation there will be three asexually reproducing females that can have two female offspring each. In contrast, the sexually reproducing female will have only one female daughter, so in the next generation there will be only two females reproducing, having two offspring each—only one of which will be female. Run this thought exercise through three or four cycles and compare the numbers of offspring produced.

Asexual reproduction limits genetic diversity

A disadvantage of asexual reproduction is that the offspring are genetically identical to one another and to their parents. Thus asexual reproduction does not generate genetic diversity. Genetic diversity is the raw material that enables natural selection to shape adaptations in response to environmental change. When environmental changes occur, lack of genetic diversity can be disadvantageous to a population. Asexual reproduction is, however, a good way to preserve a successful genotype in a stable environment. Aphids are an example of a species that has it both ways (**Figure 41.1**). In the spring, the aphids that hatch on rose bushes from overwintering eggs are all females. Each of those aphids reproduces asexually to produce many more females—all genetically identical. This is a time when there is plenty of food and the environment is stable. When the conditions change due to drought

Figure 41.1 Aphids Are Sexual and Asexual When environmental conditions are favorable, such as in a rose garden in the summer, aphids make the most of resources by rapidly reproducing asexually. They are actually making identical copies of themselves. But when environmental conditions are unsure, such as in the fall, aphids reproduce sexually and thereby increase their genetic diversity in the face of changing, unpredictable conditions.

or season, the females still reproduce asexually, but some of the offspring develop into males. The ensuing sexual reproduction introduces genetic variation into the eggs that will remain dormant until favorable conditions return.

Three common modes of asexual reproduction are budding, regeneration, and parthenogenesis.

Budding and regeneration produce new individuals by mitosis

Some simple multicellular animals produce offspring by **budding**. New individuals form as outgrowths or buds from the bodies of older animals. A bud grows by mitotic cell division of somatic cells that dedifferentiate. The cells of the bud differentiate into the cell types of the new individual before the bud breaks away from the parent (**Figure 41.2A**). The bud is genetically identical to the parent, and it may grow as large as the parent before it becomes independent.

Regeneration is usually thought of as the replacement of damaged tissues or lost limbs, but in some cases pieces of an organism can regenerate complete individuals. Echinoderms, for example, have remarkable abilities to regenerate. If sea stars are cut into pieces, each piece that includes an arm and a portion of the central disc can grow into a new animal (**Figure 41.2B**). In

(A) *Hydra littoralis*

Budding

(B) *Linckia multifora*

Regeneration

Figure 41.2 Two Forms of Asexual Reproduction **(A)** Budding: a new individual forms as an outgrowth from an adult hydra. **(B)** Regeneration: a single severed arm and a piece of the central disc of a mature sea star can regenerate into an entire animal.

the early 1900s oyster fishermen in Narragansett Bay between Rhode Island and Massachusetts tried to eliminate the sea stars that were preying on their oysters. Whenever they encountered sea stars, they cut them up with their knives and threw them back into the water. As a result, the sea star population increased explosively. A variant of regeneration called fission involves the animal splitting in half, with each half growing into a whole individual. An example is seen in sea anemones.

Regeneration can occur when an animal is broken by an outside force such as wave action in the intertidal zone. In some cases, breakage occurs in the absence of external forces. Some species of segmented marine worms develop segments with rudimentary heads bearing sensory organs. The segments then break apart and each one forms a new worm.

Parthenogenesis is the development of unfertilized eggs

Not all eggs must be fertilized to develop. A common mode of asexual reproduction in arthropods (including aphids) is the development of offspring from unfertilized eggs. This phenomenon, called **parthenogenesis**, also occurs in some species of fishes, amphibians, and reptiles. Most species that reproduce parthenogenetically also engage in sexual reproduction or at least sexual behavior at other times. In some species, parthenogenesis is part of the mechanism that determines sex. In honey bees (as well as in most ants and wasps), males develop from

unfertilized eggs and are haploid, whereas females develop from fertilized eggs and are diploid.

Parthenogenetic reproduction in some species requires sexual behavior even though sperm are not involved and eggs are not fertilized. David Crews and his students at the University of Texas extensively investigated one such case, that of parthenogenetic reproduction in a species of whiptail lizard. There are no males of this species. Females can act as males, engaging in all aspects of courtship display and mating, although no sperm are produced or transferred (**Figure 41.3**). Whether a specific female acts as a female or as a male depends on cyclical hormonal states. When her estrogen levels are high, she acts as a female. When her progesterone levels peak, she acts as a male. The stimulation resulting from the sexual activity triggers the release of eggs from the ovaries of the acting female.

(A) Sexual behavior in parthenogenetic whiptail lizards

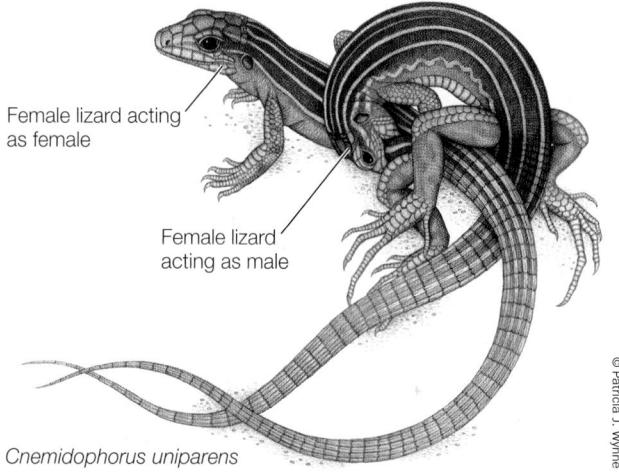

Female lizard acting as female

Female lizard acting as male

Cnemidophorus uniparens

(B) Sex role in whiptail lizards is under hormonal control

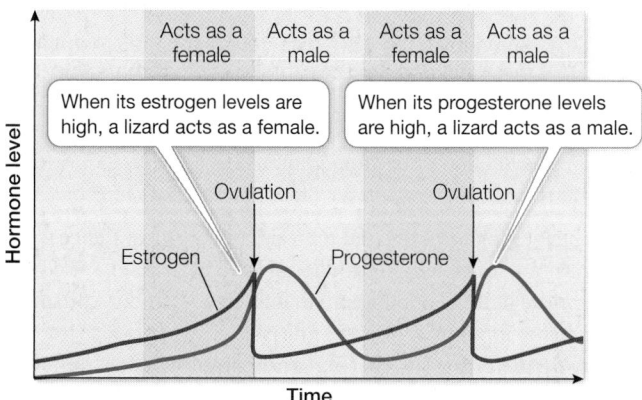

Acts as a female | Acts as a male | Acts as a female | Acts as a male

When its estrogen levels are high, a lizard acts as a female.

When its progesterone levels are high, a lizard acts as a male.

Ovulation

Ovulation

Estrogen

Progesterone

Hormone level

Time

Figure 41.3 Asexual Reproduction May Require Sexual Behavior **(A)** Parthenogenetic whiptail lizards are all females, but they take turns acting the male role in reproductive behavior. The stimulation from sexual behavior is necessary for ovulation to occur. **(B)** The cycling of ovarian hormones determines the role an individual whiptail plays. (B after D. Crews. 1988. *Psychobiology* 16: 321–334.)

Q: What selective advantages could accrue to a bisexual species becoming unisexual? What disadvantages?

41.1 Recap and Assess

Many species of animals, especially invertebrates, can reproduce asexually through budding, regeneration, or parthenogenesis. Asexual reproduction is an efficient use of resources but does not produce genetic diversity.

1. What is similar about budding and regeneration but *not* parthenogenesis?

2. Is global climate change likely to have a more negative impact on a species that reproduces asexually or one that reproduces sexually, and why?

3. The Komodo dragon is a very large, sexually breeding species of lizard that lives on the Indonesian island of Komodo. A young Komodo dragon named Flora was raised alone for many years in London Zoo. One year after reaching sexual maturity, she laid a clutch of eggs that produced several baby dragons, all males. How did Flora reproduce? What advantage might this ability have for an island-dwelling species?

Asexual reproduction is an efficient way to use resources. Since most animals reproduce sexually, however, the genetic diversity produced by sexual reproduction must confer a tremendous advantage.

KEY CONCEPT
41.2 Sexual Reproduction Involves the Union of Haploid Egg and Sperm

Learning Objectives

41.2.1 Discuss the similarities and differences between oogenesis and spermatogenesis.

41.2.2 Explain the connection between sex chromosome asymmetry and spermatocytes remaining in cytoplasmic contact.

41.2.3 Describe the interactions between sperm and eggs in sea urchins.

41.2.4 Summarize the ways that aquatic animals enhance the likelihood that sperm and eggs of the same species will meet.

41.2.5 Identify and describe conditions that favor the evolution of hermaphroditism.

Given the inefficiency of sexual reproduction, its prevalence is surprising. In most sexually reproducing species, the sex ratio is 1:1 and therefore half the population (males) do not produce offspring. Mating behaviors involve costs and risks. Costs include time and energy spent finding, attracting, and competing for a mate, as well as the "opportunity costs" of detracting from other activities such as feeding and caring for existing offspring. Risks include increased exposure to predation and the potential for physical damage. Despite these disadvantages, most eukaryotic organisms reproduce sexually. Thus it would seem that genetic diversity is an evolutionary advantage that can overwhelm the cost of sex (see Key Concepts 19.2 and 19.4).

Sexual reproduction requires the joining of two haploid sex cells to form a diploid individual. These haploid cells, or **gametes**, are produced through gametogenesis, a process that involves meiotic cell divisions. Two events in meiosis contribute to genetic diversity: crossing over between homologous chromosomes and the independent assortment of chromosomes (see Key Concepts 11.5 and 12.1). Mating behavior itself also contributes to genetic diversity. The genetic variation among the gametes of an individual and the genetic variation between any two parents produce an enormous potential for genetic variation between any two offspring of a sexually reproducing pair of individuals.

Sexual reproduction in animals consists of three steps:

1. **Gametogenesis**: making gametes

2. **Spawning** or **mating**: bringing gametes together

3. **Fertilization**: fusing gametes

The process of gametogenesis is similar across sexually reproducing animal species. Processes of fertilization are also quite similar in widely different species. Therefore, while our discussion of gametogenesis will focus generally on mammals, and our discussion of fertilization will feature sea urchins, the facts would not be dramatically different were we to consider many other animal groups. Adaptations for spawning and mating, in contrast, show incredible anatomical, physiological, and behavioral diversity across species.

Gametogenesis produces eggs and sperm

Gametogenesis occurs in the gonads: male **testes** (singular *testis*) and female **ovaries** (singular *ovary*). The tiny male gametes, **sperm**, move by beating their flagella. The larger female gametes, **eggs** or **ova** (singular *ovum*), are nonmotile.

Gametes are produced from **germ cells**, which have their origin in early cell divisions of the embryo and remain distinct from all the other cells of the body (the somatic cells). Germ cells are sequestered in the body of the embryo until its gonads begin to form. The germ cells then migrate to the developing gonads, take up residence, and proliferate by mitosis, producing **spermatogonia** (singular *spermatogonium*) in males and **oogonia** (singular *oogonium*) in females (**Figure 41.4**). Spermatogonia and oogonia are diploid, multiply by mitosis, and are stem cells. They are self-regenerating, and they produce progeny—spermatocytes and oocytes—that enter the next stage of gametogenesis.

In that next stage of gametogenesis, meiotic cell division reduces the chromosomes to the haploid number (see Key Concept 11.5). The progeny of the spermatogonia and oogonia that enter meiosis are **primary spermatocytes** and **primary oocytes**. The steps of meiosis are similar in males and females, but there are important sex differences in gametogenesis.

SPERMATOGENESIS The initial proliferation of male germ cells into spermatogonia proceeds by mitosis in the embryo. Throughout the male life span, spermatogonia continue to divide by mitosis, with one daughter cell retaining the self-regenerating capacity of a spermatogonium and the other daughter cell becoming a primary spermatocyte. As illustrated in Figure 41.4A, primary spermatocytes undergo the first meiotic division—the reduction division—to form two haploid **secondary spermatocytes**. The second meiotic division produces four haploid **spermatids** for each primary spermatocyte that enters meiosis. In mammals, the

(A) Spermatogenesis

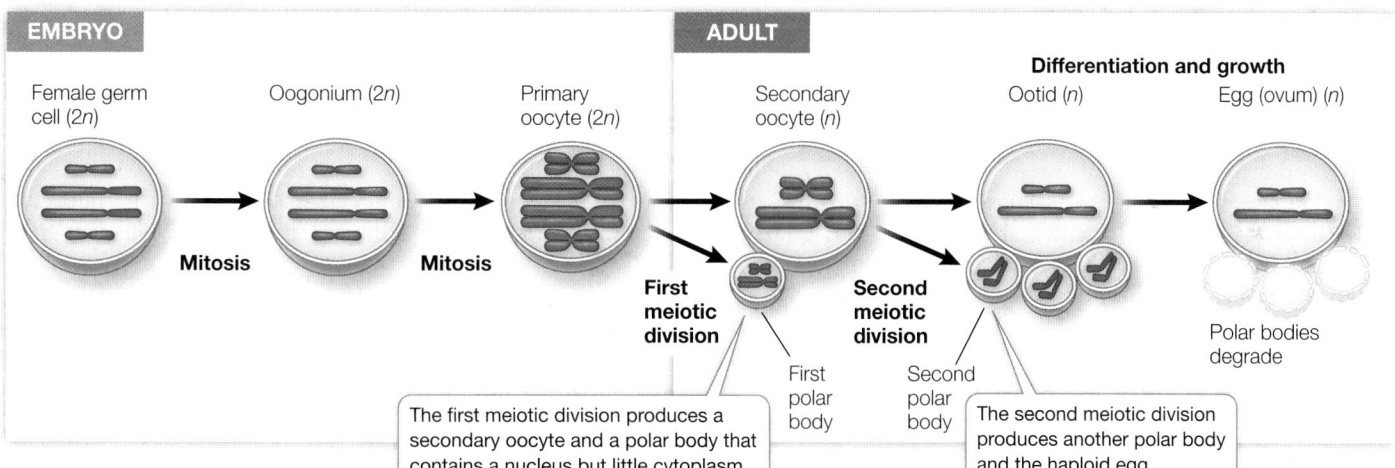

(B) Oogenesis

Figure 41.4 Gametogenesis   Male and female germ cells proliferate by mitosis and produce diploid spermatogonia and oogonia that mature into primary spermatocytes and oocytes before entering meiosis. **(A)** Spermatogonia continue to divide by mitosis in adults, producing a steady supply of spermatocytes that divide meiotically to produce haploid spermatids, which differentiate into sperm. In many species, the progeny of spermatocytes remain in contact through cytoplasmic bridges until the sperm mature. **(B)** In mammals, oogonia cease division in the embryo, and primary oocytes remain arrested in prophase I of meiosis until they are ovulated and fertilized. Each oocyte will produce one haploid ootid, which matures into an egg.

progeny of primary spermatocytes remain connected by cytoplasmic bridges after each division.

Mammalian spermatocytes remain in cytoplasmic contact throughout their development because of the asymmetry of sex chromosomes in males. Half the secondary spermatocytes receive an X chromosome, the other half a Y chromosome. The Y chromosome contains fewer genes than the X chromosome, and some of the products of genes found only on the X chromosome

are essential for spermatocyte development. By remaining in cytoplasmic contact, all four spermatocytes can share the gene products of the X chromosomes, although only half of them have an X chromosome.

A spermatid bears little resemblance to a mature sperm. Through further differentiation the spermatid becomes compact, streamlined, and develops a flagellum to become motile. We discuss the production of human sperm in Key Concept 41.3.

OOGENESIS   Oogonia, like spermatogonia, proliferate through mitosis (see Figure 41.4B). The resulting primary oocytes immediately enter prophase of the first meiotic division. In many species, including humans, the oocyte experiences developmental arrest at this point and may remain in that state for days, months, or years. In the human female, this period of arrest is at least 10 years (i.e., until puberty), and some primary oocytes remain in prophase I for more than 50 years (i.e., until menopause). In contrast, spermatogenesis continues, uninterrupted, to completion once the primary spermatocyte has differentiated.

During the prolonged prophase I, or shortly before it ends, the primary oocyte grows larger through increased production of ribosomes, RNA, cytoplasmic organelles, and energy stores. At this point the primary oocyte acquires all the energy, raw materials, and RNA that the egg will need to survive its first cell divisions after fertilization. In fact, the nutrients in the egg must maintain the embryo until it is either nourished by the maternal circulatory system or can feed on its own.

When a primary oocyte resumes meiosis, its nucleus completes the first meiotic division near the surface of the cell. The daughter cells of this division receive grossly unequal shares of cytoplasm. This asymmetry represents another major difference from spermatogenesis, in which cytoplasm is apportioned equally. The daughter cell that receives almost all the cytoplasm becomes the **secondary oocyte**, and the one that receives almost none forms the **first polar body** (see Figure 41.4B).

The second meiotic division—that of the large secondary oocyte—is also accompanied by asymmetrical division of the cytoplasm. One daughter cell forms the large, haploid **ootid** that eventually differentiates into a mature egg, and the other forms the **second polar body**. In most species the polar bodies rapidly degenerate, so the end result of oogenesis is only one mature egg for each primary oocyte that enters meiosis. However, that egg is a large, well-provisioned cell. In a few species the polar bodies have evolved specialized functions. In some species that reproduce parthenogenetically, a polar body can fuse with the egg to restore the diploid number of chromosomes. In some insect species the polar bodies form organs with specialized functions. An example is scale insects, in which cells derived from the polar bodies form a container for endosymbiotic bacteria that the insects require for life.

A second period of arrested development occurs after the first meiotic division forms the secondary oocyte. The egg may be expelled from the ovary in this condition. In many species, including humans, the second meiotic division is not completed until the egg is fertilized by a sperm.

Fertilization is the union of sperm and egg

The union of the haploid sperm and the haploid egg (fertilization) creates a single diploid cell, a **zygote** that will develop into an embryo. Fertilization does more than just restore the full genetic complement of the animal. The processes associated with fertilization help the egg and sperm get together, prevent the union of the sperm and egg of different species, and guarantee that only one sperm will enter and activate the egg. Fertilization involves a complex series of events:

1. The sperm and the egg chemically recognize each other.
2. The sperm is activated, enabling it to gain access to the cell membrane of the egg.
3. The cell membrane of the egg fuses with the cell membrane of a single sperm.
4. The egg blocks entry of additional sperm.
5. The egg is metabolically activated and stimulated to start development.
6. The egg and sperm nuclei fuse to create the diploid nucleus of the zygote.

SPECIFICITY IN SPERM–EGG INTERACTIONS   Specific recognition molecules mediate interactions between sperm and eggs. These molecules ensure that the activities of sperm are directed toward eggs and not other cells, and they help prevent eggs from being fertilized by sperm from the wrong species. The latter function is particularly important in aquatic species that release eggs and sperm into the surrounding water, where the eggs can readily be exposed to sperm of other species. The sea urchin is a good example of such a species, and sea urchin fertilization has been well studied.

Sea urchin eggs release chemical attractants that increase the motility of sperm and cause them to swim toward the egg. These chemical attractants are species-specific. For example, eggs of one species of sea urchin release a specific peptide consisting of 14 amino acids. This peptide binds to receptors present on sperm of the same species. The sperm respond by increasing their mitochondrial respiration and motility. Before exposure to the peptide, the sperm swim in tight little circles, but after binding to the peptide, they swim energetically up the concentration gradient of the peptide until they reach the egg that is releasing it.

When a sperm reaches an egg, it must get through two protective layers before it can fuse with the egg cell membrane. The eggs of sea urchins are covered with a jelly coat that surrounds a proteinaceous **vitelline envelope** (Figure 41.5A). The success of a sperm's assault on these protective layers depends on a membrane-enclosed structure at the front of the sperm head called an **acrosome**.

The acrosome contains enzymes and other proteins. When a sperm makes contact with an egg of its own species, substances in the jelly coat trigger an acrosomal reaction. This reaction begins with the breakdown of the cell membrane covering the sperm head and the underlying acrosomal membrane (Figure 41.5B). The acrosomal enzymes are released and digest a hole through the jelly coat.

The acrosomal reaction also triggers polymerization of actin in the sperm head, and an acrosomal process extends out of the front of the sperm head. This acrosomal process is coated with species-specific recognition molecules called **bindin**, and there are bindin receptors on the vitelline envelope of the egg. The interaction of bindin with their receptors enables the sperm to contact the egg cell membrane. That contact results in fusion of the sperm and egg cell membranes and the formation of a fertilization cone that engulfs the sperm head, bringing it into the egg cytoplasm. The sperm mitochondria, which largely constitute the midpiece of the sperm, are also drawn into the egg cytoplasm, but they degrade and disappear; this means that the mitochondria and mitochondrial genes of the new urchin are derived only from the egg.

(A) A sea urchin egg

Figure 41.5 Fertilization of the Sea Urchin Egg **(A)** Sea urchin eggs are protected by a jelly layer and a proteinaceous vitelline envelope. Sperm must penetrate both to reach the egg cell membrane. Many sperm attach to the vitelline envelope, but only the first one to reach the egg cell membrane achieves fertilization. The numbers match structures with the events shown in (B). **(B)** The acrosomal reaction allows a sea urchin sperm to recognize an egg of the same species and pass through its protective layers. Enzymes from the egg's cortical granules trigger the slow block to polyspermy. (After D. Epel. 1977. *Sci Am* 237: 128–138. Drawing by Carol Donner.)

▶ **View in Achieve**
   Animation 41.1 Fertilization in a Sea Urchin Egg

(B) Fertilization of the sea urchin egg

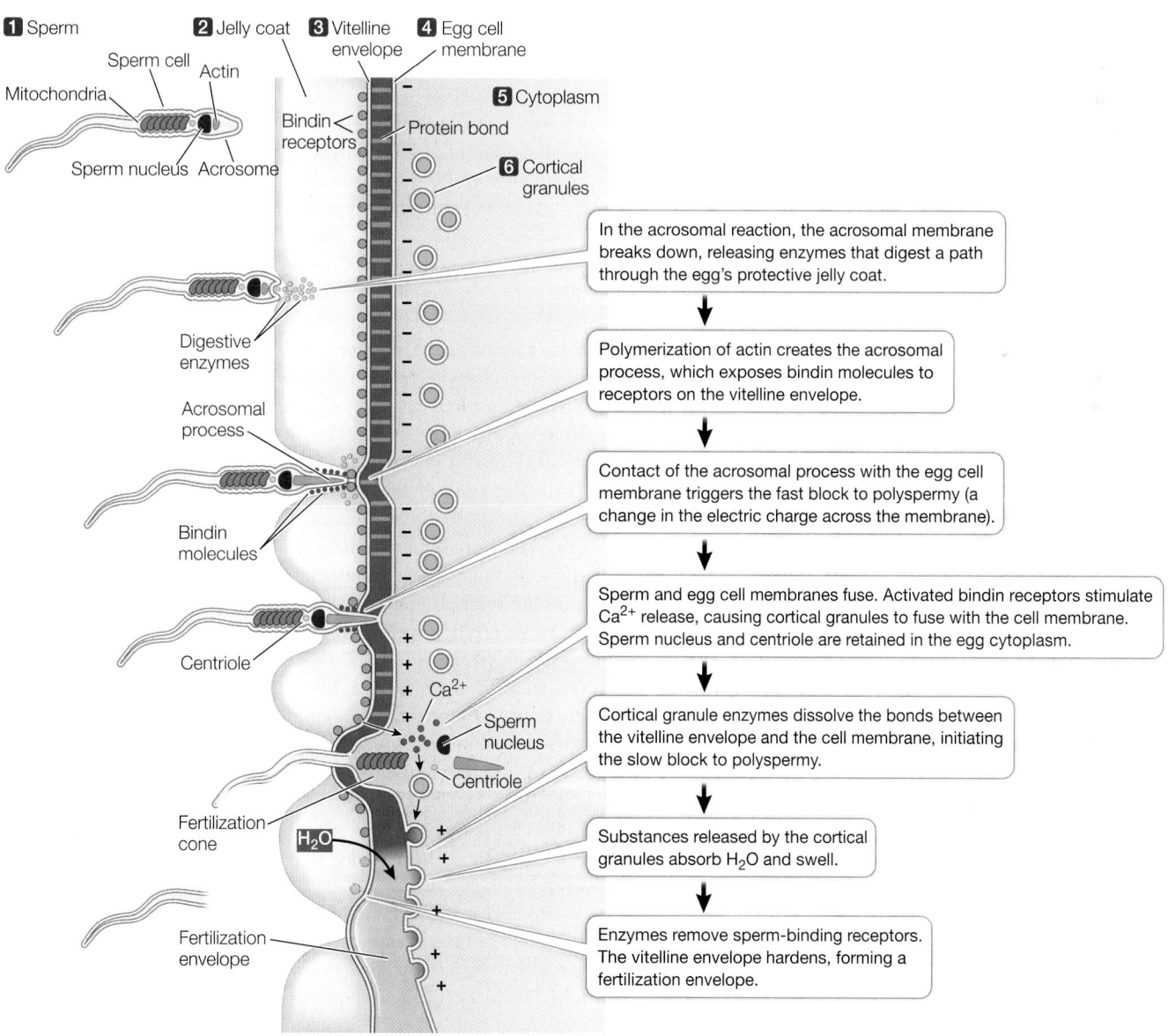

In the acrosomal reaction, the acrosomal membrane breaks down, releasing enzymes that digest a path through the egg's protective jelly coat.

Polymerization of actin creates the acrosomal process, which exposes bindin molecules to receptors on the vitelline envelope.

Contact of the acrosomal process with the egg cell membrane triggers the fast block to polyspermy (a change in the electric charge across the membrane).

Sperm and egg cell membranes fuse. Activated bindin receptors stimulate Ca^{2+} release, causing cortical granules to fuse with the cell membrane. Sperm nucleus and centriole are retained in the egg cytoplasm.

Cortical granule enzymes dissolve the bonds between the vitelline envelope and the cell membrane, initiating the slow block to polyspermy.

Substances released by the cortical granules absorb H_2O and swell.

Enzymes remove sperm-binding receptors. The vitelline envelope hardens, forming a fertilization envelope.

Connect the Concepts Because mitochondrial genes are inherited only from the mother, traits controlled by those genes are not inherited in a Mendelian fashion (see Key Concept 12.5), and they enable establishment of matrilineal phylogenies (see Key Concept 20.2).

In animals that use internal fertilization, mating behaviors help guarantee species specificity, but egg–sperm recognition mechanisms still exist. The mammalian egg is encased by the **cumulus**, a loose assemblage of maternal cells in a gelatinous matrix (**Figure 41.6**). Beneath the cumulus is a glycoprotein envelope called the **zona pellucida**, which is functionally similar to the vitelline envelope of sea urchin eggs. Mammalian sperm become activated when they are deposited in the female reproductive tract, and they are then capable of an acrosomal reaction should they encounter an egg. An activated sperm can penetrate the cumulus and interact with the zona pellucida.

Unlike the jelly coat of sea urchin eggs, the cumulus of mammalian eggs does not trigger the acrosomal reaction. When sperm make contact with the zona pellucida, a species-specific glycoprotein binds to recognition molecules on the head of the sperm. This binding triggers the acrosomal reaction, releasing acrosomal enzymes that digest a path through the zona pellucida. When the sperm head reaches the egg cell membrane, other proteins facilitate its adhesion to and fusion with the egg cell membrane.

BLOCKS TO POLYSPERMY The fusion of the sperm and egg cell membranes and the entry of the sperm into the egg initiate

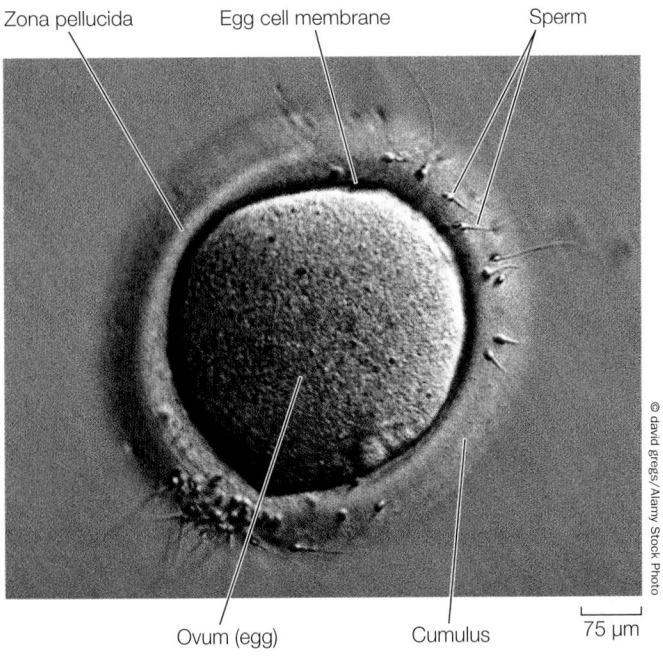

Zona pellucida   Egg cell membrane   Sperm

Ovum (egg)   Cumulus   75 μm

© david gregs/Alamy Stock Photo

Figure 41.6 Barriers to Sperm This human egg, like other mammalian eggs, is surrounded by the cumulus and zona pellucida. Sperm must penetrate both to fertilize the egg. Only one sperm will penetrate the zona pellucida and fuse with the egg cell membrane.

Q: What would be the consequences of two sperm fertilizing the egg?

a programmed sequence of events. The first responses to sperm entry are **blocks to polyspermy**: mechanisms that prevent more than one sperm from entering the egg. Survival of the embryo is unlikely if more than one sperm enters the egg. The sperm contributes a haploid set of chromosomes, so an extra set would disrupt the mitotic division of the egg and subsequent cells. In addition, in most mammals the sperm contributes a centriole to the fertilized egg, and the centriole forms the centrosome, which is critical for organizing the mitotic spindle. Having two centrosomes would disrupt mitosis of the fertilized egg.

Connect the Concepts The roles of the centriole and the centrosome in mitosis are discussed in Key Concept 11.3.

Blocks to polyspermy have been studied extensively in sea urchin eggs because they can be fertilized in a dish of seawater under a microscope. Within seconds after the sperm membrane contacts the egg membrane, an influx of sodium ions changes the electric charge difference across the egg cell membrane. This fast block to polyspermy prevents the fusion of any other sperm with the egg cell membrane, but it is transient. The change in membrane electric charge lasts only about a minute, but that is enough time to allow a slower block to sperm entry to develop.

The slow block to polyspermy involves converting the vitelline envelope to a physical barrier that sperm cannot penetrate. Before fertilization, the vitelline envelope is bonded to the egg cell membrane. Just under the cell membrane are vesicles called cortical granules (see Figure 41.5) that contain enzymes and other proteins.

The sea urchin egg, like all animal cells, sequesters calcium in its endoplasmic reticulum. Sperm entry into the egg stimulates the release of calcium ions from the endoplasmic reticulum and into the egg cytosol. This increase in cytosolic calcium causes the egg's cortical granules to fuse with the cell membrane and release their contents. Cortical granule enzymes break the bonds between the vitelline envelope and the cell membrane, and other proteins released from the cortical granules attract water into that space. As a result, the vitelline envelope rises to form a fertilization envelope. Cortical granule enzymes also degrade sperm-binding molecules on the surface of the fertilization envelope and cause it to harden. Thus additional sperm cannot contact the egg cell membrane.

In mammalian eggs, sperm entry does not cause a rapid change in membrane potential, but it does trigger a release of calcium from the endoplasmic reticulum. As in the sea urchin egg, increased calcium causes the cortical granules to fuse with the egg cell membrane. A fertilization envelope does not form around the mammalian egg, but the cortical granule enzymes destroy the sperm-binding molecules in the zona pellucida. The rise in cytosolic calcium also signals the egg to complete meiosis. The stage is set for the first cell division.

Spawning and mating behaviors get eggs and sperm together

As you have just seen, sexual reproduction requires the production of haploid gametes (gametogenesis) and the joining together of those gametes to form a diploid zygote (fertilization). Spawning and mating behaviors get eggs and sperm close enough together that fertilization can occur. Fertilization can occur externally or internally.

EXTERNAL FERTILIZATION In an aquatic environment, animals can bring their gametes together by simply releasing them into the water. This practice, called spawning, results in **external fertilization**. Many aquatic animals are not very mobile, but they produce huge numbers of gametes that can travel far from the point of release. A female oyster, for example, releases millions of eggs when she spawns, and the number of sperm produced by a male oyster is astronomical.

Numbers alone, however, do not guarantee that gametes will meet. The reproductive activities of the males and females of a population must be synchronized, since released gametes have a limited life span. Seasonal breeders may use day length, changes in temperature, or changes in weather to time the production and release of their gametes. Mutual stimulation is also important. Release of gametes into the water by one individual can stimulate others to spawn.

Behavior can play an important role in bringing gametes together even when fertilization is external. Some species travel great distances to congregate with potential mates and release their gametes at the same time in a suitable environment. Salmon are an extreme example. They hatch and develop in freshwater streams and then migrate to the ocean. They remain as oceanic fishes for years. When they are mature and ready to spawn, they travel hundreds of miles back to and then up the same stream to the region where they hatched. Males and females expend great amounts of energy to swim up the streams to the spawning grounds, where they pair up, prepare a depression in the streambed gravel, and together release their sperm and eggs. As the gametes drift down into the gravel, fertilization occurs.

INTERNAL FERTILIZATION Terrestrial animals cannot simply release their gametes into the environment. Sperm can move only through liquid, and delicate gametes released into air would dry out and die. Most terrestrial animals avoid these problems by **internal fertilization**, the release of sperm into the female reproductive tract. Some aquatic animals also practice internal fertilization, but it is ubiquitous in terrestrial animals.

Animals have evolved an astonishing diversity of behavioral and anatomical adaptations for internal fertilization. The reproductive organs together are the animal's **genitalia**. Gametogenesis occurs in the gonads, which are the **primary sex organs**. All additional components of an animal's genitalia are called **accessory sex organs**. The internal accessory sex organs include a variety of glands, tubules, ducts, and other structures. External accessory sex organs are referred to as the external genitalia. In males of many species, the external genitalia includes a **penis** that enables the male to deposit sperm in the female's **vagina**, the first segment of her reproductive tract.

Copulation is the physical joining of male and female accessory sex organs. Most male insects copulate and transfer sperm to the female's vagina through a penis. The external genitalia of insects often have species-specific shapes that match in a lock-and-key fashion to ensure a tight, secure fit between the mating pair during the prolonged period of sperm transfer. In some insect species in which females mate with more than one male, the male external genitalia includes elaborate structures that can scoop sperm deposited by other males out of the female's reproductive tract, allowing a male to replace that sperm with his own.

Transfer of sperm in internal fertilization can also be indirect. Males of some invertebrate species (e.g., mites and scorpions) and a few vertebrates (e.g., salamanders) deposit spermatophores—packets of sperm protected from desiccation—in the environment. When a female mite encounters a spermatophore from a potential mate, she straddles it and opens a pair of plates in her abdomen so that the tip of the spermatophore enters her reproductive tract and allows the sperm to enter.

Male squid and spiders play a more active role in spermatophore transfer. The male spider secretes a drop containing sperm onto a bit of web, then uses a special structure on his foreleg to pick up the sperm-containing web and insert it through the female's genital opening. Some male squid use one specialized tentacle to pick up a spermatophore and insert it into the female's genital opening.

Some individuals can function as both male and female

In most species, gametes are produced by individuals that are either male or female. Species that have separate male and female members are referred to as **dioecious** (Greek, "two houses"). In some species, however, a single individual may produce both sperm and eggs. Such species are **monoecious** ("one house"), or **hermaphroditic**.

Almost all invertebrate groups contain some hermaphroditic species. An earthworm is an example of a simultaneous hermaphrodite, meaning an individual is both male and female at the same time. When two earthworms mate, they exchange sperm, and as a result the eggs of each are fertilized (see Figure 30.12C). Some vertebrates are sequential hermaphrodites, meaning an individual may function as a male or a female at different times in its life. An example is the anemonefishes, or clownfishes, species that live in small groups within large sea anemones (**Figure 41.7**). All

Amphiprion sp.

© Jane Gould/Alamy Stock Photo

Figure 41.7 When Size Determines Sex Anemonefishes (also known as clownfishes) live in groups of about a dozen centered on a single sea anemone. All anemonefishes are born male; the largest fish in the group becomes a functional female. Thus a fish may function as a male and as a female at different times in its life.

anemone fishes are born male. The largest fish in a group becomes a functional female. If that fish is removed from the group, the next-largest male becomes a female. The second-largest fish in the group is the only male in breeding condition. The reverse situation exists in some species in which a large dominant male controls a harem of females. If the male is removed, the largest female becomes the male in the group.

What is the evolutionary advantage of hermaphroditism? Some simultaneous hermaphrodites, such as parasitic tapeworms, have a low probability of meeting a potential mate—an individual tapeworm may be the only one in its host. Tapeworms can fertilize their own eggs, but most simultaneous hermaphrodites must mate with another individual. Because every simultaneous hermaphrodite is both male and female, however, the probability of encountering a possible mate doubles. In some sequential hermaphrodites, siblings are all male or all female at the same time, thus reducing the incidence of inbreeding.

The evolution of vertebrate reproductive systems parallels the move to land

The earliest vertebrates evolved in aquatic environments. The closest living relatives of those earliest vertebrates are modern-day fishes. They remain exclusively aquatic, and most practice external fertilization. The most primitive fishes, the lampreys and hagfishes, simply release their gametes into the environment. In most fishes, however, mating behaviors bring females and males into close proximity at the time of gamete release. In sharks and rays, fins have evolved into claspers that hold the male and female together and enable sperm to be transferred directly into the female reproductive tract.

Amphibians were the first vertebrates to live in terrestrial environments. They dealt with the challenge of a dry environment by returning to water to reproduce, as most amphibians still do today.

Reptiles were the first vertebrate group to solve the problem of reproduction in the terrestrial environment (**Figure 41.8**). Their solution was the amniote egg (see Figure 31.19A). A hard

or leathery shell protects the embryo and impedes water loss while allowing the diffusion of oxygen into the egg and carbon dioxide out of the egg. The eggshell creates an obvious problem for fertilization. Sperm cannot penetrate the shell, so they must reach the egg before the shell forms. Hence internal fertilization and the evolution of accessory sex organs were necessary for the evolution of the amniote egg.

Male snakes and lizards have paired hemipenes (singular *hemipenis*) that can be engorged with blood and thereby extruded from the male's body. Only one hemipenis is inserted into the female's reproductive tract. It is usually rough or spiny at the end to achieve a secure hold while sperm are transferred down a groove on its surface. Retractor muscles pull the hemipenis back into the male's body when mating is completed. Some evolutionarily ancient bird species have erectile penises that channel sperm along a groove into the female's reproductive tract. Birds with more recent evolutionary origins, however, do not have erectile penises; instead, the male and female simply bring their genital openings (cloacae; singular *cloaca*) close together to transfer sperm. Usually this involves the male standing on the female's back (see Figure 41.8B).

All mammals practice internal fertilization. Then all except the prototherian mammals retain the developing embryo for some time in the female reproductive tract. Prototherian mammals (the monotremes; see Figure 31.26) lay eggs. The other mammals (the therians) vary enormously as to the developmental stage of their offspring at the time of birth. As you saw at the beginning of the chapter, the tammar wallaby is extremely immature at birth. By comparison, a horse foal can stand up soon after birth and is able to run within hours.

Animals with internal fertilization are distinguished by where the embryo develops

Two patterns of care and nurture of the embryo have evolved in animals: oviparity (egg laying) and viviparity (live bearing).

Oviparous animals lay eggs in the environment, and their embryos develop outside the mother's body. Oviparous terrestrial

Figure 41.8 The Shelled Egg
The terrestrial environment is desiccating. Therefore the shelled egg was a major evolutionary step that allowed reptiles to reproduce in the terrestrial environment. **(A)** A female banded krait has deposited her eggs in the sand. **(B)** The shelled egg requires that sperm meet egg before the shell forms. Therefore reptiles must practice internal fertilization, as these European Bee-eaters are doing.

(A) *Bungarus fasciatus*

(B) *Merops apiaster*

animals such as insects and reptiles—including birds—protect their eggs from desiccation with waterproof membranes or shells. Oviparity is possible because eggs are stocked with abundant nutrients to supply the needs of the embryo. Some oviparous animals engage in various forms of parental behavior to protect their eggs, but until the eggs hatch, the embryos depend entirely on the nutrients stored in the egg.

Viviparous animals retain the embryo within the mother's body during its early developmental stages. The embryo is nourished and its wastes removed through exchanges with the mother's tissues. Viviparity occurs in many vertebrate groups, and with the exception of the prototherians, it is universal in mammals. Therian mammals have a specialized portion of the female reproductive tract, the **uterus** or womb, that contains the embryo until it is born. The early embryo arriving in the uterus from the fallopian tube implants into the lining of the uterus. Implantation involves interactions between the tissues of the embryo and the uterus to form a **placenta**. Intimate contact in the placenta between the blood of the embryo and the blood of the mother facilitates the exchange of nutrients and wastes.

In most non-mammalian viviparous animals, such as garter snakes and the well-known aquarium fish the guppy, fertilized eggs are retained in the mother's body until they hatch. These embryos still receive nutrition from stores in the egg, so this reproductive adaptation is called **ovoviviparity**.

_{KEY CONCEPT}
41.2 Recap and Assess

Sexual reproduction involves gametogenesis, mating, and fertilization. Fertilization can be external or internal and involves mechanisms for ensuring that only one sperm from the right species enters the egg. Oviparous female animals lay eggs in the environment, and their embryos develop outside the mother's body. Viviparous female animals retain the developing embryo in the uterus until it is born.

1. Crossing over is the reciprocal exchange of segments in homologous chromatids. Why does it occur more frequently in human oocytes than in human spermatocytes?

2. If a mutation in a mammal eliminated the maintenance of cytoplasmic bridges between spermatids, would you expect all offspring sired by that mammal to be male or female? Explain your answer.

3. In animals that spawn, what mechanisms ensure that an egg is fertilized by sperm of the same species, and by only one sperm?

4. What are three situations in which hermaphroditism would be advantageous?

Now that we have covered some of the general aspects of gametogenesis and fertilization and have briefly discussed the great diversity of mating systems, we next consider the human reproductive systems in detail.

_{KEY CONCEPT}
41.3 Male Sex Organs Produce and May Deliver Sperm

Learning Objectives

41.3.1 Identify the different components of semen, where they are produced, and their functions.

41.3.2 Describe the anatomical and functional relationships between Leydig cells and Sertoli cells.

41.3.3 Explain the roles of NO and cGMP in the male sexual response.

41.3.4 Summarize the hormonal changes that occur during puberty in males and how they lead to the development of male secondary sexual characteristics.

This key concept describes the structures and functions of the male reproductive system in mammals, using humans as the prime example. You will also learn about the hormonal regulation of the male reproductive system. The discussion covers:

- *The primary sex organs*, testes, that produce sperm and serve endocrine functions.

- *The accessory sex organs*, including the ducts through which the sperm pass, the glands that produce and deliver secretions into those ducts, and the external genitalia.

- *Secondary sexual characteristics* that result in male appearance but are not directly involved in reproduction.

Semen is the product of the male reproductive system

Semen contains sperm and a mixture of fluids and molecules (seminal fluid) that support the sperm and facilitate fertilization. Sperm make up less than 5% of the volume of the semen. Sperm are produced in the testes, the paired male gonads, and the seminal fluid is produced by accessory glands.

Figure 41.9 illustrates the human male reproductive organs. The testes of most mammals are located outside the body cavity in a pouch of skin called the **scrotum**. Why should the testes be located outside the body cavity? The optimal temperature for spermatogenesis in most mammals is slightly lower than the normal body temperature. The scrotum keeps the testes at this optimal temperature. Muscles in the scrotum contract in a cold environment, bringing the testes closer to the warmth of the body; in a hot environment the muscles relax, cooling the testes by suspending them farther from the body.

Spermatogenesis takes place within the **seminiferous tubules** tightly coiled in each testis (**Figure 41.10A**). Between the seminiferous tubules are clusters of **Leydig cells** that produce testosterone (**Figure 41.10B**). Spermatogonia reside in the outer regions of the seminiferous tubules, just under the basement membrane. Moving inward toward the lumen of the tubule are germ cells in successive stages of spermatogenesis (**Figure 41.10C**). The germ cells are intimately associated with **Sertoli cells**, which provide nutrients for the developing sperm and secrete several things, including hormones and growth factors that

(A) Posterior view

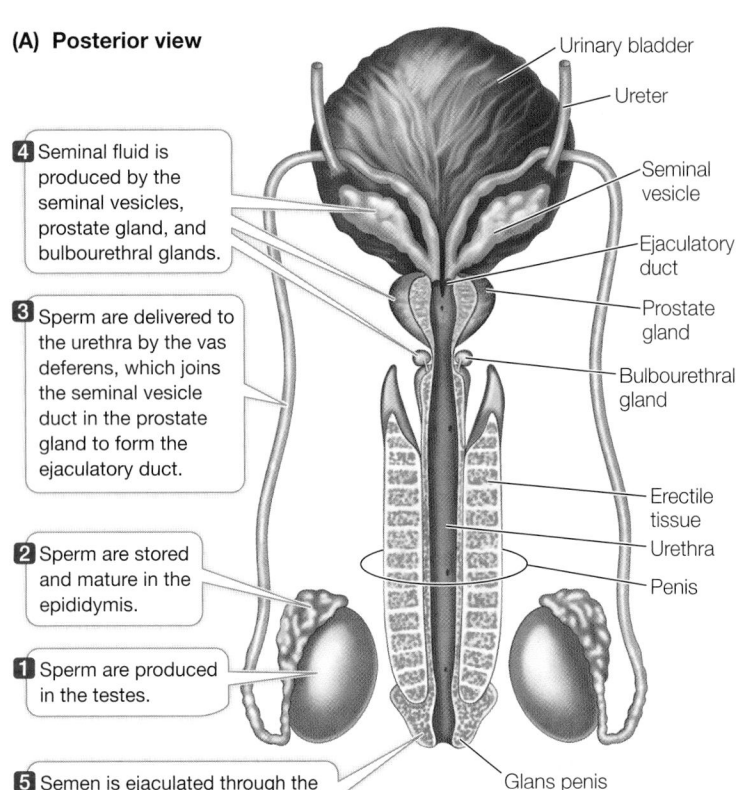

4 Seminal fluid is produced by the seminal vesicles, prostate gland, and bulbourethral glands.

3 Sperm are delivered to the urethra by the vas deferens, which joins the seminal vesicle duct in the prostate gland to form the ejaculatory duct.

2 Sperm are stored and mature in the epididymis.

1 Sperm are produced in the testes.

5 Semen is ejaculated through the male copulatory organ, the penis.

Urinary bladder
Ureter
Seminal vesicle
Ejaculatory duct
Prostate gland
Bulbourethral gland
Erectile tissue
Urethra
Penis
Glans penis

(B) Side view

Urinary bladder
Pubic symphysis
Prostate gland
Erectile tissue
Urethra
Glans penis
Foreskin
Scrotum Testis Epididymis
Vas deferens
Bulbourethral gland
Anus
Ejaculatory duct
Rectum
Seminal vesicle
Colon
Ureter (from kidney)

Figure 41.9 Reproductive Tract of the Human Male The male reproductive organs are shown (**A**) from the rear and (**B**) from the side.

Q: What problem might an enlarged prostate gland produce?

▶ **View in Achieve**
Activity 41.1 The Human Male Reproductive Tract

are necessary for spermatogenesis (which is why Sertoli cells are sometimes called "nurse cells"). Tight junctions (see Key Concept 6.2) between Sertoli cells create a blood–sperm barrier that prevents many harmful substances that can be circulating in the blood from getting to the developing sperm.

When the second meiotic division is complete, each primary spermatocyte has produced four spermatids (see Figure 41.4A). The spermatids develop into spermatozoa as they migrate toward the lumen of the seminiferous tubule. The nucleus becomes compact, and the surrounding cytoplasm is lost. A flagellum—the sperm tail—develops. The mitochondria that provide the energy for sperm motility become condensed into a midpiece between the head and tail. An acrosome forms over the nucleus in the head of the sperm. Immature sperm are shed into the lumen of the seminiferous tubule.

From the seminiferous tubules, sperm move into the **epididymis** (see Figure 41.9A), where they mature, become motile, and are stored. The epididymis connects to the **urethra** via the **vas deferens** (plural *vasa deferentia*) and the **ejaculatory duct**. The urethra originates in the bladder, runs through the penis, and opens to the outside of the body at the tip of the penis. It serves as the common final duct for urine and semen.

The components of the semen other than sperm come from three accessory glands. About 60% of the volume of semen is secreted by the paired **seminal vesicles** that secrete into the vas deferens just before it joins the urethra. Seminal fluid is thick because it contains mucus and fibrinogen, a protein also found in the blood, where it can polymerize to form blood clots. Seminal fluid also contains the monosaccharide fructose, an energy source for the sperm.

The **prostate gland** contributes about 30% of the volume of the semen. Prostate fluid is alkaline, so it neutralizes the acidity in the male and female reproductive tracts and makes these environments more hospitable to sperm. The prostate secretes a clotting enzyme that causes fibrinogen from the seminal vesicles to clot and convert the semen into a gelatinous mass that can be ejaculated into the female reproductive tract. Another prostate enzyme, fibrinolysin, dissolves the clotted semen after it is ejaculated, thereby liberating the sperm. Prostaglandins—hormones produced by the prostate—stimulate contractions of the female reproductive tract.

The **bulbourethral glands** produce a small volume of an alkaline, mucoid secretion that helps neutralize acidity in the urethra and lubricate it to facilitate the passage of semen during the climax of sexual intercourse.

The penis and the scrotum are the male external genitalia

The shaft of the penis is covered with normal skin, but the highly sensitive tip, the **glans penis**, is covered with thinner, more sensitive skin that is especially responsive to sexual stimulation. A fold of skin called the foreskin covers the glans of the human penis. The procedure known as circumcision removes a portion of the foreskin.

Sexual stimulation triggers responses in the nervous system that result in penile **erection**. This response is mediated by nerves to the penis from the central nervous system (brain and spinal cord) that release the neurotransmitter acetylcholine (ACh) onto endothelial cells lining the penile blood vessels. These

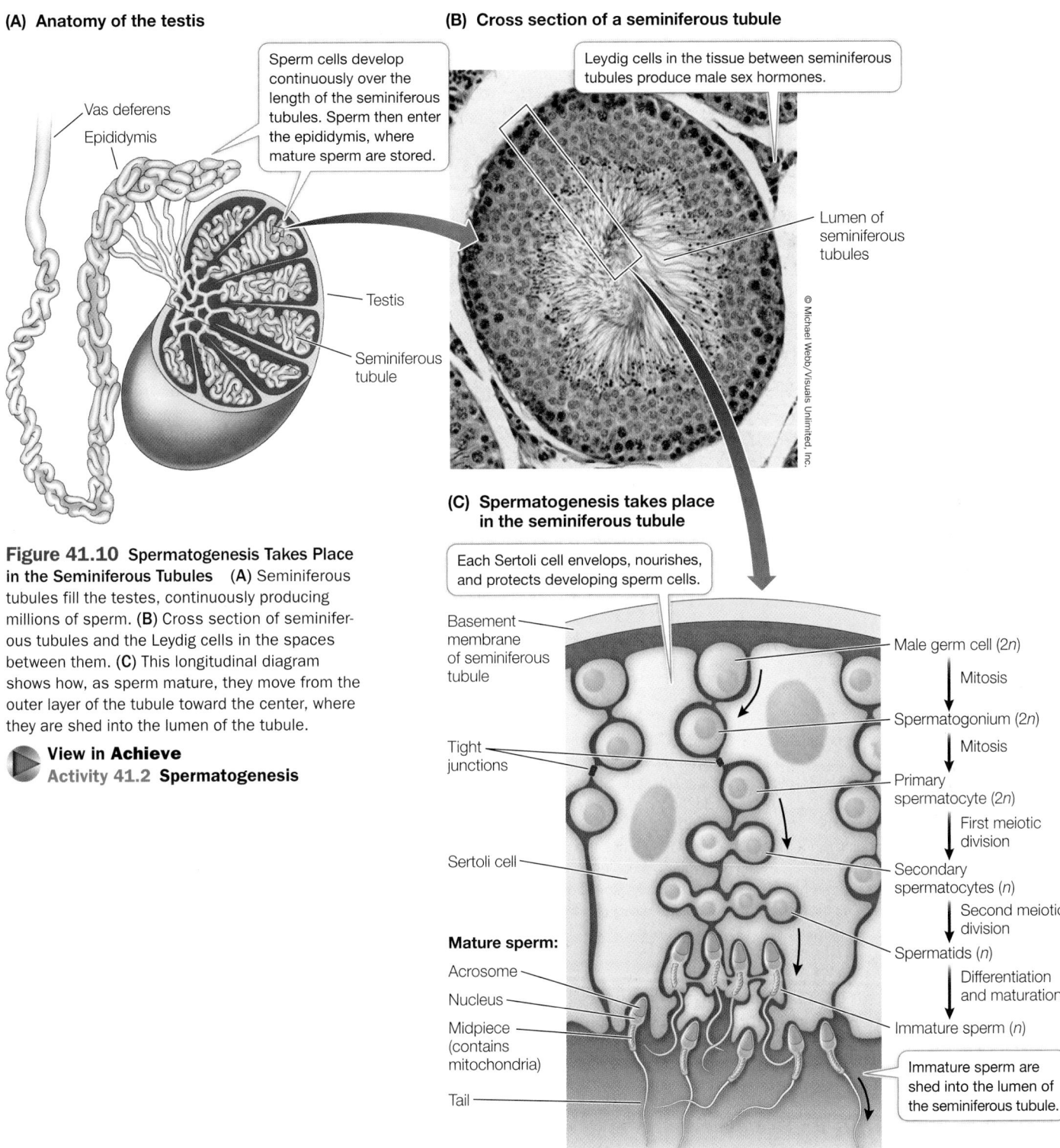

(A) Anatomy of the testis

Vas deferens

Epididymis

Sperm cells develop continuously over the length of the seminiferous tubules. Sperm then enter the epididymis, where mature sperm are stored.

Testis

Seminiferous tubule

(B) Cross section of a seminiferous tubule

Leydig cells in the tissue between seminiferous tubules produce male sex hormones.

Lumen of seminiferous tubules

© Michael Webb/Visuals Unlimited, Inc.

Figure 41.10 Spermatogenesis Takes Place in the Seminiferous Tubules **(A)** Seminiferous tubules fill the testes, continuously producing millions of sperm. **(B)** Cross section of seminiferous tubules and the Leydig cells in the spaces between them. **(C)** This longitudinal diagram shows how, as sperm mature, they move from the outer layer of the tubule toward the center, where they are shed into the lumen of the tubule.

▶ **View in Achieve**
Activity 41.2 Spermatogenesis

(C) Spermatogenesis takes place in the seminiferous tubule

Each Sertoli cell envelops, nourishes, and protects developing sperm cells.

Basement membrane of seminiferous tubule

Tight junctions

Sertoli cell

Mature sperm:

Acrosome

Nucleus

Midpiece (contains mitochondria)

Tail

Lumen

Male germ cell ($2n$)

↓ Mitosis

Spermatogonium ($2n$)

↓ Mitosis

Primary spermatocyte ($2n$)

↓ First meiotic division

Secondary spermatocytes (n)

↓ Second meiotic division

Spermatids (n)

↓ Differentiation and maturation

Immature sperm (n)

Immature sperm are shed into the lumen of the seminiferous tubule.

endothelial cells respond by synthesizing and releasing a gaseous signal—**nitric oxide (NO)** (**Figure 41.11**; see also Figure 7.13). The NO diffuses into the smooth muscle cells that control the diameter of the penile arteries and stimulates them to produce the second messenger cyclic GMP (cGMP). Increased cGMP in these muscle cells causes a decrease in cytoplasmic Ca^{2+} by closing Ca^{2+} channels and stimulating Ca^{2+} reuptake by the endoplasmic reticulum. The decrease in Ca^{2+} causes the smooth muscles to relax; the arteries dilate and carry more blood into the penis. Increased blood flow swells the shafts of spongy erectile tissue located along the length of the penis (see Figure 41.9). The enlargement of these blood-filled cavities compresses the vessels that carry blood out

Ejaculation is caused by contractions of other muscles at the base of the penis surrounding the urethra. These contractions force the coagulum of semen through the urethra and out of the penis. The muscle contractions of ejaculation are accompanied by feelings of intense pleasure known as orgasm. They are also accompanied by transient increases in heart rate, blood pressure, breathing, pupil dilation, and skeletal muscle contractions throughout the body.

After ejaculation, NO release decreases and a phosphodiesterase enzyme breaks down cGMP (see Figure 41.11). With decreased cGMP, the cytoplasmic Ca^{2+} concentration increases, causing constriction of the blood vessels carrying blood into the penis. Blood pressure in the erectile tissue decreases, relieving the compression of the blood vessels leaving the penis, and the erection declines.

Erectile dysfunction (ED), or impotence, is the inability to achieve or sustain an erection. ED may have different causes, including cardiovascular disease. Drugs such as sildenafil are used to treat ED because they inhibit the phosphodiesterase that breaks down cGMP, thus enhancing the effect of NO released in the penis and thereby improving the ability to achieve and maintain an erection.

Male sexual function is controlled by hormones

Spermatogenesis and maintenance of male secondary sexual characteristics such as facial hair and a deep voice depend on testosterone produced by the Leydig cells of the testes. As described in Key Concept 39.3, increased production of testosterone at puberty results from an increased release of gonadotropin-releasing hormone (GnRH) by the hypothalamus. GnRH stimulates anterior pituitary cells to secrete luteinizing hormone (LH) and follicle-stimulating hormone (FSH) (**Figure 41.12**). Higher levels of LH stimulate the Leydig cells to increase their production and release of testosterone. Testosterone exerts negative feedback on the anterior pituitary and the hypothalamus. At the time of puberty, the sensitivity of the hypothalamus to negative feedback from testosterone declines; as a result, the level of circulating testosterone increases.

Increased testosterone in pubertal boys causes the development of pubic and facial hair, a deeper voice, enlarged genitals, and an increased growth rate. Testosterone also promotes increased muscle mass and maturation of the testes. Continued production of testosterone after puberty is essential for the maintenance of secondary sexual characteristics and the production of sperm.

Spermatogenesis is controlled by the influence of FSH and testosterone on the Sertoli cells in the seminiferous tubules. The

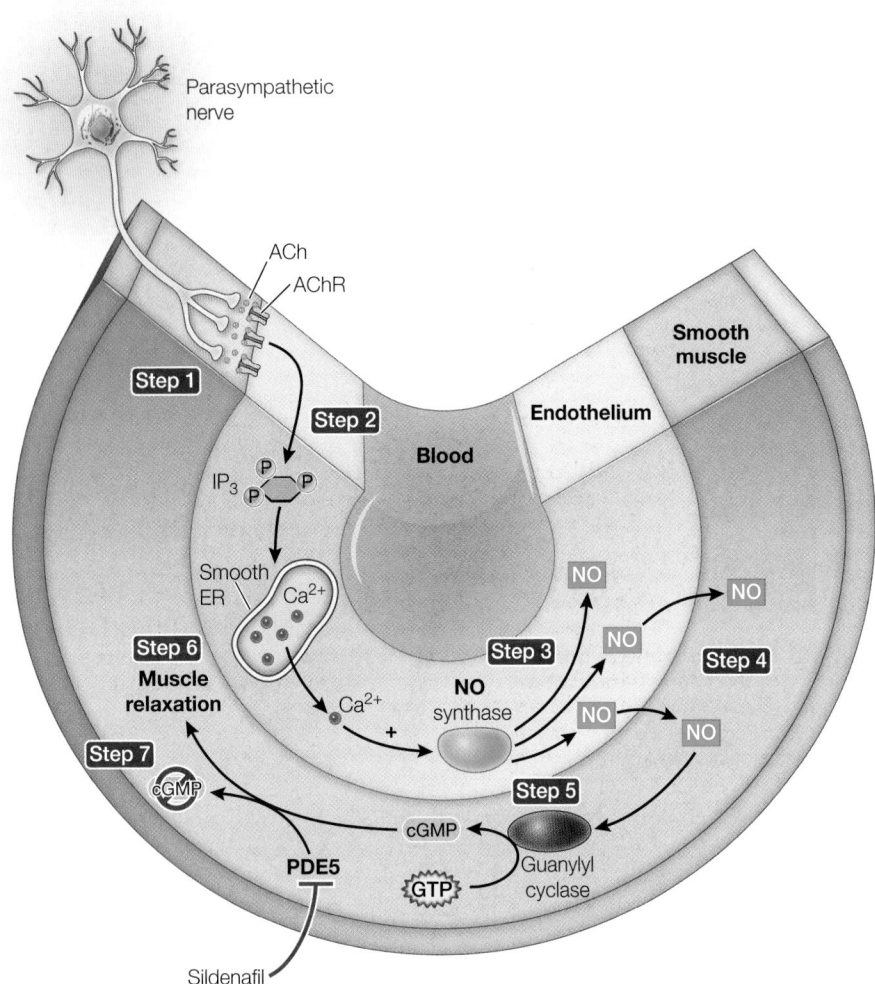

Figure 41.11 Neural Control of Erection Involves a Gaseous Signal Neural release of acetylcholine (ACh) onto endothelial cells of the penile blood vessels activates second messenger IP$_3$ (inositol triphosphate) which stimulates the synthesis and release of nitrous oxide (NO), which diffuses to the surrounding smooth muscle cells. NO induces the production of cyclic GMP (cGMP), which lowers cytoplasmic Ca^{2+}, causing the smooth muscles to relax and thereby allow greater blood flow and an erection. A phosphodiesterase breaks down the cGMP, ending the erection. Drugs such as sildenafil that inhibit phosphodiesterase prolong the erection.

of the penis, and the erectile tissue becomes engorged with blood. The penis becomes hard and erect, facilitating its insertion into the vagina. Many species of mammals (though not humans) have a bone in the penis, but these species still depend on erectile tissue for copulation.

Connect the Concepts The mechanism whereby the neurotransmitter ACh causes production of the gas NO in smooth muscle is described in Key Concept 7.3 (see Figure 7.13), and how intracellular Ca^{2+} controls smooth muscle contraction is described in Key Concept 46.1 (see Figure 46.9).

At the climax of copulation, 2–6 milliliters of semen are propelled through the vasa deferentia and the urethra in two steps, emission and ejaculation. During emission, rhythmic contractions of smooth muscles in the vasa deferentia and accessory glands move the semen into the urethra at the base of the penis.

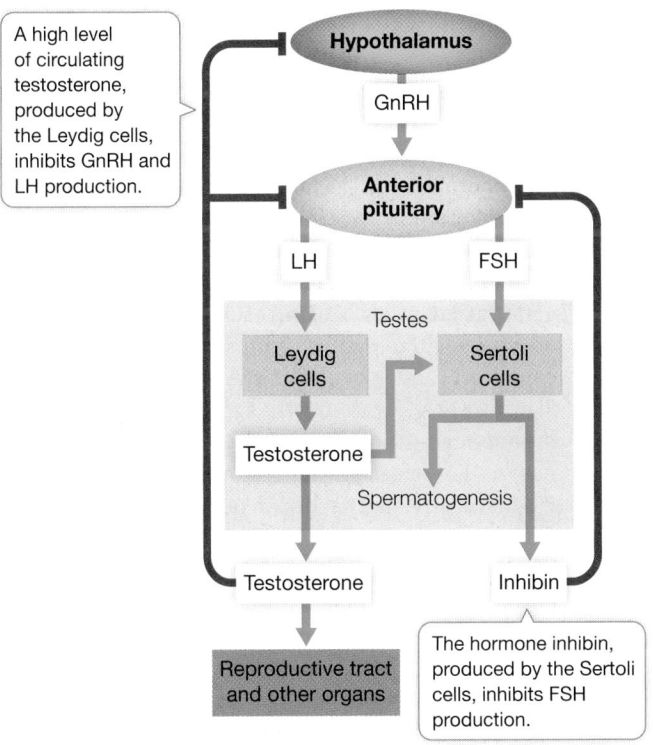

A high level of circulating testosterone, produced by the Leydig cells, inhibits GnRH and LH production.

The hormone inhibin, produced by the Sertoli cells, inhibits FSH production.

Figure 41.12 Male Reproductive Hormones The male reproductive system is under hormonal control by the hypothalamus and the anterior pituitary. Red lines indicate inhibition; green lines indicate stimulation and secretion.

Sertoli cells also produce a hormone called inhibin that exerts negative feedback on the anterior pituitary cells that produce and secrete FSH.

KEY CONCEPT
41.3 Recap and Assess

Sperm are produced in the testes and are contained in the seminal fluid produced by accessory glands. The resulting semen is ejaculated into the female reproductive tract during copulation. Prior to copulation, sexual stimulation causes the penis to become erect by increasing the blood flow into the erectile tissues. The male reproductive system is under hormonal control by the hypothalamus and anterior pituitary, with negative feedback coming from hormones produced by the testes.

1. What makes ejaculated semen thick and gelatinous, and how do sperm escape the gel to move up the female reproductive tract?
2. What are the roles of Sertoli cells in spermatogenesis?
3. How does an inhibitor of phosphodiesterase treat erectile dysfunction?
4. What is the significance of the fact that the testes of a prepubertal male are responsive to FSH and LH?

Whereas the male reproductive system produces sperm continuously throughout reproductive life, the female system produces eggs that can be fertilized by sperm periodically. We now turn to the cyclical processes by which the female reproductive system produces and releases eggs and prepares the female reproductive tract to receive a developing embryo should fertilization occur.

KEY CONCEPT
41.4
Female Sex Organs Produce Eggs and May Nurture Embryos

Learning Objectives

41.4.1 Link the events in the ovarian and menstrual cycles.

41.4.2 Explain how the number of eggs that are ovulated in each cycle is controlled.

41.4.3 Explain how the blastocyst prevents menstruation.

41.4.4 Describe how mechanical and hormonal stimuli interact during labor.

The human female reproductive system is illustrated in **Figure 41.13**. Eggs are produced in and released from the ovaries, located on each side of the lower abdominal cavity. When an egg leaves the ovary (**ovulation**), it enters the abdominal cavity, but it does not go far. The ovaries are close to the openings of the **oviducts** (also known as the fallopian tubes). The openings are surrounded by undulating, fringed tissues called fimbria that sweep the egg into the oviduct. Cilia lining the oviduct propel the egg toward the **uterus**, a muscular, thick-walled cavity shaped in humans like an upside-down pear. The uterus is where the embryo will develop if the egg is fertilized. At its bottom, the uterus narrows into a region called the **cervix**, which opens into the vagina.

Externally, the vagina is enclosed by two sets of skin folds. The inner, more delicate folds are the labia minora; the outer, thicker folds are the labia majora. At the anterior tip of the labia minora is the clitoris, a small bulb of highly sensitive erectile tissue that has the same developmental origins as the male glans penis. Clitoral tissues, homologous with the erectile tissues of the penis, extend deep under the labia minora and the walls of the vagina. The labia minora and the clitoral tissues become engorged with blood in response to sexual stimulation. Just as stimulation of the glans penis during sexual intercourse culminates in orgasm in the male, stimulation of the clitoral tissues results in orgasm in the female.

The external opening of an infant's vagina is usually, but not always, partly covered by a thin membrane, the hymen. Eventually the hymen can be torn by vigorous physical activity or by first sexual intercourse; it can sometimes make first intercourse difficult or painful for the woman.

Sperm deposited in the vagina swim and are propelled by contractions of the female reproductive tract through the cervical opening, up through the uterus, and most of the way up an oviduct, where fertilization takes place. Before meeting a sperm, the egg is still a secondary oocyte. Fertilization stimulates the egg to complete its second meiotic division. Following that division, the haploid nuclei of the sperm and the egg can fuse to produce a diploid zygote nucleus.

The zygote undergoes its first few cell divisions to become a **blastocyst** while still in the oviduct. The blastocyst moves down the oviduct to the uterus, where it attaches itself to the epithelial lining of the uterus—the **endometrium**. Once attached, the blastocyst implants in the endometrium and interacts with it to form the

(A) Front view

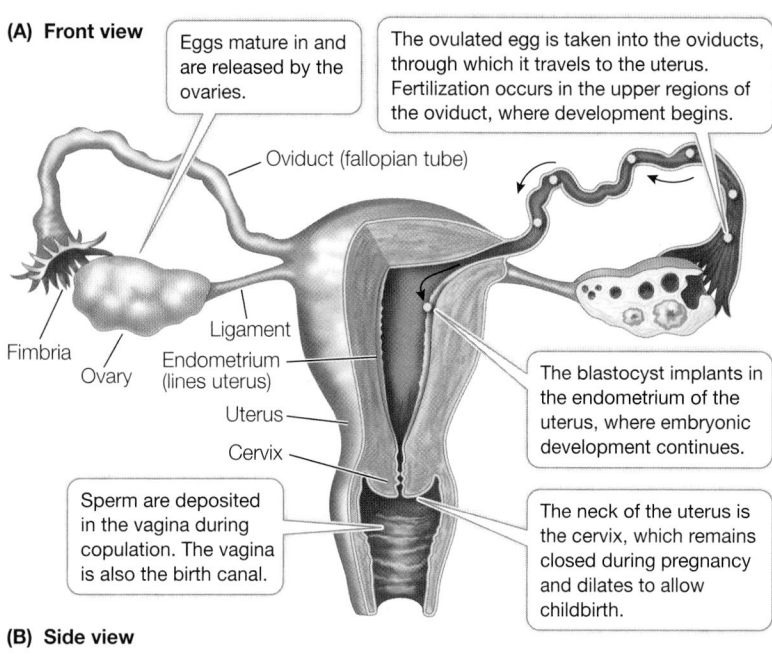

Eggs mature in and are released by the ovaries.

The ovulated egg is taken into the oviducts, through which it travels to the uterus. Fertilization occurs in the upper regions of the oviduct, where development begins.

Oviduct (fallopian tube)

Ligament

Fimbria

Ovary

Endometrium (lines uterus)

Uterus

Cervix

The blastocyst implants in the endometrium of the uterus, where embryonic development continues.

Sperm are deposited in the vagina during copulation. The vagina is also the birth canal.

The neck of the uterus is the cervix, which remains closed during pregnancy and dilates to allow childbirth.

(B) Side view

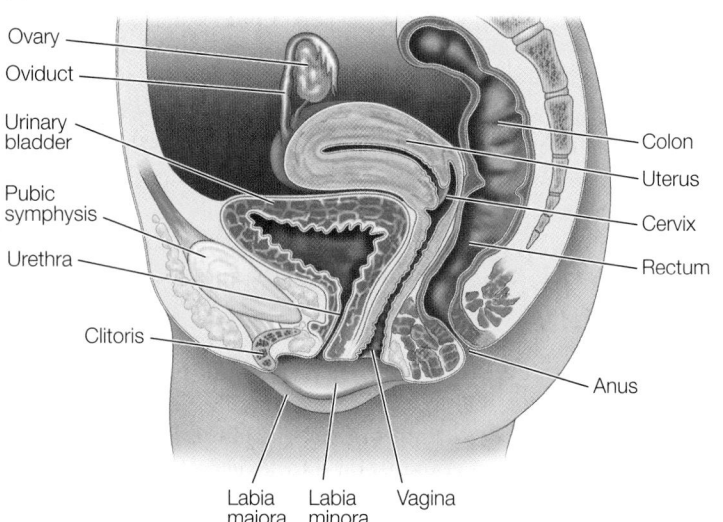

Ovary

Oviduct

Urinary bladder

Pubic symphysis

Urethra

Clitoris

Colon

Uterus

Cervix

Rectum

Anus

Labia majora   Labia minora   Vagina

Figure 41.13 Reproductive Tract of the Human Female The female reproductive organs are shown **(A)** from the front and **(B)** from the side.

View in Achieve
Activity 41.3 The Human Female Reproductive Tract

placenta, as you will see in Key Concept 42.2. The mother's body nurtures the embryo through the placenta, which also produces hormones that sustain pregnancy.

The maturation of eggs and ovulation are cyclical events in the ovaries. Changes in the uterus are also critical processes. These cycles in humans average about 28 days, but they can vary considerably in an individual and among different individuals. In anticipation of receiving a blastocyst, the endometrium thickens and develops lots of blood vessels. The endometrium regresses if a blastocyst does not arrive within a certain window of time. Thus female reproductive functions consist of two linked cycles: an **ovarian cycle** that produces eggs and hormones; and a **uterine**, or **menstrual**, **cycle** that prepares the endometrium for the arrival of a blastocyst (**Figure 41.14**).

The two cycles must be synchronized so that a blastocyst arrives in the uterus at the optimal time to implant in the endometrium and continue its development.

Ovarian cycles produce mature eggs

A newborn baby girl has about a million primary oocytes in each ovary. By the time she reaches puberty, she has only about 200,000; the rest have degenerated. During a woman's fertile years, her ovaries go through about 450 ovarian cycles. During each cycle, 10–20 primary oocytes begin to mature, but usually only one matures completely and is ovulated; the others degenerate (see Figure 41.14A). At around the age of 50, a woman reaches **menopause**—the end of fertility—and may have few oocytes left in each ovary. For more than 50 years, the gradual age-related decline in oocytes was taken as evidence that oogenesis in humans is limited to prenatal life. However, in recent years oogonial stem cells (OSCs) have been isolated from adult ovaries of mice and of humans. These OSCs have been shown to be capable of division and production of oocytes. Thus menopause may not be the absolute end of fertility.

A primary oocyte surrounded by a layer of ovarian cells is the functional unit of the ovary—the **follicle** (see the photo in Figure 41.14A). The follicle cells surrounding the oocyte supply it with nutrients and growth factors. The follicle cells are also the main site of production of the female hormones estrogen and progesterone. Usually only one follicle matures completely and reaches the stage of ovulation, releasing its egg at midcycle. Events that lead up to and follow ovulation are illustrated in Figure 41.14B. Follicle maturation occurs in the first half of the cycle, therefore called the **follicular phase**. The notable hormonal event leading up to ovulation is the gradual and then escalating increase in estrogen, which peaks just prior to midcycle (see Figure 41.14B).

The second half of the ovarian cycle is called the **luteal phase** because the follicle cells left in the ovary after the egg is ovulated develop into an endocrine gland—the **corpus luteum** ("yellow body")—secreting estrogen and progesterone. If the egg is not fertilized and does not embed into the endometrium, the corpus luteum becomes inactive and degenerates in 12–14 days.

Media Clip 41.1 Human Ovulation
Life12e.com/mc41.1

The uterine cycle prepares an environment for a fertilized egg

The uterine cycle parallels the ovarian cycle and consists of a buildup and then a breakdown of the endometrium (see Figure 41.14B). The breakdown of the endometrium, or **menstruation** (from the Latin *menses*, "months"), marks the beginning of each uterine and ovarian cycle. About 5 days after menstruation begins, the endometrium starts to thicken in preparation for receiving a blastocyst. The uterus attains its maximal state of preparedness about 5 days

(A) Changes in the ovary during the ovarian cycle

1 About once a month between puberty and menopause, 6–12 primary oocytes begin to mature. A primary oocyte and its surrounding cells constitute a follicle.

2 The surrounding follicular cells nourish the developing oocyte and release estrogen.

3 After 1 week, usually only one primary oocyte continues to develop. A meiotic division just before ovulation creates the secondary oocyte (*n*).

Primary oocyte (2*n*)

Ligament (holds ovary in place in the abdomen)

6 If pregnancy does not occur, the corpus luteum degenerates.

Ovary

5 The remaining follicle cells form the corpus luteum, which produces progesterone and estrogen.

4 At ovulation, the follicle ruptures, releasing an oocyte.

Ruptured follicle

Mature mammalian follicle

Primary oocyte   Granulosa cells   Thecal cells

© Biophoto Associates/Science Source

(B) Coordinated events in ovarian and uterine cycles

FSH stimulates the development of follicles; the LH surge causes ovulation and then the development of the corpus luteum.

Events in ovary (ovarian cycle)

Oocyte maturation   Developing follicle   Ovulation (day 14)   Corpus luteum   Developing oocyte

Estrogen and progesterone stimulate the development of the endometrium in preparation for pregnancy.

Ovarian hormones and the uterine cycle

Estrogen

Progesterone

Endometrium of uterus   Bleeding and sloughing (menstruation)   Highly proliferated and vascularized endometrium

Thickness of endometrium

FSH and LH are under control of GnRH from the hypothalamus and the ovarian hormones estrogen and progesterone.

Gonadotropins (from anterior pituitary)

Estrogen inhibits LH and FSH release | Estrogen stimulates LH and FSH release | Estrogen inhibits LH and FSH release

Luteinizing hormone (LH)

LH surge triggers ovulation.

Follicle-stimulating hormone (FSH)

0   7   14   21   28
Day of uterine cycle

Figure 41.14 The Ovarian and Uterine Cycles

(A) The ovarian cycle progresses from the development of a follicle to ovulation and then to growth and finally to degeneration of the corpus luteum.
(B) During a woman's ovarian and uterine cycles, coordinated changes occur in the development of the ovarian follicle, the release of female sex steroids, and the endometrial lining of the uterus. The release of hypothalamic GnRH stimulates the release of pituitary LH and FSH, which in turn control the development of the follicle and eventually ovulation. The cycles begin with the onset of menstruation; ovulation is at midcycle (yellow bar). **(C)** The ovarian and uterine cycles are under a complex series of positive- and negative-feedback controls involving several hormones.

Q: Hormonal contraceptive pills contain estrogen and progesterone. Which portion of the ovarian cycle do they simulate, and how do they prevent ovulation?

▶ View in **Achieve**
Animation 41.2
The Ovarian and Uterine Cycles

(C) Hormones control the ovarian and uterine cycles

Hypothalamus

GnRH

Positive feedback occurs during days 12 through 14.

Anterior pituitary

LH/FSH

Ovary

Estrogen and progesterone

Uterus

Negative feedback occurs throughout most of the cycle.

after ovulation and remains in that state for another 9 days. If a blastocyst has not arrived by that time, the endometrium breaks down and the sloughed-off tissue, including blood, flows from the body through the vagina as a menstrual discharge.

The uterine cycles of most mammals other than humans do not include menstruation; instead, the uterine lining typically is reabsorbed. In these species, the most obvious correlate of the ovarian cycle is a state of sexual receptivity called **estrus** ("heat") around the time of ovulation. You may be aware of the bloody discharge that occurs in dogs at the time of estrus. This discharge is not the same as menstruation—in fact it is exactly the opposite. Bleeding in dogs occurs during the *proliferation* of the uterine lining, which occurs just before ovulation. When the female mammal comes into estrus, she actively solicits male attention and may be aggressive to other females. Humans are unusual among mammals in that females are potentially sexually receptive throughout their ovarian cycles and at all seasons of the year.

Hormones control and coordinate the ovarian and uterine cycles

The ovarian and uterine cycles are coordinated and timed by the same hormones that initiate sexual maturation. Gonadotropins (FSH and LH) secreted by the anterior pituitary are the central elements of this control (see Figure 41.14B). Before puberty (i.e., before about 11 years of age), the secretion of FSH and LH is low and the ovaries are inactive. At puberty the hypothalamus increases its release of GnRH, stimulating the anterior pituitary to secrete FSH and LH. In response to FSH and LH, ovarian tissue grows and produces estrogen. The rise in estrogen causes the maturation of the accessory sex organs and the development of female secondary sexual characteristics. Between puberty and menopause, interactions of GnRH, gonadotropins, and sex steroids control the ovarian and uterine cycles.

A few days before menstruation begins, the anterior pituitary begins to increase its secretion of FSH and LH. In response, several follicles begin to mature in the ovaries, and these follicles steadily increase their production of estrogen. After about a week, all but one of the follicles wither away.

For the first 12 days of a 28-day ovarian cycle, estrogen exerts positive- rather than negative-feedback control on the pituitary. As a result, a surge of LH and a lesser surge of FSH occur (see Figure 41.14B). The LH surge triggers the mature follicle to rupture and release its egg, and it stimulates the cells of the ruptured follicle to develop into a corpus luteum.

Estrogen and progesterone secreted by the corpus luteum following ovulation are crucial to growth and maintenance of the endometrium. These sex steroids also exert negative-feedback control on the pituitary, inhibiting gonadotropin release and thus preventing new follicles from maturing.

If the egg is not fertilized, the corpus luteum degenerates on about day 26 of the cycle. Without production of progesterone by the corpus luteum, the endometrium sloughs off and menstruation occurs. The decrease in circulating steroids also releases the hypothalamus and pituitary from negative-feedback control, so GnRH, FSH, and LH all begin to increase. The increase in these hormones induces the next round of follicle development, and the ovarian cycle begins again.

FSH receptors determine which follicle is ovulated

Early in the ovarian cycle several follicles begin to develop, but only one reaches full maturity. What determines which one will survive? There are two types of follicle cells, arranged in two layers. The inner layer immediately surrounding the ovum is made up of **granulosa cells**, and the outer layer consists of **thecal cells**. Thecal cells are stimulated by LH to produce testosterone (similar to Leydig cells in the male). Testosterone diffuses into the granulosa cells, where the enzyme aromatase converts the testosterone to estrogen. Estrogen, along with FSH, stimulates the growth and maturation of the granulosa cells (similar to the Sertoli cells in the male). The estrogen plays two important roles in the selection of the follicle that is ovulated: (1) estrogen stimulates the granulosa cells to express more FSH and LH receptors, and (2) estrogen entering the circulation feeds back on the pituitary to decrease the production of FSH. The granulosa cells also produce inhibin (similar to Sertoli cells in the male), and inhibin also decreases the production of FSH. As FSH and LH levels fall, the follicle with the most FSH and LH receptors survives and matures while the others regress.

In pregnancy, hormones from the extraembryonic membranes take over

If the egg is fertilized and a blastocyst arrives in the uterus and implants in the endometrium, a new hormone comes into play. A layer of cells covering the blastocyst begins to secrete **human chorionic gonadotropin**, or **hCG** (**Figure 41.15**). This gonadotropin, a molecule similar to LH, stimulates the corpus luteum to continue to produce estrogen and progesterone to support the growth and maintenance of the endometrium and thereby prevent menstruation. Because it is present only in the blood of pregnant women, the presence of hCG is the basis for pregnancy testing. Pregnancy tests use an antibody to detect hCG in urine; they take only minutes and can be done at home.

Blastocyst and endometrial tissues form the placenta, which nourishes the embryo. The placenta also replaces the corpus

Figure 41.15 Hormones of Pregnancy When a fertilized ovum implants in the uterus, cells surrounding it produce human chorionic gonadotropin, which acts like LH and keeps the corpus luteum functioning as an endocrine gland. The ovarian and uterine cycles are put on hold for the duration of pregnancy. (After B. Pansky. 1982. *Review of Medical Embryology*. Macmillan: New Jersey.)

luteum as the major producer of estrogen and progesterone. Continued high levels of estrogen and progesterone prevent the pituitary from secreting gonadotropins; thus the ovarian cycle ceases for the duration of pregnancy. This mechanism underlies the action of birth control pills, which contain synthetic hormones resembling estrogen and progesterone that exert negative-feedback control on the hypothalamus and pituitary.

Breast feeding may delay the return of the ovarian cycle

Following birth, estrogen and progesterone levels drop because of the loss of the placenta, and therefore negative feedback on the hypothalamus and pituitary imposed by these hormones during pregnancy is gone. Nevertheless, women who breast feed their infants may not have their ovarian and menstrual cycles return for some time—a phenomenon called lactational delay. In Figure 39.4 you learned that the pituitary hormone prolactin stimulates the growth of the mammary glands and the production of milk. Prolactin release is stimulated by the suckling of the infant. Even the sight or sound of the infant can stimulate prolactin release in the mother. Investigations have now shown that in addition to stimulating the mammary glands, prolactin also inhibits GnRH release and LH release, possibly explaining lactational delay. Going back to the case of the tammar wallaby in the opening to this chapter, could prolactin release stimulated by the suckling of the joey in the pouch be responsible for the delayed implantation seen in this species? *Investigating Life: The Control of Diapause in the Tammar Wallaby* examines this question.

Childbirth is triggered by hormonal and mechanical stimuli

Throughout pregnancy, the muscles of the uterine wall periodically undergo slow, weak, rhythmic contractions called Braxton Hicks contractions. These contractions become stronger during the third trimester of pregnancy and are sometimes called false labor. The contractions of true labor mark the beginning of childbirth. Both hormonal and mechanical stimuli contribute to the onset of labor (**Figure 41.16A**).

Progesterone inhibits and estrogen stimulates contractions of uterine muscle. Toward the end of the third trimester, the estrogen–progesterone ratio shifts in favor of estrogen. The onset of labor is marked by increased secretion of the hormone oxytocin by the posterior pituitaries of both mother and fetus. Oxytocin is a powerful stimulant of uterine muscle contraction. Manufactured oxytocin is used to induce labor when that is necessary.

Mechanical stimuli come from the stretching of the uterus by the fully grown fetus and the pressure of the fetal head on the cervix. These mechanical stimuli increase the release of oxytocin by the mother's posterior pituitary, which in turn increases the activity of uterine muscle, causing even more pressure on the cervix. This positive-feedback loop converts the weak, slow, rhythmic Braxton Hicks contractions into stronger labor contractions.

In the early stage of labor, hormonal changes and pressure created by the contractions cause the cervix to dilate (expand) until it is large enough to allow the baby to pass through. Gradually the contractions become more frequent and more intense. This stage of labor lasts an average of 12–15 hours in a first pregnancy but is usually 8 hours or less in subsequent ones.

The second stage of labor begins when the cervix is fully dilated to a diameter of about 10 centimeters (**Figure 41.16B**). The baby's head can now move into the vagina. Passage of the fetus through the vagina is assisted by the mother's bearing down ("pushing") with her abdominal and other muscles. Once the head and shoulders of the baby clear the cervix, the rest of its body eases out rapidly, but it is still connected to the placenta by the umbilical cord. Once the baby clears the birth canal, it

(A) Signals stimulating labor and birth

(B) Delivery

Figure 41.16 Labor and Delivery (**A**) Both mechanical and hormonal signals are involved in stimulating the uterine contractions of labor and delivery. (**B**) A new person comes into the world headfirst.

▶Investigating LIFE   The Control of Diapause in the Tammar Wallaby

Experiment

Original Paper: L. A. Hinds and C. H. Tyndale-Biscoe. 2013. Daily prolactin pulse inhibits the corpus luteum during lactational quiescence in the marsupial, *Macropus eugenii*. *Reprod Fertil Dev* 25: 456–461.

In Chapter 39 (see Figure 39.4) we discussed how the hormone prolactin (PRL) has evolved to serve many physiological processes in different vertebrate groups, but these various processes all have some connection to reproduction. Since prolactin is involved in controlling lactation in mammals, could prolactin be the signal in the tammar wallaby that maintains embryonic diapause as long as suckling continues?

HYPOTHESIS▶ Pulses of prolactin in lactating female tammar wallabies prevent new embryos from developing as long as previous offspring are suckling.

METHOD▶ The hormone progesterone (P) prepares the uterine lining for implantation of an embryo and maintains the uterine lining during pregnancy. Thus measurements of blood levels of P reveal when diapause is broken in tammar wallabies. A stimulus known to break diapause in these animals is the removal of the prior young from the pouch (RYP). The RYP method was used to study the effects of prolactin on maintenance of diapause.

1. Remove young from the pouches of three groups of five wallabies.

2. Following RYP, administer the following treatments:

    Group A: Daily saline injections for 8 days following RYP (controls)

    Group B: PRL injection every 24 hr for 8 days following RYP

    Group C: PRL injection every 48 hr for 8 days following RYP

3. Take daily blood samples to measure P levels.

RESULTS▶ Data are approximate means of the actual measurements, progesterone concentrations (P) expressed in picograms per milliliter (pg/mL).

Days following RYP	P level (picograms/mL)		
	Group A	Group B	Group C
0	100	125	100
1	150	175	113
2	150	125	125
3	180	150	135
4	300	150	175
5	450	125	215
6	175	125	240
7	200	150	325
8	175	16	210
9	175	175	240
10	225	250	335
11	200	450	260
12	250	350	200
13	225	225	225
14	300	250	230
15	350	200	210
16	360	225	225

CONCLUSION▶ When tammar wallabies were treated with daily saline injections (controls), they broke diapause 4 or 5 days following RYP. However, when they were treated with daily PRL injections, they broke diapause 11 or 12 days following RYP. Hence daily PRL pulses can prolong diapause and delay implantation of a new blastocyst.

Figure: Progesterone level (pg/mL) versus Days following RYP. Group A: Daily saline injection; Group B: Daily prolactin injection.

Work with the Data

Following the experiment showing that daily pulses of PRL can maintain diapause, the investigators asked whether pulses of PRL every 2 days could maintain diapause. The data are shown in the table as Group C. Plotting the data will show if there is a difference in the response to PRL when pulses were given every other day following RYP.

QUESTION▶

1. Plot the data as was done for Groups A and B. Was the 48-hr PRL pulse effective in preventing the breaking of diapause?

Go to Achieve for a companion Data in Depth exercise.

starts breathing and is independent of its mother's circulation. The umbilical cord may then be clamped and cut. The segment still attached to the baby dries up and sloughs off in a few days, leaving behind its distinctive signature, the belly button—more properly called the umbilicus. The third stage of labor, the detachment and expulsion of the placenta and fetal membranes, takes from a few minutes to an hour, and may be accompanied by uterine contractions. A baby's suckling at the breast immediately following birth stimulates additional secretion of oxytocin, which augments uterine contractions, reduces the size of the uterus, and helps stop bleeding.

Birth as well as reproduction is timed

Reproduction in many species is seasonal. This seasonality in many species of vertebrates involves mechanisms of photoperiodism. Briefly, changes in day length enable animals to anticipate the best time of year for the rearing of young and therefore time their reproduction and birth accordingly. How do animals measure day length? As we will discuss in more detail in Chapter 51, animals have endogenous daily rhythms called circadian (*circa*, "day," + *dia*, "length") rhythms. As day length changes, sunrise and sunset occur at different phases of the circadian rhythm. The release of melatonin from the pineal gland is controlled by the circadian rhythm but is inhibited by light. Therefore as days get longer, the nightly pulse of melatonin gets shorter, and conversely as days get shorter, the melatonin pulse gets longer. Day length determines when many species come into reproductive condition and mate. That is not true for the tammar wallaby that was introduced at the beginning of this chapter. The wallaby mates at any time of year soon after it gives birth. However, diapause in the wallaby is sensitive to night length—that is, to the duration of the melatonin pulse. A non-lactating wallaby will break diapause when night length reaches 12 hours. Similarly, when non-lactating wallabies are held at a night length of 9 hours but given melatonin injections 2.5 hours before sunset, they break diapause. These results support the hypothesis that short daily melatonin pulses prolong diapause and that long daily melatonin pulses are a signal to break diapause. The significance for the nocturnal wallaby is that birth tends to be at the time of year when nights are longest.

Humans are not seasonal breeders, but there is a timing component of childbirth. Most women go into labor at night. However, it is quite common for labor to cease when women arrive in the brightly lit hospital. Bright light interrupts the nightly melatonin pulse in humans.

KEY CONCEPT
41.4 Recap and Assess

The reproductive system of women produces oocytes (eggs) and hormones, and these functions are controlled by hypothalamic and anterior pituitary hormones. The follicle is the functional unit of the ovary. Usually one follicle matures and is ovulated each month as controlled by a cyclical feedback interplay between ovarian hormones and the hypothalamic–pituitary axis. These hormonal cycles also coordinate the uterine, or menstrual, cycle so that the endometrium is prepared to receive a blastocyst should fertilization occur. A blastocyst implanted in the uterus produces hCG, which suspends the ovarian and uterine cycles by sustaining the ovarian production of progesterone and estrogen until the placenta can take over this function. Childbirth and lactation are controlled by mechanical and hormonal mechanisms.

1. What events in the ovary are responsible for the onset of menstruation and what prevents it if pregnancy occurs?
2. What are the roles of thecal cells and granulosa cells in the ovarian cycle, and how do they limit the number of eggs that are ovulated?
3. How does positive feedback between hormonal and mechanical processes play a role in childbirth?

Understanding the physiology of human reproduction has led to numerous methods and technologies for controlling reproduction, either to prevent unwanted pregnancies or to overcome infertility.

KEY CONCEPT
41.5 Fertility Can Be Controlled

Learning Objectives

41.5.1 Discuss the relative advantages and disadvantages of different contraceptive methods.

41.5.2 Compare contraception and contragestational techniques.

41.5.3 Explain how procedures that use genetic analysis and in vitro fertilization can inform decisions about therapeutic abortions.

Sexual issues and sexual behavior are dominant aspects of our society, and reproductive technologies have had huge impacts on our sexual and reproductive lives.

Humans use a variety of methods to control fertility

According to a 2011 study, 45% of the 6.1 million pregnancies that occurred in the United States that year were unintended. Although a very high number, the rate of unintended pregnancies had dropped considerably from three years earlier when it was 54% and had been around that level for many years. This considerable drop is likely due to an increase in use of highly effective contraceptive methods. Even with this encouraging decrease in unintended pregnancies, however, the number is still much too high for a modern, educated society. It is important to keep in mind, that for women of college age, a single act of unprotected intercourse in the 2 days prior to ovulation carries a chance of conception as high as 50%.

The only failure-proof methods of preventing pregnancy are complete abstinence from sexual activity or surgical removal of the gonads. Those options are not acceptable to most people, and they turn to other methods to prevent pregnancy. Many of these methods prevent fertilization or implantation (conception) and are referred to as **contraception**. Table 41.1 lists some commonly used contraceptive methods and their relative failure rates. These methods vary enormously in their effectiveness. Most methods are used by the woman; only some are used by the man.

TABLE 41.1 | Methods of Contraception

Method	Mode of action	Failure rate[a]	Comments
UNPROTECTED	No form of birth control.	85	High risk of pregnancy, especially for women 15–30.
NONTECHNOLOGICAL METHODS			
Rhythm method	The couple abstains from intercourse between days 10 and 20 of the ovarian cycle (peak fertility).	5–24	High failure rate due to miscalculation and/or variation of individual cycles.
Coitus interruptus	The man withdraws his penis prior to ejaculation, with the intention of not depositing sperm into the vagina.	4–20	Requires self-control, especially by the man. Very high failure rate.
BARRIER METHODS[b]			
Condom (male or female)	A sheath of impermeable material (often latex) is fitted over the erect penis or into the vagina. Semen is trapped in the condom, so no sperm are deposited in the vagina.	13–20	If fitted correctly, an intact condom can prevent pregnancy. Failure can be due to material failure or improper use. Condoms are the only contraceptive method that protects against sexually transmitted diseases (STDs), including HIV (AIDS).
Spermicidal jellies	Applied deep inside the vagina, these chemical compounds kill or immobilize sperm.	18–28	Used alone, spermicidal compounds have a high failure rate.
Diaphragms, cervical caps, cervical sponges containing spermicide	Inserted by the woman prior to intercourse, these devices work by blocking the cervix so that sperm cannot pass into the uterus.	15–30	Approximately the same failure rate as condom use by men, but do not protect against STDs. Can be used in conjunction with spermicidal jelly for extra protection.
HORMONE-BASED CONTRACEPTIVES			
Oral hormones ("the pill")	A daily pill for women containing a combination of synthetic estrogens and progesterone. These hormones mimic pregnancy to the extent that the ovarian cycle and ovulation are suspended. The uterine cycle can continue by including a week of non-hormone administration every 21–28 days.	0.3–7	Requires medical consultation and prescription. Taken correctly, oral contraceptives are extremely effective. In the United States, more than 12 million women use them each year; they are sometimes prescribed to treat menstrual disorders.
Non-orally administered hormones	Making use of the same hormonal actions as the pill, these methods include long-acting injections, patches that release hormones transdermally (through the skin), and a hormone-containing vaginal ring. Implantable progestin releasing tubes have a failure rate of <0.1% and can last up to 3 years.	<7	Same as oral hormones. A slightly lower failure rate because the woman does not have to remember to take a daily pill.
Progestin-only pill (Plan B®)	An oral contraceptive meant to be taken within 72 hours after unprotected sex. A high dose of progestin in two pills prevents ovulation in the same manner birth control pills do.	5–40	Not an "abortion pill"; this drug will not terminate an existing pregnancy. Currently available to women over 17 without a prescription. Failure rate varies widely depending on when taken.
IMPLANTATION BLOCKERS			
Intrauterine device (IUD)	A medical professional inserts a small plastic or metal device into the uterus. The resulting inflammation reaction (see Chapter 39) releases prostaglandins, which prevent implantation of the fertilized egg.	0.1–0.5	A highly effective contraceptive, and the most widely used birth control device in China (and hence the world). With medical monitoring, can remain in place for several years.
Contragestational pill	Mifepristone, or RU-486, is a drug that blocks the action of progesterone, which is necessary to maintain the endometrium during implantation and pregnancy.	15–40	Prevents implantation when taken up to several days after unprotected intercourse. Can terminate a pregnancy up to the time of the first missed menstrual period. In the United States, available from specialized providers.
When used with a prostaglandin analogue		1-5	
STERILIZATION			
Vasectomy	The vasa deferentia (see Figure 41.9) are cut and tied off so that sperm can no longer pass into the urethra. Sperm continue to be produced but are reabsorbed by the man's body. Male hormone levels and sexual responses are not affected.	0.1	A simple surgical procedure performed under local anesthetic in a doctor's office. Although theoretically it can be reversed, vasectomy should be considered permanent.
Tubal ligation	The oviducts (see Figure 41.13A) are tied off so that eggs cannot reach the uterus and sperm cannot reach the egg. As with vasectomy, hormone levels and sexual responses are not affected.	0.5	This surgical procedure is somewhat more complex than vasectomy. It is often performed in conjunction with childbirth when a woman has decided that her family is complete.

[a]Failure rate refers to the number of pregnancies per 100 women per year.

[b]All of these barrier methods are routinely available without medical prescription.

Sources: Centers for Disease Control. 2017. *Effectiveness of family planning methods.* (tinyurl.com/ya8t92y4); A. Sundaram, et al. 2017. *Perspectives on Sexual and Reproductive Health* 49: 7–16; O. M. Avrech et al. 1991. *Fertil Steril* 56: 385–393.

Once a fertilized egg is successfully implanted in the uterus, any termination of the pregnancy is called an **abortion**. A spontaneous abortion is the medical term for what is commonly called a miscarriage. Spontaneous abortions frequently occur early in pregnancy and are usually the result of either a chromosomal abnormality in the fetus or a breakdown in the process of implantation. Many spontaneous abortions occur before the woman even realizes she is pregnant.

Abortions that result from medical intervention may be performed either for therapeutic purposes or for fertility control. A therapeutic abortion may be necessary to protect the health of the mother, or it may be performed because prenatal testing reveals that the fetus has a severe defect. In a medical abortion, the cervix is dilated and some of the endometrium, along with the implanted fetus, is removed. When performed in the first trimester of a pregnancy, a medical abortion carries less risk of death to the mother than a full-term pregnancy. The risk rises after the first 12 weeks of pregnancy but remains less than that of a full-term pregnancy through the second trimester.

Reproductive technologies help solve problems of infertility

About 15% of couples in the United States are infertile—that is, they can't have children. The reasons for infertility are many, and are about equally distributed between men and women. Several technologies have been developed to overcome barriers to both conceiving and bearing a child. The simplest of these is **artificial insemination**, in which the physician places sperm in the woman's reproductive tract. This technique is useful if the male's sperm count is low, if his sperm lack motility, or if problems in the female's reproductive tract prevent the normal movement of sperm up the oviducts. Artificial insemination is also widely used in the production of domesticated animals such as cattle.

Assisted reproductive technologies, or **ARTs**, involve procedures that remove unfertilized eggs from the ovary, combine them with sperm outside the body, and then place fertilized eggs or egg–sperm mixtures in the appropriate location in the woman's reproductive tract for development to take place. The first successful ART was in vitro fertilization (IVF). In IVF the woman is treated with hormones that stimulate many follicles in her ovaries to mature. Eggs are collected from these follicles, and sperm are collected from the intended father. Eggs and sperm are combined in a culture medium outside the body, where fertilization takes place. The resulting embryos can be injected into the mother's uterus in the blastocyst stage or kept frozen for implantation later. The first "test tube baby" resulting from IVF was born in England in 1978. Since then, millions of babies have resulted from this ART.

A major cause of IVF failure is inability of sperm to gain access to the egg cell membrane (see Figure 41.5). To solve this problem, methods have been developed to inject a sperm cell directly into the cytoplasm of an egg. In intracytoplasmic sperm injection (ICSI), an egg is held in place by suction applied through a polished glass pipette. A slender, sharp pipette is then used to penetrate the egg and inject a sperm (**Figure 41.17**). This ART was used successfully for the first time in 1992 by researchers in Belgium;

Figure 41.17 Intracytoplasmic Sperm Injection In this procedure, a sperm is injected directly into a mature egg cell. The fertilized egg is then placed in the female reproductive tract, where it can implant and develop into a fetus.

now thousands of these procedures are performed in U.S. clinics each year, with a success rate of about 25%.

IVF, coupled with techniques of genetic analysis, can eliminate the risk that adults who are carriers of genetic diseases will produce affected children. It is now possible to take a cell from a human embryo at the four- or eight-cell stage (see Figure 42.4B) without damaging its developmental potential. The sampled cell can be subjected to molecular analysis to determine whether it carries the harmful gene. This procedure, called preimplantation genetic diagnosis (PGD), makes it possible to determine whether an embryo produced by IVF carries the genetic defect of concern.

KEY CONCEPT
41.5 Recap and Assess

Controlling fertility is an important aspect of modern human life. Decreasing the probability of pregnancy is achieved through methods that prevent sperm and egg from meeting and that prevent implantation. Pregnancies can be facilitated through technologies that extract eggs from the ovary and fertilize them in vitro before reintroducing them into the female reproductive tract.

1. Which method of contraception is the only one to offer protection against sexually transmitted diseases (STDs)? Explain why.

2. Both the contraceptive pill ("the pill") and the contragestational pill (RU-486) involve progesterone signaling. How do their mechanisms of action differ?

3. How can IVF be used to prevent transmission of a genetic disease?

The fertilized egg of a sexually reproducing organism is a single cell containing all the genetic information needed to create a new organism. Chapter 21 introduced some of the molecular aspects of the process of development in multicellular animals. Chapter 42 will describe the physiological and anatomical events of animal development.

▶InvestigatingLIFE

Q and A **What signal controls the breaking of diapause in the tammar wallaby?**

The experiment presented in Investigating Life: The Control of Diapause in the Tammar Wallaby exploited the fact that removal of the young joey from the pouch of its mother (RYP) stimulated the blastocyst in her uterus to break diapause, implant, and continue development. What diapause-breaking signal might be involved in conjunction with RYP? Researchers hypothesized that RYP resulted in cessation of prolactin release stimulated by suckling of the young, and that the absence of those prolactin pulses initiated the breaking of diapause. The test of that hypothesis was to apply RYP to groups of mother wallabies and test whether applications of prolactin could prevent the breaking of diapause. The results showed that injections of prolactin every 24 hours for 8 days following RYP delayed the progesterone rise that indicates the breaking of diapause. Prolactin injections at intervals of 48 hours or longer were less effective or ineffective in maintaining diapause. The conclusion was thus reached that prolactin pulses stimulated by suckling are a signal for the maintenance of diapause, and that the removal of

that signal results in the breaking of diapause. Another signal, melatonin, could be involved in the breaking of diapause. The prolactin experiments were all done at the time of year when night length was appropriate for the breaking of diapause.

Future directions

Reproductive success depends on many factors, including ecological, physiological, and socio-behavioral factors. It is therefore not surprising that evolutionary adaptations have exploited many kinds of information to control the timing of reproduction in various species. While these controlling factors are diverse, in vertebrates they all work through the hypothalamic, pituitary, and gonadal regulatory pathways. Therefore whatever we can learn about the physiology of reproduction in one vertebrate species may also apply to other species, or at least inform us as to what questions we should ask of other species, including humans. The answers to these questions can help us preserve endangered species, improve domesticated species, solve reproductive problems in humans, and even help control human population growth.

 VISUAL SUMMARY 41

© Tui De Roy/Minden Pictures

You should be able to relate each summary to the adjacent figures. If you go to this visual summary in **Achieve**, you can follow links to figures, animations, activities, and simulations that will help you consolidate the material.

KEY CONCEPT

41.1 Asexual Reproduction Is Efficient but Limits Genetic Variability

- Asexual reproduction produces offspring that are genetically identical to their parent.
- **Budding**, **regeneration**, and **parthenogenesis** are types of asexual reproduction.
- Budding and regeneration produce new individuals by mitotic divisions of dedifferentiated somatic cells.
- Parthenogenesis produces new individuals by development of unfertilized eggs.

Questions

1. What environmental conditions favor asexual reproduction, and why?
2. What is the role of sexual behavior in the all-female populations of whiptail lizards?

Figure 41.2

Hydra littoralis

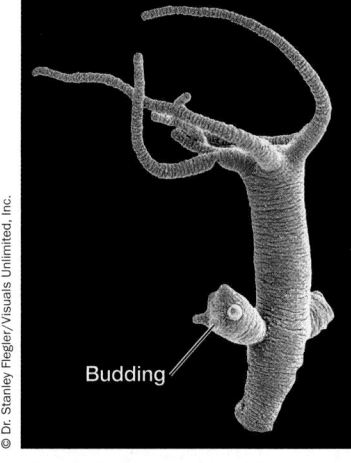

Budding

© Dr. Stanley Flegler/Visuals Unlimited, Inc.

KEY CONCEPT

41.2 Sexual Reproduction Involves the Union of Haploid Egg and Sperm   Go to Animation 41.1

- **Gametogenesis** and **fertilization** are similar in all animals, but **spawning** and **mating** include a great variety of anatomical, physiological, and behavioral adaptations.

- In **testes** and **ovaries**, the **germ cells** proliferate mitotically, undergo meiosis, and mature into **gametes**. Each **spermatogonium** can produce four **sperm**, but each **oogonium** produces only one **egg**. In humans, spermatogenesis continues throughout life, whereas oogenesis ceases before birth and oocytes undergo developmental arrest after the first meiotic division.

- Fertilization can be external or internal. Fertilization involves sperm activation, binding to the egg, digestion of a path through the coverings of the egg, and fusion of sperm and egg cell membranes. Fusion triggers **blocks to polyspermy**, and in mammals signals the egg to complete meiosis and begin development.

- **Hermaphrodites** are **monoecious**, meaning individuals have both male and female reproductive systems, either sequentially or simultaneously. **Dioecious** species have separate male and female individuals.

- The young of **oviparous** species begin development outside the mother's body. The young of **viviparous** species begin development inside the mother's body.

Questions

1. What are four differences between gametogenesis in human males and females?

2. What is the difference between a viviparous and an ovoviviparous species?

Figure 41.5

Fertilization of the sea urchin egg

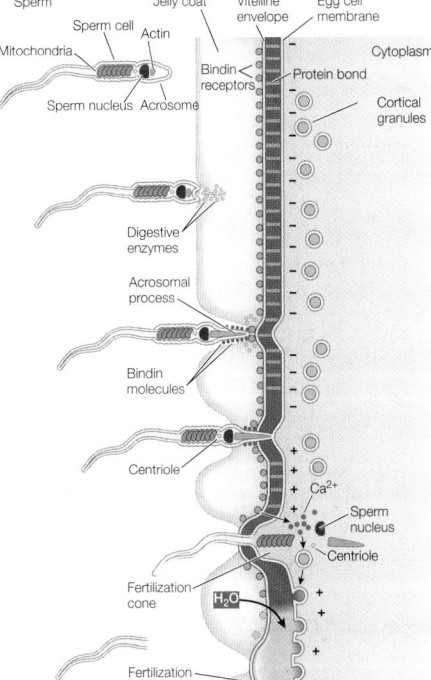

KEY CONCEPT

41.3 Male Sex Organs Produce and May Deliver Sperm   Go to Activities 41.1 and 41.2

- **Semen** consists of sperm suspended in seminal fluid. Sperm are generated in the **seminiferous tubules** of the testes, mature in the **epididymis**, and are delivered to the **urethra** through the **vasa deferentia**. Other components of semen are produced in the **seminal vesicles**, **prostate gland**, and **bulbourethral glands**. Semen is ejaculated through the erect penis by muscle contractions at the climax of copulation.

- Spermatogenesis depends on testosterone secreted by the **Leydig cells** of the testes, which are under the control of hormones produced by the hypothalamus and the anterior pituitary. The production of these hormones is controlled by negative feedback from testosterone and from inhibin, a hormone produced by the **Sertoli cells** of the testes.

Questions

1. Describe the path taken and the transitions made by a male gamete from being a spermatogonium to ejaculated sperm.

2. What are the functions of Leydig and Sertoli cells, and how are those functions controlled?

3. What are the sources and functions of the components of semen other than sperm?

Figure 41.12

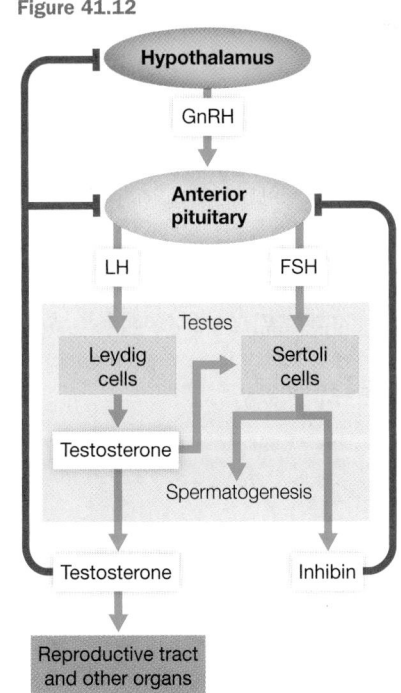

KEY CONCEPT

41.4 Female Sex Organs Produce Eggs and May Nurture Embryos

Go to Activity 41.3 and
Animation 41.2

- An ovarian **follicle** contains an oocyte surrounded by **granulosa cells** and **thecal cells**. Each month a small number of follicles respond to pituitary FSH by growing, producing estrogen, and promoting development of the oocyte, but usually only one of these follicles is ovulated

- An ovulated oocyte is picked up by the fimbria of an **oviduct**. Sperm deposited in the vagina during copulation move up through the **cervix** and uterus into the oviducts, where fertilization occurs. In humans, maturation and release of eggs constitute an **ovarian cycle**. The **uterine**, or **menstrual**, **cycle** prepares the uterus for receipt of a **blastocyst**. If no blastocyst implants, the lining of the uterus sloughs off in the process of **menstruation**. The ovarian and uterine cycles are controlled by hypothalamic and pituitary hormones, which are under feedback control of estrogen and progesterone.

- Childbirth is initiated by hormonal and mechanical stimuli that increase the contractility of uterine muscle.

Questions

1. What is the relationship between ovarian hormones and the endometrium of the uterus during the ovarian cycle?

2. Explain the role of human chorionic gonadotropin in pregnancy.

3. How does the birth process involve positive feedback?

Figure 41.14

Coordinated events in ovarian and uterine cycles

Events in ovary (ovarian cycle)

Ovarian hormones and the uterine cycle

Gonadotropins (from anterior pituitary)

KEY CONCEPT

41.5 Fertility Can Be Controlled

- Contraceptive methods and technologies decrease the probability of fertilization but differ in efficacy.

- **Assisted reproductive technologies** (**ARTs**) can increase fertility.

Questions

1. Apart from sterilization, what are the two most effective contraceptive methods?

2. What are three of the least effective contraceptive methods, and why?

3. In cases of infertility, what technology would be appropriate if the woman's oviducts are blocked? What technology would be appropriate if the man's sperm are not motile?

Figure 41.17

Pipette holding egg

Egg

Pipette injecting sperm

© AJP/Hop Américain/Science Source

Animal Development 42

© Nerthuz/Getty Images

Our internal organization is not symmetrical, and some individuals are born with the mirror-image organization of what is seen in most people—a condition called situs inversus.

KEY CONCEPTS

42.1 Fertilization Activates Development

42.2 Mitosis Divides Up the Early Embryo

42.3 Gastrulation Generates Multiple Tissue Layers

42.4 Organs Develop from the Three Germ Layers

42.5 Extraembryonic Membranes Nurture Avian and Mammalian Embryos

▶ Investigating LIFE

Go with the Flow

Place your hand over your heart. Point to your appendix; point to your pancreas. Surely your hand went to the left side of your chest, then to the right side of your lower abdomen, and last to the left side of your upper abdomen. Vertebrates are bilaterally symmetrical, but our symmetry is not absolute. Some internal organs are oriented to the left and some to the right. This bilateral asymmetry arises from events very early in the development of the embryo. However, in about 1 out of every 7,000 people, bilateral asymmetry is reversed—a condition known as situs inversus ("location inverted"). Most people with situs inversus lead normal lives and are unaware of their condition until they have diagnostic imaging or surgery.

You will learn in this chapter that a mammalian embryo goes from a single layer of cells to two layers of cells by forming a midline slit. Cells migrate through that slit to form the second cell layer. At one end of the slit is an area called the node. Each cell at the node has a primary cilium. The primary cilia of some of these cells are nonmotile and serve sensory functions. The primary cilia of other nodal cells are motile, and they beat in a clockwise motion that moves extracellular fluid across the surface of the node. That fluid movement is from right to left. Why?

Imagine that a cilium moves like the hands of a clock (but much faster!). Twelve o'clock points to the embryo's future head. The cilia protrude from the cells at an angle such that they are closest to the cell surface at the 6 o'clock position. Thus when the cilia rotate through the 6 o'clock position, they are closer to the cell surface and experience greater resistance than at the 12 o'clock position. As a result, the circular beating of cilia at the node creates left–right flow of extracellular fluid and therefore left–right positional information.

Does that simple left–right positional information generated by beating nodal cilia instruct the development of left–right anatomical asymmetry? The answer is probably yes, because in strains of mice that have no nodal cilia or have only nonmotile nodal cilia, about half of the population has reversed organ asymmetry. Similarly, in humans there is a spectrum of rare genetic disorders called Kartagener's syndrome that is characterized by nonmotile cilia. About half of these individuals have situs inversus.

 How does the embryo know left from right? (Find the answer on page 958.)

Learning Objectives

42.1.1 List the contributions of the sperm and the egg to the zygote.

42.1.2 Explain how sperm entry converts frog egg symmetry from radial to bilateral.

42.1.3 Describe how the movement of cytoplasm, proteins, and organelles following fertilization of the frog egg instructs early development.

Fertilization is the joining of sperm and egg to produce a diploid zygote. You might think of fertilization as the event that begins development. But recall two things from Chapter 41: (1) in asexually reproducing animals, development proceeds without fertilization, and (2) in sexually reproducing animals, fertilization is preceded by events in the maturing egg that set the stage for development but are paused. Thus fertilization activates multicellular development in sexually reproducing animals.

Fertilization does more than restore a full diploid complement of maternal and paternal genes. The fusion of sperm and egg cell membranes:

- triggers ion fluxes across the egg membrane.
- creates blocks to the entry of additional sperm into the egg.
- changes the pH of the egg cytoplasm.
- increases egg metabolism and stimulates protein synthesis.
- initiates the rapid series of cell divisions that produce a multicellular embryo.

We described the mechanisms of fertilization in Key Concept 41.2. Here we take a closer look at the cellular and molecular interactions of sperm and egg that are the first steps of development.

The sperm and the egg make different contributions to the zygote

Eggs are much larger than sperm. Egg cytoplasm is well stocked with organelles, nutrients, and a variety of molecules, including **cytoplasmic determinants** such as transcription factors and mRNAs. Nearly everything the embryo needs during its early stages of development comes from the mother, including its mitochondria (and therefore all of its mitochondrial DNA), its ribosomes, and other organelles. Cytoplasmic determinants in the egg play important roles in setting up the signaling cascades that orchestrate the four major events of development: determination, differentiation, morphogenesis, and growth. **Determination** involves processes that limit the patterns of gene expression in the earliest cells of the embryo, which are totipotent—each one has the capacity to develop into a whole organism. **Differentiation** is when those limited patterns of gene expression are initiated and the cells take on specialized characteristics of a tissue type, such as the appearance of contractile proteins in muscle cells. **Morphogenesis** is the stage of development when tissues interact and change shape to form organs. **Growth** is maturing and getting larger to have the size and capabilities of the adult organism.

The sperm makes only two major contributions to the zygote: its haploid nucleus and, in most species, a centriole. That centriole produces the zygote's centrosome, which organizes the mitotic spindles for subsequent cell divisions (see Figure 11.9). Centrioles are also the origin of the microtubules of the primary cilia, which are important in cell signaling, as you will see when we return to the opening question about how embryos know right from left.

 View in Achieve
Animation 42.1 Early Asymmetry in the Embryo

Fertilization sets the stage for determination

The large size of amphibian eggs and the fact that they can be fertilized and go through early stages of development in culture media make them ideal models for studying how rearrangements of egg cytoplasm lead to determination. Determination sets the developmental fates of cells and precedes differentiation—the expression of different cell properties. The molecules in the cytoplasm of the amphibian egg are not homogeneously distributed. The entry of the sperm into the egg stimulates rearrangements of the egg cytoplasm that introduce additional organization to the egg. One such cytoplasmic difference is the emergence of distinct "top" and "bottom" ends of an organism or structure, a difference that establishes **polarity**. Sperm entry establishes the polarity of the zygote, and informational molecules in the egg cytoplasm are organized with respect to that polarity. Therefore when cell divisions begin, these informational molecules—which guide subsequent development—are not divided equally among daughter cells.

Rearrangement of egg cytoplasm following fertilization is easily observed in some frog species because of pigments in the cytoplasm. The nutrients in an unfertilized frog egg are dense yolk granules that are concentrated by gravity in the lower half of the egg, called the **vegetal hemisphere**. The haploid nucleus of the egg is located at the opposite end, in the **animal hemisphere**. The outermost (cortical) cytoplasm of the animal hemisphere is more pigmented than the underlying cytoplasm. The vegetal hemisphere is not pigmented. Because of these differences, rearrangement of the cytoplasm after fertilization is easy to observe.

The unfertilized frog egg is radially symmetrical. You can turn it on its vegetal–animal pole axis, and all sides are the same. Sperm-binding sites are localized on the surface of the animal hemisphere. When a sperm binds to and enters the egg, the egg's radial symmetry is converted to bilateral (left–right) symmetry with a dorsal–ventral axis. The cortical (superficial) cytoplasm rotates toward the site of sperm entry (**Figure 42.1**). This rotation brings the animal and vegetal regions of cytoplasm into contact with each other, producing a band of lightly pigmented cytoplasm on the side opposite the site of sperm entry. This band, called the **gray crescent**, marks the location of important developmental events in some species of amphibians.

The centriole that was the sperm's contribution to the egg initiates cytoplasmic reorganization that coincides with the appearance of the gray crescent. The centriole organizes microtubules in the vegetal hemisphere cytoplasm into a parallel array that guides the movement of the cortical cytoplasm as well as proteins and organelles.

The movement of cytoplasm, proteins, and organelles changes the distribution of critical signals. A key transcription factor in

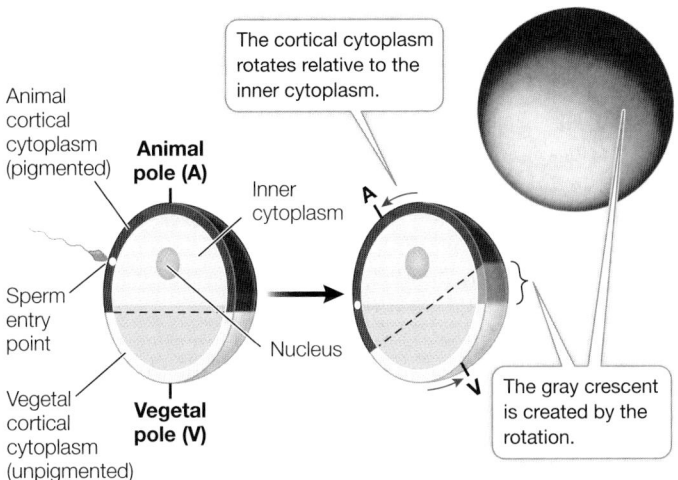

Figure 42.1 The Gray Crescent   In amphibian eggs, cortical rotation and rearrangement of the cytoplasm after fertilization create the gray crescent opposite the point of sperm entry. These events are important for specifying the body axes and other important events in later development. (After R. P. Elinson and B. Rowning. 1988. *Dev Biol* 128: 185–197.)

early development is β-catenin produced from maternal mRNA that was produced and stored in the egg while it was maturing in the ovary. β-Catenin is found throughout the egg cytoplasm (**Figure 42.2**). Also present throughout the egg cytoplasm is a protein kinase, glycogen synthase kinase-3 (GSK-3), that phosphorylates β-catenin and thereby targets it for degradation. An inhibitor of GSK-3 is localized in the vegetal cortex of the egg. After sperm entry, this inhibitor moves along microtubules to the gray crescent, where it prevents the degradation of β-catenin. As a result, the concentration of β-catenin is higher on the dorsal side of the developing embryo than on the ventral side (the side where the sperm entered). The regional differences in β-catenin concentration set up differences within the egg cytoplasm that have developmental consequences.

KEY CONCEPT
42.1 Recap and Assess

The haploid egg has a full complement of cell organelles and is stocked with nutrients and informational molecules that power and direct the early stages of development. Sperm entry into the egg contributes a haploid nucleus and a centriole to the zygote. Fertilization restores diploidy, activates the egg, and stimulates rearrangement of the cytoplasm, setting up the body axes and organizing positional information that will control determination and differentiation.

1. Apart from its nucleus, what is the major contribution of the sperm to subsequent cell signaling in the embryo?
2. How is the gray crescent generated in the fertilized frog egg?
3. How does β-catenin become more concentrated on the dorsal side of the amphibian embryo?

The uneven distribution of informational molecules in the cytoplasm of the fertilized egg is essential to later events in development. In the next key concept you will see how these informational molecules end up in different cells of the developing embryo.

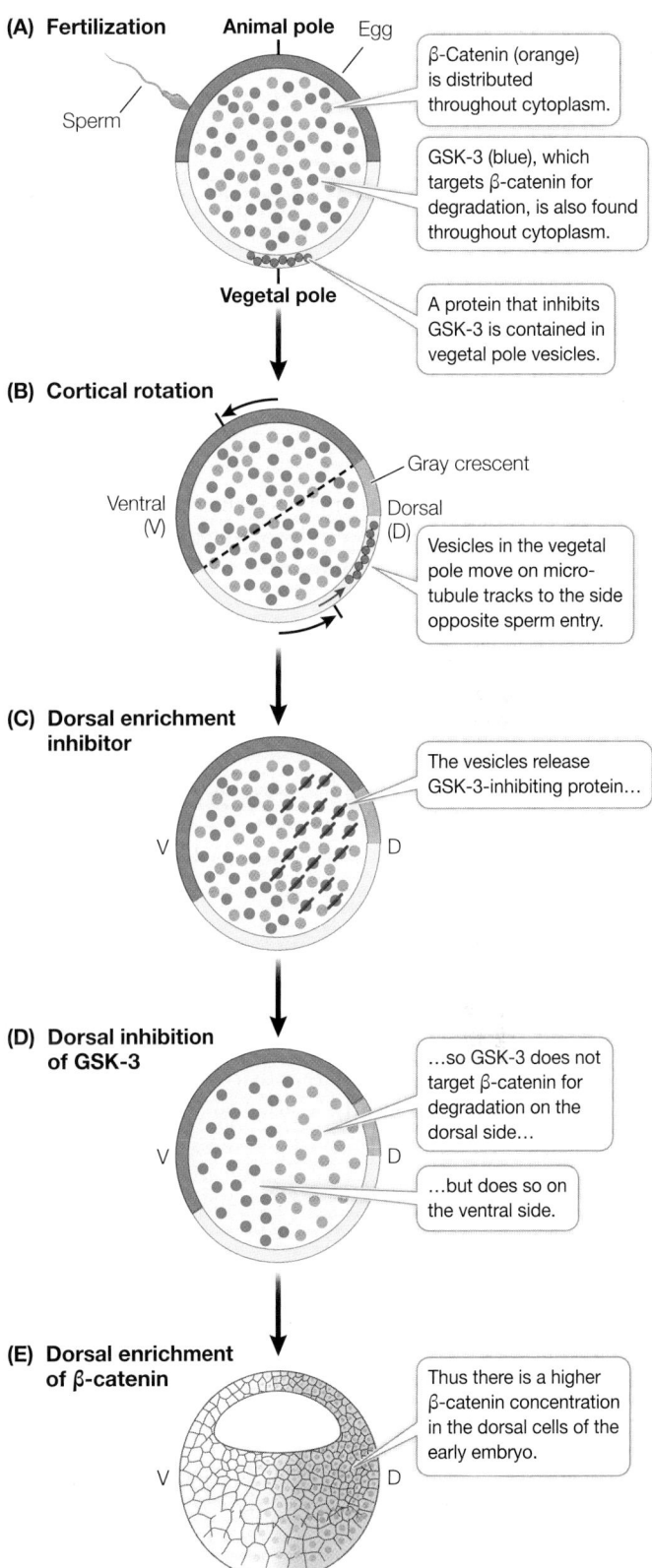

Figure 42.2 Cytoplasmic Factors Set Up Signaling Cascades
Cytoplasmic movement changes the distributions of critical developmental signals. In the fertilized frog egg, the interaction of the protein kinase, the GSK-3 inhibitor, and the protein β-catenin results in differential concentrations of β-catenin in blastomeres following cleavage, thereby specifying the dorsal–ventral axis of the embryo.

KEY CONCEPT

42.2 Mitosis Divides Up the Early Embryo

Learning Objectives

42.2.1 Compare four types of cleavage.

42.2.2 Explain the difference between regulated and autonomous specification.

42.2.3 Explain the difference between identical and non-identical twins.

42.2.4 Describe the difference between determination in reproductive germ cells and other types of cells in the embryo.

β-Catenin plays a major role in the cell–cell signaling cascade that begins the process of cell determination and the formation of the embryo. But cell–cell signaling requires more than one cell. The single-celled zygote must become a multicellular embryo.

Cleavage produces a multicellular embryo

Cleavage transforms the diploid zygote into a mass of undifferentiated cells that develop as the embryo. Zygote cytoplasm is not homogeneous, and these first cell divisions result in the differential distribution of nutrients and cytoplasmic determinants in the early embryo.

In most animals, cleavage proceeds with rapid DNA replication and mitosis but with no cell growth and little gene expression. The embryo becomes a solid ball of smaller and smaller cells. Eventually this ball forms a central fluid-filled cavity called a **blastocoel**. At this developmental stage the embryo is called a **blastula**, and its individual cells are **blastomeres**. The pattern of cleavage in different species influences the form of their blastulas.

- **Complete cleavage** occurs in eggs that have little yolk, such as the eggs of amphibians. Early cleavage furrows divide the egg completely. In the amphibian egg, the concentration of yolk in the vegetal pole causes unequal cytoplasm division, and animal hemisphere blastomeres are smaller than those in the vegetal hemisphere (**Figure 42.3A**).

- **Incomplete cleavage** occurs in eggs with a lot of yolk, and the cleavage furrows do not penetrate it completely. **Discoidal cleavage** is a type of incomplete cleavage common in fishes as well as in birds and other reptiles. In the yolk-rich eggs of these species, the embryo forms as a disc of cells, or **blastodisc**, that sits on top of the dense yolk mass (**Figure 42.3B**).

- **Superficial cleavage** is a variation of incomplete cleavage that occurs in insects such as fruit flies (*Drosophila*). Early in development, cycles of mitosis occur without cell division, producing a **syncytium**—a single cell with many nuclei (**Figure 42.3C**). The nuclei eventually migrate to the periphery of the egg, after which the cell membrane of the egg grows inward, creating a **blastoderm** by partitioning the nuclei into individual cells surrounding a core of yolk.

- **Rotational cleavage** is a unique form of complete cleavage that occurs only in placental (eutherian) mammals.

The positions of the mitotic spindles during cleavage are not random but are defined by cytoplasmic determinants produced from the maternal genome and stored in the egg. The orientation of the mitotic spindles can determine the planes of cleavage and the arrangement of the blastomeres.

In complete cleavage, if the mitotic spindles of successive cell divisions form parallel or perpendicular to the animal–vegetal axis of the zygote, a pattern of **radial cleavage** occurs. The first two cell divisions are parallel to the animal–vegetal axis, and the third is perpendicular to it (see Figure 42.3A). **Spiral cleavage** results when the mitotic spindles are at oblique angles to the animal–vegetal axis. In spiral cleavage, each new cell layer is shifted to the left or right, depending on the orientation of the mitotic spindles. Most mollusks have spiral cleavage, reflected in some species, such as snails, by a coiling shell pattern.

Cleavage in mammals is unique

Several features of early cell divisions in eutherian mammals are very different from those seen in other animal groups. (Note: unless stated otherwise, all mammals referred to in this chapter are eutherians). First, this process in mammals is very slow. Cell divisions are 12–24 hours apart, compared with tens of minutes to a few hours in non-mammalian species. Also, the cell divisions of mammalian blastomeres are not in synchrony with each other. Because the blastomeres do not undergo mitosis at the same time, the number of cells in the embryo does not increase in the regular progression (2, 4, 8, 16, 32, etc.) typical of other species. The slowness of mammalian cleavage means that genes expressed during cleavage can play roles in cleavage. In animals such as sea urchins and frogs in which cleavage progresses rapidly, very little if any gene transcription occurs in the blastomeres. Instead, cleavage is directed by molecules that were present in the egg before fertilization.

The pattern of mammalian cleavage is called **rotational cleavage**. The first cell division is parallel to the animal–vegetal axis as in radial cleavage, but in the second cell division, the two blastomeres divide at right angles to one other. One blastomere divides parallel to the animal–vegetal axis, while the other divides perpendicular to this axis (**Figure 42.4A**). As in other animals that have complete cleavage, the early cell divisions in a mammalian zygote produce a loosely associated ball of cells. After the eight-cell stage, however, the behavior of the mammalian blastomeres changes. They change shape to maximize their surface contact with one another, form tight junctions (see Figure 6.6), and become a compact mass of cells (**Figure 42.4B**).

Soon after the transition to the 32-cell stage, the cells of the mammalian embryo separate into two groups. The **inner cell mass** develops as the embryo, while the surrounding outer cells become an encompassing sac called the **trophoblast**. Trophoblast cells secrete fluid, creating a cavity—the blastocoel—with the inner cell mass at one end. At this stage the mammalian embryo is called a **blastocyst**, distinguishing it from the blastulas of other animal groups (**Figure 42.4C**). The pluripotent cells of the inner cell mass are known as **embryonic stem cells** and are the subject of much research because of their therapeutic potential.

 View in Achieve

Animation 42.2 Embryonic Stem Cells

(A) Complete cleavage (frog)

Animal pole

From H. W. Beams and R. G. Kessel, 1976. Am Sci 64: 279–290, courtesy of the authors and L. Biedler

© Dr. Lloyd M. Beidler/Science Source

© Dr. Richard Kessel & Dr. Gene Shih/Visuals Unlimited, Inc.

The first cleavage passes through the poles and site of sperm entry and bisects the gray crescent.

The second cleavage is at right angles to the first.

The third cleavage is at right angles (horizontal) to the first two and separating the animal and vegetal hemispheres. Vegetal hemisphere cells are larger.

The embryo forms as a blastodisc that sits on top of the yolk mass.

(B) Incomplete cleavage (zebrafish)

Four photos to left from H. W. Beams and R. G. Kessel, 1976. Am Sci 64: 279–290, courtesy of the authors and L. Biedler

In birds and fishes, cleavage furrows do not penetrate the large yolk mass.

(C) Superficial cleavage (fruit fly)

Nucleus

1 Mitosis (nuclear division) occurs without cell division.

3 The nuclei migrate to the edge of the cell membrane.

2 A syncytium—a single cell with many nuclei—is produced.

4 Cellularization occurs, creating a blastoderm.

S. Kotadia et al. 2010, eLS, (Ed.). doi:10.1002/9780470015902. a0001071.pub2

Figure 42.3 Some Patterns of Cleavage
Differences in patterns of early embryonic development reflect differences in the way the egg cytoplasm is organized. **(A)** The frog is a model organism representing complete cleavage in these scanning electron micrographs (SEMs). **(B)** SEMs of zebrafish (*Danio rerio*) embryos illustrate incomplete cleavage, in which the large yolk mass limits the planes of cleavage. **(C)** Nuclear staining reveals the syncytial nuclei characteristic of the early embryo of a fruit fly. These nuclei migrate to the periphery. Cleavage furrows then move inward to separate the nuclei into individual cells, forming the blastoderm.

(A) Mammalian rotational cleavage

Parallel plane of second division

Plane of first division

A

Perpendicular plane of second division

V

(B) Early cleavage in human embryo

8-Cell stage   Bleb   16-Cell stage   Compacted cells

© Dr. Yorgos Nikas/Science Source

© Dr. Yorgos Nikas/Science Source

© Petit Format/Science Source

(C) Cross section of a mammalian blastocyst

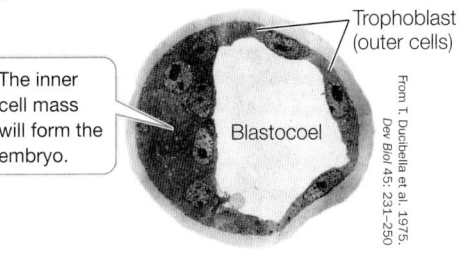

Trophoblast (outer cells)

The inner cell mass will form the embryo.

Blastocoel

From T. Ducibella et al. 1975. Dev Biol 45: 231–250

Figure 42.4 Becoming a Blastocyst **(A)** Mammals have rotational, complete cleavage, in which the plane of the first cleavage is parallel to the animal–vegetal (A–V) axis, but the second cell division involves two planes (beige) at right angles to each other. **(B)** Scanning electron micrographs (color added) of early cleavage (leading to the formation of the blastocyst) in a human embryo. The cells' outer surfaces are covered with cilia (bright yellow). The small spheres, or "blebs," of cytoplasmic material, prominent at the eight-cell stage, disintegrate as cleavage progresses. **(C)** Seen in cross section under a light microscope, a mammalian blastocyst consists of an inner cell mass adjacent to a fluid-filled blastocoel and surrounded by trophoblast cells. (A after B. J. Gulyas. 1975. *J Exp Zool* 193: 235–247. doi:10.1002/jez.1401930212)

Why is mammalian cleavage so different? A key factor is that mammalian eggs contain little or no yolk and must derive all nutrients from the mother. To support the developing embryo, a connection develops between the circulatory systems of the embryo and the mother. As you will see later in this chapter, the structures that provide this connection are the placenta and the umbilical cord. Thus the blastocyst of mammals must produce both the embryo (from the inner cell mass) and its support structures (from the trophoblast).

Fertilization in mammals occurs in the upper reaches of the oviduct, and cleavage occurs as the zygote travels down the oviduct to the uterus (**Figure 42.5**). When the blastocyst arrives in the uterus, the trophoblast adheres to the lining of the uterus (the **endometrium**), beginning the process of **implantation**. In humans, implantation begins about 6 days after fertilization and is aided by adhesion molecules and enzymes secreted by the trophoblast.

As the blastocyst moves down the oviduct to the uterus, it must not embed itself in the oviduct (fallopian tube) wall, or the result will be an ectopic, or tubal, pregnancy—a very dangerous condition. Early implantation is prevented by the zona pellucida that surrounded the egg (see Figure 41.6) and remains around the cleaving ball of cells. At about the time the blastocyst reaches the uterus, it hatches from the zona pellucida so implantation can occur.

The fates of blastomeres depend on the cytoplasm they receive during cleavage

Cleavage results in a repackaging of the egg cytoplasm into a large number of small cells surrounding the fluid-filled blastocoel. There is little gene expression during early cleavage divisions in most species with mammals being the exception. Even without gene expression, however, cells in different regions of the blastula possess different complements of the nutrients and cytoplasmic determinants that were present in the egg. For example, Figure 42.2 illustrated the processes by which β-catenin becomes localized in the region of the amphibian zygote that will become the dorsal side of the embryo.

The blastocoel prevents cells from different regions of the blastula coming into contact and interacting, but that soon changes. During the next stage of development, the cells of the blastula move around and come into new associations with one another, communicate instructions to one another, and begin to differentiate. In many animals, these movements of the blastomeres are so regular and well orchestrated that it is possible to label specific blastomeres with a dye, thus producing **fate maps** that identify the tissues and organs formed from each blastomere's progeny (**Figure 42.6**).

Blastomeres become **determined**—committed to specific fates—at different times in different species. In some species, such as roundworms, the fates of blastomeres are restricted as early as the two-cell stage. This early determination depends on informational molecules that were originally present in the egg cytoplasm and is called **autonomous specification**. If one of these blastomeres is experimentally removed, a particular portion of the embryo will not form. The resulting developmental pattern has been called **mosaic development** because each blastomere seems to contribute a specific set of "tiles" to the final "mosaic" that is the adult animal. Mosaic development is the common form of development in invertebrates.

The fates of blastomeres in most vertebrate embryos are determined by information they receive from their environment and their neighboring cells. This mechanism of determination is called **regulated specification**, and it gives rise to **regulative development**. Unlike in mosaic development, the loss of some cells during cleavage in regulative development does not affect the developing embryo, because the remaining cells compensate for the loss. A subset of the remaining cells may add a cell division, or they may even change their fate to compensate for the

16–32 Cells (3–4 days postfertilization)

Implantation of blastocyst (6–7 days postfertilization)

2–4 Cells (2 days postfertilization)

Oviduct

Fimbria

Uterus

Ovary

Site of fertilization

Cervix

Vagina

Human embryo at 9 days

Wall of uterus

Developing placenta

Inner cell mass (embryo) { Hypoblast / Epiblast

Trophoblast

Blastocoel

Uterine cavity

Endometrium

Amniotic cavity

Emerging chorionic villus

Blood vessel

Figure 42.5 A Human Blastocyst at Implantation Adhesion molecules and proteolytic enzymes secreted by trophoblast cells allow the blastocyst to burrow into the endometrium. Once the blastocyst is implanted in the wall of the uterus, the trophoblast cells send out numerous projections—the chorionic villi—which increase the embryo's area of contact with the mother's bloodstream. The inner cell mass divides into two embryonic tissues, the hypoblast and the epiblast. The epiblast splits to form the amniotic cavity.

Figure 42.6 Fate Map of a
Typical Amphibian Blastula

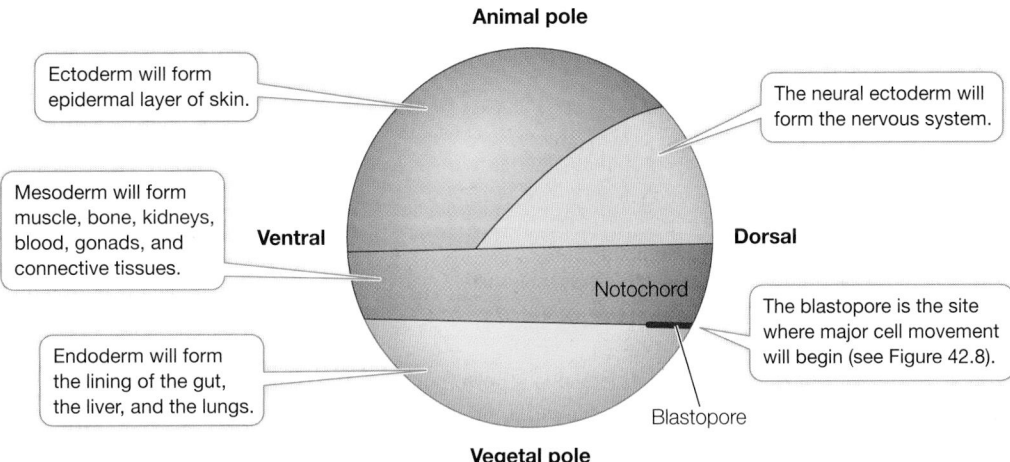

Animal pole

Ectoderm will form
epidermal layer of skin.

The neural ectoderm will
form the nervous system.

Mesoderm will form
muscle, bone, kidneys,
blood, gonads, and
connective tissues.

Ventral

Dorsal

Notochord

The blastopore is the site
where major cell movement
will begin (see Figure 42.8).

Endoderm will form
the lining of the gut,
the liver, and the lungs.

Blastopore

Vegetal pole

cells lost. Because development is regulative in humans, a single blastomere can be removed from early embryos without harming the remaining blastomeres or disrupting normal development. Cells removed from embryos produced by in vitro fertilization can be used for preimplantation genetic diagnosis to ensure that healthy embryos are selected for implantation in the mother.

If some blastomeres can change their fate to compensate for the loss of other cells during cleavage and blastula formation, can those cells form an entire embryo? Yes, in species with regulative development, they can. If during cleavage or early blastula formation, the blastomeres are physically separated into two groups, both groups can produce complete embryos. Since the two embryos come from the same zygote, they will be monozygotic twins—genetically identical.

Non-identical twins occur when two separate eggs are fertilized by two separate sperm. Thus although identical twins are always the same sex, non-identical twins have a 50% chance of being the same sex (the same chance as two non-twin siblings). If genetic or environmental factors cause the blastula or blastocyst to split partially, the result is twins who are conjoined at some point on their bodies and usually share some of their organs and limbs. Conjoined twins occur in about 1 out of 50,000 human pregnancies.

Reproductive germ cells are determined early in cleavage

Molecules present in the egg cytoplasm determine which lineage of cells will eventually populate the gonads and become the reproductive stem cells—oogonia and spermatogonia. In fruit flies, at the ninth nuclear division (recall that the egg is a multinucleate syncytium at this stage; see Figure 42.3C), a group of nuclei migrate to the posterior pole of the egg where they become surrounded by **pole plasm**—cytoplasm containing a complex mixture of fibrils, mitochondria, specific proteins, and mRNAs. As the cellularization of the blastoderm proceeds, the nuclei within the pole plasm give rise to the lineage of cells that will eventually migrate to the gonads (when they form) and produce germ cells (eggs and sperm).

As in fruit flies, the germ cell lineage in frogs starts with a special type of cytoplasm—the germ cell plasm—localized to one part of the egg. As a result of cleavage, the germ cell plasm becomes enclosed within some of the cells in the vegetal hemisphere; descendants of these cells will eventually migrate to the gonads once those structures form. Germ cell plasm includes inhibitors of transcription and translation that prevent these cells from differentiating into anything other than germ cells.

KEY CONCEPT
42.2 Recap and Assess

Cleavage divides up the cytoplasm of the zygote such that different blastomeres contain different combinations of informational molecules. The amount of nutrients stored in the egg influences the pattern of cell cleavage that produces the blastula. Blastulation in mammals is different than in other vertebrates. The cells that will give rise to germ cell lineages are set aside very early in development.

1. What characteristic of the eggs of different species relates to whether cleavage is complete or incomplete, and what is the exception?

2. Why can gene expression during cleavage play developmental roles in mammals but not in sea urchins and frogs?

3. Why can identical twins arise from a single egg in mammals but not in most invertebrates?

4. Why is there a longer time between determination and differentiation in germ cells than in skin cells?

Of the next stage of development—gastrulation—the developmental biologist Lewis Wolpert once said, "It is not birth, marriage, or death, but gastrulation which is the most important time in your life." During gastrulation, cell movements create new cell-to-cell contacts, which in turn set up signaling cascades that initiate the differentiation of cells and tissues and set the stage for the emergence of the body plan.

KEY CONCEPT
42.3
Gastrulation Generates Multiple Tissue Layers

Learning Objectives

42.3.1 Compare gastrulation in sea urchins, frogs, and reptiles.

42.3.2 Describe the experiment that revealed the role of the dorsal lip of the amphibian blastopore in embryonic development.

42.3.3 Describe cell movements that occur during gastrulation in sea urchins and amphibians.

42.3.4 Summarize how organizer cells achieve a pattern by appropriately expressing growth factor antagonists.

42.3.5 Explain the meaning of necessity and sufficiency in investigating potential inductive signals.

The blastula is typically a fluid-filled ball of cells. How does this simple ball of cells become an embryo made up of multiple tissue layers with head and tail ends and dorsal and ventral sides? **Gastrulation** is the process whereby the blastula is transformed by massive movements of cells into an embryo with multiple tissue layers and distinct body axes. The resulting spatial relationships between tissues make possible the inductive interactions between cells that trigger differentiation and organ formation.

In the triploblastic animals (see Key Concept 29.1), three **germ layers** (also called cell layers or tissue layers, and not to be confused with germ cells) form during gastrulation:

1. The **endoderm** is the innermost germ layer, created as some blastomeres move to the inside of the embryo. The endoderm gives rise to the epithelial lining of the digestive tract, respiratory tract, pancreas, thyroid, and liver.

2. The **ectoderm** is the outer germ layer, formed from those cells remaining on the outside of the embryo. The ectoderm contributes to the nervous system, including the eyes and ears; and to the epidermal layer of the skin and structures derived from skin, such as hair, feathers, nails or claws, sweat glands, oil glands, and even teeth and other tissues of the mouth.

3. The **mesoderm** is the middle layer and is made up of cells that migrate between the endoderm and the ectoderm. The mesoderm contributes to many organs, including the heart, blood vessels, muscles, and bones.

The three germ layers are illustrated for a very early embryo in the fate map shown in Figure 42.6.

Some of the most interesting and important challenges in animal development have dealt with two related questions: what directs the cell movements of gastrulation, and what is responsible for the resulting patterns of cell differentiation and organ formation? Scientists have made significant progress in answering both these questions at the molecular level. In the following discussion we begin with sea urchin gastrulation because it is the simplest to conceptualize in spatial terms. We then describe the more complex pattern of gastrulation in frogs, and then the still more complex patterns in reptiles (including birds) and mammals.

▶ **View in Achieve**
  Animation 42.3 Gastrulation

Invagination at the vegetal pole initiates gastrulation in the sea urchin

The sea urchin blastula is a hollow ball of cells only one cell layer thick. At the end of blastulation the rate of mitosis slows, and the beginning of gastrulation is marked by a flattening of the vegetal hemisphere (**Figure 42.7**). Some cells at the vegetal pole break away from neighboring cells and migrate into the cavity to become **mesenchyme**—cells of the middle germ layer,

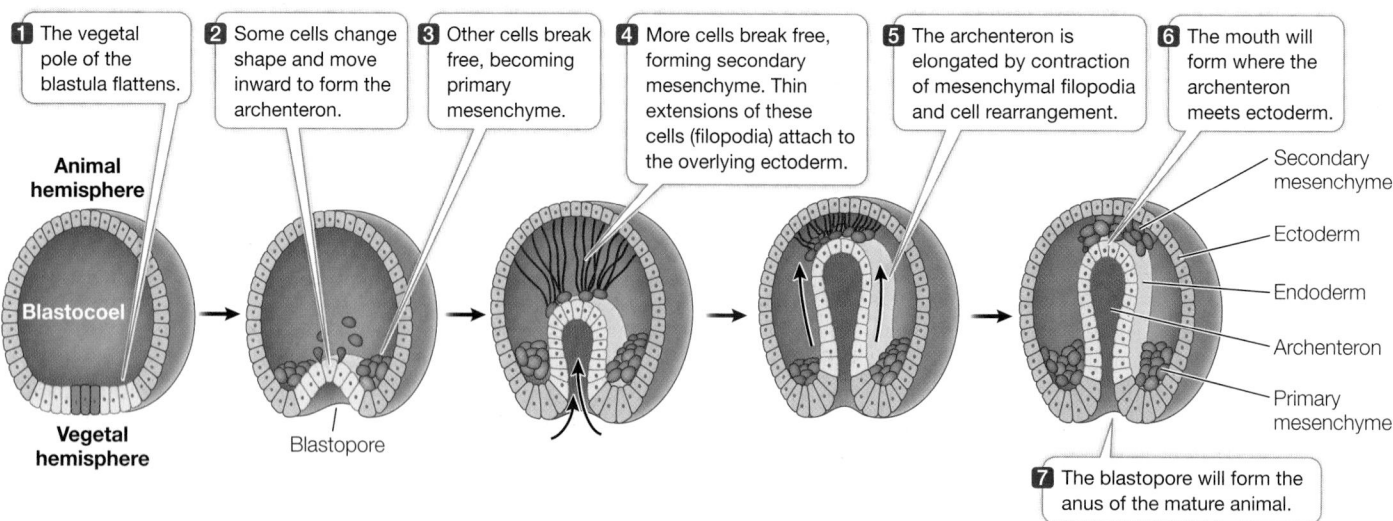

1 The vegetal pole of the blastula flattens.

2 Some cells change shape and move inward to form the archenteron.

3 Other cells break free, becoming primary mesenchyme.

4 More cells break free, forming secondary mesenchyme. Thin extensions of these cells (filopodia) attach to the overlying ectoderm.

5 The archenteron is elongated by contraction of mesenchymal filopodia and cell rearrangement.

6 The mouth will form where the archenteron meets ectoderm.

7 The blastopore will form the anus of the mature animal.

Animal hemisphere

Blastocoel

Vegetal hemisphere

Blastopore

Secondary mesenchyme

Ectoderm

Endoderm

Archenteron

Primary mesenchyme

Figure 42.7 Gastrulation in Sea Urchins During gastrulation, cells move to new positions and form the three germ layers from which differentiated tissues develop.

Q: How do cells on the surface of the vegetal pole become the cells lining the gut?

the mesoderm. Mesenchymal cells are not organized in tightly packed sheets or tubes like epithelial cells are; they act as independent units, migrating into and among the other tissue layers. These early mesenchymal cells will contribute to the skeletal structures of the sea urchin.

The flattening at the vegetal pole results from changes in the shape of individual blastomeres. These cells, which are originally rather cuboidal, become wedge-shaped, with smaller outer edges and larger inner edges. As a result, the vegetal pole bulges inward, or invaginates, as if someone were poking a finger into a hollow ball (see Figure 42.7). The invaginating cells become endoderm and form the primitive gut, called the **archenteron**. The archenteron begins as a short stubby invagination, but its cells extend, flatten, interdigitate, and migrate over one another to form a long thin tube. This process is called **convergent extension**. As the archenteron gets closer to the opposite side of the blastocoel, more mesenchymal cells migrate out of it into the blastocoel. These cells remain attached to the tip of the archenteron and send out extensions called filopodia that adhere to the overlying ectoderm. The filopodia contract and pull the archenteron toward the overlying ectoderm. The mouth of the animal will form where the archenteron makes contact with this overlying ectoderm. The opening created by the invagination of the vegetal pole is called the **blastopore**, and it will become the anus of the animal.

> **Connect the Concepts** Recall from Key Concept 29.1 that where the mouth and anus form during gastrulation distinguishes the two major groups of animals that have bilateral symmetry, the protostomes and the deuterostomes. If the blastopore becomes the mouth, the animals are classified as protostomes ("mouth first"); if the blastopore becomes the anus, the animals are classified as deuterostomes ("mouth second").

What mechanisms control the various cell movements of sea urchin gastrulation? The immediate answer is that specific properties of particular blastomeres change. For example, some vegetal cells change shape and bulge into the blastocoel, and these cells become mesenchyme. Once they lose contact with their neighboring cells on the surface of the blastula, they send out filopodia that then move along an extracellular matrix of proteins laid down by the cells lining the blastocoel.

A deeper understanding of gastrulation requires that we discover the molecular mechanisms whereby different blastomeres develop different properties. Cleavage systematically divides the cytoplasm of the egg. The sea urchin blastula at the 64-cell stage is radially symmetrical, but it has polarity and consists of tiers of cells. As in the frog blastula, the top is the animal pole and the bottom is the vegetal pole. If the embryo is cut in half horizontally, only the cells from the vegetal pole are capable of initiating the development of a complete sea urchin. Such experiments show that the different cells of the blastula already have different developmental potentials. Why is this so? We now know that many transcriptional regulatory proteins are not uniformly distributed in the egg cytoplasm, and as cleavage progresses, these proteins end up in different groups of cells. Therefore specific sets of genes are activated in different cells, determining their different developmental capacities.

Frog gastrulation begins at the gray crescent

Amphibian blastulas are more than one cell layer thick and they contain stored nutrients called yolk; gastrulation is therefore more complex in amphibians than in sea urchins. Variation is considerable across different species of amphibians, so this brief account combines results from studies done on different species to produce a generalized picture of amphibian development.

Amphibian gastrulation begins when certain cells in the gray crescent region (see Figure 42.1) change their shapes and cell-adhesion properties. These cells bulge inward toward the blastocoel while they remain attached to the outer surface of the blastula by slender necks; because of their shape, they are called bottle cells. Bottle cells mark the spot where the **dorsal lip** of the blastopore will form (**Figure 42.8**).

As the bottle cells move inward, the dorsal lip is created, and a sheet of cells moves over it into the blastocoel. This process is called **involution**. One group of involuting cells is the prospective endoderm; these cells form the primitive gut, or archenteron. Another group will move between the endoderm and the outermost cells to form mesoderm. As with the extension of the archenteron in the sea urchin, these cell rearrangements involve convergent extension. The cells elongate in the direction of growth, but they also intercalate (move in between each other). As gastrulation proceeds, cells from the animal hemisphere flatten and move toward the site of involution in a process called **epiboly**. The blastopore lip widens and spreads ventrally, and eventually forms a complete circle surrounding a "plug" of yolk-rich cells. As cells continue to move inward through the blastopore, the archenteron grows, gradually displacing the blastocoel.

As gastrulation comes to an end, the amphibian embryo consists of three germ layers: ectoderm on the outside, endoderm on the inside, and mesoderm in between. The embryo also has a dorsal–ventral and anterior–posterior organization. Most important, the fates of specific regions of the endoderm, mesoderm, and ectoderm have been determined. The beautiful experiments revealing how determination takes place in the amphibian embryo are an old but exciting story.

The dorsal lip of the blastopore organizes the formation of the amphibian embryo

In the early 1900s the German biologist Hans Spemann was studying the development of salamander eggs. He was interested in finding out whether the nuclei of blastomeres remain capable of directing the development of complete embryos or whether these nuclei lose some developmental potential. With great patience and dexterity, he formed loops from single hairs taken from his baby daughter and tied them around fertilized eggs along the plane of the first cell division, effectively dividing the eggs in half, with the nucleus restricted to one side. The side containing the nucleus went through cell divisions and developed into a salamander; the other half simply degenerated. Up until the 16-cell stage, if one nucleus escaped to the other side of the constriction, twin salamanders could develop. Thus each of the nuclei of the blastula (at least up to the 16-cell stage) was capable of directing and supporting development of the whole organism (regulative development).

1 Gastrulation begins at the junction of the animal and vegetal poles opposite the site of sperm entry into the egg. Cells in the region move inward, forming the dorsal blastopore lip.

2 Cells of the animal pole spread out, pushing surface cells below them toward and across the dorsal blastopore lip. These cells involute into the interior of the embryo, where they form the endoderm and mesoderm.

Animal pole

Blastocoel

Ectoderm

Neural ectoderm

Archenteron

Mesoderm

Blastocoel displaced

Dorsal blastopore lip

Bottle cells

Dorsal blastopore lip

Vegetal pole

Bottle cells

Endoderm

3 Involution creates the archenteron and destroys the blastocoel. The blastopore lip forms a circle, with cells moving to the interior all around the blastopore.

Mesenchyme   **Dorsal**   Ectoderm

Chordamesoderm

Dorsal blastopore lip

Archenteron (future digestive tract)

Mesoderm (notochord)

Dorsal mesoderm

Dorsal blastopore lip

Anterior   **Posterior**

Dorsal blastopore lip

Endoderm

Ectoderm

Endoderm

Ventral   Ventral mesoderm

Ventral mesoderm

Ventral blastopore lip

Ectoderm

Figure 42.8 Gastrulation in the Frog Embryo   Yellow, blue, green, and red in this diagram are matched to those colors in Figure 42.6, the frog fate map. (After R. E. Keller. 1986. In *Developmental Biology: A Comprehensive Synthesis*, Vol. 2, L. Browder (ed.), pp. 241–327. Springer: New York.)

Media Clip 42.1 Frog Gastrulation Time-Lapse
Life12e.com/mc42.1

Q: Epiboly results in the formation of which tissues in the adult frog?

As often happens in science, Spemann's bisection experiments revealed a new phenomenon. Sometimes the half of the blastula receiving an escaped nucleus did not develop. When his loops bisected the gray crescent of the egg, both halves of the zygote developed into a complete embryo. When he tied the loops so the gray crescent was on only one side of the constriction, however, only that half of the zygote developed into a complete embryo (**Figure 42.9**). When the half lacking gray crescent material received a nucleus, it underwent cell division but formed only a clump of undifferentiated cells that Spemann called a "belly piece." Spemann hypothesized that cytoplasmic factors unequally distributed in the fertilized egg were necessary for gastrulation and the development of a normal salamander.

To further test the hypothesis that cells receiving different complements of cytoplasmic factors had different developmental fates, Spemann transplanted pieces of early gastrulas to various locations on other gastrulas. Guided by fate maps (see Figure 42.6),

he was able to take a piece of ectoderm he knew would develop into the epidermis of the skin and transplant it to a region that normally becomes part of the nervous system, and vice versa.

When he performed these transplants in early gastrulas—when the blastopore was just beginning to form—the transplanted pieces always developed into tissues that were appropriate for the location where they were placed. Transplanted cells destined to become epidermis in their original location developed into nervous system tissue, and transplanted cells destined to become nervous system tissue in their original location developed into host epidermis. Thus Spemann learned that the fates of the transplanted cells had not been determined before the transplantation.

View in Achieve
Simulation 42.1 Cell Fates

In late gastrulas, however, the same experiment yielded opposite results. Transplanted cells destined to become epidermis in their original location produced patches of skin cells in the

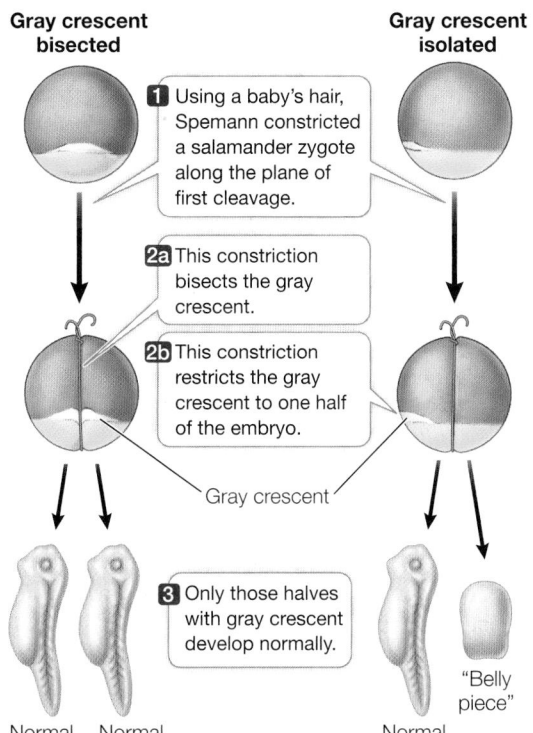

Gray crescent bisected

Gray crescent isolated

1 Using a baby's hair, Spemann constricted a salamander zygote along the plane of first cleavage.

2a This constriction bisects the gray crescent.

2b This constriction restricts the gray crescent to one half of the embryo.

Gray crescent

3 Only those halves with gray crescent develop normally.

"Belly piece"

Normal Normal

Normal

Figure 42.9 Gastrulation and the Gray Crescent Spemann's research revealed that gastrulation and subsequent normal development in salamanders depend on cytoplasmic determinants localized in the region of the blastula that corresponds to the gray crescent region in the fertilized egg. (After H. Spemann. 1938. *Embryonic Development and Induction*. Yale University Press: New Haven, CT.)

host nervous system, and the transplanted cells from regions that would develop into nervous system tissue produced nervous tissue in the skin of the recipient. At some point during gastrulation, the fates of the embryonic cells had become determined.

Spemann's next experiment, done with his student Hilde Mangold, produced momentous results: they transplanted the dorsal lip of the blastopore (**Figure 42.10**). When this small piece of tissue was transplanted into the presumptive belly area of another gastrula, it stimulated a second site of gastrulation—and a second complete embryo formed belly-to-belly with the original embryo. Because the dorsal lip of the blastopore was apparently capable of inducing the host tissue to form an entire embryo, Spemann and Mangold called the dorsal lip tissue the **primary embryonic organizer**, or simply the **organizer**. For more than 100 years, what has come to be called the Spemann–Mangold organizer has been an active area of research.

Transcription factors and growth factors underlie the organizer's actions

The primary embryonic organizer has been studied intensively with molecular methods to discover the mechanisms involved in its action. The distribution of the transcription factor β-catenin in the late blastula corresponds to the location of the organizer in the early gastrula, so β-catenin is a candidate for the initiator of organizer activity. To prove that a protein is an inductive signal, it has to be shown that it is both *necessary* and *sufficient* for the

proposed effect. In other words, the effect should not occur if the candidate protein is not present (necessity), and the candidate protein should be capable of inducing the effect where it would otherwise not occur (sufficiency).

The criteria of necessity and sufficiency have been satisfied for β-catenin. If β-catenin mRNA transcripts are depleted by injections of antisense RNA into the egg (see Key Concept 18.4), gastrulation does not occur. If β-catenin is experimentally overexpressed in another region of the blastula, it can induce a second axis of embryo formation, as the transplanted dorsal lip did in the Spemann–Mangold experiments. Thus β-catenin appears to be both necessary and sufficient for the formation of the primary embryonic organizer. But, β-catenin is only one component of a complex signaling process. How the presence of β-catenin creates the organizer, and how the organizer induces the beginnings of the body plan, involves a complex series of interactions between transcription factors and growth factors that control gene expression.

Properties of organizer cells change as they migrate from the dorsal lip

Organizer cells begin the process of formation of the dorsal lip of the blastopore. Specifically, these cells are at the center of the dorsal lip and involute, moving forward on the midline (i.e., the middle of the anterior–posterior axis). The first organizer cells to enter the embryo migrate anteriorly to become the head endoderm and head mesoderm. Here they induce neighboring cells to participate in making structures of the head. Organizer cells that involute later in gastrulation induce structures of the trunk, and the last of the organizer cells to move inward from the dorsal lip induce structures of the tail. How do the organizer cells change to enable them to induce head, trunk, or tail structures?

Inductive tissue interactions can suppress as well as activate. Goosecoid is a transcription factor expressed by early organizer cells. Goosecoid activates genes encoding certain signaling factors. As the early organizer cells move forward in the blastocoel, they come into contact with new populations of cells that produce several different growth factors. For head structures to form, certain of these growth factors have to be suppressed. The most anterior organizer cells, under the influence of Goosecoid, produce and release antagonists to those growth factors.

The induction of trunk structures requires suppression of a different set of growth factors. In organizer cells that involute later than the head organizers, Goosecoid is no longer the dominant transcription factor, and these cells express different growth factor antagonists. The induction of tail structures requires still different activities of the organizer cells that involute last. Thus the organizer cells express appropriate sets of growth factor antagonists at the right times to achieve different patterns of differentiation on the anterior–posterior axis.

The initiation of nervous system development also involves a suppressive tissue interaction. For a long time it was thought that the involuting organizer cells actively induced the overlying ectoderm to form nervous tissue rather than becoming epidermis. We now know, however, that epidermis is not the default state of the dorsal ectoderm. Rather, the underlying mesoderm secretes

Experiment

Figure 42.10   The Dorsal Lip Induces Embryonic Organization

Original Paper: H. Spemann and H. Mangold. 1924. *Roux' Arch Entw Mech* 100: 599–638. Viktor Hamburger's translation appeared in *Foundations of Experimental Embryology*, 1964, B. H. Willier and J. M. Oppenheimer (eds.), pp. 146–184. Prentice Hall, Inc.: Englewood Cliffs, NJ.

In a classic experiment, Hans Spemann and Hilde Mangold transplanted the dorsal blastopore lip tissue of an early gastrula stage salamander embryo. The results showed that the cells of this embryonic region, which they dubbed "the organizer," could direct the formation of an entire embryo.

HYPOTHESIS▶   The early dorsal blastopore lip organizes cell differentiation in amphibian embryos.

METHOD▶

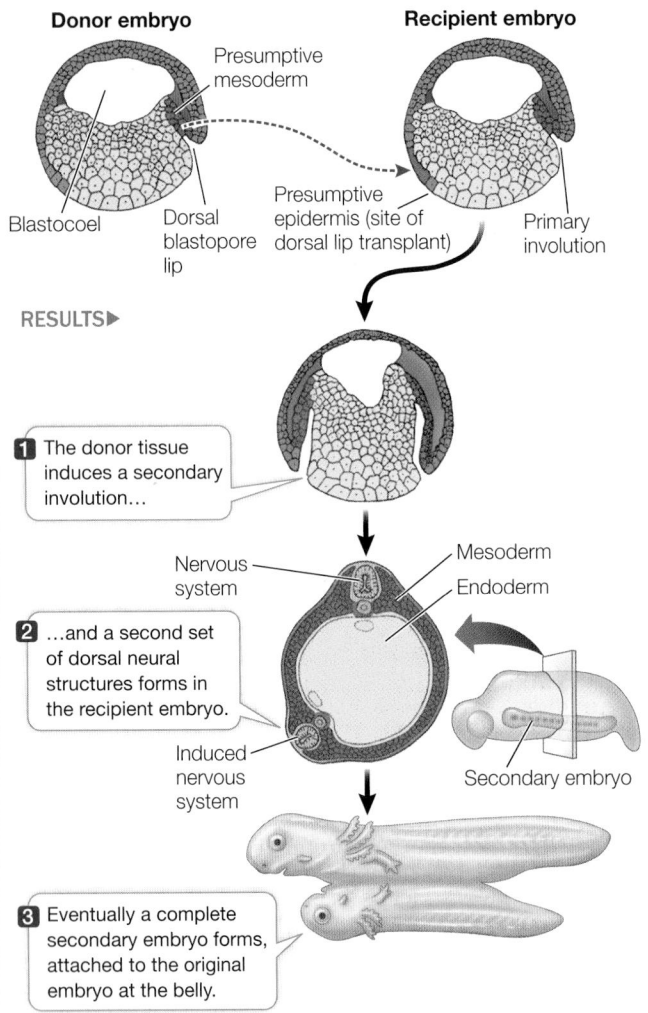

1. Excise a piece of dorsal blastopore lip of an early gastrula stage salamander embryo (the donor).

2. Transplant the donor tissue onto a recipient embryo at the same stage. The donor tissue is transplanted onto a region of ectoderm that should become epidermis (skin).

CONCLUSION▶   The cells of the dorsal blastopore lip can induce other cells to change their developmental fates.

 View in Achieve
Animation 42.4 The Primary Embryonic Organizer

---

factors called BMP proteins that induce the ectoderm to become epidermis. The role of the involuting organizer cells is to block that induction, allowing the overlying ectodermal cells to follow what is really their default pathway—differentiation into nervous tissue.

The amount of yolk influences gastrulation

The eggs of reptiles, including birds, contain a massive amount of yolk, and the blastulas of these groups develop as a disc of cells on top of the yolk (see Figure 42.3B). We will use the chicken egg to show how gastrulation proceeds in a flat disc of cells rather than in a ball of cells.

Cleavage in the chick results in a flat, circular layer of cells called a blastodisc (**Figure 42.11**). Between the blastodisc and the yolk mass is a fluid-filled space. Some cells from the blastodisc break free and move into this space. These cells come together to form a continuous layer called the **hypoblast**, which will later contribute to extraembryonic membranes that support and nourish the developing embryo. The overlying cells make up the **epiblast**, from which the embryo will form. Thus the avian blastula is a flattened structure consisting of an upper epiblast and a lower hypoblast, which are joined at the margins of the blastodisc. The blastocoel is the fluid-filled space between the epiblast and hypoblast.

Gastrulation begins with a thickening in the posterior region of the epiblast, caused by the movement of cells toward the midline and then forward along the midline (see Figure 42.11). The result is a midline ridge called the **primitive streak**. A depression called the primitive groove forms along the length of the primitive streak. The primitive groove functions as the blastopore, and cells migrate through it into the blastocoel to become endoderm and mesoderm.

In the chick embryo, no archenteron forms, but the endoderm and mesoderm migrate forward to form the gut and other structures. At the anterior end of the primitive groove is a thickening called **Hensen's node**, which is the equivalent of the dorsal lip in the amphibian blastopore. Many signaling molecules found in the frog organizer are also expressed in Hensen's node. Cells moving into the blastocoel and moving anteriorly from Hensen's node become the notochord and organize the chick embryo in a manner similar to that of the frog embryo.

Gastrulation in mammals is similar to avian gastrulation

Mammalian embryos (with the exception of protherians) derive their nourishment from the maternal circulation, and therefore mammalian eggs do not have large amounts of yolk constraining their cleavage and early development. Nevertheless, mammals evolved from reptilian ancestors, so it is not surprising that mammals and reptiles, including birds, share certain patterns of early development. Earlier we described the development of the mammalian inner cell mass (the equivalent of the avian blastodisc) and the outer trophoblast.

As in birds, in eutherians the inner cell mass splits into an upper layer called the epiblast and a lower layer called the hypoblast. The embryo forms from the epiblast, while the

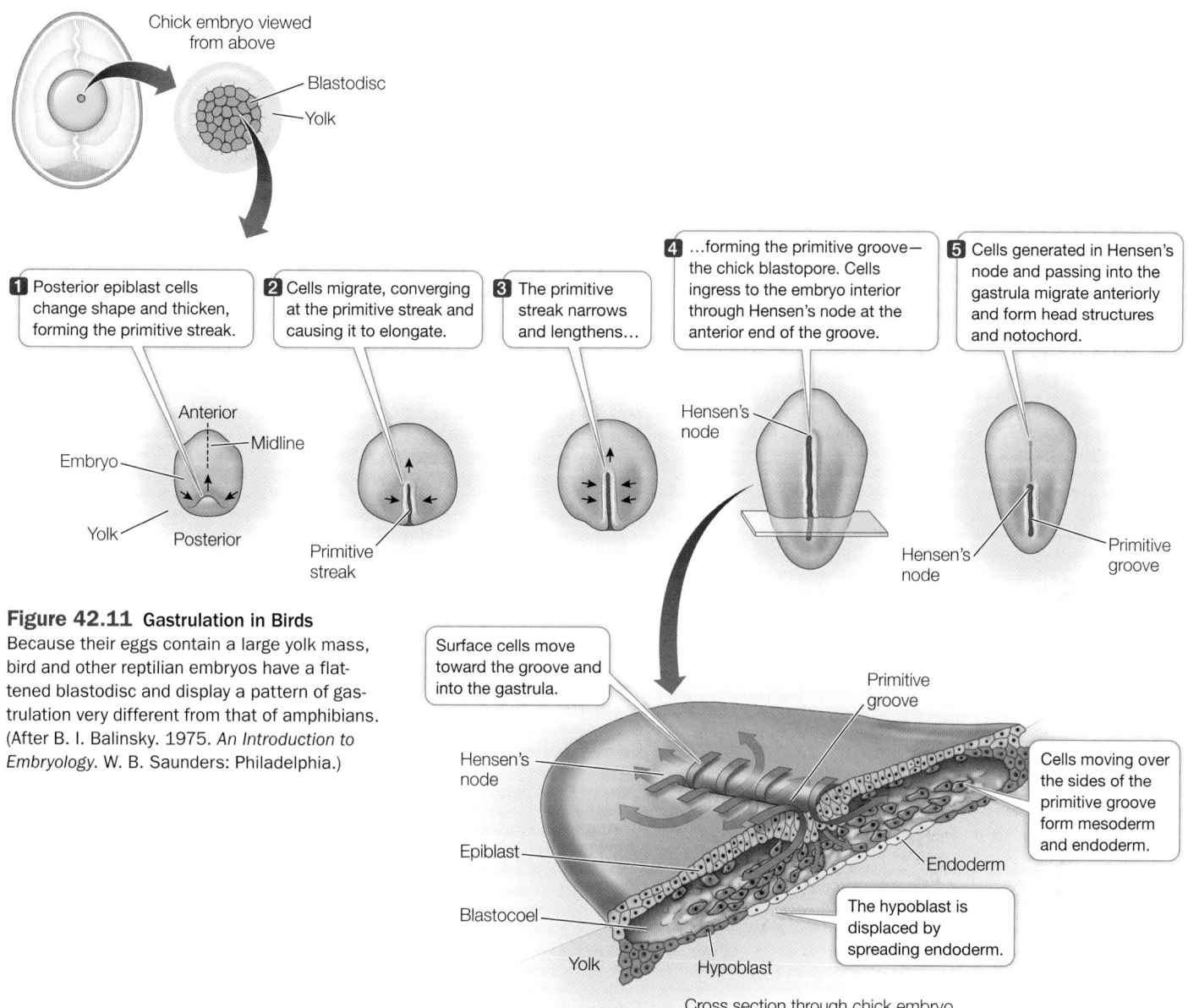

Chick embryo viewed
from above

Blastodisc

Yolk

1 Posterior epiblast cells change shape and thicken, forming the primitive streak.

2 Cells migrate, converging at the primitive streak and causing it to elongate.

3 The primitive streak narrows and lengthens...

4 ...forming the primitive groove— the chick blastopore. Cells ingress to the embryo interior through Hensen's node at the anterior end of the groove.

5 Cells generated in Hensen's node and passing into the gastrula migrate anteriorly and form head structures and notochord.

Anterior

Midline

Embryo

Yolk

Posterior

Primitive
streak

Hensen's
node

Hensen's
node

Primitive
groove

Figure 42.11 **Gastrulation in Birds**
Because their eggs contain a large yolk mass, bird and other reptilian embryos have a flattened blastodisc and display a pattern of gastrulation very different from that of amphibians. (After B. I. Balinsky. 1975. *An Introduction to Embryology*. W. B. Saunders: Philadelphia.)

Surface cells move toward the groove and into the gastrula.

Primitive
groove

Hensen's
node

Cells moving over the sides of the primitive groove form mesoderm and endoderm.

Epiblast

Endoderm

Blastocoel

The hypoblast is displaced by spreading endoderm.

Yolk

Hypoblast

Cross section through chick embryo

hypoblast contributes to the extraembryonic membranes that will encase the developing embryo and help form the placenta (see Figure 42.5). The epiblast also contributes to the extraembryonic membranes; specifically, it splits off an upper layer of cells that forms the amnion. The amnion grows to surround the developing embryo as a membranous sac filled with amniotic fluid. Gastrulation occurs in the mammalian epiblast just as it does in the avian epiblast. A primitive groove forms, and epiblast cells migrate through the groove to become layers of endoderm and mesoderm. At the top of the groove is the **node** which is homologous with Hensen's node in birds.

How is bilateral symmetry broken?

Gastrulation results in the anterior–posterior and dorsal–ventral patterning of the embryo, but all of the mechanisms discussed produce bilateral symmetry. At the opening of this chapter we introduced an early mechanism that breaks that symmetry to produce the well-known left–right asymmetries of the body. The human heart is on the left; the major lobe of the liver is on the right; the pancreas and spleen are on the left; the appendix is on the right; the major blood vessel leaving the heart, the aorta, bends to the left; the right lung has three lobes and the left lung has two; and so on. At the very beginning of gastrulation, the location where the involution of cells begins in a mammal is marked by a node of cells. The ventral surface of the node has ciliated cells. Some of these cilia are motile and others are not. The motile cilia create a leftward flow of extracellular fluid over the node. The experiments in **Investigating Life: Does the Direction of Nodal Flow Influence the Development of Left–Right Asymmetry in the Mouse Embryo?** investigate whether that directional flow is both necessary and sufficient to initiate signaling processes that break bilateral symmetry of the embryo.

▶Investigating**LIFE**   Does the Direction of Nodal Flow Influence the Development of Left–Right Asymmetry in the Mouse Embryo?

Experiment

Original Paper: S. Nonaka et al. 2002. Determination of left–right patterning of the mouse embryo by artificial nodal flow. *Nature* 418: 96–99.

HYPOTHESIS▶ The leftward flow of extracellular fluid created by the beating of nodal primary cilia is the stimulus for breaking bilateral symmetry in organ development in the mouse.

METHOD▶

1. Mount wild-type mouse embryos at different stages of development (presomite and 1, 2, or 3 somites; see Figure 42.13) in a culture medium–filled chamber with their nodal ends pointed upward.

2. Artificially pump culture medium through the chamber either from the left (normal) or from the right (reversed) and at slow or fast flow rates.

3. After 4 days assess the embryos as to the direction of looping (normal or reversed) of their developing heart tubes.

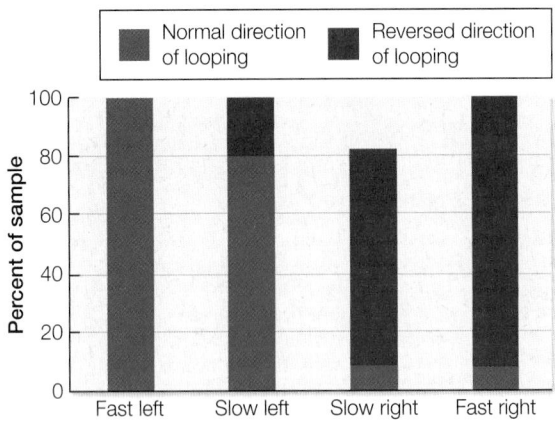

RESULTS▶ Since there were different numbers of embryos in different conditions, and some embryos did not survive, the data are displayed as percent of the total sample under each condition that showed normal or reversed direction of looping of their heart tubes. For example, in the slow left column there were 16 total embryos: 12 had normal direction of looping and 4 had reversed looping. The graph displays how heart-looping patterns were affected in the presomite stage by the direction of culture-medium flow.

Genotype, stage	Speed and direction of culture-medium flow[a]			
	Fast left	**Slow left**	**Slow right**	**Fast right**
Wild type, presomite	9N, 0R, 10T	12N, 4R, 16T	13N, 3R, 16T	2N, 21R, 24T

[a]N = normal heart looping; R = reversed looping; T = total embryos in sample.

CONCLUSION▶ When extracellular fluid moved across the node from right to left, the direction of heart-tube looping was normal. If this signal was weak (slow left flow), or if a weak reversed signal was applied (slow right flow), there was a small effect on normal direction of heart-tube looping, but when the reversed signal was strong, the heart-tube looping was in the reversed direction. These results support the conclusion that nodal flow is an important signal in breaking bilateral symmetry in the mouse embryo.

Work with the Data

The experiment illustrated in the graph was done on presomite embryos—before any somites had formed. Developmental signals usually have a time window of effectiveness given that developmental events are sequential and different events must be coordinated. Is there a time window within which nodal flow determines left–right symmetry in the embryo? To investigate the timing of sensitivity to nodal flow, another experiment was conducted using only fast right flow on early embryos at different stages of development.

Genotype, stage	Results
Wild type, presomite	2N, 21R, 24T
Wild type, 1-somite	9N, 0R, 12T
Wild type, 2-somite	22N, 0R, 22T
Wild type, 3-somite	14N, 0R, 14T

QUESTIONS▶

1. Plot the data as the percent of responses on the y axis and developmental stage on the x axis.

2. Why did this experiment not include left flow as a stimulus?

3. Do these data provide evidence for a sensitive period for nodal flow determining left–right asymmetry?

4. What do you conclude from the results on the 1-, 2-, and 3-somite wild-type embryos?

Go to **Achieve** for a companion
Data in Depth exercise.

42.3 Recap and Assess

The cell movements of gastrulation convert the blastula into an embryo with three tissue layers. New contacts between cells set up inductive signaling interactions that determine cell fates. Dorsal lip tissue is the source of organizer cells that induce development of head, trunk, and tail structures.

1. The sea urchin blastula develops into a radially symmetrical larva, but the frog blastula develops into a bilateral embryo. How does this difference relate to processes of gastrulation in these two types of animals?

2. What is meant by the criteria of necessity and sufficiency, and how have modern methods shown that the Spemann–Mangold primary embryonic organizer satisfies those criteria?

3. How do the cells of the primary embryonic organizer induce different structures on the anterior–posterior axis as they migrate from the dorsal lip to the head region of the embryo?

4. How does gastrulation in reptiles compare with that in amphibians?

We have described how the fertilized egg develops into an embryo with three germ layers and how cellular signals trigger different patterns of differentiation. In the next key concept we describe how organs and organ systems develop.

42.4 Organs Develop from the Three Germ Layers

Learning Objectives

42.4.1 Describe how nervous system development begins with neurulation.

42.4.2 Describe the formation of somites and their role in development.

42.4.3 Explain how genetic and environmental factors can influence neural tube formation.

42.4.4 Explain how a limited number of Hox genes can organize complex anterior–posterior patterning of the vertebrate embryo.

Gastrulation produces an embryo with three germ layers that are positioned to influence one another through inductive tissue interactions. During the next phase of development, called **organogenesis**, organs and organ systems develop simultaneously and in coordination with each other. In the chordates (see Key Concept 31.1), an early process of organogenesis is **neurulation**, the initiation of the nervous system. We examine neurulation in the amphibian embryo, but it occurs in a similar fashion in reptiles (including birds) and in mammals.

The organizer sets the stage for organogenesis

One group of cells that passes over the dorsal lip of the blastopore moves anteriorly and becomes the endodermal lining of the digestive tract. Another group of cells that passes over the dorsal lip on the midline becomes **chordamesoderm**, so named because it forms a rod of mesoderm—the **notochord**—that extends down

the center of the embryo. These cells also have important organizer functions (see Figure 42.8). The notochord gives structural support to the developing embryo, and in vertebrates it is replaced by the vertebral column. The organizing capacity of the chordamesoderm enables the overlying ectoderm to become neural ectoderm.

Neurulation involves the formation of an internal neural tube from an external sheet of cells. The first signs of neurulation are flattening and thickening of the ectoderm overlying the notochord; this thickened area forms the neural plate (**Figure 42.12A**). The edges of the neural plate that run in an anterior–posterior direction continue to thicken to form ridges or folds. Between these neural folds, a groove forms and deepens as the folds roll over it to converge on the midline. The folds fuse, forming a cylinder, the **neural tube**, and a continuous overlying layer of epidermal ectoderm (**Figure 42.12 B–D**).

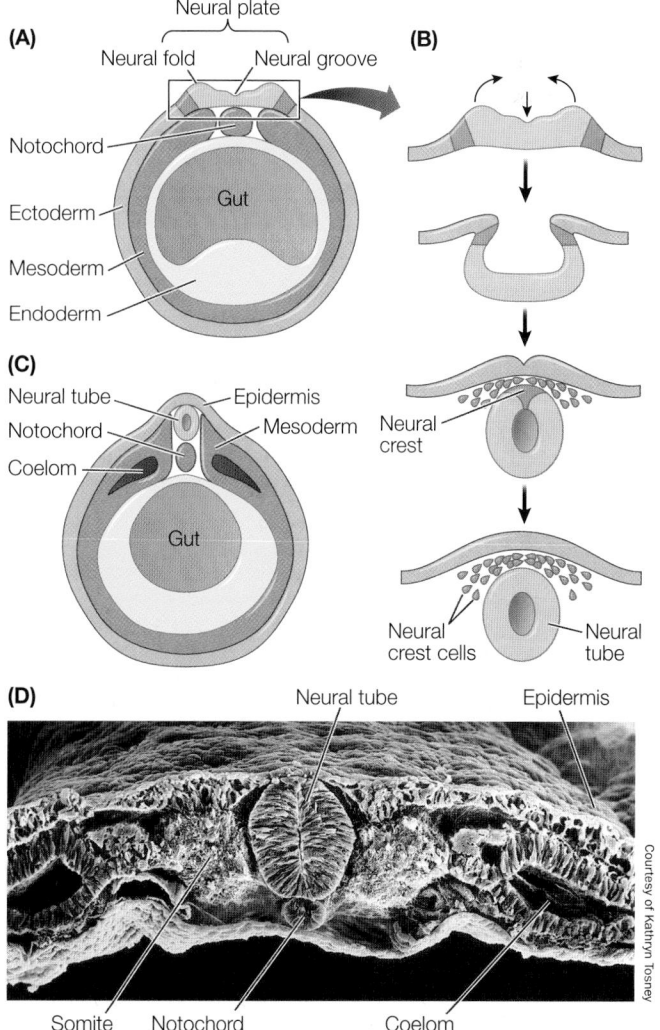

Figure 42.12 Neurulation in a Vertebrate (A) At the start of neurulation, the ectoderm of the neural plate (green) is flat. (B) The neural plate invaginates and folds, forming a tube. (C, D) The completely formed neural tube seen (C) in diagrammatic form and (D) in a scanning electron micrograph of a chick embryo.

Cells from the most lateral portions of the neural plate do not become part of the neural tube, but disassociate from it and come to lie between the neural tube and the overlying epidermis. These **neural crest cells** migrate outward to lead the development of the connections between the central nervous system (brain and spinal cord) and the rest of the body. Neural crest cells generate many diverse structures, including jaws, skull, face, pigment cells, glands, smooth muscle, and many others.

The neural tube develops bulges at the anterior end, which become the major divisions of the brain; the rest of the tube becomes the spinal cord. In humans, failure of the neural folds to fuse in this posterior region results in spina bifida, a birth defect in which the spinal cord is exposed because the vertebrae do not fuse. If the folds fail to fuse at the anterior end, an infant can develop without a forebrain (a condition called anencephaly). Although several genetic factors can cause these defects, other factors are environmental, including maternal diet. The incidence of neural tube defects in the United States in the early 1900s was as high as 1 in 300 live births; today it is less than 1 in 1,000. A major factor in this improvement has been the inclusion of folate (a B vitamin) in the mother's diet. It is essential for pregnant women to ingest sufficient folate.

Body segmentation is an early feature of vertebrate development

The vertebrate body plan, like that of arthropods, consists of repeating segments that are modified during development. These segments are most evident as the repeating patterns of vertebrae, ribs, nerves, and muscles along the anterior–posterior axis.

As the neural tube forms, mesodermal tissues gather along the sides of the notochord to form separate, segmented blocks of cells called **somites** (Figure 42.13). Somites produce cells that will become the vertebrae, ribs, muscles of the trunk, and limbs.

Nerves that connect the brain and spinal cord with tissues and organs throughout the body are also arranged segmentally. The somites help guide the organization of these peripheral nerves, but the nerves are not of mesodermal origin. As you saw earlier, when the neural tube fuses, the neural crest cells break loose and migrate inward between the epidermis and the somites and also through the somites. These neural crest cells have diverse fates, including the development of peripheral nerves.

As development progresses, the different segments of the body change. Regions of the spinal cord differ, regions of the vertebral column differ in that some vertebrae grow ribs of various sizes and others do not, forelegs arise in the anterior part of the embryo, and hind legs arise in the posterior region.

Hox genes control differentiation along the anterior–posterior axis

How is mesoderm in the anterior part of a mouse embryo programmed to produce forelegs rather than hind legs? In Key Concept 21.4 you saw how homeotic genes control body segmentation in *Drosophila*. You also learned that all homeotic genes contain a DNA sequence called the **homeobox**. In vertebrates, the homeotic

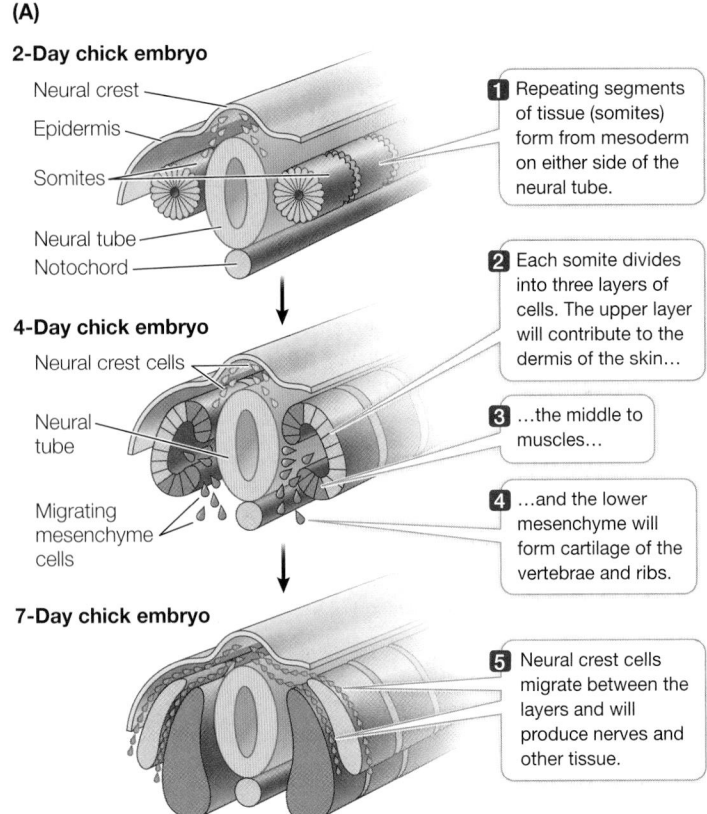

(A)

2-Day chick embryo

Neural crest
Epidermis
Somites
Neural tube
Notochord

1 Repeating segments of tissue (somites) form from mesoderm on either side of the neural tube.

4-Day chick embryo

Neural crest cells
Neural tube
Migrating mesenchyme cells

2 Each somite divides into three layers of cells. The upper layer will contribute to the dermis of the skin…

3 …the middle to muscles…

4 …and the lower mesenchyme will form cartilage of the vertebrae and ribs.

7-Day chick embryo

5 Neural crest cells migrate between the layers and will produce nerves and other tissue.

Neural tube   Somites

Somite forming

Mesodermal tissue (will become somites)

Courtesy of Kathryn Tosney

Figure 42.13 Developing Body Segmentation (**A**) Repeating blocks of tissue called somites form on either side of the neural tube. Muscle, cartilage, bone, and the inner layer of the skin form from the somites. (**B**) In this scanning electron micrograph of somite formation in a chick embryo, the overlying ectoderm has been removed and the neural tube and somites are seen from above.

genes that control differentiation along the anterior–posterior body axis are called **Hox genes**

In mammals, four Hox gene complexes reside on different chromosomes in clusters of about ten genes each. Remarkably, the temporal and spatial expression of these genes generally follows the same pattern as their linear order on their chromosome. That is, the Hox genes closest to the 3′ end of each gene complex are expressed first and in the anterior of the embryo. The Hox genes at the 5′ end of the gene complex are expressed later and in a more posterior part of the embryo. As a result, different segments of the embryo receive different combinations of Hox gene products, which serve as transcription factors (**Figure 42.14**; see also Figure 21.15).

Whereas Hox genes give cells information about their position on the anterior–posterior body axis, other genes provide information about their dorsal–ventral position. Tissues in each segment of the body differentiate according to their dorsal–ventral location. The notochord provides many of these signals.

After body segmentation develops, the formation of organs and organ systems progresses rapidly. The development of an organ involves extensive inductive interactions. An example is the ability of the chordamesoderm to induce overlying ectoderm to become neural ectoderm, and form the neural tube (see Figure 42.12). These inductive interactions are a current focus of study for developmental biologists.

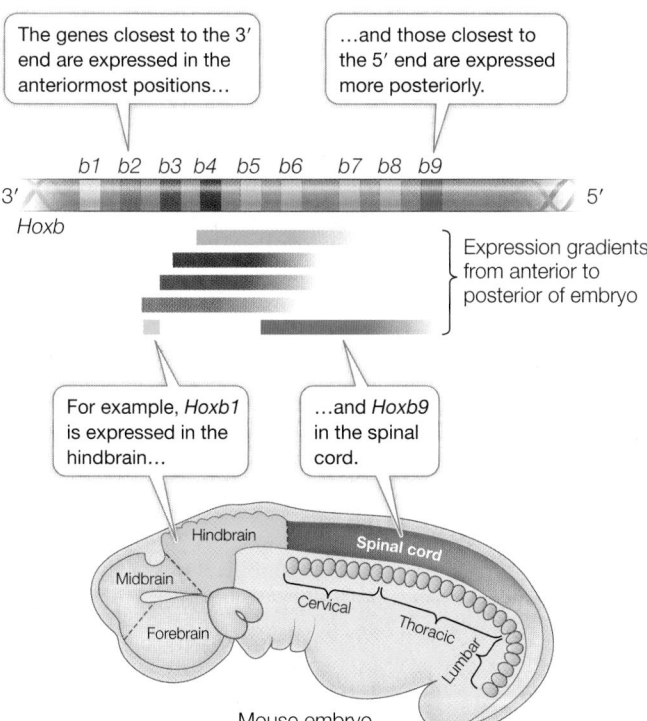

Figure 42.14 Hox Genes Control Body Segmentation Hox genes are expressed along the anterior–posterior axis of the embryo in the same order as their arrangement between the 3′ and 5′ ends of the gene complex. As a result of gene duplication during evolution, vertebrates have four copies of the Hox gene complex shown.

KEY CONCEPT
42.4 Recap and Assess

Gastrulation sets up tissue interactions that initiate organogenesis. Neurulation is initiated by organizer mesoderm that forms the notochord. Neurulation results in the formation of the central nervous system, and associated neural crest cells form the peripheral nerves. Suites of Hox genes are expressed sequentially in vertebrates, but in overlapping patterns providing a variety of signaling molecule patterns that govern differentiation on the anterior–posterior axis.

1. How does the ectoderm overlying the notochord respond to chordamesoderm signals to form a neural tube as well as neural crest cells?
2. What might be some consequences of a disruption in somite formation in the embryo?
3. How do Hox genes generate a diversity of signals sufficient to control differentiation of tissues and organs on the anterior–posterior axis?

You have seen how the basic structure of the developing embryo arises, through the establishment of the anterior–posterior and dorsal–ventral axes, the formation of the neural tube, and the emergence of a segmented body plan. In the next key concept we examine the developmental events that result in the formation of structures that support the developing embryo: the extraembryonic membranes and the placenta.

KEY CONCEPT
42.5 Extraembryonic Membranes Nurture Avian and Mammalian Embryos

Learning Objectives

42.5.1 Describe the formation of the yolk sac, amnion, chorion, and allantois, using the chick as an example.

42.5.2 Explain how the placenta forms.

42.5.3 Explain why a first-trimester embryo is particularly sensitive to environmental risks for birth defects.

There is more to a developing reptile or mammal than the embryo itself. The embryos of these vertebrates are surrounded by several **extraembryonic membranes** that originate from the embryo but are not part of it. Extraembryonic membranes function in nutrition, gas exchange, and waste removal. In mammals they interact with tissues of the mother to form the placenta. The evolutionary relationships between the extraembryonic membranes of birds and mammals were discussed in Key Concept 31.4.

Birds develop four extraembryonic membranes

The chicken provides a good example of how extraembryonic membranes form from the germ layers created during gastrulation. In the chick, four membranes form—the yolk sac, the allantois, the amnion, and the chorion. The **yolk sac** is the first to form, and it does so by extension of the hypoblast layer along with some adjacent mesoderm. The yolk sac grows to enclose the entire body of yolk in the egg (**Figure 42.15**). It constricts at the top to create a tube that is continuous with the gut of the embryo. However, yolk does not pass through this tube. Yolk is digested by the cells of the yolk sac, and the nutrients are transported to the embryo through blood vessels that form from mesoderm and line the outer surface of the yolk sac. The **allantois** is also an outgrowth of the extraembryonic endoderm plus adjacent mesoderm. It forms a sac for storage of metabolic wastes.

Ectoderm and mesoderm combine and extend beyond the limits of the embryo to form the other extraembryonic membranes.

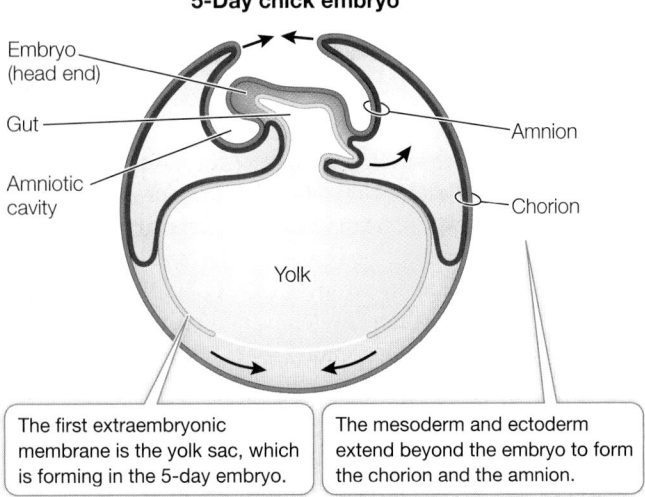

5-Day chick embryo

Embryo (head end)

Gut

Amniotic cavity

Amnion

Chorion

Yolk

> The first extraembryonic membrane is the yolk sac, which is forming in the 5-day embryo.

> The mesoderm and ectoderm extend beyond the embryo to form the chorion and the amnion.

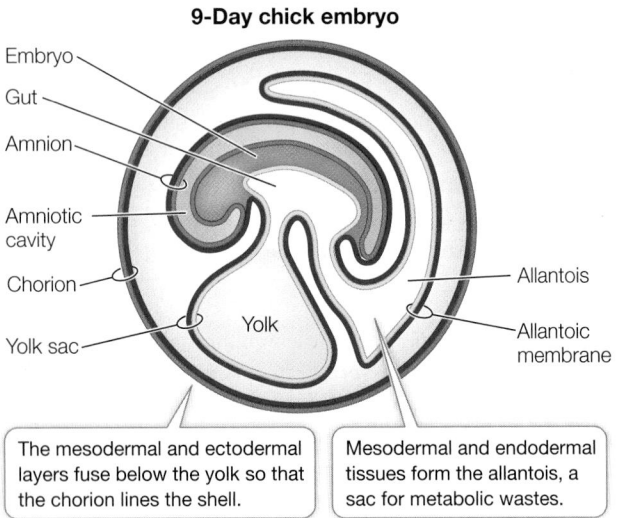

9-Day chick embryo

Embryo

Gut

Amnion

Amniotic cavity

Chorion

Yolk sac

Yolk

Allantois

Allantoic membrane

> The mesodermal and ectodermal layers fuse below the yolk so that the chorion lines the shell.

> Mesodermal and endodermal tissues form the allantois, a sac for metabolic wastes.

Figure 42.15 The Extraembryonic Membranes   In birds (and other reptiles) and mammals, the embryo constructs four extraembryonic membranes. In birds, the yolk sac encloses the yolk, and the amnion and chorion enclose the embryo. Fluids secreted by the amnion fill the amniotic cavity, providing an aqueous environment for the embryo. The chorion, along with the allantois, mediates gas exchange between the embryo and its environment. The allantois stores the embryo's waste products. (See also Figure 31.19.)

View in Achieve
Activity 42.1 Extraembryonic Membranes

Two layers of cells extend all along the inside of the eggshell, both over the embryo and below the yolk sac. Where they meet, they fuse, forming two membranes, the inner **amnion** and the outer **chorion**. The amnion surrounds the embryo, forming the amniotic cavity. The amnion secretes fluid into the cavity, providing a protective environment for the embryo. The outer membrane, the chorion, forms a continuous membrane just under the eggshell (see Figure 42.15) that limits water loss from the egg. The exchange of O_2 and CO_2 between the embryo and the environment requires diffusion of those gases across the chorion and the allantois.

The mammalian placenta forms from extraembryonic membranes

In eutherian mammals, the first extraembryonic membrane to form is the trophoblast (see Figures 42.4C and 42.5). When the blastocyst reaches the uterus and hatches from its encapsulating zona pellucida, trophoblast cells interact directly with the endometrium. Adhesion molecules expressed on the surfaces of these cells attach them to the uterine wall. By secreting proteolytic enzymes, the trophoblast burrows into the endometrium, beginning the process of implantation. Eventually the entire trophoblast is within the wall of the uterus. The trophoblast cells send out numerous projections, or villi, to increase the surface area of contact with maternal blood.

Meanwhile, the hypoblast cells proliferate to form what in the bird would be the yolk sac. But there is virtually no yolk in eggs of eutherian mammals; instead the yolk sac contributes mesodermal tissues that interact with trophoblast tissues to form the chorion. The chorion, along with tissues of the uterine wall, produces the **placenta**, the organ that exchanges nutrients, respiratory gases, and metabolic wastes between the mother and the embryo (**Figure 42.16**).

At the same time the yolk sac is forming from the hypoblast, the epiblast produces the amnion, which grows to enclose the entire embryo in a fluid-filled amniotic cavity. The rupturing of the amnion and chorion and the loss of **amniotic fluid** (the "water breaks") herald the onset of labor in humans.

An allantois also develops in mammals, but its importance depends on how well nitrogenous wastes can be removed by the blood vessels of the placenta. The human allantoic sac is small because the human placenta deals effectively with the fetal nitrogenous wastes. In contrast, the pig placenta is less effective at clearing nitrogenous wastes from the fetus, so the pig's allantoic sac is large. In humans and other eutherian mammals, the allantois contributes to the formation of the umbilical cord, by which the embryo is attached to the chorionic placenta (see Figure 31.19B). It is through the blood vessels of the umbilical cord that nutrients and oxygen from the mother reach the developing fetus, and wastes, including carbon dioxide and urea, are removed.

Human gestation is divided into trimesters

In humans, **gestation**, or pregnancy, lasts about 266 days, or 9 months. Gestation is shorter in smaller mammals (21 days in mice) and longer in larger mammals (600 days in elephants). The events of human gestation (**Figure 42.17**) are divided into three **trimesters** of roughly 3 months each. The first trimester

Figure 42.16 The Mammalian Placenta
In humans and most other mammals, nutrients and wastes are exchanged between maternal and fetal blood in the placenta, which forms from the chorion and tissues of the uterine wall. The embryo is attached to the placenta by the umbilical cord. Embryonic blood vessels invade the placental tissue to form fingerlike chorionic villi. Maternal blood flows into the spaces surrounding the villi, and placental blood flows through the villi so nutrients and respiratory gases can be exchanged between the maternal and fetal blood.

(see Figure 42.17A) is a time of rapid cell division and tissue differentiation. Because signal transduction cascades that determine sequences of developmental processes are in their early stages, the first trimester is the period when the embryo is most sensitive to damage from radiation, drugs, chemicals, and pathogens that can cause birth defects. An embryo can be damaged before the mother even realizes she is pregnant. A classic case is that of thalidomide, a drug widely prescribed in Europe in the late 1950s to treat nausea. Women who took this drug in the fourth and fifth weeks of pregnancy, when the embryo's limbs are beginning to form, gave birth to children with missing or severely malformed arms and legs.

During the second trimester the fetus grows rapidly; its limbs elongate, and its fingers, toes, and facial features become well formed (see Figure 42.17B). Eyebrows and fingernails grow, and the fetus's nervous system develops rapidly. Fetal movements are first felt by the mother early in the second trimester and become progressively stronger and more coordinated.

The fetus grows rapidly during the third trimester. As this final stage approaches its end (see Figure 42.17C), the internal organs mature. The digestive system begins to function, the liver stores glycogen, the kidneys produce urine, and the brain undergoes cycles of sleep and waking. A human infant is born when the last of its critical organs—the lungs—mature.

Although the first-trimester embryo is the most susceptible to adverse effects of drugs, chemicals, and diseases, the potential for serious effects from exposure to environmental factors exists throughout pregnancy. Protein malnutrition and exposure to alcohol and cigarette smoke are examples of factors that can result in low birth weight, intellectual disability, and other developmental complications.

(A) First trimester
4 Weeks

Actual length ~0.4 cm (4 mm)

8 Weeks

Actual length ~3 cm

(B) Second trimester
4 Months

Actual length ~10 cm

(C) Third trimester
9 Months

Actual length ~40 cm

Figure 42.17 Stages of Human Development   **(A)** At 4 weeks, most of the embryo's organ systems have been formed and the heart is beating. The body structures of this 8-week-old embryo are forming rapidly. **(B)** At 4 months, the fetus has fully formed limbs with fingers and toes and moves freely within the amniotic cavity. **(C)** This fetus is well along in its ninth month. Soon its lungs will be mature enough to trigger the onset of contractions and birth.

KEY CONCEPT
42.5 Recap and Assess

The extraembryonic membranes of reptiles and mammals sustain the growing embryo. In reptiles these membranes surround the embryo within the shelled egg. In mammals the extraembryonic membranes form the placenta, an organ that exchanges nutrients, respiratory gases, and metabolic wastes between the mother and the embryo. Human gestation lasts 9 months. At the end of the first trimester, the fetus is very small but most of its organs have begun to form. In the second trimester, limbs elongate and the fetus moves. By the end of the third trimester, most organs have begun to function.

1. Which germ layers participate in the development of the chick's yolk sac, allantois, chorion, and amnion?
2. What is the origin of the placenta in mammalian development?
3. Why is a first-trimester embryo particularly sensitive to environmental risks?

▶Investigating**LIFE**

 and A **How does the embryo know left from right?**

At the beginning of gastrulation in the mammal, when midline cells of the epiblast begin to move inward to create the primitive groove, a region called the node forms at the anterior end of the groove. Motile cilia at the node create a flow of extracellular fluid across the node. Nonmotile nodal cilia are believed to sense the direction of fluid flow across the node. There are two hypotheses about how these cilia function, one chemical and the other mechanical. Both sensory mechanisms are used by cilia elsewhere in the body. In the nose, cilia of the olfactory cells sense chemicals. In the ear, cilia are bent by sound waves, which stimulates ion channels to open. The leftward flow of fluid across the node imposes mechanical forces on the nonmotile cilia that differ on the two sides of the node. Other research, however, supports the possibility of chemical signaling. Research on the mouse node shows that the beating of the cilia causes proteins of a certain size range to form a concentration gradient across the node. More important, it was discovered that nodal cells secrete small vesicles that are swept to the left side of the node by the flow, and these vesicles burst when they contact the nonmotile cilia of surrounding cells. The contents of these vesicles could be the chemical signals that initiate left–right asymmetry in gene expression and development.

Future directions

A major player in the determination of left–right asymmetry is the primary cilium of cells in the node that forms during gastrulation. However, just about every cell in the body has a primary cilium. Until fairly recently, the primary cilia were thought to be vestigial structures or simply organelles to sequester the centriole and thereby inhibit cell division. We now know that the primary cilia of cells function widely in mechanisms of cell signaling and in transduction of physical and chemical stimuli. Just about every organ in the body uses primary cilia for essential functions. Primary cilia have been implicated in many medical conditions such as cancer, kidney disease, obesity, blindness, and developmental disorders. In the near future we will be seeing lots of new discoveries about the functions of primary cilia.

VISUAL SUMMARY 42

© Nerthuz/Getty Images

You should be able to relate each summary to the adjacent figures. If you go to this visual summary in **Achieve**, you can follow links to figures, animations, activities, and simulations that will help you consolidate the material.

KEY CONCEPT
42.1 Fertilization Activates Development

Go to Animations 42.1

- The sperm contributes a haploid nucleus and a centriole to the zygote. The egg contributes a haploid nucleus, nutrients, organelles, mRNAs, and proteins.

- The amphibian egg is radially symmetrical, with an animal and vegetal hemisphere. The site of sperm entry defines the anterior–posterior axis and therefore the left–right sides of the zygote.

- Sperm entry into the amphibian egg stimulates rotation of the cortical cytoplasm, forming the **gray crescent** on the side opposite the site of sperm entry.

- Microtubules organized by the centriole move organelles and proteins, including a GSK-3 inhibitor, from the vegetal area toward the gray crescent. GSK-3 breaks down β-catenin, so its inhibition enhances β-catenin concentration in the gray crescent area, instructing the first stages of development.

Figure 42.2

Cortical rotation

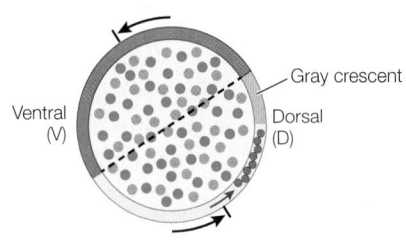

Gray crescent

Ventral (V)

Dorsal (D)

Questions

1. Why is mitochondrial DNA especially useful for investigating genealogical histories?

2. What event following sperm entry breaks the radial symmetry of the frog egg?

3. How does the sperm contribute to the formation of the gray crescent?

KEY CONCEPT

42.2 Mitosis Divides Up the Early Embryo

Go to Animations 42.2

- **Complete cleavage** completely divides the egg; **incomplete cleavage** does not, leaving the yolk undivided. Complete cleavage can be **radial**, with successive mitotic spindles at right angles, or **spiral**, with successive mitotic spindles at oblique angles. In **rotational cleavage**, the type of complete cleavage seen in mammals, the mitotic planes of the second division are at right angles to each other. **Superficial cleavage** divides nuclei, which later are partitioned into individual cells.

- Cleavage results in **autonomous specification** if the fates of individual blastomeres are **determined**, and in **regulated specification** if the fates of individual blastomeres are dependent on their environment.

- Identical twins develop from the same fertilized egg. Non-identical twins develop simultaneously from separate fertilized eggs.

- Reproductive germ cells remain undetermined and totipotent throughout development and migrate into the gonads once they have formed.

Figure 42.3

Animal pole

© Dr. Richard Kessel & Dr. Gene Shih/Visuals Unlimited, Inc.

Questions

1. In a species with autonomous specification, is it possible for an individual to have identical twins? If not, why?

2. Why is cleavage in birds and fishes called discoidal?

3. Why is it possible to genotype human blastocysts growing in culture without damaging the developing embryo?

KEY CONCEPT

42.3 Gastrulation Generates Multiple Tissue Layers

Go to Animations 42.3 and 42.4 and Simulation 42.1

- **Gastrulation** involves massive cell movements that turn a ball (sea urchin, frog) or sheet (reptile) of cells into a cellular mass with three **germ layers**: **endoderm**, **ectoderm**, and **mesoderm**.

- Transplanting the **dorsal lip** of the **blastopore** from one salamander gastrula to the belly region of another resulted in two belly-to-belly embryos and led to the concept of the **primary embryonic organizer**.

- The transcription factor β-catenin is responsible for inducing the primary embryonic organizer. If it is depleted in the egg by antisense RNA, gastrulation does not occur (demonstrating necessity), but if it is overexpressed in a region of the blastula, a second embryo forms (demonstrating sufficiency).

- As cells from the surface of the amphibian gastrula move over the dorsal lip of the blastopore and migrate forward, they release transcription factors that antagonize locally produced growth factors, thus altering the developmental fates of the cells in those areas.

Figure 42.8

Dorsal mesoderm

Dorsal blastopore lip

Endoderm

Ectoderm

Ventral mesoderm

Archenteron (future digestive tract)

Mesoderm (notochord)

Dorsal blastopore lip

Ventral blastopore lip

Questions

1. Why did Spemann's constriction of a frog egg through the gray crescent result in two tadpoles, whereas constriction that did not bisect the gray crescent resulted in only one tadpole?

2. What are the three germ layers formed by gastrulation in the frog, what are their origins, and what are their fates?

3. How and why are amphibian and avian gastrulation different?

KEY CONCEPT

42.4 Organs Develop from the Three Germ Layers

- Development of the nervous system begins by folding of the dorsal neural plate to form a **neural tube**. Mesodermal cells adjacent to the neural tube form segmentally arranged blocks of cells called **somites**, which will become skin, muscle, and bone.

- **Neural crest cells** break away from the neural tube and migrate between somites to become peripheral nerves and many other structures.

- Genetic, nutritional, and environmental factors can cause abnormalities in neural tube development.

- Anterior–posterior patterning of the vertebrate embryo is controlled by clusters of **Hox genes** that are arranged linearly on different chromosomes. Hox genes are expressed in the embryo in the same sequence as they occur on the chromosomes, which results in different segments of the embryo receiving different combinations of transcription factors.

Figure 42.12

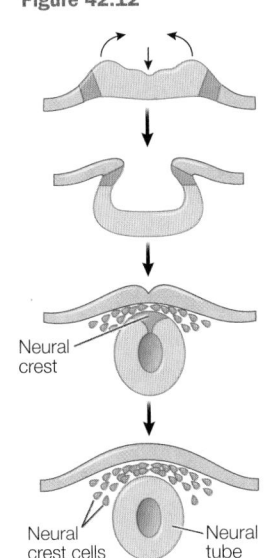

Figure 42.13

4-Day chick embryo

Questions

1. How does a plate of dorsal ectoderm become the neural tube of the amphibian embryo?

2. What are neural crest cells, and what do they do?

3. What is the relationship between the positions of Hox genes on their chromosomes and their location of expression in the embryo?

KEY CONCEPT

42.5 Extraembryonic Membranes Nurture Avian and Mammalian Embryos

Go to Activity 42.1

- The embryos of reptiles and mammals are protected and nurtured by four **extraembryonic membranes**. In reptiles the **yolk sac** surrounds the yolk and provides nutrients to the embryo, the **chorion** lines the eggshell and participates in gas exchange, the **amnion** surrounds the embryo and encloses it in an aqueous environment, and the **allantois** stores metabolic wastes.

- In mammals the chorion and the trophoblast cells interact with the maternal uterus to form a **placenta**, which provides the embryo with nutrient and gas exchange.

- The first-trimester embryo is particularly sensitive to environmental risks because this is a time of rapid cell divisions and of many signaling cascades responsible for tissue differentiation and organ formation.

- Human pregnancy, or **gestation**, lasts 9 months. The embryo forms in the first **trimester**; during this time, it is most vulnerable to environmental factors that can lead to birth defects. During the second and third trimesters the fetus grows, external features form, and the organ systems mature.

Figure 42.15

9-Day chick embryo

Questions

1. What is the function of the allantois in the avian embryo, and why is an allantois less important in the mammalian embryo?

2. Compare the function of the chorion in birds and mammals.

3. Why are fetal movements not felt by the mother in the first trimester?

Go to **Achieve** for the eBook, **LearningCurve**, animations, activities, simulations, and additional resources and assignments.

Neurons, Glia, and Nervous Systems 43

KEY CONCEPTS

43.1 Neurons and Glia Are Unique Cells of Nervous Systems

43.2 Neurons Generate and Transmit Electric Signals

43.3 Neurons Communicate with Other Cells

43.4 Neurons and Glia Form Information-Processing Circuits

Courtesy of Philip Haydon

Neurons, colored blue in this photo, code, transmit, integrate, and store information and send commands to non-neuronal cells. The activities of neurons are supported and modulated by glial cells, colored red in this photo.

▶Investigating LIFE

Balancing the Brain

Your brain enables you to learn the material in this chapter—to read the words, understand the illustrations, and store information to allow you to answer questions. You must study to master this chapter, but if you do you will learn how the brain receives and processes information.

Imagine what it would be like if you could not learn any of this material—no matter how much you poured over the book. This is the situation faced by individuals with a condition known as Down syndrome, which affects approximately 1 out of every 700 children born in the United States.

Individuals with Down syndrome are born with three copies of most of chromosome 21, one of the smallest of the human chromosomes (containing about 225 confirmed genes). Having an extra copy of these genes causes numerous developmental and functional problems, including learning disability. Can we understand the cause of this disability and perhaps find a way to remedy it?

One productive way of investigating the causes and possible treatments for a human disease or deficit is to develop an animal model. Through genetic engineering, researchers created a "Down syndrome mouse" that has most of the same genes triplicated as those in humans with Down syndrome. These mice cannot perform in mouse memory tests as normal mice do. The mouse Down

© John Birdsall/AGE Fotostock

syndrome model revealed that excess inhibition in the brain causes the learning disability. What is meant by "excess inhibition in the brain"? We tend to think mostly about the excitatory actions of the brain, likening the brain to a puppet master who pulls the strings that activate the muscles and organs of the body. In fact the brain is more like an orchestra conductor, making some sections louder, some softer, speeding up, slowing down. The brain must constantly maintain a delicate balance of excitation and inhibition, acting on some signals and ignoring others. In the brains of Down syndrome model mice there is consistently too much inhibition. When inhibition is experimentally reduced with drugs, the mice are able to learn. Research like this is a first step toward bringing potential therapies for humans into clinical trials in the hope of improving the cognitive functions of individuals with Down syndrome.

 Can learning be restored in mouse models of Down syndrome? (Find the answer on page 981.)

43.1 Neurons and Glia Are Unique Cells of Nervous Systems

Learning Objectives

43.1.1 Describe the parts of a neuron and explain their functions.

43.1.2 Describe in general terms how information is transmitted by axons and across synapses to dendrites.

43.1.3 Explain the different functions of glial cells.

Nervous systems are information systems. They encode, process, and store a wide variety of information from the external and internal environments, and they use that information to control and regulate the physiology and behavior of the organism. The nervous systems of all animals can carry out these functions because of the properties of a unique class of cells: nerve cells, or **neurons**. Vertebrate nervous systems also include another unique class of cells called glial cells, or **glia**.

There are many types of neurons, which vary in size, shape, and function, but they all generate and conduct electric signals. Glia do not generate and conduct electric signals, and there are two major types—macroglia and microglia. **Macroglia** support and modulate the functions of neurons. **Microglia** are phagocytic cells derived from blood-forming stem cells. Microglia are motile, are activated by foreign matter or damage to nervous tissue, and are the first and major immune defense mechanism in the nervous system.

Nervous systems in all but the simplest invertebrates are divided into central and peripheral divisions. The central division includes dense assemblages of neurons that process and store information and generate commands. In invertebrates these assemblages of neurons are generally called ganglia. In more complex invertebrates some large ganglia are designated as brains. In vertebrates the **central nervous system** (**CNS**) includes the brain and spinal cord. The **peripheral nervous system** (**PNS**) provides communication between the CNS and all of the rest of the body.

Vertebrate neurons and macroglia originate in the embryonic neural tube

Neurons and macroglia have a common origin in the neural tube of the early vertebrate embryo (see Figure 42.13). The neural tube contains rapidly dividing neuronal stem cells. Initially the divisions of these neural stem cells are symmetrical—all of the progeny are stem cells. Eventually, however, the cell divisions become asymmetrical, with one daughter cell remaining a stem cell and the other daughter cell becoming either a neural progenitor cell or a macroglial progenitor cell—a neuroblast or a glioblast. These progenitor cells produce the neurons and glia that together form the various structures of the nervous system.

The structure of neurons reflects their functions

Neurons vary enormously in structure and appearance, but they have a basic structure that includes four regions (**Figure 43.1**).

1. A **cell body** contains the nucleus and most of the cell's organelles.

2. Shrub-like projections called **dendrites** (Greek *dendron*, "tree") may extend from the cell body. Dendrites receive information from other neurons or sensory cells and bring it to the cell body.

3. In most neurons, one projection—the **axon**—is much longer than the others. Axons carry information from the cell body to target cells.

4. At the target cell, the axon divides into a spray of fine nerve endings. The tips of these tiny nerve endings have swellings called **axon terminals**.

Neurons have a wide variety of forms that reflect different functionalities (**Figure 43.2**). Neurons with few dendrites receive information from specific and limited sources, whereas neurons with large arrays of dendrites can collect and integrate information from a wide range of sources. Some neurons communicate over very short distances, but others communicate over extremely long distances and therefore have very long axons. For example, axons from neurons in your spinal cord control the muscles that move your toes.

Regardless of form and function, all neurons process and communicate information through changes in the electric potentials across their membranes. As in all cells, the electric charge on the inside of the neuronal cell membrane is slightly negative in comparison with the outside. Specialized neurons called sensory neurons respond to specific stimuli such as light, temperature, and pressure by changes in the flow of electrically charged ions across their cell membranes. These changes in local electric potential travel along the cell membrane to the base of the cell's axon, where a small change in membrane potential generates a large, rapidly reversed change in membrane potential that is called an **action potential** (**AP**). Axons conduct APs over long distances. Non-sensory neurons receive inputs from other neurons through connections in their

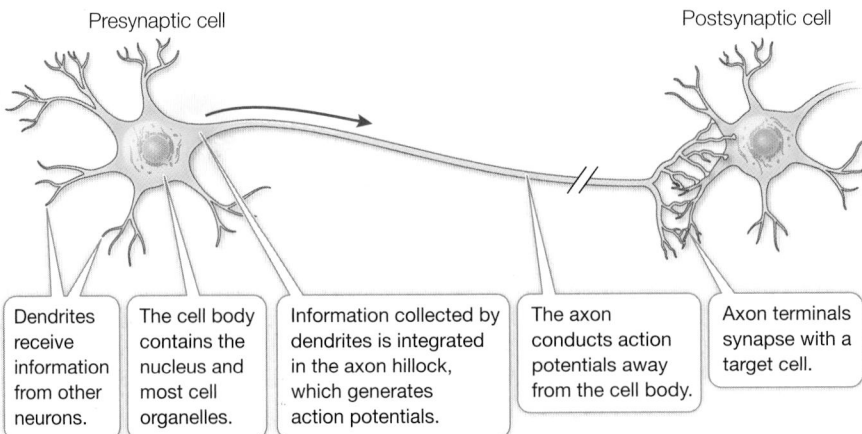

Presynaptic cell
Postsynaptic cell

| Dendrites receive information from other neurons. | The cell body contains the nucleus and most cell organelles. | Information collected by dendrites is integrated in the axon hillock, which generates action potentials. | The axon conducts action potentials away from the cell body. | Axon terminals synapse with a target cell. |

Figure 43.1 A Generalized Neuron The diagram shows the features typical of most neurons. The forms of these features, including the length of the single axon and the density and branching patterns of the dendrites, vary greatly across the many different types of neurons.

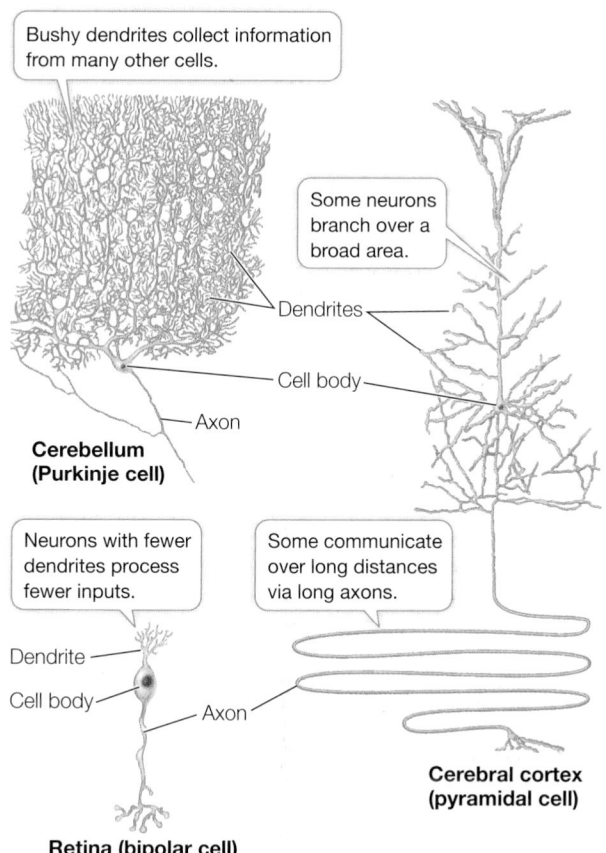

Bushy dendrites collect information from many other cells.

Some neurons branch over a broad area.

Dendrites

Cell body

Axon

Cerebellum (Purkinje cell)

Neurons with fewer dendrites process fewer inputs.

Some communicate over long distances via long axons.

Dendrite

Cell body

Axon

Cerebral cortex (pyramidal cell)

Retina (bipolar cell)

Figure 43.2 Neurons Have Many and Varied Forms The morphological differences in neurons from different parts of the mammalian nervous system are related to their specific functional adaptations. The small sample here shows two neuronal types from the human brain (a Purkinje cell and a pyramidal cell) and a sensory neuron from the retina of the human eye.

Q: Which of these neurons is likely to receive a greater number of inputs?

dendrites. Local changes in the dendrites' membrane potentials travel to the membrane of the cell body where they are summed and thereby influence the firing of APs in the neuron's axon.

In summary, a neuron receives specific stimuli (e.g., light, sound, pressure, chemicals) that cause changes in the electric potentials across the cell membranes of its dendrites. These electric signals from dendrites spread to and are averaged by the cell body. Changes in the electric potential of the membrane of the cell body at the base of its axon can cause an AP that is conducted along the axon to its terminals. APs can travel at speeds up to 100 meters per second (360 kilometers per hour), making it possible for an individual to sense, process, and act on information very quickly.

What happens when the AP reaches the axon terminals? Axon terminals come extremely close to the membrane of the target cell, which can be another neuron, a muscle cell, or a secretory cell. Structures called **synapses** form at these locations. The synapse transfers the information conveyed by the AP from the presynaptic cell to the postsynaptic cell (see Figure 43.1).

Synapses can be either electrical or chemical. Electrical synapses allow the AP to pass directly between two neurons. In

vertebrates most synapses are chemical. At chemical synapses a space about 25 nanometers wide (about 1/2000th the width of a human hair) separates the presynaptic and postsynaptic membranes. An AP arriving at an axon terminal causes it to release chemical messenger molecules called **neurotransmitters**. Neurotransmitters diffuse across the synaptic space and bind to receptors on the cell membrane of the postsynaptic (target) cell. The binding of the neurotransmitter to its receptor alters the activity of the postsynaptic neuron. Some neurotransmitter–receptor combinations inhibit activity of the postsynaptic neuron, and other neurotransmitter–receptor combinations excite it. Neurons integrate information by summing excitatory and inhibitory inputs.

Glia are the "silent partners" of neurons

The human brain has at least as many glial cells as neurons, and maybe more. A neurobiologist once said "flashy neurons get all of the attention, but glial cells do most of the brain's work and are the cause of many of its diseases." It has been easier to study the functions of neurons because their APs can be observed. The mostly silent glia are more difficult to study, and therefore we know much less about them. Our knowledge of glia will grow enormously in the years to come.

Like neurons, glia come in several forms and have diverse functions. As we mentioned earlier, microglia are macrophages (see Figure 40.4) and provide immune defense responses for the nervous system. Macroglia include Schwann cells, oligodendrocytes, astrocytes, and ependymal cells. In the brain and spinal cord, **oligodendrocytes** wrap around the axons of neurons, covering them with concentric layers of cell membrane. You can think of this wrapping as being insulation, like the insulation on electrical wires. It prevents electric current from leaking out of the axon. Outside the brain and spinal cord, **Schwann cells** provide this same function for the peripheral nerves that communicate between the brain and spinal cord and all parts of the body (**Figure 43.3**). **Myelin** is the wrapping produced by oligodendrocytes and Schwann cells, and it gives many parts of the nervous system a glistening white appearance. Not all axons are myelinated, but those that are conduct APs more rapidly than can axons that are not myelinated, for reasons described in Key Concept 43.2. **Ependymal cells** line the central fluid-filled chambers in the brain called ventricles and produce the cerebrospinal fluid that bathes the brain and spinal cord.

Diseases that affect myelin can be devastating because they impair conduction of APs. The most common of these demyelinating diseases is multiple sclerosis (MS)—literally "multiple scars"—which occurs in about 1 in 700 people in the United States. The cause of MS is not known, but it involves inflammatory autoimmune damage to the myelin in the brain and spinal cord. The symptoms of the disease depend on where in the nervous system the myelin is damaged. Motor impairment is common. An example of a demyelinating disease that attacks myelin outside the brain and spinal cord is Guillain–Barre syndrome, which is usually the result of a severe infection. Environmental factors such as pesticide exposure can also damage myelin. There are no known cures for demyelinating diseases.

(A) Schwann cells

Myelin-producing Schwann cells

Site and direction of myelin growth

Nodes of Ranvier

Nucleus of Schwann cell

(B) Cross section of a myelinated axon

Mitochondria

Axon

Multiple layers of myelin insulate the axon.

© C. Raines/Visuals Unlimited, Inc.

0.1 µm

Figure 43.3 Glial Cells Insulate Axons (A) Schwann cells produce layers of myelin, a type of cell membrane that provides electrical insulation to the axon. At the intervals between Schwann cells—the nodes of Ranvier—the axon is exposed. APs travel along the axon by "jumping" from node to node, as described in Key Concept 43.2. (B) A myelinated axon, seen in cross section through an electron microscope.

The fourth type of macroglia, **astrocytes** (so named because they look like stars), contributes to the **blood–brain barrier** that protects the brain from toxic chemicals in the blood. Blood vessels throughout the body are very permeable to many chemicals, including toxic ones that could reach the brain if this barrier did not exist. The contribution of the astrocytes to the blood-brain barrier are the end-feet of their many projections that surround the blood vessels in the brain. The barrier is not perfect, however. Because it consists of cell membranes, it is permeable to fat-soluble substances such as anesthetics and alcohol (which explains why these substances have such rapid and marked effects on the nervous system).

Recently a new function of astrocytes is being investigated: ridding the brain of metabolic wastes. In the blood–brain barrier there is a small space—the **perivascular space**—between the membranes of the blood vessels and the astrocyte end-feet that surround them. Fluid can leak out of incoming blood vessels into the perivascular spaces. The astrocyte membranes have water channels (aquaporins) that can take up fluid from the perivascular spaces and deliver it to wherever the astrocytes project. The fluid can then leave the astrocytes and enter the interstitial fluid. In a reverse process, interstitial fluid can enter the perivascular spaces around the blood vessels leaving the brain, taking metabolic waste products with it. This system of perfusion of extracellular fluid in the brain is called the **glymphatic system** (Figure 43.4).

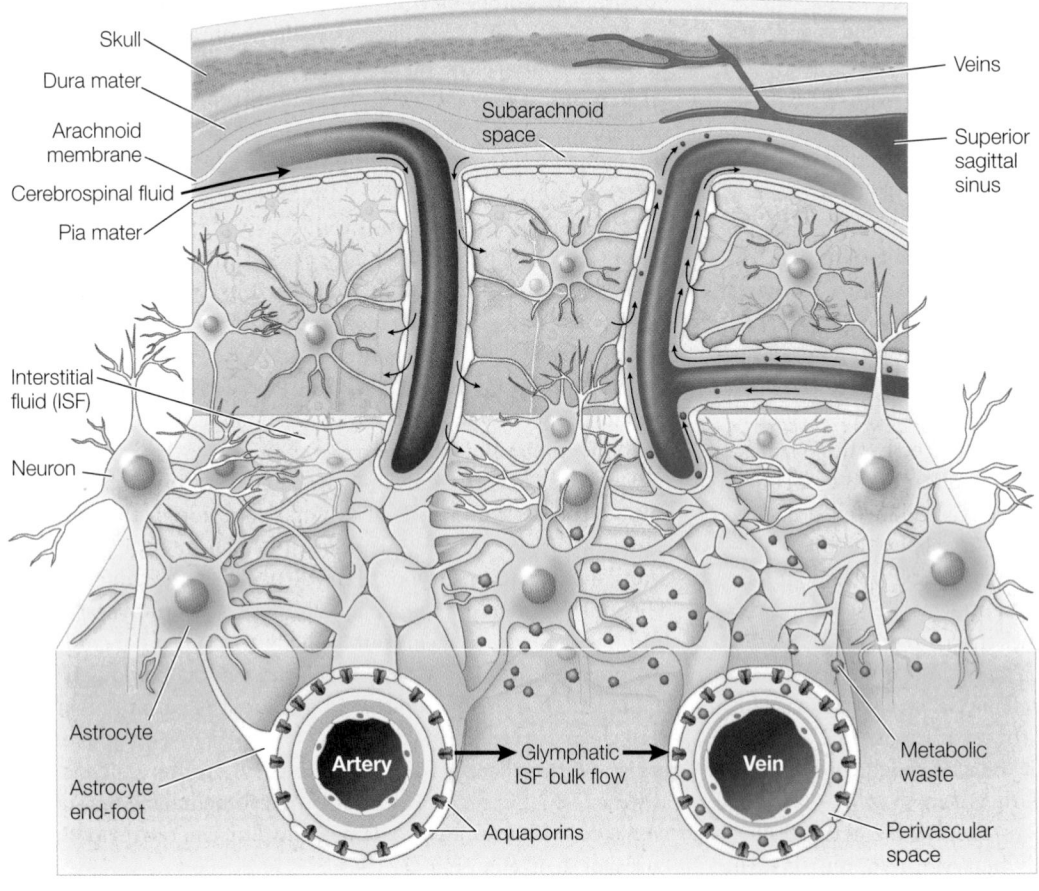

Skull

Dura mater

Arachnoid membrane

Cerebrospinal fluid

Pia mater

Subarachnoid space

Veins

Superior sagittal sinus

Interstitial fluid (ISF)

Neuron

Astrocyte

Astrocyte end-foot

Artery

Glymphatic ISF bulk flow

Vein

Metabolic waste

Aquaporins

Perivascular space

Figure 43.4 The Glymphatic System Interstitial fluid enters the brain through the perivascular spaces between the blood vessels (arteries) and the astrocytes that surround them. The astrocytes have water channels (aquaporins) that enable them to take up fluid from the perivascular spaces and distribute it to the interstitial fluid compartment of the brain. That fluid leaves the brain through the perivascular spaces of the outgoing blood vessels (veins), taking metabolic waste products with it. (After M. Nedergaard. 2013. *Science* 340: 1529–1530.)

Connect the Concepts The glymphatic system is to the brain what the lymphatic system is to the rest of the body (see Figure 40.3).

Astrocytes have several functions at the synapse:

- They can take up neurotransmitter that has been released into the synapse and thereby control communication between the pre- and postsynaptic cells.

- They can supply neurons with nutrients. Neurons have no energy reserves, but astrocytes store glycogen that they can break down to supply the neurons with fuel.

- They have signaling properties. Even though most astrocytes do not generate APs, they do release neurotransmitters that can alter the activities of neurons.

- They aid in the repair and regeneration of neurons.

- They make contact with both blood vessels and neurons and can therefore signal changes in the composition of the blood.

Astrocytes play crucial yet poorly understood roles in modulating synapse activity. The projections of a single astrocyte may make contact with more than 100,000 synapses. The contact of the astrocyte with the neuronal components of the synapse is so intimate that it has inspired the concept of the **tripartite synapse**—the idea that a synapse includes not only the pre- and postsynaptic neurons but also connections from astrocytes.

Although astrocytes do not generate APs, they do communicate with each other. They are connected to each other through electrical synapses, and the electric signals traveling across these synapses cause changes in the Ca^{2+} content of the postsynaptic astrocyte. When Ca^{2+}-sensitive dyes are applied to nervous tissue, Ca^{2+} waves can be seen traveling through extensive networks of astrocytes. The functions of these Ca^{2+} waves are not understood.

KEY CONCEPT
43.1 Recap and Assess

Nervous systems have two unique types of cells: neurons and glia. There are many types of neurons, but they can all generate and conduct electric signals, and most generate APs. A neuron has four regions: cell body, dendrites, axon, and axon terminals. Neurons communicate with target cells at synapses, which can be chemical or electrical. Although glia do not generate APs, they have a variety of functions, including contributing to the blood–brain barrier, insulating axons, modulating synaptic activity, and providing neurons with metabolic fuel.

1. Explain how a neuron integrates information received from several other neurons and communicates it to another neuron.

2. Is communication faster over chemical synapses or electrical synapses? Explain your answer.

3. What is a tripartite synapse, and how can it modulate information flow in neural circuits?

The one feature common to neurons is that they process information in the form of changes in the electric potential across their cell membranes. In the next key concept we focus on how electric signals are generated and transmitted by neurons.

KEY CONCEPT
43.2 Neurons Generate and Transmit Electric Signals

Learning Objectives

43.2.1 Describe the ionic mechanisms of resting potentials and action potentials.

43.2.2 Explain how action potentials are conducted along unmyelinated and myelinated axons.

43.2.3 Explain the difference between action potentials and graded potentials, and how each can represent quantitative information.

Ion pumps create ion concentration gradients across animal cell membranes (see Key Concept 6.4). For example, Na^+ concentrations are higher outside cells and K^+ concentrations are higher inside. The positive charges of these ions are balanced by negatively charged ions both inside and outside the cell. But across the cell membrane there is an electric charge difference, with the inside of the cell being negative relative to the outside. This electric charge is due to the cell membrane being differentially permeable to certain ions. For neurons at rest, their membranes are mostly permeable to K^+, and that permeability is primarily responsible for the electric charge across their membranes.

Because the concentration of K^+ is higher inside the cell than in the extracellular fluid, K^+ tends to diffuse out of the cell down its concentration gradient. But when K^+ leaks out of the cell, it leaves behind an unbalanced negative electric charge that tends to pull K^+ back into the cell. An equilibrium is reached when the tendency for K^+ to diffuse out is countered by the electric charge pulling K^+ back in. The resulting charge difference across the membrane is called the **membrane potential**, with the inside of the cell negative relative to the outside. Membrane potentials exist in all cells.

In neurons the steady-state membrane potential is called the **resting potential**. Stimuli that cause changes in the permeability of the cell membrane cause local changes in that membrane resting potential. These local changes can generate APs that are conducted along the axon of the neuron and convey information about the stimulus that caused the initial small change in resting potential. The AP is a sudden, large, transient change in membrane potential generated by sudden changes in permeability to Na^+ ions. Before describing the mechanisms of these permeability changes and the resulting APs in detail, it may be useful to review some simple concepts of electricity.

Simple electrical concepts underlie neuronal function

Voltage (electric potential difference) is a force that causes electrically charged particles to move between two points. Voltage is to the flow of electrically charged particles as pressure is to the flow of water. If the negative and positive poles of a battery are connected by a wire, an electric current will flow through the wire because there is a voltage difference between the two poles. This flow of electric current can be used to do work, just as a current of water can be used to do work.

In wires, electric current is carried by electrons, but in solutions and across cell membranes, electric current is carried by ions. The major ions that carry electric charges across the cell membranes of neurons are sodium (Na^+), potassium (K^+), calcium (Ca^{2+}), and chloride (Cl^-). Recall that ions with opposite charges attract one another and those with like charges repel one another. How do these basic principles of bioelectricity establish the resting potential of the neuronal cell membrane? And how is the flow of ions through membrane channels turned on and off to generate APs?

Activities of neurons are recorded as changes in membrane potential

We record electrical events in a cell using electrodes. **Figure 43.5** shows how this technique is applied across the cell membrane of a neuron to measure the resting potential, which is usually between −60 and −70 millivolts (mV). The minus sign indicates that the inside of the cell is electrically negative compared with the outside.

As just explained, the resting potential is largely due to a balance between the tendency of K^+ ions to diffuse down their concentration gradient and the electric potential that holds them back. This resting potential provides a means for a neuron to respond to stimuli. If some determinant of this balance of forces is altered, the membrane potential will change. The concentration gradient of the different ions inside and outside the neuron may not change, but if the permeability of the membrane to ions changes, the membrane potential will change. Therefore any chemical or physical stimulus that changes the permeability of the cell membrane to ions will cause a change in the cell's membrane potential. For example, what would happen to the membrane potential if there

was a sudden increase in the permeability of the membrane to Na^+ ions? Na^+ ions are more abundant outside the cell than inside. Also, the inside of the resting cell is negatively charged, which attracts the positively charged N^+ ions. Thus a sudden increase in permeability of the membrane to Na^+ would cause a change of the membrane potential in the positive direction. If that change in Na^+ permeability were transient, the membrane potential would rapidly return to its resting, negative value. Such a rapid change in membrane potential is an AP.

 View in Achieve
Animation 43.1 **The Resting Membrane Potential**

Ion transporters and channels generate membrane potentials

The cell membranes of neurons, like those of all other cells, are lipid bilayers that are impermeable to ions but contain many protein molecules that serve as ion transporters and ion channels. Ion transporters and channels are responsible for the distribution of charges across the membrane that determine membrane potential.

> **Connect the Concepts** The passive and active mechanisms that transport materials across cell membranes are discussed in Key Concepts 6.3 and 6.4. The passive mechanisms are membrane proteins that form channels (see Figure 6.11), and the active mechanisms (which require ATP) are membrane proteins engaged in active transport (see Figure 6.14).

Ion transporters require energy to move ions against their concentration or electrical gradients and are therefore called ion pumps. A

Research Tools

Figure 43.5 **Measuring the Membrane Potential** An electrode can be made from a glass pipette with a very sharp tip filled with a solution that conducts electric charges. If one electrode is placed inside the neuron and another one on the outside of the cell membrane, the difference in voltage across the cell membrane can be measured.

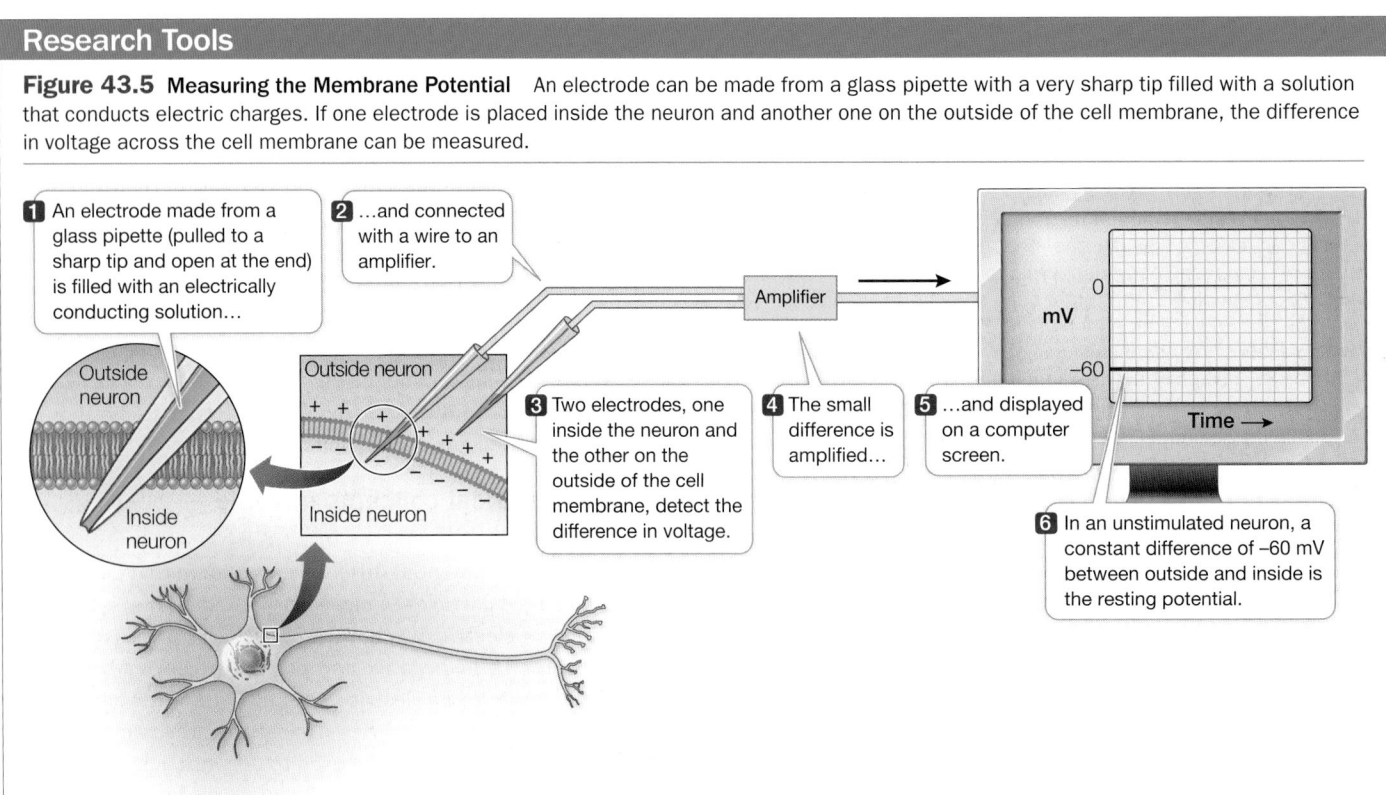

major ion transporter in the cell membranes of neurons (and all other cells) is the **sodium–potassium (Na⁺–K⁺) pump**, so called because it actively expels Na⁺ ions from inside the cell, exchanging them for K⁺ ions from outside the cell (see Figure 6.14). The Na⁺–K⁺ pump is also known as sodium–potassium ATPase, a term emphasizing that it is an enzyme complex requiring ATP to do its work. The Na⁺–K⁺ pump keeps the concentration of K⁺ inside the cell greater than the K⁺ concentration of the extracellular fluid, and the concentration of Na⁺ inside the cell less than that of the extracellular fluid. The concentration differences established by this active transporter mean that K⁺ would diffuse out of the cell and Na⁺ would diffuse in if the ions could cross the lipid bilayer. How do these concentration gradients relate to the electrical gradients we discussed earlier?

Ion channels permit the diffusion of ions across membranes. These channels are water-filled pores formed by proteins that span the lipid bilayer and are generally selective, allowing some types of ions to pass through more easily than others. Thus there are potassium channels, sodium channels, chloride channels, and calcium channels, and there are different kinds of channels for each ion. Ions can diffuse through these channels in either direction. The direction and magnitude of the net movement of ions through a channel depend on the concentration gradient of that ion type across the cell membrane, as well as on the voltage difference across that membrane. These two motive forces acting on an ion are termed its **electrochemical gradient**. The electrochemical gradient drives the movement of ions through channels, but that movement is modified by gates that open and close the channels.

Potassium channels are the most common open, or leak, channels in the cell membranes of resting (non-stimulated) neurons. As a consequence, resting neurons are more permeable to K⁺ than to any other ion. Thus open potassium channels are largely responsible for the resting membrane potential. Because the potassium channels make the cell membrane permeable to K⁺, and because the Na⁺–K⁺ pump keeps the concentration of K⁺ inside the cell much higher than that outside the cell, K⁺ tends to diffuse down its electrochemical gradient, out of the cell. But if K⁺ ions leave the cell, they leave behind unbalanced negative charges, generating an electric potential across the membrane that tends to pull K⁺ back into the cell.

The membrane potential at which the net diffusion of K⁺ out of the cell ceases (that is, the point at which K⁺ diffusion out due to the concentration gradient is balanced by its inward movement due to the negative electric potential) is the **potassium equilibrium potential**, or E_K. The value of E_K can be calculated from the concentrations of K⁺ on the two sides of the membrane using the **Nernst equation (Figure 43.6A)**. This equation, developed in the late 1800s, shows that

Research Tools

Figure 43.6A Using the Nernst Equation The Nernst equation calculates membrane potential when only one type of ion can cross a membrane that separates solutions with different concentrations of that ion.

1. Measure concentrations of ions inside and outside a neuron.

   When these experiments were first done, the scientists found that squid were the ideal experimental animals. Squid have giant neurons that control their escape response (see Figure 43.14C). It is possible to sample the cytoplasm of these axons, which are about 1 mm in diameter.

From A. L. Hodgkin and R. D. Keynes. 1956. *J Physiol* 131: 592–616.

2. Use the Nernst equation to calculate what the membrane potential would be if it were permeable to each of the ions that are differently concentrated on the two sides of the membrane: Na⁺, K⁺, Ca²⁺, and Cl⁻.

   The Nernst equation predicts the membrane potential resulting from membrane permeability to a single type of ion that differs in concentration on the two sides of the membrane. The equation is written

   $$E_{ion} = 2.3 \frac{RT}{zF} \ \log \frac{[ion]_o}{[ion]_i}$$

   where *E* is the equilibrium (resting) membrane potential (the voltage across the membrane in mV), *R* is the universal gas constant, *T* is the absolute temperature, *z* is the charge on the ion, and *F* is the Faraday constant. The subscripts o and i indicate the ion concentrations outside and inside the cell, respectively.

At this point you could just "plug and play," but do you understand this equation?

A concentration difference of ions across a membrane creates a chemical force that pushes the ions across the membrane by diffusion; however, the resulting unbalanced electric charges will pull the ions back the other way. At equilibrium, the two forces are in balance and there is no net movement of ions across the membrane.

The *chemical* energy pushing the ions will equal 2.3 *RT* log [ion]o/[ion]i

The *electric* energy pulling the ions will equal *zEF*. So at equilibrium:

$$zEF = 2.3 \ RT \ \log \frac{[ion]_o}{[ion]_i}$$

Rearranging the equation to solve for *E*, we get the Nernst equation:

$$E_{ion} = 2.3 \frac{RT}{zF} \ \log \frac{[ion]_o}{[ion]_i}$$

We can simplify the equation by picking a temperature—let's use "room temperature," or 20°C—and solving for 2.3 *RT/F*. At 20°C, 2.3 *RT/F* equals 58. Thus:

$$E_{ion} = 58/z \ \log \frac{[ion]_o}{[ion]_i}$$

3. Measuring ion concentrations in squid giant axon cytoplasm and in seawater, then solving the Nernst equation for each ion, we find:

Ion	Ion concentration (mM) in squid axon	in seawater	Predicted membrane potential (mV)
K⁺	400	20	−75
Na⁺	50	460	+56
Ca²⁺	0.5	10	+38
Cl⁻	50	560	−60

Since the measured membrane potential is −66 mV, it is clear that the resting potential of the axon is due to permeability of the membrane to more than just one type of ion.

Figure 43.6B Work with the Data follows on next page.

Work with the Data

Figure 43.6B Equilibrium Membrane Potential: The Goldman Equation

Original Papers: D. E. Goldman. 1943. Potential, impedence and rectification in membranes. *J Gen Physiol* 27: 37–60.

A. L. Hodgkin and B. Katz. 1949. The effect of sodium ions on the electrical activity of the giant axon of the squid. *J Physiol* 108: 37–77.

Figure 43.6A presented the Nernst equation, by which the membrane potential for a single ion can be determined. But you also saw (at the end of Figure 43.6A) that the equilibrium membrane potential is the product of more than one ion. The Goldman equation (frequently called the Goldman, Hodgkin, Katz equation) calculates the equilibrium membrane potential by taking into account all of the ions that can diffuse across a given membrane and the relative permeabilities of the membrane to those ions. The ions involved in mammalian neurons here are K^+, Na^+, and Cl^-, and the Goldman equation is

$$V_m = \frac{RT}{F} \ln\left(\frac{p_K\left[K^+\right]_o + p_{Na}\left[Na^+\right]_o + p_{Cl}\left[Cl^-\right]_i}{p_K\left[K^+\right]_i + p_{Na}\left[Na^+\right]_i + p_{Cl}\left[Cl^-\right]_o}\right)$$

Relative permeabilities (*p*) are expressed as ratios. The membrane's permeability to potassium ions is the highest, so $p_K = 1.0$. Then $p_{Na} = 0.05$ and $p_{Cl} = 0.43$. Bracketed elements refer to the inside and outside ion concentrations, as in the Nernst equation.

QUESTION▶

1. The table gives the intra- and extracellular ion concentrations for a mammalian neuron. Use these values and the Goldman equation to calculate the membrane potential. Refer to Figure 43.6A for a comparison with calculations based on the Nernst equation. (*Hint*: In redrafting the equation, you can substitute "2.3 *RT/F* log" for "*RT/F* ln.")

	Ion concentration (mM)	
	Intracellular	**Extracellular**
K^+	140	5
Na^+	10	145
Cl^-	20	110

Go to **Achieve** for a companion **Data in Depth** exercise.

Research Tools

Figure 43.7 Patch Clamping
The patch clamp electrode is a glass micropipette with a polished tip and is filled with an electrically conductive solution that has the same composition as extracellular fluids. When this pipette/electrode is positioned against the membrane of a cell and slight suction is applied, a seal forms. If a single ion channel or a few ion channels are within the patch of membrane bounded by the seal, the openings and closings of individual channels can be recorded by the electrode. If the pipette is retracted, it can tear the patched membrane away from the cell, and the activities of the ion channels in the patch can continue to be recorded.

Recording pipette

A recording pipette filled with an electrically conductive solution is placed in contact with a neuron's membrane.

Neuron—

Mild suction

Slight suction creates a seal between the pipette tip and a patch of the membrane.

Retracting the pipette removes the membrane patch, often with one or more ion channels in it.

Tracing of ionic current shown on computer screen

Closed

Open

The opening and closing of ion channels can be recorded through the pipette.

---

the existence of ion channels in neuronal membranes was hypothesized long before their specific structures and properties were discovered.

In the late 1940s, A. L. Hodgkin and A. F. Huxley at the University of Cambridge set out to study the electrical properties of axonal membranes. With the techniques available at the time, the necessary measurements could be made only if you had a very large axon to work with. Such an axon exists in nature—the huge neuron that controls the escape response of squid. Hodgkin and Huxley used electrodes to measure the voltage across the cell membrane of this large axon, as seen in Figure 43.6A, and to pass electric current into it to change its membrane potential. They also changed the concentrations of Na^+ and K^+ both inside and outside the squid axon and measured the resulting changes in membrane potential.

On the basis of their many careful experiments, Hodgkin and Huxley developed virtually all of our basic concepts about the electrical properties of neurons, and they shared a Nobel Prize in 1963.

The resting potential of a neuron is less negative than the E_K calculated from the Nernst equation. This means that the resting potential is not due solely to leak K^+ channels. The neuronal membrane is slightly permeable to other ions, especially Na^+ and Cl^-, and movements of these ions influence the resting potential. A different equation takes into account (1) all of the ions that can cross the membrane and (2) the relative permeability of the membrane to those ions. This equation, called the **Goldman equation**, predicts the membrane potential more accurately than does the Nernst equation (**Figure 43.6B**).

Ion channels and their properties can be studied directly

Because Hodgkin and Huxley were working long before there were laboratory techniques enabling the investigation of ion channels, they could only hypothesize ion channel properties. These hypotheses could not be tested until the late 1970s, when B. Sakmann and E. Neher developed a technique called **patch clamping**, for which they shared the Nobel Prize in 1991. Patch clamping, described in **Figure 43.7**, is widely used by neurobiologists, allowing them to record in real time the tiny electric currents caused by the openings and closings of single ion channels.

Gated ion channels alter membrane potential

The ion channels called leak channels are always open, but other ion channels in the cell membranes of neurons behave as if they contain "gates"; they are open under some conditions and closed under other conditions. **Voltage-gated channels** open or close in response to a change in the voltage across the cell membrane. **Chemically gated channels** open or close depending on the presence or absence of a specific molecule that binds to the channel protein, or to a separate receptor that in turn alters the channel protein. **Mechanically gated channels** open or close in response to mechanical force applied to the cell membrane. Gated channels play important roles in neuronal function.

Openings and closings of gated channels alter the membrane potential. Earlier, we considered what would happen if the permeability of the membrane to Na^+ suddenly increased. Such a change in local membrane permeability is generated by the opening of Na^+ channels. When those channels open, Na^+ ions move down their electrochemical gradient until the membrane approaches the equilibrium potential for Na^+ (E_{Na}). Therefore the inside of the cell becomes less negative. When the inside of a neuron becomes less negative (or more positive) than it is in its resting condition, its cell membrane is **depolarized** (**Figure 43.8**). The opposite change in the membrane potential occurs if gated K^+ channels open. Opening of these channels increases the permeability of the cell membrane to K^+, and the membrane potential becomes even more negative than when only the leak K^+ channels were open, and the cell membrane is said to be **hyperpolarized**.

The openings and closings of ion channels that result in changes in the voltage across the cell membrane are the basic mechanisms by which neurons respond to stimuli, be they electrical, chemical, or mechanical. How do such local changes in membrane potential get communicated to other parts of the cell?

A local change in membrane potential causes a flow of ions that spreads the change in membrane potential to adjacent regions of the membrane. For example, when Na^+ channels in an axon open, making that region of the axon positive, a rapid flow of ionic

Figure 43.8 Membranes Can Be Depolarized or Hyperpolarized
The resting potential is produced mostly by leak K^+ channels with a small contribution from leak Na^+ channels (not shown here). A shift from the resting potential to a less negative membrane potential caused by increased Na^+ permeability is called depolarization. Hyperpolarization occurs when the membrane potential becomes more negative, as when the permeability of the membrane to K^+ increases.

electric current in the axoplasm causes a decay in that electric potential change, and it does not spread very far.

Graded changes in membrane potential can integrate information

The flow of ionic electric current along cell membranes can only extend over a short distance, but it causes a graded change in the local membrane potential. A **graded membrane potential** is a change from the resting potential that is proportional to the magnitude of a stimulus. That stimulus can be chemical or mechanical. Graded potentials are a means of integrating stimuli because the membrane can respond with proportional amounts of depolarization or hyperpolarization to each stimulus, and those changes in membrane potential are summed. In Chapter 44 you will learn how graded potentials play important roles in sensory systems. However, the spread of graded potentials can only be local and cannot be transmitted down long axons. Therefore axons code information as discrete APs that travel along their membranes. Graded potentials, however, play an important role in the generation of APs.

Sudden changes in Na⁺ and K⁺ channels generate action potentials

APs are sudden, transient, large changes in membrane potential. In unmyelinated axons (those not wrapped in myelin by oligodendrocytes or Schwann cells), APs can be conducted at speeds of up to 2 meters per second, but in myelinated axons the conduction velocity can be 100 meters per second. Think of running the 100-meter dash—the world record is slightly under 10 seconds.

If we place the tips of a pair of electrodes on either side of the cell membrane of a resting axon and measure the voltage difference, the reading might be about −60 mV, as you saw in Figure 43.5. If these electrodes are in place when an AP travels down the axon, they register a rapid change in membrane potential, from −60 mV to about +50 mV, followed by a rapid return to the resting level of −60 mV (**Figure 43.9**).

The AP is generated by the openings and closings of voltage-gated Na⁺ and K⁺ channels in the cell membrane of the axon. At the resting potential, most of these channels are closed except for the leak K⁺ channels (balloon 1 in Figure 43.9). A slight depolarization of the membrane can cause some voltage-gated Na⁺ channels to open. Specifically, if a neuron is stimulated sufficiently to cause the membrane of its cell body to depolarize slightly, that graded potential spreads by local current flow to the **axon hillock**, the region of the cell body at the base of the axon (see Figure 43.1). Voltage-gated Na⁺ channels are concentrated in the axon hillock. A slight depolarization of the cell membrane in this area causes some of these voltage-gated channels to open briefly—for less than a millisecond (balloon 2 in Figure 43.9). When these channels open, the increased Na⁺ permeability depolarizes the membrane even more, causing more Na⁺ channels to open—a positive-feedback effect. When the membrane is depolarized about 5–10 mV above the resting potential, a **threshold** is reached; a large number of sodium channels open (balloon 3 in Figure 43.9), and the membrane potential becomes positive—an AP. The rising phase

of the AP halts abruptly in 1–2 milliseconds, and the membrane potential rapidly becomes negative once again.

What causes the axon to return to resting potential? There are two contributing factors: the voltage-gated Na⁺ channels close, and voltage-gated K⁺ channels open (balloon 4 in Figure 43.9). Voltage-gated K⁺ channels open in response to the same depolarization that triggered the Na⁺ channels, but they do so more slowly and they stay open longer, allowing K⁺ to carry excess positive charges out of the axon. As a result, the membrane potential returns to a negative value and usually becomes even more negative than the resting potential until the voltage-gated K⁺ channels close (balloon 5 in Figure 43.9).

Another feature of the voltage-gated Na⁺ channels is that once they open and close, they have a **refractory period** of 1–2 milliseconds during which they cannot open again. This property can be explained by the channels having two gates, an **activation gate** and an **inactivation gate** (see Figure 43.9). Under resting conditions, the activation gate is closed and the inactivation gate is open. Depolarization of the membrane to the threshold level causes both gates to change state, but the activation gate responds faster. As a result, the channel is open for a brief time between the opening of the activation gate and the closing of the inactivation gate. Inactivation gates remain closed for 1–2 milliseconds before they spontaneously open again, thus explaining the refractory period. By the time the inactivation gate reopens, the activation gate is closed, and the membrane is poised to generate another AP. Another contribution to the refractory period is the duration of the opening of the voltage-gated K⁺ channels, as you saw earlier. The dip in the membrane potential following an AP is called the **after-hyperpolarization** or **undershoot**.

The difference in the concentration of Na⁺ across the cell membrane and the negative resting potential constitute the "battery" that drives APs. How rapidly does the battery run down? It might seem that a substantial number of ions would have to cross the membrane for the membrane potential to change from −60 mV to +50 mV and back to −60 mV again. In fact, only a vanishingly small number of Na⁺ ions move through the channels during the passage of an active potential. Thus the effect of a single AP on the concentration gradients of Na⁺ and K⁺ is very small, and the sodium–potassium pump can keep the "battery" charged, even when the neuron is generating many APs every second.

Action potentials are conducted along axons without loss of signal

An AP is conducted over long distances with no loss of signal. If we place two pairs of electrodes at two different locations along an axon, we can record an AP at those two locations as it travels along the axon (**Figure 43.10A**). The magnitude of the AP does not change between the two recording sites. This constancy is possible because an AP is an *all-or-none, self-regenerating event*.

- An AP is *all-or-none* because of the interaction between the voltage-gated Na⁺ channels and the membrane potential. If the membrane is depolarized slightly, some voltage-gated Na⁺ channels open. Some sodium ions cross the cell

Figure 43.9 The Course of an Action Potential   APs result from rapid changes in voltage-gated Na^+ and K^+ channels.

▶ **View in Achieve**
Animation 43.2 **The Action Potential**

1 Leak K^+ channels create the resting potential. Gated channels are closed.

2 Some voltage-gated Na^+ channels open, depolarizing the cell to threshold.

3 Additional voltage-gated Na^+ channel activation gates open, causing a rapid spike of depolarization—an action potential.

4 Na^+ channel inactivation gates close; gated K^+ channels open, repolarizing and even hyperpolarizing the cell.

5 All gated channels close. The cell returns to its resting potential. Na^+ inactivation gates reopen.

membrane and depolarize it even more, opening more voltage-gated Na^+ channels, and so on, generating an AP. This positive-feedback mechanism ensures that APs always rise to their maximum value.

• An AP is *self-regenerating* because it spreads by local current flow to adjacent regions of the cell membrane. The resulting depolarization brings those neighboring areas of membrane to threshold. Therefore when an AP occurs at one location on an axon, it stimulates the adjacent region of axon to generate an

AP, and so on down the length of the axon. Although we say that the AP travels down the axon, what is really happening is that new APs are being created sequentially.

We can use an electrode to stimulate an axon, causing it to depolarize and to fire an AP that is then conducted along the axon. **Figure 43.10B** shows the changes in the ion channels in the membrane that are responsible for conducting the AP along the axon without a reduction in amplitude. Normally an AP is propagated in only one direction—away from the cell body. It cannot reverse itself because

(A)

Electrical stimulus

Point A Point B

Tracing of recorded membrane potential changes at two locations on the axon.

Amplifier

Point A

Amplifier

Point B

Time ⟶

Outside axon

Inside axon

Outside axon

Point A   Point B

(B)

1 Voltage-gated Na⁺ channels open in response to spreading membrane depolarization but have inactivation gates that close quickly.

2 A depolarizing current spreads to adjacent areas of the membranes.

Point A   Point B

Direction of action potential propagation

(C)

3 Upstream Na⁺ channels inactivate, making the membrane refractory.

4 Voltage-gated K⁺ channels open, hyperpolarizing the axon, then close.

5 As it travels down the axon, the action potential stimulates more Na⁺ channels to open in a self-extending forward stream.

Direction of action potential propagation

Point A   Point B

Figure 43.10 Action Potentials Travel along Axons **(A)** There is no loss of signal as an AP travels along an axon. **(B)** When an AP is stimulated in one region of membrane, ionic current flows to and depolarizes adjacent areas of membrane. **(C)** The advancing wave of depolarization causes more Na⁺ channels to open, and the AP is generated anew in the next section of membrane. Meanwhile, in the region where the AP has just fired, the Na⁺ channels are inactivated and the voltage-gated K⁺ channels are still open, rendering this section of the axon incapable of generating an AP. Hence the AP cannot "back up," but moves continuously forward, regenerating itself as it goes.

vertebrates mostly depend on myelination of axons to increase AP conduction velocity.

Action potentials jump along myelinated axons

In vertebrate nervous systems, increasing the speed of APs by increasing the diameter of axons is not feasible because of the huge number of axons involved. Each of our eyes, for example, has about a million axons connecting it to the brain. These axons conduct APs at about the same speed as does the squid giant axon—about 20 meters per second—yet the diameter of each is 200 times smaller than the squid axon's diameter. Imagine having optic tracts 200 times bigger. A different way of increasing conduction velocity of axons has evolved in vertebrates, and that adaptation is myelination.

When glia wrap around axons, they cover the axons with concentric layers of myelin (see Figure 43.3). However, they leave regularly spaced gaps called **nodes of Ranvier**, where the axon is not covered (see Figure 43.11). Underneath the myelin sheaths, there are no Na⁺ or K⁺ channels, and therefore APs cannot propagate under the myelin sheath. However, an AP firing at a node of Ranvier creates a local electric field inside the axon that spreads almost

the voltage-gated Na⁺ channels in the region of the membrane it came from are in their refractory period (**Figure 43.10C**).

APs are not conducted at the same speed in all axons. They travel faster in large-diameter axons than in small-diameter axons because the resistance to ionic current flow decreases as an axon's diameter gets bigger. They travel faster in myelinated than in unmyelinated axons because they can move down the axon in short "jumps" as described in the next section (**Figure 43.11**). Invertebrates depend on increased axon diameter for fast conduction, but

instantaneously to the next node of Ranvier. The resulting depolarization of that next node triggers another AP, and so on down the axon. Thus the APs appear to jump from node to node, and their conduction down the axon is very fast.

The speed of conduction is increased in these myelin-wrapped axons because electric current flows much faster through the cytoplasm than ion channels can open and close. This form of rapid impulse propagation is called **saltatory conduction** (Latin *saltare*, "to jump").

Figure 43.11 Saltatory Action Potentials APs "jump" from node to node in myelinated axons, allowing faster transmission of information.

Labels within figure:
- Nodes of Ranvier
- Myelin-forming Schwann cells
- **1** Na⁺ channels open, generating an action potential.
- **2a** Spreading current from the upstream node...
- **2b** ...brings the membrane at the next node to threshold.
- **3** Upstream Na⁺ channels inactivate, making the membrane refractory. Voltage-gated K⁺ channels open, repolarizing the axon.
- **4** The action potential jumps to the new node and continues from node to node.

KEY CONCEPT
43.2 Recap and Assess

Neurons have membrane potentials due to ion concentration differences across their membranes and the different permeabilities of the membrane to those ions created by ion channels. Leak channels generate the resting potential, and opening and closing of gated channels can create graded changes in membrane potentials depending on how many of which channel types open or close. Voltage-gated channels have threshold potentials for opening. If some voltage-gated Na⁺ channels open, they create a local depolarization that brings other Na⁺ channels to threshold—a positive-feedback mechanism that generates APs. Sudden closure of Na⁺ channels and the opening of K⁺ channels terminate the AP. APs are rapid, all-or-none changes in membrane potential that are conducted along axons from the cell body to the axon terminals. In myelinated axons, APs jump between nodes of Ranvier and conduction is more rapid than in unmyelinated axons.

1. How would the resting potential of neurons be different if the neuronal cell membrane were more permeable to Na⁺ than to K⁺, and how would the APs of such a neuron look if they were due to voltage-gated K⁺ channels with thresholds lower than the resting potential?

2. Why does the Goldman equation produce a more accurate calculation of membrane resting potential than the Nernst equation does?

3. Why is an AP self-regenerating in both unmyelinated and myelinated neurons?

4. How do graded membrane potentials enable a neuron to generate signals that reflect the inputs from many neurons?

Having described how APs are generated and transmitted along axons, we next address the question of what happens when an AP reaches the axon terminals. How is the AP's signal communicated to the next cell—which could be another neuron, a muscle cell, or a secretory cell?

KEY CONCEPT
43.3 Neurons Communicate with Other Cells

Learning Objectives

43.3.1 Describe the events at a neuromuscular junction, beginning with the action potential in the presynaptic neuron and ending with the response of the postsynaptic cell.

43.3.2 Compare the characteristics of electrical versus chemical synapses and explain why chemical synapses present a greater variety of postsynaptic responses than do electrical synapses.

43.3.3 Describe the mechanisms that make the actions of neurotransmitters transitory.

Neurons communicate with each other and with other cells at synapses. In **electrical synapses**, which are common among invertebrates, the AP spreads directly from presynaptic to postsynaptic cell. The most common type of synapse in the vertebrate nervous system is the **chemical synapse**, in which neurotransmitters released from a presynaptic cell induce changes in a membrane potential of a postsynaptic cell. This key concept begins with a discussion of the synapses between neurons and muscle cells. We then consider the diversity in synapses between neurons and how they integrate information.

The neuromuscular junction is a model chemical synapse

Neuromuscular junctions are synapses between neurons and skeletal muscle cells. They are excellent models for how chemical synaptic transmission works. Neurons that control muscles are called **motor neurons**. Like other neurons, a motor neuron has only one axon, but that axon can branch into numerous axon terminals that form many synapses with muscle cells. At each axon terminal an enlarged knob or buttonlike structure (called a synaptic bouton) contains membrane-bound vesicles filled with neurotransmitter molecules. The neurotransmitter used by motor neurons to skeletal muscles in all vertebrates is **acetylcholine** (**ACh**). ACh is released by exocytosis when the membrane of a vesicle containing this neurotransmitter fuses with the presynaptic membrane of the axon terminal.

The postsynaptic membrane of the neuromuscular junction is a modified part of the muscle cell membrane called a **motor end plate**. It appears as a depression in the muscle cell membrane, and the terminals of the motor neuron sit in the depression. The space between the presynaptic membrane and the postsynaptic membrane is the **synaptic cleft**, which in chemical synapses is about 20–40 nanometers wide. ACh released into the cleft by the presynaptic cell diffuses across to the postsynaptic membrane (**Figure 43.12**).

The arrival of an action potential causes the release of neurotransmitter

Neurotransmitter is released when an AP arrives at the axon terminal and causes the opening of voltage-gated Ca^{2+} channels in the presynaptic membrane. Because the Ca^{2+} concentration is greater outside the cell than inside, Ca^{2+} enters the axon terminal. This increase in Ca^{2+} inside the axon terminal causes the vesicles containing neurotransmitter to fuse with the presynaptic membrane and empty their contents into the synaptic cleft.

In neuromuscular synapses, vesicle fusion and emptying is all-or-none. The vesicle membrane is incorporated into the presynaptic membrane, which actually gets larger as a result—at least until the extra membrane is recycled through endocytosis. The internalized membrane is processed by the cell into new vesicles that are filled with neurotransmitter.

Synaptic functions involve many proteins

Our description of the release of neurotransmitter from the presynaptic membrane may seem simple, but it involves hundreds of proteins that are responsible for various aspects of the process: vesicle formation, transport of neurotransmitter into vesicles, anchoring of vesicles to cytoskeletal elements, docking of the vesicles with the presynaptic membrane, fusion of the vesicular and cell membranes, and endocytosis of the vesicle membrane for recycling.

Some of these proteins are the targets of toxins. For example, botulinum and tetanus toxins from bacteria of the genus *Clostridium* act on several of the proteins necessary for the docking of vesicles to the presynaptic membrane, resulting in diseases that are frequently fatal. Botulinum toxin impairs muscle contraction, whereas tetanus toxin causes uncontrolled muscle contraction. Poisons can become medicines. Botulinum toxin (in the form of Botox˚) is used therapeutically to subdue muscle spasms and cosmetically to reduce wrinkles.

The postsynaptic membrane responds to neurotransmitter

When acetylcholine is released at a synapse, some of it diffuses across the synaptic cleft and binds to ACh receptors (AChRs) on the postsynaptic membrane. The postsynaptic membrane of the motor end plate is highly folded. AChRs are on the crests of the folds, and voltage-gated cation channels are at the bottoms of the folds and in the surrounding muscle cell membrane (see Figure 43.12). The AChRs are gated channels that allow both Na^+ and K^+ to flow through, but since the electrochemical gradients favor a net influx of Na^+, the response of the motor end plate to ACh is to depolarize. The amount of depolarization depends on the number of receptors activated, and therefore the response to ACh is a graded potential. If the graded potential is sufficient, the membrane depolarization spreads to the depths of the folds of the motor end plate membrane and to the surrounding muscle cell membrane, where there are voltage-gated Na^+ channels.

The spreading depolarization of the motor end plate activates the voltage-gated Na^+ channels and causes the firing of an AP. This AP is then conducted throughout the muscle cell's system of membranes, causing the cell to contract. We will discuss the neural control of contraction of muscle cells in greater detail in Key Concept 46.1.

How much neurotransmitter is enough? Neither a single ACh molecule nor the contents of an entire vesicle (about 10,000 ACh molecules) will depolarize the membrane of a muscle cell to threshold. However, a single AP in an axon terminal releases the contents of about 100 vesicles—more than enough to fire an AP in the muscle cell and cause it to contract.

 View in Achieve
Simulation 43.1 Neurons and Synapses

Synapses can be excitatory or inhibitory

The synapses between vertebrate motor neurons and muscle cells are always excitatory. The motor end plates always respond to ACh with a graded potential that is less negative than the resting potential (depolarization). However, synapses between neurons are frequently inhibitory; such a synapse causes hyperpolarization of the postsynaptic membrane or simply makes it less likely that its membrane potential will reach threshold for the voltage-gated Na^+ channels. For example, there are more Cl^- ions outside than inside the cell. However, in a mammalian neuron the equilibrium potential for Cl^- is around −60mV. Given a resting potential that is also around −60 mV, opening of Cl^- channels will not hyperpolarize the membrane, but if these channels are open, it will make it more difficult to raise the membrane potential to the threshold for the voltage-gated Na^+ channels.

1 Action potential arrives at axon terminal.

2 Na⁺ channels open; depolarization causes voltage-gated Ca^{2+} channels to open.

Synaptic cleft

3 Ca^{2+} enters the cell and triggers fusion of ACh vesicles with the presynaptic membrane.

AChR

Postsynaptic cell
(motor end plate of muscle cell)

Motor neuron

Muscle fiber

Axon

Presynaptic cell
(motor neuron)

Axon terminal

ACh in vesicle

Na^+

Ca^{2+}

Na^+

Na^+

Ca^{2+}

Na^+

7 AChE brakes down ACh and the components are taken back up by the presynaptic cell. ACh and vesicles are recycled.

ACh

Na^+

AChR

K^+ Na^+

AChE

Action potential

6 The spreading depolarization fires an action potential in the postsynaptic membrane.

4 ACh molecules diffuse across the synaptic cleft and bind to receptors on the postsynaptic membrane.

5 When receptors bind ACh, they open their cation channels and depolarize the postsynaptic membrane.

Figure 43.12 Chemical Synaptic Transmission Begins with the Arrival of an Action Potential The neuromuscular junction is a typical chemical synapse. Events shown here are similar for other neurotransmitters at other synapses. Both chemically gated and voltage-gated ACh receptors (AChRs) are found in the motor end plate. These are nonselective cation channels but are more permeable to Na⁺ than to K⁺ (inset). When one of the chemically gated receptors binds ACh, its channel pore opens and the net increase in Na⁺ permeability of the postsynaptic membrane depolarizes it. The depolarization spreads beyond the motor end plate, activating voltage-gated Na⁺ channels in the muscle cell membrane, depolarizing it and initiating an AP. The enzyme acetylcholinesterase (AChE) breaks down ACh in the synapse, closing the chemically gated channels. The breakdown products (acetate and choline) are taken up by the presynaptic membrane and resynthesized into more ACh.

Q: If this synapse were between neurons, and the neurotransmitter were inhibitory rather than excitatory, what chemically gated channels would you expect to be on the postsynaptic membrane?

View in Achieve
Animation 43.3 **Synaptic Transmission**

Media Clip 43.1 **Put Some ACh Into It!**
Life12e.com/mc43.1

Recall that most neurons have many dendrites. Axon terminals from many other neurons can form synapses with those dendrites and with the cell body. The axon terminals of different presynaptic neurons can store and release different neurotransmitters, and the cell membrane of the dendrites and cell body of a postsynaptic neuron can have receptors for a variety of neurotransmitters. The mix of synaptic activity impinging on a neuron will cause it to have a graded membrane potential that can be either more positive or more negative than its resting potential and thereby increase or decrease its probability of firing APs.

The postsynaptic neuron sums excitatory and inhibitory input

What determines when an individual neuron fires an AP? As you just learned, the sum of excitatory and inhibitory postsynaptic potentials creates a graded membrane potential in the postsynaptic cell body. This summation ability is the major mechanism by which the nervous system integrates information. A neuron may receive 1,000 or more synaptic inputs, but it has only one output: APs in a single axon. At any one time, the information from all of the active inputs is translated into the rate at which that neuron generates APs in its axon.

For most neurons, summation takes place in the axon hillock at the base of the axon. The cell membrane of the axon hillock is not insulated by glia and has many voltage-gated Na^+ channels. Excitatory and inhibitory postsynaptic potentials from synapses anywhere on the dendrites or the cell body spread to the axon hillock by local current flow. If the resulting graded potential depolarizes the axon hillock to threshold, it fires an AP. Because postsynaptic potentials decrease in strength as they spread from the site of the synapse, a synapse at the tip of a dendrite has less influence than a synapse on the cell body, near the axon hillock.

Excitatory and inhibitory postsynaptic potentials are summed over space and over time. **Spatial summation** adds up the simultaneous influences of synapses at different sites on the postsynaptic cell (**Figure 43.13A**). **Temporal summation** adds up postsynaptic potentials generated at the same site in a rapid sequence (**Figure 43.13B**).

Electrical synapses are fast but do not integrate information well

Electrical synapses are different from chemical synapses because they couple neurons electrically. Electrical synapses contain numerous gap junctions. At these synapses, the presynaptic and postsynaptic cell membranes are separated by a space of only 2–3 nanometers, and membrane proteins called connexins link the two neurons by forming pores that connect the cytoplasm of the two cells (see Figure 7.16A). Electric current as well as ions and small molecules can pass directly from cell to cell through these pores. As a result, transmission at electrical synapses is very fast and can proceed in either direction. In comparison, transmission at chemical synapses is slow and unidirectional.

Connect the Concepts The proteins that form gap junctions between cells, including neurons, are discussed in Key Concept 6.2.

The properties of electrical synapses make them especially well adapted for processes that have to be fast—for example, escape from danger. They are also effective means of achieving synchronous activity of populations of cells. Electrical synapses are less common in the nervous systems of vertebrates than are chemical synapses. The major reason is that they offer fewer means for integration of information. Electrical synapses are almost exclusively excitatory, whereas chemical synapses are both excitatory and inhibitory. Electrical synapses are not well suited for temporal summation of inputs. Also, because of their relative simplicity of structure and function, electrical synapses offer fewer possible mechanisms for plasticity, which is the foundation of learning and memory.

The action of a neurotransmitter depends on the receptor to which it binds

More than 100 neurotransmitters are now recognized, and more will surely be discovered. Acetylcholine (ACh) is an important neurotransmitter because it is the substance the nervous system uses to signal muscles to contract. ACh also plays roles in certain synapses between neurons in the brain, but it accounts for only a small percent of the total neurotransmitter content of the brain.

The workhorse neurotransmitters of the brain are three simple amino acids: glutamate, which is usually excitatory, and glycine and γ-aminobutyric acid (GABA), which are usually inhibitory. The integration of information at the cellular level is a balance between excitation and inhibition, so it is understandable that excessive inhibition such as you saw in the Down syndrome mice described at the start of this chapter could impair an animal's ability to process and integrate new information. Indeed, when GABA's inhibitory action in these mice was reduced by a drug that blocks the GABA receptor, the learning ability of the mice improved, as described in **Investigating Life: Can Learning Be Restored in Mouse Models of Down Syndrome?**

Another important group of neurotransmitters in the brain is the monoamines, which are derivatives of amino acids. They include dopamine and norepinephrine (derivatives of tyrosine) and serotonin (a derivative of tryptophan). Peptides also function as neurotransmitters; for example, endorphins and enkephalins are the body's opiates and modulate the sensation of pain. Another peptide, substance P, transmits pain sensations. Even a gas, nitric oxide, is used by neurons as an intercellular messenger (see Figure 7.13).

Figure 43.13 The Postsynaptic Neuron Sums Information Individual neurons sum excitatory and inhibitory postsynaptic potentials over space (**A**) and time (**B**). When the sum of the potentials depolarizes the axon hillock to threshold, the neuron generates an AP.

▶InvestigatingLIFE   Can Learning Be Restored in Mouse Models of Down Syndrome?

Experiment

Original Paper: D. Colas et al. 2013. Short-term treatment with the GABA antagonist pentylenetetrazole produces a sustained procognitive benefit in a mouse model of Down's syndrome. *Br J Pharmacol* 169: 963–973.

If the learning disability in the mouse model of Down syndrome (DS) is due to overinhibition, then reducing the activity of the major inhibitory neurotransmitter, GABA, might improve learning in these mice.

HYPOTHESIS▶   The inability of DS model mice to learn and remember experiences as well as wild-type (WT) mice is due to overactive GABA signaling in their brains. If GABA signaling is reduced, the ability of mice to perform learning tasks should improve.

METHOD▶

1. Keep DS and WT mice of the same age on a 12-hour:12-hour light–dark cycle. At the same time each morning, for 2 weeks, inject the mice in the experimental group with the drug pentylenetetrazole (PTZ), which blocks the action of GABA. Use three different doses. Inject the control mice with saline. The doses are measured as mg PTZ/kg body weight of mouse.

2. Following completion of the 2-week drug-dosing protocol, evaluate the mice using the Novel Object Recognition (NOR) test. For training, place each mouse in a 4-square-foot arena that contains two objects such as chessmen or small bottles. Allow the mouse to explore the objects for 10 minutes and then return it to its home cage. An acceptable baseline is when the mouse spends the same amount of time exploring each object. Test again 1 day later, placing the mouse back in the arena but with one of the objects changed (the novel object). If the mouse spends more time exploring the novel object, that is evidence that it remembered the original object from the day before.

3. Quantify the mouse's behavior as a NOR preference (time spent exploring object A/time spent exploring objects A and B × 100%). For the testing trial, A is the novel object. A NOR preference of 50% means the mouse spent equal amounts of time with each object, and therefore did not remember the objects it explored previously. A NOR preference significantly greater than 50% means the mouse spent more time exploring the novel object and is evidence that the mouse remembered the objects it saw before.

RESULTS▶   Data are NOR preference percentages ± 1 SEM (standard error of the mean). An asterisk (*) indicates $P < 0.01$ for difference between training (blue) and testing (orange) results as determined by a *t*-test: **, $P < 0.001$.

CONCLUSION▶   The saline treatments (controls) show that the WT mice can recognize the novel object 24 hours after training and that the DS mice cannot. PTZ treatment had no effect on the WT mice. PTZ treatment at 0.3 and 0.03 mg/kg improved the ability of the DS mice to remember the familiar objects and therefore recognize the novel object, whereas treatment at 0.01 mg/kg did not.

Neurotransmission is complex in part because each neurotransmitter has multiple receptor types. ACh, for example, has two receptor types: nicotinic receptors and muscarinic receptors. All of the AChRs in skeletal muscles are nicotinic. Both types of AChRs are found in the brain and spinal cord, where nicotinic receptors tend to be excitatory and muscarinic receptors tend to be inhibitory. ACh actions can differ outside the brain and spinal cord as well. ACh acting through nicotinic receptors causes the smooth muscle of the gut to increase its motility, but ACh acting through muscarinic receptors causes cardiac muscle to hyperpolarize and therefore to slow down. There are many more examples of neurotransmitters that have different effects in different tissues, but the important thing to remember is that the action of a neurotransmitter depends on the receptor to which it binds. In addition, turning neurotransmitter action off is as important as turning it on.

View in Achieve
Activity 43.1 **Neurotransmitters**

Work with the Data

All of the PTZ injections in the experiment described above were given to the mice early in the light phase of their day. This is the time when these nocturnal animals are normally sleeping. The researchers therefore asked whether the same results could be obtained if the treatments were delivered during the dark phase of the day, when the mice are usually active and exploring. They obtained the following data. Data are NOR preference percentages ± 1 SEM. An asterisk (*) indicates $P < 0.01$ for difference between saline and PTZ treatments.

| | Treatment | |
Group	Saline	PTZ 0.3 mg/kg
WT Mice Training	55.0 ± 3.1	55.4 ± 2.4
DS Mice Training	51.9 ± 2.4	50.7 ± 2.0
WT Mice Testing	65.8 ± 5.3*	67.4 ± 4.9*
DS Mice Testing	53.7 ± 4.7	51.3 ± 6.9

QUESTIONS▶

1. How did the learning ability of the WT and DS mice compare during the dark phase of the day, and did this result differ from when the training and testing were done during the light phase?

2. Describe any difference between the effect of the PTZ treatment on the performance of the WT and DS mice on the NOR task during the light and dark phases of the day.

Go to **Achieve** for a companion Data in Depth exercise.

Synapses must be cleared of neurotransmitter to turn off responses

If released neurotransmitter molecules simply remained in the synaptic cleft, the postsynaptic membrane would become saturated and receptors would be constantly activated. The postsynaptic cell would remain hyperpolarized or depolarized and would be unresponsive to additional APs arriving at the presynaptic cell. The more rapidly neurons can respond to input, the more information they can process in a given amount of time. Thus neurotransmitter must be cleared from the synaptic cleft shortly after it is released by the axon terminal.

Neurotransmitter action can be terminated in several ways. First, enzymes can destroy the neurotransmitter. Acetylcholine, for example, is rapidly destroyed by the enzyme acetylcholinesterase (AChE), which is present in the synaptic cleft in close association with AChRs on the postsynaptic membrane (see Figure 43.12). When AChE is inhibited, ACh lingers in the synaptic cleft, causing spastic (contracted) muscle paralysis that can lead to death. Some of the most deadly nerve gases developed for chemical warfare worked by inhibiting AChE. Some agricultural insecticides, such as malathion, also inhibit AChE and can poison farm workers if used without safety precautions.

Neurotransmitter can also simply diffuse away from the cleft or be taken back up by the presynaptic membrane to be recycled. Glial cells also take up neurotransmitters. The antidepressant drug fluoxetine (commonly prescribed under the brand name Prozacˣ) slows the reuptake of the neurotransmitter serotonin, thus enhancing serotonin's activity at the synapse.

The diversity of receptors makes drug specificity possible

Many drugs used to treat the nervous system act by modulating specific synaptic interactions. Drugs that mimic or potentiate the effect of a neurotransmitter are called **agonists**; those that block the actions of neurotransmitters are called **antagonists**. For example, morphine is an agonist at the endorphin receptor and therefore blocks pain. Propranolol, a widely used beta blocker, is an antagonist of receptors in the fight-or-flight response and therefore decreases panic attacks and anxiety. A major emphasis in neurobiology is to identify neurotransmitter receptor subtypes and design drugs that selectively bind to them to have highly specific effects on nervous system activity.

KEY CONCEPT

43.3 Recap and Assess

Chemical synapses involve the release of neurotransmitter molecules stored in vesicles in the presynaptic axon terminal. APs reaching that terminal cause the fusion of vesicles with the presynaptic membrane, releasing neurotransmitter that can then bind to receptors on the postsynaptic membrane and influence its membrane potential. At excitatory synapses, the neurotransmitter causes depolarization of the postsynaptic membrane, and at inhibitory synapses the neurotransmitter hyperpolarizes or stabilizes the postsynaptic membrane potential. There is a great diversity of neurotransmitters and their receptors. At electrical synapses the AP moves directly between pre- and postsynaptic cells.

1. What are the two major types of cation channels in the motor end plate, and what are their functions?

2. How can the same neurotransmitter be excitatory to some postsynaptic neurons and inhibitory to others?

3. Sarin is a colorless, odorless liquid that can quickly evaporate into the environment and is highly lethal. It irreversibly inactivates the enzyme acetylcholinesterase (AChE). Explain why victims of sarin poisoning generally die of asphyxiation.

4. Explain why parts of nervous systems that integrate complex information use chemical rather than electrical synapses.

Now that you understand how neurons communicate with each other, let's explore how they are organized into circuits and systems that process sensory information and generate responses to that information.

KEY CONCEPT

43.4 Neurons and Glia Form Information-Processing Circuits

Learning Objectives

43.4.1 Distinguish the central from the peripheral nervous system and describe how these systems range in complexity among different species.

43.4.2 Using the knee-jerk reflex, explain how a neural circuit involves both afferent and efferent neurons.

Nervous systems can process information because their neurons are organized into **neural networks**. These networks include three functional categories of neurons that are responsible for input, output, and integration:

1. **Afferent neurons** carry sensory information into the nervous system. That information comes from specialized sensory cells that transduce (convert) various kinds of sensory stimuli (e.g., light, heat, pressure) into APs.

2. **Efferent neurons** carry commands to physiological and behavioral effectors such as muscles and glands.

3. **Interneurons** integrate and store information and communicate between afferent and efferent neurons.

Nervous systems range in complexity

Simple animals such as cnidarians (sea anemones, for example) process information with a limited number of simple neural networks that do little more than provide direct lines of communication from sensory cells to effectors; there is little integration or processing of signals (**Figure 43.14A**). The cnidarian's **nerve net** is most developed around the tentacles and the oral opening, where it facilitates detection of food or danger and causes tentacles to extend or retract.

Animals that are more complex and move about in search of food and mates must process and integrate larger amounts of information. Even earthworms fit this description, and their increased need for information processing is met by higher numbers of neurons organized into clusters of neuronal cell bodies called **ganglia** (singular *ganglion*). Ganglia serving different functions may be distributed around the body, as in earthworms (**Figure 43.14B**). In animals

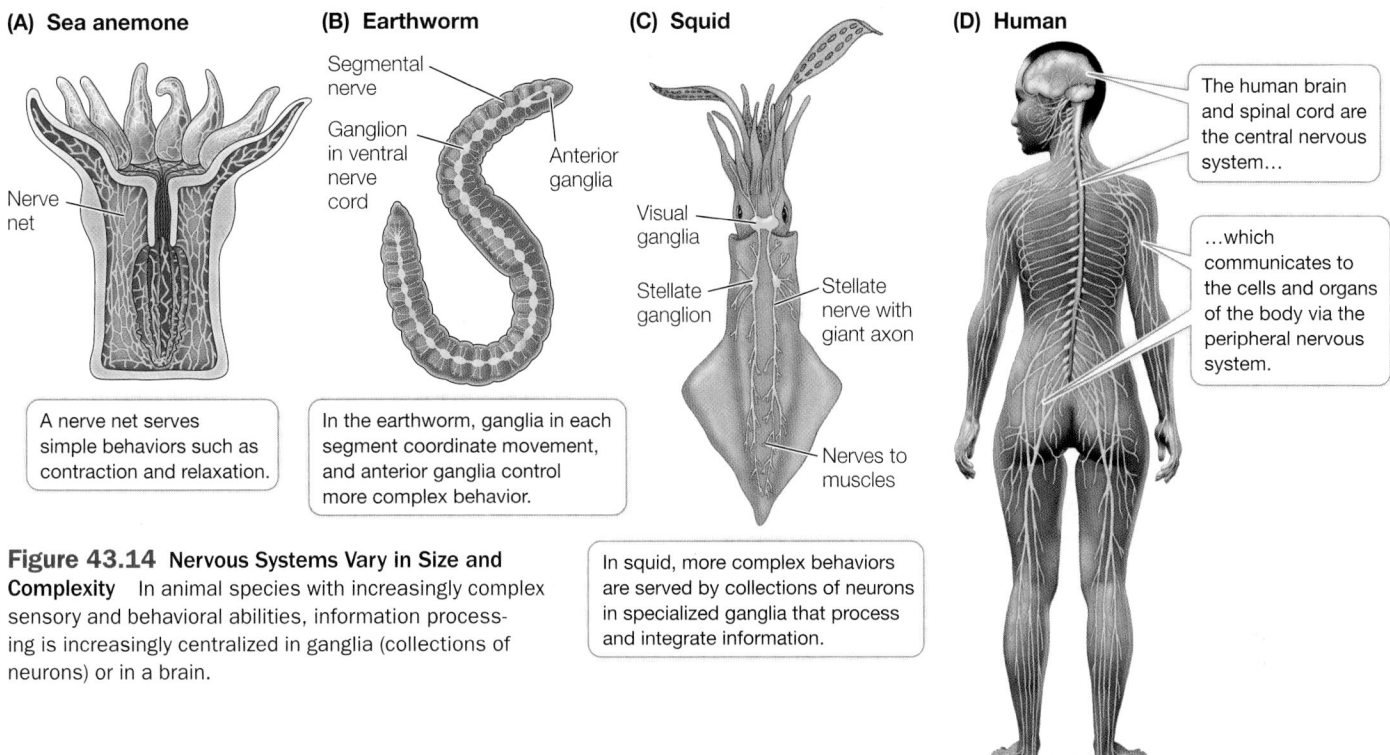

(A) Sea anemone

Nerve net

A nerve net serves simple behaviors such as contraction and relaxation.

(B) Earthworm

Segmental nerve

Ganglion in ventral nerve cord

Anterior ganglia

In the earthworm, ganglia in each segment coordinate movement, and anterior ganglia control more complex behavior.

(C) Squid

Visual ganglia

Stellate ganglion

Stellate nerve with giant axon

Nerves to muscles

In squid, more complex behaviors are served by collections of neurons in specialized ganglia that process and integrate information.

(D) Human

The human brain and spinal cord are the central nervous system...

...which communicates to the cells and organs of the body via the peripheral nervous system.

Figure 43.14 Nervous Systems Vary in Size and Complexity   In animal species with increasingly complex sensory and behavioral abilities, information processing is increasingly centralized in ganglia (collections of neurons) or in a brain.

that are bilaterally symmetrical, ganglia frequently come in pairs, one on each side of the body (**Figure 43.14C**). Also, as animals increase in complexity, some ganglia may become enlarged or fused together at the anterior end, forming a **brain**. Small nervous systems of invertebrates can be remarkably complex. Consider the nervous systems of spiders, which have programmed within them the thousands of precise movements necessary to construct an intricate web without prior experience or opportunities to learn the specific web architecture of their species.

In vertebrates, most cells of the nervous system are found in the central nervous system (CNS). The CNS includes the brain and the spinal cord, which are the sites of most information processing, storage, and retrieval (**Figure 43.14D**). Information is transmitted from sensory cells to the CNS and from the CNS to cells that respond (effectors) via neurons that extend or reside outside the brain and the spinal cord. These sensory and effector neurons and their supporting cells are the peripheral nervous system.

Reflexes are controlled by simple circuits involving sensory neurons, interneurons, and effectors

A reflex is a behavioral or physiological response that does not require conscious information processing—it is autonomic, meaning an involuntary or unconscious reaction. Examples are salivating at the sight or smell of food, and the jerk of your lower leg when a physician taps your knee with a small rubber hammer. The knee-jerk reflex involves a very simple neural circuit involving just a few neurons that connect with each other in the spinal cord. Thus it is called a **spinal reflex**. A cross section of the human spinal cord reveals a central area of gray matter in the shape of a butterfly, surrounded by areas of white matter (see Figure 43.15). In the

nervous system, **gray matter** is rich in neuronal cell bodies, and **white matter** contains myelinated axons. The gray matter of the spinal cord contains the cell bodies of the spinal neurons; the white matter contains myelinated axons that conduct information up and down the spinal cord.

Spinal nerves extend from the spinal cord at regular intervals on each side. Each spinal nerve has two roots, one connecting with the dorsal horn of the gray matter, the other with the ventral horn. The afferent (sensory) axons in a spinal nerve enter the spinal cord through the dorsal root, and the efferent (motor) axons leave through the ventral root. The neural circuit of the knee-jerk reflex is diagrammed in **Figure 43.15**. The tap of the physician's rubber hammer stretches the tendon going over the knee. That tendon attaches the muscle of the upper leg to bone in the lower leg. Stretching the tendon stretches muscle fibers in the upper leg, and stretch receptors in that muscle transduce the physical stimulus into APs. The APs are then conducted by a sensory neuron into the dorsal horn of the spinal cord. That sensory neuron goes all the way to the ventral horn and synapses onto a motor neuron, which fires APs. The axon of that motor neuron travels out through the ventral horn of the spinal cord and extends all the way to the same muscle that initially was stretched, causing that muscle to contract.

What is the function of the spinal knee-jerk reflex? This simple circuit senses increased load on a muscle and adjusts its level of contraction to match the load. Most spinal reflexes are more complex. For example, limb movement is controlled by antagonistic sets of muscles that work against each other. When one member of an antagonistic set of muscles contracts, it bends (flexes) the limb; it is therefore called a flexor. The antagonist muscle, the extensor,

Figure 43.15 A Neural Network in the Spinal Cord Generates the Knee-Jerk Reflex Sensory (afferent) information enters the spinal cord through the dorsal horns, and motor (efferent) output leaves it via the ventral horns. Information travels to the brain in white matter tracts. Interneurons make connections within the spinal cord that result in a complex, coordinated behavior pattern.

▶ View in **Achieve**
   Animation 43.4 **Information Processing in the Spinal Cord**

1 A hammer tap stretches the tendon in the knee, stretching receptors in the extensor muscle.

2 Stretch receptors fire action potentials.

3 In a monosynaptic pathway, the sensory neuron synapses with a motor neuron in the ventral horn of the spinal cord.

Dorsal root (afferent nerves)
White matter
Gray matter
Dorsal horn

Ventral root (efferent nerves)

4 The motor neuron conducts action potentials to the extensor muscle, causing contraction.

Motor neurons
Inhibitory interneuron
Ventral horn

6 The leg extends.

5 A multiple synapse pathway involving a spinal interneuron inhibits firing in the motor neuron for the antagonistic muscle.

— Sensory (afferent) pathway
— Motor (efferent) pathway
— Interneuron pathway

Human

Cerebrum

Olfactory lobe

The brain region that processes olfactory information is relatively more developed in the pig than in the human.

In humans, much of the brain is given over to integration of complex behaviors, learning, and memory.

Cerebellum
Brainstem

Pig

The cerebellum integrates sensory and motor information.

Olfactory lobe

Alligator

Brainstem structures serve basic physiological functions.

Shark

Figure 43.16 Brains Vary in Size and Complexity The brains of four vertebrate species—all of which may have a similar body mass—show immense differences. Note that the brainstem, which is involved in physiological regulation and stereotypic behavior, differs less among these species than does the cerebrum, which is responsible for complex behavior and learning.

Q: What sensory capability do you think is well developed in the pig?

straightens (extends) the limb. For a limb to move, one muscle of the pair must relax while the other contracts. Thus sensory input that activates the motor neuron of one muscle also inhibits its antagonist. This coordination is achieved by an interneuron between the sensory neuron and the motor neuron of the antagonist muscle (see Figure 43.15). Thus the reciprocal inhibition of antagonistic muscles involves at least two synapses.

The withdrawal reflex is an example of a polysynaptic spinal reflex that involves many interneurons. When you step on a tack, you immediately pull back your foot, but you don't fall over because many other muscles change your posture. The tack stimulates pain receptors in the foot, and the sensory neurons transmit APs into the dorsal horn of the spinal cord on the same side of the body. In the dorsal horn, these neurons synapse with a variety of interneurons. Some send the pain information through their axons to the brain, resulting in the conscious sensation of pain. But even before the brain is aware of the pain, other interneurons coordinate the withdrawal of the foot with actions of other muscles to shift your weight onto the other leg. Thus a rather complex suite of movements is coordinated by a network of interneurons in the spinal cord. By extension, you can appreciate how much more complex the neural networks are that enable you to execute complex movements in time with music and coordinated with another person—in other words, to dance.

The vertebrate brain is the seat of behavioral complexity

Vertebrates differ greatly in their behavioral complexity and in their physiological specializations, and their neural networks reflect this diversity. **Figure 43.16** shows the brains of four vertebrate species of similar body mass drawn to the same scale.

The current estimate for the number of neurons in the human brain is 8.6×10^{10}. A given neuron in the brain can have 1,000 or more synapses. Thus the human brain can contain 10^{14} synapses ($\sim 10^{11}$ neurons $\times \sim 10^3$ synapses per neuron). Then there are the glia currently estimated to be about the same number as neurons. A single astrocyte might participate in thousands of synapses while at the same time monitoring signals in the extracellular fluid and the blood. In addition, synapses are not constant but can be highly plastic. They can increase or decrease in number and size, and they can become more or less sensitive.

This astronomical number of neurons and synapses is divided into thousands of distinct but interacting networks that function in parallel. The possible number of information networks in the brain is almost infinite, and therein lies the incredible ability of the human brain to process information, to learn, to do complex tasks, to remember, and to have emotions.

KEY CONCEPT
43.4 Recap and Assess

Nervous systems are composed of neural networks that include afferent neurons, interneurons, and efferent neurons. Nervous systems range in complexity from simple nerve nets to the human brain. The spinal knee-jerk reflex is an example of a simple neural network, but networks that control more complex behavior are much more complicated.

1. What are ganglia, and why are they concentrated in the anterior region of many invertebrates?

2. Draw or describe the flow of information from stimulus to response in the knee-jerk reflex circuit.

3. In the knee-jerk reflex circuit, how can the same stimulus cause contraction in one muscle and relaxation in another?

▶Investigating**LIFE**

Q and A Can learning be restored in mouse models of Down syndrome?

Some neurotransmitter–receptor combinations excite activity in the postsynaptic neuron, depolarizing it and making it likely to fire an AP. Other neurotransmitter–receptor combinations inhibit the responses of the postsynaptic cell. Neurons integrate information by summing excitatory and inhibitory synaptic inputs. Overinhibition in the nervous system can arise when too much inhibitory neurotransmitter (such as GABA) is released, or if postsynaptic cells have too many receptors for inhibitory neurotransmitters. Drugs that decrease the synthesis and release of the inhibitory neurotransmitter can reduce the inhibition, as can drugs that block the receptors for such neurotransmitters. In the case of the Down syndrome model mice, drugs such as pentylenetetrazole, which blocked the GABA receptors (which function also as Cl^- channels), reduced the level of inhibition in the mouse nervous system and increased the ability of the mice to learn and form memories.

Future directions

Going from experiments on the effects of drugs on mice to a therapy for humans is a difficult path. To protect patients, the federal Food and Drug Administration (FDA) has a rigorous procedure for approving drugs for human use. After a candidate drug is shown to be effective and safe in animal models, four stages of approval must be passed before a drug is allowed on the market. In Phase 0, the first in-human trials are conducted on a small group of volunteers to study how the body absorbs, distributes, metabolizes, and excretes the drug, and whether it has any obvious side effects. In Phase 1, trials are conducted in a small group of volunteers to evaluate safety and dosage, and again to look for side effects. Phase 2 involves a larger group of subjects who have the disease that the drug is expected to treat, to see if it is effective and safe. The comparison is with a placebo. In Phase 3, trials are conducted with a large group of patients to assess the drug's effectiveness and safety, and to compare it with other commonly used treatments. Each of these phases must be reviewed by the FDA and approved before proceeding to the next phase.

VISUAL SUMMARY 43

Courtesy of Philip Haydon

You should be able to relate each summary to the adjacent figures. If you go to this visual summary in **Achieve**, you can follow links to figures, animations, activities, and simulations that will help you consolidate the material.

KEY CONCEPT
43.1 Neurons and Glia Are Unique Cells of Nervous Systems

- **Neurons** generate and conduct electric signals, and most can generate **action potentials** (**APs**). **Glia** support and modulate the activities of neurons but do not generate APs.

- A neuron receives information via its **dendrites** and transmits information via its **axon**.

- Neurons communicate with target cells at **synapses**.

Figure 43.1 Presynaptic cell   Postsynaptic cell

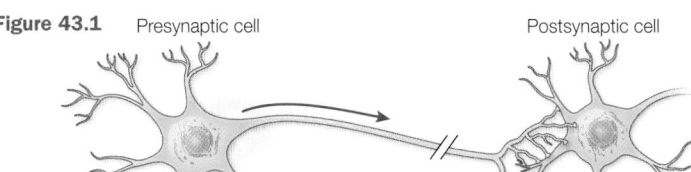

- Glia include **Schwann cells** and **oligodendrocytes**, both of which generate **myelin** sheaths on axons.

- Glia also include **astrocytes**, which support neurons metabolically, modulate synaptic signaling, and contribute to the **blood–brain barrier** and the **glymphatic system**.

Questions

1. How do neurons integrate information from multiple sources?
2. Why are neurons that communicate over chemical synapses better for integrating different inputs than are neurons that communicate over electrical synapses?
3. How does the glymphatic system remove metabolic wastes from the brain?

KEY CONCEPT
43.2 Neurons Generate and Transmit Electric Signals

Go to Animations 43.1 and 43.2

- The **sodium–potassium (Na⁺–K⁺) pump** concentrates K^+ on the inside of a neuron and Na^+ on the outside. Permeability of the membrane to K^+ allows K^+ to diffuse out, leaving behind unbalanced negative charges, creating the **resting potential**.

- The resting potential is altered by the opening or closing of ion channels that **depolarize** or **hyperpolarize** the membrane, producing a **graded membrane potential**.

- An AP is a rapid, all-or-none, transient reversal in charge across a portion of the cell membrane resulting from the sequential opening and closing of voltage-gated Na^+ and K^+ channels.

- APs are conducted down non-myelinated axons because local current brings adjacent regions of membrane to threshold. These events jump between **nodes of Ranvier** in myelinated axons.

Questions

1. Why is there a negative electric potential across neuronal membranes?
2. Why does myelination increase AP conduction speed?

Figure 43.9

Amplifier

Time →

Outside axon
+ + + +   + +   + +
– – – – – – – – – – –
Inside axon

+ + + + + + + + + +
Outside axon

KEY CONCEPT
43.3 Neurons Communicate with Other Cells

Go to Activity 43.1, Animation 43.3, and Simulation 43.1

- Neurons communicate with other cell types at **electrical synapses** or **chemical synapses**.

- The **neuromuscular junction** is a chemical synapse between a **motor neuron** and a skeletal muscle cell. Its neurotransmitter is **acetylcholine (ACh)**, which causes depolarization of the postsynaptic **motor end plate**.

- At chemical synapses, APs cause the release of neurotransmitters, which diffuse across the **synaptic cleft** and bind to postsynaptic receptors.

- Synapses between neurons can be either excitatory or inhibitory, and postsynaptic neurons can sum excitatory and inhibitory postsynaptic potentials both spatially and temporally.

- There are many different neurotransmitters and types of receptors. The action of a neurotransmitter depends on the type of receptor to which it binds.

- Neurotransmitter molecules must be cleared from the synapse to turn off responses in the postsynaptic cell.

Questions

1. How does an AP cause release of neurotransmitter at the neuromuscular synapse?
2. How do graded membrane potentials relate to integration of information by postsynaptic neurons?
3. What are four ways that neurotransmitter action can be terminated?

Figure 43.12

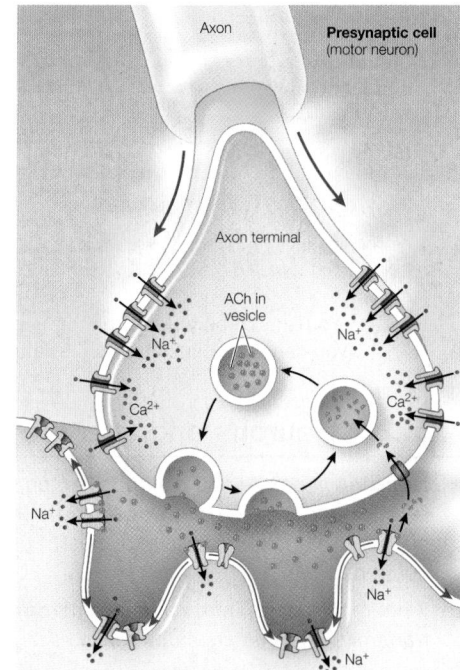

Axon

Presynaptic cell
(motor neuron)

Axon terminal

ACh in vesicle

Na^+

Ca^{2+}

Na^+

Na^+

Na^+

KEY CONCEPT

43.4   Neurons and Glia Form Information-Processing Circuits

Go to Animation 43.4

- In vertebrates, the **brain** and spinal cord form the central nervous system, which communicates with the rest of the body through the peripheral nervous system.

- The CNS increases in complexity from invertebrates to vertebrates and from fishes to mammals.

- **Neural networks** include **afferent neurons** and **efferent neurons**, generally connected through **interneurons**.

- A **spinal reflex** is a simple neural network.

Figure 43.15

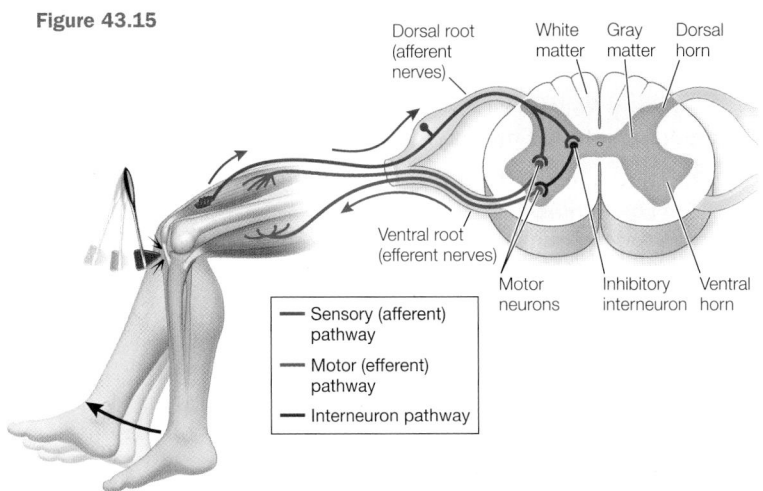

Questions

1. What are the differences between a nerve net, a ganglion, and a brain?

2. When considering fishes, then reptiles, then mammals, which part of the vertebrate brain increases most in size?

3. What are the roles of interneurons in the withdrawal reflex?

Go to **Achieve** for the eBook, **LearningCurve**, animations, activities, simulations, and additional resources and assignments.

44 Sensory Systems

KEY CONCEPTS

44.1 Sensory Receptor Cells Convert Stimuli into Action Potentials

44.2 Chemoreceptors Respond to Specific Molecules

44.3 Mechanoreceptors Respond to Physical Forces

44.4 Photoreceptors Respond to Light

The "holes" below the eyes of this rattlesnake are the pit organs that detect infrared radiation from the snake's preferred prey—small rodents—with precision, even in total darkness. The forked tongue also provides information, picking up chemical signals (odors) that are detected by a specialized organ in the roof of the snake's mouth.

© John Cancalosi/Alamy Stock Photo

▶Investigating LIFE

Seeing in the Dark

A rattlesnake can see to strike a running rodent in complete darkness. How can this be, when "seeing" means using the eyes to detect light, and "complete darkness" means no light? But these definitions are based on human capabilities. What we experience as light is only a small portion of the spectrum of electromagnetic radiation. We see wavelengths that we call red, orange, yellow, green, blue, indigo, and violet, but other animals see wavelengths humans cannot. Some insects, for example, perceive patterns on flowers that reflect ultraviolet wavelengths invisible to humans (see Figure 27.15). Similarly, rattlesnakes "see" infrared wavelengths that we cannot (although at high enough levels of intensity, humans feel infrared wavelengths as heat).

It is not the snake's eyes that perceive infrared light. Pit vipers, rattlesnakes, and their relatives have pit organs located between the nostril and the eye on each side of the head that contain high densities of infrared-sensitive neurons. The two pits are positioned in such a way that sensory receptor cells in the pits receive directional information. Information from the pit organs goes to the same region of the brain as information from the eyes, so rattlesnakes actually do "see" the world in a range of electromagnetic radiation that is different from the human visual spectrum.

Our definition of silence is as human-oriented as our definition of darkness. "Sound" is actually pressure waves in the environment, and many animals are sensitive to pressure waves with frequencies, or pitches, we cannot hear. Elephants communicate using sound waves that are below human hearing range; such long waves travel great distances, an advantage to large animals that roam over extensive areas. Bats emit incredibly loud, brief sound pulses that are above our range of hearing. A flying bat hears echoes of these pulses bouncing off objects in the environment and can therefore avoid obstacles and catch prey in total darkness.

"Reality" to us is what our eyes see, our ears hear, our noses smell, and what we touch and taste. Humans sense only a limited range of the information available. Animals with different ranges of sensitivity process different sources of information and perceive the world quite differently than we do. A challenge for neurobiologists is to understand how neurons are adapted to detect different types of information in the environment.

 How do pit vipers "see" in the dark? (Find the answer on page 1003.)

Sensory Receptor Cells Convert Stimuli into Action Potentials

Learning Objectives

44.1.1 Describe the roles of receptor potentials and action potentials in sensory systems.

44.1.2 Explain how the same membrane event, an action potential, can result in sensations of heat, light, sound, touch, or taste.

44.1.3 Describe the various ways that environmental stimuli can generate receptor potentials.

44.1.4 Explain the functional significance of sensory adaptation.

Sensory receptor cells, usually called **sensors** or **receptors**, transduce (convert) physical and chemical stimuli such as light and sound waves, pressure (e.g., touch), and odorant and taste molecules into neuronal signals. These signals are then transmitted to the central nervous system (CNS) for processing and interpretation. The first step in this process of **sensory transduction** is a change in the membrane potential of the receptor cell in response to a specific type of stimulus.

Sensory transduction involves changes in membrane potentials

Sensory transduction typically begins with a **receptor protein** that opens or closes ion channels in response to a specific stimulus such as heat, light, chemicals, mechanical force, or electric fields. The resulting change in membrane permeability to ions alters the receptor cell's membrane potential. A change in the membrane potential of a receptor cell in response to a stimulus is a **receptor potential**. Receptor potentials are graded membrane potentials that spread over only short distances. To signal over long distances in the nervous system, receptor potentials must generate action potentials, which they can do in two ways:

1. The receptor potential may trigger action potentials in the receptor cell itself.

2. The receptor potential may cause the receptor cell to release neurotransmitters that induce a postsynaptic neuron to generate action potentials.

A good model of how a receptor cell generates action potentials is the **stretch receptor** of a crayfish (**Figure 44.1**). Stretching the muscle to which the stretch receptor is attached causes receptor potentials. These receptor potentials spread to the base of the cell's axon, where they generate action potentials that travel down the axon to the CNS. The rate at which action potentials are fired depends on the magnitude of the receptor potential; that magnitude, in turn, depends on how much the muscle is stretched.

In a receptor cell that does not fire action potentials (such as the photoreceptors in the vertebrate eye), the spreading receptor potential reaches a presynaptic patch of cell membrane and induces the

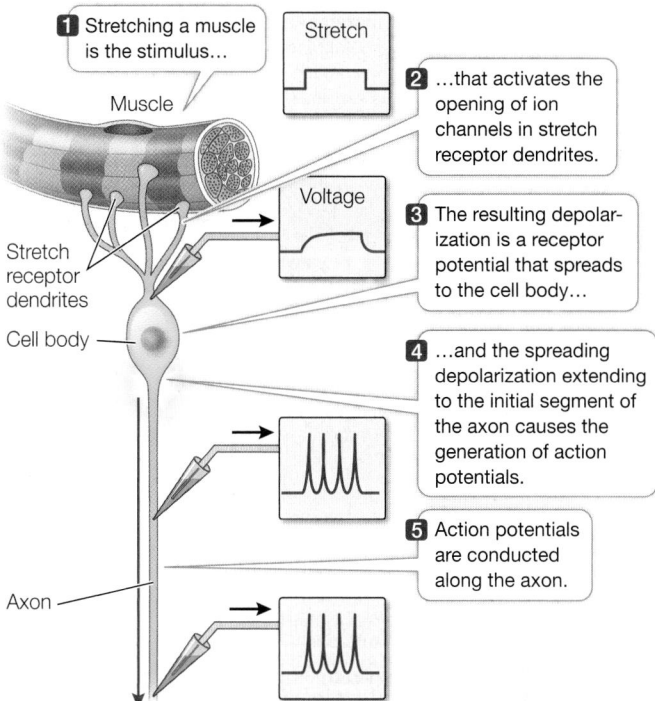

Figure 44.1 Stimulating a Sensory Cell Produces a Receptor Potential   Signal transduction in the stretch receptor of a crayfish can be investigated by measuring the membrane potential at different places on the stretch receptor neuron while stretching the muscle innervated by that sensory neuron.

release of a neurotransmitter. The intensity of the stimulus influences how much neurotransmitter is released. That neurotransmitter binds to receptor proteins on an associated sensory neuron, altering its membrane potential and causing it to increase or decrease its rate of firing action potentials. In a few cases, this second cell also does not generate action potentials, but simply changes the rate at which it releases neurotransmitter onto another neuron. Eventually, however, the stimulation of a sensory cell is always coded as a change in firing of action potentials in a sensory circuit.

Sensory receptor proteins act on ion channels

Sensory receptor proteins respond to stimuli by directly or indirectly opening or closing ion channels in the sensory cell (**Figure 44.2**), leading either to an action potential or to the release of neurotransmitter. Those sensory receptor proteins that act directly on membrane potential are either ion channels themselves or directly affect the opening of an associated ion channel. Examples are receptors that respond to physical force (mechanoreceptors) and those that respond to temperature (thermoreceptors). Electroreceptors do not have receptor proteins, but their cell membranes are sensitive to voltage changes and respond to depolarization by opening voltage-gated Ca^{2+} channels, and the Ca^{2+} triggers neurotransmitter release. Sensory receptor proteins that influence ion channels indirectly usually do so by activating G proteins and second messengers, as described in Key Concepts 7.2 and 7.3. Examples are most chemoreceptors and photoreceptors.

Figure 44.2 Sensory Cell Membrane Receptor Proteins Respond to Stimuli Mechanoreceptors and thermoreceptors have transmembrane proteins that are also cation channels. Changes in their respective stimuli, pressure or heat, alter the permeability of the channels. Electroreceptors are ion channels responsive to electric currents. Chemoreceptors and photoreceptors influence ion channels through G proteins and second messengers.

To discover the molecular mechanisms by which infrared radiation is detected, a large superfamily of receptor proteins called transient receptor potential (TRP) channel proteins are the focus of investigation. TRP channels generate large initial responses to stimuli and then gradually fade even as the stimuli remain constant. Seven classes of TRP channels have been identified, along with about 28 different molecular structures. Each type of TRP channel is specialized to respond to a different stimulus, such as stretch, pressure, temperature, light, or certain chemicals. Some respond to both physical and chemical stimuli, such as one that responds to heat, capsaicin (an active ingredient in chili peppers), and wasabi. Could a heat-sensitive TRP channel be responsible for the infrared-detection function of the pit organs of rattlesnakes? We pursue this question in **Investigating Life: How Do Pit Vipers "See" in the Dark?**

Sensation depends on which neurons receive action potentials from sensory cells

All sensory systems process information in the form of action potentials. But the sensations we perceive—heat, pressure, light, smell, sound—differ because the messages from different kinds of sensory cells arrive at different places in the CNS. Action potentials arriving in the visual cortex of the brain are interpreted as light, whereas those that arrive in the olfactory bulb are perceived as smells.

A small patch of skin on your arm contains some sensory receptor cells that increase their firing rates when the skin is warmed and others that increase their activity when the skin is cooled. Other sensory cells in the same patch of skin respond to touch, irritants such as insect bites, and painful stimuli. These receptor cells transmit their messages through axons that enter the CNS at the spinal cord. The synapses made by those axons in the spinal cord and the subsequent pathways of transmission determine whether the stimulation of the skin on your arm is perceived as warmth, cold,

touch, itch, or pain; even though the action potentials carried by all of these sensory axons are the same, the connectivity of each axon is specific for a given sensory modality. The *intensity* of a given sensation is coded by the frequency of the action potentials.

Some sensory receptors transmit information about the body's internal conditions of which we are not consciously aware. The brain continuously receives information about body temperature, the concentrations of carbon dioxide and oxygen in the blood, arterial pressure, muscle tension, and the position of the limbs. All of this information is important for homeostasis but does not necessarily result in conscious sensation.

Some sensory receptor cells are assembled with other types of cells into **sensory organs**, such as eyes, ears, and noses, that enhance the ability of sensory cells to collect, filter, and amplify stimuli. **Sensory systems** include the sensory cells, their associated organs, and the neuronal networks that process the information.

Many receptors adapt to repeated stimulation

Some sensory receptor cells give gradually diminishing responses to maintained or repeated stimulation. This phenomenon, known as **sensory adaptation**, enables an animal to ignore background or unchanging conditions while remaining sensitive to changes and new information. (Note that this use of the term "adaptation" is different from its application in an evolutionary context.) When you get dressed, you feel each item of clothing touch your skin, but the sensation of clothes touching your skin is not constantly on your mind throughout the day. You are immediately aware of new sensations, however, such as your shoe coming untied or someone touching your back.

Some sensory receptor cells adapt very little or very slowly; examples are some types of pain receptors and the mechanoreceptors that control balance. You do not want to ignore pain, which usually is signaling that something is wrong in your body, and to

▶Investigating**LIFE**   How Do Pit Vipers "See" in the Dark?

Experiment

Original Paper: E. O. Gracheva et al. 2010. Molecular basis of infrared detection by snakes. *Nature* 464: 1006–1012.

Neurons of the pit organ have their cell bodies in a neuronal ganglion in the head—the trigeminal ganglion (TG). Sensory neurons conducting information from the body of the snake have their cell bodies in neuronal ganglia associated with the spinal cord—the dorsal root ganglia (DRGs). Any receptor protein that is involved in sensing heat by the pit organ or by temperature sensors in the skin should be expressed in the TG or the DRGs, respectively.

HYPOTHESIS▶   Different transient receptor potential (TRP) channel proteins responsive to heat are expressed in the TG and the DRGs, and they have different properties.

METHOD▶   Many neurons in the TG of rattlesnakes innervate the pit organs, and therefore the RNA transcripts for any protein that is abundant in the pit organ nerve endings should be highly expressed in the TG. Similarly, RNA transcripts for sensory receptor proteins in the skin of the body should be highly expressed in the DRGs. Whole genome RNA sequencing (RNA-seq) was used to create the RNA profiles of the TG and the DRGs of the rattlesnake. Of particular interest were specific TRP RNA reads (specific RNA sequences) that were differentially expressed in the TG and the DRGs. If there are more reads for a certain TRP channel in the TG versus the DRGs, that TRP channel might play a role in the pit organ's ability to sense infrared radiation. Because the range of read values was so large, the data are plotted as logarithmic values (log–log plot).

RESULTS▶

CONCLUSION▶

1. TRPV1 and "Other TRPs" are expressed equally in the TG and the DRGs, so they probably are not responsible for the unique infrared-sensing properties of the pit organ.

2. TRPA1 is expressed more in the TG than in the DRGs. This channel could therefore serve a unique function in the pit organ.

---

maintain equilibrium you must continuously know (albeit unconsciously) the tensions and forces on all of your joints and muscles.

KEY CONCEPT
44.1 Recap and Assess

Sensory receptor cells have receptor proteins that respond to specific stimuli from the external or internal environment by directly or indirectly opening or closing ion channels, causing the generation of action potentials or neurotransmitter release in sensory neurons. How the resulting information is processed and interpreted depends on the neuronal circuitry that is activated.

1. In the crayfish stretch receptor, what creates the receptor potential? Where and how does it stimulate an action potential?

2. How are we able to perceive action potentials—all of which are essentially the same—as different sensations?

3. Peppers have a distinctive flavor, but they also can be hot if they contain the molecule capsaicin. Explain the difference in how the flavor versus the hotness of a pepper is sensed.

4. Why is adaptation or the lack thereof important in different sensory modalities?

Now that you have a general view of how sensory systems code and process information, let's turn to how sensory systems gather and filter stimuli, transduce specific stimuli into action potentials, and transmit action potentials to the CNS, which perceives them as different types of information.

Work with the Data

The data from the experiment comparing TRP channel expression in the TG and the DRGs support the conclusion that the TRPA1 channel could be the infrared (IR) sensor in the pit organ. Another piece of evidence would be finding that the *TRPA1* gene is not highly expressed in the TG of snakes without pit organs, or that it is highly expressed in snakes not closely related to rattlesnakes but that have pit organs. Accordingly, the investigators performed RNA-seq analysis of the TG and the DRGs of rat snakes (no pits) and pythons (pits).

RESULTS▶   (Simulated data, arbitrary units)

| | Rat snake | | Python | |
Channel	TG	DRGs	TG	DRGs
TRPA1	105	110	900,000	50
TRPV1	85	90	15	9

QUESTIONS▶

1. Compare the relative expression of TRPV1 and TRPA1 in the TG and the DRGs of the rat snake (no pits) and the python (pits). What is the major difference?

2. Explain how these results do or do not support the conclusion that the TRPA1 channel is the IR sensor in the pit organ.

3. What functional data on the TRPA1 channel would further support the conclusion that TRPA1 is the IR sensor in the pit organ?

Go to Achieve for a companion Data in Depth exercise.

Chemoreceptors Respond to Specific Molecules

Learning Objectives

44.2.1 Explain how a large but limited number of olfactory receptor proteins can discriminate a much larger number of odorant molecules, as well as their concentrations.

44.2.2 Explain how the five classes of taste receptors generate action potentials in their sensory neurons.

A colony of corals responds to a small amount of meat extract in seawater by extending its coral polyps and their tentacles in search of food; a solution of a single type of amino acid can stimulate this response. Conversely, a small amount of seawater in which corals were crushed will stimulate a defensive retraction of the coral polyps. Humans also react strongly to certain chemical stimuli. When you smell freshly baked bread you salivate and feel hungry, and when you smell rotting meat you feel nauseated.

All animals receive information about chemical stimuli through **chemoreceptors**, which are receptor proteins that bind to specific molecules (their **ligands**) and are responsible for smell and taste. Chemoreceptors are also responsible for monitoring some aspects of the internal environment, such as the level of carbon dioxide in the blood.

Olfaction is the sense of smell

The sense of smell, **olfaction**, depends on chemoreceptors. In vertebrates the olfactory receptors are neurons embedded in a layer of epithelial tissue in the uppermost region of the nasal cavity (**Figure 44.3**). The dendrites of these neurons project as olfactory cilia on the surface of the nasal epithelium, and their axons extend through holes in the overlying bone into the **olfactory bulb**

(the olfactory integration area of the brain). A protective layer of mucus covers the nasal cavity epithelium. Molecules from the environment must diffuse through this mucus to reach the receptor proteins on the olfactory cilia. When you have a cold, the amount of mucus in your nasal cavity increases, and the epithelium swells. With this in mind, you can easily understand why respiratory infections cause loss of your sense of smell.

An **odorant** is a molecule in the environment that binds to and activates an olfactory receptor protein on the cilia of **olfactory receptor neurons** (**ORNs**). Different olfactory receptor proteins bind specific subsets of odorant molecules. An odorant molecule binding to its receptor on an ORN activates a G protein. The G protein then activates an enzyme that causes an increase of a second messenger (cAMP in vertebrates) in the cytoplasm. The second messenger binds to and opens cation channels in the ORN's cell membrane, causing an influx of Na^+ into the ORN, which depolarizes to threshold and fires action potentials. An interesting feature of ORNs is that they are continuously regenerated. ORNs have to be constantly replaced because they are embedded in nasal epithelium, which sheds regularly, as do other epithelial linings.

Connect the Concepts Key Concept 7.2 describes how G protein-coupled receptors transmit signals from a variety of stimuli outside a cell to its interior. Ligand binding of the receptor activates the G protein on the cytoplasmic surface of the membrane. A subunit of the G protein separates and travels along the membrane to activate an effector protein.

The olfactory world has an enormous number of odors and a correspondingly large number of olfactory receptor proteins. In the 1990s Linda Buck and Richard Axel discovered a family of about 1,000 genes in mice (about 3% of the mouse genome) that code for olfactory receptor proteins. Each receptor protein that is expressed is found in a limited number of ORNs in the olfactory epithelium, and each ORN expresses just one receptor

3 Neurons in a glomerulus receive input only from receptor cells expressing the same receptor gene.

2 Action potentials generated by odorant binding are transmitted to glomeruli in the olfactory bulb.

1 Olfactory cilia have receptors that bind specific odorant molecules.

START

Olfactory bulb Glomeruli

Bone
Connective tissue
Basal cell
Olfactory receptor neuron (ORN)
Supporting cell
Dendrite

Olfactory bulb
Nasal cavity
Odorant molecules
Olfactory epithelium
Mucus film Odorant molecules

Figure 44.3 Olfactory Receptors Communicate Information Directly to the Brain The receptor cells of the human olfactory system are embedded in epithelial tissues lining the nasal cavity and send their axons to the olfactory bulb of the brain.

type. The investigators matched specific gene products with the odorants they detect. For their discoveries of the molecular nature of the olfactory system, Buck and Axel received a Nobel Prize in 2004.

Olfactory sensitivity involves discrimination of many more odorants than there are olfactory receptors. An odorant molecule can be quite complex, and different regions of that molecule may bind to different receptor proteins. The next stage of processing olfactory information occurs in the olfactory bulb, where axons from ORNs expressing the same receptor protein make synapses with olfactory bulb neurons that contribute their axons to the olfactory tract. The globular tangles of axons from ORNs and dendrites from olfactory bulb neurons are called **olfactory glomeruli** (see Figure 44.3). A complex odorant molecule can activate a unique combination of glomeruli in the olfactory bulb, so an olfactory system with hundreds of different receptor proteins can discriminate an astronomically large number of smells. The more odorant molecules that bind to ORNs, the greater the frequency of action potentials and thus the greater the intensity of the perceived smell.

Humans have a sensitive olfactory system, but in comparison with most mammals we depend far more on vision than on olfaction. The nasal epithelium of a typical dog is 15–20 times larger than a human's and has about *300 million* odorant receptors, compared with about 6 million in the average human. For some scents, the threshold sensitivity of the dog is 100,000 times lower; a dog's nose reveals a huge amount of information not available to people.

Some chemoreceptors detect pheromones

A chemical signal used for communication among conspecifics (individuals of the same species) is called a **pheromone**. Individual animals secrete pheromone molecules into the environment, triggering behavioral responses in other individuals of the species. Pheromones may attract mates, communicate alarm signals, mark food trails, or define territories, among many other uses. Their function in mate attraction illustrates the remarkable sensitivity of chemosensory systems, and the silkworm moth *Bombyx mori* is an extensively studied example.

To attract a mate, the female silkworm moth releases a pheromone called bombykol from a gland at the tip of her abdomen (**Figure 44.4A**). The male silkworm moth has about 10,000 receptors for this molecule on each of his feathery antennae (**Figure 44.4B**). A single molecule of bombykol may be sufficient to generate action potentials in the antennal nerve, which transmits the signal to the male's CNS. The extreme sensitivity of the male bombykol receptors ensures that the sexual message sent by a female moth is likely to reach any male within a huge downwind area. The rate of firing in the male's sensory nerves is proportional to the concentration of bombykol in the air, so by flying upwind he can follow an airborne concentration gradient to "home in" on the signaling female.

(A) Release of pheromone by female

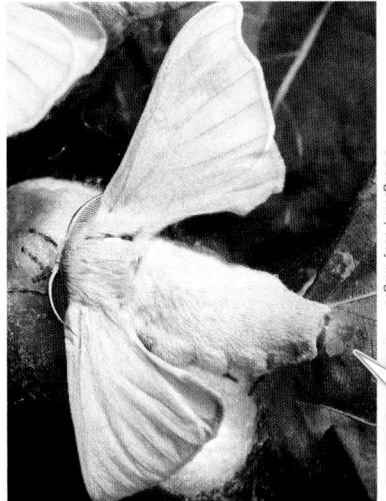

The female moth releases a pheromone from a gland at the tip of her abdomen. The pheromone can travel thousands of meters downwind.

(B) Detection of pheromone by male

A male moth detects this pheromone in the air passing over his antennae, which are covered with chemosensitive hairs.

Figure 44.4 Pheromones Can Communicate over Great Distances   Mating in silkworm moths of the genus *Bombyx* is coordinated by a pheromone called bombykol.

Q: Molecules have different diffusion coefficients. *Bombykol* has a high diffusion coefficient. How do you think its diffusion coefficient would compare with that of a territory-marking pheromone, and why might they be different?

The vomeronasal organ contains chemoreceptors

The **vomeronasal organ** (**VNO**) is a small, paired tubular structure embedded in the nasal epithelium of many species of amphibians, reptiles, and mammals (not including humans). In mammals the VNO is located on the septum dividing the two nostrils (see Figure 51.3) and has a pore that opens into the nasal cavity. The VNO pulsates and draws a sample of nasal fluid over the chemoreceptors embedded in its walls. The information from these chemoreceptors goes to an accessory olfactory bulb in the brain, and from there to brain regions involved in sexual and other instinctive behaviors. The VNO of a rodent detects pheromones that signal the sex, strain, identity, and sexual receptivity of another individual.

In snakes the VNO opens into the roof of the mouth cavity. Each time the snake's forked tongue darts in and out, the forks fit into the VNO openings and present the chemoreceptors located there with a sample of molecules from the surrounding air (see the chapter opening photo). Thus the snake uses its tongue to smell its environment, not to taste it. Why doesn't the snake simply use the flow of air to and from its lungs, as we do, to smell the environment? In snakes, air flows to and from the lungs slowly (and can even stop entirely for long periods of time), but the tongue can dart in and out rapidly. It is a quick source of olfactory information used in social communication and hunting prey.

Gustation is the sense of taste

In humans and other vertebrates, the sense of taste, **gustation**, depends on clusters of chemoreceptors called **taste buds**. The taste buds of terrestrial vertebrates are confined to the mouth cavity, but some fishes have taste buds in the skin that enhance their ability to sense their environment. Some fishes living in murky water are very sensitive to small amounts of amino acids in the water and

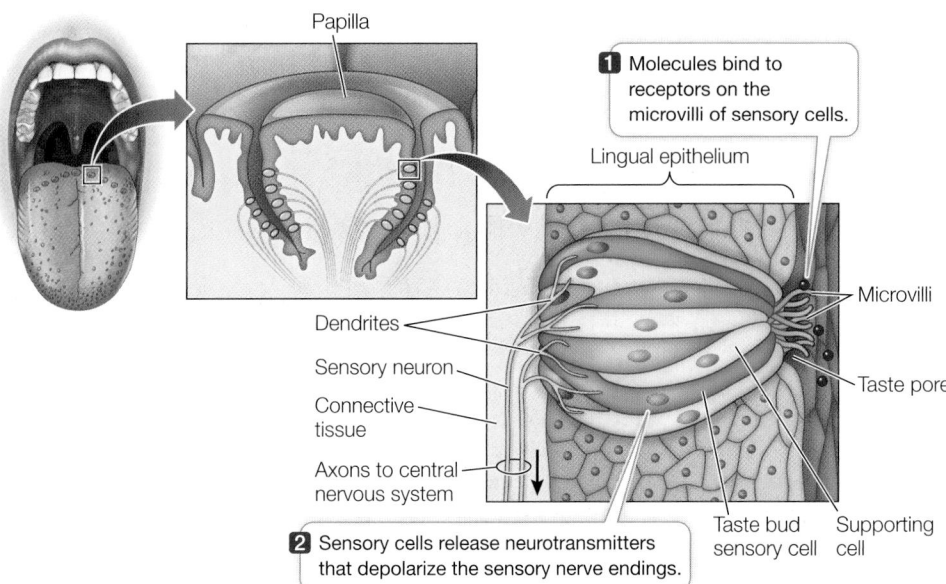

Papilla

1 Molecules bind to receptors on the microvilli of sensory cells.

Lingual epithelium

Dendrites

Sensory neuron

Connective tissue

Axons to central nervous system

Microvilli

Taste pore

2 Sensory cells release neurotransmitters that depolarize the sensory nerve endings.

Taste bud sensory cell

Supporting cell

Figure 44.5 Taste Buds Are Clusters of Sensory Cells A human tongue has as many as 10,000 taste buds, most of which are found on the raised papillae.

can find food without the use of vision. The duck-billed platypus, a prototherian mammal (see Figure 31.26B), has a similar ability as a result of taste buds on the sensitive skin of its bill.

The human tongue has 5,000–10,000 taste buds embedded in the epithelium. Most of them are found on the sides of the papillae (**Figure 44.5**). (Look at your tongue in a mirror—the papillae make it look fuzzy.) The outer surface of a taste bud has a pore that exposes the tips of the sensory receptor cells. Microvilli (tiny hairlike projections) increase the surface area of these cells where their tips converge at the pore. These chemoreceptor cells generate action potentials and release neurotransmitter at their bases, where they form synapses with sensory neurons that convey the signals to the CNS.

The tongue does a lot of hard work, so its epithelium, along with cells of its taste buds, is shed and replaced at a rapid rate. Individual taste bud cells last about 10 days before they are replaced, but the sensory neurons associated with them live on, constantly forming new synapses as new taste buds form.

Gustation begins with the membrane receptor proteins of the microvilli of the taste bud sensory cells (see Figure 44.5). Humans perceive five taste classes: sweet, salty, sour, bitter, and umami. However, taste buds can distinguish among a variety of sweet-tasting molecules and a variety of bitter-tasting molecules. Umami is a savory, meaty taste that is stimulated by amino acids, including monosodium glutamate (MSG), a commonly used flavor enhancer. Sweet, bitter, and umami tastes are the functions of a small family of G protein-coupled TRP channels. Other TRP channels related to the ones you saw associated with heat sensation in Investigating Life: How Do Pit Vipers "See" in the Dark? are responsible for spicy and hot tastes. Still other TRP channels that act as cold sensors are activated by minty, cool-tasting foods. Saltiness receptor proteins allow Na^+ to diffuse into taste bud sensory cells through open Na^+ channels, depolarizing the sensory cell. Sourness receptors are

activated by a direct effect of H^+ ions on Na^+ channels.

Various selective pressures led to the evolution of diversity in gustatory receptors. Receptors for bitter tastes may have evolved as protective mechanisms enabling animals to detect toxic plant compounds such as quinine, caffeine, and nicotine. Because many such toxic compounds evolved in plants as protections against herbivorous predators, having a variety of receptors in those herbivores is a product of the continuous "arms race" between predators and prey (see Key Concept 54.1). Also, a large number of molecules in food could indicate nutritional value, so having a variety of receptors is advantageous. The diversity of sweet receptors helps explain why it has been possible to invent many chemically distinct artificial sweeteners.

Regardless of the mechanism of taste transduction by the receptors of the taste buds, all these cells release neurotransmitter onto sensory neurons. These neurons then generate action potentials that are conducted to the CNS, where they are interpreted as specific taste sensations. The full complexity of the chemosensitivity that enables us to enjoy the subtle flavors of food comes from the combined activation of gustatory and olfactory receptors, which is why you may lose your sense of taste when you have a cold.

KEY CONCEPT
44.2 Recap and Assess

All animals receive information about chemical stimuli through chemoreceptors, which have diverse structures and bind to a tremendous variety of ligands. Chemoreceptors are the basis of the sensations of olfaction and gustation and the reception of pheromones. They also monitor some aspects of an animal's internal environment.

1. Different odorants have different cell surface receptors, but these receptors activate the same intracellular G protein signaling pathway. How does the olfactory system discriminate different odors?

2. How does the olfactory system discriminate between the whiff of a skunk, a repulsive odor of skunk, and the smell of a skunk cabbage?

3. The concentration thresholds for sensing bitter tastes are lower than for salt or sweet. Offer an evolutionary explanation for why this is so.

4. With only five classes of taste receptors, how can we discriminate so many different tastes?

You have now seen how chemoreceptors give rise to the sensations of smell and taste, and how some animals use chemoreception to communicate with others of their species. Next we describe the sensory cells that respond to mechanical forces, including the vibrations you perceive as sound.

Learning Objectives

44.3.1 Describe the various touch sensors and their unique properties.

44.3.2 Describe how tension in a muscle is sensed and adjusted for load.

44.3.3 Explain how sound waves of different frequencies are heard as sounds of different pitches.

The cell membranes of **mechanoreceptors** have cation channels that open when the membrane is disturbed by physical forces. The intensity of the physical force is registered as a graded receptor potential, which in turn leads to either the release of neurotransmitter or the generation of action potentials. The amount of neurotransmitter release or the rate of action potentials tells the CNS the strength of the stimulus to the mechanoreceptor. A diversity of mechanoreceptor cells has evolved in different sensory systems. The functions of these cells include interpreting skin sensations, sensing blood pressure, hearing, and maintaining balance.

Many different receptor cells respond to touch and pressure

Human skin (and that of other animals) is packed with diverse mechanoreceptors that generate varied sensations (**Figure 44.6**).

Figure 44.6 The Skin Feels Many Sensations Even a very small patch of skin contains a variety of sensory cells, making the skin a multimodal receptor that can sense temperature, pressure, texture, pain, touch, and itch.

The most important tactile receptors, found in both hairy and non-hairy skin of humans, are **Merkel's discs**, which adapt rather slowly and provide continuous information about anything touching the skin. **Meissner's corpuscles**, found primarily in non-hairy skin, are very sensitive but adapt rapidly; they provide information about *changes* in things touching the skin. The rapid adaptation of Meissner's corpuscles is why you roll a small object between your fingers (rather than holding it still) to discern its shape and texture: as you roll it, the object continually stimulates the Meissner's corpuscles.

Deeper in the skin, **Ruffini endings** adapt slowly and are good at providing information about vibrating stimuli of low frequencies, while **Pacinian corpuscles**, which adapt rapidly, provide information about vibrating stimuli of higher frequencies. Even deeper in the skin, the dendrites of sensory neurons wrap around hair follicles. When the surface hairs are displaced, those neurons are stimulated.

The density of tactile mechanoreceptor cells varies across the body's surface. By touching the skin with two toothpicks simultaneously (when a person's eyes are closed!), you can determine how far apart two stimuli have to be before the person can tell whether the sensations are produced by one toothpick or by two. On back skin, stimuli have to be relatively far apart before they are perceived as two discrete stimuli. But when this same "two-point spatial discrimination test" is applied to the lips or fingertips, a person can identify two stimuli as separate even when they are quite close together, because the receptor density is much greater in these regions.

Mechanoreceptors are also found in muscles, tendons, and ligaments

An animal receives information from mechanoreceptors about the position of its limbs and the stresses on its muscles and joints. These mechanoreceptors supply information continuously to the CNS, and this information is essential for postural control and the coordination of movements.

The mechanoreceptors in skeletal muscle are the **muscle spindles**. These stretch receptors are modified muscle cells embedded in connective tissue inside muscles and innervated by sensory neurons (**Figure 44.7A**). When a muscle is stretched, the muscle spindles are stretched as well, signaling the spindle neurons to transmit action potentials to the CNS. Figure 44.1 showed how crayfish stretch receptors transduce physical force into action potentials; the actions of muscle spindles are similar. The CNS uses the information from muscle spindles to adjust the strength of the muscle contraction so that it matches the load put on the muscle; thus a person can hold a mug steady while it is being filled.

Another type of mechanoreceptor, the **Golgi tendon organ**, is found in tendons and ligaments and provides information about the force generated by a contracting muscle (**Figure 44.7B**). When a contraction becomes too forceful, action potentials from the Golgi tendon organ inhibit the spinal cord motor neurons innervating that muscle, causing the muscle to relax and protecting it from tearing. (You may recall a cell organelle called the Golgi apparatus. What these two very different structures have in common is their discovery in the late nineteenth century by the Italian anatomist Camillo Golgi.)

Figure 44.7 Stretch Receptors
Stretch receptors provide information about the stresses on muscles and joints in an animal's limbs. **(A)** Signals from muscle spindles to the CNS initiate muscle contraction. **(B)** Golgi tendon organs in tendons and ligaments inhibit a contraction that becomes too forceful, triggering a reduction in muscle tension and protecting the muscle from tearing.

(A) Signals from muscle spindles

Muscle

Muscle spindle

Sensory neuron

Muscle

Tendon

Load

1 Muscle spindles are stretch receptors. When muscle spindles are stretched…

2 …sensory neurons associated with them transmit action potentials to the CNS. These signals stimulate motor neurons that initiate muscle contraction.

Stretch

Firing of sensory neuron

Time

(B) Signals to and from Golgi tendon organs

Muscle

Collagen fibers

Golgi tendon organ

Sensory neuron

Tendon

1 Golgi tendon organs sense load and measure the force of muscle contraction. When contraction becomes too forceful…

2 …the sensory neurons send action potentials to the CNS that inhibit motor neurons, and the muscle relaxes.

Load on muscle

Firing of sensory neuron

Time

Hair cells are mechanoreceptors of the auditory and vestibular systems

Hair cells are the mechanoreceptors for the vertebrate auditory (sound-perceiving) and vestibular (equilibrium-maintaining) systems. Both of these systems are housed in the complex structures of the vertebrate ear. **Stereocilia**—fingerlike extensions of the cell membrane stiffened by cross-linked actin filaments—project from the surface of each hair cell like a set of organ pipes (**Figure 44.8**). Stereocilia bend in response to waves of pressure; bending of the stereocilia in one direction depolarizes the hair cell, and bending in the other direction hyperpolarizes it.

Measurements with microelectrodes have shown that the bending of stereocilia creates local electric currents near their tips, indicating that ion channels near the tips must be opening or closing. Electron microscope images reveal minute filaments that connect the tip of each stereocilium to its taller neighbor. It is hypothesized that these filaments are fine molecular attachments to the ion channels, and that they act like springs that open the channels. If the taller neighboring stereocilium is bent away, the spring tightens and the ion channel is opened. If the taller neighbor bends toward its shorter neighbor, the spring is relaxed and the channel closes (see Figure 44.8).

Auditory systems use hair cells to sense sound waves

The stimuli that animals perceive as sounds are pressure waves. Auditory systems use mechanoreceptors to convert pressure waves into receptor potentials. Auditory systems include special structures that gather sound waves, direct them to the sensory organ, and amplify their effect on the mechanoreceptors. A good example of an auditory system is the human ear (**Figure 44.9**), which can be divided into three major areas: the outer, middle, and inner ear (see Figure 44.9A).

OUTER EAR   The outer ear consists of the pinna (plural *pinnae*) and the auditory canal. The pinnae collect sound waves and direct them into the auditory canals; watch a dog change the orientation of its ears to focus on a particular sound to get the idea of the role pinnae play in hearing. Covering the end of the auditory canal is the **tympanic membrane** (commonly called the eardrum), which vibrates in response to pressure waves traveling down the canal, thus converting the pressure waves to physical forces in the middle ear.

MIDDLE EAR   On the other side of the tympanic membrane is the middle ear, an air-filled cavity connected to the throat at the back of the mouth through the **eustachian tube** (also called the pharyngotympanic tube). Because the eustachian tube is also filled with air, pressure can equilibrate between the middle ear and the environment. When you have a cold, the tube can be blocked by mucus or tissue swelling and you may have difficulty equilibrating the pressure in the middle ear with the outside air pressure (as you have to do when changing altitude in an airplane).

Figure 44.8 Hair Cells Have Mechanosensors on Their Stereocilia Hair cells have stereocilia that are connected to each other by small filaments. When a cilium is bent in one direction, the filament opens a cation channel at the tip of the neighboring cilium, resulting in depolarization of membrane potential. When depolarized, the hair cell releases neurotransmitter onto a sensory neuron. Movement of the hair cell in the opposite direction closes the cation channel and the cell hyperpolarizes, causing a reduction in its release of neurotransmitter.

The middle ear contains the **ossicles**, three delicate bones individually named the malleus ("hammer"), incus ("anvil"), and stapes ("stirrup") (see Figure 44.9B). The ossicles transmit the vibrations of the tympanic membrane to another flexible membrane, the **oval window**. The ossicles act as a lever (like a hammer pulling out a nail), translating a large movement of the tympanic membrane into a smaller movement of the oval window, but a movement of greater force. Because the oval window is much smaller than the tympanic membrane, the pressure the stapes transmits to the oval window is more than 20 times greater than the pressure exerted by a sound wave on the tympanic membrane.

Behind the oval window lies the fluid-filled inner ear. Movements of the oval window impart pressure changes to that enclosed fluid. These pressure waves are transduced into action potentials.

INNER EAR   The inner ear is a bony structure consisting of two sets of canals. One is the organ of balance, the **vestibular system**, and the other is the organ of hearing, the **cochlea**. The cochlea ("snail" or "spiral shell") is a long, tapered, coiled structure. A cross section of the cochlea reveals that it is composed of three parallel canals separated by two membranes, the vestibular membrane and the basilar membrane (see Figure 44.9C). Sitting on the basilar membrane is the **organ of Corti**, which transduces pressure waves into action potentials. The organ of Corti contains hair cells with stereocilia (see Figure 44.8). The tips of the hair cells are embedded in a gelatinous overhanging shelf called the tectorial membrane all enclosed in the cochlear canal (see Figure 44.9D).

Stereocilia are not motile, but because their tips are attached to the more rigid tectorial membrane, stereocilia bend when the basilar membrane flexes. As shown in Figure 44.8, when the stereocilia are bent in one direction, the hair cell is depolarized by an inflow of K^+ ions. This effect of opening K^+ channels happens because the fluid in the cochlear canal has a higher K^+ concentration than does the intracellular fluid of the hair cell. The response of the hair cell is a graded membrane potential. The hair cells do not fire action potentials, but the changes in their membrane potential alter the rate at which the hair cells release neurotransmitter onto the sensory neurons. Those sensory neurons fire action potentials, and their axons, which make up the auditory nerve, transmit those action potentials to the brain.

The vestibular and tympanic canals are separate until they reach the apical end of the cochlea (the end farthest from the oval window), where they join; thus they form one continuous canal that turns back on itself (see Figure 44.10). Just as the oval window is a flexible membrane at the beginning of the vestibular canal, the **round window** is a flexible membrane at the end of the tympanic canal. When the oval window vibrates, the waves of fluid pressure create traveling waves of flexion in the basilar membrane.

Flexion of the basilar membrane is perceived as sound

What causes the basilar membrane to flex, and how does this mechanism distinguish sounds of different frequencies? Air is highly compressible but fluids are not; therefore a pressure wave can travel through air without displacing much air, whereas a pressure wave in fluid displaces that fluid. When the stapes pushes on the oval window, the fluid in the vestibular canal is displaced. If the movement of the oval window occurs very slowly, the cochlear fluid pressure wave travels down the vestibular canal, around the bend, and back through the tympanic

(A) Overview of the human auditory system

(B) The middle and inner ear

Figure 44.9 Structures of the Human Ear **(A)** The pinnae direct sound waves down the auditory canal to impinge on the tympanic membrane. The tympanic membrane mechanically transmits these pressure waves into movements of the ossicles in the middle ear. **(B)** The ossicles transmit their movement into pressure waves in the fluid of the cochlea at the oval window. **(C)** The cochlea is divided into fluid-filled canals; pressure waves from the ossicles cause the membranes between the canals to flex. **(D)** Flexing of the basilar membrane bends stereocilia on hair cells in the organ of Corti.

Q: How can the ears detect directionality of a sound source?

 View in Achieve
Activity 44.1 Structures of the Human Ear

canal (**Figure 44.10**). At the end of the tympanic canal, the displacement pressure is dissipated by the outward bulging of the round window.

The basilar membrane is not uniform—it is thicker and stiffer at its base and wider and thinner at its apical end. Pressure waves in the cochlear fluid have different frequencies and set up different patterns of traveling waves. High-frequency waves cause maximal flexion at the basal end of the basilar membrane, whereas low-frequency pressure waves result in maximal flexion at the apical end (see Figure 44.10). Thus different frequencies of pressure waves flex the basilar membrane at different locations and activate different sets of hair cells. Action potentials stimulated by different sets of hair cells along the organ of Corti code for different frequencies of sound and send that information along the cochlear nerve to the auditory cortex, where those action potentials are interpreted as different pitches of sound.

Various types of damage can result in hearing loss

There are two general types of acquired hearing loss, or deafness. Conduction deafness is caused by the loss of function of

(C) Cross section of the cochlea

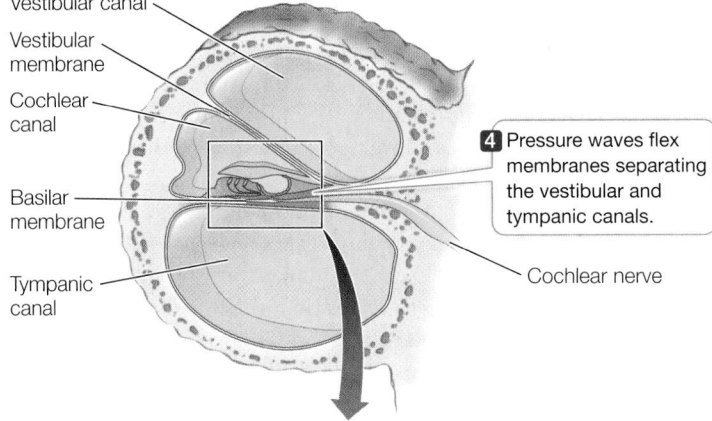

(D) The organ of Corti

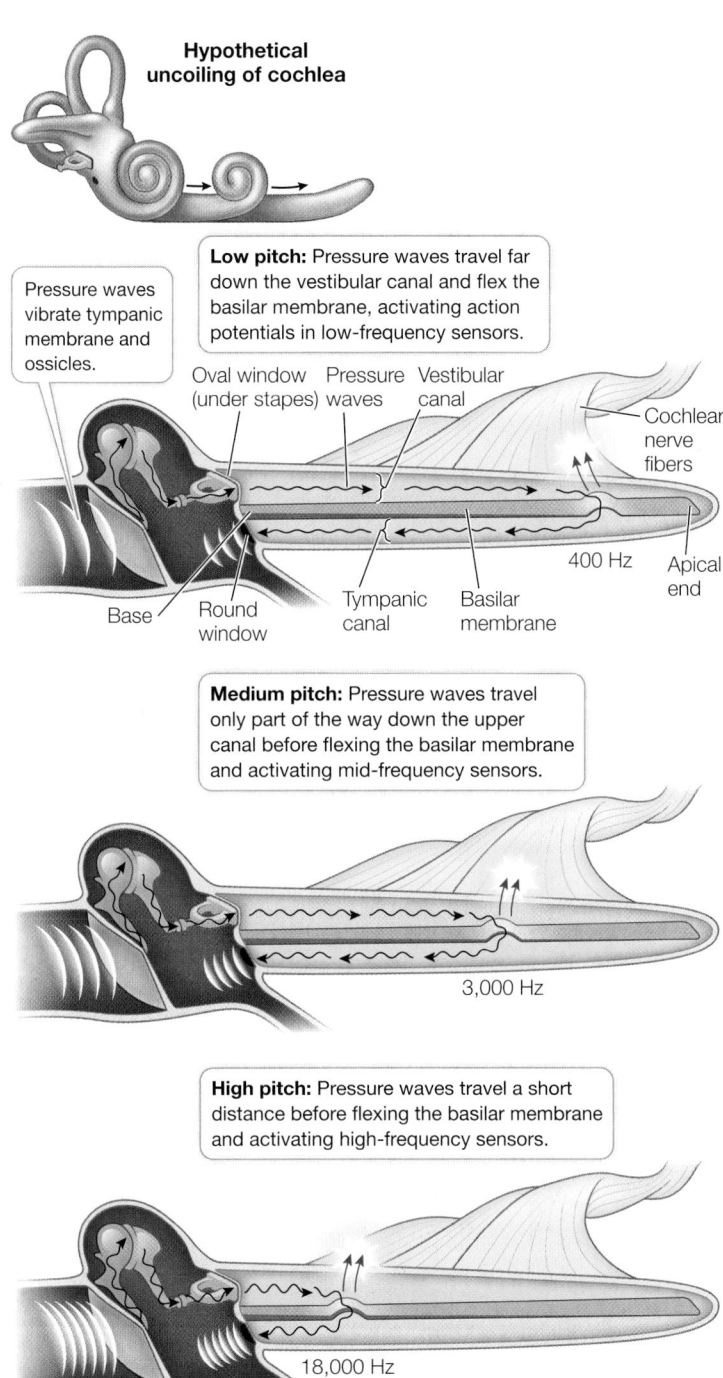

Hypothetical uncoiling of cochlea

Pressure waves vibrate tympanic membrane and ossicles.

Low pitch: Pressure waves travel far down the vestibular canal and flex the basilar membrane, activating action potentials in low-frequency sensors.

Oval window (under stapes) Pressure waves Vestibular canal

Cochlear nerve fibers

400 Hz Apical end

Base Round window Tympanic canal Basilar membrane

Medium pitch: Pressure waves travel only part of the way down the upper canal before flexing the basilar membrane and activating mid-frequency sensors.

3,000 Hz

High pitch: Pressure waves travel a short distance before flexing the basilar membrane and activating high-frequency sensors.

18,000 Hz

Figure 44.10 Sensing Pressure Waves in the Inner Ear Pressure waves of different frequencies flex the basilar membrane at different locations. Information about sound frequency is specified by which hair cells are activated. For simplicity, this representation illustrates the cochlea as uncoiled.

 View in Achieve
Animation 44.1 **Sound Transduction in the Human Ear**

the tympanic membrane or the ossicles of the middle ear. Repeated infections of the middle ear can cause scarring of the tympanic membrane and stiffening of the connections between the ossicles. The consequence is less efficient conduction of sound

waves from the tympanic membrane to the oval window. With increasing age, the ossicles inevitably stiffen, resulting in a gradual loss of the ability to hear high-frequency sounds.

Nerve deafness is caused by damage to the inner ear or the auditory pathways. A common cause of nerve deafness is damage to the hair cells of the delicate organ of Corti by exposure to loud sounds such as jet engines, pneumatic drills, or highly amplified music. Consistent exposure to sounds above 85 decibels can damage hearing; this damage is cumulative and irreversible. Even using earphones can put you at risk for hearing loss because they generate high-pressure sound waves close to the tympanic membrane. Personal stereo earphones can reach 120 decibels, and people commonly use them at 100 decibels (equivalent to being at a rock concert).

The vestibular system uses hair cells to detect forces of gravity and momentum

Hair cells in the vestibular system of the inner ear detect the position and movement of the head—information essential for maintaining equilibrium (balance). Information from the vestibular system is also crucial for the control of eye movements. When you look at something, you can move your head while staying focused on the object because of your vestibulo-ocular reflex.

In the mammalian inner ear, the vestibular system consists of three bony **semicircular canals** and a bony chamber called the **vestibule**. Within each canal is a membranous semicircular duct, and within the vestibule are the membranous saccule and the utricle. The ducts and the saccule and utricle are filled with fluid. In the semicircular ducts, the fluid shifts when the head changes position (**Figure 44.11A**). Since the three semicircular canals have different orientations, the fluid in their ducts responds differentially to the direction of movement. Projecting into the base of each duct is a **cupula**, a gelatinous swelling enclosing a cluster of hair cell stereocilia. When the shifting fluid pushes on the cupula, it bends the stereocilia and causes a graded potential in the hair cell membranes.

The stereocilia in the saccule and utricle are bent in a different way. These stereocilia are embedded in gelatinous membranes that contain **otoliths** ("ear stones"), which are crystals of calcium carbonate. When the head changes position or when it accelerates or decelerates, gravitational forces are exerted on the otoliths and the stereocilia bend (**Figure 44.11B**).

As in the cochlea, the hair cells of the vestibular system do not fire action potentials, but they release neurotransmitter at synapses with sensory neurons, which in turn fire action potentials.

Motion sickness is a common malady experienced when riding in a boat, car, plane, or amusement park ride, or when experiencing any situation in which the vestibular system and the visual system produce conflicting information. The vestibular system may be indicating movement when the visual system is not, or vice versa.

 View in Achieve
Simulation 44.1 **Mechanoreceptors**

(A) Looking through a semicircular canal to the cupula

Semicircular canals

Duct of semicircular canal

Utricle

Saccule

Macula

Vestibule

Ampulla

Flow of fluid through semicircular duct

Semicircular duct

Hair cells

Cupula

In the semicircular ducts, the gelatinous cupulae of hair cells are pushed one way or the other when changes in the position of the head cause the fluid in the canals to shift.

Cupula

Stereocilia

Support cell

Vestibular nerve fibers

Direction of body movement

(B) Sterocilia dynamics in the saccule and utricle

Force of gravity

Otoliths ("ear stones") are granules of calcium carbonate on the top surface of a gelatinous substance (the otolith membrane).

Stereocilia

Hair cell

Vestibular nerve fibers

Support cell

Force of gravity

Direction of body movement

Due to inertial mass of otoliths, when the head changes position, accelerates, or decelerates, the gelatinous otolith membrane bends hair cells.

Figure 44.11 Organs of Equilibrium The vestibular system consists of bony chambers and fluid-filled canals. **(A)** Each semicircular duct has a cupula containing stereocilia. When fluid moves against the cupula, the stereocilia bend. **(B)** In the maculae of the saccule and utricle, vestibular nerve endings synapse with hair cells whose stereocilia are embedded in a gelatinous layer covered with otoliths. Forces that move the otoliths bend the stereocilia.

KEY CONCEPT
44.3 Recap and Assess

Sensations that derive from mechanoreceptors include touch, tickle, pressure, joint position, muscle load, hearing, and equilibrium. The membranes of mechanoreceptors have ion channels that are opened by distortion of the membrane, resulting in graded receptor potentials that cause the cell to release neurotransmitter or to fire action potentials. Hair cells involved in hearing and equilibrium have stereocilia that are bent by pressure waves, resulting in receptor potentials.

1. Why are there different types of mechanoreceptor cells that have different rates of adaptation?

2. Explain the role of specific mechanoreceptors when you are (a) holding a glass that is being filled and (b) lifting heavy furniture.

3. How do different frequencies of pressure waves in the air result in action potentials being fired in different acoustic neurons?

We next turn to vision, perhaps the most elaborate of the senses.

KEY CONCEPT
44.4 Photoreceptors Respond to Light

Learning Objectives

44.4.1 List the steps whereby a photon of light is transduced into a change in membrane potential.

44.4.2 Describe the properties and locations of rod and cone cells in the retina.

44.4.3 Describe the structural adaptations enabling movement detection and visual acuity.

44.4.4 Explain ganglion cell receptive fields in terms of the lateral processing afforded by the horizontal and amacrine cells.

Sensitivity to light—**photosensitivity**—confers on the simplest animals the ability to orient to the Sun and sky, and it gives more complex animals rapid and extremely detailed information about objects in their environments. Photosensitivity is ubiquitous in the animal kingdom, and the molecular basis for that sensitivity is a family of visual pigments that have been evolutionarily conserved.

These photosensitive pigments are contained in **photoreceptor cells** in the eyes, the organs that gather light energy and initiate its conversion into action potentials. The photoreceptors in the eyes are associated with several additional cell types that integrate the information from the visual receptors. Visual pigments with different spectral sensitivities enable color vision.

 View in Achieve
Animation 44.2 **Photosensitivity**

Invertebrates have a variety of visual systems

Photoreceptors and visual pigments are incorporated into a variety of visual systems, from simple to complex. Flatworms obtain directional information about light from photoreceptor cells that are organized into **eye cups**—paired, bilateral structures, each partly shielded from light by a layer of pigmented cells lining the cup. The photoreceptors on the two sides of the animal are unequally stimulated unless the animal is facing directly toward or away from a light source. The flatworm generally uses directional information from the eye cups to move away from light.

Arthropods have **compound eyes** that provide them with information about patterns in the environment. These eyes are called compound because each eye consists of many optical units called **ommatidia** (singular *ommatidium*), each with its own narrow-angle lens (**Figure 44.12**). In contrast, a vertebrate eye consists of just one optical unit with a wide-angle lens. The number of ommatidia in a compound eye varies from only a few in some ants to 800 in fruit flies and to 30,000 in some dragonflies.

Each ommatidium has a lens that directs light onto photoreceptor cells. Flies, for example, have eight elongated photoreceptors in each ommatidium. The inner borders of the photoreceptors are covered with microvilli that contain a photosensitive pigment that traps light. Axons from the photoreceptors send the light information to the nervous system. Since each ommatidium of a compound eye is directed at a slightly different part of the visual world, only a low-resolution (pixilated) image can be communicated from the compound eye to the CNS.

Image-forming eyes evolved independently in vertebrates and cephalopods

Both vertebrates and cephalopod mollusks (such as squid and octopuses) have eyes with exceptional abilities to form detailed images of the visual world. Like cameras, both of these eye types focus inverted images on an internal surface that is sensitive to light. Considering that they evolved completely independently of

© Susumu Nishinaga/Science Photo Library/Getty Images

Figure 44.12 **Ommatidia: The Functional Units of Insect Eyes**   (A) The micrograph shows the compound eye of a fruit fly. (B) The rhodopsin-containing retinula cells are the photoreceptors in ommatidia. (B after M. Friedrich. 2006. *Arthropod Struct Dev* 35: 357–378.)

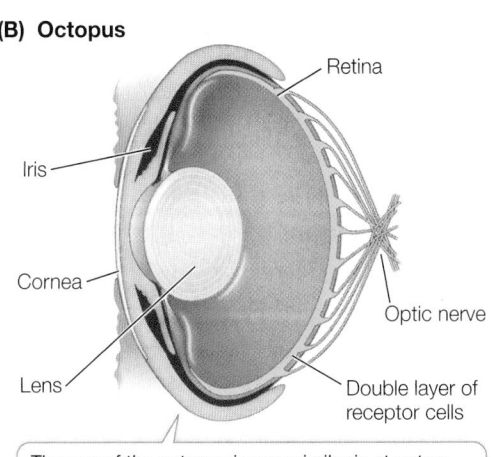

Figure 44.13 **Convergent Evolution of Eyes**   The lenses of vertebrate (A) and cephalopod (B) eyes focus images on layers of photoreceptor cells.

Q: Humans commonly experience "floaters" in their eyes—tissue fragments that float around in the field of vision. Where in the structure of the eye would you expect floaters to exist?

The eye of the octopus is very similar in structure to the vertebrate eye, but it evolved independently—an example of convergent evolution.

each other, their degree of similarity is remarkable (**Figure 44.13**).

The vertebrate eye (see Figure 44.13A) is a spherical, fluid-filled structure bounded by a tough connective tissue layer called the **sclera**. The sclera at the front of the eye forms the transparent **cornea**, through which light passes to enter the eye. Just inside the cornea is the pigmented **iris**, which gives the eye its color. The iris controls the amount of light that reaches the photoreceptor cells at the back of the eye. The central opening of the iris is the **pupil**. The iris is under neural control. In bright light, the iris constricts and the pupil is very small. As light levels fall, the iris opens and the pupil enlarges.

Behind the iris is the crystalline protein **lens** that makes fine adjustments in the focus of images falling on the photosensitive layer—the **retina**—at the back of the eye. The cornea and the gel-like mass (vitreous humor) within the eye bend light rays passing through them so that they are focused on the retina. The lens makes fine adjustments to the focus and allows the eye to accommodate—that is, to focus on objects at various locations in the near visual field. To focus a camera on objects close at hand, you adjust the distance between the lens and the internal surface sensitive to light. Fishes, amphibians, and non-avian reptiles accommodate in a similar manner, moving the lenses of their eyes closer to or farther from their retinas. Mammals and birds use a different method; they alter the shape of the lens.

The mammalian lens is contained in a connective tissue sheath that tends to keep it in a spherical shape, but the sheath is attached to suspensory ligaments that pull the lens into a flatter shape. Circular ciliary muscles counteract the pull of the suspensory ligaments, permitting the lens to round up. When the ciliary muscles are at rest, the flatter lens has the correct optical properties to focus distant images on the retina. Contracting the ciliary muscles rounds up the lens, changing its light-bending properties to bring close images into focus (**Figure 44.14**).

Lenses become less elastic with age, so we lose the ability to focus on objects close at hand without the help of corrective lenses. Most people over the age of 45 need the assistance of reading glasses or bifocal lenses.

 View in Achieve
Activity 44.2 Structure of the Human Eye

The vertebrate retina receives and processes visual information

During embryonic development, nervous tissue grows out from the brain to form the retina. In addition to a layer of photoreceptor cells, the retina includes other cells arranged in layers that process visual information from the photoreceptors (see Figure 44.20). Light must pass through all the layers of retinal cells before being captured by photosensors. In humans and other day-active animals, the light that is not captured is absorbed by a black-pigmented epithelial tissue layer behind the retina.

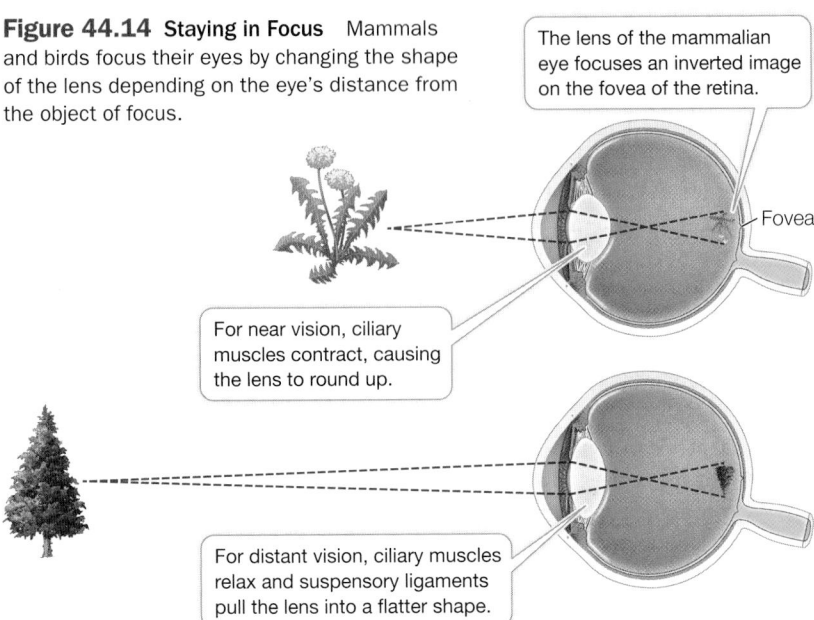

Figure 44.14 Staying in Focus Mammals and birds focus their eyes by changing the shape of the lens depending on the eye's distance from the object of focus.

The lens of the mammalian eye focuses an inverted image on the fovea of the retina.

Fovea

For near vision, ciliary muscles contract, causing the lens to round up.

For distant vision, ciliary muscles relax and suspensory ligaments pull the lens into a flatter shape.

In contrast, nocturnal animals such as deer and raccoons have an iridescent reflective layer behind their retinas, which maximizes the capture of photons by reflecting them back onto the photoreceptors. This is why a deer in the headlights or your pet dog or cat in a flash photo appears to have bright white eyes. In contrast, humans do not have a white reflective layer in the retina, so flash photographs often have a "red-eye effect," caused by the flash being reflected by the abundant blood vessels in the retina.

Opsins are the universal photoreceptor molecule in animals

Photosensitivity in animals depends on the ability of **opsin** molecules to absorb photons of light and activate a G protein. Opsins are proteins that are not themselves photosensitive, but they contain covalently bound functional groups called 11-*cis*-retinal (**Figure 44.15**). **Retinal** absorbs photons of light, and the color of light it receives depends on the structure of its opsin. There are several different opsins. The most common one that gives humans sensitivity to low levels of light, but not color, is called **rhodopsin**.

When 11-*cis*-retinal absorbs a photon of light energy, it changes into a different isomer of retinal, called all-*trans*-retinal. This change puts a strain on the bonds between retinal and opsin, changing the conformation of opsin and signaling the detection of light. In vertebrate eyes, the retinal and the opsin eventually separate from each other (a process called bleaching), which causes the opsin to lose its photosensitivity. A series of enzymatic reactions returns the all-*trans*-retinal to the 11-*cis* isomer, which then recombines with opsin so that it once again becomes photosensitive.

How does the conformational change of opsin transduce light into a cellular response? After retinal is converted from the 11-*cis* to the all-*trans* form, its interactions with opsin pass through several unstable intermediate stages. One of these stages triggers

3 When all-*trans*-retinal returns to 11-*cis* conformation, it is photoresponsive again.

Light

1 11-*cis*-retinal is sensitive to light...

11-*cis*-retinal

Activated transducin

Transducin (G protein)

All-*trans*-retinal

2 ...and when it absorbs a photon it becomes all-*trans*-retinal. After passing through unstable intermediates, all-*trans*-retinal activates a G protein (transducin) that mediates a change in membrane potential (see Figure 44.18).

Opsin

11-*cis*-retinal covalently bound to protein

Cell membrane

Figure 44.15 Light Changes the Conformation of Rhodopsin The light-absorbing molecule 11-*cis*-retinal bonds with the protein opsin to form the vertebrate visual pigment rhodopsin.

a G protein signaling cascade that results in the alteration of membrane potential that is the photoreceptor cell's response to light.

Rod and cone cells are the photoreceptors of the vertebrate retina

The photoreceptors of the vertebrate retina are two types of modified neurons called **rod cells** and **cone cells** based on their shapes (**Figure 44.16**). Rod cells are highly light-sensitive and perceive shades of gray in dim light. Cone cells function at high light levels and are responsible for high-acuity color vision. The human retina has about 5 million cones and 100 million rods, but the density of each type varies across the retina.

ROD CELLS   Rod cells do not produce action potentials, but they release neurotransmitter from their bases, where they form synapses with the next neurons in the visual pathway. Each rod cell has an outer segment, an inner segment, and a synaptic terminal (see Figure 44.16). The highly specialized outer segment contains stacks of discs made up of cell membranes densely packed with rhodopsin. These discs capture photons of light. The inner segment contains the cell nucleus, mitochondria, and other organelles. The synaptic terminal is where the rod cell communicates with other neurons.

To see how a rod cell responds to light, we can penetrate a single rod cell with an electrode and record its membrane potential in the dark and in the light, as shown in **Figure 44.17**. From what you have learned about other types of sensory receptors, you might expect that stimulation of the rod cell by light would make its membrane potential less negative, but the opposite is true—it becomes more negative, that is, it becomes hyperpolarized.

Rod cell outer segments have cyclic GMP (cGMP) gated sodium channels. In the dark, abundant cGMP in the cell keeps these channels open, creating the dark current. When light is flashed on the dark-adapted rod cell, these Na^+ channels close in proportion to the intensity of the light, and the cell's membrane potential becomes more negative—it hyperpolarizes (see Figure 44.17). The rate of neurotransmitter release from the base of the cell changes as membrane potential changes. As the rod cell hyperpolarizes, its release of neurotransmitter decreases.

How does the absorption of light by rhodopsin hyperpolarize the rod cell? As illustrated in Figure 44.15, when rhodopsin is excited by light it undergoes conformational changes that initiate a signaling cascade. The dark-adapted rod cell has open Na^+ channels—the depolarizing dark current (**Figure 44.18**). Light photons excite rhodopsin, which activates a G protein called transducin. Activated transducin activates a phosphodiesterase (PDE). Activated

Rod cells   Cone cells

Rod photoreceptor

Cone photoreceptor

Outer segment

Membranous discs containing photopigment

Inner segment

Cell bodies

Synaptic terminal

© Omikron/Science Source

Figure 44.16 Rods and Cones This scanning electron micrograph of photoreceptors in the retina of a mud puppy (an amphibian) shows cylindrical rods and tapered cones.

Experiment

Figure 44.17   How Light Stimulates Rod Cells

Original Paper: D. A. Baylor et al. 1979. The Membrane Current of Single Rod Outer Segments. *J Physiol* 288: 589-611.

The cell membrane of a rod cell hyperpolarizes—becomes more negative—in response to a flash of light. Rod cells do not fire action potentials, but in response to the absorption of light energy, the rod cell undergoes a change in membrane potential.

HYPOTHESIS▶   When a rod cell absorbs photons (light energy), its membrane potential changes in proportion to the strength of the light stimulus.

METHOD▶

1. Record membrane potentials from the inner segment of a rod cell.

2. Stimulate the rod cells with light flashes of varying intensity and record the results.

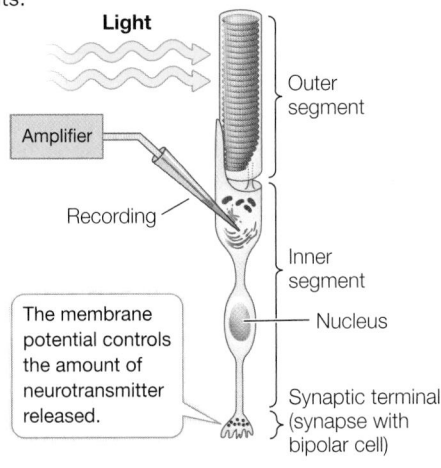

The membrane potential controls the amount of neurotransmitter released.

RESULTS▶

A dim light stimulus results in a slight hyperpolarization.

Medium light

A bright light stimulus results in a strong hyperpolarization.

CONCLUSION▶   The membrane potential of rod cells is depolarized in the dark and hyperpolarizes in response to light.

PDE converts cGMP to GMP, which causes the cGMP gated Na⁺ channels to close, changing the balance between the inward flow of Na⁺ and the outward flow of K⁺ and causing the cell to hyperpolarize.

This cascade may seem like a roundabout way of doing business, but its advantage is its enormous amplification ability. Each molecule of light-excited rhodopsin can activate several hundred transducin molecules, thus activating a large number of PDE molecules. The catalytic capacity of PDE is great—one PDE molecule can hydrolyze several hundred molecules of cGMP per second. The bottom line is that a single photon of light can result in the closure of a huge number of Na⁺ channels.

CONE CELLS   Cone cells are responsible for the high-acuity color vision of day-active vertebrates such as humans. It is therefore logical that the highest density of cone cells is in the area of the retina that receives light from the center of the visual field, a region called

Figure 44.18 Light Absorption Closes Sodium Channels   The absorption of light by rhodopsin initiates a signaling cascade that hyperpolarizes the rod cell.

Figure 44.19 Absorption Spectra of Cone Cells The three kinds of cone cells contain slightly different visual pigments that absorb different wavelengths of light. (After J. K. Bowmaker et al. 1980. *J Physiol* 298: 131–143.)

the **fovea** (see Figure 44.13A). The human fovea has about 160,000 cones per square millimeter. But humans are not the champions of high-acuity vision; a hawk's fovea has almost twice that number of cones, making the hawk's vision much sharper than ours. Birds also have *two* foveae in each eye; one receives light from straight ahead, the other from a more lateral field of vision. The forward-looking foveae make binocular vision possible, while the lateral-looking foveae provide high-acuity vision. Birds use both sets of foveae by frequently turning their heads slightly; they cannot move their eyes in the sockets as humans can.

Cones have low sensitivity to light and contribute little to night vision. Night vision depends mostly on rod cells, which is why vision in dim light is mostly in shades of gray and acuity is low. You may have trouble seeing a small object at night when you are looking straight at it—that is, when its image is falling on your fovea. If you look a little to the side, so that the image falls on a rod-rich area of your retina, you see the object better. Astronomers looking for faint objects in the sky learned this trick a long time ago. The retinas of nocturnal animals, such as flying squirrels, contain a high percentage of rods. By contrast, some animals that are active only during the day (such as chipmunks) have mostly cones in their retinas.

The human retina usually has three kinds of cone cells, each containing slightly different opsin molecules that differ in the wavelengths of light they absorb best. Although the same 11-*cis*-retinal group is the light-absorber in all three kinds of cones, its molecular interactions with opsin determine the spectral sensitivity of the cone cell as a whole (**Figure 44.19**). Those that absorb maximally around 419 nanometers (nm) are called S-cones for short wavelength (blue range). Those that absorb maximally around 531 nm are called M-cones for medium wavelength (green range), and those that absorb maximally around 559 nm are called L-cones for long wavelength (yellow–red range). Because different wavelengths of light are differentially absorbed by the different cone cell visual pigments,

the brain interprets the relative inputs from the different classes as a full range of color. Color blindness in humans results from the absence or dysfunction of one or more of the three classes of cone cells. Since the genes for the medium (green) and short (yellow/red) opsins are on the x chromosome in humans, and males have only one x chromosome, it is more likely that men will be colorblind for red and/or green than will women.

Information is integrated by the layers of neurons in the retina

The human retina is organized into layers of neurons that receive visual information and process it before sending it to the brain (**Figure 44.20**). Closest to the lens (and thus to light input) is a layer of **ganglion cells**; a central layer contains three neuronal

Figure 44.20 The Human Retina Five layers of neurons receive and process visual information. The rods and cones are photoreceptors. The other four layers are the ganglion cells, the bipolar cells, the horizontal cells, and the amacrine cells, all of which are involved in transmitting light signals received by the photoreceptors to the brain.

Media Clip 44.1 Into the Eye
Life12e.com/mc44.1

View in Achieve
Activity 44.3 **Structure of the Human Retina**

types, **bipolar cells**, **horizontal cells**, and **amacrine cells**; and at the "rear" of the retina lie the photoreceptors (rods and cones). The layers of cells between the photoreceptors and the ganglion cells process information about the visual field.

GANGLION AND BIPOLAR CELLS   From our discussion of rod cells, you know that the photoreceptor cells at the back of the retina hyperpolarize in response to light and do not generate action potentials. The ganglion cells at the front of the retina do, however, fire action potentials. The axons of ganglion cells form the **optic nerves** that travel to the brain.

The ganglion cells are connected to the photoreceptors by bipolar cells. Changes in the membrane potential of rods and cones in response to light alter the rates at which the rods and cones release neurotransmitter at their synapses with the bipolar cells. In response to this neurotransmitter, the membrane potentials of the bipolar cells change, altering the rate at which they release neurotransmitter onto ganglion cells. The neurotransmitter release from the bipolar cells determines the rate at which ganglion cells fire action potentials. Thus the direct flow of information in the retina is from photoreceptor to bipolar cell to ganglion cell. The ganglion cells send the information to the brain via the optic nerves.

Each human eye contains about 1.2 million ganglion cells but more than 100 million rods and cones. Therefore there must be convergence of information as it passes from the photoreceptors to the ganglion cells. A given bipolar cell can receive input from multiple rods or multiple cones, but not from both. The relationship among photoreceptors, bipolar cells, and ganglion cells depends on their location on the retina. In the fovea, a ganglion cell may receive input from as few as five photoreceptors, but in the periphery of the retina, a ganglion cell may receive input from thousands of photoreceptors. Visual acuity is a reflection of these quantitative relationships.

The patch of photoreceptors that communicates with a ganglion cell forms a circular receptive field. When light falls on a receptive field, its ganglion cell can be either excited or inhibited. As already mentioned, each ganglion cell sends an axon to the brain in an optic nerve. Thus the information coming from the retina to the brain is about the pattern of patches of light and dark falling on the retina. We'll return to a discussion of how the brain constructs the visual field from the input from receptive fields in Chapter 45.

HORIZONTAL AND AMACRINE CELLS   The other two cell layers, the horizontal cells and the amacrine cells, consist of interneurons that communicate laterally across the retina. Horizontal cells form synapses with neighboring photoreceptors and bipolar cells. Thus light falling on one photoreceptor can influence the sensitivity of its neighbors to light. This lateral flow of information enables the retina to sharpen the perception of contrast between light and dark patterns. Amacrine cells form local interconnections between bipolar cells and ganglion cells. Some amacrine cells are highly sensitive to changing illumination or to motion. Others assist in adjusting the sensitivity of the eyes according to the overall level of light falling on the retina. When background light levels change, amacrine cell connections to the ganglion cells adjust the range of intensities to which they are sensitive. Thus even with large changes in background illumination such as going from outdoors into a building, the eyes are still sensitive to small, rapid changes in the pattern of light falling on the retina. The light reflected from this page can vary by nine orders of magnitude (1,000,000,000-fold) between a sunny outdoor environment and a moonless night. Even though our eyes function best over a light-intensity range of only two orders of magnitude, modulation by amacrine cells can rapidly shift that functional range to accommodate a wide range of light intensities.

KEY CONCEPT
44.4 Recap and Assess

Vertebrates have image-forming eyes in which a lens focuses incoming light onto the photosensitive retina. Opsin molecules are responsible for light sensitivity in all animals, and in vertebrates opsins are contained in receptor cells called rods and cones. Slight differences in the opsin molecules result in differences in spectral sensitivity, which is the basis for color vision. Rods and cones do not fire action potentials, but their graded membrane potentials alter neurotransmitter release onto retinal bipolar cells. The bipolar cells in turn influence ganglion cells that do fire action potentials in their axons, which travel in the optic nerves to the brain. Two other types of retinal cells, horizontal and amacrine cells, sharpen contrast and adjust sensitivity of the retina, respectively.

1. Explain why a compound eye is better at detecting movement than at forming images.

2. How do photons of light change the receptor potential of rod cells?

3. Explain how rods and the various cones differ in their spectral sensitivity.

4. If you are looking straight ahead and someone holds up a colored card on your right or left side, why can't you tell what the color is?

5. Give two reasons why your vision is impaired when you come from bright outside light into a dimly lit room.

Knowing the path of information from sensory receptor cells to the CNS still does not tell us how that information is processed by the brain. What does the eye tell the brain, for example, in response to a pattern of light falling on the retina? In Chapter 45 you will learn how the mammalian brain reassembles sensory information into our perception of the world.

►Investigating**LIFE**

Q and A   How do pit vipers "see" in the dark?

The pit organs of rattlesnakes are the infrared detectors that signal the presence of warm-blooded prey. In this chapter we considered how the pit organs transduce infrared radiation into neuronal information. Infrared is a portion of the electromagnetic radiation spectrum, as is visible light. So could the receptor cells in the pit organs be modified photoreceptors? Or have they evolved from the types of sensory neurons in the skin that sense temperature? The temperature-sensitive neuron theory seems more likely since there is no rhodopsin in the pit organs. But how did such neurons acquire an acute sensitivity to minute changes in temperature of the pit organ caused by distant infrared emitters? The experiments covered in **Investigating Life: How Do Pit Vipers "See" in the Dark?** identified a particular TRP channel that is highly expressed in the trigeminal ganglia but not in the dorsal root ganglia of rattlesnakes. These experiments also revealed that the TRPA1 channel is not highly expressed in the TG or DRGs of non-pit snakes, but is highly expressed in a distantly related

pit snake, the python. In the online exercise to **Investigating Life: How Do Pit Vipers "See" in the Dark?** it was determined that expression of the *TRPA1* gene in frog oocytes causes them to have a steep temperature sensitivity in the range of 34°C–42°C. Thus we can conclude that the TRPA1 channel has evolved along with the pit organ to enable pit vipers such as the rattlesnake to detect warm-blooded prey.

Future directions

The identification of specific genes that convey specific sensory capabilities—for example, identification of the different opsin genes for color vision and the *TRPA1* gene for infrared detection—raises the possibility that genetic engineering efforts could be directed toward expanding the sensory capabilities of animals, including humans. What would it be like to be able to see in the infrared and ultraviolet ranges or to hear infrasound and ultrasound? Would the human brain be able to process and integrate that huge amount of additional information? How would our conscious perception of reality be changed?

VISUAL SUMMARY 44

© John Cancalosi/Alamy Stock Photo

You should be able to relate each summary to the adjacent figures. If you go to this visual summary in **Achieve**, you can follow links to figures, animations, activities, and simulations that will help you consolidate the material.

KEY CONCEPT

44.1   Sensory Receptor Cells Convert Stimuli into Action Potentials

- **Receptor potentials** are graded membrane potentials that can generate action potentials or cause the release of neurotransmitter.

- **Receptor proteins** cause ion channels to open or close, affecting the receptor cell's membrane potential. Different receptor proteins respond to physical forces, light, chemicals, temperature, or electric charge.

- Transient receptor potential (TRP) genes are responsible for many modalities of **sensory transduction**.

- **Sensory adaptation** enables the nervous system to ignore irrelevant or continuous stimuli while remaining responsive to relevant or new stimuli.

Questions

1. What is a graded membrane potential, and how can it integrate inputs from multiple receptor proteins?

2. Which would generate a faster response, an electroreceptor or a chemoreceptor? Why?

3. Which type of receptor protein enables a pit viper to see in the dark?

Figure 44.1

KEY CONCEPT

44.2   Chemoreceptors Respond to Specific Molecules

- **Chemoreceptors** are responsible for **olfaction**, **gustation**, and the sensing of pheromones.

- There are thousands of olfactory receptor genes, but each mammalian **olfactory receptor neuron (ORN)** expresses only one of these genes. A molecule binding to that receptor protein causes the cell to fire an action potential.

- ORNs project to the **olfactory bulb** of the brain, and ORNs for a particular **odorants** project to specific olfactory glomeruli.

- **Pheromones** communicate information among individuals of the same species.

- **Taste buds** in the mouth cavities of terrestrial vertebrates are responsible for gustation. The five basic tastes are sweet, salty, sour, bitter, and umami.

Questions

1. What is the function of a glomerulus in the olfactory bulb?

2. How can pheromones released by a female silkworm moth provide directional information enabling a male to find her?

3. What are similarities and differences in which taste receptors detect and signal sweet versus salty tastes?

Figure 44.3

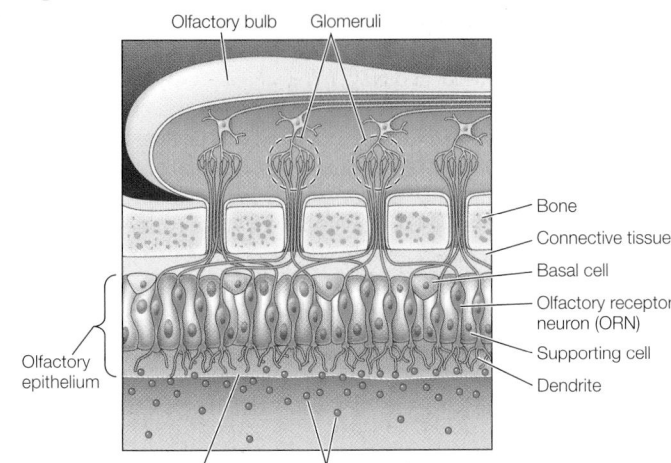

KEY CONCEPT

44.3   Mechanoreceptors Respond to Physical Forces

Go to Activity 44.1, Animation 44.1, and Simulation 44.1

- Skin **mechanoreceptors** respond to touch and pressure. The density of mechanoreceptors determines the sensitivity of a skin area.

- Stretch receptors in **muscle spindles** and in **Golgi tendon organs** inform the CNS of the positions of and loads on parts of the body.

- In mammals, ear pinnae collect and direct sound waves to the **tympanic membrane**, which vibrates in response to sound waves. The movements of the tympanic membrane are amplified by the **ossicles** that conduct the vibrations to the **oval window**. Movements of the oval window create pressure waves in the fluid-filled **cochlea**.

- Pressure waves of different frequencies in the cochlea flex its basilar membrane in different locations. These flexions bend the stereocilia of the hair cells in the **organ of Corti** causing them to cells to release neurotransmitter onto auditory sensory neurons that fire action potentials in the auditory nerve.

- Hair cells are also the mechanoreceptors in the organs of equilibrium in the mammalian **vestibular system**—the **semicircular canals** and the saccule and utricle.

Figure 44.8

Questions

1. Ruffini endings adapt slowly, whereas Pacinian corpuscles adapt rapidly. Both of these mechanoreceptors sense vibrations applied to the skin. Which one is best at sensing high-frequency vibrations, and why?

2. You read that the muscle spindle has a sensory neuron. It also has motor neurons that cause the spindle fibers to contract and stretch their mechanosensors. What would be the response of the arm flexor muscle in response to action potentials in the motor neurons to its muscle spindles?

3. What is the function of otoliths, and how do they achieve that function?

KEY CONCEPT

44.4 Photoreceptors Respond to Light

Go to Activities 44.2 and 44.3 and Animation 44.2

- **Eye cups** of flatworms sense the direction of a light source. **Compound eyes** of arthropods detect shapes, patterns, and movement. Eyes of vertebrates and cephalopods form high-resolution images.

- Vertebrate and cephalopod eyes focus images of the visual field onto dense arrays of **photoreceptor cells** that transduce the image into neuronal signals.

- Photons of light are absorbed by **opsins**, visual pigments that bind light-absorbing 11-*cis*-retinal. Absorption of light changes conformation of **retinal**, resulting in changes in the membrane potential of the photoreceptor cell.

- Vertebrates have two types of photoreceptors, **rod cells** and **cone cells**.

- **Rhodopsin** is the visual pigment of rod cells. Cone cells have three different opsins, which gives them different spectral sensitivities.

- The photoreceptor cells of vertebrates are at the rear of the **retina**. They communicate with **ganglion cells** through **bipolar cells**. Ganglion cell axons form the **optic nerves**.

Figure 44.20

Five cell layers in the retina

Questions

1. If you had an electrode in a rod cell and you shone a light on the cell, what would you see in the recording from that electrode, and how would that response be communicated to the next retinal cell involved in visual transduction?

2. If you are trying to put a key in a lock in very dim light, why does it help to look a little bit to the side of the keyhole?

3. What is transducin and how does it work?

Go to **Achieve** for the eBook, **LearningCurve**, animations, activities, simulations, and additional resources and assignments.

45 The Mammalian Nervous System: Structure and Higher Functions

KEY CONCEPTS

45.1 Functions Are Localized in the Nervous System

45.2 Nervous System Functions Rely on Neural Circuits

45.3 Higher Brain Functions Involve Integration of Multiple Systems

© Jason Hawkes/Getty Images

The extraordinary ability of taxicab drivers in London to navigate its maze of streets and byways prompted a study that revealed London cabbies to have larger than normal posterior hippocampi—a brain region implicated in the memory of spatial relationships in the environment.

▶ InvestigatingLIFE

The Brains of Taxi Drivers

Compare Google maps of London and New York City at the same scale. In which city do you think it is easier to drive a taxi? Eleanor Maguire at University College London was so impressed with the navigational abilities of London taxi drivers that she investigated whether there was anything "special" about their brains. Using magnetic resonance imaging, Maguire and her colleagues examined the brains of taxi drivers with varying numbers of years of experience and compared them with each other and with the brains of control subjects who were not taxi drivers. The studies revealed significant differences in the sizes of a brain region called the hippocampus.

The hippocampus is involved in learning and memory. The posterior hippocampus in particular is implicated in the memory of spatial relationships among objects in the environment. Maguire found that the posterior hippocampi of taxi drivers were larger than those of control subjects and that, among the cab drivers, there was a positive correlation between the size of the posterior hippocampus and years of driving experience.

In Matt Wilson's lab at the Massachusetts Institute of Technology, researchers record the activity of hippocampal neurons of rats running in a maze. Specific neurons called "place cells" fire action potentials only when the rat is at a particular location in the maze. Thus when the rat runs the maze from beginning to end, a sequence of cell firing is recorded. Sometimes when the rat is resting, the same sequence is recorded but is speeded up about 20 times, or the reverse sequence is recorded. It seems as if the recordings are reflecting what the resting rat is thinking—where it has been, where it is going to go. In a maze with a choice point (go right or go left), the sequence recorded when the rat is resting at the start position frequently predicts which direction it will turn.

The hippocampus is important for acquiring memories and consolidating them into long-term memory. We also know that sleep is important for learning. What is happening in the hippocampus during sleep to promote memory?

Can recordings of hippocampal place cells reveal processes of memory consolidation during sleep? (Find the answer on page 1023.)

Functions Are Localized in the Nervous System

Learning Objectives

45.1.1 Classify the types of afferent information to and efferent information from the nervous system.

45.1.2 Explain the developmental relationships between the major brain regions, starting with the forebrain, midbrain, and hindbrain and ending with structures such as the amygdala, hypothalamus, primary motor cortex, reticular-activating system, and other components of the adult brain.

45.1.3 Sketch and/or list the five lobes of the cerebrum and identify the primary sensory and motor areas.

45.1.4 Describe the relationship between body size and brain size in humans and other vertebrates.

The organization of the mammalian nervous system can be described anatomically and functionally. In anatomical terms, all vertebrate nervous systems consist of three parts: a brain, a spinal cord, and a set of peripheral nerves that reach all parts of the body. As discussed in Key Concept 43.4, the brain and spinal cord are the **central nervous system**, or **CNS**, and the neurons that connect the CNS to all the tissues and sensors of the body are the **peripheral nervous system**, or **PNS**. An additional division of the nervous system exists in the gut; we will discuss this **enteric nervous system** in Chapter 49.

Recall from Key Concept 43.1 that a neuron is an electrically excitable cell that communicates via an axon. When used in the context of a nervous system, the term **nerve** refers to a bundle of axons in the PNS that carry information about many things simultaneously. Some axons in a nerve may be carrying information to the CNS while other axons in the same nerve are carrying information from the CNS to the body's organs. An understanding of the functional organization of the nervous system requires knowledge of these paths of information flow. In this chapter we divide the anatomy of the mammalian brain, spinal cord, and PNS into smaller, discrete functional units.

Functional organization is based on flow and type of information

Figure 45.1 illustrates the major avenues of information flow through the human nervous system. The white boxes identify four divisions of the PNS; two of these bring information from the periphery to the CNS, and two transmit information from the CNS to the periphery.

1. The **afferent** portion of the PNS (see Figure 45.1, left) carries information from sensory receptor cells to the CNS. We are *conscious* of much of this information (e.g., light, sound, skin temperature, limb position), but we are usually *unconscious* of the information involved in physiological regulation (e.g., blood pressure, deep body temperature, blood oxygen levels).

2. The **efferent** portion of the PNS (see Figure 45.1, right) carries information from the CNS to the muscles and glands of the body. Efferent pathways are divided into a *voluntary* division that executes our conscious movements; and an *involuntary*, or *autonomic*, division that controls physiological functions.

In addition to the neural information it receives from the PNS, the CNS receives chemical information from hormones circulating in the blood. In turn, neurohormones released by neurons enter the circulation and affect neurons and other cells distant from the site of release (see Key Concept 39.1).

The anatomical organization of the CNS emerges during development

Early in the development of a vertebrate embryo, a tube of nervous tissue forms (see Key Concept 42.4). At its anterior end, this neural tube forms three swellings that become the **forebrain**, **midbrain**, and **hindbrain**. The rest of the neural tube becomes the spinal cord. Peripheral nerves sprout from the midbrain and hindbrain (the cranial nerves) and from the spinal cord (the spinal nerves). From these early stages we see the linear axis of information flow in the nervous system. Although the developing brain will fold and become a complex structure, the information flow in the adult nervous system will follow paths that emerge from the simple, linear neural tube.

Each of these three regions of the embryonic brain develops into several structures in the adult brain (**Figure 45.2**). From the

Figure 45.1 Organization of the Nervous System The peripheral nervous system carries information to (afferent) and from (efferent) the central nervous system (center circle in the diagram). The CNS also receives hormonal inputs and produces hormonal outputs (see Key Concept 39.2).

Q: How do hormonal inputs reach the CNS and hormonal outputs leave the CNS?

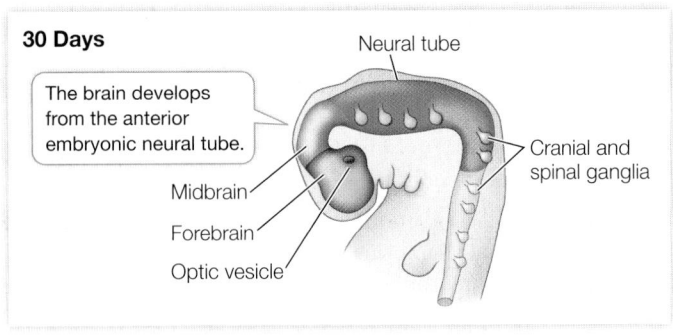

30 Days

The brain develops from the anterior embryonic neural tube.

Neural tube

Midbrain

Forebrain

Optic vesicle

Cranial and spinal ganglia

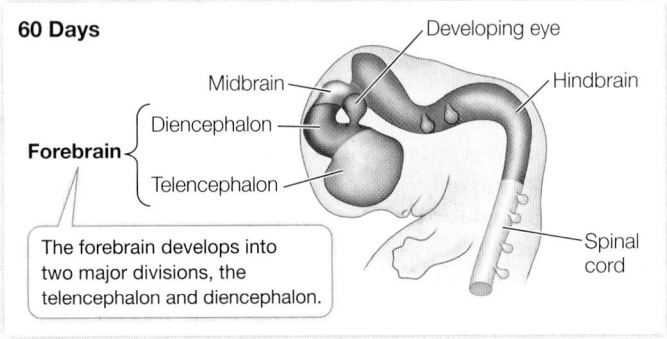

60 Days

Developing eye

Midbrain

Forebrain {
Diencephalon

Telencephalon
}

Hindbrain

Spinal cord

The forebrain develops into two major divisions, the telencephalon and diencephalon.

180 Days

The telencephalon develops into the cerebrum.

The hindbrain develops into three major divisions: the cerebellum, pons, and medulla.

Cerebrum

Cerebellum

Pons

Medulla

Spinal cord

Adult brain (midsagittal section)

The diencephalon develops into the thalamus and hypothalamus.

Thalamus

Hypothalamus

Pituitary

Brainstem {
Midbrain

Pons

Medulla
}

Right cerebral hemisphere

Cerebellum

Spinal cord

Figure 45.2 Development of the Central Nervous System
In vertebrate embryos, the anterior end of the hollow neural tube differentiates into forebrain, midbrain, and hindbrain. Each of these regions develops into several structures of the adult brain. The remainder of the neural tube becomes the spinal cord.

embryonic midbrain come structures that integrate information from the different senses and coordinate motor responses. From the hindbrain come the **medulla**, the **pons**, and the **cerebellum**. The medulla is continuous with the spinal cord, the pons is anterior to the medulla, and the cerebellum is a dorsal outgrowth of the pons. The medulla and pons contain distinct groups of neurons involved in controlling physiological functions such as breathing, circulation, and basic motor patterns such as swallowing and vomiting. All information traveling between the spinal cord and higher brain areas must pass through the pons, the medulla, and the midbrain, which are collectively known as the **brainstem**.

One function of the cerebellum is coordinating muscle activity and maintaining balance. It is like the director of a movie; the cerebellum receives a "script" of the commands going to the muscles from higher brain areas, and it receives information about the actual performance coming up the spinal cord from the "actors"—the joints and muscles. The cerebellum compares the "script" with the performance and refines motor commands accordingly. Damage to the cerebellum results in loss of fine motor control and coordination.

The embryonic forebrain develops a central region called the **diencephalon** and a surrounding structure called the **telencephalon**. The diencephalon is the core of the forebrain and consists of an upper structure, the **thalamus**, and a lower structure, the **hypothalamus**. The thalamus is the final relay station for sensory information going to the telencephalon. The hypothalamus receives a lot of physiological information of which we are not conscious, and it uses that information to regulate many physiological functions and biological drives. A major function of the hypothalamus is to control the pituitary gland (see Key Concept 39.2).

Connect the Concepts Key Concept 39.2 explains how the endocrine system and nervous system work together.

The embryonic telencephalon gives rise to the **cerebrum**, consisting of the left and right **cerebral hemispheres**. The outer layer of the cerebrum is the **cerebral cortex**, a thin layer rich in cell bodies. If we compare vertebrate groups from fishes through amphibians, reptiles, and mammals, the cerebrum increases in size, complexity, and importance—an evolutionary trend called telencephalization (see Figure 43.16). In humans, the cerebrum is by far the largest part of the brain and plays major roles in sensory perception, learning, memory, and conscious behavior.

The spinal cord transmits and processes information

The spinal cord conveys information to and from the brain. However, the spinal cord is more than an information pipe. As you saw in Key Concept 43.4, the spinal cord carries out integrative functions as well. The knee-jerk reflex (see Figure 43.15) is an example of a circuit between the PNS and the spinal cord that controls a behavioral function. That simple circuit can be built on to control more complex behaviors such as the withdrawal reflex, which involves readjusting tension in many muscles on both sides of the body to coordinate movement and maintain balance.

The brainstem carries out many autonomic functions

Swallowing, salivating, breathing, eye movements, blood pressure regulation, and gut activity are only a few of the many autonomic functions that are localized in the medulla, the pons, and the midbrain. To carry out these functions, the brainstem has its own components of the PNS, the 12 paired **cranial nerves**. You encountered the olfactory nerve, the optic nerve, and the auditory nerve (cranial nerves I, II, and VIII) in Chapter 44. Another one, cranial nerve X, is called the vagus ("wandering") nerve because it travels into the body cavity and communicates with many of the organs, including the heart and the gut. You will encounter the vagus nerve in subsequent chapters.

Anatomically distinct groups of neurons in the CNS that work together as a unit are called a **nucleus** (not to be confused with the nucleus of a single cell). Axons from the neurons of many brainstem nuclei extend to various regions of the brain and modulate brain activity; for example, brainstem nuclei are involved in keeping the higher brain areas awake or allowing them to sleep. All of the sensory information coming up the neural axis from the spinal cord passes through the brainstem on its way to the forebrain, and many of these ascending neuronal tracts give off branches to the awake-promoting nuclei in the brainstem. Because the neuronal circuitry in this part of the brain is so complicated and because activity in these ascending sensory pathways can promote wakefulness, the core of the brainstem has been termed the **reticular-activating system** ("reticular" means netlike). Damage to the brain or spinal cord below the reticular-activating system can result in paralysis but leave sleep–wake cyclic behavior normal. Damage above the level of the reticular-activating system can interrupt ascending wake-promoting activity, resulting in a coma.

The core of the forebrain controls physiological drives, instincts, and emotions

As mentioned earlier, the diencephalon consists of the thalamus and the hypothalamus. The thalamus communicates sensory information to the cerebral cortex; the hypothalamus receives information about physiological conditions in the body and regulates many homeostatic functions. Key Concept 38.5 described how the hypothalamus is involved in regulating body temperature, and Key Concept 39.2 discussed the intimate association between the hypothalamus and the pituitary gland in the control of many homeostatic functions.

The forebrain of vertebrates includes a phylogenetically old, complex set of structures called the **limbic system** (Figure 45.3). The limbic system is responsible for some basic instincts and drives such as hunger and thirst, sexual behavior, and emotions. Within the limbic system there are areas that, when stimulated with small electric currents, can cause intense sensations of pleasure, pain, or rage.

Pleasure and pain centers in the limbic system play roles in learning and in physiological drives. One component of the limbic system—the **amygdala**—is involved in fear and fear memory. If a certain portion of the amygdala is damaged or chemically blocked, an animal becomes tame and cannot learn to be afraid of a situation that would normally induce a strong fear reaction.

Figure 45.3 The Limbic System The evolutionarily primitive parts of the forebrain are referred to as the limbic system. The hippocampus is involved in forming long-term memory. The amygdala triggers fear emotions and fear memories.

The amygdala is involved in post-traumatic stress disorder (PTSD). Another part of the limbic system, the **hippocampus**, is involved in the transfer of certain types of short-term memory to long-term memory, as discussed in the chapter opener and in **Investigating Life: Place Cells Reveal Processes of Memory Consolidation during Sleep.**

The cerebrum is responsible for complex behavior and consciousness

The cerebrum is the dominant structure in the mammalian brain. In humans it is so large that it covers all other parts of the brain except the cerebellum (**Figure 45.4A**). Layers of cells at the surface of the cerebrum form the cerebral cortex, which is about 4 millimeters thick and is folded into ridges (**gyri**; singular *gyrus*) and valleys (**sulci**; singular *sulcus*). If the cortex were flattened out, it would be about 1 square meter, but the foldings, or **convolutions**, enable that extensive surface area of cortex to fit within the skull.

As we explore the infoldings of the cerebral cortex and other parts of the brain, we will occasionally mention an individual whose brain was damaged by an accident or other unfortunate event. Until about 50 years ago the study of such individuals was the main source of functional information about the human brain, but developments of imaging technologies such as positron emission tomography (PET) and magnetic resonance

▶InvestigatingLIFE   Place Cells Reveal Processes of Memory Consolidation during Sleep

Experiment

Original Paper: A. K. Lee and M. A. Wilson. 2002. Memory of sequential experience in the hippocampus during slow wave sleep. *Neuron* 36: 1183–1194.

Multiple hippocampal cells were recorded while a rat ran a maze. Individual cells fired only when the rat was at particular locations in the maze; thus the rat's progress through the maze can be represented by a specific sequence of firing of these "place cells." Since memory is consolidated during sleep, are the sequences of place cells expressed during the maze-running experience replayed and processed into long-term memory during sleep?

HYPOTHESIS▶ Memory of the maze-running experience is represented by a sequence of firing of hippocampal place cells. This sequence is repeated during sleep as part of the process of memory consolidation.

METHOD▶

1. Record from multiple hippocampal neurons while a rat is running through a maze.

2. Identify sequences of cell firing that reoccur whenever the rat runs the maze.

3. Continue to record the neuronal activity during sleep and determine if similar sequences are occurring with a probability greater than expected from random activity in that group of cells.

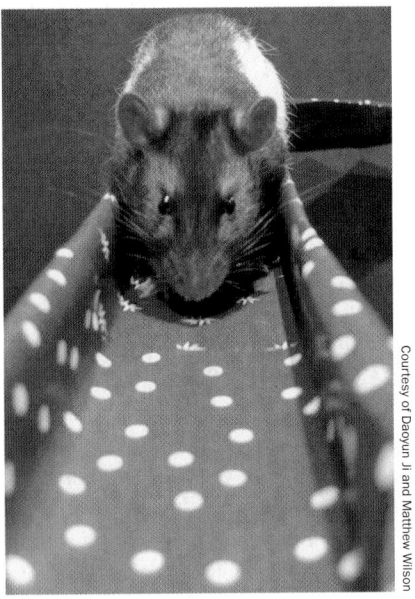

Courtesy of Daoyun Ji and Matthew Wilson

RESULTS▶

1 After 30 runs through the maze, a group of nine place cells are identified that fire in the same order correlating with position in the maze.

2 The peak firing rate of each neuron can be calculated as a function of position in the maze. When the neurons are arranged in the temporal order of their peak firing rates, you can think of each neuron as being a "letter" in a "word" that codes spatial information about the maze.

3 Subsequent recordings while the animal is awake, at rest, or asleep are analyzed for the occurrence of the same or similar "words"— complete or partial sequences of place-cell activity in the same order as the base sequence. Thus a similar word to a nine-letter (nine-neuronal) sequence might be a sequence of seven cells firing in the same order as in the original nine-letter sequence.

CONCLUSION▶

1. Sequences of hippocampal-cell firing that correspond to locations in the maze were highly repeatable and probably represent the coding of that place information in the hippocampus.

2. During sleep, bursts of cell firing sometimes occurred that correspond wholly or partially to the sequences recorded when the rat was running in the maze.

Work with the Data

To conclude that a particular sequence of cell firing observed during sleep is a significant event—meaning that it could be a replay of the waking experience—we have to compare it with the probability that it would occur by random chance. And we need to consider whether an observed sequence that includes some but not all of the components of the baseline "word" is nevertheless a significant event.

What is the minimum number of elements that would have to match the baseline sequence for it to be considered a significant event with $P < 0.01$? To find out, we need to calculate the probabilities of the recorded neurons firing randomly and creating the sequence matches. First, let's consider the probability of a recurrence by chance of the exact nine-"letter" baseline sequence being recorded in a single burst of that group of nine cells. The total number of possible combinations of those nine letters can be calculated as the factorial 9!:

$$9! = 9 \times 8 \times 7 \times 6 \times 5 \times 4 \times 3 \times 2 \times 1 = 362,880$$

In other words, the probability of repeating the entire nine-letter sequence would be 1 out of 362,880. That repeat would have an extremely low probability of occurring and would therefore be a highly significant event. But what if the recorded sequence has only six of the nine cells firing in the proper order? How do you determine the probability of that? First, calculate the probability of

a combination of six cells out of the nine. So for the first cell you have nine choices, for the second you have eight choices, and so forth. Then you have to calculate the probability of that combination of six cells being in the proper sequence, and that will be 1 out of the total number of possible arrangements of those six cells, or 6!. Then what do you do for probabilities of successive events? You multiply the probabilities. For example, if you flip a coin, the probability of heads is 0.5. If you flip it twice, the probability of getting heads both times is 0.5×0.5, or 0.25.

QUESTIONS ▶

1. What is the probability of the sequence 1, 4, 6, 7, 8, 9 out of a random firing of nine cells?

2. What is the probability of a sequence of four letters occurring out of a random firing of nine cells?

3. Are both of the recordings from Questions 1 and 2 low-probability events?

4. What do you note about the time frame of the sequence during sleep versus during wakefulness?

Go to **Achieve** for a companion Data in Depth exercise.

---

imaging (MRI) greatly expanded opportunities to study the human brain. Advances in imaging technologies are contributing to rapid progress in neurobiology.

A curious feature of the human nervous system is that the left side of the body is served (in both sensory and motor aspects) mostly by the right side of the brain, and the right side of the

body is served mostly by the left side of the brain. Thus sensory input from the right hand goes to the left cerebral hemisphere, and sensory input from the left hand goes to the right cerebral hemisphere. The exception is the head, where the left side is controlled by the left cerebral hemisphere and the right side by the right cerebral hemisphere. The two hemispheres are not symmetrical with

(A) The lobes of the cerebrum

The highly convoluted cerebral cortex, viewed here from the left side, covers all of the other structures of the forebrain.

Central sulcus

Parietal lobe

Frontal lobe

Occipital lobe

Olfactory bulb

Cerebellum

The insular cortex, or lobe, is an involution of the cortex between the temporal and the frontal/parietal lobes.

Spinal cord

Temporal lobe

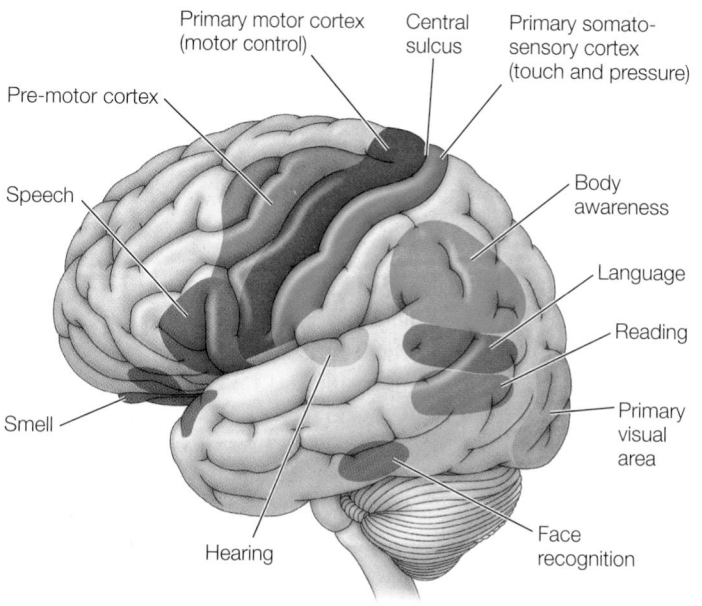

(B) Functions of selected regions of the cerebral cortex

Primary motor cortex (motor control)

Central sulcus

Primary somato-sensory cortex (touch and pressure)

Pre-motor cortex

Speech

Body awareness

Language

Reading

Smell

Primary visual area

Hearing

Face recognition

Figure 45.4 The Human Cerebrum   **(A)** Each cerebral hemisphere is divided into frontal, temporal, parietal, occipital, and insular lobes. **(B)** Different functions are localized in particular areas of the five cerebral lobes.

▶ **View in Achieve**
Activity 45.1 The Human Cerebrum

respect to all functions. Language abilities, for example, reside predominantly in the left hemisphere in most people.

Different regions of the cerebral cortex have specific functions (**Figure 45.4B**). Some of those functions are easily defined, such as receiving and processing sensory information or generating motor commands, but in humans most of the cortex is involved in higher-order information processing that is less easy to define. These latter areas are given the general name of **association cortex**, because they integrate, or *associate*, information from different sensory modalities and from memory.

To understand the cerebral cortex, it helps to have an anatomical road map. Viewed from the left side, the left cerebral hemisphere looks like a boxing glove for the right hand with the fingers pointing forward, the thumb on the side, and the wrist at the rear. The "thumb" area is the **temporal lobe**, the fingers the **frontal lobe**, the back of the hand the **parietal lobe**, and the wrist the **occipital lobe** (see Figure 45.4A). What you can't see from an external view is the **insular lobe**, which is folded in between the thumb and finger areas of the boxing glove (between the frontal/parietal and the temporal lobes). The right cerebral hemisphere shows a mirror image of this arrangement. We will look at each lobe separately.

THE TEMPORAL LOBE   The upper region of the temporal lobe receives and processes auditory information. The association areas of this lobe are involved in recognizing, identifying, and naming objects. Damage to the temporal lobe results in disorders called agnosias, in which the individual is aware of an object but cannot identify it.

Damage to a specific region of the temporal lobe results in the inability to recognize faces. Even old acquaintances cannot be identified by facial features, although they may be identified by other attributes such as voice, body features, and posture. Damage to other association areas of the temporal lobe can cause deficits in understanding spoken language, although speaking, reading, and writing abilities may be intact.

THE FRONTAL LOBE   The frontal and parietal lobes are separated by a deep valley called the central sulcus. A strip of the frontal lobe cortex just in front of the central sulcus is called the **primary motor cortex** (see Figure 45.4B). The neurons in this region control muscles in specific parts of the body; the parts of the body map onto the primary motor cortex, with the head represented in the lower outside region and the legs and feet in the top region near the midline. The graphic drawing of body parts overlying the diagram of the cortex is called a homunculus, and its distortion represents disproportionate innervation (**Figure 45.5**). Parts of the body with fine motor control, such as

the face and hands, have disproportionate representation (see Figure 45.5A). Electrical stimulation of neurons in different regions of the primary motor cortex causes specific muscles of the body to twitch. Just anterior to the primary motor cortex is the **pre-motor cortex**, which is involved in planning more complex and coordinated movements.

The association functions of the frontal lobe are diverse and best described as having to do with feeling and planning. They are said to have **executive function** and they contribute significantly to personality. People with frontal lobe damage have drastic alterations of personality and difficulty planning future events. A dramatic case of frontal lobe damage is that of Phineas Gage, who in 1848 was an industrious and responsible young railroad construction foreman. Then a blasting accident shot a meter-long, 3-centimeter-wide iron tamping rod through his brain. The rod entered Gage's head below his left eye, passed through his frontal lobe, and exited the top of his head (**Figure 45.6**).

Remarkably, Gage survived, but he had a different personality. In the years following his recovery, he was quarrelsome, impatient, obstinate, and used profane language, which he did not do before. He lost his railroad job and earned money by telling his story and exhibiting his scars (and the tamping iron). Several years later,

Figure 45.5 **The Body Is Represented in Primary Motor and Primary Somatosensory Cortexes**   Neurons in the primary motor cortex (**A**) control muscles in specific parts of the body, while neurons in the primary somatosensory cortex (**B**) receive information from specific parts of the body. The locations of these neurons within each cortex correspond to "maps" on which regions of the body are represented in proportion to the amount of innervation they receive. (After W. Penfield and T. Rasmussen 1950. *The Cerebral Cortex of Man: A Clinical Study of Localization of Function.* The Macmillan Company: New York.)

however, he took a job as a stage coach driver in Chile—a challenging job indicating considerable behavioral recovery. He died of a seizure in 1860, at the age of 38. If you are in Boston, you can pay him a visit—his skull, death mask, and the tamping iron are on display in the Warren Anatomical Museum of Harvard Medical School.

THE PARIETAL LOBE The strip of parietal lobe cortex just behind the central sulcus is the **primary somatosensory cortex** (see Figure 45.4B). This area receives touch and pressure information relayed from the body through the thalamus.

As with the primary motor cortex, the entire body surface can be mapped onto the primary somatosensory cortex (see Figure 45.5B). Areas of the body that have a high density of tactile mechanoreceptors and are capable of making fine discriminations in touch (such as the lips and fingers) have disproportionately large representation. If a very small area of the primary somatosensory cortex is stimulated electrically, the subject reports feeling specific sensations, such as touch, in a localized part of the body.

A major association function of the parietal lobe is attending to complex stimuli. Damage to the right parietal lobe causes a condition called contralateral neglect syndrome, in which the individual tends to ignore stimuli from the left side of the body or the left visual field. Such individuals have difficulty performing complex tasks, such as dressing the left side of the body; an afflicted man may not shave the left side of his face unless he is reminded to do so. When asked to copy simple drawings, a person who exhibits this syndrome can do well with the right side of the drawing but not the left. When reading, the person will tend to start from the middle of the page rather than the left margin of the page.

The parietal cortex is not symmetrical with respect to its role in attention. Damage to the left parietal cortex does not cause the same degree of neglect of the right side of the body. You will see similar asymmetries in cortical function later in the chapter when we discuss language.

THE OCCIPITAL LOBE The occipital lobe receives and processes visual information. The association areas of the occipital cortex are essential for making sense of the visual world and translating visual experience into language. Some deficits resulting from damage to these areas are specific. In one case, a woman with limited damage was unable to see motion. Her vision was intact, but she could see a waterfall only as a still image, and an approaching car only as a series of a stationary object at different distances.

THE INSULAR CORTEX The insular cortex, buried deep in the forebrain, receives a great variety of afferent information. The posterior regions receive somatosensory information (e.g., touch, pain, temperature); the middle region combines that with autonomic regulatory information and drives (e.g., hunger, thirst, sex); and the anterior region, which is well developed in more complex primates, elephants, and marine mammals, receives information about social interactions. Thus in mammals the insular cortex appears to integrate

Figure 45.6 A Mind-Altering Experience Phineas Gage miraculously survived a nineteenth-century railroad construction accident that blew an iron rod through his brain. His personality, however, was permanently altered from that of a responsible foreman to a sometimes quarrelsome drifter.

physiological information from all over the body to create a sensation of how the body "feels," and in more complex mammals it may extend that function into a sense of self.

The size of the human brain is off the curve

Humans are sometimes called "big-brain primates," and that is an accurate characterization. Across vertebrate species there is a correlation between body size and brain size (**Figure 45.7**). More complex primates such as chimpanzees, baboons, and gorillas all

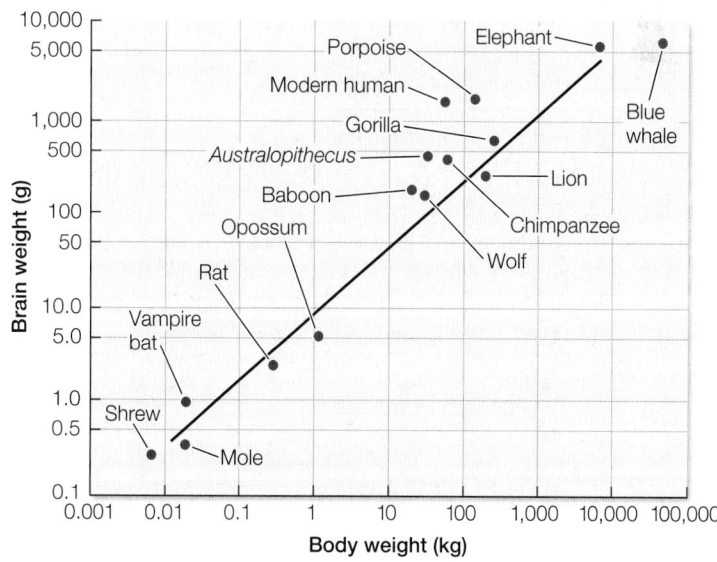

Figure 45.7 Evolution of the Human Brain Brain size scales to body size across a wide range of vertebrates. The more complex primates have larger brains than predicted by the correlation, and humans stand outside this relationship with much bigger brains. The increase in brain size in humans is due mostly to an increase in the cerebral cortex. The human brain is also highly convoluted, and more of it is devoted to associative functions. (After H. J. Jerison. 1969. *Am Nat* 103: 575–588; data from G. Crile and D. P. Quiring. 1940. *Ohio J Sci* 40: 219–259.)

fall above this regression line, but humans stand out because they are so far above the regression line. Gorillas are much larger than humans, but they have smaller brains. Elephants and whales have large brains, but they fall closer to the regression line. Porpoises and humans stand out as having much larger brains than would be predicted by their body sizes.

> **Connect the Concepts** Key Concept 31.5 described how human brains became larger as jaws became smaller.

The correlation of brain size to body size does not tell the whole story of human brain evolution, however. In Figure 43.16, which compares the brains of four vertebrates, we see that in mammals the forebrain is larger than other brain regions, and another feature is the degree of convolution of the cortex. Since the cortex is a layered, two-dimensional array of neurons, the area of cortex is increased by convolutions, which are greatest in humans. And finally, the percent of the cortex that is association cortex (i.e., devoted to the integration of information) is by far the greatest in humans. It is these evolutionary changes, primarily in the cortex, that provide the resources for the intellectual capacity of humans—a topic to which we will return at the end of the chapter.

KEY CONCEPT
45.1 Recap and Assess

The central nervous system communicates with the rest of the body through the peripheral nervous system. We are conscious of some sensory information coming into the CNS, but we are not conscious of other afferent information used in physiological regulation. The brain develops from the anterior region of the embryonic neural tube. The forebrain gives rise to the cerebrum, which is divided into five lobes. Specific functions such as somatosensation, vision, hearing, motor control, smell, and speech are localized in specific cortical areas. At the center of the cerebrum is the limbic system, which contributes to the processing of emotions, inborn responses, and some types of memory. Underneath the cerebrum is the hypothalamus, responsible for many autonomic functions, and the thalamus, which directs ascending information to the cortex. The midbrain and hindbrain constitute the brainstem, within which are many nuclei that support autonomic functions, including sleep and wakefulness. Evolution of the human brain has resulted in a greatly increased cerebral cortex devoted to integration of information.

1. Given your understanding of afferent and efferent systems operating in the nervous system, give an example of a brain–body feedback loop that influences each of the following:

   a. Voluntary behavior through a conscious sensory stimulus.

   b. Involuntary response through a conscious sensory stimulus.

   c. Involuntary response through an unconscious stimulus.

2. What is significant about the location of the reading and language areas of the cerebral cortex as shown in Figure 45.4B?

3. Key Concept 44.3 described the two-point spatial discrimination test. How do the typical results of that test relate to Figure 45.5B?

4. The brain size of humans is significantly above the regression line for mammalian brain size as a function of body size. Why is this observation an understatement of the difference in cerebral cortical capacity in humans as compared with other mammals?

Having briefly described the structure and function of different regions of the nervous system, we now explore some examples of how information is processed by the neural circuitry in some specific brain regions.

KEY CONCEPT
45.2 Nervous System Functions Rely on Neural Circuits

Learning Objectives

45.2.1 Predict the outcome on effector organs when specific peripheral nerves of the sympathetic or parasympathetic divisions of the autonomic nervous system are damaged or stimulated.

45.2.2 Explain how receptive fields are generated in the retina through the interactions among photoreceptors, bipolar cells, ganglion cells, horizontal cells, and amacrine cells.

45.2.3 Describe how neural connections between the eyes and the visual cortex produce three-dimensional vision.

Specific functions are localized in specific parts of the nervous system and depend on the neural circuits, or networks, in those structures. A major focus of modern neuroscience is to understand how the various functions of the nervous system, ranging from simple reflexes to complex learning and memory, are accomplished by the interactions of neurons in circuits. Two extensively studied examples of how neuronal networks process information are the autonomic nervous system (an output pathway) and the visual system (an input pathway).

Pathways of the autonomic nervous system control involuntary physiological functions

The **autonomic nervous system**, or **ANS**, includes CNS and PNS components and controls many involuntary functions, such as heart rate, blood flow, sweating, and digestive activities. Its control of diverse organs and tissues is crucial to homeostasis. The ANS has two divisions, **sympathetic** and **parasympathetic**, that work in opposition to each other in their effects on most organs (**Figure 45.8**). The sympathetic and parasympathetic divisions are distinguished by their anatomy, neurotransmitters, and actions.

The best-known functions of the ANS are those of the sympathetic division that produce the **fight-or-flight response**: increasing heart rate, blood pressure, and cardiac output—all of which prepare the body for emergencies (see Figure 39.3). In contrast, the parasympathetic division slows the heart and lowers blood pressure; its actions have been characterized as "rest and digest." It is tempting to think of the sympathetic division as speeding things up and the parasympathetic division as slowing things down, but it is not that simple; for example, the sympathetic division slows down the digestive system whereas the parasympathetic division accelerates it.

Both sympathetic and parasympathetic efferent pathways begin with cholinergic neurons (neurons that use acetylcholine as their neurotransmitter) whose cell bodies are in the brainstem or spinal cord. These cells are called preganglionic neurons because the

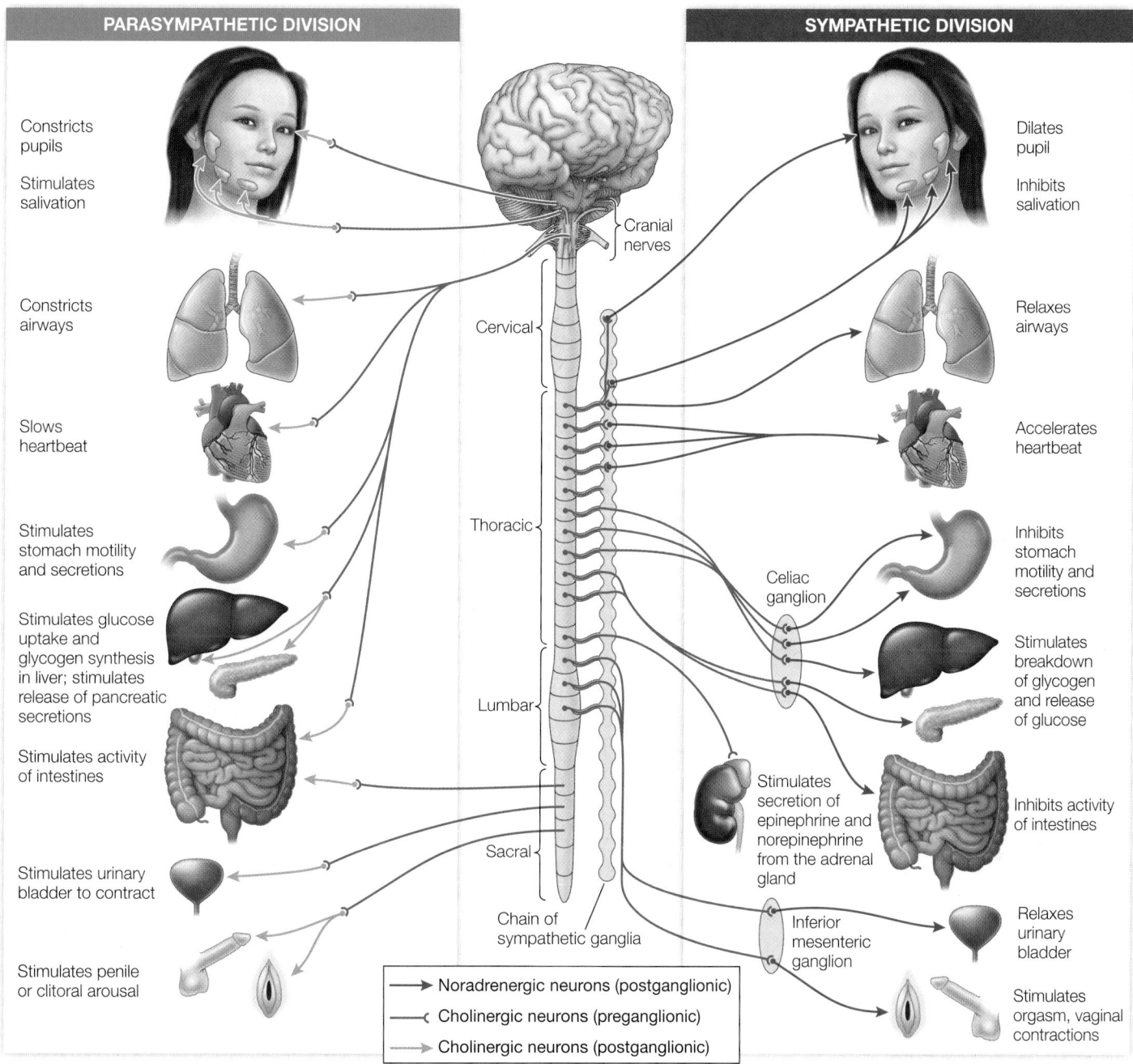

PARASYMPATHETIC DIVISION

Constricts pupils

Stimulates salivation

Constricts airways

Slows heartbeat

Stimulates stomach motility and secretions

Stimulates glucose uptake and glycogen synthesis in liver; stimulates release of pancreatic secretions

Stimulates activity of intestines

Stimulates urinary bladder to contract

Stimulates penile or clitoral arousal

SYMPATHETIC DIVISION

Dilates pupil

Inhibits salivation

Relaxes airways

Accelerates heartbeat

Inhibits stomach motility and secretions

Stimulates breakdown of glycogen and release of glucose

Inhibits activity of intestines

Relaxes urinary bladder

Stimulates orgasm, vaginal contractions

Cranial nerves

Cervical

Thoracic

Celiac ganglion

Lumbar

Sacral

Chain of sympathetic ganglia

Stimulates secretion of epinephrine and norepinephrine from the adrenal gland

Inferior mesenteric ganglion

→ Noradrenergic neurons (postganglionic)
⊰ Cholinergic neurons (preganglionic)
→ Cholinergic neurons (postganglionic)

Figure 45.8 The Autonomic Nervous System   The autonomic nervous system is divided into the sympathetic and parasympathetic divisions. The two divisions work in opposition to each other in their effects on most organs; one results in an increase and the other a decrease in activity.

Q: Why does a person get an extremely dry mouth when speaking in public?

second neurons in these pathways reside in collections of neurons outside the CNS called **ganglia** (singular *ganglion*). The second neurons are called postganglionic neurons because their axons extend out from the ganglia. The axon of a postganglionic neuron synapses with cells in the target organs (see Figure 45.8).

The postganglionic neurons of the sympathetic division mostly use norepinephrine as their neurotransmitter. In contrast, the postganglionic neurons of the parasympathetic division are mostly cholinergic. In organs that receive both sympathetic and

parasympathetic input, the target cells respond in an opposite manner to norepinephrine and to acetylcholine. This happens, for example, in a region of the heart called the pacemaker, which initiates the heartbeat. Stimulating the sympathetic nerve to the heart or dripping norepinephrine onto pacemaker cells increases their firing rate and causes the heart to beat faster. In contrast, stimulating the parasympathetic nerve to the heart or dripping acetylcholine onto pacemaker cells decreases their firing rate and causes the heart to beat more slowly (see Figure 48.8).

The sympathetic and parasympathetic divisions of the ANS can also be distinguished by anatomy. The preganglionic neurons of the parasympathetic division come from the cranial nerves of the brainstem and the sacral (lowest) region of the spinal cord; those of the sympathetic division come from the thoracic and lumbar regions of the spinal cord (see Figure 45.8). Most of the ganglia of the sympathetic division are lined up and interconnected in two chains, one on either side of the spinal cord. The parasympathetic ganglia are close to the target organs and are not interconnected.

The ANS is an important link between the CNS and many physiological functions. Its control of diverse organs and tissues is crucial to homeostasis. Despite the complexity of the ANS, work by neurobiologists and physiologists over many decades has made it possible to understand its functions in terms of neuronal properties and circuits.

The visual system is an example of information integration by the cerebral cortex

The visual system is one of the most-studied input pathways to the CNS. Key Concept 44.4 described how light falling on the retina produces signals that are transmitted through the cellular circuits of the retina, resulting in action potentials in the optic nerve. But how does the brain use this information to represent the visual world?

RETINAL RECEPTIVE FIELDS   Key Concept 44.4 described how a retinal ganglion cell collects information from several photoreceptors—an example of "convergence of information." Each ganglion cell is communicating to the brain something more than simply the presence or absence or intensity of light falling on a portion of the retina.

The question of what information the retinal ganglion cell extracts from the photoreceptors was addressed in classic experiments by Stephen Kuffler at Johns Hopkins University. He used electrodes placed in the retinas of anesthetized cats to record the activity of single ganglion cells while stimulating their retinas with spots of light (**Figure 45.9**). Kuffler's experiments revealed that each ganglion cell has a well-defined **receptive field** composed of a group of photoreceptor cells that receive light from a small area of the entire visual field. Stimulating these photoreceptors with light activates the ganglion cell, which sends action potentials to the thalamus and on to the visual cortex (the area of the occipital lobe where visual information is processed; see Figure 45.4). Information from many photoreceptors is therefore communicated to the brain as a single message. Individual photoreceptors may contribute to the receptive fields of multiple ganglion cells, so that receptive fields overlap.

The receptive fields of most ganglion cells are circular, but whether a spot of light falling on a receptive field excites or inhibits its ganglion cell depends both on the nature of the receptive field and on where the spot of light falls on it. Receptive fields have a center and a concentric surround, and can be either "on-center" or "off-center." Light falling on the center of an on-center receptive field excites the ganglion cell, and light falling

on the center of an off-center receptive field inhibits the ganglion cell. Light falling on the surround has the opposite effect: the surround for an on-center receptive field inhibits the ganglion cell, and the surround for an off-center field is excitatory. Thus the activity of the ganglion cell reflects how much of the light stimulus is on the center and how much is on the surround of its receptive field (see Figure 45.9).

Center effects are always stronger than surround effects. Thus a small dot of light directly on the center of a receptive field has the maximum effect, and a larger light stimulus illuminating the center and parts of the surround has a smaller effect. A uniform patch of light falling equally on the center and surround has very little effect on the firing rate of the ganglion cell for that receptive field. The center and surround almost exactly cancel one another, even though the area of the surround is much larger.

 View in Achieve
Simulation 45.1 Visual Receptive Fields

As is seen in Figure 45.9, photoreceptors synapse onto bipolar cells and bipolar cells onto ganglion cells. This is the pattern of connectivity between photoreceptors in the center of a receptive field, their bipolar cells, and their ganglion cells. In contrast, the photoreceptors in the surround areas modify communication between the center photoreceptors and their bipolar cells through the lateral connections of horizontal cells and amacrine cells. Thus the receptive field of a ganglion cell results from the integration of synaptic activity between photoreceptors, horizontal cells, amacrine cells, and bipolar cells. A general lesson to learn from this seemingly confusing chain of events is that inhibition can be as important as excitation in neural circuits.

In summary, the neural circuitry of the retina results in the generation of signals in the ganglion cell axons traveling in the optic nerve that communicate simple information about the contrasting patterns of light and dark falling on different parts of the retina. But once the action potentials in the optic nerve reach their destinations, how does the brain integrate them to construct visual images of the outside world?

View in Achieve
Animation 45.1 Information Processing in the Retina

RECEPTIVE FIELDS OF CELLS IN THE VISUAL CORTEX   The axons of the optic nerves terminate in a region of the thalamus that is a relay station receiving information from both the right and left eyes. From the thalamus, the information encoded in the activity of axons in the optic nerves is relayed to the visual cortex in the occipital lobes at the back of the brain. In the 1960s David Hubel and Torsten Wiesel of Harvard University studied the activity of neurons in the visual cortex by shining spots and bars of light on retinas of cats while recording the activities of single cells in the cortex. They found that many neurons in the visual cortex, like retinal ganglion cells, have receptive fields with regions that are mutually antagonistic.

Hubel and Wiesel discovered that neurons in the visual cortex respond selectively to bars of light of different orientations falling on the retina, and in some cases to movement of those bars of light in different directions. The concept that emerges from these experiments is that the brain assembles a mental image of

Experiment

Figure 45.9   What Does the Eye Tell the Brain?

Original Paper: S. W. Kuffler. 1953. Discharge patterns and functional organization of mammalian retina. *J Neurophysiol* 16: 37–68.

Stephen Kuffler's experiments recorded the activity of single ganglion cells in the eyes of cats. These groundbreaking experiments revealed the existence of a circular receptive field for each of the retina's ganglion cells. Signals from photoreceptor cells in a receptive field are either excitatory or inhibitory to the ganglion cell, which sends action potentials via the optic nerve to the brain.

HYPOTHESIS▶   Retinal ganglion cells are excited or inhibited by light and dark stimuli falling on local areas of the retina.

METHOD▶

1. Place electrodes next to an individual retinal ganglion cell.

2. Stimulate the retina with different combinations of light and dark stimuli and record the responses of the ganglion cell.

3. Continue recording and move the stimuli around the retina to find the area of sensitivity—the receptive field—for a specific ganglion cell.

Optic nerve

Fine light beams are used to stimulate small regions of the retina.

Recording of action potentials in axon of ganglion cell

Electrode   Horizontal cells

Axons of ganglion cells   Ganglion cells   Amacrine cells   Bipolar cells   Photoreceptors

RESULTS▶

| Stimulus patterns on retina | Action potentials in on-center ganglion cell | Action potentials in off-center ganglion cell |

Complete darkness

Small spot falling on center of receptive field

Large spot covering receptive field

Ring of light excluding center of receptive field

↑ Stimulus ↑
On / Off

↑ Stimulus ↑
On / Off

An on-center ganglion cell is maximally stimulated by light falling on its receptive field's center and is inhibited by a ring of light falling on its receptive field's surround.

An off-center ganglion cell is maximally stimulated by light falling on its receptive field's surround and is inhibited by light falling on its center.

CONCLUSION▶   Ganglion cells use a center-surround dichotomy to encode patterns of contrast between light and dark.

Q: Why is there a blind spot in each eye?

the visual world by analyzing edges in patterns of light falling on the retina. Each retina sends a million axons to the brain, but there are *hundreds of millions* of neurons in the visual cortex. The action potentials from one retinal ganglion cell are received via the thalamus by hundreds of cortical neurons, each responsive to a different combination of orientation, position, color, and movement of contrasting lines in the patterns of light and dark falling on the retina.

Three-dimensional vision results from cortical cells receiving input from both eyes

How do we perceive objects in three dimensions? The short answer is that our two eyes see overlapping, yet slightly different, visual fields—that is, humans have **binocular vision**. A person who is blind in one eye has difficulty discriminating distances. Animals whose eyes are on the sides of the head rather than facing front have minimal overlap in their fields of vision and, as a result, poor

depth vision except for a narrow field straight ahead; however, they can see predators creeping up from all sides.

The story of how the brain integrates information from two eyes begins with the paths of the optic nerves. The two optic nerves run along the underside of the brain, join just under the hypothalamus, and then separate again (**Figure 45.10**). The place where they join is called the **optic chiasm**. Axons from the half of each retina closest to the nose cross in the optic chiasm and go to the opposite side of the brain. The axons from the outer half of each retina do not cross over at the optic chiasm; axons from the outer left retina go to the left side of the brain, and vice versa for axons from the outer right retina.

The functional consequence of the optic chiasm is that all of the visual information from the left side of your field of vision when you are looking straight ahead goes to the right side of your brain, and all of the visual information from the right side of your field of vision goes to the left side of your brain.

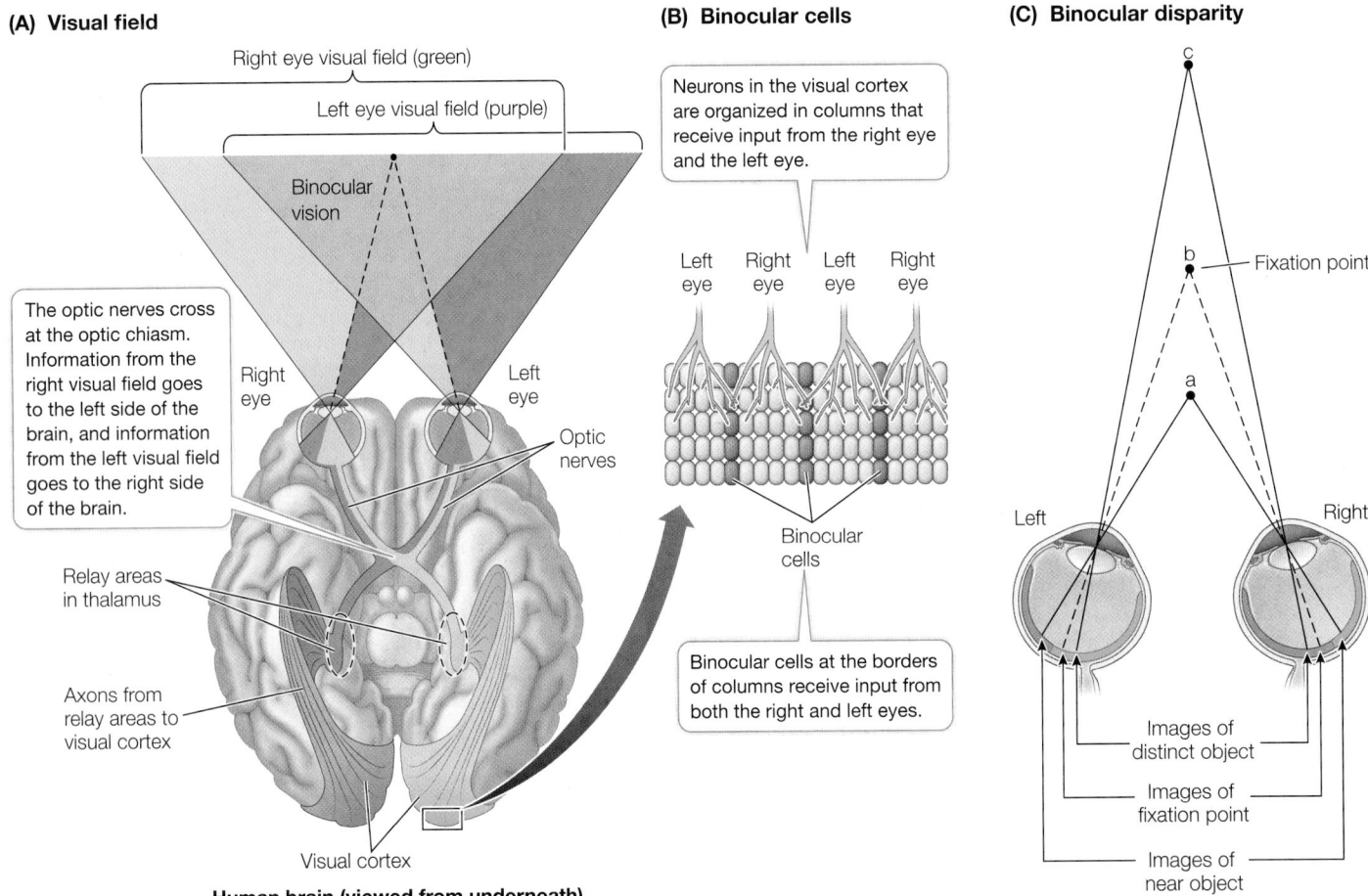

Figure 45.10 How Do We See in Three Dimensions? (**A**) Our eyes have largely overlapping visual fields, and both eyes transmit information to both sides of the brain. However, because the axons from the inner sides of the retinas cross at the optic chiasm, information from the visual space to the left of straight ahead goes to the right side of the brain, and information from the visual space to the right of straight ahead goes to the left side of the brain. (**B**) Between these left and right eye columns of neurons are neurons that receive input from both eyes.

These are the binocular cells. (**C**) Light from objects that are different distances away will fall at different locations on the retinas. These disparities between where the image of the fixation point and the images of other objects fall on the retina mean that different binocular cells will receive input from different retinal axons depending on how far away the object is. These disparity-sensitive cells enable depth perception and three-dimensional vision.

However, there is a large area of overlap between the visual fields of the two eyes. These relationships are shown in purple and green in Figure 45.10.

Because of the overlap between the visual fields of the two eyes, there can be neurons in the visual cortex that receive input from both the left and the right eye. These are called binocular cells, and they can detect disparity between where the image of an object falls on the two retinas. What is disparity? Hold your finger out in front of you and look at it closing one eye and then the other. Your finger appears to jump back and forth because its image falls on a different position on each retina. Repeat the exercise with a distant object. It doesn't jump back and forth as much because there is less disparity in the positions of the image on the two retinas. Certain binocular cells respond optimally to a stimulus falling on both retinas with a particular disparity. Which set of binocular cells is stimulated depends on how far away the stimulus is.

When we look at something, we can detect its shape, color, depth, and movement. Where does all this information come together? Is there a single cell that fires only when a red sports car drives by? The answer to that is probably no. Visual experience comes from simultaneous activity in many different cells. In addition, most visual experiences are enhanced by information from the other senses and from memory, which helps explain why about 75% of the cerebral cortex is association cortex.

KEY CONCEPT
45.2 Recap and Assess

Information in the nervous system is processed by cellular interactions in neuronal networks. The opposing actions of the sympathetic and parasympathetic divisions of the ANS can be understood in terms of neural pathways consisting of just two neurons. Vision begins with retinal photoreceptors organized into circular retinal receptive fields that influence the activity of retinal ganglion cells. Information from ganglion cells is transmitted in the optic nerves to the thalamus and relayed from there to the visual cortex. The left visual field from both eyes is represented in the right visual cortex, and vice versa for the right visual field. Receptive fields of cortical cells represent input from multiple ganglion cells, and binocular, disparity-sensitive cortical cells enable depth perception.

1. Explain how a knife wound to left side of the neck can result in pupillary constriction in the left eye.

2. How does the ANS differ in its control of heart rate versus digestive activity?

3. Why can a small spot of light on the retina cause a larger response in a retinal ganglion cell than a large spot of light falling on the same area of retina?

By studying the neural circuitry of the visual system and the ANS, you have gained some understanding of how information reaches the CNS and how the CNS controls various functions of the body. But what about the higher functions of the mammalian CNS—the complex functions between input and output, such as language, learning, memory, and dreams?

KEY CONCEPT
45.3
Higher Brain Functions Involve Integration of Multiple Systems

Learning Objectives

45.3.1 Describe the EEG, EOG, and EMG characteristics associated with wake, non-REM and REM sleep and how they change throughout the daily sleep-wake cycle.

45.3.2 Describe the flow of information when speaking a written or a heard word, and specify which areas of the brain are involved in speech processing.

45.3.3 Explain how the modification of synaptic strength in hippocampal place cells produces a spatial map in the hippocampus.

45.3.4 Discuss how evolutionary changes in brain structures led to the development of self-awareness.

The higher brain functions discussed in the remaining pages of this chapter are undeniably complex. Nevertheless, neuroscientists, using a wide range of techniques, are making considerable progress in understanding these functions in terms of their cellular, molecular, and network properties. The following discussion addresses several aspects of brain and behavior that present challenges to neuroscientists: sleep and dreaming, learning and memory, language use, and consciousness.

Sleep and dreaming are reflected in electrical patterns in the cerebral cortex

A dominant feature of behavior is the daily cycle of sleep and waking. All birds and mammals, probably all other vertebrates, and also many invertebrates, sleep. We humans spend one-third of our lives sleeping, yet we do not know why or how. We do know, however, that we need to sleep. Loss of sleep impairs alertness and performance. Many people in our society—certainly most college students—are chronically sleep-deprived. Accidents and serious mistakes that endanger lives can be attributed to impaired alertness caused by lack of sleep. Insomnia (difficulty in falling or staying asleep) is one of the most common medical complaints.

THE ELECTROENCEPHALOGRAM A common tool of sleep researchers is the **electroencephalogram**, or **EEG**. Rather than recording the activity of single neurons, the EEG characterizes activity in huge numbers of neurons. EEG electrodes are much larger than the fine electrodes used to detect single cell activity. Placed at different locations on the head and scalp, EEG electrodes record fluctuations in the electric potential differences between electrodes over time (**Figure 45.11A**). These differences reflect the electrical activity of the neurons in the brain regions under the electrodes, primarily regions of the cerebral cortex. Usually the electrical activity of one or more skeletal muscles is also recorded; this record is called an electromyogram (EMG). Movements of the eyes are recorded as an electrooculogram (EOG).

EEG, EMG, and EOG patterns reveal the transition from being awake to being asleep. They also reveal that there are different

(A)

(B)

(C)

Figure 45.11 Stages of Sleep **(A)** Electrical activity in the cerebral cortex is detected by electrodes that are placed on the head and record changes in voltage between the electrodes through time. **(B)** The resulting record is an electroencephalogram, or EEG. **(C)** Humans cycle through different stages of sleep throughout the night. (B after A. Rechtschaffen and A. Kales. 1968. *A manual of standardized terminology, techniques and scoring system for sleep stages of human subjects.* NINDB Neurological Information Network (U.S.). Bethesda, MD.)

states of sleep. In mammals other than humans, two major sleep states are easily distinguished: **slow-wave sleep** and **rapid eye movement (REM) sleep**. Slow-wave sleep gets its name from the high-amplitude, slow-frequency waves in the EEG. REM sleep gets its name from jerky movements of the eyeballs that occur during this state. In humans, sleep states are characterized as non-REM sleep and REM sleep. Human non-REM sleep is divided into three stages.

When you fall asleep, you first enter stage 1 non-REM sleep, which then progresses through stage 2 to stage 3 (**Figure 45.11B**). Stage 3 is deep, restorative, slow-wave sleep. This first full cycle of non-REM sleep is followed by an episode of REM sleep. Throughout the night you experience four or five cycles of non-REM and REM sleep (**Figure 45.11C**). About 80% of your sleep is non-REM sleep. The most vivid dreams and nightmares occur during the 20% of sleep that is REM sleep.

CELLULAR CHANGES DURING SLEEP   When we are awake, several nuclei (groups of neurons) in the brainstem reticular-activating system (see Key Concept 45.1) are continuously active. Axons from neurons in these nuclei extend to the thalamus and throughout the cerebral cortex, where they release depolarizing neurotransmitters (acetylcholine, norepinephrine, and serotonin). These broadly distributed neurotransmitters keep the resting potential of the neurons of the thalamus and cortex close to threshold and sensitive to synaptic inputs, thereby maintaining the responsiveness of the brain that characterizes being awake.

With the onset of sleep, activity in these brainstem nuclei decreases, and their axon terminals release less neurotransmitter. With the withdrawal of these depolarizing neurotransmitters, the resting potentials of the cells of the thalamus and cortex become more negative (hyperpolarized), and the cells are less sensitive to

excitatory synaptic input. Their processing of information is inhibited, and consciousness is lost. You have probably experienced this as "nodding off." As you enter non-REM sleep, cells of the cortex begin to fire action potentials in bursts. The synchronization of these bursts over broad areas of cerebral cortex results in the EEG slow-wave pattern that characterizes deep non-REM sleep.

At the transition from non-REM to REM sleep, dramatic changes occur. Some of the brainstem nuclei that were inactive during non-REM sleep become active again, causing a general depolarization of cortical neurons. Thus in REM sleep the synchronized bursts of firing cease, and the EEG resembles that of the awake brain. Because the resting potentials of the neurons return to near threshold levels, the cortex can process information, and vivid dreams occur.

So why don't we act out our dreams? During REM sleep the brain inhibits both afferent (sensory) and efferent (motor) pathways; we are paralyzed during REM sleep. Limb twitches and the jerky eye movements are motor signals breaking through the inhibition. The bizarre nature of dreams may be due to the lack of sensory feedback to the cortex from the body and the outside world. In other words, a functioning cortex is out of touch with reality. The function of muscle paralysis during REM sleep may be to prevent the acting out of dreams.

Knowing the cellular mechanisms of sleep has not yet led to an understanding of its function. Many questions remain. Why do we have two sleep states with very different neurophysiological characteristics? Why does non-REM sleep always occur first? Why do the two states cycle during the rest phase? We know sleep is essential for life, but we don't know why. One set of hypotheses is that sleep is necessary for the maintenance and repair of neural connections and for the neural changes involved in learning and memory—and forgetting. These hypotheses are supported by many experiments showing that performance of a learned task or recall of declarative information on the day following training is impaired if sleep is prevented, and is best following a good night's sleep. Another possible function of sleep was introduced in Key Concept 43.1, and that was the clearing of the brain of metabolic waste products by the newly described glymphatic system. Understanding the function, or more likely functions, of sleep is a major challenge for neuroscientists.

Language abilities are localized in the left cerebral hemisphere

No aspect of brain function is as integrally related to human consciousness and intellect as is language. Therefore brain mechanisms that underlie the acquisition and use of language are extremely interesting to neuroscientists. A curious observation about language ability is that it resides principally in one cerebral hemisphere—which in 97% of people is the left hemisphere. This phenomenon is referred to as the **lateralization** of language functions.

Fascinating research on this subject was conducted by Roger Sperry and his colleagues at the California Institute of Technology. The two cerebral hemispheres are connected by a tract of white matter called the corpus callosum. Recall from Key Concept 43.4 that white matter tracts are bundles of myelin-coated axons transmitting neural information from one area of the CNS to another. In one severe form of epilepsy, bursts of action potentials causing seizures travel between hemispheres via the corpus callosum. Cutting the tract eliminates the problem, and patients function well following surgery. However, these "split-brain" patients display interesting deficits in language ability.

After the surgery, if an object is shown in the right visual field and the left eye is closed (see Figure 45.10), the patient can describe it verbally and in writing. If the object is shown in the left visual field and the right eye is closed, the patient cannot describe it either verbally or in writing, but can use his or her left hand to point to a picture of the object. Without the connecting tissue between the two hemispheres, knowledge or experience of the right hemisphere can no longer be expressed in language.

Individuals who have suffered damage to the left hemisphere frequently suffer from some form of **aphasia**, a deficit in the ability to use or understand words. Studies of such individuals have identified several language areas in the left hemisphere.

- **Broca's area**, located in the frontal lobe just in front of the primary motor cortex, is essential for speech. Damage to Broca's area results in halting, slow, poorly articulated speech or even complete loss of speech, but the patient can still read and understand language.

- **Wernicke's area**, located in the temporal lobe close to its border with the occipital lobe, is more involved with sensory than with motor aspects of language. Damage to Wernicke's area can cause a person to lose the ability to speak sensibly while retaining the abilities to form the sounds of normal speech and to imitate its cadence. Such a patient cannot understand spoken or written language.

- The **angular gyrus**, located near Wernicke's area, is involved in integrating spoken and written language.

Normal language ability depends on the flow of information among various areas of the left cerebral cortex. Input from spoken language travels from the auditory cortex to Wernicke's area (**Figure 45.12A**). Input from written language travels from the visual cortex to the angular gyrus to Wernicke's area (**Figure 45.12B**). Commands to speak are formulated in Wernicke's area and travel to Broca's area and from there to the primary motor cortex. Damage to any one of those areas or the pathways between them can result in aphasia. Using methods of brain imaging such as functional magnetic resonance imaging (fMRI) or positron emission tomography (PET), it is possible to see the metabolic activity in different brain areas when the brain is using language (**Figure 45.13**).

Some learning and memory can be localized to specific brain areas

Learning is the modification of behavior by experience. Memory is the ability of the nervous system to retain what is learned and experienced. Even very simple animals can learn and remember, but

(A) Repeating a heard word

(B) Speaking a written word

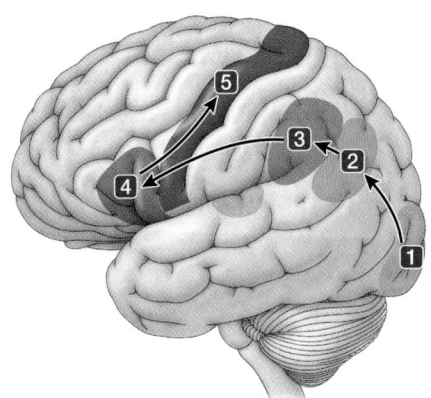

Figure 45.12 Language Areas of the Cortex   Different regions of the left cerebral cortex participate in the processes of (**A**) repeating a word that is heard and (**B**) speaking a written word.

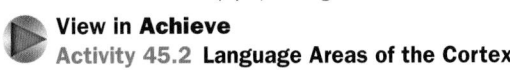

View in **Achieve**
Activity 45.2 **Language Areas of the Cortex**

Listening to words

Passively viewing words

Speaking words

Generating word associations

From M. I. Posner and M. E. Raichle. 1994. Images of Mind. W. H. Freeman: New York

Figure 45.13 **Imaging Techniques Reveal Active Parts of the Brain**   Positron emission tomography (PET) scanning reveals the brain regions activated by different aspects of language use. Radioactively labeled glucose is given to the subject. Brain areas take up radioactivity in proportion to their metabolic use of glucose. The PET scan visualizes levels of radioactivity in specific brain regions when a particular activity is performed. The red, yellow, and white areas are the most active.

these two abilities are most highly developed in humans. Consider the amount of information associated with learning a language, and then the much greater amount of information that language enables our brains to store and to process. The capacity of memory and the rate at which memories can be retrieved are remarkable features of the human nervous system.

Learning that leads to long-term memory and modification of behavior must involve long-lasting synaptic changes. A phenomenon that may explain how long-term synaptic changes might arise is **long-term potentiation**, or **LTP**. LTP results from high-frequency electrical stimulation of certain identifiable circuits that makes these circuits more sensitive to subsequent stimulation. In contrast, continuous, repetitive, low-level stimulation of these same circuits reduces their responsiveness, a phenomenon that has been called **long-term depression** (**LTD**). LTP and LTD may be fundamental cellular or molecular mechanisms involved in learning and memory.

Above the level of the synapse, memory involves interactions between several brain areas, as we discussed in the opener to this chapter and in **Investigating Life: Places Cells Reveal Processes of Memory Consolidation during Sleep**. Some of the first insights into memory processes came from surgical treatment of patients with severe seizures. That treatment involves destruction of the excessively active brain area triggering the seizures. To find the right area, the surgery is done under local anesthesia, with the patient remaining conscious. As different regions of the brain are electrically stimulated with electrodes, the patient reports the resulting sensations. Stimulation of some regions of the association cortex

elicits recall of vivid memories. Such observations provided the first evidence that specific areas in the brain are associated with specific memories and that memory can be attributed to networks of neurons. Destroying a small area of the brain does not completely erase a memory, however, so it is postulated that memory is a function distributed over many brain regions and can be stimulated via many different routes.

You experience several forms of memory everyday. You have **immediate memory** for events that are happening now. Immediate memory is almost perfectly photographic but lasts only seconds. **Short-term memory** contains less information but lasts longer—on the order of 10–15 minutes. When you are introduced to a group of several new people, you probably will have forgotten their names in an hour or so if you have not written them down, used them in a conversation, or made a conscious effort to repeat them. Repetition, use, or reinforcement by something that gets your attention (a title such as "President," for example) facilitates the transfer of short-term memory to **long-term memory**, which can last for days, months, years, or a lifetime. There is also intermediate-term memory, which lasts about a day.

Knowledge about neural mechanisms for the transfer of short-term memory to long-term memory—memory consolidation—has come from observations of persons who have lost parts of the limbic system, notably the hippocampus. A famous case is that of the man identified as H.M., whose hippocampus on both sides of the brain was removed to control his severe epilepsy. After the surgery, H.M. was unable to transfer information to long-term memory. If someone was introduced to him, had a conversation with him, and then left the room for several minutes, when that person returned, H.M could not recognize him—it was as if the conversation had never taken place. Up until his death 55 years later, H.M. remembered events that happened before his surgery but could not remember post-surgery events for more than 10–15 minutes.

The studies of H.M., other such patients, and experiments on animals and even London taxi drivers show that the hippocampus plays an essential role in the acquisition of **declarative memories**—those that involve people, places, things, and events. The study featured in the opener to this chapter revealed the mapping of spatial information by neuronal networks in the rat, and the replay of that information when the rat is resting before or after running a maze. Subsequent experiments revealed the replay of the same spatial information during sleep, possibly revealing a process that is consolidating the memory and transferring it into long-term storage (see Investigating Life: Place Cells Reveal Processes of Memory Consolidation during Sleep).

 Media Clip 45.1 The Man with No Short-Term Memory
Life12e.com/mc45.1

We still cannot answer the question "What is consciousness?"

This chapter has only scratched the surface of the organization and functions of the human brain. Even with all of our knowledge of the human brain, and with all of the sophisticated new research tools, we still cannot answer the question "What is consciousness?"

The word "consciousness" is used in everyday language to refer to being awake in contrast to being asleep or in a coma. Here we are referring to being mentally aware of yourself, your environment, and events going on around you in such a way that you can plan for future events and make decisions based on experience, evidence, value systems, and predicted consequences. Speculations about consciousness have been the realm of philosophers, but we are getting closer to a neurobiological understanding.

One requirement for conscious experience is a perception of self that can be integrated with information from the physical and social environment and information from past experience. The basis for a perception of self derives from the huge amount of somatosensory and visceral information that comes from all parts of the body. This information is used for motor control and for homeostatic regulation. It enables animals to find food, seek mates, seek warmth, avoid cold, avoid danger, and so on. Different modes of this afferent information go to appropriate control and regulatory systems in the brainstem and forebrain. But these diverse sources of information also go to the insular cortex. The insular lobe appears to integrate physiological information from all over the body to create a sensation of how the body "feels." Thus when an animal's actions restore homeostasis, it "feels" better, and this is motivation to do the right thing for well-being.

In humans and the great apes, the insular lobe is greatly expanded and its circuitry communicates with parts of the brain involved in planning and decision making. In imaging studies, the insular cortex is activated by a great diversity of situations that involve strong feelings such as pleasure, disgust, humor, pain, lust, craving, humiliation, guilt, or empathy. Damage to the insular lobe causes apathy, loss of the ability to enjoy music, loss of sexual responsiveness, and even loss of the ability to distinguish good food from spoiled food. Humans and the few other species (great apes, elephants, and some marine mammals) that have expanded insular lobes are unique in that they can recognize themselves in a mirror. Could it be that this very discrete part of our brains and its circuitry are the neurobiological basis for self-awareness?

KEY CONCEPT
45.3 Recap and Assess

Complex functions of the nervous system can be understood in terms of the properties of neurons and neuronal networks. Language functions are lateralized to the left cerebral hemisphere. Since information about objects seen in the left visual field is processed in the right visual cortex, patients with a severed connection between their left and right cerebral hemispheres can see and recognize objects in their left visual field, but not describe them in words. Imaging shows the integration of different brain areas in the hearing, reading, and speaking of words. REM and non-REM sleep and awake states involve very different activities in many areas of the brain. Sleep states have a regular organization of expression during the daily rest phase. At the cellular level, learning and memory involve changes in synaptic strength, and memory processes involve interactions of neuronal networks from different brain areas. Declarative memories are acquired through the hippocampus. Consciousness may involve creation of a perception of the self in the insular cortex.

1. What is the significance of paralysis of skeletal muscles during REM sleep?

2. If a person with a severed corpus callosum is shown an object in his left visual field, how will he be able to communicate to an observer what that object is?

3. What does the case of H. M. tell us about the brain mechanisms underlying the acquisition of declarative memories?

4. How might the insular lobe of humans contribute to the phenomenon of consciousness?

 View in Achieve
Activity 45.3 Concept Matching: The Mammalian Nervous System

 ▶Investigating**LIFE**

QandA Can recordings of hippocampal place cells reveal processes of memory consolidation during sleep?

Unfortunately we cannot give a rat an exam to ask what it remembers. However, we can look in other brain areas for electrophysiological patterns of activity that correlate with the hippocampal place-cell patterns. Wilson and colleagues described the fast replay of the hippocampal place-cell patterns as a unique EEG signal called "ripples." They observed that these ripples were tightly coupled to slower EEG brainwaves that spread to cortical areas of the brain. When they recorded in some of these areas of the cortex, they found similar patterns of firing (i.e., ripples) in those areas that were synchronized to the hippocampal ripples. They hypothesized that the ripples represent memory transcripts that are transferred to and stored in areas of the cortex.

Future directions

The neurophysiological studies of the acquisition and consolidation of declarative memories bring us closer to understanding the physical nature of a memory. The synaptic strengthening known as LTP (long-term potentiation) lasts a long time in contrast to action potentials, but not nearly as long as a memory that can last a lifetime. We can think of a memory as a piece of information that is stored in the brain. We have used the word "information" a lot in this chapter, but we really do not know what "information" is in the brain. It is not simply action potentials; they are brief, transient events. It is not patterns of synapses; they are constantly being altered. It must involve patterns of connectivity in and between neuronal networks in the brain; but what maintains those networks over years? We have much to learn about how our brains work.

You should be able to relate each summary to the adjacent figures. If you go to this visual summary in **Achieve**, you can follow links to figures, animations, activities, and simulations that will help you consolidate the material.

KEY CONCEPT

45.1 Functions Are Localized in the Nervous System

Go to **Activity 45.1**

- The brain and spinal cord make up the **central nervous system** (**CNS**); the cranial and spinal nerves make up the **peripheral nervous system** (**PNS**).

- The vertebrate brain forms from three swellings at the anterior end of the embryonic neural tube that become the **hindbrain**, **midbrain**, and **forebrain**. The forebrain consists of the **telencephalon** and **diencephalon**. The telencephalon develops into the **cerebrum** (**cerebral hemispheres**). The diencephalon develops into the **thalamus** and **hypothalamus**. The midbrain and hindbrain develop into the **brainstem** and the **cerebellum**.

- The spinal cord and the cranial nerves communicate information between the brain and the rest of the body.

- The **limbic system** is involved in emotions, mood, physiological drives, instincts, and memory.

- The cerebral hemispheres can be divided into the **temporal**, **frontal**, **parietal**, **occipital**, and **insular lobes**. Layers of neurons on the surfaces of these lobes are the **cerebral cortex**, different regions of which have specific functions.

Figure 45.1

Cerebral hemispheres
Cingulate gyrus
Thalamus
Olfactory bulbs
Hypothalamus
Pituitary
Amygdala
Hippocampus

Questions

1. What major structures of the adult brain develop from the embryonic forebrain?

2. Per square centimeter, which has greater representation in the primary somatosensory cortex, the hand or the foot? What does that mean?

3. What are the major functions associated with each of the five cerebral lobes?

KEY CONCEPT

45.2 Nervous System Functions Rely on Neural Circuits

Go to **Animation 45.1** and **Simulation 45.1**

- The **autonomic nervous system** (**ANS**) controls physiological functions of organs and organ systems. Its **sympathetic** and **parasympathetic** divisions are characterized by their anatomy, neurotransmitters, and effects on target tissues.

- Information from retinal ganglion cells is communicated via the optic nerve to the thalamus and then to the visual cortex. The visual cortex assembles an image of the visual world by analyzing edges of patterns of light.

- **Binocular vision** results from information from both eyes being communicated to binocular cells in the visual cortex. These cells interpret distance by measuring the disparity between where the same stimulus falls on the two retinas.

Figure 45.9

Optic nerve
Electrode
Horizontal cells
Recording of action potentials in axon of ganglion cell
Axons of ganglion cells
Ganglion cells
Amacrine cells
Bipolar cells
Photoreceptors

Stimulus patterns on retina

Ring of light excluding center of receptive field

Action potentials in on-center ganglion cell

Stimulus
On   Off

Action potentials in off-center ganglion cell

Stimulus
On   Off

Questions

1. What are three major differences between sympathetic and parasympathetic pathways?

2. What are the five cell types in the layered organization of the retina, and what role does each play?

3. How does binocular vision enable perception of distance?

VISUAL SUMMARY 45

KEY CONCEPT
45.3 Higher Brain Functions Involve Integration of Multiple Systems

Go to Activities 45.2 and 45.3

- Humans, like other mammals and birds, have daily cycles of wake and sleep. Sleep can be divided into **rapid eye movement** (**REM**) sleep and non-REM sleep.

- Language abilities are **lateralized** mostly in the left cerebral hemisphere. Different areas of the left hemisphere—including **Broca's area**, **Wernicke's area**, and the **angular gyrus**—are responsible for different aspects of language.

- Learning and memory processes are localized to specific brain areas. **Long-term potentiation** (**LTP**) and **long-term depression** (**LDP**) are important processes in learning and memory.

- Complex memories can be elicited by stimulating small regions of association cortex. Damage to the hippocampus can destroy the ability to form long-term **declarative memory**.

Figure 45.11

Both photos courtesy of Compumedics

Questions

1. What are the differences between non-REM and REM sleep at the level of cortical neurons, EEG recordings, and behavior?

2. Learning to do a behavioral task like riding a bike is forming a procedural memory. Interpret the fact that patient H.M. could get better at a behavioral task over days but could not remember having practiced it.

3. Why is it proposed that the insular lobe of the cerebrum is responsible for a generalized perception of feeling good or bad?

Figure 45.12

Repeating a heard word

Broca's area
Primary motor cortex (motor control)
Wernicke's area
Angular gyrus
Primary visual area
Speech
Hearing

Go to **Achieve** for the eBook, **LearningCurve**, animations, activities, simulations, and additional resources and assignments.

46 Musculoskeletal Systems

KEY CONCEPTS

46.1 Interactions of Actin and Myosin Cause Muscles to Contract

46.2 Many Factors Affect Muscle Performance

46.3 Muscles and Skeletal Systems Work Together

© Michael Durham/Minden Pictures

Relative to their size, many animals have more impressive jumping skills than humans. This red-legged frog (*Rana aurora*) can leap distances up to 20 times its body length.

▶Investigating**LIFE**

Champion Jumpers

The women's long jump Olympic record is 7.4 meters, set in 1988 by Jackie Joyner-Kersee. Another world-record long jump was set two years earlier by Rosie the Ribeter, who jumped 6.5 meters. Rosie was a frog competing in the Calaveras County Jumping Frog Contest. Rosie's jump is more impressive—it was 20 times her body length, whereas Jackie's was 5 times her body length. And Rosie jumped from a sitting, crouched position, while Jackie's jump was propelled by a sprint.

Both jumps were powered by skeletal muscle. The cellular mechanisms of muscle contraction are the same in frog and human, so why is the frog's jump more impressive? The answer involves the concept of *leverage*—muscles and skeletal elements working together. Muscles pull on bones that are connected at joints to make levers. With a lever you can use the same force to move a large mass a small distance or a small mass a large distance. The ratio of leg length to body mass is greater for the frog than for the human. Thus the frog's long legs can move its small body mass a long distance.

The power for the frog's jump comes from a single contraction of its leg muscles (there is no sprint), and those muscles

contract only a very short distance compared with the length of the jump. One species of frog, *Rana pipiens*, has a body length of only 11 centimeters, but longer legs. The muscles that power the jump are only about 3.5 centimeters long and shorten by just 0.75 centimeters (21%) when the frog jumps. Once again leverage comes into play. The thigh muscles are attached to the lower leg bones close to the knee joint and thus can move the opposite ends of those bones over a longer distance and more quickly than if they were attached farther away from the joint. There is a trade-off, however, in terms of force and speed. To use a shovel, you have one hand near the end of the shaft and the other hand farther down the shaft. With hands close together, you move the shovel blade fast, but can't pick up a heavy load of dirt. With hands farther apart, you can't move the blade as fast, but you can pick up a heavier load.

 What adaptations optimize the jumping muscles of the frog?
(Find the answer on page 1044.)

KEY CONCEPT
46.1 Interactions of Actin and Myosin Cause Muscles to Contract

Learning Objectives

46.1.1 Describe changes in sarcomere structure and appearance as muscle contraction occurs.

46.1.2 Explain the molecular events underlying the sliding filament model of muscle contraction.

46.1.3 Describe how ATP is involved in muscle contraction.

46.1.4 Beginning with an action potential in a motor neuron, describe the sequence of events at the molecular level that leads to skeletal muscle contraction.

46.1.5 Discuss why gap junctions are important for cardiac and smooth, but not skeletal, muscle functions.

Behavior and most physiological functions of animals, such as beating of the heart and moving of food through the digestive tract, depend on muscle contraction. Wherever tissues contract, muscle cells are responsible. As you saw in Figure 38.2, there are three types of vertebrate muscle:

1. **Skeletal muscle** is responsible for all voluntary movements, such as running or playing a piano. It is also involved in many involuntary actions, including breathing, shivering, and maintaining posture.

2. **Cardiac muscle** is responsible for the beating of the heart.

3. **Smooth muscle** creates movement in many hollow internal organs, such as the digestive system, bladder, and blood vessels, and is under the control of the autonomic (involuntary) nervous system.

Skeletal and smooth muscle occur in all animal phyla, but cardiac muscle is unique to vertebrates. All three muscle types share the same underlying molecular mechanisms for generating force. We will use vertebrate skeletal muscle as our primary example. Later in this key concept we discuss the differences in cardiac and smooth muscle that adapt them to their particular functions, and at the end of Key Concept 46.2 we describe interesting specializations of insect muscle.

Sliding filaments of actin and myosin cause skeletal muscle to contract

Skeletal muscles are so named because they attach to skeletal elements and make most movements of the body possible. Skeletal muscles are frequently called **striated muscles** because of their striped appearance (**Figure 46.1**; also see Figure 38.2). Skeletal muscle cells, called **muscle fibers**, are large and long and have many nuclei. These multinucleate cells form in development through the fusion of many individual embryonic muscle cells called **myoblasts**. A specific muscle such as your biceps (which bends your arm) is composed of hundreds or thousands of muscle fibers bundled together by connective tissue.

Muscle contraction is due to the interaction of the contractile proteins **actin** and **myosin**, which exist as long filaments within muscle cells. Actin filaments are thin and myosin filaments are thick, and they lie parallel to each other. When muscle contraction is triggered, the actin and myosin filaments slide past each other in a telescoping fashion.

Connect the Concepts Key Concept 5.3 discussed how microfilaments made of polymerized actin are elements of the cytoskeleton that are involved in maintaining cell shape and cell movements in all eukaryotic cells.

Thin actin and thick myosin filaments are bundled together in an orderly fashion as **myofibrils**. A muscle cell (fiber) contains many myofibrils (see Figure 46.1). A longitudinal view of a myofibril reveals why skeletal muscle appears striated. The myofibril consists of repeating units called **sarcomeres**. Each sarcomere is made of overlapping bundles of actin and myosin filaments that create a distinct banding pattern (see Figure 46.1). Before the molecular nature of the muscle banding pattern was known, the bands were given names that are still used today. Each sarcomere is bounded by Z lines, which anchor the thin actin filaments. Centered in the sarcomere is the A band, which contains the myosin filaments. The light-appearing H zone and I band are regions where actin and myosin filaments do not overlap in the relaxed muscle. The dark stripe within the H zone is the M band; it contains proteins that hold the myosin filaments in their regular arrangement.

The bundles of myosin filaments are held in a centered position within the sarcomere by a protein called **titin** (see Figure 46.2). Titin is the largest protein in the body; it runs the full length of the sarcomere from Z line to Z line. Each titin molecule runs right through a myosin bundle. Between the ends of the myosin bundles and the Z lines, titin molecules are very stretchable, like bungee cords. In a relaxed skeletal muscle, resistance to stretch is mostly due to the elasticity of the titin molecules.

As the muscle contracts, the sarcomeres shorten and the band pattern changes. The H zone and the I band become much narrower, and the Z lines move toward the A band as if the actin filaments were sliding into the H zone, the region occupied by only myosin filaments (**Figure 46.2**). In the mid-1950s this observation independently led two teams of British biologists to propose the **sliding filament model** of muscle contraction.

It is not uncommon in science for critical breakthroughs to be made simultaneously in different laboratories, but in this case the coincidences are remarkable. The leaders of the two teams were named Hugh Huxley and Andrew Huxley—but they were not related. Andrew Huxley was a faculty member at Cambridge University in the early 1950s, and Hugh Huxley was a graduate student working in a different laboratory. Both were interested in the structure of muscle and the mechanism of contraction. Hugh Huxley moved to MIT as a postdoctoral fellow where he worked with Jean Hanson using electron microscopy. Andrew Huxley, joined by Rolf Niedergerke, used a new form of light microscopy that the two developed. The two groups proposed the

Figure 46.1 The Structure of Skeletal Muscle
A skeletal muscle is made up of bundles of muscle fibers. Each muscle fiber is a multinucleate cell containing numerous myofibrils, which are highly ordered assemblages of thick myosin and thin actin filaments. The arrangement of the actin and myosin filaments gives skeletal muscle fibers their characteristic striated appearance.

▶ **View in Achieve**
Activity 46.1
The Structure of a Sarcomere

Twisting around the actin chains is another protein, **tropomyosin**, and attached to tropomyosin at intervals are molecules of **troponin**. We discuss these two proteins later in this key concept.

The myosin heads bind reversibly to specific sites on actin and thereby form cross-bridges between the myosin and the actin filaments. When a myosin head binds to an actin filament, the head's conformation changes. As the head bends, it exerts a tiny force that causes the actin filament to move 5–10 nanometers relative to the myosin filament. When the myosin heads are bound to actin, they can bind and hydrolyze ATP. The energy released when this happens changes the conformation of the myosin head, causing it to release the actin and return to its extended position, from which it can bind to actin again.

Together these details explain the cycle of events that cause the actin and myosin filaments to slide past each other and shorten the sarcomere. They also explain rigor mortis—the stiffening of muscles soon after death. ATP binding causes myosin to release from actin, so when ATP production stops with death, myosin cannot release and the muscles stay contracted. Eventually, however, the proteins lose their integrity and the muscles soften. The timing of these events in different muscles helps a medical examiner estimate the time of death.

We have been discussing the cycle of contraction in terms of a single myosin head. But each myosin filament has many myosin heads at both ends and is surrounded by six actin filaments; thus the contraction of the sarcomere involves a great many cycles of interaction between actin and myosin molecules. That is why when a single myosin head breaks its contact with actin, the actin filaments do not slip backward.

sliding filament model at the same time, and both papers were published in the same issue of the journal *Nature*.

Actin–myosin interactions cause filaments to slide

To understand the mechanism causing the actin and myosin filaments to slide past each other, we must first examine the structures of actin and myosin (**Figure 46.3**). A myosin molecule consists of two long polypeptide chains coiled together, each ending in a large globular head. A myosin filament is made up of many myosin molecules arranged in parallel, with their heads projecting sideways at each end of the filament like a bunch of golf clubs.

An actin filament consists of actin monomers polymerized into long chains that look like two strands of beads twisted together.

Actin–myosin interactions are controlled by calcium ions

Like neurons, muscle cells are excitable—that is, their cell membranes generate and conduct action potentials. Skeletal muscle action potentials are initiated by motor neurons releasing

Figure 46.2 Sliding Filaments
The banding pattern of the sarcomere changes as it shortens, as seen in electron micrographs. These observations led to the sliding filament model of muscle contraction.

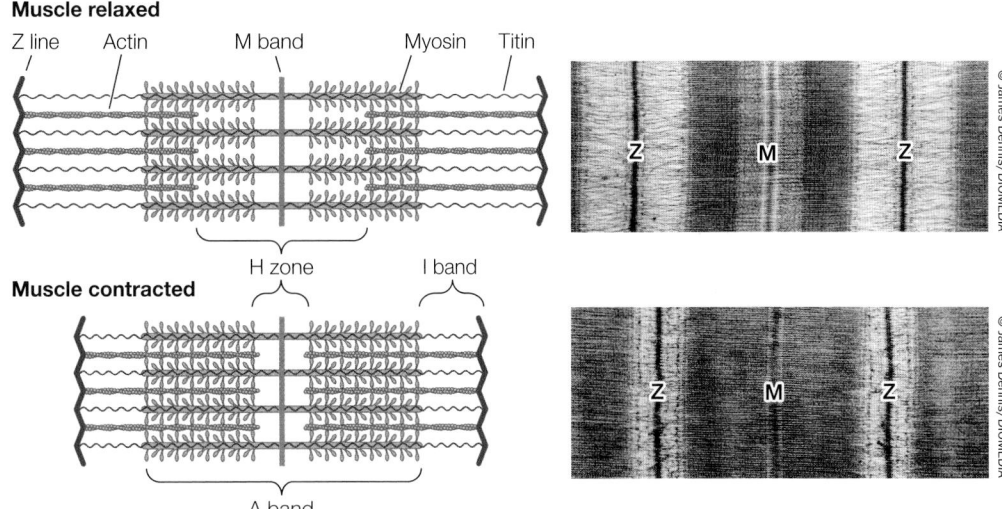

neurotransmitter at **neuromuscular junctions** (see Key Concept 43.3). The axon terminals of motor neurons are generally highly branched and form synapses with hundreds of muscle fibers (**Figure 46.4**). A motor neuron and all of the fibers with which it synapses constitute a **motor unit**. The fibers contract simultaneously when the unit's motor neuron fires. One muscle can consist of many motor units. Thus there are two ways to increase a muscle's strength of contraction—increase the firing rate of an individual motor neuron, or recruit more motor neurons.

When an action potential arrives at a neuromuscular junction, acetylcholine is released from the motor neuron terminals, diffuses across the synaptic cleft, binds to receptors in the postsynaptic membrane, and causes ion channels in the motor end plate to open (see Figure 43.12). Most of the ions that flow through these channels are Na^+, and therefore the motor end plate is depolarized. The depolarization spreads to the surrounding cell membrane of the muscle fiber, which contains voltage-gated sodium channels. When thresholds for those channels are reached, the cell membrane fires an action potential that is conducted rapidly to all points on the surface of the muscle fiber.

An action potential in a muscle fiber also travels deep within the cell. The cell membrane is continuous with a system of **T**

tubules that descend into the muscle fiber cytoplasm (also called the **sarcoplasm**). The "T" stands for "transverse." The contents of the T tubules are outside the cell. The T tubules are like the indentations created in a water-filled balloon by poking your finger into it. The action potential that spreads over the surface membrane of the fiber also spreads through this system of T tubules (**Figure 46.5**).

The T tubules come very close to the endoplasmic reticulum (ER) of the muscle cell. In muscle cells the ER is called the **sarcoplasmic reticulum**, and it is a closed compartment surrounding every myofibril. Calcium pumps in the sarcoplasmic reticulum take up Ca^{2+} from the sarcoplasm. Therefore when the muscle fiber is at rest, there is a high concentration of Ca^{2+} in the sarcoplasmic reticulum and a low concentration of Ca^{2+} in the sarcoplasm.

Spanning the space between the T tubule membrane and the sarcoplasmic reticulum are two proteins. One protein, the dihydropyridine (DHP) receptor, is located in the T tubule membrane; it is voltage-sensitive and changes its conformation in response to an action potential spreading through the T tubule system. The other protein, the ryanodine receptor, is located in the sarcoplasmic reticulum membrane and is a Ca^{2+} channel.

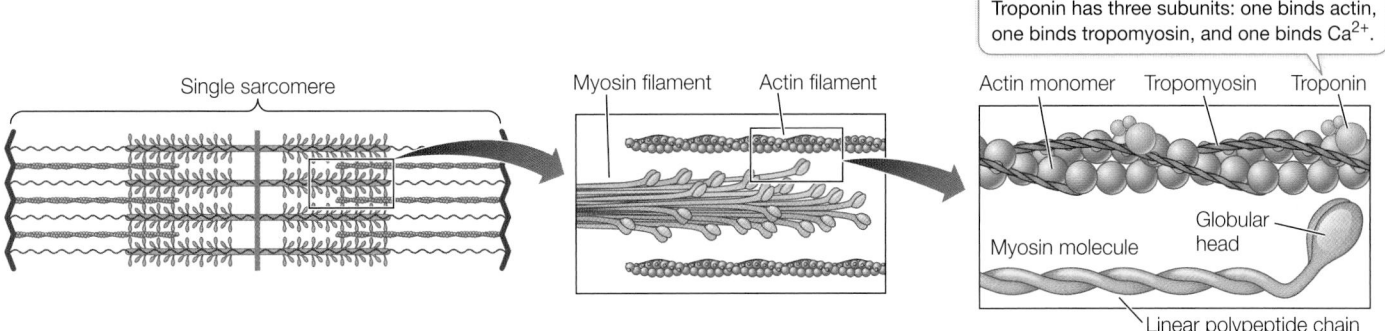

Figure 46.3 Actin and Myosin Filaments Overlap to Form Myofibrils
Myosin filaments are bundles of molecules with globular heads and polypeptide tails; the protein titin holds these filaments centered within the sarcomeres. Actin filaments consist of two chains of actin monomers twisted together. They are wrapped by chains of the polypeptide tropomyosin and are studded at intervals with another protein, troponin.

Axon

Skeletal muscle fiber

Axon terminals

10 μm

© M. I. Walker/Science Source

Figure 46.4 The Neuromuscular Junction Axons branching from a single motor neuron end in terminals that innervate multiple skeletal muscle fibers.

Q: Is there a relationship between the number of fibers that a motor neuron innervates and fine motor control, between the number of fibers innervated and the exertion of force?

These two proteins are physically connected. When the DHP receptor changes its conformation due to an action potential, it opens the ryanodine Ca^{2+} channels, and Ca^{2+} flows from the sarcoplasmic reticulum into the sarcoplasm. Ca^{2+} ions diffusing through the sarcoplasm surrounding the actin and myosin filaments trigger the interaction of actin and myosin and the sliding of the filaments. How do the Ca^{2+} ions do this?

An actin filament, as you have seen, is a helical arrangement of actin monomers. Twisted around the actin filament are two strands of the protein tropomyosin (**Figure 46.6**; see also Figure 46.3). At regular intervals, the filament also includes a globular protein, troponin. The troponin molecule has three subunits: one binds actin, one binds tropomyosin, and one binds Ca^{2+}.

When the muscle is at rest, the tropomyosin strands are positioned so that they block the myosin binding sites on the actin filaments. When Ca^{2+} is released into the sarcoplasm, it binds to troponin, changing its conformation. Because the troponin is bound to the tropomyosin, this conformational change twists the tropomyosin

Figure 46.5 T Tubules Spread Action Potentials into the Fiber An action potential at the neuromuscular junction spreads throughout the muscle fiber via a network of T tubules, triggering the release of Ca^{2+} from the sarcoplasmic reticulum.

View in Achieve
Activity 46.2 The Neuromuscular Junction

Action potential

Neuromuscular junction

T tubule

Sarcoplasmic reticulum

Myofibril

Cell membrane

Action potential

Ca^{2+} channel

Motor neuron

ACh

1 Action potentials (red arrows) open voltage-gated Ca^{2+} channels in the axon terminal. Influx of Ca^{2+} initiates release of acetylcholine (ACh) from presynaptic membrane.

Action potential

Muscle fiber

K^+

Na^+

T tubule

Motor end plate

2 Action potentials generated by the postsynaptic membrane are conducted along the muscle fiber membrane and spread down T tubules...

Sarcoplasmic reticulum

Ca^{2+}

ATP
ADP

ATP
ADP

Calcium pump

Ryanodine receptor

DHP (dihydropyridine) receptor

3 ...which causes a change in the conformation of the DHP receptor and ryanodine receptor, releasing Ca^{2+} stored in the sarcoplasmic reticulum.

ATP
ADP

ATP
ADP

4 Released Ca^{2+} diffuses in sarcoplasm, stimulating muscle contraction.

ATP
ADP

ATP
ADP

5 Ca^{2+} is taken up by the sarcoplasmic reticulum, terminating muscle contraction.

1 Ca^{2+} is released from the sarcoplasmic reticulum.

2 Ca^{2+} in the sarcoplasm binds to troponin, causing a conformation change that exposes mysosin binding sites on the actin.

Ca^{2+}

Troponin

Tropomyosin

Myosin filament

ADP—P$_i$

3a Myosin heads bind to actin;...

Myosin binding site

ADP—P$_i$

3b ...release of P$_i$ initiates power stroke.

P$_i$

ADP

7 If Ca^{2+} is returned to the sarcoplasmic reticulum, the muscle relaxes.

8 If Ca^{2+} remains available, the cycle repeats and muscle contraction continues.

ADP—P$_i$

ATP

ATP

ADP

4 In the power stroke, the myosin head changes conformation; filaments slide past one another.

5 ADP is released at the end of the power stroke. ATP binds to myosin, causing it to release actin.

6 Hydrolysis of ATP returns the myosin head to its "cocked" position.

ADP—P$_i$

Figure 46.6 Release of Ca^{2+} from the Sarcoplasmic Reticulum Triggers Muscle Contraction When Ca^{2+} binds to troponin, it changes the conformation of troponin, exposing myosin binding sites on the actin. As long as binding sites and ATP are available, the cycle of actin and myosin interactions continues and the filaments slide past each other. Note that in the relaxed condition, the myosin heads are energized.

Q: What are three roles that ATP plays in skeletal muscle contraction?

View in Achieve
Animation 46.1
Molecular Mechanisms of Muscle Contraction

enough to expose the actin–myosin binding sites, and the cycle of making and breaking actin–myosin bonds is initiated. The filaments pull past each other, and the muscle fiber contracts. When the calcium pumps in the sarcoplasmic reticulum membranes remove the Ca^{2+} ions from the sarcoplasm, the conformation of the tropomyosin reverts and again blocks the binding of myosin heads to actin, and the muscle fiber returns to its resting condition. Figure 46.6 summarizes this cycle.

Cardiac muscle is similar to and different from skeletal muscle

Like skeletal muscle, cardiac muscle appears striated because of the regular arrangement of actin and myosin filaments into sarcomeres (**Figure 46.7**). Cardiac muscle cells are smaller than skeletal muscle fibers and have only one nucleus each (uninucleate). Cardiac muscle cells branch, and the branches of adjoining cells interdigitate, forming a meshwork resistant to tearing. As a result, the heart walls can withstand high pressures while pumping blood, without the danger of developing leaks. Adding to the strength of cardiac muscle are **intercalated discs** that provide strong mechanical adhesions between adjacent cells. Gap junctions are an important feature of cardiac muscle. These structures in the intercalated discs allow cytoplasmic continuity between cells (see Figure 7.16A). Because of gap junctions, cardiac muscle cells are electrically coupled. An action potential initiated at one point in a sheet of cardiac muscle spreads rapidly, causing a large number of cardiac muscle cells to contract simultaneously.

Certain cardiac muscle cells are specialized for generating and conducting electric signals. These pacemaker and conducting cells have a low density of actin and myosin filaments, but they initiate and coordinate the rhythmic contractions of the

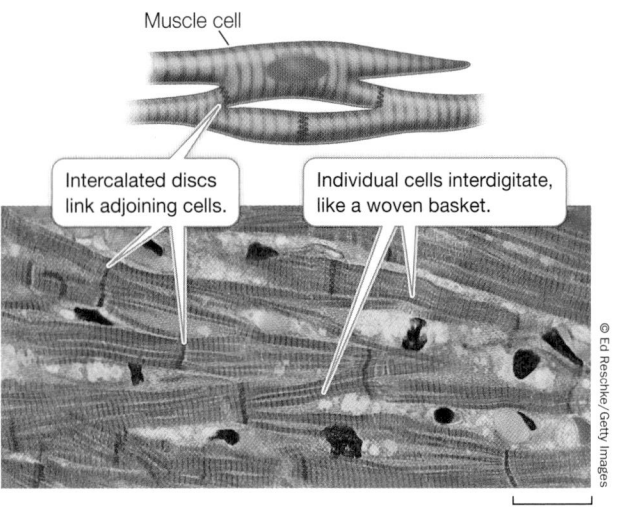

Muscle cell

Intercalated discs link adjoining cells.

Individual cells interdigitate, like a woven basket.

© Ed Reschke/Getty Images

15 μm

Figure 46.7 Cardiac Muscle Cells Form a Strong Meshwork Cardiac muscle cells branch and interdigitate, forming a tear-resistant mesh that can withstand the blood pressure generated by the contraction of the heart muscle.

heart. (The molecular basis for this pacemaking function is covered in Key Concept 48.3.) Pacemaker cells make the vertebrate heartbeat autorhythmic, meaning the heartbeat is generated by the heart muscle itself. A heart removed from a vertebrate can continue to beat with no input from the nervous system. Input from the autonomic nervous system modifies the *rate* at which pacemaker cells fire, but it is not essential for their continued rhythmic function.

The mechanism of excitation–contraction coupling in cardiac muscle cells is different from that in skeletal muscle cells. The T tubules are larger, and the DHP receptor proteins in the T tubules are Ca^{2+} channels. The DHP receptors in the cardiac T tubules are not physically connected with the ryanodine receptors in the sarcoplasmic reticulum. Instead, when an action potential spreads down the T tubules, it causes the voltage-gated DHP channels to open, allowing extracellular Ca^{2+} to flow into the sarcoplasm. That increased sarcoplasmic Ca^{2+} binds to the ryanodine receptors, causing their Ca^{2+} channels to open. The resulting huge rise in sarcoplasmic Ca^{2+} concentration stimulates fiber contraction. This mechanism is called Ca^{2+}-induced Ca^{2+} release.

 Media Clip 46.1 Be Still My Beating Stem Cell Heart Life12e.com/mc46.1

Smooth muscle causes slow contractions of many internal organs

Smooth muscle provides the contractile force for most of our internal organs, which are under the control of the autonomic nervous system. Smooth muscle moves food through the digestive tract, controls the flow of blood through blood vessels, and empties the urinary bladder. Smooth muscle also generates "goose bumps" on the skin and causes the hair on the back of a dog or cat to stand erect when the animal is being aggressive or defensive. Structurally, smooth muscle cells are the simplest

muscle cells. They are smaller than skeletal muscle cells, usually long and spindle-shaped, and each has a single nucleus. They appear "smooth" because the actin and myosin filaments are not as regularly arranged as they are in skeletal and cardiac muscle, and so do not produce the striated appearance.

Some smooth muscle tissue, such as that from the wall of the digestive tract, is arranged in sheets, and individual cells in a sheet are in electrical contact with one another through gap junctions, as they are in cardiac muscle. As a result, an action potential generated in one smooth muscle cell spreads to all the cells in that sheet of tissue, and the sheet contracts in a coordinated fashion.

The cell membranes of smooth muscle cells are sensitive to stretch, with important consequences. For example, if the wall of the digestive tract is stretched in one location (as by a mouthful of food passing down the esophagus to the stomach), the membranes of the stretched cells depolarize, reach threshold, and fire action potentials, which cause the cells to contract. Thus smooth muscle contracts after being stretched, and the harder it is stretched, the stronger it contracts. This behavior of smooth muscle is important for moving food through the digestive system.

The walls of blood vessels—except capillaries—contain much smooth muscle, especially on the arterial side where the blood is under higher pressure. Changes in vascular smooth muscle tone are responsible for controlling the distribution of blood in the body.

The neural influences on smooth muscle come from the two divisions of the autonomic nervous system (see Figure 45.8). The neurotransmitters of the sympathetic and parasympathetic postganglionic cells alter the membrane potential of smooth muscle cells. For example, in the digestive tract acetylcholine causes smooth muscle cells to depolarize, making them more likely to fire action potentials and contract. Antagonistically, norepinephrine causes these muscle cells to hyperpolarize and thus be less likely to fire action potentials and contract (**Figure 46.8**). In contrast, norepinephrine acting through G protein-coupled receptors causes the smooth muscle in arteries serving the gut to contract. Remember that the action of the neurotransmitters depends on the receptors in the target tissues. Sympathetic activity is high in a fight-or-flight situation. In an emergency you don't need to digest your lunch, but shunting blood from the gut to tissues such as major skeletal muscles could be critical for your survival.

Smooth muscle cell contraction is not controlled by the troponin–tropomyosin mechanism, but calcium still plays a critical role. A Ca^{2+} influx into the sarcoplasm of a smooth muscle cell can be stimulated by action potentials, hormones, or stretching. The Ca^{2+} that enters the sarcoplasm combines with a protein called calmodulin. The Ca^{2+}–calmodulin complex activates an enzyme called myosin kinase that phosphorylates myosin heads. When the myosin heads in smooth muscle are phosphorylated, they undergo cycles of binding and releasing actin, causing muscle contraction. As Ca^{2+} is removed from the sarcoplasm, it dissociates from calmodulin, and the activity of myosin kinase falls. An additional enzyme, myosin phosphatase, dephosphorylates the myosin to help reduce actin–myosin interactions (**Figure 46.9**).

 View in Achieve **Animation 46.2 Smooth Muscle Action**

(A) Overview of the experiment

1 A strip of intestinal smooth muscle is anchored to a device that measures contractile force.

2 A pipette drips acetylcholine or norepinephrine onto the strip.

3 An electrode detects action potentials in a muscle cell.

4 Muscle membrane potential and action potentials are recorded.

© SPL/Science Source

Measuring electrode

Display screen

Amplifier →

Time

Reference electrode (outside cell)

Force transducer →

Measures muscle contractions

Time

Intestinal muscle   Saline bath

5 The force of contraction of the muscle is measured by a force transducer.

(B) Experimental results

When acetylcholine is dripped onto the muscle, the cells depolarize, fire action potentials more rapidly, and increase their force of contraction.

Norepinephrine, by contrast, causes the cells to hyperpolarize, decrease their rate of firing, and decrease their force of contraction.

Apply acetylcholine   Wash out acetylcholine   Apply norepinephrine   Wash out norepinephrine

Membrane potential (mV)

+25
0
−25
−50

Force →

Muscle contracts

Muscle relaxes

Time

Figure 46.8 How do Autonomic Nervous System Neurotransmitters Control the Firing Rate of Smooth Muscle Cells? **(A)** When a strip of intestinal smooth muscle is mounted in an incubation bath so that its generation of action potentials and its force of contraction can be recorded, it is possible to test the effects of sympathetic and parasympathetic neurotransmitters on that tissue. **(B)** Acetylcholine depolarizes (makes less negative) the membranes and increases action potentials; norepinephrine hyperpolarizes (makes more negative) the membranes and decreases action potentials. (B after T. B. Bolton et al. 1979. *Physiol Rev* 59: 606–718.)

Figure 46.9 The Role of Ca²⁺ in Smooth Muscle Contraction

When a smooth muscle cell is depolarized by an action potential, a neurotransmitter, or stretch, Ca^{2+} enters the sarcoplasm and binds to calmodulin, which in turn activates an enzyme that phosphorylates the myosin heads, causing them to bind to actin. As long as the myosin remains phosphorylated, actin and myosin go through cycles of binding and release. Thus in smooth muscle the Ca^{2+}-mediated change is on myosin, whereas in skeletal and cardiac muscle it is on the actin–tropomyosin filament.

KEY CONCEPT
46.1 Recap and Assess

The three types of muscle are skeletal, cardiac, and smooth. The contractile ability of muscle derives from interactions between actin and myosin filaments. Contraction depends on control by Ca^{2+} in the sarcoplasm. Tropomyosin and troponin are controlling elements in skeletal and cardiac muscle. Calmodulin is the controlling element in smooth muscle.

1. In terms of the arrangement of actin and myosin filaments in the sarcomere, why do the H zone and I band get smaller when the skeletal muscle contracts, and why does the A band stay the same?

2. What roles do the three subunits of troponin play in the control of skeletal muscle contraction?

3. Why does rigor mortis—the stiffening of muscles after death— occur first in muscles with the least glycogen content?

4. The insecticide malathion destroys the enzyme acetylcholinesterase. Accidental exposure can cause extreme rigid muscle paralysis. Why?

5. Why are gap junctions important to the function of cardiac and smooth muscle, but not skeletal muscle?

Now that you understand how muscles generate force, let's look at what determines the characteristics of a muscle, its performance, and how individual muscles can change their characteristics with regular use and conditioning.

KEY CONCEPT
46.2 Many Factors Affect Muscle Performance

Learning Objectives

46.2.1 Explain what determines how much force or tension is generated by a muscle.

46.2.2 Describe how muscle fiber types contribute to performance abilities in aerobic and anaerobic work.

46.2.3 Explain why peak running performance declines with distance of the event.

The various functions that muscles perform place different demands on them. Some muscles, such as postural muscles, must sustain a load continuously over long periods of time. Muscles used in walking or running must rapidly vary their strength of contraction over a wide range of positions. In contrast, the jumping muscles of the frog must exert maximum force instantaneously. The muscles that control your fingers generally do not have to sustain long, strong contractions, but they must be able to undergo quick yet graded contractions for fine manual dexterity. What is "quick" for humans, however, doesn't begin to compare with insect flight muscles that can contract as fast as 1,000 times per second. How are different muscles adapted for specific functions and demands?

The strength of a muscle contraction depends on how many fibers are contracting and at what rate

The arrival of an action potential at a neuromuscular junction of a skeletal muscle fiber causes an action potential in that fiber. That action potential is conducted through the muscle fiber's T tubule system and causes a minimum unit of contraction, called a **twitch**. A twitch can be measured in terms of the tension, or force, it generates (**Figure 46.10A**). A single action potential stimulates a single twitch, but the ultimate force generated by an action potential varies enormously depending on how many muscle fibers it reaches. The level of tension an entire muscle generates depends on two factors: the number of motor units activated, and the frequency at which those motor units fire.

In muscles responsible for fine movements, such as those of the fingers, a motor neuron may innervate only one or a few muscle fibers, but in a muscle that produces large forces, such as the biceps, a motor neuron innervates a large number of muscle fibers.

At the level of a muscle fiber, a single action potential stimulates a single twitch. If action potentials reaching the muscle fiber are adequately separated in time, each twitch is a discrete, all-or-none phenomenon. If action potentials are fired more rapidly, however, new twitches are triggered before the myofibrils have a chance to return to their resting condition. As a result, the twitches sum, and

the tension generated by the fiber increases and becomes more sustained. Thus an individual muscle fiber can show a graded response to increased levels of stimulation by its motor neuron.

Twitches sum at high levels of stimulation because the calcium pumps in the sarcoplasmic reticulum (see Figure 46.5) are unable to clear the Ca^{2+} ions from the sarcoplasm between action potentials. Eventually a stimulation frequency can be reached that results in the continuous presence of Ca^{2+} in the sarcoplasm at high enough levels to cause continuous activation of the contractile machinery—a condition known as **tetanus** (**Figure 46.10B**). (Do not confuse this condition with the disease tetanus, which is caused by a bacterial toxin and is characterized by spastic contractions of skeletal muscles.)

How long a muscle fiber can maintain a tetanic contraction depends on its supply of ATP. Eventually the contracting fiber will become fatigued and be unable to sustain the contraction. It may seem paradoxical that the *lack* of ATP causes fatigue, since the action of ATP is to break actin–myosin bonds. But remember that the energy released from the hydrolysis of ATP "re-cocks" the myosin heads, allowing them to cycle through another power stroke. When a muscle is contracting against a load, the cycle of making and breaking actin–myosin bonds must continue in order to prevent the load from stretching the muscle. The situation is like rowing a boat upstream. You cannot maintain your position relative to the stream bank by just holding the oars out against the current; you have to keep rowing. Likewise, actin–myosin bonds have to keep cycling to maintain tension in the muscle.

Many muscles of the body maintain a low level of tension even when the body is at rest. For example, the muscles of the neck, trunk, and limbs that maintain our posture against the pull of gravity are always working, even when we are standing or sitting still. Muscle tone comes from the activity of a small but changing number of motor units in a muscle; at any one time, some of the

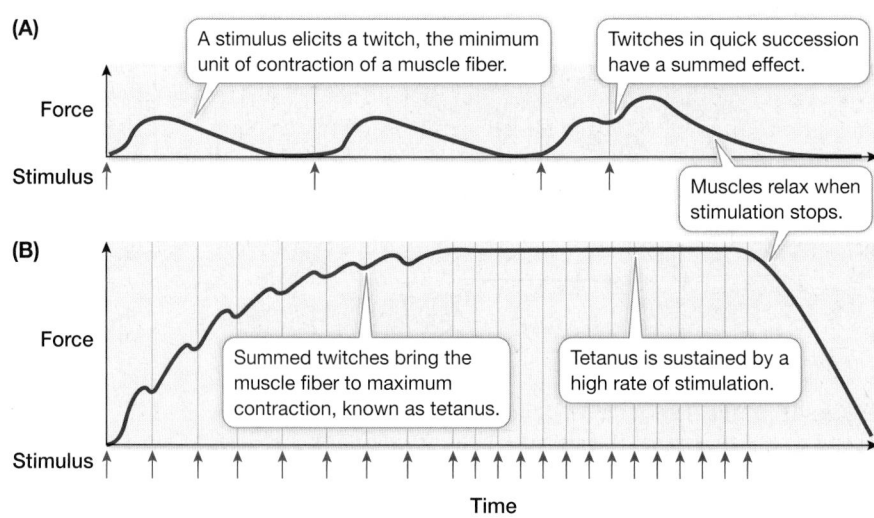

(A)

A stimulus elicits a twitch, the minimum unit of contraction of a muscle fiber.

Twitches in quick succession have a summed effect.

Force

Stimulus

Muscles relax when stimulation stops.

(B)

Force

Summed twitches bring the muscle fiber to maximum contraction, known as tetanus.

Tetanus is sustained by a high rate of stimulation.

Stimulus

Time

Figure 46.10 Twitches and Tetanus **(A)** Action potentials from a motor neuron cause a muscle fiber to twitch. Twitches in quick succession can be summed. **(B)** Summation of many twitches can bring the muscle fiber to the maximum level of contraction, known as tetanus.

muscle's fibers are contracting and others are relaxed. The nervous system is constantly readjusting muscle tone.

Muscle fiber types determine endurance and strength

Not all skeletal muscle fibers are alike, and a single muscle often contains more than one type of fiber. The two major types of skeletal muscle fibers express different genes for their myosin molecules, and these myosin variants have different rates of ATPase activity. Those with high ATPase activity can recycle their actin–myosin cross-bridges rapidly and are therefore called **fast-twitch fibers**; those with lower ATPase activity are called **slow-twitch fibers**, and they develop tension more slowly but can maintain it longer (**Figure 46.11A**).

Slow-twitch fibers are also called oxidative or red muscle because they contain especially large amounts of **myoglobin** (an oxygen-binding protein similar to the hemoglobin in red blood cells), have many mitochondria, and are well supplied with blood vessels. These characteristics increase the fibers' capacity for oxidative metabolism and result in their red appearance. The maximum tension a slow-twitch fiber produces is low and develops slowly but is highly resistant to fatigue. Slow-twitch fibers have substantial reserves of fuel, mostly lipids, so they can maintain steady, prolonged production of ATP as long as oxygen is available. Muscles with high proportions of slow-twitch fibers are good for long-term aerobic work (work that requires oxygen). Long-distance runners, swimmers, cyclists, and other athletes whose activities require endurance have leg and arm muscles consisting mostly of slow-twitch fibers (**Figure 46.11B**).

Fast-twitch fibers, also called glycolytic or white muscle, have few mitochondria, little or no myoglobin, and fewer blood vessels; thus they look pale. Their major energy source is glycolysis, and therefore their major stored fuel is glycogen. Fast-twitch glycolytic fibers can develop maximum tension more rapidly than slow-twitch fibers can, and that maximum tension is greater. However, fast-twitch fibers fatigue rapidly (see Figure 46.11A). The myosin of these fibers puts the energy of ATP to work very rapidly, but the fibers cannot replenish ATP quickly enough to sustain contraction for a long time. Fast-twitch fibers are especially good for short-term work that requires maximum strength, such as sprinting (see Figure 46.11B).

The types of fibers that make up a muscle influence the performance properties of that muscle, and different muscles have different fiber compositions depending on their function. Postural muscles that maintain continuous contractions are mostly composed of slow-twitch fibers. An example is the soleus muscle that runs up the back of the leg from the heel. Its contraction extends the foot and is therefore used in walking, but its continuous contraction is required for standing. If the soleus muscle fatigued, we would fall forward. We can walk or stand for a long period of time because the soleus muscle is resistant to fatigue. In contrast, a muscle that is used mostly for short-term work, such as the biceps, has a higher percentage of fast-twitch fibers than does the soleus. We can use our biceps to pick up a heavy

(A) Force sustained by fast- and slow-twitch fibers

(B) Fiber type and performace

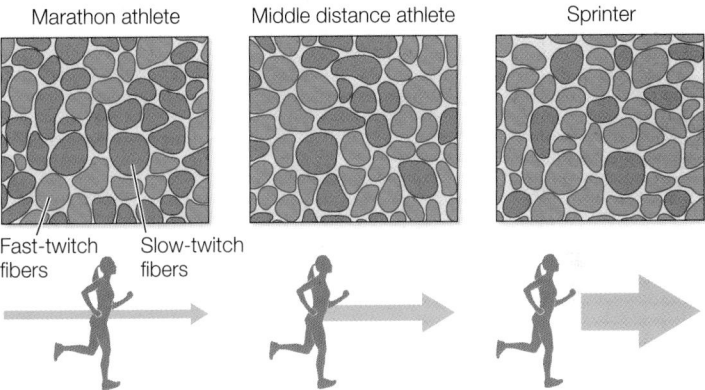

Figure 46.11 Fast- and Slow-Twitch Muscle Fibers (A) Fast-twitch fibers generate a large force quickly but fatigue rapidly. Slow-twitch fibers generate smaller forces, and do so more slowly, but can sustain them for a longer time. (B) The skeletal muscles in these three panels show slow-twitch fibers as red and fast-twitch fibers as blue. Arrows represent the duration (length) and speed (thickness) of running.

Q: What would you expect the muscle fiber distribution to be in a champion weight-lifter?

weight, but we cannot hold that weight in a given position for a long period of time.

Can you change the fiber composition of your muscles to optimize your performance in a particular activity? To a limited extent, you can alter the properties of your muscle fibers through training. There are fast-twitch fibers that are somewhat oxidative and therefore intermediate in their properties between slow-twitch and fast-twitch fibers. These intermediate fibers can become more oxidative with endurance training and more glycolytic with strength training. However, the most important determinant of your muscle fiber types is your genetic heritage. There is some truth to the statement that champions are born, not made. A person born with a high proportion of fast-twitch fibers in her legs is unlikely to become a champion marathon runner, and a person born with a high proportion of slow-twitch fibers in her legs is unlikely to become a champion sprinter.

A muscle has an optimal length for generating maximum tension

Two parts of a pull-up exercise are especially difficult. When your arms are fully extended, it is hard to start the pull-up; and when your chin has almost reached the bar, the last little bit is difficult. The structure of the sarcomere is the reason.

When a muscle changes length the sarcomeres also change length, and the spatial relationship between the actin and myosin filaments changes (**Figure 46.12**). If there is no actin–myosin overlap, cross-bridges cannot form and the sarcomere can't generate force. This is almost the situation when you are hanging from the pull-up bar. At the other extreme, when the muscle is fully contracted, the actin filaments are overlapping and the myosin filaments are bumping up against the Z lines, so additional force cannot be generated. With these considerations, you can ask how well a specific muscle—such as the frog jumping muscle—will function given a range of sarcomere lengths. In **Investigating Life: What Is the Optimal Resting Position for the Jumping Muscle of the Frog?**, we examine an experiment done to identify the optimal sarcomere length for a forceful frog jump. As you review this experiment, think about how it applies to deciding on the best starting position for a sprint.

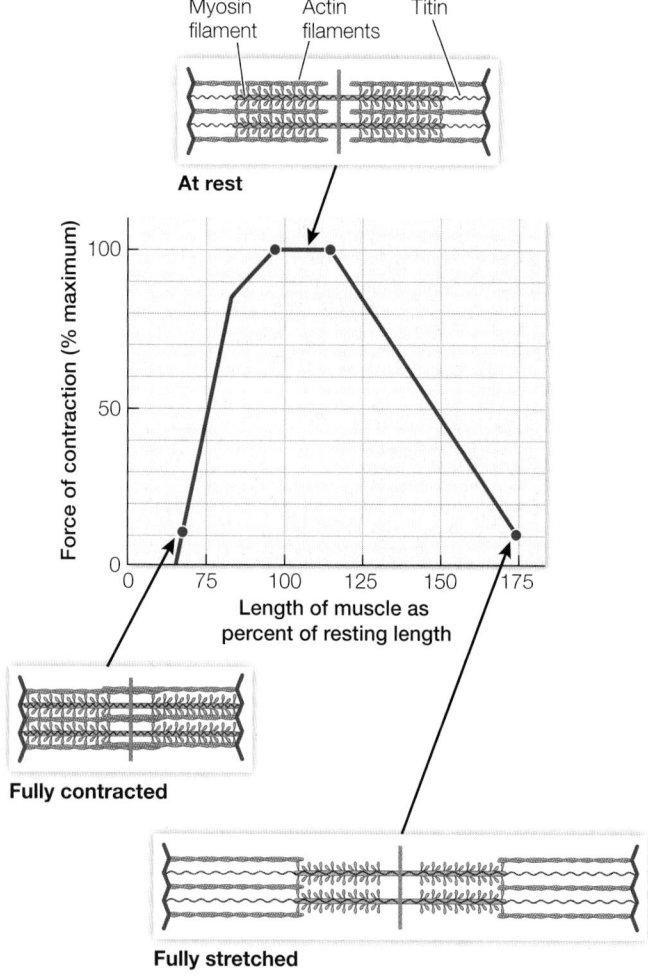

Figure 46.12 Force and Length The amount of force a sarcomere can generate depends on its resting length. When a muscle is stretched and its sarcomeres lengthened, there is less overlap between the actin and myosin filaments, and less force can be produced. When a muscle is fully contracted, the myosin filaments are bumping up against the Z lines of the sarcomeres, so further contraction is not possible. (After A. M. Gordon et al. 1996. *J Physiol* 184: 170–192.)

Exercise increases muscle strength and endurance

Different types of exercise produce different physical conditioning responses. In general, anaerobic activities such as weight-lifting increase strength, and aerobic activities such as jogging increase endurance. Strength is the maximum force a muscle can exert, and endurance is work capacity or how long a given workload can be sustained. What are the physiological bases for these differences?

Strength is a function of the volume of the muscles: the more actin and myosin filaments in a muscle fiber, and the more muscle fibers in a muscle, the more tension it can produce. When athletes undertake strength training, they use weights or exercises such as pull-ups or bench presses to repeatedly contract specific muscles under heavy loads. Repetitions are usually done until the muscle is completely fatigued. Such stress on a muscle does minor tissue damage—hence the soreness the day or two after a hard work-out—but it also induces the formation of new actin and myosin filaments in existing muscle fibers. The muscle fibers, and hence the muscles, get bigger and stronger. In extreme cases, and after serious muscle damage, new muscle fibers can also be produced from stem cells called satellite cells in the muscle. In general, however, the major effect of strength training is to produce bigger, rather than more, muscle fibers.

Aerobic exercise has a completely different effect on muscles: it enhances their oxidative capacity. This effect comes from increases in the number of mitochondria, in enzymes involved in energy use, and in the density of capillaries that deliver oxygen to the muscle. Myoglobin also increases in skeletal muscle cells. Myoglobin is similar to hemoglobin, but it has a higher affinity for oxygen. Therefore myoglobin accepts oxygen from the blood, facilitates the diffusion of oxygen throughout the muscle, and provides a store of oxygen for use when oxygen delivery by the blood is insufficient. By increasing the capacity of muscle to use oxygen to produce ATP, aerobic training increases the length of time that a given workload can be sustained.

Muscle ATP supply limits performance

Muscles have three systems for supplying the ATP they need for contraction:

1. The *immediate system* uses preformed ATP and creatine phosphate.

2. The *glycolytic system* metabolizes carbohydrates to lactate and pyruvate.

3. The *oxidative system* metabolizes carbohydrates or fats all the way to H_2O and CO_2.

The capacity of these three systems and the rates at which they can produce ATP determine both work capacity and endurance of a muscle (**Figure 46.13**).

ATP is present in muscles in very small amounts. However, muscle fibers also contain a storage compound called **creatine phosphate (CP)**. This molecule stores energy in a phosphate bond that it can transfer to ADP. The total energy available in all the muscles of your body in the form of ATP and CP—the immediate energy system—is only about 10 kilocalories. When at rest, you metabolize a kilocalorie of energy in less than a minute. Even

▶Investigating**LIFE** What Is the Optimal Resting Position for the Jumping Muscle of the Frog?

Experiment

Original Paper: G. J. Lutz and L. C. Rome. 1994. Built for jumping: The design of the frog muscular system. *Science* 263: 370–372.

The force propelling a frog's jump should be greatest when there is optimal overlap between the actin and myosin filaments and not when the muscle is stretched. The following experiment attempted to determine the resting sarcomere length that allows a frog to achieve a maximal jump.

QUESTION▶ If you want to get the maximum force out of a slingshot, you stretch it as far as you can. Would the frog's jump be greater if the jumping muscle were stretched when the frog was crouched before the jump?

METHOD▶

1. Through anatomical studies, measure sarcomere length at different resting positions observed in frogs before they jump and also measure the changes in muscle length and sarcomere length during jumps.

2. Excise frog jumping muscle from a frog and mount it in a tissue culture chamber so that the muscle can be held at different lengths and electrically stimulated to contract. Attach one end of the muscle to a force transducer that measures the force generated by the contraction. With this experimental setup you can determine the relationship between sarcomere length and maximum force the muscle can generate.

3. Compare the sarcomere length measurements with the forces measured in muscles held at different lengths.

4. Measure velocity of contraction of the muscle under different load conditions.

RESULTS▶

1. With methods not described here, it was determined that the jumping muscle shortened from 33.6 mm to 26.1 mm during a jump, and the resting sarcomere lengths varied from 2.34 μm to 1.82 μm.

2. The relative forces generated by isometric contraction at different sarcomere lengths corresponded well with a previously determined strength–length curve (data points shown in the graph).

CONCLUSION▶ During the jump, the sarcomeres of the frog shortened over the optimal range for generation of force.

Work with the Data

The resting position of the sarcomeres and the extent of their shortening during a jump maximize the force that the frog's muscle can generate to power the jump. But in physical terms, power is a force applied over a specific time. Therefore the velocity of contraction (measured as muscle length/second [ML/s]) will influence the maximum power the muscle can generate, and the velocity of contraction depends on the load. If the load is too great, the contraction is isometric (velocity = 0). If the load is negligible, the velocity of contraction can be maximal. **Figure A** shows the relationship between force and velocity of contraction in a frog jumping muscle under different loads. The mean jump velocity is indicated. **Figure B** shows the change in muscle length (millimeters) during a jump (milliseconds).

QUESTIONS▶

1. Power is work/time and work is force × displacement. Displacement/time = velocity. Therefore power = force × velocity. Using the data in Figure A, plot a curve that shows power as a function of contraction velocity for the frog muscle.

2. What is the velocity of contraction of the frog jumping muscle in muscle lengths/second? Use the data in Figure B.

3. Are the speed and force of the frog muscle optimal for generating the most powerful jump?

Go to Achieve for a companion Data in Depth exercise.

(A) Three systems that supply ATP

1 Preformed ATP and creatine phosphate are immediately available but rapidly exhausted.

2 Glycolysis comes on line within seconds but has limited capacity.

3 Sustained ATP production by oxidative metabolism kicks in after about 1 minute.

(B) Timing of ATP replenishment systems

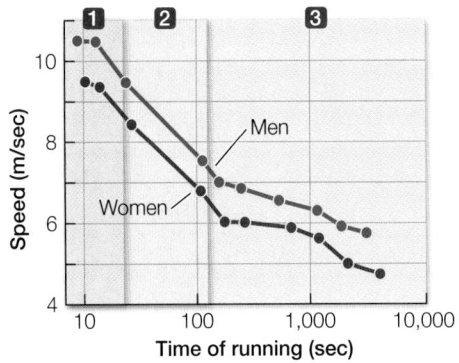

Figure 46.13 Supplying Fuel for High Performance (A) Muscles have three systems for obtaining the ATP they need for contraction during exertion such as running. (B) Looking at a plot of world-record times for running events of different durations, you can see that the performance of the athletes corresponds to the time courses of the three energy systems. (B data from the International Association of Athletics Federations. https://www.iaaf.org/records/by-category/world-records. Accessed 10/2/2019.)

Q: Figure 46.13B shows how maximum speed decreased as the duration of the running events got longer. Explain why there are three different slopes for this curve.

though the energy available from ATP and CP is limited, it is available immediately, and it enables fast-twitch fibers to generate a lot of force quickly. During burst activity, the immediate system is exhausted in seconds.

The glycolytic system activates within a few seconds to replace the ATP depleted at the onset of muscle activity. The glycolytic enzymes are located in the cytoplasm of the muscle fiber, and therefore the ATP they generate is rapidly available to the myosin filaments. However, as noted in Chapter 9, glycolysis alone is an inefficient way to produce ATP, and it leads to the accumulation of lactate, which slows the process. Thus the glycolytic system and the immediate system together provide the energy needed by active muscles for less than a minute (see Figure 46.13). Fortunately, oxidative metabolism becomes fully active in about a

Work with the Data

Does Heat Cause Muscle Fatigue?

Original Paper: D. A. Grahn et al. 2012. Work volume and strength training responses to resistive exercise improve with periodic heat extraction from the palm. *J Strength Cond Res* 26: 2558–2569.

Physical conditioning requires repeated intense physical activity, and the capacity of such workouts is limited by muscle fatigue. Because metabolic heat production raises the temperature of muscles during workouts, it is possible that the rise in temperature contributes to muscle fatigue and limits the capacity of workouts. To test this idea, investigators used rapid-cooling technology to extract heat from subjects during 3-minute rests between ten sets of pull-ups twice a week. In each of the ten sets of pull-ups, the subjects worked until muscle failure—the inability to complete an additional pull-up. The control condition was 3-minute rests without cooling. Each subject was his own control; the subjects were randomly assigned to begin with 6 weeks of training with cooling or 6 weeks of training without cooling, followed by a reversal of the treatments. The results are shown in the figure.

The Effect of Cooling on Workout Capacity (A) The results for individual subjects. Open symbols indicate control treatment, closed symbols indicate cooling treatment; different colors indicate different subjects. (B) The slopes of the lines in Figure A show the rates of increase in workout capacity over the course of the experiment. Mean ± standard deviation of rate of change in pull-ups per set during the two treatment phases (N = 6, P < 0.001 paired t-tests).

QUESTIONS▶

1. What do these data indicate about the possible role of muscle temperature in muscle fatigue?

2. What do these data indicate about the relationship between workout capacity and physical conditioning effects?

minute, producing relatively huge amounts of ATP because it can completely metabolize carbohydrates and fats to CO_2 and water. However, oxidative metabolism requires many reactions, and it takes place in the mitochondria, so O_2 and substrate must get into the mitochondria, and the formed ATP must get from the mitochondria to the myosin filaments in the muscle. These processes are not instantaneous, so the rate at which oxidative metabolism can make ATP available to do work is slower than the rate at which the other two systems can supply ATP.

The fuel resources available to the muscles influence how long someone can sustain a high level of aerobic exercise. From the circulating blood, muscle receives glucose and free fatty acids that it metabolizes to generate ATP. At high levels of aerobic exercise, however, most of the fuel used by muscles to produce ATP comes from the reserve of glycogen stored in the muscle itself. Depletion of muscle glycogen contributes to fatigue.

Connect the Concepts The work performance curves for different activities reflect the complexity of the biochemical processes by which different fuel sources are metabolized to produce ATP. Glycolysis supports anaerobic activities and it only entails ten enzymatic steps, so it can come on fast (see Key Concept 9.2). For aerobic activity, the citric acid cycle and the respiratory chain reactions add more steps and limit the rate of ATP production.

The rate at which muscle glycogen is replenished depends on diet. Glycogen is quickly replenished with a high-carbohydrate diet, but slowly replenished with a high-fat diet. A method used to maximize muscle glycogen is called carbo-loading. About 1 week before an athletic endurance event, athletes typically exercise for 3–5 days at a level that depletes muscle glycogen. Then, 2–3 days before the event, they taper down their level of training and eat a diet rich in complex carbohydrates. The result can be glycogen supercompensation, in which the restoration of muscle glycogen stores "overshoots" and reaches above-normal levels.

Insect muscle has the greatest rate of cycling

Insect flight muscle can produce a wingbeat frequency of up to 1,000 cycles per second. Since neuronal action potentials last 1–3 milliseconds, that number of cycles per second would exceed the capacity of motor neurons, let alone the mechanism of cycling of striated muscle contraction and relaxation. The extremely fast wingbeat of a hummingbird may be only about 50 cycles per second. How do insects do it?

Vertebrate skeletal muscle and much of invertebrate skeletal muscle is called "synchronous" because the cycling of the contractile mechanism is linked to the firing of the motor neurons. Insect flight muscle does not contract in tandem with the firing of motor neurons, however, and is thus called "asynchronous" muscle. The firing of action potentials in the insect flight motor neurons is not particularly fast, but it does cause depolarization of the muscle cell membrane, the spreading of an action potential throughout the membrane, and the release of Ca^{2+} from the sarcoplasmic reticulum. However, once the asynchronous muscle fiber is stimulated, its cycle of contraction and relaxation proceeds at its own characteristic frequency as long as Ca^{2+} is

available to bind to the troponin. Thus contractile cycling and the resulting wingbeat frequency are not tied to the firing rate of the flight motor neurons.

Regardless of how much force a muscle can generate, how long it can sustain a workload, or how fast it can contract and relax, a muscle needs something to pull on; otherwise it would just be a lump of pulsating, quivering tissue. Let's look now at how muscle and skeletal elements work together to produce movement.

KEY CONCEPT
46.3 Muscles and Skeletal Systems Work Together

Learning Objectives

46.3.1 Compare the features of hydrostatic skeletons, exoskeletons, and endoskeletons.

46.3.2 Explain why molting is a universal characteristic of arthropods but not of vertebrates.

46.3.3 Describe how osteoblasts, osteoclasts, and osteocytes work together to maintain bone structure.

46.3.4 Discuss how the load and force arm ratio gives different endoskeletal joints different capabilities.

Muscles can contract and exert force, or they can relax. To create significant movement, they must have something to pull on and something that stretches the muscle back to a longer position. In some cases muscles pull on each other, as in the elephant's trunk or the arms of an octopus. In most cases, however, **skeletal systems** are the rigid supports against which muscles pull to create directed movement. In this key concept we examine the three types of skeletal systems: hydrostatic skeletons, exoskeletons, and endoskeletons.

Hydrostatic skeletons depend on pressure differences

Cnidarians, annelids, and other soft-bodied invertebrates have **hydrostatic skeletons** consisting of a volume of fluid enclosed in a body cavity surrounded by muscle (see Key Concept 29.1). When

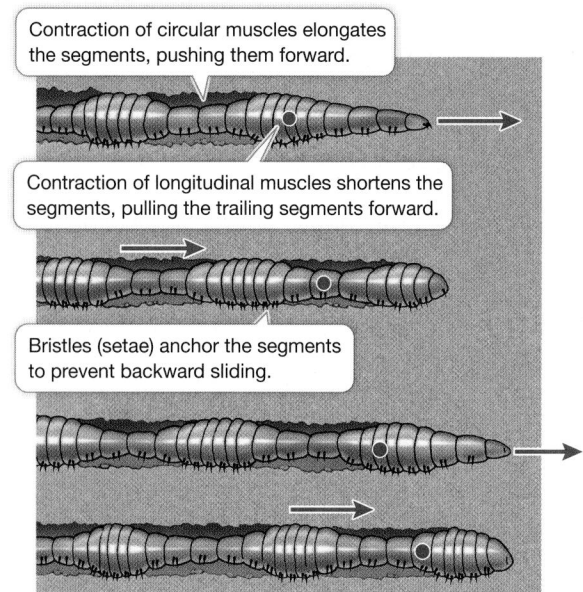

Figure 46.14 A Hydrostatic Skeleton Alternating waves of muscle contraction move the earthworm through the soil. The red dot enables you to follow the changes in one segment as the worm moves forward.

muscles oriented in one direction contract, the fluid-filled body cavity bulges out in a perpendicular direction.

An earthworm uses its hydrostatic skeleton to crawl (**Figure 46.14**). The earthworm's body cavity is divided into separate segments filled with extracellular fluid. The body wall surrounding each segment has two muscle layers: a circular layer and a longitudinal layer. If the circular muscles in a segment contract, that segment constricts and elongates. If the longitudinal muscles in a segment contract, it shortens and bulges outward. Alternating contractions of the earthworm's circular and longitudinal muscles create waves of narrowing and widening, lengthening and shortening, that travel down the body. Bulging, shortened segments serve as anchors as long, narrow segments project forward and longitudinal contractions pull other segments forward. Bristles help the widest parts of the body to hold firm against the substrate, so the body moves forward.

Exoskeletons are rigid outer structures

An **exoskeleton** is a hardened, rigid outer surface to which muscles can be attached. Contractions of the muscles cause jointed segments of the exoskeleton to move relative to each other. The simplest example of an exoskeleton is the shell of a mollusk. Some marine mollusks, such as clams, have shells composed of protein strengthened by crystals of calcium carbonate (a rock-hard material). These shells can be massive, affording significant protection against predators. The shells of terrestrial snails contain less calcium carbonate, and are therefore lighter.

The most complex exoskeletons are found among the arthropods (see Key Concept 30.1). A type of exoskeleton called a **cuticle** covers the outer surfaces of the arthropod body, including its appendages. It is made up of **chitin** (a nitrogen-containing

Figure 46.15 The Human Endoskeleton Cartilage and bone make up the internal skeleton of a human.

polysaccharide) secreted by a layer of cells just below the exoskeleton. Chitin stiffens and hardens the cuticle everywhere except at the joints, where flexibility must be retained. Muscles attached to the inner surfaces of the arthropod cuticle move its parts around the joints (see Figure 30.4). Growth of animals with exoskeletons is accommodated by molting (see Figure 30.3). Soft-shelled crabs, a gourmet delicacy, are crabs caught while they are molting.

Vertebrate endoskeletons consist of cartilage and bone

The **endoskeleton** of vertebrates is an internal scaffolding. Muscles are attached to it and pull against it. Endoskeletons are composed of rodlike, platelike, and tubelike bones connected to one another at a variety of joints that allow a wide range of movements. An advantage of endoskeletons over the exoskeletons of arthropods is that bones in the body can grow without the animal shedding its skeleton.

The adult human skeleton consists of 206 bones, some of which are shown in **Figure 46.15**. It can be divided into an axial skeleton, which includes the skull, vertebral column, sternum, and ribs; and an appendicular skeleton, which includes the pectoral girdle, pelvic girdle, and bones of the arms, legs, hands, and feet.

The vertebrate endoskeleton consists of two kinds of connective tissue, cartilage and bone, which are produced by two kinds of connective tissue cells that produce extensive extracellular matrices. **Cartilage** cells produce a matrix that is a tough, rubbery mixture of polysaccharides and proteins—mainly fibrous collagen. Collagen fibers run in all directions like reinforcing cords through the gel-like matrix and give it the well-known strength and resiliency of gristle in meat. Cartilage is found in parts of the endoskeleton where both stiffness and resiliency are required, such as on the surfaces of joints where bones move against one another. Cartilage is also the supportive tissue in stiff but flexible structures such as the larynx (voice box), nose, and ear pinnae. Sharks and rays are called cartilaginous fishes because their skeletons are composed entirely of cartilage. In most other vertebrates, cartilage is the principal component of the embryonic skeleton, but during development most of it is gradually replaced by bone.

Bone also contains collagen fibers, but it gets its rigidity and hardness from an extracellular matrix of insoluble calcium phosphate crystals. Bone serves as a reservoir of calcium for the rest of the body and is in dynamic equilibrium with soluble calcium in the extracellular fluids of the body. This equilibrium is under the control of calcitonin and parathyroid hormone (see Figure 39.15). If too much calcium is taken from the skeleton, the bones are significantly weakened.

The living cells of bone—osteoblasts, osteocytes, and osteoclasts—are responsible for the constant dynamic remodeling of bone (**Figure 46.16**). **Osteoblasts** lay down new matrix material on bone surfaces. These cells gradually become surrounded by matrix and eventually become enclosed within the bone, at which point they cease laying down matrix but continue to exist within small lacunae (cavities) in the bone. In this state they are called **osteocytes**. Despite the vast amounts of matrix between them, osteocytes remain in contact with one another through long cellular extensions that run through tiny channels in the bone. Communication between osteocytes is important in controlling the activities of the cells that are laying down or removing bone.

The cells that break down bone and release calcium into the extracellular fluid are called **osteoclasts**. They are derived from the same cell lineage that produces white blood cells. Osteoclasts erode bone, forming cavities and tunnels. Osteoblasts follow osteoclasts, depositing new bone. Thus the interplay of osteoblasts and osteoclasts continuously replaces and remodels the bones, allowing a bone to recover from damage and adjust to the forces placed on it.

A dramatic finding from the early days of manned space missions was that the bones of astronauts who spent long periods in zero gravity decalcified. Conversely, in athletes certain bones thicken during training. Both thickening and thinning of bones are experienced by anyone who has had a leg in a cast for a long time: the bones of the uninjured leg carry the person's weight and thicken while the bones of the inactive leg in the cast thin. We now know that there are multiple mechanisms in bone that transduce

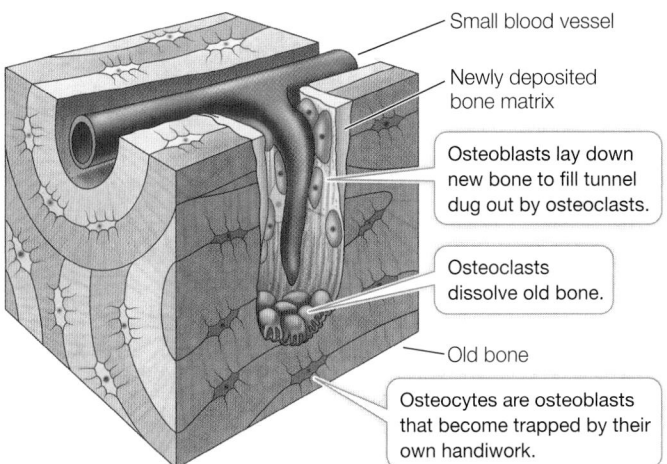

Small blood vessel

Newly deposited bone matrix

Osteoblasts lay down new bone to fill tunnel dug out by osteoclasts.

Osteoclasts dissolve old bone.

Old bone

Osteocytes are osteoblasts that become trapped by their own handiwork.

Figure 46.16 Bone Is Living Tissue Bones are constantly being remodeled by osteoblasts, which lay down bone, and osteoclasts, which break down bone.

physical stress into activation of various cell signaling mechanisms that can control the bone remodeling responses to those stressors.

Because of the positive effects of physical stress on bone deposition, weight-bearing exercise is effective in preventing and treating osteoporosis, which is the loss of bone density (and hence strength). More than 25 million people in the United States suffer from this debilitating condition. Although osteoporosis is most commonly a problem for postmenopausal women, it can occur in younger people as a result of malnutrition. For example, the condition known as female athlete triad includes eating disorders, cessation of menstrual cycling, and osteoporosis. These are interactive conditions in which the eating disorder and excessive training lead to malnutrition that can result in endocrine disruption and osteoporosis. Excessive training and malnutrition can lead to bone loss in males as well.

Bones develop from connective tissues

Bones are divided into two types on the basis of how they develop. **Membranous bone** forms on a scaffold of connective tissue membrane. **Cartilage bone** forms first as a cartilaginous structure resembling the future mature bone, then gradually hardens, or ossifies, to become bone. The outer bones of the skull are membranous bones; the bones of the limbs are cartilage bones.

Cartilage bones can grow throughout the ossification process. The long bones of the legs and arms, for example, ossify first at the centers and later at each end (**Figure 46.17**). The cartilage between these ossification centers forms **epiphyseal plates**. Growth can continue until these areas of ossification join, eliminating the epiphyseal plates. The membranous bones forming the skull cap grow until their edges meet. The large soft spot on the top of a baby's head, called a fontanel, is a point where the skull bones have not yet joined. There are multiple fontanels in the neonate where the skull bones eventually join.

The structure of bone may be **compact** (solid and hard) or **cancellous** (having numerous internal cavities that make it appear spongy, although it is rigid). The architecture of a specific bone depends on its position and function, but most bones have both

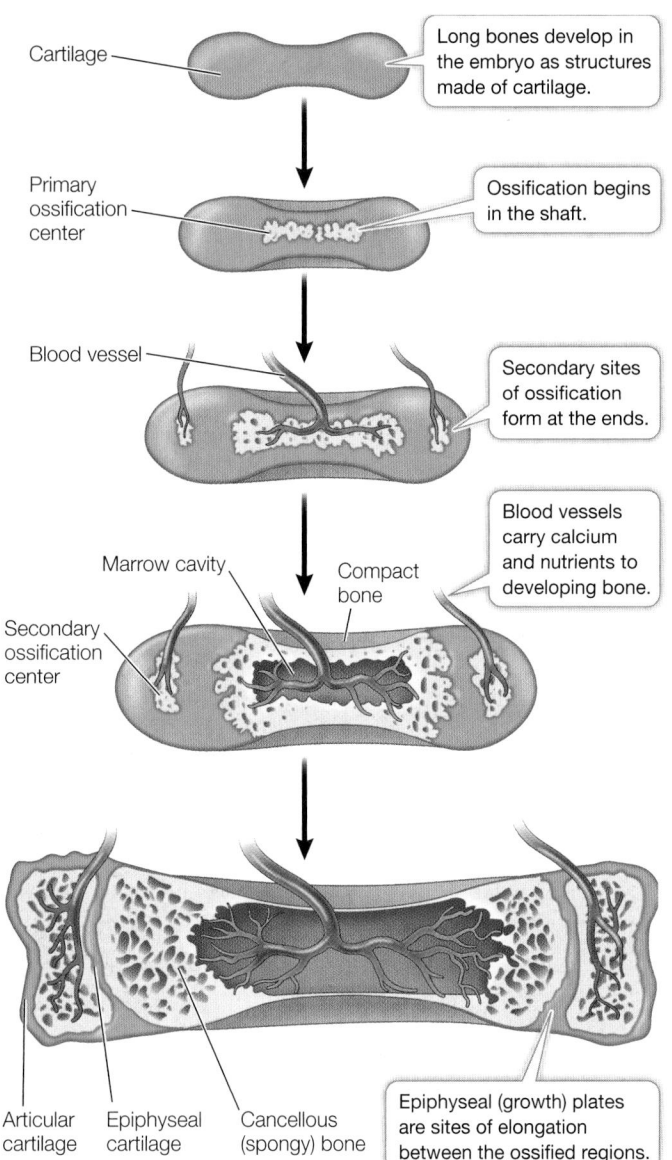

Cartilage — Long bones develop in the embryo as structures made of cartilage.

Primary ossification center — Ossification begins in the shaft.

Blood vessel — Secondary sites of ossification form at the ends.

Marrow cavity — Compact bone

Secondary ossification center — Blood vessels carry calcium and nutrients to developing bone.

Articular cartilage — Epiphyseal cartilage — Cancellous (spongy) bone — Epiphyseal (growth) plates are sites of elongation between the ossified regions.

Figure 46.17 **The Growth of Long Bones** In the long bones of human limbs, ossification occurs first at the centers and later at each end.

Osteoblasts lay down bone in layers. In long bones these layers form concentric tubes parallel to the long axis of the bone.

Haversian canals contain blood vessels and nerves (which convey pain when we break a bone).

Glue line

0.5 mm

© Ed Reschke/Getty Images

Figure 46.18 **Most Compact Bone Is Composed of Haversian Systems** A micrograph of a section of a long bone shows Haversian systems with their central canals. Glue lines separate Haversian systems. Osteocytes reside in small spaces and are in communication by means of thin cell processes running through small channels.

compact and cancellous regions. The shafts of the long bones of the limbs, for example, are cylinders of compact bone surrounding central cavities that contain fatty bone marrow called yellow bone marrow. The rigid, tubelike shaft of compact bone can withstand compression and bending forces. Architects and nature alike use hollow tubes as lightweight structural elements.

The ends of the long bones are cancellous (see Figure 46.17). Cancellous bone is lightweight because of its numerous cavities. These cavities contain the red bone marrow responsible for red blood cell formation as well as other cellular elements of the blood. Cancellous bone is also strong because its internal meshwork constitutes a support system. It can withstand considerable forces of compression.

Most compact bone in mammals is called Haversian bone because it is composed of structural units called **Haversian systems** (**Figure 46.18**). Each Haversian system is a set of thin, concentric bony cylinders that surround a narrow Haversian canal that contains blood vessels and nerves. Osteocytes are arranged in small spaces between the concentric circles of bone surrounding the canals. Adjacent Haversian systems are separated by boundaries called glue lines. Haversian bone is resistant to fracturing because cracks tend to stop at glue lines.

Bones that have a common joint can work as a lever

Muscles and bones work together around **joints**, where two or more bones come together. Different kinds of joints allow motion in different directions (**Figure 46.19**), but muscles can exert force in only one direction. Therefore muscles create movement around joints by working in antagonistic pairs: when one muscle contracts, the other relaxes. When both contract, the joint becomes rigid (which is important for maintaining posture, for example).

With respect to a particular joint, such as the knee, we refer to the muscle that bends, or flexes, the joint as the **flexor**, and the muscle that straightens, or extends, the joint as the **extensor**. The bones that meet at the joint are held together by **ligaments**, which are flexible bands of connective tissue. Other straps of connective tissue, called **tendons**, attach the muscles to the bones. In **Figure 46.20**, which shows the knee joint, you can see a tendon that connects a flexor muscle in the upper leg (biceps femoris) to a bone in the lower leg. You can also see a tendon connecting the extensor muscle (quadriceps) to the kneecap (patella) and

Ball-and-socket joint

Pivot joint

Saddle joint

Ellipsoid joint

Hinge joint

Plane joint

Figure 46.19 Types of Joint Motions The designs of joints are similar to mechanical counterparts and enable a variety of movements.

 View in **Achieve**
Activity 46.3 **Joints**

the patellar ligament that connects the patella to the lower leg bone. It is the patellar ligament that is tapped when testing the knee-jerk reflex (see Figure 43.15).

Bones constitute a system of levers that are moved around joints by the muscles. Levers have three parts: load arm, force arm, and fulcrum. The joint is the fulcrum, and the length of the force arm relative to the load arm depends on where the muscle attaches to the bone. Three classes of levers are defined based on the location of the fulcrum (**Figure 46.21**). In a class 1 lever, the fulcrum is between the load and force arms, as in a seesaw. An example is the joint between the skull and the spinal cord. A class 2 lever is like a wheelbarrow, with the load in the middle. An example is the ankle joint and the muscle in the back of the leg that enables you to walk and stand on tiptoe. In a class 3 lever, the force arm is between the fulcrum and the load. An example is your elbow or your knee. The length ratio of the load and force arms determines whether a particular lever can exert a lot of force over a short distance or is better at translating force into large or fast movements. Think of the powerful jaws of carnivores that can easily crack bones. In contrast, the force arm of the lower legs of Rosie the Ribeter and Jackie Joyner-Kersee, featured in the opener to this chapter, is short relative to the load arm, so they can jump fast and high.

Flexor and extensor muscles work antagonistically to operate the joint.

Flexor muscle (biceps femoris)

Femur

Fibula

Tibia

Extensor muscle (quadriceps)

Tendons attach muscle to bone.

Quadriceps tendon

Patella (kneecap)

Cartilage

Patellar ligament

Ligaments attach bone to bone.

Figure 46.20 Joints, Ligaments, and Tendons A side view of the knee shows the interactions of muscle, bone, cartilage, ligaments, and tendons at this crucial and vulnerable human joint.

Class 1 lever

Force arm   Load arm

Fulcrum is located between the load and the point of force application. Load moves in opposite direction as the application of force. The position of the fulcrum determines the ratio of the load arm to the force arm, which in this case is 1:1.

Class 2 lever

Force arm

Load arm

Load is located between the fulcrum and the point of force application, making it possible to move heavy objects a short distance (e.g., standing on your tip-toes). Ratio of load arm to force arm here is 1:2.

Class 3 lever

Force arm   Load arm

→ Force direction
↑ Load movement
▲ Fulcrum

Point of force application is located between the fulcrum and the load, making it possible to move the load over a large distance with speed (e.g., throwing a ball). Ratio of load arm to force arm here is 5:1.

Figure 46.21 Bones and Joints Work as Levers   The three classes of levers are defined by the relationship between the fulcrum and the load and force arms. For each class of lever, the load and force arm ratio determines whether force or speed of movement is maximized.

Q: What class of lever is the knee joint?

46.3 Recap and Assess

Muscles can only contract and relax; to achieve organized movement, they must pull against rigid structures—other muscles, hydrostatic skeletons, exoskeletons, or endoskeletons. Endoskeletons consist of cartilage and bone. Bone is continuously resorbed by osteoclasts and laid down by osteoblasts. Joints give directionality to movements, and muscle–joint combinations act as levers.

1. Why is molting a universal characteristic of arthropods but not of vertebrates?

2. What changes in the activities of bone cells might explain the loss of bone mass in astronauts who spend long periods at the International Space Station, and what mechanism in the bone might be responsible?

3. What is the significance of the fact that the ratio of the force arm to the load arm is much greater in the jaw joint than in the elbow joint?

▶ InvestigatingLIFE

Q and A   What adaptations optimize the jumping muscles of the frog?

Rosie the Ribeter was an exceptional jumper judged by the length of time her record remains unbeaten, but frogs in general are remarkable jumpers. This ability is not due to the molecular structure of their muscles, as the arrangement of sarcomeres is very similar across a wide cross section of animals, and in all cases the sarcomeres and therefore the muscles only contract by about 25%–30% of their length. So how can a muscle only a few centimeters long produce a jump of many meters? One answer, which is considered in the experiment described in **Investigating Life: What Is the Optimal Resting Position for the Jumping Muscle of the Frog?**, involves maximizing force and power. First, you saw that the resting posture of the frog maintains the sarcomere length where it can generate the maximum force when it contracts. Then by using the measured force/velocity curve, you saw that the velocity of the jump was at the level that maximized the power of the jump. This rather fast velocity of contraction is possible because the jumping muscle contains mostly fast-twitch fibers. As mentioned in the opening story, and further explained in Key Concept 46.3, the legs operate as class 3 levers to move the body mass. Because the legs of the frog are long, the load arms of those levers are long in comparison with the force arms—that is, the length ratio

of the load and force arms is high. A frog's long legs and big feet have another advantage as well. Muscles must have something to exert force against to maximize power, and once the frog leaves the ground, its muscles can no longer generate power. Long legs and feet ensure that as the jumping muscles contract, the feet remain in contact with the ground for a longer time, thus maximizing the power of the jump.

Future directions

Understanding how muscles and skeletal structures work together to generate movements of different types is essential in the growing field of robotics. Robots that repeat the same movement over and over are quite common in manufacturing, but more and more robotic systems are being created to do more variable and complex tasks that mimic and frequently augment the abilities of humans and other animals. For example, robots have been developed to travel over rough terrain, even while carrying heavy loads. Robots have been developed to do household chores such as washing dishes and folding laundry. Robotic systems are improving the functionality of prosthetic limbs for amputees. And melding of robotic systems with normal human functionality is leading to technologies called "exoskeletons" that greatly enhance the physical abilities of humans. The starting point in all of these engineering efforts is a thorough characterization of how the biological musculoskeletal system works.

© Michael Durham/Minden Pictures

You should be able to relate each summary to the adjacent figures. If you go to this visual summary in **Achieve**, you can follow links to figures, animations, activities, and simulations that will help you consolidate the material.

KEY CONCEPT
46.1 Interactions of Actin and Myosin Cause Muscles to Contract

Go to **Activities 46.1 and 46.2 and Animations 46.1 and 46.2**

- **Skeletal muscle** fibers are multinucleate cells containing **myofibrils**, which are regularly arranged bundles of **actin** and **myosin** filaments forming **sarcomeres** as the functional units of contraction.

- A motor neuron and the fibers it activates constitute a **motor unit**. The synapse between a motor neuron and a muscle fiber is a motor end plate.

- Action potentials generated at the motor end plate spread across the muscle cell membrane and through the **T tubules**, causing Ca^{2+} to be released from the **sarcoplasmic reticulum**.

- Ca^{2+} binds to **troponin** and changes its conformation, pulling the **tropomyosin** strands away from myosin binding sites on the actin filament.

- **Cardiac muscle** cells are striated, uninucleate, branching, and electrically connected by gap junctions.

- **Smooth muscle** cells are uninucleate and connected by gap junctions.

Figure 46.6

Questions

1. How does an action potential in the T tubule initiate skeletal muscle contraction?

2. Why do skeletal muscles stiffen soon after death?

3. What are the structural and functional differences between skeletal, cardiac, and smooth muscle?

KEY CONCEPT
46.2 Many Factors Affect Muscle Performance

- In skeletal muscle, an action potential causes a minimum unit of contraction called a **twitch**. Twitches occurring in rapid succession can be summed to achieve graded levels of contraction. Sustained maximal contraction is known as **tetanus**.

- **Slow-twitch fibers** are used for extended aerobic work; **fast-twitch fibers** generate maximum forces for short periods of time. Mixtures of slow- and fast-twitch fibers suit different muscles for different functions.

- Anaerobic exercise stimulates the enlargement of muscle fibers through production of new filaments. Aerobic exercise stimulates greater oxidative capacity of muscle fibers.

- Muscle performance depends on a supply of ATP.

Figure 46.11

Fiber type and performace

Marathon athlete   Middle distance athlete   Sprinter

Fast-twitch fibers   Slow-twitch fibers

Questions

1. If you compared the fiber composition of the large leg muscles of a champion sprinter and a cross-country skier, what differences would you expect to find?

2. A high-fat diet results in lower levels of muscle glycogen. If a weight-lifter and a mile-runner went on a high-fat diet, which one would see the greatest decrease in performance, and why?

3. Why is it harder to do pull-ups if you go to full extension between pull-ups?

Figure 46.13   **Three systems that supply ATP**

KEY CONCEPT

46.3 Muscles and Skeletal Systems Work Together

Go to Activity 46.3

- **Hydrostatic skeletons** are fluid-filled body cavities that are squeezed by muscles.

- **Exoskeletons** are hardened outer surfaces to which internal muscles are attached.

- **Endoskeletons** are internal systems of rigid rodlike, platelike, and tubelike supports, consisting of **bone** and **cartilage** to which muscles are attached.

- Bone is continually remodeled by **osteoblasts**, which lay down new bone, and **osteoclasts**, which resorb bone.

- Bones develop from connective tissue membranes (**membranous bone**) or from cartilage (**cartilage bone**) through ossification.

- Bone is **compact** (solid and hard) or **cancellous** (containing numerous internal spaces). Most compact bone of mammals is composed of **Haversian systems**.

- **Joints** enable muscles to power movements in different directions.

- **Tendons** connect muscles to bones; **ligaments** connect bones to one another.

Figure 46.20

Questions

1. Earthworm bodies are divided into separate segments. Why is this important for their locomotion?

2. Why is the human skull divided into epiphyseal plates?

3. Is height an advantage or a disadvantage to a football kicker, and why?

Go to **Achieve** for the eBook, **LearningCurve**, animations, activities, simulations, and additional resources and assignments.

Gas Exchange 47

KEY CONCEPTS

47.1 Respiratory Gas Exchange Is Governed by Physical Factors

47.2 Enhancing Diffusion Maximizes Respiratory Gas Exchange

47.3 Humans Have Tidal Respiration

47.4 Respiratory Gases Are Transported by the Blood

47.5 Breathing Is Homeostatically Regulated

Northern elephant seals (*Mirounga angustirostris*) are champion breath-hold divers. Diving repeatedly, they may spend only 20% of their time at the surface.

▶Investigating**LIFE**

The Breath of Life

Northern elephant seals (*Mirounga angustirostris*) on a beach are impressive. Typical adult males are 5 meters long and weigh 2,500 kilograms. They fight viciously to defend areas of beach where the females come out of the water to give birth and rear their young. The beach masters are really defending their opportunities to father the next generation.

Physiologically, these animals are even more impressive in the water. Female elephant seals, half the size of the males and therefore easier and safer to manage for experiments, have been fitted with instruments to record the depth and duration of their dives after they leave the beach where they gave birth. They spend up to 7 months at sea, and during that entire time they dive continually—day and night—to feed on eels, skates, rays, squid, and other prey. Most dives are 300–600 meters deep and last 20 minutes, but dives lasting over an hour and exceeding 2,000 meters have been recorded. The seals spend only 4–5 minutes at the surface between dives. Thus for the 80% of their lives that they spend at sea, they are breathing only about 20% of the time—12 minutes per hour!

The best human divers are perhaps the pearl divers of Japan and Korea. They dive repeatedly during their workday to about 20 meters, and their dives last about a minute. Record breath-hold dives for humans resting facedown in a pool are about 10 minutes, but that is a one-time event that cannot be repeated for many hours. The elephant seals are not resting—they are descending and ascending great distances and pursuing prey.

How can these behemoths spend so much time not breathing? How can they survive such crushing depths? How can they not get the bends, which is a serious danger for human divers? How much oxygen do these animals need to carry out their normal behavior? How much oxygen can they store in their bodies during the short times they spend at the surface? And what adaptations do they have to make those oxygen stores last as long as they do? To answer these questions, elephant seals and other diving animals have been studied in unique laboratory facilities and in the field.

 What adaptations make seals champion breath-hold divers? (Find the answer on page 1066.)

47.1 Respiratory Gas Exchange Is Governed by Physical Factors

Learning Objectives

47.1.1 Describe the concept of partial pressures of gases and how they relate to concentrations of gases in air and water.

47.1.2 Explain adaptations for respiratory gas exchange in terms of Fick's law of diffusion.

47.1.3 Compare water and air as respiratory media.

47.1.4 Describe three factors that make it more difficult for fishes to satisfy their respiratory needs at higher temperatures.

47.1.5 Explain how elevation influences respiratory gas exchange.

The **respiratory gases** that animals must exchange are oxygen (O_2) and carbon dioxide (CO_2). Cells need to obtain O_2 from the environment to produce an adequate supply of ATP by cellular respiration (see Chapter 9). CO_2 is an end-product of cellular respiration, and it must be removed from the body to prevent toxic effects. Gas exchange systems of animals consist of (1) specialized body surface areas where these gases can move between the body and the external environment, (2) **ventilation** mechanisms that move air or water over the environmental sides of those surfaces, and (3) **perfusion** mechanisms that circulate extracellular fluids on the internal sides.

Diffusion is the only means by which respiratory gases are exchanged between an animal's internal body fluids and the outside medium (air or water). There are no active transport mechanisms to move respiratory gases across biological membranes. Because diffusion is a physical process, knowing what physical factors influence rates of diffusion helps us understand the diverse adaptations of gas exchange systems. (You may want to review the coverage of diffusion in Key Concept 6.3.)

Diffusion of gases is driven by partial pressure differences

Diffusion is due to the random motion of molecules, and it results in a net movement of molecules from areas of higher concentration to areas of lower concentration. In other words, diffusion evens out the distribution of molecules. Diffusion of respiratory gases occurs either in water or in air. Concentrations of gases in water or air vary with pressure because gases are compressible, a relationship described in physics by Boyle's law. For example, there are twice as many gas molecules in a liter of gas at 2 atmospheres of pressure as there are in a liter of gas at 1 atmosphere of pressure. And if that gas is in contact with a liquid such as water, twice as many gas molecules will enter into solution when the gas pressure is 2 atmospheres than when it is 1 atmosphere.

The concentrations of different gases in a mixture are described as the **partial pressures** of those gases. To calculate the partial pressure of a gas such as oxygen in a mixture of gases such as air, we have to know the total pressure. The total pressure of air inhaled by air-breathing animals is the atmospheric pressure. At sea level, atmospheric pressure is about 760 millimeters of mercury (mm Hg), depending on the weather. Because dry air is 20.9%

O_2, the partial pressure of oxygen (P_{O_2}) at sea level is 20.9% of 760 mm Hg, or about 159 mm Hg. If two gas mixtures are separated by a membrane permeable to O_2, O_2 will diffuse from the mixture where its partial pressure is higher to the mixture where its partial pressure is lower.

To calculate the concentration of O_2 in the environment of a water breather, we have to know two things: the partial pressure of O_2 in the air in contact with the water, and the solubility of O_2 in water. The amount of a gas that dissolves in a liquid depends both on its partial pressure in the gas phase in contact with the liquid *and* on its solubility in that liquid. The *diffusion* of a gas between the gas phase and the liquid phase is a function of its partial pressures in those two phases; the gas diffuses from the phase with the higher partial pressure to the phase with the lower partial pressure until equilibrium is reached—the point at which the partial pressures in the two phases are equal. However, the *amount* of the gas that can be contained in the liquid depends on the solubility of that gas in that liquid. Furthermore, the solubility of a gas in a particular liquid can vary widely depending on conditions. What follows is a practical illustration of these facts.

Solubility of a gas in a liquid, such as oxygen in water, is a function of temperature—solubility is higher at low temperatures. Think of opening a bottle of warm soda in comparison with a bottle of cold soda. When the pressure is relieved by opening the bottle, more gas comes out of solution—there is more fizz—in the warm soda. So if we have similar containers of water in equilibrium with air, but at different temperatures, the concentrations of oxygen in these water containers will be different (less O_2 in the warmer one), but the partial pressures of oxygen will be the same. Thus for water-breathing animals, the warmer the water is, the less O_2 there is per liter of water. The important point is that for a gas in solution, its concentration is not the same as its partial pressure, but partial pressures are what drive diffusion. Thus in our continuing discussions of respiratory gas exchange, we will always use partial pressure rather than concentration when referring to the diffusion of respiratory gases.

Fick's law applies to all systems of gas exchange

Whether in air or water, the diffusion rates of respiratory gases between an animal and its respiratory medium—air or water—depend on the partial pressure gradients across the gas exchange surfaces and on other factors that are described quantitatively with a simple equation called **Fick's law of diffusion**. All environmental variables that limit respiratory gas exchange and all adaptations that maximize respiratory gas exchange are reflected in one or more components of this equation. Fick's law is written as

$$Q = DA \frac{P_1 - P_2}{L}$$

where

- Q is the rate at which a gas such as O_2 diffuses between two locations.

- D is the diffusion coefficient, which is a characteristic of the diffusing substance, the medium, and the temperature. For example, perfume has a higher D than motor oil vapor, and all substances diffuse faster at higher temperatures and faster in air than in water. Temperature is not expressed explicitly in Fick's law because diffusion coefficients are usually determined at room temperature (about 20°C).

- *A* is the area across which the gas is diffusing.
- P_1 and P_2 are the partial pressures of the gas at the two locations.
- *L* is the path length, or distance, between the two locations.
- $(P_1 - P_2)/L$ is a partial pressure gradient.

The strict dependence of animals on diffusion for gas exchange with their environments has selected for various adaptations that maximize *Q*, many of which we describe in this chapter. Animals can maximize *D* for respiratory gases by using air rather than water as their gas exchange medium whenever possible. All other adaptations for maximizing respiratory gas exchange must influence the surface area (*A*) for gas exchange or the partial pressure gradient across that surface area.

Air is a better respiratory medium than water

The slower diffusion of O_2 molecules in water than in air affects both air- and water-breathing animals. Diffusion of O_2 in water is so slow that even animal cells with low rates of metabolism cannot function more than a few millimeters away from a good source of environmental O_2. Therefore there are severe size and shape limits on the many species of invertebrates that lack internal systems for distributing O_2. Most of these species are small or, like marine flatworms, have evolved a flat, thin body with a large external surface area (**Figure 47.1A**). Another strategy is seen in sponges, which have bodies made of cells surrounding water channels through which the external medium flows (**Figure 47.1B**; also see Figure 29.2B). Critical factors enabling larger, more complex animal bodies are (1) the evolution of specialized respiratory structures with large surface areas that are highly permeable to respiratory gases (**Figure 47.1C**) and (2) internal systems that facilitate the movement of respiratory gases between the respiratory exchange surfaces and the tissues of the body.

Respiratory systems of air-breathing animals also have had to evolve adaptations to minimize the path length for diffusion of respiratory gases in aqueous media. Eukaryotic cells carry out cellular respiration in their mitochondria, which are located in the cytosol, a gel-like substance. Cells are bathed in extracellular fluid—also an aqueous medium. All respiratory surfaces consist of cells, and to protect them from drying out, they are covered by a thin film of fluid. O_2 must diffuse through all of these aqueous respiratory barriers. So even in air-breathing animals, the slow rate of O_2 diffusion in water limits the efficiency of O_2 distribution from the environment to the sites of cellular respiration.

O_2 can be obtained more easily from air than from water for several reasons:

- *The O_2 content of air is much higher than the O_2 content of an equal volume of water.* The maximum O_2 content of a bubbling stream in equilibrium with air is less than 10 milliliters (mL) of O_2 per liter of water. The O_2 content of the air over the stream is about 200 mL of O_2 per liter of air.
- *O_2 diffuses about 8,000 times more rapidly in air than in water.* That is why the O_2 content of a stagnant pond can be zero only a few millimeters below the surface.

- *An animal has to work (expend energy) to ventilate its gas exchange surfaces with water or air.* More energy is required to move water than air because water is 800 times denser than air and about 50 times more viscous.

You can appreciate how important these facts were for the evolutionary transition of life to the terrestrial environment, because they meant that there were fewer constraints on the evolution of higher metabolic rates.

High temperatures create respiratory problems for aquatic animals

Animals that use water for their respiratory exchange medium are in a double bind when environmental temperatures rise. Most water-breathing animals are ectotherms—their body temperatures are closely tied to the temperature of the water around them. As the water temperature rises, an ectotherm's body temperature and metabolic rate rise (see Figure 38.8). Thus water breathers need more O_2 as their environment gets warmer (**Figure 47.2**). But as mentioned earlier, warm water holds less dissolved gas than cold water does. In addition, since a water-breathing animal performs work to move water across its gas exchange surfaces, it must expend more energy to breathe as water temperature rises. Therefore as water temperature goes up, a water-breathing animal must extract more and more O_2 from an environment that is increasingly O_2 deficient, and has a lower percentage of that O_2 available to support activities other than breathing.

(A) *Maiazoon orsaki*   **(B)** *Callyspongia plicifera*

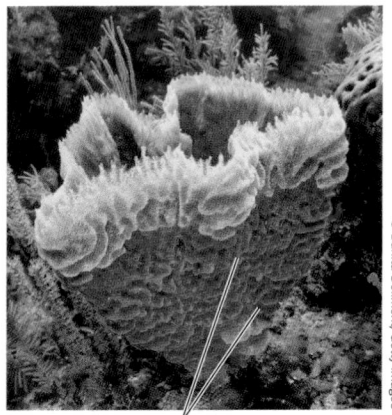

Channels

(C) *Triturus* sp.   Gills

Figure 47.1 Keeping in Touch with the Medium **(A)** No cell in the leaflike body of this marine flatworm is more than a millimeter away from seawater. **(B)** Sponges have body walls perforated by many channels, which allow water to flow between the outside world and a central cavity. No cell in the sponge is more than a millimeter away from seawater. **(C)** A feathery fringe of gills on this larval aquatic salamander provides a large surface area for gas exchange. Blood circulating through the gills comes into close contact with the respiratory medium.

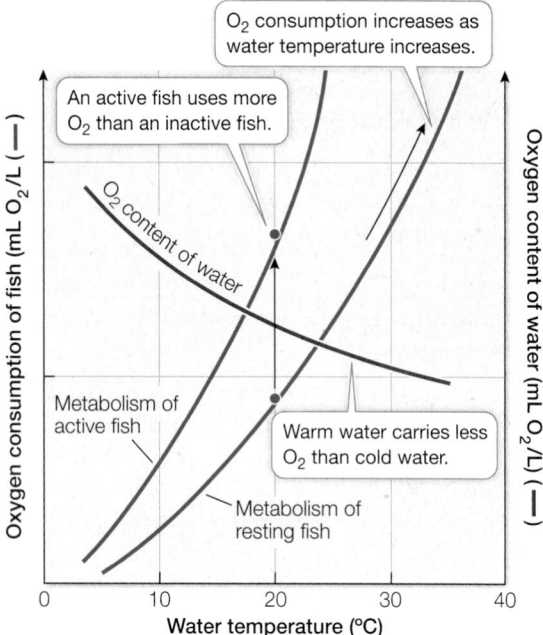

Figure 47.2 The Double Bind of Water Breathers   Fishes need more O_2 when the water is warmer, but warm water carries less O_2 than cold water.

O_2 availability decreases with elevation

Just as a rise in water temperature reduces the supply of O_2 available to water-breathing animals, an increase in elevation reduces the O_2 supply for air breathers. At all elevations, O_2 makes up 20.9% of the dry air; however, as you go up in elevation, the total amount of gas per unit of volume decreases, as reflected by the atmospheric pressure. For example, at 5,800 meters, atmospheric pressure is only half what it is at sea level, so the P_{O_2} at that elevation is only about 80 mm Hg. At the summit of Mount Everest (8,850 m), P_{O_2} is only about 50 mm Hg—roughly one-third what it is at sea level.

Because diffusion of O_2 across respiratory gas exchange surfaces and into the body depends on the P_{O_2} difference between the air and the body fluids, the reduced P_{O_2} in the air at high elevations constrains O_2 uptake. Because of this, mountain climbers attempting peaks such as Mount Everest or K2 usually breathe O_2 from pressurized bottles.

CO_2 is lost by diffusion

Respiratory gas exchange is a two-way process: CO_2 diffuses out of the body as O_2 diffuses in. The direction and rate of diffusion of the respiratory gases across the exchange surfaces depend on the partial pressure gradients of the gases. The partial pressure gradients of O_2 and CO_2 across these exchange surfaces are quite different. The amount of CO_2 in the atmosphere is extremely low (0.03%), so for air-breathing animals there is always a large concentration gradient for diffusion of CO_2 from the body to the environment. Whereas the partial pressure gradient for O_2 decreases with increasing elevation, the gradient driving CO_2 out of the body hardly changes. The partial pressure of carbon dioxide (P_{CO_2}) in the atmosphere is close to zero both at sea level and atop Mount Everest.

In general, getting rid of CO_2 is not a problem for water-breathing animals because CO_2 is more soluble in water than is O_2. Even in stagnant water, where the P_{CO_2} is higher than in moving water,

the lack of O_2 becomes a problem for an animal long before CO_2 exchange difficulties arise.

47.1 Recap and Assess

Respiratory gases are exchanged only by diffusion and are therefore a function of partial pressure gradients. All factors influencing respiratory gas exchanges are components of Fick's law of diffusion. Air is a better respiratory medium than water because a given volume of air has more O_2 than the same volume of water. O_2 diffuses faster in air than in water, and less work is required to move air over respiratory exchange surfaces. CO_2 exchange with the external environment occurs readily because of a large concentration gradient from the body to the environment and because CO_2 is highly soluble in water.

1. What is the partial pressure of oxygen in inhaled air at sea level; at 2,000 meters above sea level, where atmospheric pressure is 80% that of sea level; and while breathing air at the same pressure as the environment at 10 meters (= an additional 1 atmosphere of pressure) underwater?

2. Flatworms (see Figure 47.1A) are invertebrates that do not have respiratory systems. What two components of Fick's law enable flatworms to satisfy their need for oxygen?

3. The O_2 content of water decreases with an increase in water temperature, but the gill ventilation rate of a fish increases much more than is necessary to match that decrease in O_2 availability. Why?

4. In terms of Fick's law, describe differences between the ability to exchange O_2 and CO_2 at sea level and at high elevation.

Now that we have discussed the physical factors that influence diffusion rates of respiratory gases between animals and their environments, let's look at some of the adaptations that have evolved for maximizing respiratory gas exchange.

47.2 Enhancing Diffusion Maximizes Respiratory Gas Exchange

Learning Objectives

47.2.1 Explain how insects can sustain high levels of activity without active respiratory systems.

47.2.2 Explain the concept and adaptive significance of countercurrent exchange, using fish gills as the example.

47.2.3 Describe how the avian respiratory system maximizes the partial pressure gradient for O_2 uptake.

47.2.4 Determine the total lung capacity (including residual volume) of a human.

Adaptations to maximize respiratory gas exchange are reflected in the values of Fick's law of diffusion $Q = DA(P_1 - P_2)/L$. Such adaptations have to do with one or more of the following:

- Increase the surface area for gas exchange (A)

- Maximize the partial pressure difference driving diffusion ($P_1 - P_2$)

- Minimize the diffusion path length (L)

- Minimize the diffusion that takes place in an aqueous medium (maximize D)

With these factors in mind, we now look at four different respiratory systems: those of insects, fishes, birds, and mammals.

Respiratory organs have large surface areas

A variety of anatomical adaptations maximize the specialized body surface areas (A) for respiratory gas exchange. Water-breathing animals generally have gills, and air-breathing animals have tracheae or lungs. Gills are highly branched and folded extensions of the body surface that provide a large surface area for gas exchange. Because gills consist of thin, delicate tissues, they minimize the path length (L) traversed by diffusing molecules of O_2 and CO_2. **External gills** are found in larval amphibians and in the aquatic larvae of many insects (**Figure 47.3A**; see also Figure 47.1C). External gills are vulnerable to damage and are tempting morsels for predators, so in many animals protective body cavities for gills have evolved. Such **internal gills** are found in many mollusks such as clams, many arthropods such as crabs and lobsters (**Figure 47.3B**), and in all fishes.

Lungs are highly divided internal cavities with large surface areas for respiratory gas exchange with air (**Figure 47.3C**). Because lung tissue is elastic, lungs can be inflated with air and deflated as a means of ventilating the respiratory exchange surfaces.

Insects have a respiratory gas exchange system consisting of a network of air-filled tubes called **tracheae** that branch through all tissues of the insect's body (**Figure 47.3D**). The tracheae branch into smaller tracheoles that further branch into extremely fine air capillaries. These air capillaries, which are the respiratory gas exchange surfaces, are so numerous that they have an enormous surface area compared with the external surface area of the insect's body.

Ventilation and perfusion of gas exchange surfaces maximize partial pressure gradients

Partial pressure gradients, $(P_1 - P_2)/L$, drive diffusion across gas exchange surfaces; the larger the gradient, the greater the rate of gas exchange. These gradients can be maximized in several ways:

(A) External gills **(B) Internal gills**

(C) Lungs **(D) Tracheae**

Figure 47.3 Gas Exchange Systems Large surface areas for the diffusion of respiratory gases (tan in these diagrams) are common features of animals. External **(A)** and internal **(B)** gills are adaptations for gas exchange with water. Lungs **(C)** and tracheae **(D)** are adaptations for gas exchange with air.

- *Minimizing path length*: Very thin tissues in gills and lungs reduce the diffusion path length (L).
- *Ventilating*: Actively moving the external medium over the gas exchange surfaces (i.e., breathing) regularly exposes those surfaces to fresh respiratory medium containing maximum O_2 and minimum CO_2 concentrations. This maximizes the partial pressure gradients.
- *Perfusing*: Actively moving the internal medium (e.g., blood) over the internal side of the exchange surfaces transports CO_2 to those surfaces and O_2 away from them, thus maximizing the partial pressure gradients driving diffusion.

Insects have airways throughout their bodies

The tracheal system that enables insects to exchange respiratory gases extends to all tissues in the insect body. Thus respiratory gases diffuse through air most of the way to and from every cell. The insect respiratory system communicates with the outside environment through gated openings called spiracles in the sides of the abdomen and thorax (**Figure 47.4A,B**). The spiracles open to allow gas exchange and then close to decrease water loss. They open into tubes called tracheae that branch into even finer tubes,

(A) Trachea Air sacs Abdominal spiracles

Muscle fiber

Tracheole

Tracheae

Thoracic spiracles

Spiracle

Figure 47.4 The Tracheal Gas Exchange System of Insects **(A)** In insects, respiratory gases diffuse through a system of air sacs and tubes (tracheae) that open to the external environment through holes called spiracles. **(B)** The spiracles of a hawkmoth larva run down its sides. **(C)** A scanning electron micrograph shows an insect trachea dividing into smaller tracheoles and still finer air capillaries.

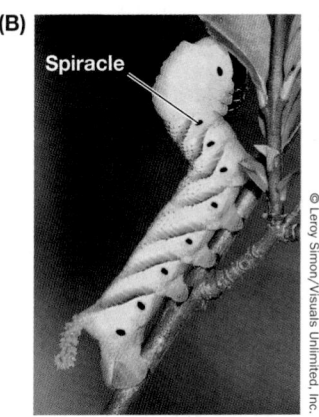

(B)

Spiracle

Acherontia atropos

© Leroy Simon/Visuals Unlimited, Inc.

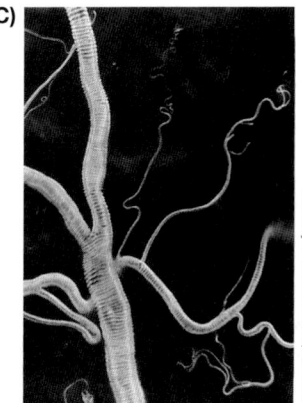

(C)

Courtesy of Thomas Eisner, Cornell U.

the tracheoles, that end in tiny air capillaries—the actual gas exchange surfaces (**Figure 47.4C**).

Fish gills use countercurrent flow to maximize gas exchange

The internal gills of fishes are supported by gill arches that lie between the mouth cavity and the protective opercular flaps on the sides of the fish just behind the eyes (**Figure 47.5A**). Water flows unidirectionally into the fish's mouth, over the gills, and out from under the opercular flaps. Thus there is a constant one-way flow of oxygenated water over the gills, maximizing the P_{O_2} on the external gill surfaces. On the internal side of the gill membranes, the circulation of blood minimizes the P_{O_2} by sweeping O_2 away as rapidly as it diffuses across.

Gills have an enormous surface area for gas exchange because they are so highly subdivided. Each gill consists of hundreds of ribbonlike gill filaments (**Figure 47.5B**). The upper and lower flat surfaces of each gill filament are covered with rows of evenly spaced folds, or lamellae (**Figure 47.5C**). The lamellae are the actual gas exchange surfaces. Because the lamellae are exceedingly thin, the path length (L) for diffusion of gases between blood and water is minimized. The surfaces of the lamellae consist of highly flattened epithelial cells, so the water and the fish's red blood cells are separated by little more than 1–3 micrometers.

The flow of blood perfusing the inner surfaces of the lamellae, like the flow of water over the gills, is unidirectional. **Afferent** blood vessels bring deoxygenated blood to the gills, while **efferent** blood vessels take oxygenated blood away from the gills (see Figure 47.5C). However, blood flows through the lamellae in the opposite direction to the flow of water over the lamellae. This **countercurrent flow** maximizes the transfer of O_2 from water to blood because at all points along the exchange surface there is a P_{O_2} gradient between water and blood. In other words, the P_{O_2} in the water and the blood never come into equilibrium as they would if the two parallel streams flowed in the same direction (concurrent flow) (**Figure 47.6**). Thus even though the concentration gradient at any one point along the gill filament is not large, the effective concentration gradient across the entire length of the gill filament is maximal.

Some fishes, including anchovies, tuna, and certain sharks, ventilate their gills by swimming almost constantly with their mouths open. Most fishes, however, ventilate their gills by means of a two-pump mechanism. The closing and contracting of the mouth cavity pushes water over the gills, and the expansion of the opercular cavity prior to opening of the opercular flaps pulls water over the gills. In both cases the ventilation of the gills is unidirectional and continuous, thus maximizing the P_{O_2} on the water side of the lamellar membranes.

These adaptations for maximizing the surface area (A) for diffusion, minimizing the path length (L) for diffusion, and maintaining the a P_{O_2} gradient along the entire length of the lamellae allow fishes to efficiently extract O_2 from meager environmental sources.

(A) Gill arches

Gill arches (under opercular flap)

Water enters when mouth is open.

Horizontal section through head

(B) Filaments of gill arches

Blood vessels carry blood to and from the gills.

Gill arch
Filament

Mouth
Gill arch

Opercular flap   Gill slit   Gill filament

Water flow

(C) Lamellae on gill filaments

Deoxygenated (afferent) blood enters the gills (P_{O_2} low)

Oxygenated (efferent) blood leaves the gills (P_{O_2} high)

Water leaves, P_{O_2} is low.

Water with high P_{O_2} ventilates gills.

Water flow

O_2 diffuses from water into the blood over the entire length of a lamella.

© Dr. Fred Hossler/Visuals Unlimited, Inc.

Lamella

Deoxygenated blood

Blood perfusion of the lamellae is countercurrent to the flow of water over the lamellae.

Oxygenated blood

Afferent blood vessel

Efferent blood vessel

Figure 47.5 Fish Gills (A) Water flows unidirectionally over the gills of a fish, in through the mouth and out through the opercular opening. (B) Gill filaments have a large surface area and thin membranes. (C) Gill filaments are lined with lamellae, which are the gas exchange surfaces. Blood flows through the lamellae (left to right in this drawing; small blue and red arrows) countercurrent to the direction of the flow of water across the gills (right to left in this drawing; large blue arrows).

(A) Concurrent flow

Oxygen saturation (%)

Gill lamella

Blood in 20 30 40 50 50 50 50 50 50 50 50 50

Water in 100 80 70 60 50 50 50 50 50 50 50 50 50

Equilibrium (no more gas exchange)

(B) Countercurrent flow

Exchange is more complete with countercurrent flow.

Oxygen saturation (%)

Blood in 30 35 40 45 50 55 60 65 70 75 80 85 90 95 100

Water out 35 40 45 50 55 60 65 70 75 80 85 90 95 100

In the countercurrent exchanger, a gradient of O_2 saturation exists over the full length of exchange surfaces.

Figure 47.6 Countercurrent Flow Enables More Complete Exchange In these models of concurrent and countercurrent gas exchange, the numbers represent the O_2 saturation percentages of blood and water. **(A)** In a concurrent exchanger, the saturation percentages of blood and water reach equilibrium halfway across the exchange surface. **(B)** A countercurrent exchanger allows more complete gas exchange because the water always has a higher P_{O_2} than the blood; thus gradients of P_{O_2} support diffusion of O_2 into the blood across the entire length of the exchanger.

Q: What could make the concurrent exchanger achieve the same maximum O_2 saturation as the countercurrent exchanger?

Birds use unidirectional ventilation to maximize gas exchange

Birds are remarkable for their ability to sustain high levels of activity for a long time—on long-distance flights for example —even at high altitudes where mammals cannot even survive. The first team to climb Mount Everest (8,850 meters) was surprised to see birds flying over the mountain when they themselves could barely move without supplemental O_2. Bar-headed Geese (*Anser indicus*) regularly migrate over Mount Everest and surrounding peaks, but the highest recorded flight of a bird is that of a Ruppell's Vulture (*Gyps rueppelli*) that was sucked into a jet engine at 11,278 meters. Humans cannot survive at such elevations without supplemental O_2. Yet the lungs of a bird are smaller than the lungs of a similar-sized mammal, and bird lungs expand and contract less during a breathing cycle than do mammalian lungs. Most different from mammalian lungs is that the volume of bird lungs decreases during inhalation and increases during exhalation. How do birds accomplish such remarkable feats of respiratory gas exchange?

Figure 47.7 The Respiratory System of a Bird **(A)** Air sacs in the body cavity (and air spaces in the bones) are unique to birds. **(B)** Air comes in through the trachea, which divides into a left and a right primary bronchus. The primary bronchi go to the posterior air sacs. Secondary bronchi connect the posterior air sacs to the lungs. Air flows unidirectionally through the lungs in numerous parabronchi and flows in secondary bronchi from the lungs to the anterior air sacs, then out through the trachea. **(C)** Air capillaries running between the parabronchi are the site of gas exchange.

The structure of bird lungs allows air to flow unidirectionally through the lungs, rather than bidirectionally through all the same airways, as it does in tidally ventilating mammals (discussed in the next section). Because mammalian lungs are never completely emptied of air during exhalation, there is always some lung volume that is not ventilated with fresh air. The air remaining in lungs and airways after exhalation is called **dead space**. Bird lungs, by contrast, have very little dead space, and the fresh incoming air is not mixed with stale air. In this way, a high P_{O_2} gradient is maintained.

Air sacs are an important and unique feature of the avian respiratory system, and they occupy much of the body cavity of the bird (**Figure 47.7A**). They can be divided into a group of anterior

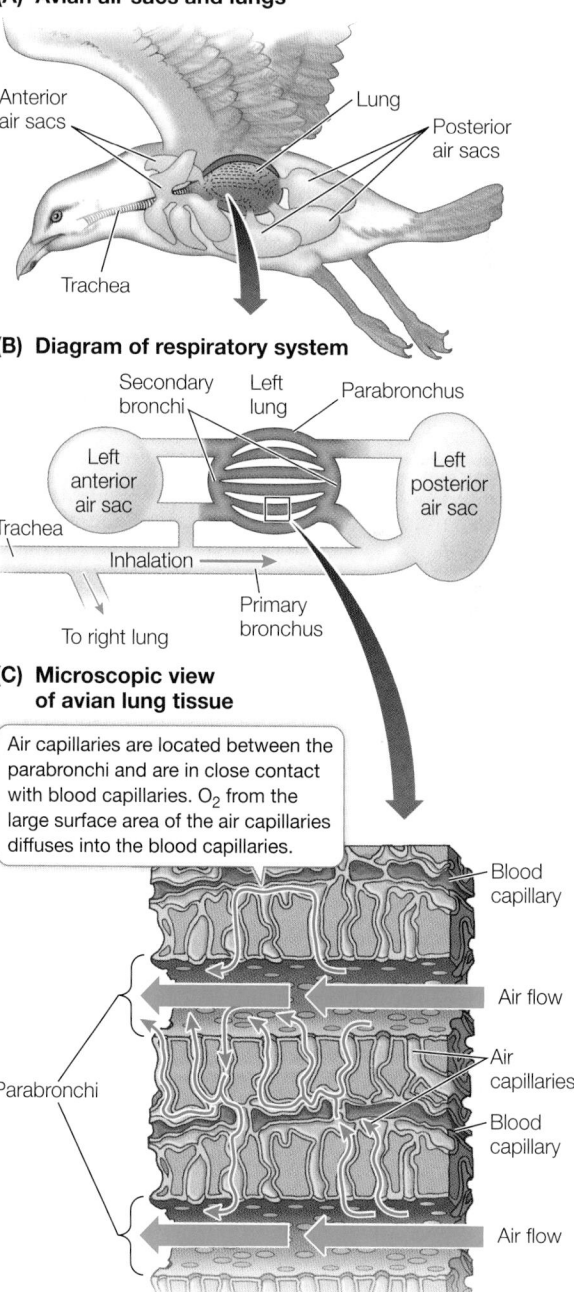

(A) Avian air sacs and lungs

Anterior air sacs

Lung

Posterior air sacs

Trachea

(B) Diagram of respiratory system

Secondary bronchi

Left lung

Parabronchus

Left anterior air sac

Left posterior air sac

Trachea

Inhalation

To right lung

Primary bronchus

(C) Microscopic view of avian lung tissue

Air capillaries are located between the parabronchi and are in close contact with blood capillaries. O_2 from the large surface area of the air capillaries diffuses into the blood capillaries.

Blood capillary

Air flow

Air capillaries

Blood capillary

Parabronchi

Air flow

air sacs and a group of posterior air sacs. The air sacs are interconnected with each other, with the lungs, and with air spaces in some of the bones. The air sacs are not gas exchange surfaces; rather, they act as bellows to maintain a unidirectional flow of air through the lungs.

As in other air-breathing vertebrates, air enters and leaves a bird's gas exchange system through the **trachea** (commonly known as the windpipe, and not to be confused with the air-conducting tracheae of insects) (**Figure 47.7B**). The trachea divides into two smaller airways, the **primary bronchi** (singular *bronchus*). The primary bronchi extend all the way to the posterior air sacs and also branch into **secondary bronchi**. The posterior air sacs also have connections to the secondary bronchi. Secondary bronchi divide into tubelike **parabronchi** that run parallel to one another through the lungs in a posterior to anterior direction.

Branching off the parabronchi and running between them are numerous tiny air capillaries (**Figure 47.7C**). Air flows through the parabronchi and diffuses into the air capillaries, which are the gas exchange surfaces. The air capillaries are so numerous that they provide an enormous surface area for gas exchange. The blood capillaries are in close contact with the air capillaries, and oxygen from the air diffuses into the blood. The parabronchi coalesce into larger bronchi that take the air out of the lungs and into anterior air sacs and then back to the trachea. Thus the anatomy of a bird's airways allows air to flow unidirectionally through the lungs: trachea, bronchi, posterior air sacs, parabronchi, bronchi, anterior air sacs, trachea.

The puzzle of how birds breathe was solved by placing small O_2 sensors at different locations in birds' air sacs and airways. The birds were then allowed to inhale pure O_2 for just a single breath, which made it possible to track that particular breath by recording when each of the O_2 sensors registered a peak value. The experiment showed that a single breath remains in a bird's respiratory system for two cycles of inhalation and exhalation. During inhalation, the air sacs expand and air flows through the trachea into the posterior air sacs. At the same time, the lungs are contracting as air moves from the lungs into the anterior air sacs. During exhalation, the air sacs contract. The posterior air sacs push air into the lungs, which are expanding, and the anterior air sacs push air into the trachea and out of the respiratory system. This bellows-like action of the air sacs maintains a continuous, unidirectional flow of fresh air through the lungs (**Figure 47.8**).

The advantages of the avian respiratory system are similar to those of fish gills. The air sacs keep fresh air flowing unidirectionally over the gas exchange surfaces without interruption. Thus those gas exchange surfaces are constantly exposed to a P_{O_2} that is very close to that of the ambient air. Even at high elevations where the P_{O_2} of the ambient air may be only slightly above that of the blood, O_2 can still diffuse continuously from air to blood.

Tidal ventilation produces dead space that limits gas exchange efficiency

Lungs evolved in early lungfishes as outpocketings of the digestive tract. Although lung structure has evolved considerably, lungs remain dead-end sacs in all air-breathing vertebrates except birds (and likely their extinct reptilian ancestors). Ventilation of dead-end sacs with common passageways for inflow and outflow cannot be constant and unidirectional but must be

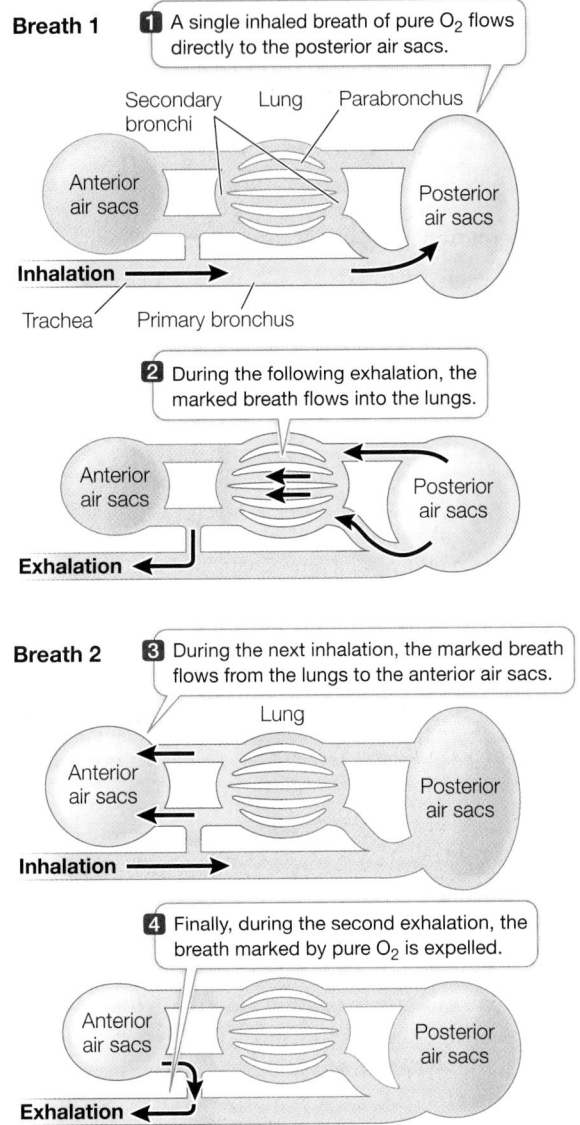

Breath 1

1 A single inhaled breath of pure O_2 flows directly to the posterior air sacs.

Secondary bronchi — Lung — Parabronchus

Anterior air sacs — Posterior air sacs

Inhalation →

Trachea — Primary bronchus

2 During the following exhalation, the marked breath flows into the lungs.

Anterior air sacs — Posterior air sacs

Exhalation →

Breath 2

3 During the next inhalation, the marked breath flows from the lungs to the anterior air sacs.

Lung

Anterior air sacs — Posterior air sacs

Inhalation →

4 Finally, during the second exhalation, the breath marked by pure O_2 is expelled.

Anterior air sacs — Posterior air sacs

Exhalation ←

Figure 47.8 An Experiment to Describe Airflow in the Avian Respiratory System Oxygen sensors placed in different locations in the avian respiratory system trace the flow of a single breath of pure oxygen (blue) through the system. A single breath remains in the system for two breathing cycles.

 View in Achieve
Animation 47.1 Airflow in Birds

tidal: air flows in and exhaled gases flow out by the same route. Since the lungs and airways can never be completely emptied of air, they always contain dead space. We can easily measure the volumes of air exchanged during breathing, but we have to use an indirect method to measure the dead space contained in the lungs and airways. Measures of dead space are important in assessing lung health and disease.

A flowmeter measures the volume of air breathed in and out (**Figure 47.9**). Using a human as an example, the amount of air that moves either in or out per breath when at rest is called the **tidal volume** (**TV**) (about 500 mL for an average human adult). When we breathe in as much as possible, the additional volume

Figure 47.9A **Measuring Lung Ventilation**   A flowmeter measures the volume of air a person breathes through a mouthpiece. The combined tidal volume, inspiratory reserve volume, and expiratory reserve volume are the lungs' vital capacity. The vital capacity plus the residual volume are the total lung capacity.

The person breathes through the mouthpiece of the flowmeter...

...and the computer records and displays the volume of air flow as changes in lung volume.

Flowmeter

Mouthpiece of flowmeter

Inspiratory reserve volume is an additional capacity of the lungs that enables the deepest breath.

Vital capacity

Total lung capacity

Liters

Maximum exhalation

Tidal volume is the normal amount of air exchanged in breathing when at rest.

Expiratory reserve volume is the additional air that can be forcefully exhaled.

Residual volume is the amount of air left in the lungs after maximum exhalation.

Figure 47.9B **Measuring Lung Ventilation**

A patient complains of always being short of breath. Using a flowmeter, the physician determines that the patient's tidal volume is 0.3 liter (L) and his expiratory reserve volume is 1.5 L. The physician decides to use the Helium dilution method to measure the patient's residual volume. She attaches the flowmeter to a 30-L air reservoir containing 5% helium. Using a two-way valve, she can have the patient breathe room air or the air in the reservoir. At the end of a tidal exhalation, the physician turns the valve and lets the patient take 10 breaths from the reservoir. She then switches the patient to room air at the end of a tidal exhalation. She determines that the volume of the reservoir is still 30 L, but the helium concentration in the reservoir is now 4.4%.

QUESTIONS▶

1. What is the patient's residual volume?

2. Why do you think the patient complains of always being short of breath?

Go to **Achieve** for a companion **Data in Depth** exercise.

---

is the **inspiratory reserve volume** (**IRV**). Conversely, if we forcefully exhale as much air as possible, the additional amount of air expelled is the **expiratory reserve volume** (**ERV**). The maximum capacity for air exchange in one breath, or the **vital capacity** (**VC**), is the sum of TV + IRV + ERV. The vital capacity of an athlete is generally greater than that of a nonathlete, and vital capacity decreases with age because of stiffening of the lung tissue.

Vital capacity is not the entire lung volume because of the dead space, also called the **residual volume** (**RV**). We can't measure RV directly with the flowmeter, but we can measure it indirectly using the helium dilution method. The flowmeter is attached to a closed reservoir of air of a known volume (V_{res}) so that a person can breathe in and out from that reservoir. If this reservoir has a known amount of helium (He) in it, and a subject breathes the air in that reservoir through several breathing cycles, the helium will become distributed in the reservoir and in the subject's respiratory system. Helium is not absorbed into the body from the lungs, so the total amount of helium at the beginning of a test (He_i) will equal the total amount at the end of the test (He_f)—it will just be distributed over a larger volume and therefore be less concentrated. The following formula quantifies that relationship:

Initial amount of He = final amount of He

We start the subject breathing from the reservoir at an end-tidal breath, and we end the breathing from the reservoir at an end-tidal breath. Since the V_{res} does not change, the decrease in helium

concentration [He] enables us to calculate the subject's **functional residual volume** (**FRV**), which is the ERV + RV.

$$V_{res} \times [He]_i = (V_{res} + FRV) \times [He]_f$$

Since we *can* measure the ERV with the flowmeter, we can subtract the ERV from the FRV to obtain the RV.

Why is the RV important? Referring to Figure 47.9, you will see that for a normal person the ERV is about 1,000 mL and the RV is 1,000 mL. Thus the FRV is 2,000 mL, but the tidal volume is only 500 mL; this means that the air that reaches the alveoli (the actual gas exchange surfaces) with each breath consists of only 500 mL of fresh air diluted by 2,000 mL of stale air. The maximum P_{O_2} in this mixed air is much below the P_{O_2} of the outside air, and because of the tidal ventilation pattern, the P_{O_2} in the alveoli is steadily dropping during the breathing cycle. The RV is important because it contributes to the FRV and to the dilution of the O_2 in the inhaled air. Any disease or condition that increases the RV (such as emphysema or pulmonary fibrosis) compromises a patient's respiratory ability. Similarly, considering the mixing of fresh air with the FRV, you can understand why reductions in tidal volume can be a problem—and therefore why patients recovering from surgery are encouraged to breathe deeply, even if it hurts.

Small residual volume prevents the bends in seals

In the opening of this chapter we discussed the remarkable abilities of elephant seals to dive to great depths for long times and then spend only minutes breathing at the surface. We asked how elephant seals avoid getting the bends, a very painful condition that develops in scuba divers who surface too rapidly after spending time at depths. The pressure of the water on the body increases by 1 atmosphere for every 10 meters of depth. Body tissues are not compressible, but air in the respiratory system is, so scuba divers breathe air through a regulator that equalizes the air pressure in their lungs to the pressure of the water on the body. As the total air pressure goes up, the partial pressures of the component gases go up, increasing their rate of diffusion into the tissues. Eighty percent of the air is nitrogen, so the amount of nitrogen dissolved in tissues increases. If the diver comes up too rapidly, the dissolved nitrogen comes out of solution in the tissues, creating small bubbles that block blood vessels, damage tissues, cause pain, and can even result in death. To avoid the bends, divers use decompression tables that tell them how to ascend depending on how deep and how long their dives have been. For example, if a diver has spent 1 hour at a depth of 60 meters, he would have to spend 3 hours gradually ascending to shallower and shallower depths to allow the nitrogen dissolved in his tissues to diffuse out through the respiratory system rather than form bubbles in his tissues. Why does a seal that makes repeated dives not face the same consequences? The seal exhales before diving and the residual air in its respiratory system gets compressed into its airways, which are not respiratory exchange surfaces. So when seals dive they do not have compressible air in their lungs that can be forced into tissues at depth and then come out of solution upon resurfacing.

KEY CONCEPT

47.2 Recap and Assess

The major adaptations that increase efficiency of respiratory gas exchange are large surface areas for exchange and maximized partial pressure gradients across those surfaces. Fishes have countercurrent exchange across their gill filaments. Fish and avian respiratory systems have continuous and unidirectional ventilation of their respiratory exchange surfaces. Mammals have tidal ventilation, resulting in residual volumes of low-P_{O_2} air that dilutes the incoming fresh air.

1. Given constant rates of ventilation and perfusion of fish gills, how can the directionality of blood flow inside the gill lamellae and directionality of water flow on the outside the lamellae influence the maximum O2 exchange that can occur?

2. How do birds maintain a constant and unidirectional flow of air through their lungs?

3. Find the functional residual volume of a person who yields the following data while breathing through a flowmeter from a closed reservoir that has a volume of 30 liters (L) and an initial gas mixture of 20% O_2, 75% nitrogen (N), and 5% helium (He). Beginning with an inhalation, the person inhales and exhales 20 times. The final concentration of He in the flowmeter is 4.6%.

Despite their limitations, mammalian lungs serve the respiratory needs of mammals well. Offsetting the inefficiencies of tidal breathing, mammalian lungs have an enormous surface area and a very short path length for diffusion. Next we look at the human respiratory system as an example.

KEY CONCEPT

47.3 Humans Have Tidal Respiration

Learning Objectives

47.3.1 Explain the roles of surface tension and surfactant in breathing.

47.3.2 Explain how changes in volume and pressure in the thoracic cavity are involved in ventilation.

47.3.3 Describe the changes (in arbitrary units) in tension between the pleural membranes and the pressure in the alveoli, and airflow during a breathing cycle.

The respiratory exchange surfaces in mammalian lungs are the very thin-walled alveoli that cluster around a huge number of finely branching terminal airways. To understand how these respiratory surfaces are ventilated and perfused, we first examine the functional anatomy of the whole respiratory system (**Figure 47.10**).

Lungs are ventilated through a branching system of airways

Air enters the lungs through the oral cavity or through the nasal passages, which join together in the **pharynx** (see Figure 47.10A). Below the pharynx, the esophagus conducts food to the stomach, and the trachea conducts air to the lungs. At the beginning of this airway is the **larynx**, or voice box, which houses the vocal cords. The larynx is the lump that you can see or feel on the front of your neck. The trachea is about 2 centimeters in diameter. C-shaped bands of cartilage prevent the thin walls of the trachea from collapsing as air pressure changes during the breathing cycle. If you run your fingers down the front of your neck just below your larynx, you can feel a few of these bands of cartilage.

The trachea branches into two primary **bronchi**, one leading into the right lung and one into the left. The right lung has three lobes and the left lung has two, so there is an asymmetry in the secondary bronchi, with three on the right and two on the left. The bronchi branch repeatedly to generate treelike structures of progressively smaller airways extending to all regions of the lungs. After four branchings, the cartilage supports disappear, marking the transition to **bronchioles**. After about 16 branchings, the bronchioles are less than a millimeter in diameter, and tiny, thin-walled air sacs called **alveoli** begin to appear. Alveoli are the sites of gas exchange. After the first alveoli there are about six more branchings of the airways that end in clusters of alveoli (see Figure 47.10B). Because the airways conduct air only to and from the alveoli and do not themselves participate in gas exchange, their volume is dead space.

Human lungs have about 300 million alveoli. Although each alveolus is very small, their combined surface area for diffusion of respiratory gases is about 70 square meters—about one-fourth the size of a basketball court. The walls of each alveolus are made of very thin cells. Wrapped around the alveoli are networks of capillaries that also have very thin walls. Thus where capillary meets alveolus, the diffusion path length between air and blood is less than 2 micrometers (see Figure 47.10C).

Diseases of the bronchioles and alveoli are the fourth leading cause of death in the United States as of 2019 Among these

(A) Respiratory system

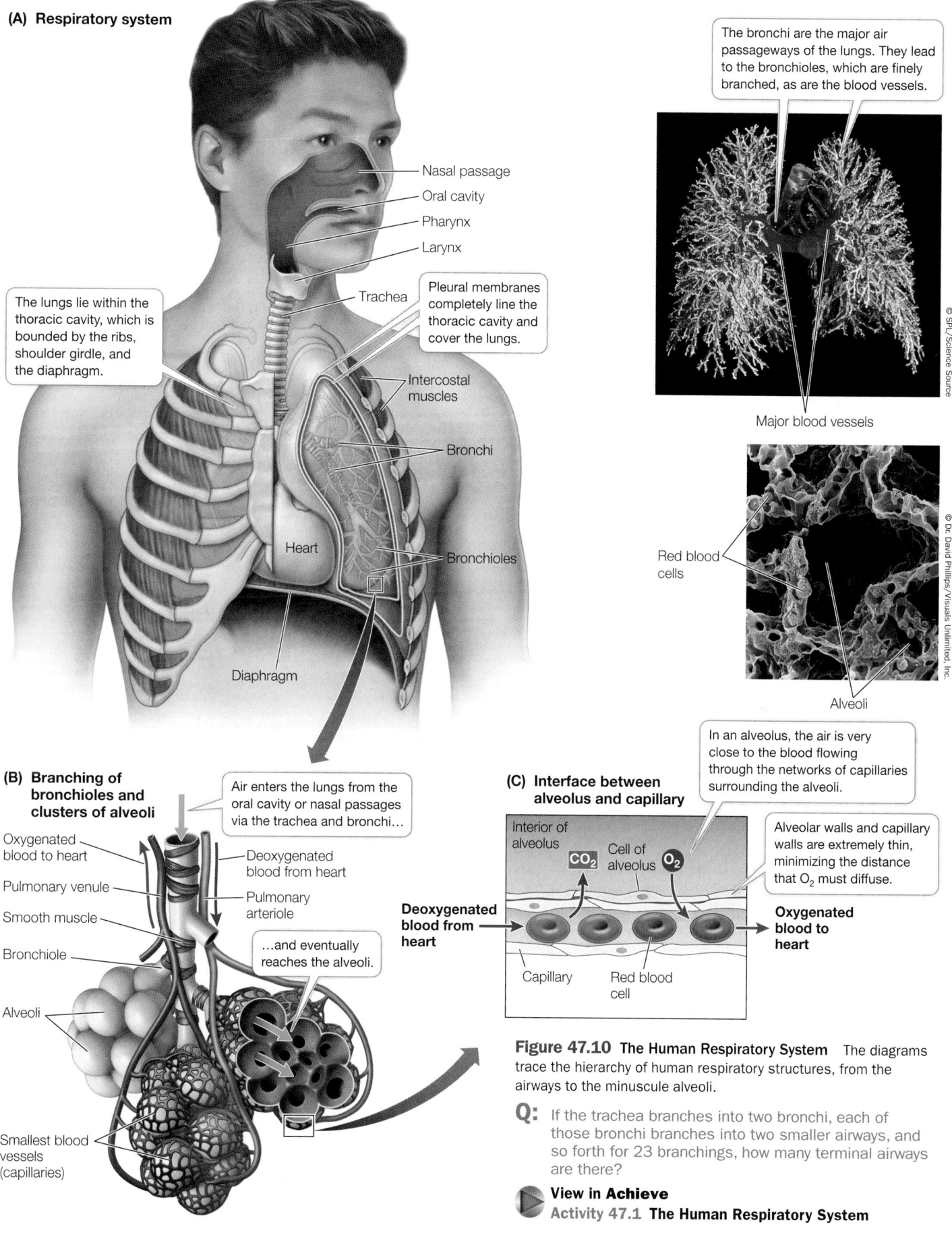

The bronchi are the major air passageways of the lungs. They lead to the bronchioles, which are finely branched, as are the blood vessels.

The lungs lie within the thoracic cavity, which is bounded by the ribs, shoulder girdle, and the diaphragm.

Nasal passage
Oral cavity
Pharynx
Larynx
Trachea

Pleural membranes completely line the thoracic cavity and cover the lungs.

Intercostal muscles

Bronchi

Heart

Bronchioles

Diaphragm

Major blood vessels

Red blood cells

Alveoli

(B) Branching of bronchioles and clusters of alveoli

Air enters the lungs from the oral cavity or nasal passages via the trachea and bronchi...

Oxygenated blood to heart
Pulmonary venule
Smooth muscle
Bronchiole

Deoxygenated blood from heart
Pulmonary arteriole

...and eventually reaches the alveoli.

Alveoli

Smallest blood vessels (capillaries)

(C) Interface between alveolus and capillary

In an alveolus, the air is very close to the blood flowing through the networks of capillaries surrounding the alveolus.

Interior of alveolus

CO_2 Cell of alveolus O_2

Alveolar walls and capillary walls are extremely thin, minimizing the distance that O_2 must diffuse.

Deoxygenated blood from heart

Oxygenated blood to heart

Capillary Red blood cell

Figure 47.10 The Human Respiratory System The diagrams trace the hierarchy of human respiratory structures, from the airways to the minuscule alveoli.

Q: If the trachea branches into two bronchi, each of those bronchi branches into two smaller airways, and so forth for 23 branchings, how many terminal airways are there?

▶ **View in Achieve**
Activity 47.1 The Human Respiratory System

© SPL/Science Source

© Dr. David Phillips/Visuals Unlimited, Inc.

diseases, the most lethal is emphysema, a condition in which inflammation damages and eventually destroys the walls of the alveoli. As a result, the lungs have fewer but larger alveoli, the lungs lose elasticity, and the RV increases. A principal cause of emphysema is smoking and another is air pollution.

Respiratory tract secretions aid ventilation

Mammalian lungs produce two secretions that do not directly influence their gas exchange but do affect the process of ventilation: mucus and surfactant.

Many cells lining the airways produce sticky mucus that captures bits of dirt and microorganisms that are inhaled. Other cells lining the airways have cilia that beat continually and sweep the mucus, with its trapped debris, up toward the pharynx, where it is swallowed or spit out. This phenomenon, called the mucus escalator, can be adversely affected by inhaled pollutants. Smoking one cigarette can immobilize the cilia of the airways for hours. A smoker's cough results from the need to clear the obstructing mucus from the airways when the mucus escalator is out of order.

A **surfactant** is a substance that reduces the surface tension of a liquid. **Surface tension** gives the surface of a liquid the properties of an elastic membrane, and it is why certain insects, such as water striders, can walk on water. As discussed in Key Concept 2.4, surface tension is the result of chemical forces of attraction between water molecules. The attractive forces working on the water molecules at the surface pull from below and from the sides but not from above. This imbalance of forces creates surface tension. The thin film of fluid covering the air-facing surfaces of the alveoli has surface tension that contributes to the lungs' elasticity. To inflate the lungs, enough force has to be generated to overcome both the elasticity of the lung tissue and the surface tension in the alveoli.

Lung surfactant is a fatty lipoprotein complex substance that reduces the work necessary to inflate the lungs. Certain cells in the alveoli release these surfactant molecules. If a baby is born more than a month prematurely, these cells may not have developed the ability to produce surfactant. A baby with this condition, known as respiratory distress syndrome (RDS), will have great difficulty breathing and may die from exhaustion and lack of O_2. RDS is the leading cause of death for premature babies, but current treatment protocols have greatly reduced mortality due to RDS. Those treatments include application of synthetic or animal-derived surfactants directly into the infant's lungs. Positive airway pressure applied through nasal tubes also helps ventilate the infant's lungs.

Laundry detergent is also a surfactant, but lung surfactant differs in a very important way. Detergent dissolves in water; lipoprotein surfactant does not, and remains at the water–air interface. Therefore as the alveoli expand, the surfactant molecules are more thinly distributed over a larger surface area and have less of an effect on surface tension. Why is this property important?

Have you ever wondered how a tiny fan can hold up a collapsible cover over a tennis court or a swimming pool? The answer is **LaPlace's law**, which describes the relationships between pressure (P), tension (T), and radius (r) of bubbles: $P = 2T/r$. The larger the radius, the less pressure it takes to overcome the tension. Alveoli are not all the same size, so according to LaPlace's law, inhalation should preferentially inflate the larger alveoli and not the smaller ones. The unique property of lung surfactant solves this problem because as the larger alveoli inflate, their surface tension increases, favoring the inflation of the smaller alveoli. Also, the increased surface tension in the inflated lungs adds to the recoil during exhalation, facilitating the emptying of the lungs.

Lungs are ventilated by pressure changes in the thoracic cavity

Human lungs are suspended in the **thoracic cavity**, a closed compartment bounded on the bottom by a sheet of muscle called the **diaphragm** (see Figure 47.10A). Each lung is covered by a continuous sheet of tissue called the **pleural membrane** that also lines the thoracic cavity adjacent to the lung. A thin film of fluid between the pleural membranes of the lung and the thoracic cavity lubricates the inner surfaces of the pleural membranes so they can slip and slide against each other. As with surface tension, there are forces of attraction between the molecules of fluid covering the pleural membranes. As a result, it is difficult to pull the pleural membranes apart. Think of two wet panes of glass or two wet microscope slides; you can slide them past each other, but it is difficult to separate them. While the inner surfaces of the pleural membranes are "stuck" to each other by surface tension, they can move relative to each other during breathing movements.

Inhalation and exhalation involve changes in the volume of the thoracic cavity (**Figure 47.11**). Because the pleural membranes covering the cavity wall and the lung surface are stuck to each other by surface tension, any attempt to increase the volume of the thoracic cavity increases the tension between the pleural membranes. Even between breaths, there is tension between the pleural membranes because the rib cage is pulling outward and the elasticity of the lung tissue is pulling inward. This slight negative pressure keeps the alveoli partly inflated even at the end of an exhalation. If the thoracic cavity is punctured—by a knife wound, for example—air can leak into the space between the pleural membranes and cause the lung to deflate. If the wound is not sealed, breathing movements pull air in between the pleural membranes rather than into the lung (a "sucking chest wound"), and there is no ventilation of the alveoli in that lung—a condition called "collapsed lung."

At rest, inhalation is initiated by contraction of the muscular diaphragm (see Figure 47.11A). As the domed diaphragm contracts, it pulls down, expanding the thoracic cavity and pulling on the pleural membranes. Since the pleural membranes cannot separate, they pull on the lungs, increasing their volume and decreasing the alveolar pressure. As a result, air rushes in through the trachea from the outside. Exhalation begins when contraction of the diaphragm ceases. As the diaphragm relaxes, the elastic recoil of the lung tissues pulls the diaphragm up and pushes air out through the airways (see Figure 47.11B). When a person is at rest, inhalation is an active process and exhalation is a passive process.

The diaphragm is not the only muscle that can change the volume of the thoracic cavity. Between the ribs are two sets of **intercostal muscles** (see Figure 47.11C). The external intercostal muscles expand the thoracic cavity by lifting the ribs up and

(A) Inhalation

Air in

Thoracic cavity

Thoracic cavity expands during inhalation.

Lung

Lung

Heart

Pleural cavity

Diaphragm

During inhalation:
- Diaphragm contracts
- Thoracic cavity expands
- Intrapleural pressure becomes more negative
- Lungs expand
- Intra-alveolar pressure becomes more negative
- Air rushes in

(B) Exhalation

Air out

Thoracic cavity contracts during exhalation.

During exhalation:
- Diaphragm relaxes
- Thoracic cavity contracts
- Intrapleural pressure becomes less negative
- Lungs contract
- Gases in lungs are expelled

(C) Intercostal muscles

Rib

Innermost intercostal

Internal intercostal

External intercostal

(D)

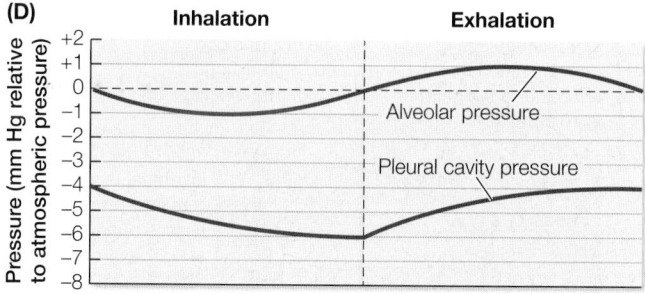

Inhalation   Exhalation

Pressure (mm Hg relative to atmospheric pressure)

Alveolar pressure

Pleural cavity pressure

Figure 47.11 Into the Lungs and Out Again (A) Inhalation is an active process spurred by contraction of the diaphragm. (B) Exhalation generally is a passive process as the diaphragm relaxes. (C) Strong inhalations and exhalations also involve the external and internal intercostal muscles. (D) Between breaths, the intra-alveolar pressure is the same as the external barometric pressure, but the interpleural pressure is still negative and keeps the lungs from collapsing. During inhalation the interpleural pressure becomes more negative, expanding the lungs and causing the intra-alveolar pressure to become negative, which pulls air into the lungs.

 View in Achieve
Animation 47.2 Airflow in Mammals

outward. The internal intercostal muscles decrease the volume of the thoracic cavity by pulling the ribs down and inward. During strenuous exercise, the external intercostal muscles increase the volume of air inhaled, making use of the inspiratory reserve volume, and the internal intercostal muscles increase the amount of air exhaled, making use of the expiratory reserve volume. The abdominal muscles can also aid in breathing. When they contract, they cause the abdominal contents to push up on the diaphragm and thereby contribute to the expiratory reserve volume.

Remember that ventilation and perfusion work together to maximize the partial pressure gradients across the alveolar membranes (see Figure 47.11D). Ventilation delivers O_2 to the environmental side of the exchange surface, where it diffuses across and is swept away by the perfusing blood, which carries it to the tissues. The reverse is true for CO_2. Perfusion delivers CO_2 to the exchange surface, where it diffuses across and is swept away by ventilation.

KEY CONCEPT
47.3 Recap and Assess

The mammalian respiratory system consists of a highly branching system of airways that lead to alveoli—the gas exchange surfaces. Respiratory muscles ventilate the alveoli by creating pressure differences between the lungs and the outside air. Alveolar surfactant decreases the work of inflating the lungs, and surface tension in the alveoli contributes to elastic recoil, facilitating emptying of the lungs. CO_2 and O_2 are exchanged across thin capillary and alveoli walls by diffusion.

1. In terms of LaPlace's law, explain the functional significance of the unique properties of lung surfactant.

2. Explain why a puncture wound of the chest causes a collapsed lung.

3. In the breathing cycle, what is the alveolar pressure when the tension between the pleural membranes is maximal? Explain your answer.

Having discussed how respiratory gases get to and from the environmental side of the gas exchange membranes through ventilation, we now look at how these gases get to and from the internal side of those membranes through perfusion.

KEY CONCEPT

47.4 Respiratory Gases Are Transported by the Blood

Learning Objectives

47.4.1 Describe the functional properties of the hemoglobin–oxygen dissociation curve.

47.4.2 Explain the significance of the effects of 2,3-bisphosphoglycerate and pH on the O_2-binding properties of hemoglobin.

47.4.3 Explain how the same enzyme, carbonic anhydrase, catalyzes both the loading of CO_2 from cells into the blood and the off-loading of CO_2 from the blood to the alveoli.

Perfusion of the lungs is one of the functions of the circulatory system. The circulatory system uses a pump (the heart) and a network of vessels to transport blood around the body. Circulatory systems are the subject of Chapter 48, so here we discuss only one aspect of perfusion: how blood transports respiratory gases.

The liquid part of blood, the plasma, carries some O_2 in solution, but its ability to transport this nonpolar molecule is limited. The blood plasma of a human can contain in solution about 3 mL of O_2 per liter of plasma, which is inadequate to support even basal metabolism. However, the blood of vertebrates and of many invertebrates contains molecules that bind and release O_2 and thus augment its transport capacity. These molecules pick up O_2 where P_{O_2} is high and release it where P_{O_2} is lower. There are many O_2 transport molecules in the animal kingdom, but in vertebrates this role is played by hemoglobin, a protein contained in red blood cells (RBCs). The percent of the blood volume consisting of RBCs is called the **hematocrit**. The hematocrit of human males averages 45% and that of females 40%. Hemoglobin enables the blood to carry 60 times more oxygen than it could carry just in solution, making high rates of metabolism possible.

Red blood cells are produced in the bone marrow

RBCs are the most abundant human cells in the body. They are produced in the bone marrow at a rate of about 2 million per second, and they circulate around the body for 100–120 days before they are destroyed. Each circuit around the body takes about a minute when at rest. RBCs are among the smallest cells of the body. They have to pass through the tiniest blood vessels, the capillaries. To be so small yet carry a lot of hemoglobin (at least 25% of their volume), RBCs lose their nuclei and most cell organelles prior to being released into the circulation. Because they have no mitochondria, they depend on glycolysis for energy.

Connect the Concepts In Key Concept 9.2, glycolysis is described as a sequence of reactions that by the sixth step has converted one molecule of glucose to two molecules of 1,3-bisphosphoglycerate (see Figure 9.7) and by the tenth step to two molecules of pyruvate in addition to a net gain of two molecules of ATP. However, some of the 1,3-bisphosphoglycerate can be enzymatically converted to 2,3-bisphosphoglycerate, which plays an important role in regulating the oxygen-binding properties of hemoglobin, as we discuss later in this key concept.

Hemoglobin combines reversibly with O_2

RBCs contain enormous numbers of **hemoglobin (Hgb)** molecules. Hgb is a protein consisting of four polypeptide subunits, each of

Figure 47.12 Binding of Oxygen to Hemoglobin Depends on P_{O_2} (A) The sigmoidal shape of the hemoglobin–oxygen binding/dissociation curve reflects positive cooperativity among hemoglobin's subunits. (B) Hemoglobin in blood leaving the lungs is 100% saturated (four O_2 molecules are bound to each hemoglobin molecule). Most hemoglobin molecules drop only one of their four O_2 molecules as they circulate through the body and are still 75% saturated when the blood returns to the lungs. The steep portion of this O_2-binding/dissociation curve comes into play when tissue P_{O_2} falls below 40 mm Hg, which is a normal mixed venous blood P_{O_2}.

which surrounds a heme group—an iron-containing ring structure that can reversibly bind a molecule of O_2. Thus each Hgb molecule can bind and release up to four O_2 molecules, enabling the blood to carry a large amount of O_2 to the body's tissues.

Hgb's ability to pick up or release O_2 depends on the P_{O_2} in its environment. When the P_{O_2} of the blood plasma is high, as it usually is in the lung capillaries, each Hgb molecule can carry its maximum load of four O_2 molecules. As the blood circulates through the rest of the body, it releases some of the O_2 it carries when it encounters lower P_{O_2} values in tissues.

The relationship between P_{O_2} and the amount of O_2 bound to Hgb is not linear but S-shaped (sigmoidal). The hemoglobin–oxygen binding/dissociation curve reflects interactions between the four subunits of the Hgb molecule. At low P_{O_2} values, only one subunit will bind an O_2 molecule (**Figure 47.12A**). When it does so, the shape of that subunit changes, altering the quaternary structure of the entire Hgb molecule. That structural change makes it easier for the other subunits to bind an O_2 molecule; that is, their O_2 *affinity* is increased. Therefore a smaller increase in P_{O_2} is necessary to get the Hgb molecule to bind a second O_2 molecule (to become 50% saturated) than was necessary to get it to bind one O_2 molecule (to become 25% saturated). This change in affinity is reflected in the increased steepness of the O_2-binding curve. The influence of O_2 binding to one Hgb subunit on the O_2 affinity of the other subunits is called **positive cooperativity**.

Once the third O_2 molecule is bound, the relationship seems to change, as a larger increase in P_{O_2} is required for the Hgb to reach 100% saturation. This upper bend of the sigmoid curve is due to a probability phenomenon. The closer we get to having all subunits occupied, the less likely it is that any particular O_2 molecule will find a place to bind. Therefore it takes a relatively greater P_{O_2} to achieve 100% saturation.

The O_2-binding/dissociation properties of Hgb help get O_2 to the tissues that need it most (**Figure 47.12B**). In the lungs, where the P_{O_2} is about 100 mm Hg, Hgb is 100% saturated. The P_{O_2} in blood returning to the heart from the body (at rest) is usually about 40 mm Hg. You can see that at this P_{O_2} the Hgb is still about 75% saturated. This means that as the blood circulates around the body, it releases only about one in four of the O_2 molecules it carries. This system seems inefficient, but because the Hgb keeps 75% of its O_2 in reserve, it can meet the demands of highly active tissues.

When a tissue becomes starved of O_2 and its local P_{O_2} falls below 40 mm Hg, the Hgb flowing through that tissue is on the steep portion of its binding/dissociation curve. That means relatively small decreases in P_{O_2} below 40 mm Hg will result in the release of lots of O_2 to the tissue. Thus Hgb is very effective in making O_2 available to tissues precisely when and where it is needed most.

The O_2 transport function of Hgb can rapidly and tragically be disrupted by a common by-product of incomplete combustion: carbon monoxide (CO). If CO from a faulty heating system, engine exhaust, or burning charcoal accumulates in a closed space, the results can be deadly. Because CO binds to Hgb with a 240-fold higher affinity than O_2, it can prevent Hgb from transporting O_2. In the United States, up to 500 people die each year from CO poisoning.

View in Achieve
Simulation 47.1 Hemoglobin Loading

Figure 47.13 **Oxygen-Binding Adaptations**   Myoglobin and the different hemoglobins have different O_2-binding properties adapted for different circumstances. Fetal hemoglobin, for example, has a higher affinity for O_2 than does adult hemoglobin, facilitating O_2 transfer in the placenta. When high metabolism lowers the pH of the blood, or low O_2 increases 2,3- bisphosphoglycerate (2,3-BPG), hemoglobin releases more of its O_2.

Q: How would breathing some carbon monoxide affect the hemoglobin–oxygen binding curve?

  View in Achieve
Activity 47.2 Oxygen-Binding Curves

Myoglobin holds an O_2 reserve

Muscle cells have their own O_2-binding molecule, **myoglobin**. Myoglobin consists of just one polypeptide chain associated with an iron-containing ring structure that can bind one O_2 molecule. Myoglobin has a higher affinity for O_2 than Hgb does, so it picks up and holds O_2 at P_{O_2} values at which Hgb is releasing its bound O_2 (**Figure 47.13**).

> **Connect the Concepts** The evolutionary relationships between myoglobin and the various hemoglobin subunits are shown in Figure 21.10.

Myoglobin facilitates the diffusion of O_2 in muscle cells and provides an O_2 reserve for times when metabolic demands are high and blood flow is interrupted. Interruption of blood flow in muscles is common because contracting muscles squeeze blood vessels. When tissue P_{O_2} values are low and Hgb can no longer supply more O_2, myoglobin releases its bound O_2. Diving mammals such as seals have high concentrations of myoglobin in their muscles, which is one reason they can stay underwater for so long (**Investigating Life: Seals Are Champion Breath-Hold Divers**). Even in nondiving animals, muscles called on for extended periods of work frequently have more myoglobin than do muscles that are used for short, intermittent periods, as noted in Key Concept 46.2.

Hemoglobin's affinity for O_2 is variable

Various factors influence the O_2-binding/dissociation properties of Hgb, thereby influencing O_2 delivery to tissues. Three of these factors are the chemical composition of the Hgb, the blood pH, and the presence of 2,3-bisphosphoglycerate (2,3-BPG) in RBCs.

►Investigating**LIFE**   Seals Are Champion Breath-Hold Divers

Experiment

Original Paper: M. A. Castellini et al. 1992. Metabolic rates of freely diving Weddell seals: Correlations with oxygen stores, swim velocity, and diving duration. *J Exper Biol* 165: 181–194.

Weddell seals (*Leptonychotes weddellii*) live near the edges of the ice in Antarctica where they feed by diving in the surrounding ocean. The ice-covered ocean presents a unique opportunity to study the diving and breathing behaviors of these seals if they have to return to the same breathing hole in the ice.

QUESTION►   How do metabolic requirements of a freely diving seal correlate with its oxygen stores?

METHOD►

1. Transport Weddell seals several kilometers away from the ice edge, but still on the extensive Antarctic ice sheet.

2. Fit the seals with distance and depth gauges to calculate the metabolic costs of individual dives.

3. Make a hole in the ice and release the seals so they can return to the sea through the hole.

4. Allow the seals to dive and feed naturally.

5. When seals return to the hole to breathe, measure O_2 consumption and CO_2 release and determine each seal's metabolic rate (MR).

RESULTS►   Most dives were only a few minutes long, but many were over 30 minutes and the longest was 82 minutes. MR was also measured when the seals rested and slept. Seals frequently do not breathe during sleep. The longest sleep episode without breathing was 13.5 minutes. Mean MR is listed with ± standard deviation (See Appendix B for discussion of statistical concepts.)

© Aurora Photos/Alamy Stock Photo

Condition	Mean MR (mL O_2/min kg) (± SD)
Rest	4.1 (0.3)
Sleep	3.5 (0.6)
All dives	4.5 (0.9)
Short dives	5.0 (0.9)
Long dives	3.4 (0.6)

CONCLUSION►

1. There were no significant differences in MR during rest, sleep, and the mean for all dives taken together. The relatively consistent measurements of MR indicate a very low metabolic cost of diving and activities during the dives. Going from resting to diving resulted in only a 10% increase in MR. (In humans, by contrast, going from resting to standing involves a 16% increase in MR.)

2. MRs during long dives were lower than at rest, but MRs during short dives (<15 minutes) were significantly higher than during long dives, indicating the capacity of the seals to conserve O_2 supplies to extend dive duration.

Work with the Data

How do the seal's oxygen stores compare with its oxygen demands? To calculate the oxygen reserves of a Weddell seal, we have to assess the amount of oxygen in its blood and in the myoglobin in its muscles at the beginning of the dive. The amount of oxygen in its lungs is irrelevant since a seal exhales before diving, so there is little oxygen available in its alveoli during the dive.

The problem requires calculating the amount of O_2 in the arterial and venous blood and myoglobin at the beginning of the dive that is available to support the seal's MR.

Assume the following:

- Average body mass: 355 kg
- Blood volume: 14.8% of mass (7% in humans)
- Hematocrit: 58% (human averages 42%)
- Hemoglobin content of red blood cells: 23.7%
- O_2 holding capacity of hemoglobin: 1.34 mL/g
- Blood: 34% is arterial, 95% saturated at beginning of dive, can desaturate to 20%

Available O_2 in arterial blood is calculated as follows:

Total arterial blood = 355 kg × 0.148 × 0.34 = 17.9 kg

Total arterial hemoglobin = 17.9 kg × 0.58 × 0.24 = 2.49 kg

Maximum O_2 content = 3.34 L

Arterial O_2 available = 3.34 × (95% − 20%) = 2.5 L

QUESTIONS►

1. Calculate the available O_2 in the venous blood. Assume venous blood is 66% of total blood volume, and that it is 90% saturated at the beginning of the dive and can desaturate to 0%.

2. Calculate the available O_2 in myoglobin. Assume 33% of body mass is muscle, myoglobin content of seal muscle is 45 g/kg (20–25 g/kg for humans), and O_2 holding capacity of myoglobin is 1.34 mL O_2/g.

3. What are the total O_2 reserves at the beginning of the dive?

4. Given the MR values found in the experiment, what do you predict would be the maximum duration of no breathing during sleep?

5. Using the table of MR values for all dives in the results portion of the experiment, predict the maximum duration of a Weddell seal dive.

Go to Achieve for a companion Data in Depth exercise.

HEMOGLOBIN COMPOSITION   There is more than one type of Hgb because the chemical composition of the polypeptide chains that form the Hgb molecule varies. The normal Hgb of adult humans has two each of two kinds of polypeptide chains—two α-globin chains and two β-globin chains. This normal adult Hgb has the O_2-binding characteristics shown in Figure 47.13.

Before birth, the human fetus has a different form of Hgb, consisting of two α-globin and two γ-globin chains. The functional difference between fetal and adult Hgb is that fetal Hgb has a higher affinity for O_2. Therefore the fetal hemoglobin–oxygen binding/dissociation curve is shifted to the left compared with the adult curve (see Figure 47.13). You can see from these curves that if both types of Hgb are at the same P_{O_2} (as they are in the placenta), fetal Hgb will pick up O_2 that the adult Hgb releases. This difference in O_2 affinities enables the efficient transfer of O_2 from the mother's blood to the fetus's blood.

HEMOGLOBIN AND pH   The O_2-binding properties of Hgb are also influenced by physiological conditions. The influence of pH on the function of Hgb is known as the **Bohr effect**. As blood passes through metabolically active tissue such as exercising muscle, it picks up acidic metabolites. As a result, blood pH falls. The excess H^+ ions bind preferentially to deoxygenated Hgb and decrease its affinity for O_2, and the O_2-binding/dissociation curve of Hgb shifts to the right (see Figure 47.13). This shift means the Hgb will release more O_2 in tissues where pH is low—another way that O_2 is supplied where and when it is most needed.

2,3-BISPHOSPHOGLYCERATE   1,3-BPG is an intermediate in glycolysis (see Figure 9.7), and therefore an important source of energy for cells. However, 1,3-BPG can be converted to 2,3-BPG by an enzyme in the RBC. 2,3-BPG is an important regulator of Hgb function. Like excess H^+, 2,3-BPG reversibly combines with deoxygenated Hgb and lowers its affinity for O_2. The result is that

at any P_{O_2}, Hgb releases more of its bound O_2 than it otherwise would. In other words, 2,3-BPG shifts the O_2-binding/dissociation curve of mammalian Hgb to the right.

When humans go to high elevations, or when they cease being sedentary and begin to exercise, the level of 2,3-BPG in their RBCs goes up, making it easier for Hgb to deliver more O_2 to tissues. During pregnancy, a woman has about a 30% increase in 2,3-BPG, which makes more O_2 available in the placenta to be picked up by the fetal Hgb. In addition, fetal Hgb has a left-shifted O_2-binding/dissociation curve because its γ-globin chains have a lower affinity for 2,3-BPG than do the β-globin chains of adult Hgb.

Most CO_2 is transported as bicarbonate ions in the blood

Delivering O_2 to tissues is only half the respiratory function of blood. Blood also carries CO_2, a metabolic waste product, away from tissues (**Figure 47.14**). CO_2 is highly soluble and readily diffuses through cell membranes, moving from its site of production in the tissues into the blood, where P_{CO_2} is lower. However, only about 5% of the CO_2 carried by the blood is dissolved CO_2. About 20% of the CO_2 carried to the lungs in the blood is in chemical combination with Hgb. And most CO_2 produced by the tissues is transported to the lungs in the form of bicarbonate ions (HCO_3^-). CO_2 diffusing from cells is converted to HCO_3^-, transported to the lungs, and then converted back to CO_2 to be exhaled.

When CO_2 dissolves in water, some of it slowly reacts with the water molecules to form carbonic acid (H_2CO_3), some of which then dissociates into a proton (H^+) and a bicarbonate ion (HCO_3^-). This reversible reaction is expressed as follows:

$$CO_2 + H_2O \rightleftharpoons H_2CO_3 \rightleftharpoons H^+ + HCO_3^-$$

In the extracellular fluid, the reaction between CO_2 and H_2O proceeds slowly. But it is a different story in the endothelial cells of the capillaries and in the RBCs, where the enzyme **carbonic**

Figure 47.14 Carbon Dioxide Is Transported as Bicarbonate Ions
The left panel represents the circulation through the tissues of the body where carbonic anhydrase (CA) in capillary endothelial cells and in RBCs facilitates conversion of CO_2 produced in the tissues to bicarbonate ions (HCO_3^-) in the blood. The right panel shows the process reversing in the lungs as CO_2 diffuses from blood to alveolar air and is exhaled.

anhydrase (**CA**) speeds up the conversion of CO_2 to H_2CO_3. The newly formed H_2CO_3 dissociates, and the resulting bicarbonate ions enter the blood plasma in exchange for Cl^- (see Figure 47.14). By converting CO_2 to H_2CO_3, carbonic anhydrase reduces the P_{CO_2} in these cells and in the blood plasma, facilitating the diffusion of CO_2 from tissue cells to endothelial cells, blood plasma, and RBCs.

In the lungs, the reactions involving CO_2 and bicarbonate ions are reversed. Remember that an enzyme such as carbonic anhydrase only speeds up a reversible reaction; it does not determine its direction. The direction is determined by concentrations of reactants and products. Ventilation keeps the P_{CO_2} in the alveoli low, so CO_2 diffuses from the blood plasma into the alveoli, lowering the P_{CO_2} in the blood, which favors the conversion of HCO_3^- into CO_2. Also, the oxygenation of Hgb in the alveoli decreases its affinity for CO_2, a phenomenon known as the Haldane effect.

KEY CONCEPT
47.4 Recap and Assess

O_2 is transported from the lungs to the body's tissues in reversible combination with Hgb. Each Hgb molecule can reversibly combine with four O_2 molecules; the percent saturation of the binding sites is a function of the P_{O_2} in the Hgb's environment. The hemoglobin–oxygen binding/dissociation curve is shifted by the concentration of H^+ and the level of 2,3-BPG in the blood. CO_2 is transported by the blood mostly in the form of HCO_3^-.

1. The P_{O_2} of atmospheric air at sea level is about 159 mm Hg. What is the functional significance of the fact that human Hgb fully saturates with O_2 at a P_{O_2} of 100 mm Hg and returns to the heart in venous blood with a P_{O_2} of about 40 mm Hg, reflecting 75% saturation?

2. When RBCs are stored in the blood bank, they will eventually use their 1,3-BPG for energy. What will be the consequence for their ability to function after transfusion into a patient?

3. Why do HCO_3^- ions leave the RBCs in systemic venous blood but enter RBCs in the alveolar circulation?

We must breathe every minute of our lives, but most of us usually don't worry about it, or even think about it very often. In the next key concept we examine how the regular breathing cycle is generated and controlled by the central nervous system.

KEY CONCEPT
47.5 Breathing Is Homeostatically Regulated

Learning Objectives

47.5.1 Explain the roles of the dorsal and ventral groups of respiratory neurons in the medulla.

47.5.2 Apply knowledge about the physiological processes underlying breathing to explain the body's response to intense exercise and to decreases in P_{O_2}.

47.5.3 Describe where chemosensitive cells are located and how they participate in negative feedback control of breathing.

Breathing is an involuntary function of the central nervous system (CNS). The breathing pattern is adjusted around other activities

(such as speech and eating), and breathing rates change to match the metabolic demands of the body. How is this accomplished?

Breathing is controlled in the brainstem

The basic breathing rhythm is an involuntary function that is modified by feedback information that conveys the body's need for an adequate O_2 supply and CO_2 elimination. Breathing is driven by a rhythm-generating neural circuit in the brainstem, but where? Breathing ceases if the spinal cord is severed in the neck region, showing that breathing is generated in the brain. If the brainstem is cut just above the pons, breathing is normal. If the brainstem is cut between the pons and the medulla (the segment of the brainstem just above the spinal cord), the breathing pattern becomes irregular (**Figure 47.15**). Electrophysiological recordings reveal a group of respiratory motor neurons in the dorsal medulla that increase their firing rates just before and as an inhalation occurs. The axons of these neurons leave the CNS in the neck region to form the phrenic nerve that innervates the diaphragm. As more and more of these neurons fire—and fire faster and faster—the diaphragm contracts. All of a sudden these neurons stop firing, the diaphragm relaxes, and exhalation begins. Exhalation is usually a passive process that depends on the elastic recoil of the lung tissues. Another group of respiratory motor neurons is found in the ventral medulla, and they become active when breathing demand is high. These motor neurons communicate through thoracic spinal nerves to the intercostal muscles between the ribs. By expanding and contracting the rib cage, the intercostal muscles increase both the inhalation and the exhalation volumes.

Neurons in the lower region of the pons help regularize the basic respiratory rhythm. Still higher brain areas modify breathing to accommodate speech, ingestion of food, coughing, and emotional states.

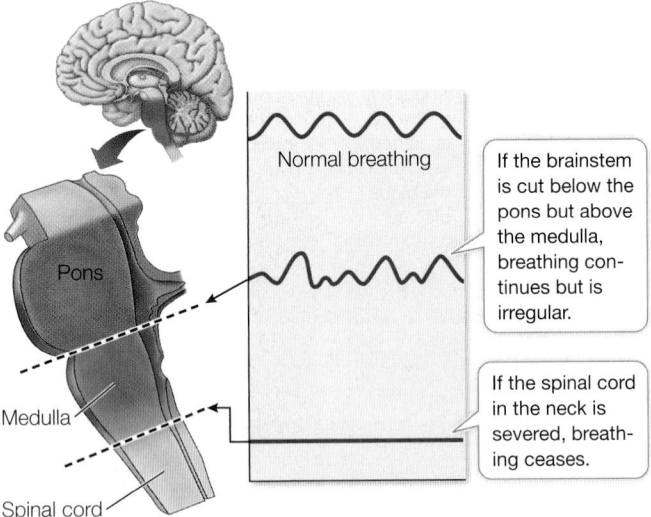

Figure 47.15 Breathing Is Controlled in the Brainstem The basic breathing rhythm is generated in the medulla and is modified by neurons in or above the pons.

Media Clip 47.1 Sea Bed Hunting on One Breath
Life12e.com/mc47.1

Regulating breathing requires feedback

When breathing or metabolism changes, the P_{O_2} and P_{CO_2} in the blood change as well. It is reasonable to surmise that the blood levels of one or both of these gases provide feedback information to the breathing rhythm generator in the medulla. Humans and other mammals are remarkably insensitive to falling levels of O_2 in arterial blood but are extremely sensitive to increases in CO_2. Arterial P_{O_2} can deviate considerably from normal without causing much of an increase in ventilation rate, but even a small rise in arterial P_{CO_2} causes a large increase in ventilation (**Figure 47.16**). This relationship is reversed for water-breathing animals, in which O_2 is the primary feedback stimulus for gill ventilation.

The lack of O_2 sensitivity in humans was tragically demonstrated by an accident at the Kennedy Space Center in 1981 prior to the first flight of the Space Shuttle Program. The space shuttle *Columbia* was being prepared for launch, and to reduce the danger of fire, the engine compartment was purged with nitrogen and sealed. Unaware of the nitrogen, workers opened a hatch to the compartment for inspection. The first worker to enter became unconscious, and others followed him in a rescue attempt. Three of these workers died, and two others who were stricken recovered. When exposed to lack of oxygen, there is no alerting, emergency response—there is simply loss of consciousness.

Where are partial pressures of gases in the blood sensed? The major site of P_{CO_2} sensitivity is an area on the ventral surface of the medulla that is in contact with the cerebrospinal fluid that surrounds the brain. The primary sensitivity of these chemosensitive

cells is not, however, to CO_2. It is H⁺ ions that stimulate these cells. The H⁺ ion concentration in the environment of these cells is a direct reflection of the P_{CO_2} of the blood, but not of the pH of the blood. The cerebrospinal fluid is extracellular fluid, and extracellular fluid has less protein content than the blood plasma. The high protein content of the blood plasma buffers its pH (see Figure 2.18). But, where the P_{CO_2} of the blood is higher than that of the extracellular fluid, CO_2 diffuses out of the blood. This CO_2 interacts with H_2O in the extracellular fluid to form carbonic acid (H_2CO_3), which dissociates into H⁺ ions and HCO_3^- ions (see Figure 47.14, which describes this same reaction in the RBCs). It is the H⁺ ions produced by the dissociation of carbonic acid that stimulate the chemosensitive cells on the ventral surface of the medulla that increase respiratory gas exchange. Thus even though we measure blood P_{CO_2} as the stimulus for breathing, the major stimulus is an increase in H⁺ ion concentration (lowered pH).

We do have physiological sensitivity to blood P_{O_2} in nodes of neural tissue on the large blood vessels leaving the heart: the aorta and the carotid arteries (**Figure 47.17**). These **carotid bodies** and **aortic bodies** are chemosensors. If the blood supply to these structures decreases, or if the blood P_{O_2} falls dramatically, the chemosensors are activated and send nerve impulses to the breathing control center. Although we are not very sensitive to changes in blood P_{O_2}, the carotid and aortic bodies can stimulate increases

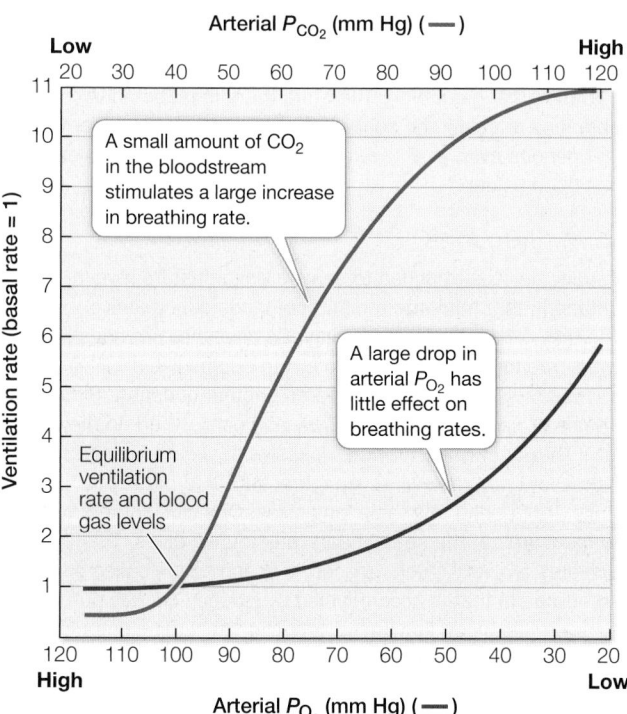

Figure 47.16 Arterial P_{CO_2} Affects Breathing Rate More Than Low O_2 Altering arterial P_{CO_2} or P_{O_2} by breathing air with different concentrations of those gases shows that the regulation of human breathing is more sensitive to increased levels of CO_2 in arterial blood than to decreased amounts of O_2.

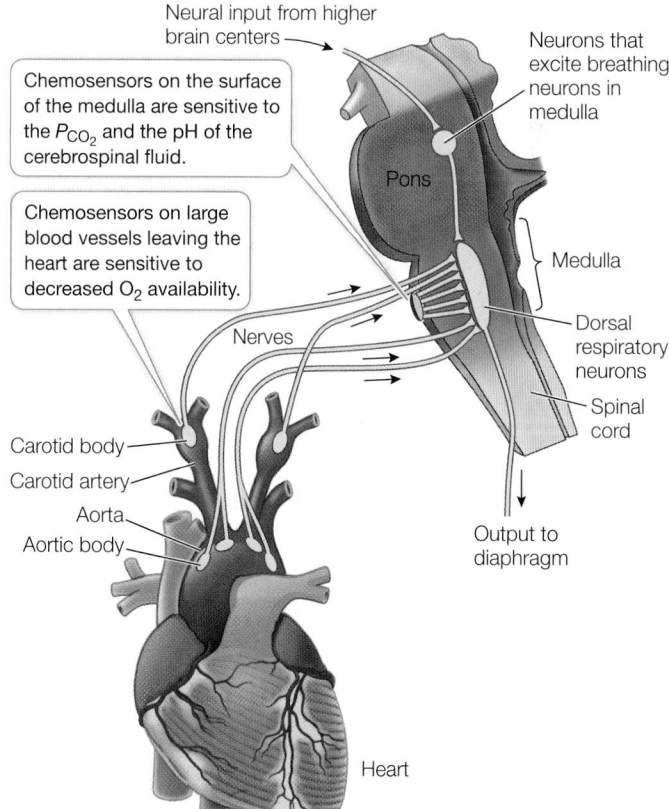

Figure 47.17 Feedback Information Controls Breathing   The body uses feedback information from chemosensors in the great arteries leaving the heart and on the ventral surface of the medullary brainstem to match breathing rate to metabolic demand.

in breathing during exposure to high elevations or when blood volume or blood pressure is very low. Also, there is a synergism between CO_2 and O_2 sensing. When blood P_{CO_2} increases, there is an increased sensitivity to low O_2, and vice versa.

KEY CONCEPT

47.5 Recap and Assess

The rhythmic contractions of the respiratory muscles that drive breathing are generated by neurons in the brainstem. Breathing is regulated predominantly in response to the P_{CO_2} of the blood. Respiratory chemosensors are cells on the ventral surface of the medulla that are sensitive to the blood P_{CO_2}, and the carotid and aortic bodies on the large arteries leaving the heart that are sensitive to the blood P_{O_2} or to a decrease in the blood they are receiving.

1. In terms of respiratory motor neurons and respiratory muscle groups, what changes occur in transitioning from breathing at rest to breathing during exercise that uses more of the lungs' vital capacity?

2. When you go rapidly to high elevation, you may experience a breathing pattern in which periods of no breathing alternate with periods of fast breathing. Explain that response in terms of diffusion gradients for O_2 and CO_2 and the feedback signals regulating breathing.

3. Cells in the carotid and aortic bodies have high metabolic rates, and they are sensitive either to a decrease in blood flow or to a decrease in the P_{O_2} of the blood. How are these two facts related?

 View in Achieve
Activity 47.3 Concept Matching: Gas Exchange

InvestigatingLIFE

Q_and_**A** **What adaptations make seals champion breath-hold divers?**

Seals have remarkable abilities to dive deep and long and to spend only minutes at the surface to breathe between dives. In the chapter opener about elephant seals, we posed several questions that apply to all seals: Why aren't seals crushed by the water pressure at extreme depths? Why don't they get the bends? What are their O_2 demands? And what are their O_2 reserves? The answers to the first two questions are related. Only air-filled structures of the body are compressible, and the seals exhale at the beginning of a dive. Their residual volume is restricted to their airways, where gas exchanges do not occur. Thus the high pressure of the small amount of gas in their respiratory system does not drive dissolved nitrogen into their tissues. **Investigating Life: Seals Are Champion Breath-Hold Divers** presented metabolic rate (MR) measurements for Weddell seals resting, sleeping, and diving. No significant differences in MR for various activities were observed, leading to the conclusion that the metabolic costs of diving are very low. In fact, MRs during dives were only about 10% higher than at rest—not much different than for humans going from sitting to standing.

In spite of the low metabolic expenditures of seals, how do they maintain O_2 reserves sufficient to support them during dives? The calculations made in the Work with the Data exercise in **Investigating Life: Seals Are Champion Breath-Hold Divers** showed that the O_2 reserve of a sleeping seal would permit it to not breathe for a maximum of 12.8 minutes, which corresponds well with the maximum episodes of sleep observed—13.5 minutes. Using the MR value for all dives, calculations show that the seals' O_2 reserves would only support dives that were under 10 minutes in duration. Therefore there must be additional adaptations enabling the seals to remain active underwater for longer periods even at an average MR similar to what they experience during sleep.

Future directions

Recording devices attached to seals diving in nature reveal adaptations that minimize their O_2 demands during a dive. Because they exhale at the beginning of a dive, they are negatively buoyant, meaning they can drift down to depths like a falling leaf. These recordings also answered another question. Since the seals at sea dive continually day and night, when do they sleep? They spend much of their passive descent time sleeping, thus lowering their MR even more. Yet more metabolic savings are needed to enable long dives. One clue comes from measures of the seals' heart rates during dives. Their heart rates are very much reduced, a phenomenon called diving bradycardia that is accompanied by reduced cardiac output (total systemic blood flow). This reduction in cardiac output is achieved by shutting off blood flow to many tissues that can switch to anaerobic metabolism and in response to low levels of O_2 become hypometabolic. The result is that available O_2 in the blood is reserved for heart and brain, which are highly sensitive to lack of O_2.

You should be able to relate each summary to the adjacent figures. If you go to this visual summary in **Achieve**, you can follow links to figures, animations, activities, and simulations that will help you consolidate the material.

KEY CONCEPT

47.1 Respiratory Gas Exchange Is Governed by Physical Factors

- Exchange of **respiratory gases** occurs only by diffusion, and any adaptation to maximize gas exchange must influence a factor in **Fick's law of diffusion**.

- Diffusion coefficients depend on the diffusing substance, the medium, and the temperature.

- For aquatic organisms, increases in water temperature raise O_2 requirements and decrease its availability.

Questions

1. In terms of Fick's law, how does elevation affect respiratory gas exchange?

2. Why is water a worse respiratory gas exchange medium than air?

3. Why does a rise in water temperature put fishes in a double bind?

$$Q = DA \frac{P_1 - P_2}{L}$$

Figure 47.2

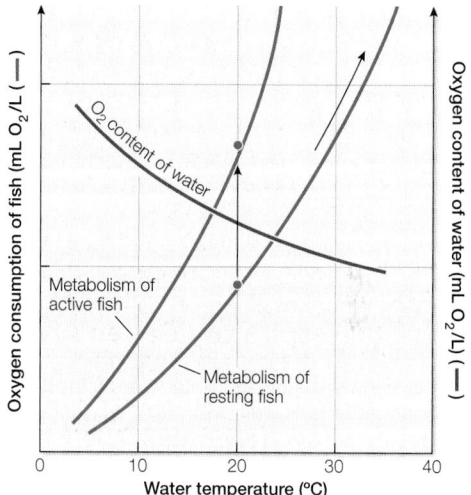

KEY CONCEPT

47.2 Enhancing Diffusion Maximizes Respiratory Gas Exchange

Go to Animation 47.1

- O_2 delivery to cells of the insect body is by diffusion in air. The gills of fishes have large gas exchange surfaces that are ventilated continuously and unidirectionally with water flowing countercurrent to the flow of blood inside the gills. Air inhaled by birds flows continuously and unidirectionally through airways, **air sacs**, **parabronchii**, and air capillaries and is in the system for two breathing cycles.

- Except for birds, air-breathing vertebrates have **tidal** ventilation, creating **dead space** and resulting in mixing of incoming fresh air with stale air.

Questions

1. How does countercurrent flow maximize gas exchange in fish gills?

2. What is the main functional difference between parabronchi of birds and bronchi of mammals?

3. How would you measure the difference between vital capacity and total lung volume in a human?

Figure 47.5

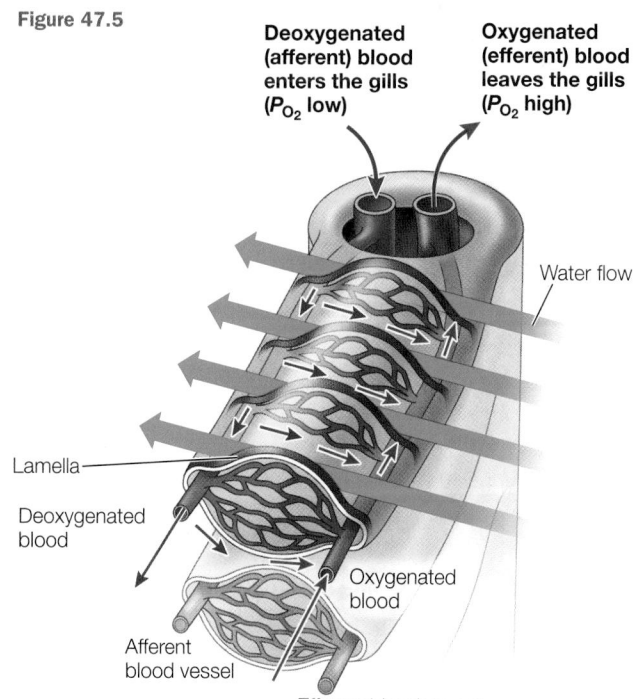

KEY CONCEPT

47.3 Humans Have Tidal Respiration

Go to **Activity 47.1** and **Animation 47.2**

- **Alveoli** are the respiratory exchange surfaces of mammalian lungs and are ventilated through a branching system of **bronchi** and **bronchioles** and are surrounded by capillaries.

- Lung **surfactant** reduces **surface tension** in alveoli, thereby decreasing the pressure necessary to inflate them.

- Contractions of the **diaphragm** and **intercostal muscles** drive inhalation and exhalation by changing the pressure in the **thoracic cavity**.

Questions

1. Describe the path taken by air during breathing.

2. How are the properties of lung surfactant important for both inhalation and exhalation?

3. How do alveolar pressure and pleural cavity pressure change relative to the outside air pressure during the breathing cycle?

Figure 47.11

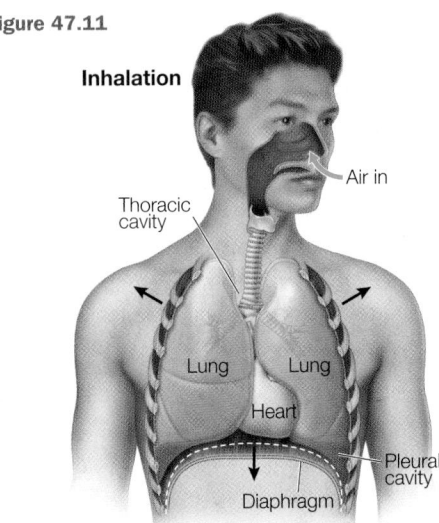

KEY CONCEPT

47.4 Respiratory Gases Are Transported by the Blood

Go to **Activity 47.2** and **Simulation 47.1**

- Oxygen reversibly binds to **hemoglobin** (**Hgb**) in red blood cells, and percent saturation depends on the P_{O_2} to which the Hgb is exposed. **Myoglobin** serves as an O_2 reserve in muscle.

- The affinity of Hgb for O_2 is altered by the composition of the Hgb, by pH, and by the presence of 2,3-bisphosphoglycerate (2,3-BPG). CO_2 is transported in the blood principally as bicarbonate ions (HCO_3^-).

Questions

1. What is the significance of the fact that mixed venous blood can have a P_{O_2} of 40 mm Hg and its Hgb is still 75% saturated?

2. Why is it important that fetal Hgb has a higher affinity for 2,3-BPG than does adult Hgb?

3. What is the role of carbonic anhydrase (CA) in eliminating CO_2 from the body?

Figure 47.13

KEY CONCEPT

47.5 Breathing Is Homeostatically Regulated

Go to **Activity 47.3**

- Breathing movements are generated by neurons in the medulla and modulated by higher brain centers.

- The breathing rhythm is altered by feedback from chemosensors on the ventral surface of the medulla and in the **carotid** and **aortic bodies** on the large vessels leaving the heart.

- The most important feedback stimulus for breathing is the P_{CO_2} in the blood.

Questions

1. What are the locations and roles of respiratory group neurons?

2. What is the relationship between P_{CO_2} and pH in the regulation of breathing?

3. What roles do carotid and aortic bodies play in the regulation of breathing?

Figure 47.17

Neural input from higher brain centers

Neurons that excite breathing neurons in medulla

Pons

Medulla

Inputs from aortic and carotid bodies

Dorsal respiratory neurons

Spinal cord

Output to diaphragm

Go to **Achieve** for the eBook, **LearningCurve**, animations, activities, simulations, and additional resources and assignments.

Circulatory Systems 48

© Andrew Yates/Stringer/Getty Images

KEY CONCEPTS

48.1 Circulatory Systems Are Transport Systems

48.2 Vertebrate Circulatory Systems Evolved from Single to Double Circuits

48.3 Heart Function Depends on Properties of Cardiac Muscle

48.4 Circulatory System Functions Depend on Blood and Blood Vessels

48.5 Circulation Is Controlled by Hormonal and Neuronal Signals

Fabrice Muamba (on the right) was a lucky survivor of cardiac arrest caused by hypertrophic cardiomyopathy, the most common cause of death among young athletes. What causes this condition, and can it be prevented or treated?

▶Investigating LIFE

Athletes with Big Hearts

Fabrice Muamba is a much-loved and now retired professional soccer player. On March 17, 2012, during a championship quarterfinal match, 23-year-old Fabrice suddenly collapsed on the field. He was immediately attended to by team physicians and a cardiologist who happened to be a spectator at the match. Fabrice received numerous defibrillator shocks, cardiopulmonary resuscitation, and was rushed to a hospital, but still his heart stopped for 78 minutes. Remarkably he survived, but many young, fit athletes have died from cardiac arrest during physical exertion. Sudden cardiac arrest is the most common cause of death for athletes. In most cases the cause is not a heart attack, but a condition known as hypertrophic cardiomyopathy (HCM).

Your heart is a muscular pump. At rest it beats an average of 60–70 times per minute. With each beat, it circulates about 70 milliliters of blood through your body. Without adding the increases due to work or exercise, that is 300 liters per hour, 7,200 liters per day, 2.6 million liters per year—no time-outs.

Heart failure is the leading cause of death in the United States, accounting for some one-fourth (about 600,000) of the deaths each year. Heart failure most commonly results from

blockage of the blood vessels called coronary arteries that supply the heart muscle with blood, and the risk for blockage of these vessels increases with age. HCM has a different cause, originating with gene mutations that affect the contractile proteins of the heart. About 1,000 such mutations have been identified, and they exist in about 1 in 500 people. Most people with one of these mutations live normally, so why are they so dangerous in athletes? The mutations decrease the efficiency of the contractions of the heart muscle, so the heart has to work much harder. Especially in athletes, the heart gets bigger to compensate for its inefficiency. The walls of the heart can get so thick that they impede the blood from leaving the heart, and the thick walls can interfere with the signals that coordinate the contractions of the heart muscle. The result is cardiac arrest. Assessment of HCM risk is improving, and many afflicted athletes are choosing to retire rather than taking a chance of dying from cardiac arrest.

 Are there potential therapies that could treat HCM? (Find the answer on page 1092.)

KEY CONCEPT
48.1 Circulatory Systems Are Transport Systems

Learning Objectives

48.1.1 List the diverse functions of circulatory systems.

48.1.2 Explain why some animals can function without a circulatory system.

48.1.3 Describe the differences between hemolymph, blood plasma, and interstitial fluid.

48.1.4 Explain why a closed circulatory system can be more efficient than an open circulatory system.

A **circulatory system** consists of a muscular pump (heart), a fluid (blood), and a series of conduits (blood vessels) through which the fluid is pumped throughout the body. Heart, blood, and vessels are also known collectively as a **cardiovascular system** (Greek *kardia*, "heart," + Latin *vasculum*, "vessel"). The function of a circulatory system is to transport things around the body. Preceding chapters discussed how circulatory systems transport heat, hormones, respiratory gases, blood cells, platelets, and cells and molecules of the immune system. Succeeding chapters will add nutrients and waste products to that list. In this key concept we describe the general types of circulatory systems found in animals.

Some animals do not have a circulatory system

Single-celled organisms serve all of their needs through direct exchanges with the environment. Such organisms are found mostly in aquatic or very moist terrestrial environments. Similarly, many multicellular aquatic organisms are small or thin enough that all of their cells are close to the external environment (see Figure 47.1A). Such species may not have a circulatory system because nutrients, respiratory gases, and wastes can diffuse directly between the cells of their bodies and the environment.

Connect the Concepts Key Concept 47.1 explains how Fick's law of diffusion describes all of the physical factors that control rates of diffusion.

The internal cells of some larger aquatic multicellular animals without a circulatory system are served by highly branched central cavities called **gastrovascular systems** that bring the external environment into the animal. All the cells of a sponge are in contact with, or very close to, the water that surrounds the animal and circulates through its central cavity (see Figure 47.1B). Very small animals without a circulatory system can maintain high levels of metabolic activity, but larger animals without a circulatory system such as sponges, jellyfishes, and flatworms tend to be inactive, slow, or even sedentary. Large, active animals require circulatory systems.

Circulatory systems can be open or closed

The cells of large, mobile animals are supported by extracellular fluid. All requirements of cells—oxygen, fuel, nutrients, essential molecules—come from that fluid, and the waste products of cell metabolism go into it. Circulatory systems have muscular chambers, or **hearts**, that move the extracellular fluid through the body.

In open circulatory systems, extracellular fluid is the same as the fluid in the circulatory system and is called **hemolymph**. This fluid leaves the vessels of the circulatory system, percolates between cells and through tissues, and then flows back into the heart or vessels of the circulatory system to be pumped out again. In contrast, closed circulatory systems completely contain the circulating fluid (blood) in a continuous system of vessels. Blood cells and large molecules stay within the system, but water and low-molecular-weight solutes leak out of the smallest vessels, which are highly permeable.

In animals with a closed circulatory system, **extracellular fluid** refers to both the fluid in the circulatory system and the fluid outside it. The fluid in the circulatory system is the blood plasma; the extracellular fluid outside the circulatory system is the **interstitial fluid**. A 70-kilogram person has a total extracellular fluid volume of about 14 liters. Less than one-fourth of it—about 3 liters—is the blood plasma.

Connect the Concepts Key Concept 38.2 and Figure 38.4 describe the different extracellular fluid compartments that constitute the internal environment that supports all of the metabolic needs of the cells of the body.

Open circulatory systems move extracellular fluid

Open circulatory systems are found in arthropods, mollusks, and some other invertebrate groups. In these systems a heart moves the hemolymph through vessels leading to different regions of the body. The fluid leaves the vessels to filter through the tissues before returning to the heart. In the arthropod shown in **Figure 48.1A**, the fluid returns directly to the heart through openings called **ostia**. Ostia have valves that allow hemolymph to enter the relaxed heart but prevent it from flowing in the reverse direction when the heart contracts. In a mollusk such as a clam, open vessels collect hemolymph from different regions of the body and return it to the heart (**Figure 48.1B**).

Lest you think that open circulatory systems are inefficient and can support only sluggish lifestyles such as those of mollusks, remember that locusts swarming over crops, yellow jackets buzzing around your picnic, and scorpions dashing across the desert all have open circulatory systems.

Closed circulatory systems circulate blood through a system of blood vessels

In **closed circulatory systems**, blood vessels separate blood from interstitial fluid. Blood is pumped through this vascular system by one or more hearts, and cellular and macromolecular components of the blood never leave the vessels. Closed circulatory systems characterize vertebrates and some invertebrate groups, among them annelids.

A simple example of a closed circulatory system is that of the earthworm (**Figure 48.1C**). One large ventral blood vessel carries blood from the worm's anterior end to its posterior end. Smaller vessels branch off and transport the blood to even smaller vessels serving the tissues in each body segment. In the smallest vessels, respiratory gases, nutrients, and metabolic wastes diffuse between the blood and interstitial fluid. The blood then flows from these vessels into larger vessels that lead into one large, muscular dorsal vessel that carries the blood from the posterior to the anterior end of the body. Five pairs of muscular vessels

(A) Arthropod circulation

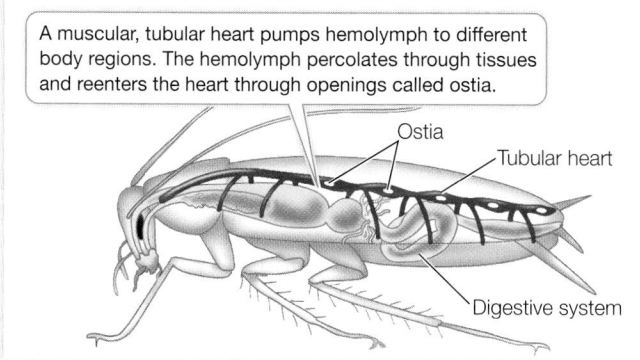

A muscular, tubular heart pumps hemolymph to different body regions. The hemolymph percolates through tissues and reenters the heart through openings called ostia.

Ostia
Tubular heart
Digestive system

(B) Mollusk circulation

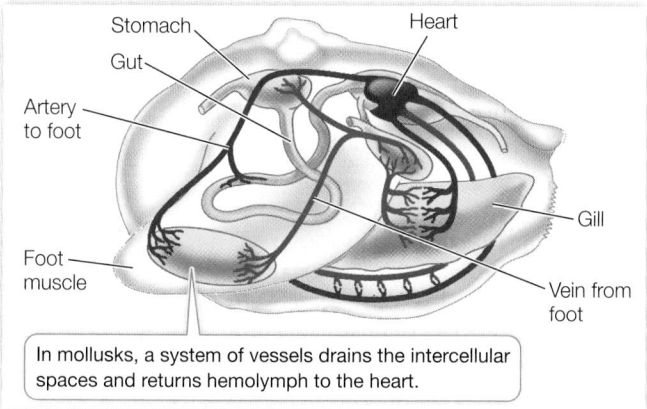

Stomach
Gut
Heart
Artery to foot
Foot muscle
Gill
Vein from foot

In mollusks, a system of vessels drains the intercellular spaces and returns hemolymph to the heart.

(C) Annelid worm circulation

In annelids, muscular hearts pump blood through a system of closed vessels.

Dorsal vessel

Smaller vessels are sites of exchange of materials between blood and interstitial fluid.

Hearts (connecting vessels)
Ventral vessel

Figure 48.1 Circulatory Systems Arthropods, illustrated here by a grasshopper (**A**), and mollusks, illustrated by a clam (**B**), have open circulatory systems. Hemolymph is pumped by a tubular heart and directed to different regions of the body through vessels that open into the intercellular environment. (**C**) Annelids, illustrated here by an earthworm, contain the cellular and macromolecular elements of their blood in the vessels of a closed circulatory system that includes muscular hearts. Earthworms exchange respiratory gases across their skin. The circulation distributes those gases between the skin and the deeper tissues.

connect the large dorsal and ventral vessels in the anterior end, thus completing the circuit. The dorsal vessel and the five connecting vessels serve as hearts for the earthworm; their contractions keep the blood circulating. The direction of circulation is determined by one-way valves in the dorsal vessel.

Closed circulatory systems have several advantages compared with open systems:

- Fluid can flow more rapidly through vessels than through intercellular spaces and can therefore transport things to and from tissues more rapidly.

- By changing the diameter (and hence the resistance) of specific vessels, closed systems can control the flow of blood to selective tissues and organs to match their needs.

- Specialized cells and large molecules that aid in transporting hormones, nutrients, and oxygen can be kept in the vessels but can drop their cargo in the tissues where it is needed.

With all of these "advantages" of closed circulatory systems, you might wonder how some species with open circulatory systems can sustain such high levels of activity. In the case of insects, the answer is clear: insects do not depend on their circulatory systems for respiratory gas exchange (see Figure 47.4).

KEY CONCEPT
48.1 Recap and Assess

Circulatory systems consist of a pump and an open or closed set of vessels through which a fluid transports oxygen, nutrients, wastes, and a variety of other substances. Flow to and from tissues in closed systems of vessels can be more rapid and can be directed to specific tissues according to their needs.

1. Describe three ways that circulatory systems support exercising muscles.

2. A sponge is neither small nor thin. How can it survive without a circulatory system?

3. Explain the importance of extracellular fluid in large mobile animals.

4. How does a closed circulatory system facilitate the fight-or-flight response?

Our overview of the open and closed systems found among invertebrates introduced some basic concepts about circulatory systems. Next we turn to describing the closed circulatory systems of vertebrates.

KEY CONCEPT
48.2 Vertebrate Circulatory Systems Evolved from Single to Double Circuits

Learning Objectives

48.2.1 Diagram the single circuit of the circulatory system of fishes.

48.2.2 Describe how a lungfish distributes oxygen to its tissues in both water and air environments.

48.2.3 Explain how and why the circulatory systems of ectothermic reptiles are unique in their control of pulmonary and systemic circulation.

48.2.4 Describe how the avian and mammalian four-chambered hearts maintain separate but linked pulmonary and systemic circuits operating at different pressures.

Vertebrates have a closed circulatory system that includes a heart with multiple chambers. When heart chambers contract, they squeeze the blood, putting it under pressure and causing it to flow. One-way valves prevent backflow of blood as the heart chambers cycle between contraction and relaxation. Blood flows out of the heart and into vessels called **arteries** that carry blood away from the heart. Arteries branch into smaller **arterioles** that feed blood into capillary beds. **Capillaries** are tiny, thin-walled vessels where materials are exchanged between blood and the interstitial fluid. Small vessels called **venules** drain capillary beds. The venules join to form the larger **veins** that ultimately deliver blood back to the heart.

We can trace the evolutionary history of vertebrate circulatory systems by comparing the circulatory systems of fishes, lungfishes, amphibians, reptiles (including crocodilians), birds, and mammals (**Figure 48.2**). These comparisons show that as circulatory systems became more complex, they evolved from a single circuit (heart, gills, body, heart) to a double circuit (heart, lungs, heart, body, heart). Through this progression of vertebrates, the blood flowing to the gas exchange organs (gills or lungs; see Figure 47.3) becomes increasingly separated from the blood flowing to the rest of the body.

Fishes have a four-chambered heart that pumps blood through the gills to be oxygenated and then throughout the tissues of the body and back to the heart—a single circuit. In birds and mammals, blood is pumped from the heart to the lungs and back to the heart in a **pulmonary circuit**, and then from the heart to the rest of the body and back to the heart in a **systemic circuit**. In amphibians and ectothermic reptiles (i.e., all reptiles except birds) we see various adaptations that incompletely separate the blood flow into pulmonary and systemic circuits.

Circulation in fishes is a single circuit

Since fishes are phylogenetically the oldest vertebrates, their circulatory systems reflect the most primitive vertebrate circulatory systems. Frequently it is stated that fish have a two chambered heart. That is wrong, the fish heart has four chambers that are connected in series (see Figure 48.2A). Blood returning from all parts of the body collects in a **sinus venosus** that feeds into the muscular **atrium**. The atrium pumps blood into the more muscular chamber, the **ventricle**. Contraction of the ventricle pushes blood into the last chamber, the **bulbus arteriosus**, a highly elastic chamber. The pressure imparted to the blood by the ventricle stretches the bulbus arteriosus, and its elastic recoil dampens the blood pressure oscillations generated by the beating of the heart. The arterial blood leaving the bulbus arteriosus under pressure flows through the gills, where respiratory gases are exchanged. Blood leaving the gills collects in a large dorsal artery, the **aorta**, which distributes blood to smaller arteries and arterioles leading to all the organs and tissues of the body. In the tissues, blood flows through beds of tiny capillaries, collects in venules and veins, and eventually returns to the sinus venosus of the heart. The unidirectional flow of blood in this circuit is enabled by one-way valves between the sinus venosus and the atrium, between the atrium and the ventricle, and between the ventricle and the bulbus arteriosus.

Most of the pressure imparted to the blood by the contraction of the ventricle is dissipated as a result of resistance to flow in the many narrow spaces in the gill lamellae (see Figure 47.5). Therefore blood leaving the gills and entering the aorta is under low pressure, limiting the capacity of the fish circulatory system to supply the tissues with oxygen and nutrients. In spite of this limitation on arterial blood pressure, some species, such as tunas and marlins, can swim at remarkably high speeds for considerable distances.

The evolutionary transition from breathing water to breathing air had important consequences for the vertebrate circulatory system. An example of how the system changed to serve a primitive lung can be seen in the African lungfishes.

Lungfishes evolved a gas-breathing organ

Lungfishes have descended from a lineage that predates the rise of tetrapod vertebrates. Present-day lungfishes are exposed periodically to water with low oxygen content or to situations in which their aquatic environment dries up. The adaptation that enables them to survive these conditions is an outpocketing of the gut just behind the mouth cavity. This outpocketing forms a lung structure that runs most of the length of the animal. Air is gulped into this lung and oxygen is picked up by the blood flowing through the many capillaries in its walls.

How does the lungfish circulatory system take advantage of this new organ? In fishes the gills are arranged on supportive pairs of gill arches (see Figure 47.5A,B). In most fishes the gills on all the gill arches are similar. Deoxygenated blood from the heart flows through thin gill filaments, where it picks up oxygen, and then flows into the aorta, which distributes the oxygenated blood throughout the body. The circulatory anatomy in lungfishes is quite different. Of the six pairs of gill arches, only the posterior three have fine gill filaments that enable the blood to take up oxygen from the water. The blood leaving these three pairs of gill arches can flow into the dorsal aorta or into a pulmonary artery to the lung. Thus even if the blood has picked up little oxygen in the gills, it can pick up considerable oxygen in the lung from the air that the fish has gulped. The oxygenated blood from the lung returns to the atrium of the heart. From the atrium, the blood flows into the ventricle, which pumps it into the bulbous arteriosus. From there, the oxygenated blood mostly flows into the anterior three pairs of gill arches. These gills do not have fine filaments for gas exchange; instead they are modified to be low-resistance vessels that enable the oxygenated blood to flow directly into the dorsal aorta.

But doesn't the oxygenated blood from the lung completely mix with the deoxygenated blood from the systemic circulation? The answer is no, because the lungfish heart partially, but effectively, separates the flow of blood into pulmonary and systemic circuits. The atrium is partially divided by a tissue fold (see Figure 48.2B). The left side receives oxygenated blood from the lung, and the right side receives deoxygenated blood from the body via the sinus venosus. The ventricle and the bulbous arteriosus also have tissue folds and septa that keep the oxygenated and deoxygenated bloodstreams mostly separate. As a result, the oxygenated blood from the lung goes mostly to the low-resistance, high-throughput anterior gill arches leading to the dorsal aorta, and deoxygenated blood goes mostly to the posterior gill arches that have functional gill filaments. The blood leaving those posterior gill arches can flow to the dorsal aorta or

(A) Fish heart

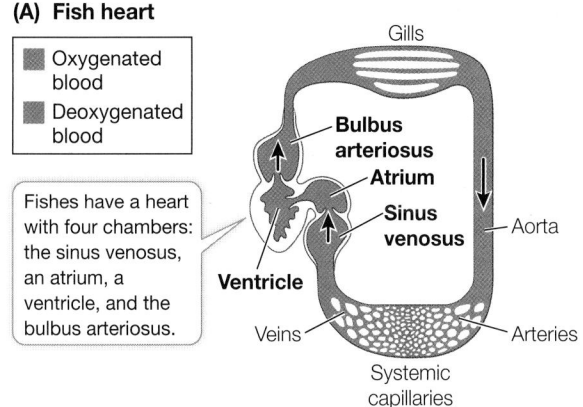

Oxygenated blood
Deoxygenated blood

Fishes have a heart with four chambers: the sinus venosus, an atrium, a ventricle, and the bulbus arteriosus.

Gills
Bulbus arteriosus
Atrium
Sinus venosus
Aorta
Ventricle
Veins
Arteries
Systemic capillaries

(B) Lungfish heart

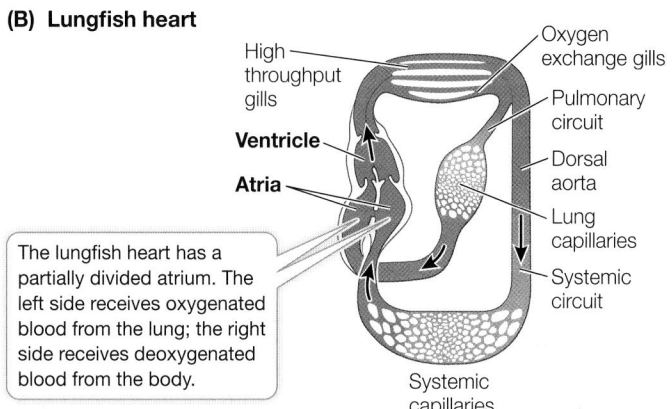

High throughput gills
Ventricle
Atria
Oxygen exchange gills
Pulmonary circuit
Dorsal aorta
Lung capillaries
Systemic circuit

The lungfish heart has a partially divided atrium. The left side receives oxygenated blood from the lung; the right side receives deoxygenated blood from the body.

Systemic capillaries

(C) Amphibian heart

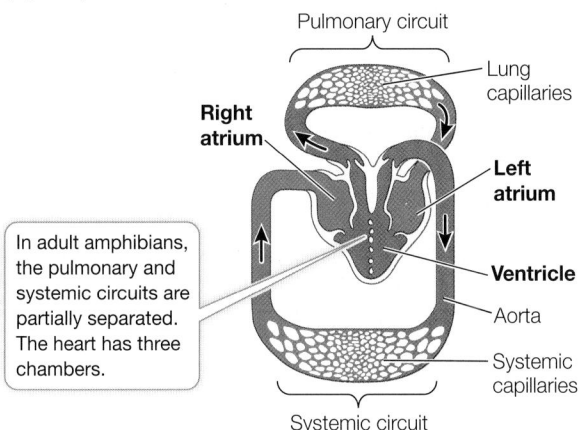

Pulmonary circuit
Lung capillaries
Right atrium
Left atrium
Ventricle
Aorta
Systemic capillaries

In adult amphibians, the pulmonary and systemic circuits are partially separated. The heart has three chambers.

Systemic circuit

(D) Hearts of most ectothermic reptiles

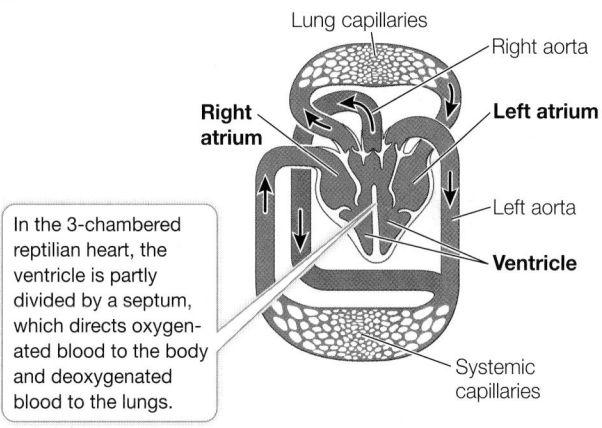

Lung capillaries
Right aorta
Right atrium
Left atrium
Left aorta
Ventricle
Systemic capillaries

In the 3-chambered reptilian heart, the ventricle is partly divided by a septum, which directs oxygenated blood to the body and deoxygenated blood to the lungs.

(E) Crocodilian heart

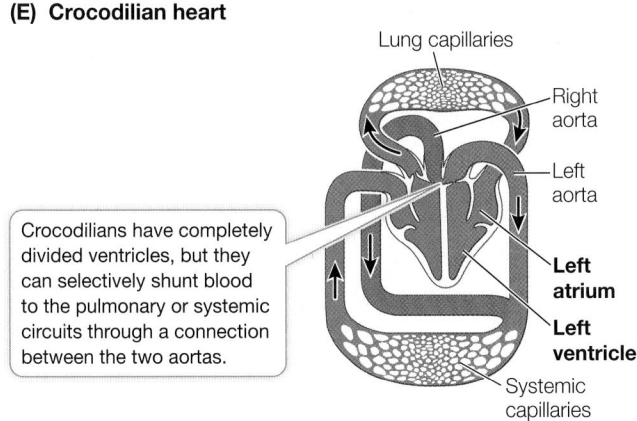

Lung capillaries
Right aorta
Left aorta
Left atrium
Left ventricle
Systemic capillaries

Crocodilians have completely divided ventricles, but they can selectively shunt blood to the pulmonary or systemic circuits through a connection between the two aortas.

(F) Bird and mammal hearts

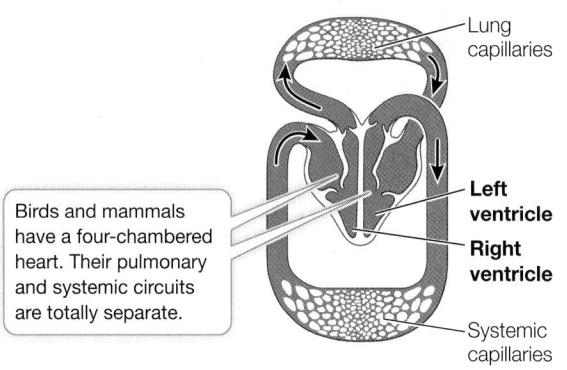

Lung capillaries
Left ventricle
Right ventricle
Systemic capillaries

Birds and mammals have a four-chambered heart. Their pulmonary and systemic circuits are totally separate.

Figure 48.2 Comparing Circulatory Systems of Vertebrates (A) The general fish heart has a single muscular ventricle that pumps blood first through the gills and then through the systemic blood vessels. (B) Lungfish hearts can pump blood through the gills or to a lung that the fish fills by gulping air. (C) Amphibians have three chambered hearts that incompletely separate blood flow to lungs and to the rest of the body. (D) Most ectothermic reptilian hearts have an incomplete separation of left and right ventricles and they have two aortas, thus they can either send blood returning to the right ventricle from the systemic circulation to the lungs if they are breathing or back into the systemic circuit if they are not breathing. (E) The crocodilian heart has fully divided ventricles, but communication between their left and right aortas can shunt blood from the pulmonary to the systemic circuits. (F) Bird and mammal hearts have fully divided pulmonary and systemic circuits.

to the lung. Thus the dorsal aorta can receive oxygenated blood either from the lung (via the anterior gill arches) or from the gill filaments of the posterior gill arches.

We can conclude that the lungfish lung evolved as a means of supplementing oxygen uptake from the gills. When the water is oxygenated, the lungfish can obtain oxygen through its gills; but in oxygen-depleted water, it can depend on getting oxygen from its lung. Associated modifications of the lungfish vascular system set the stage for the evolution of separate pulmonary and systemic circulations in all tetrapod vertebrates.

Amphibians have partial separation of systemic and pulmonary circulation

In adult amphibians, a single ventricle pumps blood to the lungs and the rest of the body, but two atria receive blood returning to the heart (see Figure 48.2C). The left atrium receives oxygenated blood from the lungs, and the right atrium receives deoxygenated blood from the body. Because both atria deliver blood to the same ventricle, the oxygenated and deoxygenated blood could mix, in which case blood going to the tissues would not carry a full load of oxygen. Mixing is limited, however, because, as in lungfishes, anatomical features of the ventricle direct the flow of deoxygenated blood from the right atrium primarily to the pulmonary circuit and the flow of oxygenated blood from the left atrium primarily to the aorta. Partial separation of pulmonary and systemic circulation has the advantage of allowing blood destined for the tissues to sidestep the large pressure drop that occurs in the gas exchange organ. Blood leaving the amphibian heart for the tissues moves directly to the aorta, and hence to the body, at a higher pressure than if it had first flowed through the lungs as it does in fishes.

Some amphibians have another adaptation for oxygenating their blood: they can pick up a considerable amount of oxygen in blood flowing through small blood vessels in their skin.

Reptiles have exquisite control of pulmonary and systemic circulation

As described in Chapter 31, the reptiles include turtles, snakes, lizards, crocodilians, and birds (see Figures 31.21 and 31.22). Crocodilians and birds have circulatory systems with two completely separated ventricles. All other reptiles have ventricles that are not completely separated into left and right chambers. Are incompletely separated ventricles in reptiles a disadvantage or an adaptation?

Consider the behavior, ecology, and physiology of ectothermic reptiles. Many are active, powerful, fast animals, but their activity comes in bursts that are interspersed with long periods of inactivity. At these times the animals' metabolic rates are much lower than the resting metabolic rates of the endothermic birds and mammals. So enormous is the range of metabolic demand in ectothermic reptiles that they do not need to breathe continuously. Some species are accomplished divers and spend long periods under water, where they cannot breathe air.

When these animals are not breathing, it would be a waste of energy for them to pump blood through their lungs. Thus they pump blood to the lungs and the rest of the body when they are breathing, but when they are not breathing, they bypass the pulmonary circuit and pump blood just to the body. How do they do this?

In ectothermic reptiles with a three-chambered heart—that is, the turtles, snakes, and lizards—the ventricle is partially divided into left and right halves by a septum (see Figure 48.2D). Oxygenated blood from the lungs enters the left side of the ventricle through the left atrium. Deoxygenated blood from the body enters the right side of the ventricle through the right atrium. These species have two aortas, left and right. The left aorta is positioned so that it receives oxygenated blood from the left side of the ventricle. The right aorta, however, is positioned so that it can receive blood from either the right or left side of the ventricle.

When the animal is breathing air, the resistance in the pulmonary circuit is lower than the resistance in the systemic circuit, so blood from the right side of the ventricle tends to flow into the pulmonary artery rather than the right aorta. When the animal is not breathing, pulmonary vessels constrict, resistance in the pulmonary circuit goes up, and blood from the right side of the ventricle tends to flow into the right aorta. As a result, blood from both sides of the ventricle flows through the two aortas to the systemic circuit.

Crocodilians, like birds, have two completely separated ventricles. Unlike birds, they have two aortas, one originating in each ventricle. But there is a connection between the two aortas just as they leave the heart, and this connection enables them to alter the proportions of blood going to their pulmonary and systemic circuits (see Figure 48.2E). When a crocodilian is breathing and resistance in the pulmonary circuit is low, backpressure from the stronger left ventricle closes the valve between the right ventricle and the right aorta, forcing all of the blood from the right ventricle to flow into the pulmonary circuit. When the animal stops breathing, pulmonary vessels constrict, resistance in the pulmonary circuit rises, and pressure in the right ventricle overcomes the backpressure in the right aorta from the left ventricle. As a result, the blood from the right ventricle flows into the right aorta. This ability of all ectothermic reptiles to direct blood to their pulmonary or systemic circuits is highly adaptive for their lifestyle of intermittent breathing.

Birds and mammals have fully separated pulmonary and systemic circuits

The four-chambered hearts of birds and mammals have completely separate pulmonary and systemic circuits (see Figure 48.2F). Separate circuits have several advantages for these active animals with continuously high metabolic rates:

- Oxygenated and deoxygenated blood cannot mix; therefore the systemic circuit always receives blood with the highest oxygen content.

- Respiratory gas exchange is maximized because the blood with the lowest oxygen content and highest CO_2 content is sent to the lungs.

- Separate systemic and pulmonary circuits can operate at different pressures.

The tissues of birds and mammals have high nutrient demands and thus a very high density of blood vessels, requiring the heart to generate a high blood pressure to perfuse all the vessels of the systemic circuit. The pulmonary circuit of these animals receives a blood flow equal to that of the systemic circuit, but the lungs have far fewer blood vessels. Thus the pulmonary circuit of birds and mammals can function at lower pressures, and the four-chambered heart makes that possible. Additionally, the high pressure in the systemic circuit increases the ability to direct blood to tissues that need it the most, through controlled changes in resistance in arterioles.

 View in Achieve
Activity 48.1 Vertebrate Circulatory Systems

KEY CONCEPT
48.2 Recap and Assess

The closed circulatory system of vertebrates has evolved from a single circuit in fishes to separate pulmonary and systemic circuits in birds and mammals. A key step was the evolution of a primitive lung in a lineage of air-breathing fishes. Further adaptations increasingly separated the flows of oxygenated and deoxygenated blood in separate circuits, as seen in amphibians and reptiles. Ectothermic reptiles retained the ability to direct blood to either the pulmonary or systemic circuit, but birds have complete division of those two circuits, as do mammals, allowing the circuits to function at different pressures.

1. The bulbous arteriosus of fishes is less muscular than the ventricle but has more elastic fibers. Given the location of the bulbous arteriosus in the fish circulatory system, what could be its function?

2. A lungfish brooding in stagnant water can increase the oxygen content in the water immediately surrounding its eggs. How is this possible?

3. Explain how and why ectothermic reptiles shunt blood from the pulmonary circuit when not breathing.

4. The ductus arteriosus in a human fetus connects the dorsal aorta with the pulmonary artery, allowing blood to bypass the fluid-filled lungs. This connection normally closes at birth. What are the consequences if it does not?

We turn now to the structure and function of the mammalian heart, focusing in particular on human cardiac function.

KEY CONCEPT
48.3 Heart Function Depends on Properties of Cardiac Muscle

Learning Objectives

48.3.1 Trace the path of blood through both sides of the mammalian heart, naming the major blood vessels and heart valves.

48.3.2 Explain how heart valves function.

48.3.3 Describe and diagram the cardiac cycle in terms of left ventricular volume and pressure, aortic pressure, and heart sounds.

48.3.4 Explain the differences between pacemaker potentials and ventricular muscle potentials and their ionic bases.

In this key concept we describe in detail the structure and function of the mammalian heart, using the human heart as the example. We first trace the paths of blood flow through the heart and the body, and then we examine the unique electrical properties of cardiac muscle that result in the rhythmic contractions of the heart.

The mammalian heart has four chambers—a right and a left atrium and a right and a left ventricle (**Figure 48.3**). The right atrium receives blood from the systemic circuit, and the left atrium receives blood from the pulmonary circuit. The right ventricle pumps blood through the pulmonary circuit, and the left ventricle pumps blood through the systemic circuit.

One-way valves between the atria and ventricles, the **atrioventricular (AV) valves**, prevent backflow of blood into the atria when the ventricles contract. The right AV valve is called the **tricuspid valve** because it has three leaves. The left AV valve is called the **bicuspid valve** because it has two leaves. The bicuspid valve is also called the **mitral valve** because it has the shape of a religious headdress called a miter. There are also one-way valves between the ventricles and the arteries leaving the heart. The **pulmonary valve** goes to the lungs, and the **aortic valve** goes to the aorta. These two valves are also called **semilunar valves** because their separate leaves are shaped like half-moons.

Blood flows from right heart to lungs to left heart to body

The **superior** (upper) **vena cava** and the **inferior** (lower) **vena cava** (see Figure 48.3) are the large veins that return deoxygenated blood from the upper and lower body to the right atrium. The veins of the heart itself also drain into the right atrium. From the right atrium, the blood flows through the tricuspid valve into the right ventricle. The filling of the ventricle is mostly passive flow while the heart is relaxed between beats. At the end of this phase of passive ventricular filling, the atrium contracts and adds a little more blood to the ventricular volume. The right ventricle then contracts, causing the tricuspid valve to close and pumping the blood into the **pulmonary artery** leading to the lungs.

Pulmonary veins return the oxygenated blood from the lungs to the left atrium, from where the blood enters the left ventricle through the bicuspid valve. As on the right side of the heart, most left ventricular filling is passive, and is only topped off when the atria contract.

The walls of the ventricles are powerful muscles that contract around the blood with a wringing motion starting from the bottom. When pressure in the left ventricle is high enough to push open the aortic valve, blood rushes into the aorta to begin its circulation throughout the body. In Figure 48.3 observe that the walls of the left ventricle are thicker than those of the right ventricle. The left ventricle has to propel blood through many more kilometers of blood vessels than does the right ventricle, and must therefore push against more resistance, even though both ventricles pump the same volume of blood.

It is the left ventricle that creates the condition of hypertrophic cardiomyopathy (HCM) that you learned about at the beginning of this chapter. Mutations that reduce the efficiency of contraction of the cardiac muscle result in an increased workload of the left ventricle, so the ventricular muscle compensates by getting bigger (hypertrophy). When the heart is repeatedly stressed by high levels of activity, as is common in athletes, the hypertrophy can become extreme (**Figure 48.4**). The consequences can be blockage of blood flowing into the aorta and disruption of the signals that coordinate the contractions of the ventricular muscles.

Both sides of the heart contract at the same time. Contraction of the two atria, followed by contraction of the two ventricles and then relaxation, is the **cardiac cycle**. The cardiac cycle is divided into two phases: **systole** (pronounced sís-toll-ee), when the ventricles contract, and **diastole** (die-ás-toll-ee), when the ventricles

(A) The human circulatory system

Internal jugular vein

Common carotid artery

Subclavian artery and vein

Aorta

Superior vena cava

Pulmonary artery

Pulmonary veins

Inferior vena cava

Hepatic veins

Hepatic portal vein

Renal vein and artery

Common iliac vein and artery

Vessels shown in red bring oxygenated blood from the lungs to the left side of the heart, which pumps it to the rest of the body.

Vessels shown in blue bring deoxygenated blood from the body to the right side of the heart, which pumps it to the lungs for oxygenation.

(B) The human heart

Aorta

Superior vena cava

To lung

From lung

Pulmonary artery

To lung

Pulmonary veins

From lung

Inferior vena cava

Descending aorta

Closed

Pulmonary valve

Open

Aortic valve

1 Deoxygenated blood from the tissues of the body enters the right atrium…

2 …and flows through the right AV valve (tricuspid valve) into the right ventricle.

3 The right ventricle pumps the blood through the pulmonary valve into the pulmonary circuit.

4 From the pulmonary circuit, the oxygenated blood returns to the left atrium…

5 …and flows through the left AV valve (bicuspid valve) into the left ventricle.

6 The left ventricle pumps blood through the aortic valve into the systemic circuit.

Figure 48.3 The Human Heart and Circulation **(A)** The major blood vessels of the body either carry blood away from the heart (arteries) or return blood to the heart (veins). **(B)** In the human heart, blood flows from the right side of the heart to the lungs, back to the left side of the heart, and then out to the body. The atrioventricular valves prevent blood from flowing back into the atria when the ventricles contract. The pulmonary and aortic valves prevent blood from flowing back into the ventricles from the arteries when the ventricles relax.

▶ **View in Achieve**
Activity 48.2 The Human Heart

Figure 48.4 Hypertrophic Cardiomyopathy
(A) Comparison of a normal and a hypertrophic heart.
(B) Micrographs of the ventricular heart muscle fibers of a normal and a hypertrophic heart. The organization of the muscle fibers is irregular, causing inefficient contractions.

(A) Normal heart   Hypertrophic heart

(B) Normal   Hypertrophic

Both photos from B. K. McConnell et al. 1999. *J Clin Inv* 104: 1235–1244

relax (**Figure 48.5**). At the very end of diastole (step 1 in Figure 48.5), just before the ventricles contract, the atria contract and top off the volume of blood in the ventricles.

The sounds of the cardiac cycle—the "lub-dup" heard through a stethoscope—are created by the heart valves slamming shut. The closing and opening of these valves are simple mechanical events resulting from pressure differences on the two sides of the valves. As the ventricles begin to contract (step 2 in Figure 48.5), the pressure in them rises above the pressure in the atria, so the

AV valves close ("lub"). When the ventricles begin to relax (step 4 in Figure 48.5), the high pressures in the aorta and pulmonary artery close the aortic and pulmonary valves ("dup").

Defective valves that do not close completely produce turbulent blood flow and the sounds known as heart murmurs. For example, if an AV valve does not close completely, blood will flow back into the atrium with a "whoosh" at the beginning of systole.

Blood pressure changes associated with the cardiac cycle can be measured in the large artery in your arm by using an inflatable

(A) The filling and emptying of the ventricles

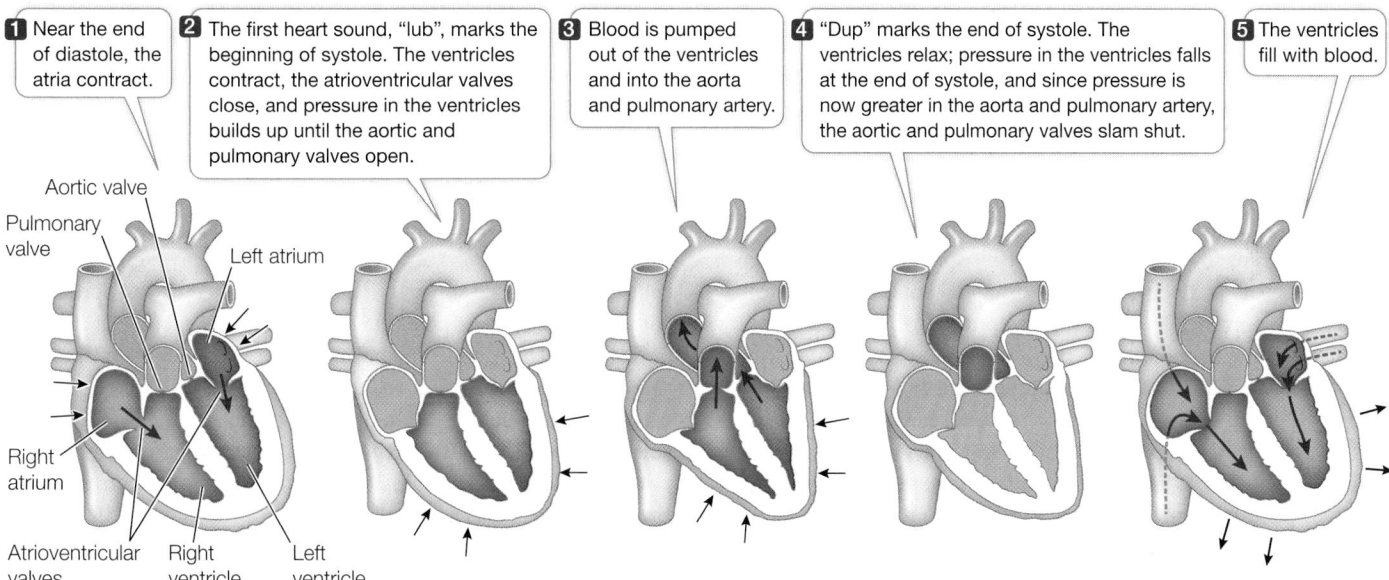

(B) Pressure and volume changes during the cardiac cycle

Figure 48.5 The Cardiac Cycle (A) The rhythmic contraction (systole) and relaxation (diastole) of the ventricles is called the cardiac cycle. (B) During diastole, the ventricles fill and pressure is low. During systole, the ventricular pressure rises and the ventricles empty. The representation here shows pressure and volume changes for the left ventricle only. The dashed lines represent the maximum and minimum volumes of blood in the left ventricle.

Q: If these curves were for the right ventricle instead of the left ventricle, how would they differ and how would they be the same?

 View in Achieve
Animation 48.1 The Cardiac Cycle

pressure cuff and a pressure gauge, together called a sphygmoma-nometer, and a stethoscope (**Figure 48.6**). This method measures the minimum pressure necessary to compress an artery so blood does not flow through it at all (the systolic pressure) and the maximum pressure that allows continuous flow through the artery (the diastolic pressure). A conventional blood pressure reading is expressed as the systolic pressure placed over the diastolic pressure. Healthy values for a young adult might be 120 millimeters of mercury (mm Hg) during systole and 70 mm Hg during diastole, or 120/70. Modern blood pressure measuring devices such as you might encounter in a drugstore are automated so that the stethoscope is unnecessary.

The heartbeat originates in the cardiac muscle

Some cardiac muscle cells are **pacemaker cells** that initiate action potentials without stimulation from the nervous system. These specialized muscle cells do not contract, but they generate rhythmic sequences of action potentials that spread to neighboring cardiac muscle cells that do contract. Since cardiac muscle cells are in electrical contact with one another through gap junctions, the action potentials from the pacemaker cells spread rapidly through a large mass of cardiac muscle, causing it to contract in unison. Coordinated contraction is essential for pumping blood effectively.

The primary pacemaker of the heart is a group of modified cardiac muscle cells, the **sinoatrial node**, located at the junction of the superior vena cava and right atrium (see Figure 48.9). The resting membrane potentials of these cells are less negative than those of other cardiac muscle cells and are not stable; instead they gradually become even less negative until they reach threshold for initiating an action potential. The action potentials of pacemaker cells are very different from those of neurons and other muscle cells (see Figure 43.9). They are slower to rise; they are broader; and they are slower to return to resting potential (**Figure 48.7A**). These properties of pacemaker cells are due to the ion channels in their membranes.

Pacemaker potentials involve Na^+, Ca^{2+}, and K^+ channels (**Figure 48.7B**). As discussed in Key Concept 43.2, when Na^+ or Ca^{2+} channels open, positive charges flow into the cell and the membrane potential becomes less negative. When K^+ channels open, positive charges flow out of the cell and the membrane potential becomes more negative. Because the Na^+ channels of pacemaker cells are open more of the time than are those of other cardiac muscle cells, the pacemaker resting potential is less negative. The action potential of pacemaker cells is due to voltage-gated Ca^{2+} channels rather than to voltage-gated Na^+ channels as in neurons, skeletal muscle, and the contractile cardiac muscle cells. These Ca^{2+} channels open and close more slowly than voltage-gated Na^+ channels, explaining the rounded shape of pacemaker action potentials.

The unstable resting potential of pacemaker cells is due to the behavior of cation channels. As in neurons and skeletal muscle cells, the rise of the action potential is followed by the opening of voltage-gated K^+ channels. The increased permeability of the cells to K^+ brings the membrane potential back to a negative level. But that restoration of a negative membrane potential causes a unique class of voltage-gated Na^+ channels to open. At the same time, the voltage-gated K^+ channels that restored the negative membrane potential are gradually closing. The opening Na^+ channels and closing K^+ channels cause the membrane potential to drift upward (become less negative) (see Figure 48.7B).

Figure 48.6 Measuring Blood Pressure
Blood pressure in the major artery of the arm can be measured with a device called a sphygmomanometer, which combines an inflatable cuff and a pressure gauge. A stethoscope or an automatic sensor is used to detect sounds created by the blood vessels in response to changes in pressure during the cardiac cycle.

1 The cuff is inflated to shut off all blood flow to the arm.

2 Pressure in the cuff is gradually lowered until the sound of a pulsing flow of blood through the constriction in the artery is heard. At this time, pressure in the cuff is just below the peak systolic pressure in the artery.

3 Pressure is further lowered until the sound becomes continuous. At this time, the cuff is just below the diastolic pressure in the artery. This person's blood pressure is 120/70.

Pulsing sounds

Pulsing sound gives way to smooth "whoosh" of blood flow

Figure 48.7 The Pacemaker Potential (A) The resting potential of the pacemaker cells of the sinoatrial node gradually drifts upward between action potentials. The pacemaker action potential is slow to rise and is broad. These characteristics are due to properties of Na⁺, K⁺, and two types of Ca²⁺ channels. (B) At rest, sinoatrial pacemaker cells are more permeable to Na⁺ than are neurons or other muscle cells. During rest, the K⁺ channels gradually close, but voltage-gated T-type Ca²⁺ channels open. When a threshold is reached, the L-type Ca²⁺ channels open, generating the action potential. Opening of the K⁺ channels helps the membrane potential return to its most negative value. (From E. P. Widmaier et al. 2008. *Vander's Human Physiology*, 11th Edition. McGraw-Hill: New York.)

(A) The pacemaker potential

1 A slow influx of first Na⁺, then Ca²⁺ causes a gradual depolarization of pacemaker cells.

2 Once threshold is reached, a major influx of Ca²⁺ generates an action potential.

3 Opening of K⁺ channels allows K⁺ to exit and the cell repolarizes.

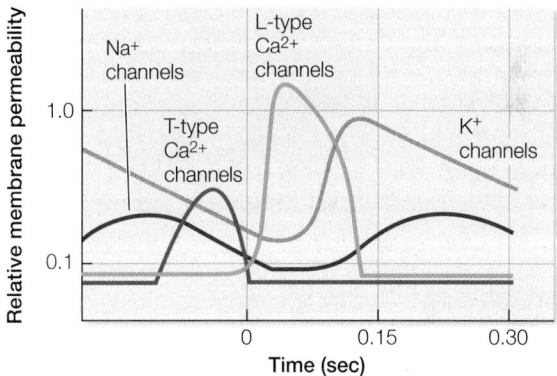

(B) Ion channel activity of pacemaker cells

The gradual rise in membrane potential closes the channels that allow Na⁺ to move into the cell, but as the membrane becomes less negative, some Ca²⁺ channels open, causing the membrane potential to continue its gradual rise. These Ca²⁺ channels are called T-types because they open transiently. Eventually the rising membrane potential reaches threshold for the major voltage-gated Ca²⁺ channels to open. These Ca²⁺ channels are called L-types because their opening is long-lasting. It is the opening of these L-type Ca²⁺ channels that generates the pacemaker action potential. The intricate interaction of these ion channels through their effects on membrane potential causes the rhythmic generation of action potentials that characterizes pacemaker cells.

The autonomic nervous system controls the heartbeat (speeds it up or slows it down) by influencing the rate at which the membrane potentials of pacemaker cells drift upward (**Figure 48.8**). Norepinephrine (NE) released onto pacemaker cells by sympathetic nerves increases the permeability of the Na⁺ channels and the Ca²⁺ channels. The result is that the resting potential of the pacemaker cells drifts up more rapidly, the interval between action potentials is decreased, and the heart beats faster. Conversely, the parasympathetic neurotransmitter acetylcholine (ACh) has opposite effects. ACh increases the permeability of K⁺ channels so that the membrane potential becomes even more negative following an action potential and rises more slowly. ACh also decreases the permeability of the Ca²⁺ channels so that the rate of rise of the membrane potential slows, the interval between pacemaker action potentials lengthens, and the heart slows down.

A conduction system coordinates the contraction of heart muscle

A normal heartbeat begins with an action potential in the sinoatrial node (**Figure 48.9**). This action potential spreads rapidly throughout the electrically coupled cells of the atria, causing them to contract in unison. Because there are no gap junctions between the cells of the atria and those of the ventricles, the action potential does not spread directly to the ventricles. Therefore the ventricles do not contract in unison with the atria.

How does the action potential move from the atria to the ventricles? Situated at the junction of

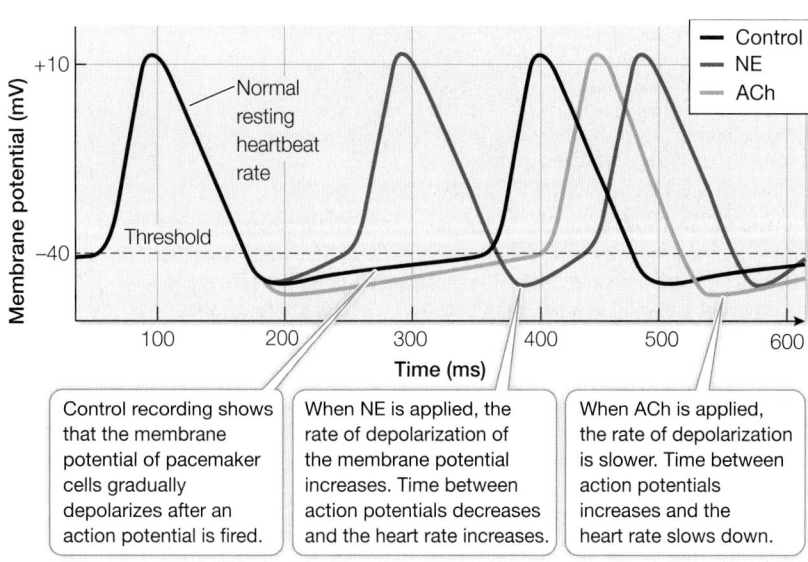

Control recording shows that the membrane potential of pacemaker cells gradually depolarizes after an action potential is fired.

When NE is applied, the rate of depolarization of the membrane potential increases. Time between action potentials decreases and the heart rate increases.

When ACh is applied, the rate of depolarization is slower. Time between action potentials increases and the heart rate slows down.

Figure 48.8 The Autonomic Nervous System Controls Heart Rate Neurotransmitters from the two divisions of the autonomic nervous system either speed up (norepinephrine, NE) or slow down (acetylcholine, ACh) the rate at which the pacemaker membrane potential drifts upward, thereby controlling the rate at which pacemaker cells fire action potentials.

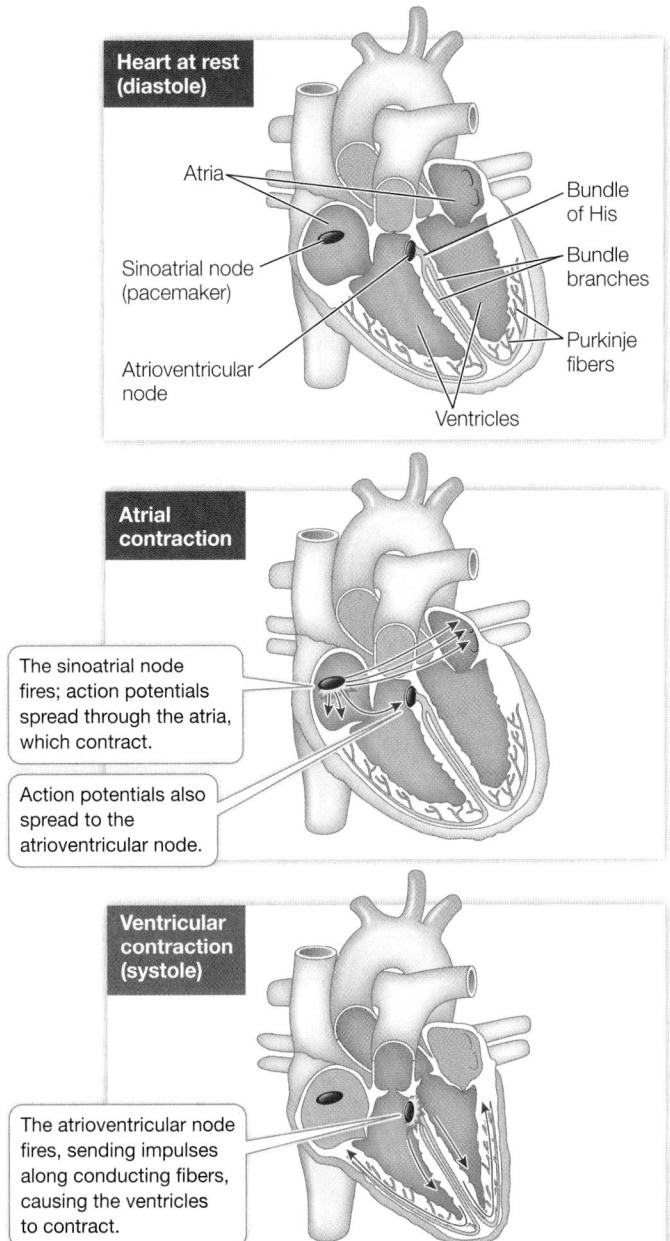

Heart at rest (diastole)

Atria

Bundle of His

Sinoatrial node (pacemaker)

Bundle branches

Atrioventricular node

Purkinje fibers

Ventricles

Atrial contraction

The sinoatrial node fires; action potentials spread through the atria, which contract.

Action potentials also spread to the atrioventricular node.

Ventricular contraction (systole)

The atrioventricular node fires, sending impulses along conducting fibers, causing the ventricles to contract.

Figure 48.9 The Heartbeat Pacemaker cells in the sinoatrial node initiate the heartbeat by firing action potentials that spread through the electrically coupled atrial muscle. The atrial action potential spreads to the atrioventricular node which, with a delay, conducts it through the bundle of His and Purkinje fibers to the cells of the ventricles.

the atria and the ventricles is a nodule of modified cardiac muscle cells—the **atrioventricular node**—which is stimulated by the depolarization of the atria. With a slight delay, the AV node generates action potentials that are conducted to the ventricles via the **bundle of His**, which consists of modified cardiac muscle fibers that do not contract but do conduct action potentials. These fibers course down the septum between the left and right ventricles and divide into right and left bundle branches. The branches of conducting fibers run to the tips of the ventricles and then spread throughout the ventricular muscle mass as **Purkinje fibers**. This

system of conducting fibers ensures that the cardiac action potential spreads rapidly and evenly throughout the ventricular muscle mass, starting at the very bottom of the ventricles. The short delay in the spread of the action potential imposed by the atrioventricular node ensures that the atria contract before the ventricles do, so that the blood passes progressively from the atria to the ventricles to the arteries.

HCM can disrupt conduction

Returning to the case of HCM introduced at the beginning of this chapter, consider in Figure 48.9 how HCM can impair the function of the left ventricle. First, in many cases the septum between the ventricles is greatly modified by the hypertrophy, and this can disrupt the conducting fibers that run down through the septum. Second, the thickening of the septum near the aorta can block the entrance to the aorta and therefore impede blood flow and the emptying of the ventricle. How can these effects be prevented? In **Investigating Life: Silencing Mutant Myosin Genes** we describe a recent study on mice that have been genetically engineered to carry mutations of a gene for one of the myosin chains of cardiac muscle that is associated with a large percentage of human HCM cases. These mice develop the pathologies that are seen in humans who inherit the genes causing HCM. The investigators found that by using RNA interference to silence the mutated genes, they could prevent the development of the HCM pathology.

> **Connect the Concepts** The use of RNA interference to block gene expression at the mRNA level is discussed in Key Concept 18.4.

Electrical properties of ventricular muscles sustain heart contraction

Ventricular muscle fibers can contract for about 300 milliseconds—much longer than skeletal muscle fibers. As in neuronal and skeletal muscle action potentials, the rising phase of the ventricular muscle cell action potentials is due to the opening of voltage-gated Na^+ channels. Unlike neurons and skeletal muscle fibers, however, ventricular muscle cells remain depolarized for a long time due to sustained opening of voltage-gated Ca^{2+} channels (**Figure 48.10**). Like other muscle, cardiac muscle is stimulated to contract when Ca^{2+} is available to bind with troponin (see Figure 46.6). As long as Ca^{2+} remains in the sarcoplasm, the ventricular muscle cells continue to contract.

To terminate systole and allow the ventricles to fill again, Ca^{2+} must be cleared from the sarcoplasm of the ventricular muscle cells. Ca^{2+} pumps in the sarcoplasmic reticulum membrane and the cell membrane actively transport Ca^{2+} ions out of the sarcoplasm and into the sarcoplasmic reticulum or into the interstitial fluid. Thus Ca^{2+} in the sarcoplasm is maintained at a low level until the next action potential triggers another round of Ca^{2+} release and muscle contraction. The rate of cycling of Ca^{2+} into and out of the sarcoplasm puts limits on the heart rate and strength of contraction of the ventricle.

The ECG records the electrical activity of the heart

Electrical events in the cardiac muscle during the cardiac cycle are recorded by electrodes placed on the surface of the body. Such a

►Investigating LIFE   Silencing Mutant Myosin Genes

Experiment

Original Paper: J. Jiang et al. 2013. Allele-specific silencing of mutant *Myh6* allele in mice suppresses hypertrophic cardiomyopathy. *Science* 342: 111–114.

Hypertrophic cardiomyopathy (HCM) is caused by mutations in myosin genes. A similar mutation has been engineered into mice, and they develop HCM. In addition, it was shown that treatment of these mice with cyclosporine A (CsA) exacerbates their development of HCM. Since the HCM model mice are heterozygous for the mutated gene (as are most afflicted humans), and since there are multiple myosin genes, the question arose as to whether or not the selective silencing of the mutant gene would allow the normal alleles to correct the disorganization of the cardiac muscle due to the mutant allele.

HYPOTHESES►

1. Mice genetically engineered to carry a mutation in the myosin gene most commonly responsible for HCM in humans will show the HCM phenotype, and it will be exacerbated by treatment with CsA.

2. Silencing expression of the mutant gene will prevent the development of the HCM phenotype.

METHOD►

1. Using genetic engineering techniques, generate a mouse model that carries a mutation in one of its myosin genes. The heterozygotes are viable, but the homozygotes are not.

2. Using the wild-type mice as a comparison, measure left ventricular wall thickness in mutant mice with and without treatment with CsA to exacerbate the development of left ventricular wall hypertrophy.

3. Develop an interference RNA (RNAi) that will silence expression of the mutant gene in vitro.

4. Transfect mice heterozygous for the mutation with the RNAi construct and at a later time assess them for hypertrophy of their left ventricular walls. Some mice are also treated with CsA, which exacerbates the development of hypertrophy in the mutant mice.

5. Calculate the means and standard deviations for each cohort of mice. Then do non-paired *t*-tests to see if there are significant differences.

RESULTS► Data in the graph are simulated based on reported means and standard deviations.

Mutant mice, not CsA treated

Mutant mice, CsA treated

From J. H. Jiang, et al. 2013. *Science* 342: 111–114

In untreated mice, cardiac muscle cells are disorganized.

Treated mice have normal cardiac muscle cells.

CONCLUSION► The mice carrying the mutation show a significant ($P < 0.003$) increase in left ventricular wall thickness. The mutant mice treated with CsA show a larger increase in left ventricular wall thickness ($P < 0.001$) in comparison with the mutant mice not treated with CsA. Thus the mutation has the expected effect of promoting the development of HCM symptoms, and the effect is exacerbated by treatment with CsA.

Work with the Data

The second hypothesis posed in the Investigating Life experiment is that treatment of the mutant mice with interference RNA (RNAi) targeted to the mutant myosin gene will reduce the development of the HCM phenotype. The data are listed in the table. All values are for left ventricular wall thickness (mm) of individual mice and are simulated based on the reported means and standard deviations.

QUESTIONS►

1. Comparing mutant mice that did not receive CsA, did the treatment with RNAi significantly reduce their left ventricular wall thickness?

2. Comparing mutant mice that did receive CsA, did the treatment with RNAi significantly reduce their left ventricular wall thickness?

Go to **Achieve** for a companion Data in Depth exercise.

CsA treated	Not CsA treated	RNAi and CsA treated	RNAi but not CsA treated
1.60	0.96	0.87	0.63
1.34	0.98	0.82	0.68
1.50	1.01	0.87	0.85
1.39	0.89	0.91	0.65
1.50	0.86	0.74	0.68
1.44	0.91	0.83	
1.42		0.92	

(A)

1 The rising phase of the ventricular cell action potential is due to opening of voltage-gated Na^+ channels and closure of K^+ channels.

2 The plateau phase is due to the prolonged opening of voltage-gated Ca^{2+} channels.

3 The falling phase is due to the closure of Ca^{2+} channels and opening of K^+ channels.

Figure 48.10 The Action Potential of Ventricular Muscle Fibers
(A) The three phases of the action potential of ventricular muscle fibers are due to the opening and closing of voltage-gated channels. (B) At the initiation of the action potential, voltage-gated Na^+ channels open rapidly but briefly. At the same time, but more slowly, K^+ channels are closing and Ca^{2+} channels are opening. The open Ca^{2+} channels sustain the depolarization. Repolarization occurs when the Ca^{2+} channels close, and the slow opening of the K^+ channels also contributes to the repolarization. (After D. E. Mohrman and L. J. Heller. 2002. *Cardiovascular Physiology*, Fifth Edition. Langer Medical Books/McGraw-Hill: New York.)

Q: Why is the broadening of the ventricular muscle action potential important?

recording is an **electrocardiogram**, or **ECG** or **EKG** reflecting the Greek spelling (*kardia*). The ECG is an important tool for diagnosing heart problems (**Figure 48.11A**).

The action potentials that sweep through the muscles of the atria and ventricles before they contract are massive, localized electrical events causing electric currents to flow throughout the body. Electrodes placed at different locations on the skin detect those currents at different times and register a voltage difference between them. The appearance of the ECG depends on the placement of the electrodes. Electrodes placed on the right wrist and

(A) ECG setup

© Phanie/Alamy Stock Photo

(B) Typical ECG recording with corresponding arterial pressures and heart sounds

P corresponds to the depolarization of the atrial muscle.

Q, R, and S correspond to the depolarization and therefore the contraction of the ventricles as well as the repolarization of the atria.

T corresponds to the repolarization and therefore the relaxation of the ventricles.

The sounds heard through a stethoscope occur at the beginning and end of ventricular systole.

Figure 48.11 The Electrocardiogram   (A) An electrocardiogram (abbreviated as ECG or EKG) is used to monitor heart function. Electrodes attached to the person record an ECG that is amplified and displayed on a monitor. (B) Variations from the normal pattern shown here can be used to diagnose heart problems.

Q: Abnormal ECG patterns are characteristic of HCM hearts. If there were an occasional or a long-lasting block of the AV node, what would you expect to see in the ECG?

left ankle produced the normal ECG shown in **Figure 48.11B**. The wave patterns of the ECG are designated P, Q, R, S, and T, each letter representing a particular event in the cardiac muscle, as shown in the figure.

48.3 Recap and Assess

The mammalian heart has two atria and two ventricles. The right atrium and ventricle serve the pulmonary circuit, and the left atrium and ventricle serve the systemic circuit. Valves that are open and shut by pressure differences prevent the backflow of blood. Modified cardiac muscle tissue in the right atrium functions to spontaneously generate pacemaker action potentials. Other modified cardiac muscle tissue between the atria and ventricles and throughout the ventricles conducts those signals and coordinates the heart contraction. Broad action potentials in ventricular muscle reflect Ca^{2+} cycling in the ventricular muscle cells and make sustained contractions possible. The depolarization and repolarization of cardiac muscle during the cardiac cycle create electrical events that can be recorded by electrodes placed on the skin to generate an ECG.

1. Valves of the heart can become stiff and calcified, limiting the flow of blood through them in a condition called stenosis. What would be the consequences of aortic valve stenosis and of pulmonary valve stenosis?

2. Digitalis is a drug that causes an increase in Ca^{2+} concentration in the cardiac muscle cells. Why is it used to treat patients with a weakened heart?

3. Heart valve stenosis impedes blood flow, whereas heart valve prolapse allows blood to flow backward (regurgitation). Both of these conditions can be detected as heart murmurs when a stethoscope is used to listen to heart sounds. When in the cardiac cycle could a heart murmur indicate aortic valve stenosis, and when could it indicate aortic valve prolapse? Explain your answer.

Next we consider the composition of the blood and the characteristics of the vessels through which blood circulates around the body, illustrating once again how structure serves function. We also consider the role of the lymphatic vessels that return interstitial fluid to the blood.

KEY CONCEPT
48.4 Circulatory System Functions Depend on Blood and Blood Vessels

Learning Objectives

48.4.1 Describe the features, life cycle, and function of a red blood cell.

48.4.2 Describe the blood-clotting process as a flow diagram.

48.4.3 Explain the role of arterioles in the control of blood flow.

48.4.4 Explain the forces that cause water to leave and reenter the capillaries.

48.4.5 Describe the factors that affect the return of blood in veins to the heart.

Blood is a connective tissue. Like all connective tissues, it consists of cells suspended in an extracellular matrix. Different blood cell types serve different functions, and the extracellular matrix has a complex composition that is highly regulated. Blood is a fluid tissue circulating through a system of closed vessels. The properties of the different classes of vessels reflect their functions.

Blood cells can be separated from the fluid matrix, called blood plasma, by centrifugation (**Figure 48.12**). If a sample of blood is spun in a centrifuge, all the cells move to the bottom of the tube, leaving the clear, straw-colored blood plasma on top. The packed-cell volume, or hematocrit, is the percentage of the blood volume made up by red blood cells (RBCs). Normal hematocrit is about 42% for women and 46% for men, but these values can vary considerably. The hematocrits of people living and working at high elevations are usually greater than in people living and working at low elevations, because exposure to low oxygen stimulates the production of more RBCs. Between the blood plasma and the packed RBCs there is a very thin layer—less than 1% of the blood volume—called the buffy coat that contains most of the white blood cells and platelets. **Platelets** are pinched-off fragments of a class of bone marrow cells. Here we consider the RBCs and the platelets. White blood cells, or leukocytes, are cells of the immune system, discussed in Chapter 40.

Red blood cells transport respiratory gases

Most blood cells are RBCs—also called **erythrocytes**. Mature RBCs are biconcave, flexible discs that lack nuclei but are packed with hemoglobin. Their function is to transport respiratory gases (see Key Concept 47.4). The shape of RBCs gives them a large surface area for gas exchange, and their flexibility enables them to squeeze through narrow capillaries. Men have 4.5–6.0 million RBCs per microliter of blood, and women have 3.5–5.0 million.

RBCs, as well as all the other cellular components of blood, are generated by stem cells in the bone marrow, particularly in the ribs, breastbone, pelvis, vertebrae, and the long bones of the limbs. RBC production is controlled by a hormone, **erythropoietin** (**EPO**), released by cells in the kidneys in response to low oxygen—**hypoxia**. Many tissues respond to hypoxia by expressing a transcription factor called hypoxia-inducible factor 1 (HIF-1). When the kidneys become hypoxic and express HIF-1, one of the actions of the transcription factor is to activate the gene encoding erythropoietin. Increased circulating erythropoietin extends the lives of mature RBCs and stimulates production of new RBCs in the bone marrow. For the discovery of HIF and its mechanisms of action, William G. Kaelin Jr., Sir Peter J. Ratcliffe, and Gregg L. Semenza of Harvard, Oxford, and Johns Hopkins Universities respectively were awarded the 2019 Nobel Prize in Physiology or Medicine.

Under normal conditions, your bone marrow produces about 2 million RBCs every second. Developing RBCs divide many times while still in the bone marrow, and during this time they produce hemoglobin. When hemoglobin makes up about 25% of the volume of the immature RBC, the nucleus is extruded from the cell and other cell organelles are also lost. This process is almost complete when the newly mature RBC squeezes between the endothelial cells of blood vessels in the bone marrow and enters the

Figure 48.12 The Composition of Blood Blood consists of a complex aqueous solution (the blood plasma) and numerous cell types and cell fragments. The hematocrit (arrow) is a measure of the volume of red blood cells as a percentage of total blood volume. At the surface of the packed cells is the thin buffy coat that contains leukocytes and platelets. Major classes of leukocytes are shown, but a more complete list along with their functions can be found in Key Concept 40.1.

circulation. Loss of nuclei from the RBCs occurs in most mammalian species, but the RBCs of a few mammals and of all other vertebrates are nucleated.

Each RBC circulates for about 120 days. As it gets older, its membrane becomes less flexible and more fragile, so older RBCs are more likely to rupture as they bend to fit through narrow capillaries. RBCs are particularly squeezed in the **spleen**, an organ that sits near the stomach in the upper left side of the abdominal cavity. The spleen has many sinuses (cavities) that serve as reservoirs for RBCs. To get into the sinuses, however, the RBCs must squeeze between spleen cells. When old RBCs are ruptured by this squeezing, their remnants are taken up and degraded by macrophages (a class of white blood cells that ingest debris and foreign materials; see Key Concept 40.3).

Platelets are essential for blood clotting

Besides producing erythrocytes and leukocytes, the bone marrow stem cells described in Key Concept 40.1 also produce cells called **megakaryocytes**. Megakaryocytes are large cells that remain in the bone marrow and release platelets into the circulation. A platelet is a tiny fragment of a cell without cell organelles, but packed with enzymes and chemicals necessary for its function: sealing leaks in blood vessels and initiating **blood clotting** (Figure 48.13).

Damage to a blood vessel exposes collagen fibers. An encounter with collagen fibers activates platelets. The platelet swells, becomes irregularly shaped and sticky, and releases chemicals that activate other platelets and initiate the clotting of blood. The sticky platelets also form a plug at the damaged site.

Blood clotting requires many steps and many clotting factors, most of which are circulating in the blood in an inactive form. The absence of any one of these proteins can impair clotting, resulting in excessive bleeding. Because the liver produces most of the clotting factors, liver diseases such as hepatitis and cirrhosis can result in excessive bleeding. People with hemophilia experience uncontrolled bleeding because of a genetic inability to produce a clotting factor.

Blood clotting factors participate in a cascade of chemical activations of other substances circulating in the blood. The cascade begins with damage to a blood vessel or other tissue that exposes the blood to proteins such as collagen that are normally separated from the blood by endothelial cells lining the blood vessels. This exposure activates platelets and initiates the clotting factor cascade. The end result of this cascade is to convert an inactive circulating enzyme, **prothrombin**, to its active form, **thrombin**. Thrombin is a protease that acts on molecules of **fibrinogen**, a blood plasma protein, to create insoluble threads of **fibrin**. The fibrin threads form a meshwork that binds platelets, seals the vessel, and provides a scaffold for the formation of scar tissue (see Figure 48.13).

Arteries withstand high pressure, arterioles control blood flow

The walls of the large arteries have many extracellular collagen and elastin fibers that enable them to withstand the high blood

(A)

An injury to the lining of a blood vessel exposes collagen fibers; platelets adhere and become sticky.

Platelets release substances that cause the vessel to contract. Sticky platelets form a plug and initiate the formation of a fibrin clot.

The fibrin clot seals the wound until the vessel wall heals.

Platelet

Red blood cell

Collagen fibers

Platelet plug

(B)

Fibrin meshwork

Clotting factors:
1. Released from platelets and injured tissue
2. Blood plasma proteins synthesized in liver and circulated in inactive form

Prothrombin circulating in blood plasma

Thrombin

Fibrinogen circulating in blood plasma

Fibrin

© Science Photo Library/Alamy Stock Photo

Figure 48.13 Blood Clotting **(A)** Damage to a blood vessel initiates a cascade of events that produce a fibrin meshwork. **(B)** As the meshwork forms, red blood cells are enmeshed in the fibrin threads, forming a clot, as shown in this color-enhanced electron micrograph.

pressures generated by the heart (**Figure 48.14A**). These elastic tissues have another important function: they are stretched during systole, and thereby store some of the energy imparted to the blood by the heart. Elastic recoil during diastole returns this energy to the blood by squeezing it and pushing it forward. As a result, even though pressure in the arteries pulsates with the beating of the heart, the flow of blood is smoother than it would be through a system of rigid pipes.

Contraction of smooth muscle cells in the walls of the arteries constricts the vessels, and relaxation of the smooth muscle dilates them. When the diameter of a vessel changes, its resistance to blood flow changes, and the amount of blood flowing through it changes as a result. Neural and hormonal mechanisms act on smooth muscle cells in the walls of the arteries and arterioles, controlling the flow of blood through these vessels. The arterioles are referred to as resistance vessels because their resistance can vary to control the blood flow to specific tissues.

Materials are exchanged in capillary beds by filtration, osmosis, and diffusion

Beds of capillaries lie between arterioles and venules (**Figure 48.14B**). Most cells are not more than a few cell diameters away from a capillary. The needs of cells are served by the exchange of materials between blood and interstitial fluid across the capillary walls. Capillary walls are thin and permeable to water and many solutes. Also, blood flows slowly through capillaries, allowing time for exchange.

It may seem strange that blood flows through the large arteries rapidly at high pressures, but when it reaches the small capillaries

the pressure and rate of flow decrease (**Figure 48.14C**). When you constrict the opening of a garden hose, the pressure in the hose and the velocity of the water spraying out increase. But keep in mind that the arteries branch into many arterioles that serve huge numbers of capillaries. Even though each capillary has a diameter so small that red blood cells pass through in single file, there are so many capillaries that their total cross-sectional area is much greater than that of any other class of vessel. As a result, all the capillaries together have a much greater capacity for blood than do the arterioles.

Capillary walls consist of a single layer of endothelial cells (**Figure 48.15**). Capillaries are permeable to water, some ions, and some small molecules but not to large molecules such as proteins, and certainly not to red blood cells. At the arterial (high-pressure) end, blood pressure squeezes water and small solutes out through spaces between the cells of the capillary walls into the surrounding intercellular space.

How is the blood volume maintained if fluid is continuously leaking out of the capillaries? An answer to this question was put forth more than 100 years ago by the physiologist E. H. Starling. Starling suggested that water movement across capillary walls is a result of two opposing forces, which are now known as **Starling's forces**:

1. Blood hydrostatic pressure squeezes water and small solutes out of the capillaries.

2. Blood osmotic pressure pulls water back into the capillaries.

Blood hydrostatic pressure is high at the arterial end of a capillary bed and steadily drops as blood moves toward the venous

(A) The tissue layers of blood vessels

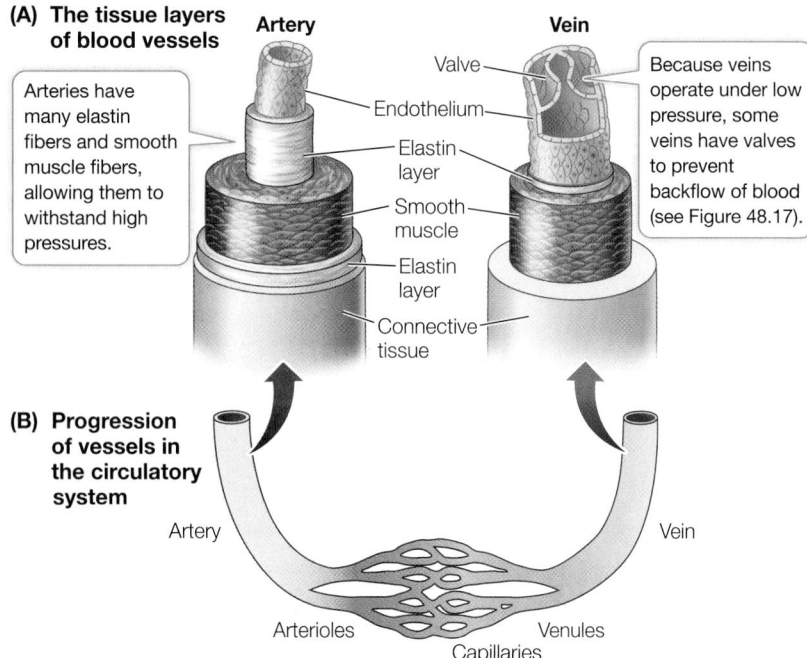

Arteries have many elastin fibers and smooth muscle fibers, allowing them to withstand high pressures.

Because veins operate under low pressure, some veins have valves to prevent backflow of blood (see Figure 48.17).

Artery

Vein

Valve
Endothelium
Elastin layer
Smooth muscle
Elastin layer
Connective tissue

(B) Progression of vessels in the circulatory system

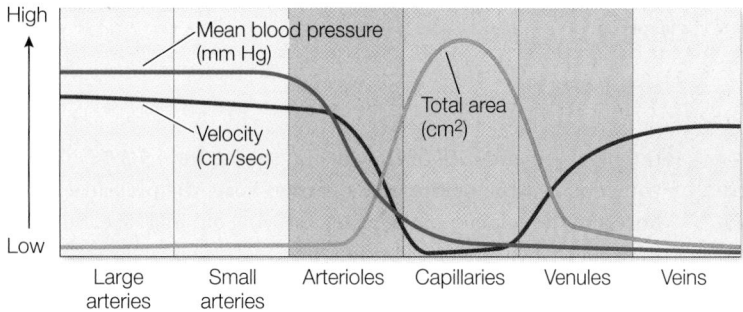

Artery

Vein

Arterioles

Venules

Capillaries

(C) Characteristics of classes of vessels

High

Mean blood pressure (mm Hg)

Velocity (cm/sec)

Total area (cm²)

Low

Large arteries | Small arteries | Arterioles | Capillaries | Venules | Veins

Figure 48.14 Anatomy of Blood Vessels **(A)** The different anatomical characteristics of arteries and veins match their functions. **(B)** Blood from the arterial system feeds into capillary beds where exchanges with the interstitial fluid occur. The venous system returns the blood to the heart. **(C)** The cross-sectional area encompassed by each vessel type is graphed along with the pressure and velocity of the blood within it.

▶ **View in Achieve**
   Activity 48.3 Structure of Blood Vessels

end (**Figure 48.16**). Blood osmotic pressure is due to the large protein molecules that cannot leave the capillaries, and it is relatively constant along the capillaries. As long as the blood hydrostatic pressure is above the blood osmotic pressure, fluid leaves the capillaries. At the venule end of most capillaries, blood hydrostatic pressure falls below blood osmotic pressure, so fluid returns to the capillaries. The actual numbers for a normal capillary bed in a resting person suggest that there would be a *slight* net loss of fluid to the intercellular spaces. This lost fluid, about 4 liters per day, percolates between cells as the interstitial fluid before it returns to the venous blood via the **lymphatic system**, which we discuss later in this key concept.

Recent research suggests that in addition to large protein molecules in the blood, bicarbonate ions (HCO_3^-) may also contribute significantly to pulling water back into the capillaries. The CO_2 produced by cellular metabolism diffuses into the endothelial cells lining the capillaries, where it is converted into HCO_3^- and released into the blood plasma. When an individual is at rest, the increasing HCO_3^- concentration can cause the blood osmotic pressure at the venous end to be 30 mm Hg higher than at the

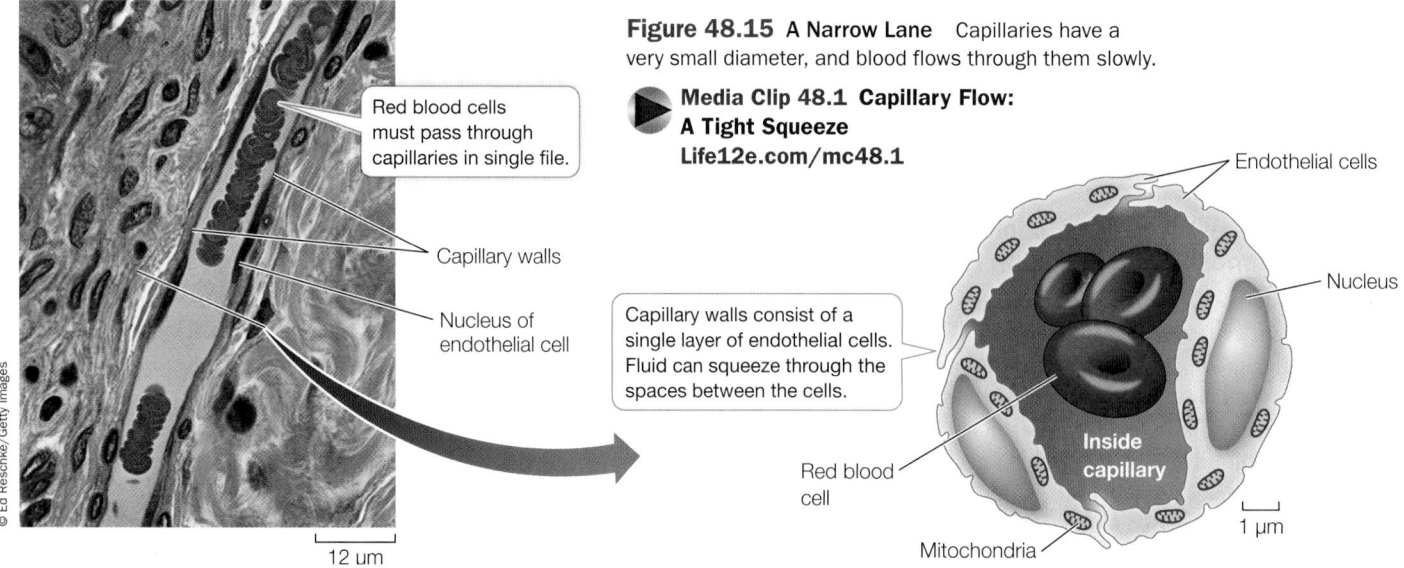

Red blood cells must pass through capillaries in single file.

Capillary walls

Nucleus of endothelial cell

Capillary walls consist of a single layer of endothelial cells. Fluid can squeeze through the spaces between the cells.

© Ed Reschke/Getty Images

12 um

Figure 48.15 A Narrow Lane   Capillaries have a very small diameter, and blood flows through them slowly.

▶ **Media Clip 48.1 Capillary Flow: A Tight Squeeze**
   Life12e.com/mc48.1

Endothelial cells

Nucleus

Inside capillary

Red blood cell

Mitochondria

1 μm

(A)

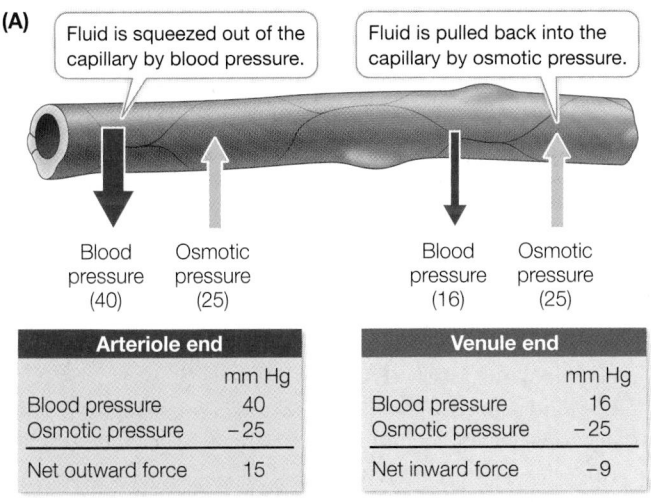

Fluid is squeezed out of the capillary by blood pressure.

Fluid is pulled back into the capillary by osmotic pressure.

Blood pressure (40)　Osmotic pressure (25)　Blood pressure (16)　Osmotic pressure (25)

Arteriole end	
	mm Hg
Blood pressure	40
Osmotic pressure	−25
Net outward force	15

Venule end	
	mm Hg
Blood pressure	16
Osmotic pressure	−25
Net inward force	−9

(B)

Net driving force for fluid to leave capillary

Blood pressure

Osmotic pressure

Net driving force for fluid to reenter capillary

Pressure (mm Hg): 0, 25, 50

Figure 48.16 Starling's Forces Starling's model explains fluid balance in capillary beds. **(A)** When blood hydrostatic pressure is greater than blood osmotic pressure, fluid leaves the capillaries; when blood hydrostatic pressure falls below blood osmotic pressure, fluid returns to the capillaries. **(B)** The balance of these two forces changes over the capillary bed as blood hydrostatic pressure falls.

Blood flow through veins that are above the level of the heart is assisted by gravity. Below the level of the heart, however, venous return is against gravity. The most important force propelling blood from these regions is the squeezing of the veins by the contractions of surrounding skeletal muscles. As muscles contract, the veins are compressed and blood is squeezed through them. Blood flow may be temporarily obstructed during a prolonged muscle contraction, but when muscles relax, blood is free to move again. One-way valves in the veins of the extremities prevent backflow of blood. Thus when veins are squeezed, blood is propelled forward toward the heart (**Figure 48.17**).

When a person is sitting, gravity causes blood accumulation in the veins of the lower body and exerts backpressure on the capillary beds. This backpressure shifts the balance between blood hydrostatic pressure and osmotic pressure, causing increased loss of fluid to the intercellular spaces. That is why your feet swell during a long airline flight.

arterial end, and during strenuous exercise this difference can be higher. Thus it appears that CO_2 and HCO_3^- are factors that pull water back into the capillaries.

All capillaries are permeable to O_2, CO_2, and small ions. Lipid-soluble substances readily pass through the capillary walls. Water and small solutes pass through intercellular spaces in the capillary wall, and through holes called **fenestrations** in the endothelial cells. More permeable and less selective capillaries are found in the digestive tract, where nutrients are absorbed, and in the kidneys, where wastes are filtered. Capillary endothelial cells also contain transporters that can facilitate the passage of specific molecules, such as glucose and lactate.

The capillaries of the brain are a special case, being rather impermeable and wrapped by glia. Not much can pass through them other than lipid-soluble substances (including alcohol and anesthetics). This high selectivity of brain capillaries is known as the **blood–brain barrier**. Even in the brain, however, there are specific regions where the capillaries are more permeable, enabling the brain to detect non-lipid-soluble hormones.

Blood flows back to the heart through veins

The pressure of the blood flowing from capillaries to venules is low and insufficient to propel blood back to the heart. The walls of veins are more expandable than the walls of arteries, and blood tends to accumulate in veins. Sixty percent of your total blood volume may be in your veins when you are resting. Because of their capacity to stretch and store blood, veins are called capacitance vessels.

Contractions of skeletal muscles squeeze the veins.

Valve closed　Valve open

Muscle contracts:

This squeezing moves the blood in the veins toward the heart because of one-way valves that prevent backflow.

Valve open　Valve closed

Muscle relaxes:

Blood is propelled forward by muscle contractions and, in some body regions, by gravity.

Backpressure is due to contractions of atria, contractions of muscles, and, in some regions, gravity.

Figure 48.17 One-Way Flow Veins of the extremities have valves that prevent blood from flowing backward, and contractions of skeletal muscle help move blood toward the heart.

Because of the one-way valves in the veins of the legs, the contractions of leg muscles act as auxiliary vascular pumps when an animal walks or runs and facilitate the return of blood to the heart from the lower body. As a greater volume of blood is returned to the heart, the heart contracts more forcefully and its pumping action is enhanced. The heartbeat gets stronger because of a property of cardiac muscle cells described by the **Frank–Starling law**: if the cardiac muscle cells are stretched, as they are when the volume of returning blood increases, they contract more forcefully.

The actions of breathing also help return venous blood to the heart. The muscles involved in inhalation create negative pressure that pulls air into the lungs (see Figure 47.11), and this negative pressure also pulls blood toward the chest, increasing venous return to the right atrium. In addition, some of the largest veins closest to the heart contain smooth muscle that contracts at the onset of exercise. Contraction of veins can rapidly increase venous return and stimulate the heart in accord with the Frank–Starling law, increasing cardiac output.

Lymphatic vessels return interstitial fluid to the blood

The interstitial fluid contains water and other small molecules, but no RBCs, and less protein than found in blood plasma. A separate system of vessels—the lymphatic system—returns interstitial fluid to the blood. Each capillary bed contains at least one blind-ended lymph capillary.

Connect the Concepts The lymphatic system was introduced in conjunction with the immune system in Key Concept 40.1.

Interstitial fluid that enters the lymphatic vessels is called **lymph**. Fine lymphatic capillaries merge into progressively larger vessels and ultimately into the right and left **lymphatic ducts** that empty into large veins at the base of the neck (see Figure 40.3). The left lymphatic duct, also known as the **thoracic duct**, carries most of the lymph from the lower part of the body and is larger than the right lymphatic duct. Lymphatic vessels, like veins, have one-way valves that keep the lymph flowing toward the lymphatic ducts. Therefore lymph, like blood, is propelled toward the heart by skeletal muscle contractions and breathing movements. **Lymph nodes** along the major lymphatic vessels are a major site of lymphocyte production and of the phagocytic action that removes microorganisms and other foreign materials from the circulation.

Vascular disease is a killer

As mentioned at the beginning of this chapter, cardiovascular disease is responsible for about one-fourth of all deaths each year in the United States, and the same is true in Europe. The immediate cause of most of these deaths is not a defect in heart muscle as in cases of HCM, but is heart attack or stroke—both of which are usually the result of a disease called **arteriosclerosis** ("hardening of the arteries") that begins many years before symptoms are detected.

Healthy arteries have a smooth internal lining of endothelial cells (**Figure 48.18A**) which can be damaged by chronic high blood pressure, smoking, a high-fat diet, or microorganisms. Deposits called **plaque** begin to form at sites of endothelial damage, initiating an early stage of arteriosclerosis called **atherosclerosis**.

First, the damaged endothelial cells attract certain white blood cells to the site. These cells are then joined by smooth muscle cells migrating from the deeper layers of the arterial wall. Lipids, especially cholesterol, are deposited in these cells, so that the developing plaque becomes fatty. Fibrous connective tissue made by the invading smooth muscle cells in the plaque, along with deposits of calcium, gradually makes the artery wall less elastic—hence "hardening of the arteries." Plaque deposits narrow the artery and causes turbulence in the blood flow. Blood platelets stick to the plaque (see Figure 48.13) and initiate formation of an intravascular blood clot, a **thrombus** (plural *thrombi*) that can block the artery (**Figure 48.18B**).

The blood supply to the heart muscle flows through the **coronary arteries**, which are highly susceptible to atherosclerosis. As these arteries narrow, blood flow to the heart muscle decreases, causing the symptoms of chest pain and shortness of breath during mild exertion. A person with atherosclerosis is at high risk of forming a thrombus in a coronary artery. This condition, called **coronary thrombosis**, can totally block the vessel, causing a **myocardial infarction** (heart attack).

A piece of a thrombus that breaks loose, called an **embolus** (plural *emboli*), is likely to become lodged in a vessel of smaller diameter, blocking its flow (an **embolism**). Arteries already narrowed by plaque formation are likely places for an embolism. An embolism in an artery in the brain causes the cells fed by that artery to die. This event is a **stroke**. The specific damage resulting from a stroke, such as memory loss, speech impairment, or paralysis, depends on the location of the blocked artery in the brain.

(A) Healthy

Smooth muscle

Endothelium

(B) Atherosclerotic

Thrombus

Plaque

Smooth muscle

Figure 48.18 Atherosclerotic Plaque **(A)** A healthy, clear artery. **(B)** An atherosclerotic artery, clogged with plaque and a thrombus.

Important risk factors for developing atherosclerosis are your genetic predisposition and your age. Environmental risk factors also play a large role. These include high-fat and high-cholesterol diets, smoking, and a sedentary lifestyle. Certain untreated medical conditions such as hypertension (high blood pressure), obesity, and diabetes are also risk factors for atherosclerosis. For those who have a genetic predisposition to atherosclerosis, it is even more important to minimize environmental risk factors. Changes in diet and behavior and treatment of predisposing medical conditions can prevent and reverse early atherosclerosis and help fend off this silent killer.

KEY CONCEPT
48.4 Recap and Assess

Blood is a fluid tissue with cellular components that play roles in transport of respiratory gases, immune system function, and blood clotting. The properties of the arteries, arterioles, capillaries, venules, and veins reflect their functions. Exchanges between the blood and interstitial fluids occur in the smallest of those vessels, the capillaries. These exchanges are governed by Starling's forces and the movement of HCO_3^- into the blood. Lymphatic vessels return interstitial fluid to the blood. Blockage of arteries by plaque, thrombi, or emboli are major causes of heart disease and stroke.

1. Why do athletes train at high elevations?
2. Why is the blood-clotting process called a cascade?
3. Why are arterioles called resistance vessels and veins called capacitance vessels, and what do these terms imply about function?
4. In advanced starvation, the body breaks down its blood plasma proteins for energy. At this stage of disease, fluid accumulates in the abdomen and the extremities. What is the connection between these two consequences of starvation?

Every tissue in the body requires an adequate flow of oxygen-saturated blood. Blood flow depends on the maintenance of an appropriate blood pressure, and the distribution of blood flow throughout the body depends on control of the resistance in the blood vessels supplying different tissues.

KEY CONCEPT
48.5 Circulation Is Controlled by Hormonal and Neuronal Signals

Learning Objectives

48.5.1 Describe the mechanisms underlying autoregulation of local blood flow and how it influences mean arterial pressure (MAP).

48.5.2 Explain the role of the autonomic nervous system in regulating MAP.

48.5.3 Explain how an increase or a decrease in the firing rate of baroreceptors causes a change in MAP.

48.5.4 Discuss the roles of positive and negative feedback in controlling blood pressure.

When we investigate how a physiological process is regulated, we start by identifying the critical components of that process,

how they can be controlled, and the information used to govern that control. Because blood flow depends on pressure, we can identify the mean arterial pressure (MAP) as a critical variable of the circulatory system.

Pressure in the aorta oscillates between systole and diastole, and the duration of diastole is usually twice as long as that of systole (see Figure 48.5). Therefore a simple way of estimating MAP is to take the diastolic pressure and add to it one-third of the difference between systolic and diastolic pressure. However, to understand the physiological mechanisms that control MAP, we have to consider the factors that determine it. MAP is determined by the cardiac output (CO) and the resistance to flow in the blood vessels, or total peripheral resistance (TPR):

$$MAP = CO \times TPR$$

Since CO is equal to the heart rate (HR) times how much blood the heart pumps with each beat (stroke volume [SV]), the critical relationships can be expressed as:

$$MAP = HR \times SV \times TPR$$

HR, SV, and TPR are controlled by neural and hormonal mechanisms at both the local and systemic levels.

At the local level, each tissue controls its own blood flow through **autoregulatory mechanisms** that alter the diameter and therefore the resistance of the arterioles serving it. The collective autoregulatory actions in the arterioles in all tissues of the body influence TPR and therefore MAP. If many arterioles suddenly dilate, TPR goes down and MAP falls. If many arterioles constrict, TPR goes up and MAP goes up. Therefore changes in MAP provide information about changing needs of the body. In addition, as blood flows through capillary beds, its composition changes—its CO_2 content goes up and its O_2 content goes down. Thus blood composition also provides information the body uses to regulate the circulatory system.

The nervous and endocrine systems respond to changes in MAP and blood composition by changing breathing rate, heart rate, stroke volume, and peripheral resistance to match the metabolic needs of the body.

 View in Achieve
Simulation 48.1 **Blood Pressure and Heart Rate**

Autoregulation matches local blood flow to local need

The amount of blood that flows through a capillary bed is controlled by contraction or relaxation of the smooth muscle of the arteries and arterioles feeding that bed. **Figure 48.19** illustrates the flow of blood in a typical capillary bed. Blood flows into the bed from an arteriole. Smooth muscle "cuffs," or **precapillary sphincters**, on the arteriole can shut off the supply of blood to the capillary bed. When the precapillary sphincters are relaxed and the arteriole is open, blood flow through the capillaries increases.

Autoregulation depends on the sensitivity of the smooth muscle to its local chemical environment. Low O_2 concentrations and high CO_2 concentrations cause the smooth muscle to relax, thus increasing the supply of blood, which brings in more O_2 and

Blood flow through a capillary bed is controlled by the constriction of smooth muscle in the arteries and arterioles.

Vein

Artery

Arteriole

Capillary

Muscle fibers (cells)

Bed open

Venule

Throughfare vessel

Bed closed

Precapillary sphincters can open in response to low O_2, low pH, or cytokines...

...or they can constrict and shut off blood supply to the capillary bed.

Figure 48.19 Local Control of Blood Flow Low O_2 concentrations or high levels of metabolic by-products cause the smooth muscle of the arteries and arterioles to relax, thus increasing the supply of blood to the capillary bed.

START

Arterial pressure falls

Kidney blood pressure declines

Firing in arterial stretch sensors decreases

Autoregulation results in positive feedback

Kidney releases renin

Negative feedback

Autoregulatory widening of vessels

Decreased blood flow to tissue

Negative feedback

ADH released from posterior pituitary

Local accumulation of metabolic wastes

Circulating renin activates angiotensin

ADH stimulates water resorption by kidneys

Angiotensin causes vessels to constrict and stimulates thirst

Arterial pressure rises

Figure 48.20 Control of Blood Pressure through Local and Systemic Mechanisms A drop in arterial pressure reduces blood flow to tissues, resulting in local accumulation of metabolic wastes. This change in the extracellular environment stimulates autoregulatory opening of the arterioles. A fall in central blood pressure is prevented by negative-feedback mechanisms (including the release of antidiuretic hormone, ADH) that constrict arterioles in less essential tissues and stimulate maintenance of blood volume and blood pressure.

carries away CO_2—a response known as hyperemia, which means "excess blood." Increases in other by-products of metabolism, such as lactic acid, hydrogen ions, potassium, and adenosine (all of which increase in exercising muscle), also promote hyperemia. Hence activities that increase the metabolism of a tissue also induce hyperemia in that tissue. Regional autoregulation, however, sets up a dangerous positive-feedback loop (**Figure 48.20**). A fall in MAP decreases blood flow to tissues. Decreased local blood flow generates autoregulatory decreases in resistance in the arterioles serving those tissues, contributing to decreased TPR that further decreases MAP. Systemic regulatory mechanisms must counter the positive feedback caused by autoregulation.

Arterial pressure is regulated by hormonal and neural mechanisms

Control and regulation of the circulation of the blood begin with the local autoregulatory mechanisms that alter the resistance of arteries and arterioles feeding capillary beds. The demands of the capillary beds influence MAP and blood composition. Both of these provide information for the control of systemic endocrine and neural responses that return blood pressure and composition to normal. Thus circulatory functions are matched to the regional and to the overall needs of the body.

Arteries and arterioles are innervated by the autonomic nervous system, particularly the sympathetic division. The sympathetic postganglionic neurotransmitter norepinephrine binds to receptors in smooth muscle in blood vessels in the gut and other tissues not essential for "fight or flight" and causes these vessels to constrict, resulting in reduced blood flow through them and an elevation in MAP. As we discussed earlier in this chapter, increased sympathetic activity increases heart rate, and by increasing the strength of the cardiac muscle contraction, it also increases stroke volume. Thus the actions of sympathetic activation increase MAP.

Hormones also play a role in regulating arterial pressure. Epinephrine has actions similar to those of norepinephrine and is released from the adrenal medulla during massive sympathetic activation stimulated by a fall in arterial pressure or by activation of the fight-or-flight response to a dangerous threat. Another hormone, **angiotensin**, is activated when blood pressure in the kidneys falls (see Figure 48.20). In response to the fall in blood pressure, the kidneys release an enzyme, **renin**, into the circulation. Renin and another enzyme in the lungs converts a circulating protein, angiotensinogen into the active hormone angiotensin. Angiotensin has several actions: constricting arterioles located in peripheral tissues, stimulating thirst, and increasing release of another hormone **aldosterone** from the adrenal gland. Aldosterone increases Na⁺ reabsorption. All of these responses protect

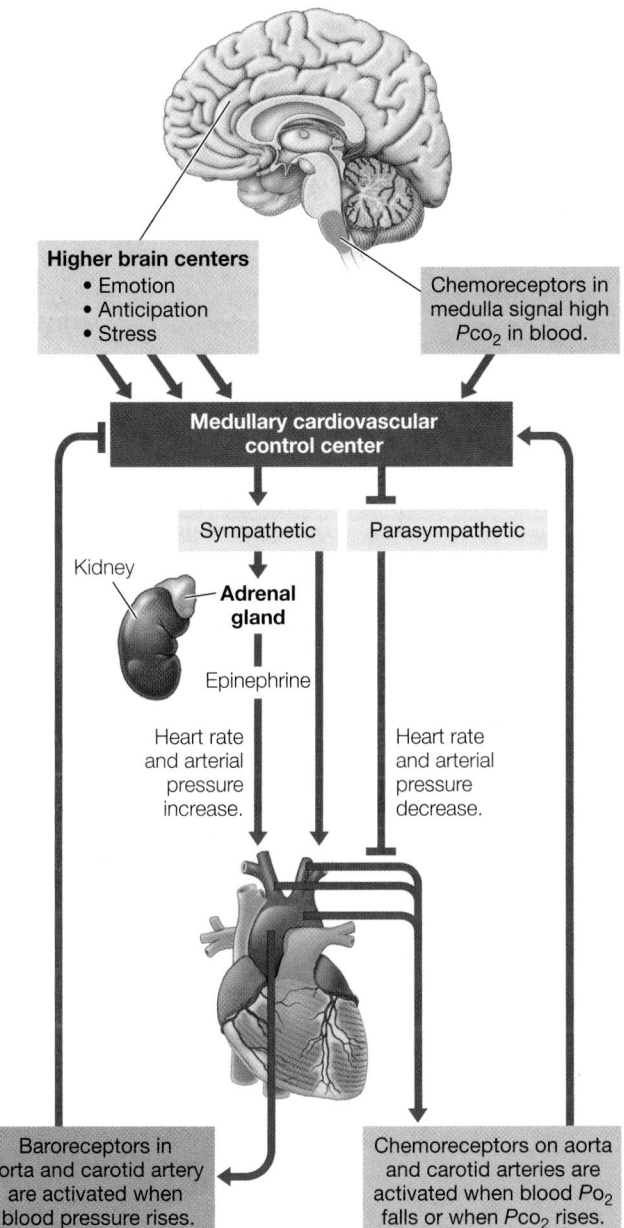

Figure 48.21 Regulating Cardiac Output The autonomic nervous system controls heart rate in response to information about blood pressure and blood composition originating in baroreceptors and chemoreceptors shown at the bottom of the figure. Information from these sensors goes to the cardiovascular control center in the medulla, where it is integrated with other information. The medullary center generates responses in the sympathetic and parasympathetic nervous systems that control cardiac output.

or increase blood volume and therefore central blood pressure necessary to maintain adequate blood flow to essential organs such as the heart, brain, and kidneys.

The autonomic nervous system activity that controls heart rate and constriction of blood vessels originates in a cardiovascular control center in the medulla. Many inputs converge on this central integrative network and influence the commands it issues via parasympathetic and sympathetic nerves (**Figure 48.21**).

Of special importance is incoming information about changes in blood pressure from **baroreceptors** (stretch receptors) in the walls of the large arteries leading to the brain—the aorta and the carotid arteries.

Increased activity in baroreceptors of the large arteries signals rising blood pressure and inhibits sympathetic nervous system signaling to arteries and arterioles while increasing parasympathetic signaling to the heart's pacemaker. As a result, the heart slows and arterioles in peripheral tissues dilate, reducing blood pressure. If pressure in the large arteries falls, the activity of the baroreceptors decreases, stimulating sympathetic output to the arteries and arterioles while reducing parasympathetic output to the heart's pacemaker. As a result, the heart beats faster and the arterioles in peripheral tissues constrict, increasing blood pressure.

Another hormone that helps stabilize blood pressure is **antidiuretic hormone** (**ADH**, also called **vasopressin**), which is secreted by the posterior pituitary in response to a fall in the activity of the baroreceptors, signaling a fall in MAP. ADH causes the kidneys to reabsorb more water and thereby maintain blood volume and increase blood pressure (see Figure 50.14). Increased activity of the baroreceptors inhibits the release of ADH, and as a result the kidneys excrete more water, reducing blood volume and contributing to a fall in arterial pressure (see Figure 48.20).

Other information that causes the cardiovascular control center to increase heart rate and blood pressure comes from chemoreceptors in the medulla, aorta, and the carotid arteries. The information from the chemoreceptors, from the baroreceptors, and from the kidney constitutes negative-feedback signals that serve to regulate MAP at optimal levels in spite of greatly changing demands of the body.

Connect the Concepts Key Concept 47.5 discusses the mechanisms for sensing CO_2 and O_2 concentrations in the blood. The medullary chemoreceptors are activated by increases in CO_2 levels and decreases in pH, and the carotid and aortic bodies are activated by falling O_2 levels. Chemoreceptors send signals to the cardiovascular regulatory center as well as to the respiratory regulatory center.

KEY CONCEPT
48.5 Recap and Assess

The delivery of blood to specific regional tissues is controlled locally by autoregulatory mechanisms that dilate or constrict arterioles. These local actions are translated into alterations in central blood pressure and composition. Those changes generate neural and hormonal negative-feedback signals that mediate corrective cardiovascular adjustments.

1. Why is autoregulation in Figure 48.20 described as a positive-feedback loop?

2. Distinguish between the roles of the two divisions of the autonomic nervous system (ANS) in regulating MAP?

3. Baroreceptor neurons have a range of firing rates depending on their degree of stretch, and at rest they are firing at the midpoint of that range. Why is this adaptive?

4. Explain how local autoregulatory controls of blood flow can stimulate hormonal adjustments of MAP.

Q and A — Are there potential therapies that could treat HCM?

Many organs of your body can shut down for a while and you can recover—but not your heart. Cardiac arrest lasting only minutes can result in death. But why should the heart of a healthy, physically fit, top-performing athlete stop? Just as physical conditioning results in making skeletal muscles bigger and stronger, it does the same for the heart. The heart responds to increased demand by getting bigger and stronger. However, if an individual has mutations in genes responsible for proteins involved in contractions of cardiac muscle, that muscle will be less efficient. To compensate for that inefficiency, the heart gets bigger than a normal heart would when repeatedly challenged by excessive exercise. Hypertrophy of the walls of the left ventricle can have two serious consequences: (1) The opening of the aorta is at the top of the heart next to the septum that divides the two ventricles. Enlargement of that septum can block the entrance to the aorta, so the cardiac output falls. (2) The bundle of His and the left and right bundle branches that convey the pacemaker potential to the ventricular muscle course down through the septum. Hypertrophy of the septum can interfere with

conduction of these critical signals. If advanced conditions of HCM are discovered, there are surgical procedures that remove some of the heart muscle to increase blood flow.

Future directions

The mutations responsible for the development of HCM are not rare, but most people who carry them live their entire lives without even knowing they are at risk for HCM. Why? Most people do not place the excessive demands on their hearts that athletes do. So what can be done to reduce the risk of death by HCM? Preventative measures such as genetic screening could allow carriers of the mutations to make decisions about whether or not to pursue extreme physical activity. Physical examinations including ECGs, sonograms, and even magnetic resonance imaging (MRI) would enable diagnosis and recommendations to decrease levels of physical exertion. The work presented in **Investigating Life: Silencing Mutant Myosin Genes** suggests a potential future treatment through gene therapy. If safe reagents could be developed to silence the mutant genes, and those reagents were applied before severe HCM developed, they could have a protective benefit.

VISUAL SUMMARY 48

You should be able to relate each summary to the adjacent figures. If you go to this visual summary in **Achieve**, you can follow links to figures, animations, activities, and simulations that will help you consolidate the material.

KEY CONCEPT

48.1 Circulatory Systems Are Transport Systems

- **Circulatory systems** consist of muscular pumps (**hearts**) that move **extracellular fluid** through vessels to serve tissues of the body. These systems can be **open** or **closed**.

- Circulatory systems transport nutrients, respiratory gases, heat, signaling molecules, immune system elements, and metabolic wastes throughout the body.

Questions

1. What are the relationships and differences between extracellular fluid, hemolymph, blood, and interstitial fluid?

2. What advantages does a closed circulatory system have for an active species? Why are insects an exception?

3. How does an animal with a closed circulatory system respond to changing demands for oxygen in its different tissues?

Figure 48.1

Mollusk circulation

Annelid worm circulation

KEY CONCEPT
48.2 Vertebrate Circulatory Systems Evolved from Single to Double Circuits

Go to **Activity 48.1**

- Vertebrate hearts pump blood through **arteries** and **arterioles** to **capillaries**, the site of exchange between blood and interstitial fluid. Blood returns to the heart through **venules** and **veins**.

- Vertebrate circulatory systems evolved from single circuits in fishes to partially or completely separate **pulmonary circuits** and **systemic circuits** in amphibians, reptiles, and mammals.

- Ectothermic reptiles shunt blood from the pulmonary to the systemic circuit when they are not breathing.

- Pulmonary and systemic circuits are completely separate in birds and mammals and operate at different pressures.

Figure 48.2

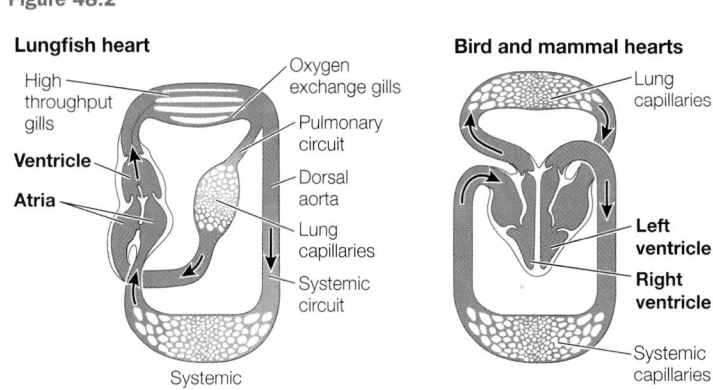

Questions

1. Explain how a lungfish can breathe in water or in air.

2. How does blood flow change in an ectothermic reptile when it isn't breathing?

3. Trace the flow of blood through a mammalian circulatory system.

KEY CONCEPT
48.3 Heart Function Depends on Properties of Cardiac Muscle

Go to **Activity 48.2** and **Animation 48.1**

- The ventricles of the mammalian heart fill mostly passively during **diastole** and pump blood into the pulmonary and systemic circuits during **systole**. Valves in the heart prevent the backflow of blood.

- The heartbeat is due to interactions of unique Ca^{2+}, Na^+, and K^+ channels that generate rhythmic action potentials in cardiac muscle **pacemaker cells**.

- Action potentials in the **sinoatrial node** cause atrial muscle to contract and the **atrioventricular node** to fire.

- Action potentials from the atrioventricular node are conducted throughout the ventricular muscle by the **bundle of His** and **Purkinje fibers**.

Figure 48.9

Pacemaker potentials spread electrotonically in atrial muscle

Figure 48.10

Ion channel changes in a ventricular muscle cell

- Sustained contraction of ventricular muscle cells is due to Ca^{2+} channels.

- The **electrocardiogram** (**ECG** or **EKG**) reflects electrical events in the heart.

Questions

1. Explain the heart sounds ("lub"/"dup") in terms of events occurring in the heart.

2. Explain how the different functions of pacemaker cells and ventricular muscle cells are due to their unique ion channels.

3. How are the contractions of the atria and the ventricles coordinated?

KEY CONCEPT

48.4 Circulatory System Functions Depend on Blood and Blood Vessels

Go to Activity 48.3

- Blood consists of plasma containing protein and ionic solutes, cells of the immune system (leukocytes), red blood cells carrying oxygen, and **platelets** that form blood clots.

- The functions of arteries as resistance vessels and of veins as capacitance vessels are reflected in their structural differences.

- Extracellular fluid filters out of capillaries where blood pressure is higher than osmotic pressure and flows back into capillaries where blood pressure is lower than osmotic pressure.

- Valves in veins and in **lymphatic ducts** enable muscle contraction to propel blood back to the heart and interstitial fluid back to the circulation, respectively.

- Buildup of **plaque** and of **thrombi** (blood clots) in arteries can block blood flow, causing heart attack and **stroke**.

Questions

1. How do platelets initiate blood clotting?

2. Capillaries are permeable to water, and blood is under pressure, so why doesn't interstitial fluid accumulate in tissues?

3. What is the progression of a healthy cardiac artery with a smooth endothelial lining to one that causes a myocardial infarction?

Figure 48.14

The tissue layers of blood vessels

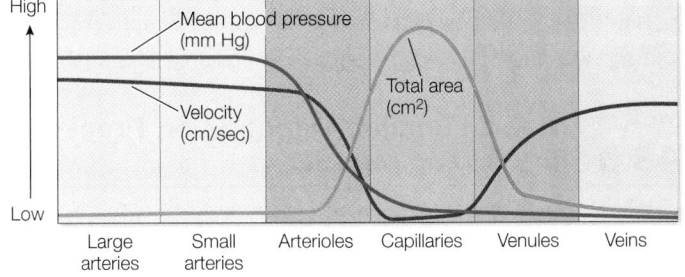

Characteristics of classes of vessels

KEY CONCEPT

48.5 Circulation Is Controlled by Hormonal and Neuronal Signals

Go to Simulation 48.1

- To meet local needs, blood flow through capillary beds is controlled by local **autoregulatory mechanisms**.

- Mean arterial pressure (MAP) depends on cardiac output and total peripheral resistance (TPR).

- **Baroreceptors** provide negative-feedback information on MAP.

- Chemoreceptors provide negative-feedback information on composition of the blood.

- **Antidiuretic hormone** (**ADH**, also called **vasopressin**) and **angiotensin** act to raise MAP.

Questions

1. What neural and hormonal mechanisms raise MAP?

2. How does cardiovascular regulation respond to variations in local autoregulation of capillary beds?

3. How do chemoreceptors and baroreceptors contribute to the regulation of MAP?

Figure 48.21

Regulation of the heart

Go to **Achieve** for the eBook, **LearningCurve**, animations, activities, simulations, and additional resources and assignments.

Nutrition, Digestion, and Absorption 49

© Yaacov Dagan/Alamy Stock Photo

KEY CONCEPTS

49.1 Food Provides Energy as well as Materials for Biosynthesis

49.2 Diverse Adaptations Support Ingestion and Digestion of Food

49.3 The Vertebrate Gastrointestinal System Is a Disassembly Line

49.4 Nutrient Availability Is Controlled and Regulated

In Pima populations, historic occurrences of food deprivation may have imposed selection for genes that improve the efficiency of managing the energy obtained from food. With modern diets and lifestyles, these "thrifty genes" can contribute to obesity and diabetes.

▶Investigating**LIFE**

Thrifty Phenotypes

For millennia the Pima of southwestern North America were hunter–gatherers, supplementing their diet with subsistence agriculture. Their environment was arid, so they developed sophisticated irrigation systems; even so, they frequently encountered drought and subsequent starvation. Today most ethnic Pima in North America are clinically obese. As a population they are one of the heaviest in the world.

Obesity contributes to health problems such as diabetes, high blood pressure, and heart disease. Diabetes incidence in the Pima is seven times the national average. Two-thirds of Pima adults over age 40 are diabetic, and diabetes is occurring in younger individuals than previously seen. What has caused such a radical health change in the population? Two interacting factors are involved: genetics and lifestyle.

Geneticists hypothesize that recurring episodes of starvation produce strong selective pressure for "thrifty genes"—particular alleles of the genes involved in digestion, absorption, and energy storage that result in above-average efficiency in converting food into fat. Thrifty genes would carry a strong selective advantage when food is scarce. The Pima display a "thrifty" phenotype. They have low resting metabolic rates and convert food into fat readily. Insulin facilitates conversion of dietary sugar into fat. For

many Pima, consuming a standard amount of glucose causes their insulin levels to rise three times higher than it does in people of European ancestry.

Lifestyle also plays a role in the Pima obesity epidemic. Instead of eating their traditional diet, the Pima now eat a high-calorie, high-fat Western diet, and they engage in less physical activity than their ancestors did. A population of Pima living in northern Mexico are genetically the same as the Arizona population. However, they eat traditional foods and live a traditional lifestyle that involves much physical activity. Obesity and diabetes are not prevalent among the Mexico Pima.

A high-calorie diet and sedentary lifestyle affect not just the Pima but contribute to the overall obesity epidemic in the U.S. Recently an additional factor that might contribute to obesity and diabetes has been discovered—the type of food that is eaten. The composition of the diet influences the populations of gut microbes, and those microbes influence outcomes of digestion. Apparently calories are not all equal; their impact depends on their origin.

 If the nutritional values were the same, could different foods have different impacts on health? (Find the answer on page 1117.)

KEY CONCEPT
49.1 Food Provides Energy as well as Materials for Biosynthesis

Learning Objectives

49.1.1 Describe energy storage adaptations in animal species.

49.1.2 Explain challenges related to obtaining all essential amino acids from the diet.

49.1.3 Describe mineral macro- and micronutrients and their functions.

49.1.4 Give examples of water-soluble and fat-soluble vitamins and their effects on an animal's body.

Animals are **heterotrophs**—they derive their nutrition from eating other organisms. In contrast, **autotrophs** (most plants, some bacteria, some archaea, and some protists) can use solar energy or inorganic chemical energy to synthesize all of their components. Of course, some plants are also heterotrophs.

Connect the Concepts Carnivorous and parasitic plants are discussed in Key Concept 34.4.

Directly and indirectly, heterotrophs take advantage of—indeed, depend on—the organic synthesis carried out by autotrophs and have evolved an enormous diversity of adaptations to exploit this resource (**Figure 49.1**). In this key concept we describe how animals use food, be it plants or other animals, to obtain energy and building blocks of complex molecules. We also consider the need for special mineral nutrients and organic molecules and the diseases that result when they are lacking in the diet.

Energy needs and expenditures can be measured

Energy—the capacity to do work—comes in different forms, including electric, heat, chemical, and nuclear energy. A calorie (note the small *c*) is a unit of heat energy; specifically, it is the amount of heat necessary to raise the temperature of 1 gram of water 1 degree Celsius. Because this is such a tiny amount of energy, physiologists commonly use the **kilocalorie** (**kcal**) as a unit of measure (1 kcal = 1,000 calories). Nutritionists also use the kilocalorie as a standard unit of energy, but they traditionally refer to it as the **Calorie** (**Cal**), which is capitalized to distinguish it from the single calorie.

Just about any food container you pick up in the United States carries the label "Nutrition Facts," which includes the item "Calories." How do Calories (or kcal) relate to the discussion in Chapter 9 about how energy in the chemical bonds of food molecules is transferred to the high-energy phosphate bonds of adenosine triphosphate (ATP) and is then used to do cellular work? And why do we use heat energy as a measure of nutrition?

The reason is found in the laws of thermodynamics, which state that energy cannot be created or destroyed, but can be converted from one form to another. However, every energy conversion is inefficient; a large portion of the original energy always ends up as heat. Whether we are using the energy in glucose to make ATP or are using that ATP to power muscle contraction or ion transport, most of the available chemical energy is lost as heat. The bottom line is that if an animal is not growing, not doing any external work, and

not changing its body temperature, the heat it loses to the environment is a measure of its total energy expenditure, or metabolism.

Connect the Concepts The laws of thermodynamics and their application to biological energetics are described in Key Concept 8.1.

An animal's energy needs must be met by the ingestion, digestion, and assimilation of food. The basal energy expenditure (basal metabolic rate, BMR) of a human is 1,300–1,490 Cal/day for an adult female and 1,600–1,800 Cal/day for an adult male. Any physical activity adds to the BMR. For a person doing sedentary work, about 30% of the total Calories expended are used for skeletal muscle activity; for a person doing heavy physical labor, more than 95% of caloric expenditure is for skeletal muscle activity.

Macronutrients are the components of food that provide energy. They are fats, carbohydrates, and proteins. Fats yield 9.5 Cal/gram, carbohydrates 4.2 Cal/gram, and proteins about 4.1 Cal/gram. **Figure 49.2** shows some equivalences of food, energy, and energy consumption.

(A)

(B)

Figure 49.1 Heterotrophs Get Energy from Autotrophs
(A) Herbivores get their energy directly from autotrophs. The large herbivores of the African grasslands must consume huge amounts of plant matter to fulfill their nutritional needs. **(B)** A carnivore's energy is indirectly obtained from autotrophs, since the energy stored in a prey animal was originally obtained from autotrophs.

Figure 49.2 **Food Energy and How We Use It**   Estimates of the energy contained in four common food items is shown at the left. Note: Caloric contents of these food examples can vary conciderably. The graphs indicate about how long it would take a person with a basal energy requirement of about 1,800 Cal/day to use the equivalent amount of energy while resting, walking, or jogging.

Even though the units calorie, kilocalorie, and Calorie remain in popular use, most scientists now use the International System of Units (ISU). In this system the basic unit of energy is the joule: 1 joule (J) = 0.239 calories, and the measure of energy use is 1 J/second = 1 watt. You are familiar with lightbulb ratings, so think about that when you convert kcal/day into watts. The 1,700 Cal/day energy expenditure of the average man converts to 82 watts (note that a watt includes the time dimension, so it is a rate of energy use).

Thus it is possible to quantify the caloric value of any food an animal eats. It is also possible to quantify the caloric expenditure of any activity or behavior an animal performs. By comparing calories consumed with calories expended, we can construct **energy budgets** that allow ecologists and evolutionary biologists to apply a cost–benefit analysis to feeding behavior.

> **Connect the Concepts** Any behavior involves energetic costs, opportunity costs, and risk costs and can be measured in terms of its effect on reproductive success. Key Concept 51.4 explores costs and benefits of various behaviors, illustrating how measures of metabolism permit quantitative analysis of evolutionary adaptations.

Sources of energy are stored in the body

Although cells of the body use energy continuously, most animals do not eat continuously and so must store fuel molecules that can be released as needed between meals. Carbohydrates are stored in the liver and in muscle cells as glycogen, but the total glycogen stored represents only about a day's basal energy requirement. Fat is the most important form of stored energy in the bodies of animals. Not only does fat have more energy per gram than glycogen, but it can be stored with little associated water, making it more compact and less expensive to carry. Migrating birds store energy as fat to fuel their long flights; if they had to store the same amount of energy as glycogen, they would be too heavy to fly. Proteins are not used as energy storage compounds, but the body's proteins can be metabolized as an energy source of last resort.

If an animal takes in too little food to meet its energy requirements, it starts to metabolize some of the molecules of its own body. This "self-consumption" begins with the energy storage compounds glycogen and fat. Once fat reserves are seriously depleted, the body increases its metabolism of proteins for energy (**Figure 49.3A**). The first proteins to be sacrificed are those of the blood plasma. The loss of plasma proteins decreases the osmotic concentration of the plasma, resulting in increased loss of fluid from the blood to the interstitial spaces (edema). Accumulation of fluid in the extremities and abdomen is the classic sign of kwashiorkor, a disease caused by chronic protein deficiency (**Figure 49.3B**). Continued protein loss damages the body's organs, eventually leading to death.

When an animal consistently takes in more food than it needs to meet its energy requirements, the excess nutrients are stored as increased body mass. First glycogen reserves build up; then additional dietary carbohydrates, fats, and proteins are converted to body fat. In some species, such as those that hibernate, seasonal overnutrition is an important adaptation for surviving periods when food is not available. In humans, however, overnutrition can be a serious health hazard, increasing the risk of high blood pressure, heart attack, diabetes, and other disorders, as seen in the Pima that we discussed in the chapter opener.

Food provides carbon skeletons for biosynthesis

Every animal must take in certain organic molecules that it cannot synthesize for itself but needs to serve as building blocks for its own complex organic molecules. The acetyl group (CH_3CO-) is one such required building block, supplying the **carbon skeleton** of larger organic molecules (**Figure 49.4**). Animals cannot synthesize acetyl groups from carbon, oxygen, and hydrogen molecules but must obtain them from food. Acetyl groups can be derived from the metabolism of almost any food, but they originate in plants.

Acetyl groups are never in short supply for an adequately nourished animal. However, some groups supplying carbon

(A)

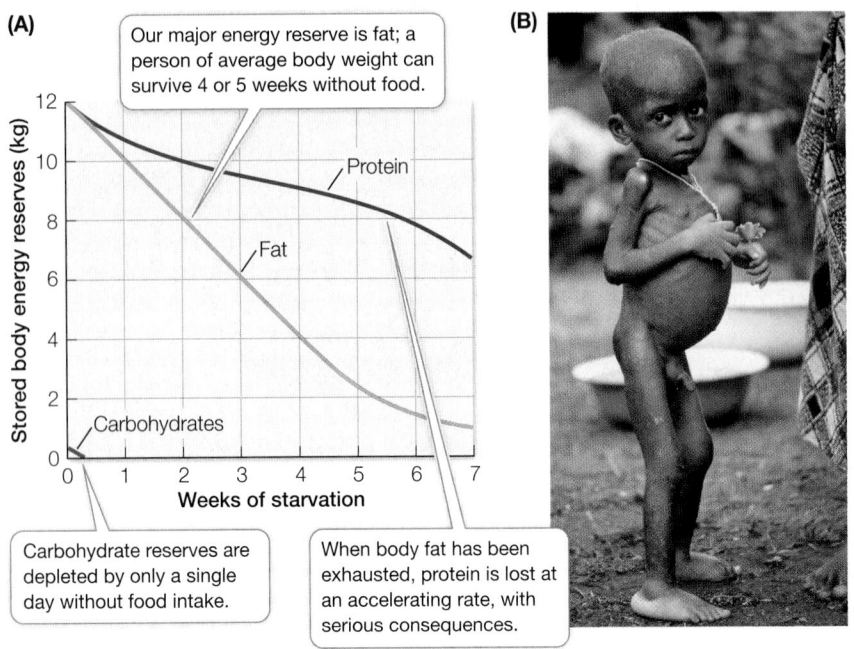

Our major energy reserve is fat; a person of average body weight can survive 4 or 5 weeks without food.

Carbohydrate reserves are depleted by only a single day without food intake.

When body fat has been exhausted, protein is lost at an accelerating rate, with serious consequences.

(B)

© Jean-Claude Sauer/Paris Match/Getty Images

Figure 49.3 The Course of Starvation (A) When a person is subjected to undernutrition, the body's energy reserves are depleted. (B) The swollen abdomen, hands, and feet of this boy are due to edema. Along with his spindly limbs, these are symptoms of kwashiorkor, a disease resulting from the body breaking down blood proteins and muscle tissue to fuel metabolism. (A after A. C. Guyton. 1971. *Basic Human Physiology: Normal Function and Mechanisms of Disease*. W. B. Saunders: Philadelphia.)

skeletons can be deficient in an animal's diet even if caloric intake is adequate. One such group includes certain amino acids, the building blocks of proteins. Animals can synthesize some of their own amino acids by using carbon skeletons from acetyl or other groups and transferring to them amine groups ($-NH_2$) derived from other amino acids. However, most animals cannot synthesize all the amino acids they need and thus must obtain certain **essential amino acids** from food. If an animal does not take in enough of even one of its essential amino acids, its protein

synthesis is impaired and therefore its capacity to maintain many functions such as tissue repair and synthesis of many molecules such as enzymes, ion channels, transporters, hormones, etc. is compromised.

Essential amino acids vary by species. Most researchers agree that adult humans must obtain eight essential amino acids from their food: isoleucine, leucine, lysine, methionine, phenylalanine, threonine, tryptophan, and valine. All eight are available in milk, eggs, meat, and soybean products, but most plant foods do not contain adequate quantities of all eight, so a strict vegetarian diet carries a risk of protein malnutrition. A **complementary diet** of plant foods, however, supplies all eight essential amino acids (**Figure 49.5**). In general, grains (such as rice, wheat, and corn) are complemented by legumes (such as beans and peas). Long before the chemical basis for complementarity was understood, societies with little access to meat developed complementary diets. Many Central and South American peoples traditionally eat beans with corn, and the native peoples of North America complemented their beans with squash.

Human infants are thought to require four additional amino acids in their diets: histidine, tyrosine, cysteine, and arginine. Also, some amino acids are required by individuals with certain metabolic disorders who cannot synthesize them adequately. For example, individuals with the genetic disease phenylketonuria lack the enzyme for converting phenylalanine to tyrosine (see Key Concept 15.2) and must obtain tyrosine from their diets. They must keep their dietary intake of phenylalanine low to prevent its accumulation to toxic levels.

Why are dietary proteins completely digested to their constituent amino acids before being used by the body? Wouldn't it

Figure 49.4 The Acetyl Group Is an Acquired Carbon Skeleton Animals cannot synthesize the acetyl group for themselves, but they ingest it in their food and use it to synthesize a wide variety of molecules.

Animals use acetyl groups obtained from their food to build more complex organic molecules.

The acetyl group is present in virtually all of the foods animals ingest.

Protein, carbohydrate, or fat metabolism

Steroid hormones

Acetyl group carbon skeleton

Oxaloacetate

Citrate

Amino acids, heme, and other compounds

Fatty acids

Figure 49.5 A Strategy for Vegetarians By combining cereal grains with legumes, an adult vegetarian can obtain all eight essential amino acids.

be more energy-efficient to reuse some dietary proteins directly? There are several reasons why ingested proteins are not used "as is":

- Macromolecules such as proteins are not readily absorbed by the cells of the gut, but their constituent monomers (such as amino acids) are readily absorbed.

- Protein structure and function are highly species-specific. A protein that functions optimally in one species might not function well in another.

- Foreign proteins entering the body directly from the gut would be recognized as invaders and would be attacked by the immune system.

Humans can synthesize almost all the lipids required by the body using acetyl groups obtained from food (see Figure 49.4), but we must have a dietary source of two **essential fatty acids**—linoleic acid and alpha-linolenic acid—that we cannot synthesize. Linoleic acid is needed by mammals to synthesize other unsaturated fatty acids, such as arachidonic acid, which is a component of several signal molecules, including prostaglandins. Essential fatty acids are also necessary components of membrane phospholipids. A deficiency of linoleic acid can lead to problems such as infertility and impaired lactation, but because it is commonly present in vegetable oils, a deficiency is unlikely in an adequately nourished individual.

Animals need mineral elements for a variety of functions

Principal mineral elements that animals require are listed in Table 49.1. Elements required in large amounts are called **mineral macronutrients**; those required in only tiny amounts (generally less

TABLE 49.1 | Mineral Elements Required by Animals

Element	Source in human diet	Major functions
MINERAL MACRONUTRIENTS		
Calcium (Ca)	Dairy foods, eggs, green leafy vegetables, whole grains, legumes, nuts, meat	Found in bones and teeth; blood clotting; nerve and muscle action; enzyme activation
Chlorine (Cl)	Table salt (NaCl), meat, eggs, vegetables, dairy foods	Water balance; digestion (as HCl); principal negative ion in extracellular fluid
Magnesium (Mg)	Green vegetables, meat, whole grains, nuts, milk, legumes	Required by many enzymes; found in bones and teeth
Phosphorus (P)	Dairy foods, eggs, meat, whole grains, legumes, nuts	Component of nucleic acids, ATP, and phospholipids; bone formation; buffers; metabolism of sugars
Potassium (K)	Meat, whole grains, fruits, vegetables	Nerve and muscle action; protein synthesis; principal positive ion in cells
Sodium (Na)	Table salt, dairy foods, meat, eggs	Nerve and muscle action; water balance; principal positive ion in extracellular fluid
Sulfur (S)	Meat, eggs, dairy foods, nuts, legumes	Found in proteins and coenzymes; detoxification of harmful substances
MINERAL MICRONUTRIENTS		
Chromium (Cr)	Meat, dairy foods, whole grains, legumes, yeast	Glucose metabolism
Cobalt (Co)	Meat, tap water	Found in vitamin B_{12}; formation of red blood cells
Copper (Cu)	Liver, meat, fish, shellfish, legumes, whole grains, nuts	Found in active site of many redox enzymes and electron carriers; production of hemoglobin; bone formation
Fluorine (F)	Most municipal water supplies	Found in teeth; helps prevent tooth decay
Iodine (I)	Fish, shellfish, iodized salt	Found in thyroid hormones
Iron (Fe)	Liver, meat, green vegetables, eggs, whole grains, legumes, nuts	Found in active sites of many redox enzymes and electron carriers, hemoglobin, and myoglobin
Manganese (Mn)	Organ meats, whole grains, legumes, nuts, tea, coffee	Activates many enzymes
Molybdenum (Mo)	Organ meats, dairy foods, whole grains, green vegetables, legumes	Found in some enzymes
Selenium (Se)	Meat, seafood, whole grains, eggs, milk, garlic	Fat metabolism
Zinc (Zn)	Liver, fish, shellfish, and many other foods	Found in some enzymes and some transcription factors; insulin physiology

than 100 mg/day) are called **mineral micronutrients**. Some mineral micronutrients are required in such minute amounts that deficiencies are never observed, but the elements are nevertheless essential.

Calcium is an example of a mineral macronutrient. It is the fifth most abundant element in the body; a 70-kg person contains about 1.2 kg of calcium. Calcium phosphate is the principal structural material in bones and teeth. Muscle contraction, neural function, and many other intracellular functions in animals require calcium ions (Ca^{2+}). The turnover of calcium in the extracellular fluid is high, as bones are constantly being remodeled and calcium is constantly entering and leaving cells. Calcium is lost from the body in urine, sweat, and feces, so it must be replaced regularly. Adult humans require 800–1,000 mg of calcium per day in their diet.

Connect the Concepts Many physiological processes are affected by Ca^{2+}; therefore it is essential that the blood levels stay between 9 and 11 mg/100 mL. This is only 0.1% of the Ca^{2+} in the body. About 1% is intracellular and 99% is in the bones; thus it is a challenge to maintain tiny, but critical, blood levels in the face of such huge reservoirs. Hormonal regulation of blood Ca^{2+} is discussed in Key Concept 39.4, and the roles of Ca^{2+} in muscle function are discussed in Key Concept 46.1.

Iron is an example of a mineral micronutrient. It is found throughout the body because it is the oxygen-binding atom in hemoglobin and myoglobin and is a component of enzymes in the respiratory chain. Nevertheless, the total amount of iron in a 70-kg person is only about 4 g, and since iron is recycled efficiently in the body and is not lost in the urine, we require only about 15 mg per day in our food. Despite the small amount required, insufficient iron is the most common mineral nutrient deficiency in the world today. Iron deficiency leads to anemia, a condition that renders individuals weak and tired all the time.

View in **Achieve**
Activity 49.1 **Mineral Elements Required by Animals**

Animals must obtain vitamins from food

Like essential amino acids and fatty acids, **vitamins** are carbon compounds that an animal requires for growth and metabolism but cannot synthesize for itself. Most vitamins function as coenzymes or parts of coenzymes (see Key Concept 8.4).

Each species has its own vitamin requirements. Primates, for example, require vitamin C (ascorbic acid). While most mammals can make their own ascorbic acid, primates (including humans) cannot, so for primates, ascorbic acid is a vitamin. If we do not get vitamin C in our food, we develop scurvy, a disease characterized by bleeding gums, loss of teeth, subcutaneous hemorrhages, and slow wound healing. Scurvy was a frequently fatal problem for sailors on long voyages until late in the eighteenth century when a Scottish physician, James Lind, discovered that the disease could be prevented if the sailors ate fresh greens and citrus fruit. The British Admiralty made limes standard provisions for its ships (and British sailors have been called "limeys" ever since). When the active ingredient in limes was isolated, it was named ascorbic ("without scurvy") acid.

Humans require 13 vitamins; these are divided into two groups, water-soluble and fat-soluble (**Table 49.2**). When water-soluble vitamins are ingested in excess of the body's needs, they are simply eliminated in the urine. (This is the fate of much of the large doses of vitamin C that people take.) Fat-soluble vitamins, however, can accumulate in body fat and may build up to toxic levels in the liver if taken in excess.

The fat-soluble vitamin D (calciferol), which is essential for absorbing and metabolizing calcium, is a special case because the body can synthesize it. (As noted in Key Concept 39.4, vitamin D is by definition a hormone.) Certain lipids present in the human

TABLE 49.2 | Vitamins in the Human Diet

Vitamin	Source	Function	Deficiency symptoms
WATER-SOLUBLE			
B_1 (thiamin)	Liver, legumes, whole grains	Coenzyme in cellular respiration	Beriberi, loss of appetite, fatigue
B_2 (riboflavin)	Dairy foods, meat, eggs, green leafy vegetables	Coenzyme in FAD	Lesions in corners of mouth, eye irritation, skin disorders
B_3 (niacin)	Meat, fowl, liver, yeast	Coenzyme in NAD and NADP	Pellagra, skin disorders, diarrhea, mental disorders
B_5 (pantothenic acid)	Liver, eggs, yeast	Found in acetyl CoA	Adrenal problems, reproductive problems
B_6 (pyridoxine)	Liver, whole grains, dairy foods	Coenzyme in amino acid metabolism	Anemia, slow growth, skin problems, convulsions
B_7 (biotin)	Liver, yeast, bacteria in gut	Found in coenzymes	Skin problems, loss of hair
B_{12} (cobalamin)	Liver, meat, dairy foods, eggs	Formation of nucleic acids, proteins, red blood cells	Pernicious anemia
Folic acid	Vegetables, eggs, liver, whole grains	Coenzyme in formation of heme and nucleotides	Anemia
C (ascorbic acid)	Citrus fruits, tomatoes, potatoes	Formation of connective tissues; antioxidant	Scurvy, slow healing, poor bone growth
FAT-SOLUBLE			
A (retinol)	Fruits, vegetables, liver, dairy foods	Found in visual pigments	Night blindness
D (calciferol)	Fortified milk, fish oils, sunshine	Absorption of calcium and phosphate	Rickets
E (tocopherol)	Meat, dairy foods, whole grains	Muscle maintenance, antioxidant	Anemia
K (menadione)	Intestinal bacteria, liver	Blood clotting	Blood-clotting problems

body can be converted into vitamin D by the action of ultraviolet light on the skin. Thus vitamin D must be obtained in the diet by individuals with inadequate exposure to the Sun.

The need for vitamin D may have been an important factor in the evolution of skin color. For humans living in equatorial and low latitudes, dark skin pigmentation is adaptive, as it protects against the damaging effects of ultraviolet radiation. These peoples generally expose extensive areas of skin to the Sun on a regular basis, so their skin synthesizes adequate amounts of vitamin D. Most races that adapted to life in the higher latitudes lost this dark skin pigmentation, probably because lighter skin facilitates vitamin D production in the relatively small areas of skin exposed to sunlight during the short days of winter. The dark-skinned Inuit peoples of the Arctic are an exception to the correlation between latitude and skin pigmentation, but the Inuit obtain ample vitamin D from the large amounts of animal fat (especially whale blubber) and fish oils in their diet.

 View in Achieve
Activity 49.2   Vitamins in the Human Diet

Nutrient deficiencies result in diseases

The lack of an essential nutrient in the diet produces a state of **malnutrition**, and chronic malnutrition leads to a characteristic **deficiency disease** (see Table 49.2). We discussed kwashiorkor (protein deficiency) and scurvy (vitamin C deficiency). Another deficiency disease, beriberi, was directly involved in the discovery of vitamins.

Beriberi, which means "extreme weakness," became prevalent in Asia in the nineteenth century when it became standard practice to mill rice to a white polish and discard the hulls present in brown rice. A critical observation was that chickens and pigeons developed beriberi-like symptoms when they were fed only polished rice. In 1912 Casimir Funk, a Polish scientist working in England, cured pigeons of beriberi by feeding them discarded rice hulls.

At the time of Funk's discovery, all diseases were thought either to be caused by microorganisms or to be inherited. Funk suggested that beriberi and some other diseases are dietary in origin and result from deficiencies in specific substances. Funk coined the term "vitamines" from "vital amines" because he mistakenly thought that all these substances vital for life were compounds with amine groups. In 1926 thiamin (vitamin B_1)—the substance lost in the rice milling process—was the first vitamin to be isolated in pure form.

Deficiency diseases can also result from an inability to absorb or process an essential nutrient even if it is present in the diet. Vitamin B_{12} (cobalamin), for example, is present in all foods of animal origin. Since plants neither use nor produce vitamin B_{12}, a strictly vegetarian diet (not supplemented with dairy products or vitamin pills) can lead to a B_{12} deficiency disease called pernicious anemia, characterized by a failure of red blood cells to mature. The most common cause of pernicious anemia, however, is not a lack of vitamin B_{12} in the diet but an inability to absorb it. Normally cells in the stomach lining secrete a peptide called intrinsic factor that binds to vitamin B_{12} and makes it absorbable by the small intestine. Conditions that damage the stomach lining, such as alcoholism or gastritis, can thus lead to pernicious anemia.

Inadequate mineral nutrition can also lead to deficiency diseases. Examples are hypothyroidism and goiter resulting from iodine deficiency (see Key Concept 39.4), and anemia resulting

from iron deficiency. Iodine deficiency is almost unheard of in the developed world because we add iodide to salt. However, it is still a major health problem in large segments of the human population.

49.1 Recap and Assess

As heterotrophs, animals must obtain the energy and molecular building blocks for biosynthesis from their food. Energy can come from the metabolism of carbohydrates, fats, and proteins. Molecular building blocks include carbon skeletons, vitamins, and minerals. Lack of essential nutrients results in deficiency diseases.

1. Gray whales (*Eschrichtius robustus*) migrate each year from their summer range in the Bering and Chukchi Seas to their winter range off Mexico (see Figure 51.13). During their migrations and their stay in Mexican waters, they eat very little, if anything. What is their energy source over this long time, and what are the advantages of this energy source?

2. Inuit peoples do not eat the liver of polar bears (*Ursus maritimus*) because it contains so much vitamin A that consuming it produces a serious disease called hypervitaminosis A. Why isn't there a disease called hypervitaminosis C?

3. Anemia is lack of the mineral micronutrient iron. The incidence of anemia is greater in premenopausal women than in men. Why?

4. A comatose patient is fed a nutrient mix through a food tube into the stomach, but a patient with a nonfunctional gastrointestinal system will receive a nutrient mix via blood vessels. Mixes delivered into the stomach include proteins, but mixes delivered into blood vessels do not. Explain why, and what must take the place of proteins in the mix delivered into blood vessels.

We have surveyed the essential elements of nutrition in animals. Next we look at various methods and adaptations by which animals obtain the food they need, and the mechanisms they use to extract nutrients from their food.

49.2 Diverse Adaptations Support Ingestion and Digestion of Food

Learning Objectives

49.2.1 Compare the feeding and digestive adaptations of different species.

49.2.2 Relate structural features of animal guts to their functions and adaptive significance in digestion.

49.2.3 Describe digestive enzymes that are present in animal guts.

49.2.4 Explain the importance of the microbiome in the digestion of food.

Heterotrophic organisms can be classified by how they acquire their nutrition. **Saprobes** (also called saprotrophs) are organisms that absorb nutrients from dead organic matter. Most saprobes are either protists or fungi. **Detritivores**, or **decomposers**, such as earthworms and crabs, actively feed on dead organic material. Animals that feed on living organisms are **predators: herbivores** prey on plants, **carnivores** prey on animals, and **omnivores** prey on both. **Filter feeders**, such as clams and blue whales (*Balaenoptera musculus*), prey on small organisms by filtering them from the aquatic environment. **Fluid feeders** include mosquitoes, aphids, leeches, and hummingbirds. The anatomical adaptations that enable a species to exploit a particular source of nutrition are usually obvious, but physiological and biochemical adaptations are also important.

The food of herbivores is often low in energy and hard to digest

Most vegetation is coarse, difficult to break down, and has low energy content. Therefore herbivores spend a great deal of time feeding and processing their food. Many have striking adaptations for feeding, such as the trunk (a flexible, gripping nose) of the elephant or the huge bill of the fruit-eating toucan, which can be half as long as its body. Many types of grinding, rasping, cutting, and shredding mouthparts have evolved in invertebrates for ingesting plant material, and the teeth of herbivorous vertebrates have been shaped by selection to tear, crush, and grind coarse plant matter.

The elephant provides an example of the importance of teeth. Elephants have six chewing teeth per quadrant, which appear one at a time. The first is present at birth, and subsequent ones appear at the back of the jaw and move forward as the elephant ages. The first falls out at 2–3 years of age, the second at 4–6 years of age, and so forth until the last, and biggest, one (20 cm long and 4 kg) is worn out sometime past 60 years of age. With the loss of that last tooth, the elephant starves and dies.

The digestive processes of herbivores can be quite specialized. An example is the koala (*Phascolarctos cinereus*), which almost exclusively eats leaves of eucalyptus trees. These leaves are very fibrous, low in usable energy and protein, and high in toxic chemicals. The koala has strong jaws for grinding the leaves, a very long gut for fermenting them, enzymes in its liver for detoxifying chemicals in the leaves, and a low metabolic rate (i.e., it expends little energy) to compensate for low energy intake.

Carnivores must find, capture, and kill prey

The predatory behaviors of many carnivores are legendary—the hunting skills of hawks, wolves, and tigers, for example. Carnivores have evolved stealth, speed, power, large jaws, sharp teeth, and strong gripping appendages. They also have evolved remarkable means of detecting prey. Bats use echolocation, pit vipers sense infrared radiation from the warm bodies of their prey (see the Chapter 44 opener), and certain fishes detect electric fields created in the water by their prey. There are many fascinating examples of adaptations for capturing prey, such as the immobilizing venom of many snakes, the long sticky tongues of chameleons, and the webs of spiders.

Some predators digest their prey externally. For example, a spider injects insect prey with digestive enzymes and then sucks out the liquefied contents, leaving behind the empty exoskeletons frequently seen in old spider webs. The majority of animals, however, digest their food internally. For many, the process of digestion begins with the physical breaking down of the food items by the teeth.

Vertebrate species have distinctive teeth

Teeth are adapted for the acquisition and initial processing of specific types of foods. Because they are among the hardest structures of the body, an animal's teeth remain in the environment long after it dies. Paleontologists use teeth to identify animals that lived in the distant past and to deduce their feeding behavior.

In general, teeth of all vertebrates have the same, three-layered structure (Figure 49.6A). An extremely hard material called **enamel**, composed principally of calcium phosphate, covers the crown of the tooth. Both the crown and root contain a layer of bony material called **dentine**, inside of which is a **pulp cavity** containing blood vessels, nerves, and the cells that produce the dentine.

There is a great deal of homology in the dentition of mammals, but the shapes and organization of mammalian teeth are

(A)

(B)

Figure 49.6 Mammalian Teeth **(A)** A mammalian tooth has three layers: enamel, dentine, and a pulp cavity. **(B)** The teeth of different mammalian species are specialized for different diets. This illustration depicts the teeth of the lower jaw, viewed from above.

View in Achieve
Activity 49.3 Mammalian Teeth

adaptations to different diets (**Figure 49.6B**). In general, incisors are used for cutting, chopping, and gnawing; canines are used for stabbing, gripping, and ripping; and molars and premolars (the cheek teeth) are used for shearing, crushing, and grinding. The highly varied diet of humans is reflected in our multipurpose set of teeth, as is common among omnivores.

Digestion usually begins in a body cavity

Animals take food into a body cavity that is continuous with the outside environment. They secrete digestive enzymes into that cavity, and the enzymes break down the food into nutrient molecules that can be absorbed by the cells lining the cavity.

The simplest digestive system is found in the simplest animals such as sponges. Water flows from the environment through the body of the sponge in water channels, and individual cells capture food particles from the water (see Figure 29.2B). A slightly more specialized digestive system is a **gastrovascular cavity**, which connects to the outside world through a single opening. Cnidarians, such as jellyfishes, capture prey using stinging nematocysts and use their tentacles to cram the prey into their gastrovascular cavities. Enzymes in the gastrovascular cavity partially digest the prey. Cells lining the cavity take in small food particles by endocytosis. The vesicles created by endocytosis then fuse with lysosomes containing digestive enzymes, and intracellular digestion completes the breakdown of the food. Nutrients are released to the cytoplasm as the vesicles break down.

Tubular guts have an opening at each end

Animals classified as bilaterians (see Key Concept 29.1) have a tubular digestive system called a **gastrointestinal system** or simply **gut**. The gut begins with a mouth that takes in food. The food is moved through the length of the gut as it is sequentially disassembled or digested, and the smallest units of the digested food are absorbed across the gut wall. Solid digestive wastes are eliminated through an **anus**. Different regions in the tubular gut are specialized for particular functions (**Figure 49.7**). These functions must be coordinated so they occur in the proper sequence, and they must be regulated so they occur slowly enough to allow complete digestion but quickly enough to supply the energy needs of the animal.

In the mouth cavity, food may be physically fragmented by teeth (in many vertebrates), by a **radula** (in snails), or by **mandibles** (in many arthropods). In most birds, food is ground by small stones in an early, muscular portion of the gut called the **gizzard**. Some animals, such as snakes, simply ingest whole prey with little or no fragmentation. Teeth in these species are angled backward to keep the prey moving in only one direction while being slowly swallowed. **Stomachs** and **crops** are storage chambers that enable animals to ingest relatively large amounts of food when it is available, and then digest it gradually. In these storage chambers, food may be further fragmented and mixed, and in most vertebrates it is an important site of digestion. Food delivered into the next section of the gut, the **intestine**, is in small particles, well mixed, and usually partially digested.

Most digestion occurs in the intestine, and nutrients, water, and ions are absorbed across its walls. Glands secrete digestive enzymes into the intestine, and other enzymes are produced and secreted by cells lining the intestine. The final segment of the intestine recovers

Earthworm

Cockroach

Rabbit

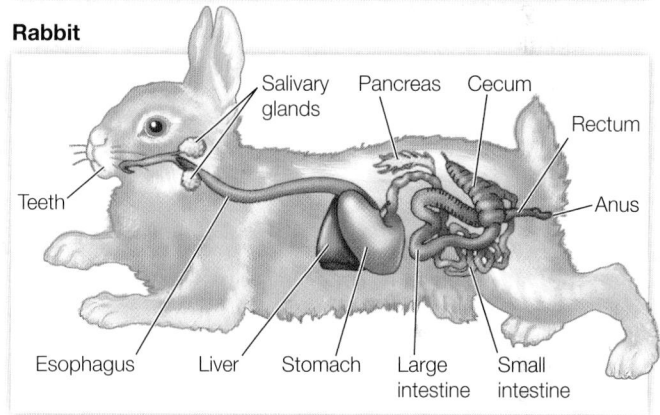

Figure 49.7 Compartments for Digestion and Absorption Most invertebrates and all vertebrates have a tubular gut that begins with a mouth where food is taken in, and ends in an anus where waste is eliminated. Between these two structures are specialized regions for digestion and nutrient absorption; the structures in these regions are adapted to different diets and vary from species to species.

water and ions and stores undigested wastes, or **feces**, so they can be released to the environment at an appropriate time or place. A muscular **rectum** near the anus assists in expelling feces.

In many animals, the parts of the gut that absorb nutrients have greater surface areas than would be expected of a simple tube. The simplest way to increase the surface area of a tube without changing its diameter is to produce an infolding. Such an infolding of the gut, called a typhlosole, is seen in earthworms (**Figure 49.8A**). Sharks, which have large stomachs but short intestines, have a unique adaptation called a spiral valve (**Figure 49.8B**). The lower region of the intestine is enlarged and has an internal structure that forces the food to pass through it in a spiral fashion (like going down a spiral staircase). The walls of the spiral present a large surface area for absorption of nutrients. This spiral passage, however, will not accommodate large chunks of food or undigestible matter, so food remains in the stomach for a long time to

(A) Intestinal infolding in the earthworm

Earthworms have a typhlosole, a longitudinal infolding of the intestinal wall.

Intestine

(B) The spiral valve in the shark

Sharks have relatively short intestines, but the lower region has an internal structure—the spiral valve—that increases surface area.

(C) Intestinal folds and villi in the human gut

In most vertebrates, an enormous absorptive surface is achieved by the sheer length of the tubular small intestine...

...and the folding of its lining.

Intestinal folds

Villi

Blood vessels

Capillaries

Villus

Lacteal (see p. 1111)

Fingerlike villi increase the surface area of these folds...

...and microvilli cover the villi, vastly increasing the absorptive surface area.

Microvilli

Epithelial cell

Lymphatic vessel

© Biophoto Associates/Science Source

Figure 49.8 Intestinal Surface Area and Nutrient Absorption
Maximizing the surface area of the gut increases an animal's ability to absorb nutrients.

be broken down, and some larger, undigestible items leave the stomach only by regurgitation.

The wall of the intestine in humans and most other vertebrates is highly folded, with the individual folds bearing legions of tiny fingerlike projections called **villi** (Figure 49.8C). The cells that line the surfaces of the villi, in turn, have microscopic projections called **microvilli**. The microvilli give the intestine an enormous internal surface area for absorbing nutrients.

Digestive enzymes break down complex food molecules

Protein, carbohydrate, and fat macromolecules are broken down into their simplest monomeric units by hydrolytic enzymes produced at different locations in the digestive tract. Many are secreted into the lumen of the gut, and others remain associated with the membranes of the microvilli. All of these enzymes cleave the chemical bonds of macromolecules through hydrolysis, a reaction that adds a water molecule (see Figure 3.4B). Digestive enzymes are classified according to the substances they hydrolyze: **proteases** break the bonds between adjacent amino acids in proteins; **carbohydrases** hydrolyze carbohydrates; **peptidases** break down peptides; **lipases**, fats; and **nucleases**, nucleic acids. We discuss the digestive enzymes of humans in detail in Key Concept 49.3.

The gut microbiome contributes to digestion

The gut is colonized by a huge population of microorganisms, mostly bacteria. Collectively the foreign species associated with an organism are called its **microbiota**, and their cumulative genomes are called the organism's **microbiome**. The microbiomes of the skin are different from the microbiomes of the mouth, gut, respiratory tract, and urogenital tracts. The microbiota of the gut obtain their nutrition from the food passing through the gut while contributing to the host's digestive processes. For example, members of the leech genus *Hirudo* produce no enzymes that can digest the proteins in the blood they suck from vertebrates; instead they depend on bacteria to perform this service. The resulting amino acids are subsequently used by both the leech and the bacteria. The microbiota of the human gut also provide important services in digestion, prevent the establishment of harmful microorganisms, and even produce some vitamins (vitamin K and biotin). It is estimated that the human body consists of 37×10^{13} cells, but our guts contain probably three times that number of unicellular organisms representing at least 490 different species (see Figure 24.19). Recent studies have revealed that gut microbiomes are not constant, but are influenced by diet and other factors, including medications we ingest. The effects of different microbiomes may go far beyond simply facilitating digestion (**Investigating Life: How Does the Gut Microbiome Contribute to Obesity and Metabolic Disease?**).

►Investigating LIFE How Does the Gut Microbiome Contribute to Obesity and Metabolic Disease?

Experiment

Original Paper: R. Caesar et al. 2015. Crosstalk between gut microbiota and dietary lipids aggravates WAT inflammation through TLR signaling. *Cell* 22: 658–668.

Fats differ in fatty acid composition, and fatty acids differ in the number of single or double bonds between their carbon atoms (see Key Concept 3.4). Saturated fatty acids have no double bonds, and unsaturated fatty acids do. Diets rich in saturated fatty acids are implicated in several health concerns, but what is it about saturated fatty acids that is unhealthy? Recent research examines the effect of diet on the gut microbiome, and in turn, the effect of the microbiome on health. Does the amount of saturated fat in the diet influence the composition of the microbiome, and does the microbiome influence the health consequences of a diet rich in saturated fats? We examine the first question in the experiment below, and the second question in an online companion Data in Depth exercise.

HYPOTHESIS► The type of fat in the diet can influence the composition of the gut microbiome.

METHOD►

1. Raise two groups of 15 mice on isocaloric diets rich in saturated fats (lard) or unsaturated fats (fish oil).

2. Each week, record the mice's body weight.

3. At the end of 11 weeks, compare the mice's microbiomes (by sequencing the ribosomal RNA genes) and body weight gain.

RESULTS►

Using a statistical test called principle components (PC) analysis, the microbiomes of the two groups of mice were compared by sequencing. The ribosomal RNA genes of the two microbiomes were shown to be significantly different.

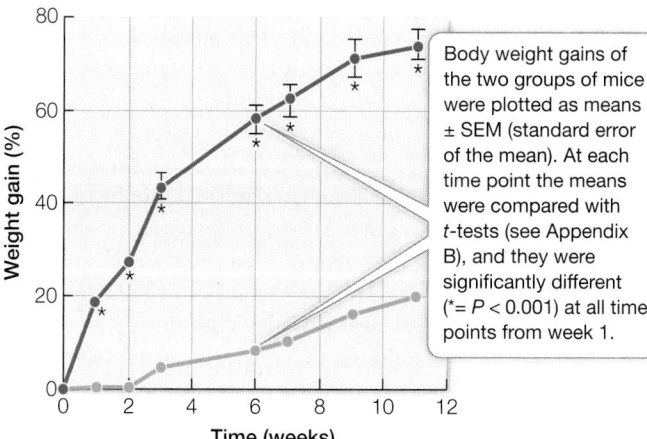

Body weight gains of the two groups of mice were plotted as means ± SEM (standard error of the mean). At each time point the means were compared with *t*-tests (see Appendix B), and they were significantly different (*= *P* < 0.001) at all time points from week 1.

CONCLUSION►

1. The fat composition of the diet influenced the composition of the microbiome.

2. Mice on the diet containing saturated fats gained more weight and gained weight faster than mice on the isocaloric diet containing unsaturated fats.

Work with the Data

The researchers hypothesized that mice consuming more saturated fats would have a higher probability of becoming obese and developing symptoms of diabetes. To test for dietary effects on the development of metabolic disease, the researchers collected additional data from the two cohorts of mice: fasting blood glucose levels (measured in millimolars, mM) and fasting blood insulin levels (measured in nanograms per milliliter, ng/mL). They also did an insulin tolerance test (effect of a dose of insulin on blood glucose level). Data are reported as means (± SEM).

Fasting blood glucose (mM)		Fasting blood insulin (ng/mL)	
Lard (*N* = 14)	Fish oil (*N* = 14)	Lard (*N* = 10)	Fish oil (*N* = 14)
11 (0.22)	10.32 (0.23)	3.96 (0.36)	1.09 (0.17)

	Blood glucose (% of the time 0 level)	
Time after insulin injection (min)	Lard	Fish oil
0	100	100
30	59.8 (3.05)	49.8 (4.09)
60	54.5 (3.51)	37.2 (4.07)
90	63.1 (3.91)	39.1 (4.09)
120	75.6 (3.06)	56.9 (3.31)

QUESTIONS►

1. Using a *t*-test, determine whether the difference in the fasting blood glucose levels for the lard-fed and fish-oil-fed mice is significant.

2. Using a *t*-test, determine whether the difference in the fasting blood insulin levels for the lard-fed and fish-oil-fed mice is significant.

3. Plot the glucose over time data. Did the two groups of mice differ in their response to the same dose of insulin? At which time points?

4. What conclusions can you make about the effect of the type of dietary fat on carbohydrate metabolism?

Go to Achieve for a companion **Data in Depth** exercise.

49.2 Recap and Assess

Heterotrophs have diverse adaptations for acquiring food. Once captured or ingested, food is digested extracellularly by secreted enzymes to release nutrients that are absorbed into the animal's body, usually via a tubular gut. The gut microbiome plays a role in digestion.

1. Why do herbivores typically spend more time feeding than do carnivores?

2. What do the actions of all digestive enzymes have in common?

3. Why is it common for individuals to have digestive problems after antibiotic therapy?

4. When people with celiac disease eat food containing gluten, their immune system damages their intestinal villi. If undiagnosed, such people are likely to experience bloating, abdominal pain, diarrhea, fatty stool, loss of body weight, and iron deficiency. Why do these symptoms occur?

Once ingested by an animal, food may be fragmented and moved into the gut for digestion by hydrolytic enzymes. The processes of digestion release nutrients that are absorbed into the animal's body. Next we focus on how those processes occur in vertebrates.

KEY CONCEPT
49.3 The Vertebrate Gastrointestinal System Is a Disassembly Line

Learning Objectives

49.3.1 Explain the mechanisms moving food through the vertebrate digestive system.

49.3.2 Discuss the role of stomach acid and how it is produced.

49.3.3 Describe the role of autocatalysis in digestion.

49.3.4 Explain the role of bile in digestion.

49.3.5 Discuss the roles of microbiota in the digestive systems of different vertebrates.

Digestion in vertebrates occurs in the gastrointestinal system, which includes a tubular gut running from mouth to anus and several accessory structures that produce secretions that play important roles in digestion (**Figure 49.9**). In this key concept we consider three important processes of this system: the movement of food through it, the sequential steps of digestion, and the absorption of nutrients. We use as our primary example a typical vertebrate, the human.

The vertebrate gut consists of concentric cellular layers

Tissues of the vertebrate gut are arranged in concentric layers that have a similar organization throughout its length (**Figure 49.10**). The **mucosa** lines the internal cavity, or **lumen**, of the gut. The mucosa consists of delicate epithelial cells with underlying connective tissue. Some cells of this mucosal epithelium secrete mucus to lubricate and protect the walls of the gut; some

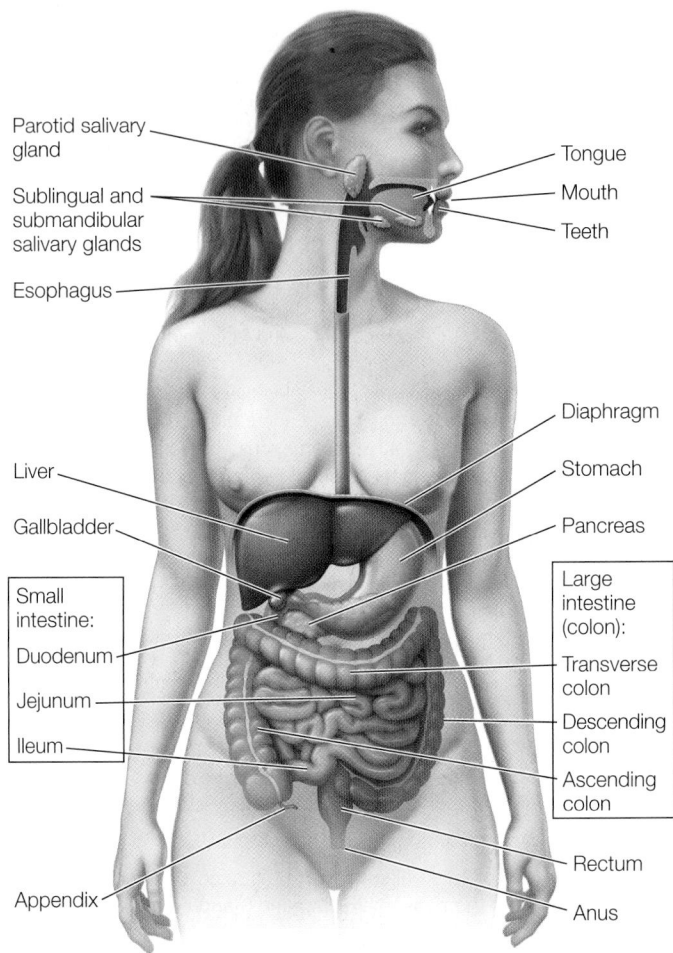

Figure 49.9 The Human Digestive System   Different compartments in the long tubular gut specialize in digesting food, absorbing nutrients, and storing and expelling wastes. Accessory organs contribute secretions containing enzymes and other molecules.

  View in Achieve
Activity 49.4 The Human Digestive System

secrete digestive enzymes; and some secrete hormones. Mucosal epithelial cells in the stomach secrete hydrochloric acid, and as we noted in Key Concept 49.1, some secrete intrinsic factor to aid the absorption of vitamin B_{12}. In some regions of the gut, nutrients are absorbed by mucosal epithelial cells. The apical cell membranes of these absorptive cells have microvilli that increase the surface area over which absorption can take place (see Figure 49.8C).

At the base of the mucosa there is a thin layer of smooth muscle cells with random orientations. The function of this cell layer is to move the mucosal epithelium to maximize its contact with the gut contents. Just under the mucosa is the submucosal tissue layer where blood and lymph vessels pick up nutrients to transport to the rest of the body. The **submucosa** also contains a network of nerves; the neurons in this network have sensory functions (responsible for stomach aches) and also control various secretory functions of the gut.

External to the submucosa are two layers of smooth muscle responsible for large movements of the gut. Innermost is the circular muscle layer, with its cells oriented around the gut; outermost is the longitudinal muscle layer, with its cells oriented along the

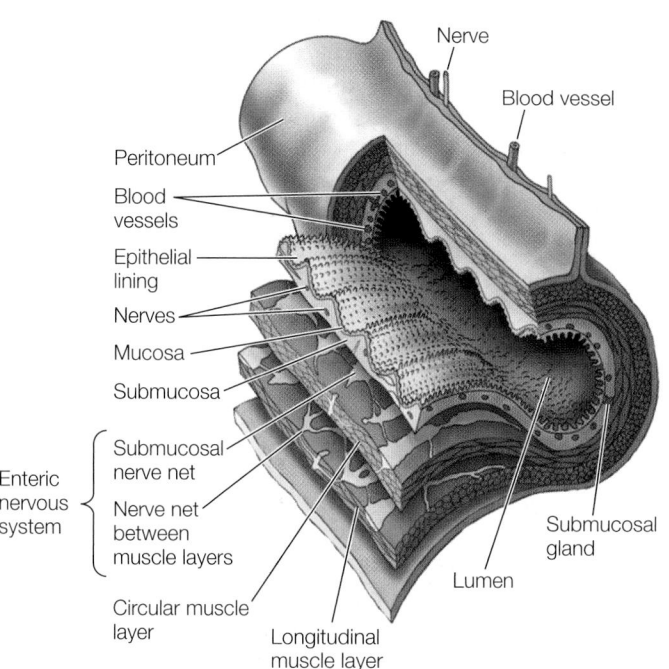

Figure 49.10 **Tissue Layers of the Vertebrate Gut** The organization of tissue layers is the same in all compartments of the gut, but specialized adaptations of specific tissues characterize different regions.

length of the gut (see Figure 49.10). The circular muscles constrict the gut, and the longitudinal muscles shorten it. Between the two layers of smooth muscle is another nerve network that controls and coordinates the movements of the gut. The coordinated activity of the two smooth muscle layers mixes contents of the gut and moves them continuously toward the anus.

 Media Clip 49.1 Following Food from Mouth to Gut
Life12e.com/mc49.1

Nerve nets in the submucosa and between the smooth muscle layers are called the **enteric nervous system**, and they are unusual. The cell bodies of most peripheral nerves are in the central nervous system (CNS)—in the brain or spinal cord. The only exceptions are the postganglionic cells of the autonomic nervous system and the cells of the enteric nervous system. In addition, most neurons of the peripheral nervous system either receive synapses from neurons in the CNS or contribute synapses to neurons in the CNS. In contrast, most of the neurons in the enteric nervous system form synapses only with other neurons in their network. Thus they are responsible for communication within the gut. The CNS can influence activity in the enteric nervous system and receive information from it, but the gut truly has "a mind of its own."

A tissue membrane called the **peritoneum** surrounds the gut and most of the organs of the abdominal cavity as well as lining the wall of the cavity. The peritoneum includes connective and epithelial tissues that secrete a lubricating fluid that enables the organs to easily slide against each other in the body cavity.

Gut motility moves food through the gut and aids digestion

In humans and most other mammals, food is chewed in the mouth and mixed with saliva. Periodically the tongue pushes a bolus (mass) of the chewed food toward the throat. By making contact with the soft palate at the back of the mouth cavity, the food bolus initiates swallowing, which is a complex series of reflexes. Swallowing propels the food through the pharynx (where the mouth cavity and nasal passages join) and into the **esophagus** (food tube). To prevent food from entering the trachea (windpipe), the larynx (voice box) closes, and a flap of tissue called the **epiglottis** covers the entrance to the larynx (**Figure 49.11A**).

Once a bolus of food enters the esophagus, it is moved toward the stomach both by gravity and by waves of muscle contraction called **peristalsis** (**Figure 49.11B**). The muscle of the upper region

(A) Swallowing

Food
Soft palate
Pharynx
Tongue
Epiglottis
Larynx
Glottis
Trachea (windpipe)
Upper esophageal sphincter
Esophagus

1 Food is chewed and the tongue pushes the bolus of food to the back of the mouth. Sensory nerves initiate the swallowing reflex.

2 The soft palate is pulled up as the vocal cords are pulled together to close the larynx.

3 The larynx is pulled up and forward and is covered by the epiglottis. The esophageal sphincter relaxes. The bolus of food enters the esophagus.

(B) Peristalsis

Esophagus
Circular muscles contract
Food bolus
Circular muscles relax
Longitudinal muscles contract
Lower esophageal sphincter
Pyloric sphincter
Stomach

4 Peristaltic contractions propel the food to the stomach.

Figure 49.11 **Swallowing and Peristalsis** (A) Food pushed to the back of the mouth triggers the swallowing reflex. (B) Once a food bolus enters the esophagus, peristalsis propels it from mouth to anus by coordinated actions of the circular and longitudinal muscle layers of the gut.

of the esophagus is striated (i.e., skeletal muscle) and is controlled by the CNS reflexes of swallowing. The muscles of the rest of the esophagus are smooth muscles controlled by the autonomic and enteric nervous systems.

Smooth muscles of the gut contract in response to being stretched. When a bolus of food reaches the smooth muscle region of the esophagus and stretches it, the muscle responds by contracting, thus pushing food toward the stomach. Why doesn't the contraction of the esophageal smooth muscle push food back toward the mouth? The nerve net between the two smooth muscle layers coordinates the muscles so that when a region of the gut smooth muscle contracts, the circular smooth muscle just beyond it relaxes. This action, controlled by the enteric nervous system, is called an anticipatory wave of relaxation. The contractions of smooth muscles behind the relaxing area push food into it—in the direction of the anus. The resulting stretch of that region stimulates its circular smooth muscle to contract as the anticipatory wave of relaxation causes the smooth muscle of the next region to relax. The peristaltic waves of contraction and relaxation of the gut smooth muscle move food along the gut from the mouth to the anus.

At the junction of the esophagus and stomach is an esophageal **sphincter**, a ring of circular smooth muscle that is usually constricted. Waves of peristalsis cause the sphincter to relax enough to let food pass from the esophagus into the stomach. Sphincter muscles are found elsewhere in the digestive tract as well: the pyloric sphincter governs the passage of stomach contents into the small intestine; the ileocaecal sphincter controls the flow of food between the small and large intestines; and the anal sphincter relaxes to allow defecation.

Some movements of the stomach are not as coordinated as the peristaltic movements of the esophagus and serve to move the contents of the stomach around and mix them with the digestive juices. However, peristaltic waves of contraction reorganize in the lower region of the stomach and push the semi-digested material up against the pyloric sphincter which controls the opening to the small intestine. In the small intestine, peristaltic activity continues to move the contents of the gut toward the large intestine.

Chemical digestion begins in the mouth and the stomach

Salivary glands secrete the enzyme **amylase** into the mouth where it is mixed with the food being chewed. Amylase hydrolyzes bonds between glucose monomers that make up carbohydrate molecules. The action of amylase is what makes a chewed piece of bread or cracker taste slightly sweet if you hold it in your mouth and chew it long enough.

The main role of the stomach is to store food, continue its enzymatic digestion, and deliver it to the small intestine at an appropriate rate so that digestion can occur more slowly than ingestion. The stomach produces secretions that facilitate digestion and also kill potential pathogens that are ingested with food. **Gastric pits** in the stomach walls (**Figure 49.12A,B**) have three types of secretory cells: (1) mucus-secreting cells, (2) **parietal cells** that secrete hydrochloric acid (HCl), and (3) **chief cells** that secrete the inactive proteolytic enzyme pepsinogen (**Figure 49.12C**). The low pH of the stomach juices kills most microorganisms that are ingested

with food; denatures proteins, making them more accessible to the hydrolytic actions of pepsin; and converts pepsinogen to pepsin by cleaving away a sequence of amino acids that masks the active site of the enzyme. Newly activated pepsin activates other pepsinogen molecules, creating a positive-feedback process called **autocatalysis**. Acid and the proteolytic enzyme pepsin could damage the stomach walls, but the mucus-secreting cells provide a protective coating for the walls of the gastric pits and stomach.

The production of HCl by gastric pit parietal cells is impressive. It amounts to about 2 liters of a highly concentrated solution per day—enough to bring the pH of the stomach contents below 1, which is the same as battery acid and ten times more acidic than pure lemon juice. This means that across their cell membranes, parietal cells create a H^+ ion concentration difference of 3 million-fold. Such a feat of transport is not seen anywhere else in the body. How do the gastric pits do it? Enzymes and transporters are involved.

The enzyme carbonic anhydrase in parietal cells catalyzes the hydration of CO_2 to H_2CO_3, which dissociates into H^+ and a bicarbonate ion (HCO_3^-). An antiporter transport protein (see Figure 6.13) exchanges HCO_3^- for Cl^- on the blood side of the gastric pits, and an antiporter on the gastric pit side exchanges H^+ for K^+ (**Figure 49.12D**). However, K^+ leaks out of the parietal cell down its concentration gradient. Thus the inward transport of K^+ acts like an endless conveyer belt moving H^+ out into the stomach lumen. Cl^- also passively leaks out of the gastric lumen side of the parietal cells to maintain electrical neutrality.

The stomach gradually releases its contents to the small intestine

The acidic, fluid mixture of gastric juice and partly digested food in the stomach is called **chyme**. A few substances can be absorbed across the stomach wall, including alcohol (hence its rapid effects), aspirin, and caffeine, but even these substances are absorbed in rather small quantities from the stomach; most absorption takes place in the small intestine. At the bottom of the stomach, peristaltic contractions push the chyme against the pyloric sphincter. Associated waves of anticipatory relaxation cause the pyloric sphincter to relax briefly so that little squirts of chyme enter the small intestine. The human stomach empties gradually over a period of approximately 4 hours. This slow introduction of food into the small intestine enables it to work on a little material at a time.

Most chemical digestion occurs in the small intestine

In the **small intestine**, digestion of carbohydrates and proteins continues, and digestion of fats and absorption of nutrients begin. The small intestine takes its name from its diameter; it is in fact a very large organ, about 6 meters long in an adult human. Given its length and the folds, villi, and microvilli of its epithelial cells, its inner surface area is roughly the size of a tennis court. Across this surface the small intestine absorbs the nutrient molecules derived from food.

The small intestine of humans has three sections. The initial section (about 25 cm long) is called the **duodenum** and is the site of most digestion; the **jejunum** and the **ileum** (together about 600 cm) carry out 90% of the absorption of nutrients (see Figure 49.9).

(A) Stomach anatomy

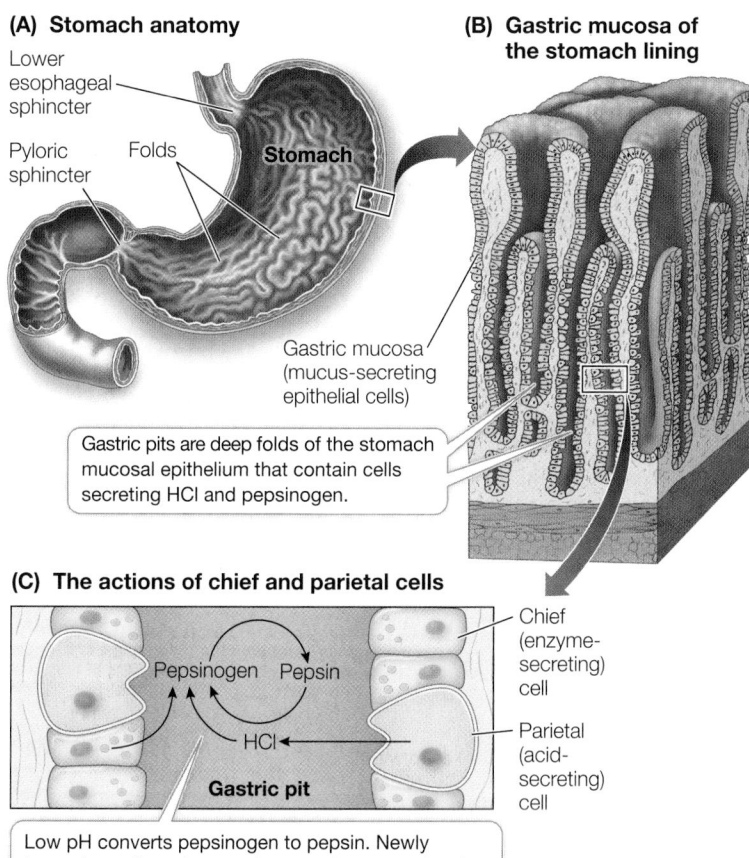

Lower esophageal sphincter

Pyloric sphincter

Folds

Stomach

Gastric mucosa (mucus-secreting epithelial cells)

Gastric pits are deep folds of the stomach mucosal epithelium that contain cells secreting HCl and pepsinogen.

(B) Gastric mucosa of the stomach lining

(C) The actions of chief and parietal cells

Pepsinogen   Pepsin

HCl

Gastric pit

Chief (enzyme-secreting) cell

Parietal (acid-secreting) cell

Low pH converts pepsinogen to pepsin. Newly formed pepsin activates other pepsinogen molecules.

(D) Active transport of H⁺ ions

1 Carbonic anhydrase catalyzes formation of carbonic acid (H_2CO_3), which dissociates into H^+ and HCO_3^-.

Blood vessel

Lumen of gastric pit

$H_2O + CO_2$

H_2CO_3

Cl^- Cl^-

HCO_3^-

HCO_3^- H^+ H^+

Cl^- Cl^-

K^+ K^+

K^+

K^+

4 K^+ and Cl^- leak out of the cell.

Parietal cell

2 Bicarbonate is actively transported out of the blood side of the cell in exchange for Cl^-.

3 H^+ is actively transported into the lumen of the gastric pit in exchange for K^+.

Figure 49.12 Action in the Stomach   **(A)** The human stomach stores ingested food and mixes it with digestive secretions. **(B)** Gastric pits are folds in the stomach lining. **(C)** Parietal cells in the gastric pits secrete hydrochloric acid (HCl), and chief cells secrete pepsinogen. HCl and autocatalysis convert inactive pepsinogen into active pepsin. **(D)** Parietal cells create a tremendous H^+ concentration difference between the gut lumen and the extracellular fluid by actively transporting into the lumen of the gastric pit H^+ ions produced through the catalytic action of carbonic anhydrase.

Digestion in the small intestine involves many specialized enzymes, as well as several other secretions. Two accessory organs that are not part of the digestive tract—the liver and the pancreas—produce most of these secretions and deliver them to the lumen of the intestine through ducts.

LIVER   The **liver** synthesizes **bile** from cholesterol. Bile also includes other substances, such as phospholipids and bilirubin (the breakdown product of hemoglobin). Bile flows from the liver through the hepatic duct. A side branch off the hepatic duct called the cystic duct goes to the **gallbladder**, where bile is stored. Below this junction, the hepatic duct is called the common bile duct. Before it reaches the duodenum, the common bile duct is joined by the pancreatic duct (**Figure 49.13**).

Fat entering the duodenum stimulates cells of the duodenal epithelium to release the hormone **cholecystokinin (CCK)**, which stimulates the walls of the gallbladder to contract rhythmically. As a result, bile is squeezed out of the gallbladder and through the cystic duct to the common bile duct. Peristalsis moves the bile down the bile duct, and a small sphincter at the junction of the common bile duct with the duodenum relaxes in response to waves of peristalsis and allows squirts of bile to enter the duodenal lumen.

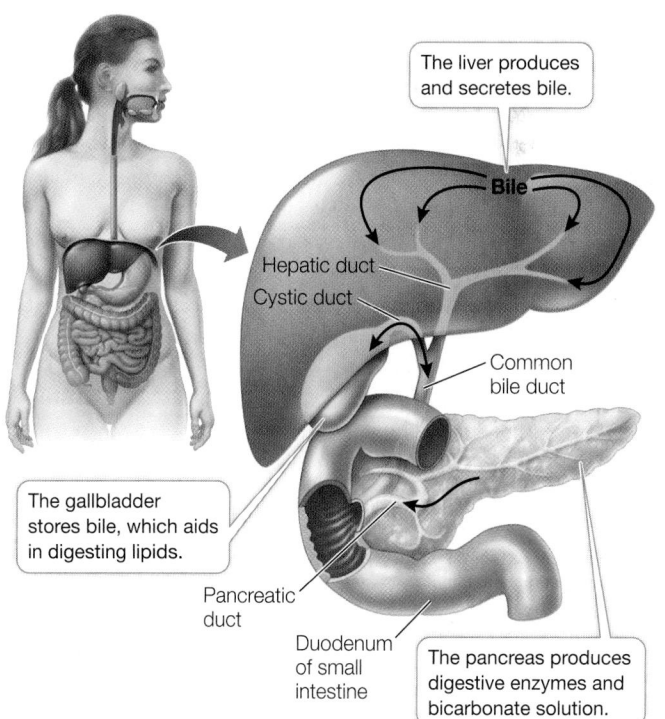

The liver produces and secretes bile.

Bile

Hepatic duct

Cystic duct

Common bile duct

The gallbladder stores bile, which aids in digesting lipids.

Pancreatic duct

Duodenum of small intestine

The pancreas produces digestive enzymes and bicarbonate solution.

Figure 49.13 Ducts of the Gallbladder and Pancreas   Bile produced in the liver flows from the liver via the hepatic duct. Branching off this duct is the gallbladder, which stores bile. Below the gallbladder, the hepatic duct is called the common bile duct and is joined by the pancreatic duct before entering the duodenum.

To understand the role of bile in fat digestion, think of an oil-and-vinegar salad dressing. Oil is hydrophobic and tends to aggregate in large globules. For that reason, many salad dressings include an emulsifier—something that prevents oil droplets from aggregating. Mayonnaise, for example, is oil and vinegar with egg yolk added as an emulsifier. Bile emulsifies fats in the chyme. One end of each bile molecule is lipophilic (soluble in fat), and the other end is hydrophilic (soluble in water). The lipophilic ends of bile molecules merge with the fat droplets, leaving their hydrophilic ends sticking out. As a result, bile prevents small fat droplets from congealing together into large fat droplets, and thereby the surface area of the fats exposed to the fat-digesting enzymes (lipases) is greatly enlarged. The very small fat particles that result from emulsification by bile are called **micelles** (**Figure 49.14A**).

PANCREAS The **pancreas** is a large gland that lies just behind and below the stomach (see Figures 49.9 and 49.13). It is both an endocrine gland (secreting hormones into the circulation; see Key Concept 39.1) and an exocrine gland (secreting digestive juices through the pancreatic duct to the gut lumen). The exocrine tissues of the pancreas produce a host of digestive enzymes, including lipases, amylases, proteases, and nucleases (**Table 49.3**). As in the stomach, the protease enzymes are released in inactive forms called **zymogens**; if proteases were not in this inactive state, they would digest the pancreas and its ducts before ever reaching the duodenum. Once in the duodenum, the zymogen trypsinogen is activated by the enzyme enterokinase (secreted by cells lining the duodenum) to produce the active protease **trypsin**. Trypsin cleaves other zymogens, releasing other proteases as well as more active trypsin.

The mixture of zymogens produced by the pancreas can be dangerous if the pancreatic duct is blocked or if the pancreas is injured by infection or physical trauma such as a blow to the abdomen. A few activated trypsin molecules can initiate a chain reaction of enzyme activity that digests the tissues of the pancreas (a condition called pancreatitis), destroying both its endocrine and exocrine functions.

The ducts of the pancreas produce a secretion rich in bicarbonate ions (HCO_3^-). Bicarbonate ions are alkaline (basic) and neutralize the acidic pH of the chyme that enters the duodenum from the stomach. Intestinal enzymes function best at a neutral or slightly alkaline pH. The production of bicarbonate and its secretion into the pancreatic ducts is similar to the production of H^+ ions and their secretion into the gastric pits—but with opposite spatial orientations. In both types of secretory cells, carbonic anhydrase catalyzes the hydration of CO_2 to produce H_2CO_3 that dissociates into H^+ and HCO_3^- ions. Whereas in the gastric pits the H^+ is secreted into the lumen of the pit, in the pancreatic duct it is the HCO_3^- that is secreted into the lumen, and the H^+ is transported into the circulation.

Nutrients are absorbed in the small intestine

The final step in digesting proteins and carbohydrates and absorbing their components occurs among the intestinal microvilli. Mucosal epithelial cells produce peptidases that cleave small peptides into absorbable amino acids. These epithelial cells also produce

(A) Digestion of fats

Large lipid droplet

Bile

Micelles

1 Dietary fats are emulsified into tiny droplets called micelles through physical disruption and the action of bile in the intestinal lumen.

2 Pancreatic lipase hydrolyzes fats in the micelles to produce fatty acids and monoglycerides.

Monoglycerides

Fatty acids

(B) Absorption of fats

3 Fatty acids and monoglycerides enter the cell by diffusion. They are resynthesized into triglycerides in the endoplasmic reticulum.

Endoplasmic reticulum

4 Triglycerides are packaged with cholesterol and phospholipids in protein-coated chylomicrons.

Intestinal epithelial cell

5 Chylomicrons are enclosed in vesicles. They leave the cell by exocytosis and enter the lymphatic system.

Lymphatic vessel

Figure 49.14 Digesting Fats **(A)** Dietary fats are broken up by bile into small micelles that present a large surface area to lipases. **(B)** The products of fat digestion are absorbed by intestinal mucosal cells, where they are resynthesized into triglycerides and exported to lymphatic vessels.

Q: A small percentage of people who have had their gallbladders removed must thereafter eat a low-fat diet, or they will experience diarrhea. Why?

 View in Achieve
Animation 49.1 **The Digestion and Absorption of Fats**

the enzymes maltase, lactase, and sucrase that cleave the common disaccharides into absorbable monosaccharides—glucose, galactose, and fructose. There is also some lipase activity that facilitates fat digestion.

Many humans stop producing the enzyme lactase in childhood and thereafter have difficulty digesting lactose (the sugar in milk). Lactose is a disaccharide and cannot be absorbed without being cleaved into its constituents, glucose and galactose. Unabsorbed lactose is metabolized by bacteria in the large intestine, causing gas, diarrhea, and abdominal cramps.

The mechanisms by which cells of the intestinal epithelium absorb nutrients and inorganic ions are diverse and include diffusion, facilitated diffusion, active transport, and secondary active

TABLE **49.3** | Major Digestive Enzymes of Humans	
Source/enzyme	**Action**
SALIVARY GLANDS	
Salivary amylase	Starch → Maltose
STOMACH	
Pepsin	Proteins → Peptides; autocatalysis
PANCREAS	
Pancreatic amylase	Starch → Maltose
Lipase	Fats → Fatty acids and glycerol
Nuclease	Nucleic acids → Nucleotides
Trypsin	Proteins → Peptides; zymogen activation
Chymotrypsin	Proteins → Peptides
Carboxypeptidase	Peptides → Shorter peptides and amino acids
SMALL INTESTINE	
Aminopeptidase	Peptides → Shorter peptides and amino acids
Dipeptidase	Dipeptides → Amino acids
Enterokinase	Trypsinogen → Trypsin
Nuclease	Nucleic acids → Nucleotides
Maltase	Maltose → Glucose
Lactase	Lactose → Galactose and glucose
Sucrase	Sucrose → Fructose and glucose

transport. Many inorganic ions such as sodium, calcium, and iron are actively transported by these cells. For example, active Na^+ transporters exist on the basal and lateral sides of the epithelial cells. They maintain a low concentration of Na^+ in those cells so that Na^+ can diffuse in from the chyme in the intestinal lumen. About 30 grams of Na^+ are transported this way every day, and Cl^- follows.

The transport of Na^+ and other ions is important for water absorption because it creates an osmotic concentration gradient. At least 7–8 liters of water per day move through the spaces between the epithelial cells in response to this osmotic gradient. Because the water moves through spaces between the cells and not through the cells themselves, it can carry with it nutrients that are in solution—a transport mechanism called **solvent drag** or **bulk transport**.

Many different kinds of transport proteins function in epithelial cell membranes. Some, such as the transport protein for fructose, only facilitate diffusion, and that requires a concentration gradient. Once fructose enters the cell it is converted to glucose, so the concentration of fructose in the cell is always low and the concentration gradient is maintained. Transport proteins known as symporters (see Figure 6.13) exploit the concentration gradient of Na^+ between the inside and outside of the cell that is maintained by the Na^+–K^+ pump common to all cells (see Figure 6.14). Symporters combine the transport of Na^+ and another molecule, such as glucose, galactose, or an amino acid. As Na^+ moves down its concentration gradient into the cell, the "hitchhiking" molecules are carried along with it.

The absorption of the products of fat digestion is relatively simple. Triglycerides are hydrolyzed to diglycerides, monoglycerides,

and fatty acids, all of which are lipid-soluble and thus able to pass through the cell membranes of the microvilli. Once these molecules are in the intestinal epithelial cells, they are resynthesized into triglycerides, combined with cholesterol and phospholipids, and coated with protein to form water-soluble **chylomicrons** (**Figure 49.14B**). Rather than enter the blood directly, chylomicrons pass into blind-ended lymph vessels called **lacteals** that are inside each villus (see Figure 49.8C). The chylomicrons then flow through the lymphatic system and enter the bloodstream through the thoracic ducts at the base of the neck. After a meal rich in fats, chylomicrons can be so abundant in the blood that they give the blood plasma a milky appearance. Chylomicrons deliver their triglyceride and cholesterol cargo as they circulate through tissues.

The bile molecules that emulsify fats are not absorbed along with the monoglycerides, diglycerides, and fatty acids, but are shuttled back and forth between the gut contents and the microvilli. In the ileum, bile is actively reabsorbed and returned to the liver via the bloodstream.

Absorbed nutrients go to the liver

Blood leaving the digestive tract flows to the liver in the **hepatic portal vein**. This large vein delivers the blood to small spaces called sinusoids between groups of liver cells. These cells absorb the nutrients coming from the digestive tract and either store them or convert them to molecules the body needs. Glucose, galactose, and fructose are used to synthesize glycogen. Amino acids are used to build proteins. Lipids from the chylomicrons are either stored as triglycerides or used to make lipoproteins that are released by the liver and carry the triglycerides and cholesterol to other tissues (as we discuss in Key Concept 49.4).

Water and ions are absorbed in the large intestine

The motility of the small intestine gradually pushes its contents through another sphincter—the ileocaecal sphincter—and into the large intestine, or **colon**. Most of the available nutrients have been removed from the chyme that enters the colon, but it contains a lot of water and inorganic ions. A major type of motility in the colon is called segmentation movements. These movements are mostly due to contractions of circular muscles that repeatedly divide the colon into separate segments. Functionally, segmentation movements cause the chyme to slosh around in the colon and promote absorption of ions and water by increasing contact between the chyme and the epithelium of the colon. As ions and water are absorbed, the chyme becomes a semisolid mass that forms feces. Absorption of too much water from the colon can cause hard feces and constipation. The opposite condition, diarrhea, results if too little water is absorbed. Excessive diarrhea caused by diseases such as cholera can produce such rapid loss of water and electrolytes that death can occur in hours. Simple rehydration therapy with electrolytes can save lives.

Fecal matter is stored in the descending colon and in the rectum until defecation occurs. This is usually once a day and is preceded by strong peristaltic activity. The distension of the walls of the rectum by fecal matter initiates a parasympathetic reflex, causing the rectal muscle to contract and the internal anal sphincter to relax. In addition, there is an external anal sphincter that is under conscious control so that defecation is not entirely an involuntary act.

Herbivores rely on their microbiota to digest cellulose

Cellulose is the primary component of plant cell walls, and is therefore the principal component of the food of herbivores. Most herbivores, however, cannot produce cellulases, the enzymes that break down cellulose. (Exceptions include earthworms, ship-worms, and the silverfishes that eat books and stored papers.) From termites to cattle, herbivores rely on the microbiota of their digestive tracts to digest cellulose.

Ruminants (cud chewers) such as cattle ferment their plant-based food in special stomachs before digestion. Their stomachs are large, four-chambered organs (**Figure 49.15**). The first two chambers, the **rumen** and the **reticulum**, are packed with endosymbiotic microorganisms that break down cellulose by fermentation. The ruminant periodically regurgitates the contents of the rumen (the cud) into the mouth for more chewing. When swallowed again, the vegetal fibers present more surface area to the microorganisms. The microorganisms metabolize cellulose and other nutrients to simple fatty acids that are nutrients for their host.

Enormous numbers of microorganisms leave the rumen along with the partially digested food. This mass is concentrated by water absorption in the **omasum** before it enters the true stomach, the **abomasum**, where the microorganisms are killed by secreted hydrochloric acid, partially digested by proteases, and passed on to the small intestine for further digestion and absorption. A cow derives more than 100 grams of protein per day from digestion of its microbiota. The rate of multiplication of microorganisms in the rumen offsets their loss, so a well-balanced, mutually beneficial relationship is maintained.

Some mammalian herbivores have a microbial fermentation chamber called a **cecum** extending from the large intestine. An example is the rabbit (see Figure 49.7). Since the cecum empties into the large intestine, absorption of nutrients produced by the microorganisms in the cecum is inefficient because of the limited surface area of the large intestine. Such species frequently produce two kinds of feces—ones that are pure waste and ones that contain cecal material. In a behavior known as **coprophagy**, these species reingest the cecal feces directly from the anus so they can digest and absorb the nutrients that would otherwise be lost. In humans the cecum is small and ends in the vestigial **appendix** which serves no digestive function.

KEY CONCEPT
49.3 Recap and Assess

The vertebrate gastrointestinal system is a tubular gut that is adapted to ingest food, fragment it, digest it, and absorb nutrients. Peristalsis moves food through the gut. Segmentation movements mix the gut contents. Enzymatic digestion and then absorption of nutrients occur mostly in the small intestine; water and ions are absorbed in the large intestine.

1. Explain why in the weightlessness of space, food still travels from the mouth to the stomach.

2. When some biochemists ground up a piece of stomach wall and stimulated it with the hormone that causes the stomach to secrete HCl, no change in the pH of the solution occurred. Why not?

3. How does bile assist in the digestion of fats, and why aren't equivalent molecules necessary to facilitate transport of lipids in the lymph and blood?

4. Explain why the gut microbiota is a significant source of nutrition for ruminants but not for humans.

5. Explain why in the ruminant digestive system HCl is secreted in the abomasum but not in the rumen, the reticulum, or the omasum.

6. Why would the autocatalytic property of pepsin foster a positive-feedback mechanism of protein hydrolysis in the stomach?

Figure 49.15 A Ruminant's Stomach Bison (*Bison bison*), like their relatives domestic cattle, have a specialized stomach with four compartments that enables them to obtain energy from coarse plant material through bacterial fermentation of the otherwise indigestible plant material. The bacteria themselves become an important source of nutrition.

The rumen and the reticulum have abundant cellulose-fermenting microorganisms.

The contents of the rumen are periodically regurgitated into the mouth for rechewing.

Esophagus

Rumen

Reticulum

The mixture of fermented food and microorganisms passes through the omasum, where it is concentrated by water absorption.

The abomasum is the "true" stomach, secreting HCl and proteases. The microorganisms are killed by the HCl, digested by the proteases, and passed on to the small intestine for further digestion.

Q: Functionally, why do the rumen and reticulum come before the true stomach, the abomasum?

The steps included in the ingestion and digestion of food—from fragmentation in the mouth to the digestive processes in the stomach and intestines—make the nutrients in food available for absorption and ultimately for metabolism. We look next at how the processes of digestion are controlled and at how nutrients are handled by the body once food has been digested.

KEY CONCEPT 49.4 Nutrient Availability Is Controlled and Regulated

Learning Objectives

49.4.1 Describe how hormones control the rate of delivery of chyme to the small intestine and how they control secretions of digestive juices.

49.4.2 Explain how the metabolic interconversions that take place in the liver and muscles meet the body's demands for glucose.

49.4.3 Describe the classes of lipoproteins.

49.4.4 Explain the effects of insulin on skeletal muscle cells, adipose cells, and liver cells.

49.4.5 Cite evidence that supports the role of leptin as a satiety signal and ghrelin as a hunger signal.

49.4.6 Interpret results from experiments designed to elucidate the mechanisms underlying regulation of body mass and food-intake behaviors.

As stated earlier, the vertebrate gut is a disassembly line, and as with a standard assembly line, control of the sequential processes is critical. Neuronal and hormonal controls coordinate digestive processes. And once the products of digestion are absorbed, their availability to the cells of the body must also be controlled and regulated.

Salivation at the sight or smell of food is an autonomic reflex, as is swallowing. Other autonomic reflexes include the release of digestive juices and increased stomach motility stimulated by good food smells. Reflexes also initiate gagging at the smell of rotting meat. These reflexes are called the "cephalic phase" of control of digestive processes because they involve the CNS. Most of the control of digestive processes, however, involves neural and hormonal mechanisms that are intrinsic to the gut.

Neuronal messages travel from one region of the digestive tract to another in the enteric nervous system. One function of the gut's nervous system is coordinating the movement of food through the gut. Of course, this intrinsic nervous system communicates information to the CNS and receives input from the CNS, but its most important role is to coordinate actions throughout the digestive tract. In spite of this marvelous intrinsic nervous system, however, much of the control and regulation of the digestive system and nutrient management involves hormonal mechanisms.

Hormones control many digestive functions

Several hormones control the activities of the digestive tract and its accessory organs (**Figure 49.16**). The first hormone ever discovered came from the duodenum; it was called **secretin** because it causes the pancreas to secrete digestive juices. We now know that secretin is only one of several hormones that control pancreatic secretion; specifically, secretin stimulates the cells of the pancreatic ducts to secrete a solution rich in bicarbonate ions.

The stimulus that causes the duodenum to release secretin is the low pH of the acidic chyme from the stomach. Similarly, the presence of fats and proteins in the chyme stimulates the release of cholecystokinin (CCK), the hormone that stimulates the gallbladder to release bile. CCK also stimulates the pancreas to release

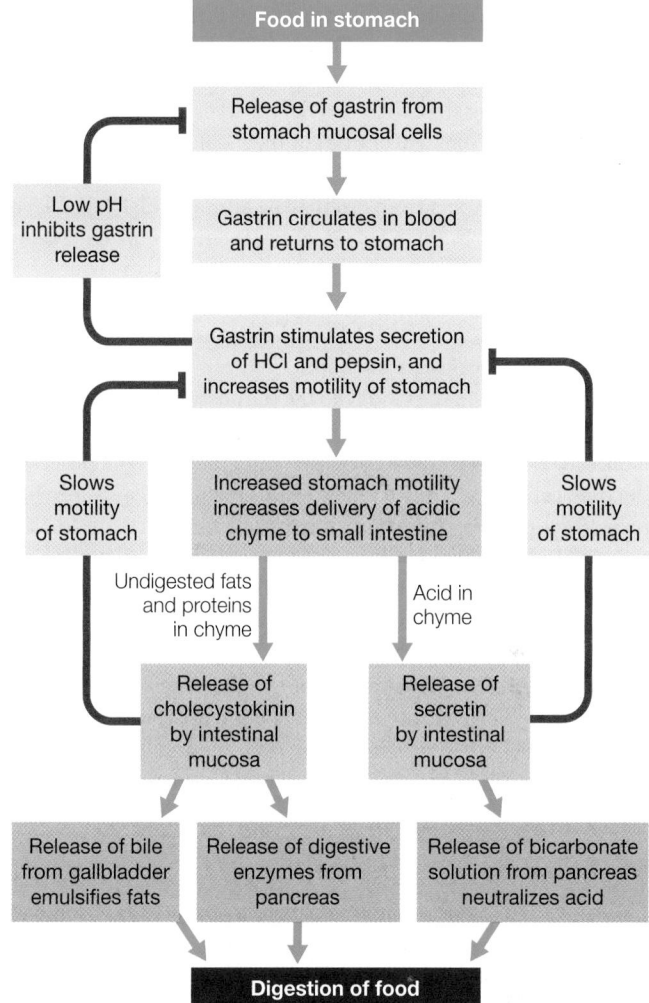

Figure 49.16 Hormones Control Digestion The hormones gastrin, cholecystokinin (CCK), and secretin are involved in feedback loops that control the sequential processing of food in the digestive tract. Red lines indicate inhibitory actions; green lines indicate stimulatory actions.

Q: Why do secretin and CCK stimulate the pancreas but inhibit the stomach?

digestive enzymes. Both CCK and secretin have negative-feedback effects on the stomach. They slow the movements of the stomach, thus slowing the delivery of chyme into the small intestine to allow more complete digestion in the duodenum.

The presence of food in the stomach stimulates cells in the lower region of the stomach to secrete a hormone called **gastrin**. Gastrin returns to the stomach in the blood and stimulates the secretion of digestive juices and also increases the motility of the stomach. Gastrin release begins to be inhibited when the pH of the stomach contents falls below 3—another example of negative feedback.

The liver stores and releases the molecules that fuel metabolism

Most animals do not eat continuously, so they can be in either an **absorptive state** (food in the gut) or a **postabsorptive state** (no food in the gut). Nutrient requirements for energy metabolism and biosynthesis are continuous, however. Thus nutrient traffic must be controlled so that during the absorptive state energy reserves accumulate in the liver, muscle, and adipose (fat) tissue, and during the postabsorptive state these energy reserves are used efficiently. When fuel molecules are abundant in the blood, the liver stores them in the form of glycogen and fats. The liver also synthesizes blood plasma proteins from circulating amino acids. When levels of fuel molecules in the blood decline, the liver taps its reserves and delivers nutrients into the blood.

The liver has an enormous capacity to interconvert fuel molecules. Liver cells convert monosaccharides into either glycogen or fats during the absorptive state and then can reverse the process, returning glucose to the blood during the postabsorptive state. The liver can also convert certain amino acids and some other molecules, such as pyruvate and lactate, into glucose—the process of gluconeogenesis (see Key Concept 9.5). Gluconeogenesis provides an indirect pathway for exercising muscle to contribute to blood glucose levels. At high levels of aerobic activity, muscle cells break down their stores of glycogen to provide glucose for metabolic fuel. The glucose released from muscle glycogen, however, has to be used in the cells that produce it. Glucose cannot leave muscle cells as it can leave liver cells. However, when the activity of the muscle becomes anaerobic, pyruvate and lactate build up, leave muscle cells, and enter the circulation. Circulating pyruvate and lactate are taken up by the liver and converted to glucose that can then move out of the liver cells, circulate in the blood, and be taken up by muscle cells.

The liver produces lipoproteins

The liver is the major controller of fat metabolism through its production of lipoproteins. A **lipoprotein** is a particle made up of a core of hydrophobic fat and cholesterol with a covering of hydrophilic protein that allows it to be suspended in the extracellular fluids. Lipoproteins are the most abundant fuel reserve in the body, and they move fats from sites of absorption or synthesis to sites of storage, and from sites of storage to sites of use. You saw in Key Concept 49.3 how bile in the intestine solves the problem of processing hydrophobic fats in an aqueous medium. Transport of fats in the circulatory system presents the same problem, and lipoproteins provide the solution.

The chylomicrons produced by the mucosal cells of the intestine are the largest lipoprotein particles in the blood. As the circulation carries chylomicrons through muscle, adipose tissue, and liver, lipoprotein lipases attached to the endothelial cells of capillaries break down the chylomicrons' triglycerides so that the component fatty acids, monoglycerides, and glycerol can be taken up by the cells. The chylomicron remnants have lipid cores with a lot of cholesterol, and they are taken up by liver cells.

Lipoproteins different from chylomicrons are synthesized in the liver. These lipoproteins can be classified according to their density. Fat has a low density (it floats on water) and protein has a high density, so the greater the fat-to-protein ratio in the lipoprotein, the lower its density.

- **High-density lipoproteins** (**HDLs**) transport lipids and cholesterol from tissues to the liver where the cholesterol can be used to synthesize bile. HDL consists of about 49% protein, 35% lipids,

and 15% cholesterol. These are called good lipoproteins, and their levels are higher in people who exercise and are fit.

- **Low-density lipoproteins** (**LDLs**) transport cholesterol around the body for use in biosynthesis and for storage. LDL consists of about 25% protein, 25% lipids, and 49% cholesterol. These lipoproteins are associated with a high risk for cardiovascular disease.

- **Very low-density lipoproteins** (**VLDLs**) transports triglycerides and cholesterol from the liver to peripheral cells that use the triglyerides for fuel and the cholesterol for membrane synthesis. These lipoproteins contain mostly triglycerides, and are about 2% protein, 94% lipids, and 3% cholesterol. As they give up their triglyceride, they become LDLs. VLDLs are associated with obesity and diabetes as well as a high risk for cardiovascular disease.

Insulin and glucagon control fuel metabolism

During the absorptive state, blood glucose levels rise as carbohydrates are digested and absorbed (**Figure 49.17**). During this time, the pancreas releases the hormone **insulin**, which plays a major role in directing glucose to where it will be used or stored. In Key Concept 49.3 we mentioned that the pancreas has both an exocrine function (secretions involved in digestion) and endocrine functions. The endocrine functions are located in clusters of cells in the pancreas called the islets of Langerhans. One class of islet cells, the beta cells, produces and releases insulin. Another class, the alpha cells, produces and releases the hormone **glucagon** (discussed shortly). The actions of insulin vary in different tissues, but they are all aimed at promoting the use of glucose for metabolic fuel and directing the excess glucose into storage as either glycogen or fat.

Glucose enters cells by diffusion. This diffusion is facilitated by transporters, but they are not active transporters—they require a concentration gradient, which is why it is important to regulate blood glucose levels so there is always an adequate glucose concentration gradient across the cell membranes. There are several kinds of glucose transporters, and those in skeletal muscle and adipose tissues are normally sequestered in cytoplasmic vesicles until insulin binds its receptors on the cell surface and triggers the insertion of transporters into the cell membrane.

Insulin plays many roles in controlling how cells use the glucose they take up from the circulation. In adipose cells, insulin inhibits lipase and promotes fat synthesis from glucose. In the liver, insulin activates an enzyme, glucokinase, that phosphorylates glucose as it enters the liver cell so it cannot diffuse back out again, thereby enhancing the overall diffusion of glucose into the cells. At the same time, insulin inhibits the enzyme glucose phosphatase that enables glucose to leave the cell. Insulin also activates glycogen synthase, an enzyme in liver cells that catalyzes the incorporation of glucose into glycogen, and activates enzymes that increase the flow of glucose into glycolysis (**Figure 49.18**).

To maintain blood glucose levels during the postabsorptive state, liver cells break down their stored glycogen, releasing glucose into the blood. The multiple processes that make it possible for the liver to release glucose depend on a fall in blood insulin levels (see Figure 49.18). Falling insulin inhibits the enzyme

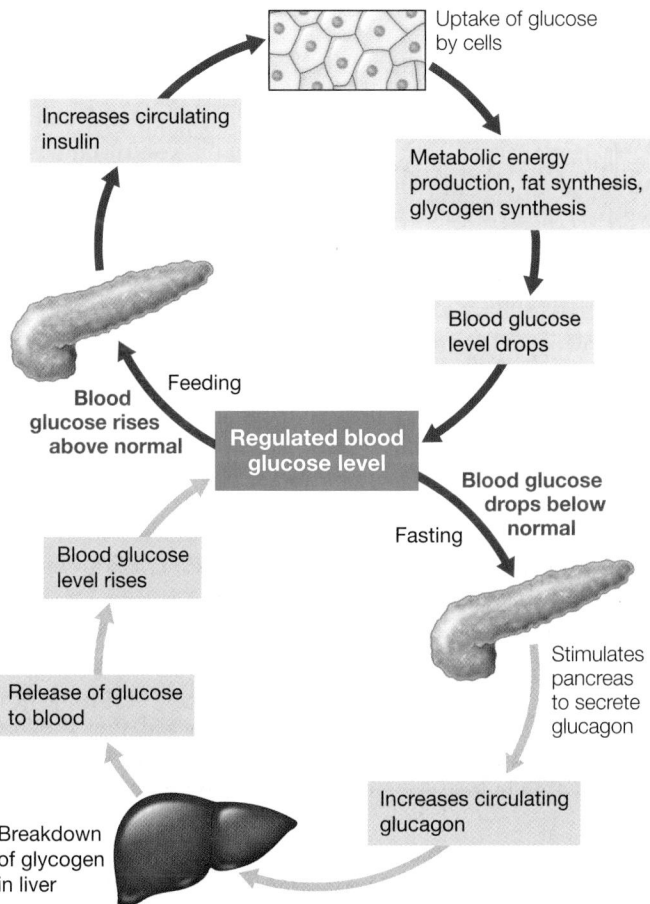

Figure 49.17 Regulating Glucose Levels in the Blood The hormone insulin (blue) acts to promote glucose use and storage and thereby lower blood glucose. The hormone glucagon (brown) acts on the liver to break down glycogen and release glucose into the blood.

Q: The nervous system depends on a constant supply of glucose, yet none of the actions of insulin or glucagon in this figure refer to supplying glucose to the nervous system. Why?

▶ **View in Achieve**
Animation 49.2 Insulin and Glucose Regulation

responsible for glycogen synthesis and activates the enzyme that breaks down glycogen. Also, with less insulin, the enzyme that phosphorylates glucose is inhibited and activity of glucose phosphatase is increased. The result is a breakdown of glycogen and the return of glucose to the blood. Another consequence of the fall in insulin levels is the increased activity of lipases in the liver and adipose tissue, releasing fatty acids to the blood. Most cells preferentially use fatty acids as their metabolic fuel during the postabsorptive state. *Overall, the most important control of fuel metabolism in the postabsorptive state is the lack of insulin.*

One tissue that does not switch fuel sources when an animal is postabsorptive is the nervous system. The cells of the nervous system require a constant supply of glucose and can use other fuels only to a limited extent. Most neurons do not require insulin to absorb glucose from the blood, but they do need an adequate glucose concentration gradient to drive the facilitated diffusion

of glucose across their cell membranes. Therefore it is critical that blood glucose levels are maintained when an animal is postabsorptive. The overall dependence of neural tissues on glucose, and their requirement for constant blood glucose levels, are the reasons it is so important for other cells of the body to shift to fat metabolism during the postabsorptive state.

The metabolism of fuel molecules during the postabsorptive state is mostly controlled by the lack of insulin, but if blood glucose falls below a certain level, glucagon is released from the pancreas. Glucagon's effect is opposite that of insulin: it stimulates liver cells to break down glycogen and to carry out gluconeogenesis. Thus, under the influence of glucagon, the liver produces glucose and releases it into the blood. Note that under conditions that stimulate glucagon release, the effects of low insulin are already in play—low glycogen synthase activity, low glucokinase activity, and high glucose phosphatase activity.

The brain plays a major role in regulating food intake

Multiple brain areas and signals are involved in the regulation of food intake. Long ago it was discovered that damaging a region in the rat hypothalamus close to the midline (the ventromedial hypothalamus) resulted in the rats increasing their food intake and becoming obese. Damage to the lateral hypothalamus, however, led to decreased food intake and the rats became thin. In both cases the rats eventually reached a new equilibrium body weight; thus it appeared that a capacity for regulation remained, but the set point was altered.

Figure 49.18 Insulin Controls Glucose Traffic in the Liver
Glucose freely enters and leaves liver cells by diffusion. But when insulin is present (green arrows), glucose is phosphorylated and cannot leave the cell. The glucose 6-phosphate either enters glycolysis or is synthesized into glycogen. Insulin activates the enzymes of glycogen synthesis. Without insulin (red arrows), glucokinase is inhibited and glycogen phosphorylase and glucose phosphatase are activated. Thus glycogen is broken down to glucose phosphate, which is dephosphorylated so that it can leave the cell and enter the blood. Other monosaccharides—galactose and fructose—can also diffuse into the cell and be converted to glucose through these pathways.

Experiment

Figure 49.19 A Single-Gene Mutation Leads to Obesity in Mice

Original Papers: D. L. Coleman and K. P. Hummel. 1969. Effects of parabiosis of normal with genetically diabetic mice. *Am J Physiol* 217: 1298–1304.

D. L. Coleman. 1973. Effects of parabiosis of obese with diabetes and normal mice. *Diabetologia* 9: 294–297.

In mice the *Ob* gene codes for the protein leptin, a satiety factor that signals the brain when enough food has been consumed. The recessive *ob* allele is a loss-of-function allele, so *ob/ob* mice do not produce leptin; they do not experience satiety and become obese. The *Db* gene encodes the leptin receptor, so mice homozygous for the recessive loss-of-function allele *db*, even if they produce leptin, cannot use it and so become obese.

HYPOTHESIS▶ Mice that cannot produce the satiety signal protein leptin will not become obese if they are able to obtain leptin from an outside source.

METHOD▶

1. Create two strains of genetically obese laboratory mice, one that lacks functional leptin (genotype *ob/ob*) and one that lacks the receptor for leptin (genotype *db/db*).
2. Create parabiotic pairs by surgically joining the circulatory systems of a non-obese (wild-type) mouse with a partner from one of the obese strains.
3. Allow mice to feed at will.

Parabiotic pair

Wild-type mouse   Genetically obese mouse
(*Ob/–* and *Db/–*)   (either *ob/ob* or *db/db*)

RESULTS▶ Parabiotic *ob/ob* mice obtain leptin from the wild-type (WT) partner and lose fat. Parabiotic *db/db* mice remain obese because they lack the leptin receptor and thus the leptin they obtain from their partner has no effect.

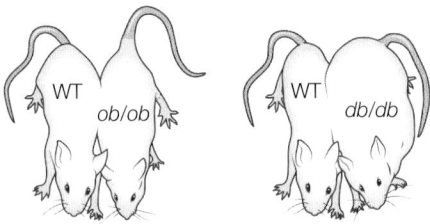

CONCLUSION▶ The protein leptin is a satiety signal that acts to prevent overeating and resultant obesity.

▶ **View in Achieve**
Simulation 49.1 Parabiotic Mice

We now know that another region of the hypothalamus, the **arcuate nucleus**, plays an important role in integrating a variety of feedback signals that influence food intake and body mass. Cells within the arcuate nucleus send axons to the ventromedial and dorsal hypothalamus, as well as to other brain areas that influence food intake and metabolism. One group of arcuate neurons projects to brain areas that inhibit food intake, while the other projects to brain areas that stimulate food intake. But what stimulates or inhibits the activity of the arcuate neurons?

Several factors have been identified that reflect the body's energy balance. Three of these are the proteins insulin, leptin, and ghrelin. Insulin, as detailed earlier, is released when blood glucose levels are high, and it induces a decline in food intake. **Leptin** (Greek *leptos*, "thin") is released by fat cells in proportion to how much lipid they contain. Evidence that leptin is a satiety signal is described in **Figure 49.19**. **Ghrelin** is released by the stomach when it is empty; its levels rise before meals and fall after meals. In the arcuate nucleus, insulin and leptin activate the neurons that inhibit feeding and inhibit the neurons that stimulate feeding. Ghrelin has the opposite effect on these two groups of neurons.

An integrative signal that could be playing a central role in regulation of feeding is the enzyme AMP-activated protein kinase (AMPK). When most cells are nutrient deprived, they produce AMPK, which stimulates the oxidation of substrates to replenish ATP. Fasting increases AMPK levels in the hypothalamus, and feeding reduces them. Insulin and leptin decrease AMPK activity in the hypothalamus, and ghrelin increases it. Thus AMPK could be a common pathway for various signals controlling food intake.

KEY CONCEPT
49.4 Recap and Assess

The major factors controlling gut function are autonomic reflexes, the enteric nervous system, and the hormones gastrin, secretin, and cholecystokinin. Insulin is the major hormonal controller of fuel metabolism through its effects on liver, muscle, and adipose tissues. The hypothalamus controls food intake by generating sensations of hunger and satiety influenced by feedback from blood glucose and hormones, including insulin, leptin, and ghrelin.

1. For various reasons, patients may be fed through a tube going into their stomach or a tube going all the way to their jejunum, the middle region of their small intestine. How would the feeding formula used in the jejunal tube have to differ from the one used in the stomach tube?

2. How do the three classes of lipoproteins differ in structure and function?

3. How are the effects of high and low insulin levels the same and different in liver and muscle?

4. In the experiments in which the lateral or the ventromedial hypothalamus was lesioned, what result enabled the conclusion that the regulation of body mass was altered rather than just the ability to produce satiety or hunger by the nutritional state of the body?

5. When exercising muscles do not have an adequate supply of oxygen, they continue to produce small amounts of ATP through glycolysis, but they also produce pyruvate and lactate. Explain how this pyruvate and lactate can help support continuing glycolysis.

6. What evidence supports the hypothesis that leptin influences satiety?

▶Investigating**LIFE**

Q and A **If the nutritional values were the same, could different foods have different impacts on health?**

The Pima of Arizona were among the first communities to be examined with a genome-wide survey. Many candidate genes were shown to be associated with obesity, but weakly so. The conclusion was that there are genetic contributions to the propensity to develop obesity, but except for a few rare cases, obesity is a multigenic trait that is highly influenced by environment. One aspect of the environment is physical activity, but another one is diet. The caloric content of the diet is obviously an important factor, but what about the composition of the diet? The experiments described in **Investigating Life: How Does the Gut Microbiome Contribute to Obesity and Metabolic Disease?** show that the composition of the diet can influence the composition of the gut microbiome, and the gut microbiome can influence the nutritional and other health effects of the diet. Thus, apart from differences in caloric intake, the consequences of the

Pima switching from a traditional diet to a high-fat Western diet could have resulted in changes in their microbiomes that have contributed to obesity and diabetes.

Future directions

It would be of interest to compare the microbiomes of the Arizona and the Mexican Pima peoples, and to compare those with the microbiomes of other populations on similar and different diets. If a particular microbiome profile is associated with the obesity–diabetes phenotype, it might be possible to change that microbiome through dietary change to promote better health. Just as we now do genomic screening to identify health risks, we might consider microbiome screening. Whereas we cannot change our genetic makeup, we could change our microbiome either through diet, or even therapeutically by uses of antibiotics and microbiome transplants. A new branch of medicine could develop around the testing, diagnosis, and therapy of the gut microbiome.

VISUAL SUMMARY 49

You should be able to relate each summary to the adjacent figures. If you go to this visual summary in **Achieve**, you can follow links to figures, animations, activities, and simulations that will help you consolidate the material.

KEY CONCEPT

49.1 Food Provides Energy as well as Materials for Biosynthesis

Go to **Activities 49.1** and **49.2**

- Animals are **heterotrophs** that directly or indirectly derive energy and molecular building blocks from **autotrophs**.

- Carbohydrates, fats, and proteins in food are **macronutrients** that provide energy. Energy content of food is measured in **kilocalories** (**kcal**), and excess caloric intake is stored as glycogen and fat.

- Food provides essential **carbon skeletons** that animals cannot synthesize themselves.

- Animals must obtain **vitamins** and **essential amino acids** and **fatty acids** from their diet. They also need **mineral macronutrients** (in large amounts) and **mineral micronutrients** (in small amounts).

- **Malnutrition** results when any essential nutrient is lacking from the diet. Chronic malnutrition causes **deficiency diseases**.

Figure 49.5

Eight essential amino acids for adult humans

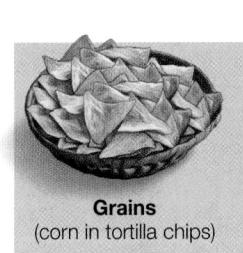

Grains
(corn in tortilla chips)

Tryptophan
Methionine
Valine
Threonine
Phenylalanine
Leucine
Isoleucine
Lysine

Legumes
(beans in bean dip)

Questions

1. Why is the energy content of food measured in quantities of heat (kcal)?

2. Why does severe starvation result in a swollen abdomen, hands, and feet?

3. What are the differences between macronutrients and mineral macro- and micronutrients?

KEY CONCEPT

49.2 Diverse Adaptations Support Ingestion and Digestion of Food

Go to **Activity 49.3**

■ Animals are characterized by how they acquire nutrients and include **saprobes**, **detritivores**, **filter feeders**, **herbivores**, and **carnivores**.

■ Digestion is the breakdown of complex food molecules into monomers that can be absorbed and used by cells.

■ Vertebrate guts are characterized by a large surface area for nutrient absorption.

■ The **microbiome** of the gut participates in digestive processes, makes certain nutrients available for absorption, and can be altered by diet and other factors.

Questions

1. Why are fossil teeth of great interest to paleontologists?

2. What is meant when someone claims that most of the DNA in our bodies is not human?

3. What are four features of the human gut that maximize its surface area for nutrient absorption?

Figure 49.8

Intestinal infolding in the earthworm

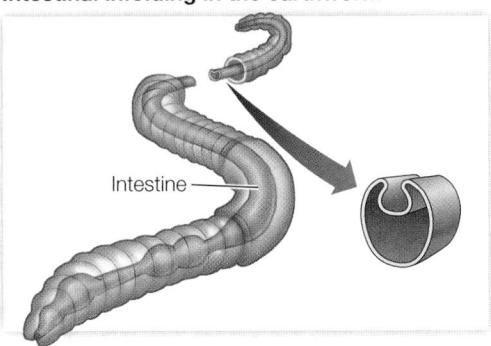

Intestine

KEY CONCEPT

49.3 The Vertebrate Gastrointestinal System Is a Disassembly Line

Go to **Activity 49.4** and **Animation 49.1**

■ Swallowing is a neural reflex. **Peristalsis** and segmentation movements move gut contents through the entire length of the gut.

■ **Sphincters** block the gut at certain locations but are opened by peristaltic waves of anticipatory relaxation.

■ Salivary **amylase** begins carbohydrate digestion in the mouth; pepsin and hydrochloric acid begin digestion of protein in the stomach. Mucus secretion facilitates food processing and protects the lining of the gut.

■ Pancreatic enzymes carry out most digestion in the duodenum, where bicarbonate ions from the pancreatic ducts neutralize the pH of the gut contents.

■ **Bile** from the **liver** and **gallbladder** emulsifies fats into **micelles**.

Questions

1. How do parietal cells in the stomach mucosa acidify the stomach contents?

2. Carbonic anhydrase also catalyzes the hydration of CO_2 in pancreatic ducts. How does this process differ from that in the gastric pits?

3. Explain two ways in which active transport of Na^+ ions by gut mucosal cells results in the movement of nutrients such as glucose into the body.

Figure 49.13

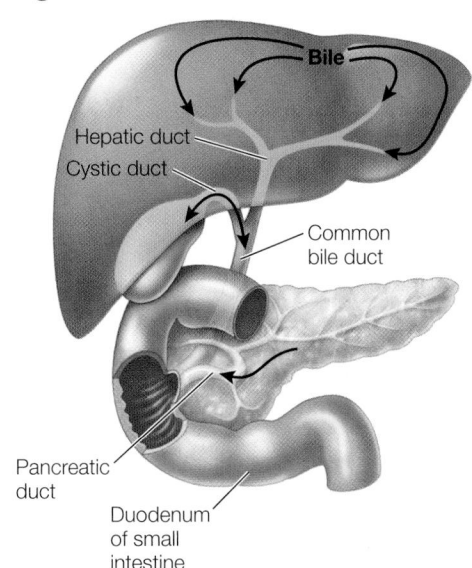

Bile

Hepatic duct
Cystic duct

Common
bile duct

Pancreatic
duct

Duodenum
of small
intestine

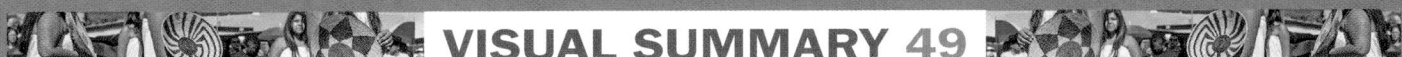

KEY CONCEPT

49.4 Nutrient Availability Is Controlled and Regulated

Go to Animation 49.2 and Simulation 49.1

- Actions of the stomach and small intestine are largely controlled by the hormones **gastrin**, **secretin**, and cholecystokinin (**CCK**).

- Fat and cholesterol are shipped out of the liver as **very low-density lipoproteins** (**VLDLs**). **Low-density lipoproteins** (**LDLs**) transport cholesterol around the body. **High-density lipoproteins** (**HDLs**) bring cholesterol back to the liver.

- **Insulin** promotes glucose uptake and storage as glycogen and fat during the **absorptive state**. In the **postabsorptive state**, lack of insulin blocks the uptake and use of glucose by most cells of the body except neurons. If blood glucose levels fall, **glucagon** secretion increases, stimulating the liver to break down glycogen and release glucose to the blood.

- Sensations of hunger and satiety are controlled by feedback signals that include insulin, **leptin**, and **ghrelin**.

Questions

1. What does gastrin control, and what controls gastrin?
2. How do secretin and CCK speed up and slow down digestive processes?
3. What are the roles of lipoproteins in lipid management?
4. How does insulin control the management of glucose in the liver?

Figure 49.16

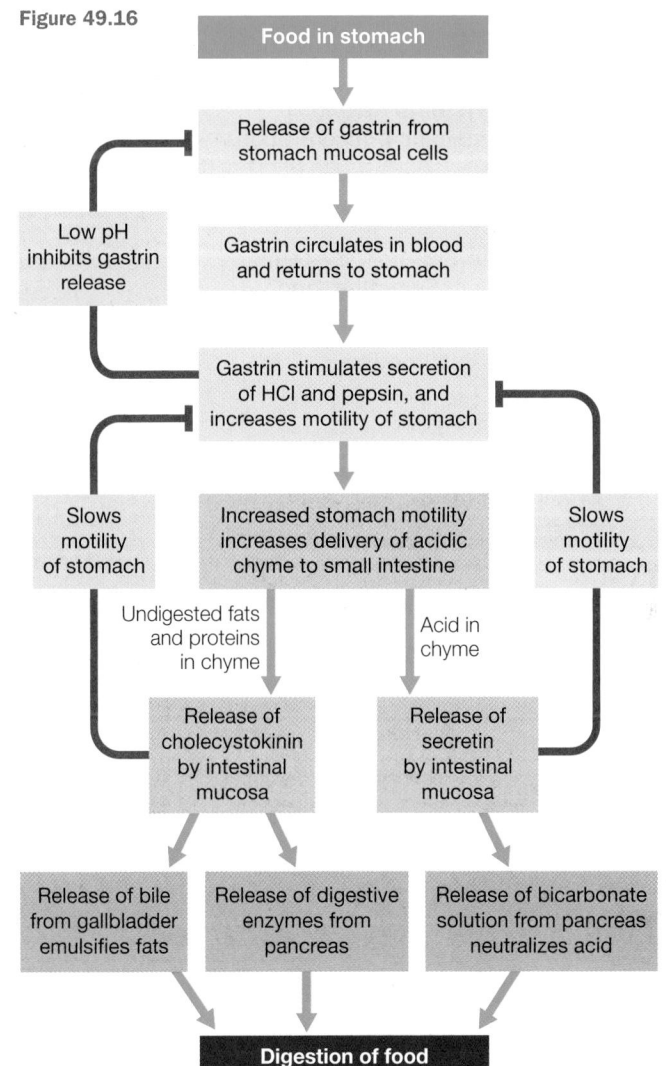

50 Salt and Water Balance and Nitrogen Excretion

KEY CONCEPTS

50.1 Excretory Systems Regulate Osmotic and Ionic Concentrations

50.2 Animals Excrete Nitrogen as Ammonia, Urea, or Uric Acid

50.3 Invertebrate Excretory Systems Use Filtration, Secretion, and Reabsorption

50.4 The Nephron Is the Basic Functional Unit of Vertebrate Excretory Systems

50.5 The Mammalian Kidney Can Produce Concentrated Urine

50.6 Kidney Function Is Regulated

© Michael & Patricia Fogden/Minden Pictures

The common vampire bat (*Desmodus rotundus*) is able to adjust its excretory physiology rapidly from water-excreting to water-conserving, depending on whether it is ingesting or digesting its blood meal.

▶Investigating LIFE

How Vampire Bats Use Blood as Fast Food

Blood, sweat, and tears have the composition of extracellular fluid and taste salty. The composition and volume of the extracellular fluid are regulated by the excretory system. Challenges to an animal's excretory system depend on its environment and lifestyle. Some desert animals rarely encounter free water, so they must conserve water by excreting their excess ions and nitrogenous wastes with minimal water loss. Animals living in fresh water have the opposite challenge: water continuously enters their bodies by osmosis and with their food, so they must excrete water and conserve ions. Most vertebrate animals living in the ocean face a challenge similar to that of the desert dwellers; they lose body water by osmosis and therefore need to conserve water and excrete ions.

Adaptations animals have to maintain salt and water balance are similar, but they are used in different ways to solve the problems unique to each species. Consider vampire bats feeding on the blood of animals such as goats and cattle. The bats use their sharp incisor teeth to make a small incision (usually on the ankle or leg of a sleeping victim) and then lap up the blood. A vampire bat feeds only once a day, and has to do so quickly, before the victim awakens and shakes it off.

Blood contains nutritious protein but is mostly water. To meet its daily energy needs, a vampire bat must take in a huge volume of blood relative to its body size, and it has to be able to fly back to its roost. To maximize protein intake and still be able to fly, the bat gets rid of water fast as a copious flow of dilute urine.

Back in the roost, the bat's challenge is reversed. To digest a high-protein meal, the bat must excrete a lot of nitrogenous waste with minimal loss of water, as it may not get more water until its next meal. Within a few hours, the bat's excretory system has to switch from rapid excretion of water to conservation of water, in spite of the need to excrete lots of nitrogenous wastes. The vampire bat's excretory system rapidly switches from producing lots of dilute urine to producing small amounts of concentrated urine.

 How does the excretory system of vampire bats process their high-protein liquid diet?
(Find the answer on page 1139.)

Excretory Systems Regulate Osmotic and Ionic Concentrations

Learning Objectives

50.1.1 Describe the roles of filtration, secretion, and reabsorption in the excretory systems of animals with closed circulatory systems.

50.1.2 Determine the osmoregulatory characteristics of a species from data about the composition of its extracellular fluid and its environment.

Homeostasis of the extracellular fluid (the blood plasma and interstitial fluid; see Key Concept 38.2) is critical because:

- The solute concentration of the extracellular fluid determines the water balance of the cells of the body.

- The specific ionic composition of the extracellular fluid influences many cell functions.

- The health of cells requires the elimination of nitrogenous wastes.

The problems that have to be solved to maintain homeostasis of the extracellular fluid depend on the environment in which a species lives (salt water, fresh water, or terrestrial) and its lifestyle, as you saw in the case of the vampire bat in the opening story. Animals depend on **excretory systems** to maintain the volume, concentration, and composition of their extracellular fluids, and to excrete wastes.

Osmosis causes water to enter or to leave cells

The volume of a cell depends on whether it takes up water from or loses water to the extracellular fluid. The movement of water across cell membranes via osmosis depends on differences in solute concentration on the two sides of the membrane and on the permeability of the membrane (see Key Concept 6.3). If the solute concentration of the extracellular fluid is less than that of the cytoplasm, water moves into the cells, causing them to swell and possibly burst (see Figure 6.10). If the solute concentration of the extracellular fluid is greater than that of the cytoplasm, the cells lose water and shrink. Thus the solute concentration of the extracellular fluid affects both the volume and the solute concentrations of the cells.

Animal physiologists use the term **osmolarity** in discussing osmosis. The osmolarity of a solution is the number of **moles** of osmotically active solutes per liter of solvent. Thus a 1-molar solution of glucose is also a 1-osmolar (1 osmole per liter) solution, but a 1-molar solution of sodium chloride (NaCl) is a 2-osmolar solution, because each NaCl molecule dissociates into two osmotically active ions.

Connect the Concepts As described in Key Concept 2.4, a mole is the amount of a substance in grams that is numerically equal to its molecular weight.

Excretory systems control extracellular fluid osmolarity and composition

Excretory systems control the osmolarity and composition of the extracellular fluids by excreting solutes that are present in excess (such as NaCl when we eat lots of salty food) and conserving solutes that are valuable or in short supply (such as glucose and amino acids). Excretory systems also eliminate the toxic waste products of protein metabolism. The output of the excretory system is **urine**.

Three basic processes are common to a wide variety of animal excretory systems: **filtration**, **secretion**, and **reabsorption**. Filtered extracellular fluid contains no cells or large molecules, such as proteins. In animals with a closed circulatory system, the blood plasma is filtered from capillaries into associated tubules. The walls of the capillaries and of the tubules are the filter, and the filtration is driven by blood pressure. As the filtrate flows through the tubules, its composition and concentration are modified through processes of secretion and reabsorption to form the urine that leaves the body.

In all of the discussions that follow about the movement of water across membranes, *it is important to remember that there are no mechanisms for the active transport of water*. The movement of water is due either to a pressure difference (filtration) or to a difference in solute concentration (osmosis). Water molecules move down a pressure gradient or up a solute concentration gradient.

Aquatic invertebrates are either ionic conformers or regulators

Most invertebrates that live in seawater conform to the osmotic concentration of their environment over a fairly wide range of salinities and are therefore called **osmoconformers** (Figure 50.1). The osmolarity of seawater in the open ocean is about 1,000 milliosmoles/liter (mOsm/L), but it can vary quite a bit in estuaries where it is diluted by an influx of fresh water or in evaporating tide pools as the salt gets concentrated. Osmoconformity can result in considerable energetic savings, as it costs metabolic energy to move ions across membranes to achieve osmotic regulation.

Osmoconformity is not an option for freshwater animals. No cell can do without ions or nutrients, so freshwater animals always have to expend energy to conserve salts and excrete water.

Some marine invertebrates maintain a rather constant osmolarity of their extracellular fluids as the osmolarity of the environment changes, and these animals are therefore called **osmoregulators** (see Figure 50.1). Osmoregulators in the marine environment mostly maintain their osmotic concentration considerably below that of the environment and are therefore engaged in **hypotonic regulation**. Occasionally, however, seawater is diluted by an influx of fresh water, as in estuaries, and animals must maintain their osmotic concentrations above that of the environment—a process called **hypertonic regulation**.

The brine shrimp *Artemia* illustrated in Figure 50.1 is an osmoregulator with an enormous range of tolerances. *Artemia* are found in huge numbers in extremely salty environments, such as Utah's Great Salt Lake and in coastal evaporation ponds where salt is concentrated for commercial purposes (see Figure 24.17)

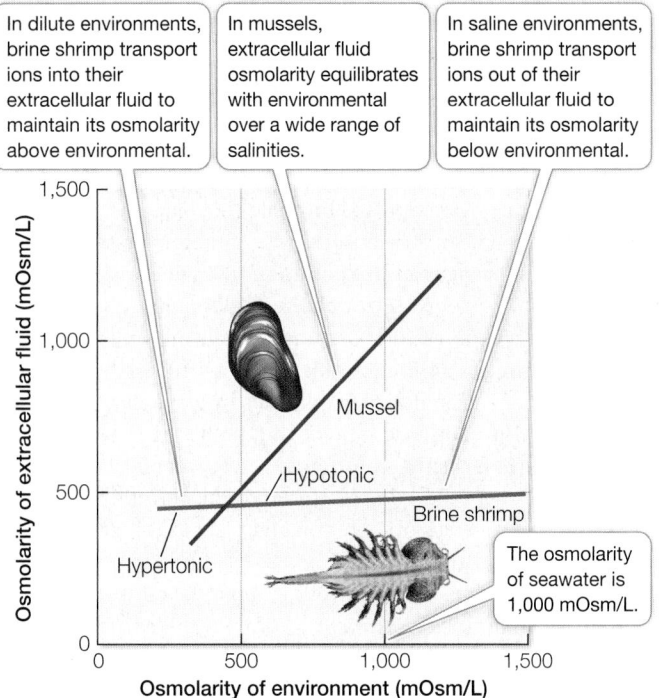

In dilute environments, brine shrimp transport ions into their extracellular fluid to maintain its osmolarity above environmental.

In mussels, extracellular fluid osmolarity equilibrates with environmental over a wide range of salinities.

In saline environments, brine shrimp transport ions out of their extracellular fluid to maintain its osmolarity below environmental.

The osmolarity of seawater is 1,000 mOsm/L.

Figure 50.1 Some Marine Invertebrates Osmoregulate Some aquatic animals, such as mussels, experience an extreme range of salt concentrations in their environment and are osmoconformers over much of that range. Other aquatic animals, such as brine shrimp, are osmoregulators in that they maintain a relatively constant osmolarity of their extracellular fluids as environmental salinity varies. (Mussel: After W. T. W. Potts and G. Parry, 1964. *Osmotic and Ionic Regulation in Animals.* Pergamon, Oxford; Brine Shrimp: P. C. Croghan. 1958. *J Exp Biol* 35: 219–233.)

and can reach an osmolarity of 2,500 mOsm/L. No animal could survive with internal osmolarities that high; such a solute concentration would cause proteins to denature. *Artemia* are able to exploit these environments because of their ability to regulate hypotonically by actively transporting NaCl from their extracellular fluid out across their gill membranes to the environment. *Artemia* cannot survive in fresh water, but they can live in dilute seawater by reversing the direction of transport of NaCl across their gill membranes to maintain the osmolarity of their extracellular fluids above that of the environment, thus becoming hypertonic regulators.

Invertebrates that are osmoconformers still have to be ionic regulators with respect to certain ions. Although the concentrations of Na^+ and Cl^- in their extracellular fluids may be the same

(A)

Salt glands are located in depressions in the skull above the eyes. They are bundles of secretory tubules served by parallel arrangements of arterioles and venules.

Each bundle of tubules drains into a central canal.

The central canal drains into the nasal cavity.

$Na^+/K^+/Cl^-$ ions are co-transported into tubule cells from the extracellular fluid. K^+ flows out of the cell in K^+ channels on the lateral cell membranes and is transported back in by Na^+/K^+ transporters. Cl^- flows into the tubule on the apical sides of the cells. Negative charged Cl^- ions pull Na^+ into the tubule from the intercellular spaces. Water follows and the tubule fluid is drained into the nasal cavity.

(B) *Macronectes giganteus*

Note the secretion at the tip of the bird's beak.

© Don Paulson/Alamy Stock Photo

Figure 50.2 Nasal Salt Glands Excrete Excess Salt (A) Marine birds have nasal salt glands that excrete the excess salt they ingest with their food. (B) This Southern Giant Petrel (*Macronectes giganteus*) has returned from a feeding trip at sea and is secreting salt through its nasal salt gland.

as in seawater, many other ions are regulated at different levels. For example, the concentration of K^+ is usually higher, and the concentrations of Mg^{2+} and of SO_4^{2-} are usually lower, in the extracellular fluids than in the seawater. Active transporters maintain the regulated ions in the extracellular fluid at optimal concentrations.

Vertebrates are osmoregulators and ionic regulators

All aquatic vertebrates, with the exception of two classes, regulate the osmolarity of their extracellular fluids at around 300 mOsm/L. In doing so, they are selective in which ions they conserve and which ions they excrete; thus they are ionic regulators and osmoregulators. The exceptions are the hagfishes and the cartilaginous fishes (sharks and rays). Hagfishes are an ancient vertebrate group of jawless fishes (see Figure 31.11). Hagfishes are osmoconformers as well as ionic conformers for most of the ions found in seawater. The cartilaginous fishes are osmoconformers, but in a unique way. They retain in their extracellular fluid two organic solutes, urea and trimethylamine oxide (TMAO), that are products of protein metabolism. As a result, their extracellular fluid is slightly hypertonic to the seawater and they gain water by osmosis rather than lose water to their salty environment.

Terrestrial vertebrates obtain their salts mostly from food, and they regulate the ionic composition of their extracellular fluids by conserving some ions and excreting others. For example, herbivores have to conserve Na^+ because most plants have low concentrations of Na^+. In contrast, birds that feed on marine animals must excrete the excess sodium they ingest with their food. Such birds, which include penguins and gulls, excrete excess salt through nasal salt glands. These glands are activated by parasympathetic innervation in response to increased osmolarity of the blood. The glands consist of bundles of secretory tubules in close relationship to blood vessels and emptying into central canals (**Figure 50.2**). Activation causes opening of potassium channels on the lateral membranes of the tubule cells and opening of Cl^- channels on the apical side of the cells (facing into the tubule). Activation also stimulates $Na^+/K^+/Cl^-$ cotransporters on the basal sides of the cells (in contact with interstitial fluid). Increased Na^+ in the cells is transported out of the lateral cell membrane in exchange K^+. The Cl^- leaving the apical membranes creates an electrochemical gradient that pulls the excess Na^+ in the lateral spaces between the tubule cells to flow into the tubule lumen through intercellular junctions. The resulting concentrated solution of NaCl flows into a series of canals that empty into the nasal cavity. These birds can be seen frequently sneezing or shaking their heads to get rid of the salty droplets excreted from their nasal salt glands.

50.1 Recap and Assess

Excretory systems control water and salt balance and the excretion of nitrogenous waste products through three mechanisms: filtration of body fluids to form urine, active secretion of substances into the urine, and active reabsorption of substances from the urine. Animals can be osmoconformers or osmoregulators.

1. What is the significance of a closed circulatory system for osmoregulation in a freshwater vertebrate?

2. Why is it important for an animal like *Artemia* that lives in the intertidal zone to be able to osmoregulate, and how does *Artemia* do that at the extremes of salinities in its environment?

3. How does water get into the nasal salt gland ducts of marine birds?

In addition to maintaining salt and water balance, animals must eliminate the waste products of metabolism from their extracellular fluids. The major problem is nitrogen. When nitrogen-containing molecules are broken down by metabolism, the end-product can be toxic.

50.2 Animals Excrete Nitrogen as Ammonia, Urea, or Uric Acid

Learning Objectives

50.2.1 Discuss the properties of ammonia, urea, and uric acid as nitrogenous waste products.

50.2.2 Describe the relative advantages and disadvantages of excreting nitrogenous waste as urea or as uric acid.

The end-products of the metabolism of carbohydrates and fats are water and carbon dioxide, which are not difficult to eliminate. Proteins and nucleic acids, however, contain nitrogen, so their metabolism produces nitrogenous wastes in addition to water and carbon dioxide.

Ammonia is toxic

The most common nitrogenous waste is **ammonia** (NH_3). Ammonia is highly toxic, so it must be excreted continuously to prevent its accumulation or it must be detoxified by conversion into **urea** or **uric acid** (**Figure 50.3**). Ammonia is highly soluble in water and diffuses rapidly, so its continuous excretion is relatively simple for many aquatic animals that continuously lose ammonia from their blood to the environment by diffusion across their gill membranes. Animals that excrete ammonia, such as aquatic invertebrates and bony fishes, are called **ammonotelic**.

Ammonia can also be lost by diffusion across the alveolar membranes of air-breathing animals, but with tidal ventilation, the buildup of ammonia in the extracellular fluids would be greater and therefore toxic. Therefore these animals detoxify ammonia by converting it into urea or uric acid.

Urea is highly soluble in water

Mammals, amphibians, cartilaginous fishes (sharks and rays), and hagfishes excrete urea as their principal nitrogenous waste product and are therefore called **ureotelic**. Urea is quite soluble in water, but its excretion can result in a large loss of water that many animals can ill afford. Mammals have somewhat solved this problem through the evolution of excretory systems that can produce urine with a high concentration of urea, thereby decreasing the water loss associated with excretion of urea. Also, recall from Key Concept 50.1 that sharks and rays solve the water loss problem of living in seawater by

Figure 50.3 Nitrogenous Waste Products of Metabolism
The metabolism of proteins and nucleic acids produces nitrogenous wastes. Many aquatic animals, including most fishes, excrete nitrogenous wastes as ammonia, which is highly diffusible and soluble in an aqueous environment. Most terrestrial animals and some aquatic animals excrete either urea or uric acid. Urea is more soluble in water and is the major nitrogenous excretory product for mammals, amphibians, and some fishes. Uric acid is not very soluble in water and is the major nitrogenous excretory product for reptiles (including birds), insects, and some amphibians.

retaining high concentrations of urea and TMAO in their extracellular fluid, so that it is hyperosmotic to seawater.

Uric acid is not very soluble in water

A single molecule of uric acid eliminates twice the amount of nitrogen as does a molecule of urea (see Figure 50.3), but uric acid is not very soluble in water. Therefore it tends to precipitate out of solution and form a colloidal suspension in the urine, requiring it to be excreted as a semisolid (for example, the whitish material in bird droppings). Because of the precipitation of the uric acid out of solution in the excretory system, water can be reabsorbed from the urine and thereby reduce the water loss necessary to excrete the nitrogenous waste. Animals that excrete uric acid are **uricotelic**, and they include insects, reptiles (including birds), and some amphibians. Many uricotelic species live in very arid environments.

Most species produce more than one nitrogenous waste

Humans are ureotelic, but we also excrete uric acid. The uric acid in human urine comes largely from the metabolism of nucleic acids. If uric acid levels in the extracellular fluid rise too high, uric acid can precipitate in joints, causing the age-old malady gout. Because solubility goes down with temperature, uric acid usually precipitates first in the extremities, especially the big toe. Pain in the big toe is a telltale symptom of gout. The risk for developing gout goes up with excessive consumption of protein, beer, and spirits (less so with wine) and in general with obesity and insulin resistance. Therefore in the past it was called "the disease of rich men." Gout has been around for a very long time; the first documented case was in Egypt around 2500 BCE.

Humans can also excrete ammonia, which is an important mechanism for regulating the pH of the extracellular fluids. As you will see later in this chapter, excreted ammonia buffers the urine and enables the excretion of excess hydrogen ions.

Species that live in different habitats at different developmental stages may use more than one mechanism of nitrogen excretion. The tadpoles of frogs and toads, for example, excrete ammonia across their gill membranes, but adult frogs and toads generally excrete urea. Some adult amphibians that live in arid habitats excrete uric acid.

KEY CONCEPT
50.2 Recap and Assess

Ammonia is a common metabolic waste product of nitrogen-containing molecules. Most aquatic animals excrete ammonia by diffusion into the water. Terrestrial animals and some aquatic animals detoxify ammonia by converting it to urea or uric acid.

1. When amino acids are broken down, a first step is removal of the amine group, forming ammonia. Why is it important to get rid of that ammonia, and how do fishes and mammals achieve this excretion?

2. Why do sharks and rays produce urea rather than uric acid to raise the osmotic concentration of their extracellular fluids?

3. For terrestrial animals, what is the advantage of excreting uric acid as the nitrogenous waste product?

Animals exhibit a variety of adaptations for dealing with the challenges of salt and water balance in different environments. All of these adaptations, however, are based on two basic mechanisms—namely, filtration and tubular processing of the filtrate to conserve some solutes and excrete others.

KEY CONCEPT
50.3 Invertebrate Excretory Systems Use Filtration, Secretion, and Reabsorption

Learning Objectives

50.3.1 Describe the structure and function of a protonephridium.

50.3.2 Diagram the process of urine formation by a metanephridium.

50.3.3 Explain how Malpighian tubules enable insects to live in very arid habitats.

Freshwater and terrestrial invertebrates have a wide variety of adaptations for maintaining salt and water balance and excreting nitrogen. Here we explore three examples of invertebrate excretory systems: protonephridia, metanephridia, and Malpighian tubules. Each of these systems produces an extract of interstitial fluid lacking large molecules. They then change the solute composition (ions and small molecules) of that fluid to form an excretory product.

Protonephridia of flatworms excrete water and conserve salts

Many free-living flatworms, such as *Planaria*, live in fresh water. These animals excrete water through an elaborate network of

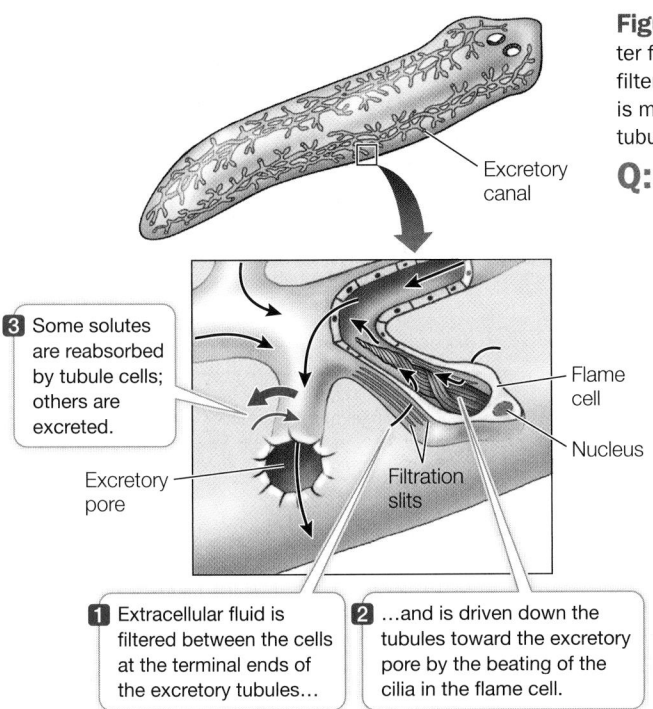

Figure 50.4 **Protonephridia in Flatworms** The protonephridia of the freshwater flatworm *Planaria* consist of tubules ending in flame cells. Extracellular fluid is filtered through the filtration slits in the flame cells. The composition of the filtrate is modified as it flows down the tubule. Black arrows indicate direction of flow of tubular fluid.

Q: Do you expect the fluid coming out of the excretory pore to be hypertonic or hypotonic to the flatworm's interstitial fluid?

Excretory canal

Flame cell

Nucleus

3 Some solutes are reabsorbed by tubule cells; others are excreted.

Excretory pore

Filtration slits

1 Extracellular fluid is filtered between the cells at the terminal ends of the excretory tubules…

2 …and is driven down the tubules toward the excretory pore by the beating of the cilia in the flame cell.

tubules running throughout their bodies. The tubules end in flame cells, so called because each cell has a tuft of cilia projecting into its tubule (**Figure 50.4**). The beating of the cilia gives the appearance of a flickering flame. A flame cell and a tubule together form a **protonephridium** (plural *protonephridia*; Greek *proto*, "before," + *nephros*, "kidney"). Flame cells are also called cap cells because they cap off the tubule.

Extracellular fluid enters the tubules by filtration through slits in the flame cells. The beating of the cilia causes a slight negative pressure in the tubule, and movements of the animal create positive pressure in the extracellular fluid. This pressure difference causes extracellular fluid to be filtered through the filtration slits in the flame cells. The filtrate flows toward the animal's excretory pore, and along the way the cells of the tubules modify the composition of the fluid by reabsorption and secretion of specific ions and molecules. Because more ions are reabsorbed than are secreted, the urine that leaves the flatworm's body is less concentrated than the extracellular fluid. Thus the protonephridium conserves ions and excretes water and wastes.

Metanephridia of annelids process coelomic fluid

Filtration of body fluids and modification of urine by tubules are highly developed processes in annelids such as the earthworm. Annelids are segmented, and in each segment they have a fluid-filled body cavity called a coelom (see Figure 30.11). Annelids have a closed circulatory system through which blood is pumped under pressure. The pressure causes the blood to be filtered across the thin, permeable capillary walls into the coelom. Some waste products, such as ammonia, diffuse directly from the tissues into the coelom. Where does this coelomic fluid go?

Each segment of the earthworm contains a pair of **metanephridia** (singular *metanephridium*; Greek *meta*, "akin to"). Each metanephridium begins as a ciliated, funnel-like opening called a nephrostome. The nephrostome resides in one segment and continues as a tubule in the next segment. The tubule ends in a pore, called a nephridiopore, that opens to the outside of the animal (**Figure 50.5**). Coelomic fluid is swept into the metanephridia through the ciliated nephrostomes. As the fluid passes through the tubules, their cells actively reabsorb certain molecules from it and actively secrete other molecules into it. What leaves the animal through the nephridiopores is a dilute urine containing nitrogenous wastes and other solutes.

Capillaries   Bladder   Coelomic cavity

Metanephridium

Collecting tubules

Nephridiopore

Urine

Nephrostome

1 Coelomic fluid is swept into the metanephridium by cilia surrounding the nephrostome.

2 The tubule cells of the metanephridium alter the composition of the fluid as it flows through the tubule…

3 …producing a dilute urine that is excreted through the nephridiopore.

Figure 50.5 **Metanephridia in Earthworms** The metanephridia of annelids are arranged segmentally. The cross section at the left end shows a pair of metanephridia. Three longitudinal sections (right) show only one metanephridium of the two in each segment. Coelomic fluid enters the nephrostome and flows through tubules leading to the nephridiopore. A close association of the tubules and blood capillaries facilitates the active exchange of substances between the blood and the tubular fluid.

View in Achieve
Activity 50.1 Annelid Metanephridia

Figure 50.6 Malpighian Tubules in Insects The blind, thin-walled Malpighian tubules are attached to the junction of the insect's midgut and hindgut and project into the spaces containing extracellular fluid. This system makes it possible to excrete wastes with very little loss of water.

Q: Why are Na^+ and K^+ ions transported into the Malpighian tubule but then transported out of the hindgut and rectum?

Malpighian tubules of insects use active transport to excrete wastes

Insects can excrete nitrogenous wastes with very little loss of water and can therefore live in the driest habitats on Earth. The insect excretory system consists of **Malpighian tubules**. An individual insect has from 2 to more than 100 of these blind-ended tubules that open into the gut between the midgut and hindgut (**Figure 50.6**).

Insects have an open circulatory system and therefore cannot use a pressure difference to filter extracellular fluids into the Malpighian tubules. Instead, the cells of the tubules actively transport uric acid, potassium ions, and sodium ions from the extracellular fluid into the tubules. The high concentration of solutes in the tubules causes water to follow osmotically, which flushes the tubule contents toward the gut.

The epithelial cells of the hindgut and rectum actively transport sodium and potassium ions from the gut contents back into the extracellular fluid. This local transport of salts creates an osmotic gradient that pulls water out of the rectal contents. As its concentration increases, the uric acid forms a colloidal suspension, freeing even more water to be reabsorbed. Remaining in the rectum is the uric acid mixed with other wastes; this semisolid matter is what the insect excretes. If you ever park your car under a tree being visited by bees, you will find the little excretory droplets from the bees all over the car. The Malpighian tubule system is a highly effective mechanism for excreting nitrogenous wastes and some salts without giving up much water.

KEY CONCEPT
50.3 Recap and Assess

Protonephridia and metanephridia work by creating a filtrate of the body fluids that is modified by the secretion and reabsorption of specific substances before being excreted. Insect Malpighian tubules actively secrete uric acid and other solutes into closed tubules.

1. How do protonephridia enable flatworms to live in fresh water?
2. What are the relationships among blood plasma, coelomic fluid, and urine in an annelid worm?
3. How does the insect excretory system conserve water?

Having described how several invertebrate groups handle nitrogen excretion, we next consider the nephron—the basic unit of the vertebrate excretory system—and how it evolved to be able to respond to a variety of salt- and water-balance challenges and maintain a relatively constant internal environment.

KEY CONCEPT
50.4 The Nephron Is the Basic Functional Unit of Vertebrate Excretory Systems

Learning Objectives

50.4.1 Discuss the structural and behavioral characteristics of amphibians and reptiles that enable them to minimize water loss.

50.4.2 Diagram and/or describe the organization of blood vessels in the nephron.

50.4.3 Explain the mechanism of filtration of blood plasma from the glomerular capillaries into Bowman's capsule.

50.4.4 Explain why the renal filtrate changes in composition as it passes through the nephron.

The main excretory organ of vertebrates is the **kidney**, and the functional unit of the kidney is the **nephron**, which has a blood vessel component and a tubule component. The blood vessel (vascular) component begins with a knot of capillaries that are highly permeable and filter the blood into the tubule component. Processes of secretion and reabsorption in the tubules produce urine, which differs in composition from the extracellular fluids of the body.

The evolution of vertebrates is thought to have begun with a marine ancestor that moved into fresh water. The excretory system of this vertebrate ancestor would have evolved to excrete large quantities of water while conserving salts. But if the early vertebrate excretory system evolved in response to the need to excrete water, how did subsequent vertebrate lineages adapt to environments where water must be conserved and salts excreted? The answer to this question differs among vertebrate groups. Even among marine fishes, the excretory adaptations of the bony fishes differ from those of the cartilaginous fishes. Reptiles, including birds, and mammals have excretory systems that conserve water. The reptiles achieve this mainly by being uricotelic and producing a semisolid excretory product that contains little water. Mammals, in contrast, are ureotelic; they excrete a liquid waste product but have evolved the ability to produce highly concentrated urine.

Marine fishes must conserve water

Marine bony fishes osmoregulate their extracellular fluids to maintain them at one-third to one-half the osmolarity of seawater. Thus marine bony fishes must conserve water, which they are constantly losing through osmosis, and must excrete excess solutes. Marine bony fishes cannot produce urine that is more concentrated than their extracellular fluids, so they minimize water loss by producing very little urine. In contrast, freshwater fishes produce lots of dilute urine.

How do marine bony fishes deal with the large salt loads they ingest with food? Marine bony fishes do not absorb from their guts some of the ions they take in, especially divalent ions such as Mg^{2+} and SO_4^{2-}. NaCl, the major salt ingested, is actively excreted across the gill membranes. As mentioned earlier, bony fishes can lose their nitrogenous waste, ammonia, by diffusion across their gill membranes.

Sharks and rays are osmoconformers but not ionic conformers. As mentioned earlier, they raise the osmolarity of their body fluids by retaining urea and TMAO, making their extracellular fluids hyperosmotic to seawater. These species have adapted to a concentration of urea in the body fluids that would be toxic to other vertebrates. Sharks and rays still have the problem of excreting the large amount of salts they take in with their food. They solve this problem by having a gland in the rectum that actively secretes NaCl by a mechanism similar to that of the nasal salt glands of seabirds.

Terrestrial amphibians and reptiles must avoid desiccation

Most amphibians live in or near fresh water, and they usually stay in humid habitats when they do venture from the water. Like freshwater fishes, most amphibians produce large amounts of dilute urine and conserve salts. Some amphibians, however, have adapted to habitats that require water conservation.

Amphibians living in dry terrestrial environments have skin with a reduced permeability to water. Some secrete a waxy substance over the skin for waterproofing. Several species of frogs that live in arid regions of Australia burrow into the ground and remain there during long dry periods. They enter **estivation**, a state of very low metabolic activity and therefore low water turnover. When it rains, the frogs come out of estivation, feed, and reproduce. Their most interesting adaptation is an enormous urinary bladder. Before entering estivation, they fill the bladder with dilute urine, which can amount to one-third of their body weight. This dilute urine serves as a water reservoir that is gradually reabsorbed into the blood during the long period of estivation. Aboriginal peoples have learned to locate these buried frogs and use them as an emergency source of water.

Reptiles occupy habitats ranging from aquatic to extremely hot and dry. In fact, snakes, lizards, and birds are among the most prominent members of many desert faunas. Three major adaptations have freed reptiles from needing to have a close association with water (see Key Concept 31.4):

1. Reptiles are amniotes that do not need fresh water to reproduce because they employ internal fertilization and lay eggs with shells that retard evaporative water loss.

2. Reptiles have a dry epidermis (skin) that retards evaporative water loss.

3. Reptiles excrete nitrogenous wastes as uric acid semisolids, losing little water in the process.

Mammals can produce highly concentrated urine

Mammals occupy diverse habitats, many of which present special excretory system challenges. The most challenging environments are those in which water is severely limited. Mammals have a variety of adaptations to conserve water, but chief among them is the ability to produce urine that is more concentrated than their extracellular fluids. They are able to concentrate their urine because of adaptations of their kidneys that we explore in detail in Key Concept 50.5. To understand how these adaptations work, you must first know the structure and function of the vertebrate nephron.

The nephron is the functional unit of the vertebrate kidney

Urine formation in vertebrate nephrons involves three main processes (**Figure 50.7**):

1. *Filtration.* Each nephron has a dense knot of capillaries called a **glomerulus** (plural *glomeruli*). The glomerulus is highly permeable to water, ions, and small molecules but impermeable to large molecules. Blood pressure drives the movement of water and small-molecular-weight solutes out of the glomerular capillaries.

2. *Tubular reabsorption.* The filtrate from the glomerulus flows into the **renal tubule**. Cells in the renal tubule modify the filtrate by reabsorbing specific ions, nutrients, and water, returning these to the blood, and leaving behind and concentrating excess ions and waste products such as urea.

3. *Tubular secretion.* The filtrate in the renal tubule is further modified by tubule cells transporting substances into the tubule. These are substances that the body needs to excrete.

Blood enters the glomerular capillaries via an **afferent arteriole** and leaves the glomerulus in an **efferent arteriole**. This short vessel is called an arteriole because it feeds another capillary bed,

1 An afferent arteriole supplies blood under pressure to the glomerulus.

2 The glomerulus, a knot of capillaries, is the site of blood filtration.

3 Bowman's capsule receives the glomerular filtrate.

Filtration

Bowman's capsule

4 An efferent arteriole carries blood from the glomerulus.

Renal tubule

Reabsorption and secretion

5 Renal tubule cells alter the composition of glomerular filtrate through reabsorption and secretion of solutes.

7 The renal venule drains the peritubular capillaries.

6 Peritubular capillaries bring materials to the tubules that will be secreted into the urine and carry away reabsorbed substances.

Peritubular capillaries

Excretion

8 The processed filtrate (urine) of the individual nephrons enters collecting ducts and is delivered to a common duct leaving the kidney.

Urine

Figure 50.7 The Vertebrate Nephron   The vertebrate nephron consists of a renal tubule closely associated with two capillary beds, the glomerulus and the peritubular capillaries.

 View in Achieve
Activity 50.2 The Vertebrate Nephron

called the **peritubular capillaries**. These capillaries intimately surround the renal tubules and deliver substances to the renal tubules that the cells of the tubules secrete into the urine. The peritubular capillaries also carry away substances that the tubule cells reabsorb from the urine.

Blood is filtered into Bowman's capsule

The renal tubule begins with **Bowman's capsule** (see Figure 50.7), which encloses the glomerulus (**Figure 50.8A,B**). The glomerulus appears to be pushed into Bowman's capsule much like a fist pushed into an inflated balloon. The cells of the capsule that are in direct contact with the glomerular capillaries are called **podocytes** (**Figure 50.8C**). These highly specialized cells have numerous extensions, each with hundreds of fine processes. The podocytes wrap around the capillaries so that their processes interdigitate and intimately cover the capillaries.

The glomerulus filters the blood, producing a fluid (the renal filtrate) that lacks cells and large molecules. The walls of the capillaries, the basal lamina of the capillary endothelium, and the podocytes of Bowman's capsule all participate in filtration. Fenestrations in the walls of the capillaries (see Key Concept 48.4) allow water and many solute molecules, but not red blood cells, to pass through. The meshwork of the basal lamina and the spaces

(A) Bowman's capsule

Proximal renal tubule

© CNRI/Science Source

Podocytes   Capillaries   Bowman's capsule

(B) Multiple glomeruli

Afferent arterioles   Glomeruli

© Susumu Nishinaga/Science Source

(C) Tubule cells

Podocyte

© Science Photo Library RF

Podocyte processes

(D) Cells of the glomerular filter

Podocyte   Podocyte processes

Filtrate

Basal lamina

Capillary wall

Blood plasma   Fenestration

© Dr. Donald Fawcett & D. Friend/Visuals Unlimited, Inc.

Figure 50.8 A Tour of the Vertebrate Nephron   Scanning electron micrographs illustrate the anatomical basis for blood filtration in the kidneys. **(A)** This cross section of an intact glomerulus shows the tubule cells that form Bowman's capsule surrounding the glomerular capillaries. **(B)** In a preparation showing only the blood vessels (tubular tissue has been digested away), the glomeruli appear as balls of capillaries served by arterioles. **(C)** Higher magnification of a glomerulus with the tubule cells intact shows the podocytes that wrap around the glomerular capillaries. **(D)** The glomerular filter has three layers: the fenestrated endothelial cells of the capillaries, the meshwork of collagen fibers making up the basal lamina, and the filtration slits between the podocyte processes. All three layers have negative charges, which contribute to their ability to prevent the passage of protein molecules.

between the processes of the podocytes are even finer and prevent large molecules from leaving the capillaries (Figure 50.8D). The arterial pressure of the blood entering the permeable capillaries causes the filtration of water and small molecules out of the glomerular capillaries and into Bowman's capsule. The glomerular filtration rate is high because blood pressure in the glomerular capillaries is high, and because the capillaries of the glomerulus, along with their covering of podocytes, are more permeable to water than are other capillary beds in the body.

Recall that marine bony fishes produce very little urine. The explanation for this is that their kidneys have evolved to have few if any glomeruli, whereas the kidneys of freshwater fishes have many glomeruli.

The renal tubules convert glomerular filtrate to urine

The composition of the filtrate that enters the renal tubule is similar to that of the blood plasma, except the filtrate lacks high-molecular-weight solutes such as proteins. Reabsorption and secretion cause the composition of this fluid to change as it passes down the renal tubule. Cells of the tubule actively reabsorb certain molecules from the tubule fluid (which are returned to the blood flowing through the peritubular capillaries). For example, glucose and amino acids are reabsorbed. Most NaCl is reabsorbed. Other substances in the blood of the peritubular capillaries are actively secreted into the tubule fluid. An example is para-aminohippuric acid (PAH), which is produced in the liver from benzoic acid, a common food preservative. Because of the actions of the renal tubules, the excreted urine is very different from the original glomerular filtrate. As you learn all the things that renal tubules do, keep in mind that renal tubules all consist of a single layer of epithelial cells

KEY CONCEPT
50.4 Recap and Assess

The kidney is the major excretory organ of vertebrates. Its functional unit is the nephron, which includes a glomerulus that filters blood and a renal tubule that secretes and reabsorbs solutes, modifying the filtrate to produce urine. As seen in freshwater fishes, the nephron evolved as a mechanism for excreting excess water while conserving valuable solutes. Vertebrates have various adaptations for conserving water. Marine bony fishes produce very little urine but lose nitrogenous waste as ammonia across their gills and also excrete salts from their gill membranes. Marine cartilaginous fishes produce urea and retain it, so their extracellular fluids are hyperosmotic to the environment and therefore take up water by osmosis. Many terrestrial vertebrates conserve water by excreting nitrogenous waste as uric acid, by minimizing evaporative water loss, and by active secretion of salts. Mammals have the ability to conserve water by producing urine that is more concentrated than their extracellular fluid.

1. What is the connection between the need to conserve water and the evolution of internal fertilization?

2. What are the roles of the afferent and efferent arterioles in the nephron?

3. What are the anatomical components of the filtration mechanism in the glomerulus?

4. How does the composition of the urine become different from the composition of the blood?

The adaptations that enable the mammalian kidney to produce urine more concentrated than extracellular fluids were important steps in vertebrate evolution, and they were largely achieved through changes in the structure and regional functions of the renal tubules. These changes converted a kidney that evolved to excrete water into an organ that conserves water.

KEY CONCEPT
50.5 The Mammalian Kidney Can Produce Concentrated Urine

Learning Objectives

50.5.1 Summarize the internal organization of the mammalian kidney.

50.5.2 Describe the mechanism whereby most of the glomerular filtrate is reabsorbed in the proximal convoluted tubule.

50.5.3 Explain how the loop of Henle maintains a concentration gradient in the extracellular fluid of the medulla of the kidney.

50.5.4 Describe how the mammalian excretory system is involved in regulating pH of the extracellular fluid.

Mammals have high body temperatures and high metabolic rates, and therefore have the potential for a high rate of water loss and a high level of nitrogenous waste production. Having an excretory system that minimizes water loss made it possible for these highly active species to occupy arid habitats.

 Media Clip 50.1 Inside the Bladder
Life12e.com/mc50.1

Kidneys produce urine and the bladder stores it

Mammalian excretory systems are similar, so we will use that of humans as our example. Humans have two kidneys at the back of the upper region of the abdominal cavity (Figure 50.9A). Each kidney filters blood, processes the filtrate into urine, and releases that urine into a duct called the **ureter**. The ureter of each kidney leads to the **urinary bladder**, where the urine is stored until it is excreted through the **urethra**, a short tube that opens to the outside of the body.

Two sphincter muscles surrounding the base of the urethra control urination. One of these sphincters is a smooth muscle and is controlled by the autonomic nervous system. As the bladder fills, stretch receptors in the walls of the bladder trigger a spinal reflex that relaxes this sphincter. This reflex is the only control of urination in infants, hence their frequent "accidents." The other sphincter is a skeletal muscle and is controlled by the voluntary nervous system. When the bladder is *very* full, only deliberate conscious effort prevents urination. Toilet training of children teaches them to control this sphincter.

Nephrons have a regular arrangement in the kidney

The kidney is shaped like a kidney bean. When sliced along its long axis on the midline, its key anatomical features are revealed (Figure 50.9B). The ureter and the **renal artery** and **renal vein** enter

(A) Organs of the excretory system

- Adrenal gland
- Kidney
- Ureter
- Urinary bladder
- Urethra

(B) Cross section of the kidney

- Cortex
- Medulla
- Renal artery
- Renal vein
- Pelvis
- Renal pyramid
- Ureter

(C) Nephrons in a mammalian kidney

- Glomerulus
- Afferent arteriole
- Efferent arteriole
- Distal convoluted tubule
- Cortex
- Bowman's capsule
- Proximal convoluted tubule
- Peritubular capillaries
- Medulla
- Vein
- Artery
- Loop of Henle (thick ascending limb)
- Venule
- Loop of Henle (thin ascending limb)
- Loop of Henle (descending limb)
- Vasa recta (capillaries)
- Collecting duct

Figure 50.9 The Human Excretory System **(A)** The kidneys lie against the back wall of the abdominal cavity, in the region of the middle back. The adrenal glands (see Figure 39.18) are positioned on top of the kidneys; they are the source of the hormone aldosterone, which plays a role in the regulation of kidney function. **(B)** A highly organized internal structure is the basis for kidney function. Certain parts of the nephrons are in the organ's outer region, the cortex; other parts are in the internal region, the medulla. **(C)** The glomeruli and the proximal and distal convoluted tubules are located in the cortex of the kidney. The loops of Henle run in parallel as straight sections down into the renal medulla and back up to the cortex. Collecting ducts run from the cortex to the inner surface of the medulla, where they open into the ureter. The vasa recta are peritubular capillaries that parallel the loops of Henle and are permeable to salts and water.

Q: How do you think the osmolarity of the blood in the vasa recta compares with the osmolarity of the interstitial fluid at different levels of the medulla?

 View in Achieve
Activity 50.3 The Human Excretory System

the kidney on its concave (punched-in) side. Inside the kidney, the ureter is continuous with structures that envelop kidney tissues called **renal pyramids**. The renal pyramids make up the internal core, or **medulla**, of the kidney. The medulla is covered by an outer layer, or **cortex**, that has a granular appearance because it contains all of the glomeruli. Between the cortex and the medulla, the renal artery divides into the many arterioles that serve the nephrons. In this same region, the renal vein collects blood from the many venules that drain the peritubular capillaries.

The organization of nephrons within the kidney is very regular. All of the glomeruli with their Bowman's capsules are located in the cortex. The initial segments of the renal tubules that come from Bowman's capsules are called the **proximal convoluted tubules**—"proximal" because they are closest to the glomerulus, and "convoluted" because they are twisted (**Figure 50.9C**). All of the proximal convoluted tubules are located in the cortex.

At the point at which the proximal convoluted tubule enters the medulla, it becomes thin, straight, and descends directly down toward the tip of a renal pyramid. In the medulla the tubule makes a hairpin turn and ascends back to the cortex, forming what is called a **loop of Henle**. Some nephrons have longer loops of Henle than others. Some 20%–30% of human nephrons that have glomeruli deep in the cortex (i.e., near the border with the medulla) have long loops of Henle that go deep into the medulla.

Nephrons that have glomeruli farther up in the cortex generally have short loops of Henle that descend only a short distance into the medulla. As you will see, the long loops are the critical adaptation of the mammalian nephron that enables the kidney to concentrate the urine.

The ascending limb of the loop of Henle becomes the **distal convoluted tubule** when it reaches the cortex—"distal" because it is farther from the glomerulus. The distal convoluted tubules of many nephrons join a common **collecting duct** in the cortex. The collecting ducts descend back down through the renal pyramid, parallel to and past the tips of the loops of Henle, and empty into a funnel-shaped structure called the pelvis. Divisions of the pelvis that surround each renal pyramid join together to leave the kidney as the ureter (see Figure 50.9B).

The organization of the blood vessels of the kidney closely parallels the organization of the nephrons (see Figure 50.9C). Smaller arteries branch from the renal artery and radiate into the cortex, forming the afferent arterioles that carry blood to each glomerulus. Each glomerulus is drained by an efferent arteriole that gives rise to the peritubular capillaries, most of which surround the proximal and distal convoluted tubules. The intimate associations of the glomerular and peritubular capillaries with the renal tubules enable exchanges between the blood and the specialized regions of the tubules.

Some of the peritubular capillaries run into the medulla in parallel with the loops of Henle and the collecting ducts, forming a vascular network called the **vasa recta**. All of the peritubular capillaries from a nephron join back together into a venule that joins with venules from other nephrons and eventually leads to the renal vein. The concentrating ability of the mammalian kidney depends on water reabsorption in the renal medulla, and the vasa recta are the avenue by which that water gets out of the renal medulla and back into the circulation.

Most of the glomerular filtrate is reabsorbed by the proximal convoluted tubule

Most of the water and solutes filtered by the glomerulus are reabsorbed and do not appear in the urine. We can reach this conclusion by comparing the rate of filtration by the glomeruli with the rate of urine production. The kidneys receive about 1 liter of blood per minute, or about 1,500 liters of blood per day. How much of this huge volume is filtered out of the glomeruli? The answer is about 12%. This is still a large volume—180 liters per day! We normally urinate less than 2 liters per day, so about 99% of the fluid volume that is filtered out of the glomerulus is returned to the blood. Where and how is this enormous amount of fluid reabsorbed?

The proximal convoluted tubule (PCT) is responsible for most of the reabsorption of water and solutes from the glomerular filtrate. The cells of this section of the renal tubule have many microvilli that increase their apical (facing into the tubule) surface area for reabsorption, and they have many mitochondria—an indication that they are metabolically active. PCT cells actively transport Na^+ (with Cl^- following) and other solutes, such as glucose and amino acids, out of the tubule fluid.

Almost all glucose and amino acid molecules that are filtered from the blood are actively reabsorbed by PCT cells and transported into the extracellular fluid. The active transport of solutes from the proximal tubule into the interstitial fluid causes water to follow osmotically. The water and solutes moved into the interstitial fluid are taken up by the peritubular capillaries and returned to the venous blood. These processes accomplish the reabsorption of more than 75% of the fluid that initially enters the nephron.

Despite the bulk reabsorption of water and solutes by the PCT, the overall osmolarity of the fluid flowing through the PCT does not change. Thus the process that is occurring in the PCT is called isosmotic reabsorption. The fluid that enters the loop of Henle has the same osmolarity as the blood plasma, although its composition is different. How then does the kidney produce urine that is more concentrated than the blood plasma?

The loop of Henle creates a concentration gradient in the renal medulla

Humans can produce urine that is four times more concentrated than their blood plasma. The vampire bat you encountered at the beginning of this chapter can produce urine that is 15 times more concentrated than its blood plasma (**Investigating Life: How Can Vampire Bats Use Blood as Fast Food?**). The concentrating ability of the mammalian kidney arises from a **countercurrent multiplier** mechanism made possible by the anatomical arrangement of the loops of Henle. The term "countercurrent" refers to the opposing

directions of fluid flow in the descending and ascending limbs. The term "multiplier" refers to the ability of this system to create a solute concentration gradient in the renal medulla.

The loops of Henle do not themselves produce concentrated urine; rather, they increase the osmolarity of the extracellular fluid in the medulla in a graduated way. In humans, for example, the extracellular fluid at the top of the medulla bordering the cortex will be about 300 mOsm/L (the concentration of blood plasma). But at the bottom of the medulla, where the loops of Henle make their hairpin turns, the extracellular fluid can be 1,200 mOsm/L (**Figure 50.10**). How do the loops produce this effect?

The cells that make up the different segments of the loop of Henle differ anatomically and functionally. Cells of the descending limb and the initial cells of the ascending limb are thin, with no microvilli and few mitochondria. They are not specialized for transport. Partway up the ascending limb, the cells become specialized for active transport. These cells are thick and have many mitochondria. Accordingly, the segments of the loop of Henle are named the thin descending limb, the thin ascending limb, and the thick ascending limb (see Figure 50.9C).

The countercurrent multiplier mechanism is best understood by first considering events occurring in the thick ascending limb (see Figure 50.10, note 1). The apical (luminal side) membranes of the cells of the thick ascending limb cotransport $Na^+/K^+/Cl^-$ from the tubule fluid into the tubule cells, and cotransport K^+/Cl^- out of the basal membranes into the interstitial fluid. The basal membranes also actively transport Na^+ out and K^+ into the cells. The end result is a reabsorption of Na+ and Cl- from the thick ascending tubule into the interstitial fluid. (In the following discussion, we distinguish between the two components of extracellular fluid—the blood plasma and the interstitial fluid.) The thick ascending limb is not permeable to water, so the reabsorption of Na^+ and Cl^- from the tubular fluid raises the concentration of those solutes in the surrounding interstitial fluid and decreases the concentration of the tubular fluid entering the distal convoluted tubule.

The thin descending limb, in contrast, is highly permeable to water but not very permeable to Na^+ and Cl^-. Since the local interstitial fluid has been made more concentrated by the Na^+ and Cl^- reabsorbed from the neighboring thick ascending limb, water is withdrawn osmotically from the fluid in the descending limb. Therefore the fluid in the descending limb becomes more concentrated as it flows toward the hairpin turn at the bottom of the renal medulla (see Figure 50.10, note 2).

The thin ascending limb, like the thick ascending limb, is not permeable to water. It is, however, permeable to Na^+ and Cl^-. As the concentrated tubule fluid flows up the thin ascending limb, it is more concentrated than the surrounding interstitial fluid, so Na^+ and Cl^- diffuse out. When the tubule fluid reaches the thick ascending limb, active transport continues to move Na^+ and Cl^- from the tubule fluid to the interstitial fluid.

Because of this countercurrent multiplier mechanism, the tubule fluid reaching the distal convoluted tubule is less concentrated than the blood plasma (see Figure 50.10, note 3), and the solutes that have been left behind in the renal medulla have created a concentration gradient in the interstitial fluid of the medulla (indicated by the background color gradient in Figure 50.10).

▶InvestigatingLIFE   How Can Vampire Bats Use Blood as Fast Food?

Experiment

Original Paper: C. Busch. 1988. Consumption of blood, renal function and utilization of free water by the vampire bat, *Desmodus rotundus. Comp Biochem Physiol A Mol Integr Physiol* 90: 141–146.

You learned at the beginning of the chapter that vampire bats feed once a day. After sunset they fly out, search for a victim, and then return to their roost. This nightly excursion generally takes less than 2 hours. Therefore in a very short time these small animals must take in a large enough volume of their liquid blood diet to supply their energy and water needs for a 24-hour period. How do they do it?

HYPOTHESIS▶   Vampire bats maximize their food intake by rapidly excreting water, but they then conserve water by producing a highly concentrated urine while digesting their protein meal.

METHOD▶

1. Offer a colony of captive vampire bats a beef blood meal once a day for 2 hours, to mimic the natural once-a-day feeding behavior of the bats.

2. Do not allow bats access to free water.

3. Measure the daily amount of blood consumed and the time course of subsequent urine volume and concentration.

RESULTS▶   The table shows the average body mass and average amount of blood consumed by nine vampire bats over a period of 5–8 days.

Average body mass (g)	Average amount of blood consumed (g)
25.0	19.7
26.3	11.3
26.4	13.6
28.6	16.8
29.6	15.7
30.3	17.8
32.4	24.7
36.0	24.4
36.2	18.6

CONCLUSION▶   In a short daily feeding period, vampire bats consume on average 60% of their body mass.

Work with the Data

To consume 60% of body mass and still be able to fly, the bats must rapidly excrete a large percentage of the water content of their food. The time course of urine flow and its concentration were measured during and after daily feeding for three vampire bats for 1 week and averaged. The data are shown in the table (—, no data reported). Create a double plot of the flow and concentration data as a function of time.

Time after beginning to feed (min)	Average urine flow rate (g/g body mass/hr)	Average urine osmolarity (Osm)
10	0.13	0.5
20	0.24	0.25
45	0.17	0.40
90	0.05	0.70
150	0.01	—
210	0.01	—
270	0.005	—
330	0.003	3.3
390	0.02	3.4

QUESTIONS▶

1. If you averaged the urine flow rates over the first 45 min following the beginning of the meal, and you assumed that the total blood intake was 60% of body mass and body mass was 30g, what percentage of the ingested volume would be excreted in that first 45 min?

2. Considering that the normal osmolarity of interstitial fluid in a mammal is 300 mOsm, what is the maximum concentrating factor in the vampire bats in this experiment?

3. Three data points are missing in the urine osmolarity curve. Would it be reasonable to plot these data by connecting the 90-minute sample and the 330-minute sample with a straight line? Why or why not?

*Go to **Achieve** for a companion
Data in Depth exercise.*

You may wonder why the blood flow through the medulla does not wash out the concentration gradient established by the loops of Henle. The parallel arrangement of the descending and ascending peritubular capillaries in the medulla—the vasa recta—helps preserve the concentration gradient in the medulla. These capillaries are permeable to both salts and water. Therefore as blood flows down the descending limb of the vasa recta into the increasingly concentrated interstitial fluid of the medulla, it loses water and gains solutes. As blood flows up from the bottom of the medulla in the ascending limb of the vasa recta, the opposite happens (water is gained and solutes are lost) because now the blood is more concentrated than the surrounding interstitial fluid (see Figure 50.10, notes 4–6). The dynamics of this countercurrent exchange of salts and water between the blood in the vasa recta and the interstitial fluids result in little net change in the composition of the interstitial fluid in the medulla.

Figure 50.10 Concentrating the Urine A countercurrent multiplier mechanism enables the mammalian kidney to produce urine that is far more concentrated than the blood plasma. The composition—but not the concentration—of the filtrate is changed by the proximal convoluted tubule, which reabsorbs valuable ions and molecules (including Na⁺/Cl⁻). Bulk reabsorption of water follows osmotically. The urine concentration process begins in the thick ascending limb of the loop of Henle, which reabsorbs Na⁺/Cl⁻ but is impermeable to H₂O. This reabsorbed Na⁺/Cl⁻ creates an osmotic differential that pulls water out of the thin descending limb; also can diffuse into the thin descending limb, making the fluid in that limb more concentrated. Through this continuous process, a concentration gradient in the interstitial fluid of the renal medulla is created as indicated by the gradient of color in the medulla. As urine in the collecting duct passes through this concentration gradient, it can lose water osmotically, becomes more concentrated as indicated by the shading of color, and can become almost as concentrated as the interstitial fluid at the bottom of the renal medulla.

Q: What would be the effect of a drug called a "loop diuretic" that blocks the Na⁺ transport in the thick ascending limb of the loop of Henle?

▶ **View in Achieve**
Animation 50.1 The Mammalian Kidney

Water permeability of kidney tubules depends on water channels

We have noted that some tubule regions, such as the PCT, are highly permeable to water whereas others, such as the thick ascending limb of the loop of Henle, are impermeable to water. What causes these differences in water permeability in different regions of the nephron? Aquaporins are a class of membrane proteins that form water channels. Regions of the nephron that are highly permeable to water have greater numbers of aquaporins. Thus aquaporins are abundant in kidney PCT cells and in descending limbs of the loops of Henle, but not in the ascending limbs of the loop of Henle.

Connect the Concepts As explained in Key Concept 6.3, water does not cross cell membranes easily, but aquaporins are protein channels that make cells permeable to water.

As an interesting evolutionary note, aquaporins are also important in maintaining water balance in amphibians. Many amphibians can gain water from a moist substrate because they have

Figure 50.11 The Kidney Excretes Acids and Conserves Bases
(A) Bicarbonate ions are filtered out of the blood at the glomerulus, and renal tubule cells secrete hydrogen ions into the tubule fluid. In the renal tubule, the filtered bicarbonate buffers the secreted hydrogen ions and keeps the urine from becoming too acidic. The CO_2 formed by the reaction of bicarbonate and hydrogen ions is converted back to bicarbonate by the renal tubule cells and transported back into the interstitial fluid.
(B) Excretion of ammonium ions (NH_4^+) by renal tubule cells is also important for acid–base balance.

(A) The HCO_3^- buffer system in the renal tubule

1 Na^+ and HCO_3^- are filtered in the glomerulus.

2 Renal tubule cells secrete H^+ in exchange for Na^+.

5 Na^+/HCO_3^- symporter carries Na^+ and HCO_3^- across basal membrane of tubule cell.

Glomerulus

Renal tubule lumen

Renal tubule cell

Interstitial fluids

Blood capillary

Renal tubule

$HCO_3^- + H^+$

H_2CO_3

$H_2O + CO_2$

Na^+ Na^+

H^+

$H^+ + HCO_3^-$

$CO_2 + H_2O$

Carbonic anhydrase

Na^+

HCO_3^-

3 CO_2 is formed by the reaction of HCO_3^- and H^+ and diffuses into the tubule cell.

4 CO_2 is converted back to HCO_3^- in the renal tubule cell.

(B) Excretion of ammonia

Glutamine

$Cl^- + NH_4^+$ $2 NH_4^+$ $2 HCO_3^-$ HCO_3^-
Na^+ Na^+

aquaporins in the epithelial cells of their belly skin. Thus water can cross their skin into the interstitial fluid by osmosis.

The distal convoluted tubule fine-tunes the composition of the urine

The first portion of the distal convoluted tubule is similar to the thick ascending limb of the loop of Henle. Na^+ and Cl^- are transported out of the tubule fluid, and water cannot follow. As a result, the tubule fluid becomes even more dilute. The later sections of the distal convoluted tubule, however, can be permeable to water, and therefore water can be osmotically drawn from the hypotonic tubule fluid into the interstitial fluid. As the tubule fluid flows through the distal tubule to the collecting duct, it equilibrates with the osmolarity of the blood plasma.

An important function of the distal tubule is the fine-tuning of the ionic composition of the urine. Even though bulk reabsorption of substances such as calcium, phosphate, bicarbonate, and potassium occurs in the proximal convoluted tubule, changes in the concentrations of these substances occur in the distal convoluted tubule. In the case of potassium, for example, if a person is potassium depleted, this ion is reabsorbed in the distal convoluted tubule, but if a person has an abundance of potassium, this ion is secreted in the distal convoluted tubule. As you will see in Key Concept 50.6, this exchange of K^+ is controlled by the hormone aldosterone. Another example is reabsorption of Ca^{2+} in the distal convoluted tubule, which is controlled by the actions of vitamin D. The fine-tuning of urine composition continues in the collecting duct. As you can imagine, the list of ion transporters in the distal convoluted tubule is large.

Urine is concentrated in the collecting duct

The tubule fluid entering the collecting duct is at about the same solute *concentration* as the blood plasma, but its solute *composition* is considerably different from that of the plasma. The major solute in the tubule fluid is now urea, since salts were reabsorbed earlier in the nephron. As the tubule fluid flows down the collecting duct, it loses water osmotically to the interstitial fluid, and that water returns to the circulatory system via the vasa recta (see Figure 50.10, note 4).

The concentration gradient established in the renal medulla by the countercurrent multiplier actions of the loops of Henle creates the osmotic potential that withdraws water from the collecting ducts. The collecting ducts begin in the renal cortex and run through the renal medulla before emptying into the ureter at the tips of the renal pyramids. During this journey, the solute concentration of the surrounding interstitial fluid increases, and more and more water can be absorbed from the urine in the collecting duct. By the time the urine reaches the ureter, it can become greatly concentrated, with urea as the major solute.

As water is withdrawn from the collecting duct, some urea also leaks out into the medullary interstitial fluid, adding to its osmotic potential. This urea diffuses back into the loop of Henle and is returned to the collecting duct. The recycling of urea in the renal medulla contributes significantly to the concentration gradient and therefore the ability of the kidney to concentrate the urine in the collecting duct. The ability of a mammal to concentrate its urine is determined by the maximum concentration gradient it can establish in its renal medulla.

START

1 Arterial blood is taken from the patient.

2 The blood is dialyzed across a semi-permeable membrane bathed with a solution similar in composition to blood plasma.

3 Used dialysis solution containing metabolic wastes is discarded.

Blood pump

Dialyzer

4 Blood is returned to the body in a vein.

Bubble trap

Fresh dialysis solution   Constant-temperature bath

Figure 50.12 Renal Dialysis Patients with kidney failure can have their blood cleansed of wastes by renal dialysis machines. Blood flows through channels of semipermeable membranes that allow diffusion of waste molecules from the blood to a dialysis fluid.

© Horizon International Images Limited/Alamy Stock Photo

The kidneys help regulate acid–base balance

Besides regulating salt and water balance and excreting nitrogenous wastes, the kidneys have another important role: they regulate the hydrogen ion concentration (the pH) of the extracellular fluids. pH is a critical variable because it influences the structure and function of proteins.

One way to minimize pH changes in a chemical solution is to add a buffer—a substance that can either absorb or release hydrogen ions (see Key Concept 2.4). The major buffer in the blood is bicarbonate ions (HCO_3^-; see Figure 47.14) that are formed from the dissociation of carbonic acid, which in turn is formed by the hydration of CO_2 according to the following equilibrium reaction:

$$CO_2 + H_2O \rightleftharpoons H_2CO_3 \rightleftharpoons H^+ + HCO_3^-$$

From this equation, you can see that if excess hydrogen ions are added to this reaction mixture, the reaction will move to the left and absorb the excess H^+. If hydrogen ions are removed from the reaction mixture, however, the reaction will move to the right and supply more H^+.

The HCO_3^- buffer system is important for controlling the pH of the blood, and therefore of the interstitial fluids as well, because the reaction can be pushed to the right and pulled to the left physiologically. The lungs control the levels of CO_2 in the blood, thus altering the acid portion of the reaction. CO_2 is considered the acid portion of the reaction because if you add additional CO_2, the reaction shifts to the right, producing more H^+ ions. The kidneys control the base portion of the reaction by removing H^+ from the blood and returning HCO_3^- to the blood. How does this occur?

HCO_3^- is filtered in the glomerulus and is therefore present in the tubule fluid. As illustrated in **Figure 50.11A**, tubule cells

transport H^+ into the tubule fluid in exchange for Na^+. In the tubule, the excreted H^+ combines with the filtered HCO_3^- to produce H_2CO_3 that then disassociates into H_2O and CO_2. The CO_2 diffuses into the tubule cells, where in the presence of the enzyme carbonic anhydrase it produces HCO_3^- that is transported out of the basal end of the cell into the interstitial fluid and thence to the blood. Thus for each H^+ secreted into the tubule fluid, a HCO_3^- ion is released into the blood.

Another mechanism for H^+ secretion and HCO_3^- reabsorption involves ammonium ions (NH_4^+). The metabolism of glutamine in tubule cells produces NH_4^+ and HCO_3^- (**Figure 50.11B**). The HCO_3^- is reabsorbed into the interstitial fluid. The NH_4^+ is transported into the tubule fluid and combines with Cl^-, which is excreted in the urine. This process results in the addition of a new HCO_3^- ion to the blood. The NH_4^+ is transported into the tubules by means of an NH_4^+ transporter.

Kidney failure is treated with dialysis

Loss of kidney function (renal failure) results in the retention of salts and water (hence high blood pressure), retention of urea (uremic poisoning), and a decreasing pH (acidosis). A person who suffers complete renal failure will die within 2 weeks if not treated. A drastic but highly successful treatment is kidney transplant, but it is usually necessary to sustain a patient for considerable time while waiting for a kidney to become available. Therefore artificial kidneys, or renal dialysis machines, are essential modes of treatment.

In a dialysis machine, the patient's blood flows through many small channels made of semipermeable membranes (**Figure 50.12**). A dialysis solution flows on the other side of these membranes, through which small molecules can diffuse. Molecules and ions diffuse from an area of higher concentration to an area of lower concentration, so the composition of the dialysis fluid is crucial. The concentrations of the molecules or ions that need to be conserved must be at the same concentration in the dialysis fluid as they are in the blood. The concentrations of molecules and ions that need to be removed from the blood are zero in the dialysis fluid. The total osmotic potential of the dialysis fluid must equal that of the blood plasma.

About 500 milliliters of the patient's blood is in the dialysis machine at any one time, and the unit processes several hundred milliliters of blood per minute. A patient with no kidney function must be on the dialysis machine for 4–6 hours three times a week.

KEY CONCEPT
50.5 Recap and Assess

The anatomical organization of nephrons makes it possible for the mammalian kidney to produce a urine more concentrated than the blood, thereby conserving water to maintain extracellular fluid volume. Bulk reabsorption of salts, other valuable solutes, and water takes place in the proximal convoluted tubule. The loops of Henle act as a countercurrent multiplier, creating a concentration gradient of the interstitial fluids in the renal medulla. Collecting ducts run through the renal medulla and lose water osmotically to the surrounding interstitial fluids, concentrating the urine. The renal tubules contribute to acid–base balance by excreting H^+ ions.

1. If you could measure the concentration of mitochondria in mammalian kidney tissues, where would you find the highest concentration, the lowest concentration, and an intermediate concentration? Explain your answer.

2. How do the loops of Henle act as a countercurrent multiplier?

3. If you compared a water rat and a desert rat of the same size, how would you expect their kidneys to differ in anatomical structure? Explain your answer.

4. How does the active secretion of H^+ ions by the renal tubule cells result in an increase in the bicarbonate concentration in the blood?

The kidneys contribute to homeostasis in several ways, including regulating extracellular fluid volume, maintaining the osmotic concentration and ionic composition of the extracellular fluid, and regulating pH. As you will see next, the kidneys also play a major role in regulating blood pressure.

KEY CONCEPT
50.6 Kidney Function Is Regulated

Learning Objectives

50.6.1 Discuss how renin, angiotensin, and aldosterone affect glomerular filtration rate (GFR) and blood pressure.

50.6.2 Given an event that lowers blood pressure, predict the response of the renin–angiotensin–aldosterone system.

50.6.3 Describe ADH's role in regulating kidney function in response to changes in blood osmolarity or blood pressure.

50.6.4 Explain the mechanisms whereby the afferent and efferent arterioles regulate the GFR, and how those responses are controlled.

Several regulatory mechanisms act on the kidneys to maintain blood pressure, blood osmolarity, and blood composition. We discuss these mechanisms separately, but keep in mind that they are always working together.

Glomerular filtration rate is regulated

If the kidneys stop filtering blood, they cannot accomplish any of their functions. The maintenance of a constant **glomerular filtration rate (GFR)** depends on an adequate blood supply to the kidneys at an adequate blood pressure. Renal arteries usually deliver blood to the kidneys at high pressure because they are early branches off the aorta. In addition, autoregulatory mechanisms ensure adequate blood supply and blood pressure for kidney function regardless of what is happening elsewhere in the body. The kidney's autoregulatory adjustments compensate for decreases in cardiac output or decreases in blood pressure so that the GFR remains constant.

One autoregulatory mechanism is the dilation (expansion) of the afferent renal arterioles when blood pressure falls. This dilation decreases the resistance in the arterioles and helps maintain blood pressure in the glomerulus. If arteriole dilation does not keep the GFR from falling, the kidney releases an enzyme, **renin**, into the blood. Renin converts a circulating protein, angiotensinogen, into angiotensin I, which is then acted on by angiotensin-converting enzyme (ACE) in the lungs and other tissues to form the active hormone angiotensin II, or simply **angiotensin (Figure 50.13)**. Angiotensin has several effects that help restore the GFR to normal:

- It constricts the efferent renal arterioles, raising the resistance for blood leaving the glomerulus. Like putting a finger over the end of a garden hose, this restriction of drainage elevates blood pressure in the glomerular capillaries.

- It constricts peripheral blood vessels all over the body, an action that elevates blood pressure.

- It stimulates the adrenal cortex to release the hormone **aldosterone**. Aldosterone stimulates sodium reabsorption by the kidney, making its reabsorption of water more effective. Enhanced water reabsorption helps maintain blood volume and therefore blood pressure.

- It acts on the brain to stimulate thirst. Increased water intake in response to thirst increases blood volume and blood pressure.

Thus the renin–angiotensin–aldosterone system, or RAAS, coordinates many responses to maintain blood pressure and kidney function.

Regulation of GFR uses feedback information from the distal tubule

A remarkable anatomical feature of the nephron is that where its renal tubule returns to the cortex and becomes the distal convoluted tubule, it makes contact with the afferent and efferent arterioles of its glomerulus. At this location the cells of the tubule are modified to form a structure called the macula densa (see Figure 50.13), and the arteriole cells are also modified and are called juxtaglomerular cells. The macula densa cells sense the concentration of NaCl in the fluid entering the distal convoluted tubule. If GFR is high, flow through the loop of Henle is high and the cells of the thick ascending limb cannot reabsorb all of the NaCl passing through it. If GFR

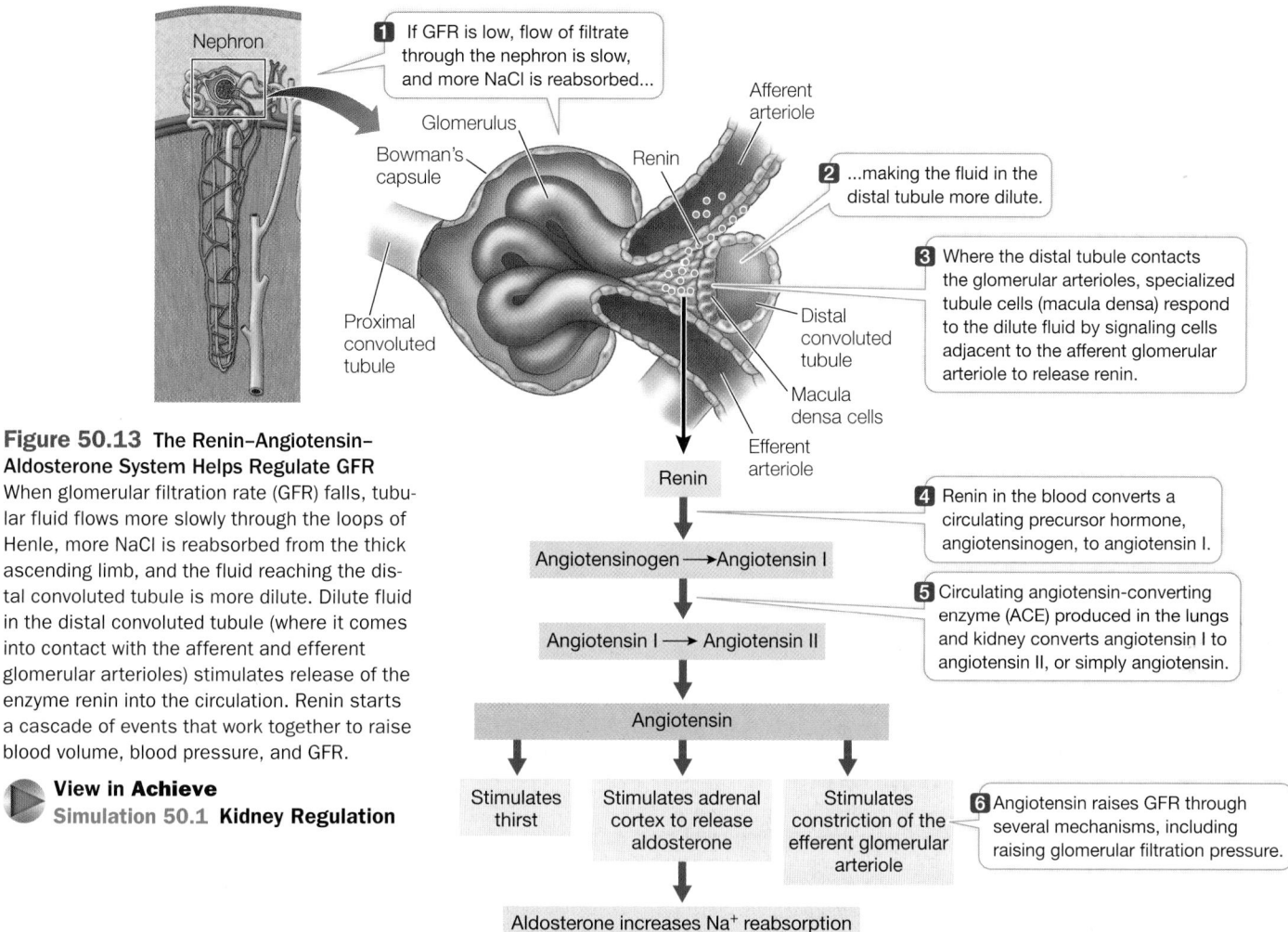

Figure 50.13 The Renin–Angiotensin–Aldosterone System Helps Regulate GFR
When glomerular filtration rate (GFR) falls, tubular fluid flows more slowly through the loops of Henle, more NaCl is reabsorbed from the thick ascending limb, and the fluid reaching the distal convoluted tubule is more dilute. Dilute fluid in the distal convoluted tubule (where it comes into contact with the afferent and efferent glomerular arterioles) stimulates release of the enzyme renin into the circulation. Renin starts a cascade of events that work together to raise blood volume, blood pressure, and GFR.

▶ View in **Achieve**
Simulation 50.1 **Kidney Regulation**

is low, flow through the loop of Henle is slower and the cells of the thick ascending limb can reabsorb more of the NaCl. If the NaCl level in the distal convoluted tubule drops too low, the macula densa cells signal the juxtaglomerular cells to release renin and trigger the RAAS response. Thus the concentration of NaCl in the fluid passing over the macula densa is a function of GFR and is information that enables fine control of the RAAS.

Blood osmolarity and blood pressure are regulated by ADH

Cells in the hypothalamus can stimulate the release of a hormone called **antidiuretic hormone** (**ADH**, also called vasopressin) from the posterior pituitary. ADH stimulates cells of the collecting duct to insert aquaporins (water channels) into their cell membranes. The aquaporins increase the permeability of these membranes to water, and therefore more water is reabsorbed from the collecting duct fluid into the interstitial fluid of the renal medulla. The higher the circulating levels of ADH, the greater the number of aquaporins. Various factors can stimulate or inhibit the release of ADH. Of key importance to kidney function are (1) osmoreceptors that monitor blood osmolarity and (2) baroreceptors that monitor blood pressure (**Figure 50.14**).

Osmoreceptor neurons in the hypothalamus are activated by a rise in blood osmolarity, and they increase the release of ADH. ADH helps regulate blood osmolarity by controlling water reabsorption. The osmoreceptors also stimulate thirst. The resulting water retention and water intake dilute the blood as they expand blood volume.

Baroreceptors in the walls of the aorta and the carotid arteries (see Figure 48.21) that detect an increase in blood pressure will *inhibit* the release of ADH. With less circulating ADH, less water is reabsorbed, which increases urine volume and decreases blood volume, hence lowering blood pressure.

If blood pressure falls, as when you lose blood volume through hemorrhage or excessive evaporative water loss, activity of the baroreceptors in the aorta and carotid arteries decreases. Input via cranial nerves to the hypothalamus from these receptors inhibits the release of ADH, so when the firing rates of these baroreceptors fall, ADH release increases. More ADH results in more efficient water reabsorption and therefore a protection of blood volume and blood pressure.

Alcohol inhibits ADH release, explaining why excessive beer drinking leads to excessive urination and dehydration, which contribute to the symptoms of a hangover.

Blood osmolarity

Rise in blood osmolarity

Osmoreceptors in the hypothalamus detect an increase in osmolarity and stimulate ADH release.

Renal excretion of solutes and reabsorption of H_2O decrease blood osmolarity.

In the kidney: ADH increases permeability of collecting duct cells and distal tubule cells to H_2O.

→ Stimulation
⊣ Inhibition

Hypothalamus

Anterior pituitary

Posterior pituitary

Release of ADH in bloodstream

Resorption of water helps maintain blood volume and blood pressure.

Blood pressure

Rise in blood pressure

Baroreceptors in the aorta and carotid artery detect increases in blood pressure and inhibit ADH release.

Decrease in blood pressure lessens the inhibition and promotes ADH release.

Fall in blood pressure

Figure 50.14 Antidiuretic Hormone Increases Blood Pressure and Promotes Water Reabsorption ADH is produced by neurons in the hypothalamus and released from nerve endings in the posterior pituitary. The release of ADH is stimulated by hypothalamic osmoreceptors and inhibited by baroreceptors in the large arteries. Red lines indicate inhibitory actions; green lines show stimulatory actions.

As already mentioned, the presence of aquaporins in cell membranes determines their water permeability. Aquaporins play an important and unique role in the collecting duct. Several members of the aquaporin family of water channels are found in the cell membranes of the collecting duct cells. At least two aquaporins (AQP-3 and AQP-4) are localized in the basolateral membranes (facing the blood vessels). A different aquaporin, AQP-2, is found in the apical cell membranes (facing into the tubule). The presence of AQP-2 in these membranes is controlled by ADH (**Figure 50.15**).

When ADH levels are low, such as when a person is well hydrated, most of the AQP-2 protein is sequestered in the membranes of intracellular vesicles, and the collecting duct permeability is low. A rise in ADH levels stimulates the insertion of these vesicles along with their AQP-2 channels into the apical cell membranes. As a result, the membranes become more permeable to water. Water that enters the collecting duct cells passes into the interstitial fluid through the aquaporins in the basolateral membranes. ADH also stimulates the synthesis of new AQP-2 proteins. Thus circulating ADH controls the number of AQP-2 water channels in the cell membranes of the collecting duct cells, and therefore the permeability of the collecting duct to water.

Experiment

Figure 50.15 ADH Induces Insertion of Aquaporins into Cell Membranes

Original Paper: S. Nielsen et al. 1995. Vasopressin increases water permeability of kidney collecting duct by inducing translocation of aquaporin-CD water channels to plasma membrane. *Proc Natl Acad Sci USA* 92: 1013–1017. © 1995. National Academy of Sciences, U.S.A.

Aquaporin proteins make some regions of renal tubules permeable to water. One aquaporin, AQP-2, is responsible for the permeability of the collecting duct cells. M. A. Knepper and colleagues did an experiment to find out how antidiuretic hormone acts on these proteins to control the level of permeability in renal cells.

HYPOTHESIS▶ Antidiuretic hormone (ADH) controls the location of aquaporin proteins.

METHOD▶

1. Isolate collecting ducts from rat kidney.

2. Use immunochemical staining to localize the AQP-2 aquaporins in collecting duct cells both with and without the presence of ADH. Also localize the aquaporins after ADH is applied and then washed away.

AQP-3/AQP-4 — Collecting duct cell — Inside collecting duct

Without ADH, AQP-2 is mostly found in membranes of intracellular vesicles.

But, with ADH, AQP-2 is mostly found in the luminal membranes of collecting duct cells.

After ADH washout, AQP-2 is again sequestered in intracellular vesicles.

Vesicle

H_2O ← → H_2O

AQP-2

Basolateral membrane — Apical membrane

3. Measure the water permeability of the collecting duct cells under the same three conditions.

RESULTS▶ Error bars indicate ± 1 standard deviation.

The change in AQP-2 location is accompanied by increased permeability of duct cells.

Permeability (μmol/sec)

Without ADH · With ADH · After ADH washout

CONCLUSION▶ In the absence of ADH, AQP-2 is sequestered intracellularly. When ADH is present, AQP-2 channels are inserted into cell membranes, making the cells more permeable to water.

The heart produces a hormone that helps lower blood pressure

You may not think of the heart as an endocrine organ, but it is. When blood volume is high, blood pressure is high, putting strain on the heart. Under these conditions, the increased venous return stretches the atria of the heart. When the atrial muscle fibers are overstretched, they release a peptide hormone called **atrial natriuretic peptide (ANP)**. This peptide hormone enters the circulation, and in the kidney it decreases the reabsorption of sodium. If less sodium is reabsorbed, less water is reabsorbed, and more passes into the urine. Thus ANP has the effect of lowering blood volume and therefore blood pressure.

KEY CONCEPT
50.6 Recap and Assess

Glomerular filtration is essential for kidney function and is sustained by autoregulatory mechanisms. These autoregulatory mechanisms include changes in dilation and constriction of the glomerular afferent arterioles and hormonal control over constriction of the efferent glomerular arteriole mediated by the renin–angiotensin–aldosterone system (RAAS). Angiotensin controls the release of aldosterone, which controls sodium reabsorption. Sensors that monitor blood pressure and blood osmolarity stimulate or inhibit the release of ADH, which controls the water permeability of the collecting duct.

1. What are the mechanisms whereby the afferent and efferent arterioles regulate the GFR, and how are those responses controlled?

2. Aldosterone stimulates activity of the Na^+/K^+ exchangers in the distal convoluted tubule and the initial segments of the collecting ducts. Aldosterone release is triggered by angiotensin. Given this information, what is the significance of the fact that the Na^+/K^+ exchanger in the tubule cells secretes two K^+ ions for every three Na^+ ions it reabsorbs?

3. If you drank a lot of salty chicken broth that had an osmotic concentration of 300 mOsm/L, what two mechanisms would play roles in the response of your kidneys to excrete the excess fluid volume and excess Na^+? Explain your answer.

 View in Achieve
Activity 50.4 The Major Organ Systems

▶Investigating**LIFE**

Q and **A** How does the excretory system of vampire bats process their high-protein liquid diet?

As we described in the opening story, vampire bats conserve water by producing urine that can be as much as 15 times more concentrated than their blood. For comparison, the maximum urine concentration of humans is about four times that of the blood.

Recall from Key Concept 50.5 that the mammalian body's ability to produce concentrated urine depends on the concentration gradient set up in the renal medulla by the loops of Henle. An important adaptation for increasing the concentration gradient is to increase the lengths of the loops of Henle relative to overall kidney size. Some tiny desert gerbils, for example, have such long loops of Henle that the renal pyramid (each of the rodent kidneys has only one, in contrast to humans) extends far out of the concave surface of the kidney and into the ureter (Figure 50.16). The large concentration gradient that results draws most of the water out of the urine as it passes down the collecting duct. Desert gerbils are so effective in conserving water that they can survive on the water released by the metabolism of their food.

The vampire bat kidney is also particularly good at concentrating urea. Within minutes after feeding, the urea concentration in its urine can increase by more than 500-fold.

Future directions

Understanding the diverse mechanisms whereby physiological systems are controlled and regulated can contribute to the discovery and development of new pharmaceuticals. The renal system is an example. Many diseases involve problems with salt and water balance. A common problem is water retention. A large number of drugs have been developed that increase the excretion of water in urine, such as occurs naturally in vampire bats. These drugs are called diuretics, and since they act through different mechanisms, they have different effects on Na^+, K^+, and Ca^{2+} levels in the blood, which can cause serious side effects. Excessive loss of K^+, for example, can lead to heart arrhythmia, muscle weakness, and paralysis. Excessive retention of K^+ can also lead to heart arrhythmia, along with muscle cramps and paralysis. Loss of too much Na^+ can result in central nervous system deficits. Too much Ca^{2+} has many negative side effects, ranging from depression and fatigue to vomiting and gout. Thus it is important to understand how drugs work on physiological systems, to avoid negative side effects.

(A) Desert gerbil   **(B) Laboratory rat**

Renal cortex   Renal medulla   Loops of Henle (many)   Loops of Henle   Renal medulla

From L. Bankir and C. de Rouffignac. 1985. *Am J Physiol* 249: R643–R666

Figure 50.16 The Ability to Concentrate The ability of the mammalian kidney to concentrate urine depends on the lengths of its loops of Henle relative to the overall size of the kidney. **(A)** The kidney of a desert gerbil has a single renal pyramid with loops of Henle so long that the pyramid extends far into the ureter (ureter not shown). **(B)** An ordinary laboratory rat has much shorter loops of Henle.

Q: Do you think the vampire bat has loops of Henle resembling those of the laboratory rat or the desert gerbil?

You should be able to relate each summary to the adjacent figures. If you go to this visual summary in **Achieve**, you can follow links to figures, animations, activities, and simulations that will help you consolidate the material.

KEY CONCEPT

50.1 Excretory Systems Regulate Osmotic and Ionic Concentrations

- **Excretory systems** maintain the **osmolarity** and volume of the extracellular fluids and eliminate the waste products of nitrogen metabolism through the processes of **filtration**, **secretion**, and **reabsorption**. **Urine** is the output of excretory systems.

- Marine animals can be **osmoconformers** or **osmoregulators**. Freshwater animals must be osmoregulators. Terrestrial animals are osmoregulators, but the nature of their regulation depends on their environment and lifestyle.

- Apart from regulating osmolarity of cells and extracellular fluids, animals must also regulate their ionic composition by conserving some ions and secreting others. Salt glands are adaptations for secretion of Na^+ and Cl^-.

Figure 50.2

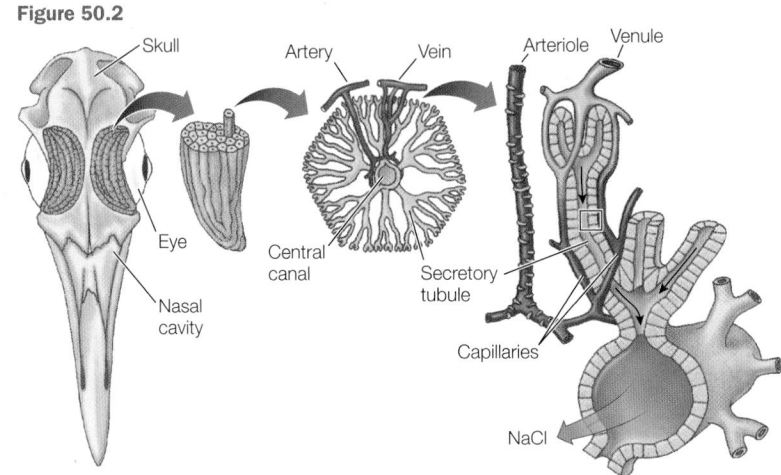

Questions

1. What are the two factors that cause water to move across biological membranes?

2. How can a marine shark be an osmoconformer and still have an extracellular NaCl concentration less than that of seawater?

3. Why are there limits to osmoconformity in marine invertebrates?

KEY CONCEPT

50.2 Animals Excrete Nitrogen as Ammonia, Urea, or Uric Acid

- Aquatic animals that breathe water can eliminate nitrogenous wastes such as **ammonia** by diffusion across their gill membranes. Terrestrial animals and some aquatic animals detoxify ammonia by converting it to **urea** or **uric acid** before excretion.

- Depending on the form in which they excrete their nitrogenous wastes, animals are classified as **ammonotelic**, **ureotelic**, or **uricotelic**.

Questions

1. Why don't water-breathing animals have to detoxify the waste product ammonia?

2. Why are many terrestrial animals that live in arid habitats uricotelic?

3. Historically, why was gout was called the disease of kings?

Figure 50.3

Ammonia	Urea	Uric acid

Ammonotelic animals (aquatic invertebrates and most bony fishes)

Ureotelic animals (mammals, most amphibians, cartilaginous fishes)

Uricotelic animals (birds, insects, non-avian reptiles)

KEY CONCEPT
50.3
Invertebrate Excretory Systems Use
Filtration, Secretion, and Reabsorption

Go to Activity 50.1

■ The **protonephridia** of flatworms consist of flame cells and excretory tubules. Extracellular fluid is filtered into the tubules, which process the filtrate to produce dilute urine.

■ In annelid worms, blood pressure causes filtration of the blood across capillary walls. The filtrate enters the coelomic cavity, where it is taken up by **metanephridia**, which alter the composition of the filtrate by active transport mechanisms.

■ The **Malpighian tubules** of insects receive ions and nitrogenous wastes by active transport across the tubule cells.

Questions

1. What is the function of metanephridia?

2. Why is filtration not a function of the insect excretory system?

Figure 50.5

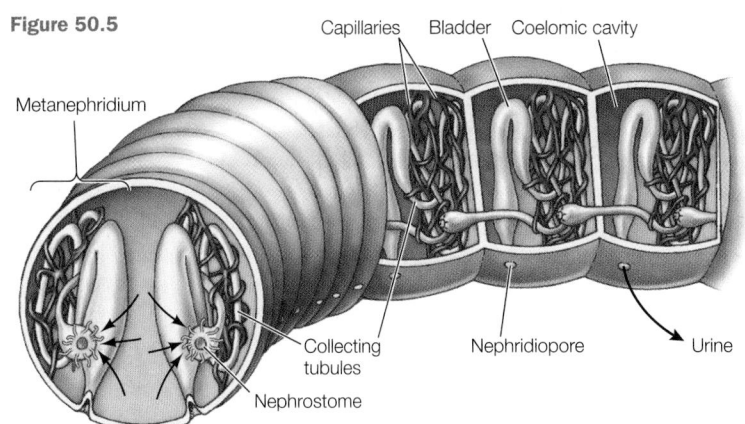

Metanephridium · Capillaries · Bladder · Coelomic cavity · Collecting tubules · Nephridiopore · Urine · Nephrostome

KEY CONCEPT
50.4
The Nephron Is the Basic Functional
Unit of Vertebrate Excretory Systems

Go to Activity 50.2

■ Marine bony fishes produce little urine.

■ Reptiles, including birds, have skin with low water permeability and excrete nitrogenous wastes as uric acid in a semisolid form.

■ Mammals produce urine that is more concentrated than their extracellular fluids.

■ The **nephron**, the functional unit of the vertebrate **kidney**, consists of a **glomerulus,** which filters the blood, a **renal tubule**, which use active secretion and reabsorption to convert the glomerular filtrate into urine, and a system of **peritubular capillaries**, which surround the tubule and support its functions of secretion and reabsorption.

Questions

1. Why do marine bony fishes have few glomeruli?

2. What is a podocyte?

3. Why does the glomerulus have an efferent arteriole rather than a venule?

Figure 50.7

Filtration · Bowman's capsule · Renal tubule · Reabsorption and secretion · Peritubular capillaries · Excretion · Urine

KEY CONCEPT

50.5 The Mammalian Kidney Can Produce Concentrated Urine

Go to Activity 50.3 and Animation 50.1

■ The glomeruli and the **proximal** and **distal convoluted tubules** are located in the **cortex** of the kidney. Certain molecules are actively reabsorbed from the glomerular filtrate by the tubule cells, and other molecules are actively secreted. Straight sections of renal tubules called **loops of Henle** and **collecting ducts** are arranged in parallel in the **medulla** of the kidney.

■ Salts, water, and valuable molecules such as glucose and amino acids are reabsorbed in the proximal convoluted tubule without the renal filtrate becoming more concentrated, although its composition changes.

■ The loops of Henle create a concentration gradient in the interstitial fluid of the renal medulla by a **countercurrent multiplier** mechanism. Urine flowing down the collecting ducts to the **ureter** is concentrated by the osmotic reabsorption of water caused by the concentration gradient in the surrounding interstitial fluid.

Figure 50.9

Questions

1. Where in the nephron does the greatest reabsorption of water and solutes occur?
2. Which part of the nephron is not permeable to water?
3. Acetazolamide is a carbonic anhydrase inhibitor used to treat altitude sickness. Explain why one of its side effects is increased urine production.

KEY CONCEPT

50.6 Kidney Function Is Regulated

Go to Activity 50.4 and Simulation 50.1

■ Kidney function in mammals is controlled by autoregulatory mechanisms that maintain a constant high **glomerular filtration rate (GFR)** even if blood pressure varies.

■ The renin–angiotensin–aldosterone system (RAAS) is an important autoregulatory mechanism. **Renin** is released by the kidney when blood pressure falls. Renin activates **angiotensin**, which causes the constriction of efferent glomerular arterioles and peripheral blood vessels, causes the release of **aldosterone** (which enhances water reabsorption), and stimulates thirst.

■ Changes in blood pressure and osmolarity influence the release of **antidiuretic hormone (ADH)**, which controls the permeability of the collecting duct to water and therefore the amount of water that is reabsorbed from the urine.

Figure 50.13

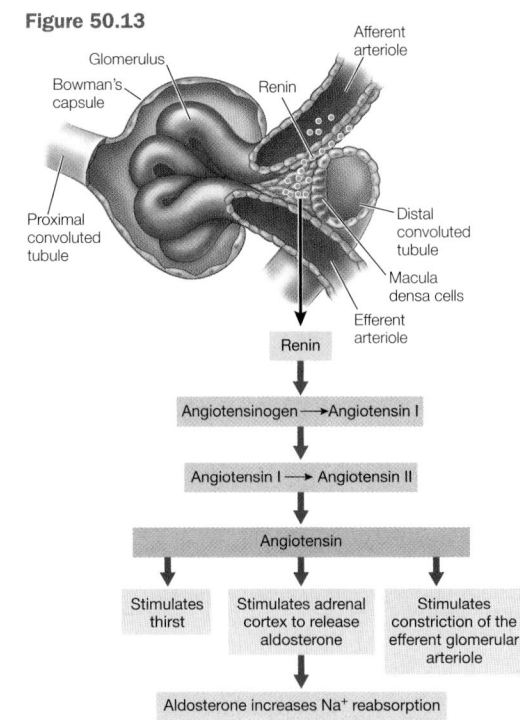

Questions

1. How does a fall in blood pressure result in a signal that increases activation of angiotensin?
2. How does angiotensin raise GFR?
3. How does ADH change the permeability of the collecting duct to water?

Go to **Achieve** for the eBook, **LearningCurve**, animations, activities, simulations, and additional resources and assignments.

Animal Behavior

© David Shaw/Alamy Stock Photo

KEY CONCEPTS

51.1 Ethology Led to Modern Behavioral Biology

51.2 Behavior Can Be Genetically Determined

51.3 Behavior Can Be Studied Developmentally

51.4 Selective Pressures Shape Behavior

51.5 Behavior Can Be Studied Mechanistically

51.6 Social Interactions Shape the Evolution of Behavior

The male songbird claims and defends his territory through song and attracts a mate through song, and the female selects her mate based on the quality and vigor of his song. Birdsong involves genetic determinants, learning, physiological conditions, and social interactions.

▶InvestigatingLIFE

An Instinct to Learn

A springtime joy is hearing birds sing. Why do they do it? Male songbirds use species-specific song to compete with other males for territory. They also sing to attract mates. Females may not sing, but they recognize the songs of their own species. Males of most species, such as the White-crowned Sparrow (*Zonotrichia leucophrys*), must learn their song, but *what* they can learn is influenced by their genes, and *when* they can learn it is influenced by their physiology. A hatchling in the nest hears his father and other White-crowned Sparrows singing. He also hears the songs of many other bird species. He does not sing until he approaches sexual maturity almost a year later, and when he does, he sings his father's type of song and not that of other species. His first attempts at song are poor, but by trial and error he gradually matches his song to the one stored in his memory, even though other species are singing in his environment. His singing talent depends on two critical conditions: he must hear his species-specific song in the first 2 months of life, and he must be able to hear himself as he develops his song. These are both learning experiences, but the bird's genes play an important role too.

Male White-crowned Sparrows raised alone in the laboratory and exposed to recordings of unrelated species will not learn any of those song templates even if they are played over and over. But if in that cacophony of songs, a bird's species-specific song is played just a few times, he will sing that song the following spring. Thus male White-crowned Sparrows must learn their song, but a genetic predisposition ensures that they learn the song of their own species.

An important reason why males learn only their species-specific song is that the females also listen to their father's songs when they are nestlings. When they mature, they choose mates that sing like their fathers did. But how does one female choose her specific mate? There is variation in male songs, and some components of songs seem sexier than others. Also, the way the songs are performed may differ among individuals and in different social contexts. As in humans, variability surely plays a role in mate choice.

 How does social context influence the learning and expression of birdsong?
(Find the answer on page 1167.)

51.1 Ethology Led to Modern Behavioral Biology

Learning Objectives

51.1.1 Identify the origins and differences between behaviorism and ethology.

51.1.2 Discuss the significance of deprivation experiments.

51.1.3 Explain what proximate and ultimate causes of behavior are, using examples.

Humans have studied animal behavior since prehistoric times. Understanding the habits of potential prey, as well as those of their predators, was of great value to hunters. Appreciation of behavioral traits led to the domestication of animal species. Accounts of animal behaviors such as seasonal appearances and disappearances, mating displays, aggression, prey capture, parental care, and communication are found throughout recorded history. Yet the scientific study of animal behavior did not truly get under way until the early 1900s.

Conditioned reflexes are a simple behavioral mechanism

In the late 1800s the Russian physiologist Ivan Pavlov used dogs to study the neural control of digestive juice secretion. His dogs, like all dogs, salivated when they smelled food, but Pavlov observed that they also salivated whenever the technician who routinely fed the dogs entered the room—even when no food was present. Following up this observation, Pavlov substituted a sound stimulus for the technician; a metronome ticked while the dogs were fed. After several trials, the dogs salivated when they heard the metronome, even if no food was offered.

Salivation in response to the sight, smell, or taste of food is a natural reflex response to a stimulus, but salivation in response to a sound was a learned response. The pairing of a sound with the experience of receiving food conditioned the dogs' nervous systems to generate a response, which Pavlov dubbed the **conditioned reflex** (Figure 51.1). The natural stimulus—food in this case—became known as the unconditioned stimulus, and the unnatural stimulus was termed the conditioned stimulus. Pavlov received a Nobel Prize in 1904 for his work showing that a simple behavior controlled by the nervous system could be modified through experience. This work stimulated much new research because Pavlov had developed an experimental model of learning.

Going beyond the conditioning of autonomic reflexes, the psychologist B. F. Skinner showed that many behaviors could become conditioned responses to stimuli if a reward was associated with the action and the stimulus. A rat, for example, could be conditioned to press a lever in response to a stimulus if it got a reward when it pressed the lever. Because the animal was conditioned to perform an *operation* on its environment, this experimental protocol was called **operant conditioning** and became another model of learning.

The experimental approaches to behavior initiated by Pavlov and Skinner stimulated much research on animal behavior, but the focus of that research was mostly controlled laboratory experiments

(A) Before conditioning

Food is an unconditioned stimulus that produces an unconditioned response (salivation).

Sound is a neutral stimulus that produces no response.

(B) Conditioning

Conditioning results from repeatedly presenting the unconditioned stimulus immediately following presentation of the neutral stimulus.

(C) After conditioning

The neutral stimulus has become a conditioned stimulus that by itself produces the conditioned reflex (salivation).

Figure 51.1 The Conditioned Reflex (A) Prior to conditioning, there is no response to the neutral stimulus. Ivan Pavlov discovered that when a normal response is paired with an artificial or neutral stimulus (B), an animal learns to produce the response even when only the artificial stimulus is presented (C).

on learning and memory in only a few species—mostly the white rat. This field of animal behavior became known as **behaviorism**.

Ethologists focused on the behavior of animals in their natural environment

An alternative approach to the study of animal behavior arose at the same time as behaviorism and focused on the various behaviors of animals in their natural environments. This field of study became known as **ethology** (Greek *ethos*, "character," + *logos*, "study"). Ethologists were interested in a wide variety of species, their evolutionary relationships, and the ways in which their behaviors were adapted to their environments. The leaders of the ethology movement were Karl von Frisch, who discovered the dance language of honey bees (*Apis* spp.); Konrad Lorenz, who discovered that the strong bond between parent and offspring develops during a "critical period" following birth; and Niko Tinbergen, who studied inborn patterns of behavior commonly known as instincts. These three scientists shared the Nobel Prize in 1973 for "their discoveries concerning organization and elicitation of individual and social behavior patterns." Their work laid the foundation for modern research on animal behavior.

Ethologists were mainly interested in species-specific or instinctive behaviors that therefore had to have genetic components. Behaviors were thought to be genetically determined if they:

- are performed without learning.
- are stereotypic (that is, they are performed the same way each time).
- cannot be modified by learning.

The ethologists called such behaviors **fixed action patterns**.

Ethologists performed **deprivation experiments** to demonstrate the genetic determination of a behavior. They raised animals in an environment devoid of opportunities to learn their species-specific behavior, and then looked for the expression of that behavior. The web spinning of a spider is an example of a natural deprivation experiment. The parents of a young spider die before it hatches, and in a seasonal environment it has no model webs to copy when it spins its first web. Web construction requires thousands of stereotyped sequential movements. Yet a young spider creates a perfect, species-specific web the first and every time it spins a web. Thus the information for the web spinning behavior has to be genetically programmed into its nervous system.

Fixed action patterns are usually responses to specific stimuli. The ethologists carefully characterized such stimuli, which they called **releasers**. In general, releasers are simple subsets of the information available in the environment. For example, Tinbergen

studied the begging behavior of Herring Gull (*Larus argentatus*) chicks. An adult Herring Gull has a red dot on its lower bill. When a parent returns to the nest to feed its chicks, the chicks peck on its red dot, which stimulates the parent to regurgitate food (**Figure 51.2A**). Experimenters investigated what stimulated the chicks to peck a parent's bill. Models of gull heads of different shapes and colors were tested (**Figure 51.2B**), as were models of a beak without a head. The results showed that the red dot was necessary for the release of chick pecking behavior. In fact, a pencil with a red eraser elicited a more robust pecking response than did an accurate model of a gull head without a red dot on its bill.

Ethologists probed the causes of behavior

The ethologists demonstrated the genetic basis for fixed action patterns by interbreeding closely related species. Konrad Lorenz studied the courtship behaviors of different species of dabbling ducks. Some of these species, such as Mallards (*Anas platyrhynchos*), teals, pintails, and Gadwalls (*Mareca strepera*), are closely related and can interbreed, but they rarely do so in nature. Each male duck performs a courtship display consisting of a precise series of movements that is typical of his species. A female is not likely to accept him unless the entire display is successfully and correctly completed.

Lorenz crossbred these duck species and found that the hybrid offspring expressed some elements of each parent's courtship display, but in novel combinations. Furthermore, Lorenz observed that hybrids sometimes exhibited display elements that were not in the repertoire of either parent species but were seen in other dabbling duck species. Lorenz's interbreeding studies demonstrated that the stereotypic motor patterns of the courtship displays are inherited. The observation that females were not interested in males performing hybrid displays was evidence that sexual selection had shaped these genetically determined behaviors to be reproductive isolating mechanisms.

(A) *Larus marinus*

(B)

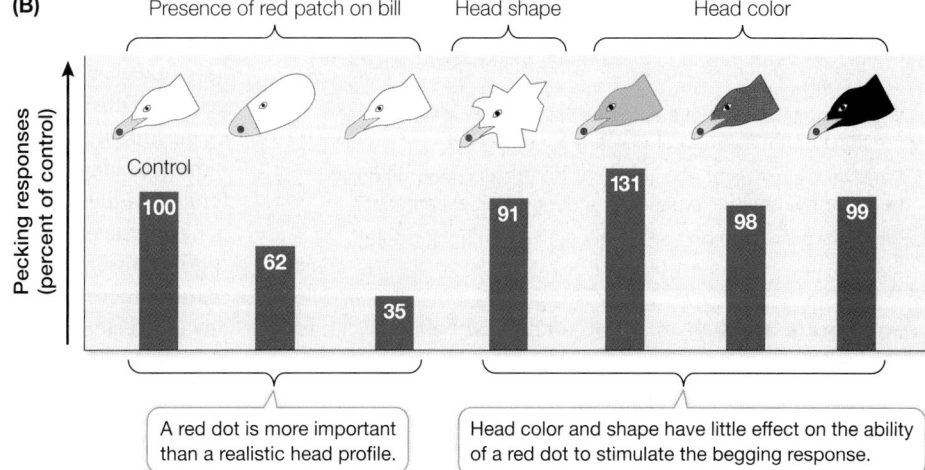

Presence of red patch on bill   Head shape   Head color

Pecking responses (percent of control)

Control

100   62   35   91   131   98   99

A red dot is more important than a realistic head profile.

Head color and shape have little effect on the ability of a red dot to stimulate the begging response.

© FLPA/Alamy Stock Photo

Figure 51.2 Releasing a Fixed Action Pattern (A) In many gull species, chicks instinctively peck at the red dot on the parent's lower bill, a behavior that induces the parent to regurgitate food into the chick's mouth. (B) Tinbergen's work showed that the red dot on the parent's lower bill is the critical component that releases the pecking response. (B after N. Tinbergen and A. C. Perdeck. 1950. *Behaviour* 3: 1–39.)

Q: Why do you think sign stimuli are rather simple components of all of the sensory information available?

Connect the Concepts The evolution of populations into different species occurs when hybrids of the two populations have lower fitness. In those cases, selection favors mechanisms that prevent hybridization, and behavioral reproductive isolating mechanisms are the most common, as described in Key Concept 22.4.

The ethologists laid the foundation for the application of modern biological methods to the study of animal behavior. Tinbergen outlined the challenges for investigators as four questions:

1. *Causation*: What is the mechanism underlying the behavior, and how can the relationship between mechanisms and behavior be modified by learning?

2. *Development*: What experiences are necessary for a behavior to be displayed, and how does the behavior change with age?

3. *Function*: How does the behavior affect the animal's chances for survival and reproduction?

4. *Evolution*: How does the behavior compare with similar behaviors in related species, and how might it have evolved?

The first two questions refer to the **proximate causes** of behavior: the immediate genetic, physiological, neurological, and developmental mechanisms that determine how an individual is behaving at a particular time. The third and fourth questions refer to the **ultimate causes** of behavior: the evolutionary processes that produced the animal's capacity and tendency to behave in particular ways. In the key concepts that follow, we describe many experiments on animal behavior. For each one, ask yourself which of Tinbergen's four questions it addresses and whether it focuses on proximate or ultimate causes of behavior.

KEY CONCEPT
51.1 Recap and Assess

Early scientific studies of animal behavior took two approaches. Behaviorists focused on the study of conditioned behavior in a few species of laboratory animals and asked questions about learning. Ethologists studied genetically determined behavior in many species in their natural environments and asked evolutionary questions.

1. What distinguishes fixed action patterns from behaviors resulting from Pavlovian or operant conditioning?

2. What variables might account for a genetically determined behavior not being expressed in a deprivation experiment?

3. What are proximate and ultimate causes of mating-display behavior?

The work of the ethologists left no doubt that behavior can be genetically determined, but how? Genes code for proteins, whereas behaviors are highly complex traits involving sensory input and intricate patterns of control over responses to that input. Is it reasonable to think that a single gene can have a specific effect on a behavior?

KEY CONCEPT
51.2 Behavior Can Be Genetically Determined

Learning Objectives

51.2.1 Describe an example of a single gene influencing a behavior.

51.2.2 Discuss the kinds of evidence that support the claim that single genes can influence behavior.

51.2.3 Explain the evolutionary benefit of a gene expression cascade that influences behavior.

The work of ethologists showed the strong genetic basis for most animal behaviors. Of course, *most* animals are insects and other invertebrates, and even among the vertebrates *most* are not mammals, let alone primates. So even though the controversy over the relative influences of nature versus nurture in human behavior has raged for many years, the dominant role played by genes in shaping behavior is amply documented by research on other species. Genetically determined complex behaviors such as the web spinning of spiders or the mating behaviors of dabbling ducks mentioned previously must surely depend on many genes. Yet with the rapid development of genomic analytical technologies, comparisons of genomes and gene expression patterns of animals with different behavioral phenotypes are producing many examples of single gene alterations that produce behavioral differences.

Single gene mutations can alter behavioral phenotypes

Are you a morning person or a night person? Some people are early risers and function best in the morning, and others have their best work hours late at night. It is possible that this big difference in the behavior of individuals could be due to differences in a single gene. This story begins with fruit flies, *Drosophila*. Fruit flies, like virtually all organisms, have daily rhythms that continue even if all external time cues are taken away. But without external time cues, these rhythms do not span exactly 24 hours, which is why they are called circadian (*circa*, "about," + *dies*, "a day"). Investigators using chemicals to randomly mutate genes in *Drosophila* found one gene that controlled the duration, or period, of the circadian rhythms of the flies. This gene was named *per* for period, and variants of this gene caused short or long circadian periods. We now know that there are many more genes involved in circadian rhythms, and that these genes are highly conserved in organisms ranging from *Drosophila* to humans. One variant of the *per* gene in humans results in familial advanced sleep phase syndrome. The affected individuals have short circadian rhythms and tend to go to sleep and wake up earlier than others.

That single genes can influence even complex behaviors should not be surprising. Many behaviors depend on a particular signaling molecule or a particular receptor molecule, and a change in the gene for that signal or receptor could therefore dramatically change the behavior. For example, mutation in a gene for an olfactory receptor could result in the ability to sense a different odorant. Even changes in the expression pattern of a gene can alter a complex behavior. As discussed at the beginning of Chapter 7, prairie voles (*Microtus ochrogaster*) are highly monogamous, and both sexes give much parental care to their young. Montane voles (*M. montanus*), in contrast, do not form pair bonds, are promiscuous, and provide a shorter period of maternal care than prairie voles. The difference between these two species lies in the expression of the receptors for the neuropeptides vasopressin (males) and oxytocin (females): there are far fewer receptors for these neuropeptides in the brains of montane voles, and their expression patterns in the brain are different. We'll return to the social systems of voles in Key Concept 51.6.

Knockout experiments reveal the roles of specific genes

As discussed in Chapter 18, in a knockout experiment, one of an organism's genes is made nonfunctional ("knocked out") to see what effect its elimination has on the organism's phenotype. Knocking out genes involved in sensory pathways can have pronounced effects on behavior. One example is a gene for a specific olfactory receptor in mice.

As we discussed in Key Concept 44.2, mice have two olfactory organs: the nasal olfactory epithelium common to all mammals, and a small organ in the nasal passages called the vomeronasal organ, or VNO (**Figure 51.3**). Catherine Dulac at Harvard University discovered that pheromone receptors are expressed in that organ. Pheromones are signal molecules that are released into the environment and are used for communication between individuals of the same species. Dulac hypothesized that when sex pheromones produced by female mice bind to the receptors in the male's VNO, they stimulate mating behavior. To test this hypothesis, Dulac created a genetically engineered male mouse in which a gene for VNO receptor signaling was knocked out. Contrary to the hypothesis, the knockout males in fact did pursue and mate with females placed in their cages. However, they

also pursued and tried to mate with males placed in their cages. Normally a male mouse reacts aggressively to a strange male, but the knockout male could not discriminate between males and females placed in his cage. Thus proper functioning of this one VNO receptor is essential not for sexual attraction, but for sex identification. You can imagine how selection working on this one gene could modify the intensity of male–male aggression and lead to changes in social behavior.

Gene cascades can control complex behavioral phenotypes

Male courtship behavior in the fruit fly (*Drosophila*) is stereotypic, species-specific, and requires no learning—a classic fixed action pattern. When a male encounters a potential mate, he follows her, taps her body with his foreleg, extends and vibrates one wing, and licks her genitals (**Figure 51.4A**). The development of this complex male behavior is under the control of a single gene, called *fruitless* (*fru*), and the development of male anatomy is under the control of another gene, called *doublesex* (*dsx*). In both males and females, these two genes are part of gene expression cascades that differ in the splicing of the mRNA in the two sexes. Those splicing differences result in different *dsx* and *fru* gene products in males and females (**Figure 51.4B**). The female version of the Dsx protein controls the development of female anatomy, and the expression of *fru* in the male nervous system results in the organization of the neural circuitry controlling male sexual behavior.

There are two take-home lessons from this example. First, genes that control aspects of behavior, like other genes, are generally embedded in gene cascades that offer opportunities for simple genetic changes to alter the phenotype of even complex behaviors. Second, certain genes, such as *dsx* and *fru*, influence a range of other genes that contribute to complex behaviors. Modifications in any one of those genes or its expression can alter behavior. Thus even though no behavior is coded for by a single gene, alterations in single genes can influence behavior in ways that affect an animal's fitness.

(A) The mouse VNO

(B)

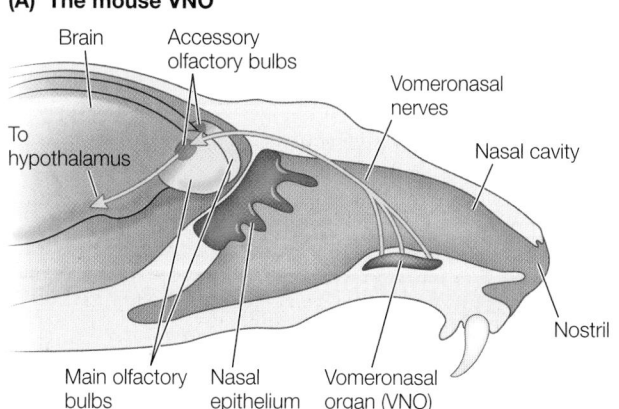

Figure 51.3 The Mouse Vomeronasal Organ Identifies Sex
(A) The mouse VNO is located in the nasal passages. It contains pheromone receptors whose input travels to a specific region of the olfactory bulb (the accessory olfactory bulb). Projections from the accessory

olfactory bulb go only to areas of the brain involved in sexual behavior, whereas projections from the main olfactory bulb go to many different areas of the brain (not shown). (B) In male mice, information from the VNO is crucial in identifying gender and thus a potential sexual partner.

(A) Fruit fly courtship behavior

Female fruit flies are XX...

...and males are XY.

Orienting

Tapping

Wing vibration

Licking

Attempted copulation

Copulation

(B) Genes responsible for sexual differentiation

1 Sex-determining pre-mRNAs are spliced in one specific way in female flies...

2 ...and another way in males.

| Female-specific mRNA | Gene | Male-specific mRNA |

Transcription and mRNA splicing

sxl mRNA

sex-lethal (sxl)

Transcription and mRNA splicing

Female Sxl protein

Stop codon

Default splicing

No functional Sxl protein

3 Female *sxl* and *tra* mRNAs make proteins that control mRNA splicing in the expression of genes in the female-specific hierarchy.

transformer (tra)

Female Tra protein

Stop codon

No functional Tra protein

4 Male *sxl* and *tra* mRNAs have stop codons that terminate translation.

doublesex (dsx)

Female Dsx protein

Male Dsx protein

5 The default splicing of *dsx* mRNAs controls male anatomy...

fruitless (fru)

Introns (noncoding DNA)

Female Fru protein

Male Fru protein

6 ...and male-specific splicing of *fru*, which results in male courtship behavior.

Figure 51.4 The *fruitless* Gene **(A)** Male fruit flies display stereotypic, species-specific court-ship behavior. **(B)** Sexual differentiation in *Drosophila* is controlled by a cascade of gene expression, including the *fru* gene, whose expression results in male sexual behavior.

KEY CONCEPT

51.2 Recap and Assess

There are strong genetic determinants of behavior in most species. Gene manipulations such as mutations and knockouts show that a single gene can play a large role in the development and expression of a behavior. Although most behaviors are controlled by multiple genes, those genes frequently function in signaling cascades, so a single gene modification can influence even a complex behavior controlled by many genes.

1. A method has been developed to increase the expression of oxytocin and vasopressin genes in montane voles. What difference might that treatment make in the behavior of these animals? If the expected result is not seen, what could be the reason?

2. If you interbred two individuals from separate populations that bred true for a trait that differed between the two, and all of the offspring resembled one of the parents, what would you conclude about the genetic basis for that behavior?

3. What could be an evolutionary reason for a species-specific mating behavior being controlled by a gene expression cascade, such as in *Drosophila*?

How can the genetic cascades that underlie complex behaviors be programmed to respond selectively to specific sets of stimuli? How can their expression be limited to appropriate times in an animal's life? The answers to these questions can be found by studying how behaviors develop over the life span.

KEY CONCEPT

51.3 Behavior Can Be Studied Developmentally

Learning Objectives

51.3.1 Discuss examples of how hormones can affect the timing and expression of behavior.

51.3.2 Describe the evidence supporting the claim that genetics plays an important role in bird singing behavior.

51.3.3 Explain the evolutionary benefit of variability in the singing behavior of a bird species.

The emergence of behavior as an animal develops and matures depends on the development of the nervous system as well as on the growth and maturation of other body systems. But even with anatomical and physiological competence, specific behaviors may not be expressed. Behaviors that are adaptive at one stage in an animal's life may not be adaptive at other stages. Behaviors typical of juvenile animals, such as begging for food, may disappear and new behavior patterns of a mature individual, such as courtship displays, appear.

Hormones can determine behavioral potential and timing

Hormones can determine the development of a behavioral potential at an early age and the expression of that behavior at a later age. An excellent example of this is sexual behavior in rats (**Figure 51.5**). Normally, adult male and female rats exhibit different patterns of sexual behavior: females adopt a sexually receptive posture, called lordosis, in the presence of males, and males copulate with receptive females. Neither sex expresses these behaviors until they reach adulthood. Experiments in which newborn and adult rats were neutered (to remove the influence of sex steroids naturally produced by their gonads) and artificially treated with hormones led to the following conclusions:

- Development of male sexual behavior requires that the brain of the newborn rat be exposed to low levels of testosterone. Female sexual behavior development does not require exposure to estrogen.

- Testosterone masculinizes the nervous systems of both genetic males and genetic females.

- Exposure to sex steroids in adulthood is necessary for the expression of sexual behavior, but testosterone produces male sexual behavior only in adult rats whose brains were masculinized when they were newborns, and estrogen produces female sexual behavior only in adult rats whose brains were not masculinized when they were newborns.

Thus the sex steroids that are present at birth determine which pattern of behavior develops, and the sex steroids that are present in adulthood determine when that pattern is expressed.

Some behaviors can be acquired only at certain times

Responsiveness to simple releasers is sufficient for certain behaviors such as begging behavior in gull chicks, but more complex information that cannot be genetically programmed is required for other behaviors. An example is parent–offspring recognition. When animals live in close proximity to other individuals, as in a herd or a nesting colony, it is important for parent and offspring to learn each other's

Figure 51.5 Hormonal Control of Sexual Behavior   Experimental hormone treatments of rats demonstrated that the sex steroids present during early development determine which sexual behavior patterns develop, whereas the sex steroids present in adulthood control the expression of those behavior patterns. The elimination of sex steroids during early postnatal development reveals that the default pattern of behavioral development is female. (After S. Levine. 1966. *Sci Am* 214: 84–90. Based on illustrations by Bunji Tagawa.)

(A) Sex hormone manipulations of female rats

(B) Sex hormone manipulations of male rats

identity soon after birth so they will be able to find each other in a crowded situation. In many such cases, a parent–offspring bond is formed by **imprinting**. What characterizes imprinting is that an animal learns a specific set of stimuli during a limited time called a **critical period**, also known as a **sensitive period**.

Konrad Lorenz demonstrated that young Graylag Geese imprint on their parents between 12 and 16 hours after hatching. By positioning himself to be present during this critical period, Lorenz succeeded in imprinting goslings on himself. The imprinted goslings followed him around as if he were their parent (**Figure 51.6A**). In a subsequent experiment his assistants wore boots with different patterns on them. The goslings imprinted on the boots, and even in a situation that mixed different groups of goslings, they always sorted themselves out by following their "parental" boots.

Imprinting requires only a brief exposure, but its effects are strong and long-lasting. Emperor Penguins reproduce during the coldest, darkest time of year in Antarctica. The adults walk up to 150 kilometers inland to form a dense colony, where the female lays her egg. She then walks back to the ocean to feed while her mate incubates the egg. By the time she returns, the chick has hatched. The female then takes over the chick's care and feeding, and the father walks back to the ocean to feed. Generally he is away so long that the mother must leave to find food to avoid starvation. Thus after being away for weeks, the father must find his chick in a crowded, milling colony of chicks, all calling for their parents (**Figure 51.6B**). Yet he can unerringly locate his own offspring by recognizing its call, on which he imprinted before he left to feed.

(A) *Anser anser*

(B) *Aptenodytes forsteri*

Figure 51.6 Imprinting Helps Parents and Offspring Recognize Each Other **(A)** Graylag Geese that imprinted on Konrad Lorenz as hatchlings followed him everywhere he went. **(B)** Imprinting allows a male Emperor Penguin to find his own chick among many others.

The critical period for imprinting may be determined by a brief hormonal state. For example, if a mother goat does not nuzzle and lick her newborn within 10 minutes after its birth, she will not recognize it as her own offspring later. This critical period is associated with peaking levels of the hormone oxytocin in the mother's circulatory system at the time she gives birth and at the same time she is sensing the olfactory cues emanating from her newborn kid. A female goat rendered incapable of smelling before giving birth is unable to differentiate between her own kid and other kids after giving birth.

Birdsong learning involves genetics, imprinting, development, and social interactions

The study of White-crowned Sparrow singing at the beginning of this chapter is a classic case of how genetics, physiology, and experience come together in the development and expression of behavior. Genetics endows the birds with a neural template that must be matched by experience during early development. That type of learning—imprinting—is limited to a critical period by processes of developmental physiology. Months later, the onset of sexual maturation motivates the birds to sing, initiating a second phase of learning that requires the birds to use auditory experience to develop the motor patterns required for the full expression of species-specific song (**Figure 51.7**). At the end of this learning phase, the song becomes permanent, or crystalized. Thus the overall process of transmission of a complex species-specific behavior necessary for reproductive success is well adapted to preserving constancy of the behavior. But variation is an important component of evolution.

Variation in birdsong is evident in nature. There are subtle differences between the songs of any two males, including those in neighboring territories. Regionally, White-crowned Sparrows have dialects, and a bird migrating into an area that has a different dialect can adopt that song pattern. There are even observations of White-crowned Sparrows singing the songs of closely related species. In a laboratory experiment, White-crowned Sparrows were raised in isolation but exposed to the sight and song of a male of a closely related species while recordings of White-crowned Sparrow song played on speakers in the background. When those birds matured, they sang the song of the closely related species. The ability to incorporate variation into an individual bird's song may relate to social interactions such as fitting into a regional norm, displaying individual qualities to a potential mate, and maintaining a bond between mates.

To investigate questions about the adaptive significance of variations in the male singing behavior, it is necessary to take female choice into consideration. Sarah Woolley and Allison Doupe at the University of California, San Francisco did that with Zebra Finches (*Taeniopygia guttata*), a species that has become a valuable model system for studying the neurobiology of birdsong. When male Zebra Finches sing in isolation, their song is variable ("undirected"), almost as if they are improvising and trying out new motifs. In the presence of females, however, they sing "directed" song (directed to a female) that is less variable. Woolley and Doupe conducted experiments to see which songs female Zebra Finches preferred (**Investigating Life: Practice Makes Perfect**). The females preferred directed song, and if mated, they preferred the directed songs of

(A) Control or wild bird

(B) Isolated hand-reared bird

(C) Deafened bird

Time (sec)

Figure 51.7 Critical Periods for Song Learning (A) Sonogram showing the species-specific song of an adult male White-crowned Sparrow (*Zonotrichia leucophrys*). (B) Song of an adult male raised in isolation (never having heard the song as a nestling). (C) Song of an adult male that heard the song as a nestling but was deafened prior to ever singing himself. Experiments showed that the bird must first acquire a song memory by hearing the song as a nestling, and must then be able to hear himself as he attempts to match his singing to that song memory. (From M. Konishi. 1965. *Z Tierpsychol* 22: 770–783.)

their mates. Thus the ability to incorporate variations into the species-specific song may be important to establish individuality and influence mate choice, but the nature of the singing depends on the social context.

Timing and expression of birdsong are under hormonal control

Both male and female songbirds hear their species-specific song as nestlings, but only the males of many species sing as adults, and most do so only in spring. Hormones underlie both the difference in song expression between male and female songbirds and the timing of song expression. When investigators injected adult female songbirds with testosterone in spring, those females sang their

---

▶Investigating**LIFE** Practice Makes Perfect

Experiment

Original Paper: S. C. Woolley and A. J. Doupe. 2008. Social context-induced song variation affects female behavior and gene expression. *PLOS Biology* 6(3): e62/CC BY 4.0

When male Zebra Finches (*Taeniopygia guttata*) sing alone, they improvise (undirected song), but when they sing in the presence of a female, they sing a stereotyped (directed) song. Woolley and Doupe asked whether the quality of the song influenced the behavior of the female.

HYPOTHESIS▶ Female Zebra Finches have a preference for directed over undirected song, and can identify the song of their mate.

METHOD▶

1. Record males singing alone and singing in the presence of their mate.

2. Place a female in the center chamber of a three-chamber apparatus; the female should be able to move between the chambers. Play recordings of her mate's directed song in one end-chamber and of her mate's undirected song in the other end-chamber.

3. Record the amount of time the female spends in the different chambers.

Recording of mate's undirected song

The female Zebra Finch can choose either compartment.

Recording of mate's directed song

RESULTS▶ Females spent a higher percentage of time in the chamber in which their mate's directed song was played. The data show results for 17 females with means and standard deviations. The *P*-value from a paired *t*-test is < 0.001.

CONCLUSION▶ Females can discriminate between their mate's directed and undirected songs and are more attracted to the directed song.

Investigating**LIFE** Work with the Data follows on the next page.

Work with the Data

Since the experiment showed that female Zebra Finches could distinguish between the directed and undirected songs of their mate, the next question was whether they could distinguish between the directed song of their mate and the directed song of other males. A second experiment used the same protocol as did the first one, but the two songs that were played to each female were the directed song of her mate and the directed song of an unfamiliar male. The results are shown in the table.

Percent time spent close to:	
Unfamiliar directed song	**Mate's directed song**
25	55
15	81
8	43
7	78
6	92
6	92
5	90
5	50
5	86
4	85
4	84
3	83
3	81
3	80
2	73
1	72
1	97
0	98

QUESTIONS▶

1. If you hypothesized that the female's preference for her mate's directed song was a factor in pair bonding rather than just a mating stimulus, what data would test this hypothesis?

2. Plot the data as bar graphs. Show the means and standard deviations, and do a paired *t*-test to determine the significance level. Can females distinguish their mate's directed song from the directed song of an unfamiliar male?

3. What do these results suggest about the mating system of the Zebra Finch?

4. What hypotheses can you suggest about the function of undirected song?

Go to Achieve for a companion Data in Depth exercise.

How does testosterone cause a songbird to sing? Each spring an increase in circulating testosterone levels causes certain parts of the male's brain necessary for learning and developing song to grow larger. Individual neurons in those regions of the brain increase in size and grow longer extensions, and the number of neurons in those regions increases. Thus hormones can control behavior by changing brain structure as well as brain function, both developmentally and in response to environmental cues.

KEY CONCEPT
51.3 Recap and Assess

Genetics can determine what behaviors can be learned, and hormones can determine the critical period when they can be learned as well as the motivational states that trigger their expression. Imprinting ensures the ability of individuals to recognize other individuals or species at a later time. Some capacity for variation of genetically determined and imprinted behaviors enables behavior to be shaped by social context.

1. Why is female considered to be the default pathway for the development of sexual behavior in rats?

2. Explain why a songbird deafened in adulthood can sing its song, but a songbird deafened before reaching sexual maturity cannot.

3. Under what conditions might variability in a species-specific behavior be adaptive or not be adaptive?

Complex behaviors are the product of interactions of genetic, physiological, and environmental factors. Many genes are involved in shaping behavior, and therefore there are multiple opportunities for selection to favor behavioral modifications. Questions about how changes in behavior adapt animals to environmental conditions are the province of an evolution-based field called **behavioral ecology**.

KEY CONCEPT
51.4 Selective Pressures Shape Behavior

Learning Objectives

51.4.1 Describe how a cost–benefit approach is applied to investigating animal behavior.

51.4.2 Describe different types of territorial behaviors and the cost and benefit factors that shape their evolution.

51.4.3 Explain why aggressive territorial behavior is associated with some essential resources but not others.

51.4.4 Explain how foraging involves trade-offs between nutrients acquired and the costs of energy required, opportunity loss, and risk.

species-specific song just as males did. Females as well as males form a memory of their species-specific song when they are nestlings, and they have the physical capacity to sing, but under normal circumstances they lack the necessary hormonal stimulation.

Most of the behaviors we have discussed so far involve interactions among individuals. The individual also interacts with its environment, and many behaviors have evolved as adaptations to the environment. Environmental conditions can be highly variable over time and space. Behavioral ecologists strive to discover the relationships between behavior and environment, with the intent of understanding the selective pressures shaping the evolution of specific behaviors. Here we offer just a few examples.

Animals are faced with many choices

Animal behavior is largely a sequence of choices: where and when to move, where to build a nest, what to eat, when to fight and when to flee, with whom to associate, with whom to mate. Making wrong choices reduces fitness. Behavioral ecologists seek to discover what information animals use to make behavioral choices and how that information relates to the environmental conditions that influence fitness.

Where an animal lives is referred to as its **habitat**. In most cases the habitat provides not only protected nest sites, but also food and access to mates. The environmental cues animals use to select their habitats may be quite simple. For example, seabirds select cliffs or offshore rocks for nesting, and both of those sites offer protection from predators. Animals with very specialized food requirements select habitats where those foods are abundant. The general hypothesis that guides behavioral ecologists is that the cues animals use to select habitats are reliable predictors of conditions suitable for future survival and reproduction.

For many species, the presence of **conspecifics**—other members of the same species—can be a valuable cue. Observing conspecifics can provide animals with information about the quality of a habitat. You can't argue with success. During the breeding season, European Collared Flycatchers (*Ficedula albicollis*) are nosy neighbors, regularly visiting the nests of conspecifics. Researchers hypothesized that this behavior allows the flycatchers to assess the quality of the habitat by seeing how well their neighbors are faring. To test this hypothesis, they created some areas with supersized broods—normally an indication of abundant food—by taking young birds from some nests and adding them to nests in another area. The next year, flycatchers preferentially settled in the areas where broods had been artificially enlarged.

Behaviors have costs and benefits

A cost–benefit approach can be used to investigate the relationships between behavior, environment, and fitness. A **cost–benefit approach** assumes that an animal has only a limited amount of time and energy, and therefore cannot afford to engage in behaviors that cost more to perform than they return in benefits. A cost–benefit approach provides a framework that can be used to construct hypotheses and design experiments to investigate why behavior patterns evolve as they do.

The benefits of a behavior are measured in terms of the enhancement in fitness an animal accrues by performing the behavior. The cost of a behavior typically has three components:

1. **Energetic cost** is the energy the animal expends performing the behavior.
2. **Risk cost** is the increased chance of being injured or killed.
3. **Opportunity cost** consists of the benefits the animal forgoes by not being able to perform other behaviors at the same time.

Territorial behavior carries significant costs

Territorial behavior is a good subject for cost–benefit analysis. Territoriality is aggressive behavior that actively denies other animals access to a habitat or resource. Optimal habitats and resources may be in short supply, so conspecifics have to compete for them. Many animals—usually males—defend all-purpose territories that provide a nest site, food, and access to mates. The territory holder stakes out his boundaries by engaging in aggressive interactions with neighbors, and must then patrol those boundaries constantly and respond to trespassers. These aggressive interactions usually consist of highly stereotypic, species-specific displays such as birdsong. Through territorial behavior, the male obtains the resources he needs for reproductive success, but he also pays a price.

Territorial displays require considerable expenditure of energy, they make a male more vulnerable to predation, and they detract from the time he has for feeding or engaging in parental behavior. Catherine Marler and Michael Moore at Arizona State University performed an experiment to estimate the costs incurred by male Yarrow's spiny lizards (*Sceloporus jarrovii*) when defending a territory. These lizards defend territories that include the home ranges of several females. Their territorial behavior is normally most intense during September and October when circulating testosterone levels of the males are high and the females are most receptive to mating. The researchers varied the intensity of the lizards' territorial behavior by implanting testosterone capsules in some males in summer, when they are not normally highly territorial (**Figure 51.8**).

Testosterone-treated males spent more time patrolling their territories, performed more displays, and expended about one-third more energy than control males (energetic cost). They had less time to feed (opportunity cost), captured fewer insects, stored less energy, and had a higher death rate (risk costs). In summer, when females are not normally receptive, these high costs of vigorous territorial defense outweigh the reproductive benefits of territoriality. Thus natural selection has favored seasonal variation in the level of the hormone controlling territorial behavior in this species.

 View in Achieve
Animation 51.1 **The Costs of Defending a Territory**

The cost–benefit approach explains the diversity of territorial behaviors seen in different species. Even if a resource is essential to an animal, if it cannot be defended economically, the animal will not engage in territorial behavior. Food is essential for all animals, but if the food is widely distributed in space or fluctuating in availability, there is no benefit to offset the high costs of defending it. For example, the distribution of food in the open ocean is highly variable, so there is no benefit to seabirds from trying to defend a patch of ocean. But safe nest sites on islands or rocky cliffs are in short supply, and they can be defended. The territories of seabirds may be no larger than the distance the birds can reach while sitting on their nests (**Figure 51.9A**).

In some cases the resource that is defended is the female herself. Northern Elephant Seals spend most of their lives at sea, but females come to land at traditional beach sites to give birth to their pups. Male elephant seals arrive at these sites ahead of time

Experiment

Figure 51.8 The Costs of Defending a Territory

Original Papers: C. A. Marler and M. C. Moore. 1988. Evolutionary costs of aggression revealed by testosterone manipulations in free-living male lizards. *Behav Ecol Sociobiol* 23: 21–26.

C. A. Marler and M. C. Moore. 1989. Time and energy costs of aggression in testosterone-implanted free-living male mountain spiny lizards (*Sceloporus jarrovii*). *Physiol Zool* 62: 1334–1350.

By using testosterone implants to increase territorial behavior, Catherine Marler and Michael Moore measured the costs to male Yarrow's spiny lizards (*Sceloporus jarrovii*) of defending a territory during the summer, when they do not normally do so.

HYPOTHESIS▶ Yarrow's spiny lizards do not defend a territory during summer because the energetic costs of territorial behavior in that season outweigh the benefits.

METHOD▶

1. During the summer, when female lizards are not sexually receptive, insert testosterone capsules under the skin of some males; other males received empty capsules to serve as controls.

2. Observe the patterns of territorial behavior and the survival rate of the two groups of males.

RESULTS▶

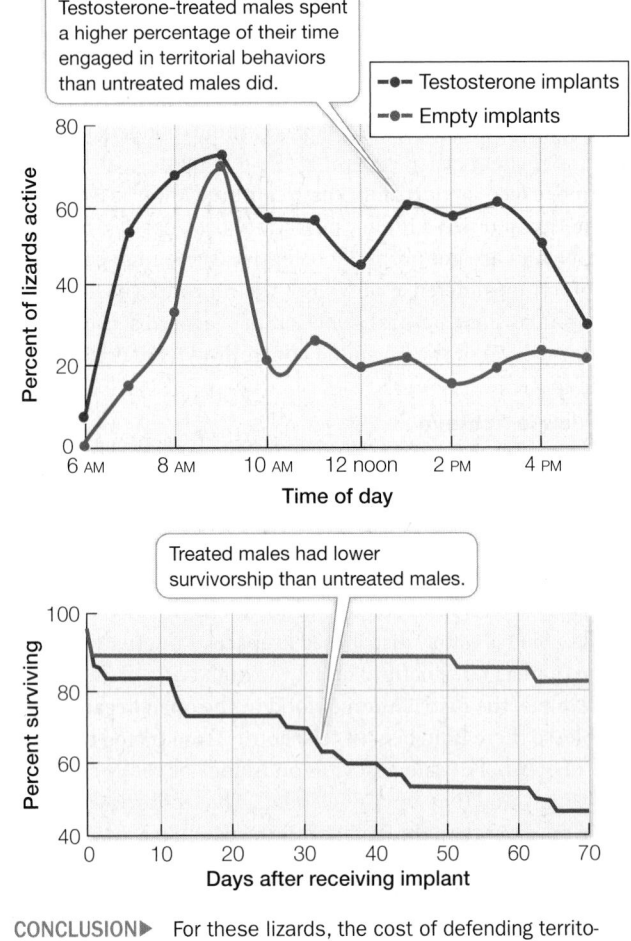

Testosterone-treated males spent a higher percentage of their time engaged in territorial behaviors than untreated males did.

Treated males had lower survivorship than untreated males.

CONCLUSION▶ For these lizards, the cost of defending territories during summer significantly reduces their survival rate.

and stake out territories through vigorous fighting (**Figure 51.9B**). When the females arrive on the beaches, they have to enter the territories of the males. As long as the male territory holder can fend off challengers, he will be able to mate with all the females using his piece of the beach.

One unusual form of male territorial behavior arises in situations in which neither food, nest sites, or females are defended. A **lek** is an area where males gather for the purpose of engaging in intense displays of their territorial prowess, aimed at impressing females and winning the opportunity to mate. Even though space is not limited, each male defends a small piece of real estate on which he performs a display (**Figure 51.9C**). Those territories closest to the center of the lek are the prime sites, and males compete intensely for those locations. The females visit the lek, observe the males, and generally mate with the males holding the prime sites. The benefit of this system to the female is that she is inseminated by a strong, successful competitor, and therefore her offspring will carry the genes that contributed to his success. This is another example of sexual selection (see Key Concept 19.2). The costs of lekking to males are high, as they engage in continuous, intense territorial behavior that precludes eating, drinking, and sleeping until they are displaced. The benefit to the male is the chance to maximize his fitness by mating with many females.

Foraging behavior has costs and benefits

Searching for food (foraging) involves many decisions: how much time to spend in each location, what is edible, and which potential foods should be eaten and which should be ignored. A cost–benefit approach to feeding behavior has resulted in an **optimal foraging theory**, which aims at identifying the fitness value of feeding choices. The primary benefits of foraging are nutrition: energy, minerals, and vitamins (see Key Concept 49.1). The costs of foraging are similar to those of other behaviors: energy expended, time lost from other activities that could enhance fitness, and the risk of increased exposure to predators.

 View in Achieve
Animation 51.2 Foraging Behavior

Animals frequently make choices among food items that may differ not only in terms of energy content, but also abundance or ease of acquisition and processing. Optimal foraging theory predicts that in such situations, animals will make choices that will maximize the rate at which they obtain energy. The more rapidly a foraging animal satisfies its energetic requirements, the lower the opportunity costs and risk costs of foraging.

The energy maximization hypothesis considers food items in terms of the energy they provide, but animals have nutrient requirements in addition to energy that can play a role in shaping their foraging behavior. Essential minerals, for example, are in short supply in some animals' diets, and those animals may incur large energetic costs and risks to obtain them (**Figure 51.10**). Some foods may also be sought for their medicinal value. Chimpanzees (*Pan troglodytes*), for example, have been observed eating the pith of the plant *Vernonia amygdalina*. The pith contains small quantities of a secondary metabolite, vernonioside B1, that is toxic to chimps at high concentrations, but at low concentrations

(A) *Thalassarche melanophris*

(B) *Mirounga angustirostris*

(C) *Centrocercus urophasianus*

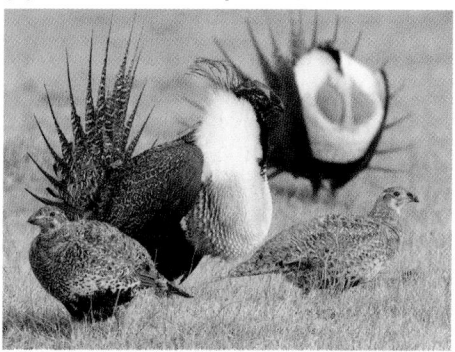

Figure 51.9 Animals Defend Territories of Different Sizes **(A)** The nesting territories of many seabirds, such as these Black-browed Albatrosses, consist of only as much space as the birds can defend without leaving the nest. **(B)** Male Northern Elephant Seals fight vigorously to defend areas of beach where females haul out of the water to give birth to their pups. **(C)** Male Greater Sage-Grouse gather at a lek in Colorado to perform displays aimed at impressing females and winning the opportunity to mate.

(A) *Ara chloropterus*

(B)

Figure 51.10 Herbivores Seek Out Unusual Sources of Minerals **(A)** Red-and-Green Macaws of the Amazon jungle obtain essential minerals by eating dried clay. **(B)** Heliconian butterflies obtain needed salts by drinking secretions from the skin and nostrils of a caiman.

vernonioside can kill their intestinal parasites. Chimps that consume this plant material have fewer parasites.

KEY CONCEPT

51.4 Recap and Assess

Many behaviors are shaped by environmental conditions that influence the decisions animals must make. Decisions can result in benefits that increase reproductive fitness, but they also involve costs, including energetic costs, opportunity costs, and risk costs. Cost–benefit analysis can be applied to territorial and foraging behaviors.

1. Male Red-winged Blackbirds prefer to build nests in marshes, but they feed in upland meadows. What costs and benefits most likely shaped these behaviors?

2. Cichlid fishes have dominant males that have colorful markings and defend territories. There are also nondominant males that are plain and do not defend territories but occasionally dash in when a female is spawning to try to fertilize some of her eggs. What are the costs and benefits of these two male phenotypes?

3. Elephant seals defend big pieces of beach as mating territories, whereas prairie-chickens defend small pieces of grassland as mating territories. Male elephant seals are much larger than the females and viciously fight with one another over their territories. Male prairie-chickens are not much larger than females; they have elaborate displays, and they don't fight viciously with neighboring males. What selective pressures have shaped the behaviors of these two different kinds of animals that defend mating territories?

4. Consider a species that has a choice of two potential sources of food. One is calorie-rich but is dispersed in a sparse environment. The other is calorie-poor but occurs in dense patches in a protected environment. What selective pressures would likely shape the food preference of this species?

Behavioral ecologists are interested in understanding how the natural environment influences the fitness value of behavioral choices—the ultimate causes of those behaviors, in Tinbergen's terms. Other behavioral biologists focus on the physiological mechanisms that underlie the proximate causes of behavior.

KEY CONCEPT
51.5 Behavior Can Be Studied Mechanistically

Learning Objectives

51.5.1 Describe characteristics of circadian rhythms.

51.5.2 Explain the concept of a time-compensated solar compass.

51.5.3 Describe the different forms of animal communication and their advantages and disadvantages.

51.5.4 Evaluate the effectiveness of various forms of animal communication in specific circumstances.

Control of behavior involves the nervous and endocrine systems. Execution of behavior involves the musculoskeletal system as well as other effector mechanisms, such as those that produce secretions, color changes, electrical impulses, sound, and even light. We have already considered many of the physiological systems that are involved in these processes, including hormones, reproductive systems, nervous systems, sensory systems, and feeding mechanisms. The field of behavioral physiology, which encompasses aspects of all of these systems, is enormous, so here we dig deeper into just three different phenomena studied by behavioral physiologists: the timing of behavior, navigation, and communication.

Biological rhythms coordinate behavior with environmental cycles

Earth rotates on its axis once every 24 hours, generating daily cycles of light and dark, temperature, humidity, and tides. In addition, Earth is tilted on its axis, so the timing of light and dark changes as Earth revolves around the Sun. These daily and seasonal cycles profoundly influence the physiology and behavior of animals. Animal species are usually active either during the day (diurnal) or at night (nocturnal) and have sensory capabilities appropriate to this distinction. Therefore it is adaptive to organize behavior on a cycle that corresponds with the environmental cycle of light and dark. Similarly, a behavior that is adaptive at one time of year (such as midsummer) may not be adaptive at another time (midwinter). Thus it is important for animals to organize their behavior with respect to time of the day or year and to be able to anticipate those times.

CIRCADIAN RHYTHMS Experimental animals kept under constant conditions with no daily time cues such as light and dark, temperature cycles, or episodic availability of food and water still have daily cycles of activities such as locomotor activity, sleeping, eating, drinking, learning, and just about anything else that can be measured. The persistence of these daily cycles in the absence

of environmental time cues suggests that animals have an internal clock. As we mentioned earlier, because these daily cycles are not exactly 24 hours long, they are known as **circadian rhythms**.

A biological rhythm can be viewed as a series of cycles, and the length of one of those cycles is the period of the rhythm. Any point in the cycle is a phase of that cycle. When two rhythms completely match, they are in phase, and if a rhythm is shifted (as in the resetting of a clock), it is phase-advanced or phase-delayed. Because the period of a circadian rhythm is not exactly 24 hours, it must be phase-advanced or phase-delayed each day to remain in phase with the daily cycle of the environment. In other words, the rhythm has to be **entrained** to the environmental cycle of light and dark.

The circadian rhythm of an animal held under constant conditions will run according to its natural period—it will be **free-running**. If the period is less than 24 hours, the animal will begin its activity a little earlier each day (**Figure 51.11**). The period of the free-running circadian rhythm is under genetic control. Different species may have different average periods, and within a species, mutations can lead to different period lengths.

Under natural conditions, environmental time cues, such as the onset of light or dark, entrain the free-running rhythm to the light–dark cycle of the environment. In the laboratory it is possible to entrain the circadian rhythms of free-running animals with short pulses of light or dark administered every 24 hours (see the bottom panel of Figure 51.11).

In mammals, the master circadian "clock" consists of two clusters of neurons just above the optic chiasm (the area of the brain where the optic nerves come together). These structures are called the **suprachiasmatic nuclei** (frequently referred to in the singular, or **SCN**). If the SCN of a mammal is destroyed, it becomes arrhythmic (loses its circadian rhythm) and is just as likely to eat, drink, sleep, or wake at any time of day.

A notable study by Martin Ralph and his colleagues, then at the University of Virginia, demonstrated that the SCN is both *necessary* and *sufficient* for circadian rhythms of mammals. In preparation for their experiment, the scientists bred two lines of hamsters. For one line they always crossed males and females with the shortest circadian periods in the population, and for the other line they crossed males and females with the longest circadian periods in the population. After many generations they had one lineage of hamsters that always produced offspring with short circadian periods and one that always produced offspring with long circadian periods. As in previous experiments, when the SCN of adult hamsters from either lineage was destroyed (lesioned), the animals became arrhythmic, showing that the SCN was *necessary* for circadian rhythmicity. After several weeks of arrhythmic behavior, the researchers transplanted SCN tissue from short-period hamster fetuses into the lesioned long-period hamsters' brains (**Figure 51.12**). They also did the opposite experiment of transplanting SCN tissue from long-period hamster fetuses into lesioned short-period adult hamsters (data not shown). These experiments produced two remarkable results showing that the SCN was *sufficient* for circadian rhythms. First, the transplanted SCN tissue restored circadian rhythmicity in the lesioned animals. Second, the restored rhythms had the period of the donor lineage. Thus the transplanted tissues did not just stimulate a recovery

On a cycle of 12 hours light/12 hours dark, the mouse is mostly active in the dark and has a rest–activity cycle of 24 hours.

In constant dark, the mouse still expresses a daily cycle of rest and activity, but the period of the cycle is less than 24 hours. As a result, the mouse starts its activity and ends its activity earlier each day.

If the mouse is given 20 minutes of light at 24-hour intervals, its rest–activity cycle becomes entrained to that 24-hour period.

Figure 51.11 Circadian Rhythms Are Entrained by Environmental Cues The activity–rest cycle of a laboratory mouse (a nocturnal animal) responds to the light–dark cycle under which it is kept. The gray bars indicate times when the mouse is running on an activity wheel. Two days of activity are represented on each horizontal line. Thus day 1 is 0–24 and day 2 is 24–48. Then on the next line day 2 is replotted as 0–24 and day 3 is 24–48, and so on. This double plotting makes patterns easier to see.

Q: In going from the last activity tracing in the second panel to the light-pulse experiment in the third panel, does this transition and its effects on the circadian clock seem more similar to what you experience if you are recovering from jet lag after traveling from San Francisco to New York, or in the opposite direction?

▶ **View in Achieve**
  Animation 51.3 Circadian Rhythms

response in the host animals, but took over the clock function in these animals and gave them the phenotype of the donor.

The molecular mechanism of the circadian clock involves negative-feedback loops. Although there are quite a few genes involved, including the *per* gene discussed in Key Concept 51.2, we can generalize about the mechanism by saying that when certain "clock genes" are expressed in SCN cells, the mRNA enters the cytoplasm, where it is translated. The resulting proteins combine, and the dimer returns to the nucleus as a transcription factor that shuts off the expression of the clock genes until the transcription factor is degraded. The period of this cycle is about a day. These findings show that it is possible to understand circadian rhythms of behavior at all levels, from the molecular rhythm generators to the environmental stimuli that entrain them to the daily cycle of light and dark.

CIRCANNUAL RHYTHMS   Seasonal changes in the environment present challenges to many species. Most animals reproduce most

successfully if they time their reproductive behavior to coincide with the most favorable time of year for the survival of their offspring. Many species require considerable advance preparation for reproduction. Migratory animals must arrive on their breeding grounds at the right time, and animals that have specialized structures used in mating displays, such as the antlers of deer, moose, and caribou, must grow these structures before the breeding season arrives.

For many species, a change in day length—the photoperiod—is a reliable indicator of seasonal changes to come. For others, however, change in day length is not a reliable seasonal cue. Hibernators, for example, spend long months in dark burrows underground but must be physiologically prepared to breed almost as soon as they emerge in the spring. A bird overwintering near the equator cannot use changes in photoperiod as a cue to time its migration to its temperate-zone breeding grounds. When held under constant laboratory conditions, such animals show endogenous circannual rhythms that keep track of the time of year. Unlike for circadian rhythms, the neural basis for circannual rhythms is unknown.

Figure 51.12 **The Circadian Clock in the Brain Can Be Transplanted** In this experiment, the activity rhythm of a wild-type (i.e., genetically typical) hamster was measured; this animal had a circadian period of 24.5 hours (top of bar). After its SCN was removed (lesioned), the hamster became arrhythmic. SCN tissue from a fetal "short-period" hamster (an experimental strain with a 19-hour circadian period) was then transplanted into the region where the lesion was made in the wild-type hamster. The transplanted tissues restored circadian rhythm in the lesioned hamster, but the restored rhythm had the period of the donor animal. (After M. R. Ralph et al. 1990. *Science* 247: 975-978.)

Connect the Concepts Photoperiodism is also a common phenomenon in plants that have to anticipate seasonal changes, and many do so by being sensitive to the length of the night. See Key Concept 36.2.

Figure 51.13 **Piloting** Gray whales (*Eschrichtius robustus*) migrate south in winter from the Bering Sea to the coast of Baja California by piloting, in part by following the western coast of North America.

Animals must find their way around their environment

To locate suitable habitats, find food and mates, and avoid predators and bad weather, an animal needs to be able to find its way around its environment. Within its local habitat, an animal can orient to landmarks. But what if its destination is a considerable distance away?

PILOTING: ORIENTATION BY LANDMARKS Most animals find their way by knowing and remembering the structure of their environment, a form of navigation called **piloting**. Gray Whales, for example, migrate seasonally between the Bering Sea and the coastal lagoons of Mexico (**Figure 51.13**). They find their way in part by following the western coast of North America. The rules are simple: keep the land on your right when traveling north and on your left when traveling south. Coastlines, mountain chains, rivers, water currents, and wind patterns can all serve as piloting cues for animals. But many remarkable cases of long-distance orientation and movement cannot be explained by piloting.

HOMING: RETURN TO A SPECIFIC LOCATION The ability to return to a nest site, burrow, or other specific location is called **homing**. Homing can be accomplished by piloting in a known environment, but some animals that travel long distances through unfamiliar territory perform much more sophisticated homing. The ability of pigeons to return to their home loft even after being transported to remote sites is well known. How do they find their way home? Experiments have shown that pigeons use the Sun as a compass, but they can still find their way home when the Sun is not visible. Other experiments have shown that pigeons equipped with frosted contact lenses can find their way home, suggesting that visual cues are not essential. Most amazing has been the demonstration that pigeons can detect Earth's magnetic field and orient to it much as a human orients with a compass. Taken together, the studies of homing by pigeons suggest that they can use multiple, redundant sources of directional information and can switch among those sources depending on the circumstances.

 View in Achieve
Simulation 51.1 **Homing**

MIGRATION: NAVIGATION OVER GREAT DISTANCES For as long as humans have inhabited high latitudes, they have been aware that entire populations of animals, especially birds, disappear and reappear seasonally. Not until the early nineteenth century, however, were patterns of migration traced by marking individual birds with identification bands around their legs. Only when individuals could be unmistakably identified was it possible to show that the same birds and their offspring returned to the same breeding grounds year after year, and that these same birds could be found during the nonbreeding season at locations hundreds or even thousands of kilometers from their breeding grounds.

Many homing and migrating species take direct routes to their destinations through environments they have never experienced because they use mechanisms of navigation other than piloting. Humans use two major forms of navigation:

1. *Distance–direction navigation* requires knowing in what direction and how far away the destination is. With a compass to determine direction and a means of measuring distance, humans navigate.

2. *Bicoordinate navigation*, also known as true navigation, requires knowing the latitude and longitude (the map coordinates) of both the current position and the destination, as well as a compass to determine direction.

Many animals seem to have a "compass sense" that allows them to use environmental cues to determine direction, and some seem to have a "map sense" that allows them to determine their position.

The behavior of some animals suggests that they are capable of bicoordinate navigation. Gray-headed Albatrosses, for example, breed on oceanic islands in the Southern Hemisphere. When a young albatross leaves its parents' nest, it flies widely over the southern oceans for 8–9 years. After those wandering years, it reaches reproductive maturity and flies back to the island where it was raised, where it mates and builds a nest (**Figure 51.14**). How can the bird find a tiny island in an enormous ocean after years of wandering? We don't know the answer, but the albatross provides strong circumstantial evidence that an animal can be capable of bicoordinate navigation, as were sailors before the days of global positioning satellites.

The ability to locate a position by calculating the angles between celestial objects such as the Sun and stars and the horizon at specific times of day is called celestial navigation. During the day, the Sun can serve as a compass if you know what time it is, and animals can use their circadian clocks for that information. This capacity has been demonstrated by "clock-shifting" experiments such as the one shown in **Figure 51.15**. Similar experiments have shown that many animal species can orient by means of a time-compensated solar compass.

▶ **View in Achieve**
Animation 51.4 **Time-Compensated Solar Compass**

Many animals are normally nocturnal; in addition, many diurnal bird species migrate at night and thus cannot use the Sun to determine direction. The stars offer two sources of information about direction: moving constellations and a fixed point. The positions of constellations (like that of the Sun) change because Earth is rotating. With a star map and a clock, direction can be determined using any constellation. But one point that does not change position during

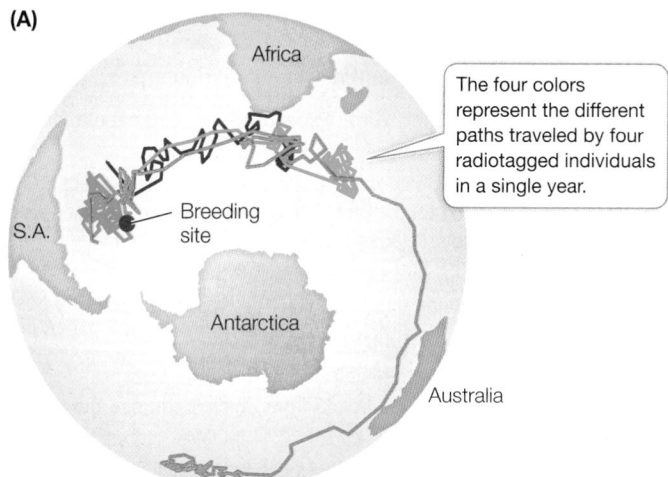

(A)

The four colors represent the different paths traveled by four radiotagged individuals in a single year.

(B) *Thalassarche chrysostoma*

© Tui De Roy/Minden Pictures

Figure 51.14 Coming Home **(A)** Gray-headed Albatrosses are born on islands in the subantarctic oceans. Young birds roam widely over the southern oceans for 8–9 years. **(B)** Once they reach maturity, the birds return to the island where they were hatched to mate and raise their own young. (A after J. P. Croxall et al. 2005. *Science* 307: 249-250.)

the night is the point directly over the axis on which Earth turns. In the Northern Hemisphere, the star Polaris—the "North Star"—lies in that region of the sky and reliably indicates north.

Stephen Emlen at Cornell University showed that birds can learn to use the stars for orientation. As the time of year approaches when young birds would normally migrate to their winter range, young captive birds become more active and orient their activity in the direction they would fly. How do they know that direction? If these birds are raised in a planetarium with a natural star pattern, but one that does not rotate, the birds do not learn to orient, and their premigratory activity is random. However, if the planetarium sky rotates, and even if it rotates around a different point than the North Star, the birds orient their premigratory activity as if the fixed point in the sky were north.

Experiment

Figure 51.15   **A Time-Compensated Solar Compass**

Original Paper: G. Kramer. 1952. Experiments on bird orientation. *Ibis* 94: 265–285.

Experiments show that pigeons use the Sun to establish directions for navigation and finding food. "Clock-shifting" experiments demonstrate that the birds' circadian clocks factor into their ability to judge direction correctly based on the Sun's position.

HYPOTHESIS▶   Pigeons determine compass direction from the position of the Sun with respect to their internal circadian clocks.

METHOD▶

1. Place a pigeon in a circular cage from which it can see the Sun and sky, but not the horizon or any other visual cue.

2. Surround the cage with multiple food bins but place food only in the southernmost bin, thus training the bird to look for food in the south. (Rotating the cage but always placing the food in the southernmost bin confirms that the bird is navigating to find south.)

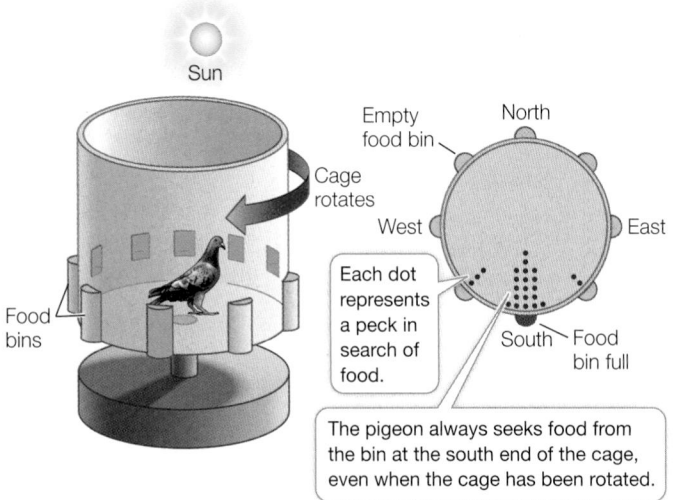

Each dot represents a peck in search of food.

The pigeon always seeks food from the bin at the south end of the cage, even when the cage has been rotated.

3. Place the trained pigeon in a room with a controlled light cycle for 2 weeks. Turn the lights on at midnight and off at noon to phase-advance its circadian rhythm by 6 hours (i.e., 6 AM feels like noon to the bird).

4. Return the pigeon to the circular cage under natural light and observe its food-seeking behavior.

RESULTS▶   A 6-hour shift in the circadian clock results in a 90-degree error in the pigeon's orientation.

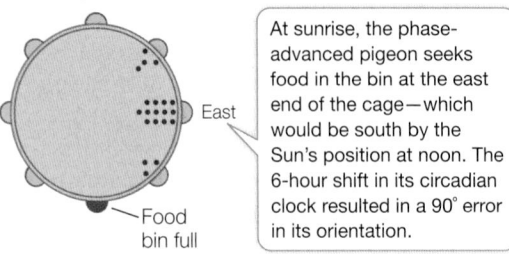

At sunrise, the phase-advanced pigeon seeks food in the bin at the east end of the cage—which would be south by the Sun's position at noon. The 6-hour shift in its circadian clock resulted in a 90° error in its orientation.

CONCLUSION▶   Pigeons have the ability to determine direction using time of day and the position of the Sun as a compass.

Animals use multiple modalities to communicate

As individual animals interact, they exchange information; therefore animal behaviors can evolve into systems of information exchange, or **communication**. The behaviors of individuals may become elaborated into communication signals, but only if the transmission of information benefits both the sender and the receiver. To understand why these conditions must be met, consider male courtship displays, which can be quite bizarre, time- and energy-consuming, and involve risk. Nevertheless, natural selection will favor them if they increase the males' probability of mating and passing on their genes. The displays can produce that result if they convey information to the females (the receivers) about the qualities of the males as potential fathers.

Animals communicate using a variety of sensory modalities that vary in the nature of the signal produced, the specificity of the information conveyed, the speed and persistence of the signal, and its suitability in different environments. Behavioral physiologists interested in communication must take into consideration the sensory and motor characteristics of their study animals, the physics of the communication modalities they use, and the environment in which the communication takes place.

CHEMICAL SIGNALS   Because of the diversity of their molecular structures, **pheromones** can communicate very specific, information-rich messages (see Key Concept 44.2). Pheromones are effective day and night, and they can cover a broad range of transmission distances. Pheromones used in different types of communication vary in their volatility (ease of vaporization) and diffusibility; these chemical properties are functions of the nature and size of the pheromone molecule. Pheromones that act as alarm signals, for example, are highly volatile and diffusible, so their message spreads rapidly but disappears rapidly. Territory-marking and trail-marking pheromones have low volatility and diffusibility and remain effective for a long time, so they can convey directional information. Sex pheromones, such as that of silkworm moths (see Figure 44.4), are intermediate in these properties, so they can spread a long distance but do not disappear rapidly.

Pheromones are an effective way to exchange species-specific information, and because the recipient must have the proper receptor molecule to detect the pheromone, it is not a signal that is easily intercepted by predators. Pheromonal signals cannot be changed rapidly, but they can convey static, complex information. Mammals that mark their territories with pheromones reveal a great deal of information about themselves: species, individual identity, reproductive status, size (indicated by the height of the marking), and how recently the animal has been in the area (indicated by the strength of the scent).

VISUAL SIGNALS   Visual signals offer the advantage of rapid delivery of information over considerable distances (depending on the environment and the visual acuity of the receiver); they also convey the exact position of the signaler. Signal content can be enhanced by movements (as in a courtship display) or by different postures. Effective visual signals, however, require sufficient light, and the receiver must be looking at the signaler. Thus visual communication is not particularly useful at night or in environments that lack light, such as caves and ocean depths. Some species have overcome this constraint with light-emitting mechanisms. Fireflies, for example, use an enzymatic mechanism to create flashes of light. By emitting flashes in species-specific patterns, fireflies advertise for mates at night.

Another drawback of visual signals is that they can be intercepted by other species. There are predatory firefly species, for example, that mimic the flash pattern of females of other species. A male that approaches the mimicking "female" becomes a meal rather than a mate. Thus deception can be part of animal communication systems, just as it is part of human communication.

ACOUSTIC SIGNALS Sound cannot convey complex information as rapidly as visual signals can. But acoustic signals, unlike visual signals, can be used at night and in dark environments. They are not hindered by objects that would interfere with visual signals, so they can be transmitted in complex environments such as forests. They are often better than visual signals at getting the attention of a receiver because the receiver does not have to be looking at the signaler for the message to be received. Sounds are also useful for communicating over long distances. Even though the intensity of a sound decreases with distance from the source, loud sounds can transmit information over much longer distances than visual signals can. The complex songs of humpback whales (*Megaptera novaeangliae*), when produced at ocean depths of about 1,000 meters, can be heard hundreds of kilometers away, allowing these whales to locate one another across vast expanses of ocean. Humpback whale populations that feed during the summer in the north Pacific Ocean migrate thousands of kilometers to winter breeding areas in either the eastern Pacific Ocean, the mid-Pacific Ocean (Hawaii), or the western Pacific Ocean (see Figure 53.4). Long-distance communication among individuals spread over such enormous expanses of open ocean is important if they are to congregate in rather limited breeding areas at the same time of year.

The information content of acoustic signals can be increased by varying their frequency, as you can see in the sonograms of the species-specific song of White-crowned Sparrows shown in Figure 51.7, and as you practice in your own speech. However, acoustic signals place the signaler at risk for detection by predators. This danger can be minimized by adjustments of frequency and signal structure that decrease the directional information the receiver can extract from the signal. Alarm calls tend to be pure tones (a single frequency) without much temporal structure (starts and stops). It is very difficult to localize such calls. By contrast, territorial calls tend to cover a broad frequency range and have temporal structure. These calls are easy to localize. The frequencies and structures of acoustic signals are also adapted to specific habitats. Different vegetation types, for example, have different sound-absorbing properties: pure tones at lower frequencies carry better in forests, and more complex calls at higher frequencies carry well in open habitats.

MECHANOSENSORY SIGNALS Animals in close contact with one another can communicate by touch. A classic case of mechanosensory communication is the dance of honey bees, first described by Karl von Frisch. Honey bees have a spectacular ability to navigate and can accurately communicate the location of food sources as far away as 10 kilometers. When a forager bee finds food, she returns to the hive and communicates her discovery to her hivemates by performing a vigorous **waggle dance** in the dark hive on the vertical surface of the honeycomb. Other bees follow the dancer and receive her message.

The waggle dance conveys information about both the distance and the direction of the food source. The dancing bee repeatedly traces out a figure-eight pattern as she runs on the honeycomb. She alternates half-circles to the left and right with vigorous wagging of her abdomen in the short, straight run between turns (**Figure 51.16**). Bees use the Sun as their compass, and the angle of the straight run indicates the direction of the food source relative to the position of the Sun projected down to the horizon. Even under cloudy conditions, the forager can provide directions to

Figure 51.16 The Honey Bee Waggle Dance (A) A honey bee (*Apis* spp.) runs straight up on the vertical surface of the honeycomb in the dark hive while wagging her abdomen to tell her hivemates that there is a food source in the direction of the Sun. (B) When her waggle runs are at an angle from the vertical, the other bees know that the same angle separates the direction of the food source from the direction of the Sun. (After T. D. Seeley. 1985. *Honeybee Ecology: A Study of Adaptation in Social Life*. Princeton University Press: Princeton, NJ.)

View in Achieve
Activity 51.1 Honey Bee Dance Communication

the food source because she can see polarized light. The bee's circadian clock allows the dancer to adjust her dance to take into account the Sun's movement during her return flight. The clocks of the recruits enable them to adjust their flight direction to accommodate the Sun's changing position.

The distance to the food source is communicated by the duration of the waggle portion of the dance. The farther away the food source is, the longer the duration of each waggle run. When food is close to the hive, the waggle portion of the dance becomes so short that it appeared to von Frisch that it was a different dance, which he called a round dance. Thus the honey bee has a dance language that communicates both the distance and the direction to a food source.

When challenged to prove that the bees were not simply using an odor trail to find the indicated food source, von Frisch responded with a very commonsense observation. Bees returning from a new food source fly around barriers such as buildings, but the recruits going out to the food source fly over the barriers in a "beeline," which would be impossible if they were following an odor trail. Careful observation is still one of the best tools for studying behavior.

COMMUNICATION IN MULTIPLE SENSORY MODALITIES
Avoiding ambiguity is a high priority in any signaling system. Signal specificity is enhanced if multiple sensory modalities are used. Courtship behavior in fruit flies, for example, involves visual, tactile, chemical, and acoustic signals (see Figure 51.4A). The male fruit fly orients toward the female's line of vision (visual signal) and taps her body with his foreleg (tactile signal). Upon detecting pheromones in her cuticle (chemical signal), the male begins to vibrate one wing, producing a species-specific courtship song (acoustic signal). The male then extends his mouthparts to taste the female's genitalia (chemical and tactile signals); if she is receptive, he initiates copulation. If at any point sensory feedback indicates to either the male or the female that their pairing is inappropriate, the courtship abruptly ends.

KEY CONCEPT
51.5 Recap and Assess

Biological rhythms allow an animal to anticipate changes in its environment. In mammals, a circadian clock located in the suprachiasmatic nuclei generates a rhythm that is entrainable by environmental information. The navigational abilities of animals range from simple piloting by landmarks to distance–direction and bicoordinate navigation. Behaviors may evolve into communication signals if the transmission of information benefits both the sender and the receiver.

1. What is a free-running circadian rhythm, and how is it entrained by light to the 24-hour day?

2. Why is it important for honey bees to have a time-compensated solar compass, and how does that mechanism influence the waggle dance?

3. Which forms of communication are most efficient for interindividual communication and for broader population-level communication? Explain your answer.

When behaviors involve interactions between multiple individuals, we have to consider how natural selection operates on all of the interacting parties, whether they are sending signals or receiving them. This concern becomes particularly relevant in the case of social behaviors.

KEY CONCEPT
51.6 Social Interactions Shape the Evolution of Behavior

Learning Objectives

51.6.1 Apply concepts of fitness to explain the evolution of social behaviors related to reproduction.

51.6.2 Explain how haplodiploidy relates to eusociality.

51.6.3 Identify costs and benefits of social behaviors.

Our discussion of behavior has focused mostly on behavior in individual animals. We've covered, for example, fixed action patterns, deprivation experiments, genetic determinants, development, and physiological mechanisms. Yet most behavior takes place in a social context. Social behavior and its evolution became a field of study in its own right in 1975, with the publication of E. O. Wilson's landmark book *Sociobiology*. Mating, parenting, group behaviors such as migration, and group living such as in animal colonies all involve interactions among individuals, and selection operates on all participants in these interactions.

Mating systems evolve to maximize fitness

We begin consideration of this enormous field of social behavior with mating behavior involving a single male and a single female. Because natural selection is always operating to maximize the reproductive success of both the male and the female of the species, an amazing array of mating systems has evolved.

MONOGAMY AND PROMISCUITY   At the start of Chapter 7 you learned about the mating behavior of two species of voles. Prairie voles are monogamous, forming strong pair bonds that can last for life, and both parents participate in rearing the young. In contrast, montane voles are promiscuous: males try to mate with many females, and the young are raised by the female alone. Behavioral physiologists have explained the proximate mechanisms behind these stark behavioral differences in terms of the release of neurohormones and the distribution of the receptors for those hormones in the brains of the two species. The ultimate question—and the one asked here—is why two such different mating systems evolved in two species that are so closely related.

There is an asymmetry in the contributions of male and female animals to their offspring at the time of fertilization. Females produce a limited number of eggs, and each egg is generously stocked with resources. Males produce an almost infinite number of sperm, which contain next to no resources. So the energetic and opportunity costs of reproduction are greater for the female than for the male. In mammals this asymmetry increases throughout gestation as the female bears most of the costs. By the time of birth or hatching, the female's investment in the young is much greater than the male's investment, and the main way for the female to maximize her fitness is to make sure her young are healthy and survive to pass on her genes.

The male has different options for maximizing his fitness. He can simply move on after inseminating the female and seek additional mates as a means of maximizing his reproductive success—as in the case of the montane vole. Or he can stay with the female he inseminated, protect her, and help care for their young—as in the case of the prairie vole. Which strategy maximizes male fitness in these species depends on several factors that are influenced by the environment, such as the likelihood that a female and her offspring will survive without a male's help, and a male's likelihood of finding another fertile female. Thus sociobiologists seek to quantify these factors in nature as a means of explaining observed differences in mating systems.

POLYGYNY Mating systems in which a male has more than one mate generally involve a male that manages to sequester a group of females from other males. The **polygynous** male increases his fitness by increasing the number of females in his group. As you saw in Key Concept 51.4, male elephant seals accomplish this by protecting an area of beach where females give birth. Male baboons do so by herding females. Male Red-winged Blackbirds (*Agelaius phoeniceus*) may acquire more than one mate by defending high-quality nesting territories where females prefer to build their nests. Since sex ratios in all these species are close to 50:50, a large differential in male fitness is established, with some males having high reproductive success while many males have none. Thus selection favors males that are successful in competing with other males to obtain and protect access to many females. In general, the bigger, stronger males are the winners, and sexual dimorphism in body size evolves. The elephant seals are an extreme example: males may weigh more than three times as much as females. When species with polygynous mating systems are compared, there is a strong correlation between the number of females a male controls and the degree of sexual dimorphism.

Why do females participate in these polygynous mating systems? Why doesn't a female seek out a nice, kind, noncompetitive male? In some cases, such as the female elephant seal, she has no choice. If a female Red-winged Blackbird wants to nest in an optimal territory, she will have to share the attentions of the territory owner with other females. Even if the female has a choice of mates, she is likely to maximize her fitness by mating with a male that is strong and dominant enough to control a number of females. Why? If her mate is a dominant male, her male offspring are likely to have their father's traits, become dominant males, and give her more grandchildren. Nonrandom mate choice by females based on male characteristics produces sexual selection. An extreme result of sexual selection is the lek mating system (see Figure 51.9C), in which the *only* thing a male offers a female is the display of his dominance over other males.

Connect the Concepts Charles Darwin recognized the phenomenon of sexual selection leading to the evolution of traits that could compromise the health and survival of the individual. See Key Concept 19.2.

POLYANDRY Mating systems in which one female mates with multiple males are relatively rare, but **polyandry** is seen in some birds and a few mammal species in which paternal care for the

Leontopithecus rosalia

© Tui De Roy/Minden Pictures

Figure 51.17 **Polyandry in a Small Primate** The endangered golden lion tamarins of Brazil are small primates whose unique life history has given rise to polyandry in some groups, with males playing a major role in rearing the young.

young can have a large effect on fitness. An example of a polyandrous species is the golden lion tamarin (*Leontopithecus rosalia*), a primate native to Brazil's tropical rainforests (**Figure 51.17**). Tamarins are small—adults weigh less than 1 kilogram and face high predation pressure. Females usually give birth to twins, and newborns constitute a higher percentage of maternal weight than is typical of other primates. The young also grow more rapidly than other primates, so nursing costs are high. For all these reasons, young tamarins cared for by their mother alone are unlikely to survive.

What can a male tamarin do to help guarantee his reproductive success? Watching out for predators is one obvious contribution; gathering food for the female and her young is another. Like other primate parents, tamarins carry their young most of the time, but most other primates have single offspring. When tamarin mothers are carrying twins, they spend 92% of the time resting, compared with 58% of the time when they are not carrying young. Resting is not compatible with foraging and filling the mother's high energy requirements. When a male is present, however, he carries the young about one-third of the time, so the mother has much more time for foraging and feeding.

If one male tamarin is helpful in protecting and raising young, then two should be even more helpful. Some females can attract a second mate by being sexually receptive to him. Neither male can be sure that any eventual offspring are his, so it is in the best interest of both to help in their rearing. Of the tamarin families observed in field studies, only 22% had one male and one female, whereas 61% had multiple males and one female.

Fitness can include more than your own offspring

As humans, we readily understand the concept of extended family—brothers, sisters, aunts, uncles, nieces, nephews. Extended families are a common form of social organization in other species as well, and members of these families may cooperate in territory defense, predator avoidance, foraging, and rearing of young. If behavior is favored when it increases the fitness of the individual performing it, then how can we explain the evolution of social behaviors that do not lead to the performer having more offspring and that may even appear to be **altruistic**—benefiting another individual at a cost to the performer?

An individual's fitness is increased by having offspring because those offspring carry the parent's genes into the next generation. Fitness gained by producing offspring is referred to as **direct fitness**. However, an individual's genes are carried into the next generation by more than his or her own offspring. In diploid organisms, two offspring of the same parents share, on average, 50% of the same alleles, and an individual is likely to share 25% of its alleles with its siblings' offspring (nieces or nephews). Therefore by helping parents and other relatives raise their offspring, an individual increases the transmission of those shared alleles to the next generation. **Inclusive fitness** is the individual's direct fitness plus its **indirect fitness**: the reproductive success of the individual's relatives, to the extent that those relatives share the individual's alleles.

The maximization of inclusive fitness is the mechanism driving **kin selection**, selection for behaviors that increase the reproductive success of relatives even when they come at a cost to the performer. One example is "helping at the nest" behavior, which was studied extensively in Florida Scrub-Jays. Scrub-jay pairs mate for life and establish large territories, which they defend aggressively. The mating pair may be assisted in rearing their young by three to five helpers (**Figure 51.18**). The helpers guard against predators, feed the young, clean the nest, and fly with fledglings. Why are these birds helping others rather than rearing their own young? A long-term study established several important facts:

- The helpers are prior offspring of the mating pair and are usually 1–3 years old.

- Young birds that attempt to breed have almost zero reproductive success.

- Mating pairs with helpers have approximately three times the reproductive success of those without helpers.

These results support the conclusion that helper scrub-jays are maximizing their inclusive fitness by helping their parents raise siblings until they are mature enough to have a reasonable probability of successfully raising their own offspring.

The concept of kin selection was formalized by W. D. Hamilton in what has become known as **Hamilton's rule**. He argued that, for an apparent altruistic behavior to be adaptive, the fitness benefit of that act to the recipient times the degree of relatedness between the performer and the recipient has to be greater than the cost to the performer. This relationship was clearly stated years before by the eminent geneticist J. B. S. Haldane, who said during an argument about altruism that he would not be willing to risk his life to save his brother, but for two brothers or eight cousins, he would consider it.

Eusociality is the extreme result of kin selection

Hamilton's rule can be applied to explain **eusociality**: social groups that include nonreproductive members (that is, members that as individuals do not reproduce). The most obvious examples of eusociality occur among the Hymenoptera, an insect group that includes wasps, bees, and ants. In a honey bee colony, for example, the thousands of individuals in the colony are sterile females.

 Media Clip 51.1   Eusocial Animals
Life12e.com/mc51.1

The key to understanding the evolution of eusociality in hymenopterans is their sex-determination mechanism, **haplodiploidy**, in which diploid individuals are female and haploid individuals are male. The queen carries a lifetime supply of sperm obtained during her single mating flight, and she controls whether her eggs are

Aphelocoma coerulescens

Figure 51.18 Helpers at the Nest   Young Florida Scrub-Jays often forego reproduction in their first few years of adulthood to help their parents raise their siblings. These young birds help their parents feed the nestlings, defend the territory, and protect the nest from predators. (After E. O. Wilson. 1975. *Sociobiology, The New Synthesis*. Harvard University Press: Cambridge, MA.)

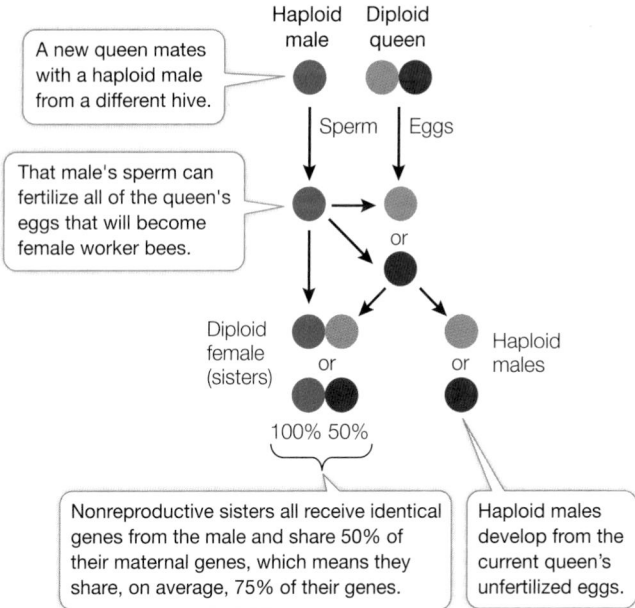

A new queen mates with a haploid male from a different hive.

Haploid male   Diploid queen

Sperm   Eggs

That male's sperm can fertilize all of the queen's eggs that will become female worker bees.

or

Diploid female (sisters)

or   or   Haploid males

100% 50%

Nonreproductive sisters all receive identical genes from the male and share 50% of their maternal genes, which means they share, on average, 75% of their genes.

Haploid males develop from the current queen's unfertilized eggs.

Figure 51.19 Favoring Sisters over Daughters Female honey bees are diploid and males are haploid. Thus if a female worker bee were to reproduce, she would share approximately 50% of her genes with her daughters. However, she shares an average of 75% of her genes with her sisters. In terms of inclusive fitness, then, a sister is more valuable than a daughter for this species.

fertilized or not. An unfertilized egg develops into a haploid male; a fertilized egg develops into a diploid female. The queen's daughters share all of their father's genes and, on average, half of their mother's genes. As a result, the sterile female workers in the hive—all sisters—share, on average, 75% of their alleles (**Figure 51.19**). The basic unit of reproductive success in eusocial insects is the creation of new colonies around a new queen. If a new queen developed from a worker's offspring, the worker would share fewer genes with the new queen than if the new queen developed from a sister.

Heterocephalus glaber

© J. Jarvis/Visuals Unlimited, Inc.

Figure 51.20 A Eusocial Mammal Naked mole-rats live in a large colony with one reproductive female and a few reproductive males. Their home is an elaborate tunnel system excavated by the colony over time.

Haplodiploidy is not essential for the evolution of eusociality. Nearly all eusocial animals construct elaborate nests or burrow systems within which their offspring are reared. Such a structure represents an enormous investment of resources. Naked mole-rats are eusocial mammals that live in elaborate underground tunnel systems (**Figure 51.20**). A colony may include 70–80 individuals but only 1 reproductive female and a few reproductive males. The other colony members are sterile workers that dig and maintain the tunnels, guard against intruders, harvest food (tubers), and use their feces to feed the queen and her offspring. Individuals attempting to found new colonies have a high risk of failing or of being captured by predators. When chances of individual reproductive success are practically zero, an individual can best maximize its inclusive fitness by staying with and helping maintain the colony.

Group living has benefits and costs

Apart from their direct influences on reproductive success, social systems can contribute to survival in many ways, but they can also involve costs. Thus the cost–benefit approach of behavioral ecology is relevant to understanding the evolution of social behavior.

An obvious example of a benefit of group living is improved foraging efficiency. By hunting in packs, African wild dogs (*Lycaon pictus*) (see Figure 57.17) employ cooperative strategies that enable them to bring down larger prey than could a single dog. The larger the pack, the greater the hunting success rate. Once the prey is killed, the presence of conspecifics also reduces the risk that the wild dogs will lose their prey to larger scavengers, such as hyenas.

Living in a group can also reduce the risk of individuals becoming prey themselves. Many small birds forage in flocks. To test the hypothesis that flocking provides protection against predators, R. E. Kenward released a trained Northern Goshawk (*Accipiter gentilis*) near wild Common Wood-Pigeons (*Columba palumbus*) in England. The hawk was most successful when it attacked solitary pigeons. Its success in capturing a pigeon in a flock decreased as the number of pigeons in the flock increased (**Figure 51.21A**). The larger the flock, the sooner some individual in the flock spotted the hawk and flew away. This escape behavior stimulated other individuals in the flock to take flight as well creating a distraction for the hawk.

Alarm calling is another means of reducing predation risk, but the caller incurs a risk cost by calling attention to itself. Belding's ground squirrels live in large colonies in open meadows. When one squirrel announces the presence of a predator with loud, sharp barks, all the nearby squirrels dive into their burrows (**Figure 51.21B**). Paul Sherman of Cornell University showed that callers double their risk of being preyed on—so why do they do it? Research by Sherman and by others has shown that this altruistic behavior is a product of kin selection. In this polygynous species, males establish large territories in the spring that include the territories of several females, whom they inseminate. The females then drive off the males. Female offspring settle near their mothers, so neighboring females in a colony tend to be sisters, and they defend each other's young. Sherman showed that males are less likely to give alarm calls than females, and that females are more likely to give alarm calls when related individuals are nearby.

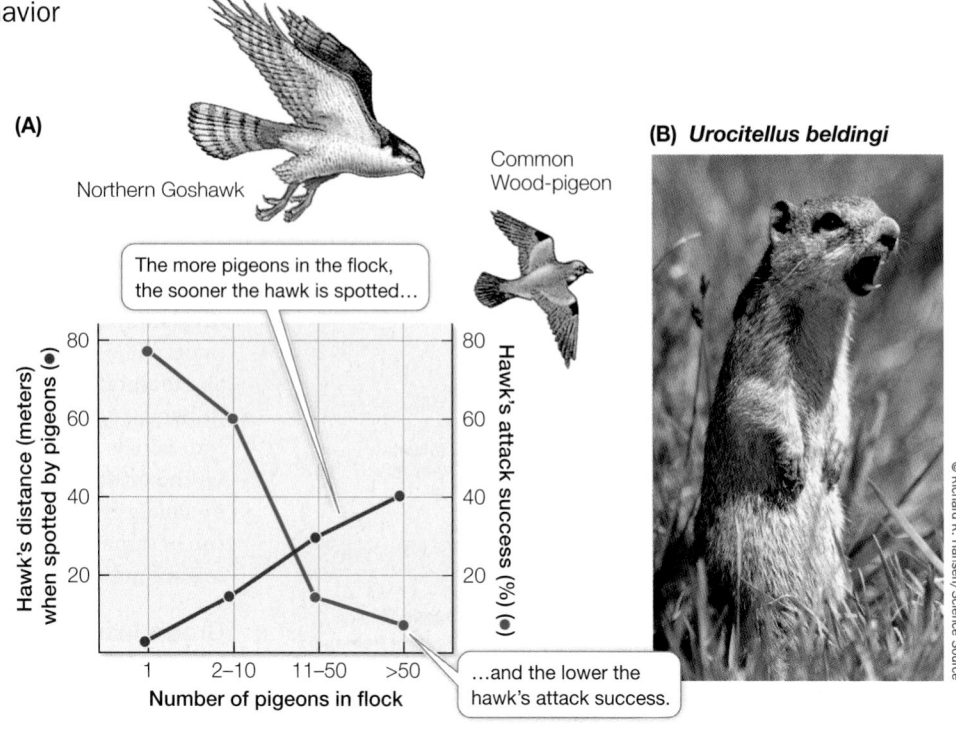

Figure 51.21 Group Living Provides Protection from Predators   Animals that live in groups can spread the cost of looking out for predators. **(A)** The larger the number of Common Wood-Pigeons in a flock, the greater the chances that one of the pigeons will spot a predatory Northern Goshawk before it attacks, and the lower the chances that the hawk will capture one of the pigeons. **(B)** A male Belding's ground squirrel gives an alarm call upon spotting a predator. Although this behavior increases his individual risk of becoming prey, he increases the survival chances of many of his close relatives. (A, graph after R. E. Kenward. 1978. *J Anim Ecol* 47: 449–460.)

Social behavior has many costs as well as benefits. Foraging in a group may reduce the amount of food available to each individual, and the foraging individuals may interfere with one another's foraging activities. Individuals living in groups may face more competition for mates, as well as for food, than solitary individuals would. A large group may actually attract the attention of predators. And living at high population densities can increase the risk of disease transmission. The study of disease transmission in wild animal populations is a relatively new field, but such studies have made it apparent that species living in social groups are more prone to outbreaks of disease than are solitary species.

Can the concepts of sociobiology be applied to humans?

With the publication of E. O. Wilson's *Sociobiology*, applications of the concepts of evolutionary genetics to human behavior were controversial. The intensity of the debate stemmed from false impressions that sociobiological approaches resembled previously discredited pseudoscientific movements such as social Darwinism, biological determinism, and eugenics, all of which have been used as rationales for racism and discrimination. However, sociobiology is an objective science; questions of "what is" should not be conflated with questions of "what ought to be." For example, we can demonstrate the genetic basis of sexual dimorphism in body size and muscle mass in humans, and we can compare this dimorphism with that in other mammals. However, any attempt to use such data as a political or legal defense for the cultural practice of polygamy would not be science and should not be confused with science.

The fact that our biochemistry, our cell biology, physiology, and anatomy are shaped by our genes is beyond argument. However, it is clear that these genetically shaped characteristics are also influenced by factors such as environment, nutrition, social interactions, and culture. Why should it be different for behavior? Studies of identical twins reared apart have produced evidence for inheritance of uncanny similarities in behavioral propensities. Studies of isolated human cultures around the world have also revealed remarkable similarities in social organization. None of these studies, however, would challenge the dominant role of learning and culture in the shaping of human behavior.

KEY CONCEPT

51.6 Recap and Assess

Social behavior can be understood by asking how it contributes to the fitness of all the individuals involved. Asymmetry between the sexes in parental investment is a key factor in the evolution of mating systems. According to the theory of kin selection, an individual can increase its fitness by helping related individuals with whom it shares alleles. In extreme cases, kin selection has given rise to eusociality.

1. Explain the selective pressures that favor an individual being a helper at the nest rather than engaging in reproduction.

2. What is the relationship between haplodiploid sex determination and the evolution of eusociality in ants, wasps, and bees?

3. Many species of small birds respond to the presence of a much larger predator by joining together to mob the predator and drive it off. What do you see as the risks and benefits of this behavior, and what hypotheses could you propose about the individuals taking part in an incidence of mobbing behavior?

 View in Achieve
Activity 51.2 Concept Matching: Animal Behavior

▶Investigating LIFE

Q and A How does social context influence the learning and expression of birdsong?

Birdsong is the classic example of how genetic determinants, development, physiology, and learning can interact to generate and control even complex behaviors. As you saw with the White-crowned Sparrow, the nestlings must experience their species-specific song if they are going to sing it (males) and respond to it (females) as adults. But there is a genetically determined template of what they can and will learn. With physiological maturation, they begin to sing poorly and must hear themselves and practice to be able to sing their species-specific songs. Social context also plays a role in learning small variations of dialects in song that may play a role in population as well as individual identity. Social context also influences what and when singing occurs. Singing intensifies in the presence of competitors and also potential or current mates. The experiments by Woolley and Doupe on Zebra Finches showed that even though there were only small differences between songs when males sang alone or in the presence of a female, these differences were clearly recognized by females and influenced their behaviors. Studies of birdsong emphasize the importance of considering the evolution of a behavior from the angles of all of the different individuals involved, and at the various levels of biological organization that contribute to the behavior.

Future directions

Language is considered a unique characteristic of humans. Many animals use simple acoustic signals to communicate, but the fine motor control necessary to produce precise, fine-tuned, rapid complex vocalizations is found only in humans and songbirds. Whereas birdsong is recognized to be an elaborate but highly stereotyped territorial and mating signal, studies like those of Woolley and Doupe show that small variations in song can convey more detailed information about the identity of the individual, its intentions, and the social context in which it is behaving. Can birdsong be used to convey more complex information? Can birdsong be a form of simple language? If so, we have much more to learn about the cognitive abilities of birds. Language is used to construct our views of ourselves and of our position in our physical and social environments, and to be able to project those views into the past and into the future—the essence of consciousness. Could birds be better models for human cognitive processes than the mammals typically used in laboratory studies?

VISUAL SUMMARY 51

You should be able to relate each summary to the adjacent figures. If you go to this visual summary in **Achieve**, you can follow links to figures, animations, activities, and simulations that will help you consolidate the material.

KEY CONCEPT

51.1 Ethology Led to Modern Behavioral Biology

- Studies of **conditioned reflexes** and **operant conditioning** led to an approach to animal behavior called **behaviorism** that mainly carried out laboratory experiments on rats.

- **Ethology** focuses on both the **proximate causes** of behavior (the immediate causes of the behavior, and how the behavior develops) and the **ultimate causes** (how the behavior affects the animal's evolutionary fitness).

- A major focus of ethologists was **fixed action patterns** and their **releasers**. They performed **deprivation experiments** as well as crossbreeding experiments to demonstrate that certain behaviors are genetically determined.

Figure 51.2

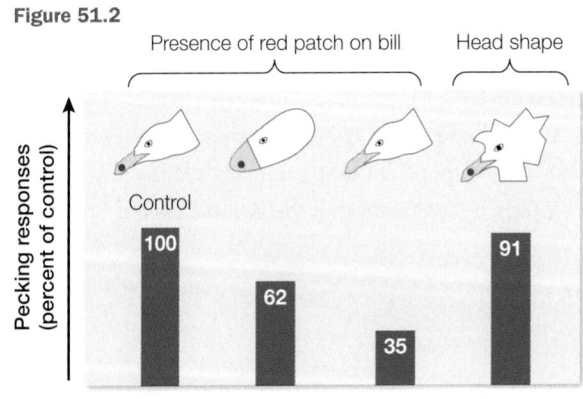

Questions

1. An airport sniffer dog is rewarded with a food treat when it detects drugs, guns, or other illicit substances. Is this type of training an example of operant conditioning or Pavlovian conditioning? Explain your answer.

2. What are Tinbergen's four questions for studying animal behavior? Cite an example of each from this chapter.

KEY CONCEPT

51.2 Behavior Can Be Genetically Determined

- Genetic manipulations such as gene knockouts can reveal the roles of specific genes underlying a behavioral phenotype.

- Most behaviors are complex traits involving many genes that function in cascades, offering many points for a change in a single gene to influence behavior.

Questions

1. What is the function of the vomeronasal organ (VNO) in mice?

2. How does posttranscriptional splicing of mRNA determine sex development in *Drosophila*?

Figure 51.4

Fruit fly courtship behavior

Wing vibration

Licking

Genes responsible for sexual differentiation

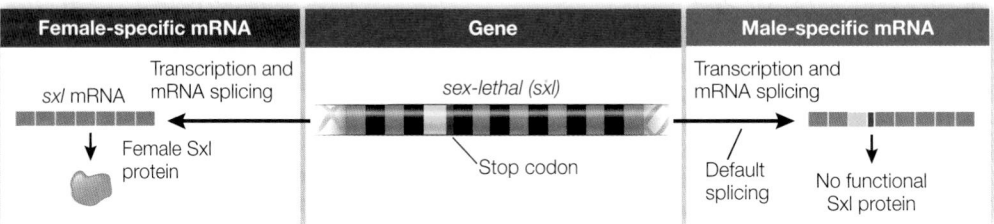

KEY CONCEPT

51.3 Behavior Can Be Studied Developmentally

- Hormones can determine the pattern of behavior that develops and the timing of its expression.

- **Imprinting** is a process by which an animal learns a specific set of stimuli during a limited **critical**, or **sensitive**, **period**. That critical period may be determined by hormones.

- The development and expression of song in White-crowned Sparrows involve a genetic predisposition to learn the species-specific song, a critical period for imprinting of a song memory, and hormonally controlled timing of song expression. Social interactions may also play a role.

- The ability to incorporate variations into species-specific behaviors may be important in establishing individuality and influencing mate choice.

Investigating Life: Practice Makes Perfect

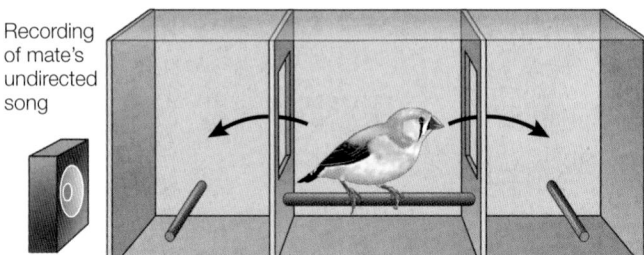

Recording of mate's undirected song

Recording of mate's directed song

Questions

1. What supports the conclusion that female is the default sex-developmental pathway in rats?

2. Why is it important that a nestling White-crowned Sparrow hear its father's song?

3. Why is it significant that the White-crowned Sparrow can introduce variations in its species-specific song?

KEY CONCEPT

51.4 Selective Pressures Shape Behavior

Go to Animations 51.1 and 51.2

Figure 51.9

Thalassarche melanophris

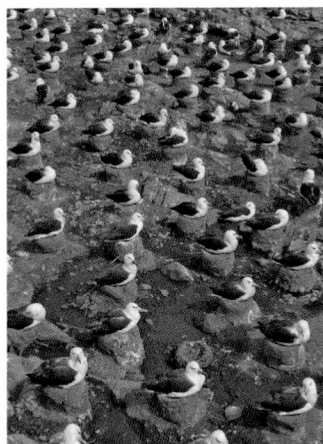

© Pete Oxford/Minden Pictures

- An animal's behavior involves choices that influence its fitness. Animals use environmental cues that are reliable predictors of the potential effects of their choices on their fitness.

- The **cost–benefit approach** can be used to investigate the fitness value of specific behaviors. The cost of a behavior includes **energetic cost**, **risk cost**, and **opportunity cost**.

- **Optimal foraging theory** states that feeding behaviors should maximize energetic gain at the least cost.

Questions

1. What are the costs and benefits to male and female Yarrow's spiny lizards of having seasonal cycles of reproductive hormone levels?

2. What is the selective advantage for many seabirds of defending small and tightly packed spaces that are not much larger than their nests?

3. Beaches on islands are preferred by dominant male elephant seals, whereas nondominant males form territories on mainland beaches. What are two reasons why female elephant seals prefer to give birth on island rather than mainland beaches?

KEY CONCEPT

51.5 Behavior Can Be Studied Mechanistically

Go to Activity 51.1,
Animations 51.3 and 51.4, and Simulation 51.1

Figure 51.16

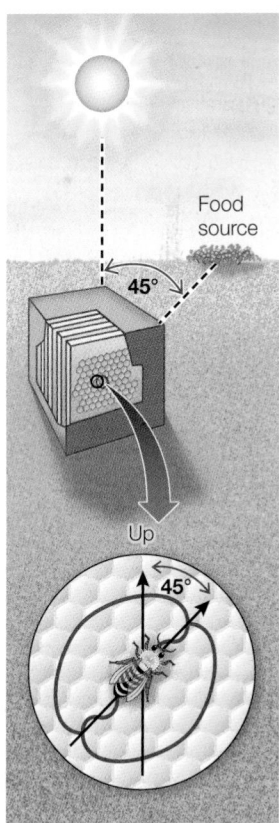

- **Circadian rhythms** are endogenous cycles that **free-run** with a period not equal to 24 hours and are **entrained** by environmental light–dark cycles.

- Endogenous circannual rhythms enable animals to anticipate seasonal changes.

- Forms of animal navigation include **piloting**, **homing**, distance–direction navigation, and bicoordinate navigation. Cues include star patterns, Earth's magnetic field, and the position of the Sun.

- Behaviors become **communication** signals if the information they convey benefits both the sender and the receiver.

- Chemical communication signals (**pheromones**) can be highly specific and have different time courses. Visual signals can convey complex messages rapidly but directionally. Acoustic signals can travel over long distances. Tactile signals can convey complex messages.

Questions

1. What is the role of circadian rhythms in solar compass navigation?

2. Explain why the SCN transplant experiment showed that the SCN was both necessary and sufficient for circadian rhythms.

3. How does the waggle dance of the honey bee convey information about distance and direction to a food source?

KEY CONCEPT

51.6   Social Interactions Shape the Evolution of Behavior

Go to Activity 51.2

- **Polygynous** mating systems result in great variation in male reproductive success.
- Monogamy and **polyandry** can evolve in circumstances in which males can maximize their reproductive fitness by helping to care for their young.
- Individual reproductive success is **direct fitness**, and it can be augmented by reproductive success of relatives (**indirect fitness**), resulting in **inclusive fitness**.
- **Kin selection** may favor **altruistic** behavior toward relatives if it increases the performer's inclusive fitness.
- **Eusocial** behavior in hymenopterans is favored because of their **haplodiploid** sex determination, but it has also arisen in diploid species.

Questions

1. Why is sexual dimorphism most common in polygynous species?

2. In genetic terms, define altruism and explain three social systems in which it evolved.

3. Belding's ground squirrels live in colonies of mostly females and their offspring. Adult females have been observed killing offspring of neighbors and also protecting offspring of neighbors. How could you explain these behaviors?

Figure 51.19

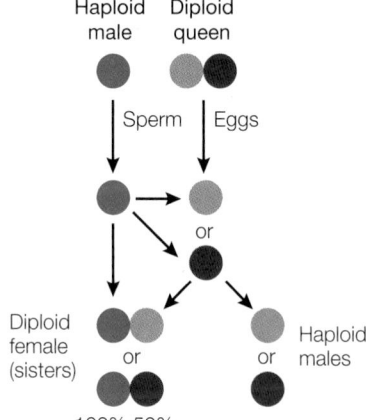

Go to **Achieve** for the eBook, **LearningCurve**, animations, activities, simulations, and additional resources and assignments.

The Physical Environment and Biogeography of Life 52

Amazonian forests, such as this, contain half of all the described species on Earth.

KEY CONCEPTS

52.1 Ecology Is the Study of the Interrelationships among Organisms and the Environment

52.2 Global Climate Is a Fundamental Component of the Physical Environment

52.3 Topography, Vegetation, and Humans Modify the Physical Environment

52.4 Biogeography Is the Study of How Organisms Are Distributed on Earth

52.5 Geographic Area and Humans Affect Regional Species Diversity

© Morley Read/Alamy Stock Photo

▶Investigating LIFE

The Largest Experiment on Earth

Most people know that there are many species on Earth, and that new species are being discovered every day, but not everyone knows that roughly half of all species worldwide reside in one place: the tropical rainforests of the Amazon Basin. The statistics are staggering: an estimated 390 billion trees representing 16,000 species grow in Amazonia, one in five bird species globally resides there, and one-fifth of all fresh water falls on its slopes and valleys. The Amazon Basin is by far the largest watershed on Earth, with thousands of tributaries leading to the Amazon River and then out to sea. To date, 2,200 freshwater fish species have been described, which is more than all the fish species in the Atlantic Ocean.

It is reasonable to assume, then, that when the Amazon Basin is threatened by human activities, so, too, is global biodiversity. By far, the main destructive force is deforestation, which began about 50 years ago. As roads pushed their way into Amazonia's forests, more rainforest was logged and converted to agriculture and settlements. It is estimated that nearly 20% of the Amazon Basin has been clear-cut. Because soil fertility is generally poor in tropical rainforests, the cleared land is often useful only for a decade or less, resulting in abandonment and new cycles of deforestation and fragmentation.

How does habitat fragmentation affect the species living in the Amazon Basin? Fragmentation makes habitats smaller, and it isolates populations. Deforestation forces species to sustain themselves in a smaller area or move to more suitable areas. In the late 1970s, some ecologists asked a deceptively simple question about Amazon deforestation: What is the minimum area needed to maintain species diversity within a rainforest fragment? They wanted to know whether the species remaining in the forest fragments could maintain themselves there, whether the sizes of the forest fragments mattered to this maintenance, and whether species would venture from one fragment to another. These ecologists conducted a large and long-running experiment in the Amazon forests near Manaus, Brazil. As you will see in Key Concept 52.5, the size of the fragments and the ability of species to move across the deforested landscape are key to maintaining the extraordinary diversity left in the Amazon Basin.

How do geographic area and isolation affect the biogeography of life on Earth?
(Find the answer on page 1194.)

KEY CONCEPT

52.1
Ecology Is the Study of the Interrelationships among Organisms and the Environment

Learning Objectives

52.1.1 Distinguish between ecology and environmentalism, and give examples of each.

52.1.2 Explain the levels of organization in ecology, and be able to distinguish them from one another based on spatial scale.

52.1.3 Describe the research methods used by ecologists, and identify how and why ecological studies might differ from studies in other scientific fields.

Whether you notice ants collecting crumbs on a sidewalk or watch a video of polar bears hunting on sea ice, you are studying ecology. From simple experiences such as these, most people know that organisms on Earth are interconnected with one another and with their environment. **Ecology** is the exploration of these interconnections and is most simply defined as the study of the interrelationships among organisms and the physical environment. Ecologists study these interactions at different scales and with different methods, but they all agree that ecology is a scientific endeavor, first and foremost.

"Ecology" is sometimes equated with "environmentalism," but the two terms are different. Ecology is a science that generates knowledge about interactions in the natural world. **Environmentalism** is the use of ecological knowledge, along with economics, ethics, and many other considerations, to inform both personal decisions and public policy related to stewardship of the natural world. So while an ecologist might study the number of bluefin tuna in the world's oceans, the environmentalist would focus on the social, economic, and political capital needed to enforce a sustainable harvest or, alternatively, to ban bluefin tuna fishing altogether.

Ecology is a relatively new branch of the biological sciences; in fact, it did not have a formal name until 150 years ago when Ernst Haeckel, a German biologist, constructed the new word "ecology," from the Greek root *oikos*, meaning "household."

Modern ecology has a more "use-inspired" focus

Although it was recognized in Darwin's day that humans could affect the natural world, and that human populations were undergoing unprecedented growth, for the most part early ecologists believed they were studying pristine systems largely untouched by human activities. Today most ecologists have a much greater awareness of ways in which humans shape the natural world, be it in the form of global climate change, the introduction of novel species to new locations, or the logging of Earth's tropical forests. Because of the dominant role that humans play in almost every ecological system on Earth, a "use-inspired" motivation often shapes ecologists' research and teaching. They understand that scientific knowledge of ecology greatly improves our ability to grow food for ourselves reliably and sustainably, to manage pests and diseases safely and effectively, and to deal with natural disasters such as floods and fires. The greater our understanding of ecological connections, the more likely it is that we can accomplish these things without causing a cascade of unanticipated consequences for ourselves and the other life on Earth.

Ecology is studied at many levels of organization

Ecology is studied at many levels of organization, from molecules to the entire globe. Some ecologists work at the level of genes to understand how individuals might adapt to a changing environment, while other researchers seek to understand how temperature might modify nutrient cycling at the ecosystem level. The work of ecologists focuses on many scales or levels of organization: individuals, populations, communities, ecosystems, landscapes, or the global biosphere (**Figure 52.1**).

As prior chapters have conveyed, a **population** is a group of individuals of the same species within a given area that have the potential to interbreed and interact with one another. For example, the individual sea stars in Figure 52.1 make up a population at this particular rocky shore location. The sea star population in turn interacts with other species, including its prey, sessile mussels, and its competitors, whelks and other sea star species. These species form a **community**, which is an assemblage of interacting species living together at the same place and time.

Ecological studies often encompass both the living, or **biotic**, and the nonliving, or **abiotic**, components of the environment. The biotic components of an organism's environment are other organisms, so ecology includes the study of interactions within and among species. The abiotic components of an organism's environment are the myriad physical and chemical characteristics of the system. For example, in the rocky shore community, tides are a key abiotic factor because they limit where sea stars can feed on mussels and compete with whelks.

The term **ecosystem** is often used when describing a community of organisms in which their physical environment is explicitly taken into account. Ecosystem ecology particularly focuses on the movement of energy and nutrients through a group of organisms. The movement of energy and nutrients, as well as organisms, can affect higher levels of organization, including **landscapes**, geographic areas that include multiple ecosystems (sometimes referred to as meta-ecosystems). Ultimately, meta-ecosystems are linked to one another at larger geographic scales to form the **biosphere**, consisting of all living organisms on Earth plus their respective environments.

Answering ecological questions requires observations, experiments, and models

Just as in other fields in biology, ecologists use a mixture of observations, experiments, and models to test ecological theories (see Key Concept 1.3). Ecologists are unique, though, in using a wide range of venues and scales in their experiments, including short laboratory experiments, long-term field manipulations, and even decades-long ecosystem-wide experiments, such as the Biological Dynamics of Forest Fragments Project described in Key Concept 52.5. However, at large spatial scales or over long periods of time, well-replicated and controlled experiments are usually not possible. For example, when studying the ecological effects of climate change on a particular species, ecologists might have to combine observations of the temperature range of that species with short-term experiments on the effects of warming on the species' distribution and then use models to project how distributions could change with continued warming. Often this type of research requires multiple techniques and collaborative efforts to be successful.

Figure 52.1 **Scale Is Important to Ecological Systems**   These photos from the Oregon coast of the United States illustrate how ecological systems can be studied at multiple scales, from the individual to the biosphere.

Courtesy of Sally Hacker

Courtesy of Sally Hacker

© Konrad Wothe/Minden Pictures

© Jean Carter/AGE Fotostock

NASA image by Reto Stöckli, based on data from NASA and NOAA

KEY CONCEPT
52.1 Recap and Assess

Ecology is the scientific study of the interrelationships among organisms and the environment. Ecology is studied at multiple levels of organization, from individuals to the biosphere. Ecologists use a mixture of observations, experiments, and models to test ecological theories.

1. Compare how an ecologist versus an environmentalist might approach an environmental problem.

2. Using observations, experiments, and models at different levels of organization, describe how you might test the hypothesis that the widespread death of the ochre sea star (*Pisaster ochraceus*) (shown in Figure 52.1) is the result of a disease.

We will begin our study of ecology in the spirit of the discipline in Haeckel's time, focusing on variations in the distribution and abundance of organisms worldwide and the factors that determine these patterns. Our first step will be to examine attributes of the physical environment, which is the most basic determinant for where organisms can live. We'll begin with climate.

KEY CONCEPT
52.2
Global Climate Is a Fundamental Component of the Physical Environment

Learning Objectives

52.2.1 Compare weather and climate, and give examples of both.

52.2.2 Given that Earth is a sphere, has an atmosphere, and rotates around its axis, explain the latitudinal variation in temperature, precipitation, and prevailing winds.

52.2.3 Relate Earth's prevailing wind patterns to ocean currents, and explain how ocean currents affect climate.

52.2.4 Connect the tilt of Earth's axis and its orbit to the existence of seasons on Earth, and explain why the Northern and Southern Hemispheres have opposite seasonal patterns.

The terms "weather" and "climate" both refer to atmospheric conditions—temperature, humidity, precipitation, and wind direction and velocity—but they consider different time scales. **Weather** is the short-term state of atmospheric conditions at a particular place and time, whereas **climate** refers to the average atmospheric conditions, and the extent of their variation, at a particular place over a longer time (years to millennia). Climate is what you expect given past conditions; weather is what you get on any one day. For example, a warming climate will cause glaciers to melt over decades or centuries (see Figure 1.17), whereas a single large snowstorm is unlikely to slow that retreat. In addition, the responses of organisms to weather are usually short-term—seeking shelter from a sudden rainstorm, for example, or shivering to keep warm when the temperature drops. Climate, by contrast, acts as a sort of filter for organisms, ultimately determining their distribution and abundance. If organisms cannot tolerate the climate of a particular

Figure 52.2 Radiant Energy Warms the Planet   Solar energy input (yellow arrows) is absorbed by Earth's atmosphere and surface. Much of this energy is radiated from Earth's surface in the form of heat (orange arrows). Of that absorbed at the surface, most is prevented from escaping back into space by greenhouse gases in the atmosphere. The widths of the arrows are roughly proportional to the sizes of the energy fluxes. (After K. E. Trenberth et al. 2009. *Bull Am Meteorol Soc* 90: 311–323;

Lindsey, R. 2009. Climate and Earth's energy budget. Earth Observatory, EOS Project Science Office, NASA Goddard Space Flight Center. Greenbelt, MD.)

Q: What effect do greenhouse gases have on Earth's energy balance?

View in Achieve
Animation 52.1 Radiant Energy Balance

place, they will not be found there. Here we consider the processes that create climate patterns.

Solar radiation drives global climate patterns

The energy that drives global climate patterns ultimately originates from the Sun. Of the solar radiation that hits Earth, about 30% is reflected back to space by clouds, atmospheric gases, and Earth's surface (**Figure 52.2**). The rest is absorbed either by the atmosphere (20%) or the surface of Earth (50%). The **atmosphere**, a thin layer of gases surrounding Earth composed of nitrogen gas (N_2, 78%), oxygen (O_2, 21%), argon (0.9%), carbon dioxide (CO_2, 0.037%), and traces of hydrogen, helium, ozone, methane (CH_4), and many other gases, moderates Earth's surface temperatures by trapping heat energy. If Earth had no atmosphere, its average surface temperature would be about −18°C, rather than its actual +17°C. Carbon dioxide, methane, nitrous oxide (N_2O), water vapor, and certain other gases in the atmosphere are known as **greenhouse gases** because they allow sunlight into Earth's atmosphere but trap heat radiating back out toward space (see Figure 52.2).

The amount of radiation received on Earth varies with latitude and with the seasons. These differences are driven by some well-known characteristics of Earth: it is a sphere that orbits the Sun, it spins on a tilted axis, and

it has both land and water. As you will see, it is the combination of these factors that determines the climate we experience on Earth.

Earth is a sphere, creating latitudinal variation in global temperature and precipitation

Because Earth is a sphere, the intensity of solar radiation hitting its surface varies with latitude. This latitudinal variation in solar energy depends primarily on the angle of the Sun's rays striking

Figure 52.3 Solar Energy Input Varies with Latitude   The angle of incoming sunlight affects the intensity of solar energy that reaches a given unit of Earth's surface. (After C. D. Ahrens. 2005. *Essentials of Meteorology: An Invitation to the Atmosphere.* Brooks/Cole, Cengage Learning: USA.)

(A) Average annual air temperature

(B) Average annual precipitation

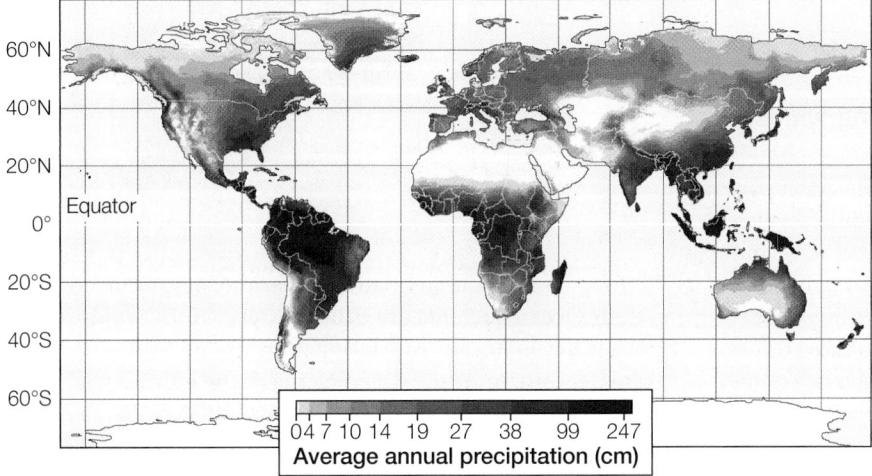

Figure 52.4 **Global Temperature and Precipitation Vary with Latitude**   Average annual air temperature **(A)** and precipitation **(B)** vary with Earth's latitude but can be modified by topography (i.e., Earth's shape and surface features) (see Figure 52.9). (A, after Berkeley Earth. 2016. *Land and Ocean Baseline Comparison Map.* http://www.berkeleyearth.org/; B, courtesy of the Nelson Institute Center for Sustainability and the Global Environment [SAGE], through their "Atlas of the Biosphere," https://nelson.wisc.edu/sage/data-and-models/atlas/. University of Wisconsin-Madison.)

Earth. At high latitudes (i.e., areas toward the North and South Poles), incoming solar energy is distributed over a larger area (and thus is less intense) than at the equator, where sunlight strikes the surface perpendicularly (**Figure 52.3**). Moreover, when the Sun's radiation comes in at an angle, it must pass through more of Earth's atmosphere, resulting in more of its energy being absorbed or reflected before reaching Earth's surface. Differences in solar energy input explain why the average global temperature varies with latitude, with warmer temperatures at the equator and colder temperatures at the poles (**Figure 52.4A**). The average air temperature over the course of a year decreases about 0.76 degrees Celsius for every degree of latitude (~110 km) at sea level.

In addition to there being a latitudinal variation in temperature, the Northern Hemisphere is slightly warmer (by ~2 degrees Celsius) and more variable in temperature (by a range of ~7 degrees

Celsius) than the Southern Hemisphere (see Figure 52.4A). Although the reasons for this difference are uncertain, one hypothesis is that because land heats up the air above it more than does the ocean (which absorbs more heat), the greater proportion of land to ocean in the Northern Hemisphere creates warmer air temperatures than those in the Southern Hemisphere. This is particularly true in summer, when the temperature difference is at its greatest. In light of global warming, it is worth noting that temperatures are increasing faster in the Northern Hemisphere than in the Southern Hemisphere.

Besides controlling temperature, solar energy input also determines atmospheric circulation and associated precipitation patterns. As you saw earlier, air in the region surrounding the equator receives the greatest input of solar energy. When a parcel of air is warmed, it expands, becomes less dense, and rises (see Figure 52.5A). As it rises, however, it starts to cool at higher elevations. Cool air cannot hold as much water vapor as warm air, so the expanding, cooling air releases moisture in the form of precipitation. This is particularly evident in the tropics, where there is abundant rainfall year-round (**Figure 52.4B**). Eventually the rising air at the equator reaches the boundary between the troposphere, the atmospheric layer above Earth's surface, and the stratosphere, the next layer up. The stratosphere is warmer than the troposphere at this boundary, causing the tropical air to stop rising and eventually move either north or south as newly warmed air rises to replace it (**Figure 52.5A**). Eventually this air starts to cool as it exchanges heat with the atmosphere and meets colder air traveling from higher latitudes. When this cool, dry air, which lost its moisture as it rose over the equator, reaches latitudes of about 30°N and 30°S, it begins to sink under high atmospheric pressure, making the climate at these latitudes dry (**Figure 52.5B**). Earth's great deserts—including the Sahara of Africa, the Gobi of China, and the deserts of Australia and the North American Southwest—are located at these latitudes (see Figure 52.5B).

While some of the descending air flows back toward the equator, some of it flows toward the poles, setting up another atmospheric cell of air circulation at higher latitudes. At about 60° latitude, air rises again due to its warming at Earth's surface (see Figure 52.5B). As this air rises, it cools and releases precipitation, creating wet climate conditions at temperate latitudes. Eventually this air reaches the stratosphere and moves north or south. The cold, dry air traveling at higher latitudes eventually reaches the cold polar region, where it descends. Despite the amount of snow and ice at the poles, high latitudes at or near 90° actually receive little precipitation and can be thought of as "polar deserts" (see Figure 52.5B).

Figure 52.5 **Air Circulation in Earth's Atmosphere Drives Climate**   **(A)** Solar energy drives patterns of atmospheric circulation. **(B)** The differential heating of Earth's surface by solar radiation gives rise to atmospheric circulation cells, which influence atmospheric pressure, air temperatures, and precipitation worldwide. (After C. D. Ahrens. 2005. *Essentials of Meteorology: An Invitation to the Atmosphere.* Brooks/Cole, Cengage Learning: USA.)

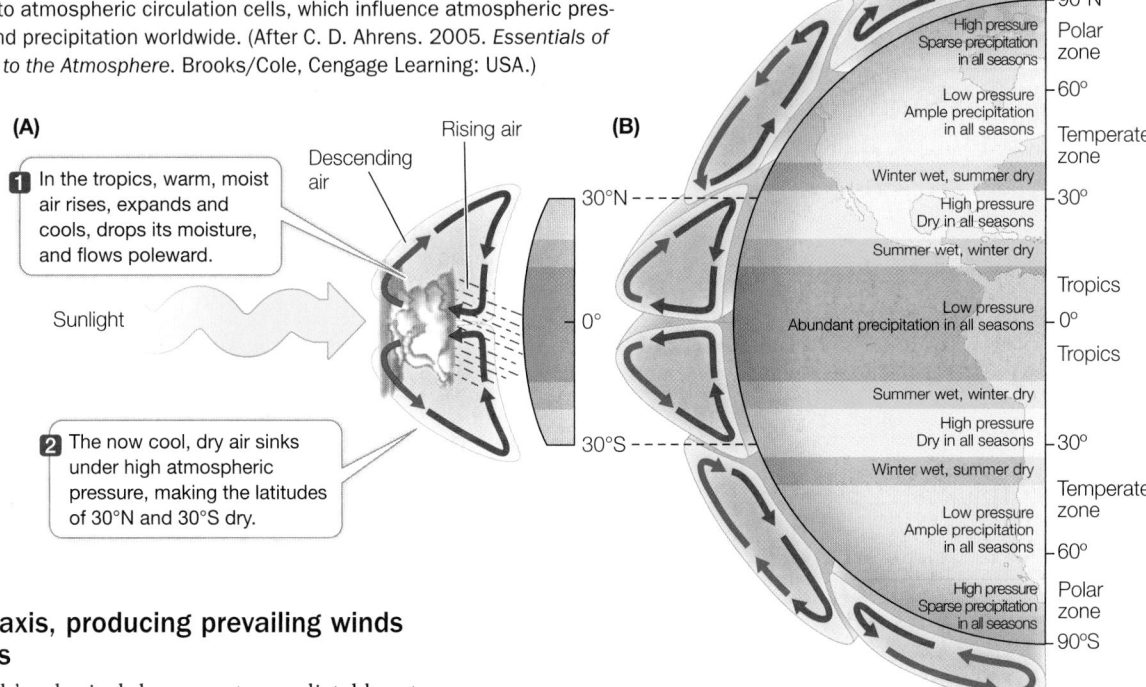

Earth spins on an axis, producing prevailing winds and ocean currents

You have seen that Earth's spherical shape creates predictable patterns of temperature and precipitation, but Earth's rotation, which moves east to west, is responsible for generating global wind and ocean currents. Because Earth is a sphere, the velocity of its rotation around its axis is fastest at the equator, where its diameter is greatest, and is slowest close to the poles. This difference creates the **Coriolis effect**, which is the deflection of air or water as a result of differences in Earth's rotational speed at different latitudes. For example, air traveling toward the equator (driven by the circulation patterns described above and in Figure 52.5) moves at a slower speed than that of the planet beneath it and is thus deflected to the west. Conversely, air traveling toward either pole is moving faster than that of the surface beneath it and is deflected to the east. This interaction of Earth's rotation and north–south air mass movement sets up a pattern of circulating surface air referred to as **prevailing winds** (Figure 52.6). Prevailing winds blow from east to west in the tropics (the **trade winds**); from west to east in mid-latitudes (the **westerlies**); and from east to west again above 60°N or 60°S latitude (the **easterlies**).

How, then, are the circulation patterns of ocean currents generated? Ocean currents are driven by prevailing winds, which move water by means of frictional drag. The trade winds, for example, cause currents to converge at the equator and move westward until they encounter a continent (**Figure 52.7**). At that point, the strong Equatorial Countercurrent brings some of the water back eastward. The remaining water divides, some moving northward and some southward along continental shores.

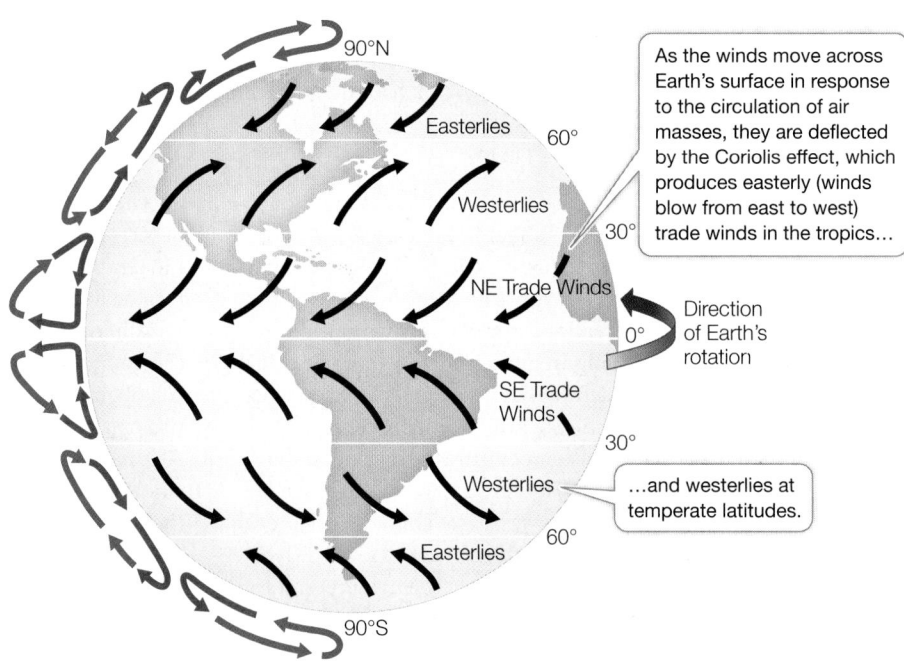

Figure 52.6 **Prevailing Winds Created by Earth's Rotation and Atmospheric Circulation**   The deflection of air as a result of differences in Earth's rotational speed at different latitudes (also known as the Coriolis effect) coupled with atmospheric circulation of air masses combine to create a global pattern of prevailing surface winds across the planet.

Figure 52.7 Oceanic Circulation Created by Winds and Continents
The surface currents of the ocean are driven by the prevailing winds (see Figure 52.6), Earth's rotation, and the placement of the continents. Red arrows indicate warm surface water, and blue arrows indicate cold surface water.

These patterns of water movement set up rotating circulation patterns called **gyres** (Greek *gyros*, "spiral"), which rotate clockwise in the Northern Hemisphere and counterclockwise in the Southern Hemisphere.

Because ocean currents transport heat, they have a tremendous effect on Earth's climates. The poleward movement of warm water from the tropics transfers large amounts of heat to high latitudes. The Gulf Stream, for example, carries warm water from the tropical Atlantic Ocean (including the Gulf of Mexico) north across the Atlantic to northern Europe, making Europe's climate considerably milder than that of some corresponding latitudes in North America. Similarly, currents flowing toward the equator from high latitudes bring cool, wet winters to some western coastal regions that are otherwise warm and dry.

The tilt of Earth's axis and its orbit result in seasons

The tilt of Earth's axis, coupled with Earth's orbit around the Sun, is responsible for seasonal changes in climate. Earth's axis is tilted at an angle of 23.5 degrees, changing the amount of sunlight a particular region receives over the course of a year as Earth orbits the Sun (**Figure 52.8**). This tilt causes seasonal variation in

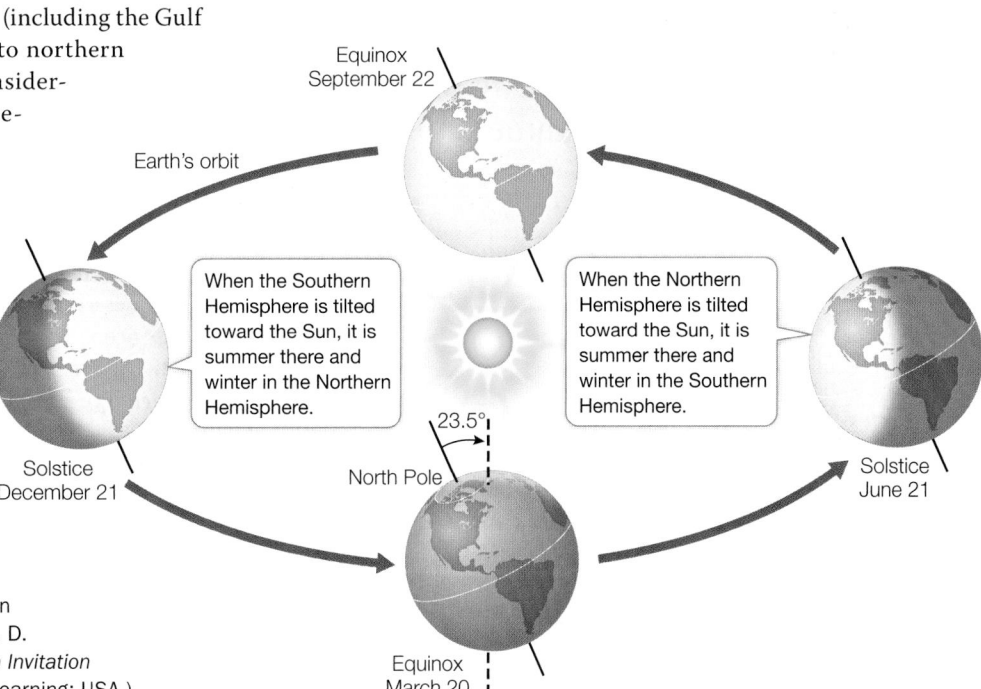

Figure 52.8 Seasonal Change Is the Result of the Tilt of Earth's Axis and Its Orbit Because Earth's axis of rotation is tilted, orientation relative to the Sun changes over the course of a year as the planet orbits the Sun. The resulting variation in solar radiation creates seasonal climate variation. (After C. D. Ahrens. 2005. *Essentials of Meteorology: An Invitation to the Atmosphere*. Brooks/Cole, Cengage Learning: USA.)

temperature and day length. Higher latitudes experience greater seasonal variation than lower latitudes do. Around the equator, day length and seasonal temperatures change only slightly over the course of the year, although there are seasonal shifts in precipitation patterns.

KEY CONCEPT
52.2 Recap and Assess

Climate and weather both refer to atmospheric conditions, but climate represents conditions over years whereas weather represents conditions over a span of days. Earth is a sphere, has an atmosphere, and rotates around its axis, which creates latitudinal variation in solar radiation, temperature and precipitation, and prevailing winds and ocean currents. Earth's tilt and orbit around the Sun result in the seasons.

1. Does a month of extremely hot weather tell us that Earth's climate is warming? Explain your answer.

2. Refer to Figure 52.3. Why does solar energy input into Earth's atmosphere vary with latitude? What are the consequences for global climate?

3. Refer to Figures 52.6 and 52.7. If you were sailing, using wind power only, from the east coast of North America to Europe across the Atlantic Ocean, describe the best route given winds and currents.

4. Explain why Earth's Northern and Southern Hemispheres have opposite seasons.

We have considered large, global patterns in climate, but we know that the physical environment can vary within certain regions or even locally. Just travel across a large mountain range and you can experience lush forests on one side and bone-dry deserts on the other. We will turn next to what controls smaller, more regional and local variation in the physical environment, both on land and in water.

KEY CONCEPT
52.3 Topography, Vegetation, and Humans Modify the Physical Environment

Learning Objectives

52.3.1 Explain and compare the causes and effects of rain shadows and temperature inversions.

52.3.2 Describe how ocean-floor topography creates variable marine environments.

52.3.3 Compare and contrast the effects of vegetation on temperature and precipitation at local and regional scales.

52.3.4 Describe and contrast ways in which agriculture and urbanization may transform local and regional climates.

Three main factors can modify the pattern of global climate, determining regional and local variation in climate and other aspects of the physical environment: (1) Earth's topography, (2) vegetation, and more recently, (3) the effects of humans.

Earth's topography affects the local and regional physical environment

Earth's **topography**, meaning its shape and surface features, has been formed over geological time and provides the basis for much of the variation in local and regional physical conditions. Here we consider how topography modifies the physical environment with respect to land, oceans, rivers, and lakes.

LAND   The topography of land plays a large role in the regional and local physical environment, including climate. Mountains create elevational gradients in temperature, precipitation, and sunlight. For example, mountains show progressively colder temperatures and greater precipitation at higher elevations, creating different environmental conditions over relatively short distances. When a mountain range occurs adjacent to an ocean, a **rain shadow** is often created, whereby one side of the mountain has a wet climate and the other side has a dry climate (**Figure 52.9A**). Rain shadows occur when winds deliver moist air evaporated from the ocean to the windward side of the mountain, where the air rises, cools, and releases rain or snow. On the leeward side of the mountain (that is, opposite from the direction of the winds), the now-dry air descends, warms, and produces arid conditions. The High Desert, on the leeward side of the Cascade Range in the Pacific Northwest of the United States, is one such area.

Other topographic features, such as canyons and valleys, also modify local climate in significant ways. Valleys can experience **temperature inversions**, extremes in temperature that produce morning fog and intense afternoon heat. Temperature inversions occur when the valley concentrates heat from solar radiation during the day. As that heat rises, it forms an inversion layer that traps cold, dense, and moisture-laden air that descends into the valley overnight and produces fog (**Figure 52.9B**).

OCEANS   Beneath the oceans, which make up 70% of Earth's surface, dramatic differences in topography influence the marine environment. If you could drain the oceans, you would notice major differences in topography, ranging from the Hawaiian island Mauna Loa, the tallest "mountain" on Earth at 9,170 meters high from base to peak, to the Mariana Trench, the deepest "valley" at 10,994 meters deep. Variations in water depth affect light penetration, water temperature, water pressure, and water movement (i.e., waves and tides). These physical discontinuities create distinct zones that are identified principally by their physical conditions and the characteristic biota they contain, similar to biomes on land (see Key Concept 52.4). The depth of an ocean basin varies from the shoreline to the relatively shallow continental shelf and to the deepest part of the ocean, sometimes known as the abyssal plain (**Figure 52.9C**). Water depth affects how much light is available to sustain the photosynthetic organisms that form the base of the marine food chain. In both marine and freshwater environments, roughly 90% of all aquatic life is found in the **photic zone**, the layer of water reached by enough sunlight to support photosynthesis.

Other zones that vary in environmental conditions include the **coastal zone**, which extends from the shoreline to the edge of the continental shelf, and the **ocean zone**, which extends beyond the coastal zone (see Figure 52.9C). The coastal zone is diverse and

(A) Rain shadow

Winds pick up moisture over the ocean.

On the windward side, air rises, cools, and releases moisture as rain or snow, creating a wet climate.

On the leeward side, dry air descends and warms, resulting in little rain and arid conditions.

(B) Temperature inversion

Cool air
7°C

Inversion layer

10°C

7°C

Fog
4°C

Warm air (inversion layer) traps cold and moisture-laden air that descends into the valley overnight, producing fog.

(C) Aquatic zones

Intertidal zone   Coastal zone   Ocean zone   Photic zone

200

2,000

Continental shelf

Pelagic zone

4,000

Benthic zone

6,000

8,000

Abyssal plain

10,000

Water depth (m)

(D) Ocean upwelling

A prevailing wind blows parallel to the coast.

The wind, along with the Coriolis effect, creates a surface current flowing away from the coast.

Wind

Deep, cool water rises to replace the surface water.

14°
13°
12°
11°

Figure 52.9 Effects of Earth's Topography on the Physical Environment   Earth's topography can affect both land and oceans. Mountains and valleys create rain shadows **(A)** and temperature inversions **(B)**. Ocean topography affects water depth, which creates aquatic zones that vary in light, temperature, and water pressure **(C)**, and along with wind, produces ocean upwelling **(D)**. (B after M. Schroeder and C. Buck. 1970. *Fire Weather: A Guide for Application of Meterological Information to Forest Fire Control Operations*, p. 29. USDA Forest Service,

Agriculture Handbook 360. D after C. D. Ahrens. 2005. *Essentials of Meteorology: An Invitation to the Atmosphere*. Brooks/Cole, Cengage Learning: USA.)

Q: What kind of weather conditions would you expect to produce temperature inversions? How about ocean upwelling?

 View in Achieve
Animation 52.2 Rain Shadow

highly productive, supporting high densities of pelagic, or floating, plankton and fishes. On the benthos or bottom of the ocean, the coastal zone has a variety of living and nonliving habitats such as rocky reefs, soft sediment flats, coral reefs, and kelp beds. The portion of the benthic coastal zone lying between the high and low tide levels is the **intertidal zone**, where tidal movements create conditions of highly variable light and temperature, alternately exposing organisms to air and water. Intertidal zones can occur on the open coast as sandy or rocky beaches, or in more protected bays as estuaries. **Estuaries** form where rivers meet the sea, creating variability in salinity, sediment, and light conditions.

In some coastal zones, where the continental shelf drops off steeply and prevailing winds are parallel to the coastline, upwelling can affect ocean and climate conditions. **Upwelling** is a process in which offshore winds in combination with the Coriolis effect push warmer surface waters away from the shore, allowing deeper,

colder, and nutrient-rich bottom water to rise to the surface (**Figure 52.9D**). Upwelling affects local and regional climate on the coast by creating cooler and moister conditions. In addition, upwelled waters support high rates of primary production by phytoplankton, which in turn support dense consumer populations. Most of the world's great fisheries are concentrated in upwelling zones.

As we move away from the coastline, most of the ocean's physical environment is made up of vast amounts of water that is, with the exception of the photic zone (which can extend to 200 meters in some regions), mostly dark, cold, and under tremendous pressure from the weight of the water above. Little photosynthesis can take place, and many of the organisms inhabiting these regions subsist on decaying organic matter that sinks down from the photic zone. Deep-ocean trenches and rift valleys support hydrothermal vent ecosystems sustained by chemoautotrophic prokaryotes that can metabolize the nutrients without the aid of sunlight (see Key Concept 24.3).

RIVERS AND LAKES   In contrast to the vast oceans, freshwater lakes and rivers make up less than 3% of Earth's surface, but they are home to about 10% of all aquatic species. Earth's topography influences freshwater environments just as it does marine environments—through the depth of the water—but it also influences the degree and direction of movement of fresh water. A river is water that flows downhill from its point of origin (the source) over the land surface as a result of gravity until it reaches either the ocean or a depression in Earth's surface, where it forms a lake or pond. The headwaters (those close to the source) tend to be cool, fast-flowing, and well oxygenated. As a river flows downstream, it widens, it slows down, it warms, and sediment accumulates, reducing light penetration and oxygen levels.

The Amazon River, mentioned in the chapter opening, offers a dramatic example of river dynamics. The Amazon is one of the longest rivers on Earth, at approximately 7,000 km. Eventually this source water reaches the Atlantic Ocean, where discharge is the largest of any river on Earth—the Amazon's mouth is 240 km wide and is referred to as "the River Sea."

Vegetation affects the local and regional physical environment, especially climate

Earth's climate would be very different without the influence of organisms, including humans. Organisms can "engineer" the environment in multiple ways that affect the surrounding climate and physical conditions. The most obvious influence comes from vegetation, especially forests, which can have large effects on temperature and precipitation at local and even regional scales. For example, measurements of energy exchange in tropical forests that have been converted to pastureland show that forests make the climate cooler and moister (**Figure 52.10**). While forests absorb heat by reflecting less sunlight (reflection of solar radiation is known as the **albedo effect**) and decrease convective heat loss by acting as a wind screen, this is more than balanced by the cooling effect produced by **evapotranspiration**: the evaporative transfer of heat and water from the surfaces of plants into the atmosphere, which reduces air temperature and increases moisture. When forests are cut and replaced by vegetation such as grasses, the albedo effect and convective heat loss intensify while evapotranspiration decreases, causing overall air temperatures to rise and precipitation to decrease, creating more arid conditions. The climate changes associated with deforestation have been seen in the Amazon Basin, where massive forest clearing makes way for cattle ranching.

Oceans have their own "forests"—coastal areas dominated by seaweeds such as giant kelps or sea grasses that create calmer waters, promote sedimentation, and provide habitat for fishes and invertebrates. In warmer coastal waters, corals generate complex reef structures that support ecosystems rivaling rainforests in diversity. In Chapter 56 you will learn more about organisms that engineer their environment, but for now let's turn to the final topic in this key concept: the effects of humans on climate and the physical environment.

Humans have transformed their physical environment, including urban climate

It is estimated that humans have transformed more than 50% of Earth's land surface, replacing it with infrastructure and agriculture needed to support our burgeoning population. You have already seen how the conversion of forestland to pastureland can change regional climate, and in Chapter 56 you will learn more about how humans have changed global climate through the burning of fossil fuels. Structures such as dams, bridges, and nuclear power plants can dramatically transform rivers and lakes. Urban areas, in particular, modify not only the immediate physical environment but also the surrounding climate. A survey of 60 U.S. cities in 2014

Figure 52.10 Deforestation Can Affect Climate Evapotranspiration by trees reduces air temperatures and increases precipitation. When land is deforested and the trees are gone, the cooling effects of the albedo (reflection of solar radiation) and of convective heat loss are not enough to outweigh the warming effects of reduced evapotranspiration. The widths of the arrows are roughly proportional to the sizes of the fluxes. (After J. A. Foley, et al. 2003. *Front Ecol Environ* 1: 38–44.)

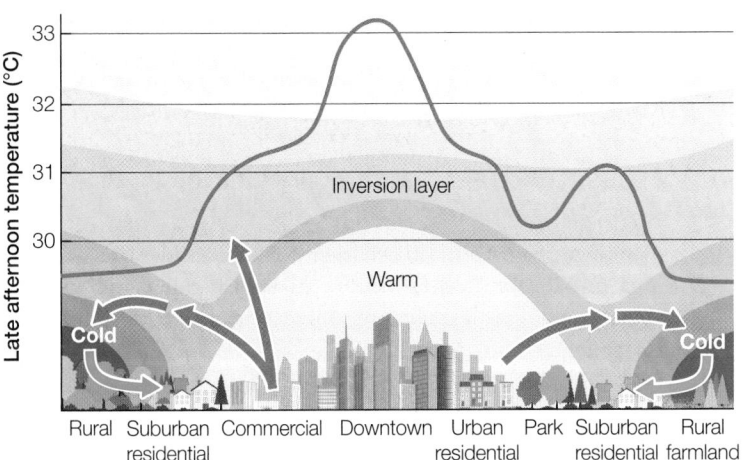

Figure 52.11 Cities Can Create Heat Islands and Country Breezes
As this hypothetical urban heat island profile shows, cities and suburbs typically have higher temperatures than rural, park, or agricultural areas. Country breezes form when warm air from cities and suburbs is replaced by cool air from rural areas. (After D. Reidel. 2004. In *Climate Change Impacts and Adaptation: A Canadian Perspective*, D. S. Lemmen and F. J. Warren (Eds.), p. 157. Ottawa, ON: Climate Change Impacts and Adaptation Program, Natural Resources Canada; and H. E. Landsberg. 1970. *Science* 170: 1265–1274.)

showed that urban summer temperatures were on average 1.5 degrees Celsius hotter than rural summer temperatures, with the top 10 cities having an average urban–rural temperature differential of 5 degrees Celsius. The cause of this so-called urban heat island effect is simple: concrete, asphalt, and even the dark roofs of buildings absorb heat from solar radiation and radiate that heat in the evening hours (Figure 52.11). Cities also produce more heat through the burning of fossil fuels from cars, factories, and buildings. Parks can serve to cool the surrounding air through the evapotranspiration of trees and other vegetation. In addition, the temperature differential between cities and the surrounding countryside can create "country breezes," air movement generated as rising warm air from the city is replaced by cold surface air from surrounding rural areas.

KEY CONCEPT
52.3 Recap and Assess

Earth's topography is responsible for rain shadows and temperature inversions, producing variation in temperature and precipitation. In the oceans, topographical variability produces differences in water depth, which affects light penetration, water temperature, water pressure, and water movement. Vegetation, especially forests, affects climate through the process of evapotranspiration. Cities can create their own climate; cities are on average hotter than rural areas.

1. What are some of the major ways that Earth's topography affects land and ocean physical conditions?

2. Why are cities warmer than rural areas, and what are country breezes? How and why could the temperature in a city be changed with the establishment of a large forested park?

With an understanding of how Earth's physical environment, including climate, is determined at a variety of spatial scales, we will turn next to biogeography: how the physical environment and other

geographic and historical processes determine the global distribution of organisms on Earth.

KEY CONCEPT
52.4
Biogeography Is the Study of How Organisms Are Distributed on Earth

Learning Objectives

52.4.1 Describe the principle characteristics of each major biome, including climate, latitude and/or continent(s), and representative plants and animals.

52.4.2 Use the observations and insights of Alfred Russel Wallace to explain how biogeography might influence the distribution of plants and animals.

52.4.3 Compare and contrast the hypotheses posed for latitudinal patterns of species diversity, including species diversification rate, species diversification time, and productivity.

Biogeography is the scientific study of the distribution and diversity of organisms on Earth. "Distribution" is simply where organisms are found. "Diversity," however, has multiple facets, which we will explore in more detail in Chapter 56, but for now you can think of it simply as the number and composition of species or higher taxa. For centuries, the processes that control these biogeographic patterns have puzzled naturalists. Why do species vary in their distributions around Earth, and what controls this variability?

Patterns of biogeography are interconnected across a hierarchy of spatial and temporal scales

The patterns of biogeography play out over global, regional, landscape, and local spatial scales (Figure 52.12). Spatial scales are interconnected in a hierarchical way, with patterns at one scale setting the conditions for patterns at other scales.

At the global scale, species are isolated from one another by continents or oceans, and for long periods of time. Thus the rates of three processes—speciation, extinction, and dispersal—help determine differences in biogeography across the globe (see Figure 52.12A). At the regional scale, large-scale climate conditions are relatively uniform and species are limited by their ability to disperse, or move between locations (see Figure 52.12B). All the species that are limited to a region are part of the **regional species pool** (also called **gamma diversity**). At the landscape scale, there are multiple community types—for example, lakes, rivers, forests, and prairies—arranged in a spatially heterogeneous way across the region (see Figure 52.12C). The change in the number of species from one community to another across the landscape is known as **beta diversity**. Finally, the local scale (also called **alpha diversity**) typically encompasses a single community—a group of species assembled together as the result of the physical environment, biotic interactions with other species, and the regional species pool (see Figure 52.12D).

(A) Global scale

Global patterns of species diversity and composition are the result of variation in speciation, extinction, and dispersal at the spatial scale of continents and at evolutionary time scales.

(B) Regional scale

Within regions, patterns of species diversity and composition (gamma diversity) are driven by dispersal and extinction across the landscape.

(C) Landscape scale

Local and regional scales are connected by turnover, which is the difference in species diversity and composition (beta diversity) when moving across the landscape from one community type to another.

(D) Local scale

Local patterns of species diversity and composition (alpha diversity) are driven by physical conditions and species interactions.

Figure 52.12 Biogeography Depends on Interconnected Spatial and Temporal Scales The arrows represent the relationship between, and processes important to, species diversity and composition at **(A)** global, **(B)** regional, **(C)** landscape, and **(D)** local scales.

Q: At what scales is the regional species pool important to species diversity and composition?

In the remainder of this chapter we will consider the distributional and diversity patterns of organisms at global and regional biogeographic scales. Chapter 55 will consider the causes and consequences of diversity at community and local scales.

Terrestrial biomes reflect global patterns of temperature and precipitation

Biomes are groupings of ecologically similar organisms shaped by the environment in which they are found. The classification of biomes is most often and easily applied to terrestrial systems. Ecologists classify terrestrial biomes principally by the growth forms of their dominant plants, which reflect the evolution of those plants under annual patterns of temperature and precipitation.

The same classic types of biomes may be widely separated, occurring on different continents, depending in large part on the presence of suitable climatic conditions (**Figure 52.13**). For example, the desert biome occurs in such distant locations as Arizona in the North American Southwest and the Namib Desert in Africa;

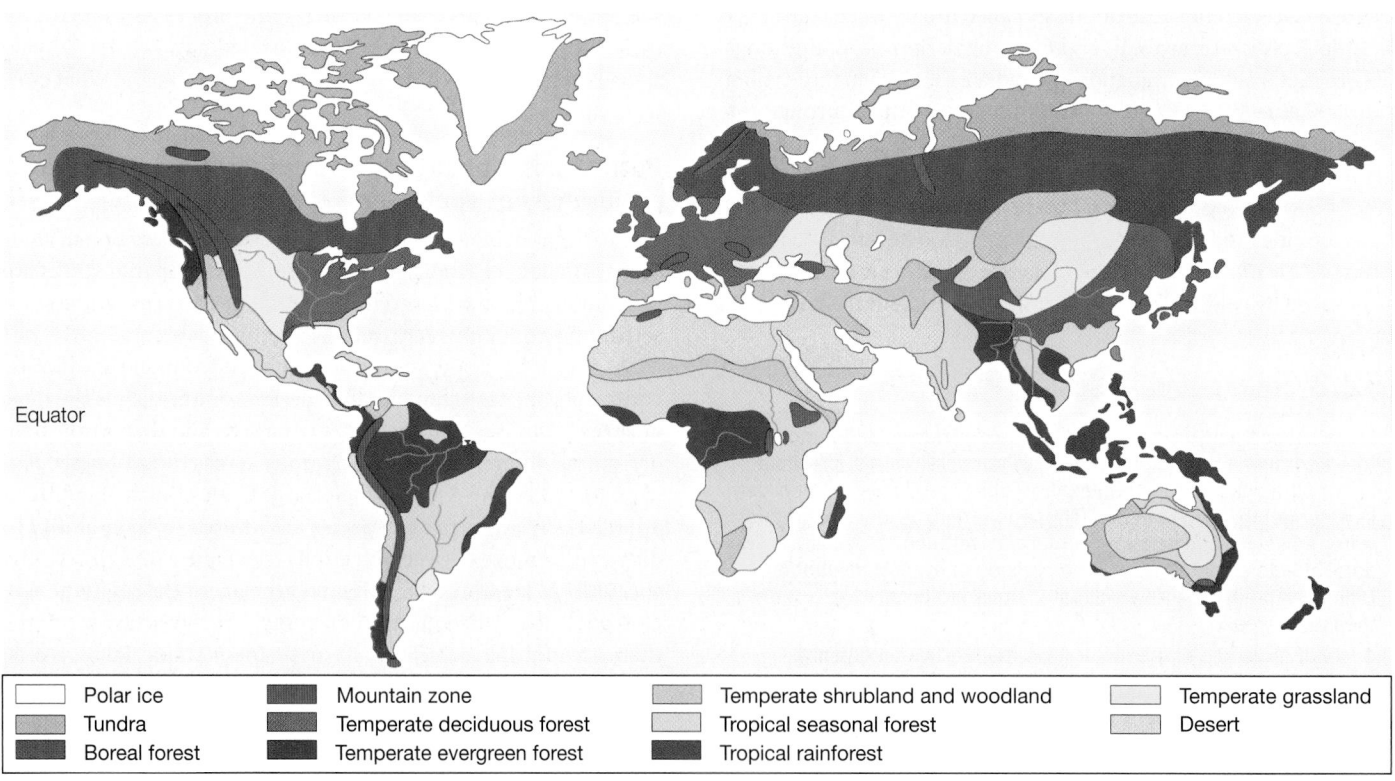

Equator

Polar ice	Mountain zone	Temperate shrubland and woodland
Tundra	Temperate deciduous forest	Tropical seasonal forest
Boreal forest	Temperate evergreen forest	Tropical rainforest

Temperate grassland
Desert

Figure 52.13 Global Distribution of Terrestrial Biomes The distribution of terrestrial biomes is determined primarily by annual patterns of temperature and precipitation.

Q: Does the Northern or Southern Hemisphere have a greater number of biome types? What do you think might determine this difference?

▶ **View in Achieve** Activity 52.1 **Terrestial Biomes**
View in Achieve Activity 52.2 **Aquatic Biomes**

Tropical Rainforest

Equator

There are over 200 bird species in this tropical rainforest at Lambir Hills National Park, on the island of Borneo, Malaysia.

Bromeliads commonly grow on trees in tropical rainforests, such as this ceibo tree in Ecuador, but can also be found in desert biomes.

The mountain gorilla (*Gorilla beringei beringei*) is a critically endangered species. This family lives in the tropical rainforest of Volcanoes National Park, Rwanda.

Yanganbi, D.R.C.
0°
Average annual temperature 24.6°C
Total annual precipitation 1,828 mm

Note that the scale changes above 100 mm of precipitation.

Temperature (°C) (---○---)

Precipitation (mm) (——●——)

Month

© Morley Read/Alamy Stock Photo

© Michael Doolittle/Alamy Stock Photo

© Thomas Marent/Minden Pictures

Data from NOAA GHCN-Monthly version 2: T. C. Peterson and R. S. Vose. 1997. *Bull Am Meteorol Soc* 78: 2837–2849

Go to **Achieve** for a companion **Data in Depth** exercise.

both locations are extremely dry and dominated by succulent plants such as cacti and by drought-tolerant shrubs and grasses. Why use plants as a way of classifying biomes? Because plants are immobile, they must adapt to environmental conditions in order to be successful over long periods of time. Thus the growth forms of plants strongly reflect their environment in ways that can be compared around the world. Furthermore, by providing three-dimensional structure, by modifying physical conditions near the ground, and by providing food, dominant plants strongly influence the organisms living there.

Connect the Concepts Key Concept 37.1 describes how plants growing in a particular type of environment (e.g., the desert) may display similar growth forms (e.g., succulence).

In the following pages we briefly describe seven terrestrial biomes (a subset of those shown in Figure 52.13). For each, a plot of the seasonal patterns of temperature and precipitation—known as a **Walter climate diagram**—is included. Devised by the German biogeographers Heinrich Walter and Helmut Lieth, this graphic technique plots temperature and precipitation data in a simple way that visualizes a "growing season"—those months when average temperatures are above freezing (0°C) and when average precipitation is sufficient for plant growth. Walter climate diagrams are predicated on the "rule of thumb" that plant growth requires temperatures above 0°C and at least 2 mm of precipitation for each 1-degree-Celsius rise in temperature. They have two y-axis scales, one for temperature and one for precipitation; these axes align 0 mm of precipitation with 0°C

Desert

Equator

A desert biome in Namibia, Africa, is home to the gemsbuck, a large antelope in the *Oryx* genus.

© Paula French/EyeEm/Getty Images

Sonoran desert in bloom with saguaro (*Carnegiea gigantea*) and cholla (*Cylindropuntia* sp.) cacti and poppies at Organ Pipe Cactus National Monument, Arizona, USA.

© Terry Donnelly/Alamy Stock Photo

When the precipitation curve falls below the temperature curve (yellow area), water availability limits plant growth.

Ouargla, Algeria
31°N
Average annual temperature 22.3°C
Total annual precipitation 39 mm

Data from NOAA GHCN-Monthly, version 2; T. C. Peterson and R. S. Vose. 1997. *Bull Am Meteorol Soc* 78: 2837–2849

© ZSSD/Minden Pictures

A desert tortoise (*Gopherus agassizii*) in its native habitat, the Mohave Desert, California, USA.

of temperature. The x axis shows 12 months, with the summer solstice placed in the center of the axis.

TROPICAL RAINFOREST   The tropical rainforest biome is found in equatorial regions where rainfall and temperatures are high year-round. With no season unsuitable for growth, it is the most productive and species-rich of all biomes. In some areas, there are up to 500 species of trees per square kilometer. Although historically these forests covered 12% of Earth's surface, and are now reduced through deforestation, they are home to more than half of all known species. These forests are home to many

epiphytes—plants that grow on other plants, deriving their nutrients and moisture from air and water rather than soil.

Tropical rainforests provide humans with a range of products, including fruits, nuts, medicines, fuel, pulp, and furniture wood. Rainforests, however, are currently being cut down or converted to agriculture at a rate of almost 1% per year. In some cases, rainforests are recovering, but the soils are often nutrient-poor, hindering regrowth.

DESERT   The desert biome is concentrated in two belts, centered around 30°N and 30°S latitude (where warm, dry air sinks under

Temperate Grassland

The vast expanse of the Sand Hill grasslands at Valentine National Wildlife Refuge, Nebraska, USA.

Equator

The blue area between the two curves represents subfreezing average monthly temperatures.

Denison, Nebraska, USA
41°N
Average annual temperature 9.1°C
Total annual precipitation 727 mm

Temperature (°C)

Precipitation (mm)

J F M A M J J A S O N D
Month

Data from NOAA GHCN-Monthly, version 2; T. C. Peterson and R. S. Vose. 1997. *Bull Am Meteorol Soc* 78: 2837–2849

A Przewalski's horse (*Equus ferus przewalskii*), a rare and endangered subspecies of the wild horse, is native to the grassland steppe of Mongolia.

The wild black-footed ferret (*Mustela nigripes*) was reintroduced back into its native habitat at Grasslands National Park, Saskatchewan, Canada.

high atmospheric pressure; see Figures 52.4 and 52.5). The driest of these regions, where rains rarely fall, are far from the oceans, as in the center of Australia and the middle of the Sahara in Africa.

Desert plants have several structural and physiological adaptations that help them conserve water, as described in Key Concept 37.1. Small desert animals are inactive during the hottest part of the day, remaining in underground burrows. Desert mammals have physiological adaptations for conserving water, including a reduced number of sweat glands and kidneys that produce highly concentrated urine. Many desert animals require no water beyond what they can extract from the carbohydrates in their food.

Humans have used deserts for livestock grazing and agriculture for centuries. Deserts can be irrigated from deep wells or distant mountains, but such efforts typically fail as a result of salinization, the buildup of salts from the evaporation of irrigation water.

TEMPERATE GRASSLAND   Temperate grasslands are found in many parts of the world, all of which are relatively dry for much of the year. Most grasslands, such as the pampas of Argentina, the veldt of South Africa, and the Great Plains of North America, have hot summers and relatively cold winters. In some grasslands, most of the precipitation falls in winter (as in California grasslands); in others, the majority falls in summer (as in the Great Plains and the Russian steppe).

Grassland vegetation is structurally simple but rich in species of perennial grasses and forbs (herbaceous plants). Grassland plants support herds of large grazing mammals and are adapted to grazing and to fire. They store much of their energy underground and resprout quickly after being burned or grazed. There are comparatively few trees in temperate grasslands because trees cannot survive the periodic fires or the dry conditions.

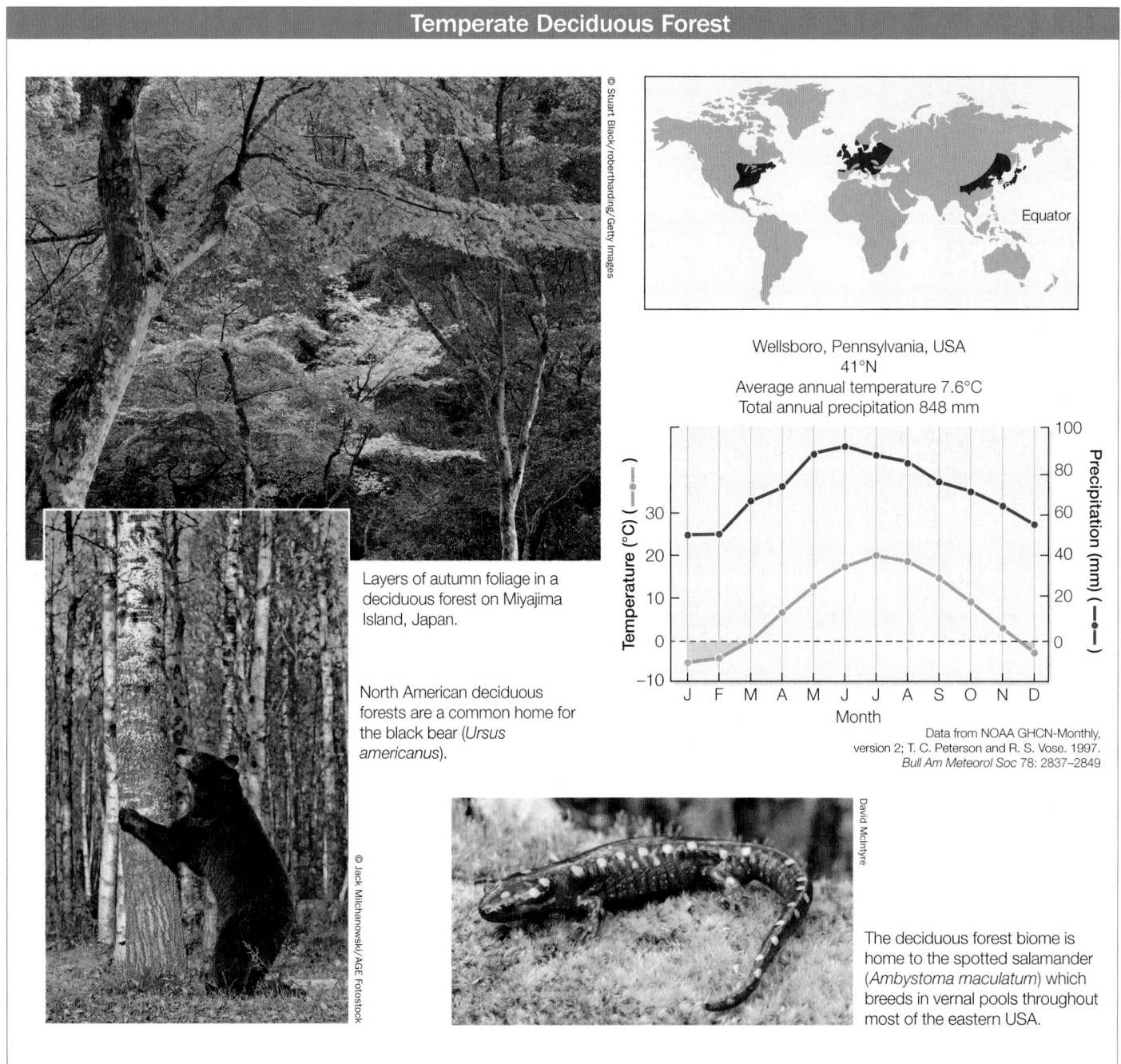

Temperate Deciduous Forest

Layers of autumn foliage in a deciduous forest on Miyajima Island, Japan.

North American deciduous forests are a common home for the black bear (*Ursus americanus*).

Wellsboro, Pennsylvania, USA
41°N
Average annual temperature 7.6°C
Total annual precipitation 848 mm

Data from NOAA GHCN-Monthly, version 2; T. C. Peterson and R. S. Vose. 1997. *Bull Am Meteorol Soc* 78: 2837–2849

The deciduous forest biome is home to the spotted salamander (*Ambystoma maculatum*) which breeds in vernal pools throughout most of the eastern USA.

The topsoil of grasslands is usually rich and deep, and thus exceptionally well suited to growing crops such as corn and wheat. As a consequence, most of the world's temperate grasslands have been turned over to agriculture and no longer exist in their natural state.

TEMPERATE DECIDUOUS FOREST The temperate deciduous forest biome is found in eastern North America, eastern Asia, and Europe. Temperatures in these regions fluctuate dramatically between summer and winter, although precipitation is fairly evenly distributed throughout the year. The deciduous trees that dominate these forests lose their leaves during the cold winters and produce new leaves during the warm, moist summers.

Temperate deciduous forests have many more species than boreal forest ecosystems. Those with the highest species richness occur in the southern Appalachian Mountains of the United States and eastern China and Japan—areas that were not covered by glaciers during the Pleistocene. Many plant genera are shared among the three geographically separate regions where this biome is found.

Although many animals are permanent residents of deciduous forests, some (including many birds) migrate to find food resources and escape the winter cold. Others that remain through the winter hibernate (see Key Concept 38.5), often in underground burrows. Many insects pass the winter in a state of diapause (suspended

Boreal Forest and Temperate Evergreen Forest

Temperate evergreen forests are found along the coasts.

Equator

© All Canada Photos/Alamy Stock Photo

A boreal forest scene in Gros Morne National Park, Newfoundland, Canada.

The boreal forests of Alaska are home to moose (*Alces americanus*), the largest North American terrestrial herbivore.

© Shin Yoshino/Minden Pictures

Fort Simpson, Northwest Territories, Canada
61°N
Average annual temperature −4.6°C
Total annual precipitation 333 mm

Data from NOAA GHCN-Monthly, version 2; T. C. Peterson and R. S. Vose, 1997. *Bull Am Meteorol Soc* 78: 2837–2849

© Javier Fernández Sánchez/Getty Images

A Great Gray Owl (*Strix nebulosa*) is camouflaged against a boreal forest tree in Finland.

development), the onset of which is triggered by the decreasing hours of daylight—a reliable predictor of winter.

BOREAL FOREST AND TEMPERATE EVERGREEN FOREST

The boreal forest biome (also known as taiga) occurs just above 50°N but below Arctic tundra, and at elevations below alpine tundra on temperate-zone mountains. Winters in the boreal forest are long and very cold; summers are short, although often relatively warm. The boreal forests of the Northern Hemisphere are dominated by coniferous trees such as spruces and firs. The short summers favor evergreen leaves, which are ready to photosynthesize as soon as temperatures warm. In winter, downward-drooping limbs allow the trees to shed snow easily.

The dominant mammals of the boreal forest, such as moose and hares, eat leaves, whereas the seeds in conifer cones support a variety of rodents, birds, and insects. Many small mammals hibernate in winter, but voles, lemmings, and mice remain active under the snowpack, serving as food for predators such as foxes and owls.

The temperate evergreen forest biome occurs along the coasts of continents in both hemispheres at middle to high latitudes, where winters are mild and wet and summers are cool and dry. In the Northern Hemisphere, the dominant trees in temperate evergreen forests are conifers, some of which are the world's most massive tree species (including the giant sequoia and coast redwood). In the Southern Hemisphere, the dominant trees are southern beeches (*Nothofagus*), some of which are evergreen.

Tundra

Arctic tundra is found at high latitudes.

Equator

The muskox (*Ovibos moschatus*) was introduced to the tundra biome of Dovrefjell National Park, Norway, in 1932.

© Peter van der Veen/NIS/Minden Pictures

A brilliant autumn tundra scene at Thorofare Pass in Denali National Park and Preserve, Alaska, USA.

© imageBROKER/Alamy Stock Photo

The Arctic fox (*Vulpes lagopus*) has a white coat that serves as camouflage in the winter.

© David W. Hamilton/Getty Images

Olenek, Russia
73°N
Average annual temperature −14.3°C
Total annual precipitation 184 mm

Data from NOAA GHCN-Monthly, version 2; T. C. Peterson and R. S. Vose, 1997. *Bull Am Meteorol Soc* 78: 2837–2849

TUNDRA   The tundra biome is found at high latitudes (above 65°) characterized by low temperatures and a short growing season. This biome is underlain by permafrost—soil permeated with permanently frozen water. The top few centimeters of the soil thaw during the short summers, when the Sun may be above the horizon 24 hours a day. Thus even though there is little precipitation near the poles, the soil in lowland Arctic tundra is wet because water cannot drain through the permafrost. As a result, trees cannot grow in the tundra biome because their roots cannot penetrate the permafrost. Instead, the tundra biome is characterized by sedges, forbs, grasses, and low-growing shrubs such as heaths, willows, and birches. Lichens and mosses are also important vegetation.

Tundra plants have several structural and physiological adaptations that help them conserve heat, as described in Key Concept 37.1. Most animals are either summer migrants or are dormant for much of the year. Resident birds and mammals, such as the Willow Ptarmigan (*Lagopus lagopus*) and Arctic fox (*Vulpes lagopus*), have thick feathers or fur that may change color with the seasons, from brown in summer to white in winter.

Biogeographic regions reflect evolutionary isolation

Climate interacts with local abiotic features to influence where and how organisms live, but these are not the only factors determining where organisms are found. Evolutionary history—where and when species originated and diverged—is key to determining their biogeography.

Until European naturalists traveled the globe in the nineteenth century, they had no way of knowing how organisms were distributed in other parts of the world. Alfred Russel Wallace, who along with Charles Darwin advanced the idea that natural selection could account for the evolution of life on Earth (see Key Concept

19.1), was one of those global travelers. Wallace spent seven years in the Malay Archipelago, where he noticed some remarkable patterns in the distributions of species. For example, he described the dramatically different species that inhabited the adjacent islands of Bali and Lombok. He pointed out that the differences could not be explained by the physical environment, because Bali and Lombok are only 24 kilometers apart.

Wallace saw that, based on the distributions of plant and animal species, he could draw a line that divided the Malay Archipelago into two distinct halves. He correctly deduced that the dramatic differences in flora and fauna were related to the depth of the channel separating Bali and Lombok. This channel is so deep that it would have remained full of water, and thus would have been a barrier to the movement of terrestrial animals, even during the glaciations of the Pleistocene, when sea level dropped more than 100 meters and Bali and the islands to the west were connected to the Asian mainland.

With these insights, Wallace established the conceptual foundations of biogeography. In *The Geographical Distribution of Animals*, published in 1876, he detailed the factors known at the time that influence the distributions of animals, including past glaciation, land bridges, deep ocean channels, and mountain ranges. He earned some measure of scientific immortality in that the Malay

discontinuity that first piqued his curiosity is known to this day as Wallace's Line (see Figure 52.14).

The biotas of different parts of the world differ enough to allow us to divide Earth into many continental-scale areas called **biogeographic regions** (Figure 52.14), each containing characteristic assemblages of species. The boundaries of the biogeographic regions in Figure 52.14 were originally proposed by Wallace, and represent assemblages of species that change dramatically, often over short distances. A major process controlling the formation of these biogeographic regions is continental drift. For example, we now know that over the course of the Triassic and Jurassic, the supercontinent Pangaea separated into two great land masses, Laurasia and Gondwana (see Figure 23.14), which subsequently separated into the continents we know today. After the land masses broke up, the descendants of the organisms widely disturbed across Pangaea evolved independently, forming new species and new species assemblages. The legacy of these continental movements can be found in several existing taxonomic groups and in the fossil record. For example, the modern southern beeches—trees of the genus *Nothofagus*—are found in both the Neotropical and the Australasian biogeographic regions. Evidence of fossilized *Nothofagus* pollen from 55 to 34 million years ago has also been found in Australia, New Zealand, western Antarctica, and South

Figure 52.14 Earth's Biogeographic Regions   Wallace identified six major biogeographic regions that are separated by climatic, topographic, or aquatic barriers to dispersal that cause their biotas to differ strikingly from one another. The red arrows on the map show the time (in millions of years) since land masses came together. Black arrows show the time since land masses separated. These areas roughly correspond to Earth's major tectonic plates. (After H. Kreft and W. Jetz. 2010. *J Biogeogr* 37: 2029–2053.)

Q: As land masses separated, would you expect speciation to increase? Explain.

 View in Achieve
Activity 52.3 Major Biogeographic Regions

America, suggesting that beeches originated in Gondwana during the Cretaceous and were geographically separated by the breakup of that land mass 100 million years ago (see Figure 52.14).

> **Connect the Concepts**   Key Concepts 23.2 and 23.3 describe how Earth's land masses have undergone continental drift over the millennia as a result of plate tectonics, shaping major patterns of biogeography.

The evolutionary separation of species can be attributed to two basic processes, vicariance and dispersal. **Vicariance** occurs when a physical barrier prevents dispersal and divides a species into two or more discontinuous populations. Dispersal occurs when the members of a species cross an existing barrier and establish a new population elsewhere.

Given that the processes of vicariance and dispersal both influence distribution patterns, how can biogeographers determine the role of each process when reconstructing the evolutionary history of a particular species? As you saw in Chapter 20, taxonomists have developed powerful molecular methods of reconstructing the phylogenetic relationships among organisms that can be used to understand how organisms came to occupy their present-day distributions. Phylogenetic trees can be used to discover whether the distribution of an ancestral species was influenced by a vicariant event, such as continental drift or a change in sea level, or was simply the result of a dispersal event.

 Media Clip 52.1 Rafting to Madagascar
Life12e.com/mc52.1

Diversity varies with latitude and longitude

About 200 years ago, the German explorer and naturalist Alexander von Humboldt spent 5 years traveling around Latin America. He remarked in the account of his voyages that "the nearer we approach the tropics, the greater the increase in the variety of structure, grace of form, and mixture of colors, as also in perpetual youth and vigour of organic life." Humboldt and other nineteenth-century scientific explorers such as Wallace and Darwin became keenly aware of this pattern as they collected thousands of species in the tropics and compared them with their more meager collections from Europe. As more observations and collections have been made over the last 200 years, the latitudinal gradient in species diversity has been established for a wide variety of taxa, including some groups of birds, mammals, flowering plants, and insects such as swallowtail butterflies (**Figure 52.15A**). Significant variation in species diversity is also seen with longitude, but the number of species depends largely on the longitudes chosen.

There are intriguing exceptions to the classic latitudinal patterns of species diversity just described. Some taxa show a positive relationship between species number and latitude (**Figure 52.15B**). That is, among some taxa—for example, seabirds—species number increases at higher latitudes. This pattern of seabird diversity correlates with marine net primary productivity, which is substantially higher in temperate and polar oceans than in the tropics.

Figure 52.15 Latitudinal Gradients in Diversity   **(A)** Among swallowtail butterflies (Papilionidae), species richness decreases with latitude both north and south of the equator. **(B)** Seabirds, by contrast, show a positive relationship between species diversity and latitude: the number of seabird species increases at higher latitudes. (A after J. M. Scriber. 1973. *Psyche* 80: 355–373; B graph data from P. Harrison 1987. *A Field Guide to Seabirds of the World*. Penguin Random House: London.)

Connect the Concepts   Key Concept 56.2 describes net primary production (NPP) as the amount of biomass incorporated into the tissues of primary producers and as the base of all food chains.

We consider productivity differences along with other explanations of latitudinal gradients in diversity in the next section.

Geographic variation in diversity is explained by multiple factors

Although most ecologists agree that latitudinal gradients in diversity exist, there is much less consensus as to why they exist. Dozens of hypotheses have been proposed to explain these patterns, but they are hard to evaluate—in part because there are multiple and confounding differences in such factors as geographic area, climate, and productivity with latitude. More important, because these factors operate at large spatial scales and over evolutionary time, it is impossible to conduct experiments to isolate the factors and separate correlation from causation.

Here we present three well-known hypotheses that have been advanced to account for latitudinal gradients in diversity. Corroborative evidence can be found for each of these hypotheses, varying with taxon, locality, and scale, which suggests that none of these hypotheses is mutually exclusive. Multiple factors, working at multiple spatial scales, are likely responsible for common biogeographic patterns.

SPECIES DIVERSIFICATION RATE   This hypothesis proposes that in the tropics the rate of speciation is higher and the rate of extinctions is lower, resulting in overall higher species diversity than in temperate or polar regions. Two factors could account for a higher speciation rate in the tropics: a larger geographic area (this is the widest part of the planet, so it encompasses the greatest amount of area) and a warm and stable climate. The rationale is that a larger geographic area with a consistent climate should promote speciation because species will have larger geographic ranges, giving them a greater chance of reproductive isolation (see Key Concept 22.2). In addition, these large and stable areas should reduce extinctions. The net result should be an increase in the number of species in the tropics.

SPECIES DIVERSIFICATION TIME   This hypothesis proposes that the amount of time over which speciation has taken place is greatest in the tropics—in other words, that the tropics have a longer evolutionary history than temperate or polar regions. First championed by Wallace in 1878, this hypothesis proposes that tropical regions, because they are more climatically stable over time, have more time to diversify than temperate or polar regions, where severe climate conditions (such as ice ages) could have decreased speciation and increased extinction. Thus even if the rates of speciation and extinction are the same worldwide, the tropics should have accumulated more species over time simply because of the lack of dramatic changes in climate.

PRODUCTIVITY   This hypothesis proposes that species diversification is promoted by higher productivity, which allows species more resources and thus decreased risk of species extinction due to

competition. The productivity hypothesis might explain the positive relationship between seabird diversity and increasing latitude, given that ocean productivity is generally higher at temperate and polar latitudes. As you will see in Chapter 55, the role of productivity can more easily be explored at smaller spatial scales, where experiments can give us a better idea of its role in determining species diversity.

KEY CONCEPT
52.4 Recap and Assess

Biogeographic patterns are interconnected across a hierarchy of scales ranging from global to local. Three strong biogeographic patterns can be seen: (1) biomes, or groupings of ecologically similar organisms, are shaped by the environment, (2) diversity varies from continent to continent, forming biogeographic regions, and (3) diversity varies with latitude.

1. What are the differences and similarities between the tropical rainforest biome and the temperate evergreen forest biome?

2. Refer to Figure 52.14. Why did Wallace's Line help explain what controls the formation of biogeographic regions?

3. Over Earth's history, ice sheets extended into temperate latitudes. Does this fact better support the species diversification rate or the species diversification time hypothesis proposed to explain latitudinal variation in diversity? Explain.

As you have seen, an important aspect of biogeography is the relationship between diversity and geographic area. We have considered this relationship at global scales. We turn now to smaller regional scales, to understand in more detail the importance of geographic area to patterns of biogeography.

KEY CONCEPT
52.5 Geographic Area and Humans Affect Regional Species Diversity

Learning Objectives

52.5.1   Discuss the species–area relationship and use the theory of island biogeography to explain the pattern.

52.5.2   Describe how humans have affected biogeographic patterns.

52.5.3   Describe specific ways in which habitat fragmentation negatively affects species diversity.

Biogeographers have repeatedly documented what is termed the **species–area relationship**, in which species diversity increases with increasing area. The relationship has most often been measured for islands or islandlike habitats—any isolated area surrounded by a "sea" of dissimilar habitat. In addition to showing a pattern of increasing species diversity with increasing area, islands also show a pattern of decreasing species number with distance from the source of those species, or the species pool (**Figure 52.16**). How do island area and distance act together to produce species–area relationships?

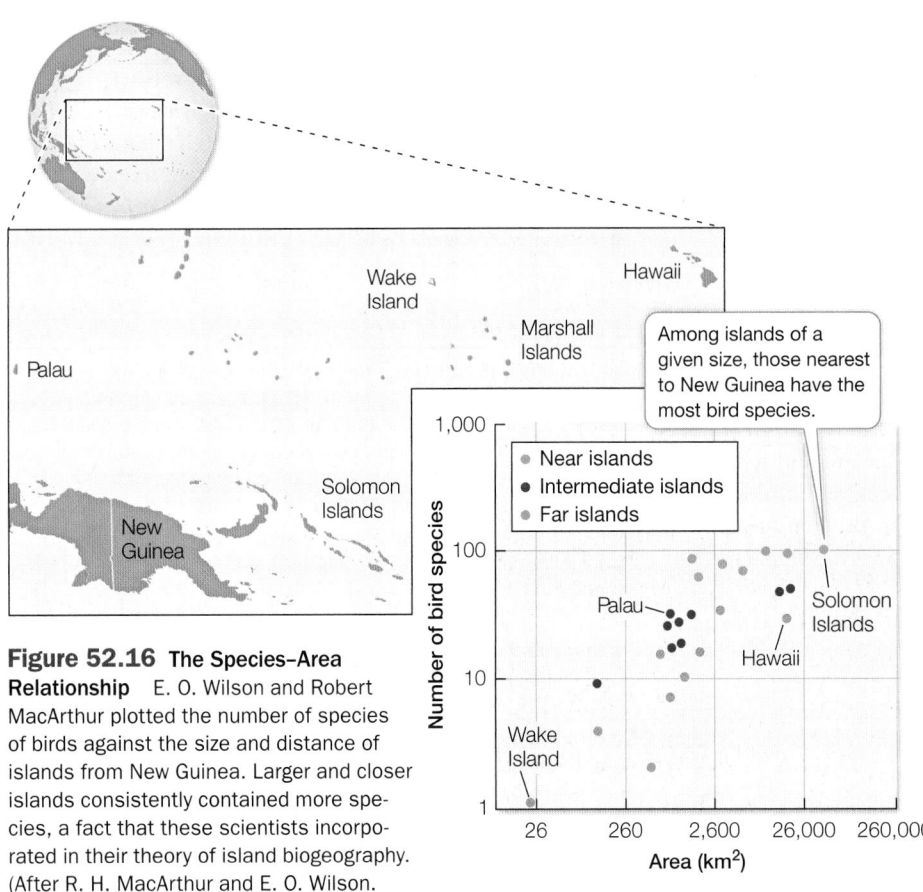

Figure 52.16 The Species–Area Relationship   E. O. Wilson and Robert MacArthur plotted the number of species of birds against the size and distance of islands from New Guinea. Larger and closer islands consistently contained more species, a fact that these scientists incorporated in their theory of island biogeography. (After R. H. MacArthur and E. O. Wilson. 1963. *Evolution* 17: 373–387.)

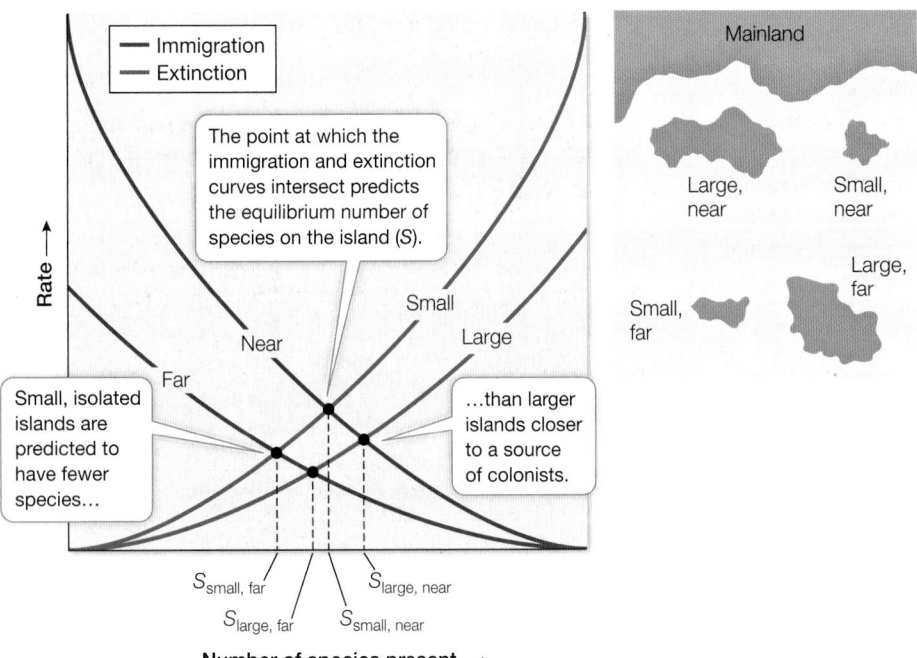

Figure 52.17 The Equilibrium Theory of Island Biogeography   MacArthur and Wilson's theory emphasized the balance between species immigration rates and species extinction rates for islands of different sizes and at different distances from a source of colonizing species. (After R. H. MacArthur and E. O. Wilson. 1963. *Evolution* 17: 373–387.)

View in Achieve
Simulation 52.1 Biogeography

The biologist Edward O. Wilson was struck by the species–area relationship from his research on ant biogeography and was looking for explanations. He teamed up with Robert MacArthur, a gifted mathematical ecologist, to develop the **theory of island biogeography** to explain this pattern. They based their theory on just two processes: the immigration of new species to an island and the extinction of species already present on that island (**Figure 52.17**). The premise of island biogeography is that the number of species on an island represents a balance between the rate at which species immigrate to and colonize the island and the rate at which resident species become locally extinct.

The rate of immigration is determined in part by the number of species in the regional species pool. In the case of oceanic islands, the species pool comprises all the species on the nearest mainland location. Not all species that reach the island will persist there, however. The more species there are on an island, the greater the likelihood that some will go extinct, either due to chance or the inability to coexist with other species on the island. The number of species that will be sustained on any particular island is determined by the balance of the immigration rate and the extinction rate for that island. Even though species will come and go over time (i.e., immigrate and become extinct), that turnover will always result in some equilibrium number of species, assuming a constant species pool and natural extinction events.

The actual number of species on an island will ultimately depend on two factors:

1. *The size (area) of the island.* The smaller the island, the fewer resources it provides, the greater the potential for competition, and the higher the extinction rate will be (see Figure 52.17). Larger islands provide more resources and can sustain larger populations (which tend to have lower extinction rates than small populations).

2. *Distance of the island from the species pool.* The farther the island is from the source of immigrants, the lower the immigration rate—the rate at which new species arrive—will be (see Figure 52.17).

Between 1966 and 1969, Wilson and his student Daniel Simberloff conducted an experiment to test the theory of island biogeography, using arthropods living on mangrove islands in the Florida Keys. You can view this experiment and the results online.

 View in Achieve
Animation 52.3 **Island Biogeography in the Florida Keys**

Humans exert a powerful influence on biogeographic patterns

The theory of island biogeography has provided surprising insight into the role human's play in regional biogeographic patterns. As you saw in Key Concepts 52.3 and 52.4, Earth's biomes are becoming smaller and more fragmented by local- and regional-scale forces such as agriculture, deforestation, and urbanization. They are being transformed into islandlike habitats—isolated patches of suitable habitat such as parks or forest fragments, surrounded by extensive areas of unsuitable habitat similar to the cattle pastures of Amazonia described at the opening of this chapter.

The fragmentation of the Amazon rainforest led Thomas Lovejoy and his colleagues to initiate, in 1979, one of the largest and longest-running ecological experiments ever conducted to investigate the effects of tropical forest fragmentation on species diversity (**Investigating Life: The Largest Experiment on Earth**). The Biological Dynamics of Forest Fragments Project (BDFFP) took

---

▶Investigating**LIFE**   The Largest Experiment on Earth

Experiment

Original Paper: G. Ferraz et al. 2003. Rates of species loss from Amazonian forest fragments. *Proc Natl Acad Sci USA* 100: 14069–14073. © 2003 National Academy of Sciences U.S.A.

Thomas Lovejoy and his colleagues asked what was the minimum area needed to maintain species diversity in the rainforest fragments created by logging near Manaus, Brazil. They conducted an experiment, starting in 1979, that took advantage of an existing Brazilian law that required landowners who cut rainforest to leave half of it untouched. In 2003, Ferraz and colleagues reported on one particular aspect of the experiment: the number of forest understory birds living in different-sized forest fragments surrounded by deforested land.

HYPOTHESIS▶ The number of understory bird species will decline faster after the isolation of the fragment, and in smaller rainforest fragments compared with larger rainforest fragments.

METHOD▶

1. Starting in 1979, fragments of three sizes (1, 10, and 100 ha) were established 80 km north of Manaus. The fragments were separated from continuous forest by at least 100 meters of cleared land.

2. Birds were captured in mist nests placed in the fragments prior to deforestation and then for 12 years after fragment establishment. The mist nets were placed in roughly the same locations throughout the study.

3. Each newly captured bird was recorded for species, given an individually numbered band, and released back into the rainforest from which it was caught.

4. The data gathered were used in species-loss curves for each fragment, and a scaling factor (i.e., a number that scales, or multiplies, by some quantity) was estimated to determine the time it takes to lose half of the bird species (t_{50}) in fragments of different sizes.

 View in Achieve
Animation 52.4 **Edge Effects**

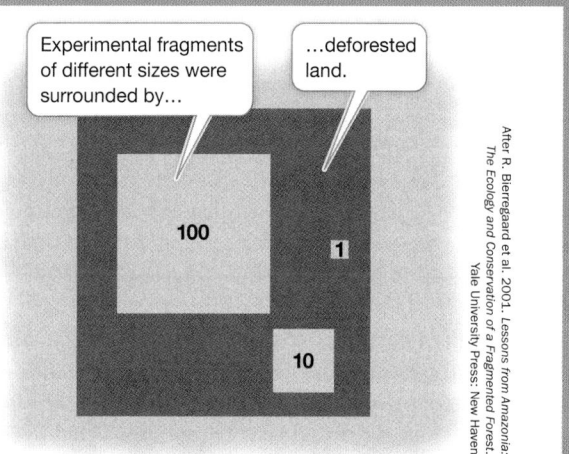

After R. Bierregaard et al. 2001. Lessons from Amazonia: The Ecology and Conservation of a Fragmented Forest. Yale University Press: New Haven

RESULTS▶ The average initial number of species was 83 for the 1-ha fragment, 92 for the 10-ha fragment, and 113 for the 100-ha fragment. Despite finding a total of 164 understory bird species in the fragments over the course of 13 years, there was a significant drop in the number of species over time. The t_{50} was shortest in the 1-ha fragments and longest in the 100-ha fragments. Fragments of 100 ha were predicted to lose half of their species in 12 years.

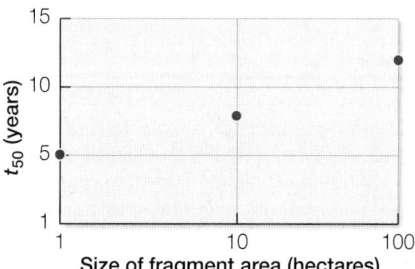

CONCLUSION▶ The number of understory bird species declined after the fragmentation of tropical rainforest habitat by deforestation. Smaller rainforest fragments lost species faster than larger forest fragments. Even the largest fragments were predicted to lose half of their bird species.

Investigating**LIFE** Work with the Data **follows on the next page.**

Work with the Data

The data in the graph shown in the experiment can be used to calculate a scaling factor for the time it takes to lose half of the bird species within a fragment. The scaling factor shows that to increase the t_{50} (i.e., the time it takes fragments to lose half their species) by 10-fold, fragment area would need to increase 1,000-fold. Here you will use this scaling factor and other data provided in the graph to determine the area needed for the conservation of understory birds in the Amazon forests outside Manaus, Brazil.

QUESTIONS▶

1. Graph the initial numbers of bird species by the size of the fragment area. Do these fragments follow the species–area relationship?

2. Suppose you are consulting for the Brazilian government on the conservation of rainforests near Manaus. Assuming that the t_{50} for 1 ha is 5 years, what is the minimum size that a rainforest fragment in the Manaus area needs to be to ensure that half of the bird species remain 50 years after the deforestation event that isolated them? How about a century after deforestation?

3. Suppose it takes 100 years for rainforests to fully recover after a deforestation event in the Manaus region. Given that the average size of a rainforest fragment in this area is no bigger than 1,000 ha, will the number of species decline by half before the recovery of rainforest occurs around the largest fragments?

Go to **Achieve** for a companion Data in Depth exercise.

---

advantage of an existing Brazilian law that required landowners who cut rainforest to leave half of it untouched. Lovejoy was able to survey the species diversity in different-sized fragments (either 1, 10, or 100 hectares [ha] in size surrounded by deforested land). Among several results, his group found that, after more than 30 years of isolation, even the largest deforested fragments surveyed (100 ha) had lost half of their bird species diversity. The researchers were also surprised by two additional findings. First, even minimal distances of 80 meters between fragments resulted in strong avoidance of the clearings, and thus isolation, by birds, insects, and tree-dwelling mammals that lived in the fragments. Second, the fragmentation exposed species within a fragment to a variety of potential hazards, including extreme heat, fires, hunting, predators, diseases, and invasive species. These so-called **edge effects** not only reduce the immigration rate from one fragment to another, thus contributing to a smaller species pool, but they effectively reduce the size of the fragment, thus increasing the extinction rate, by making the edge of the fragment much less hospitable habitat.

KEY CONCEPT

52.5 Recap and Assess

Species–area relationships, in which species diversity increases with increasing area, have been shown for islands and islandlike habitats. Smaller islands have higher extinction rates and lower immigration rates compared with larger islands. Earth's biomes are becoming smaller and more fragmented by human activities, leading to lower diversity in the remaining habitats.

1. Why do island size and distance from a species pool affect island biogeography?

2. Why is habitat fragmentation by human activities threatening species diversity? Besides ceasing the activity altogether, what can be done to reduce this threat?

▶Investigating LIFE

 How do geographic area and isolation affect the biogeography of life on Earth?

At the opening of the chapter, we asked how geographic area and isolation might affect the biogeography of life on Earth. You have seen that this question is highly relevant at different spatial scales—from whole continents to small islands—and also over different time scales—from millions of years to months. Because the spatial and temporal scales at which biogeographic patterns manifest themselves are so wide and interconnected, it can be hard to test theories of biogeography with experiments that are large and long enough to be meaningful. The Biological Dynamics of Forest Fragments Project (BDFFP), an experiment conducted in the most species-rich region of the world, and at arguably the largest scale ever attempted, offers support for theories proposed nearly 200 years ago by explorers such as Humboldt, Wallace, and Darwin, who hypothesized that the distribution of species on Earth is highly influenced by the geographic area and isolation those species have experienced. The question remains, in the case of the Amazon Basin, whether species will ultimately adapt to the changing biogeographic landscape or become a casualty of an extinction event that would be unrivaled in human history.

Future directions

One of the major findings of the BDFFP is the importance of connectivity in maintaining species diversity. Management and permitting of forest clearing are focusing on creative ways to connect forest fragments by taking advantage of existing landscape features to increase connectivity of disturbed habitat. For example, in Amazonia strong laws exist to prohibit clearing forest along rivers and steep slopes, providing strips of land that can serve to connect fragments around newly cleared land.

You should be able to relate each summary to the adjacent figures. If you go to this visual summary in **Achieve**, you can follow links to figures, animations, activities, and simulations that will help you consolidate the material.

KEY CONCEPT 52.1

Ecology Is the Study of the Interrelationships among Organisms and the Environment

- **Ecology** differs from **environmentalism**, which involves the use of ecological knowledge to inform our stewardship of natural resources.

- Ecologists have a use-inspired focus to their research, motivated by a desire to address Earth's ecological problems.

- Ecology is studied at multiple levels of organization, ranging from individuals to the **biosphere**.

Questions

1. Define the difference between ecology and environmentalism.

2. What is meant by "use-inspired" ecological research?

3. How are individuals connected to communities?

Figure 52.1

Courtesy of Sally Hacker

Courtesy of Sally Hacker

© Konrad Wothe/Minden Pictures/Getty Images

KEY CONCEPT 52.2

Global Climate Is a Fundamental Component of the Physical Environment

Go to Animation 52.1

- Climate and weather both refer to atmospheric conditions, but **climate** represents conditions over years to millennia whereas **weather** represents conditions over days to weeks.

- Solar radiation drives global climate. Of the solar radiation that hits Earth, some is reflected back to space (30%) and the rest is absorbed by the **atmosphere** (20%) or by Earth's surface (50%). **Greenhouse gases** trap heat radiating back out toward space.

- Latitudinal differences in solar energy input drive patterns of atmospheric circulation.

- The interaction of Earth's rotation and north–south air mass movements generate **prevailing winds**, which in turn drive ocean currents.

- The seasons are a consequence of Earth's tilt and orbit around the Sun.

Questions

1. Does a week of extreme cold weather tell us that Earth's climate is not warming?

2. Why are the tropics warm and wet and the poles cold and dry?

3. What direction do ocean currents flow as a result of trade winds?

Figure 52.5

Figure 52.6

KEY CONCEPT
52.3 Topography, Vegetation, and Humans Modify the Physical Environment

Go to **Animation 52.2**

- Earth's land **topography** creates **rain shadows** and **temperature inversions**, producing variation in temperature and precipitation.

- Ocean-floor topography affects water depth, which affects light penetration and water temperature, pressure, and movement, creating aquatic zones and ocean **upwelling**.

- Vegetation, especially forests, affects climate through the process of **evapotranspiration**.

- Humans have transformed their environment, including urban climate.

Figure 52.9

Questions

1. How does a rain shadow affect climate on either side of a mountain range?

2. How do winds and ocean-floor topography create ocean upwelling?

3. Why would planting more trees in an urban area help with urban climate warming?

KEY CONCEPT
52.4 Biogeography Is the Study of How Organisms Are Distributed on Earth

Go to **Activities 52.1–52.3**

- Patterns of **biogeography** are interconnected across a hierarchy of scales, ranging from global to regional to landscape to local.

- **Terrestrial biomes** are groupings of ecologically similar dominant plants shaped by patterns of temperature and precipitation.

- Earth's diversity varies from continent to continent, forming **biogeographic regions** and reflecting evolutionary isolation as a consequence of Earth's geological history.

- Earth's diversity varies with latitude. Hypotheses explaining this variation rely on multiple factors, including geographic area, time, climate, and productivity.

Figure 52.12

Questions

1. How does the regional scale determine local community species diversity and composition?

2. What criteria are used to determine Earth's terrestrial biomes?

3. Earth's diversity varies by continent and by latitude. How do evolutionary processes contribute to these patterns?

Figure 52.14

KEY CONCEPT
52.5

Geographic Area and Humans Affect Regional Species Diversity

Go to **Animations 52.3** and **52.4**
and **Simulation 52.1**

- **Species–area relationships**, in which species diversity increases with area, have been shown for islands and area fragments.

- The **theory of island biogeography** states that the number of species on an island is a balance between immigration and extinction rates, which vary by island size and distance from the species pool.

- As humans fragment Earth's biomes through agriculture, deforestation, and urbanization, remaining habitats become more isolated, or islandlike.

Questions

1. Describe why species diversity increases with increasing island or fragment area.

2. Using Figure 52.17, explain why the small and far islands have lower species numbers than the large and near islands.

Figure 52.17

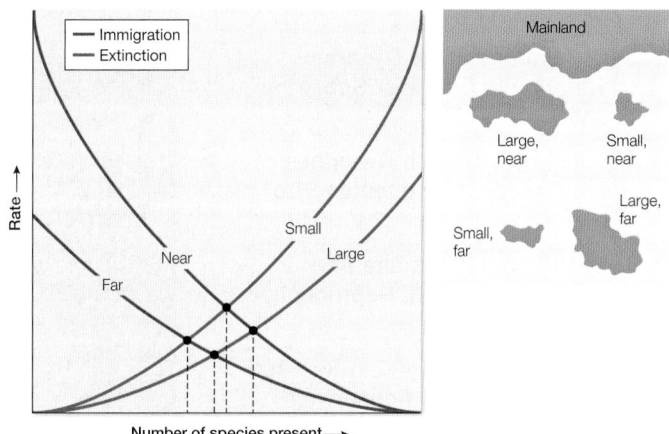

Go to **Achieve** for the eBook, **LearningCurve**, animations, activities, simulations, and additional resources and assignments.

53 Populations

KEY CONCEPTS

53.1 Populations Show Dynamic Variation in Size over Space and Time

53.2 Population Growth Describes the Change in Population Size over Time

53.3 Life History Is the Lifetime Pattern of Growth, Reproduction, and Survival

53.4 Population Biology Can Be Used in Managing and Conserving Populations

The human population crossed the 7.7 billion mark in 2019.

© Michael Warren/Getty Images

▶Investigating LIFE

Earth's Human Carrying Capacity

In 1798 Thomas Robert Malthus, in his *Essay on the Principle of Population*, pointed out that the human population was growing exponentially but its food supply was not, and argued that at some point, famine and death would be the ultimate fate of the human race. Malthus could not have anticipated the technological innovations over the next 200 years that would greatly enhance our food production and health care. Today, however, the size of the human population is once again a serious concern as we confront the effects of our contributions to climate change, pollution, habitat destruction, and species extinctions.

For thousands of years, Earth's capacity to support human populations was low because of the relative inefficiency with which we could obtain food and water. The development of social systems and communication, the domestication of plants and animals, ever-increasing crop and livestock yields due to ongoing technological advances, and our increasing proficiency at managing diseases all contributed to unprecedented growth of the human population. It took more than 200,000 years for the human population to reach 1 billion people, which happened in the early nineteenth century. Today, a mere 200 years later, the planet is home to roughly 7.7 billion human beings.

Many believe that human populations will (if they have not already) reach some maximum size (known as the population's carrying capacity) above which continued population growth is unsustainable. Food production is critical to human population growth and currently uses large amounts of land, water, fertilizers, and energy. Housing and quality health care require advances in infrastructure and drug production, and these too are highly energy-intensive. In addition, if Earth's ecosystems continue to be degraded by climate change, human populations may experience a general breakdown of Earth's life support systems.

Luckily, population growth rate has slowed from its high after World War II, but with a base of 7.7 billion, even minimal population growth rate means millions more individuals each year. As you will see later in the chapter, population biologists have used census data and standard population growth models to predict human population sizes into the future.

 What is the human population growth projected to be in the next century, and how will that affect population size? (Find the answer on page 1214.)

 Media Clip 53.1 World Population Growth
Life12e.com/mc53.1

KEY CONCEPT
53.1   Populations Show Dynamic Variation in Size over Space and Time

Learning Objectives

53.1.1 Describe how species are divided into populations, metapopulations, and geographic ranges.

53.1.2 Describe how populations vary in space and time and compare the three main factors that control population dynamics.

53.1.3 List and describe major approaches that ecologists use to estimate population size and extent.

Species, whether they are humans, yeast, or giant redwood trees, are divided into groups of individuals, or populations. A **population** is a group of individuals of the same species within a given area that have the potential to interbreed and interact with one another. As you might expect, populations vary in their **population size**—the numbers of individuals within a population. Well before ecology became a distinct biological discipline, humans were interested in **population dynamics**, the patterns and processes of population change over space and time. Growing crops, raising livestock, and controlling pests all involve paying attention to population dynamics. To this day, game wardens, park managers, and conservation biologists aim to maintain stable populations of fishes, wildlife, and threatened or endangered species in the face of change. Here we consider population dynamics in more detail.

Part of the dynamism that populations show is a consequence of their distribution across the landscape (**Figure 53.1A**). For example, distribution maps of the herbaceous perennial *Clematis fremontii* show that it is patchily distributed across Missouri, Kansas, and Nebraska. Here populations are restricted to dry, rocky meadows formed on particular limestone outcrops within the region. Populations, such as those of *Clematis*, rarely occur in isolation from one another and are usually connected through dispersal. **Dispersal** is simply the movement of individuals into (**immigration**) or out of (**emigration**) an existing population. A group of geographically isolated populations linked together by dispersal is known as a **metapopulation**. For example, a cluster of meadows might be considered a metapopulation if *Clematis* seeds from one meadow had the potential to disperse to another meadow. At larger spatial scales, the entire **geographic range**, or distribution, of a species might consist of one or multiple metapopulations, depending on the extent of the area occupied by a species.

Species differ greatly in their geographic ranges—they can be as wide-ranging as the acorn barnacle *Semibalanus balanoides*, which extends along both North American coasts and the European Atlantic coast. However, even though dispersal links populations, most species have fairly restrictive geographic ranges, such as we see for *Clematis*. We call such species **endemic** because they occur in one particular location and nowhere else on Earth. Thus *Clematis* can be said to be endemic to the central United States because its geographic range is restricted to that region.

Within a population, the spatial arrangement of individuals may vary in what are known as **dispersion patterns**. Ecologists recognize three basic dispersion patterns: (1) **regular** (or **uniform**) **dispersion**, characterized by evenly spaced individuals, (2) **random dispersion**, in which individuals are randomly spaced, and (3) **clumped dispersion**, in which individuals tend to be clustered in groups (**Figure 53.1B**). As we will consider later in this key concept, multiple processes such as resource availability, species interactions, and dispersal can shape the dispersion patterns we see in nature.

(A) Spatial scales of populations

Geographic range

Nebraska

Kansas

Missouri

A group of populations (metapopulation)

15 kilometers

A population

100 meters

(B) Dispersion patterns of populations

Regular   Random   Clumped

© Zoonar/P Himmelhuber/AGE Fotostock

Clematis fremontii

Figure 53.1 Many Populations Have Patchy Distributions
The abundance of the herbaceous perennial *Clematis fremontii* is patchy over different spatial scales. **(A)** Populations occur within limestone meadows. A group of populations makes up a metapopulation, and multiple metapopulations make up the geographic range (in this case, Missouri, Kansas, and Nebraska). **(B)** Individuals within a population show one of three different dispersion patterns. (A after R. Erickson 1945. *Ann MO Bot Gard* 32: 413–460.)

Populations can vary over time as well. For example, some populations may show "boom and bust" cycles, such as we see for bacteria, yeast, and phytoplankton, in which the population size can vary over just a few minutes to days. Species that show wide fluctuations in population size tend to have reproductive strategies that allow them to respond rapidly to changing resources. They may also have predators that are able to take advantage of these outbursts in growth. For example, aphids engage in parthenogenetic reproduction—a type of asexual reproduction resulting in genetically identical individuals—which allows them to become very abundant very quickly. If overcrowding occurs and food resources become limiting, populations can crash, leaving behind a few individuals that may ultimately serve to increase the population size through rapid clonal reproduction (**Figure 53.2**). Predatory insects such as the insidious flower bug can dampen these large swings in aphid population size, resulting in decreased resource limitation. Thus extrinsic factors such as predation can provide checks on populations, thereby limiting outbreaks.

Population dynamics are controlled by the physical environment, biological interactions, and dispersal

Even though we know that populations fluctuate in space and time, determining the factors responsible for this variation can be challenging. Ecologists recognize three main factors that affect population dynamics and that act simultaneously to set limits for populations and species: the physical environment, biological interactions, and dispersal.

As you saw in Chapter 52, the distribution and abundance of species are highly dependent on the physical environment; factors such as climate, topography, and even human infrastructure set physiological limits for species. Thus it makes sense that the physical features of the environment strongly limit a population's geographic extent and size through time. You saw this for *Clematis*, whose populations are restricted to dry, rocky limestone soils, resulting in a patchy distribution pattern (see Figure 53.1).

Likewise, many types of biological interactions affect population dynamics. Interbreeding among individuals within populations affects their size and extent—in fact, many populations can be defined by the genetic similarity of the individuals within a given area (see Key Concept 19.4). For example, populations of wild endangered salmon, which look nearly identical to hatchery-raised salmon, can be assessed for population size using genetic techniques that allow differentiation among populations. In addition, because individuals within populations share similar resources, **intraspecific competition** (competition for shared resources by individuals of the same species) can be critical in controlling population size, as you will see in Key Concept 53.2. **Interspecific interactions** (interactions among individuals of different species) are another important factor in controlling population dynamics.

> **Connect the Concepts** Chapter 54 describes how interspecific interactions such as competition, predation, and positive interactions (i.e., mutualisms and commensalisms) often set the upper limits on the number of individuals within populations.

Finally, dispersal can be a critical factor controlling population dynamics. Dispersal comes in many forms. It can be active when movement is controlled by the individual, such as you might see with elephants; passive when movement is controlled by the physical environment, as in corals and dandelions; or facilitated by active agents, such as birds or bats dispersing seed-laden fruits (**Figure 53.3**). Dispersal is a mechanism that can reduce competition for resources, either with a parent or another individual within the population. In addition, dispersal allows individuals to escape a harsh physical environment. Thus dispersal serves as a mechanism to reduce the probability of local extinctions of populations by spreading the risk among multiple populations that are geographically separated (see Key Concept 53.4).

A specific type of dispersal is migration. **Migration** typically occurs in response to seasonal variation in resources, involves round-trip movement, and includes the whole population. For example, North Pacific populations of the humpback whale migrate more than 4,800 kilometers between their winter breeding grounds in the south (Mexico, Hawaii, and Japan) and their summer feeding grounds in the north (Northeast Pacific coast and Gulf of Alaska) (**Figure 53.4**). Scientists determine whale migration patterns and population numbers by taking photographs and collecting genetic material to follow and compare individuals in the feeding and breeding grounds. A 2006 survey of North Pacific humpback whales determined that close to 20,000 individuals in five separate populations make the migration every year. Remarkably, there were only 1,400 North Pacific humpback whales in 1966, when commercial whaling of these populations was banned.

© Nigel Cattlin / Alamy Stock Photo

Figure 53.2 Population Fluctuations of Aphids and Their Predators A population of soybean aphids (*Aphis glycines*) fluctuates more when its insect predator, the insidious flower bug (*Orius insidiosus*), is excluded than when it is present. Without the predator, soybean aphids cost soybean growers hundreds of millions of dollars in damage per year. (Graph after N. Desneux et al. 2006. *Environ Entomol* 35: 1342–1349.)

(A)

(B)

(C)

(D)

Figure 53.3 Different **Dispersal Mechanisms of Organisms** **(A)** Elephants actively disperse, **(B, C)** corals and dandelions disperse passively, and **(D)** seeds within fruits are typically dispersed by an active agent, in this case a Toco Toucan (*Ramphastos toco*).

As you can see, whale biologists use various techniques to estimate the population sizes of humpback whales. Let's consider in more detail the variety of approaches ecologists use to measure population size.

Figure 53.4 **Migration of North Pacific Humpback Whales** North Pacific populations of the humpback whale (*Megaptera novaeangliae*) migrate between their winter breeding grounds off Mexico, Hawaii, and Japan and their summer feeding grounds in the Gulf of Alaska and Northeast Pacific coast. A 2006 survey of North Pacific humpback whales determined that close to 20,000 individuals migrate in five separate populations (represented by different colored arrows). (After https://hawaiihumpbackwhale.noaa.gov/explore/humpback_whale.html. Migration data from SPLASH Research.)

Ecologists use a variety of approaches to estimate population size and extent

Accurately measuring the size and extent of a population is harder than you might think. One challenge is determining the boundary of the population. If the area is self-contained and small enough, you might be able to simply count all the individuals of a particular species to get the population size. Biologists performed this type of count, called a **full census**, on the African bush elephant (*Loxodonta africana*) population of Samburu and Buffalo Springs National Reserves in Kenya. By monitoring the elephants for 21 months, the biologists learned to recognize each of the 760 individuals in the population, primarily by their unique and distinctive ear markings. But populations are often too large and too mobile for a full census; often the extent of the range of a population is not perfectly known. In these cases, ecologists instead determine the **population density**, or the number of individuals within a given area (or volume, for organisms living in water), and then extrapolate from these samples to estimate the total population size.

As you might imagine, estimating population densities is easiest for sessile organisms. Investigators need only count the individuals in a sample of representative locations and extrapolate the counts to the entire geographic range of the population. Individuals may be counted within a measured area

Research Tools

Figure 53.5A The Mark–Recapture Method The method described here is used to estimate animal population sizes for highly mobile species (such as *Ixodes scapularis*, the black-legged tick). Once a sampling area has been determined, investigators capture, mark, and then release the animals back into the population. The proportion of marked individuals recaptured in a second sample is assumed to be the same as the proportion of the total individuals in that sample to the population size within the area.

1 Capture a random sample of individuals from the population of interest. Mark each captured individual.

2 Release the marked individuals and allow an appropriate amount of time for them to merge completely with unmarked individuals in the population.

3 Capture a second random sample of individuals. Determine both the total number of individuals captured and the number of marked individuals in this sample.

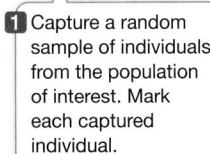

4 Estimate the total population size N using the equation

$$N = \frac{n_1 \times n_2}{M}$$

where

n_1 = the total number of individuals in the first sample (captured, marked, and released)

n_2 = the total number of individuals in the second sample

M = the number of marked individuals recaptured in the second sample

 View in **Achieve**
Animation 53.1 The Mark–Recapture Method

called a **quadrat** or along a **transect**—a line drawn across an area within the range of the population (often designated by a tape measure marked at regular intervals). By making repeated counts with either of these methods, investigators can use these surveys to make reasonably good estimates of the size of a population.

Counting mobile organisms is more difficult because individuals move into and out of sampling areas, as you saw in the humpback whale example. In such cases, investigators may use the **mark–recapture method** (Figure 53.5). They begin by capturing, marking, and then releasing a number of individuals. Later, after the marked individuals have had time to mix with unmarked individuals in the population (but before enough time has elapsed for births, deaths, and individual movement to affect the population size significantly), another sample of individuals is captured. This sample is then used to obtain an estimate of the total size of the population in the sampling area. The extrapolation is achieved by applying the equation described in Figure 53.5A, which assumes that the *proportion* of marked individuals in the second sample (i.e., individuals that were captured and marked in the first sample) is about the same as the proportion of individuals in the sampling area that were captured in the first sample.

More recently, ecologists have used DNA analysis to determine how many unique individuals might be contained within a population. In some cases, instead of capturing individuals and collecting DNA, ecologists collect the next best thing—tissues, fur, or feces left behind by animals in their natural habitat to be analyzed for DNA signatures. In a novel twist on sample collection,

Work with the Data

Figure 53.5B Monitoring Tick Populations

Original Paper: R. C. Falco and O. Fish. 1988. Prevalence of *Ixodes dammini* near the homes of Lyme disease patients in Westchester County, New York. *Am J Epidemiol* 127: 826–830.

Lyme disease is a chronic and debilitating condition caused by spirochete bacteria of the genus *Borrelia*, which infect humans by way of the bite of an intermediate host, the black-legged tick (*Ixodes scapularis*), also known as the deer tick. (In 1993 *I. dammini* and *I. scapularis* were found to be one species.) The incidence of Lyme disease has increased dramatically in the past 25 years, particularly in the Northeast and upper Midwest of the United States. In order to assess the risk of exposure to this disease in Westchester County, New York, investigators measured the abundance of deer ticks in suburban lawns near wooded areas using the mark–recapture method described in Figure 53.5A. (Ticks are typically collected by dragging a white cloth along the ground; the ticks latch onto the cloth in much the same way they would to a passing leg.) By drag-sampling one representative lawn, the researchers collected the data shown in the table.

	Original capture event	Second capture event (3 weeks later)
Adult ticks captured	180	33
No. of marked ticks	180[a]	8

[a]All ticks captured in the first event were marked with acrylic paint and released.

QUESTIONS▶

1. Refer to Figure 53.5A. Using the equation and other information described in that figure, estimate the total number of adult ticks in the sampled lawn from the data table above.

2. The lawn was approximately 700 m² in size. What is the approximate density of ticks per square meter?

3. What do you think might be the implications of this study for residents of this neighborhood?

Go to Achieve for a companion Data in Depth exercise.

some ecologists have even trained dogs to locate feces of some hard-to-find species such as orca whales (*Orcinus orca*). With enough samples, the extent and size of populations can then be determined for species that are hard to survey in the wild.

53.1 Recap and Assess

Species are divided into groups of individuals, or populations, that can vary spatially across their geographic range. All populations change in size and spatial extent due to the physical environment, biological interactions, and dispersal. Ecologists use a variety of approaches to estimate population sizes, including full censuses, surveys using quadrats or transects, mark–recapture methods, and DNA analyses.

1. Refer to Figure 53.4. Draw a diagram showing which populations of humpback whales interact on their summer feeding grounds. Do you think all five populations make up one metapopulation during the summer? Explain.

2. Refer to Figure 53.2. What type of species interaction appears to have caused the aphid population to fluctuate in size? What type of species interaction keeps the population size from fluctuating?

3. A researcher wants to determine how many leopard frog tadpoles are present in a pond in the spring. Later, after the tadpoles have metamorphosed, she wants to compare this number with the size of the frog population. What method should the researcher use to determine the population sizes? Explain your answer.

Quantifying population sizes in space and time provides valuable information on the dynamics of a species, but those observations alone cannot explain how, when, and why populations change in size. In order to understand and predict population sizes through time, ecologists characterize population growth, or the change in population size over time, using quantitative methods.

53.2 Population Growth Describes the Change in Population Size over Time

Learning Objectives

53.2.1 Devise equations for exponential and logistic population growth, and explain each of the terms of the equation.

53.2.2 Use exponential and logistic population growth equations to predict population size at some time in the future.

53.2.3 Distinguish between density-dependent and density-independent factors in population growth.

53.2.4 Interpret a life table, and explain and calculate the type of information it can provide about a population.

It is clear from Key Concept 53.1 that populations are constantly changing in size. **Population growth** describes the change in population size over time. For example, you read that North Pacific

humpback whales experienced dramatic declines in population size from commercial whaling, but when hunting was banned, the populations rebounded from 1,400 whales in 1966 to nearly 20,000 in 2006. Measuring how a population changes over time requires following its **demography**: births, deaths, immigration, and emigration.

Births increase and deaths decrease population size over time

Over any given interval of time, the size of a population increases by the number of individuals added to the population by births and by immigration (the movement of individuals into the population from elsewhere) and decreases by the number of individuals lost from the population by deaths and by emigration (individuals leaving the population to go elsewhere). This relationship is expressed mathematically as

$$N_t = N_0 + (B - D) + (I - E) \tag{53.1}$$

where N_t = the population size at time t, N_0 = the population size at time 0, B = the number of individuals born between time 0 and time t, D = the number that died between time 0 and time t, I = the number that immigrated between time 0 and time t, and E = the number that emigrated between time 0 and time t.

As you saw earlier, population size rarely remains the same but instead changes over time. We can use Equation 53.1 to estimate how population size changes over the interval of time 0 to t and get a **population growth rate**, or the rate of change in population size over time. This can be expressed mathematically as

$$\Delta N = (B - D) + (I - E),$$
or the change in N (ΔN) for the time interval 0 to t

To understand population growth rate from births and deaths alone, ecologists often assume a "closed system" that does not include immigration and emigration. This simplifies the equation to

$$\Delta N = (B - D) \tag{53.2}$$

The change in population size can then be calculated if one knows the number of births (B) and deaths (D) that have occurred over a given period of time. The birth and death numbers will naturally depend on the size of the population and the time interval considered. As a result we need to convert B and D into rates that will allow us to estimate population growth for any change in population size over time. Therefore we can further express B and D as

$$B = bN_0$$

where B is the product of the **per capita birth rate** (**b**) (i.e., the number of births per individual per unit of time) and N_0 (population size at time 0). Likewise, the death rate can be calculated as

$$D = dN_0$$

where D is the product of the **per capita death rate** (**d**) (i.e., the number of deaths per individual per unit of time) and N_0 (population size at time 0).

The term "per capita" literally translates to "per head" and is meant to indicate births and deaths per individual in the population. The change in the total number of births and deaths can then be calculated by multiplying the per capita birth and death rates by the population size at N_0. Here's what that looks like mathematically:

$$\Delta N = bN_0 - dN_0 \text{ or } \Delta N = (b - d)N_0$$

The difference between the per capita birth and death rate $(b - d)$ is the **per capita growth rate** (r). Substituting r for $(b - d)$, we get

$$\Delta N = rN_0 \qquad (53.3)$$

This simple model reflects why populations change in size. A population will increase in size if the per capita birth rate exceeds its per capita death rate; that is, if $b > d$, then $r > 0$. Likewise, the population will decline in size if $b < d$, or $r < 0$. If $b = d$, then $r = 0$, and the population will not change in size.

Ecologists use differential calculus to express the change in population size (ΔN) over very short, instantaneous periods of time (dN/dt). In this way, they are assuming that population growth is continuous, meaning the time interval is infinitely small and the growth curve will be smooth. This is expressed by

$$dN/dt = rN_0 \qquad (53.4)$$

Once we have a value for r, and we know population size, we can use it to characterize patterns of growth in populations through time. One pattern of growth that occurs when populations are not limited by resources is exponential growth, which we discuss next.

All populations have the potential for exponential growth

You know from Equation 53.4 that a population will grow, over some time period, as long as the per capita growth rate, r, is greater than zero (that is, when $b > d$). During this time period, the population will add a number of individuals that is r times its initial size. As the number of individuals in a population (N_0) increases, the number of new individuals added per unit of time accelerates—that is, rN_0 increases—even though the per capita growth

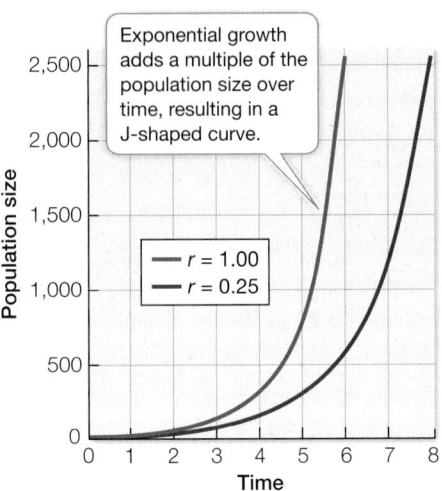

Figure 53.6 Exponential Population Growth Rate Exponential population growth occurs when the size of a population changes by a constant proportion over time. This graph compares the exponential growth of two populations that vary in their values of *r*.

Q: Which curve, blue or red, has the faster population growth rate?

View in Achieve
Simulation 53.1 Exponential Population Growth

rate (r) remains constant (**Figure 53.6**). This multiplicative pattern is known as **exponential growth**. It is also clear from Figure 53.6 that the value of r can make a big difference in the rate of growth of the population—a population with $r = 1.00$ will have a much faster rate of growth than a population with $r = 0.25$, even though both populations will display an exponential growth pattern.

Equation 53.4 gives us the exponential growth of a population, but it does not allow us to predict the size of a population at a later time. Using calculus, we can integrate Equation 53.4 and get

$$N_t = N_0 e^{rt} \qquad (53.5)$$

where N_t = the population size at time t, N_0 = the population size at time 0, e = a constant, the base of the natural log (e = 2.718), r = per capita growth rate, and t = the time interval between time 0 and time t. Knowing the starting population size and the per capita growth rate, we can use Equation 53.5 to forecast the population size at some later time, assuming exponential growth. This is similar to the equation that banks use to calculate compound interest on a loan.

One application of projecting population sizes into the future comes in the form of predicting human population growth. The human population increased relatively slowly until 1825, when it was 1 billion, and now stands at 7.7 billion (**Figure 53.7**). United Nations data show that world population growth rates have fallen from a high of 2.30%

Year	Population (billions)
1825	1
1930	2
1975	4
2019	7.7

Figure 53.7 Explosive Growth of the Human Population Human population growth was relatively slow until 1825, but advances in technology since then have allowed it to grow at an exponential rate. (Based on estimates by the History Database of the Global Environment (HYDE) and the United Nations. Visualization from OurWorldinData.org. CC BY-SA 4.0/Max Roser. Retrieved from: https://ourworldindata.org/world-population-growth.)

▶InvestigatingLIFE   Will the Global Human Population Growth Rate Decline?

Experiment

Original Paper: United Nations, Department of Economic and Social Affairs, Population Division. 2019. *World Population Prospects 2019*: Highlights (ST/ESA/SER.A/423).

Understanding the demographic changes in human populations over the coming years is critical in anticipating and planning for such challenges as food production, energy and water consumption, emerging diseases, and climate change facing our planet. The 2019 revision of World Population Prospects is the U.N.'s 26th round of official population estimates and projections. It builds on the previous reports by incorporating results from the most up-to-date national population censuses as well as findings from recent demographic and health surveys that have been carried out around the world.

HYPOTHESIS▶   World population growth rates have declined since 1950 and will continue to decline in the next century.

METHOD▶

1. Census and demographic survey data on survivorship, fertility, and international migration were gathered for 201 countries over the period 1950 to 2019.

2. The demographic data were used to establish parameters for life tables (similar to Table 53.1) in order to determine human population growth rates from 1950 to 2019.

3. To project the change in population growth rate values up to 2100,

demographic data were used to make assumptions on future trends in human survivorship, fertility, and international migration. Because the future is uncertain, several different projections were produced to understand their possible variability and arrive at a "best estimate" of the change in population growth.

RESULTS▶   Population growth rates fluctuated after 1950 but dropped from a high of 2.30% in the early 1960s to 1.10% in 2019. Projections indicate that human population growth rates will continue to decline to 0.50% in 2050 and to 0.10% in 2100. Note that the percent population growth rate is equivalent to $r \times 100$.

CONCLUSION▶   Population growth rates have dropped substantially in the last 69 years and are projected to continue this trend into 2100.

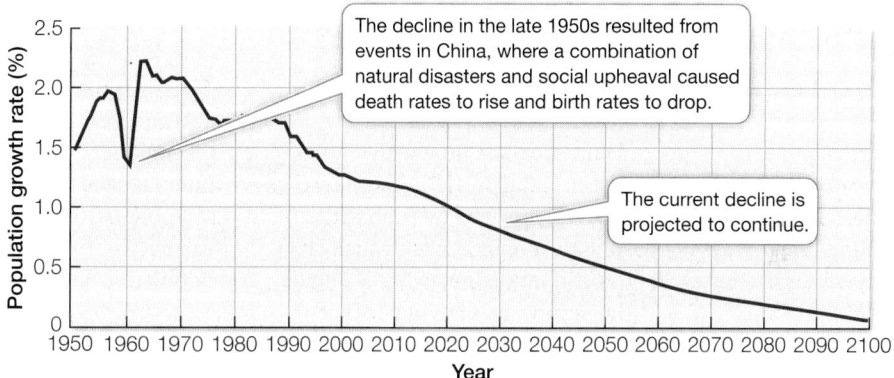

The decline in the late 1950s resulted from events in China, where a combination of natural disasters and social upheaval caused death rates to rise and birth rates to drop.

The current decline is projected to continue.

Data from U.S. Census Bureau, International Data Base, 2018; United Nations, Department of Economic and Social Affairs, Population Division (2019). *World Population Prospects 2019*: Highlights (ST/ESA/SER.A/423). Graph after Max Roser et al. 2019. *World Population Growth*. Published online at OurWorldInData.org. CC BY-SA 4.0

(note that the percent population growth rate is $r \times 100$) in the early 1960s to 1.10% today (**Investigating Life: Will the Global Human Population Growth Rate Decline?**). Projections indicate that human population growth rates will continue to decline to 0.50% in 2050 and to 0.10% in 2100, leading to a "best estimate" population size of 9.7 billion by 2050 and 11 billion by 2100. These projections in human population size beg the question: will world resources be able to sustain such large populations into the future? Is 11 billion above the maximum number of humans that can be supported sustainably on Earth? We will consider these questions at the end of the chapter.

Some populations may grow at rates close to their maximum, depending on the circumstances. During the 39 years following the ban on commercial whaling, North Pacific humpback whale populations grew exponentially at a rate of 5%–7% per year. Since the whales were released from hunting, they have had ample habitat, abundant food, and no predators, so there appeared to be little limiting their population growth at that time. However, changes in ocean conditions and thus food resources, entanglement in fishing gear, ship strikes, whale-watching harassment, and harvesting for scientific purposes all pose potential threats to humpback whale population recovery. In addition, there will always be some limit to the population sizes whales can attain, given intraspecific competition for food resources and breeding areas.

Work with the Data

Here you will use the population growth rate from above to project the human population size on Earth in the future.

QUESTIONS▶

1. Using Equation 53.5, the population size in 2019 (7.7 billion), and the population growth rate for 2019 (1.10%), estimate what the world's population size will be in 2100.

2. Projections indicate that if the human population growth rate declines to 0.50% in 2050, the population size will be 9.1 billion by 2050 and 10 billion by 2080. Using the projected population size and growth rate in 2080, project the human population size in 2100.

3. Suppose the carrying capacity of Earth is 12 billion people. Using Equation 53.7, project the human population size in 2100, given the 2019 data and 2080 data.

4. Given your calculations in Questions 1, 2, and 3, which parameter (population growth rate or carrying capacity) is projected to most reduce population size by 2100?

Go to Achieve for a companion Data in Depth exercise.

We will turn next to what happens to population growth when limiting resources affect the number of births and deaths within a population.

Logistic growth occurs as a population approaches its carrying capacity

What would happen if all the offspring produced by a population survived and reproduced? The prospects are alarming. In 1911 L. O. Howard, then chief entomologist of the U.S. Department of Agriculture, estimated that if all the offspring of the common house fly (*Musca domestica*) were to survive, a pair of flies beginning to reproduce on April 15 would produce a population of 5,598,720,000,000 adults by September 10 of the same year. Given such amazing reproductive capacities, it is clear that forces exist to limit the growth of fly populations (and populations of every other organism).

No real population can maintain exponential growth for long periods of time. As a population increases in density, the resources it requires—such as food, nest sites, and shelter—become depleted, causing birth rates to drop and death rates to rise. In other words, birth rates and death rates are dependent on the density of the population. Populations may initially grow rapidly when the population is small, but as populations increase in size, density-dependent birth and death rates cause r to decline toward zero, a pattern of population growth called **logistic growth**. Eventually when $r = 0$, the population stops changing in size because births equal deaths. Thus instead of continuing to increase exponentially, population growth slows down and the population eventually levels off at some size known as the **carrying capacity**, or **K** (Figure 53.8). K can be thought of as the number of individuals that any particular environment can sustain indefinitely. If the number of individuals in the population exceeds K, then r will be negative until population size reaches K once again. Likewise, if the number of individuals falls below K, then r will be positive until population size reaches K.

To model logistic growth, the exponential growth equation is modified by adding a term, $(K - N_0)/K$, which represents the fraction of the carrying capacity (K) that is available for population growth. As long as the population size is less than the carrying

capacity (i.e., $N_0 < K$), only a fraction of the available resources are being used. As the population size approaches the carrying capacity, however, the fraction of resources available for any new individual becomes smaller. The logistic growth equation is simply the exponential growth rate rN_0 multiplied by $(K - N_0)/K$ to get

$$\frac{dN}{dt} = rN_0 \left(\frac{K - N_0}{K} \right) \tag{53.6}$$

Population growth should stop when $N_0 = K$ because at that point, $K - N_0 = 0$, so $(K - N_0)/K = 0$, and thus $dN/dt = 0$ and the population will remain at a constant size.

Just as you saw with Equation 53.5, we can integrate Equation 53.6 to allow us to predict the population size at some later time, assuming logistic growth. When we do this we get

$$N_t = \frac{K}{1 + \left[\left((K - N_0)/N_0 \right) \right] e^{-rt}} \tag{53.7}$$

where N_t = the population size at time t, N_0 = the population size at time 0, K = carrying capacity, e = a constant, the base of the natural log (e = 2.718), r = per capita growth rate, and t = the time interval between time 0 and time t. In this case, knowing the starting population size, the per capita growth rate, and the carrying capacity of the population, we can use Equation 53.7 to forecast population size at some later time, assuming logistic growth.

 View in Achieve
Simulation 53.2 **Logistic Population Growth**

Factors limiting population growth can be density-dependent or density-independent

As you just saw, the density of a population can have large effects on population growth and ultimately the size of a population through time. **Density-dependent** factors can include:

- *Limiting resources.* As a population increases, it depletes its resources as a result of intraspecific competition.

- *Predators* may be attracted to areas with high densities of their prey, allowing them to capture a larger proportion of individuals and causing the death rate of the prey population to rise.

- *Pathogens* may spread more easily in dense populations than in populations with fewer individuals, resulting in a rise in the death rate.

It is important to note that density does not always cause a decline in population growth. Some populations grow better, albeit up to some limit, when population densities are higher rather than lower; this is known as the **Allee effect** (named after the ecologist W. C. Allee, who first described it). Sometimes individuals survive better in a group than on their own, as you saw with the predator avoidance strategies used by wood-pigeons and ground squirrels living within groups (see Figure 51.21).

Moreover, not all factors that change population size act in a density-dependent manner. A period of extreme cold, or an exceptionally strong hurricane, may kill a large number of individuals in a population regardless of the population's density; such an event is **density-independent** and may be a significant factor in depressing growth and keeping populations from reaching their carrying capacity.

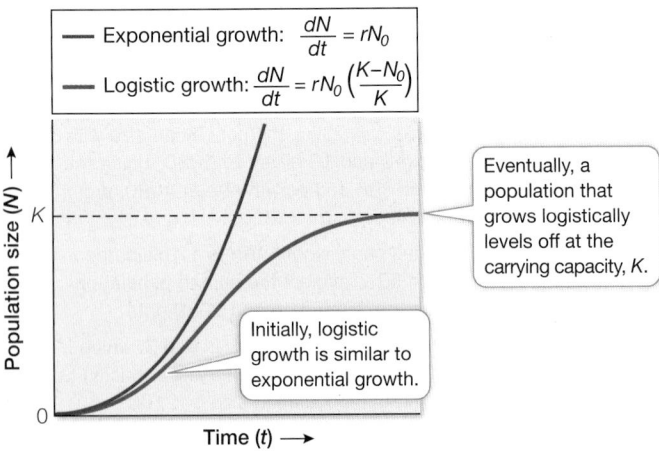

Figure 53.8 **Population Growth Models: Exponential versus Logistic Growth** Exponential population growth (red J-shaped curve) is much faster than logistic population growth (blue S-shaped curve), which is limited by the density or carrying capacity of the population.

 View in Achieve
Activity 53.1 **Population Growth**

Life tables keep track of demographic events

Up to this point we have assumed that individuals within a population do not vary in their birth and death rates. This is a big assumption given that we know real populations are made up of individuals of different ages, sizes, and sexes, which vary in their capacity to reproduce or survive. For example, a newborn whale or human cannot reproduce immediately, and must mature to reproductive age. Likewise, the likelihood of death will vary depending on the age of the individual. Ecologists use a form of accounting, known as a **life table**, to keep track of how demography will affect the growth rate of the population. Life tables summarize how survival and reproductive rates vary with the age, size, or sex of the individuals within a population. These summaries can then be used to predict future population trends and develop strategies for managing populations of commercial or ecological value. They are also used by life insurance companies to determine how much to charge people of different ages for insurance policies.

Let's consider an example of a life table from the literature. Table 53.1 shows a cohort life table using data from the acorn barnacle *Balanus glandula* on the shorelines of Scotland. A **cohort life table** uses a cohort—a group of individuals born within the same time frame—from the larger population to estimate growth rate. The two columns on the left show the number of individuals surviving and the number of offspring produced at different ages (x) through time. As the individuals within the cohort die, N_x decreases from 1 million barnacles to only 2 barnacles after 8 years. The proportion of individuals that survive, known as **survivorship** (l_x), can be calculated by simply dividing N_x by N_0, the number of barnacles originally born into the cohort (represented by age 0). In addition, we can calculate the **fecundity** (m_x), or mean number of barnacle offspring produced per surviving adult barnacle per age class, by dividing the total number of offspring ($N_{x \, offspring}$) by the number of individuals (N_x) that produce those offspring. Multiplying survivorship (l_x) by fecundity (m_x) gives us the number of offspring produced for individuals within a particular age class within the population. The sum of these values for all the age classes gives us the **net reproductive rate**, R_0, which is simply the mean number of offspring produced per individual in the cohort, adjusted for survival:

$$R_0 = \text{sum } (l_x \, m_x) \tag{53.8}$$

If R_0 is greater than 1.0, there is a net increase in offspring produced each generation, and assuming the birth and death rates do not change over time, the population should increase exponentially. If R_0 is less than 1.0, and individuals are not replaced as they die, the population declines eventually to extinction. If R_0 is 1.0, then the births and deaths balance out and the population will not change in size.

We can use R_0 to estimate the per capita growth rate, r, of a cohort by scaling R_0 to account for the generation time of the cohort. The **generation time**, G, is the average age of the parents of all the offspring produced within the cohort (see Table 53.1 for equation). To estimate r, we simply divide the natural log (ln) of R_0 by G and get

$$r = (\ln R_0)/G \tag{53.9}$$

Cohort life tables follow individuals from birth to death as a function of calendar year or life stage (e.g., eggs, larvae, pupae, and adults in insects). This is relatively easy to do if the organisms are easily followed—for example, if they are sessile and short-lived as we saw in the barnacle example. For organisms that are harder to track, a **static life table** can be constructed by sampling a population at a single slice of time. Here the numbers of individuals and their reproduction for different age classes are recorded at one time and used in a similar way as those data in Table 53.1 to calculate the net reproductive rate and per capita growth rate of the population.

The construction of life tables has allowed ecologists to observe common life history patterns, reflecting common solutions to ecological challenges, across a tremendous diversity of organisms. For example, the number of individuals surviving through each life stage (survivorship, l_x) can be taken from a life table and plotted graphically to construct a **survivorship curve**. Typically, a survivorship curve is constructed for a hypothetical cohort, usually of 1,000 individuals, by plotting the numbers of individuals expected to survive to reach each age category on a logarithmic scale.

TABLE **53.1** | Cohort Life Table for the Barnacle *Balanus glandula* [a]						
Age (x)	Number of individuals (N_x)	Number of offspring (N_x offspring)	Survivorship (l_x)	Fecundity (m_x)	$l_x \, m_x$	$x \, l_x \, m_x$
0	1,000,000	0	1	0	0	0
1	62	285,200	0.000062	4,600	0.285	0.285
2	34	295,800	0.000034	8,700	0.296	0.592
3	20	232,000	0.000020	11,600	0.232	0.696
4	15	190,500	0.000015	12,700	0.191	0.764
5	11	139,700	0.000011	12,700	0.140	0.700
6	6	76,200	0.000006	12,700	0.076	0.456
7	2	25,400	0.000002	12,700	0.025	0.175
8	2	25,400	0.000002	12,700	0.025	0.200

1 To estimate the per capita growth rate, r, sum all l_x by m_x values to get the net reproductive rate, R_0. $R_0 = \text{sum } (l_x \, m_x) = 1.27$

2 Then, sum all l_x by m_x by x values and divide by R_0 to get the generation time, G. $G = \text{sum } (x \, l_x \, m_x)/R_0 = 3.05$

3 Finally, divide the natural log of R_0 by G to get the intrinsic rate of increase, r. $r = (\ln R_0)/G = 0.08$

Source: Data from J. H. Connell. 1970. *Ecol Monogr, Ecological Society of America* 40: 49–78.

[a]The life history of barnacles involves releasing larvae into the water column, where they feed and undergo a series of larval stages. Eventually they settle back on the rock and metamorphose into a juvenile barnacle, which grows into a reproductive adult.

(A)

(B)

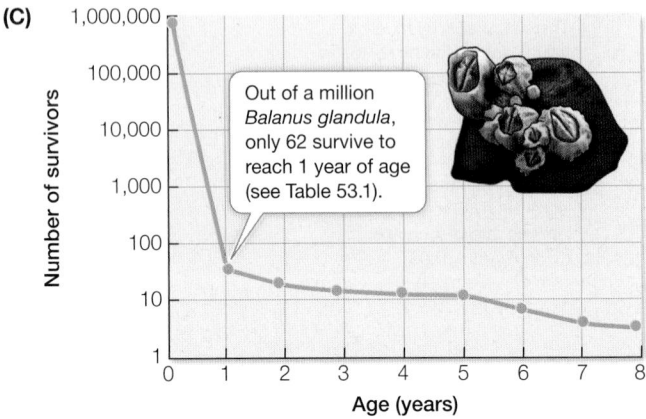

(C)

Figure 53.9 Survivorship Curves   Ecologists recognize three general types of survivorship curves. Notice that the number of survivors has been plotted on a logarithmic scale. Three species provide real-world examples of the three types of life histories. (A, B after E. S. Deevey. 1947. *Q Rev Biol* 22: 283–314; C after J. H. Connell. 1970. *Ecol Monogr, Ecological Society of America* 40: 49–78.)

Q: What type of survivorship curve do humans have?

View in Achieve
Simulation 53.3 Age Structure and Survivorship

Survivorship curves tend to take one of three general shapes:

1. Species with **type I survivorship curves** experience high overall survivorship through adulthood but steep declines late in life (the curve is concave) (**Figure 53.9A**). Species with this type of survivorship curve (humans, elephants, whales, and many other large mammals) typically have low reproduction rates but provide parental care to their offspring, which reduces the risk of death in early stages of development.

2. Species with **type II survivorship curves** face a constant risk of mortality at all ages (the curve is linear) (**Figure 53.9B**). Many birds, fishes, and plants display this pattern.

3. Species with **type III survivorship curves** experience low survivorship early in life and higher survivorship once they reach maturity (the curve is convex) (**Figure 53.9C**). Species with this type of survivorship curve (most insects; marine invertebrates, including the barnacle in Table 53.1; and annual plants) tend to produce many offspring but provide little or no parental care.

Species survivorship curves help us classify how mortality plays out in populations over time, but many species have patterns of survivorship somewhere in between these extremes. For example, some organisms show a "stair-stepped" curve, with bouts of mortality during vulnerable periods of their life, followed by periods of relatively low mortality.

KEY CONCEPT
53.2 Recap and Assess

Population growth is the change in population size over time, as reflected by the number of births, deaths, and migrants in and out of the population. Exponential (multiplicative) growth occurs when the per capita growth rate, r, is constant over time. Logistic growth occurs in an environment in which resources are limited and a population reaches its carrying capacity, K. Factors limiting population growth can be density-dependent (e.g., competition for food or space) or density-independent (e.g., environmental conditions). Life tables summarize how survival and fecundity vary with the age, size, or sex of the individuals in a population, and predict how these demographic events affect population growth.

1. Write an equation that describes how births, deaths, immigration, and emigration affect population size. Define each variable.

2. Suppose you are asked to predict what the population size of an endangered bird will be in 2040.

   a. Complete the following cohort life table, and calculate the R_0, G, and r of this cohort.

Year	Age (x)	Number of female birds (N_x)	Number of female offspring ($N_{x\ offspring}$)	Survivorship (l_x)	Fecundity (m_x)	Net reproductive rate ($l_x m_x$)	Generation time ($x\ l_x m_x$)
2017	0	100	0				
2018	1	50	75				
2019	2	40	80				
2020	3	30	60				

b. Calculate what the population size, N_t, of this cohort will be in 2040, assuming exponential population growth and $N_0 = 120$.

c. To add more realism to these calculations, suppose that K (carrying capacity) = 300 for this cohort. What will the population size be, assuming logistic growth, in 2040?

3. Plot the number of birds surviving with age for the cohort in Question 2. What type of survivorship curve does this cohort have?

4. Describe some density-dependent and density-independent factors that could control the population growth of the bird cohort in Question 2.

Life tables reflect the ways in which organisms partition their time and energy among growth, maintenance, and reproduction. Comparisons across individuals, populations, and species reveal different patterns of partitioning, which allow organisms to cope with different environmental challenges. Let's move on to discuss how life history traits arise and the types of strategies organisms employ.

KEY CONCEPT 53.3 Life History Is the Lifetime Pattern of Growth, Reproduction, and Survival

Learning Objectives

53.3.1 Distinguish between the relative contributions of environment and genetics to life history traits in specific situations.

53.3.2 Describe how and why life history trade-offs might arise in a species or population.

53.3.3 Distinguish between *r*-strategists and *K*-strategists, and identify specific situations in which evolution might favor one strategy over the other.

We know as humans that individuals vary widely in when they mature, when and how many children they have, and when they die. This lifetime pattern of growth, reproduction, and survival is known as an individual's **life history**. In addition to the variation we see in life history patterns at the individual level, all species have a common **life history strategy** that helps define the average timing and nature of important life history events (**Figure 53.10**). Life history strategies are shaped by the way individuals within and among species allocate resources to growth, reproduction, and survival based on genetic and environmental factors. For example, in the case of humans today, the average age of puberty is 11 years, the average woman has one child at a time (except in the rare cases of multiple births), and the average life span is 70 years. These life history statistics are a product of the environmental and genetic constraints placed on humans in the twenty-first century. But they also belie the fact that human life history traits have changed dramatically from historical times and vary widely among populations around the world. Thus as you will see, life history patterns not only vary within and among species but also through time.

Life history strategies can vary at species and population levels

Life history strategies can vary among species, even for species that are taxonomically closely related, as a consequence of environmental differences. For example, on Mount Kenya two species of unusual plants in the genus *Lobelia* live in different types of habitats (**Figure 53.11**). One species, *Lobelia telekii*, lives on the dry rocky slopes of the mountain, where it reproduces only once (a strategy called **semelparity**), produces vast numbers of small seeds, and has a short life span. In the moist valley bottoms, another species, *Lobelia keniensis*, reproduces more than once (a strategy called **iteroparity**), produces fewer but larger seeds per reproductive event, and lives longer. Semelparity is typical of organisms whose probability of dying remains high even when they reach adulthood; it is seen in

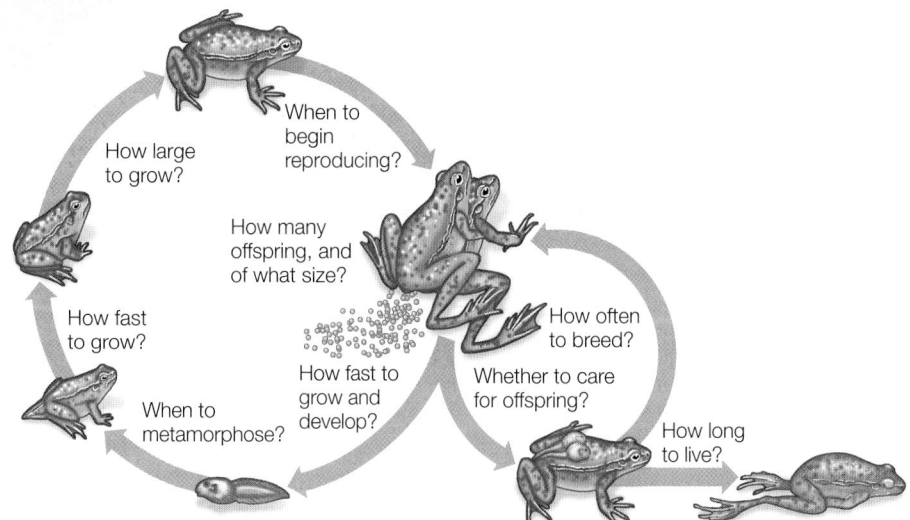

Figure 53.10 A Life History Strategy
The timing and nature of life history events shape the overall life cycle of an organism. The life history strategy of this frog species reflects how environmental and genetic factors affect strategies to optimize growth, reproduction, and survival.

How large to grow?
When to begin reproducing?
How many offspring, and of what size?
How fast to grow?
How often to breed?
Whether to care for offspring?
When to metamorphose?
How fast to grow and develop?
How long to live?

(A) *Lobelia telekii*

(B) *Lobelia keniensis*

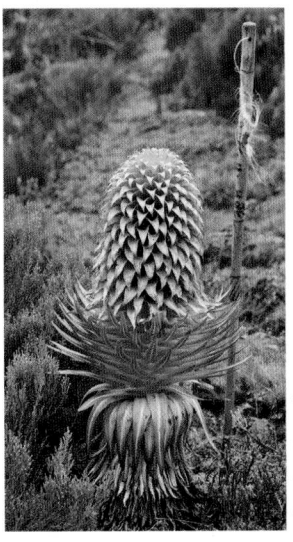

Figure 53.11 Related Species with Vastly Different Life History Strategies   On Mount Kenya, Africa, **(A)** *Lobelia telekii* lives on the dry rocky slopes of the mountain, where it reproduces once (is semelparous), produces many seeds, and has a short life span. In the moist valley bottoms, **(B)** *Lobelia keniensis* reproduces multiple times (is iteroparous), produces fewer but larger seeds, and lives longer.

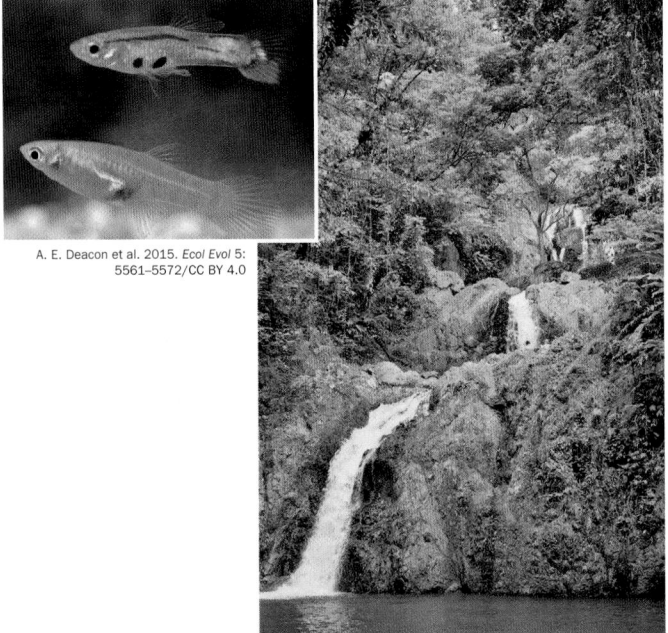

A. E. Deacon et al. 2015. *Ecol Evol* 5: 5561–5572/CC BY 4.0

Figure 53.12 Predation Affects the Life History of Guppies   In Trinidad, populations of guppies (*Poecilia reticulata*) from high-predation stream sites below the falls matured earlier, reproduced more frequently, and produced more offspring per brood compared with guppies from low-predation stream sites above the falls, no matter how many resources the guppies were given.

Q: Are the life history strategies of the two guppy populations, one from high-predation streams and the other from low-predation streams, likely genetically determined? Why?

some fishes, many insects, and all annual plants. In contrast, iteroparity is typical of organisms with long life spans. For example, because environmental conditions within the nests of social insects such as honey bees and ants are remarkably stable, iteroparity is the rule among these species; some queens live 10 years or longer and reproduce over their entire adult lives.

Life history strategies can also vary within species at the population level. For example, some populations of guppies (*Poecilia reticulata*) in Trinidad live in streams where they are attacked and eaten by larger fishes (**Figure 53.12**). But some streams have waterfalls that predatory fishes are unable to negotiate. Guppies that live in the predator-free areas upstream from those waterfalls have lower death rates compared with guppies below the falls. To see whether the risk of being eaten by a predator influenced the life history strategies of these guppies, David Reznick and his colleagues collected guppies from high-predation and low-predation sites and raised them in the laboratory. Some guppies from each group were provided with plentiful food, and others with limited food, to simulate the variation the fish would typically encounter in their home streams. In the laboratory, where no predators were present, guppies from high-predation sites matured earlier, reproduced more frequently, and produced more offspring in each brood than did guppies from low-predation sites, no matter how much food the guppies received. The investigators concluded that predation had genetically selected for early and frequent reproduction in the guppies living below the falls.

Perhaps the best-studied example of how life history traits can vary not only among populations, but also among individuals, is the case of human life span. Human life span varies widely around the world and between the sexes (**Figure 53.13**). Today, humans live on average to 87 years in Japan, Hong Kong, and many European countries, and to 35–50 years in some African countries (e.g., Sierra Leone, Democratic Republic of the Congo, and Somalia) where HIV infection, famine, and war are common. In the United States, average life span is 80 years, with women outliving men by 5 years. Research has shown that the factors contributing to lower life expectancy rates in men include higher rates of homicide, accidental death, and parasitic and infectious diseases.

For the most part, the large variability in life span we see in humans can be attributed to environmental factors. If you lived during the Bronze Age, your life expectancy was 28 years, and it was not much better even in the early nineteenth century (about 35 years). Reduction in infant mortality has accounted for most of the increase in life expectancy, but since the end of the 1950s the mortality rate of those older than 80 years has decreased by 1.5% each year. Much of the increase in life expectancy that we enjoy today is the result of modern advances in human health and nutrition, which begs the question: is there a limit to human life expectancy? One study, which plotted human life-span data over time, shows a remarkable linear relationship with no leveling off yet, which could indicate an upper limit (**Figure 53.14**). In fact, because life span has increased by 2.5 years every decade for the last 150 years, one possible scenario is that 60 years from now the average person's life span will reach 100 years! While some limit on human life span is almost certain, these predictions suggest that human life expectancy is a highly flexible life history trait indeed.

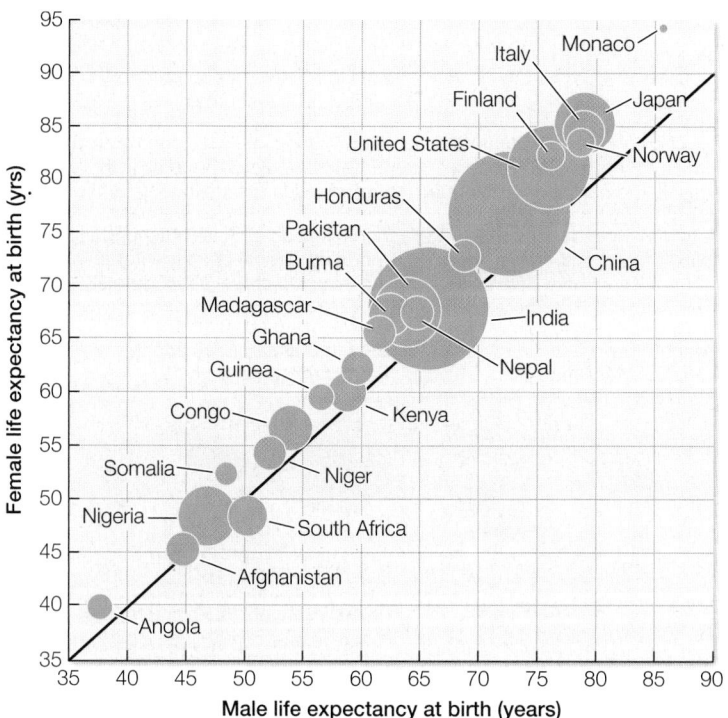

Figure 53.13 Human Life Expectancy around the World Comparison of recent male and female life expectancy at birth for a variety of countries. The solid black line corresponds to equal female and male life expectancy. The sizes of the bubbles are linearly proportional to the population of the country. (Data from The World Factbook 2016-17. Washington, DC: Central Intelligence Agency, 2016. https://www.cia.gov/library/publications/the-world-factbook/index.html)

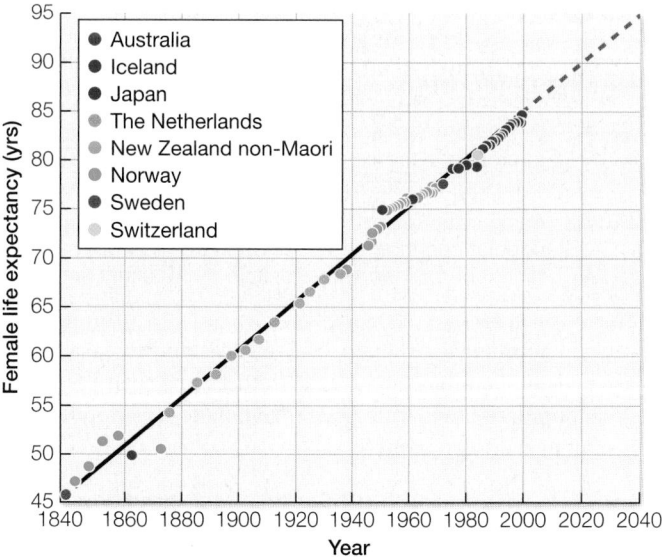

Figure 53.14 Human Life Expectancy—Past, Present, and Future Recorded human female life expectancy from 1840 to the present. The linear trend in life expectancy is depicted by the bold line, and the extrapolated trend by the dashed gray line. Based on the trend, in 2040 the average woman might have a life span of 95 years. (After J. Oeppen and J. W. Vaupel. 2002. *Science* 296: 1029–1031.)

Q: Compare the differences in female life expectancy between 1840–1940 and 1940–2040. Is the rate of change in life expectancy predicted to increase?

Life history strategies arise from constraints on growth, reproduction, and survival

As it should be clear by now, the fitness of a population or species is highly dependent on its life history strategy in relationship to its surrounding environment. Thus it makes sense that genes that maximize growth, reproduction, and survival would be favored by natural selection, resulting in an optimal life history strategy for that species or population. However, there are constraints on optimality, resulting in **trade-offs** in life history traits that put limits on the possible life history outcomes for species.

Connect the Concepts Key Concept 21.5 describes how constraints on optimality include genetic variation for evolution to act on, as well as the mediating effects of the physical and biological environment.

Trade-offs include allocation of resources to such traits as growth versus reproduction or number of offspring versus their body size. Energy devoted to one life history trait can reduce the amount available for others. For example, the growth of Douglas fir trees (*Pseudotsuga menziesii*) measured using annual growth ring size is negatively correlated with cone production. The more cones the tree produces, the narrower the width of the rings, suggesting that the allocation to reproduction takes energy from growth. Another trade-off that can have dramatic consequences for population growth is that of survival and reproduction. An example of this occurs in the giant Pacific octopus (*Enteroctopus dofleini*), which lives only 3–5 years and dies soon after significant parental investment in its thousands of offspring.

As you have seen, much of the variation in life history traits appears to result from an evolutionary response to environmental variability. Generally, unpredictable environments are associated with greater allocation to reproducing quickly, shorter life spans, and correspondingly high per capita growth rates. Conversely, predictable environments, where organisms must compete for high-quality resources, are associated with lower fecundity, longer life spans, and correspondingly lower per capita growth rates. Species whose life history strategies allow for high population growth rates are called *r*-strategists, and species whose life history strategies allow them to persist at or near the carrying capacity (*K*) of their environment are called *K*-strategists (Figure 53.15). Keep in mind, however, that these categories are extremes; most species fall along a continuum between these two strategies.

For *r*-strategists, life is uncertain. Individuals tend to reproduce only once and to produce large numbers of offspring, most of which are expected to die early in life (that is, they have a type III survivorship curve; see Figure 53.9C). They can generally use a wide variety of resources and tolerate a wide range of conditions. *K*-strategists are adapted to predictable conditions, are long-lived, and reproduce several times; their smaller numbers of offspring have a high probability of surviving to adulthood (that is, they have a type I or II survivorship curve; see Figure 53.9A,B). *K*-strategists tend to be good at enduring competition for resources, but this sometimes leads to trade-offs in reproduction.

Level	*r*-strategists	*K*-strategists
Habitat	Tolerate unpredictable conditions by using a wide variety of resources	Thrive in predictable environments but compete for high-quality resources
Reproductive strategy	Typically reproduce once (semelparity), but greater allocation to reproduction than growth results in large numbers of offspring	Reproduce more than once (iteroparity), but greater allocation to growth than reproduction results in fewer offspring
Survivorship	Short life span, density-independent mortality, typical of a type III survivorship curve (see Figure 53.9C)	Long life span, density-dependent mortality, typical of a type I or II survivorship curve (see Figure 53.9A, B)
Population growth	Period of exponential growth (*r*) followed by periodic or seasonal population declines	Slowly rising population growth that stabilizes at or near carrying capacity (*K*)
Examples		

© BillionPhotos.com/ Fotolia   © Sergii Figurnyi/ Fotolia   © sonsedskaya/ Fotolia   © Zerbor/ Shutterstock.com   © Steve Byland/ Fotolia   © Ilya Akinshin/ Fotolia

That life history trade-offs can evolve is suggested by genetic correlations among suites of life history traits. Such genetic correlations imply either simultaneous selection on two or more life history traits or linkages among the genes that code for those traits. Across *Drosophila melanogaster* strains, for example, a high per capita rate of growth is correlated with the ability to reproduce under starvation conditions and with the ability to develop on a variety of media in the laboratory—both of which are consistent with the *r* strategy of tolerating a wide range of resources and conditions.

Connect the Concepts Key Concept 12.4 describes how linked genes occur together on the same chromosome and thus are inherited together.

KEY CONCEPT
53.3 Recap and Assess

An organism's life history is characterized by its lifetime pattern of growth, reproduction, and survival. All species have a characteristic life history strategy, which arises from genetic and environmental constraints on life history traits. Two extremes of life history strategies include species with high population growth rates (*r*-strategists) and species that persist at or near their carrying capacity (*K*-strategists). Most species fall along a continuum between these two strategies.

1. Refer to Figure 53.14.
   a. Does the change in life expectancy for humans over the past 180 years suggest a genetic or an environmental cause?
   b. Given your answer, are the large differences in human life span for Japan versus Angola, shown in Figure 53.13, likely the result of genetic or environmental factors? Explain.

2. Why are species unable to maximize growth, reproduction, and survival? In other words, why are there life history trade-offs?

3. Refer to Figures 53.11 and 53.12. What life history strategy types characterize *Lobelia telekii* versus *L. keniensis*? How about guppies in high-predation versus low-predation stream sites?

For millennia, humans have tried to increase populations of desirable or useful species and reduce populations of species they consider undesirable. Such efforts are most successful if they are based on knowledge of how those populations grow and what determines their densities.

KEY CONCEPT
53.4 Population Biology Can Be Used in Managing and Conserving Populations

Learning Objectives

53.4.1 Describe the possible density-dependent population approaches to managing both desirable and undesirable species.

53.4.2 Analyze the importance of source and sink populations in a metapopulation in terms of their function in conserving a species from extinction.

If we want to manage other species—that is, to increase or decrease their populations—we need to understand their life histories and population dynamics. We turn now to how populations can be managed to our benefit.

Management plans should take life history strategies into account

Knowing the life history strategy of a species can be helpful in managing populations of commercial value. The black rockfish (*Sebastes melanops*), an important game fish that lives off the Pacific coast of North America, provides one such example. Rockfish have an indeterminate growth pattern—they continue to grow throughout their lives. As in many other animals, the number of eggs a female rockfish produces is proportional to her size, so larger females produce more eggs than smaller females. In addition, older, larger females are better able to provision the eggs they produce with oil droplets, which provide energy to the newly hatched larvae, giving them a head start in life. Larvae from eggs with larger oil droplets, produced by larger females, grow faster and survive better than do larvae from eggs with smaller oil droplets. These life history traits have important implications for the management of rockfish populations.

Because fishermen prefer to catch big fish, intensive fishing off the Oregon coast from 1996 to 1999 reduced the average age of female rockfish from 9.5 to 6.5 years. Thus the females reproducing in 1999 were, on average, smaller than the females reproducing in 1996. This change decreased the average number of eggs produced by females and reduced the average growth rate of larvae by about 50%. This reduction in reproductive ability was linked to a decrease in the ability of the rockfish population to recover from intensive fishing. Maintaining productive populations of rockfish may require regulating the number or size of fish caught, the fishing season, and/or setting aside no-fishing zones where some females can be protected from fishing and allowed to grow to large sizes.

Management plans should be guided by the principles of population dynamics

If we look at a logistic growth curve (see Figure 53.8), we can see that the number of births tends to be highest when a population is well below its carrying capacity. Therefore if we wish to maximize the number of individuals that can be harvested from a population, we should manage the population so that it is far enough below the carrying capacity to have a high birth rate. Hunting and fishing regulations are established with this objective in mind.

Fishes can, however, be overharvested, as illustrated by the story of the black rockfish. Many fish populations have been greatly reduced because so many individuals were harvested that the few surviving reproductive adults could not maintain the population. For example, Georges Bank, off the northeast coast of North America—a source of cod, haddock, and other prime food fishes—was exploited so heavily during the twentieth century that many fish stocks have been reduced to levels insufficient to support a commercial fishery (**Figure 53.16**). With fishing restrictions the haddock population has rebounded, but the cod population has not.

Many rapidly reproducing species can recover if overharvesting is stopped, but recovery is more difficult for slowly reproducing species. Just as they did with the humpback whale, twentieth-century whalers hunted the blue whale (*Balaenoptera musculus*), Earth's largest animal, nearly to extinction. These whales reproduce very slowly: they live up to 10 years before becoming reproductively mature, produce only one offspring at a time, and have long intervals between births. As opposed to humpback whales, however, blue whale populations have recovered more slowly.

Whether we want to manage the sizes of populations of desirable species for sustainable harvesting or of undesirable species for control purposes, the same principles apply. **Biological control** is the use of natural enemies (predators, parasites, or pathogens) to reduce the population density of an economically damaging species. In many cases the target species is a pest only because it has been introduced to a new

area. Natural enemies used for biological control are often obtained from the native region of the pest species. Biological control became popular in the nineteenth century after an outbreak of cottony-cushion scale (*Icerya purchasi*), an Australian insect that attacks citrus, appeared in citrus groves in California. A predaceous ladybeetle and a parasitic fly were then introduced from Australia. Within a year of their release, these insects brought the scales under control.

Sometimes, however, introduced natural enemies not only fail to have any effect on the pest they were imported to control but also, freed of their own enemies, become pests themselves. This fact underlies the horror story of the cane toad (*Rhinella marina*) in Australia. This Central American toad was introduced to control cane beetles attacking Australian sugarcane fields. But Australian cane beetles stay high on the upper stalks of the plants; the toads could not reach that high, and thus had no effect on the beetle population. Unfortunately, they had massive effects on other species.

All stages of the *R. marina* life cycle are poisonous, and Australian reptiles (including snakes and lizards) and mammals that eat them usually die. With no enemies to limit their population growth, cane toads grow fast and outcompete native amphibian species for resources. The toads have spread from northern Australia down the east coast, where they threaten native frog species by preying on them as well as by competing with them. The Australian government is forced to spend millions of dollars in attempting to reduce their numbers.

Knowledge of metapopulation dynamics helps us conserve species

Ecologists have used information on metapopulation dynamics to conserve endangered species. We know from mathematical models that the risk of extinction for a species can depend on the number and size of its populations within a metapopulation, and on the rates of dispersal among them. In some metapopulations there are **source populations**, which serve as a net source of individuals for **sink populations**, which receive more immigrants than they produce. Thus

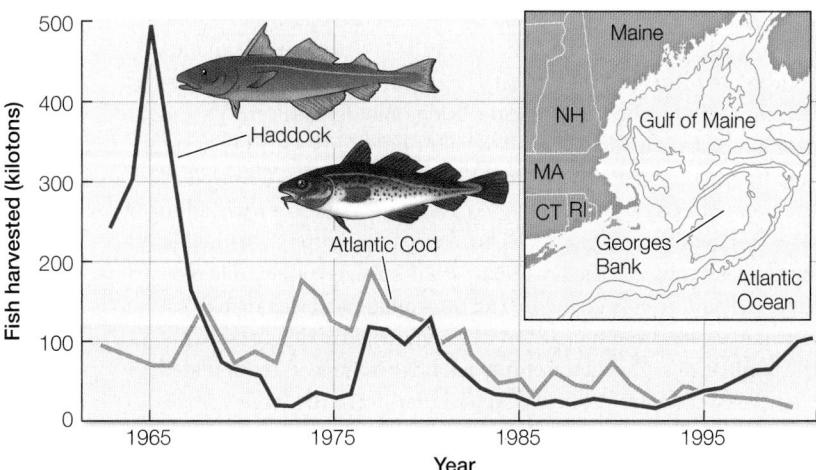

Figure 53.16 Overharvesting Can Reduce Fish Populations   Harvests of Atlantic cod (*Gadus morhua*) and haddock (*Melanogrammus aeglefinus*) on Georges Bank (map inset) have led to dramatic population declines of both species. Fishing regulations on haddock have allowed its stock to rebound enough to once again support a commercial fishery. (After C. Safina et al. 2005. *Science* 309: 707–708.)

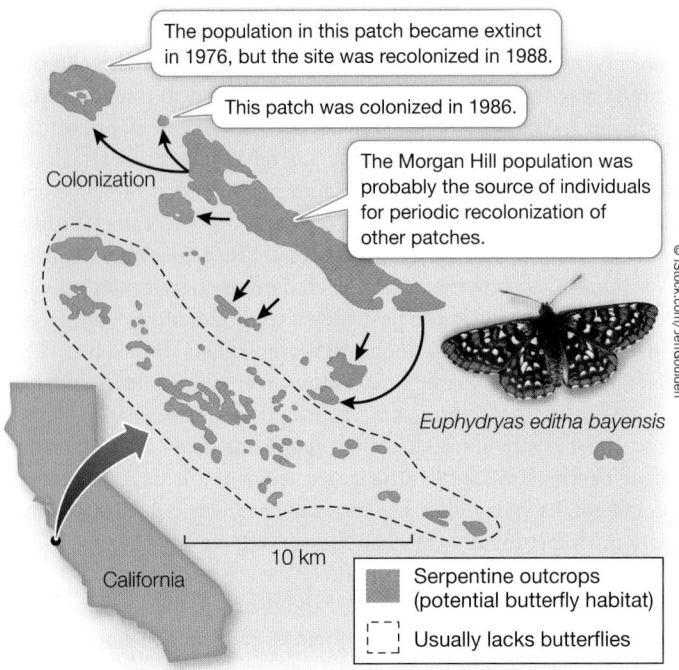

The population in this patch became extinct in 1976, but the site was recolonized in 1988.

This patch was colonized in 1986.

The Morgan Hill population was probably the source of individuals for periodic recolonization of other patches.

Colonization

California

10 km

Euphydryas editha bayensis

© iStock.com/JeffGoulden

 Serpentine outcrops (potential butterfly habitat)

 Usually lacks butterflies

Figure 53.17 **A Metapopulation of Checkerspots**   The San Francisco Bay area metapopulation of Edith's checkerspot butterfly is divided into several populations confined to patches of suitable habitat on serpentine rock outcrops that contain the food plants of the species. Arrows indicate colonization events. (After S. Harrison et al. 1988. *Am Nat* 132: 360–382.)

▶ **View in Achieve**
Simulation 53.4 **Metapopulation**

although some individual populations may undergo severe decline as a consequence of natural or human-caused factors, source populations within a metapopulation can serve to rescue them.

A dramatic example of such metapopulation dynamics is provided by Edith's checkerspot butterfly (*Euphydryas editha bayensis*). This endangered subspecies feeds on only two species of annual plants (California plantain [*Plantago erecta*] and purple owl's clover [*Castilleja exserta*]) that are endemic to outcrops of serpentine rock on hills south of San Francisco. In 1960 Paul Ehrlich and his colleagues at Stanford University began studying a population of this butterfly in the nearby Jasper Ridge Biological Preserve and discovered that it was one of several populations within a large, very fragmented metapopulation (**Figure 53.17**). They followed all the populations over several years and found that they varied in size. During drought years, the butterfly populations declined in size because most of the host plants that the caterpillars relied on died early in the spring, before the caterpillars had a chance to eat them. A severe drought in 1975–1977 led to extinctions of some of the populations. One of the empty habitat patches was repopulated a few years later, most likely by individuals from the largest single population, Morgan Hill, which as late as 1989 contained several hundred thousand butterflies. In 1998, however, the Morgan Hill population, which had historically been the largest in the metapopulation, went extinct. Ehrlich and his colleagues examined 70 years of climate data for the region and concluded that increasing climate variation accounted for the extinction. They also concluded that without a large, stable source population to provide emigrants for recolonization, as the Morgan Hill population did during the

1970s drought, it is unlikely that any of the other populations, which are sink populations, will persist without human intervention.

KEY CONCEPT
53.4 Recap and Assess

Efforts to manage populations are more likely to be successful if they are based on an understanding of life histories and population and metapopulation dynamics. Biological control is the use of natural enemies to reduce the population density of an economically damaging species. Metapopulations can conserve endangered species if source populations, which supply a source of individuals to sink populations, can rescue those populations from extinction.

1. Describe an effective strategy for recovering the population size of a desirable species that has a *K*-strategist life history.

2. Refer to Figure 53.17.

   a. Describe factors responsible for the metapopulation size of the Edith's checkerspot butterfly in the San Francisco Bay area.

   b. Given the 1998 extinction of the Morgan Hill population, what is the likely fate of the metapopulation? Explain your answer.

▶Investigating LIFE

Q and A   **What is the human population growth projected to be in the next century, and how will that affect population size?**

You have seen that this question is highly dependent on the factors that ultimately control the number of births and deaths, or population growth, of humans over time. If the population growth rate projections are correct, there will be roughly 11 billion humans in 2100. Is 11 billion above the carrying capacity of humans? Estimates of the carrying capacity published in 1994 varied tenfold: from less than 3 billion to 44 billion, with the median estimated at 12 billion. As opposed to the carrying capacities of other species, human carrying capacity depends not only on natural constraints important to all species, but also on individual and collective choices concerning the distribution of material goods, the use of technology, and the right to political, economic, and cultural freedoms. The number of people that can live on Earth will depend in part on how many will own cars, eat meat, or have air conditioning. For example, estimates suggest that if the carrying capacity values for the population in the United States were applied worldwide, Earth's carrying capacity would be limited to 1.2 billion. Compare this with the estimated values for India, where the worldwide carrying capacity could be extrapolated to 14 billion. Given that the current population size on Earth is 7.7 billion, it is clear that the vast majority of humans do not, and will not, experience the quality of life inherent to many in the United States.

Future directions

Some have argued that the number of people that can ultimately live on Earth will depend on the ability of humans to continue to expand their carrying capacity through technological innovations and greater efficiencies in food production and energy generation. These technological innovations will require that we increase food production and natural resource extraction without a heavy reliance on fossil fuels, which have a limited supply and adverse effects on the climate. Ultimately, to believe that no ceiling to human population size is inevitable defies what we know about natural populations.

© Michael Warren/Getty Images

You should be able to relate each summary to the adjacent figures. If you go to this visual summary in **Achieve**, you can follow links to figures, animations, activities, and simulations that will help you consolidate the material.

KEY CONCEPT 53.1 — Populations Show Dynamic Variation in Size over Space and Time

Go to **Animation 53.1**

- Species are divided into groups of individuals, or **populations**, that can vary spatially across their **geographic range**.

- A group of geographically isolated populations linked together by **dispersal** is known as a **metapopulation**.

- All populations vary in their **dispersion patterns** and fluctuate in size over time due to the physical environment, biological interactions, and dispersal.

- Ecologists use a variety of approaches to estimate population sizes, including **full censuses**, surveys using **quadrats** or **transects**, **mark–recapture methods**, and DNA analysis.

Figure 53.1

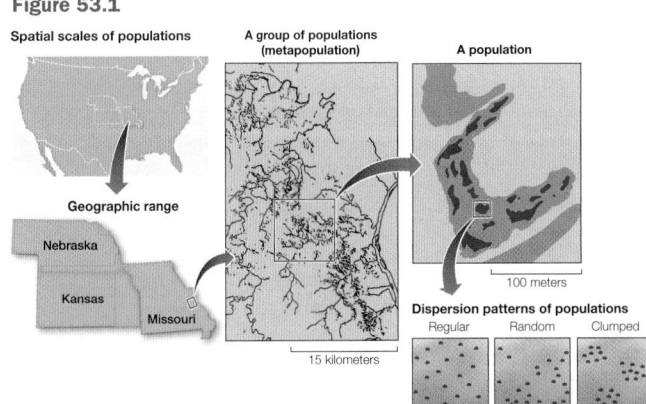

Questions

1. What is the difference between a population and a metapopulation?

2. What are the three basic dispersion patterns, and what are the main factors that influence them?

3. What are some of the ways in which population size and geographic extent of organisms can be measured?

KEY CONCEPT 53.2 — Population Growth Describes the Change in Population Size over Time

Go to **Activity 53.1** and **Simulations 53.1–53.3**

- **Population growth** is the change in population size over time, as reflected by the number of births, deaths, and migrants in and out of the population.

- **Exponential growth** occurs when the rate of change in population size is constant over time. **Logistic growth** occurs when resources are limited, slowing growth to a population's maximum size (**carrying capacity**, or **K**).

- Factors limiting population growth can be **density-dependent** when intraspecific competition between individuals affects population growth. **Density-independent** factors are those that act independently of the population density, such as physical conditions.

- **Life tables** summarize how **survivorship** and **fecundity** vary with the age, size, or sex of individuals within a population, and incorporate how these demographic events affect population growth.

- Species have different types of **survivorship curves** that reflect mortality patterns over time.

Figure 53.8

Exponential growth: $\frac{dN}{dt} = rN_0$

Logistic growth: $\frac{dN}{dt} = rN_0 \left(\frac{K-N_0}{K} \right)$

Figure 53.9

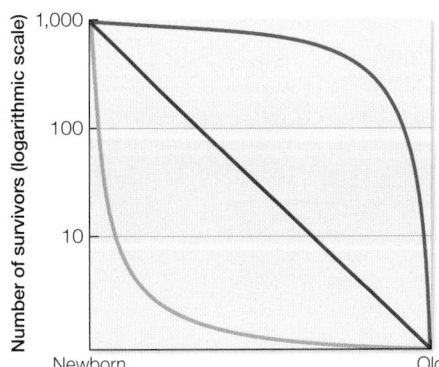

Questions

1. How does exponential growth differ from logistic growth?

2. Describe some density-dependent and density-independent factors that can control population growth.

3. How does life table analysis improve the measurements of population growth? Refer to Table 53.1. What type of survivorship curve is characteristic of barnacles?

KEY CONCEPT

53.3   Life History Is the Lifetime Pattern of Growth, Reproduction, and Survival

- **Life history strategies** are characterized by lifetime patterns of growth, reproduction, and survival, and can vary at the species and population levels.

- Life history **trade-offs** arise from genetic and environmental constraints on optimal growth, reproduction, and survival.

- Extremes in life history strategies of species allow for high growth rates (**r-strategists**) or for persistence at or near the carrying capacity (**K-strategists**), but most species fall along a continuum between these two strategies

Questions

1. What are life history traits, and why can they vary among individuals, populations, and species?

2. Describe why there are trade-offs in life history strategies.

3. How do r-strategists and K-strategists differ?

Figure 53.10

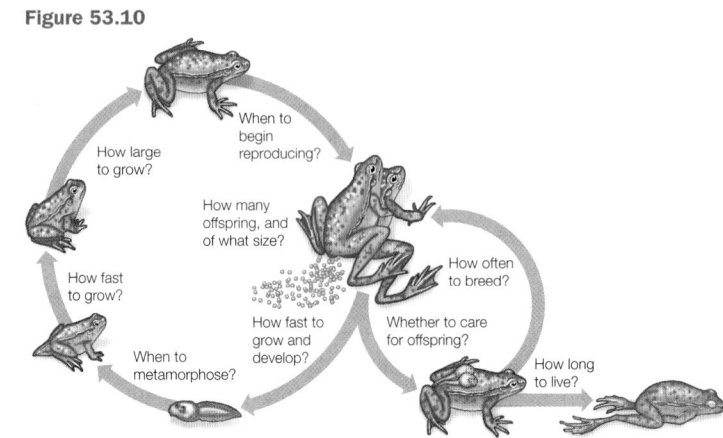

KEY CONCEPT

53.4   Population Biology Can Be Used in Managing and Conserving Populations

Go to Simulation 53.4

- Efforts to manage populations are more likely to be successful if they are based on an understanding of life histories and population and metapopulation dynamics.

- **Biological control** is the use of natural enemies to reduce the population density of an economically damaging species.

- Metapopulations can conserve endangered species if **source populations**, which serve as a source of individuals to **sink populations**, can rescue those populations from extinction.

Questions

1. Describe some ways that population dynamics can be managed for desirable and undesirable species.

2. How do source and sink populations within a metapopulation help species avoid extinction?

Figure 53.17

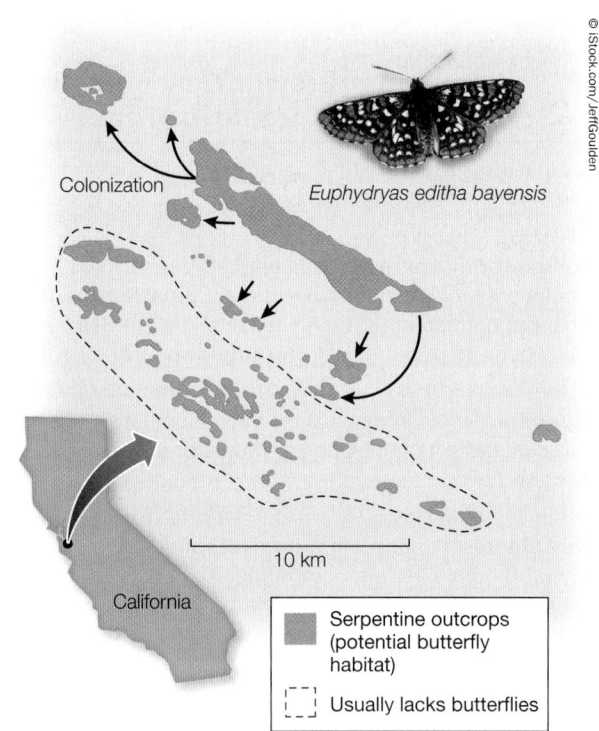

© iStock.com/JeffGoulden

Species Interactions 54

KEY CONCEPTS

54.1 Species Interactions Vary in Direction and Strength across a Continuum

54.2 Predation Is a Trophic Interaction in which Predators Benefit and Prey Are Harmed

54.3 Competition Is a Negative Interaction in which Species Overlap in the Use of Some Limiting Resource

54.4 Positive Interactions Occur When at Least One Species Benefits and None Are Harmed

Lionfishes (*Pterois* spp.), native to the Indo-Pacific region, have invaded the Atlantic Ocean and are drastically reducing native coral-reef fish populations using a novel feeding strategy.

© Georgette Douwma/Getty Images

▶ Investigating LIFE

The Lionfish King

The coral reefs surrounding the Bahamas have endured the effects of human activity for centuries, but for the last three decades they have faced a threat unlike any other—the invasion of two species of beautiful but highly destructive lionfishes (*Pterois volitans* and *P. miles*). Lionfishes, first spotted off the coast of Florida in the mid-1980s, are native to the Indo-Pacific region and are popular aquarium fishes. How they came to their new habitats is uncertain, but DNA evidence suggests that they were released into the Atlantic Ocean by unsuspecting aquarium owners. Over the last three decades, lionfish populations have thrived, successfully invading the Western Atlantic, the Caribbean and Gulf of Mexico, and now as far south as Brazil. The invasion has progressed to the point that the density of lionfishes in the Atlantic is greater than in their native Pacific range; in some locations, 450 lionfishes per hectare (2.5 acres) have been recorded.

The invasion of marine habitats by fish predators is extremely rare. What, then, allows lionfishes to be so successful? Part of their success has to do with their ability to tolerate a variety of tropical and subtropical temperatures and salinities—from the warm waters of shallow reefs, mangroves, and sea-grass beds to the colder waters of deep reefs and offshore currents. But the real story lies in their interactions with other species—they are dominant predators and competitors in their introduced range. A survey of lionfish populations at nine sites off the coast of the Bahamas showed that their abundance increased 2.5-fold from 2008 to 2010, despite the presence of 16 species of similar native competitor fishes (which declined by 44% during that period). Gut analyses of lionfishes showed that they are voracious generalist predators; the increase in lionfish abundance coincided with a 65% decline in small-bodied coral-reef fishes representing 42 different species. Other studies have shown similar results, reinforcing the notion that lionfishes may be among the most damaging marine invaders known.

Explaining the success and devastating impact of these invaders requires an understanding of the ecology and evolution of species interactions, the subject of this chapter. We will return to the example of the lionfishes' extraordinary success in capturing their prey at the end of this chapter.

 Why are small coral-reef fish species so vulnerable to lionfish predation, and what can be done about it? (Find the answer on page 1233.)

KEY CONCEPT
54.1 Species Interactions Vary in Direction and Strength across a Continuum

Learning Objectives

54.1.1 Distinguish among predation, competition, positive interactions (mutualism and commensalism), and amensalism.

54.1.2 Define asymmetrical species interactions and evaluate possible reasons for the asymmetry.

54.1.3 Explain how species interactions can result in genetic and coevolutionary changes.

One of life's certainties is that every species on Earth will encounter and interact with other species. These interactions have consequences that affect not only individuals but populations, and ultimately the distribution and abundance of species. Over the long term, they can lead to evolutionary change in one or more of the interacting species. For ease of description, we will focus on two-way relationships, such as one species eating another or two species competing for the same limiting resources. In reality, species interact with multiple species as part of an integrated ecological community. We will explore these community dynamics in Chapter 55.

Ecologists characterize species interactions based on the effects species have on each other—positive (+), negative (–), or neutral (0)—and whether that effect is **trophic** (feeding) or not (**Figure 54.1**). In addition, species interactions may include a **symbiosis**, a condition in which one of the species lives in or on the other species. As you will see, symbioses can occur whether the interaction is positive or negative. Four broad categories into which species interactions fall are predation, competition, positive interactions, and amensalism.

1. **Predation** is a trophic interaction in which an individual of one species (a **predator**) kills and/or consumes individuals (or parts of individuals) of another species (its **prey**). Predation includes **carnivory**, in which the predator and prey are both animals; **herbivory**, in which the predator is an animal and the prey is a plant or algae; and **parasitism**, in which the predator (a **parasite**) lives symbiotically on or in the prey (its **host**) and consumes only certain tissues without necessarily killing the host. Some parasites are pathogens that cause disease in their hosts.

2. **Competition** is a nontrophic interaction in which two or more species overlap in the use of at least some of the same required limiting resources, negatively affecting their growth, reproduction, and/or survival. Competition can occur under a variety of circumstances: between predators that depend on the same prey species (such as you saw in the lionfish example), between herbivores that feed on the same host plant, or between pathogenic microbes attacking the same host. The limiting resource need not be food; species may compete for water, space, nesting sites, or even (in the case of plants) sunlight.

(A)

Type of interaction	Effect on species 1	Effect on species 2
Predation (predator–prey)	+	–
Carnivory (animal–animal)	+	–
Herbivory (animal–plant)	+	–
Parasitism (parasite–host)	+	–
Competition	–	–
Positive interactions (facilitations)	+	0 or +
Mutualism	+	+
Commensalism	+	0
Amensalism	–	0

(B)

Parasitism, Predation, Mutualism
The buffalo's hide is infested with parasitic ticks. Oxpecker birds eat the ticks, to the mutual benefit of the birds and the buffalo.

Herbivory
The African buffalo feeds on the grasses of the savanna.

Amensalism, Commensalism
The large mammal unwittingly destroys insects and their nests. The white cattle egrets feed on insects disturbed by the buffalo's passage.

Courtesy of Andrew D. Sinauer

Predation
Carnivores such as wolves hunt and kill herbivorous mammals.

Competition
The grizzly bear is attempting to take over the wolves' kill.

© Michael Mauro/Minden Pictures

Figure 54.1 Types of Species Interactions Interactions among species can be grouped into categories based on whether their influence on each of the interacting species is positive (+), negative (–), or neutral (0). Species interactions are an everyday occurrence within communities.

Q: Are any of the species interactions featured in the photos trophic or symbiotic? If so, which ones?

 View in Achieve
Activity 54.1 Ecological Interactions

3. **Positive interactions** (also known as **facilitations**) are trophic or nontrophic interactions in which at least one species benefits from the interaction and none are harmed. Positive interactions include **mutualisms**, in which both species benefit from the interaction, sometimes in a highly dependent and symbiotic manner. **Commensalism** is a type of positive interaction in which one participant benefits but the other is unaffected; it includes a wide range of interactions that typically encompass the provisioning of food and habitat that improve conditions for the commensal organism.

4. **Amensalisms** occur when one participant is harmed but the other is not affected. An example is a herd of elephants moving through a forest and trampling vegetation; the elephants are not affected by this event, but the plants clearly are. Another example includes small understory plants that grow under trees. The understory plants are deprived of light but likely have no effect on the trees.

Species interactions are not always clear-cut

Although ecologists find it useful to classify interactions among species into a few basic categories, the boundaries between groupings are not always clear. In reality, the interaction categories described in this key concept are part of a continuum in how strongly each species affects the other (**Figure 54.2**). The continuum is a consequence of the variable strength in species interactions and their asymmetrical nature. For example, competition between the native Eurasian red squirrel (*Sciurus vulgaris*) and the non-native eastern gray squirrel (*S. carolinensis*) in the United Kingdom is highly asymmetrical, with the gray squirrel having a much stronger effect on the red squirrel than vice versa. This asymmetry is the result of the gray squirrel's ability to better obtain limiting food resources, particularly oak acorns, causing the red squirrel's population sizes to decline. The red squirrel is also declining because of a fatal disease spread by the gray squirrel.

Species interactions can be difficult to classify because of the different ways in which interactions affect particular species. For example, sea anemones in the Pacific Ocean sting and eat small fishes, but a select few fish species (mostly in the genus *Amphiprion*) live within the tentacles of sea anemones and are unaffected by their stings. Safe from its predators, an anemonefish moves freely among the stinging tentacles to scavenge the leavings of the anemone (**Figure 54.3**).

Anemonefishes must acclimate to the anemone's venom, and the anemone, in turn, must acclimate to the fishes. The acclimation process appears to involve a change in the mucus coat of the fishes; wiping off the mucus of an acclimated fish results in immediate stinging, whereas anemones do not sting fishes with intact mucus. The benefits of this relationship to the anemonefishes are clear: they escape their own predators by hiding behind the anemone's stinging tentacles, and they have no need to forage widely for food. But does the anemone benefit from the association? By defecating while in residence, the anemonefishes may provide nitrogen-rich nutrients to the anemone. However, the fishes may occasionally steal the anemone's prey, which has a negative effect on the anemone's fitness. Thus the net outcome

of the interaction depends on the ecological circumstances under which it occurs, including the influence of other species and the existing physical conditions.

Some interactions result in evolutionary change in the species involved

All types of interactions have the potential to influence the population sizes of interacting species. By contributing to the differential survival or reproduction of individuals with different traits, they can also alter genotype frequencies within the interacting populations over time. Thus these interactions have both ecological consequences, as when they affect the distribution and abundance of a species, and evolutionary consequences, as when they lead to evolutionary change. Darwin observed that evolutionary change occurs not only in response to physical conditions, as described in

Effects of species 1 on species 2

Amensalism   Competition   Amensalism

Effects of species 2 on species 1

Figure 54.2 A Continuum of Competitive Effects   Species interactions, such as competition, vary in their strength (represented by the thickness of the bars) and symmetry depending on the effects of one species on the other species. Amensalism occurs when one species suffers a negative effect from the interaction but the other species is not affected.

Q: Suppose the Eurasian red squirrel described in the text is species 1 and the eastern gray squirrel is species 2. Indicate which pairs of interactions between species 1 and 2 would best represent their relationship.

Amphiprion percula

Figure 54.3 Interactions between Species Are Not Always Clear-Cut   Ecologists long believed that the relationship between sea anemones and anemonefishes was a commensalism: that the fishes, by living among the anemone's stinging tentacles, gained protection from their predators. But it could also be considered a mutualism, if the fishes' feces provide the anemone with beneficial nutrients.

Chapter 52, but also in response to interactions among species. In his introduction to *On the Origin of Species*, Darwin pointed out that woodpeckers have feet, tails, beaks, and tongues "admirably adapted to catch insects under the bark of trees" as a result of their long-standing interactions with their insect prey.

While abiotic factors also act as agents of selection, they differ in a fundamental way from biotic agents of selection in that they do not themselves undergo change as a result of the interaction. Snow and ice do not become more deadly as a result of encountering cold-resistant organisms, but predators can, over evolutionary time, become swifter, more powerful, or more efficient at capturing their prey. In response, prey species may become swifter, tougher, less conspicuous, or more poisonous, all of which decrease their likelihood of being consumed. This back-and-forth evolutionary response between interacting species is known as **coevolution**.

The types of interactions most likely to lead to coevolution are those that occur predictably and with high frequency over time and that have a strong effect on the fitness of individuals. Thus species involved in amensal and commensal interactions are less likely to experience coevolutionary change as a result of the interaction than are species involved in predatory, competitive, and mutualistic interactions.

 View in Achieve
Simulation 54.1 **Coevolution**

KEY CONCEPT
54.1 Recap and Assess

Species interactions may be classified into four basic categories: predation (a trophic interaction in which a predator kills and/or consumes its prey, or part of its prey), competition (a nontrophic interaction in which species use some of the same limiting resources and have negative effects on one another), positive interactions (trophic or nontrophic interactions in which at least one species benefits from the interaction and none are harmed), or amensalism (a nontrophic interaction in which one species is harmed but the other is not affected). Species interactions are not always clear-cut but instead fall along a continuum in which species vary in how strongly they affect one other. Some species interactions result in evolutionary change.

1. Classify each of the following species interactions as carnivory, herbivory, parasitism, competition, amensalism, mutualism, or commensalism.
   a. Leafcutter ants harvest and transport leaf fragments to their nests, where the vegetation will support fungus, which the ants consume.
   b. Elephant seals lie on rocks, crushing and detaching algae underneath them.
   c. Head lice inhabit the human scalp and feed on blood.
   d. Wolves and cougars both prey on the same deer population, which is limiting to both predators.
2. Name some conditions that can modify or change the outcome of a two-species interaction.
3. Do you think the interactions between lionfishes and their fish prey in the Atlantic Ocean have resulted in evolutionary change for the prey? Explain.

Trophic interactions are critical to life on Earth. As a result, the variety of ways that heterotrophic organisms acquire food plays a critical role in the success of every species on Earth. In the next key concept we will consider how predation influences the ecology and evolution of both predator and prey species.

KEY CONCEPT
54.2 Predation Is a Trophic Interaction in which Predators Benefit and Prey Are Harmed

Learning Objectives

54.2.1 Describe the types of strategies prey use to avoid being captured and eaten by predators.

54.2.2 Explain why many herbivore–plant and parasite–host relationships have evolved to be specialized species interactions.

54.2.3 Describe why some predator–prey populations are linked and cycle in response to one another.

54.2.4 Explain how predators can have dramatic effects on communities.

Predator–prey interactions are probably the most familiar, and perhaps the most dramatic, type of species interaction. Even though carnivory, herbivory, and parasitism all involve the simple interaction of one species eating another species, they often defy categorization. For example, a carnivore might sometimes function like an herbivore by eating berries and roots, or an insect might be considered an herbivore or a parasite if it spends its entire life feeding on a single tree. In addition, predators can differ considerably in the ways they affect their prey's population dynamics if the prey species is not killed in the process. Despite these complications, we will explore predation by considering carnivory, herbivory, and parasitism separately. We will end by considering some generalities regarding population and community consequences of predation.

Carnivory results in a range of capture and avoidance mechanisms

Given that carnivores almost always kill the prey they consume, the interests of both predator and prey are at stake: the best strategy for carnivores is to maximize their ability to capture and consume prey, while the best strategy for prey is to minimize the likelihood of being eaten. We first consider the strategies carnivores use to obtain food and then examine how prey avoid being eaten.

What strategies do carnivores use to obtain food? The success of carnivores depends on balancing the cost of pursuing, capturing, and handling prey against the energetic benefit of consuming them, as discussed in Key Concept 51.4. At one extreme, carnivores use strength and swiftness to actively search for and capture high-quality prey. The "active pursuit" strategy is used by predators of all sizes: both orca whales (*Orcinus orca*) pursuing gray whales (*Eschrichtius robustus*) and foxes pursuing birds are fast, powerful predators and are equipped with strong jaws (**Figure 54.4A**). At the other extreme, an ability to look inconspicuous allows the stealthy predator to ambush prey

(A) *Vulpes vulpes fulva*

(B) *Ceratophrys* sp.

Figure 54.4 Active Searcher or Stealthy Ambusher Predators can be **(A)** active searchers such as the swift and strong red fox or **(B)** stealthy ambushers such as this seemingly inconspicuous wide mouthed frog.

"Playing possum," a term that is sometimes applied to this strategy, refers to the ability of opposums to simulate death.

CHEMICAL DEFENSES Many animals use chemical defenses to escape or repel their predators. Chemical defenses are generally used by animal prey that are small, weak, sessile, or otherwise unprotected. Many insects produce sprays, oozes, or froths when attacked. Bombardier beetles, for example, eject a hot (100°C) noxious chemical spray from the tip of their abdomen that can be fatal to attacking insects.

▶ **Media Clip 54.1 Bombardier Beetle Sprays Its Enemies**
Life12e.com/mc54.1

Predators may evolve adaptions to overcome their prey's chemical defenses, as you saw in the case of the rough-skinned newt (*Taricha granulosa*) and the garter snakes (*Thamnophis sirtalis*) that have become insensitive to the newt's protective toxin (see Figure 19.20). Some predators ingest and sequester their prey's defensive chemicals and use them as defenses against their own predators. For example, some sea slug species incorporate toxic chemicals from their sponge prey, whereas others, which feed on hydrozoans, incorporate the stinging cells into their own bodies (**Figure 54.5C**). Likewise, poison dart frogs from Central and South America sequester toxins from their prey, which include ants, mites, and other small invertebrates (**Figure 54.5D**).

unlucky enough to pass its way (**Figure 54.4B**). Various other predation strategies have evolved in predators that are smaller than their prey. For example, the jaws of some snakes open wide enough to allow them to swallow prey larger than their head. The tiny short-tailed shrews (*Blarina* spp.), among the smallest mammalian predators, produce venomous saliva that paralyzes earthworms and snails but also prey much larger than the shrews, including mice and small birds.

Prey species have in turn developed a variety of defenses against predators. Some escape from predators simply by flying or running away. Others have morphological defenses; tough skin, shells, spines, or hair can foil even a determined predator (**Figure 54.5A**). Various other defenses that prey have evolved to avoid capture are described next.

AVOIDING DETECTION Prey species can often escape predators by hiding. One form of hiding is camouflage, also known as **crypsis**. Crypsis allows species to resemble objects that their predators consider inedible. The katydid in **Figure 54.5B**, for example, looks very much like a dead leaf, even down to the likeness of a spot of fungal decay.

Because the vision of many types of predators is adapted to spot moving prey, many prey species simply stop moving if they are being pursued.

(A) *Hystrix cristata*

(B) *Typophyllum* sp.

(C) *Chromodoris* sp.

(D) *Dendrobates reticulatus*

Figure 54.5 Adaptations to Avoid Being Eaten **(A)** Porcupines have a coat of sharp spines, or quills, that protect them from predators. **(B)** Birds searching for insect prey are likely to bypass a katydid that looks like a partially eaten leaf. **(C)** Nudibranchs (sea slugs) are mollusks without protective shells that may possess stinging nematocysts acquired from their hydrozoan prey. **(D)** Poison dart frogs of Central and South America sequester highly toxic chemicals in their brightly colored skin.

WARNING SIGNALS   Some prey species that defend themselves with toxic chemicals advertise that fact with a **warning signal**. Warning signals may be visual (many toxic species are brightly colored) or acoustical (the rattlesnake's warning rattle, for example), depending on what sensory cues their predators use to find prey.

Many toxic prey, such as the nudibranchs and frogs in Figures 54.5C and D, sport bright colors or striking patterns to protect themselves against visually orienting predators. Such warning coloration increases the probability that a predator will learn to recognize and avoid the toxic species. Some vertebrate predators that rely on visual cues can learn quickly to associate certain color patterns with an unpleasant feeding experience.

MIMICRY SYSTEMS   There are two general types of mimicry systems that have evolved repeatedly in nature: Batesian mimicry and Müllerian mimicry. In **Batesian mimicry**, a benign, edible species (the mimic) closely resembles a dangerous, toxic species (the model). The mimic benefits from the avoidance behavior of predators of the model (**Figure 54.6A**). In **Müllerian mimicry**, two or more species converge on a common warning signal; all benefit from providing a stronger recognition signal to predators. Many of the Neotropical longwing butterflies (*Heliconius*), which as caterpillars feed on toxic passionflower plants and incorporate the plant toxins into their bodies, are Müllerian mimics. *Heliconius* species living together in a particular geographic region are likely to have similar coloration and share a common warning pattern (**Figure 54.6B**). Genome sequencing of *Heliconius* Müllerian mimics has identified one gene, *optix*, that codes for a transcription factor that can, by changing gene expression patterns, create the same color patterns in *Heliconius* species that are not very closely related.

BEHAVORIAL MECHANISMS   Prey often use behavioral mechanisms to avoid predation. For example, as you saw in Key Concept 51.2 and Figure 51.21, group behaviors such as flocking and alarm vocalizations can provide protection from predators. In the lionfish example introduced in the chapter opening, the evolutionary change in behavior that predator and prey may experience has not yet had time to develop. In **Investigating Life: The Lionfish King** we describe research showing that the small reef-fish prey of lionfishes are likely experiencing a novel predatory behavior not previously encountered, and thus may be defenseless in the face of lionfish predation. Lionfishes slowly approach their prey and direct jets of water toward them. Confused or distracted by the jets, the prey are often taken by headfirst capture. The highly efficient predatory behavior of lionfishes doubtless contributes to their success as invasive species in tropical Western Atlantic and Caribbean coral reefs.

Herbivory is a widespread but specialized interaction

Herbivory is a widespread interaction, with the vast majority of herbivores being insects. Of those herbivorous insects, more than 90% are specialists that feed on just one or a few, often taxonomically related, plant species. Generalist herbivores, in contrast, feed on as many as hundreds of unrelated plant species. Vertebrate herbivores are usually generalists; a cow grazing in a pasture, for example, can consume many different plant species in a single

(A) Batesian mimics

This harmless blenny...

...closely resembles a venomous related species.

Petroscirtes breviceps   *Meiacanthus grammistes*

(B) Müllerian mimics

In each pair, *Heliconius melpomene* appears on top, *H. erato* is below. Both species are toxic.

The appearances of both species vary geographically but are always linked.

Figure 54.6 Truth in Labeling?   **(A)** Batesian mimics are vulnerable species that gain protection by mimicking the warning signals of dangerous species. The appearance of the harmless blenny species *Petroscirtes breviceps* closely resembles that of the fanged striped blenny, which possesses a pair of grooved fangs with associated venom glands. **(B)** The shared warning coloration of Müllerian mimics is an honest advertisement of their toxicity. As caterpillars, all of the longwing butterflies (genus *Heliconius*) of South America feed on toxic passionflower plants and incorporate the toxins into their adult bodies. The *Heliconius* species living together in a particular region have similar warning coloration. (Map: *The World Factbook* 2016-17. Washington, DC: Central Intelligence Agency, 2016. https://www.cia.gov/library/publications/the-world-factbook/index.html.)

afternoon. There are exceptions to this pattern, however. Australian koalas (*Phascolarctos cinereus*) famously feed exclusively on the foliage of eucalyptus trees, and the diet of giant pandas (*Ailuropoda melanoleuca*) is made up almost entirely of bamboo.

▶InvestigatingLIFE   The Lionfish King

Experiment

Original Paper: M. A. Albins and P. J. Lyons. 2012. Invasive red lionfish *Pterois volitans* blow directed jets of water at prey fish. *Mar Ecol Prog Ser* 448: 1–5.

Mark Albins and his colleagues asked what feeding behaviors the invasive lionfish *Pterois volitans* might use to be a successful predator on Atlantic and Caribbean coral-reef fishes. They conducted field observations of lionfish feeding on small reef fishes and noticed that lionfish typically face their prey, flaring their pectoral fins and moving very slowly within striking distance of the prey. During the approach, lionfish produced a strong, pulsed jet of water from their mouths and directed it toward the prey. To investigate this novel feeding behavior, Albins and his colleagues conducted feeding trials on lionfish and native goby prey.

HYPOTHESIS▶   The novel feeding method of lionfish—in which jets of water are directed at their prey—disorients prey, allowing for easier headfirst capture.

METHOD▶

1. Using hand nets, capture lionfish and two species of native goby prey (*Coryphopterus glaucofraenum* and *Gnatholepis thompsoni*) from coral reefs and sea-grass beds in the Bahamas.

2. Acclimate lionfish and gobies to a flow-through aquarium and film their feeding behavior using a digital video camera.

3. Present lionfish with gobies in two ways: (i) release lionfish into an open aquarium setting containing the gobies, and (ii) release lionfish into an aquarium that holds the gobies in transparent containers so the lionfish can see but not consume them.

4. Use a glass pipette to release food-grade dye in front of the lionfish to visualize the movement of water around its mouth.

5. Examine digital videos of all feeding trials to measure characteristics of water jets and response of the prey.

RESULTS▶   In all of the open aquarium trials, lionfish produced directed water jets at goby prey. Seven of the eight trials resulted in headfirst strikes. In the container trials, the lionfish produced an average of 18 water-jet pulses before striking at the prey. The maximum distance from the mouth of the lionfish that a visible jet-front reached was 10 cm.

Goby in container

Dye

Glass pipette

The lionfish produces jets of water (indicated by the spread of the dye) to disorient its goby fish prey.

M. A. Albins and P. J. Lyons. 2012. *Mar Ecol Prog Ser* 448: 1–5

CONCLUSION▶   What would you conclude about the feeding behavior of lionfishes and the responses of prey from the Atlantic Ocean versus the Pacific Ocean? Explore this question in the following Work with the Data exercise.

Work with the Data

In addition to the aquarium experiments, the researchers conducted field observations of the feeding behavior of lionfishes in different locations—their native Pacific Ocean and their non-native Atlantic Ocean. They found that, in the Atlantic Ocean, most successful captures by lionfishes did not require them to blow jets of water at their prey (only 18% of the captures involved this behavior). However, in the Pacific Ocean, they found that 56% of successful captures by lionfishes involved them blowing jets of water at their prey. The researchers also reported that an extensive literature search showed that blowing jets of water at prey appears to be unique to lionfishes.

QUESTIONS▶

1. Refer to Method step 3 in the experiment. Why do you suppose the researchers conducted lionfish aquarium feeding trials with

free-swimming fish prey? Alternatively, what did the containers containing the fish prey afford the researchers?

2. Given what you know about the feeding behavior of lionfishes, would you expect them to produce more or fewer water jets to capture fish prey in the Atlantic Ocean compared with the Pacific Ocean? Would the distance the water jet had to travel be shorter or longer for the Atlantic Ocean prey compared with the Pacific Ocean prey?

3. Based on all the lionfish feeding behavior information presented here, what is the most plausible hypothesis to explain why lionfishes are such effective predators on coral-reef fishes in the Atlantic Ocean compared with the Pacific Ocean?

 Media Clip 54.2 Lionfish "Strike" Again!
Life12e.com/mc54.2

Go to **Achieve** for a companion Data in Depth exercise.

Herbivores, particularly insects, generally consume only parts of their food plants and usually do not kill them. In most natural ecosystems, insects rarely remove more than a small percentage of the plant biomass. For that reason, some ecologists have questioned the ability of herbivores to exert strong selection pressure on plant traits. Mortality is not, however, the only form of selection that leads to evolutionary change; herbivores can reduce plant fitness if the plants they attack produce fewer offspring.

PLANT DEFENSES AGAINST HERBIVORES   Plant chemistry is one of the principal defense mechanisms against herbivores. Plants in the mustard family (Brassicaceae) offer just one example of the strategy of producing secondary metabolites as a mechanism to reduce herbivory. The amazing variety of secondary metabolites produced by plants to defend themselves against herbivores is considered in Key Concept 37.3.

Some plants and algae protect themselves by being physically difficult to eat. For example, thorns and spines are highly effective deterrents to browsing vertebrate herbivores. Coralline algae contain calcium carbonate within their tissues, which deters many marine herbivores. An exception is some sea urchin species that have powerful articulated jaws and teeth and long coiling guts that can process less nutritious chalky tissue.

RECIPROCAL ADAPTATIONS IN HERBIVORES AND PLANTS   A spectacular variety of adaptations to plant defenses has evolved in herbivores. Many herbivores circumvent plant defenses by behavioral means. For example, the secondary metabolites produced by a plant called Saint-John's-wort (*Hypericum perforatum*) require exposure to sunlight for optimal toxicity, so some insects that feed on this plant roll its leaves into a light-impervious cylinder and feed in comfort in the dark. Large herbivores such as deer and horses graze on a wide variety of plant species, minimizing their exposure to any particular defensive chemical. Long-lived and with relatively good memories, they can learn to avoid plants with an unpleasant taste.

Unlike large mammalian herbivores, caterpillars and many other insect herbivores may spend their entire lives feeding on a single individual plant. Such exclusive diets are associated with highly specialized detoxification systems. The caterpillar of the diamondback moth (*Plutella xylostella*) eats plants in the cabbage family, which are rich in toxic mustard oil glycosides. In its gut is an enzyme that breaks down the glycosides into harmless by-products.

Some herbivores take resistance a step further by storing, or sequestering, plant toxins in specialized organs or tissues that are insensitive to those toxins. This strategy also makes the sequestered chemicals available for defense against the herbivores' own enemies. The caterpillar of the monarch butterfly (*Danaus plexippus*), for example, is insensitive to the neurotoxic glycosides in its milkweed host plants, but most of its enemies, including insect-eating birds, cannot tolerate these compounds.

Most parasites specialize on hosts, and most hosts house many species of parasites

Parasitism is an interaction in which a predator (a parasite) lives on or in the prey (its host) and consumes only certain tissues.

Many parasite–host relationships are symbiotic. Effects of parasite–host interactions can vary dramatically in magnitude, from having weak effects to causing the death of the host. While parasites typically feed on only one or a few host species, hosts typically house many species of parasites (**Figure 54.7**). Parasites can also have their own parasites. This specialization helps explain why there are so many parasite species; it is estimated that roughly 50% of the species on Earth are parasites.

Parasites can be classified as **microparasites**, which include viruses, bacteria, and protists, or **macroparasites**, which are larger and include such groups as worms and insects.

MICROPARASITES   Microparasites are many orders of magnitude smaller than their hosts and generally live and reproduce inside their hosts. Multiple generations may reside within a single individual, and a host may harbor thousands or millions of them. Many microparasites, in the process of acquiring nutrients at the expense of their host, cause symptoms of disease and thus are considered pathogens. Host mechanisms that can limit pathogen proliferation include the immune system in animals (see Chapter 40) and biochemical defenses in plants (see Key Concept 37.3).

Just as with other predator–prey interactions, hosts and pathogens can place strong selective pressure on one another. If a pathogen strain is to persist in a host population, the pathogens must continually infect new host individuals. A less deadly strain that kills a smaller proportion of host individuals may be able to infect a larger number of new hosts. Thus pathogen and host may reach a state of coexistence as increased host resistance (ability to withstand the effects of a pathogen) and decreased pathogen virulence

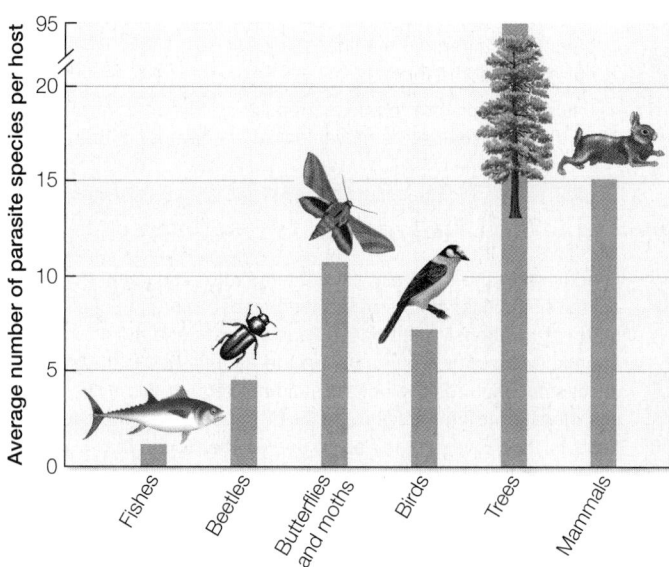

Figure 54.7 Why Are There So Many Parasites?   It is estimated that roughly 50% of the species on Earth are parasites. Most parasites specialize on host species, most host species have multiple parasite species, and most parasites have their own parasites. This specialization may help explain why there are so many species of parasites. (After P. D. Stiling. 2002. *Ecology: Theories and Applications*, 4th ed. Prentice-Hall: Upper Saddle River, NJ.)

(ability to cause disease) evolve. Yet new virulent strains may also arise, reminding us that evolution is constantly occurring.

An example of the complex interactions between host and pathogen comes from Australia, where the myxoma virus was introduced to control the exploding population of European rabbits (*Oryctolagus cuniculus*), which were devastating the rangeland vegetation used by cattle and sheep. The virus, which is transmitted by mosquitos, causes infections and blindness in rabbits, eventually leading to starvation and death. After the introduction of the virus in 1950, 99.8% of infected rabbits died. Millions of rabbits died over the following decades, but the rabbits slowly evolved resistance to the virus. The virus is still used to control rabbit populations, but this requires introducing new, more lethal strains of the virus to ultimately be effective.

MACROPARASITES   While microparasites generally live and reproduce inside their hosts, macroparasites are not always intimately associated with their hosts. Macroparasites rarely cause the same kinds of disease symptoms that pathogenic microparasites cause, but they may nevertheless affect host survival and reproduction and can thereby act as agents of selection on their hosts. **Ectoparasites** are macroparasites that live outside the bodies of their hosts. **Endoparasites**, such as the tapeworms described in Key Concept 29.2, are macroparasites that spend at least part of their life cycle inside the bodies of their hosts.

Some ectoparasites, such as leeches and mosquitoes, are only casually associated with their hosts, interacting with them just long enough to eat their fill and then moving on. Ectoparasites that spend their entire lives on their hosts have several attributes that keep them attached to their hosts. Whale lice, which are generally found in skin lesions, nostrils, and eyes of marine mammals, have claws on the tips of their legs that pierce the skin of the whale or dolphin host (**Figure 54.8A**). Most whale lice are associated with a single species of whale and spend their entire lives on one individual whale. The lice feed on algae or flaking skin on the whale's body, causing minor skin damage but no significant health risks.

Most hosts actively work to rid themselves of their ectoparasites. Grooming behavior—an important component of the social interactions of many primates—may have evolved in response to ectoparasites. The Japanese macaque (*Macaca fuscata*), for example, is prone to infestation by two species of lice, which tend to lay their multitudinous eggs on the outer surfaces of their host's back, arms, and legs. To keep louse populations in check, macaques form and maintain social bonds that ensure the consistent presence of grooming partners (**Figure 54.8B**). Some biologists believe that hairlessness in humans is an evolutionary response to ectoparasites.

Predator populations can cycle with their prey populations

The interaction between predators and prey, including parasites and hosts, not only influences the adaptations that species develop but also their population dynamics. Some predator–prey populations are linked and oscillate in response to one another. What controls such patterns of cycling?

(A) *Cyamus* sp.

(B) *Macaca fuscata*

Figure 54.8 Ectoparasites Hang On   **(A)** Ectoparasites such as these whale lice on the body of a gray whale are flattened and equipped with strong claws for gripping the body of their host. Each individual whale has its own population of lice. **(B)** Grooming behaviors among primates are believed to have evolved in response to ectoparasites. Japanese macaques form social groups in which this behavior plays a significant role.

Consider the classic example of predator–prey cycling in the Canada lynx (*Lynx canadensis*) and the snowshoe hare (*Lepus americanus*), which makes up a large portion of the lynx diet. Long-term records from Hudson's Bay Company, a Canadian retailer with a long history in the fur-trading business, show that the numbers of lynx and hares trapped over time reflect a regular cycle in the population sizes of each species, with peak abundances occurring every 10 years but falling to low abundances in the intervening years (**Figure 54.9**). In addition, the peak in the lynx population lags behind that of the hare population by 2–3 years. Models of predator–prey interactions suggest that this cycling is the result of a tight coupling between prey and predator: as prey increase in abundance, predators do as well, causing prey numbers to decline as a result of increased mortality. When prey decline, so do predators, causing both predator and prey populations to decrease. At some point, the prey population starts to increase again due to the lack of predation, which then allows the predator population, which lags behind, to increase as well. However, in the case of lynx and hare populations, it is likely more complicated.

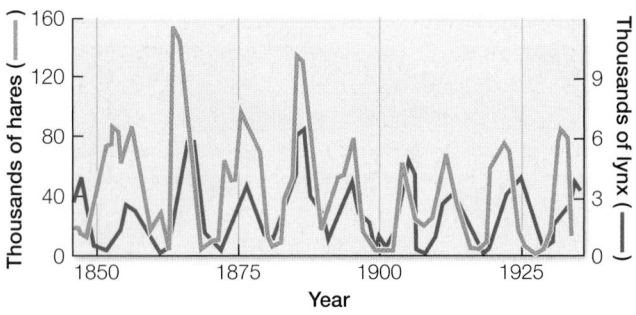

Figure 54.9 Lynx and Hare Population Cycles Historical trapping data from the Hudson's Bay Company show that numbers of both hares and lynx fluctuate in a 10-year cycle that is offset by 2–3 years. (After D. A. MacLulich. 1937. *Fluctuations in the Number of the Varying Hare* (Lepus americanus). University of Toronto Press: Toronto.)

Q: Does the peak number of hares typically occur before or after the peak number of lynx? Why is this so?

A long-term study by Charles Krebs and colleagues showed that if lynx are absent or food is added for the hares, predator and prey populations continue to cycle, suggesting that the underlying cause of the cycling may be controlled by environmental factors such as large-scale variability in climate.

 View in Achieve
Simulation 54.2 Predator-Prey System

(A) Sea stars of the Pacific Northwest

Following sea star removal at Mukkaw Bay, the number of sessile invertebrate species decreased from 15 to 8.

Courtesy of Sally Hacker

(B) Sea stars of New Zealand

At the New Zealand study site, the number of species decreased from 20 to 14.

Courtesy of Sally Hacker

Predators can have dramatic effects on communities

As you might imagine, given the reduced growth, reproduction, and survival of prey, predators (including parasites) can have dramatic effects not only on populations but also on communities.

One classic experiment, conducted by Robert Paine in the mid-1960s, showed the strong role that sea star predation has on rocky shore communities of the Pacific Northwest of North America. Paine noticed that one species in the community, the mussel *Mytilus californianus*, dominated in certain zones of the intertidal when the density of its sea star predator (*Pisaster ochraceus*) was low. Through the continual removal of *Pisaster* from the rocky shoreline, Paine showed that sessile invertebrate species number declined as the mussel monopolized space in the absence of its predator. After nearly 3 years, the experimental plots had roughly half the number of sessile invertebrate species compared with the natural condition where *Pisaster* was present (**Figure 54.10A**). Subsequent experimental removal of sea stars on New Zealand rocky shores, which share no species in common with the Pacific Northwest, resulted in similar reductions in sessile invertebrates (**Figure 54.10B**). Paine's research on the sea star–mussel interaction showed not only that predation can affect the number of species in a community but that the effect can be controlled by one or a few species, which Paine called **keystone species** (named after the single wedge-shaped stone in the center of an archway called the "keystone" that holds all the other stones in place). Keystone species have large effects, not because of their abundance but because of the important role they play in communities. You'll learn more about keystone species in Chapter 55.

Some of the most compelling examples of the effects of predation on communities come from human-caused events such as the extinction (or near extinction) of predators, as in the case of wolves living in Yellowstone National Park (see Key Concept 55.3), or from the introduction of novel predators into communities. As you saw in the opening of this chapter, the inadvertent introduction of lionfishes to the Atlantic Ocean from the Pacific Ocean has led marine ecologists to hypothesize that there may be drastic effects for reef communities.

KEY CONCEPT
54.2 Recap and Assess

Predation is a fundamental species interaction because all animals must eat. Predator–prey interactions result in the evolution of a range of capture mechanisms (extremes of swift pursuer to inconspicuous ambusher) and avoidance mechanisms (including avoiding detection, chemical defenses, warning

Figure 54.10 Sea Star Predation on Mussels Has Community-Wide Effects Along the coasts of the Pacific Northwest of North America and New Zealand, sea stars preferentially feed on mussels, creating bare space for other sessile invertebrates such as acorn and gooseneck barnacles. Experiments by Robert Paine demonstrated that when sea stars were removed from the rocky shore, mussels outcompeted other sessile invertebrates for space, resulting in a decline in the number of invertebrate species in both **(A)** the Pacific Northwest and **(B)** New Zealand. (A after R. T. Paine. 1966. *Am Nat* 100: 65–75; B after R. T. Paine. 1971. *Ecology* 52: 1096–1106.)

signals, mimicry, and behavior). Most parasites specialize on hosts, and most hosts have many species of parasites. Predator populations can cycle with their prey and can have dramatic effects on communities.

1. Given what you know about lionfish feeding behavior, describe some avoidance mechanisms that might evolve in small reef fishes in the Atlantic, to avoid being eaten by lionfishes.

2. What characteristics of herbivory and parasitism are likely important in promoting specialization?

3. Suppose the number of grass species in an alpine meadow is maintained by herbivory by hares. By feeding on the dominant space-occupier, the hares allow less dominant grass species to thrive (similar to the sea star–mussel example in Figure 54.10). Now suppose lynx predators are introduced into the system. When, in the population cycle of lynx and hare (see Figure 54.9), would you predict the number of grass species to be highest? When would it be lowest?

Predator–prey interactions are intrinsically compelling; the idea of a lionfish "vacuuming up" tiny reef fishes naturally captures our attention. But at the same time, lionfishes are not the only predators of reef fishes; sharks, barracudas, and even turtles hunt small reef fishes, potentially reducing the food available for lionfishes. Whenever any shared resource is limiting, organisms may compete to varying degrees to get that resource. In the next key concept we will consider how competition influences the ecology and evolution of species that overlap in their use of a limiting resource.

KEY CONCEPT 54.3 Competition Is a Negative Interaction in which Species Overlap in the Use of Some Limiting Resource

Learning Objectives

54.3.1 Compare and contrast the concepts of fundamental niche and realized niche.

54.3.2 Distinguish between interference competition and exploitation competition.

54.3.3 Describe some of the important processes that maintain competitive coexistence.

Virtually no species has exclusive access to any given set of resources. All species must compete with other species for at least some resources. **Resources** are simply the components of the environment—such as food, water, light, and space—that are required by all species. The full set of these resources, in part, determines the **niche** of a species, defined as the physical and biological conditions required for growth, reproduction, and survival. Thus a species' niche defines where it can and cannot live. Although a species might be physiologically able to live under a wide range of conditions, competitors may restrict its use of those resources. Thus every species has a **fundamental niche**, defined by its physiological capabilities, and a **realized niche**, defined by its interactions with other species. As you saw in Key Concept 53.1, intraspecific competition for resources is the main reason why populations do not grow indefinitely, and instead eventually reach some limit defined by

their carrying capacity. Interspecific competition—competition among different species—affects individuals in much the same way. At some point an essential resource, or set of resources, may be in such short supply that competition becomes a factor in a population's growth. Such a resource that is in short supply is referred to as a **limiting resource**. At one extreme, if a species can prevent another species from using essential resources, the inferior competitor may become locally extinct, a result called **competitive exclusion**. In reality, though, most species show some sort of **competitive coexistence**, or the ability to coexist with one another despite sharing limiting resources. Competitive coexistence is maintained through a variety of ecological processes.

Assuming competitive coexistence occurs, competition can manifest itself either directly or indirectly. **Interference competition** occurs when one species directly interferes with or excludes another species' access to a limiting resource. Interference competition can take many forms, from physical exclusion to chemical warfare among the competitors. A graphic example involves two ant species: the desert ant *Dorymyrmex bicolor* and the honeypot ant *Myrmecocystus mexicanus*. These species occupy the same habitat type—arid areas containing little vegetation—and they feed on similar foods—the sugary excretions of aphids and other sap-feeding insects. When *D. bicolor* workers find the entrance of a honeypot ant nest, they pick up small stones in their mandibles, carry them to the rim of the nest opening, and drop them down the hole—up to 200 stones in a 5-minute interval. This activity stops the honeypot ants from foraging and temporarily limits competition for food with the desert ant.

Exploitation competition occurs when a limiting resource is available to all competitors but the outcome of the interaction depends on the relative efficiency with which each species uses the resource. Exploitation competition affects the availability of a resource for another species but not in an exclusionary way, as we see with interference competition. Exploitation competition may lead to coexistence, provided that the species relying on the same resource have ways to divide up, or partition, that resource. For example, in the American Southwest at least three species of bees consume the nectar of the shin dagger agave (*Agave schottii*). The three bee species differ in where and when they collect shin dagger nectar. Honey bees tend to forage in places with the greatest numbers of shin dagger flowers, bumblebees in places with intermediate numbers of flowers, and carpenter bees where flowers are few and far between. Honey bees also tend to be most active when nectar output is greatest. With their larger nests and greater numbers of offspring to support, honey bees require greater foraging efficiency and greater energy intake. Foraging sites that are not worth their time are left to the other bees.

The bee–shin dagger agave example is one in which closely related bee species compete for agave nectar. But competition is not limited to closely related species; it commonly occurs among distantly related species as well. Bats and hummingbirds also visit shin dagger agave for its nectar. Even humans harvest agave (albeit the leaves rather than the nectar) to be used as an alternative for sugar.

Another important aspect of competition is that it is often asymmetrical (unequal): one species can be more negatively affected by the interaction than the other. Clearly this is the case under conditions of competitive exclusion, when one species drives the other

(A) Competition slows population growth

(B) Competition can result in local extinction

Figure 54.11 Competitive Exclusion or Coexistence? G. F. Gause grew three species of *Paramecium* in tubes filled with medium containing bacteria and yeast. **(A)** When *P. caudatum* and *P. bursaria* were grown alone, they showed logistic population growth and reached a stable carrying capacity. When grown together, each species showed slower population growth but were able to coexist by feeding on different food items. **(B)** When *P. caudatum* was grown with *P. aurelia*, it experienced local extinction. (A after G. F. Gause. 1935. *Vérifications Expérimentales de la Théorie Mathématique de la Lutte pour la Vie*. Hermann et Cie: Paris; B after G. F. Gause. 1934. *The Struggle for Existence*. Williams and Wilkins: Baltimore.)

Q: Predict what would happen if *P. caudatum* and *P. bursaria* both fed mainly on yeast cells.

▶ **View in Achieve**
Simulation 54.3 Species Interactions and Population Dynamics

to local extinction. But even when species coexist under competition, competitive success forms a continuum, as you saw with red and gray squirrels in the United Kingdom (see Figure 54.2). The effects of competition can vary for many reasons. Morphological, physiological, or behavioral differences can affect a species' ability to obtain limiting resources. In addition, the magnitude of competitive interactions can vary depending on environmental conditions and how they affect the competitive ability of individual species. We'll discuss how the outcome of competitive interactions can be modified by environmental factors shortly, but first let's consider the ways in which species can divide limiting resources to reduce their competitive effects on one another.

Resource partitioning allows species to coexist despite overlapping use of limiting resources

Even though the potential for intense competition is high, various ecological and evolutionary mechanisms reduce competition. As you saw with the bee–shin dagger agave example, one way is through **resource partitioning**, the sharing of limiting resources by using them in different ways. Another example of resource

partitioning comes from the classic experiments performed by G. F. Gause in the 1930s using *Paramecium*, a single-celled protist. Gause grew three species of *Paramecium* in test tubes filled with growth medium that contained bacteria and yeast for food. When grown alone, *P. caudatum* and *P. bursaria* showed logistic population growth and reached a stable carrying capacity (**Figure 54.11A**). When grown together, each species showed slower population growth but were able to coexist. However, when *P. caudatum* was grown with *P. aurelia*, it experienced local extinction in the test tubes (**Figure 54.11 B**). The difference in outcome, Gause suggested, was a consequence of *P. caudatum* and *P. aurelia* both competing for bacteria as a food source, while *P. bursaria* avoided competition by eating the other food source, yeast. Thus *P. caudatum* and *P. bursaria* partitioned their food resource in the presence of one another and were able to coexist as a result.

Connect the Concepts Key Concept 53.2 describes logistic population growth, which occurs when intraspecific competition causes population growth to slow down and eventually level off at some size known as the carrying capacity.

In some cases individuals within a species evolve different behaviors or morphologies depending on whether they are competing for resources with other species. Darwin remarked in *On the Origin of Species* that "Natural Selection leads to divergence of character; for more living beings can be supported on the same area the more they diverge in structure, habits, and constitutions." This "divergence of character" is referred to today as **character displacement**. On some of the islands of the Galápagos archipelago, for example, certain cactus species are pollinated exclusively by the Small Ground-Finch (*Geospiza fuliginosa*), for which cactus nectar is an important food source (see Figure 22.8). On other islands, a carpenter bee (*Xylocopa darwinii*) competes with the finches for cactus nectar; the birds consequently feed more often on seeds and insects. On the islands where bees are absent, the nectar-feeding birds have smaller wingspans, presumably to make it easier for them to negotiate the flowers.

Sometimes organisms respond to competition by moving. The African wild dog (*Lycaon pictus*) (see Figure 57.17) is a carnivore that lives and forages in packs (groups of related individuals). Frequent vocalizations, called twitters, function to keep the pack together, but these acoustical signals also can alert the dogs' competitors, African lions (*Panthera leo*), to the presence of prey. Lions hearing the dogs' twitters can use them to locate dog packs and steal their kills. The dogs avoid competing with lions by selecting areas for their dens where the likelihood of being overheard by lions is low. The wild dog is considered a **fugitive species**—a species that leaves an otherwise suitable habitat in order to avoid competition with another species.

The physical environment, disturbance, and predation can each alter the outcome of competition

The outcome of competition among species can be changed by a variety of factors, including the influence of the physical environment and processes such as disturbance and predation, which may injure or kill some individuals. These factors can cause a weakening or even a reversal of competitive outcomes between species if they negatively affect the competitively dominant species. By reducing the growth or survival of the competitively superior species, the physical environment, disturbance, or predation can allow the competitively inferior species a chance to acquire limiting resources, gain a foothold, and potentially increase its population size.

In an example from a Rhode Island salt marsh, Mark Bertness and colleague showed how competition could be altered by the effect of daily tides on the interaction between a rush, *Juncus gerardii*, and a shrub, *Iva frutescens*. Through a series of *Juncus* and *Iva* removal experiments in each tidal zone, the researchers found that in the relatively physically benign high intertidal, *Iva* is the competitive dominant, shading *Juncus* and causing it to have lower biomass (**Figure 54.12**). However, in the low intertidal, where salinity and waterlogging from the tides are greater, *Iva* cannot compete with *Juncus* because it is physiologically intolerant of the physical conditions in this zone. In fact, the competitive relationship is turned into a positive one, in which *Iva* is dependent on *Juncus* to survive in the low intertidal. We'll discuss the role of positive interactions in the next key concept, but it is clear from examples such as this that the outcomes of species interactions depend on the particular circumstances, or context, under which they occur.

Figure 54.12 **Species Interactions in a Salt Marsh** Plant species removal experiments showed that the shrub *Iva frutescens* competitively dominates the rush *Juncus gerardii* in the high intertidal where physical conditions are benign. But the interaction switches to a positive one in the low intertidal, where the tides flood on a daily basis and *Iva* grows better in the presence of *Juncus*. (After M. D. Bertness and S. D. Hacker. 1994. *Am Nat* 144: 363–372.)

Competition can affect species' distributions

Competition can be important in determining where species are found. As you saw earlier, although species may be physiologically able to live under a wide range of conditions, competitors may restrict their use of resources to particular locations. An example of how competition can affect species distributions comes from the rocky intertidal zone of Scotland. Two species of barnacles, the acorn barnacle *Semibalanus balanoides* and Poll's stellate barnacle (*Chthamalus stellatus*), compete for space on the rocky shorelines of the North Atlantic Ocean. The planktonic larvae of both species settle in the intertidal zone and metamorphose into sessile adults. The smaller stellate barnacles generally live at higher levels in the intertidal zone, where they face longer periods of exposure and desiccation (drying out) than do acorn barnacles, which live at lower levels. There is little overlap between the areas occupied by adults of the two species (**Figure 54.13**). What explains their distinct distributions in the intertidal zone?

In a famous study conducted nearly 60 years ago, Joseph Connell experimentally removed one or the other species of barnacle from its characteristic zone and observed the response of the remaining species. Stellate barnacle larvae normally settle in large numbers throughout much of the intertidal zone, including the lower levels where acorn barnacles are found (their fundamental niche), but they thrive at those lower levels only when acorn

Semibalanus is excluded from the top of the intertidal zone by its sensitivity to desiccation.

Chthamalus adult distribution

Semibalanus adult distribution

Chthamalus is excluded from the lower portions of the intertidal zone by competition with *Semibalanus*.

High tide

Low tide

Figure 54.13 Interspecific Competition Can Restrict a Species' Range Interspecific competition with acorn barnacles (*Semibalanus*) restricts stellate barnacles (*Chthamalus*) to a smaller portion of the intertidal zone than they could otherwise occupy. Larvae of both species settle throughout the intertidal, but at lower levels acorn barnacles grow much faster and eliminate the stellate barnacle larvae. In the upper reaches of the intertidal, however, the greater susceptibility of acorn barnacles to desiccation (drying out) allows stellate barnacles to outcompete them. The two species can coexist in a small portion of the intertidal zone. (After J. H. Connell. 1961. *Ecology* 42: 710.)

barnacles are not present (their realized niche). Connell found that the acorn barnacles grew so fast they smothered, crushed, or undercut the stellate barnacle juveniles. However, removing stellate barnacles from their spots higher in the intertidal zone did not lead to their replacement by acorn barnacles; the acorn barnacles are less tolerant of desiccation and failed to thrive there even when stellate barnacles were absent. The result of the competitive interaction between the two species is a distinctive pattern of intertidal zonation, with stellate barnacles restricted in their distribution by competition and acorn barnacles restricted in their distribution by their physiological limitations.

KEY CONCEPT
54.3 Recap and Assess

Competition occurs when species overlap in their use of limiting resources, either through interference or exploitation. At one extreme, if a superior competitor prevents another species from using essential resources, the inferior species may be competitively excluded. In reality, most species show competitive coexistence, which is maintained through a variety of ecological processes, including resource partitioning, environmental conditions, disturbance, and predation. The distribution of a species may be affected by competition when another species restricts the use of limiting resources to a particular location.

1. The fundamental niche of the native Eurasian red squirrel includes all of the United Kingdom. Since the introduction of the eastern gray squirrel, a non-native competitor, the Eurasian red squirrel's distribution has been restricted to the northern regions of Scotland and Ireland. How has the realized niche of the red

squirrel changed in response to the species' interactions with the gray squirrel?

2. Suppose you are sharing a milkshake with a friend. You each have a straw. Under scenario 1, you both drink from your straws, eventually consuming the entire milkshake together. Under scenario 2, your friend takes both straws and drinks the whole milkshake. Which scenario is an example of interference competition and which is an example of exploitation competition?

3. Refer to Question 3 in the Key Concept 54.2 recap. What species interaction controls the coexistence of competing grass species? Explain how this interaction can promote species diversity.

Prior to the 1990s, most ecologists believed that positive interactions were interesting, unusual phenomena, but of limited importance to populations and communities. Most of their focus was on the role of negative interactions such as predation and competition. But research over the last few decades has shown that just like negative interactions, positive interactions can have important consequences for the growth, reproduction, and survival of species, especially under stressful conditions. Let's turn our attention to how positive interactions might promote the coexistence of species.

KEY CONCEPT
54.4 Positive Interactions Occur When at Least One Species Benefits and None Are Harmed

Learning Objectives

54.4.1 Discuss why the types of mutualistic interactions, from generalized to specialized and from obligate to facultative, have evolved.

54.4.2 Explain why stressful environments are more likely to give rise to positive species interactions.

54.4.3 Describe why positive interactions have important effects on both population growth and community structure.

Positive interactions, or facilitations, are ubiquitous on Earth. Consider the simple fact that most vascular plants have beneficial pollinators, seed dispersers, and root-associated fungi and bacteria that are key to their survival. Consider all the species that provide essential habitat for other species. These positive interactions, while common, were often overlooked or underappreciated until recently.

As mentioned in Key Concept 54.1, there are two types of positive interactions: mutualisms, in which both species benefit from the interaction, and commensalisms, in which one species benefits and the other is unaffected. Some positive interactions are symbiotic. In addition, some interactions can be **obligate** (necessary) while others are **facultative** (optional).

Table 54.1 lists mutualistic interactions that range from highly specialized obligate symbioses to highly generalized facultative nonsymbioses. Mutualistic interactions allow organisms to access limiting resources and often involve an exchange of food for housing or defense. Plants and their mycorrhizal fungi (see Key Concept 28.2 and Figure 28.9), corals and their photosynthetic endosymbionts (see Key Concept 24.4), and lichens formed from fungi and photosynthetic algae (see Key Concept 28.2 and Figure 28.8) all provide examples of obligate and/or facultative mutualistic interactions in which food is exchanged for housing and nutrients.

Some common mutualisms occur between sessile organisms—particularly flowering plants—and mobile animal species that can pollinate flowers or disperse their offspring. These interactions can be highly specialized or very general and facultative. For example, about three-fourths of the more than 300,000 flowering plant species on Earth require the transport of pollen by an animal partner. The benefit from the plant's perspective is clear: the animals move pollen from one plant to another and thereby promote sexual reproduction and thus genetic diversity. The most direct reward for pollinators is the pollen itself, which serves as food. Plant reproduction would not be served, however, if pollinators were to eat *all* of a plant's pollen; thus plants have evolved various adaptations to ensure that they benefit from the exchange. For example, some plants have two types of anthers: feeding anthers to produce pollen for pollinators, and fertilization anthers to produce pollen for reproduction.

Plants not only need to attract pollinators, but must also ensure that those pollinators carry their pollen to other members of the same species. Repeat visits by a pollinator to different individuals of a particular plant species increase the likelihood that the pollen will end up on the appropriate stigma; thus some plants have adaptations to encourage repeat visits by a given animal, while discouraging others. The nectar of tobacco flowers, for example, contains trace amounts of nicotine, an insecticidal neurotoxin. Many flower visitors, including hummingbirds, can ingest only tiny amounts of nicotine-laced nectar before moving on to other flowers. To other pollinators, however, nicotine may actually be addictive. Putting small amounts of a potentially addictive substance in nectar may be one way tobacco plants improve their odds of a repeat visit by the right pollinator species.

Many animals that eat fruits (called **frugivores**) provide a valuable service to the plants that produce those fruits by dispersing seeds. Seed dispersal by animals not only offers plants the advantages of delivery to potential germination sites away from the parent plant (described in Key Concept 36.1), but comes with the bonus of organic fertilizer for the seeds. Interactions between plants and frugivores, however, are not always reciprocal; in many cases, one party benefits more than the other. Whereas the frugivore is paid "in advance" for its transportation services, the seeds may never reach an appropriate destination for germination (your windshield, for example, will not do). From the plant's perspective, its partnership with frugivores requires a delicate balance between discouraging them from eating fruits before the seeds are capable of germinating and attracting them when the seeds are ready. In addition, the plant must protect the seeds from destruction in the frugivore's digestive tract and defend them against inappropriate consumers that would damage the seeds or fail to disperse them at all.

Positive interactions are more common in stressful environments

It is clear from the previous examples that positive interactions arise out of net positive benefits accrued by one or more species involved in the interaction. Over the last two decades studies have repeatedly shown that positive interactions, be they mutualisms or commensalisms, are more likely to occur in stressful environments such as deserts, salt marshes, and alpine communities. In these environments, where physical conditions can limit fitness, some species provide benefits for those species that lack mechanisms to deal with the stressful conditions.

A comprehensive study conducted by Ray Callaway and an international group of ecologists testing for the influence of positive interactions in alpine plant communities around the world illustrates the benefits of these interactions in stressful environments (**Figure 54.14**). The experiment was conducted on 11 mountain ranges and involved either removing neighboring plants around target plants or keeping them in place as controls (in total, 115 plant species were used). The experiment was conducted at both high-mountain elevations where temperatures are lower and at low-mountain elevations where temperatures are higher. A year later, the relative effect of the neighbor on the growth of the target plants was measured. Researchers found that target plants benefitted from their plant neighbors at high elevations simply as a consequence of the thermal protection that living close together provides under cold temperatures. In contrast, target plants competed with neighboring plants at low elevations, where temperatures are moderate and the same dense plant growth resulted in competition. Whether the observed positive interactions were mutualisms or commensalisms is unknown because the effects of the target species on the neighboring plant species were not measured. Nonetheless, in this and other studies (e.g., see Figure 54.12) it is clear that positive interactions can arise under a variety of stressful conditions.

Positive interactions can have dramatic effects on populations and communities

You have seen how positive interactions influence the physiology, behavior, and growth of species. Research has shown that positive interactions have effects at the population and community levels as well.

TABLE 54.1 | Examples of Mutualistic Interactions

Interaction	Obligate symbiosis	Facultative symbiosis	Obligate nonsymbiosis	Facultative nonsymbiosis
Plants–mycorrhizal fungi	x	x	x	x
Corals–algal endosymbionts	x	x		
Lichens (algae–fungi)	x			
Plants–insect pollinators			x	x
Plants–animal dispersers			x	x

RNE

Low High Low High Low High Low High Low High Low High

In most regions, neighbors decreased target species performance at low-elevation sites...

...but increased it at high-elevation sites.

RNE

Low High Low High Low High Low High Low High

Elevation

© robroll/Getty Images

Figure 54.14 Positive Plant Interactions Are More Common at Higher Elevations The species interactions of alpine plants were experimentally measured (using the relative neighbor effect [RNE], defined as the growth of the target plant species with neighboring plants present minus its growth with neighboring plants removed) in 11 mountain ranges worldwide. RNE values greater than zero (in blue) indicate that neighbors increased the growth of target species; RNE values less than zero (in red) indicate that neighbors decreased the growth of target species. Plants generally benefited from neighbors at high elevations where temperatures were colder and competed with them at lower elevations where temperatures were warmer. (After R. M. Callaway et al. 2002. *Nature* 417: 844–848.)

As you know from population biology, any interaction that affects the survival of individuals can affect population growth. One example of the effects of a mutualism on population growth comes from an interaction between ants and acacia trees in Central America. In 1874, in Nicaragua, the naturalist Thomas Belt observed a peculiar interaction between bullhorn acacia trees (*Acacia cornigera*) and *Pseudomyrmex* ants. Bullhorn acacias get their common name from the enlarged, hollow thorns, in which the ants build nests. The trees also produce rewards for the ants, both in nectar-producing extrafloral structures and modified leaflet tips that are rich in oil and protein. These structures have no apparent purpose other than providing food for ants.

Belt suggested that the notoriously aggressive acacia ants defend the plants against herbivores in exchange for food and shelter. This idea was tested by Daniel Janzen in 1966 when he removed ants from some acacias with insecticide, and showed that trees without ants suffered a reduction in growth and an increase in mortality (**Figure 54.15**). If a bullhorn acacia tree lacks an ant

colony, the repeated loss of its leaves and growing tips to herbivores often kills the plant within 6–12 months. Since Janzen conducted his experiment, additional work on ants and acacias has revealed that ants do more than simply defend the plant against herbivorous enemies; they also clip weeds from around the base of the plants, presumably reducing competition. Thus the ant–acacia mutualism has considerable effects on the population size of each partner.

 View in Achieve
Animation 54.1 Mutualism

Finally, possibly one of the most important types of positive interactions is that of species that provide habitat for other species and thus have widespread community effects. These dominant species mostly include plants such as trees or kelps but can include animals such as corals and sponges. For example, coral reefs are home to many species of fishes that cannot survive outside the reef environment. Likewise, species that are forest specialists cannot survive outside the cool and shaded environment of trees. Most tree species facilitate many other types of species by

Experiment

Figure 54.15 Are Ants and Acacia Mutualists?

Original Paper: D. H. Janzen. 1966. Coevolution of mutualism between ants and acacias in Central America. *Evolution* 20: 249–275.

Bullhorn acacia trees (*Acacia cornigera*) have numerous structures that provide food and shelter for acacia ants (*Pseudomyrmex*). Daniel Janzen's experiments demonstrated that the trees benefit from their association with these ants and that the energy expended in growing ant-attractive structures is repaid with increased growth and survival.

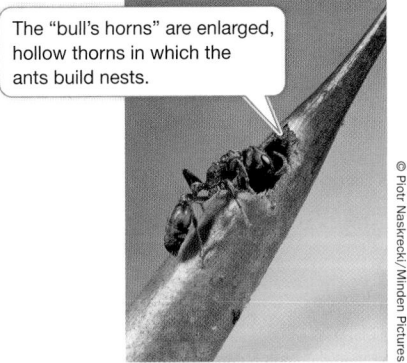

The "bull's horns" are enlarged, hollow thorns in which the ants build nests.

© Piotr Naskrecki/Minden Pictures

HYPOTHESIS▶ *Acacia cornigera* trees deprived of their *Pseudomyrmex* ant populations will have lower growth and survival than trees populated by ant colonies.

METHOD▶

1. Define a population of *A. cornigera* trees; randomly designate some of them as untreated controls and the rest as experimental subjects.

2. Fumigate the experimental trees with insecticide to eliminate all *Pseudomyrmex* ants.

3. Apply Tanglefoot (a sticky material) to the base of the experimental trees to prevent ants from recolonizing them.

4. Record the growth and survival of the trees in both groups over a 10-month period.

RESULTS▶ After 10 months, control trees (with ants) had considerably higher growth and survival than did trees without ant populations.

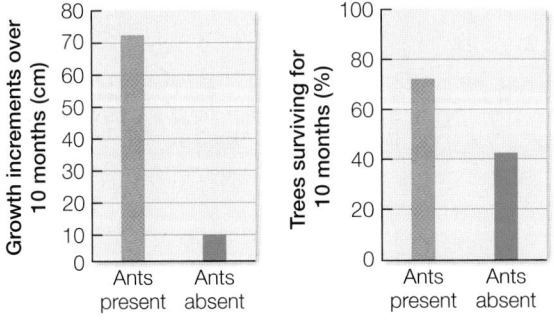

CONCLUSION▶ *Pseudomyrmex* ants provide substantial fitness benefits to *Acacia cornigera* trees.

simply providing sites for attachment, shelter from extreme environmental conditions, or hiding places from predators. Many of these species have no direct effect on the trees in which they live,

and thus have a commensalism with the trees. In all these cases, these dominant plants and animals are the very foundation of the community, which would not exist without them.

KEY CONCEPT
54.4 Recap and Assess

Positive interactions, when at least one species benefits from an interaction and none are harmed, play a key role in enhancing coexistence among species. Positive interactions are more common in stressful environments, where physical conditions can limit the population growth of some species. Positive interactions can have dramatic effects on populations and communities, especially by providing habitat for other species.

1. Offer reasons for why insect pollinators and animal dispersers might evolve obligate versus facultative mutualistic relationships with plants.

2. Refer to Figure 54.13. Where in the rocky intertidal might *Semibalanus* benefit from positive interactions with other species? How about *Chthamalus*? Explain your answer.

3. Give an example of how species that provide habitat could affect the number of species in a community.

▶Investigating LIFE

 Why are small coral-reef fish species so vulnerable to lionfish predation, and what can be done about it?

You have seen that this question is greatly informed by understanding the power that species interactions have on shaping the behavior, physiology, and morphology of interacting species. It is clear that the longer species are exposed to one another, the more likely it is that they will develop strategies that allow coexistence. When lionfishes were inadvertently introduced to coral reefs in the Atlantic Ocean, native coral-reef fishes were exposed to a simple but novel predator behavior for which they currently have no viable defense mechanisms. It is unclear whether native coral-reef fishes will evolve defensive mechanisms before coral-reef fish communities are irreparably damaged. One potential strategy to slow the invasion may be to introduce predators of lionfishes. Unfortunately, however, lionfishes are well defended by frilly fin rays with venomous spines and a zebralike barred coloration that provides crypsis. To make matters worse, populations of predators that might control lionfish populations (such as sharks) are drastically declining as a consequence of overfishing. Fortunately lionfishes are relatively easy to catch, and the future may lie in controlling the population through systematic harvesting by humans.

Future directions

Some people have argued that the best way to control lionfishes is through commercial fishing. Lionfishes are attracted to lobster traps and can also be easily speared. The only risk to harvesters is in being poked by the spines, but this can be avoided if the fishes are handled with care. After some initial skepticism, restaurant owners are realizing that lionfishes are very good eating; the meat has a light, buttery flavor. Efforts are now ramping up to create a market for this destructive invader. Lionfish and chips, anyone?

You should be able to relate each summary to the adjacent figures. If you go to this visual summary in **Achieve**, you can follow links to figures, animations, activities, and simulations that will help you consolidate the material.

KEY CONCEPT
54.1 Species Interactions Vary in Direction and Strength across a Continuum

Go to Activity 54.1

- Species vary in the effects they have on each other (positive, negative, neutral). Species interactions may involve feeding (**trophic**) effects and/or living in close association (**symbiosis**).

- The four main categories of species interactions are **predation** (**predator** kills and/or consumes all or part of its **prey**), **competition** (at least two species use some of the same limiting resources and have negative effects on one another), **positive interactions**, or **facilitations** (at least one species benefits from the interaction and none are harmed), and **amensalism** (one species is harmed but the other is not affected).

- Species interactions are not always clear-cut but instead fall along a continuum in which species vary in how strongly they affect one other.

- Some species interactions result in reciprocal evolutionary change over time, known as **coevolution**.

Questions

1. Explain the difference between the following species interactions: carnivory, herbivory, parasitism, competition, mutualism, commensalism, and amensalism.

2. Name some factors that can produce variable, or asymmetrical, species interactions.

3. What is coevolution, and what types of species interactions are most often involved?

Figure 54.1

Type of interaction	Effect on species 1	Effect on species 2
Predation (predator–prey)	+	–
Carnivory (animal–animal)	+	–
Herbivory (animal–plant)	+	–
Parasitism (parasite–host)	+	–
Competition	–	–
Positive interactions (facilitations)	+	0 or +
Mutualism	+	+
Commensalism	+	0
Amensalism	–	0

Figure 54.2

Effects of species 1 on species 2

Amensalism   Competition   Amensalism

Effects of species 2 on species 1

KEY CONCEPT
54.2 Predation Is a Trophic Interaction in which Predators Benefit and Prey Are Harmed

Go to Simulations 54.1 and 54.2

- Predator–prey interactions result in the evolution of a range of capture and avoidance mechanisms.

- Herbivory (animals preying on plants) and parasitism (parasites feeding and living on or in hosts) are widespread but specialized interactions that usually do not result in the death of the prey.

- Population sizes of predators and their prey tend to cycle as a result of predator–prey interactions over time.

- Some predators, called **keystone species**, can have dramatic effects on communities by preying on competitively dominant species.

Questions

1. What types of strategies do predators use to catch prey and do prey use to avoid being captured?

2. Why are herbivore–plant and parasite–host relationships likely to be specialized species interactions?

3. How do predator–prey cycles arise? How can predators have community-wide effects?

Figure 54.9

KEY CONCEPT
54.3   Competition Is a Negative Interaction in which Species Overlap in the Use of Some Limiting Resource

Go to **Simulation 54.3**

- The **fundamental niche** determines where a species can live physiologically, but the **realized niche** depends on interactions with other species, especially competitors.

- **Interference competition** occurs when one species directly interferes with or prevents another species' access to a **limiting resource**. **Exploitation competition** occurs when all competitors have access to the limiting resource but the outcome depends on their relative efficiency at using the resource.

- **Competitive exclusion** occurs when a species prevents another species from using essential resources, which may cause the inferior competitor to become locally extinct.

- Most competing species show **competitive coexistence** through the processes of **resource partitioning**, disturbance, stress, and/or predation. Competitive coexistence can extends species' ranges.

Questions

1. What is the difference between a fundamental niche and a realized niche?

2. How does interference competition differ from exploitation competition?

3. Competition results in exclusion or coexistence. What factors allow competitive coexistence, and how do they affect species' distributions?

Figure 54.11

KEY CONCEPT
54.4   Positive Interactions Occur When at Least One Species Benefits and None Are Harmed

Go to **Animation 54.1**

- The two types of positive interactions are mutualisms, in which both species benefit from the interaction, and commensalisms, in which one species benefits and the other is unaffected. Some positive interactions are symbiotic relationships. Some positive interactions are **obligate** (necessary), while others are **facultative** (optional).

- Positive interactions are more common in stressful environments, where physical conditions can limit the abundance and distribution of some species.

- Positive interactions can have dramatic effects on populations and communities, especially by providing habitat for other species.

Questions

1. How have obligate versus facultative mutualistic interactions evolved?

2. Why are positive interactions more common in stressful environments?

3. How do positive interactions affect population growth and community structure?

TABLE **54.1** | Examples of Mutualistic Interactions				
Interaction	**Obligate symbiosis**	**Facultative symbiosis**	**Obligate nonsymbiosis**	**Facultative nonsymbiosis**
Plants–mycorrhizal fungi	X	X	X	X
Corals–algal endosymbionts	X	X		
Lichens (algae–fungi)	X			
Plants–insect pollinators			X	X
Plants–animal dispersers			X	X

55 Communities

KEY CONCEPTS

55.1 Communities Are Groups of Interacting Species Occurring Together in Space and Time

55.2 Community Membership Depends on Species Supply, Environmental Conditions, and Species Interactions

55.3 Communities Are Complex Networks of Species Interactions That Vary in Strength and Direction

55.4 Communities Are Always Changing

55.5 Relationships between Species Diversity and Community Function Are Often Positive

©Images & Volcans/Science Source

Since its eruption on May 18, 1980, Mount St. Helens has provided a unique opportunity to study community recovery.

▶Investigating**LIFE**

Rising from the Ashes

When Mount St. Helens in Washington State erupted at 8:30 AM on May 18, 1980, almost all living things for miles around were obliterated in an instant. A huge magma-filled bulge that had been forming for months exploded, creating the largest avalanche in recorded history. Mud and rock flowed down Mount St. Helens and were deposited on alpine meadows, lush forests, and crystal-clear lakes and ponds, tens of meters deep in some areas. The bulk of the avalanche traveled to the North Fork Toutle River, where it scoured the entire valley, from floor to rim, with volcanic material. A huge pile of vegetation was deposited downstream. The blast also produced a cloud of hot air that burned forests to ash near the mountain, blew down trees over a large area, and left dead but standing trees for miles.

Volcanic eruptions are so rare that studying the aftereffects of the Mount St. Helens eruption gave ecologists an unprecedented view into how ecological communities respond to extreme natural catastrophes and the recovery processes they undergo. The event created brand-new environmental conditions to which colonizing species had to respond. At one extreme was the Pumice Plain, a large, gently sloping area close to the lava dome that had once been covered in alpine meadows and forests. Pelted with hot, sterilizing pumice (a light and porous volcanic rock), it was now a harsh moonscape-like environment that lacked life and organic matter of any form. In the aptly named Blowdown Zone, covering most of the mountain's slopes, the destruction was less catastrophic. Here there was hope of a biological legacy buried beneath the piles of downed trees and vegetation covered in mud and ash. Beyond the Blowdown Zone, forests were covered in debris and ash that spewed from the mountain for months.

Shortly after the eruption, helicopters delivered the first scientists to the mountain. A few fortunate ecologists collected baseline data on the sequence of biological changes that began soon after the eruption. Now, 40 years later, hundreds of ecologists have studied the reemergence of life on Mount St. Helens. Much of what has been learned has been unexpected and has changed the way we view the resiliency and recovery of communities after catastrophic events.

 How have ecological communities on Mount St. Helens responded to the eruption, and what processes have been important to their recovery? (Find the answer on page 1254.)

Communities Are Groups of Interacting Species Occurring Together in Space and Time

Learning Objectives

55.1.1 Explain why, and the different ways in which, ecologists subdivide communities.

55.1.2 Define and compare food webs and interaction webs.

55.1.3 Define and know how to measure species richness, species evenness, and species diversity, including calculating the Shannon index.

55.1.4 Discuss how biodiversity differs from species diversity.

In ecological terms, a **community** is a group of species living together at the same place and time. Interactions among multiple species and their physical environment give communities their character and function. Although each species has unique interactions with the other species in its community (as you saw in Chapter 54), ecologists often find it useful to study the properties of the community as a whole.

The definition of a community is more theoretical than practical, in part because communities vary greatly in size and scope. For example, communities can be small and contained, such as that living within the purple pitcher plant (*Sarracenia purpurea*), a species common in North American wetlands (**Figure 55.1A**). Pitcher plants collect rainwater and are home to a thriving community of bacteria, protists, rotifers, and mosquito larvae. A community can also encompass a large geographic area, such as a desert (**Figure 55.1B**), where the borders of the community are not always well delineated. When borders become unclear, ecologists may designate boundaries somewhat arbitrarily, based on their ability to study the community.

Another practical problem in defining communities is determining the number of species present. Most communities contain thousands if not hundreds of thousands of species, from microscopic bacteria to towering trees. Some species are easily identified, but many others are not. Additionally, some species are present only at certain times of the year, for certain life stages, or tend to move among communities. Creating a species list for a community is a huge undertaking—one that is essentially impossible to complete, especially if all small or relatively unknown species are considered. Taxonomists have officially described about 1.8 million species on Earth, but we know from sampling studies of tropical insects and microorganisms that this number greatly underestimates the actual number, which could be 15 million or even more. For this reason, and because of the difficulty of studying many species at one time, ecologists often restrict their definition and study of communities to a particular subset of species.

Ecologists often use a subset of species to define communities

A community can be subdivided on the basis of taxonomic affinity—that is, by groups of organisms classified together because of evolutionary lineage (**Figure 55.2A**). For example, all the amphibians in a set of ponds on Mount St. Helens could be considered to be part of an amphibian community. A community can also be subdivided by resource usage. A **guild** is a group of species, often taxonomically distinct, that use similar resources (**Figure 55.2B**). For example, bats, birds, and bees all feed on pollen, forming a pollen-feeding guild. Yet another way to subdivide a community is by **functional group**—species that function in similar ways but may or may not use similar resources (**Figure 55.2C**). For example, nitrogen-fixing plants (legumes) can be placed in the same functional group.

Ecologists also organize communities into a **food web**, a representation of the trophic or energetic connections among species, as illustrated in **Figure 55.3** for Yellowstone National Park. Most communities contain so many species interacting in so many different ways that it is impossible to enumerate (or even identify) all of the links in a food web. Nevertheless, simplified food webs are useful in envisioning the kinds of interactions and sequence of energy flow occurring in a community. Food webs are generally divided by **trophic levels**, with each level including species that have similar ways of interacting and obtaining energy. Primary producers start the chain of trophic levels. At the next level are **primary consumers**—the herbivores that feed on primary producers. Organisms that eat herbivores, called **secondary consumers**, are the next trophic level. Those that eat secondary consumers are tertiary consumers, and so on. Some species, known as **omnivores**, feed on multiple trophic levels. For example, a bird might eat both insects and seeds. Finally, the waste products and dead bodies of organisms (known as **detritus**) provide another source of energy. Organisms that consume such materials are called **detritivores** or **decomposers** and serve an important function by returning nutrients back to the community through the uptake of primary producers. **Scavengers** eat larger dead organisms and are typically not considered detritivores.

(A)

(B)

© Sharon Wigg/Alamy Stock Photo

© tonda/Getty Images

Figure 55.1 Defining Communities Communities exist at a variety of spatial scales. The community within a single pitcher plant (*Sarracenia Purpurea*) contains microorganisms and tiny invertebrates **(A)**, whereas a desert community might contain plants and animals over a large, hard-to-delineate, geographic area **(B)**.

Figure 55.2 Subsets of Species in Communities Ecologists often use subsets of species to define communities. **(A)** All the amphibian species in a community could be grouped together by taxonomic affinity. **(B)** All the species that use pollen as a resource form a guild. **(C)** All the legumes (e.g., vetch, clover, and peas) that have nitrogen-fixing bacteria could be placed in the same functional group. Species within functional groups may or may not use the same resources.

(A) Taxonomic affinity   **(B) Guild**   **(C) Functional group**

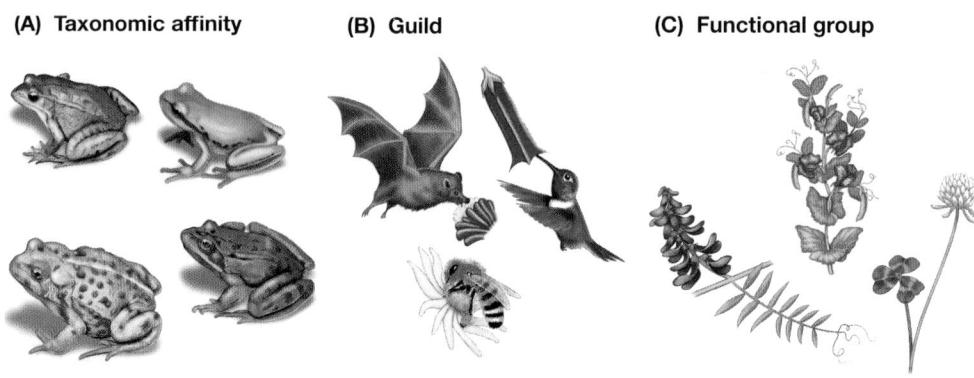

Food web depictions can sometimes include nontrophic interactions such as competition and positive interactions (mutualisms and commensalisms). These so-called **interaction webs** provide a more realistic view of all the species interactions that might be important in the community. Overall, the food web concept, regardless of whether it includes nontrophic interactions, is a useful visual representation of the important consumer relationships in a community. You will learn more about food webs later in this chapter and in Chapter 56.

▶ **Media Clip 55.1 A Food Web in Africa**
  Life12e.com/mc55.1

Species diversity and composition are important descriptors of community structure

Communities vary widely in species number and **species composition** (the kinds of species) present. A coral-reef community in the Great Barrier Reef, for example, has many more species of fish than one in the Caribbean. As you saw in Chapter 52, ecologists have devoted considerable effort to measuring the variation in species diversity and species composition at multiple spatial and temporal scales (see Figure 52.12). Patterns at the community or local scale are important descriptors of what ecologists call **community structure**. Documenting community structure is an important first step in generating

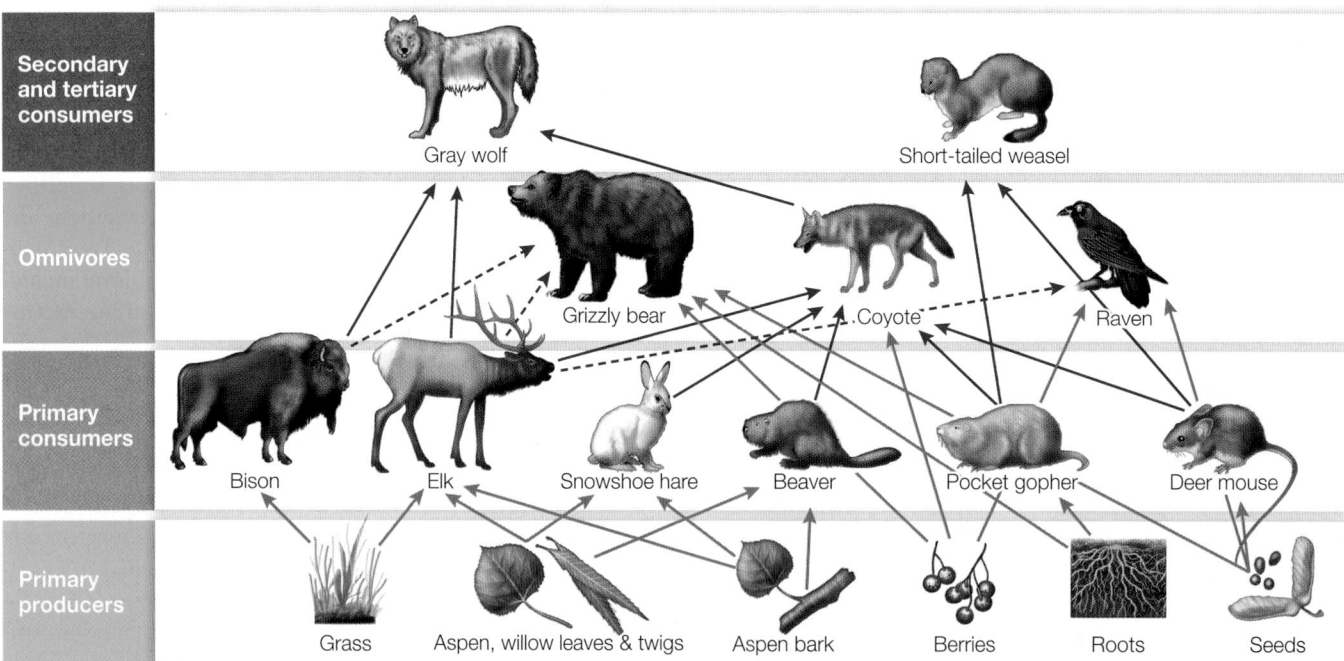

Figure 55.3 Food Webs Show Trophic Interactions in a Community This simplified food web for the meadows and forests of Yellowstone National Park includes only some vertebrates and the plants on which they depend. The arrows show trophic interactions and energetic connections. Herbivores whose sole source of food is plants (green arrows) are primary consumers. Carnivores that kill and eat animals (purple arrows) are secondary and tertiary consumers. Omnivores such as grizzly bears, coyotes, and ravens eat both plant and animal tissues; ravens and grizzlies also eat carrion (dashed purple arrows), so these species are also scavengers.

▶ **View in Achieve**
  Activity 55.1 The Major Trophic Levels

hypotheses about how communities work. Let's first consider the different ways that one metric of community structure—species diversity—is measured.

We have thus far used the term "species diversity" to describe the number of species in a sample, community, or region, but ecologists have a more technical definition. **Species diversity** is a measure that combines the number of species (**species richness**) and their relative abundances compared with that of other species (**species evenness**).

The contribution of both species richness and evenness to species diversity is illustrated in the following example from Mount St. Helens (**Figure 55.4**). Imagine that we collect samples of 20 individual amphibians in each of two different ponds on Mount St. Helens 3 years after its eruption. Our sample from Pond A contains 17 individuals of one species (Pacific tree frog, *Pseudacris regilla*) and only 1 individual of each of the other three species (an uneven distribution). Our sample from Pond B, however, contains 5 individuals of each of four amphibian species (an even distribution of individuals). Even though the species richness of the two communities is the same (four species), Pond A is less diverse because the less abundant species are encountered less frequently compared with the single most abundant species.

There are several ways to measure species diversity quantitatively. One common measure is the **Shannon index**,

$$H = -\sum_{i=1}^{s} p_i \ln\left(p_i\right)$$

where

H = the Shannon index value
p_i = the proportion of individuals found in the ith species
$\ln$ = the natural logarithm
s = the number of species in the community

The lowest possible value of H is zero; higher values represent greater species diversity. **Table 55.1** calculates the Shannon index for amphibians in the two Mount St. Helens pond communities shown in Figure 55.4. These calculations show that Pond A has the

Pond A

> In pond A, the abundance of one species (Pacific tree frog) is high relative to the other species, so this community has low species evenness.

> In pond B, each species has the same abundance, so this community has high species evenness.

Pond B

Figure 55.4 Species Richness and Evenness These two hypothetical amphibian pond communities have the same number of species (species richness) but different relative abundance of those species (species evenness).

Q: Which pond, A or B, has higher species diversity as measured using the Shannon index (see Table 55.1)? Explain.

 View in Achieve
Activity 55.2 Measures of Species Diversity

Species	Abundance	Proportion (p_i)	$\ln(p_i)$	$p_i \ln(p_i)$
POND A				
Pacific tree frog	17	0.85	−0.163	−0.139
Western toad	1	0.05	−2.996	−0.150
Cascades frog	1	0.05	−2.996	−0.150
Northern red-legged frog	1	0.05	−2.996	−0.150
Total	20	1.00		−0.589
POND B				
Pacific tree frog	5	0.25	−1.386	−0.347
Western toad	5	0.25	−1.386	−0.347
Cascades frog	5	0.25	−1.386	−0.347
Northern red-legged frog	5	0.25	−1.386	−0.347
Total	20	1.00		−1.388

TABLE 55.1 | Calculation of Species Diversity for Ponds A and B Using the Shannon Index

> To calculate the Shannon index (H), the natural logarithm (ln) is applied to p_i for each species (i)…

> …and then this value is multiplied by p_i once again.

> All the values are summed for all the species in the community and multiplied by −1 to get H.

$$H = -\sum_{i=1}^{s} p_i \ln\left(p_i\right) = 0.589$$

> Community B has higher species diversity than community A.

$$H = -\sum_{i=1}^{s} p_i \ln\left(p_i\right) = 1.388$$

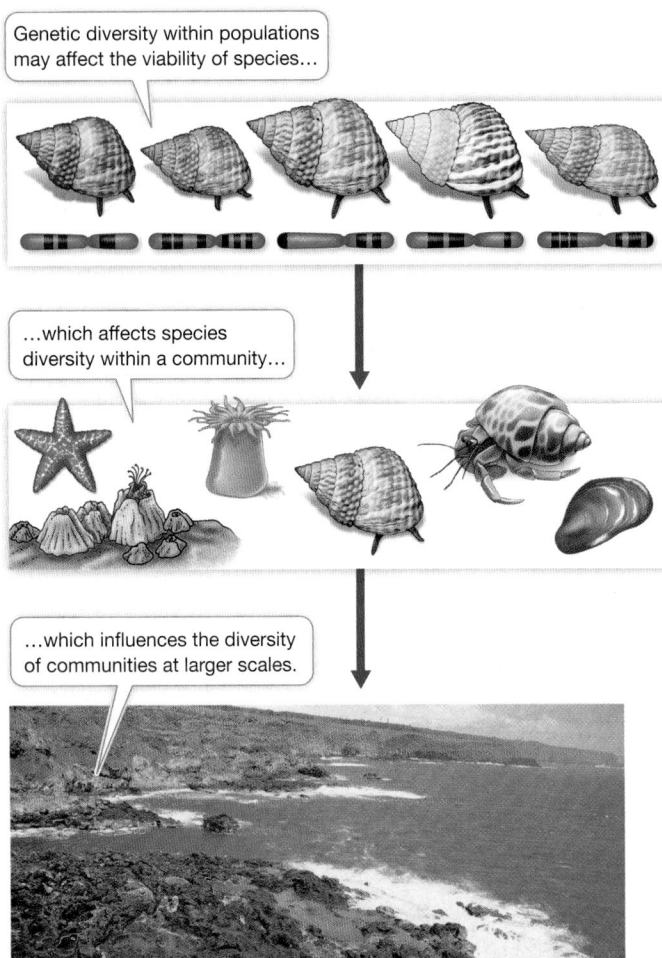

Genetic diversity within populations may affect the viability of species...

...which affects species diversity within a community...

...which influences the diversity of communities at larger scales.

© Ryan McVay/Getty Images

Figure 55.5 Biodiversity Considers Multiple Spatial Scales
Diversity can be measured at spatial scales that range from genes to species to communities. The term "biodiversity" encompasses diversity at all of these scales.

lower Shannon index value (*H*), confirming mathematically that this community has lower species diversity than Pond B. Given that both communities have the same species richness, the difference in species diversity is driven by the lower species evenness in Pond A.

How does the term "biodiversity" relate to species diversity? **Biodiversity** is used in reference to various levels of diversity, from genes to species to communities (**Figure 55.5**). Implicit in this term is the interconnectedness of different scales of diversity. For example, you saw in Chapter 19 that greater genetic diversity can lead to greater fitness of populations, which in turn can promote species diversity. The greater number of different types of communities can also lead to greater diversity at larger regional and continental scales, as you saw in Chapter 52.

KEY CONCEPT
55.1 Recap and Assess

A community is a group of species that occur together at the same place and time. Communities are often defined by a subset of species based on similar taxonomy, resource use (guild), ecological functions (functional group), or trophic and energetic connections (food webs). Species diversity and composition are descriptors of community structure. Species diversity is a measure that combines the number of species (species richness) and their relative abundances (species evenness). Biodiversity is a term that describes multiple scales of diversity, from genes to species to communities.

1. Why are subsets of species used to define communities? What type of community subset was used to define the frogs and toads in ponds on Mount St. Helens?

2. What types of species interactions are missing from the food web depicted in Figure 55.3?

3. Refer to Table 55.1. Replace the abundance of amphibians in Pond A with the following values (Pacific tree frog = 6, western toad = 8, northern red-legged frog = 4, Cascades frog = 2), recalculate the values in the other three columns in the table accordingly, and then calculate a new Shannon index value. Which pond has the higher species diversity, Pond A or Pond B?

Measuring community structure prompts us to consider many interesting questions about communities. Why do communities differ in the number and composition of species? What processes determine community membership? In the next key concept we will explore how community membership is shaped by which individuals get to the community, deal with the environmental conditions there, and form interactions with other individuals.

KEY CONCEPT
55.2
Community Membership Depends on Species Supply, Environmental Conditions, and Species Interactions

Learning Objectives

55.2.1 Describe how regional species supply and dispersal ability, environmental factors, and biotic interactions can contribute to community membership.

55.2.2 Explain why studying introduced non-native species provides a unique test of community membership.

Suppose you are looking across the landscape of Mount St. Helens. You see lakes and ponds, alpine meadows, and forests. There is no doubt that these communities vary not only in their species composition but also their species richness. The lakes might be dominated by fishes, amphibians, and freshwater algae; the alpine meadows by various species of grasses, flowering plants, and rodents; and the forests by trees, shrubs, and birds. Even though some species might move from one community to another, the three communities would still be very different. How is it that species come together to form different communities?

Community membership depends on three basic factors: (1) the regional species pool and dispersal ability (species supply), (2) physical and chemical environmental conditions (abiotic conditions), and (3) species interactions (biotic conditions). Each factor acts as a "filter" that excludes or includes species in particular communities (**Figure 55.6**). Let's consider each of these filters in more detail.

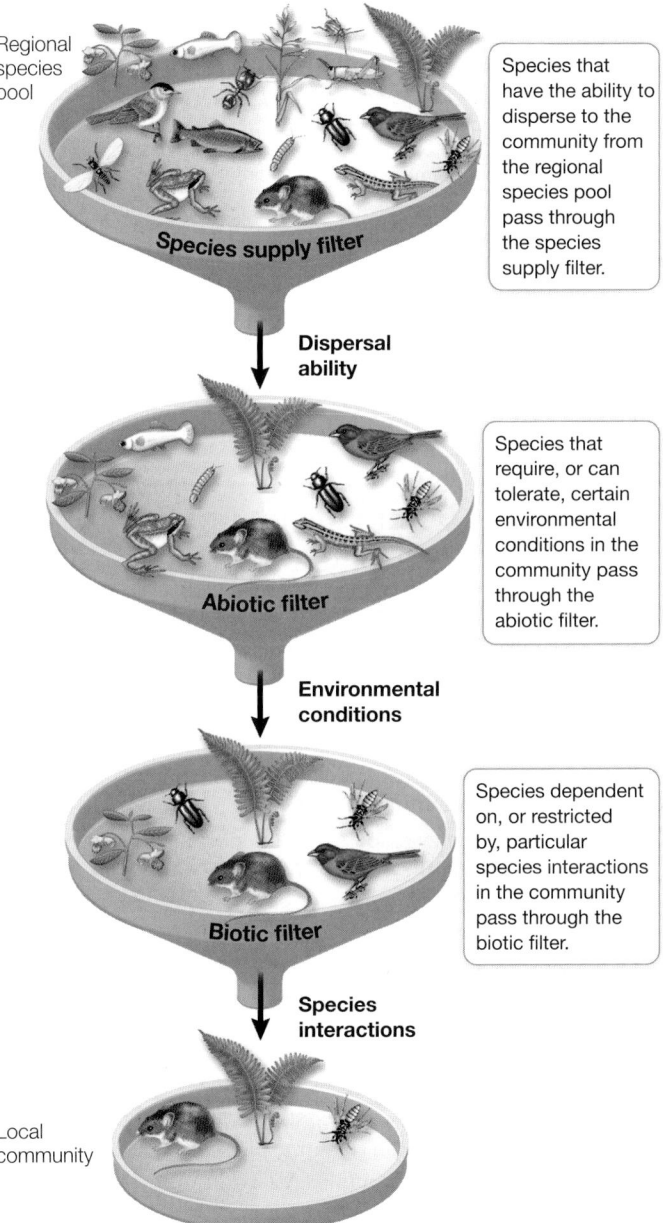

Figure 55.6 Filters Determine Community Membership
Species members are included or excluded in a local community by passing through a set of "filters." Species are lost at each filter, so local communities contain a fraction of the species in the regional pool. In practice, all the filters work at the same time, rather than in series as the figure suggests. (After J. H. Lawton. 2000. *Community Ecology in a Changing World. Excellence in Ecology.* 11: XI–227. The International Ecology Institute: Oldendorf/Luhe, Germany.)

Q: Would it make sense for the fish and frog species in the regional species pool to be present in the local community shown in the figure? Explain.

Community membership depends on species supply

In Chapter 52 we established that regional species pools provide the upper limits on the numbers and types of species that can live within communities (see Figure 52.12). An obvious first step to community membership is the presence of species at the regional level, and their ability to disperse to the community. For example, as communities started to recover from the Mount St. Helens eruption, they began to gain species supplied from the regional species pool of the Pacific Northwest of North America. Because they were able to disperse to the mountain, these species began to colonize the new and unique environments created in the aftermath of the devastation.

Maybe the best examples of how species supply affects community membership are seen in the introduction of novel species to communities. Humans have greatly expanded regional species pools, allowing new and potentially invasive species to enter communities. Chapter 54 described the catastrophic effects of the unintentional release of invasive lionfishes in Atlantic Ocean and Caribbean coral-reef communities. The lionfish invasion demonstrates that "getting there" is a critical first step to community membership. All it took was the release of these predators, and their extraordinary ability to prey on reef fishes, to dramatically change coral-reef communities.

Environmental conditions are critical to community membership

As you might expect, all species in a regional species pool do not end up becoming members of every community in that region. A species may make it to a community but fail to become a member because of unsuitable environmental conditions there. You might think of the influence of the environment as an "abiotic filter" that restricts species that are physiologically incapable of surviving in a given community. The lakes in the Mount St. Helens area, for example, have environmental attributes that accommodate fishes, amphibians, and aquatic insects but not trees.

The physical environment can be a significant barrier to introduced non-native species. Consider, for example, marine organisms that are often introduced into foreign ports via ballast water (seawater that is pumped into and out of ballast tanks to stabilize large cargo-carrying ships). Ballast water picked up outside one port and then dumped in another can potentially release organisms (from bacteria to planktonic larvae to fishes) that can colonize nearshore communities. While most ballast-water organisms do not survive the thermal, salinity, or light regimes of their new environment, a small percentage are not physiologically constrained by such conditions and may gain a foothold, especially if they are introduced multiple times.

Community membership can shift with changing environmental conditions. For example, growing evidence indicates that climate change—in particular, rising temperatures—may improve conditions for some non-native species, increasing their ability to thrive. Jay Stachowicz and his colleagues found that the recruitment and growth of invasive marine invertebrates known as ascidians (sea squirts) in New England were dependent on warm winter and summer water temperatures (**Figure 55.7A**). Warmer temperatures gave

(A) *Botryllus schlosseri*

© Paul Kay/Getty Images

(B) *Carcinus maenas*

© blickwinkel/Alamy Stock Photo

Figure 55.7 Species Invasions Can Depend on Environmental Conditions (A) Invasive sea squirts in New England depend on warmer water temperatures to grow and outcompete native sea squirts. (B) The recruitment of European green crabs to U.S. Pacific Northwest estuaries depends on warm water conditions such as those that occur during El Niño.

the non-native organisms an earlier start in spring and increased the magnitude of their growth relative to that of native sea squirts. A similar story can be told for the European green crab (*Carcinus maenas*), whose recruitment to estuarine communities along the Pacific Northwest coast is dependent on warm water temperatures during El Niño conditions (Figure 55.7B).

The final requirement for species membership is the ability to coexist with other species. Let's consider the mediating effects of species interactions on the inclusion (or exclusion) of species in communities.

Resident species can restrict or promote community membership

Even if a species makes it to a community and is able to tolerate its environmental conditions, it must be able to live with all the other species in that community. It must be able to obtain food, survive without being eaten, and cope with competitors. Thus whether a species is successful in a new community will depend on the presence of resident species that either promote or restrict species membership.

The ability of resident species to exclude or slow the population growth of non-native species is called **biotic resistance**. While there are a handful of studies showing that competitors and herbivores can slow down the spread of non-native plant species, confirmed examples of biotic resistance are few. Identifying whether biotic resistance is common in nature may reflect the fact that many failed introductions of non-native species go undetected. Nevertheless, the evidence from the invasive species literature suggests that the influence of resident species may be a

fairly porous filter when it comes to restricting species from, or promoting species to, communities.

55.2 Recap and Assess

Community membership is a consequence of regional species pools, environmental conditions, and species interactions. These three factors act as "filters" that control community membership. Biotic resistance—the process by which species interactions exclude or slow the population growth of colonizing species—is rarely documented.

1. Refer to Figure 55.6. Which factor is most limiting to the species membership of the local community? Explain.

2. If you were trying to reduce the number of non-native species colonizing Mount St. Helens, what one best general management action would you employ?

Once a species is part of a community, how is it able to coexist with other species there? In the next key concept we will consider theories and examples that seek to explain how species interactions help form communities of varying composition and diversity.

KEY CONCEPT
55.3 Communities Are Complex Networks of Species Interactions That Vary in Strength and Direction

Learning Objectives

55.3.1 Describe the role of indirect interactions in determining community structure, particularly in the case of trophic cascades.

55.3.2 Explain how resource partitioning and disturbance can regulate community structure.

55.3.3 Define and compare keystone, foundation, and ecosystem engineering species.

55.3.4 Discuss how lottery, or neutral, models explain the role of chance in regulating community structure.

So far we have presented a rather static view of communities as groups of species residing in the same place at the same time. But communities are actually complex networks of species with connections that vary in their strength (i.e., magnitude) and direction (i.e., positive, negative, or neutral). Every species in a community experiences multiple direct and indirect interactions.

Indirect interactions are important to community structure

A **direct interaction** is one that occurs between just two species. **Indirect interactions** occur when the direct relationships between two species are mediated by a third (or more) species (Figure 55.8). The addition of a third species to a two-species interaction has the possibility of dramatically changing the outcome of the original interaction.

(A) Direct interaction

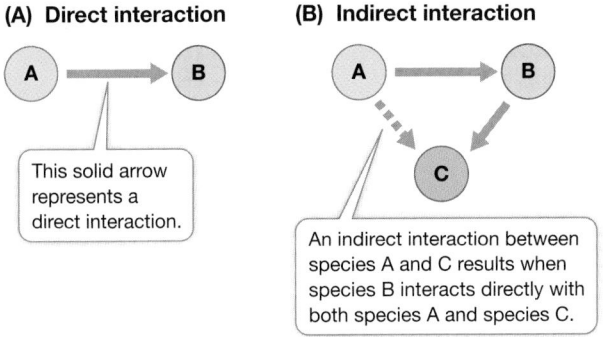

This solid arrow represents a direct interaction.

(B) Indirect interaction

An indirect interaction between species A and C results when species B interacts directly with both species A and species C.

Figure 55.8 Direct and Indirect Species Interactions (**A**) A direct interaction occurs between two species. (**B**) An indirect interaction (dashed arrow) occurs when the direct relationship between two species is mediated by a third species.

Indirect interactions were observed by Charles Darwin in *On the Origin of Species* (1859). Having described the role of bees in flower pollination and seed production of plants in the region of England where he lived, Darwin hypothesized that the number of bees in the region was dependent on the number of field mice that prey on their combs and nests. Noting that mice, in turn, are eaten by cats, Darwin wrote, "Hence it is quite credible that the presence of a feline animal in large numbers in a district might determine, through the intervention first of mice and then of bees, the frequency of certain flowers in that district!"

Today the term "trophic cascade" would be applied to Darwin's observations. A **trophic cascade** occurs when the rate of consumption at one trophic level results in a change in species abundance or composition at lower trophic levels. For example, a carnivore eats an herbivore (a direct interaction) and decreases its abundance, causing an indirect positive effect on the primary producer eaten by the herbivore. One example of a trophic cascade is the indirect regulation of U.S. Rocky Mountain meadow and forest communities by wolves, which were reintroduced into Lamar Valley in Yellowstone National Park in 1995. William Ripple and his colleagues at Oregon State University have studied this system extensively.

The simplified food web in Yellowstone National Park depicted in Figure 55.3 shows that gray wolves (*Canis lupus*) in the park feed on elk (*Cervus canadensis*), bison (*Bison bison*), and coyotes (*Canis latrans*). Although they share some of these prey species with coyotes and grizzly bears (*Ursus arctos*), wolves exert particularly strong effects on the structure and dynamics of the community. We know this mostly because of how differently the community was structured in their absence, after wolves were hunted to extinction in Yellowstone in 1926. In the absence of wolves, the park service culled elk herds to prevent their populations from exploding. In 1968, in response to public pressure, the selective killing was stopped and the elk population rapidly increased (**Figure 55.9A**). The elk browsed aspen trees so intensely that the number of young trees recruited (added to the population) declined precipitously; once elk culling stopped, no new trees were recruited at all (**Figure 55.9B**). The elk also

(A)

In the absence of wolves and culling, elk populations grew rapidly.

Wolves eliminated (1926)

Elk culling suspended (1968)

Wolves restored (1995)

(B)

Wolves present | Wolves absent

In the absence of wolves, browsing by elk prevented the recruitment of young aspens.

After wolves were restored, aspen forests began to regenerate.

Wolves eliminated (1926)

Wolves restored (1995)

Figure 55.9 Wolves Initiated a Trophic Cascade in Yellowstone National Park (**A**) Number of elk in Wyoming's Yellowstone National Park. (**B**) Aspen recruitment (new trees) in the presence and absence of wolves. (A after W. J. Ripple and R. L. Beschta. 2004. *BioScience* 54: 755–766; B after J. Halofsky and W. Ripple. 2008. *Forestry* 81: 195–207.)

Media Clip 55.2 How Wolves Change Rivers
Life12e.com/mc55.2

severely browsed streamside willows, with the result that beavers (*Castor canadensis*), which depend on willows for food, were mostly gone from Lamar Valley. In regions of the park where elk were absent, however, aspen and willow trees flourished. This observation suggested that the decline of the trees in Lamar Valley was indeed due to elk browsing rather than to climate conditions or other factors.

In 1995, after wolves had been absent for 70 years, park managers reintroduced them to Yellowstone, and their population grew rapidly. The wolves preyed primarily on elk. The elk population of Lamar Valley dropped, and elk avoided the aspen groves, where they were especially vulnerable to wolf predation. Young aspen began to grow, willows regrew along streams, and the number of beaver colonies increased from one in 1996 to seven in 2003. Thus the presence or absence of a single predator influenced not only populations of its prey but also, indirectly, its prey's food resource and other species that depended on that resource. It is clear that wolves have a dramatic effect on the structure of meadow and forest communities through the trophic cascade they create.

Strongly interacting species often regulate community structure

The example of wolves in Yellowstone National Park offers clear evidence that species interactions vary considerably in their strength and direction, influencing the structure of communities. Some species have strong negative or positive effects on community structure, while others may have almost no effect at all. We can measure the **interaction strength**, or the effect of one species on the abundance of another species, by experimentally removing the "interactor" species and observing the response of the "target" species. If removing the interactor species causes a sharp decline in the population of the target species, we know that the interaction is a strong positive one. Alternatively, the interaction is strongly negative if the removal results in a large increase in the target species. If the removal has little or no effect on the abundance of the target species, then there is no interaction.

Some species can have strong negative effects on a community by excluding or diminishing populations of other species through competition for limiting resources. As we discussed in Key Concept 54.3, competition is often asymmetrical: one species can be more negatively affected by the interaction than another. Asymmetrical competition leads either to competitive exclusion of the more negatively affected species (resulting in fewer species in the community than would be predicted by environmental conditions or dispersal alone) or to various mechanisms that promote coexistence, such as **resource partitioning** (the sharing of limiting resources by using them in different ways), thus promoting coexistence (see Key Concept 54.3 for the bee–shin dagger agave example).

Competition among species can also be mediated by factors that affect the dominant species' ability to acquire resources, so-called **resource-mediated coexistence**. For example, if events in the physical environment such as disturbance or stress affect the growth or survival of a dominant species, competitively inferior species may gain access to limiting resources. We will consider some specific examples of disturbance and stress in Key Concept 55.4. Here we consider how those effects can influence community structure.

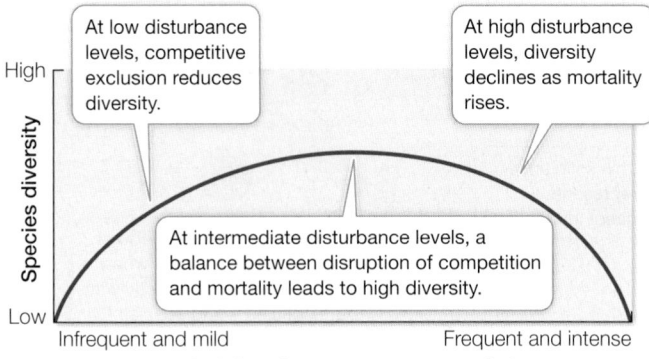

Figure 55.10 The Intermediate Disturbance Hypothesis Species diversity is expected to be greatest at intermediate levels of disturbance (an abiotic process that injures or kills individuals). (After J. H. Connell 1978. *Science* 4335: 1302–1310.)

The **intermediate disturbance hypothesis** describes how varying degrees of disturbance (an abiotic process that injures or kills individuals) affect species diversity in communities (**Figure 55.10**). Joseph Connell, the author of the classic work on barnacle competition (see Key Concept 54.3), noted that the level of disturbance (both frequency and intensity) experienced by a community could have strong effects on its species diversity. He hypothesized that species diversity would be greatest in communities with intermediate disturbance and lowest in communities with low or high disturbance. At low levels of disturbance, competition from dominant species would lead to competitive exclusion of the inferior species, resulting in lower species diversity in the community. At the other extreme, a major disturbance would cause high mortality rates, leading to the extinction of some species in the community and resulting in lower species diversity. At intermediate levels of disturbance, species diversity would be greatest because (1) the influence of the dominant species is reduced by the disturbance, allowing the subordinate species to coexist, and (2) the mortality rates are not as high, so extinction events are less likely to occur.

Here we consider three other types of species that have large effects on community structure.

KEYSTONE SPECIES   As described in Key Concept 54.2, **keystone species** can have strong community-wide effects, not because of their size or abundance but because of the important role they play in communities (**Figure 55.11**). Keystone species mostly act by creating trophic cascades. For example, top predators such as wolves and sea stars are keystone species because they have a large influence over community species richness, abundance, and composition, even though keystone species may be small in size and their abundance is relatively low.

Sea otters (*Enhydra lutris*) that inhabit kelp forests on the west coast of North America illustrate how important keystone species can be in regulating community structure. Sea otters feed on sea urchins (*Strongylocentrotus* spp.), which feed on kelp, establishing a trophic cascade. Without predation by sea otters, sea urchin populations can explode, resulting in voracious consumption of kelp. Stretches of nearshore habitat that become nearly devoid

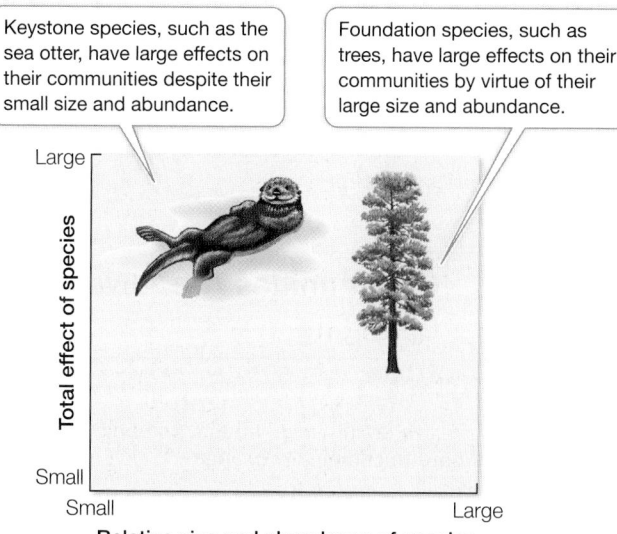

Keystone species, such as the sea otter, have large effects on their communities despite their small size and abundance.

Foundation species, such as trees, have large effects on their communities by virtue of their large size and abundance.

Figure 55.11 Keystone versus Foundation Species Species that have large effects on their communities do so by virtue of their relative size and abundance. (After M. E. Power et al. 1996. *BioScience* 46: 609–620.)

of kelp beds, called "urchin barrens," can no longer support the diversity of life that is supported when kelp habitat is present.

FOUNDATION SPECIES Some strongly interacting species are capable of providing habitat and food for other species. These **foundation species** have a large effect on communities as a consequence of their large size or great abundance (see Figure 55.11). Trees are a good example of foundation species. For example, fig trees in tropical forests provide physical habitat for several thousand species of insects, non-avian reptiles, birds, and rodents in their canopy. Fig trees also serve as an important food source for species by producing fruits several times every year, especially at times when few, if any, other trees are fruiting. Dozens of frugivores depend on figs when no other fruits are present. Fig-eating animals include fruit bats, parrots, toucans, pigeons, flycatchers, trogons, orioles, rodents, howler monkeys, and even fishes, which eat figs that fall into nearby streams. All of these animals represent prey for a diverse community of predators.

ECOSYSTEM ENGINEERING SPECIES Some species are specifically known for creating, modifying, or maintaining physical habitat for themselves and other species. These **ecosystem engineering species** can be either keystone or foundation species. These are species whose primary effect is to engineer the physical environment (rather than providing food), and they do not necessarily

have great size or abundance in the community. For example, beavers create new habitats by cutting down (and killing) trees and using them to dam streams and create ponds and wetlands that provide habitat for species that would otherwise be unable to live in the area (**Figure 55.12**).

Species with similar effects on one another may coexist by chance

We have thus far discussed instances in which communities are composed of a few strongly interacting species and many weakly interacting species. But sometimes species in a community have relatively similar effects on one another. How is species diversity maintained when species vary little in their ability to obtain resources?

Over the last few decades, ecologists have proposed and tested so-called **lottery**, or **neutral**, **models** that emphasize the role of chance in the maintenance of species diversity. Like the name suggests, these models assume that when resources are made available, they are used at random by individuals of different species who happen to be in the "right place at the right time." As long as all individuals have similar chances of obtaining resources (or "winning the lottery"), and no clear advantage in dispersal ability or population growth, then their presence in the community should be maintained by chance events that free up resources for individuals competing for those resources. If there is a large disparity among species in their ability to obtain resources, the dominant competitor will always have a greater chance of obtaining resources and will eventually monopolize them. So for lottery models to work, the element of equal chance for all individuals to obtain resources is paramount to coexistence.

Minnesota

In 1940, beavers were nearly extinct in this region, and there were few wetlands (red).

By 1986, beavers had recolonized the region, and wetland area (red) had increased 13-fold.

1940   1961   1986

© Pete Ryan/National Geographic Stock

Figure 55.12 Beavers Are Ecosystem Engineers By damming streams, beavers created networks of different types of wetlands (shown in red) in a 45-square-kilometer watershed on Minnesota's Kabetogama Peninsula, thus increasing species diversity in the region. (Maps after R. J. Naiman et al. 1988. *BioScience* 38: 753–762.)

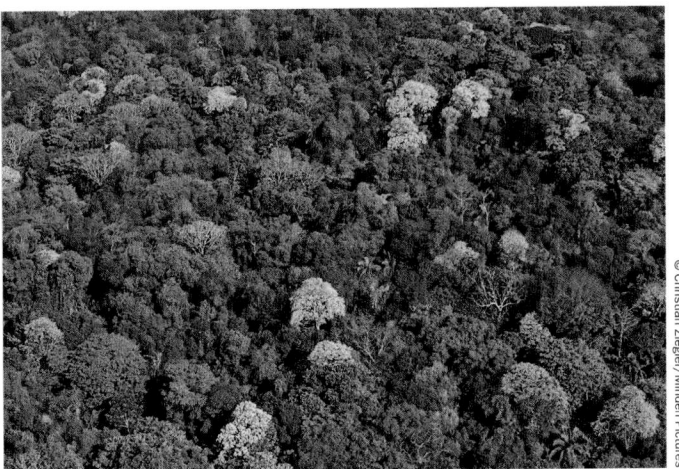

© Christian Ziegler/Minden Pictures

Figure 55.13 Lottery Models Emphasize the Role of Chance
Highly diverse tropical rainforests have hundreds of tree species that overlap in their resource requirements. As long as all individuals have similar chances of obtaining those resources (or "winning the lottery"), and no clear advantage in dispersal ability or population growth, then their presence in the community should be maintained by chance events.

The role of chance in maintaining species diversity, especially in unpredictable environments, has intuitive appeal. As long as individuals of species win the lottery every once in a while, they will continue to reproduce and grow their population. Lottery models have most often proven useful when applied to highly diverse communities such as coral-reef fishes and tropical rainforest trees, where hundreds of species overlap in their resource requirements (**Figure 55.13**).

Ecologists are pursuing various, and sometimes conflicting, hypotheses to explain why certain species coexist in space and time. It is unlikely that any one theory can provide a wholly satisfactory explanation of the mechanisms that drive structure in all communities.

KEY CONCEPT
55.3 Recap and Assess

Communities are complex networks of direct and indirect species interactions that vary in strength and direction. Trophic cascades, resource partitioning, and intermediate disturbance have been proposed to explain species diversity through their mediation of strong species interactions. Some of those strongly interacting species include keystone species, foundation species, and ecosystem engineering species, which regulate community structure through their interactions with other species. In communities where species interactions are more equivalent, chance plays a greater role in determining community structure.

1. Suppose wolves were once again excluded from Yellowstone National Park. What direct and indirect interactions would change, and what effect would this have on aspen forests?

2. Make an argument for why beavers could be considered ecosystem engineering species and keystone species but not foundation species.

3. Using the lottery model as your guide, explain how species that depend on the same set of limiting resources can coexist.

When Mount St. Helens erupted in 1980, it was clear that the surrounding ecological communities would change forever. Change is a regular feature of all communities, but not all changes are as dramatic as those involving a volcanic eruption. In the next key concept we will consider how both subtle and catastrophic factors change communities over time.

KEY CONCEPT
55.4   Communities Are Always Changing

Learning Objectives

55.4.1 Explain how disturbance, stress, and abiotic factors contribute to community change.

55.4.2 Describe the difference between primary and secondary succession in communities.

55.4.3 Explain how facilitation and inhibition influence succession in communities.

55.4.4 Discuss the concept of alternative states, or regime shifts, including how such states might arise.

Imagine that you could look back in time and observe the change in a typical forest on Mount St. Helens (**Figure 55.14**). Over the last few decades, you would have seen both subtle and catastrophic changes. Subtle changes would involve a slow replacement in species composition as a consequence of competition, predation, and facilitation. More catastrophic changes would include volcanic eruptions and deforestation, resulting in the destruction of some species and replacement with others over time. The community at any one time is the result of these various changes both natural and human-caused.

Change in communities can be caused by abiotic and biotic factors

How a community changes in species composition over time is known as **succession**. Succession is the result of both abiotic (physical and chemical) and biotic factors.

A **disturbance** is an abiotic event that physically or chemically injures or even kills some individuals, creating opportunities for other individuals to grow and/or reproduce. Some ecologists also consider biotic events, such as elephants trampling vegetation or beavers felling trees, to be disturbances. The magnitude of a disturbance can vary enormously. Many disturbances are limited to small areas—for example, a log carried by waves may crush algae and animals on a rocky shore. In contrast, hurricanes, forest fires, and volcanic eruptions can affect communities over hundreds or thousands of hectares. Although small-scale disturbances are far more frequent, the occasional large-scale event is often responsible for most of the changes in a community. For example, a single volcanic eruption on Mount St. Helens felled many more trees than multiple storm events ever did, even over decades.

Stress, in contrast to disturbance, occurs when some abiotic factor reduces the growth, reproduction, and/or survival of some individuals. A common stress on the mountain communities of Mount St. Helens is the effect of temperature on the growth and

Species interactions, such as competition, herbivory, and disease, can cause the gradual replacement of species over time.

© Konrad Wothe/Minden Pictures

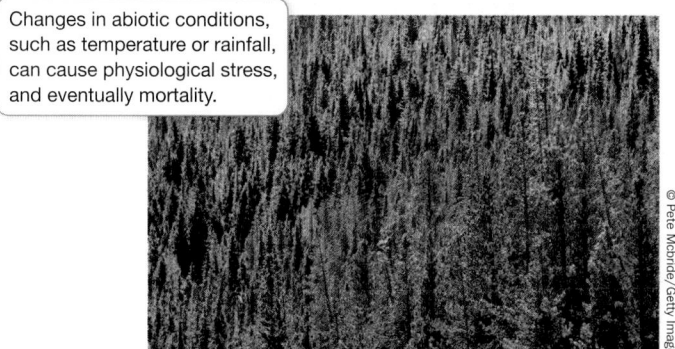

Changes in abiotic conditions, such as temperature or rainfall, can cause physiological stress, and eventually mortality.

© Pete Mcbride/Getty Images

Catastrophic disturbances, such as the eruption of Mount St. Helens or clear-cuts, can cause massive injury and death in forests.

Courtesy of J. Hughes/USDA Forest Service

Figure 55.14 Changes on Mount St. Helens Forest communities on Mount St. Helens have experienced significant changes over hundreds of years. The types of change have been both subtle and catastrophic.

reproduction of plants. As temperatures decrease with increasing elevation on the mountain, you might expect plants at higher elevations to experience more stress than those at lower elevations. But as illustrated in Figure 54.14, the stress that alpine plants experience at higher elevations can be tempered by the presence of neighboring plants. That is, some types of interactions can mitigate the effects of stress.

Biotic factors can influence community change as well. On Mount St. Helens, change might be driven by competition among different tree species, with the most dominant tree species surviving over time (see Figure 55.14). Herbivory by elk is another example of a species interaction that can initiate change. By preferentially browsing on certain species such as willow and aspen, elk can shift the trajectory of plant community succession from forest to meadow, as happened in Yellowstone National Park (see Figure 55.9).

Succession is a process of change in communities over time

Traditionally ecologists have viewed succession as a progression of stages in which species come and go until a climax community arises. The **climax community** is thought to be a stable assemblage of species that experiences little change until an intense disturbance wipes out the community, sending it back to its initial stages again. As you will see later in this key concept, whether some communities reach a true stable end point is questionable. Let's consider the mechanics of succession in more detail.

Succession is probably most easily observed after a catastrophic disturbance kills all the organisms in a community, leaving an environment devoid or nearly devoid of life. This type of change is known as **primary succession**. Glaciers, volcanic activity, and in some cases floods or landslides cause disturbance that initiates primary succession. Primary succession by its very nature can be slow because the early arrivals (known as **pioneer** or **early successional species**) must deal with extreme conditions. Many pioneer species deal with these conditions by employing certain life history strategies or species interactions to their favor.

> **Connect the Concepts** Key Concept 53.3 describes how life history strategies are the lifetime patterns of growth, reproduction, and survival of a species. Pioneer species tend to have life history strategies that maximize population growth (*r*-strategists).

One of the best-known examples of primary succession is that seen in plant communities in the wake of the retreat of glaciers in Glacier Bay, Alaska (**Figure 55.15A**). Captain George Vancouver first recorded the location of glacial ice there in 1794, while exploring the west coast of North America. Over the last 200 years, the glaciers have retreated up the bay, scraping the landscape down to bare rock and leaving a series of moraines—gravel deposits dropped where the glacial front was stationary for a number of years. No human observer was present to observe changes over the entire 200-year period, but ecologists have inferred the temporal pattern of succession by studying the vegetation on moraines of different ages (**Figure 55.15B**). The youngest moraines, closest to the current glacial front, are populated with bacteria, fungi, and photosynthetic microorganisms that can support themselves on bare rock. Slightly older moraines farther from the glacial front are home to pioneer communities containing lichens, mosses, willows, and cottonwoods, which break down rocks and, when they die, decompose and contribute to the buildup of soil. Mosses and a few species of shallow-rooted shrubs in the genus *Dryas* eventually become established and contribute to soil building as they die and decompose. Still farther from the glacial front, successively older moraines have deeper soil layers that support shrubby willows and alder trees. Finally, a century after glacial retreat, a mature Sitka spruce (*Picea sitchensis*) forest dominates, fostering a diverse array of forest species.

Nitrogen is virtually absent from glacial moraines, so the plants that grow best on recently formed moraines at Glacier Bay are *Dryas* and alders, both of which have nitrogen-fixing bacteria in nodules on their roots (see Figure 34.8B). Nitrogen fixation by these plants improves the soil so that spruce trees can grow (see

Figure 55.15 Succession in Glacier Bay, Alaska **(A)** Over more than 200 years, the melting of glaciers has exposed bare rock and glacial moraines to colonization and succession. **(B)** As the community occupying a glacial moraine changes from an assemblage of pioneer plants such as *Dryas* to a spruce forest, soil depth increases and nitrogen accumulates in the soil. (After F. S. Chapin et al. 1994. *Ecol Monograph* 64: 149–175.)

Q: Based on the locations of the glaciers over time, describe where the oldest and youngest communities (black dots) are located.

▶ **View in Achieve**
Animation 55.1 Primary Succession on a Glacial Moraine

Figure 55.15B). Spruces then outcompete and displace the early colonists. If the local climate does not change dramatically, a climax community dominated by spruce trees is likely to persist for many centuries on old moraines at Glacier Bay.

On Mount St. Helens, ecologists have had a unique opportunity to study primary succession from its inception. As described in the opening story, the alpine communities surrounding the lava dome experienced the greatest destruction; they were the first to be hit by an avalanche of mud and hot water and then pelted by hot, sterilizing pumice. This created the so-called Pumice Plain, an area completely lacking life, including any traces of organic matter. The first plant species to arrive, a year after the eruption, was the dwarf lupine (*Lupinus lepidus*). Dwarf lupines, like *Dryas* and alders, use the nitrogen produced by bacterial symbionts in root nodules to colonize the sterile environment of the Pumice Plain. They subsequently facilitated other species of plants by trapping seeds and detritus and increasing the overall nutrient content of the soil. By providing safe sites for seedlings

to become established, the dwarf lupines greatly increased the rate of primary succession on Mount St. Helens. Because of the early inroads made by dwarf lupine, researchers documented roughly 20 plant species living on the Pumice Plain 20 years after the eruption.

A surprising discovery about primary succession on Mount St. Helens was the important role of animals in directing change. For example, scientists observed that newly formed and isolated ponds and lakes were colonized by amphibians at a faster rate than one might predict given the surrounding harsh conditions. Ecologists discovered that frogs and salamanders were using tunnels created by the northern pocket gopher (*Thomomys talpoides*) as refuges when they made their way from pond to pond across the dry landscape (**Figure 55.16**). Pocket gophers successfully survived the eruption by living in tunnels under the mud. They also benefitted by the expansion of their preferred habitat—grassy meadows—after the eruption. Pocket gophers facilitated plant succession through their burrowing activities,

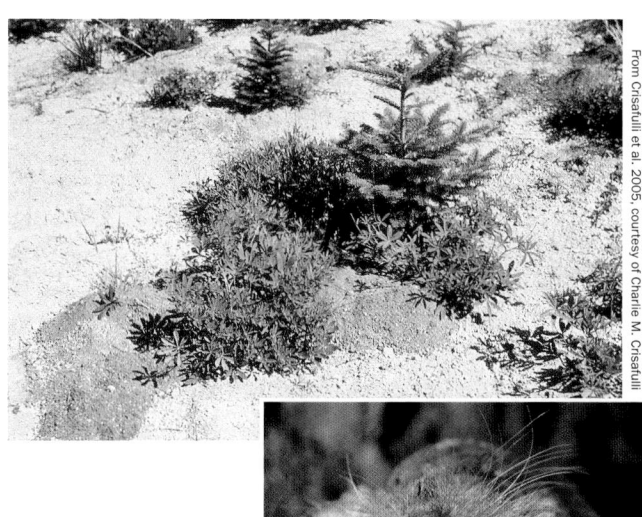

Figure 55.16 Pocket Gophers to the Rescue The burrowing activity of northern pocket gophers, some of which survived the eruption underground, resulted in tunnels that amphibians used to move from one pond to another. It also brought organic matter, seeds, and fungal spores to the soil surface, creating microhabitats, like this one in the Pumice Plain, where plants can grow.

Q: Are pocket gophers keystone species, foundation species, or ecosystem engineering species?

which brought to the surface organic matter, seeds, and fungal spores buried deep under the pumice.

The other type of succession, known as **secondary succession**, involves the reestablishment of a community when most, but not all, organisms have been destroyed. Secondary succession is often initiated by human activities (such as clear-cutting) as well as by natural disasters (such as storms and fires). Secondary succession is more common, and it progresses more rapidly than primary succession. For example, even though the eruption of Mount St. Helens completely destroyed some areas near the blast zone, there were large areas where organisms survived and secondary succession took place.

Ecologists compared primary and secondary succession on Mount St. Helens by following small mammals in the community. As we mentioned in the chapter opening, different Mount St. Helens communities experienced different levels of disturbance from the eruption. **Investigating Life: Rising from the Ashes** describes research by Charles Crisafulli and colleagues at the USDA Forest Service, showing that the recovery of small mammal populations on Mount St. Helens varied significantly between primary and secondary successional habitats. The Pumice Plain (primary successional habitat completely devoid of life after the eruption) had the lowest species richness of small mammals, a pattern that persisted for at least 20 years. In contrast, small mammal populations recovered relatively quickly in the Blowdown Zone and the

Tephra-fall Zone (secondary successional forest in which some life survived under downed trees and ash fall). In fact, within a few years, the number of small mammals in these two zones was similar to that in the undisturbed reference area 21 kilometers away. This comparison makes clear that the starting conditions characterizing secondary succession are critical in giving communities a "head start" in their recovery.

Both facilitation and inhibition influence succession

The progress of succession greatly depends on the activity of successive colonists, each of which modifies the environment to either facilitate or inhibit the colonization by other species. Facilitation is seen, for example, in the fixation of nitrogen by *Dryas* and alders that allows spruce trees to become established in Glacier Bay (see Figure 55.15B). At later stages of succession, though, competition by spruce trees for nitrogen, light, and water inhibits other tree species from establishing themselves. Likewise, dwarf lupines helped facilitate the establishment of later successional plants but, in turn, were inhibited by multiple insect herbivores, which were able to control the pace of primary succession.

Why do we see this interplay between facilitation and inhibition as succession progresses? In most post-disturbance successional sequences, the early pioneer species are exposed to physically challenging conditions that can be tolerated only with the help of other species. For example, in secondary succession, many of the first organisms to arrive on bare soil after a disturbance are detritivores, which process dead organic matter and release nutrients, thus facilitating the establishment of early colonizing plants. Early successional species that can disperse to these habitats and tolerate and modify the abiotic environment will likely facilitate other species without those capabilities. As succession progresses, species that are less stress-tolerant but are larger, longer-lived, and competitively superior will likely come to dominate as the conditions improve, inhibiting earlier pioneer species. While there is typically a transition from early facilitation to later inhibition in most successional sequences, as species diversity increases, a variety of both positive and negative interactions naturally arise, further shaping the pattern of succession.

Alternative successional pathways result in variations in community composition

The trajectory of succession in any community is not necessarily a repeatable and predictable process. Succession often occurs over long periods of time—longer than the life span of any one researcher—making it hard to know whether the changes in species composition are repeatable over time. For example, suppose dwarf lupines had not successfully colonized the Pumice Plain of Mount St. Helens because of intense herbivory. Might later successional stages, such as growth of Douglas fir forests, never develop? Possibly. What is the chance that different, alternative communities could be established after a similar disturbance? Ecologists use the term **alternative states** to refer to the different community assemblages that could develop at the same location under similar environmental conditions.

The theory behind alternative states can be visualized by imagining a landscape full of valleys, each of which represents a

▶Investigating LIFE   Rising from the Ashes

Experiment

Original Paper: C. M. Crisafulli et al. 2005. Small mammal survival and colonization on the Mount St. Helens Volcano: 1980–2002. *In Ecological Responses to the Eruption of Mount St. Helens*. V. H. Dale et al. (eds.), pp. 199–218. Springer: New York.

Charles Crisafulli and his colleagues were some of the first ecologists to study the successional processes on Mount St. Helens after the eruption. They concentrated on the recovery of small mammals in three types of communities that the eruption had disturbed in different ways: a primary successional community named the Pumice Plain, which experienced complete destruction of all living things, and two secondary successional communities: the Blowdown Zone, in which trees fell and the area was covered in mud but some life remained underground, and the Tephra-fall Zone, where the intact forests and meadows were covered in volcanic debris.

An undisturbed reference area, 21 kilometers away from the mountain, was used as a control. To compare the initial survival and subsequent recovery of small mammals in primary versus secondary successional communities, the researchers conducted extensive trapping between 1982 and 2000 at several locations on Mount St. Helens and in the reference area.

HYPOTHESIS▶ As a result of the variation in disturbance from the eruption, the primary successional community will have lower mammal species richness than the secondary successional communities, or the reference area, both initially and through time.

METHOD▶

1. Starting in 1982, several sites were established in the reference area and in three volcanically disturbed areas (Pumice Plain, Blowdown Zone, and Tephra-fall Zone). Trapping sessions were conducted at the sites up to four times a year, from June to October.

2. At each site, live traps baited with rolled oats and peanut butter were set up in multiple plots in a grid pattern. To capture northern pocket gophers, which remain underground, PVC pipe traps were constructed and placed in their burrows.

3. During a trapping session, the traps were checked each morning. Captured animals were identified, uniquely marked, weighed,

Blowdown Zone

Courtesy of Lyn Topinka/USGS

Tephra-fall Zone

Courtesy of Charlie M. Crisafulli

Washington

Pumice Plain

Courtesy of Dan Miller/USGS

N ↑

Toutle River

Spirit Lake

Reference area
21 km away

Mount St. Helens

© *Kevin Schafer/Alamy Stock Photo*

Blowdown Zone
Tephra-fall Zone
Pumice Plain
Lakes
Streams and rivers

5 km

examined to determine sex and reproductive conditions, and released.

RESULTS▶ Early trapping efforts showed that a total of 17 species of small mammals survived the eruption, with most located in the reference area. Over time, small mammal species richness increased in all the communities but proportionally more so in the Blowdown and Tephra-fall Zones (see graph). By 2000, the two secondary successional communities had species richness values roughly equivalent to those in the reference area. The Pumice Plain had only one year (1987) when more than one species of small mammal was present.

CONCLUSION▶ Numerous small mammal species survived and thrived in the post-eruption secondary successional communities of Mount St. Helens. In comparison, the primary successional community showed little recovery of small mammal richness over the 20-year period.

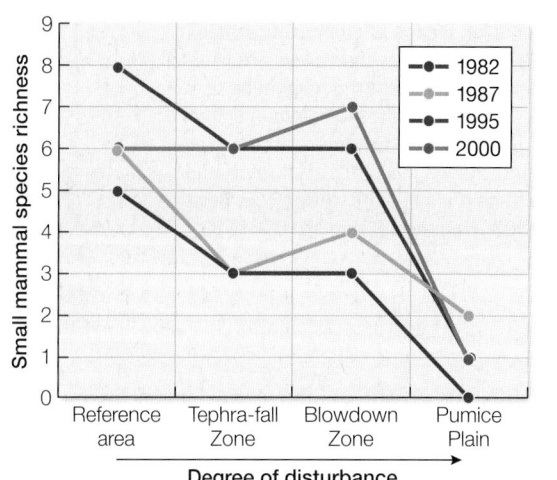

Work with the Data

In addition to examining small mammal species richness, Crisafulli and his team were interested in the composition of those species and their abundance—data that could give them additional insights into the processes important to the species' recovery (or lack thereof). The table shows capture data from 2000 on the small mammal species composition and proportional abundance in the four different post-eruption communities.

	Proportion of Individuals			
Small mammal species	**Pumice Plain**	**Blowdown Zone**	**Tephra-fall Zone**	**Reference area**
Deer mouse (*Peromyscus maniculatus*)	1.00	0.20	0.25	0.10
Yellow-pine chipmunk (*Tamias amoenus*)	0	0.40	0	0
Cascade golden-mantled ground squirrel (*Spermophilus saturatus*)	0	0.05	0	0
Creeping vole (*Microtus oregoni*)	0	0.10	0	0
Shrew mole (*Neurotrichus gibbsii*)	0	0.05	0	0
Trowbridge's mole (*Sorex trowbridgii*)	0	0.10	0	0.05
Montane shrew (*Sorex monticolus*)	0	0.10	0.15	0.10
Southern red-backed vole (*Clethrionomys gapperi*)	0	0	0.45	0.65
Townsend's chipmunk (*Tamias townsendii*)	0	0	0.05	0
Ermine (*Mustela erminea*)	0	0	0.05	0
Northern flying squirrel (*Glaucomys sabrinus*)	0	0	0.05	0
Vagrant shrew (*Sorex vagrans*)	0	0	0	0.05
Northern water shrew (*Sorex palustris*)	0	0	0	0.05

Go to **Achieve** for a companion Data in Depth exercise.

QUESTIONS▶

1. Using the data in the table, calculate the species diversity of each of the post-eruption communities using the Shannon index (see Table 55.1). Which community has the lowest species diversity and which has the highest? How does this pattern compare with that of the species richness values for the four communities?

2. Plot species diversity versus the degree of disturbance from the eruption for the four communities. How well do the data fit the intermediate disturbance hypothesis (see Figure 55.10)? Explain.

3. Consider the presence or absence of particular species in the four communities. Which species is present in all the communities? What does that suggest about its life history?

4. The Blowdown Zone, Tephra-fall Zone, and reference area all have similar species richness (7, 6, and 6 species, respectively), but how do they compare in terms of species composition? Do they appear to be similar? If not, why do you think this is the case?

different community type or state (**Figure 55.17A**). Imagine, for example, valleys on the Pumice Plain of Mount St. Helens, each of which represents a community that might potentially form there. Impose upon this landscape changes in local conditions—such as the presence or absence of a particularly strongly interacting species—that might influence a community to migrate out of one valley (or state) and into another (**Figure 55.17B**). Intense grazing

by herbivores could, for example, influence where dwarf lupine becomes established on the Pumice Plain. If lupine does not become established in a "new" valley, a different successional trajectory may be established, leading to an alternative state for the community. Now, what if conditions change again, and revert back to those of the initial state? Interestingly, even if original conditions are restored, the community may not revert

Figure 55.17 Alternative States
(A) A community is represented by a ball that moves within a landscape of community states (valleys). **(B)** In this analogy the valleys are shallower or deeper according to the magnitude of change (ΔX) needed to shift the community from one state to another. **(C)** Hysteresis occurs when reversal of the change ($-\Delta X$) does not return the community to its original state. (After B. E. Beisner et al. 2003. *Front Ecol Environ* 1: 376–382.)

(A) Stability

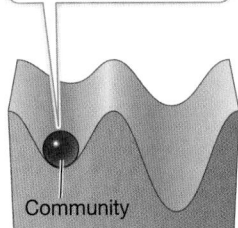

Stability occurs when the community resides within a state (valley).

Community

(B) Change

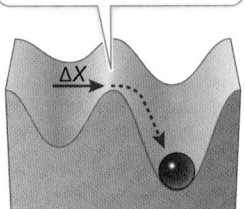

A change in some factor (ΔX) may cause the community to move to another state (valley).

ΔX

(C) Hysteresis

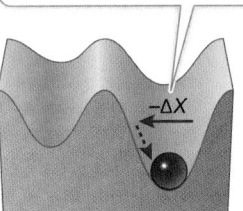

Reversal of the change ($-\Delta X$) may not result in a return to the original conditions if the initial shift was sufficiently large.

$-\Delta X$

to the initial state. If the change experienced by the original community was sufficiently large, the successional trajectory of the community can be irrevocably changed (**Figure 55.17C**). For example, removing herbivores from the system might not bring back dwarf lupine. The system is said to show **hysteresis** when the community is unable to shift back to its initial state even when the original conditions are restored.

Communities that have undergone alternative states, or what are sometimes called regime shifts, have become increasingly of interest as it becomes clear that human activities, such as habitat destruction, species introductions, and overharvesting, are shifting communities to alternative states. Once communities have shifted to a new regime, it is often unclear whether the original community can be restored or whether hysteresis will occur. Reintroducing wolves to Yellowstone National Park did successfully result in the recolonization of aspen as a consequence of elk population control (see Figure 55.9). But will protection of sea otter populations help reestablish kelp forests? Will Atlantic Ocean and Caribbean coral-reef fish communities recover if lionfishes are eradicated there (see Chapter 54, Investigating Life: The Lionfish King)? These are questions whose answers may be found in better understanding the factors that drive alternative states and the role that restoration plays in reversing the effects of those factors.

KEY CONCEPT
55.4 Recap and Assess

Communities constantly undergo change in species composition over time as a result of abiotic and biotic factors, a process known as succession. Abiotic-induced changes to communities come in two forms: disturbance and stress. There are two types of succession: primary succession is the recovery of a community after a catastrophic disturbance kills all the organisms in it, and secondary succession is the reestablishment of a community when most, but not all, organisms have been destroyed. Both facilitation and inhibition influence succession. Communities under similar environmental conditions are sometimes subject to alternative successional pathways, leading to variations in community composition (alternative states).

1. Describe the types of biotic and abiotic changes that have affected forest communities on Mount St. Helens.

2. True or false? "Primary succession is controlled only by facilitation." Explain your answer.

3. Define and give an example from the chapter of an alternative state, or regime shift.

We have focused thus far on the dynamic nature of community structure and on the factors on which community membership depends. In the next key concept we will consider whether the successful functioning of communities depends on the number of species they contain. In other words, how does species richness affect community productivity and stability?

KEY CONCEPT
55.5 Relationships between Species Diversity and Community Function Are Often Positive

Learning Objectives

55.5.1 Summarize the relationship among species diversity, community function, and stability.

55.5.2 Describe how and why growing polycultures can increase agricultural productivity.

As more and more species have either become extinct or are threatened with extinction, ecologists are increasingly interested in understanding what a loss in species diversity means for communities and the way in which they function. Let's next consider research designed to understand how species diversity affects communities as well as agricultural crops.

Community function describes the way a community works and can be measured using metrics such as plant productivity, soil fertility, or water availability. Another measure of how well a community functions is its resistance to (or recovery from) disturbance, known as its **stability**. Ecologists have hypothesized that communities with more species function better than communities with fewer species. The argument is that no two species in a community uses resources in exactly the same way such that a community with more species will show more complete and efficient resource use. Also, should environmental conditions change, a species-rich community is more likely to contain some species that can persist under the new conditions. Thus a species-rich community should be more stable—that is, less likely to change over time in either productivity or species composition—than a species-poor community. Let's examine these assumptions with some experiments.

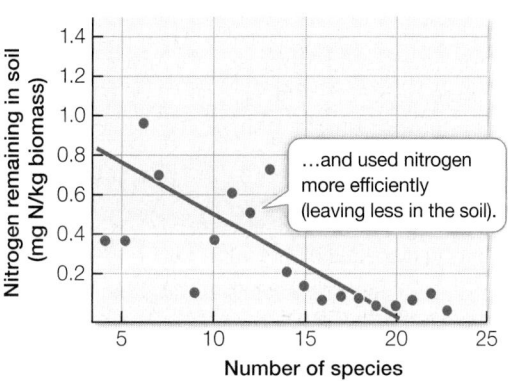

Figure 55.18 Species Richness Enhances Community Productivity David Tilman and his colleagues cultivated a total of 120 grassland plots, containing from 1 to 24 grassland species, for 11 years. **(A)** Total plant cover (a measure of grass biomass, and thus of net primary production). **(B)** The amount of nitrogen remaining in the soil is a measure of resource use efficiency. (After D. Tilman, et al. 1996. *Nature* 379: 718–720.)

Species diversity is associated with productivity and stability

To test the hypothesis that species-rich communities are more stable than species-poor communities, David Tilman and his colleagues at the University of Minnesota cleared 120 outdoor plots, in which they planted grasses in mixtures ranging from 1 to 24 grass species. At the end of each growing season, they measured total plant cover (a measure of grass biomass, and thus of net primary production) and the population densities of all the grasses in each plot. Over a period of 11 years, which included a serious drought, the plots with more species were more productive (**Figure 55.18A**), and their productivity was less variable from year to year. These findings were consistent with the hypothesis that species richness promotes productivity and keeps productivity stable. Moreover, in the plots with greater species richness, soil nitrogen was used more efficiently (**Figure 55.18B**). However, the population densities of *individual* species in the plots were not stable over the years (regardless of a plot's species richness) because different species performed better during drought years and wet years. In other words, higher species richness increased the stability of plant production in the plots, but not the stability of their species composition.

Researchers continue to debate whether species diversity is responsible for maintaining stability or is simply correlated with stability. This question is important because many of the alterations that humans have made in the structure of natural communities have reduced their species richness, and many of these human-altered communities—notably agricultural communities—are notoriously unstable.

Diversity, productivity, and stability differ between natural and managed communities

Although ecologists have been debating the relationships among species diversity, productivity, and stability for only a few decades, humans have been experimenting with those relationships, albeit inadvertently, for millennia—since plants were domesticated and agriculture was invented. Since the dawn of agriculture, crops have been susceptible to diseases and insect outbreaks: massive (often sudden) increases in populations of species that destroy or damage crops.

The practice of growing crops as **monocultures**—plantings of a single crop species—is one reason why managed agricultural communities are particularly unstable. Most farmers have little

tolerance for the presence of any potential competitors for their crops and actively eliminate weeds (and the herbivore species that live with them) from their fields. Thus a typical agricultural community has very low species diversity. So the answer to the question of whether diversity causes or is merely correlated with stability may be sought in modern farming practices. The predisposition of agricultural communities to play host to outbreaks may well result from human influences on community structure.

For the last 20 years, ecologists have been using traditional subsistence agricultural plots as experimental models for testing the relationships between diversity and stability. Throughout the world, many farmers with small land holdings grow **polycultures** or multiple crops on the same plot. In Costa Rica, farmers often grow corn together with sweet potato. Such corn–sweet potato dicultures contain fewer sweet potato pests and more parasitoid wasps (which feed on those pests) than do sweet potato monocultures. Wasps feed on the corn pollen, and the tall corn plants act as a structural barrier, shade plant, and source of disruptive chemical signals that interfere with the ability of the sweet potato pests to find their host plants.

Recently, such applications of community ecology have been paying dividends. Although monoculture is overwhelmingly the dominant agricultural practice, polycultures are under development for agricultural production systems as varied as carp and shrimp farming, vermicomposting (raising worms for compost), and biofuel feedstock production.

KEY CONCEPT
55.5 Recap and Assess

Studies show that the relationships between species diversity and community function (measured as productivity and stability) are often positive. Species diversity enhances productivity because species use resources in slightly different ways; mixtures of species tend to result in a more complete use of limiting resources. Species diversity is hypothesized to enhance stability (a measure of resistance to, or recovery from, disturbance) because the more species a community contains, the more likely some species can persist under variability. These species diversity–community function relationships can be used in agricultural settings to increase crop productivity.

1. Why do Costa Rican farmers often grow multiple crops on the same plot, and why might this be a good strategy under drought conditions?

▶Investigating**LIFE**

Q and **A** How have ecological communities on Mount St. Helens responded to the eruption, and what processes have been important to their recovery?

A similar question was asked by a group of ecologists who convened a week-long field camp on the twentieth anniversary of the eruption in 2000. Many of the participants had spent their entire careers studying the successional patterns on the disturbed landscapes of the mountain. When they left, they agreed to write a book, and 5 years later *Ecological Responses to the 1980 Eruption of Mount St. Helens* was published. The book offers unique insights into the successional processes that communities undergo. One important discovery was that the eruption created disturbances that varied in their effects both on the survival of organisms and their subsequent recovery. Because the eruption occurred in spring, many species were dormant under the winter snows and were able to survive the initial eruption. The recovery of some dormant species such as small mammals has been surprisingly quick. A second important discovery was the role that survivors played in controlling the pace and pattern of succession. Unlikely alliances were formed that hastened succession, as you saw with the northern pocket gopher and amphibians. Finally, the researchers realized that multiple mechanisms were responsible for the pattern of succession on Mount St. Helens. Dispersal, abiotic conditions, and species interactions all played a role in the successional process. The variety of ways in which species responded, and the resulting community assemblages, surprised the ecologists lucky enough to have studied the rise of these communities from the ashes.

Future directions

Despite decades of data and discoveries, research on Mount St. Helens has just begun. Will communities there follow paths of succession that are predictable and repeatable? Or will they form alternative states that are highly dependent on their historical legacies? Unfortunately, succession is a long process spanning many lifetimes of scientists. Steps have been taken to continue the "succession" of research on Mount St. Helens. One of the first steps was to secure Mount St. Helens, in 1982, as a National Volcanic Monument dedicated to research, recreation, and education. This designation, along with coordinated research funding, has set the foundation for long-term study sites and data collection and preservation. In addition, the early "pioneer" scientists have cultivated a strong collaborative culture that brings together young scientists who study different levels of biological organization—from molecules to ecosystems. The collaboration is renewed periodically with "science pulse" camps—week-long events attended by dozens of scientists from around the world who gather benchmark data on a diversity of plants, animals, and microbes. Around the campfire at night, the scientists share observations and recruit the next generation of those who will continue the scientific legacy and storytelling into the future.

VISUAL SUMMARY 55

You should be able to relate each summary to the adjacent figures. If you go to this visual summary in **Achieve**, you can follow links to figures, animations, activities, and simulations that will help you consolidate the material.

KEY CONCEPT
55.1 **Communities Are Groups of Interacting Species Occurring Together in Space and Time**

Go to **Activities 55.1 and 55.2**

- **Communities** vary in size and scope, and it is often impractical to define their boundaries. Ecologists often focus on a subset of species in a community based on similarities in taxonomy, resource use (**guilds**), function (**functional groups**), or trophic and energetic connections (**food webs**).

- Food webs can be divided into **trophic levels** based on how groups of species interact and obtain energy. Food webs identify primary producers, **primary consumers** (herbivores), **secondary consumers** (carnivores), and so on. **Omnivores** feed on multiple trophic levels, and **detritivores** feed on the waste products and dead bodies of organisms.

- **Species diversity** and composition are important descriptors of **community structure**. The **Shannon index** is a measure of species diversity that combines the number of species

Figure 55.2

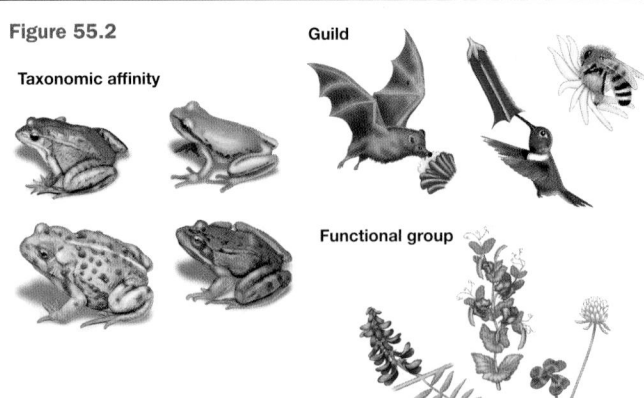

(**species richness**) and their relative abundances compared with other species (**species evenness**).

■ **Biodiversity** is a term used to span multiple scales of diversity, from genes to species to communities.

Questions

1. What are the different ways ecologists subdivide communities?

2. What is a food web, and how does it differ from an interaction web?

3. What is species diversity, and how does it differ from biodiversity?

Figure 55.3

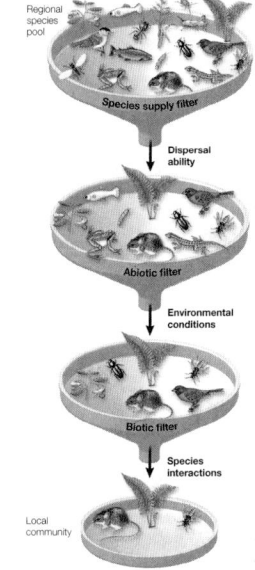

KEY CONCEPT
55.2
Community Membership Depends on Species Supply, Environmental Conditions, and Species Interactions

■ The three basic factors responsible for community membership are (1) the regional species pool and dispersal ability (species supply), (2) physical and chemical environmental conditions (abiotic conditions), and (3) species interactions (biotic conditions). These three factors act as "filters" that exclude (or include) species in communities.

Questions

1. Which regional scale processes versus local scale processes determine community membership?

2. Why is studying introduced non-native species useful in testing community membership?

Figure 55.6

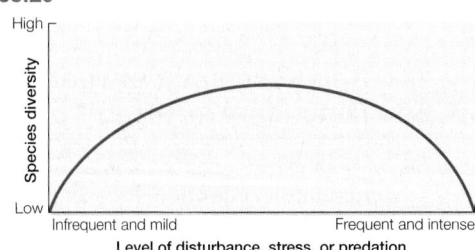

KEY CONCEPT
55.3
Communities Are Complex Networks of Species Interactions That Vary in Strength and Direction

■ **Direct interactions** occur between two species. **Indirect interactions** occur when the direct relationships between two species are mediated by a third (or more) species.

■ A **trophic cascade** occurs when the rate of consumption at one trophic level results in a change in species abundance or composition at lower trophic levels.

■ Some species have especially strong negative effects on community structure, resulting in **resource partitioning** or **resource-mediated coexistence**. The **intermediate disturbance hypothesis** proposes that disturbance promotes species diversity, in part by reducing the negative effects of dominant competitive species.

■ **Keystone species** influence community structure disproportionally to their size or abundance, producing trophic cascades. **Foundation species**, by providing food and habitat for other species, have a large effect on communities as a consequence of their large size or great abundance. **Ecosystem engineering species** affect community structure by creating, modifying, or maintaining physical habitat for themselves and other species irrespective of their size or abundance.

Figure 55.10

Figure 55.11

■ In communities where species interactions are more equivalent, **lottery**, or **neutral**, **models** propose that as long as all individuals have similar chances of obtaining resources, and no clear advantage in dispersal ability or population growth, then their presence in the community should be maintained by chance events that free up resources for competing individuals.

Questions

1. How do the indirect interactions of trophic cascades determine community structure?

2. How do keystone, foundation, and ecosystem engineering species differ?

3. How do resource partitioning, intermediate disturbance, and the lottery model differ?

KEY CONCEPT

55.4   Communities Are Always Changing

Go to **Animation 55.1**

■ Communities constantly undergo change in species composition over time as a result of abiotic and biotic factors, a process known as **succession**. Disturbance and stress are two significant forms of abiotic-induced community change. A **disturbance** is an abiotic event that physically or chemically injures or kills individuals, whereas **stress** occurs when some abiotic factor reduces the growth, reproduction, or ultimately survival of individuals.

■ There are two types of succession: **primary succession** is the recovery of a community after a catastrophic disturbance kills all the organisms in it, and **secondary succession** is the reestablishment of a community when most, but not all, organisms have been destroyed.

■ Facilitation and inhibition influence primary and secondary succession.

■ The outcome of succession is not always predictable; alternative states, or regime shifts, lead to different community assemblages under similar environmental conditions. **Hysteresis** occurs when a community is unable to shift back to its original state even when the original conditions are restored.

Figure 55.15

Pioneer plants · *Dryas* · Alders · Climax (spruce forest)

Glacial front · Youngest moraine · Slightly older moraine · Older moraine · Oldest moraine

Figure 55.17

Stability · Change · Hysteresis

Community · ΔX · $-\Delta X$

Questions

1. What are the biotic and abiotic factors that induce change in communities?

2. What are the types of succession, and how do they differ?

3. Describe alternative states and the process of hysteresis.

KEY CONCEPT

55.5   Relationships between Species Diversity and Community Function Are Often Positive

■ Studies show that the relationships between species diversity and **community function** (measured as productivity and stability) are often positive. **Stability** is a measure of resistance to, or recovery from, disturbance.

■ Species diversity–community function relationships can be used in agricultural settings to increase crop productivity.

Figure 55.18

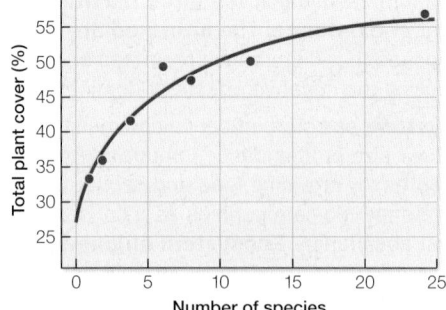

Plant cover

Total plant cover (%) vs. Number of species

Questions

1. How is species diversity associated with community function and stability?

2. How can species diversity–community function relationships be used to increase crop productivity?

Go to **Achieve** for the eBook, **LearningCurve**, animations, activities, simulations, and additional resources and assignments.

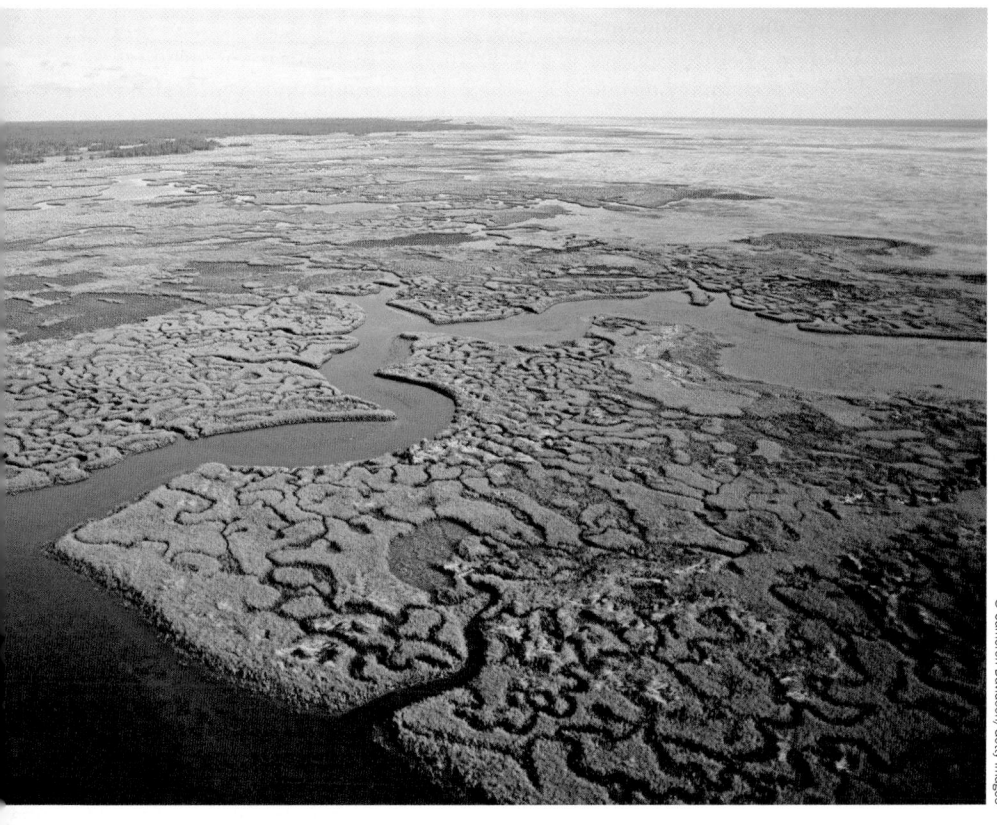

© Cameron Davidson/Getty Images

Estuaries, where the river meets the sea, provide food and habitat for commercially important fishes and shellfishes.

▶ Investigating LIFE

Food Webs in an Acidic and Warming Ocean

There is no dispute that the burning of fossil fuels over the last two centuries has increased Earth's atmospheric CO_2 concentrations. Estimates show that oceans are absorbing about 48% of all atmospheric CO_2. Marine primary producers use some of the human-caused CO_2 in photosynthesis, but the remainder reacts chemically with seawater, lowering its pH and causing oceans to become more acidic. Ocean acidification can have negative effects on calcifying organisms such as corals, mollusks, and crustaceans, which rely on calcium carbonate for the accretion and maintenance of their external shells. But the negative effects of increasing CO_2 and acidification are not universal. For example, primary producers such as phytoplankton, algae, and sea grasses are known to increase their production under elevated CO_2. Increasing photosynthesis increases O_2 production, which can potentially counteract growing acidity in surrounding seawater. Research is under way on the effects of ocean acidification on single species, but studies on how ocean acidity affects marine ecosystems and food webs are also needed. Moreover, along with the acidification of oceans, water temperatures are rising, potentially creating multiple stressors for organisms.

Estuaries are places where the dual effects of ocean acidification and temperature on primary producers and their food webs

may be particularly relevant. Among the most productive ecosystems on Earth, estuaries support a diverse array of marine organisms, including commercially important fish species. Because estuaries are at the interface between land and sea, they have been highly affected by humans through intense overfishing, habitat destruction, and pollution from rivers. Estuaries also experience warm water temperatures, a condition that could intensify with global warming. But estuaries may also be places where the effects of ocean acidification could be mitigated if primary producers such as macroalgae and sea grasses are able to sequester CO_2 and provide more food and habitat for higher trophic levels.

Research on estuaries was conducted by a group of researchers on the western coast of Sweden. The group focused on a food web that includes algae primary producers and invertebrate consumers and exposed this food web to different conditions of CO_2 and temperature. What they found suggests that ocean acidification and temperature affect food webs in complex ways that may be hard to predict.

 How will food webs respond to the multiple effects of ocean acidification and warming in marine ecosystems? (Find the answer on page 1276.)

KEY CONCEPT
56.1 Ecosystem Science Considers How Energy and Nutrients Flow through Biotic and Abiotic Environments

Learning Objectives

56.1.1 Compare and contrast ecosystems and communities.

56.1.2 List sources of energy in ecosystems, and associate each source with the processes that produce it.

56.1.3 Explain how nutrients cycle between living organisms and the abiotic environment.

In Chapter 55 we considered communities and the roles that species play in shaping their structure and function. In this chapter we will consider how energy flows and nutrients cycle through communities, a branch of ecology known as **ecosystem science**. An **ecosystem** is all the organisms living in a given area and their physical and chemical environment. The term was first coined by A. G. Tansley, a plant ecologist who was interested in how the flow of energy and chemicals was influenced by both the biotic and abiotic components of the environment.

Just like communities, ecosystems occupy a wide range of spatial scales, making them hard to delineate precisely (see Key Concept 55.1). For that reason, ecologists often define an ecosystem using subsets of species and components of the physical and chemical environment based on the questions they are investigating. For example, a soil ecosystem might include only the bacteria that transform nitrogen into forms plants can use. Or an estuarine ecosystem might be confined to the cycling of carbon through a food web of algae and their consumers, as you saw in the opening story.

Energy flowing through ecosystems originates with sunlight and inorganic and organic compounds

The flow of energy through ecosystems comes in a variety of forms (**Figure 56.1**). The most obvious source is the Sun, which delivers radiant energy that warms Earth and provides energy for photosynthesis. Autotrophs such as plants, algae, and photosynthetic bacteria capture that radiant energy and fix it into organic compounds that make up the tissues of organisms (see Figure 56.1A). Energy can also come from the oxidation of inorganic nutrients by archaea and bacteria through the process of **chemosynthesis**, which involves using energy from inorganic compounds to take up CO_2 and produce carbohydrates (see p. 552). Chemosynthesis typically occurs in ecosystems that lack sunlight and have high concentrations of particular inorganic

compounds, such as hydrothermal vents, hot springs, and soils. These two forms of energy capture and carbon fixation are both involved in a process known as primary production. Ecologists use the term "primary productivity" to indicate the rate of primary production over time.

A third source of energy in an ecosystem is the product of primary production—the organic compounds synthesized through photosynthesis and chemosynthesis—that is made available for organisms at higher trophic levels in food webs (see Figure 56.1B). This source of energy, known as **secondary production**, is contained within the tissues of organisms and

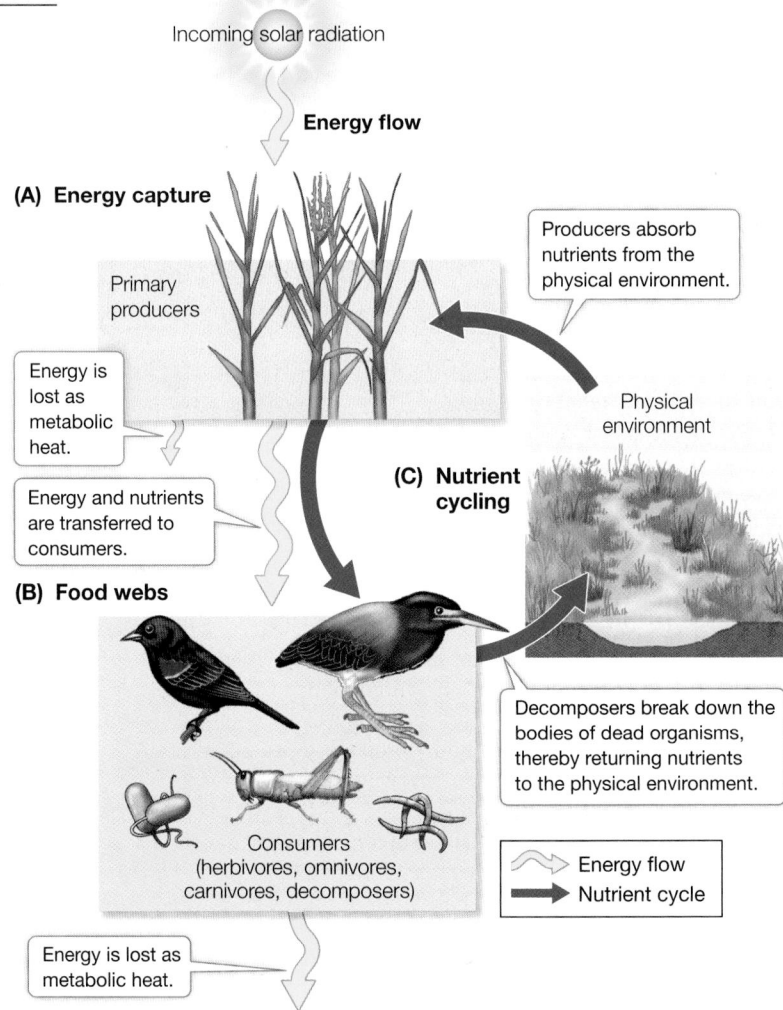

Figure 56.1 Energy Flows and Chemical Nutrients Cycle through Ecosystems (A) The flow of energy through ecosystems comes mostly from the Sun, which delivers radiant energy for photosynthesis by primary producers. (B) Primary producers then provide energy to organisms at higher trophic levels in food webs, but some of that energy is lost as metabolic heat. (C) Nutrients continually cycle between living organisms and the physical components of ecosystems.

Q: Why does energy "flow" but nutrients "cycle" through ecosystems?

 View in Achieve
Activity 56.1 Energy Flow through an Ecosystem

is used to power the metabolism of heterotrophs, or the consumers within food webs, which include herbivores, carnivores, omnivores, parasites and pathogens, and eventually decomposers. Metabolism involves converting the organic compounds in food into useable energy—primarily ATP—by processes such as glycolysis (see Key Concept 9.1). The main by-products of metabolism are inorganic compounds, CO_2, and water. The energy generated by metabolism to support the "work" that organisms do in their daily life is eventually lost from the ecosystem in the form of metabolic heat.

Nutrients cycling through ecosystems originate in soil, water, and the atmosphere

In contrast to energy, which is ultimately lost from an ecosystem as heat, nutrients continually cycle between living organisms and the abiotic components of ecosystems (see Figure 56.1C). Organisms require 30–40 different nutrients, including the macronutrients carbon, hydrogen, nitrogen, calcium, phosphorus, potassium, and magnesium, and micronutrients such as iron, manganese, zinc, and copper. All the chemical components in the bodies of organisms ultimately originate from soil, water, or the atmosphere, but organisms acquire these materials in many different ways. Autotrophs such as plants take up certain elements directly from soil, water, and the atmosphere and incorporate them in their tissues. Heterotrophs generally acquire elements by consuming the biomass of other organisms, and then reassemble them via chemical reactions. Some heterotrophs acquire some elements from mutualistic microbes that convert them into forms that are usable by their hosts.

Gas exchange by living organisms returns certain elements to the atmosphere as gases. After organisms die, the materials in their bodies become detritus and are broken down by decomposers into simpler biochemical components, which then can be used by autotrophs once again. Elements not used by autotrophs can accumulate in soil, water, or sediments.

KEY CONCEPT
56.1 Recap and Assess

An ecosystem is all the organisms in a given area and their physical and chemical environment. Autotrophs such as plants, algae, and photosynthetic bacteria capture sunlight and fix it into organic compounds (primary production). Energy is also derived through chemosynthesis: the oxidation of inorganic nutrients by archaea and bacteria. Energy captured through primary production is in turn available for organisms at higher trophic levels in food webs (secondary production). Nutrients continually cycle between living organisms and the abiotic environment.

1. An ecologist measures the number of species in an ecosystem. Is she conducting ecosystem science? Explain.

2. Describe the two ways that energy and carbon are converted into primary production.

For the remainder of this chapter we will consider in more detail how energy flows and nutrients cycle through ecosystems as depicted in Figure 56.1. We will start with primary production, whereby energy and nutrients are first captured in ecosystems.

KEY CONCEPT
56.2 Energy and Nutrients in Ecosystems Are First Captured by Primary Producers

Learning Objectives

56.2.1 Explain the difference between gross primary production and net primary production.

56.2.2 Describe the variation in NPP by latitude and biome type in terrestrial and aquatic ecosystems.

56.2.3 Explain the factors important to NPP in terrestrial and aquatic ecosystems.

56.2.4 Discuss the causes and effects of eutrophication in aquatic ecosystems.

The overwhelming majority of the primary production on Earth comes from photosynthesis. Plants, algae, and bacteria fix carbon by capturing energy from the Sun (or inorganic nutrients, in the case of chemosynthesis) and using that energy to convert carbon dioxide into carbon compounds that can then be used by higher trophic levels.

Net primary production is the amount of carbon remaining in plants after respiration

Fixed carbon, be it from photosynthesis or chemosynthesis, is the currency used to measure primary production. The total amount of carbon fixed by primary producers in an ecosystem is called **gross primary production** (**GPP**). Not all GPP becomes living plant matter, or biomass, because primary producers use some of that energy for their own respiration and other metabolic processes. Thus **net primary production** (**NPP**), the amount of biomass incorporated into the tissues of primary producers after respiration, is the most common metric used to describe an ecosystem's carbon fixation. This relationship is represented mathematically as

$$NPP = GPP - respiration$$

The carbon not used in respiration is then allocated to such important processes as growth, reproduction, and survival in the face of physical stress, herbivory, or diseases (see Chapter 38).

Patterns of primary production vary with latitude and ecosystem type

Large-scale geographic variation in primary production is one of the most obvious ecological patterns on Earth. Only recently, however, have ecologists been able to reliably quantify patterns of production at global scales. Satellite-based optical sensing techniques now help scientists detect the amount of primary production on land and in the ocean at global scales. How do terrestrial and oceanic ecosystems compare, and how is NPP distributed across the globe?

Estimates of global NPP show that the total amount of carbon taken up by terrestrial ecosystems (52%) is slightly higher than that taken up by the oceans (48%), even though oceans make up a greater percentage (70%) of Earth's surface. This difference arises because terrestrial ecosystems have a much higher per-area NPP (426 g C/m^2/year) than do oceans (140 g C/m^2/year).

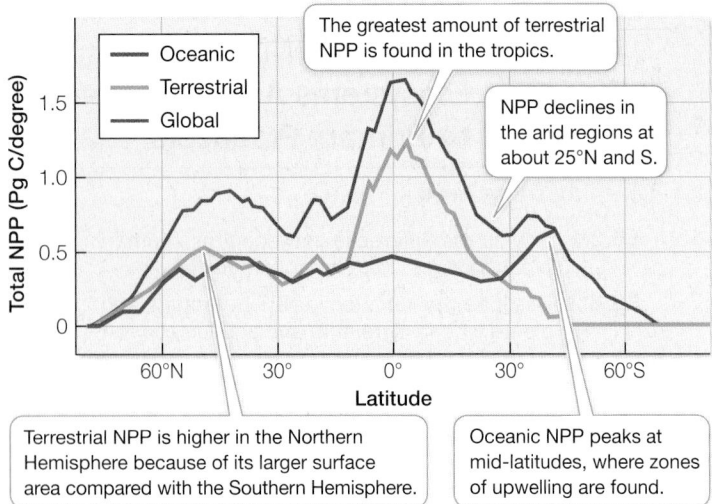

Figure 56.2 Estimates of Total Oceanic, Terrestrial, and Global NPP by Latitude On land, NPP is highest in the tropics and declines at higher latitudes. In the oceans, NPP does not vary much with latitude except at mid-latitudes, especially in the Southern Hemisphere. (1 petagram or Pg = 10^{15} g.) (After C. B. Field et al. 1998. *Science* 281: 237–240.)

have some of the highest average net primary production, but their small geographic areas make their contributions to global NPP modest. It is important to note, however, that the primary producers in these ecosystems contribute substantially to local and regional NPP and thus are critical to marine food webs.

Not surprisingly, the patterns of primary production that we see on land versus ocean, and among ecosystem types, can be explained by separate factors that control primary production in terrestrial versus aquatic systems. We will now consider these factors in more detail—first on land, and then in oceans and lakes.

Precipitation and temperature largely control terrestrial primary production

The strong latitudinal patterns in terrestrial NPP reflect variation in global climate, particularly rainfall and temperature, across latitudes and seasons. NPP increases as average annual rainfall increases up to a maximum (approximately 240 cm per year), but then declines in most ecosystems (**Figure 56.5A**). The decrease in NPP with high rainfall can occur

Satellite imaging has also shown that NPP is distributed differently on land than in the ocean. NPP on land varies dramatically with latitude, whereas oceans show much less latitudinal variation (**Figure 56.2**). On land, NPP is highest in the tropics and declines at higher latitudes. Arid regions such as those in deserts (30° latitude) and at the poles (90° latitude) show extremely low NPP (**Figure 56.3A**). NPP rises slightly at mid-latitudes, especially in the Northern Hemisphere, where land area is larger than in the Southern Hemisphere (see Figure 56.2). In the oceans, NPP is highest at mid-latitudes and along coastal zones, especially those that experience upwelling (**Figure 56.3B**). NPP is also higher in the Southern Hemisphere, where ocean area is larger than in the Northern Hemisphere (see Figure 56.2).

Remote sensing has also revealed variation in NPP among different ecosystem types or biomes. Tropical rainforest ecosystems have the second-highest average NPP, even though they make up only a little over 3% of Earth's surface (**Figure 56.4**). In comparison, open ocean ecosystems have a low average NPP, despite the large area over which they occur. Some marine ecosystems such as estuaries and algal beds and coral reefs

Figure 56.3 Geographic Variation in Terrestrial and Oceanic NPP Maps of NPP based on satellite sensor data. (**A**) Terrestrial NPP is highest in the tropics and lowest in arid regions and at the poles. Gray areas represent relatively unvegetated land masses, including deserts and ice caps. (**B**) Oceanic NPP is highest at mid-latitudes and in coastal and upwelling zones. (A, after MODIS GPP/NPP Project [MOD17]. Numerical Terradynamic Simulation Group [NTSG], The University of Montana, Missoula. http://www.ntsg.umt.edu/project/modis/mod17.php; B, image by Robert Simmon, NASA GSFC Earth Observatory, based on data provided by Watson Gregg, NASA GSFC.)

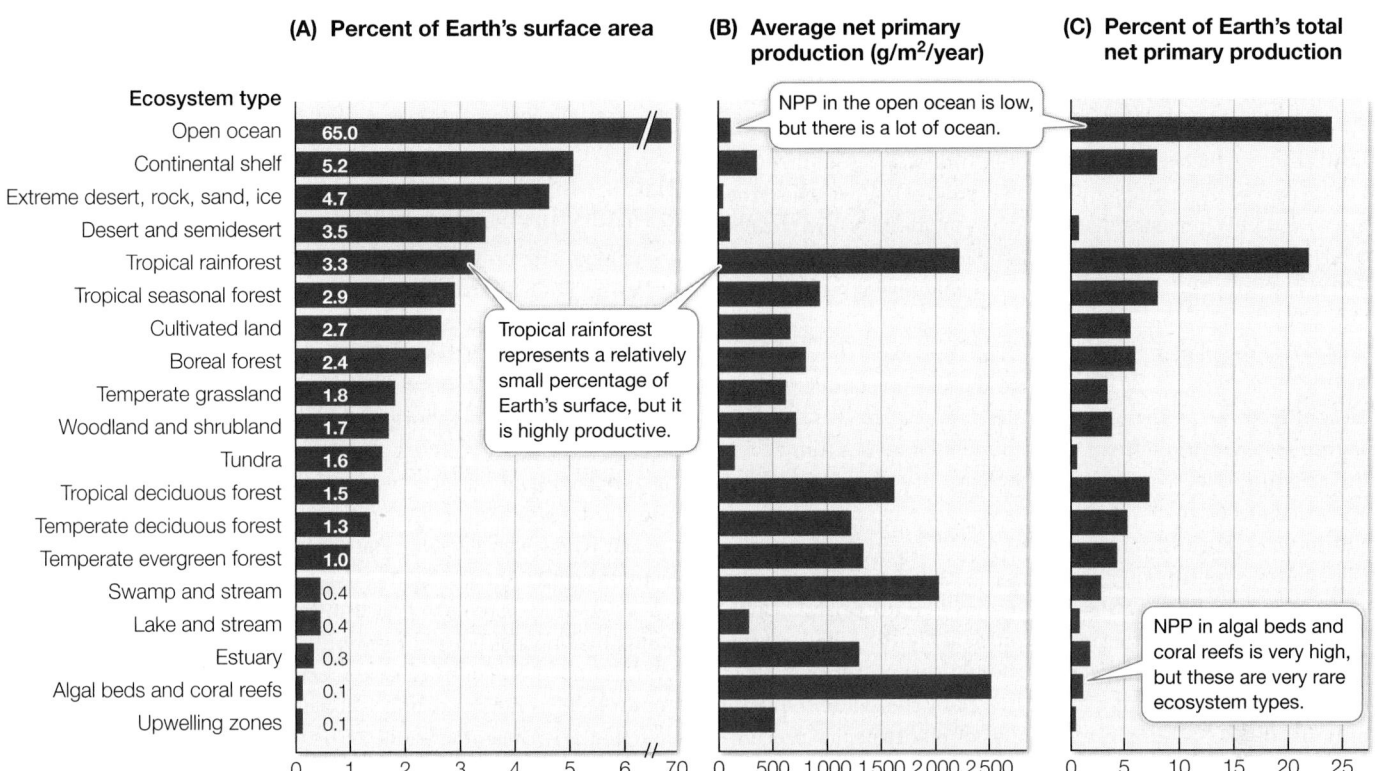

Figure 56.4 Ecosystems Differ in NPP The contribution of different ecosystem types to global NPP can be measured by (A) their geographic extent and (B) their average net primary production. (C) Combining these two measures gives the proportional contribution of each ecosystem type to Earth's total NPP. (Data primarily based on R. H. Whittaker and G. E. Likens. 1973. *Hum Ecol* 1: 357–369 and R. H. Whittaker and G. E. Likens. 1975. In *Primary Productivity of the Biosphere*, H. Lieth and R. H. Whittaker [Eds.], pp. 305–328. Springer-Verlag: New York.)

because of sunlight being reduced by cloud cover over long periods of time or as a consequence of nutrient loss or flooding. NPP also increases with average annual temperature (**Figure 56.5B**). Thus it makes sense that close to the equator, where temperatures and rainfall are high throughout the year, conditions are ideal for primary producers. In deserts, even though temperatures can be high, plant growth is limited by a lack of rainfall. At higher latitudes or elevations, even though moisture is generally available, NPP is low because it is relatively cold for

much of the year and the growing season is shorter than at lower latitudes or elevations.

In addition to being affected by global climate, terrestrial NPP is also affected by nutrient availability and atmospheric CO_2 concentrations. How these two factors affect primary production is of special interest given the increasing use of artificial fertilizers and rising atmospheric CO_2 concentrations from the burning of fossil fuels (see Key Concept 56.4). A looming question is whether plants, by taking up CO_2, might be able to offset increasing CO_2

Figure 56.5 Global Patterns of Terrestrial NPP Correlate with Climate The plots show the relationships between NPP for different terrestrial ecosystems and (A) precipitation and (B) temperature of those ecosystems worldwide. (1 megagram or Mg = 10^6 g.) (After E. A. G. Schuur. 2003. *Ecology* 84: 1165–1170.)

emissions. An ambitious experiment exploring this possibility was conducted in 1996. The FACE (*free-air* CO_2 *enrichment*) experiment involved artificially increasing CO_2 concentrations within arenas constructed around pine trees in North Carolina (**Figure 56.6A**). To test whether nutrients were a limiting factor, nitrogen was added to half the plots. By late 2000, trees showed a slight increase in NPP (measured as woody tissue biomass) in the elevated CO_2 plots compared with the ambient plots (**Figure 56.6B**). The increase in NPP, however, was significant only in the fertilized plots, suggesting that nutrients are a limiting factor in the assimilation of CO_2 by plants. Since the initial FACE experiment, more than 12 similar large-scale experiments have been conducted in a variety of ecosystems, including grasslands and agricultural crops. The results generally confirm those found in North Carolina, but there are differences. Trees are generally more responsive than herbaceous species to elevated CO_2 concentrations, and grain crop yields increase far less than anticipated.

The FACE experiments remind us that terrestrial ecosystems can vary widely in their NPP, as you saw in Figure 56.4. Clearly some of this variability is a simple consequence of global and regional climate promoting the formation of certain types of ecosystems and biomes, as you saw illustrated by the Walter climate diagrams in Chapter 52. But the types of plant species present can also determine the NPP of an ecosystem. For a given set of environmental conditions, plant species can vary widely in their NPP depending on their photosynthetic pathway (e.g., C_3 versus C_4 plants, or trees versus shrubs versus grasses), which regulates their rate of photosynthesis. Moreover, nutrient limitation can play a major role in NPP in certain ecosystems. For example, in lowland tropical forests, NPP is often limited by phosphorus, calcium, and potassium. In temperate and arctic ecosystems, nitrogen and phosphorus can be limiting.

Connect the Concepts As discussed in Key Concept 10.4, C_3 and C_4 plants differ in how they fix CO_2 and can be distinguished according to whether the first product of CO_2 fixation is a three- or four-carbon molecule (see Figure 10.16).

Light and nutrients combine to control aquatic primary production

Chapter 52 described how Earth's topography affects water depth, creating gradients in light, temperature, water pressure, and nutrient availability. The main primary producers in aquatic ecosystems—phytoplankton and algae—are most limited by light and nutrients along continental margins (coastal zones) and in the surface waters of oceans and lakes (photic zones) (see Figure 52.9C,D). Oceanic NPP peaks at mid-latitudes and along the continental margins (see Figure 56.3B) because these are regions where nutrient concentrations from ocean upwelling are high. Higher NPP is associated with estuaries as well, where nutrients can be "outwelled" from watershed runoff to coastal zones.

In aquatic systems, NPP is limited primarily by iron, nitrogen, and phosphorus. The relative importance of these three nutrients varies depending on the aquatic ecosystem. In much of the open ocean, NPP is limited primarily by nitrogen. But in some locations, particularly the equatorial Pacific Ocean where excess nitrogen has been detected in surface waters, NPP by phytoplankton may be more limited by iron. In a series of experiments in the mid-1990s, biological oceanographers added iron sulfite to the surface waters off the Galápagos archipelago and in the Southern Ocean to test the hypothesis that oceanic NPP, and thus the potential of the ocean to take up CO_2 and combat global warming and ocean acidification (see p. 1270), was limited primarily by iron. The experiments showed that NPP was as much as four- to tenfold higher in the plume of water that received the iron additions. While the experiments show that iron limitation is a major factor in reducing the ability of the ocean to absorb CO_2 from the atmosphere, large-scale fertilization of the oceans is impractical at best, and may be somewhat counteracted by respiration of CO_2 by zooplankton and bacteria feeding on phytoplankton.

In lake ecosystems, NPP is limited primarily by phosphorus. The effect of phosphorus on lake NPP was first studied in connection with the declining water quality of lakes in North America and Europe. Wastewater and sewage were implicated in a dramatic increase in **eutrophication**, a process of ecosystem change initiated by an increase in nutrients consumed by phytoplankton, cyanobacteria, and algae in aquatic systems. Eutrophication can result in the explosive growth of algae (algal blooms). Decomposition of large volumes of dead algae by bacteria can in turn severely deplete oxygen needed by aquatic life (hypoxia). To understand which nutrients were most important to the blooms, David Schindler and colleagues conducted whole lake fertilization experiments,

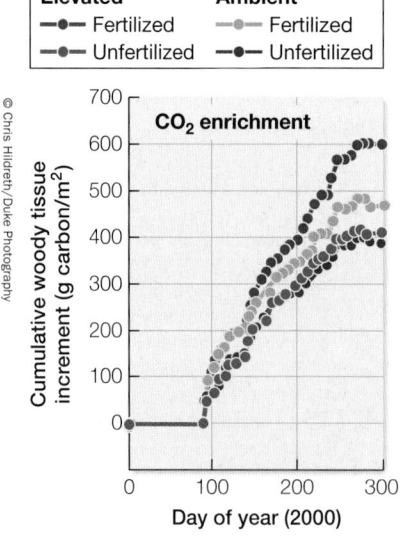

Figure 56.6 FACE Experiment: Effects of CO_2 and Nutrients on NPP **(A)** The free-air CO_2 enrichment (FACE) experiment involved releasing CO_2 from towers constructed around pine trees. **(B)** The trees grew better under conditions of elevated CO_2 (550 parts per million) and nutrients than they did under ambient conditions. Without added nutrients, elevated CO_2 had a minimal effect on tree growth. (After R. Oren et al. 2001. *Nature* 411: 469–472.)

© Chris Hildreth/Duke Photography

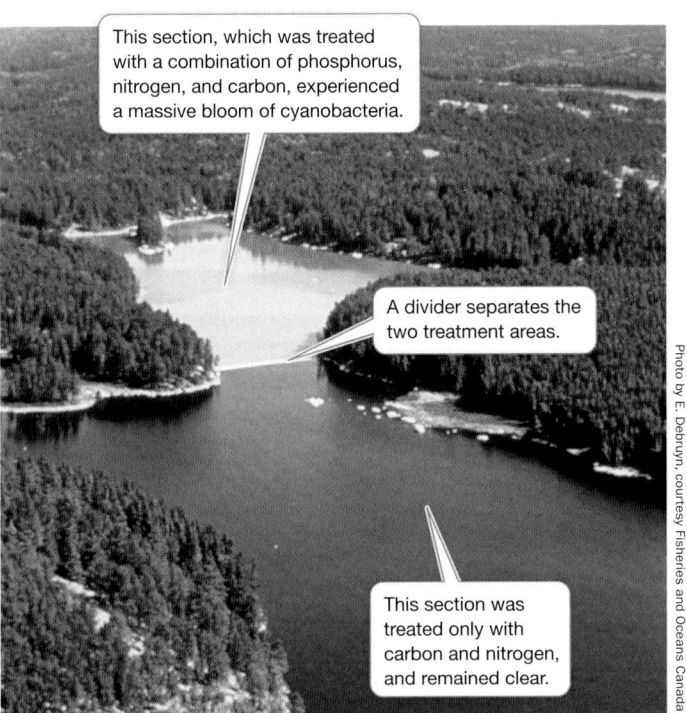

This section, which was treated with a combination of phosphorus, nitrogen, and carbon, experienced a massive bloom of cyanobacteria.

A divider separates the two treatment areas.

This section was treated only with carbon and nitrogen, and remained clear.

Photo by E. Debruyn, courtesy Fisheries and Oceans Canada.

Figure 56.7 Lake NPP Responds to Phosphorus Fertilization Experiments show that the addition of phosphorus to a lake causes massive phytoplankton and cyanobacteria blooms.

starting in 1969, in a set of small lakes in Ontario, Canada. They added nitrogen, carbon, and phosphorus to all or half of several lakes and found that phosphorus was the major trigger for phytoplankton and cyanobacteria blooms (**Figure 56.7**). These experiments set in motion a campaign to reduce phosphorus in wastewater by recommending the banning of phosphates in detergents and stripping them chemically in sewage treatment plants.

KEY CONCEPT

56.2 Recap and Assess

Fixed carbon, be it from photosynthesis or chemosynthesis, is used to measure primary production. Net primary production is the amount of biomass incorporated into the tissues of primary producers after respiration, and it varies with latitude and ecosystem type. On land, NPP is highest in the tropics where temperatures are high year-round and rainfall is abundant. In the oceans, NPP peaks along continental margins and in areas of upwelling, where the main primary producers—phytoplankton and algae—have access to light and nutrients. Nutrient runoff from agriculture and wastewater can cause eutrophication in aquatic systems, resulting in algal blooms and deadly low oxygen conditions (hypoxia).

1. Consider Figure 56.4. How does the average net primary production differ between the open ocean and algal beds and coral reefs? Why, then, does the open ocean account for such a high percentage of Earth's total NPP?

2. Atmospheric CO_2 concentrations are rising at unprecedented rates. Is it reasonable to assume that primary producers on land and in the oceans will be able to appreciably lower global CO_2 concentrations? What evidence is there to support your answer?

3. Describe the process of eutrophication and name the nutrient most responsible for this process in lake systems.

Once the energy captured by primary producers is fixed as NPP, consumption by heterotrophs transfers a fraction of that energy to higher trophic levels. Next we will consider in more detail the factors important to the movement and loss of energy between trophic levels.

KEY CONCEPT

56.3 Food Webs Transfer Energy and Nutrients from Primary Producers to Consumers

Learning Objectives

56.3.1 Describe the factors important in net secondary production, and how production efficiencies differ for ectotherms and endotherms.

56.3.2 Discuss why trophic efficiencies are higher in aquatic than in terrestrial ecosystems, and explain how this affects production throughout the food web.

56.3.3 Explain why the flow of energy in food webs is influenced by the relative contributions of bottom-up and top-down forces, the number of trophic levels, and the presence of omnivory.

56.3.4 Provide hypotheses that explain the factors important to trophic level length.

You know from Chapter 55 that food webs can be constructed to represent the interactions and energy transfers that occur between different species and trophic levels. For example, the food web presented in Figure 55.3 shows the connections among primary producers and consumers in Yellowstone National Park. While the arrows indicate the trophic connections among species, they do not show how much energy is actually being transferred up the food web and converted into secondary production. We will now consider the factors important to secondary production.

Key Concept 8.1 described how, during energy transfer, some energy is lost as "unusable" to the system (second law of thermodynamics) and thus is unavailable to do work. For food webs, the consequence of this loss is that only part of the primary production consumed by heterotrophs is converted into heterotroph biomass. What factors are important to this movement and loss of energy from primary to secondary production? **Net secondary production**, or the amount of biomass obtained from the consumption of other organisms, depends on how much plant tissue is consumed (**consumption efficiency**), how much of the consumed food can actually be digested versus released as feces and urine (**assimilation efficiency**), and how much of the digested food is used in metabolic activities and released as CO_2 through respiration versus stored as biomass (**production efficiency**) (**Figure 56.8**). We can think of production efficiency as the percentage of energy stored in assimilated food that is used to produce new biomass.

Consumers can vary dramatically in production efficiency. For example, endotherms have much lower production efficiencies than ectotherms (**Table 56.1**). Because endotherms have to maintain high body temperatures, they have higher metabolic rates than ectotherms, and thus have less energy left over to devote to

Figure 56.8 Energy Flow and Net Secondary Production in an Herbivore
The proportion of energy transferred between a caterpillar and its plant food depends on efficiencies of consumption, assimilation, and production.

Q: Why do you think herbivores have lower production efficiencies than carnivores?

growth and reproduction. Moreover, endotherms vary in production efficiency depending on body size and metabolism. Larger mammals have lower metabolic rates and higher production efficiencies compared with smaller mammals and birds, whose greater surface area-to-biomass ratios result in more heat loss and higher metabolic rates (see Key Concept 38.5).

Because production efficiency affects the growth and reproduction of consumers, changes in the quality and quantity of food can

TABLE **56.1** | Production Efficiencies of Consumers	
Consumer group	**Production efficiency (%)**
ENDOTHERMS	
Birds	1.3
Small mammals	1.5
Large mammals	3.1
ECTOTHERMS	
Fishes and social insects	9.8
Nonsocial insects	40.7
Herbivores	38.8
Detritivores	47.0
Carnivores	55.6
Non-insect invertebrates	25.0
Herbivores	20.9
Detritivores	36.2
Carnivores	27.6

Source: Data from W. F. Humphreys. 1979. *J Anim Ecol* 48: 427–453.

lead to population declines. Research on Steller sea lions (*Eumetopias jubatus*) in the Gulf of Alaska and the Aleutian Islands offers a case in point. Sea lion populations declined by 85% over a 25-year period starting in the early 1970s. Surveys of sea lion individuals showed that they were smaller and had lower birth rates compared with individuals before the decline, suggesting that food was a limiting factor. Prior to the decline, sea lions mostly fed on herring, rich in fats, along with lesser amounts of cod and pollock. But when herring populations declined in the 1970s, the sea lion diet consisted mostly of cod and pollock. The energy per gram of biomass of pollock and cod is roughly half that of herring, so sea lions would have needed to eat twice as much pollock and herring to make up for the loss in herring calories. While plenty of fish were available, consumption of a greater percentage of inferior food represented a decline in production efficiency, which in turn translated into a decline in sea lion populations.

The amount of energy transferred within food webs depends on trophic efficiency

In addition to understanding how energy flows between individual consumers, we can also consider how it flows between trophic levels. **Trophic efficiency** is a measure of the amount of energy at one trophic level divided by the amount of energy at the trophic level immediately below it. Trophic efficiency varies among ecosystems as well as trophic levels. Pyramid diagrams such as those in **Figure 56.9** illustrate the proportions of energy transferred from each trophic level to the next, making it possible to compare energy flow in different ecosystems. Pyramid diagrams can also be used to illustrate the amount of biomass found at each trophic level. As seen in Figure 56.9A,B, terrestrial ecosystems progressively lose energy from one trophic level to the next through trophic inefficiencies, especially between the primary producer and primary consumer levels. Note also that terrestrial ecosystems support less biomass at higher trophic levels than at lower trophic levels. Forest ecosystems have lower trophic efficiency than grasslands because much of the biomass in forests is in the form of wood, most of which is unavailable to primary consumers.

In aquatic systems, trophic efficiencies are much higher. Here pyramid diagrams also show a progressive loss of energy at higher trophic levels, as in terrestrial systems, but the corresponding biomass pyramids are inverted (see Figure 56.9C). Why might this be? The phytoplankton that are the primary producers in aquatic ecosystems grow and reproduce much more rapidly than do the zooplankton and small fishes that consume them, so their smaller biomass, with its rapid rate of primary production, can actually support a larger biomass of primary consumers. In part, this difference between terrestrial and aquatic systems explains why land is green but oceans are blue. Terrestrial ecosystems have primary production that far exceeds rates of herbivory,

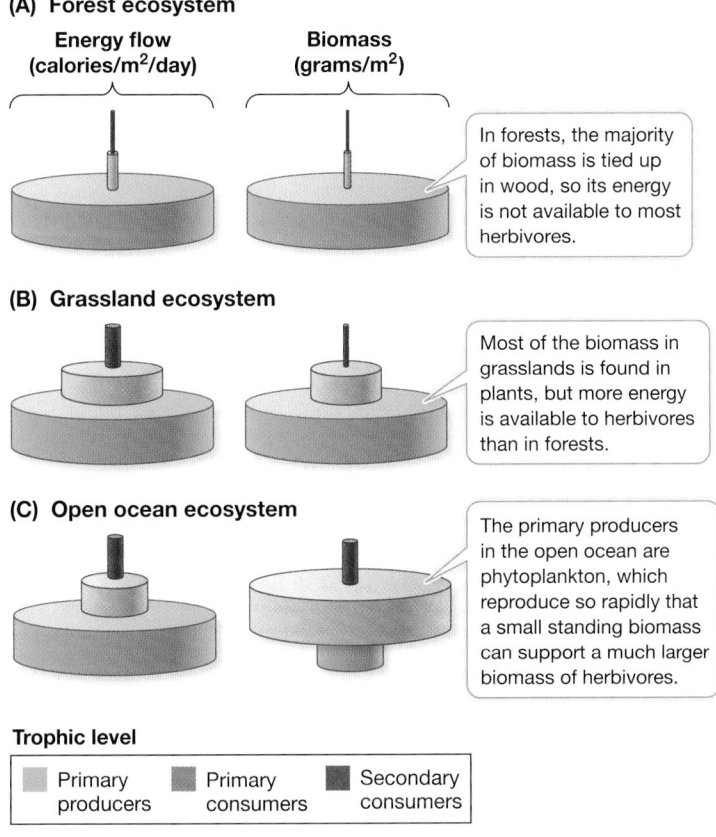

(A) Forest ecosystem

Energy flow
(calories/m²/day)

Biomass
(grams/m²)

In forests, the majority of biomass is tied up in wood, so its energy is not available to most herbivores.

(B) Grassland ecosystem

Most of the biomass in grasslands is found in plants, but more energy is available to herbivores than in forests.

(C) Open ocean ecosystem

The primary producers in the open ocean are phytoplankton, which reproduce so rapidly that a small standing biomass can support a much larger biomass of herbivores.

Trophic level

Primary producers	Primary consumers	Secondary consumers

Figure 56.9 Pyramid Diagrams Show Energy Flow and Biomass in Food Webs   Pyramid diagrams allow ecologists to compare patterns of energy flow and biomass in food webs. **(A)** Forest ecosystems have lower trophic efficiency than **(B)** grasslands because much of the biomass in forests is wood, and thus unavailable to most primary consumers. **(C)** In open oceans, the rapid rate of primary production can support a larger biomass of primary consumers.

while the opposite is true for large portions of the ocean. Overall, estimates suggest that, on average, only 13% of terrestrial biomass is consumed by primary consumers, compared with 35% in aquatic ecosystems.

Food webs are controlled by bottom-up and top-down forces

The control of energy flow in an ecosystem occurs in two ways. First, as we discussed in Key Concept 56.2, the amount of energy entering a food web can depend on the NPP of that system, which depends on such factors as rainfall, temperature, light, and nutrients. The more NPP entering the system, the more energy that is passed up the food web to consumers. This flow of energy is referred to as "bottom-up" control because it comes from the "bottom," or primary producer trophic level (**Figure 56.10A**). The other type of control on energy flow can come from consumers at higher trophic levels, who regulate the amount of NPP by feeding on lower trophic levels. This control is referred to as "top-down" control because it comes from the "top," or the secondary consumer trophic level.

All food webs are controlled by both bottom-up and top-down pathways, but the relative importance of that control can vary depending on the food web in question. For example, food webs that experience a trophic cascade driven by a keystone predator, as you saw in the examples of gray wolves (*Canis lupus*) in Yellowstone National Park (see Figure 55.9) and sea otters (*Enhydra lutris*) in kelp forests, are dominated by top-down control (see Key Concept 55.3). In those two cases, it was the top predator that controlled the prevalence of primary producers (aspen and kelp, respectively), rather than limiting resources per se.

There are also clear examples of bottom-up control in food webs. For example, in a study of pelagic ecosystems

Figure 56.10 Bottom-up and Top-down Control of Food Webs   **(A)** Production in an ecosystem can be viewed as mostly being controlled by limiting resources (bottom-up) or by consumers at higher trophic levels (top-down). **(B)** A three-level food web, in which the secondary consumer affects the primary consumer's abundance, has higher NPP (represented by the size of the green circle) than a two- or four-level food web. **(C)** A three-level food web with omnivory has lower NPP than a food web without omnivory.

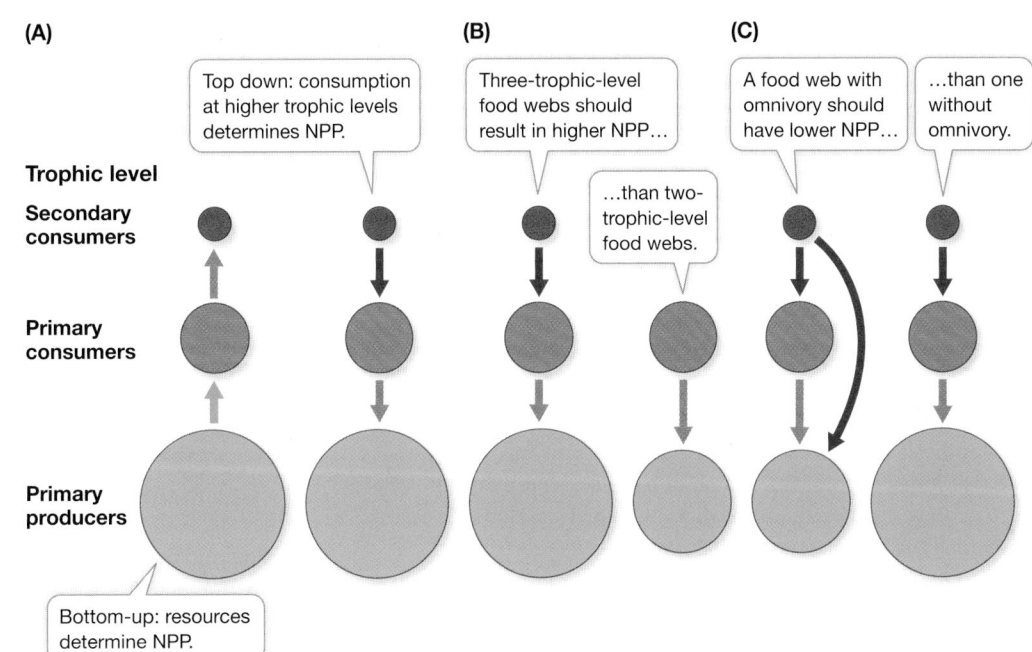

(A)

Top down: consumption at higher trophic levels determines NPP.

(B)

Three-trophic-level food webs should result in higher NPP...

...than two-trophic-level food webs.

(C)

A food web with omnivory should have lower NPP...

...than one without omnivory.

Trophic level

Secondary consumers

Primary consumers

Primary producers

Bottom-up: resources determine NPP.

off the coast of western North America, researchers found a strong positive correlation between phytoplankton abundance, zooplankton abundance, and fish production (measured from fisheries-catch data). Phytoplankton abundance in this region is largely controlled by ocean upwelling, which brings nutrients to the light-saturated surface waters for use by phytoplankton. The intensity of upwelling varies along the coast, thus creating "hotspots" of productivity that are reflected in the fish populations of the region.

The number of trophic levels can control the flow of energy through food webs

In the previous section we learned that changes in the abundance of organisms at one trophic level can influence the energy flow at multiple trophic levels. You might imagine that the number of trophic levels in a food web could be important in the magnitude of that influence. Indeed, all things being equal, a three-level food web, in which the secondary consumer affects the primary consumer's abundance, should have higher NPP than a two- or four-level food web in which primary consumers have less secondary consumer control (**Figure 56.10B**). Omnivory, or feeding on more than one trophic level, can also change the way energy is transferred in food webs by essentially "collapsing" trophic levels on one another. For example, a three-level food web with a secondary consumer feeding on both the primary consumer and primary producer should have lower NPP than a three-level food web without omnivory (**Figure 56.10C**). That's because even though the secondary consumer indirectly benefits the primary producer by feeding at the primary consumer level, it partially negates this effect by directly feeding on the primary producer as well.

While the number of trophic levels in foods webs can vary, most food webs have three or four trophic levels, with the rare exception of five or more in some systems. What factors might be important in limiting the number of trophic levels in food webs? Several factors have been hypothesized to be important:

- *The amount of NPP entering the system*: This hypothesis suggests that bottom-up factors can influence trophic structure. Given that a large amount of energy is lost from one trophic level to the next (see Figure 56.9), the number of trophic levels will be limited by the amount of energy that can sustain populations at higher trophic levels.

- *The amount of disturbance*: This hypothesis suggests that longer food webs are less likely to recover from disturbances than shorter food webs, which can presumably reassemble more quickly given the fewer trophic levels, and species, involved.

- *The evolutionary constraints on top predators*: This hypothesis focuses on the idea that no organisms on Earth today, with the exception of humans, have evolved to capture apex predators such as birds of prey, sharks, orcas (*Orcinus orca*), and polar bears (*Ursus maritimus*). With evolutionary constraints maintaining top predators at the pinnacle of food webs, the number of higher trophic levels is limited.

Once energy captured by primary producers is fixed as NPP, consumption by heterotrophs transfers a fraction of that energy to higher trophic levels (net secondary production). Terrestrial systems have lower trophic efficiencies than aquatic systems, where the rapid rate of primary production supports greater secondary production. The flow of energy in food webs is influenced by the relative contribution of bottom-up and top-down forces, the number of trophic levels, and the presence of omnivory. Food webs are typically restricted to three or four trophic levels because of energy limitations at higher trophic levels, the effects of disturbance, and/or evolutionary constraints on top predators.

1. Suppose there are two food webs, one in a forest and the other in a lake. All else being equal, which food web would have the higher trophic efficiency, and why? Comparing different species, which would have the higher production efficiency, a bear or a crayfish? Explain your answer.

2. Now compare two food webs in different lakes. One has three trophic levels, and the other has four. All else being equal, which would have the higher NPP? Why? If you added omnivory to the top level of the food web with four trophic levels, how would it differ in NPP compared with the food web without omnivory?

3. Compare a tropical rainforest food web that has five trophic levels with a desert food web having three trophic levels. What hypothesis might best explain the difference in trophic level length between the two ecosystems?

We've considered how energy flows from primary producers to consumers, and the implications of that flow for food webs. Besides energy, a key component of the metabolism and growth of organisms is nutrients (including water). Earlier in the chapter you read that nutrients continually cycle between living organisms and the abiotic environment via nutrient cycling (see Figure 56.1C). We will consider nutrient cycling next.

KEY CONCEPT
56.4 Nutrient Cycling in Ecosystems Involves Chemical and Biological Transformations

Learning Objectives

56.4.1 Define biogeochemical cycles and understand decomposition and mineralization in nutrient cycling.

56.4.2 Discuss the hydrologic cycle, including residence times of water molecules.

56.4.3 Describe Earth's carbon cycle and how burning fossil fuels is changing Earth's climate and oceans.

56.4.4 Explain the basics, and the relative roles of microbes versus geological processes, in the nitrogen, phosphorus, and sulfur cycles.

All nutrients that make up the tissues of organisms originate from either soil, water, or the atmosphere, and then cycle between organisms and their environment through (1) primary and secondary production and (2) decomposition (**Figure 56.11**). We considered production in the last two key concepts, but not decomposition. **Decomposition** occurs when detritus, or dead organisms and

Figure 56.11 Nutrient Cycles A generalized nutrient cycle, showing the movement of nutrients among biotic and abiotic compartments of an ecosystem and the potential pathways for inputs and losses.

Because geological, chemical, and biological processes are all important in moving materials around the planet, the pattern of movement of an element is called its **biogeochemical cycle**. The cycles are considered in terms of pools—the amount of elements within certain parts of the abiotic and biotic environment—and fluxes, or the rates of movement between pools. We will consider the biogeochemical cycling of water, carbon, nitrogen, phosphorus, and sulfur at the global scale because of their functional roles in biological systems and their roles as pollutants in the environment.

Water cycles rapidly around the globe

We start our discussion of global biogeochemical cycles with the water cycle—known as the **hydrologic cycle**—not only because water serves as an essential element for organisms but because it plays an important role in transporting nutrients between compartments (**Figure 56.12**). Energy from the Sun drives the hydrologic cycle by evaporating water from the vast surfaces of the oceans. Most of the water is returned to the oceans as rainfall, but a smaller fraction is transported

their waste products, are broken down by bacteria and fungi into energy and nutrients. Decomposition releases nutrients in a soluble form that can then be taken up by primary producers and microorganisms. Detritus can come in many forms, including plants and animals, but is mostly made up of plant or algal matter. Detritus must first be broken down into smaller fragments by detritivores such as worms and arthropods before it can undergo mineralization (see Figure 56.11). **Mineralization** is the process by which animals, bacteria, and fungi convert organic compounds into inorganic soluble nutrients. Along the way, some of the nutrients may be lost to the system as gas to the atmosphere or minerals to ground water. The nutrient cycle is complete when the inorganic soluble nutrients produced through mineralization are used once again by primary producers or bacteria.

The movement of nutrients through food webs from uptake to decomposition—that is, through the biotic components of ecosystems—occurs primarily on a local scale. In contrast, abiotic processes can move nutrients far beyond the boundaries of the local ecosystem. Each of the chemical elements that organisms use in large quantities cycles in a distinctive way through the globe.

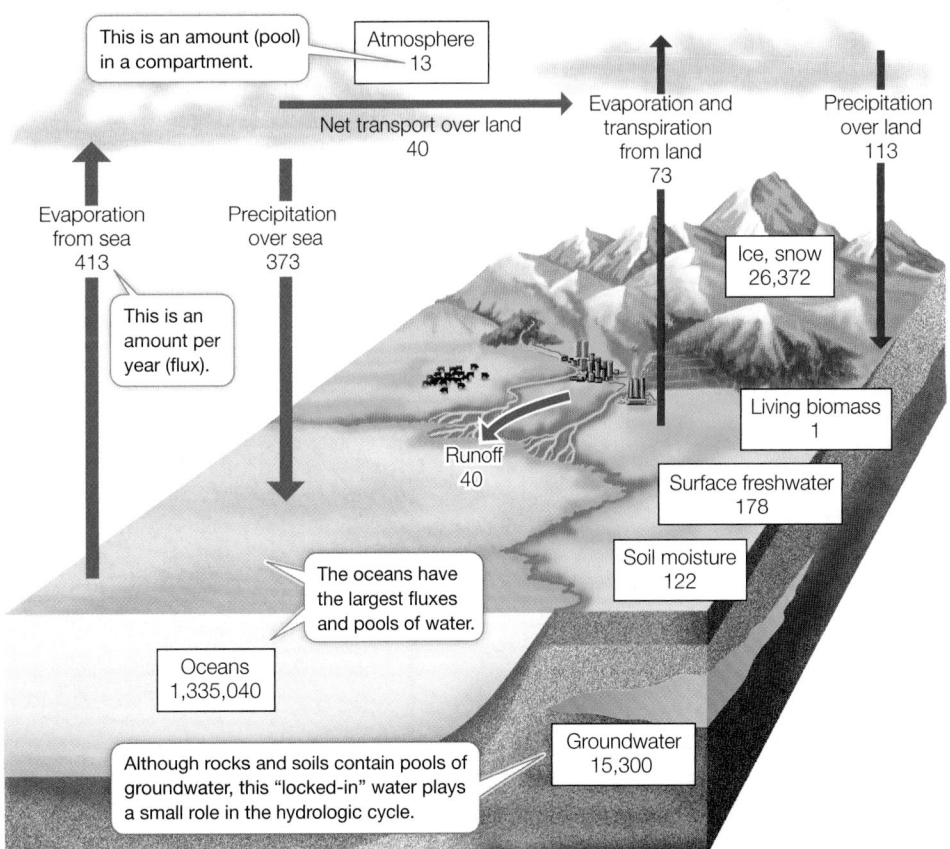

Figure 56.12 The Global Hydrologic Cycle Water is essential for life on Earth. The estimated pools in major compartments (white boxes) and the annual fluxes between compartments (arrows) are expressed in units of 10^{18} grams. (After K. E. Trenberth et al. 2007. *J Hydrometeor* 8: 758–769; F. S. Chapin et al. 2002. *Principles of Terrestrial Ecosystem Ecology*, p. 351. Springer-Verlag: New York.)

 View in Achieve
Animation 56.1 The Global Hydrologic Cycle

over land. Ocean water vapor combines with terrestrial water vapor from soils, lakes and rivers, and plants as a consequence of evapotranspiration, and falls as precipitation over land. Terrestrial precipitation eventually returns to the oceans via streams, coastal runoff, and groundwater flows. More than half of this volume of water is carried back to the oceans by Earth's four largest rivers: the Amazon in South America, the Nile in Africa, the Mississippi in North America, and the Yangtze in Asia.

Connect the Concepts In Key Concept 52.3, evapotranspiration is defined as the evaporative transfer of heat and water from the surfaces of plants into the atmosphere, which reduces air temperature and increases moisture.

Despite their relatively small volume, rivers play a disproportionate role in the hydrologic cycle because the average residence time of a water molecule in rivers is only a few years. By comparison, the average residence time of a water molecule in lakes ranges from a few years to centuries. The larger the lake, the longer the residence time; the residence time for water in the top portion of Lake Superior, for example, is 1,500–2,000 years, and the water at the bottom of this massive lake cycles over much longer time scales. In the oceans the average residence time of a water molecule is about 3,000 years. Other pools of water include glaciers (with residence times of 20–100

years), seasonal snow cover (a few months), and soil moisture (1–2 months). The average residence time of water in the bodies of organisms is particularly brief, averaging just under a week.

Although large amounts of groundwater are present in underground pools called **aquifers**, this water has a long residence time underground and plays only a small role in the hydrologic cycle. In some places, however, aquifers are being depleted because humans are using groundwater more rapidly than it can be replaced, primarily for irrigation. On the North China Plain, depletion of shallow aquifers is forcing people to sink wells more than 1,000 meters deep to reach groundwater. If current water consumption patterns continue, it has been estimated that by 2025 at least 48% of the current world population will live in areas with inadequate water supplies.

The carbon cycle is being altered by human activities, resulting in climate change

All of the important macromolecules that make up living organisms contain carbon, and much of the energy that organisms use to fuel their metabolic activities is stored in carbon-containing (organic) compounds. On land, biological processes move carbon directly between organisms and the atmosphere as terrestrial organisms take up carbon during photosynthesis and return it to the atmosphere through respiration and metabolism (**Figure 56.13**). In contrast,

Figure 56.13 The Global Carbon Cycle Carbon is the basis of the organic molecules and energy essential for life. The estimated pools in major compartments (white boxes) and the annual fluxes between compartments (arrows) are expressed in units of 10^{15} grams. (After P. Ciais et al. 2013. In *Climate Change 2013: The Physical Science Basis. Contribution of Working Group I to the Fifth Assessment Report of the Intergovernmental Panel on Climate Change*, T. F. Stocker et al. [Eds.], pp. 466–570, Cambridge University Press, Cambridge, UK and New York, NY, USA; W. H. Schlesinger and E. S. Bernhardt. 2013. In *Biogeochemistry: An Analysis of Global Change 3rd ed.* W. H. Schlesinger and E. S. Bernhardt [Eds.], pp. 445–467. Academic Press: Cambridge, MA; F. S. Chapin et al. 2002. *Principles of Terrestrial Ecosystem Ecology*, p. 336. Springer-Verlag: New York.)

The atmosphere is the immediate source of inorganic carbon for terrestrial organisms.

Atmosphere (CO_2, CH_4) 830

Biomass burning 11.6

Fossil fuel burning, cement manufacture 7.8

Altered land use 1.1

Photosynthesis 123

Respiration 119

Outgassing 78   Dissolution 80

Plant biomass 550

60

Soils 2,000

0.9   Runoff

Marine biomass 3

Dissolved CO_2 in the photic zone is available for aquatic primary producers.

50

37

Detritus 11

Ocean waters 38,000

Sand, detritus 1,200

Carbonate precipitation 0.2

Carbonate compounds in rocks 18×10^6 Fossil fuels 25×10^6

Sediments 1,750

The two largest reservoirs of carbon are carbon-containing minerals in rocks and fossil fuels.

▶ **View in Achieve**
Animation 56.2
The Global Carbon Cycle

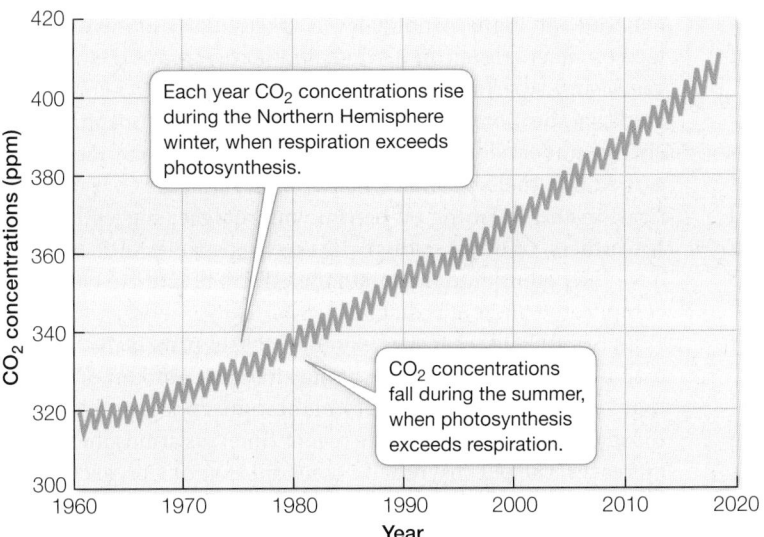

Figure 56.14 Atmospheric CO₂ Concentrations Are Increasing Carbon dioxide concentrations have been recorded since 1960 on top of Mauna Loa, Hawaii, far from most sources of human-generated CO₂ emissions. Although concentrations vary seasonally, the trend has been consistently upward. (After C. D. Keeling et al. 2001. I. Global aspects, SIO Reference Series, No. 01–06. Scripps Institution of Oceanography. San Diego. Last updated June 2019.)

 Media Clip 56.1 Time-Lapse of Global CO₂ Emissions
Life12e.com/mc56.1

carbon dioxide moves into ocean waters from the atmosphere primarily by simple diffusion at the ocean surface; this dissolved CO_2 is the source of the carbon used by marine primary producers. Even taken together, however, the amounts of carbon in the atmosphere, in soils, and in living and dead organisms are dwarfed by the vast quantities of carbon stored in terrestrial rocks, in fossil fuels, in marine sediments, and in seawater in the form of carbonate ions (CO_3^{-2}) or bicarbonate ions (HCO_3^{-}) (see Figure 56.13).

Over the span of life's existence on Earth, quantities of carbon were removed from active cycling when organisms died in large numbers and were buried in sediments lacking oxygen. In such

anaerobic environments, with few detritivores to reduce organic carbon to CO_2, organic molecules accumulate and are eventually transformed into deposits of oil, natural gas, coal, or peat—the **fossil fuels** that modern humans use as a combustible source of energy. Humans have discovered and used these fossil fuels at ever-increasing rates during the past 150 years. As a result, CO_2, one of the final products of burning fossil fuels, is being released into the atmosphere faster than it is absorbed in the oceans or incorporated into terrestrial biomass. Measurements of CO_2 on the top of Mauna Loa, Hawaii, show that, even though atmospheric CO_2 varies seasonally because of the change in NPP, it has steadily increased over the last 60 years of data collection (**Figure 56.14**).

ATMOSPHERIC CO₂ AND GLOBAL CLIMATE CHANGE

Carbon dioxide is a greenhouse gas, so we would expect increasing atmospheric CO_2 concentrations to trap more heat in Earth's atmosphere and raise temperatures at Earth's surface (see Figure 52.2). What evidence do we have that this is occurring? Measurements of gases in air trapped in the Antarctic and Greenland ice caps show that temperatures have been warmer when atmospheric CO_2 concentrations have been higher and cooler when they have been lower (**Figure 56.15**). For example, the atmospheric CO_2 concentration was very low at the end of the last glaciation (180 parts per million [ppm]), 18,000 years ago, when temperatures were much colder than they are today. In contrast, during a warm interval between 11,000 years ago and the start of the Industrial Revolution (1750), the concentration of CO_2 in Earth's atmosphere was between 260 ppm and 280 ppm. In 2019, atmospheric CO_2 concentration is just over 414 ppm (see Figure 56.14), the highest recorded in the last 800,000 years. The increase in CO_2 (and two other greenhouse gases, CH_4 and N_2O) from the burning of fossil fuels has resulted in a roughly 1-degree Celsius (1.8-degree Fahrenheit) rise in global temperatures compared with those from 1981 to 2010 (a comparison known as a "temperature anomaly").

Figure 56.15 Higher Atmospheric CO₂ Concentrations Correlate with Warmer Temperatures Atmospheric concentrations of CO_2 (measured in air bubbles trapped in Antarctic ice) have varied with temperatures over Antarctica (estimated with oxygen isotope analysis) for more than 800,000 years. "Temperature anomaly" is the change in Antarctic temperatures compared with modern temperatures. (After D. Lüthi et al. 2008. *Nature* 453: 379–382.)

How global climates and ecosystems will change in response to this rapid warming is a subject of intense investigation. Global warming has already resulted in the shrinking of Arctic sea ice, which is currently the lowest ever recorded. As temperatures continue to rise and glacial ice melts, sea level rises (because of both thermal expansion of ocean waters and the addition of glacial meltwater), increasing flooding of coastal cities and agricultural lands, especially during extreme storm events. Nearly one-third of the world's population lives in coastal regions, which make up only 4% of Earth's total land area.

Even though atmospheric CO_2 is increasing as the result of burning fossil fuels, less than half of the CO_2 released into the atmosphere by human activities remains in the atmosphere. Where does the rest of the CO_2 wind up? Much of it is absorbed by the oceans in inorganic forms. Over decades to centuries, the oceans exert a large influence over atmospheric CO_2 concentrations. Of the CO_2 absorbed by the ocean, some is used in photosynthesis by phytoplankton in the surface waters. These organisms remove dissolved CO_2 from water, thereby increasing the rate at which atmospheric CO_2 is absorbed by surface waters, but as you saw earlier, there are limits to this absorption given nutrient limitation in vast parts of the open ocean. In addition, many marine organisms (including clams, oysters, corals, and planktonic foraminiferans) incorporate carbon in their shells and other structures in the form of calcium carbonate ($CaCO_3$), which is synthesized by combining bicarbonate ions (HCO_3^-) and calcium ions (Ca^{2+}) dissolved in seawater. When these organisms die, those shells and their embedded carbon sink to the ocean floor.

Today's oceans absorb millions of tons of CO_2 from the atmosphere each day—more than at any time during the past 20 million years. As a result, water near the ocean surface is becoming more acidic. As CO_2 concentrations in the atmosphere rise, more of the gas diffuses into the water at the ocean surface, where it reacts with water to form carbonic acid (H_2CO_3). As levels of carbonic acid rise, the pH of seawater drops. This increase in acidity can have negative effects on many marine organisms, particularly corals. The combination of decreasing pH and increasing water temperature to which corals are being exposed results in coral bleaching and sometimes the death of corals. Because so many other reef species depend on corals and the structure they provide, an entire reef community can collapse if its corals fail to thrive.

Connect the Concepts As described in Investigating Life: Corals in Hot Water in Chapter 1, coral bleaching occurs when corals are exposed to warm and/or acidic waters, causing expulsion of their photosynthetic algal symbionts.

But as you read in the opening story, the effects of CO_2 and ocean acidification vary depending on the organisms or ecosystems considered. **Investigating Life: Food Webs in an Acidic and Warming Ocean** describes research in Sweden by marine ecologists interested in the effects of ocean acidification and warming on an ecologically critical but predominately primary-producer-dominated ecosystem: estuaries. In this system, the researchers focused on benthic microalgae, an important food source for a diversity of sediment-dwelling herbivores, including crustaceans, snails, and worms. Benthic microalgae indirectly

benefit from higher trophic levels, particularly omnivores that feed on macroalgae competitors and herbivores of the microalgae. Using experimental manipulations, the researchers discovered that the biomass of benthic microalgae did not appreciably change under elevated CO_2 and warming manipulations. As it turned out, the consumers mediated the effects of ocean acidification and warming on benthic microalgae, suggesting that consumers, or other strongly interacting species in food webs, have the potential to modulate the effects of climate change in complicated and unpredictable ways.

In terrestrial ecosystems, photosynthesis, principally in tropical forests, typically absorbs about the same amount of carbon that is released by terrestrial plants, microbes, and animals through metabolism. In more recent times, as atmospheric CO_2 increases, the photosynthetic consumption of CO_2 exceeds its metabolic production, which means Earth's terrestrial vegetation is storing carbon that would otherwise be increasing atmospheric CO_2 concentrations—but as we saw in the FACE experiment, we cannot count on terrestrial vegetation to store the vast amounts of excess CO_2 that human activities produce. Furthermore, climate warming (another result of increasing atmospheric CO_2 concentrations, as you have already seen) increases plant metabolism and is thus likely to increase the flux of CO_2 from vegetation into the atmosphere.

The nitrogen cycle is dominated by biotic processes

Nitrogen gas is the most abundant gas in Earth's atmosphere, but most organisms cannot use nitrogen in its gaseous form. Nitrogen enters the system as atmospheric N_2 and is fixed by bacteria into ammonia (NH_3) (**Figure 56.16**). Ammonia is rapidly transformed into ammonium (NH_4^+), which can then be used by plants and bacteria. Nitrifying bacteria can transform ammonium to nitrite (NO_2^-) and then nitrate (NO_3^-), both forms of nitrogen that plants and bacteria can use. Denitrifying bacteria take nitrate and convert it back to N_2 and N_2O gases, which are then released back into the atmosphere. Along the way, plants and bacteria incorporate the nitrogen into their tissues, making it available to higher trophic levels as secondary production and eventually to decomposers. Collectively this microbial processing of nitrogen accounts for about 95% of all natural nitrogen flux on Earth, making it a mostly biologically driven cycle (**Figure 56.17**).

All living organisms require nitrogen, and the inability of the vast majority of organisms to use N_2 means that usable nitrogen is often in short supply. Populations of nitrogen-fixing organisms rarely increase in abundance to the extent that nitrogen is no longer limiting, because the end products of their nitrogen fixation are rapidly lost from ecosystems (ammonia by vaporization and denitrification; and nitrate, which is highly water-soluble, by leaching).

Human activities that fix nitrogen, such as the manufacture of artificial fertilizers, have had large and unanticipated effects on the nitrogen cycle. The extensive use of artificial fertilizers on agricultural crops, coupled with the burning of fossil fuels (which generates nitric oxide and nitrogen dioxide), has resulted in total nitrogen fixation by humans being nearly equal to global natural nitrogen fixation (see Figure 56.17). This human-generated

Experiment

Original Paper: C. Alsterberg et al. 2013. Consumers mediate the effects of experimental ocean acidification and warming on primary producers. *Proc Natl Acad Sci USA* 110: 8603–8608.

Christian Alsterberg and his colleagues considered how the food web in an estuarine ecosystem on the western coast of Sweden was influenced by ocean acidification and warming. The researchers chose to focus on benthic microalgae (single-celled algae) and their interactions with macroalgae and consumers. In this system, omnivores (i.e., a guild of medium-sized crustaceans and snails that feed on two trophic levels) affect the productivity of benthic microalgae in two ways: (1) they increase the light available to microalgae by feeding on macroalgae, and (2) they prey on herbivores of microalgae (i.e., a guild of small crustaceans, snails, and worms). To estimate the importance of ocean acidification and increased warming in a multispecies food web, the researchers conducted an experiment on the estuarine community in which CO_2, temperature, and omnivores were manipulated.

HYPOTHESIS▶   Increasing CO_2 and temperature will increase the biomass of macroalgae competitors, causing a decline in the biomass of benthic microalgae.

METHOD▶

1. Fill 30-liter buckets with seawater and add microalgae, macroalgae, and herbivores.

2. Apply three treatments:
   a. two levels of seawater temperature (ambient and increased)
   b. two levels of CO_2 (ambient and increased)
   c. two levels of omnivores (present and absent)

3. At the end of a 5-week period over the summer, measure the biomass of benthic microalgae (as Chl *a* concentrations), macroalgae, and herbivores.

RESULTS▶   To simplify, the results (means ± SEs) from the following treatments are presented: ambient CO_2 and temperature and increased CO_2 and temperature, each with and without omnivores

The researchers found that benthic microalgae biomass did not change under increased CO_2 and temperature. This was true regardless of whether omnivores were present. However, the removal of

omnivores did cause a decline in benthic microalgae under ambient conditions, as would be predicted from the food web shown here.

Omnivore removal caused an increase in the biomass of macroalgae competitors and herbivores, which then led to a decline in benthic microalgae. Interestingly, even though there was no effect of increased CO_2 and temperature on microalgae biomass, the results showed that both macroalgae and herbivores increased in biomass under these conditions compared with under ambient conditions. This was especially the case when omnivores were removed.

CONCLUSION▶   What can you conclude about the effects of increased CO_2 and temperature on benthic microalgae in this estuarine food web? Explore this question in the following Work with the Data.

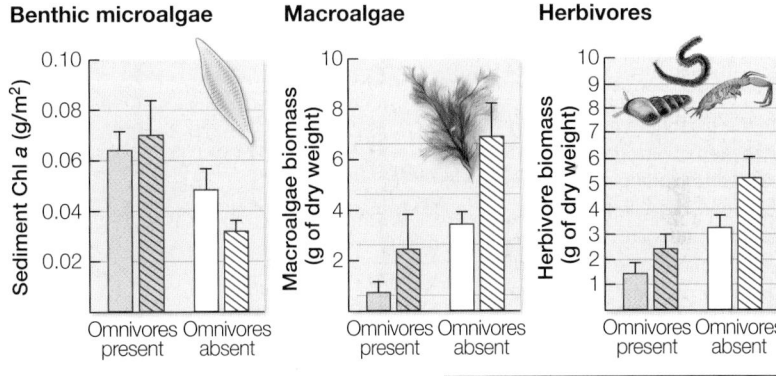

Work with the Data

To interpret the Alsterberg et al. study, we consider why benthic microalgae biomass did not change under increased CO_2 and temperature within the context of the experimental manipulation of the food web.

QUESTIONS▶

1. Draw two food webs for this system, one with and one without the omnivores. Use arrows to indicate the direct (solid) and indirect (dashed) interactions and symbols to indicate negative (–) or positive (+) interactions.

2. Now, using data from the graphs in the experiment, modify the two food webs to show how increased CO_2 and temperature will affect the strength and direction of the food web interactions.

Vary the width of the arrows to indicate the relative strength of the interactions, and use symbols to indicate whether the interactions are negative (–) or positive (+). Indicate in writing whether benthic microalgae increase, decrease, or stay the same compared with under ambient conditions.

3. Using the food webs you drew for Question 2, explain why increased CO_2 and temperature had no effect on microalgae biomass compared with the ambient conditions.

4. Under increased CO_2 and temperature, what would happen to benthic microalgae biomass if the omnivores ceased feeding on macroalgae and just preyed on herbivores?

Go to **Achieve** for a companion Data in Depth exercise.

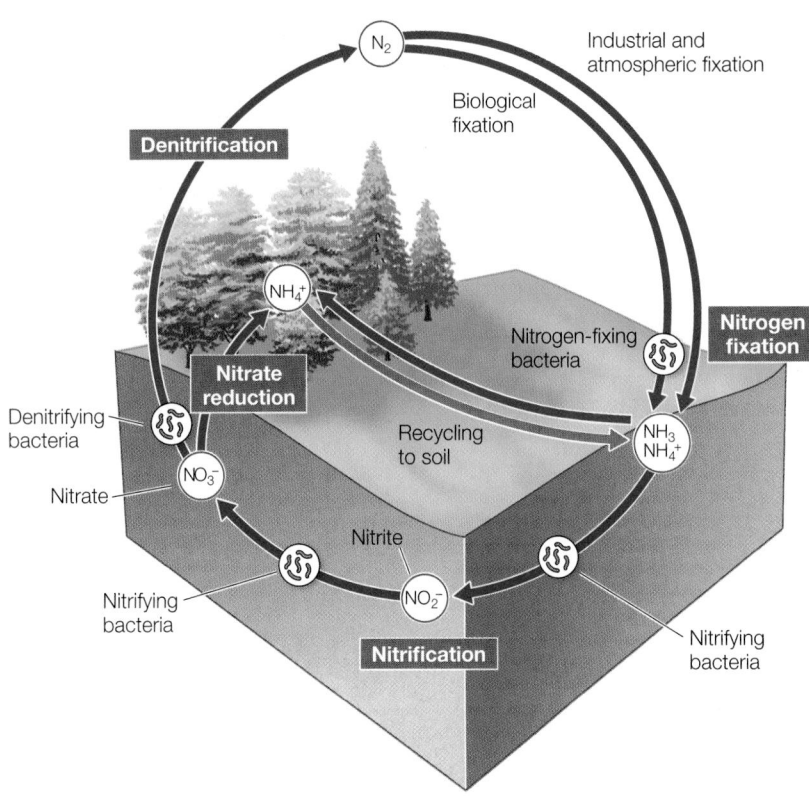

Figure 56.16 The Nitrogen Cycle Nitrogen fixation, nitrification, nitrate reduction, and denitrification are components of an essential chemical cycle that coverts atmospheric nitrogen gas into ammonium ions and nitrate ions—forms of nitrogen that can be taken up by plants—and returns N_2 to the atmosphere.

nitrogen flux has been increasing over the past half-century and is expected to continue to increase.

One consequence of artificial fertilizer production is an increase in the greenhouse gas nitrous oxide (N_2O), resulting in more tropospheric ozone (O_3) and smog. Trophospheric ozone is itself a greenhouse gas and thus can contribute to global climate change.

Some of the nitrous oxide that enters the atmosphere falls back to land in precipitation or as dry particles. This deposition of nitrogen from the atmosphere has increased dramatically during recent decades. Nitrogen deposition could affect the composition of terrestrial vegetation by favoring those plant species that are best adapted to take advantage of high nutrient levels, and which may then outcompete other species.

Figure 56.17 The Global Nitrogen Cycle The largest pool of nitrogen is in the atmosphere in the form of nitrogen gas, N_2. Nitrogen cycles through the biosphere primarily via the processes of nitrogen fixation, which converts inorganic nitrogen to an organic form usable by plants, and denitrification, which returns N_2 to the atmosphere. The estimated pools in major compartments (white boxes) and the annual fluxes between compartments (arrows) are expressed in units of 10^{12} grams. (Data from J. N. Galloway et al. 2004. *Biogeochemistry* 70: 153–226; C. C. Cleveland et al. 1999. *Global Biogeochem Cycles* 13: 623–645; Illustration after F. S. Chapin et al. 2002. *Principles of Terrestrial Ecosystem Ecology*, p. 344. Springer-Verlag: New York.)

Q: How does the industrial fixation of nitrogen (as a percentage) compare with the other forms of fixation on land?

View in Achieve
Animation 56.3
The Global Nitrogen Cycle

Another consequence of nitrogen fertilizers is eutrophication, a process we considered in Key Concept 56.2 for phosphorus additions in lake ecosystems. In this case, when more nitrogen fertilizer is applied to agricultural lands than can be taken up by the crops, the excess nitrogen moves out of the system in surface runoff, or downward into groundwater, and ultimately ends up in rivers, lakes, and oceans. So-called dead zones have formed near the mouth of the Mississippi River in the Gulf of Mexico as a result of the drainage from interior agricultural fields carrying high concentrations of nitrogen fertilizer.

 Media Clip 56.2 Tracking Dead Zones from Space
Life12e.com/mc56.2

The global phosphorus cycle is dominated by geochemical processes

Phosphorus accounts for only about 0.1% of Earth's crust, but it is an essential nutrient for all life forms. It is a key component of cell membranes, DNA, RNA, and ATP. Unlike the other biogeochemical cycles discussed thus far, the phosphorus cycle does not have a significant atmospheric component, although some phosphorus is transported by dust particles. Most of Earth's phosphorus is in the form of phosphate in rocks and deep-sea sediments, and it cycles very slowly through the geological system because it requires sedimentary rock formation, uplift, and weathering. In contrast, phosphorus in organisms cycles rapidly, and it is often a limiting factor for their growth, particularly for plants. As you learned in Key Concept 56.2, runoff of phosphorus from fertilizers and detergents into aquatic systems can result in eutrophication.

The burning of fossil fuels affects the sulfur cycle

Sulfur is required by all organisms because it is critical in the production of proteins and lignin. Most of Earth's sulfur supply is locked up in rocks on land and as sulfate salts in deep-sea sediments, but sulfur moves to the atmosphere in a variety of ways. Roughly 10%–20% of atmospheric sulfur is produced in volcanic eruptions. In terrestrial systems, when sulfur in the soil comes in contact with atmospheric oxygen, it is converted to sulfate salts, which can be taken up by plants and eventually incorporated into their tissue. This sulfur ultimately is returned to the atmosphere as H_2S via microbial decomposition. In marine systems, many phytoplankton and seaweeds manufacture large quantities of a sulfur-containing compound (dimethylsulfoniopropionate, or DMSP) to maintain their salt and water balance. When broken down, DMSP releases dimethyl sulfide (CH_3SCH_3), the principal odorant of rotting seaweed. Because the quantities of phytoplankton in the oceans are enormous, dimethyl sulfide production accounts for about half of the biotic component of the global sulfur cycle.

Atmospheric sulfur exists in gaseous and particulate forms and plays an important role in global climate. Cloud formation is dependent on small particles around which water can condense. Dimethyl sulfide is a major component of such particles, so increases in atmospheric sulfur concentrations increase cloud cover and reduce the amount of incoming solar radiation, affecting Earth's temperature. In addition, SO_2 and NO_2 produced by humans from the burning of coal and oil react with water molecules in the atmosphere to form sulfuric acid (H_2SO_4) and nitric acid (HNO_3),

respectively. These acids can travel hundreds of kilometers in the atmosphere before they are released as **acid rain**. Acid rain can damage forests and lakes, affecting the food webs they support. Restriction on the emissions of sulfur in North America and Europe has resulted in significant reductions in acid rain. Research shows that once acidity is reduced, forest and aquatic systems can quickly recover. Acid rain remains a problem in some countries such as China and India, where rapid industrialization and the lack of restrictions create high sulfur emissions.

 View in Achieve
Activity 56.2 The Phosphorus and Sulfur Cycles

KEY CONCEPT
56.4 Recap and Assess

Nutrient cycling in ecosystems and global biogeochemical cycles involves chemical and biological transformations through production, decomposition, and mineralization. The hydrologic cycle is not only crucial in making water available to organisms but also in transporting nutrients within ecosystems. Carbon moves through biological systems and returns to the atmosphere through respiration. Burning of fossil fuels increases the carbon dioxide and sulfur in the atmosphere, which is implicated in global warming and acidic conditions in lakes and oceans. The nitrogen cycle is dominated by biotic transformations controlled by bacteria, whereas phosphorus and sulfur cycles are dominated by geochemical processes.

1. The residence time of a water molecule is short in organisms, soil, and rivers and is much longer in lakes, glaciers, and oceans. Why?

2. Why is the concentration of CO_2 rising in the atmosphere and oceans? How does this rise in CO_2 affect climate and ocean chemistry?

3. Explain how the nitrogen cycle is dominated by biological processes whereas the phosphorus and sulfur cycles are dominated by geochemical processes.

As you have seen, biogeochemical cycles are intimately involved in how ecosystems function. Just as human alterations of those cycles are affecting ecosystems worldwide, the resulting changes could have important effects on humans as well.

KEY CONCEPT
56.5
Ecosystems Provide Important Services and Values to Humans

Learning Objectives

56.5.1 Describe the four categories of ecosystem services and how degradation of these services can lead to trade-offs.

56.5.2 Define sustainability and its relationship to ecosystem services and values.

Although it seems obvious today that humans depend on ecosystems for survival, explicit recognition of the services they provide and their value is rather recent. Environmental writers introduced the idea of "natural capital" in the 1940s; it was in 1970 that ecosystems were first said to provide people with a variety of "goods and services." Here we consider more recent efforts to understand the importance of ecosystems to humans.

Ecosystems services are the benefits people obtain from ecosystems. Ecologists recognize four different categories of services depending on their role in the ecosystem:

1. *Provisioning services* provide products such as food, clean water, timber, and fiber.

2. *Regulating services* regulate events such as hurricanes, floods, disease outbreaks, and water and air quality.

3. *Supporting services* function in such processes as soil formation, carbon sequestration via net primary production, and nutrient cycling.

4. *Cultural services* provide nonmaterial benefits such as recreational activities and aesthetic and spiritual enrichment.

Most of these benefits are either irreplaceable, or the technology necessary to replace them is prohibitively expensive. For example, fresh drinking water can be provided by desalinating seawater, but only at great cost. The aesthetic, spiritual, and recreational benefits of ecosystems are less tangible, but no less important, and no more easily replaced.

Although humans have been altering ecosystems for millennia, the pace and scope of human alterations to ecosystem services have increased considerably in the past century. For example, the 2005 Millennium Ecosystem Assessment estimated that approximately 60% of the ecosystem services identified in its study are being degraded or used unsustainably, including fresh water, wild-caught fisheries, air and water purification, and the regulation of regional and local climate, natural hazards, and pests.

Human alteration of ecosystems has had many positive effects on human health and prosperity, but it necessarily involves trade-offs. Agriculture, for example, feeds and employs huge numbers of people. But the spread of agriculture into marginal lands may degrade soils and compromise the ability of ecosystems to provide clean water, as when overuse of artificial fertilizers results in eutrophication. Extensive use of pesticides controls insect pests, but also reduces populations of pollinators and the services they provide to both crops and native plants.

Similarly, the loss of wetlands and other natural buffers has reduced the ability of ecosystems to regulate flooding and other natural hazards. The damage from the tsunami that hit Indonesia and other Southeast Asian countries in December 2004 was greater in many places than it would have been had the mangrove forests that protect the coast not been cut down and converted to shrimp aquaculture farms. Hurricane Katrina, which struck the U.S. Gulf Coast less than a year later, would not have caused as much flooding in New Orleans had the wetlands surrounding the city been intact. Katrina's devastating effects were due in part to a situation that had been developing for decades.

New Orleans is located on the Mississippi River delta. Much of the city lies below sea level, buffered by dams and levees constructed by the Army Corps of Engineers. The upstream dams that protect New Orleans from flooding also prevent the river from depositing the sediments that have sustained the surrounding delta wetlands for centuries. Oil and natural gas producers have cut thousands of small canals through those wetlands in order to lay pipelines and install drilling rigs, and the extraction of oil and gas from beneath the land has caused it to sink. Increased dredging of shipping lanes and rising sea levels have contributed to a rise in salinity, killing off many of the great cypress tree swamps. These extensive alterations resulted in the loss of more than 80% (1.2 million acres) of the delta wetlands between 1930 and 2005. By the time Katrina made landfall, those wetlands could no longer protect New Orleans from flooding. Storm surges raced along the paths carved by canals and shipping lanes to breach the levees, inundating much of the city.

The value of ecosystem services can be measured

Practices that allow us to conserve or enhance ecosystems so as to benefit from specific ecosystem goods and services without compromising others are referred to as **sustainable**. To develop more sustainable practices, there has been growing interest in determining the economic value of ecosystem services. **Ecosystem values** are measures of how important ecosystem services are to people—that is, what they are worth. Placing a value on ecosystem services involves estimating the amount we are willing to pay to preserve or enhance ecosystem services. Ecosystem service valuation involves determining (1) the human drivers of ecosystem change, (2) the ecosystem processes or functions that are affected by those changes, (3) how those processes or functions influence all the goods and services of an ecosystem, and then (4) using a variety of economic and social evaluation tools to value those goods and services (**Figure 56.18**). Valuing ecosystem services can be difficult, because while it is relatively easy to place a value on certain goods such as fish or timber, it is harder to value nonmarket services such as the existence of an endangered species or the ability to walk in an old-growth forest. Much of ecosystem service valuation involves determining through public surveys and census data the willingness of people to pay for such nonmarket services.

For those ecosystems in which services have been valued, in many cases the total economic value of a sustainably managed ecosystem is higher than that of a converted or intensively exploited ecosystem (**Figure 56.19**). For example, the value of coastal ecosystems such as mangroves can be driven largely by the coastal protection that mangroves provide from extreme storm or tsunami events, even though the short-term monetary gains from converting mangroves to shrimp farms can be substantial.

An important aspect of valuing ecosystem services is changing the impression that ecosystem services are "public goods" with no market value. People who do not stand to profit from the services provided by ecosystems have no incentive to pay for them, whereas individuals who convert ecosystems reap great economic benefits. Government action may be needed to create incentives that encourage sustainable ecosystem management. Raising public awareness is essential to the implementation of sustainable management programs. Most people do not realize the long-term value of ecosystem goods and services or understand how human activities affect the functioning of ecosystems. Maintaining and enhancing ecosystem goods and services that have no established market value is especially difficult. Perhaps one of the most difficult ecosystem services to maintain and value is that of biodiversity. The final chapter of this book is devoted to this important topic.

Figure 56.18 Key Steps to Ecosystem Service Valuation Placing a value on ecosystem services, such as this mangrove ecosystem used for shrimp farming, involves determining (1) the human drivers of ecosystem change, (2) the ecosystem processes or functions affected by those changes, (3) how those processes or functions affect the delivery of goods and services of an ecosystem, and (4) the willingness of people to pay for those goods and services.

Ecosystem processes, functions, and controlling components

Human drivers of ecosystem change

Ecosystem goods and services

Values

© Jan Wlodarczyk/Alamy Stock Photo

© National Geographic Creative/Alamy Stock Photo

© Kevin Schafer/Alamy Stock Photo

© Ania Blazejewska/Getty Images

KEY CONCEPT

56.5 Recap and Assess

Ecosystems provide benefits to humans in the form of goods and services. Ecologists recognize different categories of services depending on their role in the ecosystem. Ecosystem service valuation, important to establish sustainable practices, involves determining the market value or the willingness of people to pay for the services.

1. Suppose you want to maximize the coastal protection service of mangroves with shrimp aquaculture farming (which requires removing the mangrove trees to create ponds). What sustainable solution might you devise to maximize the value of this ecosystem?

View in Achieve
Activity 56.3 **Concept Matching: Ecosystems**

Figure 56.19 The Economic Value of Sustainability Managed Ecosystems Many types of ecosystems are able to provide more goods and services, and thus have a higher value, when they are sustainably managed than when they are completely converted to human use. (From Millennium Ecosystem Assessment, 2005. *Ecosystems and Human Well-being: Synthesis.* Island Press: Washington, DC. © 2005 World Resources Institute.)

▶Investigating**LIFE**

Q and A   How will food webs respond to the multiple effects of ocean acidification and warming in marine ecosystems?

Much of the ocean acidification research to date has focused on the responses of single species to increasing CO_2 and warming. While we know that ocean acidification and warming can have negative effects on calcifying organisms, potentially affecting already compromised coral-reef ecosystems, we know much less about the potentially counteracting effects of elevated CO_2 on primary producers and their consumers. Is it possible that organisms, placed within the context of their food webs, gain some resilience from the effects of climate change? The study of a Swedish estuary showed that the response of this ecosystem to ocean acidification and warming is modulated by complex food web interactions. The implications of this study may be wide-ranging if changes in food webs decrease the ability of ecosystems to respond to climate change. Will the loss of top consumers make ecosystems less resilient to climate change? This is a question that needs to be considered as both food webs and global climate change.

Future directions

While the Swedish estuary experiment shows that a consumer can affect an ecosystem's response to climate change, climate change can also affect a consumer's role in an ecosystem. A good example is the recent dramatic shift in polar bear and orca observations in the Canadian Arctic. Sea ice in the Arctic is melting at unprecedented rates as the result of global warming. Polar bears need this sea ice to stalk their prey, mainly seals, and have been driven to inland hunting grounds with the loss of ice. Orcas, by contrast, are unable to hunt their preferred prey—other species of whales—in ice-covered waters. As ice continues to melt, orcas have been spotted in areas of the Arctic where they have never been seen before. Some people have suggested that this shift from seal predation to whale predation could have important ecosystem-level effects as the food webs shift in response to the decline of sea ice.

VISUAL SUMMARY 56

© Cameron Davidson/Getty Images

You should be able to relate each summary to the adjacent figures. If you go to this visual summary in **Achieve**, you can follow links to figures, animations, activities, and simulations that will help you consolidate the material.

KEY CONCEPT
56.1   Ecosystem Science Considers How Energy and Nutrients Flow through Biotic and Abiotic Environments

Go to Activity 56.1

- An **ecosystem** includes all the organisms in a given area and their physical and chemical environment.

- Energy flowing through ecosystems originates with sunlight and inorganic and organic compounds. It involves the processes of photosynthesis, **chemosynthesis**, and **secondary production**.

- Energy is lost from ecosystems as metabolic heat.

- Nutrients originate in soil, water, and the atmosphere and cycle through ecosystems via the processes of production and decomposition.

Questions

1. How are ecosystems the same and different from communities?

2. What are the sources of energy that flow through ecosystems?

3. How do nutrients cycle through ecosystems?

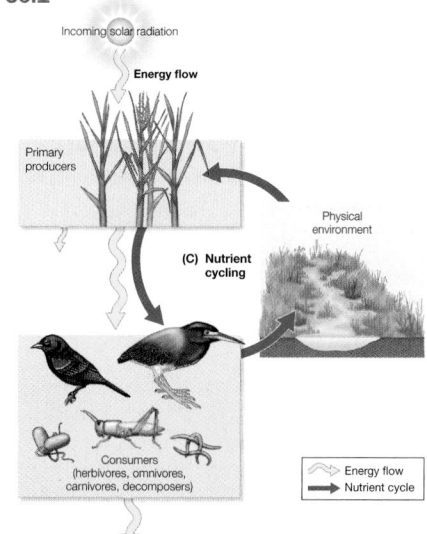

Figure 56.1

KEY CONCEPT

56.2 Energy and Nutrients in Ecosystems Are First Captured by Primary Producers

- **Net primary production** (**NPP**) is the amount of carbon remaining in plants after respiration, and varies with latitude and ecosystem type.

- Terrestrial NPP is highest in the tropics where temperatures are high year-round and rainfall is abundant.

- Oceanic NPP varies little with latitude but peaks at mid-latitudes and in coastal zones and areas of upwelling where the main primary producers—phytoplankton and algae—have access to light and nutrients.

- In aquatic systems, nutrient runoff from agriculture and wastewater can cause **eutrophication**, resulting in algal blooms and low oxygen conditions (hypoxia) for aquatic life.

Figure 56.2

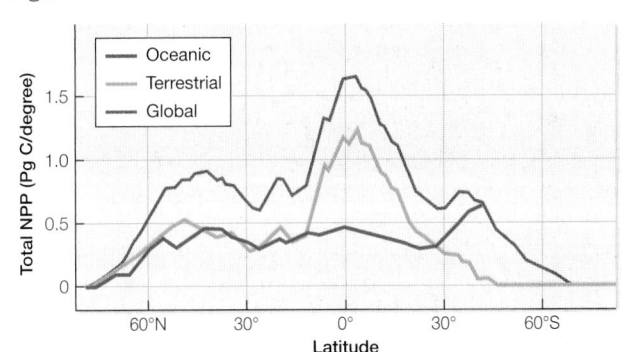

Questions

1. How does net primary production differ from gross primary production?

2. What are the latitudinal patterns and processes important to net primary production in terrestrial versus oceanic ecosystems?

3. What are the causes and consequences of eutrophication in aquatic systems?

KEY CONCEPT

56.3 Food Webs Transfer Energy and Nutrients from Primary Producers to Consumers

- Once energy captured by primary producers is fixed as NPP, consumption by heterotrophs transfers a fraction of that energy to higher trophic levels, creating **net secondary production**.

- Organisms differ in their **production efficiency**—the percentage of energy stored in assimilated food that is used to produce new biomass.

- The amount of energy transferred within food webs depends on **trophic efficiency**—the amount of energy used at one trophic level divided by the amount used at the trophic level below it.

- The flow of energy in food webs is influenced by the relative contribution of bottom-up (NPP passing up the food web) and top-down (consumers regulating NPP) forces, the number of trophic levels, and the presence of omnivory.

- Most food webs have just three or four trophic levels because of energy limitations at higher trophic levels, the effects of disturbance, or the evolutionary constraints on top predators.

Figure 56.8

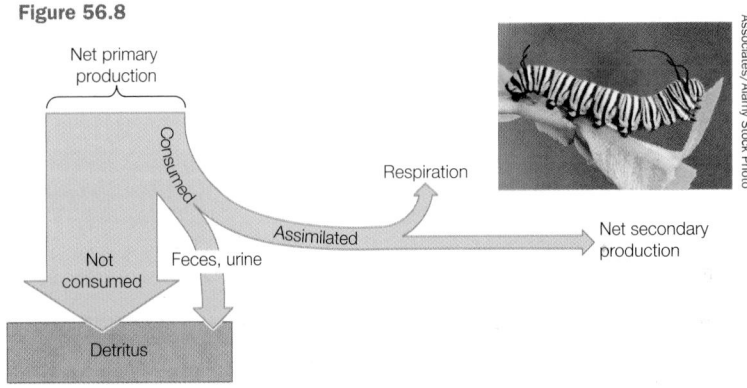

© Marvin Dembinsky Photo Associates/Alamy Stock Photo

Figure 56.10

Trophic level

Secondary consumers

Primary consumers

Primary producers

Questions

1. How and why do production efficiencies differ between ectotherms and endotherms?

2. How is energy flow in food webs influenced by the relative contributions of bottom-up and top-down forces, number of trophic levels, and the presence of omnivory?

3. What are three factors hypothesized to be important in determining food chain length?

KEY CONCEPT
56.4 Nutrient Cycling in Ecosystems Involves Chemical and Biological Transformations

Go to **Activity 56.2 and
Animations 56.1–56.3**

- Nutrients move through the biotic parts of ecosystems via production and **decomposition**.

- At a global scale, nutrients move through geological, atmospheric, and biological pools, making up **biogeochemical cycles**.

- Water cycles rapidly through the globe as part of the **hydrologic cycle**, transporting nutrients and serving as an essential requirement for organisms.

- Carbon moves through biological systems and returns to the atmosphere through respiration.

- Burning of **fossil fuels** increases the carbon dioxide and sulfur in the atmosphere, causing global warming and acidic conditions in oceans and lakes.

- The nitrogen cycle is dominated by biotic transformations controlled by bacteria, whereas the phosphorus and sulfur cycles are dominated by geochemical processes.

Questions

1. What is the role of decomposition and mineralization in nutrient cycling?

2. Describe Earth's carbon cycle and how fossil-fuel burning is raising global temperatures.

3. Describe the role of microbes versus that of geological processes in global nitrogen, phosphorus, and sulfur cycles.

Figure 56.11

Figure 56.16

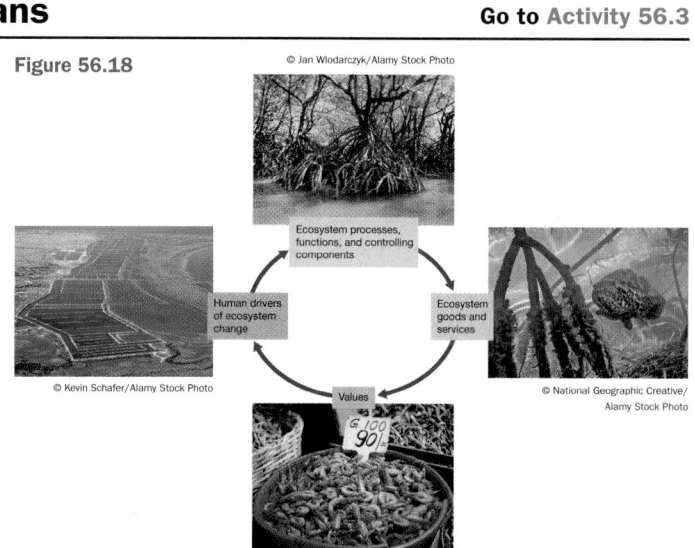

KEY CONCEPT
56.5 Ecosystems Provide Important Services and Values to Humans

Go to **Activity 56.3**

- **Ecosystem services** benefit humans and can be categorized as providing provisioning, regulating, supporting, or cultural services.

- Most ecosystem services are either irreplaceable or prohibitively expensive to replace.

- **Ecosystem values** are measures of how important ecosystem services are to people—that is, what they are worth.

- Ecosystem services can be valued by determining the market value or the willingness of people to pay for the services.

Questions

1. Describe the four categories of ecosystem services.

2. How can humans promote sustainability and reduce ecosystem service trade-offs?

Figure 56.18

© Jan Wlodarczyk/Alamy Stock Photo

© Kevin Schafer/Alamy Stock Photo

© National Geographic Creative/Alamy Stock Photo

© Ania Blazejewska/Getty Images

Go to **Achieve** for the eBook, **LearningCurve**, animations, activities, simulations, and additional resources and assignments.

A Changing Biosphere 57

© Dr. Paul A. Zahl/Science Source

A small population of the harlequin toad (*Atelopus varius*), a species in Costa Rica that was presumed extinct in 1996, was found in a mountainous protected area in 2003.

KEY CONCEPTS

57.1 Human Activities Are Changing the Biosphere, Resulting in Biodiversity Loss

57.2 Most Biodiversity Loss to Date Is Caused by Habitat Loss and Degradation

57.3 Protecting Biodiversity Requires Conservation and Management Strategies

▶Investigating LIFE

Fatal Fungus Final Fate for Frogs?

Most of us have at some point in our life encountered a frog in a local pond or park. Maybe more than almost any other wild animals, amphibians are commonly encountered by human beings. But since the late 1980s, ecologists have documented a sharp global decline in amphibian species—more than in any other major taxonomic group on Earth. Some regions show greater declines than others, but a 2019 study by the International Union for Conservation of Nature (IUCN) showed that amphibians are more threatened than either birds or mammals, with 40% of species (2,123) being globally threatened and 159 species believed to be extinct in the wild.

The decline has been particularly worrisome to scientists for a few key reasons: the sudden and global nature of the decline, the undisturbed nature of the areas where some of the declines have occurred (for example, mountainous rainforest preserves in Costa Rica, where 40% of the amphibians have become extinct), and the reputation of amphibians as "biological indicators" of environmental conditions. Amphibians have permeable skin, live their lives in water and on land, and typically do not move long distances, factors that make them particularly susceptible to changes in their immediate environment. The IUCN study showed

that most amphibian declines were caused by habitat loss, habitat degradation, and overexploitation, but for 48% of the rapidly declining species, there was no clear explanation. What factors might be contributing to the rapid decline of these species?

Over the past two and a half decades, a highly lethal and infectious skin disease called chytridiomycosis, caused by a fungal pathogen (*Batrachochytrium dendrobatidis*), has been linked to mass mortalities of amphibians, especially in the regions where amphibian declines have been most dramatic. The disease was first discovered in 1993 in dead frogs in Australia and then seemed to appear suddenly in the Americas, Africa, Europe, and New Zealand. However, it is not clear how or why the fungal disease has emerged as a threat, and whether humans have contributed to its spread. An increasing number of studies are looking for reasons why this deadly disease has emerged and how it might be prevented.

 Is the most recent dramatic decline of amphibians the result of a novel fungal pathogen, and if so, what can be done about it? (Find the answer on page 1296.)

KEY CONCEPT

57.1

Human Activities Are Changing the Biosphere, Resulting in Biodiversity Loss

Learning Objectives

57.1.1 Describe the value of biodiversity and how its loss at one scale affects loss at other scales.

57.1.2 Explain the concept of effective population size and the various ways that small population sizes can lead to extinction.

57.1.3 Discuss why it is difficult to determine the number of species on Earth and their extinction rates.

57.1.4 Explain the methods used to estimate the probability of species extinction.

Throughout Part Nine we have described the dramatic ways in which the biosphere is changing as a result of human activities. The causes of these changes have been varied, and include habitat destruction and degradation, overharvesting of species, species invasions and emerging diseases, and now climate change. One of the largest ecological consequences of these changes has been the rapid decline of biodiversity, or the loss of diversity at genetic, population, species, ecosystem, and global scales.

Biodiversity has great value to human society

The escalating loss of Earth's biodiversity is of great concern for many reasons:

- *Humans depend on thousands of species and their ecosystems for ecosystem goods and services.* As you learned in Key Concept 56.5, species and ecosystems provide humans with important goods (e.g., food, timber, and fiber) and services (e.g., regulating and supporting services such as coastal protection, water and air quality, soil formation, and carbon sequestration).

- *Humans derive enormous psychological benefits, including aesthetic pleasure, from interacting with other organisms.* These aesthetic benefits are the reason we surround ourselves with parks and recreate in the wilderness.

- *Living in ways that cause the extinction of other species raises ethical issues.* Loss of biodiversity is of concern to anyone who believes humans have an ethical obligation to the natural world.

- *Extinctions deprive the public and scientific community of opportunities to study and understand ecological relationships among organisms.* The more species that are lost, the more difficult it will be to understand the biosphere, as it exists today.

Recognizing the importance of biodiversity propels us to develop strategies for protecting and managing it and has spawned the development of **conservation biology**—an integrative scientific discipline that relies on principles of ecology, economics, social science, and policy to protect and manage Earth's biodiversity. As you will see, we will refer to many ecological concepts from other chapters to establish, first, how and why biodiversity is being lost

and, second, the role of conservation biology in protecting against and managing its further loss.

Diversity loss at one scale affects diversity loss at other scales

As you saw in Key Concept 55.1, biodiversity is central to the interconnectedness of various levels of biological organization, from genes to species to communities. Thus the loss of diversity at one scale affects the loss of diversity at other scales (**Figure 57.1**).

Human-caused habitat destruction, overharvesting, species invasions and emerging diseases, and climate change cause the loss of individuals...

...leading to smaller and less genetically diverse populations, which are more susceptible to extinction (see Figure 57.2). The fewer populations there are, the smaller the metapopulations and the greater the risk of species extinction.

Once species are lost, species diversity can decline if those species play critical roles in the ecosystem.

Declines in species diversity in ecosystems lead to losses at regional, continental...

...and global scales.

Figure 57.1 Biodiversity Loss Is Interconnected across Scales Human activities have caused the rapid decline of biodiversity, or the loss of diversity at genetic, population, species, ecosystem, and global scales. Implicit in biodiversity loss is the concept that the loss of diversity at one scale affects the loss of diversity at other scales (see Figure 55.5).

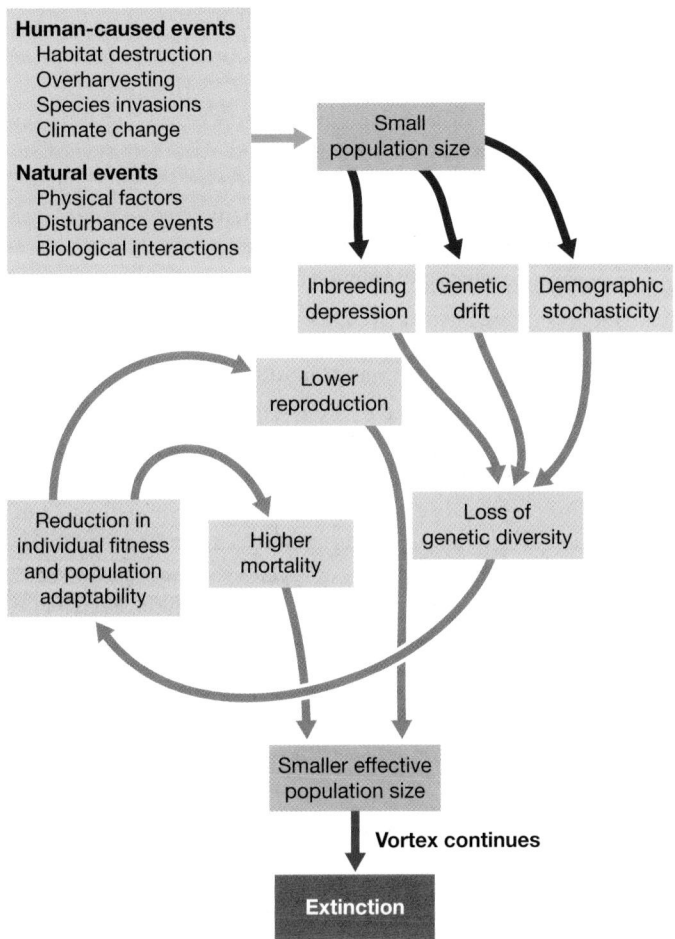

Figure 57.2 Extinction Vortex   Human-caused and natural events can reduce the effective population size (number of individuals that can contribute offspring to the next generation) of species, eventually leading to population and species extinctions.

Q: Explain how the chytrid fungal pathogen described in the opening story could cause the extinction of a species such as the harlequin frog.

For example, when human-caused activities reduce the number of individuals in a population, they reduce what is called the **effective population size**, or the number of individuals that can contribute offspring to the next generation, resulting in further population size decline, or what has been termed an "extinction vortex" (**Figure 57.2**). How does the effective population size continue to decline? First, small populations are more likely to experience genetic drift and inbreeding, which can lead to lower genetic diversity and inbreeding depression. Second, when population sizes are small, there is also a greater chance of **demographic stochasticity**, or fluctuations in population size as the result of random differences among individuals in reproduction and survival. For example, a small population might have, by chance, fewer females than males, resulting in fewer offspring than expected if the sex ratio were reversed. Finally, external mortality events such as extreme weather or habitat destruction can have devastating effects on small populations by increasing their chance of extinction even if only a small number of individuals are killed.

Biodiversity loss is also connected at higher metapopulation, species, and ecosystem levels (see Figure 57.1). For example, you know from Key Concept 53.4 that the larger the metapopulation, the greater the chance that dispersal among source populations can rescue sink populations from extinction. As more local populations become extinct, and as more metapopulations are compromised, there is a greater risk that species will become extinct as well. Unfortunately, if some of those species play critical roles in their ecosystems—if they are, for example, keystone or foundation species—the possibility exists that other species will be threatened with extinction as well. As species diversity declines in ecosystems, biodiversity loss manifests itself at larger regional, continental, and even global scales (see Figure 57.1).

There are many examples of how a series of unfortunate events at different levels of biodiversity has led to the extinction of species—or subspecies, in the case of the Heath Hen (*Tympanuchus cupido cupido*), a large bird in the grouse family (**Figure 57.3A**). Heath Hens were common from Maine to Virginia prior to the 1800s but were hunted extensively for food. By 1830 only one population, on the island of Martha's Vineyard, Massachusetts, was left. By 1908 only 50 birds remained, and a reserve was established to recover the population, which eventually grew to several thousand birds. Unfortunately, in 1916 a fire and a series of environmental factors that included a hard winter, an influx of predators, and a poultry disease caused the population size to decline dramatically. By 1928 demographic stochasticity and inbreeding depression set in, leaving only 13 individuals—2 females and 11 males. Four years later, the Heath Hen was extinct.

Species diversity is being lost at unprecedented rates

The loss of the Heath Hen and other extirpations caused by humans (see Figure 57.3) remind us of the finality inherent in species extinctions. However, over the scope of Earth's history extinction has been a constant theme; most of the species that have lived on Earth are extinct today. Extinctions have occurred throughout Earth's history at what is referred to as a "background" rate as changes in environmental conditions have favored some species and negatively affected others. But the rate of extinctions taking place today rivals those of the five great mass extinction events, which were the result of cataclysmic natural disturbances rather than human activities (see Table 23.1 and Figure 23.2). One estimate, from renowned evolutionary biologist Edward O. Wilson, suggests that Earth is losing some 30,000 species per year, putting us in the midst of a sixth mass extinction event.

This mass extinction event has been ongoing for some time. For example, research suggests that when humans first arrived in North America from Siberia about 15,000 years ago, they

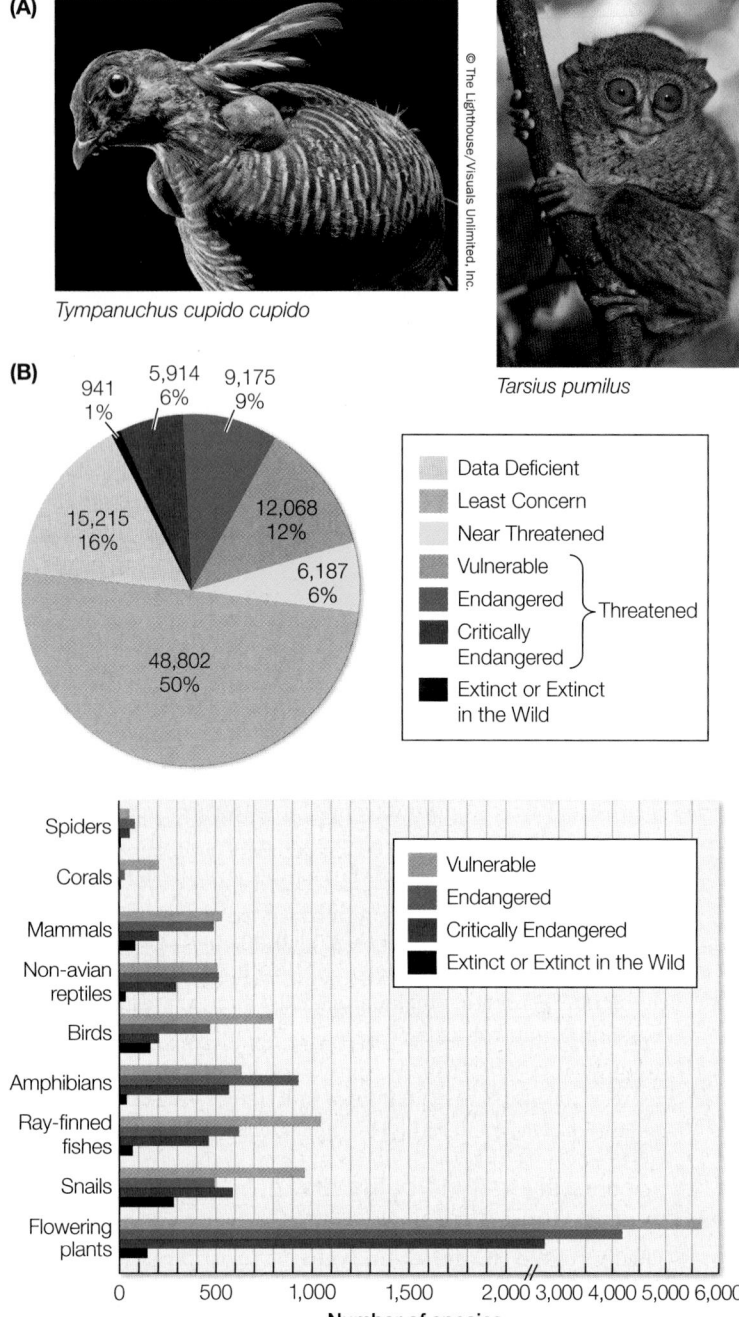

Tympanuchus cupido cupido

Tarsius pumilus

Figure 57.3 Species Extinctions: Going, Going …   (A) The Heath Hen (above left) became extinct in 1932. In 2008 the pygmy tarsier (above right) was discovered in an Indonesian national park after having been presumed extinct for 85 years. **(B)** The pie chart shows the breakdown by risk category of 98,302 animal, plant, and fungi species that are either Extinct or Threatened as assessed by the International Union for Conservation of Nature. The bar graph shows examples of animal and plant taxonomic groups from that assessment that are experiencing heightened extinction or risk of extinction. (B after IUCN 2019. *The IUCN Red List of Threatened Species. Version 2019-1.* http://www.iucnredlist.org. Downloaded on 16 May 2019.)

Q: What percentage of species are categorized as Extinct versus Threatened? Of those species, which taxonomic group has experienced the most extinction and which can be categorized as most Threatened? Of the animal groups, which can be categorized as most Threatened?

encountered a diverse and spectacular group of large mammals, including saber-toothed cats, dire wolves (*Canis diris*), mammoths, mastodons, giant ground sloths, and giant beavers. Most of this "megafauna" became extinct within a few thousand years after humans arrived. Although several hypotheses have been advanced to account for the rapid and simultaneous disappearance of so many large animals, overhunting by humans is the most likely explanation. Losses of megafauna coinciding with the arrival of humans have been documented worldwide, most notably in Australia, New Zealand, and Madagascar. Tracking and predicting extinctions are, however, difficult for several reasons:

- *We do not know how many species live on Earth today.* Many species that are likely to become extinct in the near future have not been named and described by scientists. Insects provide a case in point: although more than 1 million species have been described (see Key Concept 30.4), estimates of the number of species yet to be discovered range from 2 million to more than 15 million. Even for larger organisms, our understanding of diversity is incomplete. For example, worldwide, an annual inventory of newly described species reported 19,232 species discovered in 2009 alone; this list included 9,738 insects, 2,184 plants, 1,360 fungi, 71 mammals, and 7 birds.

▶ **Media Clip 57.1**
New Species Found in the Twenty-First Century
Life12e.com/mc57.1

- *The distributions of most described species, particularly those that are small, reclusive, and rare, are poorly known.* One tiny North American true bug, *Corixidea major* (so rare it has no common name), had been found in only one location near Clarksville, Tennessee, until entomologists using lights to collect insects at night discovered it in Virginia and Florida, extending the species' known range by more than 1,000 kilometers.

- *It is difficult to determine whether a species is truly extinct.* Rarely is the death of the last surviving member of a species recorded with certainty, as it was in the case of the last Passenger Pigeon (*Ectopistes migratorius*), a female named Martha, that died in the Cincinnati Zoo on September 1, 1914. The status of rare, reclusive species with poorly known life histories is much more difficult to determine, as has been the case with the pygmy tarsier (*Tarsius pumilus*) (see Figure 57.3A). This tiny primate, weighing less than 60 grams, was thought to have become extinct in its native cloud forests on the island of Sulawesi in Indonesia. In 2008—85 years after the last reported sighting of a living *T. pumilus*—a research team discovered individuals of this species living in one of the island's national parks.

- *We rarely know all of the interactions among species.* The loss of one species—be it as a member of a food web or as habitat for species—can place other species at risk. How many species are at risk as a result of their interactions with other species is hard to characterize and often requires detailed ecological knowledge.

We can predict the effects of human activities on biodiversity

Despite gaps in our understanding of biodiversity, methods exist for estimating the extinction probability of species, taking into account their population sizes, genetic variation, life history traits, and ecology. The IUCN has published categories that define the risk of extinction of species. Species in imminent danger of extinction in all or most of their range are classified as "Critically Endangered" or "Endangered"; those believed to be susceptible to extinction in the near future are classified as "Vulnerable." Biologists consider species in any one of these three categories to be "Threatened" (**Figure 57.3B**).

Rarity in and of itself is not always a cause for concern. Some species may be specialized for rare and unusual habitats and not be particularly abundant by nature. But as you saw earlier, "newly rare" species are of concern because large and rapid reductions in population sizes can lead to smaller effective population sizes through a variety of mechanisms (see Figure 57.2).

Certain aspects of species' life histories (see Key Concept 53.3) can be important in predicting the ability of species to recover from declines. In fishes and mammals, for example, one of the best predictors of extinction risk is age at maturity, a life history trait that influences the rate of reproduction. Ecological requirements can also influence the ability of species to recover from rapid declines. Species with specialized habitat or dietary requirements, for example, are more likely to become extinct than are species with more generalized requirements.

Ecologists can apply the principles of the species–area relationship and the theory of island biogeography (see Key Concept 52.5) to predict the effects of habitat loss on species—a major cause of extinction today. By measuring the rate at which species richness decreases with decreasing habitat patch size, they can estimate how many species that live in and depend on that habitat may be lost. We examined the connection between habitat area and species loss in Investigating Life: The Largest Experiment on Earth in Chapter 52.

KEY CONCEPT
57.1 Recap and Assess

Biodiversity has great value to human society in the form of goods and services. Human activities have resulted in a rapid loss of biodiversity, a decline detectable at genetic, population, species, ecosystem, and global scales. Species extinctions can occur when human and natural events reduce effective population sizes and cause inbreeding depression, genetic drift, and demographic stochasticity. Methods exist for estimating the extinction probability of species that take into account their population sizes, genetic variation, life history traits, and ecology.

1. What are some of the values that humans place on biodiversity?

2. Using the extinction vortex concept as your guide, describe how the Heath Hen became extinct in 1932.

3. Figure 57.3B shows the number of extinct species in various taxonomic groups. What types of animals have shown the most extinction, and why might this be the case?

We've said that human activities have played a major role in the loss of biodiversity. In the next key concept we will describe the types of human activities that most threaten biodiversity.

KEY CONCEPT 57.2   Most Biodiversity Loss to Date Is Caused by Habitat Loss and Degradation

Learning Objectives

57.2.1 Describe how habitat loss, fragmentation, and degradation have caused species extinctions.

57.2.2 Explain the effect that overharvesting of species has had on species extinctions and food webs.

57.2.3 Describe how the introduction of non-native species has threatened many species.

57.2.4 Provide evidence of how climate change is linked to declines of species and ecosystems.

Global Biodiversity Outlook 4, a report published by the United Nations in 2014, identified four principal pressures on biodiversity: (1) habitat loss and degradation, (2) overharvesting of biological resources, (3) species invasions and emerging diseases, and (4) climate change. Here we consider each of these pressures separately while keeping in mind that the threats to biodiversity are often not mutually exclusive.

Habitat loss and degradation endanger species

Most scientists agree that, up to this point in human history, **habitat loss** (reduction in habitat quantity) and **habitat degradation** (reduction in habitat quality) have been the major culprits in biodiversity loss. Our human footprint is large—it is estimated that we have transformed 50%–60% of the land surface, primarily for agriculture, timber, and livestock grazing. The building of infrastructure, such as cities, transportation corridors, and utilities (including hydroelectric dams), has altered another 2%–3% of Earth's surface.

As humans increasingly dominate the planet, the transformations they are causing affect whole biomes and the species dependent on them. For example, the current rate of loss of tropical rainforest—Earth's most species-rich biome—is about 2% of the remaining forest each year due to the increasing demands of a rapidly expanding human population for forest products and cleared agricultural land. Most of the rainforests of Asia have already been reduced to small fragments, with the only extensive remaining tracts being found on the islands of New Guinea and, to a much lesser extent, Borneo (**Figure 57.4**). As of 2019, the greatest amount of tropical rainforest deforestation had taken place in Brazil. If the current rate of loss continues, millions of rainforest species could become extinct before the end of this century.

Physical destruction of habitat, as when tropical rainforests are cut down or wetlands are drained and converted to agricultural use, has significant effects on the distributions and abundances of species. Reductions in suitable habitat have contributed to the extinction of thousands of species. As the remaining habitat gets divided into smaller and smaller fragments, it can become further degraded by edge effects (as you saw in Investigating Life: The Largest Experiment on Earth in Chapter 52 and Animation 52.4, Edge Effects). Recall that as habitat fragments become smaller,

Boulikhamsai, Southeast Asia

Brazil, South America

Swaziland, Africa

Figure 57.4 The Disappearing Tropical Forest Rainforests, the most abundant tropical forests, have long been recognized as centers of biodiversity that harbor vast numbers of species (see tropical rainforest biome, p. 1183). Since the 1950s, tropical forests have been cleared for agriculture, highways, timber resources, and other needs of an exploding human population. Map based on data from 2005. (After S. L. Pimm and C. Jenkins. 2005. *Sci Am* 293: 66–73.)

proportionally more land is exposed to edge effects (see Key Concept 52.5). The physical conditions at the edges of habitats often are more similar to those of the new habitat than to the original habitat, and this can be physically stressful for species acclimatized to the original habitat. In addition, species from surrounding habitats can colonize the edges, where they may compete with or prey on the species living in the fragment.

One effect of forest fragmentation in much of North America has been an increase in the abundance of the Brown-headed Cowbird (*Molothrus ater*), a brood parasite that lays its eggs in the nests of other bird species. Nestlings of a brood parasite are raised by the host parents, to the detriment of their own young (**Figure 57.5A**). Historically, cowbirds followed bison (*Bison bison*) and other grazing mammals, feeding on insects kicked up by the herds; thus their eggs were laid primarily in nests of grassland host species. Forest fragmentation has opened up new opportunities for the cowbirds, which can now lay their eggs in the nests of forest birds in habitat edges, affecting nestling mortality and fledging success (**Figure 57.5B**). Fragmented forests, with relatively more edge than intact forest, thus favor the proliferation of cowbirds at the expense of forest birds.

Pollution is another cause of habitat loss and degradation. The negative effects of acid rain (see Key Concept 56.4), for example, have greatly affected lake and forest ecosystems. Among the most troublesome toxic pollutants in ecosystems today are heavy metal waste products of mining and manufacturing, and synthetic organic chemicals (pesticides) released into the environment to control pests. Multiple studies have implicated a variety of pesticides in the decline of amphibian species, particularly in areas with intense agriculture such as California and the Midwestern United States.

A relatively hidden form of pollution comes from nondegradable plastic garbage in open ocean habitats (**Figure 57.6**). One garbage patch in the middle of the Pacific Ocean is estimated to be the size of Texas. Plastic is broken up into smaller pieces and when ingested by marine birds, mammals, or fishes can be a choking hazard or can disrupt endocrine functions such as reproduction, neural development, and immune function. Plastic or abandoned fishing nets can also entangle marine organisms, including marine mammals, resulting in death.

Overharvesting has driven many species to extinction and changed food webs

Overharvesting occurs when single species, or groups of similar species, are harvested for human use. Overharvesting for such resources as food, clothing, ornamentation, pets, and medicines was once the most important and rapid cause of species extinction. For example, it has been estimated that overharvesting is responsible for roughly 40% of the approximately 150 bird species that have become extinct since the 1500s. Maybe one of the most egregious examples of overharvesting of birds came from "plume hunting" in the late nineteenth century. Feathers were harvested for ornamentation on hats and clothing—during the heyday, 5 million birds were killed each year, including 95% of Florida's shorebirds.

(A)

(B)

Forest edge

Distance edge effect
penetrates into forest

Distance from edge of forest (m)

Figure 57.5 Cowbird Parasitism at Forest Edges **(A)** Cowbirds are nest parasites—they lay their eggs (black speckled) in the nests of host bird species and depend on them to raise their young (note the large cowbird chick). **(B)** At forest edges, host birds have higher nestling loss and lower fledging success as a result of cowbird parasitism. (B after J. E. Gates and L. W. Gysel. 1978. *Ecology* 59: 871–883.)

of Africa and Asia because of markets for ivory tusks and horns. A recent study estimated that in central Africa alone, regional elephant population sizes have declined by 64% because of illegal killing within the last decade (**Figure 57.7**). On a continental scale, the study showed that between 2010 and 2012, 40,000 elephants were killed illegally, a rate of 8% per year.

Massive and lucrative international trade in exotic pets such as birds, non-avian reptiles, frogs, mammals, aquarium fishes and corals, and ornamental plants threatens many species. It is estimated that 2–5 million birds and 2–3 million non-avian reptiles are captured live each year. In addition, it has been estimated that more than 1 billion ornamental fishes comprising more than 4,000 freshwater and 1,400 marine species are traded internationally each year. For example, the Banggai cardinalfish (*Pterapogon kauderni*) is on the brink of extinction entirely because of the pet trade; almost a million of these critically endangered fish are caught annually near

The plumes of white egrets sold for $32 per ounce in 1915, which was the same price as gold.

Even today, overharvesting is still of great concern for critically endangered species that are not yet extinct but have a high probability of becoming so within the century, particularly as their habitat declines or is further degraded. Recently there has been an alarming uptick in illegal poaching of what might be considered charismatic megafauna, or species with widespread popular appeal. One example is the illegal poaching of elephants and rhinoceroses in much

Figure 57.6 Plastic Ocean
Large amounts of plastic garbage have accumulated in the North Pacific Gyre, degrading the pelagic environment. Inset is a photo of tiny bits of plastic comingled with a sample of water taken from the vicinity of the North Pacific Gyre garbage patch. (After Marine Debris Division/NOAA, US Department of Commerce. https://marinedebris. noaa.gov/sites/default/files/ GPmap_2012_NOAAMDP.jpg. Accessed 4/8/2019.)

Figure 57.7 Mass Killing of Elephants One of the largest known mass elephant killing events took place in Bouba Njida National Park, Cameroon, in 2012. Poachers killed more than 300 elephants with AK-47s and grenades.

Sulawesi, Indonesia, to satisfy the demand from saltwater aquarium enthusiasts. The exotic pet trade is worrisome from multiple aspects—harvesting and transporting species not only cause the decline of rare or endangered species but also can unintentionally

lead to disease transmission or species invasions, as you saw with the lionfishes example in Chapter 54.

Even though we tend to think of the oceans as boundless, they too are affected by overharvesting. Burgeoning human populations in need of food are placing unprecedented pressure on species harvested from the wild. Humans have fished for at least 40,000 years, but in recent centuries innovations in technology and increasing demand have accelerated overharvesting. A recent comprehensive study of fisheries found that nearly 14% of fished taxa collapsed between 1950 and 2007 (**Figure 57.8A**). The effects of fish harvesting vary widely across the globe, in part because restrictions in some locations have been implemented to encourage the recovery of overfished species (**Figure 57.8B**). Top predators such as sharks, bluefin tunas, and groupers, which are preferentially harvested, are at particular risk of extinction. These long-lived species show slow population recovery, and because they are keystone species, their losses are likely to have more lasting ecosystem ramifications.

What are some of the consequences of single-species overharvesting, particularly of species that are long-lived or top predators? First, species such as elephants and rhinoceroses that are characterized by slow population growth show slower recovery. Blue whales (*Balaenoptera musculus*) are at greater risk of extinction than are humpbacks (*Megaptera novaeangliae*), even though both species experienced chronic overharvesting in the nineteenth

(A)

(B)

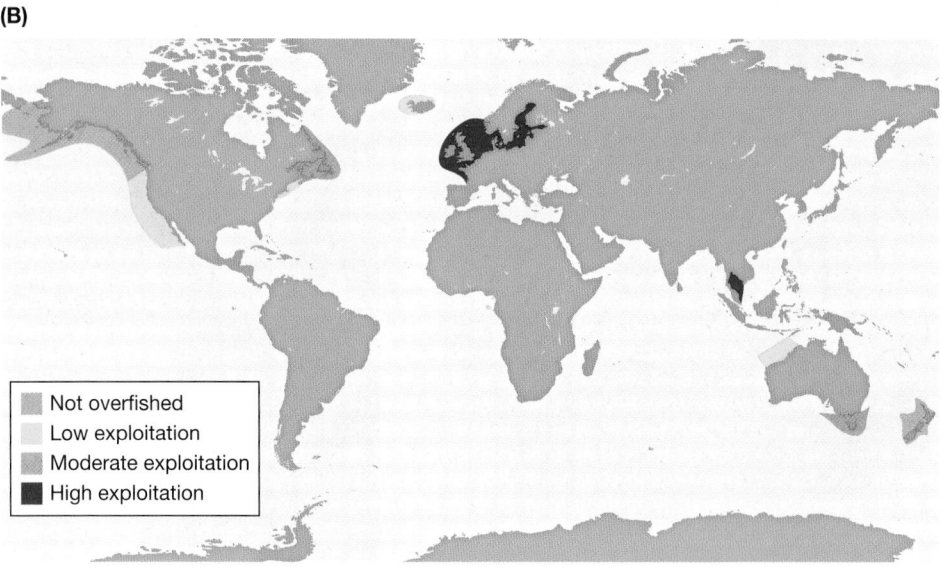

Not overfished
Low exploitation
Moderate exploitation
High exploitation

Figure 57.8 Overharvesting Has Caused Fisheries Collapses, but Some Recovery Is Occurring (A) The number of collapsed fished taxa (estimated as a decline of biomass of the fished taxa to less than 10% of their unfished biomass) increased steadily from 1950 to 2007. (B) Worldwide status of exploited fish populations. (After B. Worm et al. 2009. *Science* 325: 578–585.)

Q: Using the map, indicate which regions of the world are experiencing the highest fisheries exploitation.

century. You saw in Key Concept 53.4 that while humpback whales have been recovering relatively quickly with the cessation of hunting, blue whale populations have lagged behind because of their lower reproductive rates. Recovery of populations of the black rockfish (*Sebastes melanops*), which we introduced in Key Concept 53.4, has been extremely slow because older, larger females were preferentially harvested, and the remaining smaller females produce fewer and smaller larvae.

Second, consider what happens when an overharvested species plays an important keystone or foundation role in its community. A recent study by William Ripple and colleagues considered the status and ecological consequences of the decline of 31 of the world's largest carnivores. Most of the species studied have experienced substantial population declines over the past two centuries as the result of overharvesting, persecution (culling because of conflicts with humans), and habitat loss. Using data from several studies, the researchers showed that when top large carnivores declined, trophic cascades were interrupted, dramatically changing the abundance of herbivore and primary producer species (**Figure 57.9**). This research suggests that large carnivores are necessary to maintain biodiversity and ecosystem function in some ecosystems.

Invasive predators, competitors, and pathogens threaten many species

Deliberate or inadvertent introductions of non-native species have increased exponentially over the last 200 years. It is estimated that 50,000 species have been introduced to the United States alone. Many of these species were intentionally introduced to provide food, natural resources, or other important services for humans. But roughly 10% of these species have become **invasive**—that is, they reproduce rapidly, spread widely, and have mostly negative effects on the native species or ecosystems of the region. As you saw in Key Concept 55.2, once an introduced species arrives in a new community, a successful invasion usually involves multiple introduction events and the ability to cope with the physical environment and coexist with other species in the community.

While arguments can be made for the positive side of some species invasions, most invasions have had negative effects on species and ecosystems. For example, estimates suggest that 400 of the 958 species (42%) listed under the U.S. Endangered Species Act are at risk primarily because of predation, competition, or disease transmission by invasive species. Invasive species also can have dramatic effects on the functions and services of ecosystems, affecting fire cycles, water availability, and coastal sedimentation (**Figure 57.10**).

Invasive species have even changed the genetic diversity of native species through hybridization events with wild populations (e.g., non-native rainbow trout [*Oncorhynchus mykiss*] and native cutthroat trout [*Oncorhynchus clarkii*] in Montana). The total cost estimate for dealing with undesirable invasive species in the United States alone was roughly $120 billion per year.

Non-native species are spread in a variety of ways. Over the past 400 years, Europeans colonizing new continents have deliberately introduced plants and animals to reconstruct their once familiar surroundings. Many of these introductions have had disastrous effects on native flora and fauna. In Australia the introduction of European rabbits (*Oryctolagus cuniculus*) and foxes for sport hunting and of dogs and cats as pets has led to the extermination of nearly half the small- to medium-sized native marsupials over the last 100 years. As you saw in Key Concept 53.4, the use of biological control, or the deliberate introduction of species to control other invasive species, can sometimes cause even greater problems. Examples include the introduction of small predators such as mongoose to Hawaii to control rabbits and stoat (*Mustela erminea*, a type of weasel) to New Zealand to control rats. Instead of curbing the population sizes

Figure 57.9 Large Carnivores Are Declining, Changing Food Webs   Examples of the effects of large-carnivore decline on the change in abundance of species in their food webs. The blue bars represent the direct effects and the red bars represent the indirect effects. The number of years refers to the time since the carnivore species ceased to exist at the study site. (After W. J. Ripple et al. 2014. *Science* 343: 1241484; Sea otter © iStock.com/dstone6; Dingo © John Carnemolla/Shutterstock.com; Gray wolf © age fotostock/Alamy Stock Photo; Puma © iStock.com/John Pitcher; Lion and leopard courtesy of Andrew D. Sinauer.)

(A) Changes in fire cycle

Bromus tectorum

Courtesy of Leslie J. Mehrhoff, University of Connecticut/Bugwood.org

© Chris Lunesky/Alamy Stock Photo

(B) Changes in hydrology

Tamarix ramosissima

David McIntyre

© Jordana Meilleur/Alamy Stock Photo

(C) Changes in sedimentation

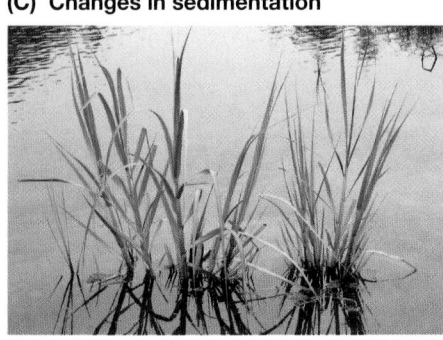

Spartina anglica

Courtesy of Sally Hacker

Courtesy of Sally Hacker

Figure 57.10 Species Invasions Can Change Ecosystem Functions and Services Three examples of the effects that invasive species can have: **(A)** cheatgrass increases the fire cycle in sagebrush habitat, **(B)** salt cedar draws down water in desert streams, and **(C)** English cordgrass leads to sedimentation, transforming coastal mudflats into salt marshes.

of rabbits and rats, these predators have been the major cause of bird species extinctions on these islands.

Sometimes invasions have occurred out of ignorance in what people believe are unlikely events of releasing non-native species (as was the case with the lionfishes described in Chapter 54). It can be difficult for people to imagine that species that are desirable and attractive in their place of origin can "go rogue" in a new region. Some of today's most noxious weeds were deliberately transported and planted in new places for their beauty, fragrance, or culinary value.

A more inadvertent mechanism of introduction comes from species that stow away during transportation. For example, you saw in Key Concept 55.2 how non-native species are transported in ballast water. The brown tree snake (*Boiga irregularis*) arrived on Guam in air cargo shortly after World War II and today can be found at densities up to 5,000 individuals per square kilometer. The snake has exterminated 15 species of land birds, including 3 found only on Guam.

Introduced pathogens have also wreaked havoc among native species, as exemplified by the fungal pathogen *Batrachochytrium dendrobatidis*, or *Bd* for short, which is implicated in the dramatic worldwide declines of amphibians over the last 25 years. As described in the story opening this chapter, the disease may be responsible for the large percentage of amphibian declines recorded globally and for which there has been no clear explanation (the others being a result of some combination of habitat loss, overharvesting, exposure to UV radiation, or pollution). Such "rapidly declining" events have taken place on all the major continents and occur within well-protected areas such as Yosemite National Park (USA), Monteverde Cloud Forest Reserve (Costa Rica), and Eungella National Park (Australia). Most of the mass mortality

events in which *Bd* has been implicated have not been observed because they happen so rapidly. Generally, researchers return to a site to find that population sizes are drastically reduced, or that some species are missing altogether, and discover the fungus present in some remaining individuals.

Researchers studying amphibian declines are interested in whether *Bd* is a novel and highly virulent pathogen that was recently introduced into wild populations ("novel pathogen hypothesis") or if *Bd* existed prior to the declines but emerged as a serious pathogen as a result of human-caused environmental changes to climate or UV radiation ("emerging endemic hypothesis"). Although *Bd* seems to thrive under fairly specific environmental conditions (high-elevation streams with permanent water sources and temperatures between 12°C and 27°C), most of the evidence now suggests that *Bd* is a non-native pathogen likely introduced through the global trade in amphibians for food, for use as laboratory animals, or for use as pets or display animals. **Investigating Life: Exploring the Decline of Central American Frogs** describes research by Karen Lips and colleagues on the 20-year decline of four species of frogs in the genus *Atelopus* at multiple sites in Costa Rica and Panama. Their data suggest that the *Bd* pathogen traveled as an "invasion front" from infected to uninfected populations over time and that, based on microscopic tissue analyses of frogs collected prior to the declines, *Bd* was probably never present in this region of the world until its introduction in the 1980s. Of the four *Atelopus* species considered in this study, three species (*A. chiriquiensis, A. senex,* and *A. zeteki*) are likely extinct, and one species (*A. varius*; photo at chapter opening), thought to be extinct in 1996, likely exists only in a small population near Quepos, Costa Rica.

Experiment

Original Paper: K. Lips et al. 2008. Riding the wave: Reconciling the roles of disease and climate change in amphibian declines. *PLOS Biol* 6: e72. CC BY 4.0.

Karen Lips and her colleagues studied the spread of the fungal pathogen *Batrachochytrium dendrobatidis* (*Bd*), implicated in the dramatic declines of frogs in the genus *Atelopus* seen in the moist and mountainous regions of lower Central America (Costa Rica and Panama) starting in the late 1980s. They compiled biogeographic reports of *Atelopus* declines and conducted microscopic tissue analyses to test whether *Bd* was a non-native pathogen species recently introduced to Central America or an existing disease that emerged as the result of changes in climate or the environment.

HYPOTHESIS► Amphibian declines in Central America are caused by the non-native species invasion of the *Bd* pathogen rather than by an environmentally induced emergence of *Bd* as an existing pathogen.

METHOD►

1. The researchers mapped the location and approximate year of decline as a result of *Bd* infection for populations of four species of *Atelopus* at numerous sites in Costa Rica and Panama using data from published studies, the Global Amphibian Assessment, and their own fieldwork.

2. The distance of *Bd* spread was plotted against the years since *Bd* first caused a decline in *Atelopus* populations.

3. Sixty-four frogs, collected before 1987 in Monteverde, Costa Rica, were examined for *Bd* to determine if the pathogen was present prior to the decline.

RESULTS►

1. The *Bd* pathogen was not found in frogs collected prior to 1987.

2. The map of *Atelopus* decline from *Bd*'s first appearance in 1987 to nearly 20 years later in 2006 shows that *Bd* spread from Costa Rica to Panama in a wavelike pattern from northwest to southeast.

3. There is a positive linear relationship between *Bd* travel distance and the years since *Bd* infection was detected (see inset on map).

CONCLUSION► The analyses of the prevalence of *Bd* in lower Central America over nearly 20 years support a classic pattern of a novel invasive disease spread across naive populations rather than the environmentally induced emergence of an already existing disease.

Work with the Data

The researchers were able to combine the distributional data of *Bd* infection from lower Central America with a much larger data set from South America to determine the percentage of *Atelopus* species that became extinct as a function of elevation. They found the following frog species extinctions with elevation:

Elevation (m)	Species extinctions (%)
0–199	30
200–1,000	85
1,001–4,000	100

QUESTIONS►

1. The data from the results portion of the experiment can be used to calculate the rate of spread (km/year) of *Bd* by dividing the distance between pairs of locations (distance interval) by the number of years between the dates of decline. Calculate the rate of spread of the *Bd* pathogen between pairs of locations of frog declines (time interval). Is the rate of *Bd* spread similar among locations, or does it differ?

2. Calculate the average rate of spread for the *Bd* pathogen in lower Central America. Predict how far and in what direction *Bd* could travel by 2020 (14 years).

3. Using the map elevations in the results section of the experiment, and the species extinction data in the table here, do you think is it likely that the *Bd* pathogen will spread, and cause species extinctions, in the direction and distance estimated in your answer to Question 2? If so, what is your best estimate of the percentage of species that would become extinct? Explain.

Go to **Achieve** for a companion Data in Depth exercise.

Species and ecosystems are already being affected by climate change

As you saw in Key Concept 56.4, human-generated emissions of greenhouse gases are contributing to global climate warming, sea level rise, increased storminess, and ocean acidification, all of which are likely to become increasingly important causes of habitat loss and degradation, and ultimately species extinctions. Across North America, for example, average annual temperatures are predicted to increase by 2–5 degrees Celsius by the end of the twenty-first century. If the climate warms to that extent, model projections show that the average temperature found at any given location in North America today could shift 500–800 kilometers to the north. Those species that cannot adapt to the warmer climate will have to shift their geographic ranges to stay within their physiological and ecological ranges. The shift in distributional range that organisms experience could result in habitat loss and fragmentation, especially if appropriate habitat does not shift as well or is lost altogether.

For example, as the globe warms, sea level is rising as a result of melting polar glaciers and warming seas. The Intergovernmental Panel on Climate Change (IPCC) estimates that the current rate of global sea level rise is 3.4 millimeters per year, resulting in a projected rise of 0.65 meters by 2100. As the seas slowly inundate the coast, coastal ecosystems will become increasingly flooded, putting them at great risk for habitat loss. Likewise, as polar regions warm, sea ice ecosystems are disappearing at an alarming rate, affecting species such as polar bears (*Ursus maritimus*) and seals dependent on that habitat (see the "Future directions" discussion in Chapter 56). Global warming has also been implicated in causing more frequent and extreme storm events, as seas warm and winds increase in intensity. Extreme storms such as Hurricane Irma in 2017 are causing flooding and erosion hazards for both human and natural coastal communities. Finally, as discussed in Investigating Life: Food Webs in an Acidic and Warming Ocean in Chapter 56, as the ocean absorbs more atmospheric CO_2, seas become more acidic, leading to a host of individual species and ecosystem changes.

Scientists are beginning to explore how species and ecosystems will respond to climate change by predicting how it may affect organisms and looking for ways to mitigate those effects. Their research activities include analyses of past climate changes and studies of sites currently undergoing rapid climate change. It would be helpful to know, for example, how rapidly species responded to the end of the most recent ice age. Which species did and did not keep pace with the warming climate and rising seas? How much, and in what ways, do past ecological communities differ from those of today as a result of changes in climate?

Species that can disperse easily, such as birds, insects, and fishes that can move considerable distances, may be able to shift their ranges as rapidly as the climate changes, provided they can find appropriate habitats. However, the ranges of other species, particularly plants, are likely to shift more slowly. For example, after the glaciers started to retreat in North America about 18,000 years ago, the ranges of plant communities slowly shifted northward (**Figure 57.11**). In addition, roughly 12,000 years ago, some novel, or what are termed "no analog," plant communities formed under unique climate conditions that do not exist today. Thus it

may be that as climate rapidly changes, unique combinations of species will come together to form similar novel communities.

Modern-day scientific observations have shown that for a wide variety of organisms, latitudinal and elevational distributions are

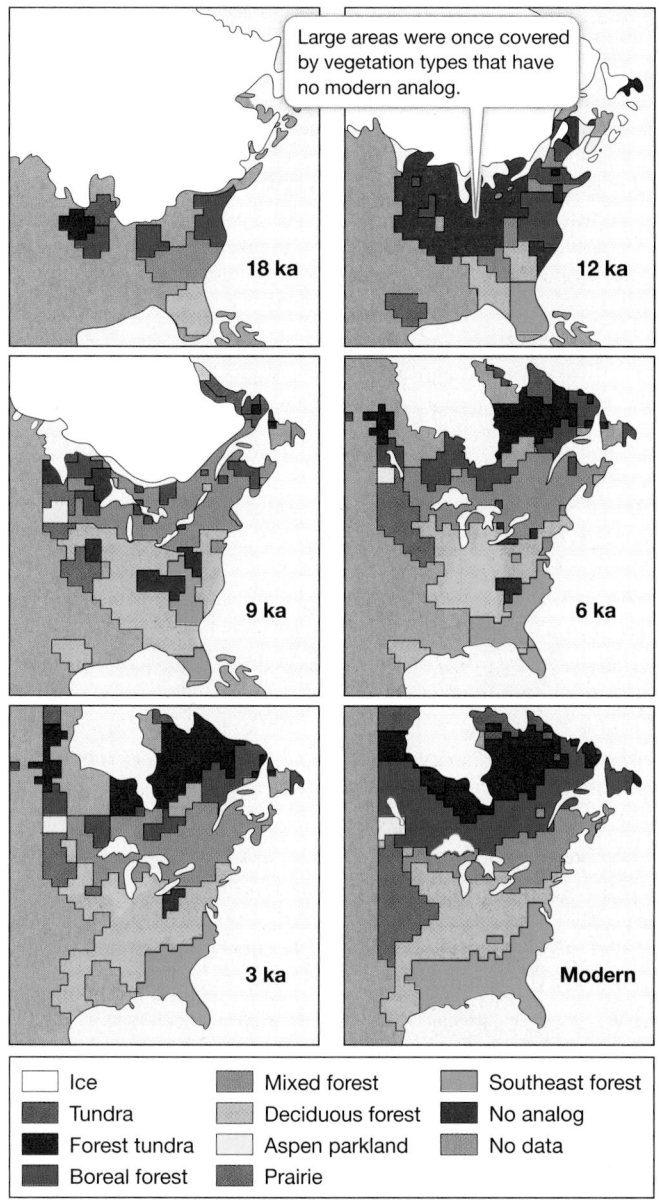

Figure 57.11 Past Changes in Plant Communities Due to Climate Vegetation types in eastern North America have changed since the last glacial maximum, 18,000 years ago (ka, thousands of years ago). Vegetation composition was determined from pollen preserved in sediments. (After J. T. Overpeck et al. 1992. *Geology* 20: 1071–1074; Mapped paleogeography and Laurentide ice sheet after A. S. Dyke and V. K. Prest. 1987. *Géographie physique et Quaternaire* 41: 237–263 and G. H. Denton and T. J. Hughes. 1981. *The Last Great Ice Sheets.* John Wiley & Sons: New York.)

Q: After the glaciers first started to retreat 18,000 years ago, what has been the pattern of plant community change with latitude? What were the "no analog" plant communities, and how did they form?

TABLE 57.1 | Recent Latitudinal and Elevational Range Shifts That Likely Result from Climate Change

Community or taxon	Location	Observed changes	Climate link
Tree line	Europe, New Zealand	Elevational shifts from lower to higher mountain zones	Increased air temperature
Alpine plants	European alps	Elevational shifts of 1–4 m per decade	Increased air temperature
Zooplankton, intertidal invertebrate, and fish communities	California coast, North Atlantic Ocean	Increasing abundance of warm-water species	Increased ocean temperature
39 butterfly species	North America, Europe	Northward range shifts up to 200 km over 27 years	Increased air temperature
Lowland birds	Costa Rica	Elevational shifts from lower to higher mountain zones	Decreased dry-season mist frequency
12 bird species	Britain	Northward range shifts up to 19 km over 20 years	Increased winter air temperature
Red fox (*Vulpes vulpes*), Arctic fox (*Alopex lagopus*)	Canada	Northward range shift of red fox and simultaneous southward range shift of Arctic fox	Increased air temperature

Source: G.-R. Walther et al. 2002. *Nature* 416: 389–395.

shifting in ways that are consistent with climate change (**Table 57.1**). For example, a study that considered the range shifts in alpine plants in the European alps showed that plant species have been moving to higher elevations consistent with increasing temperature. Researchers compared current plant community species richness with historical data from the eighteenth and nineteenth centuries. They found that alpine plant species richness increased over time, suggesting that plants were moving from lower elevations to higher elevations. Likewise, observations of the distribution of nonmigratory butterfly species in Europe and North America showed that of the 39 species examined, 63% had moved their ranges northward, while only 3% had moved southward.

Along with the shifts in distribution, evidence is mounting that important life history events are also occurring earlier in the spring (**Table 57.2**). The observations suggest that increases in temperature are triggering species to breed or migrate earlier than they have in the past few decades. There can also be physiological changes that reduce growth and reproduction. For example, since the mid-1980s the average minimum nightly temperature at La Selva Biological Station in the Caribbean lowlands of Costa Rica has increased from about 20°C to 22°C. On warmer nights, trees use more of their energy reserves to maintain themselves. As a result, even this small rise in temperature has reduced the average growth rate of six different tree species by about 20%.

Finally, climate change has the potential to cause species extinctions, although to date, none have been directly and definitively linked to this cause. However, as you saw in Figure 57.2, effects of climate change such as habitat loss or changes in life history or physiology could lead to lower effective population sizes, increased population extinctions, and eventually species extinctions.

 View in Achieve
Animation 57.1 The Effects of Climate Change

KEY CONCEPT
57.2 Recap and Assess

Biodiversity loss is the result of four major, and potentially interacting, factors. First, habitat loss and degradation (including pollution) have been primary culprits contributing to the extinction of tens of thousands of species. Second, overharvesting for food, clothing, ornamentation, pets, and medicines has eased for some species, but others are still under threat. Third, deliberate or inadvertent introduction of non-native species has increased exponentially, with some becoming invasive—meaning they reproduce rapidly, spread widely, and have mostly negative effects on native species. Finally, some species are already affected by climate change through distributional changes, timing of life history events, and decreased growth and reproduction and will continue to be affected as climate change progresses.

1. Describe how invasive species can cause habitat loss and habitat degradation.

2. Refer to Figure 55.9. Describe how the loss of gray wolves (*Canis lupus*) has likely resulted in a decrease in hardwood trees in Yellowstone National Park (see Figure 57.9).

3. Suppose you have ecological data for a species of butterfly over the last 50 years. The data show that this species' range has moved north by 100 km and that its emergence occurs 4 days earlier than 50 years ago. Do these data suggest the butterfly species is responding to climate warming? Explain.

TABLE 57.2 | Recent Advances in the Timing of Life History Events That Likely Result from Climate Change

Taxon	Location	Observed changes	Period over which change occurred
Numerous plant species	Europe	Earlier flowering and leaf unfolding by 1.4–3.1 days per decade	30–48 years
	North America	Earlier flowering and leaf unfolding by 1.2–2.0 days per decade	35–63 years
18 butterfly species	United Kingdom	Earlier appearance by 2.8–3.2 days per decade	23 years
Amphibians	United Kingdom	Earlier breeding	25 years
Numerous bird species	Europe, North America	Earlier spring migration by 1.3–4.4 days per decade and earlier breeding by 1.9–4.8 days per decade	30–60 years

Source: G.-R. Walther et al. 2002. *Nature* 416: 389–395.

A major objective of understanding how and why biodiversity loss is occurring is to determine how conservation and management strategies might help preserve species. In the next key concept we will consider some positive steps that are being taken to recover and protect biodiversity.

KEY CONCEPT

57.3

Protecting Biodiversity Requires Conservation and Management Strategies

Learning Objectives

57.3.1 Discuss the guiding principles behind establishing protected areas and promoting sustainable coupled human–natural practices.

57.3.2 Explain how restoration ecology can be used to reestablish the original structure and function of degraded ecosystems.

57.3.3 Discuss the benefits and limitations of captive breeding programs as a method for preserving endangered species.

57.3.4 Describe what can be done to end the trade of endangered species, control invasive species, and make biodiversity a marketable commodity.

As you have seen multiple times in this chapter, human activities play an integral role in biodiversity loss. Consequently, it falls to humans to develop, strengthen, and defend policies that conserve biodiversity. Biodiversity conservation integrates interests from ecological, institutional, and socioeconomic contexts into the

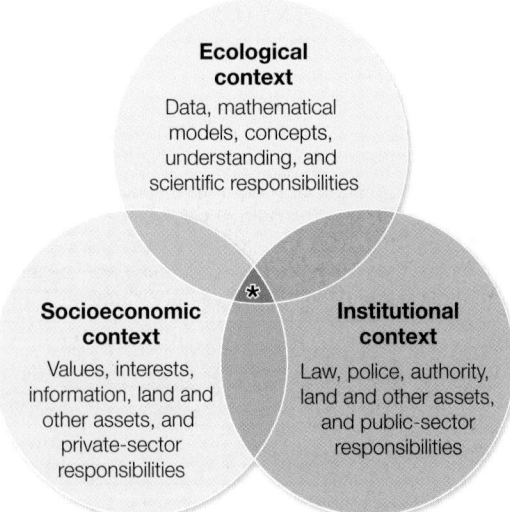

Figure 57.12 Humans Are an Integral Part of Protecting and Managing Biodiversity Protecting and managing biodiversity involves integrating interests from ecological, institutional, and socioeconomic contexts. Partnerships that incorporate these multiple contexts (*) often result in conservation plans with the most support. (From Dennis A. Schenborn, personal communication.)

decision-making process (**Figure 57.12**). Ecologists use scientific theory, empirical data, and tools from a variety of disciplines to help inform the protection and management of endangered and threatened species and ecosystems. They identify the factors that present risks to species and ecosystems and provide that information to managers, landowners, politicians, lawyers, nonprofit agencies, and the general public so that appropriate decisions can be made and action plans can be devised. Partnerships that incorporate these multiple contexts and stakeholders often result in conservation plans with the most support. Here we consider some conservation actions designed to protect and manage biodiversity in more detail.

Protected areas preserve habitat and curtail biodiversity loss

The establishment of **protected areas**, in which habitat loss or degradation is restricted or prohibited, is probably the most important component of efforts to conserve and manage biodiversity. Protected areas allow populations of multiple species to maintain themselves in the preserved habitat and may also serve as nurseries from which individuals can disperse into unprotected areas, replenishing populations that might otherwise become extinct. Without proper habitat, the long-term preservation of biodiversity will be nearly impossible.

Deciding which areas to protect usually involves a complex array of decisions by stakeholders. From an ecological perspective, two criteria need to be met: (1) the candidate habitat must support viable populations of the species it is meant to protect, and (2) the original ecosystem functions and services of the candidate habitat must be mostly intact.

DESIGNING PROTECTED AREAS   The first element in nature-preserve design involves identifying a large area that is relatively undisturbed and can serve as the core of the protected area (**Figure 57.13A**). This core natural area should allow populations of endangered species to maintain themselves and potentially serve as source individuals for populations outside the core area. This typically means that the core area should be large and compact with as little edge habitat as possible, to reduce edge effects.

The second element in designing a protected area involves buffer zones around the core area (**Figure 57.13B**). Buffer zones have some features required by the species of concern but involve less stringent controls on land use. For example, buffer zones allow some resource extraction (e.g., timber, food, or medicines) or recreation while maintaining some of the original habitat.

The third element in nature-preserve design involves habitat connectivity (**Figure 57.13C**), which keeps populations from becoming isolated from the greater metapopulation and thus subject to extinction (see Key Concept 53.4). Traveling from one protected habitat to another requires habitat corridors, or patches that connect blocks of suitable habitat. Insight into the importance of corridors has led to new regional conservation initiatives, among the most notable of which is the Yellowstone to Yukon Conservation Initiative. This joint Canada–United States nonprofit organization has as its goal the sustainable preservation of the mountain ecosystem extending from Yellowstone National Park in the United States to Yukon, Canada. This stretch of land, the largest intact ecosystem of its kind on the planet, contains high-quality habitat

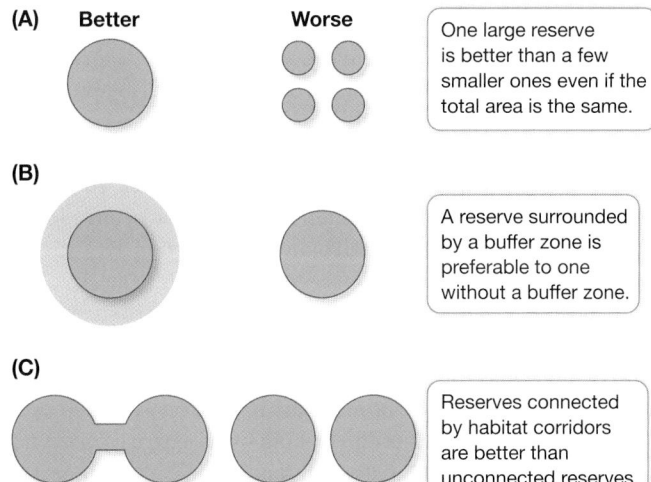

(A) Better   Worse

One large reserve is better than a few smaller ones even if the total area is the same.

(B)

A reserve surrounded by a buffer zone is preferable to one without a buffer zone.

(C)

Reserves connected by habitat corridors are better than unconnected reserves.

Figure 57.13 Nature-Reserve Designs Based on Ecological Principles Some spatial configurations are better than others when designing reserves for fostering biodiversity. (After J. C. Williams et al. 2005. *Environ Model Assess* 10: 163–181.)

for many of North America's most imperiled animals, including grizzly bears (*Ursus arctos*), gray wolves, lynx, and native fishes. The initiative works with landowners to find sustainable ways of preserving high-quality, well-connected wildlife habitat in the region. For example, Banff National Park has 40 human-made corridors for wildlife that cross an 83-kilometer stretch of the Trans-Canada Highway (**Figure 57.14**). Managing the entire region in this way will not only provide passageways to habitat for these species, but will also provide room for their populations to shift in response to global climate change.

▶ **View in Achieve**
Animation 57.2 Habitat Corridors

COUPLED HUMAN–NATURAL SYSTEMS Establishing protected areas is an essential component of efforts to maintain biodiversity, but this action alone is insufficient to stem global biodiversity loss. The extensive landscapes in which people live and extract resources should be integrated into biodiversity conservation efforts. Even urban and suburban areas can contribute to the conservation of species and habitats. The practice of encouraging biodiversity and sustainability in systems where humans and nature are intricately linked is known as **coupled human–natural system ecology**.

Research into coupled human–natural systems builds on the disciplines of ecology, physical sciences, social sciences, and economics. It is based on the principle that most ecosystem services are provided locally, and that people are motivated to work to protect their local interests. In practice, encouraging linkages between humans and nature comes in many forms. For example, the National Wildlife Federation has established a successful program in which people petition to have their backyards certified as wildlife-friendly. Criteria for certification include planting shrubs that provide food for birds and refraining from applying pesticides. In the case of coastal developments exposed to flooding hazards during extreme storms or sea level rise, humans are encouraging the protection and restoration of coastal wetlands and

dunes, so-called green infrastructure, which provide important ecosystem services such as coastal protection, biodiversity, and recreation. Peregrine Falcons (*Falco peregrinus*), once endangered by pesticide use, are thriving in urban settings where tall buildings mimic the cliffs that peregrines naturally nest on, and non-native pigeons are a main prey item. Green roofs, which are roofs covered with soil and native vegetation, are a way of creating parks and habitat, cooling buildings, and dealing with storm-water runoff, all important ecosystem services to humans. France passed a law in 2015 that requires all new buildings constructed in commercial areas to be partially covered by green roofs or solar panels.

Even some industrial sites can support biodiversity. The Turkey Point power plant in southern Florida uses large amounts of water to cool its generating units. To cool the heated water before discharging it, the Florida Power & Light Company dug a system of 38 canals that covers 2,428 hectares. These cooling canals are separated by low-lying berms that support a variety of native and non-native plants. Red mangroves (*Rhizophora mangle*) grow along the edges of the canals. Today they support a thriving population of American crocodiles (*Crocodylus acutus*), a highly endangered species. Crocodiles living in the canals yield about 10% of all young crocodiles born in the United States.

Degraded ecosystems can be restored

When a species is endangered as a consequence of habitat degradation rather than outright habitat loss, protecting the species may require restoring the habitat to a more natural state. Without human assistance, many degraded ecosystems recover very slowly, if at all. **Restoration ecology** involves renewing degraded ecosystems by active human intervention. Ideally, restoration involves reestablishing the original structure and function of native ecosystems through such techniques as active removal of pollutants or non-native species, revegetation to reestablish habitat and food resources, reintroduction of native species, and reestablishment of hydrological processes or disturbance regimes. For example, many

Figure 57.14 Habitat Corridors: Passageways to Recovery
Grizzly bears and other wildlife can use this overpass to travel safely over the Trans-Canada Highway and gain access to more protected area in Banff National Park, Canada.

species depend on particular patterns of disturbance, such as fire or windstorms, to maintain their populations (see Key Concept 55.4).

Recognition of the need for periodic disturbance to maintain healthy ecosystems is a relatively new dimension of conservation biology. We know, for example, that many plant species require periodic fires for successful establishment and survival, but for many years the official policy of the U.S. Forest Service, symbolized by the iconic mascot Smokey Bear, was to suppress all forest fires. Today, however, controlled burning is common, particularly in western North America. In order to use fire as an ecosystem management tool, it is important to know the historical pattern of fires in an area, which can be determined in part by studies of the annual growth rings and fire scars of trees. A schedule of controlled burning that recreates the historical pattern can reduce forest floor litter, avoiding a buildup of fuel that can lead to intense, tree-killing canopy fires.

Sometimes restoration involves using species that act as ecosystem engineers to help restore the original ecosystem. For example, as Key Concept 55.3 and Figure 55.12 described, the recolonization of beavers (*Castor canadensis*), once hunted to near extinction on Minnesota's Kabetogama Peninsula, resulted in more wetlands and higher species diversity as a consequence of the beavers' dam-building activities. You've seen also how vegetation such as grasses can be planted to facilitate sediment capture, accretion, and ultimately the restoration of sea-grass beds, salt marshes, and sand dunes for habitat and coastal protection.

A large-scale terrestrial grassland restoration project—coined the "American Serengeti"—is under way in northeastern Montana. The goal of the project, which is run by the World Wildlife Fund and American Prairie Reserve in cooperation with public land managers and several other private conservation organizations, is to restore and conserve the native prairie and its fauna over a 1.2-million-hectare area near the Missouri River (**Figure 57.15**). When Lewis and Clark mapped this region more than 200 years ago, they saw large herds of bison, elk (*Cervus canadensis*), deer, and pronghorn (*Antilocapra americana*) as well as abundant populations of their predators. But by the middle of the twentieth century, most North American prairies had been converted to cropland or were heavily grazed by domestic livestock, reducing the herds of large mammals to small remnant populations. Most of these populations are too small to maintain their genetic diversity or to function in their original ecological roles. However, the species have survived, so opportunities exist to reintroduce them if their habitat can be restored.

This ambitious restoration and protection project is feasible for three reasons. First, the private land in the area is owned by a small number of ranchers, each of whom owns extensive grazing leases on public lands administered by either U.S. federal agencies or the State of Montana. Second, most of the land has never been plowed, so native vegetation may recover rapidly when grazing pressures are reduced. Third, the area's human population is decreasing. Ranchers are aging, and some of their children are leaving for careers in urban settings. Now that free-ranging herds of several thousand bison and large numbers of elk—along with their predators (wolves)—have established in the Reserve, it is generating millions of dollars to the local economy from tourism alone.

Captive breeding programs can maintain a few species

A few of the world's endangered species can be maintained in captivity while the external threats to their persistence are reduced or removed. However, captive propagation is only a temporary measure that buys time to deal with those threats. Zoos, aquariums, and botanical gardens do not have enough space to maintain adequate populations of more than a small fraction of Earth's endangered and threatened species. Nonetheless, captive propagation can play an important role by maintaining species and their genetic diversity during critical periods, providing a source of individuals for reintroduction into the wild, and raising public awareness of threatened and endangered species.

The California Condor, North America's largest bird, survives today only because of captive propagation (**Figure 57.16**). Two centuries ago, condors ranged from British Columbia to northern Mexico, but by 1978 the wild population was plunging toward extinction. Many of the birds, which are scavengers, had died from ingesting animal carcasses containing lead shot or bullets. To save the condor from certain extinction, the Endangered Species Act was evoked and biologists captured all the remaining condors—only 22 individuals—and initiated a captive breeding program in 1983.

(A)

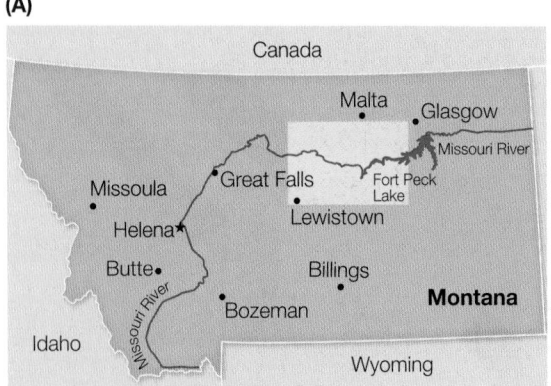

Courtesy of Dennis J. Lingohr/ American Prairie Reserve

(B)

(C) *Bison bison*

© Brandon Smith/Alamy Stock Photo

Figure 57.15 Restoring a North American Prairie
(A) A major prairie restoration project (yellow area) is under way north of the Missouri River in Montana.
(B) Restoration of prairie ecosystems can be as simple as removing fences that restrict large herds of native grazers such as bison. **(C)** The first bison were reintroduced to the area in 2005. (Area map courtesy of American Prairie Reserve.)

The first captive-bred birds were released in the mountains north of Los Angeles in 1992. Since that time, there have also been releases in northern Arizona and Baja California. Today captive-bred birds use the same roosting sites, bathing pools, and mountain ridges that their wild-born predecessors did. In 2003 a wild-born chick fledged in the wild for the first time in more than two decades. By 2017 the number of condors living in the wild had reached 290 with another 170 living in captivity. Most of the major threats to condor survival, including power lines, pesticides, and museum collectors, have been mitigated. Lead poisoning is still a problem, but as of July 1, 2008, under the Ridley–Tree Condor Preservation Act, California hunters are required to use non-lead bullets when hunting in the condor's range. Passage of this legislation marks a change in public attitudes from the days when cattle ranchers, in the mistaken belief that the condors killed livestock, opposed their reintroduction into the wild.

Ending trade is crucial to saving some species

Most endangered species cannot survive any further reductions in their breeding populations, so it is important to prevent their exploitation. The legal mechanism for prohibiting trade in these species or their products is an international agreement called the Convention on International Trade in Endangered Species (CITES). CITES currently prohibits international trade in items such as whale meat, rhinoceros horns, and many species of parrots, orchids, and other animals and plants.

The recent history of elephant poaching for ivory illustrates how complex it can be to prevent hunting of endangered species. CITES instituted a ban on international trade in African elephant ivory in 1989, but demand for ivory remains strong, especially in Asia. As a result, as we described in Key Concept 57.2, poaching of elephants continues in the forests of central and east Africa, where the animals are threatened. However, some countries, including Malawi and Zambia, have so many elephants that government officials kill them to control populations and prevent the animals from damaging crops. This excess of elephants led to the controversial decision to sanction sales of ivory from Namibia, Botswana, Zimbabwe, and South Africa in 2008, the first such sales in close to a decade. More than 100 tons of elephant tusks—the equivalent of 20,000 dead elephants—were auctioned off to authorized buyers from China and Japan and generated $15 million for elephant conservation efforts. Although the 2008 sales were monitored by CITES, concerns remain that the flood of legal ivory will be intermingled with poached ivory.

Species invasions must be controlled or prevented

The best way to reduce the damage caused by invasive species is to prevent their introduction or eradicate them earlier in their establishment phase. Given the tremendous volume of global trade, curtailing it might seem impossible, but some promising strategies do exist. For example, transoceanic transport of invasive species in ballast water could be largely eliminated by the simple procedure of deoxygenating ballast water before it is pumped out. This practice not only kills most organisms in the water but also extends the life of ballast tanks—an economic benefit to shippers.

In 1996 the U.S. Congress responded to concerns about ballast water with legislative action. After years of wrangling, in 2012 the

(A)

(B) *Gymnogyps californianus*

Courtesy of the U.S. Fish and Wildlife Service

© kenowolfpack/Getty Images

Figure 57.16 California Condors Make a Comeback   (A) California Condors raised in captivity are fed by humans wearing hand puppets so that the birds will not imprint on their human captors and will be able to survive in the wild. **(B)** Numbered wing tags allow conservation biologists to identify and track released adult condors. The survival of North America's largest bird depends on this captive propagation project.

U.S. Coast Guard amended its regulations on managing ballast water to set standards for "the allowable concentration of living organisms in ballast water discharged from ships in waters of the United States." Despite the adoption of these strict standards for protecting U.S. waterways, transport of invasive aquatic organisms in ballast water is an international problem whose potential solutions continue to run up against political and economic barriers.

Biodiversity can be conserved as a consequence of its economic value

As we've discussed previously, biodiversity can benefit humans in profound ways, providing important goods and services. You learned in Key Concept 56.5 that ecosystem goods and services can be valued by using a variety of methods to determine what people are willing to pay for them. Some goods such as timber or products from the animal trade are relatively easy to value, but nonmarket services such as the existence of an endangered species or the ability to visit a unique ecosystem are much harder to value. The following examples provide a sense of the nonmarket benefits of conserving rare or endangered species.

WILD DOGS AND ECOTOURISM   Environmentally responsible travel to natural areas, the proceeds of which support conservation efforts and the economic well-being of the local communities, is a major source of income for many developing nations. For example, tourists visiting Africa often express interest in seeing wild dogs (*Lycaon pictus*) (**Figure 57.17**). However, diseases such as rabies and canine distemper, along with habitat loss, road kills, deliberate extermination due to a perceived threat to livestock, and many other factors have decimated wild dog populations, making this the second-most endangered carnivore in Africa. (Another canid, the Ethiopian wolf, *Canis simensis*, is first.) South Africa is home to about 400 of Africa's remaining 5,000 wild dogs, most of which

Figure 57.17 Tourists Are Willing to Pay to See Wildlife
The wild dog (*Lycaon pictus*) is the second-most endangered carnivore in Africa. Tourists come to Kruger National Park in South Africa to catch a glimpse of this rare species.

live in Kruger National Park. Their endangered status has piqued tourist interest in these charismatic animals; a survey of visitors to South Africa revealed that nearly three-fourths of them would be willing to pay an extra U.S. $12 for the opportunity to see wild dogs. Conservation biologists are working with lodge owners and ranchers elsewhere in South Africa and in Kenya to encourage them to reestablish wild dogs in areas from which they have disappeared.

POLLINATORS AND COFFEE   Taylor Ricketts and colleagues at Stanford University assessed the economic value of the pollination services provided by the bees that live in, and depend on, tropical forest patches adjacent to a coffee plantation in Costa Rica. They found that coffee production was highest at the sites that were closest to forest patches. They also hand-pollinated some coffee plants to show that the difference in production was a result of pollination services rather than other environmental conditions. The investigators calculated that the value of pollination services to the plantation on which the experiments were carried out was about $60,000 per year, more than the current conservation incentive payments offered to landowners to preserve forest patches.

KEY CONCEPT
57.3 Recap and Assess

Ecologists use scientific theory, empirical data, and tools from a variety of disciplines to help inform socioeconomic and institutional sectors in the protection and management of biodiversity. To achieve these biodiversity conservation goals, various strategies are employed, including creating protected areas, restoring degraded habitat, breeding endangered species in captivity, ending trade of endangered species, controlling species invasions, and making biodiversity a marketable commodity.

1. Given the principles of reserve design and an understanding of how global warming can affect the distribution of species, design the best possible but realistic protected area for the conservation of terrestrial biodiversity today and in the future.

2. Using the example of the California Condor, describe how species recovery is dependent on the integration of ecological information, socioeconomic interests, and institutional authority.

View in **Achieve**
Activity 57.1 Concept Matching: A Changing Biosphere

▶Investigating LIFE

Q and A **Is the most recent dramatic decline of amphibians the result of a novel fungal pathogen, and if so, what can be done about it?**

The research to date suggests that amphibian declines are caused by multiple human-instigated factors, including habitat loss and pollution, overharvesting, and even exposure to UV radiation, but that the final fatal blow may be the unintended introduction of the novel chytrid fungal pathogen *Batrachochytrium dendrobatidis*, or *Bd*. Population declines and species extinctions of amphibians have occurred at such alarming rates, and in areas that are considered undisturbed, that it can be hard to know how the *Bd* invasion can be stopped or realistically treated in the wild. Despite these hurdles, scientists are recommending several measures to help control the pathogen's destructive effects. The first and foremost recommendation is to reduce the volume of amphibian trade and ensure that amphibians transported long distances are required by law to undergo disease testing and quarantine procedures. Second, improvements in diagnostics and knowledge of the disease are needed in both wild and captive settings. Recently, a method using polymerase chain reaction (PCR) has been developed to definitively identify the fungus in the water and on the skin of potentially infected animals. Third, the risk of spread can be minimized by restricting the movement of captive amphibians, especially to the wild, and by disinfecting footwear and collecting equipment when working in aquatic environments. A variety of strategies that integrate ecological research, socioeconomic interests, and institutional authority will likely be required to save the remaining amphibian species that are susceptible to this highly fatal disease.

Future directions

Although it is tragic that the harlequin frog (*Atelopus varius*), once ubiquitous in the mountains of Costa Rica, and the golden frog (*Atelopus zeteki*), the national symbol of Panama, could disappear so fast, hope still remains. An active area of research involves understanding why some amphibian species, such as the American bullfrog (*Rana catesbeiana*) and African clawed frog (*Xenopus laevis*), are more resistant to *Bd* while other species are highly susceptible. Some mechanisms that could explain species resistance to the disease are (1) the presence of specific types of bacteria or antimicrobial compounds that discourage *Bd* growth, (2) inherent genetic resistance to *Bd*, and (3) certain less virulent strains of *Bd*. More research will be needed to understand the complexities of the disease. In the meantime, captive breeding programs are under way for both the harlequin frog and golden frog so that they might one day be reintroduced into the Costa Rican and Panamanian nature preserves designed to protect them.

© Dr. Paul A. Zahl/Science Source

VISUAL SUMMARY 57

You should be able to relate each summary to the adjacent figures. If you go to this visual summary in **Achieve**, you can follow links to figures, animations, activities, and simulations that will help you consolidate the material.

KEY CONCEPT

57.1 Human Activities Are Changing the Biosphere, Resulting in Biodiversity Loss

- Biodiversity has great value to human society in the form of goods and services, but human activities have caused its rapid decline at genetic, population, species, ecosystem, and global scales.

- Human-caused events coupled with natural events can reduce a species' **effective population size** (number of individuals that can contribute offspring to the next generation), leading to population and species extinctions. Ever-smaller effective population sizes are affected by inbreeding depression, genetic drift, and **demographic stochasticity**.

- Humans are causing biodiversity loss at unprecedented rates, rivaling that of the five previous mass extinction events, which were the result of cataclysmic natural disasters.

- We can estimate the extinction probability of species by taking into account their population sizes, genetic variation, life history traits, and ecology.

Questions

1. How does the loss of biodiversity at one scale affect its loss at other scales?

2. How can reducing a species' effective population size result in population and species extinction?

3. Why is it difficult to determine how many species are extinct, and what factors indicate that a species could be at risk of extinction?

Figure 57.2

Human-caused events
- Habitat destruction
- Overharvesting
- Species invasions
- Climate change

Natural events
- Physical factors
- Disturbance events
- Biological interactions

→ Small population size

Inbreeding depression | Genetic drift | Demographic stochasticity

Lower reproduction

Reduction in individual fitness and population adaptability | Higher mortality | Loss of genetic diversity

Smaller effective population size

Vortex continues

Extinction

KEY CONCEPT

57.2 Most Biodiversity Loss to Date Is Caused by Habitat Loss and Degradation

Go to Animation 57.1

- **Habitat loss** (reduction in habitat quantity) and **habitat degradation** (reduction in habitat quality) have been the major causes of biodiversity loss. Estimates are that humans have transformed and fragmented 50%–60% of the land surface, primarily for agriculture, timber, and livestock grazing.

- Overharvesting of species for food, clothing, ornamentation, pets, and medicines was once the most important and rapid cause of species extinction and is still a concern for some species, and their food webs, if conservation measures are not enacted.

- Deliberate or inadvertent introductions of non-native species have increased exponentially over the last 200 years, with roughly 10% of those species becoming invasive.

- **Invasive** species can endanger native species through predation, competition, and disease. They can cause changes to ecosystem functions or genetic diversity through hybridization with wild populations.

- Human-generated emissions of greenhouse gases are contributing to global climate warming, sea level rise, increased storminess, and ocean acidification, all of which are becoming increasingly important causes of biodiversity loss.

Figure 57.5

© Ed Reschke/Getty Images
© Rolf Nussbaumer Photography/Alamy Stock Photo

Forest edge

Distance edge effect penetrates into forest

Nestling loss (%)

Fledging success (%)

Distance from edge of forest (m)

- Scientific evidence shows that some species have been, or are currently being, affected by climate change through distributional changes, timing of life history events, and decreased growth and reproduction.

Figure 57.9

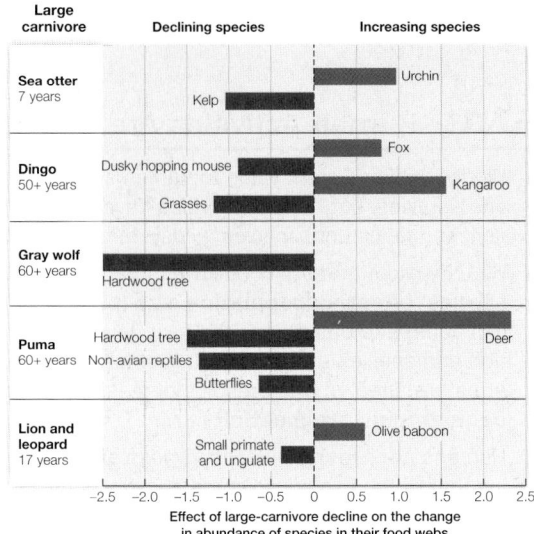

Questions

1. How do habitat loss, degradation, and fragmentation contribute to the extinction of species?

2. Give three reasons why invasive species can have negative effects on biodiversity and ecosystems.

3. Describe how overharvesting and climate change could affect a large carnivore species and its food web.

KEY CONCEPT
57.3 Protecting Biodiversity Requires Conservation and Management Strategies

Go to Activity 57.1 and Animation 57.2

- Ecologists use scientific theory, empirical data, and tools from a variety of disciplines to help inform socioeconomic and institutional sectors in the protection and management of biodiversity.

- Creating **protected areas** and restoring degraded habitat can curtail biodiversity loss. Creating viable protected areas requires establishing core natural areas, buffer zones surrounding them, and habitat corridors connecting them.

- **Restoration ecology** involves renewing degraded ecosystems by re-establishing their original structure and function through active removal of pollutants or non-native species, revegetation to reestablish habitat and food resources, reintroduction of native species, or reestablishment of important processes such as disturbance.

- Captive breeding programs and ending trade can help conserve and manage a few highly threatened or charismatic species.

- The best way to reduce the damage caused by invasive species is to either prevent their introduction through trade restrictions or eradicate them in their early establishment phase.

- Biodiversity can be conserved because of the economic value of the goods and services it provides.

Questions

1. Using ecological principles, what are the best spatial configurations for nature-reserve designs?

2. How can restoration ecology be used to reestablish the original structure and function of degraded ecosystems?

3. What are the best ways to reduce the damage caused by invasive species?

Figure 57.12

Ecological context
Data, mathematical models, concepts, understanding, and scientific responsibilities

Socioeconomic context
Values, interests, information, land and other assets, and private-sector responsibilities

Institutional context
Law, police, authority, land and other assets, and public-sector responsibilities

Figure 57.13

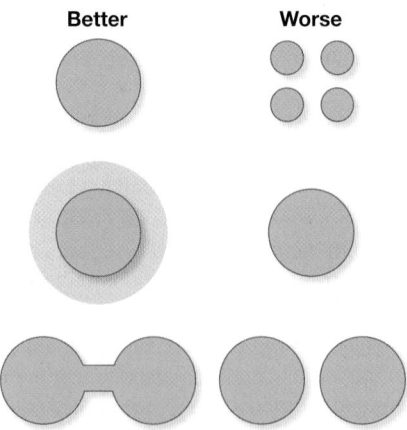

Better   Worse

Go to **Achieve** for the eBook, **LearningCurve**, animations, activities, simulations, and additional resources and assignments.

Appendix A
The Tree of Life

Phylogeny is the organizing principle of modern biological taxonomy. A guiding principle of modern phylogeny is monophyly. A monophyletic group is considered to be one that contains an ancestral lineage and all of its descendants. Any such group can be extracted from a phylogenetic tree with a single cut.

The trees shown here provide a guide to the relationships among the major groups of extant (living) organisms in the tree of life as we have presented them throughout this book. The position of the branching "splits" indicates the relative branching order of the lineages of life, but the time scale is not meant to be uniform. In addition, the groups appearing at the branch tips do not necessarily carry equal phylogenetic "weight." For example, the ginkgo [78] is indeed at the apex of its lineage; this gymnosperm group consists of a single living species. In contrast, a phylogeny of the eudicots [86] could continue on from this point to fill many more trees the size of this one.

The glossary entries that follow are informal descriptions of some major features of the organisms described in Part Six of this book. Each entry gives the group's common name, followed by the formal scientific name of the group (in parentheses). Numbers in square brackets reference the location of the respective groups on the tree.

It is sometimes convenient to use an informal name to refer to a collection of organisms that are not monophyletic but nonetheless all share (or all lack) some common attribute. We call these "convenience terms"; such groups are indicated in these entries by quotation marks, and we do not give them formal scientific names. Examples include "prokaryotes," "protists," and "algae." Note that these groups cannot be removed with a single cut; they represent a collection of distantly related groups that appear in different parts of the tree. We also use quotation marks here to designate two groups of fungi that are not believed to be monophyletic.

Go to **Achieve** for interactive versions of these trees, with links to photos, distribution maps, species lists, and identification keys.

Figure A1

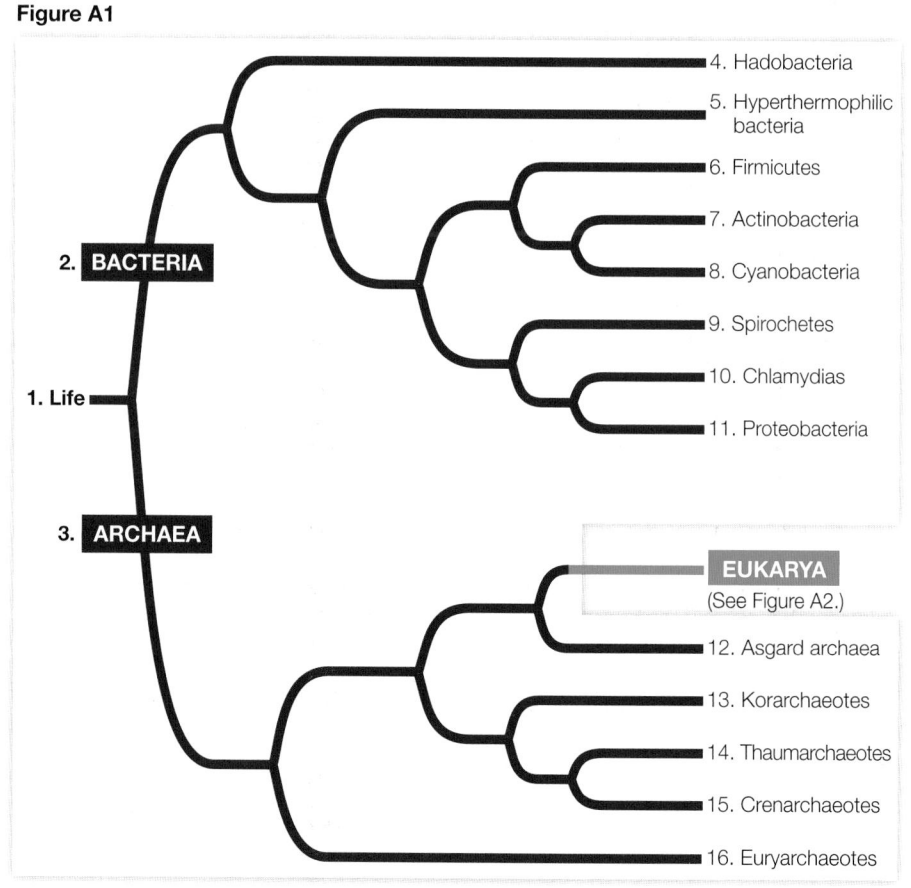

Figures A1 and A2 The Tree of Life
In this rendition, the prokaryotic lineages are shown in Figure A1 and the eukaryotic lineages are in Figure A2. Among the eukaryotes, the microbial lineages are shown in teal. The eukaryote groups that contain major radiations of large multicellular organisms are shown in brown (brown algae), green (Plantae), orange (fungi), and red (animals).

 See the **Interactive Tree of Life**
Life12e.com/tree

Figure A2

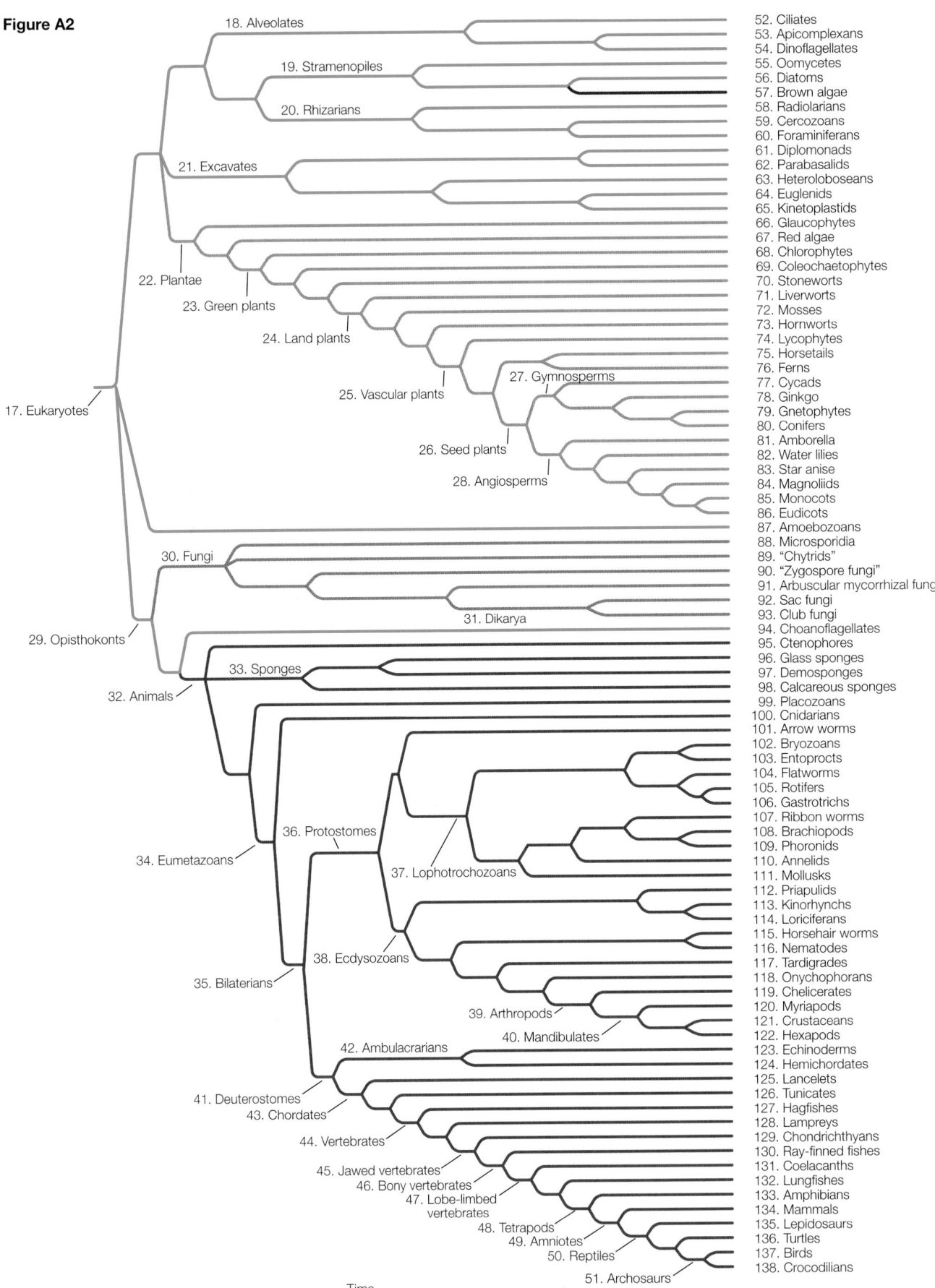

18. Alveolates
19. Stramenopiles
20. Rhizarians
21. Excavates
22. Plantae
23. Green plants
24. Land plants
25. Vascular plants
26. Seed plants
27. Gymnosperms
28. Angiosperms
17. Eukaryotes
30. Fungi
31. Dikarya
29. Opisthokonts
33. Sponges
32. Animals
34. Eumetazoans
36. Protostomes
37. Lophotrochozoans
38. Ecdysozoans
35. Bilaterians
39. Arthropods
40. Mandibulates
42. Ambulacrarians
41. Deuterostomes
43. Chordates
44. Vertebrates
45. Jawed vertebrates
46. Bony vertebrates
47. Lobe-limbed vertebrates
48. Tetrapods
49. Amniotes
50. Reptiles
51. Archosaurs

52. Ciliates
53. Apicomplexans
54. Dinoflagellates
55. Oomycetes
56. Diatoms
57. Brown algae
58. Radiolarians
59. Cercozoans
60. Foraminiferans
61. Diplomonads
62. Parabasalids
63. Heteroloboseans
64. Euglenids
65. Kinetoplastids
66. Glaucophytes
67. Red algae
68. Chlorophytes
69. Coleochaetophytes
70. Stoneworts
71. Liverworts
72. Mosses
73. Hornworts
74. Lycophytes
75. Horsetails
76. Ferns
77. Cycads
78. Ginkgo
79. Gnetophytes
80. Conifers
81. Amborella
82. Water lilies
83. Star anise
84. Magnoliids
85. Monocots
86. Eudicots
87. Amoebozoans
88. Microsporidia
89. "Chytrids"
90. "Zygospore fungi"
91. Arbuscular mycorrhizal fungi
92. Sac fungi
93. Club fungi
94. Choanoflagellates
95. Ctenophores
96. Glass sponges
97. Demosponges
98. Calcareous sponges
99. Placozoans
100. Cnidarians
101. Arrow worms
102. Bryozoans
103. Entoprocts
104. Flatworms
105. Rotifers
106. Gastrotrichs
107. Ribbon worms
108. Brachiopods
109. Phoronids
110. Annelids
111. Mollusks
112. Priapulids
113. Kinorhynchs
114. Loriciferans
115. Horsehair worms
116. Nematodes
117. Tardigrades
118. Onychophorans
119. Chelicerates
120. Myriapods
121. Crustaceans
122. Hexapods
123. Echinoderms
124. Hemichordates
125. Lancelets
126. Tunicates
127. Hagfishes
128. Lampreys
129. Chondrichthyans
130. Ray-finned fishes
131. Coelacanths
132. Lungfishes
133. Amphibians
134. Mammals
135. Lepidosaurs
136. Turtles
137. Birds
138. Crocodilians

Time

A

acoels (*Acoela*) A group of reduced bilaterians [35] of uncertain phylogenetic relationships. Placed variously among the protostomes [36], deuterostomes [41], or as a sister group of all other bilaterians [35].

actinobacteria (*Actinobacteria*) [7] High G-C Gram-positive bacteria [2] with genomes that have a high ratio of G-C to A-T nucleotide base pairs.

"algae" A term of convenience encompassing various distantly related groups of aquatic, photosynthetic eukaryotes [17].

ambulacrarians (*Ambulacraria*) [41] The echinoderms [123] and hemichordates [124].

amniotes (*Amniota*) [49] Mammals, reptiles, and their extinct close relatives. Characterized by many adaptations to terrestrial life, including an amniote egg (with a unique set of membranes—the yolk sac, amnion, chorion, and allantois), a water-repellant epidermis (with epidermal scales, hair, or feathers), and in males, a penis that allows internal fertilization.

amoebozoans (Amoebozoa) [87] A group of eukaryotes [17] that use lobe-shaped pseudopods for locomotion and to engulf food. Major amoebozoan groups include the loboseans, plasmodial slime molds, and cellular slime molds.

amphibians (*Amphibia*) [133] Tetrapods [48] with glandular skin that lacks epidermal scales, feathers, or hair. Many amphibian species undergo a complete metamorphosis from an aquatic larval form to a terrestrial adult form, although direct development is also common. Major amphibian groups include frogs and toads (anurans), salamanders, and caecilians.

annelids (*Annelida*) [110] Segmented worms, including earthworms, leeches, and polychaetes. One of the major groups of lophotrochozoans [37].

anthozoans (*Anthozoa*) One of the major groups of cnidarians [100]. Includes the sea anemones, sea pens, and corals.

apicomplexans (*Apicomplexa*) [53] Parasitic alveolates [18] characterized by having an apical complex at some stage in the life cycle.

arbuscular mycorrhizal fungi (*Glomeromycotina*) [91] A group of fungi [30] that associate with plant roots in a close symbiotic relationship.

archaea (*Archaea*) [3] One of the two primary divisions of life [1], and one of the three domains of life. The term is often used only for the prokaryotic archaea, which are unicellular organisms that lack a nucleus and lack peptidoglycan in the cell wall. Recent studies indicate that eukaryotes [17] are most closely related to the lokiarchaeotes [12] among the archaea.

archosaurs (*Archosauria*) [51] A group of reptiles [50] that includes dinosaurs and crocodilians [138]. Most dinosaur groups became extinct at the end of the Cretaceous; birds [137] are the only surviving dinosaurs.

arrow worms (*Chaetognatha*) [101] Small planktonic or benthic predatory marine worms with fins and a pair of hooked, prey-grasping spines on each side of the head.

arthropods (*Arthropoda*) The largest group of ecdysozoans [38]. Arthropods are characterized by a stiff exoskeleton, segmented body, and jointed appendages. Includes the chelicerates [119], myriapods [120], crustaceans [121], and hexapods (insects and their relatives) [122].

Asgard archaea [12] A group of recently discovered archaeal lineages (including lokiarchaeotes) that are the closest known prokaryotic relatives of eukaryotes.

B

bacteria (*Bacteria or Eubacteria*) [2] One of the two primary divisions of life [1], and one of the three domains of life. Unicellular organisms lacking a nucleus, possessing distinctive ribosomes and initiator tRNA, and generally containing peptidoglycan in the cell wall. Different bacterial groups are distinguished primarily on the basis of nucleotide sequence data.

bilaterians (*Bilateria*) [35] Those animal groups characterized by bilateral symmetry and three distinct tissue types (endoderm, ectoderm, and mesoderm). Includes the protostomes [36] and deuterostomes [41].

birds (*Aves*) [137] Feathered, flying (or secondarily flightless) tetrapods [48].

bivalves (*Bivalvia*) A major mollusk [111] group; clams, oysters, and mussels. Bivalves typically have two similar hinged shells that are each asymmetrical across the midline.

brachiopods (*Brachiopoda*) [108] Lophotrochozoans [37] with two similar hinged shells that are each symmetrical across the midline. Superficially resemble bivalve mollusks, except for the shell symmetry.

brown algae (*Phaeophyta*) [57] Multicellular, almost exclusively marine stramenopiles [19] generally containing the pigment fucoxanthin as well as chlorophylls *a* and *c* in their chloroplasts.

bryozoans (*Ectoprocta or Bryozoa*) [102] A group of marine and freshwater lophotrochozoans [37] that live in colonies attached to substrates; also known as ectoprocts or moss animals.

C

cellular slime molds (*Dictyostelida*) Amoebozoans [87] in which individual amoebas aggregate under stress to form a multicellular pseudoplasmodium.

cephalopods (*Cephalopoda*) Active, predatory mollusks [111] in which the molluscan foot has been modified into muscular hydrostatic arms or tentacles. Includes octopuses, squid, and nautiluses.

cercozoans (*Cercozoa*) [59] Unicellular eukaryotes [17] that feed by means of threadlike pseudopods. Group together with foraminiferans [60] and radiolarians [58] to make up the rhizarians [20].

chelicerates (*Chelicerata*) [119] A major group of arthropods [39] with pointed appendages (chelicerae) used to grasp food (as opposed to the chewing mandibles of most other arthropods). Includes arachnids, horseshoe crabs, sea spiders, and extinct sea scorpions.

chitons (*Polyplacophora*) Flattened, slow-moving mollusks [111] with a dorsal protective calcareous covering made up of eight articulating plates.

chlamydias (*Chlamydiae*) [10] A group of very small Gram-negative bacteria; they live as intracellular parasites of other organisms.

chlorophytes (*Chlorophyta*) [68] The most abundant and diverse group of green algae, including freshwater, marine, and terrestrial forms; some are unicellular, others colonial, and still others multicellular. Chlorophytes use chlorophylls *a* and *c* in their photosynthesis.

chondrichthyans (*Chondrichthyes*) [129] One of the two main groups of jawed vertebrates [45]; includes sharks, rays, and chimaeras. They have cartilaginous skeletons and paired fins.

chordates (*Chordata*) [43] One of the three major groups of deuterostomes [41], characterized by the presence (at some point in development) of a notochord, a hollow dorsal nerve cord, and a post-anal tail. Includes the lancelets [125], tunicates [126], and vertebrates [44].

"chytrids" [89] A term of convenience used for a paraphyletic group of mostly aquatic, microscopic fungi [30] with flagellated gametes. Some exhibit alternation of generations.

ciliates (*Ciliophora*) [52] Alveolates [18] with numerous cilia and two types of nuclei (micronuclei and macronuclei).

clitellates (*Clitellata*) Annelids [110] with gonads contained in a swelling (called a clitellum) toward the head of the animal. Includes earthworms (oligochaetes) and leeches.

club fungi (*Basidiomycota*) [93] Fungi [30] that, if multicellular, bear the products of meiosis on club-shaped basidia and possess a long-lasting dikaryotic stage. Some are unicellular.

cnidarians (*Cnidaria*) [100] Aquatic, mostly marine eumetazoans [34] with specialized stinging organelles (nematocysts) used for prey capture and defense, and a blind gastrovascular cavity. The sister group of bilaterians [35].

coleochaetophytes (*Coleochaetales*) [69] Multicellular green algae characterized by a flattened growth form composed of thin-walled cells. Thought to be the sister group to the stoneworts [70] plus land plants [24].

conifers (*Pinophyta or Coniferophyta*) [80] Cone-bearing, woody seed plants [26].

craniates (*Craniata*) Some biologist exclude the hagfishes [127] from the vertebrates [44], and use the term craniates to refer to the two groups combined.

crenarchaeota (*Crenarchaeota*) [15] A major and diverse group of archaea [3], defined on the basis of rRNA base sequences. Many are extremophiles (inhabit extreme environments), but the group may also be the most abundant archaea in the marine environment.

crocodilians (*Crocodylia*) [138] A group of large, predatory, aquatic archosaurs [51]. The closest living relatives of birds [137]. Includes alligators, caimans, crocodiles, and gharials.

crustaceans (*Crustacea*) [121]   A major group of marine, freshwater, and terrestrial arthropods [39] with a head, thorax, and abdomen (although the head and thorax may be fused), covered with a thick exoskeleton, and with two-part appendages. Crustaceans undergo metamorphosis from a larva. Includes decapods, isopods, krill, barnacles, amphipods, copepods, and ostracods.

ctenophores (*Ctenophora*) [95]   Radially symmetrical, gelatinous marine animals [32], with eight rows of fused plates of cilia (called ctenes).

cyanobacteria (*Cyanobacteria*) [8]   A group of unicellular, colonial, or filamentous bacteria that conduct photosynthesis using chlorophyll *a*.

cycads (*Cycadophyta*) [77]   Palmlike gymnosperms with large, compound leaves.

cyclostomes (*Cyclostomata*)   This term refers to the possibly monophyletic group of lampreys [128] and hagfishes [127]. Molecular data support this group, but morphological data suggest that lampreys are more closely related to jawed vertebrates [45] than to hagfishes.

D

deuterostomes (*Deuterostomia*) [41]   One of the two major groups of bilaterians [35], in which the mouth forms at the opposite end of the embryo from the blastopore in early development (contrast with protostomes). Includes the ambulacrarians [42] and chordates [43].

diatoms (*Bacillariophyta*) [56]   Unicellular, photosynthetic stramenopiles [19] with glassy cell walls in two parts.

Dikarya [31]   A group of fungi [30] in which two genetically different haploid nuclei coexist and divide within the same hypha; includes the club fungi [93] and sac fungi [92].

dinoflagellates (*Dinoflagellata*) [54]   A group of alveolates [18] usually possessing two flagella, one in an equatorial groove and the other in a longitudinal groove; many are photosynthetic.

dinosaurs (*Dinosauria*)   A group of archosaurs [51] that includes birds [137] as well as many extinct groups from the Mesozoic. Extinct Mesozoic dinosaurs included some of the largest terrestrial vertebrates that have ever lived. Informally, many people use the term to refer only to the extinct Mesozoic species.

diplomonads (*Diplomonadida*) [61]   A group of eukaryotes [17] lacking mitochondria; most have two nuclei, each with four associated flagella.

dry-nosed primates (*Haplorhini*)   A group of primate mammals [134] that includes apes, monkeys, and tarsiers.

E

ecdysozoans (*Ecdysozoa*) [38]   One of the two major groups of protostomes [36], characterized by periodic molting of their exoskeletons. Nematodes [116] and arthropods [39] are the largest ecdysozoan groups.

echinoderms (*Echinodermata*) [123]   A major group of marine deuterostomes [41] with fivefold radial symmetry (at some stage of life) and an endoskeleton made of calcified plates and spines. Includes sea stars, crinoids, sea urchins, sea cucumbers, and brittle stars.

embryophytes   *See* land plants [24].

entoprocts (*Entoprocta*) [103]   A group of marine and freshwater lophotrochozoans [37] that live as single individuals or in colonies attached to substrates. They are the sister group of bryozoans, from which they differ in having both their mouth and anus inside the lophophore (the anus is outside the lophophore in bryozoans).

euglenids (*Euglenida*) [64]   Flagellated excavates [21] characterized by a pellicle composed of spiraling strips of protein under the cell membrane; the mitochondria have disc-shaped cristae. Some are photosynthetic.

eukaryotes (*Eukarya*) [17]   A group of organisms made up of one or more complex cells in which the genetic material is contained in nuclei. Includes all plants [22], fungi [30], and animals [32]. One of the three main domains of life.

euphyllophytes (*Euphyllophyta*)   The group of vascular plants [25] that is sister to the lycophytes [74] and which includes all plants with megaphylls.

euryarchaeotes (*Euryarchaeota*) [16]   A major group of archaea [3], diagnosed on the basis of rRNA sequences. Includes many methanogens, extreme halophiles, and thermophiles.

eutherians (*Eutheria*)   A group of viviparous mammals [134], well developed at birth (contrast with prototherians and marsupials, the other two groups of mammals). Most familiar mammals outside the Australian and South American regions are eutherians (see Table 31.1).

excavates (*Excavata*) [21]   A diverse group of unicellular, flagellated eukaryotes, many of which possess a feeding groove; some lack mitochondria.

F

firmicutes (*Firmicutes*) [6]   Mostly low-GC Gram-positive bacteria [2] with genomes that have a low ratio of G-C to A-T nucleotide base pairs.

flatworms (*Platyhelminthes*) [104]   A group of dorsoventrally flattened and generally elongated soft-bodied lophotrochozoans [37]. May be free-living or parasitic, found in marine, freshwater, or damp terrestrial environments. Major flatworm groups include the tapeworms, flukes, monogeneans, and turbellarians.

foraminiferans (*Foraminifera*) [60]   Amoeboid organisms with fine, branched pseudopods that form a food-trapping net. Most produce external shells of calcium carbonate.

G

gastropods (*Gastropoda*)   The largest group of mollusks [111]. Gastropods possess a well-defined head with two or four sensory tentacles (often terminating in eyes) and a ventral foot. Most species have a single coiled or spiraled shell. Common in marine, freshwater, and terrestrial environments.

gastrotrichs (*Gastrotricha*) [106]   Tiny (0.06–3.0 mm), elongated acoelomate lophotrochozoans [37] that are covered in cilia. They live in marine, freshwater, and wet terrestrial habitats. They are simultaneous hermaphrodites.

ginkgo (*Ginkgophyta*) [78]   A gymnosperm [27] group with only one living species. The ginkgo seed is surrounded by a fleshy tissue not derived from an ovary wall and hence not a fruit.

glaucophytes (*Glaucophyta*) [66]   Unicellular freshwater algae with chloroplasts containing traces of peptidoglycan, the characteristic cell wall material of bacteria. Thought to be the sister group to the rest of Plantae.

gnathostomes (*Gnathostomata*)   *See* jawed vertebrates [45].

gnetophytes (*Gnetophyta*) [79]   A gymnosperm [27] group with three very different lineages; all have wood with vessels, unlike other gymnosperms.

green plants (*Viridiplantae*) [23]   Organisms with chlorophylls *a* and *b*, cellulose-containing cell walls, starch as a carbohydrate storage product, and chloroplasts surrounded by two membranes.

H

hadobacteria (*Hadobacteria*) [4]   A group of extremophilic bacteria [2] that includes the genera *Deinococcus* and *Thermus*.

hagfishes (*Myxini*) [127]   Elongated, slimy-skinned vertebrates [44] with three small accessory hearts, a partial cranium, and no stomach or paired fins. *See also* craniates; cyclostomes.

hemichordates (*Hemichordata*) [124]   One of the two primary groups of ambulacrarians [42]; marine wormlike organisms with a three-part body plan.

heteroloboseans (*Heterolobosea*) [63]   Colorless excavates [21] that can transform among amoeboid, flagellated, and encysted stages.

hexapods (*Hexapoda*) [122]   A major group of arthropods [39] characterized by a reduction (from the ancestral arthropod condition) to six walking appendages, and the consolidation of three body segments to form a thorax. Includes insects and their relatives (see Table 30.2).

hornworts (*Anthocerophyta*) [73]   Nonvascular land plants with sporophytes that grow from the base. Cells contain a single large, platelike chloroplast.

horsehair worms (*Nematomorpha*) [115]   A group of very thin, elongated, wormlike fresh-water ecdysozoans [38]. Largely nonfeeding as adults; as larvae, they are parasites of insects and crayfishes.

horsetails (*Sphenophyta* or *Equisetophyta*) [75]   Vascular plants [25] with reduced megaphylls in whorls.

hydrozoans (*Hydrozoa*)   A group of cnidarians [100]. Most species go through both polyp and medusa stages, although one stage or the other is eliminated in some species.

hyperthermophilic bacteria [5]   A group of thermophilic bacteria [2] that live in volcanic vents, hot springs, and underground oil reservoirs; includes the genera *Aquifex* and *Thermotoga*.

I

insects (*Insecta*)   The largest group within the hexapods [122]. Insects are characterized by exposed mouthparts and one pair of antennae containing a sensory receptor called a Johnston's organ. Most have two pairs of wings as adults.

There are more described species of insects than all other groups of life [1] combined, and many species remain to be discovered. The major insect groups are described in Table 30.2.

J

jawed vertebrates (*Gnathostomata*) [45] A major group of vertebrates [44] with jawed mouths. Includes chondrichthyans [129], ray-finned fishes [130], and lobe-limbed vertebrates [47].

K

kinetoplastids (*Kinetoplastida*) [65] Unicellular, flagellated organisms characterized by the presence in their single mitochondrion of a kinetoplast (a structure containing multiple, circular DNA molecules).

kinorhynchs (*Kinorhyncha*) [113] Small (< 1 mm) marine ecdysozoans [38] with bodies in 13 segments and a retractable proboscis.

korarchaeotes (*Korarchaeota*) [13] A group of archaea [3] known only by evidence from nucleic acids derived from hot springs.

L

lampreys (*Petromyzontiformes*) [128] Elongated, eel-like vertebrates [44] that often have rasping and sucking discs for mouths.

lancelets (*Cephalochordata*) [125] A group of weakly swimming, eel-like benthic marine chordates [43].

land plants (*Embryophyta*) [24] Plants with embryos that develop within protective structures; also called embryophytes. Both sporophytes and gametophytes of land plants are multicellular. Land plants possess a cuticle. Major groups are the liverworts [71], mosses [72], hornworts [73], and vascular plants [25].

lepidosaurs (*Lepidosauria*) [135] Reptiles [50] with overlapping scales. Includes tuataras and squamates (lizards, snakes, and amphisbaenians).

liverworts (*Hepatophyta*) [71] Nonvascular land plants lacking stomata; the stalk of the sporophyte elongates along its entire length.

lobe-limbed vertebrates (*Sarcopterygii*) [47] One of the two major groups of bony vertebrates [46], characterized by jointed appendages (paired fins or limbs).

loboseans (*Lobosea*) A group of unicellular amoebozoans [87]; includes the most familiar amoebas (e.g., *Amoeba proteus*).

lokiarchaeotes (*Lokiarchaeota*) [12] A group of archaea [3] known from deep-sea hydrothermal vents. Among the known archaea, they are among the closest relatives of the eukaryotes [17]. See Asgard archaea.

lophotrochozoans (*Lophotrochozoa*) [37] One of the two main groups of protostomes [36]. This group is morphologically diverse, and is supported primarily by information from gene sequences. Includes bryozoans [102], entoprocts [103], flatworms [104], rotifers [105], gastrotrichs [106], ribbon worms [107], brachiopods [108], phoronids [109], annelids [110], and mollusks [111].

loriciferans (*Loricifera*) [114] Small (< 1 mm) ecdysozoans [38] with bodies in four parts, covered with six plates.

lungfishes (*Dipnoi*) [132] A group of aquatic lobe-limbed vertebrates [47] that are the closest living relatives of the tetrapods [48]. They have a modified swim bladder used to absorb oxygen from air, so some species can survive the temporary drying of their habitat.

lycophytes (*Lycopodiophyta*) [74] Vascular plants [25] characterized by microphylls; includes the club mosses, spike mosses, and quillworts.

M

magnoliids (*Magnoliidae*) [84] A major group of angiosperms [28] possessing two cotyledons and pollen grains with a single opening. The group is defined primarily by nucleotide sequence data; it is more closely related to the eudicots and monocots than to three other small angiosperm groups.

mammals (*Mammalia*) [134] A group of tetrapods [48] with hair covering all or part of their skin; females produce milk to feed their developing young. Includes the prototherians, marsupials, and eutherians.

mandibulates (*Mandibulata*) [40] Arthropods [39] that include mandibles as mouthparts. Includes myriapods [120], crustaceans [121], and hexapods [122].

marsupials (*Marsupialia*) Mammals [134] in which the female typically has a marsupium (a pouch for rearing young, which are born at an extremely early stage in development). Includes such familiar mammals as opossums, koalas, and kangaroos.

microsporidia (*Microsporidia*) [88] A group of parasitic unicellular relatives of fungi [30] that lack mitochondria and have walls that contain chitin.

mollusks (*Mollusca*) [111] One of the major groups of lophotrochozoans [37], mollusks have bodies composed of a foot, a mantle (which often secretes a hard, calcareous shell), and a visceral mass. Includes monoplacophorans, chitons, bivalves, gastropods, and cephalopods.

monilophytes (*Monilophyta*) A group of vascular plants [25], sister to the seed plants [26], characterized by overtopping and possession of megaphylls; includes the horsetails [75] and ferns [76].

monoplacophorans (*Monoplacophora*) Mollusks [111] with segmented body parts and a single, thin, flat, rounded, bilateral shell.

mosses (*Bryophyta*) [72] Nonvascular land plants with true stomata and erect, "leafy" gametophytes; sporophytes elongate by apical cell division.

mycoplasmas Firmicutes [6] that lack cell walls and are among the smallest known cellular organisms.

myriapods (*Myriapoda*) [120] Arthropods [39] characterized by an elongated, segmented trunk with many legs. Include centipedes and millipedes.

N

nematodes (*Nematoda*) [116] A large group of elongated, unsegmented ecdysozoans [38] with thick, multilayer cuticles. They are among the most abundant and diverse animals, although most species have not yet been described. Includes free-living predators and scavengers, as well as parasites of most species of land plants [24] and animals [32].

neopterans (*Neoptera*) The largest group of flying (winged) hexapods [122], recognizable by the fact that they can fold their wings close to their body upon landing.

O

oomycetes (*Oomycota*) [55] Water molds and relatives; absorptive heterotrophs with nutrient-absorbing, filamentous hyphae.

opisthokonts (*Opisthokonta*) [29] A group of eukaryotes [17] in which the flagellum on motile cells, if present, is posterior. Includes the fungi [30], animals [32], and choanoflagellates [94].

P

parabasalids (*Parabasalia*) [62] A group of unicellular eukaryotes [17] that lack mitochondria; they possess flagella in clusters near the anterior of the cell.

phoronids (*Phoronida*) [109] A small group of sessile, wormlike marine lophotrochozoans [37] that secrete chitinous tubes and feed using a lophophore.

placozoans (*Placozoa*) [99] A poorly known group of structurally simple, asymmetrical, flattened, transparent animals found in coastal marine tropical and subtropical seas. Most evidence suggests that placozoans are secondarily simplified eumetazoans [34].

plantae (*Plantae*) [22] The most broadly defined plant group, corresponding to the group that descended from the primary endosymbiotic event that gave rise to chloroplasts. Includes green plants [23] as well as glaucophytes [66] and red algae [67]. In most parts of this book, we use the word "plant" as synonymous with "land plant" [24], a more restrictive definition.

plasmodial slime molds (*Myxogastrida*) Amoebozoans [87] that in their feeding stage consist of a coenocyte called a plasmodium.

pogonophorans (*Pogonophora*) Deep-sea annelids [110] that lack a mouth or digestive tract; they feed by taking up dissolved organic matter, facilitated by endosymbiotic bacteria in a specialized organ (the trophosome).

polychaetes (*Polychaeta*) A group of mostly marine annelids [110] with one or more pairs of eyes and one or more pairs of feeding tentacles; parapodia and setae extend from most body segments. May be paraphyletic with respect to the clitellates.

priapulids (*Priapulida*) [112] A small group of cylindrical, unsegmented, wormlike marine ecdysozoans [38] that take their name from their phallic appearance.

primates (*Primates*) A group of mammals [134] that includes apes, monkeys, tarsiers, lemurs, and lorises.

progymnosperms (*Progymnospermophyta*) An extinct group of seedless, vascular plants [25] that were among the first large, woody trees; lived from the middle Devonian to the early Carboniferous.

"prokaryotes"   Unicellular organisms that do not have nuclei. Not a monophyletic group; as commonly used, includes the bacteria [2] and archaea [3]. A term of convenience encompassing all cellular organisms that are not eukaryotes. (Contrast with eukaryotes.)

proteobacteria (*Proteobacteria*) [11]   A large and extremely diverse group of Gram-negative bacteria that includes many pathogens, nitrogen fixers, and photosynthesizers. Includes the alpha, beta, gamma, delta, and epsilon proteobacteria.

"protists"   A term of convenience used to encompass a large number of distinct and distantly related groups of eukaryotes, many but far from all of which are microbial and unicellular. Essentially a "catch-all" term for any eukaryotic group not contained within the land plants [24], fungi [30], or animals [32].

protostomes (*Protostomia*) [36]   One of the two major groups of bilaterians [35]. In protostomes, the mouth typically forms from the blastopore (if present) in early development (contrast with deuterostomes). The major protostome groups are the lophotrochozoans [37] and ecdysozoans [38].

prot[o]therians (*Prototheria*)   A mostly extinct group of mammals [134], common during the Cretaceous and early Cenozoic. The five living species—four echidnas and the duck-billed platypus—are the only extant egg-laying mammals.

pterygotes (*Pterygota*)   Flying (winged) insects, the largest group of hexapods [122].

R

radiolarians (*Radiolaria*) [58]   Amoeboid organisms with needlelike pseudopods supported by microtubules. Most have glassy internal skeletons.

ray-finned fishes (*Actinopterygii*) [130]   A highly diverse group of freshwater and marine bony vertebrates [46]. They have reduced swim bladders that often function as hydrostatic organs and fins supported by soft rays (lepidotrichia). Includes most familiar fishes.

red algae (*Rhodophyta*) [67]   Mostly multi-cellular marine and freshwater algae characterized by the presence of phycoerythrin in their chloroplasts.

reptiles (*Reptilia*) [50]   One of the two major groups of extant amniotes [49], supported on the basis of similar skull structure and gene sequences. The term "reptiles" traditionally excluded birds [137], but the resulting group is then clearly paraphyletic. As used in this book, living reptiles include turtles [136], lepidosaurs [135], birds [137], and crocodilians [138].

rhizarians (*Rhizaria*) [20]   Mostly amoeboid unicellular eukaryotes with pseudopods, many with external or internal shells. Includes the foraminiferans [60], cercozoans [59], and radiolarians [58].

rhyniophytes (*Rhyniophyta*)   A group of early vascular plants [25] that appeared in the Silurian and became extinct in the Devonian. Possessed dichotomously branching stems with terminal sporangia but no true leaves or roots.

ribbon worms (*Nemertea*) [107]   A group of unsegmented lophotrochozoans [37] with an eversible proboscis used to capture prey. Mostly marine, but some species live in fresh water or on land.

rotifers (*Rotifera*) [105]   Tiny (< 0.5 mm) lophotrochozoans [37] with a pseudocoelomate body cavity that functions as a hydrostatic organ, and a ciliated feeding organ called the corona that surrounds the head. Rotifers live in freshwater and wet terrestrial habitats.

S

sac fungi (*Ascomycota*) [92]   Fungi that bear the products of meiosis within sacs (asci) if the organism is multicellular. Some are unicellular.

scyphozoans (*Scyphozoa*)   Marine cnidarians [100] in which the medusa stage dominates the life cycle. Commonly known as jellyfishes.

"seed ferns"   A paraphyletic group of loosely related, extinct seed plants that flourished in the Devonian and Carboniferous. Characterized by large, frondlike leaves that bore seeds.

simians (*Simiiformes*)   A group of primate mammals [134] that consists of apes and monkeys.

spirochetes (*Spirochaetes*) [9]   Motile, Gram-negative bacteria with a helically coiled structure and characterized by axial filaments.

sponges (*Porifera*) [33]   A group of relatively asymmetrical, filter-feeding animals that lack a gut or nervous system and generally lack differentiated tissues. Includes the glass sponges [96], demosponges [97], and calcareous sponges [98].

squamates (*Squamata*)   The major group of lepidosaurs [135], characterized by the possession of movable quadrate bones (which allow the upper jaw to move independently of the rest of the skull) and hemipenes (a paired set of eversible penises, or penes) in males. Includes the lizards (a paraphyletic group), snakes, and amphisbaenians.

staphylococci (*Staphylococcus*)   Firmicutes [6] that are abundant on the surface of the human body; can cause skin diseases and respiratory, intestinal, and wound infections.

stoneworts (*Charales*) [70]   Multicellular green algae with branching, apical growth and plasmodesmata between adjacent cells. The closest living relatives of the land plants [24], they retain the egg in the parent organism.

stramenopiles (*Heterokonta* or *Stramenopila*) [19]   Organisms having, at some stage in their life cycle, two unequal flagella, the longer possessing rows of tubular hairs. Chloroplasts, when present, are surrounded by four membranes. Major stramenopile groups include the brown algae [57], diatoms [56], and oomycetes [55].

streptophytes (*Streptophyta*)   All green plants [23] other than chlorophytes [68].

T

tardigrades (*Tardigrada*) [117]   Small (< 1.5 mm) ecdysozoans [38] with fleshy, unjointed legs and no circulatory or gas exchange organs. They live in marine sands, in temporary freshwater pools, and on the water films of plants. Also called water bears.

tetrapods (*Tetrapoda*) [48]   The major group of lobe-limbed vertebrates [47]; includes the amphibians [133] and amniotes [49]. Named for the presence of four jointed limbs (although limbs have been secondarily reduced or lost completely in several tetrapod groups).

thaumarchaeotes (*Thaumarchaeota*) [14]   A group of archaea [3] known from hot environments and marine surface waters; they oxidize ammonia and are thought to play an important role in the nitrogen cycle.

therians (*Theria*)   Mammals [134] characterized by viviparity (live birth). Includes the eutherians and marsupials.

theropods (*Theropoda*)   Archosaurs [51] with bipedal stance, hollow bones, a furcula ("wishbone"), elongated metatarsals with three-fingered feet, and a pelvis that points backward. Includes many well-known extinct dinosaurs (such as *Tyrannosaurus rex*), as well as the living birds [137].

tracheophytes   See vascular plants [25].

trilobites (*Trilobita*)   An extinct group of arthropods [39] related to the chelicerates [119]. Trilobites flourished from the Cambrian through the Permian.

tuataras (*Rhyncocephalia*)   A group of lepidosaurs [135] known mostly from fossils; there is only one living tuatara species. The quadrate bone of the upper jaw is fixed firmly to the skull. The sister group of the squamates.

tunicates (*Tunicata*) [126]   A group of chordates [43] that are mostly saclike filter feeders as adults, with motile larval stages that resemble tadpoles.

turtles (*Testudines*) [136]   A group of reptiles [50] with a bony carapace (upper shell) and plastron (lower shell) that encase the body in a fashion unique among the vertebrates.

V

vascular plants (*Tracheophyta*) [25]   Plants with xylem and phloem. Major groups include the lycophytes [74] and euphyllophytes.

velvet worms (*Onychophora*) [118]   Elongated, segmented ecdysozoans [38] with many pairs of soft, unjointed, claw-bearing legs.

vertebrates (*Vertebrata*) [44]   The largest group of chordates [43], characterized by a rigid endoskeleton supported by the vertebral column and an anterior skull encasing a brain. Includes hagfishes [127], lampreys [128], and the jawed vertebrates [45], although some biologists exclude the hagfishes from this group. *See also* craniates.

W

wet-nosed primates (*Strepsirrhini*)   A group of primate mammals [134] that includes lemurs and lorises.

X

xenoturbellids (*Xenoturbellida*)   Wormlike organisms that feed on or parasitize marine mollusks. Relationships uncertain; thought to be a sister group of either ambulacrarians [42] or bilaterians [35].

Z

"zygospore fungi" (*Zoopagomycota*, if monophyletic) [90]   A term of convenience for a probably paraphyletic group of fungi [30] in which hyphae of differing mating types conjugate to form a zygosporangium.

Making Sense of Data: A Statistics Primer

This appendix is designed help you understand the analysis of biological data in a statistical context. We outline major concepts involved in the collection and analysis of data, and we present basic statistical analyses that will help you interpret, understand, and complete the problems throughout this book as well as understand and interpret scientific studies in general. We present formulas for some common statistical tests as examples, but the main purpose of this appendix is to help you understand the purpose and reasoning behind statistical tests. Once you understand the basis of an analysis, you may wish to use one of many free, online websites for conducting the tests (such as http://vassarstats.net).

Why Do We Need Statistical Analysis?

ALMOST EVERYTHING VARIES   We live in a variable world, but within the variation we see among biological organisms there are predictable patterns. We use concepts and methods from the field of statistics to find and analyze these patterns. Consider any group of common things in nature—all women aged 22, all the cells in your liver, or all the blades of grass in your yard. Although they will have many similar characteristics, they will also have important differences. Men aged 22 tend to be taller than women aged 22, but of course not every man will be taller than every woman in this age group.

Natural variation can make it difficult to find general patterns. For example, scientists have determined that smoking increases the risk of getting lung cancer. But we know that not all smokers will develop lung cancer and not all nonsmokers will remain cancer-free. If we compare just one smoker with just one nonsmoker, we may end up drawing the wrong conclusion. So how did scientists discover this general pattern? How many smokers and nonsmokers did they examine before they felt confident about the risk of smoking?

Statistics helps us detect and describe general patterns in nature, and draw conclusions from those patterns.

AVOIDING FALSE POSITIVES AND FALSE NEGATIVES When a woman takes a pregnancy test, there is some chance that it will be positive even if she is not pregnant, and there is some chance that it will be negative even if she is pregnant. We call these kinds of mistakes "false positives" and "false negatives."

Doing science is a bit like taking a medical test. We observe patterns in the world, and we try to draw conclusions about how the world works from those observations. Sometimes our observations lead us to draw the wrong conclusions. We might conclude that a phenomenon occurs, when it actually does not; or we might conclude that a phenomenon does not occur, when it actually does.

For example, planet Earth has been warming over the past century (see Key Concept 56.4). Ecologists are interested in whether plant and animal populations have been affected by global warming. If we have long-term information about the locations of species and about temperatures in certain areas, we can determine whether shifts in species distributions coincide with temperature changes. Such information, however, can be very complicated. Without proper statistical methods, one may not be able to detect the true impact of temperature, or instead may think a pattern exists when it does not.

Statistics helps us avoid drawing the wrong conclusions.

How Does Statistical Analysis Help Us Understand the Natural World?

Statistical analysis is essential to scientific discovery. Most biological studies involve five basic steps, each of which involves aspects of statistical analysis.

- **Step 1: Experimental Design**
  Clearly define the scientific question and the methods necessary to tackle the question.

- **Step 2: Data Collection**
  Gather information about the natural world through observations and experiments.

- **Step 3: Organize and Visualize the Data**
  Use tables, graphs, and other useful representations to gain intuition about patterns in the data.

- **Step 4: Summarize the Data**
  Summarize the data with a few key statistical calculations.

- **Step 5: Inferential Statistics**
  Use statistical methods to draw general conclusions from the data about the world and the ways it works.

Step 1: Experimental Design

We make observations and conduct experiments to gain knowledge about the world. Scientists come up with scientific ideas based on prior research and their own observations. These ideas start as a question such as "Does smoking cause cancer?" From prior experience, scientists then propose possible answers to the question in the form of hypotheses such as "Smoking increases the risk of cancer." Experimental design then involves devising comparisons that can test predictions of the hypotheses. For example, if we are interested in evaluating the hypothesis that smoking increases cancer risk, we might decide to compare the incidence of cancer in nonsmokers and smokers. Our hypothesis would predict that the cancer incidence is higher in smokers than in nonsmokers. There are various ways we could make that comparison. We could compare the smoking history of people newly diagnosed with cancer with that of people whose tests came out negative for cancer. Alternatively, we could assess the current smoking habits of a sample of people and see whether those who smoke more heavily are more likely to develop cancer in, say, 5 years. Statistics provides us with tools for assessing which approach will provide us with an answer with smaller costs in time and effort in data collection and analysis.

We use statistics to guide us in planning exactly how to make our comparisons—what kinds of data and how many observations we will need to collect.

Step 2: Data Collection

TAKING SAMPLES When biologists gather information about the natural world, they typically collect representative pieces of information, called **data** or observations. For example, when evaluating the efficacy of a candidate drug for medulloblastoma brain cancer, scientists may test the drug on tens or hundreds of patients, and then draw conclusions about its efficacy for all patients with these tumors. Similarly, scientists studying the relationship between body weight and clutch size (number of eggs) for female spiders of a particular species may examine tens to hundreds of spiders to make their conclusions.

We use the expression "sampling from a population" to describe this general method of taking representative pieces of information from the system under investigation (**Figure B1**). The pieces of information together make up a **sample** of the larger system, or **population**. In the cancer therapy example, each observation was the change in a patient's tumor size 6 months after initiating treatment, and the population of interest was all individuals with medulloblastoma tumors. In the spider example, each observation was a pair of measurements—body weight and clutch size—for a single female spider, and the population of interest was all female spiders of this species.

▶ **View in Achieve**
  Simulation B.1 Population Sampling

Sampling is a matter of necessity, not laziness. We cannot hope (and would not want) to collect and weigh *all* of the female spiders of the species of interest on Earth! Instead, we use statistics to determine how many spiders we must collect to confidently infer something about the general population and then use statistics again to make such inferences.

DATA COME IN ALL SHAPES AND SIZES In statistics we use the word "variable" to mean a measurable characteristic of an individual component of a system. Some variables are on a numerical scale, such as the daily high temperature or the clutch size of a spider. We call these **quantitative variables**. Quantitative variables that take on only whole number values (such as spider clutch size) are called **discrete variables**, whereas variables that can also take on a fractional value (such as temperature) are called **continuous variables**.

Other variables take categories as values, such as a human blood type (A, B, AB, or O) or an ant caste (queen, worker, or male). We call these **categorical variables**. Categorical variables with a natural ordering, such as a final grade in Introductory Biology (A, B, C, D, or F), are called **ordinal variables**.

Each class of variables comes with its own set of statistical methods. We will introduce a few common methods in this appendix that will help you work on the problems presented in this book, but you should consult a biostatistics textbook for more advanced tests and analyses for other data sets and problems.

Step 3: Organize and Visualize the Data

Your data consist of a series of values of the variable or variables of interest, each from a separate observation. For example, **Table B1** shows the weight and length of 34 fish (*Abramis brama*) from Lake Laengelmavesi in Finland. From this list of numbers, it's hard to get a sense of how big the fish in the lake are, or how variable

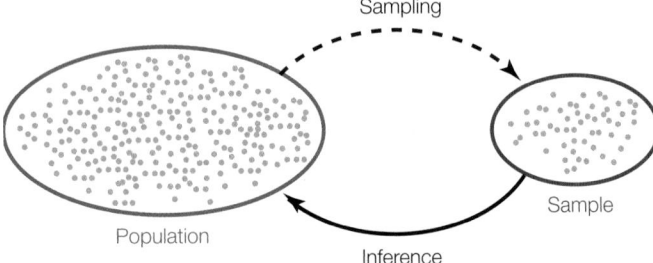

Figure B1 Sampling from a Population Biologists take representative samples from a population, use descriptive statistics to characterize their samples, and then use inferential statistics to draw conclusions about the original population.

TABLE **B1** | Weight and Length Measurements for a Sample of *Abramis brama* from Lake Laengelmavesi

Individual number	Fish weight (g)	Fish length (cm)
1	242	30.0
2	290	31.2
3	340	31.1
4	363	33.5
5	390	35.0
6	430	34.0
7	450	34.7
8	450	35.1
9	475	36.2
10	500	34.5
11	500	36.2
12	500	36.2
13	500	36.4
14	575	38.7
15	600	37.3
16	600	37.2
17	610	38.5
18	620	39.2
19	650	38.6
20	680	39.7
21	685	39.5
22	700	37.2
23	700	38.3
24	700	40.6
25	714	40.6
26	720	40.9
27	725	40.5
28	850	41.5
29	920	42.6
30	925	44.0
31	950	45.9
32	955	44.1
33	975	45.3
34	1,000	41.6

Source: fishcatch.txt from http://jse.amstat.org/jse_data_@archive.htm

TABLE **B2**	Summary of Fish Weights of *Abramis brama* from Lake Laengelmavesi	
Weight (g)	Frequency	Relative frequency
201–300	2	0.06
301–400	3	0.09
401–500	8	0.24
501–600	3	0.09
601–700	8	0.24
701–800	3	0.09
801–900	1	0.03
901–1,000	6	0.18
Total	34	1.0

TABLE **B3**	Poinsettia Colors	
Color	Frequency	Proportion
Red	108	0.59
Pink	34	0.19
White	40	0.22
Total	182	1.0

they are in size. It's much easier to gain intuition about your data if you organize them. One way to do this is to group (or bin) your data into **classes**, and count up the number of observations that fall into each class. The result is a **frequency distribution**. Table B2 shows the fish weight data as a frequency distribution. For each 100-gram weight class, Table B2 shows the number, or frequency, of observations in that weight class, as well as the relative frequency (proportion of the total) of observations in that weight class. Notice that the data take up much less space when organized in this fashion. Also notice that we can now see that most of the fish fall in the middle of the weight range, with relatively few very small or very large fish.

 Media Clip B.1 Interpreting Frequency Distributions
Life12e.com/mcB.1

It is even easier to visualize the frequency distribution of fish weights if we graph them in the form of a **histogram** such as the one in **Figure B2**. When grouping quantitative data, it is necessary to decide how many classes to include. It is often useful to look at multiple histograms before deciding which grouping offers the best representation of the data.

 View in Achieve
Simulation B.2 Frequency Distributions

Frequency distributions are also useful ways of summarizing categorical data. Table B3 shows a frequency distribution of the colors of 182 poinsettia plants (red, pink, or white) resulting from an experimental cross between two parent plants. Notice that, as with the fish example, the table is a much more compact way to present the data than a list of 182 color observations would be. For categorical data, the possible values of the variable are the categories themselves, and the frequencies are the number of observations in each category. We can visualize frequency distributions of categorical data like this by constructing a **bar chart**. The heights of the bars indicate the number of observations in each category (**Figure B3**). Another way to display the same data is in a **pie chart**, which shows the proportion of each category represented like pieces of a pie (**Figure B4**).

Sometimes we wish to compare two quantitative variables. For example, the researchers at Lake Laengelmavesi investigated the relationship between fish weight and length, from the data presented in Table B1. We can visualize this relationship using a **scatter plot** in which the weight and length of each fish is represented as a single point (**Figure B5**). These two variables have a **positive relationship** since the slope of a line drawn through the points is positive. As the length of a fish increases, its weight tends to increase in an approximately linear manner.

Tables and graphs are critical to interpreting and communicating data, and thus should be as self-contained and understandable as possible. Their content should be easily understood simply by looking at them. Axes, captions, and units should be clearly

Figure B2 Histograms Depict Frequency Distributions of Quantitative Data   This histogram shows the relative frequency of different weight classes of fish (*Abramis brama*).

Figure B3 Bar Charts Compare Categorical Data   This bar chart shows the frequency of three poinsettia colors that result from an experimental cross.

Figure B4 **Pie Charts Show Proportions of Categories** This pie chart shows the proportions of the three poinsettia colors presented in Table B3.

labeled, statistical terms should be defined, and appropriate groupings should be used when tabulating or graphing quantitative data.

Step 4: Summarize the Data

A **statistic** is a numerical quantity calculated from data, whereas **descriptive statistics** are quantities that describe general patterns in data. Descriptive statistics allow us to make straightforward comparisons among different data sets and concisely communicate basic features of our data.

DESCRIBING CATEGORICAL DATA   For categorical variables, we typically use proportions to describe our data. That is, we construct tables containing the proportions of observations in each category. For example, the third column in Table B3 provides the proportion of poinsettia plants in each color category, and the pie chart in Figure B4 provides a visual representation of those proportions.

DESCRIBING QUANTITATIVE DATA   For quantitative data, we often start by calculating **measures of center**, quantities that roughly tell us where the center of our data lies. There are three commonly used measures of center:

• The **mean**, or average value, of our sample is simply the sum of all the values in the sample divided by the number of observations in our sample (**Figure B6**).

Figure B5 **Scatter Plots Contrast Two Variables** Scatter plot of *Abramis brama* weights and lengths (measured from nose to end of tail). These two variables have a positive relationship since the slope of a line that could be drawn through the points is positive.

• The **median** is the value at which there are equal numbers of smaller and larger observations.

• The **mode** is the most frequent value in the sample.

> **View in Achieve**
> **Simulation B.3** **Measures of Center**

It is often just as important to quantify the variation in the data as it is to calculate its center. There are several statistics that tell us how much the values differ from one another. We call these **measures of dispersion**. The easiest one to understand and calculate is the **range**, which is simply the largest value in the sample minus the smallest value. The most commonly used measure of dispersion is the **standard deviation**, which calculates the extent to which the data are spread out from the mean. A deviation is the difference between an observation and the mean of the sample. The standard deviation is a measure of how far the average observation in the sample is from the sample mean. Two samples can have the same range, but very different standard deviations if observations in one are clustered closer to the mean than in the

---

Research Tools

Figure B6 Descriptive Statistics for Quantitative Data

Below are the equations used to calculate the descriptive statistics we discuss in this appendix. You can calculate these statistics yourself, or use free internet resources to help you make your calculations.

Notation:

$x_1, x_2, x_3, \ldots x_n$ are the n observations of variable X in the sample.

$\sum_{i=1}^{n} x_i = x_1 + x_2 + x_3, \ldots + x_n$ is the sum of all of the observations. (The Greek letter sigma, Σ, is used to denote "sum of.")

In regression, the independent variable is X, and the dependent variable is Y. b_0 is the vertical intercept of a regression line. b_1 is the slope of a regression line.

Equations

1. Mean: $\bar{x} = \dfrac{\sum_{i=1}^{n} x_i}{n}$

2. Standard deviation: $s = \sqrt{\dfrac{\Sigma(x_i - \bar{x})^2}{n-1}}$

3. Correlation coefficient: $r = \dfrac{\Sigma(x_i - \bar{x})(y_i - \bar{y})}{\sqrt{\Sigma(x_i - \bar{x})^2 (y_i - \bar{y})^2}}$

4. Least-squares regression line: $Y = b_0 + b_1 X$
   where $b_1 = \dfrac{\Sigma(x_i - \bar{x})(y_i - \bar{y})}{\Sigma(x_i - \bar{x})^2}$ and $b_0 = \bar{y} - b_1 \bar{x}$

5. Standard error of the mean: $SE_{\bar{x}} = \dfrac{s}{\sqrt{n}}$

Figure B7 Measures of Dispersion   Two samples with the same mean (black horizontal lines) and range (blue vertical line). Red lines show the deviations of each observation from the mean. Samples with large deviations have large standard deviations. Sample 1 has a smaller standard deviation than sample 2.

other. In **Figure B7**, for example, sample 1 has a smaller standard deviation ($s = 2.6$) than does sample 2 ($s = 3.6$), even though the two samples have the same means and ranges.

To demonstrate these descriptive statistics, let's return to the Lake Laengelmavesi study (see the data in Table B1). The mean weight of the 34 fish (see equation 1 in Figure B6) is:

$$\bar{x} = \frac{\text{sum of the weight of all fish in sample}}{\text{number of fish in sample}} = \frac{21,284\,\text{g}}{34} = 626\,\text{g}$$

Since there is an even number of observations in the sample, then the median weight is the value halfway between the two middle values:

$$\frac{610\,\text{g} + 620\,\text{g}}{2} = 615\,\text{g}$$

The mode of the sample is 500 g, which appears four times. The standard deviation (see equation 2 in Figure B6) is:

$$s = \sqrt{\frac{\sum(x_i - \bar{x})^2}{n-1}} = 206.6\,\text{g}$$

and the range is 1,000 g – 242 g = 758 g.

DESCRIBING THE RELATIONSHIP BETWEEN TWO QUANTITATIVE VARIABLES   Biologists often are interested in understanding the relationship between two different quantitative variables: How does the height of an organism relate to its weight? How does air pollution relate to the prevalence of asthma? How does lichen abundance relate to levels of air pollution? Recall that scatter plots visually represent such relationships.

We can quantify the strength of the relationship between two quantitative variables using a single value called the Pearson product–moment **correlation coefficient** (see equation 3 in Figure B6).

This statistic ranges between –1 and 1 and tells us how closely the points in a scatter plot conform to a straight line. A negative correlation coefficient indicates that one variable decreases as the other increases; a positive correlation coefficient indicates that the two variables increase together; and a correlation coefficient of zero indicates that there is no linear relationship between the two variables (**Figure B8**).

One must always keep in mind that *correlation does not mean causation*. Two variables can be closely related without one causing the other. For example, the number of cavities in a child's mouth correlates positively with the size of his or her feet. Clearly cavities do not enhance foot growth; nor does foot growth cause tooth decay. Instead the correlation exists because both quantities tend to increase with age.

Intuitively, the straight line that tracks the cluster of points on a scatter plot tells us something about the typical relationship between the two variables. Statisticians do not, however, simply eyeball the data and draw a line by hand. They often use a method called least-squares **linear regression** to fit a straight line to the data (see equation 4 in Figure B6). This method calculates the line that minimizes the overall vertical distances between the points in the scatter plot and the line itself. These distances are called **residuals** (**Figure B9**). Two parameters describe the regression line: b_0 (the vertical intercept of the line, or the expected value of variable Y when $X = 0$), and b_1 (the slope of the line, or how much values of Y are expected to change with changes in values of X).

Step 5: Inferential Statistics

Data analysis often culminates with statistical inference—an attempt to draw general conclusions about the system under investigation—the larger population—from observations of a representative sample (see Figure B1). When we test a new medulloblastoma brain cancer drug on ten patients, we do not simply want to know the fate of those ten individuals; rather, we hope to predict the drug's efficacy on the much larger population of all medulloblastoma patients.

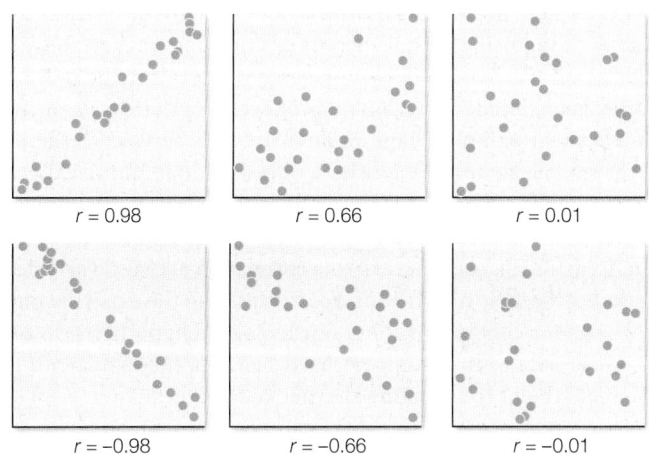

Figure B8 Correlation Coefficients   The correlation coefficient (*r*) indicates both the strength and the direction of the relationship.

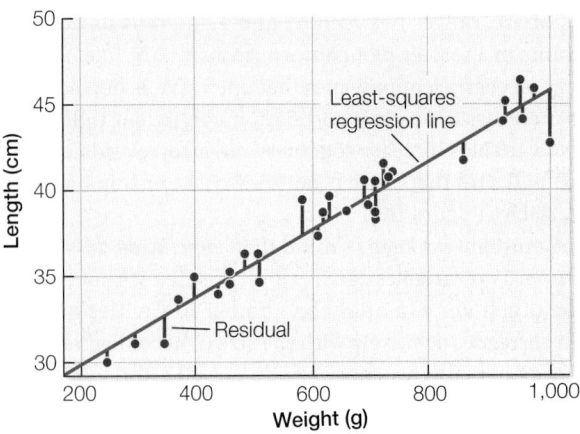

Figure B9 Linear Regression Estimates the Typical Relationship between Two Variables Least-squares linear regression line for *Abramis brama* weights and lengths (measured from nose to end of tail). The regression line (blue line) is given by the equation $Y = 26.1 + 0.02X$. It is the line that minimizes the sum of the squares of the residuals (red lines).

View in **Achieve**
Simulation B.4 **Linear Regression**

STATISTICAL HYPOTHESES   Once we have collected our data, we want to evaluate whether or not they fit the predictions of our hypothesis. For example, we want to know whether or not cancer incidence is greater in our sample of smokers than in our sample of nonsmokers, whether or not clutch size increases with spider body weight in our sample of spiders, or whether or not growth of a sample of fertilized plants is greater than that of a sample of unfertilized plants.

Before making statistical inferences from data, we must translate our "whether or not" question into a pair of opposing statistical hypotheses. Often our "whether" hypothesis is difficult to translate because it does not make specific predictions such as *how much* greater the cancer incidence should be in smokers compared with nonsmokers, or *how much* clutch size will increase with body weight, or *how big* the growth advantage of fertilized plants will be. For this reason, scientists often evaluate the "whether" hypothesis indirectly by calculating the fit of the data to an opposing "or not" hypothesis that does make a specific prediction. This "or not" hypothesis is often called the **null hypothesis** (denoted H_0) because it proposes that there is *no difference* between sample means, or *no correlation* between variables in the sample, or *no difference* between our sample and an expected frequency distribution. The statistical **alternative hypothesis** (denoted H_A) is often our biological hypothesis: that there *is* a difference in means, or that there *is* a correlation between variables, or that the sample distribution *does* differ from the expected one. We base our conclusion about our biological hypothesis on the fit of our data to the null hypothesis because it is so difficult to calculate the fit to the many alternative hypotheses.

Suppose, for example, we would like to know whether or not a new vaccine is more effective than an existing vaccine at immunizing children against influenza. We have measured flu incidence in a group of children who received the new vaccine and want to compare it with flu incidence in a group of children who received the old vaccine. Our statistical hypotheses would be as follows:

H_0: *Flu incidence was the same in both groups of children.*

H_A: *Flu incidence was different between the two groups of children.*

In the next few sections we will discuss how we decide when to reject the null hypothesis in favor of the alternative hypothesis.

View in **Achieve**
Simulation B.5 **Hypothesis Testing**

JUMPING TO THE WRONG CONCLUSIONS   There are two ways that we can draw incorrect conclusions from a statistical test (**Figure B10**). We can reject the null hypothesis when it is actually true (**Type I error**), or we can accept the null hypothesis when it is actually false (**Type II error**). These kinds of errors are analogous to false positives and false negatives in medical testing, respectively. If we mistakenly reject the null hypothesis when it is actually true, then we falsely endorse the incorrect alternative hypothesis. If we mistakenly accept the null hypothesis when it is actually false, then we falsely reject the correct alternative hypothesis.

Fortunately, statisticians have developed statistical tests to minimize the chance of committing these kinds of errors and to increase our confidence in the reliability of our conclusions. The methods are based on calculating the probabilities of obtaining different possible data values. Although you may have heard or even used the word "probability" on multiple occasions, it is important that you understand its mathematical meaning. A **probability** is a numerical quantity that expresses the chance of making a particular observation. It ranges between 0 and 1; 0 means that the observation never occurs, and 1 that the observation always occurs. This makes sense only if there is an element of chance—that is, if alternative observations are possible. For example, in a coin flip, heads and tails are possible observations. Similarly, when we select an individual from a human population, we may select a female or a male, or when we select an *Abramis brama* from Lake Laengelmavesi, its length can take on any number of values.

Probability is at the core of statistics. To draw conclusions about the real world (the population) from our sample, we first calculate the *probability of obtaining the data in our sample if the null hypothesis is true*. We refer to this probability as the **P-value** of our test. Specifically, we ask "What is the probability of observing what we see or measure in our random sample from the total population if the null hypothesis is true?" If our sample

	The real world	
	Null hypothesis true (*not more females*)	Null hypothesis false (*more females*)
Null hypothesis true (*not more females*)	√	Type II error (*false negative*)
Null hypothesis false (*more females*)	Type I error (*false positive*)	√

Figure B10 Two Types of Errors Possible outcomes of a statistical test. Statistical inference can result in correct and incorrect conclusions about the population of interest.

is highly improbable under the null hypothesis, then we gain confidence in the alternative hypothesis.

To take an example, suppose we would like to know whether there are equal numbers of females and males in a population of 10,000 students. To determine the makeup of the population, we choose 20 individuals at random and record their sex. Our null hypothesis is that the sex ratio in the population is 50:50, and our alternative hypothesis is that the sex ratio is not 50:50. Suppose that our sample contains 5 women and 15 men. The probability by chance alone of a sex ratio that skewed or more, if the sex ratio is really 50:50, turns out to be 0.02 (that is, 2%). (We will explain below how to arrive at this P-value.)

What sense can we make of this result and its P-value? We are justified in being skeptical that the population from which we drew the sample really has a 50:50 sex ratio. Yes, it's possible to randomly choose 5 women and 15 men if the null hypothesis is true, but we would expect this outcome in only 2% of all samples of 20 students that we could take. Said another way, if we are wrong and the sex ratio is actually 50:50, we have made a Type I error, but the chance of doing that is only 2%. We will likely go ahead to reject the null hypothesis and instead conclude that the sex ratio is not 50:50 in the population of 10,000 students.

Now, suppose instead that our sample of 20 students contains 8 women and 12 men. Here $P = 0.44$ (that is, 44%). What can we conclude from this result? We are much less certain about rejecting the null hypothesis that the sex ratio is 50:50. The P-value means that 44% of samples would be this skewed, or more, if the sex ratio were 50:50.

With a result like this, we are tempted to conclude that the sex ratio indeed is 50:50, and it is a common practice to accept the null hypothesis when the P-value is moderate. But this action might very well represent a Type II error (accepting a false hypothesis). Note that a probability of 44% of obtaining our result if the sex ratio is 50:50 is not very strong support for that specific null hypothesis. Other hypotheses, such as a hypothesis that the student population actually contains 40% women and 60% men (the observed proportions) fit the data even better than the null hypothesis of a 50:50 sex ratio.

For this reason, it is better to conclude simply that we cannot reject the null hypothesis when we obtain a moderate P-value. How moderate does the P-value have to be for us to conclude this? It has become conventional to use $P = 0.05$ (5%) as a cutoff, and to label a result with $P < 0.05$ as "significant" and one with $P > 0.05$ as "not significant." You should keep in mind, however, that $P = 0.05$ is not some magic number that determines whether one or another hypothesis is absolutely "proved" or "falsified."

What can we do to go further, with the example of $P = 0.44$ for our sample sex ratio? If possible, we could obtain additional samples (for example, of 20 individuals) from the overall population, to gather more information on the underlying sex ratio. But this sort of replication of sampling may often be impossible or impractical. Fortunately, it may not matter in many cases, because what often is critical is to minimize the chance of making a Type I error of rejecting a true null hypothesis. Once again, think of a clinical trial of a new drug, using a sample of patients. If we obtain a very small P-value—a very small chance of a Type I error—when we compare patients chosen at random to receive the drug with those receiving a

placebo, then we gain confidence that the drug works. If the P-value is relatively large, then we accept the null hypothesis that the drug is not effective, and we aren't very concerned about a Type II error of accepting a false null hypothesis in this case. We are looking to see whether the drug has a strong beneficial effect. If it does not have a strong effect, we are not so interested in finding out whether its effect is exactly zero or just close to zero.

This agrees with our intuition. When choosing 20 people randomly from an evenly divided population, we would be surprised if almost all of them were female, but we would not be surprised at all if we ended up with a few more females than males (or a few more males than females). Exactly how many females do we need in our sample before we can confidently infer that they make up the majority of the population? And how confident are we when we reach that conclusion? Statistics allows us to answer these questions precisely.

STATISTICAL SIGNIFICANCE: AVOIDING FALSE POSITIVES

Whenever we test hypotheses, we calculate the probability just discussed, and refer to this value as the P-value of our test. Specifically, the P-value is the probability of getting data as extreme as our data (just by chance) if the null hypothesis is in fact true. In other words, it is the probability that chance alone would produce data that differ from the null hypothesis as much as our data differ from the null hypothesis. How we measure the fit of our data to the null hypothesis depends on the kind of data in our sample (categorical or quantitative) and the nature of the null hypothesis (assertions about proportions, single variables, multiple variables, differences between variables, correlations between variables, etc.).

For many statistical tests, P-values can be calculated mathematically. One option is to quantify the extent to which the data depart from the null hypothesis and then use look-up tables (available in most statistics textbooks or on the internet) to find the probability that chance alone would produce a difference of that magnitude. Most scientists, however, find P-values primarily by using statistical software rather than hand calculations combined with look-up tables. Regardless of the technology, the most important steps of the statistical analysis are still left to the researcher: constructing appropriate null and alternative hypotheses, choosing the correct statistical test, and drawing correct conclusions.

After we calculate a P-value from our data, we have to decide whether it is small enough to conclude that our data are inconsistent with the null hypothesis. This is decided by comparing the P-value to a threshold called the **significance level**, which is often chosen even before making any calculations. We reject the null hypothesis only when the P-value is less than or equal to the significance level, denoted α. This ensures that, if the null hypothesis is true, we have at most a probability α of rejecting it when it is true. Therefore the lower the value of α, the less likely you are to make a Type I error (see the lower left cell of Figure B10). The most commonly used significance level is $\alpha = 0.05$, which limits the probability of a Type I error to 5%.

If our statistical test yields a P-value that is less than our significance level α, then we conclude that the effect described by our alternative hypothesis is statistically significant at the level α and we reject the null hypothesis. If our P-value is greater than α, then we conclude that we are unable to reject the null hypothesis.

POWER: AVOIDING FALSE NEGATIVES The **power** of a statistical test is the probability that we will correctly reject the null hypothesis when it is false (see the lower right cell of Figure B10). Therefore the higher the power of the test, the less likely we are to make a Type II error (see the upper right cell of Figure B10). The power of a test can be calculated, and such calculations can be used to improve your methodology. Generally, there are several steps that can be taken to increase power and thereby avoid false negatives:

- **Increase the value of α.** The lower the value of α (our significance level), the harder it is to reject the null hypothesis, even if it is actually false.

- **Increase the sample size.** The more data one has, the more likely one is to find evidence against the null hypothesis, if it is actually false.

- **Decrease variability in the sample**. The more variation there is in the sample, the harder it is to discern a clear effect (the alternative hypothesis) when it actually exists.

 View in Achieve
Simulation B.6 Power of Statistical Tests

It is always a good idea to design your experiment to reduce any variability that may obscure the pattern you seek to detect. For example, it is possible that the chance of a child contracting influenza varies depending on whether he or she lives in a crowded (e.g., urban) environment or one that is less so (e.g., rural). To reduce variability, a scientist might choose to test a new influenza vaccine only on children from one environment or the other. After you have minimized such extraneous variation, you can use power calculations to choose the right combination of α and sample size to reduce the risks of Type I and Type II errors to desirable levels.

There is a trade-off between Type I and Type II errors: as α decreases, the risk of a Type I error decreases but the risk of a Type II error increases. As discussed above, scientists tend to be more concerned about Type I than Type II errors. However, there are many real-world scenarios in which it would be worse to make a Type II error than a Type I error. For example, suppose a new cold medication is being tested for dangerous (life-threatening) side effects. The null hypothesis is that there are no such side effects. A Type II error might lead regulatory agencies to approve a harmful medication that could cost human lives. In contrast, a Type I error would simply mean one less cold medication among the many that already line pharmacy shelves. In such cases, policymakers take steps to avoid a Type II error, even if, in doing so, they increase the risk of a Type I error.

STATISTICAL INFERENCE WITH QUANTITATIVE DATA Statistics that describe patterns in our samples are used to estimate properties of the larger population. Earlier we calculated the mean weight of a sample of *Abramis brama* in Lake Laengelmavesi, which provided us with an estimate of the mean weight of all the *Abramis brama* in the lake. But how close is our estimate to the true value in the larger population? Our estimate from the sample is unlikely to exactly equal the true population value. For example, our sample of *Abramis brama* may, by chance, have included an excess of large individuals. In this case, our sample would overestimate the true mean weight of fish in the population.

The **standard error** of a sample statistic (such as the mean) is a measure of how close it is likely to be to the true population value. The **standard error of the mean**, for example, provides an estimate of how far we might expect a sample mean to deviate from the true population mean. It is a function of how much individual observations vary within samples (the standard deviation) and the size of the sample (*n*). Standard errors increase with the degree of variation within samples, and they decrease with the number of observations in a sample (because large samples provide better estimates about the underlying population than do small samples). For our sample of 34 *Abramis brama*, we would calculate the standard error of the mean using equation 5 in Figure B6:

$$SE_{\bar{x}} = \frac{s}{\sqrt{n}} = \frac{206.6\,\text{g}}{\sqrt{34}} = 35.4\,\text{g}$$

The standard error of a statistic is related to the **confidence interval**—a range around the sample statistic that has a specified probability of including the true population value. The formula we use to calculate confidence intervals depends on the characteristics of the data, and the particular statistic. For many types of continuous data, the bounds of the **95% confidence interval** of the mean can be calculated by taking the mean and adding and subtracting 1.96 times the standard error of the mean. Consider our sample of 34 *Abramis brama*, for example. We would say that the mean of 626 grams has a 95% confidence interval from 556.6 grams to 695.4 grams (626 ± 69.4 grams). If all our assumptions about our data have been met, we would expect the true population mean to fall in this confidence interval 95% of the time.

Researchers typically use graphs or tables to report sample statistics (such as the mean) as well as some measure of confidence in them (such as their standard error or a confidence interval). This book is full of examples. If you understand the concepts of sample statistics, standard errors, and confidence intervals, you can see for yourself the major patterns in the data, without waiting for the authors to tell you what they are. For example, if samples from two groups have 95% confidence intervals of the mean that do not overlap, then you can conclude that it is unlikely that the groups have the same true mean.

 View in Achieve
Simulation B.7 Standard Deviations, Standard Errors, and Confidence Intervals Simulation

Biologists conduct statistical tests to obtain more precise estimates of the probability of observing a given difference between samples if the null hypothesis that there is no difference in the populations is true. The appropriate test depends on the nature of the data and the experimental design. For example, we might want to calculate the probability that the mean weights of two different fish species in Lake Laengelmavesi, *Abramis brama* and *Leusiscus idus*, are the same. A simple method for comparing the means of two groups is the *t*-test, described in **Figure B11**. We looked earlier at data for *Abramis brama*; the researchers who collected these data also collected weights for six individuals of *Leusiscus idus*: 270, 270, 306, 540, 800, and 1,000 grams. We begin by stating our hypotheses and choosing a significance level:

Research Tools

Figure B11 The *t*-test

What is the *t*-test? It is a standard method for assessing whether the means of two groups are statistically different from each another.

Step 1: State the null and alternative *hypotheses*:
H_0: The two populations have the same mean.
H_A: The two populations have different means.

Step 2: Choose a significance level, α, to limit the risk of a Type I error.

Step 3: Calculate the *test statistic*:

$$t_s = \frac{\bar{y}_1 - \bar{y}_2}{\sqrt{\frac{s_1^2}{n_1} + \frac{s_2^2}{n_2}}}$$

Notation: $\bar{y}_1$ and $\bar{y}_2$ are the sample means; s_1 and s_2 are the sample standard deviations; and n_1 and n_2 are the sample sizes.

Step 4: Use the test statistic to assess whether the data are consistent with the null hypothesis:
Calculate the *P-value* (*P*) using statistical software or by hand using statistical tables.

Step 5: Draw conclusions from the test:
If $P \leq \alpha$, then reject H_0, and conclude that the population distribution is significantly different.
If $P > \alpha$, then we do not have sufficient evidence to conclude that the means differ.

H_0: *Abramis brama* and *Leusiscus idus* have the same mean weight.

H_A: *Abramis brama* and *Leusiscus idus* have different mean weights.

$\alpha = 0.05$

The test statistic is calculated using the means, standard deviations, and sizes of the two samples:

$$t_s = \frac{626 - 531}{\sqrt{\frac{207^2}{34} + \frac{310^2}{6}}} = 0.724$$

We can use statistical software or one of the free statistical sites on the internet to find that the *P*-value for this result is *P* = 0.497. Since *P* is considerably greater than α, we fail to reject the null hypothesis and conclude that our study does not provide evidence that the two species have different mean weights.

You may want to consult an introductory statistics textbook to learn more about confidence intervals, *t*-tests, and other basic statistical tests for quantitative data.

STATISTICAL INFERENCE WITH CATEGORICAL DATA   With categorical data, we often wish to ask whether the frequencies of observations in different categories are consistent with a hypothesized frequency distribution. We can use a **chi-square goodness-of-fit** test to answer this question.

Figure B12 outlines the steps of a chi-square goodness-of-fit-test. As an example, consider the data described in Table B3. Many plant species have simple Mendelian genetic systems in which parent plants produce progeny with three different colors of flowers in a ratio of 2:1:1. However, a botanist believes that these particular poinsettia plants have a different genetic system that does not produce a 2:1:1 ratio of red, pink, and white plants. A chi-square goodness-of-fit can be used to assess whether or not the data are consistent with this ratio, and thus whether or not this simple genetic explanation is valid. We start by stating our hypotheses and significance level:

H_0: The progeny of this type of cross have the following probabilities of each flower color:

$$\Pr\{\text{Red}\} = .50, \Pr\{\text{Pink}\} = .25, \Pr\{\text{White}\} = .25$$

Research Tools

Figure B12 The Chi-Square Goodness-of-Fit Test

What is the chi-square goodness-of-fit test? It is a standard method for assessing whether a sample came from a population with a specific distribution.

Step 1: State the null and alternative *hypotheses*:
H_0: The population has the specified distribution.
H_A: The population does not have the specified distribution.

Step 2: Choose a significance level, α, to limit the risk of a Type I error.

Step 3: Determine the *observed frequency* and *expected frequency* for each category:
The observed frequency of a category is simply the number of observations in the sample of that type.
The expected frequency of a category is the probability of the category specified in H_0 multiplied by the overall sample size.

Step 4: Calculate the *test statistic*:

$$\chi_s^2 = \sum_{i=1}^{C} \frac{(O_i - E_i)^2}{E_i}$$

Notation: C is the total number of categories, O_i is the observed frequency of category *i*, and E_i is the expected frequency of category *i*.

Step 5: Use the test statistic to assess whether the data are consistent with the null hypothesis:
Calculate the *P-value* (*P*) using statistical software or by hand using statistical tables.

Step 6: Draw conclusions from the test:
If $P \leq \alpha$, then reject H_0, and conclude that the population distribution is significantly different than the distribution specified by H_0.
If $P > \alpha$, then we do not have sufficient evidence to conclude that population has a different distribution.

View in Achieve
Simulation B.8 Chi-Square Goodness-of-Fit Test

H_A: At least one of the probabilities of H_0 is incorrect.

$$\alpha = 0.05$$

We next use the probabilities in H_0 and the sample size to calculate the expected frequencies:

	Red	Pink	White
Observed	108	34	40
Expected	(.50)(182) = 91	(.25)(182) = 45.5	(.25)(182) = 45.5

Based on these quantities, we calculate the chi-square test statistic:

$$\chi_s^2 = \sum_{i=1}^{C} \frac{(O_i - E_i)^2}{E_i} = \frac{(108-91)^2}{91} + \frac{(34-45.5)^2}{45.5} + \frac{(40-45.5)^2}{45.5} = 6.747$$

We find the P-value for this result to be $P = 0.034$ using statistical software. Since P is less than α, we reject the null hypothesis and conclude that the botanist is likely correct: the plant color patterns are not explained by the simple Mendelian genetic model under consideration.

This appendix is meant to provide only a brief introduction to the concepts of statistical analysis, with a few example tests. **Figure B13** summarizes some of the commonly used statistical tests that you may encounter in biological studies.

Figure B13 **Some Common Methods of Statistical Inference**
This flowchart shows some of the commonly used methods of statistical inference for different combinations of data. Detailed descriptions of these methods can be found in most introductory biostatistics textbooks.

▶ **View in Achieve**
Simulation B.9 **Methods of Statistical Inference**

Some Measurements Used in Biology

Measures of	Unit	Equivalents	Metric—English conversion
Length			
	meter (m)	base unit	1 m = 39.37 inches = 3.28 feet = 1.196 yards
	kilometer (km)	1 km = 1000 (10^3) m	1 km = 0.62 miles
	centimeter (cm)	1 cm = 0.01 (10^{-2}) m	1 cm = 0.39 inches
	millimeter (mm)	1 mm = 0.1 cm = 10^{-3} m	1 mm = 0.039 inches
	micrometer (μm)	1 μm = 0.001 mm = 10^{-6} m	
	nanometer (nm)	1 nm = 0.001 μm = 10^{-9} m	
Area			
	square meter (m^2)	base unit	1 m^2 = 1.196 square yards
	hectare (ha)	1 ha = 10,000 m^2	1 ha = 2.47 acres
Volume			
	liter (L)	base unit	1 L = 1.06 quarts
	milliliter (mL)	1 mL = 0.001 L = 10^{-3} L	1 mL = 0.034 fluid ounces
	microliter (μL)	1 μL = 0.001 mL = 10^{-6} L	
Mass			
	gram (g)	base unit	1 g = 0.035 ounces
	kilogram (kg)	1 kg = 1000 g	1 kg = 2.20 pounds
	metric ton (mt)	1 mt = 1000 kg	1 mt = 2,200 pounds = 1.10 ton
	milligram (mg)	1 mg = 0.001 g = 10^{-3} g	
	microgram (μg)	1 μg = 0.001 mg = 10^{-6} g	
Temperature			
	degree Celsius (°C)	base unit	°C = (°F − 32)/1.8
			0°C = 32°F (water freezes)
			100°C = 212°F (water boils)
			20°C = 68°F ("room temperature")
			37°C = 98.6°F (human internal body temperature)
	Kelvin (K)*	K = °C − 273	0 K = −460°F
Energy			
	joule (J)		1 J ≈ 0.24 calorie = 0.00024 kilocalorie[†]

*0 K (−273°C) is "absolute zero," a temperature at which molecular oscillations approach 0—that is, the point at which motion all but stops.

[†]A *calorie* is the amount of heat necessary to raise the temperature of 1 gram of water 1°C. The *kilocalorie*, or nutritionist's calorie, is what we commonly think of as a calorie in terms of food.

Glossary

3′ end   (3 prime) The end of a DNA or RNA strand that has a free hydroxyl group at the 3′ carbon of the sugar (deoxyribose or ribose).

5′ cap   (5 prime) Methylated guanine nucleotide bonded to the 5′ end of eukaryotic mRNA.

5′ end   (5 prime) The end of a DNA or RNA strand that has a free phosphate group at the 5′ carbon of the sugar (deoxyribose or ribose).

A

A horizon   *See* topsoil.

abiotic   (a′ bye ah tick) [Gk. *a*: not + *bios*: life] Nonliving. In ecology, the nonliving components of the environment, including its physical and chemical characteristics. (Contrast with biotic.)

abomasum   (a bo mey′ sum) The fourth of the four chambers of the stomach in ruminants; the true stomach.

aboral   Pertaining to the side of the body opposite or away from the mouth and that contains the anus. (Contrast with oral.)

abortion   Any termination of pregnancy, whether induced or natural (in which case it is called a spontaneous abortion), that occurs after a fertilized egg is successfully implanted in the uterus.

abscisic acid (ABA)   (ab sighs′ ik) A plant hormone. Causes stomata to close; involved in a plant's response to salt and drought stress.

abscission   (ab sizh′ un) [L. *abscissio*: break off] The process by which leaves, petals, and fruits separate from a plant.

absorption spectrum   A graph of light absorption versus wavelength of light; shows how much light is absorbed at each wavelength.

absorptive heterotrophs   Organisms (primarily fungi) that feed by **absorptive heterotrophy**, i.e., by secreting digestive enzymes into the environment to break down large food molecules, then absorbing the breakdown products.

absorptive heterotrophs   Organisms (primarily fungi) that feed by **absorptive heterotrophy**, i.e., by secreting digestive enzymes into the environment to break down large food molecules, then absorbing the breakdown products.

absorptive state   The state in which food is in the gut and nutrients are being absorbed. (Contrast with postabsorptive state.)

accessory fruit   A fruit in which some of the flesh develops from tissue exterior to the carpel.

accessory sex organs   Anatomical structures that allow transfer of sperm from male to female for internal fertilization. (Contrast with primary sex organs.)

acclimation   Refers to increased tolerance for environmental extremes (e.g., extreme cold) after prior exposure to them.

acclimatization   The change in an individual's phenotype that results from long-term exposure to a new environment. A form of phenotypic plasticity. Sometimes used only to describe responses in a natural (non-laboratory) setting. (*See also* acclimation.)

acetyl CoA   A compound that reacts with oxaloacetate to produce citrate at the beginning of the citric acid cycle; a key metabolic intermediate in the formation of many compounds. Sometimes called **acetyl coenzyme A**.

acetyl coenzyme A   *See* acetyl CoA.

acetylcholine (ACh)   A neurotransmitter that carries information across vertebrate neuromuscular junctions and some other synapses. It is then broken down by the enzyme acetylcholinesterase (AChE).

acid   [L. *acidus*: sharp, sour] A substance that can release a proton in solution. (Contrast with base.)

acid growth hypothesis   The hypothesis that auxin increases proton pumping, thereby lowering the pH of the cell wall resulting in wall loosening. Proposed to explain auxin-induced cell expansion in plants.

acid rain   Rain that has a lower pH than normal as a result of acid-forming precursor molecules introduced into the atmosphere by human activities.

acoelomate   Lacking a coelom. (Contrast with coelomate, pseudocoelomate.)

acoels   *See* Appendix A.

acquired immune deficiency syndrome (AIDS)   A condition caused by human immunodeficiency virus (HIV) in which the body's T-helper cells are reduced, leaving the infected individual subject to opportunistic diseases.

acrosome   (a′ krow soam) [Gk. *akros*: highest + *soma*: body] The structure at the forward tip of an animal sperm, which is the first part to fuse with the egg membrane and enter the egg cell.

actin   [Gk. *aktis*: ray] A protein that makes up the cytoskeletal microfilaments in eukaryotic cells and is one of the two contractile proteins in muscle. (*See also* myosin.)

actinobacteria   *See* Appendix A.

action potential (AP)   An electric signal that is generated by a neuron and transmits information via waves of depolarization or hyperpolarization of the cell membrane. (Contrast with resting potential.)

action spectrum   A graph of a biological process versus light wavelength; shows which wavelengths are involved in the process.

activation energy (E_a)   The energy barrier that blocks the tendency for a chemical reaction to occur.

activation gate   The property of a voltage-gated Na^+ ion channel that increases its permeability to Na^+ ions when the membrane is depolarized. (Contrast with inactivation gate.)

activator   A transcription factor that stimulates transcription when it binds to a regulatory sequence for a gene. (Contrast with repressor.)

active site   The region of an enzyme or ribozyme where the substrate binds, and where catalysis occurs.

active transport   The energy-dependent transport of a substance across a biological membrane against a concentration gradient—that is, from a region of low concentration (of that substance) to one of high concentration. (*See also* primary active transport, secondary active transport. Contrast with facilitated diffusion, passive transport.)

adaptation   (1) In evolutionary biology, a particular structure, physiological process, or behavior that makes an organism better able to survive and reproduce. Also, the evolutionary process that leads to the development or persistence of such a trait. (2) In sensory neurophysiology, a sensory cell's loss of sensitivity as a result of repeated stimulation.

adaptive defenses   A type of defense against pathogens that is aimed at specific pathogens. Present in some prokaryotes (involving CRISPR-Cas) and in vertebrates (involving antibodies and T cell receptors). (Contrast with innate defenses.)

adaptive radiation   A series of evolutionary events that results in an array (radiation) of related species that live in a variety of environments, differing in the adaptations each uses to exploit those environments.

addition rule   The rule that the probability of two or more events that are mutually exclusive is the sum of their independent probabilities. (Contrast with multiplication rule.)

adenine (A)   (a′ den een) A nitrogen-containing base found in nucleic acids, ATP, NAD, and other compounds.

adenine (A)   (a′ den een) A nitrogen-containing two-ringed base found in nucleic acids, ATP, NAD, and other compounds.

adeno-associated virus   A small, non-pathogenic virus with a single-stranded DNA genome, which can be used for gene therapy in humans and does not integrate into the host chromosomes.

adhesion   The binding of one cell or substance to another.

adrenal cortex   The outer region of the adrenal gland that produces and secretes steroid hormones.

adrenal gland   (a dree′ nal) [L. *ad*: toward + *renes*: kidneys] An endocrine gland located near the kidneys of vertebrates, consisting of two parts, the adrenal cortex and adrenal medulla.

adrenal medulla   The tissue that makes up the core of the adrenal gland and secretes epinephrine and norepinephrine.

adrenergic receptors   G protein-coupled receptor proteins that bind to the hormones epinephrine and norepinephrine, triggering specific responses in the target cells.

adrenocorticotropic hormone (ACTH) A tropic hormone produced by the anterior pituitary gland that stimulates release of cortisol and certain other hormones from the adrenal cortex.

adventitious roots   (ad ven ti′ shus) [L. *adventitius*: arriving from outside] Roots originating outside the regular progression of lateral root formation in the root; e.g. roots arising from the stem, at ground level or below; typical of the fibrous root system of monocots.

aerenchyma   In plants, parenchymal tissue containing air spaces.

aerobic   (air oh′ bic) [Gk. *aer*: air + *bios*: life] Occurring in the presence of oxygen; requiring or using oxygen (as in **aerobic metabolism**). (Contrast with anaerobic.)

aerotolerant anaerobe   A prokaryote that does not require an oxygen atmosphere for survival, but that can live while exposed to O_2.

afferent   (af′ ur unt) [L. *ad*: toward + *ferre*: to carry] Carrying to, as in neurons that carry impulses to the central nervous system (**afferent neurons**), or a blood vessel that carries blood to a structure (**afferent arteriole**). (Contrast with efferent.)

after-hyperpolarization   A fall in membrane potential below normal resting level following an action potential. Also called undershoot.

aggregate fruit   A fruit that develops from several carpels from the same flower.

agonist   A chemical substance (e.g., a neuro-transmitter) that elicits a specific response in a cell or tissue. (Contrast with antagonist.)

air sacs   Structures in the respiratory system of birds that receive inhaled air; they keep fresh air flowing unidirectionally through the lungs, but are not themselves gas exchange surfaces.

albedo effect   (al bee′ doh) [L. *albus*: white] The solar radiation reflected by Earth's surface.

alcoholic fermentation   A metabolic pathway in which glucose is catabolized in the absence of oxygen with the production of ethyl alcohol. *See* fermentation.

aldosterone   (al dohs′ ter own) A steroid hormone produced in the adrenal cortex of mammals. Promotes secretion of potassium and reabsorption of sodium in the kidney.

aleurone layer   (al yu′ rown) In some seeds, a tissue that lies beneath the seed coat and surrounds the endosperm. Secretes digestive enzymes that break down macromolecules stored in the endosperm.

algae   *See* Appendix A.

allantoic membrane   In animal development, an outgrowth of extraembryonic endoderm plus adjacent mesoderm that forms the allantois, a saclike structure that stores metabolic wastes produced by the embryo.

allantois   (al′ lun toh is) [Gk. *allant*: sausage] An extraembryonic membrane enclosing a sausage-shaped sac that stores the embryo's nitrogenous wastes.

Allee effect   An increase in the population growth rate (r) as the population density decreases.

allele   (a leel′) [Gk. *allos*: other] The alternate form of a genetic character found at a given locus on a chromosome.

allergic reaction   [Ger. *allergie*: altered] An overreaction of the immune system to amounts of an antigen that do not affect most people; often involves IgE antibodies.

allopatric speciation   (al′ lo pat′ rick) [Gk. *allos*: other + *patria*: homeland] The formation of two species from one when reproductive isolation occurs because of the interposition of (or crossing of) a physical geographic barrier such as a river. Also called geographic speciation. (Contrast with sympatric speciation.)

allopolyploidy   The possession of more than two chromosome sets that are derived from more than one species. (Contrast with **autopolyploidy**.)

allosteric regulation   (al lo steer′ ik) [Gk. *allos*: other + *stereos*: structure] Regulation of the activity of a protein (usually an enzyme) by the binding of a non-substrate molecule to a site other than the active site.

alpha diversity   Species diversity at the local or community scale. (Compare with beta diversity, gamma diversity.)

α (alpha) helix   A prevalent type of secondary protein structure; a right-handed spiral.

alternation of generations   The succession of multicellular haploid and diploid phases in some sexually reproducing organisms, notably plants.

alternative splicing   A process for generating different mature mRNAs from a single gene by splicing together different sets of exons during RNA processing.

alternative states   Different community assemblages that develop at the same location under similar environmental conditions.

altricial   Born or hatched in a relatively undeveloped state that requires care and feeding by the parents. (Contrast with precocial.)

altruistic   Pertaining to behavior that benefits other individuals at a cost to the individual who performs the behavior.

alveolus   (al ve′ o lus) (plural: alveoli) [L. *alveus*: cavity] A small, baglike cavity, especially the blind sacs of the lung.

amacrine cells   Cells in the retina that communicate laterally between ganglion and bipolar cells.

ambulacrarians   *See* Appendix A.

amensalism   A type of interaction in which one species is harmed and the other is unaffected. (Contrast with commensalism, competition, mutualism.)

amine hormones   Small hormone molecules synthesized from single amino acids (e.g., thyroxine and epinephrine).

amino acid   An organic compound containing both NH_2 and COOH groups. Proteins are polymers of amino acids.

ammonia NH_3, the most common nitrogenous waste. (Compare with urea, uric acid.)

ammonotelic   (am moan′ o teel′ ic) [Gk. *telos*: end] Pertaining to an organism in which the final product of breakdown of nitrogen-containing compounds (primarily proteins) is ammonia. (Contrast with ureotelic, uricotelic.)

amnion   (am′ nee on) The fluid-filled sac within which the embryos of reptiles (including birds) and mammals develop.

amniote egg   A shelled egg surrounding four extraembryonic membranes and embryo-nourishing yolk. This evolutionary adaptation permitted mammals and reptiles to live and reproduce in drier environments than can most amphibians.

amniotes   *See* Appendix A.

amniotic fluid   The fluid in the amniotic sac that contains mammalian and reptilian embryos.

amoebozoans   *See* Appendix A.

amphibians   *See* Appendix A.

amphipathic   (am′ fi path′ ic) [Gk. *amphi*: both + *pathos*: emotion] Of a molecule, having both hydrophilic and hydrophobic regions.

amplitude   The magnitude of change over the course of a regular cycle.

amygdala   A component of the limbic system that is involved in fear and the memory of fearful experiences.

amylase   A starch digesting enzyme.

amyloids   Aggregates of many individual molecules of a protein that self-assemble into large fibers. Associated with human diseases, such as Alzheimer's disease.

anabolic reaction   (an uh bah′lik) [Gk. *ana*: upward + *ballein*: to throw] A synthetic reaction in which simple molecules are linked to form more complex ones; requires an input of energy and captures it in the chemical bonds that are formed. (Contrast with catabolic reaction.)

anaerobic   (an ur row′bic) [Gk. *an*: not + *aer*: air + *bios*: life] Occurring without the use of molecular oxygen, O_2 (as in **anaerobic metabolism**). (Contrast with aerobic.)

anaerobic respiration   A metabolic pathway in which glucose is catabolized in the absence of oxygen.

analogous   In biology, referring to similar structures found in two or more groups of organisms, but with separate, independent evolutionary origins. An example is the wings of bats and the wings of birds, which evolved independently as wings from wingless ancestors.

ancestral trait   The trait originally present in the ancestor of a given group; may be retained or changed in the descendants of that ancestor.

anchored membrane proteins   Proteins that are associated with the membrane by covalent attachments to lipids. (Contrast with integral membrane proteins, peripheral membrane proteins.)

androgen   (an′ dro jen) Any of the several male sex steroids (most notably testosterone).

aneuploidy   (an′ you ploy dee) A condition in which one or more chromosomes are either lacking or present in excess.

angiosperms Flowering plants; one of the two major groups of living seed plants. (*See also* gymnosperms.)

angiotensin (an′ jee oh ten′ sin) A peptide hormone that raises blood pressure by causing peripheral vessels to constrict. Also maintains glomerular filtration by constricting efferent vessels and stimulates thirst and the release of aldosterone.

angiotensin (an′ jee oh ten′ sin) A peptide hormone that raises blood pressure by causing peripheral vessels to constrict. Also maintains glomerular filtration by constricting efferent vessels and stimulates thirst and the release of aldosterone.

angular gyrus A part of the human brain believed to be essential for integrating spoken and written language.

animal hemisphere The metabolically active upper portion of some animal eggs, zygotes, and embryos; does not contain the dense nutrient yolk. (Contrast with vegetal hemisphere.)

anion (an′ eye on) [Gk. *ana*: upward] A negatively charged ion. (Contrast with cation.)

annelids *See* Appendix A.

annual A plant whose life cycle is completed in one growing season. (Contrast with biennial, perennial.)

antagonist A biochemical substance (e.g., a drug) that blocks the normal action of another biochemical substance. (Contrast with agonist.)

antenna system *See* light-harvesting complex.

anterior pituitary The portion of the vertebrate pituitary gland that derives from gut epithelium. Produces tropic hormones.

anterior Toward or pertaining to the tip or headward region of the body axis. (Contrast with posterior.)

anther (an′ thur) [Gk. *anthos*: flower] A pollen-bearing portion of the stamen of a flower.

antheridium (an′ thur id′ ee um) [Gk. *antheros*: blooming] The multicellular structure that produces the sperm in nonvascular land plants and ferns.

anthozoan *See* Appendix A.

antibody *See* immunoglobulin.

anticodon The three nucleotides in transfer RNA that pair with a complementary triplet (a codon) in messenger RNA.

antidiuretic hormone (ADH) A hormone that promotes water reabsorption by the kidney. ADH is produced by neurons in the hypothalamus and released from nerve terminals in the posterior pituitary gland. Also called vasopressin.

antigen (an′ ti jun) Any substance that stimulates the production of an antibody or antibodies in the body of a vertebrate.

antigen presentation In cellular immunity, a process in which either a white blood cell ingests and digests an antigen and exposes fragments of it on its class II MHC molecules, or a nucleated cell exposes fragments of cytosolic viral proteins or abnormal proteins made by cancer cells on its class I MHC molecules

antigenic determinant The specific region of an antigen that is recognized and bound by a specific antibody. Also called an epitope.

antiparallel Referring to molecular orientation in which a molecule or parts of a molecule have opposing directions.

antiporter A membrane transport protein that moves one substance in one direction and another in the opposite direction. (Contrast with symporter, uniporter.)

antisense RNA A single-stranded RNA molecule complementary to, and thus targeted against, an mRNA of interest to block its translation.

anus An opening through which solid digestive wastes are expelled, located at the posterior end of a tubular gut.

aorta (a or′ tah) [Gk. *aorte*: aorta] The main trunk of the arteries leading to the systemic (as opposed to the pulmonary) circulation.

aortic body A chemosensor in the aorta that senses a decrease in blood supply or a dramatic decrease in partial pressure of oxygen in the blood.

aortic valve A one-way valve between the left ventricle of the heart and the aorta that prevents backflow of blood into the ventricle when it relaxes.

aphasia A deficit in the ability to use or understand words.

apical dominance In plants, inhibition by the apical bud of the growth of axillary buds.

apical hook A form taken by the stems of many eudicot seedlings that protects the delicate shoot apex while the stem grows through the soil.

apical meristem The meristem at the tip of a shoot or root; responsible for a plant's primary growth.

apicomplexans *See* Appendix A.

apomixis (ap oh mix′ is) [Gk. *apo*: away from + *mixis*: sexual intercourse] The asexual production of seeds.

apoplast (ap oh plast) In plants, the continuous meshwork of cell walls and extracellular spaces through which material can pass without crossing a cell membrane. (Contrast with symplast.)

apoptosis (ap uh toh′ sis) A series of genetically programmed events leading to cell death.

appendix A small blind-end sac that is attached to the initial segment of the colon.

aquaporin A transport protein in plant and animal cell membranes through which water passes in osmosis.

aquifer A large pool of groundwater.

arbuscular mycorrhizae Mutualistic fungi that enter the root and penetrate the cell walls of the root cells, forming arbuscular (treelike) structures inside the cell wall but outside the cell membrane. (Contrast with ectomycorrhizae.)

arbuscular mycorrhizal fungi *See* Appendix A.

archaea *See* Appendix A.

archegonium (ar′ ke go′ nee um) The multicellular structure that produces eggs in nonvascular land plants, ferns, and gymnosperms.

archenteron (ark en′ ter on) [Gk. *archos*: first + *enteron*: bowel] The earliest primordial animal digestive tract.

archosaurs *See* Appendix A.

arcuate nucleus A group of neurons in the hypothalamus that produce and secrete many neuroendocrines and are involved in regulating appetite.

arrow worms *See* Appendix A.

arteriole A small blood vessel arising from an artery that feeds blood into a capillary bed. (Contrast with venule.)

arteriosclerosis *See* **atherosclerosis**.

artery A muscular blood vessel carrying oxygenated blood away from the heart to other parts of the body. (Contrast with vein.)

arthropod *See* Appendix A.

artificial insemination An infertility treatment that involves the artificial introduction of sperm into the woman's reproductive tract.

artificial selection Selective breeding of organisms, commonly practiced by animal and plant breeders, to increase the frequency of a favored trait from one generation to the next. (Contrast with natural selection.)

ascospores Haploid spores contained within the sexual reproductive structure (the ascus) of sac fungi.

ascus (ass′ cus) (plural: asci) [Gk. *askos*: bladder] In sac fungi, the club-shaped sporangium within which spores (ascospores) are produced by meiosis.

asexual reproduction The formation of new individuals without gamete fusion (in eukaryotes) or conjugation (in prokaryotes). Often takes place by budding or fragmentation. The offspring are genetically identical to their parent.

Asgard archaea *See* Appendix A.

assimilation efficiency The proportion of ingested biomass that consumers assimilate by digestion.

assisted reproductive technologies (ARTs) Any of several procedures that remove unfertilized eggs from the ovary, combine them with sperm outside the body, and then place fertilized eggs or egg–sperm mixtures in a female's reproductive tract for development.

association cortex In the vertebrate brain, the portion of the cortex involved in higher-order information processing, so named because it integrates, or associates, information from different sensory modalities and from memory.

asthenosphere (ass thenn′ o sphere) [Gk. *asthenes*: weak] The viscous, malleable (changeable) layer of Earth's mantle. It is overlain by the solid lithospheric plates. (Contrast with **lithosphere**.)

astrocyte [Gk. *astron*: star] A type of macroglial cell that contributes to the blood–brain barrier by surrounding the smallest, most permeable blood vessels in the brain.

atherosclerosis (ath′ er oh sklair oh′ sis) [Gk. *athero*: gruel, porridge + *skleros*: hard] A disease of the lining of the arteries characterized by fatty, cholesterol-rich deposits in the walls of the arteries. When fibroblasts infiltrate these deposits and calcium precipitates in them, the disease becomes **arteriosclerosis**, or "hardening of the arteries."

atmosphere A thin layer of gases surrounding Earth composed of nitrogen gas, oxygen, argon, carbon dioxide, and traces of hydrogen, helium, ozone, methane, and many other gases.

atom [Gk. *atomos*: indivisible] The smallest unit of a chemical element. Consists of a nucleus and one or more electrons.

atomic number The number of protons in the nucleus of an atom; also equals the number of electrons around the neutral atom. Determines the chemical properties of the atom.

atomic weight The average of the mass numbers of a representative sample of atoms of an element, with all the isotopes in their normally occurring proportions.

ATP synthase An integral membrane protein that couples the transport of protons with the formation of ATP.

atrial natriuretic peptide (ANP) A hormone released by the atrial muscle fibers of the heart when they are overly stretched, which decreases reabsorption of sodium by the kidney and thus blood volume.

atrioventricular (AV) valve A heart valve between an atrium and a ventricle.

atrioventricular node A modified node of cardiac muscle that organizes the action potentials that control contraction of the ventricles.

atrium (a′ tree um) [L. *atrium*: central hall] An internal chamber. (1) In the hearts of vertebrates, the thin-walled chamber(s) entered by blood on its way to the ventricle(s). (2) The outer ear.

autocatalysis [Gk. *autos*: self + *kata*: to break down] A positive-feedback process in which an activated enzyme acts on other inactive molecules of the same enzyme to activate them.

autocrine Pertaining to a chemical signal that binds to and affects the cell that makes it. (Contrast with juxtacrine, paracrine.)

autoimmunity An immune response by an organism to its own molecules or cells.

autonomic nervous system (**ANS**) The portion of the nervous system that controls autonomic effectors (effectors other than the skeletal muscles). Also called the involuntary nervous system. The ANS has two divisions, **sympathetic** and **parasympathetic**, that work in opposition to each other. *See also* **parasympathetic division, sympathetic division**.

autonomous specification The determination of cell fates due to informational molecules originally present in the egg.

autophagy The programmed destruction of a cell's components.

autopolyploidy The possession of more than two entire chromosome sets that are derived from a single species. (Contrast with **allopolyploidy**.)

autoregulatory mechanisms In mammalian circulatory systems, local control of blood flow through capillary beds by constriction or dilation of incoming arterioles in response to local metabolite concentrations.

autosome Any chromosome (in a eukaryote) other than a sex chromosome.

autotroph (au′ tow trowf′) [Gk. *autos*: self + *trophe*: food] An organism that is capable of living exclusively on inorganic materials, water, and some energy source such as sunlight (*see* photoautotroph) or chemically reduced matter (*see* chemoautotroph). (Contrast with heterotroph.)

auxin (awk′ sin) [Gk. *auxein*: to grow] In plants, a substance (the most common being indole-3-acetic acid) that regulates growth and various aspects of development.

Avogadro's number The number of atoms or molecules in a mole (weighed out in grams) of a substance, calculated to be 6.023×10^{23}.

axillary bud A bud that forms in the angle (axil) where a leaf meets a stem.

axon [Gk. axle] The process (branching structure) of a neuron that conducts action potentials away from the cell body. (*See also* dendrites.)

axon hillock The junction between an axon and the neuron's cell body; where action potentials are generated.

axon terminal The end portion of an axon, which passes action potentials to another cell. Axon terminals can form synapses and release neurotransmitter.

B

B cell A type of lymphocyte involved in the humoral immune response of vertebrates. Upon recognizing an antigenic determinant, a B cell develops into a plasma cell, which secretes an antibody. (Contrast with T cell.)

B horizon *See* subsoil.

bacillus (bah sil′ us) [L: little rod] Any of various rod-shaped bacteria.

bacteria *See* Appendix A.

bacterial conjugation *See* conjugation.

bacteriophage (bak teer′ ee o fayj) [Gk. *bakterion*: little rod + *phagein*: to eat] Any of a group of viruses that infect bacteria. Also called phage.

bacteroids Nitrogen-fixing organelles that develop from endosymbiotic bacteria.

bark All tissues external to the vascular cambium of a plant.

baroreceptor [Gk. *baros*: weight] A pressure-sensing cell or organ. Sometimes called a stress receptor.

basal metabolic rate (BMR) The minimum rate of energy turnover in an awake (but resting) endotherm (bird or mammal) that is not expending energy for thermoregulation.

basal transcription apparatus The RNA polymerase II and general transcription factors bound to a promoter.

base (1) A substance that can accept a hydrogen ion in solution. (Contrast with acid.) (2) In nucleic acids, the purine or pyrimidine that is attached to each sugar in the sugar–phosphate backbone.

basidioma (plural: basidiomata) A fruiting structure produced by club fungi.

basidium (bass id′ ee yum) In club fungi, the characteristic sporangium in which four **basidiospores** are formed by meiosis and then borne externally before being shed.

Batesian mimicry The convergence in appearance of an edible species (the mimic) with an unpalatable species (the model).

behaviorism One of two classic approaches to the study of animal behavior, derived from

the discoveries of Ivan Pavlov and focused on conditioned behavior and controlled laboratory studies. (Contrast with ethology.)

benign Referring to a tumor that grows to a limited extent and does not spread to other parts of the body. (Contrast with malignant.)

beta diversity The change in species number and composition, or turnover of species, across a landscape. (Compare with alpha diversity, gamma diversity.)

β (beta) pleated sheet A type of protein secondary structure; results from hydrogen bonding between polypeptide regions running antiparallel to each other.

biased gene conversion A mechanism of concerted evolution in which a DNA repair system appears biased in favor of using particular nucleotide sequences as templates for repair, resulting in the rapid spread of the favored sequence across all copies of the gene. (*See* concerted evolution, unequal crossing over.)

bicuspid valve The left **atrioventricular (AV)** valve. So named because it has two leaves. Also called the mitral valve.

biennial A plant whose life cycle includes vegetative growth in the first year and flowering and senescence in the second year. (Contrast with annual, perennial.)

bilateral symmetry The condition in which only the right and left sides of an organism, divided by a single plane through the midline, are mirror images of each other.

bilaterians *See* Appendix A.

bilayer A structure that is two layers in thickness. In biology, most often refers to the phospholipid bilayer of membranes. (*See* phospholipid bilayer.)

bile A secretion of the liver made up of bile salts synthesized from cholesterol, various phospholipids, and bilirubin (the breakdown product of hemoglobin). Emulsifies fats in the small intestine.

binary fission Reproduction of a prokaryote by division of a cell into two genetically identical progeny cells.

bindin A species-specific recognition molecule on the sperm acrosomal process.

binocular vision Vision in which the visual fields of an animal's two eyes overlap, allowing the animal to see in three dimensions.

binomial nomenclature [Gk. two names] A taxonomic naming system in which each species is given a binomial, a genus name followed by a species name.

biodiversity The diversity of important ecological entities that span multiple spatial scales, from genes to populations to species to communities.

biofilm A community of microorganisms embedded in a polysaccharide matrix, forming a highly resistant coating on almost any moist surface.

biogeochemical cycle The movement of inorganic elements such as water, nitrogen, phosphorus, and carbon through living organisms and the physical environment.

biogeographic regions   Distinct regions of biota characterized by different species that occur at the continental scale. (Contrast with biome.)

biogeography   The scientific study of the distribution and diversity of organisms across Earth.

bioinformatics   The use of computer programs and mathematical approaches to analyze complex biological data, such as DNA sequences.

biological control   The use of natural enemies (predators, parasites, or pathogens) to reduce the population density of an economically damaging (pest) species.

biological species concept   The definition of a species as a group of actually or potentially interbreeding natural populations that are reproductively isolated from other such groups. (Contrast with lineage species concept; morphological species concept.)

biology   [Gk. *bios*: life + *logos*: study] The scientific study of living things.

biome   (bye′ ome) A major division of the ecological communities of Earth, characterized primarily by distinctive vegetation and annual patterns of temperature and precipitation. A given biogeographic region contains many different biomes.

biosphere   All regions of Earth (terrestrial and aquatic) and Earth's atmosphere in which organisms can live.

biota   (bye oh′ tah) All of the organisms—animals, plants, fungi, and microorganisms—found in a given area. (Contrast with flora, fauna.)

biotechnology   The use of living cells or organisms to produce materials useful to humans.

biotic   (bye ah′ tick) [Gk. *bios*: life] Living. In ecology, the living components of the environment such as organisms. (Contrast with abiotic.)

biotic resistance   The ability of resident species to exclude or slow the population growth of non-native species.

bipedal locomotion   Terrestrial locomotion by means of two rear limbs or legs.

bipolar cells   Cells in the retina that communicate between photoreceptors and ganglion cells.

birds   *See* Appendix A.

bivalves   *See* Appendix A.

blastocoel   (blass′ toe seal) [Gk. *blastos*: sprout + *koilos*: hollow] The central, hollow cavity of a blastula.

blastocyst   (blass′ toe cist) An early embryo formed by the first divisions of the fertilized egg (zygote). In mammals, a hollow ball of cells.

blastoderm   A layer of undifferentiated cells that are a very early stage of development prior to the specification of the embryonic axis.

blastodisc   (blass′ toe disk) An embryo that forms as a disc of cells on the surface of a large yolk mass; comparable to a blastula, but occurring in animals such as birds and other reptiles, in which the massive yolk restricts complete cleavage.

blastomere   Any of the cells produced by the early divisions of a fertilized animal egg.

blastopore   In animal embryos, the opening created by the invagination of the vegetal pole during gastrulation.

blastula   (blass′ chu luh) An early stage of the animal embryo; in many species, a hollow sphere of cells surrounding a central cavity, the blastocoel. (Contrast with blastodisc.)

block to polyspermy   Any of several responses to entry of a sperm into an egg that prevents more than one sperm from entering the egg.

blood clotting   A cascade of events involving platelets and circulating proteins (clotting factors) that seals damaged blood vessels.

blood plasma   The liquid portion of blood, in which blood cells and other particulates are suspended.

blood–brain barrier   The selective impermeability of blood vessels in the brain that prevents most chemicals from diffusing from the blood into the brain.

blue-light receptors   Pigments in plants that absorb blue light (450–500 nm). These pigments mediate many plant responses, including phototropism, stomatal movements, and expression of some genes.

body cavity   An internal, fluid-filled space, enclosed by mesoderm in triploblastic animals.

body plan   The general structure of an animal, the arrangement of its organ systems, and the integrated functioning of its parts.

Bohr effect   A shift in the O_2-binding curve of hemoglobin in response to excess H^+ ions such that the hemoglobin releases more O_2 in tissues where pH is low.

bone   A rigid component of vertebrate skeletal systems that contains an extracellular matrix of insoluble calcium phosphate crystals as well as collagen fibers.

Bowman's capsule   An elaboration of the renal tubule, composed of podocytes, that surrounds and collects the filtrate from the glomerulus.

brachiopods   *See* Appendix A.

brain   The centralized integrative center of a nervous system.

brainstem   The portion of the vertebrate brain between the spinal cord and the forebrain, made up of the medulla, pons, and midbrain.

brassinosteroids   Plant steroid hormones that mediate many developmental processes including light effects promoting the elongation of stems and pollen tubes.

Broca's area   A portion of the human brain essential for speech. Located in the frontal lobe just in front of the primary motor cortex.

bronchioles   The smallest airways in a vertebrate lung, branching off the bronchi.

bronchus   (plural: bronchi) The major airway(s) branching off the trachea into the vertebrate lung.

brown algae   *See* Appendix A.

brown fat   In mammals, fat tissue that is specialized to produce heat. It has many mitochondria and capillaries, and a protein that uncouples oxidative phosphorylation.

bryozoans   *See* Appendix A.

bud   A protuberance on a stem that contains an undeveloped leaf, shoot, or flower.

budding   Asexual reproduction in which a more or less complete new organism grows from the body of the parent organism, eventually detaching itself.

buffer   A substance that can transiently accept or release hydrogen ions and thereby resist changes in pH.

bulbourethral glands   Secretory structures of the human male reproductive system that produce a small volume of an alkaline, mucoid secretion that helps neutralize acidity in the urethra and lubricate it to facilitate the passage of semen.

bulbus arteriosus   The last chamber of the fish heart.

bulk flow   The movement of a solution from a region of higher pressure potential to a region of lower pressure potential.

bulk transport   *See* solvent drag.

bundle of His   Fibers of modified cardiac muscle that conduct action potentials from the atria to the ventricular muscle mass.

bundle sheath cell   Part of a tissue that surrounds the veins of plants, and where the fixed CO_2 is released for use in the Calvin cycle.

C

C horizon   *See* parent rock.

C_3 plants   Plants that produce 3PG as the first stable product of carbon fixation in photosynthesis and use ribulose bisphosphate as a CO_2 receptor.

C_4 plants   Plants that produce oxaloacetate as the first stable product of carbon fixation in photosynthesis and use phosphoenolpyruvate as a CO_2 acceptor. C_4 plants also perform the reactions of C_3 photosynthesis.

calcitonin   A hormone produced by the thyroid gland; lowers blood calcium and promotes bone formation. (Contrast with parathyroid hormone.)

calcitriol   A hormone derived from vitamin D and whose actions include stimulating the cells of the digestive tract to absorb calcium from ingested food.

calorie   [L. *calor*: heat] The amount of heat required to raise the temperature of 1 gram of water by 1 degree Celsius. Physiologists commonly use the kilocalorie (kcal) as a unit of measure (1 kcal = 1,000 calories). Nutritionists also use the **kilocalorie**, but refer to it as the **Calorie** (capital C).

Calvin cycle   The stage of photosynthesis in which CO_2 reacts with RuBP to form 3PG, 3PG is reduced to a sugar, and RuBP is regenerated, while other products are released to the rest of the plant. Also known as the Calvin–Benson cycle.

Cambrian explosion   The rapid diversification of multicellular life that took place during the Cambrian period.

cAMP (cyclic AMP)   A compound formed from ATP that acts as a second messenger.

cancellous bone   A type of bone with numerous internal cavities that make it appear spongy, although it is rigid. (Contrast with compact bone.)

capacitance vessels   A name given to veins because their walls are more stretchable than arteries and therefore can contain different amounts (capacities) of blood.

capillary   [L. *capillaris*: hair] In the circulatory system, a microscopic blood vessel with walls composed of a single layer of epithelial cells. Capillaries are permeable and therefore the principal sites of exchange between blood and other tissues in animals with closed circulatory systems. **Capillary beds** are networks of capillaries where materials are exchanged between the blood and the interstitial fluid.

capsid   The outer shell of a virus that encloses its nucleic acid.

capsule   In some prokaryotes, a dense layer of polymers that surrounds the cell wall.

carbohydrases   Digestive enzymes that break down carbohydrates.

carbohydrates   Organic compounds containing carbon, hydrogen, and oxygen in the ratio 1:2:1 (i.e., with the general formula $C_nH_{2n}O_n$). Common examples are sugars, starch, and cellulose.

carbon skeleton   The chains or rings of carbon atoms that form the structural basis of organic molecules. Other atoms or functional groups are attached to the carbon atoms.

carbon-fixation reactions   The phase of photosynthesis in which chemical energy captured in the light reactions is used to drive the reduction of CO_2 to form carbohydrates.

carbonic anhydrase (CA)   An enzyme that catalyzes the hydration of CO_2 to produce carbonic acid.

carboxylase   An enzyme that catalyzes the addition of carboxyl functional groups (O=C—OH) to a substrate.

cardiac cycle   The alternating contraction and relaxation of the heart. In a mammal, contraction of the two atria of the heart, followed by contraction of the two ventricles and then by relaxation until the next contraction begins. *See also* diastole, systole.

cardiac muscle   A type of muscle tissue that makes up, and is responsible for the beating of, the heart. Characterized by branching cells with single nuclei and a striated (striped) appearance. (Contrast with smooth muscle, skeletal muscle.)

cardiovascular system   [Gk. *kardia*: heart + L. *vasculum*: small vessel] The heart, blood, and vessels of a circulatory system.

carnivore   [L. *carn*: flesh + *vorare*: to devour] An organism that eats animal tissues. (Contrast with detritivore, herbivore, omnivore.)

carnivorous plant   A plant capable of trapping and digesting animals to obtain nutrients.

carnivory   An act of predation in which the predator and prey are both animals. (Contrast with herbivory, omnivory, parasitism).

carotid body   A chemosensor in the carotid artery that senses a decrease in blood supply or a dramatic decrease in partial pressure of oxygen in the blood.

carpel   (kar' pel) [Gk. *karpos*: fruit] The organ of the flower that contains one or more ovules.

carrier proteins   Proteins that bind another substance to transport it from one location to another; carriers bind small molecules and transport them across membranes.

carrying capacity (*K*)   The maximum number of individuals in a population (i.e., maximum population size) that can be supported by the resources present in a given environment.

cartilage bone   A type of bone that begins its development as a cartilaginous structure resembling the future mature bone, then gradually hardens into mature bone. (Contrast with membranous bone.)

cartilage   In vertebrates, a tough connective tissue found in joints, the outer ear, and elsewhere. Forms the entire skeleton in some animal groups.

Casparian strip   A band of cell wall containing suberin and lignin, found in the endodermis. Restricts the movement of water across the endodermis.

caspase   One of a group of proteases that catalyze cleavage of target proteins and are active in apoptosis.

catabolic reaction   (kat uh bah' lik) [Gk. *kata*: to break down + *ballein*: to throw] A synthetic reaction in which complex molecules are broken down into simpler ones and energy is released. (Contrast with anabolic reaction.)

catabolite repression   In the presence of abundant glucose, the diminished synthesis of catabolic enzymes for other energy sources.

catalyst   In chemistry, a substance that speeds up a reaction without being permanently altered itself.

cation   (cat' eye on) An ion with one or more positive charges. (Contrast with anion.)

cation exchange   The process in soil by which cations bound to soil particles are released from the particles and made available to plant roots in soil water through the binding of hydrogen ions to the soil particles.

cDNA   *See* complementary DNA.

cDNA library   A collection of complementary DNAs derived from mRNAs of a particular tissue at a particular time in the life cycle of an organism.

cecum   (see' cum) [L. blind] A blind branch off the large intestine. In many non-ruminant mammals, the cecum contains a colony of microorganisms that contribute to the digestion of food.

cell   The simplest structural unit of a living organism. In multicellular organisms, many individual cells serve as the building blocks of tissues and organs.

cell adhesion   The binding of one cell to another, often mediated by noncovalent forces.

cell body   The portion of the neuron that contains the nucleus and gives rise to dendrites and an axon.

cell cycle checkpoints   Points of transition between different phases of the cell cycle, which are regulated by cyclins and cyclin-dependent kinases (CDKs).

cell cycle   The stages through which a cell passes between one mitotic division and the next. Includes all stages of interphase (G1, S and G2 phases), mitosis and cytokinesis (M phase). (*See* mitosis.)

cell division signals   The one or more signals required to initiate cell division. The signals may originate from either inside or outside the cell.

cell junctions   Specialized structures associated with the cell membranes of epithelial cells. Some contribute to cell adhesion, others to intercellular communication.

cell membrane   The membrane that surrounds the cell, regulating the entry and exit of molecules and ions. Every cell has a cell membrane.

cell recognition   The specific binding of cells to one another mediated by membrane proteins or carbohydrates.

cell theory   The theory that cells are the basic structural and physiological units of all living organisms, and that all cells come from preexisting cells.

cell wall   A relatively rigid structure that encloses cells of plants, fungi, many protists, and most prokaryotes, and which gives these cells their shape and limits their expansion in hypotonic media.

cell-free system   A test-tube or similar vessel in which the contents of cells are released and studied, after the cells are lysed by destruction of the integrity of the cell membrane.

cellular immune response   The immune system response mediated by T cells and directed against parasites, fungi, intracellular viruses, abnormal proteins produce by cancer cells and foreign tissues (grafts). (Contrast with humoral immune response.)

cellular respiration   The catabolic pathways by which electrons are removed from various molecules and passed through intermediate electron carriers to O_2, generating H_2O and releasing energy.

cellular slime molds   *See* Appendix A.

cellular specialization   In multicellular organisms, the division of labor such that different cell types become responsible for different functions (e.g., reproduction or digestion) within the organism.

cellulose   A straight-chain polymer of glucose molecules, used by plants as a structural supporting material.

central dogma   The premise that information flows from DNA to DNA, from DNA to RNA, and from RNA to polypeptide (protein).

central nervous system (CNS)   The portion of the nervous system that is the site of most information processing, storage, and retrieval; in vertebrates, the brain and spinal cord. (Contrast with peripheral nervous system.)

centriole   (sen' tree ole) A paired organelle that helps organize the microtubules in animal and protist cells during nuclear division.

centromere   (sen' tro meer) [Gk. *centron*: center + *meros*: part] The region where sister chromatids join and microtubules attach to chromosomes.

centrosome   (sen' tro soam) The major microtubule organizing center of an animal cell. Contains a pair of centrioles.

cephalization   (sef ah luh zay' shun) [Gk. *kephale*: head] The evolutionary trend toward increasing concentration of brain and sensory organs at the anterior end of the animal.

cephalopods   *See* Appendix A.

cercozoans   *See* Appendix A.

cerebellum   (sair uh bell' um) [L. diminutive of *cerebrum*: brain] The brain region that controls muscular coordination; located at the anterior end of the hindbrain.

cerebral cortex   The thin layer of gray matter (neuronal cell bodies) that overlies the cerebrum.

cerebral hemispheres   The bilateral divisions of the cerebrum.

cerebrum   (su ree' brum) [L. brain] The dorsal anterior portion of the forebrain, making up the largest part of the brain of mammals; the chief coordination center of the nervous system and the major information-processing areas of the vertebrate brain, consisting of two cerebral hemispheres, each comprised of five lobes.

cervix   (sir' vix) [L. neck] The opening of the uterus into the vagina.

channel protein   An integral membrane protein that forms an aqueous passageway across the membrane in which it is inserted and through which specific solutes may pass.

chaperone   A protein that guards other proteins by counteracting molecular interactions that threaten their three-dimensional structure.

character   In genetics, an observable feature, such as eye color. (Contrast with trait.)

character displacement   An evolutionary phenomenon in which species that compete for the same limiting resources diverge in morphology and/or behavior.

chelicerates   *See* Appendix A.

chemical bond   An attractive force stably linking two atoms.

chemical equilibrium   A state of no net change, occurring when the forward and reverse reactions in a system take place at the same rate.

chemical evolution   The theory that life originated through the chemical transformation of inanimate substances.

chemical reaction   The change in the composition or distribution of atoms of a substance, with consequent alterations in properties.

chemical synapse   A type of synapse at which neurotransmitter molecules released from a presynaptic cell induce changes in a postsynaptic cell. (Contrast with electrical synapse.)

chemically gated channel   A type of membrane channel that opens or closes depending on the presence or absence of a specific molecule that binds either to the channel protein itself or to a separate receptor that alters the three-dimensional shape of the channel protein.

chemiosmosis   The formation of ATP in mitochondria and chloroplasts, resulting from a pumping of protons across a membrane (against a gradient of electric charge and of pH), followed by the return of the protons through a protein channel with ATP synthase activity.

chemoautotroph   An organism that obtains energy by oxidizing inorganic substances, using some of that energy to fix carbon. (Contrast with chemoheterotroph, photoautotroph, photoheterotroph.)

chemoheterotroph   An organism that must obtain both carbon and energy from organic substances. (Contrast with chemoautotroph, photoautotroph, photoheterotroph.)

chemoreceptor   A receptor protein that binds to specific molecules (such as odorant molecules or pheromones) in the environment.

chemosynthesis   The use of energy from inorganic chemical compounds by archaea and bacteria to fix CO_2 and produce carbohydrates using the Calvin cycle.

chiasma   (kie az' muh) (plural: chiasmata) [Gk. cross] An X-shaped connection between paired homologous chromosomes in prophase I of meiosis. A chiasma is the visible manifestation of crossing over between homologous chromosomes.

chief cells   One of three types of secretory cells found in the gastric pits of the stomach wall. Chief cells secrete the protein-digesting enzyme pepsin. (*See also* parietal cells.)

chitin   (kye' tin) [Gk. *kiton*: tunic] The characteristic tough but flexible organic component of the exoskeleton of arthropods, consisting of a complex, nitrogen-containing polysaccharide. Also found in cell walls of fungi.

chitons   *See* Appendix A.

chlamydias   *See* Appendix A.

chlorophyll   (klor' o fill) [Gk. *kloros*: green + *phyllon*: leaf] Any of several green pigments associated with chloroplasts or with certain bacterial membranes; responsible for trapping light energy for photosynthesis.

chlorophytes   *See* Appendix A.

chloroplast   [Gk. *kloros*: green + *plast*: a particle] An organelle bounded by a double membrane containing the enzymes and pigments that perform photosynthesis. Chloroplasts occur only in eukaryotes.

choanocyte   (ko' an uh site) The collared, flagellated feeding cells of sponges.

cholecystokinin (CCK)   (ko' luh sis tuh kai' nin) A hormone produced and released by the lining of the duodenum when it is stimulated by undigested fats and proteins. It stimulates the gallbladder to release bile and slows stomach activity.

chondrichthyans   *See* Appendix A.

chordamesoderm   Tissue of the vertebrate embryo that will form the notochord and somite mesoderm, and plays roles in organizing the embryonic axis.

chordates   *See* Appendix A.

chorion   (kor' ee on) [Gk. *khorion*: afterbirth] In mammals and reptiles (including birds), the outermost of the membranes protecting the embryo; in mammals it forms part of the placenta.

chromatin   The nucleic acid–protein complex that makes up eukaryotic chromosomes.

chromosomal rearrangements   Large changes in the sequence of DNA caused by breakage and rejoining of DNA molecules. Includes deletions, duplications, inversions and translocations.

chromosome   [Gk. *kroma*: color + *soma*: body] In bacteria and viruses, the DNA molecule that contains most or all of the genetic information of the cell or virus. In eukaryotes, a structure composed of DNA and proteins that bears part of the genetic information of the cell.

chylomicrons   (ky low my' crons) Particles of lipid coated with protein, produced in the gut from dietary fats and secreted into the extracellular fluids.

chyme   (kime) [Gk. *kymus*: juice] Created in the stomach; a mixture of ingested food with the digestive juices secreted by the salivary glands and the stomach lining.

chytrids   *See* Appendix A.

cilia   (singular: cilium) [L. eyelashes] Hairlike organelles used for locomotion by many unicellular organisms and for moving water and mucus by many multicellular organisms. Generally shorter than flagella.

ciliates   *See* Appendix A.

circadian rhythm   (sir kade' ee an) [L. *circa*: approximately + *dies*: day] A rhythm of growth or activity that recurs about every 24 hours.

circulatory system   A physiological system of vessels that distribute a fluid (blood or hemolymph) around the body. It can be open or closed to the interstitial fluid and include a muscular pump. (*See also* cardiovascular system)

cis-trans isomers   In molecules with a double bond (typically between two carbon items), identifies on which side of the double bond similar atoms or functional groups are found. If they are on the same side, the molecule is a *cis* isomer; in a *trans* isomer, similar atoms are on opposite sides of the double bond. (*See* isomers.)

clade   [Gk. *klados*: branch] A monophyletic group made up of an ancestor and all of its descendants.

class I MHC proteins   Cell surface proteins that participate in the cellular immune response directed against virus-infected cells and cancer cells.

class II MHC proteins   Cell surface proteins of monocyte-derived cells and B that present antigens to T-helper cells of the humoral immune response.

class switching   Occurs when a B cell changes the immunoglobulin class it synthesizes (e.g., a B cell making IgM switches to making IgG).

cleavage   The first few cell divisions of an animal zygote. (*See also* complete cleavage, incomplete cleavage.)

climate   The long-term average atmospheric conditions (temperature, precipitation, humidity, wind direction and velocity) at a particular place over longer time (years to millennia). (Contrast with weather.)

climax community   The final stage of succession; a community that is capable of perpetuating itself under local climatic and soil conditions and persists for a relatively long time.

clinal variation   [Gk. *klinein*: to lean] Gradual change in the phenotype of a species over a geographic gradient.

clitellates   *See* Appendix A.

clonal deletion   Inactivation or destruction of B or T cell clones that would produce immune reactions against an animal's own body.

clonal lineages   Asexually reproduced groups of nearly identical organisms.

clonal selection   A mechanism by which exposure to antigen results in the activation of selected T or B cell clones, resulting in an immune response.

clone   [Gk. *klon*: twig, shoot] (1) Genetically identical cells or organisms produced from a common ancestor by asexual means. (2) To produce many identical copies of a DNA sequence by its introduction into, and subsequent asexual reproduction of, a cell or organism.

closed circulatory system   A circulatory system in which the circulating fluid is contained within a continuous system of vessels. (Contrast with open circulatory system.)

club fungi   *See* Appendix A

clumped dispersion   The spatial arrangement of individuals within a population, characterized by clumped spatial patterns. (Compare with random dispersion, regular [uniform] dispersion.)

cnidarians   *See* Appendix A.

CO (CONSTANS)   A gene coding for a transcription factor that activates the synthesis of florigen; involved in the induction of flowering.

co-repressor   In the regulation of bacterial operons, a molecule that binds to the repressor, causing it to change shape and bind to the operator, thereby inhibiting transcription.

co-transport   *See* secondary active transport.

coastal zone   The marine life zone that extends from the shoreline to the edge of the continental shelf. Characterized by relatively shallow, well-oxygenated water and variable temperatures and salinities.

coccus   (kock' us) (plural: cocci) [Gk. *kokkos*: berry, pit] Any of various spherical or spheroidal bacteria.

cochlea   (kock' lee uh) [Gk. *kokhlos*: snail] A spiral tube in the inner ear of vertebrates; it contains the sensory cells involved in hearing.

codominance   A condition in which two alleles at a locus produce different phenotypic effects and both effects appear in heterozygotes.

codon   The three nucleotides in messenger RNA that direct the placement of a particular amino acid into a polypeptide chain. (Contrast with anticodon.)

coelomate   Possessing a coelom. (Contrast with acoelomate, pseudocoelomate.)

coenocyte   (see' no site) An organism that contains many nuclei within each cell membrane.

coenocytic   (seen' a sit ik) [Gk. *koinos*: common + *kytos*: container] Referring to the condition of "cells" containing many nuclei but enclosed by a single cell membrane. Results from nuclear division without cytokinesis.

coenzyme   A nonprotein carbon-containing molecule that is required for the action of one or more enzymes.

cohesion   The tendency of molecules (or any substances) to stick together.

cohort life table   A life table in which the fate of a group of individuals born during the same time frame (a cohort) is followed from birth to death.

coleochaetophytes   *See* Appendix A.

coleoptile   A sheath that surrounds and protects the shoot apical meristem and young primary leaves of a grass seedling as they move through the soil.

collagen   [Gk. *kolla*: glue] A fibrous protein found extensively in bone and connective tissue.

collecting duct   In vertebrates, a tubule that receives urine produced in the nephrons of the kidney and delivers that fluid to the ureter for excretion.

collenchyma   (cull eng' kyma) [Gk. *kolla*: glue + *enchyma*: infusion] A type of plant cell, living at functional maturity, which lends flexible support by virtue of primary cell walls typically thickened at the corners. (Contrast with parenchyma, sclerenchyma.)

colon   [Gk. *kolon*] The portion of the gut between the small intestine and the anus. Also called the large intestine.

commensalism   [L. *com*: together + *mensa*: table] A type of positive interaction in which one species benefits from the interaction while the other is unaffected. (Contrast with amensalism, competition, mutualism.)

communication   A signal from one organism (or cell) that alters the functioning or behavior of another organism (or cell).

community   A group of species living together at the same place and time.

community function   The way a community works as measured by metrics such as plant productivity or stability.

community structure   The set of characteristics or patterns that describes a community, including the number, composition, and abundance of species.

compact bone   A type of bone with a solid, hard structure. (Contrast with cancellous bone.)

companion cell   In angiosperms, a specialized cell found adjacent to a sieve tube element.

comparative experiment   An experiment in which data from various unmanipulated samples or populations are compared, but in which variables are not controlled or even necessarily identified. (Contrast with controlled experiment.)

comparative genomics   Computer-aided comparison of DNA sequences both within and between species to address a variety of topics, such as the identity of shared genes, rates of sequence divergence, and how species are related to one another.

comparator   In a regulatory system, the mechanism for comparing a feedback variable to a set point to generate command signals to effector organs.

competition   A nontrophic interaction in which two or more species overlap in the use of at least some of the same required limiting resources, negatively affecting their growth, reproduction, and/or survival. (Contrast with amensalism, commensalism, mutualism.)

competitive coexistence   The ability of species to coexist with one another despite sharing limiting resources. (Contrast with competitive exclusion.)

competitive exclusion   A result of competition between species for resources, in which one species completely eliminates the other from a given habitat. (Contrast with competitive coexistence.)

competitive inhibitor   A non-substrate that inhibits the activity of an enzyme by binding to its active site, preventing substrate binding. (Contrast with noncompetitive inhibitor.)

complement system   A group of more than 20 proteins that play a role in some reactions of the vertebrate immune system. The complement proteins are not immunoglobulins.

complementary base pairing   The A-T (or A-U), T-A (or U-A), C-G, and G-C pairing of bases in double-stranded DNA, in transcription, and between tRNA and mRNA.

complementary diet   A mixture of foods that supplies all essential nutrients.

complementary DNA (cDNA)   DNA formed by reverse transcriptase acting with an RNA template; an essential intermediate in the reproduction of retroviruses; used as a tool in recombinant DNA technology; lacks introns.

complete cleavage   A pattern of cleavage that occurs in eggs that have little yolk. Early cleavage furrows divide the egg completely, and the blastomeres are of similar size. (Contrast with incomplete cleavage.)

complete metamorphosis   A change of state during the life cycle of an organism in which the body is almost completely rebuilt to produce an individual with a very different body form. Characteristic of insects such as butterflies, moths, beetles, ants, wasps, and flies. (Contrast with direct development, incomplete metamorphosis.)

complex ions   Groups of covalently bonded atoms that carry an electric charge (e.g., NH_4^+, the ammonium ion).

complex life cycle   In reference to parasitic species, a life cycle that requires more than one host to complete.

composite transposon   Two transposable elements located near one another that transpose together and carry the intervening DNA sequence with them. (*See* transposable element.)

compound   (1) A substance made up of atoms of more than one element. (2) Made up of many units, as in the **compound eyes** of arthropods.

concentration gradient   A difference in concentration of an ion or other chemical substance from one location to another, often across a membrane. (*See* active transport, facilitated diffusion.)

concerted evolution   The common evolution of a family of repeated genes, such that changes in one copy of the gene family are replicated in other copies of the gene family, and thus evolve "in concert." (*See* biased gene conversion, unequal crossing over.)

condensation reaction   A chemical reaction in which two molecules become connected by a covalent bond and a molecule of water is released (AH + BOH → AB + H_2O.) (Contrast with hydrolysis reaction.)

conditional mutation   A mutation that results in a characteristic phenotype only under certain environmental conditions.

conditioned reflex   A form of associative learning first described by Ivan Pavlov, in which a natural response (such as salivation in response to food) becomes associated with a normally unrelated stimulus (such as the sound of a bell or a metronome).

conduction   The transfer of heat from one object to another through direct contact.

cone   In conifers, a reproductive structure consisting of spore-bearing scales extending from a central axis. (*See also* megastrobilus, microstrobilus.)

cone cells   In the vertebrate retina, photoreceptor cells responsible for color vision.

conidium   (ko nid′ ee um) (plural: conidia) [Gk. *konis*: dust] A type of haploid fungal spore borne at the tips of hyphae, not enclosed in sporangia.

conifers   *See* Appendix A.

conjugation   (kon ju gay′ shun) [L. *conjugare*: yoke together] (1) A process by which DNA is passed from one cell to another through a conjugation tube, as in bacteria. (2) A nonreproductive sexual process by which *Paramecium* and other ciliates exchange genetic material.

connective tissue   A type of tissue that connects or surrounds other tissues; its cells are embedded in a collagen-containing matrix. One of the four major tissue types in multicellular animals, including cartilage, bone, blood, and fat.

connexon   In a gap junction, a protein channel linking adjacent animal cells.

consensus sequences   Short stretches of DNA that appear, with little variation, in many different genes, or other locations, that have the same function (e.g., at intron splice sites).

conservation biology   An integrative scientific discipline that relies on principles of ecology, economics, social science, and policy to protect and manage Earth's biodiversity.

conspecifics   Individuals of the same species.

constant region   The portion of an immunoglobulin molecule whose amino acid composition determines its class and does not vary among immunoglobulins in that class. Also, the portion of a T-cell receptor molecule that does not vary. (Contrast with variable region.)

constitutive   Always present; produced continually at a constant rate. (Contrast with inducible.)

constitutive proteins   Proteins that an organism produces all the time, and at a relatively constant rate. (Contrast with inducible proteins.)

consumption efficiency   The proportion of available biomass that is ingested by consumers.

continental drift   The gradual movements of the world's continents that have occurred over billions of years.

contraception   Birth control methods that prevent fertilization or implantation (conception).

contractile vacuole   (kon trak′ tul) A specialized vacuole that collects excess water taken in by osmosis, then contracts to expel the water from the cell.

controlled experiment   An experiment in which a sample is divided into groups whereby experimental groups are exposed to manipulations of an independent variable while one group serves as an untreated control. The data from the various groups are then compared to see if there are changes in a dependent variable as a result of the experimental manipulation. (Contrast with comparative experiment.)

controlled system   A set of components in a physiological system that is controlled by commands from a regulatory system. (Contrast with regulatory system.)

convection   The transfer of heat to or from a surface via a moving stream of air or fluid.

convergent evolution   Independent evolution of similar features from different ancestral traits.

convergent extension   Movements of cells in the sea urchin blastula that form the archenteron. These cells elongate, flatten, and interdigitate to form a tubular structure.

convolutions   Foldings of the vertebrate brain's cerebral cortex into ridges called gyri and valleys called sulci. The level of cortical convolution increases taxonomically and is especially extensive in humans.

coprophagy   The consumption of feces.

copulation   Reproductive behavior that results in a male depositing sperm in the reproductive tract of a female.

coral bleaching   The loss of color in coral colonies, usually because of the loss or decline of symbiotic zooxanthellae.

Coriolis effect   The deflection of air or water as a result of differences in Earth's rotational speed at different latitudes.

cork cambium   [L. *cambiare*: to exchange] In plants, a lateral meristem that produces secondary growth, mainly in the form of waxy-walled protective cells, including some of the cells that become bark.

cornea   The clear, transparent tissue that covers the eye and allows light to pass through to the retina.

corolla   (ko role′ lah) [L. *corolla*: a small crown] All of the petals of a flower, collectively.

coronary artery   An artery that serves the cardiac muscles.

coronary thrombosis   A blood clot in a blood vessel of the heart.

corpora allata   The insect endocrine gland that secretes juvenile hormone.

corpora cardiaca   The insect endocrine gland that secretes **prothoracicotropic hormone (PTTH)**.

corpus luteum   (kor′ pus loo′ tee um) (plural: corpora lutea) [L. yellow body] A structure formed from a follicle after ovulation; produces hormones important to the maintenance of pregnancy.

cortex   [L. *cortex*: covering, rind] (1) In plants, the tissue between the epidermis and the vascular tissue of a stem or root. (2) In animals, the outer tissue of certain organs, such as the adrenal gland (adrenal cortex) and the brain (cerebral cortex).

corticosteroids   Steroid hormones produced and released by the cortex of the adrenal gland.

corticotropin-releasing hormone (CRH)   A hormone produced by the hypothalamus and that controls the release of cortisol from the anterior pituitary.

cortisol   A corticosteroid that mediates stress responses.

cost–benefit approach   An approach to evolutionary studies that assumes an animal has a limited amount of time and energy to devote to each of its activities, and that each activity has fitness costs as well as benefits. (*See also* trade-off.)

cotyledon   (kot′ ul lee′ dun) [Gk. *kotyledon*: hollow space] A "seed leaf." An embryonic organ that stores and digests reserve materials; may expand when the seed germinates.

countercurrent flow   An arrangement that promotes the maximum exchange of heat, or of a diffusible substance, between two fluids by having the fluids flow in opposite directions through parallel vessels close together.

countercurrent heat exchange   The exchange of heat that occurs between two closely juxtaposed fluid streams that are flowing in opposite directions (e.g., blood flowing in opposite directions in two juxtaposed blood vessels).

countercurrent multiplier   The mechanism that increases the concentration of the interstitial fluid in the mammalian kidney through countercurrent flow in the loops of Henle and selective permeability and active transport of ions by segments of the loops of Henle.

coupled human–natural system ecology   The practice of encouraging biodiversity and sustainability in systems where humans and nature are intricately linked.

coupled transporters   Membrane proteins that transport two substances across a membrane, often with the transport of one energetically driving the transport of another.

covalent bond   A chemical bond based on the sharing of electrons between two atoms.

CpG islands   DNA regions rich in C nucleotides adjacent to G nucleotides. Especially abundant in promoters, these regions are where methylation of cytosine usually occurs.

cranial nerves   The 12 pairs of nerves that go directly from the brain to different parts of the body without going down the spinal cord.

craniates   *See* Appendix A.

crassulacean acid metabolism (CAM)   A metabolic pathway enabling the plants that possess it to store CO_2 at night and then perform photosynthesis during the day with stomata closed.

creatine phosphate (CP)   A phosphorylated creatine molecule that is abundant in skeletal muscle and can shuttle high-energy phosphate from mitochondria to myofibrils.

Crenarchaeota   *See* Appendix A

CRISPR   In some prokaryotes, *c*lustered *r*egularly *i*nterspaced *s*hort *p*alindromic *r*epeat sequences in DNA that are adjacent to sequences from invading viruses. When the two sequences are transcribed, the RNA binds a complementary RNA that binds a nuclease, CAS9, that can cleave and inactivate the genome of the invading virus. This mechanism can be adapted for inactivating and mutating any gene.

critical period   The life stage during which some particular type of learning must take place, or during which it occurs much more easily than at other times. Also called a sensitive period.

crocodilians   *See* Appendix A.

crop   A simple food storage sac, the first of two stomachlike organs in many animals (including reptiles, earthworms, and various insects). (*See also* gizzard.)

crossing over   The mechanism by which linked genes undergo recombination. In general, the term refers to the reciprocal exchange of corresponding segments between two homologous chromatids.

crosstalk   Interactions between different signal transduction pathways.

crustaceans   *See* Appendix A.

crustose   A growth form of organisms, such as lichens, in which the organism forms a thin, close, tight bond with the surface of a rock, tree, or other object.

crypsis   [Gk. *kryptos*: hidden] The resemblance of an organism to some part of its environment, which helps it escape detection by enemies.

cryptochromes   [Gk. *kryptos*: hidden + *kroma*: color] Photoreceptors mediating some blue-light effects in plants and animals.

ctene   (teen) [Gk. *cteis*: comb] In ctenophores, a comblike row of cilia-bearing plates. Ctenophores move by beating the cilia on their eight ctenes.

ctenophores   *See* Appendix A.

cumulus   A thick gelatinous layer that protects a mammalian ovum.

cupula   A gelatinous swelling in the semicircular canals of the vestibular system. A cupula encloses hair cell stereocilia that react to shifting fluid in the canal ducts.

cuticle   (1) In plants, a waxy layer on the outer body surface that retards water loss. (2) In ecdysozoans, an outer body covering that provides protection and support and is periodically molted.

cyanobacteria   *See* Appendix A.

cycads   *See* Appendix A.

cyclic AMP   *See* cAMP.

cyclic electron transport   In photosynthetic light reactions, the flow of electrons that produces ATP but not NADPH or O_2.

cyclin   A protein that activates a cyclin-dependent kinase, bringing about transitions in the cell cycle.

cyclin-dependent kinase (CDK)   A protein kinase whose target proteins are involved in transitions in the cell cycle and that is active only when complexed with additional protein subunits, called cyclins.

cyclostomes   *See* Appendix A.

cytokine   A regulatory protein made by immune system cells that affects other target cells in the immune system.

cytokinesis   (sy′ toe kine ee′ sis) [Gk. *kytos*: container + *kinein*: to move] The division of the cytoplasm of a dividing cell. Occurs at end of M phase after mitosis and after replication in binary fission.

cytokinins   (sy′ toe kine′ in) A class of plant growth substances that play roles in senescence, cell division, and other phenomena.

cytoplasm   The contents of the cell, excluding the nucleus.

cytoplasmic streaming   The flow of cytoplasm around fungal and plant cells.

cytosine (C)   (site′ oh seen) A nitrogen-containing base found in DNA and RNA.

cytoskeleton   The network of microtubules and microfilaments that gives a eukaryotic cell its shape and its capacity to arrange its organelles and to move.

cytosol   The fluid portion of the cytoplasm, excluding organelles and other solids.

cytotoxic T (T_C) cell   A type of T cell of the cellular immune system that binds to cells presenting antigens on class I MHC molecules and causes their death. The recognized antigen can be from a virus in infected cells or from an abnormal protein in cancer cells. (Contrast with T-helper cell.)

D

daily torpor   A daily reduction in metabolic rate and body temperature to conserve energy.

dalton (DA)   A measure of mass for atoms equal to the atomic mass unit.

data   Quantified observations about a system under study.

daughter chromosomes   During mitosis, the separated chromatids from the beginning of anaphase onward.

dead space   The lung volume that fails to be ventilated with fresh air (because the lungs are never completely emptied during exhalation).

declarative memory   Memory of people, places, events, and things that can be consciously recalled and described.

decomposer   *See* detritivore.

decomposition   The physical and chemical breakdown of detritus by bacteria and detritivores, leading to the release of nutrients and energy.

deductive logic   A logical thought process that starts with a premise believed to be true, then predicts what facts would also have to be true to be compatible with that premise. (Contrast with inductive logic.)

defensin   A type of protein made by phagocytes that kills bacteria and enveloped viruses by insertion into their cell membranes.

deficiency disease   A condition (e.g., scurvy, beriberi) caused by chronic lack of any essential nutrient.

deficiency symptom   A characteristic displayed by a plant when it is deficient in an essential element.

delayed hypersensitivity   An allergic response in which a T cell clone resulting from binding to an antigen-presenting cell releases cytokines over a period of hours to days, resulting in such effects as inflammation and rash. (Contrast with immediate hypersensitivity.)

deletion   A mutation resulting from the loss of a continuous segment of a gene or chromosome. Such mutations almost never revert to wild type. (Contrast with duplication, point mutation.)

demethylase   An enzyme that catalyzes the removal of the methyl group from cytosine, reversing DNA methylation.

demographic stochasticity   Fluctuations in population size as a result of random differences among individuals in reproduction and survival.

demography   The study of how births, deaths, immigration, and emigration affect population changes over time.

denaturation   The loss of activity of an enzyme or nucleic acid molecule as a result of structural changes induced by heat or other means.

dendrites   [Gk. *dendron*: tree] Branching fibers (processes) of a neuron. Dendrites are usually relatively short compared with the axon, and commonly carry information to the neuronal cell body.

denitrifiers   Bacteria that release nitrogen to the atmosphere as nitrogen gas (N_2).

density-dependent   Pertaining to any factor or interaction that varies with density. For example, individual survival and reproductive success often change as population density changes. (Contrast with density-independent.)

density-independent   Pertaining to any factor or interaction that varies independent of density. For example, an exceptionally strong hurricane may kill a large number of individuals in a population regardless of the population's density. (Contrast with density-independent.)

dentine   The layer of dense bony material beneath the enamel of a tooth.

deoxyribose   A five-carbon sugar found in nucleotides and DNA.

depolarization   A change in the resting potential across a membrane so that the inside of the cell becomes less negative, or even positive, compared with the outside of the cell. (Contrast with hyperpolarization.)

deprivation experiments   Experiments that involve raising an animal in an environment devoid of behavioral models from which it could learn a species-specific behavior, to see if the behavior is still expressed.

derived trait   A trait that differs from the ancestral trait. (Contrast with synapomorphy.)

dermal tissue system   The system of cells that forms the outer covering of a plant, consisting of epidermis in the young plant and periderm in a plant with extensive secondary growth. (Contrast with ground tissue system, vascular tissue system.)

descent with modification   Darwin's premise that all species share a common ancestor and have diverged from one another gradually over time.

desmosome   (dez′ mo sowm) [Gk. *desmos*: bond + *soma*: body] An adhering junction between animal cells.

desmotubule   In plants, the tubule inside a plasmodesma, through which small metabolites and ions move between plant cells. *See* plasmodesmata.

determinate growth   A growth pattern in which the growth of an organism or organ ceases when an adult state is reached; characteristic of most animals and some plant organs. (Contrast with indeterminate growth.)

determination   In development, the process whereby the fate of an embryonic cell or group of cells (e.g., to become epidermal cells or neurons) is set (becomes **determined**).

detritivore   (di try′ ti vore) [L. *detritus*: worn away + *vorare*: to devour] An organism that obtains its energy from the dead bodies or waste products (**detritus**) of other organisms, releasing nutrients and energy. (Contrast with carnivore, herbivore, omnivore.)

detritus   (di try′ tus) The dead bodies or waste products of organisms.

deuterostomes   *See* Appendix A.

development   The process by which a multicellular organism, beginning with a single cell, goes through a series of changes, taking on the successive forms that characterize its life cycle.

diabetes mellitus   Several diseases involving abnormalities in how the body manages blood glucose levels. Type I is characterized by lack of insulin and Type II is characterized by decreased responsiveness to insulin. Both can lead to excess glucose in the urine.

diacylglycerol (DAG)   In hormone action, the second messenger produced by hydrolytic removal of the head group of certain phospholipids.

diaphragm   [Gk. *diaphrassein*: barricade] (1) A sheet of muscle that separates the thoracic and abdominal cavities in mammals; responsible for breathing. (2) A shallow silicone cup that is inserted in the vagina and covers a woman's cervix, blocking the entry of sperm; a form of birth control.

diastole   (dye ass′ toll ee) [Gk. dilation] The phase of the cardiac cycle when the heart muscle relaxes. (Contrast with systole.)

diatoms   *See* Appendix A.

dichotomous   (dye cot′ oh mus) [Gk. *dichot*: split in two + *tomia*: removed) A branching pattern in which the shoot divides at the apex, producing two equivalent branches that subsequently never overlap.

diencephalon   The portion of the vertebrate forebrain that develops into the thalamus and hypothalamus.

differentiation   The process whereby originally similar cells follow different developmental pathways; the actual expression of determination.

diffusion   The random movement of molecules or other particles, resulting in even distribution of the particles when no barriers are present. (Contrast with active transport, diffusion.)

digestive vacuole   In protists, an organelle specialized for digesting food ingested by endocytosis.

dihybrid cross   A mating in which the parents differ with respect to the alleles of two loci of interest.

Dikarya   *See* Appendix A.

dikaryon   (di care′ ee ahn) [Gk. *di*: two + *karyon*: kernel] A cell or organism carrying two genetically distinguishable nuclei. Common in fungi.

dinoflagellates   *See* Appendix A.

dinosaurs   *See* Appendix A.

dioecious   (die eesh′ us) [Gk. *di*: two + *oikos*: house] Pertaining to organisms in which the two sexes are "housed" in two different individuals, so that eggs and sperm are not produced in the same individuals. Examples include humans, fruit flies, date palms. (Contrast with monoecious.)

diploblastic   Having a body derived from only two embryonic cell layers (ectoderm and endoderm, but no mesoderm). (Contrast with monoblastic, triploblastic.)

diploid   (dip′ loid) [Gk. *diplos*: double] Having a chromosome complement consisting of two copies (homologs) of each chromosome. Designated 2*n*. (Contrast with haploid.)

diplomonads   *See* Appendix A.

direct development   A pattern of development (notably among insects) in which hatchlings look like miniature versions of adults. (Contrast with metamorphosis.)

direct fitness   The component of fitness resulting from an organism producing its own offspring. (*Contrast with:* indirect fitness and inclusive fitness.)

direct interaction   An interaction that occurs between two species, such as predation, competition, or a positive interaction. (Compare with indirect interaction.)

directional selection   Selection in which phenotypes at one extreme of the population distribution are favored. (Contrast with disruptive selection, stabilizing selection.)

disaccharide   A carbohydrate made up of two monosaccharides (simple sugars).

discoidal cleavage   In animal development, a type of incomplete cleavage that is common in fishes and reptiles (including birds), the eggs of which contain a dense yolk mass.

dispersal   The movement of individuals into (immigration) or out of (emigration) an existing population.

dispersion patterns   The spatial arrangement of individuals in space within a population. (*See* clumped dispersion, random dispersion, regular [uniform] dispersion.)

disruptive selection   Selection in which phenotypes at both extremes of the population distribution are favored. (Contrast with directional selection, stabilizing selection.)

dissociation constant (K_D)   An equilibrium constant measuring the tendency of two substances that are bound together to separate into two smaller components. In cell signaling, the two substances are a ligand and receptor.

distal convoluted tubule   The portion of a renal tubule from where it reaches the renal cortex, just past the loop of Henle, to where it joins a collecting duct. (Contrast with proximal convoluted tubule.)

disturbance   An abiotic event that physically or chemically injures or kills some individuals, creating opportunities for other individuals to grow or reproduce. (Contrast with stress.)

disulfide bridge   The covalent bond between two sulfur atoms (–S—S–) linking two molecules or remote parts of the same molecule.

DNA (deoxyribonucleic acid)   The fundamental hereditary material of all living organisms. In eukaryotes, stored primarily in the cell nucleus. A nucleic acid using deoxyribose rather than ribose.

DNA fingerprinting   The identification of individuals based on their unique pattern of allele sequences, commonly short tandem repeats and single nucleotide polymorphisms.

DNA helicase   An enzyme that unwinds the double helix.

DNA ligase   An enzyme that seals breaks in DNA strands during replication and recombination.

DNA methyltransferase   An enzyme that catalyzes the methylation of DNA.

DNA microarray   A small glass or plastic square onto which hundreds of thousands of single-stranded DNA sequences are fixed so that hybridization of cell-derived RNA or DNA to the target sequences can be performed.

DNA polymerase   Any of a group of enzymes that catalyze the formation of DNA strands from a nucleic acid template.

DNA replication   The creation of a new strand of DNA in which DNA polymerase catalyzes the exact reproduction of an existing (template) strand of DNA.

DNA segregation   The separation of two DNA molecules formed by replication into two new cells during cell division.

DNA testing   In human genetics, the determination of genotype by analysis of DNA sequence.

Dobzhansky–Muller model   A genetic model that describes how reproductive isolation between two physically isolated populations can develop through the accumulation of incompatible genes or chromosomal arrangements.

domain   (1) An independent structural element within a protein. Encoded by recognizable nucleotide sequences, a domain often folds separately from the rest of the protein. Similar domains can appear in a variety of different proteins across phylogenetic groups (e.g., "homeobox domain," "calcium-binding domain"). (2) In phylogenetics, the three major groups of life (Bacteria, Archaea, and Eukarya).

dominant   In genetics, the phenotype (or trait) that is expressed, and its associated allele, in a heterozygote that has the same phenotype as one of the two homozygotes. (Contrast with recessive.)

dormancy   A condition in which normal activity is suspended, as in some spores, seeds, and buds.

dorsal   [L. *dorsum*: back] Toward or pertaining to the back or upper surface. (Contrast with ventral.)

dorsal lip   In amphibian embryos, the dorsal tissue surrounding the blastopore. Also called the organizer, this region directs the development of nearby embryonic regions.

double fertilization   In angiosperms, a process in which the nuclei of two sperm fertilize one egg. One sperm's nucleus combines with the egg nucleus to produce a zygote, while the other combines with the same egg's two polar nuclei to produce the first cell of the triploid endosperm (the tissue that will nourish the growing plant embryo).

dry-nosed primates   *See* Appendix A.

duodenum   (do′ uh dee′ num) The beginning portion of the vertebrate small intestine. (*See also* ileum, jejunum.)

duplication   A mutation in which a segment of a chromosome is duplicated, often by the attachment of a segment lost from its homolog. (Contrast with deletion, point mutation.)

dynein   A type of protein that binds to microtubules and causes bending in cilia and flagella.

E

early successional species   See pioneer species.

easterlies   The prevailing winds that blow from east to west at high latitudes. (Compare with westerlies.)

ecdysone   (eck die′ sone) [Gk. *ek*: out of + *dyo*: to clothe] In insects, a hormone that induces molting.

ecdysozoans   *See* Appendix A.

echinoderms   *See* Appendix A.

ecology   [Gk. *oikos*: house] The scientific study of the interrelationships of organisms with their living (biotic) and nonliving (abiotic) environments.

ecosystem   The organisms of a particular community together with the physical and chemical environment in which they live.

ecosystem engineering species   A species that creates, modifies, or maintains physical habitat for itself and other species, and can be a keystone or foundation species as well.

ecosystem science   The branch of ecology that considers how energy flows and nutrients cycle through communities.

ecosystem services   The benefits that humans obtain from ecosystems, such as natural products, protective and regulating services, and recreational, aesthetic, and spiritual enrichment.

ecosystem values   Measures of the economic and biophysical values of ecosystem services to humans.

ectoderm   [Gk. *ektos*: outside + *derma*: skin] The outermost of the three embryonic germ layers first delineated during gastrulation. Gives rise to the skin, sense organs, and nervous system.

ectomycorrhizae   Mutualistic fungi that cover the roots of plants and assist in the uptake of water and minerals from the soil by the plant. (Contrast with arbuscular mycorrhizae.)

ectoparasite   A parasite that lives on the surface of its host organism. (Compare with endoparasite.)

ectotherm   [Gk. *ektos*: outside + *thermos*: heat] An animal that is dependent on external heat sources for regulating its body temperature (Contrast with endotherm.)

edge effects   The abiotic and biotic changes to the edge of a habitat that are brought about by habitat fragmentation.

effective population size   The number of individuals in a population that can contribute offspring to the next generation.

effector   (1) A component of a physiological system that responds to information by *effecting* changes (making change happen) in the internal environment; examples include muscles and the secretory cells of the digestive tract. (2) In plants, a pathogen-produced elicitor that triggers plant R proteins to initiate the specific immunity response.

effector cells   In cellular immunity, B cells and T cells that attack an antigen, either by secreting antibodies that bind to the antigen or by releasing molecules that destroy any cell bearing the antigen.

effector mechanisms   Adaptations that enable an organism to alter its physiological or behavioral state.

effector protein   In cell signaling, a protein responsible for the cellular response to a signal transduction pathway.

efferent   (ef′ ur unt) [L. *ex*: out + *ferre*: to bear] Carrying outward or away from, as in neurons that carry impulses outward from the central to the peripheral nervous system (**efferent neurons**), or a blood vessel that carries blood away from a structure (**efferent arteriole**). (Contrast with afferent.)

egg   In all sexually reproducing organisms, the female gamete; in reptiles (including birds) and some other vertebrates, a structure within which early embryonic development occurs. (*See also* amniote egg, ovum.)

ejaculatory duct   The duct that carries semen from the seminal vesicle to the urethra.

electrical synapse   A type of synapse at which action potentials spread directly from presynaptic cell to postsynaptic cell. (Contrast with chemical synapse.)

electrocardiogram (ECG or EKG)   A graphic recording of electrical potentials from the heart.

electrochemical gradient   The concentration gradient of an ion across a membrane plus the voltage difference across that membrane.

electroencephalogram (EEG)   A graphic recording of electrical potentials from the brain.

electromagnetic radiation   A self-propagating wave that travels through space and has both electrical and magnetic properties.

electron   A subatomic particle outside the nucleus carrying a negative charge and very little mass.

electron shell   The region surrounding the atomic nucleus at a fixed energy level in which electrons orbit.

electronegativity   The tendency of an atom to attract electrons when it occurs as part of a compound.

element   A substance that cannot be converted to a simpler substance by ordinary chemical means.

elicitors   Molecules associated with plant pathogens that attach to specialized receptors in plants to initiate a defensive response.

elongation   (1) In molecular biology, the addition of monomers to make a longer DNA, RNA or protein during transcription or translation. (2) Growth of a plant axis or cell primarily in the longitudinal direction.

embolus   (em′ buh lus) [Gk. *embolos*: stopper] A circulating blood clot. Blockage of a blood vessel by an embolus or a bubble of gas is called an **embolism**. (Contrast with thrombus.)

embryo   [Gk. *en*: within + *bryein*: to grow] A young animal, or young plant sporophyte, while it is still contained within a protective structure such as an egg, uterus, or seed.

embryo sac   In angiosperms, the female gametophyte. Found within the ovule, it consists of eight or fewer cells, membrane-bounded but without cellulose walls between them.

embryonic stem cell (ESC)   A pluripotent cell in the blastocyst.

embryophytes   *See* Appendix A.

emigration   The dispersal of individuals out of an existing population. (Contrast with immigration.)

enamel   The hard material, composed primarily of calcium phosphate, that covers a tooth.

endemic   (en dem′ ik) [Gk. *endemos*: native] A species that occurs in a particular location and nowhere else on Earth.

endergonic   Referring to a chemical reaction in which the products have higher free energy than the reactants, thereby requiring free energy input to occur. (Contrast with exergonic.)

endocrine gland   (en′ doh krin) [Gk. *endo*: within + *krinein*: to separate] An aggregation of secretory cells that secrete hormones into the blood. The endocrine system consists of all endocrine cells and endocrine glands in the body that produce and release hormones. (Contrast with exocrine gland.)

endocrines   Chemical signals released by cells that enter the blood and affect cells anywhere in the body that have appropriate receptors. Also known as hormones.

endocytosis   A process by which liquids or solid particles are taken up by a cell through invagination of the cell membrane. (Contrast with exocytosis.)

endoderm   [Gk. *endo*: within + *derma*: skin] The innermost of the three embryonic germ layers delineated during gastrulation. Gives rise to the digestive and respiratory tracts and structures associated with them.

endodermis   In plants, a specialized cell layer marking the inside of the cortex in roots and some stems. Frequently a barrier to free diffusion of solutes.

endogenous retroviruses   Retroviruses that have been incorporated into the host's genome.

endomembrane system   A system of intracellular membranes that exchange material with one another, consisting of the Golgi apparatus, endoplasmic reticulum, and lysosomes when present.

endometrium   The epithelial lining of the uterus.

endoparasite   A parasite that spends at least part of its life cycle inside the body of its host organism. (Compare with ectoparasite.)

endophytic fungi   Fungi that live within the aboveground portions of plants without causing obvious harm to the host plant.

endoplasmic reticulum (ER)   [Gk. *endo*: within + L. *reticulum*: net] A system of membranous tubes and flattened sacs found in the cytoplasm of eukaryotes. Exists in two forms: rough ER, studded with ribosomes; and smooth ER, lacking ribosomes.

endorphins   Molecules in the mammalian brain that act as neurotransmitters in pathways that control pain.

endoskeleton   [Gk. *endo*: within + *skleros*: hard] An internal skeleton covered by other, soft body tissues. (Contrast with exoskeleton.)

endosperm   [Gk. *endo*: within + *sperma*: seed] A specialized triploid seed tissue found only in angiosperms; contains stored nutrients for the developing embryo.

endospore   [Gk. *endo*: within + *spora*: to sow] In some bacteria, a resting structure that can survive harsh environmental conditions.

endotherm   [Gk. *endo*: within + *thermos*: heat] An animal that can control its body temperature by the expenditure of its own metabolic energy. (Contrast with ectotherm.)

endotoxin   A lipopolysaccharide that forms part of the outer membrane of certain Gram-negative bacteria that is released when the bacteria grow or lyse. (Contrast with exotoxin.)

energetic cost   The difference between the energy an animal expends in performing a behavior and the energy it would have expended had it rested. (Contrast with opportunity cost, risk cost.)

energy   The capacity to do work or move matter against an opposing force. The capacity to accomplish change in physical and chemical systems.

energy budget   A quantitative description of all paths of energy exchange between an animal and its environment.

enhancer   Regulatory DNA sequences that bind transcription factors that either activate or increase the rate of transcription.

enkephalins   Molecules in the mammalian brain that act as neurotransmitters in pathways that control pain.

enteric nervous system   The nerve nets in the submucosa and between the smooth muscle layers of the vertebrate gut.

enthalpy (H)   The total energy of a system.

entoprocts   *See* Appendix A.

entropy (S)   (en′ tro pee) [Gk. *tropein*: to change] A measure of the degree of disorder in any system. Spontaneous reactions in a closed system are always accompanied by an increase in entropy.

enveloped virus   A virus enclosed within a phospholipid membrane derived from its host cell.

environmental genomics   A sequencing technique used when biologists are unable to work with the whole genome of a prokaryote species but instead examine individual genes collected from a random sample of the organism's environment.

environmentalism   The use of ecological knowledge, along with economics, ethics, and many other considerations, to inform both personal decisions and public policy relating to stewardship of natural resources and ecosystems.

enzyme   (en′ zime) [Gk. *zyme*: to leaven (as in yeast bread)] A catalytic protein that speeds up a biochemical reaction.

enzyme–substrate complex (ES)   An intermediate in an enzyme-catalyzed reaction; consists of the enzyme bound to its substrate(s).

ependymal cell   A type of macroglial cell that lines the central fluid-filled ventricles in the brain and produces the cerebrospinal fluid that bathes the brain and spinal cord.

epiblast   The upper or overlying portion of the avian blastula which is joined to the hypoblast at the margins of the blastodisc.

epiboly   The movement of cells over the surface of the blastula toward the forming blastopore.

epididymis   (epuh did′ uh mus) [Gk. *epi*: over + *didymos*: testicle] Coiled tubules in the testes that store sperm and conduct sperm from the seminiferous tubules to the vas deferens.

epigenetics   The scientific study of changes in the expression of a gene or set of genes that occur without change in the DNA sequence.

epiglottis   The flap of tissue that covers the entrance of the larynx to prevent food and liquid from entering the trachea.

epinephrine   (ep i nef′ rin) [Gk. *epi*: over + *nephros*: kidney] The "fight-or-flight" hormone produced by the medulla of the adrenal gland; it also functions as a neurotransmitter. Also known as adrenaline.

epiphyseal plates   Plates of cartilage near the ends of long bones where bone growth occurs up to adolescence, when growth ceases.

epistasis   Interaction between genes in which the presence of a particular allele of one gene determines whether or how another gene is expressed.

epithelial tissue   A type of animal tissue, made up of sheets of cells, that lines or covers organs, makes up tubules, and covers the surface of the body; one of the four major tissue types in multicellular animals.

epitope   *See* antigenic determinant.

epoch   A subdivision of a period in a geological time scale.

erection   The state of the penis in which it is stiffened by engorgement with blood.

error signal   In regulatory systems, any difference between the set point of the system and its current condition.

erythrocyte   (ur rith′ row site) [Gk. *erythros*: red + *kytos*: container] A red blood cell.

erythropoietin (EPO)   (ur rith′ row poi′ i tn) A hormone produced by the kidney in response to lack of oxygen that stimulates the production of red blood cells.

esophagus   (i soff′ i gus) [Gk. *oisophagos*: gullet] The part of the gut between the pharynx and the stomach.

essential amino acids   Amino acids that an animal cannot synthesize for itself and must obtain from its food.

essential element   A mineral nutrient required for normal growth and reproduction in plants and animals.

essential fatty acids   Fatty acids that an animal cannot synthesize for itself and must obtain from its food.

ester linkage   A condensation (water-releasing) reaction in which the carboxyl group of a fatty acid reacts with the hydroxyl group of an alcohol. Lipids, including most membrane lipids, are formed in this way. (Contrast with ether linkage.)

estivation   (ess tuh vay′ shun) [L. *aestivalis*: summer] A state of dormancy and hypometabolism that occurs during the summer; usually a means of surviving drought or intense heat. (Contrast with hibernation.)

estrogen   Any of several female steroid sex hormones found in all vertebrates and some invertebrates; produced chiefly by the ovaries in mammals and by the placenta during pregnancy.

estrus   (es′ trus) [L. *oestrus*: frenzy] The period of heat, or maximum sexual receptivity, in some female mammals. Ordinarily, estrus is also the time of release of eggs in the female.

estuary   An aquatic habitat in which salt water and fresh water mix, as when a river meets the ocean. Includes such ecosystems as salt marshes, mangrove forests, mudflats, and sea-grass beds.

ether linkage   The linkage of two hydrocarbons by an oxygen atom (HC—O—CH). Ether linkages are characteristic of the membrane lipids of archaea. (Contrast with ester linkage.)

ethology   [Gk. *ethos*: character + *logos*: study] One of two classic approaches to the study of animal behavior, focused on studying species in natural environments and addressing questions about the evolution of behavior. (Contrast with behaviorism.)

ethylene   One of the plant growth hormones, the gas $H_2C{=}CH_2$. Involved in fruit ripening and other growth and developmental responses.

etiolated   Referring to a flowering plant grown in the absence of light and characterized by long weak stems, smaller leaves due to longer internodes, and a pale yellow color.

euchromatin   Diffuse, uncondensed chromatin. Contains active genes that will be transcribed into mRNA. (Contrast with heterochromatin.)

eudicots   Angiosperms with two embryonic cotyledons; one of the two largest clades of angiosperms. (*See also* monocots.)

euglenids   *See* Appendix A.

Eukarya   The formal taxonomic name for eukaryotes (*See* Appendix A).

eukaryotes   (yew car′ ree oats) [Gk. *eu*: true + *karyon*: kernel or nucleus] Organisms whose cells contain their genetic material inside a nucleus. Includes all life other than the viruses, archaea, and bacteria. (Contrast with prokaryotes, *See* Appendix A.)

euphyllophytes   *See* Appendix A.

Euryarchaeota   *See* Appendix A.

eusociality   A type of social group in which some adults are infertile and aid the reproduction of other, fertile adults.

eustachian tube   A connection between the middle ear and the throat that allows air pressure to equilibrate between the middle ear and the outside world. Also called the pharyngotympanic tube.

eutherians   *See* Appendix A.

eutrophication   (yoo trofe′ ik ay′ shun) [Gk. *eu*: truly + *trephein*: to flourish] A process in aquatic ecosystems initiated by a pulse of nutrients that results in an increase of algal growth that may lead to decomposition and depleted oxygen conditions (hypoxia).

evaporation   The transition of water from the liquid to the gaseous phase.

evapotranspiration   The evaporative transfer of heat and water from the surfaces of plants into the atmosphere, which reduces air temperature and increases moisture.

evolution Any gradual change. Most often refers to organic or Darwinian evolution, which is the genetic and resulting phenotypic change in populations of organisms from generation to generation. (*See* macroevolution, microevolution. Contrast with speciation.)

evolutionary radiation The proliferation of many species within a single evolutionary lineage.

evolutionary reversal The reappearance of an ancestral trait in a group that had previously acquired a derived trait.

evolutionary theory The understanding and application of the mechanisms of evolutionary change to biological problems.

ex vivo gene therapy Alteration of the human genome sequence in cells removed from the body and then reimplanted into the body for medical benefit.

excavates *See* Appendix A.

excision repair A DNA repair mechanism that removes damaged DNA and replaces it with the appropriate nucleotide(s).

excretory system In animals, the organs that maintain the volume, solute concentration, and composition of the extracellular fluid by excreting water, solutes, and nitrogenous wastes in the form of urine.

executive functions Cognitive processes (e.g., attentional control, inhibitory control, reasoning, problem solving, planning) that allow goal-directed control of thought and behavior.

exergonic Referring to a chemical reaction in which the products of the reaction have lower free energy than the reactants, resulting in a release of free energy. (Contrast with endergonic.)

exocrine gland (eks' oh krin) [Gk. *exo*: outside + *krinein*: to separate] Any gland, such as a salivary gland, that secretes to the outside of the body or into the gut. (Contrast with endocrine gland.)

exocytosis A process by which a vesicle in a cell fuses with the cell membrane and releases its contents to the outside. (Contrast with endocytosis.)

exon A portion of a gene that is present in mature mRNA. Exons encode polypeptide sequence. (Contrast with intron.)

exoskeleton (eks' oh skel' e ton) [Gk. *exos*: outside + *skleros*: hard] A hard covering on the outside of the body to which muscles are attached. (Contrast with endoskeleton.)

exotoxin A highly toxic, usually soluble protein released by living, multiplying bacteria. (Contrast with endotoxin.)

expanding triplet repeat A three-base-pair sequence in a human gene that is unstable and can be repeated a few to hundreds of times. Often, the more the repeats, the less the activity of the gene involved. Expanding triplet repeats occur in some human diseases such as Huntington's disease and fragile-X syndrome.

expiratory reserve volume (ERV) The amount of air that can be forcefully exhaled beyond the normal tidal expiration. (Contrast with inspiratory reserve volume, tidal volume, vital capacity.)

exploitation competition Competition in which both species reduce the quantities of their shared but limited resources. (Contrast with interference competition.)

exponential growth A pattern of population growth characterized by a multiplicative pattern in which, as the number of individuals increases, the number of new individuals added per unit of time accelerates. (Contrast with logistic growth.)

expression vector A DNA vector, such as a plasmid, with a DNA sequence that allows for the expression of an inserted gene into mRNA and protein in a host cell.

expressivity The degree to which a genotype is expressed in the phenotype; may be affected by the environment.

extensor A muscle that extends an appendage. (Contrast with flexor.)

external fertilization Fertilization that occurs after the release of sperm and eggs into the external environment (a practice called spawning); typical of aquatic animals. (Contrast with internal fertilization.)

external gills Highly branched and folded extensions of the body surface that provide a large surface area for gas exchange with water; typical of larval amphibians and many larval insects.

extracellular fluid In a closed circulatory system, both the fluid in the circulatory system and the fluid outside it.

extracellular matrix A material of heterogeneous composition surrounding cells and performing many functions, including adhesion of cells.

extraembryonic membranes Four membranes that support but are not part of the developing embryos of reptiles (including birds) and mammals, defining these groups phylogenetically as amniotes. (*See* amnion, allantois, chorion, yolk sac.)

extreme halophiles A group of euryarchaeotes that live exclusively in very salty environments.

extremophiles Archaea and bacteria that live and thrive under conditions (e.g., extremely high temperatures) that would kill most organisms.

exudates In plants, any compounds that are exuded (secreted) by the plant—for example, compounds secreted into the soil environment by plant roots that influence the type and abundance of organisms living near the roots.

eye cups Photosensory organs in flatworms; components of one of the simplest visual systems in animals.

F

F_1 The first filial generation; the immediate progeny of a parental (P) mating.

F_2 The second filial generation; the immediate progeny of a mating between members of the F_1 generation.

facilitated diffusion Passive movement through a membrane involving a specific carrier protein; does not proceed against a concentration gradient. (Contrast with active transport, diffusion.)

facilitation *See* positive interaction.

facultative Referring to a type of species interaction that is optional for at least one species involved in the interaction. (Compare with obligate.)

facultative anaerobe A prokaryote that can shift its metabolism between anaerobic and aerobic modes depending on the presence or absence of O_2. Alternatively, facultative aerobe. (Compare with obligate anaerobe.)

facultative parasite An organism that can parasitize other living organisms but is also capable of growing independently.

fast-twitch fibers Skeletal muscle fibers that can generate high tension rapidly, but fatigue rapidly ("sprinter" fibers). Characterized by an abundance of enzymes of glycolysis. (Contrast with slow-twitch fibers.)

fat (1) A triglyceride that is solid at room temperature. (Contrast with oil.) (2) Adipose tissue, one type of connective tissue. (*See* brown fat.)

fate map A diagram of the blastula showing which cells (blastomeres) are "fated" to contribute to specific tissues and organs in the mature body.

fatty acid A molecule made up of a long nonpolar hydrocarbon chain and a polar carboxyl group. Found in many lipids.

fauna (faw' nah) All the animals found in a given area. (Contrast with flora.)

FD (FLOWERING LOCUS D) A gene coding for a transcription factor in the shoot apical meristem that binds to florigen; involved in the induction of flowering.

feather A structure growing from the skin of theropods (living birds and their extinct relatives) that consists of a hollow shaft fringed with vanes of barbs. Functions to support flight, plumage display, and thermoregulation.

feces [L. *faeces*: dregs] Waste excreted from the digestive system.

fecundity (m_x) The average number of offspring produced by each individual (or female) within the population.

feedback In regulatory systems, information about the relationship between the set point of the system and its current state. (Contrast with feedforward information.)

feedforward information In regulatory systems, information that changes the set point of the system. (Contrast with feedback.)

fenestrations Small holes in the walls of some capillaries.

fermentation [L. *fermentum*: yeast] The anaerobic degradation of a substance such as glucose to smaller molecules such as lactic acid or alcohol with the extraction of energy.

fertilization The union of gametes.

fertilizer Any of several substances added to soil to improve the soil's capacity to support plant growth. May be organic or inorganic.

fiber In angiosperms, an elongated, tapering sclerenchyma cell, usually with a thick cell wall, that serves a support function in xylem. (*See also* muscle fiber.)

fibrin A protein that polymerizes to form long threads that provide structure to a blood clot.

fibrinogen A circulating protein that can be stimulated to fall out of solution and provide the structure for a blood clot.

fibrous root system   A root system typical of monocots composed of numerous thin adventitious roots that are all roughly equal in diameter. (Contrast with taproot system.)

Fick's law of diffusion   An equation that describes the factors that determine the rate of diffusion of a molecule from an area of higher concentration to an area of lower concentration.

fight-or-flight response   A rapid physiological response to a sudden threat that is mediated by the hormone epinephrine.

filament   In flowers, the part of a stamen that supports the anther.

filter feeder   An organism that feeds on organisms much smaller than itself, and that are suspended in water or air, by means of a straining device. Also called suspension feeder.

filtration   A process that separates a mixture of solids and fluids by passing the mixture through a material that only allows the solids below a certain size to pass.

firmicutes   *See* Appendix A.

first filial generation   *See* F_1.

first polar body   The small daughter cell from the first meiotic division of a primary oocyte. (*See also* **secondary oocyte.**)

fitness   The contribution of a genotype or phenotype to the genetic composition of subsequent generations, relative to the contribution of other genotypes or phenotypes. (*See also* inclusive fitness.)

fixed   The condition in which a particular allele is the only allele present at a genetic locus within a population (i.e., there is no genetic variation at the locus).

fixed action pattern   In animal behavior, a genetically determined behavior that is performed without learning, is stereotypic (performed the same way each time), and is not modifiable by learning.

flagellum   (fla jell′ um) (plural: flagella) [L. *flagellum*: whip] A long, whiplike appendage that propels cells. Prokaryotic flagella differ greatly from those found in eukaryotes.

flatworms   *See* Appendix A.

flexor   A muscle that flexes an appendage. (Contrast with extensor.)

flora   (flore′ ah) All of the plants found in a given area. (Contrast with fauna.)

floral meristem   In angiosperms, a meristem that forms the floral organs (sepals, petals, stamens, and carpels).

florigen   A plant hormone involved in the conversion of a vegetative shoot apex to a flower.

flower   The sexual structure of an angiosperm.

fluid mosaic model   A molecular model for the structure of biological membranes consisting of a fluid phospholipid bilayer in which suspended proteins are free to move in the plane of the bilayer.

foliose   Having a leafy growth form.

follicle   [L. *folliculus*: little bag] In female mammals, an immature egg surrounded by nutritive cells.

follicle-stimulating hormone (FSH)   A gonadotropin produced by the anterior pituitary.

follicular phase   In human females, the first half of the ovarian cycle, when follicle maturation occurs. (Contrast with luteal phase.)

food web   A representation of the trophic or energetic connections among species within a community.

foraminiferans   *See* Appendix A.

forebrain   The region of the vertebrate brain that comprises the cerebrum, thalamus, and hypothalamus. (Compare with hindbrain, midbrain.)

fossil fuels   Fuels, including oil, natural gas, coal, and peat, formed over geologic time from organic material buried in anaerobic sediments.

foundation species   A species that has large, community-wide effects as a consequence of its large size and abundance, and its provision of habitat or food for other species.

founder effect   Random changes in allele frequencies resulting from establishment of a population by a very small number of individuals.

fovea   [L. *fovea*: a small pit] In the vertebrate retina, the area of most distinct vision.

frame-shift mutation   The addition or deletion of a single or two adjacent nucleotides in a gene's sequence. Results in the misreading of mRNA during translation and the production of a nonfunctional protein. (Contrast with loss-of-stop mutation, missense mutation, nonsense mutation, silent mutation.)

Frank–Starling law   The principle that the stroke volume of the heart increases with increased return of blood to the heart.

free energy (G)   Energy that is available for doing useful work, after allowance has been made for the increase or decrease of disorder.

free-running   A descriptor of an endogenous rhythm that is not entrained by an environmental cue.

frequency-dependent selection   Selection that changes in intensity with the proportion of individuals in a population having the trait.

frontal lobe   The largest of the brain's cerebral lobes in humans; involved with problem solving, memory, language, cognition, emotional expression, judgment, and planning functions; includes the primary motor cortex.

frugivore   [L. *frugis*: fruit + *vorare*: to devour] An animal that eats fruit.

fruit   In angiosperms, a ripened and mature ovary (or group of ovaries) containing the seeds. Sometimes applied to reproductive structures of other groups of plants.

fruticose   Having a shrubby growth form.

FT (*FLOWERING LOCUS T*)   A gene that codes for florigen, a small, diffusible protein involved in the induction of flowering.

fugitive species   A species that leave an otherwise suitable habitat in order to avoid competition with another species.

full census   A count of every individual in a population.

functional genomics   The assignment of functional roles to the proteins encoded by genes identified by sequencing entire genomes.

functional group   (1) A characteristic combination of atoms that contributes specific properties (such as charge or polarity) when attached to larger molecules (e.g., carboxyl group, amino group). (2) A group of species that function in similar ways, whether or not they use the same resources. (Compare with guild.)

functional residual volume (FRV)   The residual volume plus the expiratory reserve volume.

fundamental niche   A species' niche as defined by its physiological capabilities. (Contrast with realized niche.)

G

G protein   A membrane protein involved in signal transduction; characterized by binding GDP or GTP.

G protein-coupled receptors   A class of receptors that change configuration upon ligand binding such that a G protein binding site is exposed on the cytoplasmic domain of the receptor, initiating a signal transduction pathway.

G0   A resting phase in which a cell is not preparing for the cell division cycle.

G1 phase   In the cell cycle, the gap between the end of cytokinesis and the onset of S phase.

G1-to-S transition   In the cell cycle, the point at which G1 phase ends and S phase begins.

G2 phase   In the cell cycle, the gap between S phase and the onset of mitosis.

gain-of-function mutation   A mutation that results in a protein with a new function. (Contrast with loss-of-function mutation.)

gallbladder   In the human digestive system, an organ in which bile is stored.

gametangium   (gam uh tan′ gee um) (plural: gametangia) [Gk. *gamos*: marriage + *angeion*: vessel] Any plant or fungal structure within which a gamete is formed.

gamete   (gam′ eet) [Gk. *gamete/gametes*: wife, husband] The mature sexual reproductive cell: the egg or sperm.

gametogenesis   (ga meet′ oh jen′ e sis) The specialized series of cellular divisions that leads to the production of gametes. Called oogenesis when referring to processes in the ovary, and spermatogenesis in the testis.

gametophyte   (ga meet′ oh fyte) In plants and photosynthetic protists with alternation of generations, the multicellular haploid phase that produces the gametes. (Contrast with sporophyte.)

gamma diversity   Species diversity within a geographic region; sometimes called the regional species pool. (Compare with alpha diversity, beta diversity.)

ganglion   (gang′ glee un) (plural: ganglia) [Gk. lump] A cluster of neurons that have similar characteristics or function.

ganglion cells   Cells at the front of the human retina that transmit information from the bipolar cells to the brain.

gap genes   In *Drosophila* development, segmentation genes that define broad areas along the anterior–posterior axis of the early embryo. Part of a developmental cascade that includes maternal effect genes, pair rule genes, segment polarity genes, and Hox genes.

gap junction   A 2.7-nanometer gap between cell membranes of two animal cells, spanned by protein channels. Gap junctions allow chemical substances or electric signals to pass from cell to cell.

gastric pits   Deep infoldings in the walls of the stomach that are lined with secretory cells.

gastrin   A hormone secreted by cells in the lower region of the stomach that stimulates the secretion of digestive juices as well as movements of the stomach.

gastrointestinal system   *See* gut.

gastropods   *See* Appendix A.

gastrotrichs   *See* Appendix A.

gastrovascular cavity   A body cavity that has one opening to the environment and serves both digestion ("gastro") and circulation ("vascular"); in particular, the central cavity of the body of Cnidarians and Platyhelminthes.

gastrovascular system   A branching body cavity in Cnidaria and Platyhelminthes that has one opening to the environment and serves to digest food and distribute nutrients to the body.

gastrulation   The development of a blastula into a gastrula. In embryonic development, the process by which a blastula is transformed by massive movements of cells into a gastrula, an embryo with three germ layers and distinct body axes.

gated channel   A membrane protein that changes its three-dimensional shape, and therefore its ion conductance, in response to a stimulus. When open, it allows specific ions to move across the membrane.

gel electrophoresis   (e lek′ tro fo ree′ sis) [L. *electrum*: amber + Gk. *phorein*: to bear] A technique for separating molecules (such as DNA fragments) from one another on the basis of their electric charges and molecular weights by applying an electric field to a gel.

gene   [Gk. *genes*: to produce] A unit of heredity. Used here as the unit of genetic function that carries the information for a polypeptide or RNA.

gene duplication   The generation of extra copies of a gene in a genome over evolutionary time. A mechanism by which genomes can acquire new functions.

gene expression   The transcription and translation into a protein of the information (nucleotide sequence) contained in a gene.

gene family   A set of similar genes derived from a single parent gene by duplication; need not be on the same chromosomes. The vertebrate globin genes constitute a classic example of a gene family.

gene flow   The exchange of genes between populations through migration of individuals or movements of gametes.

gene pool   All of the different alleles of all of the genes existing in all individuals of a population.

gene therapy   Treatment of a genetic disease by providing patients with cells containing functioning alleles of the genes that are nonfunctional in their bodies.

gene tree   A graphic representation of the evolutionary relationships of a single gene in different species or of the members of a gene family.

gene-for-gene resistance   In plants, resistance that is triggered when the products of a pathogen's *Avr* genes are directly or indirectly recognized by proteins encoded by a plant's *R* genes.

general transcription factors   In eukaryotes, transcription factors that bind to the promoters of most protein-coding genes and are required for their expression. Distinct from specific transcription factors, which have regulatory effects only at certain promoters or classes of promoters.

generation time (G)   The average age of the parents of all the offspring produced within a cohort.

genetic code   The list of all possible 64 triplet mRNA sequences (codons) and the amino acids they encode. Used during translation to convert a linear sequence of nucleotides into a linear sequence of amino acids.

genetic drift   Changes in gene frequencies from generation to generation as a result of random (chance) processes.

genetic marker   (1) In gene cloning, a gene of identifiable phenotype that indicates the presence of another gene, DNA segment, or chromosome fragment. (2) In general, a DNA sequence such as a single nucleotide polymorphism whose presence is correlated with the presence of other linked genes on that chromosome.

genetic screen   A technique for identifying genes involved in a biological process of interest. Involves creating a large collection of randomly mutated organisms and identifying those individuals that are likely to have a defect in the pathway of interest. The mutated gene(s) in those individuals can then be isolated for further study.

genetic structure   The frequencies of different alleles at each locus and the frequencies of different genotypes in a Mendelian population.

genetic switches   Mechanisms that control how the genetic toolkit is used, such as promoters and the transcription factors that bind them. The signal cascades that converge on and operate these switches determine when and where genes will be turned on and off.

genetic toolkit   A set of developmental genes and proteins that is common to most animals and is hypothesized to be responsible for the evolution of their differing developmental pathways.

genetics   The scientific study of the structure, functioning, and inheritance of genes, the units of hereditary information.

genitalia   The reproductive organs, especially the external accessory sex organs.

genome   (jee′ nome) The complete DNA sequence for a particular organism or individual.

genome sequencing   Determination of the nucleotide sequence of the entire genome of an organism.

genomic library   All of the cloned DNA fragments generated by the breakdown of genomic DNA into smaller segments.

genomics   The scientific study of entire sets of genes and their interactions.

genotype   (jean′ oh type) [Gk. *gen*: to produce + *typos*: impression] The alleles carried by an individual, either with respect to a single gene, or locus, or with respect to numerous genes, or loci. (Contrast with phenotype.)

genus   (jean′ us) (plural: genera) [Gk. *genos*: stock, kind] A group of related, similar species recognized by taxonomists with a distinct name used in binomial nomenclature.

geographic range   The entire region within which a species occurs.

germ cell   [L. *germen*: to beget] A reproductive cell or gamete of a multicellular organism. (Contrast with somatic cell.)

germ layers   The three embryonic layers formed during gastrulation (ectoderm, mesoderm, and endoderm). Also called cell layers or tissue layers.

germ line gene therapy   Alteration of the human genome sequence in the gametes or cells giving rise to gametes, for medical benefit. (Contrast with somatic cell gene therapy.)

germ line mutation   A mutation in a cell that produces gametes (i.e., a germ line cell). (Contrast with somatic mutation.)

germination   The sprouting of a seed or spore.

gestation   (jes tay′ shun) [L. *gestare*: to bear] The period during which the embryo of a mammal develops within the uterus. Also known as pregnancy.

ghrelin   A hormone produced and secreted by cells in the stomach that stimulates appetite.

gibberellins   (jib er el′ lin) A class of plant growth hormones that play roles in stem elongation, seed germination, flowering of certain plants, and other processes.

ginkgo   *See* Appendix A.

gizzard   [L. *gigeria*: cooked chicken parts] The second of two stomachlike organs in reptiles, earthworms, and various insects; grinds up food, sometimes with the aid of fragments of stone. (*See also* crop.)

glans penis   The highly sensitive tip of the mammalian penis.

glaucophytes   *See* Appendix A.

glia   (glee′ uh) [Gk. *glia*: glue] One of the two classes of neural cells (along with neurons, with which glia interact). Glia typically do not generate and conduct action potentials. *See also* macroglia and microglia.

glomerular filtration rate (GFR)   The rate at which the blood is filtered in the glomeruli of the kidney.

glomerulus   (glo mare′ yew lus) (plural: glomeruli) [L. *glomus*: ball] Sites in the kidney where blood filtration takes place. Each glomerulus consists of a knot of capillaries served by afferent and efferent arterioles.

glucagon   A hormone produced by alpha cells of the pancreatic islets of Langerhans. Glucagon stimulates the liver to break down glycogen and release glucose into the circulation.

gluconeogenesis   The biochemical synthesis of glucose from other substances, such as amino acids, lactate, and glycerol.

glucose [Gk. *gleukos*: sugar, sweet wine] The most common monosaccharide; the monomer of the polysaccharides starch, glycogen, and cellulose.

glyceraldehyde 3-phosphate (G3P) A phosphorylated three-carbon sugar; an intermediate in glycolysis and photosynthetic carbon fixation. Also called triose phosphate.

glycerol (gliss′ er ole) A three-carbon alcohol with three hydroxyl groups; a component of phospholipids and triglycerides.

glycogen (gly′ ko jen) [Gk. *glyk*: sweet] An energy storage polysaccharide found in animals and fungi; a branched-chain polymer of glucose, similar to starch.

glycolipid A lipid to which sugars are attached.

glycolysis (gly kol′ li sis) [Gk. *gleukos*: sugar + *lysis*: break apart] The enzymatic breakdown of glucose to pyruvic acid.

glycoprotein A protein to which sugars are attached.

glycosidic bond A bond between carbohydrate (sugar) molecules through an intervening oxygen atom (–O–).

glycosylation The addition of a carbohydrate to another type of molecule, such as a protein.

glymphatic system A waste clearing system in the vertebrate brain that allows cerebrospinal fluid to mix with brain interstitial fluids and then flow out along with metabolic wastes through venous perivascular spaces.

glyoxysome (gly ox′ ee soam) A plant organelle in which stored lipids are converted to carbohydrates.

gnathostomes *See* Appendix A.

gnetophytes *See* Appendix A.

goiter Swelling in the neck resulting from an enlarged thyroid gland.

Goldman equation An equation that calculates membrane potential by taking into consideration the concentration differences of all ions on both sides of the membrane and the relative permeability of the membrane to those ions.

Golgi apparatus (goal′ jee) A system of concentrically folded membranes found in the cytoplasm of eukaryotic cells; functions in secretion from the cell by exocytosis.

Golgi tendon organ A mechanoreceptor found in tendons and ligaments; provides information about the force generated by a contracting muscle.

gonad (go′ nad) [Gk. *gone*: seed] An organ that produces gametes in animals: either an ovary (female gonad) or testis (male gonad).

gonadotropin-releasing hormone (GnRH) A hormone produced by the hypothalamus that stimulates the anterior pituitary to secrete gonadotropins.

gonadotropins Tropic hormones secreted by the anterior pituitary gland that control activity of gonadal endocrine cells and support and maintain gonadal functions including gamete production.

Gondwana The large southern land mass that existed from the Cambrian (540 mya) to the early Cretaceous (138 mya). Present-day remnants are South America, Africa, India, Australia, and Antarctica.

graded membrane potential A small local change in membrane potential caused by opening or closing of ion channels.

grafting The artificial transplantation of tissue from one organism to another. In horticulture, the transfer of a bud or stem segment from one plant onto the root of another as a form of asexual reproduction.

Gram-negative bacteria Bacteria that appear red when stained using the Gram-staining technique. These bacteria have an outer membrane outside the relatively thin peptidoglycan layer of the cell wall.

Gram-positive bacteria Bacteria that appear blue to purple when stained using the Gram-staining technique. These bacteria have an outer cell wall consisting of a thick layer of peptidoglycan.

Gram stain A differential purple stain useful in characterizing bacteria. The peptidoglycan-rich cell walls of Gram-positive bacteria stain blue to purple; cell walls of Gram-negative bacteria generally stain red.

granulosa cells In mammals, the inner layer of cells of the ovarian follicle that surround and nurture the oocyte. (Contrast with **thecal cells**.)

gravitropism [L. *gravitas*: weight, force + Gk. *tropos*: to turn] A directed plant growth response to gravity.

gray crescent In frog development, a band of diffusely pigmented cytoplasm on the side of the egg opposite the site of sperm entry. Arises as a result of cytoplasmic rearrangements that establish the anterior–posterior axis of the zygote.

gray matter In the nervous system, tissue that is rich in neuronal cell bodies. (Contrast with white matter.)

green plants *See* Appendix A.

greenhouse gases Gases in the atmosphere, such as carbon dioxide and methane, that are transparent to sunlight but trap heat radiating from Earth's surface, causing heat to build up at Earth's surface.

gross primary production (GPP) The total amount of carbon fixed by primary producers in an ecosystem. (Compare with net primary production.)

ground tissue system Those parts of the plant body not included in the dermal or vascular tissue systems. Ground tissues function in storage, photosynthesis, and support.

growth An increase in the size of the body and its organs by cell division and cell expansion.

growth factor A chemical signal that stimulates cells to divide.

growth hormone (GH) A peptide hormone released by the anterior pituitary that stimulates many anabolic processes.

growth hormone–inhibiting hormone (GHIH) A peptide hormone produced in the hypothalamus that inhibits the activity of growth hormone–secreting and thyroid hormone stimulating cells in the anterior pituitary. Also called somatostatin. GHIH produced by the pancreas slows digestive functions.

guanine (G) (gwan′ een) A nitrogen-containing base found in DNA, RNA, and GTP.

guard cells In plants, specialized, paired epidermal cells that surround and control the opening of a stoma (pore).

guild A group of species, often taxonomically distinct, that use the same resources. (Compare with functional group.)

gustation The sense of taste.

gut An animal's digestive tract.

gymnosperms Seed plants that do not produce flowers or fruits; one of the two major groups of living seed plants. (*See also* angiosperms.)

gyres Large-scale circular ocean currents caused by prevailing winds and Earth's rotation.

gyri (singular: gyrus) The ridges (folds) in the cerebral cortex.

H

habitat The particular environment in which an organism lives.

habitat degradation The conversion of an ecosystem that reduces habitat quality. (Compare with habitat loss.)

habitat loss The conversion of an ecosystem that reduces habitat quantity. (Compare with habitat degradation.)

hadobacteria *See* Appendix A.

hagfishes *See* Appendix A.

hair cell A type of mechanoreceptor in animals. Detects sound waves and other forms of motion in air or water.

half-life The time required for half of a sample of a radioactive isotope to decay to its stable, nonradioactive form, or for a drug or other substance to reach half its initial dosage.

halophyte An organism that can grow in high salinity.

Hamilton's rule The principle that, for an apparent altruistic behavior to be adaptive, the fitness benefit of that act to the recipient times the degree of relatedness of the performer and the recipient must be greater than the cost to the performer.

haplodiploidy A sex determination mechanism in which diploid individuals (which develop from fertilized eggs) are female and haploid individuals (which develop from unfertilized eggs) are male; typical of hymenopterans.

haploid (hap′ loid) [Gk. *haploeides*: single] Having a chromosome complement consisting of just one copy of each chromosome; designated $1n$ or n. (Contrast with diploid.)

Hardy–Weinberg equilibrium In a sexually reproducing population, the allele frequency at a given locus that is not being acted on by agents of evolution; the conditions that would result in no evolution in a population.

haustorium (haw stor′ ee um) (plural: haustoria) [L. *haustus*: draw up] A specialized hypha or other structure by which fungi and some parasitic plants draw nutrients from a host plant.

Haversian systems Units of organization in compact bone that reflect the action of intercommunicating osteoblasts.

heart In circulatory systems, a muscular pump that moves extracellular fluid around the body.

heat of vaporization The energy that must be supplied to convert a molecule from a liquid to a gas at its boiling point.

heat shock proteins Chaperone proteins expressed in cells exposed to high or low temperatures or other forms of environmental stress.

hematocrit The proportion of the blood volume that consists of red blood cells.

hemichordates *See* Appendix A.

hemiparasite A parasitic plant that can photosynthesize but derives water and mineral nutrients from the living body of another plant. (Contrast with holoparasite.)

hemizygous (hem′ ee zie′ gus) [Gk. *hemi*: half + *zygotos*: joined] In a diploid organism, having only one allele for a given trait, typically the case for X-linked genes in male mammals and Z-linked genes in female birds. (Contrast with heterozygous, homozygous.)

hemocoel The primary body cavity of many invertebrates, which contains circulatory fluid.

hemoglobin (Hgb) (hee′ mo glow bin) [Gk. *heaema*: blood + L. *globus*: globe] An oxygen-transporting protein found in the red blood cells of vertebrates (and found in some invertebrates).

hemolymph The extracellular fluid in an open circulatory system.

Hensen's node In avian embryos, a structure at the anterior end of the primitive groove; determines the fates of cells passing over it during gastrulation.

hepatic portal vein The vein that begins in capillary beds in the gut and ends in capillary beds in the liver.

herbivore (ur′ bi vore) [L. *herba*: plant + *vorare*: to devour] An animal that eats plant tissues. (Contrast with carnivore, detritivore, omnivore.)

herbivory (ur′bi vor e) [L. *herba*: plant + *vorare*: to devour] Predation in which the predator is an animal and the prey is a plant or algae. (Contrast with carnivory, omnivory, parasitism.)

hermaphroditic (her maf row di′ tik) Having both female and male sex organs in the same organism.

heterochromatin Densely packed, dark-staining chromatin; any genes it contains are usually not transcribed. (Contrast with euchromatin.)

heterochrony [Gk. different time] Alteration in the timing of developmental events, contributing to the evolution of different phenotypes in the adult. (Contrast with heterometry, heterotypy.)

heterocyst A large, thick-walled cell type in the filaments of certain cyanobacteria that performs nitrogen fixation.

heteroloboseans *See* Appendix A.

heterometry [Gk. different measure] Alteration in the level of gene expression, and thus in the amount of protein produced, during development, contributing to the evolution of different phenotypes in the adult. (Contrast with heterochrony, heterotypy.)

heteromorphic (het′ er oh more′ fik) [Gk. different form] Having a different form or appearance, as two heteromorphic life stages of a plant. (Contrast with isomorphic.)

heterosis The superior fitness of heterozygous offspring as compared with that of their dissimilar homozygous parents. Also called hybrid vigor.

heterosporous (het′ er os′ por us) Producing two types of spores, one of which gives rise to a female megaspore and the other to a male microspore. (Contrast with homosporous.)

heterotherm An animal that regulates its body temperature at a constant level at some times but not others, such as a hibernator.

heterotroph (het′ er oh trof) [Gk. *heteros*: different + *trophe*: feed] An organism that requires preformed organic molecules as food. (Contrast with autotroph.)

heterotypic Pertaining to the binding of the same types of cells, due to the interaction of the same molecules on the cell surfaces. (Contrast with homotypic.)

heterotypy [Gk. different kind] Alteration in a developmental regulatory gene itself rather than the expression of the genes it controls. (Contrast with heterochrony, heterometry.)

heterozygous (het′ er oh zie′ gus) [Gk. *heteros*: different + *zygotos*: joined] In diploid organisms, having different alleles of a given gene on the pair of homologs carrying that gene. (Contrast with hemizygous, homozygous.)

hexapods *See* Appendix A.

hexose [Gk. *hex*: six] A sugar containing six carbon atoms.

hibernation [L. *hibernum*: winter] The state of inactivity of some animals during winter; marked by a drop in body temperature and metabolic rate. (Contrast with estivation.)

high-density lipoproteins (HDLs) Lipoproteins that remove cholesterol from tissues and carry it to the liver; HDLs are the "good" lipoproteins associated with good cardiovascular health.

high-throughput sequencing Rapid DNA sequencing on a micro scale in which many fragments of DNA are sequenced in parallel.

highly repetitive sequences Short (less than 100 bp), nontranscribed DNA sequences, repeated thousands of times in tandem arrangements.

hindbrain The region of the developing vertebrate brain that gives rise to the medulla, pons, and cerebellum. (Compare with forebrain, midbrain.)

hippocampus [Gk. sea horse] A part of the forebrain that takes part in long-term memory formation.

histamine (hiss′ tah meen) A substance released by mast cells and basophils in response to tissue damage or to allergens. Histamine increases vascular permeability, leading to edema (swelling).

holometabolous Undergoing complete metamorphosis.

holoparasite A fully parasitic plant (i.e., one that does not perform photosynthesis). (Contrast with hemiparasite.)

homeobox A 180-base-pair segment of DNA found in certain homeotic genes. A specific sequence within the homeobox—the homeodomain—regulates the expression of other genes and through this regulation controls large-scale developmental processes. (*See* homeotic genes.)

homeodomain *See* homeobox.

homeostasis (home′ ee o sta′ sis) [Gk. *homos*: same + *stasis*: position] The maintenance of a steady state, such as a constant temperature, by means of physiological or behavioral feedback responses.

homeotherm An animal that regulates its body temperatures within a narrow range when confronted with a much greater range of environmental temperatures.

homeotic genes Genes that act during development to determine the formation of an organ from a region of the embryo. (Compare with Hox genes.)

homeotic mutation A mutation in a homeotic gene that results in the formation of a different organ than that normally made by a region of the embryo.

homing In animal navigation, the ability to return to a nest site, burrow, or other specific location.

hominins Modern humans (*Homo sapiens*) and their extinct ancestors (e.g., australopithecines, *Homo erectus*).

homolog (1) In cytogenetics, one of a pair (or larger set) of chromosomes having the same overall genetic composition and sequence. In diploid organisms, each chromosome inherited from one parent is matched by an identical (except for mutational differences) chromosome—its homolog—from the other parent. (2) In evolutionary biology, one of two or more features in different species that are similar by reason of descent from a common ancestor.

homologous pair A pair of matching chromosomes made up of a chromosome from each of the two sets of chromosomes in a diploid organism.

homology (ho mol′ o jee) [Gk. *homologia*: of one mind, agreement] A similarity between two or more features that is due to inheritance from a common ancestor. The structures are said to be **homologous**, and each is a **homolog** of the others.

homoplasy (home′ uh play zee) [Gk. *homos*: same + *plastikos*: shape, mold] The presence in multiple groups of a trait that is not inherited from the common ancestor of those groups. Can result from convergent evolution, evolutionary reversal, or parallel evolution.

homosporous Producing a single type of spore that gives rise to a single type of gametophyte, bearing both female and male reproductive organs. (Contrast with heterosporous.)

homotypic Pertaining to adhesion of cells of the same type. (Contrast with heterotypic.)

homozygous (home′ oh zie′ gus) [Gk. *homos*: same + *zygotos*: joined] In diploid organisms, having identical alleles of a given gene on both homologous chromosomes. An individual may be a homozygote with respect to one gene and a heterozygote with respect to another. (Contrast with hemizygous, heterozygous.)

horizons   The horizontal layers of a soil profile, including the topsoil (A horizon), subsoil (B horizon) and parent rock or bedrock (C horizon).

horizontal cells   Cells in the retina that communicate laterally between photoreceptors and bipolar cells.

hormone   [Gk. *hormon*: to excite, stimulate] A chemical signal produced in minute amounts at one site in a multicellular organism and transported to another site where it acts on target cells.

hornworts   *See* Appendix A.

horsehair worms   *See* Appendix A.

horsetails   *See* Appendix A.

host   An organism that harbors a parasite or symbiont and provides it with nourishment.

Hox genes   Conserved homeotic genes found in vertebrates, *Drosophila*, and other animal groups. Hox genes contain the homeobox and specify pattern and axis formation in these animals.

human chorionic gonadotropin (hCG)   A hormone secreted by the placenta that sustains the corpus luteum and helps maintain pregnancy.

Human Genome Project   A publicly and privately funded research effort, successfully completed in 2003, to produce a complete DNA sequence for the entire human genome.

human immunodeficiency virus (HIV)   The retrovirus that causes acquired immune deficiency syndrome (AIDS).

humoral immune response   The response of the immune system mediated by B cells that produces circulating antibodies active against extracellular bacterial and viral infections. (Contrast with cellular immune response.)

humus   (hew' mus) The partly decomposed remains of plants and animals on the surface of a soil.

hybrid vigor   *See* heterosis.

hybrid zone   A region of overlap in the ranges of two closely related species where the species may hybridize.

hydrogen bond   A weak electrostatic bond which arises from the attraction between the slight positive charge on a hydrogen atom and a slight negative charge on a nearby oxygen or nitrogen atom.

hydrogen molecule   A molecule containing only hydrogen and carbon atoms.

hydrologic cycle   The movement of water from the oceans to the atmosphere, to the soil, rivers, and lakes, and back to the oceans.

hydrolysis reaction   (high drol' uh sis) [Gk. *hydro*: water + *lysis*: break apart] A chemical reaction that breaks a bond by inserting the components of water ($AB + H_2O \rightarrow AH + BOH$). (Contrast with condensation reaction.)

hydrophilic   (high dro fill' ik) [Gk. *hydro*: water + *philia*: love] Having an affinity for water. (Contrast with hydrophobic.)

hydrophobic   (high dro foe' bik) [Gk. *hydro*: water + *phobia*: fear] Having no affinity for water. Uncharged and nonpolar groups of atoms are hydrophobic. (Contrast with hydrophilic.)

hydrophobic interaction   A weak chemical interaction caused when molecules that are not attracted to water interact to exclude water.

hydroponic   Pertaining to a method of growing plants with their roots suspended in nutrient solutions instead of soil.

hydrostatic skeleton   A fluid-filled body cavity that transfers forces from one part of the body to another when acted on by surrounding muscles.

hydrozoans   *See* Appendix A.

hyperpolarization   A change in the resting potential across a membrane so that the inside of a cell becomes more negative compared with the outside of the cell. (Contrast with depolarization.)

hypersensitive response   A defensive response of plants to viral or microbial infection in which phytoalexins and pathogenesis-related proteins are produced and the infected tissue undergoes apoptosis to isolate the pathogen from the rest of the plant.

hyperthermophilic bacteria   *See* Appendix A.

hypertonic   Having a higher solute concentration; said of one solution in comparing it with another. (Contrast with hypotonic, isotonic.)

hypertonic regulation   The maintenance of body fluids at a greater solute concentration than the environment. (Contrast with hypotonic regulation.)

hypha   (high' fuh) (plural: hyphae) [Gk. *hyphe*: web] In fungi and oomycetes, any single filament.

hypoblast   The lower tissue portion of the avian blastula which is joined to the epiblast at the margins of the blastodisc.

hypothalamus   The part of the brain lying below the thalamus; it coordinates water balance, reproduction, temperature regulation, and metabolism.

hypothermia   Below-normal body temperature.

hypothesis   A tentative answer to a question, from which testable predictions can be generated. (Contrast with theory.)

hypotonic   Having a lower solute concentration; said of one solution in comparing it with another. (Contrast with hypertonic, isotonic.)

hypotonic regulation   The maintenance of body fluids at a lesser solute concentration than the environment. (Contrast with hypertonic regulation.)

hypoxia   A deficiency of oxygen.

hysteresis   The inability of a community that has undergone change to shift back to the initial community type, even when the original conditions are restored.

I

igneous rocks   Rocks solidified from lava or magma.

ileum   The final segment of the small intestine. (*See also* duodenum, jejunum.)

imbibition   Water uptake by a seed; the first step in germination.

immediate hypersensitivity   A rapid, extensive overreaction of the immune system against an allergen, resulting in the release of large amounts of histamine. (Contrast with delayed hypersensitivity.)

immediate memory   A form of memory for events happening in the present that is almost perfectly photographic but lasts only seconds. (Contrast with long-term memory, short-term memory.)

immigration   The dispersal of individuals into an existing population. (Contrast with emigration.)

immunoglobulins   A class of proteins containing a tetramer consisting of four polypeptide chains—two identical light chains and two identical heavy chains—held together by disulfide bonds; active as receptors and effectors in the immune system. Also called antibodies.

immunological memory   The capacity to more rapidly and massively respond to a second exposure of an antigen than occurred on the first exposure.

imperfect flower   A flower lacking either functional stamens or functional carpels. (Contrast with perfect flower.)

implantation   The process by which the early mammalian embryo becomes attached to and embedded in the lining of the uterus.

imprinting   In animal behavior, a rapid form of learning in which an animal learns, during a brief critical period, to make a particular response (which is then maintained for life) to some object or other organism.

in vitro evolution   A method based on natural molecular evolution that uses artificial selection in the laboratory to rapidly produce molecules with novel enzymatic and binding functions.

in vivo gene therapy   Alteration of the human genome sequence in cells in the body, for medical benefit.

inactivation gate   The property of a voltage-gated Na^+ ion channel that decreases its permeability to Na^+ when the membrane is depolarized. (Contrast with activation gate.)

inbreeding   Breeding of two closely genetically related individuals.

inbreeding depression   The reduction of fitness in offspring produced by breeding of two closely genetically related individuals.

inclusive fitness   The sum of an individual's genetic contribution to subsequent generations both via production of its own offspring and via its influence on the survival of relatives who are not direct descendants. (*See also* indirect fitness, kin selection. Contrast with direct fitness.)

incomplete cleavage   A pattern of cleavage that occurs in many eggs that have a lot of yolk, in which the cleavage furrows do not penetrate all of it. (*See also* discoidal cleavage, superficial cleavage. Contrast with complete cleavage.)

incomplete dominance   The condition in which the heterozygous phenotype is intermediate between the two homozygous phenotypes.

incomplete metamorphosis   Insect development in which changes between instars are gradual. (Contrast with direct development, complete metamorphosis.)

independent assortment   During meiosis, the random separation of genes carried on nonhomologous chromosomes into gametes so that inheritance of these genes is random. This principle was articulated by Mendel as his second law.

indeterminate growth   An open-ended growth pattern in which an organism or organ continues to grow as long as it lives; characteristic of some animals and of plant shoots and roots. (Contrast with determinate growth.)

indirect fitness   The component of inclusive fitness due to the reproductive success of related individuals times the percentage of shared genes between those individuals (e.g., 50% for a sibling). (*See also* direct fitness, inclusive fitness, kin selection.)

indirect interaction   An interaction in which the relationship between two species is mediated by a third (or more) species. (Compare with direct interaction.)

induced fit   A change in the shape of an enzyme caused by binding to its substrate that exposes the active site of the enzyme.

induced mutation   A mutation resulting from exposure to a mutagen from outside the cell. (Contrast with spontaneous mutation.)

inducer   (1) A compound that stimulates the synthesis of a protein. (2) In embryonic development, a substance that causes a group of target cells to differentiate in a particular way.

inducible   Produced only in the presence of a particular compound or under particular circumstances. (Contrast with constitutive.)

inducible proteins   Proteins that an organism produces only when they are needed. (Contrast with constitutive proteins.)

inductive logic   A logical thought process that involves making observations and then formulating one or more possible scenarios—hypotheses—that might explain those observations. (Contrast with deductive logic.)

inferior vena cava   The large vein that returns deoxygenated blood to the right atrium from the lower body.

inflammation   A nonspecific defense against pathogens; characterized by redness, swelling, pain, and increased temperature.

inflorescence   A structure composed of a few to many flowers.

inflorescence meristem   A meristem that produces floral meristems as well as other small leafy structures (bracts.)

ingroup   In a phylogenetic study, the group of organisms of primary interest. (Contrast with outgroup.)

initials   Cells that perpetuate plant meristems, comparable to animal stem cells. When an initial divides, one daughter cell develops into another initial, while the other differentiates into a more specialized cell.

initiation complex   In protein translation, a combination of a small ribosomal subunit, an mRNA molecule, and the tRNA charged with the first amino acid, usually methionine, coded for by the mRNA; formed at the onset of translation.

initiation site   The place within a promoter where transcription begins.

innate defenses   In animals, one of two general types of defenses against pathogens. Nonspecific and present in most animals. (Contrast with adaptive defenses.)

inner cell mass   A group of internal cells in the mammalian blastula (blastocyst) that gives rise to the embryo proper (via the epiblast) and to the yolk sac, allantois, and amnion (via the hypoblast). (Contrast with trophoblast.)

inorganic fertilizer   A chemical or combination of chemicals applied to soil or plants to make up for a plant nutrient deficiency. Often contains the macronutrients nitrogen, phosphorus, and potassium (N-P-K). (Contrast with organic fertilizer.)

inositol trisphosphate (IP$_3$)   An intracellular second messenger derived from membrane phospholipids.

insects   *See* Appendix A.

inspiratory reserve volume (IRV)   The amount of air that can be inhaled above the normal tidal inspiration. (Contrast with expiratory reserve volume, tidal volume, vital capacity.)

instar   (in' star) An immature stage of an insect between molts.

insular cortex   The outer layers of the insular lobe.

insular lobe   One of five lobes of the brain's cerebral hemisphere, folded in between the temporal lobe and the overlying frontal and parietal lobes. Integrates many sources of information to generate a percept of the self.

insulin   [L. *insula*: island] A hormone synthesized in islet cells of the pancreas that promotes the conversion of glucose into the storage material, glycogen.

integral membrane proteins   Proteins that are at least partially embedded in the cell membrane. (Contrast with anchored membrane proteins, peripheral membrane proteins.)

integrin   In animals, a transmembrane protein that mediates the attachment of epithelial cells to the extracellular matrix.

integument   [L. *integumentum*: covering] A protective surface structure. In gymnosperms and angiosperms, a layer of tissue around the ovule that will become the seed coat.

interaction strength   A measure of the effect of one species (the interactor) on the abundance of another species (the target species).

interaction web   A concept that describes both the trophic (vertical) and nontrophic (horizontal; such as competition, mutualism, commensalism) interactions among the species in a food web.

intercalated discs   Structural features of cardiac muscle cells that connect cells together and provide electrical continuity through gap junctions.

intercostal muscles   Muscles between the ribs that can augment breathing movements by elevating and suppressing the rib cage.

interference competition   Competition in which one species actively interferes with another species' access to a limiting resource. (Contrast with exploitation competition.)

interferons   Glycoproteins produced by virus-infected animal cells; interferons increase the resistance of neighboring cells to the virus.

intermediate disturbance hypothesis   A hypothesis describing how varying degrees of disturbance (or stress or predation) affect species diversity within communities. Species diversity is greatest at intermediate levels of disturbance because competitive exclusion at low levels of disturbance and mortality at high levels of disturbance reduce species diversity.

intermediate filaments   A part of the cytoskeleton that includes filaments intermediate in diameter between microtubules and microfilaments.

internal environment   In multicellular organisms, the extracellular body fluids (interstitial fluids, or tissue fluids) that bathe the cells of the body and therefore constitute the immediate environment of the cells.

internal fertilization   Fertilization that occurs inside the body of the female after sperm are deposited into the female reproductive tract and encounter ova there; typical of terrestrial animals. (Contrast with external fertilization.)

internal gills   Gills enclosed in protective body cavities; typical of mollusks, arthropods, and fishes.

internal membrane   A membrane that is enclosed within a membrane-bound organelle. Examples include membranes around thylakoids in chloroplasts and the inner mitochondrial membrane.

internal skeleton   See endoskeleton.

interneuron   A neuron that communicates information between two other neurons.

interphase   In the cell cycle, the period between successive nuclear divisions during which the chromosomes are diffuse and the nuclear envelope is intact. During interphase the cell is most active in transcribing and translating genetic information.

interspecific interactions   Interactions among members of two or more species.

interstitial fluid   Extracellular fluid that is not contained in the vessels of a circulatory system.

intertidal zone   The portion of the benthic coastal zone lying between the high and low tide levels that is periodically exposed to the air as the tides rise and fall.

intestine   The portion of the gut following the stomach, in which most digestion and absorption occurs.

intracellular receptor   A receptor that binds its ligand inside the cell. An example is the estrogen receptor in mammals.

intraspecific competition   Competition for shared limited resources by individuals of the same species.

intron   A portion of a gene within the coding region that is transcribed into pre-mRNA but is spliced out during mRNA processing, prior to translation. (Contrast with exon.)

invasive species   A non-native species that reproduces rapidly and spreads widely, often to the detriment of the native species or ecosystems of the region to which it has been introduced.

inversion   A rare 180-degree reversal of DNA sequence within a segment of a gene or chromosome.

involution   Cell movements that occur during gastrulation of frog embryos, giving rise to the archenteron.

ion   (eye′ on) [Gk. *ion*: wanderer] An electrically charged particle that forms when an atom gains or loses one or more electrons.

ion channel   An integral membrane protein that allows ions to diffuse across the membrane in which it is embedded.

ionic bond   An electrostatic attraction between positively and negatively charged ions.

iris   (eye′ ris) [Gk. *iris*: rainbow] The round, pigmented membrane that surrounds the pupil of the eye and adjusts its aperture to regulate the amount of light entering the eye.

islets of Langerhans   Clusters of hormone-producing cells in the pancreas.

isomers   Molecules consisting of the same numbers and kinds of atoms, but differing in the bonding patterns by which the atoms are held together.

isomorphic   (eye so more′ fik) [Gk. *isos*: equal + *morphe*: form] Having the same form or appearance, as when the haploid and diploid life stages of an organism appear identical. (Contrast with heteromorphic.)

isotonic   Having the same solute concentration; said of two solutions. (Contrast with hypertonic, hypotonic.)

isotope   (eye′ so tope) [Gk. *isos*: equal + *topos*: place] Isotopes of a given chemical element have the same number of protons in their nuclei (and thus are in the same position on the periodic table) but differ in the number of neutrons.

isozymes   Enzymes of an organism that have somewhat different amino acid sequences but catalyze the same reaction.

iteroparity   A type of reproductive life history in which individuals are physiologically capable of reproducing multiple times in a lifetime. (Contrast with semelparity.)

J

jasmonic acid (jasmonate)   A plant hormone involved in triggering responses to pathogen attack as well as other processes.

jawed vertebrates   See Appendix A.

jejunum   (jih jew′ num) The middle division of the small intestine, where most absorption of nutrients occurs. (*See also* duodenum, ileum.)

joint   In skeletal systems, a junction between two or more bones.

juvenile hormone   In insects, a hormone maintaining larval growth and preventing maturation or pupation.

juxtacrine   Pertaining to a chemical signal that binds to and affects only cells adjacent to it and with which it is in direct contact. (Contrast with autocrine, paracrine.)

K

***K*-strategist**   A species whose life history strategy allows it to persist at or near the carrying capacity (*K*) of its environment. (Contrast with *r*-strategist.)

karyogamy   The fusion of nuclei of two cells. (Contrast with plasmogamy.)

karyotype   The number, forms, and types of chromosomes in a cell.

K_D   *See* dissociation constant.

keystone species   A species that has a strong community-wide effect despite its small size and abundance.

kidneys   A pair of excretory organs in vertebrates.

kilocalorie (kcal)   *See* calorie.

kin selection   Selection for behaviors that increase the reproductive success of relatives even when they come at a cost to the performer.

kinesin   A type of protein that binds to microtubules and also to vesicles. By moving along the microtubules, kinesins act as motor proteins to move attached vesicles.

kinetic energy   (kuh-net′ ik) [Gk. *kinetos*: moving] The energy associated with movement. (Contrast with potential energy.)

kinetochore   (kuh net′ oh core) A specialized structure on a centromere to which microtubules attach.

kinetoplastids   *See* Appendix A.

kinorhynchs   *See* Appendix A.

Koch's postulates   A set of rules for establishing that a particular microorganism causes a particular disease.

Korarchaeota   *See* Appendix A.

L

lacteals   The smallest vessels of the lymphatic system.

lactic acid fermentation   A metabolic pathway in which glucose is catabolized in the absence of oxygen with the production of lactic acid.

lagging strand   In a DNA replication fork, the daughter strand that is synthesized in discontinuous stretches. (*See* Okazaki fragments. Contrast with leading strand.)

lampreys   *See* Appendix A.

lancelets   *See* Appendix A.

land plants   *See* Appendix A.

landscape   A geographic area consisting of multiple ecosystems or habitats.

LaPlace's law   An equation that describes the relationships between pressure (*P*), tension (*T*), and radius (*r*) of spherical or tubular containers.

larva   (plural: larvae) [L. *lares*: guiding spirits] An immature stage of any animal that differs dramatically in appearance from the adult.

larynx   A structure between the pharynx and trachea that contains the vocal cords.

lateral gene transfer   The transfer of genes from one species to another, common among bacteria and archaea.

lateral meristem   Either of the two meristems, the vascular cambium and the cork cambium, that give rise to a plant's secondary growth.

lateral root   A root extending outward from the taproot in a taproot system; typical of eudicots.

lateralization   A phenomenon in humans in which language functions come to reside in one cerebral hemisphere, usually the left.

laticifers   (luh tiss′ uh furs) In some plants, elongated cells containing secondary plant products such as latex.

Laurasia   The northernmost of the two large continents produced by the breakup of Pangaea.

law of independent assortment   *See* independent assortment.

law of mass action   The principle that the rate of a chemical reaction is directly proportional to the concentrations of the reacting substances.

law of segregation   *See* segregation.

laws of thermodynamics   [Gk. *thermos*: heat + *dynamis*: power] Laws derived from studies of the physical properties of energy and the ways energy interacts with matter.

LDP   *See* long-day plant.

leaching   In soils, a process by which mineral nutrients in upper soil horizons are dissolved in water and carried to deeper horizons, where they are unavailable to plant roots.

leading strand   In a DNA replication fork, the daughter strand that is synthesized continuously. (Contrast with lagging strand.)

leaf   (plural: leaves) In plants, the chief organ of photosynthesis.

leaf primordium   (plural: primordia) An outgrowth on the side of the shoot apical meristem that will eventually develop into a leaf.

leghemoglobin   In nitrogen-fixing plants, an oxygen-carrying protein in the cytoplasm of nodule cells that transports enough oxygen to the nitrogen-fixing bacteria to support their respiration, while keeping free oxygen concentrations low enough to protect nitrogenase.

lek   A display ground within which male animals compete for and defend small display areas as a means of demonstrating their territorial prowess and winning opportunities to mate.

lens   In the vertebrate eye, a crystalline protein structure that makes fine adjustments in the focus of images falling on the retina.

lenticels   Small porous regions on the bark of woody stems and roots in eudicots.

lepidosaurs   *See* Appendix A.

leptin   A hormone produced by fat cells that is believed to provide feedback information to the brain about the status of the body's fat reserves.

leukocytes   *See* white blood cells.

Leydig cells   The cells between the seminiferous tubules of the testes that secrete testosterone.

lichen   (lie′ kun) An organism resulting from the symbiotic association of a fungus and either a cyanobacterium or a unicellular alga.

life history   The lifetime pattern of growth, reproduction, and survival for an average individual.

life history strategy   The way in which individuals within and among species allocate resources to growth, reproduction, and survival based on genetic and environmental factors.

life table   A summary of how survival and reproductive rates vary with the age, size, or sex of individuals within a population, and used to estimate population growth rate.

ligament A band of connective tissue linking two bones in a joint.

ligand (lig′ and) Any molecule that binds to a receptor site of another (usually larger) molecule.

light reactions The initial phase of photosynthesis, in which light energy is converted into chemical energy.

light-harvesting complex In photosynthesis, a group of different molecules that cooperate to absorb light energy and transfer it to a reaction center. Also called antenna system.

lignin A complex, hydrophobic polyphenolic polymer in plant cell walls that cross-links other wall polymers, strengthening the walls, especially in wood.

limbic system A group of evolutionarily primitive structures in the vertebrate telencephalon that are involved in emotions, drives, instinctive behaviors, learning, and memory.

limiting resource A required resource whose supply (or lack thereof) strongly influences the size of a population.

lineage A series of populations, species, or genes descended from a single ancestor over evolutionary time.

lineage species concept The definition of a species as a branch on the tree of life, which has a history that starts at a speciation event and ends either at extinction or at another speciation event. (Contrast with biological species concept, morphological species concept.)

linkage analysis Genetic analysis in which a gene and its alleles are linked to an unknown gene and its alleles and the location of the latter is determined by its co-segregating with the former in genetic crosses.

lipases Digestive enzymes that break down fats.

lipid bilayer See phospholipid bilayer.

lipids [Gk. *lipos*: fat] Nonpolar, hydrophobic molecules that include fats, oils, waxes, steroids, and the phospholipids that make up biological membranes.

lipoproteins Lipids packaged inside a covering of protein, which allows them to be circulated in the blood.

liposome (lip′ o zome) A spherical structure contained by a membrane of phospholipids. Can be used to deliver drugs to cells.

lithosphere (lith′ o sphere) [Gk. *lithos*: strong] The crust of sold rock plates that overlays the viscous mantle of Earth. The movements of the lithosphere are the source of plate tectonics. (Contrast with asthenosphere.)

liver A large digestive gland. In vertebrates, it secretes bile and is involved in the formation of blood.

liverworts See Appendix A.

loading In phloem, the process of transferring the products of photosynthesis, usually sugars, into sieve tubes.

loam A type of soil consisting of a mixture of sand, silt, clay, and organic matter. One of the best soil types for agriculture.

lobe-limbed vertebrates See Appendix A.

loboseans See Appendix A.

locus (low′ kus) (plural: loci, low′ sigh) In genetics, a specific location on a chromosome. Sometimes used synonymously with gene.

logistic growth A pattern of population growth characterized by a multiplicative pattern that eventually levels off as density-dependent processes slow growth at some carrying capacity. (Contrast with exponential growth.)

Lokiarchaeota See Appendix A.

long-day plant (LDP) A plant that requires long days (actually, short nights) in order to flower. (Compare with short-day plant.)

long-term depression (LTD) A long-lasting decrease in the responsiveness of a neuron that results from a period of prior stimulation. (Contrast with long-term potentiation.)

long-term memory Information that is maintained in the brain and is accessible for long periods of time—hours to years. (Contrast with immediate memory, short-term memory.)

long-term potentiation (LTP) A long-lasting increase in the responsiveness of a neuron that results from a period of intense stimulation. (Contrast with long-term depression.)

loop of Henle (hen′ lee) A long, hairpin loop of the mammalian renal tubule that runs from the cortex down into the medulla and back to the cortex; creates a concentration gradient in the interstitial fluids in the medulla.

lophophore A U-shaped fold of the body wall with hollow, ciliated tentacles that encircles the mouth of animals in several different groups. Used for filtering prey from the surrounding water.

lophotrochozoans See Appendix A.

loriciferans See Appendix A.

loss-of-function mutation A mutation that results in the loss of a functional protein. (Contrast with gain-of-function mutation.)

loss-of-stop mutation A mutation that results in a change from a stop (nonsense) codon to a sense codon, causing additional amino acids to be added to the end of the protein. (Contrast with frame-shift mutation, missense mutation, nonsense mutation, silent mutation.)

lottery model A hypothesis proposing that species diversity in communities is maintained by a "lottery" in which resources, made available by the effects of disturbance, stress, or predation, are captured at random by individuals of different species. Also called neutral model.

low-density lipoproteins (LDLs) Lipoproteins that transport cholesterol around the body for use in biosynthesis and for storage; LDLs are the "bad" lipoproteins associated with a high risk of cardiovascular disease.

lower critical temperature The environmental temperature at which a resting endotherm must increase its metabolic rate to avoid a drop in its body temperature.

lumen (loo′ men) [L. *lumen*: light] The open cavity inside any tubular organ or structure, such as the gut or a renal tubule.

lung An internal organ specialized for respiratory gas exchange with air.

lungfishes See Appendix A.

luteal phase In human females, the second half of the ovarian cycle, when the follicle cells remaining in the ovary after ovulation develop into the corpus luteum. (Contrast with follicular phase.)

luteinizing hormone (LH) A gonadotropin produced by the anterior pituitary and that stimulates the gonads to produce sex hormones.

lycophytes See Appendix A.

lymph [L. *lympha*: liquid] A fluid derived from blood and other tissues that accumulates in intercellular spaces throughout the body and is returned to the blood by the lymphatic system.

lymph node A specialized structure in the vessels of the lymphatic system. Lymph nodes contain lymphocytes, which encounter and respond to foreign cells and molecules in the lymph as it passes through the vessels.

lymphatic duct One of two large lymphatic vessels that drain lymph into a subclavian vein.

lymphatic system An elaborate system of vessels, separate from the blood vascular system, that picks up excess interstitial fluid (lymph) and returns it to the blood.

lymphocytes One of the three major groups of white blood cells; includes T cells, B cells, and natural killer cells.

lysogeny A form of viral replication in which the virus becomes incorporated into the host chromosome and remains inactive. Also called a lysogenic cycle. (Contrast with lytic cycle.)

lysosomal storage diseases A class of human diseases, invariably harmful or fatal, that are caused by the failure of lysosomes to digest specific cellular components. An example is Tay-Sachs disease.

lysozyme (lie′ so zyme) An enzyme made by cells in the mucous membranes (for example, in saliva, tears, nasal secretions, and breast milk) that hydrolyzes bacterial cell walls.

lytic cycle A viral reproductive cycle in which the virus takes over a host cell's synthetic machinery to replicate itself, then bursts (lyses) the host cell, releasing the new viruses. (Contrast with lysogeny.)

M

macroevolution [Gk. *makros*: large] Evolutionary changes occurring over long time spans and usually involving changes in many traits. (Contrast with microevolution.)

macroglia One of the two major types of glia; support and modulate the functions of neurons. Macroglia include astrocytes, ependymal cells, oligodendrocytes, and Schwann cells. (Contrast with microglia.)

macromolecule A giant (molecular weight > 1,000) polymeric molecule. The macromolecules are the proteins, polysaccharides, and nucleic acids.

macronutrient (1) In plants, a mineral element required in concentrations of at least 1 milligram per gram of plant dry matter. (Contrast with micronutrient.) (2) In animals, the components of food that provide energy: fats, carbohydrates, and proteins. (Contrast with mineral macronutrient, mineral micronutrient.)

macroparasites Relatively large parasite species, such as arthropods and worms. (Compare with microparasites.)

magnoliids See Appendix A.

maintenance methylase   An enzyme that catalyzes the methylation of the new DNA strand when DNA is replicated.

major histocompatibility complex (MHC) A complex of linked genes, with multiple alleles, that encode cell surface proteins involved in antigen presentation. Class I MHC proteins are present on all nucleated cells and mismatches between donor and recipient can lead to graft rejection.

malignant   Referring to a tumor that can grow indefinitely or spread from the original site of growth to other locations in the body. (Contrast with benign.)

malnutrition   A condition caused by lack of any essential nutrient.

Malpighian tubule   (mal pee′ gy un) A type of protonephridium found in insects.

mammals   See Appendix A.

mandible   A crushing part of arthropod mouthparts; in mammals, the lower jaw bone; in birds, the upper or lower part of the beak.

mandibulates   See Appendix A.

mantle   (1) In mollusks, a fold of tissue that covers the organs of the visceral mass and secretes the hard shell that is typical of many mollusks. (2) In geology, Earth's crust below the solid lithospheric plates.

mark–recapture method   A method of estimating population sizes of mobile organisms by capturing, marking, and releasing a sample of individuals, then capturing another sample at a later time.

marsupials   See Appendix A.

mass   A measure of the quantity of matter present; the greater the mass, the greater the quantity of matter.

mass extinction event   A period of evolutionary history during which rates of extinction are much higher than during intervening times.

mass number   The sum of the number of protons and neutrons in an atom's nucleus.

mast cell   A type of white blood cell, typically found in connective tissue, that releases histamine in response to tissue damage or to allergens.

maternal effect genes   Genes coding for morphogens that determine the polarity of the egg and larva in fruit flies. Part of a developmental cascade that includes gap genes, pair rule genes, segment polarity genes, and Hox genes.

mating   The joining of individuals for the purpose of reproduction.

mating type   In fungi, a particular strain of a species that is incapable of sexual reproduction with another member of the same strain but capable of sexual reproduction with members of other strains of the same species.

maximum likelihood   A statistical method of determining which of two or more hypotheses (such as phylogenetic trees) best fit the observed data, given an explicit model of how the data were generated.

mechanically gated channel   A molecular channel that opens or closes in response to mechanical force applied to the cell membrane in which it is inserted.

mechanoreceptor   A cell that is sensitive to physical movement and generates action potentials in response.

mediator   A regulatory protein composed of multiple subunits that interacts with the general transcription factors and RNA polymerase II of the basal transcription apparatus and with specific transcription factors.

medulla   (meh dull′ luh) (1) The inner, core region of an organ, as in the adrenal medulla (adrenal gland) or the renal medulla (kidneys). (2) The portion of the brainstem that connects to the spinal cord.

medusa   (plural: medusae) In cnidarians, a free-swimming, sexual life cycle stage shaped like a bell or an umbrella.

megagametophyte   In heterosporous plants, the female gametophyte; produces eggs. (Contrast with microgametophyte.)

megakaryocyte   A bone marrow cell that produces blood platelets.

megaphyll   The generally large leaf of a fern, horsetail, or seed plant, with several to many veins. (Contrast with microphyll.)

megasporangia   The plant structures that bear megaspores.

megaspore   [Gk. *megas*: large + *spora*: to sow] In plants, a haploid spore that produces a female gametophyte.

megastrobilus   In conifers, a female (seed-bearing) cone. (Contrast with microstrobilus.)

meiosis   (my oh′ sis) [Gk. *meiosis*: diminution] The division of a diploid nucleus to produce four haploid daughter cells. The process consists of two successive nuclear divisions of a cell that has undegone only one cycle of chromosome replication. In meiosis I, homologous chromosomes separate but retain their sister chromatids. The second division, meiosis II, is similar to mitosis, in which sister chromatids separate.

meiosis I   See meiosis.

meiosis II   See meiosis.

Meissner's corpuscles   Rapidly adapting skin mechanoreceptors sensitive to light touch and vibration. Found primarily in non-hairy skin; provide continuous information about changes in things touching the skin.

melanocyte-stimulating hormone (MSH) A pituitary peptide hormone that stimulates melanocytes to produce the pigment melanin.

melatonin   A hormone released by the pineal gland. Involved in photoperiodicity and circadian rhythms.

membrane   A phospholipid bilayer forming a barrier that separates the internal contents of a cell from the nonbiological environment, or enclosing the organelles within a cell. The membrane regulates the molecular substances entering or leaving a cell or organelle.

membrane potential   The difference in electric charge between the inside and the outside of a cell, caused by a difference in the distribution of ions.

membranous bone   A type of bone that develops by forming on a scaffold of connective tissue. (Contrast with cartilage bone.)

memory cells   Long-lived B and T cells that are produced after exposure to antigen. They persist in the body and are able to mount a rapid response to subsequent exposures to the antigen.

menopause   In human females, the end of fertility and menstrual cycling.

menstrual cycle   A term for the uterine cycle of humans that refers to the monthly sloughing of the uterine lining, or menses.

menstruation   In human and other primate females, the process by which the endometrium breaks down (after a failure of pregnancy to occur) and the sloughed-off tissue, including blood, flows from the body.

meristem culture   A method for the asexual propagation of plants, in which pieces of shoot apical meristem are cultured to produce plantlets.

Merkel's discs   Slowly adapting skin mechanoreceptors that provide continuous information about anything touching the skin.

mesenchyme   (mez′ en kyme) [Gk. *mesos*: middle + *enchyma*: infusion] Embryonic or unspecialized cells derived from the mesoderm.

mesoderm   [Gk. *mesos*: middle + *derma*: skin] The middle of the three embryonic germ layers first delineated during gastrulation. Gives rise to the skeleton, circulatory system, muscles, excretory system, and most of the reproductive system.

mesoglea   (mez′ uh glee uh) [Gk. *mesos*: middle + *gloia*: glue] A thick, gelatinous noncellular layer that separates the two cellular tissue layers of ctenophores, cnidarians, and scyphozoans.

mesophyll   (mez′ uh fill) [Gk. *mesos*: middle + *phyllon*: leaf] Chloroplast-containing, photosynthetic cells in the interior of leaves.

messenger RNA (mRNA)   The transcript, after processing in eukaryotes, of a region of one of the strands of DNA for a gene; it carries information (as a sequence of codons) for the synthesis of one or more proteins.

metabolic pathway   A series of enzyme-catalyzed reactions so arranged that the product of one reaction is the substrate of the next.

metabolism   (meh tab′ a lizm) [Gk. *metabole*: change] The sum total of the chemical reactions that occur in an organism, or some subset of that total (as in respiratory metabolism).

metabolome   The quantitative description of all the small molecules in a cell or organism.

metagenomics   The practice of analyzing DNA from environmental samples without isolating intact organisms.

metamorphosis   (met′ a mor′ fo sis) [Gk. *meta*: between + *morphe*: form, shape] A change occurring between one developmental stage and another, as for example from a tadpole to a frog. (See also complete metamorphosis, incomplete metamorphosis; contrast with direct development.)

metanephridia   (singular: metanephridium) [Gk. *meta*: akin to] The paired excretory organs of annelids.

metapopulation   A group of geographically isolated populations linked together by dispersal.

metastasis   The spread of tumor cells to regions of the body away from the primary tumor.

methanogens Methane-producing microbes.

methylation The addition of a methyl group (—CH$_3$) to a molecule.

micelle A particle of lipid covered with bile salts that is produced in the duodenum and facilitates digestion and absorption of lipids.

microbial eukaryotes *See* Appendix A.

microbiome The diverse community of bacteria that lives on or within the body of an organism and is essential to bodily function.

microbiota The diverse communities of bacteria that live on or within the body.

microevolution Evolutionary changes below the species level, affecting allele frequencies. (Contrast with macroevolution.)

microfilament In eukaryotic cells, a fibrous structure made up of actin monomers. Microfilaments play roles in the cytoskeleton, in cell movement, and in muscle contraction.

microgametophyte In heterosporous plants, the male gametophyte; produces sperm. (Contrast with megagametophyte.)

microglia One of the two major types of glia; act as macrophages and mediators of inflammatory responses in the central nervous system. Microglia are motile and are the first and major immune defense mechanism in the nervous system. (Contrast with macroglia.)

micronutrient In plants, a mineral element required in concentrations of less than 100 micrograms per gram of plant dry matter; in animals, a mineral element required in concentrations of less than 100 micrograms per day. (Contrast with macronutrient.)

microparasites Parasite species too small to be seen with the naked eye, such as viruses, bacteria, protists, and fungi. (Compare with macroparasites.)

microphyll A small leaf with a single vein, found in club mosses and their relatives. (Contrast with megaphyll.)

micropyle (mike' roh pile) [Gk. *mikros*: small + *pylon*: gate] An opening in the integument(s) of a seed plant ovule through which pollen grows to reach the female gametophyte within.

microRNA (miRNA) A small, noncoding RNA molecule, typically about 21 bases long, that binds to mRNA to inhibit its translation.

microsporangia The plant structures that bear microspores.

microspore [Gk. *mikros*: small + *spora*: to sow] In plants, a haploid spore that produces a male gametophyte.

microsporidia *See* Appendix A.

microstrobilus In conifers, a male (pollen-bearing) cone. (Contrast with megastrobilus.)

microtubules Tubular structures found in the centrioles, spindle apparatus, cilia, flagella, and cytoskeleton of eukaryotic cells. Microtubules play roles in the motion and maintenance of shape of eukaryotic cells.

microvilli (singular: microvillus) Projections of epithelial cells, such as the cells lining the small intestine, that increase their surface area.

midbrain One of the three regions of the vertebrate brain. Part of the brainstem, it serves as a relay station for sensory signals sent to the cerebral hemispheres. (Compare with forebrain, hindbrain.)

migration The round-trip movement of individuals within a population as a consequence of seasonal variation in resources.

mineral macronutrient In animals, an element required in large amounts.

mineral micronutrient In animals, an element required in only tiny amounts (generally less than 100 mg/day).

mineral nutrients Inorganic ions required by organisms for normal growth and reproduction.

mineralization The process by which animals, bacteria, and fungi convert organic compounds into inorganic soluble nutrients.

mismatch repair A mechanism that scans DNA after it has been replicated and corrects any base-pairing mismatches.

missense mutation A change in a gene's sequence that changes the amino acid at that site in the encoded protein. (Contrast with frame-shift mutation, loss-of-stop mutation, nonsense mutation, silent mutation.)

missense substitution A change in a gene from one nucleotide to another that results in a change to the corresponding amino acid in the encoded protein. (Contrast with synonymous substitution.)

mitochondria (my' toe kon' dree uh) (singular: mitochondrion) [Gk. *mitos*: thread + *chondros*: grain] Energy-generating organelles in eukaryotic cells that contain the enzymes of the citric acid cycle, the respiratory chain, and oxidative phosphorylation.

mitogen A signal that stimulates mitosis.

mitosis (my toe' sis) [Gk. *mitos*: thread] Nuclear division in eukaryotes leading to the formation of two daughter nuclei, each with a chromosome complement identical to that of the original nucleus. With cytokinesis, makes up M phase of cell cycle.

mitosomes Reduced structures derived from mitochondria found in some organisms.

mitral valve *See* bicuspid valve. So named because it has a similar shape to a miter (a religious headdress).

model organisms Also known as **model systems**, these include the small group of species that are the subject of extensive research. They are organisms that adapt well to laboratory situations, and findings from experiments on them can apply across a broad range of species. A few examples include mice, zebrafish, fruit flies (*Drosophila*), and *E. coli* bacteria.

moderately repetitive sequences DNA sequences repeated 10–1,000 times in the eukaryotic genome. They include the genes that code for rRNAs and tRNAs, as well as the DNA in telomeres.

molds Sac fungi composed of filamentous hyphae that do not form large ascomata.

mole A quantity of a compound whose weight in grams is numerically equal to its molecular weight expressed in atomic mass units. Avogadro's number of molecules: 6.023×10^{23} molecules.

molecular clock The approximately constant rate of divergence of macromolecules from one another over evolutionary time; used to date past events in evolutionary history

molecular evolution The scientific study of the mechanisms and consequences of the evolution of macromolecules.

molecular weight The sum of the atomic weights of the atoms in a molecule.

molecule A chemical substance made up of two or more atoms joined by covalent bonds or ionic bonds.

mollusks *See* Appendix A.

molting The process of shedding part or all of an outer covering, as the shedding of feathers by birds or of the entire exoskeleton by arthropods.

monilophytes *See* Appendix A.

monoblastic Having a body derived from a single embryonic cell layer. (Contrast with diploblastic, triploblastic.)

monocots Angiosperms with a single embryonic cotyledon; one of the two largest clades of angiosperms. (*See also* eudicots.)

monoculture In agriculture, a large-scale planting of a single crop species. (Contrast with polyculture).

monoecious (mo nee' shus) [Gk. *mono*: one + *oikos*: house] Pertaining to organisms in which both sexes are "housed" in a single individual that produces both eggs and sperm. (In some plants, these are found in different flowers within the same plant.) Examples include corn, peas, earthworms, hydras. (Contrast with dioecious.)

monohybrid cross A mating in which the parents differ with respect to the alleles of only one gene of interest.

monomer [Gk. *mono*: one + *meros*: unit] A small molecule, two or more of which can be combined to form oligomers (consisting of a few monomers) or polymers (consisting of many monomers).

monophyletic (mon' oh fih leht' ik) [Gk. *mono*: one + *phylon*: tribe] Pertaining to a group that consists of an ancestor and all of its descendants. (Contrast with paraphyletic, polyphyletic.)

monoplacophorans *See* Appendix A.

monosaccharide A simple sugar. Oligosaccharides and polysaccharides are made up of monosaccharides.

monosomic Pertaining to a cell or organism with only one copy of a chromosome that should be in two (or more) copies.

morphogen A diffusible substance whose concentration gradient determines a developmental pattern in embryonic animals and plants.

morphological species concept The definition of a species as a group of individuals that look alike. (Contrast with biological species concept, lineage species concept.)

morphology (more fol' o jee) [Gk. *morphe*: form + *logos*: study, discourse] The scientific study of organic form, including both its development and function.

mosaic development   A pattern of animal embryonic development in which each blastomere contributes a specific part of the adult body. (Contrast with regulative development.)

mosses   *See* Appendix A.

motile   (mo' tul) Able to move from one place to another. (Contrast with sessile.)

motor end plate   The depression in the postsynaptic membrane of the neuromuscular junction where the terminals of the motor neuron sit.

motor neuron   A type of efferent neuron that carries signals from the central nervous system to a skeletal muscle, stimulating the muscle to contract.

motor proteins   Specialized proteins that use energy to change shape and move cells or structures within cells.

motor unit   A motor neuron and the muscle fibers it controls.

mucosa   The first layer of the gut that lines the luminal surface.

mucus   A viscous substance secreted by mucous membranes (e.g., mucosal epithelium). A barrier defense against pathogens in innate immunity in animals and a protective coating in many animal organ systems.

Muller's ratchet   The accumulation—"ratcheting up"—of deleterious mutations in the nonrecombining genomes of asexual species.

Müllerian mimicry   The convergence in appearance of two or more unpalatable species.

multifactorial   Referring to the interaction of many genes and proteins with one or more factors in the environment. For example, cancer is a disease with multifactorial causes.

multiple fruit   A fruit that develops from several carpels of multiple flowers.

multiplication rule   The rule that the probability of two or more independent events occurring together is the product of their independent probabilities. (Contrast with addition rule.)

muscle fiber   A single muscle cell. In the case of skeletal muscle, a syncitial, multinucleate cell.

muscle spindles   Mechanoreceptors embedded in skeletal muscle that sense changes in the length of the muscle.

muscle tissue   Excitable tissue that can contract through the interactions of actin and myosin; one of the four major tissue types in multicellular animals. There are three types of vertebrate muscle tissue: skeletal, smooth, and cardiac.

mutagen   (mute' ah jen) [L. *mutare*: change + Gk. *genesis*: source] Any agent (e.g., a chemical, radiation) that increases the mutation rate.

mutation   A change in the genetic material not caused by recombination.

mutualism   A type of positive interaction in which both species benefit from the interaction, sometimes in a highly dependent and symbiotic manner. (Contrast with amensalism, commensalism, competition.)

mutualistic   Referring to a relationship that benefits both partners.

mycelium   (my seel' ee yum) [Gk. *mykes*: fungus] In fungi, a mass of hyphae.

mycologists   Scientists who study fungi.

mycoplasmas   *See* Appendix A.

mycorrhiza   (my' ko rye' za) (plural: mycorrhizae) [Gk. *mykes*: fungus + *rhiza*: root] An association of the root of a plant with the mycelium of a fungus.

myelin   (my' a lin) Concentric layers of oligodendrocyte or Schwann cell membrane that form a sheath around some axons; myelin provides the axon with electrical insulation and increases the rate of transmission of action potentials.

myoblast   An embryonic type of stem cell that gives rise to muscle cells.

myocardial infarction   Blockage of an artery that carries blood to the heart muscle; a "heart attack."

myofibril   (my' oh fy' bril) [Gk. *mys*: muscle + L. *fibrilla*: small fiber] A polymeric unit of actin or myosin in a muscle.

myoglobin   (my' oh globe' in) [Gk. *mys*: muscle + L. *globus*: sphere] An oxygen-binding molecule found in muscle. Consists of a heme unit and a single globin chain; carries less oxygen than hemoglobin.

myosin   One of the two contractile proteins of muscle. (*See also* actin.)

myriapods   *See* Appendix A.

myxamoeba   An independent, unicellular, haploid life stage of cellular slime molds.

N

natural killer cell   A type of lymphocyte that attacks virus-infected cells and some tumor cells as well as antibody-labeled target cells.

natural selection   The differential contribution of offspring to the next generation by various genetic types belonging to the same population. The mechanism of evolution proposed by Charles Darwin. (Contrast with artificial selection.)

nauplius   (naw' plee us) [Gk. *nauplios*: shellfish] A bilaterally symmetrical larval form typical of crustaceans.

necrosis   (nec roh' sis) [Gk. *nekros*: death] Premature cell death caused by external agents such as toxins.

negative feedback   In regulatory systems, information that decreases a regulatory response, returning the system to the set point. (Contrast with positive feedback.)

negative regulation   A type of gene regulation in which the binding of a repressor protein to DNA prevents transcription. (Contrast with positive regulation.)

negative-sense RNA   A strand of RNA that is complementary to mRNA.

nematocyst   (ne mat' o sist) [Gk. *nema*: thread + *kystis*: cell] An elaborate, threadlike structure produced by cells of jellyfishes and other cnidarians, used chiefly to paralyze and capture prey.

nematodes   *See* Appendix A.

neopterans   *See* Appendix A.

nephron   (nef' ron) [Gk. *nephros*: kidney] The functional unit of the kidney, consisting of a structure for receiving a filtrate of blood and a tubule that reabsorbs selected parts of the filtrate.

Nernst equation   A mathematical statement that calculates the potential across a membrane permeable to a single type of ion that differs in concentration on the two sides of the membrane.

nerve   A structure consisting of many neuronal axons and connective tissue.

nerve net   A diffuse, loosely connected aggregation of nervous tissue in certain non-bilaterian animals such as cnidarians.

nervous tissue   Tissue specialized for processing and communicating information; one of the four major tissue types in multicellular animals.

net primary production (NPP)   The amount of energy or biomass incorporated into the tissues of primary producers after respiration. (Compare with gross primary production.)

net reproductive rate (R_0)   The mean number of offspring produced by an individual in a population during its lifetime.

net secondary production   The consumption of other organisms, taking into account consumption efficiency, assimilation efficiency, and production efficiency.

neural crest cells   During vertebrate neurulation, cells that migrate outward from the neural plate and give rise to connections between the central nervous system and the rest of the body.

neural network   An organized group of neurons that contains three functional categories of neurons—afferent neurons, interneurons, and efferent neurons—and is capable of processing information.

neural tube   An early stage in the development of the vertebrate nervous system consisting of a hollow tube created by two opposing folds of the dorsal ectoderm along the anterior–posterior body axis.

neurohormone   A chemical signal produced and released by neurons that subsequently acts as a hormone.

neuromuscular junction   The synapse (point of contact) where a motor neuron axon stimulates a muscle fiber cell.

neurons   (noor' ons) [Gk. *neuron*: nerve] One of the two classes of neural cells (along with glia). Neurons can generate and conduct action potentials along an axon to a synapse with another cell.

neurotransmitter   A biochemical substance produced in and released by a neuron (the presynaptic cell) that diffuses across a synapse and excites or inhibits another cell (the postsynaptic cell).

neurulation   The stage in vertebrate development when the nervous system begins to form.

neutral model   *See* lottery model.

neutral theory   A view of molecular evolution that postulates that most mutations do not affect the amino acid being coded for, and that such mutations accumulate in a population at rates driven by genetic drift and mutation rates.

neutron (new′ tron) One of the three fundamental particles of matter (along with protons and electrons), with mass slightly larger than that of a proton and no electrical charge.

niche (nitch) [L. *nidus*: nest] The set of physical and biological conditions a species requires to grow, reproduce, and survive.

nitrate reduction The process by which nitrate (NO_3^-) is reduced to ammonia (NH_3).

nitric oxide (NO) A gaseous molecule that serves as s neurotransmitter.

nitrification The oxidation of ammonia (NH_3) to nitrate (NO_3^-) in soil and seawater, carried out by chemoautotrophic bacteria (nitrifiers).

nitrifiers Prokaryotes that can convert ammonium into nitrate.

nitrogen fixation The conversion of atmospheric nitrogen gas (N_2) into a more reactive and biologically useful form (ammonia), which makes nitrogen available to living things. Carried out by nitrogen fixers—bacteria, some of them free-living and others living within plant roots.

nitrogen fixers Organisms capable of fixing atmospheric N_2 to form NH_3.

nitrogenase An enzyme complex found in nitrogen-fixing bacteria that mediates the stepwise reduction of atmospheric N_2 to ammonia and which is strongly inhibited by oxygen.

node [L. *nodus*: knob, knot] (1) In plants, a (sometimes enlarged) point on a stem where a leaf is or was attached. (2) A region at the anterior end of the primitive grove—the site of ingression of cells during gastrulation. In mammals and birds it serves a function similar to the dorsal lip of the blastopore in amphibians. (3) In phylogenetics, a split in a phylogenetic tree when one lineage diverges into two.

node of Ranvier A gap in the myelin sheath covering an axon; the point where the axonal membrane can fire action potentials.

non-REM sleep In humans and other mammals, one of two major sleep states. Human non-REM sleep is divided into three stages, the last of which is deep sleep characterized by high-amplitude, slow-frequency waves in the EEG. (*See also* rapid eye movement sleep, slow-wave sleep.)

noncompetitive inhibitor A non-substrate that inhibits the activity of an enzyme by binding to a site other than its active site. (Contrast with competitive inhibitor.)

noncyclic electron transport In photosynthesis, the flow of electrons that forms ATP, NADPH, and O_2.

nondisjunction The failure of sister chromatids to separate in meiosis II or mitosis, or of homologous chromosomes to separate in meiosis I. Results in aneuploidy.

nonpolar covalent bond A covalent bond between atoms that has equal sharing of electrons.

nonpolar Having electric charges that are evenly balanced from one end to the other. (Contrast with polar.)

nonsense codon *See* stop codon.

nonsense mutation A change in a gene's sequence that prematurely terminates translation by changing one of its codons to a stop codon.

(Contrast with frame-shift mutation, loss-of-stop mutation, missense mutation, silent mutation.)

nonsense substitution A change in a gene from one nucleotide to another that prematurely terminates translation by changing one of its codons to a stop codon. (Contrast with synonymous substitution.)

nonsynonymous substitution A change in a gene from one nucleotide to another that changes the amino acid specified by the corresponding codon (i.e., AGC → AGA, or serine → arginine). (Contrast with synonymous substitution.)

nonvascular land plants All land plants that lack a vascular system.

norepinephrine A neurotransmitter found in the central nervous system and also at the postganglionic nerve endings of the sympathetic nervous system. Also called noradrenaline.

notochord (no′ tow kord) [Gk. *notos*: back + *chorde*: string] A flexible rod of gelatinous material serving as a support in the embryos of all chordates and in the adults of tunicates and lancelets.

nuclear envelope A double membrane that encloses the cell nucleus.

nucleases Digestive enzymes that break down nucleic acids.

nucleic acid (new klay′ ik) A polymer made up of nucleotides, specialized for the storage, transmission, and expression of genetic information. DNA and RNA are nucleic acids.

nucleic acid hybridization A technique in which a single-stranded nucleic acid probe is made that is complementary to, and binds to, a target sequence, either DNA or RNA. The resulting double-stranded molecule is a hybrid.

nucleoid (new′ klee oid) The region that harbors the chromosomes of a prokaryotic cell. Unlike the eukaryotic nucleus, it is not bounded by a membrane.

nucleolus (new klee′ oh lus) A small, generally spherical body found within the nucleus of eukaryotic cells. The site of synthesis of ribosomal RNA.

nucleoside A nucleotide without the phosphate group; a nitrogenous base attached to a sugar.

nucleosome A portion of a eukaryotic chromosome, consisting of part of the DNA molecule wrapped around a group of histone molecules, and held together by another type of histone molecule. A chromosome is made up of many nucleosomes.

nucleotide The basic chemical unit in nucleic acids, consisting of a pentose sugar, a phosphate group, and a nitrogen-containing base.

nucleus (new′ klee us) [L. *nux*: kernel or nut] (1) In cells, the centrally located compartment of eukaryotic cells that is bounded by a double membrane and contains the chromosomes. (2) In the brain, an identifiable group of neurons that share common characteristics or functions.

null hypothesis In statistics, the premise that any differences observed in an experiment are simply the result of random differences that arise from drawing two finite samples from the same population.

nutrient A food substance; or in the case of mineral nutrients, an inorganic element required for completion of the life cycle of an organism.

O

obligate aerobe An organism that requires an oxygen atmosphere to live.

obligate anaerobe An anaerobic prokaryote that cannot survive exposure to O_2. (Compare with facultative anaerobe.)

obligate parasite An organism that can only survive and grow in or on another living organism, to the detriment of the host.

obligate Referring to a type of species interaction that is necessary for at least one species involved in the interaction. (Compare with facultative.)

occipital lobe One of five lobes of the brain's cerebral hemisphere; processes visual information.

ocean zone The marine life zone that extends from the coastal zone into open ocean. Characterized by deep water that varies in its oxygenation and relatively stable temperatures and salinities.

odorant A molecule that can bind to an olfactory receptor.

oil A triglyceride that is liquid at room temperature. (Contrast with fat.)

Okazaki fragments Newly formed DNA making up the lagging strand in DNA replication. After primer removal, DNA ligase links Okazaki fragments together to make a continuous strand.

olfaction (ole fak′ shun) [L. *olfacere*: to smell] The sense of smell.

olfactory bulb A structure in the vertebrate forebrain that receives and processes input from olfactory receptor neurons.

olfactory glomeruli Collections in the olfactory bulb of axonal terminals from olfactory receptor neurons that share a common olfactory receptor type.

olfactory receptor neurons (ORNs) Neurons with receptors for odorant molecules.

oligodendrocyte A type of macroglial cell that myelinates axons in the central nervous system.

oligopeptide *See* peptide.

oligosaccharide A polymer containing a small number of monosaccharides.

omasum The third of the four chambers of the stomach in ruminants; concentrates food by water absorption before it enters the true stomach (abomasum).

omega-3 fatty acid An unsaturated fatty acid with a C=C bond at position 3.

ommatidia [Gk. *omma*: eye] The units that make up the compound eye of some arthropods.

omnivore [L. *omnis*: everything + *vorare*: to devour] An organism that feeds on multiple trophic levels; also an organism that feeds on animals and primary producers. (Contrast with carnivore, detritivore, herbivore.)

oncogene [Gk. *onkos*: mass, tumor + *genes*: born] A gene that codes for a protein product that stimulates cell proliferation. Mutations in oncogenes that result in excessive cell proliferation can give rise to cancer. (Contrast with tumor supressor.)

one gene–one polypeptide   The idea, now known to be an oversimplification, that each gene in the genome encodes only a single polypeptide—that there is a one-to-one correspondence between genes and polypeptides.

one-gene, one-enzyme hypothesis   *See* one gene–one polypeptide.

one-gene, one-polypeptide relationship   *See* one gene–one polypeptide.

oogonium   (oh′ eh go′ nee um) (plural: oogonia) (1) In some algae and fungi, a cell in which an egg is produced. (2) In animals, the diploid progeny of a germ cell in females.

oomycetes   *See* Appendix A.

ootid   In oogenesis, the daughter cell of the second meiotic division that differentiates into the mature ovum. (*See also* second polar body.)

open circulatory system   A circulatory system in which extracellular fluid leaves the vessels of the circulatory system, percolates between cells and through tissues, and then flows back into the circulatory system to be pumped out again. (Contrast with closed circulatory system.)

open reading frames   Sequences of DNA within genes that begin with a start codon and end with a stop codon.

operant conditioning   Using a reward or a punishment to control the expression of a behavior by an animal in response to an unrelated stimulus.

operator   The region of an operon that acts as the binding site for the repressor.

operon   A genetic unit of transcription, consisting of two or more structural genes that are transcribed together; the operon contains at least two control regions: the promoter and the operator.

opisthokonts   *See* Appendix A.

opportunity cost   The sum of the benefits an animal forfeits by not being able to perform some other behavior during the time when it is performing a given behavior. (Compare with energetic cost, risk cost.)

opsin   (op′ sin) [Gk. *opsis*: sight] The protein portion of vertebrate visual pigments; associated with the pigment molecule 11-*cis*-retinal. (*See also* rhodopsin.)

optic chiasm   [Gk. *chiasma*: cross] A structure on the lower surface of the vertebrate brain where the two optic nerves come together.

optic nerve   The nerve that carries information from the retina of the eye to the brain.

optical isomers   Two molecular isomers that are mirror images of each other.

optimal foraging theory   The theory, based on a cost–benefit approach to feeding behavior, that animals will make feeding choices that maximize energetic gain at the least cost.

oral   [L. *os*: mouth] Pertaining to the mouth, or that part of the body that contains the mouth. (Contrast with aboral.)

orbital   A region in space surrounding the atomic nucleus in which an electron is most likely to be found.

organ   [Gk. *organon*: tool] A body part, such as the heart, liver, brain, root, or leaf. Organs are composed of different tissues integrated to perform a distinct function. Organs, in turn, are integrated into organ systems.

organ identity genes   In angiosperms, genes that specify the different organs of the flower.

organ of Corti   A structure in the inner ear that transforms mechanical forces produced from pressure waves ("sound waves") into action potentials that are sensed as sound.

organ system   An interrelated and integrated group of tissues and organs that work together in a physiological function.

organelle   (or gan el′) Any of the membrane-enclosed structures within a eukaryotic cell. Examples include the nucleus, endoplasmic reticulum, and mitochondria.

organic fertilizer   A substance added to soil to improve the soil's fertility; derived from partially decomposed plant material (compost) or animal waste (manure). (Contrast with inorganic fertilizer.)

organizer   The region of the early amphibian embryo that directs early embryonic development. Also known as the primary embryonic organizer and the dorsal lip of the blastopore.

organogenesis   The formation of organs and organ systems during development.

origin of replication (ori)   A DNA sequence at which helicase unwinds the DNA double helix and DNA polymerase binds to initiate DNA replication.

ortholog   [Gk. *ortho*: true, direct] A homologous gene whose divergence can be traced to speciation events. (Contrast with paralog.)

osmoconformer   An aquatic animal that equilibrates the osmolarity of its extracellular fluid to be the same as that of the external environment. (Contrast with osmoregulator.)

osmolarity   The concentration of osmotically active particles in a solution.

osmoregulator   An aquatic animal that actively regulates the osmolarity of its extracellular fluid. (Contrast with osmoconformer.)

osmosis   (oz mo′ sis) [Gk. *osmos*: to push] The movement of water across a differentially permeable membrane, from one region to another region where the water potential is more negative.

ossicles   Three bones in the middle ear that transmit vibrations from the tympanum to the oval window of the inner ear. Individually named the malleus ("hammer"), incus ("anvil"), and stapes ("stirrup").

osteoblast   (oss′ tee oh blast) [Gk. *osteon*: bone + *blastos*: sprout] A cell that lays down the protein matrix of bone.

osteoclast   (oss′ tee oh clast) [Gk. *osteon*: bone + *klastos*: broken] A cell that dissolves bone.

osteocyte   (oss′ tee oh site) [Gk. *osteon*: bone + *kytos*: cell] An osteoblast that has become enclosed in lacunae within the bone it has built.

ostia   Pores or openings such as the openings of the tracheal system on the sides of insects.

otoliths   (oh′ teliths) [Gk. *ous*: ear + *lithos*: stones] Crystals of calcium carbonate in the inner ear. Also called ear stones.

outer membrane   In organelles that have two membranes such as chloroplasts and mitochondria, the outer membrane encloses the entire organelle.

outgroup   In phylogenetics, a group of organisms used as a point of reference for comparison with the groups of primary interest (the ingroup).

oval window   The flexible membrane that, when moved by the bones of the middle ear, produces pressure waves in the inner ear.

ovarian cycle   (oh var′ ee un) In human females, the monthly cycle of events by which eggs and hormones are produced. (Contrast with uterine cycle.)

ovary   [L. *ovum*: egg] Any female organ, in plants or animals, that produces an egg.

overtopping   A plant growth pattern in which one branch differentiates from and grows beyond the others.

oviduct   In mammals, the tube serving to transport eggs to the uterus or to the outside of the body.

oviparity   Reproduction in which eggs are released by the female and development is external to the mother's body. (Contrast with viviparity.)

ovoviviparity   Reproduction in which fertilized eggs develop and hatch within the mother's body but are not attached to the mother by means of a placenta.

ovulation   The release of an egg from an ovary.

ovule   (oh′ vule) In plants, a structure comprising the megasporangium and the integument, which develops into a seed after fertilization.

ovum   (oh′ vum) (plural: ova) [L. egg] The female gamete.

oxidation   The relative loss of electrons in a chemical reaction; either outright removal to form an ion, or the sharing of electrons with substances having a greater affinity for them, such as oxygen. Most oxidations, including biological ones, are associated with the liberation of energy. (Contrast with reduction.)

oxidation–reduction (redox) reaction   A reaction in which one substance transfers one or more electrons to another substance. (*See* oxidation, reduction.)

oxidative phosphorylation   ATP formation in the mitochondrion, associated with the flow of electrons through the respiratory chain.

oxygenase   An enzyme that catalyzes the addition of oxygen to a substrate from O_2.

oxytocin   A hormone released by the posterior pituitary that promotes social bonding.

ozone layer   A layer of Earth's atmosphere, 20–30 km above the surface and containing a high concentration of ozone (O_3). Absorbs much of the Sun's damaging ultraviolet radiation and prevents it from reaching Earth's surface.

P

pacemaker cells   Cardiac cells that can initiate action potentials without stimulation from the nervous system, allowing the heart to initiate its own contractions.

Pacinian corpuscles   (puh sin′ ee uhn) Encapsulated mechanoreceptors in deep skin sensitive to pressure and vibration.

pair rule genes   In *Drosophila* development, segmentation genes that divide the early embryo into units of two segments each. Part of a developmental cascade that includes maternal effect genes, gap genes, segment polarity genes, and Hox genes.

pancreas   A gland located near the stomach of vertebrates that secretes digestive enzymes into the small intestine and releases insulin into the bloodstream.

parabasalids   *See* Appendix A.

parabronchi   Passages in the lungs of birds through which air flows.

paracrine   [Gk. *para*: near] Pertaining to a chemical signal that binds to and affects nearby cells. (Contrast with autocrine, juxtacrine.)

paralog   A homologous gene whose divergence can be traced to gene duplication events. (Contrast with ortholog.)

paraphyletic   (par′ a fih leht′ ik) [Gk. *para*: beside + *phylon*: tribe] Pertaining to a group that consists of an ancestor and some, but not all, of its descendants. (Contrast with monophyletic, polyphyletic.)

parasite   [Gk. *parasitos*: one who eats at another's table] An organism that kills and/or consumes parts of an organism much larger than itself (known as its host). Parasites sometimes, but not always, kill their host.

parasitic plants   Plants that obtain some of their nutrition by growing on other plants.

parasitism   Predation in which the predator (a parasite) lives symbiotically on or in the prey (its host) and consumes only certain tissues without necessarily killing the host. (Contrast with carnivory, herbivory, omnivory.)

parasympathetic division   A division of the vertebrate autonomic nervous system that is connected to the central nervous system via cranial and sacral nerves; the parasympathetic and sympathetic divisions tend to exert opposing controls on autonomic effectors. (Contrast with sympathetic division.)

parathyroid glands   Four glands on the posterior surface of the thyroid gland that produce and release parathyroid hormone.

parathyroid hormone (PTH)   A hormone secreted by the parathyroid glands that stimulates osteoclast activity and raises blood calcium levels. Also called parathormone. (Contrast with calcitonin.)

parenchyma   (pair eng′ kyma) A type of relatively unspecialized plant cell without secondary walls. (Contrast with collenchyma, sclerenchyma.)

parent rock   The soil horizon consisting of the rock that is breaking down to form the soil. Also called bedrock or the C horizon.

parental (P) generation   The individuals that mate in a genetic cross. Their offspring are the first filial (F_1) generation.

parietal cells   One of three types of secretory cells found in the gastric pits of the stomach wall. Parietal cells produce hydrochloric acid (HCl),

creating an acidic environment that destroys many of the harmful microorganisms ingested with food. (*See also* chief cells.)

parietal lobe   One of five lobes of the brain's cerebral hemisphere; processes complex stimuli and includes the primary somatosensory cortex.

parsimony principle   The principle that states that the preferred explanation of observed data is the simplest explanation.

parthenocarpy   The formation of fruit from a flower without fertilization.

parthenogenesis   [Gk. *parthenos*: virgin] Production of an organism from an unfertilized egg.

partial pressures   In a mixture of gasses at a specific pressure, the contribution of each gas to that total pressure.

passive transport   Diffusion across a membrane; may or may not require a channel or carrier protein. (Contrast with active transport.)

patch clamping   A technique for isolating a tiny patch of membrane to allow the study of ion movement through a particular channel.

pathogen   (path′ o jen) [Gk. *pathos*: suffering + *genesis*: source] An organism that causes disease.

pathogen associated molecular patterns (PAMPs)   The molecules produced by pathogens that are recognized by pattern recognition receptors of the host.

pathogenesis-related (PR) genes   Plant genes that encode proteins that are produced in response to attack by bacteria, fungi, or viruses.

pattern recognition receptors (PRRs)   Proteins expressed by cells of the innate immune system in animals or plants that bind to molecules from pathogens containing pathogen associated molecular patterns (PAMPs).

peat   Partly decomposed vegetable matter, especially of sphagnum moss, that is typically formed in acidic bogs.

pedigree   The pattern of inheritance of a genetic trait within a family.

penetrance   The proportion of individuals with a particular genotype that show the expected phenotype.

penis   An accessory sex organ of male animals that enables the male to deposit sperm in the female's reproductive tract.

pentaradial symmetry   Symmetry in five or multiples of five; a feature of adult echinoderms.

pentose   [Gk. *penta*: five] A sugar containing five carbon atoms.

PEP carboxylase   The enzyme that combines CO_2 with PEP to form a four-carbon dicarboxylic acid at the start of C_4 photosynthesis or of crassulacean acid metabolism (CAM).

peptidases   Digestive enzymes that break down peptides.

peptide   A short polymer of 20 or fewer amino acids. Also called an oligopeptide.

peptide bond   The bond between amino acids in a protein; formed between a carboxyl group and amino group (—CO—NH—) with the loss of water molecules.

peptide hormones   Hormone molecules made up of chains of 2–50 amino acids (upper size arbitrary); encoded by genes and produced by translation.

peptidoglycan   The cell wall material of many bacteria, consisting of a single enormous molecule that surrounds the entire cell.

peptidyl transferase   A catalytic function of the large ribosomal subunit that consists of two reactions: breaking the bond between an amino acid and its tRNA in the P site, and forming a peptide bond between that amino acid and the amino acid attached to the tRNA in the A site.

per capita birth rate (*b*)   In population growth models, the average number of offspring that an individual produces over some time interval.

per capita death rate (*d*)   In population growth models, the average individual's chance of dying in some time interval.

per capita growth rate (*r*)   In population growth models, the average individual's contribution to total population growth rate. In mathematical terms, r is the difference between per capita birth rate (b) and per capita death rate (d), or ($b - d$).

perennial   (per ren′ ee al) [L. *per*: throughout + *annus*: year] A plant that survives from year to year. (Contrast with annual, biennial.)

perfect flower   A flower with both stamens and carpels; a hermaphroditic flower. (Contrast with imperfect flower.)

perfusion   The flow of blood through a tissue or organ.

pericycle   [Gk. *peri*: around + *kyklos*: ring or circle] In plant roots, tissue just within the endodermis but outside the root vascular tissue. Meristematic activity of pericycle cells produces lateral root primordia.

period   (1) A category in the geological time scale. (2) The duration of a single cycle in a cyclical event, such as a circadian rhythm.

periodic table   The arrangement of elements in order of increasing atomic number, with vertical groupings of similar valence electrons.

peripheral membrane proteins   Proteins associated with but not embedded within the cell membrane. (Contrast with anchored membrane proteins, integral membrane proteins.)

peripheral nervous system (PNS)   The portion of the nervous system that transmits information to and from the central nervous system, consisting of neurons that extend or reside outside the brain or spinal cord and their supporting cells. (Contrast with central nervous system.)

peristalsis   (pair′ i stall′ sis) Wavelike muscular contractions proceeding along a tubular organ, propelling the contents along the tube.

peritoneum   The mesodermal lining of the body cavity in coelomate animals.

peritubular capillaries   Small blood vessels that surround the renal tubules.

perivascular space   Fluid filled spaces between blood vessels and the organ tissues they serve. In the central nervous system perivascular spaces exist between blood vessels and the macroglial cells that surround them as part of the blood brain barrier.

peroxisome   An organelle that houses reactions in which toxic peroxides are formed and then converted to water.

petal   [Gk. *petalon*: spread out] In an angiosperm flower, a sterile modified leaf, nonphotosynthetic, frequently brightly colored, and often serving to attract pollinating insects.

P$_{fr}$ *See* phytochrome.

pH   The negative logarithm of the hydrogen ion concentration; a measure of the acidity of a solution. A solution with pH = 7 is said to be neutral; pH values higher than 7 characterize basic solutions, while acidic solutions have pH values less than 7.

phage   *See* bacteriophage.

phage therapy   The therapeutic use of bacteriophages to treat pathogenic bacterial infections.

phagocytosis   The process by which a cell uses its cell membrane to enclose and engulf a macromolecule or particle in the extracellular environment.

pharmacogenomics   The study of how an individual's genetic makeup affects his or her response to drugs or other agents, with the goal of predicting the effectiveness of different treatment options.

pharming   The use of genetically modified animals or plants to produce medically useful products.

pharynx   [Gk. throat] The part of the gut between the mouth and the esophagus.

phenotype   (fee' no type) [Gk. *phanein*: to show] The observable properties of an individual resulting from both genetic and environmental factors. (Contrast with genotype.)

pheromone   (feer' o mone) [Gk. *pheros*: carry + *hormon*: excite, arouse] A chemical substance used in communication between organisms of the same species.

phloem   (flo' um) [Gk. *phloos*: bark] In vascular plants, the vascular tissue that transports sugars and other solutes from sources to sinks.

phloem sap   The liquid contents of the phloem tubes.

phoronids   *See* Appendix A.

phosphatidyl inositol-bisphosphate (PIP$_2$)   A phospholipid in the cell membrane that is involved in cell signaling after a ligand binds to a nearby receptor.

phosphodiester bond   The connection in a nucleic acid strand, formed by linking two nucleotides. Two covalent bonds through a phosphate group link the sugars of adjacent nucleotides.

phosphoenolpyruvate (PEP)   The phosphorylated salt of a three-carbon acid, formula OPO$_3$H$_2$—CO—CO—COOH, that is an intermediate in metabolic pathways such as glycolysis.

phospholipid   A lipid containing a phosphate group; an important constituent of cellular membranes. (*See* lipid.)

phospholipid bilayer   The basic structural unit of biological membranes; a sheet of phospholipids two molecules thick in which the phospholipids are lined up with their hydrophobic "tails" packed tightly together and their hydrophilic, phosphate-containing "heads" facing outward. Also called a lipid bilayer.

phosphorylation   The addition of a phosphate group to a molecule.

photic zone   The life zone in lakes and oceans that is penetrated by light and therefore supports photosynthetic organisms.

photoautotroph   An organism that obtains energy from light and carbon from carbon dioxide. (Contrast with chemoautotroph, chemoheterotroph, photoheterotroph.)

photoheterotroph   An organism that obtains energy from light but must obtain its carbon from organic compounds. (Contrast with chemoautotroph, chemoheterotroph, photoautotroph.)

photomorphogenesis   In plants, a process by which physiological and developmental events are controlled by light.

photon   (foe' ton) [Gk. *photos*: light] A quantum of visible radiation; a "packet" of light energy.

photoperiodism   Control of an organism's physiological or behavioral responses by the length of the day or night (the **photoperiod**).

photophosphorylation   The mechanism for ATP formation in chloroplasts in which electron transport is coupled to the transport of hydrogen ions (protons, H$^+$) across the thylakoid membrane. (Contrast with chemiosmosis.)

photoreceptors   (1) In plants, pigments that trigger a physiological response when they absorb a photon. (2) In animals, the sensory receptor cells that sense and respond to light energy. (*See* cone cells, rod cells.)

photorespiration   The fixation of O$_2$ instead of CO$_2$ in chloroplasts on hot, sunny days, resulting in the release of some CO$_2$ fixed in photosynthesis.

photosensitivity   Sensitivity to light.

photosynthates   The carbohydrate products of photosynthesis.

photosynthesis   (foe tow sin' the sis) [Gk. creating from light] The metabolic processes carried out by green plants and some microorganisms by which visible light is trapped and the energy used to synthesize compounds such as ATP and glucose.

photosynthetic lamellae   The internal membrane system of the cyanobacteria.

phototropins   Blue light photoreceptors in plants that are composed of a proteinaceous component bound to light-absorbing chromophores.

phototropism   [Gk. *photos*: light + *trope*: turning] A directed plant growth response to light.

phycoerythrin   A red protein pigment that occurs in red algae.

phylogenetic tree   A graphic representation of the lines of descent among organisms or their genes.

phylogeny   (fy loj' e nee) [Gk. *phylon*: tribe, race + *genesis*: source] The evolutionary history of a particular group of organisms or their genes.

phytoalexins   Substances toxic to pathogens, produced by plants in response to fungal or bacterial infection.

phytochrome   (fy' tow krome) [Gk. *phyton*: plant + *chroma*: color] A photoreceptor, composed of a proteinaceous component bound to a light-absorbing chromophore, that regulates a large number of developmental and other phenomena in plants. It has two isomers: P$_r$, which absorbs red light, and P$_{fr}$, which absorbs far-red light. P$_{fr}$ is the active form.

pigment   A substance that absorbs visible light.

piloting   A form of navigation in which an animal finds its way by remembering landmarks in its environment.

pilus   (plural: pili) A structure that links prokaryote cells at the beginning of conjugation.

pineal gland   A gland located between the cerebral hemispheres that secretes melatonin.

pinocytosis   Endocytosis by a cell of liquid containing dissolved substances within vesicles.

pioneer species   Species that arrive first to primary successional habitats and must deal with extreme conditions; they tend to have life history strategies that maximize population growth (see *r*-strategist). Also called early successional species.

pistil   [L. *pistillum*: pestle] The structure of an angiosperm flower within which the ovules are borne. May consist of a single carpel, or of several carpels fused into a single structure. Usually differentiated into ovary, style, and stigma.

pith   In plants, relatively unspecialized tissue found within a cylinder of vascular tissue.

pituitary gland   A small gland attached to the base of the brain in vertebrates. Its hormones control the activities of other glands.

placenta   (pla sen' ta) The organ in female mammals that provides for nourishment of the fetus and elimination of the fetal waste products.

placozoans   *See* Appendix A.

plankton   Aquatic organisms that float in the water column, dependent on currents and wind for movement. Plankton include many protists, some algae, and larval animals.

Plantae   *See* Appendix A.

planula   (plan' yew la) [L. *planum*: flat] A free-swimming, ciliated larval form typical of the cnidarians.

plaque   (plack) [Fr. a metal plate or coin] (1) A circular clearing in a layer (lawn) of bacteria growing on the surface of a nutrient agar gel. (2) An accumulation of prokaryotic organisms on tooth enamel. Acids produced by these microorganisms cause tooth decay. (3) A region of arterial wall invaded by fibroblasts and fatty deposits.

plasma cell   An antibody-secreting cell that develops from a B cell; the effector cell of the humoral immune system.

plasmid   A DNA molecule distinct from the chromosome(s); that is, an extrachromosomal element. Found in many bacteria. May replicate independently of the chromosome.

plasmodesmata   (singular: plasmodesma) [Gk. *plassein*: to mold + *desmos*: band] In plants, membrane-lined channels that extend through the cell walls and connect the cytoplasms of adjacent cells.

plasmodial slime mold   *See* Appendix A.

plasmogamy   The fusion of the cytoplasm of two cells. (Contrast with karyogamy.)

plate tectonics   [Gk. *tekton*: builder] The scientific study of the structure and movements of Earth's lithospheric plates, which are the cause of continental drift.

platelet   A membrane-bounded body without a nucleus, arising as a fragment of a cell in the bone marrow of mammals. Important to blood-clotting action.

pleiotropy   (plee′ a tro pee) [Gk. *pleion*: more] The determination of more than one character by a single gene.

pleural membrane   [Gk. *pleuras*: rib, side] The membrane lining the outside of the lungs and the walls of the thoracic cavity. Inflammation of these membranes is a condition known as pleurisy.

pneumatophores   Roots that grow upward out of water or mud to reach the air and obtain oxygen for the root systems of trees that live in swampy or tidal habitats.

podocytes   Cells of Bowman's capsule of the nephron that cover the capillaries of the glomerulus, forming filtration slits.

pogonophorans   *See* Appendix A.

poikilotherm   An animal whose body temperature is largely dependent on environmental temperature.

point mutation   A mutation that results from the gain, loss, or substitution of a single nucleotide. (Contrast with deletion, duplication.)

polar   Referring to a molecule with separate and opposite electric charges at two ends, or poles; the water molecule (H_2O) is the most prevalent example. (Contrast with nonpolar.)

polar covalent bond   A covalent bond in which the electrons are drawn to one nucleus more than the other, resulting in an unequal distribution of charge.

polar nuclei   In angiosperms, the two nuclei in the central cell of the female gametophyte; following fertilization they give rise to the endosperm.

pole plasm   Cytoplasm at one end of an insect egg that determines that the cells that form at that location will become germ cells.

pollen   [L. *pollin*: fine flour] In seed plants, the male gametophytes that contain the male gametes (microspores).

pollen tube   A structure that develops from a pollen grain through which sperm are released into the female gametophyte.

pollination   The process of transferring pollen from an anther to the stigma of a pistil in an angiosperm or from a strobilus to an ovule in a gymnosperm.

poly A tail   A long sequence of adenine nucleotides (100–300) added after transcription to the 3′ end of most eukaryotic mRNAs.

polyandry   A mating system in which one female mates with multiple males. (Contrast with polygyny.)

polychaetes   *See* Appendix A.

polyculture   In agriculture, a large-scale planting of multiple crop species. (Contrast with monoculture.)

polygyny   A mating system in which one male mates with multiple females. (Contrast with polyandry.)

polymer   [Gk. *poly*: many + *meros*: unit] A large molecule made up of similar or identical subunits called monomers. (Contrast with monomer.)

polymerase chain reaction (PCR)   An enzymatic technique for the rapid production of millions of copies of a particular stretch of DNA where only a small amount of the parent molecule is available.

polymorphic   (pol′ lee mor′ fik) [Gk. *poly*: many + *morphe*: form, shape] Referring to the coexistence in a population of two or more alleles at a locus or gene.

polyp   (pah′ lip) [Gk. *poly*: many + *pous*: foot] In cnidarians, a sessile, asexual life cycle stage.

polypeptide   A large molecule made up of 20 or amino acids joined by peptide bonds. Large polypeptides are called proteins.

polypeptide chain   *See* polypeptide.

polyphyletic   (pol′ lee fih leht′ ik) [Gk. *poly*: many + *phylon*: tribe] Pertaining to a group that consists of multiple distantly related organisms, and does not include the common ancestor of the group. (Contrast with monophyletic, paraphyletic.)

polyploidy   (pol′ lee ploid ee) The possession of more than two entire sets of chromosomes.

polyribosome   A complex consisting of a threadlike molecule of messenger RNA and several (or many) ribosomes. The ribosomes move along the mRNA, synthesizing polypeptide chains as they proceed. Also called a polysome.

polysaccharide   A macromolecule composed of many monosaccharides (simple sugars). Common examples are cellulose and starch.

polysome   *See* polyribosome.

pons   [L. *pons*: bridge] The region of the brainstem anterior to the medulla.

population   (1) In biology, any group of organisms coexisting at the same time and in the same place and capable of interbreeding with one another. (2) In statistics, a study group of interest.

population bottleneck   A period during which only a few individuals of a normally large population survive.

population density   The number of individuals in a population per unit of area or volume.

population dynamics   The patterns and processes of change in populations over space and time.

population growth   The change in population size over time.

population growth rate   The rate of change in population size over time.

population size   The total number of individuals in a population.

portal blood vessels   Blood vessels that begin and end in capillary beds.

positive cooperativity   Occurs when a molecule can bind several ligands and each one that binds alters the conformation of the molecule so that it can bind the next ligand more easily. The binding of four molecules of O_2 by hemoglobin is an example of positive cooperativity.

positive feedback   In regulatory systems, information that amplifies a regulatory response, increasing the deviation of the system from the set point. (Contrast with negative feedback.)

positive interaction   A trophic or nontrophic interaction between two species in which one or both species benefit and neither is harmed. Also called facilitation. (*See also* commensalism, mutualism.)

positive regulation   A form of gene regulation in which the binding of an activator protein to DNA increases transcription; in its absence, transcription will not occur. (Contrast with negative regulation.)

positive selection   Natural selection that acts to establish a trait that enhances survival in a population. (Contrast with purifying selection.)

postabsorptive state   The state in which no food remains in the gut and thus no nutrients are being absorbed. (Contrast with absorptive state.)

posterior   Toward or pertaining to the rear. (Contrast with anterior.)

posterior pituitary   The portion of the pituitary gland derived from neural tissue; involved in the storage and release of antidiuretic hormone and oxytocin.

postzygotic isolating mechanisms   Barriers to the reproductive process that occur after the union of the nuclei of two gametes. (Contrast with prezygotic isolating mechanisms.)

potassium equilibrium potential (E_K)   The negative membrane potential that balances the tendency for K^+ ions to diffuse out of the cell down their concentration gradient.

potential energy   Energy not doing work but with the potential to do so, such as the energy stored in chemical bonds. (Contrast with kinetic energy.)

P_r   *See* phytochrome.

pre-motor cortex   The region of the frontal lobe of the cerebrum that is anterior to the primary motor cortex.

pre-mRNA (precursor mRNA)   The initial gene transcript before it is modified to produce functional mRNA. Also known as the primary transcript.

Precambrian   The first and longest period of geological time, during which life originated.

precapillary sphincter   A cuff of smooth muscle that can shut off the blood flow to a capillary bed.

precocial   Born or hatched in a relatively advanced state that allows a high degree of independence from the parents. (Contrast with altricial.)

predation   A trophic or feeding interaction in which an individual of one species (a predator) kills and/or consumes individuals (or parts of individuals) of another species (its prey).

predator   An organism that kills or consumes individuals (or parts of individuals) of another species (its prey).

pressure flow model   A model for phloem transport in angiosperms. It holds that sieve element transport is driven by an osmotically generated pressure gradient between source and sink.

pressure potential (Ψ_p)   The hydrostatic pressure of an enclosed solution in excess of the surrounding atmospheric pressure. (Contrast with solute potential, water potential.)

prevailing winds   The circulation of air (wind) that moves across Earth's surface in a predominately single direction.

prey   [L. *praeda*: booty] An organism killed and/or consumed by a predator as an energy source.

prezygotic isolating mechanisms   Barriers to the reproductive process that occur before the union of the nuclei of two gametes (Contrast with postzygotic isolating mechanisms.)

priapulids   *See* Appendix A.

primary active transport   Active transport in which ATP is hydrolyzed, yielding the energy required to transport an ion or molecule against its concentration gradient. (Contrast with secondary active transport.)

primary bronchi   The first airways that branch off the trachea in the vertebrate lung.

primary cell wall   In plant cells, a structure that forms at the middle lamella after cytokinesis, made up of cellulose microfibrils, hemicelluloses, and pectins. (Contrast with secondary cell wall.)

primary consumer   An organism (herbivore) that feeds on primary producers.

primary embryonic organizer   *See* organizer.

primary endosymbiosis   The engulfment of a cyanobacterium by a larger eukaryotic cell that gave rise to the first photosynthetic eukaryotes with chloroplasts.

primary growth   In plants, growth that is characterized by the lengthening of roots and shoots and by the proliferation of new roots and shoots through branching. (Contrast with secondary growth.)

primary immune response   The first response of the immune system to an antigen, involving recognition by B and T cells and the production of effector cells and memory cells. (Contrast with secondary immune response.)

primary lysosome   A lysosome before fusion with an endosome. (Contrast with secondary lysosome.)

primary oocyte   (oh′ eh site) [Gk. *oon*: egg + *kytos*: container] The diploid progeny of an oogonium. In many species, a primary oocyte enters prophase of the first meiotic division, then remains in developmental arrest for a long time before resuming meiosis to form a secondary oocyte and a polar body.

primary producer   A photosynthetic or chemosynthetic organism that synthesizes complex organic molecules from simple inorganic ones.

primary sex determination   The genetic determination of gametic sex, male or female.

primary sex organs   The testes and ovaries.

primary somatosensory cortex   An area of the parietal lobe that receives touch and pressure information from mechanoreceptors throughout the body; neurons in this area are arranged according to the parts of the body with which they communicate.

primary spermatocyte   The diploid progeny of a spermatogonium; undergoes the first meiotic division to form secondary spermatocytes.

primary structure   The specific sequence of amino acids in a protein. (Contrast with secondary, tertiary, quaternary structure.)

primary succession   Succession of ecological communities that begins in an area devoid of life, such as on recently exposed glacial till or lava flows. (Contrast with secondary succession.)

primase   (prigh′ maze) An enzyme that catalyzes the synthesis of an RNA primer for DNA replication.

primates   *See* Appendix A.

primer   A strand of nucleic acid, usually RNA, that is the necessary starting material for the synthesis of a new DNA strand, which is synthesized from the 3′ end of the primer.

primitive streak   A midline ridge that forms in the avian blastula and that will become the blastopore.

probe   A segment of single-stranded nucleic acid used to identify DNA molecules containing the complementary sequence.

proboscis   An elongated nose or sucking mouthpart that is typically tubular and flexible.

processive   Referring to an enzyme that catalyzes many reactions each time it binds to a substrate, as DNA polymerase does during DNA replication.

product   A molecule that results from the completion of a chemical reaction.

production efficiency   The proportion of assimilated biomass used to produce new consumer biomass or net secondary production.

progesterone   [L. *pro*: favoring + *gestare*: to bear] A female sex hormone that maintains pregnancy.

progymnosperms   *See* Appendix A.

prokaryotes   Unicellular organisms that do not have nuclei or other membrane-enclosed organelles. Includes Bacteria and Archaea. (Contrast with eukaryotes.) (*See* Appendix A.)

promoter   A DNA sequence to which RNA polymerase binds to initiate transcription.

proofreading   During DNA replication, a mechanism that excises a base that is incorrectly inserted across from the template (e.g., an A opposite a template G) and inserts the correct base (e.g., C opposite template G).

prop roots   Adventitious roots in some monocots that function as supports for the shoot.

prophage   (pro′ fayj) The noninfective viral genome that is present in the chromosome of the host bacteria and multiplies with it but do not cause dissolution of the cell. Prophage can enter into the lytic phase to complete the virus life cycle.

prostaglandins   A group of specialized lipids with hormone-like functions. Prostaglandins interact with nerve endings and are partly responsible for the pain caused by inflammation.

prostate gland   In human males, the gland surrounding the urethra at its junction with the vas deferens; supplies an acid-neutralizing fluid to the semen.

proteases   Digestive enzymes that break the bonds between adjacent amino acids in proteins.

proteasome   In the eukaryotic cytoplasm, a huge protein complex that binds to and digests cellular proteins that have been tagged by ubiquitin.

protected area   An area in which habitat loss or degradation by human activity is restricted or prohibited.

protein   [Gk. *protos*: first] A long-chain polymer of amino acids with 20 different common side chains. Occurs with its polymer chain extended in fibrous proteins, or coiled into a compact macromolecule in enzymes and other globular proteins. The component amino acids are encoded in the triplets of messenger RNA, and proteins are the products of genes.

protein hormones   Large hormone molecules made up of chains of generally more than 50 amino acids; encoded by genes and produced by translation.

protein kinase   (kye′ nase) An enzyme that catalyzes the addition of a phosphate group from ATP to a target protein.

protein kinase cascade   A series of reactions in response to a molecular signal, in which a series of protein kinases activate one another in sequence, amplifying the signal at each step.

proteobacteria   *See* Appendix A.

proteoglycan   A glycoprotein containing a protein core with attached long, linear carbohydrate chains.

proteolysis   [protein + Gk. *lysis*: break apart] The enzymatic digestion of a protein or polypeptide.

proteome   The complete set of proteins that can be made by an organism. Because of alternative splicing of pre-mRNA, the number of proteins that can be made is usually much larger than the number of protein-coding genes present in the organism's genome.

prothoracic gland   A gland in insects that secretes the molting hormone ecdysone.

prothoracicotropic hormone (PTTH)   An insect hormone that controls the prothoracic gland.

prothrombin   The inactive form of thrombin, an enzyme involved in blood clotting.

protists   *See* Appendix A.

protocell   A self-organized sphere of lipids proposed as a stepping-stone to the origin of life.

proton   (pro′ ton) [Gk. *protos*: first, before] (1) A subatomic particle with a single positive charge. The number of protons in the nucleus of an atom determines its element. (2) A hydrogen ion, H^+.

proton pump   An active transport system that uses ATP energy to move hydrogen ions across a membrane, generating an electric potential.

proton-motive force   A force generated across a membrane having two components: a chemical potential (difference in proton concentration) plus an electric potential due to the electrostatic charge on the proton.

protonephridium   (plural: protonephridia) [Gk. *proto*: before + *nephros*: kidney] The excretory organ of flatworms, made up of a tubule and capped with a flame cell.

protostomes   *See* Appendix A.

prototherians   *See* Appendix A.

provirus   Double-stranded DNA made by a virus that is integrated into the host's chromosome and contains promoters that are recognized by the host cell's transcription apparatus.

provirus   Double-stranded DNA made by a virus that is integrated into the host's chromosome and contains promoters that are recognized by the host cell's transcription apparatus.

proximal convoluted tubule   The initial segment of a renal tubule, closest to the glomerulus. (Contrast with distal convoluted tubule.)

proximate causes   In animal behavior, the immediate genetic, physiological, neurological, and developmental mechanisms responsible for a behavior or morphology. (Contrast with ultimate causes.)

pseudocoelomate   (soo' do see' low mate) [Gk. *pseudes*: false + *koiloma*: cavity] Possessing a body cavity, called a pseudocoel, consisting of a fluid-filled space in which many of the internal organs are suspended, but which is enclosed by mesoderm only on its outside. (Contrast with acoelomate, coelomate.)

pseudogene   [Gk. *pseudes*: false] A DNA segment that is homologous with a functional gene but is not functional, and often not expressed, because of changes to its sequence or changes to its location in the genome.

pseudoplasmodium   An aggregation of myxamoebas that resembles a plasmodium.

pterygotes   *See* Appendix A.

pulmonary arteries   In vertebrates, blood vessels that carry blood from the heart to the lungs.

pulmonary circuit   The portion of the circulatory system by which blood is pumped from the heart to the lungs or gills for oxygenation and back to the heart for distribution. (Contrast with systemic circuit.)

pulmonary valve   A one-way valve between the right ventricle of the heart and the pulmonary artery that prevents backflow of blood into the ventricle when it relaxes.

pulmonary veins   Veins that return oxygenated blood from the lungs to the left atrium.

pulp cavity   The space in the interior of a tooth that contains blood vessels, nerves, and dentine-producing cells.

Punnett square   A method of predicting the results of a genetic cross by arranging the gametes of each parent at the edges of a square.

pupil   The opening in the vertebrate eye through which light passes.

purifying selection   The elimination by natural selection of detrimental characters from a population. (Contrast with positive selection.)

purine   (pure' een) One of the two types of nitrogenous bases in nucleic acids. Each of the purines—adenine and guanine—pairs with a specific pyrimidine.

Purkinje fibers   (pur kin' jee) Specialized heart muscle cells that conduct excitation throughout the ventricular muscle.

pyrimidine   (pe rim' a deen) One of the two types of nitrogenous bases in nucleic acids. Each of the pyrimidines—cytosine, thymine, and uracil—pairs with a specific purine.

pyruvate   The ionized form of pyruvic acid, a three-carbon acid; the end-product of glycolysis and the raw material for the citric acid cycle.

Q

Q_{10}   A value that compares the rate of a biochemical process or reaction over 10° Celsius temperature ranges. A process that is not temperature-sensitive has a Q_{10} of 1; values of 2 or 3 mean the reaction speeds up as temperature increases.

quadrat   A four-sided measurement area of any size, used to count the individuals within the area.

qualitative   Based on observation of an unmeasured quality of a trait, as in brown vs. blue.

qualitative traits   Traits that differ from one another by discrete qualities (e.g., black vs. white or smooth vs. wrinkled).

quantitative   Based on numerical values obtained by measurement, as in quantitative data.

quantitative trait   Traits that show *continuous* quantitative variation rather than *discrete* qualitative variation.

quantitative trait loci   A set of genes determining a complex character that exhibits quantitative variation (variation in amount rather than in kind).

quaternary structure   The specific three-dimensional arrangement of protein subunits. (Contrast with primary, secondary, tertiary structure.)

quorum sensing   The use of chemical communication signals to trigger density-linked activities such as biofilm formation in prokaryotes.

R

R genes   *See* resistance genes.

R group   The distinguishing group of atoms of a particular amino acid. Also called a side chain.

R proteins   *See* resistance proteins.

r-strategist   A species whose life history strategy allows for a high intrinsic rate of population increase (*r*). (Contrast with *K*-strategist.)

radial cleavage   Embryonic development in which the planes of cell division are parallel and perpendicular to the animal–vegetal axis of the embryo. (Compare with spiral cleavage.)

radial symmetry   The condition in which any two halves of a body are mirror images of each other, providing the cut passes through the center;

a cylinder cut lengthwise down its center displays this form of symmetry.

radiation   The transfer of heat from warmer objects to cooler ones via the exchange of infrared radiation. (*See also* electromagnetic radiation, evolutionary radiation.)

radicle   An embryonic root.

radioactive decay   The spontaneous disintegration of a substance with the emission of ionizing radiation.

radioisotope   A radioactive isotope of an element. Examples are carbon-14 (^{14}C) and hydrogen-3, or tritium (^{3}H).

radiolarians   *See* Appendix A.

radiometric dating   A method for determining the age of objects such as fossils and rocks based on the decay rates of radioactive isotopes.

radula   A rasplike structure used for scraping food particles off a surface.

rain shadow   The relatively dry area on the downwind side of a mountain range.

random dispersion   The spatial arrangement of individuals within a population, characterized by random spatial patterns. (Compare with clumped dispersion, regular [uniform] dispersion.)

rapid eye movement (REM) sleep   In humans and other mammals, one of two major sleep states, characterized by skeletal muscle relaxation and rapid eye movements. In humans, the most vivid dreams and nightmares occur during REM sleep. (*See also* non-REM sleep, slow-wave sleep.)

ray-finned fishes   *See* Appendix A.

reabsorption   The active reuptake of a substance that was eliminated from the body by filtration. In particular the reuptake of molecules filtered into the glomerular tubular fluid by cells making up the renal tubules.

reactant   A chemical substance that enters into a chemical reaction with another substance.

reaction center   A group of electron transfer proteins that receive energy from light-absorbing pigments and convert it to chemical energy by redox reactions.

realized niche   A species' niche as defined by its interactions with other species. (Contrast with fundamental niche.)

receptive field   The area of visual space that activates a particular cell in the visual system.

receptor   *See* receptor protein, sensor.

receptor potential   The change in the resting potential of a sensory cell when it is stimulated.

receptor protein   A protein that can bind to a specific molecule, or detect a specific stimulus, within the cell or in the cell's external environment.

receptor-mediated endocytosis   Endocytosis initiated by macromolecular binding to a specific membrane receptor.

recessive   In genetics, the phenotype (or trait) that is not expressed, and its associated allele, in a heterozygote that has the same phenotype as one of the two homozygotes. (Contrast with dominant.)

recognition sequence   *See* restriction site.

recombinant chromatid   In meiosis, a chromatid that has exchanged parts with a nonsister homologous chromatid.

recombinant DNA   A DNA molecule made in the laboratory that is derived from two or more genetic sources.

recombinant frequency   The proportion of gametes, usually scored using offspring phenotypes, of a genetic cross that have genotypes different from the parental genotypes due to indepependent assortment or crossing over between linked genes during gamete formation.

rectum   The terminal portion of the gut, ending at the anus.

red algae   See Appendix A.

reduction   The gain of electrons by a chemical reactant. (Contrast with oxidation.)

refractory period   The time interval after an action potential during which another action potential cannot be elicited from an excitable membrane.

regeneration   The development of a complete individual from a fragment of an organism.

regional species pool   All the species that are limited to a geographic region; sometimes called gamma diversity.

regular (uniform) dispersion   The spatial arrangement of individuals within a population, characterized by evenly spaced individuals. (Compare with clumped dispersion, random dispersion.)

regulated specification   Determination of cell fates due to signals mostly received from neighboring cells.

regulative development   A pattern of animal embryonic development in which the fates of the first blastomeres are not absolutely fixed. (Contrast with mosaic development.)

regulatory sequence   A DNA sequence to which the protein product of a regulatory gene binds.

regulatory system   A system that uses feedback information to maintain a physiological function or parameter at an optimal level. (Contrast with controlled system.)

regulatory T cells (Tregs)   The class of T cells that mediates tolerance to self antigens.

reinforcement   The evolution of enhanced reproductive isolation between populations due to natural selection for greater isolation.

releaser   A sensory stimulus that triggers performance of a stereotyped behavior pattern.

renal artery   The main artery supplying the kidney.

renal pyramids   Tissue of the renal medulla that projects into and releases urine into the renal pelvis which is drained by the ureter.

renal tubule   A structural unit of the kidney that collects filtrate from the blood, reabsorbs specific ions, nutrients, and water and returns them to the blood, and concentrates excess ions and waste products such as urea for excretion from the body.

renal vein   The main vein carrying blood from the kidney.

renin   An enzyme released from the kidneys in response to a drop in the glomerular filtration rate. Together with angiotensin-converting enzyme, converts an inactive protein in the blood into angiotensin.

replication fork   A point at which a DNA molecule is replicating. The fork forms by the unwinding of the parent molecule.

replicon   A region of DNA replicated from a single origin of replication.

reporter gene   A genetic marker whose expression is easily observed; often included in recombinant DNA to indicate the presence of the recombinant DNA in a host cell.

repressor   A transcription factor that reduces or prevents transcription when it binds to a regulatory sequence for a gene. (Contrast with activator.)

reproductive isolation   A condition in which two divergent populations are no longer exchanging genes. Can lead to speciation.

reptiles   See Appendix A.

residual volume (RV)   In tidal ventilation, the dead space that remains in the lungs at the end of exhalation.

resistance (R) genes   Plant genes that confer resistance to specific strains of pathogens.

resistance (R) proteins   In plants, receptor proteins encoded by R genes that confer resistance to pathogens that produce corresponding Avr proteins.

resource partitioning   The sharing of limiting resources by using them in different ways.

resource-mediated coexistence   A type of coexistence among competitors in which factors such as disturbance, stress, or predation acting on the dominant competitor allow inferior competitors access to limiting resources.

resources   Components of the environment such as food, water, light, and space that are required by all species.

respiratory chain   The terminal reactions of cellular respiration, in which electrons are passed from NAD or FAD, through a series of intermediate carriers, to molecular oxygen, with the concomitant production of ATP.

respiratory gases   Oxygen (O_2) and carbon dioxide (CO_2); the gases that an animal must exchange between its internal body fluids and the outside medium (air or water).

resting potential   The membrane potential of a living cell at rest. In cells at rest, the interior is negative to the exterior. (Contrast with action potential.)

restoration ecology   The science and practice of restoring damaged or degraded ecosystems by active human intervention.

restriction digestion   An enzymatic reaction in which a molecule of DNA is fully cleaved by a restriction enzyme.

restriction enzyme   Any of a type of enzyme that cleaves double-stranded DNA at specific sites; extensively used in recombinant DNA technology. Also called a restriction endonuclease.

restriction point (R)   The specific time during G1 phase of the cell cycle at which the cell becomes committed to undergo the rest of the cell cycle.

restriction site   A specific DNA base sequence that is recognized and acted on by a restriction endonuclease. Also called a recognition sequence.

reticular-activating system   [L. *reticulum*: net] A central region of the vertebrate brainstem that includes complex fiber tracts conveying neural signals between the forebrain and the spinal cord, with collateral fibers to a variety of nuclei that are involved in autonomic functions, including arousal from sleep.

reticulation   In a phylogenetic tree, a combining of lineages (through hybridization of gene capture, for example).

reticulum   The second of the four chambers of the ruminant stomach. Along with the rumen, it is where food is partially digested with the assistance of gut bacteria.

retina   (rett' in uh) [L. *rete*: net] The light-sensitive layer of cells in the vertebrate or cephalopod eye.

retinal   One of many forms of vitamin A that is a chromophore bound to opsin proteins to form light sensitive molecules, which are the chemical basis for animal vision.

retrovirus   An RNA virus that contains reverse transcriptase. Its RNA serves as a template for cDNA production, and the cDNA is integrated into a chromosome of the host cell.

reverse transcriptase   An enzyme that catalyzes the production of DNA (cDNA), using RNA as a template; essential to the reproduction of retroviruses.

reverse transcription   The production of DNA using an RNA template.

reversible reaction   A chemical transformation that can occur in either direction, so that reactants become products and vice versa.

reversion mutation   A second- or third-round mutation that reverts the DNA to its original sequence or to a new sequence that results in a non-mutant phenotype.

rhizarians   See Appendix A.

rhizoids   (rye' zoids) [Gk. root] Hairlike extensions of cells in mosses, liverworts, and a few vascular plants that serve the same function as roots and root hairs in vascular plants. The term is also applied to branched, rootlike extensions of some fungi and algae.

rhizome   (rye' zome) An underground stem (as opposed to a root) that runs horizontally beneath the ground.

rhizosphere   The region of soil close enough to a root to be affected by the presence of the root. The composition of the rhizosphere changes over time depending on the environment and state of the plant.

rhodopsin   A vertebrate visual pigment involved in transducing photons of light into changes in the membrane potential of certain photoreceptor cells.

rhyniophytes   See Appendix A.

ribbon worms   See Appendix A.

ribose   A five-carbon sugar in nucleotides and RNA.

ribosomal RNA (rRNA)   Several species of RNA that are incorporated into the ribosome. Involved in peptide bond formation.

ribosome   A small particle in the cell that is the site of protein synthesis.

ribozyme   An RNA molecule with catalytic activity.

ribulose bisphosphate carboxylase/ oxygenase   *See* rubisco.

risk cost   The increased chance of being injured or killed as a result of performing a behavior, compared with resting. (Compare with energetic cost, opportunity cost.)

RNA (ribonucleic acid)   An often single-stranded nucleic acid whose nucleotides use ribose rather than deoxyribose and in which the base uracil replaces thymine found in DNA. Serves as genome for some viruses. (*See* messenger RNA, ribosomal RNA, ribozyme, transfer RNA.)

RNA polymerases   Enzymes that catalyze the formation of RNA from a nucleic acid (usually DNA) template.

RNA processing   The modification of RNA primary transcripts; for example, the splicing out of introns.

RNA sequencing (RNA-seq)   The sequencing of all the complementary DNA in a sample, obtained from the RNA by reverse transcription.

RNA splicing   The last stage of RNA processing in eukaryotes, in which the transcripts of introns are excised through the action of small nuclear ribonucleoproteins (snRNPs).

rod cells   Light-sensitive cells in the vertebrate retina; these sensory receptor cells are sensitive in extremely dim light and are responsible for dim-light, black-and-white vision.

root   (1) The organ responsible for anchoring the plant in the soil, absorbing water and minerals, and producing certain hormones. Some roots are storage organs. (2) In phylogenetics, the base (oldest) part of a phylogenetic tree.

root apical meristem   A group of cells at the apex of the root that gives rise to the organs of the root.

root cap   A thimble-shaped mass of cells, produced by the root apical meristem, that protects the meristem; the organ that perceives the gravitational stimulus in root gravitropism.

root hair   A long, thin process from a root epidermal cell that absorbs water and minerals from the soil solution.

root nodule   A swelling on the root of a leguminous plant, such as soybean, that contains nitrogen-fixing rhizobia bacteria.

root system   The organ system that anchors a plant in place, absorbs water and dissolved minerals, and may store products of photosynthesis from the shoot system.

rotational cleavage   The form of complete cleavage that occurs in mammals. The first cleavage plane is parallel to the animal–vegetal axis, but the two second cleavage planes are at right angles to each other.

rotifers   *See* Appendix A.

rough endoplasmic reticulum (RER)   The portion of the endoplasmic reticulum whose outer surface has attached ribosomes. (Contrast with smooth endoplasmic reticulum.)

round window   A flexible membrane at the end of the lower canal of the cochlea in the human ear. (*See also* oval window.)

RT-PCR   A laboratory manipulation of RNA in which the RNA is first incubated with reverse transcriptase (RT) to make cDNA and then the cDNA amplified for analysis by the polymerase chain reaction (PCR).

rubisco   Contraction of ribulose bisphosphate carboxylase/oxygenase, the enzyme that combines CO_2 or O_2 with ribulose bisphosphate to catalyze the first step of photosynthetic carbon fixation or photorespiration, respectively.

Ruffini endings   Slowly adapting stretch receptors in the skin.

rumen   The first of the four chambers of the ruminant stomach. Along with the reticulum, it is where food is partially digested with the assistance of gut bacteria.

ruminants   Herbivorous, cud-chewing mammals, such as cows and sheep, characterized by a stomach that consists of four compartments: the rumen, reticulum, omasum, and abomasum.

S

S phase   In the cell cycle, the stage of interphase during which DNA is replicated. (Contrast with G1 phase, G2 phase.)

sac fungi   *See* Appendix A.

salt glands   (1) In plants, glands on the leaves of some halophytes that secrete salt, thereby ridding the plants of excess salt. (2) In marine birds, nasal glands that excrete excess salt they ingest with their food.

saltatory conduction   [L. *saltare*: to jump] The rapid conduction of action potentials in myelinated axons; so called because action potentials appear to "jump" between nodes of Ranvier along the axon.

saprobe   [Gk. *sapros*: rotten] An organism (usually a bacterium or fungus) that obtains its carbon and energy by absorbing nutrients from dead organic matter. Also called a saprotroph.

saprobic   Feeding on dead organic matter.

sarcomere   (sark′ o meer) [Gk. *sark*: flesh + *meros*: unit] The contractile unit of a skeletal muscle.

sarcoplasm   The cytoplasm of a muscle cell.

sarcoplasmic reticulum   The endoplasmic reticulum of a muscle cell.

saturated fatty acid   A fatty acid in which all the bonds between carbon atoms in the hydrocarbon chain are single bonds—that is, all the bonds are saturated with hydrogen atoms. (Contrast with unsaturated fatty acid.)

scavenger   An animal that eats larger dead organisms but is not typically considered a detritivore.

Schwann cell   A type of macroglial cell that myelinates axons in the peripheral nervous system.

scion   In horticulture, the bud or stem from one plant that is grafted to a root or root-bearing stem of another plant (the stock).

sclera   The white outer layer of the eyeball continuous with the cornea.

sclereid   One of the principle types of cells in sclerenchyma.

sclerenchyma   (skler eng′ kyma) [Gk. *skleros*: hard + *kymus*: juice] A type of plant cell with heavily thickened cell walls. The principal types of sclerenchyma cells are fibers and sclereids. (Contrast with parenchyma, collenchyma.)

scrotum   In most mammals, a pouch outside the body cavity that contains the testes.

scyphozoans   *See* Appendix A.

SDP   *See* short-day plant.

second filial generation   *See* F_2.

second messenger   A compound, such as cAMP, that is released within a target cell after a hormone (the first messenger) has bound to a surface receptor on a cell; the second messenger triggers further reactions within the cell.

second polar body   In oogenesis, the daughter cell of the second meiotic division that subsequently degenerates. (*See also* ootid.)

secondary active transport   A form of active transport that does not use ATP as an energy source; rather, transport is coupled to ion diffusion down a concentration gradient established by primary active transport. Also called co-transport. (Contrast with primary active transport.)

secondary bronchi   The airways branching off the primary bronchi in the vertebrate lung.

secondary cell wall   A thick, cellulosic structure internal to the primary cell wall formed in some plant cells after cell expansion stops. (Contrast with primary cell wall.)

secondary consumer   An organism (carnivore) that feeds on herbivores or primary consumers. (Contrast with primary consumer.)

secondary endosymbiosis   The engulfment of a photosynthetic eukaryote by another eukaryotic cell that gave rise to certain groups of photosynthetic eukaryotes (e.g., euglenids).

secondary growth   In plants, growth that contributes to an increase in girth. (Contrast with primary growth.)

secondary immune response   A rapid and intense response to a second or subsequent exposure to an antigen, initiated by memory cells. (Contrast with primary immune response.)

secondary lysosome   A membrane-enclosed organelle formed by the fusion of a primary lysosome with a phagosome, in which macromolecules taken up by phagocytosis are hydrolyzed into their monomers. (Contrast with primary lysosome.)

secondary metabolite   A compound synthesized by a plant that is not needed for basic cellular metabolism. Typically has an antiherbivore or antiparasite function.

secondary oocyte   In oogenesis, the daughter cell of the first meiotic division that receives almost all the cytoplasm. (*See also* first polar body.)

secondary production   The source of energy for organisms and ecosystems that is derived from the consumption of organic compounds produced by other organisms.

secondary sex characteristics   The outward expression of sex determination in organs and tissues, such a body hair and stature in humans, that are not directly part of the reproductive system.

secondary spermatocyte   One of the products of the first meiotic division of a primary spermatocyte.

secondary structure   In a protein, the localized regularities of structure, such as the α helix and the β pleated sheet. (Contrast with primary, tertiary, quaternary structure.)

secondary succession   The reestablishment of a community when most, but not all, organisms have been destroyed. (Contrast with primary succession.)

secretin   A peptide hormone secreted by the upper region of the small intestine when acidic chyme is present. Stimulates the pancreatic duct to secrete bicarbonate ions.

secretion   1. The release of substances from a cell, tissue, or organ either within the body or from the body. 2. The active transport of molecules from the interstitial fluid of the body to the outside of the body such as into the renal tubules.

sedimentary rock   Rock formed by the accumulation of sediment grains on the bottom of a body of water. Often contains stratified fossils that allow geologists and biologists to date evolutionary events relative to each other.

seed   A fertilized, ripened ovule of a gymnosperm or angiosperm. Consists of the embryo, nutritive tissue, and a seed coat.

seed ferns   *See* Appendix A.

seedling   A plant that has just completed the process of germination.

segment polarity genes   In *Drosophila* development, segmentation genes that determine the boundaries and anterior–posterior organization of individual segments. Part of a developmental cascade that includes maternal effect genes, gap genes, pair rule genes, and Hox genes.

segmentation   The division of an animal body into segments.

segmentation genes   Genes that determine the number and polarity of body segments.

segregation   In genetics, the separation of alleles, or of homologous chromosomes, from each other during meiosis so that each of the haploid daughter nuclei produced contains one or the other member of the pair found in the diploid parent cell, but never both. This principle was articulated by Mendel as his first law.

selectable marker   A gene, such as one encoding resistance to an antibiotic, that can be used to identify (select) cells that contain recombinant DNA from among a large population of untransformed cells.

selective permeability   The characteristic of membranes that allows certain substances to pass through while other substances are excluded.

self-incompatability   In plants, the possession of mechanisms that prevent self-fertilization.

semelparity   A type of reproductive life history in which individuals are physiologically capable of reproducing only once in a lifetime. (Contrast with iteroparity.)

semen   (see' men) [L. *semin*: seed] The thick, whitish liquid produced by the male reproductive system in mammals, containing the sperm.

semicircular canals   Three canals in the human inner ear that form part of the vestibular system.

semiconservative replication   The way in which DNA is synthesized. Each of the two partner strands in a double helix acts as a template for a new partner strand. Hence, after replication, each double helix consists of one old and one new strand.

semilunar valves   The valves of the pulmonary artery and the aorta that prevent back flow of blood into the ventricles.

seminal vesicles   Male accessory sex glands that contribute most of the volume of the semen, including mucus, fibrinogen, and fructose.

seminiferous tubules   The tubules within the testes within which sperm production occurs.

sensitive period   *See* critical period.

sensor   A cell that is responsive to a particular type of physical or chemical stimulation. Also called a receptor.

sensory adaptation   The diminishing response by sensory receptor cells to maintained or repeated stimulation.

sensory mechanisms   The means by which internal or external stimuli are converted into neural signals.

sensory organs   Structures that convert types of internal or environmental energy into electric signals used by the nervous system.

sensory system   A set of organs and tissues for detecting a stimulus; consists of sensory cells, the associated structures, and the neural networks that process the information.

sensory transduction   The transformation of environmental stimuli or information into neuronal signals.

sepal   (see' pul) [L. *sepalum*: covering] One of the outermost structures of the flower, usually protective in function and enclosing the rest of the flower in the bud stage.

septate   [L. wall] Divided, as by walls or partitions.

septum   (plural: septa) (1) A partition or cross-wall appearing in the hyphae of some fungi. (2) The bony structure dividing the nasal passages.

sequence alignment   A method of identifying homologous positions in DNA or amino acid sequences by pinpointing the locations of deletions and insertions that have occurred since two (or more) organisms diverged from a common ancestor.

Sertoli cells   Cells in the seminiferous tubules of the testes that nurture the developing sperm.

sessile   (sess' ul) [L. *sedere*: to sit] Permanently attached; not able to move from one place to another. (Contrast with motile.)

set point   In a regulatory system, the threshold sensitivity to the feedback stimulus.

sex chromosome   In organisms with a chromosomal mechanism of sex determination, one of the chromosomes involved in sex determination (in humans and many other animals, these are the X and Y chromosomes).

sex pilus   A thin connection between two bacteria through which genetic material passes during conjugation.

sex-linked   Referring to a gene that is carried on a sex chromosome, such as the X chromosome in mammals.

sex-linked inheritance   A pattern of inheritance characteristic of genes located on the sex chromosomes of organisms having a chromosomal mechanism for sex determination.

sexual reproduction   Reproduction involving the union of gametes.

sexual selection   Selection by one sex of characteristics in individuals of the opposite sex. Also, the favoring of characteristics in one sex as a result of competition among individuals of that sex for mates.

Shannon index   The quantitative index most commonly used to describe species diversity that includes measures of both species richness and species evenness.

shoot apical meristem   A group of cells at the apex of the shoot that gives rise to the organs of the shoot.

shoot system   In plants, the organ system consisting of the leaves, stem(s), and flowers.

short tandem repeats (STRs)   Short (1–5 base pairs), moderately repetitive sequences of DNA. The number of copies of an STR at a particular location varies between individuals and is inherited.

short-day plant (SDP)   A plant that flowers when nights are longer than a critical length specific for that plant's species. (Compare with long-day plant.)

short-term memory   Information that is maintained in the brain and can be accessed for a short period of time—seconds to minutes. (Contrast with immediate memory, long-term memory.)

side chain   *See* R group.

sieve plates   The end walls of sieve tube elements, containing pores that form connections with neighboring cells.

sieve tube element   The characteristic conducting cell of the phloem in angiosperms, which contains cytoplasm but relatively few organelles, and whose end walls (sieve plates) contain pores that form connections with neighboring cells.

sigma factor   In prokaryotes, a protein that binds to RNA polymerase, allowing the complex to bind to and stimulate the transcription of a specific class of genes (e.g., those involved in sporulation).

signal peptide   *See* signal sequence.

signal sequence   The sequence within a protein that directs the protein to a particular organelle. Also called the signal peptide.

signal transduction pathway   The series of biochemical steps whereby a stimulus to a cell (such as a hormone or neurotransmitter binding to a receptor) is translated into a response of the cell.

signaling mechanisms   The means of transferring information between cells, organs, or organisms.

silencer   A gene sequence binding transcription factors that repress transcription. (Contrast with enhancer.)

silent mutation   A change in a gene's sequence that has no effect on the amino acid sequence of a protein either because it does not change the amino acid specified by the corresponding codon. (Contrast with frame-shift mutation, loss-of-stop mutation, missense mutation, nonsense mutation.)

silent substitution   *See* synonymous substitution.

simians   *See* Appendix A.

similarity matrix   A matrix used to compare the degree of divergence among pairs of objects. For molecular sequences, constructed by summing the number or percentage of nucleotides or amino acids that are identical in each pair of sequences.

simple diffusion   Diffusion that does not involve a direct input of energy or assistance by carrier proteins.

simple fruit   A fruit that develops from a single carpel in a single flower.

single nucleotide polymorphisms (SNPs)   Inherited variations in a single nucleotide base pair in DNA that differ among individuals.

single-stranded binding protein   In DNA replication, a protein that binds to single strands of DNA after they have been separated from each other, keeping the two strands separate for replication.

sink   In plants, any organ that imports the products of photosynthesis, such as roots, developing fruits, and immature leaves. (Contrast with source.)

sink population   A population that receives more immigrants from other populations within a metapopulation than it produces. (Compare with source population.)

sinoatrial node   (sigh' no ay' tree al) [L. *sinus*: curve + *atrium*: chamber] The pacemaker of the mammalian heart.

sinus venosus   The first chamber of the fish heart that opens into the atrium.

sister chromatid   Each of a pair of newly replicated, genetically identical (except for new mutations) chromatids.

sister clades   Two clades that are each other's closest relatives.

sister species   Two species that are each other's closest relatives.

skeletal muscle   A type of muscle tissue characterized by multinucleated cells containing highly ordered arrangements of actin and myosin microfilaments. Also called striated muscle. (Contrast with cardiac muscle, smooth muscle.)

skeletal systems   Organ systems that provide rigid supports—**skeletons**—against which muscles can pull to create directed movements. (*See also* endoskeleton, exoskeleton.)

sliding DNA clamp   A protein complex that keeps DNA polymerase bound to DNA during replication.

sliding filament model   A mechanism of muscle contraction based on the formation and breaking of cross-bridges between actin and myosin filaments, causing the filaments to slide together.

slow-twitch fibers   Skeletal muscle fibers specialized for sustained aerobic work; contain myoglobin and abundant mitochondria, and are well supplied with blood vessels. Also called oxidative or red muscle fibers. (Contrast with fast-twitch fibers.)

slow-wave sleep   *See* non-REM sleep.

small interfering RNAs (siRNAs)   Short, double-stranded RNA molecules used in RNA interference.

small intestine   The portion of the gut between the stomach and the colon; consists of the duodenum, the jejunum, and the ileum.

smooth endoplasmic reticulum (SER)   The portion of the endoplasmic reticulum that lacks ribosomes and has a tubular appearance. (Contrast with rough endoplasmic reticulum.)

smooth muscle   Muscle tissue consisting of sheets of mononucleated cells innervated by the autonomic nervous system. (Contrast with cardiac muscle, skeletal muscle.)

sodium–potassium (Na⁺–K⁺) pump   An antiporter responsible for primary active transport; it pumps sodium ions out of the cell and potassium ions into the cell, both against their concentration gradients. Also called a sodium–potassium ATPase.

soil fertility   The ability of a soil to sustain plant growth, in terms of the soil's concentration of available plant nutrients.

soil solution   The aqueous portion of soil, from which plants take up dissolved mineral nutrients.

soils   The upper layers of Earth's surface that support plant growth.

solute   A substance that is dissolved in a liquid (solvent) to form a solution.

solute potential (Ψ_s)   A property of any solution, resulting from its solute contents; it may be zero or have a negative value. The more negative the solute potential, the greater the tendency of the solution to take up water through a semi-permeable membrane. (Contrast with pressure potential, water potential.)

solution   A liquid (the solvent) and its dissolved solutes.

solvent   The liquid in which a substance (solute) is dissolved to form a solution.

solvent drag   A transport mechanism in which solutes move across a tissue layer through intercellular spaces by a flow of water (solvent). Also called bulk transport.

somatic cell gene therapy   Alteration of the human genome sequence in somatic cells, for medical benefit. (Contrast with germ line gene therapy.)

somatic cells   [Gk. *soma*: body] All the cells of the body that are not specialized for reproduction. (Contrast with germ cell.)

somatic mutation   A permanent genetic change in a somatic cell (as opposed to a germ cell, the egg or sperm). These mutations affect only the individual; they are not passed on to offspring. (Contrast with germ line mutation.)

somatostatin   A peptide hormone made principally in the hypothalamus and the pancreas. Hypothalamic somatostatin, also called Growth Hormone Inhibiting Hormone, inhibits the release of growth hormone and thyroid stimulating hormone from the pituitary. Pancreatic somatostatin slows digestive processes.

somite   (so' might) One of the segments into which an embryo becomes divided longitudinally, leading to the eventual segmentation of the animal as illustrated by the spinal column, ribs, and associated muscles.

soredia   (singular: soredium) Propagules of lichens consisting of one or a few photosynthetic cells bound by fungal hyphae.

sorus   (plural: sori) A spore-producing structure on the underside of a fern frond.

source   In plants, any organ that exports the products of photosynthesis in excess of its own needs, such as a mature leaf or storage organ. (Contrast with sink.)

source population   A population that serves as a net source of individuals to other populations within a metapopulation. (Compare with sink population.)

spatial summation   In the production or inhibition of action potentials in a postsynaptic cell, the summation of depolarizations and hyperpolarizations produced at different sites on the postsynaptic cell. (Contrast with temporal summation.)

spawning   Among aquatic animals, the release of gametes into the water, resulting in external fertilization. (*See also* external fertilization.)

speciation   (spee' see ay' shun) The process of splitting one population into two populations that are reproductively isolated from one another. (Contrast with evolution.)

species   (spee' sees) [L. kind] The base unit of taxonomic classification, consisting of an ancestor–descendant group of populations of evolutionarily closely related, similar organisms. The more narrowly defined "biological species" consists of individuals capable of interbreeding with each other but not with members of other species.

species composition   The kinds of species present in a community.

species concepts   The ways that biologists think about the category of species.

species diversity   A measure that combines the number of species (species richness) in a community and their relative abundances compared with one another (species evenness).

species evenness   The relative abundances of species compared with one another.

species richness   The total number of species within an area.

species–area relationship   The relationship between the size of an area and the numbers of species it supports.

specific heat   The amount of energy that must be absorbed by a gram of a substance to raise its temperature by one degree centigrade. By convention, water is assigned a specific heat of one.

specific transcription factors   In eukaryotes, transcription factors that have specific regulatory effects only at certain promoters or classes of promoters. (Contrast with general transcription factors.)

sperm   [Gk. *sperma*: seed] The male gamete.

sperm cells   *See* sperm.

spermatid   One of the products of the second meiotic division of a primary spermatocyte; four haploid spermatids, which remain connected by cytoplasmic bridges, are produced for each primary spermatocyte that enters meiosis.

spermatogonium   (plural: spermatogonia) In animals, the diploid progeny of a germ cell in males.

sphincter   [Gk. *sphinkter*: something that binds tightly] A ring of muscle that can close an orifice, for example, at the anus.

spicule   [L. arrowhead] A hard, calcareous skeletal element typical of sponges.

spinal reflex   The conversion of afferent to efferent information in the spinal cord without participation of the brain.

spindle   The array of microtubules emanating from both poles of a dividing cell during mitosis and playing a role in the movement of chromosomes at nuclear division. Named for its shape.

spiral cleavage   A form of complete cleavage in which the cleavage planes are at oblique angles to the animal–vegetal axis. (Compare with radial cleavage.)

spirillum   Any of various spiral-shaped bacteria.

spirochetes   *See* Appendix A.

spleen   An organ that serves as a reservoir for venous blood and eliminates old, damaged red blood cells from the circulation.

sponges   *See* Appendix A.

spontaneous generation   The idea that under ordinary circumstances, living organisms can form from nonliving materials.

spontaneous mutation   A genetic change caused by internal cellular mechanisms, such as an error in DNA replication. (Contrast with induced mutation.)

sporangiophore   A stalked reproductive structure produced by zygospore fungi that extends from a hypha and bears one or many sporangia.

sporangium   (spor an' gee um) (plural: sporangia) [Gk. *spora*: seed + *angeion*: vessel or reservoir] In plants and fungi, any specialized structure within which one or more spores are formed.

spore   [Gk. *spora*: seed] (1) Any asexual reproductive cell capable of developing into an adult organism without gametic fusion. In plants, haploid spores develop into gametophytes, diploid spores into sporophytes. (2) In prokaryotes, a resistant cell capable of surviving unfavorable periods.

sporocytes   Specialized cells of the diploid sporophyte that divide by meiosis to produce four haploid spores. Germination of these spores produces the haploid gametophyte.

sporophyte   (spor' o fyte) [Gk. *spora*: seed + *phyton*: plant] In plants and protists with alternation of generations, the diploid phase that produces the spores. (Contrast with gametophyte.)

sporulation   The formation of spores, or resting stages.

squamates   *See* Appendix A.

stability   The resistance of an ecological community to (or recovery from) a disturbance.

stabilizing selection   Selection against the extreme phenotypes in a population, so that the intermediate types are favored. (Contrast with directional selection, disruptive selection.)

stamen   (stay' men) [L. *stamen*: thread] A male (pollen-producing) unit of a flower, usually composed of an anther, which bears the pollen, and a filament, which is a stalk supporting the anther.

standard free energy   The energy associated with a chemical reaction that can be used to do work. The sum of the enthalpy and the product of temperature and entropy.

staphylococci   *See* Appendix A.

starch   [O.E. *stearc*: stiff] A polymer of glucose; used by plants to store energy.

Starling's forces   The two opposing forces responsible for water movement across capillary walls: blood pressure, which squeezes water and small solutes out of the capillaries, and osmotic pressure, which pulls water back into the capillaries.

start codon   The mRNA triplet (AUG) that acts as a signal for the beginning of translation at the ribosome. (Contrast with stop codon.)

static life table   A life table that records the survival and reproduction of individuals of different ages during a single time period.

stele   (steel) [Gk. pillar] The central cylinder of vascular tissue in a plant stem.

stem   In plants, the organ that holds leaves and/or flowers and transports and distributes materials among the other organs of the plant.

stereocilia   Fingerlike extensions of hair cell membranes whose bending initiates sound perception. (*See* hair cell.)

steroid hormones   Steroid molecules that circulate in the blood and affect cells with appropriate receptors. Examples are testosterone and estrogen.

sticky ends   On a piece of two-stranded DNA, short, complementary, single-stranded regions produced by the action of a restriction endonuclease. Sticky ends facilitate the joining of segments of DNA from different sources.

stigma   [L. *stigma*: mark, brand] The part of the pistil at the apex of the style that is receptive to pollen, and on which pollen germinates.

stock   In horticulture, the root or root-bearing stem to which a bud or piece of stem from another plant (the scion) is grafted.

stoma   (plural: stomata) [Gk. *stoma*: mouth, opening] A small opening in the plant epidermis that permits gas exchange; bounded by a pair of guard cells whose osmotic status regulates the size of the opening.

stomach   An organ that physically (and sometimes enzymatically) breaks down food, preparing it for digestion in the midgut.

stomatal crypt   In plants, a sunken cavity below the leaf surface in which a stoma is sheltered from the drying effects of air currents.

stoneworts   *See* Appendix A.

stop codon   Any of the three mRNA codons that signal the end of protein translation at the ribosome: UAG, UGA, UAA. Also called nonsense codon. (Contrast with start codon.)

stramenopiles   *See* Appendix A.

stratigraphy   The study of geological strata.

stratum   (plural: strata) [L. *stratos*: layer] A layer of rock laid down at a particular time in the past.

streptophytes   *See* Appendix A.

stress   An abiotic factor that reduces the growth, reproduction, or survival of some individuals. (Contrast with disturbance.)

stress-relaxation cycle   The process by which plant cells increase in size. Changes in the structure of the cell wall result in a decrease in stress within the wall, thereby lowering turgor pressure in the cell and allowing more water to enter.

stretch receptor   A modified muscle cell embedded in the connective tissue of a muscle that acts as a mechanoreceptor in response to stretching of that muscle.

striated muscle   *See* skeletal muscle.

strigolactones   Signaling molecules produced by plant roots that attract the hyphae of mycorrhizal fungi.

strobilus   (plural: strobili) One of several conelike structures in various groups of plants (including club mosses, horsetails, and conifers) associated with the production and dispersal of reproductive products.

stroke   An embolism in an artery in the brain that causes the cells fed by that artery to die. The specific damage, such as memory loss, speech impairment, or paralysis, depends on the location of the blocked artery.

structural gene   A gene that encodes the primary structure of a protein not involved in the regulation of gene expression.

structural isomers   Molecules made up of the same kinds and numbers of atoms, in which the atoms are bonded differently.

structural motif   A three-dimensional structural element that is part of a larger molecule. For example, the helix-turn-helix motif in many DNA-binding proteins.

style   [Gk. *stele*: pillar or column] In the angiosperm flower, a column of tissue extending from the tip of the ovary, and bearing the stigma or receptive surface for pollen at its apex.

subduction   In plate tectonics, the movement of one lithospheric plate under another.

submucosa   (sub mew koe' sah) The tissue layer just under the epithelial lining of the lumen of the digestive tract.

subsoil   The soil horizon lying below the topsoil and above the parent rock (bedrock); the zone of infiltration and accumulation of materials leached from the topsoil. Also called the B horizon.

substrate   (1) The molecule(s) on which an enzyme exerts catalytic action. (2) The base material on which a sessile organism lives.

succession   The gradual, sequential series of changes in the species composition of an ecological community following a disturbance.

succulence In plants, the possession of fleshy, water-storing leaves or stems; an adaptation to dry environments.

sulci (singular: sulcus) The valleys between the folds of the cerebral cortex.

superficial cleavage A variation of incomplete cleavage in which cycles of mitosis occur without cell division, producing a syncytium (a single cell with many nuclei).

superior vena cava The large vein that returns deoxygenated blood to the right atrium from the upper body.

suprachiasmatic nuclei (SCN) In mammals, two clusters of neurons just above the optic chiasm that act as the master circadian clock.

surface area-to-volume ratio For any cell, organism, or geometrical solid, the ratio of surface area to volume; this is an important factor in setting an upper limit on the size a cell or organism can attain.

surface tension The attractive intermolecular forces at the surface of a liquid; an especially important property of water.

surfactant A substance that decreases the surface tension of a liquid. Lung surfactant, secreted by cells of the alveoli, is mostly phospholipid and decreases the amount of work necessary to inflate the lungs.

survivorship (l_x) The fraction of individuals that survive from birth to a given life stage or age.

survivorship curve A plot of the number of individuals surviving through each life stage (survivorship, l_x) for a hypothetical cohort, usually of 1,000 individuals; includes three general curves called type I, II, and III survivorship curves.

suspension feeder *See* filter feeder.

suspensor In the embryos of seed plants, the stalk of cells that pushes the embryo into the endosperm and is a source of nutrient transport to the embryo.

sustainable Pertaining to the use and management of ecosystems in such a way that humans benefit over the long term from specific ecosystem goods and services without compromising others.

swim bladder An organ in fishes used primarily to regulate buoyancy.

symbiosis (sim' bee oh' sis) [Gk. *sym*: together + *bios*: living] The living together of two or more species in a prolonged and intimate relationship.

symbiotic Referring to a relationship in which two or more organisms live in close association with one another.

symmetry Pertaining to an attribute of an animal body in which at least one plane can divide the body into similar, mirror-image halves. (*See* bilateral symmetry, radial symmetry.)

sympathetic division A division of the vertebrate autonomic nervous system that is connected to the central nervous system via thoracic and lumbar spinal nerves; the sympathetic and parasympathetic divisions tend to exert opposing controls over autonomic effectors. (Contrast with parasympathetic division.)

sympatric speciation (sim pat' rik) [Gk. *sym*: same + *patria*: homeland] Speciation due to reproductive isolation without any physical separation of the subpopulation. (Contrast with allopatric speciation.)

symplast The continuous meshwork of the interiors of living cells in the plant body, resulting from the presence of plasmodesmata. (Contrast with apoplast.)

symporter A membrane transport protein that carries two substances in the same direction. (Contrast with antiporter, uniporter.)

synapomorphy A trait that arose in the ancestor of a phylogenetic group and is present (sometimes in modified form) in all of its members, thus helping delimit and identify that group. Also called a shared derived trait. (Contrast with derived trait.)

synapse (sin' aps) [Gk. *syn*: together + *haptein*: to fasten] A specialized type of junction where a neuron meets its target cell (which can be another neuron or some other type of cell) and information in the form of neurotransmitter molecules is exchanged across a synaptic cleft.

synapsis (sin ap' sis) The highly specific parallel alignment (pairing) of homologous chromosomes during meiosis I.

synaptic cleft The space between the presynaptic cell and the postsynaptic cell in a chemical synapse.

syncytium A single cell with many nuclei, produced as a result of superficial cleavage.

synonymous (silent) substitution A change of one nucleotide in a sequence to another when that change does not affect the amino acid specified (i.e., UUA → UUG, both specifying leucine). (Contrast with missense substitution, nonsense substitution, nonsynonymous substitution.)

systematics The scientific study of the diversity and relationships among organisms.

systemic acquired resistance In plants, a general resistance to many plant pathogens throughout the plant following infection at a single location.

systemic circuit The portion of the circulatory system by which oxygenated blood from the lungs or gills is distributed throughout the rest of the body and returned to the heart. (Contrast with pulmonary circuit.)

systems biology The scientific study of an organism as an integrated and interacting system of genes, proteins, and biochemical reactions.

systole (sis' tuh lee) [Gk. contraction] The phase of the cardiac cycle when the ventricles contract, driving blood forward in the circulatory system. (Contrast with diastole.)

T

T cell A type of lymphocyte involved in the cellular immune response. The final stages of its development occur in the thymus gland. (*See also* cytotoxic T cell, T-helper cell. Contrast with B cell.)

T cell receptor A protein on the surface of a T cell that recognizes the antigenic determinant for which the cell is specific.

T tubules A system of tubules that runs throughout the cytoplasm of a muscle fiber, through which action potentials spread.

T-helper (T_H) cell A type of T cell that stimulates events in both the cellular and humoral immune responses by binding to the antigen on an antigen-presenting cell that uses class II MHC molecules for presentation; target of the HIV-1 virus, the agent of AIDS. (Contrast with cytotoxic T cell.)

taproot The largest plant root from which other roots sprout laterally.

taproot system A root system typical of eudicots and consisting of a primary root (taproot) that extends downward by tip growth and outward by initiating lateral roots. (Contrast with fibrous root system.)

tardigrades *See* Appendix A.

taste bud A structure in the epithelium of the tongue that includes a cluster of chemoreceptors innervated by sensory neurons.

TATA box An eight-base-pair sequence, found about 25 base pairs before the starting point for transcription in many eukaryotic promoters, that binds a general transcription factor and thus helps initiate transcription.

taxon (plural: taxa) [Gk. *taxis*: put in order] A biological group (typically a species or a clade) that is given a name.

telencephalon The outer, surrounding structure of the embryonic vertebrate forebrain, which develops into the cerebrum.

telomerase An RNA-dependent DNA polymerase that catalyzes the addition of telomeric sequences lost from chromosomes during DNA replication.

telomeres (tee' lo merz) [Gk. *telos*: end + *meros*: units, segments] Repeated DNA sequences at the ends of eukaryotic chromosomes.

temperature inversions Foggy conditions created when cold air is trapped within a warm inversion layer that forms over valleys during warm days.

template A molecule or surface on which another molecule is synthesized in complementary fashion, as in the replication of DNA.

temporal lobe One of five lobes of the brain's cerebral hemisphere; receives and processes auditory and visual information; involved in recognizing, identifying, and naming objects.

temporal summation In the production or inhibition of action potentials in a postsynaptic cell, the summation of depolarizations and hyperpolarizations produced by rapidly repeated stimulation of a single point on the postsynaptic cell. (Contrast with spatial summation.)

tendon A collagen-containing band of tissue that connects a muscle with a bone.

termination In molecular biology, the end of transcription or translation.

territorial behavior Aggressive actions engaged in to defend a habitat or resource such that other animals are denied access.

tertiary endosymbiosis The mechanism by which some eukaryotes acquired the capacity for photosynthesis; for example, a dinoflagellate that apparently lost its chloroplast became photosynthetic by engulfing another protist that had acquired a chloroplast through secondary endosymbiosis.

tertiary structure   In a protein, the relative locations in three-dimensional space of all the atoms in the molecule. The overall shape of a protein. (Contrast with primary, secondary, quaternary structure.)

test cross   The mating of a dominant phenotype individual (who may be either heterozygous or homozygous) with a homozygous recessive individual.

testis   (tes′ tis) (plural: testes) [L. *testis*: witness] The male gonad; the organ that produces the male gametes.

tetanus   [Gk. *tetanos*: stretched] (1) A state of sustained maximal muscular contraction caused by rapidly repeated stimulation. (2) In medicine, an often fatal disease ("lockjaw") caused by the bacterium *Clostridium tetani*.

tetrapods   See Appendix A.

thalamus   [Gk. *thalamos*: chamber] A region of the vertebrate forebrain; involved in integration of sensory input.

thallus   The body of a fungus or plant that is not differentiated into stem and leaves and lacks true roots and a vascular system.

Thaumarchaeota   See Appendix A.

thecal cells   In mammals, the outer layer of cells of the ovarian follicle that bound the follicle and secrete the hormone testosterone. (Contrast with **granulosa cells**.)

theory   [Gk. *theoria*: analysis of facts] A far-reaching explanation of observed facts that is supported by such a wide body of evidence, with no significant contradictory evidence, that it is scientifically accepted as a factual framework. Examples are Newton's theory of gravity and Darwin's theory of evolution. (Contrast with hypothesis.)

theory of endosymbiosis   [Gk. *endo*: within + *sym*: together + *bios*: life] The theory that the eukaryotic cell evolved via the engulfing of one prokaryotic cell by another.

theory of island biogeography   A theory proposing that the number of species on an island (or in another geographically defined and isolated area) represents a balance, or equilibrium, between the rate at which species immigrate to the island and the rate at which resident species go extinct.

therians   See Appendix A.

thermogenin   Also called uncoupling protein 1 (UCP1). A protein in the mitochondria of brown fat that uncouples oxidative phosphorylation.

thermoneutral zone   [Gk. *thermos*: temperature] The range of temperatures over which an endotherm does not have to expend extra energy to thermoregulate.

thermoregulatory adaptations   Physiological and behavioral mechanisms for altering the heat content of the body.

theropods   See Appendix A.

thoracic cavity   [Gk. *thorax*: breastplate] The portion of the mammalian body cavity bounded by the ribs, shoulders, and diaphragm. Contains the heart and the lungs.

thoracic duct   The connection between the lymphatic system and the circulatory system.

threshold   The level of depolarization that causes an electrically excitable membrane to fire an action potential.

thrombin   An enzyme involved in blood clotting; cleaves fibrinogen to form fibrin.

thrombus   (throm′ bus) [Gk. *thrombos*: clot] A blood clot that forms within a blood vessel and remains attached to the wall of the vessel. (Contrast with embolus.)

thylakoid   (thigh′ la koid) [Gk. *thylakos*: sack or pouch] A flattened sac within a chloroplast. Thylakoid membranes contain all of the chlorophyll in a plant, in addition to the electron carriers of photophosphorylation. Thylakoids stack to form grana.

thymine (T)   A nitrogen-containing single-ringed base found in DNA.

thyroid gland   [Gk. *thyreos*: door-shaped] A two-lobed gland in vertebrates. Produces the hormone thyroxine.

thyroid-stimulating hormone (TSH)   A hormone produced by the anterior pituitary that stimulates the thyroid gland to produce and release thyroxine. Also called thyrotropin.

thyrotropin   See thyroid-stimulating hormone (TSH).

thyrotropin-releasing hormone (TRH)   A hormone produced by the hypothalamus that stimulates the anterior pituitary to release thyrotropin.

thyroxine   A hormone produced by the thyroid gland; controls many metabolic processes.

tidal ventilation   The bidirectional form of ventilation used by all vertebrates except birds; air enters and leaves the lungs by the same route.

tidal volume (TV)   The volume of air inhaled and exhaled by a resting individual. (Contrast with expiratory reserve volume, inspiratory reserve volume, vital capacity.)

tight junction   A junction between epithelial cells in which there is no gap between adjacent cells.

tissue   A group of similar cells organized into a functional unit; usually integrated with other tissues to form part of an organ.

titin   A protein that holds bundles of myosin filaments in a centered position within the sarcomeres of muscle cells. The largest protein in the human body.

Toll-like receptors (TLRs)   Proteins on cell membranes with extracellular domains that recognize characteristic molecules (pathogen-associated molecular patterns) from microbial pathogens.

topography   The shape and surface features of Earth, in the form of mountains, valleys, ocean basins, etc.

topsoil   The uppermost soil horizon; contains most of the organic matter of soil, but may be depleted of most mineral nutrients by leaching. Also called the A horizon.

totipotent stem cells   Stem cells that have the capacity to develop into any other cell type .

trachea   (tray′ kee ah) [Gk. *trakhoia*: tube] (1) In a vertebrate lung, the principal tube leading into the lungs from the mouth cavity. (2) In insects,

one of the air-filled tubes (**tracheae**) in the tracheal breathing network that branches through all tissues of the body.

tracheary element   Either of two types of xylem cells—tracheids and vessel elements—that undergo apoptosis before assuming their transport function.

tracheid   (tray′ kee id) A type of tracheary element found in the xylem of nearly all vascular plants, characterized by tapering ends and walls that are pitted but not perforated. (Contrast with vessel element.)

tracheophytes   See Appendix A.

trade winds   The prevailing winds that blow from east to west across the tropics.

trade-off   The relationship between the fitness benefits conferred by an adaptation and the fitness costs it imposes. For an adaptation to be favored by natural selection, the benefits must exceed the costs.

trait   In genetics, a specific form of a character: eye color is a character; brown eyes and blue eyes are traits. (Contrast with character.)

trans fat   A fat with fatty acids whose double bonds are in the trans, rather than the cis, configuration. While some rare fatty acids are trans, more commonly trans fats are produced as a byproduct when cis fats are treated chemically to saturate them.

transcription   The synthesis of RNA using one strand of DNA as a template.

transcription factors   Proteins that assemble on a eukaryotic chromosome, allowing RNA polymerase II to perform transcription. (*See also* general transcription factors, specific transcription factors.)

transcriptome   The subset of the genome that is expressed as RNA in a particular cell or tissue at a particular time.

transect   A linear measurement of any length used to count individuals along the stretch of the line.

transfection   The insertion of recombinant DNA into animal cells.

transfer RNA (tRNA)   A family of folded RNA molecules. Each tRNA carries a specific amino acid and an anticodon that will pair with the complementary codon in mRNA during translation.

transformation   (1) A mechanism for transfer of genetic information in bacteria in which pure DNA from a bacterium of one genotype is taken in through the cell surface of a bacterium of a different genotype and incorporated into the chromosome of the recipient cell. (2) Insertion of recombinant DNA into a host cell. *See also* transfection.

transgenic   Containing recombinant DNA incorporated into the genetic material.

transgenic organism   An organism engineered to contain, and usually express, a gene from another organism.

transition   In genetics, a base pair substitution such that a purine base is converted to the other purine (e.g., adenine to guanine) and its matching pyrimidine is converted to the other pyrimidine (e.g., thymine to cytosine).

transition state   In an enzyme-catalyzed reaction, the reactive condition of the substrate after there has been sufficient input of energy (activation energy) to initiate the reaction.

translation   The synthesis of a protein (polypeptide). Takes place on ribosomes, using the information encoded in messenger RNA.

translocation   (1) In genetics, a rare mutational event that moves a portion of a chromosome to a new location, generally on a nonhomologous chromosome. (2) In vascular plants, the movement of solutes in the phloem.

transmembrane domain   A protein region rich in hydrophobic amino acids that spans the phospholipid bilayer.

transmembrane protein   An integral membrane protein that spans the phospholipid bilayer.

transpiration   [L. *spirare*: to breathe] The evaporation of water from plant leaves and stem, driven by heat from the Sun, and providing the motive force to raise water (plus mineral nutrients) from the roots.

transposable element (transposon)   A segment of DNA that can move to, or give rise to copies at, another location on the same or a different chromosome.

transversion   In genetics, a base pair substitution such that a purine base is converted to a pyrimidine (e.g., adenine to cytosine) and its matching pyrimidine is converted to a purine (e.g., thymine to guanine).

tree of life   A term that encompasses the evolutionary history of all life, or a graphic representation of that history.

tricuspid valve   The right **atrioventricular (AV)** valve. So named because it has three leaves.

triglyceride   A simple lipid in which three fatty acids are combined with one molecule of glycerol.

trilobites   *See* Appendix A.

trimesters   The three stages of human pregnancy, approximately 3 months each in length.

tripartite synapse   The idea that a synapse includes not only the pre- and postsynaptic neurons involved but also encompasses many connections with glial cells called astrocytes.

triploblastic   Having a body derived from three embryonic cell layers (ectoderm, mesoderm, and endoderm). (Contrast with diploblastic, monoblastic.)

triploid (3*n*) cell   A cell containing three sets of an organism's chromosomes.

trochophore   (troke' o fore) [Gk. *trochos*: wheel + *phoreus*: bearer] A radially symmetrical larval form typical of annelids and mollusks, distinguished by a wheel-like band of cilia around the middle.

trophic   [Gk. *trophes*: nourishment] Referring to feeding.

trophic cascade   A series of trophic interactions within a food web in which the rate of consumption at one trophic level results in a change in species abundance or composition at lower trophic levels.

trophic efficiency   A measure of the amount of energy or biomass at one trophic level divided by the amount of energy at the trophic level immediately below it.

trophic level   A subdivision of a food web that includes species that have similar ways of interacting and obtaining energy.

trophoblast   [Gk *trophes*: nourishment + *blastos*: sprout] At the 32-cell stage of mammalian development, the outer group of cells that will become part of the placenta and thus nourish the growing embryo. (Contrast with inner cell mass.)

tropic hormones   Hormones produced by the anterior pituitary that control the secretion of hormones by other endocrine glands.

tropomyosin   (troe poe my' oh sin) One of the three protein components of an actin filament; controls the interactions of actin and myosin necessary for muscle contraction.

troponin   One of the three components of an actin filament; binds to actin, tropomyosin, and Ca^{2+}.

trypsin   A protein-digesting enzyme. Secreted by the pancreas in its inactive form (trypsinogen), it becomes active in the duodenum of the small intestine.

tuataras   *See* Appendix A.

tube feet   A unique feature of echinoderms; extensions of the water vascular system, which functions in gas exchange, locomotion, and feeding.

tubulin   A protein that polymerizes to form microtubules.

tumor   [L. *tumor*: a swollen mass] A disorganized mass of cells. Malignant tumors spread to other parts of the body.

tumor necrosis factor   A cytokine protein that kills target cells and activates immune cells.

tumor suppressor   A gene that codes for a protein product that inhibits cell proliferation; inactive in cancer cells. (Contrast with oncogene.)

tunicates   *See* Appendix A.

turgid   Swollen or distended. In plants, a cell is turgid when its water potential is lower than that of the surrounding environment.

turgor pressure   [L. *turgidus*: swollen] The force exerted by a plant cell against the cell wall when it has taken up water by osmosis. (*See* pressure potential.)

turtles   *See* Appendix A.

twitch   A muscle fiber's minimum unit of contraction, stimulated by a single action potential.

tympanic membrane   [Gk. *tympanum*: drum] The eardrum.

type I survivorship curve   A survivorship curve in which individuals experience high overall survivorship through adulthood but a steep decline late in life. (Compare with type II survivorship curve, type III survivorship curve.)

type II survivorship curve   A survivorship curve in which individuals experience a constant chance of surviving at all ages. (Compare with type I survivorship curve, type III survivorship curve.)

type III survivorship curve   A survivorship curve in which individuals experience low survivorship early in life and higher survivorship once they reach maturity. (Compare with type I survivorship curve, type II survivorship curve.)

U

ultimate causes   In animal behavior, the evolutionary processes that produce an animal's capacity and tendency to behave in particular ways. (Contrast with proximate causes.)

uncompetitive inhibitor   An enzyme inhibitor that binds to the enzyme–substrate complex, preventing the complex from releasing products.

undershoot   *See* after-hyperpolarization.

unequal crossing over   The displacement in alignment of a highly repeated gene sequence during meiotic crossing over, so that one chromosome receives many copies of the sequence while the second chromosome receives fewer copies. One of the mechanisms of concerted evolution. (*See also* biased gene conversion.)

uniporter   [L. *unus*: one + *portal*: doorway] A membrane transport protein that carries a single substance in one direction. (Contrast with antiporter, symporter.)

unloading   In phloem, the process of transferring sugars and other molecules in the phloem to adjacent plant tissues.

unsaturated fatty acid   A fatty acid whose hydrocarbon chain contains one or more double bonds. (Contrast with saturated fatty acid.)

upper critical temperature   The environmental temperature at which a resting endotherm must actively increase its heat loss to avoid a rise in its body temperature.

upwelling   A process by which offshore winds in combination with the Coriolis effect push warmer surface water away from the shore, allowing cold, nutrient-rich water from deeper waters to rise to the surface.

uracil (U)   A pyrimidine base found in nucleotides of RNA.

urea   (you ree' uh) A compound that is the main form of nitrogen excreted by many animals, including mammals. (Compare with ammonia, uric acid.)

ureotelic   Pertaining to an organism in which the final product of the breakdown of nitrogen-containing compounds (primarily proteins) is urea. (Contrast with ammonotelic, uricotelic.)

ureter   (your' uh tur) A long duct leading from the vertebrate kidney to the urinary bladder or the cloaca.

urethra   (you ree' thra) In most mammals, the canal through which urine is discharged from the bladder and which serves as the genital duct in males.

uric acid   A compound that serves as the main excreted form of nitrogen in some animals, particularly those that must conserve water, such as reptiles and insects. (Compare with ammonia, urea.)

uricotelic   Pertaining to an organism in which the final product of the breakdown of nitrogen-containing compounds (primarily proteins) is uric acid. (Contrast with ammonotelic, ureotelic.)

urinary bladder   A structure in which urine is stored until it can be excreted to the outside of the body.

urine   (you′ rin) In vertebrates, the fluid waste product containing the toxic nitrogenous by-products of protein and nucleic acid metabolism.

uterine cycle   Cyclical changes in the uterus of mammals that prepares the endometrium for the arrival of a blastocyst. In humans, also called the menstrual cycle. (Contrast with ovarian cycle.)

uterus   (yoo′ ter us) [L. *utero*: womb] In mammals, a specialized portion of the female reproductive tract that receives the fertilized egg and nurtures the embryo in its early development. Also called the womb.

V

vaccination   The injection of virus or bacteria or their proteins into the body, to induce immunity. The injected material is usually attenuated (weakened) before injection and is called a vaccine.

vacuole   (vac′ yew ole) A membrane-enclosed organelle in plant cells that can function for storage, water concentration for turgor, or hydrolysis of stored macromolecules.

vagina   (vuh jine′ uh) [L. sheath] In female animals, the entry to the reproductive tract.

valence shell   The outermost energy shell of an atom, containing the valence electrons involved in chemical reactivity.

van der Waals forces   Weak attractions between atoms resulting from the interaction of the electrons of one atom with the nucleus of another. This type of attraction is about one-fourth as strong as a hydrogen bond.

variable region   The portion of an immunoglobulin molecule or T cell receptor that includes the antigen-binding site and is responsible for its specificity. (Contrast with constant region.)

vas deferens   (plural: vasa deferentia) The duct that transfers sperm from the epididymis to the urethra.

vasa recta   Blood vessels that parallel the loops of Henle and the collecting ducts in the renal medulla of the kidney.

vascular bundle   In vascular plants, a strand of vascular tissue, including xylem and phloem as well as thick-walled fibers.

vascular cambium   (kam′ bee um) [L. *cambiare*: to exchange] In plants, a lateral meristem that gives rise to secondary xylem and phloem.

vascular plants   *See* Appendix A.

vascular tissue system   The transport system of a vascular plant, consisting primarily of xylem and phloem. (Contrast with dermal tissue system, ground tissue system.)

vasopressin   *See* antidiuretic hormone (ADH).

vector   (1) An agent, such as an insect, that carries a pathogen affecting another species. (2) A plasmid or virus that carries an inserted piece of DNA into a bacterium for cloning purposes in recombinant DNA technology.

vegetal hemisphere   The lower portion of some animal eggs, zygotes, and embryos, in which the dense nutrient yolk settles. The vegetal pole is to the very bottom of the egg or embryo. (Contrast with animal hemisphere.)

vegetative   Nonreproductive, nonflowering, or asexual.

vegetative cells   (1) Generally: nonreproductive cells. (2) The photosynthesizing cells of a cyanobacterial colony.

vegetative meristem   An apical meristem that produces leaves.

vegetative reproduction   Asexual reproduction through the modification of stems, leaves, or roots.

vein   [L. *vena*: channel] A blood vessel that returns blood to the heart. (Contrast with artery.)

velvet worms   *See* Appendix A.

ventilation   The forced flow of air or water over or through structures used for breathing (external respiration).

ventral   [L. *venter*: belly, womb] Toward or pertaining to the belly or lower side. (Contrast with dorsal.)

ventricle   A muscular heart chamber that pumps blood through the lungs or through the body.

venule   A small blood vessel draining a capillary bed that joins others of its kind to form a vein. (Contrast with arteriole.)

vernalization   [L. *vernalis*: spring] Events occurring during a required chilling period, leading eventually to flowering.

vertebral column   [L. *vertere*: to turn] The jointed, dorsal column that is the primary support structure of vertebrates.

vertebrates   *See* Appendix A.

very low-density lipoproteins (VLDLs)   Lipoproteins that consist mainly of triglyceride fats, which they transport to fat cells in adipose tissues throughout the body; associated with excessive fat deposition and high risk for cardiovascular disease.

vesicle   Within the cytoplasm, a membrane-enclosed compartment that is associated with other organelles; the Golgi apparatus is one example.

vessel element   A type of tracheary element with perforated end walls; found only in angiosperms. (Contrast with tracheid.)

vestibular system   (ves tib′ yew lar) [L. *vestibulum*: an enclosed passage] Structures in the inner ear that sense changes in position or momentum of the head, affecting balance and motor skills.

vestibule   A central part of the inner ear involved in balance.

vicariance   (vye care′ ee uns) [L. *vicus*: change] The evolutionary separation of species due to a barrier that results in the geographic isolation of species that once were connected to one another.

villi   (vil′ li) (singular: villus) [L. *villus*: shaggy hair or beard] Hairlike projections from a membrane; for example, from many gut walls.

virus   Any of a group of ultramicroscopic particles constructed of nucleic acid and protein (and sometimes lipid) that require living cells in order to reproduce. Viruses evolved multiple times from different cellular species.

visceral mass   The bulk of the digestive, reproductive, excretory, and respiratory systems of mollusks, contained within the shell.

vital capacity (VC)   The maximum capacity for air exchange in one breath; the sum of the tidal volume and the inspiratory and expiratory reserve volumes.

vitamin   [L. *vita*: life] An organic compound that an organism cannot synthesize but nevertheless requires in small quantities for normal growth and metabolism.

vitamin D   A fat soluble vitamin that is actually produced endogenously as a result of UV light falling on the skin. Vitamin D is involved in regulation of Ca^{2+} and phosphate in the blood and is critical for bone mineralization and growth.

vitelline envelope   The inner, proteinaceous protective layer of a sea urchin egg.

viviparity   (vye vi par′ uh tee) Reproduction in which fertilization of the egg and development of the embryo occur inside the mother's body. (Contrast with oviparity.)

vivipary   Premature germination in plants.

voltage   A measure of the difference in electric charge between two points.

voltage-gated channel   A type of gated channel that opens or closes when a certain voltage exists across the cell membrane in which it is inserted.

vomeronasal organ (VNO)   A chemosensory structure embedded in the nasal epithelium of amphibians, reptiles, and many mammals. Often specialized for detecting pheromones.

W

waggle dance   A behavior of honey bees that communicates to hivemates the direction and distance to a food source or a location for a new colony.

Walter climate diagram   A graphic technique that plots temperature and precipitation data to visualize a growing season for plants (those months when average temperatures are above freezing and average precipitation is sufficient for plant growth).

warning signal   A visual or acoustical defense mechanism used by prey species to advertise to predators that they may be toxic.

water potential (Ψ, psi)   In osmosis, the tendency for a system (a cell or solution) to take up water from pure water through a differentially permeable membrane. Water potential has two major components relevant to water flow between neighboring cells: pressure potential and solute potential.

water vascular system   In echinoderms, a network of water-filled canals that functions in gas exchange, locomotion, and feeding.

wavelength   The distance between successive peaks of a wave train, such as electromagnetic radiation.

weather   The short-term state of atmospheric conditions (temperature, precipitation, humidity, wind direction and velocity) at a particular place and time. (Contrast with climate.)

Wernicke's area   A region in the temporal lobe of the human brain that is involved with the sensory aspects of language.

westerlies   The prevailing winds that blow from west to east across the mid-latitudes. (Compare with easterlies.)

wet-nosed primates   *See* Appendix A.

white blood cells   Cells in the blood plasma that play defensive roles in the immune system. Also called leukocytes.

white matter   In the central nervous system, tissue that is rich in axons. (Contrast with gray matter.)

wild type   Geneticists' term for standard or reference type. Deviants from this standard, even if the deviants are found in the wild, are usually referred to as mutant. (Note that this terminology is not usually applied to human genes.)

wood   Secondary xylem tissue.

X

xenoturbellids   *See* Appendix A.

xerophyte   (zee′ row fyte) [Gk. *xerox*: dry + *phyton*: plant] A plant adapted to an environment with a limited water supply.

xylem   (zy′ lum) [Gk. *xylon*: wood] In vascular plants, the tissue that conducts water and minerals; xylem consists, in various plants, of tracheids, vessel elements, fibers, and other highly specialized cells.

xylem sap   The liquid contents of the xylem.

xylem vessels   The continuous tubes that conduct water in plants.

Y

yeasts   Microscopic fungi consisting of single oval cells that reproduce by budding.

yolk   [M.E. *yolke*: yellow] The stored food material in animal eggs, rich in protein and lipids.

yolk sac   In reptiles (including birds) and mammals, the extraembryonic membrane that forms from the endoderm of the hypoblast; it encloses and digests the yolk.

Z

zeatin   A cytokinin originally purified from corn kernels.

zona pellucida   A jellylike substance that surrounds the mammalian ovum when it is released from the ovary.

zone of cell differentiation   The part of a plant root, generally above the zone of cell elongation, where cells are differentiating. Also called the maturation zone.

zone of cell division   The region close to a root tip in which cell division takes place; the source of all cells of the root's primary tissues.

zone of cell elongation   The part of a plant root, generally above the zone of cell division, where cells are expanding (growing), primarily in the longitudinal direction.

zygospore   A multinucleate, diploid cell that is a resting stage in the life cycle of zygospore fungi.

zygospore fungi   *See* Appendix A.

zygote   (zye′ gote) [Gk. *zygotos*: yoked] The cell created by the union of two gametes, in which the gamete nuclei are also fused. The earliest stage of the diploid generation.

zymogen   The inactive precursor of a digestive enzyme; secreted into the lumen of the gut, where a protease cleaves it to form the active enzyme.

Index

Numbers in *italic* indicate the information will be found in a figure, caption, or table.

A

A band, 1027, *1028, 1029*
A horizon, 767, 768
Aardvark, *716, 718*
ABA. *See* Abscisic acid
ABC model of flowering, 809–810
Abdomen, muscular segmentation, *651*
Abiotic environment, 1172
ABO blood group, 257–258
Abomasum, 1112
Aboral, 697
Abortion, 935
Abscisic acid (ABA)
  effects on seed dormancy and germination, 787
  plant acclimation to salinity, 826
  plant response to water stress, 757, 823–824
  seed development and, 808
  structure and typical activities, *785*
Abscission, 790–791
Abscission zone, 790
Absorption spectra
  cone cells, *1001*
  defined, 200
  photosynthetic pigments, 200–201
  phototropin, *795*
  phytochromes, 797, *798*
Absorptive heterotrophy, 568, 624
Absorptive state, 1113–1114
Acacia cornigera (bullhorn acacia), 1232, *1233*
Acanthamoeba polyphaga mimivirus (APMV), *555, 556*
Acanthostega, 709
Accessory fruits, 615, *616*
Accessory olfactory bulb, 989
Accessory sex organs, 921, 923
Accipiter gentilis (Northern Goshawk), 1165, *1166*
Acclimation, to environmental stress by plants, 823–824, 825–827
Acclimatization, 848–849
Accommodation, 998
ACE. *See* Angiotensin-converting enzyme
Acetaldehyde, *44*
Acetate, 180
Acetic acid, *44*
Acetyl coenzyme A (acetyl CoA), 180, 181, 190, 192
Acetyl group, 166, 1097–1098
Acetylcholine (ACh)
  clearing from the synapse, 978
  effects on heartbeat, 1079
  effects on smooth muscle, 142, *143*, 1032, *1033*
  importance as a neurotransmitter, 976
  neuromuscular junctions, 974, *975*
  parasympathetic division and, 1015
  penile erection and, 924, *926*

skeletal muscle contraction and, 1029, *1030*
sleep and, 1020
Acetylcholine receptor, 137, 142, *143*
Acetylcholinesterase (AChE), *975*, 978
Acetylsalicylic acid, 152, 166
ACh. *See* Acetylcholine
ACh receptors (AChRs), 974, *975*, 977
AChE. *See* Acetylcholinesterase
AChRs. *See* ACh receptors
Acid growth hypothesis, 791
Acid rain, 1273, 1284
Acid–base catalysis, 163
Acidophilic thermophiles, 546
Acidosis, 1135
Acids, 38–40
Acoelomates, 650, 669
Acoels, *654, 664*, 697, *698*
Acorn barnacles, 1199, 1207, *1208*, 1229–1230
Acorn worms, 700
Acoustic signals, 1161, 1162
Acquired immunodeficiency syndrome (AIDS)
  anti-HIV drugs, 364
  course of, 907–908
  dating the origin of HIV, 457–458
  fungal diseases and, 627
  HIV protease inhibitors and, 319
  phylogenetic analyses of HIV, 454–455
  prevalence, 908
  treatment, 908
Acrosomal process, 918, *919*
Acrosomal reaction, 918, *919*, 920
Acrosome, 918, *919*, 924, *925*
ACTH. *See* Adrenocorticotropic hormone
Actias selene, 429
Actin
  acrosomal reaction and, 918, *919*
  contractile ring, 229
  microfilaments, *101*, 102
  sliding filament model of skeletal muscle contraction, 1027–1031
  smooth muscle contraction, 1032, *1033*
Actin filaments. *See* Microfilaments
Actin-binding proteins, 102
Actinobacteria, *537*, 542–543
Actinomyces, 542
Action potentials (AP)
  an all-or-none, self-generating event, 970–971
  bioelectrical concepts underlying, 965–966
  cardiac muscle contraction, 1032
  defined, 962, 965
  dendrites and, 963
  electrical synapses, 973–974
  electrocardiograms, 1082–1083
  generation of, 970, *971*
  heartbeat and, 1078, 1080
  muscle twitch and, 1034
  neuronal summation of excitatory and inhibitory input and, 975–976

neurotransmitter release and, 974
rapid cycling of asynchronous muscle and, 1039
saltatory conduction, 972, *973*
sensory perception and, 985, 986
skeletal muscle contraction, 1028–1029, 1030
spinal reflexes, 979
Action spectra
  defined, 200
  photosynthetic pigments, 200–201
  phototropism in coleoptiles, *795*
  phytochromes, 796
Activation energy (E_a), 160, 162–163
Activation gate, 970, *971*
Activator proteins, 351, 354–355
Active pursuit strategy, 1220
Active site, of enzymes, 160, 163, 164, 169
Active transport, 119, 125–127, 751
Adaptations
  defined, 10, 427
  to environmental stress by plants, 823, 824–825, 826, *827*
  natural selection and, 427, *428–429*
  trade-offs between cost and benefits, 439–440
Adaptive defenses
  cellular immune response, 894–895, 903–906
  clonal selection and deletion, 895, *896*
  defined, 887
  humoral immune response, 894–895, 899–902
  immunological memory and vaccines, 894, 896–898
  innate immune system and, 887, 895
  key features of, 893–894
  mammals, 888
  natural killer cells, 892
Adaptive radiations, 509–510
Addison's disease, 882–883
Addition rule, 253
Adenine
  Chargaff's rule for DNA, 278–279
  complementary base pairing, 68–70, *71*, 279, 280
  in DNA, 68, *69*, 70, 279, 280, *281*
  genetic code and, 308–309
  in RNA, 68, *69, 70*
  structure, *68*
  synthesis from ribose 5-phosphate, *170*
  wobble base pairing and, 312
Adeno-associated virus, 346
Adenosine, *69, 136*, 137
Adenosine diphosphate (ADP), 157, 158, *159*, 175
Adenosine receptor, *136*, 137
Adenosine triphosphate (ATP)
  active transport and, 125, *126*
  allosteric regulation of glycolysis, 191
  allosteric regulation of the citric acid cycle, 191–192
  biochemical energetics of, 157–159

biological nitrogen fixation and, 773
in C_4 photosynthesis, *210*, 211
Calvin cycle and, *207*
cAMP and, 141
charging transfer RNAs with an amino acid, 312, *313*
functions, 72
heat-induced muscle fatigue and, 849
hydrolysis (*see* ATP hydrolysis)
muscle supplies, 1036, 1038–1039
production (*see* ATP production)
role in catalyzed reactions, *164*
synthesis in mitochondria, 97
tetanic muscle contraction and, 1034
Adenylyl cyclase, 141, 143
ADH. *See* Antidiuretic hormone
Adhesion, 37
Adiantum, 596
Adiponectin, 192
Adipose tissue, 174, *844, 868*, 1116
  See also Brown adipose tissue; White adipose tissue
Adrenal cortex, *868*, 882–874
Adrenal gland
  adrenal cortex, *868*, 882–883
  adrenal medulla (*see* Adrenal medulla)
  fight-or-flight response, 866
  hormones of, *868*
  hypothalamus-pituitary-adrenal axis, 870–871, 882–883
  location, 880
Adrenal medulla
  control of, 880, 882
  hormones of, *868*, 880, 883
  regulation of blood flow, 1090, *1091*
  responses to stress, 883
Adrenalin. *See* Epinephrine
Adrenergic receptors, 883
Adrenocorticotropic hormone (ACTH), *868*, 870, *871*, 882
Adventitious roots, 737
Aegilops tauschii, 832
Aequorea victoria, 405, 445
Aerenchyma, 826, *827*
Aerobes, 552
Aerobic exercise, 863, 1036, 1039
  See also Exercise
Aerobic metabolism
  atmospheric oxygen concentration and, 5, 522
  cellular respiration, 175–176, 177, *178*
  citric acid cycle, 180–181
  glycolysis, 179–180
  overview, 179
  oxidative phosphorylation, 182–187
  pyruvate oxidation, 180
  yields of cellular respiration and fermentation compared, 188, *189*
Aerotolerant anaerobes, 552
Afferent blood vessels, 1052, 1127–1128, 1130, 1136, *1137*
Afferent nerves, 1007
Afferent neurons, 978, 979, *980*
Aflatoxins, 331, 639